Preview *The American Nation Videodisc Program* for 60 days.

...OLOGY?

...g teachers what they
...as and advice became our

...s available today share a
...lum. Most of them were
... and ROM, but not very
...rs: frustration and hours of

...um since 1866, we know
...e technology. That's why
...l your curriculum, and that's
...mages you can access in 30
...characterize every product
...o to identify these
...not an extra; it's part of an

...d this is your opportunity to
...makes when a technology
...hine's.

...*tion Videodisc Program* —

...*t to fit your curriculum*

...*ccessfully*

...*use the program* —
...*codes* —

...*rpassed*

...today, please let us send
...complete the attached

NO POSTAGE
NECESSARY
IF MAILED
IN THE
UNITED STATES

BUSINESS REPLY MAIL
FIRST-CLASS MAIL PERMIT NO. 6767 AUSTIN TX

POSTAGE WILL BE PAID BY ADDRESSEE

ATTN: MULTIMEDIA MARKETING / RL
HOLT RINEHART AND WINSTON, INC.
1120 S CAPITAL OF TEXAS HWY STE II 100
AUSTIN TX 78746-9507

NO POSTAGE
NECESSARY
IF MAILED
IN THE
UNITED STATES

BUSINESS REPLY MAIL
FIRST-CLASS MAIL PERMIT NO. 6767 AUSTIN TX

POSTAGE WILL BE PAID BY ADDRESSEE

ATTN: MULTIMEDIA MARKETING / RL
HOLT RINEHART AND WINSTON, INC.
1120 S CAPITAL OF TEXAS HWY STE II 100
AUSTIN TX 78746-9507

▦ Boyer's
The American Nation

CONTENT REVIEWERS

Richard D. Brown
  University of Connecticut
  Early America

John Buenker
  University of Wisconsin,
    Parkside
  Progressive era

Joyce E. Chaplin
  Vanderbilt University
  Colonial America

Clifford Clark
  Carleton College
  Cultural and intellectual history

John Milton Cooper, Jr.
  University of Wisconsin,
    Madison
  *South; late 19th- and early
    20th-century U.S.*

Carlos E. Cortés
  University of California,
    Riverside
  *Multiculturalism; Latin
    America*

Edward Countryman
  Southern Methodist University
  American Revolution

Lynn Dumenil
  Occidental College
  Modern U.S.

Eric Foner
  Columbia University
  Civil War and Reconstruction

William Freehling
  State University of New York,
    Buffalo
  Antebellum America

Ellis Hawley
  University of Iowa
  20th-century U.S.

George Herring
  University of Kentucky
  U.S. foreign relations; Vietnam

Michael Holt
  University of Virginia
  19th-century U.S.

Mary Kelley
  Dartmouth College
  U. S. intellectual history

Robin Kelley
  University of Michigan
  African American history

Lawrence Frederick Kohl
  University of Alabama
  Antebellum America

Bruce Laurie
  University of Massachusetts,
    Amherst
  Labor history

Jean B. Lee
  University of Wisconsin,
    Madison
  Early America

John Marszalek
  Mississippi State University
  Civil War

William H. McNeil
  Emeritus, University of Chicago
  History

Reid Mitchell
  University of Maryland,
    Baltimore County
  Civil War

Gary Mukai
  Stanford Program on
    International and Cross-
    Cultural Education
  Asia/Asian American issues

Mary Neth
  Virginia Tech
  Social history; women's history

James Oakes
  Northwestern University
  19th-century U. S.

Mary Odem
  Emory University
  *Late 19th- and 20th-century
    U. S.; women's history*

David Oshinsky
  Rutgers University
  Modern U. S.

Colin Palmer
  University of North Carolina
  African diaspora

B. Marie Perinbam
  University of Maryland,
    College Park
  West African history

Carla Rahn Phillips
  University of Minnesota
  Early modern Europe

Morton Rothstein
  University of California, Davis
  *Agricultural history; economic
    history*

Neal Salisbury
  Smith College
  *Colonial America; American
    Indian history*

Linda K. Salvucci
  Trinity University
  *Spanish American and Mexican
    history*

Linda Schott
  University of Texas, San Antonio
  Women's history

John Selby
  College of William and Mary
  Colonial America

J.C.A. Stagg
  University of Virginia
  *Early America; diplomatic
    history*

Ronald Walters
  Johns Hopkins University
  *Early national U.S.; African
    American history*

Richard White
  University of Washington
  *American West; American
    Indian history*

William M. Wiecek
  Syracuse University
  Legal and constitutional history

Marilyn Young
  New York University
  U.S.–East Asian relations

CONTRIBUTORS

Alice Kessler-Harris
  Rutgers University
  Women and labor history

Paul Hutton
  University of New Mexico
  U.S. history; military history

Carol Karlsen
  University of Michigan
  *Early American social and
    cultural history; women's
    history*

Joseph Kett
  University of Virginia
  American cultural history

Edward Linenthal
  University of Wisconsin,
    Oshkosh
  *Religion and American culture;
    war and memory*

Richard Salvucci
  Trinity University
  Latin American economic history

Holly Shulman
  University of Maryland
  20th-century U. S.

Sterling Stuckey
  University of California,
    Riverside
  African American history

EDUCATIONAL REVIEWERS

Dean C. Brink
  Chair, History Department,
    Roosevelt High School
  Seattle, Washington

Michele Forman
  Middlebury Union High School
  Middlebury, Vermont

Elizabeth Hartung-Cole
  LEP Program Specialist, Long
    Beach Unified School
    District
  Long Beach, California

Dr. Karen Hoppes
  Lakeridge High School
  Lake Oswego, Oregon

Dr. Frances J. Powell
  Montgomery College
  Takoma Park, Maryland
  Social Studies Curriculum
    Director, District of
    Columbia Public Schools
    (Ret.)
  Washington, D.C.

Susan Reeder
  Port St. Lucie High School
  Port St. Lucie, Florida

Steven Seto
  Muriel S. Snowden
    International School
  Boston, Massachusetts

Dr. D. William Tinkler
  Administrator, Webb Bridge
    Middle School, Fulton
    County School System
  Alpharetta, Georgia

FIELD TEST TEACHERS

Charles W. Davis
  Catholic High School
  Baton Rouge, Louisiana

Pamela S. Hunt
  Starkville High School
  Starkville, Mississippi

Bonnie C. Feig
  Starkville High School
  Starkville, Mississippi

Mark A. Dragoo
  Chattanooga School for Arts
    and Sciences
  Chattanooga, Tennessee

Robert L. Neely, Jr.
  George Washington High School
  Charleston, West Virginia

Dennis Payne
  West High School
  Knoxville, Tennessee

Pete Meszaros
  Capital High School
  Charleston, West Virginia

Diane Greer
  McCallum High School
  Austin, Texas

Randall Ittner
  Upland High School
  Upland, California

Patricia B. Blagg
  George Washington High School
  Charleston, West Virginia

Gloria Fox Foster
  Upland High School
  Upland, California

Karen E. Hoppes
  Lakeridge High School
  Lake Oswego, Oregon

Anita L. Phillips
  Lubbock High School
  Lubbock, Texas

Charles L. Palmer, III
  Thomas Worthington High
    School
  Worthington, Ohio

Evelyn J. Hunt
  Northeast High School
  Kansas City, Missouri

George W. Allan, Jr.
  John Ehret High School
  Marrero, Louisiana

Sandra Ditschle
  Linden-McKinley High School
  Columbus, Ohio

Philip J. Perry
  Abraham Lincoln High School
  Denver, Colorado

B. Paul Haskell
  Thomas Edison High School
  Alexandria, Virginia

FIELD TEST MATERIALS REVIEWER

John S. Wenrick
  Upland High School
  Upland, California

∷ Boyer's
The American Nation

PAUL BOYER

HOLT, RINEHART AND WINSTON
Harcourt Brace & Company

Austin • New York • Orlando • Atlanta • San Francisco • Boston • Dallas • Toronto • London

About the Author
PAUL BOYER

*P*aul Boyer is Merle Curti Professor of History at the University of
Wisconsin, Madison, and director of the university's Institute for Research
in the Humanities. He is also a member of the executive board of the
Organization of American Historians, of the national advisory board of the PBS
American Experience series and is editor-in-chief of the forthcoming *Oxford
Companion to United States History.* Dr. Boyer has held visiting professorships
at UCLA and Northwestern University and received Guggenheim and
Rockefeller Foundation fellowships.

Awarded a Ph.D. from Harvard in 1966, Dr. Boyer is the author of
numerous articles, essays, reviews, and books. *Salem Possessed: The Social
Origins of Witchcraft,* which he co-authored with Stephen Nissenbaum, won
the John H. Dunning prize of the American Historical Association.

Cover Photo: © Tony Stone Images, Reza Estakhrian.

Copyright © 1998 by Holt, Rinehart and Winston, Inc.

For acknowledgments, see page 1090, which is an extension of the
copyright page.

Printed in the United States of America

ISBN 0-03-050789-8

1 2 3 4 5 6 7 8 9 032 00 99 98 97

As we approach a new century and think about all of our nation's possibilities, dreams, and aspirations, examining our past is even more important. *Boyer's The American Nation* is the best tool for exploring the traditions that have helped to define America's past and will continue to influence the course of American history.

In addition to providing a solid foundation of knowledge about the people, places, and dates important to our country, *Boyer's The American Nation* gives you the ability to choose the combination of materials that best helps you meet your the instructional objectives and the needs of your students. Now all your students can see, hear, and experience history like never before!

Boyer's
The American Nation

❖ Makes history meaningful by exploring the traditions that have shaped America's past and will continue to mold its future

❖ Provides in-depth content and makes the study of history meaningful by helping students understand history and make connections between the past and present

❖ Examines the role that geography has played in influencing our past and present

❖ Gives students the background they need to put recent history in context

❖ Encourages students to become active historians by developing critical-thinking skills

❖ Captures the emotion of history with stunning artwork, compelling quotes, and moving literature

❖ Integrates multimedia support directly into the text with on-page barcodes in the *Annotated Teacher's Edition*

No matter how well you know America's story, *Boyer's The American Nation* will intrigue you and your students. An exciting narrative filled with firsthand accounts, distinguished quotes, and stirring primary source readings creates a memorable experience for students while calling attention to the critical traditions that have become the foundation of the American nation.

In-depth Content

Boyer's: The American Nation examines events from multiple points of view, helping students realize that history is a record of the past that belongs to all of us.

A wealth of teacher's materials provides complete support for each chapter and the flexibility to choose materials that fit your own needs and the needs of all of your students.

UNIT 2

American Letters

Revolutionary Literature

The Revolutionary era inspired many writers to take up the cause of liberty. Fiery orator and author Thomas Paine wrote pamphlets and songs urging the American colonists to fight for their freedom from Great Britain. During the war, women writers—among them dramatist and poet Mercy Otis Warren—encouraged American women to participate in the struggle. After the war, African American mathematician and almanac writer Benjamin Banneker argued that the liberty fought for in the Revolution should be applied to enslaved African Americans.

▲ Mercy Otis Warren

Liberty Tree

by Thomas Paine

In a chariot of light from the regions of day,
   The Goddess of Liberty came;
Ten thousand celestials[1] directed the way,
   And hither conducted the dame.
A fair budding branch from the gardens above,
   Where millions with millions agree,
She brought in her hand as a pledge of her love,
   And the plant she named *Liberty Tree*.

he celestial exotic struck deep in the ground,
   Like a native it flourish'd and bore;
fame of its fruit drew the nations around,
       bore.

But hear, O ye swains,[4] 'tis a tale most profane,
   How all the tyrannical powers,
Kings, Commons and Lords, are uniting amain,[5]
   To cut down this guardian of ours;
From the east to the west blow the trumpet to arms,
   Thro' the land let the sound of it flee,
Let the far and the near all unite with a cheer,
   In defense of our *Liberty Tree*. ❖

1 angels
2 endowed
3 British coin made of silver, worth four pennies
4 country youths
5 with strength and speed

From *To the Hon. J. Winthrop, Esq.'*

AMERICAN LETTERS

features use primary sources—including literature, poetry, and song lyrics—to give students a different view of the United States.

CUBAN MISSILE CRISIS

In October 1962 President Kennedy issued an ultimatum to the Soviet Union, demanding that it remove all its missiles from Cuba. For several days the world held its breath as it teetered on the brink of nuclear war. In the end, the Soviets agreed to remove the missiles. Soviet Premier Nikita Khrushchev relates his memory of the crisis:

THROUGH OTHERS' EYES

"It had been, to say the least, an interesting and challenging situation. The two most powerful nations of the world had been squared off against each other, each with its finger on the button. You'd have thought that war was inevitable. But both sides showed that if the desire to avoid war is strong enough, even the most pressing dispute can be solved by compromise. . . . I'll always remember the late President [Kennedy] with deep respect because, in the final analysis, he showed himself to be sober-minded and determined to avoid war. He didn't let himself become frightened, nor did he become reckless. He didn't overestimate America's might, and he left himself a way out of the crisis. . . . It was a great victory for us, though, that we had been able to extract from Kennedy a promise that neither America nor any of her allies would invade Cuba. "

THROUGH OTHERS' EYES

bring a personal perspective to American history as seen by individuals outside of the United States.

Thinking Critically About History

Strategies for Success

INTERPRETING EDITORIAL CARTOONS

Editorial cartoons are drawings that present points of view on the issues, ideas, people, and events of the day. They usually appear in the editorial sections of newspapers and newsmagazines. Although some express a positive outlook, many are critical of a person or policy.

To communicate their message, editorial cartoonists frequently use caricature and symbolism. A *caricature* is a drawing that exaggerates or distorts physical features. *Symbolism* is the use of one thing to stand for something else. For instance, cartoonists often use Uncle Sam to repre-

4. Consider the cartoonist's purpose. Identify the points of view being expressed in the speech balloons or caption. Try to determine the cartoonist's message.

Applying the Strategy

Andrew Jackson was a popular subject for editorial cartoonists of his day. In the cartoon on this page, Jackson is shown wearing a crown and kingly robe, holding a scepter like a club and a "veto" as if it were a royal decree. Tattered papers labeled "Constitution of the United States," "Internal Improvements," and "U.S. Bank" and a book titled *Judiciary of the U. States are stre...*

Practicing the Strategy

Study the editorial cartoon on page 266 of your textbook. Then, on a separate sheet of paper, answer the following questions.

1. Who are the central figures in the cartoon? Are they portrayed realistically, or are they caricatures?
2. What symbols does the cartoon contain?
3. How do the labels and the title help make the cartoonist's point of view and message clear?
4. What is (a) the cartoonist's point of view and (b) the cartoon's message?

▼ Criticizing Andrew Jackson

STRATEGIES FOR SUCCESS

features develop students' critical-thinking skills and provide activities to apply these skills. In addition, the *Skills Handbook* teaches and reviews important skills such as identifying main ideas, building vocabulary, reading primary and and secondary sources, identifying cause and effect, and writing about history.

Studying the past teaches students valuable lessons that will enable them to make intelligent, informed decisions. *Boyer's The American Nation* teaches students those lessons through a comprehensive program designed to develop critical thinking, decision-making, and map, chart, and graph skills while strengthening reading and writing skills.

Linking Geography to History

AMERICA'S GEOGRAPHY

features explore a wide range of social studies themes, using maps and charts to show the influence of geography on American history.

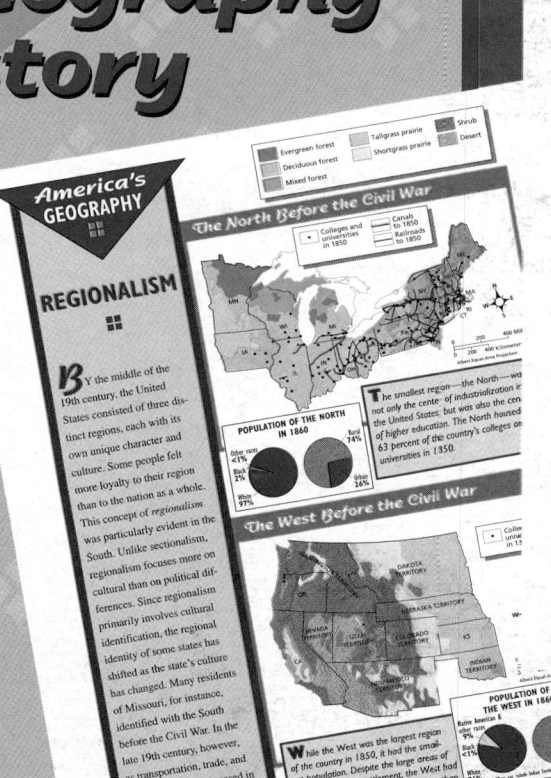

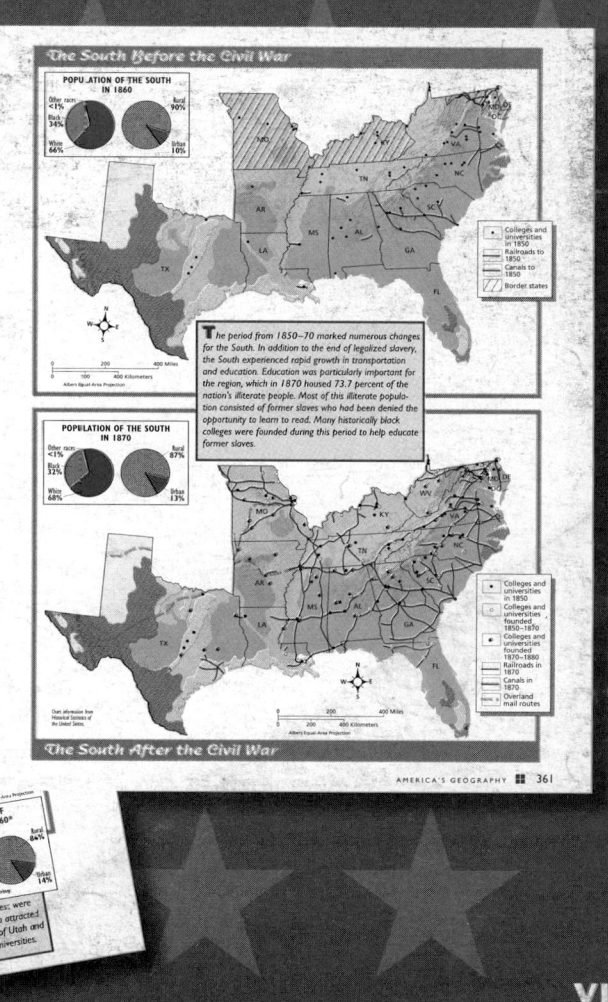

Complete Teacher Support

❖ All teaching materials for **Boyer's The American Nation** are integrated into the *Annotated Teacher's Edition* for ease of planning and instruction. The *Annotated Teacher's Edition* includes:

❖ *Chapter Planning Guides* to organize all materials and make planning easier and more effective.

❖ *Teaching Strategies* to help students understand and apply what they are learning

❖ Many other suggestions to help teachers and students such as *Historical Sidelights, Global Connections, Cooperative Learning, Building Vocabulary, Building Your Portfolio, Link to Today,* and more!

This comprehensive *Annotated Teacher's Edition,* along with the other teacher resource materials available, give you the flexibility to customize instruction.

Components

❖ **Geography Teaching Strategies and Worksheets** synthesize and apply information from the *America's Geography* feature in the textbook to provide students with opportunities to practice key skills.

❖ **Daily Quizzes** provide a short objective assessment for each section of every chapter.

❖ **Building Your Portfolio Worksheets and Review Worksheets** assist students in completing unit portfolio projects.

❖ **Literature Worksheets** reinforce chapter themes and main ideas through historical prose and poetry and introduce students to key literary figures in American history.

❖ **Social Studies Skills Worksheets** reinforce the skills that are emphasized throughout the program.

❖ **Graphic Organizers** visually organize and reinforce each chapter's content and themes and help improve student understanding.

❖ **Chapter Tests**—two per chapter—combine objective and essay questions for a quick and comprehensive evaluation of student learning.

❖ **Writing About American History** develops and improves students' skills in historical research, writing, and test-taking.

❖ **Alternative Assessment Forms** offer teachers options for effectively evaluating student knowledge and progress through various types of self-assessment, peer assessment, portfolio assessment, and teacher assessment.

❖ **World and Regional Outline Maps** contain outline maps of the continents, major subcontinents, and the world to provide students with opportunities to practice map skills and reinforce important location concepts.

❖ **American Almanac Posters and Worksheets** provide illustrated time lines and worksheets, requiring students to analyze and apply information found on the Posters.

❖ **American History Visual Resources** include *Linking History and Geography* transparencies and worksheets, and *Everyday Life in America* transparencies and worksheets. These transparencies are supported by an *Answer Key and Teacher's Notes.*

❖ *Boyer's The American Nation Test Generator* permits custom-designed tests on Macintosh or IBM-compatible hardware so that your tests can match what you teach.

❖ *The American Nation Videodisc Program* offers an array of still images and video segments in English or Spanish. The videodiscs are supported by a *Teacher's Guide* that includes lesson plans and worksheets that provide students with an unparalleled opportunity to experience American history.

Additional Program Resources

❖ *Art in American History* includes 49 four-color transparencies with teacher notes and student worksheets to help students gain an appreciation of American art.

❖ *Eyewitnesses and Others* provides two volumes of primary source readings in American history to give students an opportunity to read the words and understand the thoughts of those who shaped and lived our history.

Introduction to the Program

The study of American history, like history itself, is an ever-evolving process. Over the course of the 20th century, historians have expanded their inquiry beyond the analysis of important events and great leaders to include an examination of the contributions of all members of society to America's story. Central to this enriched historical inquiry is an appreciation of the importance of cultural diversity, geography, democratic values, economics, global relations, and technology in shaping America's past, present, and future. American history today is multidisciplinary. **Boyer's The American Nation** is a reflection of this broadened perspective. **The American Nation** draws on political history, social history, geography, literature, and economics to paint a more complete and accurate picture of America's history.

Boyer's The American Nation program has three major goals for students. The first goal is to inform and excite them about the study of our nation's past. The second is to enable them to appreciate and respect the nation's rich cultural diversity and the many contributions of diverse peoples to its history. The third goal of the program is to strengthen students' critical thinking skills, study skills, and map and chart skills—skills that are vital to subjects across the curriculum and crucial to effective participation in a democratic society. The components of **The American Nation** program—the Pupil's Edition, the Annotated Teacher's Edition, the Core Resource Booklets, the Visual Resources Binder, and a variety of other program resources—all work together to achieve these goals.

Program Components

THE PUPIL'S EDITION

The Pupil's Edition provides comprehensive coverage of American history from prehistory to the present. The text consists of 33 chapters divided chronologically into 9 units. Each chapter presents a blending of political and social history to provide students with a broad view of America's past and present. Through the consistent use of a wide variety of primary sources, a lively and clear writing style, and vivid maps, charts, photographs, and other images, *Boyer's The American Nation* brings history alive for students.

The book's commitment to telling the history of all Americans is reinforced through in-text **Biographies** and **Commentaries** and through such features as **American Letters, Through Others' Eyes, Then and Now, Changing Ways, History in the Making,** and **Presidential Lives.** Geographic coverage is woven into the running text and is reinforced in the map skills program, in the **America's Geography** feature, and in chapter review exercises. Seven broad themes in American history—Global Relations, Constitutional Heritage, Democratic Values, Technology and Society, Cultural Diversity, Geographic Diversity, and Economic Development—are examined in the running text and in chapter opener and review questions to help students see connections between events over time. Critical thinking and study skills are taught and reinforced in the **Strategies for Success** unit feature, the **Skills Handbook,** and all section and chapter reviews. And a wide range of review and assessment questions and activities, including portfolio assessment, are presented in the section, chapter, and unit reviews.

THE ANNOTATED TEACHER'S EDITION

The Annotated Teacher's Edition (ATE) of *Boyer's The American Nation* is designed to reduce teacher preparation time and to provide full instructional support for every element of the Pupil's Edition. *The American Nation* ATE contains all Pupil's Edition pages, slightly reduced in size to create side and top margins. An **interleaf** at the beginning of each chapter helps the teacher to organize and to plan chapter instruction. Within each chapter, page margins contain a variety of point-of-use instructional strategies and resources. ATE top text provides **teaching strategies** correlated to each section's learning objectives. Side-margin **annotations** include a wealth of supplementary information to engage students and to enhance their understanding of major concepts.

Planning and Resources

The two-page **chapter interleaf** facilitates effective planning and teaching. The chapter's main points are overviewed, and the Pupil's Edition themes are explored. Alternative strategies are suggested for meeting individual students' needs.

A **Chapter Planning Guide** in the interleaf lists ancillaries that support chapter instruction and identifies which of the program's resources might be used to introduce or review the chapter. These print and multimedia materials are also correlated for chapter or section use in **resource organizers** on the opening pages of each chapter and section in the ATE. In addition, transparencies and videodisc segments are cited in ATE side margins at their suggested points of use.

Teaching from the Annotated Teacher's Edition

Each chapter in *Boyer's The American Nation* ATE begins in the same way. Specialized strategies tie chapter content to previous learning and introduce students to the chapter's main ideas, events, and themes.

Section lessons also follow an identical format. A **Preview Workshop** lists the important people, places, and terms that will be encountered in the reading. The Pupil's Edition Focus questions are restated as **learning objectives.** Following these introductory elements is the lesson itself.

Answers to all chart, graph, and map questions, section reviews, and chapter reviews are provided in the ATE at point of appearance in the Pupil's Edition.

THE TEACHING LESSON

The teaching lesson for each section is based on a six-step instructional model—**Motivating, Teaching, Practice, Review** and **Assessment, Closure,** and **Extension:**

1 MOTIVATING activities engage students by tying their own experiences, previous learning, or current knowledge to the content of the upcoming section.

2 TEACHING THE SECTION strategies address each section learning objective. They may be teacher-directed; require students to work independently, in pairs, or as a class; or involve cooperative learning or other group efforts. They also encourage students to be imaginative and self-expressive, both orally and in writing.

3 PRACTICE strategies for each section begin with a **Guided Practice,** which allows the teacher to model, monitor, and remediate students' learning or skills. An accompanying **Independent Practice** asks students, in class or as homework, to individually utilize the Guided Practice model without teacher direction.

4 REVIEW AND ASSESSMENT exercises check students' achievement of section objectives and then evaluate the learning that has taken place. Reteaching strategies are provided for students who need remediation.

5 CLOSURE strategies tie section objectives together and apply or evaluate learning.

6 EXTENSION offers activities to enrich or extend learning.

Side-Margin Annotations

The side margins of *The American Nation* ATE include a variety of enrichment and extension materials at points appropriate to the content of textbook pages. Among the frequently appearing annotations are **Global Connections,** which place American history in a global context, and **Cultural Patterns** and **Voices in History,** which offer observations of ethnic Americans and insights from other cultures about the American experience. Point-of-use references to *The American Nation* **Videodisc Program** and the *American Civics Citizenship Skills* **Videocassette** or **Videodisc** provide barcodes and information about disc number, side, location, and length of video segments that support instruction.

THE TEACHER'S RESOURCES

The teacher's resources for *Boyer's The American Nation* provide a variety of effective materials for extending and enriching learning, reinforcing and reteaching content, and evaluating student performance.

Core Resource Booklets

The following **Core Resource Booklets** provide reproducible blackline masters and answer keys to all worksheets:

AMERICAN ALMANAC POSTER WORKSHEETS require students to analyze and apply information found on each unit's American Almanac poster.

GEOGRAPHY TEACHING STRATEGIES AND WORKSHEETS explore the links between geography and important chapter themes and ideas and synthesize and apply information from the textbook's America's Geography feature.

DAILY QUIZZES provide a short objective assessment for each section of the chapter.

BUILDING YOUR PORTFOLIO WORKSHEETS and **REVIEW WORKSHEETS** assist students in completing a unit portfolio project and in reorganizing and reviewing each chapter's content, providing students with another chance to master its main ideas.

LITERATURE WORKSHEETS reinforce chapter themes and main ideas through historical prose and poetry.

SOCIAL STUDIES SKILLS WORKSHEETS reinforce skills that are emphasized throughout the program.

GRAPHIC ORGANIZERS visually organize and reinforce each chapter's content and themes.

CHAPTER TESTS, FORMS A and **B** provide two comprehensive tests, combining objective and essay questions, for each chapter.

Also included are the following program-wide booklets:

WRITING ABOUT AMERICAN HISTORY develops students' skills in historical research, writing, and test-taking.

ALTERNATIVE ASSESSMENT FORMS include student and teacher guidelines for various types of self-assessment, peer assessment, portfolio assessment, and teacher assessment.

OUTLINE MAPS contain outline maps of the continents, major subcontinents, and the world.

VIDEODISC RESOURCES provide correlations and barcodes for *The American Nation* Videodisc Program.

Visual Resources Binder

The **Visual Resources Binder** provides 36 four-color **LINKING HISTORY AND GEOGRAPHY** transparencies, including overlays and worksheets. It also contains 33 **EVERYDAY LIFE IN AMERICA** social history transparencies and worksheets, and an Answer Key and Teacher's Notes for both transparency packages.

Program Resources

Other resources available for use with *Boyer's The American Nation* include the following:

AMERICAN CIVICS CITIZENSHIP SKILLS **VIDEOCASSETTE OR VIDEODISC** includes eight segments that help develop citizenship skills and Teacher's Guide.

THE AMERICAN NATION **TEST GENERATOR** permits custom-designed tests on Macintosh or IBM-compatible hardware.

THE AMERICAN NATION **VIDEODISC PROGRAM** offers video lessons in English or Spanish, support segments, and still images on two discs with Teacher's Guide.

ART IN AMERICAN HISTORY is a package of 49 four-color transparencies with teacher notes and student worksheets.

EYEWITNESSES AND OTHERS provides two volumes of primary source readings in American history.

CONTENTS

Toltec carving of Quetzalcoatl

UNIT 4

War and Reunification

1845–1900   334

Teacher with students (1866)

Painting (1889) of the First Battle of Bull Run

UNIT 5

The Nation Transformed

1860–1910   **422**

Building the transcontinental railroad

The Scott family outside their Nebraska home, 1889

UNIT 7 Prosperity and Crisis

1919–1945   618

Life magazine cover (1926)

The Granger Collection, New York

Reference Section

Features

CONTENTS

Mess equipment from a
doughboy's pack

Charts and Maps

CONTENTS

Themes in American History

*B*oyer's *The American Nation* begins every chapter with a set of theme questions. These questions are drawn from seven broad themes central to American history: global relations, our Constitutional heritage, democratic values, technology and society, cultural diversity, geographic diversity, and economic development. They provide a context for the historical events in each chapter. This context will help you understand the connections between historical events and see how past events are relevant to today's social, political, and economic concerns.

As you begin each chapter, examine the theme questions and answer them based on your own experiences or prior knowledge. At the end of each chapter, you will be asked to answer another set of theme questions, this time using specific facts learned from studying the chapter. This process will help you develop critical thinking skills and encourage you to synthesize the information you have learned. In addition, by tracing the themes through the book, you will be able to see how each theme has developed over time.

■ GLOBAL RELATIONS

This theme asks you to explore the global context in which the United States exists. From its settlement by Asian immigrants tens of thousands of years ago to the first arrival of European, African, and later Asian immigrants to today, America has influenced and been influenced by other parts of the world. Your exploration of the Global Relations theme will help you understand how the relations the United States has maintained with other countries over time have affected our nation's political, social, and economic development. It also will help you appreciate the problems and possibilities of living in an interdependent world community.

■ CONSTITUTIONAL HERITAGE

The study of American history would not be complete without an exploration of the Constitution, the legal framework that structures our democratic government. The Constitutional Heritage theme questions ask you to think about the origin of the Constitution and the ways in which the Constitution has been interpreted and amended over time. You will explore how the laws and government institutions established in the 18th century have evolved through amendments, Supreme Court rulings, and congressional actions. Your examination of this theme will encourage you to understand the part individuals play in promoting the goals—such as justice and democratic rights—enshrined in the Constitution's preamble.

■ DEMOCRATIC VALUES

This theme concerns the continuing struggle to define and protect such democratic values as individual liberty, political representation, freedom of religion, and freedom of speech. The Democratic Values theme questions ask you to consider the impact of changing social, economic, and political conditions on these values. For example, in the years before the Civil War, enslavement of African Americans—a violation of the democratic value of individual liberty—was practiced in the South. Some slaveholders justified this practice by arguing that the democratic value of right to property should be the overriding concern. It took a bloody civil war to settle the issue. Conflicts over democratic values recur throughout American history, and this theme explores the attempts at resolution.

■ TECHNOLOGY AND SOCIETY

From computers in your homes and classrooms to communications satellites orbiting the earth, technology influences many aspects of society. The Technology and Society theme questions ask you to trace technological developments and explore their influence on the economy and our lives.

■ CULTURAL DIVERSITY

Different ethnic, racial, and religious groups have all contributed to the creation of America's rich and unique culture. The Cultural Diversity theme questions ask you to explore how the United States has dealt with diversity from the days of the first encounters between Native Americans and Spanish and English settlers to its status today as a haven for immigrants from all over the world.

■ GEOGRAPHIC DIVERSITY

The majestic old-growth forests of the Pacific Northwest, the rich coal deposits of the Appalachian and Rocky mountains, the oil fields of Texas and Alaska, and the tropical plantations on the volcanic islands of Hawaii have enriched the U.S. economy. The Geographic Diversity theme questions ask you to consider how the development of the nation's diverse natural resources has shaped U.S. society, politics, and the economy. The questions also explore how government and public awareness of the effects of natural resource development on the environment has changed over time.

■ ECONOMIC DEVELOPMENT

The United States has developed one of the world's strongest economies. The Economic Development theme explores the influence of the nation's economy on domestic politics and social life and on international relations. The theme questions ask you to explore the implications of such economic issues as trade, depression and expansion, poverty, taxation, government regulation, and the status of workers.

Chapter Opener

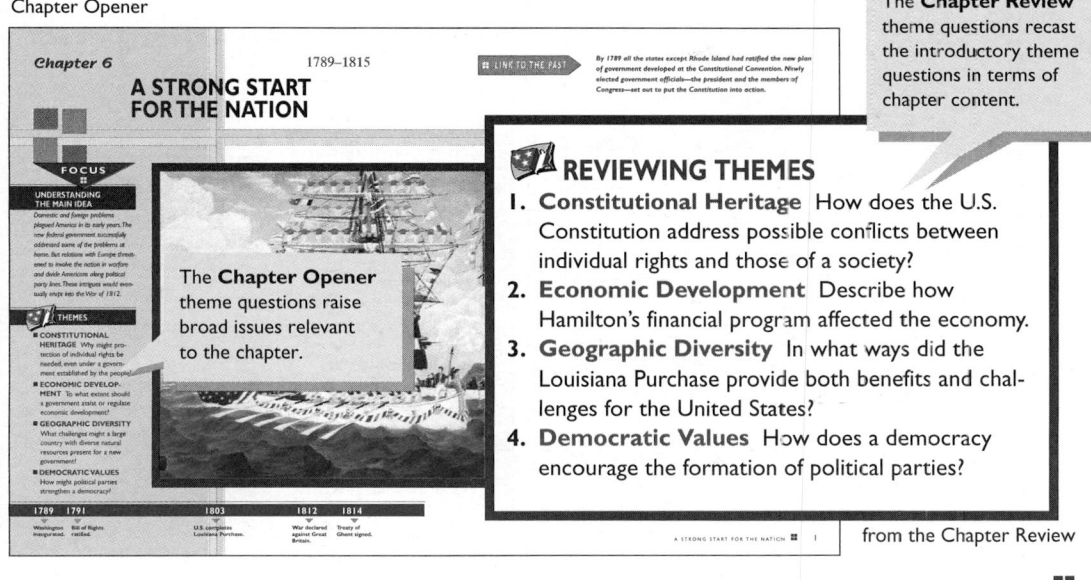

The **Chapter Opener** theme questions raise broad issues relevant to the chapter.

The **Chapter Review** theme questions recast the introductory theme questions in terms of chapter content.

⚑ REVIEWING THEMES

1. **Constitutional Heritage** How does the U.S. Constitution address possible conflicts between individual rights and those of a society?
2. **Economic Development** Describe how Hamilton's financial program affected the economy.
3. **Geographic Diversity** In what ways did the Louisiana Purchase provide both benefits and challenges for the United States?
4. **Democratic Values** How does a democracy encourage the formation of political parties?

from the Chapter Review

Critical Thinking and the Study of History

Throughout *Boyer's The American Nation*, you are asked to think critically about the events and issues that have shaped U.S. history. Critical thinking is the reasoned judgment of information and ideas. People who think critically study information to determine its accuracy. They evaluate arguments and analyze conclusions before accepting them. Critical thinkers are able to recognize and define problems and develop strategies for resolving them.

The development of critical thinking skills is essential to effective citizenship. Such skills empower you to exercise your civic rights and responsibilities. For example, critical thinking skills equip you to judge the messages of candidates for office and to evaluate news reports.

Helping you develop critical thinking skills is an important goal of *Boyer's The American Nation*. The following 14 critical thinking skills appear in the section reviews and chapter reviews. Additional skills strategies can be found in each unit's Strategies for Success and in the Skills Handbook, which begins on page 988.

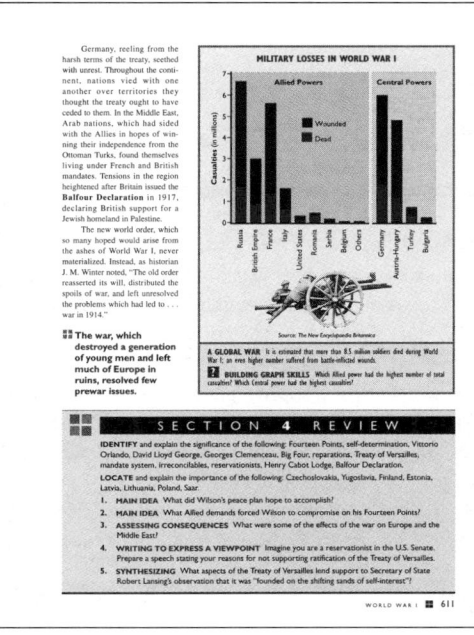

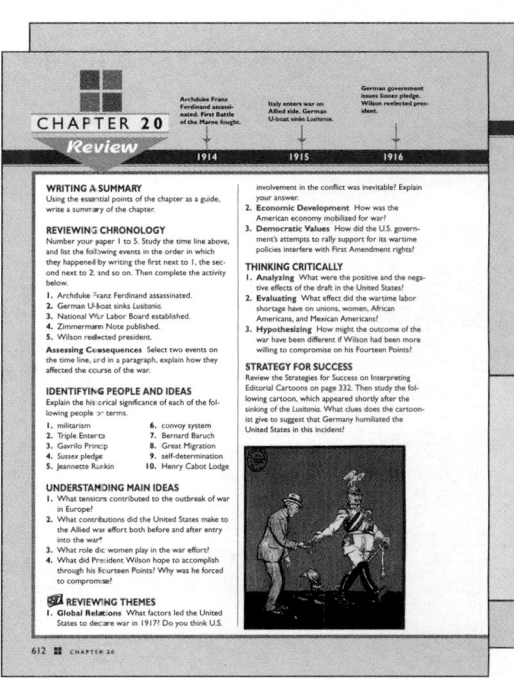

Union mortar battery

the Americas. They encountered a land already settled by people with rich cultures.

3 **Recognizing Point of View** means identifying the factors that color the outlook of an individual or group. A person's point of view includes beliefs and attitudes that are shaped by factors such as age, gender, religion, race, and economic status. This thinking skill helps us examine why people see things as they do and reinforces the realization that people's views may change over time, or with a change in circumstances. When a point of view is highly personal or based on unreasoned judgment, it is considered *bias*.

1 **Using Historical Imagination** is mentally stepping into the past to consider an event or situation as people at the time would have considered it. In putting yourself in their place, you might note whether they lived *before* or *after* historical turning points. Ask yourself: Did these people live before or after major medical advances such as penicillin? before or after technological advances such as the automobile? before or after World War II? Keep in mind what the people of the time knew and did not know. For example, to grasp the experience of a soldier wounded in the Civil War, you need to understand that little was known then about the causes of disease and infection.

4 **Comparing and Contrasting** is examining events, situations, or points of view for their similarities and differences. *Comparing* focuses on both the similarities and the differences. *Contrasting* focuses on only the differences. For example, a comparison of early Irish and Chinese immigrants to the United States would point out that both groups were recruited to help build the transcontinental railroad and that both groups faced discrimination and experienced difficulties in finding well-paying jobs. In contrast, language and racial barriers generally proved more of a problem for Chinese immigrants. Other factors to compare and contrast could include reasons for immigrating to the United States.

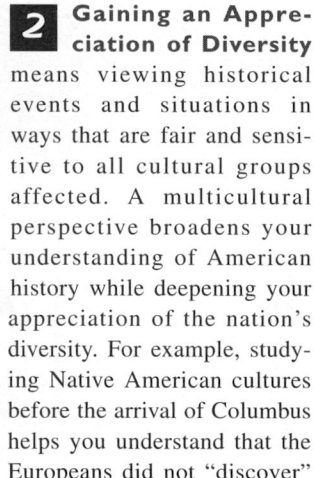

2 **Gaining an Appreciation of Diversity** means viewing historical events and situations in ways that are fair and sensitive to all cultural groups affected. A multicultural perspective broadens your understanding of American history while deepening your appreciation of the nation's diversity. For example, studying Native American cultures before the arrival of Columbus helps you understand that the Europeans did not "discover"

Mayan pillar

Railroad laborers

example, you might study a map such as the one on this page. Analyzing the results state by state shows how Woodrow Wilson won a majority in the electoral college without winning a majority of the popular vote.

7 **Assessing Consequences** means studying an action, an event, or a trend to predict its long-term effects—and to judge the desirability of those effects. *Consequences* often are effects that are indirect and unintended. They may appear long after the event that led to them. An example of assessing consequences is the federal government's weighing of the positive and negative elements of a new drug or medical procedure before permitting its use. Consequences include side effects and other possible risks, as well as benefits.

Struggle at Concord Bridge

5 **Identifying Cause and Effect** is part of interpreting the relationships between historical events. A *cause* is any action that leads to an event; the outcome of that action is an *effect*. To explain historical developments, historians may point out multiple causes and effects. For instance, the actions of the colonists as well as those of the British government brought about the American Revolution, which in turn had many far-reaching effects. (For a more detailed discussion of Identifying Cause and Effect, see page 989.)

6 **Analyzing** is the process of breaking something down into its parts and examining the relationships between them. Analysis enables you to better understand the whole. To analyze the outcome of the 1912 presidential election, for

Election of 1912

WILSON'S STRENGTH Wilson's strength was in the South. Although he won the electoral vote by a landslide, the only states outside the old Confederacy where he won at least half the popular vote were Kentucky, Maryland and Oklahoma.

? **LOCATION** Which state split its electoral vote?

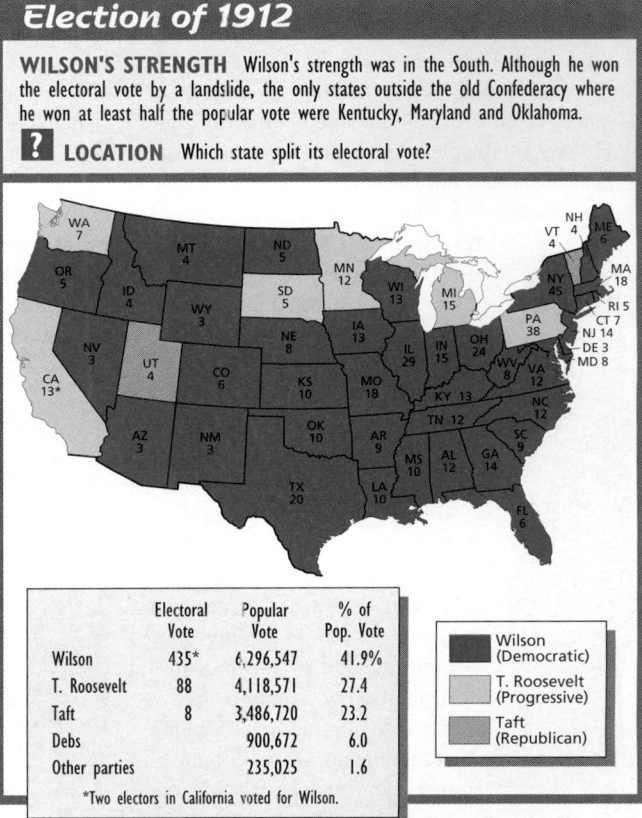

	Electoral Vote	Popular Vote	% of Pop. Vote
Wilson	435*	6,296,547	41.9%
T. Roosevelt	88	4,118,571	27.4
Taft	8	3,486,720	23.2
Debs		900,672	6.0
Other parties		235,025	1.6

*Two electors in California voted for Wilson.

Wilson (Democratic)

T. Roosevelt (Progressive)

Taft (Republican)

8 **Distinguishing Fact from Opinion** means separating the facts about something from what people say about it. A fact can be proved or observed; an opinion, on the other hand, is a personal belief or conclusion. We often hear facts and opinions mixed in everyday conversation—as well as in advertising, in political debate, and in historical sources. Although some opinions can be supported by facts, in an argument opinions do not carry as much weight as facts. (For a more detailed discussion of Distinguishing Fact from Opinion, see page 990.)

9 **Identifying Values** involves recognizing the core beliefs that a person or group holds. Values are more deeply held than opinions and are less likely to change. Values commonly concern matters of right and wrong and may be viewed as desirable in and of themselves. The values of freedom and justice, for example, motivated the struggle to abolish slavery, just as the value of equality has been a foundation of the civil rights and women's movements.

10 **Hypothesizing** is forming a possible explanation for an event, a situation, or

American buffalo

a problem. A hypothesis is not a proven fact. Rather it is an "educated guess" based on available evidence and tested against new evidence. A historian, for instance, might hypothesize that the Civil War was primarily the result of a power struggle between the ruling classes of the North and the South over control of the United States' western frontier. The historian would then organize the evidence to support this hypothesis and challenge other explanations of the war's causes.

L. J. Cranstone's painting depicting a slave auction

Migrant Mother, photographed by Dorothea Lange during the Great Depression

You would then propose and evaluate possible solutions or courses of action, selecting the one you think best and giving the reasons for your choice.

13 **Evaluating** is assessing the significance or overall importance of something, such as the success of a reform movement or the legacy of a president. You should base your judgment on standards that others will understand and are likely to share. An evaluation of the early women's movement, for example, might assess the short- and long-term effects of the focus on women's suffrage.

Woman suffragist

11 **Synthesizing** is combining information and ideas from several sources or points in time to gain a new understanding of a topic or event. Much of the narrative writing in *Boyer's The American Nation* is a synthesis. It pulls together historical data from many sources into a chronological story of our nation. Synthesizing the history of the Great Depression, for example, might involve studying photographs and economic statistics from the 1930s, together with interviews of Americans who lived through the period.

14 **Taking a Stand** is identifying an issue, deciding what you think about it, and persuasively expressing your position. Your stand should be based on specific information. In taking a stand, even on controversial or emotional issues, state your position clearly and give reasons to support it.

12 **Problem Solving** is a process of reviewing a situation and making decisions and recommendations for improving or correcting it. Before beginning, however, the problem must be identified and stated. For instance, in considering a solution to the nation's drug-abuse crisis, you might state the problem in terms of the relationship of drug addiction to violent crime.

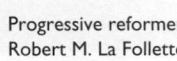

Progressive reformer Robert M. La Follette

PAUL BOYER

To the Reader of *Boyer's The American Nation*

When I studied American history in high school, we used a textbook by a historian named David S. Muzzey. My teacher called him "Fuzzy Muzzey." Muzzey wrote in a lively style, but his history was limited. He focused mainly on politicians, military leaders, and other notables, most of them white males whose ancestors had come from the British Isles or northern Europe. Today's history is far richer in social texture, including not just elites but all Americans: men and women, Native Americans, and immigrants from Europe, Latin America, Africa, Asia, and all other parts of the world.

But my introduction to history did not come from a textbook. History begins in stories. I first learned history from grandparents who recalled their childhoods in Ohio in the 1870s and 1880s. My Grandfather Boyer once told me how he heard of the assassination of President James Garfield in 1881! My father remembered World War I. As a young man of German immigrant origins who held religious beliefs against war, he was forced to recite the Pledge of Allegiance by fellow workers who suspected him of disloyalty. My Aunt Ann, born in 1894, told me stories of her grandfather, a 19th-century healer who treated the ill with herbs. Aunt Ann also spoke proudly of an American Indian ancestor in our family line. These are all strands of our American history, and they begin in family memories.

But why study history at all? History is to a nation what memory is to an individual. A person without memory is sad and tragic. A society that ignores its past and lives only in the present loses a vital element of what we call civilization. History can tell us how far we have come as a nation— and how far we have yet to go. Through history we can see the achievements. as well as the failures, of those who have gone before.

I hope this book will help spur for you a lifelong interest in the past. Its aim is not to provide all the answers, but to raise questions. History is not something fixed forever in concrete. There is no single version of "what really happened." Historians continually find new dimensions of the past to probe and explore. This is the appeal and sometimes the frustration of historical research.

But above all, history can be fascinating. The experiences of Americans of earlier generations were as gripping and vital for them as our lives are for us. History comes alive as we begin to grasp that vivid reality. When you move beyond the textbook to original documents, letters, diaries, and films and recordings, the past comes even more sharply alive.

This book brings the story of our national experience near to the present. The next chapter will be written by you and your generation. As you write that chapter, a knowledge of the past will provide guidance and perspective.

Sincerely,

Paul Boyer

Paul Boyer

Introducing the Unit

- **Chapter 1**
  THE WORLD BY 1500
  Prehistory–1500
- **Chapter 2**
  EMPIRES OF THE AMERICAS
  1492–1800
- **Chapter 3**
  THE ENGLISH COLONIES
  1620–1763

UNIT OVERVIEW

The first Americans migrated from Asia to North America between 12,000 and 60,000 years ago. Over the centuries, they spread throughout the Americas and, isolated from the rest of the world, developed distinct cultures. During the 1400s the people of Europe began to look beyond their own borders, undertaking voyages of exploration that eventually brought them to the Americas. The Spanish and, later, the English built huge colonial empires in the Americas. In the process, they drove the Native Americans from their lands and established the practice of enslaving Africans. In the 1700s struggles between European powers drew the American colonies into a number of wars. Britain emerged victorious, gaining control of North America east of the Mississippi River.

CORE RESOURCES

- **American Almanac Poster** and **Worksheet 1**
- **Building Your Portfolio Worksheet 1**
  You may wish to preview the Unit 1 Review and Building Your Portfolio performance assessment activities on p. 99.

Using the American Almanac Posters

Begin the unit by displaying the American Almanac Poster and discussing entries with students. In addition to the worksheet, the annotations that follow provide additional information about the entries and suggest questions and activities.

Then, as students study the unit, have them work in small groups to create their own almanacs—using the same six headings—on pieces of butcher paper. At the end of the unit, call on groups to display and discuss their almanacs.

Chapter 1
THE WORLD BY 1500
Prehistory–1500

Chapter 2
EMPIRES OF THE
AMERICAS 1492–1800

Native American Life

Point out that many Native American tribes used isolation and fasting as part of the initiation into manhood. A boy remained alone without food or drink until he experienced a revelation through visions or dreams. This revelation served as a guideline for the boy in his adult life. Girls, too, were isolated during their initiation into adulthood.

While in seclusion the girls received instruction from female elders in the duties and obligations of womanhood.

■■ Have students identify religious "initiation rites" to adulthood that exist in society today.

Beginnings
Prehistory–1800

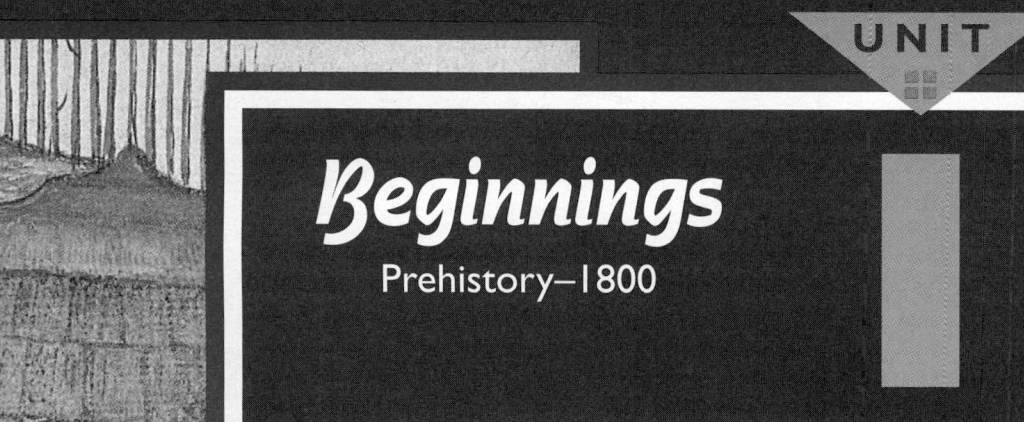

The first Americans migrated from Asia to North America thousands of years ago, spreading throughout the Americas and developing distinct cultures. Then in the 1400s, Europeans began undertaking voyages of exploration that ultimately led to new migrations to the Americas. The Spanish and, later, the English built empires in the lands they claimed. In the process, they drove Native Americans from their lands and established the practice of enslaving Africans. In the 1700s, European nations drew their colonies into a series of wars. Victorious, Britain gained control of North America east of the Mississippi.

◀ *The Towne of Pomeiock*, watercolor by John White, 1585

Chapter 3

THE ENGLISH COLONIES
1620–1763

The Early Economy

The barter system in America applied even to colonial law enforcement. In Virginia, for example, failure to attend church regularly was punishable by a fine of 50 pounds of tobacco.

■■ Ask students if they would be willing to be paid in goods or services rather than in money.

Food for Thought

Note that Native Americans also showed settlers how to tap maple trees for syrup. This practice, however, did not become popular among settlers until well into the 1700s.

■■ Have students identify other common foods that are of Native American origin.

Colonial Life

In 1648, among crimes in Massachusetts that were punishable by death were blasphemy, cursing of a parent by a child over age 16, and a third offense of robbery or burglary. Public confession by the criminal, however, could cause his or her life to be spared.

■■ Ask students how the crimes noted in the almanac (Colonial Life, 1656) are looked upon today.

THE WORLD BY 1500

Prehistory–1500

THE AMERICAN NATION VIDEODISC PROGRAM
A variety of still images, short videos, and activities are available for you to use as you teach this chapter. See Correlation to *The American Nation Videodisc Program* for barcode correlations and suggestions for using the program.

Chapter Overview

Most archaeologists believe the Americas were uninhabited until sometime during the last Ice Age, when people crossed from Asia to North America. Over time, these people spread throughout the Americas. Isolated from the rest of the world, Native Americans developed a variety of distinct cultures.

Native Americans would not remain isolated forever. By the late Middle Ages, Europe, Asia, and Africa were linked by trade. The Europeans' desire for easier access to Asian markets launched them on voyages of exploration that would eventually bring them to the Americas.

Chapter Planning Guide

CHAPTER 1	CORE RESOURCE BOOKLETS	AUDIOVISUAL RESOURCES	PROGRAM RESOURCES
INTRODUCTION pp. 2–3	■ Geography Worksheet 1 ■ Building Your Portfolio Worksheet 1		
TEACHING THE CHAPTER pp. 4–31	■ Graphic Organizer 1 ■ Social Studies Skills Worksheet 1 ■ Literature Worksheet 1 ■ Outline Maps 1, 2, 3, 7, 8, 11, 12, 13, 14, 17, 19, 20	■ *The American Nation* Videodisc: Inquiry and Exploration ■ Linking Geography and History Transparencies and Worksheets 1, 2, 3, 4, 5 ■ Everyday Life in America Transparency and Worksheet 1	■ Art in American History Transparencies and Worksheets 1, 2
REVIEW AND ASSESSMENT pp. 32–33	■ Chapter 1 Daily Quizzes ■ Review Worksheet 1 ■ Chapter 1 Tests ■ Alternative Assessment Forms		■ Test Generator

Additional Resources

BOOKS FOR TEACHERS

Davidson, Basil. *The Lost Cities of Africa.* Revised ed. Little, Brown, 1988. Summarizes sub-Saharan African history prior to European colonialism.

Hourani, Albert. *A History of the Arab Peoples.* Warner Books, 1991. Explores Arab history from the founding of Islam to the present.

Josephy, Alvin M., Jr., ed. *America in 1492.* Newberry, 1991. Examines Native American civilizations before the arrival of Columbus.

BOOKS FOR STUDENTS

*Adams, Simon. *The Middle Ages: A.D. 456–1450.* Warwick Press, 1990. Reviews medieval times in Africa, the Americas, China, Europe, and the Islamic world.

*Garlake, Peter. *The Kingdoms of Africa.* 2nd ed. Bedrick Books, 1991. Illustrated exploration of African history.

Waldman, Carl. *Atlas of the North American Indian.* Facts on File, 1989. Examines Native American civilizations.

* for students reading below grade level

MULTIMEDIA MATERIALS

Africa Before the Europeans, 100–1500. Video, 26 min. Landmark Films. Examines pre-1500 civilizations in Africa.

Archaeology: The Process of Discovery. Film, 11 min. University of New Hampshire Audio Visual Center. Illustrates techniques used by archaeologists.

Native Americans: The History of a People, Volume 1. Video, 25 min. Knowledge Unlimited/SSSS. Historical overview of Native Americans before arrival of Europeans.

THEMES IN AMERICAN HISTORY

USE WITH PAGES 2–3

Listed on the right are the themes emphasized in Chapter 1. The questions in boldface type stimulate critical thinking and provide students with an opportunity to discuss the themes within a broadened context. The questions also appear in the pupil's edition on p. 2.

■ CULTURAL DIVERSITY

In what ways might a culture be affected by contact with other cultures? Students might consider the kinds of contact that cultures have with one another. When one culture defeats another in war, the losing side may be forced to adopt the customs of the conquerors. When cultures meet peacefully, each may willingly adopt elements of the other's culture. In either case, contact and exchanges are likely to alter both cultures to some degree.

■ ECONOMIC DEVELOPMENT

How might extensive contact with other societies both benefit and harm a society's economic development? Students may suggest that a society might benefit from contact by gaining needed items through trade or by acquiring new skills or technologies. However, if the society becomes totally dependent on trade for too many items, it might have difficulty sustaining its own economic development.

■ TECHNOLOGY AND SOCIETY

What impact might technological advances have on trade and exploration? Students might suggest that new technologies could lead to better forms of transportation and navigation. These changes, in turn, could make it possible for traders and explorers to travel into previously inaccessible or unknown places.

CHAPTER STRATEGIES FOR MEETING INDIVIDUAL NEEDS

LIMITED ENGLISH PROFICIENT LEARNERS

Organize students in small groups and assign each group a section from the chapter. Have groups develop definitions for the Preview Workshop terms for their section. Then ask groups to write sentences and draw sketches, using each term. Have groups share their work with the class.

TACTILE/KINESTHETIC LEARNERS

Guide students to work in groups to make large wall maps showing the major geographic movements—migrations, trade routes, cultural diffusion— discussed in the chapter.

LEARNERS HAVING DIFFICULTY

After students have read the chapter, have them work in pairs, assigning each pair an Essential Point from the chapter. Ask pairs to expand on their topic by writing brief explanations or creating visuals. Have pairs share their explanations or visuals.

AUDITORY LEARNERS

Suggest that students work individually or in groups to prepare (and tape-record, if possible) a dramatic reading on one of the major events discussed in the chapter. Have students present their readings to the class.

VISUAL LEARNERS

Have students work in small groups to develop illustrated time lines. Time lines should consist of four sections—one each for the Americas, Africa, Asia, and Europe—and should include events discussed in this chapter.

GIFTED LEARNERS

Ask students to research and write an essay comparing the religious practices, political structures, social organizations, or economic systems of two cultures discussed in the chapter.

USING THE CHAPTER FOCUS

■ **UNDERSTANDING THE MAIN IDEA**

Call on a volunteer to read the Understanding the Main Idea paragraph aloud. Then ask students to suggest, using a world map, why some early civilizations had little or no contact. *(separated by great distances and physical barriers such as mountain ranges and oceans)* Have students speculate about what developments broke the isolation. *(desire to trade, technological innovations, desire to explore)* List student responses on a flip chart. Have students evaluate their responses after they have completed the chapter.

🎖 **THEMES**
Have students work individually or in small groups to answer the questions under Themes. Save students' responses so that they can compare them with their responses after studying the chapter. (See p. 1B for suggested answers.)

■ **THE TIME LINE**
Have students list the timeline entries in their notebooks. Have students note each entry's significance as they read the chapter. Upon completing the chapter, have students compare notes.

CORE RESOURCES

- **Graphic Organizer 1**
- **Geography Worksheet 1**
- **Outline Maps 1, 2, 3, 7, 8, 11, 12, 13, 14, 17, 19, 20**
- **Building Your Portfolio Worksheet 1**

ABOUT THE ILLUSTRATION

Machu Picchu stands as a testament to the engineering and construction skills of the Incas. The walls of the city's nearly 200 rooms were made of huge granite blocks. No mortar was used to hold these blocks together. Rather, carved ridges and grooves locked the stones to one another. Built in the Andes at an elevation of about 10,000 feet, Machu Picchu may have served as the Incas' last stronghold against the Spanish conquistadors. Ask students how this city might demonstrate the complexity of Incan society.

Chapter 1

Prehistory–1500

THE WORLD BY 1500

▼ **FOCUS**

UNDERSTANDING THE MAIN IDEA

For thousands of years great civilizations rose and fell throughout Europe, Asia, Africa, and the Americas. Some of these civilizations had little or no contact with one another. During the Middle Ages, however, people from diverse cultures increasingly came together to trade goods. By the 1400s the desire for an all-sea route to Asia inspired Europeans to explore beyond the frontiers of their known world.

🎖 **THEMES**

■ **CULTURAL DIVERSITY**
In what ways might a culture be affected by contact with other cultures?

■ **ECONOMIC DEVELOPMENT** How might extensive contact with other societies both benefit and harm a society's economic development?

■ **TECHNOLOGY AND SOCIETY** What impact might technological advances have on trade and exploration?

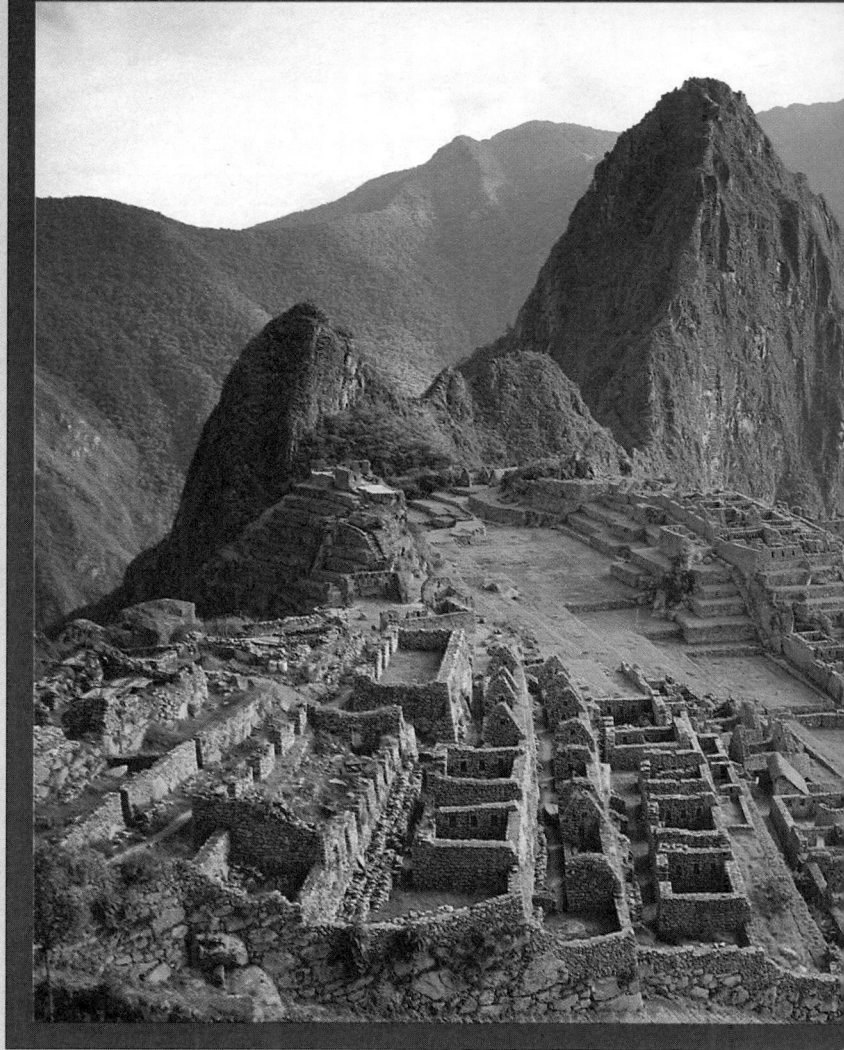

c.3500	c.1000 B.C.	A.D. 610	1096	1324	1498
▼ Rise of farming in desert Southwest.	▼ Kush founded.	▼ Muhammad founds Islam.	▼ Crusades begin.	▼ Mansa Mūsā makes pilgrimage to Mecca.	▼ Vasco da Gama sails to India.

LINK TO THE FUTURE

On a large wall map of the world, point out the world known to Europeans, Asians, and Africans in the mid-1400s and the world known to peoples of the Americas in the same period. Then suggest that students speculate on what developments might bring about greater interaction between these two "worlds" and what impact this interaction might have on them both.

LINK TO THE FUTURE

World maps of the 1400s showed only three continents—Africa, Asia, and Europe. Many Europeans had some idea of the geography of Africa and Asia and had probably heard fabulous stories about the continents' riches. Likewise, many Africans and Asians knew of each other and of Europeans. Until the late 1400s, however, few knew that two other inhabited landmasses—the Americas—existed.

Incan ruins at Machu Picchu, Peru

*T*his chapter may seem an odd way to begin an American history book. Why discuss the Ice Age hunters who crossed from Asia to North America tens of thousands of years ago? Why tell the story of their descendants, who wove a tapestry of Native American cultures over two continents? Why examine Europe, Asia, and Africa during the Middle Ages?

We start in prehistory, before the time of written records, because American history is more than a chronicle of wars, laws, politics, and economic changes. It is the story of a continent and its people and their rich cultures. That story begins with the Ice Age hunters—the first Americans—and their Native American descendants.

We focus on Europe, Asia, and Africa in the Middle Ages in order to understand what drove early explorers into the unknown. In 1492, Europe was at the dawn of a new age, ready to break free of its geographic isolation. As Europeans reached out beyond their borders, they met Asians and Africans engaged in trade. The desire to share in this trade launched Europeans on a remarkable journey of exploration that eventually brought them to the shores of the Americas.

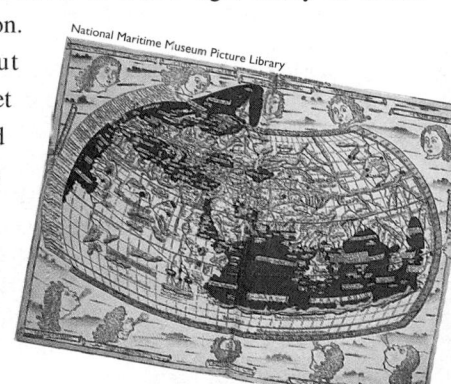

National Maritime Museum Picture Library

World map published in 1486

CULTURAL PATTERNS

Incan communities such as Machu Picchu tended to be highly organized. The basic unit of Incan social organization was the *ayllu,* a kinship group whose members descended from a common ancestor and married within the group. The Incas considered a common heritage and common language to be very important to maintaining a stable community. Today, the Incan language, *Quechua,* is still spoken by five sixths of the residents of the central Andes region.

Chapter 1

SECTION 1

Introducing the Section

FOCUS OBJECTIVES

- Identify when and how the first people arrived in the Americas.

- Describe how the changing environment influenced the first Americans.

- Identify some of the effects of the Agricultural Revolution.

- Explain what the five themes of geography explore.

BUILDING VOCABULARY

The prefix *paleo,* often used in terms that refer to things prehistoric is derived from *palaiós,* a Greek word meaning "old" or "ancient."

CORE RESOURCES

- **Section 1 Daily Quiz**

AV RESOURCES

- **Linking Geography and History Transparencies** and **Worksheets 1, 2**

4

PREVIEW WORKSHOP

Following is a list of the significant places and terms in this section. You may wish to use this list as a section preview.

Places
- Beringia

Terms
- Paleo-Indians
- environment
- hunter-gatherers
- domestication
- cultural diffusion
- subsistence farming

MOTIVATING: STUDENT EXPERIENCES

Call on volunteers to use their own experiences to give brief physical descriptions of their neighborhoods and cities, or of regions of North America they have visited. Then, as students read this section, have them compare these descriptions to the depiction of North America prior to the arrival of Europeans.

Section 1

PEOPLING THE AMERICAS

FOCUS

- **When and how did the first people arrive in the Americas?**
- **How did the changing environment influence the first Americans?**
- **What were some of the effects of the Agricultural Revolution?**
- **What do the five themes of geography explore?**

*L**ong after Europe, Africa, and Asia were populated, the American continents remained empty of human life. From the frozen lands of the Arctic to the southernmost tip of South America, no human voice had ever echoed through the wilderness; no human foot had ever left a print in the soil. Sometime during the last Ice Age, however, men and women began crossing from Asia into North America. Over time, they spread throughout the Americas, adopting ways of life that were suitable to the environments they found.*

Prehistoric rock carving of hunter, found in Michigan

THE FIRST AMERICANS

Most archaeologists—the scientists who study the remains of past cultures—agree that the first people who discovered the vast American wilderness came from Asia during the last Ice Age, when glaciers, or thick sheets of ice, covered much of northern Asia, North America, and Europe. The glaciers locked up so much of the world's water that the sea level dropped by several hundred feet. This drop in sea level exposed a wide land bridge—**Beringia**—between Siberia and what is now Alaska. The first Americans, whom

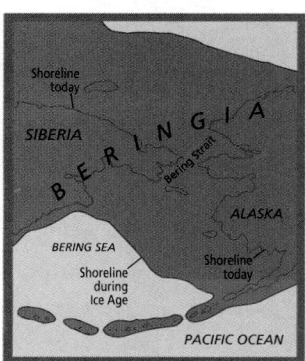

▼ **Beringia land bridge**

(map labels: Shoreline today, SIBERIA, BERINGIA, Bering Strait, ALASKA, BERING SEA, Shoreline during Ice Age, Shoreline today, PACIFIC OCEAN)

archaeologists call **Paleo-Indians**, probably followed animal herds across Beringia to their new home in North America.

Archaeologists do not know exactly when—or in how many waves—these men and women came to North America. Estimates place the date for the first arrivals between 12,000 and 50,000 years ago. Nor do scientists know whether the migration ended when the glaciers began to melt around 10,000 years ago. Some archaeologists believe that when the land bridge disappeared beneath the rising waters of the Bering Strait, Asian immigrants paddled to America in skin boats or wooden dugouts or walked across the ice in winter.

Why is it not possible to talk with certainty about the Paleo-Indians? With no written records to guide them, archaeologists must rely on human and animal remains and on artifacts such as weapons, tools, pots, and jewelry for clues. The methods for analyzing these clues are not precise. Thus,

Teaching the Section

THE FIRST AMERICANS

Call on volunteers to describe the arrival of the first Americans: who they were; where they came from; when and how they came; and what they found. Record responses on the chalkboard for the class. Have students use a large wall map to point out locations, routes, and so on, that they mention.

MIGRATION ROUTES

Point out that as they migrated from Beringia, the first Americans probably followed mountain ranges and river valleys throughout the Americas. Provide students with outline maps of the Americas, and have them use atlases to mark on the maps possible migration routes taken by the first Americans. Have students compare their maps with the map in the America's Geography feature on pp. 34–35.

scholars can paint a broad picture of Paleo-Indian cultures, but details are often beyond their grasp.

■■ **Most scholars agree that during the last Ice Age, the first Americans crossed from Asia to North America by way of a land bridge called Beringia.**

LIFE IN A NEW LAND

Archaeologists have learned that the Paleo-Indians brought with them skills that were well suited to the **environment**, or physical surroundings, of their new homeland. They knew how to make fire and how to find food and shelter in a harsh environment.

The Paleo-Indians were **hunter-gatherers** who stalked whatever game their stone-tipped weapons could kill—bears, bison, and other mammals. The animals provided them with food as well as with furs and skins for clothing. In the few weeks of summer, when the vegetation of the tundra briefly flourished, the Paleo-Indians gathered roots, berries, and other edible plants. Like other hunter-gatherers, they lived as nomads, moving from place to place in search of food. They camped in caves or beneath rock overhangs on the vast treeless plains of the tundra.

The changing environment. Sometime between 10,000 and 5000 B.C., the climate of the Americas grew hotter and drier. This climatic change dramatically transformed the landscape, leaving the continents much as they must have appeared to the first European explorers (see map on page 6). Conifers—evergreen trees such as pine, fir, and spruce—and broadleaf trees—such as oak, hickory, and maple—eventually covered much of North America east of the Mississippi River. In what is today southern Florida, lush swamp vegetation thrived.

Much of the area between the Mississippi River and the Rocky Mountains became meadowland where tall prairie grasses and flowers grew, broken in places by cottonwood trees marking courses of rivers. Closer to the mountains, meadows gave way to the flat, treeless lands of the Great Plains. The Rockies, a snow-covered range with peaks rising more than 10,000 feet, marked the western edge of the Great Plains.

▼ Fern fossil

Coniferous and broadleaf forests spread over much of the land between the foothills of the Rockies westward to the Pacific coast. Giant fir trees, some soaring more than 150 feet above the ground, grew in the north. To the south, in present-day northern California, there were forests of redwoods, with some trees as large as 30 feet in diameter and as tall as a 30-story building.

Farther south, the coastal forests gave way to scrub forests of small trees and bushes. This landscape contrasted starkly with the bare desert of what is today the southwestern United States and northern Mexico. There, only cacti, sparse grasses, and small hardy plants could survive in the dry climate.

Tropical forests dominated the landscape of present-day southern Mexico and Central America as well as northern and eastern South America. Flat grasslands covered much of central South America, giving way in the far west to a vast stretch of scrub forest and desert. Cutting through this region were the majestic Andes Mountains, with peaks reaching 20,000 feet and foothills rising higher than the Appalachian Mountains of eastern North America.

Cultural adaptations. As the climate changed, groups of Paleo-Indians slowly moved south. In a migration that took many thousands of years, they spread throughout the Americas.

▲ Fish fossil

MAKING CONNECTIONS

Science

Scholars employ a number of scientific techniques to study prehistory. For example, carbon dating, a commonly used procedure to determine the age of an object, combines principles of biology and chemistry. All living things contain radiocarbons. After an organism dies, radiocarbons break down and are released at a constant and uniform rate. By measuring how much radiocarbon remains in a bone fragment, piece of wood, or other organic substance, scientists can date objects that are up to around 75,000 years old.

𝒯eaching the 𝒮ection

ENVIRONMENTAL INFLUENCES

Using a physical wall map of the Americas or the **Linking Geography and History Transparency 1**, point to various regions mentioned in the section, and call on volunteers to describe the environment that Paleo-Indians would have found in each region around 5000 B.C. Then call on other volunteers to speculate about how each of these environments might have influenced how the first Americans lived.

Map Caption Answer
tundra, coniferous forest, mixed forest

CULTURAL PATTERNS

Archaeologists note that as Paleo-Indians moved throughout the Americas, they adapted their tools to suit their surroundings. This led to regional differences. Paleo-Indians living in forest environments, for instance, developed strong axes, while those living on the open plains fashioned bows and arrows to kill the game they could stalk only from a distance.

AV **TRANSPARENCY**

Linking Geography and History Transparency and **Worksheet 1**

Americas Landscape Map

CLIMATE The type of vegetation that is found in a region depends largely on its climate.

? **PLACE** Which vegetation regions found in North America are not widely found in South America?

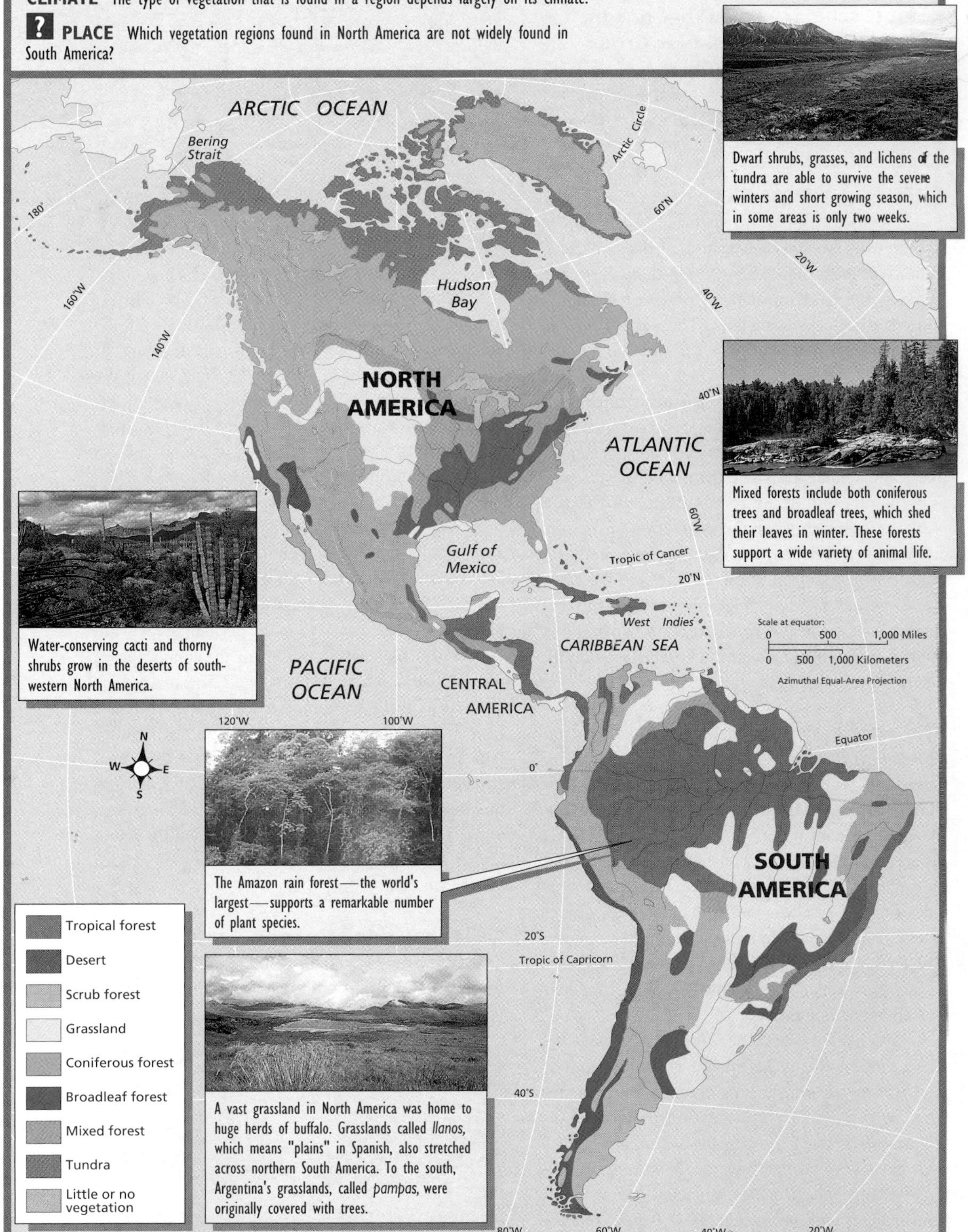

ARCTIC OCEAN
Bering Strait
Arctic Circle
180°
160°W
140°W
60°N
40°W
20°W
Hudson Bay
NORTH AMERICA
40°N
ATLANTIC OCEAN
60°W
Gulf of Mexico
Tropic of Cancer
20°N
West Indies
CARIBBEAN SEA
PACIFIC OCEAN
CENTRAL AMERICA
120°W
100°W
Equator
0°
20°S
Tropic of Capricorn
SOUTH AMERICA
40°S
80°W
60°W
40°W
20°W

Dwarf shrubs, grasses, and lichens of the tundra are able to survive the severe winters and short growing season, which in some areas is only two weeks.

Mixed forests include both coniferous trees and broadleaf trees, which shed their leaves in winter. These forests support a wide variety of animal life.

Water-conserving cacti and thorny shrubs grow in the deserts of southwestern North America.

The Amazon rain forest—the world's largest—supports a remarkable number of plant species.

A vast grassland in North America was home to huge herds of buffalo. Grasslands called *llanos*, which means "plains" in Spanish, also stretched across northern South America. To the south, Argentina's grasslands, called *pampas*, were originally covered with trees.

Scale at equator:
0   500   1,000 Miles
0   500   1,000 Kilometers
Azimuthal Equal-Area Projection

N W E S

Tropical forest
Desert
Scrub forest
Grassland
Coniferous forest
Broadleaf forest
Mixed forest
Tundra
Little or no vegetation

THE AGRICULTURAL REVOLUTION

On the chalkboard draw the outline of a cause-and-effect diagram titled *Agricultural Revolution.* Ask volunteers to list the effects of the Agricultural Revolution. Fill in the diagram with their responses. *(domestication→settlement→division of labor→social classes)* Then organize students into small groups and have groups illustrate each effect with an appropriate visual image.

GEOGRAPHY'S FIVE THEMES

Ask students to suggest examples of how each of the five themes of geography is illustrated in this section. *(for example, the migration of Paleo-Indians across Beringia as an example of movement)* Note their responses on the chalkboard. Then ask students to write five sentences—one for each theme—explaining how the themes help scholars understand life in prehistoric America.

▶

These men and women found lands rich in wildlife. Water from the melting glaciers had formed fast-flowing rivers and huge lakes teeming with fish. Musk-oxen, reindeer, mammoths, and giant bison roamed the vast lowland regions, while the hills and mountains abounded with saber-toothed tigers, mountain lions, and bears.

Many of the Paleo-Indians throughout North America and Central America hunted with spears armed with stone tips called Clovis points. Named after Clovis, New Mexico, where archaeologists first found them, these points were more effective against large game than earlier spear tips. Abundant wildlife and an effective method of hunting provided a plentiful and reliable supply of food for the Paleo-Indians.

Eventually the mammoths and other big game died out, perhaps hunted to extinction. Consequently, the Paleo-Indians had to develop new skills to help them adjust to the changing environment. The men and women of the eastern woodlands, for example, burned large areas of forest to make it easier to spot and track small game such as rabbit and deer. They also broadened their food-gathering activities to include trapping fish and birds and collecting a wider variety of plants.

■■ **The Paleo-Indians responded to the changing environment by adapting their hunting and gathering methods.**

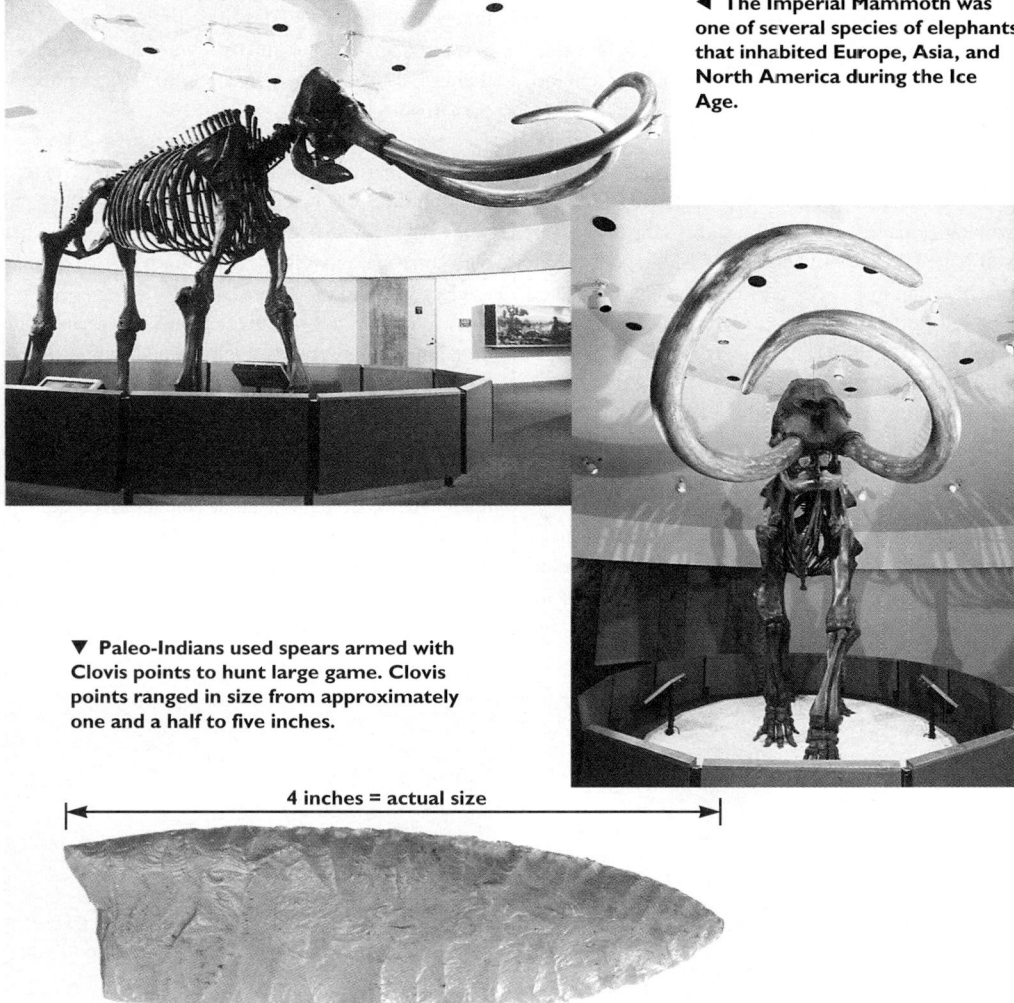

◀ **The Imperial Mammoth was one of several species of elephants that inhabited Europe, Asia, and North America during the Ice Age.**

▼ **Paleo-Indians used spears armed with Clovis points to hunt large game. Clovis points ranged in size from approximately one and a half to five inches.**

◀———— 4 inches = actual size ————▶

Practice

GUIDED PRACTICE

Organize students into small groups. Ask groups to use the five themes of geography to organize information about the Paleo-Indians into a chart. Suggest that groups present and compare their charts in prepara-tion for an individual writing assignment based upon them.

INDEPENDENT PRACTICE

Ask students to choose one of the themes from their chart and write a poem that illus-trates the connection between the history of the first Americans and a geographic theme.

Review and Assessment

REVIEW Have students write a brief pas-sage explaining why and how Paleo-Indian cultures changed over time. Call on volun-teers to read their paragraphs aloud. Then assign the Section 1 Review on p. 9.

ASSESS Assign the **Section 1 Daily Quiz** in *Core Resources.*

GLOBAL CONNECTIONS

Archaeologists offer many theories on the worldwide origins of domestication. One theory holds that the first groups to shift from hunting and gathering to domestication were those living in environmentally diverse areas rich in wild plants and animals. Over time, these groups moved from managing their wild food sources to actively domesticating them. Domes-tication then spread from these environmentally di-verse areas to less diverse areas as population pres-sures and crop failures forced people to move.

HISTORICAL SIDELIGHTS

Agriculture

Evidence suggests that the earliest domesticated plant in Mesoamerica, and in the Andes region, was the bot-tle gourd. Unsuitable for eating, it was used as a con-tainer and as a float for fish-nets. Scientists suggest that Mesoamericans experiment-ed with the cultivation of food plants such as beans, squash, pumpkins, chili peppers, and maize.

AV **TRANSPARENCY**

Linking Geography and History Transparency and **Worksheet 2**

THE AGRICULTURAL REVOLUTION

The most revolutionary change made by Paleo-Indians, however, was the shift from hunting and gathering to the **domestication**, or adaptation and control, of plants and animals. This shift occurred worldwide as the big game died out, first in Africa, Asia, and Europe, and finally in the Americas.

Some historians speculate that the first peo-ple to move from gathering seeds to planting them in the ground were women. Because women did the bulk of gathering in hunter-gatherer societies, they were the most familiar with plants and the most likely to notice that the seeds that fell to the ground sprouted new plants.

Archaeologists continue to debate the dates for the spread of agriculture, but they generally believe that people in southwestern Asia had domesticated wheat and barley by 8000 B.C. and that those in southeastern Asia were growing rice by about 6000 B.C. No one knows exactly when the first Americans turned to farming, but archaeolo-gists have found evidence that by 8000 B.C. com-munities in Mexico were growing maize (corn), and by 2000 B.C. people in the Andes region were growing potatoes. By 1500 B.C. farming was well established throughout much of Mexico, Central America, and the Andes region.

Farther to the north, the people of the desert Southwest began farming around 3500 B.C. Archaeologists believe that the desert people learned about farming techniques from their south-ern neighbors. The process of spreading cultural practices or beliefs from one group to another is called **cultural diffusion**.

Cultivating crops and domesticating animals transformed life and made it possible for human populations to increase. As people settled down to grow their own food, small villages formed. At

▲ The corn we eat today (left) evolved from smaller, earlier hybrids. The five cobs at the right were excavated from Bat Cave, Mexico, and date from as far back as 2000 B.C. to around A.D. 250.

first most people practiced **subsistence farming**— growing just enough crops for survival. Over time, though, many groups developed techniques—such as using animals to pull plows—that increased their food production. As a result, village popula-tions rose.

As populations grew, villages gave way to cities. The first cities appeared in southwestern Asia about 3500 B.C. Over the next few thousand years, this "urban revolution" took place in other parts of Asia as well as in northern Africa, south-ern Europe, and the Americas.

With the rise of cities came a more elaborate division of labor. Some men farmed, while others became artisans, soldiers, laborers, merchants, scholars, physicians, priests, and government offi-cials. Women took on such important tasks as spin-ning, weaving, baking, and raising children. As a result, the basic equality that characterized hunter-gatherer and simple farming societies gave way to the development of social classes. In most societies men became more powerful than women; and the small number of priests, government officials, and

► Paleo-Indians ground maize on stone slabs, or *metates.*

RETEACH Organize students into four groups and assign each group one of the Focus questions on p. 4. Have group members discuss and write an answer to their question. Ask group representatives to share their answers with the other groups.

Closure

Have students work in small groups to design a museum exhibit titled *Peopling the Americas.* Suggest that they divide the exhibit into four sections: *The Arrival of the First Americans, Early Life-styles, Environmental Changes and Changes in Life-style, The Agricultural Revolution.* Have students present their exhibit plans.

Extension

CREATE Have students create maps showing North American archaeological sites that provide evidence of the historical stages covered in the section. Maps should include descriptive captions for each site.

INVESTIGATE Suggest that students research and report on a dating method used by archaeologists, such as radiocarbon or stratigraphic dating.

successful merchants became more powerful than the masses of farmers, laborers, and artisans.

■■ **The Agricultural Revolution led to the rise of cities, an elaborate division of labor, and the development of social classes.**

HISTORY AND GEOGRAPHY

Many terms in this section may seem better suited to a geography book. But history and geography are closely linked. History describes the events that make up the human story from the earliest times to the present day. Geography, especially the branch called cultural geography, describes how physical environments influence human events and how human beings affect their surroundings. Therefore, to present the unfolding drama of people and events without placing them in their physical settings is to tell only part of the story. Geographers have developed a number of themes to help them organize information. Five common themes are location, place, human-environment interaction, movement, and region.

Location describes a site's position and can be expressed in two ways: absolute location and relative location. *Absolute location* describes the exact point on the earth that a site occupies. It is most often presented in terms of latitude and longitude. The absolute location of Chicago, for example, is 41°52′ north latitude and 87°37′ west longitude. *Relative location,* on the other hand,

describes the position of a site in relation to other sites. Chicago's relative location might be given as the southwest shore of Lake Michigan or as about 355 miles south-southeast of Minneapolis.

Place refers to the physical features and human influences that define a site and make it different from other areas. Physical features include landscape, climate, and vegetation. Human influences include land use, architecture, and population size.

Human-environment interaction deals with all the ways in which people interact with their natural environments, such as clearing forests, irrigating the land, and building cities. This theme is especially important to the study of history since it shows how people shape and are shaped by their surroundings.

Movement describes the way people interact as they travel, communicate, and trade goods and services. Movement includes human migration as well as the exchange of goods and ideas.

To better study and understand the earth, geographers divide it into *regions.* Geographers might distinguish one region from another by comparing physical characteristics, such as landforms or climate, or by comparing cultural features like dominant languages or religions.

■■ **The geographic themes of location, place, human-environment interaction, movement, and region explore the interplay between people and their environment.**

SECTION REVIEW ANSWERS

IDENTIFY

For significance, see the following pages:
Paleo-Indians (p. 4)
environment (p. 5)
hunter-gatherers (p. 5)
domestication (p. 8)
cultural diffusion (p. 8)
subsistence farming (p. 8)

LOCATE

For location, see the map on p. 4.

1. *during the last Ice Age (12,000–50,000 years ago); crossed from Asia to North America by way of Beringia*
2. *migrated south; adapted their hunting and gathering methods to new locations*
3. *location, place, human-environment interaction, movement, region; explore interplay between people and their environment*
4. *Paragraphs should mention that the Agricultural Revolution led to rise of cities, elaborate division of labor, and formation of social classes.*
5. *More successful hunting with Clovis points led to short supply of big game, larger population, and new methods of tracking animals and gathering food.*

■■ **S E C T I O N 1 R E V I E W**

IDENTIFY and explain the significance of the following: Paleo-Indians, environment, hunter-gatherers, domestication, cultural diffusion, subsistence farming.

LOCATE and explain the importance of the following: Beringia.

1. **MAIN IDEA** According to most scholars, when might the first people have arrived in the Americas? What route did they probably follow?

2. **MAIN IDEA** How did the Paleo-Indians respond to the changing environment?

3. **LINKING HISTORY AND GEOGRAPHY** What are the five themes of geography? How do they help explain historical events?

4. **WRITING TO EXPLAIN** Write a paragraph explaining how the Agricultural Revolution changed the structure of ancient societies.

5. **EVALUATING** How did the development of the Clovis point alter the culture of the Paleo-Indians?

Following is a list of the significant people, places, and terms in this section. You may wish to use this list as a section preview.

People
- Olmecs
- Mayas
- Toltecs
- Aztecs

- Incas
- Anasazi

Places
- Mexico
- Guatemala
- Tikal
- Tenochtitlán
- Peru
- Cuzco

- Cahokia

Terms
- Mesoamerica
- glyph

FOCUS OBJECTIVES

- Outline the characteristics of the Aztec and Incan cultures.

- Explain why there was so much variation among early North American cultures.

- Discuss why some scholars believe that there was contact between the Americas and other cultures before the late 1400s.

CULTURAL PATTERNS

Most Native American peoples originally gave themselves names that meant "people," or "human beings." The names by which Native American peoples call themselves usually differ from the names given to them by others. The name *Navajo*, for example, is the Spanish name for one tribe whose members prefer to call themselves *Dinneh*. Likewise the name *Hopi* is an English mispronunciation of the tribal name *Hopiti*.

CORE RESOURCES

- **Geography Worksheet 1**
- **Section 2 Daily Quiz**

AV RESOURCES

- **Linking Geography and History Transparency and Worksheet 3**

Section 2

NATIVE AMERICAN CULTURES

FOCUS
- **What were the characteristics of the Aztec and Incan cultures?**
- **Why was there so much variation among early North American cultures?**
- **Why do some scholars believe that there was contact between the Americas and other cultures before the late 1400s?**

*B*y 1200 B.C. the Native American societies that would one day intrigue European explorers were already forming. In Central America and South America, advanced farming societies created beautiful cities that were home to tens of thousands of people. Farther north, in what is now the southwestern United States, farmers built impressive cliff dwellings high above the desert floor. Over much of North America the abundance of wild animals and plants enabled large groups to support themselves through hunting, fishing, and gathering or by combining these activities with farming.

Toltec-carved figurine of plumed serpent Quetzalcoatl

VARIED CULTURES

Historians do not know how many people lived in the Americas before the arrival of Christopher Columbus in 1492. Population estimates for the late 1400s range from 8.4 million to 112.5 million. Historians do know, however, that the areas where the Agricultural Revolution had first taken hold—Mexico, Central America, and the Andes region—supported the largest populations. More than half the population of the Western Hemisphere may have lived in these regions.

Today it is common to refer to the early people of the Americas and their descendants as *Native Americans* or *American Indians*. They did not, however, consider themselves a single people. By the 1400s there were probably over 650 groups living in the Americas, each with a distinct culture and language.

THE CULTURES OF MESOAMERICA

Central America and the southern and central regions of Mexico—the area archaeologists call **Mesoamerica**, or Middle America—was home to some of the largest of the early cultures. It is estimated that at its height the region boasted a population of some 25 million who shared a common cultural heritage.

The Olmecs and the Mayas. The first great Mesoamerican culture was that of the Olmecs, who thrived on the fertile coastal lowlands along the Gulf of Mexico from about 1200 to 400 B.C. Historians call it the mother culture of Mesoamerica because it so strongly influenced later societies.

Like the Mesoamerican people who followed them, the Olmecs were farmers. They practiced

MOTIVATING: PRIOR KNOWLEDGE

Write the following on the chalkboard: *Environment→Way of Life*. Have volunteers recall the ways in which the environment influenced how early Americans lived. Write their responses on the chalkboard. Direct students to copy the list and, as they read the section, note which items on their lists apply to the cultures discussed.

Teaching the Section

WELLSPRING OF CULTURES

Suggest that students work individually or in pairs to design an illustrated chart that shows the major features of Olmec culture and that also indicates Olmec influence on other Mesoamerican cultures. Explain that the completed work should illustrate why the Olmec civilization is called the "Mother Culture" of Mesoamerica. Students may wish to include their illustrated charts in their portfolios.

▲ The Olmecs carved these jade and serpentine figures and buried them at La Venta. The figures were found in this arrangement.

slash-and-burn agriculture: toward the end of the dry season, the Olmecs cut down and burned sections of the jungle. Then, before the rainy season came, they planted maize, beans, chili peppers, and squash in the ash-enriched soil.

Olmec farms usually surrounded a large ceremonial center where priests, government officials, merchants, and artisans lived. The ceremonial center included a raised courtyard on which stood a pyramid of packed earth. Olmec priests probably used the mound as a place of worship. Monuments at these centers also included large stone heads—believed to portray Olmec rulers.

Excavations of Olmec sites have revealed that the Olmecs worshipped many gods—who were usually portrayed with a combination of human and animal features—and that the Olmec played a form of the sacred ball game, which became an important feature of later Mesoamerican civilizations. They also developed the beginnings of a calendar and writing.

About 400 B.C., for reasons that are unclear to archaeologists, the Olmec civilization began to fade. However, the Olmec way of life had influenced others in Mesoamerica. The Mayas, who rose to prominence about A.D. 300, were probably the direct descendants of the Olmecs. The Maya flourished for more than 500 years, primarily in present-day Mexico and Guatemala.

The Mayas improved upon the Olmecs' accomplishments. Mayan astronomers developed a calendar that was more accurate than the one used in Europe. Mayan mathematicians devised a number system that included zero long before Europeans adopted the concept from the Arabs.

Mayan scholars developed a form of **glyph**, or picture, writing that included ideograms—characters that represented ideas—and phonograms—characters that represented words or syllables.

The Mayas also improved upon Olmec farming techniques. For example, they developed an intricate water-management system that ensured a steady supply of water even during the dry season. This allowed the Mayas to produce more food and support a larger population. In Guatemala the great ceremonial center Tikal (ti-KAHL)—with its six magnificent temple-pyramids and more than 3,000 other structures—is believed to have been home to some 100,000 people.

By about A.D. 900, however, the Mayas had abandoned Tikal and their other cities. Over time they merged with other cultures in the area. As with the Olmec, archaeologists are unsure why the Mayan civilization declined.

The Toltecs and the Aztecs. In the century before the Mayas' decline, invading groups from the north descended upon the Valley of Mexico. About A.D. 900, one of these groups, the Toltecs (TOHL-teks), came to dominate the area. Adopting the customs of the peoples they conquered, the Toltecs built a great city-state at Tula in central Mexico. Under the leadership of a warrior class, the Toltecs gradually extended their domain. During the 12th century, however, internal conflicts weakened the Toltec empire. As a result, it soon fell to invading groups from the north.

▼ This photograph shows part of the ruins of the ancient Toltec city of Tula in the present-day state of Hidalgo, Mexico. The inset shows one of the pillars atop the ruin.

MAKING CONNECTIONS

Anthropology

No one knows for sure why the Mayas abandoned their cities, but archaeologists have offered a variety of theories. Most theories center on some crisis befalling the Mayan people. Among the suggested crises are a peasant revolt against the priests and nobles, a fatal epidemic, crop failures resulting from climatic changes, food shortages brought on by rapid population growth, and foreign invasion or prolonged warfare.

Teaching the *Section*

INCAS AND AZTECS

Ask students to write on index cards one question—and answer—concerning either the Aztec or the Incan culture. Encourage students to write questions that compare or contrast these cultures. Collect the index cards and organize students into four teams. Ask the questions and have teams compete to provide answers.

HISTORICAL SIDELIGHTS

Aztec Agriculture

The Aztecs practiced farming on *chinampas*—artificial islands made of reeds anchored at the bottom of the lake, then piled high with earth and fertilizer. These "floating gardens" yielded rich crops of vegetables and flowers.

HISTORICAL SIDELIGHTS

Terrace Farming

The Incas greatly increased the land available for planting by constructing terraces, or flat ledges cut into hillsides and held in place by stone walls. Terraces consisted of a base of compost covered with soil and fertilizer. The Incas cultivated an array of crops—squash, beans, corn, avocados, peppers, peanuts, tomatoes, and potatoes—on these terraces.

HISTORICAL SIDELIGHTS

Incan Accounting Methods

The Incas kept accounts with a *quipu,* a series of knotted strings attached to a larger cord. Each knot on a string indicated a particular amount. The Incas used *quipus* to record everything from personal wealth to population statistics.

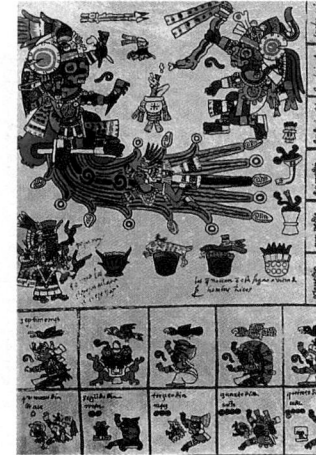

▲ **Aztecs created artwork with colorful figures and glyphs, such as this piece depicting the rain god Tlaloc.**

The conquerors of the Toltecs fought among themselves until one group, the Aztecs, emerged victorious. Although they were a warrior society, the Aztecs, or Mexicas, as they called themselves, settled down and adopted the ways of the local people. They built their capital, Tenochtitlán (tay-nawch-tee-TLAHN)—the site of present-day Mexico City—on an island in Lake Texcoco (tay-SKOH-koh). Eventually Tenochtitlán grew into a magnificent city with hundreds of buildings, an elaborate system of canals, and an estimated population of 300,000.

Warfare continued to dominate Aztec life. Huge, well-trained Aztec armies conquered neighboring kingdoms. Over a period of two centuries, the Aztecs gained control of an empire of five million people. The Aztecs demanded tribute in gold, silver, and precious stones from those they conquered. They also took thousands of captives as sacrifices to their war god, Huitzilopochtli (wee-tsee-loh-POHCH-tlee).

Human sacrifice was central to the Aztec religion. The Aztecs believed that the world had been destroyed four times, each time by the death of a sun. To keep the present sun from dying, the Aztecs sacrificed captives to nourish it. By the time of the Spanish conquest in the early 1500s, thousands of prisoners had been sacrificed on Tenochtitlán's altars.

*T*HE INCAS OF SOUTH AMERICA

As the cultures of Mesoamerica were developing, similar advances were taking place in South America. Farming cultures arose on the Pacific coastal plains, in the high valleys of the Andes, and along the upper Amazon. By the mid-1400s one group, the Incas, had gained control of the whole region.

The Incan state, based in the capital city of Cuzco (KOO-skoh), high in the Andes, was founded in the 11th century. Around 1440, the Incas began

a great campaign of expansion and conquest. Within 35 years the Incas controlled an immense realm that covered much of present-day Chile, Peru, Bolivia, and Ecuador. Until the arrival of the Spanish, it was the largest empire in the Americas—with an estimated six to nine million people who spoke more than 20 languages.

Unlike the Aztecs, the Incas did not force their subjects to pay tribute, but they did require their labor. With this labor they filled their armies and built palaces, temples, bridges, and the thousands of miles of roads that linked their empire.

Like many other advanced agricultural societies, Incan society was organized into strict social classes. The working class—the farmers, laborers, and artisans—made up the bulk of Incan society. Above them was the noble class— priests, teachers, military leaders, and government officials. At the top was the supreme ruler, the "Sapa Inca," who represented the Sun God.

Incan silver llama with gold trim

▪▪ **The Incas of South America, like their contemporaries the Aztecs of Mesoamerica, were empire builders.**

*E*ARLY CULTURES OF NORTH AMERICA

The population of North America was too small and spread over too large an area to support societies of the size found in Mesoamerica and South America. Few groups north of Mesoamerica numbered more than a few thousand people. But because tribes living in the same region made similar adaptations to the environment and often traded with one another, they generally shared many characteristics. For example, peoples in the southwestern region and peoples in the eastern half of the present-day United States developed distinct regional cultures.

Southwestern cultures. Native Americans who settled in the barren hills and deserts of the Southwest began to cultivate maize and other

CULTURAL VARIETY IN NORTH AMERICA

Have students compare the American landscape map on p. 6 with the Native American cultures map on p. 15. Ask students how the physical environment might have influenced the ways of life adopted by people in North America. Note students' suggestions on the chalkboard. Then ask students how this information reflects the general relationship between environment and culture.

▶

Then and Now — SACRED OR SCIENTIFIC SITES?

Early Native Americans practiced a variety of burial customs and rituals to honor their dead. The Navajos, for example, buried treasured possessions with the deceased so that they would be content in their graves and not return to haunt the living. The Hurons placed their dead in mass graves lined with beaver robes and gifts. They believed that mingling their departed relatives' bones encouraged the living to exist in harmony.

Over the years many of these burial sites have been unearthed and even destroyed as bones and artifacts are removed from graves for research. This practice has led to a bitter conflict between some American Indians and the anthropologists and archaeologists doing the digging.

To these researchers, grave sites are windows into history that provide a glimpse of past cultures and clues to changes in peoples' ways of life over time. Researchers argue that studying skeletal remains

and the objects buried with them reveals much about Native American cultures that might otherwise remain unknown. For example, the amulets (charms), prayer sticks, and figurines found buried with the corpses shed light on the religious life of early American Indians. Other objects show the kinds of foods they ate and the utensils they made.

Researchers also argue that analyses of human skeletons can promote medical research. Bones—even those that are centuries old—provide a physical record tracing the development and spread of many diseases. They also show the effects of diet, pollution, and other factors on health. This

▲ **Bowl from a burial site in New Mexico**

information is useful in preventing and treating diseases today. "Indians living today," argues one anthropologist, "stand to benefit from our conclusions."

But to many Native Americans, the burial sites are sacred places not to be disturbed. They believe that excavation of the sites shows a disregard for their cultural traditions. As an attorney for an American Indian tribe in New Mexico asks: "Why single out Indians? Why not dig up everybody's ancestors?"

There is a growing respect for the Native American point of view. Through recent lawsuits, some Native Americans have succeeded in obtaining the return of their ancestors' remains for reburial. They have also successfully applied political pressure to close museum exhibits displaying certain Indian relics. American Indians have been assisted in their efforts by the Native American Grave Protection and Repatriation Act, which Congress passed in 1990. The act requires federally funded museums to grant Indian tribes with the opportunity to retrieve selected items.

crops about 3500 B.C. Their farming methods, pottery styles, and social practices show very strong Mesoamerican influences.

One of these groups was the Anasazi (ahn-uh-SAHZ-ee). Between A.D. 800 and 1100 the Anasazi began to construct multistory rock and adobe dwellings—many nestled against cliffs and some containing as many as 800 rooms. Some of these rooms served as living quarters and others as ceremonial centers, or *kivas.* Spanish explorers

later called these huge buildings *pueblos* (villages). Each pueblo housed not only farmers but also weavers, potters, builders, and storytellers.

Archaeologists believe that a crisis of some kind caused the Anasazi to abandon their communities. By the mid-1400s they had ceased to exist as a distinct people. Researchers believe, however, that the Anasazi were probably the ancestors of the Pueblo Indians, whom the Spanish encountered in the 1500s.

Teaching the Section

THE AMERICAS BY 1500

Organize students into three groups and assign each group one of the following areas: North America, Mesoamerica, South America. Ask groups to design a "Century in Review" page showing the cultural development of their area by 1500. Suggest that they use maps and other illustrations, with captions, for their pages. Display students' finished work on the bulletin board.

EARLY CONTACT

Ask students to list and discuss the different scholarly views concerning the extent of cultural contact between Native American groups and people from Europe, Asia, and Africa prior to the arrival of Columbus.

▲ The Anasazi built their homes against cliffs to provide defense against enemies. These ruins are located in Mesa Verde National Park in Colorado.

Eastern cultures. The Adena and Hopewell cultures of the eastern woodlands and the Mississippian culture of the Southeast combined hunting and gathering with farming to support relatively large populations.

The Adenas and the Hopewells, who dominated the eastern region for about 1,700 years, are often called the Mound Builders because of the distinctive earthworks they created. Originating in the Ohio River Valley about 1000 B.C., the Adenas eventually occupied an area extending from present-day Kentucky to New York. About 300 B.C., however, the Hopewells began to push the Adenas out of the region. The Hopewell culture dominated the area until the more advanced Mississippian culture replaced it about A.D. 700.

Beginning in the lower Mississippi River Valley, the Mississippian culture spread out to occupy much of the Southeast and Midwest. Huge temple mounds, resembling Mesoamerican pyramids, dominated their villages. The largest Mississippian settlement was located at Cahokia (kuh-HOH-kee-uh), near present-day St. Louis. It extended six miles and contained 85 burial and temple mounds, the largest of which covered 16 acres and stood more than 100 feet high.

By A.D. 1200, Cahokia's population may have numbered about 40,000. Its rulers controlled a network of trade routes that stretched from the Great Lakes to the Gulf of Mexico and into Mesoamerica. Perhaps because of climate changes or crop failures, the Mississippians abandoned Cahokia during the 1200s, but their culture continued to flourish elsewhere for several centuries.

■■ **There was great variety in North American cultures, in large part because of the effect the environment had on diet, housing, and social structure.**

*N*ORTH AMERICAN CULTURE AREAS

By the time of European contact, the Native American population of North America was divided into hundreds of different groups—none as large as the earlier mound-building societies. For the purposes of comparison, scholars often organize

▲ The Adenas and Hopewells built elaborate earthen mounds in the shape of animals as burial places for their dead. This aerial photograph shows the Great Serpent Mound, near present-day Hillsboro, Ohio.

Practice

GUIDED PRACTICE

Organize students into five groups to study the following: the Olmecs and Mayas, the Toltecs and Aztecs, the Incas, the southwestern cultures of North America, and the eastern woodland and southeastern cultures of North America. Have each group list the achievements of its assigned cultures. After the groups have finished, work with the class to produce a chart that incorporates the lists and shows each culture in its relative time frame.

INDEPENDENT PRACTICE

Have students use the information on the Guided Practice chart to write a paragraph comparing cultural development in each region.

Review and Assessment

REVIEW Have students work in small groups to develop an outline or a table of contents for a book titled *Native American Cultures*. Ask group members to present and explain their ideas to the class. Then assign the Section 2 Review on p. 16.

ASSESS Assign the **Section 2 Daily Quiz** in *Core Resources.* ▶

AV **TRANSPARENCY**
Linking Geography and History Transparency and **Worksheet 3**

COOPERATIVE LEARNING

Organize the class into eight groups and assign each group one of the North American cultural areas listed on p. 16. Ask groups to create a two-page picture essay on their cultural area. Students should divide tasks—research, design and art, caption writing. Have groups display their work on the bulletin board.

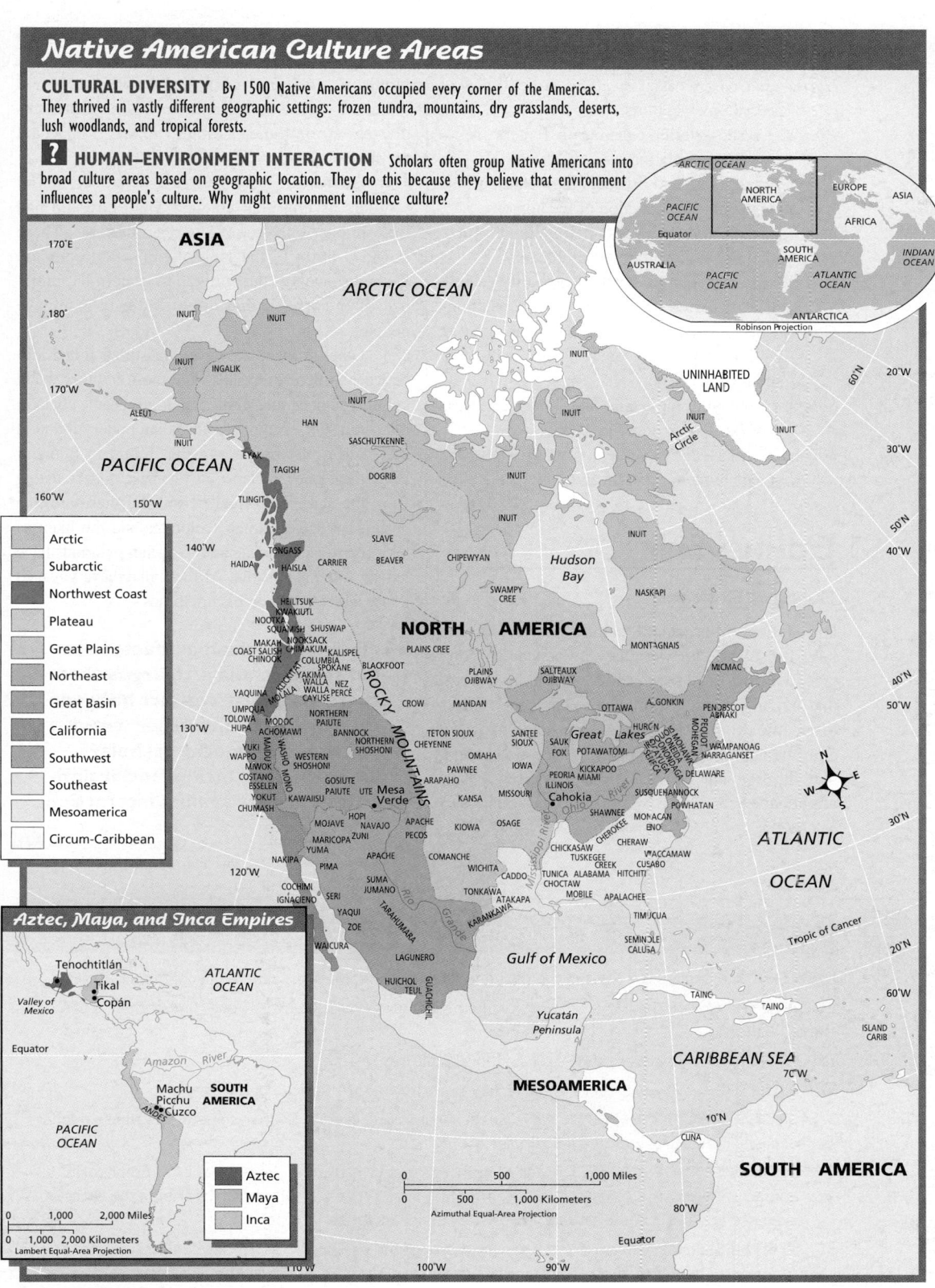

Native American Culture Areas

CULTURAL DIVERSITY By 1500 Native Americans occupied every corner of the Americas. They thrived in vastly different geographic settings: frozen tundra, mountains, dry grasslands, deserts, lush woodlands, and tropical forests.

? **HUMAN–ENVIRONMENT INTERACTION** Scholars often group Native Americans into broad culture areas based on geographic location. They do this because they believe that environment influences a people's culture. Why might environment influence culture?

Legend:
- Arctic
- Subarctic
- Northwest Coast
- Plateau
- Great Plains
- Northeast
- Great Basin
- California
- Southwest
- Southeast
- Mesoamerica
- Circum-Caribbean

Aztec, Maya, and Inca Empires
- Aztec
- Maya
- Inca

RETEACH Refer students to the Essential Point statements in the section. For each Essential Point, have students write a few sentences that provide supporting evidence for the statement. Ask students to share sentences with the group.

Closure

Refer students to the map on p. 15. Ask them to identify the Native American culture areas. Then have them generalize about the life-styles of the early peoples who lived in each region.

Extension

CREATE Encourage students to create a diagram of a typical community in one of the cultures discussed in the section.

RESEARCH Have students work in pairs to research and report on a pre-1500 Native American culture in their state. Encourage students to contact local historical societies and visit museums in their search.

SECTION REVIEW ANSWERS

IDENTIFY

For significance, see the following pages:
Mesoamerica (p. 10)
Olmecs (p. 10)
glyph (p. 11)
Mayas (p. 11)
Toltecs (p. 11)

LOCATE

For locations, see the maps on p. 15 and pp. 1012–1013.

1. *were agricultural societies that built large empires*
2. *The influence of different environments on diet, housing, and social structure led to a variety of cultures.*
3. *Anasazi—similar farming methods, pottery styles, and social practices; Mound Builders—similar architecture*
4. *Reports should mention similar artwork and architecture as evidence of contact.*
5. *Mesoamerica—farmed, built ceremonial centers, developed writing and number systems; South America—farmed, built a vast empire, had strict social classes; eastern North America—hunted, gathered food, farmed, built earthworks; southwestern North America—farmed, built multistory dwellings*

---

these groups into broad cultural areas on the basis of geographical location and shared characteristics:

Northwest Coast: coastal dwellers; fishers; developed complex culture

Plateau: river dwellers; primarily fishers; relatively low population

Great Plains: grassland dwellers; nomadic buffalo hunters after introduction of the horse

Northeast: forest dwellers; primarily hunter-gatherers, but also farmers and fishers

Great Basin: desert basin dwellers; primarily gatherers due to barren surroundings; low population

California: desert, mountain, river, or coastal dwellers depending on location; primarily gatherers and fishers

Southwest: canyon, mountain, and desert dwellers; either farmers or nomadic hunters

Southeast: river-valley dwellers; primarily farmers, but also hunter-gatherers and fishers

COMMENTARY

Cultural Contacts

Did Native Americans develop their varied cultures in isolation, or were they influenced by contacts with the outside world? Most scholars agree that Asians probably continued to cross the Bering Strait into North America for thousands of years after the land bridge disappeared. They also accept that ships plying the Atlantic and Pacific oceans might have been blown by storms to the Americas.

Most scholars also believe that about A.D. 1000, Vikings—Scandinavian people from Sweden, Norway, and Denmark—reached the North American coast at Vinland (most likely present-day Newfoundland, Canada) nearly 500 years before Columbus.

Despite this consensus, however, many scholars assume that contacts were rare and had little impact on Native American cultures. These scholars point to the lack of important common elements, such as the cultivation of corn or similar use of the wheel, that might indicate extensive contact.

Other scholars, however, insist that similarities between American artifacts and those of other world cultures suggest that significant transoceanic contacts did occur. For example, both Indian pottery found in the Pacific Northwest and that found in Ecuador bear striking resemblance to Japanese pottery dating from the same historical period. Furthermore, the designs of some Olmec sculptures and the likeness between Mesoamerican and Egyptian pyramids have led some to suggest that Africans may have voyaged to Mesoamerica in prehistoric times.

■■ **Native American artifacts have led some scholars to argue that there was early contact between the Americas and other world cultures, while other scholars insist that the lack of social similarities argues against interaction.**

SECTION 2 REVIEW

IDENTIFY and explain the significance of the following: Mesoamerica, Olmecs, glyph, Mayas, Toltecs.

LOCATE and explain the importance of the following: Mexico, Guatemala, Tikal, Tenochtitlán, Peru, Cuzco, Cahokia.

1. **MAIN IDEA** How were the Aztec and Incan cultures similar?

2. **MAIN IDEA** Why was there great variety in early North American cultures?

3. **GEOGRAPHY: MOVEMENT** How do the Anasazi and Mound Builder societies provide evidence of the spread of Mesoamerican culture?

4. **WRITING TO DESCRIBE** You are an archaeologist investigating the possibility of prehistoric contact between the Americas and other continents. Write a brief report describing the types of evidence you might look for and how that evidence might be interpreted.

5. **SYNTHESIZING** What were the general traits of the early cultures of Mesoamerica, South America, eastern North America, and southwestern North America?

PREVIEW WORKSHOP

Following is a list of the significant people, places, and terms in this section. You may wish to use this list as a section preview.

People
- Johannes Gutenberg

Places
- Jerusalem
- Portugal
- France
- England
- Iberian Peninsula

Terms
- feudalism
- manor
- serfs
- Crusades
- bourgeoisie
- Magna Carta
- Renaissance
- *Reconquista*

Section 3

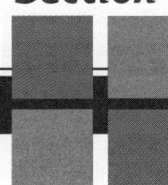

EUROPE IN THE MIDDLE AGES

FOCUS

- **What led to the rise and fall of feudalism?**
- **How did the Crusades affect European society?**
- **What was the Renaissance?**
- **What factors led to the rise of nations in Europe?**

The fall of the Roman Empire in the fifth century A.D. led to cultural turmoil in Europe. During the Middle Ages (roughly A.D. 500–1500), Europe transformed itself from a warring group of small, isolated kingdoms operating under a strict class system to a continent of powerful trading nations.

14th-century Italian moneylenders and borrowers

THE EARLY MIDDLE AGES

By A.D. 500 the once-powerful Roman Empire lay in ruin in western Europe, victim of repeated attacks by nomadic tribes from northern Europe and Asia. In its place arose a multitude of small warring kingdoms. Within a few centuries most of the wonders of the Roman Empire—its laws, literature, and learning—disappeared. Its vast network of roads fell into disrepair. Cities shrank and trade slowed as lawlessness made travel dangerous. Fields went unplanted as peasants fled from the invaders.

Among the most feared of the attackers were the Vikings. These skilled seafarers sailed thousands of miles to raid and colonize. About A.D. 800 the Vikings moved into northern England and Ireland. By the early 900s many had settled in northern France—where they were called Normans—and others had ventured west to Iceland and Greenland.

The rise of feudalism. To combat the Vikings and other invaders, many European rulers enlisted the aid of nobles under a system known as **feudalism**. The nobles pledged their military assistance and their loyalty to the rulers in return for land and protection.

The land a noble received was called a **manor**. Each manor was a self-sufficient estate, which included a manor house, pastures, fields, and a village. Most of those who lived on the manor were **serfs**, men and women bound to the land by their labor. Serfs were required to work their lord's land in exchange for a share of the crops they grew and for protection from attack by outsiders.

▲ **This scene from a medieval calendar shows serfs reaping grain in the fields.**

FOCUS OBJECTIVES

- Explain what led to the rise and fall of feudalism.
- Determine how the Crusades affected European society.
- Describe the Renaissance.
- Identify the factors that led to the rise of nations in Europe.

BUILDING VOCABULARY

The word *feudalism* derives from the Latin *feudum, feudālis,* meaning "a feud or fief." Feuds or fiefs were lands rented from a lord in return for service to him. Mention of the manorial system—the basis of feudalism—first appears in French documents dating from the 9th century.

MOTIVATING: STUDENT EXPERIENCES

Ask students what they know about medieval Europe from books, television, and films. Record student responses on a flip chart so that later they can see if their preconceptions are supported by information in the section.

Teaching the Section

THE RISE OF FEUDALISM

Discuss with students the factors that led to the rise of feudalism. Then have students draw an organizational chart of feudal society. Suggest that they include labeled arrows between the various classes to show the system of loyalty. Have volunteers present their charts. Call on other students to describe the life-styles of nobles and serfs. Students may wish to include their charts in their portfolios.

HISTORICAL SIDELIGHTS

Medicine
Apart from the very occasional ministrations of visiting barbers, who practiced blood-letting and tooth-pulling as well as shaving, serfs were left to their own devices. They treated practically every ailment with remedies made from herbs and roots. For the most part, these were as effective as the medications a physician of the time might provide.

[AV] TRANSPARENCY

Everyday Life in America Transparency and **Worksheet 1**

🌐 GLOBAL CONNECTIONS

At about the same time that feudalism was rising in Europe, a similar system was developing in Japan. The breakdown of Japan's central government in the 800s affected its society in much the same way that the collapse of the Roman Empire affected Europe. In Japan, landed nobles called *daimyō* employed bands of warriors called *samurai* to protect their great estates and the peasants who worked on them. Japanese feudalism hung on much longer than the European version, however, lasting until the 1860s.

▦ The collapse of the Roman Empire and the continued threat of invasion led to the development of feudalism.

Feudal society operated under a rigid class system. At the top of society was the noble class. Noblemen spent their days managing their estates, hunting, or engaging in battle. Men held most of the power, although some women obtained positions of influence by inheriting land from male relatives. Most noblewomen married in their early teens and generally had large families. They spent their days directing the servants in such duties as cooking, cleaning, spinning, weaving, brewing, and caring for livestock.

Life for the serfs was more difficult than it was for nobles. Most spent their days in unending physical labor. Both men and women worked in the fields, and women had to perform the household tasks as well. Although the lords received the largest portion of the crops grown by the serfs, many also required their workers to pay them fees, such as marriage or inheritance taxes.

Some serfs were able to obtain their freedom, but most remained tied to the land. They were considered property—part of the estate—and their status was passed on to their children. Most serfs lived in small one-room cottages. Their diet consisted mainly of soup, bread, and ale, with some occasional meat. Life was difficult and short. Few serfs lived beyond age 40.

The role of the church. Most of the people living in feudal Europe had no sense of national identity and little awareness of the outside world. In fact, few people ever traveled more than 25 miles from their homes. Life centered around the manor and the church.

The Roman Catholic church, led by the pope, was the most important political and social force in medieval Europe. The village church was the center of social activity for the manor. All of the important events in a person's life took place there. Parish priests led the mass, conducted baptisms, weddings, and funerals, and performed acts of charity.

On a wider scale, the Roman Catholic church was the only institution in Europe that carried on the traditions of the Roman Empire. In monasteries and convents, the monks and the nuns worshiped, studied the scriptures, and preserved the writings of the ancient Greeks and Romans. The medieval church promoted art and culture, leaving a rich heritage of religious music, tapestries, illuminated manuscripts, and great cathedrals.

Most important, the Roman Catholic church, under the direction of the pope, played a leading role in guiding the politics of Europe. It often stepped in to settle disputes between warring Christian kingdoms, help negotiate political alliances, or suggest various courses of action.

Decline of feudalism. Beginning about 1100, a series of changes brought about a gradual end to feudal society. New farm equipment—such as heavy plows that could turn the

◀ In this 16th-century fresco by Sodoma, St. Benedict is shown supervising the completion of the abbey of Monteoliveto Maggiore Siena—one of the 12 monasteries he built in the 6th century.

THE FALL OF FEUDALISM

Have students write a diary entry from the viewpoint of a European nobleman or noblewoman lamenting the decline of feudalism and listing the causes of this decline. Ask volunteers to read their entries to the class. Students may wish to include their diary entries in their portfolios.

THE IMPACT OF THE CRUSADES

On the chalkboard, draw a chart with the following headings: *Political, Economic, Social, Intellectual.* Have students suggest changes in these areas of European society brought about by the Crusades. Enter responses in the appropriate columns. Suggest to students that they copy the chart in their notebooks for future reference.

▶

rich, marshy soil of northern Europe and padded horse collars that allowed horses to pull heavier loads—increased the amount of land that could be farmed. Farm laborers could now produce enough food to sustain large armies and a growing number of townspeople as well.

As the military strength of the kingdoms grew, the Vikings and other invaders were less likely to attempt to take by force what they could get by trade. Soon trading towns and cities replaced manors as the focus of economic activity. As a result, many serfs moved from manors to towns, where they could either work for wages or farm rented plots on land surrounding the town.

▪▪ **Feudalism declined because of new farming technology, the rise of medieval towns, and the expansion of trade.**

𝒯HE CRUSADES AND TRADE

The shift away from feudalism was further aided by the series of wars known as the **Crusades**. Between 1096 and the late 1200s, waves of Christian crusaders fought Muslims for control of the Holy Land, an area of Southwest Asia sacred to Jews, Christians, and Muslims. Various groups of Muslims—followers of Islam, the religion founded by the prophet Muhammad about A.D. 610—had held the Holy Land since the 600s. In 1071 the area fell to the Seljuk (SEL-jook) Turks, Muslims from Central Asia. Unlike earlier groups, the Turks prevented Christians from visiting the holy city of Jerusalem.

In the First Crusade in the 11th century, Christian invaders from Europe captured Jerusalem and established several kingdoms in the area. (The city was retaken by Muslims in the late

BUILDING VOCABULARY

Crusaders were committed to the defeat of all "enemies of the Cross." Indeed, the word *crusade* derives from the Latin word *crux,* meaning "a cross." Today, the term is often used to describe a concerted action for some cause or idea, or against some form of injustice.

Map Caption Answer
Atlantic Ocean and Mediterranean Sea

CULTURAL PATTERNS

Muslims had controlled the Holy Land since the 7th century. For most of that time, they lived in relative harmony with those of other religious faiths. Although Muhammad had commanded his followers to spread the faith, few early Muslims had any interest in actively converting those living under their rule. Many people influenced by the culture did eventually convert, however. The Seljuk Turks were much more conservative and strict than early Muslims. They believed in actively converting others. This desire to spread the faith led them to exert greater control over their territory, including monitoring access to Jerusalem.

Viking and Crusade Routes

CRUSADES The religious wars for control of the Holy Land introduced Europeans to the riches of the Arab world and led to expanded trade.

❓ **MOVEMENT** Which bodies of water did the English members of the Third Crusade cross to reach Jerusalem?

Spanish Reconquista, 1492

Teaching the Section

THE RENAISSANCE

On the chalkboard draw a word web with *Renaissance* at the center and *Desire for Learning, Technological Developments, Exploration, Printing, Art,* and *Commerce* around it. Ask volunteers to describe the relationship of each satellite word or phrase to the Renaissance.

NATIONS RISE IN EUROPE

Ask a volunteer to cite factors that led to the rise of nations in Europe. *(warfare, marriages between royal families)* Then ask students to draw political cartoons that depict how Ferdinand and Isabella unified and changed their kingdoms. Ask volunteers to present their cartoons to the class. Students may wish to include their cartoons in their portfolios.

🌐 GLOBAL CONNECTIONS

The goods imported from the East by Italian traders traveled to the outskirts of Europe by way of markets and fairs. The center of exchange was the French province of Champagne, which held fairs approximately six times a year. There, exotic goods from Byzantium and Africa, Flemish cloth, French wine, English wool, and a profusion of other products changed hands in a frenzy of trade.

■ Ask students to compare modern shopping centers to medieval fairs.

PRIMARY SOURCE

Description of Change: excerpted
Rationale: excerpted to focus on main idea

BUILDING VOCABULARY

The term *bourgeoisie* comes from the Old French word *borjois* (later *bourgeois*) meaning "the middle class." The root of both words is the Old French *bourg*, a medieval village or town. It is also related to the suffix *burg* seen in the names of many American towns and cities.

1100s, however.) Though later Crusades were never as successful for the Europeans, the wars had important consequences for trade. Banks and merchants in the Italian city-states of Venice, Genoa (JEN-uh-wuh), and Pisa funded the Crusades in return for trading privileges. Italian traders brought back from the Muslim lands rare spices, fine silks, and many other exotic goods. Europeans responded by demanding more.

The impact of trade helped change Europe's political and social order. The merchants who organized trading voyages and the bankers who financed these voyages formed a new social class—the **bourgeoisie** (boohzh-wah-ZEE), or middle class. They knew that political stability was needed for trade to flourish. Feudal nobles, who often fought with one another, could not provide this stability. However, central government under a strong king or queen could. Thus the bourgeoisie generally threw their support to the monarchs.

▲ **The Seljuk Turks captured the city of Antioch in 1085, but it was retaken by Crusaders 13 years later. The recapture of Antioch is the subject of this 15th-century painting by Vincent de Beauvais.**

The bourgeoisie's support came at a price, however: they demanded a greater degree of economic and political freedom for themselves and their cities. Kings and lords reluctantly granted towns self-government, and some of them even organized meetings attended by nobles and the leading people from each town. The delegates to these assemblies—the forerunners of modern parliaments—helped the monarchs decide on taxes and government policies.

The move toward greater political representation was under way even before the first parliament in Europe was called, toward the close of the 13th century. In 1215, for instance, English nobles who were angered over new taxes forced King John to sign the **Magna Carta**, a charter limiting the power of the monarch. In addition to guaranteeing basic liberties for nobles, the charter protected trade:

> 66 All merchants shall have safe and secure conduct to go out of, and to come into, England . . . by land as by water, for buying and selling by the ancient and allowed customs, without any unjust tolls, except in time of war. 99

■ **The Crusades spurred trade, which led to the rise of the middle class and the introduction of representative government.**

---

*T*HE RENAISSANCE

In addition to spurring trade and political reform, the Crusades also promoted a rebirth of European learning and artistic creativity known as the **Renaissance**. During the early centuries of the Middle Ages, much of Europe had been closed off intellectually from the rest of the world. The Crusades helped end this isolation. Crusaders and traders brought back classical Greek and Roman works and new ideas in science, technology, art, and philosophy from the Byzantine Empire (the eastern half of the former Roman Empire) and from the Islamic world.

Inspired, European scholars sought to learn the secrets of the physical world. The Catholic Church encouraged the study of the natural order as one way of understanding God. The works of classical and

Practice

GUIDED PRACTICE

Have students work in small groups to write a *You Are There* newscast on the return to Europe of a crusader ship from Muslim lands. Newscasts should include interviews with crusaders and descriptions of items the crusaders have brought with them. Have groups "broadcast" their newscasts to the class.

INDEPENDENT PRACTICE

Ask students to write medieval "editorials" about how the items described in the Guided Practice might affect life in Europe.

Review and Assessment

REVIEW Have students write a paragraph on Europe in the Middle Ages, using the terms listed under Identify in the Section Review. Ask for volunteers to read their paragraphs to the class. Then assign the Section 3 Review on p. 22.

ASSESS Assign the **Section 3 Daily Quiz** in *Core Resources*.

▶

▲ This 16th-century painting shows Muslim astronomers observing the sky from the tower of Galata in Constantinople (now Istanbul).

Muslim thinkers also inspired scholars. Arab advances in mathematics and the sciences provided clues to the workings of nature, while Arab geographic studies provided pictures of the world beyond Europe's borders. Inventions like the compass and the astrolabe—used to observe and calculate the positions of the planets and the stars—became important tools for world exploration.

The Renaissance began in Italy in the 14th century and soon spread to the rest of Europe. A major factor in this cultural diffusion was the work of a German printer, Johannes Gutenberg. His invention, in the 1450s, of a printing press that used moveable type made it possible to print a large number of books quickly—and thus to spread ideas far and wide.

Commerce also played a role in promoting the Renaissance. European cities, whose banks and treasuries were overflowing with profits from trade, tried to outdo one another by funding building projects and by supporting artists. Such Renaissance artists as Leonardo da Vinci and Michelangelo were supported by wealthy sponsors.

■■ Trade, a renewed thirst for knowledge, and the invention of the printing press helped spark the Renaissance—a rebirth of European art and learning.

THE RISE OF NATIONS

The other great transformation of the Middle Ages was the rise of nations. Feudal kingdoms, independent city-states, and church-controlled lands slowly gave way to national monarchies in most of western Europe. Most often these changes were accomplished through years of warfare, and at other times by marriage between royal families. By the 1400s national monarchies existed in Portugal, France, England, Spain, Denmark, Norway, Sweden, Poland, and Hungary.

Among the first to achieve national unity during this period were Portugal, France, and England. Portugal, which had won its independence from the Spanish kingdom of Castile (kas-TEEL) in the 12th century, was unified under King John I in the early 1400s. The various French provinces were unified under the rule of Louis XI by the time his reign ended in 1483. And England was unified under Henry VII in 1485 after 30 years of bloody fighting.

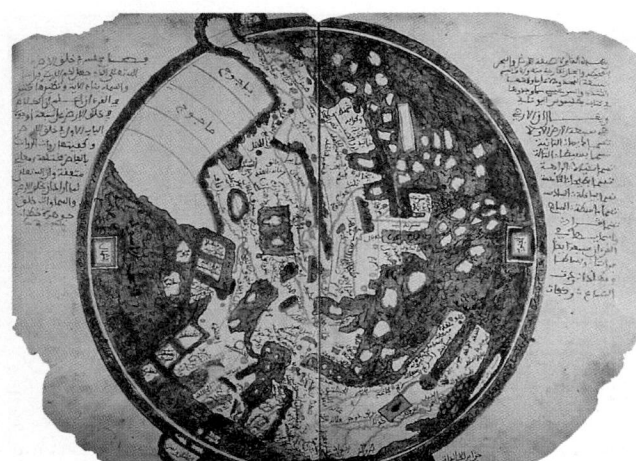

◀ The 12th-century Arab geographer Abū al-Idrīsī developed a map of the world that consisted of many different sections. One section displaying the "Seven Climatic Zones" is shown here.

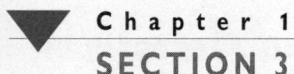

RETEACH Organize students in small groups and assign each group a subsection of Section 3. Have group members work together to prepare a summary of the main points of their subsection, accompanied by a visual such as a chart or map. Ask group representatives to read their summaries.

Closure

Organize students into four groups and assign each group one of the following topics: Feudalism, the Crusades, the Renaissance, the Rise of Nations. Have students draw a cartoon that illustrates an important concept concerning their assigned topic. Have groups present their cartoons in chronological order, explaining the rationale behind their drawings.

Extension

COMPARE Have students research and write an essay comparing European feudalism with the feudal system of medieval Japan.

EVALUATE Suggest that students evaluate the impact of the Crusades on life in Europe and the Holy Land by drawing an annotated map titled *The Crusades and Trade*. Display maps on the bulletin board.

SECTION REVIEW ANSWERS

IDENTIFY

For significance, see the following pages:
feudalism (p. 17)
manor (p. 17)
serfs (p. 17)
Crusades (p. 19)
bourgeoisie (p. 20)
Magna Carta (p. 20)
Renaissance (p. 20)
Johannes Gutenberg (p. 21)
Reconquista (p. 22)

LOCATE

For locations, see the map on p. 19.

1. *rise—collapse of Roman Empire, continued threat of invasion; decline—new farming technology, expansion of trade, rise of medieval towns*
2. *political—spurred trade, gave rise to representative government; social—created middle class, rebirth of art and learning*
3. *Royal marriages and wars led to rise of monarchies that ruled nations.*
4. *Essays should mention a period fostering learning and artistic creativity in Europe; better maps, compass, astrolabe, printing press.*
5. *Yes, because nations were united and trade was expanded. No, because warfare increased and ethnic diversity decreased.*

▲ This detail from the *Fall of Granada* by Pradilla shows Ferdinand and Isabella receiving the surrender of the Kingdom of Granada from the Moors in 1492.

the ongoing battle to recapture Spanish lands from the Moors. The *Reconquista* ended in 1492, when Spain defeated the Moors in Granada.

Isabella and Ferdinand believed that the best way to truly unify their kingdoms—and to gain the approval of the pope—was to make Spain a completely Catholic nation by driving non-Christians from their lands. In March 1492 they ordered all Jews to convert to the Catholic faith or leave Spain.

The action did much to achieve the monarchs' goal of an all-Catholic Spain. But it carried a price for the country that was not immediately obvious. Among the nearly 150,000 departing Jews were some of the nation's leading scholars, bankers, merchants, and government officials. These people settled throughout Europe and the Muslim world, strengthening Spain's enemies. But in 1492 Spain's future looked bright as it joined other European nations in the search for new trade routes and the riches they would bring.

Spain faced a special problem, however. Four Christian kingdoms—Portugal, Castile, Navarre (nuh-VAHR), and Aragon—controlled most of the Iberian Peninsula. But the Moors—Muslims who were originally from North Africa—still held the kingdom of Granada in the southernmost part of the peninsula. The Moors, in fact, had controlled much of southwestern Europe during the Middle Ages.

The first step toward unification occurred when Isabella of Castile and Ferdinand II of Aragon married in 1469. They did not unite their kingdoms until 1479, but they did quickly join forces in the *Reconquista* (re-kawng-KEE-stah)—

■■ **Through royal marriages and warfare, monarchies built nations from feudal kingdoms, independent city-states, and church-controlled lands.**

SECTION 3 REVIEW

IDENTIFY and explain the significance of the following: feudalism, manor, serfs, Crusades, bourgeoisie, Magna Carta, Renaissance, Johannes Gutenberg, *Reconquista*.

LOCATE and explain the importance of the following: Jerusalem, Portugal, France, England, Iberian Peninsula.

1. **MAIN IDEA** What factors led to the rise of feudalism? What factors contributed to its decline?
2. **MAIN IDEA** In what ways did the Crusades change political and social life in Europe?
3. **MAIN IDEA** What caused the rise of nations in Europe?
4. **WRITING TO INFORM** In a short essay, explain what the Renaissance was and describe some of the technological advances that came to Europeans during the period.
5. **TAKING A STAND** Were the national monarchies that developed in the Middle Ages better for Europe than the old systems? Why or why not?

Section 4

ASIA AND AFRICA IN THE MIDDLE AGES

FOCUS OBJECTIVES

- Describe how Islamic religion and culture spread during the Middle Ages.

- Explain how China was opened to world trade.

- Assess the role trade played in the development of African kingdoms.

FOCUS

- **How did Islamic religion and culture spread during the Middle Ages?**
- **How did China become open to world trade?**
- **What role did trade play in the development of African kingdoms?**

*A*s feudalism gave way to nation-states in Europe, large cultures flourished in Asia and Africa. When Europeans began to venture beyond their borders in search of trade, they encountered a commercial world dominated by merchants from these societies. As the different groups came together, they exchanged ideas and cultural practices as well as commercial goods. This exchange expanded the Europeans' knowledge of the world, stimulated their desire for more goods, and influenced the course of world events.

Bronze figurine of a flute player from Benin, West Africa

THE ISLAMIC WORLD

Trade between Asia and Africa had existed for centuries. Horses, cloth, and luxury goods from Asia were exchanged for ivory and gold—and slaves—from Africa. After 900, much of this trade was controlled by Muslim merchants.

Muhammad, the prophet of Islam, had commanded his followers to convert all nonbelievers—by force if necessary. Although Muslim armies did much to spread the faith, many people were drawn to Islam by merchants. Carrying the **Qur'an** (kuh-RAN)—the holy book of Islam—Muslim merchants tirelessly preached their religion wherever they went. The traders' devotion proved to be as potent a weapon as the sword in spreading Islamic faith and culture. By the late Middle Ages, vast areas of Asia, Africa, and Europe had become part of the Muslim empire.

■■ Muslim soldiers and merchants spread their religion and culture throughout Asia, Africa, and Europe during the Middle Ages.

The pursuit of knowledge flourished in the Islamic world during the Middle Ages. In the 10th and 11th centuries, two Muslim physicians, Rāzī (RAH-zee) and Ibn Sīnā (IB-uhn SEE-nah), compiled medical encyclopedias that quickly became the basis for teaching medicine in the educational centers of Baghdad. Muslim scholars excelled at mathematics and perfected algebra. Using knowledge gained from the mathematicians of India, they refined the Arabic numeral system and the concept of zero. Muslim geographers used travelers' observations and astronomical calculations to advance the art of cartography, or mapmaking. Through trade many of these advances found their way to cultures outside the Muslim world.

Teaching the Section

ISLAMIC RELIGION & CULTURE

Ask a volunteer to describe how the Islamic religion was spread during the Middle Ages. Then draw a chart on the chalkboard using various disciplines—medicine, astronomy, geography, and so on—as headings. Ask students to give examples of Islamic developments in these disciplines and to record them on the chart. Then have volunteers explain how each development might have affected learning in medieval Europe.

Write the following words on the chalkboard and ask students what they have in common: *cotton, muslin, sherbet, sofa, lemon, orange, almanac, algebra, giraffe. (All have Arabic origins.)* Then have students speculate how these words entered the English language.

CULTURAL PATTERNS

The Chinese called their country *Zhongguo,* or "Middle Kingdom," because they believed that they were the core of the civilized world.

■■ Ask students to give examples from recent news stories that suggest whether or not China remains an insular society today.

PRIMARY SOURCE

Description of Change: excerpted
Rationale: excerpted to focus on main idea

HISTORICAL SIDELIGHTS

Admiral Zheng He
The Chinese maritime expeditions were commanded by Admiral Zheng He. On his first expedition he sailed with a fleet of more than 300 vessels—some as big as 444 feet long and 186 feet wide—carrying a crew of more than 27,000.

CHINA

Trade also played a role in spreading the culture of China to other parts of the world. For much of China's early history, the towering Himalayas (him-uh-LAY-uhz) of central Asia and the dry, barren Gobi (GOH-bee) Desert cut off the Chinese society from contact with other cultures. Because they were insulated from outside influences, the Chinese developed a distinctive culture, which was maintained through the moral code and philosophy of Confucianism. Confucius (551–479 B.C.) taught that people should strive to build a peaceful, well-ordered society.

In time, the Chinese developed a sense of cultural superiority, a belief that their country stood at the center of everything important. Their technological and cultural achievements lent support to this self-image. Among other things, the Chinese either invented or improved the compass, the water mill, the wheelbarrow, the horse harness, gunpowder, and paper. In addition, they made the world's first known printed book, the *Diamond Sutra,* in A.D. 868.

China's isolation ended in the 1200s, when invaders from Mongolia overran the country. The Mongol leader Kublai Khan (KOO-bluh KAHN)—the Great Khan—set up as his capital what is now the city of Beijing (Peking) in 1264. Under his rule China became the largest land empire in the world. It also opened up dramatically to the Western world. The Mongols protected the trade routes across Asia so that travelers were safe from raiding bands. As a result, trade flourished.

Among the Europeans to visit China between 1270 and 1300 was a young Italian, Marco Polo, an adventurer and merchant from Venice. Polo spent more than 20 years traveling through China and central Asia. In a chronicle about his travels, *Description of the World,* Polo wrote of the magnificent Mongol Empire, including the royal city now called Beijing:

66 This new city is a perfect square, with each side six miles long. The wall of the city has 12 gates, 3 on each side of the square. The whole city was laid out by line. The streets are so straight that if you stand above one of the gates, you can see the gate on the opposite side of the city. . . . Everything that is most rare and valuable in all the world finds its way here. This is especially true of India, which supplies precious gems, pearls, and spices. 99

■■ **The Mongols under Kublai Khan protected Asian trade routes and opened China to world trade.**

After Kublai Khan's death in 1294, the Mongols' power declined, and the Chinese regained control. The new leaders, wanting to return to the nation's ancient traditions, reintroduced Confucianism. To protect their culture from foreign influences, the Chinese once again sought to isolate their society from the world.

China did not withdraw from outside contact completely, however. Beginning in 1405, the nation launched a series of seven maritime expeditions. The expeditions—the largest and most far-reaching the world had ever seen—sailed to present-day Vietnam, Indonesia, Ceylon (now Sri Lanka), India, the Arabian Peninsula, and numerous East African ports. The purpose of this vast undertaking was not to claim and conquer foreign territories, but to trade and to explore new lands. The Chinese also wanted to show the world their nation's wealth and achievements.

In 1433, however, China halted trade with the outside world. But China's withdrawal from trade did not reduce the West's desire for exotic Chinese goods. Dreams of trade with Asia still fueled European imaginations.

The Granger Collection, New York

◀ **This detail from a Chinese scroll drawn during the Ming dynasty (1368–1644) shows the Chinese navy sailing against Japanese pirates.**

CHINA AND WORLD TRADE

Draw a time line on the chalkboard with the following dates relating to China: *551 B.C.* (birth of Confucius), *1264* (Kublai Khan establishes capital), *1270* (Marco Polo visits), *1294* (death of Kublai Khan), *1405* (maritime expeditions begin), *1433* (China halts foreign trade). Have volunteers state the significance of each date. Then have students characterize China between each date as seeking isolation or as open. Ask what social and geographic factors may have encouraged China's isolation. Conclude by working with the class to develop a generalization, based on the time line, about factors that opened China to world trade.

AFRICAN KINGDOMS AND TRADE

Provide students with outline maps of Africa to create maps showing major West African kingdoms and East African city-states. Have them fill in the maps with principal trade routes and key goods traded. Then ask students to write a paragraph on the role trade played in the development of African kingdoms. ▶

Map Caption Answer
the Himalayas

MAKING CONNECTIONS
Geography

Leaving the East African coast, traders sailed across the Indian Ocean, taking advantage of the southerly summer monsoon winds. In the winter months, when the monsoon winds blew out of the north, they returned to Africa.

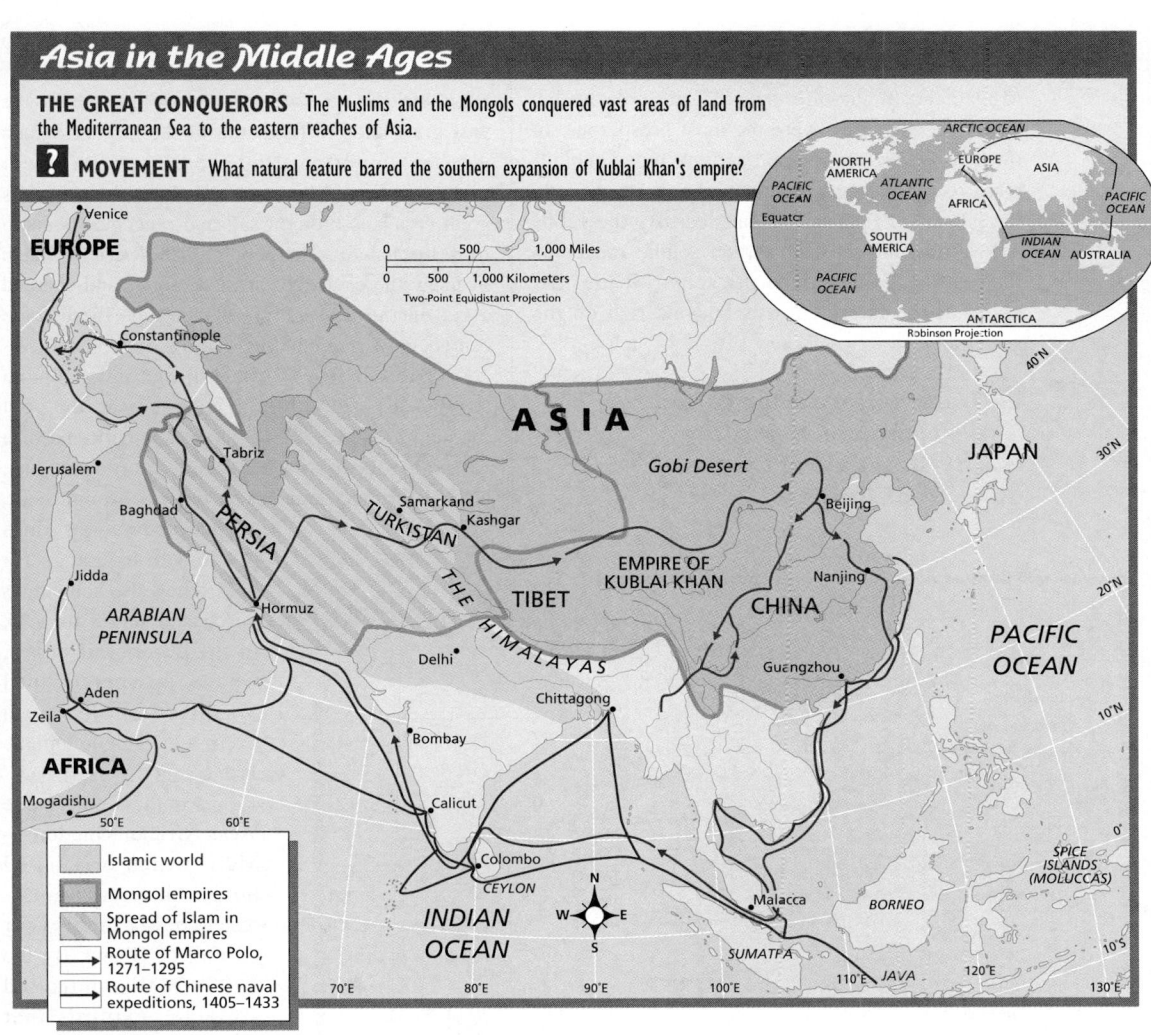

Asia in the Middle Ages

THE GREAT CONQUERORS The Muslims and the Mongols conquered vast areas of land from the Mediterranean Sea to the eastern reaches of Asia.

? MOVEMENT What natural feature barred the southern expansion of Kublai Khan's empire?

Legend:
- Islamic world
- Mongol empires
- Spread of Islam in Mongol empires
- Route of Marco Polo, 1271–1295
- Route of Chinese naval expeditions, 1405–1433

𝒯HE AFRICAN TRADING KINGDOMS

Trade also was instrumental in the development of great kingdoms in East and West Africa. Early kingdoms—such as Kush (1000 B.C.–A.D. 350) and Axum (A.D. 50–600)—controlled highly developed trade networks and established the trading practices that later empires adopted. During the Middle Ages the city-states on the East African coast thrived on trade with Asia. In West Africa, kingdoms grew rich by trading in gold and salt.

East African city-states. During the 700s many of the people in what are today Somalia, Kenya, and Tanzania (tan-zuh-NEE-uh) moved to the coastal areas and became involved in trade between Africa and Asia. Most of the people specialized in mainland trade, or the bringing of goods from the interior to the coast. Other traders then shipped the goods to the Arabian Peninsula, where they would be traded to merchants from China. Many different goods were brought to the coast, but the most sought-after item was gold, which formed a large part of the trade.

Most of the traders who shipped goods to the Arabian Peninsula were Arabs who had come to East Africa after fleeing political and religious upheaval in their homelands. Over time the mix of newcomers and original inhabitants created a unique African culture. The people spoke **Swahili** (swah-HEE-lee), a form of Bantu that showed strong Arabic influences. (*Swahili* is an Arabic word meaning "of the coast.")

Over the years, trade between Africa and Asia expanded, and many East African trading

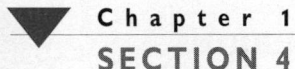

Practice

GUIDED PRACTICE

Have groups of students role-play merchants from China, East Africa, West Africa, and the Islamic world. Ask groups to explain how they exchange ideas, cultural practices, and goods with other parts of the world.

INDEPENDENT PRACTICE

Have students use information gained from the Guided Practice to write a Middle Ages travel brochure expounding the cultural diversity of China or an African city-state.

Review and Assessment

REVIEW Have students work in pairs to make three cause-event-effect charts that show how trade led to cultural exchanges among the Islamic world, China, and Africa. Call on volunteer pairs to present their charts to the class. Then assign the Section 4 Review on p. 27.

ASSESS Assign the **Section 4 Daily Quiz** in *Core Resources.*

HISTORICAL SIDELIGHTS

A Center of Learning

In Mecca, Mansa Mūsā met with the leading Islamic scholars, many of whom he persuaded to go back with him to Mali. Sankoré University, in the city of Tombouctou, quickly became a major center of learning, drawing students and teachers from throughout North Africa and the Middle East.

PRIMARY SOURCE

(for source on p. 27)
Description of Change: excerpted and bracketed
Rationale: excerpted to focus on main idea; bracketed to clarify meaning

Map Caption Answer
Nile River

villages grew into powerful and wealthy city-states. At first, northern city-states such as Mogadishu (mahg-uh-DISH-oo)—the present-day capital of Somalia—were the most prosperous. In time, however, commercial activity moved southward to Malindi, Mombasa (mahm-BAHS-uh), and the islands of Pemba and Zanzibar. By the 1200s Kilwa, on another island farther south, ranked as the leading East African port city. Meanwhile, many of the interior towns became rich on the gold trade.

■■ **Trade with Asia led to the development of wealthy city-states along the east coast of Africa.**

West African kingdoms. Trade also became an important activity early in the history of West Africa. In the western area of the Sudan—the vast grasslands to the south of the mighty Sahara —many important trade routes crisscrossed: traders with gold headed north from the Sudan as great caravans brought salt and other goods south from the Sahara. The people of the western Sudan oversaw the exchange of these goods and charged a tax on the transactions. Over time these trade centers grew into bustling trading kingdoms.

The earliest of these kingdoms—Ghana (GAHN-uh)—developed from a trading post founded around A.D. 300 at the southern end of a caravan route from Morocco (muh-RAHK-oh). North Africans and desert traders brought salt, copper, and various kinds of cloth to exchange for gold. They also sometimes purchased slaves to work in the desert salt mines. Ghana prospered until Muslims from the north overran the kingdom in the 11th century.

Another remarkable West African kingdom— Mali, which originated in the 7th century A.D.— rose to power shortly after the fall of Ghana. By the 1300s Mali controlled a huge empire that stretched from the upper Niger (NY-juhr) River westward to the Atlantic coast. Mali's best-known leader was Mansa Mūsā, who ruled from 1307 to 1332. A devout Muslim, he undertook a *hajj* (pilgrimage) to Mecca in 1324. Mansa Mūsā saw this journey to the holy city as an opportunity to display Mali's wealth. The ruler was accompanied by thousands of other pilgrims—among them 500 slaves, each of whom carried a four-pound gold bar.

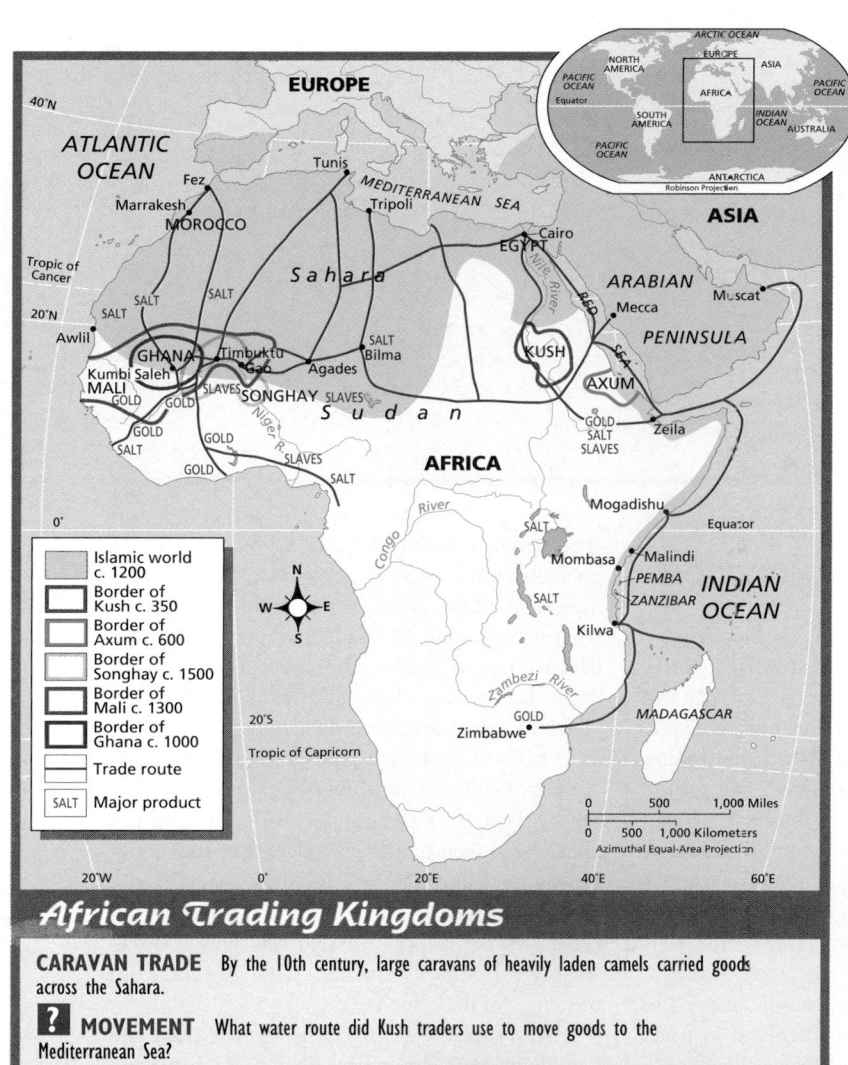

African Trading Kingdoms

CARAVAN TRADE By the 10th century, large caravans of heavily laden camels carried goods across the Sahara.

? **MOVEMENT** What water route did Kush traders use to move goods to the Mediterranean Sea?

RETEACH Organize students into small groups. Tell each group to divide the section material, by subsections, among its members. Direct students to write questions about the main ideas presented in their assigned material. Have group members quiz one another with the questions.

*C*losure

Have volunteers summarize how Muhammad, Marco Polo, Kublai Khan, and Mansa Mūsā each demonstrates the existence of cultural diffusion in the world of his time.

*E*xtension

CREATE Suggest that students work in small groups to research and create an annotated map of the Silk Road, the great trade route that linked Europe and Asia.

INVESTIGATE Have students investigate the advances made by Muslim geographers and astronomers who improved navigation in the Middle Ages.

Mansa Mūsā's trip was widely reported, and his fame spread far beyond the Muslim world. An atlas made for King Charles V of France showed a black man seated on a throne and clutching a huge gold nugget. Accompanying the picture was this inscription:

> ❝ This black lord is called [Mansa Mūsā], lord of the negroes of Guinea [Mali]. The gold which is found in his country is so abundant that he is the richest and noblest lord in all the region. ❞

After Mansa Mūsā died in 1332, Mali slowly lost its powerful position in the region.

In the mid-1300s, as Mali declined, the relatively weak state of Songhay (SAWNG-hy)—once under Mali's rule—won its independence. Songhay eventually became the dominant power in West Africa, growing rich on the trade in gold, ivory, and slaves. It also flourished as a center of Islamic learning. The city of Timbuktu was home to three universities and 180 Islamic schools. The universities, which housed large collections of Greek, Roman, and Arabic manuscripts, taught religion, poetry, astronomy, and medicine. By the mid-1500s, education rivaled trade as Timbuktu's major activity.

▪▪ A succession of powerful kingdoms in West Africa controlled the major north-south trade routes.

▲ **Detail showing Mansa Mūsā from atlas of Charles V**

Despite the presence of large cities like Timbuktu, the majority of people in West Africa lived in small villages. They believed that many things in nature were sacred. They also placed great importance on family ties and on respect for their ancestors, which led to a strong sense of family loyalty and communal values. This whole world, however, would soon change with the arrival of the Europeans.

SECTION REVIEW ANSWERS

IDENTIFY

For significance, see the following pages:
Muhammad (p. 23)
Qur'an (p. 23)
Confucius (p. 24)
Diamond Sutra (p. 24)
Kublai Khan (p. 24)
Marco Polo (p. 24)
Swahili (p. 25)
Mansa Mūsā (p. 26)
hajj (p. 26)

LOCATE

For locations, see the maps on pp. 25 and 26.

1. *Muslim merchants carried the Qur'an, spreading their religion and culture as they traveled through Asia, Africa, and Europe.*
2. *The Mongols protected Asian trade routes and opened China to world trade.*
3. *locations beneficial to trade—either on coast or on trade routes; became major trading centers*
4. *Journal entries will vary but should describe the technological and cultural achievements of the Mongol Empire.*
5. *Essays should balance the desire to limit foreign influences and to maintain ancient traditions against the economic benefits of expanded trade.*

▪▪ S E C T I O N 4 R E V I E W

IDENTIFY and explain the significance of the following: Muhammad, Qur'an, Confucius, *Diamond Sutra*, Kublai Khan, Marco Polo, Swahili, Mansa Mūsā, *hajj*.

LOCATE and explain the importance of the following: Beijing, Mogadishu, Sahara, Ghana, Mali, Tombouctou.

1. **MAIN IDEA** What role did trade play in spreading Islamic culture?
2. **MAIN IDEA** How did the Mongol invasion affect trade between China and the rest of the world?
3. **LINKING HISTORY AND GEOGRAPHY** How did the location of East and West African city-states prove important to their development?
4. **WRITING TO DESCRIBE** Imagine you are a member of Marco Polo's expedition. Write a journal entry that describes your impressions of the Mongol Empire.
5. **USING HISTORICAL IMAGINATION** As a Chinese citizen in the year 1300, write a brief essay expressing your view on either expanding trade or returning to isolationism.

PREVIEW WORKSHOP

Following is a list of the significant people, places, and terms in this section. You may wish to use this list as a section preview.

People
- Prince Henry
- Gomes Eanes de Zurara
- Bartolomeu Dias
- Vasco da Gama

Places
- Spice Islands
- Genoa
- Venice
- Sagres
- Black Sea
- Mediterranean Sea
- Madeira Islands
- Cape Verde Islands
- Sierra Leone
- Cape of Good Hope

Terms
- monopoly
- African diaspora

FOCUS OBJECTIVES

- Explain why Europeans sought a new route to the East.

- Determine the origins of Portugal's involvement in the slave trade.

- Examine how Portugal gained control of East-West trade.

HISTORICAL SIDELIGHTS

Paid in Pepper
Pepper was recognized in Europe as legal tender, just like silver or gold, and workers sometimes accepted pepper as wages. Two to three weeks' work on a farm, for example, might earn a pound of pepper.

CORE RESOURCES
- **Social Studies Skills Worksheet 1**
- **Section 5 Daily Quiz**

AV RESOURCES
- *The American Nation* **Videodisc: Inquiry and Exploration**
- **Linking Geography and History Transparencies and Worksheets 4, 5**

28

Section 5

THE LURE OF TRADE AND EXPLORATION

F O C U S
- **Why did Europeans seek a new route to the East?**
- **What were the origins of Portugal's involvement in the slave trade?**
- **How did Portugal gain control of East-West trade?**

Europe was greatly enriched by the flow of ideas and technology from Africa and Asia. But Europeans were most interested in goods: grain and gold from Africa and perfumes, spices, and silks from Asia. By the early 1400s most of these items were readily available in Europe, but very costly. Goods coming from Asia and Africa were controlled by Muslim trading empires and Italian city-states. The newly emerging nation-states of Europe wanted to share in this wealth. To do so, however, they needed to find other routes to these distant markets. The seafaring nation of Portugal led the way in this great enterprise.

Detail from woodcarving of Venice, 15th century

EAST–WEST TRADE

Wealthy Europeans wanted Syrian fabrics and Chinese silk to make fine clothes and Persian rugs and Chinese glass and porcelain to decorate their homes. They also wanted cloves, cinnamon, and nutmeg from the Spice Islands of the Indies, ginger from China, and pepper from India to flavor and preserve their foods.

But trade routes overland from China or by sea from the Indies were long and dangerous. On the journey from the East, goods might change hands a dozen times, their prices marked up each time. Some of the profit went to the Muslim traders who controlled the Asian trade routes. Much more, however, went to the Italian merchants from Genoa and Venice who bought the goods from Muslim traders in North Africa or in Black Sea ports and shipped them across the Mediterranean Sea to be sold in Europe.

Hungry for trade goods and envious of Genoa and Venice's **monopoly**, or exclusive

◀ During the 13th century Genoa became the chief trading center in the Mediterranean region. This view of the city and its harbor was painted about 1481.

Have students recall trade arrangements that existed in the Mediterranean region in the 1400s. *(trade controlled by Italian and Muslim merchants)* Then point out that Section 5 explains how this situation gave rise to the age of exploration.

SEEKING A NEW ROUTE

Ask students to pretend to be European merchants. Direct them to write petitions to the merchants in the Italian city-states, listing their grievances and explaining why they intend to circumvent the Italian merchants in the future. Ask volunteers to read their petitions to the class.

Have students create an annotated map or an illustrated time line to show the various stages in Portugal's search for an all-water route to the East. Captions and entries should indicate the development of the slave trade, areas explored, and goods exchanged. Have students display their maps and time lines on the bulletin board. Students may wish to include their work in their portfolios.

▶

control, of East-West trade, other European merchants began looking for ways to get Asian goods more cheaply. An all-sea route to the East seemed the most promising answer.

■■ **The control of trade by Muslim and Italian merchants made Asian goods very costly, causing Europeans to look for new routes to the East.**

*P*ORTUGAL LEADS THE WAY

Portugal, a small country with a long seafaring tradition, led the way in exploration. A strong desire to seize a share of the East-West trade drove the Portuguese of the early 1400s to seek a new route to Asia. Their country's geographic location, on the west coast of the Iberian Peninsula, determined the route the Portuguese

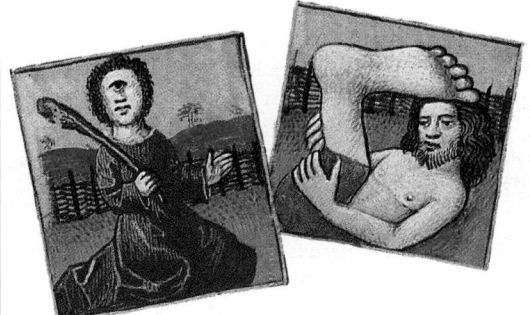

▲ These pictures from a 1492 book, *On the Nature of Created Things,* show two monsters that seafarers imagined could be found in mysterious lands across the Atlantic Ocean.

took—southward into the Atlantic Ocean and around Africa.

What knowledge of the world did the Portuguese possess as they set out on their voyages of exploration? Most Portuguese sea captains were aware of the works of Arab geographers and of books written by European travelers to the East. Much of the information contained in these

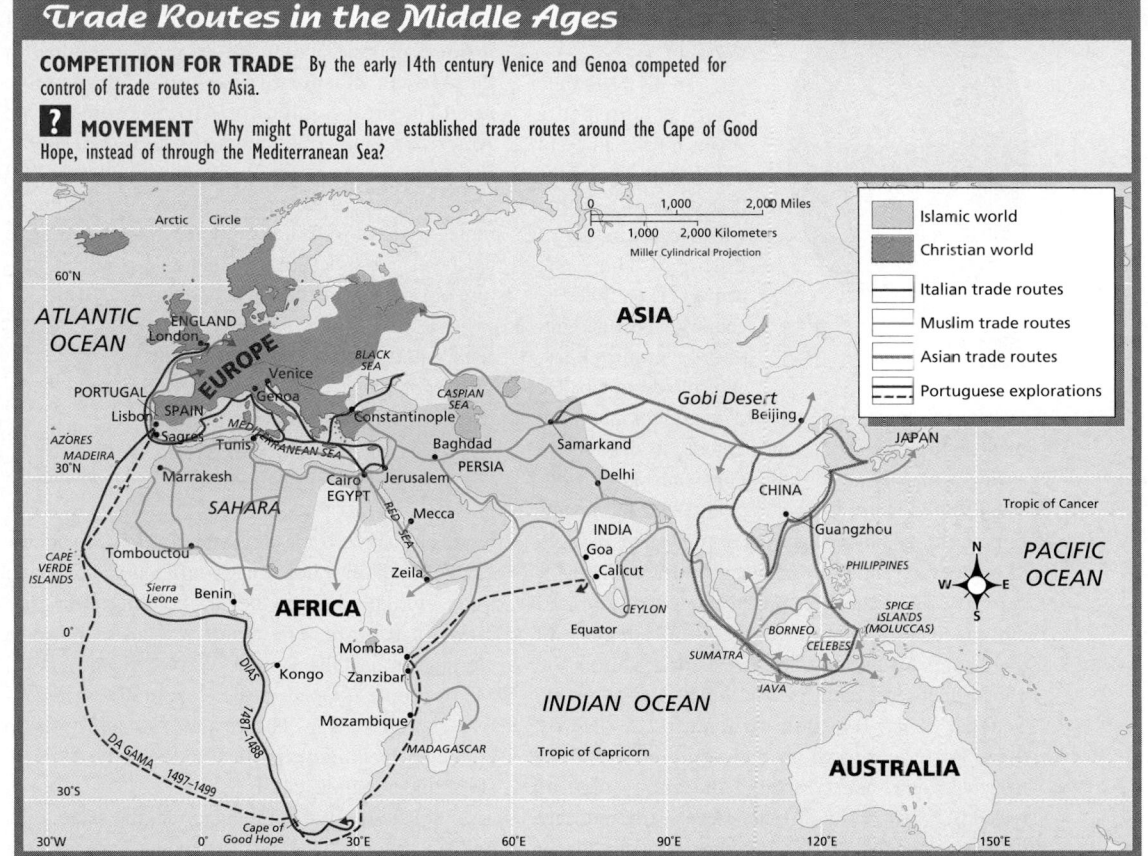

*T*rade *R*outes in the *M*iddle *A*ges

COMPETITION FOR TRADE By the early 14th century Venice and Genoa competed for control of trade routes to Asia.

? **MOVEMENT** Why might Portugal have established trade routes around the Cape of Good Hope, instead of through the Mediterranean Sea?

0   1,000   2,000 Miles
0   1,000   2,000 Kilometers
Miller Cylindrical Projection

- Islamic world
- Christian world
- Italian trade routes
- Muslim trade routes
- Asian trade routes
- Portuguese explorations

Arctic Circle
60°N
ATLANTIC OCEAN
ENGLAND
London
EUROPE
BLACK SEA
PORTUGAL
Venice
Genoa
CASPIAN SEA
ASIA
Gobi Desert
Beijing
JAPAN
Lisbon
SPAIN
Constantinople
AZORES
Sagres
Tunis
MEDITERRANEAN SEA
Baghdad
Samarkand
MADEIRA
30°N
Marrakesh
Cairo
EGYPT
Jerusalem
PERSIA
Delhi
CHINA
SAHARA
RED SEA
Mecca
Guangzhou
Tropic of Cancer
CAPE VERDE ISLANDS
Tombouctou
INDIA
Goa
Callicut
PACIFIC OCEAN
Sierra Leone
Benin
AFRICA
CEYLON
PHILIPPINES
N W E S
0°
Equator
BORNEO
SPICE ISLANDS (MOLUCCAS)
CELEBES
DIAS
Mombasa
SUMATRA
Kongo
Zanzibar
JAVA
INDIAN OCEAN
Mozambique
MADAGASCAR
DA GAMA
1481–1488
1497–1499
Tropic of Capricorn
AUSTRALIA
30°S
30°W
Cape of Good Hope
0°
30°E
60°E
90°E
120°E
150°E

Practice

GUIDED PRACTICE

Write the following on the chalkboard: *Italian city-states, monopoly, Portugal, Prince Henry, exploration, slave trade, East-West trade.* Have students work together to design and complete a graphic organizer on the chalkboard, showing the relationship of these terms. Call on volunteers to explain the significance of each relationship.

INDEPENDENT PRACTICE

Have students work individually to write "help wanted" ads for geographers, mapmakers, ship designers, and others to work at Prince Henry's study center at Sagres. Ads should include the terms from the Guided Practice.

Review and Assessment

REVIEW Organize the class into teams and assign each team a subsection of the section. Ask teams to write several questions and answers about the main ideas in their subsection. Have teams "face off" to ask each other questions. Then assign the Section 5 Review on p. 31.

ASSESS Assign the **Section 5 Daily Quiz** in *Core Resources.*

PRIMARY SOURCE

Description of Change: excerpted
Rationale: excerpted to focus on main idea

BIO GRAPHY | PERSONALITIES IN HISTORY

Prince Henry wanted to locate the legendary "Prester John," a great lord who supposedly ruled a Christian kingdom somewhere in Africa. With his aid Prince Henry hoped to drive the Muslims out of the Holy Land.

AV TRANSPARENCY

Linking Geography and History Transparency and **Worksheet 5**

CULTURAL PATTERNS

Many of the West African states that became part of the slave trade had been heavily influenced by Islamic traders. Thus, many African slaves were devout Muslims well versed in the Arabic language and writing system. These slaves often relied upon their faith to help them through the difficult separation from their family and culture. Often they continued to practice their faith in secret during their captivity, despite European efforts to convert them to Christianity.

---

sources, however, was quite fanciful. For example, according to the popular 14th-century *Travels of Sir John Mandeville,* seafarers who survived the rough seas of the Atlantic might come upon lands inhabited by strange creatures:

> 66 In one, there is a race of great stature, like giants, foul and horrible to look at; they have one eye only, in the middle of their foreheads. . . . In another part, there are ugly folk without heads, who have eyes in each shoulder; their mouths are round, like a horseshoe, in the middle of their chest. . . . And there are in another place folk with flat faces, without noses or eyes. 99

BIO GRAPHY Common sense, reason, and order were brought to the study of geography and exploration by Prince Henry of Portugal. Henry was born in 1394, the third son of King John I and Philippa of Lancaster. His burning desire was to find the African "gold kingdoms" he had heard of while fighting in Morocco. He also yearned to find an all-sea route to Asia.

In 1419 Prince Henry established a center for the study of navigation at Sagres (SAH-greesh), on the southwestern tip of Portugal. There, he brought together the country's best geographers, mapmakers, and ship designers. He

Prince Henry

oversaw all their work, encouraging them to experiment with new navigation methods, to draw more accurate maps, and to build ships capable of withstanding the stormy Atlantic. Henry put the results to practical use by sponsoring a number of voyages of exploration southward down the African coast.

By 1430 the Portuguese had explored and colonized the Madeira (muh-DIR-uh) Islands and the Azores off Africa's northwest coast. During the 1450s they reached the Cape Verde Islands off the Senegal coast. By 1462, two years after Henry died, Portuguese sailors had ventured as far as Sierra Leone, nearly around the great bulge of western Africa. Prince Henry never sailed on any of these voyages, but his immense contribution to

Portugal's seafaring efforts earned him the nickname "the Navigator."

THE AFRICAN SLAVE TRADE

The first Portuguese to visit Africa's Atlantic coast were interested in trading for the spices that were in such great demand back home. They also sought gold, which they had heard frequently mentioned in tales about the continent. In time, however, another business—the trade in human slaves—came to dominate their dealings with Africa.

Slavery was not unknown to Africans, but its form was different from what it would eventually become under the Europeans. Many slaves in West African society were either criminals or captives taken in war. Their rights were restricted, but they did have some protection under the law. Most could marry, and their children did not become slaves. Moreover, slavery was usually temporary—individuals could obtain their freedom.

Portugal's role in the slave trade was relatively small in the late 1400s. But by the end of the following century, the slave trade had become a major economic activity. It eventually resulted in the **African diaspora** (dy-AS-pruh)—the forcible resettlement of millions of African people to the Americas from the 1500s through the 1800s. Estimates suggest that in the approximately 400 years the slave trade operated, some 10 million or more Africans were transported across the Atlantic as slaves. Countless more died as a result of capture or on the horrible voyage to the Americas.

■■ **Portuguese traders, first attracted to Africa's gold and other natural resources, soon became interested in the profitable slave trade.**

The slave trade devastated African society. Because of the enormous profits that the slave trade brought, villages began targeting their enemies for capture. The result was an increase in warfare among the various West African nations. Many people trapped in the slave trade were captives taken in war. The rest were usually those abducted by raiding parties and swiftly taken to slave traders on the coast.

It is hard to imagine the effect the slave trade had on those who experienced the capture of a

RETEACH Organize students into small groups and assign each a subsection of the section. Tell each group to create a poster, drawing, or cartoon that illustrates the main idea of its subsection. Have each group explain its creation.

Closure

Have students work individually or in small groups to write a generalization explaining how and why Europeans set out to explore the world at the end of the 1400s and some of the consequences. Have students or groups present and explain their generalizations to the class.

Extension

CREATE Encourage students to research and draw diagrams of a navigational or sailing development made at Prince Henry's center at Sagres.

RESEARCH Have students work in pairs to research one of the people mentioned in this section. Then ask the pair to perform as the interviewer and the subject.

The Granger Collection, New York.

▲ **The slave market at Yemen is the subject of this illustration from a 13th-century Arabic manuscript.**

friend or family member. The experience would be devastating to anyone, but in a culture that placed such strong emphasis on family ties, it was especially painful. In 1444 Gomes Eanes de Zurara (GOH-mish A-nush duh zoo-RAH-ruh), the official reporter for the Portuguese king, described one of the miseries brought about by the traffic in human slaves:

66 Mothers would clasp their infants in their arms, and throw themselves on the ground to cover them with their bodies, disregarding any injury to their own persons, so that they could prevent their children from being separated from them. 99

A ROUTE TO THE INDIES

The profits from the African trade prompted further searches for new routes to Asia. During the mid-1480s, Portuguese sailors discovered the mouth of the Congo River and charted the southwest coast of Africa. In 1488 Bartolomeu Dias rounded Africa's southernmost tip, but he went no farther. His crew, fearing the great expanse of unknown ocean that lay ahead of them, forced the ship to turn back.

In 1497 a fleet of four ships outfitted by Dias and commanded by Vasco da Gama set out from Portugal to complete the African voyage. By early 1498 da Gama had rounded the Cape of Good Hope at Africa's southernmost tip and made his way to India. Over the next half century, the Portuguese established trading forts in West and East Africa, India, the Spice Islands (now the Moluccas of Indonesia), and southern China, thereby gaining control of East-West trade. Other powerful nation-states of Europe, envious of Portugal's success, soon began to sponsor voyages of their own.

■■ **Pioneering voyages of exploration around Africa and to Asia gave Portugal control of East-West trade.**

PRIMARY SOURCE
Description of Change: excerpted
Rationale: excerpted to focus on main idea

SECTION REVIEW ANSWERS

IDENTIFY

For significance, see the following pages:
monopoly (p. 28)
Prince Henry (p. 30)
African diaspora (p. 30)
Gomes Eanes de Zurara (p. 31)
Bartolomeu Dias (p. 31)
Vasco da Gama (p. 31)

LOCATE

For locations, see the map on p. 29.

1. *Muslim and Italian merchants controlled trade, making goods costly; a new trade route*
2. *gave Portugal control of East-West trade*
3. *Portugal's location at western tip of Iberian Peninsula put it closest to southern sea routes around Africa.*
4. *Reports should indicate how slave trade arose and mention the consequences—the people who died during the voyage, increased warfare in Africa, and the separation of friends and family.*
5. *established study center, encouraged development of new navigation methods, sponsored exploration*

■ ■ SECTION 5 REVIEW

IDENTIFY and explain the significance of the following: monopoly, Prince Henry, African diaspora, Gomes Eanes de Zurara, Bartolomeu Dias, Vasco da Gama.

LOCATE and explain the importance of the following: Spice Islands, Genoa, Venice, Sagres, Black Sea, Mediterranean Sea, Madeira Islands, Cape Verde Islands, Sierra Leone, Cape of Good Hope.

1. **MAIN IDEA** Why were most European nations unhappy with the trade system in the early 1400s? What was their solution?

2. **MAIN IDEA** Why were the voyages of Bartolomeu Dias and Vasco da Gama important to Portugal?

3. **GEOGRAPHY: LOCATION** Why did Portugal, rather than Italy, Spain, or England, lead the way in exploring the East?

4. **WRITING TO PERSUADE** Imagine that you are Gomes Eanes de Zurara. Write a report to the Portuguese king explaining how the slave trade began and why Portugal should abandon its involvement.

5. **EVALUATING** How did Prince Henry of Portugal improve the study of geography and exploration?

Chapter Review Answers

WRITING A SUMMARY
See Essential Points in each section for main ideas.

REVIEWING CHRONOLOGY
1, 4, 5, 2, 3
Linking History and Geography
Each of the five events selected should illustrate one of the five themes of geography.

IDENTIFYING PEOPLE AND IDEAS

1. *physical surroundings*
2. *process of spreading cultural practices or beliefs from one group to another*
3. *multistory rock and adobe dwelling built by Anasazi*
4. *class system in which nobles pledged military assistance and loyalty to rulers in return for land and protection*
5. *series of wars fought between European Christians and Arab Muslims for control of the Holy Land*
6. *holy book of Islam, carried by followers of the prophet Muhammad as they spread their faith throughout Asia, Africa, and Europe*
7. *Chinese philosopher who taught that people should try to build a peaceful, well-ordered society*
8. *Italian merchant-adventurer who visited China and described Mongol Empire*
9. *forcible resettlement of Africans to the Americas from the 1500s through the 1800s*
10. *Portuguese explorer who circumnavigated Africa and established trade route to Asia*

UNDERSTANDING MAIN IDEAS

1. *Climate and physical resources influenced migration patterns, food-producing activities, and shelter construction.*
2. *economic—expansion of trade; political—feudalism, Crusades, rise of nations; social—exploration, formation of middle class, Renaissance*
3. *Answers will vary but should use examples from the chapter to assess the effects of trade on the culture group selected.*

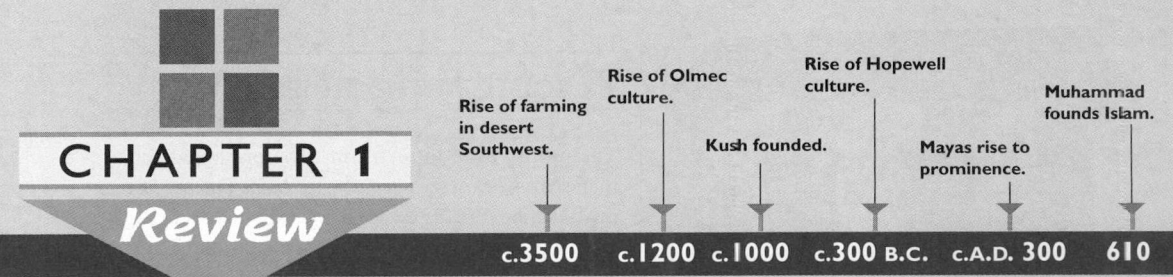

CHAPTER 1
Review

Rise of farming in desert Southwest. — c.3500
Rise of Olmec culture. — c.1200
Kush founded. — c.1000
Rise of Hopewell culture. — c.300 B.C.
Mayas rise to prominence. — c.A.D. 300
Muhammad founds Islam. — 610

WRITING A SUMMARY
Using the essential points of the chapter as a guide, write a summary of the chapter.

REVIEWING CHRONOLOGY
Number your paper 1 to 5. Study the time line above, and list the following events in the order in which they happened by writing the first next to 1, the second next to 2, and so on. Then complete the activity below.

1. Rise of farming in the desert Southwest.
2. Prince Henry's navigation center established.
3. Vasco da Gama sails to India.
4. Muhammad founds Islam.
5. Crusades begin.

Linking History and Geography Pick five events on the time line and tell how each illustrates one of the five themes of geography.

IDENTIFYING PEOPLE AND IDEAS
Explain the historical significance of each of the following people or terms.

1. environment
2. cultural diffusion
3. pueblo
4. feudalism
5. Crusades
6. Qur'an
7. Confucius
8. Marco Polo
9. African diaspora
10. Vasco da Gama

UNDERSTANDING MAIN IDEAS
1. What effect did geography and the changing environment of the Americas have on Paleo-Indian culture?
2. What were the major economic, political, and social changes in Europe during the Middle Ages?
3. Describe the role of trade in one of the following: the spread of Islamic culture; relations between China and the West; the development of African kingdoms; or Portuguese exploration.

REVIEWING THEMES
1. **Cultural Diversity** What evidence suggests that cultural diffusion occurred between Native American cultures in Mesoamerica and in North America?
2. **Economic Development** How did the Crusades benefit European economies?
3. **Technology and Society** How did technological advances influence cultural development in medieval Europe?

THINKING CRITICALLY
1. **Evaluating** Why do historians consider the advent of farming in the Americas such an important event?
2. **Synthesizing** Describe daily life in feudal society, including the role of the Roman Catholic church.
3. **Analyzing** How did Muslims influence cultural diffusion between Africa, Asia, and Europe?

STRATEGY FOR SUCCESS
Review the *Skills Handbook* entry on Reviewing Map Basics on page 992. Then study the map below of Black Mesa in Arizona. A mesa is a flat-topped natural elevation, much like a plateau. The shaded area represents the site of an ancient Native American village. According to the map, approximately how far is Kayenta from Rough Rock? What features of the region might have encouraged Native Americans to settle there?

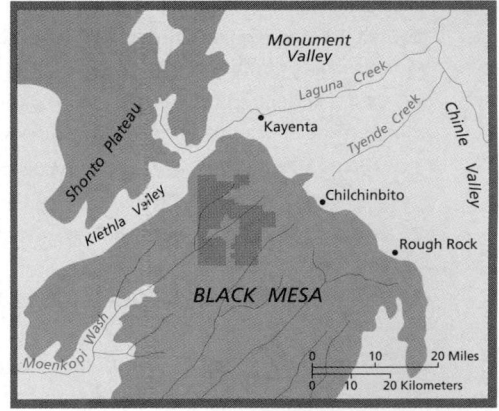

Monument Valley
Laguna Creek
Shonto Plateau
Kayenta
Tyende Creek
Chinle Valley
Chilchinbito
Klethla Valley
Rough Rock
BLACK MESA
Moenkopi Wash
0   10   20 Miles
0   10   20 Kilometers

REVIEWING THEMES

1. Cultural diffusion led to an exchange of agricultural methods, trade goods, social roles, language, and customs.
2. strengthened economy by increasing trade profits
3. New equipment increased farm production and contributed to the fall of feudalism; printing press spread knowledge to the masses.

THINKING CRITICALLY

1. because it represented control over the food source, permitting a shift from nomadic hunter-gatherer existence to more permanent communities; encouraged trade and other cultural exchanges
2. Noblemen managed estates, hunted, and fought in battles; noblewomen married, had large families, and directed servants; serfs labored in manor's fields and household; church was center of village social life.
3. Africa—influenced development of Swahili language; Asia—refined Arabic numeral system and concept of zero, advanced art of cartography; Europe—influenced mathematics and science, used compass and astrolabe in exploration

WRITING ABOUT HISTORY

Answers will vary but should express the accomplishments of the culture chosen.

USING PRIMARY SOURCES

oral historian who passed along traditions and knowledge of tribe to other generations; instructed kings in history of ancestors; resolved quarrels between tribes

LINKING HISTORY AND GEOGRAPHY

Charts will vary but should identify the culture area, the Native American groups present, the features of each group, the place characteristics, and the traces of each group still evident.

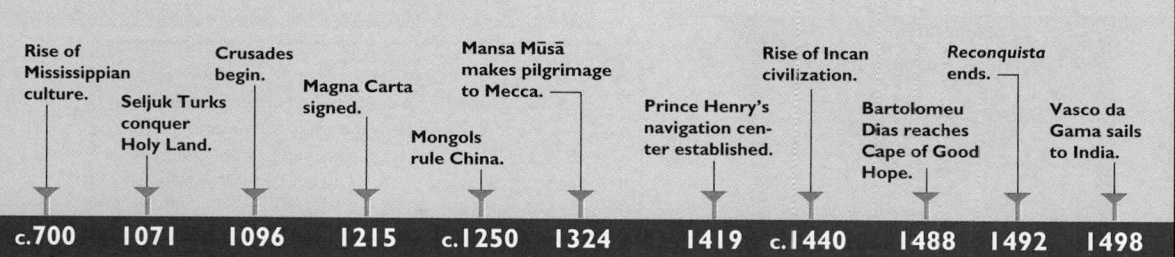

Rise of Mississippian culture.	Seljuk Turks conquer Holy Land.	Crusades begin.	Magna Carta signed.		Mansa Mūsā makes pilgrimage to Mecca.	Mongols rule China.	Prince Henry's navigation center established.	Rise of Incan civilization.	Bartolomeu Dias reaches Cape of Good Hope.	Reconquista ends.	Vasco da Gama sails to India.
c.700	1071	1096	1215	c.1250	1324		1419	c.1440	1488	1492	1498

WRITING ABOUT HISTORY

Writing to Create Research the ceremonies, social roles, or artistic expressions of one culture described in the chapter. Then write a poem or song celebrating the accomplishments of this culture.

USING PRIMARY SOURCES

Africa has a rich tradition of oral, or spoken, literature, such as the epic poem. One of the best-known African epic poems is *Sundiata*, the story of the 13th-century founder of the empire of Mali. The narrator is a *griot*, an oral historian named Mamoudou Kouyaté (KOO-yah-tai). Read the poem, then write a paragraph explaining the role of the griot in African culture.

Sundiata

I am a griot. It is I, Djeli Mamoudou Kouyaté, son of Bintou Kouyaté and Djeli Kedian Kouyaté, master of the art of eloquence [speaking]. Since time immemorial the Kouyates have been in the service of the Keita princes of Mali; we are vessels of speech, we are the repositories which harbour secrets many centuries old. . . . Without us the names of kings would vanish into oblivion, we are the memory of mankind; by the spoken word we bring to life the deeds and exploits of kings for younger generations. . . .

I teach kings the history of their ancestors so that the lives of the ancients might serve them as an example, for the world is old, but the future springs from the past.

My word is pure and free of all untruth; it is the word of my father; it is the word of my father's father. I will give you my father's words just as I received them; royal griots do not know what lying is. When a quarrel breaks out between tribes it is we who settle the difference, for we are the depositaries [people entrusted with something] of oaths which the ancestors swore.

Listen to my word, you who want to know; by my mouth you will learn the history of Mali.

—Translated by D. T. Niane

LINKING HISTORY AND GEOGRAPHY

Study the map on page 15. Locate the culture area in which your community is found. Then prepare a chart listing the Native American groups who lived in your area in 1500, the main features of each group, the major place characteristics of the area, and the influences of these groups that still exist locally—either through place-names, artifacts, or customs.

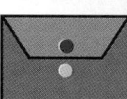

BUILDING YOUR PORTFOLIO

Complete the following projects independently or cooperatively.

1. **TRADE** Imagine you are a trader in the late 1400s. Prepare a map that shows trade routes between Europe, Africa, and Asia. Draw symbols on the map to indicate major items of trade.

2. **CULTURAL EXCHANGES** Imagine you are a museum researcher preparing an exhibit on cultural exchanges in the Americas. Select two groups that appear to have had cultural contact prior to 1500. Create a wall chart that illustrates the nature of the contact.

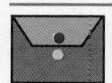

BUILDING YOUR PORTFOLIO

Have students refer to **Building Your Portfolio Worksheet 1**, assigned at the beginning of Unit 1. Use the worksheet to help students monitor their progress on the portfolio projects.

Assessment

Core Resources
- Review Worksheet 1
- Chapter 1 Tests
- Alternative Assessment Forms

Test Generator

A MEETING OF CULTURES

HISTORICAL SIDELIGHTS

The Horse

Fossilized remains of the modern horse's ancestors have been found in the Mississippi Valley area. The prehistoric breed became extinct for reasons not yet known, and horses did not reappear in the Americas until the Spanish brought them from Europe in the 1500s. Other species that became extinct in North America before the arrival of Europeans include the early camel, long-horned bison, tapir, dire wolf, and giant ground sloth.

America's GEOGRAPHY

THE COLUMBIAN EXCHANGE

::

THE exchange of goods across the Atlantic Ocean that Columbus started transformed the world. Even the distribution of the world's flora and fauna was affected. The first European explorers and settlers were struck by the differences between the plants and animals of Europe and those of the Americas. They responded to the unfamiliar environment by introducing familiar food crops and livestock, hoping to transform the Americas into another Europe.

Food plants from the Americas were also quickly introduced into Africa, Europe, and Asia. Many of these plants were particularly useful because they produced higher yields and could tolerate a wider range of climates than could the old staples, wheat and rice.

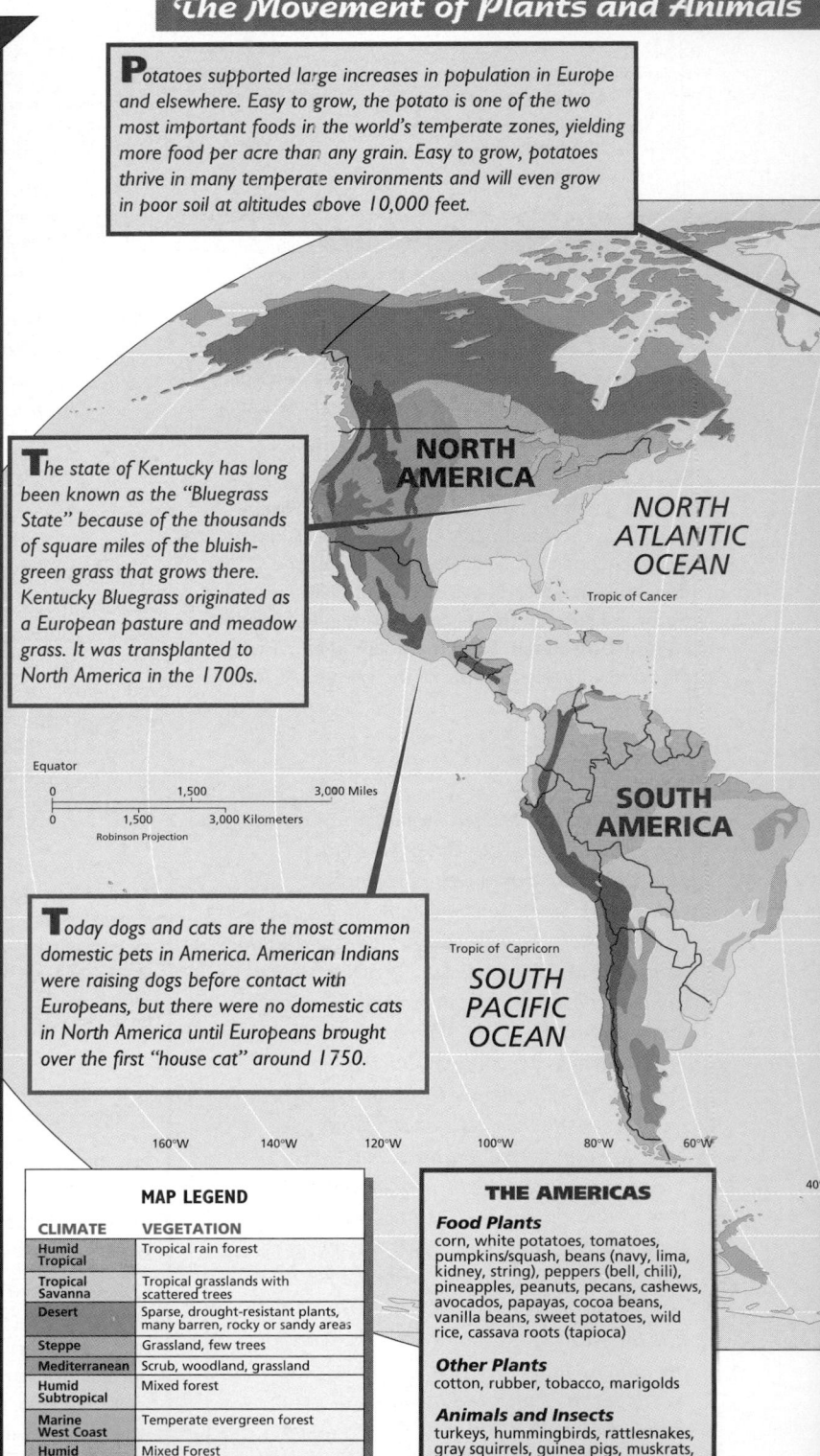

The Movement of Plants and Animals

Potatoes supported large increases in population in Europe and elsewhere. Easy to grow, the potato is one of the two most important foods in the world's temperate zones, yielding more food per acre than any grain. Easy to grow, potatoes thrive in many temperate environments and will even grow in poor soil at altitudes above 10,000 feet.

The state of Kentucky has long been known as the "Bluegrass State" because of the thousands of square miles of the bluish-green grass that grows there. Kentucky Bluegrass originated as a European pasture and meadow grass. It was transplanted to North America in the 1700s.

Today dogs and cats are the most common domestic pets in America. American Indians were raising dogs before contact with Europeans, but there were no domestic cats in North America until Europeans brought over the first "house cat" around 1750.

NORTH AMERICA

NORTH ATLANTIC OCEAN

Tropic of Cancer

Equator

| 0 | | 1,500 | | 3,000 Miles |
| 0 | 1,500 | | 3,000 Kilometers | |

Robinson Projection

SOUTH AMERICA

Tropic of Capricorn

SOUTH PACIFIC OCEAN

160°W   140°W   120°W   100°W   80°W   60°W

40°

MAP LEGEND

CLIMATE	VEGETATION
Humid Tropical	Tropical rain forest
Tropical Savanna	Tropical grasslands with scattered trees
Desert	Sparse, drought-resistant plants, many barren, rocky or sandy areas
Steppe	Grassland, few trees
Mediterranean	Scrub, woodland, grassland
Humid Subtropical	Mixed forest
Marine West Coast	Temperate evergreen forest
Humid Continental	Mixed Forest
Subartic	Northern evergreen forest
Tundra	Moss, lichens, low shrubs
Highland	Forest to tundra vegetation, varies with altitude

THE AMERICAS

Food Plants
corn, white potatoes, tomatoes, pumpkins/squash, beans (navy, lima, kidney, string), peppers (bell, chili), pineapples, peanuts, pecans, cashews, avocados, papayas, cocoa beans, vanilla beans, sweet potatoes, wild rice, cassava roots (tapioca)

Other Plants
cotton, rubber, tobacco, marigolds

Animals and Insects
turkeys, hummingbirds, rattlesnakes, gray squirrels, guinea pigs, muskrats, potato beetles

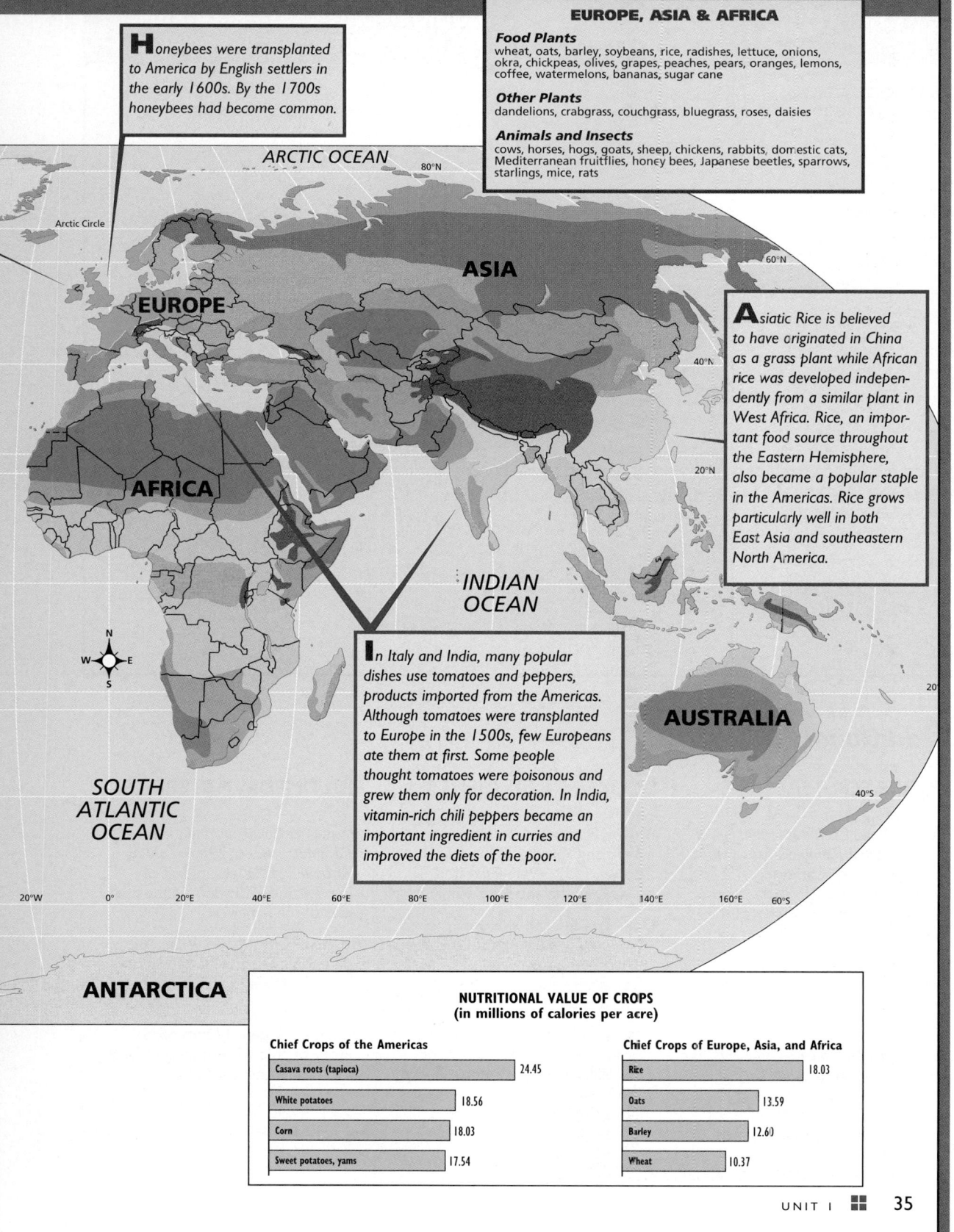

Honeybees were transplanted to America by English settlers in the early 1600s. By the 1700s honeybees had become common.

ARCTIC OCEAN

Arctic Circle

80°N

EUROPE, ASIA & AFRICA

Food Plants
wheat, oats, barley, soybeans, rice, radishes, lettuce, onions, okra, chickpeas, olives, grapes, peaches, pears, oranges, lemons, coffee, watermelons, bananas, sugar cane

Other Plants
dandelions, crabgrass, couchgrass, bluegrass, roses, daisies

Animals and Insects
cows, horses, hogs, goats, sheep, chickens, rabbits, domestic cats, Mediterranean fruitflies, honey bees, Japanese beetles, sparrows, starlings, mice, rats

ASIA

EUROPE

60°N

40°N

Asiatic Rice is believed to have originated in China as a grass plant while African rice was developed independently from a similar plant in West Africa. Rice, an important food source throughout the Eastern Hemisphere, also became a popular staple in the Americas. Rice grows particularly well in both East Asia and southeastern North America.

20°N

AFRICA

N W E S

INDIAN OCEAN

In Italy and India, many popular dishes use tomatoes and peppers, products imported from the Americas. Although tomatoes were transplanted to Europe in the 1500s, few Europeans ate them at first. Some people thought tomatoes were poisonous and grew them only for decoration. In India, vitamin-rich chili peppers became an important ingredient in curries and improved the diets of the poor.

AUSTRALIA

SOUTH ATLANTIC OCEAN

40°S

20°W   0°   20°E   40°E   60°E   80°E   100°E   120°E   140°E   160°E   60°S

ANTARCTICA

NUTRITIONAL VALUE OF CROPS
(in millions of calories per acre)

Chief Crops of the Americas		Chief Crops of Europe, Asia, and Africa	
Casava roots (tapioca)	24.45	Rice	18.03
White potatoes	18.56	Oats	13.59
Corn	18.03	Barley	12.60
Sweet potatoes, yams	17.54	Wheat	10.37

Pesky Products

Not all the plants and animals transported to Europe from the Americas were as beneficial as corn or turkeys. An American vine aphid, or small insect, threatened France's valuable grape crop during the 1860s. North American gray squirrels have almost completely displaced British red squirrels. Muskrats, which Europeans introduced in 1905 and hoped would provide an inexpensive and fashionable source of fur, practically overran the continent before worried citizens embarked on a control program in 1917.

EMPIRES OF THE AMERICAS

1492–1800

Chapter Overview

Until the late 1400s the Americas remained insulated by two broad oceans, virtually unknown to the rest of the world. Although the native peoples of the Americas had experienced some contact with other cultures before 1492, they were unprepared for the European invasion that followed Columbus's voyage. By the mid-1500s Spain controlled a vast American empire; however, by the end of the century Spain's power was beginning to decline. England, fresh from its victory over the Spanish Armada, began building its own colonial empire in North America.

Chapter Planning Guide

CHAPTER 2	CORE RESOURCE BOOKLETS	AUDIOVISUAL RESOURCES	PROGRAM RESOURCES
INTRODUCTION pp. 36–37	■ Literature Worksheet 2 ■ Building Your Portfolio Worksheet 1		
TEACHING THE CHAPTER pp. 38–61	■ Graphic Organizer 2 ■ Social Studies Skills Worksheet 2 ■ Geography Worksheet 2 ■ Outline Maps 8, 9, 11, 12, 13, 14	■ *The American Nation* Videodisc: The Spanish Mission System ■ Linking Geography and History Transparency and Worksheet 6 ■ Everyday Life in America Transparency and Worksheet 2	■ Art in American History Transparency and Worksheet 4 ■ *Eyewitnesses and Others*, Volume 1: Readings 1, 2, 3, 4, 6
REVIEW AND ASSESSMENT pp. 62–63	■ Chapter 2 Daily Quizzes ■ Review Worksheet 2 ■ Chapter 2 Tests ■ Alternative Assessment Forms		■ Test Generator

Additional Resources

BOOKS FOR TEACHERS

Curtin, Philip D. *The Rise and Fall of the Plantation Complex: Essays in Atlantic History.* Cambridge University Press, 1990. In-depth study by leading historian of the slave trade.

Davies, Nigel. *The Aztec Empire.* University of Oklahoma Press, 1987. Discussion of Aztec history and culture.

Wright, Ronald. *Stolen Continents: The Americas Through Indian Eyes Since 1492.* Houghton Mifflin, 1992. Examines European colonization from the Native American perspective.

BOOKS FOR STUDENTS

Brown, Dale, ed. *Aztecs: Reign of Blood and Splendor.* Time-Life Books, 1992. Well-illustrated history of the ancient culture.

Dor-Ner, Zvi, and William Scheller. *Columbus and the Age of Discovery.* William Morrow, 1991. Companion volume to PBS documentary.

*Marrin, Albert. *Inca and Spaniard: Pizarro and the Conquest of Peru.* Macmillan Children's Book Group, 1989. Illustrated history of the Incan empire and its conquest.

* for students reading below grade level

MULTIMEDIA MATERIALS

Christopher Columbus and the Great Adventure. Video, 28 min. Video Knowledge. Traces impact of European exploration on the peoples of the Americas.

The Incas Remembered. Video, 60 min. SSSS. Documentary explores the achievements of the Incan people.

Jamestown. Video, 14 min. SSSS. Story of colony's founding through its abandonment.

THEMES IN AMERICAN HISTORY

USE WITH PAGES 36–37

Listed on the right are the themes emphasized in Chapter 2. The questions in boldface type stimulate critical thinking and provide students with an opportunity to discuss the themes within a broadened context. The questions also appear in the pupil's edition on p. 36.

■ GLOBAL RELATIONS

What positive and negative effects might result from interactions between countries? Students' examples of positive effects could include increased trade and the exchange of technological developments and new crops. Negative effects might include conflicts over control of resources and the domination of one country over the other.

■ ECONOMIC DEVELOPMENT

How might devoting energy to overseas exploration and conquest help or hurt a nation's economy? Students might consider that overseas exploration could drain money from a country's economy. However, overseas exploration could also bring new resources and establish new markets for products.

■ CULTURAL DIVERSITY

How do people's values and experiences affect their contacts with people of other cultures? Students might discuss how people's values could cause them to attempt to impose their way of life on other groups. They might mention ignorance of other cultures as a factor in people feeling that their own culture is superior, and that such feelings could lead to conflict with people of other cultures.

CHAPTER STRATEGIES FOR MEETING INDIVIDUAL NEEDS

LIMITED ENGLISH PROFICIENT LEARNERS

As students read through the chapter, have them work in pairs to select an illustration from each section. Ask pairs to write a caption for each illustration, explaining its significance and tying it to the section content.

TACTILE/KINESTHETIC LEARNERS

Have students work in groups to create a large map of the voyages of exploration. Assign each group a specific voyage to chart and annotate.

LEARNERS HAVING DIFFICULTY

Have students work in pairs to create biography cards of the chapter's key people and groups. One side should list the name of the person or group; the other should list pertinent actions, events, and issues. Have students use the cards to quiz each other.

AUDITORY LEARNERS

Pair students and assign each pair a person discussed in the chapter. Have pairs write statements that might have been said by their assigned person. Call on volunteers to read their statements and have the class identify the person.

VISUAL LEARNERS

Have students use materials in the school and public libraries to locate visual materials of the period covered in this chapter. Have volunteers share their visuals.

GIFTED LEARNERS

Have students write an illustrated report chronicling Columbus's voyages to the Americas or Magellan's voyage of circumnavigation.

USING THE CHAPTER FOCUS

■ UNDERSTANDING THE MAIN IDEA

After students read Understanding the Main Idea, ask them to speculate about how people's lives around the world changed after Columbus's voyages.

THEMES

Have students work individually or in small groups to answer the questions under Themes. Save students' responses so that they can compare them with their responses after studying the chapter. (See p. 35B for suggested answers.)

■ THE TIME LINE

In the year that Columbus sailed to the Americas, Martin Behaim, a German navigator and geographer, constructed the oldest existing globe of the earth—a round ball with a parchment map pasted to it. The globe reflected current cartographic knowledge; there was nothing between the European and Asian coasts but Japan and a few scattered islands. Ask students how much time passed between Columbus's landing in the Americas and Spain's conquest of the Aztecs, and from Columbus's landing to the founding of England's colony at Jamestown.

CORE RESOURCES

- Graphic Organizer 2
- Literature Worksheet 2
- Social Studies Skills Worksheet 2
- Outline Maps 8, 9, 11, 12, 13, 14
- Building Your Portfolio Worksheet 1

ABOUT THE ILLUSTRATION

This view of Columbus's landing in the Americas was printed by 16th-century Flemish engraver and publisher Theodor de Bry. This engraving, as with most artistic representations of early European-American contact, shows how the artist imagined the event taking place, for few eyewitness portrayals exist. Ask students to speculate about how the Spaniards and the Native Americans reacted upon first seeing each other.

Chapter 2

1492–1800

EMPIRES OF THE AMERICAS

FOCUS

UNDERSTANDING THE MAIN IDEA

Christopher Columbus's landing in the Americas in 1492 marked a turning point in world history. The event forever altered the lives of people around the globe as the cultures of Europe, Africa, Asia, and the Americas came into contact with one another. Much of this encounter brought conflict; but it also united many separate societies into one connected world.

THEMES

■ GLOBAL RELATIONS
What positive and negative effects might result from interactions between countries?

■ ECONOMIC DEVELOPMENT How might devoting energy to overseas exploration and conquest help or hurt a nation's economy?

■ CULTURAL DIVERSITY
How do people's values and experiences affect their contacts with people of other cultures?

1492	1519	1565	1607	1612	1779
Columbus lands in the Americas.	Conquest of Aztecs begins.	St. Augustine founded.	Jamestown established.	Rolfe introduces tobacco in Jamestown.	Gaspar de Portolá founds San Diego.

Have students list the technological advances made during the Middle Ages that aided navigation. Discuss how these advances contributed to the search for quicker trading routes to Asia and to other voyages of exploration.

■ Ask students what recent technological advances have "connected" the world. *(satellite communication, computers, fax machines)*

HISTORICAL SIDELIGHTS

The Myth of Paradise

Many European explorers were intrigued by an age-old legend about an earthly paradise that lay somewhere beyond the western horizon. Looking upon the exotic beauty of the Indies for the first time, Columbus and his sailors may have thought that they had discovered that mythic land.

■ **LINK TO THE PAST**

In the 1400s, Europeans sought an eastward sea route to Asia to replace the long, dangerous, and expensive overland routes. Years of trading in the Mediterranean and the Atlantic had given many merchants valuable sailing experience. Moreover, scientific and technological advances had taken some of the guesswork out of navigation.

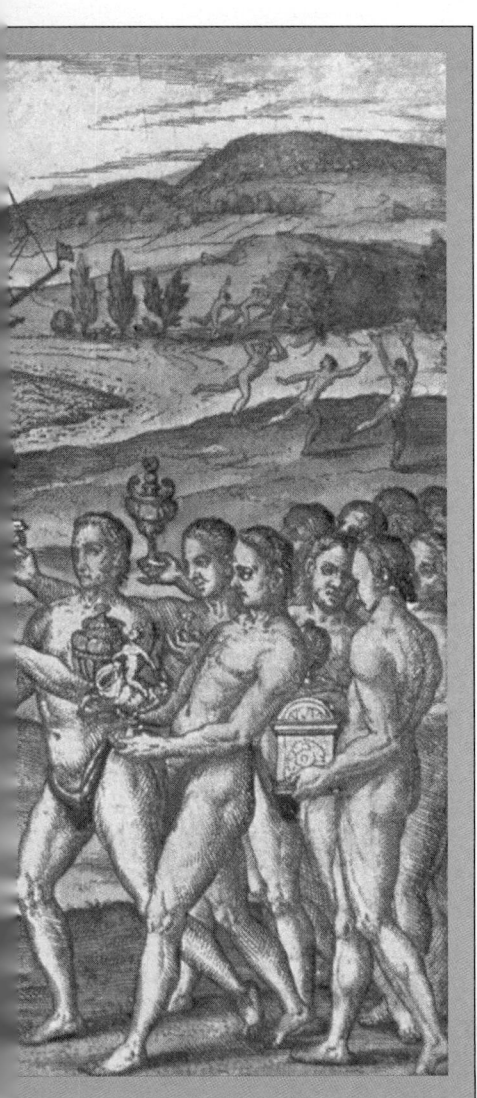

First contact between Columbus and Native Americans, 1492

𝓕ew dates in American history are as instantly recognizable as 1492. It was a year that shaped the destiny of continents. With Christopher Columbus's daring voyage, worlds apart became worlds in contact—and conflict.

On Friday, October 12, 1492, Columbus landed on an island in the Bahamas and "broke out the royal banner, and the captain's two flags with the green cross." These actions staked Spain's first claims in the Americas.

Columbus and his captains admired the beauty and abundance of this land: "Once ashore they saw very green trees and many ponds and fruits of various kinds." Columbus and the Europeans who followed him saw these lands as theirs for the taking. In their zeal to spread their cultures and enrich their treasuries, many Europeans imposed their ways of life on the original inhabitants of the Americas. Rich and varied Native American cultures were changed or destroyed as a result.

Still, Columbus's voyages and those of later explorers were remarkable feats. These first explorers and colonists carved out new lives for themselves, often in harsh environments. In the process, they created new American cultures and brought great riches to Europe.

Flora and fauna of the Americas

SECTION

1

Introducing the Section

FOCUS OBJECTIVES

- Explain why Columbus sailed west from Europe.

- Analyze the purpose of the *encomienda* system and explain how it affected Native Americans.

- Identify the reforms Las Casas urged the Spanish Crown to undertake.

- Describe some of the results of the Columbian exchange.

**BIO
GRAPHY** **PERSONALITIES
IN HISTORY**

Columbus was an expert in a navigational skill called "dead reckoning," which calculates a ship's position by estimating course and speed. Columbus measured the ship's speed by watching the flow of water along the hull while assessing the effects of winds and currents.

CORE RESOURCES

• Section 1 Daily Quiz

PREVIEW WORKSHOP

Following is a list of the significant people, places, and terms in this section. You may wish to use this list as a section preview.

People
- Christopher Columbus
- Tainos
- Guacanagarí
- Bartolomé de Las Casas

Places
- Bahamas
- Hispaniola
- La Navidad

Terms
- viceroy
- *encomienda*
- Columbian exchange

Section 1

FIRST CONTACT

F O C U S

- **Why did Columbus sail west from Europe?**
- **What was the purpose of the *encomienda* system? How did it affect Native Americans?**
- **What reforms did Las Casas urge the Spanish Crown to undertake?**
- **What were some of the results of the Columbian exchange?**

*B*y the 15th century, Europeans desired a cheaper, faster trade route to the East. Portugal took the lead, concentrating on finding a sea passage around the southernmost tip of Africa. But Spain, largely because of the boldness and imagination of one man—Christopher Columbus—looked westward. Columbus's landing introduced the Americas to the rest of the world, thus beginning a new era of trade, colonization, and cultural exchange.

Portuguese astrolabe

CHRISTOPHER COLUMBUS

In 1492 a mariner named Christopher Columbus set sail from Spain on the first in a series of historic Atlantic crossings. He understood that the earth was round and concluded that if he sailed far enough west, he could establish a more direct trade route to Asia.

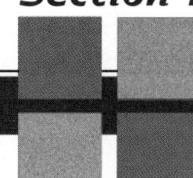

Columbus grew up in Genoa, a bustling port city on Italy's western coast. Fascinated by the sea, the adventurous youth sailed on Genoese trading vessels. He became an excellent navigator and learned to handle a caravel—a small, lightweight vessel most often used in sea trade. A former shipmate recalled Columbus's skill: "By a

Christopher Columbus

simple look at the night sky, he would know what route to follow or what weather to expect."

Eventually Columbus made his way to Lisbon, Portugal, the center of European knowledge about sea travel. While in Lisbon, he studied charts of contemporary geographers and astronomers and read ancient Greek and Roman texts, the Bible, and Marco Polo's exciting account of his travels in Asia. As a result of his studies, Columbus developed a theory about a westward route to Asia. He concluded that the western sea could not be very large and that the great trading cities of Asia lay about 2,400 miles west of Portugal.

■■ Columbus believed that by sailing west from Europe, he could find a more direct route to Asia.

In the 1480s Columbus tried to persuade various European monarchs to sponsor a westward voyage across the Atlantic Ocean. He had little success. King John II of Portugal rejected the plan because he doubted Columbus's calculation of the

MOTIVATING:
STUDENT EXPERIENCES

Ask students to brainstorm about what they would want to know before setting off on a trip to a place they had never visited. Ask what feelings they might have about such a trip and what risks might be involved. Then discuss what information they think Columbus had before setting out on his journey, how he might have felt, and what risks he faced.

Teaching the Section

SAILING WEST FROM EUROPE

Have students write a letter from Columbus to Ferdinand and Isabella, explaining why he wants to sail west from Europe, what he hopes to find, and why he feels he is qualified to make the journey. Have volunteers read their letters to the class. Students may wish to include their letters in their portfolios.

distance to Asia. In fact, the actual distance to Asia proved to be about five times greater than Columbus had calculated.

Initially Columbus had no better luck with the Spanish monarchs, Ferdinand and Isabella. They devoted most of their energy and money to the *Reconquista,* the reconquest of Spain from the Moors. But Columbus persisted. He described to them the golden palaces and temples of Asia mentioned in Marco Polo's tales and tempted them with visions of the riches that could belong to Spain.

Columbus also vowed to take the Catholic faith to the peoples of foreign lands, a task for which he believed God had chosen him. This idea impressed the deeply religious Isabella. Nevertheless, it was only after the monarchs had defeated the Moors at Granada in January 1492 that they were willing to back an expedition. On April 17, 1492, the king and the queen authorized the necessary funding for Columbus's journey.

To reward Columbus for his future discoveries, Ferdinand and Isabella agreed that the mariner would be knighted, appointed admiral, and made **viceroy,** or governor, over all the lands he might discover. After his death these titles would be passed on to his descendants. In addition, he was to receive at least 10 percent of the riches he obtained on Spain's behalf.

THE FATEFUL FIRST VOYAGE

Columbus outfitted three vessels—the *Santa María,* the *Niña,* and the *Pinta*—and recruited an experienced crew of 90 sailors, most of whom were Spaniards. At dawn on August 3, 1492, Columbus and his crew departed from Palos, Spain. The small fleet first journeyed some 800 miles southwest to the Canary Islands, Spain's westernmost possession. Then in September the three vessels set out across the uncharted sea.

Imagine them one month later: Somewhere in the vast Atlantic, three small ships sail slowly westward. The men aboard have not sighted land since leaving the Canaries. The crew's patience is wearing thin, their hopes having risen like the waves with every sign of land—birds, green weeds, cloudbanks—only to be dashed. Many sailors demand that the ships turn back. Then, as the lookout on the lead ship scans the horizon in the early morning hours of October 12, he gives the long-awaited cry: "*Tierra!*" Land!

The October 12th entry in Columbus's *Journal,* his diary of the voyage, reads: "[At] daylight Friday . . . they reached an islet . . . which was called Guanahani [gwahn-uh-HAHN-ee]. . . . Soon they saw naked people, and the Admiral went ashore in his armed longboat." (The *Journal* survives only in a secondhand summary, which explains why Columbus is referred to as "the Admiral.")

The people of the Indies. Columbus and his men had struck land on a tiny coral island in the central Bahamas, about 400 miles southeast of present-day Florida. Columbus named it San Salvador (Holy Savior). Confident that he had reached Asia, the Admiral called the island dwellers "Indios," the Spanish word for inhabitants of the Indies.

The Native Americans Columbus encountered called themselves "Tainos" (TEE-nohs), the word for "good" or "noble" in their Arawak language. The Tainos were farmers who lived in settlements of some 100 to 300 people. Some groups traded salt, shells, and other goods peacefully with their neighbors. Other groups participated in raids against other islands. Taino war chiefs increased their power through successful raids.

On the larger islands of the Caribbean—such as present-day Cuba, Puerto Rico, Jamaica, and Hispaniola (his-puhn-YOH-luh)—lived groups with a more complex social and political organization. They built larger settlements with leaders living in a central area surrounded by the villagers' houses. They exported tobacco, salt, and handicrafts as far as the mainland.

The Spanish praised the Tainos' generosity. "They invite you to share anything that they possess, and show as much love as if their hearts went

▲ **This drawing by Gonzalo Fernández de Oviedo y Valdés shows the type of building in which Taino chiefs lived.**

GLOBAL CONNECTIONS

The day before Columbus set sail, numerous other ships were leaving Spain. Shortly after the *Reconquista,* the Crown forced Jews to leave Spain by August 2, 1492, unless they converted to Roman Catholicism.

MAKING CONNECTIONS
Science

Advances in navigation were reflected in the *Niña,* the *Pinta,* and the *Santa María.* When running before the wind, the vessels' swiftness was notable, often surpassing that of present-day yachts. The 33 days that the vessels took to get from the Canary Islands to the Bahamas would impress even today's navigators.

Teaching the Section

THE *ENCOMIENDA* SYSTEM

Ask volunteers to define the *encomienda* system. Have students compare the *encomienda* system with earlier feudalism in Europe. (If necessary, refer students to pp. 17 and 18 in their textbooks.) Touch on the relationship in each system between landowner, workers, and land; the role of the Roman Catholic church; and so on. Then pair students to role-play a conversa-tion between an *encomendero* and a Native American worker. The worker should complain to the *encomendero* about the hardships of the *encomienda* system. The *encomendero* should defend the system by explaining its purpose. Select pairs to present their exchanges to the class.

with it," Columbus noted. He believed that they would make easy converts to the Catholic faith. But he also took the Tainos' generosity to mean that they "could all be subjugated [conquered] and compelled to do anything one wishes."

The search for gold. Because some of the Tainos wore gold ornaments, Columbus concluded that gold mines were close at hand. Over the next month Columbus and his men sailed from island to island—naming and claiming each for Spain—in search of gold. Then on Christmas Eve, 1492, the *Santa María* struck a coral reef off the island that Columbus had named Hispaniola—the site of present-day Haiti and the Dominican Republic. The crew was forced to abandon ship. Believing that the shipwreck was a sign from God, Columbus decided to establish the first Spanish colony here. He named the settlement La Navidad (The Nativity), in honor of the day of its founding.

Like the inhabitants of Guanahani, the Indians of Hispaniola were generous to the Spanish. Their chief, Guacanagarí (gwah-KAHN-uh-gah-REE), showered Columbus with gold nuggets and ornaments—even promising "a statue of pure gold" the size of Columbus himself. This impressive display convinced some of Columbus's men to remain in the settlement.

Columbus sailed back to Spain in January 1493, taking with him two dozen Taino captives and evidence of the riches of the Indies. Ferdinand and Isabella gave him a hero's welcome and speedily approved a second voyage.

The captive islanders were objects of both sympathy and curiosity. The queen ordered that the Indians on Hispaniola and elsewhere in the Americas be treated humanely and converted to the Roman Catholic faith. But she left open the possibility that anyone who resisted the authority of the Spanish Crown could be enslaved.

COLUMBUS THE COLONIZER

When Columbus returned to La Navidad 11 months later, he found the colony destroyed. All the Spaniards were dead or gone. Some probably had left to find gold elsewhere, but most either had fallen victim to illness or had died in disputes with one another or with the Tainos. Most likely, the colonists' excessive demands for gold and food had worn down the generosity of the Tainos, causing conflicts.

Columbus and some 1,500 male colonists—most of whom were craftsmen, builders, or farmers—built another settlement: Isabela. Columbus left the settlement under the care of his brother Bartolomé and spent the next three years sailing the Caribbean searching for gold. While Columbus was away, the pressure the colonists put on the Indians to provide food and gold led the Indians to revolt. Violent disputes over land and Indian labor also broke out between Bartolomé and the colonists. Columbus's failure to maintain order led to his eventual replacement as viceroy.

Before Columbus was replaced, he granted the colonists control over Indian labor. He thereby informally introduced to Hispaniola what would later become the *encomienda* (en-koh-mee-EN-duh) system. Under this system the colonists, or *encomenderos* (en-koh-muhn-DE-rohs), received the right to have a certain number of Indians work for them. The *encomenderos* used the Indians to mine gold, provide food, and build houses. The system required that the *encomenderos* instruct their charges in the Roman Catholic faith and permit them to grow food for themselves.

◀ This scene, entitled "Baptism of the First Indians," is taken from a *Conquista* cloth.

LAS CASAS AND REFORM

Have students work in small groups to study Las Casas's recommendations to the Crown for reforming the *encomienda* system. Then have groups draft a Spanish law to protect Indian rights. The law should incorporate Las Casas's ideas. Have groups present their proposed laws to the class and lobby for their passage. Then have the class act as an advisory body to the Crown and decide which law best addresses Las Casas's concerns. Conclude by having the class vote on which proposal to recommend to the Crown.

▶

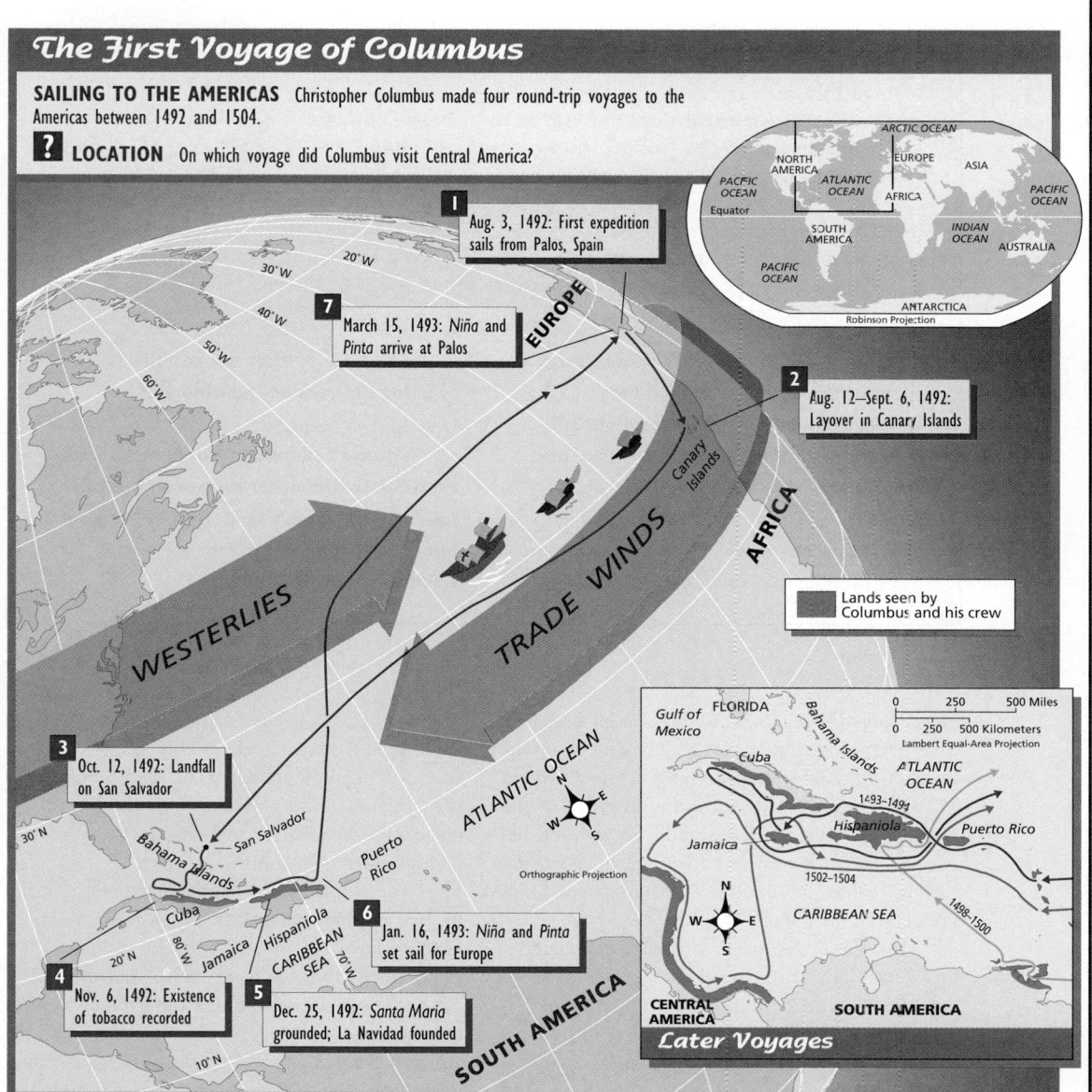

The First Voyage of Columbus

SAILING TO THE AMERICAS Christopher Columbus made four round-trip voyages to the Americas between 1492 and 1504.

? LOCATION On which voyage did Columbus visit Central America?

1 Aug. 3, 1492: First expedition sails from Palos, Spain

7 March 15, 1493: *Niña* and *Pinta* arrive at Palos

2 Aug. 12–Sept. 6, 1492: Layover in Canary Islands

WESTERLIES

TRADE WINDS

EUROPE

AFRICA

Lands seen by Columbus and his crew

3 Oct. 12, 1492: Landfall on San Salvador

ATLANTIC OCEAN

San Salvador

Bahama Islands

Puerto Rico

Cuba

Jamaica   Hispaniola

CARIBBEAN SEA

6 Jan. 16, 1493: *Niña* and *Pinta* set sail for Europe

4 Nov. 6, 1492: Existence of tobacco recorded

5 Dec. 25, 1492: *Santa Maria* grounded; La Navidad founded

SOUTH AMERICA

ARCTIC OCEAN

NORTH AMERICA   EUROPE   ASIA

PACIFIC OCEAN   ATLANTIC OCEAN   AFRICA   PACIFIC OCEAN

Equator

SOUTH AMERICA   INDIAN OCEAN   AUSTRALIA

PACIFIC OCEAN

ANTARCTICA

Robinson Projection

Gulf of Mexico   FLORIDA   Bahama Islands

Cuba   ATLANTIC OCEAN

1493–1494

Jamaica   Hispaniola   Puerto Rico

1502–1504

1498–1500

CARIBBEAN SEA

CENTRAL AMERICA   SOUTH AMERICA

0   250   500 Miles
0   250   500 Kilometers
Lambert Equal-Area Projection

Orthographic Projection

Later Voyages

The Spanish Crown formally established the *encomienda* system in the Americas in 1503. In the monarchs' eyes Native Americans were not slaves—they were supposed to be paid a small allowance for their labor. But in practice the *encomienda* system amounted to enslavement for many Indians because they were seldom paid.

The *encomienda* also disrupted Indian economies and societies. Because of excessive Spanish demands for food and labor, Indians had little time to grow food for themselves. Widespread malnutrition resulted. The Spanish were thus able to take the most fertile pieces of land away from the Indians. The Spanish also disturbed Indian societies by suppressing Indian customs and religions.

■■ **The *encomienda* system gave the Spanish control over Indian labor and disrupted Indian societies.**

LAS CASAS AND SLAVERY

Some Spaniards protested the harsh treatment of Native Americans. One prominent critic, Bartolomé de Las Casas, had spent some years as

VOICES IN HISTORY

To illustrate the cultural differences between the Spanish and the Native Americans, Las Casas told the story of Hathvey, an Indian chief who fled to Cuba from Hispaniola. Hathvey explained to the Indians that the Spaniards believed gold to have supernatural powers. He suggested that if the Indians prayed to these same powers, the Spanish might possibly be placated. Following Hathvey's advice, the Indians prayed to a gold-filled chest.

In 1511 the Spaniards traveled to Cuba, where they captured Hathvey and burned him alive for worshipping false gods. As the chief neared death, a monk extolled the glories of the Spaniards' heaven to him. Hathvey replied, "Let me go to hell that I may not come where they [the Spanish] are."

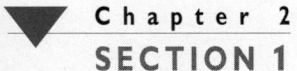
Teaching the Section

RESULTS OF THE COLUMBIAN EXCHANGE

Have students study the America's Geography feature on pp. 34–35 and the Commentary on pp. 43–44 and discuss the exchange of items. Then organize the class into four groups. Ask one group to develop a list of the pros and cons of the Columbian exchange from the American perspective. The other groups should develop similar lists from the European, Asian, and African perspectives. Have groups present and explain their lists.

■■ Ask students to give examples of ways in which the Columbian exchange affects their lives today.

THE SLAVE TRADE

Nzinga Mbemba (en-ZING uhm-BEM-buh), **"Lord of the Congo,"** was a central-African ruler who hoped to increase contact and trade between the Congo states and the leading European powers. To aid this effort, he even adopted the Christian faith and assumed a new name: Dom Afonso. His dreams turned sour, however, as he watched Portuguese slave ships take more and more of his people by force to the Americas. In 1526 he urged King John III of Portugal to curb this practice:

THROUGH OTHERS' EYES

66 We cannot reckon how great the damage is, since the . . . [slave] merchants daily seize our subjects, sons of the land and sons of our noblemen and vassals and our relatives. . . . Thieves and men of evil conscience take them . . . and cause them to be sold: and so great, Sir, is their corruption . . . that our country is being utterly depopulated. **99**

Afonso's pleas went unheeded, however. Spain and other European nations followed Portugal's lead. By 1600 several hundred thousand Africans were in bondage in the Americas.

an *encomendero* in Cuba. He spent a great deal of time giving the Indians under his care religious instruction. But after becoming a priest around 1512, he began to question the morality of the *encomienda* system. Eventually he gave up his *encomienda* and returned to Spain to plead the Indians' cause. In 1516 the Crown appointed him Protector of the Indians.

Las Casas described to European audiences how harshly the Spanish treated Native Americans and demanded an end to the *encomienda*. He urged Spanish colonists to live and work peacefully with Native Americans. He called for friars and priests to convert Indians to Catholicism gradually, through "love, gentleness, and kindness."

In the *Apologetic History of the Indies* (1566), Las Casas argued a radical idea for the time—that Indian humanity and wisdom equaled that of Europeans:

66 Not only have [the Indians] shown themselves to be very wise peoples and possessed of lively and marked understanding, . . . governing and providing for their nations . . . but they have equaled many diverse nations of the . . . past and present . . . and exceed by no small measure the wisest of all these. **99**

Las Casas argued for Indian rights at the same time that the Spanish king wanted to limit the growing independence of the colonists. To protect the Indians and to curb the colonists' power, the Spanish Crown enacted laws in 1542 restricting *encomiendas*.

The colonists resisted the new laws, refusing to give up their control of Indian labor. Within a century, however, the *encomienda* no longer supplied much labor for the Spanish. But the end of the system came not through the Crown's actions but through the catastophic decline of the Native American population. Overwork and malnutrition contributed to the decline, but disease took by far the greatest toll.

European diseases were particularly deadly because the American Indians had no immunity to them. The cold, harsh climate of Siberia, the Bering Land Bridge, and Alaska effectively prevented disease organisms from crossing with the first immigrants to the Americas. The long isolation of the Western Hemisphere from the rest of the world meant that the Native Americans had never been exposed to diseases such as chickenpox, measles, typhus, and smallpox that were common in Europe and Africa. When Europeans and Africans arrived, they unknowingly introduced the organisms that caused these diseases.

Practice

GUIDED PRACTICE

Ask students to create on the chalkboard a time line of Columbus's first voyage to the Americas. As volunteers enter dates and events on the time line, ask other students to elaborate on those events and their significance. Leave the time line on the chalkboard for students to use in the Independent Practice.

INDEPENDENT PRACTICE

Invite students to imagine that they are crew members on Columbus's first voyage and that they have kept a personal journal of the trip. Tell students to write a journal entry for each date on the Guided Practice time line, recording their thoughts and experiences for that day. Students may wish to include their entries in their portfolios.

Review and Assessment

REVIEW Have students write a paragraph completing the following thought: *The greatest impact of Spain's involvement in the Americas was. . . .* Have volunteers read their paragraphs aloud and ask the class if they agree or disagree. Then assign the Section 1 Review on p. 44.

ASSESS Assign the **Section 1 Daily Quiz** in *Core Resources*.
▶

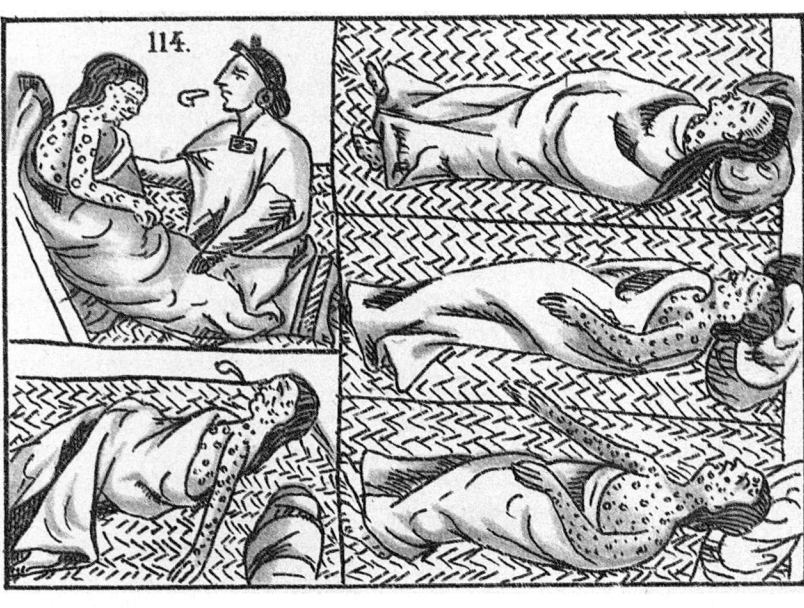

◄ This illustration from a history of New Spain written in the 1500s by a Spanish monk, Bernadinode Sahagun, shows the devastating effects of smallpox on the Aztecs. Smallpox, measles, and malaria were just a few diseases brought by Europeans that caused epidemics among Native American peoples.

PRIMARY SOURCE

Description of Change: excerpted and bracketed **Rationale:** excerpted to focus on main idea; bracketed to clarify meaning

HISTORICAL SIDELIGHTS
A "New" Continent

Vespucci published several letters in the early 1500s claiming to have sailed along the coast of a "new" continent as early as 1497. Although he probably did sail to the Americas three times, his first voyage was not until 1499, seven years after Columbus's first voyage. His letters, in which he described "a continent in those southern regions that is inhabited by more numerous peoples and animals than in our Europe, or Asia or Africa," were widely read in Europe.

HISTORICAL SIDELIGHTS
The Horse

The horse first evolved in the Americas, wandered across the land bridge to Asia, and then spread into Europe. While the horse flourished in Asia and Europe, it became extinct in the Americas.

In some areas the epidemics preceded the appearance of the Europeans, and no doubt the resulting devastation made it much easier for the Spanish to conquer the Indians. One Mayan chronicle records the dispiriting effects of an epidemic.

66 Great was the stench of the dead. After our fathers and grandfathers succumbed [died], half of the people fled to the fields. . . . The mortality was terrible. Your grandfathers died, and with them died the son of the king and his brothers and kinsmen. So it was that we became orphans, oh, my sons! So we became when we were young. All of us were thus. 99

While the death rate for Native Americans varied, in some areas their numbers declined by over 90 percent by the mid-16th century.

To replace the Indian laborers, the Spanish imported African slaves. They reached the West Indies in the early 1500s. By 1550 some 15,000 enslaved Africans had arrived in the Spanish colonies. Many worked on sugar plantations or other large farms, performing hard labor for no pay.

▪▪ **Las Casas urged the Spanish Crown to enact laws to end Spanish mistreatment of Native Americans.**

COMMENTARY

The Columbian Legacy

Historians offer different interpretations of the lasting significance of Columbus's voyages to the Americas. Some have applauded him for enlarging geographic knowledge. Yet Columbus himself died without realizing he had encountered a continent. Columbus did not even get the honor of having the continent named after him. Another navigator, Amerigo Vespucci (ahm-ay-REE-goh vay-SPOOT-chee), received that honor after he made at least two trips along the coast of present-day South America. In 1507 the German mapmaker Martin Waldseemüller (VAHLT-zay-mool-uhr) credited Vespucci with the "discovery" of America and suggested the newly encountered continent be named America in his honor.

Other people have interpreted Columbus's voyages in a negative light. They blame him for introducing the *encomienda* system to the Americas and for the drastic reduction of the Native American population. But Columbus saw himself as a faithful Christian who had won new converts to Catholicism. Las Casas, the fierce Protector of the Indians, agreed.

With such conflicting interpretations of Columbus's significance, how can we judge his impact? Perhaps the best way to understand the legacy of Columbus's voyages is to see the enormous effect they had on the world. The transfer of

RETEACH Organize students so that a roughly equal number are assigned to each subsection of the section. Direct each student to write a question about the material in his or her assigned subsection. Then use the questions to quiz the entire group.

Closure

Have students hold a panel discussion on the following topic: Columbus's voyages had negative as well as positive effects on the world.

Extension

INVESTIGATE Challenge students to investigate the impact of the Columbian exchange on European diet.

INTERPRET Have interested students write a monologue about Columbus's first voyage from the viewpoint of one of Columbus's sailors. Monologues should include descriptions of the sailor's emotions as well as sights and opinions. Encourage volunteers to perform their monologues.

SECTION REVIEW ANSWERS

IDENTIFY

For significance, see the following pages:
Christopher Columbus (p. 38)
viceroy (p. 39)
Tainos (p. 39)
Guacanagarí (p. 40)
encomienda (p. 40)
Bartolomé de Las Casas (p. 41)
Columbian exchange (p. 43)

LOCATE

For locations, see the map on p. 41.

1. *a more direct trade route between Europe and Asia*
2. *enabled Spanish to use Indian labor for mining, providing food, and building houses; took Indian lands and virtually enslaved them, disrupted their economies and societies*
3. *end to encomienda system, peaceful coexistence, conversion of Indians to Catholicism; colonists refused to give up control of Indian labor.*
4. *Essays might mention people and goods associated with Columbian exchange, effects of disease on Native Americans and slavery on African Americans, and influence of American gold and silver on European economies.*
5. *Murals should show Tainos helping Spanish and later being enslaved by them.*

people, ideas, plants, animals, and diseases between the Americas, Europe, Asia, and Africa initiated by Columbus's journeys has come to be called the **Columbian exchange** (see America's Geography feature on pages 34–35).

The Columbian exchange transformed the world. As various cultures came into contact, they transformed each other. Precious metals and other resources taken from the Americas made many European nations wealthy and powerful. Exotic agricultural products from the Americas, such as corn, potatoes, and tomatoes, soon became staples that improved the nutrition of people everywhere and often resulted in dramatic population growth. Foods crops from the Americas transformed African agriculture in particular. The plants adapted easily to the African environment and offered high yields and greater variety.

Through settlement and the slave trade, the islands and continents of the Western Hemisphere, formerly inhabited by only Native Americans, were gradually peopled with Europeans, Africans, and Asians. But the Columbian exchange involved more than the transfer of crops and people. The introduction of European animals transformed the American landscape. For example, once cattle, sheep, and pigs arrived in the Americas, they multiplied rapidly in the abundant grazing lands.

The horse, introduced to the Americas by the Spanish by 1507, proved to be particularly suited to the Americas. Horses spread from New Mexico in the 1600s throughout the West and into Canada by the late 1700s. At first the horse terrified many Native Americans, but several tribes began to use it to their advantage. Soon, the horse had transformed the cultures of many North American peoples, notably the Apaches, Cheyennes, Comanches, and Sioux. With the horse these peoples were able to give up their existence in the mountains and other areas and move onto the relatively uninhabited Great Plains. There, Native Americans hunted on horseback the plentiful buffalo, which became the cornerstone of their way of life.

The Columbian exchange also introduced deadly diseases—smallpox and measles from Europe and yellow fever and malaria from Africa. Because Native Americans lacked immunity, or resistance, to these diseases, many died. Historians have estimated that in some areas as much as 90 percent of the Native American population was wiped out. By 1600 practically all of the original inhabitants of the Caribbean were gone.

For many, the tragic impacts of disease and military conquest on Native Americans and the introduction of slavery on Africans understandably overshadow the positive aspects of the Columbian exchange. But when determining the significance of Columbus's voyages, we must take into account the global transformation he initiated.

■■ **The Columbian exchange resulted in the transfer of people, precious metals, crops, and animals between the Americas and Europe, Asia, and Africa.**

SECTION 1 REVIEW

IDENTIFY and explain the significance of the following: Christopher Columbus, viceroy, Tainos, Guacanagarí, *encomienda*, Bartolomé de Las Casas, Columbian exchange.

LOCATE and explain the importance of the following: Bahamas, Hispaniola, La Navidad.

1. **MAIN IDEA** What did Columbus hope to find by sailing west from Europe?
2. **MAIN IDEA** How did the *encomienda* system benefit the Spanish settlers? What effect did it have on Native Americans?
3. **ASSESSING CONSEQUENCES** What reforms did Las Casas request on behalf of Native Americans? Why were the reforms of only limited success?
4. **WRITING TO EVALUATE** Write an essay examining the long-term effects of Columbus's voyages.
5. **USING HISTORICAL IMAGINATION** Imagine you are a Taino living on San Salvador. Draw a plan for a mural that portrays your interactions with the Spanish explorers.

Chapter 2

SECTION

2

*Introducing
the Section*

PREVIEW WORKSHOP

Following is a list of the significant people, places, and terms in this section. You may wish to use this list as a section preview.

People
- Ferdinand Magellan
- Juan Sebastián de Elcano
- Vasco Núñez de Balboa
- Juan Ponce de León
- Álvar Núñez Cabeza de Vaca
- Estevanico
- Hernando de Soto
- Francisco Vásquez de Coronado
- Hernán Cortés
- Malintzin
- Moctezuma II
- Francisco Pizarro
- Atahuallpa

Places
- Line of Demarcation

Terms
- Treaty of Tordesillas
- circumnavigate
- conquistadors

Section 2

CONQUEST OF THE MAINLAND

FOCUS
- **What were the Spanish explorers and the conquistadors seeking?**
- **What were the conquistadors' roles in building a Spanish empire in the Americas?**
- **How did Native Americans respond to the conquistadors?**

Aztec soldier

*C*olumbus's claims fueled the rivalry between Spain and Portugal. To avoid open conflict, the two nations agreed to divide all non-Christian lands in the Western Hemisphere between themselves. Within decades Spanish adventurers had conquered the Aztecs of Mexico and the Incas of Peru and expanded Spain's colonial empire to include territory in North America.

EXPLORING THE AMERICAS

Portugal viewed Columbus's voyages as a threat to its control of the Atlantic. To settle the matter of boundaries, Spain and Portugal, both Catholic countries, agreed to divide control over any newly encountered lands. They signed the **Treaty of Tordesillas** (tawrd-uh-SEE-uhs) in 1494. This treaty drew an imaginary line of demarcation, or separation, around the world: territory explored west of the line would belong to Spain; east of the line, to Portugal.

Ferdinand Magellan, a Portuguese mariner sponsored by the Spanish Crown, explored the land west of the Line of Demarcation. Magellan set out in 1519 to find a westward route to Asia. After threading through the turbulent, narrow waterway at the southern tip of South America, Magellan sailed into the Pacific Ocean. In September 1522 the *Victoria*—the only ship remaining of Magellan's five-vessel fleet—sailed into the harbor near Cádiz (KAHD-iz), Spain. Captain Juan Sebastián de Elcano (el-KAHN-oh) and his 17 shipmates—the only survivors of the original 270-person expedition—thus became the

first people to **circumnavigate**, or sail completely around, the world (see map below).

Other explorers focused on the lands of North America and South America, claiming them for Spain. In 1513 Vasco Núñez de Balboa (NOON-yays day bahl-BOH-uh) explored Panama and was probably the first European to glimpse the Pacific Ocean from the Americas. Juan Ponce de León (PAWN-say day lay-AWN) sought the mythical "Fountain of Youth" in Florida in 1513.

In the 1520s Pánfilo de Narváez (PAHM-fee-loh day nahr-BAH-ays) led an unsuccessful attempt to colonize North America's coastline along the Gulf of Mexico. A survivor of Narváez's

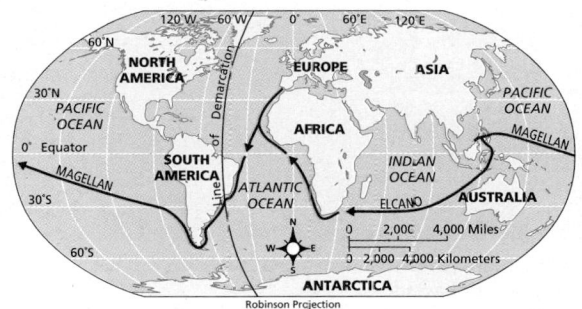

▲ **Magellan–Elcano Expedition**

FOCUS OBJECTIVES
- Identify what the Spanish explorers and the conquistadors were seeking.
- Explain the conquistadors' roles in building a Spanish empire in the Americas.
- Describe how Native Americans responded to the conquistadors.

 **GLOBAL CONNECTIONS**

Not surprisingly, the rest of Europe did not recognize the Treaty of Tordesillas. Elizabeth I of England declared that the sea was common to all nations. Foreshadowing the coming struggle between England and Spain, she added, "Since the sea belongs to everyone, it belongs to me."

CORE RESOURCES
- **Geography Worksheet 2**
- **Section 2 Daily Quiz**

MOTIVATING:
PRIOR KNOWLEDGE

Ask students to recall Columbus's return to Spain from his first voyage. Ask how he was treated and what he took back with him from the islands. Then tell students that in this section they will study the impact of other Spanish explorers who were inspired by Columbus's voyages.

Teaching the Section

MOTIVES FOR EXPLORATION

Ask students what reasons Spanish explorers and conquistadors had for coming to the Americas. List the reasons on the chalkboard as the class discusses them.

■■ Ask students how the motivations of the Spanish explorers and conquistadors compare to those of explorers of outer space and the ocean floor today.

MAKING CONNECTIONS

Religion
The Aztecs adopted the god Quetzalcoatl from the Toltecs. In legend, he taught the Aztecs the benefits of civilization. He then left for the East, prophesying that he would return when the Aztecs faced a great crisis.

BIO GRAPHY PERSONALITIES IN HISTORY

There are no Aztec descriptions of Moctezuma's appearance. His subjects were forbidden, on penalty of death, to look at him when he appeared in public. But according to one Spanish account, he "was about forty years old, . . . well proportioned, slender. . . . He had good eyes and showed in his appearance and manner often tenderness and when necessary, gravity."

BUILDING VOCABULARY

In this case *prophecy* refers to a prediction of something to come. It derives from the Greek word *prophēteia*, which means "the gift of interpreting the will of the gods."

---

expedition, Álvar Núñez Cabeza de Vaca (kah-BAY-sah day BAH-kah) explored much of present-day Texas, New Mexico, and Arizona. In 1539 another member of the expedition, Estevanico, an African, was the first non-Indian to visit the Pueblo Indians in present-day New Mexico. And in the 1540s Hernando de Soto explored southeastern North America and the Mississippi River, while Francisco Vásquez de Coronado marched through most of the present-day southwestern United States (see map on page 57).

*T*HE SPANISH ENCOUNTER THE AZTECS

In the footsteps of the early explorers came the Spanish conquerors, known as **conquistadors** (kawng-KEES-tuh-dawrs). By the early 1500s Spanish soldiers had successfully expelled the Moors from Spain. These Spanish soldiers then set out to conquer the Americas and to gain riches for themselves. They also wanted to spread the Catholic religion throughout the world.

■■ **Spanish explorers and conquistadors sought wealth and glory and hoped to win new converts to Christianity.**

Among the most able and adventurous of the conquistadors was Hernán Cortés. A professional soldier in Spain, Cortés settled in Cuba as an *encomendero*. Intrigued by stories of gold on the Mexican mainland, Cortés gathered a force of

▲ In this mural, **Hernán Cortés and Malintzin receive gifts from Aztec ambassadors.**

some 600 Spaniards and African slaves and set sail in February 1519. On the Mexican coast he engaged Indians in battle. Cortés's army defeated the Indians, and through them he learned much about the wealthy Aztec Empire.

Among the Indians was a young Aztec woman, Malintzin (mah-LINT-suhn), called Doña Marina by the Spanish, who became Cortés's valuable interpreter and adviser. She described Aztec weaknesses to Cortés, explaining that many Indian groups hated the Aztecs. Most were being taxed heavily by the empire—forced to give up the best of their crops and handicrafts. Armed with this knowledge, Cortés set off to confront the Aztec ruler, Moctezuma II (MAWK-tay-SOO-mah).

BIO GRAPHY When Cortés set foot on the mainland, Moctezuma II had already ruled the Aztec Empire for 17 years. During his reign, he presided over the expansion of Aztec territory through military conquest and the vast extension of trade routes. Like his predecessors, he maintained strict control over Aztec subjects by requiring tribute.

Moctezuma learned of Cortés's arrival almost immediately. An Aztec scout had witnessed the Spanish defeat of the coastal Indians. He raced on foot to the capital city of Tenochtitlán to tell Moctezuma of the pale-skinned men who rode "deer" (horses) taller than a house. The scout

Moctezuma II

reported that these bearded strangers even had weapons (cannons) powerful enough to crack a hole in the side of a mountain!

The deeply religious ruler contemplated this amazing news. According to an ancient prophecy, a light-skinned god called Quetzalcoatl (ket-SAHL-kwaht-uhl) would one day return to rule over the Aztecs. Moctezuma feared that the prophecy was now coming true.

Moctezuma believed that the god's arrival would mean the end of his reign. Before Cortés had even arrived on the Mexican mainland, Moctezuma had been shaken by omens, such as the appearance of a brilliant comet, that he believed foretold the terrible destruction of his people. He sent gold and other gifts to Cortés to

CONQUISTADORS' ROLES

Have students work in small groups to write reports from either Cortés or Pizarro to the Spanish Crown, describing and explaining the actions taken by the conquistadors. Suggest that groups illustrate their reports with maps and other visuals. Have volunteer groups present their reports to the class.

NATIVE AMERICANS' RESPONSE

Have students take the identity of 16th-century Native Americans and record in their "journals" the effects of Spanish conquests on their way of life and the actions they took to survive. Ask volunteers to share their entries. Students may wish to include their journal entries in their portfolios.

▶

persuade him not to come to Tenochtitlán. Instead, the gifts made Cortés even more determined to conquer the Aztecs.

CORTÉS CONQUERS THE AZTECS

To defeat the Aztecs, Cortés knew he must increase the size of his army. With Malintzin's help, he recruited Indians who had been defeated by the Aztecs. As Cortés approached the Aztec capital, his army of Indian recruits grew to several thousand.

Moctezuma realized by this time that Cortés was not the god Quetzalcoatl. Hoping to save Tenochtitlán from destruction, however, the Aztec ruler welcomed Cortés as an honored guest. Cortés responded to this hospitable welcome by imprisoning Moctezuma. Cortés let Moctezuma retain his title—though not his power—as emperor of the Aztecs.

This fragile arrangement collapsed when Cortés temporarily left Tenochtitlán. In his absence his lieutenant, Pedro de Alvarado, ordered the killing of scores of men, women, and children attending an Aztec religious ceremony. The Aztecs saw Alvarado's actions as an unprovoked attack and fought back, forcing the Spanish to retreat to their quarters. When Cortés returned, he found things in chaos. In desperation he urged Moctezuma to try to calm his angry subjects. But the Aztecs no longer trusted their ruler. When Moctezuma attempted to intervene, he was killed—Spanish and Aztec sources dispute which side murdered the emperor.

With Moctezuma dead and the Aztecs in full revolt, the Spanish knew they had no choice but to leave the capital. They tried to escape during the middle of the night by crossing the main causeway over Lake Texcoco, but a woman drawing water sounded an alarm. Thousands of Aztecs attacked

▶ During *La Noche Triste*, the Aztecs forced the Spanish to retreat from Tenochtitlán across Lake Texcoco.

the Spanish. Though the Spanish managed to leave the city, heavy casualties resulted on both sides. While the Aztecs celebrated their victory, that night in 1520 is remembered in Spanish history as *La Noche Triste* (lah NOH-chay TREES-tay), the Night of Sorrow.

In the following months Cortés regrouped his forces and obtained reinforcements. In May 1521 he attacked Tenochtitlán. This time the whole Aztec population seemed determined to fight to the death. A four-month siege by the Spaniards, however, left the Aztecs worn out and starving. The Aztecs were also weakened by a smallpox epidemic that had swept through the city. On August 13 Cortés attacked, and the great city fell. Soon he controlled all of present-day central Mexico. An Aztec poet captured his people's sadness:

> 66 Broken spears lie in the roads;
> we have torn our hair in our grief.
> The houses are roofless now, and
> their walls
> are red with blood. 99

After the conquest the Spanish leveled Aztec temples and other buildings, destroyed beautiful Aztec works of art, and melted down elaborate gold jewelry into bullion and shipped it to Spain. Over the ruins of Tenochtitlán, Cortés built Mexico City, the present-day capital of Mexico.

COOPERATIVE LEARNING

Organize the class into groups of three. Have half the groups conduct a meeting between Moctezuma II, Cortés, and an Aztec subject. The other groups should conduct a meeting between Atahuallpa, Pizarro, and an Incan subject. All group members should take turns explaining the reasons for their actions during the conquest of the Aztecs or the Incas, respectively. Encourage groups to present their meetings to the class for discussion.

PRIMARY SOURCE

Description of Change: excerpted
Rationale: excerpted to focus on main idea

Practice

GUIDED PRACTICE

Lead the class in creating a chart of the explorers and conquistadors discussed in this section. Students should chart each person's name, date(s), goals, and results.

INDEPENDENT PRACTICE

Tell students to assume the identity of a Spanish conquistador or explorer charted in the Guided Practice, and to write a letter to a relative in Spain describing their experiences in the Americas.

Review and Assessment

REVIEW Have students write brief statements that describe the Columbian exchange and its effects on the Spanish and on Native Americans. Then assign the Section 2 Review on p. 49.

ASSESS Assign the **Section 2 Daily Quiz** in *Core Resources.*

HISTORICAL SIDELIGHTS

About the Illustration

Felipe Guamán Poma de Ayala's drawing on p. 48 is part of his illustrated history of Peru, *El Primer Nueva Corónica y Buen Gobierno (The New Chronicle and Good Government).* Written sometime between 1584 and 1614, the book criticizes the Spanish treatment of the Incas and calls for governmental reforms. Despite his work as an interpreter for Spanish officials, Guamán Poma was imprisoned and banished for his views. He is thought to have died, elderly and poor, in 1616.

PRIMARY SOURCE

Description of Change: excerpted and bracketed
Rationale: excerpted to focus on main idea; bracketed to clarify meaning

THINKING CRITICALLY

Recognizing Prejudice
Ask students in what ways the Spanish showed their prejudice toward Native Americans.

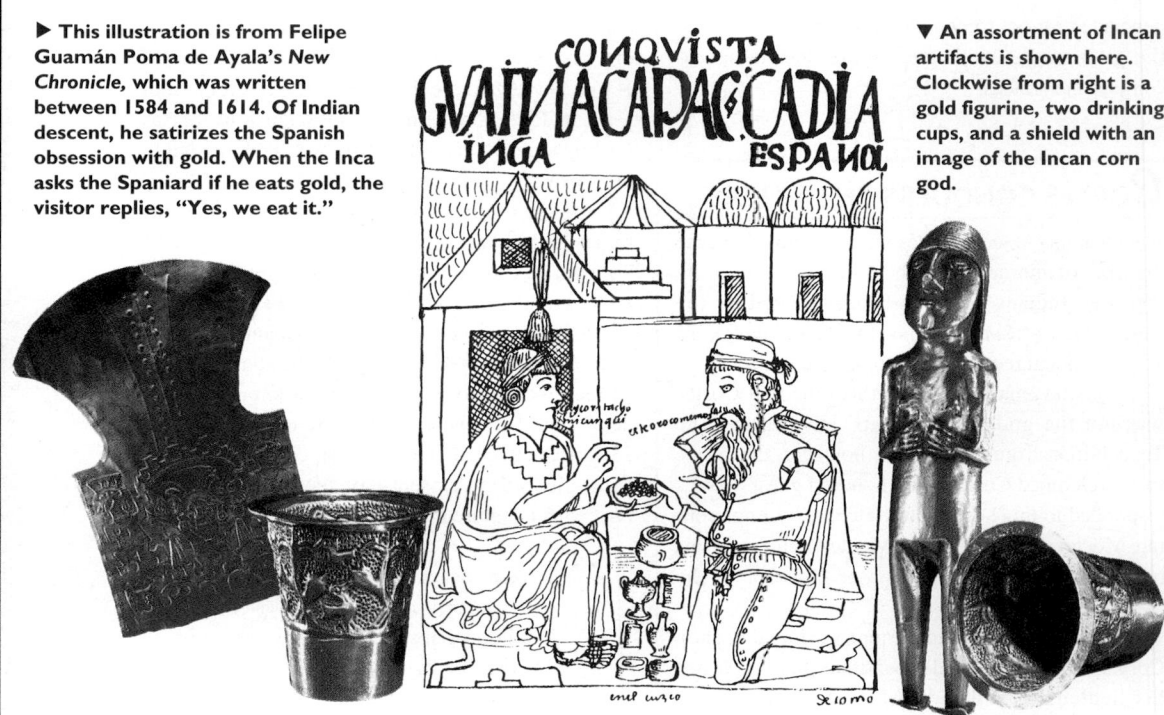

▶ This illustration is from Felipe Guamán Poma de Ayala's *New Chronicle,* which was written between 1584 and 1614. Of Indian descent, he satirizes the Spanish obsession with gold. When the Inca asks the Spaniard if he eats gold, the visitor replies, "Yes, we eat it."

▼ An assortment of Incan artifacts is shown here. Clockwise from right is a gold figurine, two drinking cups, and a shield with an image of the Incan corn god.

Cortés lived like a king within the conquered region. In 1522 the Spanish Crown appointed him viceroy. By the 1530s he was probably the wealthiest person in Spanish America. As for the Aztec people, they had fallen victim to the *encomienda* system.

PIZARRO CONQUERS THE INCAS

The Incan Empire, centered in the Andes Mountains of South America, became Spain's next target for conquest. In 1531 Francisco Pizarro (pee-SAHR-roh), a Spanish soldier and treasure hunter, led a small army to the very heart of the empire. Traveling cautiously along steep, narrow passes that snaked through rugged, snowcapped peaks, they reached the town of Cajamarca (kah-huh-MAHR-kuh) in present-day northern Peru.

Pizarro lured the Incan ruler, Atahuallpa (ah-tah-WAHL-pah), to his camp. A Spanish priest told Atahuallpa that the Incas must convert to Catholicism. Atahuallpa asked to see the book—the Bible—that "spoke" their god's words. According to an Incan account:

66 [Atahuallpa] took the book and began to leaf through its pages. And the Inca said, "Why does it not speak to me? This book tells me nothing!" And . . . [Atahuallpa] Inca threw the book from his hands. 99

The outraged Spaniards attacked the Indians and captured Atahuallpa.

To gain his freedom, Atahuallpa promised to fill his large prison quarters with gold and silver. Desperate to save their emperor-god, the Incas delivered a large ransom in gold and silver. Pizarro accepted the ransom but ordered Atahuallpa killed, not freed.

◀ Rumors of a gold-rich empire drew Francisco Pizarro to western South America, which he explored in the 1520s. Pizarro went to Spain in 1528 and convinced the Spanish king to authorize the conquest of the Incas.

The Mansell Collection

RETEACH Have students work in pairs to turn the Focus questions into statements by supplying the answers. Have pairs exchange their work and check the accuracy of the statements.

Closure

Write *Gold, Glory,* and *Christianity* on the chalkboard. Then have volunteers explain what impact each had on Spanish explorers and Native Americans in the Americas.

Extension

RESEARCH Have students research the Aztec or Incan cultures and prepare an oral report and visual display featuring images of Aztec or Incan artifacts.

CREATE Ask students to make a display about the Spanish treasures being recovered from ships that sank in the Caribbean and Gulf of Mexico. Encourage students to show pictures of artifacts, write captions, and draw maps of the ships' locations.

At the time of Pizarro's arrival in Cajamarca, the Incas were divided by an internal dispute. One group allied with Pizarro, and the other group retreated to a remote area of the Andes, where they held out against the Spanish for many years. But control of the vast South American empire finally passed into Spanish hands. Pizarro ruled until 1541, when he was murdered by one of his own men.

■■ **By conquering the Aztecs and the Incas, the conquistadors added vast territory and wealth to the Spanish American empire.**

POSTCONQUEST INDIAN SOCIETY

To maintain control over the conquered Indians, the Spanish went to great lengths to wipe out Native American cultures. They tore down Indian temples, destroyed Indian art, and reorganized Indian settlements. Native American cultures were not completely destroyed, however; they live on in the people and customs of most modern Latin American nations.

Native Americans often took up arms against the Spanish to defend their lives, lands, and religions. Some fought the Spanish to the death. Others, worn down by superior Spanish weaponry or by the unbearable toll of disease, came to terms with a force they could not drive out. Some found ways to escape or make the best of Spanish rule.

▲ This illustration, drawn sometime between 1540 and 1541, shows Native Americans from southern Mexico fleeing from the conquistadors.

For example, the Mayas in southern Mexico fled to the interior of the Yucatán (yoo-kuh-TAN) Peninsula. Others allied themselves with the Spanish and negotiated a place for themselves in the new social order.

Survival usually meant the mixing of Spanish and Native American peoples and cultures. For example, many Indians developed a new religion by mixing their rituals with Catholic rituals. Over time both Native Americans and Spaniards adopted elements of the other's language and customs. Eventually, there emerged a new culture that blended ingredients of Native American and Spanish ways of life.

■■ **The Spanish won official control over the Indians. Native Americans, however, developed ways to ensure their survival.**

SECTION REVIEW ANSWERS

IDENTIFY

For significance, see the following pages:
Treaty of Tordesillas (p. 45)
Ferdinand Magellan (p. 45)
Juan Sebastián de Elcano (p. 45)
circumnavigate (p. 45)
Vasco Núñez de Balboa (p. 45)
Juan Ponce de León (p. 45)
Álvar Núñez Cabeza de Vaca (p. 46)
Estevanico (p. 46)
Hernando de Soto (p. 46)
Francisco Vásquez de Coronado (p. 46)
conquistadors (p. 46)
Hernán Cortés (p. 46)
Malintzin (p. 46)
Moctezuma II (p. 46)
Francisco Pizarro (p. 48)
Atahuallpa (p. 48)

LOCATE

For location, see the map on p. 45.

1. *to claim new lands for Spain; to colonize; for wealth, glory, and new converts to Christianity*
2. *conquered Aztecs, Incas, and other Native Americans; transferred wealth to Spain*
3. *Some fought or escaped; others allied with Spanish, blending Spanish customs with their own.*
4. *Poems should indicate why Aztecs revolted.*
5. *possible answer—wanted to convert Indians to Catholicism; weakened it*

■ **SECTION 2 REVIEW**

IDENTIFY and explain the significance of the following: Treaty of Tordesillas, Ferdinand Magellan, Juan Sebastián de Elcano, circumnavigate, Vasco Núñez de Balboa, Juan Ponce de León, Álvar Núñez Cabeza de Vaca, Estevanico, Hernando de Soto, Francisco Vásquez de Coronado, conquistadors, Hernán Cortés, Malintzin, Moctezuma II, Francisco Pizarro, Atahuallpa.

LOCATE and explain the importance of the following: Line of Demarcation.

1. **MAIN IDEA** Why did the Spanish explorers and conquistadors come to the Americas?
2. **MAIN IDEA** How did the conquistadors help Spain build an empire in the Americas?
3. **MAIN IDEA** What were some of the strategies Native Americans used to protect their ways of life?
4. **WRITING TO CREATE** Imagine you are an Aztec whose son or daughter has died fighting the Spanish. Write a poem describing why he or she fought.
5. **HYPOTHESIZING** Why do you think the Spaniards tore down Aztec temples? What impact do you think this had on Aztec religion?

FOCUS OBJECTIVES

- Identify the extent of Spanish settlement in North America.

- Explain how missions and estates helped establish Spanish rule in the Americas.

- Describe what elements of their culture the Spanish colonists introduced to the Americas.

CULTURAL PATTERNS

The Timucuas of northern Florida lived in villages surrounded by palisades, or staked fences. For food, they fished, hunted, and raised corn. The way of life of the Timucuas changed drastically after the arrival of the Spanish. By 1819 their numbers had dwindled as diseases brought by the Europeans ravaged their populations.

CORE RESOURCES

- Literature Worksheet 2
- Section 3 Daily Quiz

AV RESOURCES

- *The American Nation* Videodisc: The Spanish Mission System
- Linking Geography and History Transparency and Worksheet 6
- Everyday Life in America Transparency and Worksheet 2

Section 3

THE SPANISH SETTLE THE AMERICAS

F O C U S

- **What was the extent of Spanish settlement in North America?**
- **How did missions and estates help establish Spanish rule in the Americas?**
- **What elements of their culture did Spanish colonists introduce to the Americas?**

Statue of the Virgin Mary, called *La Conquistadora,* taken to New Mexico in 1626

The explorations and conquests of Cortés, Pizarro, and others enabled Spain to claim vast portions of the Americas. For the next two centuries, the Spanish fanned out from Mexico City—the heart of their American empire—and from their island colonies in the Caribbean. Armed with the soldier's sword and the priest's cross, they set out to find riches and spread the Roman Catholic faith.

FLORIDA

By the early 1500s the Spanish already had turned their attention to La Florida, the entire eastern seaboard from present-day Florida to Newfoundland. Because Spanish ships from the Caribbean often sailed up the Atlantic coast on

▲ Settlers in St. Augustine tried to maintain Spanish culture and customs.

their way back to Europe, Spain wanted to establish settlements to provide safe harbors.

One of the first attempts to establish a permanent settlement in Florida took place in 1526. Lucas Vázquez Ayllón (yl-YAWN) led some 500 colonists from Hispaniola to a site on the coast of present-day South Carolina. The expedition, which included families, missionaries, and African slaves, built San Miguel de Gualdape (gwahl-DAHP-ay), but the colony did not survive the first winter. Sick and too weak to farm or to catch fish, nearly two thirds of the settlers perished. The others straggled home in early 1527.

Farther south along the Florida coast, settlers again had trouble establishing a colony. Native American groups living in the area—such as the Timucuas (tim-uh-KOO-uhs), Calusas, and Apalachees—fought the Spanish to keep them from settling in the area. In 1565, however, an expedition led by Pedro Menéndez de Avilés (may-NAYN-days day ah-bee-LAYS) succeeded in planting a permanent settlement in Florida. This was St. Augustine, the oldest city established by Europeans in what is now the United States.

MOTIVATING:
LINK TO TODAY

Have students identify Spanish influences in their lives. Encourage them to think of places, plants and animals, foods, and words that have Spanish origins. List responses on the chalkboard. Ask students to speculate on reasons that the Spanish influence is evident in the U.S. today.

Teaching the Section

SPANISH NORTH AMERICA

Organize students into four groups and assign each group one of the following: Florida, New Mexico and Arizona, Texas, or California. Have each group use the text information and the map on p. 52 of their textbook to develop a presentation of how Spanish settlement progressed in their assigned area. Have groups give their presentations in chronological order.

◀ The Pueblo Indians skillfully decorated pottery with beautiful symbols and designs.

Museum of Indian Arts and Culture, Santa Fe

MAKING CONNECTIONS
Geography

The Apalachees were an industrious and wealthy farming group. Geographic areas such as the Appalachian Mountains and Apalachicola Bay in Florida derive their names from the Apalachees. The name of the capital of Florida, Tallahassee, comes from the Apalachee word meaning "old town."

HISTORICAL SIDELIGHTS
The *Presidios*

A *presidio* in Spanish North America usually consisted of approximately 60 soldiers, their families, and servants of Native American or African descent. The soldiers were equipped with firearms and horses. Although their primary function was to defend Spanish settlers against Indian attack, the soldiers also served as military escorts, police, and mail carriers.

PRIMARY SOURCE

Description of Change: excerpted and bracketed
Rationale: excerpted to focus on main idea; bracketed to clarify meaning

NEW MEXICO AND ARIZONA

In 1609, some 1,500 miles west of St. Augustine, Pedro de Peralta (pay-RAHL-tah), the newly appointed governor of New Mexico, established its capital at Santa Fe. From this outpost the Spanish maintained a fragile hold on the northernmost borderland of New Spain for more than 200 years.

The Pueblo Indians and the Spanish struggled bitterly for control of this area, however. The Pueblos resented Spanish demands that they pay taxes and that they convert to Catholicism. In 1680 the Pueblos temporarily drove the Spanish out of Santa Fe. Under the leadership of Popé (poh-PAY), a Pueblo prophet, the Pueblos launched a series of attacks. By the time the **Pueblo Revolt** of 1680 was over, some 400 Spaniards lay dead, and some 2,000 settlers had fled south.

After the Spanish were driven out, according to Pueblo witnesses:

66 Popé . . . ordered . . . that they instantly break up and burn . . . everything pertaining to Christianity. . . . They were ordered likewise not to teach the Castilian [Spanish] language in any pueblo and to burn the seeds which the Spaniards sowed and to plant only maize and beans, which were the crops of their ancestors. 99

Popé hoped that by destroying all traces of Spanish culture, the Pueblos could reestablish their way of life. But the Pueblos regained control of their territory only temporarily. In the 1690s New Mexico's new governor, Diego de Vargas, reestablished Spanish rule. At the same time, the Spanish began moving into present-day Arizona. Father Eusebio Kino (ay-oo-SAYB-yoh KEE-noh) built missions near present-day Nogales (noh-GAL-uhs) in 1687 and Tucson in 1700. He also explored the southern reaches of the Colorado River.

During the 1700s the fear of French and British expansion prompted the Spanish to speed up their colonization of this region. They established *presidios* (forts), missions, villages, towns, and large ranches. The Spanish influence found today throughout the southwestern United States dates from this period.

TEXAS

Despite the early explorations of Cabeza de Vaca and others, Spanish settlement in present-day Texas proceeded slowly. The first permanent Spanish colony was founded at Ysleta (i-ZLAYT-uh) in 1681 by settlers driven from New Mexico by the Pueblo Revolt.

By 1690 France's colonizing activity in North America spurred Spain to strengthen its hold on Texas. The San Francisco de los Tejas mission was established near the Neches (NECH-uhz) River in 1690, and the San Antonio de Valero mission was built in 1718. A few other settlements emerged along the lower Rio Grande, but lack of mineral resources and constant raids by the Apaches and the Comanches slowed settlement.

Teaching the Section

ESTABLISHING SPANISH RULE

Have students prepare graphic organizers that show the types of settlements established by the Spanish to administer their empire in the Americas (missions, haciendas, *ranchos,* and *presidios*). Organizers should include descriptive information about each type of settlement. After volunteers present their organizers to the class, ask students to explain how each type of settlement solidified Spanish control of an area, and how each impacted the lives of the Native Americans in the area.

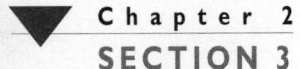

Spanish America in 1785

SPANNING TWO CONTINENTS For more than 300 years the Spanish ruled lands that stretched from northern California to Chile in South America.

? PLACE Which viceroyalty included lands that are now part of the United States?

CALIFORNIA

California was the last of Spain's northern territories to be colonized. Juan Rodríguez Cabrillo (kah-BREE-yoh) explored much of the California coastline for Spain as early as 1542. But not until the late 1700s did Spain, alarmed by Russian explorations in northern California, attempt to set up permanent settlements. In 1769 Gaspar de Portolá (pawr-toh-LAH) founded San Diego. Seven years later (as the British colonies on the eastern seaboard were declaring their independence) Juan Bautista de Anza (bow-TEE-stah day AHN-sah) founded San Francisco.

Friar Junípero Serra (hoo-NEE-pay-roh SER-rah), a scholarly Franciscan missionary, came to

California with de Portolá's expedition. Serra founded a mission at San Diego, and by the time of his death in 1784, he had founded eight more missions along the Pacific coast.

▪▪ Beginning in the mid-1500s, Spain established settlements from coast to coast in what is now the continental United States.

SPANISH AMERICA

By 1780 Spanish America was one of the largest colonial empires the world had ever known. Within its vast borders were lands of rich geographic diversity—from the coastal lowlands of Florida and the arid lands and mountains of northern Mexico to the rain forests of Panama and the Andean heights of Peru.

To oversee this huge and diverse empire, Spain organized it into viceroyalties. The first two viceroyalties established were New Spain and Peru. Each was governed by a viceroy, who acted as the king's representative and supervised lesser officials.

Colonial government worked better in theory than in practice, though. Orders issued by the Crown or the Catholic church in Spain had to be carried by messenger thousands of miles—first by ship and then by horseback or by foot—to the outposts of the empire. Government officials in Spanish America often became impatient with the delays and made their own decisions. Officials who ignored orders and laws were rarely penalized, however. Colonists, especially those in the remote corners of the empire, usually organized their own settlements and exercised some independence in local government.

Missions. The mission was one form of settlement established by the Spanish in the Americas. Historians have counted more than 150 Spanish missions founded in the present-day United States. At the center of each mission stood a simple church. Surrounding the church were living quarters and workshops where "mission Indians" worked at weaving, blacksmithing, and other crafts. In fields nearby, missionaries and Native Americans raised cattle and grew grain, grapes, and other crops.

Create three columns on the chalkboard with the following headings: *government, architecture,* and *customs.* Ask students for examples of the Spanish contribution to the Americas in each category. Suggest to the class that some contributions may fit more than one category. As responses are offered, have the class discuss them and decide under which category or categories each should be included. When lists of contributions are complete, have students survey them and identify which remain part of the Americas' Spanish heritage today.

The missionaries labored to win the Native Americans to Catholicism, to teach them Spanish ways, and to make them loyal Spanish subjects. But in their zeal they suppressed Indian culture and enforced a harsh labor system resembling the *encomienda.* Resentful of forced labor and harsh discipline, many Indians fled from the missions. Many others died from European diseases against which they had no immunity.

Haciendas and *ranchos.* Outside the missions the Spanish government divided the land into farming and ranching estates. Haciendas, some consisting of hundreds of thousands of acres, were the largest; smaller farms and ranches were called *ranchos.*

Peons, or landless laborers, most of whom were Indians, worked on the haciendas. In theory, hacienda owners paid the peons, who were free to come and go as they wished. In reality, however, many land owners kept the workers bound to the land by debts. Hacienda owners made the peons purchase daily necessities from the hacienda store, sometimes at inflated prices. Before they could seek employment elsewhere, workers had to pay off their debts—an impossible task for many. In addition, children often had to assume the debts of their deceased parents.

Most owners of *ranchos* lived on their land and worked alongside their laborers. The Spaniards who drove the cattle on haciendas and *ranchos* were excellent horsemen called *vaqueros* (vah-KER-ohs). Familiar words like *lasso, rodeo,* and *corral* originated with the *vaqueros,* whose life-style became a model for later North American cowboys.

▲ **A Mexican hacienda owner, his wife, an overseer, and a *vaquero* are shown in this watercolor from the early 1830s.**

▲ **Ysleta Indian Mission (top) in Texas and San Xavier del Bac Mission (bottom) in Arizona are two examples of Spanish architecture.**

■■ **Missions, haciendas, and *ranchos* established Spanish control over Indian labor and land.**

Colonial life. People living on haciendas, in missions, and in the bustling cities of Spanish America developed a unique social structure. *Peninsulares* (pay-nin-soo-LAHR-uhs), Spaniards born in Spain, and *criollos* (kree-OH-yohs), Spaniards born in the colonies, held the most privileged positions in the Americas. Most lived in huge houses with many servants and owned businesses and haciendas. Spaniards held high government positions and studied law, theology, or medicine.

MAKING CONNECTIONS

Language Arts

Many terms that are associated with ranching and cowboys originated in Spanish. *Lariat* comes from *la reata,* the Spanish term for rope; *chaps* from *chaparreras,* protective leggings to guard against cactus needles and brush; and *buckaroo* is the Anglo-American version of *vaquero,* meaning "cowboy."

BUILDING VOCABULARY

Peninsulares were named for the Iberian Peninsula—another name for the area occupied by present-day Portugal and Spain. *Criollo* probably derives from the Spanish word *criadillo,* meaning "unweaned infant." The French and American designation *Creole* derives from the Spanish *criollo.* *Mestizo* comes from the Latin word meaning "to mix."

AV **TRANSPARENCY**

Everyday Life in America Transparency and **Worksheet 2**

Practice

GUIDED PRACTICE

Work with students to create a chart titled *Organization of Spanish America* with column headings *Social, Economic,* and *Political*. Have volunteers suggest entries for each heading, giving a brief explanation of each.

INDEPENDENT PRACTICE

Have students imagine that they are Spanish colonists in the late 1700s. Have them write a letter to a friend in Europe, describing the extent of Spanish settlement in North America and the organization of daily life in their colony.

Review and Assessment

REVIEW Organize students into small groups, and provide each group with a piece of butcher paper. Then ask groups to draw scenes illustrating the methods established by the Spanish to rule Spanish America. Have groups display their scenes on the bulletin board. Then assign the Section 3 Review on p. 55.

ASSESS Assign the **Section 3 Daily Quiz** in *Core Resources*.

HISTORICAL SIDELIGHTS

A Literary Figure

In the convent, Sor Juana Inés de la Cruz surrounded herself with literary works, scientific treatises, and writing materials. She was an extraordinary and admired writer, but she could not completely escape the society in which she lived. At age 40, she faced opposition from the bishop of Puebla, who criticized her interest in poetry and science as irreligious and unwomanly. Although she defended her pursuits, Cruz had become a pawn in the political struggle between her patron—the viceroy—and the archbishop of Mexico. Deprived of church support, Cruz renounced her writing. She died four years later in 1695.

PRIMARY SOURCE

(for source on p. 55)
Description of Change: excerpted and bracketed
Rationale: excerpted to focus on main idea; bracketed to clarify meaning

Then and Now — THE ENCOMIENDA'S LEGACY

In 1521 Hernán Cortés first laid eyes on Cuernavaca (kwer-nuh-VAHK-uh), an Indian town some 50 miles south of Mexico City. The lush orchards and fertile valleys surrounding the town so captivated Cortés that he secured five *encomiendas* in the area. These *encomienda* grants gave him control of the labor of tens of thousands of Indians. By the mid-1530s, Spaniards controlled 30 *encomiendas* in the region and close to 180,000 Indians.

As in most of Central America and South America, the *encomienda* Indians around Cuernavaca were forced to work long hours in the fields of Spanish estates and in the mines. Indian laborers built mills, churches, roads, and even a huge palace for Cortés. The Indians provided Cortés and the other *encomenderos* with gold and daily necessities like food and wood for fuel. They also wove textiles and grew crops such as sugar, wheat, and corn, which the *encomenderos* sold for a large profit.

Today, Hernán Cortés would scarcely recognize Cuernavaca. As the capital of the Mexican state of Morelos, it is home to some 230,000 people. Cortés's palace is now a tourist attraction. No longer surrounded by fields and orchards, its modern neighbor

▲ **A Guatemalan plantation worker harvests coffee in southern Mexico.**

is, instead, a huge industrial complex. In fact, today in the entire state of Morelos, only about 30 percent of the population is involved in agriculture. Most of the old haciendas have been turned into hotels or spas for tourists.

Though many changes have come to Cuernavaca since 1521, remnants of the *encomienda* system endure. The Indians still lack control over major economic resources. Much of the agricultural land around the city remains divided into large estates owned mostly by wealthy families of European descent but worked mainly by Indians and *mestizos*. This situation persists despite both the Indian farmers' protests and the Mexican government's attempts at land reform. In industry as well, the descendants of the *encomienda* Indians work in the new factories, the vast majority of which they neither own nor control. This is the social legacy of the *encomienda* system, not only in Cuernavaca but in much of the rest of former Spanish America.

Below the Spaniards were *mestizos* (me-STEE-zohs), men and women born of European-Indian unions. If they looked more Spanish than Indian or were related to important Spanish families, *mestizos* could aspire to the highest positions in Spanish American society. But most *mestizos* lived modestly as artisans, estate supervisors, traders, or shopkeepers. Roughly equal in status to *mestizos* were mulattoes (people of African-European ancestry).

At the bottom of the social structure were Indians, Africans, and *zambos* (people of Indian-African ancestry). These groups were legally prevented from holding public office and certain jobs. Most Indians were farmers or farm laborers, though some worked as tavern keepers, wagon drivers, or sailors. Most African slaves worked as hacienda supervisors or as artisans.

Women's roles were also determined by race or family background. Spanish women—who made up only 5 to 17 percent of migrants in the early 1500s—maintained a degree of economic independence because they could own property in their own names. Many also managed family businesses,

RETEACH Have students work in pairs to outline the main ideas in Section 3, using the Essential Points and heads as a guide. Pairs should prepare brief summaries of each outline entry.

Closure

Have students each determine and record the one word that they think best describes life in Spanish America. Call on students to reveal and explain their choices.

Extension

SYNTHESIZE Ask students to research and present a "day in the life" of a *vaquero* in Spanish America. Encourage students to use pictures and drawings of a *vaquero*'s clothing, equipment, and so on.

CREATE Have students research Spanish missions and create models or detailed diagrams showing their layout and organization.

either with their husbands or, if widowed, by themselves.

Many wealthy Spanish women were taught, at home or at convent schools, to read, write, sew, and cook. But the majority of Spanish American women could not read. They were also discouraged from pursuing higher education. Juana Inés de la Cruz, a noted Mexican poet in the late 17th century, described her efforts to receive an education:

66 When I was six or seven and already knew how to read and write, . . . I discovered that in the City of Mexico there was a university . . . and as soon as I learned this I began to deluge [overwhelm] my mother with urgent and insistent pleas to change my manner of dress . . . so that I might study and take courses at the university. She refused . . . ; nevertheless, I found a way to read many different books my grandfather owned. 99

Cruz later entered a convent, a common practice for women who wanted to have the freedom for religious contemplation and study.

Indian, African, and Spanish-Indian women had even fewer opportunities to receive a formal

▲ This 18th–century painting shows a *mestizo* family in Mexico.

The Granger Collection, New York

education. Most women were taught useful skills at home such as cooking, pottery making, and weaving. This childhood training allowed them to own and run their own shops, produce clothes or textiles, sell food in markets, work as maids, or serve as midwives.

■■ **Colonists brought Spanish government, architecture, and customs to the Americas.**

■■ **SECTION 3 REVIEW**

IDENTIFY and explain the significance of the following: Lucas Vázquez Ayllón, Pedro Menéndez de Avilés, Pedro de Peralta, Popé, Pueblo Revolt, Father Eusebio Kino, Juan Rodríguez Cabrillo, Friar Junípero Serra, peons, Juana Inés de la Cruz.

LOCATE and explain the importance of the following: St. Augustine, Santa Fe, Nogales, Ysleta, San Diego, San Francisco.

1. **MAIN IDEA** Where and when did Spanish colonists found settlements in North America?
2. **MAIN IDEA** How did the Spanish use missions and estates to administer their empire in the Americas?
3. **MAIN IDEA** What elements of Spanish culture were transplanted to Spanish America?
4. **WRITING TO INFORM** You are putting on a play about the residents of St. Augustine. Write a short script that presents the lives of *peninsulares*, *mestizos*, and *zambos*.
5. **IDENTIFYING CAUSE AND EFFECT** What Spanish actions led to the Pueblo Revolt?

PREVIEW WORKSHOP

*Following is a list of the significant
people, places, and terms in this
section. You may wish to use this
list as a section preview.*

People
■ John Cabot
■ Giovanni da Verrazano
■ Jacques Cartier
■ Francis Drake

■ Sir Walter Raleigh
■ Powhatans
■ Wahunsonacock
■ Pocahontas

Places
■ St. Lawrence River
■ Roanoke
■ Jamestown

Terms
■ northwest passage
■ Protestant Reformation
■ Spanish Armada
■ inflation
■ Charter of 1606
■ joint-stock companies
■ indentured servant

FOCUS OBJECTIVES

■ Explain the importance
of the defeat of the
Spanish Armada.

■ Compare the English
method of colonization
with that of the Spanish.

■ Identify how the
Jamestown colonists sur-
vived and prospered.

■ Explain how the growth
of Jamestown affected
Native Americans'
relationships with the
settlers.

CORE RESOURCES

• Section 4 Daily Quiz

Section 4

THE ENGLISH IN NORTH AMERICA

FOCUS

■ **Why was the defeat of the Spanish Armada important?**
■ **How did the English method of colonization differ from the Spanish method?**
■ **How did the Jamestown colonists survive and prosper?**
■ **How did the growth of Jamestown affect Native Americans' relationships with the settlers?**

$\mathcal{J}$n the 1500s the Spanish began settling North America. At
the same time, other European nations—especially England
and France—began claiming large areas of the continent.
However, since the French and the English were more concerned with events in Europe, it was nearly a century before
these nations successfully colonized North America.

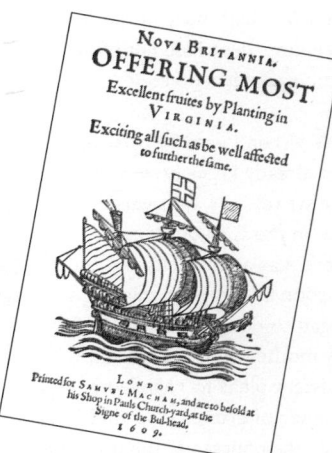

A 1609 English pamphlet
promoting colonization

EARLY CLAIMS

European contact with the Americas began well
before Columbus. In the 10th and 11th centuries
Leif Eriksson and other Viking explorers sighted
and temporarily settled parts of northeastern North
America. The remains of one Viking settlement
have been found at L'Anse aux Meadows
in Newfoundland. There are also tales of early

▲ The Vikings are believed to have sighted the North
American mainland as early as 986.

sightings and landings by Irish, Portuguese,
Chinese, African, and other sailors.

Shortly after Columbus's first voyage, other
mariners searched for a route to Asia. Another sea-
farer from Genoa, John Cabot, sailed along the
coasts of what are now Newfoundland, Nova
Scotia, and New England, first in 1497 and again
in 1498. Cabot claimed these lands for England,
which had backed his venture. In return he
received a small amount of money and some trade
privileges—little reward for the explorer who gave
England its first claim in North America.

Geographic knowledge of the Americas
slowly grew. Balboa's sighting of the Pacific Ocean
and Magellan's voyage around the tip of South
America sent explorers seeking a northern route—a
northwest passage—to the Pacific and thus to
Asia. Many European claims in North America
resulted from failed attempts to find such a passage.

French claims to North America were based
on the voyages of Giovanni da Verrazano (vayr-
raht-SAHN-oh) and Jacques Cartier (kahr-TYAY).
Verrazano, an Italian, failed in 1524 to find a

Have volunteers recall reasons the Spanish colonized in the Americas. List their responses on the chalkboard. Then have students speculate why other European countries might have had an interest in exploring and colonizing the Americas. Then tell students this section describes these countries' explorations and explains why their colonization in North America was delayed.

Teaching the Section

DEFEAT OF THE SPANISH ARMADA

Have students use the headline "Spanish Armada Defeated" to write an article that explains why Spain organized the Armada, the reasons for its defeat, and the consequences for Europe and North America. Call on volunteers to read their articles, and have the class fill in any missing details. Students may wish to include their articles in their portfolios.

▶

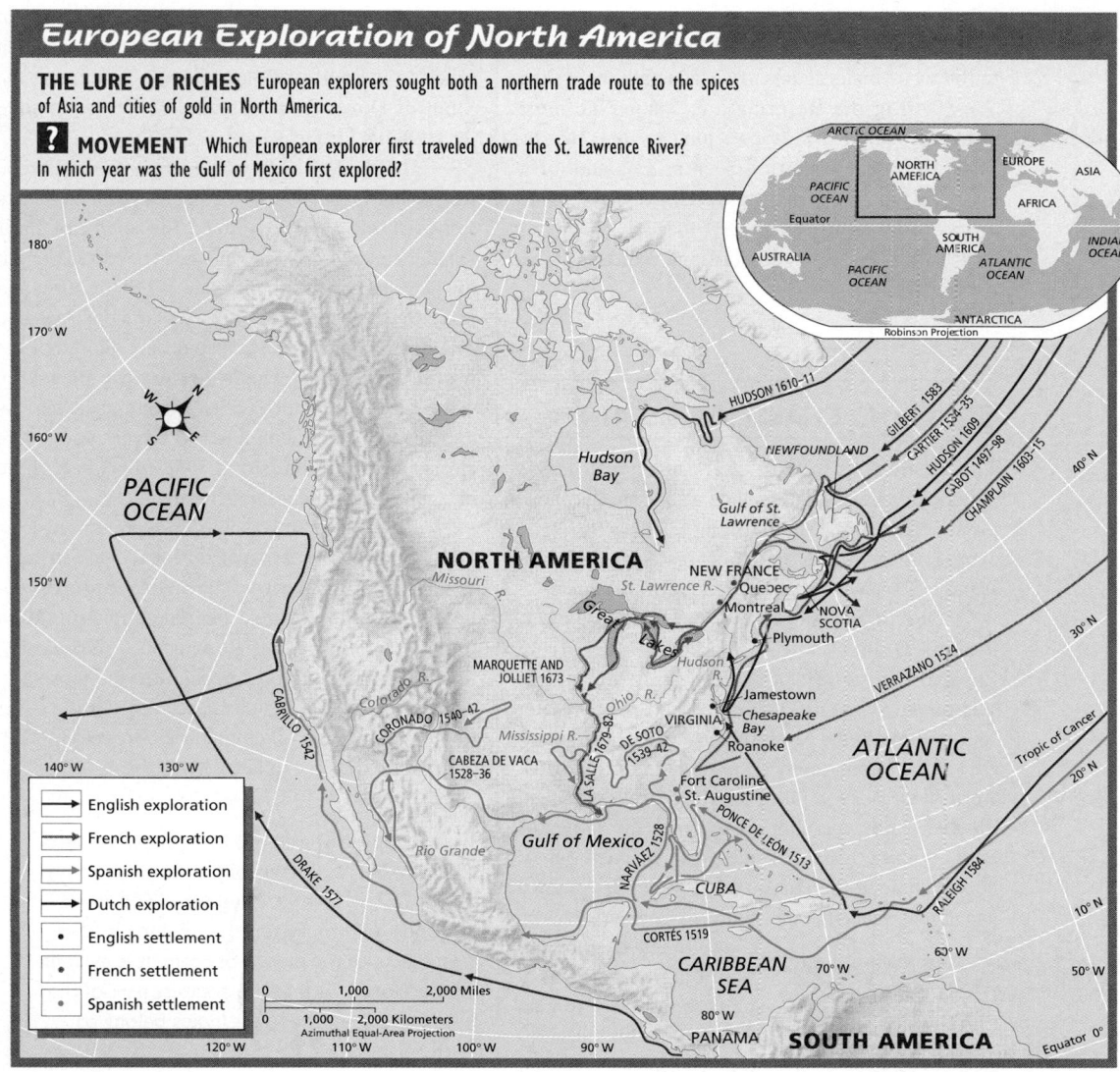

European Exploration of North America

THE LURE OF RICHES European explorers sought both a northern trade route to the spices of Asia and cities of gold in North America.

❓ MOVEMENT Which European explorer first traveled down the St. Lawrence River? In which year was the Gulf of Mexico first explored?

Map Caption Answer
Cartier; 1519

HISTORICAL SIDELIGHTS
False Diamonds

By establishing a settlement on the St. Lawrence, Cartier hoped to gain control of Saguenay, a territory somewhere to the north that was believed to be rich in precious metals. Indeed, Cartier did find quantities of what appeared to be gold and diamonds close to the settlement. On his return to France, however, his precious discoveries turned out to be nothing more than iron pyrites and quartz. This probably gave rise to the French saying "false as Canadian diamonds."

westward route to Asia. But he did claim for France lands along the North American coast. Ten years later, Cartier explored the Gulf of St. Lawrence and the St. Lawrence River as far west as present-day Montreal. Cartier's attempts to start a settlement were unsuccessful, but his efforts strengthened French claims to what is now Canada.

The European powers thus made claims to North American territory early in the 1500s but did not establish permanent colonies. At that time most European countries were more concerned with trade with Asia than with organized efforts to settle the Americas.

Another reason for the delay in colonization efforts was the religious upheaval known as the **Protestant Reformation**. The Reformation began in Germany in 1517, when Martin Luther, a German monk, protested against corruption in the Roman Catholic church. Protests quickly spread to other European countries. As a result, a number of Protestant churches were established as alternatives to Catholicism.

This conflict between Protestants and Catholics became not only a religious struggle but also a territorial and political one. For a time the Reformation commanded Europe's attention.

Teaching the Section

COMPARING ENGLISH AND SPANISH COLONIZATION

Organize students into pairs and have them create a chart in which they compare the Spanish and English methods of colonization. Ask a volunteer pair to present their chart and discuss the similarities and differences with the class.

France, for example, was too involved with a civil war (1562–1598) between Catholics and Protestants to follow up on its claims to Canada until the 1600s.

During the Reformation, Spain, the most powerful nation in Europe, clung to the Catholic faith. But other countries, such as England, officially became Protestant states. This division led to a drawn-out conflict between the two groups as each tried to achieve religious and political dominance in Europe.

ENGLAND CHALLENGES SPAIN

The earliest European challenges to Spain's American empire came in the late 1500s. European pirates—especially the English "sea dogs"—began attacking Spanish galleons as they left the Americas and seizing their cargoes of treasure.

One of the most successful sea dogs was Francis Drake. In 1577 Drake ventured from England with a fleet of swift, heavily armed vessels on a voyage of exploration and piracy. After sailing through the Strait of Magellan at the southern tip of South America, he turned north. Off the western coast of South America, Drake attacked Spanish ships carrying silver from the mines of Peru. With his vessels loaded with Spanish riches, he sailed along the Pacific coast of North America and slowly made his way home to England.

Queen Elizabeth I welcomed Drake as a hero, knighting him on the deck of his treasure-laden ship, the *Golden Hind.* The queen's action angered King Philip II of Spain, who viewed it as a defiant challenge to Spanish power.

King Philip decided to strike back. He assembled a massive force of some 130 ships

◄ The faster English ships outmaneuvered the ships of the Spanish Armada.

and 30,000 men, known as the **Spanish Armada**, to invade England. In 1588 most of the Armada sailed to the port of Calais, France, just across the Strait of Dover from England. There they waited for additional troops.

The Spanish navy had a reputation in Europe for having large, well-armed ships. But England's sea captains skillfully used the speed of their smaller ships to great advantage. They loaded eight of their ships with gunpowder, set them afire, and propelled the burning ships toward the Armada. The heavy Spanish vessels could not get out of the way in time. Many caught fire or were blown up. The rest of the Armada was driven out to sea. As the Spanish ships attempted to escape, they were smashed by a furious storm. Only about half of the original fleet made it home to Spain.

The year 1588 was a turning point in history. The defeat of the Armada revealed Spanish military weaknesses. By the 17th century, Spanish economic weaknesses also became apparent. With tons of colonial silver flowing into its treasury, Spain seemed quite prosperous. But the prosperity was deceptive. The Spanish used most of the silver to buy goods from other countries. John Campbell, an English writer, explained:

> 66 [Spanish] galleons bring the silver into Spain, but . . . it runs out as fast as it comes in. . . . The silver . . . and very little of the goods or manufactures . . . belong to the subjects of the crown of Spain. It is evident, therefore, . . . that the greatest part of the returns from the West Indies belong to . . . [foreigners]. 99

The steady flow of silver caused **inflation**, or an increase in prices, throughout Europe. When the flow of silver slowed in the 17th century, Spain found itself with few resources to buy imported goods.

In order to launch the Armada, the Spanish government had taken out loans. These debts, and the weak Spanish economy, prevented Spain from launching new plans for further American colonization. The way was thus open for the English, the French, and the Dutch to begin colonization.

▪▪ **The defeat of the Spanish Armada marked the start of England's power in the Americas.**

CONDITIONS IN JAMESTOWN

Have students work in groups and take on the roles of an interviewer, Powhatans, and Jamestown settlers. Have them prepare an interview in which the settlers describe the harsh conditions in Jamestown and the Powhatans relate the role they played in the settlers' survival. Ask volunteers to present their interviews. Then discuss with the class why such conditions existed and the roles that John Smith, John Rolfe, and Pocahontas played in the colony's success.

JAMESTOWN: CONFLICT OVER LAND

Organize the class into two groups. Have one group represent the Powhatans, explaining their side of the dispute over land use. The other group should represent the Jamestown settlers' position on the issue. Moderate a discussion of the issue, allowing each group to present its position and to challenge the views of the other side.

■■ Ask students what arguments over land use are taking place in the U.S. today.

▶

ENGLAND'S FIRST ATTEMPTS AT COLONIZATION

Even before the defeat of the Spanish Armada, English adventurers had planned to colonize the lands claimed by Cabot and others. They were eager to develop commerce with the Americas as Spain had done.

Royal permission to start an English colony first went to a soldier, Sir Humphrey Gilbert. In 1583 he sailed to Newfoundland, but on the return journey he and his ship were lost in a storm. The following year Queen Elizabeth extended the permit to Gilbert's half-brother, Sir Walter Raleigh, who explored the Atlantic seaboard for a suitable site to colonize. He named the area that he chose Virginia, in honor of Elizabeth, the "Virgin Queen."

In 1585 Raleigh sent a small group of settlers to Virginia. They settled on Roanoke Island, off the coast of present-day North Carolina. After almost a year of hardship, the colonists returned to England. In 1587 Raleigh tried again, sending 117 people, including women and children, under the command of John White. After establishing a new Roanoke colony, White headed back to England for additional supplies.

Events in Europe—such as the attack on the Spanish Armada, which interrupted all English shipping—delayed White's return. When he finally reached Roanoke in 1590, all he found were the words CRO and CROATOAN carved into trees near the original settlement. "Croatoan" was the Native American name for an island off the coast. Searchers found no other trace of the colonists. The fate of the "Lost Colony" remains a mystery.

In 1606 the English again attempted to colonize Virginia. Unlike the Spanish government, which organized settlements in the Americas, the English government did not play a direct role in colonization. Instead, King James I issued the **Charter of 1606**, which licensed two merchant

▲ **This detail is from a supply list that was issued to all prospective colonists interested in settling in Virginia.**

▲ This map of Virginia, drawn by John Smith, appeared in his 1624 book, *General historie of Virginia*.

groups to organize settlements in Virginia. The two groups, the Plymouth Company and the London Company, were **joint-stock companies**, which operated somewhat like corporations do today. Investors shared the cost of running the company; they also shared any profits or losses.

The Charter of 1606 gave the Plymouth and London companies the right to establish settlements in North America and "to dig, mine, and search for all manner of mines of gold, silver, and copper." No doubt everyone pictured the tantalizing treasures Spain had discovered in its American colonies. Like the Spanish before them, the English did not consider the land rights of Native Americans already living in the region they called Virginia.

■■ **Great Britain, unlike Spain, chartered joint-stock companies to settle colonies in North America.**

THE EXPERIMENT AT JAMESTOWN

The first settlers—some 100 men provisioned by the London Company—reached Virginia in the spring of 1607. Sailing along Chesapeake Bay, they noted the "fair meddowes and goodly tall Trees, with Fresh-waters running through the woods." They chose a location near one of these rivers. In honor of their king, they named the settlement Jamestown.

GUIDED PRACTICE

On the chalkboard, write the section's main heads, one under the other, leaving ample space between each head. Ask for volunteers to suggest how each head describes a step in the development of an English presence in North America. Write responses under the appropriate head.

INDEPENDENT PRACTICE

Have students use the information from the Guided Practice to create a cause-effect chain for the establishment of English colonies in North America.

Review and Assessment

REVIEW Organize the class into groups and assign each group a subsection. Direct each group to develop questions about the main ideas in its subsection. Then have groups exchange questions and answer them. Then assign the Section 4 Review on p. 61.

ASSESS Assign the **Section 4 Daily Quiz** in *Core Resources*.

PRIMARY SOURCES
Description of Change: excerpted
Rationale: excerpted to focus on main idea

CULTURAL PATTERNS

In August 1619 a Dutch vessel arrived at Jamestown and sold some 20 Africans to a local merchant. Since slavery was not formally established in the colony of Virginia, the Africans were considered indentured servants. Some of these African American indentured servants received land in the colony after their work period had ended.

HISTORICAL SIDELIGHTS

Tobacco Smoking
Sir Walter Raleigh helped popularize smoking. According to one story, a servant, upon first seeing Raleigh light a pipe of tobacco, threw a jug of spiced ale on him, thinking he was on fire.

The early years. Unfortunately, Jamestown rested on a low, wooded peninsula near a marsh infested with disease-carrying mosquitoes. Disease, exposure to the elements, or starvation—the settlers had arrived too late to plant a crop—killed many people the first year. After seven months only some 30 settlers were still alive. One survivor, George Percy, recalled:

> 66 Our men were destroyed with cruell diseases . . . but for the most part they died of meere famine. There were never Englishmen left in a forreigne Countrey in such miserie as wee were in this new discovered Virginia. 99

The colonists' situation was made worse by the decisions of the directors of the London Company. Hoping for quick returns on their investment, the directors insisted that the settlers concentrate on searching for gold. This demand proved foolhardy since there was no gold. Precious time that could have gone toward building better shelters and cultivating crops was therefore wasted.

The result was an appalling loss of lives. During the first three years, most of the Virginia settlers died. The death toll might have been higher had it not been for Captain John Smith. An adventurous soldier, explorer, and mapmaker, Smith was elected president of the council of settlers in 1608. He called off the fruitless hunt for gold and imposed harsh discipline. He ordered wells dug, new shelters built, land cleared, and crops planted.

The help of the local Indians, whom the English called "Powhatans," prevented total disaster. The Powhatans, actually a large confederation of some 30 small tribes under the leadership of Wahunsonacock (wah-hoohn-SUH-nuh-kahk), were skilled in agriculture and fishing. The Powhatans gave the settlers food and taught them how to cultivate corn—a crop with which the English were not familiar.

George Percy described the relief brought by the Powhatans: "Bread, Corn, Fish, and Flesh in great plenty; which was the setting up

▲ This Powhatan robe, made of tanned deerskin and decorated with shells, was possibly worn by Wahunsonacock.

▲ This portrait of Pocahontas at age 21 was painted shortly after her arrival in London in 1616.

[reviving] of our feeble men: otherwise we had all perished." Pocahontas, the daughter of Wahunsonacock, also helped the English colonists. She delivered dried corn to them and established trade between the colonists and the Native Americans.

However, relations with the Powhatans were strained when Smith returned to England. Desperate for food in the harsh winter of 1609–10, the English raided local Native American villages—stealing food, burning down shelters, and killing many of the Indians. Wahunsonacock sought a truce, saying:

> 66 Why will you take by force what you may obtain by love? Why will you destroy us who supply you with food? What can you get by war? . . . We are unarmed, and willing to give you what you ask, if you come in a friendly manner. 99

Conflicts between colonists and Native Americans continued. In 1614 an uneasy truce was reached when Pocahontas married John Rolfe, an English colonist.

Tobacco and prosperity. But additional conflicts arose over the crop that would bring the colony economic prosperity—tobacco. The profitable cultivation of tobacco requires large amounts of land. The English settlers saw the abundant land around them as theirs for the taking, since the Native Americans seemed to not fully use it. The Indians, however, wished to leave the lands uncultivated as hunting grounds.

RETEACH Organize students in small groups to chart the major ideas and events presented in the section. Direct each group to indicate on its chart how each item addresses one of the Focus questions.

Closure

Retrieve the list of speculations students made after reading the Understanding the Main Idea paragraph at the beginning of the chapter. Have the class work together to evaluate and revise their responses.

Extension

ANALYZE Ask students to research the watercolors done by John White based on his observations of Roanoke. Have them analyze and write a report on the artwork, explaining what it reveals about the region.

RESEARCH Have students research the Powhatan culture and give an oral report to the class.

When Jamestown was settled in 1607, the Caribbean islands produced all the tobacco that Europe imported. John Rolfe challenged this monopoly in 1612 by successfully adapting the desirable Caribbean tobacco to Virginia. Soon the colonists were shipping large quantities of it to England. The success of the crop allowed Virginia to grow and prosper.

▪▪ Jamestown thrived with John Smith's leadership, the Powhatans' help, and profitable tobacco cultivation.

To provide laborers for tobacco cultivation, Jamestown's backers introduced headrights: 50 acres of land for anyone who paid for workers to come to Jamestown. They also set up a new arrangement for bringing settlers to Jamestown: indentured servitude. An **indentured servant** was bound for a period of years to the person who paid his or her way to America. At first, most of those who survived their term of service (far from a certainty in Jamestown) acquired land to work for themselves. Most historians believe that the first Africans to settle in the English colonies came as indentured servants.

Warfare with Native Americans. As Jamestown's population grew, the colonists' tobacco farms expanded onto Indian hunting

▲ **Women were sent to Virginia and sold as wives to male settlers.**

The Granger Collection, New York

grounds. Native Americans viewed the taking of their lands as an act of war.

In the spring of 1522, Indians attacked Jamestown's outlying farmhouses, killing some 350 settlers—including John Rolfe—and burning most of the buildings. The English struck back fiercely. They even concluded one "peace conference" by murdering some 200 Native Americans with poisoned wine. These actions brought an end to attempts at mutual understanding between the settlers and the Indians.

▪▪ Jamestown's prosperity attracted hundreds of new settlers. The colonists' demands for additional land brought them into violent conflict with Native Americans.

SECTION REVIEW ANSWERS

IDENTIFY

For significance, see the following pages:
John Cabot (p. 56)
northwest passage (p. 56)
Giovanni da Verrazano (p. 56)
Jacques Cartier (p. 56)
Protestant Reformation (p. 57)
Francis Drake (p. 58)
Spanish Armada (p. 58)
inflation (p. 58)
Sir Walter Raleigh (p. 59)
Charter of 1606 (p. 59)
Powhatans (p. 60)
Wahunsonacock (p. 60)
Pocahontas (p. 60)
indentured servant (p. 61)

LOCATE

For locations, see the map on p. 57.

1. *revealed Spanish weakness; opened way for other European nations to colonize the Americas*
2. *assisted settlers; conflicts over land and colonists' raids*
3. *corn—saved colonists from starvation; tobacco—brought prosperity*
4. *Letters should compare Spanish Crown's direct involvement in colonization with English government's indirect method of chartering merchant groups and describe how joint-stock companies worked.*
5. *possible examples—put stop to search for gold, imposed harsh discipline, made settlers plant crops*

▪▪ SECTION 4 REVIEW

IDENTIFY and explain the significance of the following: John Cabot, northwest passage, Giovanni da Verrazano, Jacques Cartier, Protestant Reformation, Francis Drake, Spanish Armada, inflation, Sir Walter Raleigh, Charter of 1606, Powhatans, Wahunsonacock, Pocahontas, indentured servant.

LOCATE and explain the importance of the following: St. Lawrence River, Roanoke, Jamestown.

1. **MAIN IDEA** What did the defeat of the Spanish Armada mean to Europe and to North America?

2. **MAIN IDEA** How did Native Americans first respond to the settlers at Jamestown? Why did relations worsen?

3. **GEOGRAPHY: RELATIONSHIPS** What impact did the cultivation of corn and tobacco have on Jamestown?

4. **WRITING TO PERSUADE** Imagine you are an investor in the London Company. Write a letter to a Spanish friend explaining how the English colonization process differs from the Spanish process. Be sure to describe how a joint-stock company works.

5. **EVALUATING** Do you think that John Smith was an effective leader? Provide examples from the text that support your position.

9. leader of the Powhatans
10. person who contracted to work a certain number of years to pay off passage to America

UNDERSTANDING MAIN IDEAS
1. *Native Americans should be treated well and converted to Catholicism; set up encomienda to control Indian land and labor, which led to Native American enslavement and disrupted Indian economies and societies*
2. *by race and family background; to own shops, sell food, work as maids, or serve as midwives*
3. *to establish an English settlement and to search for gold, silver, and copper in North America*

DEVELOPING THEMES

Return to the Themes section on p. 36. Have students discuss these again and compare their original responses with those given now. (See p. 35B for suggested answers.)

Chapter Review Answers

WRITING A SUMMARY
See Essential Points in each section for main ideas.

REVIEWING CHRONOLOGY
4, 2, 5, 1, 3
Hypothesizing
Paragraphs will vary but should accurately describe Native American reactions to the events chosen.

IDENTIFYING PEOPLE AND IDEAS
1. *Spanish priest who opposed harsh treatment of Native Americans and who tried to end the encomienda system*
2. *night in 1520 when Aztecs temporarily drove Spanish from Tenochtitlán*
3. *Spanish conquistador who conquered the Aztecs*
4. *religious upheaval in Europe that began in 1517 and established Protestant churches as alternatives to Catholicism*
5. *Spanish conquistador who conquered Incas*
6. *licensed London Company and Plymouth Company to organize settlements and to seek riches in North America*
7. *company in which investors shared costs, profits, and losses*
8. *leader of Jamestown whose discipline helped save the settlement*

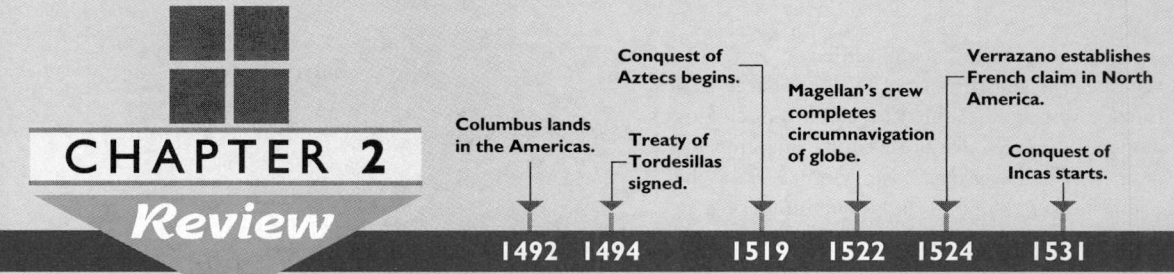

CHAPTER 2
Review

Columbus lands in the Americas. | Conquest of Aztecs begins. | Treaty of Tordesillas signed. | Magellan's crew completes circumnavigation of globe. | Verrazano establishes French claim in North America. | Conquest of Incas starts.

1492 1494   1519   1522 1524   1531

WRITING A SUMMARY
Using the essential points of the chapter as a guide, write a summary of the chapter.

REVIEWING CHRONOLOGY
Number your paper 1 to 5. Study the time line above, and list the following events in the order in which they happened by writing the first next to 1, the second next to 2, and so on. Then complete the activity below.
1. Jamestown established.
2. Conquest of Aztecs begins.
3. Pueblo Revolt drives Spanish from Santa Fe.
4. Treaty of Tordesillas signed.
5. Spanish Armada defeated.

Hypothesizing Select two events on the time line that affected Native Americans, and write a paragraph describing how Native Americans may have reacted to these events.

IDENTIFYING PEOPLE AND IDEAS
Explain the historical significance of each of the following people or terms.
1. Bartolomé de Las Casas
2. La Noche Triste
3. Hernán Cortés
4. Protestant Reformation
5. Francisco Pizarro
6. Charter of 1606
7. joint-stock company
8. John Smith
9. Wahunsonacock
10. indentured servant

UNDERSTANDING MAIN IDEAS
1. What instructions did Spain give Columbus and early settlers to guide them in their relationships with Native Americans? What changes did Spanish settlers introduce that affected Native Americans?
2. How were women's roles defined in Spanish America? What kinds of opportunities did Indian, African, and Spanish-Indian women have?
3. Why was Jamestown founded?

REVIEWING THEMES
1. **Global Relations** What were the positive and negative results of the Columbian exchange?

2. **Economic Development** How did the Spanish and English colonization of the Americas both benefit and hurt their economies?
3. **Cultural Diversity** How did differences in beliefs and values affect relations between Europeans and Native Americans?

THINKING CRITICALLY
1. **Evaluating** How successful was the Catholic church at protecting the Indians and improving their lives?
2. **Hypothesizing** Suppose the Spanish Armada had defeated the English in 1588. Do you think Spain would have continued to dominate the Americas?
3. **Analyzing** How did Native Americans respond to both Spanish and English colonization?

STRATEGY FOR SUCCESS
Review the Skills Handbook entry on Distinguishing Fact from Opinion on page 990. Read the excerpt below from a 17th-century Spanish judge's defense of Spanish treatment of Native Americans. Then identify which aspects of the argument are facts and which are opinions.

66 At each step they [critics] throw in our faces the fact that the Indians have been badly treated and that in many places they have completely disappeared. . . .
   In many places the Indians gave cause for their mistreatment or for war to be made against them, either because of their bestial [brutal] and savage customs or because of the excesses and treason that they attempted or committed against our people. . . .
   Moreover, it is not the Spaniards who have exterminated them, but their own vices and drunkenness or the earthquakes and repeated epidemics of smallpox and other diseases with which God in His mysterious wisdom has seen fit to reduce their numbers. 99

REVIEWING THEMES

1. *positive—trade, transfer of foods, animals, technologies, medicines, and ideas; negative—military conquest, enslavement, transfer of disease*
2. *Spanish benefited from increased trade and wealth, but flow of silver caused inflation; English profited from tobacco cultivation, but were unable to find gold to cover initial investment.*
3. *Europeans' land use and search for wealth often brought them into conflict with Native Americans. Religion and feelings of cultural superiority sometimes tempered and at other times aggravated these conflicts.*

THINKING CRITICALLY

1. *Answers should balance the church's success in instituting reforms with the fact that converting Indians to Catholicism helped suppress Indian culture.*
2. *Student answers should consider that inflation and Spain's debts made future colonization difficult.*
3. *Some Native Americans fled to escape contact with Europeans, others revolted against the Europeans, and some adapted European cultures to their own in order to survive.*

STRATEGY FOR SUCCESS

facts—Indians mistreated, population reduced due to earthquakes and epidemics; opinions—Indian customs, vices, and behaviors brought on wars and population decline

WRITING ABOUT HISTORY

Essays might mention the establishment of a Spanish empire in the Americas, the introduction of the encomienda system, and the impact of the Columbian exchange.

USING PRIMARY SOURCES

Paragraphs should mention the effects of famine and the mistreatment of Indians by Christians; colonization should be carried out with kindness.

LINKING HISTORY AND GEOGRAPHY

Students should consider that all the countries were located along the Atlantic coast, with direct access to a landmass immediately to their west.

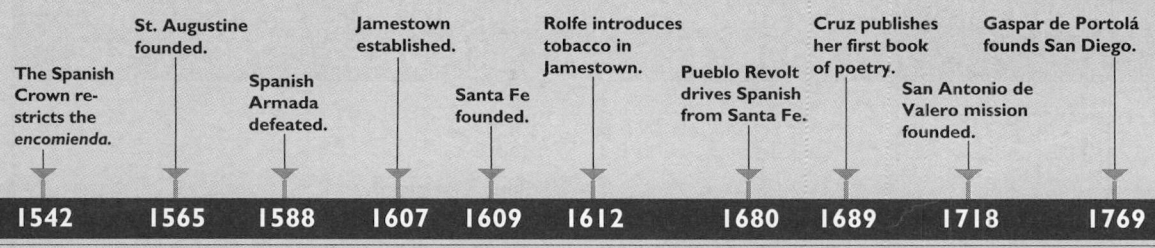

| The Spanish Crown restricts the *encomienda*. | St. Augustine founded. | Spanish Armada defeated. | Jamestown established. | Santa Fe founded. | Rolfe introduces tobacco in Jamestown. | Pueblo Revolt drives Spanish from Santa Fe. | Cruz publishes her first book of poetry. | San Antonio de Valero mission founded. | Gaspar de Portolá founds San Diego. |
| 1542 | 1565 | 1588 | 1607 | 1609 | 1612 | 1680 | 1689 | 1718 | 1769 |

WRITING ABOUT HISTORY

Writing to Evaluate Write an essay explaining why Columbus's first voyage was a turning point in history.

USING PRIMARY SOURCES

Read the following excerpt from Álvar Núñez Cabeza de Vaca's report to the Spanish king on his 8-year, 6,000-mile journey across North America. Then write a paragraph summarizing Cabeza de Vaca's experiences with Native Americans. What advice did he give the king about colonization?

❝ *We hastened through a vast territory, which we found vacant, the inhabitants having fled to the mountains in fear of Christians. With heavy hearts we looked out over the lavishly watered, fertile, and beautiful land, now abandoned and burned and the people thin and weak. . . . Not having planted, they were reduced to eating roots and bark; and we shared their famine the whole way. . . . They . . . told us how [Christians] had come through razing [tearing down] the towns and carrying off half the men and all the women and boys; those who had escaped were wandering about as fugitives. We found the survivors too alarmed to stay anywhere very long, . . . preferring death to a repetition of their recent horror. While they seemed delighted with our company, we grew apprehensive that the Indians resisting farther on at the frontier would avenge themselves on us.*

When we got there . . . they received us with the same awe and respect the others had—even more, which amazed us. Clearly, to bring all these people to Christianity and subjection to Your Imperial Majesty, they must be won by kindness, the only certain way. **❞**

LINKING HISTORY AND GEOGRAPHY

Spain, Portugal, England, and France led the exploration of the Americas. Study the maps on pages 19 and 57, noting the locations of these countries in relation to the Americas. Then, in a brief essay, explain how geographic location helped these countries lead the way to the Americas.

British Museum

Spanish coin

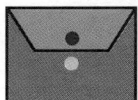

BUILDING YOUR PORTFOLIO

Complete the following projects independently or cooperatively.

1. **TRADE** In Chapter 1 you portrayed a trader. Building on that material, expand your map to include trade routes between Europe, Africa, Asia, and the Americas during the 1500s. Include symbols to represent major items of trade.

2. **SLAVERY** Imagine you are a Spanish priest opposed to slavery in the Americas. Plan a mural that conveys your concerns about the *encomienda* system and about the introduction of African slavery to the Americas.

3. **CULTURAL EXCHANGES** In Chapter 1 you portrayed a museum researcher. Building on that material, expand your exhibit to include dramatic readings of first-person accounts of exchanges between Native Americans, Africans, and Spanish conquistadors, mission priests, or colonists.

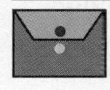

BUILDING YOUR PORTFOLIO

Have students refer to **Building Your Portfolio Worksheet 1**, assigned at the beginning of Unit 1. Use the worksheet to help students monitor their progress on the portfolio projects.

THE AMERICAN NATION VIDEODISC PROGRAM
A variety of still images, short videos, and activities are available for you to use as you teach this chapter. See Correlation to *The American Nation* Videodisc Program for barcode correlations and suggestions for using the program.

THE ENGLISH COLONIES

1620–1763

Chapter Overview

Beginning in the early 1600s, increasing numbers of immigrants left the political, economic, and religious problems of their homelands to start a new life in a new land. The freedom to live life as they pleased drew many settlers to America. But African Americans—many of whom were enslaved—and Native Americans—who were driven from their homelands—did not enjoy this opportunity.

Struggles between European powers, most notably Britain and France, over colonial empires and trade involved the American colonies in a number of wars. Britain emerged victorious, securing a vast North American empire.

Chapter Planning Guide

CHAPTER 3	CORE RESOURCE BOOKLETS	AUDIOVISUAL RESOURCES	PROGRAM RESOURCES
INTRODUCTION pp. 64–65	▪ Geography Worksheet 3 ▪ Building Your Portfolio Worksheet 1	▪ *The American Nation* Videodisc ▪ Linking Geography and History Transparency and Worksheet 7	
TEACHING THE CHAPTER pp. 66–93	▪ Graphic Organizer 3 ▪ Social Studies Skills Worksheet 3 ▪ Literature Worksheet 3 ▪ Outline Maps 8, 9, 10	▪ Linking Geography and History Transparency and Worksheet 8 ▪ Everyday Life in America Transparency and Worksheet 3	▪ *Eyewitnesses and Others*, Volume 1: Readings 7, 8, 9, 10, 11, 12, 14, 15, 16, 17, 19
REVIEW AND ASSESSMENT pp. 94–95	▪ Chapter 3 Daily Quizzes ▪ Review Worksheet 3 ▪ Chapter 3 Tests ▪ Alternative Assessment Forms		▪ Test Generator

Additional Resources

BOOKS FOR TEACHERS

Hawke, David Freeman. *Everyday Life in Early America.* HarperCollins, 1989. Shows how early European settlers adjusted to life in North America.

Lippy, Charles H., et al. *Christianity Comes to the Americas: 1492–1776.* Paragon House, 1992. Reviews role of religion in the development of British North America.

Nash, Gary B. *Red, White, and Black: The Peoples of Early North America,* 3rd ed. Prentice-Hall, 1991. Discusses race relations in colonial America.

BOOKS FOR STUDENTS

Scott, John A. *Settlers on the Eastern Shore, 1607–1750.* Facts on File, 1990. Primary source materials describe colonial life.

Weatherford, Jack. *Native Roots: How the Indians Enriched America.* Fawcett, 1992. Shows Native American influence on development of American society.

*Zeinert, Karen. *The Salem Witchcraft Trials.* Watts, 1989. Background and outcome of events at Salem.

* for students reading below grade level

MULTIMEDIA MATERIALS

As It Was in Colonial America. Video, 59 min. January Productions. Shows life-styles of colonial Americans.

The French and Indian War, 2nd ed. Video, 15 min. Coronet Instructional Films. Depicts the struggle between England and France.

The Godly Community. Video, 20 min. Films Incorporated. Re-creation of colonial life filmed at Plimoth Plantation museum.

THEMES IN AMERICAN HISTORY

USE WITH PAGES 64–65

Listed on the right are the themes emphasized in Chapter 3. The questions in boldface type stimulate critical thinking and provide students with an opportunity to discuss the themes within a broadened context. The questions also appear in the pupil's edition on p. 64.

■ CULTURAL DIVERSITY

How might the cultural backgrounds of settlers influence the development of a region? Students might note that settlers bring their cultural beliefs and practices with them. If an area is settled by people with similar beliefs and practices, the region may develop a society that is opposed to change or diversity. Areas settled by people from diverse cultures, on the other hand, might be more tolerant of differing views and practices and thus more varied and dynamic.

■ GEOGRAPHIC DIVERSITY

How might differences in environment and land use result in diverse ways of life? Students should note that environmental factors—types and abundance of resources, terrain—help determine the types of economic activities a people can pursue. This, in turn, affects the distribution of the population, the growth of cities, and the development of cultural practices.

■ ECONOMIC DEVELOPMENT

Why might a nation find it useful to regulate trade with its colonies? Students might suggest that a nation would most likely regulate colonial trade in an effort to boost its own economy.

What effect might this have on the colonies? This regulation could hurt the colonial economy or individuals or groups within the colonies if it restricted certain economic activities. But it could also help others by directing resources toward the most profitable endeavors.

CHAPTER STRATEGIES FOR MEETING INDIVIDUAL NEEDS

LIMITED ENGLISH PROFICIENT LEARNERS

Have students keep a running log of "difficult words" as they read the chapter. Have students list words they recognize but cannot define and new words. At the end of each section, have pairs of students work together to define the words in their logs.

TACTILE/KINESTHETIC LEARNERS

Have students work in groups to create an exhibit of the items and materials colonists used in their everyday lives—foods, clothing, building materials, and so on.

LEARNERS HAVING DIFFICULTY

As students read the chapter, have them outline each section using the Essential Points and headings as a guide.

AUDITORY LEARNERS

Have students listen to recordings or read aloud the lyrics of colonial American songs. (The audiocassettes *Colonial and Revolution Songs* by Keith and Rusty McNeil are a possible source.) Then, have students discuss what the songs reveal about life in colonial times.

VISUAL LEARNERS

Have students prepare an illustrated catalog of colonial American crafts. Catalog entries should include background information, dates, origins, and so on.

GIFTED LEARNERS

Have students research and write a report on a Native American group in the Plymouth area. Reports should discuss the group's way of life and its interaction with the English settlers.

ABOUT THE ILLUSTRATION

Many groups fled Europe for the Americas in search of religious freedom. One such group, the Brethren—a Protestant sect from Bohemia and Moravia—established the community of Bethlehem on the Lehigh River in Pennsylvania in the early 1740s. It was named after the town in which Jesus Christ was born. An orderly, industrious group, the Moravians, as they came to be known, won the admiration of many prominent Americans, including Benjamin Franklin and George Washington. This view of Bethlehem was drawn in 1757 by a member of the community. Ask students to suggest how the illustration shows the community's orderliness and industriousness.

Chapter 3

THE ENGLISH COLONIES

1620–1763

FOCUS

UNDERSTANDING THE MAIN IDEA

The colonists who settled North America in the 1600s and 1700s came for many reasons. Many came for religious freedom, others for wealth; and some came because they had no choice. The communities they founded developed in different ways, giving rise to distinctive societies within England's North American colonies. In the process, colonists forever changed Native Americans' lives and cultures.

THEMES

■ **CULTURAL DIVERSITY** How might the cultural backgrounds of settlers influence the development of a region?

■ **GEOGRAPHIC DIVERSITY** How might differences in environment and land use result in diverse ways of life?

■ **ECONOMIC DEVELOPMENT** Why might a nation find it useful to regulate trade with its colonies? What effect might this have on the colonies?

1620	1630	1651	1732	1754	1763
Mayflower lands.	Massachusetts Bay Colony established.	Parliament begins passing Navigation Acts.	Georgia founded.	French and Indian War begins.	Treaty of Paris signed.

◩▶ LINK TO THE PAST

Ask volunteers to recall the reasons that the English established the colony of Jamestown. Have students record responses in their notebooks. As students read the chapter, encourage them to compare these reasons with the reasons that other settlers came to America.

In the early 1600s hard times in England limited opportunities for many people. So when the chance arose to go to North America, thousands of men and women sailed west. Some hoped to make their fortune in the Virginia tobacco fields. Others wished to establish a "New England" based on their religious beliefs.

HISTORICAL SIDELIGHTS

The *Mayflower*

The *Mayflower* was about 90 feet long, weighed approximately 180 tons, and required a crew of more than 30 sailors. Before its voyage to the New World, the *Mayflower* had been used to transport cargoes such as fish, tar, timber, and wine.

A View of Bethlehem (1757) by Nicholas Garrison

𝓘n November 1620 a small ship sailing from England was blown off course into a harbor near what is now Provincetown, Massachusetts. It was the *Mayflower,* which had been bound for Virginia. The weary voyagers "fell upon their knees and blessed the God of Heaven, who had brought them over the vast and furious ocean," wrote William Bradford, a leader of the group.

The voyagers had indeed been over a "furious ocean." For more than two months, the *Mayflower* had been blown about by violent storms. The passengers were sick and weak, and they had landed far north of their destination at the wrong time of year. The "howling wilderness" terrified many of them, and the weather was cold and getting colder. While their shipmates huddled on board, some of the passengers searched for a place to settle. By mid-December they had found a site—Plymouth, named after the English port from which they had sailed. Who were these people? Why did they undertake such a voyage?

The Puritan

FOCUS OBJECTIVES

- Explain why the Pilgrims came to North America.

- Determine what drove the Puritans to leave England for North America, and describe the kind of society they tried to establish in America.

- Recognize why some colonists were forced to leave Massachusetts Bay Colony.

CULTURAL PATTERNS

At the time the Pilgrims signed the Mayflower Compact, a form of democratic government already existed in North America. The Great Law of Peace, the constitution of the Iroquois League, was more democratic than were European governmental systems of the time. Iroquois leaders were regarded as servants of the people, rather than as their masters. In addition, the Great Law of Peace endorsed freedom of speech and worship and allowed women a role in government.

CORE RESOURCES

- **Section 1 Daily Quiz**

PREVIEW WORKSHOP

Following is a list of the significant people, places, and terms in this section. You may wish to use this list as a section preview.

People
- Anne Hutchinson
- Lady Deborah Moody

Places
- Plymouth, Massachusetts
- Salem, Massachusetts
- Connecticut
- Rhode Island

Terms
- Pilgrims
- Separatists
- Puritans
- Mayflower Compact
- dissenters
- Great Migration
- covenant
- commonwealth
- freemen
- General Court
- New England Way
- Fundamental Orders of Connecticut

Section 1

THE NEW ENGLAND COLONIES

FOCUS

- **Why did the Pilgrims come to North America?**
- **What drove the Puritans to leave England for North America? What kind of society did they try to establish in America?**
- **Why were some colonists forced to leave Massachusetts Bay Colony?**

The prospect of religious freedom drew many English men and women—as it would later draw others—to North America. But not everyone came for religious reasons. Poverty plagued 17th-century England and drove many people to look for a better life elsewhere. Still, religion was vitally important to most New England colonists. They organized their close-knit communities around shared religious beliefs, creating a distinct and prosperous way of life.

Old Testament Psalms

THE PILGRIMS

In 1620 the men and women aboard the *Mayflower* reached Cape Cod Bay, near what is now Provincetown, Massachusetts, and founded Plymouth Colony. Known as **Pilgrims**, they had left England because of religious conflict. They saw themselves as wanderers who, like the "pilgrims and exiles" of the Bible, traveled in search of a place to worship God in their own way.

Conflicts over religious doctrine had raged in England since 1534 when Henry VIII broke with the Roman Catholic church to form the Church of England (Anglican church). Henry's motives had been primarily personal—the pope had refused to grant him a divorce from his first wife. At heart still a Roman Catholic, he had created a church that remained largely Catholic in form. This deeply troubled many English Christians, who longed for a truly Protestant church.

The Pilgrims were **Separatists**, so called because they had broken with the Church of England. They were the most radical of the **Puritans**, English Protestants who wished to "purify" the Anglican church of all Catholic rituals and traditions. The Puritans objected, for example, to the clergy's elaborate robes, insisting that church leaders should be known for "their purity of mind, not their adornment of person."

Some Separatists, including the Pilgrims, left England for the more religiously tolerant Netherlands after James I threatened to "harry them out of the land, or else do worse." There, forced into

Pilgrim Society, Plymouth, Massachusetts

◀ The *Mayflower* is shown covered with ice in this 19th-century painting by William Halsall.

MOTIVATING:
STUDENT EXPERIENCES

Ask students who know recent immigrants or who have read news stories about recent immigrants to explain the reasons that these newcomers moved to the U.S. As students read the section, have them compare these reasons to the reasons that the Pilgrims and Puritans came to America.

Teaching the *Section*

PILGRIMS TO NORTH AMERICA

Draw a web on the chalkboard, with *Pilgrims Come to America* as the center. Ask for volunteers to complete the web by offering reasons that these people left England for the Netherlands and then came to America. Have students copy the web into their notebooks. Leave the web on the chalkboard for use with the next teaching strategy.

▶

low-paid, unskilled work, they confronted what one Pilgrim called the "grimme & grisly face of pover-tie." Even more alarming, they faced the prospect of losing control of their children. The children were not only adopting Dutch ways but were also being led, as Pilgrim leader William Bradford saw it, by "evil examples into extravagant and dangerous courses, getting the reins off their necks and depart-ing from their parents." Seeking "some place of bet-ter advantage and less danger," Bradford and others obtained permission to settle in Virginia.

■■ **The Pilgrims came to North America for religious and economic reasons.**

*P*LYMOUTH COLONY

The Pilgrims never reached Virginia. Their ship was blown off course, and they landed far north in Massachusetts' Cape Cod Bay. Rather than risk traveling farther, they decided to stay. Because Cape Cod Bay was outside the area controlled by the London Company, the *Mayflower*'s passengers had no legal government. In an effort to maintain order in the new settlement, Pilgrim leaders drew up an agreement and asked all the men to sign it. This document, the **Mayflower Compact**, established a self-governing colony based on the majority rule of male church members:

> 66 We, whose names are underwritten, . . . Having undertaken for the Glory of God, and Advancement of the Christian Faith, and the Honour of our King and Country, a Voyage to plant the first colony in the north-ern Parts of Virginia; Do by these Presents [this document], solemnly and mutually in the Presence of God and one another, covenant and combine ourselves together into a civil Body Politick, for our better Ordering and Preservation, and Furtherance of the Ends aforesaid; And by Virtue hereof do enact, constitute, and frame, such just and equal Laws, Ordinances, Acts, Constitutions, and Offices, from time to time, as shall be thought most meet and convenient for the general Good of the Colony; unto which we promise all due Submission and Obedience. 99

The Mayflower Compact was important because it helped set a precedent for local government based on written agreements and the consent of the governed.

Once the Compact was signed, the colonists elected Bradford as their governor and turned to

Joslyn Museum, Omaha, Nebraska

▶ *Europeans Encountering Indians* is the title of this painting by an unknown artist.

BUILDING VOCABULARY

The word *compact* comes from a Latin word that means "to make an agree-ment." While *compact* can be applied to any arrange-ment or understanding between individuals, it is most often used to describe agreements between na-tions—treaties, for example.

THINKING CRITICALLY

Recognizing Prejudice
You may wish to point out to students William Brad-ford's opinion that the Pilgrims found in America "a hideous and desolate wilderness, full of wild beasts and wild men." Have students discuss on what attitudes and beliefs Bradford might have based his evaluation.

Teaching the Section

PURITANS TO NORTH AMERICA

Draw another web on the chalkboard beside the Pilgrims web, this one titled *Puritans Come to America.* Ask students to complete the web by offering reasons that the Puritans came to America. Call on volunteers to point out any similarities or differences in the Pilgrims' and the Puritans' reasons for emigrating. Have students copy the web into their notebooks.

▶ These artifacts were used by the Pilgrims in the 17th century. Clockwise from top are a christening shirt and mitts worn by William Bradford, the wicker cradle used by Peregrine White, who was born aboard the *Mayflower,* and a pair of boys' leather shoes.

Peabody & Essex Museum, Salem, Massachusetts

Peabody & Essex Museum, Salem, Massachusetts

Pilgrim Society, Plymouth, Massachusetts

the challenge of surviving the winter. But the cold climate, disease, and hunger took their toll. The colony's record for March 24, 1621, notes: "In three months past dies halfe our company . . . Of a hundred persons, scarce fifty remain, the living scarce able to bury the dead."

The colony, like Jamestown, owed its survival to Native Americans. The settlers were particularly indebted to Squanto, a member of the Patuxet band of the Wampanoags (wahm-puh-NOH-ags). He taught them where to fish and how to plant corn. He also spoke English. Kidnapped in 1614, he had lived in Spain and England before returning home in 1619. The Pilgrims viewed Squanto, in Bradford's words, as "a special instrument sent of God for their good beyond their expectation." With Squanto's aid autumn brought a bountiful harvest. The Pilgrims then invited the Indians to a harvest feast—the first Thanksgiving.

THE PURITANS AND THE GREAT MIGRATION

In contrast to the Pilgrims, most Puritans remained in England and did not leave the Anglican church. These religious **dissenters** hoped to reform the church from within.

The Crown, however, opposed reform. James I feared that Puritan demands would lead to political upheaval. Religious dissent, he declared, "as well agreeth with a Monarchy as God and the Devill. Then Jack & Tom, & Will &

Dick, shall meete and at their pleasure censure me, and my Councell, and all our proceedinges." King James's son Charles, who succeeded James in 1625, was even more determined than his father to stop dissent and suppress Protestant ministers and practices.

The English Puritans faced economic difficulties as well. England's population had dramatically increased, but employment had not. The growing profitability of wool production encouraged large landowners to turn from farming to raising sheep. They fenced their lands and drove off the tenant farmers, many of whom were Puritans. Then in the 1620s crop failures and an economic depression in the woolen industry hit Puritan farmers and weavers.

To escape both religious persecution and economic ruin, many Puritans decided to risk a move to the colonies. Beginning in 1630, in what is known as the **Great Migration**, some 60,000 people left England for the Americas. While most of them went to the West Indies, some 10,000 to 20,000 settled in Massachusetts.

Most Puritans, however, did not leave England. In 1642 the conflict between the Puritans and the Royalists, the supporters of King Charles I, erupted in civil war. Led by Oliver Cromwell, the Puritans won. During Cromwell's rule (1653–1658), Puritan emigration almost ceased.

▪▪ **The Puritans left England to escape religious conflict and economic problems.**

THE PURITAN SOCIETY

Have students assume the role of Puritan members of Massachusetts Bay Colony. Have them hold a town meeting to decide the part that their religious beliefs should play in the life of their community. Assign a number of students to act as clerks and record the results of the meeting.

MASSACHUSETTS BAY COLONY

The year before the Puritan exodus began, a group of well-to-do Puritans secured a royal charter for the Massachusetts Bay Company, allowing them to establish a colony. In 1630 the company's fleet of 11 ships carried some 1,000 settlers to Massachusetts. These Puritans did not wish to cut all ties with England or the Anglican church. Inspired by a sense of mission, they hoped to provide other Christians with an example of a model community. While still aboard ship, John Winthrop, their governor, expressed their vision and warned against failure:

▲ John Winthrop

66 We must consider that we shall be as a city upon a hill. The eyes of all people are upon us. So that if we shall deal falsely with our God in this work we have undertaken, and so cause Him to withdraw His present help from us, we shall be made a story and a byword through the world. 99

Most colonists, wrote Winthrop, expected to find in their new home more of God's "wisdom, power, goodness and truth than formerly we have been acquainted with." Their expectations arose from their belief that they had a **covenant**, or contract, with God to build a society based on the

▲ This drawing shows a meetinghouse built at Plymouth in 1683. The building contained glass windows, a Gothic-style roof, and a bell.

New England

SETTLING NEW ENGLAND Colonists spread out from Massachusetts Bay to settle much of New England.

? **PLACE** New England's rocky soil turned many colonists to the sea for a livelihood. Which colony had the least ocean shoreline?

Scriptures and a covenant with one another "to walk together in all His ways."

The Massachusetts Bay Company's charter allowed Winthrop and the other stockholders to govern the colony however they wished, so long as they did not violate English law. To fulfill their covenant with God, they established their colony as a Bible **commonwealth**, in which everyone, guided by English law and the Bible, was expected to work together for the common good. The stockholders granted voting rights to all **freemen**, that is, adult men who were church members and property owners. The freemen in each town then elected representatives to the **General Court**, or legislature, to make laws for the colony.

The Puritan commonwealth was based on cooperation between church and state. The colonists referred to this relationship as the **New England Way**. The meetinghouse, in which Puritans held both town meetings and church services, symbolized this unity. Its civil function was clearly visible: the outside walls of the plain, unpainted clapboard building served as a public notice board. Sermons delivered within on Sundays and on important occasions instructed the congregation in the New

HISTORICAL SIDELIGHTS

Crossing the Atlantic

The voyage from England to the Massachusetts Bay Colony took anywhere from 6 weeks in summer to as much as 14 weeks in the winter. Living quarters aboard the ships were cramped, and sanitary conditions were primitive at best. And the daily diet—hard biscuits, dried or heavily salted meat, cheese, peas, and, occasionally, fresh fish—was severely limited.

Map Caption Answer
New Hampshire

PRIMARY SOURCE

Description of Change: excerpted
Rationale: excerpted to focus on main idea

Teaching the Section

NEW ENGLAND LIFE

Have students imagine they are living in the Massachusetts Bay Colony in the mid-1600s. Ask them to write journal entries for a typical week in the colony. Suggest that they focus on themes such as government, education, family life, work, and trade. Have volunteers read their journals aloud. Students may wish to include their journal entries in their portfolios.

HISTORY
in the Making

THE SALEM WITCHCRAFT TRIALS

SETTING THE SCENE

A great witch hunt had taken place in Western Europe in the 16th and 17th centuries. During that time hundreds, possibly thousands, of people were burned at the stake as witches.

ADMITTING ERROR

In the years after the trials, many witnesses began to confess that they had made errors. As a result, the provincial legislature set aside January 14, 1697, as a day of fasting and repentance. In 1710 the legislature awarded damages to many of the accused witches or their families.

■■ Ask students if they know of any examples of a government admitting error and paying compensation.

HISTORY *in the Making*

BY DR. CAROL KARLSEN

The Salem Witchcraft Trials

Few questions have so baffled historians as those surrounding the Salem witchcraft trials. The answers are complicated, and no single explanation tells the whole story. But recent interpretations have profoundly changed the way we look at colonial America's most dramatic witch trials.

In the winter of 1692, several young women in Salem Village, Massachusetts, were stricken with seizures. The community attributed the seizures to demonic possession. Most people in Europe and America believed in the Devil's existence and ability to possess humans. They also believed that the Devil empowered human agents, called witches, to cause this possession.

Members of the village community pressed the possessed females to name those responsible for their afflictions. Once the young women began

identifying witches in their midst, hundreds of residents of Salem and other eastern Massachusetts towns came forward to testify that they too were victims of witchcraft. They claimed witches had used supernatural powers to kill their children, sicken their farm animals, and otherwise harm their families and property.

Witchcraft accusations and trials had taken place in New England many times prior to 1692. What made the Salem

trials so unusual was the number of people involved. In a matter of months, over 200 persons were named as witches. At least 59 were tried, 31 convicted, and 19 hanged. As in earlier times, older women were the main targets.

For a long time, many historians considered the Salem outbreak a bizarre and irrational event and argued that the young women were mentally disturbed. Other accusers, most of whom were adult men, were

▶ On August 5, 1692, a group of Salem girls accused George Jacobs (kneeling at right) of witchcraft. He was hanged two weeks later. T. H. Matteson painted this version of the trial in 1855.

England Way. First the minister explained the meaning of a Biblical text and then showed the congregation the way to apply the lesson in their spiritual and earthly lives. Such lessons were important because the Puritans believed that everyone in the community had to live a moral life; otherwise, the entire community would suffer God's wrath. When catastrophe struck, the faithful often blamed the occurrence on New England's sinfulness.

The Puritans also believed that an all-knowing God had already determined who would be saved. Just as God had entered a covenant with the saved, so New Englanders joined in a covenant with one

another to found churches and towns. The church granted full membership to those who convinced the congregation that they had undergone a "conversion experience." Those who did not were admitted to partial membership.

The New England Way depended on educated people who could understand the Scriptures. The General Court thus required parents to teach their children to read, and a law passed in 1647 required towns to maintain schools. The "Old Deluder Law," as it was known, was meant to foil the "chief project of that old deluder, Satan, to keep men from the knowledge of the Scriptures."

LEAVING MASSACHUSETTS BAY COLONY

Ask for volunteers to play the parts of Thomas Hooker, Roger Williams, and Anne Hutchinson. Have them make short speeches outlining their objections to the colony's practices. Then suggest that the rest of the class might wish to act as the Massachusetts General Court and issue an opinion about whether the views of Hooker, Williams, and Hutchinson are compatible with the New England Way.

▶

thought either to have been carried away with the hysteria of the moment or to have deliberately accused people they resented. The older women who were convicted and executed as witches were simply viewed as convenient targets.

Recent historians have challenged this view of the trials, emphasizing how the trials were rooted in the social and cultural climate of New England. The religious, economic, and family life of New England's settlers all fostered an environment in which witchcraft fears flourished and accusations were an accepted way of dealing with personal conflict and community tensions.

Ideas about witches, demons, and magical practices were a part of Puritan beliefs and popular folklore. New England ministers and their followers had brought these ideas with them from England. Rather than irrational responses, witchcraft accusations and trials were expressions of 17th-century religious thinking about the nature of society, the causes of

misfortune, the existence of sin, and the rebelliousness of the human spirit.

The outbreak also had roots in decades of community conflict and economic tensions. Salem Village lay on the edge of Salem Town, a thriving port. Some village farmers had family and economic links to the town and shared in its growing prosperity. Other villagers, however, felt pinched as farmland grew scarce. These economic tensions produced deep divisions in the community. The witchcraft accusation, egged on by several of the village's less prosperous residents, provided an outlet for resentments and grievances. The way the community divided over the witchcraft scare paralleled the village's deeper factional divisions.

But why were most of the accused women? Historically, on the basis of the Bible and a vast body of witchcraft lore, witch belief had focused mainly on females. A more immediate answer, however, lies in the contradictory view of women held by Puritan men. On the

one hand, men acknowledged women's value and held them in esteem as "helpmates." On the other hand, they feared women gaining economic and social independence. Such independence was seen as a challenge to men's power and a threat to the social order. Women who did not have brothers or sons were among the most feared. In New England, where property customarily passed from father to son, such women could and did become economically independent by inheriting property. Women without brothers and sons were the most likely targets of Salem's witchcraft trials.

With this better awareness of how witchcraft beliefs and accusations were deeply embedded in New England culture and society, the Salem outbreak appears less bizarre but no less fascinating. The story of Salem is still unfolding, however. Historians continue to reexamine the trials and reevaluate the surviving evidence, offering us new perspectives on what caused the tragic events of 1692.

MAKING CONNECTIONS

Literature

Among the judges who took part in the witch trials was a John Hathorne. The writer Nathaniel Hawthorne, one of his descendants, was haunted by the family's past, and he made sin and guilt a major theme in much of his work—most notably in his masterpiece of American literature, *The Scarlet Letter.*

LINK TO TODAY

Point out that the first use of the term *witch hunt* to describe the persecution of people who hold unpopular views or opinions came in 1938 in the writings of British author George Orwell.

▪▪ Ask students to identify a recent news item that was described as a "witch hunt."

THINKING CRITICALLY

Have students write a paragraph supporting or opposing the following statement: *The witchcraft hysteria reflected deep anxieties about social changes taking place in New England.*

▪▪ **The Puritans hoped to build a model commonwealth in which the Bible guided all aspects of life.**

NEW ENGLAND LIFE

By the time Massachusetts Bay Colony passed its school law, it had more than 20,000 inhabitants. The men who immigrated were primarily educated artisans or farmers—"godly men . . . endowed with grace and furnished with means," according to Deputy Governor Thomas Dudley.

Three out of four had paid their own way to the colony.

In contrast to the Jamestown colonists, these men brought along their wives and children. Puritans considered orderly families to be essential to a stable society. Women were expected to defer to their fathers or husbands in most aspects of life. Single people had to live with a family, and children could be removed from "disorderly" ones. Town officials inspected families on a regular basis so that "disorders may be prevented, and ill weeds nipped before they take too great a head."

Practice

GUIDED PRACTICE

Organize students into six groups; assign to each group a subsection of Section 1. Ask groups to review their subsections and then create a visual that illustrates its main idea. Visuals can be cartoons, book jackets, or maps. Have groups share their artwork.

INDEPENDENT PRACTICE

Direct students to write a paragraph that explains how their group's Guided Practice creation represents the main idea of their assigned subsection.

Review and Assessment

REVIEW Provide five groups with sheets of paper labeled *New England Settlers*. Assign each group one of these headings: *Why They Came, Where They Settled, Government, Daily Life, Objections to Way of Life*. Have groups list appropriate responses. Assign the Section 1 Review on p. 73.

ASSESS Assign the **Section 1 Daily Quiz** in *Core Resources*.

COOPERATIVE LEARNING

Organize students in small groups and have them imagine they are settlers arriving in New England. Have them draw up a plan for a new colony that addresses these issues: choosing a location, acquiring land, governing the colony, establishing laws and procedures, and assigning work duties. Each group member should handle at least one issue. Have members present their plans to the class.

HISTORICAL SIDELIGHTS

Life Expectancy

In New England in the mid-1600s the average life expectancy for males aged 21 was about 70 years. The average was slightly lower for females because of the high rate of maternal mortality—some 20 percent of adult women died in childbirth.

▲ These illustrations from the American edition of *The Book of Trades* show two colonial crafts: spinning (left) and coopering (right).

New England's environment encouraged the growth of large families. Food was plentiful, and the cold climate proved relatively hostile to some of the diseases that plagued Jamestown. As a result, some 80 percent of all children lived to adulthood. Colonist Mary Buell's tombstone shows just how large these families could be—it records that she died at age 90 leaving behind 336 living descendants.

Married in their early 20s, most women had at least six children, and families with nine or more were common. Such a large family led Sarah Ripley Stearns to lament that "the care of my Babes takes up so large a portion of my time and attention." Furthermore, because women bore children on into their 40s, a mother in New England could expect to be well into her 60s before her last child left home.

Following English custom, New England women usually did not work in the fields, although they often helped at harvesttime. Instead, they took on many other tasks required to run a farm. They made many of the things their families needed: soap, candles, yarn, clothes, butter, and cheese. Women might sell their occasional surplus in town to help support their families.

New Englanders with large families had relatively little need for indentured servants or slaves. Fathers and sons could supply all the labor needed to transform the "remote, rocky, barren, bushy, wild-woody wilderness," as Edward Johnson described it in 1653, into "a second England." However, because of long winters and the poor soil found in much of New England, farmers did not have a large surplus to market.

▪▪ New England was populated mostly by educated artisans and farmers who had immigrated with their families.

To pay for supplies and luxury items from England, some New Englanders turned to fishing, trade, and business. They distilled rum and built ships. They sold fish, grain, meat, naval stores (turpentine, pitch, and rosin), and lumber to England, Spain, Portugal, and the West Indies. New England merchants also prospered through trade with England's other American colonies. In time the merchants also earned substantial profits by selling their shipping services.

DISCONTENTED COLONISTS ESTABLISH NEW COLONIES

As Massachusetts Bay Colony prospered and grew, some colonists started new settlements. Thomas Hooker and his congregation left Massachusetts in part, they said, because its "towns were set so near to each other." To get more farmland, they moved southwest, establishing a colony in the Connecticut Valley. In 1639 Hooker's settlers adopted the **Fundamental Orders of Connecticut**, which some regard as the first written constitution in the colonies.

▶ Thomas Hooker was such a domineering figure that he was once described as a man who could put a king in his pocket. This picture shows Hooker and his congregation traveling through the wilderness.

RETEACH Organize students into small groups and assign each group a subsection. Direct each group to develop questions about the main ideas in its subsection. Then have each group exchange its questions with another group and work to answer the questions it receives.

Closure

Ask students whether they would have wanted to live in New England in the mid-1600s. In their responses, have them consider living conditions, community standards and values, and the alternative of remaining in England as religious dissenters.

Extension

INTERPRET Invite students to rewrite in modern English the excerpt from the Mayflower Compact on p. 67 and then highlight and explain the significant principles contained in the Compact.

CREATE Have students use historical atlases to create a map that shows the Great Migration of the 1600s.

Other colonists were forced to leave Massachusetts Bay Colony because they questioned Puritan ways. One such person was Roger Williams, a Puritan minister who, unlike most other Puritans, believed in strict separation of church and state. He also challenged the king's right to give Native American land to English colonists. These beliefs so angered Puritan leaders that they banished Williams. He purchased land from the Narragansets and in 1636 founded a settlement that became Providence, Rhode Island. An able politician, Williams secured a charter for the colony in 1644 that permitted its inhabitants complete religious freedom. Because of this tolerant attitude, the colony attracted those who, like Williams, held unpopular beliefs.

BIO GRAPHY Another Puritan who found refuge in Rhode Island after refusing to conform to the New England Way was Anne Hutchinson. Born in England in 1591, Hutchinson came to Boston, the capital of Massachusetts Bay Colony, in 1634 with her family. "A woman of a ready wit and bold spirit," as Governor Winthrop acknowledged, she worked as a nurse and midwife and devoted herself to Bible study and teaching. At meetings in her home, she discussed the sermons of Boston's leading ministers. She attracted a following of women and wealthy merchants, many of whom resented the ministers' authority.

Increasingly, Hutchinson expressed ideas critical of the established clergy's teachings. In 1637 she was charged with weakening the authority of the church. The fact that she was a woman added to the authorities' displeasure. Her meetings, Governor Winthrop told her, were "not tolerable . . . in the sight of God nor fitting for your sex." The Puritans found especially dangerous Hutchinson's claim that she received her religious insights directly from God. To them this claim set the individual above the community and threatened the authority of both the community and the church. Banished in 1638, she moved to Rhode Island and then to Long Island. When Hutchinson died in an Indian attack in 1643, Massachusetts ministers declared it the "just vengeance of God."

Anne Hutchinson

Hutchinson was not the only woman whose religious beliefs put her at odds with Puritan authorities. In 1643 Lady Deborah Moody and her followers left Massachusetts because of disagreements over religion. A few years later, she received permission to establish a self-governing colony on Long Island.

■ **Massachusetts Bay Colony did not tolerate differences of opinion in religious matters and banished offending colonists.**

SECTION REVIEW ANSWERS

IDENTIFY

For significance, see the following pages:
Pilgrims (p. 66)
Separatists (p. 66)
Puritans (p. 66)
Mayflower Compact (p. 67)
dissenters (p. 68)
Great Migration (p. 68)
covenant (p. 69)
commonwealth (p. 69)
freemen (p. 69)
General Court (p. 69)
New England Way (p. 69)
Fundamental Orders of Connecticut (p. 72)
Anne Hutchinson (p. 73)
Lady Deborah Moody (p. 73)

LOCATE

For locations, see the map on p. 69.

1. *religious conflict; economic difficulties*
2. *did not tolerate differences of opinion; banished offenders*
3. *Essays should mention that women married in their 20s, had large families, helped run farms, and deferred to their fathers or husbands in most aspects of life.*
4. *Pamphlets should mention the establishment of a moral society in which the Bible guides all aspects of life.*
5. *The New England Way depended on educated people who could read the Scriptures.*

SECTION 1 REVIEW

IDENTIFY and explain the significance of the following: Pilgrims, Separatists, Puritans. Mayflower Compact, dissenters, Great Migration, covenant, commonwealth, freemen, General Court, New England Way, Fundamental Orders of Connecticut, Anne Hutchinson, Lady Deborah Moody.

LOCATE and explain the importance of the following: Plymouth, Massachusetts; Salem. Massachusetts; Connecticut; Rhode Island.

1. **MAIN IDEA** What conditions in England and Europe led the Pilgrims and the Puritans to settle in North America?
2. **MAIN IDEA** How did Massachusetts Bay Colony react to colonists who challenged Puritan ways?
3. **USING HISTORICAL IMAGINATION** Write an essay describing life in New England from the perspective of a woman colonist.
4. **WRITING TO PERSUADE** Imagine you are a Puritan dissenter who wishes to leave England to found a Bible commonwealth in North America. Write a pamphlet describing the type of society you hope to create.
5. **ANALYZING** Why was education important to the Puritan community?

FOCUS OBJECTIVES

- Describe what life was like for the Chesapeake colonists in the 17th century.

- Explain why planters turned to the use of slave labor.

- Examine what the Middle Passage was like for newly captured slaves.

Section 2

SLAVERY AND THE SOUTHERN COLONIES

F O C U S
- **What was life like for the Chesapeake colonists in the 17th century?**
- **Why did planters turn to the use of slave labor?**
- **What was the Middle Passage like for newly captured slaves?**

In the Chesapeake colonies of Virginia and Maryland, people developed a way of life different from that in the New England colonies. Most Chesapeake colonists lived on scattered farms and plantations, where they grew tobacco as a cash crop. The majority of them had come to the colonies as indentured servants, obligated to work for whoever purchased their contracts. However, by the end of the 17th century, more and more planters bought African slaves to work in the tobacco fields.

Slaves loading tobacco barrels at a Virginia wharf

THE CHESAPEAKE

Within 25 years of Jamestown's founding, Virginia was a thriving colony with a population of some 2,500. Tobacco fueled the economy and remained the most valuable staple export of the lands making up British North America until 1793. The promise of huge profits led more than one wealthy Englishman to dream of establishing a colony in the Chesapeake—the land surrounding Chesapeake Bay. The first to do so was Cecilius Calvert, the second Baron Baltimore.

In 1632 Charles I made Cecilius Calvert proprietor, or owner, of

◀ **Cecilius Calvert**

millions of acres on the upper Chesapeake Bay. The colony was named Maryland, after Charles's French wife, Henrietta Maria. As proprietor, Calvert was free to dispose of the land and to govern—within loose guidelines—as he wished.

Calvert wanted to create a haven for fellow Roman Catholics who faced persecution in Protestant England. But he also hoped to make money. Because there were not enough Catholic immigrants to make his venture profitable, he opened his colony to Protestants. Soon Protestants greatly outnumbered Roman Catholics. To protect the Catholic minority's legal rights, the Maryland Assembly passed the **Toleration Act** in 1649. The act guaranteed religious freedom to all Christians.

Population. Catholic and Protestant settlers in Maryland soon followed Virginia's lead and devoted much of their land to tobacco production. As a result, both colonies developed a distinct culture in response to life in the Chesapeake.

Most white colonists in the Chesapeake came as indentured servants. Many came because

Teaching the Section

LIFE IN THE CHESAPEAKE

Ask students to imagine that they are Massachusetts Bay colonists visiting the Chesapeake region. Have them write a letter to a friend in Massachusetts, describing the Chesapeake and comparing life there to life in New England. Ask for volunteers to read their letters to the class. Students may wish to include their letters in their portfolios.

▶

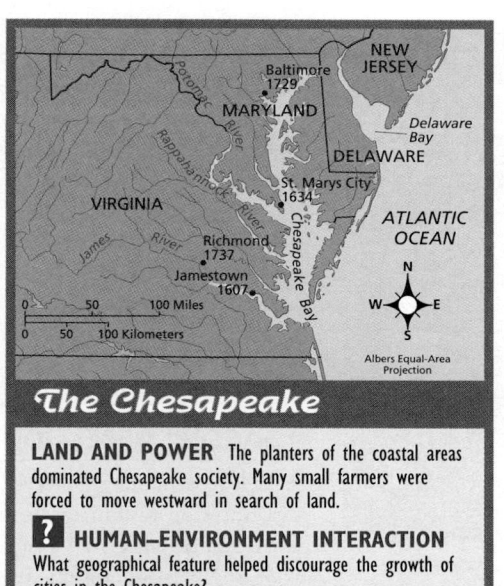

The Chesapeake

LAND AND POWER The planters of the coastal areas dominated Chesapeake society. Many small farmers were forced to move westward in search of land.

? **HUMAN–ENVIRONMENT INTERACTION**
What geographical feature helped discourage the growth of cities in the Chesapeake?

they could not find work in England. But not all came willingly. In the 17th century some men, women, and even children were "spirited" and "snared"—kidnapped—from London streets to meet the demand for servants. A 1645 report to Parliament told of gangs who "in a most barbarous and wicked manner steal away many little children." Moreover, in the 1700s England sent an estimated 30,000 to 50,000 convicts to work as servants in the Chesapeake.

One indentured servant, John Harrower, described how some servants were bought and sold once they arrived in Virginia:

66 Soul drivers. . . are men who make it their bussines to go on board all ships who have in either Servants or Convicts and buy sometimes the whole and sometimes a parcell of them, . . . and then they drive them through the Country like a parcell of Sheep untill they can sell them to advantage. 99

Of the colonists who came as indentured servants, some 75 percent were men or boys between ages 15 and 24. Even as late as 1704, the Archives of Maryland show that there were more than three times as many white men as white women living in the colony. Because there were so few white women in these early years, many men never married.

High death rates also affected the Chesapeake population. Throughout the 1600s typhoid, malaria, and other diseases ravaged the colonists. Up to 55 percent of those born in the Chesapeake died before age 20. Life expectancy slowly improved around the turn of the century as the number of native-born colonists who had better immunity to the region's diseases increased.

The high death rates gave rise to family patterns that differed from those of New England. New England's low death rates meant that most people married only once. In the Chesapeake, however, one partner in most marriages died within seven or eight years of marrying. In most cases the surviving partner quickly remarried. Second and even third marriages were common. As a result, most families included stepparents, stepsiblings, half siblings, and possibly the orphans of deceased relatives or friends.

■■ **In the 17th century, colonists in the Chesapeake suffered from high death rates, and white men greatly outnumbered white women.**

A rural society. The vast majority of colonists in the Chesapeake lived on widely scattered farms and plantations. They produced tobacco for export and grew or made many of the things they needed. Away from the coast, poor settlers on small farms grew corn and vegetables, kept chickens and hogs, hunted, and trapped.

Most of the large plantations fronted one of the many navigable rivers that flowed into

◀ This ragged London oyster seller symbolized the class of people who indentured themselves as servants in order to start over in the colonies.

Teaching the Section

THE RISE OF SLAVE LABOR

Assume the role of a legislator in colonial Virginia. Hold a meeting in your district about the indenture system in the aftermath of Bacon's Rebellion. Have students take the roles of indentured servants, small farmers, landless laborers, and planters. Encourage students, in their roles, to express opinions about the indenture system, its benefits and problems, and its role in Virginia's unrest. Conclude the activity by asking how the increased use of slave labor might have been seen as a way to alleviate the problems students have raised.

GLOBAL CONNECTIONS

In 1662, in order to maintain closer control of trade in the Chesapeake, the English government ordered Virginians to build a port town on every river. But the plague ravaged London three years later, and Virginians, fearing that the disease might be carried on ships from England, deserted the new ports. The English government abandoned the town-building plan shortly thereafter.

Graph Caption Answer
Falling tobacco prices drove many farmers into debt and led them to expand onto lands promised to American Indians. The conflict between settlers and Indians over land contributed to Bacon's Rebellion.

The Metropolitan Museum of Art

▲ *The Plantation* **was painted by an unknown American artist about 1825. The roads leading down from the manor house to the river allowed for easy transportation of goods to or from ships docked at the wharf.**

Chesapeake Bay. At first, English trading ships stopped at the planters' docks to collect the tobacco crops and to deliver goods previously ordered. Later, Scottish brokers set up stores and traded in tobacco.

The fact that planters did not need to bring their crops to a central market hindered the growth of towns. As late as 1750 the only large town in the Chesapeake was Baltimore. Without towns to provide customers, the Chesapeake was slow to develop a substantial class of independent artisans and shopkeepers.

The slow growth of towns also hindered the development of schools. Education was left to individual families who either taught their children themselves or hired tutors. Wealthy families made sure their children—both boys and girls—were educated, but they did not support schooling for others. As a result, especially when compared with those in New England, literacy rates were low. They were very low for women: from the 1600s to the mid-1700s, less than 25 percent of Chesapeake women signing legal documents could write their names. In New England in the mid-1700s, the figure was about 50 percent.

In 1671 Governor William Berkeley, who had long governed Virginia and who had enriched himself in the process, proudly reported to the English government that Virginia had "no free schools nor printing, and I hope we shall not have these [for a] hundred years." Berkeley and many

other wealthy planters agreed with the view—widely held in England—that schooling made ordinary people—particularly women—"unfit" for their "station" in life.

■■ **Most Chesapeake colonists lived on tobacco plantations or small farms.**

*B*ACON'S REBELLION

A lack of schooling, however, did not stop colonists from challenging authority. Virginia was home to an increasing number of freed indentured servants. Around 1660, tobacco prices had tumbled, and with tobacco selling for so little, it was difficult for these people to earn enough money to buy land. Most were forced to rent land or to work as wage laborers for wealthy

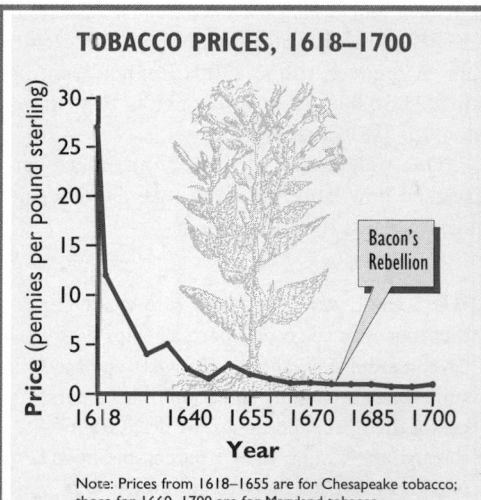

TOBACCO PRICES, 1618–1700

Illustration: The Granger Collection, New York

Note: Prices from 1618–1655 are for Chesapeake tobacco; those for 1660–1700 are for Maryland tobacco.
Source: *Historical Statistics of the United States*

MAKING ENDS MEET Between 1658 and 1660, the per-pound price of tobacco fell from 2.10 to 1.50 pennies per pound sterling. By 1676—the year of Bacon's Rebellion—the price had hit 1.05. Many farmers could not make ends meet.

[?] IDENTIFYING CAUSE AND EFFECT How might declining tobacco prices have influenced events leading to Bacon's Rebellion?

THE MIDDLE PASSAGE

Ask for volunteers to assume the role of a Quaker abolitionist. Have them prepare speeches to make to the class, denouncing the slave trade and making the cruelties of the Middle Passage the focus of their addresses. Call on volunteers to deliver their speeches in class. Then ask students to recap what the Middle Passage was like for enslaved Africans.

▶

planters. Landless laborers and small landowners grew increasingly discontented. They were in debt, taxes were high, and as far as they could see, the colonial legislature was doing nothing to help them.

This discontent erupted in violence in Virginia in 1675. Many poor farmers and laborers, believing that access to land would solve their problems, wanted to settle the area in western Virginia guaranteed to the Powhatans in a 1646 treaty. The treaty did not stop settlers from moving onto Indian lands. When whites killed a group of friendly Susquehannocks (suhs-kwuh-HAN-uhks) and no compensation was made, the Susquehannocks attacked outlying plantations. The colonists then demanded war against all Native Americans in the Chesapeake.

The governor refused, but Nathaniel Bacon was willing. Described by his enemies as "ambitious and arrogant" with a "dangerous hidden pride of heart," this well-connected young planter raised an army of settlers in 1676 and randomly attacked Indians on the frontier. As one colonist later explained, "It matters not whether they be Friends or Foews Soe they be Indians." Bacon's followers, now joined by indentured servants and enslaved

▲ Shown here is an artist's depiction of a confrontation between Nathaniel Bacon and Governor William Berkeley.

Africans, looted wealthy plantations. The rebels also seized and burned Jamestown.

Bacon's Rebellion ended with Bacon's sudden death from one of the illnesses that plagued the Chesapeake. Charles II ordered Berkeley to return to England, and the large planters in the **House of Burgesses**—Virginia's assembly—quieted opposition by cutting taxes and opening Indian lands to colonists.

SLAVERY

While Bacon's Rebellion was short-lived, it had one far-reaching effect: it strengthened the move already under way among planters to switch from indentured to slave labor. More indentured servants ultimately meant more discontented freed servants. Slaves did not pose this problem. Slaves were also becoming more plentiful and—in the long run—cheaper than indentured servants. As employment opportunities improved in England, fewer people were willing to come to the Chesapeake under terms of indenture.

Surviving court records suggest that slavery as an institution developed gradually in the Chesapeake. The first Africans brought to the Chesapeake were treated as indentured servants. After completing their periods of indenture, they were free to work for themselves, and some became landowners. However, by the 1640s some, but not all, were slaves instead of servants.

■■ **Planters turned to slave labor in response to Bacon's Rebellion and to the declining number of indentured servants.**

The slave trade. During the early years of the slave trade, African traders sold criminals and war captives. As the demand for plantation workers increased, however, first in Spanish America and later in the Chesapeake, African raiders moved farther inland in search of slaves. Their constant attacks destroyed the countryside and emptied villages. In 1700 William Bosman, an agent for a Dutch slave-trading company, observed the effects of the slave trade on the once powerful city of Benin in West Africa. It had been "very thick and close-built," he wrote, "but now the Houses stand like poor men's corn, widely distant from each other."

MAKING CONNECTIONS
Political Science

Bacon announced his rebellion by issuing "The Declaration of the People," in which he listed the grievances of the "common people" against Governor Berkeley. In an observation that would prove prophetic, he said that Berkeley's government was not lawful without the consent of the governed.

VOICES IN HISTORY

In Indian societies, oral rules and agreements were respected as binding. Yet, Native Americans observed white colonists routinely violating the laws and treaties they had put in writing. In the late 1600s, Kondiaronk, a leader of the Hurons, commented on whites and their lack of respect for the law: "What sort of men must the Europeans be . . . who must be forced to do good, and have no other prompter for the avoiding of evil than the fear of punishment. . . . Your man is rather a beaver. For man is not entitled to that character upon the force of his walking upright upon two legs, or of reading and writing, and showing a thousand other instances of his industry."

Practice

GUIDED PRACTICE

Organize students into teams of defense and prosecuting "attorneys." Ask the defense to list the grievances of the participants in Bacon's Rebellion. Ask the prosecution to argue against the rebels' actions. Call on each group's spokespersons to present its case to you as judge in a mock trial.

INDEPENDENT PRACTICE

Inform students that the losers in the Guided Practice "trial" have decided to appeal. Direct students to write "briefs" for the appeals judge as either prosecuting or defense attorneys to summarize their case and rebut the other side's arguments. Students may wish to include their "briefs" in their portfolios.

Review and Assessment

REVIEW Ask students to write a paragraph on the development of slavery in the Chesapeake region from the point of view of a slave, a wealthy planter, or an abolitionist. Ask for volunteers to read their paragraphs to the class. Then assign the Section 2 Review on p. 79.

ASSESS Assign the **Section 2 Daily Quiz** in *Core Resources.*

PRIMARY SOURCE

Description of Change: excerpted
Rationale: excerpted to focus on main idea

MAKING CONNECTIONS

Literature

The Selling of Joseph was the first antislavery pamphlet published in America. In it, Samuel Sewall (see p. 79) used the techniques of the sermon—especially long quotations from the Bible—to make his point.

BIO GRAPHY **PERSONALITIES IN HISTORY**

Equiano was born inland of the Guinea Coast in the Kingdom of Benin—an area that today is in southern Nigeria. Before his capture he had never seen the ocean nor had he heard of the existence of white men.

In 1765 an Englishman, one of the few to accompany a slave-raiding expedition, described how raiders hid "under the bushes in the day when they came near a village," and at the right opportunity, seized "every one they could see." The raiders marched the captive men, women, and children hundreds of miles to the coast. There they were inspected, branded, and held in prisons until there were enough to fill a ship.

Once on the ships, the captives were packed in, one captain wrote, until "they had not so much room *as a man in his coffin.*" As a result, many died from suffocation, disease, or violence during the dread **Middle Passage**—the voyage across the Atlantic.

Some captives killed themselves rather than face further horrors. Another captain reported that they "often leap'd . . . into the sea, and kept under water till they were drowned."

■■ **Packed into ships for the Middle Passage, many African captives died from suffocation, disease, or brutality. Some committed suicide.**

BIO GRAPHY Olaudah Equiano (oh-LOW-duh ek-wee-AHN-oh), who was kidnapped and sold into slavery in the mid-1700s, when he was 11 or 12, later described the ordeal of the Middle Passage in his autobiography. At first he was terrified that he and the other captives were "to be eaten by those white men with horrible looks, red faces, and long hair." He was eventually reassured that he would not be eaten, but new horrors confronted him when he was put below deck:

❝ There I received such a salutation in my nostrils as I had never experienced in my life: so that with the loathsomeness of the stench, and crying together, I became so sick and low that I was not able to eat, nor had I the least desire to taste any thing. I now wished for the last friend, death, to relieve me; but soon, to my grief, two of the white men offered me eatables; and, on my refusing to eat, one of them held me fast by the hands . . . and tied my feet, while the other flogged me severely. ❞

Olaudah Equiano

Soon after Equiano arrived in the Americas, a Virginia planter purchased him and then sold him to a British naval officer, Michael Pascal, who renamed him Gustavus Vassa. Equiano served with Pascal in the Seven Years' War (see page 91). At the war's end he was again sold, this time to a West Indian merchant for whom he worked as a seaman. By 1766 Equiano had earned enough money to buy his freedom. He continued to work as a seaman and even accompanied an expedition to the Arctic.

In 1777 Equiano settled in England and devoted himself to the antislavery movement. He lectured widely on the evils of slavery. His popular autobiography, published in 1789, convinced many people of the need to stop the slave trade.

Early abolitionists. Equiano was not the only person to speak out against slavery. Other blacks and a few white colonists denounced the institution. Although **abolitionists,** those who wanted slavery abolished,

National Maritime Museum, London

▲ **This watercolor shows Africans below deck on the Spanish slave ship** *Albatross,* **bound for the West Indies. A British naval officer painted this grim scene from life in 1846.**

RETEACH Organize students into small groups and have them assign one Focus question to each member. Direct students to prepare brief answers to their assigned questions and to share their answers with their group.

Closure

Ask students to suggest terms and phrases that describe the southern colonies. List responses on the chalkboard. Then work with the class to narrow the list to what it considers the most important items. Review these items with students and discuss whether each had a positive effect or a negative effect on colonial development.

Extension

CREATE Suggest that students draw an annotated plan or diagram of a typical plantation in the Chesapeake region.

RESEARCH Ask students to research Native American groups of the Chesapeake region during the 1600s and 1700s. Suggest that they present their findings on an annotated map.

did not become a force in America until the early 1800s, a group of Quakers—members of a radical Protestant sect—took a public stand against slavery as early as 1688. In 1700 Puritan judge Samuel Sewall published an anti-slavery pamphlet, *The Selling of Joseph.* In it Sewall reminded his readers that "all Men, as they are the Sons of *Adam, . . .* have equal Right unto Liberty, and all other outward Comforts of Life."

By the mid-1700s most Quakers condemned slavery. John Woolman, a Quaker tailor, traveled throughout the colonies, urging Quakers to free their slaves. He urged those who were not slaveholders to refuse to use goods, such as sugar and dyed cloth, that were the products of slave labor.

Slave codes. Despite such protests slavery was practiced in all the English colonies. As Africans became more numerous after 1660, they were—by law and by custom—treated as inferior to whites. In 1705 Virginia consolidated its various laws and customs into one "slave code." Other colonies did the same.

The slave codes were designed to prevent escape and discourage revolt. The codes forbade slaves to meet together, to leave the plantation, to learn to read or write, or to own weapons. The codes went so far as to declare that a master who

killed a slave while "correcting" him or her could not be tried for murder!

Harsh rules did not prevent rebellion, however. Newly arrived Africans often ran away. There were also a few uprisings. The largest occurred in 1739 at Stono, South Carolina. Slaves killed some 30 whites before the militia quelled the uprising. The slaves who survived the rebellion were "put to the most cruel Death." Most slaves, however, resisted in other, less direct ways, such as by destroying property or working slowly.

AFRICAN POPULATION IN BRITISH NORTH AMERICA, 1650–1760

(graph: Population in thousands vs. Year, 1660–1760)

Source: *Historical Statistics of the United States*

GROWTH OF SLAVERY The colonial economy in the South depended on a steady supply of unskilled laborers. When the number of English indentured servants began to decline in the late 1600s, the colonists increased their reliance on African slaves.

? BUILDING GRAPH SKILLS By about how much did the African population of British North America increase from 1730 to 1760?

Graph Caption Answer
about 235,000

SECTION REVIEW ANSWERS

IDENTIFY
For significance, see the following pages:
Cecilius Calvert (p. 74)
Toleration Act (p. 74)
Nathaniel Bacon (p. 77)
Bacon's Rebellion (p. 77)
House of Burgesses (p. 77)
Middle Passage (p. 78)
Olaudah Equiano (p. 78)
abolitionists (p. 78)
Samuel Sewall (p. 79)
John Woolman (p. 79)

LOCATE
For locations, see the map on p. 75.

1. *in response to Bacon's Rebellion and to the declining numbers of indentured servants*
2. *Slaves were packed into ships; they often died from suffocation, disease, brutality, or suicide.*
3. *Letters should mention high death rates, men outnumbering women, frequent remarriages, and living conditions on a tobacco plantation or a small farm.*
4. *The tobacco-based economy discouraged the development of central markets and towns; a more diversified economy might have led to more urbanization, better education, a larger middle class, and fewer slaves.*

SECTION 2 REVIEW

IDENTIFY and explain the significance of the following: Cecilius Calvert, Toleration Act, Nathaniel Bacon, Bacon's Rebellion, House of Burgesses, Middle Passage, Olaudah Equiano, abolitionists, Samuel Sewall, John Woolman.

LOCATE and explain the importance of the following: Chesapeake Bay; Baltimore, Maryland; Virginia.

1. **MAIN IDEA** Why did Chesapeake planters increasingly choose to rely on slave labor?
2. **MAIN IDEA** What were conditions like during the Middle Passage?
3. **WRITING TO DESCRIBE** Imagine you are one of the few white women living in the Chesapeake. Write a letter home to England, describing your life in the colonies.
4. **HYPOTHESIZING** How might the colonies in the Chesapeake have developed if they had had a more diversified economy?

PREVIEW WORKSHOP

Following is a list of the significant people, places, and terms in this section. You may wish to use this list as a section preview.

People
- William Penn
- James Oglethorpe
- Sir Edmund Andros

- Jonathan Edwards
- George Whitefield

Places
- North Carolina
- South Carolina
- New York
- Pennsylvania
- Delaware
- Georgia

Terms
- task system
- mercantilism
- balance of trade
- Navigation Acts
- Glorious Revolution
- Enlightenment
- Great Awakening

FOCUS OBJECTIVES

- Describe how life in South Carolina differed from life in the other Restoration colonies.

- Explain why England regulated colonial trade.

- Analyze what the Glorious Revolution accomplished.

- Determine why so many people responded to the Great Awakening.

CULTURAL PATTERNS

Missionaries tried to improve conditions for slaves in the Carolinas. They convinced some slaveholders to let their slaves attend religious services. Others agreed to give slaves time off to learn to read and write and to study the Bible. The missionaries believed they were making the lives of enslaved persons better. But the planters considered their work as a religious endorsement of slavery.

CORE RESOURCES

- **Literature Worksheet 3**
- **Section 3 Daily Quiz**

AV RESOURCES

- **Linking Geography and History Transparency and Worksheet 7**

Section 3

THE COLONIES AFTER THE RESTORATION

FOCUS
- **How did life in South Carolina differ from life in the other Restoration colonies?**
- **Why did England regulate colonial trade?**
- **What did the Glorious Revolution accomplish?**
- **Why did so many people respond to the Great Awakening?**

The colonies established after the Restoration of the English monarchy in 1660 were, like Maryland, proprietary colonies. Eager to reap profits, some proprietors and land speculators recruited colonists from Europe as well as from the British Isles. The Crown, too, expected to benefit and made efforts to control colonial trade despite the colonists' opposition. At the same time, new intellectual and religious ideas transformed colonial life.

The Fine Arts Museums of San Francisco

Detail from the 1670 painting
The Mason Children

THE CAROLINAS

After Cromwell's death and the Restoration of the monarchy, another wave of colonization began. The new king, Charles II, rewarded his supporters with grants of land. In 1663 he gave eight supporters a charter for a colony between Virginia and Spanish Florida. The colony was named Carolina in the king's honor. Later the colony was divided into North and South Carolina. The proprietors proved incompetent governors, and in the 1720s the Crown officially took over both colonies.

In North Carolina many settlers from the Chesapeake established small farms. The forests provided naval stores and furs and skins that the settlers could trade. In South Carolina the first colonists came primarily from Barbados. They and the few slaves they brought with them raised cattle, cut timber, and traded with Native Americans. Some settlers tried to grow rice but failed. However, slaves who came from Sierra Leone and other rice-growing regions of West Africa knew the proper cultivation techniques.

◀ **This extract from *Colonial Office Papers* shows the earliest land grants, beginning in 1674, given to settlers in South Carolina. By 1765 more than 11,000 names appeared on this list.**

Have students relate what they know about "Buy American" sentiments. Point out that such policies focus on buying American products, protecting American industries, and regulating and restricting foreign trade. As students read this section, ask them to compare British colonial trade policies with the "Buy American" campaign.

Teaching the Section

LIFE IN THE RESTORATION COLONIES

Organize students into four groups and assign each group one of the following colonies: South Carolina, North Carolina, Pennsylvania, Georgia. Ask groups to create murals showing life in their assigned colonies, placing special emphasis on economic activities. Have groups display and discuss their murals, noting in particular how life in South Carolina differed from life in the other Restoration colonies.

HISTORICAL SIDELIGHTS

Jewish Immigrants
The first Jewish community in North America was established in 1654, when 23 refugees fleeing persecution in Brazil landed at New Amsterdam (now New York). Peter Stuyvesant, governor of the colony, did not support religious diversity and wanted them to leave. But a group of Jews in Holland who were major stockholders in the West India Company brought their considerable economic influence to bear and persuaded the company to allow the 23 to stay.

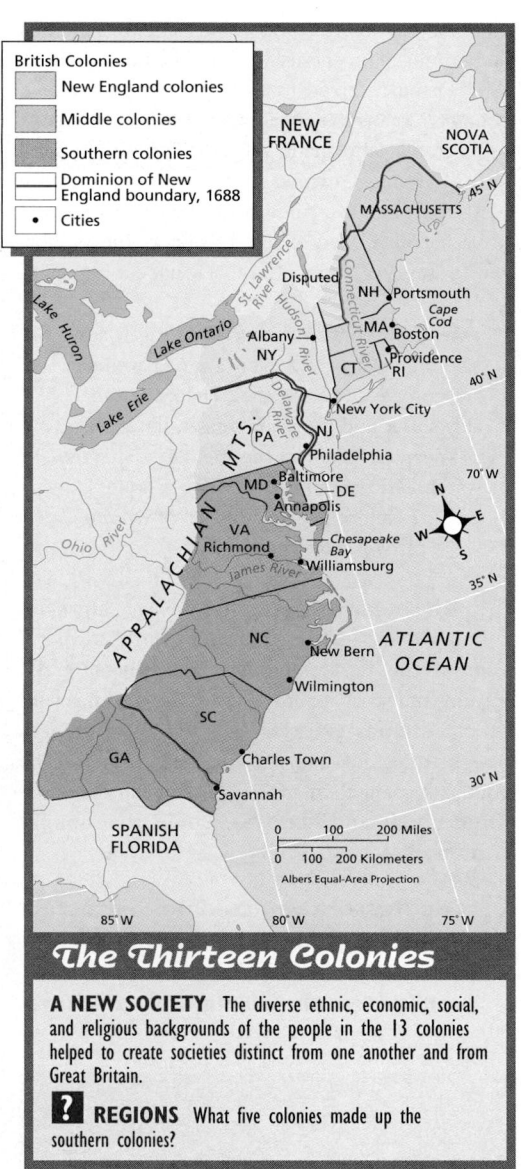

Colonial Williamsburg Foundation

▲ This late–18th-century painting by an unknown artist, entitled *The Old Plantation*, shows the merging of African and American cultures through slaves' musical instruments, dress, and dance.

British Colonies
New England colonies
Middle colonies
Southern colonies
Dominion of New England boundary, 1688
• Cities

The Thirteen Colonies

A NEW SOCIETY The diverse ethnic, economic, social, and religious backgrounds of the people in the 13 colonies helped to create societies distinct from one another and from Great Britain.

? REGIONS What five colonies made up the southern colonies?

Settlers used their slaves' knowledge and labor to transform the swampy coastal region into fabulously profitable rice plantations.

The Carolinas and the thriving port of Charles Town (Charleston) attracted Scots, Scotch-Irish, Germans, European Jews, West Indians, and in 1685, French Huguenots (Protestants) fleeing religious persecution. In South Carolina, however, the demand for plantation workers was so great that by 1720 African slaves made up about 70 percent of the population.

On the large rice plantations, the slaves had relatively little contact with whites. As a result,

they kept more African traditions than slaves in other areas kept. Even their language, Gullah, combined West African dialects and English.

Slaves on the rice plantations worked under the **task system**. Each day the slaves were assigned particular duties. Once they had completed them, the slaves could tend small plots and raise livestock. Some sold their hogs, chickens, and produce or worked for wages on their own time. A few slaves earned enough to buy their freedom. Slaveholders worried that their slaves—who now outnumbered them—were becoming too independent. Fearful of slave revolts, they urged passage of a harsh slave code.

NEW YORK AND NEW JERSEY

Besides rewarding his supporters, Charles II wanted to cripple Dutch trading interests. The Dutch West India Company, attracted by the profitable fur trade, had established a colony in North America. Its colony, New Netherland, extended inland along the Hudson River Valley and included the town of New Amsterdam, founded in 1626 on Manhattan Island. (The town was renamed New York in 1664.) Although successful at its trading activities, the Dutch West India Company had little luck attracting Dutch settlers. The company did attract others: primarily English, French Huguenots, Swedes, Jews, and free Africans. Colonists also purchased enslaved Africans. By 1750, blacks made up almost 20 percent of New York City's population.

Map Caption Answer
MD, VA, NC, SC, GA

Teaching the Section

REGULATING COLONIAL TRADE

Assign volunteers to play the following roles: New York merchant, Dutch trader, French manufacturer, Boston shipbuilder, Charleston tobacco exporter, northern logger, southern cotton planter. Have the rest of the class act as the Parliament. Tell the volunteers that they are to appear before Parliament to state their views on England's trade policies as outlined in the Navigation Acts. Instruct the members of Parliament to question each volunteer about his or her views and to respond to each volunteer's concerns by explaining why Parliament enacted the policies and how they apply to that individual.

MAKING CONNECTIONS
Language Arts
Yankee—the nickname that identifies Americans in other nations—is probably of Dutch origin. The English often referred disparagingly to Dutch seamen as *Jan Kee*—Dutch for "Little John." Later this term also referred to New England sailors. Over time *Jan Kees* became *Yankee* and, by the Revolution, the British were applying it to all American colonists.

PRIMARY SOURCE
Description of Change: excerpted
Rationale: excerpted to focus on main idea

MAKING CONNECTIONS
Sociology
German immigrants arrived at a rate of about 2,000 per year between 1727 and 1750. Almost all of them settled in Pennsylvania. Indeed, by the time of the American Revolution they probably made up one third of the colony's population. They brought with them many interesting customs—the communal barn raising, for example. Friends and neighbors would help a farmer erect a barn and then celebrate by holding a dance in the new building.

Most settlers considered their governors inept. Consequently, they refused to defend the colony when an English fleet sailed into the harbor in 1664 and demanded that the Dutch hand over New Netherland. Without a shot being fired, the colony's governor, Peter Stuyvesant, a domineering old soldier with a wooden leg, surrendered to the English.

Charles II made his brother, James, the Duke of York, proprietor of New Netherland. James kept part of the colony—renamed New York—and gave the rest—New Jersey—to two friends.

PENNSYLVANIA AND DELAWARE

In 1681 Charles II repaid the £16,000 he owed Admiral Sir William Penn by making Penn's son William proprietor of a large tract of land near New York. Penn's holdings increased the following year when the Duke of York gave him Delaware.

Penn wanted to make his colony, which the king named Pennsylvania, a haven for his fellow Quakers. Persecuted by Anglicans and Puritans alike as "violators of order," the Quakers had no formal clergy, opposed warfare, and ignored class privileges.

Penn also wanted Pennsylvania to be a "Holy Experiment," where people of different nationalities and religious beliefs "could shape their own lives" and live peacefully together. He extended his policy to Native Americans, paying them for their lands and treating them fairly.

While Penn was a man with deep religious convictions, he was also a shrewd promoter who needed to raise cash. To recruit colonists, he published pamphlets in English, Dutch, and German that described his colony in glowing terms and promised prosperity to would-be immigrants.

Often referred to as the "best poor man's country," Pennsylvania attracted thousands of poor immigrants who made the crossing on cramped ships. One German immigrant, Gottlieb Mittelberger, described how they were packed "like herrings" and endured "stench, fumes, horror, . . . scurvy, . . . mouthrot." He added:

> 66 Children from 1 to 7 years rarely survive the voyage; and many a time parents are compelled to see their children miserably suffer and die from hunger, thirst and sickness, and then to see them cast into the water. I witnessed such misery in no less than 32 children in our ship, all of whom were thrown into the sea. 99

Those who survived the voyage, however, found cheap, fertile land and a mild climate. Pennsylvania farmers produced a surplus of grain, milling much of it into flour and exporting it to other colonies and the West Indies. Butchers bought livestock and exported salted meat. The colonists spent their profits on English manufactured goods and luxuries. Some also bought African slaves.

▪▪ **The Restoration colonies attracted a diverse group of people. Most farmed their own lands, but slaves worked South Carolina plantations.**

Winterthur Museum

▶ *The Peaceable Kingdom* was one of several paintings Edward Hicks made of animals living in harmony with nature. In this version, William Penn is shown in the background, meeting with other colonists.

THE GLORIOUS REVOLUTION

Organize the class into two groups. Have students in each group conduct a "radio broadcast" about the Glorious Revolution. One group's broadcast should center on how the Glorious Revolution changed England, and the other group should focus on its impact on the colonies. In addition to hard news stories, each group's broadcast should include human interest features, editorial commentary, and interviews with government officials and private citizens.

THE GREAT AWAKENING

Randomly assign the following roles among students until all have a role: an Old Light preacher, a poor white man, an enslaved woman, a free African American, a member of the educated upper class. Have students write, from the viewpoint of their character, a letter to a friend, explaining their response to a sermon preached by George Whitefield. Ask volunteers to read their letters to the class. Students may wish to include their letters in their portfolios.

AV **TRANSPARENCY**
Linking Geography and History Transparency and **Worksheet 7**

GEORGIA

While Pennsylvania began as a "Holy Experiment," Georgia was a social experiment. This last British colony was established on the southern frontier of British North America in 1732, more than a century after Jamestown's founding. James Oglethorpe and a group of supporters planned the colony to give the English poor a fresh start. Parliament supported the project in the hope that it would "carry off the . . . poor that pester the streets of London." It also expected the colony to provide a buffer between South Carolina's prosperous plantations and Spanish Florida.

As a social experiment the colony failed. Oglethorpe and his partners wanted to aid only the most "virtuous and industrious" poor. However, very few debtors qualified, and the colony attracted few other settlers because of its rigid rules.

Oglethorpe's rules included prohibitions against rum and slavery. The trustees wanted to prevent the "Sin of Drunkenness" and believed that slaveholders "would be less disposed to labor" for themselves. But the settlers complained that without slaves they could not compete with South Carolina planters. In 1750 the founders reluctantly gave in, but the colony still did not prosper. By 1760 Georgia's European population numbered only some 6,000.

TRADE

Above all else, the founding of the Restoration colonies was driven by the Crown's faith in the economic policy of **mercantilism**. Mercantilists held that a nation's power was a product of wealth, and a nation's wealth was measured by its stock of gold and silver. The best way for a nation to obtain wealth was to maintain a favorable **balance of trade**: to export more than it imported. But only nations that were relatively self-sufficient could maintain a favorable balance of trade. Thus the colonies were vitally important as a source of raw materials and as a ready market for goods from the homeland.

Mercantilist ideas had the support of the merchant class, which was well represented in England's

▲ This illustration from a 1733 book, showing Georgia in an idealized setting, was used to help promote colonization in that region.

Parliament. In 1651 Parliament began passing a series of mercantilist laws—the **Navigation Acts**—to promote the "wealth, safety, and strength of this kingdom." In part, these acts were designed to increase English merchants' profits by limiting direct trade between the English colonies and other European nations. The acts required European goods destined for the colonies to be routed through England. In addition, all colonial products had to be carried on ships built and owned by "his Majesty's subjects of England, Ireland, and the Plantations." The acts also listed, or "enumerated," colonial products that could be exported only to England or to other destinations within the empire. The list was added to over the years and eventually included tobacco, cotton, sugar, and naval stores.

Southern colonists, who produced most of the enumerated goods, resented the restrictions because they cut into profits. But the acts helped northern shipbuilders and merchants. As British subjects they could build and sail their own ships and provide shipping services. Because timber and naval stores were so much cheaper in America than in Europe, colonial shipbuilders thrived. By the early 1770s colonists had built about one third of all merchant ships flying the British flag.

▲ Tobacco was advertised on trade cards. This one shows men smoking the long clay pipes used in the 1600s.

■■ England regulated colonial trade to achieve a favorable balance of trade and to benefit English merchants.

BUILDING VOCABULARY

The term *mercantilism* derives from the Latin *mercantilis,* which means "of a merchant or trade." The first serious discussion of the policy came in Thomas Mun's *England's Treasure by Forraign Trade,* which, although probably written in the 1630s, was not published until 1664.

Practice

GUIDED PRACTICE

On the chalkboard draw a chart with the following headings: *Colony, When Founded, Purpose, Economic Activities.* Ask for volunteers to fill in information on each of the Restoration colonies. Students may wish to copy the chart in their notebooks for future reference.

INDEPENDENT PRACTICE

Ask students to write a paragraph explaining in which of the Restoration colonies they would rather have settled and why. Students who select the same colony may compare reasons for their choice before writing the final drafts of their paragraphs.

Review and Assessment

REVIEW Instruct students to write four short paragraphs, each one responding to a Focus question for this section. Select students to read their paragraphs in class. Then assign the Section 3 Review on page 85.

ASSESS Assign the **Section 3 Daily Quiz** in *Core Resources.*

JAMES II AND THE GLORIOUS REVOLUTION

The Lords of Trade, a committee established to oversee the colonies for the Crown, sent customs agents to the colonies to enforce the Navigation Acts. The colonists were often uncooperative. Massachusetts, for example, declared that it was exempt from English restrictions on trade. In response, the English government revoked the Massachusetts charter in 1684.

The following year James, Duke of York, became King James II. To increase royal authority over the colonies, the new king ordered the Lords of Trade to organize the northern colonies into the Dominion of New England. The committee placed the dominion under the control of Sir Edmund Andros in 1686. Andros quickly angered the colonists by imposing taxes without their consent and by abolishing the Massachusetts General Court.

James II was no more popular in England than Andros was in New England. James II's Catholicism rankled English Protestants, and his habit of ruling by decree angered Parliament. In 1688 the Protestant opposition staged a bloodless rebellion: the **Glorious Revolution**. They invited the king's Protestant daughter, Mary, and her Dutch husband, William, Prince of Orange, to take the throne. Unable to rally support, James II fled to France in 1688.

To prevent future abuses of power, Parliament enacted the Bill of Rights in 1689. The act listed the rights and liberties guaranteed to every citizen and to Parliament, including regular free elections and a prohibition against taxation without Parliament's consent.

Colonists used the Glorious Revolution to rid themselves of hated officials. Protestants in Maryland got rid of wealthy Catholic officials. Massachusetts colonists sent Andros back to England. The New York militia, under Jacob Leisler's leadership, ousted the dominion's lieutenant governor. The new rulers, William and Mary, broke up the Dominion of New England and restored those representative assemblies that had been abolished. The Navigation Acts, however, largely remained in place.

■■**The Glorious Revolution limited royal power and led to the passage of England's Bill of Rights.**

THE GREAT AWAKENING

The Glorious Revolution had another important effect. It established that royal power flowed from the consent of Parliament, not from the will of God. The idea that God did not directly intervene in human affairs was not confined to politics. Europe in the 18th century was experiencing the birth of a revolution in ideas called the **Enlightenment**. Enlightenment thinkers emphasized human reason and progress. Science and logic, they believed, provided the keys to understanding nature and improving society.

Enlightenment ideas found religious expression in Deism. Deists believed that God created the universe, set it in motion, and then let it run itself according to natural law. They placed more emphasis on leading a virtuous life than on piety or religious faith. In the colonies Deism appealed to many educated people, particularly merchants and wealthy planters.

Religious revivals. Not everyone shared the Deists' belief in an orderly, predictable world. Changes in society that emphasized individual and material success rather than the common good of the community troubled many people, particularly those in rural areas. These people longed for religion that moved their hearts. They found it in a series of religious revivals—known as the **Great Awakening**—that swept through the British colonies in the mid-18th century.

Winterthur Museum

▲ This plate, depicting James II, appeared after the coronation of the new king.

RETEACH Organize students into seven groups and assign each group one of the section's subsections. Have groups write 5 to 10 true/false statements based on the content of their subsections. Ask group representatives to read statements to the class, and have class members identify them as true or false. Have students recast false statements to make them correct.

Closure

Work with the class to develop on the chalkboard advertising copy for a brochure to attract people to the colonies in the 1700s. In developing the brochure, suggest that students promote changes brought by the Glorious Revolution and Great Awakening, and economic opportunities created by the Navigation Acts. Then ask students what kinds of people their brochure would likely attract.

Extension

FORMULATE Have students hypothesize and write a scenario of how the economies of the southern colonies might have developed if no slave labor had been available. Ask for volunteers to present and explain their scenarios.

RESEARCH Ask students to research the life of one of the Great Awakening preachers. Have students present their findings to the class.

The minister often credited with launching New England's Great Awakening is Jonathan Edwards of Massachusetts. He believed in appealing to people's emotions as a way to open their hearts to God. In the 1730s a revival broke out in Edwards's church in Northampton, Massachusettes, and spread to surrounding churches.

It was, however, the English revivalist George Whitefield who, beginning with his first trip to Georgia in 1738, spread the message of the Great Awakening throughout the colonies.

▲ George Whitefield

During his several tours of the colonies, the minister inspired crowds of thousands. "Hearing him preach," wrote Nathan Cole, a farmer, "gave me a heart wound." One woman, Fanny Lewis, wrote that at a Baltimore revival "there was such a gust of the power of God, that it appeared to me the very gates of hell would give way."

The Great Awakening's effects. Not everyone, however, was a New Light—a supporter of the Great Awakening. Those who opposed it— the Old Lights—objected to the New Lights' emotional, disorderly services and to the disruptions in settled congregations caused by traveling evangelists. Such differences encouraged the growth of New Light Protestant churches, particularly the Baptists and the Methodists.

The New Light preachers also emphasized a personal relationship with God. They encouraged men, women, and even children to describe their religious experiences. These emotional services appealed to many, especially to the poor and to the enslaved—whom the established churches often neglected.

Preaching to Virginia slaves, Presbyterian Cary Allen assured them that the "Savior died and shed his blood as much for you as for your master, or any of the white people." Christ has "opened the door of heaven . . . and invites you all to enter." Many blacks responded enthusiastically to Allen and other New Light preachers. The revivalists' emphasis on emotional religious experience more closely resembled African religious tradition than Puritan or Anglican Protestantism did.

The Great Awakening challenged established religious authority. The revivalist preachers appealed to ordinary people rather than to the educated upper class. And above all, they emphasized the equality of everyone—including women and slaves—before God.

■■ **The Great Awakening revivalists appealed to people's emotions and stressed everyone's equality before God.**

■■ **SECTION 3 REVIEW**

IDENTIFY and explain the significance of the following: task system, William Penn, James Oglethorpe, mercantilism, balance of trade, Navigation Acts, Sir Edmund Andros, Glorious Revolution, Enlightenment, Great Awakening, Jonathan Edwards, George Whitefield.

LOCATE and explain the importance of the following: North Carolina, South Carolina, New York, Pennsylvania, Delaware, Georgia.

1. **MAIN IDEA** How did South Carolina's agricultural economy differ from the agricultural economies of the other Restoration colonies?

2. **MAIN IDEA** What effect did the Glorious Revolution have on England and the colonies?

3. **MAIN IDEA** Why did the Great Awakening revive people's interest in religion?

4. **WRITING TO INFORM** Imagine you are a customs agent sent to the colonies to enforce the Navigation Acts. Write a report to Parliament, outlining why England should regulate colonial trade.

5. **EVALUATING** What reasons did Charles II have for granting land in the Carolinas, New York, New Jersey, and Pennsylvania? Why was there renewed interest in founding colonies after the Restoration?

SECTION REVIEW ANSWERS

IDENTIFY

For significance, see the following pages:
task system (p. 81)
William Penn (p. 82)
James Oglethorpe (p. 83)
mercantilism (p. 83)
balance of trade (p. 83)
Navigation Acts (p. 83)
Sir Edmund Andros (p. 84)
Glorious Revolution (p. 84)
Enlightenment (p. 84)
Great Awakening (p. 84)
Jonathan Edwards (p. 85)
George Whitefield (p. 85)

LOCATE

For locations, see the map on p. 81.

1. *South Carolina's economy was based on plantation agriculture and slave labor; in other colonies, individuals farmed their own land.*

2. *England—limited royal power, prompted Bill of Rights; colonies—resulted in removal of hated authorities*

3. *appealed to people's emotions, stressed equality before God, and reached out to ordinary people*

4. *Reports should mention need to achieve favorable balance of trade and to benefit English merchants.*

5. *to reward supporters, cripple Dutch trading interests, repay debt; belief in mercantilism*

FOCUS OBJECTIVES

- Determine what pressures in the colonies pushed settlers to the frontier.

- Describe life on the frontier.

- Analyze how the fur trade and the conflicts over land affected Native American lives and cultures.

- Identify the main causes and results of the French and Indian War.

Section 4

THE FRONTIER AND THE STRUGGLE FOR LAND

FOCUS

- **What pressures in the colonies pushed settlers to the frontier?**
- **What was life on the frontier like?**
- **How did the fur trade and the conflicts over land affect Native American lives and cultures?**
- **What were the main causes and results of the French and Indian War?**

Throughout the 18th century, English colonial cities grew rapidly. Philadelphia roughly doubled in size every 20 years, eventually becoming Great Britain's largest overseas port. But despite this growth British America remained overwhelmingly rural: about 95 percent of the some two million colonists lived on farms. Hungry for new land to farm, the colonists moved onto lands claimed by Native Americans and by the French.

Frontiersman's jacket, rifle, powder horn, satchel, and trap

GROWTH AFFECTS PROSPERITY

Throughout the colonial period New England's population roughly doubled every 25 years; the Middle Colonies—New York, New Jersey, Pennsylvania, and Delaware—grew even faster. As the population increased, social differences among community members became more obvious. A few families increasingly controlled the wealth. In 1693 the richest 10 percent of Philadelphia's taxpayers owned some 45 percent of taxable wealth; by 1772 their share had risen to some 70 percent.

In the major port cities of Boston, New York, and Philadelphia, wealthy merchant families imitated the homes, dress, and manners of the English upper class. Many other city dwellers, however, were less fortunate, though some "leather apron men"—butchers, carpenters, potters, smiths, and other artisans—prospered and moved up in society. Even in the 1700s cities experienced cycles of

▲ Colonial cities soon faced the problem of growing numbers of urban poor. This 1767 engraving commemorates the opening of new almshouses and workhouses in Philadelphia.

CORE RESOURCES

- **Section 4 Daily Quiz**

AV RESOURCES

- **Linking Geography and History Transparency and Worksheet 8**

MOTIVATING:
PRIOR KNOWLEDGE

Ask students to recall and identify the reasons that early settlers came to North America. Note their suggestions on the chalkboard, underscoring responses such as *land, freedom,* and *economic opportunity.* Point out that in this section, students will observe that these underscored reasons also helped spur migration from the Restoration colonies—a migration westward.

Teaching the Section

LEAVING FOR THE FRONTIER

Have students assume one of these roles: a person living in poverty in a colonial town or a member of a family living on a small farm. Then ask students to write a letter to a friend or family member, explaining that they have decided to move to the frontier, giving reasons for this decision. Have volunteers read their letters to the class.

LIFE ON THE FRONTIER

Organize students into pairs to portray a colonist on the frontier and an eastern reporter to interview that person about his or her life. Allow students a few minutes to plan their interviews. Suggest that interview questions be appropriate to the role identity (gender, locale, economic status, daily activities, and so on) of the interviewee. Conclude by selecting students to present their interviews to the class. ▶

prosperity and hard times. Without a fortunate marriage or an ample inheritance, hard work alone sometimes offered no escape from poverty. By the 1730s all major towns had poorhouses where the very poor lived at public expense.

Farms became smaller with each generation as the same amount of land was divided among ever more heirs. As more people competed for land within existing communities, it became expensive. Many of those who wanted to live near their families but were unable to afford land worked as farm laborers.

Instead of struggling to support themselves in the cities or in their communities, townspeople and farmers had another choice: they could leave for the frontier. And many colonists did, pushing north into New York's border areas and west into other newly opened areas such as the western portions of Massachusetts, Pennsylvania, Virginia, and North Carolina.

It was not easy, however, for people to leave their families, friends, and communities. One colonist who stayed behind expressed the widely held fear that the "desire after Land" would doom the pioneers' children to a life of "heathenish ignorance and barbarisme"—and all "so they might have Elbow-room enough in the world."

█ █ Rapid population growth and economic problems encouraged many colonists to move to the frontier.

PIONEER LIFE

These were not idle fears. The frontier lacked schools and churches. Pioneer families might live in crude shelters such as one "poor, dirty hovel, with hardly anything in it but children" that Virginia planter William Byrd observed in 1733. When they were able to build more-permanent housing, pioneers often built Swedish-style log cabins, which one traveler in 1679 praised as "quite tight and warm." They were, he wrote, made of "entire trees, split through the middle, or squared out of the rough, and placed in the form of a square."

Pioneers who prospered might lay wood floors in their cabins, cut windows in the walls, and nail clapboards over the logs. They might add

American Antiquarian Society

▲ A farm family at work in the fields is the subject of this 1760s woodcut from a Pennsylvania almanac.

sleeping lofts or small rooms. But others, who moved as frequently as the soil wore out, devoted little attention to their houses. In the frontier communities, Byrd observed, "a citizen . . . is counted extravagant if he has ambition enough to aspire to a brick chimney."

From childhood on, everyone had to work hard. Besides farming, the men and women did the work of butchers, carpenters, candle makers, soap makers, and other artisans. Those who could not, a frontier minister observed in 1711, would "have but a bad time of it; for help is not to be had at any rate."

In western Virginia and Pennsylvania—the backcountry—some pioneers grazed cattle in the woods. The settlers, reported a British seaman in 1755, "drive up their Herds on Horseback . . . for their Cattle are near as wild as Deer" and they "run as they please in the Great Woods, where there are no Inclosures to stop them." Pioneer families also cleared and fenced some land and planted corn, wheat, and other crops among the stumps. Once backcountry farmers began to produce a marketable surplus, small market towns appeared.

Deep in the interior a few frontiersmen lived a roving existence. They adapted their clothing from Indian dress, wearing coarse linen hunting shirts and deerskin leggings and moccasins. They hunted for food and traded furs for supplies such as the powder and shot needed for their rifles.

█ █ Frontier families grew their own food and made almost everything they needed.

MAKING CONNECTIONS
Geography

Settlers on their way to the Pennsylvania and Virginia frontiers took the Great Wagon Road, a route that stretched about 700 miles along the eastern edge of the Appalachians from Philadelphia to Georgia. Although little more than a rutted track, it was the most traveled highway in colonial America.

HISTORICAL SIDELIGHTS
A Frontier Legend

Daniel Boone was the archetypal frontiersman. He frequently disappeared from his farm—sometimes for months—to go hunting, trapping, camping, and surveying. Boone helped open up the land west of the Appalachians to white settlement.

Teaching the Section

THE FUR TRADE

Ask students to write a speech that a Native American leader might have made, decrying the effect of the fur trade on Native American life. Tell students in preparing their speeches to focus on the social, economic, and political disruptions the fur trade brought to Native American cultures. Have volunteers deliver their speeches to the class. Students may wish to include their speeches in their portfolios.

🌐 GLOBAL CONNECTIONS

At about the same time that England was enacting the Navigation Acts and other laws to economically integrate its empire, French leaders also were adopting mercantilist policies. In the 1660s Jean-Baptiste Colbert, one of Louis XIV's chief ministers, set down a plan for New France. Canada would produce ships, iron, and naval stores for France and food for the French West Indian colonies. In turn, the island colonies would produce sugar and tobacco for France. And funds from the fur trade would finance the whole colonial operation in New France.

Map Caption Answer
for fur trade and other rich resources

THE FRENCH IN NORTH AMERICA

As frontiersmen and traders crossed the Appalachians into the Ohio Valley, they moved into territory claimed by several British colonies as well as by France. French claims to American land were based on the early voyages of Giovanni da Verrazano, who explored the coast of North America in 1524, and of Jacques Cartier, who explored the Gulf of St. Lawrence in 1534–1535. Samuel de Champlain's fur trading expeditions in 1603 and his founding of Quebec in 1608 strengthened these claims. Then in 1673 Jesuit missionary Jacques Marquette and fur trader Louis Jolliet (jahl-ee-ET) crossed the Great Lakes, made their way to the Mississippi River, and traveled down it as far as the Arkansas River. René-Robert de La Salle also explored the Mississippi, reaching the Gulf of Mexico in 1682. He claimed the Mississippi Valley for France, naming it Louisiana in honor of Louis XIV.

The founding of New Orleans in 1718 gave the French command of the Mississippi River. Control of the Mississippi, combined with their thriving colonies along the St. Lawrence River and their knowledge of a water route through the Great Lakes, put the French in a position to control the North American interior.

But New France—France's North American empire—never reached its potential strength. France claimed a huge area but settled very little of it. Most French colonists were single men in search of riches and adventure. The French *coureurs de bois* (kooh-ruhr duh BWAH), or runners of the woods, traded with Native Americans for furs. Many married Indian women.

CULTURES CLASH

The French colonial economy was tied to that of the Native Americans. Native Americans included French fur traders in their trade networks early in the 17th century. Native Americans desired European trade goods such as horses, firearms, and metal tools. To pay for those goods, they traded beaver pelts and other furs. "The beaver does everything perfectly well," one Indian explained. "It makes kettles, hatchets, swords, knifes, bread . . . in short, it makes everything."

The fur trade. The European clamor for furs, however, changed life for Native Americans, many of whom became dependent on the fur trade. For them, hunting became a commercial

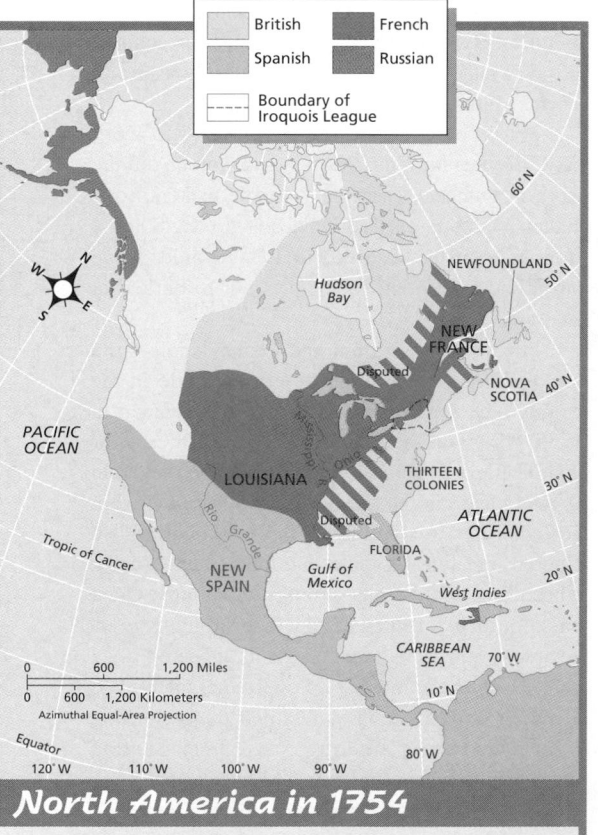

North America in 1754

Legend:
- British
- Spanish
- French
- Russian
- Boundary of Iroquois League

PACIFIC OCEAN · Hudson Bay · NEWFOUNDLAND · NEW FRANCE · NOVA SCOTIA · LOUISIANA · THIRTEEN COLONIES · Disputed · ATLANTIC OCEAN · Rio Grande · FLORIDA · NEW SPAIN · Gulf of Mexico · West Indies · CARIBBEAN SEA · Tropic of Cancer · Equator

0 600 1,200 Miles
0 600 1,200 Kilometers
Azimuthal Equal-Area Projection

OLD ENEMIES The rivalry in Europe between Great Britain and France carried over to North America.

❓ HUMAN–ENVIRONMENT INTERACTION Why do you think both France and Great Britain desired the lands of the Ohio Valley?

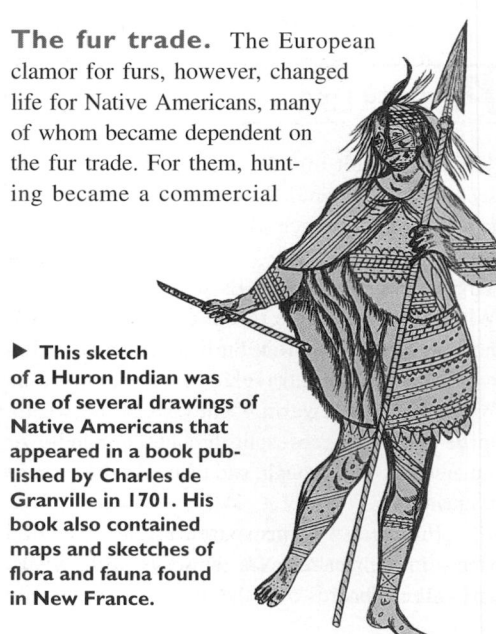

▶ **This sketch of a Huron Indian was one of several drawings of Native Americans that appeared in a book published by Charles de Granville in 1701. His book also contained maps and sketches of flora and fauna found in New France.**

TWO VIEWS OF THE LAND

Select two teams to debate the issue of land use in colonial America. Have one team argue the view of Native Americans, and the other express the opinion of European settlers. Encourage the rest of the class to join the debate by asking questions or by challenging arguments. Conclude by asking students to write a paragraph summarizing how these conflicts and the fur trade affected Native American lives and cultures.

▶

Then and Now   THE VANISHING FORESTS

A logging truck

Before European settlers arrived in North America, dense forests covered more than half of the some 7.2 million square miles of what are today the United States and Canada. The continent's abundant forests seemed endless.

Native Americans were the first to alter the forest landscape. Using fire, they cleared small patches of woodland to create space for their crops and to encourage the growth of the tender new vegetation that deer, elk, and other game preferred to eat. But American Indians cleared no more of the wooded land than was necessary for their survival.

In the 1600s the newly arrived Europeans began clearing the forests at a rapid pace. In their eyes the wilderness was to be feared or subdued. Colonists cut the forests to make room for farms, towns, and roads. They used the wood for building. Wood was also the only fuel available to many settlers.

Soon logging was a major colonial industry, providing lumber for home and ship construction and yielding other needed products such as turpentine, charcoal, and paper. Even soap making relied on lye made from wood ash.

Large-scale logging began in the deep forests of Maine. Logs were floated downriver to sawmills in the harbors along the Atlantic seaboard. In a few decades all of Maine's old-growth (original) pine and spruce forests were gone, and the industry moved progressively westward and southward.

After some 300 years of deforestation (clearing of forests), only a fraction of old-growth forests in the United States remains. Many claim that this destruction of the forests is having far-reaching environmental consequences. Clear-cutting (cutting down all trees in an area) wipes out the trees' root networks that hold soil in place and trap rainwater. The loss of forest cover can result in flooding and severe erosion, which strips away fertile topsoil. The disappearance of forests also means the loss of habitats for many wild animals, endangering or leading to the extinction of species. Deforestation even affects the air, because green plants add to the supply of oxygen in the atmosphere.

Many argue that what is needed now is more efficient management of the remaining forest lands. Old-growth forests should be selectively logged, to leave enough of the ecological system in place to generate new growth. And new-growth forests need time to mature. The challenge is to find a balance between the demand for wood and paper products—and the jobs which that demand supports—and the need to conserve our vanishing forests.

enterprise, and they killed as many animals as they could. Some villages devoted so much time to trapping and preparing furs that they had to buy food that they had once produced for themselves.

The fur trade also disrupted relations among tribes. As they killed off the beaver and other fur-bearing animals in one area, Indian trappers moved their settlements to areas where the animals were still plentiful. Thus previously distant tribes came into contact and competition with each other. Firearms made the resulting conflicts particularly deadly.

■■ Some American Indians became economically dependent on the fur trade, and competition for hunting territories caused conflict.

Conflicts over land. The European desire for land had even more disastrous consequences for Native Americans than did the European demand for furs. Indian ways of using land did not fit European concepts of landownership. Europeans thought that land that was not registered by deed,

Teaching the Section

RELATIONS WITH NATIVE AMERICANS

Instruct half the class to write paragraphs summarizing the attitudes and actions of the French colonists toward Native Americans. Tell the other half to write similar paragraphs about English actions and attitudes. Select volunteers to read their paragraphs. Then have the class identify similarities and differences in English and French behaviors. List responses on the chalkboard. Ask if French and English goals in their relations with Native Americans explain any similarities or differences in their policies. Conclude by asking if differences in French and English treatment of Native Americans made any difference in the outcome of Indian-white relations.

PRIMARY SOURCE
Description of Change: excerpted
Rationale: excerpted to focus on main idea

CULTURAL PATTERNS

The Pequot War was sparked in part by the murder of two European traders. Historians are not sure that the Pequots were actually involved in the murders, but the Pequots' Indian neighbors were quick to blame them. Most Native American groups in the area disliked the Pequots, who collected annual tribute from them by force. The weaker Indian groups saw the military power of the colonists as a chance to rid themselves of a hated foe. When war broke out the Pequots could find few Indian allies. Instead most nearby groups eagerly assisted the Puritans.

---

cleared, or built on was not owned. Since most Indian land appeared wild and unused, Europeans believed that it was there for the taking.

Native Americans viewed land differently. They recognized territorial boundaries, but not individual ownership. Individuals did have, however, the right to use land for growing crops and for hunting and gathering. The loss of the land had serious consequences because it meant losing sources of food. English agricultural practices further diminished these resources by destroying animal habitats. Miantonomo (my-an-tuh-NOH-moh), a Narraganset, observed as early as 1642:

> 66 Our plains were full of deer, as also our woods, and of turkies, and our coves full of fish and fowl. But these English having gotten our land, they with scythes cut down the grass, and with axes fell the trees; their cows and horses eat the grass, and their hogs spoil our clam banks, and we shall be starved. 99

War in New England. Less than 20 years after Plymouth Colony was founded, the Pequots and English were at war over land. The Pequot War, which began in 1636, pitted the English and their Narraganset and Mohegan allies against the Pequot, who were allied in the fur trade with the Dutch of New Netherland. It ended in 1637 when the English burned a Pequot village, killing hundreds of

▲ Metacom

people. A formal treaty was signed the following year. Friction between American Indians and white settlers increased as Massachusetts' growing population pushed onto Indian lands. War broke out again in 1675, when Metacom—whom the English named King Philip—led the Wampanoags and other Native Americans against the colonists.

Metacom's well-armed forces attacked New England settlements, destroying 12 towns. The Indian war effort collapsed, however, when Metacom was killed in battle. An estimated 3,000 Indians died in the fighting, and the Puritans sold most of the surviving Wampanoags as slaves. Ten years later, a Frenchman observed that Native Americans in New England posed little threat: "The last Wars . . . have reduced them to a small Number, and consequently they are incapable of defending themselves."

■■ **Conflicts over land led to wars that nearly wiped out the Native Americans of New England.**

THE IROQUOIS LEAGUE

In part, the New Englanders owed their victory over the Wampanoags to the Mohawks. At the urging of the

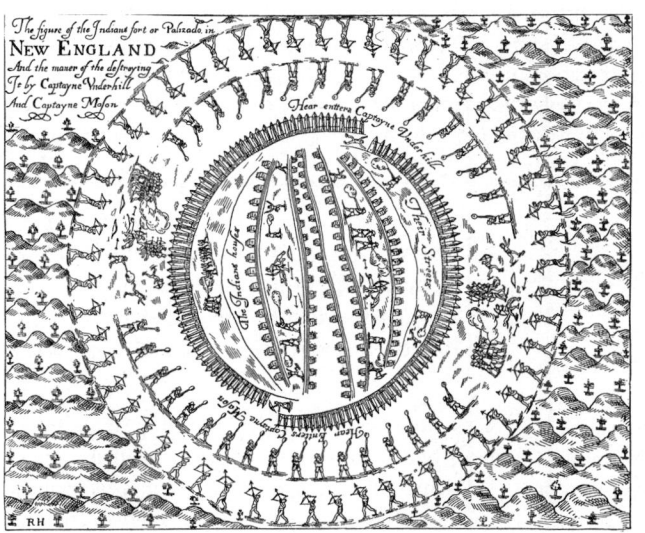
▲ The English burning of a Pequot village is the subject of this engraving.

THE FRENCH AND INDIAN WAR

Work with students to develop a chalkboard chart on the French and Indian War. Suggest that chart entries address causes, strategies and tactics, turning points, and outcomes. Then have groups of students write summary paragraphs based on the chart. Ask a representative of each group to read its paragraph to the class.

▶

governor of New York, the Mohawks had driven Metacom's forces out of New York, dealing them a crippling blow.

The Mohawks belonged to the powerful **Iroquois League**. The Senecas, Cayugas, Onondagas, Oneidas, and Mohawks of New York and Pennsylvania had formed the confederation in the 15th or 16th century. In 1722 the Tuscaroras, who had been forced out of North Carolina by settlers, joined them, and the confederation also became known as the Six Nations. Each nation kept control of its local affairs, but larger issues—such as going to war or signing treaties—required the agreement of the league's leaders.

Their combined military strength allowed the Iroquois League to dominate the fur trade, to extend its influence over American Indians to the west, and to protect its independence. The Iroquois often acted as middlemen, obtaining furs from other Native Americans and selling the furs to the English. The Iroquois maintained their independence by skillfully playing the English and the French against each other. They willingly became involved in colonial conflicts if they thought they could further their own interests—sometimes siding with the French, other times with the British.

𝓣HE FRENCH AND INDIAN WAR

France, Spain, and England were engaged in a worldwide struggle for empire, and the fighting often spilled over into North America. Between 1689 and 1748, English colonists were dragged into three wars: King William's War (1689–1697), Queen Anne's War (1702–1713), and King George's War (1744–1748). As long as the great European powers continued their rivalry, the prospect of more colonial warfare remained.

To plan for defense and to recruit the Iroquois as allies, representatives from seven colonies and the Iroquois League met in Albany, New York, June 19–July 10, 1754. At the Albany Congress the colonies' delegates adopted Benjamin Franklin's **Albany Plan of Union**, which called for a loose confederation to promote defense. The colonial assemblies, however, rejected the plan, fearing that it would raise taxes and give Great Britain too much power. The Iroquois, concluding that the English were too

THE FRENCH AND INDIAN WAR

THROUGH OTHERS' EYES

King George's War ended in Europe in 1748, but less than 10 years later, Europeans were again at war. This time, Europe's future course hinged on events happening more than 3,000 miles away in sparsely settled North America. The French and Indian War, begun in 1754 on American soil but not formally declared until 1756, expanded into a worldwide battle between Great Britain and France. At stake was control of North America as well as other colonial empires throughout the world.

At the time, the French philosopher Voltaire remarked how these increasing global connections were shaping history: "Such was the complication of political interests that a cannon-shot fired in America could give the signal that set Europe in a blaze."

disunited to defeat the French, would not commit their support.

Competition for the Ohio Valley. King William's War, Queen Anne's War, and King George's War had all been sparked by fighting elsewhere in the world. However, the next major colonial conflict—the French and Indian War (1754–1763)—began in the colonies and spread to Europe in 1756 as the Seven Years' War. Unlike the previous conflicts, which were mainly fought on New England's northern frontier and at Spanish posts in Florida, the French and Indian War broke out in the west in the Ohio Valley.

Virginia **land speculators**, who bought land expecting a quick profit from its resale, had acquired a large land grant in the Ohio Valley in 1749. To protect their interests, the Virginians began building a fort at the junction of the Ohio, Allegheny (al-uh-GAY-nee), and Monongahela (muh-nahn-guh-HEE-luh) rivers—which became the site of Pittsburgh, Pennsylvania. The French, who considered the land theirs, drove the Virginians off, completed the fort, and named it

Point out that, indeed, all the major European powers were drawn into the conflict. Austria, Saxony, Sweden, and Russia sided with France, while Prussia and Hanover allied with Great Britain.

🌐 GLOBAL CONNECTIONS

As with the French and Indian War, the colonists had names for the conflicts they fought that were different from the names that identified these wars in Europe. Europe's War of the League of Augsburg was called King William's War by the colonists. Queen Anne's War was the colonists' name for the War of the Spanish Succession. And King George's War in the colonies was the War of the Austrian Succession in Europe.

*P*ractice

GUIDED PRACTICE

At the top of a chalkboard write *Population Growth*, and at the bottom write *Moving to the Frontier*. Tell students that these headings represent the ends of a cause-and-effect chain on movement to the frontier. Ask for volunteers to come to the chalk-board and add steps in the chain to show how population growth created conditions that encouraged people to move west.

INDEPENDENT PRACTICE

Have students write a paragraph that summarizes the Guided Practice chain by explaining the relationship between population growth and westward expansion in the colonies. Students may wish to include their paragraphs in their portfolios.

*R*eview and *A*ssessment

REVIEW Have students work in small groups to develop an annotated time line of the most important events surveyed in the section. Display time lines on the bulletin board, and have students discuss similarities and differences in their time lines. Then assign the Section 4 Review on p. 93.

ASSESS Assign the **Section 4 Daily Quiz** in *Core Resources.*

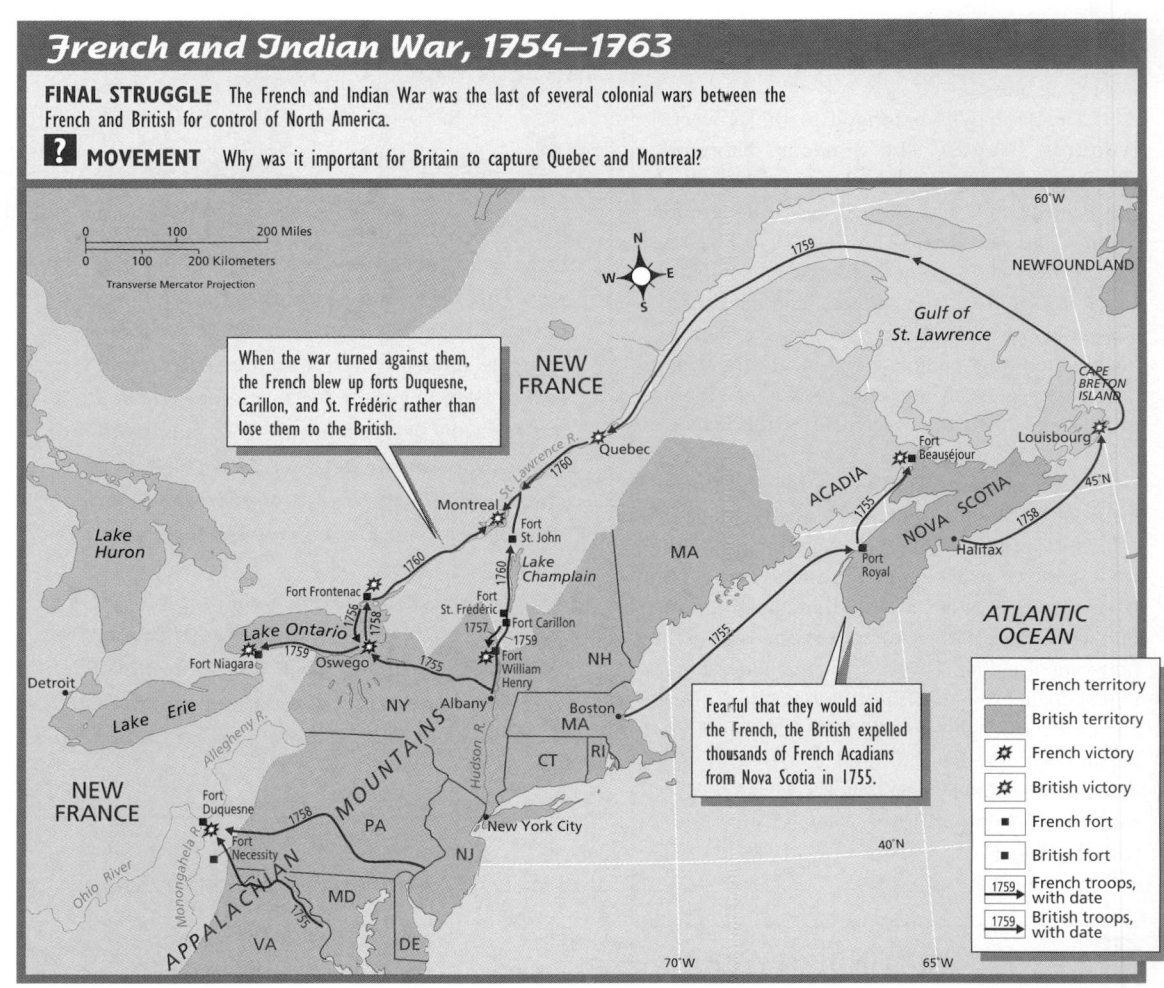

French and Indian War, 1754–1763

FINAL STRUGGLE The French and Indian War was the last of several colonial wars between the French and British for control of North America.

? **MOVEMENT** Why was it important for Britain to capture Quebec and Montreal?

When the war turned against them, the French blew up forts Duquesne, Carillon, and St. Frédéric rather than lose them to the British.

Fearful that they would aid the French, the British expelled thousands of French Acadians from Nova Scotia in 1755.

	French territory
	British territory
✸	French victory
✸	British victory
▪	French fort
▪	British fort
1759→	French troops, with date
1759→	British troops, with date

Map Caption Answer
They were centers of French power in New France and controlled access to the St. Lawrence.

PRIMARY SOURCE
Description of Change: excerpted
Rationale: excerpted to focus on main idea

Governor Robert Dinwiddie of Virginia sent young George Washington and a company of militia to expel the French from the region. But the French held fast.

The British were unwilling to give up the area to the French, however. They sent General Edward Braddock, Washington, and a large force of British and colonial soldiers to take Fort Duquesne. Inexperienced in colonial warfare, the British forces panicked when they clashed with the French and their force of Delawares, Ottawas, Abnakis, and other Native Americans in July 1755. Washington described the British defeat in a letter to his mother:

❝ The English soldiers . . . were struck with such a panic that they behaved with more cowardice than it is possible to con-ceive. . . . They broke and ran as sheep pursued by dogs. . . . I luckily escaped without a wound, though I had four bullets through my coat, and two horses shot under me. ❞

In August 1757 the British lost Oswego and Fort William Henry to the French. The "lightly cloathed and armed" French and Indians succeeded, as one colonist reported, because they are "often on all Sides of us, . . . taking the Advantage of every Tree and Bush." The Delawares, whom the British had pushed out of eastern Pennsylvania, also launched attack after attack on the backcountry settlers.

British victories. Britain's fortunes improved when British cabinet minister William Pitt assumed full control of Britain's war effort. He

RETEACH Organize students into four groups and assign each group one of the Focus questions on p. 86. Have group members discuss and write an answer to their question. Ask group representatives to share their answers with the other groups.

Closure

Offer the following proposition to the class: *Land hunger is the best explanation for the events we have studied in this section.* Ask students whether they agree or disagree with this statement. Require them to explain and defend their opinions.

Extension

RESEARCH Ask students to research the impact that the French colonial presence had on American culture. Have them present their findings in an oral report.

COMPARE Encourage students to conduct research and write a report comparing the Iroquois League to the Albany Plan of Union.

◄ **George Washington experienced his first taste of military service during the French and Indian War.**

Washington/Curtis/Lee Collection, Washington and Lee University, Lexington, Virginia

assumed full control of Britain's war effort. He poured money and troops into the North American conflict. His efforts paid off. In July 1758 a British force under General Jeffrey Amherst captured Louisbourg on Cape Breton Island, which guarded the entrance to the Gulf of St. Lawrence. Louisbourg's fall meant that the British could prevent French supplies from reaching Canada. Then in August, the British captured Fort Frontenac on Lake Ontario. When the British marched on Fort Duquesne in November, the French blew up the fort rather than surrender it to the British.

After these British military successes, the Iroquois reassessed their neutrality and lent support to the British. As the tide turned against the French, they lost their Indian allies in the Ohio Valley. Abandoning their remaining forts there, the French withdrew to Canada.

The British followed, determined to take Quebec. But General James Wolfe could not entice the French commander, General Louis-Joseph de Montcalm, into battle—that is, not until the English discovered a path that led from the St. Lawrence River up the cliff to Quebec. Under cover of night the English army climbed up and assumed battle formation outside the city. The British emerged victorious from the ensuing battle although both Wolfe and Montcalm were fatally wounded. Quebec surrendered to the English in September 1759. Montreal fell in September of the following year, and with this defeat France lost the last of its Canadian holdings.

The spoils of war. The war in North America ended in 1761, but fighting continued for two more years in other parts of the world. In 1763 the Treaty of Paris ended all hostilities and awarded territories. The victorious British claimed Canada and all French holdings east of the Mississippi River except New Orleans. Spain, which had joined the French war effort in 1762, surrendered Florida to the British. In anticipation of this loss, Spain had received France's vast Louisiana territory west of the Mississippi in the 1762 Treaty of Fontainebleau.

▪▪ **Competition for the North American interior touched off the French and Indian War. The war cost France most of its North American holdings.**

SECTION REVIEW ANSWERS

IDENTIFY

For significance, see the following pages:
Jacques Marquette (p. 88)
Louis Jolliet (p. 88)
René-Robert de La Salle (p. 88)
Metacom (p. 90)
Iroquois League (p. 91)
Albany Plan of Union (p. 91)
land speculators (p. 91)
William Pitt (p. 92)
James Wolfe (p. 93)
Louis-Joseph de Montcalm (p. 93)

LOCATE

For locations, see the map on p. 92.

1. *desire for land, rapid population growth, economic problems*
2. *Some Native Americans became economically dependent on fur trade and fought over hunting territories; land conflicts nearly wiped out the Native Americans of New England.*
3. *Conflicts over Ohio Valley sparked French and Indian War; France lost most of its holdings at end of war.*
4. *Accounts should describe settlers growing own food, making homemade items, and building log cabins.*
5. *to further their interests and play the English against the French*

▪▪ **S E C T I O N   4   R E V I E W**

IDENTIFY and explain the significance of the following: Jacques Marquette, Louis Jolliet, René-Robert de La Salle, Metacom, Iroquois League, Albany Plan of Union, land speculators, William Pitt, James Wolfe, Louis-Joseph de Montcalm.

LOCATE and explain the importance of the following: Quebec, St. Lawrence River, Fort Duquesne, Oswego, Fort William Henry.

1. **MAIN IDEA** Why did some colonists choose to move to the frontier?
2. **MAIN IDEA** How did the Europeans' desire for furs and land affect Native Americans?
3. **LINKING HISTORY AND GEOGRAPHY** How did competition for land in North America cause conflicts between England and France? How did these conflicts end?
4. **WRITING TO CREATE** Imagine you are an author living on the frontier. Write a short fictional account of frontier life. Illustrate your story by including sketches of your surroundings.
5. **ANALYZING** Why did Native Americans become involved in conflicts between the French and the English?

Return to the Themes section on p. 64. Have students discuss these again and compare their original responses with those given now. (See p. 63B for suggested answers.)

Chapter Review Answers

WRITING A SUMMARY
See Essential Points in each section for main ideas.

REVIEWING CHRONOLOGY
5, 2, 1, 4, 3
Analyzing
They hoped to establish new colonies that promoted religious freedom and economic opportunity.

IDENTIFYING PEOPLE AND IDEAS
1. *Wampanoag who helped Pilgrims survive*
2. *Puritan governor who helped develop a model commonwealth in Massachusetts*
3. *Puritan woman who established a self-governing colony*
4. *guaranteed religious freedom to Christians*
5. *ex-slave who described the Middle Passage*
6. *religious revival that made religion emotional and emphasized equality before God*
7. *bloodless rebellion that led to English Bill of Rights*
8. *English revivalist who spread Great Awakening*
9. *plan that called for the Iroquois League and a confederation of colonies to promote defense*
10. *English commander who defeated the French*

94

UNDERSTANDING MAIN IDEAS
1. *led to founding of more colonies and efforts to control colonial trade*
2. *challenged Puritan authority; challenged governor's authority in Bacon's Rebellion; criticized ministers' authority during Great Awakening; replaced unpopular officials after Glorious Revolution*
3. *economic opportunities, religious freedom, social experiments; some formed Iroquois League, others attacked the English, or played English and French against each other*

REVIEWING THEMES
1. *Primarily Puritan, New England developed a fairly uniform culture; other regions attracted a wider range of immigrants and had more diverse cultures.*
2. *New England—Healthy climate led to low death rates, large families; poor soil led colonists to turn to fishing, trade, business. Chesapeake—Climate led to high death rates; abundance of rich farmland led to plantation agriculture; ease of river transportation discouraged growth of cities.*
3. *mercantilism; cut southern colonists' profits; helped northern shipbuilders, merchants*

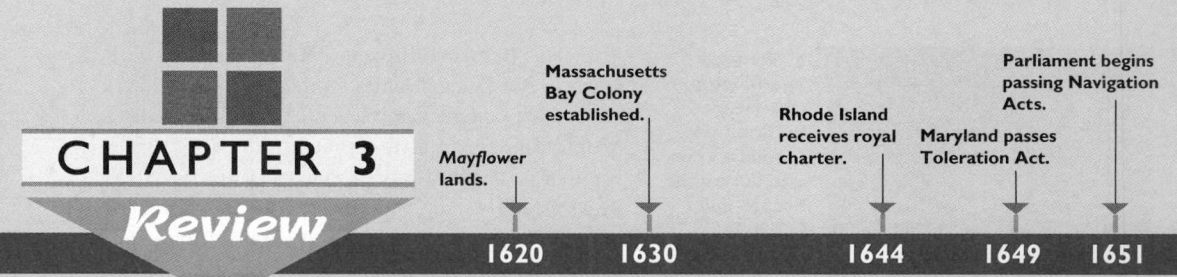

CHAPTER 3
Review

Mayflower lands.	Massachusetts Bay Colony established.		Rhode Island receives royal charter.	Maryland passes Toleration Act.	Parliament begins passing Navigation Acts.
1620	**1630**		**1644**	**1649**	**1651**

WRITING A SUMMARY
Using the essential points of the chapter as a guide, write a summary of the chapter.

REVIEWING CHRONOLOGY
Number your paper 1 to 5. Study the time line above, and list the following events in the order in which they happened by writing the first next to 1, the second next to 2, and so on. Then complete the activity below.

1. Bacon's Rebellion erupts.
2. Rhode Island receives royal charter.
3. Treaty of Paris signed.
4. Glorious Revolution occurs.
5. Massachusetts Bay Colony established.

Analyzing What common goals did the founders of Massachusetts, Maryland, Rhode Island, and Pennsylvania share?

IDENTIFYING PEOPLE AND IDEAS
Explain the historical significance of each of the following people or terms.

1. Squanto
2. John Winthrop
3. Lady Deborah Moody
4. Toleration Act
5. Olaudah Equiano
6. Great Awakening
7. Glorious Revolution
8. George Whitefield
9. Albany Plan of Union
10. General James Wolfe

UNDERSTANDING MAIN IDEAS
1. How did mercantilism affect England's relations with the colonies?
2. In what ways did some colonists challenge established authority in the colonies?
3. Why did settlers continually start new settlements? How did Native Americans react to this expansion?

REVIEWING THEMES
1. **Cultural Diversity** How did the cultural backgrounds of the colonists affect the development of the colonies in which they settled?
2. **Geographic Diversity** What influence did environmental differences have on the development of colonies in New England and the Chesapeake?

3. **Economic Development** Why did England regulate colonial trade? What effect did this regulation have on the colonists?

THINKING CRITICALLY
1. **Evaluating** How effective was the English Crown in maintaining political authority in the colonies? Give reasons for your answer.
2. **Hypothesizing** Would Massachusetts Bay Colony's Bible commonwealth have worked in the Chesapeake? Why or why not?
3. **Comparing** How did women's lives compare in the New England and southern colonies?
4. **Identifying Cause and Effect** What were the causes and effects of Bacon's Rebellion?

STRATEGY FOR SUCCESS
Review the Skills Handbook entry on Identifying the Main Idea on page 988. Read the following excerpt from a 1705 study of Native American culture. Then identify the main idea of the selection.

> ❝ *They [Native Americans] have on several accounts reason to lament [regret] the arrival of the Europeans, by whose means they seem to have lost their felicity [happiness] as well as their innocence. The English have taken away [a] great part of their country and consequently made everything less plenty amongst them. They have introduced drunkenness and luxury amongst them, which have multiplied their wants and put them up to desiring a thousand things they never dreamt of before.* ❞

THINKING CRITICALLY

1. Students should balance English efforts to control colonial trade with the colonists' efforts to limit royal authority after the Glorious Revolution.
2. Students should consider how the social and geographic characteristics of the Chesapeake would make establishing a Bible commonwealth difficult.
3. All made many things their families needed; women in the North came to the colonies with their families, had many children, usually married once; women in the South often came as servants, married several times due to high death rates, had stepchildren.

4. causes—discontent over land and tobacco prices, high taxes; effects—opened Indian lands for settlement, lowered taxes, strengthened the move to replace indentured servants with enslaved Africans

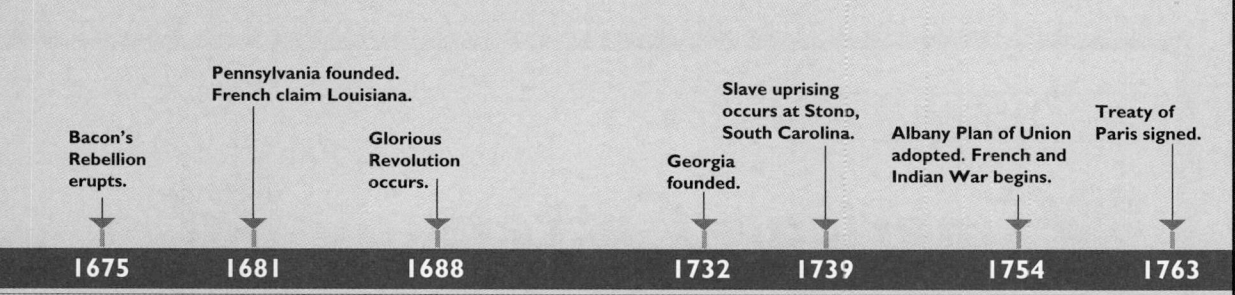

Bacon's Rebellion erupts.	Pennsylvania founded. French claim Louisiana.	Glorious Revolution occurs.	Georgia founded.	Slave uprising occurs at Stono, South Carolina.	Albany Plan of Union adopted. French and Indian War begins.	Treaty of Paris signed.
1675	1681	1688	1732	1739	1754	1763

WRITING ABOUT HISTORY
Writing to Evaluate Write an essay about the introduction of slavery into the English colonies. Be sure to include how changes in indentured servitude contributed to the introduction of slavery.

USING PRIMARY SOURCES
Colonists often resented the authority of English royal governors. Read the following excerpt from Nathaniel Bacon's "The Declaration of the People." Then write an essay evaluating whether or not Bacon's accusations against Governor William Berkeley were justified.

> ❝ *FOR HAVING UPON specious [deceptive] pretenses of Public works raised unjust Taxes upon the Commonality for the advancement of private Favorites and other sinister ends. . . .*
>
> *For having abused and rendered Contemptible the Majesty of Justice, [by] advancing to places of judicature [law courts] scandalous and Ignorant favorites.*
>
> *For having wronged his Majesty's Prerogative and Interest by assuming the monopoly of the Beaver trade.*
>
> *By having in that unjust gaine Bartered and sold his Majesty's Country and the lives of his Loyal Subjects to the Barbarous Heathen [the Indians]. . . .*
>
> *For having . . . forged a Commission by we know not what hand, not only without but against the Consent of the People, for raising and effecting of Civil Wars and distractions. . . .*
>
> *Of these the aforesaid Articles we accuse Sir William Berkeley, as guilty of each and every one of the same, and as one, who has Traitorously attempted, violated and Injured his Majesty's Interest here.* ❞

LINKING HISTORY AND GEOGRAPHY
Study the map on page 92. How might the outcome of the French and Indian War have been different if France had established colonies along the Mississippi River and in the Ohio Valley?

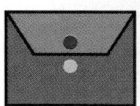 **BUILDING YOUR PORTFOLIO**

Complete the following projects independently or cooperatively.

1. **TRADE** In chapters 1 and 2 you prepared a map showing trade routes between Europe, Africa, Asia, and the Americas. Building on that material, revise your map to reflect French and English trade from North America during the 1600s. Add symbols to represent major trade items exchanged by French and English traders.

2. **SLAVERY** In Chapter 2 you planned a mural protesting slavery. Building on that material, now imagine you are a Quaker abolitionist. Prepare a newspaper advertisement or a handbill protesting the slave trade and outlining why slavery should be banned in North America.

Slaves in cargo hold

3. **CULTURAL EXCHANGES** In chapters 1 and 2 you researched cultural exchanges in the Americas. Building on that material, develop a series of drawings and captions that illustrate some of the ways in which contact between Native Americans, African slaves, and British and French colonists affected each culture.

STRATEGY FOR SUCCESS
Europeans devastated Native American cultures by taking away Indian land and resources and introduced them to "drunkenness" and to "luxury."

WRITING ABOUT HISTORY
Essays should note that former indentured servants competed for land. As servants became expensive and difficult to obtain, plantation owners turned to slavery.

USING PRIMARY SOURCES
Essays should analyze whether a royal governor is justified in acting on a broad range of issues without colonists' consent.

LINKING HISTORY AND GEOGRAPHY
Students could mention that the French presence might have prevented the English from settling beyond the Appalachians.

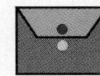 **BUILDING YOUR PORTFOLIO**
Have students refer to **Building Your Portfolio Worksheet 1**, assigned at the beginning of Unit 1. Use the worksheet to help students monitor their progress on the portfolio projects.

Assessment
Core Resources
- Review Worksheet 3
- Chapter 3 Tests
- Alternative Assessment Forms

Test Generator

NATIVE AMERICAN CREATION MYTHS

SETTING THE SCENE

Native Americans traditionally have told the story of their past through painting, sculpture, and ritual dance and music. One of the fullest and richest methods of recounting Native American history, however, is the oral tradition. Early American Indian storytellers were trained from an early age in the tribal myths, legends, and traditions. Because the storytellers were guardians of history, they were highly respected members of society. They traditionally told their stories during the winter months, believing that to practice their art at any other time might bring ill fortune.

The legends included here concern creation, but Native American oral literature deals with many other subjects—the beauty of the landscape, natural phenomena such as earthquakes and floods, and victories in battle or other notable historical events.

American Letters

Native American Creation Myths

Native Americans, the first inhabitants of the Americas, developed a rich oral literature. In the following creation myths, the Iroquois of present-day New York explain the origin of the Iroquois League, the Jicarilla-Apaches of present-day Colorado and New Mexico account for the origin of fire, and the Abnakis of present-day Maine describe the mythic origins of corn.

▲ **Storyteller pottery figurine**

From *The Origin of the Iroquois League*

Iroquois

Long, long ago, in the great past, there were no people on the earth. All of it was covered by deep water. Birds, flying, filled the air, and many huge monsters possessed the waters.

One day the birds saw a beautiful woman falling from the sky. Immediately the huge ducks held a council. . . .

After some discussion, they decided to spread out their wings and thus break the force of her fall. . . . The beautiful woman reached them safely.

Then the monsters of the deep held a council, to decide how they could protect the beautiful being from the terror of the waters. . . . The monsters decided . . . that only Giant Tortoise was big enough to bear her weight. He volunteered, and she was gently placed upon his back. Giant Tortoise magically increased in size and soon became a large island.

After a time, the Celestial Woman gave birth to twin boys. One of them was the Spirit of Good. He made all the good things on the earth and caused the corn, the fruits, and the tobacco to grow.

The other twin was the Spirit of Evil. He created the weeds and also the worms and the bugs and all the other creatures that do evil to the good animals and birds.

All the time, Giant Tortoise continued to stretch himself. And so the world became larger and larger. . . .

After many, many years had passed by, the Sky-Holder . . . decided to create some people. He wanted them to surpass all others in beauty, strength, and bravery. So from the bosom of the island where they had been living on moles, the Sky-Holder brought forth six pairs of people.

The first pair were left near a great river, now called the Mohawk. So they are called the Mohawk Indians. The second pair were told to move their home beside a large stone. Their descendants have been called the

Oneidas. Many of them lived on the south side of Oneida Lake and others in the valleys of Oneida Creek. A third pair were left on a high hill and have always been called the Onondagas.

The fourth pair became the parents of the Cayugas, and the fifth pair the parents of the Senecas. Both were placed in some part of what is now known as the State of New York. But the Tuscaroras were taken up the Roanoke River into what is now known as North Carolina. There the Sky-Holder made his home while he taught these people and their descendants many useful arts and crafts. ❖

From *Origin of Fire*

Jicarilla-Apache

Long, long ago, animals and trees talked with each other, but there was no fire at that time.

Fox was most clever and he tried to think of a way to create fire for the world. One day, he decided to visit the Geese, . . . whose cry he wished to learn how to imitate. They promised to teach him if he would fly with them. So they contrived [devised] a way to attach wings to Fox, but cautioned him never to open his eyes while flying.

Whenever the Geese arose in flight, Fox also flew along with them to practice their cry. On one such adventure, darkness descended suddenly as they flew over the village of the fireflies. . . . In midflight, the glare from the flickering fireflies caused Fox to forget and he opened his eyes—instantly his wings collapsed! His fall was uncontrollable. He landed within the walled area of the firefly village, where a fire constantly burned in the center.

Two kind fireflies came to see fallen Fox. . . .

Fox hoped to persuade the two fireflies to tell him where he could find a way over the wall to the outside. They led him to a cedar tree, which they explained would bend down upon command and catapult him over the wall if he so desired. . . .

Fox suggested to the fireflies, "Let's have a festival where we can dance and I will produce the music."

They all agreed that would be fun and helped to gather wood to build up a greater fire. Secretly, Fox tied a piece of cedar bark to his tail. Then he made a drum, probably the first one ever constructed, and beat it vigorously with a stick for the dancing fireflies. Gradually, he moved closer and closer to the fire.

Fox pretended to tire from beating the drum. He gave it to some fireflies who wanted to help make the music. Fox quickly thrust his tail into the fire, lighting the bark, and exclaimed, "It is too warm here for me, I must find a cooler place."

Straight to the cedar tree Fox ran, calling, "Bend down to me, my cedar tree, bend down!"

Down bent the cedar tree for Fox to catch hold, then up it carried him far over the wall. On and on he ran, with the fireflies in pursuit.

As Fox ran along, brush and wood on either side of his path were ignited from the sparks dropping from the burning bark tied to his tail.

Fox finally tired and gave the burning bark to Hawk, . . . who carried it to brown Crane. . . . He flew far southward, scattering fire sparks everywhere. This is how fire first spread over the earth. ❖

From **The Strange Origin of Corn**

Abnaki

A long time ago, when the Indians were first made, one man lived alone, far from any others. He did not know fire, and so he lived on roots, bark, and nuts. This man became very lonely for companionship. He grew tired of digging roots, lost his appetite, and for several days lay dreaming in the sunshine. When he awoke, he saw someone standing near and, at first, was very frightened. But when he heard the stranger's voice, his heart was glad, and he looked up. He saw a beautiful woman with long *light* hair! . . . He sang to her about her loneliness, and begged her not to leave him.

At last she replied, "If you will do exactly what I tell you to do, I will also be with you."

He promised that he would try his very best. So she led him to a place where there was some very dry grass. "Now get two dry sticks," she told him, "and rub them together fast while you hold them in the grass."

Soon a spark flew out. The grass caught fire, and as swiftly as an arrow takes flight, the ground was burned over. Then the beautiful woman spoke again: "When the sun sets, take me by the hair and drag me over the burned ground."

"Oh, I don't want to do that!" the man exclaimed.

"You must do what I tell you to do," said she. "Wherever you drag me, something like grass will spring up, and you will see something like hair coming from between the leaves. Soon seeds will be ready for your use."

The man followed the beautiful woman's orders. And when the Indians see silk on the cornstalk, they know that the beautiful woman has not forgotten them. ❖

THINKING AND WRITING ABOUT LITERATURE

1. According to the Iroquois legend, how did animals and gods create the earth and people?
2. How does Fox outsmart the fireflies in the Jicarilla-Apache story about the origin of fire?
3. How does the Abnaki legend account for the existence of corn silk?

PRIMARY SOURCES

Description of Change: excerpted and bracketed
Rationale: excerpted for space considerations; bracketed to clarfy meaning

THINKING AND WRITING ABOUT LITERATURE

1. *Giant Tortoise turned into an island and then grew larger to form the earth. The Sky-Holder took pairs of people from the island and spread them around the world.*
2. *Fox asks the fireflies to have a party. He pretends to be tired from playing the drum, approaches the fire, then lights a piece of bark hidden in his tail and escapes with it.*
3. *The corn silk is a reminder of the beautiful woman who introduced the cultivation of corn.*

INTERPRETING THE VISUAL RECORD

Write the following headings on the chalkboard: *Subject, Details, Point of View, Comparison*. Ask students to review the painting below and to provide information for each of the headings. Then have students complete the Practicing the Strategy exercise. Point out to students that since very few artists traveled to the Americas in the early years of European exploration, most paintings of European-Indian encounters were based solely on the artist's imagination. Note that in the 16th-century illustration by Theodor de Bry on pp. 36–37, the Native Americans are depicted as welcoming the Europeans. In the anonymous painting on p. 67, done around 1700, the Native Americans seem more cautious.

PRACTICING THE STRATEGY

1. **(a)** *Native Americans are presented in different settings and roles; the loincloths and hairstyles of those in the painting on p. 67 are more elaborate. The Native Americans are otherwise depicted in much the same posture.*
(b) *Artists may have relied on differing accounts of contacts with Native Americans or on descriptions of different groups. Students may also note similarities between the Europeans in the two illustrations, as well as the more dramatic differences between the Europeans and the Native Americans in both illustrations.*
2. *Students' evaluations may differ, but there is little in the illustrations to suggest significant historical inaccuracy.*

Strategies for Success

INTERPRETING THE VISUAL RECORD

Studying the visual record of a period or place can help you understand its history in ways the written word sometimes cannot. Paintings, photographs, and other types of images provide clues about an era's architecture and technology and can give the viewer a feel for the dress, work, and values of a people.

Visual artists often use their imagination and artistic freedom to add or omit details. Thus even the most realistic painting may not be an accurate record of history. In addition, artists sometimes depict a time period earlier than their own. They depend on others' accounts and may lack reliable enough information to portray the events accurately. Artists are also influenced by their own values and by social and artistic movements. Consequently, you must interpret what you view.

How to Interpret the Visual Record

1. **Determine the work's subject matter.** Note the people portrayed and any objects surrounding them. For clues about a work's theme, examine its title, if it has one.
2. **Examine the details.** Study the details and the background.
3. **Determine the artist's point of view.** Look for information in the picture that suggests the artist's purpose. Ask yourself: Is the subject depicted favorably or unfavorably?

Find out when the work was created and what contemporary influences may have shaped the artist's outlook.
4. **Use the information cautiously.** Compare what you know from other sources about the event, people, or period being portrayed.

Applying the Strategy

Study the untitled painting below of colonial Baltimore in the mid-1700s. Note the wide harbor, which made the site an appealing place to settle. The loading dock and British trading ship in the painting's center show that shipping was important to Baltimore from its founding. A striking feature of the painting is the sharp contrast between the orderly settlement and the thick woods beyond the back fence—the environment out of which the town was created. Few people are noticeably at work, but the many buildings that dot the landscape and the neat roads, fences, and rows of crops suggest how much work has gone into establishing the colony. This peaceful image of an enterprising new community was perhaps meant to attract additional colonists or to inspire others.

Practicing the Strategy

Study the images on pages 36–37 and 67 depicting European views of Native Americans during the colonial period. Then, on a separate sheet of paper, answer the following questions.

1. **(a)** How do the two illustrations differ in their presentation of Native Americans? How are they similar?
(b) To what do you attribute the difference and similarities between the illustrations?
2. Based on what you have learned about Native Americans, evaluate the historical accuracy of each illustration.

▼ **Colonial Baltimore, 1752**

BUILDING YOUR PORTFOLIO

Each portfolio project described below is the culmination of the Building Your Portfolio activities in the chapter reviews of Unit 1. First, decide whether you wish students to work individually or in groups on these unit projects. Then permit each student to choose the project on which he or she desires to work. Provide students with copies of **Building Your Portfolio Worksheet 1** from *Core Resources*. This worksheet will guide students step by step to complete their projects.

BUILDING YOUR PORTFOLIO

Outlined below are three projects. Independently or cooperatively, complete one and use the products to demonstrate your mastery of the historical concepts involved.

trade agreement to be presented at an upcoming international trade conference. Your trade proposal should take into account the interests of delegates from each participating nation.

1 TRADE

Trade became truly worldwide from the time of the Crusades through the mid-1700s, bringing diverse cultures into contact with one another. Using the portfolio materials you designed in chapters 1, 2, and 3, write a proposal for a

2 SLAVERY

The *encomienda* system and the enslavement of Africans raised public debate in Europe and the Americas. Using the portfolio materials you designed in chapters 2 and 3, create a wall display that illustrates the nature and scope of this debate. Include in your display short

biographies of Bartolomé de Las Casas, Benjamin Banneker, and other opponents of either or both systems.

3 CULTURAL EXCHANGES

Many different cultures exchanged technology, food, religion, and ideas in the Americas. Using the portfolio materials you designed in chapters 1, 2, and 3, prepare a brochure that explains the variety of cultural exchanges explored in your museum exhibit. Then present your brochure and exhibit to the class.

Video Review

In assigned groups, develop an outline for a video collage of the Americas from prehistory through 1763. Choose images that best illustrate the major topics of the period. Write a script to accompany the images. Assign narrators to different parts of the script, and present your video collage to the class.

Further Reading

Bakeless, John. *America As Seen by Its First Explorers: The Eyes of Discovery.* Dover (1989). Descriptions of North America

taken from the firsthand accounts of early explorers.

Clendinnen, Inga. *Aztecs.* Cambridge University Press (1991). Explores life in the Aztec capital in the period immediately before the arrival of the first Spanish explorers and conquistadors.

Hawke, David F. *Everyday Life in Early America.* Harper & Row (1988). Portrait of life in early New England.

Hirschfelder, Arlene, and Paulette Molin. *The Encyclopedia of Native American Religions.* Facts On File (1992). Descriptions of Native American religious customs and leaders in encyclopedia form.

Josephy, Jr., Alvin M. *America in 1492: The World of the Indian Peoples before the Arrival of Columbus.* Random House (1991). Panorama of North and South American life from prehistoric times to the early 15th century.

Nash, Gary B. *Red, White, and Black: The Peoples of Early North America.* Prentice Hall (1992). Account of interaction between Native Americans, Africans, and whites during colonial times.

Weber, David J. *The Spanish Frontier in North America.* Yale University Press (1992). Overview of Spanish exploration and colonization in North America.

PORTFOLIO ASSESSMENT

1. *Proposals should demonstrate an understanding of trade routes and networks; the exchange of products and resources; and the role of trade in the expansion, economic development, and international politics of the time period.*

2. *Wall displays should show the following: Catholic and Quaker arguments against the enslavement of Native Americans and Africans, respectively, and an understanding of the role Las Casas, Banneker, or others played in opposing injustices such as the* encomienda *system or slavery.*

3. *Brochures and exhibits should show an understanding of specific exchanges between the cultures that have influenced the Americas, including Native American, African, Hispanic, Asian, and European.*

UNIT OVERVIEW

When Britain sought to gain greater control over the colonies, the colonists objected. Tensions grew until they exploded into revolt and war. Years of struggle ended in 1781, and the colonies won independence. Prominent Americans soon devised a Constitution that established a strong central government while reserving powers for the states. The nation grew and prospered as it acquired new territory. But the political scene proved turbulent as new political parties disagreed over domestic and foreign policy. Although the nation tried to stay clear of foreign entanglements, in 1812 it was again drawn into war with Britain.

CORE RESOURCES

- **American Almanac Poster** and **Worksheet 2**
- **Building Your Portfolio Worksheet 2**
  You may wish to preview the Unit 2 Review and Building Your Portfolio performance assessment activities on p. 221.

Using the American Almanac Posters

Begin the unit by displaying the American Almanac Poster and discussing entries with students. In addition to the worksheet, the annotations that follow provide additional information about the entries and suggest questions and activities.

Then, as students study the unit, have them work in small groups to create their own almanacs—using the same six headings—on pieces of butcher paper. At the end of the unit, call on groups to display and discuss their almanacs.

Chapter 4
INDEPENDENCE!
1763–1783

Chapter 5
FROM CONFEDERATION TO FEDERAL UNION
1776–1789

Note that the graph shows life expectancy *at birth* and reflects the impact of child mortality. People who reached age 21 in the late 1700s could expect to live about 40 more years.

■■ Have students check a current almanac to determine life expectancy in the U.S. today.

Inventing America

In 1754 Banneker constructed the first clock made entirely in America—even though he had never seen a working clock before. It ran accurately for 20 years.

■■ Have students suggest why Banneker's inventions and innovations were of importance to everyday life in 18th-century America.

The Student Life

Note that teaching methods focused on memorizing material rather than on understanding it. The chief technique of learning and testing—recitation aloud—often transformed classrooms into noisy, chaotic places.

■■ Have students compare today's teaching methods with those of the late 1700s.

Town and Country

Inform students that in the years around 1800, most Americans wore homemade clothes fashioned from home-produced linen or wool. Wealthy plantation owners and city-dwellers, however, wore tailor-made clothes of fine linen, woolen broadcloth, silk, or cotton.

■■ Ask students what materials are used to make the clothes they wear today.

Symbols of a New Nation

E Pluribus Unum was officially adopted by Congress as the motto of the U.S. in 1781.

■■ Have students discuss why *E Pluribus Unum* was an appropriate motto for the new nation.

At Your Leisure

Point out that wrestling matches commonly were staged at the end of social gatherings such as barn-raisings and local militia meetings.

■■ Have students identify the leisure activities that Americans enjoy today.

UNIT 2

Creating a Nation

1763–1815

Tensions between Britain and its North American colonies exploded into revolt and war, and in 1781 the colonies won their independence. A Constitution established a strong central government, while reserving powers for the states. The new nation prospered and grew. But the political scene proved turbulent as political parties disagreed over domestic and foreign policy. Although the nation tried to avoid foreign entanglements, it was drawn into war with Britain in 1812.

◀ Assembly Room, Independence Hall

Chapter 6

A STRONG START FOR THE NATION 1789–1815

THE AMERICAN NATION
VIDEODISC PROGRAM
A variety of still images, short
videos, and activities are available for you
to use as you teach this chapter. See
Correlation to *The American Nation*
Videodisc Program for barcode correlations
and suggestions for using the program.

INDEPENDENCE!

1763–1783

Chapter Overview

Britain had paid in blood and treasure to expand its great empire, but victory created a new set of problems. To pay its war debts and cover the costs of maintaining its expanded empire, Britain imposed new taxes and restrictive laws on the American colonies. Over the years, however, American colonists had developed a way of life increasingly independent of Britain, and they considered the taxes and laws unjust. Tensions between the colonies and Britain grew, eventually exploding into war. Years of bitter fighting ended in 1781, and the colonists were officially granted their independence under the Treaty of Paris in 1783.

Chapter Planning Guide

CHAPTER 4	CORE RESOURCE BOOKLETS	AUDIOVISUAL RESOURCES	PROGRAM RESOURCES
INTRODUCTION pp. 102–103	■ Literature Worksheet 4 ■ Building Your Portfolio Worksheet 2		
TEACHING THE CHAPTER pp. 104–133	■ Graphic Organizer 4 ■ Social Studies Skills Worksheet 4 ■ Geography Worksheet 4 ■ Outline Maps 8, 9	■ *The American Nation Videodisc: Patriotism and Propaganda: The Boston Massacre* ■ Linking Geography and History Transparencies and Worksheets 8, 9 ■ Everyday Life in America Transparency and Worksheet 4	■ *Eyewitnesses and Others,* Volume 1: Readings 20, 21, 22, 23, 24, 25, 26 ■ Art in American History Transparencies and Worksheets 3, 6
REVIEW AND ASSESSMENT pp. 134–135	■ Chapter 4 Daily Quizzes ■ Review Worksheet 4 ■ Chapter 4 Tests ■ Alternative Assessment Forms		■ Test Generator

Additional Resources

BOOKS FOR TEACHERS

Berlin, Ira, and Ronald Hoffman, eds. *Slavery and Freedom in the Age of the American Revolution.* University of Illinois Press, 1986. Shows effects of Revolution on African Americans.

Middlekauff, Robert. *The Glorious Cause.* Oxford University Press, 1985. Dramatic account of crucial Revolution events.

Norton, Mary Beth. *Liberty's Daughters: The Revolutionary Experience of American Women.* Scott Foresman, 1987. Discusses women in the Revolution.

BOOKS FOR STUDENTS

*Marrin, Albert. *The War for Independence.* Atheneum, 1988. Retells Revolution events through eyes of historical characters.

Wheeler, Richard. *Voices of 1776: The Story of the American Revolution in the Words of Those Who Were There.* Meridian, 1991. Eyewitness accounts of the Revolution.

* for students reading below grade level

MULTIMEDIA MATERIALS

The American Revolution: Two Views. Video, 60 min. Educational Audio Visual, Inc. Examines the Revolution from colonial and British viewpoints.

Women in the Revolution: Legend and Reality, 20 min. Multi-Media Productions/SSSS. Examines the roles of women in the Revolution.

Making a Revolution. Video, 52 min. BBC/Time-Life. Traces how the diverse colonies drew together to fight for freedom.

THEMES IN AMERICAN HISTORY

USE WITH PAGES 102–103

Listed on the right are the themes emphasized in Chapter 4. The questions in boldface type stimulate critical thinking and provide students with an opportunity to discuss the themes within a broadened context. The questions also appear in the pupil's edition on p. 102.

■ ECONOMIC DEVELOPMENT

How might the economic interests of one country conflict with those of another? Students should note that countries try to establish economic policies—tariffs, duties, and other taxes; strategies for resource use; import and export limits; etc.—that benefit their own economic development. These policies often run counter to the economic needs and desires of their trading partners. Students might draw specific examples from U.S. trade relations with Japan, Latin America, or Canada.

■ DEMOCRATIC VALUES

In a democracy, when are individuals and groups justified in protesting taxes or specific laws? Students might note that, in a democracy, elected officials are meant to serve the will of the people. When citizens believe that the government is implementing policies that are not in the best interests of the people, they have the right to make their objections heard.

What kinds of actions are proper for people to take? Students might debate the limits of acceptable protest, considering factors such as conflicting interests, legal restraints, basic rights, and the abuse of government power.

■ GLOBAL RELATIONS

Do powerful nations have any obligations toward less-powerful nations? If so, what kinds of obligations? Students might argue that powerful nations have an obligation to assist less-powerful nations in achieving economic and political progress. They might also argue, however, that powerful nations often assist less-powerful nations out of self-interest, sometimes to the detriment of the less-powerful nations.

CHAPTER STRATEGIES FOR MEETING INDIVIDUAL NEEDS

LIMITED ENGLISH PROFICIENT LEARNERS

After they have read the chapter, have pairs of students create illustrated time lines of the chapter's major events. Students should write brief captions for each entry and present their work to the class.

TACTILE/KINESTHETIC LEARNERS

Have students work in small groups to sketch key events and scenes of the Revolutionary War. Call on volunteers to use their sketches for a "slide show" presentation on the Revolution.

LEARNERS HAVING DIFFICULTY

As students study the chapter, have them make an annotated outline using chapter, section, and subsection titles as heads.

AUDITORY LEARNERS

Have small groups of students select short readings from titles listed in Books for Students on p. 101A. One group member should read the selection to the class. Other members should explain the reading's significance.

VISUAL LEARNERS

Have students skim the chapter and locate the visual they think best illustrates the chapter title: Independence! Call on students to explain their choices to the class.

GIFTED LEARNERS

Have students write and deliver a speech by either a colonist in favor of independence or a British official justifying the government's colonial policies.

USING THE CHAPTER FOCUS

■ UNDERSTANDING THE MAIN IDEA

Call on a volunteer to read the Understanding the Main Idea paragraph aloud. Then have students jot down in their notebooks information on revolutions, political upheavals, or human rights issues that have recently appeared in the media. As students read the chapter, have them look for comparisons between these events and the American Revolution.

★⚡ THEMES

Have students work individually or in small groups to answer the questions under Themes. Save students' responses so that they can compare them with their responses after studying the chapter. (See p. 101B for suggested answers.)

■ THE TIME LINE

Point out that a Peruvian rebellion against Spanish rule from 1780 to 1782 heightened British fears of a worldwide challenge to colonial rule. Then have students list the time-line entries in their notebooks. As they read the chapter, have students write under each entry a sentence explaining the part that incident played in the struggle for American independence. Upon completion of the chapter, ask for volunteers to read their sentences to the class.

CORE RESOURCES

• **Graphic Organizer 4**
• **Literature Worksheet 4**
• **Outline Maps 8, 9**
• **Building Your Portfolio Worksheet 2**

ABOUT THE ILLUSTRATION

This detail from the painting *The Battle of Princeton* by William Mercer illustrates the Americans' ambush of British troops on January 3, 1776. In Trenton, hearing the sounds of the cannons, British commander General Charles Cornwallis realized that George Washington had outsmarted him. Ask students to locate the site of the Battle of Princeton on the map on p. 129 and to tell who finally won the battle.

Chapter 4

1763–1783

INDEPENDENCE!

▼ FOCUS

UNDERSTANDING THE MAIN IDEA

Colonial conflicts with the British eventually erupted into war. But the American Revolution was more than a war for independence. It established a new relationship between government and the governed and a new definition of human rights.

★⚡ THEMES

■ **ECONOMIC DEVELOPMENT** How might the economic interests of one country conflict with those of another?

■ **DEMOCRATIC VALUES** In a democracy, when are individuals and groups justified in protesting taxes or specific laws? What kinds of actions are proper for people to take?

■ **GLOBAL RELATIONS** Do powerful nations have any obligations toward less-powerful nations? If so, what kinds of obligations?

1763	1765	1770	1775	1776	1781	1783
Pontiac's Rebellion crushed.	Stamp Act enacted.	Boston Massacre angers colonists.	Revolutionary War begins.	Declaration of Independence issued.	British surrender at Yorktown.	Treaty of Paris signed.

LINK TO THE PAST

Ask students to list the results of the French and Indian War. Have students speculate on what problems might develop between Britain and the colonies as a consequence of these results. Have students check the accuracy of their speculations as they work through the chapter.

LINK TO THE PAST

Through their victory in the French and Indian War, the British gained control of most of North America east of the Mississippi River. They now faced the tasks of governing, protecting, and financing their expanded empire.

HISTORICAL SIDELIGHTS

Vergennes's Prediction
Vergennes played a significant role in making his prophecy about the American colonies come true. He was instrumental in persuading France's King Louis XVI to support the Americans in their revolution.

With the signing of the Treaty of Paris in 1763, Great Britain's future looked bright. Many people in Great Britain and elsewhere realized, however, that the British Empire faced new challenges. One of these observers, a French government official named Charles Gravier (grawv-yay) Comte de Vergennes (ver-ZHEN), believed that Great Britain's North American colonies would prove especially troublesome.

Mindful that France had lost its colonial claim in North America, Vergennes predicted a similar fate for Great Britain. "The American colonies stand no longer in need of England's protection," he said. "England," he continued, "will call on them to help contribute toward supporting the burden they have helped to bring on her, and they will answer by striking off all dependence."

Vergennes's prophecy would prove accurate. Thirteen years after his prediction, the British colonies along the Atlantic seaboard declared independence—and fought to win it.

Battle of Princeton

Continental soldier

FOCUS OBJECTIVES

- Explain why the Crown issued the Proclamation of 1763.

- Determine why Parliament passed the Sugar Act and the Stamp Act.

- Examine why and how the colonists protested British taxes.

PRIMARY SOURCE

Description of Change: excerpted
Rationale: excerpted to focus on main idea

VOICES IN HISTORY

The Delaware leader Pachgantschilhilas encouraged other Native Americans to end their cooperation with whites who had settled in the Ohio Valley: "I admit that there are good white men, but they bear no proportion to the bad; the bad must be the strongest, for they rule. . . . They enslave those who are not of their color. . . . They would make slaves of us if they could, but as they cannot do it, they kill us!"

CORE RESOURCES

- **Section 1 Daily Quiz**

AV **RESOURCES**

- **Linking Geography and History Transparency** and **Worksheet 8**

104

Following is a list of the significant people and terms in this section. You may wish to use this list as a section preview.

People
- Samuel Adams

Terms
- Pontiac's Rebellion

- Proclamation of 1763
- Sugar Act
- duty
- Stamp Act
- nonimportation agreements
- Sons of Liberty
- Stamp Act Congress
- Declaratory Act

Section 1

THE SEEDS OF UNREST

FOCUS

- **Why did the Crown issue the Proclamation of 1763?**
- **Why did Parliament pass the Sugar Act and the Stamp Act?**
- **Why and how did the colonists protest British taxes?**

Victory in the French and Indian War left Great Britain with a huge debt and more territory to govern and defend. British leaders expected the American colonists to help pay for administering this expanded empire. The colonists disagreed. With the French and Indian War over, the freedom many colonists sought to defend was their own. This attitude placed the colonies on a collision course with their protector.

Protests took many forms.

GOVERNING THE NEW TERRITORIES

The Treaty of Paris of 1763 forced the French to give up their North American empire. With the stroke of a pen, the British gained control of Spanish Florida, Canada, and the land between the Appalachian Mountains and the Mississippi River. It was rich land. Indian agent and trader George Croghan, who traveled through the western territory in 1765, noted in his diary that a "good hunter, without much fatigue to himself, could here daily

▲ Settlers and traders to the Ohio Valley saw many colorful and unusual species of flora, such as this wild honeysuckle painted by naturalist artist Edwin Whitefield.

supply one hundred men with meat." Croghan went on to describe the variety of the terrain:

66 We set out very early in the morning and marched through a high country, extremely well timbered, for three hours. . . . The remainder of this day we traveled through fine rich bottoms, overgrown with reeds, which make the best pasture in the world. 99

Such glowing reports drew pioneer farmers and speculators to the region. Ignoring Native American claims to the land, they demanded that the territory be opened for settlement. But British officials, fearing conflicts between pioneers and Native Americans, opposed this request.

Native American resistance. There was reason for concern. Following the war, the British had limited the amount of ammunition and rum available for trade with Native Americans. They had also abandoned the French practice of presenting annual gifts to the Indians. These changes angered many Native Americans who considered the trade goods

Point out that just as the U.S. is a world power today, Great Britain was a leading power in the mid-18th century. Then ask students to compare and contrast the way in which an 18th-century world power was expected to behave toward subject peoples with the behavior that is expected today.

Teaching the Section

THE PROCLAMATION OF 1763

Organize students into five groups and assign each group one of the following characters: a fur trader, a settler on the western frontier, a Native American in the west, a colonial governor, and a British official. Have each group prepare and deliver to the class a statement stating their character's position on the Proclamation of 1763.

---

and the presents fair payment for allowing colonists onto their lands. George Croghan warned that the Indians who "had great expectations of being very generally supplied by us" might wage war.

Native Americans' resentment grew as settlers poured into the western lands. Many Indian tribes had already had their traditional ways of life disrupted by European trade. Now they were in danger of losing their lands as well. Alarmed, Neolin, known as the Delaware Prophet, traveled among western tribes, appealing for a return to ancient practices. He denounced the use of European goods and customs, urging his audiences to drive out the settlers. "They are my enemies," he said of the British. "They are your brothers' enemies."

Pontiac, an Ottawa chief, acted upon Neolin's message. He called on the Delawares, Senecas, Shawnees, Wyandots, Ojibways, and other Indians to unite and "exterminate from our lands this nation which seeks only to destroy us." For most of 1763 war raged all along the frontier. Pontiac's forces killed some 2,000 settlers and destroyed many British forts.

Pontiac's Rebellion, however, ended when the Indians were unable to take Fort Detroit and Fort Pitt. For months they had besieged the forts. With winter approaching and ammunition in short supply, Pontiac's men began to doubt that victory was possible. Faced with disheartened warriors and no hope of French aid, Pontiac called off the siege.

The Proclamation of 1763. Pontiac's Rebellion and other Indian uprisings convinced British authorities that they could not effectively protect British settlers on the frontier. As a result, Great Britain issued the **Proclamation of 1763**, barring settlement west of the Appalachian Mountains. The law also required every fur trader to obtain royal permission before entering the territory.

The British hoped that separating settlers and Native Americans would end fighting on the frontier. But the proclamation was difficult to enforce. Land-hungry colonists resented the measure, and colonial governors, often land speculators themselves, did little to enforce it. Thus settlers continued to stream into the territory.

■■ **In the wake of Pontiac's Rebellion, the Crown issued the Proclamation of 1763 in hopes of bringing peace to the frontier.**

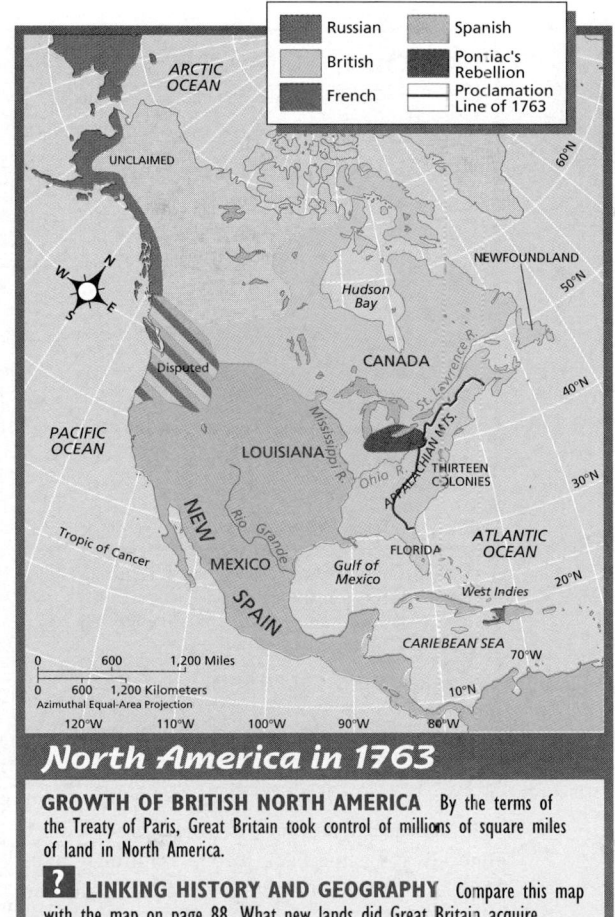

North America in 1763

GROWTH OF BRITISH NORTH AMERICA By the terms of the Treaty of Paris, Great Britain took control of millions of square miles of land in North America.

? **LINKING HISTORY AND GEOGRAPHY** Compare this map with the map on page 88. What new lands did Great Britain acquire between 1754 and 1763?

---

*F*INANCING THE EMPIRE

The royal proclamation was not the only British policy the colonists resented. They were also angered by Parliament's efforts to make them pay part of the costs of "protecting and securing" the frontier. Despite colonial protests, the government believed its position was justified. Thomas Whately stated the Crown's position in his pamphlet *Considerations on This Trade and Finances of the Kingdom:*

66 We are not yet recovered from a War undertaken . . . for their Protection . . . and . . . no Time was ever so seasonable [appropriate] for claiming their Assistance. The Distribution is too unequal, of Benefits only to the colonies, and of all the Burthens [burdens] upon the Mother Country. 99

HISTORICAL SIDELIGHTS
Germ Warfare?
A smallpox epidemic broke out among Native Americans and contributed to the failure of Pontiac's Rebellion. The epidemic may have been caused by the British giving the Native Americans blankets that had been used by smallpox victims.

Map Caption Answer
all former French and Spanish territory between the Appalachian Mountains and the Mississippi River; acquired disputed claim to formerly unclaimed territory in the far Northwest

PRIMARY SOURCE
Description of Change: excerpted and bracketed
Rationale: excerpted to focus on main idea; bracketed to clarify meaning

■■ Have students identify recent instances in which government officials have used similar arguments to justify a new policy.

𝒯eaching the 𝒮ection

SUGAR AND STAMP ACTS

Invite students to imagine that they are members of the British Parliament at the end of the French and Indian War. Ask them to study the graph on p. 106 and then to write a brief speech explaining why they intend to pass the Sugar Act and the Stamp Act. Students may wish to include their speeches in their portfolios.

THE COLONISTS PROTEST

Ask students to write protest statements addressed to Parliament, detailing the colonists' opposition to the Stamp Act. Statements should include the actions colonists will take if the act is not repealed. Call on students to read their protest statements to the class. Students may wish to include their statements in their portfolios.

Graph Caption Answer
about 4.5 million pounds

PRIMARY SOURCE
Description of Change: excerpted
Rationale: excerpted to focus on main idea

HISTORICAL SIDELIGHTS
Colonial Protests
The colonists' protests against British laws gave women a level of involvement in politics that few had previously known. In particular, women held the key to the success or failure of embargoes or boycotts of British goods. For many women, household management became a political act. Spinning thread and yarn, weaving their own cloth, and "buying American" gave women a way to defy British authority in the course of their daily activities.

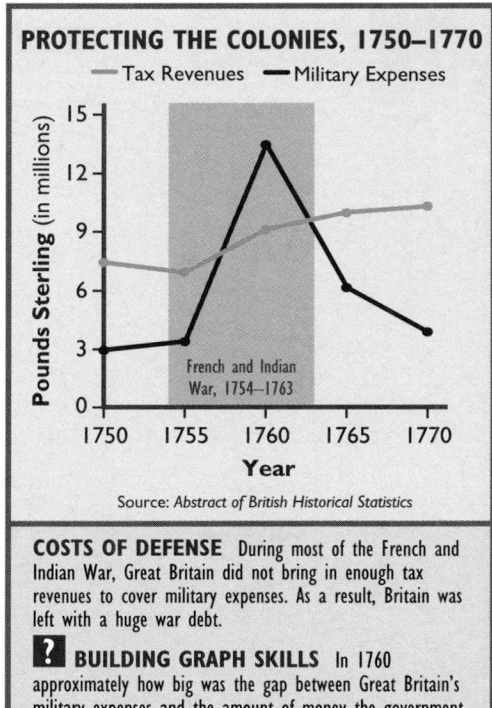

PROTECTING THE COLONIES, 1750–1770

— Tax Revenues ▬ Military Expenses

(Y-axis: Pounds Sterling (in millions), 0, 3, 6, 9, 12, 15)
(X-axis: Year, 1750, 1755, 1760, 1765, 1770)
French and Indian War, 1754–1763

Source: *Abstract of British Historical Statistics*

COSTS OF DEFENSE During most of the French and Indian War, Great Britain did not bring in enough tax revenues to cover military expenses. As a result, Britain was left with a huge war debt.

? **BUILDING GRAPH SKILLS** In 1760 approximately how big was the gap between Great Britain's military expenses and the amount of money the government collected in taxes?

The question of how to raise this needed revenue always came back to one solution—taxes. Thus as a first step to increase revenue, Parliament passed the **Sugar Act** of 1764, which set a **duty**, or import tax, on foreign sugar, molasses, and several other items entering Britain's American colonies.

This was not the first time the British had imposed a duty on foreign molasses and sugar. In fact, the new law actually lowered the existing duty on molasses. It was, however, the first time officials seriously enforced such a law. Royal inspectors searched ships, warehouses, and homes for smuggled goods. The Crown's judges presided over courts without juries to hear smuggling cases.

For colonial merchants, shipowners, and rum distillers who profited from foreign trade and smuggling, the Sugar Act meant decreased business. They angrily protested the law.

Amid these protests, Parliament passed another revenue law, the **Stamp Act** of 1765. Far more sweeping than the Sugar Act, the Stamp Act levied a tax on printed matter of all kinds: newspapers, advertisements, playing cards, and legal documents. These materials had to be printed on stamped paper or have special stamps affixed to show the tax had been paid.

■■ **The British government passed the Sugar Act and the Stamp Act in an effort to raise revenue in the colonies.**

𝒞OLONIAL PROTESTS

British officials had expected the colonists to object to the Stamp Act, but they were not prepared for the level of outcry. In the past the colonists had accepted taxes levied by the colonial assemblies. In the colonists' eyes, however, this tax was different—it had been passed by Parliament, where the colonists had no direct representation.

Colonial assemblies met in protest. In May 1765 the Virginia House of Burgesses passed a series of resolutions condemning the act. The resolutions declared that

> ❝ the taxation of the people by themselves, or by persons chosen by themselves to represent them, . . . is the only security against a burdensome taxation, and the distinguishing characteristick of British freedom. ❞

British officials countered by claiming that the colonists had "virtual representation," since Parliament represented all British subjects. Many colonists rejected this argument and decided it was time to act.

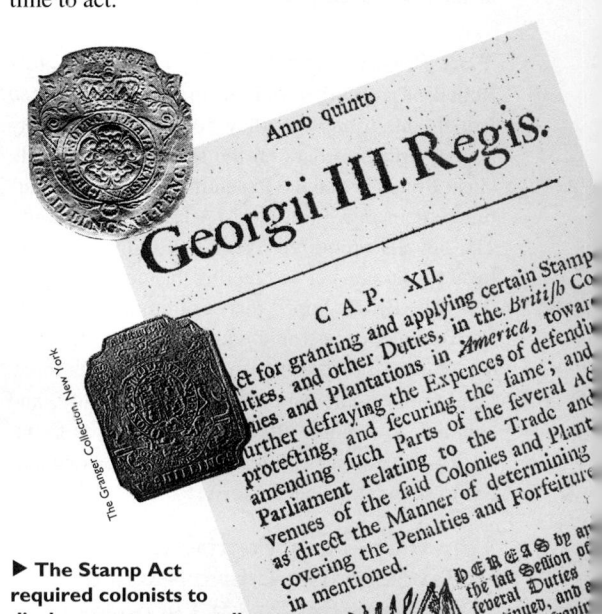

The Granger Collection, New York

▶ **The Stamp Act required colonists to display tax stamps on all printed documents.**

Practice

GUIDED PRACTICE

Have students suggest entries for a time line on events that caused increasing tensions between Britain and the colonies. Record suggestions on the chalkboard as they are offered. Have volunteers explain why each entry should be included on the time line.

INDEPENDENT PRACTICE

Have students design a handbill (containing a slogan and/or a sketch) that illustrates the colonial or British view of one of the time-line entries from the Guided Practice. Display handbills in the classroom. Students may wish to include their handbills in their portfolios.

Review and Assessment

REVIEW Have students construct a chart with the headings *Date, Purpose,* and *Results.* Ask students to make entries for the following: Proclamation of 1763, Sugar Act, Stamp Act, nonimportation agreements, Stamp Act Congress, Declaratory Act. Then assign the Section 1 Review on p. 108.

ASSESS Assign the **Section 1 Daily Quiz** in *Core Resources.* ▶

A call to action. Colonial merchants signed **nonimportation agreements**, promising not to buy or import British goods. Workers and artisans who opposed the Stamp Act took to the streets in demonstrations. Though most of these protests were peaceful, some did turn violent. One of the most violent demonstrations occurred in Boston on a hot August night in 1765. A mob led by shoemaker Ebenezer MacIntosh wrecked a building belonging to stamp agent Andrew Oliver and then beheaded an effigy—a crude likeness—of Oliver. Within two weeks the mob struck again, destroying court records and wrecking the house of the chief customs officer. They then turned their anger on the elegant mansion of Oliver's brother-in-law Thomas Hutchinson—the lieutenant governor of the colony. Throughout the colonies terrified stamp agents resigned their posts—rendering the Stamp Act almost impossible to enforce.

British officials singled out MacIntosh as the mob's leader. But they also suspected that members of the Boston Sons of Liberty were involved. The **Sons of Liberty** were secret committees made up of politicians, lawyers, merchants, and artisans, formed to protest the Stamp Act. The Sons of Liberty generally relied on petitions, public meetings, and pamphlets to rally support, but they were not above employing violence.

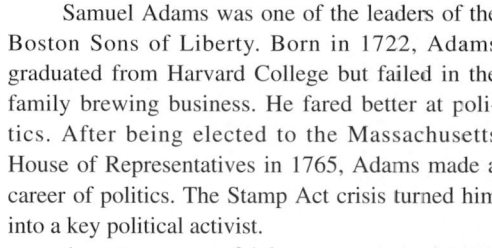

Samuel Adams was one of the leaders of the Boston Sons of Liberty. Born in 1722, Adams graduated from Harvard College but failed in the family brewing business. He fared better at politics. After being elected to the Massachusetts House of Representatives in 1765, Adams made a career of politics. The Stamp Act crisis turned him into a key political activist.

A contemporary of Adams described him as a man who "eats little, drinks little, sleeps little, thinks much, and is most decisive and indefatigable [tireless] in the pursuit of his objects." A master of propaganda, Adams often worked behind the scenes, staging demonstrations and working to control the public's perception of events. He started a club to influence local politics and wrote often for the Boston *Gazette.* Adams was particularly popular among Boston's less-prosperous artisans and shopkeepers. They responded enthusiastically to his charges that the British were stealing money from the colonists' pockets:

The Granger Collection, New York

Samuel Adams

> 66 We are told to be quiet when we see that very money which is torn from us by lawless force made use of still further to oppose us, to feed and pamper a set of infamous wretches [British officials and soldiers] who swarm like the locusts of Egypt. 99

REPEAL OF THE STAMP ACT

Led by Samuel Adams and others, the colonists made themselves heard in England. In October 1765, delegates from nine colonies gathered in New York City for the **Stamp Act Congress**. The delegates expressed the "warmest sentiments of

BIO GRAPHY

BIO GRAPHY PERSONALITIES IN HISTORY

Point out that a major reason for Samuel Adams's popularity among the less prosperous was that he passionately championed the right of all men—regardless of their financial status—to take part in the political process.

BUILDING VOCABULARY

The word *effigy* derives from the Latin *effigies,* meaning "a likeness or image." The practice of hanging or burning people in effigy as a symbolic act dates back to prehistory and is rooted in the belief (which continues in some societies today) that harm can be done to enemies by damaging images of them. In France during the 1600s and 1700s, it was customary to hang a criminal in effigy if the criminal could not be found.

PRIMARY SOURCE

Description of Change: excerpted and bracketed
Rationale: excerpted to focus on main idea; bracketed to clarify meaning

THE PENNSYLVANIA JOURNAL AND WEEKLY ADVERTISER.

◀ **Before the Stamp Act went into effect, the** *Pennsylvania Journal and Weekly Advertiser* **printed a skull and crossbones on its masthead in protest of the measure.**

Closure

Extension

RETEACH Organize students into small groups and assign each group a subsection of Section 1. Ask groups to prepare a summary of the main points of their subsection. Have groups share their summaries.

Call on volunteers to list key events between 1763 and 1766 that affected relations between Britain and the colonies. Then ask students to explain if and how, at this point, more serious conflict could have been avoided.

CREATE Encourage students to create a biographical dictionary of the American Revolution. Students should add to the dictionary as they work through the chapter.

RESEARCH Suggest that students research and report on the purpose, actions, and membership of the Sons of Liberty.

SECTION REVIEW ANSWERS

IDENTIFY
For significance, see the following pages:
Pontiac's Rebellion (p. 105)
Proclamation of 1763 (p. 105)
Sugar Act (p. 106)
duty (p. 106)
Stamp Act (p. 106)
nonimportation agreements (p. 107)
Sons of Liberty (p. 107)
Samuel Adams (p. 107)
Stamp Act Congress (p. 107)
Declaratory Act (p. 108)

1. *by issuing the Proclamation of 1763, which barred colonial settlement west of the Appalachians and required fur traders to obtain royal permission before entering the territory*
2. *to raise revenue for Great Britain; colonists protested by demonstrating and signing nonimportation agreements*
3. *Students should consider benefits of maintaining Native American customs versus adapting to European way of life.*
4. *Letters should note delegates' pledges of loyalty and protests against taxation without representation.*
5. *because of colonial protests and pressure from British merchants; because the right of Parliament to tax colonies was unresolved*

◄ This 1766 British cartoon celebrates the repeal of the Stamp Act. As members of the British government carry the dead act in a coffin, background ships show that trade with America is already beginning.

affection and duty to His Majesty's Person and Government" and pledged "all due subordination" to Parliament. Yet they also sought repeal of the Stamp Act and denied Parliament's right to tax the colonies. The congress marked an important step toward more unified resistance.

British merchants who profited from colonial trade joined in the protest. The nonimportation agreements had hurt their businesses. Fearing financial ruin, and wanting to keep the colonies "firmly attached to their mother country," they pressured Parliament to repeal the Stamp Act. Thus people on both sides of the Atlantic rejoiced when Parliament repealed the act in March 1766.

■■ **Colonists protested "taxation without representation" through petitions, nonimportation agreements, and demonstrations.**

Busy celebrating the Stamp Act's demise, most colonists ignored the passage of the **Declaratory Act** of 1766. This bold declaration asserted the "full power and authority" of Parliament "to make laws . . . to bind the colonies and people of *America*." The issue of whether Parliament had the right to tax the colonists remained unresolved.

SECTION 1 REVIEW

IDENTIFY and explain the significance of the following: Pontiac's Rebellion, Proclamation of 1763, Sugar Act, duty, Stamp Act, nonimportation agreements, Sons of Liberty, Samuel Adams, Stamp Act Congress, Declaratory Act.

1. **MAIN IDEA** How did the Crown attempt to bring peace to the frontier following Pontiac's Rebellion?
2. **MAIN IDEA** What was the purpose of the Sugar Act and the Stamp Act? How did the colonists react to these measures?
3. **USING HISTORICAL IMAGINATION** Imagine that you are a Native American living west of the Appalachian Mountains in the 1760s. Explain why you favor or oppose Neolin's message.
4. **WRITING TO EXPRESS A VIEWPOINT** You have just returned from the Stamp Act Congress. Write a letter to your colonial governor outlining the views of the congress's delegates.
5. **ANALYZING** Why did Parliament repeal the Stamp Act? Why did the repeal not solve the issue of taxation without representation?

Section 2

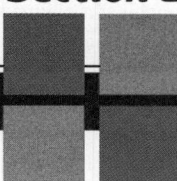

MOUNTING TENSIONS

FOCUS
■ **What events led to the Boston Massacre?**
■ **Why did the colonists stage the Boston Tea Party?**
■ **Why did the British pass the Intolerable Acts?**

*A*lthough colonial protests helped repeal the Stamp Act, they did not end Parliament's efforts to raise revenue in the colonies. When Parliament tried a new approach that did not involve direct taxes, the arguments used against the Stamp Act were also applied to these new measures. These protests were unsuccessful, setting in motion events that pushed the colonies to the brink of war.

British troops occupy Boston in 1768.

THE TOWNSHEND ACTS

The colonists had objected to the Stamp Act because Parliament had imposed it. It was, they argued, just one more example of Great Britain's meddling in colonial affairs. But Charles Townshend, Great Britain's finance minister, like many other government officials, never grasped this point. Townshend believed that the colonists had opposed the stamp tax because it was collected within the colonies. They would, he reasoned, be willing to accept a tax that would be collected at colonial ports. Parliament agreed, passing the **Townshend Acts** in 1767. The Townshend Acts placed import duties on such common items as tea, lead, glass, and dyes for paint. British customs officials revived the use of special search warrants called **writs of assistance** to enforce the law. Unlike today's search warrants, which must state the exact articles sought and the specific

▶ **Charles Townshend was responsible for passage of the Townshend Acts in 1767.**

places to be searched, writs of assistance were general warrants. Armed with a writ, a customs officer could search any vessel, warehouse, or home on the mere suspicion that it contained smuggled goods.

The writs of assistance aroused powerful opposition, and many colonial courts refused to issue them. Although the colonists accepted Great Britain's right to regulate colonial trade, they strongly objected to duties intended strictly to raise money. The Crown, troubled by renewed protests, stationed additional soldiers in the colonies. The New York assembly responded by refusing to vote money to quarter, or house and supply, these troops as the **Quartering Act** of 1765 required. The British government promptly suspended the assembly.

But the real center of protest was Boston. In February 1768 the Massachusetts legislature drafted a letter attacking taxation without representation and sent it to the other colonial assemblies for endorsement. The British government responded by dissolving the Massachusetts assembly. This only served to fuel protests and a new round of nonimportation

The Granger Collection, New York

MOTIVATING:
STUDENT EXPERIENCES

Ask students what actions they might take to protest a school rule that they regard as unfair, and write their suggestions on the chalkboard. As students study this section, have them compare these suggested actions with those used by colonists to protest British policies.

Teaching the Section

THE BOSTON MASSACRE

Create a time line on the chalkboard of the events leading to the Boston Massacre, asking how each contributed to tensions in Boston. Then organize the class into "juries" to consider the time line as evidence in the trial of soldiers accused in the shooting. After the juries deliberate, ask each for its verdict. Encourage other students to poll jury members about their decision.

TEA PARTY AND
INTOLERABLE ACTS

Organize students into groups of five. Have half the groups prepare and deliver speeches designed to persuade the Boston Sons of Liberty to stage the Boston Tea Party. Speeches should emphasize why the action is necessary and why the possible consequences are worth the risk. Have the other groups prepare and deliver speeches in Parliament in favor of the Intolerable Acts, citing reasons they should be passed.

HISTORICAL
SIDELIGHTS

The Boston Massacre

The immediate cause of the Boston Massacre continues to be unclear. Boston newspapers blamed British soldiers for parading in the streets and abusing citizens in order to provoke a confrontation. The mayor of Boston charged that it was a riot planned by leaders of the resistance. Some historians believe, however, that the incident was sparked by friction between journeymen ropemakers and "moonlighting" British soldiers who sought second jobs.

PRIMARY SOURCE

Description of Change: excerpted
Rationale: excerpted to focus on main idea

THE AMERICAN NATION
VIDEODISC PROGRAM

Patriotism and Propaganda: The Boston Massacre

```
1A    38399    3:24
```

agreements. A Massachusetts woman wrote that her friends would not touch "a Drop of Tea." Other women, rather than buy British cloth, held spinning parties to make their own. Angry demonstrators boarded and smashed British ships, attacked customs officials, and tarred and feathered anyone who informed on smugglers.

THE BOSTON MASSACRE

In 1768 General Thomas Gage dispatched British troops to Boston to quiet the protests and enforce the writs of assistance. But tensions exploded into one violent confrontation after another. On the evening of March 5, 1770, an angry crowd gathered outside a customs house. Some 50 or 60 colonists faced a small group of British soldiers. The crowd yelled insults and began throwing snowballs, rocks, oyster shells, and pieces of coal at the soldiers. Then, according to John Adams, "the motley mob of saucy boys, negroes, mulattoes, . . . and outlandish jacktars [sailors]" pressed so hard against the soldiers that there was no room to move. One soldier either slipped or was knocked down. His gun discharged, and the others opened fire on the crowd. Three colonists, including Crispus Attucks—a sailor and an escaped slave of African and Native American ancestry—lay dead. Two others died later.

News of the clash stunned the colonists. Lieutenant Governor Thomas Hutchinson claimed that "the people of Boston are run mad." Sam Adams and the Sons of Liberty promptly dubbed the incident the **Boston Massacre** and denounced British aggression. The victims received elaborate funerals and inspired poems and songs of patriotic resistance.

Months later the British soldiers were tried for murder. Josiah Quincy and John Adams—Sam's cousin—agreed to defend them. Neither man sympathized with the British, but both insisted on the soldiers' right to a fair trial. As John Adams later wrote:

> 66 Counsel ought to be the very last thing that an accused person should want [lack] in a free country; . . . and . . . persons whose lives were at stake ought to have the counsel they prefer. 99

In the end, two soldiers were convicted of a lesser charge. They were branded on their thumbs and released.

■ **Mounting tensions between the colonists and the British soldiers stationed in Boston to enforce the Townshend Acts sparked the Boston Massacre.**

▲ Crispus Attucks

◀ Boston silversmith Paul Revere engraved and printed *The Boston Massacre*, which depicts the British as the aggressors.

*P*ractice

GUIDED PRACTICE

Organize the class into two groups. Ask the first group to identify and justify the major British colonial policies between 1767 and 1774. As each policy is offered, ask the other group to offer the colonists' response.

INDEPENDENT PRACTICE

Suggest that students write a newspaper editorial about one of the British policies addressed in Guided Practice. Editorials should express either a British or a colonial point of view toward the policy. Students may wish to include their editorials in their portfolios.

*R*eview *and* *A*ssessment

REVIEW Invite students to imagine that they are colonists in 1774 and to make a list of complaints about British actions and policies. Then assign the Section 2 Review on p. 112.

■■ Ask students who have written letters to the editor to discuss the experience.

ASSESS Assign the **Section 2 Daily Quiz** in *Core Resources*.

▶

CONTINUING UNREST

When Frederick, Lord North became Great Britain's prime minister in 1770, he hoped to pacify the rebellious colonies by a partial repeal of the Townshend Acts. Parliament consented and also allowed the Quartering Act to expire. But the British retained a small duty on tea. As the king explained, there must "always be one tax to keep up the right."

The repeal quieted the general unrest, but the calm was short-lived. In 1772 the Crown announced that it—not the colonial legislature—would pay the salaries of Massachusetts' governor and judges. The Crown reasoned that if these officials did not depend on the legislature for their pay, they might more readily ignore colonial demands.

Bostonians, led by Sam Adams, challenged this latest threat. They created a 21-member **Committee of Correspondence** charged with keeping the rest of the colony—and "the World"— informed about events. From 1772 to 1776, similar committees in Massachusetts and other colonies helped shape colonial opinion.

The Tea Act of 1773. Even the business of selling tea provoked a crisis. By 1773 the powerful British East India Company was almost bankrupt. To save the ailing company, Parliament passed the **Tea Act** of 1773. The law excused the company from paying certain duties and permitted it to bypass the wholesalers and sell tea directly to American agents. As a result the price of tea in the colonies was lower than ever before.

Most of the colonists, however, opposed the Tea Act and refused to buy the tea. What concerned many of them was the possible monopoly of the tea trade by the East India Company. American wholesalers and merchants feared that other British companies would secure similar privileges from Parliament and force them out of business.

The Sons of Liberty in Philadelphia and New York threatened anyone who imported tea. But the most famous protest against the Tea Act occurred in Massachusetts. On December 16, 1773, after the governor refused demands to send three shiploads of tea back to England, colonists held a mass meeting at Boston's Old South Church. Later that night, a well-organized group of colonists "dressed in an Indian manner" boarded the tea ships anchored in Boston Harbor and

dumped 90,000 pounds of tea into the water. As one of the participants later remembered:

❝ In about three hours from the time we went on board, we had thus broken and thrown overboard every tea chest to be found. . . . We were surrounded by British armed ships, but no attempt was made to resist us. ❞

News of the **Boston Tea Party** drew widespread attention at home and abroad. Many colonists cheered the tea's destruction; others were shocked by such disregard for property rights.

■■ **Bostonians staged the Boston Tea Party to protest the Tea Act.**

The Intolerable Acts of 1774. British officials were furious. Parliament responded by passing the Coercive Acts, four laws designed to punish Boston and the rest of Massachusetts and to strengthen British control over all of the colonies. The colonists called the laws the **Intolerable Acts**.

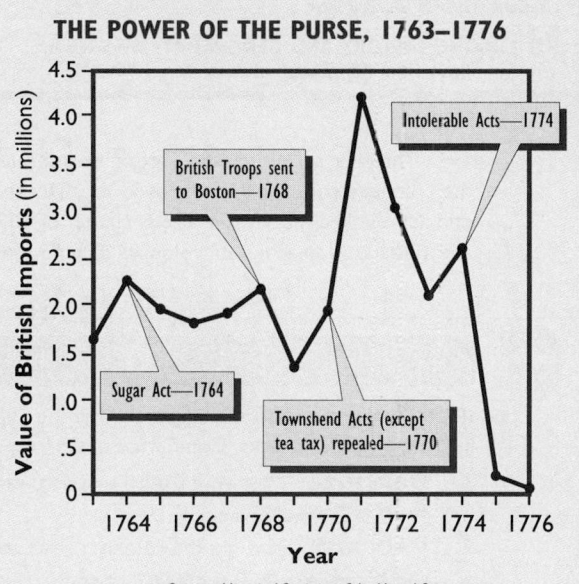

THE POWER OF THE PURSE, 1763–1776

Source: *Historical Statistics of the United States*

EFFECT OF PROTESTS Colonists reacted to British policies such as the Sugar and Stamp acts by refusing to import British goods. Parliament's repeal of the Townshend Acts resulted in a brief upsurge in imports. But soon British actions sparked new protests.

❓ **BUILDING GRAPH SKILLS** Between which two years did British imports experience the greatest drop?

PRIMARY SOURCE
Description of Change: excerpted
Rationale: excerpted to focus on main idea

MAKING CONNECTIONS
Sociology
The Revolution was reflected in colonial religious life. Congregational and Presbyterian ministers were outspoken advocates of the dissidents' position and, according to Loyalists, preached sedition. Episcopalian ministers, on the other hand, were among the most active Loyalist supporters, writing numerous pamphlets for the Loyalist position.

VOICES IN HISTORY
Women were highly visible in colonial resistance to British authority. Poems and essays written by women fostered patriotism and commitment to political principles. One poem encouraged women to: "Let the Daughters of Liberty, nobly arise,/ And tho' we've no Voice, but a negative here,/ The use of the Taxables, let us forbear./ Stand firmly resolved and bid Grenville to see/ That rather than Freedom, we'll part with our Tea."

Graph Caption Answer
1774–1775

Write this statement on the chalkboard: *Colonial opposition to British actions was justified.* Have volunteers list and evaluate the major arguments in support of and in opposition to the statement.

EVALUATE Have students report on the British East India Company's presence in India in the mid-1700s and evaluate British activities there.

RECOGNIZE Point out the bias inherent in names such as Sons of Liberty, Boston Massacre, and Intolerable Acts. Have interested students research and identify other ways that colonial dissidents attempted to shape public opinion.

RETEACH Organize students into groups of five. Give each group a large sheet of paper on which the outline of a flowchart of events titled *British Actions and Colonial Responses, 1767–1774* is drawn. Group members should fill in the chart, each one taking a turn round-robin style. Encourage students to help each other finish the chart.

Map Caption Answer
Massachusetts, Connecticut, and Virginia; land previously claimed by them was now part of Quebec

SECTION REVIEW ANSWERS

IDENTIFY

For significance, see the following pages:
Townshend Acts (p. 109)
writs of assistance (p. 109)
Quartering Act (p. 109)
Crispus Attucks (p. 110)
Boston Massacre (p. 110)
Committee of Correspondence (p. 111)
Tea Act (p. 111)
Boston Tea Party (p. 111)
Intolerable Acts (p. 111)
Quebec Act (p. 112)

1. *to quiet colonial protests and to enforce the Townshend Acts; increased tensions between colonists and British soldiers*
2. *Most colonists refused to buy tea; Bostonians staged the Boston Tea Party.*
3. *Time lines should include Townshend Acts and partial repeal, Quartering Act, committees of correspondence, Tea Act, Boston Tea Party.*
4. *Boston Massacre—should consider number of colonists killed by British; Boston Tea Party—should consider colonial fears of tea monopoly and effects of protests*
5. *deepened hostility toward the Crown and led to emergence of unique identity*

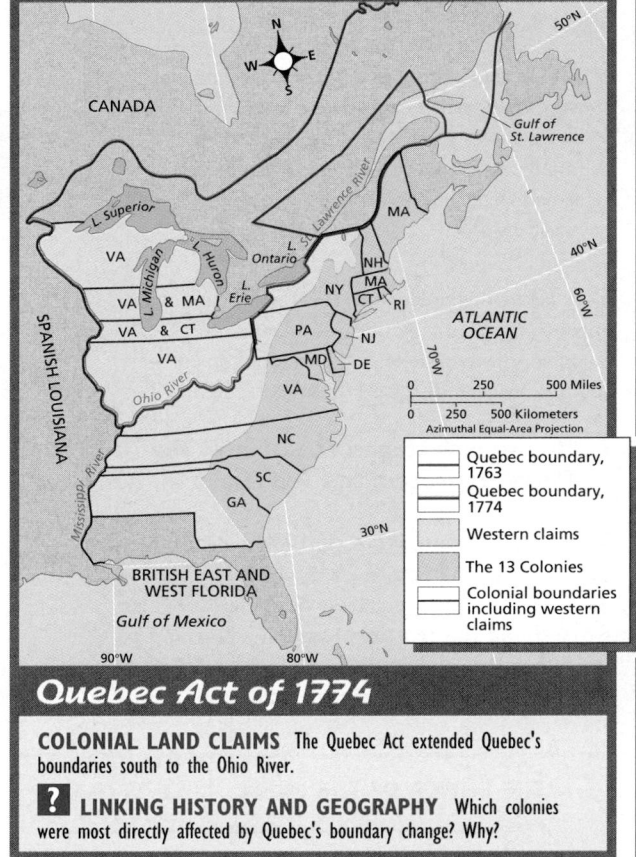

Quebec Act of 1774

COLONIAL LAND CLAIMS The Quebec Act extended Quebec's boundaries south to the Ohio River.

? **LINKING HISTORY AND GEOGRAPHY** Which colonies were most directly affected by Quebec's boundary change? Why?

The first act closed the port of Boston until the colonists paid for the destroyed tea. The second act revoked the Massachusetts charter of 1691 and forbade Massachusetts colonists to hold town meetings. The third act allowed royal officials charged with crimes related to their duties to be tried in England. Many colonists assumed the soldiers would be lightly punished or escape punishment entirely. The fourth law, a new Quartering Act, ordered local officials to provide food and housing, in private homes if necessary, for British soldiers stationed in the colonies.

■■ The British passed the Intolerable Acts to punish Massachusetts for the Boston Tea Party and to regain control over the colonies.

The Intolerable Acts deepened colonial hostility toward the Crown. Colonists everywhere responded with sympathy toward Massachusetts, while denouncing George III, the Parliament, and the threats to colonial liberty.

The **Quebec Act**, also passed in 1774, was not technically one of the Intolerable Acts, but it further inflamed colonial resentment. The law extended Quebec's boundaries south to the Ohio River, thus overriding the claims of Massachusetts, Connecticut, and Virginia to the western lands. It also granted full religious rights to French Roman Catholics, upsetting many Protestant colonists.

The movement toward colonial unity quickened after 1774. The colonists directed their anger no longer at specific British policies but at what they saw as a growing pattern of oppression. Among those who questioned loyalty to the Crown and Parliament, a new identity—not yet fully American, but no longer British—was emerging.

■ SECTION 2 REVIEW

IDENTIFY and explain the significance of the following: Townshend Acts, writs of assistance, Quartering Act, Crispus Attucks, Committee of Correspondence, Tea Act, Intolerable Acts, Quebec Act.

1. **MAIN IDEA** Why were British troops stationed in Boston? How did their presence provoke the Boston Massacre?
2. **MAIN IDEA** How did the colonists react to the Tea Act of 1773?
3. **IDENTIFYING CAUSE AND EFFECT** Create a time line showing the events leading up to the passage of the Intolerable Acts.
4. **WRITING TO DESCRIBE** Imagine that you are a member of the Sons of Liberty. In a letter to the colonists outside Massachusetts, write an account of the Boston Massacre or the Boston Tea Party that will rally them to oppose Britain.
5. **ASSESSING CONSEQUENCES** How did the Intolerable Acts and the Quebec Act help unify the colonies?

PREVIEW WORKSHOP

*Following is a list of the significant
people, places, and terms in this
section. You may wish to use this
list as a section preview.*

People
- George Washington

Places
- Lexington
- Concord

Terms
- First Continental Congress
- minutemen
- Second Continental
  Congress
- Battle of Bunker Hill
- Olive Branch Petition

FOCUS OBJECTIVES

- Describe how the
  First Continental
  Congress responded
  to British actions.

- Identify the actions
  taken by the Second
  Continental Congress.

Section 3

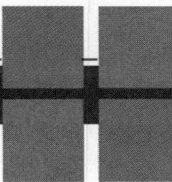

THE SHOT HEARD ROUND THE WORLD

FOCUS
- **How did the First Continental Congress respond to British actions?**
- **What actions did the Second Continental Congress take?**

*I*n 1774, delegates from 12 colonies met in
Philadelphia at the First Continental Congress
to voice their opposition to British actions. The delegates
demanded that the British government restore colonial
rights. But Great Britain ignored the demands. Delegates
called the Second Continental Congress in 1775 to plan
their next move. As the crisis deepened, war seemed inevitable.

Struggle at
Concord Bridge

THE FIRST CONTINENTAL CONGRESS

Between September 5 and October 26, 1774, representatives from every colony except Georgia attended the **First Continental Congress** in Philadelphia to discuss their grievances. Some delegates to the Congress—which was a convention, not a lawmaking body—wanted the colonies to remain part of the British Empire; others favored independence.

The delegates' efforts to compromise between these two positions were reflected in the Congress's final resolution, the Declaration of Resolves. While expressing loyalty to the British Crown, the declaration outlined the colonists' rights as British subjects and asserted the peoples' right to the "free and exclusive power of legislation in their several provincial legislatures." To put teeth in their demands, the colonists also called for a ban of all trade with Great Britain. The delegates pledged to meet again in May 1775 if their demands were not met.

▪▪ Delegates to the First Continental Congress demanded that the Crown restore colonial rights and called on the colonists not to buy British goods.

For George III the Continental Congress was the last straw. In November 1774 he wrote to Lord North: "The New England Governments are in a

◀ **George III, shown here
at age 33, reigned as king
of England for 60 years.**

CORE RESOURCES

- **Geography
  Worksheet 4**
- **Section 3 Daily Quiz**

Map Caption Answer
to avoid the British; to increase chances of success if one were captured

MAKING CONNECTIONS

Literature
"The shot heard round the world" comes from Ralph Waldo Emerson's poem "Concord Hymn": "By the rude bridge that arched the flood,/ Their flag to April's breeze unfurled,/ Here once the embattled farmers stood/ And fired the shot heard round the world." Written in 1836, the poem commemorates the completion of the Concord Monument honoring the minutemen.

VOICES IN HISTORY

As fighting began between Patriot and British forces, the Creeks proclaimed neutrality and sent the following message: "We thought that all English people were as one people but now we hear that they have a difference amongst themselves. It is our desire that they drop their disputes and not spoil one another; as all the red people are living in friendship with one another we desire that the white people will do the same."

State of Rebellion, blows must decide whether they are to be subject to this Country or independent." Acting on the king's wishes, Parliament ordered General Thomas Gage to put down the rebellion.

LEXINGTON AND CONCORD

In an effort to reassert royal authority, Gage decided to seize rebel supplies stored at Concord, Massachusetts. On April 18, 1775, under cover of darkness, British troops left Boston and rowed across the Charles River. But they were expected. Colonists waited on the far shore, watching for approaching troops. At first sight, Patriots Paul Revere and William Dawes—later joined by Samuel Prescott—galloped off shouting the alarm: "The British are coming!" Patriots throughout the countryside hurriedly headed off to confront the British.

At dawn on April 19, Captain John Parker and 70 **minutemen**—members of the militia who promised to be ready at a minute's notice—waited on the Lexington village green. When the British patrol arrived, its commander shouted, "Lay down your arms, you damned rebels, and disperse!" The colonists began departing, still holding their guns. Suddenly someone—each side accused the other—fired "the shot heard round the world." A barrage

| Revere's route | ⋯⋯▸ Prescott's route |
| - -▸ Dawes's route | ✹ Battle |

0 ——— 5 Miles
0 ——— 5 Kilometers
Transverse Mercator Projection

Concord · North Bridge · Lexington
Stopped by the British, only Prescott manages to reach Concord.
BRITISH FORCES · Charlestown
Cambridge · Charles River · Boston
N W E S · Boston Harbor

Lexington and Concord

FIRST BATTLES OF THE REVOLUTION In April 1775, on their way to seize rebel arms and ammunition at Concord, British forces clashed with colonial minutemen at Lexington. The American Revolution had begun.

❓ MOVEMENT As British troops began their march, Paul Revere and William Dawes rode off to alert the Patriots. They were later joined by Dr. Samuel Prescott. Why might Revere and Dawes have taken different routes?

of British gunfire followed. When the smoke cleared, 8 colonists lay dead, 10 others wounded.

The British marched on to Concord and destroyed the Patriot supplies. Then the British started back toward Boston. From behind stone walls minutemen fired steadily at the retreating British, whose traditional marching formations made them easy targets. The Patriots made an impressive showing, suffering fewer than 100 casualties in the day's fighting. British casualties were 273. A humbled British officer wrote: "Whoever looks upon them [the Patriots] as an irregular mob will find himself much mistaken."

THE SECOND CONTINENTAL CONGRESS

With the news of Lexington and Concord on everyone's lips, the **Second Continental Congress** opened in Philadelphia on May 10. Although radicals such as Samuel Adams pushed for an immediate declaration of independence, conservatives led by John Dickinson of Pennsylvania urged restraint. By June, however, the delegates had agreed to establish the Continental Army.

The delegates unanimously chose George Washington of Virginia to command the Continental Army. Though not a fiery orator or a profound political thinker, Washington inspired confidence. His careful judgment, dignity, and imposing stature enhanced his reputation. After meeting him Abigail Adams wrote to her husband: "The gentleman and soldier look agreeably blended in him. Modesty marks every line and feature of his face."

BIO GRAPHY Born February 22, 1732, George Washington first worked as a surveyor, later assuming control of the family's large Virginia plantation, Mount Vernon. Washington acquired military experience and a reputation for bravery while fighting for the

George Washington

British in the French and Indian War. He also served twice as a Virginia delegate to the Continental Congress. With his country now at war, Washington

GUIDED PRACTICE

Divide the class in half. Have one half work in small groups to draw editorial cartoons or design posters reflecting the Patriot view of Lexington and Concord. Do likewise with the other half, but have them show the British viewpoint. Ask volunteers to explain their group's cartoon or poster.

Have students take the viewpoint that they were assigned in the Guided Practice and write a speech about the events at Lexington and Concord that is designed to gain public support for their position. Students may choose either to deliver their speeches to the class or to turn in written versions.

REVIEW Have students write a letter to a British friend in early 1776, describing the colonial viewpoint of the major events discussed in this section. Have volunteers read their letters to the class. Ask students how the British friend might respond. Then assign the Section 3 Review on p. 116.

ASSESS Assign the **Section 3 Daily Quiz** in *Core Resources*.

▶

Changing Ways — RELIGION AND THE REVOLUTION

Many leaders of the American Revolution found their inspiration in the Enlightenment, which stressed goodness and reason over faith. But for many colonists, the Protestant religious traditions of the Great Awakening—not Enlightenment ideals—shaped their views of the struggle for independence. Evangelicalism, with its emphasis on faith and individuality over absolute authority, seemed to echo the promise of the Revolution.

Revolutionary leaders were well aware of the power of religion to sway public opinion. Patrick Henry was among those who used the evangelical style in their political speeches. These leaders often spoke of the war as a moral struggle between good and evil.

While most colonial ministers tried to distance themselves from the political upheavals of the era, some pro-independence ministers preached the Revolution's message from their pulpits. Scores of Congregationalist ministers in New England, Presbyterian ministers in the middle colonies, and Baptist ministers in Virginia openly supported the Revolution. And although most Anglican ministers in New England and the middle colonies remained loyal to the British, about a third of the Anglican clergy in Maryland and Virginia threw their support behind the struggle for independence.

▲ The fiery style of the Great Awakening ministers and their message that good could triumph over evil hit a responsive chord in Revolutionary America.

In their sermons, pro-independence ministers reinforced the Revolution's political message of the moral struggle between good and evil. Thomas Craddock, a Maryland Anglican, warned his flock:

❝ The life of every sincere Christian is a warfare against a great number of Enemies, some of them very potent, and others very politick. Virtue is a rich Prey rescued narrowly out of the Fire, the purchase of Labor and sweat of Care and Vigilance. We are too liable to loose it by our own Sloth and Treachery. ❞

Some ministers were even more pointed in supporting the Revolution. Thomas Jefferson noted that one Anglican minister in Virginia urged his congregation "to support their Liberties . . . and in a room of God save the king he cried out

God Preserve all of the Just rights and Liberties of America."

The vast majority of Anglican ministers, however, did not share the southern clergy's zeal for the Revolution. Revolutionary leaders often used the tax-sponsored Anglican church as an example of the Crown's tyranny, thus the clergy feared that the Revolution might threaten the church's existence in America. Many German Reformed and Lutheran ministers in Pennsylvania and Scots-Irish Presbyterian ministers on the frontier also feared the consequences of the Revolution. As early as 1775, German Reformed ministers warned their congregations that they lived in dangerous times, "the like of which, so far as we know, has never been seen in America." Others agreed. No matter what the outcome, war was sure to divide communities and test the limits of religious authority.

Changing Ways

RELIGION AND THE REVOLUTION

SETTING THE SCENE

John Adams credited ministers such as Jonathan Mayhew of Boston with sowing the seeds of independence long before 1776. Mayhew provided religious grounds for revolution in his 1750 pamphlet *A Discourse Concerning Unlimited Submission and Non-Resistance to the Higher Powers* when he said that while God established rulers, these rulers had no authority from God to do harm. Christians, therefore, had an obligation to resist evil rulers.

PRIMARY SOURCE

Description of Change: excerpted
Rationale: excerpted to focus on main idea

RETEACH Have students write on sheets of paper questions and answers on the major points of the section, two questions for each subsection. Collect the sheets; then use them to quiz the group in a game show format by stating the answers and having students supply the questions.

Closure

Have students list and rank the events discussed in this section according to each event's significance in the deteriorating relationship between Britain and the colonies. Ask for volunteers to read their lists and justify the order in which they placed events.

Extension

SYNTHESIZE Some believe that revolution was in the minds of the colonists long before the fighting started. Have students write a brief paper supporting or challenging this belief.

IDENTIFY Have students identify and use propaganda techniques to write newspaper headlines from the British and colonial viewpoints on George III's rejection of the Olive Branch Petition.

PRIMARY SOURCE
Description of Change: excerpted
Rationale: excerpted to focus on main idea

SECTION REVIEW ANSWERS

IDENTIFY

For significance, see the following pages:
First Continental Congress (p. 113)
minutemen (p. 114)
Second Continental Congress (p. 114)
George Washington (p. 114)
Battle of Bunker Hill (p. 116)
Olive Branch Petition (p. 116)

LOCATE

For locations, see the map on p. 114.

1. *discussed grievances; published "Declaration of Resolves" outlining colonists' rights as British subjects; called for ban on trade with Britain*
2. *prepared for war by establishing Continental Army; hoped for peace by issuing Olive Branch Petition*
3. *positioned themselves at high elevations so they could fire down on the British*
4. *Accounts will vary but should note the Patriots' shortage of ammunition and the heavy British casualties.*
5. *Students might mention cost of war in money and lives, damage to commerce, chance that British government might change its position, loyalty to Britain.*

◄ **Martha Dandridge Custis, one of the richest women in America, married George Washington in 1759.**

Washington/Custis/Lee Collection, Washington & Lee University

devoted himself and his fortune to the "glorious cause" of American independence.

After the fighting at Lexington and Concord, the Second Continental Congress moved beyond peaceful solutions and began active preparations for war.

The BATTLE OF BOSTON

On June 17, 1775, the Patriot forces were again put to the test. Atop two hills overlooking Boston Harbor—Bunker Hill and Breed's Hill—New England militiamen dug in, awaiting an onslaught of British troops. To save ammunition, an American commander ordered his men: "Don't one of you fire until you see the whites of their eyes."

British troops commanded by General Sir William Howe advanced in three bold assaults. Corporal Amos Farnsworth of the Massachusetts militia later recalled the **Battle of Bunker Hill**:

 We . . . sustained the enemy's attacks with great bravery. . . ; and after bearing, for about 2 hours, as severe and heavy a fire as perhaps ever was known, and many having fired away all their ammunition . . . we were overpowered by numbers and obliged to leave. 🙿

The British took both hills but suffered 1,054 casualties. Fewer than 450 Americans were killed or injured.

Even after the battle, conservatives worked to avoid a permanent break with Great Britain. They persuaded the Continental Congress to send a final plea to George III. This plea—the **Olive Branch Petition**—professed the colonists' loyalty to the king and asked for his help in ending the conflict.

■■ **The Second Continental Congress established the Continental Army in June 1775. But the delegates held out the hope of peace with the Olive Branch Petition.**

The king refused to accept the petition and ordered the Royal Navy to blockade all shipping to the colonies. He also sent Hessian (HESH-uhn) mercenaries—hired soldiers primarily from the German state Hesse—to help defeat the Americans.

Meanwhile, George Washington had plans of his own. In a surprise move on March 4, 1776, he positioned troops and cannon on Dorchester Heights overlooking Boston. From there, the Patriots could fire on British forces in the city. Washington hoped to force General Howe and his men to take the hill or flee Boston. General Howe chose to flee. On March 26, 1776, the British, joined by about one thousand colonists loyal to the Crown, sailed for Nova Scotia—leaving, said Washington, "in so much . . . confusion as ever troops did."

■■ SECTION 3 REVIEW

IDENTIFY and explain the significance of the following: First Continental Congress, minutemen, Second Continental Congress, George Washington, Battle of Bunker Hill, Olive Branch Petition.

LOCATE and explain the importance of the following: Lexington, Concord.

1. **MAIN IDEA** What actions did the First Continental Congress take?
2. **MAIN IDEA** Why can it be said that the Second Continental Congress both prepared for war and hoped for peace?
3. **GEOGRAPHY: LOCATION** How did the Patriots attempt to use geography to their advantage at Bunker Hill and at Dorchester Heights?
4. **WRITING TO INFORM** Imagine that you are a reporter for the Boston *Gazette*. Write a short account of the Battle of Bunker Hill for your newspaper.
5. **HYPOTHESIZING** What arguments might the conservatives at the Second Continental Congress have used to convince the other delegates to send the Olive Branch Petition to George III?

PREVIEW WORKSHOP

Following is a list of the significant people and terms in this section. You may wish to use this list as a section preview.

People
- Thomas Paine
- Richard Henry Lee
- Thomas Jefferson
- Abigail Adams
- Salem Poor
- Peter Salem
- Thayendanegea
- Margaret Corbin
- Molly Pitcher
- Deborah Sampson Gannett

Terms
- Declaration of Independence
- Loyalists

Section 4

INDEPENDENCE DECLARED

FOCUS

- **How did the Declaration of Independence justify America's break with Great Britain?**
- **What roles did Loyalists, African Americans, Native Americans, and women play in the Revolutionary War?**
- **What problems did the colonial military have to overcome?**

Fighting had begun. Yet most colonists insisted they were merely resisting unjust acts of Parliament, not waging war. Many hesitated to make a final break with Great Britain. After all, the British government maintained stability in the colonies and provided protection from France and Spain. But to others, the time was ripe for independence.

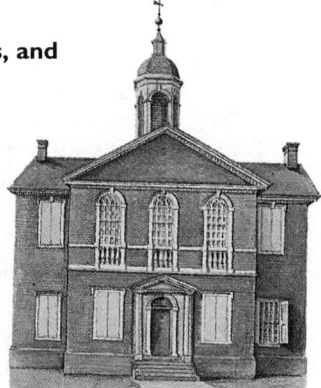

Carpenter's Hall in Philadelphia, site of Second Continental Congress

REASONS FOR INDEPENDENCE

Many colonists supported independence for two reasons. First, they believed that the British government had violated their rights as English subjects. Second, colonists had already died defending these rights.

▲ Thomas Paine

Patrick Henry and Thomas Paine were among the most eloquent supporters of independence. Henry's "Give me Liberty or Give me Death" speech in 1775 in Virginia and Paine's *Common Sense,* published in January 1776, won support for the revolution. In his pamphlet Paine wrote:

> **66** The period of debate is closed. Arms, as the last resource, must decide the contest. . . . Every thing that is right or reasonable pleads for separation. The blood of the slain, the weeping voice of nature cries, 'TIS TIME TO PART. **99**

Common Sense sold some 120,000 copies in three months. Paine helped transform a haphazard colonial rebellion into a focused crusade for independence.

◀ **Thomas Paine came to America in 1774. He settled in Philadelphia and wrote for *Pennsylvania Magazine*.**

FOCUS OBJECTIVES

- Explain how the Declaration of Independence justified America's break with Great Britain.

- Identify the roles played by Loyalists, African Americans, Native Americans, and women in the Revolutionary War.

- Examine the problems the colonial military had to overcome.

PRIMARY SOURCE

Description of Change: excerpted
Rationale: excerpted to focus on main idea

CORE RESOURCES

- **Literature Worksheet 4**
- **Section 4 Daily Quiz**

AV RESOURCES

- **Everyday Life in America Transparency** and **Worksheet 4**

MOTIVATING: STUDENT EXPERIENCES

Ask students if they have made decisions that set them on what they felt was an irreversible course. *(choosing classes, quitting a team or a job)* Have volunteers describe their decisions and reasons for making them. Then point out that in this section the colonists make an irreversible decision by declaring independence.

Teaching the Section

THE BREAK WITH GREAT BRITAIN

Divide the class with an imaginary line. Ask students on one side to list reasons the colonists should seek independence from Great Britain. Have students on the other side list reasons the colonies should remain part of the British Empire. Select students from each group to write their lists on the chalkboard. Discuss the lists.

HISTORICAL SIDELIGHTS

Editing the Declaration
The draft of the Declaration presented to the Congress was practically all Jefferson's work, for the other committee members had made only minor changes to Jefferson's original version. The Congress, however, wielded its "editor's pencil" like a butcher knife, cutting about one quarter of Jefferson's original language.

PRIMARY SOURCE

Description of Change: excerpted
Rationale: excerpted to focus on main idea

THE DECLARATION OF INDEPENDENCE

On June 7, 1776, Richard Henry Lee of Virginia introduced a resolution in the Second Continental Congress declaring "that these United Colonies are, and of right ought to be, free and independent States . . . and that all political connection between them and the State of Great Britain is . . . totally dissolved." The resolution also called for planning a confederation, or loose pact, of the states and for securing foreign alliances.

Before voting on Lee's proposal, the Congress appointed a five-man committee to draft a formal **Declaration of Independence**. Thomas Jefferson, a Virginia lawyer and planter—and at 33 one of the youngest delegates—did most of the actual writing. On June 28 the committee presented the Declaration to the Congress.

Before turning their attention to the Declaration, the Congress debated—and quickly adopted—Lee's resolution for independence, officially declaring on July 2 the new United States of America to be independent of Great Britain. Two days later, on July 4, the Congress formally adopted the Declaration of Independence.

The Declaration's immediate purpose was to win public support for independence, both at home and abroad. To undermine loyalty to King George III, the Declaration detailed his misdeeds. It also outlined basic principles of representative government, listing these "self-evident" truths:

❝ We hold these truths to be self-evident, that all men are created equal, that they are

▶ **Mum Bett, a Massachusetts slave, believed that the words "all men are created equal" should apply to her. In 1781 she successfully sued for her freedom. Her lawyer's daughter, Susan Sedgwick, painted this portrait of her.**

endowed by their Creator with certain unalienable Rights, that among these are Life, Liberty, and the pursuit of Happiness. ❞

The document also proclaimed the right of people "to alter or abolish" a government that deprived them of life, liberty, or happiness. The men who signed the Declaration of Independence knew they were now traitors in the eyes of the Crown. The price for failing to win independence might well be imprisonment or even death.

■■ **The Declaration of Independence asserted the right of people to overthrow an unjust government.**

COMMENTARY

Independence for Whom?

Thomas Jefferson's words "all men are created equal" have, almost from the beginning, been a source of controversy. What exactly did he mean? Remember that 18th-century colonial America, like Europe, was full of social, political, and economic inequalities. The delegates to the Continental Congress, as citizens of their time, would not have viewed issues of justice as we do today. Besides, they were seeking to justify a political, not a social, revolution.

Nevertheless, the Declaration and the revolution it symbolized had social consequences. Many women organized boycotts and participated in street demonstrations. During the war women took over the work of their absent husbands, fathers, and brothers, or cared for troops. As a result, some women argued for a greater voice in politics.

"I desire you would remember the ladies," Abigail Adams appealed to her husband, John, a delegate to the Continental Congress. "Be more generous and favorable to them than your ancestors." John Adams did not agree. Like most men of his day, he believed that women's power came from their influence over the men in their lives.

Whether the delegates intended the words men and mankind to include women is debatable. It is more certain that they did not intend the words to apply to slaves. This statement does not mean, however, that all of the delegates supported slavery. In Jefferson's original draft, he accused the king of violating the "sacred rights of life and

Organize students into small groups. Have each group read the Declaration of Independence (pp. 120–123) and then make a list of the colonial grievances outlined in the document. Ask volunteers to read their group's list. Have students compare the lists.

▶

liberty" of blacks "who never offended him, captivating and carrying them into slavery in another hemisphere." But some of the southern delegates objected, and the passage was stricken from the final document. Thus America's leaders for the first but not the last time sidestepped the explosive issue of slavery.

REACTIONS TO INDEPENDENCE

News of independence inspired mixed reactions throughout the colonies. Patriots rejoiced wildly—ringing "liberty bells," singing and dancing around bonfires, celebrating at banquets. In one city, Patriots tore down a huge statue of Britain's King George III. According to an independence-loving newspaper reporter, this small act of rebellion was "the just desert of an ungrateful tyrant!" On July 13 Ezra Stiles noted in his diary that "the CONGRESS have tied a . . . knot, which the Parliament will find they can neither cut nor untie. The *thirteen united Colonies* now rise into an *Independent Republic* among the kingdoms, states and empires on earth."

Some Americans opposed or simply ignored the developments. Among those who refused to celebrate were the **Loyalists**, also known as Tories. Some Tories based their loyalty to Great Britain on the long-held belief that to resist the king was to rebel against God. "It is our duty not to disturb and destroy the peace of the community by becoming . . . rebellious subjects and resisting the ordinances of God," explained one Anglican minister. Other Loyalists, such as merchants and officials, stood to lose power and wealth if royal authority were undermined. "Upon this event [the Declaration of Independence] the law, the courts, and justice itself ceased; all was anarchy, all was confusion," a Loyalist judge complained. "A usurped [unlawfully gained] kind of government took place, a medley of military law, convention ordinances, Congress recommendations and committee resolutions." Many more saw support for the king as they saw loyalty to family.

As support for independence mounted, Loyalists feared for their safety. To many a Patriot, a Loyalist was "a thing whose head is in England, and its body is in America, and its neck ought to be stretched [hanged]." More disquieting than the taunts were the threats of violence to the Loyalists, their families, and their property.

Many wealthy and influential Loyalists escaped to Canada, the British West Indies, or England. Loyalists who remained either tried to stay out of the conflict or openly aided the British forces.

■■ **During the war, Loyalists either left the colonies, hid out until the fighting ended, or supported the British.**

THE DECLARATION OF INDEPENDENCE

Thomas Paine's pamphlet Common Sense, *with its call for American independence, made for shocking reading in Great Britain. The reaction to the Declaration of Independence in 1776 was even stronger, for this was not just a call for independence but a statement of it signed by prominent Americans. Both Parliament and the king knew that it seriously challenged British rule.*

An outraged British press was first to respond. In a reply to the "DISUNITED STATES in AMERICA," *the* Morning Post *accused Americans of scorning "the duty and allegiance which in honour and in necessity they owe" to Great Britain. The British government's response—an 80-page pamphlet,* The Rights of Great Britain Against the Claims of America—*soon followed, attacking the Declaration paragraph by paragraph. The British did not see an American people struggling for independence; instead, they saw ungrateful fellow subjects betraying their mother country, which had protected them. The British government found the Americans' "pretended arguments justifying rebellion" so defiant that it saw no alternative but to crush the rebellion.*

GLOBAL CONNECTIONS

The Declaration angered British leaders, while the governments of other countries, fearing that it might spur their own subjects to rebellion, looked on it with apprehension. In a number of countries, possession of copies of the Declaration was a crime. And well into the 1800s, professors in some German states could be fired for teaching about American liberties.

COOPERATIVE LEARNING

Organize students into groups of five, and ask them to design pamphlets presenting the Declaration of Independence in a form that would be suitable for grade-schoolers. Suggest that group members divide the work as follows: design and layout, paraphrasing the document, finding or creating illustrations, final preparation of the pamphlet. Have groups present their pamphlets to the class.

HISTORICAL
Document

The Declaration of Independence

HISTORICAL
Document

The Declaration of Independence

HISTORICAL SIDELIGHTS

Selecting an Author

Jefferson thought that John Adams ought to write the first draft of the Declaration. Adams responded that Jefferson should write the document: "Reason 1st. You are a Virginian and a Virginian ought to be at the head of this business. Reason 2nd. I am obnoxious, suspected and unpopular; you are very much otherwise. Reason 3rd. You can write ten times better than I can."

Thomas Jefferson wrote the first draft of the Declaration in a little more than two weeks.

In the first paragraph, the signers are justifying why they are separating from Great Britain.

impel: force

endowed: provided

"Laws of Nature" and "Nature's God" refer to Isaac Newton's belief that certain patterns are constant and predictable. Natural or "unalienable" rights (the rights to life, liberty, and the pursuit of happiness) cannot be taken away. The signers supported John Locke's view that people created governments to protect their natural rights. A government, therefore, must have the consent of the governed. If a government abuses its powers, it is the right as well as the duty of the people to do away with that government.

usurpations: wrongful seizures of power

despotism: unlimited power

BUILDING VOCABULARY

The word *despotism* derives from the Greek word *despotēs,* which means "master" or "chief." Over the years, many of the leaders upon whom the title *despotēs* was bestowed ruled in a repressive fashion. By the late-18th century, *despot* had come to mean an absolute, tyrannical ruler.

tyranny: oppressive power exerted by a government
candid: fair

In Congress, July 4, 1776 The unanimous Declaration of the thirteen united States of America,

When in the Course of human events, it becomes necessary for one people to dissolve the political bands which have connected them with another, and to assume among the powers of the earth, the separate and equal station to which the Laws of Nature and of Nature's God entitle them, a decent respect to the opinions of mankind requires that they should declare the causes which impel them to the separation.

We hold these truths to be self-evident, that all men are created equal, that they are endowed by their Creator with certain unalienable Rights, that among these are Life, Liberty, and the pursuit of Happiness.

That to secure these rights, Governments are instituted among Men, deriving their just powers from the consent of the governed,

That whenever any Form of Government becomes destructive of these ends, it is the Right of the People to alter or to abolish it, and to institute new Government, laying its foundation on such principles and organizing its powers in such form, as to them shall seem most likely to effect their Safety and Happiness. Prudence, indeed, will dictate that Governments long established should not be changed for light and transient causes; and accordingly all experience hath shown, that mankind are more disposed to suffer, while evils are sufferable, than to right themselves by abolishing the forms to which they are accustomed. But when a long train of abuses and usurpations, pursuing invariably the same Object evinces a design to reduce them under absolute Despotism, it is their right, it is their duty, to throw off such Government, and to provide new Guards for their future security.

Such has been the patient sufferance of these Colonies; and such is now the necessity which constrains them to alter their former Systems of Government. The history of the present King of Great Britain is a history of repeated injuries and usurpations, all having in direct object the establishment of an absolute Tyranny over these States. To prove this, let Facts be submitted to a candid world.

He has refused his Assent to Laws, the most wholesome and necessary for the public good.

He has forbidden his Governors to pass Laws of immediate and pressing importance, unless suspended in their operation till his Assent should be obtained; and when so suspended, he has utterly neglected to attend to them.

He has refused to pass other Laws for the accommodation of large districts of people, unless those people would relinquish the right of Representation in the Legislature, a right inestimable to them and formidable to tyrants only.

He has called together legislative bodies at places unusual, uncomfortable, and distant from the depository of their public Records, for the sole purpose of fatiguing them into compliance with his measures.

He has dissolved Representative Houses repeatedly, for opposing with manly firmness his invasions on the rights of the people.

He has refused for a long time, after such dissolutions, to cause others to be elected; whereby the Legislative powers, incapable of Annihilation, have returned to the People at large for their exercise; the State remaining in the meantime exposed to all the dangers of invasion from without, and convulsions within.

He has endeavored to prevent the population of these States; for that purpose obstructing the Laws for Naturalization of Foreigners; refusing to pass others to encourage their migrations hither, and raising the conditions of new Appropriations of Lands.

He has obstructed the Administration of Justice, by refusing his Assent to Laws for establishing Judiciary powers.

He has made Judges dependent on his Will alone, for the tenure of their offices, and the amount and payment of their salaries.

He has erected a multitude of New Offices, and sent hither swarms of Officers to harass our people, and eat out their substance.

Here the Declaration lists the charges that the colonists had against King George III. How does the language of the list appeal to people's emotions?

relinquish: release, yield

inestimable: priceless

formidable: causing dread

Why do you think the king had his legislatures in the colonies meet in places that were hard to reach?

annihilation: destruction

convulsions: violent disturbances

naturalization of foreigners: the process by which foreign-born persons become citizens

appropriations of land: setting aside land for settlement

tenure: term

a multitude of: many

HISTORICAL SIDELIGHTS

Accusing the King

Today the list of grievances presented in the Declaration generally elicits little interest. This list, however, is the part of the document that was most debated and changed by the Continental Congress. In England attention also focused on the list of grievances. John Lind, a pamphleteer for Lord North, wrote an answer to the Declaration in which he devoted 110 out of a total of 129 pages to a consideration of the grievances.

BUILDING VOCABULARY

Tenure derives from the Latin verb *tenēre,* which means "to hold." In the Declaration *tenure* refers to the length of time judges may hold office.

◄ The Continental Congress is shown voting for independence in this painting by Robert Pine and Edward Savage.

HISTORICAL SIDELIGHTS

Rebellion to Tyrants

The sentiments expressed in the Declaration appeared in the proposals for the design of the seal of the United States. Franklin suggested that the motto "Rebellion to tyrants is obedience to God" should be used on the seal. This recommendation was eventually rejected. Jefferson, however, liked the saying so much that he adopted it as his personal motto, stamping it in the wax with which he sealed his letters.

What wrongful acts does the Declaration state have been committed by the king and the British Parliament?

The "neighboring Province" that is referred to here is Quebec.
arbitrary: not based on law
render: make

abdicated: given up

foreign mercenaries: soldiers hired to fight for a country not their own

perfidy: violation of trust

insurrections: rebellions

petitioned for redress: asked formally for a correction of wrongs

He has kept among us, in times of peace, Standing Armies without the Consent of our legislatures.

He has affected to render the Military independent of and superior to the Civil power.

He has combined with others to subject us to a jurisdiction foreign to our constitution, and unacknowledged by our laws; giving his Assent to their Acts of pretended Legislation:

For quartering large bodies of armed troops among us:

For protecting them, by a mock Trial, from punishment for any Murders which they should commit on the Inhabitants of these States:

For cutting off our Trade with all parts of the world:

For imposing Taxes on us without our Consent:

For depriving us in many cases, of the benefits of Trial by Jury:

For transporting us beyond Seas to be tried for pretended offences:

For abolishing the free System of English Laws in a neighboring Province, establishing therein an Arbitrary government, and enlarging its Boundaries so as to render it at once an example and fit instrument for introducing the same absolute rule into these Colonies:

For taking away our Charters, abolishing our most valuable Laws, and altering fundamentally the Forms of our Governments:

For suspending our own Legislatures, and declaring themselves invested with power to legislate for us in all cases whatsoever.

He has abdicated Government here, by declaring us out of his Protection and waging War against us.

He has plundered our seas, ravaged our Coasts, burnt our towns, and destroyed the Lives of our people.

He is at this time transporting large Armies of foreign Mercenaries to complete the works of death, desolation and tyranny, already begun with circumstances of Cruelty & perfidy scarcely paralleled in the most barbarous ages, and totally unworthy the Head of a civilized nation.

He has constrained our fellow Citizens taken Captive on the high Seas to bear Arms against their Country, to become the executioners of their friends and Brethren, or to fall themselves by their Hands.

He has excited domestic insurrections among us, and has endeavored to bring on the inhabitants of our frontiers, the merciless Indian Savages, whose known rule of warfare, is an undistinguished destruction of all ages, sexes and conditions.

In every stage of these Oppressions We have Petitioned for Redress in the most humble terms: Our repeated Petitions have been answered only by repeated injury. A Prince, whose character is thus marked by every act which may define a Tyrant, is unfit to be the ruler of a free people.

THE DECLARATION OF INDEPENDENCE

Nor have We been wanting in attentions to our British brethren. We have warned them from time to time of attempts by their legislature to extend an unwarrantable jurisdiction over us. We have reminded them of the circumstances of our emigration and settlement here. We have appealed to their native justice and magnanimity, and we have conjured them by the ties of our common kindred to disavow these usurpations, which would inevitably interrupt our connections and correspondence. They too have been deaf to the voice of justice and of consanguinity. We must, therefore, acquiesce in the necessity, which denounces our Separation, and hold them, as we hold the rest of mankind, Enemies in War, in Peace Friends.

We, therefore, the Representatives of the united States of America, in General Congress, Assembled, appealing to the Supreme Judge of the world for the rectitude of our intentions, do, in the Name, and by Authority of the good People of these Colonies, solemnly publish and declare, That these United Colonies are, and of Right ought to be Free and Independent States; that they are Absolved from all Allegiance to the British Crown, and that all political connection between them and the State of Great Britain, is and ought to be totally dissolved; and that as Free and Independent States, they have full Power to levy War, conclude Peace, contract Alliances, establish Commerce, and to do all other Acts and Things which Independent States may of right do.

And for the support of this Declaration, with a firm reliance on the protection of divine Providence, we mutually pledge to each other our Lives, our Fortunes and our sacred Honor.

unwarrantable jurisdiction: unjustified authority

magnanimity: generous spirit

conjured: called upon

consanguinity: common ancestry
acquiesce: consent to

rectitude: rightness

In this paragraph, the signers state their actual declaration of independence. What rights would the new United States of America now have as an independent nation?

Congress adopted the final draft of the Declaration of Independence on July 4, 1776. A formal copy, written on parchment paper, was signed on August 2, 1776.

John Hancock	Benjamin Harrison	Lewis Morris
Button Gwinnett	Thomas Nelson, Jr.	Richard Stockton
Lyman Hall	Francis Lightfoot Lee	John Witherspoon
George Walton	Carter Braxton	Francis Hopkinson
William Hooper	Robert Morris	John Hart
Joseph Hewes	Benjamin Rush	Abraham Clark
John Penn	Benjamin Franklin	Josiah Bartlett
Edward Rutledge	John Morton	William Whipple
Thomas Heyward, Jr.	George Clymer	Samuel Adams
Thomas Lynch, Jr.	James Smith	John Adams
Arthur Middleton	George Taylor	Robert Treat Paine
Samuel Chase	James Wilson	Elbridge Gerry
William Paca	George Ross	Stephen Hopkins
Thomas Stone	Caesar Rodney	William Ellery
Charles Carroll	George Read	Roger Sherman
of Carrollton	Thomas McKean	Samuel Huntington
George Wythe	William Floyd	William Williams
Richard Henry Lee	Philip Livingston	Oliver Wolcott
Thomas Jefferson	Francis Lewis	Matthew Thornton

HISTORICAL SIDELIGHTS

Signing the Declaration
Some of the signers of the Declaration were not in Philadelphia on August 2, 1776, so not all 56 signatures were affixed on that date. Evidence suggests that a few of the signers did not put their names to the document until October or November.

BUILDING VOCABULARY

John Hancock, the president of the Congress, was the first to sign the Declaration. Boldly writing his name in large letters, he declared that the king would be able to read it without his glasses. Today, *John Hancock* is a synonym for a signature or autograph.

𝒯eaching the 𝒮ection

FIGHTING FOR THE CAUSE

Colonists learned about the war from broadsides—large printed sheets of paper. Ask some students to create broadsides with news of women's contributions to the war, some to focus on African American contributions, others on Native American roles, and still others from the Loyalist viewpoint. Circulate completed broadsides so that students can read "news" of the war.

BUILDING AN ARMY

Pair students and have partners work together to make a list of the problems the Continental Army faced in 1776, as well as the possible solutions for each problem. Call on pairs to suggest problems, and have the class offer solutions.

𝟋IGHTING THE WAR

To declare independence was one thing; to fight for it was another. The lack of a central government hindered the American war effort. The Second Continental Congress had no real authority. It could *ask* the states for supplies, troops, and funds, but it could not force the states to comply.

Supply shortages and disease. Without a strong government behind it, the Continental Army constantly faced supply shortages. Some colonial merchants charged high prices for shoddy goods. Farmers sold their produce to the highest bidder, whether American or British.

Because of these problems, Washington's troops suffered, enduring bitter winters at Morristown, New Jersey, in 1777 and at Valley Forge, Pennsylvania, in 1777–78. British soldiers meanwhile wintered in comfort in nearby cities.

Another problem the Continental Army faced was disease. Even though General Washington issued orders about cleanliness and hygiene, illness plagued the camps. Poorly prepared food spread germs, and camp toilets contaminated the water

supply. Dysentery caused by these unsanitary conditions killed thousands.

Building an army. Washington also faced troop shortages. He seldom had more than 16,000 Continentals available nationwide at any one time, although about 231,000 men served in the Continental Army over the course of the war. But quality, not quantity, was the general's main complaint. "What we need is a good army, not a large one," he once remarked. In his view the lack of quality stemmed from Congress's insistence on short-term enlistments:

❝ Good God, gentlemen! Our cause is ruined if you engage men only for a year. You must not think of it. If we ever hope for success, we must have men enlisted for the whole term of the war. ❞

Most men signed on for one year, some for just three months, so training of troops was especially difficult. By the time recruits gained the experience to be good soldiers, their enlistment was up. Despite his appeals, Washington fought the war with poorly trained, short-term troops.

There were other problems. Recruiting went well only after victories, and the soldier-farmers in the ranks often deserted at planting or harvesting time. Although state militias also fought, they, too, were poorly trained. But Patriot forces enjoyed two key advantages over the British: they often fought on familiar ground, and they were inspired by a revolutionary cause.

■■ **With no central government to enforce cooperation, the military faced supply and troop shortages; it also suffered from disease.**

African Americans in the war. Despite the shortage of troops, Washington initially ordered that no black soldiers—enslaved or free— could serve in the Continental Army.

▼ **By the end of 1775, some 27,500 men were inspired by recruiting posters such as this one to enlist in the struggle for independence.**

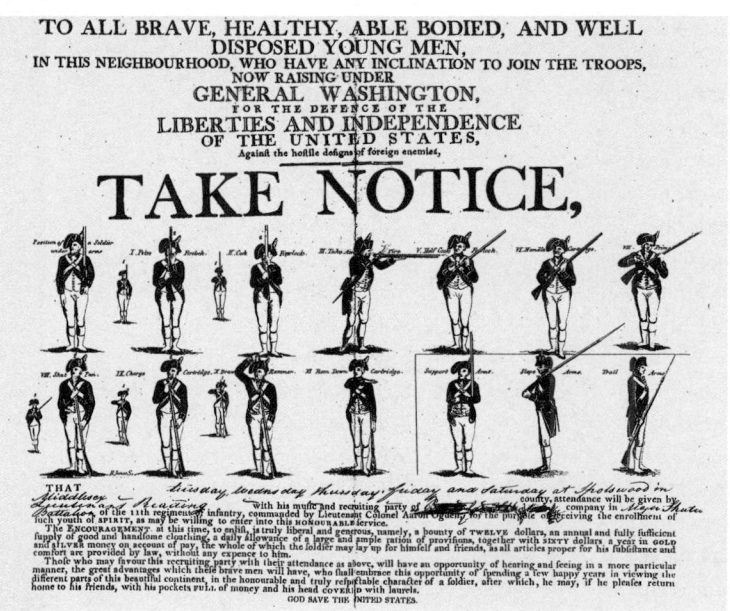

TO ALL BRAVE, HEALTHY, ABLE BODIED, AND WELL DISPOSED YOUNG MEN,
IN THIS NEIGHBOURHOOD, WHO HAVE ANY INCLINATION TO JOIN THE TROOPS,
NOW RAISING UNDER
GENERAL WASHINGTON,
FOR THE DEFENCE OF THE
LIBERTIES AND INDEPENDENCE
OF THE UNITED STATES,
Against the hostile designs of foreign enemies,

TAKE NOTICE,

GOD SAVE THE UNITED STATES.

*P*ractice

GUIDED PRACTICE

On the chalkboard, create a three-column chart titled *The Declaration of Independence*. Write the headings *Rights of the People, Purposes of Government,* and *Powers of Government* above each column; then call on volunteers to complete the chart as you list their answers in the appropriate column. Suggest that students copy the completed charts in their notebooks for use in Independent Practice.

INDEPENDENT PRACTICE

Ask students to review the Declaration of Independence (pp. 120–123), to choose one of the headings from Guided Practice, and to paraphrase in their own words those portions of the Declaration that refer to their chosen heading's topic.

*R*eview and *A*ssessment

REVIEW Organize the class into groups and assign each group a subsection of the section. Have each group develop several questions and answers about the main ideas in its assigned material. Then have each group use its questions to quiz the other groups. Then assign the Section 4 Review on p. 126.

ASSESS Assign the **Section 4 Daily Quiz** in *Core Resources*. ▶

◀ **Peter Salem was one of many African Americans who fought for the Patriots during the American Revolution.**

Some colonial leaders feared that slaves would revolt if given weapons; others believed that blacks would not make good soldiers. In late 1775, however, the British threatened to recruit African Americans, whether free or enslaved.

To counter this strategy, Washington ordered the Continental Army to enlist free blacks. Many served in fighting units alongside whites, but separate African American companies were also formed. Commanders of these all-black companies were usually white. At first, most white officers were reluctant to lead all-black groups. But the bravery of African American soldiers became so celebrated that many white officers changed their minds.

About 5,000 African American Patriots fought in the war. One Hessian noted that "no regiment is to be seen in which there are not Negroes in abundance." Numerous black soldiers, such as Salem Poor and Peter Salem, two of many African Americans who fought at Bunker Hill, received official recognition for their courage. Hundreds more served bravely but anonymously.

Native Americans in the war. Initially, both the British and the Patriots tried to keep Native Americans out of the war. Soon, however, the need for skilled fighters led each side to change its stand.

Both sides recruited members of the Iroquois League. In July 1777 the League held a council to discuss the war. The League split. Thayendanegea (thah-yuhn-dah-ne-GAY-uh), an important Mohawk chief known to whites as Joseph Brant, had received British assurances of Iroquois land rights. He was, therefore, staunchly pro-British. The Mohawks, Onondagas, Cayugas, and Senecas agreed to fight with the British under Brant; the Oneidas and Tuscaroras sided with the Patriots.

▪▪ African Americans and Native Americans fought on both sides in the war.

Women in the war. A few Patriot women fought in the war, while others undertook dangerous missions as spies or messengers. Although legends about women in the war abound, it seems certain that Margaret Corbin and Molly Pitcher took their wounded husbands' places. Young Deborah Sampson Gannett disguised herself as a man and became the "faithful and gallant soldier" Robert Shurtleff. She was said to be as "fleet as a gazelle, bounding through swamps . . . ahead of her companions." After she died in 1827, her husband was awarded a pension as the "widow" of a Revolutionary War veteran.

▲ **Thayendanegea was given a captain's commission by the British during the Revolutionary War. He commanded Native American forces during the fateful Saratoga campaign.**

RETEACH Have students write the section's headings and subheadings on a sheet of paper, allowing space to write between each. Then have them describe the main ideas under each heading and subheading. Have students compare and correct their outlines.

Closure

Have students write diary entries as colonists reacting to one of the following: the justification for the Declaration of Independence; the problems of the Continental Army; and the roles played by women, African Americans, and Native Americans in the war. Ask volunteers to read their entries aloud. Students may wish to include their diary entries in their portfolios.

Extension

ANALYZE The Declaration of Independence expounded a new theory of government. Have students research and write an essay explaining how that government differed from the British government of the time.

CREATE Have students design a billboard that reflects the Patriot or the Loyalist view of the Declaration of Independence.

SECTION REVIEW ANSWERS

IDENTIFY

For significance, see the following pages:
Thomas Paine (p. 117)
Richard Henry Lee (p. 118)
Thomas Jefferson (p. 118)
Declaration of Independence (p. 118)
Abigail Adams (p. 118)
Loyalists (p. 119)
Salem Poor (p. 125)
Peter Salem (p. 125)
Thayendanegea (p. 125)
Margaret Corbin (p. 125)
Molly Pitcher (p. 125)
Deborah Sampson Gannett (p. 125)

1. *detailed King George III's misdeeds; outlined basic principles of representative government; declared people's right to alter or abolish an unjust government*
2. *no central government to force states to support it; shortages of supplies and troops; disease*
3. *African Americans and Native Americans served as soldiers; women aided troops, served as spies or messengers, fought, and ran businesses and farms.*
4. *Letters should stress loyalty to Britain and fear that revolution would bring social and political chaos and loss of wealth, property, and status.*
5. *Students should pick phrases that rely on emotional appeals rather than on facts.*

◀ Women participated in the American Revolution in many ways. Nancy Hart is shown here defending her home from attack.

Many other women accompanied the troops and worked as laundresses, nurses, and cooks. After one bloody South Carolina battle, women nursed injured American soldiers even as "men dared not come to minister to their wants." But most Patriot women stayed behind. They supported the war effort by distributing medical supplies and by making uniforms. They also collected lead and helped in the manufacture of bullets. And with the men off to war, some women managed businesses and farms, helping to keep the colonial economy going.

Loyalist women were also caught up in the war. Many fled their homes or were exiled. Others spied for the British army, aided British prisoners, or hid British soldiers in their homes.

■■ **Patriot and Loyalist women assisted the war effort by aiding the troops, spying on the enemy, and even fighting in battles.**

 SECTION 4 REVIEW

IDENTIFY and explain the significance of the following: Thomas Paine, Richard Henry Lee, Thomas Jefferson, Declaration of Independence, Abigail Adams, Loyalists, Salem Poor, Peter Salem, Thayendanegea, Margaret Corbin, Molly Pitcher, Deborah Sampson Gannett.

1. **MAIN IDEA** What arguments did the Declaration of Independence offer in support of revolution?
2. **MAIN IDEA** What were the main problems that the Continental Army faced?
3. **MAIN IDEA** How did African Americans, Native Americans, and Patriot and Loyalist women contribute to either the American or the British war effort?
4. **WRITING TO EXPLAIN** Imagine you are a Loyalist at the outbreak of the American Revolution. Write a letter to your local newspaper editor, explaining why you support the king rather than the colonial fight for independence.
5. **ANALYZING** Historians have pointed out that the Declaration of Independence was intended, in part, to convince the colonists to support the fight for independence. Provide several examples from the Declaration that support this view.

PREVIEW WORKSHOP

*Following is a list of the significant
people, places, and terms in this
section. You may wish to use this
list as a section preview.*

People
- William Howe
- "Gentleman Johnny"
  Burgoyne
- Bernardo de Gálvez

Places
- Kings Mountain, South
  Carolina

Terms
- Battle of Trenton
- Battle of Saratoga
- Battle of Vincennes
- Battle of Camden
- guerrilla warfare

- Battle of Yorktown
- Treaty of Paris

Section 5

AN AMERICAN VICTORY

FOCUS

- **Why was the victory at Saratoga so important?**
- **How did the Americans defeat the British in the South?**
- **What were the main terms of the treaty that ended the war?**
- **What were some of the social and political effects of the American Revolution?**

*C*ounting on support from the colonists loyal to the
Crown, confident British generals planned a quick end
to the war. But British plans that looked good on paper
failed on the battlefield. Key Patriot victories at Trenton
and Saratoga fueled the momentum of the Revolution,
attracting powerful European allies, such as France, to
the American cause. When the war shifted to the South,
combined American and French forces defeated the British.
A favorable peace treaty capped the military victory.

The Granger Collection, New York

Raising the new
American flag, 1783

THE WAR HEATS UP

With General William Howe's evacuation of
Boston in March 1776, Washington knew the
British would soon strike elsewhere. New York
City, a Loyalist stronghold, seemed the most likely
possibility. Anticipating that Howe would try to
use the city as a base of operation, Washington
brought his forces from Boston to guard it.

On July 2 Howe sailed into New York
Harbor, landing his troops on Staten Island. The
British won an easy victory at Brooklyn Heights in
late August and continued to hit the Patriots hard.
As the city fell to the British, Washington tried to
regroup. Thomas Paine expressed the somber
mood in his pamphlet *The American Crisis:*

66 These are the times that try men's
souls. The summer soldier and the sunshine
patriot will, in this crisis, shrink from the

service of their country; but he that stands
it now deserves the love and thanks of man
and woman. Tyranny, like hell, is not easily
conquered. **99**

As winter neared, almost every "sunshine
patriot" departed the ranks.
To make matters worse,
most regular-army enlist-
ments were due to expire.
Washington admitted in
a letter to his brother
that without new recruits
"the game will be pretty
near up."

▶ **General William Howe
was commander in chief of
the British forces from 1775
to 1778.**

FOCUS OBJECTIVES

- Explain the impor-
  tance of the victory at
  Saratoga.

- Determine how the
  Americans defeated the
  British in the South.

- Identify the main terms
  of the treaty that ended
  the war.

- Outline the social and
  political effects of the
  American Revolution.

PRIMARY SOURCE

Description of Change:
excerpted
Rationale: excerpted to
focus on main idea

■■ Ask a volunteer to
define the term *fair-weather
friend.* Ask students how
they might feel about such
friends.

CORE RESOURCES
- **Section 5 Daily Quiz**

AV RESOURCES
- **Linking Geography
  and History
  Transparency** and
  Worksheet 9

Teaching the Section

THE BRITISH WAR EFFORT

Have students use information in the section to create a "report card" for the British war effort. Suggest that they list things such as leadership, military strategy, and others they regard as important to winning a war. Then have students assign a letter grade to each item on the report card, along with a reason for the grade. Have students compare their cards.

BUILDING VOCABULARY

The word *bayonet* comes from the French *baïonnette*, meaning "short dagger." The French word almost certainly derives from the town of Bayonne in southern France, where such weapons originally were made. The first recorded use of *bayonet* to mean "a blade attached to a rifle" came in 1672.

PRIMARY SOURCE

Description of Change:
excerpted
Rationale: excerpted to focus on main idea

*T*HE BATTLE OF TRENTON

Thinking the war was almost won, General Howe prepared to celebrate Christmas in New York. As a precaution he stationed about 1,400 Hessians at Trenton, New Jersey, to keep a close eye on the Patriots nearby. But rather than build fortifications against a possible Patriot attack, the Hessian commander Colonel Rall boasted, "Let them come. We want no trenches. We will go at them with the bayonet."

And come the Americans did. Ignoring the customary winter halt in fighting, Washington and his troops boldly ferried across the ice-choked Delaware River on Christmas night. As Thomas Rodney, one of Washington's soldiers, vividly recalled:

> 66 It was as severe a night as ever I saw, and after two battalions were landed, the storm increased so much, and the river was so full of ice, that it was impossible to get the artillery over. 99

Although Washington's troops had, in Rodney's words, "then been on duty four nights and days . . . without six hours sleep in the whole time," they surprised the Hessian camp at daybreak. Henry Knox, one of Washington's officers, wrote his wife that in the **Battle of Trenton**, the "hurry, fright and confusion of the enemy was [not] unlike that which will be when the last trump [trumpet] shall sound." The Hessians surrendered as the "poor fellows . . . saw themselves completely surrounded."

Of the 1,400 Hessian soldiers, 106 were killed or wounded, and 918 were taken prisoner. The Americans suffered no casualties in the battle.

General Charles Cornwallis, the British field commander, prepared to counterattack. But the American troops slipped away by night, leaving their campfires burning to fool the British. Washington then struck inland, boldly ambushing British regiments at Princeton. British plans to end the war quickly were, as one London official wrote, "blasted by the unhappy affair at Trenton."

▲ A surprise Patriot attack the day after Christmas led to a complete defeat of the Hessian garrison at Trenton. It was only one of a few American victories during 1776–1777.

FIGHTING THE WAR

Ask students to study the map on p. 129, and have them identify the major battles, troop movements, and other military information shown. Then have students create charts of Revolutionary War battles with the following headings: *Battle, Location, Date, American Leader, British Leader, Outcome.* Students may wish to include their charts in their portfolios.

THE IMPORTANCE OF SARATOGA

Write the following on the chalkboard: *What if Burgoyne's battle plan had worked at Saratoga?* Have students meet in groups to discuss how this might have affected the campaign in the North, the attitude of foreign governments toward the colonists, and the final outcome of the war. Have a volunteer from each group present the results of the group's discussion.

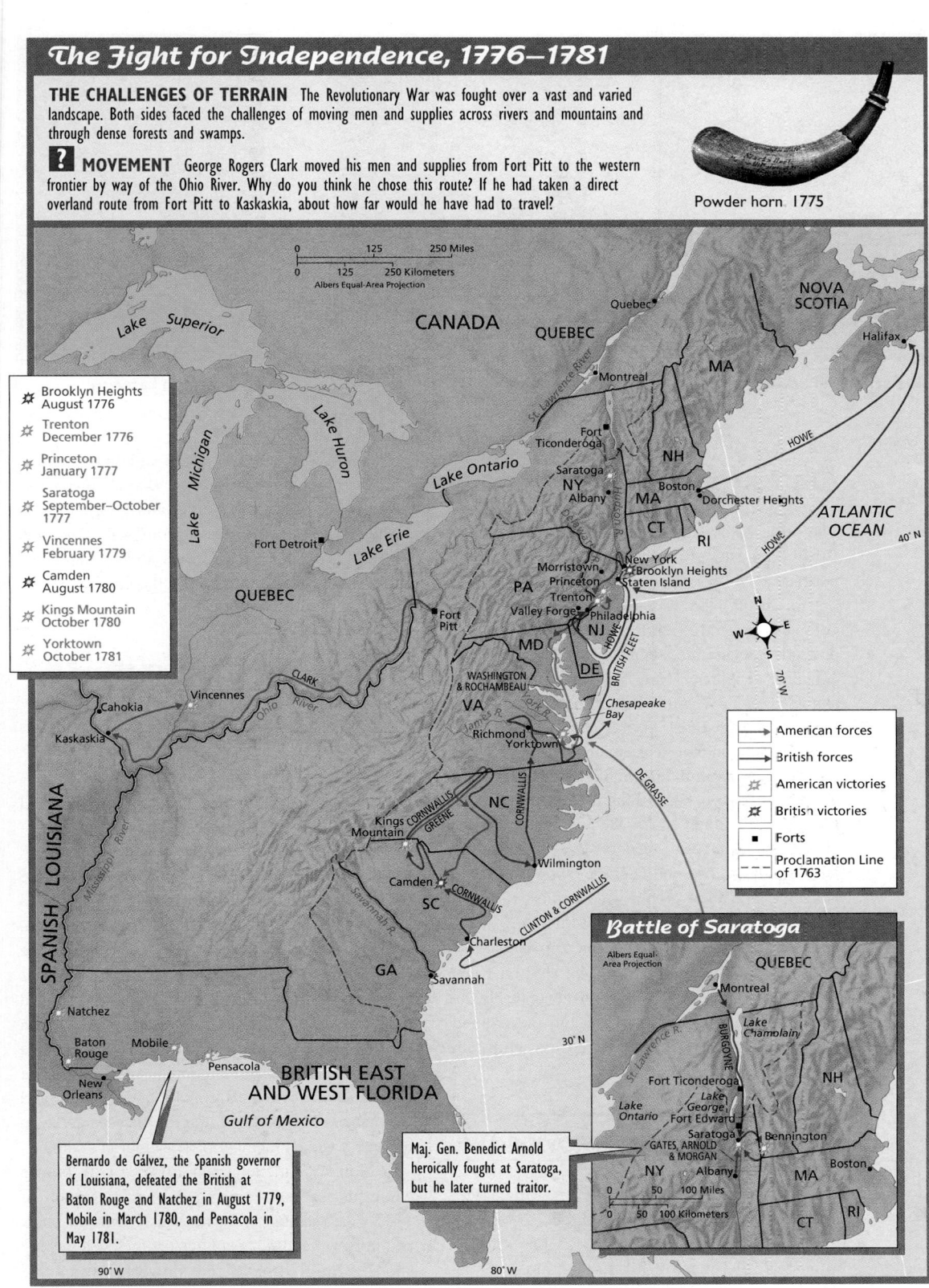

The Fight for Independence, 1776–1781

THE CHALLENGES OF TERRAIN The Revolutionary War was fought over a vast and varied landscape. Both sides faced the challenges of moving men and supplies across rivers and mountains and through dense forests and swamps.

? MOVEMENT George Rogers Clark moved his men and supplies from Fort Pitt to the western frontier by way of the Ohio River. Why do you think he chose this route? If he had taken a direct overland route from Fort Pitt to Kaskaskia, about how far would he have had to travel?

Powder horn, 1775

Brooklyn Heights
August 1776

Trenton
December 1776

Princeton
January 1777

Saratoga
September–October
1777

Vincennes
February 1779

Camden
August 1780

Kings Mountain
October 1780

Yorktown
October 1781

American forces
British forces
American victories
British victories
Forts
Proclamation Line
of 1763

Bernardo de Gálvez, the Spanish governor of Louisiana, defeated the British at Baton Rouge and Natchez in August 1779, Mobile in March 1780, and Pensacola in May 1781.

Maj. Gen. Benedict Arnold heroically fought at Saratoga, but he later turned traitor.

Battle of Saratoga

Teaching the Section

THE WAR IN THE SOUTH

Refer students to the illustration on pp. 102–103 of their textbooks and ask volunteers to characterize the style of warfare that was typical to the 18th century. Ask how Patriots' military tactics in the South varied from this style and why these different tactics were necessary to avoid defeat.

THE TREATY OF PARIS

Have students draw two maps of North America, one showing the area before the Treaty of Paris of 1783, the other showing the area after the treaty. Display maps on the bulletin board and use them as a starting point for class discussion on the land disputes settled and created by the treaty. Students may wish to include their maps in their portfolios.

VOICES IN HISTORY

The American Revolution aroused great enthusiasm for democracy among the French people. It is not enough, the Marquis de Condorcet exclaimed, that rights "should be written in the books of philosophers and in the hearts of virtuous men; it is necessary that ignorant or weak men should read them in the example of a great people. America has given us this example." In such an atmosphere, French help for the Americans came only after much deliberation. King Louis XVI understandably hesitated to aid a revolution that was based on the theory that "governments derive their just powers from the consent of the governed." In the end, however, he was unable to forgo the opportunity to disrupt the British Empire.

HISTORICAL SIDELIGHTS

Language Problems
Because Baron von Steuben knew no English, his secretary translated the drill exercises von Steuben wrote into English. Alexander Hamilton and John Laurens, members of Washington's staff, then "Americanized" the translation.

▲ **Kazimierz Pulaski**

The Historic New Orleans Collection, Museum/Research Center

▲ **Bernardo de Gálvez**

▲ **Marquis de Lafayette**

*B*RITISH DISASTER AT SARATOGA

The setbacks at Trenton and Princeton roused the British to greater effort. In control of Canada to the north and New York City to the south, the British set out to cut off New England from the other rebel colonies. General "Gentleman Johnny" Burgoyne devised the plan: three separate British forces would converge at Albany, New York. The plan seemed simple enough. What the British did not realize—or ignored—was that their lines of attack crossed lakes, swamps, hills, and forests teeming with Patriots.

Almost from the beginning Burgoyne's strategy failed. Two of the British forces—those under Lieutenant Colonel Barry St. Leger and General Howe—never arrived. General Burgoyne's troops left Canada in June and began moving southward. His long caravan of supplies and artillery moved at a crawl, hampered by blocked trails and bridges destroyed by American militiamen. In September Burgoyne and his men crossed the Hudson River, where they clashed with the Americans in the **Battle of Saratoga**. Outfoxed and outmanned, Burgoyne formally surrendered his troops on October 17, 1777.

*E*UROPEAN POWERS PROVIDE AID

Saratoga was a turning point for Americans. Encouraged by the victory, the French—who had been secretly aiding the Patriots—signed a formal alliance in February 1778. French aid provided Americans with gold, supplies, a fleet, and troops.

France also declared war on Great Britain. A year later Spain joined the war as an ally of France, followed in 1780 by the Netherlands. Bernardo de Gálvez, Spain's governor of Louisiana, aided the Patriots with needed supplies and defeated the British in several battles along the Gulf coast and the Mississippi River.

■■ **The Americans' victory at Saratoga convinced France and other European powers to support the colonists.**

New volunteers from Europe brought useful military skills. Even before the treaty, an impressive group of Europeans had aided the Patriots. From Minorca, off the coast of Spain, came George Farragut, who fought in both the army and the navy. From Prussia came Baron von Steuben, who took charge of organizing and drilling the Continental Army. From Poland came Kazimierz Pulaski (kah-ZEEM-yesh puh-LAS-kee), who trained the cavalry, and Tadeusz Kosciuszko (tah-DE-oosh kahs-ee-UHS-koh), an army engineer who planned Patriot fortifications. From France came the German-born officer Baron Johann de Kalb and 19-year-old Marquis de Lafayette (lahf-ee-ET), who became a valued member of Washington's staff.

For the Americans the alliance with France came just in time. During the severe winter of 1777–78, Washington's army was reduced to a sick and hungry handful of soldiers, some even lacking shoes. The glad news that powerful allies had joined them gave the Patriots new hope.

CONSEQUENCES OF THE REVOLUTION

Write the headings *Positive Effects* and *Negative Effects* on the chalkboard. Ask students to list results of the Revolution in each category. Remind students that many groups were involved in the Revolution and that a positive consequence for one group could be a negative result for another. Ask students to explain why each entry is positive, negative, or both.

DIVERSE VIEWS

Organize students into six groups. Assign each group one of the following roles: a Patriot woman, a Loyalist woman, an African American Patriot, an African American Loyalist, a Native American who fought for the colonists, a Native American who fought for the British. Have each group write a letter to the editor, detailing how the group's character viewed the outcome of the Revolution. Have group representatives read their letters.

▶

FIGHTING IN THE WEST AND SOUTH

Things were going better for the Patriots in the West. Lieutenant Colonel George Rogers Clark of Virginia, with a small group of frontier fighters and Native Americans, overran British posts at Kaskaskia (ka-SKAS-kee-uh), Cahokia (kuh-HOH-kee-uh), and Vincennes (vin-SENS) in 1778. The British recaptured Vincennes by year's end, only to lose it again to Clark in the **Battle of Vincennes** in February 1779. Clark's army went on to take control of the western lands.

Late in 1778 the British focused their attacks on the southern colonies, where they anticipated strong Tory support. Backed by their navy, the British occupied the seaport towns: Savannah, Georgia, fell in December 1778; Charleston, South Carolina, in May 1780. From Charleston, General Cornwallis attacked inland. After crushing the Americans in the **Battle of Camden** (South Carolina) in 1780, British forces marched toward North Carolina.

Cornwallis did not find the support he expected. Although companies of Loyalist militia terrorized the Carolina countryside, bands of Patriots retaliated in kind. Patriot hostility toward the Loyalists was never more apparent than at Kings Mountain, South Carolina, in October 1780. In that battle the victorious Patriots savagely killed the wounded who were trying to surrender.

It was a new Patriot commander, Nathanael Greene of Rhode Island, however, who stopped the British advances. Greene was a master of the tactics of **guerrilla warfare**—wearing down the enemy in hit-and-run skirmishes while avoiding direct battles. Even in defeat Greene bragged, "We fight, get beat, rise, and fight again." Using forest cover and the element of surprise, the Patriots made the most of their limited numbers and frustrated British hopes of winning in the South.

■■ **Americans used guerrilla warfare to defeat the British army and its Loyalist supporters in the South.**

VICTORY AT YORKTOWN

During the summer of 1781, Cornwallis moved his army into Yorktown, Virginia, located on the peninsula between the York and James rivers. There he had access to the British fleet and

▶ In 1779 Jones's ship, the *Bonhomme Richard*, engaged the British ship *Serapis* in battle. With his own warship about to sink, Jones lashed the two ships together and in desperate fighting won the victory.

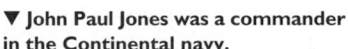

▼ John Paul Jones was a commander in the Continental navy.

The Granger Collection, New York

The Granger Collection, New York

Practice

GUIDED PRACTICE

On the chalkboard under the title *Revolutionary War*, create two columns, one headed *Setbacks* and the other *Solutions*. Organize the class into two teams: members of one team take turns listing problems or setbacks that faced the colonists; members of the second team have no more than three minutes to write the solutions to these problems.

INDEPENDENT PRACTICE

Have students write a paragraph explaining how, despite numerous setbacks, the Americans were able to prevail in the Revolutionary War.

Review and Assessment

REVIEW For each subsection in the section, have students write a sentence that summarizes the main idea. Select students to read their statements aloud. Have the class choose the best summary sentence for each subsection. Then assign the Section 5 Review on p. 133.

ASSESS Assign the **Section 5 Daily Quiz** in *Core Resources*.

MAKING CONNECTIONS
Music

One verse of "The World Turned Upside Down" ends: "If summer were spring and the other way round,/ Then all the world would be upside down." Ask students to explain why this was an appropriate song for the British to play at Yorktown.

HISTORICAL SIDELIGHTS
Casualties of War

Historians estimate that there were no less than 25,000 American military deaths in the Revolutionary War. More than 6,800 died in battle, about 10,000 died from diseases, and some 8,500 prisoners died.

GLOBAL CONNECTIONS

The Revolutionary War played a role in founding a new nation far from America—Australia. For years Britain had dumped its surplus prison population in the American colonies. With American independence, however, this practice ended. Its prisons once again overflowing, Britain sent a fleet of prison ships to found a penal colony at Botany Bay in 1788 in the South Pacific. In time, that penal colony grew into the nation of Australia.

◄ **John Trumbull painted a series of scenes from the Revolutionary War. Shown here is the surrender of Lord Cornwallis at Yorktown in October 1781.**

Yale University Art Gallery, Trumbull Collection

supplies. A small Patriot army led by generals Lafayette, von Steuben, and "Mad Anthony" Wayne kept close watch on the British but did not attack.

On August 14 a dispatch reached General Washington's New York headquarters: Admiral François de Grasse, the French naval commander in the West Indies, was moving his fleet north to block Chesapeake Bay. Meanwhile, Washington's army, along with a French force under Comte de Rochambeau (raw-shahn-boh), rushed south to Yorktown, completing the trap. Boxed in by the French fleet, the British faced vastly greater numbers of American and French troops.

After numerous attempts on land and sea failed to break the blockade, Cornwallis admitted defeat. On October 19, 1781, as their band played the old English folk tune "The World Turned Upside Down," the British surrendered their weapons. Cornwallis wrote to General Clinton to inform him of the disastrous outcome of the **Battle of Yorktown**: "I have the mortification [shame] to inform your Excellency that I have been forced to . . . surrender the troops under my command."

THE TREATY OF PARIS OF 1783

Although some fighting continued in the South and on the frontier, Cornwallis's surrender marked the end of the war. In the peace talks that followed, American negotiators Benjamin Franklin, John Adams, and John Jay won generous terms. The **Treaty of Paris**, signed on September 3, 1783, granted the United States (1) independence, (2) the land from the Atlantic coast westward to the Mississippi River and from the Great Lakes south to Florida, and (3) fishing rights in the Gulf of Saint Lawrence and off the coast of Newfoundland.

The treaty declared that Americans should pay debts owed to the British. The American negotiators also pledged that the Congress would "earnestly recommend" to the states that all property seized from Loyalists be returned. (The states chose to ignore this request.)

■■ **The Treaty of Paris recognized American independence and greatly expanded the nation's boundaries.**

Fortunately for the new nation, the American delegates negotiated with only Great Britain. If they had been forced to sit at a peace table with delegates from Spain and France as well, the Americans would have won their independence, but little else.

Spain wanted to confine the United States of America to the land east of the Appalachians. Having regained Florida in the negotiations ending the war, Spain hoped to expand northward to the Ohio Valley. However, George Rogers Clark's campaign in the West had established the new nation's presence within the region. His victories were important in shaping postwar America.

RETEACH Ask students to write who, what, when, where, or why questions and answers for each of the headings of the section. Collect question sheets and use them to quiz students on section content.

*C*losure

Ask students to design a time capsule for the American Revolution. Have them make suggestions for artifacts to place in the time capsule. Ask them to explain why these artifacts should be included.

*E*xtension

INTERPRET Have students debate the following statement, made by French foreign minister Count Vergennes, on the terms of the Treaty of Paris: "The English buy peace rather than make it."

EVALUATE Have students evaluate the outcome of the American Revolution by writing a paragraph answering the following question: *Did the Revolution attain all its goals?*

*C*OMMENTARY

Consequences of the American Revolution

The American Revolution had important social and economic effects, both immediate and long-term. As a result of the war, many great fortunes were destroyed. Many were built, as well. In the early years of the Revolution, political writer Thomas Paine commented, "the necessities of an army create a new trade." Americans made money and contributed to the nation's economic development as they rushed to supply this growing demand.

Almost 100,000 Loyalists fled the colonies by war's end; few of these people ever returned. The British government provided lands in Canada as compensation, but many Tories, especially the wealthy, chose to start new lives in Great Britain.

Social implications. As you have read, the war for independence was not a fight for independence for everyone. American women continued to be excluded from political life. Many slaves fought for and gained their freedom, but slavery did not end.

Native Americans also failed to benefit. Many lost their lands and homes. The war destroyed the Iroquois League; the split in 1777 caused member groups to fight against each other as well as against whites. Sadly, few Native Americans were recognized by either side for their assistance.

Political implications. Few Americans at the end of the war dwelt on the Revolution's unfulfilled promise. To them, the overwhelming fact was independence from Great Britain. Inexperienced Patriot forces (aided by foreign allies) had defeated the world's greatest military power. An American doctor stated the collective joy in simple terms when he learned of the British surrender at Yorktown. "This is," he wrote, "a most glorious day." The Americans had won the fight for representative government. Their Revolution created and strengthened a new national unity.

Equally important, the Revolution began to change Americans' ideas about who had the right to rule. They no longer believed that only the well born should rule. This belief would eventually lead to the expansion of democratic rights to include all Americans, whatever their sex, race, or economic condition. This historic change in attitude is the Revolution's greatest legacy. Harrison Gray Otis, a Massachusetts politician, later wrote to a friend: "You and I did not imagine, when the . . . war with Britain was over, that revolution was just begun."

■■ **The Revolution achieved its goal—independence and self-government. But women, African Americans, and Native Americans did not share equally in the hard-won freedoms.**

SECTION REVIEW ANSWERS

IDENTIFY

For significance, see the following pages:
William Howe (p. 127)
Battle of Trenton (p. 128)
"Gentleman Johnny" Burgoyne (p. 130)
Bernardo de Gálvez (p. 130)
Battle of Vincennes (p. 131)
Battle of Camden (p. 131)
guerrilla warfare (p. 131)
Battle of Yorktown (p. 132)

LOCATE

For location, see the map on p. 129.

1. ended British attempt to cut off New England from other colonies; won French and other European powers' support for the colonies
2. guerrilla warfare
3. recognized independence, set U.S. boundaries, granted U.S. fishing rights, required Americans to pay debts to British; France and Spain would have limited territorial gains by U.S.
4. social—little changed for women, slavery not ended, Native Americans lost lands and homes; political—independence achieved, created and strengthened national unity, changed Americans' ideas about who had the right to rule
5. unprepared for guerrilla warfare tactics and the Patriots' use of terrain

---

■■ **S E C T I O N   5   R E V I E W**

IDENTIFY and explain the significance of the following: William Howe, Battle of Trenton, "Gentleman Johnny" Burgoyne, Bernardo de Gálvez, Battle of Vincennes, Battle of Camden, guerrilla warfare, Battle of Yorktown.

LOCATE and explain the importance of the following: Kings Mountain, South Carolina.

1. **MAIN IDEA** How did the American victory at Saratoga affect the course of the war?

2. **MAIN IDEA** What tactics did the Americans use to defeat the British in the South?

3. **MAIN IDEA** What were the terms of the Treaty of Paris? Why might the terms have been less favorable to the United States if France and Spain had been included in the treaty negotiations?

4. **WRITING TO EVALUATE** Write an essay explaining the social and political significance of the American Revolution.

5. **ASSESSING CONSEQUENCES** British soldiers were well trained in traditional military procedures and tactics. How might this have been a disadvantage in the Revolutionary War?

Chapter Review Answers

WRITING A SUMMARY

See Essential Points in each section for main ideas.

REVIEWING CHRONOLOGY

4, 3, 5, 1, 2
Identifying Cause and Effect
Answers will vary but should make the cause and effect of events clear.

IDENTIFYING PEOPLE AND IDEAS

1. *regulated fur trading and barred colonial settlement west of the Appalachians; designed to reduce conflict with Native Americans*
2. *Ottawa chief who tried to unite Native Americans against British and colonists*
3. *law taxing printed items; protested as taxation without representation*
4. *colonist whose writings helped focus colonial drive for independence*
5. *general warrants allowing customs officers to search for hidden smuggled goods*
6. *African American Patriot who died in Boston Massacre*
7. *as commander, led Continental Army to victory*
8. *hit-and-run battle technique used effectively by colonists, particularly in the South*

134

UNDERSTANDING MAIN IDEAS

1. *Because of huge debts, British expected colonies to help pay for the costs of their protection.*
2. *restrictions on westward expansion; quartering of soldiers in peacetime; taxation without representation; attacks on self-government*
3. *through petitions, demonstrations, and nonimportation agreements*
4. *to proclaim freedom; to gain domestic and foreign support; to undermine loyalty to British Crown; to list reasons for rebellious actions; and to assert right of citizens to overthrow an unjust government*
5. *These victories took British by surprise, inspired Americans, and assured European support.*

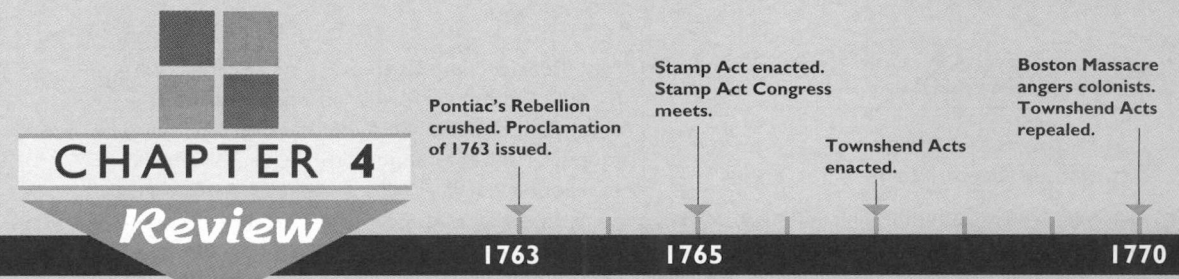

CHAPTER 4
Review

Pontiac's Rebellion crushed. Proclamation of 1763 issued.

Stamp Act enacted. Stamp Act Congress meets.

Townshend Acts enacted.

Boston Massacre angers colonists. Townshend Acts repealed.

1763　　　**1765**　　　　　　　**1770**

WRITING A SUMMARY
Using the essential points of the chapter as a guide, write a summary of the chapter.

REVIEWING CHRONOLOGY
Number your paper 1 to 5. Study the time line above, and place the following events in the order in which they happened by writing the first next to 1, the second next to 2, and so on. Then complete the activity below.

1. Intolerable Acts passed.
2. Declaration of Independence issued.
3. Stamp Act enacted.
4. Pontiac's Rebellion crushed.
5. Boston Massacre angers colonists.

Identifying Cause and Effect Select two events on the time line, and in a paragraph, explain the cause-and-effect relationship between them.

IDENTIFYING PEOPLE AND IDEAS
Explain the historical significance of each of the following people or terms.

1. Proclamation of 1763
2. Pontiac
3. Stamp Act
4. Thomas Paine
5. writs of assistance
6. Crispus Attucks
7. George Washington
8. guerrilla warfare

UNDERSTANDING MAIN IDEAS

1. How and why did the British attitude toward the colonies change after 1763?
2. What were the main reasons the colonists protested British actions?
3. How did the colonists protest British policies?
4. Why did the Second Continental Congress issue the Declaration of Independence?
5. Why were the American victories at Trenton and Saratoga so important?

⚑ REVIEWING THEMES

1. **Economic Development** How did British attempts to raise revenues in the colonies conflict with colonial interests?

2. **Democratic Values** What role did democratic values play in colonial protests?
3. **Global Relations** How was the Revolutionary War affected by global relations?

THINKING CRITICALLY

1. **Evaluating** Some historians claim that wise leaders could have resolved the differences between Great Britain and the colonies before 1775. Do you agree? Explain.
2. **Hypothesizing** Explain how the war might have been different if the Loyalists had organized more effectively and in greater numbers.
3. **Analyzing** What theories of government were outlined in the Declaration of Independence?

WRITING ABOUT HISTORY
Using Historical Imagination Imagine that you are a Loyalist or a Patriot woman. Write a letter to a friend explaining why you chose the side you did and how you are attempting to help the war effort.

STRATEGY FOR SUCCESS
Review the Strategies for Success on Interpreting the Visual Record on page 98. Then study the 1774 picture below entitled *Bostonians Paying the Excise Man*. On a separate sheet of paper, explain the artist's point of view, using specific examples from the picture.

The Granger Collection, New York

REVIEWING THEMES

1. British revenue measures cut into colonial profits from trade and smuggling; colonists objected to being taxed by Parliament, where they had no representation.
2. Colonists argued that they had the natural right to oppose—and even overthrow—leaders who hampered self-government.
3. Britain's European rivals—France, Spain, and the Netherlands—provided military and financial aid to the Americans.

THINKING CRITICALLY

1. Students should consider how leaders could have balanced the Crown's need for revenue against the colonists' desire for self-government.
2. possible effects of organized support: guerrilla warfare against Patriots, spying, propaganda campaigns, and military aid
3. All men are created equal, and governments derive power from consent of the governed.

WRITING ABOUT HISTORY

Letters might consider patriotic reasons, support of family, and personal beliefs that actions might promote a new equality for women.

STRATEGY FOR SUCCESS

The artist is pro-British; examples include presence of Liberty Tree with hangman's noose on it, Patriots portrayed as mob, excise man being tarred and feathered, sarcastic title.

USING PRIMARY SOURCES

Hamilton planned to enlist slaves in the army and to grant them freedom. He hoped this plan would secure the overall loyalty of African Americans for the rebellion. He feared his plan would be opposed because of prejudice and the refusal of slaveholders to cooperate.

Patriots stage Boston Tea Party.

Intolerable Acts passed. First Continental Congress meets.

British and Patriots clash at Lexington, Concord, and Bunker Hill. Second Continental Congress meets.

Declaration of Independence issued. Patriots win at Trenton.

British defeated at Saratoga.

British surrender at Yorktown.

Treaty of Paris signed.

1775   **1780**   **1783**

USING PRIMARY SOURCES

At first some Patriot leaders opposed enlisting African Americans in the fight for freedom. However, when soldiers were needed for the southern campaign, Washington's aide, Alexander Hamilton, suggested recruiting African Americans. Read the following excerpt from a letter by Hamilton, in which he outlines his plan. Then write a summary of the points outlined in the letter.

Head Quarters March 14th 79

Dear Sir:

Colonel Laurens, who will have the honor of delivering you this letter, is on the way to South Carolina on a project . . . to raise two[,] three[,] or four batalions of negroes . . . by contributions from owners in proportion to the number they possess. . . .

I have not the least doubt, that the negroes will make excellent soldiers, with proper management. . . .

I foresee that his project will have to combat much opposition from prejudice and self-interest. The contempt we have been taught to entertain for the blacks, makes us fancy many things that are founded neither in reason nor experience. . . .

An essential part of the plan is to give them their freedom with their muskets. This will secure their fidelity, animate their courage, and I believe will have a good influence upon those who remain, by opening a door to their emancipation [freedom]. . . .

—*Alexander Hamilton*

Purple Heart

LINKING HISTORY AND GEOGRAPHY

British forces fought the Revolutionary War in physical settings that were often unfamiliar to them. Study the map on page 129. Select one of the battles or campaigns included on the map and indicate how geography might have helped or hurt British efforts.

British soldier, 1778

LINKING HISTORY AND GEOGRAPHY

Students should describe the terrain and discuss its impact on battle tactics and the movement of men and supplies.

BUILDING YOUR PORTFOLIO

Complete the following projects independently or cooperatively.

1. **WAR** Imagine you are a member of the Second Continental Congress assigned to oversee the American war effort. Create a poster aimed at recruiting Native Americans and free blacks for the Continental Army. Your poster should indicate reasons why both groups would benefit by joining the Patriot war effort.

2. **DEMOCRATIC RIGHTS** Imagine you are a reporter for a colonial newspaper. Select a specific tax, such as the stamp tax or sugar tax, and interview a British official responsible for collecting that tax and a colonist opposed to the tax. Your interview should include questions that examine Great Britain's point of view.

BUILDING YOUR PORTFOLIO

Have students refer to **Building Your Portfolio Worksheet 2**, assigned at the beginning of Unit 2. Use the worksheet to help students monitor their progress on the portfolio projects.

Assessment

Core Resources
- Review Worksheet 4
- Chapter 4 Tests
- Alternative Assessment Forms
Test Generator

FROM CONFEDERATION TO FEDERAL UNION

1776–1789

Chapter Overview

The Articles of Confederation, the framework of the new nation, reflected Americans' past experiences with government. A weak central government, however, was unable to solve the nation's problems, especially its economic ones. Shays's Rebellion demonstrated that change was necessary. Instead of revising the Articles, however, delegates to the Constitutional Convention decided to establish a completely new framework. The Constitution—a result of compromises about representation, slavery, and trade—established a strong national government but limited its power in a number of ways.

Chapter Planning Guide

CHAPTER 5	CORE RESOURCE BOOKLETS	**AV** AUDIOVISUAL RESOURCES	PROGRAM RESOURCES
INTRODUCTION pp. 136–137	■ Literature Worksheet 5 ■ Building Your Portfolio Worksheet 2		
TEACHING THE CHAPTER pp. 138–157	■ Graphic Organizer 5 ■ Social Studies Skills Worksheet 5 ■ Geography Worksheet 5 ■ Outline Maps 8, 9	■ Linking Geography and History Transparency and Worksheet 8 ■ Everyday Life in America Transparency and Worksheet 5	■ *Eyewitnesses and Others,* Volume 1: Readings 27, 28, 29, 30
REVIEW AND ASSESSMENT pp. 158–159	■ Chapter 5 Daily Quizzes ■ Review Worksheet 5 ■ Chapter 5 Tests ■ Alternative Assessment Forms		■ Test Generator

Additional Resources

BOOKS FOR TEACHERS

Bernstein, Richard B. and Kym S. Rice. *Are We to Be a Nation? The Making of the Constitution.* Harvard University Press, 1987. Perspectives on the Constitutional Convention.

Gillespie, Michael A. and Michael Lienesch, eds. *Ratifying the Constitution.* University Press of Kansas, 1989. Essays on ratification arranged by states.

Kerber, Linda K. *Women of the Republic: Intellect and Ideology in Revolutionary America.* Norton, 1986. Examines women's political role.

BOOKS FOR STUDENTS

Collier, Christopher and James L. *Decision in Philadelphia: The Constitutional Convention 1787.* Ballantine, 1987. Lively account of Constitutional Convention.

*Faber, Doris and Harold. *We the People: The Story of the United States Constitution since 1787.* Macmillan, 1987. Recounts history of the Constitution to the present.

Holder, Angela R. *The Meaning of the Constitution,* 2nd ed. Barron, 1987. Clause-by-clause explanation of the Constitution.

* for students reading below grade level

MULTIMEDIA MATERIALS

The Constitution: Relevant for Today? Video, 57 min. Close-Up Foundation/SSSS. Students discuss Constitution's relevance today.

The Constitution of the United States, 2nd ed. Video, 19 min. Britannica. Depicts Constitutional Convention from James Madison's viewpoint.

The Constitution: The Compromise That Made a Nation. Video, 27 min. Learning Corporation of America/SSSS. Award-winning film dramatizes debate over equal representation.

THEMES IN AMERICAN HISTORY

USE WITH PAGES 136–137

Listed on the right are the themes emphasized in Chapter 5. The questions in boldface type stimulate critical thinking and provide students with an opportunity to discuss the themes within a broadened context. The questions also appear in the pupil's edition on p. 136.

■ CONSTITUTIONAL HERITAGE

How does the organization of government affect the way power is distributed and exercised? Students should note that government organization determines how power is distributed and exercised. In an absolute monarchy or a dictatorship, power is concentrated at the top of the government in the hands of a few. In a democracy, power ultimately rests with the people. How that power is translated into government responsibilities depends on the government's structure. In the U.S. these responsibilities are shared between a strong federal government and the states.

■ ECONOMIC DEVELOPMENT

How might a government's policies affect the economic well-being of groups or individuals within a society? Students should consider how specific laws, such as tariffs or taxes, might help or hurt various groups in society. They might note that governments often impose special import restrictions in an effort to help specific businesses or industries. These restrictions sometimes harm other businesses, workers, or consumers within the society. Similarly, taxation to help one group, or to provide for the general welfare of all citizens, might place extra hardships on some groups within society.

■ DEMOCRATIC VALUES

How can a nation ensure that every citizen has a voice in government? Students might suggest that a nation can ensure that citizens have a voice in government by giving them the right to vote, to petition the government with their grievances, and to speak out for or against government actions. Students also might note that the concept of representative government also gives citizens a voice in their rule.

CHAPTER STRATEGIES FOR MEETING INDIVIDUAL NEEDS

LIMITED ENGLISH PROFICIENT LEARNERS

Organize students into small groups and assign each group a section from the chapter. Have groups develop sketches for two of the boldfaced terms in their assigned section. Encourage students to present and explain the significance of their work.

TACTILE/KINESTHETIC LEARNERS

Refer students to the illustration at the top of p. 151. Ask them to design a float or a poster that could have been used at a rally celebrating the ratification of the Constitution.

LEARNERS HAVING DIFFICULTY

As they read through the chapter, have students work in pairs to construct an annotated outline, section by section. Encourage pairs to compare their outlines.

AUDITORY LEARNERS

Read to students selections from Madison's *Notes of Debates in the Federal Convention of 1787.* Then ask students to write summaries of the arguments presented in each selection.

VISUAL LEARNERS

Have students construct an illustrated cause-and-effect chart with *End of the Revolutionary War* and *Ratification of the Constitution* as the first and last entries. Ask for volunteers to present and explain their charts to the class.

GIFTED LEARNERS

Suggest that students research the ideas of Enlightenment thinkers as well as documents and institutions providing the foundations for self-government. Ask students to explain how these ideas influenced the framers of the Constitution.

USING THE CHAPTER FOCUS

■ UNDERSTANDING THE MAIN IDEA

Ask students to review the colonists' main complaints against Britain in the pre-Revolutionary period. Have a volunteer record responses on the chalkboard, grouping them into general categories (political representation, economic policy, executive power). Discuss how colonists' experiences with Britain may have affected the kind of governments established after independence.

★ THEMES

Have students work individually or in small groups to answer the questions under Themes. Save students' responses so that they can compare them with their responses after studying the chapter. (See p. 135B for suggested answers.)

■ THE TIME LINE

Tell students that in 1784 Hungary suspended its constitution—at about the same time that Americans were trying to establish their government. Hungary's action, coupled with Americans' colonial experiences, made colonists fearful of strong central government. Ask students how long the nation functioned under the Articles of Confederation. Ask what event on the time line hints at the weakness of the new government.

CORE RESOURCES

- **Graphic Organizer 5**
- **Literature Worksheet 5**
- **Outline Maps 8, 9**
- **Building Your Portfolio Worksheet 2**

ABOUT THE ILLUSTRATION

Howard Chandler Christy's 20- by 30-foot canvas of the signing of the Constitution in Independence Hall on September 17, 1787, now hangs at the east stairway of the House wing of the Capitol. In the painting George Washington, who presided over the signing, is standing on the platform. Benjamin Franklin, in the foreground, is listening to Alexander Hamilton at his right. James Madison is sitting at Franklin's left. Ask students to describe the mood depicted in the painting.

Chapter 5

1776–1789

FROM CONFEDERATION TO FEDERAL UNION

▼ FOCUS

UNDERSTANDING THE MAIN IDEA

During the war the colonies replaced their royal charters with republican constitutions. The Continental Congress then drafted the Articles of Confederation to guide the new nation. Soon after the Revolution, however, political problems led the Congress to call for revision of the Articles. In response, the Constitutional Convention drafted the Constitution of the United States of America.

★ THEMES

- **■ CONSTITUTIONAL HERITAGE** How does the organization of government affect the way power is distributed and exercised?

- **■ ECONOMIC DEVELOPMENT** How might a government's policies affect the economic well-being of groups or individuals within a society?

- **■ DEMOCRATIC VALUES** How can a nation ensure that every citizen has a voice in government?

1776	1777	1781	1786	1788
Congress urges states to draft new constitutions.	Articles of Confederation adopted.	States officially become "The United States of America."	Shays's Rebellion begins.	U.S. Constitution ratified.

Call on volunteers to identify the problems the Continental Congress faced in governing the country during wartime. *(had no real authority, could only ask states for assistance, inability to regulate finances, and so on)* As students read the chapter, have them compare these problems with problems faced by the government under the Articles of Confederation.

■ **LINK TO THE PAST** ►

Disagreements between the British government and its colonies in North America resulted in war. Recognizing the need for unity in their fight for independence, the colonies united under the leadership of the Continental Congress.

HISTORICAL SIDELIGHTS

Washington's View

Washington's opinion of the young nation was similar to Hamilton's. "I see one head gradually changing into thirteen," Washington wrote. "I see the powers of Congress declining too fast for the. . . respect which is due to them as the grand representative body of America, and I am fearful of the consequences."

Scene at the Signing of the Constitution of the United States (1940) by Howard Chandler Christy

Within a few years of the American victory at Yorktown, influential Revolutionary leaders despaired for the future of the United States. In 1786 George Washington warned James Madison of an "impending storm" and sadly remarked: "No morn ever dawned more favorably than ours did; and no day was ever more clouded than the present." Madison wrote to James Monroe that if something was not done soon, "our case may become desperate."

These statesmen were alarmed by the quarreling among the states. Only five years after defeating the British, Americans were fighting one another!

What had happened? By the end of the war, the former colonies had united in a "firm league of friendship." But the league was not friendly in practice. Alexander Hamilton accurately described the league as "a number of petty states, with the appearance only of union, jarring, jealous and perverse, without any determined direction." This disunity was also apparent to Great Britain's foreign minister, who chose not to send any ambassador to the fragile American republic, remarking that it would be too expensive to send 13! The crisis of the 1780s put in jeopardy the future of the young nation that John Adams believed was "destined beyond a doubt to be the greatest power on earth . . . within the life of [a] man." If the newly independent states did not remain united, what would become of the Revolution's goals?

Great Seal of the Supreme Court

FOCUS OBJECTIVES

■ Describe the issues that the new state constitutions addressed.

■ Explain why the Land Ordinances of 1785 and 1787 were passed.

■ Analyze the weaknesses of the Articles of Confederation, and identify the problems these weaknesses caused.

■ Determine the causes and consequences of Shays's Rebellion.

BUILDING VOCABULARY

Republic derives from the Latin term *rēs pūblica*, which means "the public interest." The first recorded use of *republic* to mean "representative government" came in 1604 in Robert Cawdrey's *The Table Alphabetical of Hard Words.*

PRIMARY SOURCE

Description of Change: excerpted
Rationale: excerpted to focus on main idea

CORE RESOURCES

• **Section 1 Daily Quiz**

AV RESOURCES

• **Linking Geography and History Transparency** and **Worksheet 8**
• **Everyday Life in America Transparency** and **Worksheet 5**

PREVIEW WORKSHOP

Following is a list of the significant people, places, and terms in this section. You may wish to use this list as a section preview.

People
■ John Locke
■ Judith Sargent Murray
■ Daniel Shays

Places
■ Northwest Territory

Terms
■ republic
■ Virginia Statute for Religious Freedom
■ Articles of Confederation
■ Land Ordinance of 1785
■ Northwest Ordinance

■ Northwest Territory
■ depression
■ Shays's Rebellion

Section 1

THE ARTICLES OF CONFEDERATION

FOCUS

■ **What issues did the new state constitutions address?**

■ **Why were the Land Ordinances of 1785 and 1787 passed?**

■ **What were the weaknesses of the Articles of Confederation? What problems did these weaknesses cause?**

■ **What were the causes and consequences of Shays's Rebellion?**

𝒯he American experiment in self-government began even before the Declaration of Independence. In May 1776 the Second Continental Congress urged the colonies to begin drafting new constitutions to replace their British royal charters. To unify the new state governments, the Congress adopted a plan for a national government in November 1777. This new form of self-government would face severe tests during the nation's first decade.

Articles of Confederation cover

𝒯HE STATE CONSTITUTIONS

The American Revolution brought an end to monarchical rule in America. The colonists' open rebellion forced royal governors from office. To fill this void, the Second Continental Congress advised the colonies "under the authority of the people" to form new governments. John Adams conveyed the optimism many felt:

66 You and I . . . have been sent into life at a time when the greatest lawgivers of antiquity would have wished to live. How few of the human race have ever enjoyed an opportunity of making . . . government . . . for themselves or their children! 99

Between 1776 and 1780 all of the states except Connecticut and Rhode Island drafted and ratified new constitutions. (Connecticut and Rhode Island revised their royal charters.) Despite differences in economy, geography, and population, the states adopted similar constitutions. All of the constitutions defined executive power and voting rights, and many states took steps to separate church and state. Many states also included a bill of rights that guaranteed freedom of speech, trial by jury, and the right to assemble.

The republican spirit. To form the new governments, the state legislatures relied on republican theory. A **republic** is a form

◀ Many American statesmen used the political theories of John Locke when framing state constitutions.

MOTIVATING: PRIOR KNOWLEDGE

Have students recall the aims of the American Revolution. Then point out that Benjamin Rush, a signer of the Declaration of Independence, suggested that the Revolutionary War was simply "the first act of the great drama" of revolution. Ask students what they think Rush meant by this statement. Have them speculate as to what acts would complete the drama.

Teaching the Section

THE STATE CONSTITUTIONS

Poll students on whether they agree or disagree with the following statement: *The state constitutions drafted during the Revolution reflected Americans' strong belief in democracy and individual rights.* Call on volunteers to explain their opinions. Then lead a class discussion on how the major issues addressed by the states in the development of their constitutions were a result of their experiences under British rule.

of government in which political leaders receive from the citizens their authority to make and enforce laws.

The ideas of self-government were not new to Americans. The Mayflower Compact of 1620 had incorporated these ideas. Americans were also familiar with the works of Enlightenment thinkers such as John Locke, the English philosopher who developed the theory of "natural rights." Locke believed that all people were born with the rights of life, liberty, and property and that the role of the government was to protect these rights.

American republicanism, however, went further than Locke's theory did in challenging older forms of political and social order. Americans took the radical step of rejecting monarchical government and began participating actively in politics. Americans had absorbed ideas of natural rights and self-government from reading popular newspapers and pamphlets and participating in revolutionary committees and public meetings. With this knowledge and experience, Americans were confident that they could govern their own communities.

Limits on executive power. Many Americans had resented the powerful royal governors, who had often overturned laws the elected assemblies had passed. As a result, most of the new state constitutions limited the powers of governors. Nine states limited governors to one-year terms and denied them power to overturn laws. In other states the governors shared power with the legislatures. New York and Massachusetts had the most powerful governors. But in both states governors were elected rather than appointed.

Separation of church and state. Besides curbing the powers of governors, many state constitutions reduced the influence the church had over government. Before the Revolution, several New England colonies had collected taxes to support the Congregational church. New York and some southern colonies used tax money to support the Anglican, or English, church. People were required to pay the taxes even if they did not belong to the church.

Baptist and Presbyterian dissenters and liberal thinkers such as Thomas Jefferson opposed this close relationship between the government and one particular religious affiliation. Such a bond, they argued, often led to abuses of political power and to religious wars.

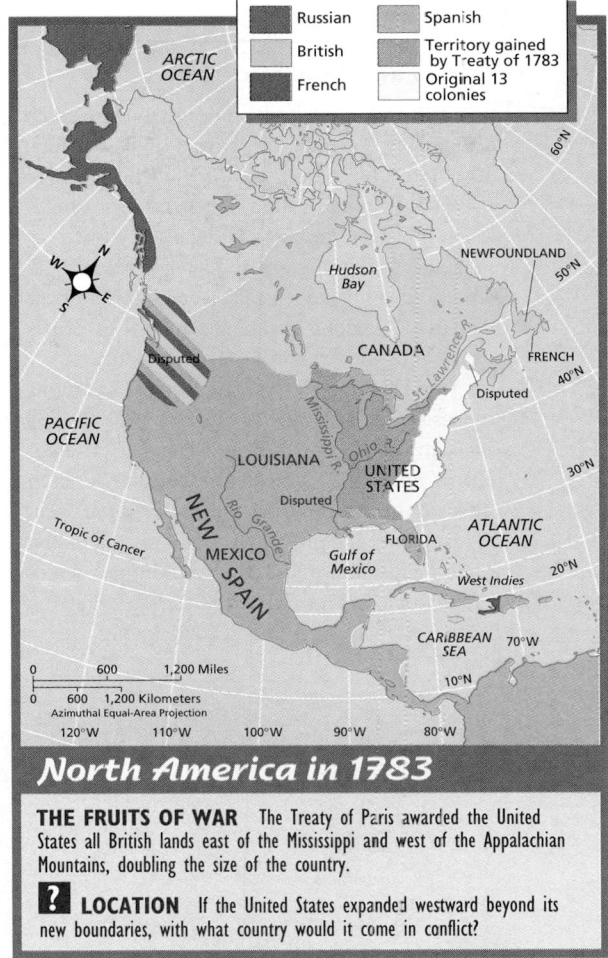

North America in 1783

THE FRUITS OF WAR The Treaty of Paris awarded the United States all British lands east of the Mississippi and west of the Appalachian Mountains, doubling the size of the country.

? LOCATION If the United States expanded westward beyond its new boundaries, with what country would it come in conflict?

In 1779 Thomas Jefferson drafted the **Virginia Statute for Religious Freedom**. The statute began "Whereas Almighty God has created the mind free; . . . legislators and rulers . . . have assumed dominion over the faith of others." It went on to argue that forcing a citizen to give money in support of "opinions which he disbelieves is sinful and tyrannical. . . . No man shall be compelled to . . . support any religious worship. . . . All men shall be free to profess . . . their opinion in matters of religion." Virginia adopted the statute in 1786. By 1833 all of the states had forbade the establishment of official state churches supported by tax dollars.

:: The state constitutions defined executive power and voting rights. Many also took steps to separate church and state.

HISTORICAL SIDELIGHTS
Separation of Church and State

American Jews, many of whom had lent invaluable support to the Revolution, were among those who supported the separation of church and state. In 1783 several members of the Philadelphia synagogue, including Haym Salomon, a Polish Jew who had immigrated to America in 1772 and lent hundreds of thousands of dollars to the American government, wrote a petition opposing a state requirement that members of the General Assembly "acknowledge the scriptures of the old and new Testament to be given by divine inspiration." The provision effectively prevented Jews from sitting in the assembly and, in the eyes of the synagogue members, showed state bias toward one religious viewpoint.

Map Caption Answer
Spain

Teaching the Section

WOMEN AND REPUBLICANISM

Direct students to write summaries, in their own words, of Judith Sargent Murray's reflection on p. 140 about the status of women in the early republic. Ask volunteers to read their summaries aloud.

■■ Have students compare the roles and opportunities for women in the U.S. in the 1780s to the roles and opportunities that American women have today.

PRIMARY SOURCE

Description of Change: excerpted and bracketed

Rationale: excerpted to focus on main idea; bracketed to clarify meaning

HISTORICAL SIDELIGHTS

A View of Women

In his essay *Republicanism,* Jefferson scholar John Howe writes, "Women, in Jefferson's judgment, possessed neither the economic nor the personal independence essential to political judgment." Judith Sargent Murray, on the other hand, argued that it was unfair for men like Jefferson to so judge women's political abilities when women had been denied the educational opportunities open to men. "We can only reason from what we know," she wrote, "and if opportunity of acquiring knowledge hath been denied us, the inferiority of our sex cannot fairly be deduced from thence."

■■ Call on volunteers to compare Jefferson's assessment with Murray's. Ask students how these arguments might be applied to the average American today.

COMMENTARY

Women and Republicanism

The republican state constitutions, though much more democratic than the British royal charters, did not grant full citizenship to women. The state constitutions limited voting rights and office-holding to white male property owners. Most men, as well as many women, opposed women's participation in politics, believing that women should contribute to the republic by taking care of their homes and educating their children to be good citizens.

This teaching duty created both limitations and possibilities for women. Most people expected women to devote themselves exclusively to their families and their homes. But because women were responsible for their children's education, this responsibility provoked calls for expanding women's education. Judith Sargent Murray, one of the first women playwrights in America, argued in 1790 that women and men had equal minds:

66 While we are pursuing the needle, or the superintendency [management] of the family, I repeat, that our minds are at full liberty for reflection; that imagination may exert itself in full vigor; and that if a just foundation [be] early laid, our ideas will then be worthy of rational beings. . . . Is it reasonable, that [women] . . . should at present . . . be allowed no other ideas, than those which are suggested by the mechanism of a pudding, or the sewing of the seams of a garment? 99

This debate led to the founding of several women's academies, or high schools. The opening of educational opportunities for women and the recognition of women's contributions laid the basis for an expanded role for women in public life in the next century.

Winterthur Museum

▲ This engraving advising women that their place was within the home reflected the attitudes of many men and women during the early republic.

A PLAN FOR CONFEDERATION

The state constitutions established frameworks of government for the former colonies. But no such framework existed on the national level. The Continental Congress had been fulfilling the duties of a national government since 1774, but it lacked real authority. To secure national unity, the Congress knew that it had to create a plan for a central government.

Adoption of the Articles. The states were willing to join in a loose union but were reluctant to give up many powers to a national government. In 1776 a congressional committee began the difficult task of drafting a plan for national unity that the states would accept.

On July 12, 1776, the committee presented its plan—the **Articles of Confederation**—to the other congressional delegates. For 16 months the delegates debated this plan for a "Perpetual Union," finally adopting it on November 15, 1777. The Articles created a confederation, or an alliance, of states while guaranteeing each state its "sovereignty, freedom, and independence." (A sovereign nation or state has supreme power over its own affairs.) All powers not "expressly delegated" to Congress were retained by the states.

The Articles authorized Congress to borrow and coin money, conduct foreign affairs, set policy toward Native Americans, and settle disputes between the states. In addition, Congress could ask, but not compel, the states to contribute money to the central government and to provide recruits for the military. The Articles allowed each state one vote in Congress.

The problem of land. For the plan to take effect, all 13 states had to ratify, or approve, it. One major issue blocked ratification: control of the land between the Appalachian Mountains and the Mississippi River. On the basis of their old royal charters, several states claimed vast tracts of western land. States without land claims wanted the other states to surrender their holdings to the new national government.

Part of the problem was money. Each state was expected to help pay the war debt. States with western lands had additional sources of revenue. States without surplus land faced the prospect of raising taxes—never a popular course of action.

▼ Surveyors used equipment such as a compass and a protractor when dividing land into tracts and sections. This set of equipment belonged to George

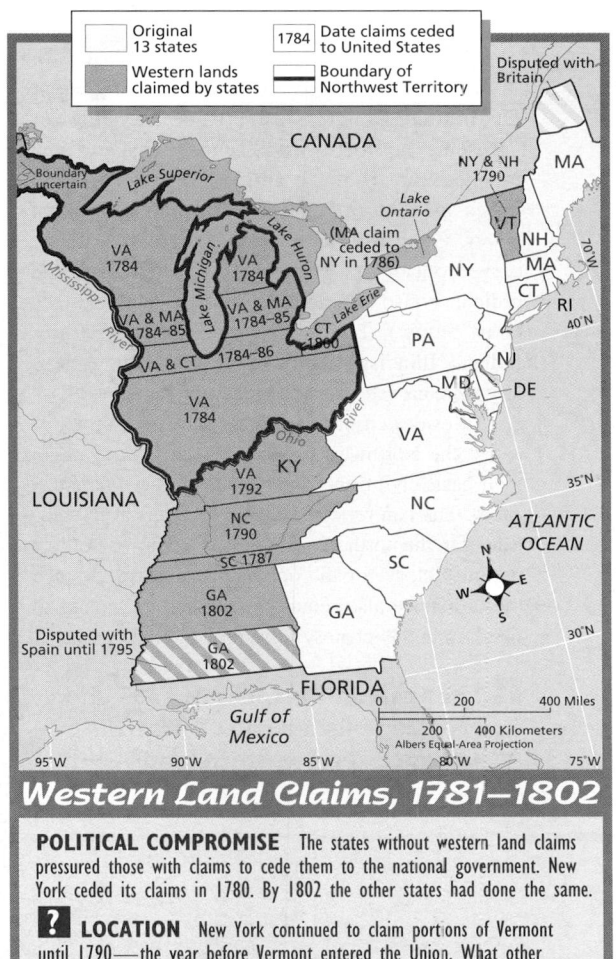

Western Land Claims, 1781–1802

| | Original 13 states | | 1784 Date claims ceded to United States |
| | Western lands claimed by states | | Boundary of Northwest Territory |

POLITICAL COMPROMISE The states without western land claims pressured those with claims to cede them to the national government. New York ceded its claims in 1780. By 1802 the other states had done the same.

? LOCATION New York continued to claim portions of Vermont until 1790—the year before Vermont entered the Union. What other state claimed part of Vermont?

To promote national unity, New York and Virginia—the two states with the largest landholdings—yielded their land claims to Congress. Other states eventually followed suit. By 1781 all of the states had agreed to enter the Confederation. The states were now officially "The United States of America."

The Confederation knew, however, that the problem of western lands remained. To regulate the disposal of the land, Congress passed the **Land Ordinance of 1785**. The ordinance marked off the land into townships and divided each township into 640-acre sections. The ordinance permitted the cash sale of 640-acre tracts for not less than a dollar an acre and reserved one section of each township for the establishment of a school. This provision in the ordinance marked the first government aid given to public education.

Teaching the Section

PROBLEMS UNDER THE ARTICLES

Organize the class into four groups and assign each group one of the following roles: merchants, farmers, artisans, and bankers. Have group members work together to write a handbill or press release that identifies a problem faced by the group they represent and that ties the problem to weaknesses in the Articles of Confederation. Have representatives from each group present and explain their handbills or press releases to the class.

SHAYS'S REBELLION

Invite students to work in groups to prepare "news broadcasts" on Shays's Rebellion. Ask groups to include in their "broadcasts" interviews with farmers, merchants, Massachusetts officials, and wealthy citizens about the causes of the rebellion and its consequences. Then have groups present their "broadcasts" to the class.

VOICES IN HISTORY

The Northwest Ordinance pledged that Native Americans would always be treated with the "utmost of good faith," and that "their land and property [would] never be taken away from them without their consent." Many settlers ignored these promises, however, moving onto Indian lands or violating treaties and agreements in other ways. In 1794 Mohawk leader Thayendanegea warned that Native Americans' patience with the settlers was wearing thin. Emphasizing Indian rights to use the land, he said, "We, as the original inhabitants of this country, and sovereigns of the soil, look upon ourselves as . . . independent, and free as any other nation. . . . This country was given to us by the Great Spirit above; we wish to enjoy it."

Two years later, with the Land Ordinance of 1787, commonly referred to as the **Northwest Ordinance**, Congress established a system for governing the **Northwest Territory**. This vast area extended north of the Ohio River to the Great Lakes and west of Pennsylvania to the Mississippi River. Congress intended that states would be carved out of the Northwest Territory. Thus the ordinance also outlined the steps to statehood (see chart below). The present-day states of Ohio, Indiana, Illinois, Michigan, and Wisconsin eventually were carved out of the territory.

Besides ensuring eventual self-rule in the territory, the Northwest Ordinance guaranteed settlers their basic civil rights and banned slavery in the territory. The ban reflected a growing antislavery sentiment in the northern states. But the ban was only a partial victory for the opponents of slavery, since the ordinance also required that slaves escaping to freedom in the territory be returned to their owners.

■■ **The Land Ordinances of 1785 and 1787 established rules for settling and governing western lands.**

WEAKNESSES IN THE CONFEDERATION

The land ordinances established a pattern of land settlement for the next 75 years and marked an important achievement for the Confederation. But Congress could point to few other noteworthy accomplishments.

On paper the Confederation government enjoyed broad powers, but in reality it was weak. Proposed changes to the Articles needed the consent of all 13 states. Major new legislation needed the approval of at least 9 states. Agreements were hard to reach because northern and southern delegates often had conflicting interests. The fragile bonds that had united the states during the war were weakening during peacetime.

The Confederation government also had financial problems. Congress desperately needed cash to pay the war debt. But it could only ask the states for funds; it could not tax the people directly. Some states hid behind their independent status to avoid paying their share of the debt.

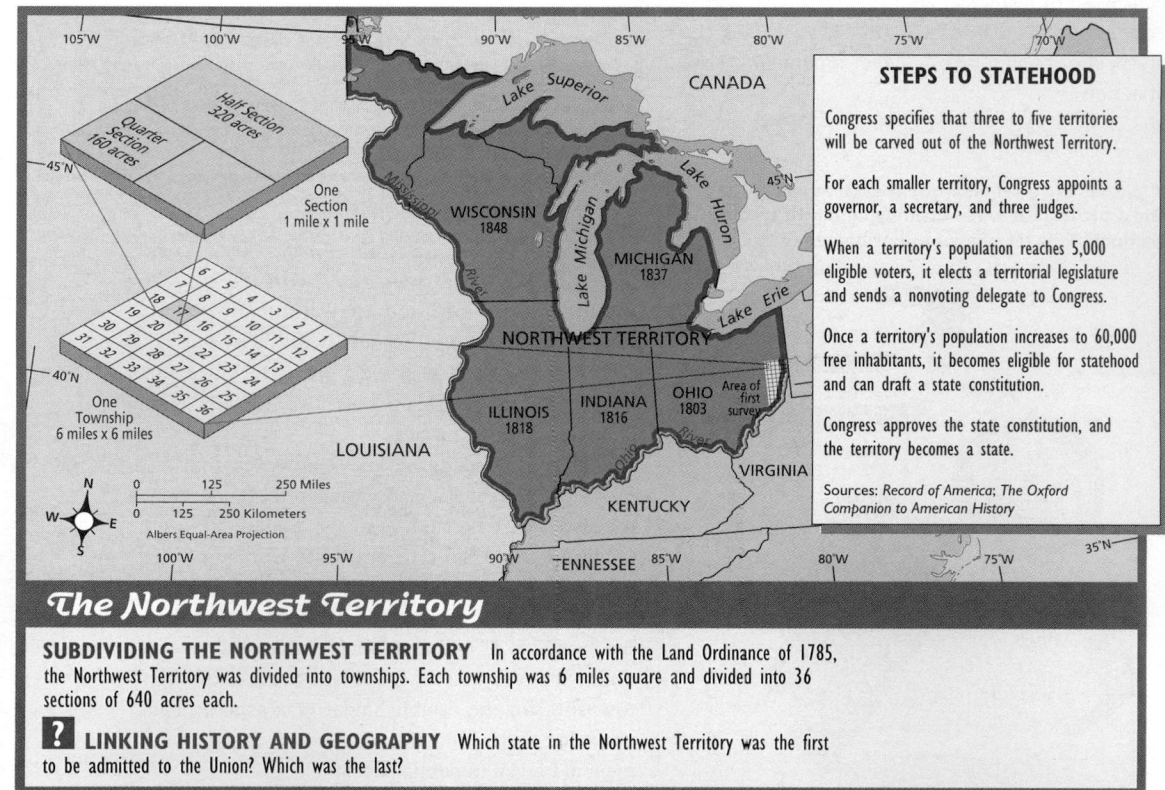

STEPS TO STATEHOOD

Congress specifies that three to five territories will be carved out of the Northwest Territory.

For each smaller territory, Congress appoints a governor, a secretary, and three judges.

When a territory's population reaches 5,000 eligible voters, it elects a territorial legislature and sends a nonvoting delegate to Congress.

Once a territory's population increases to 60,000 free inhabitants, it becomes eligible for statehood and can draft a state constitution.

Congress approves the state constitution, and the territory becomes a state.

Sources: *Record of America; The Oxford Companion to American History*

The Northwest Territory

SUBDIVIDING THE NORTHWEST TERRITORY In accordance with the Land Ordinance of 1785, the Northwest Territory was divided into townships. Each township was 6 miles square and divided into 36 sections of 640 acres each.

❓ LINKING HISTORY AND GEOGRAPHY Which state in the Northwest Territory was the first to be admitted to the Union? Which was the last?

Map Caption Answer
Ohio; Wisconsin

GUIDED PRACTICE

Draw a two-column chart on the chalkboard with the headings *Weaknesses* and *Problems*. Organize the class into two groups. Ask one group to identify weaknesses of the Articles. Then ask the other group to identify problems resulting from each weakness. List replies on the chalkboard. Then ask the entire class to suggest how these weaknesses might be corrected.

INDEPENDENT PRACTICE

Ask students to select a problem identified in the Guided Practice. Direct them to write a letter about the problem to their representative in the Confederation Congress. The letter should indicate why the problem is the result of one of the Articles' weaknesses and suggest how that specific weakness could be corrected. Students may wish to include their letters in their portfolios.

Review and Assessment

REVIEW Have students work in pairs to prepare newspaper headlines summarizing the main events in Section 1. Then assign the Section 1 Review on p. 144.

ASSESS Assign the **Section 1 Daily Quiz** in *Core Resources*.

 The Continental Congress had authorized states to print paper money to finance the Revolution. By 1779 more than $441 million in Continentals had been issued. The dollars shown here were printed in Philadelphia in 1779.

Congress responded to the revenue shortage by printing paper money. The financial consequences were disastrous. These dollars, called "Continentals," were not backed by gold or silver, so merchants and lenders refused to accept them at face value. In 1779 it took about 38 Continentals to purchase a product worth a dollar in gold. By 1781 the price had skyrocketed to 100 Continentals! The widespread inflation frustrated many Americans. The popular expression "not worth a Continental" reflected Americans' anger over their nearly worthless currency.

The Confederation's economic worries multiplied. In 1786 the nation experienced a **depression**, a sharp drop in business activity accompanied by rising unemployment. The primary cause of the depression was the loss of British markets. Before the war American merchants had traded with Great Britain and other colonies within the British Empire. After the war Great Britain closed some of its colonial markets to American commerce.

To make matters worse, Great Britain and France were flooding the United States with inexpensive goods. Struggling American merchants and artisans could not match the prices and survive. Congress was powerless to help since the Articles did not give it the authority to draft international trade policies.

The young nation also faced challenges in international diplomacy. Great Britain refused to abandon its forts in North America on the grounds that Americans were not honoring the terms of the 1783 Treaty of Paris. Under the Articles the U.S. government could not force individuals or states to honor the treaty. As a result, few Americans paid their prewar debts to British merchants, even though the treaty required such payment. As one Virginian remarked, "If we are now to pay the debts due to British merchants, what have we been fighting for all this while?" The treaty also called for compensation to Loyalists for property seized during the war, but few states complied.

■■ The limitations on congressional power under the Articles caused serious economic and diplomatic problems.

SHAYS'S REBELLION

The weak Confederation also proved unable to help farmers, who had been particularly hard hit by the war and its aftermath. The depression and widespread inflation left farmers with fewer markets in which to sell their goods and little money to pay their debts. Instead of extending credit, merchants demanded hard money—gold or silver—which farmers seldom had in their possession.

In Massachusetts the merchant-controlled legislature passed a law that imposed a heavy tax on land. If a landowner did not pay the tax, the state would seize the property. Outraged farmers in western Massachusetts sent petitions to the legislature, complaining of "taxation without representation." These western farmers asked the legislature to issue more paper money and to put a stop to the foreclosures. "Our property is torn from us," one petition complained, "our Gaols [jails] filled & still our Debts are not discharged."

The closing of some of its traditional markets forced the U.S to search for new trading partners. Among the most profitable new trade arrangements was that with China. In the early 1800s some 30 to 40 ships sailed to China each year carrying furs, tar, turpentine, wine, and ginseng—a root that the Chinese believed had medicinal properties. The ships returned with cargoes of silk, tea, and porcelain.

HISTORICAL SIDELIGHTS

Creditors and Judges

It is estimated that from 1784 to 1786 almost a third of American males over the age of 16 were brought to court over unpaid debts. Hundreds of those sent to prison were farmers. The farmers' creditors were often the judges who sent them to prison or the officers who led the militia that enforced acts of the state government.

RETEACH Ask students to write the section's headings and subheadings on a sheet of paper, leaving a space between each. Then have them list in the appropriate space the main ideas of each heading and subheading. Suggest that students compare their main ideas.

Closure

Have students reread George Washington's remark on p. 137. Call on volunteers to explain what Washington meant by these words. Then ask students if they think that Washington was being unnecessarily pessimistic.

Extension

RESEARCH Have students research and prepare reports on the views of Abigail Adams and Mercy Otis Warren on women's rights.

ANALYZE Ask students to read their present-day state constitution and outline how it addresses the issues that were of concern to Americans of the 1770s and 1780s.

SECTION REVIEW ANSWERS

IDENTIFY

For significance, see the following pages:
republic (p. 138)
John Locke (p. 139)
Virginia Statute for Religious Freedom (p. 139)
Judith Sargent Murray (p. 140)
Articles of Confederation (p. 140)
Northwest Ordinance (p. 142)
depression (p. 143)
Daniel Shays (p. 144)

LOCATE

For location, see the map on p. 141 or p. 142.

1. 1785—divided western lands into townships and sections for sale; 1787—established system for governing Northwest Territory, outlined steps to statehood, banned slavery in territory
2. needed 13 states to change Articles and 9 to add new laws, could not tax; led to economic and diplomatic problems
3. anger over high taxes and heavy debts; call for stronger central government
4. Essays should mention defining governors' powers, separation of church and state, voting requirements, and protection of individual rights.
5. take care of home and educate children to be good citizens; limited political activities, but expanded educational opportunities

When the Massachusetts legislature adjourned in July 1786 without addressing the tax or debt issues, farmers rebelled. Under the leadership of such men as Daniel Shays, a former Revolutionary War captain, angry farmers took up arms to dramatize their grievances and to demand a greater voice in Massachusetts politics. In what became known as

▲ This 1884 painting by Howard Pyle shows Daniel Shays and his mob taking possession of a courthouse.

Shays's Rebellion, farmers shut down debtor courts and stopped property auctions.

The most serious threat to peace began in late 1786. On December 26, Shays and some 1,200 farmers set out for Springfield, Massachusetts, intent on seizing the federal arsenal. Worried that Shays's forces would overrun the militiamen guarding the arsenal, the governor quickly called for more than 4,000 additional recruits.

Shays and his men launched their attack in late January. However, when cannon fire killed four of the farmers, Shays's men fled. By the end of February the militia had crushed the rebellion.

Despite Shays's defeat, the rebellion helped the farmers. The Massachusetts legislature did away with direct taxes and passed debtor-relief legislation that prevented creditors from seizing household goods and tools.

The rebellion's most important legacy, though, was its effect on public opinion. The unrest frightened the wealthy and raised doubts about the government's ability to deal with civil unrest and to bring about national unity. As a result many people who had previously objected to a strong central government began calling for new powers for the Confederation.

■■ **Farmers, angry over high taxes and heavy debts, launched Shays's Rebellion. The revolt led to calls for a stronger central government.**

 SECTION **1** REVIEW

IDENTIFY and explain the significance of the following: republic, John Locke, Virginia Statute for Religious Freedom, Judith Sargent Murray, Articles of Confederation, Northwest Ordinance, depression, Daniel Shays.

LOCATE and explain the importance of the following: Northwest Territory.

1. **MAIN IDEA** How did the Land Ordinances of 1785 and 1787 help regulate the settlement of western territories?
2. **MAIN IDEA** What limits did the Articles of Confederation place on federal power? What were some of the consequences of these limits?
3. **IDENTIFYING CAUSE AND EFFECT** Why did farmers launch Shays's Rebellion? What was the rebellion's most important legacy?
4. **WRITING TO DESCRIBE** Write an essay describing what provisions the states wrote into their new constitutions.
5. **EVALUATING** What role did republicanism assign to women? How did this influence women's activities and opportunities?

Section 2

DRAFTING AND RATIFYING THE CONSTITUTION

FOCUS

- **Why did delegates to the Constitutional Convention agree to keep the proceedings secret?**
- **What major compromises are reflected in the Constitution?**
- **What kind of government did the Federalists want? Why did the Antifederalists oppose the Federalist position?**

In February 1787, Congress requested that the 13 states name delegates to revise the Articles of Confederation. The delegates created a national document, the Constitution, which outlined a new structure of government. Its acceptance was not a foregone conclusion, and heated debates followed as the citizens of each state struggled over ratification.

Woodcut commemorating ratification of the Constitution, 1788

THE CALL TO PHILADELPHIA

Striking evidence of the disunity of the Confederation came in September 1786. A meeting held in Annapolis, Maryland, to work out a cooperative trade agreement failed because only five states sent delegates. This disappointment, followed soon after by Shays's Rebellion, made Congress consider the weaknesses of the Articles of Confederation. Congressional leaders issued a call for a **Constitutional Convention** to strengthen the government. The convention was to be held in Philadelphia beginning May 14, 1787.

The convention. By the appointed day only the delegates from Pennsylvania and Virginia had arrived. Others straggled in, delayed by muddy roads. By May 25 enough delegates were on hand to convene the proceedings.

The convention met in the Pennsylvania State House (now called Independence Hall), in the same room where the leaders of the American Revolution had signed the Declaration of Independence. The delegates agreed to keep the proceedings secret, believing that it would be easier to debate and resolve their differences behind closed doors. Despite the sweltering heat, even the windows were kept tightly closed.

▲ **Delegates to the Constitutional Convention** walked to the **City Tavern** (extreme left) for meals or to discuss events of the day. This engraving was done by **William Russell Birch and Thomas Birch** between 1799 and 1800.

MOTIVATING: STUDENT EXPERIENCES

Call on volunteers to describe situations in which they have compromised to reach an agreement. Discuss why compromise is a valuable life skill and an important factor in politics. Then ask students to identify recent examples of political compromises.

Teaching the Section

SECRET PROCEEDINGS

Have students draft a memorandum to George Washington from the viewpoint of a delegate at the Constitutional Convention, explaining why the proceedings of the convention should or should not be kept secret. Ask volunteers to read their memoranda to the class. Then encourage students to discuss whether they think the delegates' decision to hold secret proceedings was a

wise one. Students may wish to include their memoranda in their portfolios.

■■ Ask students how difficult they think it would be today to keep secret the proceedings of such an important gathering.

Turgot felt that the U.S. could serve as a model for other nations, as long as it did not develop into another Europe, which he described as "a heap of divided powers quarreling over territory or trade profits."

HISTORICAL SIDELIGHTS

Madison's Preparation
Several months before the beginning of the Constitutional Convention, Madison had written to Jefferson in Paris, asking for a "literary cargo" of books about republican government. Jefferson sent about 200 volumes in English and French, and Madison pored over them in preparation for the convention.

PRIMARY SOURCE

Description of Change: excerpted
Rationale: excerpted to focus on main idea

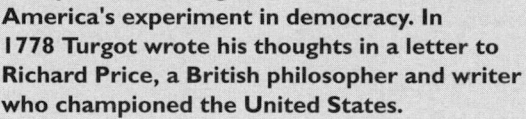

THE AMERICAN EXPERIMENT

Anne-Robert-Jacques Turgot (toor-GOH), a retired French government official, was among the many Europeans watching America's experiment in democracy. In 1778 Turgot wrote his thoughts in a letter to Richard Price, a British philosopher and writer who championed the United States.

"The fate of America is already decided," Turgot wrote. *"Behold her independent beyond recovery. But will she be free and happy?"* Turgot worried whether the 13 separate states would be able to work together. He also wondered whether people could be governed *"only by nature, reason and justice"* without falling prey to the greed and self-interest of individuals.

Despite his doubts Turgot wished the experiment well. Of the Americans he wrote, *"They are the hope of the world."*

The delegates took seriously their vow of secrecy. When someone accidentally dropped some notes on the floor outside the meeting room, George Washington, the presiding officer, erupted in anger:

> 66 Gentlemen, I am sorry to find that some member of the body has been so neglectful to the secrets of the Convention as to drop in the State House a copy of their proceedings. . . . I know not whose paper it is, but here it is, let him who owns it take it. 99

Throwing the notes on the desk, Washington stalked from the room. Not surprisingly, none of the convention delegates made a move to claim the document.

The delegates. George Washington and the 54 other convention delegates were a remarkable collection of politicians. Most had helped to write their state constitutions. All had held public

office, many as delegates to the Continental Congress. They were a young group: James Madison of Virginia was 36; Alexander Hamilton of New York, 32. The youngest delegate, Jonathan Dayton of New Jersey, was only 26. At 81, Benjamin Franklin was the elder statesman of the convention.

Several prominent Americans were absent from the convention, however. Thomas Jefferson and John Adams were in Europe on diplomatic missions. Patrick Henry refused to attend. Saying he "smelled a rat," Henry claimed that the delegates were plotting to undermine states' rights. He feared that "the tyranny of Philadelphia may be like the tyranny of George III."

Generally wealthy and well educated, most delegates represented the privileged ranks of society. Many were merchants, planters, and bankers; more than half were lawyers. Although the delegates were hardly "average" citizens, there was no public outcry against their appointment. Few Americans of the day questioned the assumption that the wealthy were best qualified to govern.

■■ Convention delegates debated issues in secret because they believed it would make it easier to resolve differences.

FEDERAL POWER VERSUS STATES' RIGHTS

Although charged by Congress to revise the Articles of Confederation, some delegates believed that the Articles should be replaced with a new plan of government. At issue were relations among the states and between the states and the central government.

On May 29, Governor Edmund Randolph of Virginia started a heated debate when he presented James Madison's **Virginia Plan**. Madison's proposal to restructure the government was a bold departure from the Articles. His plan shifted political power away from the states and toward the central government. The central government would coordinate the states' activities for the benefit of the entire nation. The plan expressed Madison's belief that the nation's survival depended on **federalism**, or the division of powers between a strong central government and the state governments.

Suggest that students imagine they are delegates to the Philadelphia Convention. Ask them to assume the backgrounds and economic positions of typical delegates and prepare a short speech describing their values, their view of the purpose of government, and their reason for attending the convention. Select students to deliver their speeches to the class. Ask class members to analyze the content of each speech and to make inferences from it about the delegate's social and economic background.

▶

▲ Governor Edmund Randolph of Virginia presented Madison's Virginia Plan to the Constitutional Convention.

BIO GRAPHY James Madison was born in 1751 to a prominent Virginia family of planters, lawyers, and judges. He was frail in childhood and prone to vague ailments affecting his "nerves." Ill health prompted Madison to concentrate on strengthening his mind rather than his body.

A contemporary described Madison as being "no bigger than half a piece of soap." He was so quiet and reserved that an acquaintance called him "a gloomy, stiff creature." Nevertheless, Madison had a distinguished political career, helping draft Virginia's state constitution and ably serving as a member of the Continental Congress. Madison's leadership at the Constitutional Convention earned him the name "father of the Constitution."

James Madison

Madison's Virginia Plan gave Congress vast powers, including the rights to overturn state laws, tax the states, and "bring the force of the Union against any [state] . . . failing to fulfill its duty." Such a drastic move away from states' rights alarmed some delegates. Charles Pinckney of South Carolina feared that such a powerful federal government would "abolish the State Governments altogether."

The Virginia Plan called for a federal government made up of three branches: executive, judicial, and legislative. Under this plan the legislature would be **bicameral**—made up of two houses. Voters would elect representatives to the lower house, who would then choose members of the upper house. State populations would determine the number of representatives in each house.

A dispute quickly arose over the number of representatives each state could send to the legislature. States with large populations, such as Virginia and Pennsylvania, naturally favored representation based on population. States with small populations insisted on an equal number of representatives for each state. Said a delegate from tiny Delaware: "We would sooner submit to a foreign power than . . . be thrown under the domination of the large states."

William Paterson of New Jersey offered an alternative to the Virginia Plan. Paterson's New Jersey Plan provided for a unicameral, or one-house, legislature in which each state would have one vote. Madison and others objected to Paterson's plan because they believed that it did not correct the weaknesses of the Articles.

COMPROMISE AT THE CONVENTION

Arguments raged over the Virginia and New Jersey plans. By the end of June the convention was in danger of collapsing.

To balance the interests of large and small states, Roger Sherman of Connecticut fashioned a compromise. He proposed a two-house legislature that would allow for both equal representation and representation based on population. This **Great Compromise** granted each state, regardless of size, an equal voice in the upper house. In the lower house, representation would be according to population. The delegates narrowly approved this proposal, ending what Madison later described as "the most serious and threatening excitement" of the convention.

The Three-Fifths Compromise. The delegates resolved one dispute only to see another emerge. They now debated whether slaves should be counted as part of a state's population to

Teaching the Section

CONVENTION COMPROMISES

Organize the class into three groups and assign each group one of the three major divisive issues debated at the Constitutional Convention: representation in Congress, slavery, and control of commerce. Direct groups to role-play the debates over these issues for the class. Have students who observe each debate explain why the solution to each issue was a compromise.

determine representation. Southern delegates insisted that the slave population be included. Northern delegates strongly objected to this demand. Some deeply opposed slavery on moral grounds and argued that it violated the republican ideal of liberty. Others objected to including slaves for political reasons. Southern states would be able to increase their representation in the lower house if slaves were included in population counts.

In the end, northern and southern delegates accepted a compromise. The final agreement, known as the **Three-Fifths Compromise**, counted only three fifths of the slave population in determining total state population.

Compromises over commerce. The states also clashed over control of commerce. Northern delegates favored giving the national government the power to regulate all trade with foreign nations and among the states. Southern delegates opposed such broad powers.

The southern economy depended on exports of tobacco, rice, and cotton to Europe and to northern states. Southerners feared that if the national government imposed **tariffs**, or taxes, on exports, overseas buyers would have to pay more for southern agricultural products. If buyers refused to pay higher prices, sales would be hurt. Southern opposition finally forced another compromise.

Delegates agreed that Congress could levy tariffs on imports but not on exports.

Once again, however, problems arose. Planters now worried that Congress might use its power to tax imports to restrict or abolish the slave trade. Bowing to southern pressure, convention delegates voted to permit the slave trade until the end of 1807. They also gave slaveholders the right to pursue runaway slaves across state lines.

Some northern delegates agreed to the compromises because they feared the South would withdraw from the union if planters thought their property and rights were threatened. James Madison argued that great as the evils of the slave trade were, "dismemberment of the union would be worse." Others agreed to the compromise because they mistakenly believed that slavery was a dying institution. Little did they know that more than 70 years of bitter debate and a civil war lay ahead before Americans would see slavery end.

■■ **The Constitution included compromises over political representation, commerce, and slavery.**

Completing the Constitution. On July 26, 1787, five delegates began drafting the Constitution, which they presented to the full convention on August 6. Between August 6 and

▲ This detail from an 18th-century map shows enslaved African Americans working on an indigo plantation in South Carolina. By 1775 some 35 percent of South Carolina's exports involved shipments of indigo, a blue dye.

September 10, the delegates debated the draft, hammering out such specifics as the terms of office for the president and for the members of both houses. Another five-delegate committee then prepared the finished document.

On September 17, 1787, the committee presented to the other delegates the final version of the Constitution, neatly handwritten by Gouverneur Morris of Pennsylvania. Some of the 55 delegates had already left Philadelphia, but of those remaining, 39 signed it. With the convention over, the Constitution went to the states for ratification.

THE FEDERALISTS AND THE ANTIFEDERALISTS

To win ratification, the Constitution required the approval of 9 of the 13 states. Most convention delegates, however, hoped for unanimous approval as a show of national unity.

When local newspapers printed copies of the Constitution, many Americans were shocked by what they read. They expected a revision of the Articles; what they saw was a new framework of government. Citizens soon divided over the issue of ratification.

One group, who called themselves **Federalists**, favored ratification. Wealthy merchants, planters, and lawyers generally were Federalists. They advocated a strong national government that would assure a sound currency and protect property rights. Many Americans who were not wealthy also supported the Constitution, believing that a strong national government would provide stability and security against political unrest like Shays's Rebellion. Speaking before the Massachusetts ratifying convention, a farmer explained his reason for supporting the Constitution:

▲ This 1788 print by engraver Amos Doolittle shows George Washington encircled by the seals of the 13 states and the seal of the United States. The joined circles symbolize the unity of the states.

66 I have lived in a part of the country where I have learned the worth of good government by the lack of it. There was a black cloud of rebellion that rose in the east last winter and spread over the west. . . . Our distress was so great that we should have been glad to grab at anything that looked like a government. . . . Now when I saw this Constitution, I found it was a cure for these disorders. 99

▶ *The Pennsylvania Packet, and Daily Advertiser* was one of several newspapers that carried the full text of the Constitution on September 19, 1787. The preamble to the Constitution is shown here.

The Pennsylvania Packet, and Daily Advertiser.

[Price Four-Pence.]   WEDNESDAY, September 19, 1787.   [No. 2690.]

WE, the People of the United States, in order to form a more perfect Union, establish Justice, insure domestic Tranquility, provide for the common Defence, promote the General Welfare, and secure the Blessings of Liberty to Ourselves and our Posterity, do ordain and establish this Constitution for the United States of America.

CELEBRATING THE CONSTITUTION

Ask students to study the illustration on p. 151. Then have them work in small groups to develop a "news broadcast" on the ratification celebrations in New York City. Suggest that they include in their "broadcasts" descriptions of the scene, interviews with people on the street, and commentaries on the Constitution by political experts. Call on groups to "air" their "broadcasts" for the class.

MAKING CONNECTIONS

Government

Antifederalists, believing that state officials probably would not be happy about surrendering some of their powers to a stronger national government, wanted state legislatures to vote on ratification. The Federalists instead argued for, and succeeded in setting up, state ratifying conventions, made up of delegates chosen by the voters.

PRIMARY SOURCE

Description of Change: excerpted

Rationale: excerpted to focus on main idea

The other group, called **Antifederalists** by their opponents, feared a powerful national government. One Antifederalist described the Constitution as "a beast, dreadful and terrible" that "devours, breaks into pieces, and stamps [the states] with his feet."

The Antifederalists offered three objections to ratification. First, they argued that delegates to the Constitutional Convention had conspired under "a thick veil of secrecy" to create a new form of government. In doing so, the delegates had gone beyond what they had been charged to do. Second, the Antifederalists claimed that a strong national government would destroy states' rights. Third, they argued that the new system of government resembled a monarchy because of its concentration of power, and thus violated the principle of liberty that had guided the Revolution.

■■ **The Federalists wanted a strong national government. The Antifederalists believed that such a government threatened the liberty of the states.**

▼ *The Federalist* contained a collection of essays by Hamilton, Madison, and Jay in support of the Constitution. The book appeared in two volumes in 1788.

THE

FEDERALIST:

ADDRESSED TO THE

PEOPLE OF THE STATE OF
NEW-YORK.

NUMBER I.

Introduction.

AFTER an unequivocal experience of the inefficacy of the subsisting federal government, you are called upon to deliberate on a new constitution for the United States of America. The subject speaks its own importance; comprehending in its consequences, nothing less than the existence of the UNION, the safety and welfare of the parts of which it is composed, the fate of an empire, in many respects, the most interesting in the world. It has been frequently remarked, that it seems to have been reserved to the people of this country, by their conduct and example, to decide the important question, whether societies of men are really capable or not, of establishing good government from reflection and choice, or whether they are forever destined to depend, for their political constitutions, on accident and force. If there be any truth in the remark, the crisis, at which we are arrived, may with propriety be regarded as the æra in which

A   that

The Granger Collection, New York

The Antifederalists pointed to the election procedures outlined in the Constitution as proof that the new national government was undemocratic. Under the Constitution, voters did not elect the president and the vice president—**electors** would choose them. Moreover, voters would not necessarily choose the electors; state legislatures would select them, just as they chose U.S. senators. Voters would elect only members of the lower house of Congress, the House of Representatives. But even then, Antifederalists pointed out, the Senate had the power to take this authority away as well.

The anonymous "Cato" (believed by many to have been Governor George Clinton of New York) challenged citizens to consider the dangers of such a system:

❝ For what did you throw off the yoke of Britain and call yourselves independent? Was it from a disposition fond of change, or to procure new masters? . . . This new form of national government . . . will be dangerous to your liberty and happiness. ❞

The Federalists answered their critics in a series of 85 essays written by James Madison, Alexander Hamilton, and John Jay. Between the fall of 1787 and the spring of 1788, 77 of the essays appeared in newspapers throughout the states. The essays were later published in book form as *The Federalist*, also known as the *Federalist Papers*. The writers intended the essays to sway the ratification vote in New York, but they also influenced public opinion in other states. Today the essays are regarded as the most authoritative commentary on the Constitution.

THE RATIFICATION STRUGGLE

The question of federalism versus states' rights was at the heart of the ratification struggle. Another crucial issue was individual rights. Unlike most state constitutions, the U.S. Constitution did not contain a bill of rights. This omission outraged the Antifederalists, some of whom refused to sign the Constitution.

Ordinary citizens joined the debate over ratification. Amos Singletary, a Massachusetts farmer, argued that the Constitution would take away individual rights, just as Great Britain had done.

Practice

GUIDED PRACTICE

Organize students into small groups and randomly assign among the groups the major divisive issues debated at the Constitutional Convention. Have each group write a statement of its position on the assigned issue. Invite groups to read their statements to the class.

INDEPENDENT PRACTICE

Instruct students to create political cartoons that illustrate a position on the issue assigned to their group in the Guided Practice. Students may wish to include their political cartoons in their portfolios.

Review and Assessment

REVIEW Have students write a Federalist or Antifederalist position paper comparing the Articles of Confederation with the new Constitution. Call on volunteers to read their papers aloud. Students may wish to include their papers in their portfolios. Then assign the Section 2 Review on p. 152.

ASSESS Assign the **Section 2 Daily Quiz** in *Core Resources*.   ▶

The Granger Collection, New York

▲ On July 23, 1788, the people of New York City celebrated the adoption of the Constitution. The ship on wheels was pulled by a team of horses and represented the new "ship of state."

HISTORICAL SIDELIGHTS

A Bitter Debate

In Virginia a bitter personal exchange between Edmund Randolph and Patrick Henry enlivened the debate over ratification. Randolph had played a major role in drafting the Constitution. Although he refused to sign the completed document, he later championed its ratification. Henry, who had expressed skepticism about the Constitution from the beginning, openly ridiculed Randolph for changing his mind. Randolph, visibly angry, responded with a sarcastic rejection of Henry's arguments. At the end of the exchange, both men seemed ready to settle their differences in a duel. Tempers cooled, however, and the duel did not take place.

PRIMARY SOURCE

Description of Change: excerpted and bracketed
Rationale: excerpted to focus on main idea; bracketed to clarify meaning

❝ We contended [fought] with Great Britain . . . because they claimed a right to tax us and bind us in all cases whatever. And does not this Constitution do the same? Does it not take away all we have—all our property? Does it not lay *all* taxes, duties, imposts [import fees], and excises? . . . These lawyers, and men of learning, and moneyed men . . . expect to be managers of this Constitution, and get all the power and all the money into their own hands, and then they will swallow up all us little folks. ❞

The Federalists claimed that the state constitutions adequately protected the rights of American citizens. But several states, including Virginia and New York, agreed to ratify the Constitution only if a bill of rights was added. Although by June 21, 1788, enough states had ratified the Constitution for it to take effect, a union without these two large states had little chance of succeeding.

The debates were bitter in both states' ratifying conventions. In Virginia, Patrick Henry eloquently argued against the Constitution, while James Madison and George Washington strongly urged the convention delegates to vote for ratification. New York Federalists, strongest in New York City, threatened to withdraw the city from the state if the state did not ratify the Constitution. In the end the Federalists won in both states, but only by very narrow margins.

The last state to ratify was Rhode Island, which had even refused to send delegates to the Constitutional Convention. After the Constitution had been drafted, the state legislature initially refused to call for a ratifying convention, prompting some towns to consider seceding. When the state—threatened with an economic boycott by Congress—finally did call a convention, the vote was so close that the governor had to break the tie.

The battle had been long, the final vote close, but with ratification most Americans embraced the Constitution. They had endured the Revolution and the turmoil of the Confederation years. They could now hope to launch constitutional government in the United States with solid prospects for success.

RETEACH

Organize students into small groups and have each group write on a sheet of paper questions for the section's headings and subheadings. Have groups exchange sheets and write answers to the questions. Question-and-answer sheets should be handed back to original groups for marking.

Closure

Organize students into two groups. Have one group make a list of reasons for supporting ratification of the Constitution and the other group reasons for opposing ratification. Groups should draw on the Americans' experiences in the Revolutionary War and under the Articles of Confederation. Have groups present their lists. Then poll the class as to whether they would have supported or opposed ratification.

Extension

CREATE Suggest that small groups of students create maps of the original states and dates of ratification. Have groups conduct research to find areas of Federalist and Antifederalist support and offer reasons for differences of opinion among geographical areas.

ANALYZE Have students read *The Federalist, No. 10*. Then ask students to write a critique of the essay.

IDENTIFY

For significance, see the following pages:
Constitutional Convention (p. 145)
Virginia Plan (p. 146)
federalism (p. 146)
James Madison (p. 146)
bicameral (p. 147)
Great Compromise (p. 147)
Three-Fifths Compromise (p. 148)
tariffs (p. 148)
Federalists (p. 149)
Antifederalists (p. 150)
electors (p. 150)
The Federalist (p. 150)

1. *to work out differences more easily*
2. *Delegates compromised over political representation, commerce, and slavery.*
3. *Speeches will vary but should show understanding of the Federalist or Antifederalist view of government power.*
4. *limitations—granted full political rights only to free white male property owners, protected slavery; revolutionary implications—laid foundation for future political and social reforms*

COMMENTARY

Evaluating the Constitution

The men who wrote the Constitution knew that their gathering in Philadelphia in 1787 had revolutionary implications far greater than the war for independence. Yet their goal was not to remake the United States but to set the young nation on more stable political, economic, and social foundations by reforming the structure of government.

In this sense many of these men were conservatives, worried about maintaining their own status in a quickly changing world. Their concern was to preserve what they had created, rather than to carry out what they thought would be rash and dangerous innovations. They did not, for example, wish to grant political power to all members of society. Such a move would at once overturn long-standing social conventions and decentralize political and economic power. Women, servants, free blacks, and slaves could not vote or hold political office. Only free white men of property, according to the prevailing wisdom, were full members of political society and, therefore, equal.

One of the reasons that the limitations seem so startling today is that we view the Constitution in relation to the Revolution. Why did the democratic values that gave rise to the fight for independence not find full expression in the Constitution?

The answer lies in a society in transition. The republican spirit that fueled the Revolution called into question many traditional social patterns. The convention delegates had to walk a fine line between the old order and a new order that was still emerging.

The motives of the delegates and the limitations of the Constitution as first drafted should not cloud the fact that the document is a grand achievement. The government it created was like no other of its time—headed by an elected president, limited in its powers over individuals and state governments, and held in check by laws and courts. Since its ratification the Constitution has served as an enduring example of the promise of self-government for nations around the world.

The Constitution also had revolutionary implications. As the antislavery and women's movements would show, the radical promise of the Constitution was not lost on those excluded from power. In pressing for the same rights and liberties granted to free white men, all groups stood to benefit from the vision of republican government contained in the Constitution.

Quill pen

SECTION 2 REVIEW

IDENTIFY and explain the significance of the following: Constitutional Convention, Virginia Plan, federalism, James Madison, bicameral, Great Compromise, Three-Fifths Compromise, tariffs, Federalists, Antifederalists, electors, *The Federalist*.

1. **MAIN IDEA** Why did delegates to the Constitutional Convention believe it was best to keep the convention a secret?

2. **MAIN IDEA** The Constitution is sometimes called "a bundle of compromises." What were the major compromises that came out of the convention?

3. **WRITING TO PERSUADE** Imagine you are a Federalist or an Antifederalist delegate to a state ratifying convention. Write a speech supporting or opposing ratification of the Constitution. Be sure to address the concerns of the opposing side in your speech.

4. **ANALYZING** Why can it be said that the Constitution had both limitations and revolutionary implications?

PREVIEW WORKSHOP

Following is a list of the significant terms in this section. You may wish to use this list as a section preview.

Terms
- delegated powers
- reserved powers
- concurrent powers
- supremacy clause

- separation of powers
- checks and balances
- impeachment
- veto
- override
- elastic clause
- judicial review

Section 3

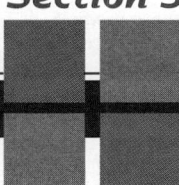

THE CONSTITUTION: A LIVING DOCUMENT

FOCUS

- **Why did the framers of the Constitution include a list of powers delegated to the federal government?**
- **Why did the framers of the Constitution provide for separation of powers and checks and balances?**
- **How is the Constitution able to adapt to changing conditions?**

Detail from *Triumph of Liberty*

The men who convened in Philadelphia in 1787 are often referred to as the framers *of the Constitution. They framed, or built, a new structure of national government. To prevent conflicts between the national government and the state governments, the framers identified specific powers for each. To avoid possible abuses of power by the national government, the delegates divided and limited the powers of the federal government. In doing so they created a flexible and enduring system of government.*

FEDERALISM

Drawing on their experiences with British rule and with the Confederation, the delegates to the Constitutional Convention worked to form a

▲ **This woodcut, entitled *The federal Ship Union,* was made by an unknown artist to celebrate passage of the Constitution.**

stronger federal government. James Madison spoke eloquently of the need for the new government:

> **If** men were angels, no government would be necessary. If angels were to govern men, neither external nor internal controls on government would be necessary. In framing a government which is to be administered by men over men, the great difficulty is this: You must first enable the government to control the governed; and in the next place, oblige it to control itself. **"**

Thus the delegates worked to frame a constitution that would provide for a strong central government while protecting states' rights.

Delegated, reserved, and concurrent powers. Once the delegates settled on a federal system of government, they had to decide which powers would fall to the federal government and

FOCUS OBJECTIVES

- Explain why the framers of the Constitution included a list of powers delegated to the federal government.

- Analyze reasons that the Constitution's framers provided for separation of powers and checks and balances.

- Identify how the Constitution is able to adapt to changing conditions.

PRIMARY SOURCE

Description of Change: excerpted
Rationale: excerpted to focus on main idea

MOTIVATING: LINK TO TODAY

Ask students to identify current issues that involve differences of opinion between Congress and the president. Also ask about controversies involving Supreme Court rulings. Point out that this section explains how the Constitution's framers provided

guidelines for handling disagreements among the three branches of the federal government, as well as guidelines for assuring that no one branch becomes too powerful.

POWERS OF THE FEDERAL GOVERNMENT

Write the following terms on the chalkboard: *delegated powers, reserved powers, concurrent powers.* Call on volunteers to define and list examples of each type of power. Then ask students to speculate why the framers of the Constitution felt it necessary to grant only delegated powers to the national government.

COOPERATIVE LEARNING

Organize students into groups of four or five. Ask groups to create a four- to eight-page illustrated handbook that outlines the major features of the Constitution. Suggest that group members allocate various tasks—research, art, design, writing, and so on—among themselves. Have groups present and explain their handbooks to the class.

MAKING CONNECTIONS

Political Science

The distinction between state and federal powers enabled state governments to discriminate against groups that, under a unitary form of government, would have been protected under the Constitution's Bill of Rights. For example, New Jersey, which in 1776 had granted women the right to vote, revoked women's suffrage in 1807, largely because women were voting against incumbent candidates.

Chart Caption Answer

to balance the interests of the states with those of the national government

◄ **This depiction of Federal Hall, where the first Congress met under the Constitution, was completed in 1789.**

which powers the states would retain. They decided to give the federal government authority in matters of concern to all the people. These **delegated powers**, which are outlined in the

Constitution, include the rights to coin money, to regulate trade with foreign nations and among the states, and to raise and support an army and a navy.

All powers not specifically granted to the federal government or denied to the states are kept, or reserved, by the states. These **reserved powers** are guaranteed by the Tenth Amendment, adopted in 1791. Examples of the states' reserved powers include establishing local governments, overseeing schools, conducting elections, and making marriage laws.

The powers that are held jointly by the federal government and the state government are called **concurrent powers**. Examples of concurrent powers include levying and collecting taxes, borrowing money, providing for the public welfare, and establishing courts to apply and enforce laws.

DELEGATED, RESERVED, AND CONCURRENT POWERS

Powers Delegated to National Government	Powers Reserved to States
Declare war	Establish and maintain schools
Maintain armed forces	Establish local governments
Regulate interstate and foreign trade	Conduct elections
Admit new states	Create corporate laws
Establish post offices	Regulate business within the state
Set standard weights and measures	Make marriage laws
Coin money	Provide for public safety
Establish foreign policy	Assume other powers not delegated to the national government or prohibited to the states
Make all laws necessary and proper for carrying out delegated powers	

Powers Shared (Concurrent Powers)

Maintain law and order	Charter banks
Levy taxes	Establish courts
Borrow money	Provide for public welfare

FEDERALISM The division of power between a national government and the states is called *federalism.* The Constitution delegates certain powers to the national government, reserves other powers for the states, and allows some powers to be shared jointly.

? **EVALUATING** Why might the delegates to the Constitutional Convention have supported a division of powers?

SEPARATION OF POWERS

On the chalkboard draw a chart, titled *Separation of Powers/Checks and Balances,* with the following headings: *Power, Held By, Checked By, Check On.* Begin the table by entering *impeachment, veto,* and *override* in the *Power* column. Then call on volunteers to complete the chart for these powers. Ask students to copy the chart into their notebooks and add entries for other powers mentioned in the text. Have students compare their completed charts. Then ask students why the framers created this system to separate and balance the powers of the national government.

■■ Ask students if the principles of separation of powers and of checks and balances are present in their student government or other student organizations to which they might belong. Call on volunteers to give examples.

CONSTITUTIONAL FLEXIBILITY

Guide students in writing a class letter to one of the framers of the Constitution. In their letter students should update the framer on use of the amendment process, the elastic clause, and judicial review, explaining how these provisions have enabled the federal government to adapt to changing conditions.

▶

▲ The state seals of Massachusetts, New York, and North Carolina are shown here. State legislatures use seals such as these on official public documents.

■■ **The Constitution identifies the powers of the federal government in order to define the scope of federal authority.**

National supremacy. The delegates to the Constitutional Convention recognized that the national government exercising its powers at the same time as the state governments could lead to problems. Which laws would have ultimate authority?

To help eliminate conflicts, the delegates added a clause to the Constitution, clearly stating that the federal constitution and all federal laws outrank state constitutions and state laws: "This Constitution, and the laws . . . and all treaties . . . of the United States, shall be the supreme law of the land." This clause, defined in Article VI of the Constitution, is called the **supremacy clause**.

SEPARATION OF POWERS

To prevent the federal government from abusing its powers, the framers separated the government into three branches: legislative, executive, and judicial. Each branch has specific powers the other branches cannot claim. The legislative branch makes laws, the executive branch sees that they are carried out, and the judicial branch interprets them and punishes lawbreakers. This **separation of powers** prevents any part of the federal government from becoming too powerful.

Checks and balances. The separation of powers is upheld by a system of **checks and balances** that gives each branch the means to restrain the powers of the other two. Congress, for example, has the responsibility to check presidential power. The Constitution's many checks on executive power reflect the framers' bitter experience with British royal governors. The most extreme restraint on presidential authority is the legal process of **impeachment**. The House of Representatives may impeach, or charge, a president who is thought to be guilty of "treason, bribery, or other high crimes and misdemeanors." An impeached president would then be tried by the Senate and, if found guilty, removed from office.

There are other checks and balances between the legislative and the executive branches. The president has the power to make treaties, but a two-thirds vote of the Senate is necessary to ratify them. Similarly, the president can appoint ambassadors, federal judges, and other important officials, but only with the "advice and consent" of the Senate. Congress can also check the president through "the power of the purse"—because it has the authority to appropriate government monies and approve the federal budget, it can slow or stop a presidential action that requires funding.

The president, in turn, can curb the powers of Congress. The president can **veto**, or reject, laws passed by Congress. Although Congress possesses the power to **override**, or overrule, a presidential veto, the two-thirds majority necessary to do so is often difficult to obtain.

The president can also check congressional power through influence and pressure. The Constitution grants the president the authority to call Congress into special session to deal with a national crisis. The president can also adjourn Congress if its members cannot agree when to end

Practice

GUIDED PRACTICE

Work with the class to define each of the terms in the section's Preview Workshop. Have students write the class definition for each term in their notebooks.

INDEPENDENT PRACTICE

Have students use the terms defined in the Guided Practice to write newspaper headlines that summarize for Americans of the 1790s the major features of the Constitution.

Review and Assessment

REVIEW Organize students into three groups. Provide each group with a set of cards on which various powers conferred by the Constitution are written—one power per card. Have groups classify the powers into the three major categories: delegated, reserved, and concurrent. Then assign the Section 3 Review on p. 157.

ASSESS Assign the **Section 3 Daily Quiz** in *Core Resources*.

HISTORICAL SIDELIGHTS

Constitutional Heritage

Delegates argued for a long time over granting the president the power of the veto. The Virginia Plan had called for giving this power to a council made up of the president and members of the national judiciary. The existing provision, like many others, was the result of compromise.

BUILDING VOCABULARY

In this context *lobbying* involves conducting activities aimed at influencing public officials, and especially members of a legislative body, on legislation. This use of the word probably derived from the large entrance hall to the British House of Commons. As early as the 17th century, this hall was called the Lobby. There citizens could talk to and try to influence Parliament members.

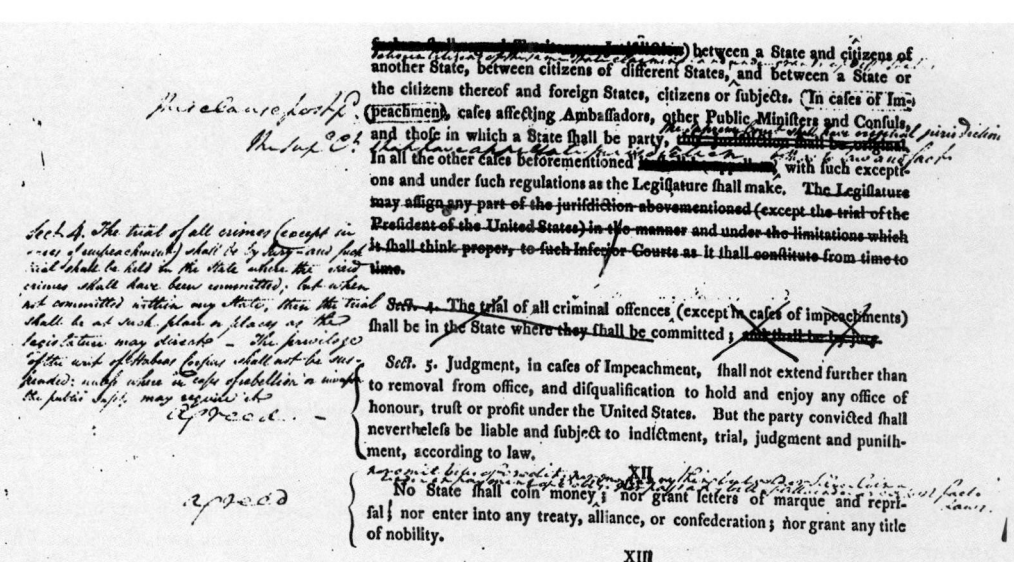

▲ George Washington made numerous editorial changes on an early draft of the Constitution. The wording of Article III, Section 3, regarding trial by jury, is largely unchanged from his handwritten suggestions in the margin. The section that follows on impeachment, which he marked as "agreed," was later moved to Article I, Section 3 of the finished document.

a session. In addition, the president can exert pressure on Congress by recommending measures "necessary and expedient" to maintaining effective government or by lobbying for specific legislation. The chief executive can also influence the thinking of Congress through annual State of the Union messages and through press conferences and public speeches.

The executive and legislative branches balance judicial power. The judicial selection process provides the most basic check. The Senate must approve all federal judges. Just as Congress has the power to impeach the president, it has the power to impeach judges for "high crimes and misdemeanors." In addition, Congress can propose constitutional amendments that overturn earlier court rulings. Similarly, the president can pardon or delay the punishment of persons convicted of federal crimes. But neither the president nor Congress can remove unpopular judges from the bench. Unless impeached and removed for "high crimes," federal judges may hold their offices for life.

Drawbacks of checks and balances. The framers built the system of checks and balances into the structure of government to keep any government branch from exercising too much power. The system, however, has always had its critics.

Some argue that checks and balances permit political disputes to hold up the workings of government. For example, a president who belongs to one political party and a Congress dominated by another party may not agree on necessary legislation. One branch may continually block the actions of the other. Nevertheless, the system has prevented what the framers of the Constitution feared most: unrestricted governmental power.

■■ **Separation of powers and checks and balances prevent any branch of government from becoming too strong.**

FLEXIBILITY AND CHANGE

The Constitution has remained effective for more than 200 years because it is a living document that can adapt to changes in our society. The Constitution works as well today for an industrialized nation of 50 states and some 265 million people as it did in 1790 for an agricultural nation of 13 states and fewer than 4 million people.

The continued effectiveness of the Constitution owes much to its flexibility. James Madison had urged his colleagues to consider "the changes which

RETEACH List on the chalkboard the terms from the Preview Workshop at the beginning of this section. Have students respond to the section's Focus questions with sentences containing the terms.

*C*losure

Remind students of Madison's words on p. 153: "You must first enable the government to control the governed; and in the next place, oblige it to control itself." Have students discuss whether the Constitution satisfies Madison's criteria, and if so, how.

*E*xtension

COMPARE Encourage students to research the constitution of another country and compare it with the U.S. Constitution. Ask students to construct a chart comparing the two documents' contents.

ANALYZE Point out that Thomas Jefferson once wrote that constitutions must "keep pace with the times." Have students comment on whether the work of the framers satisfies Jefferson's requirements.

ages will produce." To allow for needed amendments, the framers specified a procedure by which the Constitution may be changed. The framers deliberately made the amendment process difficult, intending it to be used only when a change is critical (see page 164). Only 27 amendments have been added to the Constitution since 1789.

The Constitution's **elastic clause** has increased the document's flexibility. To the specific powers granted to Congress, this clause adds the power "to make all Laws which shall be necessary and proper for carrying into Execution the foregoing Powers." The elastic clause allows Congress to stretch its powers in ways not specifically outlined in the Constitution.

The Supreme Court's power of **judicial review**—the right to determine whether or not laws violate the Constitution—also ensures the Constitution's continued effectiveness. The framers did not write judicial review into the Constitution. Legal scholars, however, believe that the framers intended the Supreme Court to have such power. James Madison often argued that the Supreme Court could declare any law void if the justices found that the law violated the Constitution. But, Madison continued, the Court would still be compelled to uphold all laws "however unjust."

In *The Federalist* Number 78, Alexander Hamilton, in arguing for judicial independence, stated the problem that might arise from judicial review:

66 The interpretation of the laws is the proper and peculiar province of the courts. . . . It therefore belongs to them to ascertain . . . the meaning of any particular

▲ **The first two sessions of the Supreme Court were held in the Water Street Exchange, a building in New York City.**

act. . . . The courts must declare the sense of the law; and if they should be disposed to exercise WILL instead of JUDGMENT, the consequence would be . . . the substitution of their pleasure to that of the legislative body. 99

Although judicial review has the potential for being abused, it remains one of the safeguards of individual rights in a changing society.

■■ **The amendment process, the elastic clause, and judicial review allow the Constitution to adapt to changing conditions.**

PRIMARY SOURCE
Description of Change: excerpted
Rationale: excerpted to focus on main idea

SECTION REVIEW ANSWERS

IDENTIFY
For significance, see the following pages:
delegated powers (p. 154)
reserved powers (p. 154)
concurrent powers (p. 154)
supremacy clause (p. 155)
separation of powers (p. 155)
checks and balances (p. 155)
impeachment (p. 155)
veto (p. 155)
override (p. 155)
elastic clause (p. 157)
judicial review (p. 157)

1. *to define the scope of federal authority*
2. *to prevent the abuse of power by one branch over another*
3. *because amendment process, elastic clause, and judicial review allow it to adapt to changing conditions*
4. *Essays should discuss the uses of veto, override powers, and judicial review.*
5. *by causing a stalemate between government branches*

■ ■
■ ■ **SECTION 3 REVIEW**

IDENTIFY and explain the significance of the following: delegated powers, reserved powers, concurrent powers, supremacy clause, separation of powers, checks and balances, impeachment, veto, override, elastic clause, judicial review.

1. MAIN IDEA Why were the federal government's powers listed in the Constitution?

2. MAIN IDEA Why were checks and balances and the separation of powers written into the Constitution?

3. MAIN IDEA Why can the Constitution be considered a flexible, living document?

4. WRITING TO EXPLAIN Write an essay explaining how the executive, the legislative, and the judicial branches use the system of checks and balances.

5. ASSESSING CONSEQUENCES How might a system of checks and balances prevent government from being effective at times?

Chapter Review Answers

WRITING A SUMMARY
See Essential Points in each section for main ideas.

REVIEWING CHRONOLOGY
4, 1, 3, 2, 5
Identifying Cause and Effect
Answers will vary but should make clear the cause and effect of events.

IDENTIFYING PEOPLE AND IDEAS
1. *James Madison's plan to restructure the government*
2. *English philosopher who developed the idea of "natural rights"*
3. *document drafted by Jefferson against state support of churches*
4. *original plan to govern the Union, with weak national government*
5. *series of essays written by Hamilton, Madison, and Jay to sway ratification vote in New York*
6. *author of Virginia Plan and "father of the Constitution"*
7. *system giving each branch of government the means to restrain the powers of the other two*
8. *compromise in which three-fifths of slave population counted in determining state population*
9. *leader of farmers' revolt against high taxes and heavy debts*
10. *clause stating that federal laws outrank state laws*

UNDERSTANDING MAIN IDEAS
1. *States were reluctant to give up powers to a national government; confederation lacked authority to resolve economic and diplomatic problems.*
2. *structure of and representation in Congress; three-fifths of slaves counted in determining state population; tariffs set only on imports; slave trade permitted until end of 1807*
3. *separation of powers; system of checks and balances*
4. *National government was given power to collect taxes, to coin money, and to regulate trade.*
5. *1785—marked off the land into townships and sections for sale; 1787—provided for division of Northwest Territory into states, outlined steps to statehood, guaranteed settlers basic civil rights, and banned slavery*

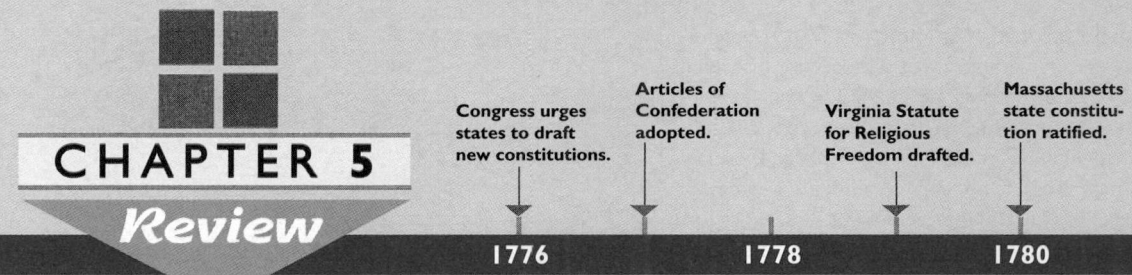

CHAPTER 5
Review

Congress urges states to draft new constitutions.	**Articles of Confederation adopted.**	**Virginia Statute for Religious Freedom drafted.**	**Massachusetts state constitution ratified.**
1776	**1778**	**1780**	

WRITING A SUMMARY
Using the essential points of the chapter as a guide, write a summary of the chapter.

REVIEWING CHRONOLOGY
Number your paper 1 to 5. Study the time line above, and list the following events in the order in which they happened by writing the first event next to 1, the second next to 2, and so on. Then complete the activity below.

1. Virginia Statute for Religious Freedom drafted.
2. Congress passes Northwest Ordinance.
3. Congress passes Land Ordinance of 1785.
4. Articles of Confederation adopted.
5. U.S. Constitution ratified.

Identifying Cause and Effect Select two events on the time line, and in a paragraph, explain the cause-and-effect relationship between them.

IDENTIFYING PEOPLE AND IDEAS
Explain the historical significance of each of the following people or terms.

1. Virginia Plan
2. John Locke
3. Virginia Statute for Religious Freedom
4. Articles of Confederation
5. *The Federalist*
6. James Madison
7. checks and balances
8. Three-Fifths Compromise
9. Daniel Shays
10. supremacy clause

UNDERSTANDING MAIN IDEAS
1. Why did colonial leaders create a weak national government in the Articles of Confederation, and why did this cause problems for the new nation?
2. What were the main compromises reached during the Constitutional Convention?
3. What elements of the Constitution addressed concerns over governmental abuse of power?
4. How did the framers of the Constitution propose to solve economic problems caused by weaknesses in the Articles of Confederation?
5. What were the provisions of the ordinances to organize and govern the Northwest Territory?

REVIEWING THEMES
1. **Constitutional Heritage** How does the way the government was organized reflect concern about a powerful national government?
2. **Economic Development** How did the government's economic policies lead to Shays's Rebellion?
3. **Democratic Values** How might the framers of the Constitution have helped ensure that more citizens had a voice in government?

THINKING CRITICALLY
1. **Analyzing** What factors shaped the republican spirit?
2. **Hypothesizing** What might have happened if the framers of the Constitution had outlawed slavery?
3. **Evaluating** The proceedings at the Constitutional Convention were secret. Do you think such government activities should be open to the public? Explain your answer.
4. **Identifying Cause and Effect** How did colonial experiences influence the actions of the framers of the state constitutions?

STRATEGY FOR SUCCESS
Review the Skills Handbook entry on Building Vocabulary on page 991. Then define the following terms, and write a sentence using each word.

republic	depression
separation of powers	judicial review
federalism	delegated powers
reserved powers	concurrent powers
bicameral	impeachment
veto	override

WRITING ABOUT HISTORY
Writing to Persuade Imagine you are a business owner in New England who supports the Constitution. Write a letter to the editor of your local newspaper, explaining why you support the new plan of government over the Articles of Confederation.

REVIEWING THEMES

1. Responsibilities were shared between the federal government and the states, each with defined powers.
2. "Continentals" led to inflation; loss of British trade led to depression; land tax burdened farmers, so they rebelled.
3. by not restricting the vote to white male property owners

THINKING CRITICALLY

1. John Locke's "natural rights," idea of self-government, and America's negative experience with monarchy in Great Britain

2. Students may mention that the South might have rejected the Constitution outright, or that the ban might have resolved the slavery issue entirely.
3. Students should balance the need for secrecy with the desire of citizens to have the opportunity to influence political decisions.
4. Their experience with colonial royal governors caused them to limit executive powers.

STRATEGY FOR SUCCESS

For definitions, see the following pages:
republic (p. 138)
separation of powers (p. 155)

federalism (p. 146)
reserved powers (p. 154)
bicameral (p. 147)
veto (p. 155)
depression (p. 143)
judicial review (p. 157)
delegated powers (p. 154)
concurrent powers (p. 154)
impeachment (p. 155)
override (p. 155)
Sentences should reflect accurate use of terms.

WRITING ABOUT HISTORY

Letters might mention how the national government would now have the power to regulate trade with foreign nations and among all states, thereby preventing loss of foreign markets and trade conflicts.

USING PRIMARY SOURCES

that they loaned money; provided food, clothing, and blankets to soldiers; were robbed by British; sacrificed own comfort; that Congress should grant citizens liberty by repaying money owed to them

LINKING HISTORY AND GEOGRAPHY

1. DE 2. PA 3. NJ 4. GA
5. CT 6. MA 7. MD 8. SC
9. NH 10. VA 11. NY
12. NC 13. RI
For ratification dates (dates of admission) see p. 1018.

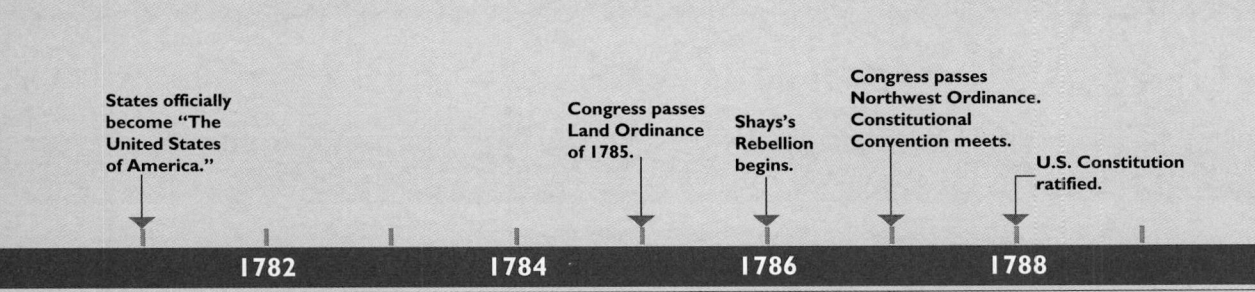

States officially become "The United States of America." — 1782

Congress passes Land Ordinance of 1785. — 1784

Shays's Rebellion begins. — 1786

Congress passes Northwest Ordinance. Constitutional Convention meets. — 1788

U.S. Constitution ratified.

USING PRIMARY SOURCES

The following is an excerpt from a petition submitted to the Continental Congress in 1786 by elderly widow Rachel Wells. Like many patriots, Wells had bought loan certificates from the state of New Jersey during the Revolution. Wells appealed to the Congress to grant her payment on the certificates. Read the excerpt from her petition. What does she reveal about the contribution of ordinary citizens to the war and the government's responsibility to live up to the ideals of the Revolution?

To the Honorable Congress,
I, Rachel, do make this complaint, who am a Widow far advanced in years & Dearly have occasion [need] of the Interest for that Cash I Lent the States. . . . I Lent the State a considerable Sum of Moneys & had I justice done me it might be Sufficient to support me in the country where I am now, near Burdentown [New Jersey]. I lived here then . . . but Being . . . so Robbed by the Britains & others I went to Phila[delphia] to try to get a Living . . . & was There in the year 1783 when our assembly was pleased to pass a Law that No one should have any Interest that lived out of Jersey States. . . .
Now, gentlemen, is this Liberty? . . . I have done as much to carry on the War as many that Sit now at the helm of government. . . . My dear Sister . . . wrote to me to be thankful that I had it in my Power to help on the War, which is well enough, but then this is to be Considered—that others get their Interest & why then a poor old widow be put of[f]? . . .
If She did not fight She threw in all her might, which bought the Soldiers food & Clothing & Let Them have Blankets & Since that She has been obliged to Lay upon Straw & glad of that.

LINKING HISTORY AND GEOGRAPHY

Study the map, noting the numbers on it. The map shows the order in which the states ratified the Constitution. Number your paper 1 to 13. Identify each state on the map and write the correct name of each state next to the corresponding number on your paper, along with the date each state ratified the Constitution.

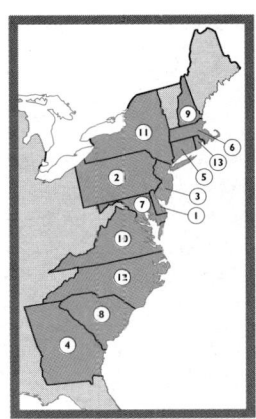

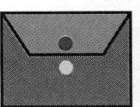 **BUILDING YOUR PORTFOLIO**

Complete the following projects independently or cooperatively.

1. **DEMOCRATIC RIGHTS** In Chapter 4 you served as a reporter interviewing people about taxes. Building on that material, now imagine you are one of Shays's rebels. Create a poster that communicates your position on taxes.

2. **THE CONSTITUTION** Imagine you are a woman interested in including women's rights in the new Constitution. Write a letter to the Constitutional Convention suggesting ways to represent women in the Constitution.

3. **POLITICS** Imagine you are attending a governors conference in 1790. Prepare a speech outlining the issues of concern to your region.

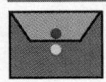 **BUILDING YOUR PORTFOLIO**

Have students refer to **Building Your Portfolio Worksheet 2**, assigned at the beginning of Unit 2. Use the worksheet to help students monitor their progress on the portfolio projects.

Assessment

Core Resources
• Review Worksheet 5
• Chapter 5 Tests
• Alternative Assessment Forms
Test Generator

Constitution
Handbook

*on defense, promote the general Welfare, and se...
...titution for the United States of America.*

Constitution Handbook

66 We the People of the United States, in Order to form a more perfect Union, establish Justice, insure domestic Tranquility, provide for the common defense, promote the general Welfare, and secure the Blessings of Liberty to ourselves and our Posterity, do ordain and establish this Constitution for the United States of America. 99

—Preamble to the Constitution

The delegates who met in the spring of 1787 to revise the Articles of Confederation included many of the ablest leaders of the United States. Convinced that the Confederation was not strong enough to bring order and prosperity to the nation, they abandoned all thought of revising the Articles. Instead, they proceeded to draw up a completely new Constitution. Patrick Henry called this action "a revolution as radical as that which separated us from Great Britain." Out of their long political experience, their keen intelligence, and their great learning, the framers of the Constitution fashioned a blueprint for a truly united nation—the United States of America.

CULTURAL PATTERNS

Long before the settlement of North America by European immigrants, the Iroquois League developed its own unwritten constitution, called the Great Law of Peace. Some provisions of the Great Law are similar to those found in the U.S. Constitution. Under the Great Law, each Indian nation in the league managed its own internal affairs but looked to the league to govern in external and common matters. The Great Law also provided a system of checks and balances, a council with representatives from each nation, and a method for impeaching leaders who abused their powers.

MAKING CONNECTIONS

World History

In many other countries, major revolutions often have been followed by periods of bloodshed, as in the French Revolution of 1789 and the Russian Revolution of 1917. Before the American Revolution, the distance between the colonies and the British monarch taught Americans how to solve many of their own problems through discussion, debate, and compromise. This experience allowed for a peaceful transition to nationhood.

F O C U S

■ **What do the first three Articles of the Constitution describe?**
■ **How do the Articles attempt to protect people's civil liberties?**
■ **What does the Bill of Rights protect?**

An observer once referred to the Constitution as "the most wonderful work ever struck off at a given time by the brain and purpose of man." Revised, modified, and amended, the Constitution has served the American people for more than 200 years, becoming a model for representative government throughout the world. The Constitution has successfully survived the years for two reasons. First, it lays down rules of procedure and guarantees of rights and liberties that must be observed even in times of crisis. Second, it is a "living" document, capable of being revised to meet changing times and circumstances.

U.S. Constitution commemorative stamps

To FORM A MORE PERFECT UNION

The framers of the Constitution wished to establish a strong central government, one that could unite the country and help it meet the challenges of the future. At the same time, however, they feared a government that was too strong. The memories of the troubled years before the Revolution were still fresh. They knew that unchecked power in the hands of individuals, groups, or branches of government could lead to tyranny.

The framers response was to devise a system of government in which power is divided between, in the words of James Madison, "two distinct governments"—the states and the federal government—and then within each government. In *The Federalist* Number 51, Madison described the advantages of such a system:

66 In the compound republic of America, the power surrendered by the people is first divided between two distinct governments, and then the portion allotted to each subdivided among distinct and separate departments. Hence a double security arises to the rights of the people. The different governments will control each other, at the same time that each will be controlled by itself. 99

The seven Articles that make up the first part of the Constitution provide the blueprint for this system. To help guard against tyranny and to keep any one part of the federal government from becoming too strong, the framers divided the government into three branches—the legislative branch (Congress), the executive branch (the president and vice president), and the judicial branch (the federal courts)—each with specific powers. As a further safeguard, the framers wrote a system of checks and balances into the Constitution (see Chapter 5). Articles I, II, and III outline the powers of each branch of government and the checks and balances.

■■ **Articles I, II, and III outline the rights and responsibilities of the legislative, executive, and judicial branches.**

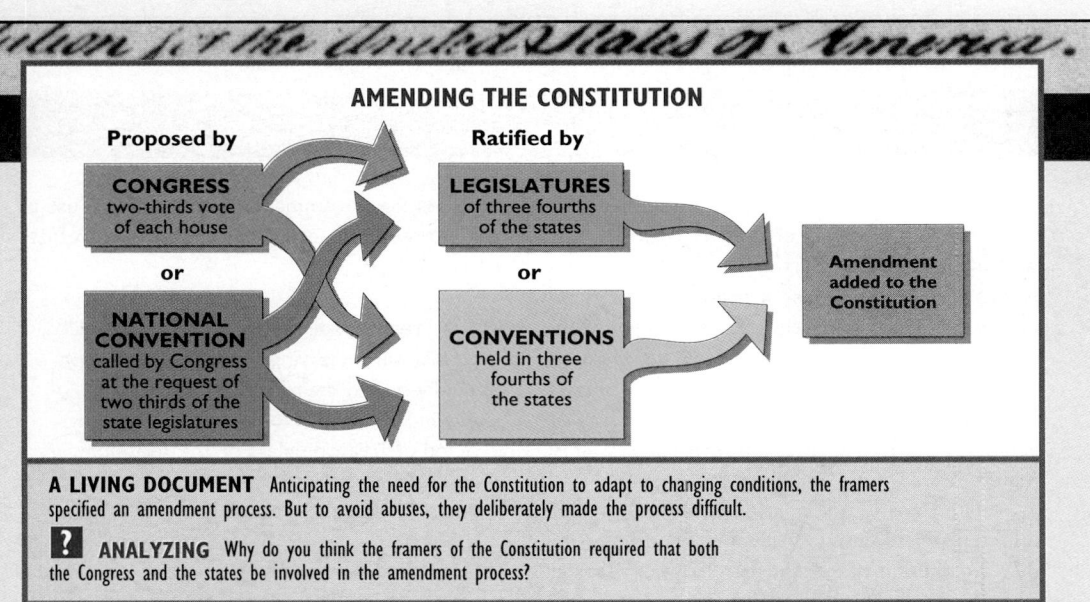

AMENDING THE CONSTITUTION

Proposed by

CONGRESS
two-thirds vote
of each house

or

**NATIONAL
CONVENTION**
called by Congress
at the request of
two thirds of the
state legislatures

Ratified by

LEGISLATURES
of three fourths
of the states

or

CONVENTIONS
held in three
fourths of
the states

**Amendment
added to the
Constitution**

A LIVING DOCUMENT Anticipating the need for the Constitution to adapt to changing conditions, the framers specified an amendment process. But to avoid abuses, they deliberately made the process difficult.

? ANALYZING Why do you think the framers of the Constitution required that both the Congress and the states be involved in the amendment process?

Article IV outlines the relations between the states and between the states and the federal government. Among the issues addressed are each state's recognition of other states' public records and citizens' rights, the admission of new states, and the rights and responsibilities of the federal government in relation to the states.

Article V specifies the process by which the Constitution can be amended. The framers purposely made the process slow and difficult. They feared that if the process was too easy, the Constitution—the fundamental law of the land—would soon carry no more weight than the most minor law passed by Congress.

Article VI includes one provision that addressed the immediate concerns of the framers and two that have lasting significance. The short-term provision promises that the United States under the Constitution will honor all public debts entered into under the Confederation. The two long-term provisions declare the Constitution the supreme law of the land and prohibit religion being used as a qualification for holding public office.

Article VII is the framers' attempt to ensure ratification of the Constitution. The Constitutional Convention was summoned by the Congress to amend the Articles of Confederation. Under the Articles of Confederation, amendments had to be approved by all 13 states. Realizing that it would be difficult to get the approval of all the states—Rhode Island, for example, had not even sent delegates to Philadelphia—the framers specified that the Constitution would go into effect after ratifica-

tion by only 9 states, not all 13. (This provision led opponents of the Constitution to claim that it had been adopted by unfair means.)

PROTECTING INDIVIDUAL LIBERTY

Opposition to a strong central government was in part a concern over states' rights. But it was also rooted in the desire to protect individual liberties. American colonists had always insisted on the protection of their **civil liberties**—their rights as individuals against the power of the government. The Articles of the Constitution contain many important guarantees of civil liberties. On a broad level, the separation of powers and the system of checks and balances help safeguard citizens against the abuse of government power. But the Articles also contain provisions that speak directly to an individual's right to due process of law. For example, Section 9 of Article I prohibits both *ex post facto* laws and bills of attainder.

An *ex post facto* **law** is a law passed "after the deed." Such a law sets a penalty for an act that was not illegal when it was committed. A **bill of attainder** is a law that punishes a person by fine, imprisonment, or seizure of property without a court trial. If Congress had the power to adopt bills of attainder, lawmakers could punish any American at will, and that person could do nothing to appeal the sentence. Instead, the Constitution provides that only the courts can impose punishment for unlawful acts, and then only by following the duly established law.

MAKING CONNECTIONS
Government
The Constitution has always been a political symbol as well as a political document. The United States, having neither a long history of nationhood nor the bonds of monarchy, aristocracy, or established church, needed a symbol of its new political order. Other icons that had emerged—George Washington, the Stars and Stripes, and the Declaration of Independence—did not reflect the political structure of the new nation. The Constitution, however, by standing for the rule of law, invoked the principles by which the American nation lived. It also served as a visible reminder of invisible ideals and linked the individual to the political order. Thus, the Constitution became an important symbol of national identity.

HISTORICAL
Document

HISTORICAL SIDELIGHTS

George Mason and the Bill of Rights

George Mason of Virginia was one of three delegates to Philadelphia who refused to sign the Constitution. His greatest objection was that the Constitution did not protect and define individual rights, and unlike Thomas Jefferson he could not overcome his concern. Earlier, Mason had helped draft a major portion of the Virginia Constitution of 1776 and he had been almost solely responsible for writing its Declaration of Rights. This early bill of rights served as the model for the first part of the Declaration of Independence and later for the Bill of Rights added to the federal Constitution.

Chart Caption Answer
61 years between ratification of the Twelfth and Thirteenth amendments.

Section 9 of Article I also protects a citizen's right to the **writ of** *habeas corpus.* The writ of *habeas corpus* is a legal document that forces a jailer to release a person from prison unless the person has been formally charged with, or convicted of, a crime. The Constitution states that "the privilege of the writ of *habeas corpus* shall not be suspended, unless when in cases of rebellion or invasion the public safety may require it."

The Constitution also gives special protection to people accused of **treason**. The framers of the Constitution knew that the charge of treason was an old device used by tyrants to get rid of persons they did not like. Such rulers might bring the charge of treason against persons who merely criticized the government. To prevent such use of this charge, Section 3 of Article III carefully defines treason:

❝ Treason against the United States shall consist only in levying War against them, or in adhering to their Enemies, giving them Aid and Comfort. No Person shall be convicted of Treason unless on the Testimony of two Witnesses to the same overt Act, or on Confession in open Court. ❞

The Article also protects the innocent relatives of a person accused of treason. Only the convicted person can be punished. No penalty can be imposed on the person's family.

▪▪ The Articles protect civil liberties by guaranteeing individuals due process of law.

𝒯HE BILL OF RIGHTS

Despite the safeguards written into the Articles of the Constitution, some states at first refused to ratify the framework because it did not offer greater protection to the rights of individuals. They finally agreed to ratification after they had been promised that a bill of rights would be added to the Constitution by amendment when Congress was called into session following ratification.

In 1789 the first Congress of the United States wrote the ideals of the Declaration of Independence into the Bill of Rights, the first 10 amendments to the Constitution. The Bill of Rights protects individuals

AMENDMENTS TO THE CONSTITUTION

Amendment	Year Enacted	Subject
1st	1791	Personal and political freedoms
2nd	1791	Right to keep weapons
3rd	1791	Quartering of troops
4th	1791	Search and seizure; search warrants
5th	1791	Rights of accused persons
6th	1791	Speedy trial
7th	1791	Jury trial
8th	1791	Bails, fines, punishments
9th	1791	Rights of the people
10th	1791	Powers of the states
11th	1798	Suits against states
12th	1804	Election of president and vice president
13th	1865	Abolition of slavery
14th	1868	Rights of citizens; privileges and immunities, due process, and equal protection
15th	1870	Extension of suffrage to black males
16th	1913	Income tax
17th	1913	Direct election of senators
18th	1919	Prohibition on liquor
19th	1920	Women's suffrage
20th	1933	Change in dates for presidential and congressional terms of office
21st	1933	Repeal of prohibition
22nd	1951	Two-term limit on presidential tenure
23rd	1961	Right to vote in presidential elections for residents of the District of Columbia
24th	1964	Poll tax banned in federal elections
25th	1967	Presidential disability and succession
26th	1971	Lowering of voting age to 18
27th	1992	Legislative salaries

THE AMENDMENT PROCESS The supreme law of the land has proven very durable. The Constitution has only been amended 27 times in over 200 years.

❓ **BUILDING GRAPH SKILLS** What is the longest interval between ratification of two consecutive amendments?

against any action by the federal government that may deprive them of life, liberty, or property without "due process of law."

Among the guarantees of liberty in the Bill of Rights, several are especially important. The First Amendment guarantees freedom of religion, speech, press, assembly, and petition. The Fourth Amendment forbids unreasonable searches and seizures of any person's home. The Fifth, Sixth, and Eighth amendments protect individuals from arbitrary arrest and punishment by the federal government.

▪▪ The Bill of Rights protects the rights of individuals against abuses of government power.

The Bill of Rights was ratified by the states in 1791. It has remained one of the best-known features of the Constitution. The American people have turned to it for support whenever their rights as individuals have seemed to be in danger. No document in American history, except, perhaps, the Declaration of Independence, has been cherished more deeply.

▼ Supreme Court justices (from left) Antonin Scalia, Ruth Bader Ginsburg, Anthony Kennedy, John Paul Stevens, Chief Justice William Rehnquist, Harry Blackmun, Sandra Day O'Connor, David Souter, and Clarence Thomas meet with President Clinton (center).

Contents of the Constitution

Bill of Rights

Civil War Amendments

HISTORICAL SIDELIGHTS
Nationalization of the Bill of Rights

For most of our history, the Bill of Rights applied to the use of power by the federal government but not by state and local governments. Only state constitutions and laws prevented local governments from encroaching upon basic liberties such as the freedoms of speech, press, and religion. In 1897 the Supreme Court first began to extend the protections guaranteed in the Bill of Rights. Using the due process clause, the Supreme Court ruled in *Chicago, Burlington & Quincy Railroad Co.* v. *Chicago* that states must give property owners just compensation when taking private property for public use. Over the next 70 years, the Supreme Court gradually applied the Bill of Rights to other uses of power by state and local governments. This process is referred to as the "nationalization" of the Bill of Rights.

MAKING CONNECTIONS

Government

The "most numerous branch" of a state legislature is the one with the most members. If a person is eligible to vote for members of the "most numerous branch," he or she is eligible to vote for members of Congress. All states except Nebraska have a two-house legislature. With certain constitutional restrictions or restrictions of federal law, the states decide who can vote for state legislators. The Fifteenth, Nineteenth, Twenty-fourth, and Twenty-sixth amendments forbid the states to deny or restrict a citizen's right to vote because of race, sex, failure to pay a tax, or age (if the person is at least 18 years old).

Preamble
The short and dignified Preamble explains the goals of the new government under the Constitution.

Legislative Branch
Article I explains how the legislative branch, called Congress, is organized. The chief purpose of the legislative branch is to make the laws. Congress is made up of the Senate and the House of Representatives. The decision to have two bodies of government solved a difficult problem during the Constitutional Convention. The large states wanted the membership of Congress to be based entirely on population. The small states wanted every state to have an equal vote. The solution to the problem of how the states were to be represented in Congress was known as the Great Compromise.

The number of members of the House is based on the population of the individual states. Each state has at least one representative. The current size of the House is 435 members, set by Congress in 1929. If each member of the House represented only 30,000 American people, as the Constitution states, the House would have more than 6,000 members.

The Constitution of the United States of America

PREAMBLE

*W*e the People of the United States, in Order to form a more perfect Union, establish Justice, insure domestic Tranquility, provide for the common defense, promote the general Welfare, and secure the Blessings of Liberty to ourselves and our Posterity, do ordain and establish this Constitution for the United States of America.*

ARTICLE I

Section 1. All legislative Powers herein granted shall be vested in a Congress of the United States, which shall consist of a Senate and House of Representatives.

Section 2. The House of Representatives shall be composed of Members chosen every second Year by the People of the several States, and the Electors in each State shall have the Qualifications requisite for Electors of the most numerous Branch of the State Legislature.

No Person shall be a Representative who shall not have attained to the Age of twenty-five Years, and been seven Years a Citizen of the United States, and who shall not, when elected, be an inhabitant of that State in which he shall be chosen.

Representatives and direct Taxes shall be apportioned among the several States which may be included within this Union, according to their respective Numbers, ~~which shall be determined by adding to the whole Number of free Persons, including those bound to Service for a Term of Years, and excluding Indians not taxed, three fifths of all other Persons.~~ The actual Enumeration shall be made within three Years after the first Meeting of the Congress of the United States, and within every subsequent Term of ten Years, in such Manner as they shall by Law direct. The Number of Representatives shall not exceed one for every thirty Thousand, but each State shall have at Least one Representative; ~~and until such enumeration shall be made, the State of New Hampshire shall be entitled to choose three; Massachusetts eight; Rhode Island and Providence Plantations one; Connecticut five; New York six; New Jersey four; Pennsylvania~~

* Parts of the Constitution that have been ruled through are no longer in force or no longer apply.

Pennsylvania eight; Delaware one; Maryland six; Virginia ten; North Carolina five; South Carolina five; and Georgia three.

When vacancies happen in the Representation from any State, the Executive Authority thereof shall issue Writs of Election to fill such Vacancies.

The House of Representatives shall choose their Speaker and other Officers; and shall have the sole Power of Impeachment.

Section 3. The Senate of the United States shall be composed of two Senators from each State, chosen by the Legislature thereof, for six Years; and each Senator shall have one Vote.

Immediately after they shall be assembled in Consequence of the first Election, they shall be divided as equally as may be into three Classes. The Seats of the Senators of the first Class shall be vacated at the Expiration of the second Year, of the second Class at the Expiration of the fourth Year, and of the third Class at the Expiration of the sixth Year, so that one third may be chosen every second Year; and if Vacancies happen by Resignation, or otherwise, during the Recess of the Legislature of any State, the Executive thereof may make temporary Appointments until the next Meeting of the Legislature, which shall then fill such Vacancies.

No Person shall be a Senator who shall not have attained to the Age of thirty Years, and been nine Years a Citizen of the United States, and who shall not, when elected, be an Inhabitant of that State for which he shall be chosen.

The Vice President of the United States shall be President of the Senate, but shall have no Vote, unless they be equally divided.

The Senate shall choose their other Officers, and also a President pro tempore, in the Absence of the Vice President, or when he shall exercise the Office of President of the United States.

The Senate shall have the sole Power to try all Impeachments. When sitting for that Purpose, they shall be on Oath or Affirmation. When the President of the United States is tried, the Chief Justice shall preside: And no Person shall be convicted without the Concurrence of two thirds of the Members present.

Judgment in Cases of Impeachment shall not extend further than to removal from Office, and disqualification to hold and enjoy any Office of honor, Trust or Profit under the United States: but the Party convicted shall nevertheless be liable and subject to Indictment, Trial, Judgment and Punishment, according to Law.

Section 4. The Times, Places and Manner of holding Elections for Senators and Representatives, shall be prescribed in each State by the Legislature thereof; but the Congress may at any time by Law make or alter such Regulations, except as to the Places of choosing Senators.

The Congress shall assemble at least once in every Year, and such Meeting shall be on the first Monday in December, unless they shall by Law appoint a different Day.

Every state has two senators. Senators serve a six-year term, but only one third of the senators reach the end of their terms every two years. In any election, at least two thirds of the senators stay in office. This system ensures that there are experienced senators in office at all times.

The only duty that the Constitution assigns to the vice president is to preside over meetings of the Senate. Modern presidents have given their vice presidents more and varied responsibility.

The House charges a government official of wrongdoing, and the Senate acts as a court to decide if the official is guilty.

Congress has decided that elections will be held on the Tuesday following the first Monday in November of even-numbered years. The Twentieth Amendment states that Congress shall meet in regular session on January 3 of each year. The president may call a special session of Congress whenever necessary.

Qualifications to Serve

In 1806 Henry Clay of Kentucky was appointed to fill an unexpired term in the Senate. He was only 29, a few months younger than the minimum age, but no one challenged his appointment. In 1793 Albert Gallatin was elected to the Senate from Pennsylvania. He was barred from taking office because he had not been a citizen for the required nine years.

HISTORICAL SIDELIGHTS

Compensation

Section 6 prohibits members of Congress from creating jobs to which they can be appointed, from raising the salaries of jobs they hope to hold in the future, and from holding office in other branches of government. In 1909 Senator Philander C. Knox resigned from the Senate to become secretary of state, but the salary of the secretary of state had been increased during Knox's term as senator. So that Knox might accept the post, Congress withdrew the salary increase for the period of Knox's unfinished term.

Congress makes most of its own rules of conduct. The Senate and the House each have a code of ethics that members must follow. It is the task of each house of Congress to discipline its own members. Each house keeps a journal, and a publication called the *Congressional Quarterly* records what happens in congressional sessions. The general public can learn how their representatives voted on bills by reading the *Congressional Quarterly*.

The framers of the Constitution wanted to protect members of Congress from being arrested on false charges by political enemies who did not want them to attend important meetings. The framers also wanted to protect members of Congress from being taken to court for something they said in a speech or in a debate.

The power of taxing is the responsibility of the House of Representatives. Because members of the House are elected every two years, the framers felt that representatives would listen to the public and seek its approval before passing taxes.

Section 5. Each House shall be the Judge of the Elections, Returns and Qualifications of its own Members, and a Majority of each shall constitute a Quorum to do Business; but a smaller Number may adjourn from day to day, and may be authorized to compel the Attendance of absent Members, in such Manner, and under such Penalties as each House may provide.

Each House may determine the Rules of its Proceedings, punish its Members for disorderly Behavior, and, with the Concurrence of two thirds, expel a Member.

Each House shall keep a Journal of its Proceedings, and from time to time publish the same, excepting such Parts as may in their Judgment require Secrecy; and the Yeas and Nays of the Members of either House on any question shall, at the Desire of one fifth of those Present, be entered on the Journal.

Neither House, during the Session of Congress, shall, without the Consent of the other, adjourn for more than three days, nor to any other Place than that in which the two Houses shall be sitting.

Section 6. The Senators and Representatives shall receive a Compensation for their Services, to be ascertained by Law, and paid out of the Treasury of the United States. They shall in all Cases, except Treason, Felony and Breach of the Peace, be privileged from Arrest during their Attendance at the Session of their respective Houses, and in going to and returning from the same; and for any Speech or Debate in either House, they shall not be questioned in any other Place.

No Senator or Representative shall, during the Time for which he was elected, be appointed to any civil Office under the Authority of the United States, which shall have been created, or the Emoluments whereof shall have been increased during such time; and no Person holding any Office under the United States, shall be a Member of either House during his Continuance in Office.

Section 7. All Bills for raising Revenue shall originate in the House of Representatives; but the Senate may propose or concur with Amendments as on other Bills.

Every Bill which shall have passed the House of Representatives and the Senate, shall, before it become a Law, be presented to the President of the United States; If he approve he shall sign it, but if not he shall return it, with his Objections to that House in which it shall have originated, who shall enter the Objections at large on their Journal, and proceed to reconsider it. If after such Reconsideration two thirds of that House shall agree to pass the Bill, it shall be sent, together with the Objections, to the other House, by which it shall likewise be reconsidered, and if approved by two thirds of that House, it shall become a Law. But in all such Cases the Votes of both Houses shall be determined by Yeas and Nays, and the Names of the Persons voting for and against the Bill shall be entered on the

Journal of each House respectively. If any Bill shall not be returned by the President within ten Days (Sundays excepted) after it shall have been presented to him, the Same shall be a Law, in like Manner as if he had signed it, unless the Congress by their Adjournment prevent its Return, in which Case it shall not be a Law.

Every Order, Resolution, or Vote to which the Concurrence of the Senate and House of Representatives may be necessary (except on a question of Adjournment) shall be presented to the President of the United States; and before the Same shall take Effect, shall be approved by him, or being disapproved by him, shall be repassed by two thirds of the Senate and House of Representatives, according to the Rules and Limitations prescribed in the Case of a Bill.

Section 8. The Congress shall have Power To lay and collect Taxes, Duties, Imposts and Excises, to pay the Debts and provide for the common Defense and general Welfare of the United States; but all Duties, Imposts and Excises shall be uniform throughout the United States;

To borrow Money on the credit of the United States;

To regulate Commerce with foreign Nations, and among the several States, and with the Indian Tribes;

To establish an uniform Rule of Naturalization, and uniform Laws on the subject of Bankruptcies throughout the United States;

To coin Money, regulate the Value thereof, and of foreign Coin, and fix the Standard of Weights and Measures;

To provide for the Punishment of counterfeiting the Securities and current Coin of the United States;

To establish Post Offices and post Roads;

To promote the Progress of Science and useful Arts, by securing for limited Times to Authors and Inventors the exclusive Right to their respective Writings and Discoveries;

To constitute Tribunals inferior to the supreme Court;

To define and punish Piracies and Felonies committed on the high Seas, and Offenses against the Law of Nations;

To declare War, grant Letters of Marque and Reprisal, and make Rules concerning Captures on Land and Water;

To raise and support Armies, but no Appropriation of Money to that Use shall be for a longer Term than two Years;

To provide and maintain a Navy;

To make Rules for the Government and Regulation of the land and naval Forces;

To provide for calling forth the Militia to execute the Laws of the Union, suppress Insurrections and repel Invasions;

To provide for organizing, arming, and disciplining, the Militia, and for governing such Part of them as may be employed in the Service of the United States, reserving to the States respectively, the

The veto power of the president and the ability of Congress to override a presidential veto are two of the important checks and balances in the Constitution.

The framers of the Constitution wanted a national government that was strong enough to be effective. This section lists the powers given to Congress. The last sentence in Section 8 (see page 170) contains the famous "elastic clause," which can be stretched (like elastic) to fit many different circumstances. The clause was first disputed when Alexander Hamilton proposed a national bank. Thomas Jefferson said that the Constitution did not give Congress the power to establish a bank. Hamilton argued that the bank was "necessary and proper" in order to carry out other powers of Congress, such as borrowing money and regulating currency. This argument was tested in the court system in 1819 in the case of *McCulloch* v. *Maryland*, when Chief Justice Marshall ruled in favor of the federal government. Powers given to the government by the "elastic clause" are called implied powers.

HISTORICAL SIDELIGHTS

Undeclared Wars

Only Congress can officially declare war. More than one president, as commander in chief of the armed forces, has engaged the United States in war without a declaration by Congress. The major undeclared war in American history was the Vietnam War. The Korean War and the Persian Gulf War were also undeclared but were fought under United Nations auspices.

HISTORICAL SIDELIGHTS

Slave Trading

As a compromise, Congress was not allowed to ban the importation of slaves for 20 years. In 1807 President Thomas Jefferson signed a law prohibiting the importation of slaves. The law went into effect in 1808, but illegal slave trading continued for several decades. In 1860 Captain Nathaniel Gordon was arrested and tried after attempting to bring 900 West African slaves to the United States. Found guilty of breaking the slave trade law, Gordon was executed. Captain Gordon was the only American slave trader ever executed by the United States.

If Congress has implied powers, then there also must be limits to its powers. Section 9 lists powers that are denied to the federal government. Several of the clauses protect the people of the United States from unjust treatment. For instance, Section 9 guarantees the writ of *habeas corpus* and prohibits bills of attainder and *ex post facto* laws (see page 163).

Section 10 lists the powers that are denied to the states. In our system of federalism, the state and federal governments have separate powers, share some powers, and are denied other powers. The states may not exercise any of the powers that belong to Congress.

Appointment of the Officers, and the Authority of training the Militia according to the discipline prescribed by Congress.

To exercise exclusive Legislation in all Cases whatsoever, over such District (not exceeding ten Miles square) as may, by Cession of particular States, and the Acceptance of Congress, become the Seat of the Government of the United States, and to exercise like Authority over all Places purchased by the Consent of the Legislature of the State in which the Same shall be, for the Erection of Forts, Magazines, Arsenals, dock-Yards, and other needful Buildings;—And

To make all Laws which shall be necessary and proper for carrying into Execution the foregoing Powers, and all other Powers vested by this Constitution in the Government of the United States, or in any Department or Officer thereof.

Section 9. ~~The Migration or Importation of such Persons as any of the States now existing shall think proper to admit, shall not be prohibited by the Congress prior to the Year one thousand eight hundred and eight, but a Tax or duty may be imposed on such Importation, not exceeding ten dollars for each Person.~~

The Privilege of the Writ of Habeas Corpus shall not be suspended, unless when in Cases of Rebellion or Invasion the public Safety may require it.

No Bill of Attainder or ex post facto Law shall be passed.

No Capitation, or other direct, Tax shall be laid, unless in Proportion to the Census or Enumeration herein before directed to be taken.

No Tax or Duty shall be laid on Articles exported from any State.

No Preference shall be given by any Regulation of Commerce or Revenue to the Ports of one State over those of another: nor shall Vessels bound to, or from, one State, be obliged to enter, clear, or pay Duties in another.

No Money shall be drawn from the Treasury, but in Consequence of Appropriations made by Law; and a regular Statement and Account of the Receipts and Expenditures of all public Money shall be published from time to time.

No Title of Nobility shall be granted by the United States: And no Person holding any Office of Profit or Trust under them, shall, without the Consent of the Congress, accept of any present, Emolument, Office, or Title, of any kind whatever, from any King, Prince, or foreign State.

Section 10. No State shall enter into any Treaty, Alliance, or Confederation; grant Letters of Marque and Reprisal; coin Money; emit Bills of Credit; make any Thing but gold and silver Coin a Tender in Payment of Debts; pass any Bill of Attainder, ex post facto Law, or law impairing the Obligation of Contracts, or grant any Title of Nobility.

No State shall, without the Consent of the Congress, lay any Imposts or Duties on Imports or Exports, except what may be absolutely necessary for executing its inspection Laws: and the net Produce of all Duties and Imposts, laid by any State on Imports or Exports, shall be for the Use of the Treasury of the United States; and all such Laws shall be subject to the Revision and Control of the Congress.

No State shall, without the Consent of Congress, lay any Duty of Tonnage, keep Troops, or Ships of War in time of Peace, enter into any Agreement or Compact with another State, or with a foreign Power, or engage in War, unless actually invaded, or in such imminent Danger as will not admit of delay.

ARTICLE II

Section 1. The executive Power shall be vested in a President of the United States of America. He shall hold his Office during the Term of four Years, and, together with the Vice President, chosen for the same Term, be elected, as follows.

Each State shall appoint, in such Manner as the Legislature thereof may direct, a Number of Electors, equal to the whole Number of Senators and Representatives to which the State may be entitled in the Congress: but no Senator or Representative, or Person holding an Office of Trust or Profit under the United States, shall be appointed an Elector.

~~The Electors shall meet in their respective States, and vote by Ballot for two Persons, of whom one at least shall not be an Inhabitant of the same State with themselves. And they shall make a List of all the Persons voted for, and of the Number of Votes for each; which List they shall sign and certify, and transmit sealed to the Seat of the Government of the United States, directed to the President of the Senate. The President of the Senate shall, in the Presence of the Senate and House of Representatives, open all the Certificates, and the Votes shall then be counted. The Person having the greatest Number of Votes shall be the President, if such Number be a Majority of the whole Number of Electors appointed; and if there be more than one who have such majority, and have an equal Number of Votes, then the House of Representatives shall immediately choose by Ballot one of them for President; and if no Person have a Majority, then from the five highest on the List the said House shall in like Manner choose the President. But in choosing the President, the Votes shall be taken by States, the Representation from each State having one Vote; A quorum for this Purpose shall consist of a Member or Members from two thirds of the States, and a Majority of all the States shall be necessary to a Choice. In every Case, after the Choice of the President, the Person having the greatest Number of Votes of the Electors shall be the Vice President. But if there should~~

Executive Branch
The president is the chief of the executive branch. It is the job of the president to enforce the laws. The framers wanted the president and vice president's term of office and manner of selection to be different from those of members of Congress. They decided on four-year terms, but they had a difficult time agreeing on how to select the president and vice president. The framers finally set up an electoral system, which varies greatly from our electoral process today. The Twelfth Amendment changed the process by requiring that separate ballots be cast for president and vice president. The rise of political parties has since changed the process even more.

GLOBAL CONNECTIONS

The framers of the Mexican Constitution of 1824 were greatly influenced by the success of the U.S. system of government, and they modeled their constitution after that of the United States. The Mexican constitution established a federal government with powers divided among the executive, legislative, and judicial branches. The legislature was bicameral, with an upper house consisting of two senators per state, and a lower house consisting of one representative per 80,000 residents. Important differences included the election of the president and vice president by state legislatures and the establishment of the Catholic Church as the official state church.

In 1845 Congress set the first Tuesday after the first Monday in November of every fourth year as the general election date for selecting presidential electors.

The youngest elected president was John F. Kennedy; he was 43 years old when he was inaugurated. (Theodore Roosevelt was 42 when he assumed office after the assassination of McKinley.) The oldest elected president was Ronald Reagan; he was 69 years old when he was inaugurated.

Emolument means "salary, or payment." In 1969 Congress set the president's salary at $200,000 per year. The president also receives an expense account of $50,000 per year. The president must pay taxes on both.

The oath of office is administered to the president by the chief justice of the United States. Washington added "So help me, God." All succeeding presidents have followed this practice.

The framers wanted to make sure that an elected representative of the people controlled the nation's military. Today the president is in charge of the army, navy, air force, marines, and coast guard. Only Congress can decide, however, if the United States will declare war. This section also contains the basis for the formation of the president's cabinet. Every president, starting with George Washington, has appointed a cabinet.

Most of the president's appointments to office must be approved by the Senate.

~~remain two or more who have equal Votes, the Senate shall choose from them by Ballot the Vice President.~~

The Congress may determine the Time of choosing the Electors, and the Day on which they shall give their Votes; which Day shall be the same throughout the United States.

No Person except a natural born Citizen, ~~or a Citizen of the United States, at the time of the Adoption of this Constitution,~~ shall be eligible to the Office of President; neither shall any Person be eligible to that Office who shall not have attained to the Age of thirty-five Years, and been fourteen Years a Resident within the United States.

In Case of the Removal of the President from Office, or of his Death, Resignation, or Inability to discharge the Powers and Duties of the said Office, the Same shall devolve on the Vice President, and the Congress may by Law provide for the Case of Removal, Death, Resignation or Inability, both of the President and Vice President, declaring what Officer shall then act as President, and such Officer shall act accordingly, until the Disability be removed, or a President shall be elected.

The President shall, at stated Times, receive for his Services, a Compensation, which shall neither be increased nor diminished during the Period for which he shall have been elected, and he shall not receive within that Period any other Emolument from the United States, or any of them.

Before he enter on the Execution of his Office, he shall take the following Oath or Affirmation:—"I do solemnly swear (or affirm) that I will faithfully execute the Office of President of the United States, and will to the best of my Ability, preserve, protect and defend the Constitution of the United States."

Section 2. The President shall be Commander in Chief of the Army and Navy of the United States, and of the Militia of the several States, when called into the actual Service of the United States; he may require the Opinion, in writing, of the principal Officer in each of the executive Departments, upon any Subject relating to the Duties of their respective Offices, and he shall have Power to grant Reprieves and Pardons for Offenses against the United States, except in Cases of Impeachment.

He shall have Power, by and with the Advice and Consent of the Senate, to make Treaties, provided two thirds of the Senators present concur; and he shall nominate, and by and with the Advice and Consent of the Senate, shall appoint Ambassadors, other public Ministers and Consuls, Judges of the supreme Court, and all other Officers of the United States, whose Appointments are not herein otherwise provided for, and which shall be established by Law: but the Congress may by Law vest the Appointment of such inferior Officers, as they think proper, in the President alone, in the Courts of Law, or in the Heads of Departments.

The President shall have Power to fill up all Vacancies that may happen during the Recess of the Senate, by granting Commissions which shall expire at the End of their next Session.

Section 3. He shall from time to time give to the Congress Information of the State of the Union, and recommend to their Consideration such Measures as he shall judge necessary and expedient; he may, on extraordinary Occasions, convene both Houses, or either of them, and in Case of Disagreement between them, with Respect to the Time of Adjournment, he may adjourn them to such Time as he shall think proper; he shall receive Ambassadors and other public Ministers; he shall take Care that the Laws be faithfully executed, and shall Commission all the Officers of the United States.

Section 4. The President, Vice President and all civil Officers of the United States, shall be removed from Office on Impeachment for, and Conviction of, Treason, Bribery, or other high Crimes and Misdemeanors.

ARTICLE III

Section 1. The judicial Power of the United States, shall be vested in one supreme Court, and in such inferior Courts as the Congress may from time to time ordain and establish. The Judges, both of the supreme and inferior Courts, shall hold their Offices during good Behavior, and shall, at stated Times, receive for their Services, a Compensation, which shall not be diminished during their Continuance in Office.

Section 2. The judicial Power shall extend to all Cases, in Law and Equity, arising under this Constitution, the Laws of the United States, and Treaties made, or which shall be made, under their Authority;—to all Cases affecting Ambassadors, other public Ministers and Consuls;—to all Cases of admiralty and maritime Jurisdiction;—to Controversies to which the United States shall be a Party;—to Controversies between two or more States;— between a State and Citizens of another State; between Citizens of different States;—between Citizens of the same State claiming Lands under Grants of different States, and between a State, or the Citizens thereof, and foreign States, Citizens or Subjects.

In all Cases affecting Ambassadors, other public Ministers and Consuls, and those in which a State shall be Party, the supreme Court shall have original Jurisdiction. In all the other Cases before mentioned, the supreme Court shall have appellate Jurisdiction, both as to Law and fact, with such Exceptions, and under such Regulations as the Congress shall make.

The Trial of all Crimes, except in Cases of Impeachment, shall be by Jury; and such Trial shall be held in the State where the said Crimes shall have been committed; but when not committed within

Every year the president presents to Congress a State of the Union message. In this message, the president explains the legislative plans for the coming year. This clause states that one of the president's duties is to enforce the laws.

Judicial Branch
The Articles of Confederation did not make any provisions for a federal court system. One of the first things that the framers of the Constitution agreed upon was to set up a national judiciary. With all the laws that Congress would be enacting, there would be a great need for a branch of government to interpret the laws. In the Judiciary Act of 1789, Congress provided for the establishment of lower courts, such as district courts, circuit courts of appeals, and various other federal courts. The judicial system provides a check on the legislative branch; it can declare a law unconstitutional.

HISTORICAL SIDELIGHTS
State of the Union Addresses
Presidents George Washington and John Adams delivered their State of the Union messages to Congress in person. For more than 100 years after that, most presidents sent a written message that was read in Congress. President Woodrow Wilson delivered his messages in person, as did President Franklin D. Roosevelt and all presidents after Roosevelt. The presidents' messages often have great influence on public opinion and thus on Congress.

BUILDING VOCABULARY
Cases in which the Supreme Court has *original jurisdiction* are those that go directly to the Supreme Court. Such cases include those affecting the representatives of foreign countries and those in which a state is a party. In those cases in which the Supreme Court has *appellate jurisdiction,* the cases are tried first in a lower court and may come up to the Supreme Court for review. Congress cannot take away or modify the original jurisdiction of the Supreme Court, but it can create exceptions to the right to appeal to that court and set the conditions one must meet to present an appeal.

HISTORICAL
Document

BUILDING VOCABULARY

A *republican government* is one in which the people elect representatives to govern. The Supreme Court ruled that Congress, not the courts, must decide whether a government is republican. According to the Supreme Court, if Congress admits a state's senators and representatives, that action indicates that Congress considers the government to be republican.

Congress has the power to decide the punishment for treason, but it can punish only the guilty person. *Corruption of blood* refers to the effect of an attainder, which prohibits inheriting, keeping or transmitting an estate. Thus punishing the family of a person who has committed treason is expressly forbidden.

The States
States must honor the laws, records, and court decisions of other states. A person cannot escape a legal obligation by moving from one state to another.

Section 3 permits Congress to admit new states to the Union. When a group of people living in an area that is not part of an existing state wishes to form a new state, it asks Congress for permission to do so. The people then write a state constitution and offer it to Congress for approval. The state constitution must set up a representative form of government and must not in any way contradict the federal Constitution. If a majority of Congress approves of the state constitution, the state is admitted as a member of the United States of America.

any State, the Trial shall be at such Place or Places as the Congress may by Law have directed.

Section 3. Treason against the United States, shall consist only in levying War against them, or in adhering to their Enemies, giving them Aid and Comfort. No Person shall be convicted of Treason unless on the Testimony of two Witnesses to the same overt Act, or on Confession in open Court.

The Congress shall have Power to declare the Punishment of Treason, but no Attainder of Treason shall work Corruption of Blood, or Forfeiture except during the Life of the Person attainted.

ARTICLE IV

Section 1. Full Faith and Credit shall be given in each State to the public Acts, Records, and judicial Proceedings of every other State. And the Congress may by general Laws prescribe the Manner in which such Acts, Records and Proceedings shall be proved, and the Effect thereof.

Section 2. The Citizens of each State shall be entitled to all Privileges and Immunities of Citizens in the several States.

A Person charged in any State with Treason, Felony, or other Crime, who shall flee from Justice, and be found in another State, shall on Demand of the executive Authority of the State from which he fled, be delivered up, to be removed to the State having Jurisdiction of the Crime.

~~No Person held to Service of Labor in one State, under the Laws thereof, escaping into another, shall, in Consequence of any Law or Regulation therein, be discharged from such Service or Labor, but shall be delivered up on Claim of the Party to whom such Service or Labor may be due.~~

Section 3. New States may be admitted by the Congress into this Union; but no new State shall be formed or erected within the Jurisdiction of any other State; nor any State be formed by the Junction of two or more States, or Parts of States, without the Consent of the Legislatures of the States concerned as well as of the Congress.

The Congress shall have Power to dispose of and make all needful Rules and Regulations respecting the Territory or other Property belonging to the United States; and nothing in this Constitution shall be so construed as to Prejudice any Claims of the United States, or of any particular State.

Section 4. The United States shall guarantee to every State in this Union a Republican Form of Government, and shall protect each of them against Invasion; and on Application of the Legislature, or of the Executive (when the Legislature cannot be convened) against domestic Violence.

HISTORICAL SIDELIGHTS

Religious Tests

At the time that the Constitution was written, all but two states—New York and Virginia—had religious qualifications for state officeholders. Delaware, for example, would let only "Protestants who accepted the Holy Trinity" serve in the state legislature. Pennsylvania required its state officers to have a "belief in God and the inspiration of the Scriptures." When Charles Pinckney III of South Carolina proposed that the Constitution specifically prohibit these religious tests, a heated debate followed. Some delegates believed that electing officials who espoused Christian beliefs would help ensure that their leaders would rule fairly. The majority of delegates, however, favored the ban on religious tests. Pinckney's motion passed.

ARTICLE V

The Congress, whenever two thirds of both Houses shall deem it necessary, shall propose Amendments to this Constitution, or, on the Application of the Legislatures of two thirds of the several States, shall call a Convention for proposing Amendments, which, in either Case, shall be valid to all Intents and Purposes, as Part of this Constitution, when ratified by the Legislatures of three fourths of the several States, or by Conventions in three fourths thereof, as the one or the other Mode of Ratification may be proposed by the Congress; Provided that no Amendment which may be made prior to the Year One thousand eight hundred and eight shall in any Manner affect the first and fourth Clauses in the Ninth Section of the first Article; and that no State, without its Consent, shall be deprived of its equal Suffrage in the Senate.

The Amendment Process
America's founders may not have realized just how enduring the Constitution would be, but they did make provisions for changing or adding to the Constitution. They did not want to make it easy to change the Constitution. There are two different ways in which changes can be proposed to the states and two different ways in which states can approve the changes and make them part of the Constitution (see the chart on page 163).

ARTICLE VI

All Debts contracted and Engagements entered into, before the Adoption of this Constitution, shall be as valid against the United States under this Constitution, as under the Confederation.

This Constitution, and the Laws of the United States which shall be made in Pursuance thereof; and all Treaties made, or which shall be made, under the Authority of the United States, shall be the supreme Law of the Land; and the Judges in every State shall be bound thereby, any Thing in the Constitution or Laws of any State to the Contrary notwithstanding.

The Senators and Representatives before mentioned, and the Members of the several State Legislatures, and all executive and judicial Officers, both of the United States and of the several States, shall be bound by Oath or Affirmation, to support this Constitution; but no religious Test shall ever be required as a Qualification to any Office or public Trust under the United States.

National Supremacy
One of the biggest problems facing the delegates to the Constitutional Convention was the question of what would happen if a state law and a national law conflicted. Which law would be followed? Who decided? The second clause of Article VI answers those questions. When a national and state law disagree, the national law overrides the state law. The Constitution is the supreme law of the land. This clause is often called the "supremacy clause."

ARTICLE VII

The Ratification of the Conventions of nine States, shall be sufficient for the Establishment of this Constitution between the States so ratifying the Same.

DONE in Convention by the Unanimous Consent of the States present the Seventeenth Day of September in the Year of our Lord one thousand seven hundred and Eighty seven and of the Independence of the United States of America the Twelfth. IN WITNESS whereof We have hereunto subscribed our Names.

George Washington—
President and deputy from Virginia

Ratification
The Articles of Confederation called for all 13 states to approve any revision to the Articles. The Constitution required that the vote of 9 out of 13 states would be needed to ratify the Constitution. The first state to ratify was Delaware, on December 7, 1787. The last state to ratify the Constitution was Rhode Island, which finally did so on May 29, 1790, almost two and a half years later.

HISTORICAL
Document

rut our Posterity, UO ordain and establish that

New Hampshire	**Delaware**
John Langdon	*George Read*
Nicholas Gilman	*Gunning Bedford, Jr.*
	John Dickinson
Massachusetts	*Richard Bassett*
Nathaniel Gorham	*Jacob Broom*
Rufus King	
	Maryland
Connecticut	*James McHenry*
William Samuel Johnson	*Daniel of St. Thomas Jenifer*
Roger Sherman	*Daniel Carroll*
New York	**Virginia**
Alexander Hamilton	*John Blair*
	James Madison, Jr.
New Jersey	
William Livingston	**North Carolina**
David Brearley	*William Blount*
William Paterson	*Richard Dobbs Spaight*
Jonathan Dayton	*Hugh Williamson*
Pennsylvania	**South Carolina**
Benjamin Franklin	*John Rutledge*
Thomas Mifflin	*Charles Cotesworth Pinckney*
Robert Morris	*Charles Pinckney*
George Clymer	*Pierce Buttler*
Thomas FitzSimons	
Jared Ingersoll	**Georgia**
James Wilson	*William Few*
Gouverneur Morris	*Abraham Baldwin*

Attest: *William Jackson*, Secretary

Bill of Rights
One of the conditions set by several states for ratifying the Constitution was the inclusion of a Bill of Rights. Many people feared that a stronger central government might take away basic rights of the people that had been guaranteed in state constitutions. If the three words that begin the preamble, We the people—were truly meant, then the rights of the people needed to be protected.

THE AMENDMENTS

ARTICLES in addition to, and Amendment of the Constitution of the United States of America, proposed by Congress, and ratified by the Legislatures of the several states, pursuant to the fifth Article of the original Constitution.

[The First through Tenth amendments, now known as the Bill of Rights, were proposed on September 25, 1789, and declared in force on December 15, 1791.]

First Amendment

Congress shall make no law respecting an establishment of religion, or prohibiting the free exercise thereof; or abridging the freedom of speech, or of the press; or the right of the people peaceably to assemble, and to petition the Government for a redress of grievances.

The First Amendment protects freedom of speech and thought, and forbids Congress to make any law "respecting an establishment of religion" or restraining the freedom to practice religion as one chooses.

Second Amendment

A well regulated Militia, being necessary to the security of a free State, the right of the people to keep and bear Arms, shall not be infringed.

Third Amendment

No Soldier shall, in time of peace, be quartered in any house, without the consent of the Owner, nor in time of war, but in a manner to be prescribed by law.

Fourth Amendment

The right of the people to be secure in their persons, houses, papers, and effects, against unreasonable searches and seizures, shall not be violated, and no Warrants shall issue, but upon probable cause, supported by Oath or affirmation, and particularly describing the place to be searched, and the persons or things to be seized.

A police officer or sheriff may enter a person's home with a search warrant, which allows the law officer to look for evidence that could convict someone of committing a crime.

Fifth Amendment

No person shall be held to answer for a capital, or otherwise infamous crime, unless on a presentment or indictment of a Grand Jury, except in cases arising in the land or naval forces, or in the Militia, when in actual service in time of War or public danger; nor shall any person be subject for the same offense to be twice put in jeopardy of life or limb; nor shall be compelled in any criminal case to be a witness against himself, nor be deprived of life, liberty, or property, without due process of law; nor shall private property be taken for public use, without just compensation.

The Fifth, Sixth, and Seventh amendments describe the procedures that courts must follow when trying people accused of crimes. The Fifth Amendment guarantees that no one can be put on trial for a serious crime unless a grand jury agrees that the evidence justifies doing so. It also says that a person cannot be tried twice for the same crime.

Sixth Amendment

In all criminal prosecutions, the accused shall enjoy the right to a speedy and public trial, by an impartial jury of the State and district wherein the crime shall have been committed, which district shall have been previously ascertained by law, and to be informed of the nature and cause of the accusation; to be confronted with the witnesses against him; to have compulsory process for obtaining witnesses in his favor, and to have the Assistance of Counsel for his defense.

The Sixth Amendment makes several promises, including a prompt trial and a trial by a jury chosen from the state and district in which the crime was committed. The Sixth Amendment also states that an accused person must be told why he or she is being tried and promises that an accused person has the right to be defended by a lawyer.

Seventh Amendment

In Suits at common law, where the value in controversy shall exceed twenty dollars, the right of trial by jury shall be preserved,

The Seventh Amendment guarantees a trial by jury in cases that involve more than $20, but in modern times, usually much more money is at stake before a case is heard in federal court.

MAKING CONNECTIONS

Government

The First Amendment prohibits Congress from setting up or supporting an *established* or official church. The amendment also forbids Congress from passing laws limiting religious worship, and it has been interpreted to forbid government endorsement of religious doctrines. The guarantee of freedom of religion does not mean, however, that all religious practices must be allowed. In the 1800s some Mormons believed that it was a man's religious duty to have more than one wife. The Supreme Court ruled that Mormons had to obey the laws forbidding that practice.

HISTORICAL SIDELIGHTS

Due Process of Law

The due process clause is one of the most important in the Constitution. The statement expresses the idea that life, liberty, and property are not subject to the uncontrolled power of the government. Until the mid-1900s, the Court used the due process clause to strike down laws that prevented people from using their property as they wished. Today the courts use the due process clause primarily to strike down laws that interfere with personal liberty.

HISTORICAL SIDELIGHTS

Capital Punishment

In the 1972 case *Furman* v. *Georgia,* the Supreme Court ruled that capital punishment (death penalty), as it was then imposed, violated the Eighth Amendment. The Court held that capital punishment was cruel and unusual punishment because it was not applied fairly and uniformly. After that decision, many states adopted new capital-punishment laws designed to meet the objections of the Supreme Court. The Court has ruled that the death penalty may be imposed if certain standards are applied to guard against arbitrary results in capital cases.

The Ninth and Tenth amendments were added because not every right of the people or of the states could be listed in the Constitution.

The Twelfth Amendment changed the election procedure for president and vice president. This amendment became necessary because of the growth of political parties. Before this amendment, electors voted without distinguishing between president and vice president. Whoever received the most votes became president, and whoever received the next highest number of votes became vice president. A confusing election in 1800, which resulted in Thomas Jefferson's becoming president, caused this amendment to be proposed.

and no fact tried by a jury shall be otherwise reexamined in any Court of the United States, than according to the rules of the common law.

Eighth Amendment

Excessive bail shall not be required, nor excessive fines imposed, nor cruel and unusual punishments inflicted.

Ninth Amendment

The enumeration in the Constitution, of certain rights, shall not be construed to deny or disparage others retained by the people.

Tenth Amendment

The powers not delegated to the United States by the Constitution, nor prohibited by it to the States, are reserved to the States respectively, or to the people.

Eleventh Amendment

[Proposed March 4, 1794; declared ratified January 8, 1798]

The Judicial power of the United States shall not be construed to extend to any suit in law or equity, commenced or prosecuted against one of the United States by Citizens of another State, or by Citizens or Subjects of any Foreign State.

Twelfth Amendment

[Proposed December 9, 1803; declared ratified September 25, 1804]

The Electors shall meet in their respective states and vote by ballot for President and Vice President, one of whom, at least, shall not be an inhabitant of the same state with themselves; they shall name in their ballots the person voted for as President, and in distinct ballots the person voted for as Vice President, and they shall make distinct lists of all persons voted for as President, and of all persons voted for as Vice President, and of the number of votes for each, which lists they shall sign and certify, and transmit sealed to the seat of the government of the United States, directed to the President of the Senate;—The President of the Senate shall, in the presence of the Senate and House of Representatives, open all the certificates and the votes shall then be counted;—The person having the greatest number of votes for President, shall be the President, if such number be a majority of the whole number of Electors appointed; and if no person have such majority, then from the persons having the highest numbers not exceeding three on the list of those voted for as President, the House of Representatives shall choose immediately, by ballot, the President. But in choosing the President, the votes shall be taken by states, the representation from each state having one vote; a quorum for this purpose shall consist of a member or members from two thirds of the states, and a majority of all the states shall be necessary to a choice. ~~And if the House of Representatives shall not choose a President whenever the right of choice shall devolve upon them, before the fourth day of March next following, then the Vice President shall act as President, as in the case of the death or other constitutional disability of the President;~~ The person having the greatest number of votes as Vice President, shall be the Vice President, if such number be a majority of the whole number of Electors appointed, and if no person have a majority, then from the two highest numbers on the list, the Senate shall choose the Vice President; a quorum for the purpose shall consist of two thirds of the whole number of Senators, and a majority of the whole number shall be necessary to a choice. But no person constitutionally ineligible to the office of President shall be eligible to that of Vice President of the United States.

Thirteenth Amendment

[Proposed January 31, 1865; declared ratified December 18, 1865]

Section 1. Neither slavery nor involuntary servitude, except as a punishment for crime whereof the party shall have been duly convicted, shall exist within the United States, or any place subject to their jurisdiction.

Section 2. Congress shall have power to enforce this article by appropriate legislation.

Fourteenth Amendment

[Proposed June 13, 1866; declared ratified July 28, 1868]

Section 1. All persons born or naturalized in the United States and subject to the jurisdiction thereof, are citizens of the United States and of the State wherein they reside. No State shall make or enforce any law which shall abridge the privileges or immunities of citizens of the United States; nor shall any State deprive any person of life, liberty, or property, without due process of law; nor deny to any person within its jurisdiction the equal protection of the laws.

Section 2. Representatives shall be apportioned among the several States according to their respective numbers, counting the whole number of persons in each State, ~~excluding Indians not taxed.~~ But when the right to vote at any election for the choice of electors for President and Vice President of the United States, Representatives in Congress, the Executive and Judicial officers of a State, or the members of the Legislature thereof, is denied to any of the ~~male~~ inhabitants of such State, being ~~twenty-one years of age, and~~ citizens of the United States, or in any way abridged, except for participation in rebellion, or other crime, the basis of representation therein shall be reduced in the proportion which the number of such ~~male~~ citizens shall bear to the whole number of ~~male~~ citizens ~~twenty-one years of age~~ in such State.

Section 3. No person shall be a Senator or Representative in

Although some slaves had been freed during the Civil War, slavery was not abolished until the Thirteenth Amendment took effect.

In 1833 Chief Justice John Marshall ruled that the Bill of Rights limited the national government but not the state governments. This ruling meant that states were able to keep African Americans from becoming state citizens. If African Americans were not citizens, they were not protected by the Bill of Rights. The Fourteenth Amendment defines citizenship and prevents states from interfering in the rights of citizens of the United States.

MAKING CONNECTIONS

Government

The phrase "due process of law" has been construed to prohibit states from violating most rights protected by the Bill of Rights. It also has been interpreted as protecting other rights by its own force. The statement that a state cannot deny anyone "equal protection of the laws" has provided the basis for many Supreme Court rulings on civil rights. For example, the Court has outlawed segregation in public schools, declaring that "equal protection" means that all children, regardless of race, must have an equal opportunity to be educated.

HISTORICAL
Document

HISTORICAL
Document

MAKING CONNECTIONS

Government

African Americans who had been enslaved became citizens under the terms of the Fourteenth Amendment, but the Fifteenth Amendment does not specifically say that they must be allowed to vote. The amendment states that a voter cannot be denied the ballot because of race. However, the states are free to set qualifications for voters, and some states attempted to deny the ballot to African Americans through indirect means, such as the poll tax. Such measures have been overturned by Supreme Court decisions, by federal laws, and by the Twenty-fourth Amendment.

The Fifteenth Amendment extended the right to vote to African American males.

The Sixteenth Amendment made legal the income tax described in Article I.

The Seventeenth Amendment required that senators be elected directly by the people instead of by the state legislature.

Congress, or elector of President and Vice President, or hold any office, civil or military, under the United States, or under any State, who, having previously taken an oath, as a member of Congress, or as an officer of the United States, or as a member of any State legislature, or as an executive or judicial officer of any State, to support the Constitution of the United States, shall have engaged in insurrection or rebellion against the same, or given aid or comfort to the enemies thereof. But Congress may by a vote of two thirds of each House, remove such disability.

Section 4. The validity of the public debt of the United States, authorized by law, including debts incurred for payment of pensions and bounties for services in suppressing insurrection or rebellion, shall not be questioned. But neither the United States nor any State shall assume or pay any debt or obligation incurred in aid of insurrection or rebellion against the United States, ~~or any claim for the loss or emancipation of any slave;~~ but all such debts, obligations and claims shall be held illegal and void.

Section 5. The Congress shall have power to enforce, by appropriate legislation, the provisions of this article.

Fifteenth Amendment

[Proposed February 26, 1869; declared ratified March 30, 1870]

Section 1. The right of citizens of the United States to vote shall not be denied or abridged by the United States or by any State on account of race, color, or previous condition of servitude.

Section 2. The Congress shall have power to enforce this article by appropriate legislation.

Sixteenth Amendment

[Proposed July 12, 1909; declared ratified February 25, 1913]

The Congress shall have power to lay and collect taxes on incomes, from whatever source derived, without apportionment among the several States, and without regard to any census or enumeration.

Seventeenth Amendment

[Proposed May 13, 1912; declared ratified May 31, 1913]

The Senate of the United States shall be composed of two Senators from each State, elected by the people thereof, for six years; and each Senator shall have one vote. The electors in each State shall have the qualifications requisite for electors of the most numerous branch of the State legislatures.

When vacancies happen in the representation of any State in the Senate, the executive authority of such State shall issue writs of election to fill such vacancies: *Provided,* That the legislature of any

State may empower the executive thereof to make temporary appointments until the people fill the vacancies by election as the legislature may direct.

~~This amendment shall not be so construed as to affect the election or term of any Senator chosen before it becomes valid as part of the Constitution.~~

Eighteenth Amendment

[Proposed December 18, 1917; declared ratified January 29, 1919; repealed by the Twenty-first Amendment December 5, 1933]

~~*Section 1.* After one year from the ratification of this article the manufacture, sale, or transportation of intoxicating liquors within, the importation thereof into, or the exportation thereof from the United States and all territory subject to the jurisdiction thereof for beverage purposes is hereby prohibited.~~

~~*Section 2.* The Congress and the several States shall have concurrent power to enforce this article by appropriate legislation.~~

~~*Section 3.* This article shall be inoperative unless it shall have been ratified as an amendment to the Constitution by the legislatures of the several States, as provided in the Constitution, within seven years from the date of the submission hereof to the States by the Congress.~~

Although many people felt that Prohibition was good for the health and welfare of the American people, the amendment was repealed 14 years later.

Nineteenth Amendment

[Proposed June 4, 1919; declared ratified August 26, 1920]

The right of citizens of the United States to vote shall not be denied or abridged by the United States or by any State on account of sex.

Congress shall have power to enforce this article by appropriate legislation.

Abigail Adams was disappointed that the Declaration of Independence and the Constitution did not specifically include women. It took almost 150 years and much campaigning by women's suffrage groups for women to finally achieve voting privileges.

Twentieth Amendment

[Proposed March 2, 1932; declared ratified February 6, 1933]

Section 1. The terms of the President and Vice President shall end at noon on the 20th day of January, and the terms of Senators and Representatives at noon on the 3rd day of January, of the years in which such terms would have ended if this article had not been ratified; and the terms of their successors shall then begin.

Section 2. The Congress shall assemble at least once in every year, and such meeting shall begin at noon on the 3rd day of January, unless they shall by law appoint a different day.

Section 3. If, at the time fixed for the beginning of the term of the President, the President elect shall have died, the Vice President elect shall become President. If a President shall not have been chosen before the time fixed for the beginning of his term, or if the President elect shall have failed to qualify, then the Vice President

In the original Constitution, a newly elected president and Congress did not take office until March 4, which was four months after the November election. The officials who were leaving office were called "lame ducks" because they had little influence during those four months. The Twentieth Amendment changed the date that the new president and Congress take office. Members of Congress now take office on January 3, and the president takes office on January 20.

HISTORICAL SIDELIGHTS

Voting Rights

The debate over the Fourteenth and Fifteenth amendments gave suffragists the hope that women would be given the vote along with African Americans. The Fourteenth Amendment, however, defined an eligible voter as a male over 21 years of age, and for the first time, women thus were specifically excluded from the vote. Until then, voting rights had been considered a state matter, and it had been possible to interpret some state laws to include women as citizens and voters. Some women property owners previously had voted, often in local elections. The direct exclusion of women by the Fourteenth Amendment angered and disappointed suffragists, who ultimately would have to work 50 more years to gain the vote.

elect shall act as President until a President shall have qualified; and the Congress may by law provide for the case wherein neither a President elect nor a Vice President elect shall have qualified, declaring who shall then act as President, or the manner in which one who is to act shall be selected, and such persons shall act accordingly until a President or Vice President shall have qualified.

Section 4. The Congress may by law provide for the case of the death of any of the persons from whom the House of Representatives may choose a President whenever the right of choice shall have devolved upon them, and for the case of the death of any of the persons from whom the Senate may choose a Vice President whenever the right of choice shall have devolved upon them.

~~*Section 5.* Sections 1 and 2 shall take effect on the 15th day of October following the ratification of this article.~~

~~*Section 6.* This article shall be inoperative unless it shall have been ratified as an amendment to the Constitution by the legislatures of three fourths of the several States within seven years from the date of its submission.~~

The Twenty-first Amendment is the only amendment that has been ratified by state conventions rather than by state legislatures.

Twenty-first Amendment
[Proposed February 20, 1933; declared ratified December 5, 1933]

Section 1. The eighteenth article of amendment to the Constitution of the United States is hereby repealed.

Section 2. The transportation or importation into any State, Territory, or possession of the United States for delivery or use therein of intoxicating liquors, in violation of the laws thereof, is hereby prohibited.

~~*Section 3.* This article shall be inoperative unless it shall have been ratified as an amendment to the Constitution by conventions in the several States, as provided in the Constitution, within seven years from the date of the submission hereof to the States by the Congress.~~

From the time of President Washington's administration, it was a custom for presidents to serve no more than two terms of office. Franklin D. Roosevelt, however, was elected to four terms. The Twenty-second Amendment made into law the old custom of a two-term limit for each president, if reelected.

Twenty-second Amendment
[Proposed March 24, 1947; declared ratified March 1, 1951]

Section 1. No person shall be elected to the office of the President more than twice, and no person who has held the office of President, or acted as President, for more than two years of a term to which some other person was elected President shall be elected to the office of the President more than once. ~~But this Article shall not apply to any person holding the office of President when this Article was proposed by the Congress, and shall not prevent any person who may be holding the office of President, or acting as President, during the term within which this Article becomes operative from holding the office of President or acting as President during the remainder of such term.~~

~~Section 2. This Article shall be inoperative unless it shall have been ratified as an amendment to the Constitution by the legislatures of three fourths of the several States within seven years from the date of its submission to the States by the Congress.~~

Twenty-third Amendment

[Proposed June 16, 1960; declared ratified April 3, 1961]

Section 1. The District constituting the seat of Government of the United States shall appoint in such manner as the Congress may direct:

A number of electors of President and Vice President equal to the whole number of Senators and Representatives in Congress to which the District would be entitled if it were a State, but in no event more than the least populous State; they shall be in addition to those appointed by the States, but they shall be considered, for the purposes of the election of President and Vice President, to be electors appointed by a State; and they shall meet in the District and perform such duties as provided by the twelfth article of amendment.

Section 2. The Congress shall have power to enforce this article by appropriate legislation.

Twenty-fourth Amendment

[Proposed August 27, 1962; declared ratified February 4, 1964]

Section 1. The right of citizens of the United States to vote in any primary or other election for President or Vice President, for electors for President or Vice President, or for Senator or Representative in Congress, shall not be denied or abridged by the United States or any State by reason of failure to pay any poll tax or other tax.

Section 2. The Congress shall have power to enforce this article by appropriate legislation.

Twenty-fifth Amendment

[Proposed July 6, 1965; declared ratified February 23, 1967]

Section 1. In case of removal of the President from office or of his death or resignation, the Vice President shall become President.

Section 2. Whenever there is a vacancy in the office of the Vice President, the President shall nominate a Vice President who shall take office upon confirmation by a majority vote of both Houses of Congress.

Section 3. Whenever the President transmits to the President pro tempore of the Senate and the Speaker of the House of Representatives his written declaration that he is unable to discharge the powers and duties of his office, and until he transmits to them a written declaration to the contrary, such powers and duties shall be discharged by the Vice President as Acting President.

Until the Twenty-third Amendment, the people of Washington, D.C., could not vote in presidential elections.

The illness of President Eisenhower in the 1950s and the assassination of President Kennedy in 1963 were the events behind the Twenty-fifth Amendment. The Constitution did not provide a clear-cut method for a vice president to take over for a disabled president or for the death of a president. This amendment provides for filling the office of the vice president if a vacancy occurs, and it provides a way for the vice president to take over if the president is unable to perform the duties of that office.

BUILDING VOCABULARY

A *poll tax* is a tax collected equally from everyone. Some states once used such taxes to keep poor people and African Americans from voting. The term *poll tax* does not mean a tax on voting. It comes from the word *poll* meaning "head."

HISTORICAL SIDELIGHTS

Appointing a Vice President

In 1973 Gerald R. Ford became the first person ever chosen vice president under the terms of the Twenty-fifth Amendment. He was nominated by President Richard M. Nixon after Vice President Spiro Agnew resigned. In 1974 Nixon resigned and Ford became president. Nelson Rockefeller then became the new vice president under the new procedure. For the first time, the United States had both a president and a vice president who had not been elected to their offices. Before this amendment, tradition and practice dictated that vacancies in the vice presidency remain unfilled until the next presidential election.

5. freedom of speech, freedom of press; freedom of religion; freedom of assembly; right to bear arms; prohibitions regarding search and seizure; various judicial protections
6. to allow for new legal and political developments without framing new Constitution; to maintain authority of Constitution
7. Nineteenth Amendment; August 26, 1920
8. Thirteenth, Fourteenth, and Fifteenth amendments; Thirteenth—abolished slavery, Fourteenth—extended citizenship to former slaves, Fifteenth—granted suffrage to African Americans

9. override presidential vetoes, impeach presidents for "high crimes and misdemeanors"; propose amendments that overturn earlier court rulings
10. interpret laws; try government officials
11. habeas corpus, bills of attainder, ex post facto laws; definition of treason and prohibition against unfair prosecution
12. form more perfect union, establish justice, insure domestic tranquillity, provide for common defense, promote general welfare, secure blessings of liberty
13. 25 years of age, seven years as U.S. citizen, resident of state from which elected; 30 years of age,

IDENTIFYING PEOPLE AND IDEAS

1. explains goals of new government
2. prohibits imprisonment without formal charges
3. protects individual liberties
4. rights of individuals against the power of government
5. law passed "after the deed" to set penalties for acts not illegal at time of law's passage
6. law punishing person without court trial
7. charge strictly defined by Constitution to provide for protection of accused
8. a framer of Constitution, co-author of The Federalist

UNDERSTANDING MAIN IDEAS

1. execute laws; serve as commander in chief of military; make treaties; appoint ambassadors, Supreme Court justices, and other officials
2. to guard against tyranny and keep any one branch from becoming too strong
3. declare laws unconstitutional; declare presidential actions unconstitutional
4. Chief responsibilities include levying taxes, declaring war, coining money, and establishing and maintaining military forces.

HISTORICAL Document

THE CONSTITUTION

The Voting Act of 1970 tried to set the voting age at 18 years old. But the Supreme Court ruled that the act set the voting age for national elections only, not state or local elections. This ruling would make necessary several different ballots at elections. The Twenty-sixth Amendment gave 18-year-old citizens the right to vote in all elections.

Section 4. Whenever the Vice President and a majority of either the principal officers of the executive departments or of such other body as Congress may by law provide, transmit to the President pro tempore of the Senate and the Speaker of the House of Representatives their written declaration that the President is unable to discharge the powers and duties of his office, the Vice President shall immediately assume the powers and duties of the office as Acting President.

Thereafter, when the President transmits to the President pro tempore of the Senate and the Speaker of the House of Representatives his written declaration that no inability exists, he shall resume the powers and duties of his office unless the Vice President and a majority of either the principal officers of the executive department or of such other body as Congress may by law provide, transmit within four days to the President pro tempore of the Senate and the Speaker of the House of Representatives their written declaration that the President is unable to discharge the powers and duties of his office. Thereupon Congress shall decide the issue, assembling within forty-eight hours for that purpose if not in session. If the Congress, within twenty-one days after receipt of the latter written declaration, or, if Congress is not in session, within twenty-one days after Congress is required to assemble, determines by two-thirds vote of both Houses that the President is unable to discharge the powers and duties of his office, the Vice President shall continue to discharge the same as Acting President; otherwise, the President shall resume the powers and duties of his office.

Twenty-sixth Amendment
[Proposed March 23, 1971; declared ratified July 5, 1971]

Section 1. The right of citizens of the United States, who are eighteen years of age or older, to vote shall not be denied or abridged by the United States or by any State on account of age.

Section 2. The Congress shall have power to enforce this article by appropriate legislation.

Twenty-seventh Amendment
[Proposed September 25, 1789; declared ratified May 7, 1992]

No law, varying the compensation for the services of the Senators and Representatives, shall take effect, until an election of Representatives shall have intervened.

REVIEW

The Constitution

+ reflective writing

REVIEWING CHRONOLOGY

Create an illustrated time line showing the dates of passage of the Bill of Rights and the remaining 17 amendments.

IDENTIFYING PEOPLE AND IDEAS

Explain the historical significance of each of the following people or terms.

1. Preamble
2. writ of *habeas corpus*
3. Bill of Rights
4. civil liberties
5. *ex post facto* law
6. bill of attainder
7. treason
8. James Madison

UNDERSTANDING MAIN IDEAS

1. According to Article II, what are the chief responsibilities of the president?
2. What is the purpose of the separation of powers in government?
3. How can the judicial branch check the power of the legislative branch? of the executive branch?
4. According to Article I, what are the chief responsibilities of the legislative branch?
5. What protections are listed in the Bill of Rights?
6. Why did the framers of the Constitution provide for an amendment process? Why did they make the process difficult?
7. Which amendment deals with women's suffrage? When was it ratified?
8. Which amendments are termed the Civil War Amendments? What does each cover?
9. How can the legislative branch check the power of the executive branch? of the judicial branch?
10. According to Article III, what are the chief responsibilities of the judicial branch?
11. What civil liberties are addressed in Section 9 of Article I? in Section 3 of Article III?
12. What six goals of government are listed in the Preamble?
13. According to the Constitution, what are the qualifications for becoming a representative? for becoming a senator? the president?
14. How can the executive branch check the power of the legislative branch? of the judicial branch?
15. Which two amendments deal with Prohibition? When was each ratified?
16. According to Article III, what are the chief responsibilities of the judicial branch?
17. Which part of the Constitution addresses possible conflicts between federal and state laws?
18. Which Article outlines the amendment process? According to the Article, how can the Constitution be amended?
19. What are some of the ways in which the Constitution protects the rights of the states?
20. Why did the framers of the Constitution include Article VII?

THINKING CRITICALLY

1. **Analyzing** In what ways does the Constitution reflect the reasons that Americans fought the Revolutionary War?
2. **Identifying Cause and Effect** Why were the framers of the Constitution especially interested in protecting civil liberties?
3. **Synthesizing** Using the information presented in Section 7 of Article I, create a diagram showing the steps involved in passing a bill.
4. **Comparing** Describe the connections between the Preamble to the Constitution and the theory of government that is described in the Declaration of Independence.
5. **Analyzing** How do the civil liberties guaranteed in the Constitution help to prevent abuses of power?
6. **Classifying** Classify the 27 amendments to the Constitution according to whether they protect rights, extend rights, or solve problems.

LINKING HISTORY AND GEOGRAPHY

Why was it important for the framers of the Constitution to include provisions for new states to enter the Union?

THE AMERICAN WEST

HISTORICAL SIDELIGHTS

The Western Movie

The fascination with the American West and its myths is demonstrated by the popularity of novelists Zane Grey, Louis L'Amour, and Larry McMurtry, and by the enduring popularity of western films. Movie interpretations of the West have varied over the years, from the idolization of the outlaw in *Billy the Kid* (1930) to recent examinations of Native American culture in *Dances with Wolves* (1990) and the negative effects of violence in *Unforgiven* (1992).

Ask students if they have seen any westerns on television or at a movie theater recently. Then ask whether they think the West was portrayed realistically, and why or why not.

America's GEOGRAPHY

THE AMERICAN WEST

POPULAR views of the American West have changed greatly over time. As the United States expanded its borders from east to west, the area that most Americans once thought of as an uninviting wilderness became an exciting new land of opportunity. Yet many travelers, from Native American groups to Spanish missionaries and French soldiers, were drawn to the West long before citizens of the United States began to settle there. Today the West continues to be one of the most culturally and ethnically diverse regions of the nation, attracting visitors and new settlers from throughout the world.

The West, 1790

In 1790 most Americans considered the Trans-Appalachian West—the area between the Appalachian Mountains and the Mississippi River—to be "The West." Few dared move beyond the Mississippi River. Spain claimed most of the territory west of the Mississippi. With the exception of a few small Spanish and French settlements, this territory remained the free domain of Native Americans.

	American territory
	Spanish territory
	British territory
	Northwest Territory
▪	Spanish settlements and missions
▪	French forts and settlements
YAKIMA	Native American tribe

▲ As Americans moved west, they often adapted customs that closely resembled those of Native Americans. Just as some Native Americans built dwellings out of caves and soil, western settlers often lived in dugouts—homes dug out of the sides of hills or ravines—and sod homes built from bricks of soil.

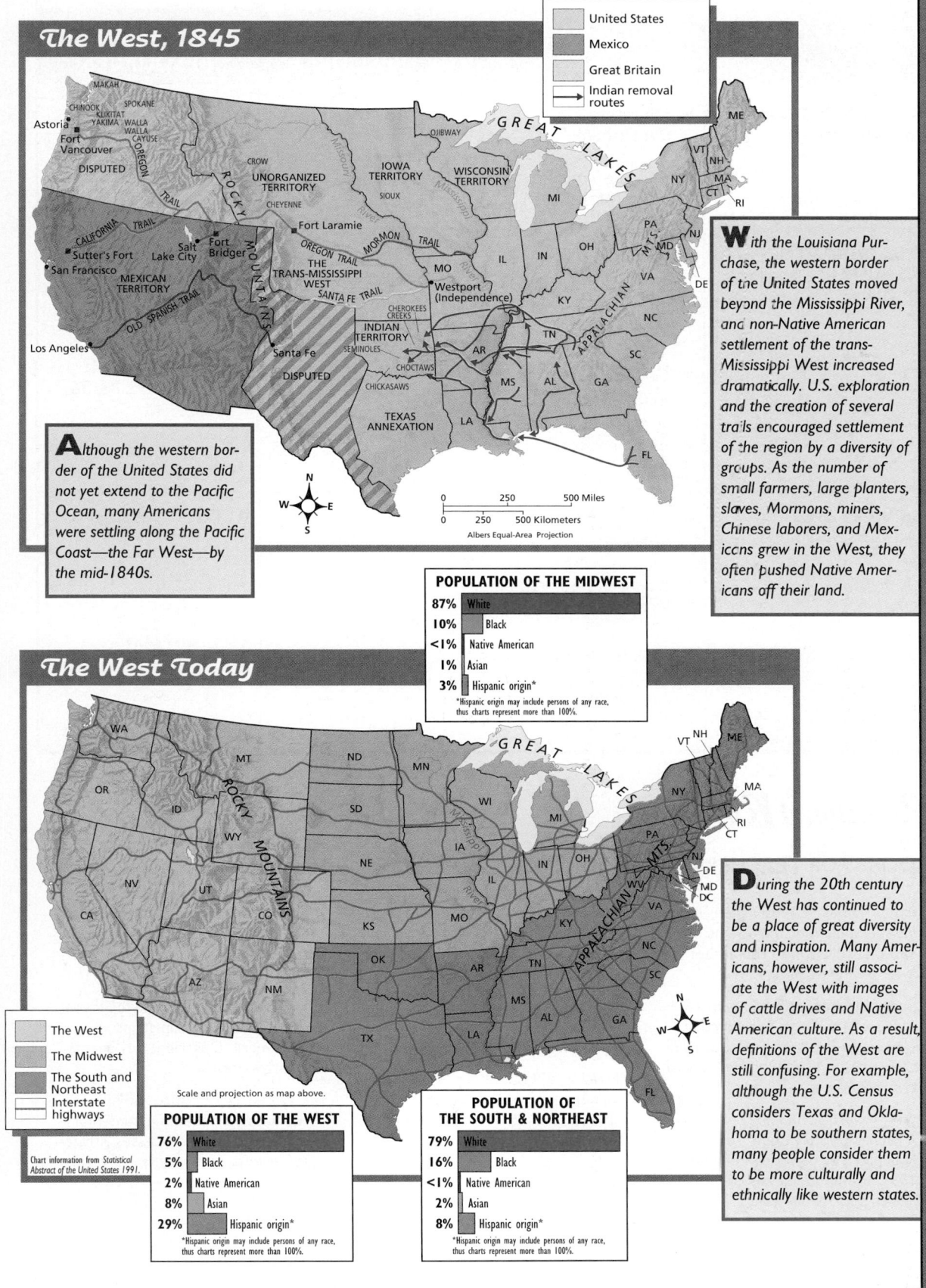

The West, 1845

Legend:
- United States
- Mexico
- Great Britain
- → Indian removal routes

MAKAH, CHINOOK, KLIKITAT, YAKIMA, WALLA WALLA, CAYUSE, SPOKANE, Astoria, Fort Vancouver, DISPUTED, CROW, OREGON, CALIFORNIA TRAIL, ROCKY MOUNTAINS, Sutter's Fort, San Francisco, Salt Lake City, Fort Bridger, MEXICAN TERRITORY, Los Angeles, OLD SPANISH TRAIL, OREGON TRAIL, THE TRANS-MISSISSIPPI WEST, MORMON TRAIL, Santa Fe, DISPUTED, SANTA FE TRAIL, UNORGANIZED TERRITORY, CHEYENNE, Fort Laramie, SIOUX, IOWA TERRITORY, WISCONSIN TERRITORY, MI, Westport (Independence), MO, CHEROKEES, CREEKS, INDIAN TERRITORY, SEMINOLES, CHOCTAWS, CHICKASAWS, TEXAS ANNEXATION, IL, IN, OH, KY, TN, AR, MS, AL, LA, GA, FL, VA, NC, SC, APPALACHIAN, PA, NJ, NY, VT, NH, MA, CT, RI, ME, MD, DE, OJIBWAY, GREAT LAKES

0 250 500 Miles
0 250 500 Kilometers
Albers Equal-Area Projection

Although the western border of the United States did not yet extend to the Pacific Ocean, many Americans were settling along the Pacific Coast—the Far West—by the mid-1840s.

With the Louisiana Purchase, the western border of the United States moved beyond the Mississippi River, and non-Native American settlement of the trans-Mississippi West increased dramatically. U.S. exploration and the creation of several trails encouraged settlement of the region by a diversity of groups. As the number of small farmers, large planters, slaves, Mormons, miners, Chinese laborers, and Mexicans grew in the West, they often pushed Native Americans off their land.

POPULATION OF THE MIDWEST
87%	White
10%	Black
<1%	Native American
1%	Asian
3%	Hispanic origin*

*Hispanic origin may include persons of any race, thus charts represent more than 100%.

The West Today

WA, MT, OR, ID, ROCKY MOUNTAINS, NV, CA, UT, WY, CO, AZ, NM, ND, SD, NE, KS, OK, TX, MN, WI, IA, MO, AR, LA, MS, AL, TN, KY, IN, IL, MI, OH, GA, FL, SC, NC, VA, WV, PA, NY, VT, NH, ME, MA, RI, CT, NJ, DE, MD, DC, APPALACHIAN MTS, GREAT LAKES

Legend:
- The West
- The Midwest
- The South and Northeast
- Interstate highways

Scale and projection as map above.

Chart information from *Statistical Abstract of the United States 1991.*

During the 20th century the West has continued to be a place of great diversity and inspiration. Many Americans, however, still associate the West with images of cattle drives and Native American culture. As a result, definitions of the West are still confusing. For example, although the U.S. Census considers Texas and Oklahoma to be southern states, many people consider them to be more culturally and ethnically like western states.

POPULATION OF THE WEST
76%	White
5%	Black
2%	Native American
8%	Asian
29%	Hispanic origin*

*Hispanic origin may include persons of any race, thus charts represent more than 100%.

POPULATION OF THE SOUTH & NORTHEAST
79%	White
16%	Black
<1%	Native American
2%	Asian
8%	Hispanic origin*

*Hispanic origin may include persons of any race, thus charts represent more than 100%.

HISTORICAL SIDELIGHTS
California Culture
Many people consider Texas and Oklahoma to be more western than southern, and others argue that the diverse population and culture of California sets it apart as a region all its own. The writer O. Henry once said of the state, "East is East and West is San Francisco, according to Californians. Californians are a race of people; they are not merely inhabitants of a state."

187

A STRONG START FOR THE NATION

1789–1815

Chapter Overview

The formative years of the nation were turbulent, marked by conflict at home and abroad. At home, by the time Washington retired from the presidency, opposing factions had formed political parties. The two parties—Republicans and Federalists—disagreed over domestic and foreign policies. However, power was transferred peacefully from Adams's Federalist administration to Jefferson's Republican one. The young nation under Jefferson about doubled in size with the Louisiana Purchase.

In foreign affairs, Washington and Adams kept the nation out of war, but during Jefferson's tenure, the country clashed with the Barbary pirates. Then under Madison, continuing conflicts with Britain finally erupted into the War of 1812.

THE AMERICAN NATION VIDEODISC PROGRAM
A variety of still images, short videos, and activities are available for you to use as you teach this chapter. See Correlation to *The American Nation Videodisc Program* for barcode correlations and suggestions for using the program.

Chapter Planning Guide

CHAPTER 6	CORE RESOURCE BOOKLETS	AUDIOVISUAL (AV) RESOURCES	PROGRAM RESOURCES
INTRODUCTION pp. 188–189	■ Literature Worksheet 6 ■ Building Your Portfolio Worksheet 2	■ Everyday Life in America Transparency and Worksheet 6	
TEACHING THE CHAPTER pp. 190–215	■ Graphic Organizer 6 ■ Social Studies Skills Worksheet 6 ■ Geography Worksheet 6 ■ Outline Maps 1, 2, 8, 9, 14, 19	■ *The American Nation* Videodisc: Designing a Nation; A Native American Confederacy	■ Art in American History Transparency and Worksheet 5 ■ *Eyewitnesses and Others*, Volume 1: Readings 32, 33, 36, 38, 39, 40
REVIEW AND ASSESSMENT pp. 216–217	■ Chapter 6 Daily Quizzes ■ Review Worksheet 6 ■ Chapter 6 Tests ■ Alternative Assessment Forms		■ Test Generator

Additional Resources

BOOKS FOR TEACHERS

Flexner, James T. *Washington: The Indispensable Man*. NAL-Dutton, 1984. Distillation of the author's award-winning biography.

Koch, Adrienne. *Jefferson and Madison: The Great Collaboration*. University Press of America, 1987. Examination of the joint efforts of two presidents.

Smith, Page. *The Shaping of America: A People's History of the Young Republic*, Vol. 3. Viking Penguin, 1989. In-depth analysis of the nation's formative years.

BOOKS FOR STUDENTS

*Bober, Natalie. *Thomas Jefferson: Man on a Mountain*. Macmillan Children's Book Group, 1988. Examines public and personal life of Jefferson.

Eckert, Allen. *Tecumseh*. Eclipse Books, 1992. Biography of the Native American hero.

*Meltzer, Milton. *George Washington and the Birth of Our Nation*. Watts, 1986. Critique of Washington's life and career.

* for students reading below grade level

MULTIMEDIA MATERIALS

The Louisiana Purchase. Video, 15 min. Media Basics Video. Examines background, acquisition, and impact of the Louisiana Purchase.

A New Nation: The Struggle to Survive 1789–1815. Two filmstrips. Benchmark. Describes key events of early national era.

The War of 1812. Video, 20 min. Media Basics Video. Documentary describing the war's causes, strategies, events, and results.

THEMES IN AMERICAN HISTORY

USE WITH PAGES 188–189

*L*isted below are the themes emphasized in Chapter 6. The questions in boldface type stimulate critical thinking and provide students with an opportunity to discuss the themes within a broadened context. The questions also appear in the pupil's edition on p. 188.

■ CONSTITUTIONAL HERITAGE

Why might protection of individual rights be needed, even under a government established by the people? Students should consider that a nation is made up of people with diverse points of view, economic interests, and personal values. A democratic nation must protect the right of individuals to maintain these differences within the context of the larger society and find ways to balance the rights of people with opposing views.

■ ECONOMIC DEVELOPMENT

To what extent should a government assist or regulate economic development? Students should explore the advantages of a free-enterprise system versus government regulation, protection, and planning in promoting economic growth.

■ GEOGRAPHIC DIVERSITY

What challenges might a large country with diverse natural resources present for a new government? Students should consider the challenges of developing plans for both utilizing and protecting resources and for mediating when groups come into conflict over the proper uses of land and resources.

■ DEMOCRATIC VALUES

How might political parties strengthen a democracy? Students might note that in a democracy such as the U.S., the people rule through their elected representatives. Political parties allow people with similar views on social issues or needs to band together to make their demands heard. Students might also note that political parties allow elected officials to band together to effect change on behalf of their constituents.

CHAPTER STRATEGIES FOR MEETING INDIVIDUAL NEEDS

LIMITED ENGLISH PROFICIENT LEARNERS

Have students work in small groups to write the chapter's boldfaced terms on one set of index cards and short definitions or sketches on another set. Then have students play a "concentration" game to match the cards.

TACTILE/KINESTHETIC LEARNERS

Organize students into five groups, assigning each group one of the chapter's five sections. Have the groups create skits reflecting the main idea of their sections. Ask them to present the skits to the class and have class members interpret.

LEARNERS HAVING DIFFICULTY

As the class moves through each section, ask students to write questions about events and concepts of which they are not certain. Have them work in pairs to find answers and quiz each other.

AUDITORY LEARNERS

Organize students into small groups and assign each group a pertinent passage from titles listed in Books for Students on p. 187A. Have each group study the passage and choose a member to read it to the class. Group members should then field any questions.

VISUAL LEARNERS

Have students look at the illustrations in the chapter. Ask them to do library research to find additional images that relate to the chapter content and to share their findings with the class.

GIFTED LEARNERS

Have students research and write essays discussing how the economic interests of different groups in U.S. society affected U.S. domestic and foreign policy from 1789 to 1815.

USING THE CHAPTER FOCUS

■ UNDERSTANDING THE MAIN IDEA

Have students identify some present-day domestic and foreign challenges facing the U.S. Write responses on the chalkboard. Then have students group these issues into broader categories such as politics, economics, and foreign relations. Ask students to speculate how the same general issues might have caused conflict in the nation's early years. Write responses on a flip chart and have students evaluate them after they complete the chapter.

THEMES
Have students work individually or in small groups to answer the questions under Themes. Save students' responses so they can compare them with their responses after studying the chapter. (See p. 187B for suggested answers.)

■ THE TIME LINE
Ask students to jot down important points about each time-line event as they study each section. When the chapter is completed, ask volunteers to discuss the points they noted.

CORE RESOURCES

- **Graphic Organizer 6**
- **Literature Worksheet 6**
- **Outline Maps 1, 2, 8, 9, 14, 19**
- **Building Your Portfolio Worksheet 2**

AV RESOURCES

- **Everyday Life in America Transparency** and **Worksheet 6**

ABOUT THE ILLUSTRATION

Following his inauguration, President George Washington is saluted by the American navy as he is rowed through New York harbor. The painting by L. M. Cooke was created in the late 19th century and now belongs to the National Gallery of Art in Washington, D.C. Invite students to write a brief newspaper article that might have appeared at the time of the inauguration, describing the scene.

Chapter 6

A STRONG START FOR THE NATION

1789–1815

FOCUS

UNDERSTANDING THE MAIN IDEA

Domestic and foreign problems plagued America in its early years. The new federal government successfully addressed some of the problems at home. But relations with Europe threatened to involve the nation in warfare and divide Americans along political party lines. These intrigues would eventually erupt into the War of 1812.

THEMES

■ **CONSTITUTIONAL HERITAGE** Why might protection of individual rights be needed, even under a government established by the people?

■ **ECONOMIC DEVELOPMENT** To what extent should a government assist or regulate economic development?

■ **GEOGRAPHIC DIVERSITY** What challenges might a large country with diverse natural resources present for a new government?

■ **DEMOCRATIC VALUES** How might political parties strengthen a democracy?

1789	1791	1803	1812	1814
Washington inaugurated.	Bill of Rights ratified.	U.S. completes Louisiana Purchase.	War declared against Great Britain.	Treaty of Ghent signed.

Ask students to recall problems faced by the Constitutional Convention. Remind them that writing and ratifying the Constitution were only the first steps in forming a new government. Ask students to speculate on the issues that the young nation would face in implementing the Constitution and to suggest why George Washington's responsibilities would be particularly difficult.

■■ Ask students if they think Washington's responsibilities were greater than the responsibilities facing a president today.

HISTORICAL SIDELIGHTS

The President's Oath

The oath that Robert Livingston administered to George Washington is set forth in Article 2, Section 1 of the Constitution: "I do solemnly swear (or affirm) that I will faithfully execute the Office of President of the United States, and will to the best of my Ability, preserve, protect and defend the Constitution of the United States."

Tell students that "I swear so help me God" was added by Washington after he had taken the required oath.

■ LINK TO THE PAST

By 1789 all the states except Rhode Island had ratified the new plan of government developed at the Constitutional Convention. Newly elected government officials—the president and the members of Congress—set out to put the Constitution into action.

Salute to George Washington in New York harbor

National Gallery of Art

It is April 30, 1789. In New York City, the nation's temporary capital, a crowd gathers on Wall Street to witness the inauguration of the first president of the United States. On the balcony of Federal Hall stands George Washington. The people fall silent while Washington takes the oath of office. As the last words echo in the air, the crowd bursts into wild cheers.

We do not know what Washington was thinking that day as he gazed on the sea of admiring faces. Perhaps he was weighing the new government's chances for success. Washington knew that America was not yet truly a nation. Most Americans still thought of themselves as members of individual states rather than as citizens of the United States.

If Washington's thoughts were on the nation's future, he was not alone in his concerns. John Adams, the new vice president, feared that the Republic might not last beyond his lifetime. Both men realized that the United States was, in Washington's words, an "experiment entrusted to the hands of the American people." Only time would tell how successful the experiment would be.

Between 1789 and 1815 the American people and their leaders laid the foundations for the "American experiment." They built new political, social, and economic institutions. They battled external threats to their way of life. In the process they built what Thomas Jefferson called "the empire of liberty." Yet as settlers pushed farther into the interior of the continent, they disrupted Native American societies that existed there.

Sampler celebrating Washington's inauguration

Museum of the City of New York

Section 1

A FEDERAL GOVERNMENT IS ESTABLISHED

FOCUS

- **What steps did the First Congress take to establish the federal government?**
- **How did Alexander Hamilton propose that Congress strengthen the nation's finances?**
- **What controversies surrounded Hamilton's financial program?**

In early 1789 newly elected federal officials gathered to organize the government. They relied on their experiences in colonial administration, the examples of historical and contemporary European governments, and the new federal Constitution. The Constitution provided only the outline of government. Congress and the president still had to fill in the details.

Painting of American eagle

St. Paul's Chapel, Parish of Trinity Church, City of New York

THE FIRST PRESIDENT

When Congress opened the ballots from the states on April 6, 1789, the unanimous choice for president was George Washington. The choice was not surprising. Washington's popularity had soared since the victory at Yorktown. Several states that had been unwilling to ratify the Constitution did so with the expectation that Washington would serve as the first president.

Yet, he said he was reluctant to accept this honor. Washington doubted his abilities and feared that people would think

◄ **"Hail, Columbia," composed for the inaugural, was performed as Washington crossed Trenton Bridge on his way to New York.**

The Free Library of Philadelphia

that he wanted to be a king. Leaving Mount Vernon for his inauguration, he said he felt like "a culprit who is going to the place of his execution." The muddy trip, though, was a triumph. Crowds cheered; towns celebrated.

But the festivities were soon over. President Washington and the other elected officials got down to work. They knew that each step they took set a **precedent**, or guide, for future leaders.

THE FIRST CONGRESS

Although Washington had the spotlight, the task of molding the new government belonged to the First Congress. The people's representatives faced a crowded agenda.

The first order of business was to add a protection of individual liberties to the Constitution—a promise that supporters of the Constitution had made during the struggle for ratification. From the 210 proposed amendments, 12 were recommended by Congress for adoption; of these, 10 were ratified

MOTIVATING:
LINK TO TODAY

Have students identify as many present-day government agencies as they can. List responses on the chalkboard. Ask students how and why they think these agencies came into being.

Teaching the Section

ESTABLISHING THE FEDERAL GOVERNMENT

Have students work with partners to list the steps taken by the First Congress to establish the federal government. *(passed Bill of Rights, created a federal court system, created three executive departments)* Have volunteers present their lists. Ask students to explain how each action was important to the success of the new government.

THE BILL OF RIGHTS

FIRST AMENDMENT guarantees freedom of religion, speech, and the press and the right to assemble peacefully and to petition the government.

SECOND AMENDMENT recognizes the necessity of state militias and thus the right to bear arms.

THIRD AMENDMENT prohibits quartering of troops without consent as regulated by law.

FOURTH AMENDMENT prohibits searches and seizures without warrants, which can be issued only upon probable cause.

FIFTH AMENDMENT requires a grand jury indictment before persons can be tried for serious criminal charges; prohibits persons from being tried twice for the same offense; prohibits forcing the accused to testify against themselves; guarantees that no one may be deprived of life, liberty, or property without due process of law.

SIXTH AMENDMENT guarantees the right to a speedy trial in criminal cases, the right to know all charges, the right to question and obtain witnesses, and the right to have counsel.

SEVENTH AMENDMENT guarantees a trial in most civil cases.

EIGHTH AMENDMENT prohibits excessive fines and bail; prohibits cruel and unusual punishment.

NINTH AMENDMENT protects individual rights not specifically mentioned in the Constitution.

TENTH AMENDMENT reserves for the states and the people those powers not delegated to the national government or prohibited by the Constitution.

▶ **The original Bill of Rights contained 12 amendments. The states ratified 10.**

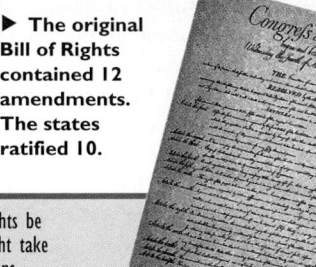

The Granger Collection, New York.

PROTECTING LIBERTY Those who insisted that the Bill of Rights be added to the Constitution feared that a strong federal government might take away the basic rights of the people guaranteed by the state constitutions.

? **ANALYZING** How does the Bill of Rights help protect against the federal government gaining too much power over individuals?

---

by the states in 1791. They became known as the **Bill of Rights**.

Another task of Congress was the creation of a federal court system. By September, Congress had passed the **Judiciary Act of 1789**, which (1) established a federal district court in each state and three circuit courts of appeal; (2) provided for a chief justice and five associate justices of the Supreme Court to be nominated by the president and approved by the Senate; and (3) defined the federal courts' powers and the relationship between the federal courts and the state courts.

During its first session Congress also created three departments to assist the president: the State Department to handle foreign affairs, the War Department to manage military affairs, and the Treasury Department to oversee the nation's finances. The president appointed the heads, or secretaries, of these departments to serve as his advisers. Over time these advisers became known as the president's **cabinet**.

Washington's first cabinet included Thomas Jefferson as secretary of state, Henry Knox as sec-retary of war, and Alexander Hamilton as secretary of the treasury. The president also appointed an attorney general, Edmund Randolph, to advise him on legal matters.

■■ **The First Congress passed the Bill of Rights, set up the federal judiciary, and established three executive departments to assist the president.**

*R*ESTORING THE NATION'S CREDIT

Next, Congress tackled the nation's finances, for the government had inherited serious financial problems. Not only did the Treasury lack funds to pay off war debts, it did not have enough money to run the country. Lawmakers turned to Secretary of the Treasury Alexander Hamilton for help. In doing so they set an important precedent: though Congress is responsible for passing laws, from its beginning it has sought guidance from the executive branch.

MAKING CONNECTIONS
Political Science

One of the 12 amendments submitted by Congress in 1789 read: "No law, varying the compensation for the services of the senators and representatives, shall take effect, until an election of representatives shall have intervened." When the amendment was not among those ratified in 1791, it seemed to die. Over the years, however, states slowly and quietly continued to approve it. In 1992 Michigan became the necessary 38th state to ratify. Thus the idea of limiting congressional pay raises became the Twenty-seventh Amendment more than 200 years after James Madison proposed it.

Chart Caption Answer
The Bill of Rights protects individual liberties.

BUILDING VOCABULARY

The word *cabinet* comes from the French and was used to describe a small, private apartment in which the king met with his advisers.

Teaching the Section

HAMILTON'S PROPOSAL

Organize students into groups of four to debate Hamilton's plan to strengthen the nation's finances. Assign students these roles: an official representing a state that has paid its debts, an official of one that has not, an original bondholder who sold his or her bonds, a northern speculator. After the debates, ask students to assess the fairness and practicality of Hamilton's plan.

FINANCIAL CONTROVERSIES

Call on students to explain the reasons why Hamilton proposed a national bank. List the responses on the chalkboard. *(safe place for government funds, uniform currency, a source for loans)* Then ask for two volunteers to role-play the Hamilton-Jefferson debate over the creation of the bank. Conclude by asking students to write a short paragraph explaining their support for either Hamilton's or Jefferson's position.

VOICES IN HISTORY

Englishman Thomas Cooper visited the U.S. and decided to stay. In 1794 he reported his views on the government of his new home: "There is little fault to find with the government of America, either in principle or in practice: we have very few taxes to pay, and those are of acknowledged necessity, and moderate in amount. . . . The government is the government *of* the people, and *for* the people. There are no tythes nor game laws: and excise laws upon spirits only."

MAKING CONNECTIONS

Geography

The District of Columbia was originally a 100-square-mile territory set aside for the seat of the federal government and made up of the towns of Alexandria, Georgetown, and Washington (the site chosen for the new capital). After Alexandria was given back to Virginia in 1846, and Georgetown annexed by Washington in 1878, the city of Washington had the same boundaries as the District of Columbia. Refer students to the maps on p. 377 and p. 387 to show the district's boundaries.

Alexander Hamilton

National Portrait Gallery

The slight, fair-haired Hamilton was one of the most brilliant, and controversial, of the nation's founders. He was born in the British West Indies in 1755, the son of a failed Scottish merchant. At an early age he went to work in a countinghouse, where his aptitude for transacting business became evident. In 1773 Hamilton went to New York City, where he attended King's College. He was ambitious in his pursuit of public praise and power. Through his writings, economic programs, and political intrigues, he exerted almost as great an influence on the young Republic as the early presidents did.

Alexander Hamilton believed that America's future depended on a strong national government controlled by the rich and well born. Although self-made, he had little faith in the ability of common people to govern. They were, he said, "turbulent and changing" and made decisions based on their immediate needs.

Hamilton's strong federalism shaped his economic plans. He believed that one of the best ways to strengthen the government, both financially and politically, was to establish economic policies that helped business and industry. If business people believed the federal government had their best interests at heart, they would support it.

The Scottish economist Adam Smith heavily influenced Hamilton's views. In his book *Wealth of Nations* (1776), Smith stated that industry and commerce—not farming—were the most important sources of wealth. Smith advocated **capitalism**—an economic system based on a free market and private ownership of property.

As a first step toward winning over the merchant class, Hamilton advised Congress to strengthen the nation's credit by paying off the **national debt**—the money that the federal government owed to its creditors. Hamilton knew that a nation that did not pay its debts would have trouble borrowing additional money. The total national debt was estimated to be a staggering $77 million.

▲ The U.S. Mint began making coins in 1792. Shown here are some of the first pieces minted.

Congress moved quickly to pay the $12 million owed to foreign nations, but Hamilton's proposal to pay the domestic debt met with strong resistance.

The Continental Congress had borrowed from individuals about $40 million during the war, mostly by selling **government bonds**—certificates issued by a government in exchange for loans of money. Each bond was the government's promise to repay the loan plus interest. But the government's credit had fallen so low that its bonds were almost worthless. Many original bondholders had panicked and sold their bonds to financial speculators at a fraction of their original value.

Hamilton's proposal to pay the bonds in full caused an uproar. His opponents rightly charged that speculators stood to make a fortune at the expense of ordinary citizens. In the end, however, Congress agreed with Hamilton that restoring the nation's credit depended on honoring these bonds.

Hamilton's next proposal—that the federal government take over about $21.5 million of the $25 million in state debts—met even stronger opposition. All the southern states except South Carolina had paid their debts and saw no reason why they should help pay the debts of other states.

Only a last-minute compromise saved the plan. In return for southern votes, Hamilton's supporters pledged that the national capital would be moved south to a site across the Potomac River from Virginia. Virginians believed this new location, later named Washington, D.C., would give them greater influence in the federal government.

HAMILTON'S BANK PROPOSAL

Establishing good credit was not the only solution to the nation's financial woes. The government also lacked the means to manage the nation's money supply. Thus, Hamilton asked Congress to create the Bank of the United States, a **national bank** consisting of a central bank with branches in major U.S. cities. Hamilton believed that such a national bank would provide (1) a safe place to deposit government funds; (2) a sound, uniform currency issued in the form of **bank notes**, or paper money; and (3) a source for loans to assist the government in times of emergency and to fuel commercial expansion.

GUIDED PRACTICE

Organize the class into two groups. Alternate asking one group to identify a problem existing when Washington took office as president and asking the other group to describe the solution to the problem.

INDEPENDENT PRACTICE

Have students prepare graphic organizers that illustrate the problems that Washington faced when he took office and the solutions found for those problems. Students may wish to include their graphic organizers in their portfolios.

*R*eview and *A*ssessment

REVIEW Have students write diary entries giving their view of the new federal government from the standpoint of either a southern farmer or a northeastern merchant. Students may wish to include their diary entries in their portfolios. Then assign the Section 1 Review on p. 194.

ASSESS Assign the **Section 1 Daily Quiz** in *Core Resources*.   ▶

■■ **Hamilton proposed that Congress pay off the national debt, assume state debts, and organize a national bank to strengthen the nation's finances.**

Hamilton argued that the nation had much to gain from the creation of a national bank. Many Americans, particularly southern planters who were short of cash, did not share his enthusiasm. They feared that the bank would be controlled by wealthy northeastern merchants.

Thomas Jefferson raised a more serious charge: the bank was illegal! Nowhere in the Constitution was the federal government given the power to set up a bank. Jefferson believed that the government could do only what the Constitution specifically allows. This philosophy of constitutional interpretation is called **strict construction**.

Hamilton, on the other hand, supported the philosophy of constitutional interpretation called **loose construction**. That is, he believed that the government can do anything the Constitution does not specifically forbid. In support of this view, he pointed to the clause in the Constitution that grants Congress the right "to make all laws . . . necessary and proper" for running the country. The government's power to collect taxes and borrow money could only be exercised, he argued, with the aid of a national bank.

Jefferson replied that the "necessary and proper" clause was meant to limit—not stretch—the power of the federal government. In his eyes a national bank was not a *necessity*, and so Congress had no authority to establish one. The members of Congress debated the issue for months. In the end, President Washington sided with Hamilton, and Congress chartered the Bank of the United States in 1791. The charter granted the Bank the right to operate for 20 years, when it would again be subject to congressional approval.

*T*AX REBELLION ON THE FRONTIER

Hamilton's next task was to raise the money to pay off the national debt. Unlike today, the government did not have the power to collect an income tax. Instead it depended on various tariffs to raise money. Hamilton knew that the tariffs could not raise enough money to pay off the debt. He

PRESIDENTIAL LIVES

GEORGE WASHINGTON
1732–1799

in office 1789–1797

As president, George Washington refused to isolate himself from the general public, saying he did not want to be shut away "like an eastern Lama [holy man]." So he set up a schedule for greeting citizens in his home. On Tuesday afternoons he met with men only. On Friday evenings he and his wife, Martha, served refreshments to men and women.

Washington also had government officials to dinner every Thursday, rotating the invitations so as not to play favorites. The dinners were not formal functions as much as they were festive occasions. Washington loved social gatherings of all kinds, from intimate tea parties to fox hunts and lavish balls. He enjoyed sharing good food, wine, and conversation, playing cards, and attending the theater.

G. Washington

therefore asked Congress to impose a tax on a few domestically produced items, most notably whiskey. The tax was to be paid by producers. When the measure passed, the cry "No taxation without representation" was again heard in the land—this time aimed at the U.S. government.

The new tax hit western farmers the hardest. Many turned corn, their most important crop, into whiskey, because it was easier to transport to the coast. News of the tax infuriated them. An anonymous poet noted the farmers' mood:

❝ Some chaps whom freedom's spirit warms
Are threatening hard to take up arms,
And headstrong in rebellion rise

COOPERATIVE LEARNING

Organize the class into groups and encourage them to research and report on a current issue, such as gun control or music censorship, from the standpoints of strict construction and loose construction of the Constitution. Each group should divide the tasks of research, report preparation, and report presentation among its members.

THE AMERICAN NATION VIDEODISC PROGRAM

Designing a Nation

| 1A | 06322 | 4:24 |

PRIMARY SOURCE
Description of Change: excerpted
Rationale: excerpted to focus on main idea

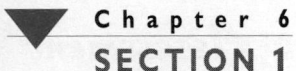

RETEACH Have students work in groups, assigning individuals or pairs the task of outlining subsections. Ask students to exchange outlines and use them to ask questions of other members of their group.

Closure

Ask students for their opinions on Hamilton's belief that America's future depended on a strong national government controlled by the rich and well born. Ask for examples of his actions as secretary of the treasury that supported his beliefs.

Extension

COMPARE Have students research the present-day Federal Reserve system and compare its structure and operation to Hamilton's national bank of the 1790s.

INVESTIGATE Ask students to research and report to the class on the various types of bonds that the government offers for public purchase today.

SECTION REVIEW ANSWERS

IDENTIFY

For significance, see the following pages:
precedent (p. 190)
Bill of Rights (p. 191)
Judiciary Act of 1789 (p. 191)
cabinet (p. 191)
Alexander Hamilton (p. 191)
capitalism (p. 192)
national debt (p. 192)
government bonds (p. 192)
national bank (p. 192)
bank notes (p. 192)
Whiskey Rebellion (p. 194)

LOCATE

For location, see the map on pp. 1016–1017.

1. *passed Bill of Rights; set up federal court system; created three executive departments*
2. *by paying off the national debt, assuming state debts, and creating a national bank*
3. *Editorials should focus on one or more of the following: fairness, constitutionality, or the nation's debts.*
4. *strict—U.S. government can do only what Constitution allows; loose—U.S. government can do anything Constitution does not prohibit. Jefferson used strict construction to argue against and Hamilton used "necessary and proper" clause to argue for the Bank.*

'Fore they'll submit to that excise:
Their liberty they will maintain,
They fought for't, and they'll
fight again.**" **

In the hot summer of 1794, farmers in western Pennsylvania did rise in rebellion. When ordered to pay the tax, they attacked federal marshals, tarring and feathering some. A group of about 500 farmers burned the home of the head revenue agent, while others talked of starting a new country.

The **Whiskey Rebellion** challenged federal authority. Hamilton urged the president to take action. Calling out the militias from neighboring states, Washington assembled a force of some 13,000, almost as large as any he had commanded during the Revolutionary War. The "Whiskey

The Granger Collection, New York

▲ **An excise officer is tarred and feathered by a mob in 1794.**

Boys" quickly melted away into the backwoods rather than confront such an army.

In its response to the rebellion, the federal government had demonstrated the effectiveness of its power, even on the remote frontier. Yet this show of force cost the government support among western farmers who believed their interests were being ignored.

■■ **Hamilton's financial program raised the issue of constitutional interpretation and led to a tax rebellion.**

EVALUATING HAMILTON'S PROGRAMS

As secretary of the treasury, Hamilton aimed to create a strong government, a stable economy, and a favorable climate for business and industry. His financial programs largely succeeded. The tax brought in needed revenue. Reducing the national debt put the nation's credit on a firm footing. The national banking system provided the United States with a single currency.

But not everyone benefited equally from these measures. Hamilton's program favored the rich, as his opponents argued. His desire to win the loyalty of the commercial class often made him act against the interests of small farmers. Nevertheless, his federalist outlook enabled business to expand while laying the foundation for a new national prosperity.

SECTION 1 REVIEW

IDENTIFY and explain the significance of the following: precedent, Bill of Rights, Judiciary Act of 1789, cabinet, Alexander Hamilton, capitalism, national debt, government bonds, national bank, bank notes, Whiskey Rebellion.

LOCATE and explain the importance of the following: Washington, D.C.

1. **MAIN IDEA** What actions did Congress take to establish the federal government?
2. **MAIN IDEA** How did Hamilton propose to solve the nation's financial problems?
3. **WRITING TO EXPRESS A VIEWPOINT** Imagine you are a newspaper editor in the 1790s. Select one controversy surrounding Hamilton's financial program. Write an editorial favoring or opposing that part of the plan.
4. **CONTRASTING** Define strict and loose construction, and explain how Jefferson and Hamilton used the philosophies in the debate over the national bank.

PREVIEW WORKSHOP

Following is a list of the significant people, places, and terms in this section. You may wish to use this list as a section preview.

People
- Edmond Genet
- Little Turtle
- "Mad Anthony" Wayne

Places
- New Orleans

Terms
- French Revolution
- impressment
- Battle of Fallen Timbers
- Treaty of Greenville
- Jay's Treaty
- Pinckney's Treaty

- right of deposit
- sectionalism

Section 2

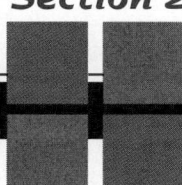

DEALING WITH A DANGEROUS WORLD

FOCUS OBJECTIVES

- Explain how conflicts in Europe affected Americans.

- Describe the significance of the Native American defeat at Fallen Timbers.

- Analyze what Jay's Treaty and Pinckney's Treaty accomplished.

- Examine how the two-party system in American politics developed.

F O C U S
- **How did conflicts in Europe affect Americans?**
- **What was the significance of the Native American defeat at Fallen Timbers?**
- **What did Jay's Treaty and Pinckney's Treaty accomplish?**
- **How did the two-party system in American politics develop?**

*H*amilton intended his financial program to strengthen the American economy. In the 1790s, however, economic independence was not yet a reality. Americans still needed British money and technology to strengthen commerce and to develop manufacturing. France provided an important market for American agricultural products. Therefore, the political upheavals and wars that engulfed Europe between 1789 and 1815 had an important impact on the United States.

U.S. cannon, 1815

THE FRENCH REVOLUTION

The American Revolution influenced events across the Atlantic. On July 14, 1789, French revolutionaries—inspired in part by Enlightenment beliefs and by the American Declaration of Independence, which put those beliefs into practice—stormed the Bastille (ba-STEEL), the old royal prison in Paris. This attack was a key turning point in the **French Revolution**.

The French revolutionaries proclaimed their goals in the ringing cry "Liberty, Equality, Fraternity," but soon the revolution turned into a bloodbath. During the period known as the Reign of Terror (1793–1794), thousands of men and women, including Louis XVI and his queen, Marie Antoinette, were beheaded.

The French revolutionaries saw themselves as champions of the people fighting against the old order. European monarchs feared that

this revolutionary spirit would spread beyond France's borders. This fear was intensified when the new French Republic declared war on Great Britain, Spain, and the Netherlands in 1793.

▲ **The Bastille was stormed and destroyed by French revolutionaries on July 14, 1789.**

The Mansell Collection

CORE RESOURCES

• **Section 2 Daily Quiz**

MOTIVATING: PRIOR KNOWLEDGE

Ask students what they know about the French Revolution from books and films. Write their responses on the chalkboard. Then have the class speculate about the American reactions to the French Revolution.

𝒯*eaching the* 𝒮*ection*

EUROPEAN CONFLICTS

Have students work in small groups to make a list of arguments for and against U.S. support of France in the European war. Ask groups to categorize possible consequences in terms of economics (effects on U.S. trade, the national debt, the overall economy), politics (divisiveness, sectional conflict), and foreign relations (U.S. susceptibility to control by another European nation).

BATTLE OF FALLEN TIMBERS

Ask students to summarize the consequences of the Battle of Fallen Timbers. List their responses on the chalkboard. Then organize the class into groups and ask them to prepare critiques of the Treaty of Greenville—half from the viewpoint of Little Turtle and half from the viewpoint of "Mad Anthony" Wayne. Have group spokespersons read the critiques to the class.

PRIMARY SOURCE

Description of Change: excerpted
Rationale: excerpted to focus on main idea

GLOBAL CONNECTIONS

The French government's debt, which tripled between 1774 and 1789, was one of the major causes of the French Revolution. Ironically, much of France's debt was incurred as a result of its support of the American Revolution.

HISTORICAL SIDELIGHTS

Citizen Genet

Genet also demanded that the U.S. immediately pay its Revolutionary War debts so that France could buy munitions. He tried to raise U.S. volunteers to invade Spanish Louisiana and Florida. When the French government recalled Genet, he feared he would be executed for his behavior. So he asked for political asylum, which Washington granted.

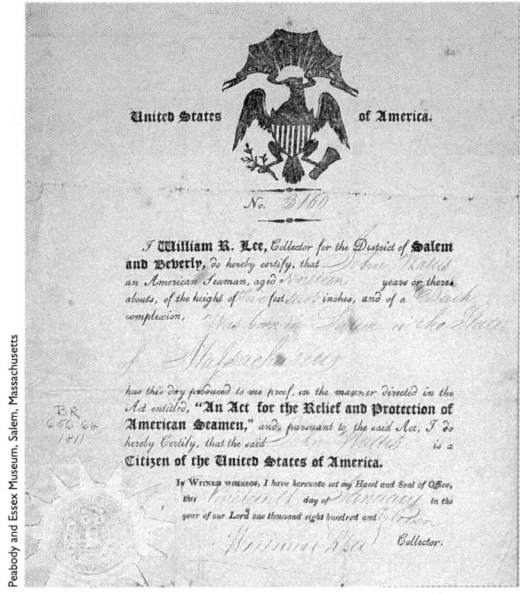

▲ American seamen took to carrying proof-of-citizenship papers to guard against possible impressment by the British navy.

Americans' reactions to these events in Europe were mixed. From Paris, Thomas Jefferson wrote excitedly to his friend James Monroe, "All the old spirit of 1776 is rekindling." Many other Americans, however, did not share Jefferson's enthusiasm. Many found it shocking that liberty depended "on the right of cutting throats."

The European conflict disrupted American trade and threatened to draw the United States into war. Both France and Great Britain ignored the American declaration of neutrality and seized American vessels bound for enemy ports.

In addition, the **impressment**—or kidnapping—of U.S. sailors by the British aroused American hostility. Between 1790 and 1812, Great Britain, claiming to be capturing deserters from British naval vessels, impressed some 10,000 American sailors.

French actions also caused resentment. In early 1793 a French diplomat, Edmond Genet (zhuh-NE), arrived in America. Citizen Genet, as he was known, toured the nation, organizing "revolutionary clubs" and trying to persuade Americans to honor their 1778

▲ The arrival of fiery French diplomat Edmond Genet in 1793 caused many Americans to choose sides.

---

military alliance treaty with France. Years later, John Adams—with some exaggeration—recalled the frightening passions that Genet excited:

> 66 Ten thousand people in the streets . . . threatened to drag Washington out of his house, and effect a revolution in the government, or compel it to declare war in favor of the French revolution and against England. 99

Washington, knowing that the United States was unprepared for war, refused to give in to pressure. On April 22, 1793 he issued a proclamation forbidding American support for any nation at war. Genet defied this neutrality policy by arming a ship in a U.S. port and sending it out to attack British shipping. Washington demanded that France recall its diplomat. Genet was replaced in 1794, but the divisions he created remained.

■■ **Conflicts in Europe caused political tension in the United States, disrupted trade, and strained U.S. diplomatic relations.**

𝒯ROUBLE ON THE FRONTIER

Washington managed to avoid foreign entanglements, but trouble brewed in the Northwest Territory. By the terms of the Treaty of Paris, which had ended the Revolutionary War in 1783, the British granted the United States the Northwest Territory. But Native Americans considered the territory theirs and battled settlers to keep it. In response, President Washington sent federal troops against American Indians.

To defend their homes, some 1,500 Miamis, Shawnees, Iroquois, Sauks (SAWKS), Fox, and Potawatomis (pahd-uh-WAHD-uh-mees) joined together in a loose confederation. Miami chief Michikinikwa (mi-chee-ken-EEK-wah), known as Little Turtle, led the group. He was a gifted strategist, and his leadership helped the confederation win several battles against American troops in 1790 and 1791.

The tide turned when President Washington sent some 3,000 well-trained and well-supplied soldiers under the command of Revolutionary War hero "Mad Anthony" Wayne to defeat the confederation.

JAY'S & PINCKNEY'S TREATIES

Organize students into groups. Assign each group one of these topics: Jay's Treaty, Pinckney's Treaty. Ask groups to list circumstances that led to the treaty and to create a map with a legend showing the results of the assigned treaty. Then call on group members to present their lists and maps.

A TWO–PARTY SYSTEM

Explain to students that early newspapers often were closely connected to political parties. Then organize students into groups. Tell them to imagine that they publish either a Federalist or a Republican newspaper. Have each group list the following about its paper: name, place published, editorial philosophy, description of readers, and topics for articles that it would publish. Call on each group to present and explain its list.

▶ **Little Turtle led Native Americans in successful battles against American troops in the Northwest Territory during 1790–1791.**

Realizing that the Native Americans were outnumbered, Little Turtle advised his allies:

> 66 We have beaten the enemy twice under different commanders. We cannot expect the same good fortune to attend us always. The Americans are now led by a chief who never sleeps. Like the blacksnake, the day and the night are alike to him for during all the time he has been marching on our villages . . . we have not been able to surprise him. . . . It would be prudent to listen to his offers of peace. 99

The other chiefs in the confederation rejected his advice, so Little Turtle refused to remain in command. In the summer of 1794, the confederation clashed with Wayne's army in the **Battle of Fallen Timbers**, near present-day Toledo, Ohio. As Little Turtle had predicted, the fighting ended in defeat for the confederation. After the battle, Wayne's men burned Indian villages and fields.

The Battle of Fallen Timbers dealt a severe blow to American Indian resistance in the territory. In 1795 over 1,000 chiefs, including Little Turtle, entered negotiations with the U.S. government. The result was the **Treaty of Greenville** (1795), which gave the United States title to Native American lands making up much of present-day Ohio and part of Indiana. In exchange Native Americans received $20,000 worth of goods and a formal acknowledgment of their claim to the lands they still held.

■■ **The Battle of Fallen Timbers weakened Native American resistance and led to the surrender of Indian lands.**

NEGOTIATING PEACE

Little Turtle's confederation had received weapons from British forts in the Northwest Territory. The existence of these British forts violated the 1783 Treaty of Paris. This situation further strained America's tense relations with Great Britain. Hoping to avert a war that he believed the United States could not win, President Washington sent Chief Justice John Jay to Great Britain in 1794 to negotiate a settlement. Among the terms of the resulting treaty, known as **Jay's Treaty**, the British agreed to abandon their forts. In return the U.S. government agreed to pay debts owed to the British.

Great Britain, however, did not stop arming American Indians, impressing American sailors, or seizing U.S. ships. These acts angered many Americans who thought Jay had sold out to the British. Mobs burned Jay in effigy, and the nation's political divisions deepened. Congress, nevertheless, ratified the treaty. Washington had realized his major goal—preventing war with Great Britain.

Jay's Treaty came just as Spain shifted alliances, joining France against Great Britain. Spain feared an American alliance with Britain could threaten Spanish territory in North America. Thus Spain moved quickly to settle its disputes with the United States. The result was **Pinckney's Treaty**, negotiated in 1795 by Thomas Pinckney of South Carolina. Pinckney's Treaty set the southern boundary of the United States near Florida at the 31st parallel.

Ohio Historical Society

▲ **General Anthony Wayne led the attack on Native Americans during the Battle of Fallen Timbers. The entire battle lasted about 40 minutes.**

PRIMARY SOURCE

Description of Change: excerpted
Rationale: excerpted to focus on main idea

VOICES IN HISTORY

After the Treaty of Greenville was signed, non-Indian hunters, trappers, and horse thieves continued to push onto American Indian lands, destroying the Indians' sources of livelihood. Shawnee leaders urged the U.S. government to "Stop your people from killing our game. At present they kill more than we do." The government suggested that the Indians take up farming rather than hunt. At the same time, the government pushed for additional land cessions by the Indians. These actions led to rebellion by some Indians.

HISTORICAL SIDELIGHTS

Jay's Treaty

When Hamilton spoke in favor of Jay's Treaty in New York, he was stoned from the platform. Later, in response to Republican goading, he offered to duel the Republicans, one at a time. Although the Republicans accepted, the duels never took place.

Practice

GUIDED PRACTICE

Create a class time line on the chalkboard of the major events in this section. Instruct students to phrase each entry as a newspaper headline. Have students suggest elements for a newspaper article that might elaborate each time-line entry, instructing the class to take notes for the Independent Practice activity.

INDEPENDENT PRACTICE

Have students choose one of the entries from the Guided Practice time line and, using their notes from the Guided Practice, write a news story that might appear under that headline. Students may wish to include their news stories in their portfolios.

Review and Assessment

REVIEW Encourage students to outline those events in the section that support the section's title, "Dealing with a Dangerous World." Then assign the Section 2 Review on p. 199.

ASSESS Assign the **Section 2 Daily Quiz** in *Core Resources.*

◀ Frontier farmers carried their goods on large flatboats down the Mississippi River to New Orleans.

The Historic New Orleans Collection

keenly aware that dangers threatened the young nation. In his farewell address he urged maintaining neutrality abroad and unity at home. "The great rule of conduct for us . . . is . . . to steer clear of permanent alliances with any portion of the foreign world."

Washington also warned of the dangers posed by political parties and regional interests:

❝ In contemplating the causes which may disturb our Union, it occurs as a matter of serious concern that . . . designing [plotting] men may endeavor to excite a belief that there is a real difference of local interests and views. . . . You cannot shield yourselves too much against the jealousies and heartburnings which spring from these misrepresentations. They tend to render alien to each other those who ought to be bound together by fraternal affection. ❞

Pinckney's Treaty also guaranteed American navigation rights on the Mississippi River. In an era dominated by water transportation, the Mississippi was the superhighway linking the American West to the rest of the nation and the world. Frontier farmers and merchants used the Mississippi and its westward-flowing tributaries, such as the Ohio River, to move their produce to New Orleans. From there goods were shipped to markets around the world. Pinckney's Treaty gave Americans the **right of deposit**—the right to temporarily unload goods at the port of New Orleans without paying a duty to Spain.

▪▪ **Jay's Treaty and Pinckney's Treaty prevented war and won important military and economic advantages for the United States.**

DOMESTIC BATTLES

In 1796 President Washington announced that he would not seek a third term—setting an informal precedent for later presidents that was not broken until 1940. He had overseen the organization of the new government and had skillfully handled several crises in foreign affairs. Still, the president was

But Washington's warning was not heeded. By the mid-1790s heated debates over whether to side with Great Britain or France had already deepened political differences and aided in shaping the first American political parties. Washington also had underestimated the extent of regional and economic differences. In the mid-1790s **sectionalism**, or loyalty to a particular part of the country, helped to create two parties: the Federalists (the party of Hamilton and Adams) and the Democratic-Republicans (the party of Jefferson and Madison). As Americans sided with one party or the other, the two-party system that is still with us today took shape.

Merchants, manufacturers, lawyers, and church leaders from New England and the Atlantic seaboard—Americans whom Federalist John Adams called "the rich, the well-born, and the able"—tended to support the Federalist party. Federalists expected the rich to provide national

RETEACH Organize students into four groups and assign each group one of the Focus questions on p. 195. Have group members discuss their question and write a group answer. Ask a volunteer from each group to share the group's answer with the other groups.

Closure

Write this statement on the chalkboard: *Events abroad influenced the course of the new nation during Washington's presidency.* Ask students if they support or contest this statement and have them explain why.

■■ Ask students what events abroad are presently influencing the U.S.

Extension

RESEARCH Have students research the Indian confederation led by Little Turtle and its confrontations with western pioneers during the 1780s and 1790s.

EVALUATE Suggest that students find and read Washington's complete Farewell Address and write an essay explaining what his reaction might be to some U.S. foreign policies today.

► The Republican party believed in an agricultural America full of orderly farms, such as the one shown here.

Abby Aldrich Rockefeller Folk Art Center

► The Federalist party drew its supporters from the ranks of wealthy men, such as cloth merchant Elijah Boardman.

The Metropolitan Museum of Art

leadership. As one leading Federalist said: "Those who own the country ought to govern it." Besides favoring a strong national government, Federalists wanted to promote the development of commerce, especially with Great Britain.

In contrast, the Democratic-Republican party (the name was soon shortened to Republican party) included planters, small farmers, and wage earners. The party (which has no historical connection to today's Republican party) was particularly strong on the frontier and in the South. Supporters favored agriculture over manufacturing and believed that farmers, who made up most of the population, deserved the most say in government.

But the party also found support in the North, especially in the middle states. Here, various groups who had little political power saw the Republican party as a means of challenging established leadership. These artisans, workers, and tradespeople were resentful of the rich and power-

ful Federalists. They sought, instead, the political equality promised them by the Revolution.

Both northern and southern Republicans were drawn together by common beliefs. Their main aim was to protect states' rights and individual liberties by limiting the federal government. They had a deep fear of a strong national government and the financial and political powers that could create such a system. Because they distrusted the aristocratic British, they tended to be pro-French.

■■ **The two-party political system arose from the rivalry between Federalists and Republicans and from the growing sectionalism of the nation.**

SECTION REVIEW ANSWERS

IDENTIFY

For significance, see the following pages:
French Revolution (p. 195)
impressment (p. 196)
Edmond Genet (p. 196)
Little Turtle (p. 196)
"Mad Anthony" Wayne (p. 196)
Treaty of Greenville (p. 197)
right of deposit (p. 198)
sectionalism (p. 198)

LOCATE

For location, see the map on pp. 1016–1017.

1. *U.S. trade was disrupted; events threatened to draw the U.S. into the European war; impressment caused resentment.*
2. *Jay's—British agreed to abandon frontier forts; Pinckney's—set southern boundary of U.S., guaranteed navigation rights on Mississippi River, gained right of deposit*
3. *Native American resistance was weakened; Indian lands were forcibly surrendered.*
4. *Ads should consider each party's economic and political philosophies and the groups to whom each party appealed.*
5. *Washington warned against foreign involvement, political parties, and sectionalism, all of which were issues facing the U.S. at the time.*

■■ ## SECTION 2 REVIEW

IDENTIFY and explain the significance of the following: French Revolution, impressment, Edmond Genet, Little Turtle, "Mad Anthony" Wayne, Treaty of Greenville, right of deposit, sectionalism.

LOCATE and explain the importance of the following: New Orleans.

1. **MAIN IDEA** How did foreign events of the early 1790s affect Americans?
2. **MAIN IDEA** What did the United States gain through Jay's Treaty and Pinckney's Treaty?
3. **MAIN IDEA** How were Native Americans affected by the Battle of Fallen Timbers?
4. **WRITING TO INFORM** Write an advertisement that describes the Federalist party in 1796, telling why it came into existence and urging Americans to join the party. Then write a similar advertisement for the Republican party.
5. **ANALYZING** How did Washington's Farewell Address reflect the state of U.S. affairs at the time?

**MOTIVATING:
PRIOR KNOWLEDGE**

Have students list what they know of
John Adams (actions, character traits,
background, party affiliation). Next
to each listed item, have them predict
how each item might help or hinder
Adams in the presidency and in this
period. As students study the section,
have them check to see if their predictions were correct.

FOCUS OBJECTIVES

■ Explain why relations
  with France worsened
  in the 1790s.

■ Explain why Congress
  passed the Alien and
  Sedition Acts.

■ Analyze the arguments
  on who should rule on
  matters of constitutionality that were presented
  in the Kentucky and
  Virginia Resolutions.

■ Describe how Chief
  Justice John Marshall
  influenced the develop-
  ment of American law.

Section 3

FEDERALISTS DOMINATE PARTY POLITICS

F O C U S
■ **Why did relations with France worsen in the 1790s?**
■ **Why did Congress pass the Alien and Sedition Acts?**
■ **According to the Kentucky and Virginia Resolutions, who should rule on
  matters of constitutionality?**
■ **How did Chief Justice John Marshall influence the development
  of American law?**

*The formation of political parties created problems for
the American electoral system. The process for electing a
president and vice president, which was outlined in the
Constitution, proved flawed on two separate occasions.
Furthermore, the struggle between the Federalist and
Republican parties had a major impact on both domestic
politics and foreign affairs.*

John Adams campaign button, 1796

THE ELECTION OF 1796

President Washington's decision not to seek
reelection in 1796 set in motion the first real competition for the presidency. In that election
Federalists John Adams and Thomas Pinckney
faced off against Republicans Thomas Jefferson
and Aaron Burr.

Envious of Adams, Alexander Hamilton
schemed to keep his rival from winning. Acting
from behind the scenes, he persuaded a few southern Federalist electors to vote only for Pinckney.
According to the Constitution, whoever received
the most votes became president; the runner-up
became vice president. Hamilton's plot backfired,
however, when northern Federalists discovered the
plan and responded by not voting for Pinckney, a
southerner. When the votes were counted, Adams
was president, and Jefferson—his Republican
opponent—was vice president!

ON THE VERGE OF WAR

President Adams faced the same challenges as
Washington. While maintaining America's status
as an independent nation, Adams also sought to
protect America's access to world markets. In
addition, he wanted to improve relations with
France. The French viewed Jay's Treaty and the
U.S. policy of neutrality as evidence of pro-British
leanings. In response, the French navy had begun
to seize American ships bound for British ports.

The XYZ affair. In 1797 President Adams sent
three diplomats to Paris to negotiate a new treaty
with France. Charles-Maurice de Talleyrand,
France's foreign minister, spurned direct negotiations with the Americans. Instead, he sent three
agents with his demands. Before talks could begin,
the United States would have to (1) apologize publicly for anti-French remarks that Adams had made;

U.S. RELATIONS WITH FRANCE

Begin a flowchart on the chalkboard with the heading *U.S. Relations with France.* Call on students to cite the events that caused U.S. relations with France to deteriorate. List students' responses on the flowchart. Then discuss and add to the chart the events in France that led to peaceful negotiations with the U.S. Complete the chart by adding the results of the negotiations. Students may wish to copy the chart and include it in their notebooks for future reference and review.

THE ALIEN AND SEDITION ACTS

Assign students to work in pairs to create an editorial cartoon that supports or opposes passage of the Alien and Sedition Acts. Have pairs exchange their completed cartoons. Then ask each pair to interpret for the class the cartoon it received and tell whether it likely would have appeared in a Republican or a Federalist newspaper.

▶

---

(2) grant France a multimillion-dollar loan; and (3) pay Talleyrand a bribe of $240,000. Diplomatic bribes were common in the 1700s, but the huge size of the bribe shocked the American diplomats, who refused to pay.

President Adams published the French demands—substituting *X, Y,* and *Z* for the names of Talleyrand's agents. Americans responded with fury against France, rallying around the slogan "Millions for defense, but not one cent for tribute." President Adams and Congress responded to the **XYZ affair** with a flurry of war preparations: creating the Navy Department, building warships, fortifying harbors, and strengthening the army. Congress also imposed taxes to pay for the military buildup. Although the United States had not declared war, U.S. warships began capturing French vessels.

Pro-British Federalists delighted in this growing anti-French sentiment. Here was a chance to smash revolutionary France and cement an economic and political alliance with Great Britain. Moreover, it was an opportunity to discredit the Republicans. Voters were dropping from the pro-French Republican party "like windfalls from an apple tree in September," wrote one happy Federalist.

War avoided. While many in his own party demanded military action, Adams was reluctant to go to war. He discounted the likelihood of a French attack, saying, "At present there is no more prospect of seeing a French army here than there is in Heaven."

▲ Many Americans were shocked and angered by the XYZ affair. France is symbolized as a multi-headed monster in this cartoon.

In 1799 Adams sent another peace mission to France. The timing was fortunate. Shortly before the delegation arrived in Paris, General Napoléon Bonaparte had overthrown the revolutionary government and made himself dictator of France. Napoléon recognized that French intrigue and hostility had pushed the United States closer to Great Britain.

Eager to forestall a stronger alliance between Great Britain and the United States, Napoléon worked out an agreement with the Americans. The terms required France to abandon the troublesome alliance treaty of 1778. In return the United States would drop claims against France for seized ships and cargo.

PRESIDENTIAL LIVES

JOHN ADAMS
1735–1826

in office
1797–1801

As the nation's second president, John Adams found that following in George Washington's footsteps was no easy task. Comparisons of the two men were inevitable: Adams's often irritating manner and fiery outbursts contrasted sharply with Washington's calm and stately disposition.

Yet John Adams possessed impressive credentials of his own. A brilliant lawyer and

experienced diplomat, he had great self-discipline and a supreme confidence in his opinions and abilities. Adams was also a practical man. This practical nature helped him during his presidency. When Adams found his salary too small to keep the White House pantry fully stocked, he brought in meat, vegetables, and apple cider from his Massachusetts farm to keep down expenses.

John Adams

Teaching the Section

KENTUCKY AND VIRGINIA RESOLUTIONS

Have students work in groups of four to summarize the Kentucky and Virginia Resolutions. One student should chart the provisions of the resolutions, one the arguments for and against, and another the outcome of the debate. The fourth student should present the group's chart to the class.

MARSHALL & JUDICIAL REVIEW

Organize the class into five groups. Instruct two groups to write "briefs" for Marbury's case in *Marbury* v. *Madison*, and two others to prepare briefs of Madison's position. Assign the fifth group to write the Supreme Court's decision in the case. Then have each group present its work. Conclude by asking students to speculate about the relative powers of each branch of government today had the Court not decided this case in this way.

MAKING CONNECTIONS

Sociology

In the 18th century, clothing expressed people's political views. Federalist men dressed traditionally, wearing kneebreeches and silk stockings, and powdering their hair or wearing wigs. Republican men cut their hair slightly above their collars, letting it fall naturally. They also adopted trousers, a style previously worn mainly by farmers and European peasants.

THINKING CRITICALLY

Recognizing Prejudice

The Alien and Sedition Acts reflected a strong antiforeign sentiment in the U.S. during this period. Discuss with students why countries often feel threatened by immigrants and other "foreign" groups.

■■ Ask students to identify any antiforeign movements currently active in the world.

■■ **Jay's Treaty, U.S. neutrality, and diplomatic intrigues strained U.S. relations with France in the 1790s, but war was avoided.**

Pleased with the settlement, President Adams later wrote, "I desire no other inscription over my gravestone than: 'Here lies John Adams, who took upon himself the responsibility of the peace with France in 1800.' "

*T*HE ALIEN AND SEDITION ACTS

The crisis with France increased the bad blood between the Federalists and the Republicans. The Federalists viewed the pro-French Republicans as traitors. The Republicans, on the other hand, suspected the Federalists of using the crisis to retain power. Charges and countercharges finally gave way to action. In 1798 the Federalist majority in Congress passed the **Alien and Sedition Acts**, a series of laws aimed not only at protecting the country but also at weakening the Republicans.

The Alien Act and the Alien Enemies Act authorized the president to imprison or expel "all such aliens [foreigners] as he shall judge dangerous to the peace and safety of the United States." Enforcement proved unnecessary. The threat of imprisonment drove many French citizens from the country and quieted those who remained.

The Sedition Act targeted American citizens. **Sedition** is the stirring up of discontent or rebellion against a government. Under the Sedition Act anyone who wrote, said, or printed anything "false, scandalous, and malicious" about the government, the Congress, or the president "with intent to defame" could be fined and jailed.

▶ The Virginia State legislature passed the Virginia Resolutions on December 24, 1798.

The act was aimed at Republicans. Matthew Lyon, a Republican congressman, was jailed for four months and fined $1,000 for denouncing President Adams. Throughout the country, Republican newspaper editors and politicians were arrested for sedition; 25 were indicted and 10 convicted.

■■ **Federalists passed the Alien and Sedition Acts to limit Republican power and to silence government critics.**

*K*ENTUCKY AND VIRGINIA RESOLUTIONS

Many Americans saw the Alien and Sedition Acts as attempts to curb the rights of individuals—foreigners and citizens alike. The Sedition Act interfered with freedom of the press and freedom of speech, two rights guaranteed by the First Amendment. Furious Republicans voiced their protests through the Kentucky Resolutions (written by Thomas Jefferson) and the Virginia Resolutions (written by James Madison), which were passed in 1798 and 1799 by those states' legislatures.

The **Kentucky and Virginia Resolutions** declared the Alien and Sedition Acts unconstitutional. In doing so, the resolutions raised an important question: Who should decide when a federal law or a government action violates the U.S. Constitution?—the states?—the Supreme Court? The Constitution did not say.

The resolutions came down on the side of the states. The states, they argued, had created the federal government as their agent, giving it specific powers defined by the Constitution. If the federal government exceeded those powers, it was the states' right—and duty—to declare the act unconstitutional and therefore void.

The Federalists disagreed. Firm believers

Practice

GUIDED PRACTICE

Have students work in groups, and assign one of these subjects to each group: election of 1796, XYZ affair, Alien and Sedition Acts, Kentucky and Virginia Resolutions, election of 1800, *Marbury* v. *Madison.* Help groups to develop a list of the main points for a newspaper editorial on their subject.

INDEPENDENT PRACTICE

Have students use the lists they created in Guided Practice to each write, in the role of a Federalist or a Republican, an editorial on their group's topic. Students may wish to include their editorials in their portfolios.

Review and Assessment

REVIEW Have students create an outline of the main points in Section 3. Students may wish to include their outlines in their portfolios. Then assign the Section 3 Review on p. 204.

ASSESS Assign the **Section 3 Daily Quiz** in *Core Resources.*

▲ When he was vice president of the United States, Aaron Burr fatally wounded Alexander Hamilton in a duel on July 11, 1804. The duel ended Burr's political career. The pistols shown here are dueling pistols of the period.

in a strong federal government, they argued that the Supreme Court should decide matters of constitutionality.

Because the Federalists controlled most state governments, the Kentucky and Virginia Resolutions failed to win wide support. But Jefferson and Madison had posed questions about the nature of the Union that would trouble Americans until the Civil War.

■■ **The Kentucky and Virginia Resolutions argued that it was the states' right to decide whether a federal law or action was unconstitutional.**

THE ELECTION OF 1800

By the election of 1800, the fortunes of the Federalist party were slipping. The election pitted Republicans Jefferson and Burr against Federalists Adams and Charles Pinckney (of South Carolina). Capitalizing on grievances against the Federalists, the Republicans swept to power, gaining control of Congress. However, neither the Republicans nor the Federalists had a formal ticket, as parties routinely do today. As a result, another electoral crisis

arose: Jefferson and Burr received the same number of votes for president!

In the event of a tie, the Constitution clearly authorized the House of Representatives to decide who the president would be. Ordinarily, the House would have chosen Jefferson, the Republicans' preferred candidate. But some Federalists who hated Jefferson voted for Burr instead. Thirty-five attempts to select a president failed. With Inauguration Day just weeks away, the country was still without a president-elect.

This problem might have continued indefinitely had help not come from an unexpected source. Preferring Jefferson over the "unprincipled and dangerous" Burr, Alexander Hamilton persuaded several Federalists to vote for Jefferson. Thus, with the help of his former rival, Jefferson became the third president of the United States.

The hatred that Hamilton and Burr felt toward each other deepened over the years. In 1804 Hamilton publicly criticized Burr, who was then running for governor of New York. Burr's demand for an apology led to a duel in which Burr fatally wounded Hamilton.

To prevent future electoral crises, Congress proposed the **Twelfth Amendment** to the Constitution. Ratified in 1804, this amendment requires electors to vote for presidential and vice-presidential candidates on separate ballots.

RETEACH Write each Focus question from p. 200 on a separate sheet of butcher paper. Organize students into four groups and give each group one sheet. Have each group create a chart that answers its assigned question. After each group presents its chart, ask other groups if they wish to make additions. Post completed charts.

Closure

Organize the class into "Federalists" and "Republicans," and have the two groups stand on opposite sides of the classroom. Ask questions on main topics of the section (XYZ affair, Alien and Sedition Acts, Kentucky and Virginia Resolutions, election of 1800), and call on members of each team to answer from their party's viewpoint ("We thought this and took that action.").

Extension

INTERPRET Have students research and interpret the text of the Alien and Sedition Acts. Then have them review current newspapers and copy statements that might have led to prosecution under the acts.

CREATE Suggest that students research the Marshall court and create a "who's who" diagram of the justices with short biographies of each member.

IDENTIFY

For significance, see the following pages:
Charles-Maurice de Talleyrand (p. 200)
XYZ affair (p. 201)
Napoléon Bonaparte (p. 201)
sedition (p. 202)
Twelfth Amendment (p. 203)

1. *French concern about U.S.–British alliance; capture of U.S. ships; XYZ affair*

2. *Acts authorized imprisonment or expulsion of "dangerous" foreigners and the fining and jailing of anyone who wrote, said, or printed anything false, scandalous, or malicious about the government. Federalists wanted to limit Republican power and to silence government critics.*

3. *established precedent of judicial review, which gave the Supreme Court power to decide constitutionality of federal laws*

4. *Paragraphs should note the resolutions argued states could declare a federal law unconstitutional because they had created the federal government as their agent, granting it specific powers.*

5. *freedom of press and freedom of speech*

*T*HE FEDERALISTS AND THE JUDICIARY

Knowing their days in office were numbered, the Federalists feared that their programs would be abandoned. In the months between Election Day in November and Inauguration Day in March, the Federalist majority in Congress tightened its hold on the judicial branch to "protect" the country from Jeffersonian radicalism. They pushed through the Judiciary Act of 1801, which created a number of new circuit courts and federal judgeships. President Adams worked late into the night of his last day in office, signing the papers that appointed Federalists to these posts. These last-minute appointees were nicknamed "midnight judges."

Adams's most significant appointment, though not one of the midnight judgeships, was the selection of John Marshall of Virginia as chief justice of the Supreme Court. A firm Federalist with a brilliant legal mind and a shrewd grasp of politics, Marshall dominated the Supreme Court during the more than three decades he served (1801–1835). His more than 500 opinions influenced the political and economic structure of the new nation, molding a truly national union.

During his years on the bench, Marshall established many basic principles of American constitutional law. Among these was the principle of judicial review—the right of the Supreme Court to declare an act of Congress unconstitutional. The Court first exercised this right in the case of *Marbury* v. *Madison* (1803).

▲ John Marshall was the fourth chief justice of the United States and a man of such integrity that he invariably won the support of his colleagues.

For political reasons Jefferson's Secretary of State James Madison had refused to allow William Marbury, one of the "midnight judges," to take the bench. Marbury asked the Supreme Court for relief. While the Court agreed that Marbury had a right to his appointment, the Court ruled that it could hear the case only on appeal. By denying that the Supreme Court had original jurisdiction, Marshall declared a part of the Judiciary Act of 1789 unconstitutional. With this decision Marshall initiated the Supreme Court's most important role—that of final interpreter of the Constitution.

▪▪ **John Marshall shaped the development of American law through the principle of judicial review and through his many court decisions.**

SECTION 3 REVIEW

IDENTIFY and explain the significance of the following: Charles-Maurice de Talleyrand, XYZ affair, Napoléon Bonaparte, sedition, Twelfth Amendment.

1. **MAIN IDEA** What events in the 1790s strained relations with France and increased the risk of war?

2. **MAIN IDEA** What were the provisions of the Alien and Sedition Acts and why did Congress pass them?

3. **ANALYZING** How did Chief Justice John Marshall's decision in *Marbury* v. *Madison* influence the development of American law?

4. **WRITING TO EXPLAIN** Write a paragraph outlining the arguments presented in the Kentucky and Virginia Resolutions.

5. **ASSESSING CONSEQUENCES** What democratic values did the Sedition Act violate?

PREVIEW WORKSHOP

Following is a list of the significant people, places, and terms in this section. You may wish to use this list as a section preview.

People
- Robert Livingston
- Toussaint L'Ouverture
- Sacagawea
- York

- Zebulon Pike

Places
- Haiti
- Louisiana Territory

Terms
- Trans-Appalachian West
- Louisiana Purchase
- Lewis and Clark expedition

Section 4

THE NATION EXPANDS

FOCUS

- **What policy changes did the Republican Congress make during President Jefferson's first term in office?**
- **Why did the United States purchase Louisiana from France?**
- **What did explorers of the Louisiana Territory accomplish?**
- **What were some of the positive and negative consequences of the Louisiana Purchase?**

Upon taking office, Jefferson pledged to preserve the government in its "constitutional vigor" and guard "the right of election by the people." His promise of moderation did not prevent Jefferson from taking action, though. During his two terms the United States expanded westward beyond the Mississippi River to take in the heartland of North America.

Sacagawea guides Lewis and Clark.

FOCUS OBJECTIVES

- Identify policy changes made by the Republican Congress during President Jefferson's first term in office.

- Determine why the U.S. purchased Louisiana from France.

- Examine what explorers of the Louisiana Territory accomplished.

- Explain the positive and negative consequences of the Louisiana Purchase.

JEFFERSON TAKES OFFICE

Though Thomas Jefferson later heralded the Republican victory in the 1800 election as the "Revolution of 1800," the transition of power was peaceful. This was no small achievement in an era when many shifts of political power were accompanied by chaos or war. To fulfill his promise of moderation, Jefferson left untouched some Federalist programs, including the national bank and the debt payment plan, both of which he had once opposed. He also tried to maintain the neutral course set by Washington and Adams in foreign affairs.

But Jefferson had not abandoned his view that a federal government with too much power threatened individual freedoms and states' rights. Thus he urged the Republican-controlled Congress to overturn a number of Federalist programs. Congress responded by repealing the whiskey tax and the Judiciary Act of 1801, cutting military funding, and reducing the size of the army and the

navy. Jefferson saw trimming military spending as one way to achieve his campaign promise to pay off the national debt.

■■ **The Republican Congress repealed the whiskey tax and the Judiciary Act of 1801, cut military spending, and reduced the size of the army and the navy.**

THE LOUISIANA PURCHASE

In the election of 1800, the Republicans won every state that had a frontier on the **Trans-Appalachian West**, the area between the Appalachian Mountains and the Mississippi River. Unlike Federalists, who feared that westward expansion would weaken their power in Congress, Republicans favored expansion. Jefferson imagined "distant times, when our rapid multiplication will expand [the nation] . . . & cover the whole

CORE RESOURCES

- **Geography Worksheet 6**
- **Section 4 Daily Quiz**

MOTIVATING:
STUDENT EXPERIENCES

Ask students to think of a time in their lives when duties were transferred from one person to another. *(substitute teacher, new coach, school club elections)* Ask what the effects of this transfer were. Point out that when Adams lost the presidency to Jefferson, power was transferred to the Republicans and that this section explains the effects of this transfer.

Teaching the Section

JEFFERSON'S PROGRAM

Draw lines dividing the chalkboard into three columns. In one column write *Retained,* in the next write *Eliminated,* and in the third write *Effects.* Call on volunteers to give the Federalist programs retained or eliminated by Jefferson and any effects which resulted.

HISTORICAL SIDELIGHTS

Tons of Money

Federalists criticized the Louisiana Purchase for a number of reasons, not the least of which was its cost. Federalist newspapers noted that if the $15 million were stacked up in silver dollars, the stack would be three miles high. They also marveled that it would take 25 ships to carry that much money.

◄ Americans pushed westward as new territories opened. This engraving shows a family crossing the Appalachians on their way to Pittsburgh.

The Granger Collection, New York

northern if not southern continent." This view appealed to settlers. Because frontier farming practices were hard on the soil, settlers were always hungry for new, fertile land.

Fertile land was not enough, however. Western farmers also needed access to the Mississippi River and to the port of New Orleans to get their produce to market. Events in 1800 put that access in danger. Spain had held the Louisiana Territory since 1762. Now, in a secret treaty, the French ruler Napoléon regained Louisiana from Spain. The territory covered an enormous, though vaguely defined, area: roughly the northern and western reaches of the Mississippi River basin (see map on page 209).

Rumors of this transfer reached the U.S. government in 1801, alarming Jefferson and other Americans. French control of the mouth of the Mississippi River might severely limit American trade and block westward expansion. To remedy the situation, President Jefferson ordered Robert R. Livingston, the U.S. minister to France, to negotiate with France for a U.S. port at the mouth of the Mississippi or for access to New Orleans. Talks dragged on for almost two years.

In 1803 Jefferson sent James Monroe to Paris to assist Livingston with negotiations. Jefferson had instructed Monroe to offer Napoléon as much as $10 million for New Orleans and West Florida. No sooner had Monroe arrived, however, than Napoléon's representative asked how much the United States would pay for *all* of Louisiana. The astonished American diplomats quickly agreed to pay about $15 million for the entire area. Thus, for about four cents an acre, the United States com-

pleted the **Louisiana Purchase**, probably the largest land deal in history.

Although pleased with the purchase, Jefferson had reservations. He did not believe that the Constitution granted the government specific authority to buy territory from a foreign nation. Thus, he felt that a constitutional amendment might be necessary to permit the purchase. But he knew that ratifying an amendment would mean a delay, during which Napoléon might change his mind. So Jefferson advised his attorney general to "do what is necessary *in silence*" and pushed the purchase treaty through the Senate.

Why did France sell this valuable territory? The answer lay in Napoléon's failure to build an empire in the Western Hemisphere. To defend an empire in Louisiana, Napoléon needed a strong naval base in the West Indies. The most likely place was Saint Domingue (now Haiti) on the island of Hispaniola, yet the colony was no longer under French control. In 1791 the colony's slaves had revolted. Under the leadership of Toussaint L'Ouverture (TOO-san loo-vuhr-TOOHR)—a gifted

◄ This contemporary painting of Toussaint L'Ouverture is by African American artist Jacob Lawrence. It is one in his series of paintings dealing with the Haitian Revolt.

Amistad Research Center, Tulane University

POLICY CHANGES UNDER JEFFERSON

Tell students to imagine that they are Republican members of Congress at the end of President Jefferson's first term in office. Ask them to write a brief speech praising their party's achievements during the president's first term. Call on volunteers to read their speeches to the class. Students may wish to include their speeches in their portfolios.

THE LOUISIANA PURCHASE

Have students work in pairs and select one of these assignments: Create a French sales brochure for the Louisiana Territory that describes the land for sale and reasons for selling; or, create a "want ad" by the U.S. that expresses interest in the Louisiana Territory and that lists reasons for wanting to purchase, persons who would negotiate the deal, and amount buyer is willing to pay. Have pairs share their work with the class.

▶

DR. JOSEPH KETT

Jefferson's Image

Most of us today do not think of Thomas Jefferson as a controversial figure. But in his own day he inspired both admiration and ridicule. To some he was a champion of liberty. To others he was "Mad Tom," a frenzied supporter of the bloody French Revolution. Among his enemies he could count a president, John Adams; his own vice president, Aaron Burr; a secretary of the treasury, Alexander Hamilton; and a chief justice of the Supreme Court, John Marshall.

These conflicting images of Jefferson are not that surprising. Jefferson was a man of many contradictions. He was an aristocrat who championed the plain farmer and a slaveholder who wrote in the Declaration of Independence that "all men are created equal." He was opposed to a strong national government, yet he used the executive power of the presidency to double the size of the nation through the Louisiana Purchase.

The complexity of Jefferson's personality and his actions have allowed various groups—with vastly different aims—to

use his name in support of their causes. In the 1830s those who demanded broader voting rights and other democratic reforms cast Jefferson as champion of the common people. In 1860–1861 the southern states that had seceded from the Union held Jefferson up as a believer in states' rights over federalism. In the late 1800s and early 1900s, Jefferson was a hero of social reformers fighting against big business and the negative effects of industrialization. During the Great Depression of the 1930s, Franklin Roosevelt argued that Jefferson's sympathy for the common people would have made him a supporter of Roosevelt's social-welfare policies.

A new image of Jefferson emerged during the struggle against dictatorships in World War II. Jefferson became the "Apostle of Freedom." To this end, the Jefferson Memorial in Washington, D.C., was dedicated in 1943, and his Virginia home, Monticello, became a historic site.

The enshrining of Jefferson coincided with a new interest in historical research—the exami-

nation of American society's shared values and beliefs. This new emphasis was evident in the 1948 publication of volume one of the first scholarly biography of Jefferson, Dumas Malone's *Jefferson and His Time.* Merrill Peterson's *The Jefferson Image in the American Mind* (1960) continued in the same vein.

The 1960s saw another new area of historical research emerge—social history. In the midst of the decade's social changes and conflicts, many historians turned their attention to examining the everyday lives of Americans—both famous and ordinary citizens.

From this emphasis on social history came Fawn Brodie's *Thomas Jefferson: An Intimate History* (1974). Brodie examined the rumors about a love affair between Jefferson and his slave Sally Hemings that first surfaced before the election of 1800. It is difficult to prove or disprove the story, but Brodie's revelations nonetheless caused a furor. That Brodie's allegations aroused such emotion reminds us how far Thomas Jefferson's image has come from the controversy that once enveloped the man and his views.

▲ Jefferson designed Monticello in 1769.

JEFFERSON'S IMAGE

LINK TO TODAY

Encircling the dome of his memorial in Washington, D.C., are Jefferson's words, "I have sworn upon the altar of God eternal hostility against every form of tyranny over the mind of man." Ask students which of Jefferson's actions supported or contradicted this statement.

■■ Ask students if they have had an idol, a hero, or a role model whose image changed dramatically. Ask them to explain what caused the change and how they reacted to it.

Teaching the Section

EXPLORING THE LOUISIANA TERRITORY

Have students work in groups to examine the accomplishments of the explorers of the Louisiana Territory. Ask students to research and then draw illustrated maps of the explorations of Zebulon Pike and of Lewis and Clark. Encourage students to accompany their maps with actual or imaginary diary entries describing environments and experiences. Have groups present their maps and read their diary entries.

CONSEQUENCES OF THE LOUISIANA PURCHASE

Draw two columns on the chalkboard, one subheaded *Positive* and the other *Negative* under the major head *Louisiana Purchase*. Invite students to suggest positive and negative consequences of the Louisiana Purchase as you list their answers on the chalkboard in appropriate columns.

THROUGH OTHERS' EYES

Discuss with students whether Casa Irujo's prediction about the impact of the Louisiana Purchase on the U.S. came true.

VOICES IN HISTORY

The Mandans had lost many of their people to smallpox and conflicts with the Sioux. When a party of Sioux attacked late in November 1804, Lewis and Clark, who were spending the winter nearby, offered to protect the Mandans. Welcoming the assistance, a Mandan named Oheenaw replied: "Two Ricaras [Pawnees] came here and told us that two of their villages were making moccasins, that the Sioux were stirring them up against us, and that we ought to take care of our horses; yet these very Ricaras we sent home . . . lest our people should kill them in . . . grief for their murdered relatives. . . . If you will conduct us in the spring, when the snow has disappeared, we will assemble all the surrounding warriors and follow you."

PRIMARY SOURCE

Description of Change: excerpted

Rationale: excerpted to focus on main idea

THE LOUISIANA PURCHASE

THROUGH OTHERS' EYES

Spain was unpleasantly surprised to discover in 1803 that France planned to sell the Louisiana Territory to the United States. Earlier, Spain had transferred the land to France on the condition that the French never part with it. Spain feared that if the United States acquired the territory, the young nation would threaten Spain's other colonies in North America, such as California and Mexico.

The Marques de Casa Irujo (eer-OO-hoh), Spain's minister to the United States, wrote a harsh letter to Secretary of State James Madison denying the United States' right to buy Louisiana: "The sale of that province to the United States is founded on the violation of a promise so absolute that it ought to be respected—a promise without which the king, my master, would not under any circumstances have let Louisiana go."

In a letter to his own government, Casa Irujo called the Louisiana Purchase "truly an evil" for the United States. He predicted the U.S. government would be unable to hold such a vast territory of diverse peoples together: "One does not need extraordinary wisdom to anticipate that the acquisition of Louisiana, far from consolidating the strength and vigor of this nation, will rather contribute to weaken it."

---

military strategist, former slave, and grandson of an African chief—blacks eventually took control of the whole colony.

In 1802 a French attempt to regain Saint Domingue ended in disaster. Although Napoléon's troops captured Toussaint (who later died in prison), his followers and the ravages of yellow fever combined to drive the French from the island. With no foothold in the West Indies from which to protect Louisiana, Napoléon decided to sell the territory—and gain $15 million to enlarge his war chest.

■■ **The United States purchased Louisiana from France in order to secure navigation rights on the Mississippi.**

EXPLORING THE LOUISIANA TERRITORY

Neither buyer nor seller knew the exact size or boundaries of the Louisiana Territory. President Jefferson assigned the task of mapping the new territory to two skilled frontiersmen, Meriwether Lewis and William Clark. The **Lewis and Clark expedition**, numbering about 45 men, left St. Louis in May 1804. In response to the president's instructions to record all observations "with great care and accuracy," Lewis and Clark kept detailed journals of their travels. Typical is the following entry from May 23, 1805:

66 The river has become more rapid, the country much the same as yesterday, except that there is rather more rocks on the face of the hills, and some small spruce pine appears among the pitch. The wild roses are very abundant and now in bloom; they differ from those of the United States only in having the leaves and the bush itself of a somewhat smaller size. We find the mosquitoes troublesome, notwithstanding the coolness of the morning. The buffalo is scarce to-day, but the elk, deer, and antelope, are very numerous. 99

Native Americans—particularly the Mandans and Shoshonis (shuh-SHOHN-ees)—aided the expedition. After their first winter Lewis and Clark hired a French-Canadian fur trader and his Shoshoni wife, Sacagawea (sak-uh-juh-WEE-uh), as guides and interpreters. Sacagawea proved invaluable to the expedition. She showed members of the expedition the best places to fish, to hunt game, and to forage for wild vegetables. As an interpreter, she helped the expedition obtain needed supplies at critical moments. For example, when the expedition reached the Rocky Mountains, Sacagawea helped Lewis and Clark purchase horses from the Shoshonis. Without these horses the expedition could not have made the crossing through the high passes of the Rockies before snow blocked the way.

GUIDED PRACTICE

Divide the chalkboard into two columns, labeled *Domestic* and *Foreign*. Fill in the columns by calling on volunteers to give examples of Jefferson's domestic and foreign policies and actions.

INDEPENDENT PRACTICE

Ask students to write two paragraphs, one stating Jefferson's most important domestic policy or action, the other stating his most important foreign policy or action. Both paragraphs should include students' reasons for their choices. Students may wish to include their paragraphs in their portfolios.

Review and Assessment

REVIEW Have students write letters to the editor of a newspaper, giving opinions of Jefferson's administration from the viewpoint of either a Federalist or a Republican. Students should use specific policies as examples. Then assign the Section 4 Review on p. 210.

ASSESS Assign the **Section 4 Daily Quiz** in *Core Resources*.

▶

Relations with Native Americans were further enhanced by the presence of York, a slave. In his journal Clark observed that the Indians were "much astonished" by York, "who did not lose the opportunity of [displaying] his powers Strength etc." Apparently, they "never Saw a black man before."

The Lewis and Clark expedition traveled up the Missouri River, crossed the Rocky Mountains, and canoed down the Snake and Columbia rivers to the Pacific Ocean. After nearly two and a half years, the expedition returned—bringing with it plant and animal specimens, animal bones and pelts, and various soil and mineral samples.

Before Lewis and Clark had the chance to publish the chronicles of their expedition, the reports of another explorer, Zebulon Pike, appeared in print. Pike visited the upper Mississippi Valley in 1805 and went as far west as present-day Colorado before returning home via the Spanish town of Santa Fe. Pike's descriptions gave Americans their first glimpse of the lands beyond the Mississippi and helped spur expansion into Texas and the Southwest. His depiction of the Great Plains as a huge desert, however, led many to view that region as unsuitable for settlement.

■ **Meriwether Lewis, William Clark, and Zebulon Pike mapped the Louisiana Territory and cataloged its valuable natural resources.**

THE IMPORTANCE OF THE LOUISIANA PURCHASE

The Louisiana Purchase added all or part of 13 future states to the nation. This increased size gave the United States a larger international stature. As Robert Livingston noted at the time of the purchase: "From this day the United States take their place among the powers of the first rank."

The purchase had important domestic consequences as well. In addition to removing the French threat from American soil, the purchase opened the interior of the continent to white settlement. As Americans devoted more energy to developing the

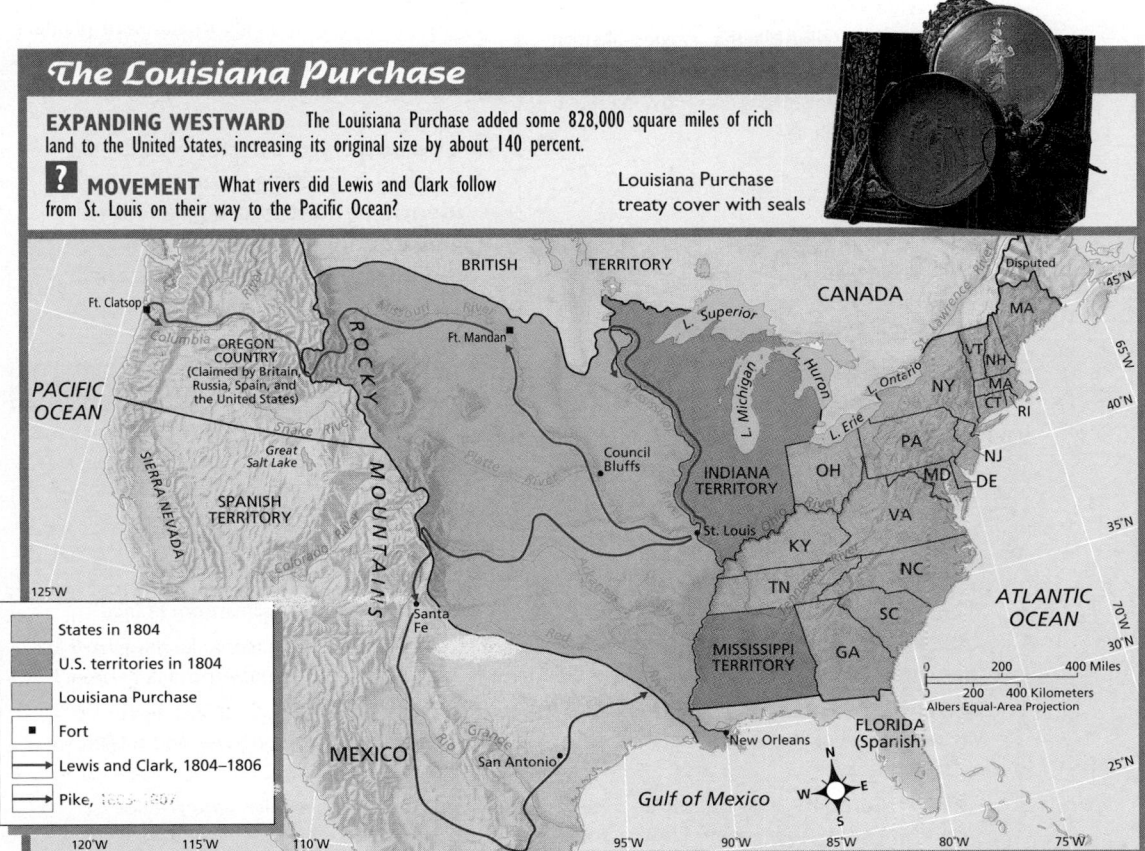

The Louisiana Purchase

EXPANDING WESTWARD The Louisiana Purchase added some 828,000 square miles of rich land to the United States, increasing its original size by about 140 percent.

❓ MOVEMENT What rivers did Lewis and Clark follow from St. Louis on their way to the Pacific Ocean?

Louisiana Purchase treaty cover with seals

States in 1804
U.S. territories in 1804
Louisiana Purchase
■ Fort
→ Lewis and Clark, 1804–1806
→ Pike, 1806–1807

RETEACH Have students work in groups to divide the section material by heads and subheads. Ask each student to write a question about the main idea of the material allocated to him or her. Then collect the questions and use them to quiz the entire group.

Closure

Discuss why the "Revolution of 1800" was a peaceful revolution. (*Both parties accepted the transfer of power and the policy changes of the new president.*) Then ask students to explain how the election of 1800 and the Louisiana Purchase were tests for the new government and to evaluate how well the government faced these trials.

Extension

RESEARCH Have students research and report on Toussaint L'Ouverture or Sacagawea.

FORMULATE Ask groups to prepare reports explaining why frontier farmers continually pushed toward new lands. Have them speculate about how the availability of land might have shaped American attitudes toward the environment and how these attitudes are changing today.

SECTION REVIEW ANSWERS

IDENTIFY

For significance, see the following pages:
Trans-Appalachian West (p. 205)
Robert Livingston (p. 206)
Louisiana Purchase (p. 206)
Toussaint L'Ouverture (p. 206)
Lewis and Clark expedition (p. 208)
Sacagawea (p. 208)
York (p. 209)
Zebulon Pike (p. 209)

LOCATE

For locations, see the maps on p. 209 and pp. 1012–1013.

1. *repealed whiskey tax and Judiciary Act of 1801; cut military funding; reduced size of army and navy*
2. *fertile land, control of Mississippi River and New Orleans*
3. *positive—increased size of U.S., increased U.S. international stature, removed French threat from American soil, opened interior to U.S. settlement, enhanced sense of national identity; negative—American Indians' land claims not considered, allowed slavery to spread by opening new lands to southern planters*
4. *Accounts will vary but should consider loss of land.*
5. *Students should consider benefits of the territory, removal of potential enemy, and fear that delay might lead Napoléon to change his mind.*

PRESIDENTIAL LIVES

THOMAS JEFFERSON
1743–1826

in office 1801–1809

Thomas Jefferson had a good-humored manner about him. He was a brilliant conversationalist who could talk just as easily about chemistry or horse racing as about politics or philosophy. He loved art, geography, and architecture and not only knew French, Italian, Spanish, Greek, and Latin but also studied some 40 Native American languages.

Though charming in person, Jefferson often hated his rivals and recorded in his diary the petty gossip he heard about them. Jefferson also struggled with a deep sense of loneliness. The death of his wife Martha Wayles Skelton and five of his six children caused him to mourn: "My evening prospects now hang on the thread of a single life."

frontier, they increasingly looked west, rather than east across the Atlantic. This shift promoted a greater sense of national identity. However, developments that followed the historic purchase were not as positive for Native Americans. When France transferred ownership of Louisiana to the United States, neither nation considered Native American claims to the land. Indian leader Sagoyewatha (suh-goh-ye-WAH-thah) (Red Jacket) lamented:

❝ There was a time when our forefathers owned this great land. Their seats [towns] extended from the rising to the setting sun. . . . Our seats were once large and yours were small. You have now become a great people, and we have scarcely a place left to spread our blankets. ❞

The purchase also had an effect on many African Americans. Historians John Hope Franklin and Alfred A. Moss, Jr., point out that the blacks of Saint Domingue, in throwing off slavery, helped make possible the purchase of Louisiana. Yet, by opening new lands to southern planters, the purchase also made possible the extension of slavery.

▪▪ **The Louisiana Purchase helped build U.S. prestige and national identity, and it had far reaching consequences for American Indians and African Americans.**

SECTION 4 REVIEW

IDENTIFY and explain the significance of the following: Robert Livingston, Louisiana Purchase, Toussaint L'Ouverture, Lewis and Clark expedition, Sacagawea, York, Zebulon Pike.

LOCATE and explain the importance of the following: Trans-Appalachian West, Haiti, Louisiana Territory.

1. **MAIN IDEA** What steps did the Republican Congress take against Federalist policies?

2. **MAIN IDEA** What did the United States hope to gain by purchasing Louisiana from France?

3. **ASSESSING CONSEQUENCES** What positive consequences did the Louisiana Purchase have for the United States? What negative impact did it have on Native Americans and African Americans?

4. **WRITING TO CREATE** Imagine you are an American Indian living in the Louisiana Territory. Write an account that expresses your feelings about white exploration, conquest, and settlement of the territory.

5. **HYPOTHESIZING** Imagine you are President Jefferson. What reasons might you give for abandoning your strict constructionist stand in the case of the Louisiana Purchase?

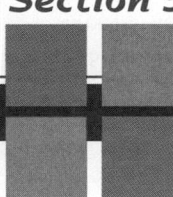

PREVIEW WORKSHOP

Following is a list of the significant people, places, and terms in this section. You may wish to use this list as a section preview.

People
- Tecumseh
- William Henry Harrison
- Andrew Jackson

Places
- the Barbary states
- Canada
- Lake Erie

Terms
- Orders in Council
- Embargo Act
- Non-Intercourse Act
- Battle of Tippecanoe

- Battle of the Thames
- Battle of New Orleans
- Treaty of Ghent
- Hartford Convention

Section 5

THE COMING OF THE WAR OF 1812

FOCUS

- **What foreign actions in the early 1800s affected U.S. trade? How did the United States respond?**
- **What were the major causes of the War of 1812?**
- **What was the significance of the outcome of the War of 1812?**

*B*y 1800, U.S. trade was expanding worldwide. Thomas Jefferson hoped to protect America's freedom of the seas. As with earlier presidents, however, this goal remained out of reach. Events across the Atlantic pulled the nation into conflicts: first off the North African coast and then—because of Napoléon's attempted conquest of Europe—on the high seas and at home.

The *Chesapeake* and the *Leopard*, 1807

THE PERILS OF WORLD TRADE

Since 1783, U.S. merchants had been trading with the Barbary states of North Africa, including Morocco, Algiers (al-JIRZ), Tunis, and Tripoli. Barbary pirates demanded protection money from all ships that sailed there. This harassment of U.S. ships convinced many Americans of the need for a powerful navy.

That conviction grew stronger as Napoléon's war in Europe spilled over into the Atlantic Ocean. In 1807 Britain passed the **Orders in Council**, which forbade neutral vessels from trading with France, or even from entering ports under French control. Napoléon reacted by threatening to seize all foreign ships that cooperated with the British navy. America was again caught in the cross fire between France and Britain.

In the summer of 1807, events took an ugly turn. Britain, facing a manpower shortage in the Royal Navy, stepped up its long-standing practice of impressment. On June 22 the captain of the

British ship H.M.S. *Leopard* demanded the right to board the U.S. *Chesapeake* to search for 4 supposed British deserters. When permission was refused, the British opened fire, killing 3 U.S. seamen and wounding 18 others.

The *Chesapeake* incident outraged many Americans. President Jefferson shared this outrage but wanted to maintain U.S. neutrality. In an effort at "peaceable coercion," Jefferson urged Congress to pass the **Embargo Act** of 1807, which stopped shipments of food and other American products to all foreign ports.

Not surprisingly, New England merchants and western farmers angrily opposed this measure, as did many others who were thrown out of work because of it. John Lane Jones, an unemployed Boston laborer, complained directly to Jefferson:

❝ You infernal villain. How much longer are you going to keep this . . . Embargo on to starve us poor people. . . . You must . . . afford us some kind of relief. . . . I wish you could feel as bad as I do. ❞

FOCUS OBJECTIVES

- Determine what foreign actions in the early 1800s affected U.S. trade and explain how the U.S. responded.

- List the major causes of the War of 1812.

- Analyze the outcome of the War of 1812.

MAKING CONNECTIONS

Economics

Many of the sailors unemployed during the embargo returned home to farms. The government gave other sailors jobs at naval installations. Some found work making naval materials. But many remained embittered, and on the embargo's first anniversary, they demonstrated by marching to funeral music and flying their ships' flags at half-mast.

PRIMARY SOURCE

Description of Change: excerpted
Rationale: excerpted to focus on main idea

CORE RESOURCES

- **Social Studies Skills Worksheet 6**
- **Literature Worksheet 6**
- **Section 5 Daily Quiz**

AV RESOURCES

- *The American Nation* **Videodisc: A Native American Confederacy**

MOTIVATING: LINK TO TODAY

Ask students for recent examples of when the U.S. has chosen military action in a dispute and why it did so. Then have students speculate why the U.S. might have gone to war in the early 1800s, noting it was a much less powerful nation than it is today.

Teaching the Section

AMERICAN TRADE POLICY

Ask volunteers to recall and summarize the colonists' use of boycotts in their relations with Great Britain. Ask students to speculate about connections between those actions and U.S. foreign policy in the early 1800s. Then work with the class to create a chalkboard chart that compares and contrasts the Embargo Act and the Non-Intercourse Act by considering their causes,

provisions, and consequences. Ask students to compare the outcomes of these policies with the results of America's bans on trade before the Revolution.

■■ Ask students how the U.S. has used embargoes in recent years and with what success.

THE AMERICAN NATION VIDEODISC PROGRAM

A Native American Confederacy

```
1A    00598    3:11
```

Map Caption Answer
All shipping into the Mediterranean had to pass through the narrow Strait of Gibraltar, which the Barbary States controlled.

 **PERSONALITIES IN HISTORY**

Tecumseh planned to recruit young men for his confederation because he believed that older chiefs and tribal leaders had been corrupted by whites. Tecumseh's father had been killed in Lord Dunmore's War, an elder brother had died during the American Revolution, and another brother was killed at the Battle of Fallen Timbers. Although he had no love for whites, Tecumseh, who was made a brigadier general, fought for the British in the War of 1812. He saw the war as an opportunity to win a homeland for all Native American groups. Tecumseh died in the Battle of the Thames in 1813.

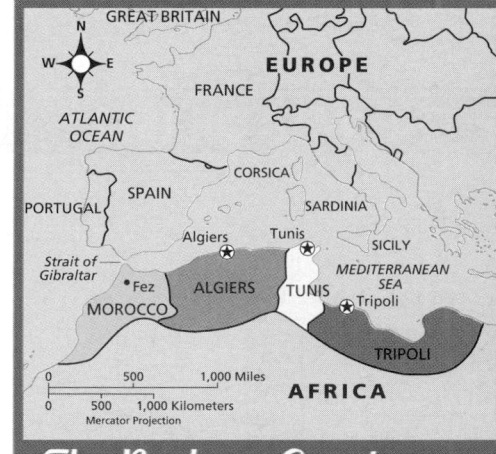

The Barbary Coast

"TO THE SHORES OF TRIPOLI" In the early 1800s the United States sent naval and marine forces to the Barbary Coast to stop the Barbary pirates' harassment of American ships.

? **PLACE** What geographical advantage enabled the Barbary States to control shipping in the Mediterranean?

James Madison, who succeeded Jefferson as president in 1809, at first kept the embargo in place. But public pressure became too great, and Congress repealed the embargo in March 1809. Congress then passed the **Non-Intercourse Act**, which only prohibited U.S. trade with Great Britain and France. The Non-Intercourse Act, like the embargo, did more harm to the American economy than to the economies of Great Britain and France. As the situation worsened, war with Britain or France, or both, seemed inevitable.

■■ **In response to harassment of U.S. ships by foreign powers, the government strengthened the navy and set limits on foreign trade.**

CONFRONTATION IN THE WEST

Problems abroad were compounded by events at home. Hunters, trappers, and farmers sought new lands in British Canada and Spanish Florida and also pushed westward into lands occupied by Native Americans.

Rapid westward expansion fueled tensions between settlers and Native Americans, who continued to look to Great Britain for assistance.

Westerners were particularly alarmed by the activities of the Shawnee leader Tecumseh (tuh-KUHM-suh).

 Settlers had a tireless and resourceful opponent in the tall, handsome Tecumseh (1768–1813). When his father was killed by whites, Tecumseh was adopted by the Shawnee chief Blackfish. As he grew older, Tecumseh became convinced that Native Americans' best hope for survival rested in a military alliance among the Indian nations.

Tecumseh

In the early 1800s Tecumseh set out to rally the Indian nations east of the Mississippi River. From the Great Lakes to the Gulf of Mexico, Tecumseh urged Native Americans not to sell land to the settlers: "Sell a country! Why not sell the air, the clouds, and the great sea? . . . Did not the Great Spirit make them all for the use of his children?"

As Tecumseh gained support, settlers pressured the government to take action. In the fall of 1811, while Tecumseh was in the South seeking support from the Creeks, Choctaws, and Cherokees, General William Henry Harrison decided to move against Tecumseh's stronghold on the Tippecanoe River in Indiana Territory. At dawn on November 7, the Indians struck the army camp first, ignoring Tecumseh's warning that the time was not yet right to fight. The **Battle of Tippecanoe** ended in defeat for Native Americans. When Tecumseh returned from the South in early 1812, he saw his dream of a united confederation shattered—replaced by isolated border wars between Native Americans and settlers.

CONGRESS DECLARES WAR

The British had supplied Tecumseh's forces with weapons. Thus, the clamor for war against Britain again arose in Congress. New congressmen, such as Henry Clay of Kentucky, John C. Calhoun of South Carolina, and Felix Grundy of Tennessee, exhibited such war fever that Congressman John Randolph of Virginia nicknamed them "War Hawks." They called for an attack on Canada in order to seize land and end the British–Native American alliance once and for all. Their cries,

CAUSES OF THE WAR OF 1812

Have groups create a cause-and-effect flowchart showing the events leading to the War of 1812. The chart should show how the actions of the British, Native Americans, southerners, and westerners influenced the decision to go to war. Ask a volunteer from each group to present the group's chart and discuss it with the class.

OUTCOME OF THE WAR OF 1812

Remind students that there were both positive and negative outcomes of the War of 1812. Write the following heads on the chalkboard: *British, Native Americans, Federalists, White Settlers.* Then ask volunteers to explain whether the war had a positive or negative effect on each and to explain why.

said Randolph, became "like the whip-poor-will, but one eternal monotonous tone—Canada! Canada! Canada!"

To reduce tensions, the British suspended the Orders in Council in June 1812. Before the news reached the United States, however, President Madison asked for a declaration of war. In his message to Congress on June 1, Madison cited repeated violations of neutral rights, continued impressment of American sailors, and British support of Native American uprisings on the frontier as reasons for the declaration. After some debate, the House voted on June 4 and the Senate on June 18 to support the declaration of war.

The vote was split almost exactly along sectional lines. The South and the West—suffering from an agricultural depression and Indian troubles that they blamed on Great Britain—overwhelmingly supported the declaration. The Middle Atlantic and the Northeast—fearing a British blockade of their coasts and the possible ruin of their shipping industry—almost unanimously opposed the declaration.

■■ **Frustration over violations of neutral rights, impressment of American sailors, and British support of Native American uprisings led to war.**

THE WAR OF 1812

The United States was ill prepared for war. The Republicans' reluctance to tax and their reduction of the military had left the American army weak and poorly equipped. Yet, despite Britain's great sea power, the American navy enjoyed the advantages of well-trained sailors and officers and a generally high morale.

Although the government made little effort to enlist blacks, African Americans—enslaved and free—took part in the war. Many fugitive slaves, hoping to win their freedom, fought for the Americans or the British. At least one tenth of the naval crewmen on the Great Lakes were African Americans.

The war's first phase. American war strategy focused on the conquest of Canada by land and sea. With the British preoccupied by their struggle

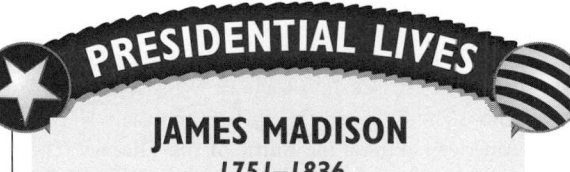

PRESIDENTIAL LIVES

JAMES MADISON
1751–1836

in office 1809–1817

One of James Madison's former professors once remarked to Thomas Jefferson, "[I] never knew him [Madison] to do, or to say, an improper thing." Jefferson delighted in teasing his friend Madison with this story, for Madison was indeed regarded as a man of great virtue.

Madison was also shy and self-conscious, often feeling out of place in social settings. At his own inauguration party, he remarked to a friend, "I would much rather be in bed." But Madison's awkward manner vanished during a good dinner with close friends. He became relaxed and charming, entertaining his companions with stories and jokes and even poking fun at himself.

James Madison

to stop Napoléon, Americans anticipated a quick victory. However, repeated attempts to invade Canada failed.

The United States, however, did enjoy early successes at sea. In the first eight months of the war, U.S. frigates won many victories against British warships. Meanwhile, American pirates seriously disrupted British commerce by raiding British ships both in the Caribbean and around the British Isles.

The U.S. navy achieved even greater success on the Great Lakes. In 1813 a small ragtag naval force commanded by Captain Oliver Hazard Perry won control of Lake Erie, helping to secure America's northwestern border. After his victory Perry notified General William Henry Harrison: "We have met the enemy and they are ours."

VOICES IN HISTORY

Native Americans were often dismayed by the European way of waging war. After witnessing the British fight the War of 1812, Black Hawk, a Sauk chief, noted in amazement that "instead of stealing upon each other, and taking every advantage to kill the enemy and save their own people . . . they march out, in open daylight, and fight, regardless of the number of warriors they may lose! After the battle is over, they . . . feast . . . as if nothing happened."

BUILDING VOCABULARY

Originally *ragtag* referred to the lower social class. In this instance *ragtag* refers to the unusual mixture of personnel who comprised Perry's naval force: militiamen, African Americans, frontier scouts, and Canadian canal men.

Practice

GUIDED PRACTICE

Organize the class into nine groups and assign each group one of these topics: Barbary pirates, *Chesapeake* incident, Embargo Act, Non-Intercourse Act, Tecumseh's confederation, Battle of Tippecanoe, Battle of New Orleans, Treaty of Ghent, Hartford Convention. Have groups discuss the relationship of their topic to the War of 1812 and present their results to the class.

INDEPENDENT PRACTICE

Ask students to create illustrated time lines of this section, using all the topics referred to in the Guided Practice. Students may wish to include their time lines in their portfolios.

Review and Assessment

REVIEW Organize the class into groups and assign each group one of the section's main heads. Ask groups to create a graphic that reflects the content of their assigned subsection. Have groups present their graphics in the order in which the topics appear in the section. Then assign the Section 5 Review on p. 215.

ASSESS Assign the **Section 5 Daily Quiz** in *Core Resources*.

Encouraged by these naval victories, General Harrison crossed into Canada. With some 4,500 troops, he defeated the British and their Native American allies at the **Battle of the Thames**. The British hold on the Northwest Territory was finally broken.

The war's second phase. Soon after ending its war against France early in 1814, Great Britain sent 14,000 reinforcements to Canada. British strategists planned a three-pronged attack. Britain would invade the United States from the north through Canada and from the south through New Orleans. They would also continue to raid points along the Atlantic coast to disrupt American commerce.

On the night of August 24, 1814, British forces struck Washington, D.C. Within a day they had captured the city, burning the executive mansion and other major public buildings before moving on. First Lady Dolley Madison escaped the mansion just minutes before the enemy crashed through the doors.

The next target for a coastal assault was the port city of Baltimore, on Chesapeake Bay. There, British vessels bombarded Fort McHenry, but the fort's brave stand—immortalized in Francis Scott Key's poem "The Star-Spangled Banner"—was a setback for the British.

Great Britain then assembled about 7,500 troops to strike at New Orleans. General Andrew Jackson, a ruthless Indian-fighter and commander of a frontier militia, led the American forces that included both whites and free African Americans. U.S. troops constructed a line of earthworks, or embankments of earth, fortified by cannons. When the invasion finally came on January 8, 1815, the well-protected U.S. sharpshooters and artillery easily won the **Battle of New Orleans**. Few Americans were killed, but British casualties topped 2,000.

Jackson had ignored the fear of many officers that it would be dangerous to arm African American troops. After the victory Jackson praised the African Americans: "I expected much from you, but you have surpassed my hopes."

The Treaty of Ghent.

Tragically, the fighting at New Orleans came after peace negotiations had produced the **Treaty of Ghent** (GENT), signed on Christmas Eve, 1814. Reports of the Americans' New Orleans victory reached Washington, D.C., at the

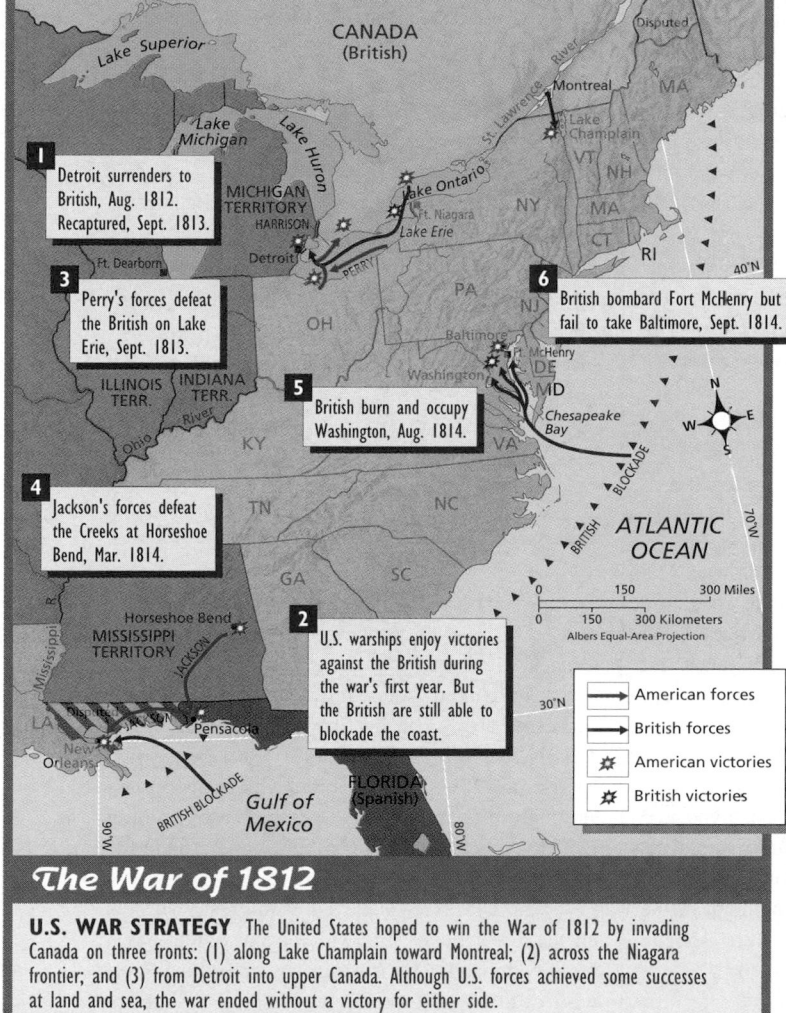

The War of 1812

U.S. WAR STRATEGY The United States hoped to win the War of 1812 by invading Canada on three fronts: (1) along Lake Champlain toward Montreal; (2) across the Niagara frontier; and (3) from Detroit into upper Canada. Although U.S. forces achieved some successes at land and sea, the war ended without a victory for either side.

? MOVEMENT What route did Jackson and his troops follow to meet the British at New Orleans?

Map labels:
- **1** Detroit surrenders to British, Aug. 1812. Recaptured, Sept. 1813.
- **3** Perry's forces defeat the British on Lake Erie, Sept. 1813.
- **4** Jackson's forces defeat the Creeks at Horseshoe Bend, Mar. 1814.
- **5** British burn and occupy Washington, Aug. 1814.
- **6** British bombard Fort McHenry but fail to take Baltimore, Sept. 1814.
- **2** U.S. warships enjoy victories against the British during the war's first year. But the British are still able to blockade the coast.

Legend:
- American forces
- British forces
- ✸ American victories
- ✸ British victories

RETEACH Have students make a flow-chart showing the events that led to war with Great Britain and a time line showing the major events of the war. Students may wish to include their flowcharts and time lines in their portfolios.

Closure

As you list their answers on the chalkboard, ask students how the U.S. responded to harassment by foreign powers in the early 1800s *(Embargo Act and Non-Intercourse Act)*. Then ask students to enumerate the major causes and effects of the War of 1812.

Extension

CREATE Ask students to research and write detailed newspaper accounts of a major event in the War of 1812 (a naval battle, the burning of Washington, the Battle of New Orleans). Encourage use of graphics, such as maps.

EVALUATE Have students write brief essays explaining in what ways the effects of Jefferson's actions as president are still evident today.

same time as news of the peace accord, leading many to assume that the victory had affected the treaty. General Jackson did nothing to correct this view and later used his fame as a war hero to win political power.

Neither side gained much by the Treaty of Ghent. By the terms of the treaty, prisoners of war were exchanged, and the territorial boundaries that existed before the war were restored. Nevertheless, the war was a turning point for the United States. It consolidated American control over the Northwest Territory through the defeat of Native Americans and the removal of their British allies. In addition, it resulted in a peace between the United States and Great Britain that marked the beginning of a long partnership.

■■ **The War of 1812 guaranteed U.S. control of the Northwest Territory while forging a new alliance between the United States and Great Britain.**

At the same time, however, the war further divided the nation along sectional lines. New England Federalists had bitterly opposed the war. So great was their discontent that they met in December 1814 at Hartford, Connecticut, to discuss seceding from the Union so that they could negotiate a separate peace with Great Britain. Moderates at the **Hartford Convention** voted down secession, suggesting instead that the Federalists push for a constitutional amendment that would limit the powers of Congress and the

▲ British troops were defeated as they attacked the line of earthworks built for the defense of New Orleans. Painted by H. Charles McBarron, Andrew Jackson is shown here mounted on a horse.

southern states. Delegates carried the proposal to Washington, D.C., but arrived just as the city learned of the peace treaty and Jackson's victory at New Orleans. Caught in the midst of the wild celebration, they slipped quietly out of town.

The Hartford Convention helped spell the end of the Federalist party. In the wake of the U.S. victory at New Orleans, the convention appeared treasonous. The party never recovered from the charge of disloyalty and collapsed a few years after the war.

SECTION REVIEW ANSWERS

IDENTIFY

For significance, see the following pages:
Orders in Council (p. 211)
Tecumseh (p. 212)
William Henry Harrison (p. 212)
Battle of Tippecanoe (p. 212)
Battle of the Thames (p. 214)
Andrew Jackson (p. 214)
Battle of New Orleans (p. 214)
Treaty of Ghent (p. 214)
Hartford Convention (p. 215)

LOCATE

For locations, see the maps on pp. 212 and 214.

1. *strengthened navy; set limits on trade with foreign powers*
2. *to protest violations of neutral rights, impressment of U.S. sailors, and British support of Native American uprisings*
3. *domestic—guaranteed U.S. control of Northwest Territory; international—forged new alliance with Great Britain*
4. *Letters should note how the Non-Intercourse Act hurts the economy in much the same way as the Embargo Act of 1807 did.*
5. *believed forming an alliance among Native American groups was best hope for survival; failed because Indians ignored his advice, attacking too soon*

■■ **SECTION 5 REVIEW**

IDENTIFY and explain the significance of the following: Orders in Council, Tecumseh, William Henry Harrison, Battle of Tippecanoe, Battle of the Thames, Andrew Jackson, Battle of New Orleans, Treaty of Ghent, Hartford Convention.

LOCATE and explain the importance of the following: the Barbary states, Canada, Lake Erie.

1. **MAIN IDEA** What actions did the United States take to prevent continued harassment of U.S. ships on the seas?
2. **MAIN IDEA** Why did the United States declare war in 1812?
3. **MAIN IDEA** How was the outcome of the War of 1812 significant for the United States domestically and internationally?
4. **WRITING TO EXPRESS A VIEWPOINT** Write a letter to President Madison explaining why you oppose the Non-Intercourse Act just as you opposed the Embargo Act of 1807.
5. **ANALYZING** Why did Tecumseh try to create an Indian confederation? Why did the confederation fail to achieve its goals?

UNDERSTANDING MAIN IDEAS

1. *added Bill of Rights; created federal judiciary; established treasury, war, and state departments*
2. *French military alliance treaty of 1778 committed U.S. as ally to France, which expected support when war broke out in Europe and disrupted U.S. trade when U.S. remained neutral.*
3. *wars in Europe; harassment of U.S. ships; impressment of U.S. sailors; Orders in Council; Chesapeake incident; British arming of Native Americans*
4. *made possible the extension of slavery by opening new lands to southern planters*

Chapter Review Answers

WRITING A SUMMARY
See Essential Points in each section for main ideas.

REVIEWING CHRONOLOGY
2, 3, 5, 4, 1
Evaluating
Paragraphs will vary but should explain the significance of the event.

IDENTIFYING PEOPLE AND IDEAS

1. *first president of the U.S.*
2. *action establishing a guide for future events*
3. *Washington's secretary of the treasury, who devised a plan to solve the nation's financial problems*
4. *right temporarily to unload goods at the port of New Orleans without paying a duty to Spain*
5. *chief justice who established basic principles of constitutional law*
6. *leader of slave revolt on Saint Domingue in 1791*
7. *Shoshoni woman who provided invaluable assistance to the Lewis and Clark expedition in Louisiana Territory*
8. *Shawnee leader who urged military alliance of Native American nations*

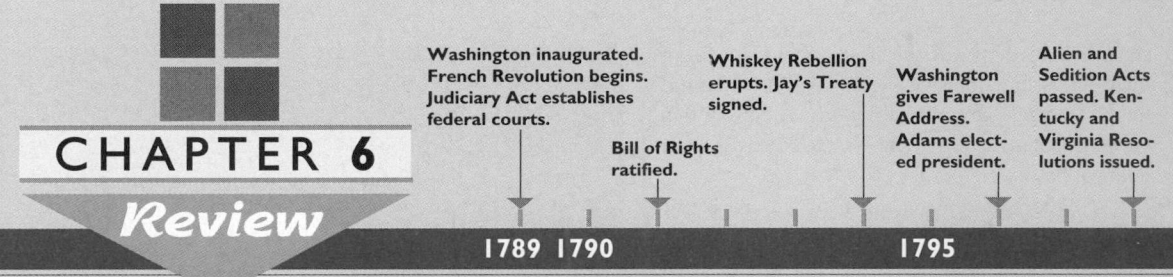

CHAPTER 6
Review

Washington inaugurated. French Revolution begins. Judiciary Act establishes federal courts.

Bill of Rights ratified.

Whiskey Rebellion erupts. Jay's Treaty signed.

Washington gives Farewell Address. Adams elected president.

Alien and Sedition Acts passed. Kentucky and Virginia Resolutions issued.

1789 1790   1795

WRITING A SUMMARY
Using the essential points of the chapter as a guide, write a summary of the chapter.

REVIEWING CHRONOLOGY
Number your paper 1 to 5. Study the time line above, and list the following events in the order in which they happened by writing the first next to 1, the second next to 2, and so on. Then complete the activity below.

1. Treaty of Ghent signed.
2. Bill of Rights ratified.
3. Washington gives Farewell Address.
4. Battle of Tippecanoe fought.
5. Alien and Sedition Acts passed.

Evaluating Select an event on the time line, and in a paragraph, state its significance in U.S. history.

IDENTIFYING PEOPLE AND IDEAS
Explain the historical significance of each of the following people or terms.

1. George Washington
2. precedent
3. Alexander Hamilton
4. right of deposit
5. John Marshall
6. Toussaint L'Ouverture
7. Sacagawea
8. Tecumseh

UNDERSTANDING MAIN IDEAS

1. What steps were taken by the First Congress to organize the federal government?
2. How did its close ties to France cause the United States problems in the 1790s?
3. What events pushed the United States toward war with Great Britain in the early 1800s?
4. Why can it be said that the Louisiana Purchase had negative effects for African Americans?

☆ REVIEWING THEMES

1. **Constitutional Heritage** How does the U.S. Constitution address possible conflicts between individual rights and those of a society?
2. **Economic Development** Describe how Hamilton's financial program affected the economy.
3. **Geographic Diversity** In what ways did the Louisiana Purchase provide both benefits and challenges for the United States?
4. **Democratic Values** How does a democracy encourage the formation of political parties?

THINKING CRITICALLY

1. **Using Historical Imagination** Why did Native Americans resist settlers moving west?
2. **Hypothesizing** What effect do you think a sedition act might have on today's press?
3. **Evaluating** Why do you think the Embargo and Non-Intercourse acts hurt the U.S. economy more than the economies of France and Britain?

STRATEGY FOR SUCCESS
Review the Skills Handbook entry on Reviewing Map Basics beginning on page 992. Then number your paper 1 to 13. Study the map below, noting the numbers on it. It illustrates the states, either in full or in part, that were formed from the Louisiana Purchase. Write the name of the state next to the corresponding number.

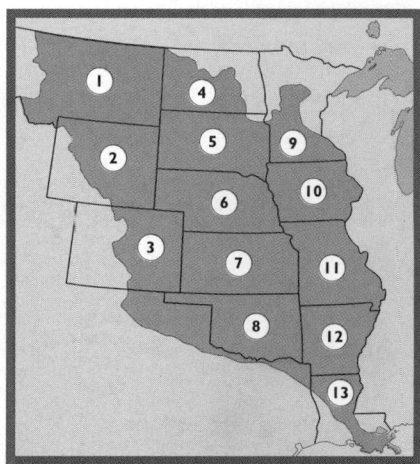

WRITING ABOUT HISTORY
Historical Imagination You are a newspaper editor in the early 1800s. Write an editorial about Tecumseh's confederation or the declaration of the War of 1812.

REVIEWING THEMES

1. Bill of Rights was added to protect individuals from possible abuse by majority or by government.
2. restored credit; reduced the national debt; provided a uniform currency; enabled business to expand
3. benefits—fertile land, abundant wildlife, access to Mississippi River, room for expansion; challenges—managing the land and resources, settling disputes between U.S. settlers and Native Americans
4. People want their views to be heard and their needs to be met; political parties provide a way for people with similar views and interests to band together to bring about change.

THINKING CRITICALLY

1. because settlers meant disruption of Indian way of life and loss of Indian land
2. Students should discuss conflict between government's controlling news and freedom of press.
3. Acts restricted foreign markets for U.S. goods and threw many laborers out of work. Britain and France had many other trading partners, including lands in their colonial empires.

STRATEGY FOR SUCCESS

1. Montana
2. Wyoming
3. Colorado
4. North Dakota
5. South Dakota
6. Nebraska
7. Kansas
8. Oklahoma
9. Minnesota
10. Iowa
11. Missouri
12. Arkansas
13. Louisiana

WRITING ABOUT HISTORY

Editorials will vary but should give specific reasons for views.

USING PRIMARY SOURCES

Statements will vary but should point out that unless the Indian peoples work together to protect their lands, the whites will destroy them one by one.

LINKING HISTORY AND GEOGRAPHY

Essays will vary but should note author's view that plentiful land and migration encouraged destruction of resources without regard for consequences.

Timeline

Jefferson elected president.

U.S. completes Louisiana Purchase.

Jefferson reelected president.

Madison elected president.

Tecumseh tries to unify Indians. Battle of Tippecanoe fought.

War declared against Great Britain.

Treaty of Ghent signed.

Battle of New Orleans fought.

1800 **1805** **1810** **1815**

USING PRIMARY SOURCES

In 1810–1811 Tecumseh traveled throughout Native American lands to seek support for his Indian Confederation. Read the following excerpts from his appeal to the Osages. Then state in your own words Tecumseh's reasons for forming a Native American confederation.

66 *Brothers—The white men are not friends to the Indians; at first, they only asked for land sufficient for a wigwam; now, nothing will satisfy them but the whole of our hunting grounds, from the rising to the setting sun.*

Brothers—My people wish for peace; . . . but where the white people are, there is no peace. . . .

Brothers—if you do not unite with us, they will first destroy us, and then you will fall an easy prey to them. They have destroyed many nations of red men because they were not united . . . we must fight each other's battles. 99

LINKING HISTORY AND GEOGRAPHY

By the late 1700s, people were pouring into Trans-Appalachia. In *America and Americans*, John Steinbeck wrote about these migrants and their uses of the land. Read Steinbeck's comments, and in a brief essay, explain how he saw the effects of western migration on America's resources.

66 It is little wonder that they [the settlers] went land-mad, because there was so much of it. They cut and burned the forests to make room for crops; they abandoned their knowledge of kindness to the land in order to maintain its usefulness. When they had cropped [worn] out a piece they moved on, raping the country like invaders. The topsoil, held by roots and freshened by leaf-fall, was left helpless to the spring

freshets [floods], stripped and eroded with the naked bones of clay and rock exposed. The destruction of the forests changed the rainfall, for the searching clouds could find no green and beckoning woods to draw them on and milk them. The merciless 19th century was like a hostile expedition for loot that seemed limitless. 99

Pioneer Mother *statue*

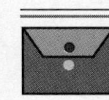

BUILDING YOUR PORTFOLIO

Complete the following projects independently or cooperatively.

1. **POLITICS** In Chapter 5 you attended a governors conference. Building on that experience, create a chart demonstrating ways in which the federal government is or is not meeting the political and economic interests of your region.

2. **THE CONSTITUTION** In Chapter 5 you focused on how women could be represented in the new Constitution. Building on that experience, imagine you are a member of a group that represents the rights of free blacks. Create a banner showing two rights you want Congress to include in the Bill of Rights.

3. **WAR** In Chapter 4 you served as a member of Congress overseeing the American war effort. Building on that experience, imagine you are a member of the War Department. Create a chart showing how you will coordinate supplies for the American army and navy during the War of 1812. Use icons to represent supplies.

BUILDING YOUR PORTFOLIO

Have students refer to **Building Your Portfolio Worksheet 2**, assigned at the beginning of Unit 2. Use the worksheet to help students monitor their progress on the portfolio projects.

Assessment

Core Resources
• Review Worksheet 6
• Chapter 6 Tests
• Alternative Assessment Forms
Test Generator

*R*EVOLUTIONARY LITERATURE

U N I T   2

American Letters

*R*evolutionary *Literature*

HISTORICAL SIDELIGHTS

Revolutionary Women
In 1780 a group of Philadelphia women began a campaign to raise funds for American soldiers in the war for independence. Organized by notable women such as Sarah Franklin Bache—Benjamin Franklin's daughter—the campaign raised some $300,000 for uniforms.

Women also took part in the Revolutionary War by boycotting British goods, a strategy urged by Mercy Otis Warren in "To the Hon. J. Winthrop, Esq." In a time when women's formal political role was proscribed, Warren argued that women's personal decisions, such as what products they bought, could also affect the course of the war for independence.

The Revolutionary era inspired many writers to take up the cause of liberty. Fiery orator and author Thomas Paine wrote pamphlets and songs urging the American colonists to fight for their freedom from Great Britain. During the war, women writers—among them dramatist and poet Mercy Otis Warren—encouraged American women to participate in the struggle. After the war, African American mathematician and almanac writer Benjamin Banneker argued that the liberty fought for in the Revolution should be applied to enslaved African Americans.

▲ **Mercy Otis Warren**

Liberty Tree

by Thomas Paine

In a chariot of light from the regions of day,
    The Goddess of Liberty came;
Ten thousand celestials[1] directed the way,
    And hither conducted the dame.
A fair budding branch from the gardens above,
    Where millions with millions agree,
She brought in her hand as a pledge of her love,
    And the plant she named *Liberty Tree.*

The celestial exotic struck deep in the ground,
    Like a native it flourish'd and bore;
The fame of its fruit drew the nations around,
    To seek out this peaceable shore.
Unmindful of names or distinctions they came,
    For freemen like brothers agree;
With one spirit endued,[2] they one friendship pursued,
    And their temple was *Liberty Tree.*

Beneath this fair tree, like the patriarchs of old,
    Their bread in contentment they ate,
Unvex'd with the troubles of silver and gold,
    The cares of the grand and the great.
With timber and tar they Old England supply'd,
    And supported her pow'r on the sea;
Her battles they fought, without getting a groat,[3]
    For the honor of *Liberty Tree.*

But hear, O ye swains,[4] 'tis a tale most profane,
    How all the tyrannical powers,
Kings, Commons and Lords, are uniting amain,[5]
    To cut down this guardian of ours;
From the east to the west blow the trumpet to arms,
    Thro' the land let the sound of it flee,
Let the far and the near all unite with a cheer,
    In defense of our *Liberty Tree.* ❖

---

1 angels
2 endowed
3 British coin made of silver, worth four pennies
4 country youths
5 with strength and speed

From *To the Hon. J. Winthrop, Esq.*[1]

by Mercy Otis Warren

    Lamira wish'd that freedom might succeed,
But to such terms what female ere[2] agreed?
To British marts forbidden to repair. . . .

    The good, the wise, the prudent, and the gay,
Mingle their tears, and sighs for sighs repay;
Deep anxious thought each gen'rous bosom fills,
How to avert the dread approaching ills;
Let us resolve on a small sacrifice,
And in the pride of Roman matrons rise;
Good as Cornelia,[3] or a Pompey's[4] wife,
We'll quit the useless vanities of life.

Liberty Displaying the Arts and Sciences, *by Samuel Jennings*

Amidst loud discord, sadness, and dismay,
Hope spread her wing, and flit across the away:
Thanks to the sex, by heavenly hand design'd,
Either to bless, or ruin all mankind.

    A sharp debate ensu'd on wrong and right,
A little warm, 'tis true, yet all unite,
At once to end the great politic strife,
And yield up all but real wants of life. ❖

1 Patriot who requested a poem urging women to boycott
  British goods
2 ever
3 Roman woman who, after the death of her husband, refused to
  remarry and was devoted to her sons and their education
4 Roman general

From *Letter to Thomas Jefferson*

by Benjamin Banneker

Maryland, Baltimore County
Near Ellicotts' Lower Mills, August 19th, 1791

Thomas Jefferson,
Secretary of State.

. . .

    Sir, suffer me to recall to your mind that time in which the arms and tyranny of the British Crown were exerted with every powerful effort in order to reduce you to a State of Servitude, look back I entreat you on the variety of dangers to which you were exposed; reflect on that time . . . and you cannot but be led to a serious and grateful sense of your miraculous and providential preservation; you cannot but acknowledge that the present freedom and tranquility which you enjoy you have mercifully received and that it is the peculiar blessing of Heaven.

    This sir, was a time in which you clearly saw into the injustice of a state of slavery and in which you had just apprehensions of the horrors of its condition, it was now, sir, that your abhorrence thereof was so excited, that you publickly held forth this true and valuable doctrine, which is worthy to be recorded and remembered in all succeeding ages. "We hold these truths to be self-evident, that all men are created equal, and that they are endowed by their creator with certain unalienable rights, that among these are life, liberty and the pursuit of happiness." . . .

    But, sir, how pitiable is it to reflect that although you were so fully convinced of the benevolence of the Father of mankind and of his equal and impartial distribution of those rights and privileges which he had conferred upon them, that you should at the same time counteract his mercies in detaining by fraud and violence so numerous a part of my brethren under groaning captivity and cruel oppression, that you should at the same time be found guilty of that most criminal act which you professedly detested in others with respect to yourselves.

    Sir, I suppose that your knowledge of the situation of my brethren is too extensive to need a recital here; neither shall I presume to prescribe methods by which they may be relieved, otherwise than by recommending to you and all others to wean yourselves from those narrow prejudices which you have imbibed with respect to them and as Job proposed to his friends, "put your souls in their souls stead." ❖

THINKING AND WRITING ABOUT LITERATURE

1. In Thomas Paine's song, what does the "Liberty Tree" stand for?
2. In Mercy Otis Warren's poem, how does the author inspire women to support the revolutionary effort?
3. What is Benjamin Banneker trying to convince Thomas Jefferson to do? Summarize his argument.

PRIMARY SOURCES

Description of Change: excerpted and footnoted
Rationale: excerpted for space considerations; footnoted to clarify meaning

THINKING AND WRITING ABOUT LITERATURE

1. *the right of freedom, which was a natural, or God-given, right*
2. *The poem gives examples of great historical figures whom women should emulate.*
3. *to free enslaved African Americans; he argues that Jefferson fought for liberty from British "servitude," yet is violating the goals proclaimed in the Declaration of Independence by keeping people in slavery*

RECOGNIZING FALLACIES IN REASONING

Guide students through the explanation of how to identify fallacies in reasoning, noting examples of each. Point out that such fallacies can occur in any type of analysis. Clip the "letters to the editor" section of your local newspaper and have students review the letters to find examples of fallacies in reasoning. Ask students to look through newspaper or magazine articles to find similar examples. Have students discuss their reactions to the fallacies: Do the fallacies undermine the writer's argument? Is the writer unintentionally overlooking information or intentionally employing fallacies to "prove" a partisan political point? Have students complete the Practicing the Strategy exercise, then ask them to conclude the exercise by giving tips on how they plan to avoid fallacies in reasoning in their own writing.

PRACTICING THE STRATEGY

1. *Single cause: The fact that Pontiac's forces did not gain French aid was not the only reason the rebellion ended; they also ran low on ammunition.*

2. *Irrelevant evidence: The timing of the passage of the Bill of Rights is not evidence that individual rights played no role in the debate over the Constitution. In fact, some states only agreed to ratify the Constitution after receiving promises that a Bill of Rights would be added.*

3. *Coincidence as cause: The Haitian revolt had already prevented Napoléon from acquiring a base from which to protect Louisiana. His decision to sell Louisiana came prior to the U.S. offer to buy it.*

Strategies for Success

RECOGNIZING FALLACIES IN REASONING

A fallacy is a mistaken idea; a fallacy in reasoning results in an unsound argument, or a mistaken, unsupported conclusion. Such fallacies in historical writing often produce statements that sound true but are not. Most reasoning errors occur either in determining cause and effect or in drawing conclusions. (You may want to review Identifying Cause and Effect beginning on page 989.) Following are some of the most common types of fallacies, with examples:

■ **Single cause** is identifying only one cause for a major event while ignoring other causes.

    Example: *The ideas of the Enlightenment were the source of Americans' revolutionary zeal.*

History is complex. Events are seldom the result of a single cause. The Revolution was driven by social, political, and economic forces as well as ideas.

■ **Coincidence as cause** means attributing the cause of one event to another that occurred earlier or at the same time—just because of the timing or *chronology* (the order) of the events.

    Example: *The U.S. victory at the Battle of New Orleans brought an end to the War of 1812.*

As you have read, the Treaty of Ghent, which ended the War of 1812, was negotiated *before* the Battle of New Orleans. But people learned of the battle and the treaty at the same time. Thus many people assumed that the battle led to the war's end.

■ **Irrelevant evidence** means basing a conclusion on information that does not apply to it. Facts that support one conclusion may be useless regarding another.

    Example: *The Constitutional Convention was a success because Thomas Jefferson and John Adams were away in Europe and unable to participate.*

Evidence must be logically presented to support a conclusion. Jefferson's and Adams's absence from the Convention is a fact, and their participation would probably have been significant. But there is no logical or relevant relationship between the Convention's success and their being in Europe.

How to Recognize Fallacies in Reasoning

1. **Read the information carefully.** Find the main ideas and evaluate them.
2. **Determine the order of events.** Decide whether the order of events contributed to a cause-and-effect relationship. Remember that chronology is not always an indicator of cause and effect.
3. **Study the reasoning.** Ask yourself: Are the arguments logical? Have cause-and-effect connections been proven? Does the conclusion follow from the facts given?

Applying the Strategy

Review the account of the War of 1812 in Chapter 6, particularly the subsection "Congress Declares War," on pages 212–13. Then analyze the following statement for a fallacy in reasoning.

> The War of 1812 came to an end in 1814, as Federalist delegates from the antiwar meeting known as the Hartford Convention arrived in Washington, D.C., to demand action.

The statement contains a fallacy of "irrelevant evidence." Tired of the armed struggle, Great Britain and the United States reached a negotiated settlement while the secret Hartford meeting was in progress. The Federalists' opposition had no effect on the war's outcome.

Practicing the Strategy

Examine the following statements for fallacies in reasoning. Then, on a separate sheet of paper, list and explain any fallacies you have found.

1. Pontiac's rebellion ended because his forces failed to acquire military aid from the French.
2. The fact that the Bill of Rights was not added until after the Constitution was ratified shows that protection of individual liberties was not a part of the debate over the Constitution.
3. The U.S. offer of $15 million lured Napoléon Bonaparte of France into selling the territory of Louisiana.

BUILDING YOUR PORTFOLIO

Each portfolio project described below is the culmination of the Building Your Portfolio activities in the chapter reviews of Unit 2. First, decide whether you wish students to work individually or in groups on these unit projects. Then permit each student to choose the project on which he or she desires to

work. Provide students with copies of **Building Your Portfolio Worksheet 2** from *Core Resources*. This worksheet will guide students step by step to complete their projects.

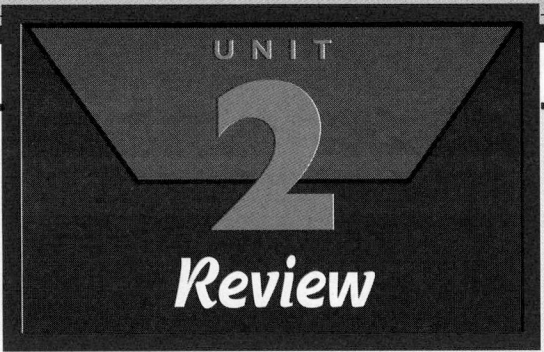

BUILDING YOUR PORTFOLIO

Outlined below are four projects. Independently or cooperatively, complete one and use the products to demonstrate your mastery of the historical concepts involved.

1 **WAR**
The United States experienced many threats to its security between 1775 and 1815. Using the portfolio materials you designed in chapters 4 and 6, create an organizational chart that illustrates how the War Department will coordinate both the recruitment of troops and the provision of necessary supplies in the future.

2 **DEMOCRATIC RIGHTS**
The right to protest is one of many rights that colonists defended during the Revolution. Using the portfolio materials you designed in chapters 4 and 5, hold a debate between government officials and protesting citizens that focuses on the government's right to tax versus the citizens' right to oppose unfair taxes.

3 **THE CONSTITUTION**
The framers of the Constitution were determined to create a representative government. Using the portfolio materials you designed in chapters 5 and 6, write a petition to your state legislature

asking members to modify the state constitution to include rights for women and free blacks.

4 **POLITICS**
Although George Washington hoped that the new nation would be spared from disunity, sectionalism encouraged the rise of political parties. Using the portfolio materials you designed in chapters 5 and 6, write a political party platform that addresses the concerns and interests of the states in your region. Your platform should outline the philosophy of the party, discuss specific issues affecting your region, and demonstrate how your party proposes to deal with those issues.

PORTFOLIO ASSESSMENT

1. *Organizational charts should show the students' understanding of the military role played by Native Americans and free blacks between 1775 and 1815 and the importance of supplies in the War of 1812.*

2. *Debates should demonstrate students' grasp of the reasons the British government taxed its colonies and the colonists' reasons for protesting the taxation.*

3. *Petitions should show an understanding of the lack of political rights of women and African Americans before 1815 and the mechanisms to achieve these rights in a democratic government.*

4. *Platforms should show the regional political and economic differences that gave rise to the Federalist and Republican parties in the early years of the nation.*

Video Review

In assigned groups, develop an outline for a video collage of America in the years between 1763 and 1815. Choose images that best illustrate the major topics of the period. Write a script to accompany the images. Assign narrators to different parts of the script, and present your video collage to the class.

Further Reading

Faber, Doris, and Harold Faber. *The Birth of a Nation.* Scribner (1989). Examination of the significant events from the organization of the U.S. federal government to the election of John Adams as president.

Hibbert, Christopher. *Redcoats & Rebels: The American Revolution through British Eyes.* Norton (1990). The War for Independence as seen through the eyes of the British.

Lavender, David S. *The Way to the Western Sea.* Doubleday (1990). Recreation of the key events surrounding Lewis and Clark's expedition.

Marrin, Albert. *1812: The War Nobody Won.* Atheneum (1985). Overview of the causes and major effects of the War of 1812.

Shorto, Russell. *Tecumseh and the Dream of an American Indian.* Silver Burdett Press (1989). Account of Tecumseh's struggle to forge an alliance among Native Americans.

Introducing the Unit

- **Chapter 7**
  NATIONALISM AND ECONOMIC GROWTH
  1815–1845
- **Chapter 8**
  SEPARATE SOCIETIES: NORTH AND SOUTH
  1820–1860
- **Chapter 9**
  WORKING FOR REFORM
  1820s–1860s
- **Chapter 10**
  EXPANSION AND CONFLICT
  1820–1860

UNIT OVERVIEW

The U.S. experienced great change as its economy grew and Americans sought new opportunities. But growth did not affect all regions the same way. In the North and the Middle West, commerce and industry brought major social and economic changes. Life in the South, however, remained largely agrarian, and the southern economy heavily dependent on cotton and slavery. The expansion of slavery became a divisive political issue as western settlers sought to bring new territories into the Union. Not all Americans welcomed the era's changes, however. Some turned to religion; others worked to reform American society.

CORE RESOURCES

- **American Almanac Poster** and **Worksheet 3**
- **Building Your Portfolio Worksheet 3**
  You may wish to preview the Unit 3 Review and Building Your Portfolio performance assessment activities on p. 333.

Using the American Almanac Posters

Begin the unit by displaying the American Almanac Poster and discussing entries with students. In addition to the worksheet, the annotations that follow provide additional information about the entries and suggest questions and activities.

Then, as students study the unit, have them work in small groups to create their own almanacs—using the same six headings—on pieces of butcher paper. At the end of the unit, call on groups to display and discuss their almanacs.

(detail), The Boatman's National Bank, St. Louis, Missouri

Chapter 7
NATIONALISM AND ECONOMIC GROWTH
1815–1845

Chapter 8
SEPARATE SOCIETIES: NORTH AND SOUTH
1820–1860

Chapter 9
WORKING FOR REFORM
1820s–1860s

The American People
Point out that in the 1860s the nation was not only sparsely populated but also rural. About 75 percent of the population lived in communities numbering less than 2,500 inhabitants or on the nation's 2.6 million farms.

■■ Ask students to find the population densities of their community, their county, and their state.

Hot off the Presses
As its name suggests, *Freedom's Journal* focused on the antislavery movement. Perhaps the most widely read African American abolitionist newspaper of the time, however, was Frederick Douglass's *North Star,* first published in 1847.

■■ Have students identify present-day publications that are associated with a particular social cause.

What Your Dollar Buys
Although the mail service would transport a half-ounce letter up to 3,000 miles for 3¢, the recipient had to pick it up from the post office or pay for it to be delivered. Free delivery of mail was not provided until 1863 in cities and 1896 in rural areas.

■■ Have students cite what the listed items cost today.

Fashion Plate
By the 1860s facial hair of all kinds—long, bushy sideburns, mustaches, goatees, or full beards—had become fashionable.

■■ Ask students to discuss if any of today's hair fashions might provoke the response that Palmer's beard received.

At Your Leisure
Mention that there was considerable opposition to gambling because of its "pernicious effects." By the 1860s antigambling views had taken hold in many areas of the country, and some forms of gaming had fallen out of favor.

■■ Ask students to cite examples of legal gambling today.

American Science and Manufacturing
Canned goods were first produced commercially in the U.S. in 1819 by Ezra Daggett and Thomas Kensett. The efficiency of canning improved after the introduction of the tin can, for which Kensett received a patent in 1825.

■■ Ask students to consider the impact that canning has had on American eating habits.

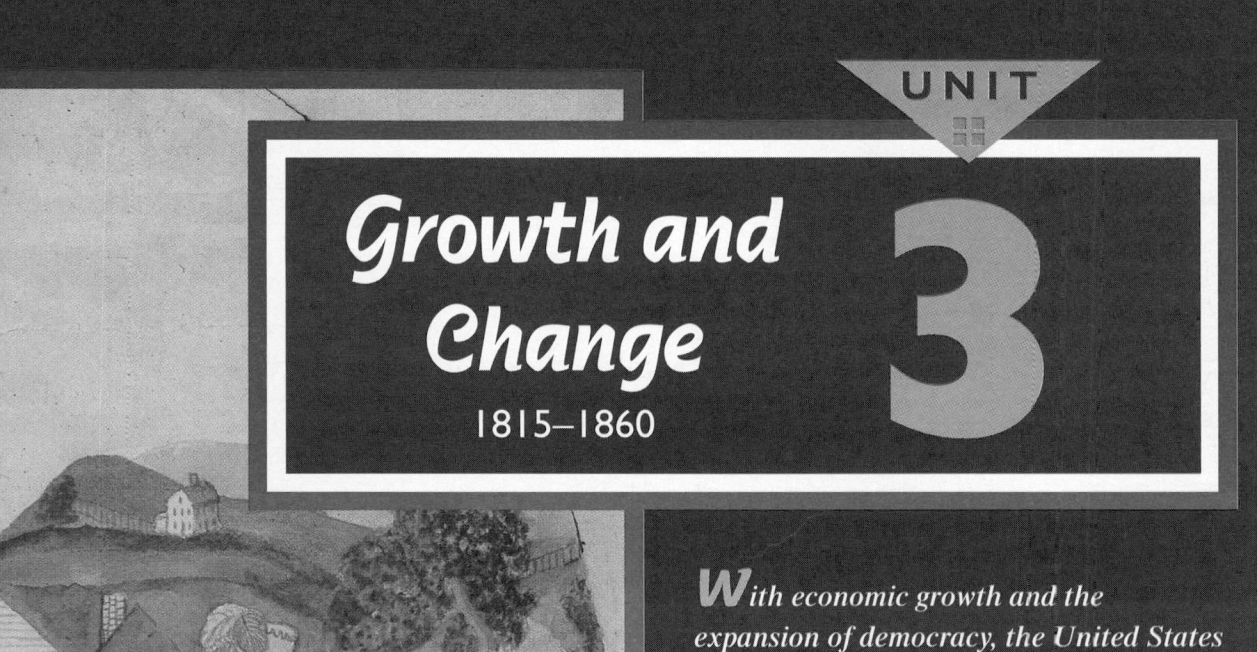

UNIT

Growth and Change

1815–1860

3

With economic growth and the expansion of democracy, the United States experienced great change, particularly in the North and Middle West. In those regions new industry and commerce brought dramatic social and economic change. In the South, however, the economy remained dependent on agriculture and slavery. The challenges presented by a rapidly changing society and by the issue of slavery led some Americans to religion and others to reform work. The expansion of slavery also became a divisive political issue as settlers sought to bring western territories into the Union.

◄ Watercolor painted by Eunice Pinney on the back of a letter, Connecticut, c. 1815

Chapter 10

EXPANSION AND CONFLICT 1820–1860

223

NATIONALISM AND ECONOMIC GROWTH

1815–1845

Chapter Overview

Having held their own in the War of 1812, Americans felt a new surge of pride in their nation. They sought to strengthen its economy, and the country assert-ed itself in foreign affairs. The U.S. joined the Industrial Revolution through invention, innovation, and a revolution in transportation.

As society changed, so did the expectations of average people. Americans began to call for increased opportunity and the expansion of democra-cy. One person, more than any other, repre-sented the new spirit and energy of America—Andrew Jackson, the hero of the "common man." Often called the first modern president, Jackson changed forever the nature of American government and politics.

Chapter Planning Guide

CHAPTER 7	CORE RESOURCE BOOKLETS	AUDIOVISUAL RESOURCES	PROGRAM RESOURCES
INTRODUCTION pp. 224–225	■ Literature Worksheet 7 ■ Building Your Port-folio Worksheet 3		
TEACHING THE CHAPTER pp. 226–249	■ Graphic Organizer 7 ■ Social Studies Skills Worksheet 7 ■ Geography Worksheet 7 ■ Outline Map 9	■ Linking Geography and History Trans-parencies and Worksheets 10, 11, 12 ■ Everyday Life in America Trans-parency 7 and Worksheet 7	■ Art in American History Trans-parency and Worksheet 10 ■ *Eyewitnesses and Others,* Volume 1: Readings 43, 47, 54, 55, 58
REVIEW AND ASSESSMENT pp. 250–251	■ Chapter 7 Daily Quizzes ■ Review Worksheet 7 ■ Chapter 7 Tests ■ Alternative Assessment Forms		■ Test Generator

Additional Resources

BOOKS FOR TEACHERS

Remini, Robert V. *The Life of Andrew Jackson.* Viking Penguin, 1990. Analysis by eminent Jackson scholar.

Sellers, Charles. *The Market Revolu-tion: Jacksonian America, 1815–1846.* Oxford, 1992. Examines the causes and consequences of the market revolution.

Wilkins, Thurman. *Cherokee Tragedy.* University of Oklahoma Press, 1989. Account of government's treatment of the Cherokees.

BOOKS FOR STUDENTS

Ehle, John. *Trail of Tears: The Rise and Fall of the Cherokee Nation.* Doubleday, 1989. Account of the Indian removal.

Hindle, Brooke, and Steven Lubar. *Engines of Change: The American Industrial Revolution, 1790–1860.* Smithsonian, 1986. Pictorial history of U.S. Industrial Revolution.

*Remini, Robert V. *The Revolutionary Age of Andrew Jackson.* Harper-Collins, 1987. Examines the Jacksonian era.

* for students reading below grade level

MULTIMEDIA MATERIALS

Andrew Jackson: The People's President. Video, 15 min. Westport Media/SSSS. Depicts the controver-sial life and career of Jackson.

Erie Canal. Video, 21 min. Phoenix/SSSS. Period music and historical illustrations tell history of Erie Canal.

Movin' On. Video, 58 min. Harold Mayer/SSSS. Details the effects of the growth of railroads.

THEMES IN AMERICAN HISTORY

USE WITH PAGES 224–225

Listed on the right are the themes emphasized in Chapter 7. The questions in boldface type stimulate critical thinking and provide students with an opportunity to discuss the themes within a broadened context. The questions also appear in the pupil's edition on p. 224.

■ ECONOMIC DEVELOPMENT

What are some of the factors that might influence a region's economic development? Students might mention natural resources, climate, geography, population size, ease of transportation, and the balance between urban and rural areas as factors that could affect a region's economic development.

Why might regions within a large country develop different economies? Students might suggest that variations in factors that influence economic development could explain development of distinct regional economies in a large country.

■ TECHNOLOGY AND SOCIETY

How might new technologies promote economic growth? Students might point out that new technologies are usually developed in response to specific problems or situations. When these problems or situations are related to economic issues (production, transportation, markets), new technologies often result in improvements or solutions that lead to economic growth.

■ DEMOCRATIC VALUES

How might economic change lead to greater political participation by certain groups? Students might mention that economic growth (such as the development or expansion of new industries) might bring more people into the work force or improve their economic standing within the work force. This change, in turn, might increase their incentive to influence the direction of government.

CHAPTER STRATEGIES FOR MEETING INDIVIDUAL NEEDS

LIMITED ENGLISH PROFICIENT LEARNERS

As the class progresses through the chapter, have students work in small groups to create a collage showing the major changes in the U.S. from 1815 to 1845. Groups should present their collages, explaining each image.

TACTILE/KINESTHETIC LEARNERS

Have students work in groups and write on index cards each of the terms in Identify in the Section Reviews. Have students take turns "acting out" the cards by using drawings or gestures. Other members of the group should identify what is on each card.

LEARNERS HAVING DIFFICULTY

Organize students in small groups, and assign to individuals or pairs sections to outline. Ask students to share outlines with others in the group and to take turns generating questions they can ask each other.

AUDITORY LEARNERS

Organize students into four groups and assign each group one of the chapter's sections. Have each group prepare and present newscasts in which they comment on major events in their section.

VISUAL LEARNERS

After they have read the chapter, have students work in groups to prepare illustrated time lines showing major events in the chapter. Ask students to prepare a caption for each event.

GIFTED LEARNERS

Have students write essays and create charts explaining how Jacksonian democracy extended and differed from Jeffersonian democracy.

USING THE CHAPTER FOCUS

■ UNDERSTANDING THE MAIN IDEA

Call on a volunteer to read aloud the Understanding the Main Idea paragraph. Ask students why a "man of the people" would have been a likely candidate for president after the War of 1812.

■■ Ask students if feelings of nationalism are evident in the U.S. today.

⭐ THEMES

Have students work individually or in small groups to answer the questions under Themes. Save students' responses so that they can compare them with their responses after studying the chapter. (See p. 223B for suggested answers.)

■ THE TIME LINE

Ask students to recall how earlier U.S. expansion affected American Indians. *(It led to battles between white settlers and American Indians, and many Indians were pushed from their lands.)* Ask students to look at the time line and speculate about the U.S. policy toward Native Americans in the mid-1800s. *(The Indian Removal Act of 1830 indicates that the policy was to continue to push the American Indians from their lands.)*

CORE RESOURCES

- **Graphic Organizer 7**
- **Literature Worksheet 7**
- **Outline Map 9**
- **Building Your Portfolio Worksheet 3**

ABOUT THE ILLUSTRATION

By the 1820s many states had removed restrictions on suffrage and allowed all white males to vote. Ask students how this fact is reflected in the painting on these two pages. Tell students that George Caleb Bingham is known for his paintings that depict scenes from everyday life on the frontier. His paintings of election scenes are keen studies of town life in the mid-1800s. Ask volunteers to characterize the general mood of the people in this painting. Then ask if they note anything missing from the scene *(women)* and if so, why. *(Women were not part of the election process at this time.)*

Chapter 7

1815–1845

NATIONALISM AND ECONOMIC GROWTH

▼ FOCUS

UNDERSTANDING THE MAIN IDEA

The War of 1812 filled Americans with national pride and confidence in the future. The U.S. government began to assert a stronger foreign policy and to promote the growth of the domestic economy. A new spirit of democracy swept the nation, as symbolized by "the man of the people," Andrew Jackson.

⭐ THEMES

■ **ECONOMIC DEVELOPMENT** What are some of the factors that might influence a region's economic development? Why might regions within a large country develop different economies?

■ **TECHNOLOGY AND SOCIETY** How might new technologies promote economic growth?

■ **DEMOCRATIC VALUES** How might economic change lead to greater political participation by certain groups?

1816	1820	1825	1830	1841
James Monroe elected president.	Missouri Compromise passed.	Erie Canal completed.	Indian Removal Act passed.	John Tyler succeeds to presidency.

Ask students to describe how the U.S. benefited from the terms of the Treaty of Ghent at the end of the War of 1812. Then ask students to speculate as to how the war's outcome might affect the American people as a nation and as individuals. Save responses on butcher paper or a flip chart so that students can check their predictions as they study the chapter.

LINK TO THE PAST

The War of 1812, although producing no clear-cut victory for the United States, proved that the country could stand up to a major European power. Americans began to believe that the United States could become a power in its own right, free from Europe's influence and control.

I n 1828 Frances Wright of Scotland, a travel writer, social reformer, and sometime U.S. resident, delivered a Fourth of July speech at New Harmony, Indiana. She praised the United States as the protector of "human liberty [and] the favored scene of human improvement." Soon, she predicted, "all mankind" would celebrate "the Jubilee of Independence."

The United States was far from granting liberty to all in 1828, as Native Americans and enslaved African Americans well knew. The nation also faced growing sectional differences. Yet most Americans of the time would have cheered Wright's speech. Americans during this period celebrated the Fourth of July with zest. Indeed, one British visitor noted that American national pride "blazes out everywhere and on all occasions."

The new confidence that burst forth in this era took many forms. The United States built new roads and canals, developed new industries, launched a period of economic growth, secured its borders, and warned Europe to stay out of Latin America.

The Boatmen's National Bank, St. Louis, Missouri

Verdict of the People (1855)
by George Caleb Bingham

Frances Wright

PREVIEW WORKSHOP

Following is a list of the significant people, places, and terms in this section. You may wish to use this list as a section preview.

People
- Henry Clay
- James Monroe

Places
- National Road
- Erie Canal
- Oregon Country
- Latin America

Terms
- nationalism
- specie
- American System

- Tariff Act of 1816
- internal improvements
- Rush-Bagot Agreement
- Convention of 1818
- Adams-Onís Treaty
- Monroe Doctrine

FOCUS OBJECTIVES

- Describe how the War of 1812 helped strengthen the U.S. economy and list the weaknesses that the war revealed.

- Analyze what the American System attempted to accomplish.

- Examine how U.S. foreign policy reflected a growing sense of nationalism.

MAKING CONNECTIONS
Economics

The refusal of Congress to recharter the Bank led to a rapid increase in the number of banks—from 88 to 208 in just four years. Many of these banks were unstable. One such bank in Ohio was known as the Saddlebag because its backer reputedly had carried all its capital resources from Pittsburgh in his saddlebags.

PRIMARY SOURCE

Description of Change: excerpted and bracketed
Rationale: excerpted to focus on main idea; bracketed to clarify meaning

Section 1

THE RISE OF NATIONALISM

FOCUS

- **How did the War of 1812 help strengthen the U.S. economy? What weaknesses did the war reveal?**
- **What did the American System attempt to accomplish?**
- **How did U.S. foreign policy reflect a growing sense of nationalism?**

The War of 1812 was a turning point for the United States. The young nation's stand against Great Britain gave Americans confidence and pride in their country. But the war also brought to light weaknesses in the nation's financial and transportation systems. Following the war, government leaders took steps to remedy these problems and to secure the nation's borders.

Flag of the United States, 1818

NATIONALISM TAKES ROOT

The United States did not gain territory from the War of 1812. But confirmation of the young Republic's independence from Europe was vastly more important than any spoils of war. The war stirred a new sense of **nationalism**, or national pride and loyalty. The United States had successfully stood up to Great Britain! Americans for the first time began to believe—not just hope—that their new nation would survive and prosper. Baltimore newspaper editor Hezekiah Niles captured the growing economic vitality of the United States in an 1815 editorial in his *Niles' Weekly Register:*

> ❝ The republic, reposing [resting] on the laurels of a glorious war, gathers the rich harvest of an honorable peace. Everywhere the sound of the axe is heard, opening the forest to the sun and claiming for agriculture the range of the buffalo. Our cities grow and towns rise up as by magic. . . . The busy hum of 10,000 wheels fills our seaports. . . . The republic lives, and in honor! ❞

The war had given U.S. manufacturing a big boost. With the flow of European products all but stopped by embargoes and naval blockades, Americans had been forced to produce goods themselves. U.S. merchants used the opportunity to build new factories. The number of New England cotton mills, for example, jumped by 94 between 1805 and 1815.

But the war also revealed weaknesses in the nation's financial system. By mid-1814 the war had drained the U.S. Treasury. Without the Bank of the United States, which Congress had refused to recharter in 1811, the Treasury had to rely on state banks for loans. Instead of borrowing from one central bank, the government had to negotiate with scores of banks.

Securing loans was only part of the problem, however. Each bank printed its own notes, often in amounts far exceeding the **specie**—the gold or silver coin—that the bank held to back up the notes. As a result, banks often refused to accept one another's notes. Thus the government ran the risk of borrowing from one bank money that it could not deposit in another. New England banks, for instance, regularly refused to accept bank notes from the South or West.

Teaching the Section

THE WAR OF 1812 AND THE ECONOMY

Divide the class into small groups. Have some groups write newspaper headlines about how the War of 1812 benefited the U.S. economy. Have other groups write newspaper headlines about the weaknesses of the country's financial system that were exposed by the war. Have groups present their headlines while the class fills in details of stories that might appear under each headline.

▶

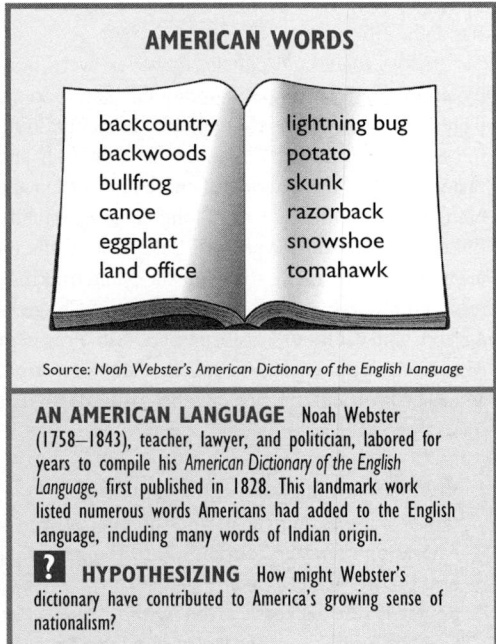

AMERICAN WORDS

backcountry	lightning bug
backwoods	potato
bullfrog	skunk
canoe	razorback
eggplant	snowshoe
land office	tomahawk

Source: *Noah Webster's American Dictionary of the English Language*

AN AMERICAN LANGUAGE Noah Webster (1758–1843), teacher, lawyer, and politician, labored for years to compile his *American Dictionary of the English Language,* first published in 1828. This landmark work listed numerous words Americans had added to the English language, including many words of Indian origin.

❓ HYPOTHESIZING How might Webster's dictionary have contributed to America's growing sense of nationalism?

Wartime also underscored the nation's transportation problems. With sea trade blocked by British ships, merchants had to transport goods over slow and costly land routes. Goods, although usually abundant and cheap where they were produced, became scarce and expensive in other areas. In 1813, for example, sugar that sold for $9 per 100 pounds in New Orleans cost $40 in New York.

By 1815 many Republicans—former opponents of a strong central government—were calling for national measures to promote manufacturing, strengthen the financial system, and improve transportation. The war won them over to the Federalist view that a strong America needed a balance among agriculture, manufacturing, and commerce. Even Jefferson had a change of heart. "To be independent for the comforts of life," he wrote a colleague, "we must fabricate [make] them ourselves. We must now place the manufacturer by the side of the agriculturist."

■■ The War of 1812 led to a boom in U.S. manufacturing but revealed weaknesses in the nation's financial and transportation systems.

*T*HE AMERICAN SYSTEM

While the War of 1812 convinced many older Republicans to support a stronger federal government, many younger party members had already been thinking in national terms. Chief among these "nationalists" was Congressman Henry Clay of Kentucky. After the war, Clay began to push for a program of federal support for economic development. Clay's program, which came to be called the **American System,** had three main features: (1) a national bank to provide sound currency and serve as the government's banker; (2) a protective tariff to encourage industrial development; and (3) a national transportation system to unite northern manufacturers, western farmers, and southern planters.

Banking and industry. By 1816 the public cry for a sound national currency was growing. Even Republican President Madison, who had opposed the First Bank of the United States, declared in his annual message to Congress that the establishment of a national bank warranted consideration.

Clay and other nationalists in Congress took this message as a sign that Republicans in Congress would no longer oppose the creation of a national bank. On January 8, South Carolina's John C. Calhoun introduced a bill to charter the Second Bank of the United States. President Madison signed the bill on April 10, 1816.

Clay's call for a protective tariff also met with approval. After the Treaty of Ghent was signed, British-made goods had again flooded American ports. New U.S. manufacturers, unable to sell their goods as cheaply as the much larger British firms, demanded protective measures. Congress responded by passing the **Tariff Act of 1816,** which put a 25 percent duty on most imported

▶ **During this period, state banks issued their own currency. A five-dollar bank note from the Bank of Cincinnati is shown here.**

MAKING CONNECTIONS

Language Arts
Noah Webster's *Spelling Book,* commonly called the "Blue-Backed Speller," was widely used in primary schools for more than a century. Webster suggested dropping the *u* from words such as *colour* and *humour.* This book, and his famous dictionary, helped standardize spelling in the U.S. Today, partly because of Webster, many English words are spelled differently in the U.S. from the way they are spelled in Great Britain. In 1859 the publisher of the Blue-Backed Speller, Appleton & Co., claimed that its aggregate sales of the speller equaled the entire population of the U.S.!

NATIONALISM AND ECONOMIC GROWTH **■■** 227

Teaching the Section

THE AMERICAN SYSTEM

Point out that the American System was intended to strengthen the nation as a whole, as well as each region. Have students identify the three main features of the American System. List them in a column on the chalkboard. Then write *North, South,* and *Middle West* in a row to create a nine-cell table. Ask the class to decide whether each section would be helped or hurt by each feature of the plan. Record class decisions in the appropriate cells of the table. Then have students debate the system's merits by assuming the roles of northern manufacturers, southern farmers, and middle western farmers.

HISTORICAL SIDELIGHTS

Fashion and the Tariff

The Tariff of 1816 virtually excluded imported cotton fabrics. As a result, New York merchants, using cheap cloth produced in New England textile mills, gradually were able to capture the American clothing market. One fashion observer noted in the 1840s that "everywhere throughout the country, New York–made clothing is popular over all others."

PRIMARY SOURCE

Description of Change: excerpted
Rationale: excerpted to focus on main idea

HISTORICAL SIDELIGHTS

Era of Good Feelings

After his inauguration Monroe traveled to the Middle Atlantic and the northern states. At every stop he spoke of national unity and the reconciliation of sectional differences. He was met with overwhelming enthusiasm. The Boston *Columbian Centinel* declared Monroe's trip the start of "the Era of Good Feelings." The label stuck, and for more than 150 years it has identified that period in American history.

▲ *The Book Bindery,* a watercolor by an anonymous American artist, shows women workers.

The Museum of Fine Arts, Boston

factory goods. This made imported goods more expensive than similar U.S.–made goods.

The tariff had wide support among northern manufacturers and among westerners and some southerners who hoped to benefit from industrial development. However, New England importers and southern planters who relied on British trade opposed the tariff. Congressman John Randolph of Virginia saw the tariff as a conflict between southern planters who "bear the whole brunt of the war and taxation" and northern manufacturers who benefited from the tariff. Arguments like Randolph's arose repeatedly after 1816 as sectional economic interests began to override calls for national economic growth. Even Calhoun, among the tariff's strongest defenders, became a champion of southern interests by the 1820s.

Internal improvements. In 1817, though, Calhoun was still a nationalist. In February he introduced a bill to fund a national system of roads and canals. "Let us . . . bind the republic together with a perfect system of roads and canals," Calhoun told Congress. "Let us conquer space." Congress was receptive. The difficulty of transporting goods and troops during the war had convinced most people of the need for such **internal improvements**.

Some progress had already been made on a national transportation system. During Jefferson's presidency, Congress had authorized a paved highway from Cumberland, Maryland, across the mountains into the western territories. In 1811 construction of the National (or Cumberland) Road began. By 1819 it reached as far as present-day

Wheeling, West Virginia. (It was later extended to Vandalia, Illinois.)

Most roads and canals, however, were built by states or by private companies (see map on page 233). New York, for example, began building the Erie Canal in 1817. Intended as a cheaper and faster route to the interior of the country than the National Road, the 363-mile-long canal eventually linked the Hudson River with Lake Erie. Calhoun argued that the great scale of such undertakings required federal aid. Enough members of Congress agreed, and Calhoun's bill passed. But President Madison opposed it. As his last act in office, Madison vetoed the bill on the grounds that it overstepped federal powers:

> 66 I am not unaware of the great importance of roads and canals and the improved navigation of water courses . . . to the general prosperity. But seeing that such a power is not expressly given by the Constitution, . . . I have no option but to withhold my signature from it. 99

■■ The American System attempted to strengthen the economy with proposals for a national bank, a protective tariff, and a national transportation system.

MONROE AND FOREIGN POLICY

In 1816 Congressional Republicans nominated Madison's secretary of state, James Monroe of Virginia, to run for president. Monroe easily defeated the Federalist candidate, Senator Rufus King of New York. The Federalist party had angered many Americans by its opposition to the War of 1812. The party was losing political power even in New England, long a Federalist stronghold.

The collapse of the Federalist party initiated a period of political harmony in the United States known as the Era of Good Feelings. President Monroe moved quickly to bring the same harmony to foreign relations.

Relations with Great Britain. After the War of 1812, the United States and Great Britain continued to sail warships on the Great Lakes.

U.S. FOREIGN POLICY

Have students work in pairs to identify the nation's foreign policy problems and the solutions provided by Monroe's treaties with Great Britain and Spain and by the Monroe Doctrine. Ask students how U.S. foreign policy reflected a growing sense of nationalism. Then ask students to refer to Washington's Farewell Address. Have the class decide whether Monroe's policies were a return to the principles set forth by Washington, and if so, how.

Monroe, fearing further conflict, ordered Acting Secretary of State Richard Rush to negotiate a disarmament plan with British foreign minister Charles Bagot. In the resulting **Rush-Bagot Agreement** of 1817, each nation pledged to limit its military presence on the lakes to a few armed ships.

Next, Monroe moved to define the northern boundary of the Louisiana Purchase. In the **Convention of 1818** Great Britain and the United States set the U.S.–Canadian border at the 49th parallel west to the Rocky Mountains. Great Britain agreed to occupy **Oregon Country**—the disputed area of the Pacific Northwest—jointly with the United States for 10 years, with a boundary to be set later. The border agreement between the two North American neighbors was one of the most important outcomes of the War of 1812.

Relations with Spain. Settling border disputes with Spain proved much trickier. In 1812 the United States incorporated West Florida (a strip of land on the Gulf of Mexico in present-day

▲ *The Intruders* (1966) by Native American artist Jerome Tiger portrays the Florida home of the Seminoles.

Mississippi and Alabama) into the Mississippi Territory on the grounds that it was part of the Louisiana Purchase. Spain, preoccupied with war in Europe at the time, only protested.

Then in 1818 General Andrew Jackson went into East Florida (present-day Florida) to pursue a group of Seminoles who had been harboring runaway slaves and attacking U.S. border settlements.

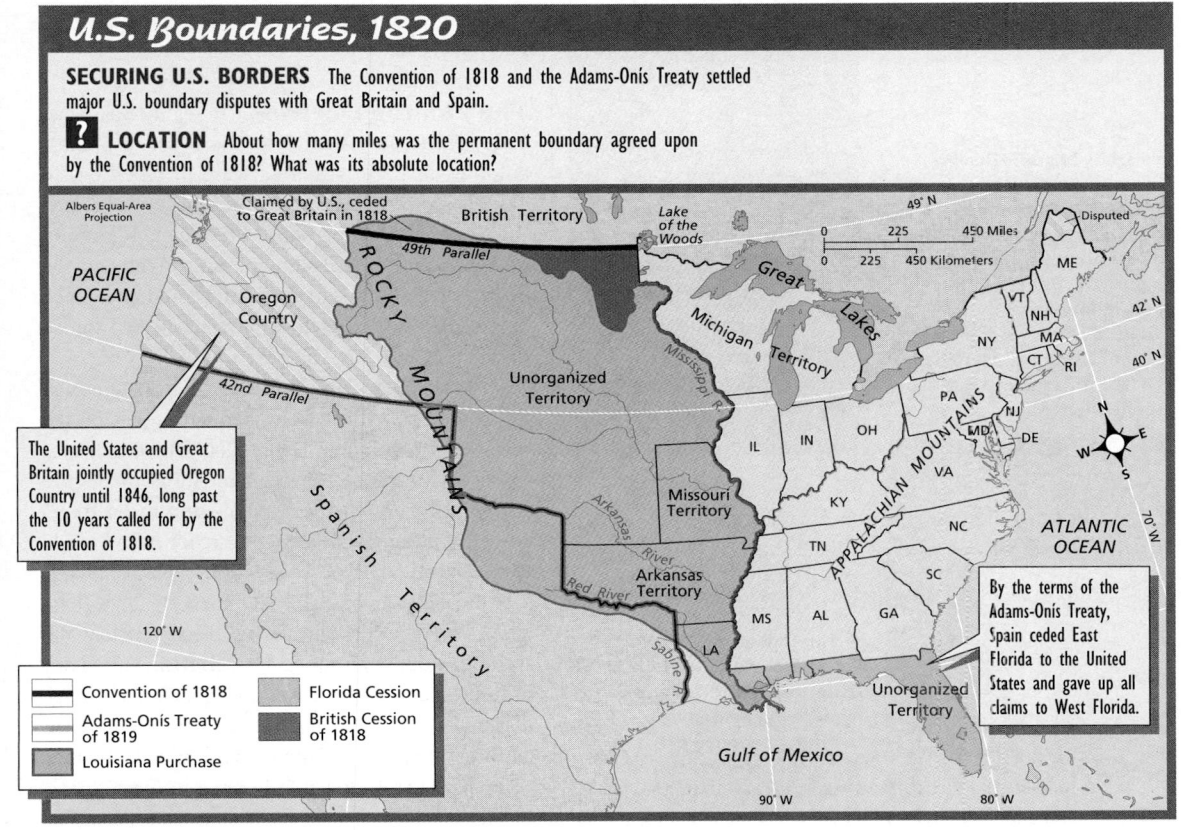

U.S. Boundaries, 1820

SECURING U.S. BORDERS The Convention of 1818 and the Adams-Onís Treaty settled major U.S. boundary disputes with Great Britain and Spain.

? LOCATION About how many miles was the permanent boundary agreed upon by the Convention of 1818? What was its absolute location?

The United States and Great Britain jointly occupied Oregon Country until 1846, long past the 10 years called for by the Convention of 1818.

By the terms of the Adams-Onís Treaty, Spain ceded East Florida to the United States and gave up all claims to West Florida.

Legend:
- Convention of 1818
- Adams-Onís Treaty of 1819
- Louisiana Purchase
- Florida Cession
- British Cession of 1818

Map Caption Answer
about 900 miles; 49th parallel from the Lake of the Woods to the Rocky Mountains

Practice

GUIDED PRACTICE

Write *Economic Policy* and *Foreign Policy* on the chalkboard. Ask students to give examples of post–1812 policies and to explain how each reflected the new spirit of nationalism. Write responses under the appropriate heading. Tell students to make notes in preparation for creating a lyrical work that illustrates these nationalistic events.

INDEPENDENT PRACTICE

Have students write songs, poems, or raps to illustrate the major domestic and foreign policy events in the U.S. after the War of 1812. Ask volunteers to perform their compositions for the class. Students may wish to include their work in their portfolios.

Review and Assessment

REVIEW Ask students to imagine they are living in the years after the War of 1812. Have them write a letter to a friend in another country, explaining why it is an exciting time to be an American. Students may wish to include their letters in their portfolios. Then assign the Section 1 Review on p. 231.

ASSESS Assign the **Section 1 Daily Quiz** in *Core Resources*.

🌐 GLOBAL CONNECTIONS

Less than a decade before the Monroe Doctrine was issued, the U.S. and Britain had been locked in war. Yet Monroe was confident of British support even before he made his announcement. British leaders feared the loss of Latin American markets if Spanish rule was reestablished. Although Britain remained in the background and allowed Monroe to set the policy, the powerful British navy was a much greater deterrent to French and Spanish ambitions in Latin America than were the American president's tough words.

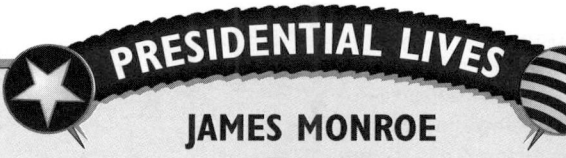

PRESIDENTIAL LIVES

JAMES MONROE
1758–1831

in office
1817–1825

James Monroe was the last president to have fought in the Revolutionary War as well as the last of the "Founding Fathers" to occupy the White House. Indeed, Monroe looked very much the 18th-century statesman. He wore a powdered wig and draped his tall frame in the fashion of an earlier age: cutaway coat, waistcoat, knee britches, long stockings, and buckled shoes.

Monroe's generally quiet and modest manner matched his elegant appearance. In fact, his longtime friend Thomas Jefferson remarked that Monroe was "a man whose soul might be turned wrong side outward, without discovering a blemish to the world."

James Monroe

Jackson, unable to catch those responsible, instead claimed the territory for the United States. Secretary of State John Quincy Adams denied that President Monroe had authorized Jackson's actions. Nevertheless, Adams offered Spain a choice: either control the Seminoles or give Florida to the United States.

► **Father Miguel Hidalgo** was a priest in Dolores, Mexico. On September 16, 1810, Hidalgo called on the townspeople to revolt against the Spanish. His speech, known as the "Grito de Dolores," or "Cry of Dolores," launched the war for Mexican independence.

◄ **Simon Bolívar,** known as "the Liberator," was a South American revolutionary leader who helped fight for the independence of Colombia, Venezuela, and Peru. The new republic of Bolivia was named after him.

Spain decided to deal. In the **Adams-Onís Treaty** (1819), Spain transferred East Florida to the United States for $5 million. In return, the United States made a promise to drop its claim to Texas. The treaty also settled the southern and western boundaries of the Louisiana Purchase. The new border ran in a stair-step fashion to the Rocky Mountains and then along the 42nd parallel to the Pacific Ocean.

The Monroe Doctrine. In reality Spain had little option but to sell Florida. Most of Spain's colonies in Latin America were in rebellion. In 1808 Napoléon, the emperor of France, had seized the Spanish throne. Latin Americans, claiming both opposition to Napoléon and loyalty to the deposed Spanish king, organized independence movements. By 1819 these movements had spread throughout Spanish America.

Most people in the United States supported the rebellions, which were inspired in part by the American Revolution. Henry Clay hailed the "glorious spectacle of eighteen millions of people struggling to burst their chains and to be free." After formal negotiations with Spain over Florida were concluded, the United States moved to recognize the new republics.

American officials knew, however, that the independence of these new Latin American nations was far from secure. Thus, they were alarmed by reports that France was prepared to supply troops to help Spain retake its former colonies. In an October 1823 letter to former president Thomas Jefferson, President Monroe wrote:

RETEACH Have students work in small groups to divide the section material by subsections. Direct each student to write questions about the main ideas under the assigned subsection. Have groups quiz each other, using the questions.

Closure

Ask students how the name that Henry Clay chose for his program, the "American System," reflected the attitudes and the feelings within the nation after the War of 1812. Then ask students to list specific examples of U.S. foreign and domestic policies that were outgrowths of these attitudes and feelings.

Extension

RESEARCH Suggest that students work in pairs to research information about the personal and professional life of Henry Clay. Then have students present their information in the form of an interview with Clay.

CREATE Have students create a model or an illustrated map of the National Road. Ask them to include captions that narrate life along the road.

"We would view an interference on the part of the European powers [into Latin America] as an attack on ourselves."

Adding to the unease was a dispute with Russia over territorial rights in the Pacific Northwest. In 1821 Russia had extended its land claims southward to the 51st parallel and had closed the surrounding coastal waters to foreign ships. In July 1823 Secretary of State John Quincy Adams warned the Russian foreign minister that the United States would not tolerate the establishment of *any* new European colonies on the American continents.

President Monroe reaffirmed this view in his annual message to Congress on December 2, 1823. In what came to be called the **Monroe Doctrine**, the president vowed that the United States would not interfere with any existing European colonies in Latin America. But he also warned Europe to keep its hands off the Latin American "governments who have declared their independence and maintained it." The United States, he said, would consider any European attempt to revive old colonies or establish new ones in the Western Hemisphere "as dangerous to our peace and safety." (See page 1004 for the Doctrine.)

■■ **The United States expressed its nationalist spirit by securing its borders and declaring the Americas off-limits to European expansion.**

Latin American Nations, 1830

NEW NATIONS Many Latin American nations became independent in the early 1800s after successful revolutions.

? LINKING HISTORY AND GEOGRAPHY What colonies did European countries still have in the Western Hemisphere in 1830?

Map Caption Answer
Cuba, Puerto Rico, British Honduras, the Bahamas, the Mosquito Coast, Jamaica, Trinidad, and the Guianas.

SECTION REVIEW ANSWERS

IDENTIFY
For significance, see the following pages:
nationalism (p. 226)
specie (p. 226)
Henry Clay (p. 227)
Tariff Act of 1816 (p. 227)
internal improvements (p. 228)
James Monroe (p. 228)
Monroe Doctrine
  (p. 231)

LOCATE
For locations, see the maps on pp. 229, 231, and 233.

1. *caused manufacturing to boom; weaknesses in financial and transportation systems*
2. *national bank, protective tariff, and national transportation system*
3. *made transport of goods to and from interior cheaper and faster*
4. *Editorials should cover Rush-Bagot Agreement, Convention of 1818, Adams-Onís Treaty, and Monroe Doctrine.*
5. *protective tariffs, internal improvements to unite regions, creation of Second Bank of the U.S., securing of U.S. borders, Monroe Doctrine*

■ SECTION **1** REVIEW

IDENTIFY and explain the significance of the following: nationalism, specie, Henry Clay, Tariff Act of 1816, internal improvements, James Monroe, Monroe Doctrine.

LOCATE and explain the importance of the following: National (Cumberland) Road, Erie Canal, Oregon Country, Latin America.

1. **MAIN IDEA** Why was the War of 1812 good for the U.S. economy? What problems did it bring to light?
2. **MAIN IDEA** What were the main features of the American System?
3. **GEOGRAPHY: LOCATION** How did the Erie Canal help promote the nation's economic growth?
4. **WRITING TO PERSUADE** Imagine that you are a newspaper editor in December 1823. Write an editorial describing and either supporting or opposing each of President Monroe's foreign policy actions.
5. **SYNTHESIZING** Provide evidence for the view that the United States entered a period of growing nationalism after the War of 1812.

Section 2

THE CHALLENGES OF GROWTH

F O C U S

- **How did the transportation and market revolutions affect the U.S. economy?**
- **How did the Industrial Revolution change the process of manufacturing goods in the United States?**
- **What led to the growth of towns and cities in the mid-1800s?**
- **What sparked the Panic of 1819?**

The United States entered a period of intense economic expansion in the mid-1800s. Advances in transportation and production allowed merchants to extend their markets, manufacturers to increase production and profit, and farmers to increase output and to transport their goods to market with greater ease. These changes also spurred the growth of towns and cities.

Leaving the Junction by Currier and Ives

THE TRANSPORTATION REVOLUTION

Before 1820 poor transportation made it difficult to sell manufactured goods and farm products between regions. Except for the National Road and a few other major routes connecting eastern cities,

▲ With the completion of Robert Fulton's *Clermont* in 1807, the era of commercial steamboat navigation began. This 1810 painting by Edward L. Henry shows the *Clermont* landing at Croton-on-Hudson, New York.

most roads between cities were little more than crude trails that turned to mud when it rained.

Middle Western farmers faced the most severe transportation problems. Flatboats could float farm products downriver but were useless in moving manufactured goods upriver. Most goods from the East were shipped to the interior of the country by wagon over mountain roads—a slow and costly process.

Canals offered one solution to the transportation problem, but they were expensive and time-consuming to build. By 1816 only about 100 miles of canals had been dug. Canal building soared, however, after New York State completed the Erie Canal in 1825. Impressed that the canal reduced the cost of moving goods between Buffalo and New York City by more than 90 percent, other states launched massive canal projects. By 1840, rivers and canals combined to provide a waterway that stretched from Illinois to the Atlantic.

Improvements in steamboat construction also aided transportation to the interior. The first steam-powered riverboat was launched in 1787, but only

MOTIVATING: PRIOR KNOWLEDGE

Write *American System* on the chalkboard. Ask volunteers to recall the provisions of this program (*national bank, protective tariff, national transportation system*) and to explain why a national transportation system was regarded as necessary. Tell students that in Section 2 they will discover how a transportation revolution affected the U.S. economy in the mid-1800s.

Teaching the Section

TRANSPORTATION AND MARKET REVOLUTIONS

Have volunteers point out on a physical map geographic obstacles to U.S. economic growth and national unity in the mid-1800s. Then have students work in small groups to discuss and chart how each new mode of transportation overcame these obstacles and affected the market for each section's products.

THE INDUSTRIAL REVOLUTION

Ask for volunteers to summarize how each of the following changed the ways products were manufactured in America: the factory system, interchangeable parts, mass production. Have students cite present-day examples of these concepts.

▶

with the completion of Robert Fulton's *Clermont* in 1807 could steamboats carry heavy loads upstream. By 1817, steamboats were moving goods up and down the Mississippi River.

Another steam-powered invention, the locomotive, came into commercial use in the 1830s. Trains had one big advantage over steamboats—they could go anywhere tracks could be laid. But they also suffered from a serious drawback—early locomotives were plagued by mechanical troubles. Thus, few people were surprised when the *Tom Thumb,* America's first commercially successful steam locomotive, lost a race against a horse-drawn train in 1830. As an observer noted, all was going well until the locomotive's engine gave out:

66 At first the gray [horse] had the best of it, . . . the engine had to wait until the rotation of the wheels set the blower to work. The horse was perhaps a quarter of a mile ahead when the safety valve of the engine lifted and the thin blue vapor issuing from it showed an excess of steam. The blower whistled, . . . the pace increased, the passengers shouted, the engine gained on the horse, . . . the race was neck and neck, nose and nose—then the engine passed the horse, and a great hurrah hailed the victory. But it was not repeated; for just at this time, . . . the band which drove the pulley, which drove the blower, slipped from the drum, the safety valve ceased to scream, and the engine for want of breath began to wheeze and pant. 99

By 1840, engineers had solved most of the trains' early mechanical problems. Over the next decade companies spent more than $200 million laying nearly 9,000 miles of track. Railroads reached many isolated parts of the country and became symbols of industrialization and the growing interdependence of the national economy.

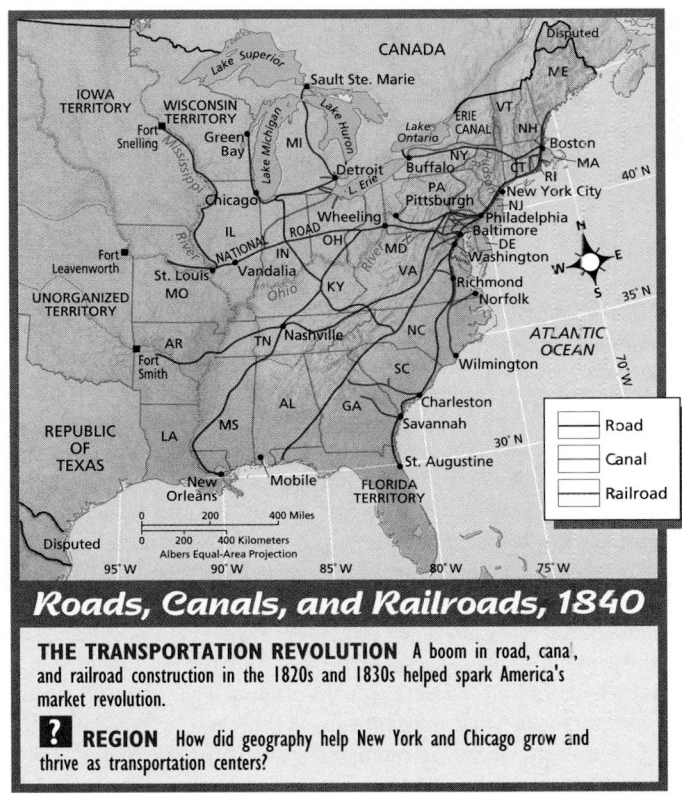

Roads, Canals, and Railroads, 1840

THE TRANSPORTATION REVOLUTION A boom in road, canal, and railroad construction in the 1820s and 1830s helped spark America's market revolution.

? **REGION** How did geography help New York and Chicago grow and thrive as transportation centers?

■■ **The transportation revolution helped promote economic growth by making it easier to transport goods.**

*T*HE MARKET REVOLUTION

By making it easier and cheaper to move farm products, raw materials, and manufactured goods long distances, new transportation systems created national markets for the first time. Regions no longer had to be relatively self-sufficient; they could import some goods and concentrate on producing what was most profitable.

The Middle West, linked to eastern markets by the Erie Canal, specialized in wheat, corn, and hog production. Southern states west of the Appalachian Mountains focused on growing cotton, much of which was shipped to market down the Mississippi to the port of New Orleans. The Northeast, with abundant waterpower, concentrated on manufacturing such products as wool and cotton textiles and specialized machinery.

Teaching the Section

URBAN GROWTH

Refer students to the graph on page 235 and discuss the answer to the question. Ask why urban growth was greatest in the Northeast. Have students recall why the graph shows no urban population for the Middle West in 1800. *(a relatively new and undeveloped area of non-Indian settlement)* Then note that by 1860, the urban populations in the Middle West and the South had increased dramatically. Ask students to explain why.

THE PANIC OF 1819

Have pairs of students create flowcharts showing the causes and effects of the Panic of 1819. Have volunteers present their completed charts to the class.

HISTORICAL SIDELIGHTS
African American Workers

The opportunities of industrialization were not shared equally. Free blacks were excluded from many trade unions and faced hostility from white workers, who feared competition for jobs. Despite great obstacles, however, by 1860 African Americans in the North were represented in engraving, photography, law, dentistry, and more than 100 other skilled trades and professions.

The Granger Collection, New York

▲ *Preparing for Market* is the title of this 1856 print by Nathaniel Currier.

This creation of profitable national markets has come to be known as the **market revolution**. The market revolution increased the profits of farmers and manufacturers and changed the way they worked and did business. Before the market revolution, for instance, entire families worked most northern farms. They grew their own food and sold the surplus locally. After the market revolution they hired laborers to help produce cash crops for the national and international markets.

The growth of the international market for cotton increased the profits of southern plantation owners. They were able to meet the increased demand for cotton because of the **cotton gin**, invented by Eli Whitney in 1793. This machine made it easier to separate, or gin, the seeds from cotton fiber. A person operating a cotton gin could clean 50 times as much cotton in a day as a person working by hand. The growing profitability of cotton also helped extend the slave system.

▪▪ **The market revolution opened profitable national and international markets for each region's products.**

EARLY INDUSTRIALIZATION

The market revolution was tied to a change in manufacturing. Before the market revolution, importers and skilled artisans provided most manufactured goods. But as markets grew, artisans could no longer keep up with demand. To produce enough goods, manufacturers reorganized production. They hired more workers and divided tasks to speed up production.

They also began to invest in new machinery that increased output.

This shift to machine production was part of the **Industrial Revolution**. The Industrial Revolution began in Great Britain in the mid-1700s with the invention of new spinning machines. The machines, some so simple that children could—and did—run them, revolutionized the textile industry by allowing for **mass production**—the manufacture of large quantities of goods.

Fearing foreign competition, the British tried to keep their new technology a secret. They outlawed the sale of textile machines abroad and kept skilled textile workers from leaving the country. But some workers, posing as ordinary laborers or farmers, managed to slip out with the machine plans memorized to the last detail.

One such worker was Samuel Slater. Slater came to America in 1789 with hopes of making a fortune. He quickly convinced Moses Brown, a Rhode Island manufacturer, to finance the construction of an English-style spinning mill. "If I don't make as good yarn as they do in England," Slater promised Brown, "I will have nothing for my services, but will throw the whole of what I have attempted over the bridge."

Slater's gamble paid off. In 1790 his spinning machine, tended by 9 children, turned out its first yarn. By 1801 the mill employed more than 100 women and children. Brown and Slater soon had factories all over Rhode Island and Massachusetts.

Inventors also contributed to the rise of U.S. industry. Chief among them was Eli Whitney, who employed **interchangeable parts** in the manufacture of firearms. He reasoned that the various musket parts could be machine-produced in mass

▼ In 1770 James Hargreaves, an English weaver, patented the spinning jenny, which transformed the manufacture of textiles and helped start the Industrial Revolution.

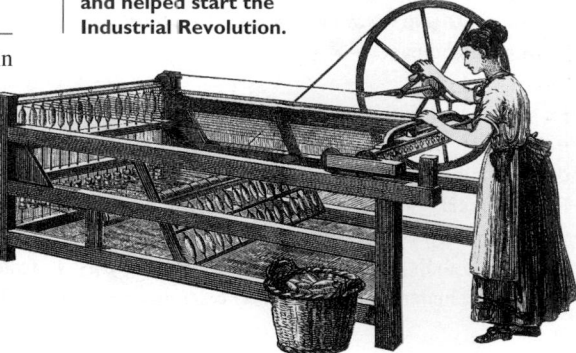

Practice

GUIDED PRACTICE

Have students work in groups to determine whether the market, Industrial, and transportation revolutions tended to unite or divide the nation. Then discuss in class the groups' findings, listing them under the headings *United* and *Divided* in preparation for writing newspaper articles.

INDEPENDENT PRACTICE

Have students write newspaper articles reporting the ways in which the market, Industrial, and transportation revolutions contributed to the unity and division of the U.S. Students may wish to include their articles in their portfolios.

Review and Assessment

REVIEW Have students imagine that they are living in the mid-1800s. Ask them to work in pairs and interview each other about why they feel optimistic or pessimistic about the nation's future. Then assign the Section 2 Review on p. 236.

ASSESS Assign the **Section 2 Daily Quiz** in *Core Resources*.

▶

quantities and used interchangeably in making individual weapons. This method would allow workers to assemble more guns in less time than it would take to make them by hand. In 1815 Seth Thomas applied the technique to the manufacture of wooden clocks. Soon workers in Thomas's factory were making some 500 clocks at a time.

New England merchant Francis Cabot Lowell introduced the next great improvement in American manufacturing. Workers in early textile mills made thread that was then delivered, or "put out," to nearby homes where women with hand looms wove it into cloth. To cut costs and increase output, Lowell had machines do everything under one roof—from spinning the thread to weaving the cloth. This system of manufacturing came to be called the **factory system**. Lowell tested the system at his mill in Waltham, Massachusetts, and his partners later applied it in Lowell, Massachusetts, which was founded after Lowell's death (see map on page 253).

■■ **The Industrial Revolution shifted manufacturing from hand labor to machines, making possible the mass production of goods.**

URBAN GROWTH

Industrialization and the market revolution led to the growth of urban areas. In the 1800s, urban areas were defined as towns or cities with 8,000 or more people. Between 1790 and 1860 America's urban population jumped from 3.3 percent to 16.1 percent of the nation's total population. This growth was seen mostly in the Northeast and the Middle West, although the southern port cities of New Orleans and Baltimore also grew tremendously during this period.

In the Northeast, Philadelphia's population tripled to more than half a million between 1820 and 1860. New York City's growth was even more spectacular. Between 1820 and 1860 the city's population increased nearly tenfold, from 123,700 to 1,080,320. New York became a major

GROWTH IN URBAN POPULATION, 1800–1860

Source: *Historical Statistics of the United States*

GROWTH OF CITIES Spurred by rapid population growth and industrialization, urban areas grew dramatically between 1800 and 1860.

? **BUILDING GRAPH SKILLS** In which part of the country was urban growth most dramatic?

commercial and manufacturing center because it had the nation's best harbor and access to the Hudson River, on which ships could travel some 150 miles inland to connect to the Erie Canal.

Equally impressive was the birth of new industrial towns, especially along the larger eastern rivers, where rapids were plentiful to run water-powered machinery. For example, the mill town of Lowell, Massachusetts, on the Merrimack River, grew from 2,500 people to 21,000 between 1825 and 1840!

The Middle West also boasted booming urban centers. Growing rapidly during this period were such towns as Buffalo, New York; Pittsburgh, Pennsylvania; Cincinnati, Ohio; and Chicago, Illinois. Initially they grew because of their location near critical points in the transportation system—major roads, rivers, canals, or railroad lines. Soon they also became important business centers, providing goods and services to Middle Western farmers and preparing farm produce for shipment to the Northeast and the South. Among the fastest growing of these cities was Chicago. Between 1833 and 1860 the city's population skyrocketed from about 150 to 109,260.

■■ **In the mid-1800s the market revolution and industrialization led to rapid urban growth, most notably in the Northeast and the Middle West.**

Graph Caption Answer
Northeast

COOPERATIVE LEARNING

Have students work in small groups to conduct research and report on the ways in which geography influenced the growth of towns and cities in the mid-1800s. Students should include Lowell, Massachusetts, as an example. Group members should divide tasks so that some members research the information, others make maps to accompany the report, and others present their findings.

[AV] **TRANSPARENCY**
Linking Geography and History Transparency and **Worksheet 11**

MAKING CONNECTIONS
Sociology
Hard times along with rapid social and economic change unleashed a wave of violent protests in the mid-1830s not seen in America since the Revolution. The most common disturbances involved laborers who were faced with low wages, poor working conditions, or unemployment.

■■ Ask students to suggest social problems today that might be related to unemployment.

RETEACH Organize students so that a roughly equal number are assigned to each subsection of the section. Direct each student to write a question about the material in his or her assigned subsection. Then use the questions to quiz the entire group.

Closure

Ask for examples from this section that support Webster's observation: "Our age is wholey [*sic*] of a different character from the past. Society is full of excitement."

Extension

CREATE Have students use models or create drawings to demonstrate how steamboats or steam trains operated.

RESEARCH Have students research and prepare a report on the Erie Canal, focusing on its location, dimensions, and purpose. Students might include a diagram or model with their report.

PRIMARY SOURCE
Description of Change: excerpted
Rationale: excerpted to focus on main idea

SECTION REVIEW ANSWERS

IDENTIFY

For significance, see the following pages:
market revolution (p. 234)
cotton gin (p. 234)
Eli Whitney (p. 234)
mass production (p. 234)
Samuel Slater (p. 234)
interchangeable parts (p. 234)
Francis Cabot Lowell (p. 235)
factory system (p. 235)

LOCATE

For locations, see the maps on pp. 233 and 253.

1. *transportation—made shipment of goods cheaper and easier; market— national markets allowed regions to specialize*
2. *manufacturing shifted from hand labor to machines, allowing mass production of goods*
3. *transportation and market revolutions, industrialization*
4. *Reports should include attempts by Second Bank of U.S. to curb state banks' lending policies, leading to foreclosures, falling prices, and bank failures.*
5. *U.S. was large with widely varying terrain, and trains could go anywhere tracks could be laid.*

THE PANIC OF 1819

By 1818, largely due to the growth of national markets, all sections of the country prospered. Increasing demand for cotton and farm products encouraged planters, farmers, and land speculators to buy up land, often at high prices. Northern manufacturers, eager for more business, built new mills and factories. To finance these enterprises, many manufacturers borrowed money from state banks, which tended to lend freely on the flimsiest security.

Late in 1818 the Second Bank of the United States attempted to bring state banks under control by ordering them to demand repayment of all loans. The Bank also required state banks to exchange their notes for gold and silver—something few banks could do. The result was the **Panic of 1819**: a chain reaction of bank failures, falling land prices, and foreclosures.

"The banking bubbles are breaking," Secretary of State John Quincy Adams wrote in his diary in May 1819. "The merchants are crumbling in ruin; the manufactures perishing, agriculture stagnating, and distress universal in every part of the country." The nation quickly sank into an economic depression that lasted several years.

■■ **The attempts of the Second Bank of the United States to curb state banks' lending policies helped trigger the Panic of 1819.**

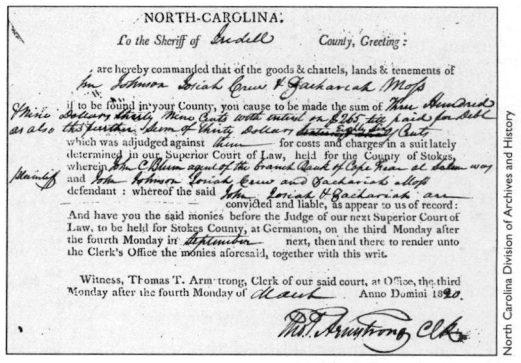

▲ Land foreclosure notices enabled the sheriff of a county to seize all property and goods to pay off debts. This notice was issued in North Carolina in 1820.

James Flint, a Scottish visitor to America, described the harsh effects of the depression on workers:

66 I think that I have seen upward of 1,500 men in quest of work within eleven months past, and many of these declared that they had no money. . . . I have seen several men turned out of boardinghouses. . . . They had no other resource left but to lodge in the woods, without any covering except their clothes. 99

For these homeless men—and many other Americans—the panic and depression ended the prosperity and optimism of the Era of Good Feelings.

■■ **SECTION 2 REVIEW**

IDENTIFY and explain the significance of the following: market revolution, cotton gin, Eli Whitney, mass production, Samuel Slater, interchangeable parts, Francis Cabot Lowell, factory system.

LOCATE and explain the importance of the following: Buffalo, New York; Waltham, Massachusetts; Lowell, Massachusetts; Pittsburgh, Pennsylvania; Chicago, Illinois.

1. **MAIN IDEA** How was the U.S. economy helped by the transportation and market revolutions?

2. **MAIN IDEA** What effect did the Industrial Revolution have on the way goods were manufactured?

3. **IDENTIFYING CAUSE AND EFFECT** What factors contributed to the boom in urban growth during the mid-1800s?

4. **WRITING TO INFORM** Imagine that you are one of President Monroe's economic advisers. Write a short report for the president outlining the causes of the Panic of 1819.

5. **LINKING HISTORY AND GEOGRAPHY** Given the geography of the United States, why were railroads a particularly effective form of transportation in the mid-1800s?

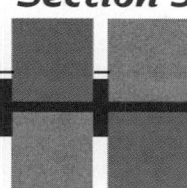

FOCUS OBJECTIVES

■ Recognize the role that the Missouri Compromise played in the dispute over slavery.

■ Examine why the election of 1824 gave rise to charges of a "corrupt bargain."

■ Explain why Jackson favored the spoils system and rotation in office.

Section 3

THE RISE OF JACKSONIAN DEMOCRACY

FOCUS
■ **What role did the Missouri Compromise play in the dispute over slavery?**
■ **Why did the election of 1824 give rise to charges of a "corrupt bargain"?**
■ **Why did Jackson favor the spoils system and rotation in office?**

E conomic developments affected national politics. The transportation revolution encouraged westward expansion, which created political conflicts over governing the new western territories. As voting laws changed, politicians had to appeal to a wider range of economic interests. After the Panic of 1819 and the depression, voters looked for politicians who could handle economic problems.

Fabric made to celebrate Jackson's inauguration in 1829

THE MISSOURI COMPROMISE

The United States faced more than economic problems in 1819. The nation was also plagued by political conflict caused by westward expansion. In that year the Missouri Territory, which counted among its population some 10,000 enslaved African Americans, applied for statehood. Because the nation was equally divided between slave states and free states, Missouri's admission as a slave state would tip the congressional balance in favor of the slaveholding South.

Congressman James Tallmadge of New York tried to amend the Missouri statehood bill to include the gradual elimination of slavery in Missouri. He argued that Congress had already exercised its power to ban slavery in the territories when it passed the Northwest Ordinance in 1787. Slaveholders, seeing this new proposal as part of a larger attempt to end slavery everywhere, reacted with alarm and anger. A Georgia congressman pointed a shaking finger at Tallmadge and cried:

"You have kindled a fire which all the waters of the ocean cannot put out, which seas of blood can only extinguish."

Free state	Slave state
Free territory	Slave territory

Missouri Compromise

EXTENSION OF SLAVERY The Missouri Compromise of 1820 permitted slavery in Missouri but outlawed it in other areas north of the Missouri Compromise Line.

? **REGIONS** How many free states were there following the compromise? How many slave states?

Map Caption Answer
12 free, 12 slave

MOTIVATING: STUDENT EXPERIENCES

Discuss recent presidential elections and ask what issues were important. Ask students if the candidates' images played a part in the campaign. Tell students that this section deals with candidates, images, and campaign issues of the early 1800s.

HISTORICAL SIDELIGHTS
The Missouri Compromise

Although the Missouri Compromise called for the admission of both Missouri and Maine, only Maine immediately became a state. Missouri's admission was delayed 17 months, until it had an acceptable state constitution. At first, a provision prohibited free blacks from entering Missouri. Not until the Missouri legislature agreed to respect the rights of all citizens did Missouri become the 24th state, in August 1821.

PRIMARY SOURCE
Description of Change: excerpted and bracketed
Rationale: excerpted to focus on main idea; bracketed to clarify meaning

MAKING CONNECTIONS
Geography

Passage of the Missouri Compromise greatly restricted the options of slaveholders who wanted to live on the frontier. Only the Arkansas Territory remained open to slavery. Consequently, southerners became increasingly interested in moving beyond the borders of the Louisiana Purchase to settle in the Mexican territory called Texas.

Teaching the Section

THE MISSOURI COMPROMISE

Organize the class into groups of free-state and slave-state representatives. Have volunteers from each group debate whether Missouri should be admitted to the U.S. as a free state or a slave state. Then discuss whether the Missouri Compromise resolved the issue.

THE ELECTION OF 1824

Point out that regional loyalties and interests played a significant role in the 1824 election. Ask volunteers to assume the roles of northern merchants, southern planters, and westerners. Have them explain how they voted and why, including their view of the charge that the election was won through a "corrupt bargain."

To end the bitter debate, Henry Clay of Kentucky led Congress in working out the **Missouri Compromise** in 1820. The agreement admitted Missouri as a slave state and Maine as a free state, thus maintaining the balance in Congress. Moreover, slavery was banned in the rest of the Louisiana Purchase north of latitude 36°30′—Missouri's southern boundary.

The Missouri Compromise calmed the sectional crisis, but many Americans still worried that the slavery issue would reemerge. Former president Thomas Jefferson later wrote:

> 66 This momentous question, like a fire-bell in the night, awakened and filled me with terror. I considered it at once as the [death] knell of the Union. It is hushed, indeed, for the moment. But . . . every new irritation will mark it deeper and deeper. 99

■■ **The Missouri Compromise resolved the crisis over Missouri statehood but left the larger issue of slavery unresolved.**

---

*T*HE ELECTION OF 1824

Westward expansion also had an effect on the election of 1824. By the 1820s voting laws were becoming more democratic, particularly in the

▲ Two campaign medallions from the 1824 election are shown here. One bears the likeness of Andrew Jackson, the other of John Quincy Adams.

Museum of American Political Life, University of Hartford.

frontier states, where most white adult males could vote. This democratization of voting rights was accompanied by growing opposition to the nomination of presidential candidates by congressional caucus. Thus, in the 1824 election, state nominating conventions played a major role in deciding the list of candidates. The result was a crowded field of regional favorites.

Five candidates—all Republicans—ended up vying for the presidency: William Crawford of Georgia, John C. Calhoun of South Carolina, John Quincy Adams of Massachusetts, Andrew Jackson of Tennessee, and Henry Clay of Kentucky. Crawford, who portrayed himself as the "southern candidate," was the early favorite. But serious

PRESIDENTIAL LIVES
JOHN QUINCY ADAMS
1767–1848

in office 1825–1829

John Quincy Adams resembled his father, John Adams, in his brilliance and self-discipline. He also inherited his father's stern and reserved personality. One observer noted that Adams seemed "hard as a piece of granite and cold as a lump of ice." Adams's coldness contributed to his frustrating and largely unsuccessful presidency.

Adams's major achievements occurred outside

his White House years. He was a Harvard graduate, successful lawyer, minister to the Netherlands, U.S. senator, minister to Russia, and secretary of state to President Monroe—all before becoming president. After his presidency, Adams returned to public service. In 1830 Massachusetts voters elected him to the House of Representatives, where he criticized the expansion of slavery.

John Quincy Adams

THE SPOILS SYSTEM

Ask students to speculate about the relationship between Jackson's status as a westerner and "man of the people" and his actions in replacing government officials with his supporters. Ask students if they agree with Jackson's belief that government workers who stay in office too long forget they are servants of the people.

■■ Tell students to imagine that they are head of the school's student government. Poll the class to see how many would choose their friends as assistants and how many would select the best-qualified students, regardless of personal feelings. Ask students to explain their positions.

▶

illness marred his candidacy. Calhoun, although a favorite in the Lower South, failed to build a nationwide following. He eventually withdrew to become the vice-presidential partner of both Adams and Jackson. Adams, an economic nationalist with antislavery views, had appeal primarily in the Northeast. Jackson, the popular military hero, represented the southern frontier. Clay, the architect of the Missouri Compromise and the American System, drew his support primarily from the Middle West.

Andrew Jackson received the most popular votes, but no candidate won a majority of the electoral votes. In such circumstances the Twelfth Amendment directs the House of Representatives to choose a president from the top three candidates. Having finished fourth, Clay was out of the running. But he was in a position to help determine the winner by recommending that his supporters back a particular candidate. Clay, who considered Jackson unqualified for the presidency, threw his support behind Adams. Adams became president. When Adams then named Clay his secretary of state, Jackson and his followers angrily accused the two men of making a "corrupt bargain." Adams and Clay denied any wrongdoing, but suspicions persisted.

■■ **When the House was forced to decide the outcome of the 1824 election, Clay threw his support behind Adams. When Adams won, Jackson charged that Adams and Clay had made a "corrupt bargain."**

President Adams supported a wide range of federal government projects, from canals and roads to a national university and a standardized system of weights and measures. Yet, owing largely to his desire to avoid "playing politics" and his unwillingness to compromise with Congress, he was unable to accomplish much during his term.

𝒯HE ELECTION OF 1828

Jackson, a sharp critic throughout Adams's presidency, resigned from the Senate in 1825 to campaign for the 1828 election. Opponents of the Adams administration rallied around the tall war hero from Tennessee.

AMERICAN POLITICS

THROUGH OTHERS' EYES

Colonel John Baillie, a British traveler to the United States in the 1820s, was fascinated by the widespread public interest in the presidential election of 1828. In Great Britain the prime minister was (and still is) elected by members of Parliament, not by ordinary voters. Baillie recorded in his journal his amazement at the American political scene:

❝𝓘 remark [that] every American of whatever condition in life is a Politician. . . . We hear nothing but Jackson and Adams. . . . These Candidates are freely talked over and their merits discussed by every man in the country. The subject is now so worn out that I am quite tired of their names. . . . A common address in a stage coach, which has been often put to me, is "I says Mister, are you for Jackson or Adams?" My answer is generally "for which you like sir."❞

Who was this man so eager to be president? Jackson was born in 1767 in a log cabin on the South Carolina frontier to Scotch-Irish immigrants. Orphaned at 14, he had little formal schooling and was a poor speller. Making his limitation a virtue, he later claimed to have no respect for anyone who knew only one way to spell a word!

After Jackson moved to the Tennessee frontier, one resident described him as a "roaring, rollicking, . . . horse-racing, card-playing, mischievous fellow." He became a successful lawyer, land speculator, and planter. In 1788 Jackson met Rachel Donelson Robards, who was then separated from her husband. Believing Rachel's divorce had been granted, the two were

BIO
GRAPHY

Andrew Jackson

THROUGH OTHERS' EYES

Point out to students that no specific British document specifies that a prime minister elected by Parliament should head the British government. This practice has come about as a result of tradition.

PRIMARY SOURCE

Description of Change: excerpted and bracketed
Rationale: excerpted to focus on main idea; bracketed to clarify meaning

VOICES IN HISTORY

In reporting their impressions of Jacksonian America, European visitors tended to focus on its democratic and egalitarian qualities. As men and women from aristocratic cultures, they were startled to encounter a society in which one's ancestry appeared to count for little or nothing. Some, like France's Alexis de Tocqueville, whose *Democracy in America* is one of the world's greatest studies of a civilization, were favorably impressed. But others, such as France's Michel Chevalier, feared "the physical force and the political power" of the masses.

Practice

GUIDED PRACTICE

Have students work in groups to create brief "newscasts" that summarize the elections of 1824 and 1828. Direct each group to prepare for its newscast presentation by reviewing for both elections these topics: campaigns and election results. Then assign half of each group the role of scriptwriters and the other half the role of news anchors (readers). Have each group present its newscast.

INDEPENDENT PRACTICE

Invite students to write letters as supporters of either Adams or Jackson, reacting to news coverage of the 1824 or 1828 election. Students may wish to include their letters in their portfolios.

Review and Assessment

REVIEW Have students work in groups and imagine that they are to write a biography of either Clay, Adams, or Jackson. Groups should choose one, justify their choice, and list the topics their biographies would cover. Have each group review its work for the class. Then assign the Section 3 Review on p. 241.

ASSESS Assign the **Section 3 Daily Quiz** in *Core Resources*.

HISTORICAL SIDELIGHTS

The People's Ticket

In some states there was support for an Adams-Jackson ticket. Supporters of what was called the "People's Ticket" created this slogan: "John Quincy Adams/Who can write/And Andrew Jackson/Who can fight."

COOPERATIVE LEARNING

Have small groups create a list of necessary and desirable qualifications for the presidency and evaluate Adams and Jackson accordingly. Direct groups to choose the candidate they would have supported in 1828, then plan a political campaign for him, highlighting his qualifications. Group members should divide tasks, such as writing speeches, designing posters, and developing platforms.

Then and Now

Have students compare the strategies of a recent presidential election campaign with that of the election of 1828. Ask students if they think attacks on a candidate's character are a legitimate campaign strategy.

married in 1791. Her divorce, however, was not finalized until two years later, at which time the Jacksons—amid much gossip—quickly renewed their vows.

Jackson was the victor at the Battle of New Orleans in the War of 1812 and a ruthless Indian-fighter in campaigns against the Creeks and Seminoles. Soldiers called him "Old Hickory" because he seemed as tough as the strong hardwood. He entered national politics as congressman and then senator from Tennessee. Although a rich lawyer and planter, Jackson

◄ This portrait of Rachel Jackson was painted by Louisa Catherine Strobel. After his wife's death, Jackson wore this miniature wherever he went.

The Hermitage: Home of Andrew Jackson

stressed his military skills and frontier origins to portray himself as a "man of the people."

Jackson's image as a "common man" won the support of farmers, laborers, and frontier settlers. His supporters, having no official name at first, eventually became known as the Democratic party (the origin of today's party of the same name).

Then and Now · CAMPAIGNING

In many ways the presidential race of 1828 was the first modern election campaign. Unlike earlier candidates who relied mainly on party supporters to campaign for them, Andrew Jackson and John Quincy Adams actively pursued votes themselves. They used mass-produced trinkets such as buttons, metal tokens, bandannas, cups, and plates to sway public opinion. Jackson in particular appealed directly to the common voter for support and began campaigning three years before the election.

Today presidential candidates still focus on reaching out to the mass public. They blanket the country with bumper stickers, buttons, and posters. Today's officeseekers also appeal directly to voters, occasionally by touring the country in buses and trains, but more often by airing television and radio commercials. And most candidates start running for office years before the election, just as Jackson did.

Jackson's 1828 campaign set another modern precedent by employing county and state campaign committees. These committees held parades, barbecues, and rallies to attract voters. Jackson also established a campaign organization of friends and advisers in Nashville to help him plot campaign strategies. His Washington-based correspondence committee was a forerunner of today's Democratic and Republican national committees. An organizational structure that was unusual in 1828 has become a political necessity in modern presidential races.

The 1828 race for president also signaled a profound change in the tone of presidential

▲ Bill Clinton and George Bush are shown debating in Missouri during the 1992 presidential campaign.

campaigns. The race has been called "spectacularly dirty," full of character assassinations and accusations. Indeed, Jackson's and Adams's campaigns focused as much on the candidates' personal qualities as on the issues. The same charge has been leveled against recent presidential campaigns. Although many years have passed since the 1828 election, Jackson and Adams might feel right at home in a modern presidential campaign.

RETEACH Have students work in groups, assigning different pairs the task of turning Section Review questions into statements by supplying answers. Ask pairs to share their work with the group.

Closure

Discuss with students how the name of the new political party led by Jackson (Democrats) reflected the changes taking place in the nation. Ask students how the issues and events discussed in Section 3 show the growing importance of the Middle West in American politics and society.

Extension

CREATE Have small groups research and then re-create hickory sticks and other 1828 campaign paraphernalia to show one reason the election is regarded as the first modern election.

RESEARCH Ask students to present reports on Remini's *The Revolutionary Age of Andrew Jackson* or the more difficult *Age of Jackson* by Schlesinger.

Like many political campaigns today, the 1828 race focused more on the candidates' personalities than on the issues. Each side used personal attacks to win votes. Adams's purchase of a chess set and billiard table for the White House raised charges that he squandered money on "gambling devices." Supporters of Adams labeled Jackson an adulterer because of the circumstances of his marriage to Rachel Robards.

In the end Jackson swept the popular and electoral vote. "The virtuous portion of the people have well sustained me," Jackson rejoiced. "I am filled with gratitude."

Once in office, Jackson showed his appreciation by giving some of his supporters government jobs. This practice became known as the **spoils system**, from the expression "to the victor belong the spoils." Jackson also took steps to reform government bureaucracy by replacing all public servants he judged "unfaithful or incompetent." He believed that government workers who stayed in office too long often forgot that they were servants of the people. Thus he favored **rotation in office**—the periodic replacement of officeholders. Yet Jackson's changes fell far short of complete rotation. During his presidency he replaced only about one tenth to one third of the bureaucracy.

■■ **Jackson backed the spoils system and rotation in office to reward his supporters and to reform government.**

COMMENTARY

Jacksonian Democracy

Jackson's political success reflected changes in American society caused by the market revolution. The old social order, led by the aristocracy, gradually gave way to a society based more on economic success than on birth. Jackson's image as a "self-made" man embodied this new sense of economic opportunity. He also held out this appealing promise for other Americans. "I believe man can be elevated," he said in a speech, "capable of governing himself."

From today's perspective, changes in the Jackson era may seem small. Full political rights, including the right to vote, were extended only to white men. Most African Americans lived under a brutal slave system; and women, American Indians, and most free blacks were denied the vote.

Yet the changes of the early 1800s were significant. Voting rolls swelled as states dropped property requirements for voting and holding office. By 1828, voters, instead of state legislatures, chose presidential electors and most public officials in almost every state. Expanding voting rights paved the way for Jackson's reelection in 1832 and continued even after he left office. In 1836, for example, around 1.5 million people voted. Just four years later, continuing the trend toward participation that Jackson had inaugurated, roughly 2.4 million citizens cast their ballots.

SECTION REVIEW ANSWERS

IDENTIFY
For significance, see the following pages:
Missouri Compromise (p. 238)
John Quincy Adams (p. 238)
Andrew Jackson (p. 238)
spoils system (p. 241)
rotation in office (p. 241)

LOCATE
For location, see the map on p. 237.

1. *because Missouri permitted slavery; through the Missouri Compromise*
2. *Clay threw support behind Adams; House selected Adams; Adams made Clay secretary of state.*
3. *Voters rather than state legislatures selected electors; Jackson's support came from laborers, farmers, and frontier settlers.*
4. *Statements should persuasively defend Jackson's support of the spoils system and rotation in office as ways to reward supporters and to reform government.*
5. *Expansion was limited primarily to adult white males; Native Americans, women, and most African Americans still could not vote.*

SECTION 3 REVIEW

IDENTIFY and explain the significance of the following: Missouri Compromise, John Quincy Adams, Andrew Jackson, spoils system, rotation in office.

LOCATE and explain the importance of the following: Missouri.

1. **MAIN IDEA** Why did Missouri's petition for statehood lead to a battle in Congress? How was the conflict resolved?

2. **MAIN IDEA** Why did Andrew Jackson charge that John Quincy Adams and Henry Clay had made a "corrupt bargain" in the election of 1824?

3. **IDENTIFYING CAUSE AND EFFECT** How did the election of 1828 signal a broadening of democratic rights?

4. **WRITING TO PERSUADE** Imagine that you are Andrew Jackson's press secretary. Write a defense of the president's support of the spoils system and rotation in office.

5. **EVALUATING** Some historians argue that Jacksonian democracy was a limited expansion of democracy at best. What evidence might have led the historians to adopt this view?

PREVIEW WORKSHOP

Following is a list of the significant people, places, and terms in this section. You may wish to use this list as a section preview.

People
■ Sequoya
■ William Henry Harrison

Places
■ Indian Territory

Terms
■ Indian Removal Act
■ Second Seminole War
■ *Worcester* v. *Georgia*
■ Trail of Tears
■ doctrine of nullification

■ pet banks
■ Specie Circular

FOCUS OBJECTIVES

■ Examine why the U.S. government forced eastern Indians to move westward, and describe how Native Americans resisted removal.

■ Explain what sparked the nullification crisis.

■ Analyze the factors that contributed to the economic crisis of the late 1830s.

■ Determine how the Whigs came to power in 1840.

Section 4

JACKSON'S POLICIES DEFINE AN ERA

F O C U S
■ **Why did the U.S. government force eastern Indians to move westward? How did Native Americans resist removal?**
■ **What sparked the nullification crisis?**
■ **What factors contributed to the economic crisis of the late 1830s?**
■ **How did the Whigs come to power in 1840?**

*A*ndrew Jackson put his stamp on a decade, and his policies shaped the nation for years to come. He pushed for the removal of Native Americans from the East and fought to preserve the Union against sectional tensions. Jackson remained popular with the American people, but by the late 1830s severe economic problems had eroded his party's strength. In 1840 an opposition party, the Whigs, emerged to vie with Jacksonian Democrats for political power.

Statue of mourning Cherokee

A QUESTION OF LAND

Thomas Jefferson had hoped that eastern Indians would become farmers and blend into American society. But European Americans' hunger for land and American Indian support for the British during the War of 1812 changed government attitudes. By 1824 many government officials were calling for the removal of all American Indians to lands beyond the United States' borders.

This change in attitudes had a profound effect on many Native American groups, particularly the Creeks, Chickasaws, Choctaws, Cherokees, and Seminoles in the Southeast. Believing that their best hope for survival lay in adapting to white culture, many had given up hunting and had become farmers. The Cherokees, for example, had shifted to farming in the late 1700s. Over the next several decades, they built towns with thriving agricultural economies. They wrote a constitution modeled on that of the United States, created a judicial system, supported schools, and formed a militia.

BIO GRAPHY

The Cherokees were greatly assisted in their efforts by the work of one man—Sequoya (si-KWOY-uh), or Sikwayi. Sequoya was born in Tennessee sometime between 1760 and 1770 to a Cherokee woman. He variously used the names George Guess and George Gist, which has led some historians to suggest he was the son of Nathaniel Gist, an English explorer and friend of George Washington. Sequoya was a silversmith, blacksmith, and painter. In 1813 he fought against the Creeks as a member of a Cherokee regiment in the U.S. Army.

Although Sequoya neither spoke nor read English, he recognized the value of a written language. He saw how literacy benefited whites by enabling them to spread ideas, keep records, and communicate over long distances. He hoped that literacy

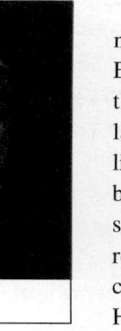

Sequoya
National Portrait Gallery

MOTIVATING:
LINK TO TODAY

Discuss with students some of the issues facing American Indians today (*land and burial ground claims, water rights, religious freedom*). Point out that some of these issues have long histories and that this section discusses Jackson's Indian policy and other policies that characterized this period.

Teaching the Section

INDIAN POLICY IN THE 1830s

Organize the class into groups and tell each group that their task is to advise President Jackson on the government's Indian policy. The policy alternatives each group is to consider are: 1) using the military to seize Native American land; 2) assimilating Native Americans into European American society; 3) protecting Native American land from white encroachment; 4) removing Native Americans to the West. Tell the groups to weigh each policy's practicality and its potential effect on European American settlers, Native Americans, and public opinion. Have a spokesperson from each group present its recommendation to the president. ▶

▶ The Cherokee primer shown here uses symbols based on the writing system created by Sequoya.

would do the same for the Cherokees. For 12 years he worked to create a writing system for the Cherokee language—a process he described as being like catching and taming a wild horse.

The system Sequoya developed contained 86 symbols based on the syllables of spoken Cherokee. Once the symbols were memorized, a person could read or write anything in Cherokee. By 1828 the Cherokees were publishing their own newspaper, the *Cherokee Phoenix*.

JACKSON'S INDIAN POLICY

American Indians' efforts to gain European Americans' acceptance made little difference. Indians in the Southeast occupied millions of acres of fertile land suitable for growing cotton. European American farmers and land speculators pressured the government to open that land to white settlement and soon found a friend in Andrew Jackson. He viewed the continued presence of Indians in the East as a barrier to "the waves of population and civilization . . . rolling westward."

Jackson cloaked his calls for removal in humanitarian terms. He claimed that Native Americans would, for their own protection, be moved westward, where "their white brothers will not trouble them." In 1830 Congress passed the **Indian Removal Act**, providing for the relocation—by force, if necessary—of Indian nations living east of the Mississippi to Indian Territory in present-day Oklahoma. Indian Territory was part of the larger Indian Country the government had set aside for relocated tribes. Jackson promised eastern Indians the land for "as long as grass grows and water runs. . . . *It will be yours forever.*"

■■ **The U.S. government forced eastern Indians to move in order to open their lands to white settlement.**

Native American resistance. By the end of the decade, most Native Americans had been driven from the Southeast. Few, however, went willingly. They had little reason to believe Jackson's promise of a permanent homeland. Georgia and other southern states had already disregarded federal treaties and limited Indian rights within state boundaries. Georgia was even seizing Indian land and selling it to white settlers.

Fearing further betrayal, many Indians opposed removal. Some wrote appeals to Congress: "Our cause is your own," began one such letter. "It is the cause of liberty and of justice. It is based upon your own principles." Osceola, a Seminole leader, was more defiant:

❝ My Brothers! . . . the white man says I shall go, and he will send people to make me go; but I have a rifle, and I have some powder and some lead. I say, we must not leave our homes and lands. If any of our people want to go west we won't let them; and I tell them they are our enemies, and we will treat them so, for the great spirit will protect us. ❞

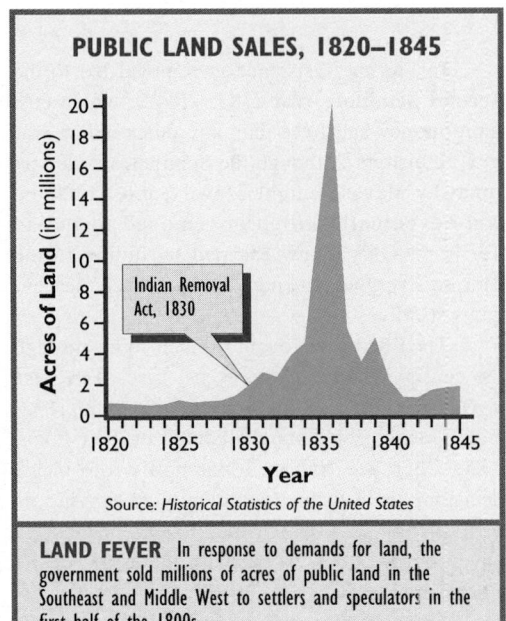

PUBLIC LAND SALES, 1820–1845

Indian Removal Act, 1830

Acres of Land (in millions)

Year

Source: *Historical Statistics of the United States*

LAND FEVER In response to demands for land, the government sold millions of acres of public land in the Southeast and Middle West to settlers and speculators in the first half of the 1800s.

? IDENTIFYING CAUSE AND EFFECT What effect do you think the Indian Removal Act of 1830 had on public land sales? Why?

BIO GRAPHY **PERSONALITIES IN HISTORY**

During his lifetime, Sequoya received a great deal of praise for developing the Cherokee writing system. (Such a system is called a syllabary—a set of characters, each of which represents a syllable.) In 1828, the people of the Cherokee Nation named Sequoya as their political envoy to Washington, and they later granted him a lifetime pension as well. Because of the beneficial results that his writing system had for the Cherokees, the U.S. government authorized a gift of $500 to Sequoya.

PRIMARY SOURCE

Description of Change: excerpted
Rationale: excerpted to focus on main idea

AV **TRANSPARENCY**

Everyday Life in America Transparency and **Worksheet 7**

Graph Caption Answer
Indian Removal Act of 1830 increased land sales by opening up fertile lands that formerly belonged to Native Americans.

Teaching the Section

NATIVE AMERICAN RESISTANCE

Ask students to cite the various ways in which Native Americans resisted removal *(appealing to Congress, making war, bringing their case to court)*. Then ask students to imagine themselves as Native Americans of the 1830s, to choose one of these courses of action, and to write a letter to President Jackson, explaining and defending their resistance.

THE TRAIL OF TEARS

Have students work in small groups, using the map in the text as the basis for creating an illustrated map of the Trail of Tears. Ask students to include topography, write captions, depict the people, and so on.

CULTURAL PATTERNS

Seminole resistance to removal was encouraged by the African Americans who lived among them. Believing the Seminoles to be a branch of the Creek nation, the U.S. government long had forced the Creeks to compensate planters for escaped slaves who sought refuge with the Seminoles. Because the government planned for the Seminoles and Creeks to live together in Indian Territory, the African Americans feared that the Creeks would seize them. Many former slaves, who had influence with Seminole leaders, were understandably reluctant to leave Florida.

PRIMARY SOURCES

Description of Change: excerpted
Rationale: excerpted to focus on main idea

AV TRANSPARENCY
Linking Geography and History Transparency and **Worksheet 12**

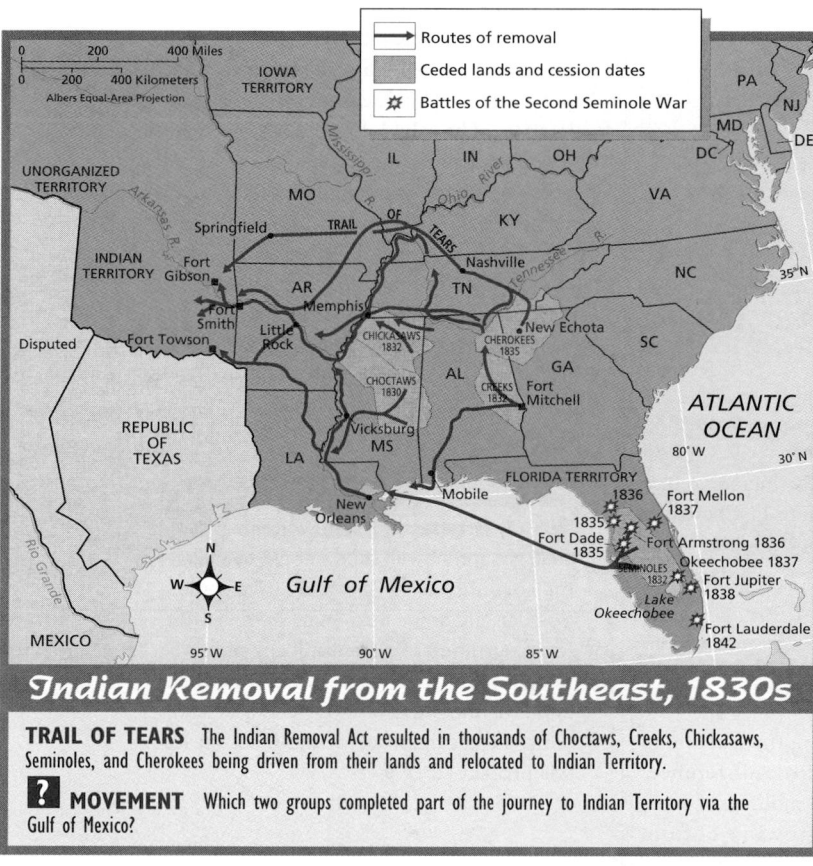

Indian Removal from the Southeast, 1830s

TRAIL OF TEARS The Indian Removal Act resulted in thousands of Choctaws, Creeks, Chickasaws, Seminoles, and Cherokees being driven from their lands and relocated to Indian Territory.

? MOVEMENT Which two groups completed part of the journey to Indian Territory via the Gulf of Mexico?

"now let him enforce it." The Cherokees, without federal protection, were unable to hold out. In 1835 they were forced to sign a treaty granting all their land to the United States in return for money and land in Indian Territory. They were ordered to move within three years.

■■ **Many Native Americans resisted removal: the Seminoles went to war; the Cherokees appealed to the U.S. Supreme Court.**

The Trail of Tears. By the 1838 deadline only a few of the some 18,000 Cherokees had moved west. Federal troops began forcing the remaining Cherokees to make the journey to Indian Territory. One U.S. soldier who witnessed the removal later recalled:

In Florida, resistance to removal led to the **Second Seminole War** (1835–1842), which cost more money and lives than any other Indian war in U.S. history. Although the Seminoles, aided by runaway slaves, fought bravely, most of them were eventually killed or removed to Indian Territory. Only a few escaped by hiding in the Florida Everglades, where some of their descendants still live.

The Cherokees fought for their rights through the courts. When the Cherokees' case, **Worcester v. Georgia**, reached the Supreme Court in 1832, Chief Justice John Marshall ruled in their favor. "The Cherokee Nation," Marshall wrote in his decision, "is a distinct community, occupying its own territory . . . which the citizens of Georgia have no right to enter, but with the assent of the Cherokees themselves."

The victory was short-lived. Georgia—with Jackson's blessing—ignored the Court's ruling and kept on seizing Cherokee land. "John Marshall has made his decision," Jackson was said to declare,

66 I saw the helpless Cherokees arrested and dragged from their homes, and driven by bayonet into the stockades. And in the chill of a drizzling rain on an October morning I saw them loaded like cattle or sheep into wagons and started toward the west. 99

An estimated 4,000 Cherokees died on the 800-mile journey that came to be known as the **Trail of Tears**. "Many fell by the wayside, too faint with hunger or too weak to keep up with the rest," remembered one of the survivors.

66 A crude bed was quickly prepared for these sick and weary people. Only a bowl of water was left within their reach, thus they were left to suffer and die alone. The little children piteously cried day after day. . . . They were once happy children. 99

Valjean Hessing, *Choctaw Removal*, (1966), 8" x 20-5/8". Philbrook Museum of Art, Tulsa

▲ In the early 1830s, under the provisions of the Indian Removal Act, the Choctaws were removed from Mississippi to Indian Territory. About one fourth of some 14,000 Choctaws died along the way. This painting of the journey, entitled *Choctaw Removal* (1966), was painted by Choctaw artist Valjean Hessing.

The Choctaws, Chickasaws, and Creeks also faced removal in the period from 1820 to 1840. During the Chickasaw removal, for example, the death rate was as high as that of the Cherokees during the Trail of Tears. Those who survived were left to rebuild their lives in the strange surroundings of Indian Territory.

THE NULLIFICATION CRISIS

Indian removal remains one of the Jacksonian era's most controversial legacies. Yet for many Americans at the time, the issue of states' rights seemed of more immediate concern. This issue, having troubled the Republic since its founding, was revived in the 1820s in debates over tariffs.

The doctrine of nullification. To protect U.S. manufacturers, Congress passed in 1828 a new tariff that doubled the rates set in 1816 for some items. Outraged southern planters charged Congress with promoting the interests of the industrial North at the expense of southern agriculture. The tariff would make British goods, on which southerners relied heavily, more expensive. Worse yet, Great Britain might fight back by buying less southern cotton. Thomas Cooper, president of South Carolina College in Columbia, warned that the South would soon have "to calculate the value of the Union, and ask of what use to us is this most unequal alliance."

By 1828 Vice President John C. Calhoun had abandoned his earlier nationalist views. He no longer believed that the national government represented the best interests of his native region, the South. Responding to this tariff, Calhoun wrote an anonymous essay outlining the South's position. The essay argued that the states, as creators of the federal union, had the right to nullify, or refuse to obey, any act of Congress they considered unconstitutional. This view became known as the **doctrine of nullification**.

South Carolina threatens secession. The tariff debate raged for the next two years. In 1830 Senator Robert Hayne of South Carolina, speaking for southern planters, argued for states' rights: "The very life of our system is the independence of the States." He called the 1828 tariff "unauthorized taxation" and warned that the South would resist.

Senator Daniel Webster of Massachusetts, widely recognized as an outstanding orator, rose to defend what he interpreted as an attack against the Northeast. Webster countered that only the Supreme Court had the power to decide whether acts of Congress were unconstitutional. In a moving speech to the Senate, Webster warned that if each state could decide which federal laws to obey, the result would be violence and needless bloodshed. Acceptance of the doctrine would shatter into "broken and dishonored fragments" the "once glorious Union." Webster closed his address with this memorable appeal: "Liberty and Union, now and forever, one and inseparable!"

■■ **Passage of a new tariff in 1828 sparked a bitter states' rights debate in Congress.**

Teaching the Section

THE ECONOMIC CRISIS OF THE LATE 1830s

Have students create political cartoons illustrating the events that contributed to the economic crisis in the 1830s. Ask students to explain their completed cartoons, and display them in the classroom. Students may wish to include their cartoons in their portfolios.

HISTORICAL SIDELIGHTS

Calhoun vs. Jackson

Relations between Jackson and Calhoun steadily declined. Calhoun, hoping to be the next president, tried to force cabinet members who did not support him to resign. Then Jackson learned that Calhoun had favored his censure during Jackson's invasion of Florida in 1819. Calhoun's doctrine of nullification was the last straw. To Jackson, it showed Calhoun was "a villain," one ready to sacrifice ideals to personal ambition.

 GLOBAL CONNECTIONS

In July 1831 the Second Bank of the U.S. had more than 4,000 stockholders. Among them were nearly 500 foreigners, some of whom were members of the British nobility. In his veto message Jackson claimed that foreigners, most of them British, held more than $8 million of the $28 million of Bank stock.

▪▪ Ask students if they have read about foreign investments in U.S. companies today. Ask their opinions about the public reaction to these investments.

Both sides eagerly awaited some indication of the president's stand on the issue. The answer was not long in coming. At a formal Washington dinner in April 1830, President Jackson rose from his chair and fixed his eyes on Vice President Calhoun. Then holding his glass in the air, he proposed a toast: "Our Union: it must be preserved!" After a moment of silence, Calhoun stood up. His hand trembling, he defiantly challenged: "The Union—next to our liberty, the most dear! May we always remember that it can only be preserved by respecting the rights of the states."

PRESIDENTIAL LIVES

ANDREW JACKSON
1767–1845

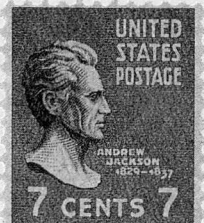

in office 1829–1837

As Andrew Jackson's presidency came to an end, well-wishers streamed into Washington, D.C., to say good-bye. "Old Hickory" received thousands of letters and many gifts as well: hats, pipes, canes, a wagon made of hickory, even a 1,400-pound cheese. On his last morning in office, Jackson rode with Martin Van Buren, the president-elect, to the inauguration. The crowds along the road did not cheer for Van Buren but removed their hats in respectful silence for Jackson instead. "For once," an observer noted, "the rising sun was eclipsed by the setting sun."

Jackson returned to the Hermitage, his plantation in Tennessee, where he remained an active, influential force in politics. Eager politicians sought his advice. Though he turned away most politicians, Jackson publicly supported his favorite candidates and causes.

Andrew Jackson

In 1832 Henry Clay attempted a compromise by pushing a slight tariff reduction through Congress. But it was too small a reduction to satisfy South Carolina. In November that state declared the 1828 and 1832 tariffs null and void. South Carolina threatened to secede if the federal government tried to collect tariffs within the state.

A furious Jackson privately warned that "if one drop of blood be shed there in defiance of the laws of the United States, I will hang the first man of them I can get my hands on to the first tree I can find." To calm tensions in South Carolina, Henry Clay convinced Congress to pass a compromise tariff in 1833 that lowered rates over a 10-year period.

At Calhoun's urging, South Carolina—with no support from other southern states—accepted the new tariff. The immediate crisis subsided, but sectional tensions continued to grow.

OPPOSING THE BANK

For all the passion around the issue of states' rights in the 1830s, the Second Bank of the United States may have caused even more excitement. Making the banking issue a personal crusade, Jackson attacked the Bank as a dangerous monopoly that benefited rich investors—many of whom were British—at the expense of the poor, the honest, and the industrious. Such a privileged group should not be allowed to control the nation's money, he

▲ This political cartoon satirizes the collapse of the Second Bank of the United States.

PANIC OF 1837

Develop a flowchart on the chalkboard, showing events leading to and resulting from the Panic of 1837. Write the events provided by students on the flowchart and discuss the relationships among the events.

■■ Have students describe how periods of economic recession may affect people their own age.

THE WHIGS COME TO POWER

Have students work in small groups to create posters for Harrison and the Whig party in the 1840 election. Encourage students to cover the campaign's issues and to include images and slogans used by the Whigs. After groups present their posters, discuss the effectiveness of the Whig campaign.

▶

---

insisted. Americans who disliked the Bank's strict lending policies or simply feared concentrated power tended to agree.

The Bank became a campaign issue when Jackson sought reelection in 1832. Opposing Jackson was Henry Clay, nominee of the National Republicans (the party of John Quincy Adams). Clay, who supported the Bank, decided to force an election-year showdown over it. Though its charter was not due to expire until 1836, in the summer of 1832 Clay pushed a bill through Congress to recharter the Bank.

Jackson vetoed the measure, sparking a great controversy, just as Clay had hoped. Clay vigorously attacked the veto during the campaign. But voters sided with Jackson. He and his running mate, Martin Van Buren of New York, won by a large margin. Jackson then moved to shut down the Bank. The fight had become bitterly personal. "The Bank is trying to kill me, but I will kill it," he grimly vowed.

Jackson stopped depositing federal funds in the national bank. New deposits went to selected state banks chosen for their officers' loyalty to the Democratic party—**pet banks**, as Jackson's enemies called them.

The Bank, however, retained much of its existing federal deposits and still had financial influence. Nicholas Biddle, who had been president of the Bank since 1823, made one final effort to save the institution. He had the Bank tighten credit to force a financial crisis, in hope of convincing Jackson and the American public of the folly of attacking such a stabilizing institution. Instead, this exercise of power by Biddle reinforced Jackson's arguments that the Bank had dangerously concentrated powers that it could use against the public good.

THE PANIC OF 1837

Jackson had won his bank war. But by weakening federal control over the banking system, he also opened the door to financial crisis. Jackson's pet banks issued their own bank notes, often in amounts far exceeding what they could back up with gold or silver. Furthermore, the amount of money in circulation more than doubled between 1830 and 1837, as many banks eased their loan requirements.

Much of the money that was lent was used for land speculation. Speculators bought millions of acres of public land in the Middle West, hoping to make quick profits by reselling it to settlers at higher prices. But as land prices increased, so did the price of everything else. To curb this inflationary spiral and slow the feverish speculation, President Jackson issued the **Specie Circular** in July 1836. This executive order instructed the Treasury to accept only gold and silver (specie) as payment for public land. Because few people had specie, land sales plunged. Many people began demanding that their banks exchange bank notes for gold or silver. As in 1819, banks that could not do so failed. By June 1837, hundreds of banks had gone under.

Contributing to the panic was the economic crisis in Great Britain. Faced with financial

PRESIDENTIAL LIVES

MARTIN VAN BUREN
1782–1862

in office 1837–1841

Martin Van Buren loved stylish living. During his administration the White House was the scene of many galas. And it was common to see him about the streets of Washington riding in his olive green carriage pulled by fine horses in silver-mounted harnesses and attended by uniformed footmen. As a friend recalled, Van Buren was "as polished and captivating a person in the social circle as America has ever known."

Despite his aristocratic tastes, Van Buren was determined to appear friendly and approachable. Thus, he was grieved by his opponents' attacks on him: "Why the deuce is it that they have such an itching for abusing me? I try to be harmless, and positively good natured, and a most decided friend of peace."

M Van Buren

HISTORICAL SIDELIGHTS
Flour Riots

Many workers became unemployed as a result of the crisis. Some demanded relief. In February 1837 at a meeting in New York City, 4,000 to 5,000 hungry and angry people demanded "Bread, Meat, Rent, Fuel." After listening to speakers denounce merchants who withheld food from starving people, a mob of almost 1,000 people stormed the warehouse of Eli Hart and Company. When the mayor tried to subdue the rioters, he was forced back by a barrage of sticks and stones. The mob dumped flour and wheat over the floor, then continued to other warehouses. The rioters were eventually subdued by the police.

Practice

GUIDED PRACTICE

On the chalkboard draw a three-column chart with these headings: *Policies, Effectiveness,* and *Effects on the Nation.* Ask students to evaluate Jackson's presidency according to the headings while you record their responses in appropriate columns. Then guide students in outlining material for a pamphlet that is either for or against one of Jackson's policies.

INDEPENDENT PRACTICE

Suggest that students use their outlines to write a pamphlet that either attacks or defends one of Jackson's policies, citing its effectiveness and its long-term effects on the nation as support for their argument. Students may wish to include their pamphlets in their portfolios.

Review and Assessment

REVIEW Have students write an editorial explaining why the period should or should not be called the Age of Jackson. Students may wish to include their editorials in their portfolios. Then assign the Section 4 Review on p. 249.

ASSESS Assign the **Section 4 Daily Quiz** in *Core Resources.*

HISTORICAL SIDELIGHTS

Van Buren vs. Harrison

In 1836, Van Buren defeated Harrison for the presidency. Things were different four years later. In presenting Harrison as a common man—he actually came from a prominent family in Virginia's planter aristocracy—the Whigs were able to paint President Van Buren as the rich aristocrat. This strategy worked well in the tough economic times of 1840. The president was turned out, and Harrison—the man Van Buren had defeated four years before—took his place.

problems at home, the British bought less southern cotton. British investors also pulled their money out of the United States, further decreasing the supply of specie. Factories closed; construction projects stood idle. Thousands of workers lost their jobs. In New York City alone, an estimated 50,000 workers were unemployed. In the cold winter of 1837–38, hungry people rioted in the streets of eastern cities. What had begun as a panic soon deepened into a depression that lasted until 1843.

■■ **The economic crisis of the late 1830s was caused by Jackson's monetary policies, easy credit, land speculation, and British economic problems.**

WILLIAM HENRY HARRISON

1773–1841

in office 1841

William Henry Harrison was a military man and war hero with little political ambition or experience. But when the Whigs offered him the party's presidential nomination in 1840, he quickly embraced the idea. After Harrison's election, his predecessor, Van Buren, remarked that Harrison "is as tickled with the Presidency as a young woman is with a new bonnet."

His opponents were not so amused. They criticized his inexperience and accused him of drunkenness, bad language, and "loose living." But Harrison had little time to answer these charges; he died of pneumonia shortly after his inauguration.

THE RISE OF THE WHIGS

Jackson left office before the inflationary bubble burst. Martin Van Buren, Jackson's vice president and handpicked successor, who was elected president in 1836, suffered the consequences of mounting economic problems. Unwilling to take steps to help the economy, Van Buren fell prey to the new Whig party when he sought reelection in 1840.

Jackson's opponents had organized the Whig party in 1834, taking their name from the old Whig party in England that had opposed the power of the king. The Whigs initially attracted people who disliked "King Andrew" Jackson's policies and use of federal power. Jackson's heavy-handed attacks on the national bank and his backing of Georgia against the U.S. Supreme Court on the issue of Indian removal, for example, led some Americans to distrust the growing power of Jackson's presidency. The Whigs did not defeat Van Buren in 1836, but their support grew over the next four years as the nation's economic problems deepened.

Rather than run Henry Clay—the acknowledged leader of the Whig party—the Whigs in 1840 nominated General William Henry Harrison, like Jackson a war hero. Clay's nomination had been opposed by such influential Whigs as Calhoun and Webster. In addition, Clay's 1839 speech attacking some abolitionists undermined his chances of winning votes in the North. Clay defended his remarks by saying, "I had rather be right than be president," but the Whigs wanted a candidate who could win. Harrison had the advantage of having few political (or sectional) enemies and thus received the party's nomination.

"My friends are not worth the powder and shot it would take to kill them," Clay bitterly said upon hearing the news of Harrison's nomination. "I am the most unfortunate man in the history of parties: always run by my friends when sure to be defeated, and now betrayed of a nomination when I, or any one, would be sure of election."

Clay's last assessment was probably right—the economic problems created during the Van Buren administration seemed to ensure the election of almost any Whig candidate. Although adopting no party platform, the Whigs targeted such economic issues as the Bank, the tariff, and especially the ongoing depression. The Whig campaign focused on presenting their candidate as a "man of

RETEACH Have students work in groups, assigning individuals or pairs the task of outlining subsections. Ask students to exchange outlines and use them to ask questions of other members of their group.

Closure

Have students use the information in Section 4 to write statements that support the title of the section, "Jackson's Policies Define an Era." Discuss statements with the class.

Extension

ANALYZE Have students research and report on the current situation of a Native American group affected by Indian removal in the 1830s. Encourage use of statistics, graphs, maps, and primary sources.

COMPARE Ask students to compare the Panic of 1837 with the Panic of 1819. Have them compare causes, government policies, and effects.

the people." They portrayed Harrison, a rich landowner, as a poor, hardworking farmer who lived in a log cabin.

Whig rallies featured miniature log cabins and flowing barrels of hard cider, the favored drink of farmers and many workers. The Whigs' chant "Tippecanoe and Tyler too" referred to the general's 1811 battle against Indians at the Tippecanoe River and to his running mate, John Tyler of Virginia. Ridiculing Van Buren, they added: "Van, Van is a used up man!"

The Whigs' reliance on slogans during the campaign echoed the election of 1828 and set unfortunate precedents for U.S. politics. After 1840 the "packaging" of candidates—emphasizing their images as much as (or even more than) their ideas or abilities—became standard practice.

But the tactic worked. Harrison won an impressive 234 electoral votes to Van Buren's 60. Harrison, however, did not enjoy his triumph for long. The 68-year-old president died of pneumonia four weeks after his inauguration, making his the shortest presidential term in U.S. history. Vice President Tyler, a states'-rights Virginian and strong opponent of Andrew Jackson, succeeded to the presidency and inherited the ongoing economic and sectional crises.

■■ **The Whigs came to power in 1840 by emphasizing economic issues—such as the Panic of 1837—and by relying on slogans and images.**

PRESIDENTIAL LIVES

JOHN TYLER
1790–1862

in office 1841–1845

John Tyler was a Virginia gentleman. A lover of music and literature, he played the violin and wrote poetry. The courtship leading up to Tyler's second marriage was so romantic that his bride's sister scolded: "You spend *so much* time in kissing, things of more importance are left undone."

In public, though, Tyler could be stubborn. When President Harrison died in 1841—the first president to die while in office—many government leaders challenged then–Vice President Tyler's right to assume full presidential duties. But Tyler was determined not to be merely a "Vice President acting as President." His bold action set a precedent for the transfer of presidential power.

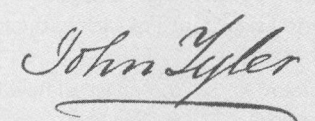

SECTION 4 REVIEW

IDENTIFY and explain the significance of the following: Sequoya, Indian Removal Act, Second Seminole War, *Worcester* v. *Georgia*, Trail of Tears, pet banks, Specie Circular, William Henry Harrison.

LOCATE and explain the importance of the following: Indian Territory.

1. **MAIN IDEA** What factors led the U.S. government to shift its policy toward Native Americans from one of coexistence to one of removal? How did Native Americans in the Southeast attempt to resist this policy shift?

2. **MAIN IDEA** How did the Whigs win the election of 1840?

3. **IDENTIFYING CAUSE AND EFFECT** Describe the relationship between the tariff of 1828, the doctrine of nullification, and South Carolina's threat to secede.

4. **WRITING TO EXPLAIN** Write a short essay explaining what led to the Panic of 1837 and the depression that followed.

5. **WRITING TO CREATE** Imagine you are a Cherokee on the Trail of Tears. Write a poem or diary entry explaining your feelings at being forced to leave your home.

SECTION REVIEW ANSWERS

IDENTIFY
For significance, see the following pages:
Sequoya (p. 242)
Indian Removal Act (p. 243)
Second Seminole War (p. 244)
Worcester v. Georgia (p. 244)
Trail of Tears (p. 244)
pet banks (p. 247)
Specie Circular (p. 247)
William Henry Harrison (p. 248)

LOCATE
For location, see the map on p. 244.

1. *land hunger, Indian support for British during war; appealing to Congress, warfare, legal action*
2. *nominated a war hero; based campaign on economic issues, slogans, and images*
3. *Southern economy was hurt by 1828 tariff; southerners responded with doctrine of nullification; South Carolina called for secession when Jackson threatened to enforce all U.S. laws, including the 1828 tariff.*
4. *Essays should address monetary policies, easy credit, land speculation, and the British economy.*
5. *Selections might express fear, anger, sadness, or anxiety.*

UNDERSTANDING MAIN IDEAS

1. brought to light weaknesses in nation's financial and transportation systems
2. In both cases bad loans led to efforts to demand repayment and exchange bank notes for gold and silver. As a result, many banks failed.
3. Slater built first American spinning machine; Whitney invented cotton gin and employed interchangeable parts; Lowell developed factory system.
4. through adoption of white culture, legal action (Worcester v. Georgia), and warfare (Second Seminole War)
5. When enough settlers had moved to the territory, Missouri applied for statehood. Northerners objected because it permitted slavery and would tip the balance between slave and free states. The Missouri Compromise was passed to satisfy the opposition.
6. A compromise tariff was passed in 1833.

DEVELOPING THEMES

Return to the Themes section on p. 224. Have students discuss these again and compare their original responses with those given now. (See p. 223B for suggested answers.)

Chapter Review Answers

WRITING A SUMMARY

See Essential Points in each section for main ideas.

REVIEWING CHRONOLOGY

3, 5, 1, 4, 2
Identifying Cause and Effect
Answers will vary but should make the cause and effect of events clear.

IDENTIFYING PEOPLE AND IDEAS

1. *called for national bank, protective tariff, transportation system*
2. *elected president 1836; succeeded by Harrison*
3. *U.S.–British arrangement to limit naval arms race on the Great Lakes*
4. *South Carolina's states' rights congressman; author of doctrine of nullification*
5. *shift from hand to machine production*
6. *created Cherokee writing system*
7. *law forcing most eastern Indians to move to Indian Territory*
8. *declaration that states could nullify federal laws*

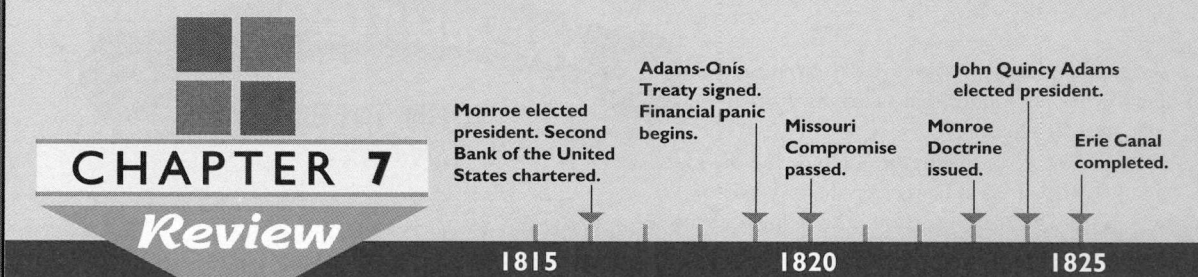

CHAPTER 7
Review

Monroe elected president. Second Bank of the United States chartered.

Adams-Onís Treaty signed. Financial panic begins.

Missouri Compromise passed.

Monroe Doctrine issued.

John Quincy Adams elected president.

Erie Canal completed.

1815   1820   1825

WRITING A SUMMARY
Using the essential points of the chapter as a guide, write a summary of the chapter.

REVIEWING CHRONOLOGY
Number your paper 1 to 5. Study the time line above, and list the following events in the order in which they happened by writing the first next to 1, the second next to 2, and so on. Then complete the activity below.

1. Jackson vetoes national bank recharter.
2. Cherokees begin Trail of Tears.
3. Missouri Compromise passed.
4. Tariff crisis resolved.
5. Monroe Doctrine issued.

Identifying Cause and Effect Select two events from the time line, and in a paragraph, explain the cause-and-effect relationship between them.

IDENTIFYING PEOPLE AND IDEAS
Explain the historical significance of each of the following people or terms.

1. American System
2. Martin Van Buren
3. Rush-Bagot Agreement
4. John Calhoun
5. Industrial Revolution
6. Sequoya
7. Indian Removal Act
8. doctrine of nullification

UNDERSTANDING MAIN IDEAS
1. How did the War of 1812 help prepare Americans for acceptance of Clay's American System?
2. How were the causes of the Panic of 1819 and the Panic of 1837 similar?
3. What roles did Samuel Slater, Eli Whitney, and Francis Cabot Lowell play in America's Industrial Revolution?
4. How did Native Americans in the Southeast resist their forced removal to Indian Territory?
5. How did westward expansion lead to passage of the Missouri Compromise?
6. Why did South Carolina not carry through on its threat to secede in the early 1830s?

REVIEWING THEMES
1. **Economic Development** How did the transportation and market revolutions lead to regional differences in economic development?
2. **Technology and Society** What were some of the ways in which 19th-century America was changed by the Industrial Revolution?
3. **Democratic Values** Why can it be said that the market revolution and industrialization aided the rise of Jacksonian democracy?

THINKING CRITICALLY
1. **Evaluating** What caused the upsurge of American nationalism after the War of 1812?
2. **Synthesizing** What did the Monroe Doctrine reveal about the way the United States viewed its role in the Western Hemisphere?
3. **Analyzing** Could industrialization and the transportation revolution have occurred without each other? Why or why not?
4. **Comparing** What did the crises over Missouri statehood and over tariffs have in common?

STRATEGY FOR SUCCESS
Following is an excerpt from the message President Jackson delivered to Congress in support of Indian removal. Review the Strategies for Success on Recognizing Fallacies in Reasoning on page 220. Then indicate what fallacy in reasoning is evident in Jackson's speech.

66 Our children by thousands yearly leave the land of their birth to seek new homes in distant regions. . . . These remove . . . at their own expense, purchase the lands they occupy, and support themselves at their new homes from the moment of their arrival. Can it be cruel . . . when . . . the Indian is made discontented in his ancient home to purchase his lands, to give him a new and extensive territory, to pay the expense of his removal, and support him a year in his new abode? 99

REVIEWING THEMES

1. *New transportation created national markets, allowing regions to specialize.*
2. *more jobs; better access to goods; increased urbanization; westward expansion*
3. *The market revolution and industrialization spurred westward expansion. Because their populations included many farmers and landless laborers, frontier states allowed most white males to vote. These "common men" were the voters who supported Jackson.*

THINKING CRITICALLY

1. *The U.S. had held its own against Britain in the war; its economy was booming.*
2. *that the U.S. viewed itself as responsible for events in its own hemisphere*
3. *No. Mass production required new forms of transportation to distribute goods; improved transportation depended upon technologies developed by industrialization.*
4. *Both reflected sectional differences and states' rights issues.*

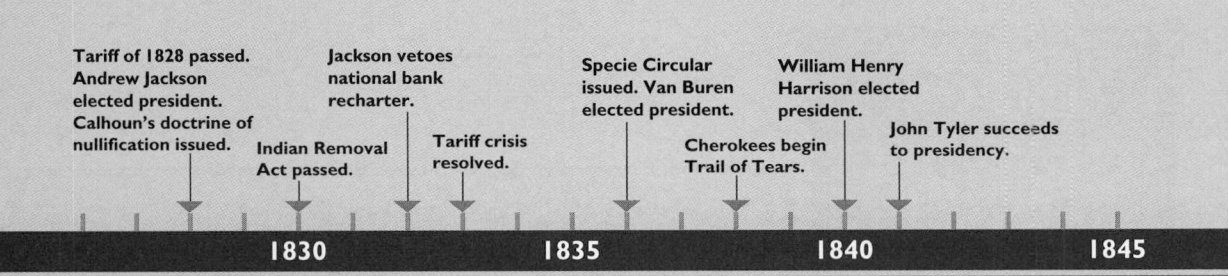

Tariff of 1828 passed. Andrew Jackson elected president. Calhoun's doctrine of nullification issued.

Jackson vetoes national bank recharter.

Indian Removal Act passed.

Tariff crisis resolved.

Specie Circular issued. Van Buren elected president.

Cherokees begin Trail of Tears.

William Henry Harrison elected president.

John Tyler succeeds to presidency.

1830   1835   1840   1845

WRITING ABOUT HISTORY

Using Historical Imagination Imagine that you are a reporter in 1828. Write a short article tracing Jackson's political career from the election of 1824 through the election of 1828.

USING PRIMARY SOURCES

When the U.S. government first began pressuring the Chickasaws to exchange their lands in the Southeast for lands in Indian Territory, the Chickasaw leaders offered the following reply. What reasons did the Chickasaws give for not wanting to move westward?

> 66 *We never had a thought of exchanging our land for any other, as we think that we would not find a country that would suit us as well as this we now occupy, it being the land of our forefathers, if we should exchange our lands for any other, fearing the consequences may be similar to transplanting an old tree, which would wither and die away, and we are fearful we would come to the same. . . .*
>
> *We have no lands to exchange for any other. We wish our father [the President] to extend his protection to us here, as he proposes to do on the west of the Mississippi, as we apprehend [fear] we would, in a few years, experience the same difficulties in any other section of the country that might be suitable to us west of the Mississippi.* 99

LINKING HISTORY AND GEOGRAPHY

Refer to the map on page 233, showing the major U.S. roads, canals, and railroads in 1840. In what parts of the country were most canals located?

Given the information on this map, why do you think the Erie Canal was so important?

"Tom Thumb" locomotive racing a horse-drawn car, 1830

The Granger Collection, New York

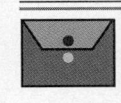

BUILDING YOUR PORTFOLIO

Complete the following projects independently or cooperatively.

1. **THE ECONOMY** Imagine you are a northern textile manufacturer. Create an illustrated chart for a new factory that shows what new technologies you will use to produce cloth from cotton and where you plan to build your factory for easy access to markets.

2. **EXPANSION** Imagine you are a reporter for the *Cherokee Phoenix*. Write a newspaper article in English that traces U.S. policy toward the Cherokee nation from 1789 to 1835. Include reasons for why these policies can be viewed as a product of U.S. expansionism.

3. **INDIVIDUAL RIGHTS** Imagine you are a western farmer supporting Andrew Jackson in the 1832 presidential election. Create a political poster that illustrates why Andrew Jackson is a "man of the people." The poster should draw on events from Jackson's first term in office.

EARLY INDUSTRIALIZATION

HISTORICAL SIDELIGHTS
Canal Towns

Just as railroad towns developed around railroad construction, canal towns developed around the construction of canals. Boat traffic was often delayed near the point of the canal locks. As a result, towns commonly grew around businesses that were established near the locks to service and repair boats that passed through. Eventually a variety of businesses moved into these towns and attracted more settlers. Long after the canal era ended, canal towns continued to live on as a legacy of the early transportation system.

■ Ask students if they know of any canals or railroads that were constructed in their area during the 19th century but are no longer in use.

America's GEOGRAPHY

EARLY INDUSTRIAL-IZATION

PATTERNS of early industrialization in the United States were largely influenced by geography. Early factories relied heavily on water power. Thus most industrial centers formed around the fall line of the eastern United States. As rivers descend from the uplands to the lowlands, they create waterfalls and rapids. A fall line is the imaginary line formed by connecting the waterfalls on numerous rivers. The fall line usually marks the farthest point that ships can travel inland. Thus many inland port cities, such as Philadelphia and Baltimore, can be found along the fall line. The multitude of waterfalls and streams in New England contributed to its becoming the leading region of early industrialization in America.

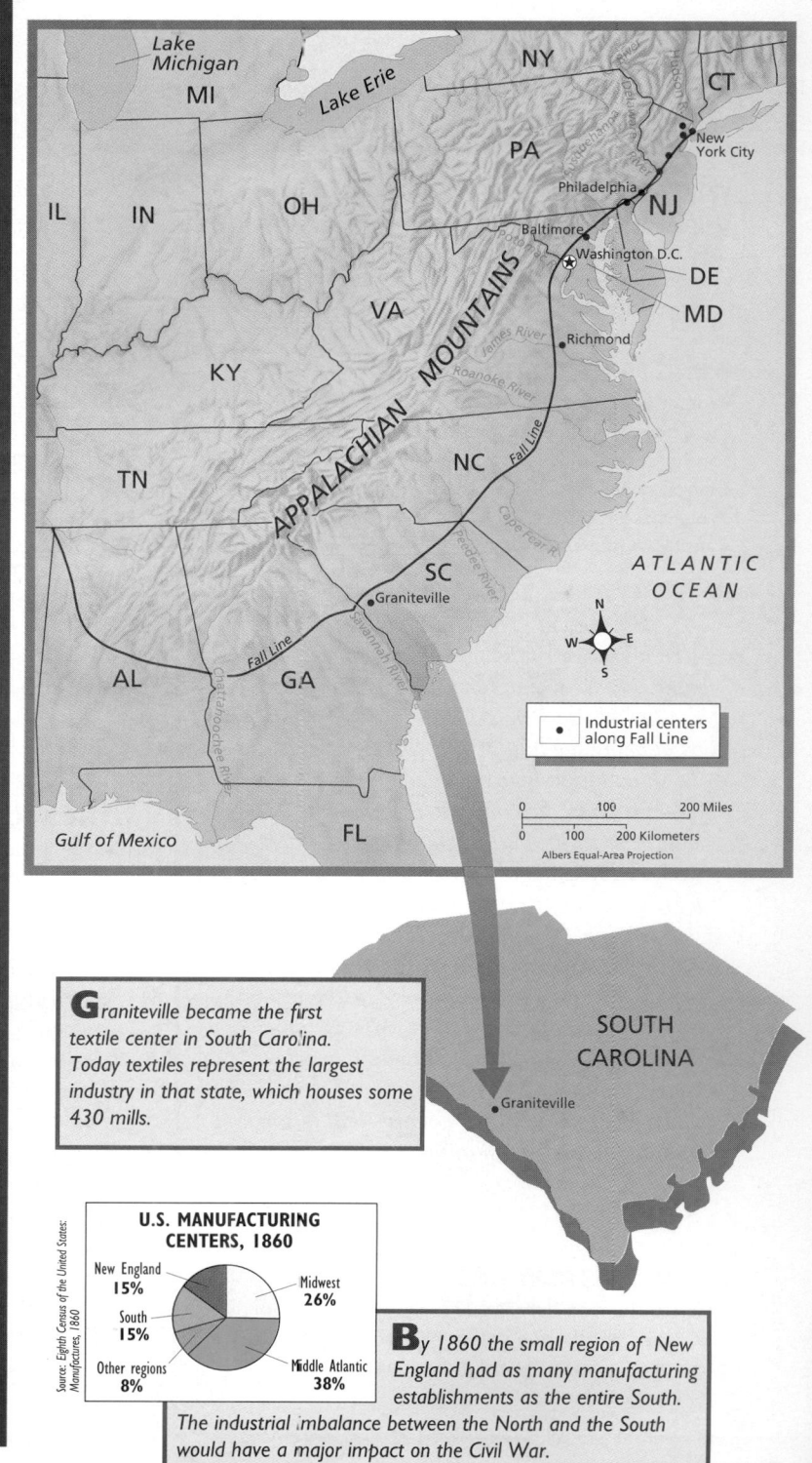

Graniteville became the first textile center in South Carolina. Today textiles represent the largest industry in that state, which houses some 430 mills.

U.S. MANUFACTURING CENTERS, 1860

Source: *Eighth Census of the United States: Manufactures, 1860*

- New England 15%
- Midwest 26%
- South 15%
- Other regions 8%
- Middle Atlantic 38%

By 1860 the small region of New England had as many manufacturing establishments as the entire South. The industrial imbalance between the North and the South would have a major impact on the Civil War.

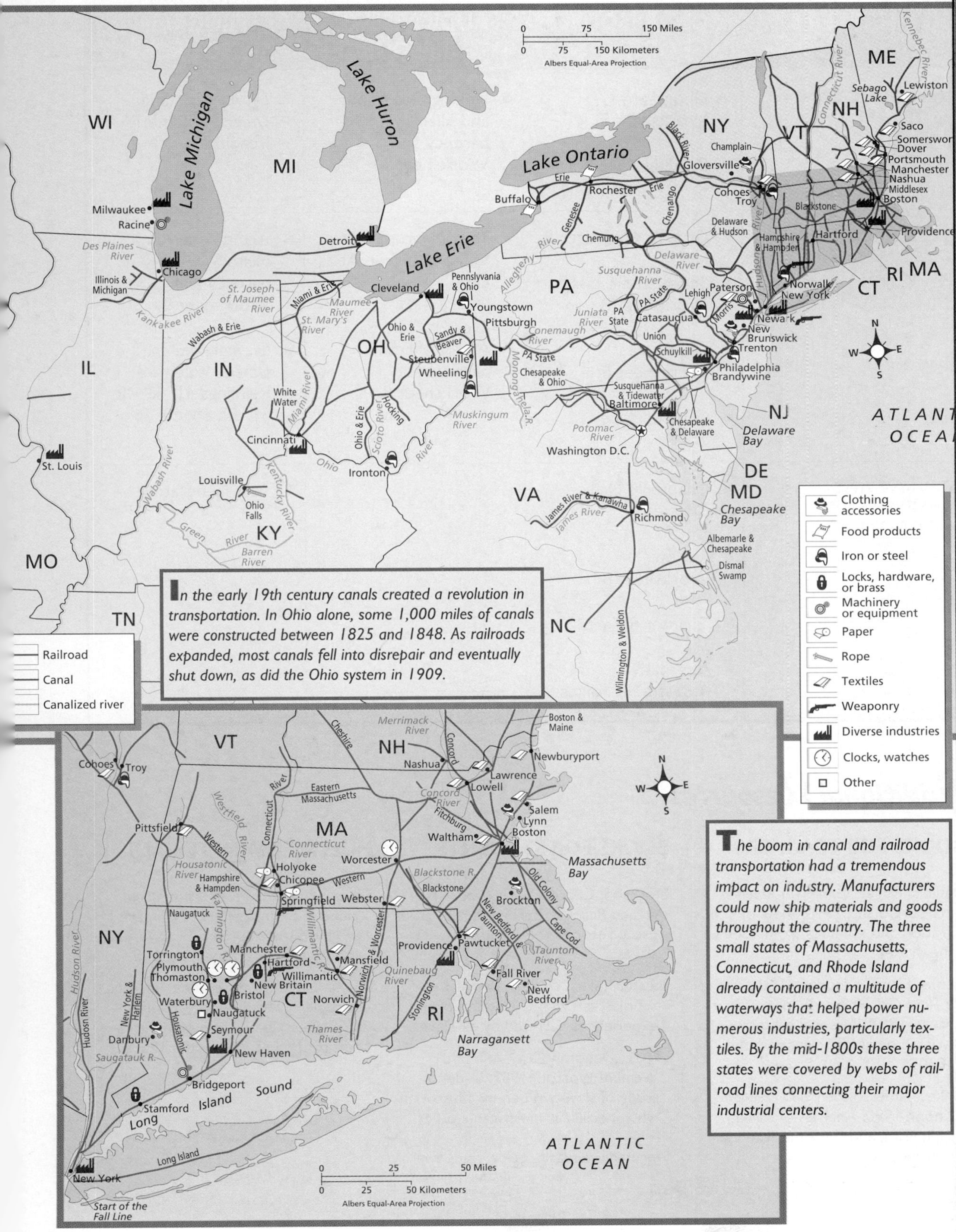

Traveling Ohio

The state of Ohio put a great deal of effort into extending its transportation systems. The canal-building project was the largest operation taken on by the state in its early history. As railroads proved cheaper and more dependable, the state shifted its efforts to railroad construction. By 1860 Ohio had the country's most extensive railroad system.

In the early 19th century canals created a revolution in transportation. In Ohio alone, some 1,000 miles of canals were constructed between 1825 and 1848. As railroads expanded, most canals fell into disrepair and eventually shut down, as did the Ohio system in 1909.

The boom in canal and railroad transportation had a tremendous impact on industry. Manufacturers could now ship materials and goods throughout the country. The three small states of Massachusetts, Connecticut, and Rhode Island already contained a multitude of waterways that helped power numerous industries, particularly textiles. By the mid-1800s these three states were covered by webs of railroad lines connecting their major industrial centers.

Legend (first map):
- Railroad
- Canal
- Canalized river

Legend (symbols):
- Clothing accessories
- Food products
- Iron or steel
- Locks, hardware, or brass
- Machinery or equipment
- Paper
- Rope
- Textiles
- Weaponry
- Diverse industries
- Clocks, watches
- Other

SEPARATE SOCIETIES: NORTH AND SOUTH

1820–1860

Chapter Overview

From 1820 to 1860 change swept through the North and the Middle West. Industrialization transformed small towns into urban centers and gave rise to a new middle class. Population increased rapidly as immigrants, mainly from Ireland and Germany, came to America to work in cities and factories and on farms.

Change came more slowly to the South, where cotton ruled over commerce and the society remained largely agrarian. Slaves provided the labor that made cotton-growing profitable on southern plantations. African Americans made many attempts to resist slavery and, in order to survive the brutalities of slave life, strengthened their family and cultural life.

THE AMERICAN NATION VIDEODISC PROGRAM A variety of still images, short videos, and activities are available for you to use as you teach this chapter. See Correlation to *The American Nation Videodisc Program* for barcode correlations and suggestions for using the program.

Chapter Planning Guide

CHAPTER 8	CORE RESOURCE BOOKLETS	AUDIOVISUAL AV RESOURCES	PROGRAM RESOURCES
INTRODUCTION pp. 254–255	■ Geography Worksheet 8 ■ Building Your Portfolio Worksheet 3	■ Linking Geography and History Transparency and Worksheet 11	■ *Eyewitnesses and Others*, Volume 1: Reading 71
TEACHING THE CHAPTER pp. 256–277	■ Graphic Organizer 8 ■ Social Studies Skills Worksheet 8 ■ Literature Worksheet 8 ■ Outline Maps 1, 2, 9, 14	■ *The American Nation Videodisc: Free At Last* ■ Everyday Life in America Transparency and Worksheet 8	■ Art in American History Transparency and Worksheet 8 ■ *Eyewitnesses and Others*, Volume 1: Readings 41, 46, 48, 51, 52, 68, 69, 76
REVIEW AND ASSESSMENT pp. 278–279	■ Chapter 8 Daily Quizzes ■ Review Worksheet 8 ■ Chapter 8 Tests ■ Alternative Assessment Forms		■ Test Generator

Additional Resources

BOOKS FOR TEACHERS

Daniels, Roger. *Coming to America.* HarperCollins, 1990. View of immigration and ethnicity from 1500 to the present.

Jacobs, Harriet. *Incidents in the Life of a Slave Girl.* Harvard University Press, 1987. Personal narrative of a woman born into slavery in the 1830s.

Oakes, James. *Slavery and Freedom.* Knopf, 1990. Analysis of slavery, capitalism, and the American ideal of freedom.

BOOKS FOR STUDENTS

Blockson, Charles L. *The Underground Railroad.* Berkley, 1989. Escape stories told by former slaves.

*Lester, Julius. *To Be a Slave.* Scholastic, 1986. Collection of experiences narrated by ex-slaves.

White, Deborah Gray. *Ar'n't I a Woman?* Norton, 1987. In-depth study of slave women by a historian who specializes in African studies.

* for students reading below grade level

MULTIMEDIA MATERIALS

Slavery: America's Peculiar Institution. Video, 32 min. Zenger. Two-part program traces origins of slavery and describes slavery in the U.S.

We All Came to America: The American Documents Series. Video, 52 min. SSSS. Describes waves of immigration to the U.S. during the 1800s.

THEMES IN AMERICAN HISTORY

USE WITH PAGES 254–255

*L*isted on the right are the themes emphasized in Chapter 8. The questions in boldface type stimulate critical thinking and provide students with an opportunity to discuss the themes within a broadened context. The questions also appear in the pupil's edition on p. 254.

■ ECONOMIC DEVELOPMENT

How might economic changes affect society?
Students might suggest that a booming economy could cause a society to expand production and investment in areas that are making the most profit. It could also encourage overall expansion and investment. A poor economy, on the other hand, could cause a society to change its focus of production and investment or to become more cautious toward expansion.

■ CULTURAL DIVERSITY

How might a people's culture be shaped by slavery?
Students might note that those who are enslaved would likely develop cultural patterns that would allow them both to resist slavery and to survive its effects. Some among those who are not enslaved might develop a culture that focuses on protecting the institution of slavery and the rights of slaveholders. Others might unite to try and end slavery. Students might also note that such differing responses would likely result in sharp divisions and conflicts within society.

■ TECHNOLOGY AND SOCIETY

What unexpected effects might a technological advance have on society?
Students should indicate how a technological advance might alter the economic focus of society, leading to industrial expansion or physical migration across the country. A technological advance in agriculture, for instance, could lead to greater crop production and increasing sale of crops for cash.

CHAPTER STRATEGIES FOR MEETING INDIVIDUAL NEEDS

LIMITED ENGLISH PROFICIENT LEARNERS

Have students create three word-webs: one with "North and Middle West" in the center, one with "South" in the center, and one with "Slave System" in the center. Ask students to identify the parts of each society or system by placing them in strands at the end of the correct word-web.

TACTILE/KINESTHETIC LEARNERS

Ask students to prepare skits showing life in the North, in the Middle West, and in the South under the slave system. Have them divide the assignment into writing scripts, finding music and quotations, and so on.

LEARNERS HAVING DIFFICULTY

Have students work in groups of six. Pair students in each group and assign each pair one of the Preview Workshops in the chapter. Have each pair make flashcards with terms on one side and definitions on the other. Then have pairs quiz each other using the flashcards.

AUDITORY LEARNERS

Have students work in pairs to simulate gathering oral histories. Have one student role-play a person living in the North or the South between 1820 and 1860 and the other act as an interviewer.

VISUAL LEARNERS

Have students work in groups to prepare a collage showing the societies and people in the chapter.

GIFTED LEARNERS

Have students write essays comparing attitudes toward business, workers, and various racial and ethnic groups from 1820 to 1860 with attitudes today.

■ UNDERSTANDING THE MAIN IDEA

Ask a volunteer to read the Understanding the Main Idea paragraph aloud. Then ask students what images they would include in drawings of life in the early 1800s in the North and the South. Have them speculate what differences in economics, populations, and ways of life would exist between the two regions.

■ THEMES

Have students work individually or in small groups to answer the questions under Themes. Save students' responses so that they can compare them with their responses after studying the chapter. (See p. 253B for suggested answers.)

■ THE TIME LINE

Point out that increased immigration to the U.S. in the mid-1800s was spurred partly by the growing demand for factory labor in the North. Ask students to name the events on the time line that are also a reflection of the rise of manufacturing in the North.

CORE RESOURCES

- **Graphic Organizer 8**
- **Geography Worksheet 8**
- **Social Studies Skills Worksheet 8**
- **Outline Maps 1, 2, 9, 14**
- **Building Your Portfolio Worksheet 3**

AV RESOURCES

- **Linking Geography and History Transparency** and **Worksheet 11**

ABOUT THE ILLUSTRATION

Early textile mills, such as the one depicted below, employed women and children to do most of the work. Workers placed spools of yarn on racks called *creels,* which fed the yarn onto rollers used in mechanical looms run by steam engines or waterwheels. The looms then wove the yarn into cloth. Ask students to spec-ulate on why textile mills might have hired so many women and children.

Chapter 8

1820–1860

SEPARATE SOCIETIES: NORTH AND SOUTH

▼ FOCUS

UNDERSTANDING THE MAIN IDEA

The market revolution changed northern and southern societies. In the North, with its growing cities and factories, a new middle class and a new working class emerged. In the South, the dominance of cotton strengthened the slave-based social order.

■ THEMES

- **ECONOMIC DEVELOPMENT** How might economic changes affect society?

- **CULTURAL DIVERSITY** How might a people's culture be shaped by slavery?

- **TECHNOLOGY AND SOCIETY** What unexpected effects might a technological advance have on society?

1831	1834	1844	1856
Nat Turner leads slave uprising.	National Trades Union founded.	Lowell Female Labor Association organized.	American party nominates Millard Fillmore for president.

LINK TO THE PAST

As early as the 1760s, the economies of the North and the South had begun to grow apart. Although farming was important in both regions, the North diversified its economy to include importing and selling manufactured goods.

MAKING CONNECTIONS
Sociology

Unlike France and other European countries, the U.S. did not have an aristocracy or upper class protected by laws or customs. This fact allowed Americans movement between classes. Birth or "good breeding" was an important ingredient for financial success in the U.S., but it did not protect one's permanent social status. As a result, Americans looked toward building successful businesses, which they could pass on to their heirs, thereby maintaining their families' social status.

Northern textile factory

In the early 19th century, new industries and growing cities changed how and where people worked. Before the market revolution, most people worked at home. People grew food and made cloth and other necessities for themselves. During the market revolution, however, people increasingly began to work outside the home—in factories, businesses, and on other people's farms. As a result, family members took on new roles.

Michel Chevalier (shuh-vahl-yay), a French visitor to America in the 1830s, noticed a new attitude among American men. The American man, he remarked, "is brought up with the idea that he will have some particular occupation, that he is to be a farmer, artisan, manufacturer, merchant, speculator, lawyer, physician . . . and that if he is active and intelligent he will make his fortune." In northern cities Chevalier noted that "men of business, instead of being scattered over the town, occupy a particular quarter, devoted exclusively to them, in which there is not a building used as a dwelling house and nothing but offices and warehouses to be seen."

Chevalier traveled to Virginia, where he observed a society in which the majority of the population—enslaved African Americans—had little choice of occupation. While Chevalier praised the flourishing tobacco and flour markets in Virginia, he also criticized southern slavery, noting that the slave "has no civil rights." Despite their lack of legal power, enslaved African Americans created a unique culture to resist and survive slavery.

Carrying cotton from southern fields

FOCUS OBJECTIVES

- Identify who made up the new middle class.

- Explain how northern workers reacted to the labor conditions they faced.

- Analyze what led to increased Irish and German immigration in this period.

- Describe how nativists reacted to Irish and German immigrants.

Section 1

THE NORTH AND THE MIDDLE WEST

FOCUS
- **Who made up the new middle class?**
- **How did northern workers react to the labor conditions they faced?**
- **What led to increased Irish and German immigration in this period?**
- **How did nativists react to Irish and German immigrants?**

The market revolution profoundly affected the North and the Middle West. The growing economy brought better living conditions for many Americans. It also attracted many Irish and German immigrants in the first half of the 19th century. But economic growth did not always improve the lives of the working class. Northern factory owners often paid low wages and provided poor working conditions, causing northern workers to call for changes.

Detail of immigrants from Samuel Waugh's *The Bay and Harbor of New York,* 1847

NORTHERN SOCIETY

The market revolution created a wide gap between the rich and the poor. Prosperous merchants, bankers, manufacturers, and their families made up the wealthy upper class. These families lived in huge, lavish homes with running water, marble mantels, elegant furnishings, and the latest in household conveniences.

The poor, by contrast, crowded into small apartments, attics, or damp cellars with little furniture and few conveniences,

◀ Some rooms in middle-class homes were heated by modern downstairs heaters rather than by old-fashioned fireplaces.

including sewers. Poor neighborhoods were plagued by crime, soot, filth, and disease.

Between the wealthy and the poor arose a new social class—the **middle class**. Prosperous farmers, artisans, shopkeepers, ministers, lawyers, and their families made up the new middle class. Some free blacks, despite facing discrimination, shared in the economic prosperity of the growing middle class. Middle-class families lived in modest but comfortable homes with conveniences such as iron cookstoves, lamps, bathing stands and bowls, and rugs.

Middle-class families had the income to buy food, clothing, and other products made available by the market revolution. Thus, families no longer worked together at home to produce their food, clothing, and other necessities. Men were expected to work outside the home to bring in money to buy these items. Women were expected to work at home and care for the children, and children were expected to go to school. These new middle-class family roles became the ideal for most families, though not all could meet this economic and social arrangement.

MOTIVATING:
STUDENT EXPERIENCES

Ask volunteers to share what they know about their ancestors and immigration. Then tell students that this section deals with the immigrants who came to the U.S. between 1820 and 1860 and the world they found in the North and the Middle West, where most of them settled.

Teaching the Section

DIFFERENCES AMONG SOCIAL CLASSES

Create a three-column chart on the chalkboard with the headings *Wealthy Upper Class, Middle Class,* and *Poor.* Call on volunteers to speculate about occupations of the members of each class between 1820 and 1860. Then ask volunteers to describe the life-styles of each class. Record responses on the chart.

 Using the chart, ask students if they think the information given still applies to life in the U.S. today.

▶

■■ **The middle class consisted of prosperous farmers, artisans, ministers, lawyers, shopkeepers, and their families.**

CHANGING WORKING CONDITIONS

The market revolution also changed how people worked. Workers still made most products, like shoes and barrels, by hand in small shops. In the early 19th century, however, workers began making more items in factories, which needed many employees. Early New England factory owners recruited whole families to work in textile mills. Such employment offers usually included housing. But the system of housing entire families became impractical when factories needed hundreds of employees.

Mill owners in Lowell, Massachusetts, overcame the problem by hiring young, single women from New England farms. Most women had the necessary skills for textile mills, since they had made cloth at home. They were also cheaper to hire. Mill owners paid single women less than male workers, since women were not seen as having to support their families.

These single women—known as **Lowell girls**—lived in closely supervised, company-owned boardinghouses. Mill owners organized cultural activities to provide "moral education" for the workers and required them to attend church. Older women acted as matrons in these boarding houses, enforcing curfews, banning alcohol, and reporting on the Lowell girls' behavior. Despite such strict supervision, recruitment was easy in the early years. "The stage-coach and canal boat came every day, always filled with new recruits," wrote former Lowell girl Harriet Robinson.

Conditions changed by the 1830s, however. Owners—searching for larger profits—cut wages, sped up production, and increased working hours. Protests and attempts to form labor unions had little success, however, as more job seekers competed for factory positions. As a result of the Panic of 1837, which had cost many workers their jobs, there were many unemployed laborers willing to work for long hours and low wages. In New York City 50,000 people—a third of the working class—were unemployed.

Even in prosperous times many workers lived on the edge of poverty. In New York City's garment-making district, entire families labored through the night, earning barely enough money to survive. They lived mainly on bread and tea; even beans were too expensive and time-consuming to prepare. "It's awful," lamented a mother of four. "I must work, else we get nothing to eat and turned into the street besides. . . . Cooking? Oh, I cook nothing, for I haven't the time."

Children often worked as hard as their parents did. Child labor was common on farms, so manufacturers took it for granted in factory work. By 1832, two out of five New England factory workers were children. These children faced especially grim working conditions. Factory superintendents often required children to run machines late into the night.

LABOR FIGHTS BACK

As conditions worsened by the 1830s, workers organized more than 60 unions. Labor leaders held their first national convention in 1834 and founded the National Trades Union, which campaigned for a 10-hour workday. President Van Buren responded in 1840 with a 10-hour workday for selected groups of federal employees. Some states passed similar legislation, but working hours remained long in many occupations.

The Granger Collection, New York

◀ **This 1836 picture shows children employed in the weaving room of a New England textile mill.**

■■ 257

ℭeaching the Section

LABOR–MANAGEMENT CONFLICTS

Tell students that they will role-play members of a labor union attending a convention in the 1830s. Organize students into small work groups, half of whom will outline the union's grievances and half of whom will draft a list of demanded reforms. Then, acting as chair of the convention, call on various "delegates" to read their lists of grievances and demands, and conduct a class vote on acceptance or rejection of the major items on these lists.

Labor unions used many methods to press for reforms. A common tactic was the **strike**— the refusal to work until employers meet union demands. During the 1830s, workers led more than 100 strikes, mostly to protest low wages or to avoid wage reductions.

Women played an important role in the early labor movement. After wages were cut in 1834, the Lowell girls went on strike, marching in the streets and shouting "Union is power." Reacting to the strike, Massachusetts legislators established a committee to investigate conditions in the textile mills. This was the first official investigation of labor conditions in the United States.

 Sarah G. Bagley, who went to work in the Lowell mills in 1836, was active in the labor movement. At first, she liked her job. In fact, in 1840 she wrote the article "Pleasures of Factory Life" for the *Lowell Offering,* a magazine published by women mill workers. But when mill owners sped up production without raising wages, Bagley urged coworkers to form a union. In 1844 she organized the Lowell Female Labor Reform Association. As its first president, Bagley denounced labor conditions and collected more than 2,000 signatures on a petition urging the Massachusetts legislature to limit the workday to 10 hours.

◄ Cover of the *Lowell Offering,* 1845

▲ This 1860 drawing accompanied an article in *Frank Leslie's Illustrated Newspaper* on a shoemakers' strike in Lynn, Massachusetts. According to the paper, 800 women led a strike procession through the city's streets on March 7, 1860.

After leaving the mill in 1845, Bagley traveled across New England, organizing other mill workers. Later she became the first woman telegraph operator in Lowell. Although Bagley did not win her fight to limit working hours, her efforts pointed the way for future labor organizers.

Most unions excluded African American workers. Whites often refused to work with blacks, sometimes calling for laws barring African Americans from particular trades. Some African American workers, such as mechanics, coach drivers, and caulkers, eventually formed organizations to promote their own interests.

▪▪ **During the mid-1800s, northern factory workers campaigned for better labor conditions.**

𝒢ROWTH IN IMMIGRATION

The labor force grew considerably in the 1830s as more than 500,000 newcomers—eager for work, land, and equality—poured into the country. By 1860 they numbered nearly 4.3 million—about 14 percent of the U.S. population. This increase was aided in part by a transportation revolution in Europe. Railways made it cheaper to reach major ports, and steamships reduced the time and cost of ocean travel.

Irish immigrants. The largest group of immigrants—more than 1.9 million—came from Ireland. Poverty, hunger, and mistreatment by the British had driven them from their homeland. British Protestants had seized much of Ireland's farmland by the 1600s, forcing most of the country's mainly

REASONS FOR IMMIGRATION

Have students work in pairs to prepare dialogues in which an Irish and a German immigrant discuss their reasons for coming to the U.S. and their hopes for improving their lives. Ask volunteers to present their dialogues to the class. Have the class take notes on the reasons given in the dialogues, and then ask the class as a whole to categorize the reasons into political, economic, or social, as you write them on the chalkboard.

▶

Roman Catholic population to rent land from Protestant landowners.

As Ireland's population nearly doubled from 1780 to 1840, the available land could no longer support the growing population. The situation worsened in the mid-1840s, when disease wiped out the potato crop—the major Irish food source—two years in a row. More than a million people (out of a population of some eight million) died from starvation or disease.

Most of those who could scrape together money for a steamship ticket left Ireland for the United States. Able to afford only the cheapest accommodations, these immigrants set off across the Atlantic Ocean, crammed together below deck in makeshift berths. Passenger Robert Smith described the conditions:

> 66 Hundreds of poor people, men, women and children of all ages, . . . huddled together without light, without air, . . . sick in body, dispirited in heart, . . . living without food or medicine, except as administered by the hand of casual charity. 99

Most Irish immigrants had been farmers, but few could afford farmland in the United States. Thus, the majority settled in crowded city slums, competing for the lowest-paying or most-dangerous jobs. Many laborers who helped build the nation's canals and railroads, mined coal, unloaded freight, and cleaned streets were Irishmen. Irishwomen cleaned the houses of the wealthy, washed and mended clothes, cared for children, and worked in factories. "You seldom see a gray-haired Irishman" became a common saying in the 19th century because the average life expectancy of Irish Americans was so short.

In addition to enduring such demanding work, the Irish often faced grim living conditions. Most lived in dark, poorly ventilated tenements. Whole families crowded into single rooms, cellars, or attics. Slum streets and yards, ankle-deep in garbage and sewage, spread diseases through Irish neighborhoods.

But Irish immigrants forged their own communities out of these conditions. They established hundreds of Catholic churches and created a vigorous and active parish life. The Irish also actively participated in local politics. By the 1880s Irish Americans ran the local governments of Boston, Chicago, Buffalo, Milwaukee, New York City, Philadelphia, and San Francisco. In return for votes Irish politicians helped poor and working-class Irish by providing them with emergency food and money, city jobs, and legal aid.

AV TRANSPARENCY

Linking Geography and History Transparency and **Worksheet 11**

PRIMARY SOURCE

Description of Change: excerpted
Rationale: excerpted to focus on main idea

GLOBAL CONNECTIONS

During the "famine years" of 1845 to 1855, more people left Ireland than in its previous recorded history. Although 75 percent of these emigrants came to the United States, hundreds of thousands settled in Britain, Australia, and Canada. The journeys were often difficult. In 1847, for example, more than one in three Irish emigrants bound for Canada died at sea or shortly after landing.

Graph Caption Answer
1851; 1854

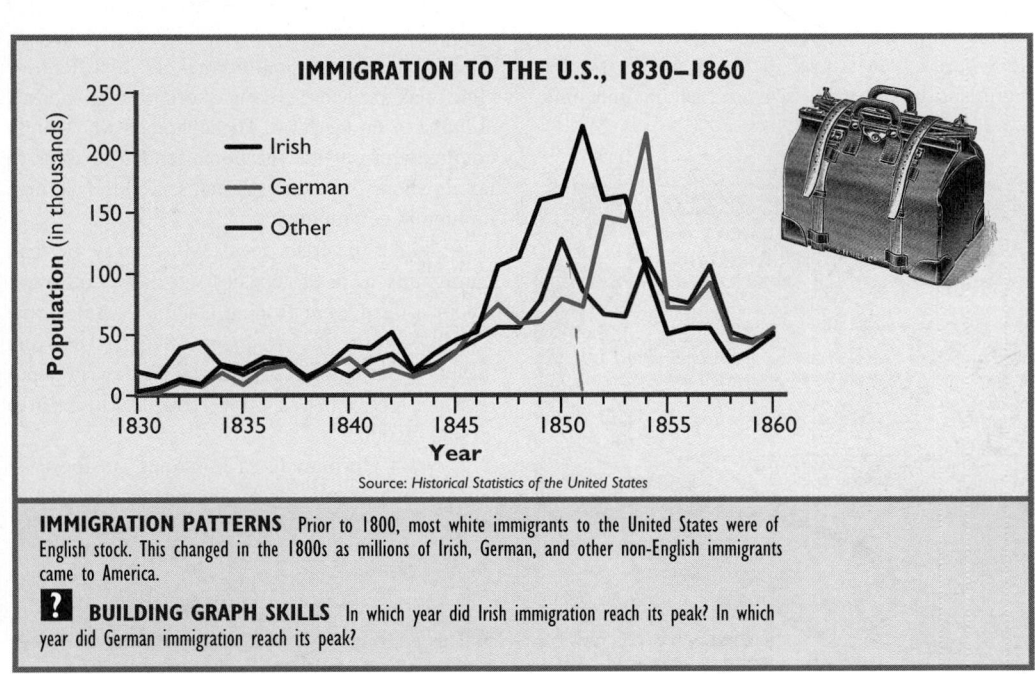

IMMIGRATION TO THE U.S., 1830–1860

— Irish
— German
— Other

Population (in thousands)

Year

Source: *Historical Statistics of the United States*

IMMIGRATION PATTERNS Prior to 1800, most white immigrants to the United States were of English stock. This changed in the 1800s as millions of Irish, German, and other non-English immigrants came to America.

? BUILDING GRAPH SKILLS In which year did Irish immigration reach its peak? In which year did German immigration reach its peak?

Teaching the Section

NATIVISM

Divide the class in half. Have one half be members of the American party, listing complaints against Irish and German immigrants and ways to limit their rights. Have the other half be Irish and German immigrants, drawing up a list of complaints against nativists. Then ask a spokesperson from each group to present the group's list. Encourage the spokespersons to lead a class discussion in response to each side's concerns. In conclusion, point out to students that nativism is a form of prejudice. Ask students if they think the reasons for this kind of prejudice have changed since the mid-1800s. Encourage them to explain their thinking.

CULTURAL PATTERNS

Realizing illiteracy's costly effects, many Irish immigrants were determined that their future generations would receive an education. They not only supported parochial schools but founded Notre Dame, Holy Cross, Villanova, Georgetown, and other colleges and universities. Have students research the founding of these colleges and universities and share their information with the class.

IMMIGRANT LIFE

Between 1820 and 1860 more than five million Europeans came to the United States in search of a better life. Although most arrived in the "promised land" with high hopes, many of them soon realized that their dreams would not come true. As competition for good jobs was stiff, skilled work was often hard to find. One Scottish immigrant expressed both despair and disappointment in this new land:

THROUGH OTHERS' EYES

❝ *America is no place for lawyers, weavers, or shoemakers, for everyone is a pettifoger [corrupt lawyer], a weaver or a shoemaker. For masons there is little use, for slaters [stone roofers] none. The houses are chiefly built with wood, and the roofs are shingled. Watch and clockmakers may stay at home [in Europe], for the Americans are regulated by the sun. It is no place for printers, there are but few readers. . . . The houses being very simply furnished, cabinet-makers are consequently not much in request. . . . In short, to gain a decent livelihood, the tradesman and labourer, must be a 'Jack of*

German immigrants. The second-largest group of immigrants in the mid-19th century was from the then-independent states that make up present-day Germany. From 1831 to 1860, more than 1.5 million Germans came to the United States. Some came for political reasons. A few thousand fled after the failed Revolution of 1848, which had tried to unify Germany. Others sought religious freedom. Most, however, came in search of economic opportunity. German industrialization had left many traditional artisans without jobs. Farmland was growing scarcer. Lacking economic opportunity at home, both groups immigrated to the United States.

▪▪ **Irish and German immigrants left economic and social hardships in Europe to seek opportunities in the United States.**

Many German immigrants went into skilled occupations, becoming brewers, bakers, butchers, machinists, tailors, cabinetmakers, distillers, or cigar makers. Most German-born women worked at home or on the farm. Those women who sought employment outside the home tended to work in family shops or businesses that served the German immigrant community.

Unlike the Irish, most 19th-century German immigrants were Protestant (especially Lutheran). About a third were Roman Catholic, while some 250,000 were Jewish. From 1825 to 1860 the influx of German Jews increased the Jewish population of New York City from about 500 to around 40,000.

Most German Jews remained on the East Coast, but other German immigrants settled in small towns and rural areas in Wisconsin, Ohio,

◀ **This photograph shows a Pennsylvania-German birth certificate from the early 19th century.**

Practice

GUIDED PRACTICE

Work with the class to develop two lists on the chalkboard—one of the benefits of being an immigrant in the U.S. in the mid-1800s, and the other reflecting the negative aspects of the immigrant experience. Ask students to choose three items on each list that would have been most important to them as immigrants of that time. Select students to explain their choices.

INDEPENDENT PRACTICE

Have students use their choices from the Guided Practice to write letters to relatives in "the old country" that tell about their lives in America. Students may wish to include their letters in their portfolios.

Review and Assessment

REVIEW Have students prepare flow-charts showing events leading to industrialization, urbanization, immigration, and growth of the labor union movement. Students may wish to include their flow-charts in their portfolios. Then assign the Section 1 Review on p. 262.

ASSESS Assign the **Section 1 Daily Quiz** in *Core Resources*.

▶

Pennsylvania, Illinois, Missouri, and Texas, and elsewhere. Those in larger cities usually lived in tightly knit German neighborhoods, complete with European-style beer gardens where families met to socialize. Many communities also published newspapers in German. In the mid-1850s, 56 German-language newspapers were published in the United States. And in some communities, public schools conducted classes in German rather than in English.

THE NATIVIST RESPONSE

Some native-born Americans were troubled by the new immigrants' customs. They disapproved of the beer gardens and the "clannishness" of the Germans. They feared the Roman Catholicism and the growing political power of the Irish. Such feeling gave rise to **nativism**—the policy of favoring native-born Americans over the foreign-born. Nativists viewed the immigrants, particularly the Irish, as politically corrupt and socially inferior. Were not, they asked, most of the people in jails Irish? Were not parts of Philadelphia, Boston, and New York controlled by Irish gangs with names like the "Dead Rabbits"? Slum conditions rooted in joblessness and low wages were blamed on the new-comers.

From the 1830s through the 1850s, anti-Catholic riots hit eastern cities such as Boston, New York, and Philadelphia. Vandalism against Catholic institutions grew so common that some insurance companies would not cover Catholic schools and churches. A Roman Catholic priest wrote in 1854 that he feared "to walk the streets after sunset":

66 Twice within the past month I have been stoned by young men. . . . The windows of the church have frequently been broken—the panels of the church door stove [smashed] in, and last week a large rock entered my chamber unceremoniously about 11 o'clock at night. 99

Some nativists urged limiting immigrants' rights to vote and to hold public office. Nativists wanted to limit Irish political power because they believed that the pope directed decisions for Irish Catholics. In 1849 a secret society of nativists, the Order of the Star-Spangled Banner, emerged. Members swore to support only native-born Protestants for public office, to lobby for a 21-year waiting period for naturalization, and to fight the Roman Catholic church. The organization soon re-formed itself as the American party. When asked about their nativist activities, party members would answer "I know nothing." They were thus dubbed

▲ This 1844 picture shows an anti-Catholic mob battling the state militia in Philadelphia.

RETEACH Have students work in small groups and assign one Focus question to each member. Direct students to prepare brief answers to their assigned questions and to share their answers with their group.

Closure

Ask students to compare the effects of the market revolution on the North and on the Middle West. Students might make a graphic organizer to show the effects on these two sections of the nation.

Extension

CREATE Suggest that students create illustrated family trees showing cultural aspects of their ancestors (food, religion, customs, dress, and so on).

RESEARCH Have students research a U.S. city in the 1840s and write a letter describing everyday life in the city to a friend living in a rural community. Letters might also include sketches of where the city dweller lives and works.

SECTION REVIEW ANSWERS

IDENTIFY

For significance, see the following pages:
middle class (p. 256)
Lowell girls (p. 257)
strike (p. 258)
Sarah G. Bagley (p. 258)
nativism (p. 261)
Know-Nothings (p. 262)

1. *prosperous farmers, artisans, shopkeepers, ministers, and lawyers*
2. *organized unions, led strikes, campaigned for 10-hour workday and better labor conditions*
3. *limits on immigrants' rights to vote and to hold public office; long waiting periods for citizenship*
4. *Essays should cover economic prosperity, comfortable but modest homes with purchased conveniences; men expected to work outside of home, women to work at home and care for children.*
5. *Irish—Most crowded into eastern slums, worked lowest paying or most dangerous jobs, commonly died young, and were involved in local politics and the Catholic church. Germans—Many became farmers, artisans, or businesspeople; spread throughout country; and often formed exclusively German communities.*

the **Know-Nothings**, and their organization was called the Know-Nothing party.

The American party, with its slogan "Americans Shall Rule America," won numerous city and state elections. In the 1856 presidential election, the party ran former Whig Millard Fillmore, who had served as president from 1850 to 1853. Fillmore carried only Maryland, and the American party—though not the nativist backlash—soon faded away.

■■ **Nativists responded to increased German and Irish immigration with violence and demands for limits on immigrants' rights.**

THE MIDDLE WEST

Many immigrants, especially Germans, Swiss, Scandinavians, and Dutch, sought opportunity in the newly prosperous Middle West. Growing northeastern factories and cities needed more farm products, which middle western farmers began to supply. Some middle western areas developed lumbering or mining, but commercial farming dominated most of the region.

As the market revolution made many manufactured products less expensive, farm families began to purchase items they had previously made at home. For example, women stopped spinning and weaving cloth, which was cheaper to buy than to make. Most middle western communities eventually had enough settlers to attract merchants selling manufactured goods. Farm families could then buy household items and new mechanized farm machines, such as Cyrus McCormick's reaper, that increased crop yields.

▲ This advertisement from a Boston company for farm equipment and seeds appeared in 1854.

With reapers and other new devices, farm families could cultivate more land with less labor. As a result, they focused on growing wheat or corn or on raising livestock for the market.

Women also began making items to sell. Farm women had long made butter and cheese for their families. Now they began making such items for sale. In Ohio, women earned so much money making butter and cheese that some farms began to specialize in dairy production.

This work was handled by women who also performed other home and farm chores. An 1862 Department of Agriculture report noted that "on three farms out of four the wife works harder [and] endures more than any other [person] on the place." Many women took pride in their ability to contribute directly to the growing family income.

 SECTION 1 REVIEW

IDENTIFY and explain the significance of the following: middle class, Lowell girls, strike, Sarah G. Bagley, nativism, Know-Nothings.

1. **MAIN IDEA** Identify some occupations that were considered part of the new middle class.
2. **MAIN IDEA** How did factory workers respond to unacceptable working conditions?
3. **MAIN IDEA** What kinds of restrictions did nativists try to impose on immigrants?
4. **WRITING TO DESCRIBE** Write an essay describing the life-style of middle-class families in the early 19th century. Include a discussion of male and female roles.
5. **CONTRASTING** How did life in America differ for Irish and German immigrants?

PREVIEW WORKSHOP

*Following is a list of the significant
people, places, and terms in this
section. You may wish to use this
list as a section preview.*

People
■ Jesse Burton Harrison
■ Thomas R. Dew

Places
■ cotton belt
■ Tredegar Iron Works

Terms
■ American Colonization
  Society
■ yeoman farmers

Section 2

THE COTTON KINGDOM

FOCUS

■ **What factors led to the rise of the Cotton Kingdom?**

■ **Why did manufacturing and cities develop more slowly in the South
than in the Northeast?**

■ **How did white southerners view the institution of slavery?**

■ **What was the class structure of southern society?**

*The market revolution helped tie the South's economy
to agriculture. In response to the increased demand
for cotton fueled by industrialization, cotton succeeded tobacco as the South's most important crop,
and the plantation system and slavery tightened
their grip on the region. This reliance on agriculture gave rise to a distinct southern social structure
of planters, small farmers, poor whites, free blacks,
and African American slaves.*

Moving cotton bales at a warehouse

KING COTTON

When tobacco prices fell in the early 1800s, many
Americans thought slavery and plantation agriculture would soon vanish. Before this could happen,
however, new machines that cut the cost and time
of cloth making sent the demand for cotton sky-
rocketing. Armed with Eli Whitney's cotton gin,
southern planters were ready to respond.

Cotton production in the South soared from
around 731,000 bales harvested in 1830 to some
2,133,000 bales in 1850. By 1859 cotton production reached a peak of some 5,387,000 bales. From
1815 to 1860 cotton represented more than half of
all American exports.

Periodic booms in the cotton export market
drove planters to open new lands for cultivation.
Cotton growers moved west from South Carolina
and Georgia into the fertile lands of Alabama,
Mississippi, Arkansas, Louisiana, and eastern
Texas. By the 1850s the cotton belt stretched in a
long crescent from central and western North
Carolina to eastern Texas.

As cotton production expanded, the demand
for slaves rose. The number of slaves grew from
about 1.5 million in 1820 to some 4 million by
1860. Because of the abolition of the international
slave trade in 1808, planters had to rely on natural
increase, or births, for more slaves. The Upper
South, with more slaves than the region needed,
sold slaves to the cotton-producing states of the
Lower South. The breakup of families that often
resulted was one of the cruelest aspects of a cruel
and inhumane system.

■■ **Booming markets, the cotton
gin, and newly cultivated lands
created the southern Cotton
Kingdom.**

FOCUS OBJECTIVES

■ Determine what factors
led to the rise of the
Cotton Kingdom.

■ Analyze why manufac-
turing and cities devel-
oped more slowly in
the South than in the
Northeast.

■ Explain how white
southerners viewed the
institution of slavery.

■ Describe the class structure of southern society.

CORE RESOURCES

• **Geography
  Worksheet 8**
• **Section 2 Daily Quiz**

AV RESOURCES

• **Linking Geography
  and History
  Transparency and
  Worksheet 11**

MOTIVATING: PRIOR KNOWLEDGE

Remind students that the South's early economy had depended on tobacco production. Ask students what invention caused cotton production to increase in the South in the early 1800s. *(cotton gin)* Then explain that this section describes the rise of the Cotton Kingdom in the South.

VOICES IN HISTORY

In the early 1850s, Marianne Finch, an English visitor to America, recognized the connection between the South's economic dependence on slavery and its defense of the institution. After visiting a Richmond, Virginia, ironworks, Finch noted: "About half the workmen were white men, and the other half slaves. The proprietor said that he would prefer all free labor if he could get it, . . . but the men were not to be had. . . . I never heard any American say slavery was right; it is always justified on the ground of expediency, like other social wrongs."

AV TRANSPARENCY

Linking Geography and History Transparency and **Worksheet 11**

Teaching the Section

THE COTTON KINGDOM

Work with students to create on the chalkboard a cause-and-effect diagram showing how the Lower South and expanding Southwest became increasingly dependent on cotton. Then have volunteers explain how these events caused manufacturing and urbanization to develop and to grow more slowly in the South than in the Northeast.

■■ Have students identify the wealthiest nations in the world today and indicate whether these nations' economies are primarily based on agriculture and commodities or industry. Discuss how industrialization generates wealth and improves standards of living.

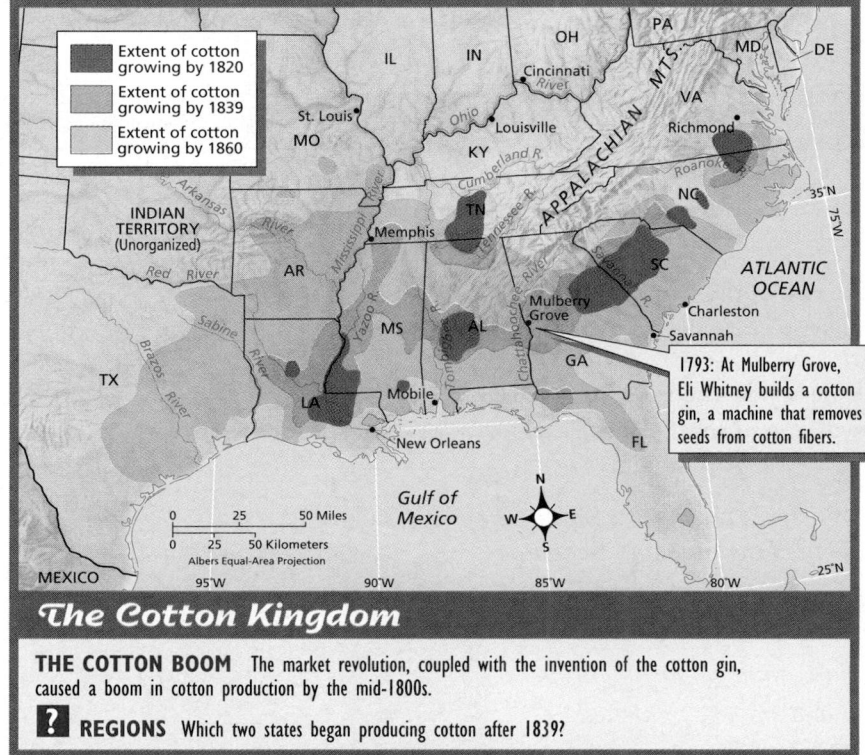

Extent of cotton growing by 1820
Extent of cotton growing by 1839
Extent of cotton growing by 1860

1793: At Mulberry Grove, Eli Whitney builds a cotton gin, a machine that removes seeds from cotton fibers.

The Cotton Kingdom

THE COTTON BOOM The market revolution, coupled with the invention of the cotton gin, caused a boom in cotton production by the mid-1800s.

? REGIONS Which two states began producing cotton after 1839?

SOUTHERN MANUFACTURING

Although cotton and other agricultural products formed the basis of the southern economy, manufacturing also played a role in economic growth, especially in the Upper South. Sawmills, ironworks, tobacco factories, textile mills, and brickyards, as well as rice, sugar, corn, and wheat mills dotted the region. The South also had one of the largest and best-equipped ironworks—the Tredegar Iron Works of Richmond, Virginia—which operated its rolling mills in the 1850s mainly by slave labor. The company manufactured steam engines for sugar mills, locomotives, cannons, railroad spikes and rails, and many other iron products.

Railroad construction and mining also added to the expanding southern economy. The Mississippi River and other inland waterways bustled with trade. Baltimore, Charleston, and Mobile were important ports. New Orleans grew to become the nation's most prosperous export center by 1840 and the fifth-largest U.S. city by 1860.

Industrialization and urbanization, however, developed more slowly in the South than in the North. The South in 1860 had 35 percent of the

nation's population but only 15 percent of the manufacturing centers. This occurred for several reasons. First, instead of investing in new factories, most southern investors continued to put their money in land and slaves. Second, planters used their influence to discourage states from passing taxes for internal improvements—improvements that might have promoted manufacturing. Third, there was a shortage of factory workers. The reliance on slave labor discouraged immigrants—the main source of cheap factory labor in the North—from coming South. Fourth, the market for manufactured goods was hurt by the fact that slaves and poor whites—the bulk of the rural population—had little or no purchasing power.

■■ **The South's continuing emphasis on plantation agriculture and slave labor slowed industrialization and urban growth.**

SOUTHERN ATTITUDES TOWARD SLAVERY

Though slave labor formed the foundation of the southern economy, some southerners criticized slavery. A few argued that an economy based on plantation agriculture and slavery was less profitable than one based on wage labor and industry. Others criticized slavery as incompatible with the American Revolution's spirit of liberty and freedom. People in the Upper South, who were less dependent on cotton, were among the most vocal critics of slavery.

Other criticisms came from southern reformers such as Jesse Burton Harrison of Virginia, who attacked the inhumanity of slavery. Fearing the upheaval that he was sure would result from

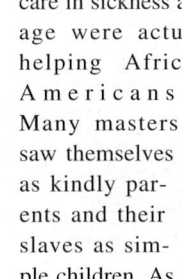

◀ Free black opponents of slavery used arguments from the Declaration of Independence to protest the enslavement of African Americans.

immediate abolition, Harrison called for a gradual end to slavery. He was not alone in his view. Most white southern abolitionists did not support immediate abolition or full equality for African Americans. Like many white abolitionists in the North, they did not believe that African Americans could fit into American society. To avoid the problem of having to accept freed blacks as citizens, many southern abolitionists joined northern abolitionists in suggesting that slaves be freed gradually and then sent to Africa. The idea of forcing freed slaves to leave the United States was especially strong among southerners who feared that free African Americans would encourage slave rebellions.

In 1817, prominent northerners and southerners founded the **American Colonization Society** for this purpose. The society's plan called for

slaveholders to free their slaves voluntarily. The society raised money to compensate slaveholders for the value of the freed slaves. Once freed, the former slaves were to be sent to Liberia—a nation the society carved out on the west coast of Africa. The impact of such efforts was limited, however. The number of slaves born in the United States in a week exceeded the number of blacks the American Colonization Society sent to Africa in a year.

One major obstacle for the colonization movement was the reluctance of African Americans to move from the United States to Africa. The idea of sending blacks "back" to Africa was a misconception. Most African Americans in the 19th-century United States had never been to Africa.

As northern attacks on slavery mounted in the 1800s, southern critics of slavery were drowned out by its supporters. Planters argued that slavery was the only way to ensure an adequate supply of field workers for southern cash crops. Slavery's defenders also insisted that planters who provided slaves with shelter, clothing, food, and care in sickness and old age were actually helping African Americans. Many masters saw themselves as kindly parents and their slaves as simple children. As

▶ In this 1832 engraving, freed slaves from the United States are shown arriving in Liberia under the sponsorship of the American Colonization Society. J. J. Roberts, the first president of Liberia, is also pictured.

The Granger Collection, New York

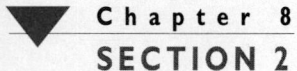
Teaching the Section

SOUTHERN SOCIETY

Work with students to create on the chalkboard a graphic organizer of the class structure of southern society. Then have volunteers describe the life-styles of each social class shown on the organizer.

PRIMARY SOURCES

Description of Change: excerpted

Rationale: excerpted to focus on main idea

COOPERATIVE LEARNING

Have students work in groups of three to discuss why most southern whites supported slavery. Assign members the following roles: wealthy planters, small farmers, and poor whites. Have each student study the text dealing with his or her assigned role and discuss his or her findings with other group members. Then ask a spokesperson from each group to summarize the group's conclusions for the class.

Thomas R. Dew, a professor at William and Mary College and noted defender of slavery, wrote:

> 66 We are well convinced that there is nothing but the mere relations of husband and wife, parent and child, brother and sister which produce a closer tie than the relation of master and servant. . . . The slaves of a good master are his warmest, most constant, and most devoted friends; they have been accustomed to look up to him as their supporter, director, and defender. 99

Another champion of slavery, southern lawyer and writer George Fitzhugh, contrasted the supposedly "secure" life of southern slaves with the sad plight of wage earners in northern and European factories and mines. Such workers, Fitzhugh argued, were at the mercy of employers who paid them little, fired them at will, and heartlessly abandoned them when they became too old or sick to work.

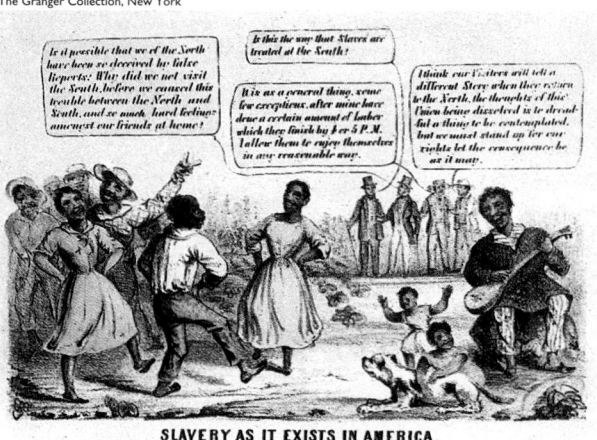

The Granger Collection, New York

▲ This 1850 cartoon compared an idealized and unrealistic image of slavery with the factory system.

Slavery mainly served the interests of the wealthiest planters. This troubled some nonslaveholding whites in the South. Most southern whites, however, supported slavery. Small farmers, even those who held no slaves, backed the institution because they hoped to become wealthy planters one day. Many poor whites supported slavery because it gave them a sense of superiority. As one white Missourian wrote in 1854:

> 66 With us, color, not money, marks the class: black is the badge of slavery; white the color of the freeman. . . . The white man, however poor, whatever be his occupation, feels himself a sovereign. 99

■■ Some southern whites opposed slavery for humanitarian or economic reasons, but most defended the institution.

SOUTHERN SOCIETY

The importance of land and slaves to the southern economy was reflected in the region's class structure. Only one in four southern whites owned slaves, but this small group dominated southern society and politics.

Planters. In 1860 less than 12 percent of the South's planters held 20 or more slaves; of these, less than 1 percent, or about 2,300, held 100 or more slaves. The 1860 census listed 14 slaveholders with as many as 500 slaves each; only one of these planters claimed control of 1,000 slaves.

The richest planters lived elegantly in beautiful tree-shaded mansions. Despite such trappings of wealth, planters often had little available cash. Much of their wealth went to brokers, mostly from the North or Great Britain, who bought their cotton and sold them household goods and farm equipment. Yet with good weather, high market prices, and skillful farm management, the cultivation of cotton or other cash crops could bring high profits.

The plantation owners' reputation for a life of ease often was more image than reality. The owners were usually quite busy managing the plantation: planning and supervising the work, assigning tasks to supervisors or slaves, keeping records of business transactions, writing to shipowners or bankers, and contracting with brokers.

Practice

GUIDED PRACTICE

Work with the class to review the South's geography, economy, and class structure in the mid-1800s. Then organize the class into groups and direct each group to prepare an outline for a report about how these factors affected southern economic development.

INDEPENDENT PRACTICE

Tell students that they are consultants hired to promote the South's economic development in the mid-1800s. Direct them to use their group's Guided Practice outline to write a report that summarizes conditions limiting economic growth and that suggests possible solutions. Students may wish to include their reports in their portfolios.

Review and Assessment

REVIEW Have students imagine they are southerners in the 1850s and write letters to the editor of their local newspaper, opposing or supporting the South's dependence on cotton. Students may wish to include their letters in their portfolios. Then assign the Section 2 Review on p. 268.

ASSESS Assign the **Section 2 Daily Quiz** in *Core Resources*.

▶

Eleanor S. Brockenbrough Library, The Museum of the Confederacy, Richmond, Virginia

▲ **Planters kept careful records of all business transactions on their plantations. A page from the 1854–56 record book of Jacob Thompson, listing the ages of his slaves, is shown here.**

The plantation mistress was not the lady of leisure depicted in myths of the Old South. In reality, she supervised the spinning, weaving, mending, housecleaning, and food preparation; cared for the sick; and often educated her children. In addition, the mistress was often expected to see to the needs of the slaves. "It is the slaves who own me," complained one mistress. "Morning, noon, and night, I'm obliged to look after them, to doctor them, and attend to them in every way."

The majority of planters, those owning less than 20 slaves, lived more modestly. Their homes were usually two-story, frame buildings with 8 to 10 rooms, deep porches, and comfortable but not luxurious furnishings.

Small farmers.
Below the planters on the social ladder were the hundreds of thousands of **yeoman farmers** who made up the majority of southern whites. Most of these small farmers lived on fertile lands but had no easy access

to markets. They built simple two-room log cabins, raised cattle and pigs, and sold some crop (often grain) for cash. They grew their own food—usually in small patches around their homes. Most small farmers owned no slaves, but some managed to afford a few. The wealth and social status of small farmers, just as that of the planters, varied considerably.

Poor whites. The poorest whites, a small percentage of the South's population, farmed the least-productive soil—the pine barrens, sand hills, and marshes. They lived in rough cabins with few material comforts. Often these families survived by hunting, fishing, and raising a few pigs.

African Americans. In 1860, the African American population in southern states varied from about 10 percent in Missouri to nearly 59 percent in South Carolina. Although most southern blacks were enslaved, by 1860 about 260,000 free blacks lived in the South. Nearly half of all free blacks made their homes in the border states of the Upper South. In Baltimore, the number of free African Americans—some 25,000 by the late 1850s—far exceeded the city's slave population of some 2,000. And in Maryland as a whole, free blacks nearly outnumbered slaves. The pattern was much different in the Lower South. Less than 2 percent of the Lower South's black population was free.

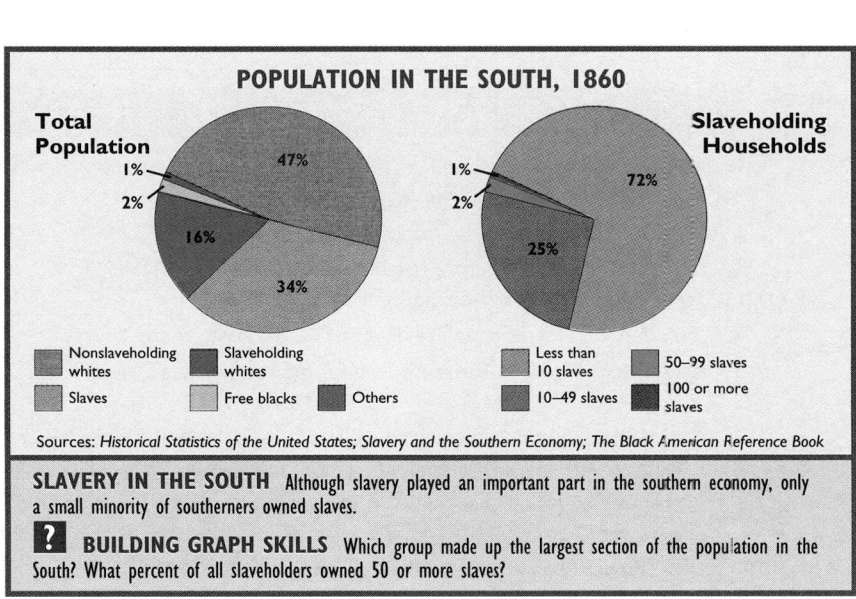

POPULATION IN THE SOUTH, 1860

Total Population
1%
2%
47%
16%
34%

Slaveholding Households
1%
2%
72%
25%

- ▮ Nonslaveholding whites
- ▮ Slaveholding whites
- ▮ Slaves
- ▮ Free blacks
- ▮ Others

- ▮ Less than 10 slaves
- ▮ 10–49 slaves
- ▮ 50–99 slaves
- ▮ 100 or more slaves

Sources: Historical Statistics of the United States; Slavery and the Southern Economy; The Black American Reference Book

SLAVERY IN THE SOUTH Although slavery played an important part in the southern economy, only a small minority of southerners owned slaves.

? **BUILDING GRAPH SKILLS** Which group made up the largest section of the population in the South? What percent of all slaveholders owned 50 or more slaves?

VOICES IN HISTORY

During the 1850s a number of Czechoslovakian immigrants settled in Texas. Most became small farmers. Some, like František Branecký, had difficulty working as wage laborers in the slave South. Branecký, who arrived in 1856, described his experiences with some landowners: "[The landowner] had me cutting brush and herding his stock, for which he paid me thirty cents a day. Of course, that was very little pay, but in those days the blacks had to work for nothing. . . . After that, my sponsor . . . bought a farm. . . . I went with him, but it turned out badly. I was with him for two years, and the money which I had brought with me had run out. Finally, I told him that we should settle up because I had grown weary of working for him. . . . He considered me a slave and said I was indebted to him and he did not want to give me anything."

Graph Caption Answer
nonslaveholding whites; 3%

RETEACH Have students work in small groups. Assign subsections to individuals or pairs. Ask students to outline the material assigned to them. Then have students trade outlines and use them to ask questions of other group members.

Closure

On the chalkboard, write this statement made by Frederick Law Olmsted, who traveled through the South in the mid-1800s: *"My own observation of the real condition of the people of our Slave States, gave me . . . an impression that the cotton monopoly in some way did them more harm than good."* Have students support or oppose the statement with examples from the section.

Extension

CREATE Have students work in pairs to research and then draw a diagram or create a model of a southern plantation, including the main house, slave quarters, and fields.

INVESTIGATE Have students work in groups to research and then prepare maps showing goods traded among the North, the South, the West, and other nations. Have them analyze the maps and write conclusions based on their findings.

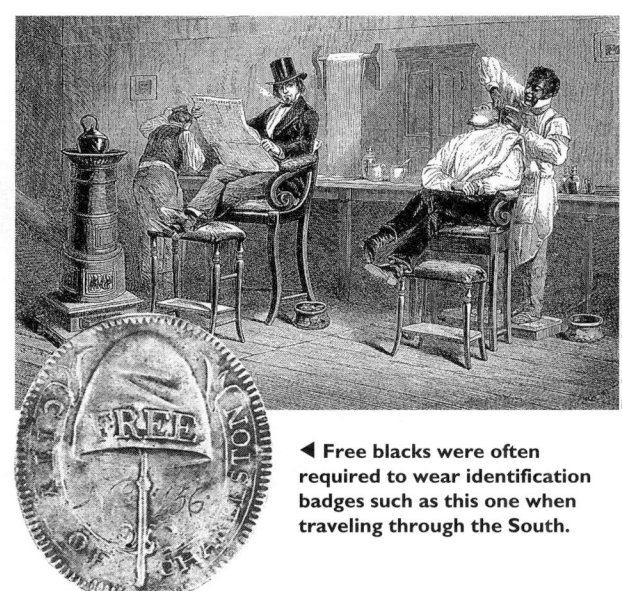

◀ Free blacks were often required to wear identification badges such as this one when traveling through the South.

◀ Some free blacks worked in skilled trades. This 1861 engraving shows a barber's shop in Richmond, Virginia.

The social and economic status of free blacks in the South, however, was never really secure. White southerners restricted the freedom of all black people. After 1830, southern legislatures severely limited the movements of free blacks, requiring them to register with local authorities and to carry identification passes proving they were not runaway slaves. Free African Americans often had to post bonds—money or a pledge of property—as a guarantee of good behavior.

Free blacks in the South could not vote, hold public meetings, speak in public, bear weapons, or testify in court against whites. In many places free African Americans were forbidden to attend all-black churches unless a white person was present. Some states denied free blacks the right to go into business for themselves or to learn how to read and write. An editorial in a black newspaper put it simply: "Though we are not slaves, we are not free."

The South's nearly four million enslaved blacks lacked even the limited rights of free African Americans. The majority of these men and women—some 55 percent—lived in the Cotton Kingdom of the Lower South, where they tended the fields and houses of the planter class.

Some free African Americans were skilled workers: mechanics, barbers, seamstresses, shoemakers, carpenters, or masons. Others found employment as cooks, waiters, laundresses, or domestic servants. Some free blacks had never been slaves, while others had worked extra hours to earn money to purchase their own freedom or were rewarded with freedom for years of dedicated service. William Ellison of South Carolina, for example, learned to repair cotton gins while a slave. After buying his own freedom, he purchased the freedom of his wife and children. A small minority of free blacks, including Ellison, became landowners and even masters of black slaves.

■■ **The southern class structure consisted of wealthy planters, small farmers, poor whites, free blacks, and slaves.**

IDENTIFY

For significance, see the following pages:
Jesse Burton Harrison (p. 264)
American Colonization Society (p. 265)
Thomas R. Dew (p. 266)
yeoman farmers (p. 267)

LOCATE

For locations, see the text and map on p. 264.

1. *cotton market boom, cotton gin, new lands; emphasis on plantation agriculture and slave labor, little investment in factories or internal improvements, few immigrant workers, low purchasing power*
2. *planters, small farmers, poor whites, free blacks, and slaves*
3. *oppose—economy based on slave labor less profitable than one based on wage labor, contrary to Revolution's ideals, inhuman; support—right to hold property, need for labor, helped protect slaves*
4. *Essays should focus on types of work and on living conditions.*
5. *economic stake in slavery, need to avoid guilt, regional bias against northern systems*

SECTION 2 REVIEW

IDENTIFY and explain the significance of the following: Jesse Burton Harrison, American Colonization Society, Thomas R. Dew, yeoman farmers.

LOCATE and explain the importance of the following: cotton belt, Tredegar Iron Works.

1. **MAIN IDEA** What factors created the southern Cotton Kingdom? Why did industries and cities grow more slowly in the South than in the North?
2. **MAIN IDEA** Identify the five different social classes in the South.
3. **CONTRASTING** What reasons did some southerners give for opposing slavery? What reasons did other southerners give for supporting slavery?
4. **WRITING TO INFORM** Write an essay about the free African Americans in southern society. Who were they? What advantages and disadvantages did they face?
5. **SYNTHESIZING** Defenders of slavery such as Thomas R. Dew and George Fitzhugh argued that slaves were better off than northern factory workers. What biases might have influenced their arguments?

PREVIEW WORKSHOP

*Following is a list of the significant
people and terms in this section.
You may wish to use this list as a
section preview.*

People
- Gabriel Prosser
- Denmark Vesey
- Nat Turner
- Harriet Tubman

Terms
- overseers
- drivers
- gang labor
- Underground Railroad
- spirituals

Section 3

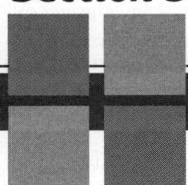

THE SLAVE SYSTEM

FOCUS

- **What was life like for slave laborers?**
- **How did slaveholders control slaves?**
- **How did African Americans resist slavery?**

*S*lavery dominated southern society. Slaveholders and slave
codes controlled the lives of enslaved African Americans, who
nevertheless continued to hope and struggle for freedom.
African Americans resisted slavery in many ways, from quiet
sabotage to outright rebellion, and strengthened family and
cultural life in efforts to survive the brutalities they suffered.

The Granger Collection, New York

Advertisement for
a runaway slave

SLAVE LABOR

Most enslaved African Americans—more than 75
percent—lived and worked on southern plantations
and farms. In the cities slaves worked as skilled
seamstresses, shoemakers, weavers, and carpenters. Slave labor was also "hired out" to employers
running coal mines, salt mines, ironworks, tobacco
factories, sugar mills, or flour mills. Some slaves

built canals, quarried rock, or drained swamps.
Still others were dockworkers, loading and unload-
ing ships in southern ports.

The life of slaves in the city was generally less
grim than that of a field hand. Field hands worked
from dawn to dusk and beyond, as many as 18–20
hours per day during the harvest. Ex-slave Peter
Clifton wrote, "The rule on the place was: Wake up
the slaves at daylight, begin work when they can
see, and quit work when they can't see." Instead of
working the fields, some slaves—especially
women—served the plantation household as maids,
cooks, or nannies. Others did sewing or laundry.
Some male slaves worked as wheelwrights, coach
drivers, gardeners, carpenters, or blacksmiths.

On small farms slaveholders usually supervised their slaves directly. On larger plantations
overseers—who were usually planters' sons,
other relatives, small farmers, or skilled workers—managed the slaves. To help supervise the
slaves, overseers used **drivers**—assistants picked
from among the slaves. Drivers occupied a difficult position between master and slave and were

◀ *Maid to the Douglas Family,* **painted by an
unknown artist in 1840, shows a slave woman who
worked in a plantation household.**

FOCUS OBJECTIVES

- Describe what life was
  like for slave laborers.

- Explain how slave-
  holders controlled
  slaves.

- Determine how
  African Americans
  resisted slavery.

CORE RESOURCES

- **Literature
  Worksheet 8**
- **Section 3 Daily Quiz**

AV RESOURCES

- *The American Nation*
  **Videodisc: Free At
  Last**

MOTIVATING:
PRIOR KNOWLEDGE

Ask students to describe the indenture system that they learned about in Chapter 3. Then have them compare that system with slavery. Guide the discussion so they recognize that both were legal institutions that addressed a need for labor, but that unlike the indenture system, slavery was involuntary and permanent. Tell students they will learn about the slave system and how enslaved persons resisted it.

even expected to handle the hated whip. A driver might be praised by the master for a job well done but be despised by the slaves for driving them too hard.

On cotton and sugar plantations, slaves were organized into tight work crews with drivers as foremen. This system of **gang labor** allowed overseers to assign groups of slaves to do specialized jobs such as plowing, hoeing, or picking, depending on the season.

■■ **Some slaves worked in manufacturing or skilled crafts, but 75 percent toiled in agriculture.**

*L*IVING CONDITIONS

To make a profit using slave labor, planters had to make sure slaves were fed, clothed, and free from illness. Masters had reason to value their human property: at an average price in 1860 of $1,200 to $1,800 each, 50 young slaves represented an investment upward of $60,000. The death or serious injury of an able-bodied slave was a major financial blow.

Many enslaved African Americans did fall victim to illnesses. Infectious disease—common among whites as well—was made worse by slaves' living and working conditions. Pneumonia and dysentery were widespread. Malnutrition frequently led to dental and other health problems.

Slave quarters were cramped and sparsely furnished. An entire family might live in a small

one-room log cabin with no more comforts than a fireplace. Gaps between the logs and the uncovered openings for doors and windows made for a cold cabin in the winter. In such homes, an observer noted, "the wind and rain will come in and the smoke will not go out."

Food was rationed on the plantation. Ben Horry, a former slave from South Carolina, explained that on Saturday every slave on the plantation lined up at the smokehouse to draw his or her share of meat, rice, grits, and meal. But these shares were seldom enough to feed slave families. To supplement their diet, slaves hunted and fished at night or on Sundays and grew greens or sweet potatoes in small gardens. House slaves sometimes received food from the planter's kitchen. Some slaves resorted to stealing food.

Slaves' clothing was simple, usually made of linsey-woolsey—a coarse woolen and linen or cotton material similar to burlap. Most slaves were given two outfits a year, one for summer and one for winter, though household slaves might receive hand-me-down clothing from the planter's family. On average, slaves got one pair of shoes a year and went barefoot when this pair wore out.

*T*REATMENT OF SLAVES

Some slaves fared better than others. Living conditions and treatment varied from plantation to plantation. Some planters used rewards instead of punishments to gain their slaves' obedience.

► *An Overseer Doing His Duty* is the title of this watercolor by Benjamin Henry Latrobe.

LIFE AS A SLAVE

Tell students to imagine that they are enslaved persons. Lead the class in brainstorming terms that might describe their lives as slaves. List students' responses on the chalkboard. Then organize the class into pairs. Direct each pair to choose 10 of the terms from the chalkboard list and to use each in a sentence that describes slavery in the South in the mid-1800s. Select pairs to read their sentences to the class.

These planters promised money, gifts of extra food or clothing, easier tasks, dances, days off, or shorter working hours to dutiful slaves. Those who obeyed orders might be granted small favors, given a garden plot, or promoted from field work to easier and more-desirable tasks in the household. Domestic slaves were generally better fed and clothed than field slaves.

▲ A slave woman is auctioned off to the highest bidder in this painting by L.J. Cranstone.

▶ An 1835 handbill advertises slaves for sale at an upcoming auction in New Orleans.

Other slaveholders relied on the use or threat of violence to control their slaves. As a planter wrote in the *Southern Patriot*, "The fear of punishment is the principle to which we must and do appeal, to keep them in awe and order."

If slaves were late getting to the fields or did not work fast or hard enough, overseers could be particularly brutal. Prince Smith, a former slave on a South Carolina plantation, recalled the use of an especially harsh form of solitary confinement—the "sweat box":

66 [The box] was made the height of the person and no larger. Just large enough so the person didn't have to be squeezed in. The box is nailed, and in summer is put in the hot sun; in winter it is put in the coldest, dampest place. 99

Sometimes slaveholders and overseers disciplined slaves with extra work or reduced rations, but whipping was the most common form of punishment. William Wells Brown, a former slave and the author of the first published novel by an African American, wrote that the whip was used "very frequently and freely, and a small offence on the part of a slave furnished an occasion for its use."

Many recipients of the lash tried to resist the master's will as best they could—often by refusing to cry out. Frederick Douglass, an escaped slave who became a prominent abolitionist, remembered one slave woman who "was not subdued, for she continued to denounce the overseer, and to call him every vile name. He had bruised her flesh, but had left her invincible spirit undaunted [determined]."

Slaves who resisted authority or showed signs of independence were whipped. If such discipline failed, they were sometimes sold "down river"—away from family and community ties.

▲ One method of slave punishment involved placing a special brace around the head to restrict the person's movement. Wilson Chinn, a slave from Louisiana, is shown here in a restrictive brace. Notice also the brand across his forehead.

PRIMARY SOURCE

Description of Change: excerpted and bracketed
Rationale: excerpted to focus on main idea; bracketed to clarify meaning

Teaching the *Section*

CONTROLLING SLAVES

Discuss with students the methods used by slaveholders to control slaves. Then ask volunteers to identify rights that were denied slaves, and list them on the chalkboard.

▪▪ Ask students to identify the rights denied to slaves that they themselves most value and to explain their answer.

HISTORICAL SIDELIGHTS

Gabriel Prosser

Gabriel Prosser advocated killing all whites—except Quakers, Methodists, and Frenchmen. He felt they were "friendly to liberty." Poor white women who had no slaves also were to be spared. Although Prosser's insurrection ended without a shot fired or any whites killed or wounded, historians estimate that 10 to 35 slaves were later executed.

PRIMARY SOURCE

Description of Change: excerpted and bracketed
Rationale: excerpted to focus on main idea; bracketed to clarify meaning

BIO GRAPHY PERSONALITIES IN HISTORY

Nat Turner's rebellion was especially shocking to whites because Southampton was considered a fairly moderate community. Over one third of Southampton's white families owned no slaves. Of those who did, many were small landowners who worked in the fields alongside their slaves.

"Marster Biggers believe in whipping and working his slaves long and hard," recalled ex-slave Peter Clifton; "then a man was scared all the time of being sold away from his wife and chillun."

Slave marriages had no legal standing in the South. Thus, slaveholders would sometimes break up a slave couple by selling one but not the other or by auctioning a husband and wife to different buyers. Since slaves brought higher prices when sold separately, slave children were often sold away from parents. Solomon Northup, a northern free black who was kidnapped and enslaved for 12 years, described an 1841 slave auction in which a mother pleaded not to be separated from her child:

 The afflicted mother . . . kept on begging and beseeching them, most piteously, not to separate the three. Over and over again she told them how she loved her boy. . . . But it was of no avail. . . . Then [the mother] ran to [her son] . . . told him to remember her—all the while her tears falling in the boy's face like rain. . . . It was a mournful scene indeed. I would have cried myself if I had dared. **99**

Laws failed to protect enslaved African Americans from brutality. On the contrary, southern slave codes—which covered all aspects of slaves' lives—rendered slaves legally powerless. Slaves were forbidden to testify in court against whites, to own property, to possess firearms, to be out after curfew, or to leave their plantations without a pass. Any white person could stop any black person and demand to see proof of either free status or permission to be away from his or her master. White patrols roamed the rural South to enforce the laws and to apprehend any slaves trying to escape.

▪▪ **Slaveholders used rewards, punishments, and laws to control slaves.**

---

*R*EBELLION AND RESISTANCE

Despite their lack of legal power, slaves used several strategies to improve their living and working conditions. From the quiet revenge of running away or working slowly to open rebellion, African Americans found ways to resist slavery.

Slave revolts. The first half of the 19th century saw several small uprisings involving slaves in the South. In 1800 a planned rebellion near Richmond involved hundreds of slaves led by Gabriel Prosser. Another plot surfaced in 1822 in Charleston. The plan, masterminded by African American Denmark Vesey, a prosperous carpenter and popular preacher, called for a massive slave uprising in Charleston and the surrounding areas.

The plan was discovered before it could be carried out, and Vesey and the other leaders were tried and executed. It nevertheless struck terror into the hearts of southern whites. Slaveholders knew that their power over slaves was based on force; they feared a massacre of the white population if slaves sought revenge. The sheer number of African Americans who might have joined the revolt—in 1820 Charleston was nearly 57 percent black—deepened whites' fears. Most of the accused slaves had been liked, respected, and trusted by their masters. Even three of the governor's own household servants had joined Vesey's revolt!

BIO GRAPHY White southerners' worst fears materialized in 1831, when Nat Turner led a violent slave uprising in Southampton County, Virginia. Turner was born in 1800 to an African-born mother. Soon after, his father ran away to freedom. Turner was very bright, and he later claimed to have taught himself to read after his mother gave him a spelling book. Turner's grandmother, who took charge of his spiritual education, told him he was destined to grow up to be a great man. He prayed, fasted, and read the Bible to discover his life's purpose.

The Granger Collection, New York

Nat Turner

The deeply religious Turner believed that he had received his answer when he began seeing visions of white and black spirits battling in the heavens: God had chosen him to free the slaves. A solar eclipse in February 1831 seemed to him a sign that it was time for action.

Turner planned to start his rebellion on July 4, Independence Day, but illness forced a delay. On August 21 Turner and a small band of followers went into action. They killed Turner's master, the

VIEWS ON SLAVE REVOLTS

Have students work in small groups to prepare newspaper headlines, introductory paragraphs, and illustrations or editorial cartoons describing one of the slave revolts as viewed by either a northern or a southern newspaper.

▶

master's family, and about 60 other whites in the area. The state militia and terrified local whites organized a hunt for Turner, killing at least 100 slaves during the two months that it took to track him down. After being captured at his hideout, a spot still called "Nat Turner's Cave," the fugitive was brought to trial. Asked why he refused to plead guilty, Turner replied, "Because I don't feel guilty." He was hanged on November 11, 1831.

Following these slave uprisings, some southern states passed stricter slave codes. These laws made it illegal to teach slaves to read and placed more restrictions on slaves' movements. Some whites took the law into their own hands, arresting, beating, and killing slaves at will. Recalled one slave woman:

66 The whites threatened to punish 'em dreadfully, if the least noise was heard. The patrols was low drunken Whites; and in Nat's time, if they heard one of the colored folks praying, or singing a hymn, they would . . . abuse 'em, and sometimes kill 'em. 99

Slave resistance. Open rebellion was rare. Slaves generally protested their bondage through individual actions. They might fake an illness, slow their work pace, or damage tools or other property in an effort to disrupt the plantation routine. In some cases, desperate slaves mutilated

Map legend:
- Counties with slave population 50% or more
- Counties with slave population 10%–50%
- Counties with slave population <10%
- Counties with slave population 0%, or no data
- → Escape route

The Underground Railroad

ROAD TO FREEDOM It is estimated that the more than 3,000 members of the Underground Railroad helped from 50,000 to 75,000 enslaved African Americans escape to freedom.

? LOCATION Why do you think Cairo, Illinois, and Cincinnati, Ohio, were important stops on the Underground Railroad?

themselves, cutting off toes or hands, hoping to avoid being sold or to escape harsh treatment and overwork. Others committed suicide.

The most tempting form of resistance was to run away, whether for only a few days or permanently. Chances of success were slim, and punishment if caught was brutal. Some aid came from the **Underground Railroad**, a network of white and black abolitionists who helped slaves escape to freedom in the North or in Canada. Escaping slaves slowly made their way out of the South, hidden in attics and haylofts by day and taken by

VOICES IN HISTORY

After escaping to freedom, J. W. Loguen went to college, became a minister, and settled in Syracuse, New York, where he assisted with the Underground Railroad. In 1859 he published an account of his life as a slave. Alerted to his whereabouts, his former owner contacted him, demanding that he return or compensate her for her loss. Loguen printed his reply in the abolitionist newspaper *The Liberator:* "You say you have offers to buy me, and that you shall sell me if I do not send you $1000, and . . . almost in the same sentence you say, 'You know we raised you as we did our own children.' Woman, did you raise your own children for the market? Did you raise them for the whipping post?"

PRIMARY SOURCE
Description of Change: excerpted
Rationale: excerpted to focus on main idea

Map Caption Answer
both located on major rivers just across the border from slave states

Teaching the Section

RESISTING SLAVERY

Have students create graphic organizers showing the different means that African Americans used to resist slavery and the obstacles they faced in each case. Ask volunteers to present their organizers to the class. Students may wish to include their organizers in their portfolios.

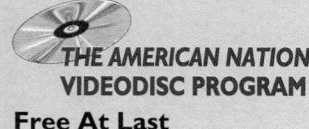

THE AMERICAN NATION VIDEODISC PROGRAM
Free At Last

| 1B | 15914 | 2:57 |

GLOBAL CONNECTIONS

Many runaway slaves fled to Canada, where they could not be captured and returned to their masters. To many slaves, *Canada* became another word for freedom. Most slaves who escaped to Canada settled in southern Ontario. One runaway slave, Josiah Henson, founded a fugitive settlement. Risking his own freedom, he returned to the South to lead slaves through the Underground Railroad to his settlement.

PRIMARY SOURCE

Description of Change: excerpted
Rationale: excerpted to focus on main idea

◄ **Harriet Tubman used the Underground Railroad to free more than 300 slaves.**

"conductors" to the next safe house at night. At first, most slaves were smuggled to safety at night and on foot. As more slaves made the attempt, covered wagons and carriages were used. Sometimes, runaway slaves were even smuggled by rail or boat, hidden inside crates. A song that inspired many slaves on their dangerous journeys expressed their hope for a new life in Canada:

> ❝ Farewell, old master
> Don't come after me.
> I'm on my way to Canada
> Where colored men are
> free. ❞

The conductors on the Underground Railroad helped thousands of slaves gain their freedom. Harriet Tubman, who escaped from a Maryland plantation in 1849, was the most famous and successful conductor. Risking her own freedom, Tubman returned to the South

▶ **This colorful quilt, which was made about 1886 by an ex-slave named Harriet Powers, depicts Biblical themes.**

19 times to lead more than 300 slaves to safety in the North.

■■ **Slave resistance took many forms, from work slowdowns and sabotage to escape and open rebellion.**

Despite the daring of the slaves and those people who aided them, many fugitives were captured and returned to their masters. But the stream of runaways never stopped.

SLAVE CULTURE

Although slaves' lives were controlled from sunup to sundown, their time was mostly their own when the workday ended. After dark and on Sundays and rare holidays, slaves devoted time to family and community, creating a unique African American culture. This culture blended to a remarkable degree customs drawn from the variety of African groups thrown together under slavery. At the center of this culture were family, religion, music, folktales, and humor.

Family and kinship bonds. Preserving family ties was a difficult challenge for enslaved African Americans. Slave marriages were not legally recognized, and slave families were always subject to being split up by the sale of individual

SLAVE CULTURE

Call on volunteers to describe the family, religion, music, folktales, and humor of the slave culture in the American South. Then have students work in pairs to write a poem or song that describes their own contemporary culture. Ask volunteers to share their work with the class.

▶

members. In response to forced separations, slaves extended their family ties to include distant as well as close relatives. Nonrelated individuals also shared significantly in a family's life and were commonly known to children as aunts and uncles.

Many slaves made valiant efforts to stay in contact with family members despite being separated. One slave told how he ran away from his master to seek his mother on a distant plantation years after their forced parting:

❝ I asked [my mother] if she knew me? she said, no. . . . I then asked her if she had any sons? she said, yes; but none so large as me. I then [described] . . . being sold into slavery, and how she grieved at my loss. . . . [Her] dire feelings on that occasion . . . rushed to her mind; she saw her own son before her, for whom she had so often wept; and, in an instant, we were clasped in each other's arms. ❞

Religion and music. Religion played a vital role in the lives of enslaved African Americans. Most worship services were a rich blend of Christian elements and traditional African beliefs, music, and dance.

Embracing the Christian belief in salvation and a heavenly future helped some slaves endure the hardships they faced. Central to the slaves' religion was their belief that they were God's chosen people who, like the Hebrews in the land of the pharaohs, would eventually reach a "promised land" free from their oppressors. The slaves' promised land was not just an afterlife of freedom; it was also a world without slavery.

Unlike white ministers who preached obedience to masters, African American preachers spoke to what was close to the hearts of slaves. For example, in 1851 a black Baptist minister named Bentley preached a sermon on the occasion of President Millard Fillmore's visit to Savannah, Georgia. According to Bentley, when the president arrived in a "grand, beautiful carriage and drove to the best house in . . . town," blacks were kept from coming too close.

❝ The great gentlemen and the rich folks went freely up the steps and in through the door and shook hands with him. Now, did Christ come in this way? Did He come only

to the rich? Did He shake hands only with them? No! Blessed be the Lord! He came to the poor! He came to us, and for our sakes, my brothers and sisters! ❞

After Nat Turner's rebellion, many masters stopped allowing slaves to congregate, even for religious meetings. Slaveholders feared that the slaves would seize every opportunity to plot a rebellion. Enslaved African Americans continued to hold gatherings, but they took to hiding in the woods to avoid detection by white patrols. To quiet the noise during these secret meetings, the slaves devised methods of muffling sound, such as making enclosures of wet quilts. With the noise thus muted, one former slave explained, they "could shout and sing all they wanted to and the noise wouldn't go outside."

Of great importance to slave religion were the haunting songs called **spirituals**. Rich in Biblical lore, these "Sorrow Songs" were sung during work, relaxation, and worship. They were modeled in part on Christian hymns and in part on traditional African rituals and musical forms. Spirituals movingly expressed the slaves' deep longing for freedom. Favorites like "Go Down, Moses," "Blow Your Trumpet, Gabriel," and "Didn't My Lord Deliver Daniel?" tell of deliverance from bondage.

John Antrobus, *Plantation Burial*, (1860) oil on canvas, The Historic New Orleans Collection

▲ *Plantation Burial*, **painted by John Antrobus in 1860, records an African American funeral on a plantation in northern Louisiana.**

PRIMARY SOURCE

Description of Change: excerpted and bracketed
Rationale: excerpted to focus on main idea; bracketed to clarify meaning

PRIMARY SOURCE

Description of Change: excerpted
Rationale: excerpted to focus on main idea

MAKING CONNECTIONS

Music
In African culture, music is used to tell history, celebrate festivals, honor the dead, and direct work. While they worked in the fields, plantation slaves sang antiphonal (call-and-response) and hymnlike songs. These songs helped the cotton pickers, cane cutters, and rice harvesters pace their work.

Practice

GUIDED PRACTICE

Ask students to review the text material on slave resistance, pp. 273–274, and, if possible, to research additional information about Harriet Tubman and the Underground Railroad. Then guide students to outline the main points in preparation for writing about this topic.

INDEPENDENT PRACTICE

Have students write a journal entry from the viewpoint of Harriet Tubman, detailing her memory of a narrow escape on the Underground Railroad and expressing her feelings about her life's accomplishments. Students may wish to include their journal entries in their portfolios.

Review and Assessment

REVIEW Organize the class into five groups and assign each group one of the section's main headings. Have each group design and interpret a quilt similar to the one shown on p. 274 that illustrates the content under their assigned heading. Then assign the Section 3 Review on p. 277.

ASSESS Assign the **Section 3 Daily Quiz** in *Core Resources.*

Then and Now

Many of the characteristics of break dancing also have roots in traditional dances of Africa. The circle formation of break dancing and the way break dancers take turns giving solo performances in the middle of the circle are characteristic of the African *juba* dance. African Americans combined the shuffle steps of the *juba* with the steps and movements of the Irish Jig to form the tap dance. Tap dance led to flash dancing, a tap-dance style that incorporates acrobatic movements such as splits and flips. Black tap dancers also experimented with dance steps borrowed from the Russians, such as drops, squats, and sweeps. Many of these tap-dance and flash-dance movements are evident in the movements and body control of break dancers.

PRIMARY SOURCE

Description of Change:
excerpted
Rationale: excerpted to focus on main idea

Then and Now — SHOUTS ACROSS THE OCEAN

When Africans were forcibly brought to North America as slaves, their culture and traditions crossed the ocean with them. Today, African influences are visible throughout American society. American dance and music, for example, have roots in the centuries-old dances and musical forms of Africa.

In much of Africa, religious and ceremonial dances are performed in a ring, with dancers slowly moving counterclockwise in a circle. Noting the subtle movements of a dancer, one observer remarked:

▲ The influence of African musical forms is still evident in African American religious ceremonies. Shown here are members of the Bradford Singers, a noted gospel group.

> ❝ It takes time to appreciate the variety and detail in the different movements and the unceasing, wave-like ripple which runs down the muscles of the back and along the arms to the finger-tips. Every part of the body dances, not only the limbs. ❞

The ring often symbolizes the life cycle—the circle of birth and death. Thus, it is an important part of many burial ceremonies, used to show respect for and a connection to one's ancestors.

The African ring dances were the source of the ring shout in American slave culture. Slaves sang, shouted, and clapped their hands as they moved counterclockwise in a circle. Barely lifting their feet from the ground, they rhythmically pounded the earth with their heels. As in Africa, the dancing and singing were forms of spiritual expression directed to ancestors.

Over time the ring shout and other African dances inspired new forms of dance in America. In the early 1900s jazz dance built on the rhythmic shuffling and pistonlike arm movements of the ring shout. But the influence of African dance was probably most widespread in the 1920s. The Charleston, which both blacks and whites danced, was wildly popular all over the country. Few people realized it was based on a religious dance in Africa.

With new forms of dance came new forms of music. Some slaves adapted songs with Christian lyrics to the ring shout. The result was the Negro spiritual, which remains an important part of many African American religious ceremonies. Several leading concert artists, such as Paul Robeson, Marian Anderson, and Leontyne Price, helped popularize spirituals.

The rhythms and emotional tones of the ring shout greatly influenced blues music as well. And the blues, in turn, shaped today's popular music. Rock musicians such as the Rolling Stones and Eric Clapton have drawn on the blues for inspiration.

Well-known performers, such as James Brown and Aretha Franklin, trained in the musical traditions of the black church, have also influenced a new generation of artists, among them Janet Jackson. In all these ways, African dance and music, like other features of African culture, have left strong and lasting imprints on American life.

—Dr. Sterling Stuckey

RETEACH Suggest that students work in small groups, with each student assigned the task of summarizing the information in a subsection by designing a poster. Have groups present their posters.

Closure

Have students explain what they think the short-term and long-term effects of slavery were on those who were enslaved.

Extension

INTERPRET Encourage students to sing or bring recordings of African American spirituals. Ask the class to interpret the feelings communicated by the words and music.

RESEARCH Students might wish to research the Underground Railroad and draw one route that shows how long the journey took, how escapees traveled, where they stayed, where they settled.

Folktales and humor. Slaves used folktales as an important means of passing on their culture. These folktales were based on African stories but related local situations, family histories, and personal experiences. Most of the tales concerned everyday human relationships, detailing the importance of friendship or a parent's love and caring. Children who misbehaved might be told the story of the chicks who disregarded their mother's warning cries and were eaten by a hawk. Moral tales warned of the pitfalls of excessive pride or stressed the ideals of cooperation and love.

Storytelling, especially the use of animal trickster tales, gave African Americans a way of talking about whites and slavery in a guarded form. In these humorous tales the attempt by the strong to trap the weak always fails. Instead, the weaker animal, such as Anansi the spider or Brer Rabbit, tricks the stronger animal and in the end gains wealth, success, and power.

Trickster tales allowed African Americans to reverse, at least in the mind, the harsh fact of the master-slave relationship. Laughter helped slaves deal with painful situations, allowing them to endure slavery, rather than be crushed by it. Wrote John Little, a former slave:

66 They say slaves are happy, because they laugh, and are merry. I myself and three or four others, have received two hundred lashes in the day, and had our feet in fetters [chains]; yet, at night, we would sing and dance, and make others laugh at the rattling

of our chains. . . . We did it to keep down trouble, and to keep our hearts from being completely broken. 99

This ability to maintain hope in the face of overwhelming abuse was perhaps enslaved African Americans' most remarkable form of resistance.

■■ **Through family ties, religion, music, and folktales, African Americans endured slavery and created a unique culture.**

▲ Joel Chandler Harris popularized animal trickster tales in books such as *Uncle Remus and Brer Rabbit*. This collage contains original A.B. Frost illustrations for Harris's stories.

PRIMARY SOURCE

Description of Change: excerpted and bracketed
Rationale: excerpted to focus on main idea; bracketed to clarify meaning

SECTION REVIEW ANSWERS

IDENTIFY
For significance, see the following pages:
overseers (p. 269)
drivers (p. 269)
gang labor (p. 270)
Gabriel Prosser (p. 272)
Denmark Vesey (p. 272)
Nat Turner (p. 272)
Underground Railroad (p. 273)
Harriet Tubman (p. 274)
spirituals (p. 275)

1. *Most were employed in agriculture.*
2. *rebellions, running away, work slowdowns, sabotage, self-mutilation*
3. *to control slaves—they believed that fear of punishment would make slaves obedient; slaves lived in fear and tried to resist violence by not crying out or showing their fear*
4. *Folktales will vary but should describe local situations, family histories, or personal experiences.*
5. *Speeches might describe the brutalities of the slave system and might also mention that Turner believed he was chosen by God to free the slaves.*

■■ **SECTION 3 REVIEW**

IDENTIFY and explain the significance of the following: overseers, drivers, gang labor, Gabriel Prosser, Denmark Vesey, Nat Turner, Underground Railroad, Harriet Tubman, spirituals.

1. **MAIN IDEA** What kind of work did most slaves perform?
2. **MAIN IDEA** What strategies did African Americans use to resist slavery?
3. **IDENTIFYING CAUSE AND EFFECT** Why did many slaveholders try to discipline slaves by using severe punishments such as whipping and the "sweat box"? How did the use of these methods affect the slave community?
4. **WRITING TO CREATE** Write a folktale that reflects the experiences of a slave living in the 1850s.
5. **USING HISTORICAL IMAGINATION** Imagine that you are Nat Turner facing trial for leading a slave rebellion in 1831. Prepare a speech to give to the jury.

Return to the Themes section on p. 254. Have students discuss these again and compare their original responses with those given now. (See p. 253B for suggested answers.)

Chapter Review Answers

WRITING A SUMMARY
See Essential Points in each section for main ideas.

REVIEWING CHRONOLOGY
4, 1, 5, 3, 2
Writing to Create
Posters will vary but should depict the events chosen.

IDENTIFYING PEOPLE AND IDEAS
1. *tactic of refusing to work until employer meets union demands*
2. *founder of Lowell Female Labor Reform Association who organized other mill workers*
3. *prejudices favoring native-born Americans over immigrants*
4. *nickname of the anti-immigrant American party*
5. *escaped slave who returned to the South to lead others to freedom*
6. *small farmers who made up the majority of southern whites*
7. *southern professor and noted defender of slavery*
8. *planters' relatives, small farmers, or skilled workers hired to manage slaves*
9. *slave who led rebellion in Virginia in 1831*
10. *slave songs modeled on Christian hymns and African musical forms*

278

UNDERSTANDING MAIN IDEAS
1. society—increased cultural diversity and labor force, increased nativist prejudices; politics—nativists tried to restrict immigration and immigrants' political rights, Irish gained hold in urban politics
2. Reapers and other devices led to commercial farming by increasing demand for Middle Western farm products in the Northeast and by providing new farm machinery that increased crop yields; provided low-cost products, resulting in farm families purchasing many goods rather than making them.

3. Slavery identified social status: wealthy planters with many slaves were distinguished from small planters with few or no slaves; free blacks were distinguished from slaves.
4. Work was harsh, hours were long, slaves lived under constant fear of punishment, housing was cramped, food was rationed, clothing was simple, and disease and illness were widespread. Slaves responded with open rebellion or quiet resistance and by developing a slave culture.

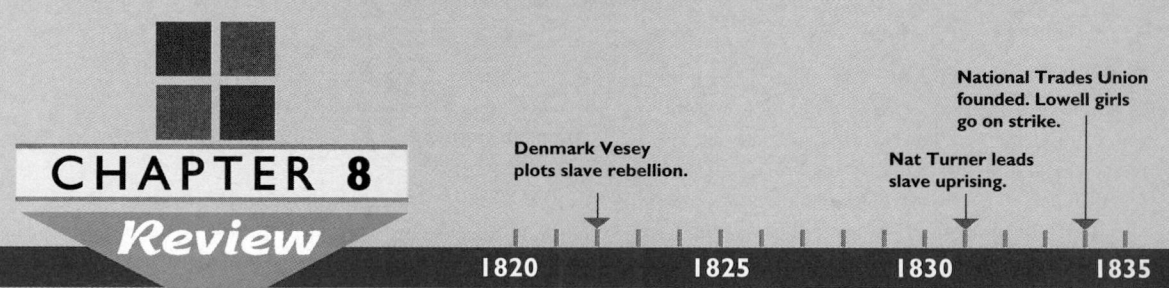

CHAPTER 8
Review

National Trades Union founded. Lowell girls go on strike.

Denmark Vesey plots slave rebellion.

Nat Turner leads slave uprising.

1820   1825   1830   1835

WRITING A SUMMARY
Using the essential points of the chapter as a guide, write a summary of the chapter.

REVIEWING CHRONOLOGY
Number your paper 1 to 5. Study the time line above, and list the following events in the order in which they happened by writing the first event next to 1, the second next to 2, and so on. Then complete the activity below.

1. National Trades Union founded.
2. American party nominates Millard Fillmore for president.
3. Order of the Star-Spangled Banner formed.
4. Nat Turner leads slave uprising.
5. President Van Buren sets 10-hour workday for federal employees.

Writing to Create Create a poster that depicts any two events on the time line.

IDENTIFYING PEOPLE AND IDEAS
Explain the historical significance of each of the following people or terms.

1. strike
2. Sarah G. Bagley
3. nativism
4. Know-Nothings
5. Harriet Tubman
6. yeoman farmers
7. Thomas R. Dew
8. overseers
9. Nat Turner
10. spirituals

UNDERSTANDING MAIN IDEAS
1. What effects did increased immigration have on American society and politics?
2. How did the market revolution and industrialization change farming and farm life in the Middle West?
3. How did the slave economy influence the South's class structure?
4. Describe the working and living conditions of slaves on southern plantations. How did slaves respond to these conditions?

REVIEWING THEMES
1. **Economic Development** What are some of the ways in which the growth of manufacturing affected northern society?
2. **Cultural Diversity** How did slavery influence African American culture in the 1800s?
3. **Technology and Society** What effect did Eli Whitney's cotton gin have on the slave economy of the South?

THINKING CRITICALLY
1. **Evaluating** What factors led to the increase in immigration to the United States from 1820 to 1860?
2. **Analyzing** How did the lives of large planters differ from those of yeoman farmers?
3. **Hypothesizing** How might slavery have been affected if industrialization in the South had advanced as it did in the North?

STRATEGY FOR SUCCESS
Review the Skills Handbook entry on Studying Primary and Secondary Sources beginning on page 998. Then study the following verses from a slave spiritual. Along with their religious meaning, how might the words relate to the life of a slave? What 19th-century people, places, and events might be represented by Moses, Israel, Egypt, and the Pharaoh and by the phrases "oppressed so hard" and "smite your first-born dead"?

> **❝**Go down Moses,
> 'Way down in Egypt land,
> Tell ole Pharaoh,
> To let my people go.
> When Israel was in Egypt land,
> Let my people go,
> Oppressed so hard they could not stand,
> Let my people go.
> Thus spoke the Lord, bold Moses said,
> Let my people go,
> If not I'll smite [strike] your first-born dead,
> Let my people go.**❞**

REVIEWING THEMES

1. created economic prosperity for new middle class; attracted immigrants to factory system; led to rise of labor unions
2. African Americans maintained family ties, religious practices, music, and folktales to help them endure slavery.
3. lowered the price and time of cloth making and thus increased cotton production; encouraged cotton cultivation in new lands across the South; helped revitalize the slave system

THINKING CRITICALLY

1. transportation revolution; poverty, hunger, political and religious oppression in Europe; economic opportunity in U.S.
2. Owners of large plantations lived elegantly, surrounded by many slaves; yeoman farmers lived in simple cabins and raised their own food, and most had no slaves.
3. Answers might mention that slavery may have ended as manufacturing increased the profitability of wage labor over slavery.

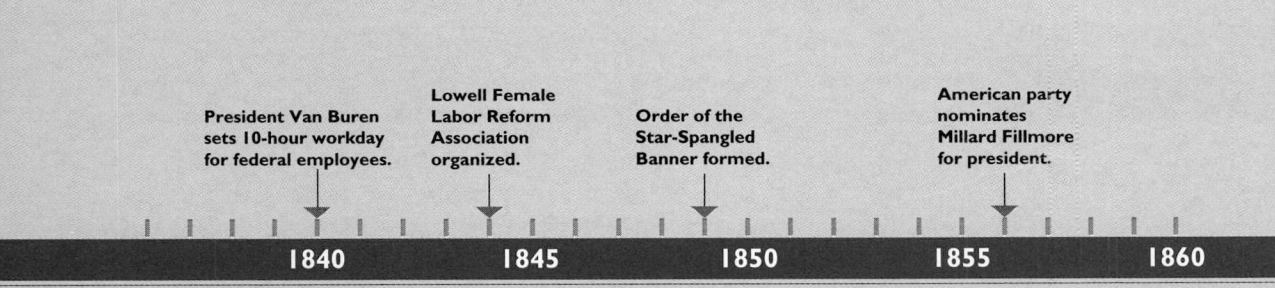

President Van Buren sets 10-hour workday for federal employees.

Lowell Female Labor Reform Association organized.

Order of the Star-Spangled Banner formed.

American party nominates Millard Fillmore for president.

1840   1845   1850   1855   1860

WRITING ABOUT HISTORY

Writing to Describe You are a "conductor" on the Underground Railroad. Write a diary entry describing your most recent efforts to help a slave family escape to freedom.

USING PRIMARY SOURCES

Many of the Lowell girls were well-educated women who found that their daily work did not provide intellectual fulfillment. To fulfill this need they established the *Lowell Offering,* a literary magazine written and edited by female mill workers. Read the following excerpt from an article written by the magazine's editors in 1845. Then write a paragraph explaining how the editors believed the *Lowell Offering* was different from other magazines and why they thought others should support them.

66 *Our magazine is the only one which America has produced, of which no other country has produced the like. The* Offering *is . . . evidence, not only of the American "factory-girls," but of the intelligence of the mass of our country. And it is in the intelligence of the mass that the permanency of our republican institutions depends.*

And our last appeal is to those who should support us, if for no other reason but their interest in "the cultivation of humanity," and the maintenance of true *democracy. There is little but this of which we, as a people, can be proud. Other nations can look upon the relics of a glory come and gone—upon their magnificent ruins. . . . We have other and better things. Let us look upon our "free suffrage,". . . our Common Schools, our Mechanics' Literary Associations, the Periodical of our Laboring Females; upon all that is indigenous [native] to our Republic, and say . . . these are our jewels.* 99

LINKING HISTORY AND GEOGRAPHY

In the period from 1820 to 1860 some cotton planters, newly arrived immigrants, and established northern farmers moved westward. Write an essay explaining the reasons for such migrations.

Mississippi cotton plantation

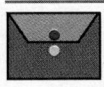
BUILDING YOUR PORTFOLIO

Complete the following projects independently or cooperatively.

1. **THE ECONOMY** In Chapter 7 you created a chart for a textile factory. Building on that material, imagine you are a southern plantation owner. Draw a map that illustrates how the transportation revolution will make it easier for you to transport your cotton to northern textile factories.

2. **IMMIGRATION** Imagine you are a newly arrived immigrant in New York City. Present an oral account of your trip to the United States, your passage through customs, and your current living and working conditions.

3. **INDIVIDUAL RIGHTS** In Chapter 7 you created a political poster. Building on that material, imagine you are a factory worker on strike. Create a speech to be given to your co-workers inspiring them to join you in protesting unfair treatment.

WORKING FOR REFORM

1820s–1860s

Chapter Overview

At the start of the 19th century, Americans were full of hope and optimism, believing that individuals and society both were capable of perfection. But many viewed the rapidly changing society around them as being far from perfect. Great numbers of Americans turned to religion for guidance, and a revivalist movement spread across the country.

Reformers applied their energy to changing society. Some helped prisoners, the mentally ill, alcoholics, or the poor, or worked to make public education a reality. Other reformers, black and white, worked to abolish slavery. And women, who were active in many reforms, began to examine their place in society and to call for greater political and social equality.

THE AMERICAN NATION VIDEODISC PROGRAM
A variety of still images, short videos, and activities are available for you to use as you teach this chapter. See Correlation to *The American Nation* Videodisc Program for barcode correlations and suggestions for using the program.

Chapter Planning Guide

CHAPTER 9	CORE RESOURCE BOOKLETS	AUDIOVISUAL (AV) RESOURCES	PROGRAM RESOURCES
INTRODUCTION pp. 280–281	■ Building Your Portfolio Worksheet 3	■ Everyday Life in America Transparency and Worksheet 9	■ *Eyewitnesses and Others*, Volume 1: Reading 53
TEACHING THE CHAPTER pp. 282–301	■ Graphic Organizer 9 ■ Social Studies Skills Worksheet 9 ■ Literature Worksheet 9 ■ Geography Worksheet 9 ■ Outline Maps 9, 19	■ *The American Nation* Videodisc: The Reform Movement	■ *Eyewitnesses and Others*, Volume 1: Readings 44, 45, 49, 59, 61, 62, 63, 64, 69
REVIEW AND ASSESSMENT pp. 302–303	■ Chapter 9 Daily Quizzes ■ Review Worksheet 9 ■ Chapter 9 Tests ■ Alternative Assessment Forms		■ Test Generator

Additional Resources

BOOKS FOR TEACHERS

Evans, Sara M. *Born for Liberty: A History of Women in America.* The Free Press, 1990. Discusses women's contributions.

Luchetti, Cathy. *Under God's Spell: Frontier Evangelists 1772–1915.* Harcourt Brace Jovanovich, 1989. Includes selections from letters and journals.

Sterling, Dorothy, ed. *We Are Your Sisters: Black Women in the Nineteenth Century.* W.W. Norton, 1985. History of black women in the 19th century.

BOOKS FOR STUDENTS

Douglass, Frederick. *My Bondage and My Freedom.* Reprint Services, 1992. Autobiography of Douglass.

* Krass, Peter. *Sojourner Truth.* Chelsea House Publishers, 1988. Examines Truth's campaign against slavery.

Schlaifer, Charles, and Lucy Freeman. *Heart's Work: The Life of Civil War Heroine and Champion of the Mentally Ill, Dorothea Dix.* Paragon House, 1991. Covers Dix's crusade to help the mentally ill.

* for students reading below grade level

MULTIMEDIA MATERIALS

Frederick Douglass: An American Life. Video, 31 min. National Park Service/SSSS. Uses excerpts from Douglass's writings to dramatize his life.

Hearts and Hands. Video, 63 min. Hearts and Hands Media Arts/SSSS. Two-part documentary on 19th-century American women.

Sojourner Truth. Video, 30 min. Library Video/SSSS. Archival visuals and period music capture Truth's life.

USE WITH PAGES 280–281

Listed on the right are the themes emphasized in Chapter 9. The questions in boldface type stimulate critical thinking and provide students with an opportunity to discuss the themes within a broadened context. The questions also appear in the pupil's edition on p. 280.

■ DEMOCRATIC VALUES

What impact might citizens' reform groups have on public policies? Students should consider the influence that such groups might have in a democratic political system. They might suggest examples of policies citizens' groups might try to change and explain why. Students should also consider how citizens' groups might try to achieve their goals.

■ CULTURAL DIVERSITY

What changes in society might lead to a new interest in religion and to an interest in new forms of community? Students might note that rapid social change commonly leads people to question values and ways of living. Such questioning might lead them to try to improve their spiritual lives and to work for social reform.

CHAPTER STRATEGIES FOR MEETING INDIVIDUAL NEEDS

LIMITED ENGLISH PROFICIENT LEARNERS

Have students work in small groups to choose a person listed in the chapter's Preview Workshops to interview for a newspaper story. Groups should write a script and present their interviews.

TACTILE/KINESTHETIC LEARNERS

Have students work in pairs to create skits about a section of the chapter. They may dramatize a meeting between real people, such as Elizabeth Cady Stanton and Frederick Douglass, or create fictional characters.

LEARNERS HAVING DIFFICULTY

As students move through the chapter, have them work in pairs to answer the basic questions of who, what, when, where, and why (whichever ones apply) for each subhead in the chapter.

AUDITORY LEARNERS

Have students choose passages in the chapter of which they are unsure. Read the selections aloud and lead a class discussion on them.

VISUAL LEARNERS

After students study the chapter, have them look in library books or magazines for visual materials that would be suitable for posters publicizing the social and political reforms discussed in the chapter.

GIFTED LEARNERS

Have students write essays on the moral, political, and economic content of the reform movements, and explain which elements were most significant with regard to changing society.

ABOUT THE ILLUSTRATION

This engraving of an antislavery meeting depicts the emotional intensity of the abolitionists. Denouncing slavery as a sin, minister Theodore Weld, a noted abolitionist organizer, used the techniques of a revival meeting to win converts to abolitionism. In the North this approach successfully contributed to changing public attitudes toward slavery. Although women were generally prohibited from speaking at such meetings, they were active in the abolitionist movement, and the artist has included many women in the crowd. Ask students to compare this engraving with that of the revival meeting included in the Chapter Review on p. 302.

Chapter 9   **1820s–1860s**

WORKING FOR REFORM

FOCUS

UNDERSTANDING THE MAIN IDEA

Industrialization and the market revolution transformed American society. Not all of the changes were positive. The rapid growth of cities was accompanied by an increase in crime and poverty. Other changes, such as the mass departure of people for the West and the flood of new immigrants, threatened the familiar social order. Alarmed, Americans launched a variety of reform movements.

THEMES

■ **DEMOCRATIC VALUES**
What impact might citizens' reform groups have on public policies?

■ **CULTURAL DIVERSITY**
What changes in society might lead to a new interest in religion and to an interest in new forms of community?

1821	1829	1841	1848	1856
First public high school opens.	Walker's *Appeal* published.	Dorothea Dix begins crusade for mentally ill.	Seneca Falls Convention held.	Wilberforce University established.

Have students recall where and how most Americans lived and worked in the late 1700s. Write responses on the chalkboard and have students speculate as to why many Americans might have been threatened by the increased industrialization, urbanization, and immigration that transformed U.S. society in the early 1800s.

■■ Ask students if it is difficult today for them to understand why people in the early 1800s might have been anxious about changes in society, and if so, ask them to explain why.

LINK TO THE PAST

During the early 1800s the United States changed with bewildering speed. Northeastern cities grew at spectacular rates as commerce quickened and new factories sprang up, attracting thousands of new residents from rural America and abroad. Boom times in the South helped tighten slavery's grip.

An antislavery meeting, 1841

One response to the rapid social change that transformed the United States in the early 1800s was an increase in religious activity. Religious revivalism swept the nation as huge crowds came together to listen to thunderous sermons, to sing hymns, and to seek God's help in reforming their lives. Many participants came away convinced of the possibility of attaining moral perfection, both for themselves and for society.

A few people formed new religions and established communities along new lines. "Americans of all ages, all conditions, and all dispositions," Alexis de Tocqueville (TAWK-veel) observed in 1831, "constantly form . . . associations of a thousand . . . kinds." The causes these associations worked for ranged from health and education reform to world peace. A variety of groups attacked slavery, and a growing movement for women's rights emerged.

Women's active participation in these reform movements brought criticism from those who insisted that women should restrict their reforming efforts to the family. But many women agreed with Sarah Grimké (GRIM-kee) that "the sphere which her Creator has assigned her" included speaking out against the sin of slavery as well as other evils.

Grimké's reform activities and those of countless other women and men—coupled with the advance of political democracy—inspired hope. Perhaps American democracy's larger vision—justice, equality, and opportunity for all—might be possible.

Tray depicting Reverend Lemuel Haynes preaching

Museum of Art, Rhode Island School of Design

PREVIEW WORKSHOP

*Following is a list of the significant
people and terms in this section.
You may wish to use this list as a
section preview.*

People
- Charles Grandison
  Finney
- Zilpha Elaw
- Jarena Lee
- Richard Allen

- "Mother Ann" Lee
- Joseph Smith
- Brigham Young
- George Ripley

Terms
- Second Great
  Awakening
- denominations
- utopias
- transcendentalists

MOTIVATING:
LINK TO TODAY

Ask students to name some well-known religious figures in the U.S. today. Write students' responses on the chalkboard, and ask volunteers to identify the religious values and ideas promoted by any figures they may know about. Tell students that in this section they will learn about religious values and beliefs in the early 19th century.

FOCUS OBJECTIVES

- Describe how 19th-century Americans renewed their enthusiasm for religion.

- Explain why Protestant church membership soared during the Second Great Awakening.

- List some common features of utopian communities.

Section 1

RELIGIOUS ZEAL AND NEW COMMUNITIES

FOCUS

- **How did 19th-century Americans renew their enthusiasm for religion?**
- **Why did Protestant church membership soar during the Second Great Awakening?**
- **What were some common features of utopian communities?**

After visiting the United States in 1831, Alexis de Tocqueville said he knew of "no country in the whole world in which the Christian religion retains a greater influence over the souls of men than in America." The America he observed was in the midst of a revival of religious faith. Revivalists established new religions, gave new life to old ones, and founded communities where they could live according to their religious values and philosophical beliefs.

Circuit rider preacher

THE SECOND GREAT AWAKENING

Americans responded by the thousands to religious revivals that swept the country beginning in the 1790s. This renewal of religious faith was known as the **Second Great Awakening**, and it was every bit as intense as the Great Awakening of the mid-1700s. These revivals caught on because ministers expressed what many people were feeling: deep religious yearnings and an optimistic belief in an individual's ability to achieve salvation and improve his or her life. This optimism was fueled by both economic growth and the heralded, although still limited, expansion of democracy.

In the frontier areas of Kentucky, Ohio, Tennessee, and South Carolina, preachers traveled from town to town, promising that all sinners could find salvation. This promise, which contrasted sharply with the common belief that only a chosen few could be saved, broadened the appeal of formal religion. Frontier revivals were usually huge outdoor camp meetings that drew up to 10,000 people eager to accept God into their lives. In 1801 James Finley, later a Methodist preacher, captured the emotional intensity of one

◀ **Religious revivals attracted people from throughout the frontier regions. This picture shows a group of Methodists traveling to a camp meeting.**

RELIGIOUS RENEWAL

Draw on the chalkboard a chart titled *Religious Revivals* with the headings *Leaders, Regions,* and *Effects.* Call on students to fill in entries to the chart and discuss them. Then ask how revivals renewed the enthusiasm of 19th-century Americans for religion and why the revival message affected church membership.

SLAVERY THREATENED?

Have students work in small groups to write short scripts for skits dramatizing the following: 1) a slaveholder and spouse arguing about whether their slaves may attend a Zilpha Elaw revival meeting—she is against it, he is in favor; or 2) two slaves discussing the same meeting—one will dare to go, the other will not. Groups should choose members to present their skits to the class.

UTOPIAN COMMUNITIES

Head three columns on the chalkboard *Shakers, Mormons,* and *Transcendentalists.* For each column, ask students to brainstorm terms to describe that group. List responses in the appropriate column. When all ideas have been exhausted, move to the next heading and repeat the process. Have the class review the three chalkboard lists and point out common features. Then ask for volunteers to add any common features of these utopian groups that are not on the lists. ▶

of the earliest revivals, held at Cane Ridge, Kentucky:

> ❝ The vast sea of human beings seemed to be agitated as if by a storm. I counted seven ministers, all preaching at one time. . . . Some of the people were singing, others praying, some crying for mercy. A peculiarly strange sensation came over me. . . . I felt as though I must fall to the ground. ❞

Revivalist ministers also spread the word of God to urban audiences in the Northeast. Charles Grandison Finney—a powerful and persuasive preacher with piercing eyes and a low, solemn voice—delivered hundreds of sermons in the 1820s and 1830s. His sermons included calls for immediate conversion that stirred many to renounce their sins:

> ❝ Let the truth take hold upon your conscience—throw down your rebellious weapons—give up your refuges of lies. . . . Another moment's delay, and it may be too late for ever. The Spirit of God may depart from you . . . and seal you over to all the horrors of eternal death. ❞

Two African American women, Zilpha Elaw and Jarena Lee, separately traveled thousands of miles to preach sermons to both black and white worshipers. Lee proclaimed that she was called to preach by a heavenly voice that told her, "Preach the Gospel; I will put words in your mouth, and will turn your enemies to become your friends." At first, Lee had reservations about her calling—especially since female Methodist ministers were unheard of at the time—but she followed her inspiration. "If a man may preach, because the Saviour died for him, why not the woman? seeing he

▲ Jarena Lee

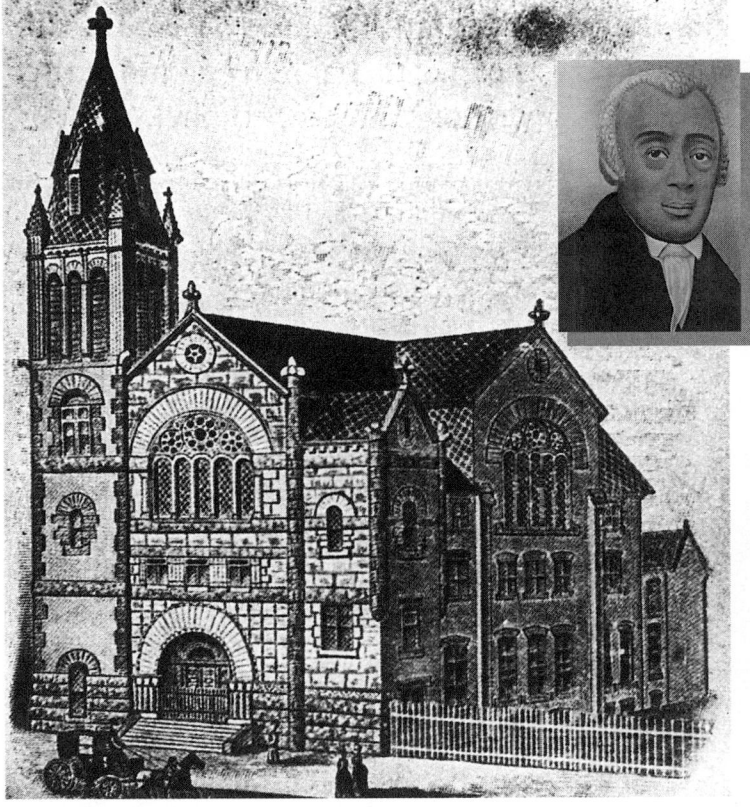

▲ The Bethel African Methodist Episcopal Church in Philadelphia is shown here, along with its founder, Richard Allen.

died for her also," Lee questioned. "Is he not a whole Saviour, instead of a half one?"

> ▌▌ **Americans rekindled their interest in religion through revivals, which captured people's energy and optimism.**

RELIGION FOR THE PEOPLE

The reawakening of religious enthusiasm sparked changes in Protestant congregations. By making salvation available to all, 19th-century churches encouraged new converts. As a result, membership soared in many Protestant **denominations**, or religious groups.

African American men and women joined Baptist and Methodist denominations in substantial numbers and formed their own churches as well. In 1794 the Reverend (later Bishop) Richard Allen founded in Philadelphia one of the first African American churches, the Bethel African Methodist Episcopal Church.

HISTORICAL SIDELIGHTS

Women Preachers

Despite the prohibition against women "preaching to men," there were women who felt compelled to preach. One of the first itinerant missionaries was Anna Nitschman, a German Moravian who rode alone through the backwoods of Pennsylvania in the early 1700s. By 1820 the United Foreign Missionary Society had sent six single women west of the Mississippi to convert American Indians to Christianity. It was more common, however, that such adventurous women were wives of missionary men. In 1836, shortly before her marriage to a preacher bound for Oregon, Mary Richardson Walker confessed: "I scarcely think of anything but becoming a missionary."

Practice

GUIDED PRACTICE

For each of the following words, have students write one sentence that expresses a main idea about religious revivalism and utopian experiments: *optimism, perfection, salvation, slavery, society, family.* Call on volunteers to read their sentences.

INDEPENDENT PRACTICE

Have students imagine that they are attending a revival meeting or living in a utopian community. Ask them to write a letter to a friend, describing and commenting on the experience. Letters should include the six words used in the Guided Practice. Students may wish to include their letters in their portfolios.

Review and Assessment

REVIEW Have students work in pairs to outline the main points of each subsection. Then assign the Section 1 Review on p. 285.

ASSESS Assign the **Section 1 Daily Quiz** in *Core Resources.*

BUILDING VOCABULARY

The utopians tried to create new, ideal worlds. Taken from the Greek *ou,* meaning "not," and *topos,* meaning "place," *utopia* means literally "not a place," i.e., not a place in existence yet.

Graph Caption Answer
Methodists

MAKING CONNECTIONS

Science
The Shakers invented several practical devices, including an apple parer, metal pen point, flat broom, and a circular buzz saw. The last was invented by a woman.

🌐 GLOBAL CONNECTIONS

The Mormons were highly successful missionaries in Denmark. Danish Mormon converts immigrated to the U.S. through the help of the Mormon Perpetual Emigration Fund, a "travel now, pay later" plan. The fund operated from 1850 to 1887, until antipolygamy sentiment caused the U.S. government to cancel the fund's charter.

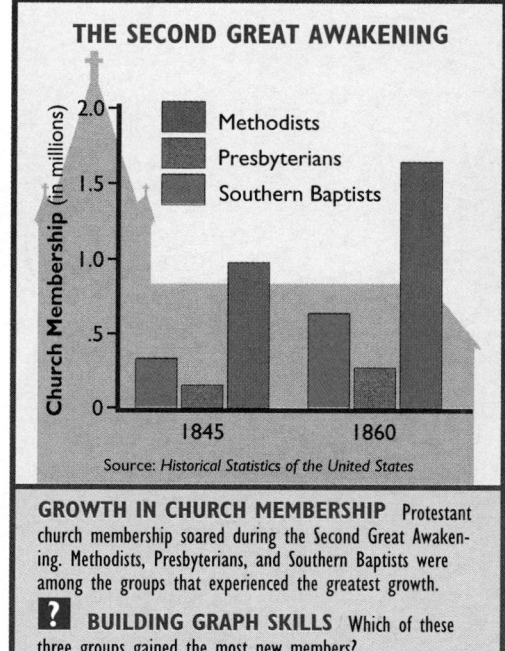

THE SECOND GREAT AWAKENING

Church Membership (in millions)

- Methodists
- Presbyterians
- Southern Baptists

2.0 — 1.5 — 1.0 — .5 — 0

1845   1860

Source: *Historical Statistics of the United States*

GROWTH IN CHURCH MEMBERSHIP Protestant church membership soared during the Second Great Awakening. Methodists, Presbyterians, and Southern Baptists were among the groups that experienced the greatest growth.

? **BUILDING GRAPH SKILLS** Which of these three groups gained the most new members?

Finney and other preachers in the industrializing Northeast attracted new members from the expanding middle class. Middle-class women, prosperous enough to hire servants to handle many household duties, generally had leisure time to devote to church activities. They led prayer groups, taught in and established Sunday schools, and supported missionary societies.

■■ Protestant churches attracted new converts by preaching that salvation was available to all.

In the South, the spread of revivalism among enslaved African Americans met with a mixed reaction among slaveholders. Some slaveholders encouraged slaves' conversion to Christianity. Many others, however, believed that recognizing a slave's soul and humanity under God contradicted the notion that a slave was property. Although Protestants stressed Bible reading, many southern states passed laws making it illegal to teach slaves to read. "Allow our slaves to read your writings [the Bible], stimulate them to cut our throats!" exclaimed South Carolina planter Jesse Hammond. "Can you believe us to be such unspeakable fools?"

UTOPIAN COMMUNITIES

The optimism that inspired revivalism also led men and women to found **utopias**—communities designed to create a better social order. More than 90 utopias sprang up in the United States between 1800 and 1850. They were influenced by a wide range of religious beliefs and philosophies. But all utopias experimented with new ways of organizing family life, work, and property ownership. Their experiments with family organization ranged from the banning of sex and marriage to "free love" communities.

The Shakers. The Shakers, or United Society of Believers in Christ's Second Appearing, founded utopian communities in the eastern United States. Led by "Mother Ann" Lee, Shakers first arrived in America from England in 1774. Lee preached that God was both male and female. Lee also claimed to be the messiah who would found a society free from sin. Shaker communities had separate but relatively equal roles for men and women, and community members jointly owned property. They also refrained from sex. Shakers saw no need to have children, since they believed that the millennium—a time in which some Christians believe Christ will reign on earth—was at hand.

▲ The Shakers were excellent woodworkers. This table is one example of their functional furniture designs.

Shakerism declined after 1860 because it became difficult to recruit new members. Shakers are remembered for their useful inventions and their simple but beautiful furniture and music.

The Mormons. The most enduring utopian venture was undertaken by the Mormons, or members of the Church of Jesus Christ of Latter-day Saints. Joseph Smith, who founded the Mormon church, claimed that divine assistance had enabled him to discover and translate buried golden plates that contained religious revelations. Smith published his translation of these revelations as the

RETEACH Ask students, working in pairs, to write sentences that explain how each entry in the Preview Workshop is related to the main idea of the subsection in which it is located. Have pairs share their sentences with the group.

Closure

Ask a volunteer to review the goals of religious and utopian communities during the Second Great Awakening.

Extension

EVALUATE Encourage students to reconsider de Tocqueville's quote on p. 282. Have them write a paragraph explaining why they think he might or might not say the same thing if he were to visit the U.S. today.

RESEARCH Have students research writings of one of the transcendentalists listed on p. 285 and find a passage that expresses the writer's philosophy to read to the class.

Book of Mormon and formed the first Mormon congregation in western New York in 1830.

Smith's religious teachings and call for group ownership of property and economic cooperation attracted many converts. These same principles also attracted strong opposition. Non-Mormons were especially outraged by the Mormon practice of having more than one wife at a time. The Mormons encountered violence wherever they tried to establish a community. In 1844 a mob in Carthage, Illinois, killed Smith.

But the Mormons did not give up. Under the leadership of Brigham Young, thousands of Smith's followers crossed the Rockies and founded successful communities in the Great Salt Lake valley. Over the years, Mormons (who no longer practice group ownership of property or allow men to have multiple wives) have spread their religion throughout the world.

Brook Farm. Perhaps the most famous utopia, Brook Farm was founded in 1841 near Boston by Unitarian minister George Ripley. He was inspired by the philosophy of the **transcendentalists**, a small group of New England intellectuals led by writers Ralph Waldo Emerson, Henry David Thoreau, and Margaret Fuller and educator Bronson Alcott. Transcendentalists believed that people could attain perfection and could acquire knowledge about God, the self, and the universe.

The Brook Farm residents retreated from industrial society to live close to nature. They shared farm and household chores in order to have

▲ Ralph Waldo Emerson once described Brook Farm as "a perpetual picnic, a French Revolution in small, an age of reason in a patty [pie]-pan."

time for study, discussion, and cultural pursuits. Dedicated to education and self-cultivation, Brook Farm was a stimulating intellectual community. But the experiment ended in 1846 after a fire destroyed part of the farm.

■■ Utopian communities experimented with new ways of organizing economic activities and family life.

By 1850 the passion for cooperative living had faded. Rather than secluding themselves from society in utopian communities, some Americans began to translate the faith in human perfection into direct attempts to perfect society. They were encouraged by those revivalists who taught that salvation could be both demonstrated and gained by working to improve society.

■ SECTION 1 REVIEW

IDENTIFY and explain the significance of the following: Second Great Awakening, Charles Grandison Finney, Zilpha Elaw, Jarena Lee, denominations, Richard Allen, utopias, "Mother Ann" Lee, Joseph Smith, Brigham Young, George Ripley, transcendentalists.

1. **MAIN IDEA** What effect did revivals have on religion in America?

2. **MAIN IDEA** Why did Protestant churches attract new members during the Second Great Awakening? What effect did this have on church membership?

3. **COMPARING** What were some characteristics that the Shakers, Mormons, and residents of Brook Farm shared?

4. **WRITING TO PERSUADE** You are a Brook Farm resident. Write an advertisement for your local newspaper to recruit new members into your community.

5. **EVALUATING** Why can it be said that the Second Great Awakening had both positive and negative consequences for African Americans?

PREVIEW WORKSHOP

*Following is a list of the significant
people and terms in this section.
You may wish to use this list as a
section preview.*

People
■ Dorothea Dix
■ Horace Mann
■ John Melvin

■ Mary Jane Patterson
■ Emma Willard
■ Mary Lyon

Terms
■ rehabilitation
■ temperance movement
■ prohibition

FOCUS OBJECTIVES

■ Describe how and
why reformers worked
to improve prisons and
other institutions.

■ Explain what moti-
vated the temperance
reformers.

■ Examine why reformers
supported free public
education.

■ Determine why reform-
ers established alterna-
tive schools for African
Americans and women.

**THE AMERICAN NATION
VIDEODISC PROGRAM**
The Reform Movement

1A   14239   4:02

CORE RESOURCES

• **Section 2 Daily Quiz**

AV RESOURCES

• *The American Nation
Videodisc: The
Reform Movement*
• **Everyday Life in
America Trans-
parency** and
Worksheet 9

Section 2

MOVEMENTS FOR SOCIAL REFORM

F O C U S
■ **How and why did reformers work to improve prisons and other
institutions?**
■ **What motivated the temperance reformers?**
■ **Why did reformers support free public education?**
■ **Why did reformers establish alternative schools for African Americans
and women?**

*M*en and women who joined the religious revivals of the
Second Great Awakening firmly believed in the possibility of
attaining individual perfection. Their optimism soon led them to
believe they could perfect society as well. Troubled by the effects
of rapid industrialization, people in the Northeast began to
direct their religious zeal toward solving social problems. Their
many concerns included better treatment of the mentally ill, prisoners, and the poor. They also tackled the problems of excessive
drinking and an inadequate educational system.

Pupil working with slate and pencil

REFORMING INSTITUTIONS

In colonial days people cared for the mentally ill in
their own homes. Criminals were punished but
rarely confined for long periods of time. And
townspeople helped the poor through informal
charity. But by the early 19th century these solutions were no longer adequate. Cities had too many
people in need of help, prisons were overcrowded,
and too few family members could offer assistance
to their kin.

Reformers responded by building new institutions and reforming existing ones for the mentally
ill, criminals, and the poor. Reformers believed they
could improve these people's lives by placing them
in institutions that taught moral values and provided
a stable environment free from the corrupting influences of city life. Middle-class women took the lead
in many of these reform efforts.

Dorothea Dix and the mentally ill. One
of these women was Dorothea Dix. A deeply religious teacher inspired by transcendentalist ideas,
she led efforts to improve treatment for the mentally

**BIO
GRAPHY** ill. Dix first became interested in the plight
of the mentally ill in 1841 when she saw
how they were treated in a Massachusetts
prison. She was horrified
to see that mentally ill
women were kept in a
damp dungeon with no
attempts made to cure
them. Dix learned that
while a few mental hospi-
tals had been established,
the most common prac-
tice was to put the men-
tally ill in prisons and
poorhouses without pro-
viding treatment.

Dorothea Dix

MOTIVATING:
PRIOR KNOWLEDGE

Ask a volunteer to recall how the Second Great Awakening was fueled by the optimistic belief that people have the ability to improve their lives. Point out that this optimism also led people to believe they could improve society as a whole. Tell students that in this section they will learn about social reform movements that were undertaken because of this belief.

Teaching the Section

REFORMING INSTITUTIONS

Organize students into groups to construct charts listing the social problems discussed in this section, the solutions that reformers implemented to address each problem, and their reasons for the reform. After groups present and discuss their charts, have students use them to develop a statement about

how each reform showed the reformers' spirit of optimism about American society.

►

Outraged, Dix spent 18 months visiting jails and poorhouses throughout Massachusetts. She found that the mentally ill were kept "in *cages, closets, cellars, stalls, pens! Chained, naked, beaten with rods, and lashed* into obedience." In January 1843 Dix collected her observations into a detailed, factual report and plea for action and delivered it to Massachusetts legislators. Her report convinced them of the need to establish more institutions in which the mentally ill could be treated humanely. Dix emphasized the need to offer the mentally ill **rehabilitation**, or treatment to restore them to a useful and constructive place in society.

New ideas about mental illness—in tune with the optimistic spirit of reform—held that mental illness was a curable disease rather than a sin or moral defect, as had previously been taught. This changed point of view helped Dix carry her crusade to other states and even to other countries. She was responsible for the founding or enlarging of more than 30 mental hospitals in the United States, Canada, Europe, and Japan.

Prisons and poorhouses. Other reformers during this period worked to rehabilitate prisoners and the poor. Reformers persuaded lawmakers to provide money to build new prisons and poorhouses. New systems of prison organization placed prisoners in individual cells so that they would think about and repent their crimes. Prisons set up strict routines for inmates to teach them how to live disciplined lives. Reformers established institutions that housed only juvenile delinquents to separate them from hardened criminals. New

AMERICAN PRISONS

In 1831 Gustave de Beaumont (goohs-tahv duh boh-mohn) and Alexis de Tocqueville, two French aristocrats, visited the United States to observe its prisons firsthand. They were surprised to find that in a country where democratic liberties were so highly valued, prisoners often suffered under horrible conditions. They concluded:

THROUGH OTHERS' EYES

❝*T*o *sum up the whole on this point it must be acknowledged that the penitentiary system in America is severe. Whilst society in the United States gives the example of the most extended liberty, the prisons of the same country offer the spectacle of the most complete despotism [oppression]. The citizens subject to the law are protected by it; they only cease to be free when they become wicked.* ❞

poorhouses taught work skills and discipline to train the poor to become self-supporting.

■■ **Reformers established mental institutions and reorganized and built prisons to offer rehabilitation to inmates.**

THROUGH OTHERS' EYES

In the early 1800s two models for prison systems existed in the U.S. Under the Pennsylvania system, prisoners were housed in complete isolation and were restricted to work that could be done inside their cells. Under the Auburn (New York) model, prisoners were permitted to work in groups but could not speak to, or even look at, one another. In both systems discipline was severe and sometimes brutal in enforcing silence, and inmates suffered a high rate of mental illness, probably from lack of human contact.

■■ Ask students to compare U.S. prisons today with the prisons described by the French visitors.

PRIMARY SOURCE

Description of Change: excerpted and bracketed **Rationale:** excerpted to focus on main idea; bracketed to clarify meaning

THINKING CRITICALLY

Recognizing Prejudice Ask students how mentally ill persons were often prejudged before Dorothea Dix crusaded for their rehabilitation.

▲ **Prison reforms included teaching inmates special skills and jobs. This 1853 image shows prisoners at Sing Sing Prison making hats.**

Teaching the Section

TEMPERANCE REFORMERS

Write *excessive drinking* in a circle on the chalkboard. Ask students to suggest effects that this problem might have had on 19th-century society. *(increased poverty, mental illness, family breakdown, crime)* Write students' responses in circles at the ends of spokes coming from the central circle. Ask volunteers to draw lines connecting any satellite circles they think are related. As students see the relationships among the problems, have them suggest how these connections would motivate the reformers and influence the approaches that they might take in solving the problems. Conclude by asking how the temperance movement highlighted religious and ethnic divisions in society.

■■ Ask students to explain how drug abuse presents similar problems today and how modern reformers attempt to deal with the problems. *(Drug abuse affects crime rate, unemployment rate, family relationships, and work-force productivity.)*

THE CRUSADE AGAINST ALCOHOL

Alcoholism was a serious problem in early America, and some reformers attacked excessive drinking. Concerned people organized the **temperance movement** to persuade others to limit alcohol consumption. Reformers blamed nearly all social ills—including mental illness, poverty, and crime—on alcohol. A popular pro-temperance novel, *Ten Nights in a Bar-Room and What I Saw There* (1854), which was later made into a play, echoed this sentiment. As a character observed, he "never knew a man to go to the almshouse that he hadn't rum to blame for his poverty."

The national temperance movement began in the 1820s. By the mid-1830s some 5,000 state and local organizations had sprung into being. Ministers won many converts to the temperance cause. In emotional sermons, they persuaded people to give up drinking completely. According to a woman who attended an 1842 revival meeting in Maryland:

❝ Upwards of 100 gallons of spirits were poured not down people's throats but on the sand and I believe there is now none in the place. Dean and Knotts [liquor sellers] have become members of the Temperance Society and are now earnestly seeking religion. ❞

▼ The American Temperance Society was founded in 1826 with the aim of preaching the benefits of total abstinence from alcohol. Some temperance supporters, however, took more active roles by demolishing liquor stocks.

Businesspeople became enthusiastic supporters of the temperance movement, in part because they saw temperance as a way of creating a more disciplined work force. Temperance women linked abstaining from alcohol to preserving the family. They saw a clear link between alcohol abuse and domestic violence.

African Americans, often excluded from white temperance organizations, formed their own temperance societies and spoke at rallies. African Americans tended to view temperance, like education, as a way to overcome prejudice and become accepted as political and social equals.

Many immigrants, on the other hand, viewed the temperance movement as an attack on their customs, which often differed from those of native-born Protestant Americans. Most German and Irish immigrants did not view alcohol consumption as a social evil. For them, beer gardens and pubs were places where people came together to socialize. Both institutions helped German and Irish immigrants preserve their cultures in the United States.

◀ As a step toward abstaining from alcohol, families were encouraged to sign temperance pledges such as the one shown here.

REFORM IN EDUCATION

Organize students into three groups to prepare five-minute investigative reports for a "TV news magazine." One group's piece should reveal why mid-19th-century reformers supported free public education. The other groups' segments should focus on why African Americans and women had to work outside the mainstream movement to achieve educational reforms. Tell groups that they may use "interviews," reenactments, news analysis, and straight reporting in their segments. After groups have completed their preparation, have the class present a 15-minute "TV feature" on mid-19th-century educational reform.

■■ Ask students if they think that the goals of public education today are the same or different from the goals of public education in the mid-19th century.

▶

■■ **Reformers supported the temperance movement as a way to eliminate many social evils.**

The temperance movement called for legal reforms to limit alcohol consumption. Some reformers went so far as to call for **prohibition**, or a ban on alcohol. In 1846 Maine became the first state to ban the sale of alcohol. A few other states followed, as did some communities. Many other states strictly licensed taverns and adopted heavy liquor taxes to help limit alcohol consumption. By the middle of the 19th century, the nationwide rate of alcohol consumption had declined substantially.

REFORMING EDUCATION

In the 1840s and 1850s, reformers turned their attention to education. Most schools established before the 1840s were private, and most children could not afford to attend them. The few public elementary schools that existed—most of them in the Northeast—had little money for books, supplies, and teachers' salaries. The curriculum was basic: reading, writing, arithmetic, and a bit of history and geography. But the quality of teaching was often poor, attendance was irregular, and many students received only a few years of schooling.

The public school movement. Reformers worried that the existing schools were inadequate to meet the needs of a growing nation and an expanding, if still limited, democracy. They argued that the nation needed public, tax-supported elementary schools to provide a free education for all students. Reformers insisted that schools were essential to educate citizens about democratic values, to unite an increasingly spread out and diverse population, and to create a literate and disciplined work force. The schools could achieve these goals, reformers hoped, by teaching a basic curriculum and instilling in students the middle-class values of hard work and respect for authority.

■■ **Reformers supported free public schools to help children become good citizens and good workers.**

Horace Mann's reform efforts in Massachusetts established the model for free public elementary education. In 1837, as Massachusetts's first secretary of education, Mann united local school districts into a state system, raised teachers' salaries, and increased spending on local schools. He also extended school terms, updated the curriculum, and established schools for training teachers. Mann's school reforms soon spread beyond Massachusetts as an increasing number of states set up state boards of education.

The Granger Collection, New York

▲ This 1857 drawing shows a rural schoolmaster with his pupils. The lessons they are reading may have come from the *American Pictorial Primer*. Pages from this primer flank the drawing.

Practice

GUIDED PRACTICE

Lead the class in outlining on the chalkboard a "grant proposal" seeking government funding for a project to reform mid-19th-century prisons. The proposal outline should identify the problem, describe the proposed reform, and explain how the reform would benefit society.

INDEPENDENT PRACTICE

Instruct students to use the Guided Practice outline as a model in writing a "grant proposal" for a project to carry out one of the other reforms they have learned about in this section.

Review and Assessment

REVIEW Have students write main idea statements for each of the headings in the section. Then assign the Section 2 Review on p. 291.

ASSESS Assign the **Section 2 Daily Quiz** in *Core Resources*.

PRIMARY SOURCE
Description of Change: excerpted and bracketed
Rationale: excerpted to focus on main idea; bracketed to clarify meaning

HISTORICAL SIDELIGHTS
Slave Schools

Laws in southern states forbade education of slaves and set punishments ranging from imprisonment to death for their teachers. Nonetheless, some slaves learned to read in underground schools taught by free blacks or whites.

VOICES IN HISTORY

Many northern whites objected to educating African Americans. When white teacher Prudence Crandall opened a school for "Young Ladies and Little Misses of Color" in Canterbury, Connecticut, local stores refused to serve her students, and people threw eggs at the girls and fouled the school's well. One student who had walked to the school from Brooklyn, New York, described her experience: "The Canterburians are *savage*—they will not sell Miss Crandall an article at their shops. . . . But the happiness I enjoy here pays me for all. The place is delightful; all that is wanting to complete the scene is civilized men."

Another educational reform during this period was the creation of the public high school. The nation's first, the English High School of Boston, opened in 1821. Free public high schools offered poor children a chance to pursue advanced courses that could prepare them for specialized careers in law or medicine.

Although these reforms provided a model for public education for all children, not all parents were pleased. Some farming and working-class families opposed public schooling because they depended on their children's labor. Also opposed were many Catholics, who viewed public schools as a means of spreading Protestant beliefs.

Educational reform had little impact on the South. The antislavery movement made the South defensive about slavery—its "peculiar institution"— and many southerners increasingly viewed all reform efforts with suspicion. As a result, the South lagged far behind the North in educational reform. Planters hired private tutors or established private schools for their own children, but they did not support public schools to educate all children.

African American education. The public school movement also failed to benefit many African American children. By the 1850s only a few towns permitted black children to attend public schools. Some northern states maintained separate schools for African American children, but these institutions were generally underfunded.

Lewis Woodson, an African American educator, knew that this situation must be changed. He hailed education:

> 66 [as a] jewel that will elevate, ennoble, and rescue the bodies of our long injured race from the shackles of bondage, and their minds from the trammels [restraints] of ignorance and vice. 99

This strong faith in education inspired free blacks to pursue an education for their children. African Americans successfully pressured a few public schools in the North to admit their children. They also set up private schools. John Melvin, an African American merchant, established Cleveland's first school for blacks and sponsored other such schools throughout Ohio in the 1830s.

Despite widespread opposition to educating African Americans, some colleges allowed free blacks to enroll. The first African American college graduate was probably Alexander Twilight, who received a degree from Vermont's Middlebury College in 1823. Within a few years other African Americans graduated from Amherst College in Massachusetts and Bowdoin College in Maine.

African Americans responded to their exclusion from most colleges by founding their own. Several colleges for black students were established in this period: Cheyney State College (1837), Avery College (1849), Lincoln University (1854), and Wilberforce University (1856).

Darius L. Donnell

Joseph S. Thompson

▲ **Lincoln University in Pennsylvania is shown here, along with photographs of two early graduates.**

Oberlin College, founded in Ohio in 1833 by ministers and abolitionists, soon became the nation's first integrated, coeducational college. In addition to its collegiate programs, Oberlin offered college preparatory courses for students who had not attended high school. By 1860, African American graduates of Oberlin, many of them fugitive slaves and the children of fugitive slaves, had gone on to become journalists, ministers, missionaries, and teachers.

Women and higher education. Women also challenged their lack of access to higher education. In 1841 the first three women to receive bachelor of arts degrees from a U.S. college graduated from Oberlin. In 1862 Mary Jane Patterson, also an Oberlin graduate, became the first African American woman to receive a college degree from a U.S. institution. These women's achievements were revolutionary because during this period women, as well as African American men, were widely considered unable to compete intellectually with white men.

Reformers realized that educational barriers prevented women from winning equal status to men. To help remedy this situation, several schools for women were established. Emma Willard founded the first women's high school, Troy Female Seminary, in New York in 1821. Two years later Catharine Beecher opened the Hartford Female Seminary, and in Alabama in 1831 the Huntsville Female Seminary opened. Mary Lyon, an accomplished teacher, founded the first women's college, Mount Holyoke Female Seminary, in 1836 in Massachusetts. The programs at Oberlin and Mount

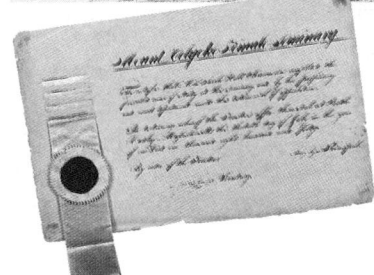

▲ **Mount Holyoke Female Seminary in Massachusetts became the model for institutions of higher education for women. A diploma is shown at left.**

Holyoke allowed women to study, for the first time, subjects that society had thought only white men could master. Women graduates from these institutions launched careers as teachers, writers, journalists, doctors, and reformers.

■■ **Reformers established alternative schools to provide African Americans and women with educational opportunities denied them by public institutions.**

SECTION 2 REVIEW

IDENTIFY and explain the significance of the following: Dorothea Dix, rehabilitation, temperance movement, prohibition, Horace Mann, John Melvin, Mary Jane Patterson, Emma Willard, Mary Lyon.

1. **MAIN IDEA** How did reformers hope to rehabilitate prisoners?
2. **MAIN IDEA** Why did reformers believe that the nation needed free public education?
3. **MAIN IDEA** How did reformers attempt to provide educational opportunities for both African Americans and women?
4. **WRITING TO INFORM** You are a 19th-century business owner with a strict temperance policy for your employees. Write a letter to the president of another company informing him or her about the advantages and disadvantages of this policy.
5. **RECOGNIZING POINTS OF VIEW** How did Dorothea Dix view the mentally ill? How did this view influence her work?

PREVIEW WORKSHOP

Following is a list of the significant people and terms in this section. You may wish to use this list as a section preview.

People
- David Walker
- William Lloyd Garrison
- Frederick Douglass

- Sojourner Truth
- Maria W. Stewart

Terms
- American Anti-Slavery Society

FOCUS OBJECTIVES

- Explain how African Americans changed the focus of antislavery efforts.

- Identify what helped spark the call for immediate abolition.

- Describe obstacles that abolitionists faced.

PRIMARY SOURCE

Description of Change: excerpted

Rationale: excerpted to focus on main idea

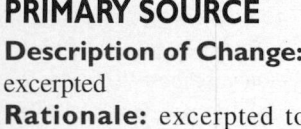

CORE RESOURCES

- **Social Studies Skills Worksheet 9**
- **Literature Worksheet 9**
- **Section 3 Daily Quiz**

292

Section 3

THE CRUSADE FOR ABOLITION

FOCUS

- **How did African Americans change the focus of antislavery efforts?**
- **What helped spark the call for immediate abolition?**
- **What obstacles did abolitionists face?**

With the transportation, market, and industrial revolutions of the early 19th century, regional economic differences heightened the existing social and political tensions between the North and the South. The division between the systems of slave and free labor became more pronounced, leading to increased support for abolition among northerners. By the 1830s influential blacks and whites joined together in a vigorous, organized campaign to end slavery.

Medallion bearing the seal of an antislavery group

EARLY OPPONENTS OF SLAVERY

Most northern states had abolished slavery by the early 1800s. After working for abolition in their own states, many antislavery northerners wanted to end slavery across the country. To achieve this goal, many northerners supported the American Colonization Society's plan for ending slavery gradually.

Unlike many of the society's southern supporters, who saw colonization as a way to rid the South of free blacks, most northern advocates genuinely wanted to rid the country of slavery. Yet both groups shared the prejudice that all African Americans, both

▲ **Henry Highland Garnet**

enslaved and free, were inferior to whites and would never fit into U.S. society. In 1829 an American Colonization Society report described free blacks as "notoriously ignorant, degraded and miserable, . . . scarcely reached in their debasement by the heavenly light."

Northern free blacks strenuously objected to this unfair characterization. They opposed the American Colonization Society's plan to banish them from their country of birth. Henry Highland Garnet, a black abolitionist, declared:

> 66 America is my home, my country, and I have no other. . . . I mourn because the accursed shade of slavery rests upon it. I love my country's flag, and I hope that soon it will be cleansed of its stains, and be hailed by all nations as the emblem of freedom and independence. 99

To provide an alternative to the American Colonization Society, free blacks founded abolitionist societies. By 1826, African Americans

MOTIVATING:
STUDENT EXPERIENCES

Ask students if they have ever seen people campaigning for a cause or issue and, if so, to explain the protest. Then tell students that in this section they will learn about people who crusaded to end slavery.

Teaching the Section

ANTISLAVERY EFFORTS

Organize students into two groups to represent the American Colonization Society and an abolitionist society founded by free blacks. Have each group state its point of view. Then allow each group to counter the other's arguments. Make sure that students recognize the similarities and differences between colonization and abolition.

CALLS FOR ABOLITION

Ask students why the appearance of books and newspapers, such as Walker's *Appeal* and Garrison's *Liberator,* would benefit a reform movement like abolition. *(increase public awareness, present a more organized attack, educate the public, mobilize and shape public opinion)*

■■ Ask students to identify and assess the role that the print and TV media play as instruments of reform today. ▶

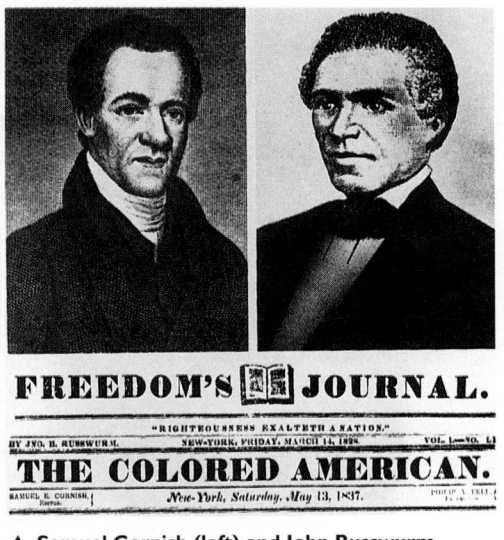

▲ Samuel Cornish (left) and John Russwurm (right) started the first African American newspaper, *Freedom's Journal,* in 1827. Cornish later served as editor of *The Colored American.*

had formed more than 143 antislavery societies. In 1827 Samuel Cornish and John Russwurm started the first African American newspaper, *Freedom's Journal,* to express African American opposition to slavery. Free blacks called on whites to join them in the fight to free "their brother[s] in chains."

These efforts helped mobilize public opinion against the American Colonization Society. By 1831 only some 1,400 African Americans had settled in Liberia, the West African republic founded by the society. The society had persuaded few slaveholders to free their slaves. And despite the discrimination that free blacks faced, few wanted to leave the United States.

■■ **Most free blacks objected to colonization efforts. They formed abolitionist societies as an alternative way to end slavery.**

THE CALL TO ACTION

Although early black and white abolitionists had not shared common strategies, in the 1830s they began to join forces to call for an immediate end to slavery. The appearance of two important publications, David Walker's *Appeal* and William Lloyd Garrison's *Liberator,* marked the start of a bold,

energetic, and more organized attack on the institution of slavery.

In 1829 David Walker, a Boston businessman and free black, published the *Appeal to the Colored Citizens of the World,* in which he demanded immediate, universal abolition. Walker bid free blacks and slaves to take action—violent action if necessary—for freedom and equality. In a blistering attack he criticized slaveholders who used the Bible to justify slavery. He urged white Americans to condemn slavery and to recognize the rights and humanity of black Americans. Before he could put his words into practice, however, Walker died in 1830 under mysterious circumstances. Nevertheless, the publication of Walker's *Appeal* represented a new mood among abolitionists. Opponents of slavery, both black and white, were becoming impatient with their lack of progress in promoting abolition.

This impatience led William Lloyd Garrison, a New England journalist, to action. With the financial backing of wealthy African American and white abolitionists, Garrison launched the abolitionist newspaper the *Liberator* in 1831. In the first issue, Garrison expressed his determination to work for the immediate abolition of slavery:

❝ I *will be* as harsh as truth and as uncompromising as justice. On this subject, I do not wish to think, or speak, or write, with moderation. . . . I am in earnest—I will not equivocate [evade the truth]—I will not excuse—I will not retreat a single inch—AND I WILL BE HEARD. ❞

▲ This colorful banner proudly displays William Lloyd Garrison's famous motto.

Garrison soon became one of the most articulate supporters of immediate abolition. He insisted that slavery was a sin and a crime because it contradicted both the Bible and the Constitution. Garrison argued that the sin of slavery should be given up immediately in order to save the country. He fiercely attacked both slavery and racial prejudice and argued that blacks should enjoy equality with whites.

■■ **Demands for immediate abolition began with the publication of the *Appeal* and the *Liberator.***

CULTURAL PATTERNS

Like David Walker, American Indians also noted contradictions between many whites' religious beliefs and their treatment of blacks. Missionaries told the chiefs of the Delaware that the Great Spirit would make them happy if they became Christians. However, the Delaware chiefs said they would wait to see if black people became happy and free in this Christian nation before they made a decision to convert.

PRIMARY SOURCE

Description of Change: excerpted and bracketed
Rationale: excerpted to focus on main idea; bracketed to clarify meaning

Teaching the Section

GET THE WORD OUT

Have students make posters or pamphlets publicizing the appearance of Garrison, Douglass, or Truth at an abolitionist meeting. Suggest that they focus on each figure's background and experiences as a way to spark public interest.

OBSTACLES TO ABOLITION

Organize the class into four groups to represent southern slaveholders, northern merchants, northern wage earners, and moderate abolitionists. Ask each group to prepare a "press release" that summarizes its opposition to the abolition movement. Post the "press releases" in the classroom. Tell students to choose one and write a letter to the group disputing its point of view.

HISTORICAL SIDELIGHTS

Quaker Abolitionists

Women were excluded from participating in the meeting convened to form the American Anti-Slavery Society. However, a group of Philadelphia women was invited to sit in the gallery as onlookers. Quaker Lucretia Mott was one of these onlookers. She and her husband, James, opposed slavery. James, a merchant, refused to handle cotton from the slave states, and Lucretia refused to use any products made with slave labor. After attending the American Anti-Slavery Society meeting in Philadelphia, Lucretia went on to organize the Philadelphia Female Anti-Slavery Society.

BIO GRAPHY PERSONALITIES IN HISTORY

Point out that Truth spent some time in a communal society, the Northampton Association of Education and Industry. This experience helped her formulate her views on abolition and women's rights.

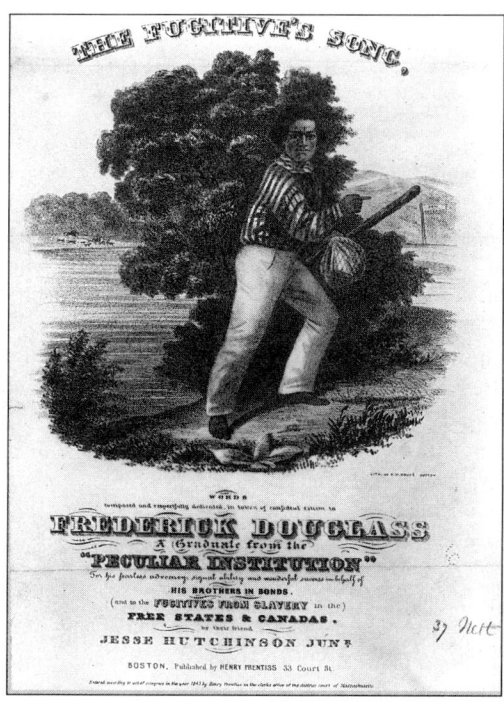

▲ Abolitionists used antislavery songs to protest the evils of slavery. One notable example was "The Fugitive's Song," composed in honor of Frederick Douglass's escape from slavery.

*T*HE AMERICAN ANTI-SLAVERY SOCIETY

In 1833, prominent black and white abolitionists formed the first national antislavery organization devoted to immediate abolition—the **American Anti-Slavery Society**. The society soon claimed more than 200 branches across the North and the Middle West. It papered the country with countless antislavery publications and organized petition drives to protest legislation supporting slavery. Most important, the society sponsored national lecture tours of abolitionists who hoped to convince Americans that slavery was morally wrong.

Frederick Douglass. Among the best at winning converts to the American Anti-Slavery Society was Frederick Douglass, a fugitive slave from Maryland. He was the first runaway to speak publicly against slavery. His moving speeches about his life as a slave who "suffered under the lash without the power of resisting" convinced many people to support abolition.

Douglass was also a powerful writer. His autobiography, *Narrative of the Life of Frederick Douglass* (1845), became a classic indictment of the slave system. In 1847 Douglass and a partner began an antislavery newspaper, the *North Star,* which was later renamed *Frederick Douglass's Paper.* Published in Rochester, New York, from 1847 to 1864, the paper won support for abolition. An editorial in the first edition urged those who had *"suffered the wrong"* to lead the abolitionist cause. "He who has *endured the cruel pangs of Slavery* is the man to *advocate Liberty.*"

Frederick Douglass's wife, Anna Murray Douglass, was also an active abolitionist. Using their home in Rochester as a depot for the Underground Railroad, she helped runaway slaves flee to Canada and freedom.

BIO GRAPHY **Sojourner Truth.** Another ex-slave who worked tirelessly for the American Anti-Slavery Society was Sojourner Truth. She was born Isabella Baumfree on the New York estate of a wealthy Dutch landowner around 1797. In 1827, the year before the mandatory abolition of slavery in New York, she managed to flee from her slaveholder. After her escape she joined religious reformers who preached on the streets of New York City. Six feet tall, extremely thin, and speaking with a Dutch accent, she made a powerful impression.

Sojourner Truth

In 1843 Baumfree said she had a religious vision in which God instructed her to find a new mission and a new identity. Adopting the name Sojourner (visitor) Truth, she traveled through New England on foot, preaching what she believed to be the truth—abolition and women's rights.

*R*ESISTANCE TO ABOLITION

By 1840, abolitionists had recruited some 200,000 northerners to their cause. Southern slaveholders, of course, felt threatened by the growing movement. But some northerners also opposed abolition. Garrison once remarked that he found "contempt more bitter, opposition more active, . . .

Practice

GUIDED PRACTICE

Guide students in listing the arguments that abolitionists used against slavery. Inform students that they will need their lists for a writing assignment in Independent Practice.

INDEPENDENT PRACTICE

Have students assume the role of a volunteer participating in a petition drive calling for legislation to abolish slavery. Ask them to write a script they would use when presenting the petition to a prospective signer. Students may wish to include their scripts in their portfolios.

Review and Assessment

REVIEW Have students chart this section's main points on a time line and briefly describe the significance of each event. Then assign the Section 3 Review on p. 296.

ASSESS Assign the **Section 3 Daily Quiz** in *Core Resources*.

Changing Ways — THE AMISTAD MUTINY

▲ The mutiny aboard the *Amistad*, the return of the captives, and the subsequent trial are depicted here in a series of three paintings.

In 1839 the Spanish ship *Amistad* set sail from Havana, Cuba, bound for a plantation on the eastern end of the island. While at sea, Joseph Cinque and some 50 other enslaved Africans on board mutinied, killing the captain and part of the crew. The Africans tried to sail back to their homeland but were picked up by a U.S. warship. They were imprisoned and charged with piracy and murder.

Abolitionists, who saw the situation as an opportunity to rally support for their cause, arranged for the Africans' defense in court. Cinque told the court that he had been kidnapped in Africa and sold into slavery. The defense then successfully argued that because Spain had outlawed the international slave trade in 1820, the accused were not slaves but free men who had acted in self-defense.

American newspapers followed the trial closely, paying particular attention to the striking figure of Cinque. One newspaper described him as "possessing the true elements of heroism," and his dignified manner throughout the trial earned him the respect and sympathy of many.

In 1841 the U. S. Supreme Court, under Chief Justice Roger B. Taney, heard the case on appeal. Former president John Quincy Adams argued for the defense. Adams told the court that the Declaration of Independence guaranteed that "every man has a right to life and liberty." In summary, he said, "I ask nothing more in behalf of these unfortunate men than this Declaration." On March 9 the Supreme Court handed down its decision, which upheld the lower court.

Abolitionists rejoiced over the verdict, which freed the Africans. The decision, however, was more narrow than it seemed. Although the trial helped to focus national attention on the issue of slavery, the decision itself said nothing about the legality of slavery. Furthermore, the ruling implied that if the defendants *had* been slaves, they would not have been entitled to such a basic human right as self-defense. The *Amistad* case foreshadowed the later *Dred Scott* v. *Sandford* case, in which Chief Justice Taney ruled that slaves were indeed "property" and therefore had no fundamental rights.

---

and apathy more frozen" in New England than in the South. He exaggerated, but not by much.

As the antislavery movement gained momentum in the 1830s, mob violence increased. In 1835 Garrison was almost killed by a Boston mob. Elijah Lovejoy, an abolitionist editor in Alton, Illinois, was killed in 1837 as he tried to prevent a mob from destroying his printing press.

Why did some northerners oppose abolition with such fury? Much of the opposition was based on prejudice against African Americans. Many northern wage earners feared competing with free blacks for jobs. Many northern merchants feared abolition would disrupt cotton production, thus cutting into the profits they made from selling cotton on the world market. One merchant warned

RETEACH Organize students into small groups and assign each a subsection of Section 3. Tell each group to create a poster, drawing, or cartoon that illustrates the main idea of its subsection. Have each group explain its creation.

Closure

Review with the class the arguments that the abolitionists used. Then ask each student to write what he or she feels is the single most important argument against slavery. Have volunteers present their selections and discuss their reasons for their choices.

Extension

COMPARE Have students conduct research in order to compare the goals of the abolitionists with the goals of the African American civil rights movement of the 1950s and 1960s.

CREATE Invite students to create posters calling for abolition. Display students' work in the classroom.

IDENTIFY

For significance, see the following pages:
David Walker (p. 293)
William Lloyd Garrison (p. 293)
American Anti-Slavery Society (p. 294)
Frederick Douglass (p. 294)
Sojourner Truth (p. 294)
Maria W. Stewart (p. 296)

1. *did not want to leave land of their birth; established abolitionist societies to fight for end of slavery*
2. *demonstrated abolitionist impatience and provided an organized attack on slavery*
3. *impressed people with their powerful personalities and moving firsthand accounts of slavery*
4. *Essays should mention male attitudes, problems caused by opposition to women within the movement, and exclusion from formal membership in the American Anti-Slavery Society.*
5. *directed movement away from colonization and toward seeking an immediate end to slavery; swayed public opinion through the press and moving speeches by former slaves*

abolitionists: "We mean, sir, to put you Abolitionists down—by fair means if we can, by foul means if we must." Anti-abolition mobs were sometimes led by local civic leaders fearful of the social disorder they associated with abolitionism.

THE MOVEMENT SPLINTERS

Abolitionists also faced problems within their movement. William Lloyd Garrison's attacks on churches and the government for condoning slavery became more fierce and frequent. He also began to denounce the Constitution as an "agreement with hell," warning abolitionists to rely on moral appeals alone to end slavery. Garrison's stubborn refusal to use other tactics angered moderates, who supported change through the ballot box.

Just as troubling to many moderates was Garrison's call for equal rights for women. Many white male abolitionists believed that women should remain in the domestic sphere. They did not appreciate women's increased visibility and political activity within the movement.

Although excluded from formal membership in the American Anti-Slavery Society, women still assumed important roles in the movement. Maria W. Stewart, an African American journalist and teacher, won converts to abolition as early as 1832—the year before the formation of the American Anti-Slavery Society. She became the first American woman to speak publicly about abolition before mixed audiences. Other women

▲ An abolitionist group is shown gathered on the porch of Lucy Stone's house. Lucy Stone was a well-known suffragist and abolitionist. Abby Kelley is seated in the middle of the top row.

organized female abolitionist societies, which sponsored petition drives and raised money.

When Garrison's supporters put a woman, Abby Kelley, on an important American Anti-Slavery Society committee in 1840, moderates formed their own organization. The split did not seriously damage the cause, however. The number of local abolitionist organizations continued to grow. By the late 1840s more than 2,000 local societies—most of them in New York, Ohio, Massachusetts, and Pennsylvania—were keeping public attention focused on abolition.

▪▪ **Abolitionists faced violent opposition from some northerners and disputes within their own movement.**

SECTION 3 REVIEW

IDENTIFY and explain the significance of the following: David Walker, William Lloyd Garrison, American Anti-Slavery Society, Frederick Douglass, Sojourner Truth, Maria W. Stewart.

1. **MAIN IDEA** Why did African Americans oppose colonization? What steps did they take to change the direction of the antislavery movement?

2. **MAIN IDEA** How did publications such as the *Appeal* and the *Liberator* affect the abolitionist movement?

3. **USING HISTORICAL IMAGINATION** Why were the appeals of Frederick Douglass and Sojourner Truth so effective in persuading people to join the abolitionist movement?

4. **WRITING TO DESCRIBE** You are a woman abolitionist in 1840. Write an essay describing the obstacles you face and your experiences in the movement.

5. **ASSESSING CONSEQUENCES** Provide evidence to support the following statement: "African Americans hastened the end of slavery by taking an active role in the abolitionist movement."

Chapter 9

SECTION 4

Introducing the Section

PREVIEW WORKSHOP

Following is a list of the significant people and terms in this section. You may wish to use this list as a section preview.

People
- Sarah Grimké
- Angelina Grimké
- Catharine Beecher
- Elizabeth Cady Stanton
- Lucretia Mott
- Susan B. Anthony

Terms
- Seneca Falls Convention
- suffrage

Section 4

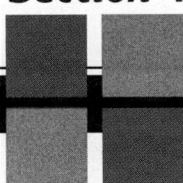

THE CAUSE OF WOMEN'S RIGHTS

FOCUS OBJECTIVES
- Examine the rights demanded by the early women's rights activists.
- Identify the reforms that the women's rights activists achieved and the issues that remained unresolved.
- Explain why middle-class women's rights groups were unable to gain wide support among African American women and white working-class women.

F O C U S
- **What rights did the early women's rights activists demand?**
- **What reforms did the women's rights activists achieve? What issues remained unresolved?**
- **Why were middle-class women's rights groups unable to gain wide support among African American women and white working-class women?**

Women played major roles in all reform movements. They ran organizations and mastered the skills of fund-raising, public speaking, and petitioning legislatures. But women still met opposition to their roles as reformers. Many women involved in reform movements realized that they needed secure economic and political rights to participate fully in society. As a result, women in the late 1840s expanded their work to include the struggle for their own rights.

Speaker for women's rights

ABOLITION AND WOMEN'S RIGHTS

The experiences of Sarah Grimké and Angelina Grimké, two early lecturers for the American Anti-Slavery Society, illustrate how supporting African Americans' rights led many women to work for their own rights. Daughters of a prominent Charleston, South Carolina, slaveholder, the Grimké sisters moved to the North in the 1820s and became abolition-ists. The sisters at first devoted their energies solely to the fight against slavery. But over time they came to view abolition and women's rights as parts of the same struggle. Angelina Grimké argued:

66 The discussion of the rights of the slave has opened the way for the discussion of other rights, and the ultimate result will most certainly be the breaking of *every* yoke . . . an emancipation far more glorious than any the world has ever yet seen. 99

The Grimkés' efforts met sharp opposition. Cath-arine Beecher, an education reformer and advocate of women's traditional roles, criticized the

PRIMARY SOURCE
Description of Change: excerpted
Rationale: excerpted to focus on main idea

▶ Sarah Grimké

◀ Angelina Grimké

CORE RESOURCES
- **Section 4 Daily Quiz**

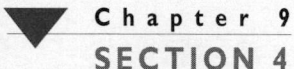

MOTIVATING:
LINK TO TODAY

Ask students to name some of the struggles and demands for which women are working today. *(equal pay for equal work, reproductive rights, child care)* Have them compare these goals with those of the early women's rights advocates as they study the section.

Teaching the Section

DEMANDS FOR WOMEN'S RIGHTS

Hold a class Seneca Falls convention. Each "delegate" is to serve on a policy group on women's suffrage, educational equity, equal employment opportunity, property rights, or domestic relations. Each group is to draft a statement that lists women's grievances in its policy area and that demands reform. Have the chairperson of each group read its statement in front of the convention.

MAKING CONNECTIONS

Medicine

In the 1800s, the idea of female doctors was so unacceptable that only one medical school—Geneva College in rural New York—would admit Elizabeth Blackwell. In 1849 she became the first woman to earn a degree from a U.S. medical school. After gaining experience in Paris and London, she opened a clinic in New York City.

HISTORICAL SIDELIGHTS

Maria W. Stewart

Maria W. Stewart, an African American, faced criticism for speaking before men and women. In response she declared that being a woman did not invalidate her message. She also pointed out that Jewish women had been among the prophets and that a woman had been chosen to announce the Resurrection of Jesus Christ. "Is not the God of ancient times the god of these modern days?" she countered.

PRIMARY SOURCE

Description of Change: excerpted
Rationale: excerpted to focus on main idea

Grimkés and other women for participating in abolitionist petition campaigns. "Petitions to congress," Beecher argued, "seem, IN ALL CASES, to fall entirely without [outside] the sphere of female duty. Men are the proper persons to make appeals to the rulers whom they appoint."

A group of Congregationalist ministers from Massachusetts echoed such sentiments. In 1837 they denounced the Grimkés for speaking before mixed audiences. The ministers said women's influence should be "unobtrusive and private" through quiet prayers and through their work at home and in Sunday schools.

But the Grimkés refused to back down. "Men and women were CREATED EQUAL," Sarah Grimké wrote. "They are both moral and accountable beings, and whatever is *right* for man to do, is *right* for woman." Her sister agreed that "it is a woman's right to have a voice in all the laws and regulations by which she is to be *governed,* whether in Church or State." She added that society's "present arrangements" on these matters "are *a violation of human rights.*"

WOMEN DECLARE THEIR RIGHTS

The link between abolition and women's rights endured as the call for equal rights for women grew stronger in the 1840s. Two noted abolitionists who became leading active supporters of women's rights were Elizabeth Cady Stanton and Lucretia Mott.

Stanton and Mott were deeply troubled by women's status in American society. Denied the right to vote, women remained second-class citizens. They had far less access to education, especially higher education, than men. Social prejudices limited women to a few professions, and women received lower wages than men. Married women had few rights to own property (even inherited property) or to keep their own earnings. Women who divorced their husbands could not get custody of their children.

Stanton and Mott became painfully aware of these injustices in 1840 when they attended the World's Anti-Slavery Convention in London. Convention officials refused to allow women to speak. As a result, Stanton and Mott agreed that after the convention they would launch a movement to end the daily discrimination women faced. Their efforts led to the first U.S. women's

▼ Elizabeth Cady Stanton

▲ Lucretia Mott

rights convention, held in Seneca Falls, New York, in 1848.

More than 300 women and men attended the **Seneca Falls Convention**, which marked the birth of the organized women's rights movement in the United States. The convention adopted a Declaration of Sentiments modeled on the democratic ideals contained in the Declaration of Independence:

> 66 We hold these truths to be self-evident: that all men and women are created equal; that they are endowed by their Creator with certain inalienable rights. . . .
> Now, . . . because women do feel themselves aggrieved, oppressed, and fraudulently deprived of their most sacred rights, we insist that they have immediate admission to all the rights and privileges which belong to them as citizens of the United States. 99

The Declaration of Sentiments also called for reforms to strengthen women's legal position.

HITS AND MISSES

Have students write editorials for 1840s newspapers arguing one of the following: *Women's rights activists have largely succeeded in their struggle for equality;* or *Women's rights activists have largely failed in their efforts to secure equality.* Remind students they should consider the reforms that activists achieved and the issues that remained unresolved. Have volunteers read their editorials to the class. Students may wish to include their editorials in their portfolios.

WOMEN'S GROUPS AT ODDS

Organize students in groups of three. Direct them to create short skits that dramatize how the interests of white middle-class women differed from those of African American women and white working-class women. Skits should show clearly why the latter two groups formed their own organizations. Characters may be real or imaginary, and skits may be serious or humorous.

▶

These reforms included granting married women the rights to control property and earnings and to be awarded custody of their children in the event of a divorce. Most important, they included granting women the right to vote.

The Declaration of Sentiments publicly voiced the discontent many women felt. Emily Collins, a woman from a small town in western New York, expressed her reaction to the convention:

> 66 I revolted in spirit against the customs of society and the laws of the State that crushed my aspirations. . . . But not until that meeting at Seneca Falls in 1848 . . . gave this feeling of unrest form and voice, did I take action. 99

Collins went on to organize the women in her town to work for women's rights.

▪▪ Women's rights activists demanded the same rights white men enjoyed.

The most fiercely debated issue at the Seneca Falls Convention was **suffrage**, the right to vote. Stanton said attaining the right to vote was crucial to winning full equality because "the power to choose rulers and make laws, was the right by which all others could be secured."

Opponents of women's suffrage said demanding the vote was too radical. Most people agreed with Catharine Beecher that women should not participate in political activities. Others believed that such an unpopular demand might jeopardize support from influential politicians.

▶ **A commemorative printing of the Declaration of Sentiments is shown here. The declaration called for legal reforms, such as granting women the right to vote, and insisted that "all men and women are created equal."**

WOMEN'S RIGHTS ACTIVISM

Although the Seneca Falls reformers agreed to work for suffrage, early activists for women's rights devoted most of their energies to attaining other legal reforms called for in the Declaration of Sentiments. To achieve these goals, the activists organized a system of linked local organizations, held national women's rights conferences, and organized a series of state conventions across the North and the Middle West. At one such convention in Akron, Ohio, in 1851, Sojourner Truth gave a speech that convinced many men in attendance that women were their equals. She eloquently recounted her own experiences:

> 66 Look at my arm! I have ploughed and planted and gathered into barns . . . and ain't I a woman? I could work as much and eat as much as a man—when I could get it—and bear the lash as well! And ain't I a woman? I have born thirteen children, and seen most of 'em sold into slavery, and when I cried out with my mother's grief, none but Jesus heard me—and ain't I a woman? 99

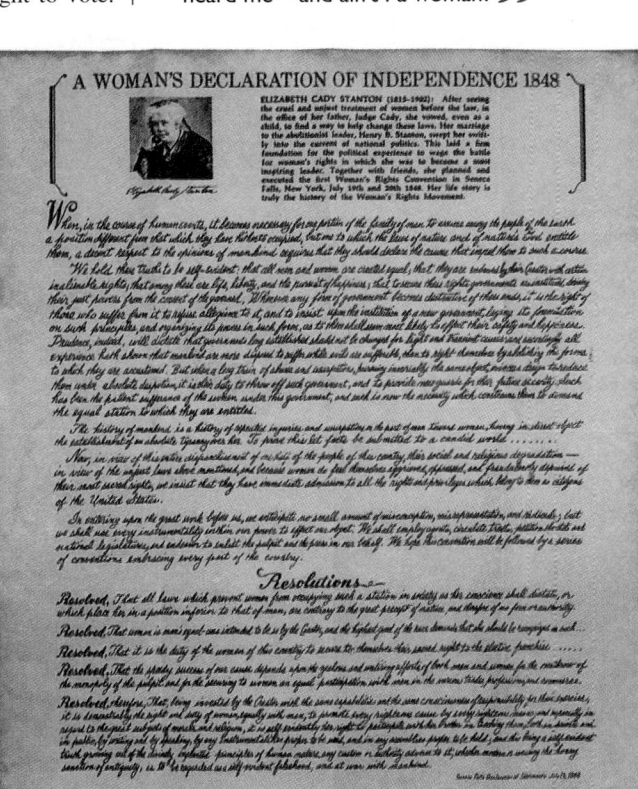

A WOMAN'S DECLARATION OF INDEPENDENCE 1848

Resolutions

🌐 GLOBAL CONNECTIONS

In 1867 John Stuart Mill, a noted British social philosopher and member of Parliament, introduced the first bill for women's suffrage in Britain. In 1869 taxpaying unmarried and widowed women were allowed to vote in municipal elections.

PRIMARY SOURCES

Description of Change: excerpted
Rationale: excerpted to focus on main idea

COOPERATIVE LEARNING

Have students work in small groups to portray the following pairs: a woman who wishes to keep her own property after marriage, and her husband; a male minister who disapproves of women speaking in public, and a female member of his congregation who wishes to do so; a congressman who disapproves of women's suffrage, and a woman who wants to vote. Have each pair prepare arguments to present to the group. Have a group reporter take notes on the major ideas presented.

Practice

GUIDED PRACTICE

On the chalkboard create a chart with the following headings: *Name, Connection to Women's Rights Movement, Actions, Ideas.* Ask students to supply information to fill in blanks in the chart, until all women mentioned in the section are covered.

INDEPENDENT PRACTICE

Assign each student one of the following names, and use the Guided Practice chart to create short biographies for a women's rights "Who's Who," telling how each fits into the movement: Sarah Grimké, Angelina Grimké, Catharine Beecher, Elizabeth Cady Stanton, Lucretia Mott, Emily Collins, Sojourner Truth, Susan B. Anthony.

Review and Assessment

REVIEW Have students role-play one of the women's rights leaders discussed in this section. Ask students to write a daily journal entry about the leader's work, the movement, and the future. Choose students to read their entries aloud until each woman in the section is covered. Then assign the Section 4 Review on p. 301.

ASSESS Assign the **Section 4 Daily Quiz** in *Core Resources.*

HISTORICAL SIDELIGHTS

Anthony's Challange

In 1872 Susan B. Anthony and other women voted in a New York election, even though they knew they could be jailed for up to three years and fined up to $500. Anthony sought legal advice before she voted, and retired Judge Henry R. Selden agreed to defend her if she was prosecuted. After the election the women voters were arrested, and bail was set at $500 each. All the women paid their bail except Anthony. She challenged the legality of her arrest, and her bail was raised to $1,000. She again refused to pay, but Judge Selden stepped in and paid her bail. Anthony was eventually found guilty and fined $100 and costs. Again, she refused to pay, and although she could have been put in jail, she was not, thereby denying her a chance to bring the case before the Supreme Court. The cases against the other women who had voted were dropped.

▲ Susan B. Anthony participated in temperance and antislavery causes, as well as those of women's rights. In 1872 she was arrested for attempting to cast a vote in the Rochester city elections.

Another important women's rights leader was Susan B. Anthony. She was raised in a Quaker family that affirmed the equality of men and women. From her involvement in temperance and abolition, Anthony learned the limits society placed on women's roles in reform movements. In 1852 she was forbidden to speak at a temperance convention because she was a woman. This event convinced her that women could not be effective in reform movements unless they won political

rights. At Elizabeth Cady Stanton's urging, Anthony dedicated the rest of her life to working for women's rights. She organized petition campaigns and meetings, gave speeches, and raised money for the cause.

Anthony, along with Stanton, Mott, and Truth, also argued for a variety of legal reforms that would benefit women. One of these reforms—women's right to own and control their property—had first been proposed by middle-class men. Some fathers had long supported this cause as a way of protecting what they saw as family property from untrustworthy sons-in-law.

In response to calls for reform, New York and other states revised their laws to permit married women to own property, file lawsuits, and retain their earnings. But political and legal equality on the national level, including the right to vote, would be slow in coming. Despite passionate demands for political rights in 1848 and the subsequent focus on suffrage, women did not gain a constitutional guarantee of voting rights until 1920. Nevertheless, the women's rights activists of the mid-1800s initiated the movement that continues today.

■■ **Women's rights activists achieved some gains in legal rights on the state level but did not win the right to vote.**

▶ Male election judges refused to accept suffragist Victoria Woodhull's ballot when she attempted to vote. In 1872 Woodhull helped form the Equal Rights party and ran unsuccessfully for president with abolitionist Frederick Douglass as her running mate.

RETEACH Organize students into small groups and assign each group a subsection of Section 4. Direct each group to develop questions about the main ideas in its subsection. Then have each group exchange its questions with another group and work to answer the questions it receives.

Closure

Write on the chalkboard this statement from the Declaration of Sentiments: *"All men and women are created equal."* Call on students to defend the viewpoint of the Declaration or to defend the traditional viewpoint of the time. Record arguments on the chalkboard. Urge students to include in their arguments all the major issues addressed in the section.

Extension

CREATE Ask students to find editorial cartoons of the period that comment on the women's rights movement. Then have students draw their own cartoons and display them in the classroom.

INVESTIGATE Have students investigate the philosophy of one of the women's rights leaders noted in the section and write a paper on how she might respond to the women's rights movement today.

COMMENTARY

Who Participated in the Women's Rights Movement?

The grievances expressed at the Seneca Falls Convention mainly reflected the concerns of white middle-class women. The demands for married women's property rights, control of wages, and custody of children were meant to cement middle-class women's social status. These rights were not the main concerns of women with few resources, such as the majority of African American women and white working-class women.

Stanton, Mott, and other white women's rights activists showed a commitment to abolition and equal rights for African Americans. However, many local women's rights activists feared a shift in focus away from women's rights and toward abolitionism. In addition, some white women believed that African Americans were inferior and did not deserve full rights. As a result, local and state organizations often discriminated against black women. When black abolitionist Sojourner Truth rose to address the Ohio convention, many people tried to keep her from speaking.

Although some African American women participated in women's rights groups, many more of them devoted their energies to building and aiding welfare and educational institutions in their own communities. In addition to these activities, they also participated in organizations devoted to abolition and equality for all African Americans.

These black women believed that the best way to improve their status as women was to focus first on improving their status as African Americans.

Although Susan B. Anthony helped draft a code of fair wages for women in 1853, most women's rights activists ignored workplace issues. As a result, most white working-class women looked to other groups for support in their struggle for better wages and working conditions. For example, when women such as Sarah Bagley organized strikes (see Chapter 8), they allied themselves with white working-class men who shared their concerns.

It is therefore important to realize that the movement created at Seneca Falls failed to include all American women. Most African American and white working-class women had concerns that differed from those of middle-class women, and therefore they did not participate in the mainstream movement. Instead, they either joined groups that shared their concerns or formed their own organizations and found a separate path to equality. At the same time, however, many of the advances won by mainstream women's rights activists were enjoyed by all women.

▪▪ Few middle-class women's rights groups addressed the needs and concerns of African American women and white working-class women.

SECTION 4 REVIEW

IDENTIFY and explain the significance of the following: Sarah Grimké, Angelina Grimké, Catharine Beecher, Elizabeth Cady Stanton, Lucretia Mott, Seneca Falls Convention, suffrage, Susan B. Anthony.

1. **MAIN IDEA** What was the goal of early women's rights activists?

2. **MAIN IDEA** How successful were women's rights activists in achieving reforms?

3. **MAIN IDEA** Why did African American women and white working-class women form their own organizations rather than join middle-class women's rights groups? What issues did these organizations tackle?

4. **WRITING TO CREATE** Write an inspirational song or poem that demonstrates the struggle for women's rights in the 1850s.

5. **ASSESSING CONSEQUENCES** How did the suffrage issue divide the women's rights movement?

Chapter Review Answers

WRITING A SUMMARY
See Essential Points in each section for main ideas.

REVIEWING CHRONOLOGY
4, 5, 3, 1, 2
Identifying Cause and Effect
Paragraphs will vary but should make the cause and effect of events clear.

IDENTIFYING PEOPLE AND IDEAS

1. *religious movement beginning in the 1790s that drew on people's optimism, sparked revival meetings, and promised salvation to all sinners*
2. *fugitive slave whose autobiography, newspaper, and speeches convinced many to support abolition*
3. *movement that fought to limit alcohol consumption*
4. *Massachusetts's first secretary of education and reformer of the public school system*
5. *published the* Liberator *and supported equal rights for African Americans and women*
6. *communities that were designed to create the perfect society*
7. *ex-slave who fought for abolition and women's rights*

8. *abolitionist and women's rights supporter whose efforts led to the Seneca Falls Convention*
9. *the right to vote*
10. *Quaker suffragist who fought for political and legal reforms for women*

UNDERSTANDING MAIN IDEAS

1. *believed literate slaves who read the Bible and other works would be led to revolt against slaveholders*
2. *Temperance, public schools, abolition, and women's rights met opposition when they threatened cus-toms, religious beliefs, prejudices, and economic interests.*
3. *formed churches; founded abolitionist societies; set up alternative schools; published newspapers; gave lectures; supported women's rights*
4. *Neither African Americans nor any women had equal rights; both movements were seen by some as part of the same struggle.*
5. *advocated teaching work skills and discipline in the poorhouses; supported temperance as a solution to poverty; favored free public education*

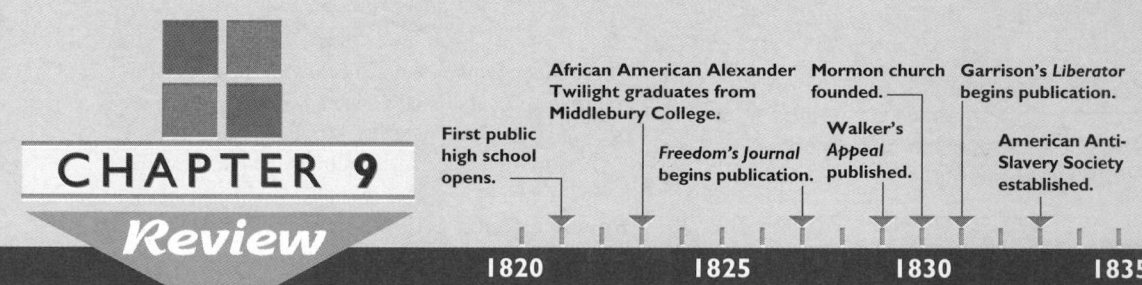

CHAPTER 9
Review

First public high school opens.

Freedom's Journal begins publication.

African American Alexander Twilight graduates from Middlebury College.

Mormon church founded.

Walker's *Appeal* published.

Garrison's *Liberator* begins publication.

American Anti-Slavery Society established.

1820   1825   1830   1835

WRITING A SUMMARY
Using the essential points of the chapter as a guide, write a summary of the chapter.

REVIEWING CHRONOLOGY
Number your paper 1 to 5. Study the time line above, and list the following events in the order in which they happened by writing the first next to 1, the second next to 2, and so on. Then complete the activity below.

1. Seneca Falls Convention held.
2. Wilberforce University founded.
3. Maine bans sale of alcohol.
4. Mormon church founded.
5. Garrison's *Liberator* begins publication.

Identifying Cause and Effect Select two events on the time line, and in a paragraph, explain the cause-and-effect relationship between them.

IDENTIFYING PEOPLE AND IDEAS
Explain the historical significance of each of the following people or terms.

1. Second Great Awakening
2. Frederick Douglass
3. temperance movement
4. Horace Mann
5. William Lloyd Garrison
6. utopias
7. Sojourner Truth
8. Lucretia Mott
9. suffrage
10. Susan B. Anthony

UNDERSTANDING MAIN IDEAS

1. Why did many southern states pass laws making it illegal to teach slaves to read?
2. Which kinds of reforms met significant opposition? Why?
3. What are some of the ways in which African Americans participated in the reform efforts of the 19th century?
4. Why were many women's rights reformers also abolitionists?
5. How did reformers work to improve the lives of poor Americans?

REVIEWING THEMES

1. **Democratic Values** In what ways were reformers successful in changing public policies that affected mental illness, prisons, schools, and women's rights?
2. **Cultural Diversity** What social factors contributed to the rise of revivalism and the spread of utopian communities in the 1800s?

THINKING CRITICALLY

1. **Synthesizing** Why did reformers tackle such a wide variety of causes during this period?
2. **Hypothesizing** What factors may have motivated reformers to persist in their efforts even under the threat of violence?
3. **Analyzing** How might the abolitionist movement have been different if William Lloyd Garrison had compromised with his opponents?

STRATEGY FOR SUCCESS
Review the Strategies for Success on Interpreting the Visual Record on page 98. Then study the painting of a camp revival meeting below. On a separate sheet of paper, describe the physical surroundings and suggest why the artist placed the meeting in an idealized setting.

The Granger Collection, New York

REVIEWING THEMES

1. *Mental illness was treated as a curable disease; prisons became more humane; public and alternative schools were created; women gained some legal rights.*
2. *expanding democratic ideals, spirit of optimism in society, desire to change an imperfect society*

THINKING CRITICALLY

1. *Slavery, increased immigration, westward expansion, industrialization, and urbanization transformed society, producing social problems as well as benefits. Religious revival and a belief that people could be perfected led reformers to work to ease social problems.*
2. *religious and moral beliefs, desire to help others, belief in the justness of their cause*
3. *Compromise might have lessened violent opposition in the North and decreased disputes within the abolitionist movement.*

STRATEGY FOR SUCCESS

Answers should describe the rural outdoor setting and mention how this idealized view emphasized the relationship between natural beauty and spiritual conversion, as well as the belief that humanity could perfect itself.

WRITING ABOUT HISTORY

Speeches will vary but should offer specific political solutions to one of the social problems.

USING PRIMARY SOURCES

Essays should point to Wright's attachment to national equality, commonality of habits and attitudes—the creation of "national institutions"—which were the goals of reform.

LINKING HISTORY AND GEOGRAPHY

Urbanization concentrated social problems and brought people and resources together to solve them.

Abolitionist Elijah Lovejoy killed.

Dorothea Dix begins crusade for mentally ill. Brook Farm founded.

Maine bans sale of alcohol.

***North Star* begins publication.**

Enslaved Africans mutiny on *Amistad*.

Douglass's autobiography published.

Seneca Falls Convention held.

Wilberforce University founded.

African American Mary Jane Patterson graduates from Oberlin.

| 1840 | 1845 | 1850 | 1855 | 1860 |

WRITING ABOUT HISTORY

Writing to Express a Viewpoint You are a politician running for office in the 1850s. Write a short speech that explains your position on one of the following issues: prohibition, public education, abolition, or women's rights.

USING PRIMARY SOURCES

Fanny Wright was a reformer who scandalized many by her outspoken views. Read the following excerpt from her lecture entitled "Of Existing Evils and Their Remedy." Then write an essay explaining why Wright advocated reform as a necessary part of a democracy.

> 66 *Great reforms are not wrought in a day. . . . A free people may boast that all power is in their hands; but no effectual power can be in their hands until knowledge be in their minds.*
>
> *But how may knowledge be imparted to their minds? Such effective knowledge as shall render apparent to all the interests of all, and demonstrate the simple truths: that a nation to be strong, must be united; to be united, must be equal in condition; to be equal in condition, must be similar in habits and feeling; to be similar in habits and in feeling, must be raised in national institutions, as the children of a common family and citizens of a common country.* 99

LINKING HISTORY AND GEOGRAPHY

Study the map at the top of the next column. Each dot represents an organization associated with a reform movement. Note that reform organizations are concentrated in the Middle West and the Northeast—areas of intense urban growth. Why do you think reform movements were most active in urban areas?

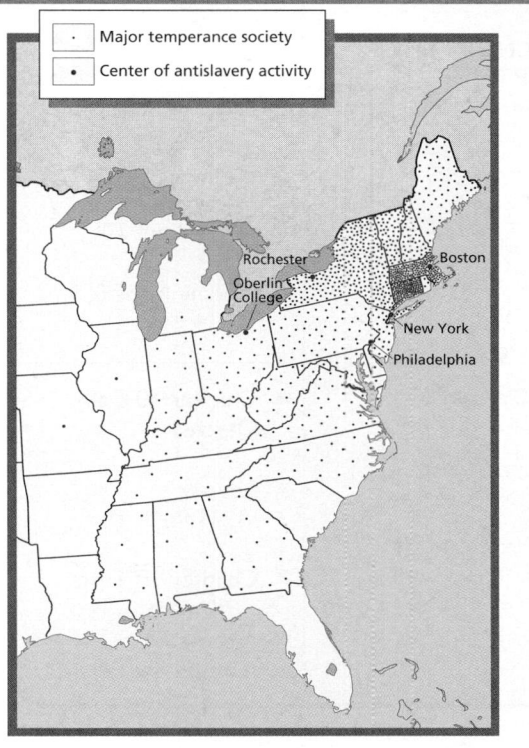

· Major temperance society
• Center of antislavery activity

Rochester
Oberlin College
Boston
New York
Philadelphia

BUILDING YOUR PORTFOLIO

Complete the following projects independently or cooperatively.

1. INDIVIDUAL RIGHTS In chapters 7 and 8 you explored individual rights. Building on that experience, imagine you are a women's rights activist. Prepare a pamphlet calling for women's rights.

2. IMMIGRATION In Chapter 8 you were a newly arrived immigrant. Building on that experience, write an editorial casting temperance as an issue of immigrants' rights.

BUILDING YOUR PORTFOLIO

Have students refer to **Building Your Portfolio Worksheet 3**, assigned at the beginning of Unit 3. Use the worksheet to help students monitor their progress on the portfolio projects.

Assessment

Core Resources
• Review Worksheet 9
• Chapter 9 Tests
• Alternative Assessment Forms
Test Generator

EXPANSION AND CONFLICT

1820–1860

Chapter Overview

In the 1820s economic depression, the lure of farmland, and opportunities for trade drove increasing numbers of Americans westward. The lands they crossed or settled were claimed by others—Mexicans, British, and American Indians. However, as pioneers spilled over the continent, many Americans began to believe it was the nation's manifest destiny to stretch to the Pacific.

By the late 1840s this goal was achieved. The Mexican War, triggered by the U.S. annexation of Texas, resulted in the U.S. acquiring the Mexican territories of California and New Mexico. Britain relinquished its claim to the southern part of Oregon Country. And American Indians were pushed back from their lands.

Chapter Planning Guide

CHAPTER 10	CORE RESOURCE BOOKLETS	AV AUDIOVISUAL RESOURCES	PROGRAM RESOURCES
INTRODUCTION pp. 304–305	■ Literature Worksheet 10 ■ Building Your Portfolio Worksheet 3	■ Everyday Life in America Transparency and Worksheet 10	■ Art in American History Transparency and Worksheet 9
TEACHING THE CHAPTER pp. 306–327	■ Graphic Organizer 10 ■ Social Studies Skills Worksheet 10 ■ Geography Worksheet 10 ■ Outline Maps 8, 9, 10, 11	■ *The American Nation* Videodisc: Community Ties: San Francisco's Chinatown ■ Linking Geography and History Transparency and Worksheet 12	■ Art in American History Transparencies and Worksheets 7, 11, 12 ■ *Eyewitnesses and Others,* Volume 1: Readings 42, 50, 56, 57, 60, 65, 66, 67
REVIEW AND ASSESSMENT pp. 328–329	■ Chapter 10 Daily Quizzes ■ Review Worksheet 10 ■ Chapter 10 Tests ■ Alternative Assessment Forms		■ Test Generator

Additional Resources

BOOKS FOR TEACHERS

Brown, Dee. *Wondrous Times on the Frontier.* HarperCollins, 1992. Describes life on the frontier.

McCaffrey, James M. *Army of Manifest Destiny: The American Soldier in the Mexican War, 1846–1848.* New York University Press, 1992. Explores the Mexican War from the viewpoint of U.S. soldiers.

Wade, L. *California: The Rush for Gold.* Rourke Enterprises, 1991. Explains effects of the gold rush on California society.

BOOKS FOR STUDENTS

Holmes, Kenneth L., ed. *Covered Wagon Women, Vol. IV, 1852: Diaries & Letters from the Western Trails, 1840–1890.* A. H. Clark, 1991. Diaries and letters of pioneers.

Mills, Bronwyn. *The Mexican War.* Facts on File, 1992. Traces events of the Mexican War.

*Van Steenwyk, Elizabeth. *California Gold Rush: West with the Forty-Niners.* Watts, 1991. Account of the gold rush in California.

*for students reading below grade level

MULTIMEDIA MATERIALS

As the Wind Rocks the Wagon: An American Odyssey. Video, 52 min. APL Educational Video/SSSS. Diaries and memoirs of pioneer women traveling the Oregon Trail.

Goldrush Country. Video, 18 min. SSSS. Examines impact of discovery of gold on development of West.

Independence—Texas Gains Its Freedom. Video, 35 min. Finley-Holiday/SSSS. Overview of the convention in Washington, Texas.

USE WITH PAGES 304–305

Listed on the right are the themes emphasized in Chapter 10. The questions in boldface type stimulate critical thinking and provide students with an opportunity to discuss the themes within a broadened context. The questions also appear in the pupil's edition on p. 304.

■ ECONOMIC DEVELOPMENT

How might individual economic choices affect a government's policies? Students should discuss how individual economic desires—such as a farmer desiring new land or a merchant seeking new markets—might lead a government to institute new policies. For example, the demand for new land might convince a government to acquire additional territory, while the desire for new markets might push a government to change its foreign or domestic policies.

■ CULTURAL DIVERSITY

Why might a nation of many cultures experience short-term conflict but emerge stronger in the long run? Students should note that, although diversity can lead to clashes between ethnic and racial groups, it also can lead to cultural enrichment. By providing a wider range of perspectives, cultural practices, and talents, diversity makes a society more vibrant, adaptive, and tolerant of differences.

■ GLOBAL RELATIONS

Why might territorial expansion lead to international as well as domestic conflicts? Students might mention that not all people may support expansion. Some people might object to expanding at another country's expense. Others might disagree over how new territory should be governed. Students should also consider that international disputes may arise when one country seizes territory from another.

CHAPTER STRATEGIES FOR MEETING INDIVIDUAL NEEDS

LIMITED ENGLISH PROFICIENT LEARNERS

Organize students into four groups and assign each group one of the chapter's sections. Have students create maps illustrating main events in their assigned section. Ask them to illustrate each event and include any relevant dates and captions.

TACTILE/KINESTHETIC LEARNERS

Have students create dioramas showing life on the trails; settlements in Oregon, Texas, and California; and events leading up to and during the Mexican War.

LEARNERS HAVING DIFFICULTY

Have students work in pairs to outline each section and then change each section's Focus questions into statements containing answers.

AUDITORY LEARNERS

Have students work in groups to prepare interviews of American settlers and other groups in Oregon, Texas, or California in the 1840s. Have groups present their interviews.

VISUAL LEARNERS

Have students work with partners to research and create illustrations of groups covered in the chapter. Have them write a caption explaining the relevance of each picture. Display illustrations on the wall.

GIFTED LEARNERS

Have students write speeches by a U.S., British, or Mexican official or by a Native American on U.S. expansion in the 1840s. Have volunteers deliver their speeches.

USING THE CHAPTER FOCUS

■ UNDERSTANDING THE MAIN IDEA

Read to the class what British author Harriet Martineau wrote in 1837: "The possession of land is the aim of all action, generally speaking, and the cure for all social ills, among men in the United States. If a man is disappointed by politics or love, he goes and buys land. If he disgraces himself, he betakes himself to a lot in the West." Have students paraphrase the quotation. Then discuss it, asking why land was so sought after in the 1800s, what it represented, and so on. Save responses on a flip chart to refer to as students study the chapter.

THEMES

Have students work individually or in small groups to answer the questions under Themes. Save students' responses so that they can compare them with their responses after studying the chapter. (See p. 303B for suggested answers.)

■ THE TIME LINE

Have students study the time line. Point out that before Texas declared its independence, it was part of Mexico. Ask students what time-line event was likely a result of Texas's independence.

CORE RESOURCES

- **Graphic Organizer 10**
- **Literature Worksheet 10**
- **Outline Maps 8, 9, 10, 11**
- **Building Your Portfolio Worksheet 3**

AV RESOURCES

- **Everyday Life in America Transparency and Worksheet 10**

304

ABOUT THE ILLUSTRATION

The arrival in Mexico City on September 14, 1847, of U.S. troops led by General Winfield Scott resulted in the surrender of Mexican troops led by General Santa Anna and the end of the Mexican War. Tell students to study the print and to imagine that they are a Mexican or an American soldier in the scene. Have them write a journal entry that describes their emotions at that moment. Ask volunteers to read their journal entries to the class. Students may wish to include their journal entries in their portfolios.

Chapter 10

1820–1860

EXPANSION AND CONFLICT

FOCUS

UNDERSTANDING THE MAIN IDEA

In the early 1800s Americans moved beyond the boundaries of the United States and into present-day Texas, New Mexico, California, and Oregon. These migrations resulted in U.S. conflicts with Mexico and Great Britain and the expansion of U.S. territory to the Pacific Ocean. This expansion disrupted the ways of life of Native Americans and Mexicans living in these areas.

THEMES

- **■ ECONOMIC DEVELOPMENT** How might individual economic choices affect a government's policies?

- **■ CULTURAL DIVERSITY** Why might a nation of many cultures experience short-term conflict but emerge stronger in the long run?

- **■ GLOBAL RELATIONS** Why might territorial expansion lead to international as well as domestic conflicts?

1836	1846	1848	1851
Texas declares independence.	U.S. Congress declares war on Mexico.	Gold discovered in California.	Treaty of Fort Laramie signed.

Have students recall the boundaries of the Louisiana Purchase. Ask a volunteer to indicate the region on a wall map of the U.S. Have another volunteer indicate what countries and groups controlled the areas surrounding the Louisiana Purchase. Tell students that this chapter deals with how the U.S. came into conflict with these groups as the nation strove to expand beyond the Louisiana Purchase.

▶ LINK TO THE PAST

The 19th century was the principal era of U.S. expansion in North America. In 1803 the Louisiana Purchase added to the United States a vast portion of the continent west of the Mississippi River. Then in 1819 the nation acquired Florida from Spain.

HISTORICAL SIDELIGHTS
Mier y Terán

Manuel Mier y Terán was a hero of the Mexican war for independence and a respected politician. He had held a seat in the Mexican congress and the post of Minister of War and Navy. After his visit to Texas, he helped author legislation in 1830 to lessen U.S. influence in the province. *Empresario* Stephen F. Austin trusted Mier y Terán to protect Texas interests, noting that "my hopes are fixed on you to save Texas."

PRIMARY SOURCE
Description of Change: excerpted
Rationale: excerpted to focus on main idea

In 1827 the Mexican government sent General Manuel Mier y Terán, a hero of the struggle for Mexican independence, to inspect Mexico's northeastern border. In a report written two years later he described the United States as hungry for more territory:

66 The North Americans have conquered whatever territory adjoins them. In less than half a century, they have become masters of extensive colonies which formerly belonged to Spain and France, and of even more spacious territories from which have disappeared the former owners, the Indian tribes. 99

Mier y Terán warned his superiors that people in the United States were already calling for the annexation of Texas. He predicted that soon U.S. settlers in Texas would begin to "incite uprisings in the territory." His words proved prophetic: in 1835, Texas settlers—both American and Mexican—rose up in revolt against the Mexican government.

Americans also moved to other territories in these years. After 1820 the search for trade and furs drew American settlers to the Mexican provinces of New Mexico and California and to Oregon Country, jointly occupied by Great Britain and the United States. These migrations caused conflicts as the United States sought to expand its boundaries to include the territories.

Carl Nebel's 1851 print of U.S. troops entering Mexico City

Covered wagon moving westward

The Shelburne Museum, Shelburne, Vermont

PREVIEW WORKSHOP

Following is a list of the significant people, places, and terms in this section. You may wish to use this list as a section preview.

People
- Tejanos
- Martín de León
- Lorenzo de Zavala
- Stephen F. Austin
- Antonio López de Santa Anna
- Sam Houston
- Henri Castro
- Prince Carl of Solms-Braunfels
- Juan Nepomuceno Seguín

Places
- San Antonio
- Goliad

Terms
- manifest destiny
- *empresarios*
- Texas Revolution
- Battle of San Jacinto

FOCUS OBJECTIVES

- Analyze the argument western expansionists used to win support for their views.

- Explain why the Mexican government invited American settlers into Texas.

- Examine the conflicts between the Texans and the Mexican government that led to revolution.

- Describe how Texas independence affected Tejanos.

PRIMARY SOURCE

Description of Change: excerpted and bracketed
Rationale: excerpted to focus on main idea; bracketed to clarify meaning

CORE RESOURCES

• Section 1 Daily Quiz

306

Section 1

THE LURE OF THE WEST

F O C U S
- **What argument did western expansionists use to win support for their views?**
- **Why did the Mexican government invite American settlers into Texas?**
- **What conflicts between the Texans and the Mexican government led to revolution?**
- **How did Texas independence affect Tejanos?**

Before 1820 few U.S. settlers ventured into the Spanish territories of Texas, California, and New Mexico. Even fewer, mainly trappers and traders, went to Oregon Country, the territory to which Great Britain and the United States shared a disputed claim. After 1820, however, U.S. settlers, driven by the search for economic opportunities and rich farmland, moved to the Far West in increasing numbers. U.S. expansionists urged them on.

Detail from *The Funeral of an Angel*

MANIFEST DESTINY

In 1845 the magazine editor John L. O'Sullivan coined the phrase **manifest destiny**, which expressed the popular belief that the United States was destined to extend its territory to the Pacific Ocean. O'Sullivan urged the United States to ignore other nations' claims to territory in North America:

❝ Away, away with all these cobweb tissues of rights of discovery, exploration, settlement. . . . The American claim is by the right of our manifest destiny to overspread and to possess the whole of the continent which Providence [God] has given us for the development of the great experiment of liberty. ❞

Many Americans supported manifest destiny. Northerners troubled by economic instability and urban crowding believed that expansion would lessen population pressures and would create new markets for U.S. products.

Southerners hungry for more land for cotton production also supported manifest destiny. To counter northern fears about the spread of slavery, they suggested that expansion would actually help end slavery in the Upper South by shifting the slave population westward. This argument appealed to northern whites who opposed slavery but did not want to see freed blacks settle in the North.

▪▪ U.S. expansionists argued that it was the nation's manifest destiny to claim all of North America.

Ask students to refer to TV programs or
their own experiences to discuss cultural
differences they have observed in American
society. Discuss why cultural differences
can sometimes create conflict. Then tell
students that this section explains how cultural differences contributed to conflicts in
Texas.

Teaching the Section

MANIFEST DESTINY AND WESTERN EXPANSIONISM

Have students work in pairs to list arguments for and against manifest destiny in
the 1840s. Then ask volunteers to debate
the issue from the standpoints of expansionists and anti-expansionists of the time.

AMERICANS IN TEXAS

Organize students into groups to develop an
immigration policy for Texas. Each group's
policy statement should tell why immigration to Texas should be encouraged, identify
potential problems with this immigration,
and suggest possible solutions. Have group
spokespersons read their policies to the
class.

▶

Not all Americans supported manifest destiny, however. Some objected to expansion because
the lands were already claimed by other nations.
Others feared that expansion would produce a
nation too large to govern. But for most
Americans, particularly those facing the sometimes
bitter realities of the market revolution, debates
over manifest destiny were of little interest. Land
and opportunity were their main concerns.

MEXICAN TEXAS

U.S. settlement of foreign territory was most
clearly visible in the Mexican territory of Texas.
By 1815 a few hundred Americans had already
crossed the Sabine and Red rivers and settled in
northeastern Texas.

This immigration increased after Mexico
won its independence in 1821. After more than 10
years of fighting Spanish rule, Mexicans established the independent Republic of Mexico.
Mexican authorities encouraged U.S. immigration
to its northern territory to boost Texas's non-Indian
population, which was about 4,000 in 1821.
Officials hoped the non-Indian settlers would serve
as a barrier between Mexico's northern settlements
and Apache and Comanche raiders.

The tactic was a calculated risk. Mexican officials feared that the United States, which had twice
tried to purchase Texas, would one day take the
territory by force. The few thousand Tejanos
(tay-HAH-nohs)—native Mex-
icans living in Texas—stood
little chance of blocking an invasion. But if Mexico could recruit
enough American settlers and
turn them into loyal Mexican citizens—something it hoped to
accomplish by making them
landowners—the country might
build a defensive force large
enough to prevent a U.S. invasion. As a precaution, however,
the Mexican government
planned to recruit other foreign
settlers to offset the American
presence.

As an additional safe-
guard, Mexico did not open settlement to everyone. Instead, it
gave generous land grants to

empresarios (em-pruh-SAH-ree-ohs), businesspeople who agreed to recruit and take responsibility
for new settlers. The *empresarios* attracted thousands of settlers to Texas. Though Mexico granted
most *empresario* contracts to Americans, it gave
some to Tejanos. Martín de León received a contract in 1824 to settle Mexican families in Texas.
He founded Victoria, Texas, as the capital of his
colony. Lorenzo de Zavala, a prominent Mexican
politician, received a grant in eastern Texas in
1829, but transferred the contract the next year.

■■ **Mexico promoted U.S. settlement in Texas to shield Mexico
from Indian raids and a possible
U.S. invasion.**

Moses Austin, a Missouri businessman hoping to rebuild his fortunes after the Panic of 1819,
was the first American granted an *empresario* contract. In 1821 the Spanish granted Austin permission to start a colony, but he died before he could
recruit any settlers. His son, Stephen F. Austin,
assumed the grant and went to Texas to select a
site for his colony.

Recruitment proved easy, since Austin sold
large lots for 12 cents an acre. (At the time, public
land in the United States sold for $1.25 an acre.)
Many of the settlers were cotton farmers who
brought enslaved African Americans with them. By
1830 Austin and the other *empresarios* had relocated some 7,000 Americans to Texas.

▲ **Shown here are Mary and John Rabb, two of the first settlers to
receive a land grant in Stephen F. Austin's colony.**

HISTORICAL SIDELIGHTS
Settlers' Challenges

Mary and John Rabb went to
Texas in 1823 and settled for
a time near present-day
Houston. Mary Rabb de-
scribed the challenges of living "where the horseflies and
mosquitoes was so bad we
had to leave and travel in the
night." Rabb immediately
"went to spinning and spun
enough thread to make forty-
six yards of mosquito barring
[netting] and wove it out in
the open air and sun."

CULTURAL PATTERNS

Mexican officials in
Texas were well aware of
the difficulty of assimi-
lating U.S. settlers. When
debating approval of
Austin's *empresario* contract, one official urged
that the U.S. colonists be
settled around San
Antonio. He argued that
if the colonists settled
there, they would in time
be assimilated by the
city's native inhabitants.
The official also stressed
the importance of the settlers' being separated
from the United States by
an expanse of unsettled
land.

Teaching the *Section*

THE TEXAS REVOLUTION

Organize the class into two groups—one representing the Mexican government and the other, Texans. Ask each group to cite the conflicts that led to the Texas Revolution. Then call on members of each group to debate the issues from the Mexican government's and the Texans' perspectives.

TEJANOS IN TEXAS

Organize students into small groups and tell them that their task is to create a "TV documentary" on the status of Tejanos in Texas after the Texas Revolution. Ask students to outline a script that includes a commentary on the status of Tejanos before and during the revolution, the reason they were discriminated against after the revolution, and the result of the discrimination.

THE TEXAS REVOLUTION

By 1830, non-Mexicans outnumbered the Tejanos by about two to one. These new arrivals made little effort to learn Spanish or adapt to Mexican culture. In 1830, Mexico, fearing a rebellion in Texas as well as a U.S. invasion, closed the Texas border to further immigration from the United States and prohibited further importation of slaves to Texas. But these measures did little to slow immigration. By 1835 approximately 25,000 Americans, including some 3,000 slaves, lived in Texas. Many of these immigrants had entered illegally.

The recent immigrants deeply resented the 1830 measures. Slaveholders feared that Mexican authorities would soon crack down on the practice of slavery. The Mexican legislature had banned slavery in 1827, but Texans had negotiated a law to classify slaves as indentured servants. If the government overturned the law, they feared that the Texas cotton industry would collapse.

In 1834 the tense situation worsened when General Antonio López de Santa Anna seized control of the Mexican government. Santa Anna eliminated state representation by replacing elected representatives with his own appointees. The loss of state power angered the residents of many Mexican states, including Texans. Outraged American settlers and Tejanos rose up in revolt the next year. Isolated clashes quickly grew into a full-scale rebellion known as the **Texas Revolution**.

■■ **Conflicts over immigration, slavery, and state power led to the Texas Revolution.**

In December 1835, Texas rebels captured San Antonio. Other volunteers soon joined them. Santa Anna, leading several thousand Mexican troops, arrived at San Antonio in February 1836 to restore Mexican rule. From the Alamo, a stronghold built by Spanish missionaries, 187 Texas rebels fought off repeated attacks by Santa Anna's troops. On March 6, Mexican troops finally overran the fort, killing all 187 rebels (but sparing some 30 civilians). The Mexicans paid a heavy price for their victory, though—some 1,500 casualties. A few weeks later, Mexican troops defeated a Texas army near Goliad (GOH-lee-ad) and executed some 350 prisoners.

The Texans, who had declared their independence on March 2, were badly shaken by these defeats. On April 21, 1836, however, a Texas army under the command of Sam Houston surprised Santa Anna near the San Jacinto River. Shouting, "Remember the Alamo!," and "Remember Goliad!," the Texans tore

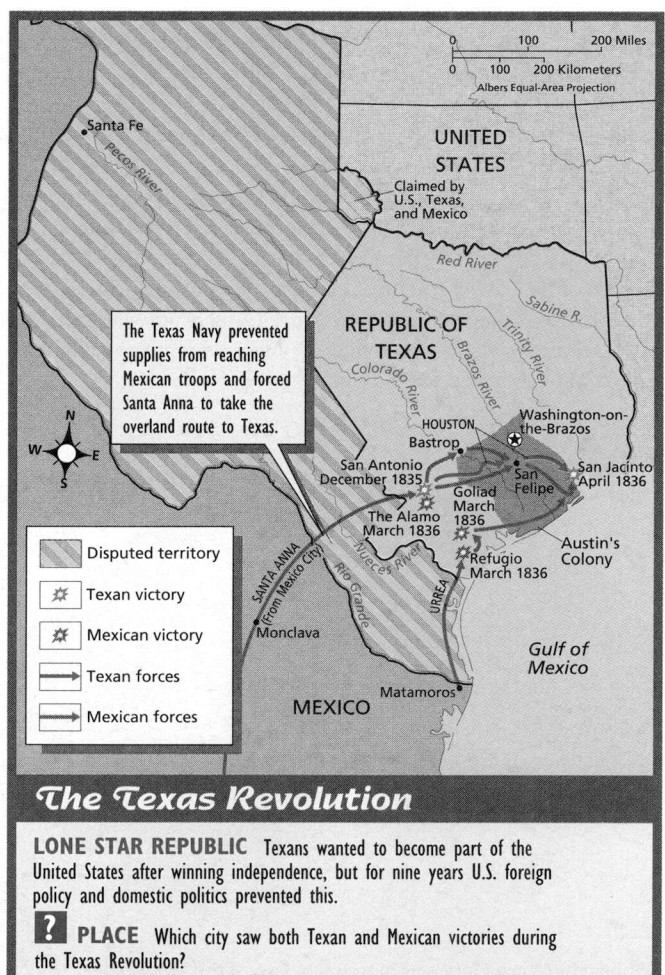

The Texas Navy prevented supplies from reaching Mexican troops and forced Santa Anna to take the overland route to Texas.

Disputed territory
✷ Texan victory
✷ Mexican victory
→ Texan forces
→ Mexican forces

The *Texas* *Revolution*

LONE STAR REPUBLIC Texans wanted to become part of the United States after winning independence, but for nine years U.S. foreign policy and domestic politics prevented this.

❓ **PLACE** Which city saw both Texan and Mexican victories during the Texas Revolution?

GUIDED PRACTICE

Create a cause-and-effect diagram with the heading *Texas Revolution* on the chalkboard. Have students suggest the causes and effects of the rebellion (including the impact of the rebellion on immigration to Texas and on the Tejanos). Add students' responses to the diagram.

INDEPENDENT PRACTICE

Have students assume the role of a Tejano or a German immigrant to Texas after the Texas Revolution. Have them use the information from the Guided Practice to write a journal entry explaining how Texas independence affected them. Students may wish to include their journal entries in their portfolios.

Review and Assessment

REVIEW Have students write a paragraph explaining how the spirit of manifest destiny was a factor in the establishment of the Republic of Texas. Students may wish to include their paragraphs in their portfolios. Then assign the Section 1 Review on p. 310.

ASSESS Assign the **Section 1 Daily Quiz** in *Core Resources*.

▲ In this painting by William H. Huddle, Santa Anna is shown surrendering to Sam Houston. Houston, who is lying on the blanket, was wounded in the ankle at the Battle of San Jacinto.

through Mexican lines, killing about 630 Mexican troops in less than 20 minutes and taking Santa Anna prisoner in the **Battle of San Jacinto**. With his troops already diminished and supplies low, Santa Anna agreed to remove his troops and grant Texas its independence. Texans set up the independent Republic of Texas, electing Sam Houston the first president and Lorenzo de Zavala the first vice president. The Mexican government refused to recognize the Republic.

LIFE IN THE REPUBLIC OF TEXAS

In 1837 Sam Houston petitioned the U.S. Congress for annexation. But northern opposition to admitting another slave state and a cautious foreign policy toward Mexico kept the U.S. Congress from granting the petition. From 1836 to 1845 Texas existed as an independent republic, known as the Lone Star Republic because its flag had a single star.

French and German immigration.

One of the Republic's first tasks was to bring more settlers to Texas. In 1842 the Texas congress awarded Henri Castro, a French banker of Portuguese descent, an *empresario* grant in central Texas. In September 1844 Castro brought his first 35 French colonists—many of them from the German-speaking region of Alsace—to found the town of Castroville just west of San Antonio. In the colony's first year, more than

2,000 settlers established farms with the seeds and supplies Castro provided.

The Texas government also allowed a German company to recruit settlers. In 1845 the company's agent, Prince Carl of Solms-Braunfels, and several German families founded New Braunfels in central Texas. From 1844 to 1847 the German company brought more than 7,000 German settlers to the land it called the "Paradise of North America."

Following a German tradition, most families in New Braunfels had a farm outside town and a small lot and house in town. Ferdinand Roemer, a German geologist and naturalist who traveled to Texas in the 1840s, described the new colony's houses:

66 The houses were of diverse architecture. . . . Some houses were of logs, some were of studding framework filled in with brick, some were frame while others were huts. . . . Several families were packed into one house, no matter how small it was. The interior of such a house, where men, women, and children were cooped up with their unpacked chests and boxes, often looked like the steerage of an immigrant ship. 99

▼ The first capitol of the new Republic of Texas, shown here in 1857, was located in Houston. The capital was later moved to Austin.

THINKING CRITICALLY

Recognizing Prejudice
Ask students what self-interest may have motivated much of the Anglo Texans' actions against the Tejanos after Texas independence. *(revenge, desire for Tejano lands and property, prejudice against Mexicans)* Discuss with students how self-serving motives can lead to discrimination and unjust actions.

 PERSONALITIES IN HISTORY

When Seguín fled to Nuevo Laredo, Mexico, in 1842, he was imprisoned. Santa Anna ordered him sent to Mexico City, but another officer suspended the order in return for Seguín's enlistment in the Mexican army. Feeling that he had no choice, Seguín joined the army and took part in an abortive Mexican attempt to regain Texas. (for p. 310)

RETEACH Organize students into pairs. Assign a subsection to each pair. Then have pairs write questions about the material in their assigned subsections. Use the questions to quiz the group.

Closure

Refer students to John L. O'Sullivan's statement on p. 306. Ask students to explain how various groups in American society (such as merchants, planters, farmers, industrial laborers, and so on) likely felt about such sentiments.

Extension

COMPARE Have students research and compare the Texas Declaration of Independence with the U.S. Declaration of Independence.

EVALUATE Ask students to write a report evaluating the policy of Mirabeau B. Lamar, the second president of the Republic of Texas, toward American Indians, especially toward the Cherokees and the Comanches.

SECTION REVIEW ANSWERS

IDENTIFY

For significance, see the following pages:
manifest destiny (p. 306)
Tejanos (p. 307)
empresarios (p. 307)
Martín de León (p. 307)
Lorenzo de Zavala (p. 307)
Stephen F. Austin (p. 307)
Antonio López de Santa Anna (p. 308)
Texas Revolution (p. 308)
Sam Houston (p. 308)
Battle of San Jacinto (p. 309)
Henri Castro (p. 309)
Prince Carl of Solms-Braunfels (p. 309)
Juan Nepomuceno Seguín (p. 310)

LOCATE

For locations, see the map on p. 308.

1. *by arguing that it would relieve population pressures, open new markets, address the slavery issue, and that the nation's manifest destiny was to claim all of North America*
2. *shield Mexico against Indian raids and build a force to deter a possible U.S. invasion*
3. *faced discrimination, lost lands to whites; postwar spirit of prejudice and revenge against all Mexicans*
4. *Stories should mention conflicts over immigration, slavery, and state power.*
5. *brought Mexican, white American, African American, and European settlers to Texas*

The families did not remain crowded for long, however, since most soon moved out of town and settled on their farms. Many families kept their homes in town, but used them only when they came into town for church or shopping.

German settlers spread their farming practices, language, and customs throughout the Hill Country of central Texas. German-language newspapers, church services, and social clubs helped them retain their language and customs for many generations.

Discrimination against Tejanos. The Tejanos did not fare as well as German settlers did in the Lone Star Republic. During the revolution, many Tejanos had fought and died alongside other Texans. After the revolution, however, a spirit of revenge against all Mexicans prevailed. Many Anglo Texans rushed to seize Tejano lands and property. Anglo Texans attacked some Tejanos and drove many others from the country.

Juan Nepomuceno Seguín (nay-poh-moo-SAY-noh se-GEEN), a member of a prominent San Antonio family and friend of Anglo settlers, was a tragic victim of prejudice. When the Texas Revolution began, Seguín joined the fight for independence and recruited Tejanos to face Santa Anna. After distinguishing himself in battle, he became a captain in the Texas cavalry.

Seguín escaped the slaughter at the Alamo only because he was sent through the Mexican lines in a desperate attempt to find help

Juan Seguín

for the besieged rebels. He then joined Houston's army and fought bravely in the Battle of San Jacinto. Seguín served as military commander of San Antonio after the war, bringing order to San Antonio and reassurance to the threatened Tejanos.

As a senator in the Texas congress and as the mayor of San Antonio, Seguín worked to improve conditions for Tejanos. "The American straggling adventurers," he later wrote of those early years, "were already beginning to work their dark intrigues against the native families, whose only crime was, that they owned large tracts of land and desirable property."

The pressure on Seguín gradually mounted. "At every hour of the day and night," he later recalled, "my countrymen ran to me for protection." In 1842 Anglo pressures forced Seguín to flee to Mexico. Seguín eventually returned to Texas for a time, but he lived out his last years in Mexico, where he died in 1890.

■■ **After independence Tejanos faced increased discrimination and lost much of their land.**

SECTION 1 REVIEW

IDENTIFY and explain the significance of the following: manifest destiny, Tejanos, *empresarios*, Martín de León, Lorenzo de Zavala, Stephen F. Austin, Antonio López de Santa Anna, Texas Revolution, Sam Houston, Battle of San Jacinto, Henri Castro, Prince Carl of Solms-Braunfels, Juan Nepomuceno Seguín.

LOCATE and explain the importance of the following: San Antonio, Goliad.

1. **MAIN IDEA** How did western expansionists try to gain support for their views?
2. **MAIN IDEA** What did the Mexican government hope to accomplish by encouraging American settlement of Texas?
3. **IDENTIFYING CAUSE AND EFFECT** Describe the conditions faced by Tejanos after the Texas Revolution. What caused these conditions?
4. **WRITING TO INFORM** Imagine you are a newspaper reporter. Write a news story giving three causes of the Texas Revolution.
5. **SYNTHESIZING** How did Texas's *empresario* policy contribute to the state's cultural diversity?

PREVIEW WORKSHOP

Following is a list of the significant people, places, and terms in this section. You may wish to use this list as a section preview.

People
■ James K. Polk
■ Zachary Taylor
■ John Slidell
■ Stephen Kearny

■ John C. Frémont
■ Winfield Scott
■ Juan Nepomuceno Cortina

Places
■ Rio Grande
■ Nueces River
■ Monterey
■ Chapultepec
■ Mexican Cession

■ Gila River

Terms
■ Mexican War
■ Bear Flag Revolt
■ Treaty of Guadalupe Hidalgo
■ Gadsden Purchase

Section 2

AMERICAN EXPANSIONISM

FOCUS OBJECTIVES

■ Analyze the issues and events that led to the war between the U.S. and Mexico.

■ Identify the territories the U.S. gained as a result of the war.

■ Describe the impact of the war on former Mexican citizens.

F O C U S

■ **What issues and events led to the war between the United States and Mexico?**

■ **What territories did the United States gain as a result of the war?**

■ **What was the impact of the war on former Mexican citizens?**

Fueled by expansionist dreams, southerners and Democrats hoped to add Texas and the northern Mexican borderlands to the United States. By 1850 the United States did indeed expand to the Pacific Ocean—but only after a bloody war with Mexico and after intense political conflicts within the United States. This expansion disrupted the lives of former Mexican citizens living in the newly conquered regions.

1846 cartoon criticizing Polk's policies

HISTORICAL SIDELIGHTS

1844 Election
The third-party candidacy of James G. Birney of the antislavery Liberty party severely damaged Clay and the Whigs. In New York, only about 15,000 votes were cast for Birney, but they were more than enough to swing the state to Polk and cost Clay the presidency in the electoral college.

TEXAS ANNEXATION

From 1836, when Texas won its independence, to 1845, the question of annexing Texas never died. Convinced of America's manifest destiny to expand westward, many citizens believed Texas should be added to the Union. The issue caused heated debate in Congress.

The debate over annexation. Supporters of Texas annexation argued that if Texas was not admitted to the Union, Great Britain might increase its influence there. Britain wanted an independent Texas as a source of cotton and as a market for British goods. Opponents of annexation, however, feared Texas's admission would increase the South's power in Congress by upsetting the balance between slave and free states.

The issue of western expansion dominated the 1844 presidential campaign, in which Whig party candidate Henry Clay of Kentucky opposed Democrat James K. Polk. A Tennessee politician, Polk called for annexation of Texas and Oregon. He became the dark horse choice of the Democrats

after they could not agree on a candidate at their convention. (A dark horse is a candidate who has not been considered a strong contender prior to the convention.)

Clay's Whig platform, on the other hand, made no mention of the Texas issue. Polk received 170 electoral votes to Clay's 105, but the popular vote was much closer. In fact, if Clay had won New York—which he lost by only 5,080 votes—he would have won the election by 7 electoral votes.

Polk's immediate call for Texas annexation pushed the United States closer to the brink of war with Mexico. Mexico had previously warned that it would consider U.S. annexation of Texas "equivalent to a declaration of war against the Mexican Republic." On March 28, 1845, in the wake of the

▶ **James and Sarah Polk were the first presidential couple to be photographed.**

CORE RESOURCES

• **Literature Worksheet 10**
• **Section 2 Daily Quiz**

MOTIVATING: LINK TO TODAY

Work with students to characterize the relationship between Mexico and the U.S. today (economic relationship, issues surrounding Mexican immigration to U.S., and so on). As students study this section, have them compare today's relationship with U.S.–Mexican relations in the 1840s.

Teaching the Section

THE MEXICAN WAR

Assign students to work in pairs to list the reasons (economic and political) for war from the viewpoints of the American and Mexican governments. Have students use their lists to explain to the class whether they believe each nation's stance made war inevitable.

COOPERATIVE LEARNING

Organize students into three groups to stage an 1844 presidential election campaign rally. Have each group represent one of the following: southern slaveholders, northern merchants, and western settlers. Ask each group to choose the candidate they will vote for in 1844. Then have each member of each group choose one of the following tasks: creating a slogan for their candidate, preparing a poster that justifies their choice of candidate, or writing a speech explaining why their candidate is the best choice for president. Call on groups to present their campaign rallies to the class.

HISTORICAL SIDELIGHTS

Attempts at Diplomacy
In February 1846, before the start of the war, Spanish American colonel Alexander J. Atocha told President Polk that Santa Anna, then in exile in Cuba, was willing to grant the U.S. territorial concessions in return for $30 million. Once back in Mexico in August, however, Santa Anna went back on his word, dashing hopes of a quick end to the war.

---

congressional resolution annexing Texas, Mexico broke diplomatic relations with the United States.

Prelude to war. Polk fueled the Mexican government's anger by demanding that it recognize the Rio Grande as Mexico's northern border. The Rio Grande was about 100 miles south of the Nueces (nooh-AY-suhs) River, which Mexico recognized as the dividing line between Texas and Mexico. To back up the demand, Polk ordered troops under General Zachary Taylor to move into the disputed territory. As Polk was well aware, a U.S. military presence south of the Nueces River would almost certainly provoke an armed clash with Mexican troops.

After receiving information that Mexico was willing to resume diplomatic relations, Polk sent politician John Slidell to Mexico in late 1845 to establish the Rio Grande as the U.S.–Mexico boundary and to purchase the remaining Mexican territories in the Southwest. When Mexican citizens learned of Slidell's mission, they reacted angrily. Giving in to public outrage, the Mexican government refused to negotiate with Slidell. Polk immediately ordered General Taylor to move deeper into the disputed area. While publicly insisting that the troops were only defending American territory, Polk hoped that Mexico would commit an act that would justify war.

*T*HE MEXICAN WAR

Months passed and Polk's impatience grew stronger. On May 9, 1846, he finally received the news he had been waiting for: Mexican troops had crossed the Rio Grande and had attacked a U.S. patrol. Polk sent his war message to Congress. "Mexico," he said, "has invaded our territory and shed American blood upon the American soil." On May 13 Congress declared war.

▪▪ The U.S. annexation of Texas and its quest for more territory led to war with Mexico.

Americans respond. Some Americans, particularly Whigs and northerners, criticized the **Mexican War**, calling it "Mr. Polk's war." Congressman Abraham Lincoln of Illinois, for example, introduced a series of "spot resolutions"

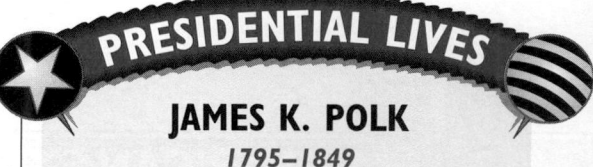

PRESIDENTIAL LIVES

JAMES K. POLK
1795–1849

in office
1845–1849

James K. Polk's contemporaries thought him unsociable—cold, formal, and closed-minded. Because of his wife's strict religious beliefs, Polk shunned the social life of Washington. Dancing was even banned in the White House. Besides, his work ethic left little time for recreation. "No President," Polk believed, "who performs his duty faithfully and conscientiously can have any leisure."

He usually rose at dawn, took a walk, and ate breakfast before most of Washington was awake. After a full day in his office, the president would return to his desk after dinner and work late into the night. Polk confided to his diary that the duties of the presidency sometimes bewildered him. After attending several elaborate diplomatic receptions, he wrote, "Such ceremonies seem very ridiculous to an American."

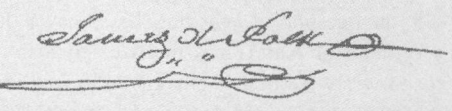

---

in December 1847 challenging the president to identify the exact spot where American blood had been spilled. If the site was indeed on American soil, he would support the war; if not, he said, the war was unjustified.

In addition, Polk's opponents charged that the war was aimed at acquiring more slave territory. The *Liberator* called the war one "of aggression, of invasion, of conquest." In Concord, Massachusetts, writer Henry David Thoreau went to jail rather than pay taxes to support the war. Abolitionist Frederick Douglass condemned the "disgraceful, cruel . . . war with our sister republic." In riveting public speeches, he demanded that Americans "leave off this horrid conflict, abandon

---

NEW TERRITORIES

Have students identify on a map of the modern U.S. the territories acquired as a result of the Mexican War. Ask students to point out Spanish place-names that indicate the extent of Hispanic settlement in the present-day U.S.

MEXICAN AMERICANS

Have students imagine they are Mexican landowners living in the Mexican Cession. Ask them to write a letter to a relative in Mexico describing their life before and after the Mexican War. Have volunteers read their letters to the class. Use student letters to develop on the chalkboard a list of ways that the war changed the lives of former Mexican citizens. Students may wish to include their letters in their portfolios.

their murderous plans, and forsake the way of blood."

Generally, however, Americans—especially southerners and westerners wanting Mexican lands—supported the war. Young men eager for adventure rushed to enlist.

The two sides clash. While Taylor pushed into northern Mexico, other U.S. forces seized New Mexico and California. In August 1846 an expedition led by Brigadier General Stephen Kearny (KAHR-nee) took Santa Fe and won control of New Mexico. Next, Kearny marched to California, where a group of U.S. settlers in northern California had recently revolted against Mexican rule. Declaring California an independent republic, the settlers raised a flag bearing the image of a grizzly bear, giving the uprising its name—the **Bear Flag Revolt**. Captain John C. Frémont, an American army officer and explorer who had led an expedition into California in 1845, helped organize the revolt after receiving a secret message from Polk.

U.S. marines under the command of Commodore John Sloat had already captured Monterrey (the capital of the province) in July. Kearny's troops first faced armed resistance at San Pasqual (puh-SKWAWL) near San Diego. After several other battles, troops led by Kearny and Commodore Robert F. Stockton defeated Mexican troops in January 1847 at San Gabriel near Los Angeles, completing the U.S. conquest of California.

Soon thereafter, fierce fighting raged in northern Mexico near the hacienda of Buena Vista. In February 1847 Taylor's force of fewer than 5,000 men battled Santa Anna's force of some 15,000. Although the battle forced Santa Anna to withdraw, Taylor felt little joy at the victory. "The great loss on both sides," he wrote, "has deprived me of everything like pleasure."

A bold siege of Mexico City marked the war's final campaign. Led by General Winfield Scott, some 10,000 U.S. troops captured the fortified castle at Veracruz on the Gulf of Mexico in March 1847. Marching from the coast, General Scott daringly maneuvered into position to attack the very heart of the Mexican nation. He avoided large-scale battles, thereby preserving both supplies and soldiers for the siege.

Mexicans valiantly defended the long, mountainous road to the capital. One wounded U.S.

The Mexican War

MEXICO LOSES A VAST TERRITORY The United States' huge acquisition in the Southwest was gained at Mexico's expense.

? MOVEMENT Why would a U.S. general want to seize Veracruz?

soldier wrote: "Nobody ever told us how them [Mexicans] could fight. We thought they'd run like sheep; instead, they turned on us like bobcats." Despite the fierce resistance, U.S. troops reached Mexico City in September. They took over the National Palace, which President Santa Anna had already abandoned. In the hilltop garrison of Chapultepec (chuh-POOL-tuh-pek), young Mexican cadets fought hard to hold off U.S. soldiers. Despite their individual heroism, Mexico City's defenders fell as U.S. troops assaulted and captured the capital on September 14.

The Treaty of Guadalupe Hidalgo. By September 1847, U.S. forces held California and New Mexico; General Taylor's troops occupied much of northern Mexico; and General Scott's soldiers held Mexico City. In February 1848 the **Treaty of Guadalupe Hidalgo** (GWAHD-uhl-oop hi-DAL-goh) ended the war on terms dictated by the United States.

VOICES IN HISTORY

The Mexican defense of Mexico City against the U.S. Army was intense until the end. A Mexican merchant described the situation: "Though we inflicted havoc and death upon the Yankees, we suffered greatly ourselves. Many were killed by the blowing up of the houses, many by the bombardment, but more by the confusion which prevailed in the city, and altogether we cannot count our killed, wounded and missing . . . at less than 4,000, among whom are many women and children. The enemy confesses a loss of over 1,000, it is no doubt much greater. What a calamity! But Mexico will yet have vengeance. God will avenge us for our sufferings."

Map Caption Answer
It opened the route to Mexico City and shortened the distance U.S. troops would have to move overland.

EXPANSION AND CONFLICT ■ 313

THE MEXICAN WAR

SETTING THE SCENE

Under the Treaty of Guadalupe Hidalgo, the land ceded to the U.S., not counting Texas, amounted to some 525,000 square miles —an area about the size of Spain, France, and Italy combined. At the end of the war Mexico was in turmoil—with Indian raids in the North, bandits on the highways, and Indian revolts in several Mexican states. This chaos led to the Mexican congress's call for Santa Anna to rule the country once again. He assumed the presidency in April 1853 and set himself up as a virtual king with the title His Most Serene Highness.

PRIMARY SOURCE

Description of Change: excerpted and bracketed
Rationale: excerpted to focus on main idea; bracketed to clarify meaning

HISTORY
in the Making

BY DR. RICHARD SALVUCCI

The Mexican War

Few Americans consider the Mexican War a major turning point in U.S. history. Even in Brownsville, Texas, the site of the battles of Resaca de la Palma and Palo Alto, no great monuments stand to mark the events.

In contrast, Mexicans view the war as a critical event in their history. Every year Mexicans make pilgrimages to a large monument in Mexico City that honors those who died in the fighting. Many streets bear the names of soldiers, and their portraits appear on Mexican currency.

Why do the Mexican and the American views differ? To answer that question, we need to look at the war through Mexican eyes. In early 1846 U.S. troops crossed into disputed territory on the border between Mexico and the United States. Mexico saw these troops as an invading force. The United States had been pushing its borders toward Mexican lands for decades. The Louisiana Purchase in 1803, the acquisition of Florida in 1819, the migration of settlers to Oregon Country, and the annexation of Texas in 1845 all convinced Mexico that Americans intended to occupy the entire continent. Mexico feared for its California and New Mexico territories.

Thus, Mexico saw the United States as a land-hungry aggressor. Mexicans believed they had no choice but to defend their homeland against the "Colossus of the North." In addition, some Mexicans hoped to reconquer Texas, whose independence and annexation by the United States Mexico had not yet formally recognized. Although Mexico believed it had "right" on its side and fought bravely, its army could not withstand the U.S. attacks.

At the war's end the United States laid claim to Mexico's northern territories— about two fifths of all Mexican land—as the spoils of war. To Mexico the terms of the Treaty of Guadalupe Hidalgo were as unfair and unjustifiable as the U.S. attack had been. As one critic of the treaty, Mexican Congress member Manuel Cresencio Rejón, cried:

> 66 With all the right on our side, I cannot see by what justification [the United States] comes to us giving us as a condition for the reestablishment of the peace . . . , the renunciation [forfeit] of our northern frontier from sea to sea, and all for the measly sum of 18,250,000 pesos [15 million dollars]. 99

According to Rejón, the sum the United States offered for this land was less than one twentieth of its value.

The war and the terms of the treaty shattered Mexico. Its California and New Mexico territories were taken, and with

▲ Detail from the 1848 Treaty of Guadalupe Hidalgo

them some 80,000 Mexican citizens and the tremendous natural resources of the regions. Tragically for Mexico, gold, which could have boosted the Mexican economy, was discovered in California just nine days before the signing of the treaty.

For many years after the war, Mexico struggled to stabilize its government and develop its economy to prevent any further losses of territory to the United States. As a result, for most of the 19th century, Mexico focused on internal rather than external affairs. This inward-looking policy delayed Mexico's full entry into the world marketplace.

In the 20th century, as Mexico's government and economy have grown stronger, some political leaders have used the Mexican War to criticize U.S. expansionism and foreign policy. Many Mexicans have expressed resentment at the United States for becoming the most powerful country in the Americas at Mexico's expense. Thus, even today the Mexican War remains an important part of Mexican consciousness.

GUIDED PRACTICE

Draw a time line on the chalkboard. Have volunteers identify and explain key events that led to U.S. acquisition of Mexican lands as you add the events to the time line.

INDEPENDENT PRACTICE

Tell students to imagine they are correspondents at one of the events on the Guided Practice time line. Direct them to write a news story of the event for their hometown newspaper. Students may wish to include their news stories in their portfolios.

Review and Assessment

REVIEW Ask students to imagine they are Americans in the 1840s. Have them write their congressperson to express and explain their support for or opposition to American attitudes and behaviors toward Mexico. Then assign the Section 2 Review on p. 316.

ASSESS Assign the **Section 2 Daily Quiz** in *Core Resources*.

▶

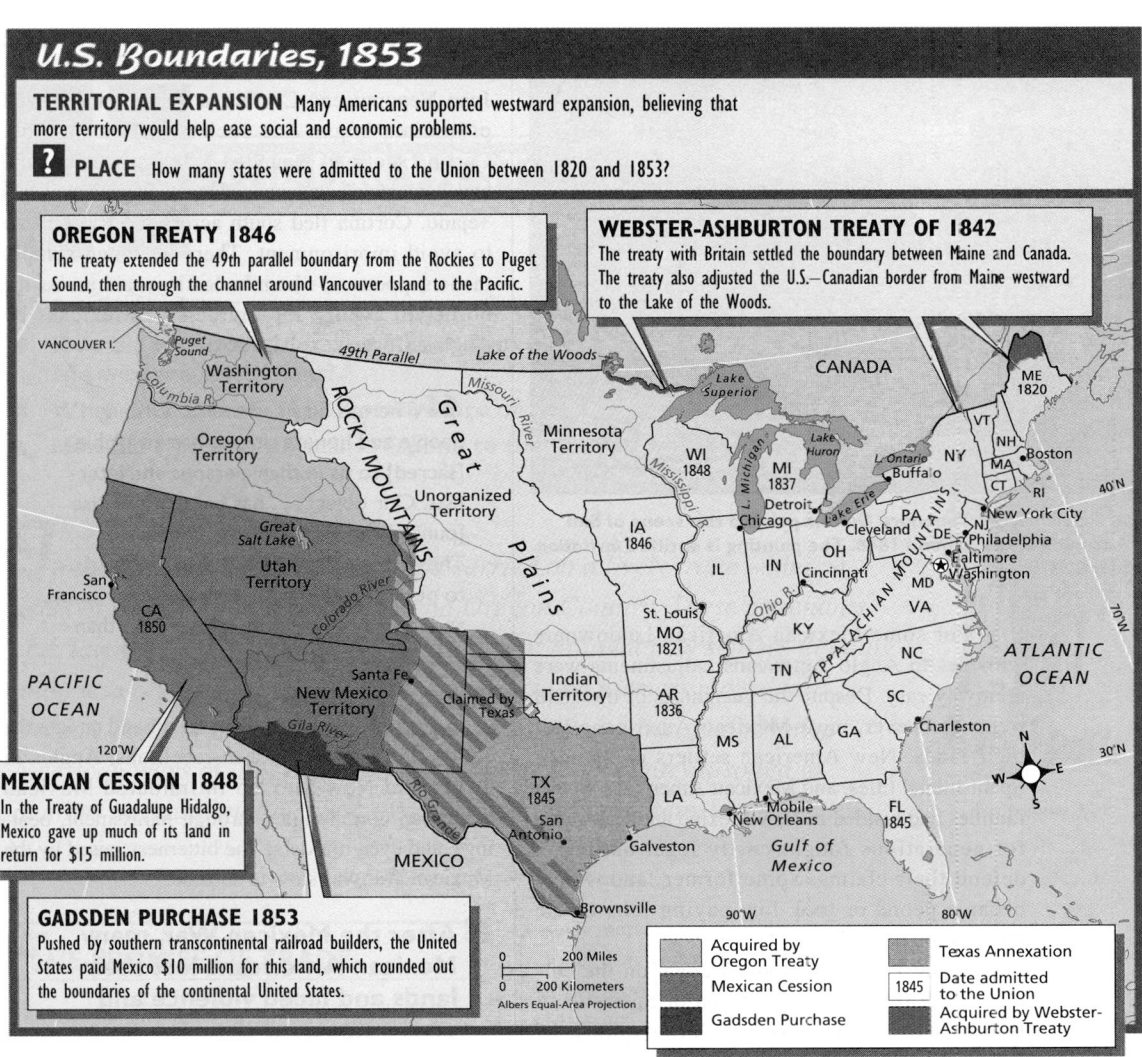

U.S. Boundaries, 1853

TERRITORIAL EXPANSION Many Americans supported westward expansion, believing that more territory would help ease social and economic problems.

? **PLACE** How many states were admitted to the Union between 1820 and 1853?

OREGON TREATY 1846
The treaty extended the 49th parallel boundary from the Rockies to Puget Sound, then through the channel around Vancouver Island to the Pacific.

WEBSTER-ASHBURTON TREATY OF 1842
The treaty with Britain settled the boundary between Maine and Canada. The treaty also adjusted the U.S.–Canadian border from Maine westward to the Lake of the Woods.

MEXICAN CESSION 1848
In the Treaty of Guadalupe Hidalgo, Mexico gave up much of its land in return for $15 million.

GADSDEN PURCHASE 1853
Pushed by southern transcontinental railroad builders, the United States paid Mexico $10 million for this land, which rounded out the boundaries of the continental United States.

Legend:
- Acquired by Oregon Treaty
- Mexican Cession
- Gadsden Purchase
- Texas Annexation
- 1845 Date admitted to the Union
- Acquired by Webster-Ashburton Treaty

Albers Equal-Area Projection

By the terms of the Treaty of Guadalupe Hidalgo, Mexico gave up all claims to Texas and surrendered the vast territory known as the **Mexican Cession**: the present-day states of California, Nevada, and Utah, and parts of Arizona, Colorado, and New Mexico. In return, the United States agreed to pay Mexico $15 million and take over payment of the damages claimed by Americans against Mexico. The United States also agreed to grant full citizenship to Mexicans in the Mexican Cession and to respect their religious beliefs and property rights.

▪▪ **Mexico surrendered present-day California, Nevada, Utah, and parts of Arizona, Colorado, and New Mexico to the United States.**

In 1853 U.S. diplomat James Gadsden negotiated a deal with Mexico to purchase an additional strip of land south of the Gila (HEE-luh) River (in present-day southern Arizona and New Mexico) for $10 million. With the **Gadsden Purchase** the United States had acquired all of Mexico's territory north of the Rio Grande.

MEXICAN AMERICANS

With the Treaty of Guadalupe Hidalgo, two fifths of Mexico's territory and some 80,000 Spanish-speaking people became part of the United States. But many of these new citizens felt, as one Mexican American explained, like "foreigners in their own land."

Map Caption Answer
nine: ME, MO, AR, MI, FL, TX, IA, WI, CA

MAKING CONNECTIONS
Literature
Richard Henry Dana's classic adventure story *Two Years Before the Mast,* published in 1840, narrates the author's life at sea as he traveled from Boston to Cape Horn and then along the Pacific Coast in the 1830s. The book is also considered to contain one of the most vivid descriptions of life in California during the last years of Mexican rule.

MOTIVATING:
STUDENT EXPERIENCES

Discuss why people move from one place to another today. Ask volunteers to explain why their friends or acquaintances have moved in the past or why they might do so in the future. List responses on the chalkboard. Tell students that this section explains why people moved to the Far West in the 1800s.

Teaching the **S**ection

FUR TRADE AND SETTLING THE FAR WEST

Organize the class into groups and instruct each group to create a graphic organizer to show how merchants, American Indians, and mountain men contributed to the growth of the fur trade. Then ask each group to explain how the advance of the fur trade helped encourage western settlement.

On the heels of the merchants came the fur trappers, or **mountain men**. Beaver pelts, which were used to make men's hats, were in great demand. American Indians helped the mountain men extend the fur trade to new areas by negotiating with other Indian groups. American Indians worked in the fur trade as trappers, guides, and interpreters. Indian women were vital to the functioning of the fur trade. They skinned and prepared the beaver pelts and provided food and special clothing for the trappers.

It was in the Rockies—along the Missouri River and its tributaries—that the fur trade proved most profitable. The Rocky Mountain fur trade succeeded in part because of the **rendezvous system** worked out by William Ashley, a Missouri politician and owner of a fur-trading business. Ashley recognized that transporting furs out of the Rockies was expensive. To cut costs, he persuaded his trappers to remain in the mountains and gather once a year to sell their furs and purchase supplies. This system increased profits.

After each rendezvous the mountain men fanned out for hundreds of miles across the Rockies trapping beavers. In the process the restless and adventurous trappers explored every inch of the mountains and pioneered the trails that settlers later used to reach the Far West.

Mountain men like Hugh Glass, Jim Bridger, and Kit Carson became American legends. African American mountain man James Beckwourth also won fame. Beckwourth spent his last years exploring and looking for gold. In 1850 he discovered a key mountain pass a few miles northwest of present-day Reno, Nevada. Today, the pass, mountain peak, valley, and nearby town bear Beckwourth's name.

■■ **Mountain men and American Indians trapped furs and blazed the trails that would take U.S. settlers to the Far West.**

SETTLING OREGON COUNTRY

The fur trade also spread west of the Rockies to Oregon Country. In 1811, U.S. fur trappers founded the fur-trading post of Astoria near the mouth of the Columbia River on the Pacific coast. Although the fur trade proved disappointing, the venture paved the way for more U.S. settlers. U.S. newspapers publicized the trappers' route to Oregon Country in 1813. This route, known as the **Oregon Trail**, followed the Platte River across treeless plains to the towering Rockies, then descended into Oregon along the Snake and Columbia rivers.

Farmers and missionaries. The new route was of particular interest to farm families who wanted to settle in Oregon Country's Willamette Valley. The first U.S. settlers in the valley were American fur traders and their families who settled as farmers just south of present-day Salem, Oregon, in 1830.

Missionaries were also attracted to the region, not for farming but as a fertile ground for converting American Indians to Christianity. In 1833 the *Christian Advocate and Journal,* a Methodist newspaper, published a letter supposedly from an American Indian requesting missionaries to instruct the

Plumas County Museum

◀ **James Beckwourth was known to exaggerate some of his daring deeds, but he did lead an interesting life. He served in two wars, lived among the Crow Indians, and established the trading post pictured here.**

ON THE OREGON TRAIL

Organize students into small groups and ask them to create skits that depict the difficulties encountered by settlers in their journey on the Oregon Trail. Ask students to present their skits to the class.

■■ Ask students what qualities they think the settlers needed to face the difficulties of the Oregon Trail. Have students speculate how well they themselves would have fared on the trail.

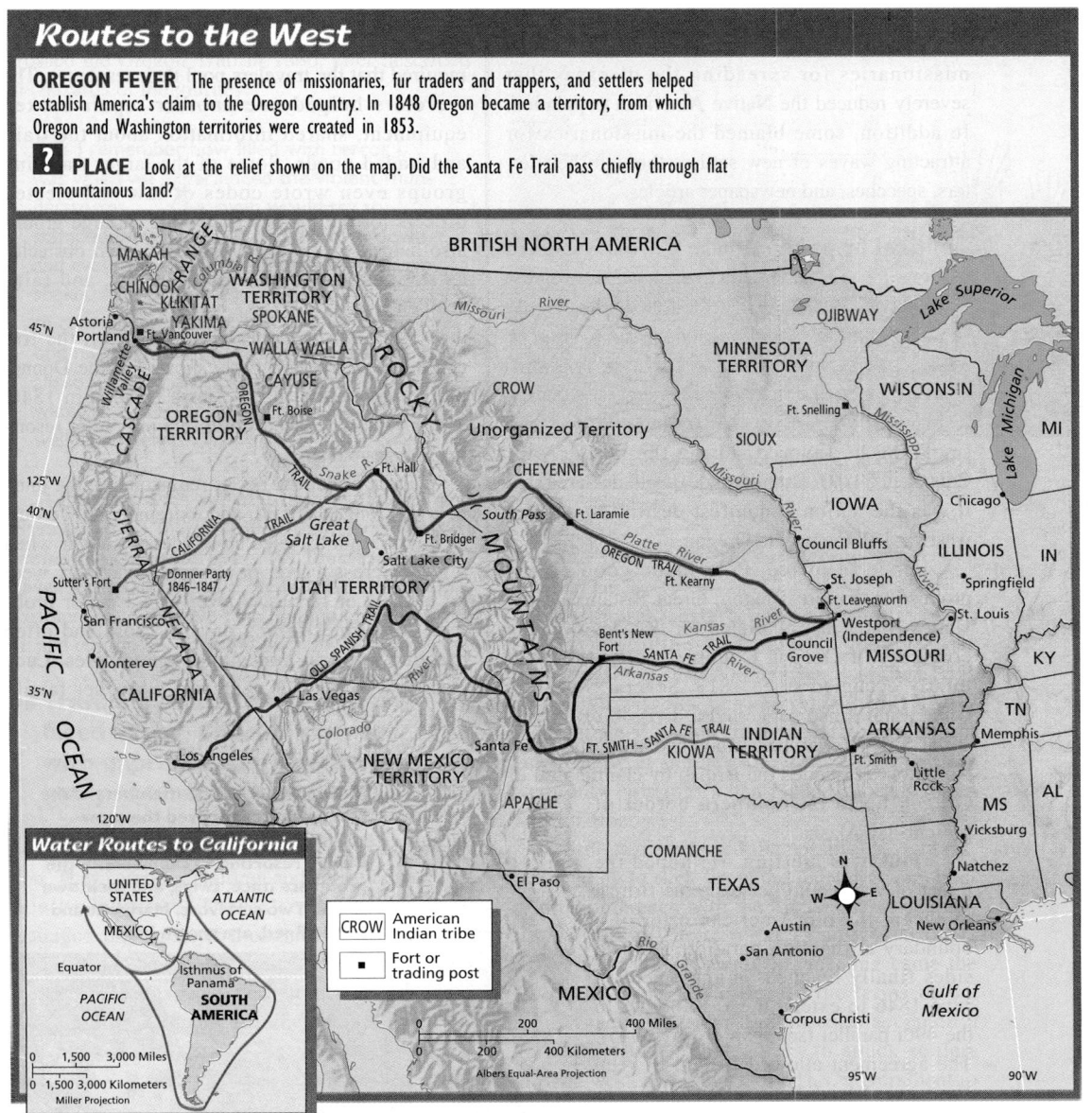

Routes to the West

OREGON FEVER The presence of missionaries, fur traders and trappers, and settlers helped establish America's claim to the Oregon Country. In 1848 Oregon became a territory, from which Oregon and Washington territories were created in 1853.

? **PLACE** Look at the relief shown on the map. Did the Santa Fe Trail pass chiefly through flat or mountainous land?

Map Caption Answer
flat land

HISTORICAL SIDELIGHTS
The Wyandot Letter
In 1831 three Nez Percés and one Flathead from Oregon Country traveled to St. Louis to learn about the white people's culture. They had accompanied fur trappers returning from the Rocky Mountains. William Walker, a Wyandot from the East, heard of the visit by the four Native Americans. More than a year later, Walker wrote a letter to a friend describing the visit. The letter was a distorted account of the visit, saying that the Native Americans were there to learn about white people's religion. The friend then passed the letter on to the *Christian Advocate and Journal.*

PRIMARY SOURCE
Description of Change: excerpted and bracketed
Rationale: excerpted to focus on main idea; bracketed to clarify meaning

Indians of Oregon Country in the Christian faith. Historians suspect that the letter was a pious hoax, but Methodist response at the time was swift. Methodist missionary Jason Lee arrived in Oregon Country in 1834. Missionaries from other Protestant denominations soon followed.

Catholic missionaries from France established a church and boarding school for Indians near present-day Portland in 1840. In her journal Sister Mary Catherine Cabareaux described the language problem the missionaries faced when trying to teach Indians about Christianity:

❝ The half Canadians were my portion. About twenty understood French, [which] I spoke simply to them. . . . Sister Mary Cornelia had the best portion, which consisted of about a dozen old Indian women who did not know a word of French, yet were requested to know their prayers in that language. Imagine, then, what a painful task for pupils as well as teachers! ❞

Missionaries had little success, though, in converting the Indians to Christianity. Besides having a natural desire to retain their own beliefs

INTERPRETING EDITORIAL CARTOONS

Guide students through the explanation of how to interpret editorial cartoons and have them complete the Practicing the Strategy exercise. Then divide students into groups of three, and have groups assign each person the task of identifying either the main symbol and its meaning, the meaning of the title and label, or the point of view of an editorial cartoon clipped from a newspaper or magazine.

Assign the class a different topic, such as a news event or a recent event in school, and ask the groups to draw an editorial cartoon about it. Have the groups present their cartoons, explaining the symbols, labels, and point of view of their drawing. Ask students to discuss what information future historians might draw from these cartoons.

PRACTICING THE STRATEGY

1. *Northern visitors to the South, southern slaveholders, enslaved African Americans, English textile workers and poor people, an English gentleman; the activities of the black slaves are caricatured*

2. *Dancing and banjo playing symbolize the supposedly happy, carefree life of slaves.*

3. *The label "Cloth Factory" is not particularly important, since the speech of the characters makes the subject of factory work clear. The title suggests a contrast is being drawn between slavery in the American South and the sad condition of textile workers and coal miners in England.*

4. **(a)** *that of a defender of slavery who is critical of industrialization* **(b)** *that enslaved African Americans in the South have a shorter workday and better working conditions, and therefore an easier life, than do the working class of England*

Strategies for Success

INTERPRETING EDITORIAL CARTOONS

Editorial cartoons are drawings that present points of view on the issues, ideas, people, and events of the day. They usually appear in the editorial sections of newspapers and newsmagazines. Although some express a positive outlook, many are critical of a person or policy.

To communicate their message, editorial cartoonists frequently use caricature and symbolism. A *caricature* is a drawing that exaggerates or distorts physical features. *Symbolism* is the use of one thing to stand for something else. For instance, cartoonists often use Uncle Sam to represent the United States, an elephant to symbolize the Republican party, and a donkey to stand for the Democrats.

Many editorial cartoons rely on labels to help identify symbols or other aspects of the picture. Most also include captions or "speech balloons," which may serve as a sort of punchline.

How to Interpret Editorial Cartoons

1. **Identify the caricatures.** Identify each figure and object. Note any distortions or exaggerations, and decide whether they cast the figure in a positive or negative light.
2. **Identify the symbols used.** Determine what each symbol stands for.
3. **Read the title and labels.** Read and determine the meaning of any title and labels.
4. **Consider the cartoonist's purpose.** Identify the points of view being expressed in the speech balloons or caption. Try to determine the cartoonist's message.

Applying the Strategy

Andrew Jackson was a popular subject for editorial cartoonists of his day. In the cartoon on this page, Jackson is shown wearing a crown and kingly robe, holding a scepter like a club and a "veto" as if it were a royal decree. Tattered papers labeled "Constitution of the United States," "Internal Improvements," and "U.S. Bank" and a book titled *Judiciary of the U. States* are strewn underfoot.

According to his critics, Jackson had abused his constitutional authority by his vetoes of bills that would have rechartered the national bank and provided for internal improvements. The cartoonist uses symbols of monarchy to accuse Jackson of acting more like a king than the president of a republic. This point is reinforced by the condition and position of the papers and by the title: "King Andrew the First."

Practicing the Strategy

Study the editorial cartoon on page 266 of your textbook. Then, on a separate sheet of paper, answer the following questions.

1. Who are the central figures in the cartoon? Are they portrayed realistically, or are they caricatures?
2. What symbols does the cartoon contain?
3. How do the labels and the title help make the cartoonist's point of view and message clear?
4. What is **(a)** the cartoonist's point of view and **(b)** the cartoon's message?

▼ Cartoon satirizing Andrew Jackson

KING ANDREW THE FIRST.

BUILDING YOUR PORTFOLIO

Each portfolio project described below is the culmination of the Building Your Portfolio activities in the chapter reviews of Unit 3. First, decide whether you wish students to work individually or in groups on these unit projects. Then permit each student to choose the project on which he or she desires to work. Provide students with copies of **Building Your Portfolio Worksheet 3** from *Core Resources*. This worksheet will guide students step by step to complete their projects.

BUILDING YOUR PORTFOLIO

Outlined below are four projects. Independently or cooperatively, complete one and use the products to demonstrate your mastery of the historical concepts involved.

1 EXPANSION
The 19th century was the period of the greatest U.S. expansion in North America. Using the portfolio materials you designed in chapters 7 and 10, conduct a panel discussion about U.S. expansion that showcases the views of Anglo settlers, Native Americans, Tejanos, and government officials from both Mexico and the United States.

2 THE ECONOMY
The market and transportation revolutions brought significant economic changes to the North, the South, and the Middle West. Using the portfolio materials you designed in chapters 7 and 8, create a board game that shows the movement of cotton from a southern plantation to a northern factory and then to various markets. Games should illustrate the impact of transportation systems, new technologies, and economic policies on new markets.

3 IMMIGRATION
Poverty, hunger, and oppression drove many immigrants from their homelands to the United States in the 19th century. Using the portfolio materials you designed in chapters 8, 9, and 10, prepare a short one-scene play about an immigrant's experiences in the United States. Plays might describe life in an ethnic community, encounters with nativists, workers' strikes, or tenement housing conditions.

4 INDIVIDUAL RIGHTS
Rapid changes in U.S. society in the first half of the 1800s led to new social problems and threats to individual liberties. Using the portfolio materials you designed in chapters 7, 8 and 9, discuss the different ways political and social reforms were carried out by presenting your posters, speeches, and pamphlets to the class.

PORTFOLIO ASSESSMENT

1. *Panel discussions should show the U.S. policy on expansion in the mid-1800s and the Native American, Mexican, and U.S. settlers' responses to U.S. acquisition of new territory.*
2. *Board games should show students' mastery of the regional economic specialization resulting from the transportation and market revolutions.*
3. *One-scene plays should show an appreciation for the opportunities and difficulties of European and Asian immigrants in America from 1820 to 1860.*
4. *Presentations of posters, speeches, or pamphlets should show an understanding of the expansion of voting rights during the Jacksonian era, the organization of the early labor movement, and the origin of the women's rights movement.*

Videodisc Review

In assigned groups, develop an outline for a video collage of America between 1815 and 1860. Choose images that best illustrate the major topics of the period. Write a script to accompany the images. Assign narrators to different parts of the script, and present your video collage to the class.

Further Reading

Ehle, John. *Trail of Tears.* Doubleday (1988). History of the Cherokees' forced removal to Indian Territory.

Fisher, Leonard E. *The Oregon Trail.* Holiday House (1990). Firsthand accounts and photographs of life on the trail.

Holliday, J. S. *The World Rushed In. The California Gold Rush Experience.* S & S Trade (1981). Eyewitness accounts of the California Gold Rush.

Johannsen, Robert W. *To the Halls of the Montezumas.* Oxford (1985). The Mexican War examined through primary sources.

Luchetti, Cathy. *Under God's Spell: Frontier Evangelists 1772–1915.* Harcourt (1989). The lives and work of frontier evangelists told through primary sources.

Mellon, James, ed. *Bullwhip Days: The Slaves Remember.* Avon Books (1988). Interviews with ex-slaves conducted in the 1930s.

War and Reunification ❖ 1845–1900

Introducing the Unit

- **Chapter 11**
  SLAVERY'S EXPANSION
  1845–1861
- **Chapter 12**
  THE CIVIL WAR
  1861–1865
- **Chapter 13**
  RECONSTRUCTION
  AND THE NEW SOUTH
  1865–1900

UNIT OVERVIEW

During the 1840s and 1850s, sectional issues, centering largely around slavery, drove the North and the South further apart. Only a series of political compromises kept the Union intact. Compromise eventually failed, however, and a number of southern states seceded. For four years the armies of the North and the South fought a bitter Civil War. Eventually, the superior resources of the North turned the tide, and it emerged victorious. After the war the nation's major political task was to bring the defeated South back into the Union. The plan that Congress adopted created bitterness among southern whites that lasted for decades. Much of their anger was vented upon the freed African Americans, who were relegated to second-class citizenship.

CORE RESOURCES

- **American Almanac Poster** and **Worksheet 4**
- **Building Your Portfolio Worksheet 4**
  You may wish to preview the Unit 4 Review and Building Your Portfolio performance assessment activities on p. 421.

Using the American Almanac Posters

Begin the unit by displaying the American Almanac Poster and discussing entries with students. In addition to the worksheet, the annotations that follow provide additional information about the entries and suggest questions and activities.

Then, as students study the unit, have them work in small groups to create their own almanacs—using the same six headings—on pieces of butcher paper. At the end of the unit, call on groups to display and discuss their almanacs.

SLAVERY'S EXPANSION
1845–1861

THE CIVIL WAR
1861–1865

RECONSTRUCTION AND
THE NEW SOUTH
1865–1900

The American People

Point out that about a third of the total population lived in the South, and more than a third of all southerners were enslaved African Americans.

■■ Have students research the present-day racial and ethnic makeup of the American population.

Course of the War

Note that Stand Watie was among the Cherokees who had been forced to take the "Trail of Tears" from Georgia to Oklahoma in the 1830s. He also was the last Confederate general to surrender.

■■ Have students investigate if and how people from their region or community were involved in fighting the Civil War.

The Home Front

Life on the home front in the South was made difficult by soaring prices. In April 1863 hundreds of women looted shops in Richmond. Jefferson Davis stopped the riots, and the leaders were briefly arrested and jailed.

■■ Ask students how the women could have more effectively expressed their grievances.

Hot off the Presses

William Wells Brown also wrote a play titled *The Escape; or, Leap to Freedom* (1856). This drama, based on his experiences as a fugitive slave, was published in narrative form in 1847.

■■ Encourage students to discuss fiction they have read or a film or TV program they have seen that addresses one of today's social issues.

Changing Times

There were more than 500,000 working women in 1850—about 8 percent of the labor force. About 330,000 of them were employed as domestic servants.

■■ Have students investigate the number and percent of women in the work force today.

A Soldier's Life

Point out that Confederate general Robert E. Lee and his troops lived on a steady diet of cornbread and cabbage. They ate meat perhaps only one or two times a week.

■■ Ask students to discuss why it might be easier to provision troops today.

UNIT 4

War and Reunification

1845–1900

In the 1840s and 1850s sectional issues—particularly slavery—drove the North and South further apart. For a time, political compromises kept the Union together. Ultimately, compromise failed, and several southern states seceded. For four years, the North and the South fought a bitter Civil War until the North's superior resources brought it victory. After the war, Congress's plan to bring the South back into the Union created long-lasting bitterness among southern whites. Much of their anger was vented upon the freed African Americans.

◀ President Lincoln and General McClellan, Antietam, 1862

SLAVERY'S EXPANSION

1845–1861

Chapter Overview

The Missouri Compromise of 1820 had temporarily quieted the debate over the extension of slavery. But the debate erupted again in the 1830s and 1840s over the admission of Texas and California and over the lands acquired as a result of the Mexican War. In an attempt to satisfy both the North and the South, Henry Clay proposed the Compromise of 1850. Its fugitive slave law, however, caused further division. Then in the 1850s, several events—the Kansas-Nebraska Act, the Dred Scott decision, and John Brown's raid on Harpers Ferry—pushed the nation further toward crisis. When the Republicans captured the presidency in 1860 without winning a single southern state, seven southern states seceded from the Union.

Chapter Planning Guide

CHAPTER 11	CORE RESOURCE BOOKLETS	AV AUDIOVISUAL RESOURCES	PROGRAM RESOURCES
INTRODUCTION pp. 336–337	■ Geography Worksheet 11 ■ Building Your Port-folio Worksheet 4		■ Eyewitnesses and Others, Volume 1: Reading 75
TEACHING THE CHAPTER pp. 338–357	■ Graphic Organizer 11 ■ Social Studies Skills Worksheet 11 ■ Literature Worksheet 11 ■ Outline Map 9	■ The American Nation Videodisc: Free At Last ■ Everyday Life in America Trans-parency and Worksheet 11	■ Eyewitnesses and Others, Volume 1: Readings 70, 73, 74
REVIEW AND ASSESSMENT pp. 358–359	■ Chapter 11 Daily Quizzes ■ Review Worksheet 11 ■ Chapter 11 Tests ■ Alternative Assessment Forms		■ Test Generator

Additional Resources

BOOKS FOR TEACHERS

Johannsen, Robert W. *The Frontier, the Union, and Stephen A. Douglas.* University of Illinois Press, 1989. Essays on issues of slavery, seces-sion, and the nature of the Union in the 1850s.

McPherson, James M. *Battle Cry of Freedom.* Ballantine, 1989. Narrative of events from Mexican War to end of Civil War.

Stampp, Kenneth M. *America in 1857: A Nation on the Brink.* Oxford, 1992. Examination of a pivotal year.

BOOKS FOR STUDENTS

Catton, William and Bruce. *Two Roads to Sumter.* Peter Smith, 1992. Study of the North and the South prior to the Civil War.

*Freedman, Russell. *Lincoln: A Photobiography.* Clarion, 1989. Photobiography of Lincoln including samples of his writings.

*Ray, Delia. *A Nation Torn: The Story of How the Civil War Began.* Lodestar, 1990. Describes crucial events that led to the Civil War.

* for students reading below grade level

MULTIMEDIA MATERIALS

The Background of the Civil War. Video, 20 min. BFA/SSSS. Sum-marizes the debate over slavery.

The Civil War: Union at Risk. Video, 25 min. Britannica. Examines pre–Civil War differences between the North and the South.

Uncle Tom's Cabin. Video, 55 min. SSSS. Condensed dramatization of the 1852 classic novel.

THEMES IN AMERICAN HISTORY

**USE WITH PAGES
336–337**

*Listed on the right are
the themes emphasized in
Chapter 11. The questions in
boldface type stimulate critical
thinking and provide students
with an opportunity to discuss
the themes within a broadened
context. The questions also
appear in the pupil's edition
on p. 336.*

■ CONSTITUTIONAL HERITAGE

**How might different
groups use the Constitu-
tion to justify deeply held
beliefs?** Students might suggest that the Constitution was
written with an eye toward
broad principles rather than
specific situations, and therefore its language is open to
interpretation. Thus, opposing
groups can often find support
for their positions.

■ DEMOCRATIC VALUES

**Majority rule is at the
heart of the democratic
system. Why is protec-
tion of the rights of those
in the minority also
essential to the system?**
Students might suggest that if
those in the minority think
that their basic rights are
ignored, they are likely to feel
that they have no stake in the
system. To protect their
rights, they may reject the
existing system and choose to
support another system.

■ GEOGRAPHIC DIVERSITY

**Why might people in dif-
ferent geographic regions
have conflicting economic
and political interests?**
Students might suggest that
a region's natural resources,
climate, availability and fertility of land, and kinds of crops
that can be grown help determine the ways in which people make their living. People's
political interests, in turn, are
often influenced by their economic interests.

CHAPTER STRATEGIES FOR MEETING INDIVIDUAL NEEDS

LIMITED ENGLISH PROFICIENT LEARNERS

Organize students in three groups and
assign each group the people in one of
the chapter's Preview Workshops. Have
groups do outside research to locate
visuals of their assigned people and then
write a caption that relates each person
to the section content.

TACTILE/KINESTHETIC LEARNERS

Have students work in groups to prepare and present skits illustrating the
chapter's main topics.

LEARNERS HAVING DIFFICULTY

Have students outline each section and
then use their outlines to write brief
summaries of each section and of the
chapter as a whole.

AUDITORY LEARNERS

Organize students into small groups and
assign each group a prominent person
discussed in the chapter. Have each
group prepare and present a speech by
its subject, stating his or her view of the
chapter's events.

VISUAL LEARNERS

Have students work in groups of six, with
pairs assigned different sections. Ask each
pair to create a cause-effect flowchart of
the section's events. Have the group as a
whole use the flowcharts to create one
graphic organizer for the chapter.

GIFTED LEARNERS

Have students hold a panel discussion
on whether the Civil War was avoidable.
Panel members should field questions
from the class.

USING THE CHAPTER FOCUS

■ UNDERSTANDING THE MAIN IDEA

Tell students that the expansion of slavery continued to fuel political competition between free states and slave states in the halls of government and throughout the nation. In 1858, Lincoln said, "[This nation] will become all one thing, or all the other." Ask students to discuss what Lincoln meant.

 ### THEMES

Have students work individually or in small groups to answer the questions under Themes. Save students' responses so that they can compare them with their responses after studying the chapter. (See p. 335B for suggested answers.)

■ THE TIME LINE

Point out that as the U.S. was grappling with the slavery issue in this period, other nations were dealing with similar issues. For example, Austria emancipated the peasants in 1848, and Czar Alexander II of Russia issued the Emancipation Edict liberating the serfs in March 1861. Ask students what event occurred in the U.S. the same year that Russia emancipated the serfs. *(Jefferson Davis elected president of the Confederacy)*

CORE RESOURCES

- **Graphic Organizer 11**
- **Geography Worksheet 11**
- **Literature Worksheet 11**
- **Social Studies Skills Worksheet 11**
- **Building Your Portfolio Worksheet 4**

ABOUT THE ILLUSTRATION

African Americans of all ages were enslaved in the South. Unlike the picture presented in this illustration, however, enslaved families were often separated and family members sold to different slaveholders. Ask students to identify the kind of crop picked by the slaves in this illustration. *(cotton)* Then ask students to describe the kinds of conditions in which slaves worked.

Chapter 11

1845–1861

SLAVERY'S EXPANSION

▼ FOCUS

UNDERSTANDING THE MAIN IDEA

The U.S. acquisition of Mexican land in 1848 reopened the fierce debate over slavery in the West. Increasingly the issue divided the North and the South as northerners tried to limit the expansion of slavery and southerners insisted that it be allowed to spread into the West.

THEMES

■ CONSTITUTIONAL HERITAGE
How might different groups use the Constitution to justify deeply held beliefs?

■ DEMOCRATIC VALUES
Majority rule is at the heart of the democratic system. Why is protection of the rights of those in the minority also essential to the system?

■ GEOGRAPHIC DIVERSITY
Why might people in different geographic regions have conflicting economic and political interests?

1845	1850	1854	1857	1861
Texas admitted to the Union.	Compromise of 1850 enacted.	Republican party formed.	*Dred Scott* case decided.	Jefferson Davis elected president of Confederacy.

LINK TO THE PAST

Ask volunteers to recall the specific terms of the Missouri Compromise of 1820 and to discuss the crisis it resolved. Tell students that in this chapter they will read how the debate over slavery rose again and helped deepen the conflict between the North and the South.

■ LINK TO THE PAST ▶

The Northwest Ordinance of 1787 prohibited slavery in the Northwest Territory. By the early 1800s, however, several southern slave states had joined the Union. To maintain the balance between slave and free states, Congress passed the Missouri Compromise in 1820. But the compromise, which banned slavery in much of the Louisiana Territory, only postponed further conflicts.

Hauling the Whole Week's Pickings (1842), a detail from one of four pieces by William Henry Brown

*A*t midcentury the deepening conflicts between the North, the South, and the West involved many issues, including immigration, trade unionism, women's rights, and public-education reform. The main issue dividing Americans, however, was slavery. In 1850 Senator William H. Seward of New York warned of slavery's ever-lengthening shadow over the life of the nation:

> 66 We are now arrived at that stage of our national progress when [the] crisis [of slavery] can be foreseen—when we must foresee it. It is directly before us. Its shadow is upon us. It darkens the legislative halls, the temples of worship, and the home and the hearth. Every question, political, civil, or ecclesiastical [religious]—however foreign to the subject of slavery—brings up slavery. . . . We hear of nothing but slavery, and we can talk of nothing but slavery. 99

The issue of slavery indeed loomed large on the nation's political agenda. Slavery troubled many Americans, but their leaders could find no solution. Failed compromises, renewed strife, and increasingly urgent attempts to hold together a divided nation characterized this period of crisis on the brink of civil war.

Detail from photograph of slave leg irons

HISTORICAL SIDELIGHTS

Defeat of the Gag Rule
Northern abolitionists showered so many antislavery petitions on Congress that its normal routine was threatened. So the House adopted a rule in 1836 that required all such petitions to be tabled without debate. Attempts of northern legislators to lift this so-called "gag rule" were repeatedly defeated until 1844, when they finally gathered the votes to repeal it—an event that allowed the disruptive issue of slavery to come directly to the floor of the House.

PRIMARY SOURCE

Description of Change: excerpted and bracketed
Rationale: excerpted to focus on main ideas; bracketed to clarify meaning

PREVIEW WORKSHOP

*Following is a list of the signifi-
cant people and terms in this
section. You may wish to use this
list as a section preview.*

People
■ Lewis Cass
■ Stephen A. Douglas
■ Zachary Taylor
■ Daniel Webster

■ Millard Fillmore

Terms
■ popular sovereignty
■ Wilmot Proviso
■ Free-Soil party
■ Compromise of 1850

FOCUS OBJECTIVES

■ Explain why the admis-
sion of Texas and new
territories created con-
troversy in Congress
and what solutions
Congress proposed.

■ Determine how the
slavery issue affected
the presidential election
of 1848.

■ Explain why proslavery
and antislavery forces
opposed passage of the
Compromise of 1850.

Section 1

AN UNEASY BALANCE

F O C U S
■ **Why did the admission of Texas and new territories create controversy
in Congress? What solutions did Congress propose?**
■ **How did the slavery issue affect the presidential election of 1848?**
■ **Why did both proslavery and antislavery forces oppose passage of the
Compromise of 1850?**

With the Missouri Compromise in 1820, the North and the South
resolved a serious clash over slavery. But many Americans realized
that a showdown had merely been postponed. By the 1840s northern
and southern members of Congress were in conflict over the admission of Texas and California to the Union. Arguments also erupted
over the extension of slavery into the western lands acquired as a
result of the Mexican War. As the conflict over slavery intensified,
Congress found forging a compromise more difficult.

Zachary Taylor campaign pin, 1848

THE DEBATE REOPENS

The Missouri Compromise did not end the debate
over the spread of slavery. Although Congress
admitted Arkansas and Michigan to the Union

▲ **This painting by Donald M. Yena portrays the
ceremony that took place on February 18, 1846,
welcoming Texas into the Union.**

without dispute in 1836 and 1837, trouble arose
when the Republic of Texas petitioned for annexation. Arkansas and Michigan had balanced each
other: Arkansas allowed slavery, Michigan did not.
The addition of Texas, which permitted slavery,
would tip the balance of power in Congress toward
the slaveholding states.

In 1845 Congress settled the dilemma on
terms favorable to the South. Congress not only
admitted Texas as a slave state but added that with
the consent of the state's legislature, Texas could
be divided into as many as five states. At the same
time, Congress extended the Missouri Compromise
line (36°30′ N) westward and barred slavery north
of the line. (This affected only the northernmost tip
of Texas.)

No sooner was the Texas question settled than
the issue of slavery again confronted the nation,
sparked this time by the prospect of victory in the
Mexican War. Should slavery be allowed in any
territory acquired from Mexico? Proslavery and
antislavery forces in Congress quickly took sides.

CORE RESOURCES

• **Geography
Worksheet 11**
• **Section 1 Daily Quiz**

AV RESOURCES

• **Everyday Life in
America Trans-
parency** and
Worksheet 11

MOTIVATING: STUDENT EXPERIENCES

Discuss current issues in which compromise played an important part. Ask students why attempts at compromise might fail, guiding students to use an experience to illustrate their point. Tell students that in this section they will study how the admission of new states and acquisition of territories reopened the debate over the expansion of slavery and how Congress compromised on these issues.

Teaching the Section

CONTROVERSY OVER NEW TERRITORY

Call on a volunteer to explain why the admission of Texas and acquisition of new territory from Mexico created conflict in Congress. Then have groups role-play a debate among supporters of each of the four solutions proposed by Congress. Have the class comment on the solutions and explain which one they support and why.

THE 1848 ELECTION

Have students create campaign leaflets that outline the platform of the Free-Soil party. Have volunteers present their leaflets. Then ask for other volunteers to explain the impact of the Free-Soil party on the 1848 election. Students may wish to include their leaflets in their portfolios.

▶

To quiet the debate, President Polk and others suggested extending the Missouri Compromise line to the Pacific Ocean. Senator Lewis Cass of Michigan and Senator Stephen A. Douglas of Illinois offered another solution—rely on **popular sovereignty** to settle the issue: let the citizens of each new territory decide whether to permit slavery.

Neither proposal satisfied the hard-liners. Congressman David Wilmot of Pennsylvania introduced an amendment—the **Wilmot Proviso**—banning slavery in all lands acquired from Mexico. Senator John C. Calhoun of South Carolina responded by introducing a series of resolutions in support of slavery. The resolutions argued, in part, that a ban on slavery was unconstitutional since the Constitution protected slaveholders' rights to their property—including slaves—in all U.S. territories.

■■ **Admitting Texas and new territories reopened the debate in Congress over the expansion of slavery. Some favored compromise; others took a hard-line position.**

*T*HE 1848 ELECTION

As the national election of 1848 approached, Congress still had not settled the issue. The Democrats chose Lewis Cass, who favored popular sovereignty, as their presidential nominee. The Whigs nominated a man whose political views, if indeed he had any, were unknown. Their choice—Mexican War hero General Zachary Taylor, "Old Rough and Ready"—had never even voted in a presidential election! The fact that Taylor held slaves, however, led both northerners and southerners to assume he was sympathetic to proslavery views.

Angered by the reluctance of each party to address the slavery issue, antislavery Whigs and Democrats formed the **Free-Soil party** in August 1848. The Free-Soilers demanded that Congress prohibit the expansion of slavery into the territories. Appealing to farmers, land reformers, and some industrial workers of the North and West, the Free-Soil platform also supported free western homesteads as well as federal funding for internal improvements. Proclaiming "Free Soil, Free Speech, Free Labor, and Free Men," the party nominated former president Martin Van Buren.

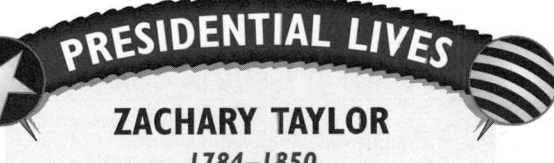

PRESIDENTIAL LIVES

ZACHARY TAYLOR
1784–1850

in office
1849–1850

As a popular U.S. Army general, "Old Rough and Ready" Zachary Taylor preferred blue denims to a uniform and led his troops with common sense and a spirit of camaraderie. The general was "perfectly unaffected by his brilliant successes" on the battlefield, one officer wrote. "[He is] plain and unassuming in his kind manners. . . . You feel at once comfortable and easy in his society."

As president, Taylor tried to run the country as he had led his troops. He dressed informally and made decisions relying on his common sense. But he needed more than common sense to grapple with the momentous issues of slavery and expansion. The politically inexperienced hero of the Mexican War had little success in the battles on Capitol Hill.

Z. Taylor

The Free-Soil party received only some 291,000 votes out of the nearly 2.9 million cast. But it won enough Democrats' votes in key northern states to enable the Whig candidate, Taylor, to win the election. Free-Soil candidates also won several seats in the House of Representatives. More important, the existence of the Free-Soil party showed that politicians could not continue to ignore the slavery question.

■■ **The Free-Soil party, formed by antislavery Democrats and Whigs, attracted enough votes in 1848 to cost the Democrats the presidency.**

HISTORICAL SIDELIGHTS

Taylor and the Military
Zachary Taylor was born in Virginia in 1784. In 1785 his family settled in Kentucky on the land that his father, Richard Taylor, received as a war bonus for serving in the Revolutionary War. Zachary Taylor's choice of a military career was influenced by his observances of Indian warfare near his home and by his father's stories about the Revolutionary War.

HISTORICAL SIDELIGHTS

Wilmot Proviso
After President Polk witnessed the strong emotions evoked in Congress by the Wilmot Proviso, he made a dire prediction. Writing in his diary, he noted that slavery "cannot fail to destroy the Democratic party, if it does not ultimately threaten the Union itself."

Teaching the Section

THE COMPROMISE OF 1850

Call on volunteers to cite the terms of Clay's proposal and write them on the chalkboard. Then create a two-column chart titled *Opposition to Compromise of 1850.* Label one column *Northern Abolitionists* and the other *Proslavery Southerners.* Have the class list each group's reasons for opposing compromise.

VOICES IN HISTORY

Frederick Douglass recognized that the effort to forge a compromise on the issue of slavery was doomed to failure. "The fact is," he noted, "the more the question has been settled, the more it has needed settling." Douglass's co-editor of the *North Star,* African American physician Martin R. Delany, was particularly incensed by the proposal for a tougher fugitive slave law. If a slave catcher appeared at his house, Delany warned, "I care not who he may be, whether constable or sheriff, magistrate or even judge of the Supreme Court . . . if he crosses the threshold of my door, and I do not lay him a lifeless corpse at my feet, I hope the grave may refuse my body a resting place."

Map Caption Answer
Louisiana, Mississippi, South Carolina

THE SLAVERY ISSUE IN CONGRESS

When Congress assembled in December 1849, tempers ran so high that members in the House voted 63 times before electing their Speaker. Congress was particularly divided over issues involving California and New Mexico—the territories of the Mexican Cession, the fruits of America's victory in the Mexican War. California wished to enter the Union as a free state, something southern members of Congress hotly opposed. In addition, Texas was claiming that its boundary extended westward into an area the federal government considered part of the New Mexico Territory. Despite opposition from southern lawmakers, the antislavery members of Congress were intent on limiting the size of Texas and on barring slavery from the New Mexico Territory.

Arguments over other questions involving slavery also echoed through the halls of Congress. Southern congressmen resisted a plan to abolish the slave trade in the District of Columbia. They also continued to block passage of the Wilmot Proviso. Some of the proviso's southern opponents even demanded that Congress adopt a resolution affirming the right of settlers to hold slaves in the New Mexico Territory. In addition, proslavery forces called for a tougher fugitive slave law. In 1842 the Supreme Court had ruled that state officials did not have to assist federal officials in capturing runaway slaves. Southerners now wanted a law that forced state officials to help.

All these issues were politically explosive— both inside and outside the halls of Congress. The debates over slavery already had split two of the nation's largest religious groups. The Methodist and Baptist churches in the South broke from their northern counterparts, forming the separate denominations of the Methodist Episcopal Church, South (1844) and the Southern Baptist Convention (1845).

CLAY'S PROPOSALS

In January and February 1850, a weary Henry Clay again urged northern and southern senators to

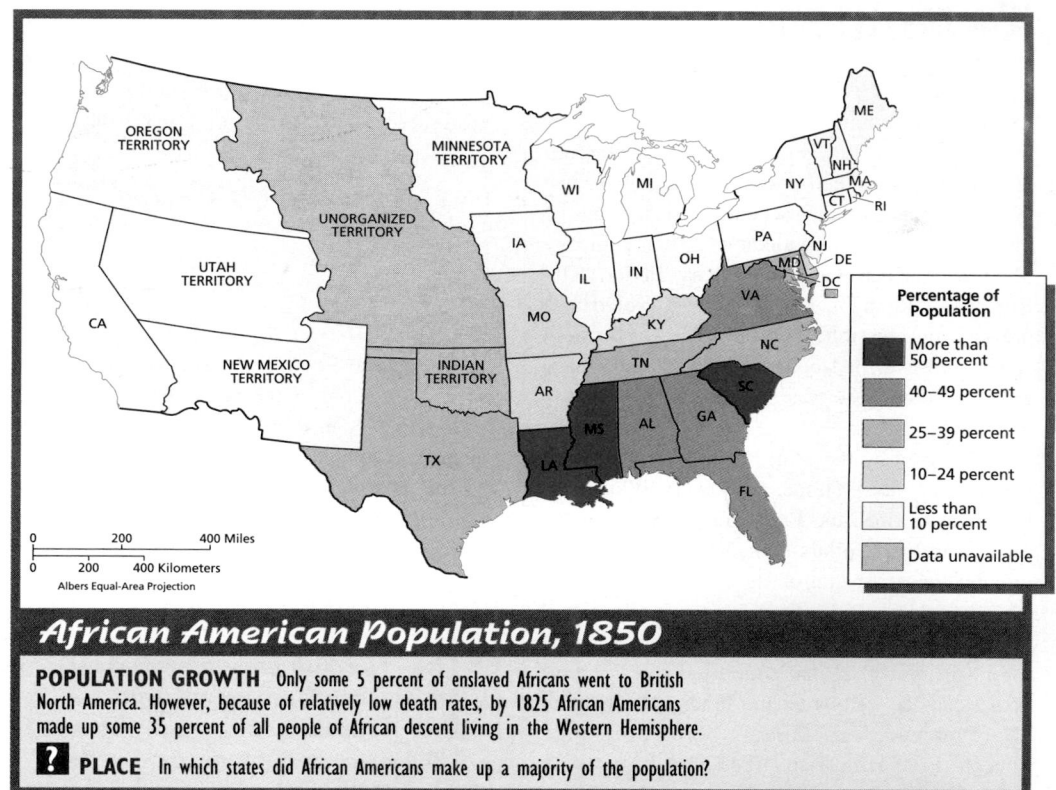

Percentage of Population	
	More than 50 percent
	40–49 percent
	25–39 percent
	10–24 percent
	Less than 10 percent
	Data unavailable

African American Population, 1850

POPULATION GROWTH Only some 5 percent of enslaved Africans went to British North America. However, because of relatively low death rates, by 1825 African Americans made up some 35 percent of all people of African descent living in the Western Hemisphere.

❓ **PLACE** In which states did African Americans make up a majority of the population?

Practice

GUIDED PRACTICE

Write on the chalkboard: *Extension of Missouri Compromise Line, Popular Sovereignty, Wilmot Proviso, Unlimited Expansion of Slavery, Compromise of 1850.* Divide the class into five groups. Assign each group one of these solutions and discuss with students how their solution would affect the territory acquired from Mexico.

INDEPENDENT PRACTICE

Instruct students to work individually or in pairs to draw maps showing how the solution their group supported, as described in the Guided Practice, would affect the territory acquired from Mexico. Students may wish to include their maps in their portfolios.

Review and Assessment

REVIEW Have students imagine that the year is 1850. Ask them to write an editorial for their local newspaper, reflecting on how the slavery issue has come to dominate national politics. Then assign the Section 1 Review on p. 342.

ASSESS Assign the **Section 1 Daily Quiz** in *Core Resources.* ▶

compromise. "All society," he explained, "is formed upon the principle of mutual concession."

To satisfy northern antislavery interests, Clay proposed admitting California as a free state, abolishing the slave trade (though not slavery itself) in the District of Columbia, and paying Texas $10 million to abandon its claim to the eastern part of the New Mexico Territory. To persuade southerners to accept these terms, Clay further proposed that the New Mexico Territory be organized into two territories—New Mexico and Utah—on the basis of popular sovereignty. Further, he proposed that Congress pass a tougher fugitive slave law. This law would force state and local officials, and even private citizens, to aid federal officials in the capture and return of escaped slaves.

The Great Debate. For months Congress angrily debated Clay's proposals. The most bitter attack came from the South's elder statesman, John C. Calhoun. On March 4, 1850, visitors to the U.S. Capitol watched intently as Calhoun, near death, was half carried into the Senate chamber. Too ill to speak, he sat in silence as his speech was read. In it Calhoun warned that the time for compromise was past. The nation could avoid civil war only if the North allowed slavery to exist in the territories:

66 If something decisive is not now done . . . , the South will be forced to choose between abolition and secession. . . . The responsibility of saving the Union rests on the North, and not the South. 99

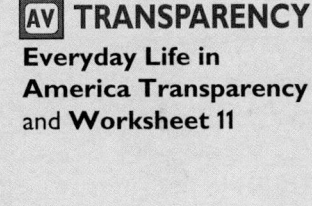

▶ John C. Calhoun defended slavery and worked to protect the rights of southern states against what he saw as the "tyranny of the majority."

Three days after Calhoun's speech, the veteran Whig leader Daniel Webster rose to support Clay's compromise measures. "I wish to speak today," Webster began, "not as a Massachusetts man, nor as a northern man, but as an American. . . . I speak today for the preservation of the Union." He argued that because the climate of the territories was unsuitable for growing cotton, slavery could not take root there. Therefore, legally barring slavery would anger southerners needlessly. Webster also endorsed Clay's proposal for a more enforceable fugitive slave law.

Many northern members of Congress, Whigs and Democrats alike, objected to Webster's speech and to Clay's compromise measures. While angrily denying that the Constitution protected slavery, they asserted that people were morally bound to "a higher law than the Constitution." They opposed stricter fugitive slave legislation and urged Congress to bar slavery from the territories. Many agreed with Senator Seward's opinion that on an issue like slavery, compromise was "radically wrong and essentially vicious."

HISTORICAL SIDELIGHTS

Opinions on Compromise
Although President Fillmore called the Compromise of 1850 "a final settlement" of sectional divisions, others, like Ohio senator Salmon P. Chase, believed that "the question of slavery in the territories has been avoided. It has not been settled."

PRIMARY SOURCE

Description of Change: excerpted
Rationale: excerpted to focus on main idea

The Granger Collection, New York

◀ Daniel Webster's controversial speech before the Senate in 1850 angered many northern lawmakers. This picture of the event was drawn in 1860.

RETEACH Have students work in small groups, with pairs assigned to answer different questions in each section's Focus. Ask pairs to share their answers with the group.

Closure

Point out that many people in Washington, D.C., on hearing that the Compromise of 1850 had been approved, rushed into the streets to celebrate. Have students explain why the settlement was considered to be so critically important and discuss whether there really was cause to celebrate.

Extension

INTERPRET Have students research the speeches of Clay, Webster, and Calhoun and prepare dramatic readings and interpretations of key passages.

ANALYZE Have students research and write a paragraph explaining why France and Great Britain urged the Republic of Texas to remain independent from the U.S.

SECTION REVIEW ANSWERS

IDENTIFY

For significance, see the following pages:
Lewis Cass (p. 339)
Stephen A. Douglas (p. 339)
popular sovereignty (p. 339)
Wilmot Proviso (p. 339)
Zachary Taylor (p. 339)
Free-Soil party (p. 339)
Daniel Webster (p. 341)
Millard Filmore (p. 342)
Compromise of 1850
(p. 342)

1. *adding Texas and new territories; extension of Missouri Compromise line, popular sovereignty, Wilmot Proviso, and extension of slavery*
2. *Reluctance of Whigs and Democrats to address slavery issue; took enough votes away from the Democrats to cost them the presidency*
3. *Northern abolitionists opposed stricter fugitive slave legislation and extending slavery into territories; proslavery southerners refused to accept any restrictions on slavery.*
4. *Speeches should outline reasons for supporting or opposing the measure chosen.*
5. *Calhoun believed that the nation could avoid civil war only if the North allowed slavery to exist in the territories, rather than forcing the South to choose between abolition and secession.*

PRESIDENTIAL LIVES

MILLARD FILLMORE
1800–1874

in office
1850–1853

Millard Fillmore was born into a poor, hardworking New York farm family. As a child he was often without decent clothes or sufficient food. To ease their economic burden and provide Fillmore with a trade, his family apprenticed him at age 14 to a clothmaker.

Fillmore was almost an adult before he owned any books beyond a few primers. At

age 17 he bought a dictionary to study while he worked. He placed the dictionary on a desk between the wooden milling machines. Each time he passed by, Fillmore looked up a word and fixed its meaning in his memory.

Fillmore's efforts paid off. With the help of his teacher—whom he later married—he, too, became a teacher, and then a lawyer, before entering politics.

 ■■ **Many northern abolitionists opposed Clay's compromise proposals on moral grounds; proslavery southerners rejected any compromise, insisting that slavery be allowed in the territories.**

The Compromise of 1850. Calhoun did not live to see the outcome of the Great Debate, nor did President Taylor, who died from a stomach ailment in July 1850. Taylor, who opposed Clay's compromise proposals, was succeeded by Vice

President Millard Fillmore, who favored them. The 73-year-old Clay, however, was too exhausted to continue the fight. Senator Douglas, the Illinois Democrat, finally pushed the compromise measures through Congress. California was admitted to the Union as a free state on September 9, 1850. By September 20, the remaining measures had passed.

Many Americans hailed the **Compromise of 1850** as a triumph for national unity. Those who looked closely at voting records, however, saw that deep sectional divisions remained. More important, the basic issue—whether slavery would be allowed to expand—remained unresolved.

■■ **SECTION 1 REVIEW**

IDENTIFY and explain the significance of the following: Lewis Cass, Stephen A. Douglas, popular sovereignty, Wilmot Proviso, Zachary Taylor, Free-Soil party, Daniel Webster, Millard Fillmore, Compromise of 1850.

1. **MAIN IDEA** What reopened the controversy over the expansion of slavery? What proposals did Congress consider to settle the controversy?

2. **MAIN IDEA** What led to the formation of the Free-Soil party, and how did the party influence the outcome of the 1848 election?

3. **MAIN IDEA** Why did many northern abolitionists oppose passage of the Compromise of 1850? Why did proslavery southerners oppose the compromise?

4. **WRITING TO PERSUADE** Imagine you are a U.S. senator in 1850. Choose one of the measures that made up the Compromise of 1850, and write a speech in which you attempt to persuade other senators to vote either for or against it.

5. **EVALUATING** Why did John C. Calhoun believe that the responsibility for saving the Union belonged to the North and not the South?

Section 2

COMPROMISE COMES TO AN END

FOCUS

■ **How did the Fugitive Slave Act of 1850 affect northerners' views on slavery?**

■ **Why did the Kansas-Nebraska Act reignite the debate over slavery? How did passage of the act affect Kansas?**

■ **What led to the formation of the Republican party?**

The relative calm produced by the Compromise of 1850 was brief. Controversy over the fugitive slave issue continued in the North, and western settlement soon renewed the national debate over the expansion of slavery. On the frontier, fierce competition for control of the new territorial government of Kansas erupted in violent conflict. Chances for compromise seemed to be fading.

Fugitive slaves escaping from Maryland

THE ELECTION OF 1852

Although many people were dissatisfied with the Compromise of 1850, most Americans hoped that it had settled the slavery question. To tap into this optimistic mood, both major political parties adopted platforms supporting the compromise, vowing to avoid further debate over slavery.

At their 1852 convention the Democrats, after 49 ballots, united behind Franklin Pierce, a New Hampshire lawyer and strong supporter of the Compromise of 1850. The likable Pierce persuaded many people on both sides of the slavery issue that he shared their views. Some Free-Soilers, convinced that Pierce could hold the South in check, returned to the Democratic party. Southerners in the meantime generally agreed that Pierce was "sound on all southern questions."

Having won the presidency in 1848 with General Taylor, the Whigs again turned to a Mexican War hero, General Winfield Scott. But many southern Whigs, angered at northern Whig

opposition to the **Fugitive Slave Act**, which was passed as part of the Compromise of 1850, refused to vote for Scott. Pierce won the election by a landslide.

In his inaugural address, the new president urged national harmony—even appointing a cabinet

▲ **Franklin Pierce was inaugurated as the 14th president of the United States on March 4, 1853.**

SLAVERY'S EXPANSION ■ 343

MOTIVATING:
LINK TO TODAY

Have students identify examples of popular sovereignty in society today. Ask students to suggest situations in which popular sovereignty might be unacceptable today.

Teaching the Section

FUGITIVE SLAVE ACT

Ask students to assume the role of a northerner who had favored the Compromise of 1850 but changed his or her mind because of the Fugitive Slave Act. Have them express their views in a letter to the editor of their local newspaper. Select volunteers to read their letters to the class. Students may wish to include their letters in their portfolios.

MAKING CONNECTIONS

Literature

In writing *Uncle Tom's Cabin,* Harriet Beecher Stowe drew upon her experiences in Cincinnati with runaway slaves and on her observances of slavery in Kentucky. Her fiction first appeared as a weekly serial in the abolitionist newspaper *National Era.*

PRIMARY SOURCE

Description of Change: excerpted
Rationale: excerpted to focus on main idea

GLOBAL CONNECTIONS

After the democratic revolutions of 1848 had been crushed throughout Europe, some Europeans looked to the United States to fulfill its potential as the beacon of democracy. In 1853 emancipationists in England sent the following message to Americans: "extinguish slavery . . . and you will at once have . . . double moral power, to reanimate the swooning liberties of Europe."

THE AMERICAN NATION VIDEODISC PROGRAM

Free At Last

| 1B | 15914 | 2:57 |

344

PRESIDENTIAL LIVES

FRANKLIN PIERCE
1804–1869

in office 1853–1857

Two months before his inauguration, Franklin Pierce and his wife witnessed a train crash in which their only child was killed. They never completely recovered from the loss.

Mrs. Pierce went into seclusion. She believed God had taken their son so that her husband would have no fatherly duties to distract him while in office. Pierce, however, interpreted the loss as punishment for his own sins and religious doubts. At his inauguration Pierce could not bring himself to swear on the Bible as was the custom. Instead, he simply raised his right hand and affirmed his loyalty to the Constitution.

Franklin Pierce

that included both southerners and northerners. But Pierce proved to be a weak leader, unable to control his diverse cabinet or to convince northerners that he was not caving in to southern pressure. Abolitionists labeled him a "northern man with southern principles."

THE FUGITIVE SLAVE ACT

The Compromise of 1850 began crumbling even before Pierce's election, largely because of the Fugitive Slave Act. The law, which made it a federal crime to assist runaway slaves and authorized the arrest of escaped slaves even in states where slavery was illegal, roused vigorous opposition in the North.

Harriet Beecher Stowe's powerful 1852 antislavery novel *Uncle Tom's Cabin* helped stir northern opposition to the law. The novel dramatized the plight of runaway slaves and showed how slavery

---

broke up black families and made a mockery of Christian morality. No previous antislavery publication approached the national impact of *Uncle Tom's Cabin,* which quickly sold over a million copies. The book convinced many northerners that the institution of slavery was morally wrong and should be abolished immediately.

Some northerners came face to face with the inhumanity of the Fugitive Slave Act. Caroline Seabury, a teacher from Massachusetts, confided to her diary the shock she felt the first time she witnessed a slave catcher at work:

> ❝ We saw . . . a man on horseback riding at a quick pace, & by his side a tall negro coming steadily along. We wondered at the perfect uniformity of his steps—until, as they came nearer us, we saw one chain going from his wrists to the saddle, another was around his ankles—giving him just room enough to walk—following them were two large thick-headed fierce-looking dogs. ❞

◀ Anthony Burns

▲ In 1854 escaped slave Anthony Burns was returned to his owner under the provisions of the Fugitive Slave Act. Shown here is a Boston mob that tried unsuccessfully to rescue him. Outraged citizens rioted and then eventually paid $1,300 for Burns's freedom a year later.

As such scenes became more common, northerners reacted with horror. Abolitionist Frederick Douglass urged "forcible resistance." A former slave himself, Douglass protested that the Fugitive Slave Act made northerners "the mere *tools* and *body-guards* of the tyrants of Virginia and Carolina." People who had supported the Compromise of 1850 were shocked at the government's enforcement of the Fugitive Slave Act. Several northern states defiantly passed "personal liberty" laws, which prevented state officials from enforcing the Fugitive Slave Act and guaranteed captured runaway slaves legal assistance. Amos A. Lawrence, a northern Democrat, voiced a common sentiment: "We have submitted to slavery long enough, and must not stand it any longer. . . . I am done catching negroes for the South."

Some northerners took direct action. In New York and Massachusetts, angry mobs freed runaway slaves taken into custody and helped them on their way to freedom in Canada. One observer wrote, "We went to bed one night old fashioned conservative Compromise Union Whigs and waked up stark mad Abolitionists."

■■ **Enforcement of the Fugitive Slave Act strengthened antislavery sentiment in the North.**

▶ Posters such as this one from 1854 were circulated by antislavery forces to protest the Fugitive Slave Act.

KIDNAPPING AGAIN!!
A MAN WAS STOLEN LAST NIGHT BY THE
Fugitive Slave Bill COMMISSIONER!
HE WILL HAVE HIS
MOCK TRIAL
ON SATURDAY, MAY 27, AT 9 O'CLOCK,
In the Kidnapper's 'Court,' before the Hon. Slave Bill Commissioner,
AT THE COURT HOUSE, IN COURT SQUARE.
SHALL BOSTON STEAL ANOTHER MAN?
Thursday, May 25, 1854.

THE KANSAS–NEBRASKA ACT

Early in 1854, Senator Stephen Douglas inflamed passions further by reigniting the debate over the spread of slavery. An enthusiastic expansionist, Douglas supported settlement on the western prairies and the construction of a railroad to the West Coast. To benefit his constituents in Illinois, he wanted the railroad to run from Chicago to the Pacific Ocean.

Construction of the railroad required Congress to organize Kansas and Nebraska—the lands of the Louisiana Purchase west of Missouri and Iowa—into territories. This meant reopening the issue of slavery in the West. Hoping to quiet

GLOBAL CONNECTIONS
Many African Americans in the North believed that the Fugitive Slave Act threatened their freedom. One result was that the black population of Ontario, Canada, doubled to 11,000 in the 1850s as free blacks and escaped slaves fled the U.S. Once in Canada, many of them became part of the Underground Railroad, helping to free other African Americans.

VOICES IN HISTORY
Charles Langston, an African American from Ohio, fought against the Fugitive Slave Act by helping a fugitive slave escape. Langston, who was tried and convicted for his actions, responded, "The law . . . is an unjust one, one made to crush the colored man, and one which outrages every feeling of humanity."

Map Caption Answer
the Kansas-Nebraska Act, which allowed the extension of slavery into a formerly "free" region if the people of those territories voted for it

---

Slave vs. Free Territory, 1850 and 1854

DEFUSING TENSIONS Passage of the Kansas-Nebraska Act convinced many northerners that the South was trying to extend slavery everywhere.

? LOCATION Compare the two maps. Which legislation allowed for the greater extension of slavery and why?

Compromise of 1850

OREGON TERRITORY
MINNESOTA TERRITORY
Unorganized Territory
UTAH TERRITORY
Missouri Compromise line (36°30'N)
CALIFORNIA
NEW MEXICO TERRITORY
Indian Terr.
Disputed
Disputed

Kansas-Nebraska Act, 1854

WASHINGTON TERRITORY
OREGON TERRITORY
NEBRASKA TERRITORY
MINNESOTA TERRITORY
UTAH TERRITORY
KANSAS TERRITORY
NEW MEXICO TERRITORY
Indian Terr.
Disputed

Legend:
- Free state
- Free territory
- Slave state
- Slave territory
- Popular sovereignty
- Change from free territory to popular sovereignty

Changing Ways

**SOUTHERN
EXPANSIONISTS
AND THE
FILIBUSTERS**

LINK TO TODAY

Ask students to identify recent world events in which a country has supported private attempts to invade another country. Have students compare the reasons for and outcomes of these events with the filibusters of the 19th century.

HISTORICAL SIDELIGHTS

The Ostend Manifesto

In the Ostend Manifesto, the three American envoys expressed the opinion that "Cuba is as necessary to the North American republic as any of its present members, and that it belongs naturally to that great family of states of which the Union is the Providential Nursery."

Changing Ways — SOUTHERN EXPANSIONISTS AND THE FILIBUSTERS

Eager to increase the South's political power and to spread slavery, southern expansionists in the mid-1800s set their sights on conquering Mexico, Central America, and the West Indies. An 1848 New Orleans publication summed up the determined ambitions of these expansionists: "We have New Mexico and California. We *will* have old Mexico and Cuba!"

The expansionists were aided in their efforts by soldiers of fortune called "filibusters" (from a Spanish word meaning freebooters, or pirates). Recruited from the ranks of penniless immigrants, frontiersmen, and Mexican War veterans, the filibusters participated in numerous attempts to conquer Latin American lands between 1848 and 1860.

One of the first targets was Cuba in 1849. Southern

▲ In 1847 the British magazine *Punch* published this satirical cartoon criticizing expansionist policies in the United States.

expansionists supported the efforts of Narciso López, a former Spanish general, to mount a revolution on the island. The attempt failed, but López tried two more times before being captured and executed in 1850.

Diplomatic efforts to obtain Cuba from Spain fared no better. Spain refused an offer of $100 million in 1848 and a second offer of $130 million in 1854. This greatly frustrated the Pierce administration, which had made acquiring Cuba a priority. At Pierce's urging, the U.S. ambassadors to Great Britain, France, and Spain met in Ostend, Belgium, in October 1854 to devise a plan for obtaining Cuba at any cost, even war. When their plan—the Ostend Manifesto—became

public, northerners were outraged. Pierce quickly withdrew his support.

Southern expansionists had no better luck acquiring lands in Mexico or Central America. In 1853 newspaper editor William Walker and a band of filibusters set sail from San Francisco for Lower California. After establishing an independent republic and declaring himself president, Walker "annexed" neighboring Sonora, Mexico. He was quickly chased out.

Undaunted, Walker joined in a Nicaraguan revolution two years later. Landing with only 58 men, in less than a year he had installed himself as dictator. One of his first official acts was to relegalize slavery, which had been abolished 30 years before. But his days in office were numbered. In April 1857, surrounded by the armies of four countries, he surrendered and was deported. Ever hopeful, he made three more attempts to invade Nicaragua, finally dying before a Honduran firing squad in 1860.

Walker's brief dictatorship in Central America was the closest any of the filibusters came to acquiring new territory for the United States. The dreams of expansionists for a new southern empire died with Walker.

► Narciso López

Teaching the Section

LIFE IN KANSAS

Have students imagine they had settled in the Kansas territory prior to the Kansas-Nebraska Act. Ask them to write a short journal entry describing and commenting on the effects of the act on their lives and their communities. Have volunteers read aloud their journal entries. Students may wish to include their entries in their portfolios.

THE REPUBLICAN PARTY

Work with students to create a graphic organizer on the chalkboard, showing the various political groups that came together to form the Republican party. Use the graphic organizer as a lead-in to a discussion of the platform, events, and developments that attracted these groups to the Republican party.

congressional debate, Douglas introduced the **Kansas-Nebraska Act**, which organized the lands on the basis of popular sovereignty.

By allowing the new states formed from the territories to "be received into the Union with or without slavery, as their constitution may prescribe at the time of their admission," the Kansas-Nebraska Act repealed the Missouri Compromise. Passage of the act in May 1854 renewed southern hopes of expanding slavery. Antislavery northerners were outraged. They called Douglas a traitor to the antislavery cause and accused him of caving in to southern pressure in an effort to gain support for a presidential bid. More and more, northerners viewed the South as intent on dominating the nation. The *New York Times* wrote that the Kansas-Nebraska Act was "part of this great scheme for extending and perpetuating the supremacy of the Slave Power."

■■ **The Kansas-Nebraska Act established popular sovereignty in the newly organized territories and overturned the Missouri Compromise.**

Not everyone opposed the Kansas-Nebraska Act on abolitionist grounds. Some critics had economic motives. These people argued that if slavery were allowed to spread to the territories, it would force out white workers. Why would employers choose to hire wage laborers when they could use slave labor? A western newspaper editor wrote:

> ❝ I am opposed to slavery not because it is a misery to the downtrodden and oppressed, but that it blights and mildews the white man whose lot is toil, and whose capital is his labor. ❞

Many people supported these arguments, increasing tension over the slavery issue.

"BLEEDING KANSAS"

The Kansas-Nebraska Act pitted antislavery and proslavery forces against one another for control of the new territories. To bolster the number of antislavery settlers, New Englanders formed the Emigrant Aid Company to help antislavery families move to Kansas. Proslavery forces countered by urging southerners to migrate to the new territories. "We are playing for a mighty stake," warned Senator David Atchinson of Missouri. "If we win, we carry slavery to the Pacific Ocean."

Proslavery forces took up the challenge in March 1855. As Kansas settlers prepared to elect

◀ Poster advertising land sales in Kansas, 1855

▶ This 1856 photograph shows a Free-State artillery battery in Topeka, Kansas, preparing to defend the territory from proslavery raiders.

PRIMARY SOURCE

Description of Change: excerpted
Rationale: excerpted to focus on main idea

COOPERATIVE LEARNING

Organize students into small groups and have them assume the roles of members of Congress in 1854. Ask each group to create a proposal for organizing the Kansas-Nebraska territories that preserves the Union. Direct each student in the group to contribute one idea for the group's proposal. Have volunteers from each group present its proposal to the class. Encourage comments from other students.

HISTORICAL SIDELIGHTS

Arming Kansas

The Emigrant Aid Company not only helped antislavery families settle in Kansas but also sent hundreds of rifles to Kansas as the division between the antislavery and proslavery factions widened and became increasingly violent.

*P*ractice

GUIDED PRACTICE

Divide the class into Free-Soilers, abolitionists, and proslavery southerners. Take turns asking a representative of each group to give a view on the Fugitive Slave Act, the Kansas-Nebraska Act, "Bleeding Kansas," or the Republican party.

INDEPENDENT PRACTICE

Have students create a poster or political cartoon that expresses one of the viewpoints presented in the Guided Practice about the Fugitive Slave Act, the Kansas-Nebraska Act, "Bleeding Kansas," or the Republican party.

*R*eview and *A*ssessment

REVIEW Have students work in small groups to create cause-event-effect graphic organizers showing the main events discussed in the section. Then assign the Section 2 Review on p. 349.

ASSESS Assign the **Section 2 Daily Quiz** in *Core Resources.*

PRIMARY SOURCE
Description of Change: excerpted
Rationale: excerpted to focus on main idea

HISTORICAL SIDELIGHTS
"Bleeding Kansas"
Although "Bleeding Kansas" cost Pierce his party's renomination in 1856, the issue lost some of its force during the later campaign, as the new territorial governor, John W. Geary, brought temporary peace to Kansas by using federal troops against agitators on both sides.

The Granger Collection, New York

▲ **A posse of proslavery men from Missouri are shown here on their way to plunder and burn Lawrence, Kansas, in 1856. Months of intense and bloody fighting followed the raid, giving rise to the phrase "Bleeding Kansas."**

their first territorial legislature, some 5,000 proslavery Missouri residents crossed into Kansas. Casting illegal votes, they helped elect a proslavery legislature, which antislavery settlers refused to accept as their legal government. The antislavery residents formed a Free State party and elected their own legislature. Kansas now had two territorial governments—one proslavery, the other antislavery!

With two rival governments vying for power, conflict was inevitable. Proslavery raiders from Missouri attacked antislavery Kansas settlers, and in May 1856 a proslavery mob of some 700 burned the town of Lawrence, Kansas. In revenge, a group led by abolitionist John Brown attacked a proslavery settlement along Pottawatomie (paht-uh-WAHT-uh-mee) Creek. They dragged five men from their beds and brutally murdered them. The **Pottawatomie Massacre** enraged southerners, shocked northerners, and sparked more violence in what newspapers began calling "Bleeding Kansas."

■■ **A bitter battle erupted between proslavery and antislavery factions for control of Kansas.**

Back in Washington the halls of Congress echoed the violence in Kansas. Among the most outspoken members of Congress was the abolitionist senator Charles Sumner of Massachusetts. In his "Crime Against Kansas" speech, delivered on

May 19–20, 1856, Sumner declared the Kansas-Nebraska Act "a swindle":

66 Slavery now stands erect, clanking its chains on the territory of Kansas, surrounded by a code of death, and trampling upon all cherished liberties. . . . It has been done for the sake of political power, in order to bring two new slaveholding senators upon this floor. 99

In addition, Sumner ridiculed the proslavery senator Andrew Butler of South Carolina. Two days later Congressman Preston Brooks of South Carolina, a relative of Butler, savagely beat Sumner with a cane until it broke. The beating was so severe that it took Sumner years to recover from his injuries. Admiring voters in Brooks's district showered him with replacement canes. Whig leader David Davis wrote, however, that Brooks's shocking attack, coupled with the violence in Kansas, "made Abolitionists of those who never dreamed they were drifting into it."

*T*HE REPUBLICAN PARTY

To carry their message to the nation, antislavery voters flocked to a new party growing in the North. In 1854 a group of antislavery Whigs and Democrats, together with some Free-Soilers, had organized a party firmly opposed to the expansion of slavery. At a July 1854 convention in Jackson, Michigan, the delegates revived the name of Thomas Jefferson's party, calling themselves Republicans.

The Republican party worked together with the Know-Nothings to defeat Democratic candidates in the election of 1854. By 1856, however, the slavery issue had split the Know-Nothing party. As a result, many antislavery Know-Nothings joined the Republican party, which was becoming a powerful force in national politics.

■■ **Antislavery Whigs and Democrats joined with Free-Soilers to form the Republican party to oppose any expansion of slavery.**

RETEACH Organize students into small groups. Tell each group to divide the section material, by subsections, among its members. Direct students to write questions about the main ideas presented in their assigned material. Have group members use the questions to quiz one another.

Closure

Ask students to describe conflicts and changes in political parties from 1850 to 1856 and then explain how these reflected conflicts and changes in the nation.

■■ Ask students to describe conflicts between present-day political parties and how they reflect conflict in the nation today.

Extension

RESEARCH Direct students to research and write an account of the Pottawatomie Massacre.

INVESTIGATE Have students investigate the Emigrant Aid Company and how it helped antislavery families move to Kansas. Then have students pretend to be a member of a family the company helped move and write thank-you letters to the company.

Running the popular western explorer John C. Frémont for president in 1856, the Republicans campaigned on the slogan "Free Soil, Free Speech, Free Men, Frémont, and Victory!" The Democrats abandoned Pierce, nominating James Buchanan of Pennsylvania. The Democratic platform praised the Kansas-Nebraska Act "as the only sound and safe solution of the slavery question" and portrayed the Republicans as a sectional party bent on destroying the Union. The remaining Whigs and the anti-immigrant, anti-Catholic Know-Nothings nominated former president Millard Fillmore.

The tactic of painting the Republicans as the party of sectionalism proved successful for Buchanan, who gathered 174 electoral votes to Frémont's 114 and Fillmore's 8. Buchanan won support in both slave and free states. Frémont, on the other hand, carried only free states, and Fillmore carried only Maryland.

Meanwhile, events in Kansas continued to boil. Early in 1857, elections were held to choose delegates for the upcoming constitutional

◀ This campaign poster appeared in 1856 in support of John C. Frémont's bid for the presidency.

convention. Suspecting that proslavery forces would rig the elections, the antislavery forces boycotted them. The constitutional convention, made up of exclusively proslavery delegates, met at Lecompton and drafted a constitution that protected the rights of slaveholders already living in Kansas. The **Lecompton Constitution** gave the voters of Kansas the right to decide only whether *more* slaves could enter the territory.

Senator Stephen Douglas attacked the Lecompton Constitution, arguing that the voters of Kansas should have the right to decide whether *any* slaves could enter their territory. This stand cost Douglas much support among southerners. Many thought that Douglas was siding with the Republicans in preventing another slave state from entering the Union. Despite the admission of Kansas as a free state in 1861, Douglas's principle of popular sovereignty had been largely discredited.

■■ **SECTION 2 REVIEW**

IDENTIFY and explain the significance of the following: Franklin Pierce, Winfield Scott, Fugitive Slave Act, Harriet Beecher Stowe, Kansas-Nebraska Act, John Brown, Pottawatomie Massacre, Charles Sumner, John C. Frémont, James Buchanan, Lecompton Constitution.

LOCATE and explain the importance of the following: Nebraska Territory, Kansas Territory.

1. **MAIN IDEA** How did the Fugitive Slave Act affect public opinion in the North?
2. **MAIN IDEA** Why was the Kansas-Nebraska Act important? What happened after Congress passed the act?
3. **LINKING HISTORY AND GEOGRAPHY** Why did passage of the Kansas-Nebraska Act result in the repeal of the Missouri Compromise?
4. **WRITING TO CLASSIFY** Imagine you are a delegate to the new Republican party's convention in Jackson, Michigan. Write a letter to a newspaper editor, explaining why your party was formed and who it hopes to attract.
5. **HYPOTHESIZING** What actions might the federal government have taken to prevent bloodshed in Kansas?

FOCUS OBJECTIVES

- Analyze what effect the Supreme Court's *Dred Scott* decision had on the national debate over slavery.

- Describe how the Lincoln-Douglas debates both helped and hurt Stephen Douglas's political career.

- Determine the importance of John Brown's raid at Harpers Ferry.

- Explain why the results of the 1860 presidential election caused a crisis and how the South justified its position.

HISTORICAL SIDELIGHTS

Opinions on *Dred Scott*
Supreme Court justices John McLean of Ohio and Benjamin Curtis of Massachusetts, neither a Democrat, wrote dissents in the *Dred Scott* decision. These became the basis for the Republican position—that Scott remained a free man because of his residency in free territory and that he was also a citizen under the Constitution.

CORE RESOURCES

• **Section 3 Daily Quiz**

350

Section 3

ON THE BRINK OF WAR

F O C U S

- **What effect did the Supreme Court's *Dred Scott* decision have on the national debate over slavery?**
- **How did the Lincoln-Douglas debates both help and hurt Stephen Douglas's political career?**
- **Why was John Brown's raid at Harpers Ferry important?**
- **Why did the results of the 1860 presidential election cause a crisis? How did the South justify its position?**

From 1857 to 1861 the slavery issue pushed the United States further toward disunion. On March 6, 1857, two days after President James Buchanan took office, the Supreme Court issued the Dred Scott *decision, which intensified the slavery controversy. The following year Democrat Stephen Douglas and Republican Abraham Lincoln of Illinois debated the issue as they campaigned for the U.S. Senate. Douglas was elected, but two years later Lincoln defeated Douglas in the presidential election. Faced with a Republican president, the Lower South made good its threat to secede.*

Stephen Douglas campaign doll

THE *DRED SCOTT* DECISION

Dred Scott was the slave of John Emerson, an army surgeon from Missouri. Scott accompanied Emerson when he served on army posts in the free state of Illinois and the free territory of Wisconsin. Eventually the two men returned to Missouri. In 1846, after Emerson's death, Scott sued for his freedom, arguing that his residence in the free state of Illinois entitled him to it.

In 1857 the case reached the U.S. Supreme Court. Chief Justice Roger B. Taney, one of five southerners on the Court, wrote the majority opinion against Scott. Taney declared that Scott was not a citizen and therefore could not bring suit in U.S. courts. The nation's founders, Taney asserted,

had viewed blacks as "beings of an inferior order" having "no rights which the white man was bound to respect."

Taney also ruled that even if Scott had a legal right to bring suit, his claim to freedom had no merit. Taney based his decision on the view that the Missouri Compromise violated the Fifth Amendment to the Constitution, which forbids Congress to deny the right to property without "due process of law." Since slaves were legally classified as property, Congress had acted unconstitutionally in barring slavery from the territory north of 36°30'.

The ***Dred Scott* decision** outraged abolitionists and all who feared the extension of slavery. African American leader Robert Purvis, speaking at a protest rally held by northern blacks,

MOTIVATING: PRIOR KNOWLEDGE

Have a volunteer review why southerners wanted a Fugitive Slave Act and what effect the act had in the North. Then tell students that in this section they will read about how new developments deepened the nation's division over slavery.

Teaching the Section

THE *DRED SCOTT* DECISION

Organize students into two groups. Direct one group to imagine that they are northerners and the other group to imagine that they are southerners. List on the chalkboard each group's arguments for or against the *Dred Scott* decision. Call on volunteers from each group to express their feelings about the *Dred Scott* decision and to respond to the other side's point of view.

▪ Ask students to identify recent Supreme Court rulings that have caused controversy and increased divisiveness among various groups in the U.S.

▶

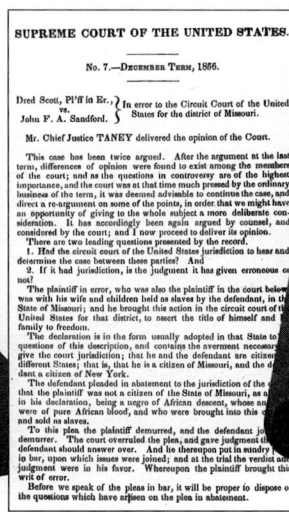

▲ The *Dred Scott* decision struck a blow for slavery and fueled bitter sectional controversy. Chief Justice Roger Taney (left) and Dred Scott (right) are shown here with a detail from the Supreme Court's decision.

expressed the angry sentiments of the free black community:

66 This atrocious decision furnishes final confirmation of the already well-known fact that, under the Constitution and government of the United States, the colored people are nothing and can be nothing but an alien, disfranchised, and degraded class. 99

After the passage of the Kansas-Nebraska Act and the Supreme Court's ruling in the *Dred Scott* case, there seemed no way to keep slavery from spreading into the territories. The struggle over slavery, declared Senator William Seward of New York, had become an "irrepressible conflict."

▪▪ **The *Dred Scott* decision intensified the sectional conflict over slavery.**

LINCOLN WINS A NATIONAL REPUTATION

The 1858 U.S. Senate race in Illinois became the forum for debate over the *Dred Scott* decision and the slavery issue—as well as a rehearsal for the 1860 presidential campaign. If Senator Douglas could win reelection, he stood a good chance of winning the Democratic party's nomination for president.

Illinois Republicans chose Abraham Lincoln to oppose Douglas. Born in 1809 in a log cabin in Kentucky, Lincoln was truly a self-made man. Although Lincoln had less than one year of formal education, he was intelligent and ambitious. During childhood he read the family Bible and walked miles to borrow books from neighbors.

In 1816 Lincoln and his family moved from Kentucky to the Indiana frontier. According to Lincoln, the move resulted in part from the family's opposition to slavery and in part from a disputed claim to their land.

Abraham Lincoln

When Lincoln was 21, his family moved to Illinois. The next year he left home and settled in New Salem, Illinois. He worked at various jobs, served in the frontier militia, and for a short time he and a partner owned a store. Although the business soon failed, Lincoln earned the respect of the townspeople and was appointed postmaster and deputy surveyor.

In 1834 he successfully ran for the Illinois legislature. A shrewd politician, Lincoln soon became the Whig floor leader. That same year he began studying law. Few law schools existed, so

HISTORICAL SIDELIGHTS

Seward's Charges
In his criticism of the *Dred Scott* decision, Seward also charged that Buchanan and Taney had conspired to further slaveholders' rights. In fact, Buchanan *had* written a letter to Supreme Court Justice Robert Grier of Pennsylvania, a Democrat, urging him to vote with the southern majority.

PRIMARY SOURCE

Description of Change: excerpted
Rationale: excerpted to focus on main idea

BIO
GRAPHY

PERSONALITIES IN HISTORY

At age 23 Lincoln ran for the Illinois state legislature, his first bid for public office. One of his campaign promises was to improve local roads and canals. He won his precinct, but lost the election.

Teaching the Section

LINCOLN–DOUGLAS DEBATES

Have students discuss the Lincoln-Douglas debates and the viewpoints of each man regarding the question of slavery. Then pair students to create two political cartoons of Stephen Douglas from a southerner's viewpoint—one that focuses on Douglas before the debates and the other after the debates. Have pairs share their cartoons with the class, explaining how the debates helped and hurt Douglas's career politically. Students may wish to include their political cartoons in their portfolios.

■■ Ask students to recall political debates they have heard in recent times. Ask them to indicate how the debates affected public opinion about the issues debated.

▲ **Robert Marshall Root's painting shows the fourth debate between Lincoln and Douglas, which took place in Charleston, Illinois. Douglas is seated to Lincoln's right.**

Lincoln—like most other aspiring attorneys—learned law by reading textbooks at home. One lawyer who lent Lincoln books said of him:

> 66 He was the most uncouth looking young man I ever saw. He seemed to have but little to say; seemed to feel timid, with a tinge of sadness visible in the countenance, but when he did talk all this disappeared for the time and he demonstrated that he was both strong and acute. He surprised us more and more at every visit. 99

Shortly after he was admitted to the bar, Lincoln moved to Springfield, Illinois. There in 1839 he began courting Mary Todd—"the very creature of excitement," as one young lawyer described her—from a well-to-do Kentucky family. After an on-again, off-again courtship, the couple married on November 4, 1842.

A successful lawyer and persuasive politician, Lincoln was elected in 1846 to the U.S. House of Representatives. While a member of Congress, Lincoln opposed the Mexican War and the slave trade in the District of Columbia. After one term in the House, he returned to practicing law but remained active in Whig party affairs.

Conflict over slavery and the Kansas-Nebraska Act prompted Lincoln's return to public life in 1854, though not as a candidate for office. In October at the Illinois state fairgrounds in Springfield, Lincoln gave a speech attacking the act, which he said would raise slavery to a "sacred right." Later that month, he delivered the speech again in Peoria, Illinois.

17.

THE LINCOLN–DOUGLAS DEBATES

For the next few years, Lincoln continued to speak out against the expansion of slavery, often in behalf of other candidates. He rose within the newly formed Republican party and was selected in 1858 as the party's candidate for the U.S. Senate seat that Douglas held. Lincoln used a quotation from the Bible as the foundation for his acceptance speech at the party's convention: "A house divided against itself cannot stand." The nation, he argued, could not remain divided into slave and free states for long:

> 66 I believe this government cannot endure permanently half slave and half free. I do not expect the Union to be dissolved; I do not expect the house to fall; but I do expect it will cease to be divided. 99

Seeking statewide exposure, Lincoln challenged Douglas to a series of seven debates between August and October 1858. Douglas accepted the challenge but acknowledged that Lincoln was "the best stump speaker in the West." Throngs of people turned out in seven Illinois towns to hear the two men debate the issues of the day.

On the platform the two men presented a startling contrast. Douglas was quite short and often called the "Little Giant." When Lincoln, at nearly 6 1/2 feet, wore the high stovepipe hat then in fashion, he towered over Douglas. Journalists described Lincoln as lank and ungainly but were impressed by his "earnest truthfulness" and "kindly sympathy."

During the debates, Lincoln attacked the *Dred Scott* decision, which seemed to grant broad constitutional protection to slavery: "I do not believe it is a constitutional right to hold slaves in a territory of the United States. I believe the decision was improperly made." Lincoln, like the Republican party, viewed slavery as "a moral, social, and political wrong." Although he was willing to tolerate slavery in the South, he firmly opposed its expansion in the territories.

In the debate at Freeport, Illinois, Lincoln challenged Douglas to explain how popular sovereignty—the method the Kansas-Nebraska Act had provided to settle the slavery issue in the new territories—was still workable in the wake of *Dred Scott.* Douglas replied that the people of a territory could still prohibit slavery simply by refusing to pass the local laws necessary to make a slave system work:

> 66 It matters not what way the Supreme Court may . . . decide. . . . The people have the lawful means to introduce [slavery] or exclude it as they please, for the reason that slavery cannot exist . . . unless it is supported by local police regulations. 99

This argument, which came to be called the **Freeport Doctrine**, helped Douglas narrowly defeat Lincoln in the U.S. Senate race. But in distancing himself from the *Dred Scott* decision, Douglas further damaged his standing with southern slaveholders. (His opposition to the Lecompton Constitution in Kansas had already enraged many southerners.) This proved to be a serious blow to Douglas's bid for the presidency in 1860.

:: The Lincoln-Douglas debates helped Douglas win the U.S. Senate race but hurt his chances of becoming president.

JOHN BROWN'S RAID

The year after the Lincoln-Douglas debates, John Brown, leader of the Pottawatomie Massacre in 1856, again grabbed national attention. This time he set out to free slaves in Virginia. With money obtained from New England abolitionists, Brown armed a band of some 20 men, including 5 blacks. On October 16, 1859, this small force seized the federal arsenal at Harpers Ferry, in what is now West Virginia. Apparently Brown planned to give the guns to slaves living nearby and to establish an independent state in the southern Appalachian Mountains. He hoped to attract both runaway slaves and free African Americans to help him liberate slaves from their masters.

Brown and his followers easily took possession of the armory and rifleworks. However, no slaves came to their aid. On October 18, federal troops under the command of Colonel Robert E. Lee assaulted Brown's position, killing half of his men and capturing the rest.

Brown was convicted of "murder, criminal conspiracy, and treason against the Commonwealth of Virginia" and was hanged on December 2, 1859. Six of his followers were later executed. One of the condemned men, African American John

▲ Thomas Hovenden painted *The Last Moments of John Brown* in 1884. This scene shows Brown being led to his place of execution on December 2, 1859.

The Metropolitan Museum of Art

VOICES IN HISTORY

Many southern slaveholders demanded that John Brown be hanged for his part in the raid on Harpers Ferry. Robert Purvis, an African American abolitionist, took a very different view. To him, Brown "nobly acted what he nobly thought, and sealed by death the lessons which he taught. He believed that the black man was a man, and he laid down his life to secure for him the rights of a man."

PRIMARY SOURCE

Description of Change: excerpted and bracketed
Rationale: excerpted to focus on main idea; bracketed to clarify meaning

ELECTION OF 1860

Create a chart on the chalkboard titled *Election of 1860* with the headings *Candidate, Party, Stand on Issues,* and *States Won*. Call on students to provide entries for the chart. Then ask students to use the chart to draw conclusions about how the election and its results reflected divisions in the nation.

MAKING CONNECTIONS

Literature

Garrison's *Liberator* called Brown's raid "a misguided, wild, and apparently insane effort." However, Herman Melville viewed Brown much as Thoreau did. Melville wrote in his poem "The Portent":

"The cut is on the crown
(Lo, John Brown),
And the stabs shall heal no more."

PRIMARY SOURCE

Description of Change: excerpted and bracketed
Rationale: excerpted to focus on main idea; bracketed to clarify meaning

HISTORICAL SIDELIGHTS

Brown's Warning

John Brown wrote the following note of warning to the nation before he was hanged: "I, John Brown, am now quite certain that the crimes of this guilty land will never be purged away but with blood. I had, as I now think, vainly flattered myself that without much bloodshed it might be done."

PRIMARY SOURCE

Description of Change: excerpted
Rationale: excerpted to focus on main idea

HARPERS FERRY

Reactions to John Brown's attack on Harpers Ferry were mixed, both in the United States and in Europe. William Edward Forster, who became a member of the British Parliament in 1861, sympathized with the abolitionist cause but was surprised by how much fear and conflict arose over Brown's small raid. The extent of the South's violent reaction only strengthened Forster's belief that the slave system would collapse. As Forster said:

THROUGH OTHERS' EYES

66*O*ne fact is quite evident, that whatever John Brown may have done toward freeing the slaves . . . he has exposed the utter weakness of the slave system—Virginia having been as much alarmed by an inroad [raid] of 22 abolitionists and colored men as England would have been by the landing of 22,000 French troops on the coast of Sussex. 99

Copeland, wrote his parents to assure them that he faced death with no regrets:

66 Remember that if I must die I die in trying to liberate a few of my poor and oppressed people from my condition of

servitude. . . . I imagine that I hear you, and all of you, mother, father, sisters, and brothers, say—"No, there is not a cause for which we, with less sorrow, could see you die." 99

Though many people questioned Brown's sanity, abolitionists saw Brown as a hero. Lydia Maria Child, a leading abolitionist writer, offered to help Brown while he was in prison. Henry David Thoreau hailed him as "an angel of light," while Ralph Waldo Emerson declared that Brown was "that new saint . . . [who] will make the gallows glorious like the cross."

In contrast, many southern whites, alarmed by the threat of slave revolts, viewed Brown as a bloodthirsty fanatic who got what he deserved. Southern secessionists, however, were actually pleased by the hysteria, believing that it helped their cause. In Congress, tension ran high. Senator James Hammond of South Carolina noted that "the only persons who do not have a revolver and a knife are those who have two revolvers."

■■ Reactions to John Brown's raid on Harpers Ferry widened the rift between the North and the South.

*T*HE ELECTION OF 1860

Thus divided, the nation approached the presidential election of 1860. Southern moderates, most of whom had been Know-Nothings or Whigs, formed the Constitutional Union party. Nominating John

▲ The 1860 Republican convention nominated Abraham Lincoln of Illinois for president and Hannibal Hamlin of Maine for vice president.

The Lincoln Museum, Fort Wayne, Indiana

354

SECESSION

Have students write newspaper headlines that describe the reaction in the South to the election of 1860. Have volunteers present their headlines. Then ask students to write an article to accompany the headline, providing details about the South's reaction to the election and reasons why the South felt justified in seceding from the Union. Call on volunteers to present their headlines and articles. Students may wish to include their headlines and articles in their portfolios.

▶

Bell of Tennessee for president, they ignored sectional differences and urged Americans to rally around the Constitution and save the Union.

The Democratic convention in Charleston, South Carolina, broke up without nominating a candidate. At a second convention in Baltimore, Stephen Douglas won the nomination he so desired. However, he no longer could count on the backing of southern Democrats, who held their own convention and nominated Senator John Breckinridge of Kentucky. Breckinridge, like many other southerners, interpreted the *Dred Scott* decision to mean that Congress would have to protect slavery in the territories.

The Republicans confidently gathered in Chicago for their nominating convention. Whigs and Know-Nothings, and even some northern Democrats, flocked to the Republican banner. Convinced that a moderate candidate from the

▲ A Lincoln-Hamlin banner and Lincoln medallions commemorate the 1860 presidential election.

Midwest stood the best chance of winning, the convention delegates chose Abraham Lincoln.

The Republican party designed its platform to attract northern industrialists and wage earners as well as midwestern farmers. It opposed slavery in the territories and called for free homesteads for western settlers. It also included federal support for the construction of roads, canals, and a transcontinental railroad and for a tariff to protect industry. Moreover, the platform supported a liberal immigration policy—a measure favored by northern factory owners seeking cheap labor.

The election results mirrored the nation's sectional divisions. Breckinridge carried every state of the Lower South. Three states of the Upper South—Virginia, Kentucky, and Tennessee—went for Bell. Douglas, though second in the popular vote, won only Missouri and three of New Jersey's electoral votes. The remaining New Jersey votes went to Lincoln, along with those of the rest of the northern states, Oregon, and California. Although Lincoln received only about 40 percent of the popular vote, his electoral victory was a landslide: 180 electoral votes to 72 for Breckinridge, 39 for Bell, and 12 for Douglas.

Election of 1860

FRAGMENTED UNION Each section voted its interests, and the result was secession.

? REGION How does the map show you that the vote followed sectional lines?

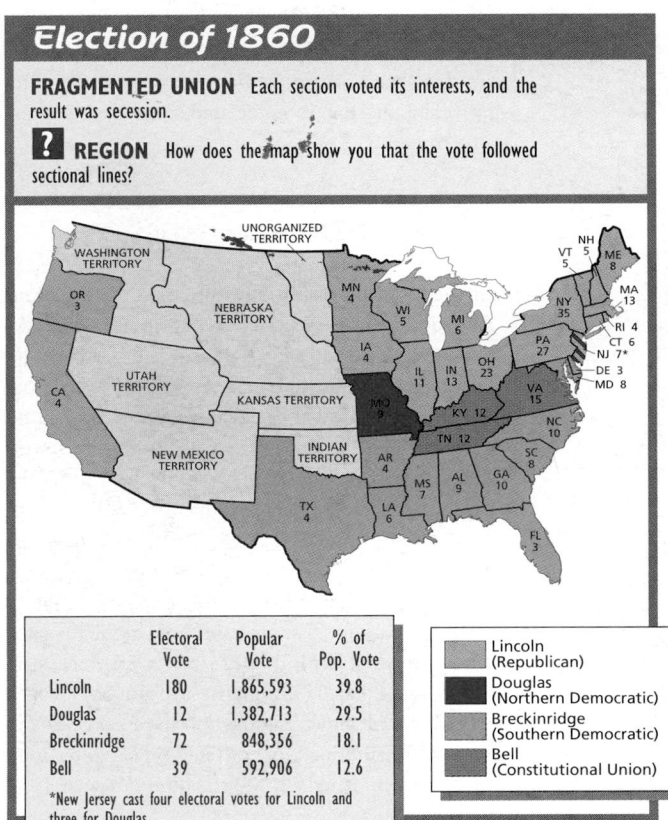

	Electoral Vote	Popular Vote	% of Pop. Vote
Lincoln	180	1,865,593	39.8
Douglas	12	1,382,713	29.5
Breckinridge	72	848,356	18.1
Bell	39	592,906	12.6

*New Jersey cast four electoral votes for Lincoln and three for Douglas.

Lincoln (Republican)
Douglas (Northern Democratic)
Breckinridge (Southern Democratic)
Bell (Constitutional Union)

MAKING CONNECTIONS

Government

Constitutional Unionists, knowing they could not win, wanted to deny Lincoln an electoral majority. With the election thrown into the House, the Unionists hoped to get Bell elected or to combine with other Democrats to elect Breckinridge, who might be forced to modify his extreme views.

HISTORICAL SIDELIGHTS

Lincoln's Beard

Today people are accustomed to seeing pictures of a bearded Lincoln. However, it wasn't until shortly before the 1860 presidential election that Lincoln grew his beard. It seems a clean-shaven Lincoln received a letter from an 11-year-old girl in Westfield, New York. She suggested that he grow a beard, saying that "you would look a great deal better for your face is so thin." Lincoln took her advice.

Map Caption Answer

Lincoln, the Republican candidate of the free-state North, carried the North, while Breckinridge, the Southern Democratic candidate representing southern interests, carried most of the South.

Practice

GUIDED PRACTICE

Call on students to identify and describe events from 1857 to 1861 that led to secession, as you write their responses on the chalkboard.

INDEPENDENT PRACTICE

Instruct students to use their responses in the Guided Practice to create a cause-event-effect flowchart. Ask them to add annotations that suggest what, if anything, might have averted secession at each step in the flowchart. Students may wish to include their flowcharts in their portfolios.

Review and Assessment

REVIEW Ask students to imagine they are northern Republicans or southern Democrats prior to the 1800 election. Have them write a journal entry that summarizes the reasons for Lincoln's growing national stature and expresses their feelings about it. Then assign the Section 3 Review on p. 357.

ASSESS Assign the **Section 3 Daily Quiz** in *Core Resources*.

SECESSION!

The outcome of the election of 1860 mobilized the Lower South. That a president had been elected without winning a single southern state confirmed the South's deepening sense of political powerlessness. Within days of the election, the South Carolina legislature called a convention to consider secession. As onlookers cheered, the delegates unanimously voted for South Carolina to leave the Union. Mississippi, Florida, Alabama, Georgia, Louisiana, and Texas soon passed similar acts of secession.

■■ Seven southern states decided to secede when Lincoln won the presidency.

Early in 1861, delegates from six of the seven seceding states met at Montgomery, Alabama, and drafted a constitution for the Confederate States of America. The Confederate

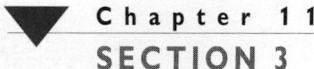

▲ The December 22, 1860, edition of *Harper's Weekly* shows members of the South Carolina delegation who voted to secede from the Union.

Constitution resembled the Constitution of the United States, with two key exceptions: the Confederate Constitution guaranteed the right to own slaves, and it stressed that each state was "sovereign and independent." The delegates chose Jefferson Davis as provisional president of the Confederacy. He won confirmation as president in an election held late in 1861. A Mississippi planter, Davis had formerly served as a U.S. senator and as the secretary of war under Franklin Pierce.

Southern support for secession was far from unanimous. Many who supported slavery and were dismayed by Lincoln's election still could not bring themselves to secede. Even Alexander Stephens, who eventually became vice president of the Confederacy, made an impassioned speech against secession to the Georgia legislature:

> 66 In my judgement, the election of no man, constitutionally chosen to that high office, is sufficient cause for any state to separate from the Union. . . . Whatever fate is to befall this country, let it never be laid to the charge of the people of the South . . . that we were untrue to our national engagements. 99

As the secession movement gained momentum, however, dissenters came under increasing pressure to yield.

CONSTITUTIONAL ISSUES

In the months before he left office, President Buchanan tried to sit on the political fence. As southern states broke from the Union, he announced that no state had the right to secede but also agreed that the federal government had no power to hold a state in the Union against its will. Caught in a dilemma, Buchanan decided to let the incoming president deal with the problem.

The southern secessionists justified their position with the doctrine of states' rights, asserting that since individual states had come together to form the Union, a state had the right to withdraw from the Union. Arguments for secession refined the doctrine originally set forth by Thomas Jefferson and James Madison in the Kentucky and Virginia Resolutions in 1798 and repeated by John C. Calhoun during the nullification crisis in 1832 (see chapters 6 and 7).

RETEACH Divide students into four groups and assign each group one of these questions: What was the Supreme Court's decision and reasoning in the *Dred Scott* case? How did Lincoln and Douglas differ in their views on slavery? Why did John Brown raid Harpers Ferry? What led to the election of a president representing one section of the country? Have groups discuss and answer their questions and then share their responses with the other groups.

Closure

Read this portion of Lincoln's Inaugural Address to students: "We are not enemies, but friends. We must not be enemies. Though passion may have strained, it must not break our bonds of affection. The mystic chords of memory, stretching from every battle-field, and patriot grave, . . . swell the chorus of the Union. . . ." Ask students to react to Lincoln's address from the viewpoint of a northern Republican and of a southern Democrat.

Extension

CREATE Have students collect poems, songs, and descriptions of John Brown's raid and produce a booklet illustrating how Brown became a symbol to different groups in the nation.

INVESTIGATE Have students investigate what happened to Dred Scott after the Supreme Court's ruling in the *Dred Scott* decision.

PRESIDENTIAL LIVES

JAMES BUCHANAN
1791–1868

in office 1857–1861

James Buchanan gave the impression of being exceptionally courteous and attentive to others. Because of his mannerism of tilting his head slightly forward and sideways in conversation to compensate for a defect in one eye, Buchanan appeared to be listening intently to the speaker's every word.

In matters of public debate, Buchanan listened to all sides. By being attentive to all, he hoped to offend no one and thereby stay out of the raging controversy over slavery. Though Buchanan detested slavery, he declared it a matter for the courts to decide, while trying to remain publicly uncommitted on the issue. As Senator Thomas Hart Benton remarked, Buchanan was "never a leading man in any high sense, but [above all] a man of peace."

■■ Southern secessionists argued that since the states had freely joined the Union, they were free to leave it.

Northerners countered this argument by saying that in ratifying the Constitution, the states had agreed to recognize it as the supreme law of the land. There could be no nation if a state were free to withdraw any time it did not like the actions of the federal government or of the majority of states. The Constitution made no provision for states to secede.

The issue went beyond states' rights, however. Also at stake was southern determination to protect slavery. Southerners feared that restricting slavery in the territories would ensure that the slave states remained a minority voting bloc. Then the northern majority in Congress could not only prohibit slavery in the territories but also abolish it in the South.

Northern Republicans, having comfortably won the election, asserted that majority rule was a fundamental principle of republican government. Abraham Lincoln, in his message to a special session of Congress, asserted that the South had to accept the election results. "When ballots have fairly and constitutionally decided," he said, "there can be no successful appeal back to bullets." Many in the South thought otherwise.

SECTION 3 REVIEW

IDENTIFY and explain the significance of the following: *Dred Scott* decision, Abraham Lincoln, Freeport Doctrine, John Bell, John Breckinridge, Jefferson Davis.

1. **MAIN IDEA** What was the Supreme Court's ruling in the *Dred Scott* case? How did it affect the relationship between the North and the South?

2. **MAIN IDEA** How did John Brown's raid affect public opinion in the North and the South? What effect did it have on the relationship between the North and the South?

3. **ASSESSING CONSEQUENCES** Why did the Lincoln-Douglas debates have both positive and negative consequences for Stephen Douglas?

4. **WRITING TO INFORM** Imagine you are a political commentator writing for a southern magazine. Write an article that explains to your readers the arguments the South has used to justify its actions after the election of 1860.

5. **SYNTHESIZING** What arguments did northerners use to counter the principle of secession?

SECTION REVIEW ANSWERS

IDENTIFY
For significance, see the following pages:
Dred Scott *decision (p. 350)*
Abraham Lincoln (p. 351)
Freeport Doctrine (p. 353)
John Bell (p. 355)
John Breckinridge (p. 355)
Jefferson Davis (p. 356)

1. *that slaves were property and had no legal rights, that Congress could not legislate against slavery; intensified the conflict between North and South*
2. *Some northerners praised Brown as a hero or saint; to southerners he was a dangerous fanatic. The raid widened the rift between the North and the South.*
3. *positive—His stand on popular sovereignty, known as the Freeport Doctrine, helped him defeat Lincoln in the U.S. Senate race. negative—By distancing himself from the Dred Scott decision, Douglas lost support of southern slaveholders, which negatively affected his bid for the presidency in 1860.*
4. *Articles should mention states' rights doctrine that held that because the states had freely joined the Union, they had the right to withdraw from it.*
5. *By ratifying the Constitution, states recognized it as supreme law; it had no provision for secession.*

Return to the Themes section on p. 336. Have students discuss these again and compare their original responses with those given now. (See p. 335B for suggested answers.)

Chapter Review Answers

WRITING A SUMMARY
See Essential Points in each section for main ideas.

REVIEWING CHRONOLOGY
3, 2, 4, 1, 5
Synthesizing
Paragraphs might mention battles in Kansas, Dred Scott decision, Lincoln-Douglas debates, and secession of southern states in 1860.

IDENTIFYING PEOPLE AND IDEAS

1. *plan to acquire Cuba*
2. *compromise plan giving settlers power to decide for or against slavery in their territory*
3. *amendment introduced to prohibit slavery in all lands acquired from Mexico*
4. *party formed by antislavery Whigs and Democrats in 1848 that opposed extension of slavery into territories*
5. *wrote* Uncle Tom's Cabin, *a novel that increased northern opposition to slavery*
6. *western explorer who became the first Republican presidential candidate in 1856*
7. *proslavery Supreme Court decision that outraged abolitionists*

8. *Republican whose victory in 1860 presidential election precipitated secession of southern states*
9. *Douglas's doctrine allowing people to exclude slavery from a region by refusing to pass legislation necessary to enforce it*
10. *abolitionist whose attacks at Pottawatomie Creek and Harpers Ferry widened rift between North and South*

UNDERSTANDING MAIN IDEAS
1. *reopened debate over expansion of slavery; extension of Missouri Compromise line, popular sovereignty, Wilmot Proviso, and extension of slavery*

2. *Both Compromise of 1850 and Kansas-Nebraska Act failed to appease those opposing extension of slavery and those demanding legal protection for slavery; Dred Scott decision made it appear there was no way to prevent the expansion of slavery.*
3. *They were debating issues of the day, including the controversial issue of the expansion of slavery.*
4. *Lincoln's victory without winning one southern state made the South feel powerless; states' rights based on states' ratification of Constitution; that by ratifying Constitution, states had recognized it as supreme, and that it contained no provisions for secession*

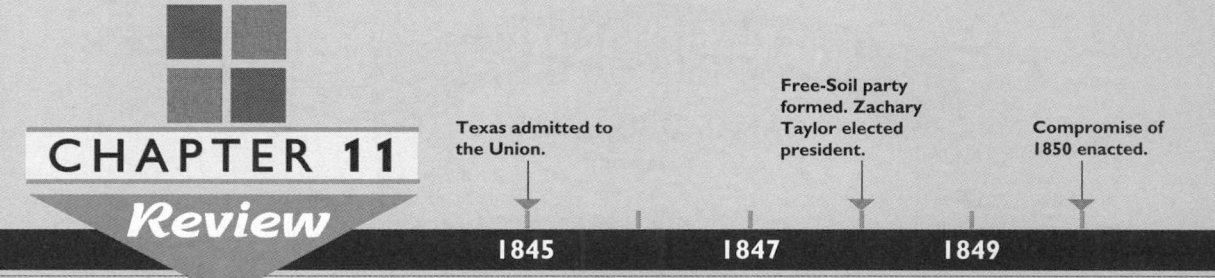

CHAPTER 11
Review

Texas admitted to the Union.

Free-Soil party formed. Zachary Taylor elected president.

Compromise of 1850 enacted.

1845   **1847**   **1849**

WRITING A SUMMARY
Using the essential points of the chapter as a guide, write a summary of the chapter.

REVIEWING CHRONOLOGY
Number your paper 1 to 5. Study the time line above, and list the following events in the order in which they happened by writing the first next to 1, the second next to 2, and so on. Then complete the activity below.

1. Lincoln-Douglas debates take place.
2. Kansas-Nebraska Act passed.
3. Compromise of 1850 enacted.
4. *Dred Scott* case decided.
5. Jefferson Davis elected president of Confederacy.

Synthesizing In a paragraph, provide evidence that neither the Compromise of 1850 nor the Kansas-Nebraska Act settled the issue of slavery in the new territories.

IDENTIFYING PEOPLE AND IDEAS
Explain the historical significance of each of the following people or terms.

1. Ostend Manifesto
2. popular sovereignty
3. Wilmot Proviso
4. Free-Soil party
5. Harriet Beecher Stowe
6. John C. Frémont
7. *Dred Scott* decision
8. Abraham Lincoln
9. Freeport Doctrine
10. John Brown

UNDERSTANDING MAIN IDEAS
1. Why did western expansion cause conflict? How did various members of Congress propose to deal with the issue?
2. How did the Compromise of 1850, the Kansas-Nebraska Act, and the *Dred Scott* decision intensify conflict over slavery?
3. Why did the Lincoln-Douglas debates receive national attention?
4. Why did the presidential election of 1860 lead to southern secession? What constitutional claims did southerners offer to justify secession? What arguments did northerners offer to counter these constitutional claims?

REVIEWING THEMES
1. **Constitutional Heritage** How did the South use constitutional arguments to try to protect its way of life?
2. **Democratic Values** How did Stephen Douglas try to use the principle of majority rule to end the debate over slavery in the territories? What other principle was in conflict?
3. **Geographic Diversity** How did geographic differences between the North and the South affect people's views on the expansion of slavery into the new territories?

THINKING CRITICALLY
1. **Hypothesizing** How might the history of the American political party system have been different if the Democrats or Whigs had taken a strong stand on the slavery issue?
2. **Evaluating** Do you think antislavery northerners were justified in disobeying the Fugitive Slave Act or supporting John Brown? Explain your answer.
3. **Problem Solving** As an aide to Senator Henry Clay in 1850, write a memorandum outlining two creative ways to settle the differences between the North and the South.

STRATEGY FOR SUCCESS
Review the Strategies for Success on Interpreting Editorial Cartoons on page 332. Then study the cartoon on the right, which appeared shortly after Lincoln was elected president. What is the cartoonist's message?

OLD ABE'S UNCOMFORTABLE POSITION
"Oh, it's all well enough to say that I must support the dignity of my high office by force—but it's darned uncomfortable sitting."

The Granger Collection, New York

REVIEWING THEMES

1. South argued that because the Constitution protected property rights and slaves were "property," Congress could not restrict the expansion of slavery.
2. Popular sovereignty would let the majority decide; property rights and the rights of the minority
3. From a region of factories and small farms, Northerners did not understand the needs of the plantation economy. Southerners needed new lands for cotton; they believed their economy could not function without slaves.

THINKING CRITICALLY

1. Students should consider how a strong stand not only might have prevented the formation of new parties but also might have increased sectional tensions between the North and the South.
2. Answers should weigh a group's goals against methods used to achieve those goals.
3. Memos might mention providing economic aid to promote industry in the South, or paying slaveholders for the loss of their slaves through a federal program of gradual emancipation.

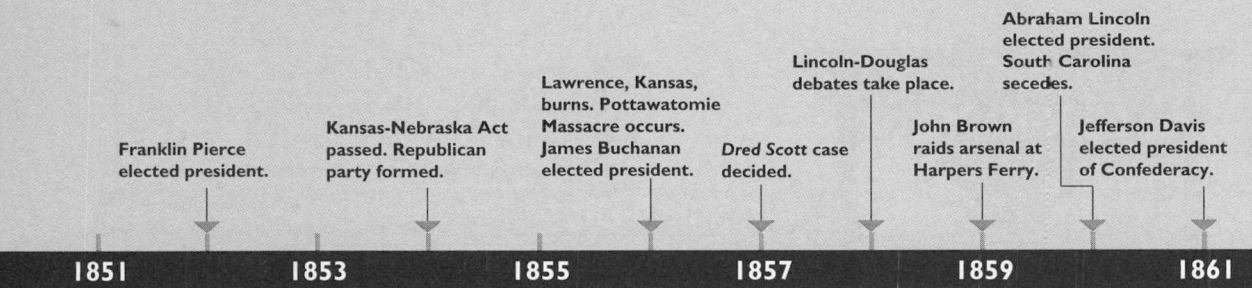

Franklin Pierce elected president.

Kansas-Nebraska Act passed. Republican party formed.

Lawrence, Kansas, burns. Pottawatomie Massacre occurs. James Buchanan elected president.

Dred Scott case decided.

Lincoln-Douglas debates take place.

John Brown raids arsenal at Harpers Ferry.

Abraham Lincoln elected president. South Carolina secedes.

Jefferson Davis elected president of Confederacy.

1851 1853 1855 1857 1859 1861

WRITING ABOUT HISTORY

Writing to Explain Frederick Douglass explained his objections to slavery by saying: "I have held all my life, that the fundamental and everlasting objection to slavery, is not that it sinks a Negro to the condition of a brute, but that it sinks a *man* to that condition." Write a brief essay explaining what Douglass's statement means to you.

USING PRIMARY SOURCES

Shortly after James Buchanan was elected president in 1856, Governor James H. Adams of South Carolina expressed the fears of many southerners that the election had not put to rest the conflict over slavery. Read the following excerpt from his *Governor's Message* of November 24, 1856. Why does Adams believe that further conflict between the North and the South is inevitable?

> 66 *Slavery and Freesoilism can never be reconciled. Our enemies have been defeated—not vanquished. A majority of the free States have declared war against the South, upon a purely sectional issue, and in the remainder of them, formidable minorities fiercely contended for victory under the same banner. The triumph of this geographical party must dissolve the confederacy, unless we are prepared to sink down into a state of acknowledged inferiority. We will act wisely to employ the interval of repose afforded by the late election, in earnest preparation for the inevitable conflict. The Southern States have never demanded more than equality and security. They cannot submit to less, and remain in the Union, without dishonor and ultimate ruin.* 99

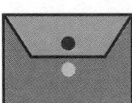

Buchanan campaign button

LINKING HISTORY AND GEOGRAPHY

Daniel Webster said that geography would limit slavery because most of the West was unsuitable for growing cotton. Write a paragraph agreeing or disagreeing with him.

Cotton field

BUILDING YOUR PORTFOLIO

Complete the following projects independently or cooperatively.

1. **SLAVERY** Imagine you are the organizer of one of the Lincoln-Douglas debates. Create a poster announcing the debate, listing highlights of the opponents' careers and summarizing their differing views on extending slavery into western territories.

2. **DEMOCRATIC RIGHTS** Imagine you are a lawyer helping Dred Scott sue for his freedom. Conduct an interview with Scott. Your interview should include questions about the circumstances of Scott's case, his views on how his rights have been violated, and the reasons why he thinks he should be set free.

STRATEGY FOR SUCCESS

Lincoln is shown on a seat of bayonets to dramatize the difficulty he will have keeping the Union together in the face of secession.

WRITING ABOUT HISTORY

Essays might mention that slavery brought out the worst in human nature, both for slaveholder and for slave.

USING PRIMARY SOURCES

Adams believed that the South was a political minority, beset by enemies in free states who would not be satisfied until the South was willing to acknowledge its minority status.

LINKING HISTORY AND GEOGRAPHY

Paragraphs should describe the environment in the West, evaluate its suitability for growing cotton, and explain how this would influence the spread of slavery.

BUILDING YOUR PORTFOLIO

Have students refer to **Building Your Portfolio Worksheet 4**, assigned at the beginning of Unit 4. Use the worksheet to help students monitor their progress on the portfolio projects.

*A*ssessment

Core Resources
• Review Worksheet 11
• Chapter 11 Tests
• Alternative Assessment Forms
Test Generator

REGIONALISM

America's GEOGRAPHY

REGIONALISM

*B*Y the middle of the 19th century, the United States consisted of three distinct regions, each with its own unique character and culture. Some people felt more loyalty to their region than to the nation as a whole. This concept of *regionalism* was particularly evident in the South. Unlike sectionalism, regionalism focuses more on cultural than on political differences. Since regionalism primarily involves cultural identification, the regional identity of some states has shifted as the state's culture has changed. Many residents of Missouri, for instance, identified with the South before the Civil War. In the late 19th century, however, as transportation, trade, and industrialization increased in the state, its culture became closely identified with that of the Midwest.

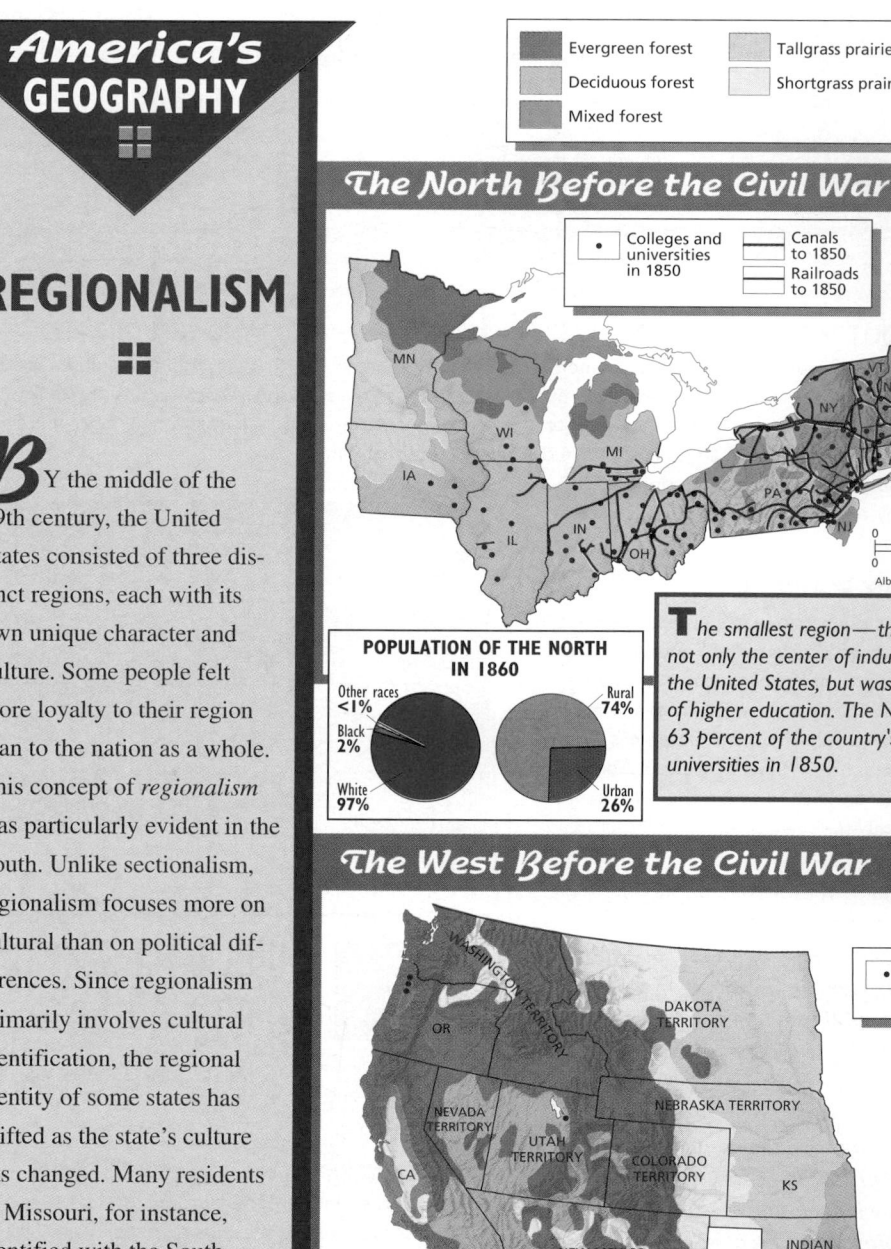

Evergreen forest   Tallgrass prairie   Shrub
Deciduous forest   Shortgrass prairie   Desert
Mixed forest

The North Before the Civil War

- Colleges and universities in 1850
— Canals to 1850
— Railroads to 1850

0   200   400 Miles
0   200   400 Kilometers
Albers Equal-Area Projection

POPULATION OF THE NORTH IN 1860
Other races <1%
Black 2%
White 97%
Rural 74%
Urban 26%

*T*he smallest region—the North—was not only the center of industrialization in the United States, but was also the center of higher education. The North housed 63 percent of the country's colleges and universities in 1850.

The West Before the Civil War

WASHINGTON TERRITORY
OR
DAKOTA TERRITORY
NEVADA TERRITORY
UTAH TERRITORY
COLORADO TERRITORY
NEBRASKA TERRITORY
CA
KS
NEW MEXICO TERRITORY
INDIAN TERRITORY

- Colleges and universities in 1850

0   200 Miles
0   200 Kilometers
Albers Equal-Area Projection

POPULATION OF THE WEST IN 1860*
Native American & other races 9%
Black <1%
White 91%
Rural 86%
Urban 14%
*Does not include Indian Territory.

*W*hile the West was the largest region of the country in 1850, it had the smallest population. Despite the large areas of land available for settlement, the West had a higher percentage of urban-dwellers than did the South as people flocked to cities such as San Francisco. Yet the first centers of education in the West were located on the frontier, not in the cities of California. As California attracted miners and other business-minded people, the Morman settlers of Utah and the followers of the Oregon Trail established the first western Universities.

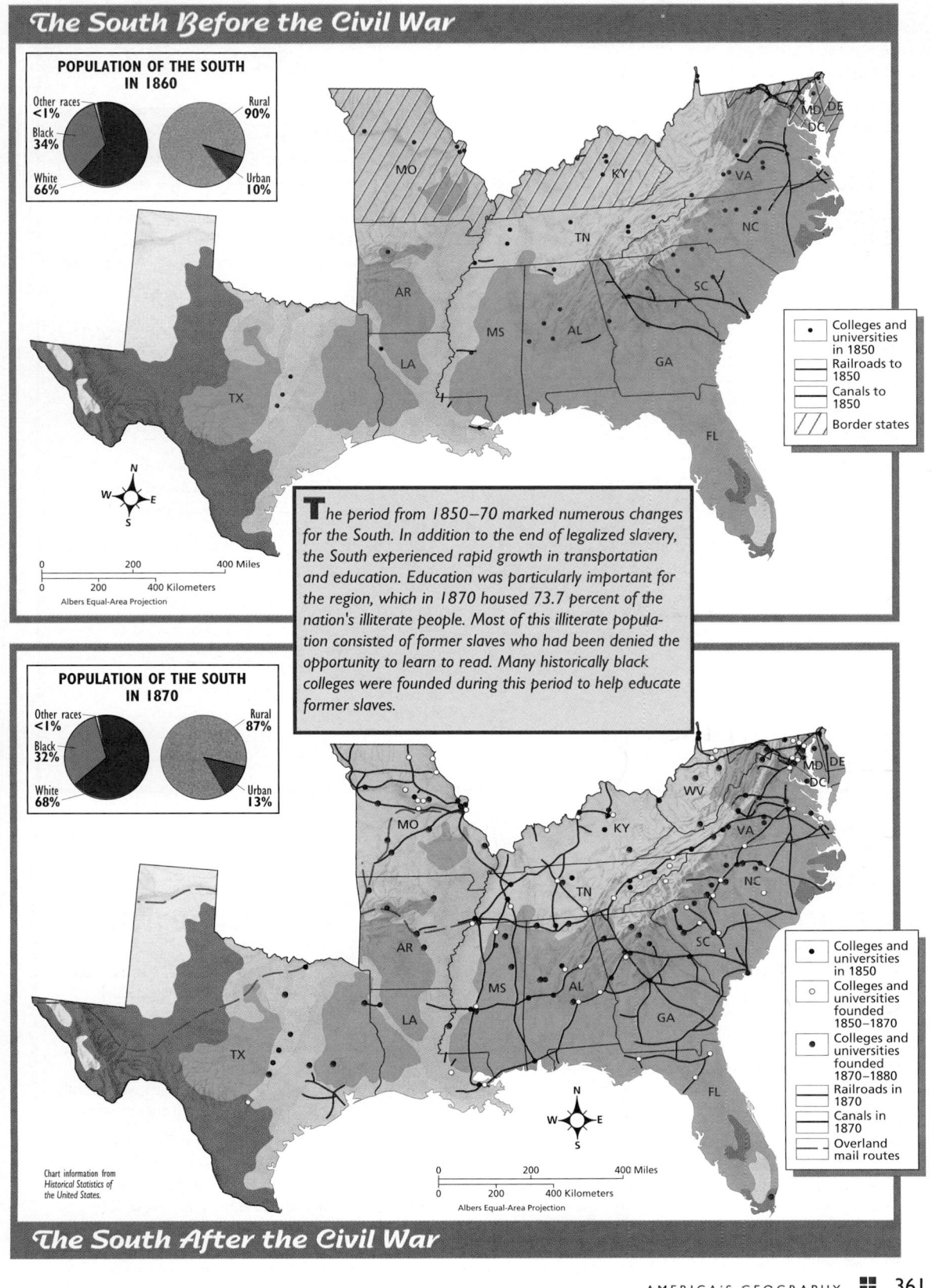

The South Before the Civil War

POPULATION OF THE SOUTH IN 1860

Other races <1%
Black 34%
White 66%
Rural 90%
Urban 10%

Legend:
- Colleges and universities in 1850
- Railroads to 1850
- Canals to 1850
- Border states

N
W E
S

0   200   400 Miles
0   200   400 Kilometers
Albers Equal-Area Projection

MO, KY, VA, TN, NC, AR, SC, MS, AL, GA, LA, TX, FL, MD, DE, DC

The period from 1850–70 marked numerous changes for the South. In addition to the end of legalized slavery, the South experienced rapid growth in transportation and education. Education was particularly important for the region, which in 1870 housed 73.7 percent of the nation's illiterate people. Most of this illiterate population consisted of former slaves who had been denied the opportunity to learn to read. Many historically black colleges were founded during this period to help educate former slaves.

POPULATION OF THE SOUTH IN 1870

Other races <1%
Black 32%
White 68%
Rural 87%
Urban 13%

Chart information from Historical Statistics of the United States.

Legend:
- Colleges and universities in 1850
- Colleges and universities founded 1850–1870
- Colleges and universities founded 1870–1880
- Railroads in 1870
- Canals in 1870
- Overland mail routes

N
W E
S

0   200   400 Miles
0   200   400 Kilometers
Albers Equal-Area Projection

The South After the Civil War

HISTORICAL SIDELIGHTS
Southern Illiteracy

The South's high illiteracy rate was attributable to its economic system. As one Mississippian recalled, "My grandfather—he raised me—figured going to school wouldn't help me pick cotton any better." This legacy of illiteracy continued to plague the South well into the 20th century. In recent years, however, dramatic improvements have been made in southern education. In Georgia, for instance, the number of illiterate citizens dropped by 45 percent between 1960 and 1970, partly because of the state's Adult Basic Education Program.

THE CIVIL WAR

1861–1865

Chapter Overview

Between 1861 and 1865, the country was torn apart by a bloody civil war between the North and the South. The war was especially devastating for the South, where most of the military campaigns took place. Although the South lacked the great industrial, financial, and population resources of the North, its defensive strategy and outstanding military leadership from Robert E. Lee and others led to several early victories for the Confederacy. Ultimately, however, northern forces under Ulysses S. Grant and others brought about a Union victory. In 1865, after four years of fighting, the South surrendered and the Union was restored.

THE AMERICAN NATION VIDEODISC PROGRAM
A variety of still images, short videos, and activities are available for you to use as you teach this chapter. See Correlation to *The American Nation* Videodisc Program for barcode correlations and suggestions for using the program.

Chapter Planning Guide

CHAPTER 12	CORE RESOURCE BOOKLETS	AUDIOVISUAL [AV] RESOURCES	PROGRAM RESOURCES
INTRODUCTION pp. 362–363	■ Building Your Portfolio Worksheet 4	■ Everyday Life in America Transparency and Worksheet 12	■ *Eyewitnesses and Others*, Volume 1: Reading 80
TEACHING THE CHAPTER pp. 364–389	■ Graphic Organizer 12 ■ Social Studies Skills Worksheet 12 ■ Literature Worksheet 12 ■ Geography Worksheet 12 ■ Outline Map 9	■ *The American Nation* Videodisc: Building an Army; The American Red Cross ■ Linking Geography and History Transparency and Worksheet 15	■ Art in American History Transparency and Worksheet 13 ■ *Eyewitnesses and Others*, Volume 1: Readings 78, 79, 81, 82, 83, 84
REVIEW AND ASSESSMENT pp. 390–391	■ Chapter 12 Daily Quizzes ■ Review Worksheet 12 ■ Chapter 12 Tests ■ Alternative Assessment Forms		■ Test Generator

Additional Resources

BOOKS FOR TEACHERS

Foner, Eric and Olivia Mahoney. *A House Divided: America in the Age of Lincoln.* Norton, 1990. Illustrated history of the war years.

McPherson, James M. *Battle Cry of Freedom.* Ballantine, 1989. Historical account of the Civil War.

Sutherland, Daniel E. *The Expansion of Everyday Life, 1860–1876.* HarperCollins, 1990. Social history from 1860 to 1876.

BOOKS FOR STUDENTS

McPherson, James M. *Marching Toward Freedom: Blacks in the Civil War, 1861–1865.* Facts on File, 1990. African Americans in the Civil War.

*Meltzer, Milton. *Voices from the Civil War.* HarperCollins, 1990. First-person accounts of the war experience.

* Ray, Delia. *Behind the Blue and Gray.* Dutton, 1991. The daily life of soldiers in the Civil War.

* for students reading below grade level

MULTIMEDIA MATERIALS

The Civil War. 9 videos, 11 hrs. PBS. Award-winning series on Civil War.

The Civil War Generals Series. 3 videos, 30 min. each. Atlas Video/SSSS. Biographies of generals Lee, Jackson, and Grant.

A Nation Asunder. 2 videos, 55 min. each. SSSS. Traces war from Fort Sumter to surrender at Appomattox.

THEMES IN AMERICAN HISTORY

USE WITH PAGES 362–363

Listed on the right are the themes emphasized in Chapter 12. The questions in boldface type stimulate critical thinking and provide students with an opportunity to discuss the themes within a broadened context. The questions also appear in the pupil's edition on p. 362.

■ GEOGRAPHIC DIVERSITY

How might geography help or hinder a war effort? Students might note that military tactics in a war, campaign, or battle are often linked to geographic features such as terrain or vegetation. They might consider the importance of rivers as a barrier to attack or in transporting troops. Also, the capture of a river could divide enemy territory or block the enemy's access to important ports. Rough terrain could make the fighting of a battle more difficult. Proximity of strategic enemy sites might make it easier to fight the war, since armies would not have to travel long distances or bring large areas under control.

■ ECONOMIC DEVELOPMENT

What positive and negative effects might war have on a nation's economy? Students should consider that nations at war might have to increase and redirect industrial production to provide needed equipment and supplies. Agricultural production might be similarly affected, and transportation systems might be expanded. On the other hand, war might destroy factories, crops, and infrastructure crucial to an economy. Thousands of people who previously contributed to the economy might be killed or permanently disabled.

CHAPTER STRATEGIES FOR MEETING INDIVIDUAL NEEDS

LIMITED ENGLISH PROFICIENT LEARNERS

Have pairs of students pick visuals from each section and explain to the class how each visual relates to the main ideas of the lesson.

TACTILE/KINESTHETIC LEARNERS

Direct students to create a series of military briefings for the media, tracking the course of the war from the First Battle of Bull Run to Appomattox. Encourage students to refer to wall maps in their briefings.

LEARNERS HAVING DIFFICULTY

Direct students to work in pairs to pick three events in each section that they consider important and to write two or three sentences explaining the importance of each event. As a class, create a time line showing all the events.

AUDITORY LEARNERS

Direct students to select a quotation from each section and write an introduction to the quote, explaining its subject, its source, and its relationship to the section. Have students read their selections and introductions to the class.

VISUAL LEARNERS

Organize students into four groups to create a photo documentary of the Civil War. Assign each group one of the chapter's sections and have students research books containing photographs that relate to their assigned section. Have groups bring their selections to class and present them.

GIFTED LEARNERS

Have students write a speech that Abraham Lincoln might have given if he had lived to see the end of the Civil War.

USING THE CHAPTER FOCUS

■ UNDERSTANDING THE MAIN IDEA

Call on a volunteer to read aloud the Understanding the Main Idea paragraph. Drawing on what they have learned in previous chapters, ask students to describe the advantages of the North and the South at the onset of the Civil War. Write responses on the chalkboard. Then have students suggest reasons for the advantages each side held and make predictions about the strategies each might use. Keep a copy of the predictions for review and further discussion after completing the chapter.

■ THEMES

Have students work individually or in groups to answer the questions under Themes. Save students' responses so they can compare them with their responses after studying the chapter. (See p. 361B for suggested answers.)

■ THE TIME LINE

Have students copy the time-line entries in their notebooks. After they read in the chapter about each time-line entry, have them write a paragraph explaining the event's significance.

CORE RESOURCES

- **Graphic Organizer 12**
- **Social Studies Skills Worksheet 12**
- **Outline Map 9**
- **Building Your Portfolio Worksheet 4**

AV RESOURCES

- **Everyday Life in America Transparency and Worksheet 12**

ABOUT THE ILLUSTRATION

Chattanooga, Tennessee's location and value to the South as an industrial center made it a target of Union strategy. In September 1863 Union general William Rosecrans took the city with little resistance. However, Confederate general Braxton Bragg positioned his forces on hills around Chattanooga and trapped Rosecrans's army. In November, Union general Ulysses S. Grant arrived to lift the siege of the city. In a fierce three-day battle, Grant's forces and troops from within Chattanooga defeated Bragg and opened the way for the Union to divide the South through Georgia. Have students study the illustration and assess the role that geography played in this battle. Ask how the illustration conveys a sense of the battle's intensity.

Chapter 12

THE CIVIL WAR

1861–1865

FOCUS

UNDERSTANDING THE MAIN IDEA

The Civil War dragged on far longer than anyone anticipated in 1861. The North was more populated and more heavily industrialized than the South, which was mostly agricultural. Consequently, the North was better prepared to fight a long war. Though the defensive strategy and superior military leadership of the South enabled it to win most of the early battles, the Confederacy was unable to overcome the staying power of the resourceful Union forces.

THEMES

■ **GEOGRAPHIC DIVERSITY** How might geography help or hinder a war effort?

■ **ECONOMIC DEVELOPMENT** What positive and negative effects might war have on a nation's economy?

1861	1862	1863	1864	1865
Fort Sumter falls.	Peninsula Campaign fails for North.	Emancipation Proclamation goes into effect.	Atlanta falls.	Lee surrenders at Appomattox.

LINK TO THE PAST

Call on volunteers to list on the chalkboard the key points of the Missouri Compromise. Have a volunteer explain why the North and the South had been willing to compromise at that time but by 1861 were once again approaching a crisis.

■ LINK TO THE PAST

The Missouri Compromise and the Compromise of 1850 had each proved only temporary solutions to the slavery issue. The Fugitive Slave and Kansas-Nebraska acts and the Supreme Court's Dred Scott decision soon reignited tensions between the North and the South. Republican Abraham Lincoln's victory in the 1860 presidential election brought the crisis to a head.

The Battle of Chattanooga, 1863

The Granger Collection, New York

On April 15, 1861, President Abraham Lincoln declared that the nation faced an armed revolt. Mary Ashton Livermore, who would soon join the war effort as a volunteer for the United States Sanitary Commission, recorded the reaction in Boston to the president's call to arms:

66 Monday dawned, April 15. Who that saw that day will ever forget it! For now . . . there rang out the voice of Abraham Lincoln calling for seventy-five thousand volunteers for three months. They were for the protection of Washington and the property of the government. . . . This proclamation was like the first peal of a surcharged thunder-cloud, clearing the murky air. The . . . whole North arose as one man. . . .

Hastily formed companies marched to camps of rendezvous, the sunlight flashing from gun-barrel and bayonet. . . . Merchants and clerks rushed out from stores, bareheaded, saluting them as they passed. Windows were flung up; and women leaned out into the rain, waving flags and handkerchiefs. Horse-cars and omnibuses halted for the passage of the soldiers, and cheer upon cheer leaped forth from [their] thronged doors and windows. . . .

I had never seen anything like this before. I had never dreamed that New England . . . could be fired with so warlike a spirit. 99

Union drum with federal eagle insignia

This "warlike spirit" pervaded the nation in early 1861. Amid the excitement, few Americans imagined the death and destruction that lay ahead.

HISTORICAL SIDELIGHTS

Raising an Army

Lincoln's call for recruits was met with an avalanche of volunteers. For example, Ohio was asked for 13 regiments but had enough volunteers for 20. The town of Flint, Michigan, had enough troops for its own regiment. The nation's immigrants formed units of Irish, Italian, and German volunteers. In New York City, some men showed support for the Union by wearing postage stamps on their hats. Some women sewed red, white, and blue ribbons on their bonnets.

PRIMARY SOURCE

Description of Change: excerpted and bracketed
Rationale: excerpted to focus on main idea; bracketed to clarify meaning

Introducing the Section

FOCUS OBJECTIVES

■ Identify some of the effects of the fall of Fort Sumter.

■ Analyze the military advantages each side possessed at the beginning of the war.

■ Explain how the draft laws affected who fought the war.

■ Describe how women contributed to the war effort.

PRIMARY SOURCE

Description of Change: excerpted

Rationale: excerpted to focus on main idea

CORE RESOURCES

• **Section 1 Daily Quiz**

AV RESOURCES

• *The American Nation* **Videodisc: Building an Army; The American Red Cross**

364

PREVIEW WORKSHOP

Following is a list of the significant people, places, and terms in this section. You may wish to use this list as a section preview.

People
■ Robert Anderson
■ Robert E. Lee
■ nuns of the battlefield
■ Elizabeth Blackwell

■ Clara Barton
■ Sally Louisa Tompkins

Places
■ Fort Sumter
■ Richmond, Virginia
■ West Virginia

Terms
■ Crittenden Compromise
■ conscription

Section 1

THE UNION DISSOLVES!

FOCUS

■ **What were some of the effects of the fall of Fort Sumter?**

■ **What military advantages did each side possess at the beginning of the war?**

■ **How did the draft laws affect who fought the war?**

■ **How did women contribute to the war effort?**

*W*hen President Abraham Lincoln took office in 1861, the nation was on the brink of collapse. The situation came to a head with the fall of Fort Sumter to the Confederates in April 1861. As war became inevitable, both sides prepared for what they believed would be a short conflict.

The Spirit of '61 recruiting poster

LAST ATTEMPTS AT COMPROMISE

By Abraham Lincoln's inauguration on March 4, 1861, seven southern states had seceded from the Union: South Carolina, Mississippi, Florida, Alabama, Georgia, Louisiana, and Texas. But the debate over secession was far from settled in the border states of the Upper South. The slave states of Delaware, Missouri, Kentucky, and Maryland all had strong economic ties to the North.

To save the Union, Senator John J. Crittenden of Kentucky proposed the **Crittenden Compromise**. The plan called for the Missouri Compromise line to be drawn west through the remaining territories. North of the line, slavery would be illegal; south of the line, slavery could expand. Lincoln quickly rejected the plan. "No spread of slavery" was the principle that held the Republican party together. Many Republicans might have turned against Lincoln if he had allowed slavery to

▲ John J. Crittenden

expand. Lincoln was willing, however, to support another part of Crittenden's plan—that slavery be protected where it already existed.

Lincoln's gesture had little effect on the secessionists, who were caught up in the excitement of creating a new nation. "It is a revolution . . . of the most intense character," wrote one southern senator. "It can no more be checked by human effort, for the time, than a prairie fire by a gardener's watering pot."

The new president was determined to preserve the Union. In his inaugural address, Lincoln was firm but cordial when he reminded southerners that secession was unconstitutional: "No State upon its own mere motion can lawfully get out of the Union." As president, he was bound to enforce the Constitution in every state. Lincoln added:

❝ There needs to be no bloodshed or violence; and there shall be none, unless it be forced upon the national authority. . . .

Teaching the Section

FORT SUMTER FALLS

Have students work in small groups to create a five-minute "TV news bulletin" on the fall of Fort Sumter. Each "bulletin" should include a report on the location of the fort; an analysis of its strategic importance to the North and the South; a background report by a Washington correspondent on Lincoln's attempts to avert a confrontation; an interview with an eyewitness to the bombardment of the fort; and predictions of the effects of the fort's fall on the Union. Have each group "broadcast" its "bulletin" during the class.

In your hands, my dissatisfied fellow countrymen, and not in mine, is the momentous issue of civil war. The government will not assail you. You can have no conflict without being yourselves the aggressors. 99

THE FALL OF FORT SUMTER

The "dissatisfied countrymen" had already demonstrated their intentions. Meeting little resistance, the Confederacy had taken over most federal forts, mints, and arsenals within its borders. However, one fort very important to the South—Fort Sumter—remained under federal control.

Fort Sumter was strategically located in the harbor of Charleston, South Carolina. The South needed the fort in order to control access to this major port city. By early March the fort's commander, Major Robert Anderson, had notified Washington that he was nearly out of supplies. Without reinforcements Sumter would soon fall to the Confederates.

The North did not want to lose the fort—it would be an admission that South Carolina was truly out of the Union. Yet Lincoln was hesitant to use force, fearing the reaction of the eight slave states that were still part of the Union. The leaders of several of these states had said that their states, too, would secede if Lincoln used force against the Confederacy.

To do nothing, however, would signify weakness. Thus, Lincoln decided to resupply Fort Sumter. If the Confederates fired on unarmed supply ships, they, not the Union, would be the aggressors.

On April 6 Lincoln sent a messenger to warn the South Carolina governor, F. W. Pickens, that supply ships were on their way. The messenger assured the governor that the ships were carrying only supplies, not troops or arms. Governor Pickens relayed the message to General P.G.T. Beauregard, local military commander of the Confederates. General Beauregard responded by ordering the federal troops to evacuate the fort. Major Anderson refused to obey the order.

At 4:30 A.M. on April 12 the Confederate forces opened fire on Fort Sumter. Abner Doubleday, Anderson's second-in-command, described the scene within the fort:

▲ The firing on Fort Sumter on April 12, 1861, marked the beginning of four long, bloody years of war.

66 Showers of balls . . . and shells . . . poured into the fort in one incessant stream, causing great flakes of masonry to fall in all directions. When the immense mortar shells, after sailing high in the air, came down in a vertical direction and buried themselves in the parade ground, their explosion shook the fort like an earthquake. 99

For 34 hours the Confederates bombarded Sumter. Finally, with much of the fort ablaze and their ammunition running low, Anderson and his men formally surrendered on April 14. Surprisingly, no one on either side was killed or seriously wounded during the fighting.

On April 15 Lincoln publicly proclaimed the existence of a rebellion "too powerful to be suppressed by the ordinary course of judicial proceedings." He asked the governors of the loyal states to provide 75,000 militiamen to put down the uprising. The recruits were to serve for just three months.

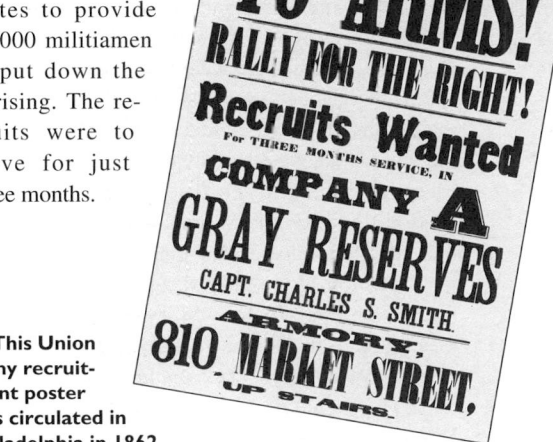

▶ This Union army recruitment poster was circulated in Philadelphia in 1862.

TO ARMS!
RALLY FOR THE RIGHT!
Recruits Wanted
For THREE MONTHS SERVICE, IN
COMPANY A
GRAY RESERVES
CAPT. CHARLES S. SMITH.
ARMORY,
810 MARKET STREET,
UP STAIRS.

PRIMARY SOURCE
Description of Change: excerpted
Rationale: excerpted to focus on main idea

VOICES IN HISTORY

Although the North refused to enlist African Americans on a large scale until 1863, a few African Americans did serve in some of the war's early campaigns. William H. Johnson, who fought in the First Battle of Bull Run, argued that if African Americans contributed to the war, they should demand that the government do more to protect their civil rights. In August 1861 he wrote: "There is much talk in high places and by leading men, of a call being made for the blacks of the North . . . to enter the army. . . . Shall we do it? Not until our rights as men are acknowledged by the government in good faith. We desire to free the slaves . . . but we must bide our own time, and choose the manner by which it shall be accomplished."

Teaching the *Section*

CHOOSING SIDES

Organize students into small groups. Ask them to study the map on p. 366 and reread the text under the heading "Choosing Sides." Have groups determine why Delaware, Missouri, Kentucky, Maryland, and northwestern Virginia were geographically vital to the Union and discuss the positions each took toward secession. Close by asking students why Maryland was particularly vital to the Union.

HISTORICAL SIDELIGHTS

Northern Firepower
The North not only outnumbered the South but also outgunned it. In 1860 New England manufactured more than $2 million worth of firearms, 60 times as much as the entire South.

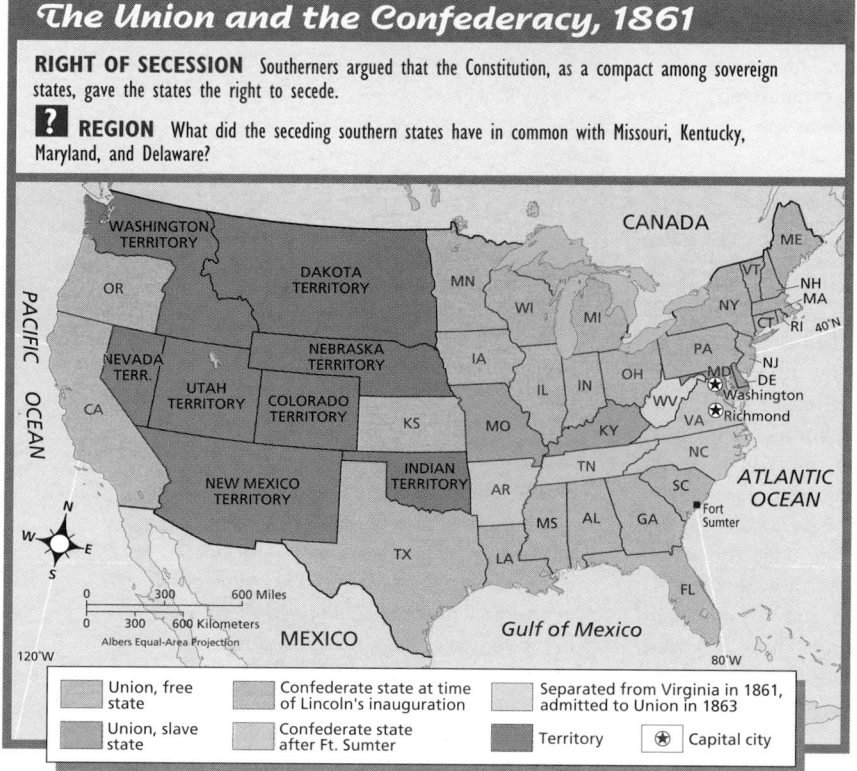

The Union and the Confederacy, 1861

RIGHT OF SECESSION Southerners argued that the Constitution, as a compact among sovereign states, gave the states the right to secede.

? **REGION** What did the seceding southern states have in common with Missouri, Kentucky, Maryland, and Delaware?

Legend:
- Union, free state
- Union, slave state
- Confederate state at time of Lincoln's inauguration
- Confederate state after Ft. Sumter
- Separated from Virginia in 1861, admitted to Union in 1863
- Territory
- ✪ Capital city

CHOOSING SIDES

Lincoln's fear of losing more states to the Confederacy quickly became a reality. Four states—Virginia, Arkansas, Tennessee, and North Carolina—responded to the president's call for troops by seceding. Richmond, Virginia, became the Confederate capital.

Four other slave states—Delaware, Missouri, Kentucky, and Maryland—remained within the Union. Secession was never a serious threat in Delaware, where there were few slaves; Delaware sympathized much more with the North than with the South. Missouri, Kentucky, and Maryland, on the other hand, were sharply divided over the issue of secession. Though the governors of both Missouri and Kentucky supported secession, neither state voted to secede. Lincoln kept Maryland in the Union by quickly securing the state with federal troops. To lose Maryland would have meant to lose the Union capital, since the state surrounded Washington, D.C., on three sides.

The mountainous counties of northwestern Virginia remained loyal to the Union as well. The people there held few slaves and had long resented the rich planter elite of the lowlands. They set up their own state government, and in 1863 the state was admitted to the Union as West Virginia.

The people of the Upper South remained divided over the issue of secession. As a result, sections of several southern states raised Union regiments to fight fellow southerners. Some families were torn apart as members fought for different sides in the war. One of John Crittenden's sons became a Union general, and another became a Confederate general. Lincoln's wife, Mary Todd, a southerner by birth, had four brothers and three brothers-in-law fighting in the Confederate army.

■■ **The fall of Fort Sumter brought on war, forcing the border states to choose sides.**

COMPARING NORTH AND SOUTH

On the face of it, the war that loomed after the fall of Fort Sumter seemed a complete mismatch. The North—with more than 22 million people—had a huge advantage in population. The South's population was only slightly more than 9 million, of whom some 3.5 million were slaves. As a result, the South had a much smaller pool of available soldiers.

The North also enjoyed an economic advantage. When the war began, the North had over 85 percent of the nation's industries and almost all the known supplies of gold, iron, copper, and other metals. With such resources the North could produce war products and replace lost or damaged

MILITARY ADVANTAGES

Have students work in small groups as northern or southern military strategists. Have each group draw up a list of its own strengths and weaknesses and its opponent's strengths and weaknesses. When lists are complete, have each group speculate on how it can best utilize its strengths and compensate for its weaknesses and how it can defend against its opponent's strengths and take advantage of any weaknesses.

Have groups put their recommendations in a strategy position paper and choose a spokesperson to read it to the class.

▶

equipment faster than the Confederacy could. Southern wealth was largely in land and slaves.

In addition, most of the nation's railroad lines were located in the Northeast and the Midwest. Thus, the Union could move troops and supplies at will. Southern routes, on the other hand, were roundabout, with few connecting lines. Furthermore, because the North manufactured most of the nation's railway equipment, the Confederacy found it increasingly difficult during the war to replace broken or worn-out railway parts and equipment.

The North also held overwhelming superiority at sea. Most of the U.S. Navy remained loyal to the Union, including such southern naval officers as David Farragut and Percival Drayton. Lacking the expertise of such experienced naval men and with no ships or submarines, the South had to build its navy from scratch.

The South, however, did have two main advantages over the North. To win, the Confederacy had only to fight a defensive war, protecting its territory until the Union tired of the struggle. The Union, on the other hand, had to conquer an area almost as large as Western Europe. The South also had excellent military

RESOURCES OF THE NORTH AND SOUTH, 1861

	North	South
Total Population	22,000,000	9,000,000*
Bank Deposits	$189,000,000	$47,000,000
Railroad Mileage	20,000 miles	9,000 miles
Number of Factories	100,500	20,600

* Southern population includes 3,500,000 slaves.

Source: *American Heritage Picture History of the Civil War, Encyclopedia of American History*

NORTH vs. SOUTH At the beginning of the Civil War, the North's abundant resources gave it a military advantage over the South.

? EVALUATING Which resource do you think had the greatest influence on the outcome of the Civil War? Why?

leadership. In fact, most southern victories resulted from the battle strategies of skillful Confederate officers.

■■ **The North had numerical and economic advantages in the war, but the South had the advantage of fighting on its own soil with skilled military leaders.**

GLOBAL CONNECTIONS

In May 1861 Britain's Prime Minister Viscount Palmerston expressed his country's attitude toward intervention in the war by quoting this rhyme:

"They who in quarrels interpose,
Will often get a bloody nose."

Students might compare this response to the American Civil War with the attitudes of U.S. politicians toward civil wars in Bosnia and Somalia in the 1990s.

THE CIVIL WAR

THROUGH OTHERS' EYES

The nations of Europe had their own aims and expectations with respect to the American Civil War. Judging that a divided United States would be less of a threat to Europe, France and England hoped the South would win. Sir Edward Bulwer-Lytton, a member of Parliament, remarked that a Confederate victory would "be attended with happy results to the safety of Europe." Believing that it was already too late to save the Union, Bulwer-Lytton noted that a united America "would have hung over Europe like a . . . thunder-cloud. No single kingdom in Europe could have been strong enough to maintain itself against a nation that had once consolidated the gigantic resources of a quarter of the globe."

Russia, on the other hand, supported the Union. Russia wanted to keep America united and strong—to help keep Great Britain and France in check and thereby maintain a balance of power in the world. Russian foreign minister Prince Gortchakov remarked to a U.S. diplomat: "We are very, very anxious . . . that any course should be pursued which will prevent the division. . . . One separation will be followed by another; you will break into fragments. You know the sentiments of Russia! We desire, above all things, the maintenance of the American Union as one indivisible nation."

Teaching the Section

DRAFT LAWS, NORTH AND SOUTH

Draw a chart on the chalkboard to contrast the Union and Confederate draft laws. Have volunteers list the date of each law, its exemptions, the rationales behind each, and the reactions of northerners and southerners to the draft. Have students suggest reasons why draft riots did not break out in the South. *(Students may suggest that many southerners recognized the need to maintain the plantation system as vital to the war's outcome.)*

▪▪ Ask students how Americans today might react to draft laws with similar exemptions.

WOMEN AND THE WAR

Have students work in pairs to create patriotic posters that celebrate women's roles in the Civil War. Tell students that the text and illustrations for their posters should inspire other women to contribute to the war effort. Have pairs explain their posters to the class.

PERSONALITIES IN HISTORY

Ask the class to cite evidence of what Lee calls his "devotion to the Union" *(long and distinguished military career)* and explain why he refused command of the Union army. *(His loyalty to his state was greater than his loyalty to the nation.)*

BUILDING VOCABULARY

The word *draft* comes from a verb meaning "to draw or pull." The term *draftee* refers to a person drafted into the army.

PRIMARY SOURCE

Description of Change: excerpted
Rationale: excerpted to focus on main idea

THE AMERICAN NATION VIDEODISC PROGRAM

Building an Army

```
1B    00600    4:27
```

Among the ablest of southern military leaders was Robert Edward Lee, who was born into a leading Virginia family in 1807. His father was Henry "Light-Horse Harry" Lee, a Revolutionary War hero. The young Robert excelled as a student at West Point. After graduating in 1829, he went on to serve first in the Army Corps of Engineers and then in the cavalry. In 1831 the young officer married Mary Custis, the great-granddaughter of Martha Washington.

Testing his military skills during the Mexican War, Lee served as a captain under General Winfield Scott and took part in the capture of Veracruz. Then in 1859, he led the federal troops that captured John Brown at Harpers Ferry.

Collection of the Corcoran Gallery of Art

Robert E. Lee

On Winfield Scott's recommendation, President Lincoln asked Lee to command the Union forces. Lee declined, resigning his commission. Although he opposed slavery and secession, he could not fight against Virginia. In a letter to his sister, he wrote:

❝ With all my devotion to the Union and the feeling of loyalty and duty of an American citizen, I have not been able to make up my mind to raise my hand against my relatives, my children, my home. I have therefore resigned my commission in the Army, and save in defense of my native State—with the sincere hope that my poor services may never be needed—I hope I may never be called on to draw my sword. ❞

Lee's wish would not be granted.

THE ARMIES

By the end of 1861, the Union had more than 527,000 soldiers, the Confederacy slightly more than 258,000. Most of these soldiers were between the ages of 18 and 29, with drummer boys as young as 9. All social classes fought, but a Confederate **conscription**, or draft, act in April 1862—the first draft law in American history—and a Union law in March 1863 put the major burden on poor farmers and working people. Wealthy men who were drafted could hire a substitute to serve for them or pay the government to be exempted from service.

In the South, anyone owning 20 or more slaves was exempt. This policy was a response to pressure from the planter class, who argued that some slaveholders had to remain at home to keep their slaves from running off. The exemption was also rooted in economics. The Confederacy needed

▶ Drummer boys not only provided music for daily calls and drills, but they also carried water, sold food to soldiers, and assisted in burying the dead.

▲ Confederate soldiers practice artillery-loading techniques near Charleston, South Carolina, in 1863.

Practice

GUIDED PRACTICE

Have volunteers identify causes and effects of the southern takeover of Fort Sumter and organize them in a diagram on the chalkboard. Discuss why Fort Sumter was symbolic in the struggle over the continuing dissolution of the Union.

INDEPENDENT PRACTICE

Have students write newspaper editorials trying to persuade citizens of a border state to remain in the Union or to secede after the fall of Fort Sumter. Suggest that editorials stress the consequences (positive or negative according to the writer's allegiance) of secession for the Union, for the South, for the state, and for individual citizens.

Review and Assessment

REVIEW Have students work in pairs to write short summaries of each of the six subsections of Section 1. Then group each pair with another pair, and ask the foursome to review each other's summaries, looking for key points that may have been missed. Then assign the Section 1 Review on p. 370.

ASSESS Assign the **Section 1 Daily Quiz** in *Core Resources*.

▶

food and cloth, but few southerners believed slaves would work without constant supervision.

The exemptions caused much resentment in both the North and the South. In the North, poor whites, many of them recent immigrants, rioted in protest. Draft riots did not break out in the South, but many whites openly criticized the draft, claiming it proved the conflict was a "rich man's war and a poor man's fight."

But resisting the war was not typical of either side. Estimates of how many men fought for the North vary because many men enlisted more than once. The U.S. government places the official wartime enlistment in the Union army at 2,672,341, with another 105,963 men enlisted in the navy or marines. Of the army's total, the government holds that some 180,000 enlistees were African Americans (of whom some 7,000 were noncommissioned officers and about 100 were commissioned officers) and that 3,530 were American Indians.

Estimates of the number of Confederate enlistments stir even greater debate, but probably some 750,000 men enlisted in the Confederate army. Included in this number are some 5,500 Cherokees, Creeks, Chickasaws, and Choctaws, many of them slaveholders lured by the promise of an all-Indian state following the war. Mexican Americans from New Mexico and Texas fought on both sides during the war.

■■ **Both sides relied on volunteers and draftees to fight the war. Most soldiers were poor farmers and laborers.**

WOMEN AND THE WAR

Women in the North and in the South threw themselves into the war effort. Some women even dressed like men so that they could fight. Cuban-born Loreta Janeta Velázquez (vay-LAHS-kays) disguised herself as a man and enlisted in the Confederate army. When she was found out for the third time and discharged, she became a spy for the South. A few other women also served as spies. Rose O'Neal Greenhow was imprisoned by the North for supplying information to the Confederacy. Elizabeth Bowser, a maid in Confederate president Jefferson Davis's home, and Harriet Tubman both supplied information to the Union from behind enemy lines.

▲ African American soldiers joined the Union cause in order to "assert their claim to freedom." Recruitment posters often were directed specifically to African Americans. The banner of the Third United States Colored Troops (bottom left) contains the slogan "Rather die Freeman than Live to be Slaves." (Image of soldier is detailed from the original photograph.)

Many more women served in medical roles. The first group of women to volunteer for medical duty were Catholic nuns, who transformed their convents into emergency hospitals throughout the North and South. Most of these neutral "nuns of the battlefield" were Irish or German immigrants. They treated all victims of the war, becoming the only group recognized by both Union and Confederate forces.

In the North, Elizabeth Blackwell, America's first professionally licensed female doctor, helped run the U.S. Sanitary Commission. The commission worked to battle the diseases and infections that killed twice as many soldiers as bullets alone. Approximately 3,000 women served in the Union army as nurses. Some, like Clara Barton, ministered to the wounded on the battlefield. After the war, Barton founded the American Red Cross, which today serves disaster victims and others in need of assistance all over the world.

HISTORICAL SIDELIGHTS

Women Warriors

About 400 women joined the army by pretending to be men. Most were discovered when they were wounded and sent to a hospital, but some went undetected for several years.

MAKING CONNECTIONS

Economics

In the South, people found clever ways to compensate for wartime shortages caused by the northern naval blockade. Women used the sap of berries for medicine, hog bristles for needles, okra or acorns for coffee, raspberry leaves for tea, cottonseed oil and ground peas for kerosene.

THE AMERICAN NATION VIDEODISC PROGRAM

The American Red Cross

1B   49210   :45

RETEACH Ask students, working in pairs, to write sentences that explain how each entry in the Preview Workshop is related to the main idea of the subsection in which it is located. Have pairs share their sentences with the group.

Closure

Have students explain how this statement by Lincoln applies to the North and the South in 1861: "Both parties deprecated [condemned] war; but one of them would *make* war rather than let the nation survive; and the other would *accept* war rather than let it perish."

Extension

RESEARCH Have students research the work of the Sanitary Commission or other relief agencies established during the Civil War.

INVESTIGATE Have students investigate the pro-Union and pro-Confederate arguments over secession that were debated in Maryland's legislature before Lincoln secured the state with federal troops.

PRIMARY SOURCE

Description of Change: excerpted
Rationale: excerpted to focus on main idea

SECTION REVIEW ANSWERS

IDENTIFY

For significance, see the following pages:
Crittenden Compromise
(p. 364)
Robert Anderson (p. 365)
Robert E. Lee (p. 368)
conscription (p. 368)
nuns of the battlefield
(p. 369)
Elizabeth Blackwell (p. 369)
Clara Barton (p. 369)
Sally Louisa Tompkins
(p. 370)

LOCATE

For locations, see the map on p. 366.

1. *brought war, Lincoln called up troops; forced border states to choose sides*
2. *North—large population, majority of industry and resources, superiority at sea; South—fought on own soil, experienced military leaders*
3. *North—ME, VT, NH, MA, CT, RI, NY, PA, NJ, OH, IN, IL, WI, MI, MN, IA, KS, CA, OR, MO, KY, WV, DE, MD; South—VA, NC, SC, GA, FL, AL, MS, TN, AR, LA, TX*
4. *The wealthy could be exempt, so burden of fighting fell on the poor.*
5. *Diary entries might mention roles as spies, nurses, doctors, office and factory workers, and volunteers.*

De Paul Provincial House

◄ **During the war, women, such as these nuns, served in medical roles. Shown here are the Daughters of Charity from New York's Satterlee Hospital, along with doctors and soldiers.**

◄ **Elizabeth Blackwell**

► **Sally Tompkins**

The Museum of the Confederacy, Richmond, Virginia

Women in the South also provided medical aid to soldiers. Sally Louisa Tompkins was among the Confederate women who founded small hospitals and clinics. She was eventually commissioned as a captain in the Confederate army so that her Richmond hospital could qualify as a military hospital. This made Tompkins the only recognized female officer in the Confederate services.

Nurses like Tompkins experienced the horrors of war firsthand. Kate Cumming, a Confederate nurse from Alabama, wrote in her diary of her experiences at a makeshift hospital:

66 The men are lying all over the house on their blankets, just as they were brought from the battlefield. . . . The foul air from this mass of human beings at first made me giddy and sick, but I soon got over it. We have to walk and, when we give the men anything, kneel in blood and water; but we think nothing of it at all. 99

Countless other women on both sides helped the war effort in vital ways, such as by organizing soldiers' aid or hospital relief societies, raising money, or making bandages. In the North the American Freedman's Aid Commission provided hundreds of women schoolteachers to educate former slaves. Many women took over in offices and factories to replace men who were off fighting the war. Nearly 450 women worked in the Treasury Department as clerks—the government's first women office workers. Some 100,000 women worked in federal factories, sewing rooms, and military arsenals.

▪▪ **A few women served as spies, but most aided the war by serving as nurses, doing volunteer work, and working in offices and factories.**

SECTION 1 REVIEW

IDENTIFY and explain the significance of the following: Crittenden Compromise, Robert Anderson, Robert E. Lee, conscription, nuns of the battlefield, Elizabeth Blackwell, Clara Barton, Sally Louisa Tompkins.

LOCATE and explain the importance of the following: Fort Sumter; Richmond, Virginia; West Virginia.

1. **MAIN IDEA** What were the immediate consequences of the fall of Fort Sumter for the Union and for the border states?
2. **MAIN IDEA** What were the North's military strengths at the beginning of the Civil War? What were the South's strengths?
3. **GEOGRAPHY: LOCATION** Refer to the map on page 366. Which states sided with the North and which states sided with the South during the Civil War?
4. **WRITING TO EXPLAIN** Write an essay on why the Civil War can be viewed as "a rich man's war and a poor man's fight."
5. **USING HISTORICAL IMAGINATION** Imagine that you are a woman in either the North or the South during the Civil War. Write a diary entry describing how you might help the war effort.

Following is a list of the significant people and terms in this section. You may wish to use this list as a section preview.

People

■ Irvin McDowell
■ Joseph E. Johnston
■ Thomas "Stonewall" Jackson

Terms

■ First Battle of Bull Run
■ Copperheads

Section 2

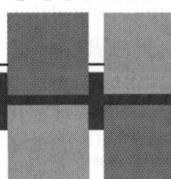

THE NORTH AND SOUTH FACE OFF

FOCUS

■ **What were the consequences of the First Battle of Bull Run?**
■ **How did the military strategies of the North and the South differ?**
■ **What were some of the daily hardships faced by soldiers?**
■ **Why did some northerners oppose the war?**

*L*ike most people, Lincoln believed that the war would be short. In mid-July 1861 he sent General Irvin McDowell and some 35,000 barely trained troops "Forward to Richmond" (a popular Union newspaper slogan). Laughing and joking along the way, the troops were joined by sightseers and reporters. The onlookers hoped to view a quick Union victory. Instead, they witnessed a Union defeat. As both sides came to realize that victory would not come easily, they began to prepare for war more seriously.

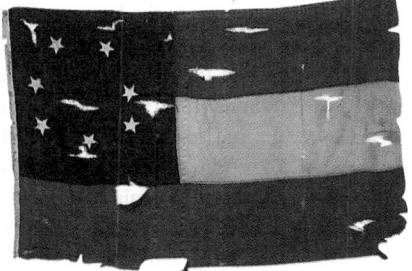

Original pattern for the Confederate flag that flew over the CSS *Virginia*

THE FIRST BATTLE OF BULL RUN

Irvin McDowell's forces never reached Richmond, Virginia. On July 21, 1861, some 35,000 Confederates met McDowell's forces near Manassas (muh-NAS-uhs) Junction, a railroad crossing about 25 miles outside Washington. Under the command of General Joseph E. Johnston, the Confederates dug in on high ground behind a creek called Bull Run. The North called the fighting that followed the **First Battle of Bull Run**; the South called it the Battle of Manassas (see map on page 377).

At first the battle went in the Union's favor. The left flank of the Confederate line came close to cracking. Had it broken, the war might well have ended. But General Thomas "Stonewall" Jackson and his men stopped the Union assault. Jackson's troops raced toward the Union line, filling the air with a terrifying scream: "Woh—who—ey!

Who—ey!" The eerie sound, which came to be known as the rebel yell, struck fear in the hearts of the enemy. "There is nothing like it on this side of the infernal region," said one Union soldier. "The peculiar corkscrew sensation that it sends down your backbone under these circumstances can never be told. You have to feel it."

▲ This 1889 painting of the First Battle of Bull Run shows Confederate soldiers on horseback breaking through Union lines.

FOCUS OBJECTIVES

■ Determine the consequences of the First Battle of Bull Run.

■ Contrast the military strategies of the North and the South.

■ Examine some of the daily hardships faced by soldiers.

■ Explain why some northerners opposed the war.

HISTORICAL SIDELIGHTS

Well-Earned Nickname

"Stonewall" Jackson earned his nickname at the First Battle of Bull Run. His stubborn defense of his position led Confederate general Barnard Bee to point to Jackson and urge his troops into battle, saying, "There is JACKSON standing like a stone wall." The name stuck.

THE CIVIL WAR ■■ 371

PREVIEW WORKSHOP

Following is a list of the significant people, places, and terms in this section. You may wish to use this list as a section preview.

People
- George B. McClellan
- John B. Magruder
- Jeb Stuart
- Ambrose E. Burnside
- Joseph Hooker
- David Farragut

Places
- Antietam
- Fredericksburg
- Chancellorsville
- Gettysburg
- Shiloh Church
- Vicksburg

Terms
- Battle of Seven Pines
- Seven Days' Campaign
- Second Battle of Bull Run
- Battle of Antietam
- Battle of Fredericksburg
- Battle of Chancellorsville
- Battle of Gettysburg
- Battle of Shiloh

FOCUS OBJECTIVES

- Compare how the North and the South fared in the eastern campaigns.

- Explain how the battles of Antietam, Fredericksburg, Chancellorsville, and Gettysburg affected northern morale.

- Analyze how the North achieved its goal of controlling the Mississippi River.

Section 3

EASTERN CAMPAIGNS AND THE WAR IN THE WEST

FOCUS

- **How did the North and the South fare in the eastern campaigns?**
- **How did the battles of Antietam, Fredericksburg, Chancellorsville, and Gettysburg affect northern morale?**
- **How did the North achieve its goal of controlling the Mississippi River?**

During 1862 and 1863 the Confederacy won many of the battles in the East. President Lincoln had no luck finding a general able to defeat Joseph E. Johnston, Robert E. Lee, and Stonewall Jackson. The Union's eastern forces had five different commanders in just one year. In the West, however, the Union forces led by Ulysses S. Grant achieved great success.

Union mortar battery

THE PENINSULA CAMPAIGN

Although the South won most of the early battles of the war, it was not because the northern army was poorly trained. In fact, the Union general George B. McClellan trained his men well, instilling in them both pride and discipline. But McClellan was overly cautious. He hesitated to commit his men to battle—much to the president's displeasure. (Lincoln once grew so frustrated with McClellan's delays that he threatened to send the general a letter asking if he could borrow the army if McClellan had no use for it.)

McClellan finally did move—in April 1862—launching a brilliant plan to take Richmond. Rather than marching directly on the city, McClellan transported more than 100,000 men, 300 cannons, and 25,000 animals by water to the peninsula between the York and James rivers. McClellan planned to hit Richmond from the southeast, where there were few fortifications. The strategy could have worked—the northern army vastly outnumbered the Confederate forces—but once again, McClellan hesitated.

◄ President Lincoln discusses war strategy with General McClellan in October 1862.

Teaching the Section

THE PENINSULA CAMPAIGN

Have students work in small groups to draw maps of Virginia, labeling Yorktown and Richmond, and the sites and dates of the Battle of Seven Pines, the Seven Days' Campaign, and the Second Battle of Bull Run. Call on groups to explain why Richmond had strategic and symbolic importance for both sides and to account for the poor showing of the North in this campaign.

▶

Union and Confederate soldiers met at Yorktown, Virginia, in the first week of April. Lincoln urged McClellan to attack, but the general refused, claiming that there were too many Confederate troops. Actually, he faced only some 13,000 Confederates, under the command of General John B. Magruder. McClellan wired Lincoln that he could only take Yorktown by siege. While McClellan waited, the Confederate general Johnston moved more troops into position.

Johnston and Magruder held on at Yorktown until the beginning of May. Just as McClellan was about to overrun the Confederate defenses, Johnston began a month-long retreat toward Richmond. McClellan soon followed. On May 31, 1862, the two sides clashed just east of Richmond at the **Battle of Seven Pines**. The South fared badly in this battle. Confederate colonel John B. Gordon wrote of the fight:

> 66 I was left alone on horseback, with my men dropping rapidly around me. . . . My field officers . . . were all dead. Every horse ridden into the fight, my own among them, was dead. Fully one half of my line officers and half my men were dead or wounded. 99

General Johnston was among the seriously wounded. Robert E. Lee assumed command of the Confederate forces and broke off fighting.

Even though the Confederates were badly weakened, McClellan again sat and waited. Lee did not. In a daring maneuver, Lee ordered a cavalry unit under the command of 29-year-old James E. B. (Jeb) Stuart to gather information on enemy positions. Armed with Stuart's information, the combined forces of Lee and Stonewall Jackson fell on the Union army in the **Seven Days' Campaign** (June 25–July 1). Union casualties numbered nearly 16,000. Although the number of Confederates killed or wounded was even higher—over 20,000—the battle was considered a victory for the South because McClellan retreated.

■■ **The Peninsula Campaign was a disappointment for the North since the ever-cautious McClellan retreated without taking Richmond.**

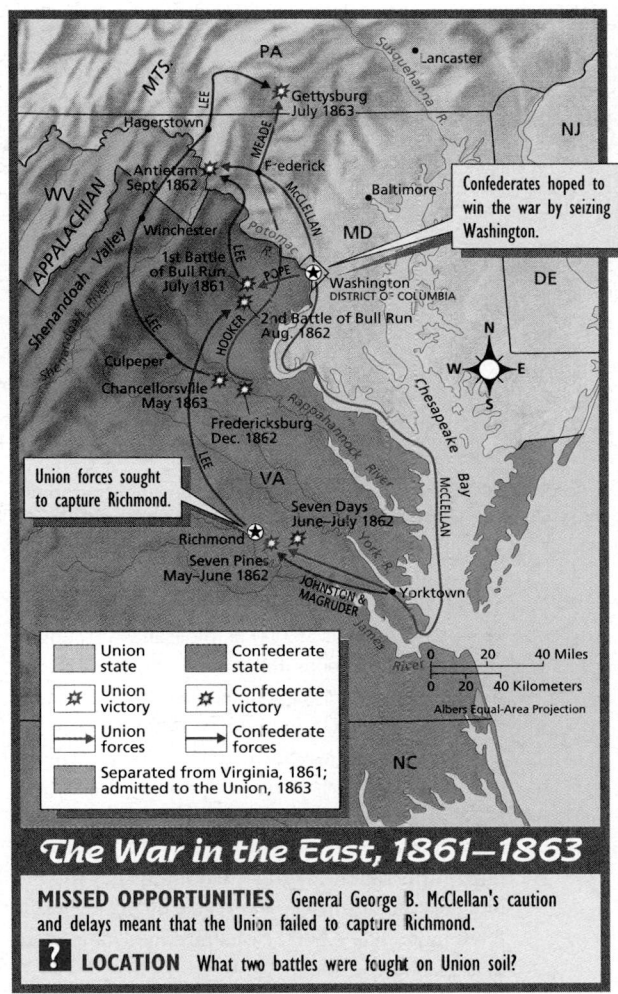

Union forces sought to capture Richmond.

Confederates hoped to win the war by seizing Washington.

The War in the East, 1861–1863

Union state
Confederate state
Union victory
Confederate victory
Union forces
Confederate forces
Separated from Virginia, 1861; admitted to the Union, 1863

MISSED OPPORTUNITIES General George B. McClellan's caution and delays meant that the Union failed to capture Richmond.

? LOCATION What two battles were fought on Union soil?

President Lincoln, furious and frustrated, ordered McClellan back to Washington. General John Pope took command of the army in the field. In late August, while marching on Richmond, Pope and his men were defeated by Lee's forces at the **Second Battle of Bull Run**. Soon after Pope's defeat, McClellan once again found himself in command of the eastern forces.

ANTIETAM

Robert E. Lee took the offensive in September 1862. Confederate diplomats believed that Great Britain might yet provide support to the Confederacy if Lee could win a major victory on Union soil. On September 4, 1862, Lee began crossing the Potomac into Maryland with some

THE CIVIL WAR ■■ 377

Teaching the Section

NORTHERN MORALE

Organize students into groups of four and assign each student in the groups one of these battles: Antietam, Fredericksburg, Chancellorsville, Gettysburg. Have each student assume the role of a civilian in the North and write a letter to a friend in the Union army explaining how morale at home has been affected by the battle. Draw a straight line on the chalkboard and write the battle names in chronological order on it. Then call on volunteers to read their letters about each battle. After each letter is read, draw a line upward or downward from the battle to indicate whether northern morale plummeted or rose due to the battle's outcome. Students might wish to include their letters in their portfolios.

AV **TRANSPARENCY**

Everyday Life in America Transparency and **Worksheet 12.**

MAKING CONNECTIONS

Music

Military bands were used to raise morale and send the troops off to battle. By the summer of 1862 Union troops had over 600 bands, most of them consisting of 22 pieces. Confederate forces had fewer bands, usually comprised of 3 to 4 pieces. Bands stationed on the front played everything from Italian opera selections to original songs created for the war, such as "Hold the Fort, For I Am Coming." During the battle of Gettysburg, musicians from North Carolina regiments played so loudly that Union soldiers fired at them.

PRIMARY SOURCE

Description of Change: excerpted and bracketed **Rationale:** excerpted to focus on main idea; bracketed to clarify meaning

▲ **Soldiers killed in the Battle of Antietam were photographed on September 17, 1862, as they were lined up for burial.**

55,000 men. (Over the next few days Lee's forces dropped to around 50,000 as thousands of hungry, tired, and sick troops fell by the wayside.) Union forces lost track of the Confederate troops for four days, until two Union soldiers found a copy of Lee's battle plans wrapped around a pack of cigars.

Armed with this information, General McClellan and some 75,000 troops met Lee at Antietam (an-TEET-uhm) Creek. The **Battle of Antietam** raged all day, becoming one of the bloodiest battles of the war. The Confederates suffered more than 13,000 casualties; the Union more than 12,000.

Although Antietam was not a clear-cut Union victory, Lee's withdrawal to Virginia raised confidence in the North. A major Confederate offensive had failed, proving that General Lee, whom many had thought was unbeatable, could be beaten. Lee's defeat cost the South any hope of support from the European countries, which did not want to risk backing the losing side in the war.

Despite the Union army's good showing at Antietam, McClellan permanently lost his command. Lincoln fired the overcautious general for allowing the Confederates to escape into Virginia.

⬛ **The Union victory at Antietam bolstered confidence in the North and dashed Confederate hopes of winning European support.**

FREDERICKSBURG AND CHANCELLORSVILLE

Lincoln's new commander, General Ambrose E. Burnside, did not want the job. He had little confidence in his abilities and knew the troops' loyalties were with McClellan. Nevertheless, he moved boldly—too boldly.

On December 11 and 12, 1862, General Burnside sent some 114,000 men across the Rappahannock (rap-uh-HAN-uhk) River near Fredericksburg, Virginia. General Lee and some 75,000 soldiers controlled the hills above the town. Reasoning that Lee would not expect a frontal attack, General Burnside ordered his men across an open plain toward the hills on the morning of December 13.

Lee took advantage of Burnside's positioning. From their high ground, the Confederates could easily pick off the Union soldiers as they crossed the open fields. As Lee's artillery commander told him, "A chicken could not live on that field when we open [fire] on it." The Union army suffered more than 12,000 casualties in the **Battle of Fredericksburg**, the Confederates some 5,000. One northerner bitterly referred to the battle as a "great slaughter pen." A Union soldier, William Lusk, wrote home:

> 66 Gone are the proud hopes, the high aspirations that swelled our bosoms a few days ago. . . . [The army] has strong limbs to march and meet the foe, stout arms to strike heavy blows, brave hearts to dare— but the brains, the brains! Have we no brains to use the arms and limbs and eager hearts with cunning? 99

The revolving door for Union generals whirled on. Lincoln transferred Burnside and gave command of the eastern forces to General Joseph ("Fighting Joe") Hooker. Although an effective general, Hooker was also opinionated. He once openly criticized President Lincoln, saying that the Union needed a dictator to win the war. Lincoln replied: "Only those generals who gain successes can set up dictators. What I now ask of you is military success, and I will risk the dictatorship."

Hooker offered a bold plan to crush Lee's forces. He proposed to divide his large army into three parts, cut off Lee's supply lines, and attack

▲ Stonewall Jackson's death in 1863 was a blow to the South. This photograph shows mourners at his grave in Virginia.

the Confederates from both flanks. The strategy seemed workable, especially since Hooker's nearly 134,000 troops outnumbered Lee's some 60,000.

By April 30, 1863, Hooker had his men positioned in a deep forest known as the Wilderness, near Chancellorsville, Virginia. But Lee once again stole the initiative from the Union army. In his most daring maneuver of the war to date, Lee divided his troops, sending Stonewall Jackson and some 30,000 men through the Wilderness to outflank Hooker. When Hooker discovered the troop movements, he assumed the Confederates were retreating. Instead, Lee and Jackson attacked the Union forces from two fronts. After several days of fighting, Hooker withdrew in defeat. Morale in the North plummeted. Once again, the South seemed unbeatable.

But the South had paid dearly for its victory at the **Battle of Chancellorsville**. Among the wounded was Stonewall Jackson. Riding back to Confederate lines after dark, Jackson was mistaken for a Union cavalryman and shot by his own men. His arm had to be amputated. Eight days later, Lee's most valued general died from pneumonia.

■■ **Morale plummeted in the North after the Union defeats at Fredericksburg and Chancellorsville.**

𝒢ETTYSBURG

Following the victory at Chancellorsville, Lee decided to invade the North again. Not only would this spare war-weary Virginia from further fighting, but it would allow Lee to resupply and feed his hungry troops as the Union had done in the South—by taking what was needed from the enemy.

In early June 1863 Lee crossed into Pennsylvania with some 75,000 troops. Lincoln urged General Hooker to attack the Confederates before they could consolidate their troops. Hooker, however, hesitated. Convinced that the government no longer had confidence in him, Hooker asked to be relieved of his command. He was replaced by General George Meade.

By the end of June the Confederates massed near the town of Gettysburg, Pennsylvania. When scouts reported that there was a supply of shoes in the town, the Confederates organized a raiding party. But the troops did not know that two Union brigades had positioned themselves on high ground northwest of Gettysburg. As the Confederate raiding party approached Gettysburg on July 1, it was met by Union fire.

On the first day of the **Battle of Gettysburg**, the Confederates pushed the Union line back to Cemetery Ridge. The Confederates held Seminary Ridge, a lower line of hills about a half mile away. But Lee knew that the fighting was not over as long as the North held the higher ground. On July 2, General Lee attacked the Union left, trying without success to capture a globe-shaped hill called Little Round Top. The next day he ordered some 15,000 men under the command of George Pickett to rush the Union center on Cemetery Ridge. Only half of the soldiers made it back.

The Granger Collection, New York

▲ The Battle of Gettysburg began when Confederates, looking for a rumored supply of shoes, clashed with a Union regiment.

Teaching the Section

THE SIEGE OF VICKSBURG

Have groups of students prepare interviews with "survivors" of the siege of Vicksburg. The interviewees can be Confederate soldiers or civilians talking about their experiences during the six-week siege, their views on the war, and their opinions on what the effects of the South's defeat at Vicksburg, and previously at New Orleans, will be. Have groups conduct their interviews for the class.

REMEMBERING GETTYSBURG

SETTING THE SCENE

In 1863 Gettysburg was a peaceful hamlet with a population of about 1,500. Gentle rolling hills covered with trees surrounded the village from which spoked several main roads—named for the towns to which they lead. West of Gettysburg lay Seminary Ridge, and to the south loomed Cemetery Ridge. The peaceful valley between the ridges consisted of cultivated farmland and orchards.

LINK TO TODAY

Have students describe ways Americans memorialize those killed in battle. *(war memorials, tombs of unknown soldiers, cemeteries for war veterans)*

▣ Ask students who have visited any war memorials to describe them and share their reactions and experiences.

THINKING CRITICALLY

Ask students if they agree with the assertion by critics that Civil War reenactments glamorize or trivialize war. Have students describe how they would like to see the 150th anniversary of the Gettysburg battle celebrated in the year 2013.

The loss of life at Gettysburg was staggering. After three days of fighting, Union casualties numbered more than 23,000; Confederate casualties more than 20,000. Although the Union army emerged victorious, it once again failed to end the war while it had the opportunity. A disappointed President Lincoln lamented, "Our Army held the war in the hollow of their hand and they would not close it." Nevertheless, the battle marked a turning point in the war. The Union army had proved that the Confederacy could be beaten.

In November 1863 President Lincoln helped dedicate a cemetery at the Gettysburg battlefield. Lincoln spoke for only a few minutes, but his Gettysburg Address remains a classic statement of democratic ideals (see page 1008).

▣▣ **The Union victory at Gettysburg proved to the North that the South could be defeated.**

THE WAR IN THE WEST

From the start the war went far better for the Union army in the West. In February 1862 General Ulysses S. Grant of Illinois led an army into Tennessee and captured two important forts that guarded the Tennessee and Cumberland rivers—Fort Henry and Fort Donelson. Moving rapidly south on the Tennessee River, Grant paused at Shiloh Church near the Mississippi state line.

HISTORY *in the Making*

BY EDWARD LINENTHAL

Remembering Gettysburg

I first visited Gettysburg during my junior year in high school. I remember standing on Cemetery Ridge, where Union troops turned back Major General George Pickett's charge. I closed my eyes to imagine the battle that raged there over a century ago and to picture President Lincoln as he stood in the nearby cemetery on November 19, 1863, to deliver the Gettysburg Address.

Lincoln said the living could not further *consecrate* Gettysburg—that is, make it sacred. Those who died there, he declared, had already "consecrated it, far above our poor power to add or detract." Yet Americans have treated Gettysburg as a special place by holding commemorations, staging vivid reenactments of the battle, and preserving the field much as it looked in 1863. It became a national military park in 1895.

Today, Gettysburg is indeed a sacred site, a powerful place of remembrance where the course of history changed. But Americans do not always agree *why* Gettysburg should be remembered. What does the battle symbolize? What lessons can we learn from it, and how should we commemorate it?

Here is how some groups of Americans have answered these questions. After the war, veterans from both sides began taking part in patriotic ceremonies at Gettysburg. Especially popular were the 50th and 75th anniversaries. The climax of these ceremonies was a meeting at the Angle, the site of Pickett's charge. As large crowds looked on, elderly veterans met and shook hands as a sign of the reborn Union. In these ceremonies Gettysburg symbolized courageous soldiers, both northern and southern.

Often neglected in these remembrances, however, was the issue at the heart of the war—slavery. In his Gettysburg Address, Lincoln had reminded the nation that the death of so many would gain meaning only if the country remained "dedicated . . . to the unfinished work which they who fought here have thus far so nobly advanced." Thus for some, Gettysburg symbolizes the movement to free the slaves

Practice

GUIDED PRACTICE

Call on volunteers to restate the war aims and strategies of the North and the South at the beginning of the war, and list their responses on the chalkboard. Then have other volunteers assess the success each side had by July 1863 in achieving these aims, citing specific battles and their effects on long-term goals.

INDEPENDENT PRACTICE

Have students imagine that they are editors of a northern or southern newspaper. Have them choose a battle from the Guided Practice and write an editorial about the effect the battle's outcome has had on their readers. Students may wish to include their editorials in their portfolios.

Review and Assessment

REVIEW Have pairs of students draw charts contrasting the war in the East with the war in the West during 1862 and 1863, focusing on geographic differences, tactics, and impact on each side's overall war aims. Then assign the Section 3 Review on p. 382.

ASSESS Assign the **Section 3 Daily Quiz** in *Core Resources*.

▶

Grant knew that Confederate generals Albert Sidney Johnston and P.G.T. Beauregard were nearby in Corinth, Mississippi. He did not, however, expect them to attack. Thus, on April 6, 1862, Grant's soldiers were caught by surprise as thousands of Confederate soldiers rushed at them. By day's end the Confederate forces had pushed Grant's men back to the Tennessee River. The Confederate commanders went to bed confident that they could finish off Grant's army the next morning.

Early the next day, however, Grant launched an attack. The **Battle of Shiloh** raged all morning. By the middle of the afternoon, Grant's forces had subdued the Confederates, and Beauregard gave the order to retreat. Both sides paid dearly: more than 13,000 Union casualties and 10,000 Confederate casualties, including General Johnston.

To achieve a decisive victory in the West, however, the Union had to gain control of the Mississippi River. Toward this end, David Farragut, commander of a Union naval squadron, moved against New Orleans. In late April 1862, Union ships entered the mouth of the Mississippi and passed the two forts defending the city. Farragut and his forces took New Orleans by the end of April.

Despite these successes, Grant knew that gaining full control of the river meant taking Vicksburg, Mississippi. Vicksburg's high river bluffs gave Confederate artillery command of the

HISTORICAL SIDELIGHTS
Lincoln's "First" General
Grant's success at Vicksburg made President Lincoln optimistic that at last the war could be won. Lincoln remarked: "Grant is the first general I have had. . . . All the rest . . . wanted me to be the general. I am glad to find a man who can go ahead without me."

and an enduring commitment to racial justice.

More recently, ceremonies have posed new questions about the meaning of the battle and of war. A few days before the 125th anniversary in 1988, a crowd of some 130,000 spectators paid to watch more than 10,000 people—each carefully dressed to play the role of a Union or Confederate soldier—reenact parts of the battle. This commercialized event portrayed the battle as glamorous and exciting. Reenactors claimed to be honoring the courage of those who fought and stimulating interest in the past. Critics, on the other hand, argued that the battle should not be presented as sport or adventure, but only as a tragic event.

The official anniversary ceremony, whose theme was "Peace Eternal in a World United," presented a different commemoration of the battle. The event took place at the

Eternal Light Peace Memorial, a monument dedicated to reconciliation by Gettysburg veterans 50 years earlier. The ceremony included a concert by an interracial choir, speeches by African American leaders, and an address by scientist Carl Sagan. Sagan told the audience that the nations of the world must heed the Gettysburg veterans' call for reconciliation "instead of the carnage and mass murder" of war.

These are some of the different, even conflicting, ways Americans commemorate Gettysburg and hold it sacred. Of course, Gettysburg is only one piece of our history. What other places have Americans consecrated and what do they symbolize? Think of places associated with the origins of the nation, of the monuments and memorials in Washington, D.C., of places sacred to American Indians, of places where admired leaders were assassi-

▲ **Gettysburg National Cemetery in Pennsylvania stands today as a grim reminder of the tremendous losses of the Civil War.**

nated. As past generations have done, we continue to consecrate the places we consider crucial to the American identity and to debate their meaning.

CULTURAL PATTERNS

American Indians from the Indian Territory also played a role in the war in the West. The Creeks fought for the North in Grant's campaign, while Cherokees, Choctaws, and Chickasaws fought for the Confederacy in such battles as Wilson's Creek, Missouri (1861) and Pea Ridge, Arkansas (1862). Cherokee leader Stand Watie became the only American Indian promoted to the rank of brigadier general in the Confederate army and was one of the last Confederate officers to surrender when the war ended.

RETEACH Have students work with partners to create a detailed, annotated time line for the years 1862 and 1863, including major battles and commanders. Pairs should include a time-line title and brief caption that summarizes the years' events and significance for both sides.

Closure

Have students debate the following comment by Civil War historian Shelby Foote: "It's my belief that the war in the West is at least as important as the one in the East."

Extension

INTERPRET Have students create diagrams or relief maps of one of the battles discussed in Section 3.

INVESTIGATE Ask students to investigate what happened to General McClellan after he was fired by President Lincoln.

Map Caption Answer
Kentucky

SECTION REVIEW ANSWERS

IDENTIFY

For significance, see the following pages:
George B. McClellan (p. 376)
John B. Magruder (p. 377)
Battle of Seven Pines (p. 377)
Jeb Stuart (p. 377)
Seven Days' Campaign
  (p. 377)
Second Battle of Bull Run
  (p. 377)
Ambrose E. Burnside (p. 378)
Joseph Hooker (p. 378)
David Farragut (p. 381)

LOCATE

For locations, see the maps on pp. 377 and 382.

1. *Have students exchange charts and check information for accuracy.*
2. *Antietam and Gettysburg—prevented South from winning European support; Fredericksburg and Chancellorsville—North experienced heavy losses*
3. *Strategy to split Confederacy required gaining full control of Mississippi River.*
4. *Time lines should include capture of Fort Henry and Fort Donelson, Battle of Shiloh, capture of New Orleans, fall of Vicksburg and Port Hudson.*
5. *hesitated to commit troops to battle, failed to follow up military advantages*

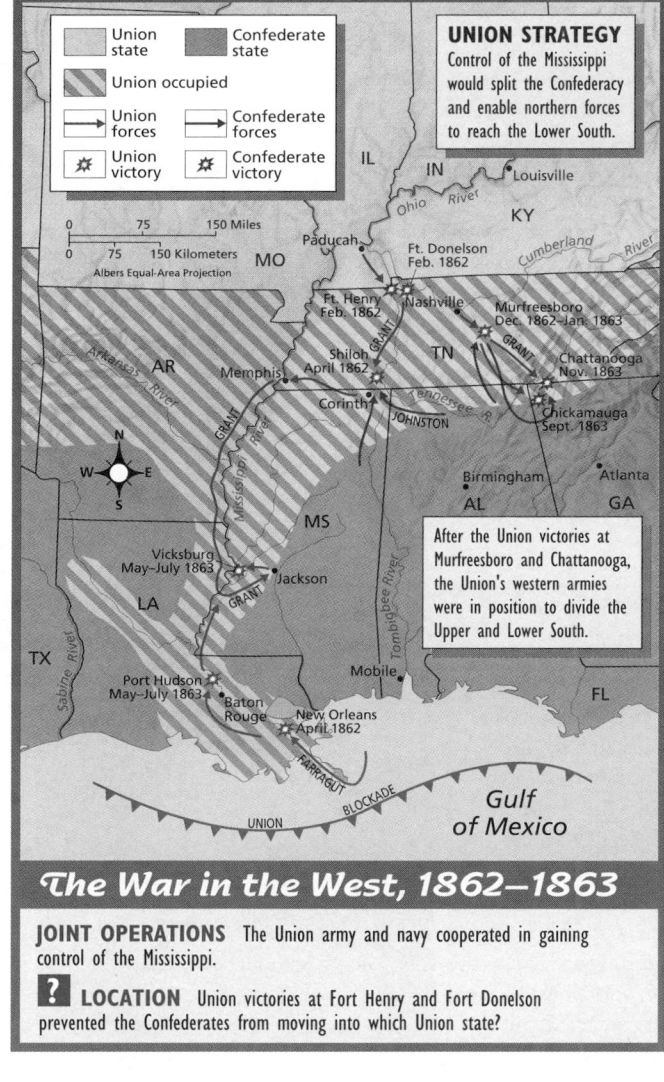

The War in the West, 1862–1863

JOINT OPERATIONS The Union army and navy cooperated in gaining control of the Mississippi.

 LOCATION Union victories at Fort Henry and Fort Donelson prevented the Confederates from moving into which Union state?

entire area. In May 1863 Grant hatched a risky but brilliant plan to take the city. Marching deep into enemy territory, he bottled up one Confederate force in Jackson, Mississippi, then raced west to trap the other enemy force inside Vicksburg.

For six weeks General Grant and his men laid siege to the town. Vicksburg's defenders devoured mules and rats to keep from starving. Finally, in late June the desperate Confederate soldiers sent a letter to their commander, urging him to surrender:

66 If you can't feed us, you had better surrender, horrible as the idea is, than suffer this noble army to disgrace themselves by desertion. 99

On July 3, 1863, General Grant and Confederate general John Pemberton met under an oak tree to discuss terms of surrender. The Confederates surrendered to Grant the next day. On July 8 the Confederate forces at Port Hudson, Louisiana, also fell. The Union now controlled the Mississippi River, thereby cutting off Arkansas, Louisiana, and Texas from the rest of the Confederacy.

■■ **The North achieved its goal of controlling the Mississippi River by capturing New Orleans and Vicksburg.**

■■ **SECTION 3 REVIEW**

IDENTIFY and explain the significance of the following: George B. McClellan, John B. Magruder, Battle of Seven Pines, Jeb Stuart, Seven Days' Campaign, Second Battle of Bull Run, Ambrose E. Burnside, Joseph Hooker, David Farragut.

LOCATE and explain the importance of the following: Antietam, Fredericksburg, Chancellorsville, Gettysburg, Shiloh Church, Vicksburg.

1. **MAIN IDEA** Create a chart that lists each battle in the eastern campaign, along with its date and location. Include a brief description of each battle and identify the victor.
2. **MAIN IDEA** Why did the battles of Antietam and Gettysburg have positive effects on northern morale? Why did those of Fredericksburg and Chancellorsville have negative effects?
3. **GEOGRAPHY: PLACE** Why was Vicksburg essential to the North's strategy in the West?
4. **WRITING TO CLASSIFY** Create a time line that lists the events leading up to the North's successful control of the Mississippi River.
5. **ANALYZING** How did McClellan contribute to the North's difficulties in the eastern campaign?

PREVIEW WORKSHOP

Following is a list of the significant people, places, and terms in this section. You may wish to use this list as a section preview.

People
- 54th Massachusetts Infantry
- Martin Delany
- Ulysses S. Grant
- William Tecumseh Sherman

Places
- Spotsylvania Court House
- Atlanta
- Savannah
- Appomattox Courthouse

Terms
- Emancipation Proclamation
- war of attrition
- total war

Section 4

THE FINAL PHASE

FOCUS

- **How and why did the Union's war aims shift?**
- **Why did the Emancipation Proclamation apply only to slaves living in areas of rebellion against the United States?**
- **What strategies did Grant and Sherman employ to win the war?**
- **What were some of the consequences of the war?**

For the North, the Civil War began as a battle to save the Union. During the first year and a half of fighting, President Lincoln stated repeatedly that preserving the Union was his only goal. To retain the support of slaveholders loyal to the Union, he pledged not to interfere with the institution of slavery anywhere. Early on, however, abolitionists demanded that the North shift its war aims from saving the Union to ending slavery.

Defeated Confederates rolling up their flag

A SHIFT IN WAR AIMS

As the months of warfare dragged on, many northerners began to question whether saving the Union without ending slavery was worth the price. Was it just or sensible, they asked, to sacrifice so much without exacting a price from the secessionist slaveholders who had caused the terrible bloodshed? Slavery, they insisted, must be destroyed. "To fight against slaveholders, without fighting against slavery," charged Frederick Douglass, "is but a half-hearted business, and paralyzes the hands engaged in it."

After fierce debate, Republicans pushed two significant acts through Congress in July 1862. One authorized African Americans to serve in the military. The other freed slaves held by Confederate soldiers or by those who aided the Confederacy. Lincoln signed the acts, but Horace Greeley, the abolitionist editor of the New York *Tribune,* soon criticized Lincoln for not making slavery the central war issue. Lincoln replied by simply restating his war aim: "My paramount object in the struggle *is* to save the Union, and is *not* either to save or to destroy slavery."

Privately, however, the president had already concluded that slavery was too important to the southern war effort to be left alone. The Confederacy depended on slaves to raise food, haul supplies, build fortifications, and work in factories. Every slave at work released a white man to fight against the Union. Lincoln hoped that if slaves heard that the North was fighting to free them, they would desert their masters, thereby weakening the South's economy.

◄ **Members of the 2nd U.S. Colored Artillery are shown loading a cannon.**

FOCUS OBJECTIVES

- Analyze how and why the Union's war aims shifted.

- Explain why the Emancipation Proclamation applied only to slaves living in areas of rebellion against the U.S.

- Describe the strategies Grant and Sherman employed to win the war.

- Identify some consequences of the war.

CORE RESOURCES

• **Section 4 Daily Quiz**

GLOBAL CONNECTIONS

One immediate effect of the Emancipation Proclamation was to end all hope of foreign support for the Confederacy. One London newspaper called the decree "a gigantic stride in the paths of Christian and civilized progress." No leaders of European governments were willing to risk public outrage by fighting against a country waging war against slavery.

PRIMARY SOURCE

Description of Change: excerpted
Rationale: excerpted to focus on main idea

THINKING CRITICALLY

Recognizing Prejudice Examine with students the belief of many Union soldiers that "freed slaves would not make good soldiers." Ask students on what this view was based. Point out that many Union soldiers changed their opinions after witnessing the performances of African American soldiers. Explain that prejudice toward a group commonly arises out of a lack of knowledge of, or personal experience with, that group.

■■ **In the hopes of weakening the South, the North enlarged its war aims to include freeing the slaves.**

THE EMANCIPATION PROCLAMATION

Lincoln lacked the constitutional authority to abolish slavery. But as commander in chief he did have the authority to institute military measures. Thus, in July 1862 Lincoln informed his cabinet that he planned to issue a new military order: As of a certain date, all slaves living in areas still rebelling against the United States would be free. To quiet constitutional concerns, he assured his cabinet that this **Emancipation Proclamation** would apply only to states that belonged to the Confederacy, not to regions under Union control. Lincoln's assurance also quelled concerns about the status of slaves in the border states.

Secretary of State William H. Seward urged Lincoln to keep the Emancipation Proclamation secret until the Union won a major victory. To issue the proclamation when the war was going badly for the Union would look like an act of desperation. Lincoln agreed. The needed victory came at Antietam on September 17, 1862. On September 22 Lincoln issued a preliminary draft of the

▼ **Poster commemorating the Emancipation Proclamation**

Emancipation Proclamation that would go into effect the first of the year.

■■ **Because of constitutional issues the Emancipation Proclamation applied only to slaves living in areas of rebellion.**

More than three years would pass before slavery was abolished everywhere in the United States. However, the institution of slavery was doomed when January 1, 1863, came and the Confederacy was still in rebellion. Lincoln's proclamation brought a decisive change in the war. The mere news of Union troops nearby inspired slaves to leave their masters to follow the Union army.

AFRICAN AMERICANS TAKE UP ARMS

Both the July 1862 act and the Emancipation Proclamation encouraged the enlistment of African American soldiers. The first official black regiments were organized in August 1862 in South Carolina. Frederick Douglass, who had been pressing for black troops since the beginning of the war, saw military service as an important step toward citizenship for African Americans:

❝ Once let the black man get upon his person the brass letters, U.S.; let him get an eagle on his button, and a musket on his shoulder and bullets in his pocket, and there is no power on earth which can deny that he has earned the right to citizenship. ❞

African American soldiers first saw serious action at Port Hudson, Louisiana, in 1863. Eight black regiments attacked a Confederate fortress seven times, suffering heavy losses. Their commander, General Nathaniel Banks, told the *New York Times*, "No troops could be more determined or more daring." By war's end nearly 180,000 African American men had served in the Union army. Some also served in the navy. The 166 all-black regiments fought in 449 engagements, including 39 major battles.

Although the Union army accepted African American volunteers, it did not offer them full

THE EMANCIPATION PROCLAMATION

Have the class role-play the House of Representatives in a debate over Lincoln's decision to limit the abolition of slavery to areas still in rebellion against the U.S. rather than to free all enslaved persons or to free none. Suggest that debaters consider the property rights and other constitutional issues that would be raised by a presidential order freeing enslaved persons within the U.S., and its military and strategic impact on the slaveholding border states.

▶

Changing Ways

THE COURAGEOUS 54TH

On July 18, 1863, the men of the 54th Massachusetts Infantry sat in camp on Morris Island in South Carolina's Charleston Harbor. Three quarters of a mile away, guarding the harbor entrance, the sloping walls of Fort Wagner rose above the sands. More than 1,700 Confederate soldiers stood ready to defend the fort.

The Confederates held not only Fort Wagner but all the forts and batteries around Charleston, South Carolina. The Union campaign to seize control of Charleston's defenses had begun on July 10. Eight days later, despite a day of Union bombardment, Fort Wagner remained in Confederate hands. So Brigadier General Truman Seymour decided to send some 6,000 Union troops in a desperate frontal attack against the fort at dusk—with the 54th Regiment in the lead.

The 54th was no ordinary regiment. It was composed of some of the first African American soldiers recruited for the Union army. And this battle represented the first time that black troops had been assigned a key role. It was up to them to break through the Confederate line, and they would undoubtedly suffer great losses. These

▲ Charles and Lewis Douglass, sons of Frederick Douglass, both served with the 54th Massachusetts, shown here charging Fort Wagner.

troops also faced a danger that white Union soldiers did not. Captured blacks were treated as outlaws—shot, hanged, or sold into slavery.

As night fell, the 54th's commanding officer, Colonel Robert Gould Shaw, gave the order "Forward!" and the troops advanced. The quiet evening exploded in a storm of gunfire. Confederate cannons all around opened fire, but somehow Colonel Shaw and his men clawed their way to the top of Fort Wagner's walls. There, they began fighting hand to hand

against the Confederate defenders inside. Shaw was killed, one of many casualties of the failed assault.

Union troops continued the siege until September 6, when Confederate forces, no longer able to hold out, finally evacuated the fort. Both armies had suffered staggering losses in the prolonged fight. Four survivors of the regiment received the Gillmore Medal for gallantry, and their courage won the 54th Regiment an honored place in U.S. military history.

equality. For much of the war, black soldiers earned less than half the pay of white soldiers. (Congress finally equalized the pay scale in June 1864, after much agitation by black soldiers and their commanding officers.) In addition, white officers commanded every black regiment. Only about 100 African Americans were commissioned as junior officers. In 1865 Martin Delany became the first African American promoted to the rank of major.

Yet the courage and dedication of African American soldiers impressed many. In 1863 Secretary of War Edwin M. Stanton noted:

66 Many persons believed, or pretended to believe, and confidently asserted, that freed slaves would not make good soldiers; that they would lack courage, and could not be subjected to military discipline. Facts have shown how groundless were these apprehensions. 99

Stanton was right. Over 20 African American soldiers and sailors won the Congressional Medal of Honor. And more than 32,000 of their black comrades gave their lives for the Union cause.

Changing Ways

THE COURAGEOUS 54TH

LINK TO TODAY

Have students contrast the roles African Americans play in the military today with their roles at the time of the Civil War. *(No longer in segregated units, African American officers may hold all ranks in the military including chairman of the joint chiefs of staff for the armed services.)*

HISTORICAL SIDELIGHTS

Treatment of Prisoners
The Civil War was governed by a variety of rules regarding the treatment of civilians, the sick or wounded, and war captives. The two sides agreed that captured white soldiers would be treated as prisoners of war. They would be humanely treated and exchanged or put into camps until the war ended. However, the Confederate Congress passed a law that stated captured white officers commanding black troops were to be put to death or "otherwise punished at the discretion of the Court."

PRIMARY SOURCE

Description of Change: excerpted
Rationale: excerpted to focus on main idea

Teaching the Section

GRANT'S WAR PLAN

Pair students to role-play Grant and Sherman. Have them write and exchange letters explaining and justifying their military tactics. Select pairs to read their letters to the class. Then discuss with students how their strategies differed from the strategies of previous Union commanders, how they built upon Union strengths and Confederate weaknesses, and what the potential costs and risks were for the Union army.

▲ **General Ulysses S. Grant, standing next to the tree at the center of the picture, and his staff were photographed at his headquarters at Cold Harbor in early June 1864.**

LINCOLN FINDS HIS GENERAL

Emancipation provided Lincoln with one key to Union success. The president found another key in General Ulysses S. Grant. This general understood that the North had advantages over the South in terms of soldiers and supplies. His strategy was to use these advantages against an enemy that was reeling from shortages. Grant told Lincoln that he would march on Richmond, take his losses, and press on. He was suggesting a **war of attrition**— to continue fighting until the South ran out of men, supplies, and will.

In May 1864 Grant, now commander of all Union forces, moved some 122,000 troops into the Wilderness near Chancellorsville, Virginia. For two days the northerners hurled themselves at some 66,000 Confederates, but the rebels held their ground. Grant's forces suffered nearly 18,000 casualties; the Confederates nearly 13,000.

Rather than rest, Grant pushed on, mile by bloody mile. "I propose to fight it out on this line if it takes all summer," he wrote. Grant swung his forces 10 miles to the south, forcing Lee to keep his weary men in the field. At Spotsylvania Court House, Virginia, Union and Confederate forces clashed several times between May 10 and May 19. As in previous battles, Union losses were heavy. Shocked by the number of casualties, a southern soldier remarked of Grant: "We have met a man this time, who either does not know when he is whipped, or who cares not if he loses his whole army."

Grant swung south yet again in order to attack Petersburg, Virginia, in mid-June. By capturing this railroad center, he hoped to cut off Richmond's supplies. But Lee held on. After three days even Grant was rattled. Since May 12 his army had suffered some 60,000 casualties. He called off the direct assault and settled down to besiege Petersburg. Grant was achieving his goal, however. Lee's army was dwindling, with no reserves available.

■■ **In 1864 General Grant began a war of attrition—wearing down the Confederates through constant attack.**

SHERMAN'S MARCH TO THE SEA

Matching Grant in determination was the Union general William Tecumseh Sherman. Moody, ambitious, and brilliant, Sherman had performed ably at Vicksburg and other battles. Grant rewarded Sherman by making him commander of the Tennessee army.

While Grant was working his way toward Richmond, Sherman moved some 100,000 troops out of Tennessee toward Atlanta, Georgia, in early May. The Confederates fell back, and Sherman entered Atlanta on September 2, 1864.

▼ **General Sherman, photographed outside of Atlanta on July 19, 1864, shortly before his army launched its attack against the city.**

TOTAL WAR

As a class examine the concept of total war, defining and comparing it with a war of attrition. Have volunteers give examples of how these war strategies were applied at the Wilderness, Spotsylvania Court House and Sherman's march to the sea. Then discuss with students what the long- and short-term impacts of such strategies might be on civilian populations.

■■ Ask students if they believe "war of attrition" and "total war" to be appropriate military strategies today. Ask students to cite some recent examples of these strategies in use.

THE WAR'S CONSEQUENCES

Divide the class into two parts. Have half write journal entries as northerners and half as southerners on how the war has affected them, their families, their friends, and their region. Have volunteers read their entries to the class. Ask the class to cite similarities and differences in the war's consequences for the North and the South.

▶

By capturing the city, General Sherman had cut the only Confederate railroad link across the Appalachians. Sherman ordered the evacuation of Atlanta and burned a significant portion of it. He defended his tactic:

66 If [southerners] raise a howl against my barbarity and cruelty, I will answer that war is war, and not popularity-seeking. If they want peace, they and their relatives must stop the war. 99

The fall of Atlanta gave a significant boost to Lincoln's reelection campaign. Up until then, it looked as if he might not even get his party's nomination. Many Republicans were upset that the war had dragged on for so long. Sherman's success, however, gave many hope that the conflict would soon be over. As a result, Lincoln won a substantial victory in the election of 1864 against Democrat General George McClellan.

After the burning of Atlanta, Sherman marched rapidly toward the port city of Savannah, Georgia. Cut off from their supply line, Sherman's

▲ Sherman's troops left a wake of destruction behind them, including torn-up railroad tracks and burned-out factories.

men stole what supplies they could and destroyed anything that might be useful to the Confederates. They uprooted crops, burned farmhouses, slaughtered livestock, and tore up railroad tracks, leaving nearly stripped a swath 60 miles wide and almost 300 miles long.

Although much of the destruction exceeded Sherman's orders, it was part of the general's tactic of fighting a **total war**. He believed that it was not enough to wage war against enemy troops. To win

PRIMARY SOURCE

Description of Change: excerpted and bracketed
Rationale: excerpted to focus on main idea; bracketed to clarify meaning

HISTORICAL SIDELIGHTS

Total War

Sherman's ideas on the conduct of war have been called the first modern view of warfare. Unlike other Civil War strategists, he viewed war as a fight between peoples, not armies, and believed that such a fight could be won only by breaking the spirit of the people of the South. He wanted to "make old and young, rich and poor, feel the hard hand of war."

■■ Ask students whether modern wars are wars between armies or peoples.

Map Caption Answer
The distance between Savannah and Columbia is about 135 miles; this averages about 8 miles a day.

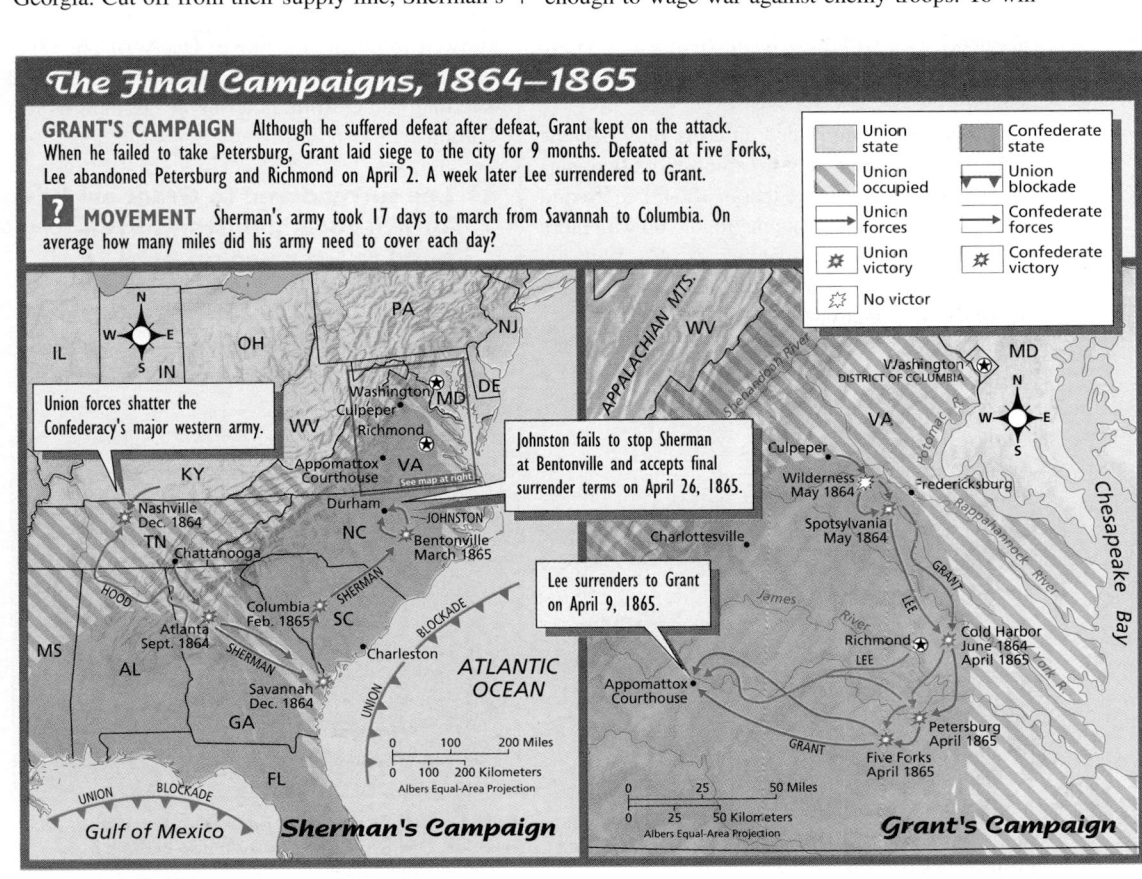

The Final Campaigns, 1864–1865

GRANT'S CAMPAIGN Although he suffered defeat after defeat, Grant kept on the attack. When he failed to take Petersburg, Grant laid siege to the city for 9 months. Defeated at Five Forks, Lee abandoned Petersburg and Richmond on April 2. A week later Lee surrendered to Grant.

? **MOVEMENT** Sherman's army took 17 days to march from Savannah to Columbia. On average how many miles did his army need to cover each day?

Union state	Confederate state
Union occupied	Union blockade
Union forces	Confederate forces
Union victory	Confederate victory
No victor	

Union forces shatter the Confederacy's major western army.

Johnston fails to stop Sherman at Bentonville and accepts final surrender terms on April 26, 1865.

Lee surrenders to Grant on April 9, 1865.

Sherman's Campaign

Grant's Campaign

Practice

GUIDED PRACTICE

Make a time line on the chalkboard for the years 1861 through 1865. Have students take turns offering significant events in headline form and add them to the time line. When the time line is complete, have students identify turning points in the war and suggest the places where a southern victory was still possible and why.

INDEPENDENT PRACTICE

Direct students to choose a headline from the time line developed in Guided Practice and write an article to accompany it. Call on volunteers to read their articles to the class. Students may wish to include their articles in their portfolios.

Review and Assessment

REVIEW Have students work in small groups turning each of the subsection headings into a question and writing answers to these questions. Then assign the Section 4 Review on p. 389.

ASSESS Assign the **Section 4 Daily Quiz** in *Core Resources*.

HISTORICAL SIDELIGHTS

The End of the War

After abandoning Richmond Lee and his army were in desperate need of rations. Instead of food, they were sent ammunition—the one thing they had in adequate supply. Lee's men were so hungry and exhausted that many fell by the wayside and waited to be captured. On April 9 Lee recognized the hopelessness of his army's situation—his troops were starving, outnumbered, and surrounded. Offering an alternative to surrender, one of Lee's men suggested that the remaining army become, in effect, guerrilla fighters. Lee, however, rejected this suggestion. He did not want to see further devastation of the countryside and his men reduced to "bands of marauders."

PRIMARY SOURCE

Description of Change: excerpted

Rationale: excerpted to focus on main idea

---

the war, the Union had to strike at the enemy's economic resources. General Sherman was successful, but his actions left deep and bitter scars across the South.

On December 10, 1864, Sherman and his men reached Savannah, where they were resupplied by the Union navy. On December 22 Sherman sent President Lincoln a message: "I beg to present you, as a Christmas gift, the city of Savannah." In February 1865 Sherman and his troops turned north to link up with Grant and fight a final battle.

■■ **General Sherman believed in fighting a total war—in defeating the enemy both militarily and economically.**

STILLNESS AT APPOMATTOX

As Sherman's army moved northward through the Carolinas, Grant's troops hammered at the doors of Richmond. On April 2, 1865, with Grant close on his heels, Lee withdrew from Richmond. Within hours Union troops poured into the Confederate capital.

Lee now commanded an army only half the size of Grant's. Knowing his troops could not survive another summer like that of 1864, Lee tried to make a run to the west, hoping to join up with more troops. But Grant cut off Lee's escape. With his once-proud army reduced to 30,000 men, many without shoes, Lee asked for terms of surrender.

Grant and Lee met in a house in the tiny village of Appomattox Court-house on April 9, 1865. Lee was in full dress uniform with a jewel-studded sword at his side. Grant wore a private's shirt, unbuttoned at the neck. For a time the two men talked about their Mexican War days. Then they turned to the business at hand. Aided by his military secretary—Lieutenant Colonel Ely Parker, a Seneca-Iroquois leader from New York—General Grant drafted the terms of surrender.

The terms were simple. Confederate officers could keep their sidearms, and all soldiers could keep their horses. "Let all the men who claim to own a horse or mule take the animals home with them to work their little farms," said Grant. "This will do much toward conciliating [uniting] our people," replied Lee.

As Lee rode off, Union troops started to cheer the Union victory, but Grant silenced them. "The war is over," he said; "the rebels are our countrymen again."

After the surrender, Lee returned to his men and quietly told them:

66 I have done for you all that it was in my power to do. You have done all your duty. Leave the result to God. Go to your homes and resume your occupations. Obey the laws and become as good citizens as you were soldiers. 99

The weary Confederates were then fed and allowed to depart for home. On April 26, 1865, General Joseph Johnston surrendered to General Sherman under similar terms at Durham, North Carolina.

■■ **Lee surrendered to Grant on April 9, 1865. Johnston surrendered to Sherman on April 26.**

▲ Tom Lovell painted this version of Lee's surrender at Appomattox. As part of the terms of surrender, Grant ordered 25,000 food rations to be given to the starving Confederate troops.

RETEACH Organize students into small groups and assign each a subsection of the section. Tell each group to compose a poem, song, or rap that expresses the main idea of its subsection. Have each group perform its composition.

Closure

Have students explain these statements from p. 386: "Emancipation provided Lincoln with one key to Union success. The president found another key in General Ulysses S. Grant." Have students suggest other keys to the Union victory.

Extension

RESEARCH Have students research and report on Civil War battles in which African American soldiers played major roles, such as Milliken's Bend, Fort Wagner, Port Hudson, and Petersburg.

COMPARE Have students learn about a recent civil war in the world and compare the causes, aims, tactics, and outcome of that conflict with the American Civil War.

THE CONSEQUENCES OF WAR

No other war on American soil has been as tragic as the Civil War in terms of human costs. Some 360,000 Union and 258,000 Confederate soldiers died during the struggle. More than a third of the young men who served during the war were killed, wounded, captured, or died of disease. More Americans were killed in the Civil War than in all other American wars combined.

Loss of life was not the war's only negative consequence, however. The war also devastated the southern economy. Southerners, including some four million enslaved African Americans who had gained their freedom as a result of the war, faced an uncertain future. Nearly all of the former slaves were without homes or jobs. Tens of thousands of white Confederate veterans were also homeless and jobless.

For the North, however, the war had many positive economic consequences. Agriculture and industry had expanded during the war to meet the needs of the military. The northern enterprises of steel, petroleum, food processing, manufacturing, and finance continued to expand after the war.

The war also finally resolved the long-debated issue of slavery. Never again would the United States government sanction the legalized enslavement of a group of people. In addition to ending slavery, the North's victory made the Republican party a dominant political force.

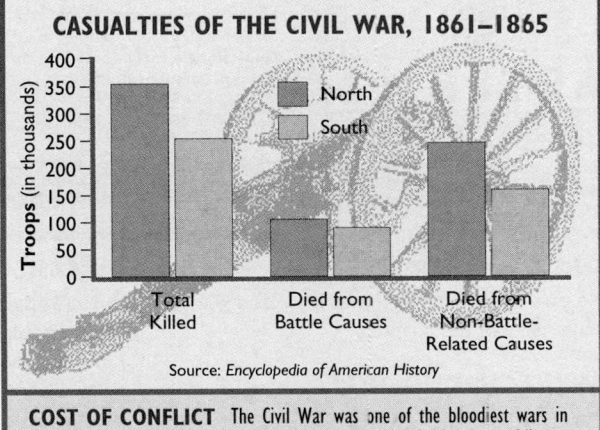

CASUALTIES OF THE CIVIL WAR, 1861–1865

Source: *Encyclopedia of American History*

COST OF CONFLICT The Civil War was one of the bloodiest wars in U.S. history. Of the more than 2.6 million Union and Confederate soldiers, more than 600,000 died during the four-year struggle.

? BUILDING GRAPH SKILLS About how many Union deaths resulted from non-battle-related causes? About how many Confederate deaths resulted from non-battle-related causes?

SECTION REVIEW ANSWERS

IDENTIFY

For significance, see the following pages:
Emancipation Proclamation (p. 384)
54th Massachusetts Infantry (p. 385)
Martin Delany (p. 385)
Ulysses S. Grant (p. 386)
war of attrition (p. 386)
William Tecumseh Sherman (p. 386)
total war (p. 387)

LOCATE

For locations, see the map on p. 387.

1. *changed from repressing rebellion to freeing slaves; hoped to weaken South by encouraging slaves to desert the South's war effort*
2. *constitutional issues; desire not to anger border states*
3. *Both strategies wore down the South militarily and economically, as well as psychologically.*
4. *North—growth of agriculture and industry; South—ruin of economy, end of slavery; both—loss of lives*
5. *Letters might mention that military service is one duty of a citizen, and by fulfilling this duty, African Americans should earn the rights of citizenship.*

SECTION 4 REVIEW

IDENTIFY and explain the significance of the following: Emancipation Proclamation, 54th Massachusetts Infantry, Martin Delany, Ulysses S. Grant, war of attrition, William Tecumseh Sherman, total war.

LOCATE and explain the importance of the following: Spotsylvania Court House, Atlanta, Savannah, Appomattox Courthouse.

1. **MAIN IDEA** How and why did the North change its war aims during the Civil War?

2. **MAIN IDEA** Why were only those slaves living in areas of rebellion against the United States affected by the Emancipation Proclamation?

3. **ASSESSING CONSEQUENCES** How did the military strategies of Ulysses S. Grant and William Tecumseh Sherman finally bring an end to the war?

4. **WRITING TO EVALUATE** Summarize the consequences of the Civil War for the North and the South.

5. **ANALYZING** Imagine you are an African American who has just enlisted in a black regiment. Write a letter to President Lincoln that explains why you believe that your military service is an important step toward citizenship.

CHAPTER 12
Review

Chapter Review Answers

WRITING A SUMMARY

See Essential Points in each section for main ideas.

REVIEWING CHRONOLOGY

5, 2, 4, 1, 3
Hypothesizing
Without a victory, it might have been viewed as an act of desperation by the Union.

IDENTIFYING PEOPLE AND IDEAS

1. commander of Confederate forces after 1862
2. first professionally licensed female doctor
3. overly cautious Union commander whose delays in moving troops led to failure
4. Confederate officer who stopped Union assault at First Battle of Bull Run
5. Northern Democrats who sympathized with South
6. first African American to rise to rank of major in Union army
7. action that freed slaves in areas of rebellion
8. Ulysses S. Grant's strategy of fighting until South ran out of men, supplies, and will
9. Union commander who practiced a strategy of total war, especially in his "march to the sea"
10. Union general whose tactics led to final victory

390

UNDERSTANDING MAIN IDEAS

1. political—changed from repressing rebellion to freeing slaves; military—shifted from dividing South to waging a war of attrition
2. South needed the river to resupply its western forces; North wanted to divide the Lower South.
3. Early optimism faded as casualties mounted; many believed the South was unbeatable; others became more determined than ever not to lose.
4. Women served as volunteers, spies, office and factory workers, and in medical roles; after July 1862, African Americans fought for the North in great numbers.
5. weakened the South economically by encouraging slaves to desert slaveholders; kept loyalty of border states by making act specific to areas of rebellion; made emancipation the central war issue
6. forced some people to serve while exempting others, favored one class while discriminating against others

---

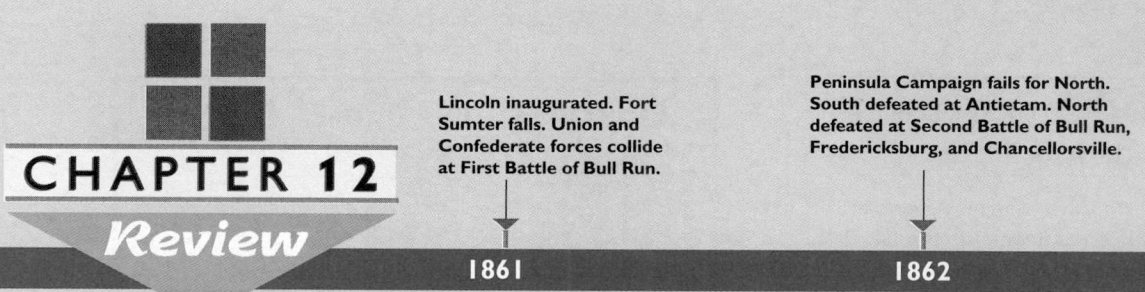

CHAPTER 12
Review

Lincoln inaugurated. Fort Sumter falls. Union and Confederate forces collide at First Battle of Bull Run.

Peninsula Campaign fails for North. South defeated at Antietam. North defeated at Second Battle of Bull Run, Fredericksburg, and Chancellorsville.

1861　　　　　　　　　　**1862**

WRITING A SUMMARY
Using the essential points of the chapter as a guide, write a summary of the chapter.

REVIEWING CHRONOLOGY
Number your paper 1 to 5. Study the time line above, and list the following events in the order in which they happened by writing the first next to 1, the second next to 2, and so on. Then complete the activity below.

1. Atlanta falls.
2. South defeated at Antietam.
3. Lee surrenders at Appomattox.
4. Emancipation Proclamation goes into effect.
5. Lincoln inaugurated.

Hypothesizing How might northerners have received the Emancipation Proclamation if it had been issued before the Battle of Antietam, rather than after?

IDENTIFYING PEOPLE AND IDEAS
Explain the historical significance of each of the following people or terms:

1. Robert E. Lee
2. Elizabeth Blackwell
3. George B. McClellan
4. Thomas "Stonewall" Jackson
5. Copperheads
6. Martin Delany
7. Emancipation Proclamation
8. war of attrition
9. William T. Sherman
10. Ulysses S. Grant

UNDERSTANDING MAIN IDEAS
1. How did the political and military goals of the North change as the war progressed?
2. Why was the Mississippi River important to both sides during the war?
3. How did early Confederate victories affect northern attitudes toward the war?
4. What contributions did women make in the war? What contributions did African Americans make?
5. What were the effects of the Emancipation Proclamation?
6. Why did some people object to the military draft?

REVIEWING THEMES
1. **Geographical Diversity** What role did geography play in helping the North win the war?
2. **Economic Development** In what ways did the Civil War both help and hurt the economies of the North and the South?

THINKING CRITICALLY
1. **Hypothesizing** How might the outcome of the Civil War have been different if European powers had aided the South?
2. **Evaluating** How did fears of alienating the border states affect northern strategy during the war?
3. **Analyzing** How did the South, with fewer supplies and resources, prevent the North from ending the Civil War quickly?

STRATEGY FOR SUCCESS
Review the Strategies for Success on Interpreting the Visual Record on page 98, then study the picture below. It shows conditions at a Confederate camp at Corinth, Mississippi, in May 1862. Then, on a separate piece of paper, list clues that suggest the artist may have painted an idealized picture of actual camp life.

Valentine Museum

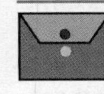
REVIEWING THEMES
1. The North was able to divide the South along the Mississippi River, weaken its economy with a naval blockade, and capture its capital, which was close to northern territory.
2. helped North by increasing industry, improving technology, and expanding transportation networks; hurt South by destroying infrastructure, crops, buildings, and ending slavery; hurt both by destroying human resources

THINKING CRITICALLY
1. Students might consider the impact of European money, manpower, and supplies in affecting the outcome.
2. helped delay making slavery an issue in the war and limited the Emancipation Proclamation to only areas in rebellion
3. waged a generally defensive war, forcing the North to fight in unfamiliar terrain; had more experienced military leaders than the North

STRATEGY FOR SUCCESS
Students might mention the absence of guns; good condition of clothing; leisurely attitude of soldiers; no sign of blood, illness, or malnutrition; and activities suggestive of a picnic rather than a war scene.

WRITING ABOUT HISTORY
Essays should balance the goal of victory against the destructive implications of total war.

USING PRIMARY SOURCES
Essays will vary, but students should express their feelings about the physical conditions of the march and the shortages of food.

LINKING HISTORY AND GEOGRAPHY
Paragraphs should mention how unreliable information about terrain may have led to difficulty in moving men and supplies and created delays in organizing military campaigns.

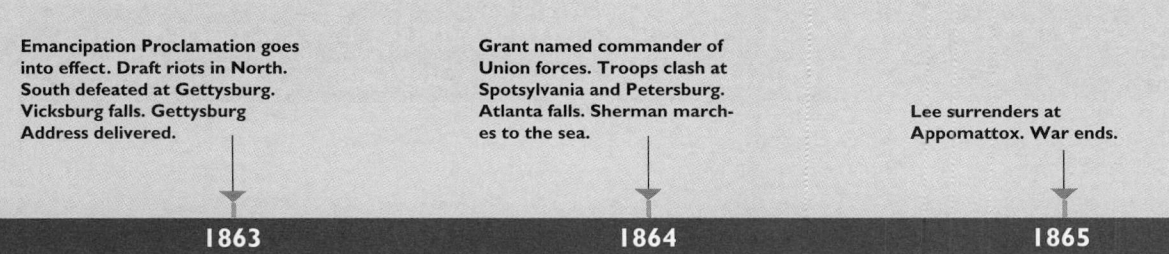

1863 — Emancipation Proclamation goes into effect. Draft riots in North. South defeated at Gettysburg. Vicksburg falls. Gettysburg Address delivered.

1864 — Grant named commander of Union forces. Troops clash at Spotsylvania and Petersburg. Atlanta falls. Sherman marches to the sea.

1865 — Lee surrenders at Appomattox. War ends.

WRITING ABOUT HISTORY
Writing to Evaluate The wisdom of Sherman's total-war tactics has been debated by historians. Write an essay evaluating whether such tactics would be practical in every war.

USING PRIMARY SOURCES
Soldiers in the Civil War fought under difficult conditions. The South, in particular, suffered from shortages of food and supplies. Read the following excerpt from a letter written by a Confederate soldier describing conditions on a march from Yorktown to Richmond in 1862. Then write an essay expressing your feelings about the passage.

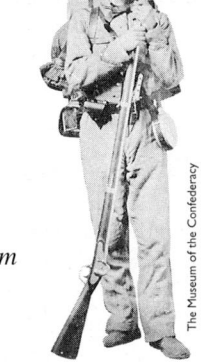

Confederate soldier

The Museum of the Confederacy

66 *I have never conceived of such trials as we have passed through. We were for days together without a morsel of food, excepting occasionally a meal of parched corn. . . . The army was kept on the march day & night and the roads were in some places waist deep in mud. . . . Many of the men became exhausted and some were actually stuck in the mud & had to be pulled out. . . .*

The men on the march ran through the gardens . . . devouring every particle of vegetables like the army worm leaving nothing at all standing. Whenever a cow or hog were found it was shot down & soon despatched. 99

LINKING HISTORY AND GEOGRAPHY
The Civil War was commanded by generals whose knowledge of the terrain was often hampered by inaccurate maps. Read the following excerpt from T. Harry Williams's *Lincoln and His Generals* (1952).

Then, in a paragraph, explain how unreliable information may have affected military campaigns in both the North and the South.

66 General Henry W. Halleck was running a campaign in the western theater in 1862 with maps he got from a book store. . . . Not until 1863 did the Army of the Potomac [the Union army] have an accurate map of northern Virginia, its theater of operations. . . . As late as 1864 there was not an office in Washington that could tell a general organizing a campaign what railroads were under military control . . . or how many men and supplies they could transport. 99

BUILDING YOUR PORTFOLIO

Complete the following projects independently or cooperatively.

1. **SLAVERY** In Chapter 11 you summarized Lincoln and Douglas's views on slavery. Building on that material, now imagine you are Frederick Douglass in 1862. Write a letter to President Lincoln urging him to take a strong stand against slavery by issuing the Emancipation Proclamation.

2. **SECTIONALISM** Imagine you are a member of a congressional committee attempting to formulate a compromise between the North and South to prevent a civil war. Create a chart that lists the political, economic, and social differences between the two sides that you think will be obstacles to an agreement and possible peaceful ways around these obstacles.

BUILDING YOUR PORTFOLIO
Have students refer to **Building Your Portfolio Worksheet 4**, assigned at the beginning of Unit 4. Use the worksheet to help students monitor their progress on the portfolio projects.

Assessment
Core Resources
• Review Worksheet 12
• Chapter 12 Tests
• Alternative Assessment Forms
Test Generator

RECONSTRUCTION AND THE NEW SOUTH

1865–1900

Chapter Overview

The Civil War freed millions of slaves but left the South devastated. Many southerners were homeless, jobless, and bitter. Lincoln's Reconstruction plan was lenient toward former Confederates, but he did not live to carry it out. His assassination put Andrew Johnson in office. Johnson's stubbornness and the South's refusal to accede to black rights allowed Radical Republicans to assume power. As a result, blacks were granted suffrage and took part in Reconstruction governments. White southerners responded by forming groups like the Ku Klux Klan and by reasserting their traditional power and control. In 1877 Reconstruction ended. In the 1880s and 1890s, blacks were disenfranchised, and segregation was legalized.

THE AMERICAN NATION VIDEODISC PROGRAM
A variety of still images, short videos, and activities are available for you to use as you teach this chapter. See Correlation to *The American Nation Videodisc Program* for barcode correlations and suggestions for using the program.

Chapter Planning Guide

CHAPTER 13	CORE RESOURCE BOOKLETS	AUDIOVISUAL RESOURCES	PROGRAM RESOURCES
INTRODUCTION pp. 392–393	■ Geography Worksheet 13 ■ Building Your Portfolio Worksheet 4		
TEACHING THE CHAPTER pp. 394–415	■ Graphic Organizer 13 ■ Social Studies Skills Worksheet 13 ■ Literature Worksheet 13 ■ Outline Map 9	■ *The American Nation* Videodisc: The Tuskegee Institute ■ Everyday Life in America Transparency and Worksheet 13	■ Art in American History Transparency and Worksheet 14 ■ *Eyewitnesses and Others*, Volume 2: Readings 3, 4, 19, 21
REVIEW AND ASSESSMENT pp. 416–417	■ Chapter 13 Daily Quizzes ■ Review Worksheet 13 ■ Chapter 13 Tests ■ Alternative Assessment Forms		■ Test Generator

Additional Resources

BOOKS FOR TEACHERS

Foner, Eric. *Short History of Reconstruction*. HarperCollins, 1990. Modern analysis of Reconstruction.

McPherson, James M. *Ordeal by Fire: the Civil War and Reconstruction*. McGraw, 1985. Account of Civil War and its aftermath.

Mellon, James, ed. *Bullwhip Days: The Slaves Remember*. Avon, 1992. Former slaves recall life in the South from slavery through Reconstruction.

BOOKS FOR STUDENTS

*Cook, Fred J. *Ku Klux Klan: America's Recurring Nightmare*. S&S Trade, 1989. Illustrated history of the Klan and its activities.

Franklin, John Hope. *Reconstruction After the Civil War*. University of Chicago Press, 1962. Classic account of American life during Reconstruction period.

* for students reading below grade level

MULTIMEDIA MATERIALS

The Background of the Reconstruction Period. Video, 20 min. BFA/SSSS. Focuses on historical and political issues of Reconstruction.

Reconstruction. Video, 35 min. EAV/SSSS. Examines Reconstruction's effects on North, South, and African Americans.

"Separate But Equal." Video, 8 min. Britannica. Describes how Jim Crow laws, KKK, *Plessy v. Ferguson* maintained inequality.

USE WITH PAGES 392–393

*L*isted on the right are the themes emphasized in Chapter 13. The questions in boldface type stimulate critical thinking and provide students with an opportunity to discuss the themes within a broadened context. The questions also appear in the pupil's edition on p. 392.

■ CONSTITUTIONAL HERITAGE

Why is it necessary that a plan of government be adaptable? Students might suggest that a plan of government must be able to adapt to changing social, economic, environmental, and other conditions because the future is unknowable.

What might happen if a plan of government cannot adapt to changes in society? If a government cannot adapt, citizens might attempt to force change on government.

■ DEMOCRATIC VALUES

Why might a nation's definition of a democratic society change over time? Students might suggest that a society's view of who should be allowed to participate in a democratic government could be altered by social changes. For example, property qualifications for voting might be lowered or eliminated if society no longer believed that only the rich were qualified to govern.

■ ECONOMIC DEVELOPMENT

How might a region's dependence on the sale of a single product limit the region's economic development? Students might note that a region with a single industry or a one-crop economy that does not diversify may find that it is too dependent on outside forces for its prosperity. Its economy could be devastated if the crop failed or if demand for its industrial products fell dramatically.

CHAPTER STRATEGIES FOR MEETING INDIVIDUAL NEEDS

LIMITED ENGLISH PROFICIENT LEARNERS

Have students work in small groups to create illustrated time lines or flowcharts identifying the main events in the chapter.

TACTILE/KINESTHETIC LEARNERS

Ask students to work in small groups to create scripts for skits about one of the main ideas in the chapter. Have them perform the skits for classmates.

LEARNERS HAVING DIFFICULTY

Help students create a chapter outline. Have them use the chapter title as the outline title; section titles for Roman numerals I, II, III, and IV; subsection titles for A, B, C, and so on; and topic sentences in the subsections for 1, 2, 3, and so on.

AUDITORY LEARNERS

Organize students in small groups, and assign individuals the names of people in the chapter's Preview Workshops. Ask students to write conversations that illustrate each person's viewpoint and actions. Invite each group to share its conversations with the class.

VISUAL LEARNERS

Have students work in groups to research and collect or draw pictures that illustrate the main ideas in the chapter. Ask them to create captions for their selections.

GIFTED LEARNERS

Encourage students to prepare and present reports on the legacy, positive *and* negative, of Reconstruction.

USING THE CHAPTER FOCUS

■ UNDERSTANDING THE MAIN IDEA

Remind students that the Civil War left the South in ruins and the nation with many of the sectional differences that existed prior to the war. Have students work in small groups, brainstorming to create a list of ideas for restoring the South to the Union in a manner that would heal divisions yet give justice and opportunity to all. Ask groups to share ideas with the class while volunteers write the ideas on a flip chart. Have students revise their list as they study the chapter.

☆ THEMES

Have students work individually or in small groups to answer the questions under Themes. Save students' responses so that they can compare them with their responses after studying the chapter. (See p. 391B for suggested answers.)

■ THE TIME LINE

Point out that Lincoln began to plan for Reconstruction two years before the Civil War ended. Then have students note how long Reconstruction lasted.

CORE RESOURCES

- **Graphic Organizer 13**
- **Geography Worksheet 13**
- **Outline Map 9**
- **Building Your Portfolio Worksheet 4**

ABOUT THE ILLUSTRATION

Although the Freedmen's Bureau was not established for the specific purpose of educating freedpeople, it became obvious that providing education was an important part of aiding them. The Freedmen's Bureau, working through religious and philanthropic organizations, supplied teachers with food, transportation, places to live, and government buildings for the schools. Ask students to compare their classroom with the one shown in the illustration.

Chapter 13

1865–1900

RECONSTRUCTION AND THE NEW SOUTH

▼ FOCUS

UNDERSTANDING THE MAIN IDEA

After the Civil War, the nation struggled to restore the southern states to the Union and determine the status of the freed slaves. The Radical and Moderate Republicans, the former slaves, and the planter aristocracy had conflicting goals for Reconstruction. Though the Union was restored, full and equal citizenship for African Americans was not achieved.

☆ THEMES

- **■ CONSTITUTIONAL HERITAGE** Why is it necessary that a plan of government be adaptable? What might happen if a government cannot adapt to changes in society?

- **■ DEMOCRATIC VALUES** Why might a nation's definition of a democratic society change over time?

- **■ ECONOMIC DEVELOPMENT** How might a region's dependence on the sale of a single product limit the region's economic development?

1865	1867	1869	1877	1896
▼	▼	▼	▼	▼
Thirteenth Amendment passed.	Reconstruction Acts passed.	Fifteenth Amendment passed.	Reconstruction ends.	Supreme Court issues ruling in *Plessy v. Ferguson.*

Ask students to recall the way of life of slaves before the Civil War. Ask students to speculate on the kinds of problems that emancipated slaves might have in the South after the Civil War. Have students review their speculations for accuracy as they study the chapter.

:: LINK TO THE PAST

Ever since the nation's founding, slavery had caused political problems. Though many Americans agreed that slavery was incompatible with democratic ideals, the nation had to fight a civil war to end the "peculiar institution." The war, however, did not solve the problem of how to include emancipated slaves in free society.

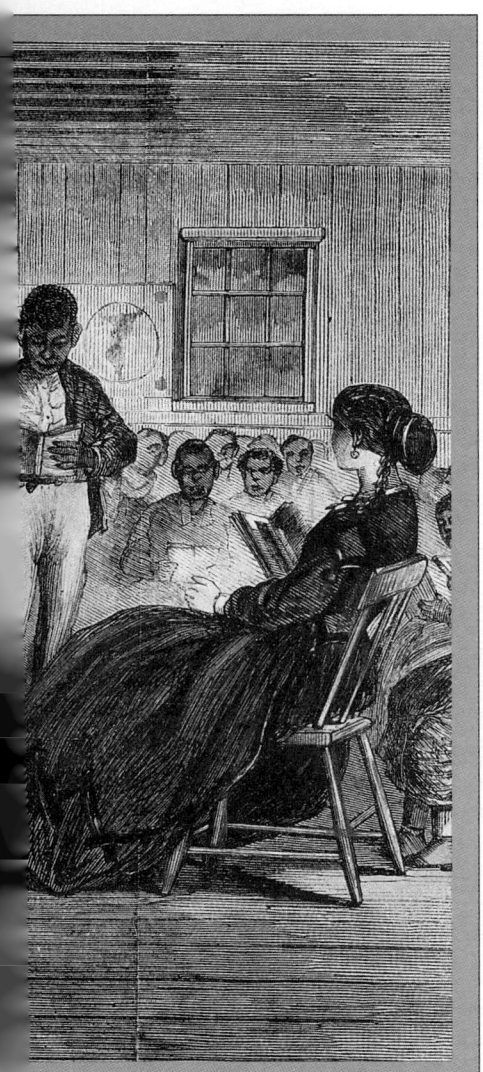

The Granger Collection, New York

Freedmen's Bureau schoolroom, 1866

In 1864 abolitionist Frederick Douglass demanded that African American men be granted suffrage:

> 66 It is said that the colored man is ignorant, and therefore he should not vote. In saying this, you lay down a rule for the black man that you apply to no other class of your citizens. . . . If he knows enough to be hanged, he knows enough to vote. If he knows an honest man from a thief, he knows much more than some of our white voters. . . . All I ask, however, in regards to blacks, is that whatever rule you adopt, whether of intelligence or wealth, as the condition of voting, you should apply it equally to the black man. 99

Douglass's appeal struck at the heart of one of the most urgent questions facing the nation: What would be the fate of the some four million newly emancipated slaves? Before this question could be answered, however, the federal government would have to confront another issue: How should the Union be restored?

Cover from
The Conquered Banner song sheet

PRIMARY SOURCE
Description of Change: excerpted
Rationale: excerpted to focus on main idea

PREVIEW WORKSHOP

Following is a list of the significant people and terms in this section. You may wish to use this list as a section preview.

People
- John Wilkes Booth
- Andrew Johnson

Terms
- Reconstruction
- amnesty
- Thirteenth Amendment
- black codes

MOTIVATING: PRIOR KNOWLEDGE

Write these categories on the chalkboard: *Transportation, Commerce, Labor, Agriculture.* Have volunteers explain how each was important to the South's economy and how each had been ravaged by the Civil War. Then tell students that Section 1 deals with the government's plans to reform and rebuild the South.

FOCUS OBJECTIVES

- Explain how the Civil War affected southern life.

- Compare and contrast Lincoln's and Congress's views on Reconstruction.

- Analyze Johnson's plan for Reconstruction.

- Determine in what ways the black codes were like a continuation of slavery.

Section 1

PRESIDENTIAL RECONSTRUCTION

F O C U S
- **How did the Civil War affect southern life?**
- **How did Lincoln and Congress differ in their views on Reconstruction?**
- **What was Johnson's plan for Reconstruction?**
- **In what ways were the black codes like a continuation of slavery?**

Republican campaign poster, 1864

Americans faced complex problems after the Civil War. Whites and blacks struggled to define the rights of freed African Americans. Politicians disagreed about how best to restore the Union. To heal the nation, President Abraham Lincoln offered generous peace terms to the former Confederate states. His successor, Andrew Johnson, was even more lenient toward the former rebels. Taking advantage of Johnson's lenience, southern legislatures restricted African Americans' rights.

PRIMARY SOURCES

Description of Change: excerpted
Rationale: excerpted to focus on main idea

THE OLD SOUTH DESTROYED

As the war ended, most of the some four million emancipated slaves found themselves without money or homes. "It came so sudden on 'em," recalled former slave Parke Johnston:

> ❝ Just think of whole droves of people, that had always been kept so close, and hardly ever left the plantation before, turned loose all at once, with nothing in the world, but what they had on their backs. ❞

◄ **This family record, showing a prosperous African American family, was marketed to former slaves after the war.**

Despite the obstacles, however, most freedpeople looked eagerly to the future. Like former slave Henry Turner, they yearned to enjoy their "rights in common with other men." They hoped to form their own churches and schools and to legalize their marriages. Many freedpeople looked forward to choosing their own livelihood rather than working as servants or as field hands for others. With freedom anything seemed possible, even finding family members who had been sold away. Former slave Hawkins Wilson sent a letter to his sister—address unknown—believing that it would somehow find its way to her. "Dear Sister Jane," he wrote:

> ❝ Your little brother Hawkins is trying to find out where you are and where his poor old mother is—Let me know and I will come to see you—I shall never forget the bag of biscuits you made for me. . . . Please send me some of Julia's hair whom I left a baby in the cradle when I was torn away from you. ❞

Call on two volunteers to role-play southerners after the Civil War. Ask one to testify about what life was like for African Americans and the other to relate what life was like for planters. The volunteers also should state what their character thinks the future might bring. Then have the remaining class members compare changes in the way of life for African Americans and southern planters after the Civil War. Encourage students to write a paragraph summarizing the class comparison. Have volunteers read their paragraphs aloud.

Have students work in pairs to make a chart that compares and contrasts Lincoln's 10 Percent Plan and the provisions of the Wade-Davis Bill. Call on volunteer pairs to copy their charts on the chalkboard. Discuss which plan was more flexible and lenient toward former Confederates.

▶

▲ After the Civil War, many southern cities lay in ruins. This 1865 photograph shows the effects of war on a district in Richmond, Virginia.

Above all, African Americans hoped, like free black Garrison Frazier, "to have land, and turn it and till it by our own labor." Most wanted land to support themselves and to protect their independence; in fact, many believed that it was their due. "Our wives, our children, our husbands, has been sold over and over again to purchase the lands we now locates upon," argued former slave Bayley Wyat; "we have a divine right to the land."

General William T. Sherman had encouraged such hopes in January 1865, when he ordered part of South Carolina to be divided into 40-acre parcels and given to freedmen. Rumors persisted that the federal government would give each freedman "40 acres and a mule."

The Union army had laid waste to parts of the South—destroying railroad lines, blowing up bridges and wells, and stripping Confederate homes, barns, and gardens. Many cities, too, lay in ruins. A visitor to Columbia, South Carolina, described "a wilderness of crumbling walls, naked chimneys, and trees killed by flames."

Disease, the grim companion of hunger and bad sanitation, swept the South. Illness ravaged the cities, where families lived in makeshift shelters and thousands died in the year after the war.

■■ At the war's end much of the South lay in ruins. Many southerners, both blacks and whites, suffered from poverty, hunger, and disease.

■■ After the Civil War, African Americans were optimistic about new possibilities for shaping their own destinies.

The planters still had land, but even they found their world "literally kicked to pieces." Mary Boykin Chesnut, a Confederate officer's wife, wrote about the despair she and many other white southerners felt:

National Portrait Gallery

▲ Mary Boykin Chesnut

❝ We are shut in here—turned with our faces to a dead wall. No mails. A letter is sometimes brought by a man on horseback, traveling through the wilderness made by Sherman. . . . We are cut off from the world—to eat out our own hearts. ❞

PRESIDENT LINCOLN AND RECONSTRUCTION

President Lincoln had gone to war not to destroy the South but to preserve the Union. Even before the fighting ended, he had begun planning for **Reconstruction**—for rebuilding the former Confederate states and reuniting the nation.

To encourage southerners to abandon the Confederacy, Lincoln had issued the Proclamation of Amnesty and Reconstruction on December 8, 1863. The proclamation offered **amnesty**—a full pardon—to all southerners (except high-ranking Confederate leaders and a few others) who would swear allegiance to the

Many African Americans spent years trying to find relatives from whom they had been separated during slavery. Well into the 1880s, African American newspapers in the North and in the South carried advertisements by former slaves requesting any information about their relatives.

GLOBAL CONNECTIONS

Economic conditions were so desperate that many former slaveholders and their families emigrated from the South after the Civil War. Some moved to the North, while others began new lives in Europe, Mexico, or Brazil. Mexico and Brazil offered large expanses of land, suitable for plantation farming, to southern plantation owners who would settle there. The emigrants were also enticed by the offer of large pools of cheap labor.

Description of Change: excerpted
Rationale: excerpted to focus on main idea

Teaching the Section

JOHNSON'S PLAN FOR RECONSTRUCTION

Call on volunteers to list the provisions of Johnson's plan for Reconstruction as you write them on the chalkboard. Then have students imagine that they are members of Congress during Reconstruction and present arguments for or against each provision.

COMPARING SLAVERY AND BLACK CODES

Ask students to imagine that they are freedpeople in the South during Reconstruction after black codes have gone into effect. Have students write letters to the editor of the local newspaper, comparing their life under black codes to life under the slave system. Select students to read their letters to the class. Students may wish to include their letters in their portfolios.

THE EMANCIPATION PROCLAMATION

In 1861, two years before President Lincoln issued the Emancipation Proclamation, Czar Alexander II of Russia promised more than 20 million Russian serfs freedom and land. Though the czar's own land policies eventually failed, in 1879 he criticized the Proclamation for having sidestepped the issue of land. The czar charged that the decree had freed the American slaves but had left them with no means to support themselves. Alexander boasted:

❝I *did more for the Russian serf in giving him land as well as personal liberty, than America did for the Negro slave set free by the Proclamation of President Lincoln. I am at a loss to understand how you Americans could have been so blind as to leave the Negro slave without tools to work out his salvation. . . . Without property of any kind he cannot educate himself and his children. I believe the time must come when many will question the manner of American emancipation of the Negro slaves in 1863.* **❞**

THROUGH OTHERS' EYES

U.S. Constitution and accept federal laws on slavery. The proclamation also permitted a state to rejoin the Union when 10 percent of the state's residents who had voted in 1860 swore their loyalty to the United States.

Many members of Congress objected to the president's "10 Percent Plan." They did not trust the rebels to become loyal citizens or to protect the rights of former slaves. Furthermore, they believed Congress should help shape Reconstruction policy.

Congress laid out its own Reconstruction plan in the Wade-Davis Bill, passed in July 1864. The bill called for the former Confederate states to abolish slavery and for a *majority* of each state's white males to take a loyalty oath. Lincoln vetoed the bill because he was not ready to "be inflexibly committed to any single plan of restoration." In his Second Inaugural Address, delivered on March 4, 1865, Lincoln made clear his underlying goal for Reconstruction:

❝ With malice toward none, with charity for all, with firmness in the right as God gives us to see the right, let us strive on . . . to bind up the nation's wounds . . . to do all which may achieve and cherish a just and lasting peace. **❞**

■■ **Unlike Congress, Lincoln favored a flexible, lenient policy toward the former Confederates.**

What course Reconstruction might have taken under Lincoln's direction will never be known. On April 14, 1865, just days after General Robert E. Lee's surrender, John Wilkes Booth, a half-crazed Confederate sympathizer, shot the president as he watched a play at Washington's Ford Theatre. Lincoln died early the following morning.

Lincoln's death was a tragic blow to the entire nation. Thousands of Americans stood beside the railroad tracks as the funeral train made its way from Washington to Lincoln's burial site in Illinois.

▲ **Mathew Brady took this photograph of Abraham Lincoln delivering his Second Inaugural Address on March 4, 1865.**

Practice

GUIDED PRACTICE

Divide the class into groups representing African Americans, members of Congress, and southern state legislators. Have groups take turns giving their views on the 10 Percent Plan, the Wade-Davis Bill, and Johnson's Reconstruction plan.

INDEPENDENT PRACTICE

Have students choose an identity from the Guided Practice and, from that person's point of view, write an evaluation of the 10 Percent Plan, the Wade-Davis Bill, or Johnson's Reconstruction plan. Students may wish to include their evaluations in their portfolios.

Review and Assessment

REVIEW Organize students to work in groups to create political cartoons or slogans that comment on the post–Civil War South; black codes; and the Reconstruction policies of Lincoln, Congress, and Johnson. Have students explain their work. Then assign the Section 1 Review on p. 398.

ASSESS Assign the **Section 1 Daily Quiz** in *Core Resources.*

▶

▲ After Lincoln's assassination, the War Department offered a reward for the capture of John Wilkes Booth. The pistol Booth used to murder Lincoln is shown here.

PRESIDENT JOHNSON AND RECONSTRUCTION

At Lincoln's death Vice President Andrew Johnson became president. Johnson—a Democrat, a one-time slaveholder, and a former U.S. senator from Tennessee—had been chosen as Lincoln's running mate in 1864 because of his pro-Union sympathies. Republican leaders had hoped he would appeal to northern Democrats and southern Unionists.

Despite his support for the Union and experience as Tennessee's military governor during the war, Johnson was ill-suited to the challenges of Reconstruction and of defining African Americans' new rights. He suffered, one contemporary observed, from "almost unconquerable prejudices against the African race." Moreover, he lacked Lincoln's tact and political skill. The opinionated Johnson refused to compromise.

The president's weaknesses were not immediately apparent. At first Johnson denounced southern treason, even suggesting that Jefferson Davis and other high-ranking Confederates be hanged as traitors. This pleased many Republicans. "Johnson, we have faith in you. By the gods, there will be no trouble now in running this government," exclaimed Senator Ben Wade of Ohio.

In May 1865, however, in a startling about-face, Johnson issued a blanket pardon to all rebels except ex-Confederate officeholders and the richest planters. These he pardoned freely on an individual basis. Johnson's leniency extended to the rebel states as well. For readmission to the Union, he required only that they nullify their acts of secession, abolish slavery, and refuse to pay Confederate government debts. (The last provision was meant to hurt wealthy southerners who had financed the Confederacy.)

Johnson's plan allowed former Confederate leaders to take charge of Reconstruction. These men dominated the new legislatures—some still proudly wore their Confederate uniforms!—and benefited

PRESIDENTIAL LIVES

ANDREW JOHNSON
1808–1875

in office
1865–1869

Andrew Johnson was a self-made man. When Johnson was three, his father died. A few years later, his mother apprenticed him to a tailor. Johnson ran away from his master and eventually went to Tennessee. He never attended school, but he probably learned to read as an apprentice. Later his wife taught him to write and to do simple arithmetic.

Johnson did well as a tailor. He was able to buy property but never identified himself with the planter class. His loyalties were to farmers and artisans, and as a politician he saw himself as an outsider. "Andy Johnson," people in East Tennessee said, "never went back on his raisin'."

He continued to make all his own clothes until he went to Washington. Even after he became president, Johnson often dropped into tailor shops for a chat.

COOPERATIVE LEARNING

Organize students into groups of six, subdivided into pairs. Direct each pair to write down a different provision of the black codes and to explain how that provision was like a continuation of slavery. Then have each pair read the provision and explanation to their group.

HISTORICAL SIDELIGHTS

American Indians After the Civil War
Because many American Indians in Indian Territory had sided with the South during the Civil War, public pressure built on Congress to punish these Indians by taking their lands. However, American Indians insisted that they had been forced to cooperate with the South, and they asked for leniency. Their leaders argued that Indians had been surrounded by the Confederacy and that the U.S. had not been able to fulfill its treaty obligations to protect them. Although some groups lost some land, the treatment of rebel groups in Indian Territory was generally less harsh than they expected.

RETEACH Organize students into small groups and assign each a subsection of the section. Tell each group to compose a poem, song, or rap that expresses the main idea of its subsection. Have each group perform its composition.

Closure

Write the following statement on the chalkboard and ask students why they agree or disagree with it: *Reconstruction of the South after the Civil War progressed swiftly because those involved in the planning of Reconstruction agreed on the methods of achieving it.*

Extension

INTERPRET Have students work in groups to find primary sources illustrating conditions for freedpeople after the Civil War. Ask groups to prepare dramatic readings from the sources.

COMPARE Have students research Russian history and compare the circumstances of former serfs to conditions encountered by emancipated slaves in the American South.

PRIMARY SOURCE
Description of Change: excerpted
Rationale: excerpted to focus on main idea

IDENTIFY

For significance, see the following pages:
Reconstruction (p. 395)
amnesty (p. 395)
John Wilkes Booth (p. 396)
Andrew Johnson (p. 397)
Thirteenth Amendment (p. 398)
black codes (p. 398)

1. *much of South in ruins; plantation system destroyed; many whites in despair and blacks hopeful for future*
2. *nullify acts of secession, abolish slavery, and refuse to pay Confederate war debts*
3. *Congress—required majority of state's white males to take loyalty oaths; Lincoln—required 10 percent of residents who had voted in 1860 to take loyalty oath*
4. *Letters might explain how black codes were like slave codes: forced former slaves into plantation labor and restricted freedom.*
5. *Farmland and a mule would help provide economic independence and protect newly gained freedom.*

---

from the president's support for "a white man's government." When they complained of the "painful humiliation" inflicted by the presence of black soldiers in the South, Johnson had the soldiers removed. When Mississippi refused to ratify the **Thirteenth Amendment**—which Congress had passed in January 1865 to abolish slavery—Johnson recognized the state's new government anyway.

▲ Newly freed slaves are shown here planting sweet potatoes on a plantation in Hilton Head, South Carolina.

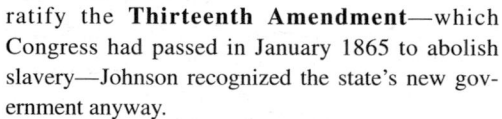 **Johnson freely granted pardons and set lenient conditions for states' readmission to the Union.**

The BLACK CODES

Johnson's actions encouraged former Confederates to adopt laws limiting the freedom of former slaves. These **black codes**, which African Americans denounced as "a disgrace to civilization," resembled prewar slave codes. Mississippi simply used its old code, substituting the word *freedman* for *slave*.

Under these laws African Americans could not hold meetings unless whites were present, travel without permits, or own guns. Blacks in New Orleans could not be on the streets after 10 o'clock at night, just one hour later than the previous slave curfew. The editor of the city's African American newspaper noted: "This additional hour is the fruit of our victories in the field. Four years of a bloody

war have been fought to gain that one hour."

Above all, the codes reestablished white control over black labor. Without slaves to do the work, "our fields everywhere lie untilled," lamented a white Mississippian in April 1865. As a way to make former slaves return to field work, some local codes forbade blacks to live in towns unless they were servants. South Carolina and Mississippi required freedpeople to sign 12-month labor contracts. Those who refused could be arrested and have their labor for the year put up for auction. One black veteran demanded: "If you call this Freedom, what do you call Slavery?"

Northerners angrily denounced the black codes. The Chicago *Tribune* reprinted the Mississippi code and proclaimed:

> 66 The men of the North will convert the State of Mississippi into a frog pond before they will allow such laws to disgrace one foot of soil in which the bones of our soldiers sleep and over which the flag of freedom waves. 99

It would be up to Congress, however, to find a way to end the rule of the "white-washed rebels."

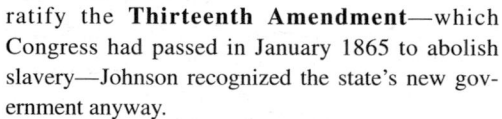 **The black codes limited the freedom of African Americans and tried to force former slaves back into plantation labor.**

 SECTION 1 REVIEW

IDENTIFY and explain the significance of the following: Reconstruction, amnesty, John Wilkes Booth, Andrew Johnson, Thirteenth Amendment, black codes.

1. **MAIN IDEA** What was southern life like after the Civil War?
2. **MAIN IDEA** Under Johnson's Reconstruction plan, how could states gain readmission to the Union?
3. **CONTRASTING** How did Congress's plan for Reconstruction differ from Lincoln's?
4. **WRITING TO DESCRIBE** Imagine you are a newly emancipated slave. Write a letter to a relative in the North describing the effects of the black codes on your life.
5. **EVALUATING** Why would "40 acres and a mule" be important to a freed slave?

Section 2

CONGRESSIONAL RECONSTRUCTION

FOCUS
■ **How did Moderate and Radical Republicans at first differ in their approaches to Reconstruction?**
■ **Why did Moderate Republicans in Congress break with Johnson and join forces with the Radicals?**
■ **How did the Fourteenth and Fifteenth amendments expand the civil rights of African Americans?**

Cartoon mocking Johnson's veto of the Freedmen's Bureau Bill

President Johnson's support of the former Confederates and his failure to protect African Americans' rights angered even Moderate Republicans, who had hoped to cooperate with the president. As a result, the Moderates in Congress deserted him and joined forces with the Radicals. Together they took over Reconstruction.

THE MODERATES VERSUS THE RADICALS

▲ Thaddeus Stevens

When Johnson took office in 1865, he did not face a united Congress. Even the Republicans were divided over the course Reconstruction should take. The Moderates, who made up the majority of the Republican party, viewed Reconstruction as a practical matter of restoring the southern states to the Union. Their main concern was keeping ex-Confederates out of government. They favored giving African Americans civil equality—which included the right to travel freely and to meet together—but not the vote.

Radical Republicans, on the other hand, insisted that African Americans be given the right to vote. For them, the proper goal of Reconstruction was to create a new South where all men would enjoy equal rights. But for this goal to be reached, warned Thaddeus Stevens, the outspoken Radical from Pennsylvania, "the whole fabric of southern society *must* be changed."

Stevens believed that land reform could change southern society. He agreed with Senator Charles Sumner of Massachusetts, who insisted that "the great plantations . . . must be broken up, and the freedmen must have the pieces." According to Stevens, economic independence for the former slaves would ensure their freedom and destroy the political power of the "proud, bloated, and defiant rebels."

Despite the efforts of Stevens and Sumner, land reform—particularly government seizure of land—never won wide support. The *New York Times* accused land reformers of starting "a war on property . . . to succeed the war on Slavery." Even many Radicals believed that the ballot, civil equality, and free labor were enough to give African Americans a chance to succeed.

FOCUS OBJECTIVES

■ Explain how Moderate and Radical Republicans at first differed in their approaches to Reconstruction.

■ Determine why Moderate Republicans in Congress broke with Johnson and joined forces with the Radicals.

■ Analyze how the Fourteenth and Fifteenth amendments expanded the civil rights of African Americans.

HISTORICAL SIDELIGHTS
Land Distribution

Thaddeus Stevens advocated federal seizure of the 400 million acres belonging to the wealthiest 10 percent of southerners. Each freedman would receive 40 acres, and the remaining land would be sold, in small lots, to the highest bidders. Proceeds from land sales would provide pensions for Civil War veterans and pay off most of the national debt.

MOTIVATING: LINK TO TODAY

Have students describe recent situations in which the president and Congress have come into conflict. Tell students that in this section they will learn about clashes between Congress and the president during Reconstruction.

Teaching the Section

REPUBLICANS DIFFER ON RECONSTRUCTION

Write the following on the chalkboard: *The main goal of Reconstruction is to restore the southern states to the Union. The main goal of Reconstruction is to create a new South in which all men enjoy equal rights.* Ask students to identify which was the goal of the Moderate Republicans and which the goal of the Radical Republicans. Then ask

volunteers to cite the approaches taken by each group to achieve its goal; write students' answers on the chalkboard.

HISTORICAL SIDELIGHTS

"Masters and Slaves"
Colonel Samuel Thomas, assistant commissioner of the Freedmen's Bureau for Mississippi, said, "The whites esteem the blacks their property by natural right, and, however much they may admit that the relations of masters and slaves have been destroyed by the war . . . they still have an ingrained feeling that the blacks at large belong to the whites at large, and whenever opportunity serves, they treat the colored people just as their profit, caprice or passion may dictate."

Map Caption Answer
Mississippi, South Carolina, North Carolina

HISTORICAL SIDELIGHTS

Grant on Freedmen
General Ulysses S. Grant had reported to Johnson that "in some form the Freedmen's Bureau is an absolute necessity until civil law is established and enforced, securing to the freedmen their rights and full protection."

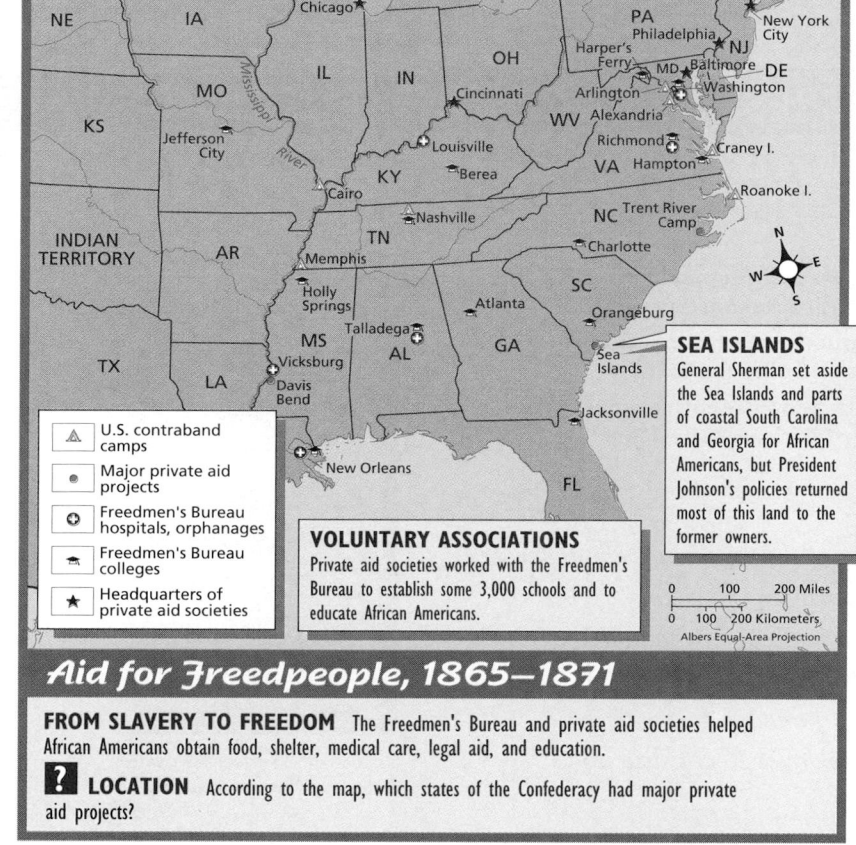

VOLUNTARY ASSOCIATIONS
Private aid societies worked with the Freedmen's Bureau to establish some 3,000 schools and to educate African Americans.

SEA ISLANDS
General Sherman set aside the Sea Islands and parts of coastal South Carolina and Georgia for African Americans, but President Johnson's policies returned most of this land to the former owners.

Map legend:
- U.S. contraband camps
- Major private aid projects
- Freedmen's Bureau hospitals, orphanages
- Freedmen's Bureau colleges
- ★ Headquarters of private aid societies

Aid for Freedpeople, 1865–1871

FROM SLAVERY TO FREEDOM The Freedmen's Bureau and private aid societies helped African Americans obtain food, shelter, medical care, legal aid, and education.

? **LOCATION** According to the map, which states of the Confederacy had major private aid projects?

■■ **At first, Moderate and Radical Republicans were divided over land reform and African American suffrage.**

CONGRESS VERSUS JOHNSON

The split between the Moderates and the Radicals was not to last, however. In early 1866 Congress began hearings on conditions in the South. Witness after witness came before the Joint Committee on Reconstruction with stories of postwar violence. African Americans recounted stories of murder and of homes, schools, and churches reduced to "ashes and cinders." Southern Unionists told of death threats. These reports and others like them convinced the Moderates to join forces with the Radicals to protect the rights and safety of the ex-slaves. Work began on legislation to extend the life of the Freedmen's Bureau and to guarantee black civil rights.

The Freedmen's Bureau. Congress had set up the **Freedmen's Bureau** in March 1865 to aid the millions of southerners left homeless and hungry by the war. The bureau distributed food and clothing, served as an employment agency, set up hospitals, and operated schools. Not surprisingly, much of the bureau's efforts were directed toward easing the plight of ex-slaves.

Congress had intended for the bureau to remain in operation for one year. In light of the hearings, however, most members now favored legislation to extend the life of the agency. African Americans largely agreed, although they thought the Freedmen's Bureau too often encouraged blacks to remain on plantations and sign labor contracts. They acknowledged, however, that the bureau's very presence forced white southerners to recognize emancipation. One black told a government official that "if the Freedman Bureau was removed, a colored man would have better sense than to speak a word in behalf of the colored man's rights, for fear of his life."

In February 1866 Congress passed the Freedmen's Bureau Bill to extend the life of the agency. Much to Congress's surprise, Johnson promptly vetoed the bill.

The Civil Rights Act of 1866. Furious with the president, Congress quickly passed the **Civil Rights Act of 1866**. The act declared that everyone born in the United States was a citizen with full civil rights. (It did not guarantee voting rights, however.) The act was designed to overturn discriminatory laws and the Supreme Court's 1857 *Dred Scott* ruling that blacks were not citizens. "If the President vetoes the Civil Rights Bill," wrote one Ohio senator, "we shall be obliged to draw our swords."

▲ This 1866 poster mocks the ineffectiveness of the Civil Rights Act of 1866. As punishment for crimes, one former slave is being sold at auction while another is being whipped.

Johnson did not heed the warning. He vetoed the bill, arguing that it would centralize power in the federal government. Johnson's veto message also underscored his racism; the president complained that the bill would "operate . . . against the white race."

Johnson's veto eroded his support in Congress and united Moderate and Radical Republicans against him. Congress overrode Johnson's veto of the Civil Rights Act. Then Congress returned to the matter of the Freedmen's Bureau, passed a new bill, and overrode yet another veto.

■■ Postwar violence and Johnson's opposition to the Freedmen's Bureau Bill and the Civil Rights Act of 1866 united Moderate and Radical Republicans.

The Fourteenth Amendment. Fearing that a future Democrat-controlled Congress might repeal the Civil Rights Act, congressional Republicans wrote its provisions into the **Fourteenth Amendment**, passed in June 1866. The amendment required states to extend equal citizenship to African Americans and all people "born or naturalized in the United States." It also denied states the right to deprive anyone of "life, liberty, or property without due process of law," and it promised all citizens the "equal protection of the laws." With its ratification in July 1868, the amendment created a national citizenship with rights—enjoyed equally by all—that were to be enforced by the federal government.

The Fourteenth Amendment did not guarantee African American voting rights. It did, however, reduce the number of representatives a state could send to Congress in proportion to the number of the state's male citizens denied the right to vote. Republicans hoped that southern states would give African Americans the right to vote rather than lose representation in Congress.

■■ The Fourteenth Amendment provided for equal citizenship for African Americans and pressured states to grant black men voting rights.

THE RADICALS COME TO POWER

Johnson tried to make the Fourteenth Amendment an issue in the 1866 congressional elections. He traveled throughout the Midwest, campaigning in support of candidates who opposed the amendment and calling the Radicals traitors.

Most voters were not receptive. Many were deeply troubled by the ongoing violence against blacks in the South. In Memphis in May 1866, white rioters killed 46 blacks and burned 12 schools and 4 churches. "If anything could reveal . . . the demoniac spirit of the southern whites toward the freedmen," one reporter noted, this violence would. On July 30 in New Orleans, more than 30 blacks and 3 white Radicals were killed in a riot. General Philip H. Sheridan, Johnson's military commander in Texas and Louisiana, called it "an absolute massacre."

▶ The August 1866 issue of *Harper's Weekly* included this illustration of the July riot in New Orleans.

*P*ractice

GUIDED PRACTICE

List the boldface terms for this section on the chalkboard. Then ask students to explain how each affected opportunities for African Americans to prosper and participate in the New South. Outline student responses on the chalkboard.

INDEPENDENT PRACTICE

Tell students to imagine that they are attorneys hired to represent African Americans in the New South who are suing for economic damages and discrimination suffered after Reconstruction. Ask students to write opening arguments for a trial.

*R*eview and *A*ssessment

REVIEW Organize students in pairs to write a conversation about the New South. Explain that the conversation is between a former slave who fled the South before the Civil War and a relative who never left the South. Encourage pairs to read their conversations to the class. Then assign the Section 4 Review on p. 415.

ASSESS Assign the **Section 4 Daily Quiz** in *Core Resources.*

PERSONALITIES IN HISTORY

Besides organizing anti-lynching societies, Ida Wells-Barnett organized local black women in Chicago to work for women's suffrage. She was also secretary of the National Afro-American Council from 1898 to 1902. She founded the Negro Fellowship League in 1910 and became its first president.

THE AMERICAN NATION VIDEODISC PROGRAM

The Tuskegee Institute

1B   33609   3:53

414

▲ **Booker T. Washington**

ruled that the Fourteenth Amendment forbade only *states,* not individuals or businesses, from discriminating against blacks. The Supreme Court went further in upholding segregation in ***Plessy v. Ferguson*** (1896), ruling that "separate but equal" facilities did not violate the Fourteenth Amendment. Only Justice John Marshall Harlan disagreed. He declared that "our Constitution is color-blind, and neither knows nor tolerates classes among citizens."

■■ **After Reconstruction, African Americans were deprived of their rights and had few economic opportunities.**

*B*LACK SOUTHERNERS ORGANIZE

Confronted by segregation and denied basic political and civil rights, some African Americans left the South for the Midwest or moved to northern cities. Most, however, stayed in the South, where their ancestors had lived for generations. To improve their lives, African Americans formed mutual aid societies, started businesses, strengthened churches, and built schools. The African Methodist Episcopal (AME) church, the AME Zion church, and black Baptist churches grew rapidly.

The key question facing African American leaders after 1877 was how to fight discrimination. Two influential leaders, Booker T. Washington, a former slave who founded Alabama's Tuskegee Institute in 1881, and Ida Wells-Barnett, a teacher

▲ **Tuskegee Institute was founded in 1881 to teach African Americans trades and professions. A dressmaking class for women and a printing class for men are shown here.**

RETEACH To students working in pairs, distribute slips of paper on which you have written one of the following four groups of Preview Workshop items: (1) sharecropping, crop-lien system; (2) poll taxes, literacy tests; (3) segregation, Jim Crow laws, *Plessy* v. *Ferguson;* (4) Booker T. Washington, Ida Wells-Barnett. Ask each pair to find the assigned words in the text and prepare statements and graphics that define and illustrate the items.

Closure

Read these words of W.E.B. Du Bois, famous African American historian, author, and educator: "The slave went free; stood a brief moment in the sun; then moved back again toward slavery." Ask students to explain what Du Bois meant. Ask students why they think that Du Bois would refer to the condition of freedpeople as "slavery."

Extension

FORMULATE Have students research Justice John Marshall Harlan's dissenting opinion in *Plessy* v. *Ferguson.* Ask students to formulate an opinion dissenting from that of the majority on the Court.

RESEARCH Invite students to read biographies and write annotations about African American leaders during the 1870s and 1880s. Compile annotations into a *Who's Who* book.

and journalist, offered different answers to the discrimination question.

Washington believed that African Americans should concentrate on economic advancement. To further blacks' economic independence—which he believed was the key to political and social equality—Washington urged blacks to seek practical training in trades and professions. He also discouraged them from protesting against discrimination, arguing that it merely increased whites' hostility. If economic and social progress was to be made, he claimed, blacks would need "the cooperation of the Southern whites" because "they control government and own the property." (Behind the scenes, however, Washington secretly provided support to groups fighting Jim Crow laws and racial violence.)

He carried his message of peaceful coexistence to white audiences as well. In an 1895 speech known as the Atlanta Compromise, he told whites that while blacks and whites could live in separate social wozrlds, they needed to cooperate for economic progress: "In all things that are purely social we can be as separate as the fingers, yet one as the hand in all things essential to mutual progress." There were, he said, "no limits to the attainments of the Negro. . . . I want to see him enter the all-powerful business and commercial world."

Some African American leaders disagreed with Washington's public position, arguing instead that blacks should protest unfair treatment. One such leader was Ida Wells-Barnett (born Ida Bell Wells). Born to a slave family in 1862, Ida Wells was educated in a Mississippi freedmen's school and became a

teacher herself at age 14. In 1884 Wells moved to Tennessee, where she taught while attending Fisk University. She lost her teaching job, however, when she began protesting discrimination and segregated schools.

Ida Wells then turned to journalism, becoming part owner of the *Memphis Free Speech.* In 1892, after whites lynched three friends of hers, she vowed to put a stop to lynching. In a fiery editorial she charged "that neither character nor standing avails the Negro if he dares to protect himself against the white man or become his rival." Angry whites destroyed her newspaper office.

Wells urged African Americans to leave the South. She herself left Memphis for New York, where she continued her crusade against lynching. She conducted investigations, wrote exposés, lectured widely in the North and in Great Britain, and organized antilynching societies. After moving to Chicago and marrying lawyer Ferdinand Barnett in 1895, she published *A Red Record,* the first statistical study of lynching. Though lynchings decreased only slightly in the early 1900s, Wells's tireless efforts kept the public's attention focused on the issue.

■■ **African Americans built their own institutions, and they adopted several approaches to fighting discrimination.**

Ida Wells-Barnett
The Granger Collection, New York

SECTION REVIEW ANSWERS

IDENTIFY
For significance, see the following pages:
sharecropping (p. 410)
crop-lien system (p. 411)
poll taxes (p. 412)
literacy tests (p. 412)
segregation (p. 413)
Jim Crow laws (p. 413)
Plessy v. Ferguson (p. 414)
Booker T. Washington (p. 414)
Ida Wells-Barnett (p. 414)

1. *rented their land and turned to sharecropping and the crop-lien system*
2. *rights still denied and still had few economic opportunities*
3. *left the South, built their own institutions, adopted strategies such as economic advancement and protest to fight discrimination*
4. *Essays may mention that the sharecropper might be no better off because of low wages and being tied to a company's housing and store.*
5. *deprived African Americans, southern Unionists, and northern carpetbaggers of power; benefited former Confederates, white Democrats, and factory owners and investors*

SECTION 4 REVIEW

IDENTIFY and explain the significance of the following: sharecropping, crop-lien system, poll taxes, literacy tests, segregation, Jim Crow laws, *Plessy* v. *Ferguson,* Booker T. Washington, Ida Wells-Barnett.

1. **MAIN IDEA** After slavery had been abolished, how did plantation owners deal with the shortage of labor?
2. **MAIN IDEA** In what ways did the New South resemble the Old South (before Reconstruction) for African Americans?
3. **MAIN IDEA** What actions did blacks take in response to their loss of rights?
4. **WRITING TO EVALUATE** Write an essay evaluating the consequences for a white sharecropper of leaving the land to seek work in a southern factory.
5. **SYNTHESIZING** How did changes in the post-Reconstruction New South harm some groups of people and benefit others?

9. state laws enforcing racial segregation
10. African American journalist who campaigned against lynching and encouraged blacks to protest unfair treatment

UNDERSTANDING MAIN IDEAS

1. Conditions included ruined property, poverty, disease and hunger, but blacks were optimistic about future; many blacks sought economic or political opportunities to improve their lives, while white planters turned to sharecroppers and tenant farmers to work their land.

2. Lincoln's and Johnson's plans were more lenient than the Radicals' plan.
3. Blacks participated in government and voted; some whites used violence and intimidation to reestablish control over them.
4. As white Democrats regained control of state governments, they passed laws to legalize segregation and to strip blacks of their newly won rights.
5. Sharecropping and crop-lien systems grew, but farmers remained poor; industrial opportunities increased, but low wages and company housing and stores kept many laborers in poverty.

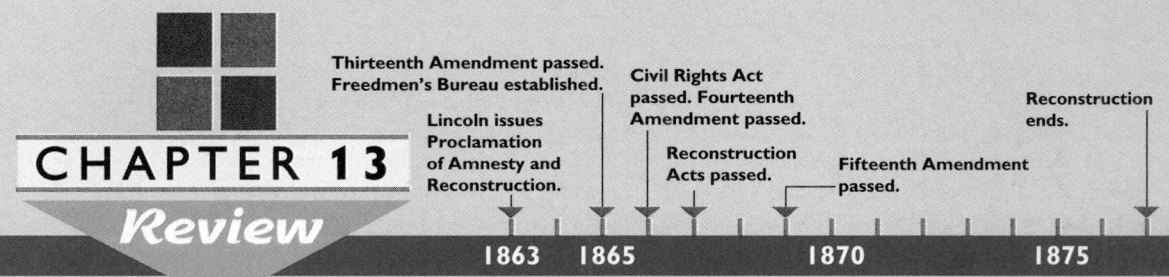

CHAPTER 13 *Review*

Lincoln issues Proclamation of Amnesty and Reconstruction.

Thirteenth Amendment passed. Freedmen's Bureau established.

Civil Rights Act passed. Fourteenth Amendment passed.

Reconstruction Acts passed.

Fifteenth Amendment passed.

Reconstruction ends.

1863   1865   1870   1875

WRITING A SUMMARY
Using the essential points of the chapter as a guide, write a summary of the chapter.

REVIEWING CHRONOLOGY
Number your paper 1 to 5. Study the time line above, and list the following events in the order in which they happened by writing the first next to 1, the second next to 2, and so on. Then complete the activity below.

1. Reconstruction Acts passed.
2. Freedmen's Bureau established.
3. Fifteenth Amendment passed.
4. Lincoln issues Proclamation of Amnesty and Reconstruction.
5. Reconstruction ends.

Assessing Consequences Choose the two events that you think had the most positive outcome for African Americans, and explain the reasons for your assessment.

IDENTIFYING PEOPLE AND IDEAS
Explain the historical significance of each of the following people or terms.

1. amnesty
2. Andrew Johnson
3. black codes
4. Thaddeus Stevens
5. Reconstruction Acts
6. carpetbaggers
7. Compromise of 1877
8. sharecropping
9. Jim Crow laws
10. Ida Wells-Barnett

UNDERSTANDING MAIN IDEAS

1. Describe conditions in the South after the Civil War, and explain how people tried to improve those conditions.
2. How did the Reconstruction plans of Lincoln, Johnson, and the Radical Republicans differ?
3. What political roles did African Americans play during Reconstruction, and how did some whites protest these new roles?
4. How did changes in the New South reverse the policies of the Reconstruction period?
5. How did conditions for southern farmers and laborers change from 1865 to 1900?

REVIEWING THEMES

1. **Constitutional Heritage** How did the Thirteenth, Fourteenth, and Fifteenth amendments attempt to adapt the U.S. Constitution to changing conditions after the Civil War?
2. **Democratic Values** How was democratic society in the U.S. expanded during Reconstruction? How did the expansion prepare for further changes in America's definition of democracy?
3. **Economic Development** In what ways did cotton continue to affect the New South?

THINKING CRITICALLY

1. **Hypothesizing** How might conditions in the New South have been different if African Americans had been given land after the war?
2. **Evaluating** Why did many southern whites react so strongly to gains made by African Americans during Reconstruction?
3. **Synthesizing** Compare and contrast the views of Booker T. Washington and Ida Wells-Barnett on the place of African Americans in society.

STRATEGY FOR SUCCESS

Review the Skills Handbook entry on Reading Charts and Graphs beginning on page 996. Then study the chart below. How did the value of cotton goods produced in the South change during this period? How did southern production compare with that of the New England and Middle Atlantic regions?

VALUE OF COTTON GOODS PRODUCED 1880–1900		
(In millions of dollars)		
Region	**1880**	**1890**	**1900**
New England	143	181	191
Middle Atlantic	29	40	48
Southern	16	41	95

Source: *The American South*

REVIEWING THEMES

1. provided framework to define some African American rights but failed to foresee how those rights would be undermined in New South
2. by extending political rights to black males; encouraged women to fight for their voting rights
3. Crop-lien system increased South's ties to cotton farming; one-crop agriculture kept South dependent on others for other goods.

THINKING CRITICALLY

1. Property ownership might have given ex-slaves more economic freedom and power, resulting in less poverty and victimization.
2. Because the changes overturned the old class structure based on race, they evoked resentment and prejudice.
3. Washington focused on economic progress and social separation; Wells-Barnett encouraged blacks to protest unfair treatment.

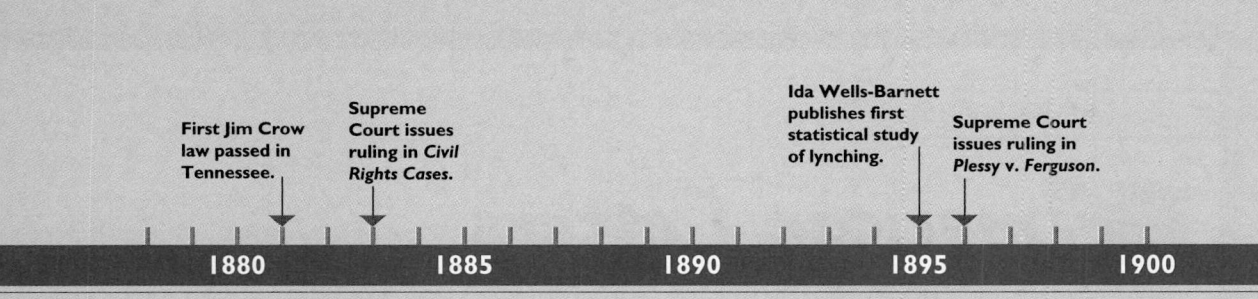

First Jim Crow law passed in Tennessee.

Supreme Court issues ruling in *Civil Rights Cases.*

Ida Wells-Barnett publishes first statistical study of lynching.

Supreme Court issues ruling in *Plessy v. Ferguson.*

1880   1885   1890   1895   1900

WRITING ABOUT HISTORY

Writing to Express a Viewpoint Imagine you are a planter in the postwar South. Write a letter to the editor of your local newspaper explaining how Reconstruction policies have affected your economic and social status and why you support the Compromise of 1877. Be sure to provide specific examples and reasons in your letter.

USING PRIMARY SOURCES

Read the following excerpt from a November 1865 letter that a group of African Americans from South Carolina wrote to the U.S. Congress. Then summarize the letter's main demands and explain the suggested basis for these demands.

❝ *We would ask for no rights or privileges but such as rest upon the strong basis of justice. . . . We ask first, that the strong arm of law and order be placed alike over the entire people of this State; that life and property be secured, and the laborer free to sell his labor as the merchant his goods.*

We ask that a fair and impartial instruction be given to the pledges of the government to us concerning the land question.

We ask that the three great agents of civilized society—the school, the pulpit, the press—be as secure in South Carolina as in Massachusetts or Vermont.

We ask that equal suffrage be conferred upon us, in common with the white men of this State.

This we ask, because "all free governments derive their just powers from the consent of the governed"; and we are largely in the majority in this State, bearing for a long period the burden of onerous taxation, without a just representation. **❞**

LINKING HISTORY AND GEOGRAPHY

Review the map on page 402. Then explain what conclusions you can draw based on the dates of states' readmission to the Union and the defeat of Radical Republican governments.

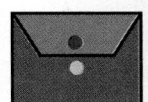 

BUILDING YOUR PORTFOLIO

Complete the following projects independently or cooperatively.

1. **SECTIONALISM** In Chapter 12 you served on a committee working on a compromise between the North and the South. Building on that experience, imagine you are a southern governor opposed to northern politicians' plans for the South during Reconstruction. Create an outline for a Reconstruction plan that would address the interests of planters, ex-soldiers, and African Americans in your state.

2. **DEMOCRATIC RIGHTS** In Chapter 11 you served as a lawyer helping Dred Scott win his freedom. Building on that experience, imagine you are working on the *Plessy v. Ferguson* case. Prepare a closing statement arguing that segregation, as practiced in "separate but equal" facilities for blacks and whites, violates the Fourteenth Amendment.

South Carolina farmer and child

The Granger Collection, New York

THE PAIN OF SLAVERY AND CIVIL WAR

UNIT 4

American Letters

The Pain of Slavery and Civil War

The tragedy of slavery and the Civil War echoed throughout the literature of the 19th century. The African American spiritual "Steal Away" and African American writer Paul Laurence Dunbar's poem capture the hardships of slave life. American poet Walt Whitman and African American poet Frances Ellen Harper explore some of the effects of the Civil War on the nation.

▲ *Walt Whitman*

Steal Away

African American spiritual

Steal away, steal away, steal away to Jesus,
Steal away, steal away home,
I ain't got long to stay here.

My Lord, He calls me,
He calls me by the thunder,
The trumpet sounds within-a my soul,
I ain't got long to stay here.

Steal away, steal away, steal away to Jesus,
Steal away, steal away home,
I ain't got long to stay here.

Green trees a-bending,
Po' sinner stands a-trembling
The trumpet sounds within-a my soul,
I ain't got long to stay here.

Steal away, steal away, steal away to Jesus,
Steal away, steal away home,
I ain't got long to stay here. ❖

Sympathy

by Paul Laurence Dunbar

I know what the caged bird feels, alas!
When the sun is bright on the upland slopes;
When the wind stirs soft through the springing grass
And the river flows like a stream of glass;
When the first bird sings and the first bud opes,
And the faint perfume from its chalice[1] steals—
I know what the caged bird feels!

I know why the caged bird beats his wing
Till its blood is red on the cruel bars;
For he must fly back to his perch and cling
When he fain[2] would be on the bough a-swing;
And a pain still throbs in the old, old scars
And they pulse again with a keener sting—
I know why he beats his wing!

I know why the caged bird sings, ah me,
When his wing is bruised and his bosom sore,—
When he beats his bars and would be free;
It is not a carol of joy or glee,
But a prayer that he sends from his heart's deep core,
But a plea, that upward to Heaven he flings—
I know why the caged bird sings! ❖

1 the cup-shaped inside of a flower
2 gladly

▼ *The Fisk University Jubilee Singers won fame for their concerts of spirituals in the late 1800s.*

Jubilee Singers, Courtesy of Fisk University

From *Beat! Beat! Drums!*

by Walt Whitman

Beat! beat! drums!—blow! bugles! blow!
Through the windows—through doors—burst like a
　　ruthless force,
Into the solemn church, and scatter the congregation,
Into the school where the scholar is studying;
Leave not the bridegroom quiet—no happiness must
　　he have now with his bride,
Nor the peaceful farmer any peace, ploughing his field
　　or gathering his grain,
So fierce you whirr and pound you drums—so shrill
　　you bugles blow. ❖

From *The Wound-Dresser*

by Walt Whitman

(Aroused and angry, I'd thought to beat the alarum,[1]
　　and urge relentless war,
But soon my fingers failed me, my face drooped and I
　　resigned myself,
To sit by the wounded and soothe them, or silently
　　watch the dead.)
Years hence of these scenes, of these furious passions,
　　these chances,
Of unsurpassed heroes, (was one side so brave? the
　　other was equally brave.) ❖

---

1 call to arms

Learning to Read

by Frances Ellen Harper

Very soon the Yankee teachers
　　Came down and set up school;
But, oh! how the Rebs did hate it,—
　　It was agin' their rule.

Our masters always tried to hide
　　Book learning from our eyes;
Knowledge didn't agree with
　　slavery—
'Twould make us all too wise.

But some of us would try to steal
　　A little from the book,
And put the words together,
　　And learn by hook or crook.

I remember Uncle Caldwell,
　　Who took pot liquor[1] fat
And greased the pages of his book,
　　And hid it in his hat.

And had his master ever seen
　　The leaves upon his head,
He'd have thought them greasy papers,
　　But nothing to be read.

And there was Mrs. Turner's Ben,
　　Who heard the children spell,
And picked the words right up by heart,
　　And learned to read 'em well.

Well, the Northern folks kept sending
　　The Yankee teachers down;
And they stood right up and helped us,
　　Though the Rebs did sneer and frown.

And I longed to read my Bible,
　　For precious words it said;
But when I begun to learn it,
　　Folks just shook their heads.

And said there is no use trying,
　　Oh! Chloe, you're too late;
But I was rising sixty,
　　I had no time to wait.

So I got a pair of glasses,
　　And straight to work I went,
And never stopped till I could read
　　The hymns and Testament.

Then I got a little cabin,
　　A place to call my own—
And I felt as independent
　　As the queen upon her throne. ❖

---

1 liquid left in a pot after cooking

THINKING AND WRITING ABOUT LITERATURE

1. African American spirituals sung by slaves often had hidden meanings. What do you think "steal away home" could have meant for slaves?
2. In Paul Lawrence Dunbar's poem, why does the "caged bird" sing?
3. What is the tone of the first Walt Whitman poem? In the second poem, how did Whitman's feelings about the war change?
4. In Frances Ellen Harper's poem, written during Reconstruction, what is the significance of reading for Chloe?

PRIMARY SOURCES

Description of Change: excerpted and footnoted
Rationale: excerpted for space considerations; footnoted to clarify meaning

THINKING AND WRITING ABOUT LITERATURE

1. *that only running away— or death—were the means of achieving freedom*
2. *to send a plea to God to free it from its cage*
3. *militant; he feels compassion and sorrow for soldiers on both sides of the war*
4. *Being able to read the Bible provides Chloe with a feeling of enrichment and independence.*

COMPARING POINTS OF VIEW

Guide students through the explanation of how to identify and compare points of view and then have them complete the Practicing the Strategy exercise. Then have students review the discussion of southern views of slavery on pp. 264–265 and northern abolitionism on pp. 292–293. Make a chart on the chalkboard with the column headings *Identity,* *Viewpoint,* and the row headings *Jesse Burton Harrison, George Fitzhugh, Henry Highland Garnet, William Lloyd Garrison.* Have students fill in the chart, noting similarities and differences in viewpoints. Ask students to speculate about the reasons for the differences in points of view.

PRACTICING THE STRATEGY

1. *Lee's; because both leaders rejected vengeance, preferring rather to look toward a restoration of national unity and peace*
2. *Lincoln, speaking before the war had ended, was deeply aware of its terrible cost. To him, only the preservation and restoration of the Union could justify the war. And as president of both North and South, he was concerned for the wounded and bereaved on both sides.*

Strategies for Success

▶ **Horace Greeley**

COMPARING POINTS OF VIEW

We all bring to our experiences a point of view, a personal frame of reference from which we see or think about things. Besides such factors as age, sex, education, and family background, historical circumstances also shape our outlook. Comparing varied views and voices gives us historical insights. It helps us understand, for example, the roots of historical conflicts.

How to Compare Points of View

1. **Note the sources.** Find out about each author or speaker. Check whether each is an authority on the subject under discussion.
2. **Do research.** Find out all you can about the event, person, or situation.
3. **Compare and contrast the main ideas.** Note similarities and differences in the main ideas being expressed.
4. **Compare supporting details.** Consider whether the ideas are supported by relevant facts, by opinions, or by a combination of both. Evaluate the logic of the supporting arguments, and look for any bias.
5. **Evaluate the points of view.** Apply your critical thinking skills to appreciate why people have different points of view and to weigh the accuracy and reliability of each view.

Applying the Strategy

When the Civil War ended, Americans seriously disagreed over how the nation should proceed, especially how the South should be treated. Read and compare the following points of view.

66 These gentlemen of the South mean to win. They meant it in 1861 when they opened fire on Sumter. They meant it in 1865 when they sent a bullet through the brain of Abraham Lincoln. They mean it now. The moment we remove the iron hand from the Rebels' throats they will rise and attempt the mastery. 99
—*Horace Greeley, editorial in the* New York Tribune, *November 15, 1865*

66 The war being at an end, the Southern states having laid down their arms and the questions at issue between them and the Northern states having been decided, I believe it to be the duty of everyone to unite in the restoration of the country and the reestablishment of peace and harmony. 99
—*Gen. Robert E. Lee, letter, September 7, 1865*

Greeley, a northerner, is pessimistic about the prospects for restoration. He fears that those he sarcastically calls "the gentlemen of the South" will rise again in rebellion. To support this view, he refers to the attack on Fort Sumter and the assassination of Lincoln. But these were the actions of only a few southerners. Greeley's worry seems exaggerated, but not totally unfounded. The war's massive destruction of the South made any new uprising unlikely; nevertheless, many ex-Confederates did regain power.

Lee's statement that the war's outcome has settled the issues that divided Americans is understandable for a military officer. Postwar struggles would prove, however, that this outlook was overly optimistic—and too simplistic as well. Many politicians and ordinary citizens, on both sides, did not share Lee's sense of duty; regional rivalries were not laid down so easily as guns.

Practicing the Strategy

Read the excerpt of President Lincoln's Second Inaugural Address on page 396, and compare it with the views quoted here. Then, on a separate sheet of paper, answer the following questions.

1. Whose point of view seems closer to Lincoln's—Greeley's or Lee's? Explain why.
2. Describe Lincoln's point of view.

◀ **Abraham Lincoln**

BUILDING YOUR PORTFOLIO

Each portfolio project described below is the culmination of the Building Your Portfolio activities in the chapter reviews of Unit 4. First, decide whether you wish students to work individually or in groups on these unit projects. Then permit each student to choose the project on which he or she desires to work. Provide students with copies of **Building Your Portfolio Worksheet 4** from *Core Resources*. This worksheet will guide students step by step to complete their projects.

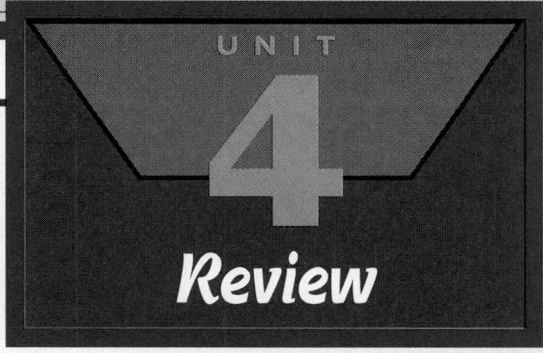

BUILDING YOUR PORTFOLIO

Outlined below are three projects. Independently or cooperatively, complete one and use the products to demonstrate your mastery of the historical concepts involved.

 SLAVERY
The Civil War ended the institution of slavery. It did not, however, end legal discrimination against African Americans. Using the portfolio materials you designed in chapters 11 and 12, hold a *New York Tribune* press conference with a representative from the Union League. Your questions at the conference should focus on the positive and negative consequences of the Civil War for African Americans.

 SECTIONALISM
Differences between the North and the South created a rift that led to the Civil War and left deep scars that Reconstruction failed to erase. Using the portfolio materials you designed in chapters 12 and 13, hold a debate arguing whether Reconstruction served the political, economic, and social interests of the North more than the South.

3 DEMOCRATIC RIGHTS
The protection of the rights of different groups in society is at the heart of a democratic system. Using the portfolio materials you designed in chapters 11 and 13, prepare a one-scene courtroom play about the segregation of schools. Characters might include Ida Wells-Barnett, northern abolitionists, ex-slaves, and southern Redeemers.

Videodisc Review

In assigned groups, develop an outline for a video collage of America in the years between 1845 and 1900. Choose images that best illustrate the major topics of the period. Write a script to accompany the images. Assign narrators to different parts of the script, and present your video collage to the class.

Further Reading

Chesnut, Mary B. *A Diary from Dixie.* Ben Ames Williams, ed. Harvard University Press (1980). Firsthand account of everyday life in the Confederate South.

Emilio, Luis F. *A Brave Black Regiment.* Bantam Books (1992). Collection of documents written about the 54th Regiment of the Massachusetts Volunteer Infantry.

Foner, Eric. *A Short History of Reconstruction, 1863–1877.* HarperCollins (1990). Overview of the Reconstruction years.

Franklin, John Hope. *Reconstruction: After the Civil War.* University of Chicago Press (1961). An account of the Radicals' efforts to legislate the South during Reconstruction.

Meltzer, Milton, ed. *Voices from the Civil War.* HarperCollins (1989). Northern and southern views of the war and its effects from 1861–1865.

Nesbitt, Mark. *35 Days to Gettysburg.* Stackpole Books (1992). Events leading up to the Battle of Gettysburg as seen through the eyes of a Union soldier and a Confederate soldier.

Stampp, Kenneth M. *America in 1857: A Nation on the Brink.* Oxford (1990). Analysis of one key year in the movement toward Civil War.

Taylor, Susie K. *A Black Woman's Civil War Memoirs.* Patricia W. Romero, ed. Talman (1988). An African American woman's account of camp life with the 33rd U.S. Colored Troops.

PORTFOLIO ASSESSMENT

1. *Press conferences should discuss the consequences for African Americans of the Emancipation Proclamation, participation in the Civil War, the devastation of the southern economy, and the rise of the Republican party.*
2. *Debate should show students' familiarity with southern and northern perspectives on Reconstruction legislation.*
3. *The courtroom play should show African American calls for education of black children, their debates about segregated schools, the support of northern abolitionists, and the opposition of southern Redeemers.*

The Nation Transformed ❖ 1860–1910

Introducing the Unit

- **Chapter 14**
  THE WESTERN CROSSROADS
  1860–1910
- **Chapter 15**
  THE TRANSFORMATION
  OF AMERICA
  1865–1910
- **Chapter 16**
  POLITICS AND PROTEST
  1865–1910

Using the American Almanac Posters

Begin the unit by displaying the American Almanac Poster and discussing entries with students. In addition to the worksheet, the annotations that follow provide additional information about the entries and suggest questions and activities.

Then, as students study the unit, have them work in small groups to create their own almanacs—using the same six headings—on pieces of butcher paper. At the end of the unit, call on groups to display and discuss their almanacs.

UNIT OVERVIEW

In the second half of the 1800s the nation underwent rapid change. Successive waves of settlers pushed the frontier westward, driving Native Americans from the land. The U.S. experienced a surge of industrial growth, with inexpensive steel, a nationwide rail network, and new sources of energy fostering a "new industrial order." During the same period, millions of immigrants came to America, spurring rapid urban growth. The late 1800s were also characterized by political scandals, graft, and other abuses of party patronage. As reformers called for an end to political corruption, other Americans sought change through labor unions. Farmers also organized to protect their political and economic interests.

Chapter 14
THE WESTERN CROSSROADS 1860–1910

Chapter 15
THE TRANSFORMATION OF AMERICA 1865–1910

UNIT

The Nation Transformed

1860–1910

5

*S*uccessive waves of settlers pushed the frontier westward during the second half of the 1800's, driving American Indians from the land. During the same period, the United States experienced a surge of industrial growth. Cities also grew rapidly as millions of immigrants came to America. The late 1800s were also marked by political scandal. As reformers called for an end to political corruption, others sought change through labor unions. Farmers also organized to protect their interests.

◀ Nat Swan in front of his sod house, Nebraska, 1886

Chapter 16
POLITICS AND PROTEST
1865–1910

THE WESTERN CROSSROADS

1860–1910

Chapter Overview

Beginning in the years after the Civil War, the American Indians of the Great Plains and Far West fought a desperate battle to maintain their homelands and ways of life. Spearheaded by the U.S. Army and supported by land-hungry settlers, the Indian wars pushed Indians from their lands and onto reservations. Land acts and the spread of railroads across the Plains greatly increased the number of non-Indian settlers in the region, who established farms and cattle ranches. Free grazing on public land created a cattle boom in the West that lasted about 20 years. Gold and silver drew thousands more westward, and eventually mining became the province of big business.

THE AMERICAN NATION VIDEODISC PROGRAM
A variety of still images, short videos, and activities are available for you to use as you teach this chapter. See Correlation to *The American Nation Videodisc Program* for barcode correlations and suggestions for using the program.

Chapter Planning Guide

CHAPTER 14	CORE RESOURCE BOOKLETS	AV AUDIOVISUAL RESOURCES	PROGRAM RESOURCES
INTRODUCTION pp. 424–425	■ Building Your Portfolio Worksheet 5	■ *The American Nation* Videodisc: Crossroads of Cultures	■ *Eyewitnesses and Others*, Volume 2: Reading 9
TEACHING THE CHAPTER pp. 426–453	■ Graphic Organizer 14 ■ Social Studies Skills Worksheet 14 ■ Literature Worksheet 14 ■ Geography Worksheet 14 ■ Outline Maps 8, 9	■ *The American Nation* Videodisc: Linking the Nation ■ Everyday Life in America Transparency and Worksheet 14 ■ Linking Geography and History Transparencies and Worksheets 10A, 12A	■ Art in American History Transparencies and Worksheets 15, 17 ■ *Eyewitnesses and Others*, Volume 1: Reading 77; Volume 2: Readings 1, 2, 5, 7, 8, 10
REVIEW AND ASSESSMENT pp. 454–455	■ Chapter 14 Daily Quizzes ■ Review Worksheet 14 ■ Chapter 14 Tests ■ Alternative Assessment Forms		■ Test Generator

Additional Resources

BOOKS FOR TEACHERS

Nabokov, Peter, ed. *Native American Testimony.* Viking Penguin, 1992. History of relations between Native Americans and whites, using Native American first-person accounts.

Painter, Nell. *Exodusters.* University Press of Kansas, 1986. Study of the African American migration to Kansas after Reconstruction.

White, Richard. *"It's Your Misfortune and None of My Own": A History of the American West.* University of Oklahoma Press, 1991. Scholarly history of the West.

BOOKS FOR STUDENTS

*Editors of Time-Life Books, *The Wild West.* Warner, 1993. Illustrated general history of the settlement of the West.

Hook, Jason. *American Indian Warrior Chiefs.* Sterling, 1990. Biographies of Crazy Horse, Chief Joseph, Geronimo, and Tecumseh.

Schlissel, Lillian, et al. *Far from Home: Families of the Westward Journey.* Schocken, 1989. Social history of western pioneers.

*for students reading below grade level

MULTIMEDIA MATERIALS

The American West: Myth and Reality. Video, 52 min. EAV/SSSS. Debunks television and movie myths about the West.

Ghost Town Hunters. Video, 50 min. SSSS. Tour of mining camps and other boom and bust towns.

Nez Percé: Portrait of a People. Video, 23 min. National Park Service/SSSS. History of the Nez Percé.

USE WITH PAGES 424–425

Listed on the right are the themes emphasized in Chapter 14. The questions in boldface type stimulate critical thinking and provide students with an opportunity to discuss the themes within a broadened context. The questions also appear in the pupil's edition on p. 424.

■ GEOGRAPHIC DIVERSITY

What strategies might people use to survive and prosper in arid or semi-arid environments? Students might consider ways people could adapt to these environments, including conserving water, raising crops and animals best suited to these regions, or devising farming methods that use the available water efficiently.

■ CULTURAL DIVERSITY

What problems might arise when one group attempts to force another group to give up its way of life? Students should discuss a group's right to retain its own values, beliefs, and practices. They should consider that forcing a group to give up its culture might result in disruption of the group's economic and social organization, perhaps accompanied by resistance to these events.

■ ECONOMIC DEVELOPMENT

How might a government promote economic development in a new territory? Students might weigh the ability of settlers to develop the economy of a new territory against the difficulty settlers might encounter with such problems as establishing transportation and communication networks, legal rights to land, or relations with people already in the territory. They might also consider the impact that a government's land policies, and its ability to protect people in the new territory, could have on the territory's economic development.

CHAPTER STRATEGIES FOR MEETING INDIVIDUAL NEEDS

LIMITED ENGLISH PROFICIENT LEARNERS

Have students work in pairs to create scenes depicting life in the West in the late 19th century. Ask volunteers to compile the finished scenes into a slide presentation for the class. You may also wish to have LEP students work with visual learners in executing that activity.

TACTILE/KINESTHETIC LEARNERS

Organize students into groups to make models, dioramas, or diagrams of a Sioux Indian encampment, a sod farmhouse, a cattle ranch, or a mining camp.

LEARNERS HAVING DIFFICULTY

Organize students into four groups. Assign each group the Focus questions for a section. Have the groups identify the pages on which information to answer the questions can be found, take notes, and put their answers in sentence form. Have groups share their answers.

AUDITORY LEARNERS

Have students pick cowboy songs for a presentation, explaining how the songs depict cowboy life. A resource for this is *Cowboy Songs and Other Frontier Ballads* by J. A. and Allan Lomax.

VISUAL LEARNERS

Have students create a series of "Western Crossroads" postage stamps showing life on the Plains for Native Americans, farmers, cowboys, and miners. They can use the people cited in each section's Preview Workshop for possible choices.

GIFTED LEARNERS

Have students research and write an essay on myths about the West. The essay should identify how these misconceptions started, any inaccuracies they contain, reasons why they gained acceptance, and any effects they caused.

USING THE CHAPTER FOCUS

■ UNDERSTANDING THE MAIN IDEA

Call on a volunteer to read aloud the Understanding the Main Idea paragraph. Ask students to identify types of people who would have been most likely to have moved west in the 1860s and after. Then ask them to describe how they think each group might have viewed the West. Discuss similarities and differences among the groups' views and speculate on potential areas of conflict among them and with groups that occupied the land.

THEMES

Have students work individually or in groups to answer the questions under Themes. Save students' responses so that they can compare them with their responses after studying the chapter. (See p. 423B for suggested answers.)

■ THE TIME LINE

Ask students to copy the events on the time line in their notebooks. After they read about each event in the chapter, ask them to write a paragraph that explains the causes and effects of that event.

CORE RESOURCES

- **Graphic Organizer 14**
- **Outline Maps 8, 9**
- **Building Your Portfolio Worksheet 5**

AV RESOURCES

- *The American Nation Videodisc:* **Crossroads of Cultures**

ABOUT THE ILLUSTRATION

Although some women mined alongside their husbands, others, like the woman in this rare 1852 photograph, only visited the mine sites. Ask students to study the photograph on these pages and read the caption. Call on volunteers to suggest, based on the photograph, the kinds of tools and supplies a prospective miner would need to buy.

Then ask them to speculate about the living and working conditions of the miners shown in the photograph.

Chapter 14

1860–1910

THE WESTERN CROSSROADS

FOCUS

UNDERSTANDING THE MAIN IDEA

After the Civil War the regions of the West—the Great Plains, the Southwest, and the Far West—played important roles in U.S. economic growth. People moved to the West, encouraged by the U.S. government's offers of free land and the promise of profits from ranching, farming, lumbering, and mining. In many years of conflict and treaty negotiations, the U.S. government forced Native Americans to give up much of their lands.

THEMES

■ GEOGRAPHIC DIVERSITY
What strategies might people use to survive and prosper in arid or semiarid environments?

■ CULTURAL DIVERSITY
What problems might arise when one group attempts to force another group to give up its way of life?

■ ECONOMIC DEVELOPMENT
How might a government promote economic development in a new territory?

1862	1869	1876	1879	1896
The Homestead Act passed.	First transcontinental railroad completed.	Battle of Little Bighorn occurs.	Exodusters trek west.	Gold discovered in Yukon Territory.

LINK TO THE PAST

The resolution of the Oregon boundary dispute in 1846 and the Treaty of Guadalupe Hidalgo in 1848 opened up millions of acres of western land for U.S. settlement. Native Americans faced increasing pressure on their lands and resources as non-Indian settlers moved to the Far West.

Miners at Auburn Ravine, California, 1852

*E*ver since the Spanish planted settlements in the present-day southwestern United States, the West has been a crossroads where Native American and Asian, African, and European cultures met and influenced each other. European horses and guns, for example, changed the culture of the Plains Indians, allowing them to hunt buffalo more successfully and to move permanently from the mountains to the Plains. The Comanches—possibly the most-skilled horse raisers of the Plains—used the guns and horses to raid settlements and to dominate other Indian groups on the southern Plains.

The Comanche way of life, however, required abundant land and buffalo. The Comanche freedom to roam the Plains was threatened after 1859, when the U.S. government stepped up its efforts to settle the Comanches on reservations in present-day Oklahoma. Ten Bears, a Comanche leader, argued against the government's plan:

> 66 When I was in Washington the Great Father told me that all the Comanche land was ours, and that no one should hinder us in living on it. So, why do you ask us to leave the rivers, and the sun, and the wind, and live in houses? 99

The federal government's reasons were overwhelmingly economic. As the U.S. government limited Native Americans to reservations, non-Indians rushed to the West to establish farms and ranches and to stake out mining claims. Soon the West began supplying the United States and the rest of the world with wheat, lumber, minerals, and cattle and sheep.

American buffalo

American Museum of Natural History

THE WESTERN CROSSROADS ■ 425

PREVIEW WORKSHOP

*Following is a list of the significant
people, places, and terms in this
section. You may wish to use this
list as a section preview.*

People
- buffalo soldiers
- Sitting Bull
- George Armstrong Custer
- Wovoka

- Chief Joseph
- Geronimo
- Helen Hunt Jackson
- Sarah Winnemucca

Places
- San Carlos Reservation

Terms
- Bureau of Indian Affairs
- Sand Creek Massacre

- Treaty of Medicine Lodge
- Battle of Rosebud
- Battle of the Little Bighorn
- Wounded Knee Massacre
- assimilation
- Dawes General Allotment
  Act
- Long Walk

FOCUS OBJECTIVES

- Analyze why the U.S.
  government adopted the
  reservation policy.

- Explain why so much
  conflict between Native
  Americans and the fed-
  eral government erupted
  in the late 1800s.

- Determine how Sarah
  Winnemucca worked to
  improve conditions for
  Native Americans.

- Describe how the feder-
  al government attempt-
  ed to "Americanize"
  Native Americans and
  how the Navajos
  responded.

CORE RESOURCES

- **Social Studies Skills
  Worksheet 14**
- **Literature
  Worksheet 14**
- **Geography
  Worksheet 14**
- **Section 1 Daily Quiz**

AV RESOURCES

- **Linking Geography
  and History
  Transparency and
  Worksheet 12A**

426

Section 1

NATIVE AMERICAN RESISTANCE

F O C U S
- **Why did the U.S. government adopt the reservation policy?**
- **Why did so much conflict erupt between Native Americans and the
  federal government in the late 1800s?**
- **How did Sarah Winnemucca work to improve conditions for
  Native Americans?**
- **How did the federal government attempt to "Americanize"
  Native Americans? How did the Navajos respond?**

*Until the 1850s most American settlers who ventured to the
West settled in California, Oregon, or Texas. By mid-century, however, settlers changed their destinations. With the U.S. government's
encouragement and the military's protection, non-Indians began settling on the Great Plains and in other parts of the West. To make
room for the settlers, the government forced Native Americans onto
reservations, provoking nearly a half century of conflict.*

Sioux doll

*I*NDIAN COUNTRY

By 1850 nearly all Native Americans—some
360,000—lived west of the Mississippi River.
Indians from the old Northwest and the Southeast
were confined to Indian Territory, in present-day
Oklahoma. On the southern Plains, the Kiowas
shared the land with the powerful Comanches.
The Sioux, Blackfeet, and Crows dominated the

northern Plains. In the Southwest the Apaches
ranged throughout New Mexico, Arizona, and
northern Mexico, while the Navajos and Hopis
lived in farming or ranching communities.

In the Far West, disease and conflict associated with nearly a century of contact with Hispanic
and other non-Indian settlers had reduced the
Native American population, including the Paiutes
(PY-oots), Pimas, Miwoks, and Maidus. In
California alone the Native American population
had dropped from an estimated 300,000 in 1769 to
some 35,000 by 1860.

In the 1851 Treaty of Fort Laramie (see
Chapter 10), the U.S. government promised Native
Americans control of the Plains—the bulk of
Indian Country. The government, however, soon
went back on its promise. Hearing tales (both

Museum of the Great Plains

◀ **Driven out of Montana by the Cheyennes and
Sioux, the Kiowas settled on the southern Plains,
in an area stretching from Kansas to Mexico.**

Ask students to recall how the attitudes of earlier settlers toward the land were different from those of Native Americans. (Areas for comparison should include attitudes toward natural resources, occupancy, land use, and land ownership.) Tell students that in this section they will learn how these differences once again became apparent in the late 1800s.

Teaching the Section

RESERVATION POLICY

Select several students to role-play a team of federal officials who are to convince a group of Native Americans to move to a reservation. Ask the rest of the class to play the Indians. The officials should attempt to convince the Indians why the move will benefit them. The Native Americans should challenge the officials about why the government wants them to move, about the benefits of reservation life, and about any government promises made to them. When the presentation is complete, have the Indians discuss among themselves whether or not to move, concluding with a vote on the issue. If the Indians vote not to move, ask them to predict possible consequences of their action. ▶

---

exaggerated and accurate) about the mineral wealth and fertile land in the West, thousands of non-Indians streamed into the territory.

In a series of new treaties, the government forced American Indians to give up their lands and move to reservations. The treaties promised permanent reservation land, money, and yearly supplies. The task of administering the reservations went to the **Bureau of Indian Affairs**, established in 1824 within the War Department. The bureau worked closely with the U.S. Army. The close ties between the army and the bureau sent a clear message: Indians who resisted confinement on reservations would be dealt with by force.

Even when American Indians went quietly to reservations, the government rarely lived up to its side of the bargain. Bureau agents—most of whom were non-Indians—often sold to non-Indians the supplies intended for Native Americans. Furthermore, the government regularly reduced the size of reservations as settlers demanded more land. As Massachusetts newspaper editor Samuel Bowles noted in 1869, the government's actions sent American Indians another clear message: "When the march of our empire demands this reservation of yours, we will assign you another; . . . so long as we choose, this is your home, your prison, your playground."

▪▪ **The U.S. government attempted to restrict American Indians to reservations to make room for non-Indian settlers.**

𝒴EARS OF STRUGGLE

Angered by the government's double-dealings, several Plains peoples, including independent groups of Cheyennes, Arapahos, Comanches, and Sioux, fought back. To them a settled life without buffalo hunting was no life at all.

The Plains peoples faced strong opposition. Some 20,000 U.S. Army troops, many of them Civil War veterans, enforced Indian removal. Some 4,000 were African Americans, often called "buffalo soldiers," who served in four segregated units. The army enlisted Indians as scouts or as soldiers by playing on rivalries among Native Americans. For example, many Pawnees, Crows, and Shoshonis helped U.S. forces battle the Sioux.

Sand Creek. One of the earliest confrontations in the West between the military and American Indians occurred in Colorado Territory. The territory's non-Indian population had been growing rapidly since the Colorado gold rush of 1858. Eager to open more land to U.S. settlers, John Evans, the territorial governor, pressured the Cheyennes and Arapahos to sell their hunting grounds and move to reservations.

In 1861 some Cheyenne and Arapaho leaders agreed to move their people to a reservation south of the Arkansas River. Other leaders and their tribes, however, refused to leave, and Evans feared a major Indian uprising. Throughout the summer of 1864, Cheyenne and Arapaho forces clashed with the local militia. By fall Black Kettle, a Cheyenne leader, had grown tired of fighting. He made his way to Fort Lyon to surrender.

When his group stopped to camp along Sand Creek, most of the men left to hunt. In their absence, some 700 troops under the command of Colonel John Chivington attacked the camp. Some 200 of Black Kettle's group, most of them women and children, were killed.

The slaughter horrified U.S. authorities. But Chivington was unrepentant. "Damn any man who sympathizes with Indians!" he exclaimed. "I have come to kill Indians, and believe it is right and honorable to use any means under God's heaven to kill Indians."

News of the **Sand Creek Massacre** swept across the Plains, prompting raids by the Arapahos and Cheyennes. The Sioux, engaged in a long-standing war against the U.S. Army, also

No Horse, *Women Honoring Warriors* (1875–1880), Collection of Heard Museum, Phoenix, Arizona

▲ Some time between 1875 and 1880, Cheyenne-Arapaho artist No Horse drew this scene, entitled *Women Honoring Warriors*.

HISTORICAL SIDELIGHTS
Buffalo Soldiers

When the Union army was reorganized after the Civil War, officers created four African American units: the 24th and 25th infantries and the 9th and 10th cavalries. All four served in the West. These regiments had the highest reenlistment rates and the lowest desertion rates of any on the frontier. A Montana newspaper wrote admiringly of them, "There are no better troops in the service."

BUILDING VOCABULARY

Many Native American groups are known today by the pejorative names given to them by their enemies. The name *Sioux*, for example, is the French version of the Chippewa word for "snake." The Sioux called themselves *Oceti Shakowin*, the "Seven Council Fires," referring to the seven tribal groups that once made up their nation.

Teaching the Section

AMERICAN INDIANS AND FEDERAL GOVERNMENT CLASH

Create a six-column chart on the chalkboard titled *The U.S.–American Indian Struggle*. Label each column as follows: *Event, Year, Participants, Causes, Outcome,* and *Consequences.* Starting with the Treaty of Fort Laramie and concluding with the Wounded Knee Massacre, have the class provide in chronological order information about battles, treaties, and other confrontations that occurred between American Indians and the government, the army, or settlers during the period. When the chart is complete, ask volunteers to generalize about why the period was characterized by so much conflict between American Indians and the government.

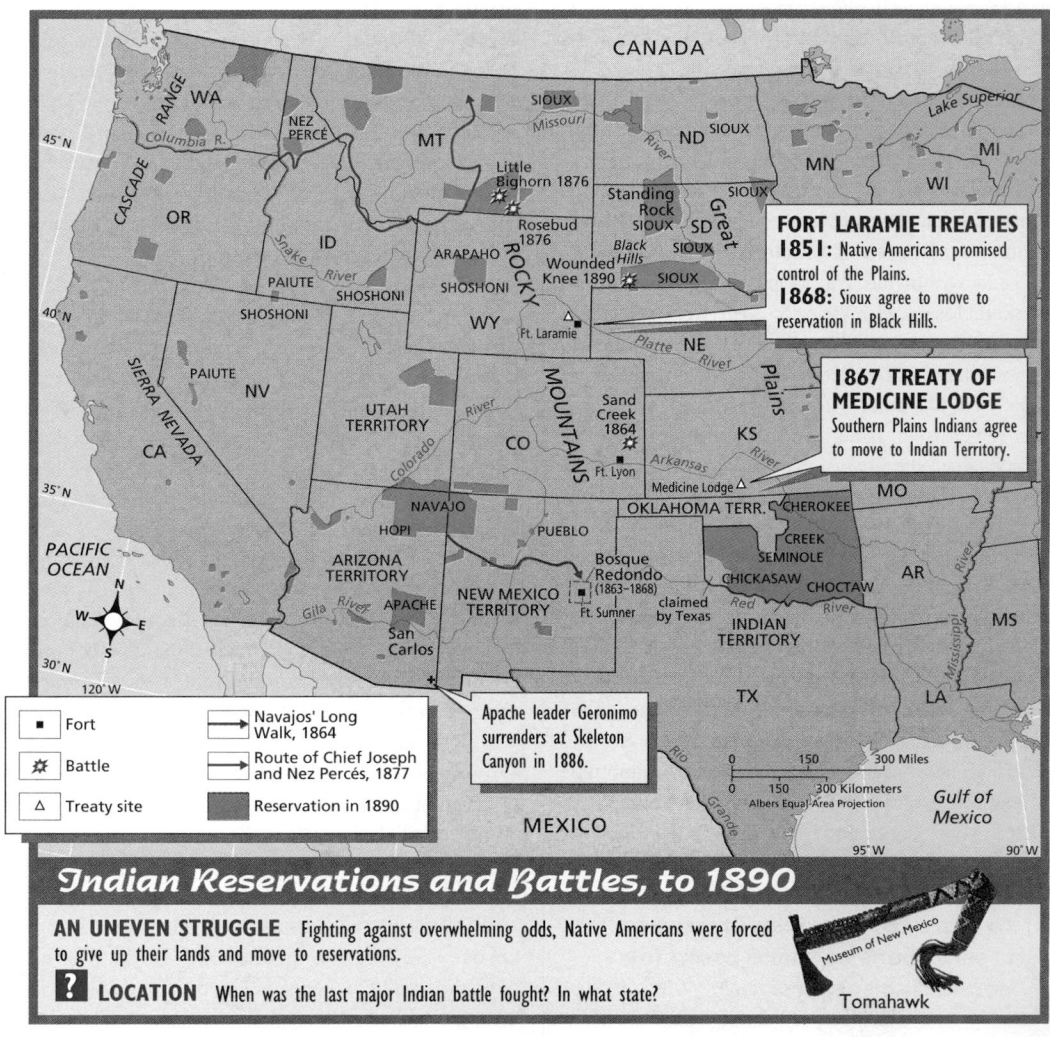

FORT LARAMIE TREATIES
1851: Native Americans promised control of the Plains.
1868: Sioux agree to move to reservation in Black Hills.

1867 TREATY OF MEDICINE LODGE
Southern Plains Indians agree to move to Indian Territory.

Apache leader Geronimo surrenders at Skeleton Canyon in 1886.

Legend:
■ Fort
☼ Battle
△ Treaty site
→ Navajos' Long Walk, 1864
→ Route of Chief Joseph and Nez Percés, 1877
Reservation in 1890

Indian Reservations and Battles, to 1890

AN UNEVEN STRUGGLE Fighting against overwhelming odds, Native Americans were forced to give up their lands and move to reservations.

? **LOCATION** When was the last major Indian battle fought? In what state?

Tomahawk

Museum of New Mexico

stepped up their efforts. But neither side emerged victorious. To end the fighting, U.S. authorities and the southern Plains leaders signed the **Treaty of Medicine Lodge** in 1867. By the terms of the treaty, southern Plains Indians agreed to give up much of their lands in exchange for reservations in Indian Territory. The following year, in a second Treaty of Fort Laramie, the Sioux agreed to move to a reservation in the Black Hills region of South Dakota and Wyoming.

The treaties did not end the fighting, however. As an editor of the *Army and Navy Journal* observed of U.S. treaty-making efforts: "One of our hands holds the rifle and the other the peace-pipe, and we blaze away

with both instruments at the same time. The chief consequence is a great *smoke*—and there it ends."

Custer's last stand. The U.S. Army waged campaigns against the Sioux in 1875. Impatient to open up the Sioux's sacred Black Hills to gold prospectors, U.S. authorities ordered the Sioux to settle near the agencies, the local offices of the Bureau of Indian Affairs. Tatanka Iyotake, a Sioux medicine man called Sitting Bull by non-Indians, urged the hunters to defy the government order.

◄ **Sitting Bull signed his name to this 1880s photograph shortly after it was taken.**

Sitting Bull

TREATY MAKING

Direct students to work in small groups and role-play U.S. government officials and Sioux or Nez Percé representatives serving as treaty negotiators. Have groups create a list of recommendations for a treaty that both sides will accept. As a spokesperson for each group shares the group's recommendations with the class, have remaining students assess the recommendations, considering their fairness and practicality.

▶

Opposed to reservation life, Sitting Bull mocked reservation Indians. "You are fools," he argued, "to make yourselves slaves to a piece of fat bacon, some hard-tack [biscuits], and a little sugar and coffee." Many agreed, and by the spring of 1876, thousands of defiant Sioux and their Cheyenne allies were camped on Rosebud Creek in southern Montana.

Inspired by Sitting Bull's prophecy of a victorious battle against the U.S. Army, several hundred Native Americans rode off to engage the enemy. Although the **Battle of Rosebud** in June 1876 did not result in an outright victory for Native Americans, they gained confidence in their strong fighting force. They proceeded west to camp near a stream the Indians called Greasy Grass and the army called Little Bighorn River. There hundreds of Indians fleeing the agencies, where food was in short supply, joined them. By late June the camp contained almost 2,000 men prepared to fight.

This time the army decided to strike first. What the army did not anticipate was the size of the Indian fighting force. The Native Americans, outnumbering the army troops by three to one and led by Ta-sunko-witko (Crazy Horse), fought off two army attacks. On the morning of June 25, General George Armstrong Custer divided his force to strike the camp from three sides. Custer himself led a battalion of over 200 men. After the final attack, which lasted for less than an hour, Custer and every soldier in his battalion lay dead.

The **Battle of the Little Bighorn** gave the Native Americans only a momentary triumph, however. Over the next several months, the Indian forces broke into smaller groups to evade army troops. Group by group, they were forced to surrender and settle near the agencies. Sitting Bull fled to Canada but eventually returned and settled on Standing Rock Reservation, in Dakota Territory, where he continued to oppose non-Indian settlement of Sioux lands.

Wounded Knee. A tragic final chapter of the Plains Indian–U.S. Army wars unfolded on the plains of South Dakota. The seeds of this conflict were planted in 1889. Wovoka (woh-VOH-kuh), a Paiute holy man from Nevada, began the Ghost Dance religion, which combined Christian and Native American beliefs. Wovoka proclaimed that white settlers would vanish, the buffalo would return, and traditional Indian ways of life would revive if Native Americans performed the Ghost Dance. A young Sioux explained why Wovoka's message appealed to him:

> 66 The rumor got about: "The dead are to return. The buffalo are to return. The Dakota [Sioux] people will get back their own way of life. The white people will soon go away, and that will mean happier times for us once more!"
>
> That part about the dead returning . . . appealed to me. To think I should see my dear mother, grandmother, brothers and sisters again! 99

Wovoka preached peace. The Sioux living on reservations in the Dakotas, however, added a militant tone to the religion by donning "Ghost Shirts," whose special symbols, they believed, could stop bullets.

▼ **While performing the Ghost Dance, dancers shuffled back and forth in a circle until one or more of them received spiritual visions and then collapsed in a trance. This photograph was taken in December 1890.**

▶ **Some Ghost Dance performers wore Ghost Shirts similar to this one. They believed that the symbols of stars, birds, and animals on the garment protected them from harm.**

Field Museum of Natural History

HISTORY
in the Making

WILL THE REAL CUSTER PLEASE STAND?

SETTING THE SCENE

In the years after the Battle of the Little Bighorn, Custer's name became inextricably linked with the last major military victory of the Plains Indians. Over the next 15 years, army recruits labeled "Custer Avengers" eagerly joined regiments to right the wrong they believed had occurred at Little Bighorn.

BLACK HILLS EXPEDITION

Custer's expedition into the Black Hills included scientists, newspaper reporters, and gold miners in addition to his troops—a total of 1,200 men and 110 wagons. After reports appeared of "gold at the roots of the grass," prospectors flooded into the area, which was sacred to the Sioux. Outraged by this intrusion, the Sioux branded Custer "the Chief of all the thieves."

HISTORY in the Making

BY DR. PAUL HUTTON

Will the Real Custer Please Stand?

Picture a dashing young soldier of the 1870s sporting fringed buckskins, a scarlet scarf, and shoulder-length, flowing blond hair. This image of George Armstrong Custer survived for almost 75 years after his death in 1876. In the minds of many Americans, Custer symbolized the army's efforts to make the West safe for U.S. settlers.

Such was the popular view of Custer—but was it the truth? How did this heroic image arise and how has it changed? Journalists, poets, novelists, playwrights, painters, and filmmakers—rather than historians—have molded the public view of Custer. Artists first created the legend of America's most famously unfortunate soldier; decades later, artists again reshaped public

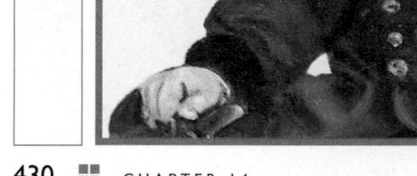

▶ **George Armstrong Custer posed for this photograph around 1870, when he was commander of the Seventh Cavalry.**

opinion of Custer—eventually destroying the legend and transforming a revered hero into a hated villain.

The real Custer was outgoing, strikingly handsome, and recklessly brave. But he was not an outstanding student: Custer graduated at the bottom of his 1861 West Point class. Upon graduation he saw immediate action in the Civil War. The young officer rose rapidly in the Union ranks through a series of field promotions, earning a brigadier general's star in 1863 at age 23. Newspapers dubbed him the "Boy General."

After the war Custer was returned to his regular rank of captain. But as the favorite officer of General

Philip Sheridan, he soon received an appointment as a lieutenant colonel in charge of the elite Seventh Cavalry. Custer's unit frequently battled the Cheyennes and Sioux on the Great Plains.

Custer's military exploits and news of his exploring expeditions into Montana's Yellowstone country in 1873 and the Dakota Territory's Black Hills in 1874 captivated the nation. Popular magazine articles and his memoir, *My Life on the Plains,* kept his name before the public. Thus the nation reeled in shock when word reached the East that Custer and every man of his detachment had been killed at the Battle of the Little Bighorn on June 25, 1876.

Though some Americans questioned Custer's motives at Little Bighorn, most held him up as a martyr. Poets, artists, and novelists promptly began to build the Custer myth. Just one day after hearing of the battle, Walt Whitman submitted his poem "A Death-Sonnet for Custer" to the *New York Tribune.* Poet Henry Wadsworth Longfellow also published his account of the battle. Both poems painted Custer in a heroic light. In addition, artists produced an endless supply of paintings of the gory battle, depicting Custer and his men as the victims of bloodthirsty Indians.

This image of Custer also appeared in the popular play *Custer's Last Charge,* which toured with Buffalo Bill's famous Wild West Show in the 1880s and 1890s. The play showed Custer fearlessly battling savage forces. He was also a favorite subject of early filmmakers. By 1941 close to 20 Custer movies had been made, all portraying Custer as a self-sacrificing defender of U.S. settlers.

Nevertheless, as early as the 1920s, Custer's image was beginning to change. From a symbol of heroic self-sacrifice in the winning of the West, he was gradually transformed into a symbol of white arrogance—a brutal conqueror of Native Americans. This change came about partly as a result of the reform movements of the early 1900s. As more people began looking at society—and its myths—with a critical eye, the treatment of Native Americans in general and the Custer legend in particular came under fire.

In the 1930s and 1940s, several novelists, such as Frederic Van de Water in *Glory-Hunter,* portrayed Custer as a vain, often brutal man. In the post–World War II era, a new wave of Custer movies re-created him as a ruthless leader of an army that slaughtered Native Americans. In such films

Southwest Museum

▲ **Kicking Bear painted this version of the Battle of the Little Bighorn. He included himself in the center of the picture, alongside Crazy Horse, Rain-in-the-Face, and Sitting Bull.**

as *Sitting Bull* (1954), *Chief Crazy Horse* (1955), *The Great Sioux Massacre* (1965), and *Little Big Man* (1970), courageous Indians defend their homelands against a cruel, glory-seeking, and even insane Custer.

Native American efforts to address their past treatment and present conditions influenced this new generation of Custer movies. Beginning in the late 1960s, such best-selling books as Vine Deloria's *Custer Died for Your Sins* (1969) and Dee Brown's *Bury My Heart at Wounded Knee* (1971) presented the Native American perspective of the Indian wars.

By the early 1970s public opinion had firmly shifted toward sympathy for the Native American view of the Battle of the Little Bighorn. In a 1971 *Life* magazine article, Alvin M. Josephy, Jr., labeled the Custer Battlefield National Monument in Montana "a sore from

America's past that has not healed." In response, Congress passed legislation in 1991 that stripped Custer's name from the national monument and authorized the construction of an Indian monument in its place. The once illustrious image of George Armstrong Custer was now thoroughly tarnished.

Early artists, writers, and filmmakers had created Custer's heroic image, "making history" in the process. Later generations of artists destroyed the myth and remade history. Twentieth-century social reformers and Native American civil rights groups forced society to take another, closer look both at Custer and at the plight of Native Americans. Artists and historians may again reinterpret and revise the Custer story, and this soldier's life and death will continue to provide Americans with lessons about their past, present, and future.

A BLEMISHED RECORD

Long before Custer's last stand, questions had been raised about his judgment and character. In 1867 he was court-martialed and removed from command for leaving his post without permission. However, his friend, General Philip Sheridan, got him reinstated. In 1868 he was accused of abandoning part of his force during the battle of the Washita, allowing them to be killed by the Cheyenne.

LINK TO TODAY

Have students identify the changes in attitudes about the past and present treatment of American Indians that have led to a reassessment of Custer.

■■ Examine with the class some of the current stereotypes of American Indians and ways they are perpetuated in TV, films, and names of sports teams.

THINKING CRITICALLY

Ask students why they think Congress decided to replace the Custer monument with an Indian monument. Have students speculate what Custer or Sitting Bull might say about Custer's current historical standing.

Teaching the Section

VOICES OF PROTEST

As a class compare the methods available to reformers such as Helen Hunt Jackson and Sarah Winnemucca for improving conditions for American Indians with the methods used by various social activists and reformers today.

■■ Ask students to suggest how Jackson and Winnemucca might have used the modern media and protest-movement tactics to raise public awareness about the conditions of American Indians.

MAKING CONNECTIONS
Art

Non-Indian artists have left a rich record of life in the West. Frederic Remington, for example, created hundreds of works during the years he worked as a cowboy and rode with the army during the Indian wars. In all, he completed more than 2,700 paintings of cowboys, American Indians, and other western subjects.

HISTORICAL SIDELIGHTS
Loss of Land

In 1855 a group of Nez Percés reluctantly signed a treaty that reduced their reservation land to 10,000 square miles. They did so out of fear they would otherwise lose their ancestral home in the Wallowa Valley. In 1863, however, U.S. officials revised the treaty, further reducing Nez Percé land from 10,000 to 1,000 square miles—and forcing the cession of the Wallowa Valley.

PRIMARY SOURCE
Description of Change: excerpted
Rationale: excerpted to focus on main idea

Government agents feared that the Ghost Dance would inspire Indian resistance. When the Ghost Dance religion spread to Standing Rock Reservation, the military ordered the arrest of Sitting Bull, who had joined the religion. When reservation police surrounded Sitting Bull's cabin on December 15, 1890, a skirmish broke out and Sitting Bull was killed. Frightened and angry, many Sioux joined the Ghost Shirt fighters farther west.

Government agents set out to arrest another Sioux leader, Big Foot. Although Big Foot had been a Ghost Shirt fighter, he decided to join Red Cloud, another Sioux leader, on Pine Ridge Reservation to end the fighting. Army troops caught up with Big Foot and some 350 members of his group. Waiting to be led to agency headquarters, the Sioux set up their tepees on Wounded Knee Creek.

The next morning—December 29—the army ordered the confiscation of Indian rifles. Mounted cavalry, reinforced by four Hotchkiss guns (which fired exploding shells), surrounded the camp. After the Indians surrendered only a few guns, the soldiers began to search the tepees. Tensions ran high. When someone fired a rifle—possibly during a scuffle, possibly as a signal—bursts of gunfire erupted between U.S. soldiers and Indians. The Hotchkiss guns ripped into the tepees, killing some 300 Sioux. About 30 U.S. soldiers were killed.

Though the **Wounded Knee Massacre** shocked many Americans, others grimly insisted that Custer had been "avenged." The battle marked the end of the Indian wars on the Great Plains.

CONFLICT IN THE FAR WEST

Native Americans west of the Great Plains also faced forced resettlement. In the Wallowa (wah-LOW-uh) River Valley of northeastern Oregon, the Nez Percés tried to avoid coming under government control. Although the Nez Percés had long maintained good relations with the U.S. government and white settlers, the government ordered the Nez Percés to move to an Idaho reservation in 1877. Chief Joseph, the Nez Percé leader, reluctantly agreed. Before his people could leave, however, a few Nez Percés killed some white settlers, whom they viewed as intruders. Joseph's group, fearing attack, fled.

Pursued by army troops for three months, the Nez Percés journeyed east and north through Idaho, Wyoming, and Montana, picking up additional

▲ Before reaching the Canadian border, Chief Joseph surrendered to Colonel Nelson A. Miles on October 5, 1877. Shown here is *Chief Joseph Rides to Surrender* by Howard Terpning.

followers along the way. The group eventually numbered from 700 to 800, including some 300 fighting men. The group's goal was to escape to Canada. But as winter approached, travel became harder. Chief Joseph surrendered only 30 miles from the Canadian border. An interpreter wept as he relayed the leader's surrender statement:

❝ I am tired of fighting. Our chiefs are killed. . . . It is cold and we have no blankets. The little children are freezing to death. . . . My heart is sick and sad. From where the sun now stands, I will fight no more forever. ❞

The Nez Percés, however, were not the last Native American group to surrender to the U.S. Army. The Apaches of the desert and canyon lands of New Mexico and Arizona mounted one of the longest campaigns against government control. The conflict began in the 1850s, when settlers began moving into Apache territory. Raids and attacks by both sides produced a climate of fear and hatred. In 1877 the U.S. government forced the seminomadic Apaches to settle on San Carlos Reservation, on the Gila River in Arizona.

Most Apaches complied, but life on the reservation proved harsh. In 1881, amid rumors of an Indian uprising, army troops moved into the territory. Fearing an attack, Geronimo, an Apache leader, fled the reservation with about 75 followers. Off and on for the next five years, Geronimo's group raided settlements and evaded

ASSIMILATION

Ask volunteers to identify ways by which the federal government attempted to "Americanize" Native Americans. List students' responses on the chalkboard. Then invite students to assume the role of an army officer at Fort Sumner assigned to direct the assimilation of the Navajos at Bosque Redondo in New Mexico. Have students write a memo from the officer to a government official explaining why the

plan for "Americanization" of the Navajos is not working. Ask volunteers to read their memo to the class. Then discuss how the government responded to the plan's failure and the resulting consequences for the Navajos.

▶

capture. But on September 4, 1886, with his followers outnumbered, Geronimo gave up. "Once I moved about like the wind," he told his captors. "Now I surrender to you and that is all." His surrender marked the end of armed resistance to the reservation system.

∷ The U.S. Army and American Indians clashed as the U.S. government took away Indian lands.

𝒱OICES OF PROTEST

By the 1880s American Indians had been forced to surrender more than 450 million acres to the U.S. government. Indians had been driven off their land and onto reservations by a number of pressures. The army had defeated many groups. In addition, U.S. settlers, whose presence increased as railroads snaked across the West, had moved onto Indian lands and killed off most of the buffalo herds. "Kill every buffalo you can," advised Colonel R. I. Dodge. "Every buffalo dead is an Indian gone." With the loss of the buffalo, Native Americans had little hope of maintaining an independent existence on the Plains.

Troubled by the treatment of American Indians, a small but active group of reformers appealed to the government to craft a more humane Indian policy. Their cause won the support of Helen Hunt Jackson, whose influential

▲ Although the buffalo population once numbered in the millions, its ranks dwindled by the 1870s as hunters were paid from one dollar to three dollars for every hide sold. An 1883 study estimated that some 13 million buffalo had been slaughtered.

book *A Century of Dishonor* (1881) attacked the government for its years of broken promises and corrupt dealings with Native Americans.

Another reformer, Thoc-me-tony (Shell-Flower), a Paiute woman known as Sarah Winnemucca, publicized the plight of American Indians. Born in Nevada around 1844, Winnemucca, who spoke English, Spanish, and several Indian languages, served for a number of years as an interpreter at U.S. forts. She also briefly taught school on the Paiute reservation in Oregon.

Although the Paiutes cooperated with the government, they often felt taken advantage of by Bureau of Indian Affairs agents. Winnemucca learned that the government had authorized two mills to be built on the Paiute reservation, but they were never constructed. She wondered:

Sarah Winnemucca

❝ The [mills] were never seen or heard of by my people, though the printed report . . . says twenty-five thousand dollars was appropriated to build them. Where did [the money] go? . . . Is it that the government is cheated by its own agents who make these reports? ❞

The Paiutes' forced removal to Yakima Reservation in Washington Territory in 1878 so outraged Winnemucca that she began lecturing on the Paiutes' behalf to non-Indian audiences. In 1880 she pleaded her cause—to allow the Paiutes to return to their lands—before President Rutherford B. Hayes. Hayes granted her request, but the bureau's agents did not carry out the president's order.

Three years later Winnemucca reached a wider audience with her book *Life Among the Piutes*. Though she died before age 50, Winnemucca helped awaken the nation to the injustices suffered by American Indians.

∷ Sarah Winnemucca brought the plight of American Indians to the nation's attention.

BIO GRAPHY **PERSONALITIES IN HISTORY**

Long before she became an advocate for the Paiutes, Winnemucca learned first-hand about prejudice against Native Americans. As a child she briefly attended a convent school in California but was told to leave because parents of some white students did not want an Indian in school with their children. She wrote her book in part to raise money for a speaking tour in the East. She spoke to more than 300 audiences and gathered thousands of signatures for a petition to change government policies toward Native Americans. [NOTE: The spelling of "Paiute" was "Piute" in the 1800s, as evidenced by Winnemucca's *Life Among the Piutes*.]

PRIMARY SOURCE
Description of Change: excerpted and bracketed
Rationale: excerpted to focus on main idea; bracketed to clarify meaning

𝒫ractice

GUIDED PRACTICE

Write the quotation from the *Army and Navy Journal* on p. 428 on the chalkboard and lead a class discussion on its meaning. Have students give examples of "rifles" and "peace-pipes" and interpret the use of the term *smoke*.

INDEPENDENT PRACTICE

Direct students to read the quote by newspaper editor Samuel Bowles on p. 427 (first column, second full paragraph). Have students write an explanation of the passage, including an interpretation of the terms "prison" and "playground."

𝑅eview and 𝐴ssessment

REVIEW Pair students and have them create illustrated time lines for the period 1850 to 1890. For each entry on the time line, have students include a brief annotation describing its impact on American Indians. Then assign the Section 1 Review on p. 435.

ASSESS Assign the **Section 1 Daily Quiz** in *Core Resources*.

 GLOBAL CONNECTIONS

Canada also adopted some assimilation policies in the late 19th century, and in 1884 passed an anti-potlatch law. Potlatch is an Indian ceremony which includes masked dancing and a lavish distribution of gifts. Some white men believed the ceremony to be barbaric and anti-Christian. A Kwakiutl Indian reacted to the law: "Do we ask the white man, 'Do as the Indian does'? No, we do not. Why then do you ask us, 'Do as the white man does'?"

▪▪ Ask students to suggest examples of ways non-Indians showed they considered American Indian cultures inferior to their own. Ask students how they think such views allowed non-Indians to justify taking Indian lands.

CULTURAL PATTERNS

When choosing their 160-acre allotments, few American Indians were concerned with their acreage's potential as farmland. Some selected acreage within traditional hunting grounds or at the site of an old encampment. Others chose land that had religious or personal significance.

𝐴SSIMILATING AMERICAN INDIANS

Many government officials and most reformers viewed **assimilation**, or the cultural absorption, of American Indians into "white America" as the only long-term way to ensure Native American survival. The federal government urged Indians to become farmers and to move out of their dwellings and live in wooden houses. The government passed laws to force Native Americans to abandon their traditional appearance and to dress like "Americans." One law even ordered Indian men to cut off their long hair. Another outlawed Indian religious practices.

To speed assimilation, the government set up a system of Indian schools. Some American Indian children attended reservation schools, while others were forced to leave their families to attend boarding schools. The Carlisle Indian School in Pennsylvania, which admitted its first class in 1879, typified the boarding school system. Students were forced to speak only English, wear "proper" clothes, and change their names to "American" ones. The school's founder summed up his aim: to "kill the Indian and save the man."

The government's most important assimilation strategy, however, was forcing Indians to give up tribal ownership of land in favor of private ownership. Private ownership, the government argued, lay at the heart of Americanization. Western settlers and developers wanted American Indians to give up tribal ownership of land for another reason: if Indians could be forced onto small plots of land, settlers and developers could then buy up surplus reservation land.

The passage of the **Dawes General Allotment Act** in 1887 established private ownership of American Indian land. The act required that Indian lands be surveyed and Indian families claim an allotment of 160 acres of reservation land for farming. The land that remained would be sold.

The Dawes Act proved to be a disaster for American Indians. In less than 50 years, they lost two thirds of their land. Some of the land was sold to settlers and developers as surplus when allotments were made. In other cases, American Indians sold or were cheated out of their allotments.

▪▪ **By outlawing Indian customs, establishing boarding schools, and enforcing private land ownership, the U.S. government attempted to assimilate American Indians.**

𝒯HE NAVAJOS: A CASE STUDY

Despite the government's hopes, few Plains Indians became farmers. Even before passage of the Dawes Act, the government had tried to force the Navajos to give up their reliance on sheep raising and become settled farmers. This plan backfired.

To carry out the government's plan, the U.S. Army waged military campaigns against the Navajos in northwestern New Mexico and

◀ The top photograph shows a group of Navajos from New Mexico arriving at the Carlisle Indian School during the 1880s. Six months later they posed for a second photograph, outfitted in school uniforms.

RETEACH Have students work in pairs to list the main topics for an outline of the section, leaving space between topics. Have pairs exchange papers to add subtopics for each main entry.

Closure

Write on the chalkboard the following statement from *Extraordinary American Indians* by Susan Avery and Linda Skinner: *"Removal and allotment were both attempts to control Indian destiny that sprang from alliances of greed and misguided humanitarian impulses."* Have volunteers explain why they agree or disagree with this statement.

Extension

INTERVIEW Direct students to research the life of one of the American Indian leaders discussed in the section. Have students present their information in the form of a question-and-answer interview.

ANALYZE Have students investigate the life of American Indians on reservations today and write editorials comparing reservation conditions in the late 1800s with conditions today.

▶ The Navajos learned the art of weaving from the Pueblos and soon produced woolen blankets of exceptional quality. This photograph of a Navajo weaver outside her hogan, or home, was taken around 1890.

Museum of New Mexico

northeastern Arizona in 1863. Soldiers destroyed Navajo houses, sheep herds, and corn crops. Without food or shelter, many Navajos surrendered in early 1864. In what came to be known as the **Long Walk**, the Navajos were forced to travel on foot to Bosque Redondo, a reservation in eastern New Mexico. Soldiers stationed at nearby Fort Sumner prevented Navajos from leaving the reservation.

The U.S. government gave the Navajos seeds and farming tools, but the land proved unsuitable for farming. Living conditions at Bosque Redondo were harsh, and many Navajos died from malnutrition or disease. Realizing its plan was unworkable, the government signed a treaty with the Navajos granting them a reservation in New Mexico and Arizona in 1868. There the Navajos rebuilt their communities, concentrating on sheep raising, weaving, and silver-

smithing. By the 1880s their economy had prospered and their population had begun to increase.

■■ After great losses, the Navajos won their battle to maintain their communities.

Although the Navajos and other American Indian groups overcame military defeat and resettlement, many groups did not. By 1890 warfare and forced assimilation had reduced the American Indian population to fewer than 250,000. Indians were commonly referred to as "vanishing Americans." Despite suffering great hardships, though, American Indians did not vanish.

SECTION 1 REVIEW

IDENTIFY and explain the significance of the following: Bureau of Indian Affairs, buffalo soldiers, Sand Creek Massacre, Treaty of Medicine Lodge, Sitting Bull, Battle of Rosebud, George Armstrong Custer, Battle of the Little Bighorn, Wovoka, Wounded Knee Massacre, Chief Joseph, Geronimo, Helen Hunt Jackson, Sarah Winnemucca, assimilation, Dawes General Allotment Act, Long Walk.

LOCATE and explain the importance of the following: San Carlos Reservation.

1. **MAIN IDEA** Why did the U.S. government attempt to resettle American Indians on reservations? How did American Indians respond to this attempt?

2. **MAIN IDEA** How did Sarah Winnemucca address the problems faced by the Paiutes?

3. **MAIN IDEA** What did the U.S. government do to try to assimilate American Indians?

4. **WRITING TO EXPLAIN** Imagine you are a Sioux who took part in the Ghost Dance religion. Write an essay explaining the meaning of the Ghost Dance and Ghost Shirt.

5. **ANALYZING** Why were Navajo communities prosperous by the 1880s?

IDENTIFY

For significance, see the following pages:
Bureau of Indian Affairs (p . 427)
buffalo soldiers (p. 427)
Sand Creek Massacre (p. 427)
Treaty of Medicine Lodge (p. 428)
Sitting Bull (p. 428)
Battle of Rosebud (p. 429)
George Armstrong Custer (p. 429)
Battle of the Little Bighorn (p. 429)
Wovoka (p. 429)
Wounded Knee Massacre (p. 432)
Chief Joseph (p. 432)
Geronimo (p. 432)
Helen Hunt Jackson (p. 433)
Sarah Winnemucca (p. 433)
assimilation (p. 434)
Dawes General Allotment Act (p. 434)
Long Walk (p. 435)

LOCATE

For location, see the map on p. 428.

1. *to make room for non-Indian settlers; clashed with U.S. Army troops*

2. *publicized their plight through lecture tours and a book; petitioned president*

3. *outlawed Indian customs, set up Indian schools, and en-forced land ownership*

4. *should mention Ghost Dance offered hope, Ghost Shirt promised protection*

5. *They were allowed to pursue activities appropriate to their geography and culture.*

PREVIEW WORKSHOP

Following is a list of the significant people, places, and terms in this section. You may wish to use this list as a section preview.

People
- Hamlin Garland

Places
- Central Pacific Railroad
- Union Pacific Railroad

Terms
- Homestead Act
- Pacific Railway Act
- Morrill Act
- Exodusters

- U.S. Department of Agriculture
- dry farming
- bonanza farm

Section 2

WESTERN FARMERS

FOCUS

- **Why did many farmers move to the West in the late 1800s?**
- **What innovations helped farmers cope with the western environments?**
- **Why and where did bonanza farms develop?**

Windmill on the western Great Plains

Attracted by the promise of free or cheap land, thousands of farmers moved to the West after the Civil War. In fact, pioneers settled some 430 million acres between 1870 and 1900. The spread of railroads across the West allowed farmers to ship crops and other farm products to the East and around the world. Although new technologies helped farmers cope with harsh environments, western farm life remained difficult.

ECONOMIC DEVELOPMENT OF THE WEST

After the southern states seceded from the Union, northern Republicans saw a chance to develop the West along northern lines. The Republicans wanted the new western states and territories to be free of slavery and populated by independent farmers who would develop the land. To attain these goals, Republicans passed a series of acts in 1862 to put public lands to productive use.

Land acts. Three government land acts increased non-Indian settlement of the Great Plains. The **Homestead Act** granted a 160-acre homestead, or farm, to any American citizen or prospective citizen willing to live in the Great Plains and cultivate the land for five years. Some 400,000 families took advantage of this offer. The **Pacific Railway Act** gave land to railroad companies to develop a transcontinental railroad linking the East and West coasts. The **Morrill Act** gave land grants to all the states to help finance agricultural colleges, which would train young farmers and thus help develop the West.

Competition for land was fierce. In Oklahoma in 1889, for example, a flood of

◄ **Daniel Freeman filed this claim in Brownsville, Nebraska, for 160 acres of land in January 1863. He received this homestead certificate after certifying that he had built a "part log & part frame" house on his claim.**

MOTIVATING: PRIOR KNOWLEDGE

Ask volunteers to recall why settlers in the early 1800s moved mainly to Texas and the Far West rather than onto the Great Plains. Then ask a volunteer to locate the Great Plains on a wall map. Have the class speculate as to why settlers in the late 1800s might have begun moving to this region.

Teaching the Section

WHY FARMERS MOVED WEST

Have students work in small groups and act as writers and artists hired by railroad companies to create full-page newspaper ads to attract settlers to Oklahoma or Kansas. Tell the groups that their ads should combine appealing images with lists of incentives that convinced farmers to settle on the Great Plains. Have groups present their completed advertisements. Then ask the class to summarize, based on the advertisements, why farmers moved to the West in the late 1800s.

▲ Although Oklahoma originally was part of Indian Territory, by the late 1880s the government opened some of the land to non-Indian settlers. This photograph shows an actual land "run" on September 16, 1893.

prospective settlers responded to a government offer of free homesteads. In March, President Benjamin Harrison announced that the acreage—former Creek and Seminole lands—would be available beginning at noon on April 22 to the first takers. By the appointed day, some 50,000 prospective homesteaders gathered to race one another for the land. At exactly noon the stampede began. Settler Hamilton S. Wicks described the difficulties involved:

> 66 The race was not over when you reached the particular lot you were content to select for your possession. The contest still was who should drive their stakes first, who would erect their little tents soonest, and then, who would quickest build a little wooden shanty. . . .
> On the morning of April 23, a city of 10,000 people, 500 houses, and innumerable tents existed where twelve hours before was nothing but a broad expanse of prairie. 99

Subsequent "runs" took place in other parts of Oklahoma—usually at the expense of Native Americans. Indians lost more than 11 million acres in Oklahoma to non-Indian settlers.

The railroads. Railroad companies also helped lure settlers to the West. Between 1869 and 1883 four transcontinental lines snaked their way across the West (see map on page 445). The federal government gave the railroad companies more than 100 million acres of public land, which they could sell to settlers to pay for the huge cost of laying the tracks. State and local governments also donated land to railroad companies.

Eager to sell this land, railroad companies advertised in the East and in Europe. The companies offered to pay the fares of buyers and sell them land on credit. Some railroad companies gave free trips to newspaper reporters. The reporters in turn wrote glowing accounts of the land and towns along the rail line. One Indiana editor wrote:

> 66 I never saw finer country in the world than that part of Kansas passed over by the Atchison, Topeka & Santa Fe road. Corn waist high, wheat in the shock [stacked], oats in fine condition, and vegetables in abundance. 99

Railroads also stimulated an important midwestern and western industry: lumbering. Vast groves of white pine in Michigan, Wisconsin, Minnesota, and eventually the Pacific Northwest supplied wood for railroad ties, railroad cars, and the houses and barns that sprang up along the railroad routes. But uncontrolled lumbering destroyed wildlife habitats, caused erosion, and had other important ecological consequences little recognized at the time.

SETTING THE SCENE

The work crews of the Central Pacific Railroad faced blizzards and other natural hazards in the winter of 1866–67, when they laid tracks over the Sierra Nevada. Many workers died when they were buried in 40-foot snowdrifts or when sudden avalanches covered entire work camps. Since few whites wanted the dangerous job of blasting through the mountains, the Chinese took these jobs. They were suspended from cliff tops in wire baskets to drill holes and plant explosives in the cliff sides. Once they lit the explosives, they faced certain death if not pulled back up in time.

THE AMERICAN NATION VIDEODISC PROGRAM

Linking the Nation

1B   29399   2:20

Who moved to the West? Migration westward after the Civil War differed from earlier migrations. The U.S. government now played a more active role in encouraging westward migration. The methods of transportation differed as well. Unlike earlier western settlers who traveled in large groups by covered wagon, these later migrants journeyed by themselves or with their families on the newly built railroads. The train rides to the West were quicker, safer, and more

Changing Ways

THE TRANSCONTINENTAL RAILROAD

In the mid-1800s there was no easy way to get from the East Coast to the West Coast. Both the overland journey from New York to San Francisco and the boat trip around the tip of South America could last several months. To help open up the West to settlers, Congress passed the Pacific Railway Act in 1862. The act awarded contracts to build a transcontinental railroad to two companies: the Central Pacific Railroad and the Union Pacific Railroad.

The track had to be laid across some 1,500 miles of wilderness—over and through mountains and across steep ravines. The Central Pacific would lay track eastward from Sacramento, California, over the towering Sierra Nevada. The Union Pacific would work westward from Omaha, Nebraska, and cross the rugged Rockies.

To encourage the companies to take on the overwhelming job, the federal government gave them land. The project soon became a contest of which company would lay more track.

The railroad companies recruited thousands of workers for the backbreaking and often perilous work. Work crews competed against nature as well as each other as they blasted, shoveled, and pickaxed their way across the North American continent. During the frigid winters huge snowdrifts and avalanches blocked mountain passes. Some laborers died doing the dangerous blasting work. Railway gangs also faced attacks by Plains Indians, who attempted to prevent the invasion of their hunting grounds by "the wagons which make a noise."

Most of the Union Pacific's 10,000 workers were Irish immigrants. After the Civil War, veterans from both sides, many still wearing remnants of their uniforms, also signed on. The Central Pacific's slightly larger work force consisted mostly of Chinese laborers. One observer called the sound of the crews' progress "a grand Anvil Chorus . . . playing across the plains and mountains, in triple time: three strokes to the spike; ten spikes to the rail; 400 rails to the mile." After seven years of exhausting labor, the railroad crews met at Promontory, Utah, on May 10, 1869.

Railroad officials, political dignitaries, infantry soldiers, and proud workers looked on as the last railroad tie—made of laurel wood, a symbol of victory in a contest of strength—was slipped into place. Leland Stanford, the president of the Central Pacific and former governor of California, then drove a golden spike to complete the railroad. The telegraph built alongside the tracks flashed the news from coast to coast that East and West were permanently linked.

◀ Laborers from different ethnic backgrounds helped build the transcontinental railroad. This 1886 photograph shows members of a Northern Pacific Railroad crew.

Teaching the Section

WHO MOVED WEST?

Organize students into eight groups. Assign each group one of the following identities: middle-class New England farmer; Confederate war veteran; African American from the South; Scandinavian, Chinese, Irish, German, or Mennonite immigrant. Have the members of each group write letters from their assigned person to a relative explaining why they are leaving their present home, why they have chosen to move west, what they think might surprise or disappoint them about life in the West, and how they expect their lives to be different in five years. Have each group choose a spokesperson to read the group's letters.

■■ Ask students to describe what expectations, surprises, disappointments, and major changes a family moving in the 1990s might face.

▶

▲ Free black settlers moved west to escape persecution and violence in the South. The Shores family lived in Custer County, Nebraska, when this photograph was taken in the late 1880s.

comfortable than the journeys on the Oregon Trail had been.

Economic motives, the search for racial tolerance, and the promise of a better life drew three main groups of people to the West: (1) white Americans from the East; (2) African Americans from the South; and (3) immigrants from Europe and Asia.

White newcomers came from more-settled areas of the United States. Because of the high cost of transporting supplies, it was mainly middle-class farmers and businesspeople who could afford to move to the West. New England farmers went west searching for more-fertile soil. Civil War veterans, especially those from the South, came to make a new start. The majority of white settlers, however, moved from states in the Mississippi Valley, where populations were growing rapidly. A Nebraska settler explained simply: "I am well satisfied that I can do better here than I can in Illinois."

For African Americans, moving west had a special appeal. In the South, blacks faced violence and persecution after the withdrawal of federal troops at the end of Reconstruction. African American settlers who ventured onto the Plains in the 1870s sent letters to their friends and families, urging them to move west. Often these letters were read aloud in black churches.

Kansas, where John Brown had first fought against slavery, especially appealed to African American settlers. The biggest rush of black set-

tlers occurred during the Kansas Fever Exodus of 1879. From 20,000 to 40,000 African Americans fled the South, where violence had broken out during elections in 1878. Seeking economic and political freedom, these black settlers, known as **Exodusters**, trekked west. With the help of established black settlers, the poor and ill-equipped Exodusters eventually settled some 20,000 acres.

European immigrants also flocked to the western United States. "America Fever" infected thousands of Norwegians, Swedes, and Danes. In 1882 alone more than 100,000 left their homes for the American West. In addition, many Irish who had helped build the railroads and a great number of Germans who had settled in the Mississippi Valley decided to move to the Plains. These Europeans were joined by Mennonites, Protestant pacifists who fled persecution in Russia. Their experience in farming wheat on the Russian steppes, or grasslands, was especially useful on the Great Plains.

Many of the Chinese immigrants who had come to California during the gold rush of 1849 had also turned to farming by 1880. In California alone some 3,200 Chinese raised crops in 1880. Throughout the West, many Chinese immigrants

▲ Shown here is a Chinese agricultural worker tending an irrigation ditch in a California orchard.

Teaching the Section

ADAPTING TO WESTERN ENVIRONMENTS

Make a three-column chart on the chalkboard labeled *Problem, Effect, Solutions.* In the first column list challenges western farmers faced, such as lack of water, lack of trees, harsh winters, strong winds, and heavy topsoil. Have students complete the chart, indicating the effects of each problem and how each problem was solved.

worked as farm laborers, sharecroppers, or produce vendors. Some owned large farms. In 1870 a Chinese farmer in Sacramento County, California, earned $9,500 from farming—an enormous profit for the time.

■■ **Farmers moved onto the Great Plains for a variety of motives, but the main incentive was readily available land.**

WESTERN ENVIRONMENTS

Although some 80 million acres of public land in the Great Plains were homesteaded between 1862 and 1900, the settlers did not immediately create a prosperous region. Though the land was free, supplies and transportation were expensive. In addition, the environments of the Southwest, the Far West, and the Great Plains posed problems for farmers. In the Southwest and the Far West, the new settlers had to learn irrigation techniques. To carve out farms from the Great Plains, the settlers relied on their resourcefulness, government support, innovative farming practices, and new technologies.

In parts of the Southwest, Hispanic and American Indian farmers had developed effective irrigation systems that used canals, sloping fields, and dams to control water flow. They had also established farms that fanned out in thin strips from water sources so that all community residents had access to water. The new settlers had to adopt these methods to survive.

The Great Plains also had few water sources. In addition, trees that could provide fuel or building materials were scarce. The climate was also difficult: bitterly cold in the winter, blazing hot in the summer, and windy much of the time.

Plains farmers worked out clever solutions to some of these problems. To cope with the lack of wood, for instance, they built houses and barns of sod chunks cut from the prairie and stacked like bricks. A few scarce pieces of wood formed the roof, topped off with a layer of sod. Building with sod was difficult, however. Wrote a Kansas settler in 1877: "The sod is heavy and when you take 3 or 4 bricks on a litter or hand barrow, and carry it 50 to 150 feet, I tell you it is no easy work." Nor was it pleasant to live with the insects that dwelled in the sod.

The **U.S. Department of Agriculture**, created in 1862, helped farmers adapt to the Plains environment. Department experts sought out and publicized new varieties of wheat suitable for the Great Plains environment. (The cold winters of the northern Plains could not support traditional winter wheat.) These new wheat crops, along with the weeds introduced with the wheat seeds, soon replaced the grasses that had once covered the Great Plains.

Department of Agriculture agents also taught **dry farming** techniques, planting and harvesting

▼ Between 1830 and 1910 some 90 percent of all pioneers west of the Missouri River lived in sod houses. Shown here is the Scott family, photographed outside their Nebraska home in 1889.

BONANZA FARMS

Ask students to write magazine articles titled "Bonanza Farms" that analyze why bonanza farms developed, where they were located, and why they eventually failed. Students may wish to include maps with their articles. Have volunteers read their articles aloud to the class. Students may wish to include their magazine articles in their portfolios.

FARM LIFE ON THE PLAINS

Have students assume the role of a member of a Plains farm family and prepare a story about life on the farm. Possible topics include participating in a land run, the railroad ride to a new and unseen homestead, building a sod house, surviving a blizzard or a drought. Then organize students into groups and have each student tell his or her story to the group.

▲ Bonanza farms applied the techniques of the factory system to agriculture. By 1890 there were some 300 farms in the Red River Valley that covered about 1,000 acres each. This photograph shows one such operation in the San Fernando Valley of California.

BUILDING VOCABULARY

Bonanza is a Spanish word that means literally "tranquil or calm weather at sea" and figuratively it means "prosperity." It comes originally from the Latin word *bonus* meaning "good." In the early 1840s a *bonanza* came to mean a lucky discovery of gold and by extension, something that is valuable, profitable, or rewarding.

HISTORICAL SIDELIGHTS

Bonanza Farms

The first bonanza farm was a 12,000-acre farm near present-day Fargo, North Dakota. It was started after the Northern Pacific Railroad used its land in Dakota Territory to pay off some stockholders after the Panic of 1873 made its bonds almost worthless. Soon after, 300 such farms could be found in Minnesota and Dakota Territory.

techniques that conserve moisture. For example, agents advised farmers to plow deep furrows to bring moisture to the surface and to break up the soil after a rainfall to prevent evaporation.

New technologies aided the Department of Agriculture's efforts to improve Plains farms. To tap water deep underground, farmers adapted drilling machinery developed by petroleum companies. Farmers also used new models of windmills—wind-powered water pumps designed to withstand the strong winds of the Plains.

New farm equipment also helped the Plains farmers. James Oliver's plow factory in South Bend, Indiana, produced thousands of plows with sharp, durable blades that could slice through the tough sod of the Plains. "Self-binding" harvesters not only cut wheat but also tied it into bundles. The combine—a sort of factory on wheels—cut wheat, separated the grain from the plant, and cleaned the grain all in one operation.

■■ **Government support, innovative farming practices, and new technologies helped make farming on the Plains possible.**

LARGE-SCALE FARMING

Efficient new farm machinery and cheap, abundant land enabled some companies to create a new kind of large-scale operation, the **bonanza farm**. Most bonanza farms were owned by large companies and run like factories, with professional managers, laborers for different tasks, and machinery. Because these large farms required from 500 to 1,000 extra workers at planting and harvesting times, most owners divided their vast enterprises into smaller units, with a foreman in charge of each.

The first bonanza farms were established in the Red River Valley in Dakota Territory and Minnesota in the mid-1870s after the completion of the Northern Pacific Railroad. Investors also organized bonanza farms as far west as California.

In California's Central Valley one of the largest wheat farms covered more than 66,000 acres, stretching for 16 miles along the Sacramento River. Although California led the country in wheat production in the 1880s, by the 1890s most farmers there had turned to more-profitable fruit and vegetable crops. Refrigerated railcars allowed California farmers to ship these crops across the country.

The era of bonanza farming soon faded. When weather conditions were favorable, bonanza farms produced large profits because of lower production costs. Since bonanza-farm owners bought seed and equipment in bulk, suppliers often gave them special deals. But in times of severe drought or low wheat prices, bonanza-farm profits fell. Family farmers, who had fewer workers to pay and less money invested in equipment, could better handle boom-and-bust cycles. Thus by the 1890s

Practice

GUIDED PRACTICE

On the chalkboard draw a two-column chart with the headings *Benefits* and *Costs*. Have students list all the possible benefits for a homesteader moving to the Great Plains. Then have them suggest the possible costs of such a change, including the social costs of isolation and initial lack of schools as well as the personal and economic risks.

INDEPENDENT PRACTICE

Have students review the chart from the Guided Practice and use it to write an essay about why they would, or would not, have moved west in the late 1800s. Students may wish to include their essays in their portfolios.

Review and Assessment

REVIEW Have students work in pairs to create an interview between a Plains farmer and a newspaper reporter on the advantages of and obstacles to farming in the West. Call on volunteers to present their interviews to the class. Then assign the Section 2 Review on p. 443.

ASSESS Assign the **Section 2 Daily Quiz** in *Core Resources*.

PRIMARY SOURCE

Description of Change: excerpted
Rationale: excerpted to focus on main idea

PRIMARY SOURCE

Description of Change: excerpted and bracketed
Rationale: excerpted to focus on main idea; bracketed to clarify meaning

HISTORICAL SIDELIGHTS

Grasshoppers
Great Plains settler Mary Lyon had this vivid memory of the grasshopper infestation, which made the day seem like night in the summer of 1874: "When they came down they struck the ground so hard it sounded almost like hail. There was a watermelon patch in our garden and the melons were quite large. . . . By the evening of the second day they were all gone."

BIOGRAPHY PERSONALITIES IN HISTORY

Garland was able to turn his anger and sadness over the harshness and drudgery of farm life into a powerful voice calling for reform. He not only campaigned for the Populist cause in Iowa, but read his book *Under the Lion's Paw* before tax-reform groups across the country.

▲ Farmers settled in areas throughout the Great Plains. Shown here is the Ellefson family outside their home in Hendricks, Minnesota.

most bonanza farms had been broken up into smaller farms.

■■ **New farm machinery, cheap land, and high wheat prices allowed bonanza farms to flourish for a time in Dakota Territory, Minnesota, and California.**

FARM LIFE ON THE PLAINS

Farm families on the Plains faced many problems for which inventors, manufacturers, and agricultural experts had no ready answers. For example, sod houses, though well insulated, windproof, and fireproof, were also dank, dirty, and far from rainproof. One woman described her efforts to keep herself and her baby dry in their sod house during a spring rainstorm:

66 The house leaked so badly that we rolled the bedding up and tied it with a rope, and put the oil cloth from the table over it to keep it dry. I put the baby on top of the roll and put the parasol over it to keep her dry. Soon the rain ran off the ribs of the parasol and soaked around the baby so I fixed a place for her in the cupboard shelf—the only dry place in the house. I walked around with a slicker, a man's hat and overshoes to keep dry. 99

Moreover, winter on the Plains brought blizzards and bone-chilling cold. A Kansas settler wrote:

66 The cold is a fierce north wind which will freeze man or beast. . . . [At night] my eyelids froze together so I picked off the ice, [and] the tops of the sheets and quilts . . . were frozen stiff with [our] breath. . . . We had not bedclothes enough to keep us warm and we piled on everything in the house. 99

Summer on the Plains could be just as fierce. Settlers described droughts during which "the earth opened in great cracks several inches across and two feet deep," and "the leaves on the trees shriveled and dried up, and every living thing was seeking shelter from the hot rays of the sun." Summer also brought cloudbursts and tornadoes. In the 1870s farmers faced swarms of grasshoppers that devoured everything in their path. Farmers killed thousands of the greedy insects, but to little

◄ Plains farmers spent many long hours in the fields. Shown here is Ella Sly, who filed a homestead claim in Kansas in 1893.

RETEACH For each subsection in the section, have students write a sentence that summarizes the main idea. Select students to read their statements aloud. Have the group choose the best summary sentence for each subsection.

Closure

Have students provide evidence from the section to support the following assessment: *Nature was sometimes the farmer's friend but more often the farmer's foe on the Great Plains.*

Extension

ANALYZE Have students research and report on an invention or innovation that helped farmers on the Plains.

INTERPRET Encourage students to read diaries and letters of homesteaders like those in Lillian Schlissel's *Women's Diaries of the Westward Journey*. Have them choose three excerpts and prepare a dramatic reading about the unique contributions women made to the settlement of the West.

effect. Moaned one homesteader: "Two new grasshoppers arrived to attend each dead one's funeral."

Even in good times, Plains farming demanded hard work from everyone in the family. Men did most of the heavy labor of building houses, fencing the land, and farming. Women, in addition to household and child-rearing tasks, often spent hours in the fields. Writing to her family in the East, one woman explained that she had been her husband's "sole help in getting up and stacking at least 25 tons of hay and oats." She might also have been responsible for tending farm animals, caring for a garden plot, and preserving fruits and vegetables.

Children had to do their share, too. They fetched water, tended gardens, and did such routine chores as churning butter. One farmer described how his two-year-old son, Baz, could "run all over, fetch up cows out of the stock fields, or oxen, carry in stove wood and climb in the corn crib and feed the hogs and go on errands down to his grandma's [house]."

BIO GRAPHY Writer Hamlin Garland described the hardships of Plains farming. Garland's father had moved from Maine to Wisconsin, where Garland was born in 1860. To his father, as Garland put it, "change was alluring," and he moved his family to Iowa and later to Dakota Territory.

Hating the drudgery of farm work, young Garland moved east to Boston. He got a job as a teacher and educated himself by reading widely. But it was a trip back to the Plains in 1887 that determined his future. He now saw through an adult's eyes the land in which he had grown up. "Nature was as beautiful as ever," he wrote, but it could not "conceal the poverty of these people, . . . the gracelessness of these homes, and the . . . mechanical daily routine of these lives." Garland wrote about his experiences to a friend, who replied, "You're the first actual farmer in American fiction— now tell the truth about it."

The Granger Collection, New York

Hamlin Garland

Garland's collection of short stories, *Main-Travelled Roads,* published in 1891, stressed the difficulties of farm life on the Plains. The book's bitterness offended many readers, who imagined farmers as happy tillers of the soil. In later years, however, this book and other works of Garland's— especially his autobiography, *A Son of the Middle Border* (1917)—won admiration for their straightforward honesty.

Difficulties overwhelmed many western farmers, forcing some to abandon their farms. But thousands stayed, forming successful communities, with churches and schools, newspapers and clubs, and even theaters and concert halls. Though harvests might be poor one year, there was always hope for better luck the next year.

SECTION REVIEW ANSWERS

IDENTIFY

For significance, see the following pages:
Homestead Act (p. 436)
Pacific Railway Act (p. 436)
Morrill Act (p. 436)
Exodusters (p. 439)
U.S. Department of Agriculture (p. 440)
dry farming (p. 440)
bonanza farm (p. 441)
Hamlin Garland (p. 443)

LOCATE

For locations, see the map on p. 445.

1. *chance for a better life; readily available land and transportation*
2. *through individual creativity, government support of innovative farming practices, and new technologies*
3. *mostly in Dakota Territory, Minnesota, and California; flourished because of lower production costs, but faded because they were unable to handle boom-and-bust crop and price cycles*
4. *Entries should mention violence and discrimination in the South and the hope for political and economic freedom in the West.*
5. *Answers should recognize that without government legislation and other assistance, and without railroads to transport people and products, Great Plains development would likely have been delayed.*

SECTION 2 REVIEW

IDENTIFY and explain the significance of the following: Homestead Act, Pacific Railway Act, Morrill Act, Exodusters, U.S. Department of Agriculture, dry farming, bonanza farm, Hamlin Garland.

LOCATE and explain the importance of the following: Central Pacific Railroad, Union Pacific Railroad.

1. **MAIN IDEA** Why did farmers move to the West in the late 19th century in such great numbers?

2. **MAIN IDEA** How were farmers able to adapt to the western environments?

3. **GEOGRAPHY: LOCATION** Where did bonanza farmers establish their operations? Why did these large-scale farms flourish and then fade?

4. **WRITING TO DESCRIBE** Imagine you are a member of an Exoduster family in Kansas in the late 1800s. Write a journal entry describing why you left the South and came to Kansas.

5. **EVALUATING** How might the development of the Great Plains have been different if the government and the railroads had not been involved?

PREVIEW WORKSHOP

Following is a list of the significant people, places, and terms in this section. You may wish to use this list as a section preview.

People
■ Basques
■ Joseph Glidden

Places
■ Abilene, Kansas
■ Dodge City, Kansas
■ Cheyenne, Wyoming
■ Ogallala, Nebraska

Terms
■ Texas longhorn
■ long drives

■ railhead
■ open range

FOCUS OBJECTIVES

■ List the factors that led to a cattle boom during the 1870s and 1880s.

■ Describe what ranch life was like for cowboys.

■ Examine the factors that brought about the end of the cattle boom.

Section 3

THE CATTLE BOOM

FOCUS

■ **What factors led to a cattle boom during the 1870s and 1880s?**
■ **What was ranch life like for cowboys?**
■ **What factors brought about the end of the cattle boom?**

attle ranchers were eager to use western lands that the government had originally reserved for Native Americans. Although Mexican settlers had been raising cattle since the 1600s, the boom era for cattle ranching arrived only after the Civil War, when railroads linked the West with growing eastern markets. The two-decade boom created cattle towns and new stresses on the Great Plains environment.

Female broncobuster

THE RISE OF THE CATTLE INDUSTRY

The earliest ranchers in the American West were Spaniards, who first imported cattle from Spain in the 1500s. By the 1850s English cattle brought to Texas by Americans interbred with Spanish cattle to produce a new breed—the **Texas longhorn**. Although their meat was tough and stringy, longhorns were hardy. They could travel long distances on little water and live year-round on grass. Equally important, longhorns were immune to a tick-born cattle disease called Texas fever.

Texas cattle ranching grew rapidly after the Civil War, spreading over the Great Plains as the buffalo vanished. As eastern cities grew, so did the demand for beef. In 1866 a steer that would bring about $4 in Texas could be sold for $40 or $50 in eastern markets.

A major problem was moving the cattle from Texas, where most of the earliest ranches were, to rail lines in Missouri and Kansas. To reach the railroads, cowboys herded as many as 3,000 cattle on **long drives**, overland treks that covered hundreds of miles and could take as long as two to four months. The long drives usually ended in Missouri. But Missouri farmers objected: unlike the longhorn, their cattle were not immune to Texas fever. Because of this opposition, later long drives avoided Missouri and headed for less-populated towns in Kansas. Over the years of the long drives, cowboys herded some four million cattle from Texas to Kansas.

On a typical long drive, a trail boss managed a crew of about 10 cowboys. The cook in the chuck wagon, which carried food and the cowboys' bedrolls, rode in front of the herd.

◄ Trail bosses were responsible for the welfare of both cattle and cowboys during the many weeks it usually took to move a herd to a rail line.

MOTIVATING: STUDENT EXPERIENCES

Have students suggest phrases and images they associate with cowboys and cattle ranching. Discuss where these impressions of western life came from and to what extent they have been influenced by movies and other media. Then tell students that in this section they can check the accuracy of their impressions against the historical reality.

Teaching the Section

CATTLE INDUSTRY: BOOM AND BUST

Have students work in several small groups to create two graphic organizers. Half the groups should create organizers showing the factors that led to the growth of cattle ranching. *(cheap land, railroads, growing eastern markets, hardy cattle)* The other groups should create organizers showing

factors that led to its decline. *(overgrazing, oversupply, price declines, barbed wire, bad weather)* Have groups present and explain their graphic organizers.

▶

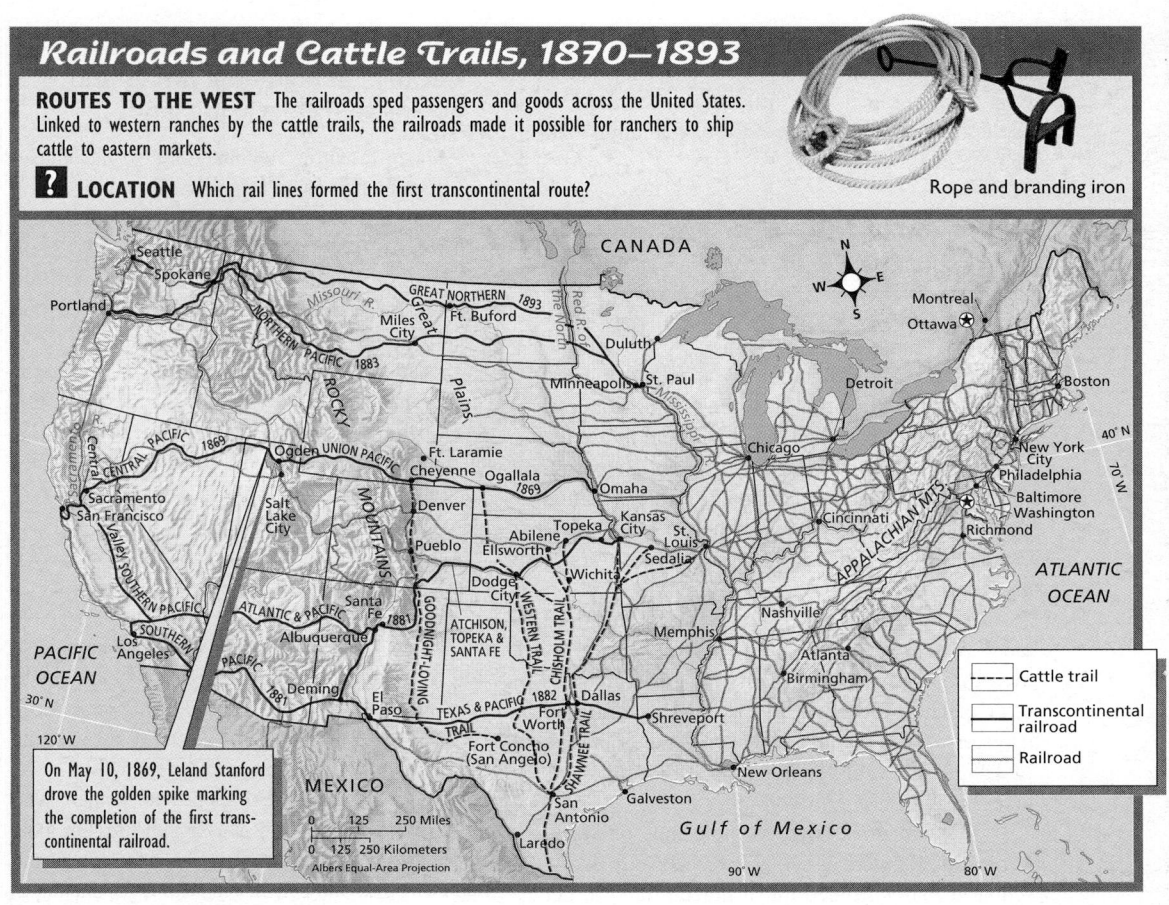

Railroads and Cattle Trails, 1870–1893

ROUTES TO THE WEST The railroads sped passengers and goods across the United States. Linked to western ranches by the cattle trails, the railroads made it possible for ranchers to ship cattle to eastern markets.

? **LOCATION** Which rail lines formed the first transcontinental route?

Rope and branding iron

On May 10, 1869, Leland Stanford drove the golden spike marking the completion of the first transcontinental railroad.

Legend:
- - - - Cattle trail
━━━ Transcontinental railroad
━━━ Railroad

0   125   250 Miles
0 125 250 Kilometers
Albers Equal-Area Projection

Managing the herd was a tough job, with the cowboys setting a brisk pace. Crossing rivers, where swift currents might drown hundreds of animals, posed one hazard. But the worst danger was a stampede. Almost any sound—a coyote's wail, a thunderclap, a sneeze—could panic the cattle.

■■ **The cattle boom developed after the Civil War, when new railroads linked western ranges to growing eastern markets.**

CATTLE TOWNS

Every long drive ended at a **railhead**, a town located along a railroad. Here, brokers bought cattle and shipped them east. The railhead stops came to be known as cattle towns; the best known were the Kansas towns of Abilene, Ellsworth, and Dodge City. Farther north and west, long drives later ended in Cheyenne, Wyoming, and Ogallala, Nebraska.

At first a typical cattle town consisted of little more than a railroad depot, a stockyard, a hotel or boardinghouse, and a general store. But if the town attracted enough cattle business, it grew. Cattle towns bustled with activity from spring to fall, when the long drives took place. Cattle brokers, railroad men, and cowboys, who were paid at the end of the long drives, were eager to spend their money. Gambling halls, saloons, clothing stores, and barbershops were just as eager to take it. As the cattle towns prospered, they attracted more businesspeople, as well as doctors, lawyers, teachers, and their families.

In a cattle town's early years, the scarcity of labor provided many opportunities for both adults and children. Because of the high demand for lodging and food, many women took in boarders or opened restaurants. Some children worked as clerks or bookkeepers in the growing businesses.

Once families arrived, the cattle towns built schools and hired police forces to keep order. Reformers, many of them women, set out to tame

Map Caption Answer
Union Pacific–Central Pacific

MAKING CONNECTIONS
Language Arts
The terms *cowpoke* and *cowpuncher* originated with the cowboys whose job it was to poke or punch the cows onto railcars with long poles. The terms soon were applied to all cowboys.

HISTORICAL SIDELIGHTS
Woman Trailblazer
In 1871 Amanda Burks was one of the first women to join one of the long drives herding longhorns. In the months that she traveled with her husband on the drive, she endured many difficulties, including severe storms, homesickness, rustlers, and extreme heat. But the freedom of outdoor life outweighed the dangers, as she reflected on her return home: "For what woman, youthful and full of spirit and the love of living, needs sympathy because of availing herself of the opportunity of being . . . in the great out-of-door world!"

𝒯eaching the 𝒮ection

CATTLE–RANCHING LIFE

Organize students into several groups. Have each group prepare a short skit on a day in the life of one of the following people: a cowboy, a ranch wife, or a ranch child. Have groups present their skits.

■■ Have students discuss how life on cattle ranches today differs from life on cattle ranches in the late 1800s. Ask students if they believe that life on cattle ranches is still romanticized in recent novels, television shows, and motion pictures.

GLOBAL CONNECTIONS

Many Europeans invested in American cattle ranches, and the introduction of English breeds of cattle such as the Devon and the Hereford led to hardier beef cattle. Herefords, for example, could withstand the wider range of temperatures of the western U.S. grasslands better than larger breeds. In contrast, the Texas longhorns grew more slowly, producing very little beef in proportion to their size.

COOPERATIVE LEARNING

Have students work in small groups and imagine they are employed by a cattletown newspaper. Assign each group a different year in the cattle boom. Students can take roles as editors, reporters, cartoonists, and headline writers. Ask each group to prepare a four-page newspaper covering activities that might have taken place during a week in the year assigned.

the rough cowboy towns by organizing poor-relief and temperance societies. Their calls for prohibition, however, met with little success as long as cattle town economies depended on gambling halls and saloons.

𝑅ANCH PROFITS

As the government converted more Indian territory into public lands, cattle ranching spread west into New Mexico and Colorado and north into Kansas, Nebraska, the Dakotas, Wyoming, and Montana. The government allowed cattle ranchers to use the public land as **open range**, or free grazing land. Access to free pasture land made cattle ranching profitable. The introduction of higher-grade cattle breeds from the East and from Europe led to even bigger profits.

Although many families established ranches, it was mainly large investment companies that took advantage of the government's offer of land. Financed by eastern and European investors, these companies created huge ranches. In 1883, for example, some 20 such companies invested $12 million in Wyoming alone.

Most ranches covered thousands of acres. Large ranches were essential because cattle on the semiarid Plains needed much grazing land to get enough feed. Ranches also needed access to water; streams, lakes, and rivers determined the size and location of ranches. "Wherever there is any water, there is a ranch," noted a Colorado cattleman.

■■ **Cattle ranching was profitable because of high beef prices and access to free grazing land.**

Sheep ranching, which was also introduced by the Spanish, was an important economic activity in the West. American Indians, particularly the Pueblos and Navajos, raised sheep in New Mexico and Arizona. After the California gold rush began, sheep by the thousands were herded to California to feed the hungry miners.

Basque shepherds, originally from southwestern France and north-central Spain, immigrated from South America and ranged flocks of sheep in California. By 1900 some 10,000 Basques lived in the West.

𝑅ANCH LIFE

Both cattle and sheep ranches demanded intense effort from ranch families. Everyone had to work to make sure the ranch prospered. A Texas sheriff explained that ranch owners "got right out with the boys on the trail" and "did just as much work."

This description also applied to women, who played an integral role in daily ranch life. On most ranches, women did housework, cooked for all the hired cowboys, and helped out with fence-mending, herding, or other chores. Many women organized their own ranch-related businesses. Ella Bird, for example, accumulated her first herd of cattle by selling hand-sewn leather gloves and vests to cowboys in exchange for yearlings.

▼ **Women were responsible for a number of chores on a ranch. Here the Becker sisters are shown branding cattle on their ranch in Colorado's San Luis Valley in 1894.**

Practice

GUIDED PRACTICE

Work with students to prepare a job description for a cowboy. On the chalkboard write the headings *Skills Needed, Benefits,* and *Major Tasks.* Have students offer entries for each heading. Then have volunteers role-play a job interview between a cattle rancher and a cowboy.

INDEPENDENT PRACTICE

Have students use the job description developed in the Guided Practice to write a help-wanted ad for a cowboy and a letter to a cattle rancher applying for the job. Students may wish to include their ads and letters in their portfolios.

Review and Assessment

REVIEW Have students make a list of topics for an encyclopedia article titled "Cowboys and the Cattle Boom." Have volunteers share their lists with the class, explaining why each topic should be included in the article. Then assign the Section 3 Review on p. 448.

ASSESS Assign the **Section 3 Daily Quiz** in *Core Resources.*

▶

Because ranches were far apart, loneliness took its toll. Susan Newcomb, a Texas ranch wife, described the loneliness of ranch life:

❝ A man that is cowhunting with a lively crowd has no idea how long and lonesome the time passes with his wife at home. . . . A man can see his friends, hear the news and pass time . . . , while his wife is at home and sees and hears nothing until he returns from a long trip tired and worn out. ❞

Ranch children often took on adult responsibilities at a young age. In addition to doing chores around the house, some children, both boys and girls, broke horses and herded cattle. Many enjoyed the freedom, though. Ralla Banta, who spent her childhood on a Texas ranch, remembered, "When we returned home in the evening we enjoyed telling where we had been, to what creek, up what branch and what we had seen." Others hated the boredom. John Norton, a young cowboy, noted that he and his brother "leaped with joy" when the cattle they were herding were finally shipped for slaughter.

Ranch life centered on the roundup. Each spring and fall, ranchers, with the help of hired cowboys, drove their cattle from the open range to some central spot. Here cowboys from each ranch "cut out," or separated, the cattle, identified by each ranch's distinctive brand. The cattle would then be rounded up for the long drive to a railhead.

Later, books, movies, and radio and television programs romanticized the life of the cowboys. Actually, their life was difficult: they worked hard in all kinds of weather and made little money. The long drives also kept them away from their families for long periods. Most cowboys worked the range for only about seven years before they settled down in towns or on farms.

▶ **Ex-slave Nat Love, also known as Deadwood Dick, claimed to have carried the marks of 14 bullet wounds on his body, "any one of which would be sufficient to kill an ordinary man."**

▲ *Vaqueros of California Roping Horses in a Corral* is the title of this 1877 painting by James Walker.

Many of the white cowboys were Confederate veterans of the Civil War. About a third of the some 35,000 cowboys were African American, Mexican, or Mexican American. Some of the African American cowboys had been brought west as slaves before the Civil War. With their experience handling longhorns, they got jobs as ranch hands after emancipation. Other black cowboys moved west after the war. In an era when most African Americans faced harsh segregation, life for a black cowboy was relatively free of discrimination. He worked, bunked, and ate alongside fellow cowboys and received the same wages they did.

Long before the days of the cattle boom, Mexican *vaqueros* had developed many ranching practices. In the 1880s most Mexican and Mexican American cowboys worked on South and West Texas ranches. They were often sons of ranchers or farmers, and sometimes owned their own ranches. Although they were paid higher wages and treated better than those who handled menial ranch jobs, Mexican cowboys faced discrimination. Many Anglo ranchers considered them inferior to Anglo cowboys. Mexican cowboys were not allowed to supervise non-Mexicans, and they worked and lived separately from Anglo cowboys.

▪▪ **Ranch life was difficult for cowboys, who worked long hours outdoors in all kinds of weather.**

THE END OF THE CATTLE BOOM

The cattle boom lasted only about 20 years. Several factors led to its early end. First, ranchers eager to make large profits filled the open range with too many cattle. This led to overgrazing, which damaged the grasslands. The vast herds also

THE WESTERN CROSSROADS ▪▪ 447

HISTORICAL SIDELIGHTS
Bill Pickett
African American cowboy Bill Pickett was described by his boss as "the greatest sweat and dirt cowhand that ever lived—bar none." He gained fame on the rodeo circuit and claimed to have invented bulldogging, a rodeo event in which a contestant wrestles a steer to the ground. In his days of rodeo stardom, Pickett's assistants included Tom Mix and Will Rogers. In 1971 Pickett was posthumously inducted into the Cowboy Hall of Fame, the first African American to receive that honor.

HISTORICAL SIDELIGHTS
Gunnysackers
In the 1880s acts of violence by cattle ranchers against sheep herders became common. Cattle ranchers maintained that sheep destroyed range grass and had an odor that upset cows. They hired gunmen, called "gunnysackers" because of the flour gunnysack masks they wore, to kill sheep, shoot sheep-dogs, and even murder herders.

RETEACH Organize students into pairs and assign each pair a subsection of the section. Tell each pair to create a poster, drawing, or cartoon that illustrates the main idea of its subsection. Have each pair explain its creation to the group.

Closure

Direct students to write epitaphs for the death of the cattle industry. Epitaphs should describe the factors that led to the cattle boom and those that led to its decline.

Extension

RESEARCH Invite students to research and report on the development of one of the prominent cattletowns of the West. Suggest that students illustrate their reports.

CREATE Have students compose a song or write a poem about life on the long drive from the viewpoint of a white, Mexican, or African American cowboy. Invite students to perform their work for the class.

PRIMARY SOURCE
Description of Change: excerpted
Rationale: excerpted to focus on main idea

SECTION REVIEW ANSWERS

IDENTIFY
For significance, see the following pages:
Texas longhorn (p. 444)
long drives (p. 444)
railhead (p. 445)
open range (p. 446)
Basques (p. 446)
Joseph Glidden (p. 448)

LOCATE
For locations, see the map on p. 445.

1. *new railroads, high eastern beef prices, and access to public land for grazing*
2. *Cowboys led difficult lives of hard work on the ranch and long drives that separated them from their families for extended periods.*
3. *Overgrazing damaged grasslands; overexpansion drove down beef prices; barbed-wire fencing restricted open-range ranching; bad weather killed cattle herds.*
4. *Narratives should mention ranch chores as well as the freedom ranch children enjoyed.*
5. *Spanish introduced cattle and sheep; Basques spread sheep ranching.*

448

▲ Barbed wire not only helped cattlemen protect their land, but also kept homesteaders away from valuable sources of water. This 1885 photograph shows a group of homesteaders cutting down wire fences.

increased the supply of beef, driving down prices—and profits. Prices crashed in 1885, as supply far exceeded demand.

Second, open-range ranching declined after the invention of barbed wire. Joseph Glidden patented this cheap method of fencing in 1874. By the 1880s farmers and cattle ranchers had erected miles of spiky networks across the open range to control access to land and water. As overgrazing thinned the grass cover, cattle needed access to more pasture lands to survive. But fencing limited the amount of open land available.

Bad weather dealt the final blow. On the southern Plains a severe winter in 1885–86 and a drought in 1886 diminished many herds. The

following year, terrible blizzards struck the northern Plains. When cowboys could finally venture out of their bunkhouses, they found the remains of thousands of starved and frozen cattle. Ranchers suffered devastating losses, some losing as much as 90 percent of their herds.

▪▪ **Boom times for cattle ranchers came to an end because of overgrazing, fencing of the open range, and bad weather.**

By the 1890s the open-range cattle boom was over. Some of the big corporations went broke. With the end of the open range, ranchers had to buy their own range land. They also had to invest more in their operations. Learning from the blizzards of the mid-1880s, they began to raise hay to feed to their cattle during the harsh winters. Sheep ranching expanded, since sheep could survive on the weeds that replaced the native grasses. The long drives ended, and the cattle towns settled down. So did many of the cowboys. A popular song of the time ended with these words:

> 66 Good-by, old trail boss, I wish you no harm;
> I'm quittin' this business to go on the farm.
> I'll sell my old saddle and buy me a plow;
> And never, no, never will I rope another cow. 99

  S E C T I O N **3** R E V I E W

IDENTIFY and explain the significance of the following: Texas longhorn, long drives, railhead, open range, Basques, Joseph Glidden.

LOCATE and explain the importance of the following: Abilene, Kansas; Dodge City, Kansas; Cheyenne, Wyoming; Ogallala, Nebraska.

1. **MAIN IDEA** What factors allowed cattle ranching to be so profitable during the boom period?
2. **MAIN IDEA** What was cowboy life like?
3. **MAIN IDEA** What factors caused the decline of the cattle boom in the West in the late 19th century?
4. **WRITING TO INFORM** Imagine you grew up on a cattle ranch in the 1890s. Write a brief narrative about the joys and difficulties of ranch life.
5. **SYNTHESIZING** What contributions did the Spanish and Basques make to cattle and sheep ranching?

PREVIEW WORKSHOP

Following is a list of the significant people, places, and terms in this section. You may wish to use this list as a section preview.

People
- William H. Seward

Places
- Pikes Peak
- Yukon Territory

- Deadwood, South Dakota

Terms
- Comstock Lode
- *patio* process
- Klondike Gold Rush
- hydraulic mining
- hard-rock mining

Section 4

A MINING BOOM

FOCUS
- Where did important mining discoveries take place in the late 1800s?
- How did early mining camps differ from more-developed mining towns?
- Why did mining become big business?

Ever since the forty-niners had flocked to California after the discovery of gold in the Sierra Nevada, miners from all over the world had been drawn to the American West. After the richest California diggings were claimed, hundreds of forty-niners moved eastward and northward into the Rockies and beyond. A few individuals prospered from new mineral discoveries. But large mining companies reaped the greatest profits.

Chinese miner in Alaska

WESTERN MINING

The first promising mining discoveries after the California gold rush were made in Colorado. Prospectors found gold near Pikes Peak late in 1858. By early 1859 thousands of people flocked to Colorado. Many of them, however, left in disappointment by midsummer.

Another center of frantic prospecting in 1859 was the Carson River Valley in present-day Nevada. In addition to gold, the area contained the famous **Comstock Lode**, one of the world's richest silver veins. Over 20 years its mines yielded more than $500 million worth of precious metals.

Some miners turned south into Arizona, where Hispanics had been mining silver since the mid-1700s. Hispanics introduced mining methods that had been developed in Mexico and South America. These included a mill for separating gold from quartz and the *patio* process—which used mercury to extract silver from the ore. The

newer arrivals used these methods to mine the Comstock Lode and in the region around Tucson. Others, trekking northward, made strikes in Idaho and Montana.

By the late 1850s others had pushed even farther north, into the Fraser River Valley of British Columbia. This movement into Canada had important consequences for Russia and the United States. Russia, which at the time owned Alaska, feared a territorial dispute with the United States. To avoid this, the Russians offered to sell Alaska to the Americans. U.S. Secretary of State William H. Seward negotiated the purchase of Alaska in 1867 for $7,200,000—about two cents an acre. Many Americans considered Alaska worthless, calling the purchase "Seward's Folly."

FOCUS OBJECTIVES

- Locate where important mining discoveries took place in the late 1800s.

- Compare early mining camps with more-developed mining towns.

- Analyze why mining became big business.

HISTORICAL SIDELIGHTS
The Comstock Lode
The Comstock Lode made Virginia City one of the most famous boomtowns in the West. About one year after the vein's discovery, Virginia City had 202 businesses. By the 1870s it had 30,000 people and more than 100 saloons. However, by the 1880s the Comstock was out of silver, and Virginia City became a ghost town.

CORE RESOURCES

• **Section 4 Daily Quiz**

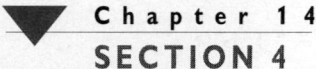
MOTIVATING: PRIOR KNOWLEDGE

Ask students to recall facts about the California gold rush of 1849. Ask volunteers to describe the forty-niners and to characterize that mining boom. Remind students to be alert for comparisons and contrasts with that boom as they study this section.

Teaching the Section

SITES OF MINING DISCOVERIES

Organize students into groups to create maps showing the locations of the major mining discoveries of the late 1800s. Have groups imagine they are novice prospectors living in San Francisco, St. Louis, or New York City. Groups should pick one of the sites on their maps for prospecting and draw on their maps the route they will take to get there. Have groups present their maps and explain their reasons for choosing a particular site, how they plan to get there, and what difficulties they might encounter along the way.

Map Caption Answer

in mountainous terrain, where veins of gold and silver ore can be seen and mined

HISTORICAL SIDELIGHTS

Many hopefuls died of cold, starvation, or disease on the way to the Klondike goldfields. Less than half of the 100,000 who started out made it; the rest died or turned back. Others reached the Yukon but returned without success. But of the 30,000 prospectors who persevered, some made as much as $1,500 a day panning for gold. In 1900 alone, $22 million worth of gold was taken out of the Klondike strike.

MAKING CONNECTIONS

Literature

Although best known for his stories of the Mississippi River, Mark Twain also captured life in a mining camp in *Roughing It*. Twain recounts the adventures he shared with his brother on their way to Carson City, Nevada, and the various schemes Twain hoped would make them rich once they got there.

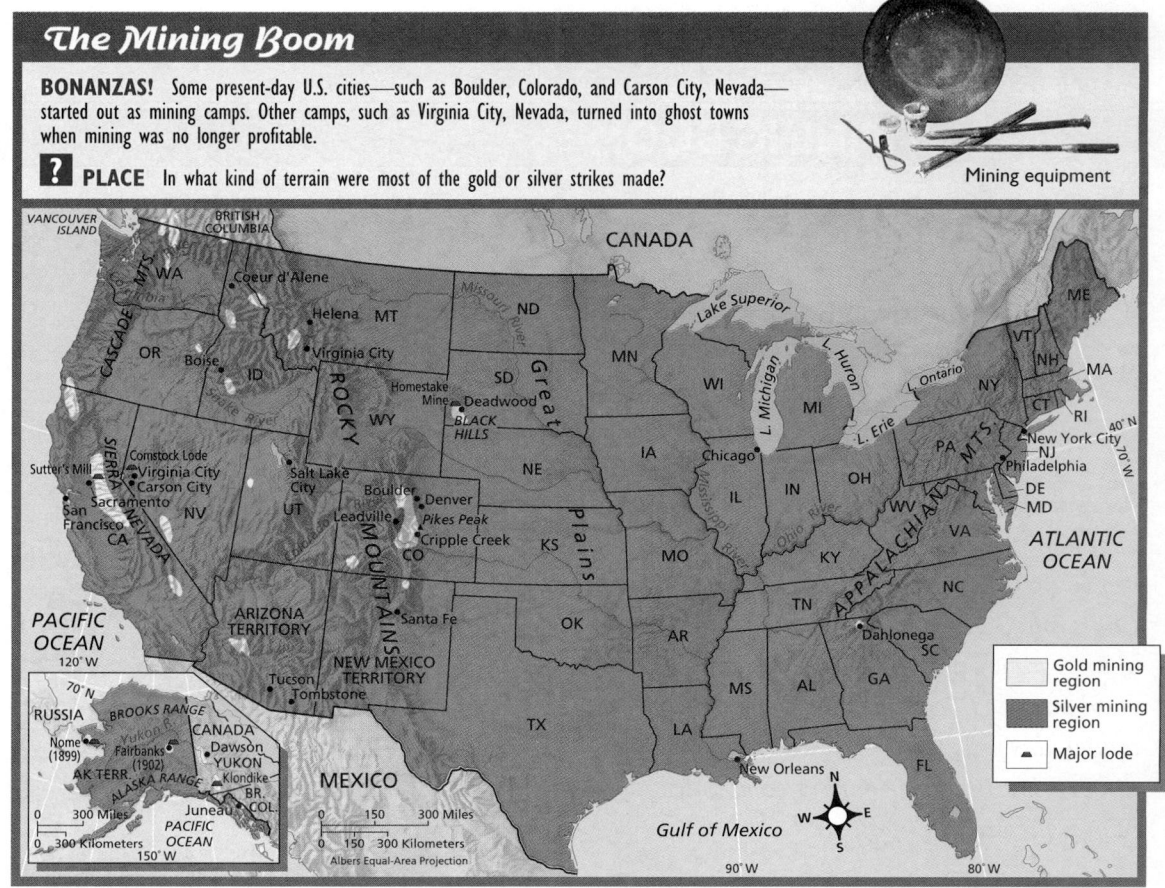

The Mining Boom

BONANZAS! Some present-day U.S. cities—such as Boulder, Colorado, and Carson City, Nevada—started out as mining camps. Other camps, such as Virginia City, Nevada, turned into ghost towns when mining was no longer profitable.

❓ PLACE In what kind of terrain were most of the gold or silver strikes made?

Mining equipment

Legend:
- Gold mining region
- Silver mining region
- ▲ Major lode

But Seward's confidence that Alaska "possesses treasures . . . equal to those of any other region of the continent" would prove correct. In 1896, prospectors discovered gold in the Klondike district of Canada's Yukon Territory, which bordered Alaska. This discovery launched the **Klondike Gold Rush**. By the summer of 1897, Yukon miners had extracted gold deposits worth more than a million dollars. From 1897 to 1899 almost 100,000 people traveled through Alaska to seek their fortunes in the Klondike. Gold discoveries in Alaska in 1898 and 1902 attracted settlers, who later established fish canneries, lumber companies, and coal and copper mining enterprises.

■■ **Mining booms attracted prospectors to present-day Colorado, Nevada, Arizona, Idaho, Montana, and Alaska.**

LIFE IN MINING COMMUNITIES

Mining camps grew up almost overnight wherever news of possible wealth brought prospectors together. Most mining communities started out inhabited almost entirely by men. Unlike ranching or farming, prospecting generally was not a family enterprise.

Mining camps drew a wide range of settlers. In the mining zones of southern California in the 1860s, Mexicans, Californios, Chileans, and Peruvians formed their own separate settlements. In other mining regions, the sometimes uneasy mixture of prospectors included U.S. citizens from all parts of the country, Irish and Chinese men who had come to work on the railroads, and miners from the Cornwall region of England. Some were drawn by the lure of quick wealth; others were fleeing difficult circumstances.

MINING CAMPS AND MINING TOWNS

Draw a two-column chart on the chalkboard labeled *Mining Camps* and *Mining Towns* and have students complete the chart, listing living conditions and activities they associate with each. Have volunteers use the completed chart to generalize about similarities and contrasts between the two types of communities. Ask students to explain how prosperity changed mining camps into permanent communities. Then have volunteers give their opinions about which factors were the most important stabilizing influences.

FROM LONE MINER TO BIG BUSINESS

Organize students into pairs to role-play a conversation between a mining engineer and a prospector. Conversations should cover the following topics: their differences in discovering and mining ore, why mining is becoming big business, and what this trend will mean for the lives of lone miners. Select pairs to reenact their conversations for the class.

▶

▲ The lure of gold and silver drew many men and eventually families to the mining camps of the West. This photograph of a mining family in Colorado was taken in the late 19th century.

At first, life in the mining camps was crude and comforts were few. J. Ross Browne described the first shelters of Virginia City, Nevada:

66 Frame shanties, pitched together as if by accident; tents of canvas, of blankets, of brush, of potato sacks and old shirts, with empty whisky-barrels for chimneys; smoky hovels of mud and stone; coyote holes in the mountain side forcibly seized and held by men. 99

Moreover, the atmosphere in most camps was one of intense competition. Prospector William Parsons remembered

66 . . . a mad, furious race for wealth, in which men lost their identity almost, and toiled and wrestled, and lived a fierce, riotous, wearing, fearfully excited life; forgetting home and kindred; abandoning old, steady habits. 99

Competition sometimes led to violence in the mining camps. Conflicts arose between different ethnic groups. Miners in the Cripple Creek camp in Colorado forcibly excluded eastern and southern Europeans as well as Hispanics. In other camps, Cornish miners fought with Irish, German, and Chinese miners. Gamblers and swindlers swarmed in, and conflicts over claims set off brawls and gunfights. The mining town of Deadwood in South Dakota gained a reputation as an especially rough town. An outlaw's haven, Deadwood became the final resting place of lawman Wild Bill Hickok, shot dead as he played cards.

But stability eventually came to the mining camps as they grew into towns. Mining towns attracted a host of businesses eager to feed and clothe the miners. In fact, owners of saloons and stores were more apt to strike it rich than miners. Cooking, cleaning, and providing lodging were especially lucrative. One industrious woman "earnt . . . nine hundred dollars in nine weeks, clear of all expenses, by washing!" Elizabeth Collins, who later became known as the "cattle queen of Montana," was offered a job as cook for 18 men at a Montana mining camp. She later wrote: "Prompted by kindness and a desire to see these hardworking men as comfortable as possible—also craving for the $75 per month—I promptly accepted the offer."

The few children in the camps had unique roles. They hunted for gold dust and stray nuggets under sidewalks or panned and scavenged for gold dust after the miners were done for the day. Much more profitable, however, was selling fresh food to the miners, who quickly grew tired of eating canned food. One brother and sister made $800 one summer selling butter and bacon to the miners.

As more families moved into the camps, many settlements turned into permanent communities. With prosperity came law and order and the establishment of schools, hospitals, churches, newspapers, and even debating societies and singing clubs. Denver and Boulder, Colorado; Carson City, Nevada; Boise, Idaho; and Helena, Montana all started out as mining camps.

⬛⬛ At first, mining camps were crude and often violent. With prosperity, however, came families, community life, and law and order.

▲ As settlement grew in the West, so did the need for schools. Blanche Lamont posed with members of her school at Hecla, Montana, in October 1893.

PRIMARY SOURCES
Description of Change: excerpted
Rationale: excerpted to focus on main idea

HISTORICAL SIDELIGHTS
Mining Strikes
In the 1860s more than half of the miners at New Almadén, a mining town a few miles south of San Jose, California, were either Mexicans or Californios. To win better working and living conditions, the Hispanic miners took part in strikes—sometimes with their fellow Cornish miners—in 1865, 1866, and 1868, requested that a school be established for their children, and established political and self-help organizations.

HISTORICAL SIDELIGHTS
Sunday Observances
Louisa Cook, a teacher who worked in Idaho mining communities in the 1860s, wrote to her family in Ohio about the lack of religious observances there. Though she was able to attend Sunday school in one town, she noted that "the school meets in . . . one of the hotels right across the street from a bowling alley where you may hear the balls rolling from morning till night."

*P*ractice

GUIDED PRACTICE

Draw a two-column chart on the chalkboard with the headings *Positive* and *Negative*. Call on volunteers to give the positive and negative effects of big business on mining. List students' responses on the chart as they are offered.

INDEPENDENT PRACTICE

Direct students to use the information from the chart developed in the Guided Practice to write an editorial for a mining-town newspaper assessing the positive and negative impacts of the takeover of mining by big businesses. Students may wish to include their editorials in their portfolios.

*R*eview and *A*ssessment

REVIEW Have students write paragraphs or draw scenes about mining life "before" and "after" big business came in, and "before" camp and "after" town. Then assign the Section 4 Review on p. 453.

ASSESS Assign the **Section 4 Daily Quiz** in *Core Resources*.

HISTORICAL SIDELIGHTS
Lawlessness

In the period that preceded the transformation of many mining towns into stable communities, mining towns often lacked law officers, and violence was a part of everyday life. "Every morning from one to three or four dead men were picked up back of the dance halls and saloons," complained one citizen. Sometimes the leading citizens of a town organized a vigilance committee to track down lawbreakers and sometimes acted as judge and jury as well.

HISTORICAL SIDELIGHTS
Western Waitresses

Some mining communities attempted to bring respectability to their towns by regulating waitresses. Waitressing was a relatively well-paying option for women in the West. However, it was not considered a respectable occupation for women; saloon waitresses were especially notorious for their skimpy attire. To reduce rowdiness in its saloons, Virginia City, Nevada, in 1878, passed an ordinance that prohibited waitresses from working between 6:00 A.M. and 6:00 P.M.

THE WILD WEST

Fantastic stories about the untamed western lands of the United States could be heard far from America's shores in the late 1800s. Fascination with outlaw gangs, shoot-outs, and man-eating wild animals lured many European travelers to America to see for themselves. But the "Wild West" rarely lived up to its reputation. Windham T. Dunraven, a British earl, wrote about what he did *not* find in the American West:

THROUGH OTHERS' EYES

"*I* never have an adventure worth a cent; nobody ever scalps me; I don't get 'jumped' by highwaymen. It never occurs to a bear to hug me, and my very appearance inspires feelings of dismay or disgust in the breast of the puma or mountain lion. It is true that I have often been horribly frightened, but generally without any adequate cause. "

*M*INING AS BIG BUSINESS

Individual prospectors roaming the West with their pack horses and hand tools made the earliest mining discoveries, or strikes. But the day of the lone miner did not last long. Within a few years after a strike, most of the easily accessible mineral deposits were "worked out." To get at the hidden ore, miners had to use one of two methods: (1) **hydraulic mining**, which used water pressure to wash away mountains of gravel and expose the minerals underneath; or (2) **hard-rock mining**, which involved sinking deep shafts to get at ore locked in veins of quartz.

Both of these methods required considerable sums of money—far beyond the resources of individual prospectors. Thus mining became the province of large, well-financed companies. These companies relied on science rather than on instinct or luck. Corps of college-educated engineers helped locate the ore and instructed the companies on how best to extract the minerals in demand by eastern factories—zinc, lead, copper, and iron.

The federal government also helped develop mineral resources. It sent out several western expeditions in the 1860s. In 1879 the government organized the U.S. Geological Survey, which gathered and coordinated data about new mines.

▪▪ **As mineral deposits became harder and more expensive to locate and extract, big business dominated mining.**

Big mining companies also changed working conditions in the mines. The big companies used new machinery and hired armies of laborers to carry out the dirty, dangerous work. These laborers sank the shafts, built the tunnels, drilled, and processed the ore. Miners, no longer spurred on by the hope of sudden riches, grew dissatisfied with wages and working conditions.

In some communities miners formed unions. Dues paid to the unions often helped workers injured in the dangerous mines or assisted the families of miners killed on the job. Unions also negotiated with or fought against owners who tried to cut wages. Many also fought against the hiring of Chinese miners, who received lower wages. Union resistance to wage cuts proved most effective during boom times. In the early 1880s, union miners at the Comstock Lode successfully maintained their four-dollar-a-day salaries and eight-hour workdays.

▼ **New mining techniques removed ore quickly from the ground, but also eroded entire hillsides.**

RETEACH Organize students into small groups and assign each group a subsection. Direct each group to develop questions about the main ideas in its subsection. Then have each group exchange its questions with another group and work to answer the questions it receives.

Closure

Copy the last statement in the Commentary on p. 453 onto the chalkboard. Call on students to cite evidence from the section to explain how the statement applies to the experiences of miners.

Extension

RESEARCH Have students research and report on the vigilante movements that sprang up in mining towns and cattletowns during the late 1800s.

CREATE Have students create a model of a mine, mining camp, or mining town.

When mining became big business, the land suffered. In their haste to extract ore, mining companies often ignored the effects of their practices on the environment. Hydraulic mining leveled mountains and often left barren, eroded hills in its wake. Hydraulic mining dumped tons of earth and rocks into rivers, thus raising riverbeds and causing flooding. Flooding in some areas swept away towns and destroyed farmland. Hardrock mining companies also destroyed forests to get wood for mine shafts.

COMMENTARY

Western Myths

The solitary miner, prospecting for gold on a remote mountain stream, is a well-known character in books, movies, and television programs. So is the cowboy who rides off alone into the sunset. Almost equally familiar is the farm or ranch family in its isolated home on the vast, empty plains. In director John Ford's classic *Stagecoach* (1939), the movie that made John Wayne a star, eight pioneers struggle alone across the southwest, dodging Indian arrows all the way. All these legendary western figures represent the American ideal of rugged individuals conquering a hostile, uninhabited land and making it productive. But these images, while powerful, are inaccurate.

Most westerners, including cowboys on ranches and prospectors in mining camps, worked for or with others. And the large companies, not the independent ranchers, farmers, or miners, generally made the biggest profits. The lands where ranchers or farmers grazed their cattle or sheep had already been settled for centuries by American Indian or Hispanic farmers, ranchers, or hunters. Mining camps were crowded and noisy places, and most were established on or near lands inhabited by Hispanics or American Indians. In addition to European Americans, the mines attracted African Americans and immigrants from Asia, South America, and other far flung places—all of whom helped make the West a meeting place for diverse cultures and ways of life.

Furthermore, Americans who settled the West could not have survived without the help of the federal government. The U.S. Army forcefully opened American Indian land for non-Indian settlement. The army also maintained forts to guard trails and protect settlements. The Department of the Interior, through its Bureau of Indian Affairs, resettled Native Americans and ran the reservations on which it placed them. The General Land Office disposed of public land at low rates. Congress subsidized the railroad development that enabled farmers and ranchers as well as mine and timber interests to ship their products to market. By 1871 Congress had granted nearly 130 million acres of western land to railroad corporations. The Department of Agriculture helped Plains farmers, and the Geological Survey aided mining interests.

Novels, songs, and traveling shows spread the myth of the "Wild West" as a region of outlaws, lone cowboys, and brave, isolated pioneers. In reality, men and women lived and worked together in a West shaped as much by technology, big business, and the federal government as by individual effort.

SECTION 4 REVIEW

IDENTIFY and explain the significance of the following: Comstock Lode, *patio* process, William H. Seward, Klondike Gold Rush, hydraulic mining, hard-rock mining.

LOCATE and explain the importance of the following: Pikes Peak; Yukon Territory; Deadwood, South Dakota.

1. **MAIN IDEA** How did later mining camps differ from earlier mining camps?
2. **MAIN IDEA** Why did mining become the domain of large companies?
3. **GEOGRAPHY: LOCATION** Where did the most important mining discoveries take place in the late 19th century?
4. **WRITING TO EXPLAIN** Write an essay contrasting the myth of the rugged individual of the West with the lives of real westerners in the late 19th century.
5. **EVALUATING** How did western mining affect the environment?

DEVELOPING THEMES

Return to the Themes section on p. 424. Have students discuss these again and compare their original responses with those given now. (See p. 423B for suggested answers.)

Chapter Review Answers

WRITING A SUMMARY

See Essential Points in each section for main ideas.

REVIEWING CHRONOLOGY

5, 3, 4, 2, 1
Identifying Cause and Effect
Answers will vary but should make the cause and effect of events clear.

IDENTIFYING PEOPLE AND IDEAS

1. *forced relocation of Navajos to Bosque Redondo*
2. *Sioux medicine man who prophesied victory over U.S. Army*
3. *Paiute leader who publicized the plight of Native Americans*
4. *1862 law granting railroads land to develop transcontinental line*
5. *black settlers who went to Kansas in 1879 to escape violence in the South*
6. *overland cattle drives from Texas to railheads in Kansas, Missouri, Nebraska, and Wyoming*
7. *immigrants who spread sheep ranching in West*
8. *one of the world's richest silver veins; discovered in 1859 in present-day Nevada*

9. *secretary of state who negotiated purchase of Alaska in 1867*
10. *mining method using water pressure to expose minerals*

UNDERSTANDING MAIN IDEAS

1. *availability of land, railroad links to eastern markets, and business opportunities*
2. *Farming was a family enterprise. Mining camps were crude and violent and initially mainly male.*
3. *mining sites—present-day states of CO, NV, AZ, ID, MT, and AK; bonanza farms—Dakota Territory, MN, and CA*
4. *Boom times ended for cattle ranching; big business dominated mining.*

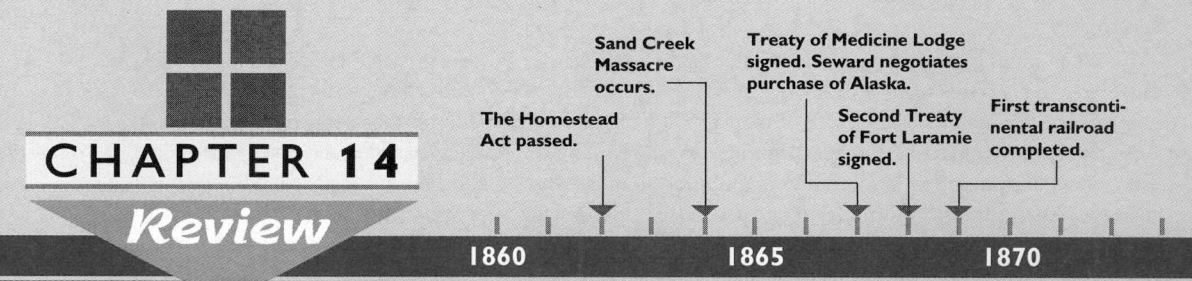

CHAPTER 14
Review

The Homestead Act passed.
Sand Creek Massacre occurs.
Treaty of Medicine Lodge signed. Seward negotiates purchase of Alaska.
Second Treaty of Fort Laramie signed.
First transcontinental railroad completed.

1860 — 1865 — 1870

WRITING A SUMMARY
Using the essential points of the chapter as a guide, write a summary of the chapter.

REVIEWING CHRONOLOGY
Number your paper 1 to 5. Study the time line above, and list the following events in the order in which they happened by writing the first next to 1, the second next to 2, and so on. Then complete the activity.

1. Beef prices crash.
2. Exodusters trek west.
3. First transcontinental railroad completed.
4. Battle of Little Bighorn occurs.
5. The Homestead Act passed.

Identifying Cause and Effect Select two events on the time line, and in a paragraph, explain the cause-and-effect relationship between them.

IDENTIFYING PEOPLE AND IDEAS
Explain the historical significance of each of the following people or terms.

1. Long Walk
2. Sitting Bull
3. Sarah Winnemucca
4. Pacific Railway Act
5. Exodusters
6. long drives
7. Basques
8. Comstock Lode
9. William H. Seward
10. hydraulic mining

UNDERSTANDING MAIN IDEAS
1. What caused settlers to travel to the West in the late 19th century?
2. How did farm life differ from life in the early mining camps?
3. In what areas were key mining sites and bonanza farms developed?
4. How had the businesses of cattle ranching and mining changed by the late 1890s?

REVIEWING THEMES
1. **Geographic Diversity** How did western farmers adapt to the weather and environment?
2. **Cultural Diversity** What problems arose from the federal government's attempt to assimilate Native Americans?

3. **Economic Development** How did the U.S. government promote western land development and settlement?

THINKING CRITICALLY
1. **Hypothesizing** How might Helen Hunt Jackson's *A Century of Dishonor* or Hamlin Garland's *Main-Travelled Roads* have shaped public opinion in the late 1800s?
2. **Evaluating** What positive and negative consequences resulted from development of the West?
3. **Synthesizing** How did different cultures influence one another in the West?

STRATEGY FOR SUCCESS
Review the Strategies for Success on Comparing Points of View on page 420. Then read the selections below. In the first selection, Priscilla Merriam Evans describes some of her responsibilities on a farm in Utah. In the second, author Hamlin Garland describes his mother's life. Compare and contrast their points of view.

66 We made our own cloth, which was mostly gray in color, for dresses. . . . With . . . Indigo . . . and other roots, I have colored beautiful fast colors. We were kept busy in those days carding, spinning, knitting, and doing all of our own sewing by hand. 99

66 All her toilsome, monotonous days rushed through my mind with a roar like a file of gray birds in the night . . . how tragically small her joys, and how black her sorrows, her toil, her tedium. 99

WRITING ABOUT HISTORY
Writing to Express a Viewpoint Imagine you are a prospector in a small mining camp. Write a speech expressing your views about the growth of big mining companies.

REVIEWING THEMES

1. used irrigation and dry-farming methods, adopted mechanized farm equipment, grew new varieties of wheat
2. Resentment over assaults on customs and tribal lands led to conflict. Harsh life on reservations caused conflict and starvation when land proved unsuitable for farming and federal agents proved corrupt.
3. provided free land to railroads and settlers, removed Indians to reservations to make more land available, supported railroad construction, aided farmers and miners by creating new government agencies

THINKING CRITICALLY

1. A Century of Dishonor might have caused people to see the need for reform of U.S. Indian policies; Main-Travelled Roads might have changed idealistic views of the West.
2. positive—economic growth through farming, ranching, and mining; negative—conflict with American Indians and damage to the environment
3. People from many culture groups provided the farmers, cowboys, miners, and other workers that brought development and change, which American Indians resisted.

STRATEGY FOR SUCCESS

Both views reflect the self-reliance of farm life, but Garland's selection shows more harshness.

WRITING ABOUT HISTORY

Speeches might mention that big companies were able to spend large sums of money on scientific mining techniques to reach ore deposits not available to prospectors, but that the companies often had a negative impact on the lifestyles of individual miners.

USING PRIMARY SOURCES

Chief Joseph expected equality and freedom for American Indians. The government limited Indians to reservations and attempted to make them give up their customs.

LINKING HISTORY AND GEOGRAPHY

Railroads opened the U.S. Southwest and Great Plains and connected the Pacific Coast with the Mississippi Valley and the East. The railroads brought non-Indian farmers, ranchers, and miners and linked the West to eastern markets.

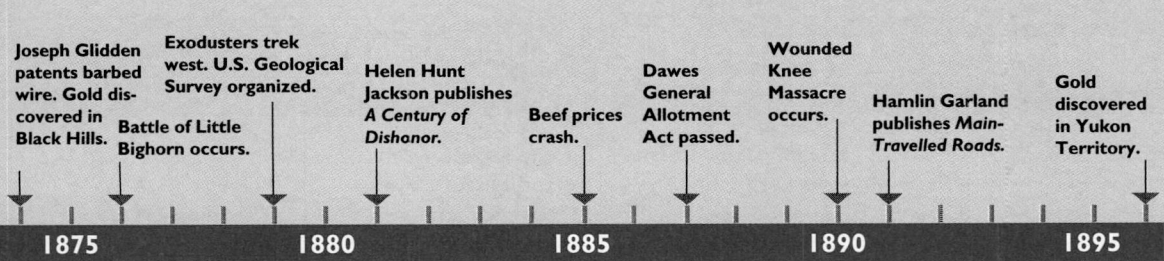

Joseph Glidden patents barbed wire. Gold discovered in Black Hills.

Battle of Little Bighorn occurs.

Exodusters trek west. U.S. Geological Survey organized.

Helen Hunt Jackson publishes *A Century of Dishonor*.

Beef prices crash.

Dawes General Allotment Act passed.

Wounded Knee Massacre occurs.

Hamlin Garland publishes *Main-Travelled Roads*.

Gold discovered in Yukon Territory.

1875   1880   1885   1890   1895

USING PRIMARY SOURCES

The following excerpt is from "Chief Joseph's Own Story," an 1879 account by the Nez Percé leader who had long been committed to peaceful relations with non-Indians. Based on the selection below, how did Chief Joseph's expectations differ from the reality of U.S. policies toward Native Americans?

❝ *We only ask an even chance to live as other men live. We asked to be recognized as men. We ask that the same law shall work alike on all men. . . .*

Let me be a free man—free to travel, free to stop, free to work, free to trade where I choose, free to choose my own teachers, free to follow the religion of my fathers, free to think and talk and act for myself—and I will obey every law, or submit to the penalty.

Whenever the white man treats the Indian as they treat each other, then we shall have no more wars. We shall be all alike— brothers of one father and one mother, with one sky above us and one country around us, and one government for all. Then the Great Spirit Chief who rules above will smile upon this land, and send rain to wash out the bloody spots made by brothers' hands upon the face of the earth. ❞

Chief Joseph

LINKING HISTORY AND GEOGRAPHY

Review the map on page 445. What areas did railroad lines open to non-Indian settlers in this period, and how did the railroads foster development of these areas?

Railroad station, c.1870s

BUILDING YOUR PORTFOLIO

Complete the following projects independently or cooperatively.

1. SOCIAL CONFLICT Imagine you are a Sioux living on the Pine Ridge Reservation in South Dakota in 1895. Compose for your grandchildren an oral account that describes how conflict between the Sioux and farmers, ranchers, and miners has affected your life and the lives of other Sioux. Be sure to work in details of the conflict.

2. TECHNOLOGY AND INDUSTRY Imagine you are a land speculator who hopes to establish a small railhead in Nebraska. Prepare a plan for the town that shows the businesses and other public buildings—stockyard, rail station, church, school, and so on—you will include to attract residents.

BUILDING YOUR PORTFOLIO

Have students refer to **Building Your Portfolio Worksheet 5**, assigned at the beginning of Unit 5. Use the worksheet to help students monitor their progress on the portfolio projects.

Assessment

Core Resources
• Review Worksheet 14
• Chapter 14 Tests
• Alternative Assessment Forms
Test Generator

THE TRANSFORMATION OF AMERICA

1865–1910

Chapter Overview

In the late 1800s the U.S. experienced a surge of industrial growth. Cheap steel, a nationwide rail network, new forms of communication, and new sources of energy fostered a "new industrial order."

During the same period, millions of immigrants, fleeing poverty or persecution at home, sought a better life in America. Many of these newcomers settled with others from their homelands in ethnic neighborhoods. They often worked long hours at exhausting, low-paying jobs.

Spurred by industrialization and immigration, American cities grew by leaps and bounds during the late 1800s, and a distinct urban culture developed.

THE AMERICAN NATION VIDEODISC PROGRAM
A variety of still images, short videos, and activities are available for you to use as you teach this chapter. See Correlation to *The American Nation* Videodisc Program for barcode correlations and suggestions for using the program.

Chapter Planning Guide

CHAPTER 15	CORE RESOURCE BOOKLETS	AV AUDIOVISUAL RESOURCES	PROGRAM RESOURCES
INTRODUCTION pp. 456–457	■ Building Your Portfolio Worksheet 5	■ Linking Geography and History Transparency and Worksheet 11A	■ *Eyewitnesses and Others*, Volume 2: Reading 27
TEACHING THE CHAPTER pp. 458–479	■ Graphic Organizer 15 ■ Social Studies Skills Worksheet 15 ■ Literature Worksheet 15 ■ Geography Worksheet 15 ■ Outline Maps 1, 2, 9, 14, 15, 20	■ *The American Nation* Videodisc: Community Ties: San Francisco's Chinatown; The Standard Oil Company ■ Linking Geography and History Transparency and Worksheet 13A ■ Everyday Life in America Transparency and Worksheet 15	■ Art in American History Transparencies and Worksheets 16, 19 ■ *Eyewitnesses and Others*, Volume 2: Readings 6, 11, 12, 16, 17, 22, 25, 31
REVIEW AND ASSESSMENT pp. 480–481	■ Chapter 15 Daily Quizzes ■ Review Worksheet 15 ■ Chapter 15 Tests ■ Alternative Assessment Forms		■ Test Generator

Additional Resources

BOOKS FOR TEACHERS

Cashman, Sean Dennis. *America in the Gilded Age*. 2nd ed. New York University Press, 1988. Thorough review of industrial, economic, political, and social history of the period.

Daniels, Roger. *Coming to America*. HarperCollins, 1991. Study of immigration to the U.S.

Schlereth, Thomas J. *Victorian America: Transformations of Everyday Life, 1876–1915*. HarperCollins, 1992. Surveys late-19th-century U.S. social history.

BOOKS FOR STUDENTS

Clark, Judith Freeman. *America's Gilded Age: An Eyewitness History*. Facts on File, 1992. Firsthand accounts of major events in the late 1880s.

Hughes, Thomas P. *American Genesis*. Viking Penguin, 1990. Focuses on technology as the driving force of the nation's development.

*James, Portia. *The Real McCoy*. Smithsonian Institution Press, 1990. Examines African American inventions and innovations.

* for students reading below grade level

MULTIMEDIA MATERIALS

The Golden Door: Our Nation of Immigrants. Video, 19 min. Knowledge Unlimited/SSSS. Shows the immigrant experience.

Industrial Revolution in Pittsburgh. Video, 20 min. Agency for Industrial Technology. Explores impact of Industrial Revolution on Pittsburgh steel industry.

Women in American Life—1880–1920. Video, 17 min. National Women's History Project. Explores changes in women's lives.

THEMES IN AMERICAN HISTORY

USE WITH PAGES 456–457

Listed on the right are the themes emphasized in Chapter 15. The questions in boldface type stimulate critical thinking and provide students with an opportunity to discuss the themes within a broadened context. The questions also appear in the pupil's edition on p. 456.

■ ECONOMIC DEVELOPMENT

How might technological change affect a nation's economy? Students may mention that a new technology might improve a nation's economy by creating new products, making existing manufacturing processes less expensive, streamlining the way businesses operate, and changing the ways that products are marketed and sold.

■ TECHNOLOGY AND SOCIETY

What role might technology play in social change? Students should note that as technology brings economic change, social change may also occur. For example, new manufacturing processes may create opportunities for some workers, yet render the job skills of others obsolete and greatly change the nature of work and the workplace. Students may express such concepts by relating them to contemporary experiences, such as the changes wrought by computers or the impact of robotics on factory work.

■ CULTURAL DIVERSITY

What challenges might an influx of people with different ways of life present to a community? Students might suggest the adjustments that some newcomers must make—finding new employment, adjusting to unfamiliar customs and behaviors, perhaps mastering a new language—and consider how these factors might impact life in a community. They may debate what responsibilities a community might have in making these adjustments easier.

CHAPTER STRATEGIES FOR MEETING INDIVIDUAL NEEDS

LIMITED ENGLISH PROFICIENT LEARNERS

This chapter introduces a number of technical terms that might be unfamiliar to LEP students. Ask pairs of students to write sentences and draw sketches that illustrate the meaning of the terms in the Preview Workshops. Have students compare their sentences and sketches.

TACTILE/KINESTHETIC LEARNERS

Have students create and perform skits about the experiences of immigrants who came to the U.S. in the late 1800s.

LEARNERS HAVING DIFFICULTY

Organize students into pairs to construct an annotated outline, section by section, as they read through the chapter. Encourage pairs to compare their outlines.

AUDITORY LEARNERS

Direct small groups of students to select short readings from the titles listed in Books for Students on p. 455A. One group member should read the selection to the class. Other members should explain the selection's significance.

VISUAL LEARNERS

Have students review the chapter to locate the visual they think best illustrates the chapter title—"The Transformation of America." Call on students to explain their choices.

GIFTED LEARNERS

Have students write and deliver a speech on poverty in the U.S. in the late 1800s that either a Social Gospel minister or a Social Darwinist might have given.

USING THE CHAPTER FOCUS

■ UNDERSTANDING THE MAIN IDEA

Ask a volunteer to read the Understanding the Main Idea paragraph aloud. Then ask students to suggest words they might use to describe the U.S. in the late 19th century. List responses on a flip chart or a piece of butcher paper. After students have completed the chapter, have them evaluate and adjust the word list.

■ THEMES

Have students work individually or in small groups to answer the questions under Themes. Save students' responses so that they can compare them with their responses after studying the chapter. (See p. 455B for suggested answers.)

■ THE TIME LINE

Ask students to cite events on the time line that provide evidence that the U.S. was in a second industrial age in the late 19th century. Then have students copy the events on the time line in their notebooks. As they read the chapter, have students write a sentence explaining the historical significance of each time-line event.

CORE RESOURCES

- **Graphic Organizer 15**
- **Outline Maps 1, 2, 9, 14, 15, 20**
- **Building Your Portfolio Worksheet 5**

AV RESOURCES

- **Linking Geography and History Transparency** and **Worksheet 11A**

456

ABOUT THE ILLUSTRATION

Tell students that although immigration from southern and eastern Europe increased substantially in the late 19th and early 20th centuries, the "old immigration" also continued. The German family in this photograph is pictured with its belongings shortly after disembarking from the ship. Have students study the photograph and point out clues that suggest this family's socio-economic status. (*It appears well-dressed and prosperous.*) Ask them to speculate about the identity of the young woman who is holding the baby. (*perhaps a relative, but more likely a nanny or other domestic servant of this family*)

Chapter 15

1865–1910

THE TRANSFORMATION OF AMERICA

FOCUS

UNDERSTANDING THE MAIN IDEA

New technologies and new forms of business organization helped usher in a second industrial age in late–19th-century America. Millions of immigrants came to the United States in this period, lured by the prospect of work. By 1900 these developments had transformed the United States into an urban nation and an industrial power.

THEMES

- **■ ECONOMIC DEVELOPMENT** How might technological change affect a nation's economy?

- **■ TECHNOLOGY AND SOCIETY** What role might technology play in social change?

- **■ CULTURAL DIVERSITY** What challenges might an influx of people with different ways of life present to a community?

1867	1876	1879	1882	1889
Christopher Sholes invents typewriter.	Alexander Graham Bell patents telephone.	Frank W. Woolworth founds first of his chain stores.	Congress passes Chinese Exclusion Act.	Jane Addams establishes Hull House.

LINK TO THE PAST

Have volunteers recall the major industrial advances and waves of immigration that took place during the first half of the 1800s. Direct students to list the major points of the discussion in their notebooks. Then, as students read the chapter, have them compare items on their list to events and developments surrounding the second industrial age and the new immigration.

LINK TO THE PAST

Industrialization and immigration helped fuel the growth of the United States in the first half of the 1800s. However, the United States remained primarily a rural nation whose people continued to depend on agriculture for a living.

Immigrants arriving from Germany

*I*n the second half of the 1800s, the United States underwent another wave of industrialization. To many this process seemed almost a natural outcome of American life. "The American mechanizes as an old Greek sculptured, as the Venetian painted," the London *Times* noted in 1878. A debate quickly developed, however, over whether the negative side effects of industrialization—such as grinding poverty existing side-by-side with great wealth—were natural outcomes as well.

Critical of the new industrial order, economist Henry George condemned the growing contrast "between the House of Have and the House of Want." He argued that the poor should not have to suffer so that a few could be rich. Yale professor William Graham Sumner took the opposite view, claiming that the rich and the poor were just where nature intended and that any change would slow progress and harm society. Not all industrialists agreed with Sumner. Some proposed that they use part of their wealth to benefit all of society. But social reformer Frederic Howe argued that if industrialists really had the well-being of society at heart, they "would stop the twelve-hour day . . . increase wages and put an end to the cruel killing and maiming" of workers. Although this debate produced no solid answers about how to reconcile the existence of poverty in the midst of great wealth, it did lead to efforts to reform the worst abuses of the industrial order.

The Edison phonograph

HISTORICAL SIDELIGHTS

America's Genius
Many Americans felt that the nation's greatest strength was in the growth of its industrial capacity. Reviewing the Machinery Hall at the 1876 Centennial Exposition in Philadelphia, novelist William Dean Howells noted "it is . . . in these things of iron and steel that the national genius most freely speaks. . . . America is voluble in the strong metals and their infinite uses."

FOCUS OBJECTIVES

■ Identify the roles that steel, railroads, and innovations in communications and energy played in the new industrial order.

■ Explain how businesses increased their profits in the late 19th century.

■ Describe how the government attempted to regulate business.

CORE RESOURCES

• **Section 1 Daily Quiz**

AV RESOURCES

• *The American Nation* **Videodisc: Standard Oil Company**
• **Everyday Life in America Transparency** and **Worksheet 15**

458

PREVIEW WORKSHOP

Following is a list of the significant people and terms in this section. You may wish to use this list as a section preview.

People
■ Granville T. Woods
■ Alexander Graham Bell
■ Thomas Edison
■ Andrew Carnegie

■ John D. Rockefeller

Terms
■ trunk lines
■ laissez-faire capitalism
■ Social Darwinism
■ proprietorships
■ partnerships
■ corporation
■ stock

■ stockholders
■ dividends
■ limited liability
■ trust
■ monopoly
■ economies of scale
■ vertical integration
■ horizontal integration
■ Sherman Antitrust Act

Section 1

INDUSTRY'S GOLDEN AGE

FOCUS

■ **What roles did steel, railroads, and innovations in communications and energy play in the new industrial order?**

■ **How did businesses increase their profits in the late 19th century?**

■ **How did the government attempt to regulate business?**

First telephone, 1876

From 1865 to 1910 the United States experienced a surge of industrial growth. These decades witnessed the beginnings of a "second industrial revolution." A "new industrial order" was created with the development of cheap steel, the completion of a nationwide rail network, the invention of the telephone and the typewriter, the introduction of new sources of energy, and the rise of big business.

TECHNOLOGICAL INNOVATIONS

America's first industrial revolution was dependent on coal and steam. Coal-fed steam engines powered the factories, which produced the goods that generated economic growth. But it was steel—not steam—that spurred industrialization in the late 1800s. The heavy machinery used to mass-produce goods, the rails that enabled trains to move people and products, the bridges that spanned the rivers, and the tall buildings that dotted the cities all required steel.

Steel was not new. Until the mid–19th century, however, the process of converting iron ore into steel was expensive. In the 1850s Henry Bessemer in England and William Kelly in the United States independently developed a method of steel making that burned off the impurities in molten iron with a blast of hot air. The Bessemer process, as it came to be called, could produce more steel in a day than the older techniques could turn out in a week. American engineer Alexander Holley adapted and improved the Bessemer process. As a result, America's annual steel

production grew from about 15 thousand tons in 1865 to over 28 million tons by 1910.

■■ **Steel provided the building blocks—the heavy machinery, rails, and beams—for industry's golden age.**

The Metropolitan Museum of Art

▲ *Forging the Shaft* by John Ferguson Weir depicts a scene from the West Point Foundry in Cold Spring, New York, during the 1870s.

Have students draw upon information from previous chapters to identify inventions and technological innovations that were important to the industrial revolution of the early 1800s. As students read the section, have them compare these inventions and innovations with those that drove the second industrial revolution.

■■ Ask students to identify the present-day inventions and technological innovations that are changing American industry.

▶

Railroads. Steel had a tremendous impact on railroad expansion. Steel rails were better than iron rails, which cracked easily. At first, steel was much more costly than iron. As steel production soared, however, prices dropped dramatically. Steel that had sold for $100 a ton in 1873 sold for $12 by the late 1890s.

The availability of cheaper steel encouraged railroads to lay thousands of miles of new track. In 1869, when Leland Stanford had hammered in a golden spike to complete the country's first transcontinental railroad, the United States had less than 50,000 miles of railroad track. By the end of the century, total mileage had skyrocketed to some 200,000. Almost a half-dozen **trunk lines**, or major railroads, crossed the Great Plains to the Pacific coast. Feeder, or branch, lines connected the trunk lines to surrounding areas. This huge railroad grid joined every state and linked remote towns to urban centers.

At the same time, technological innovations helped improve rail transportation. Bigger, more efficient locomotives made it possible to pull larger loads at greater speeds. George Westinghouse's compressed air brake increased railroad safety by enabling the locomotive and all the cars to stop at the same time. Granville T. Woods improved Westinghouse's air brake and developed a telegraph system that let trains communicate with stations.

Changes in track design also improved rail service. Double sets of tracks allowed traffic to roll in two directions at once. Equally important, the adoption in the 1880s of a standard gauge, or width between the rails, made rail transportation faster and cheaper. Passengers and freight no longer had to be transferred each time a train reached a different line.

▲ Granville T. Woods

The growth of railroads had far-reaching consequences. Railroads promoted western settlement by making travel affordable and easy. They also stimulated urban growth. Wherever the railroads went, new towns sprang up, and older towns grew into major cities.

The economic impact of the railroads was immeasurable. Not only were the railroad compa-

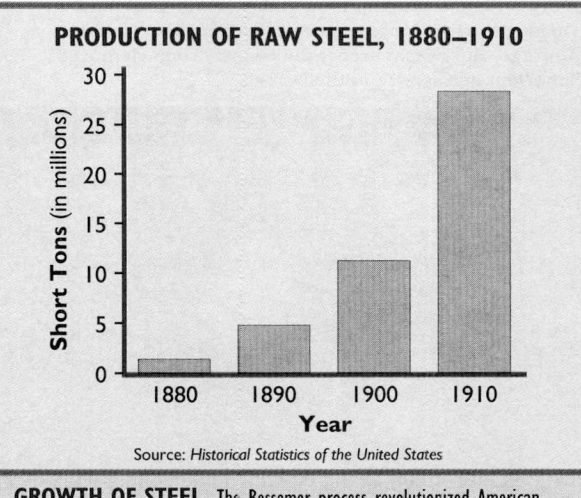

PRODUCTION OF RAW STEEL, 1880–1910

Short Tons (in millions) / Year

Source: *Historical Statistics of the United States*

GROWTH OF STEEL The Bessemer process revolutionized American industry by allowing large quantities of steel to be made more cheaply than ever before.

❓ **BUILDING GRAPH SKILLS** By about how many tons did steel production rise from 1880 to 1910?

nies the country's major employers for much of the late 1800s, they also spurred the growth of other industries. The railroads' demands for rails, locomotives, and railcars poured money into the steel industry. Innovations like refrigerated freight cars helped develop the meat-packing industry. In addition, the network of railroad lines helped build a national market. Now a Pennsylvania steel foundry could obtain iron ore from the Great Lakes region, or a Philadelphia furniture company could sell its products in small midwestern towns.

Railroads also shaped American popular culture and folk music. One ballad immortalized Casey Jones, the Illinois Central engineer killed in a spectacular crash with a freight train in 1900. Other songs celebrated famous trains like the Wabash Cannonball.

■■ **Railroad expansion spurred the growth of other industries and strengthened national markets.**

Communications. An equally remarkable transformation in communications accompanied the revolution in railroad transportation. The telegraph attracted little attention when Samuel F. B. Morse patented his version in 1837. In time, however, people saw its business potential. Using

Graph Caption Answer
by about 25 million tons

MAKING CONNECTIONS
Science
Traditionally, towns and cities set their clocks according to the movement of the sun, which meant that communities a few miles apart were also a few minutes apart. This made railroad scheduling a nightmare. Eventually, railroad officials hit upon the idea of dividing the country into four standard time zones—Eastern, Central, Mountain, and Pacific—based on the mean sun time at the meridians near Philadelphia, Memphis, Denver, and Fresno. This system went into effect at noon on November 18, 1883. However, it was not commonly accepted throughout the U.S. until Congress passed the Standard Time Act in 1918.

Teaching the Section

A NEW INDUSTRIAL ORDER

Organize the class into groups of five and provide each group with a sheet of butcher paper. Ask each group to create on the butcher paper a graphic organizer titled "Making a New Industrial Order." Suggest that they divide their organizers into four parts: contributions of steel, contributions of railroads, contributions of energy, and contributions of communications. Have groups display and explain their completed graphic organizers.

HISTORICAL SIDELIGHTS

Telephone Operators

The first telephone operators were young men. But the telephone companies found them unreliable, rowdy, and rather rude, and quickly replaced them with women. In time, women predominated in this occupation. Employers argued that women had more agreeable voices and that their smaller hands were better suited to handling the telephone equipment. A more likely reason for their predominance is that they accepted lower wages because of the few job opportunities available to women at the time.

MAKING CONNECTIONS

Language Arts

The phrase *the real McCoy*, meaning "the genuine article," may refer to an African American inventor named Elijah McCoy. In the early 1870s McCoy developed a lubricating cup that could drip oil continuously onto a locomotive engine's moving parts. Soon after, cheap copies of the device became available. Engineers asked, "Is this the real McCoy?" to make certain they were buying McCoy's invention.

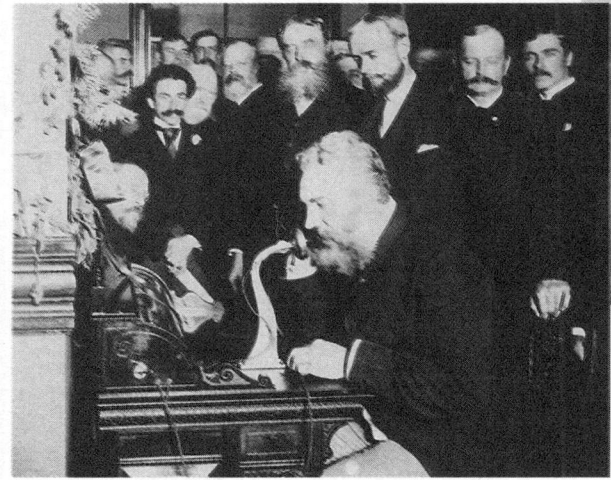

▼ This 1892 photograph shows Alexander Graham Bell making the first long-distance call from New York to Chicago. Businesses across the country soon clamored for telephone service in their cities.

▲ In 1866 Milwaukee printer and newspaper editor Christopher Sholes developed a machine that numbered book pages. This machine was the forerunner of Sholes's first typewriter. Sholes is shown here with his typewriter.

Morse's dot-and-dash code, a telegraph operator could send a business order to a distant location in minutes. By 1866 Western Union, the leading telegraph company, had over 2,000 telegraph offices.

The "talking telegraph," or telephone, which Alexander Graham Bell patented in 1876, had an even greater impact. When Bell demonstrated his gadget at the Philadelphia Centennial Exposition in June 1876, the judges pronounced it "perhaps the greatest marvel hitherto achieved by the electric telegraph." A reporter for the New York *Tribune* did not agree, asking "Of what use is such an invention?" But businesses quickly found the telephone indispensable. By the end of the 1800s, more than a million telephones had been installed in U.S. offices and homes. The telephones required operators, and many women rushed to fill these newly created jobs.

Another major achievement in communications was Christopher Sholes's development of the typewriter in 1867. After making a few improvements, Sholes sold the patent in 1873 to E. Remington & Sons. The typewriter improved communications by producing documents quickly and by making them easy to read. Carbon paper, also introduced during this period, allowed users of typewriters to produce multiple copies.

■■ **The telegraph, telephone, and typewriter aided industrialization by speeding communication.**

★ NEW SOURCES OF ENERGY

America's remarkable transportation and communications developments depended on abundant supplies of energy. In the late 1800s businesspeople and inventors began to tap into two new sources of power—oil and electricity.

The early oil industry. People in western Pennsylvania had known about oil for years. Medicine-show hucksters, seeing the chance to make a quick dollar, sold it as a miracle cure-all. But almost no one thought oil had any other uses. In the late 1850s, however, American chemist Benjamin Silliman, Jr., released a report noting that oil could be refined to make kerosene, which could be burned in lamps to produce light.

The growing demand for this inexpensive fuel prompted prospector Edwin L. Drake to drill for oil near Titusville, Pennsylvania, in 1859. At first, people questioned Drake's sanity. When the oil began to flow at a rate of some 20 barrels a day, however, other prospectors hurried to sink their own wells. By the 1880s, oil wells dotted Pennsylvania, Ohio, and West Virginia, producing more than 25 million barrels of oil in 1880 alone.

Harnessing electricity. As in the case of oil, people knew of electricity long before they put it to practical use. People considered it little more than a puzzling natural phenomenon. Then in the

NEW SOURCES OF ENERGY

Call on volunteers to cite the inventions that resulted from the two new sources of power—oil and electricity—in the late 1800s. Write responses on the chalkboard. Then organize students into small groups. Give half of the groups five minutes to brainstorm all the things they could not do if they lived without electricity. Have the other half do the same thing for petroleum. Bring the groups together and have volunteers present their ideas and list them on the chalkboard. Then use the lists to lead a class discussion on how American life in the late 1800s was changed by electricity and oil.

▶

---

mid-1800s European and American scientists and engineers developed the dynamo, or electric generator. Driven by steam, water, or other energy source, the dynamo produced enough electrical power to run a factory. An American inventor, Thomas Alva Edison, realized that the dynamo could have wide-ranging applications.

BIO GRAPHY Born in a small Ohio town in 1847, Thomas Edison had only a few months of formal schooling. At age 12 he became a newsboy and later worked as a telegraph operator. An avid amateur scientist, Edison conducted experiments and read widely in his spare time.

The Granger Collection, New York

Thomas Edison

In 1868 Edison developed an electric vote recorder. The next year, he received his first patent, for an improved stock ticker, which telegraphed stock prices. Other inventions followed, and in 1876 he went into the "invention business" full-time, opening a workshop in Menlo Park, New Jersey, where he assembled a team of researchers. Excited, Edison sent a friend the following invitation:

> 66 Brand-new laboratory . . . at Menlo Park, Western Div., Globe, Planet Earth, Middlesex County, four miles from Rahway, the prettiest spot in New Jersey, on the Penna. Railway, on a High Hill. Will show you around, go strawberrying. 99

Edison promised that he and his fellow researchers would deliver "a minor invention every ten days and a big thing every six months or so." He was as good as his word. He invented the phonograph in 1877 and the light bulb in 1879. By the time he died in 1931, the "Wizard of Menlo Park" held 1,093 patents.

Lewis Latimer–who later worked for Edison–also contributed to light bulb design. He was also a skilled draftsman and an expert in patent law. Latimer

testified in several court cases to support Edison's patents.

In 1882 Edison opened one of the world's first central electric power plants in New York City. But the plant could deliver electricity to homes and offices in only a very small area. George Westinghouse and Nikola Tesla solved this problem in the late 1880s by developing a transformer that could transmit a high-voltage current over long distances.

At the 1893 World's Columbian Exposition in Chicago, a Westinghouse-Tesla generator powered the twinkling lights outlining the major buildings. The electric lights enchanted visitors, who marveled at the "fairyland." To many it symbolized a transformation of American life. Indeed, by the end of the century, electric lights were replacing gaslights. And in many cities horse-drawn vehicles had given way to electric streetcars.

■■ **By the end of the 1800s, kerosene and electricity powered and illuminated American homes and factories.**

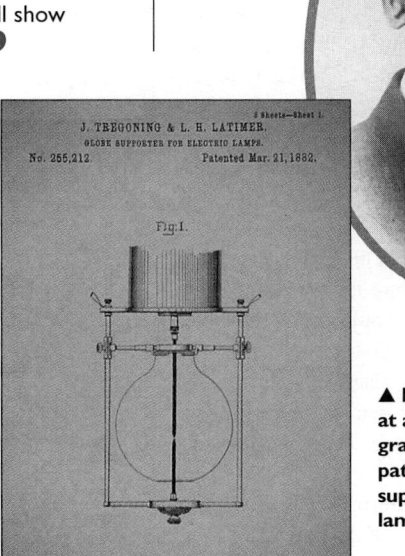

▲ Lewis Latimer is pictured at age 70 in this 1919 photograph. Shown at left is his patent drawing for a globe supporter for the electric lamp.

ᴱeaching the ˢection

FORMS OF BUSINESS CONSOLIDATION

On the chalkboard draw a chart with three columns headed *Business Form, Definition,* and *Advantages*. Have volunteers come to the board and complete the chart. Then ask students to identify for each form how its use increased profits. Have students explain which of the forms show the philosophy of Social Darwinism at work. Ask students how they would have felt about each form were they small-business owners in the late 1800s, and why.

ᵀHE RISE OF BIG BUSINESS

Along with these technological developments emerged new ideas that revolutionized the business world. The late 1800s was the age of **laissez-faire capitalism**. (*Laissez faire* is French for "let it be.") The theory of laissez-faire capitalism calls for no government regulation of economic matters. Most business leaders believed that if businesses were freed from government regulation, the economy would prosper.

Another theory, **Social Darwinism**, reinforced the laissez-faire doctrine. Originally advanced by English social philosopher Herbert Spencer, Social Darwinism applied the biological principles of natural selection and evolution to society. Social Darwinists argued that society progressed through competition. The "fittest" people (or businesses or nations) should and would rise to positions of wealth and power, while the "unfit" would fail. Social Darwinists believed that any attempts to help the poor or less capable only slowed social progress: "Nature's cure for most social and political diseases," wrote American educator and philosopher Nicholas Murray Butler, "is better than man's."

Some clergy offered religious support for Social Darwinism by suggesting that great wealth was a sign of Christian virtue. Baptist minister Russell H. Conwell declared: "You ought to get rich, and it is your duty to get rich. . . . To make money honestly is to preach the gospel."

Bigger is better. Many people did get rich during this period, particularly industrialists. Industrialists were aided in their quest for wealth by new forms of business organization. At the close of the Civil War, most businesses were **proprietorships**—small enterprises owned by individuals or families—or **partnerships**—enterprises owned by two or more people. These forms of business organization were inadequate to manage giant new industries like railroads, steel, or oil. Nor could they raise the capital needed to finance such ventures. As a result, business leaders turned to another form of business organization—the corporation—which had existed in one form or another since colonial times.

In a **corporation** organizers raise capital by selling shares of **stock**, or certificates of ownership, in the company. **Stockholders**—those who buy the shares—receive a percentage of the corporation's profits in the form of **dividends**. But the stockholders play little or no part in the corporation's daily operations.

A corporation has several advantages over a proprietorship or a partnership. First, a corporation's organizers can raise enormous sums of money by selling stock to many people. Second, unlike proprietors and partners, stockholders enjoy **limited liability**—that is, they are not responsible for the corporation's debt. Third, a corporation is a stable organization because it is distinct from its owners. A corporation continues to exist no matter who owns the stock.

Corporations needed more than organizational stability to deal with the economic climate of the late 1800s. Because competition was fierce, prices and profits fluctuated wildly. Some corporations responded by forming trusts. In a **trust**, a group of companies turn control of their stock over to a board of directors. The directors then run the companies as a single enterprise. If a trust could gain exclusive control of an industry, it could form a **monopoly**.

Carnegie and steel. Andrew Carnegie, a Scot who immigrated to the United States in 1848, established some of the first monopolies. Carnegie entered the steel business in the early 1870s. He readily admitted that he understood little about making steel, but he did know how to run a business. He surrounded himself with skillful managers and drove them relentlessly. He fitted his

▲ At age 13, Andrew Carnegie began his first job winding thread on bobbins, or spools, for $1.20 a week. When he retired from the steel industry, he was worth nearly $500 million.

▲ In 1873 Andrew Carnegie built the largest steel mill in the country, the J. Edgar Thomson Steel Works, in Pittsburgh. This interior view of a steel mill was taken in 1900.

plants with the most modern machinery. But he was also not above using questionable tactics to beat out his competitors.

Carnegie's real success, however, lay in reducing production costs. Carnegie realized that by buying supplies in bulk and producing goods in large quantities he could lower production costs and increase profits. This principle is known as **economies of scale**. Carnegie also used **vertical integration** to control costs—that is, he acquired companies that provided materials and services upon which his enterprises depended. For example, Carnegie purchased iron mines and coal mines, which provided the raw materials for his steel mills, steamship lines, and railroads. An admirer explained the great advantage:

❝ From the moment these crude stuffs were dug out of the earth until they flowed in a stream of liquid steel in the ladles, there was never a price, profit, or royalty paid to an outsider. ❞

Because Carnegie controlled businesses at each stage of production, he could sell steel at a much lower price than his competitors.

In 1889 Carnegie organized all of his companies into the Carnegie Steel Company, which dominated the steel industry. When Carnegie sold his company to banking tycoon J. P. Morgan for nearly $500 million and retired in 1901, he became the world's richest man.

Rockefeller and oil. The business career of oil tycoon John D. Rockefeller—one of the founders of Standard Oil—followed a course similar to Carnegie's. Rockefeller got into the oil-refining business in its formative years, when many small companies were in fierce competition. Arguing that such competition was inefficient, Rockefeller set out to gain control of the industry.

Like Carnegie, Rockefeller used vertical integration to make his company more competitive, eventually acquiring oil fields, barrel factories, pipelines, railroad tanker cars, and oil-storage facilities. But his main method of expansion was **horizontal integration**—one company's ownership of other companies involved in the same business, in this case, oil refining. What companies Standard Oil could not buy, it tried to control through the establishment of the nation's first trust in the early 1880s.

▶ Eastman Johnson completed this formal portrait of John D. Rockefeller in 1895.

*P*ractice

GUIDED PRACTICE

On the chalkboard write the first and last entries for a cause-effect chain on American industrialization—*Technological Innovations* and *America Becomes an Industrial Power.* Ask for volunteers to add links to the chain.

INDEPENDENT PRACTICE

Encourage students to imagine they are correspondents for a foreign business magazine. Ask them to use information from the cause-effect chain developed in the Guided Practice to write an article for their country's readers on conditions that made possible America's industrial growth in the late 1800s.

*R*eview and *A*ssessment

REVIEW Ask students, working in pairs, to write sentences that explain how each entry in the Preview Workshop is related to the main idea of the subsection in which it is located. Have pairs share their sentences with the group. Then assign the Section 1 Review on p. 465.

ASSESS Assign the **Section 1 Daily Quiz** in *Core Resources.*

PRIMARY SOURCE

Description of Change: excerpted
Rationale: excerpted to focus on main idea

HISTORICAL SIDELIGHTS

Failed Legislation
After the passage of the Sherman Antitrust Act the rate of business consolidation did not decrease, but rather, increased. Between 1893 and 1904 the number of giant business combinations grew from 12 to 318. And these 318 companies controlled about 40 percent of capital invested in manufacturing.

BUILDING VOCABULARY

The first recorded use in the U.S. of the term *department store* came in 1887 when, in an advertisement, a New York shop was listed as "H. H. Heyn's Department Store." However, the idea of dividing large stores into separate departments was at least 40 years old by that date.

AV **TRANSPARENCY**

Everyday Life in America Transparency and **Worksheet 15**

To drive his competitors out of business, Rockefeller made deals with suppliers and transporters to receive cheaper supplies and freight rates. George Rice, a small oil refiner driven out of business by Rockefeller's practices, complained to the U.S. Industrial Commission in 1899:

> ❝ I have been driven from pillar to post, from one railway line to another, for twenty years, in the absolutely vain endeavor to get equal and just freight rates with the Standard Oil Trust, . . . but which I have been utterly unable to do. I have had to consequently shut down, with my business absolutely ruined. ❞

Rice was not alone. Rockefeller forced most of his rivals to sell out. By 1899 the Standard Oil Company controlled some 90 percent of the country's petroleum refining capacity and had annual profits of some $45 million.

▪▪ Businesses used corporations, trusts, and vertical and horizontal integration to increase profits.

Government and business. Industrialists also had the government's support in making their enterprises more profitable. Although supporters of laissez-faire capitalism claimed to frown on government intervention in business activities, they welcomed the government's role in promoting the rise of the new industrial order. For instance, by placing high tariffs on imports, the federal government allowed U.S. businesses to dominate the home market. In 1875, for example, Congress increased tariff rates to make imported steel 40 percent more expensive than domestic steel.

At the same time, the government took only a few modest steps to regulate businesses, despite growing pressure from the general public. As Carnegie Steel, Standard Oil, and other large corporations grew in power, many Americans demanded that trusts be outlawed. Congress responded in 1890 by passing the **Sherman Antitrust Act**, which declared all monopolies and trusts in restraint of trade illegal. While its intentions appeared clear, the law failed to define what constituted a monopoly or trust. Thus the law proved difficult to enforce.

▪▪ The federal government adopted the Sherman Antitrust Act in an effort to eliminate monopolies.

---

*M*ASS MARKETING

Industrialists knew that cutting production costs and reducing competition were not the only ways to increase profits. They also developed new methods of marketing to sell their products.

Brand names and packaging played important roles in promoting goods. For example, the name Standard Oil conveyed the idea that the company's product set the industry standard. Other

▼ Colorful advertisements such as these for processed baby food and flour flooded newspapers and magazines by the end of the 19th century.

RETEACH Organize students into groups and assign each group a subsection of the section. Have each group develop several questions and answers about the main ideas in its assigned material. Then have each group quiz the other groups.

Closure

Have students work in small groups to draw up a list of the items they might include in a museum exhibit titled "American Industry's Golden Age." Suggest that they divide their exhibits into four sections: Technological Innovations, New Sources of Energy, The Rise of Big Business, Mass Marketing. Have groups compare their lists.

Extension

CREATE Have students research 19th-century advertising techniques and create an advertisement for a modern-day product using them. Ask for volunteers to display their advertisements on the bulletin board.

RESEARCH Ask students to research and diagram one of the inventions discussed in this section. Have them present their diagrams to the class.

companies used brightly colored packages or distinctive logos to set their products apart.

Advertising, too, became an important promotional tool. Newspapers, magazines, and roadside billboards carried advertisements urging people to buy "The Purest" soap and telephones "warranted to work *one mile,* unaffected by changes in the weather."

New types of stores sold some of these highly promoted goods. The department store carried a wide variety of products—such as shoes, clothing, hardware, and appliances—under one roof. Pioneered by John Wanamaker in Philadelphia, Marshall Field in Chicago, and R. H. Macy in New York City, the department store bought products in bulk and, as a result, could offer low prices to consumers.

Department stores became the special domain of women, both as places to work and places to shop. Wanting to create a homelike and welcoming atmosphere in their stores (and also looking for ways to cut labor costs), department-store owners hired young, mainly middle-class women to work as clerks. In addition, department-store advertisements targeted women as the chief buyers of their products.

Like department stores, chain stores—stores with branches in many cities—bought goods in large quantities. They then passed on their savings to customers. Perhaps the most famous chain store was founded by Frank W. Woolworth in 1879. By 1900 Woolworth had a network of 59 stores.

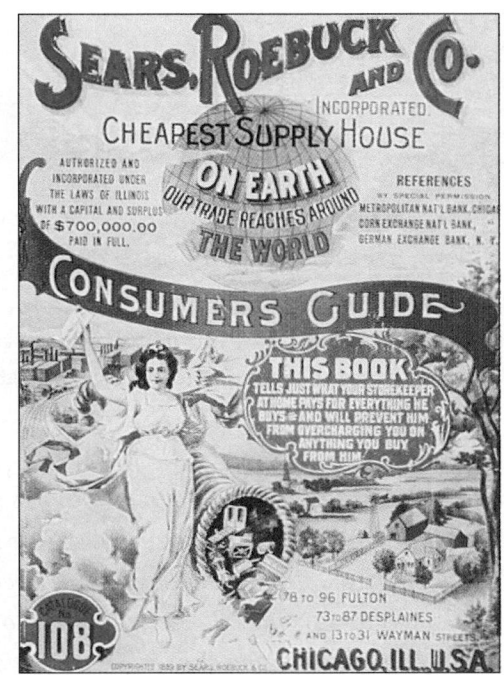

▲ Mail-order catalogs brought the latest products and inventions into homes in even the most remote rural areas.

Department stores and chain stores were a part of the urban scene. Mail-order companies like Montgomery Ward and Sears, Roebuck, and Co. catered to the rural market. Customers selected goods from a catalog, then ordered, paid for, and received the merchandise by mail.

SECTION 1 REVIEW

IDENTIFY and explain the significance of the following: trunk lines, Granville T. Woods, Alexander Graham Bell, laissez-faire capitalism, proprietorships, partnerships, corporation, stock, stockholders, dividends, limited liability, trust, monopoly, economies of scale, vertical integration, horizontal integration.

1. **MAIN IDEA** How did steel, railroads, and innovations in communications contribute to American industry?
2. **MAIN IDEA** What organizational and selling methods did businesspeople use to increase their profits in the late 1800s?
3. **MAIN IDEA** Why did Congress pass the Sherman Antitrust Act in 1890? How did the act attempt to regulate business?
4. **WRITING TO INFORM** Write an essay describing the impact of the technological advances introduced by Thomas Edison.
5. **HYPOTHESIZING** How do you think the theory of Social Darwinism shaped the business practices of Andrew Carnegie and John D. Rockefeller?

PREVIEW WORKSHOP

Following is a list of the significant people and terms in this section. You may wish to use this list as a section preview.

People
- paper sons

Terms
- old immigrants
- new immigrants
- benevolent societies
- bosses
- political machines
- Chinese Exclusion Act
- Immigration Restriction League

FOCUS OBJECTIVES

- Describe how immigration changed in the late 1800s.

- Identify the institutions that helped new immigrants adapt to American life.

- Explain why some native-born Americans objected to the new immigrants.

AV TRANSPARENCY

Linking Geography and History Transparency and **Worksheet 13A**

CORE RESOURCES

- **Literature Worksheet 15**
- **Geography Worksheet 15**
- **Section 2 Daily Quiz**

AV RESOURCES

- *The American Nation* **Videodisc: Community Ties: San Francisco's Chinatown**
- **Linking Geography and History Transparency** and **Worksheet 13A**

Section 2

THE NEW IMMIGRANTS

FOCUS

- **How did immigration change in the late 1800s?**
- **What institutions helped new immigrants adapt to American life?**
- **Why did some native-born Americans object to the new immigrants?**

Immigration is one of the dynamic forces that has shaped the United States. Immigrants fleeing persecution or poverty or seeking a better life had founded the first colonies, and immigrants had continually added to the country's population. As the 19th century drew to a close, a wave of new immigrants came to America's shores in search of opportunity.

Handbill supporting immigration, 1909

THE LURE OF AMERICA

From 1800 to 1880 more than 10 million immigrants came to the United States. Often called the **old immigrants**, many of them were Protestants from northwestern Europe—Great Britain, Ireland, Germany, and the Scandinavian countries. Then, a new wave of immigrants swept over the United States. In less than two decades, between 1891 and 1910, some 12 million immigrants came to the United States. The increase was so great that by the early 1900s, about 60 percent of the people living in the nation's 12 largest cities either were foreign-born or had foreign-born parents.

About 70 percent of these **new immigrants** were from southern or eastern Europe. They were Italians, Greeks, Poles, Czechs, Slovaks, Hungarians, and Russians. In contrast to the old immigrants, most new immigrants were Catholic, Jewish, or Greek Orthodox. French Canadians, Armenians, Arabs, Chinese, and Japanese also arrived by the thousands.

Immigration soared in the late 1800s and early 1900s. Most new immigrants were southern or eastern Europeans.

Like the old immigrants, many new immigrants came to the United States to escape poverty or persecution. Most of the Italian and Slavic immigrants were male and sought economic

◀ **This immigrant mother and her children arrived at Ellis Island, New York, around 1910.**

MOTIVATING: LINK TO TODAY

Ask volunteers to identify aspects of immigration that have become issues to some present-day Americans. List these issues on the chalkboard and have students record the list in their notebooks. As students study this section, have them compare the issues surrounding today's immigrants with those experienced by immigrants of the late 1800s and early 1900s.

Teaching the Section

IMMIGRATION—OLD AND NEW

Organize students into pairs and have each pair develop a descriptive sentence for an imaginary immigrant. (For example, "I came to America to escape poverty," or "I immigrated to America from Hungary.") As each pair reads its statement, ask other students if it likely identifies a new immigrant, an old immigrant, or both. Then ask the class to generalize, based on the statements, about ways that immigration changed in the late 1800s and ways that it remained the same.

▶

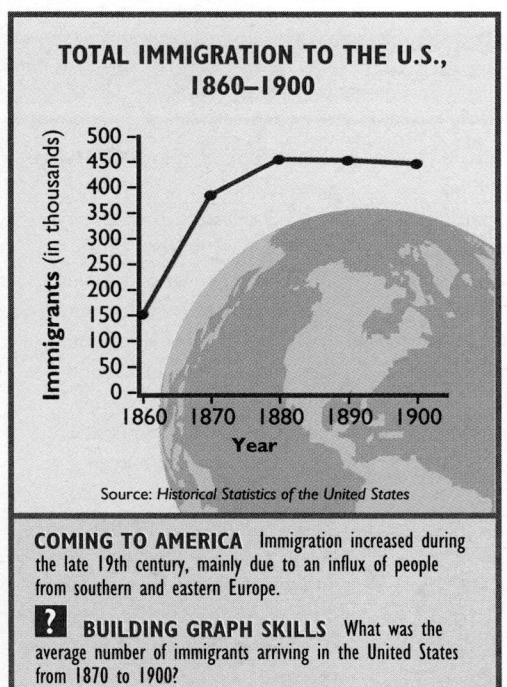

TOTAL IMMIGRATION TO THE U.S., 1860–1900

Immigrants (in thousands)

Year

Source: *Historical Statistics of the United States*

COMING TO AMERICA Immigration increased during the late 19th century, mainly due to an influx of people from southern and eastern Europe.

? **BUILDING GRAPH SKILLS** What was the average number of immigrants arriving in the United States from 1870 to 1900?

opportunities in the United States that were scarce in their home countries. Most hoped to make enough money in the United States to return home and buy land. Many did just that. Others, however, put down roots and stayed. The eastern European immigrants included Hungarian and Polish farmers and Jews from many countries. Most of the Jewish families and Armenian families fled their homelands to escape religious or political persecution.

Many immigrants learned of the opportunities available in the United States from railroad and steamship companies. In fact, convincing foreigners that the United States was *the* land of opportunity became a major business activity in the late 1800s. The agents of steamship companies and railroads swarmed over Europe, one observer noted, "as the locusts covered Egypt!" They painted a tempting—and often false—picture of America. Some railroad companies exaggerated the employment opportunities available in the United States. And the steamship lines charged rock-bottom fares to attract passengers.

Most of the millions who yielded to this hard sell found the journey to the "Promised Land" difficult and dangerous. The ocean voyage, though faster, safer, and more comfortable than in the past, was no pleasure trip for those traveling in the poorest accommodations, called steerage. One Italian immigrant asked:

> 66 How can a steerage passenger remember that he is a human being when he must first pick the worms from his food . . . and eat in his stuffy, stinking bunk, or in the hot and fetid atmosphere of a compartment where 150 men sleep? 99

A NEW LIFE

As with earlier immigrants, the vast majority of newcomers did not find paradise at the end of the voyage. Confined to dingy slums, they worked at menial jobs for low wages. Taken advantage of and harassed by some native-born Americans, newcomers often expressed disappointment. Reports about America, a Polish immigrant complained, were "all bluster [with] not a word of truth." Others, however, saw the United States as a great improvement over their home countries.

Immigrant communities. Many industrial cities of the Northeast and Midwest became a patchwork of ethnic neighborhoods as new immigrants settled among others from their homelands. Social reformer Jacob Riis (himself an immigrant from Denmark) suggested that an 1890s map of New York City, colored according to nationality, "would show more stripes than . . . a zebra, and more colors than any rainbow."

◀ The store signs in this 1910 photograph of a New York neighborhood reflect the ethnic diversity of the city.

PRIMARY SOURCE

Description of Change: excerpted
Rationale: excerpted to focus on main idea

BUILDING VOCABULARY

The passenger section on ships that was known as *steerage* was so named because it was typically located below the decks adjacent to the ship's steering gear. The first recorded use of *steerage* to designate the cheapest passenger accommodations came in a Washington Irving story published in 1804.

Graph Caption Answer *about 400,000*

HISTORICAL SIDELIGHTS

English Re-migration Large numbers of immigrants crossed the Atlantic a number of times. For example, English housepainters would travel to the U.S. in the spring to pursue their trade. They would then travel to Scotland for the summer months and return to England for the fall and winter months. They might repeat this traveling pattern for a number of years.

Changing Ways

COMING TO AMERICA

SETTING THE SCENE

Ellis Island served as the country's primary immigration center from 1892 to 1954. During that time, more than 16 million people passed through its halls. Today, about 4 of every 10 Americans claim a forebear whose first steps on American soil were at Ellis Island. Today, Ellis Island is a National Historic Site. The U.S. government abandoned the facility at Angel Island in 1940.

PRIMARY SOURCES

Description of Change: excerpted
Rationale: excerpted to focus on main idea

LINK TO TODAY

Today's immigrants are prescreened and approved by officials at a U.S. embassy or consulate in their homelands. Immigration officers check their papers when they arrive in the U.S. They are then photographed and fingerprinted. This streamlined procedure takes a fraction of the time it took to get through Ellis or Angel islands.

Changing Ways   COMING TO AMERICA

Ellis Island in New York Harbor or Angel Island in San Francisco Bay was the first sight of America for millions of newcomers in the late 1800s and early 1900s. Both islands served as immigration stations during this period.

Ellis Island opened in 1892 to receive record numbers of European immigrants. Like many other immigrants, Italian Edward Corsi arrived full of hope:

66 My first impressions of the new world will always remain etched in my memory, particularly that hazy October morning when I first saw Ellis Island. . . . All of us . . . clustered on the foredeck for fear of separation and looked with wonder on this miraculous land of our dreams.

Passengers all about us were crowding against the rail. Jabbered conversation, sharp cries, laughs and cheers—a steadily rising din filled the air. Mothers and fathers lifted up the babies so that they too could see, off to the left, the Statue of Liberty. 99

For most immigrants, however, these first feelings of joy were dampened by the confusion of the examination process. With thousands of newcomers arriving daily—many of whom spoke no English—processing at Ellis was hurried at best, impersonal and frightful at worst. Amid the noise and bustle, overworked officials sometimes misunderstood and changed immigrants' names: for example, Gardashian became Arness, and Mastroianni became Mister Yanni.

▲ **After it opened on January 21, 1910, Angel Island served as an immigration station on the West Coast.**

All newcomers who passed through Ellis were subjected to a physical exam. Those who had serious health problems, mental disorders, or contagious diseases like tuberculosis were deported. Those who passed the physicals entered a maze of crowded aisles where inspectors questioned them about their backgrounds, relatives, and job skills. Those with prison records, or without means to support themselves in America, were sent back. But the vast majority—about 99 percent in 1905—were allowed to stay.

Thousands of Asian newcomers, mostly from China, underwent similar processing on Angel Island, which opened in 1910. But many were not as fortunate as their Ellis Island counterparts. Chinese applicants faced strict immigration laws, which limited entrance to certain groups—such as students, teachers, and merchants—or to individuals who could show they were the children of American-born parents.

Some who could not meet the restrictions were deported. Others were detained on the island—some for months or even years—as they awaited a determination in their cases. Some, while imprisoned there, carved poems into the barracks' walls recording their despair:

66 Who would have expected joy to become sorrow:
Detained in a dark, crude, filthy room?
What can I do?
Cruel treatment, not one restful breath of air,
Scarcity of food, severe restrictions—all unbearable.
Here even a proud man bows his head low. 99

But for most immigrants, the anxiety they experienced on the islands soon gave way to a renewed sense of hope as they finally set foot on their adopted homeland to begin a new life.

Teaching the Section

A NEW LIFE

Have students imagine they are new immigrants to the U.S. in the late 1800s. Ask them to write a letter to a family member or friend in Europe describing life in America. Suggest that they make the process of adjusting to their new life and the institutions that helped them adapt the main focus of their letters. Ask volunteers to read their letters to the class. Students may wish to include their letters in their portfolios.

THE NATIVIST RESPONSE

Divide the class into small groups. Have each group compose a newspaper editorial presenting the nativist view of the new immigration. Then tell the groups to prepare responding editorials that challenge their previous editorials. Have two volunteers from each group read its editorials to the class.

▶

▲ Jewish immigrants strived to maintain their religious heritage after arriving in the United States. By studying the Torah, boys learned the ancient wisdom and laws of Jewish Scripture.

In these close-knit neighborhoods, residents spoke the same languages and followed the customs of the old country. Neighborhood churches and synagogues helped immigrants maintain a sense of identity and belonging.

Foreign-language papers, too, eased immigrants' transition. In the early 1900s, more than 1,000 foreign-language papers were printed in the United States. The largest, with a peak circulation of 175,000 a day, was the *Jewish Daily Forward*. Published in Yiddish—a German dialect spoken by eastern European Jews—it primarily served New York's Jewish community.

Most cities also had **benevolent societies**, or support organizations, to aid newcomers. Some organizations offered new immigrants loans to start businesses. Others set up insurance plans that provided money for families whose breadwinners were sick or had died. "We visit our sick and bury our dead" was one society's slogan.

Aid from politicians. Newly arrived immigrants also received help from political **bosses**—powerful political party leaders. Bosses headed big-city **political machines**—party organizations that used patronage, or appointments to government jobs, to control elections. Machine politicians often welcomed immigrants at dockside or at railroad stations, ready to offer assistance. One observer described a boss's methods:

❝ To this one he lends a dollar; for another he obtains a railroad ticket without payment; he has coal distributed in the depth of winter; . . . he sometimes sends poultry at Christmas time; he buys medicine for a sick person; he helps bury the dead. ❞

Of course, the bosses expected something in return for their help—the immigrants' votes. Getting party candidates elected allowed bosses to control local government. Once in power, most bosses used any means necessary—the rigging of elections, bribery, even violence—to keep it. Many also ransacked city treasuries, lining their own and their friends' pockets.

■■ **Ethnic neighborhoods, foreign-language newspapers, benevolent societies, and political machines helped immigrants adapt to American life.**

Political bosses urged new immigrants to adopt American ways. However, the Americanization process often pitted parents against children. Many older immigrants cherished their ties to the old country. Children, however, tended to view their parents' old-world language, dress, and customs as old-fashioned. A second-generation Polish immigrant expressed bittersweet feelings about his parents' way of life. It was, he

PRIMARY SOURCE

Description of Change: excerpted

Rationale: excerpted to focus on main idea

MAKING CONNECTIONS

Language Arts

Words from the new immigrants' native languages made their way into English. Yiddish, the language spoken by Eastern European Jews, provided such words as *chutzpah,* meaning "supreme self-confidence," and *schlepp,* meaning "to pull or drag." Hungarian words absorbed included *goulash* and *paprika.* Italian immigrants, too, provided a host of words related to food—*pasta, pizza, spaghetti, macaroni,* and *minestrone,* for instance.

THE AMERICAN NATION VIDEODISC PROGRAM

Community Ties: San Francisco's Chinatown

1B   40729   4:23

Museum of the City of New York

◀ For immigrant children, the Americanization process began soon after they arrived in the United States. This photograph shows the children's playground at Ellis Island.

*P*ractice

GUIDED PRACTICE

On the chalkboard draw a chart with *Old Immigrants* and *New Immigrants* as vertical headings and *From Where They Came* and *Why They Came* as horizontal headings. Ask volunteers to offer entries for the chart.

INDEPENDENT PRACTICE

Direct students to use the information from the Guided Practice chart to write a paragraph that summarizes the differences and similarities between the old and the new immigration. Suggest that students accompany their paragraphs with maps that show the regions of origin and time period of the old and new immigration.

*R*eview and *A*ssessment

REVIEW List the terms from the Preview Workshop on the chalkboard. Then have students write a summary of immigration in the late 1800s and early 1900s using these terms. Call on volunteers to read their summaries to the class. Then assign the Section 2 Review on p. 471.

ASSESS Assign the **Section 2 Daily Quiz** in *Core Resources*.

---

noted, "a slowly decaying world of aged folks living largely in a dream. One day it would pass and then there would remain only Americans whose forebears had once been Poles."

The immigrant worker. Whether they adapted to American ways or remained tied to the old world, new immigrants had a common work experience. Many did the country's "dirty work"—or, as one observer put it, "the shoveling."

Certain ethnic groups gravitated toward certain jobs, mainly because earlier arrivals had established themselves in those lines of work. For example, many Italian and Polish men worked in the building trades. Eastern European men worked in mines or steel mills. French Canadians worked in New England textile mills. Many Jewish men and women and Italian women worked in the garment industry. Most Greeks and Chinese opened businesses such as laundries and restaurants, largely because discrimination closed off other opportunities.

Whatever they did, most immigrants found working life hard. The work itself was physically exhausting, hours were long, and wages low. Contract laborers—who, in return for passage to the United States, worked for a set period—were virtual prisoners of their employers. These workers, mostly young women laboring in the sweatshops of New York's garment industry, were literally locked in until they had finished the day's required work. Some immigrants worked as many as 15 hours a day to earn a living wage. Even the best-paid workers made little more than enough to support themselves and their families.

*T*HE NATIVIST RESPONSE

While most immigrant workers enjoyed few of the rewards of their labor, they helped staff the factories that were responsible for

the vibrant U.S. economy. Yet many native-born Americans saw immigration as a threat. They agreed with Thomas Bailey Aldrich, who in his poem "The Unguarded Gates" warned against a "wild motley throng" bringing "unknown gods and rites" and speaking "accents of menace." Many felt that these newcomers were just too different ever to fit in. Others went further, blaming immigrants for all society's ills.

Nativists also opposed immigration for economic reasons. Many charged that the immigrants' willingness to work cheaply robbed native-born Americans of jobs and pushed down wages for all. With the support of labor unions, nativist workers began pressing for restrictions on immigration. They gained the most supporters and achieved the most success in the West.

For years Chinese laborers had been tolerated—and exploited—on the West Coast, especially in California. But as unemployment mounted during the Panic of 1873, the new Workingmen's Party of California angrily cried, "The Chinese must go." Party leader Dennis Kearney, who was himself an Irish immigrant, addressed crowds all over the state, working them into a frenzy. White mobs attacked the Chinese, killing some and burning the property of others.

Leaders of California's Chinese community appealed to the authorities for protection. But help was not forthcoming. In fact, the state's political leaders responded by amending the state constitution to forbid Chinese residents to own property or work at certain jobs.

▶ Chinese immigrants formed their own communities and businesses after arriving in the United States. These two photographs are of San Francisco's Chinatown district.

RETEACH For each subsection in the section, have students write a sentence that summarizes the main idea. Select students to read their sentences aloud. Have the group choose the best summary sentence for each subsection.

Closure

Organize students into groups of three. Ask groups to conduct a conversation among the following characters—a newly arrived new immigrant who talks of his or her hopes for the future; a settled new immigrant who talks of his or her experiences in America; a native-born American who talks of how the new immigration will affect his or her life. Select groups to re-create their conversations for the class.

Extension

INTERPRET Have students read "The New Colossus" by Emma Lazarus. Ask them to write a paragraph that summarizes the poem's main ideas. Ask volunteers to read their summaries to the class.

INVESTIGATE Have students investigate the Immigration Restriction League and prepare an oral report on their findings.

Then in 1882 the U.S. Congress passed the **Chinese Exclusion Act**, which denied citizenship to people born in China and prohibited the immigration of Chinese laborers. This act made conditions worse for the Chinese in America. In 1885 a mob in Rock Springs, Wyoming Territory, murdered 28 Chinese and drove away hundreds more.

Neither the act nor the violence kept Chinese immigrants from coming to the United States. After 1906, some men—dubbed "paper sons" by the Chinese—entered the country by falsely claiming to be sons of Chinese American citizens. Immigration authorities could not disprove many of the claims because the 1906 San Francisco earthquake and fire had destroyed most of the Chinese community's birth records.

But even with the proper documents, Chinese arriving in the United States were held for months while their cases were investigated. One immigrant wrote this poem on the wall of his cell:

> 66 The day I am rid of this prison and
>   attain success,
>   I must remember that this prison
>   once existed. . . .
>   All my compatriots [fellow citizens]
>   please be mindful.
>   Once you have some small gains, return
>   home [to China] early. 99

Other immigrants faced discrimination as organizations took up the anti-immigration banner. The **Immigration Restriction League**, founded in 1894 by a group of well-to-do Bostonians, sought to impose a literacy test on all immigrants. Congress passed such a measure, but President Grover Cleveland vetoed it in 1897, calling it

▲ This 1870 cartoon appeared in *Harper's Weekly* and satirizes the nativist reaction to Chinese immigration. A wall surrounds the United States that prevents immigrants from entering the country.

"illiberal, narrow, and un-American." Over the next 30 years, however, Congress tried several times—without success—to pass a similar measure.

Despite efforts to impose restrictions, immigration continued. Contrary to nativists' arguments, the new immigrants contributed to American society. America's rapid industrialization would have been impossible without immigrant workers. Their varied cultures, too, added new dimensions to American life.

■■ **Prejudice and fear prompted nativists to try to restrict immigration.**

PRIMARY SOURCE
Description of Change: excerpted and bracketed
Rationale: excerpted to focus on main idea; bracketed to clarify meaning

SECTION REVIEW ANSWERS

IDENTIFY
For significance, see the following pages:
old immigrants (p. 466)
new immigrants (p. 466)
benevolent societies (p. 469)
bosses (p. 469)
political machines (p. 469)
Chinese Exclusion Act
*   (p. 471)*
paper sons (p. 471)
Immigration Restriction League
*   (p. 471)*

1. *Immigration soared, mostly from southern and eastern Europe.*
2. *ethnic neighborhoods and newspapers, benevolent societies, political bosses and machines*
3. *thought they would take jobs and keep wages low, that they wouldn't fit in; pushed for restrictions, used mob violence*
4. *Letters might mention how the use of false identification papers, along with the destruction of the Chinese community's birth records, allowed some Chinese men to enter the U.S.*
5. *Chinese Exclusion Act restricted Chinese immigration; other legislation failed to limit immigration from other countries.*

SECTION 2 REVIEW

IDENTIFY and explain the significance of the following: old immigrants, new immigrants, benevolent societies, bosses, political machines, Chinese Exclusion Act, paper sons, Immigration Restriction League.

1. **MAIN IDEA** What changes occurred in immigration in the late 1800s?
2. **MAIN IDEA** What helped ease the new immigrants' adjustment to American life?
3. **ANALYZING** Why did nativists oppose the new immigrants? How did nativists demonstrate their bias against the new immigrants?
4. **WRITING TO EXPLAIN** Imagine you are a Chinese American citizen in 1906. Write a letter to a relative explaining how paper sons were able to come to the United States.
5. **EVALUATING** How were the new immigrants affected by new legislation?

PREVIEW WORKSHOP

Following is a list of the significant people, places, and terms in this section. You may wish to use this list as a section preview.

People
■ Jane Addams
■ Janie Porter Barrett
■ Caroline Bartlett
■ John Dewey

■ Edith Wharton
■ Samuel L. Clemens
■ Charles Chesnutt

Places
■ Hampton, Virginia
■ Columbus, Ohio

Terms
■ mass transit

■ suburbs
■ conspicuous consumption
■ philanthropy
■ settlement houses
■ Social Gospel
■ yellow journalism

Section 3

URBAN LIFE

FOCUS

■ **How did American cities change in the late 1800s?**

■ **How did urban life differ for the rich, the middle class, and the poor?**

■ **What was the aim of the settlement house and Social Gospel movements?**

*S*purred by industrialization and immigration, American cities grew dramatically during the second half of the century. In 1865 only 14 American cities had populations of more than 100,000, and only 20 percent of Americans lived in urban areas. By 1900 the nation was 40 percent urban and had 29 cities with populations in excess of 100,000. With growth came other changes, and a distinct urban culture developed.

Chicago's Masonic Temple

THE CHANGING CITY

The urban areas of the mid-1800s were compact. Few buildings were taller than two or three stories. And even in the largest cities, most people lived less than a 45-minute walk from the city center, where most businesses and industries were located. But by the late 1800s technological innovations and the great flood of people began to transform the urban landscape.

The impact of technology. Contributing to the transformation were steel, new building techniques, and Elisha Otis's mechanized elevator, all of which allowed cities to grow upward as well as outward. No longer restricted by the number of stairs people could comfortably climb, architects designed multistory buildings, or skyscrapers. Construction workers erected steel girders on which they "hung" walls of stone, brick, or concrete.

Moreover, the development of **mass transit**—trolley cars, commuter trains, and subways—made it possible for cities to spread out because workers no longer had to live within walking distance of their jobs. Frank J. Sprague, an electrical engineer who had worked with Thomas Edison, designed one of the first systems, an electric trolley that began serving Richmond, Virginia, in 1887. Other cities quickly adopted Sprague's

▶ **Trolley cars were an important part of many urban mass transit systems. This photograph was taken in New York City around 1895.**

MOTIVATING: STUDENT EXPERIENCES

Ask volunteers to explain what the phrase "urban life" means to them. List their responses on a flip chart. As students read this section, have them take notes to use in summarizing how urban life of the late 1800s compares with their ideas about urban life today. Save the flip chart for use in the Closure activity at the conclusion of the section.

Teaching the Section

CHANGES IN AMERICAN CITIES

Write these terms on the chalkboard: *elevator, skyscraper, mass transit, suburb.* Ask students to explain how each of these items brought about changes in American cities in the late 1800s. Write responses under the appropriate item. Then have students use the information on the chalkboard to write a descriptive paragraph titled "The Changing American City." Call on volunteers to read their paragraphs to the class. Students may wish to include their paragraphs in their portfolios.

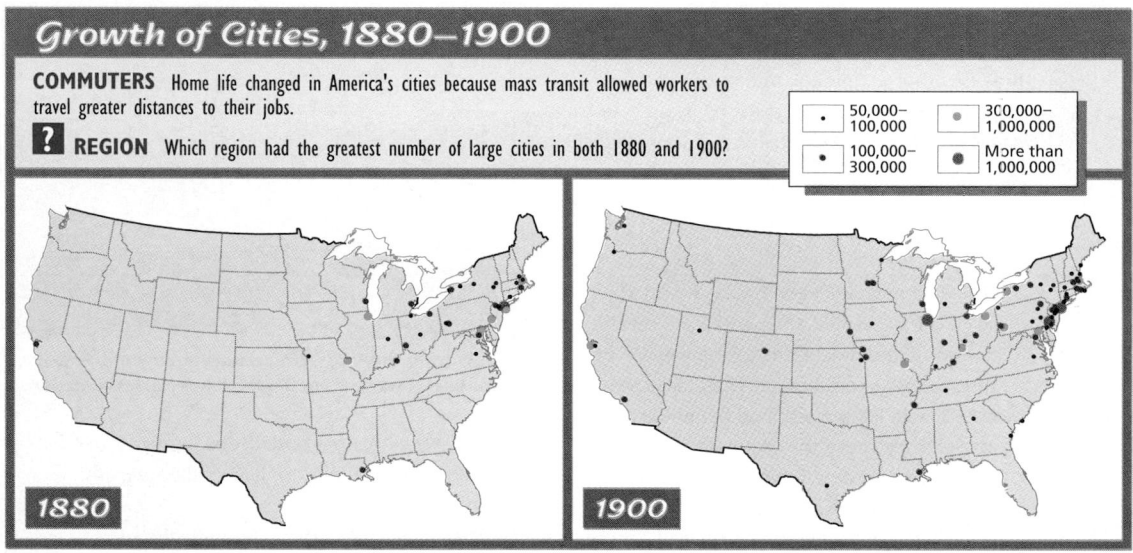

Growth of Cities, 1880–1900

COMMUTERS Home life changed in America's cities because mass transit allowed workers to travel greater distances to their jobs.

? **REGION** Which region had the greatest number of large cities in both 1880 and 1900?

| • | 50,000– 100,000 | ● | 300,000– 1,000,000 |
| • | 100,000– 300,000 | ● | More than 1,000,000 |

1880

1900

idea, and by 1895 the nation boasted over 10,000 miles of electric railways.

Mass transit led to the rise of **suburbs,** middle-class and wealthy residential areas beyond the city limits. Some social reformers applauded suburban development because it allowed people to live in "light and air." However, while middle-class and wealthy Americans could afford to enjoy the healthy life of the suburbs, many urban Americans remained trapped by poverty in crowded, and often unhealthy, tenement houses.

▪▪ The skyscraper and mass transit helped American cities grow upward and outward.

Upper-class life. The changing city also created a new group of wealthy city dwellers. There had been wealthy people in America since colonial times, but the urban upper class of the late 1800s was a new breed. The new rich made their money in the new industries, such as railroads, iron and steel, mining, or publishing. Their fortunes usually dwarfed those of the old upper-class merchants and bankers.

For the new rich, author William Dean Howells noted sarcastically, "the dollar is the measure of every value, the

stamp of every success." And the new rich spent their dollars freely so that everyone knew how successful they were. Social scientist Thorstein Veblen labeled this behavior **conspicuous consumption.**

The new rich practiced conspicuous consumption by building houses that imitated extravagantly decorated Gothic castles or Italian Renaissance palaces. In the summer they fled their city homes for equally magnificent country estates. The new rich thought nothing of paying thousands of dollars to stage one night's amusement. One

▲ Railroad baron Cornelius Vanderbilt and his wife, Alice, (left) turned their New York City home into a magnificent palace. Cornelius was named after his grandfather who founded the family's fortune.

Map Caption Answer
the Northeast

AV TRANSPARENCY
Linking Geography and History Transparency and **Worksheet 11A**

HISTORICAL SIDELIGHTS
Summer Homes
A favored summer destination for New York's wealthy was the fashionable resort town of Newport, Rhode Island. The most lavish estates in Newport were "Marble House" and "The Breakers," owned by the family of railroad baron Cornelius Vanderbilt. Decorated with precious metals and stuffed with priceless art treasures, these mansions required an army of servants—as many as 40 house servants for The Breakers alone.

Teaching the Section

THE GROWTH OF AMERICAN CITIES

Ask students to study the map titled "Growth of Cities, 1880–1900" on p. 473. Then ask them to write several sentences summarizing the trends in urbanization shown on the map. Have students compare and discuss their sentences.

---

wealthy man arranged a lavish—and unusual—party in which the guests wore riding gear and rode their horses into the dining room!

Many Americans criticized such extravagances. But Ward McAllister, a lawyer and member of the "Four Hundred"—the wealthiest group of New York's upper class—came to the defense of "fashionable people":

> 66 The mistake made by the world at large is that fashionable people are selfish, frivolous, and indifferent to the welfare of their fellow creatures. . . .The elegancies of fashionable life nourish and benefit art and artists; they cause the expenditure of money and its distribution; and they really prevent our people and country from settling down into a humdrum rut and becoming merely a money-making and money-saving people. 99

It is true that some wealthy people supported **philanthropy**—charitable efforts to promote public welfare. They financed libraries, museums, and art galleries; endowed universities; and established new theater groups, opera companies, and symphony orchestras. But, as critics quickly pointed out, not all rich men and women saw philanthropy

▲ During the late 19th century, many native-born, middle-class women began filling clerical positions.

as a way to do good. Some simply used it as another opportunity to display their wealth.

Middle-class life. As with the upper class, a middle class of doctors, lawyers, teachers, and small-business owners had existed since colonial times. However, by the late 1800s modern corporations had swelled the ranks of the middle class with managers, engineers, accountants, clerks, and salespeople. While a great show of wealth indicated success for the new rich, advancement at work measured middle-class achievement.

For the old middle class, work outside the home had been a male realm. But the rise of big

---

THE PRICE OF INDUSTRIALIZATION

In 1871 Austrian diplomat Joseph Alexander, Graf von Hübner, visited the United States. Von Hübner was impressed by the opportunities Americans enjoyed in an industrializing society. But he also saw that fierce competition in business took its toll on working people. Von Hübner said:

> 66 *In the New World man is born to conquer. Life is a perpetual struggle, . . . a race in the open field across terrible obstacles, with the prospect of enormous rewards for reaching the goal. The American cannot keep his arms folded. He must embark on something, and once embarked he must go on and on forever; for if he stops, those who follow him would crush him under their feet. His life is one long campaign, a succession of never-ending fights, marches, and countermarches.*
>
> *In such a militant existence, what place is left for the sweetness, the repose [rest], the intimacy of home or its joys? Is he happy? Judging by his tired, sad, exhausted, anxious, and often delicate and unhealthy appearance, one would be inclined to doubt it. Such an excess of uninterrupted labor cannot be good for any man.* 99

URBAN LIFE

Organize the class into thirds and assign each segment one of the three social classes discussed in the section. Have students work individually to write diary entries for a typical day in the life of a member of their assigned social class. Suggest that they discuss topics such as housing, diet, clothing, education, and daily activities in their diary entries. Ask volunteers to read their diary entries to the class. Then ask students to use the diary entries to generalize about differences in the life-styles of the urban upper, middle, and lower classes. Students may wish to include their diary entries in their portfolios.

▶

business created a whole new range of jobs, such as stenographer, salesclerk, and secretary. Business owners increasingly hired young, single middle-class women to fill these positions, paying them lower wages than men. As a result, by 1910 nearly 35 percent of the more than 1.9 million clerical workers were women.

However, most married middle-class women worked at home. Smaller families, greater reliance on purchased goods, and new household technology such as running water, water closets, and home canning changed middle-class women's domestic work. For example, ready-made clothing lightened the sewing loads of many middle-class women. The advent of hot and cold running water meant that doing laundry no longer required pumping, hauling, and heating the water. Some middle-class families could also afford to hire servants to handle many household chores. In such families, women had more free time to take part in the city's growing number of cultural events. Many women joined reading and social clubs. Others participated in and led the reform movements of the late 1800s and early 1900s (see Chapter 17).

How the poor lived. The servants who toiled in middle-class homes and the workers who labored in factories lived worlds away from the comfort of the middle class or the luxury of the wealthy. To make ends meet, working-class families often had to rent out parts of their homes or tiny apartments to boarders. The dark, airless tenement buildings sometimes housed as many as 12 families per floor. Jacob Riis described a tenement family of "honest, hard-working Germans":

> 66 All nine lived in two rooms, one about ten feet square that served as parlor, bedroom, and eating room, the other a small hall room made into a kitchen. The rent was . . . more than a week's wages for the husband and father. . . . That day the mother had thrown herself out of the window. . . . She was "discouraged," said some of the other women. 99

In New York City, a magnet for hundreds of thousands of immigrants and migrants from the countryside, some 43,000 tenement buildings housed more than 1.6 million poor people in 1900—nearly one half of the city's population.

▲ Crowded tenements, such as these lining Hester Street in New York City, sprang up as urban populations swelled.

Outside the tenements, raw sewage and piles of garbage fouled unpaved streets and alleys. Worse still, the slums usually adjoined industrial areas where factories belched pollution. "The stink is enough to knock you down," one New York resident complained. In such an environment, sickness and death were common. In some cities respiratory diseases like tuberculosis spread rapidly through tightly packed slums, killing many residents.

While the conditions faced by residents of poor neighborhoods were far from pleasant, those who experienced the greatest difficulties were African Americans. Because of widespread discrimination, most of them could get only poorly paid jobs. Moreover, African Americans had to pay outrageous rents for the most appalling apartments, and they frequently faced police harassment. Yet many preferred the North to the South. As one African American journalist explained:

> 66 They sleep in peace at night; what they earn is paid them, if not they can appeal to the courts. They vote without fear of the shot-gun, and their children go to school. 99

■■ **The rich lived in grand style; the middle class in respectable comfort. But many city dwellers faced grinding poverty.**

Teaching the Section

REFORM ORGANIZATIONS

Ask some students to imagine they are young men or women who work in settlement houses or for church-sponsored reform groups. Tell them that they are appearing at a community meeting in a poor ethnic neighborhood to inform residents about the organizations they represent. Direct the rest of the class to portray the residents, who should ask questions about the services the organizations provide and about the goals or motives of these organizations.

■■ Ask students to identify and describe institutions similar to the settlement house in their community today. Ask how the goals of today's organizations compare with the aims of the settlement houses of the late 1800s.

*T*HE DRIVE FOR REFORM

Few government programs helped the poor in the late 1800s. What assistance the poor received was limited to charitable handouts of food and clothing. Some idealistic young Americans realized that more needed to be done. To confront the problem of poverty head-on, they established and lived in **settlement houses**—community service centers—in poor neighborhoods. At the forefront of this effort was Jane Addams.

The settlement houses. Born in 1860 to a well-to-do family in Cedarville, Illinois, Jane Addams grew up in an atmosphere of politics and philanthropy. Her Quaker father was a passionate abolitionist, and as a state senator he had worked to pass social reform legislation. The young Addams set out to be a doctor, but a back problem put an end to her medical studies. Unsure about what career to pursue, she decided to recuperate and travel in Europe. Eventually, she decided to dedicate her life to helping the urban poor.

In time, Addams's work included other causes. She tirelessly worked for women's suffrage and served as president of the Women's International League for Peace and Freedom from 1919 to 1935. Worldwide recognition for her work came in 1931, when she won the Nobel Peace Prize.

Addams began her settlement-house work in 1889, when she and Ellen Gates Starr established a settlement at Hull House, a run-down mansion in one of Chicago's immigrant neighborhoods. Hull House's founding charter explained Addams's cultural and social-service mission:

Jane Addams

66 To provide a center for a higher civic and social life; to institute and maintain educational and philanthropic enterprises, and to investigate and improve the conditions in the industrial districts of Chicago. 99

Addams also hoped that Hull House would provide fulfilling careers for women. She expected that for "young women who had been given over too exclusively to study," Hull House "might restore a balance of activity" and help them "learn of life from life itself."

The volunteers who joined Addams were mostly young, college-educated women. They set up a day nursery and kindergarten for the children of working mothers and gave adult education classes. They offered recreational facilities and staffed an employment agency. And when the city failed to pick up garbage in poor neighborhoods, Addams secured an appointment as a garbage inspector to make sure the city provided the much-needed service.

Addams and other settlement workers improved services for the poor, but also learned much from their work. Addams's experiences taught her "that the things which make men alike are finer and better than the things that keep them apart, and that these basic likenesses . . . easily transcend [surpass] the less essential differences of race, language, creed, and tradition." The experience gained at settlement houses provided women such as Addams and many others with the skills

▼ As part of urban reform, settlement houses such as Hull House in Chicago improved services for immigrants and the poor.

Have students work in groups to prepare a
script outline for a "TV documentary" on
urban culture in the late 1800s. Tell groups
that their outlines should cover four topics:
Education, Journalism, Literature, and
Leisure. For each topic, the group should
prepare an introductory statement a narrator
might make, suggest possible interviewees,
and list ideas for visuals, including maps,
charts, and graphs. Call on volunteers to present their groups' script outlines to the class.

▶

and knowledge to make important contributions to social reform and politics.

Hull House served as a model for others hoping to aid the poor. In 1890 African American teacher Janie Porter Barrett founded one of the first African American settlement houses—the Locust Street Social Settlement—in Hampton, Virginia. Three years later, Lillian Wald started the Henry Street Settlement on New York's Lower East Side. By the end of the century, almost a hundred settlement houses had opened across the country.

The Social Gospel movement.
At the same time that the settlement houses began their work, a number of Protestant ministers joined the battle against poverty. They developed the idea of the **Social Gospel**, which called for people to apply Christian principles to address social problems. Washington Gladden, a Congregational minister in Columbus, Ohio, was an early leader of the Social Gospel movement. Arguing that the church had a moral duty to confront social injustice, Gladden led crusades to improve conditions for industrial workers.

Many churches attempted to implement the Social Gospel by providing libraries, classrooms, job training and counseling, and other social services. Caroline Bartlett's People's Church in Kalamazoo, Michigan, was one example of such a church. Bartlett became a Unitarian minister in 1889, the same year she began her work at the People's Church. Drawing on Social Gospel ideals, Bartlett threw open the doors of her church seven days a week. She established a free public kindergarten and a gymnasium and offered classes in domestic and industrial skills. Bartlett also set up a meals program for workers and sponsored creative activities, such as an orchestra and a literary society for African Americans.

Other religious groups joined the crusade to assist the urban poor. In 1880 the Salvation Army, an evangelical group founded in Great Britain, began offering food, clothing, shelter, and work opportunities to the poor to help put them on the path to physical and spiritual salvation.

■■ **The settlement-house and Social Gospel movements fought poverty and other social problems.**

▲ In this early 1900s photograph, nurses from New York's Henry Street Settlement House set out to help the poor and needy.

The "Gospel of Wealth."
Some Americans were troubled by the plight of the poor but viewed the Social Gospel and settlement-house movements as too radical. Steel baron Andrew Carnegie offered these people an alternative: the "Gospel of Wealth." In Carnegie's view the rich had been chosen as "stewards of wealth." Thus, they had an obligation to use their fortunes for the common good. "The man who dies . . . rich," Carnegie argued, "dies disgraced."

Carnegie, however, was also a firm believer in Social Darwinism. He opposed handouts to the poor because, he argued, such handouts rewarded equally both the unworthy beggar and the worthy worker fallen on hard times. The best way to benefit the lower class, he said, was "to place within its reach the ladders upon which the aspiring can rise." Carnegie's "ladders" included universities and libraries. Carnegie gave some $350 million to such causes during his lifetime.

HISTORICAL SIDELIGHTS
Inventor and Volunteer
At the Henry Street Settlement, African American inventor Lewis Latimer taught courses that helped immigrants adjust to living in the U.S.

MAKING CONNECTIONS
Literature
Charles Sheldon, a minister from Topeka, Kansas, applied the beliefs of the Social Gospel to fiction. His novel *In His Steps* (1896), which was published in more than 20 languages and sold more than 23 million copies, suggested that life's everyday moral dilemmas could be solved by asking: "What would Jesus do?"

HISTORICAL SIDELIGHTS
Gospel of Wealth
Carnegie believed that the rich, before disposing of their wealth, should set aside enough to live in a comfortable—but not ostentatious—fashion. Carnegie's "comfortable" life-style included a castle in Scotland with such conveniences as a 79-foot heated indoor swimming pool, a 9-hole golf course, and a huge artificial lake for fishing.

GUIDED PRACTICE

On the chalkboard write the words *Yellow Journalism.* Ask volunteers to suggest adjectives that describe what this term means. List these adjectives on the chalkboard.

Direct the class to use these adjectives to develop a one-sentence definition of yellow journalism.

INDEPENDENT PRACTICE

Have students use the adjectives and definition developed in the Guided Practice to write a newspaper article in the yellow-journalism style on one of the events, persons, or developments discussed in this section. Students may wish to include their articles in their portfolios.

*R*eview and *A*ssessment

REVIEW Ask students to write newspaper headlines that summarize the content of each heading and subheading in the section. Have students compare and discuss their headlines. Then assign the Section 3 Review on p. 479.

ASSESS Assign the **Section 3 Daily Quiz** in *Core Resources.*

🌐 GLOBAL CONNECTIONS

In 1837 Friedrich Froebel founded the world's first kindergarten in the city of Blankenburg, in present-day Germany. He later established training schools for kindergarten teachers and introduced kindergartens throughout the region. German American Margarethe Schurz, the wife of politician Carl Schurz, introduced Elizabeth Peabody to Froebel's ideas. In the 1870s Peabody popularized the idea of the kindergarten in the U.S. By the end of the 1800s there were more than 225,000 kindergartens in America.

COOPERATIVE LEARNING

Organize students into eight groups and assign each group one of the following topics: Life for the Rich, The Changing City, Middle-class Life, Life for the Poor, Reformers, Public Education, Journalism and Literature, Leisure Activities. Have groups find or create visuals that illustrate aspects of their topic. Then have groups assemble the visuals into a collage titled "Urban Life in the Late 1800s." Display the collage on the bulletin board.

*U*RBAN CULTURE

Carnegie's generosity and that of other philanthropists contributed greatly to urban cultural life during the late 1800s. Perhaps the greatest reform in this period, however, was the growth of free public education.

Public education. The growth of public education went hand in hand with the growth of the cities. After 1860 more and more states passed compulsory school attendance laws and lengthened the school year from 78 to 144 days. From 1870 to 1900 the number of students in school grew from some 7 million to more than 15 million, and high school enrollment increased almost tenfold. Many of these new students were young women: in 1900 about 60 percent of high school graduates were women. In addition, more women joined the growing number of men attending college. As a result, the number of college graduates climbed from nearly 9,400 in 1870 to some 29,000 in 1900.

As enrollments increased, educational reformers proposed that schools do more than teach reading, writing, and arithmetic by rote. One of the main reformers was philosopher John Dewey. His "Laboratory School" at the University of Chicago stressed cooperative "learning by doing" and emphasized science, art, and history. Ella Flagg Young, superintendent of schools in Chicago, worked with Dewey to implement his ideas in her schools. Most urban schools, however, were slow to take up the new methods.

In this period most public schools remained segregated by race. Despite the expansion of support for public schools, most schools for African Americans were poorly equipped, since state and local governments spent little money on them.

Popular journalism. As a result of expanded education, by 1900 some 90 percent of Americans could read. The dramatic increase in the number of daily newspapers—from almost 600 in 1870 to some 2,600 by 1910—reflected this growth in literacy.

▲ African American students attended segregated schools, where educational resources or facilities rarely equaled those of white schools. This photograph shows an African American school around 1910.

Daily newspapers in the same city often battled each other for a greater share of the reading public. The wildest circulation wars took place between Joseph Pulitzer's New York *World* and William Randolph Hearst's New York *Journal.* Pulitzer tried to win readers by running sensational news stories and by adding comic strips, advice columns, and a separate sports page. Hearst competed with even more-sensational stories under screaming headlines. The papers also vied for readers by publishing the popular cartoon series "Yellow Kid" by different artists. The cartoon provided the name for this style of reporting—**yellow journalism**.

Literature. In addition to newspapers, city dwellers read popular fiction—romances, mysteries, and westerns. Young boys favored Horatio Alger's success stories about hardworking street urchins who rose to middle-class respectability by courage—and luck. Similarly, Martha Finley's stories about the upright Elsie Dinsmore gained a huge following among young girls.

Older readers enjoyed realistic books about urban life. For example, Edith Wharton's *House of*

◀ Edith Wharton won the Pulitzer Prize in 1920 for the *Age of Innocence.*

RETEACH Have students work in small groups to create charts showing the major ideas and events presented in the section. Direct each group to indicate on its chart how each item addresses one of the section's Focus questions.

Closure

Ask students to use the flip-chart responses developed in Motivating and the notes they made during study of the section to suggest comparisons of urban life in the 1800s and urban life today.

Extension

ANALYZE Have students read selections from one of the authors mentioned in this section. Have them write a brief report explaining what the selections tell about life in America in the late 1800s.

CREATE Have students select a city and create a model or map that shows its growth patterns from the mid-1800s to the turn of the century. Have students display their maps or models.

Mirth (1905) described the conflicts between the new rich and the old elite. William Dean Howells's *Rise of Silas Lapham* (1885) wove a tale of greed and social ambition. Stephen Crane and Frank Norris depicted everyday life, including the grim side of urban experience.

Readers also favored local-color writers. The greatest of them was Samuel L. Clemens, better known as Mark Twain. In *The Adventures of Tom Sawyer* (1876) and *The Adventures of Huckleberry Finn* (1884), Twain vividly described rural adolescent life of the mid-1800s. African American writer Charles W. Chesnutt's *Conjure Woman* (1899) drew on tales told by freed slaves.

Leisure time. City dwellers also sought diversion in sports. For example, croquet and cycling—which enjoyed a great vogue in the 1890s—became especially popular activities for middle-class women. Men of all classes enjoyed playing and watching basketball, boxing, football, and baseball. Americans had been playing baseball since the 1840s, but in 1876, with the founding of the first professional league, it became a popular spectator sport as well. The *New York Times* noted that spectators "jumped like colts, clapped their hands, threw their hats into the air, slapped their companions on the back, . . . and . . . enjoyed themselves hugely."

Baseball had become, in one sportswriter's words, "the national game of the United States." But not all Americans were allowed to play in the professional leagues. In 1887 team manager Adrian "Cap" Anson, a star player in his day,

▲ Shown here is an 1866 championship game at Elysian Field, in Hoboken, New Jersey.

refused to let his team play against teams with African American players. Anson's action, and the widespread racism in the baseball leagues, led to the exclusion of African Americans from major league teams, a ban that lasted for 60 years. African Americans formed their own league, however, which produced many outstanding players.

For children, Barnum & Bailey's Circus provided "The Greatest Show on Earth." Also popular, especially among immigrant and working-class families, were amusement parks—such as Coney Island—with their roller coasters and Ferris wheels. Vaudeville shows, with roots in working-class variety acts, attracted middle-class as well as working-class audiences. Similarly, Yiddish theaters served as a source of nostalgia for Jewish immigrants.

■■ An urban culture with diverse reading, entertainment, and leisure activities developed in the late 1800s.

SECTION REVIEW ANSWERS

IDENTIFY

For significance, see the following pages:
mass transit (p. 472)
suburbs (p. 473)
conspicuous consumption (p. 473)
philanthropy (p. 474)
settlement houses (p. 476)
Jane Addams (p. 476)
Janie Porter Barrett (p. 477)
Social Gospel (p. 477)
Caroline Bartlett (p. 477)
John Dewey (p. 478)
yellow journalism (p. 478)
Edith Wharton (p. 478)
Samuel L. Clemens (p.479)
Charles Chesnutt (p.479)

LOCATE

For locations, see the map on pp. 1016–1017.

1. skyscrapers and mass transit systems built, cities spread out, rise of suburbs
2. The rich lived lavishly, the middle class comfortably, and the poor crowded in tenements.
3. Both offered social services to the poor. Addams involved herself in politics while Bartlett worked through her church.
4. Articles might mention living conditions, class distinctions, transportation, education, social services, reading, and other leisure activities.
5. Students might note Dewey's ideas about hands-on learning.

■■ **SECTION 3 REVIEW**

IDENTIFY and explain the significance of the following: mass transit, suburbs, conspicuous consumption, philanthropy, settlement houses, Jane Addams, Janie Porter Barrett, Social Gospel, Caroline Bartlett, John Dewey, yellow journalism, Edith Wharton, Samuel L. Clemens, Charles Chesnutt.

LOCATE and explain the importance of the following: Hampton, Virginia; Columbus, Ohio.

1. **MAIN IDEA** In what ways did American cities change in the late 1800s?
2. **MAIN IDEA** Describe urban life for the rich, the middle class, and the poor.
3. **COMPARING** How were Jane Addams's work at Hull House and Caroline Bartlett's at the People's Church similar? How did they differ?
4. **WRITING TO INFORM** Imagine you are a journalist from outside the United States. Write an article informing your British readers about American urban culture.
5. **HYPOTHESIZING** What impact do you think John Dewey has had on modern public education in the United States?

Chapter Review Answers

WRITING A SUMMARY

See Essential Points in each section for main ideas.

REVIEWING CHRONOLOGY

2, 5, 3, 4, 1
Evaluating
improved conditions for urban poor by providing employment assistance, day care, education, recreational facilities, and other social services in poor neighborhoods

IDENTIFYING PEOPLE AND IDEAS

1. *major railroad lines*
2. *electrician who improved air brake*
3. *inventor of phonograph and light bulb, among other products*
4. *southern and eastern European immigrants to U.S. in late 1800s and early 1900s*
5. *leaders of political machines who helped new immigrants in return for votes*
6. *1882 law that denied citizenship and restricted immigration of Chinese*
7. *social reformer who established Hull House*
8. *founder of one of the first African American settlement houses*
9. *sensational journalism style*

10. *local-color writer better known as Mark Twain, he wrote* The Adventures of Tom Sawyer, *among others*

UNDERSTANDING MAIN IDEAS

1. *Bessemer process enabled steel to be produced cheaply, thereby providing materials for mass transit and skyscrapers.*
2. *New kinds of stores appeared; gap between rich and poor grew; suburbs expanded; more leisure activities became available.*

3. *Sherman Antitrust Act declared monopolies and trusts that were in restraint of trade to be illegal.*
4. *felt that immigrants threatened jobs and social stability; pressed for legal restrictions, used violence against immigrants*
5. *to improve immigrants' well-being through community services*

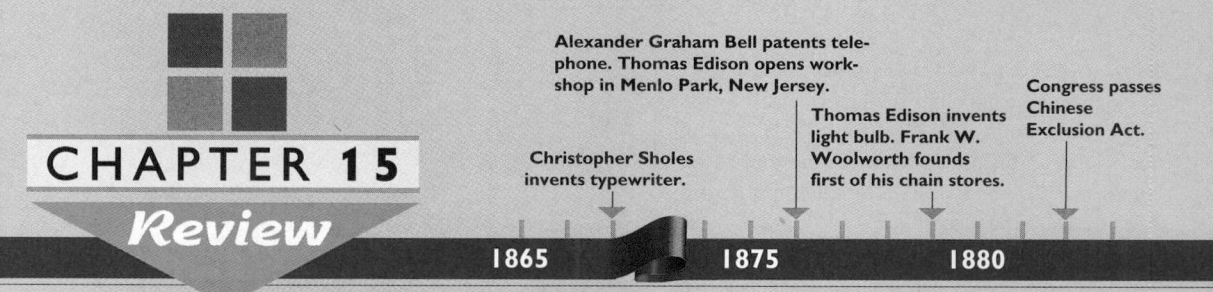

Alexander Graham Bell patents telephone. Thomas Edison opens workshop in Menlo Park, New Jersey.

Christopher Sholes invents typewriter.

Thomas Edison invents light bulb. Frank W. Woolworth founds first of his chain stores.

Congress passes Chinese Exclusion Act.

CHAPTER 15
Review

1865   1875   1880

WRITING A SUMMARY
Using the essential points of the chapter as a guide, write a summary of the chapter.

REVIEWING CHRONOLOGY
Number your paper 1 to 5. Study the time line above, and list the following events in the order in which they happened by writing the first next to 1, the second next to 2, and so on. Then complete the activity below.

1. Standard Oil's profits reach some $45 million.
2. Alexander Graham Bell patents telephone.
3. Jane Addams establishes Hull House.
4. Sherman Antitrust Act passed.
5. Congress passes Chinese Exclusion Act.

Evaluating How did the establishment of Hull House contribute to social reform?

IDENTIFYING PEOPLE AND IDEAS
Explain the historical significance of each of the following people or terms.

1. trunk lines
2. Granville T. Woods
3. Thomas Edison
4. new immigrants
5. bosses
6. Chinese Exclusion Act
7. Jane Addams
8. Janie Porter Barrett
9. yellow journalism
10. Samuel L. Clemens

UNDERSTANDING MAIN IDEAS
1. How did technological advances in steel making promote changes in American cities in the 1800s?
2. How did urban daily life change in the late 1800s?
3. How did the government attempt to restrict big business?
4. Why did nativists oppose immigration, and what actions did they take to prevent it?
5. What goals were shared by benevolent societies and by reformers involved in the settlement-house and Social Gospel movements?

REVIEWING THEMES
1. **Economic Development** How did changes in technology affect the nation's economy in the late 1800s?

2. **Technology and Society** In what ways did innovations in communication and energy change American urban life?
3. **Cultural Diversity** How did increases in immigration affect social life in the late 19th century?

THINKING CRITICALLY
1. **Evaluating** What was the impact of the new industrial order on business organization?
2. **Analyzing** How did social change contribute to the growth of department and chain stores?
3. **Synthesizing** In what ways did the second industrial age both separate people and bring them together?

STRATEGY FOR SUCCESS
Review the Skills Handbook entry on Identifying Cause and Effect on page 989. Write a paragraph tracing the rise of big business from the development of the Bessemer process to the eventual government legislation limiting monopolies and trusts. Be sure to show the connections between causes and effects.

WRITING ABOUT HISTORY
Writing to Create
Among the best-selling books of the late 19th century were dime novels, books with paper covers that sold for 10 cents. Dime novels offered plots with lots of action and suspense. Using a 19th-century tycoon, immigrant, or African American migrant as a main character, write an outline for a dime novel.

REVIEWING THEMES

1. *Technological changes made improved production, transportation, and communication possible—all changes that strengthened the economy by lowering costs, increasing profits, and expanding markets.*
2. *communication—promoted leisure activities, transportation, and communication; energy—promoted mass transit, which led to rise of suburbs and allowed upper and middle classes to leave cities*
3. *Immigrants swelled population, taxed urban services, and added to urban diversity.*

THINKING CRITICALLY

1. *Growth of large industries led to development of corporations, trusts, and other business combinations to increase efficiency or reduce competition.*
2. *The growing middle class provided employees and customers for these stores.*
3. *Unequal sharing of industrial profits created gap between rich and poor; communication innovations helped link people; railroads and mass transit had both effects.*

STRATEGY FOR SUCCESS

Paragraphs might mention the role of technology in fostering industrial growth, which led to the development of new business practices, which led to concerns over big business and to eventual government intervention.

WRITING ABOUT HISTORY

Outlines might develop the opportunities for, and obstacles to, success in the late 19th century, and the struggle of the main character against those obstacles.

USING PRIMARY SOURCES

Paragraphs might mention cultural diversity, cable cars, lights, shopping, recreation, and variety of social classes.

LINKING HISTORY AND GEOGRAPHY

Students might consider how the influx of new immigrants and African Americans provided a ready source of low-paid labor.

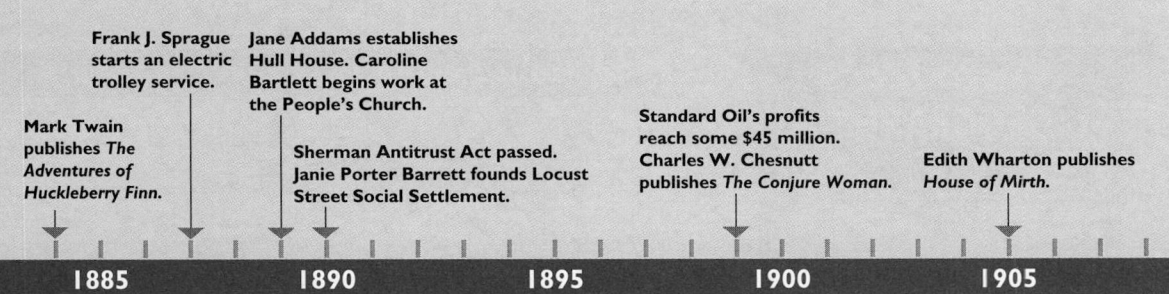

Mark Twain publishes *The Adventures of Huckleberry Finn.*

Frank J. Sprague starts an electric trolley service.

Jane Addams establishes Hull House. Caroline Bartlett begins work at the People's Church.

Sherman Antitrust Act passed. Janie Porter Barrett founds Locust Street Social Settlement.

Standard Oil's profits reach some $45 million. Charles W. Chesnutt publishes *The Conjure Woman.*

Edith Wharton publishes *House of Mirth.*

1885   1890   1895   1900   1905

USING PRIMARY SOURCES

Author Frank Norris's eye for detail makes his novels fascinating records of urban life in the late 1800s. Norris was only 22 when he wrote his first novel, *McTeague* (1899), a story of a San Francisco dentist corrupted by city influences. In the following excerpt, Norris describes McTeague's neighborhood. Write a paragraph identifying aspects of the new urban culture.

66 *From noon to evening the population of the street was of a mixed character. The street was busiest at that time; a vast and prolonged murmur arose—the mingled shuffling of feet, the rattle of wheels, the heavy trundling of cable cars. . . . Evening began; and one by one a multitude of lights, from the demoniac [devilish] glare of the druggists' windows to the dazzling blue whiteness of the electric globes, grew thick from street corner to street corner. . . . The cable cars were loaded with theatre-goers—men in high hats and young girls in furred opera cloaks. On the sidewalks were groups and couples—the plumbers' apprentices, the girls of the ribbon counters, the little families . . . the dressmakers, the small doctors,*

the harness makers—all the various inhabitants of the street were abroad, strolling idly from shop window to shop window. . . . The tamale *men appeared.* 99

LINKING HISTORY AND GEOGRAPHY

Study the map on page 473. How did the movement of people to cities lead to urban economic growth?

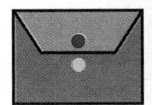

BUILDING YOUR PORTFOLIO

Complete the following projects independently or cooperatively.

1. **SOCIAL CONFLICT** In Chapter 14 you were a Sioux living on the Pine Ridge Reservation in South Dakota. Building on that experience, imagine you are an immigrant who has just arrived from southern or eastern Europe. Create a series of poems and graphics that illustrate the problems you face in your new home and your hopes for the future.

2. **TECHNOLOGY AND INDUSTRY** In Chapter 14 you were a land speculator who hopes to establish a small railhead in Nebraska. Building on that experience, develop a plan to use new technologies—such as the telephone, the dynamo, and electric lighting—and innovations in transportation to attract residents and businesses.

3. **REFORM** Imagine you are a female settlement-house worker. Create a promotional banner that shows how the reform efforts of your organization serve the needs of the entire urban community. Banners might include mottos, symbols, or slogans.

 **BUILDING YOUR PORTFOLIO**

Have students refer to **Building Your Portfolio Worksheet 5,** assigned at the beginning of Unit 5. Use the worksheet to help students monitor their progress on the portfolio projects.

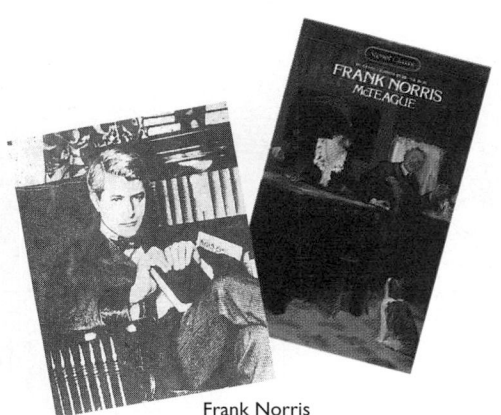

Frank Norris

Assessment

Core Resources
- Review Worksheet 15
- Chapter 15 Tests
- Alternative Assessment Forms

Test Generator

CONQUERING DISTANCE

Ordering Workers

Many Asian laborers who made their way to America in the 19th century were initially "imported" to work on American-owned plantations in Hawaii. Hawaiian plantation owners often spoke of their Asian workers as if they were property to be bought and sold. In 1890, for example, the owners of a plantation company sent a memo to a local manager requesting supplies. The order read in part as follows:

> bonemeal
> canvas
> Japanese laborers
> macaroni
> a Chinaman

America's GEOGRAPHY

CONQUERING DISTANCE

$\mathcal{T}$HE late 19th century was a period of massive population shifts for the United States. Between 1860 and 1910 some 23 million immigrants crossed the Atlantic and Pacific oceans to reach America. Many of these immigrants joined the migration across country as millions of people settled the American West. This westward migration was aided by railroad lines and improved systems of communication. These means of transportation and communication linked numerous western cities together, forming the basis of a modern transcontinental economy.

Conquering Distance Overseas

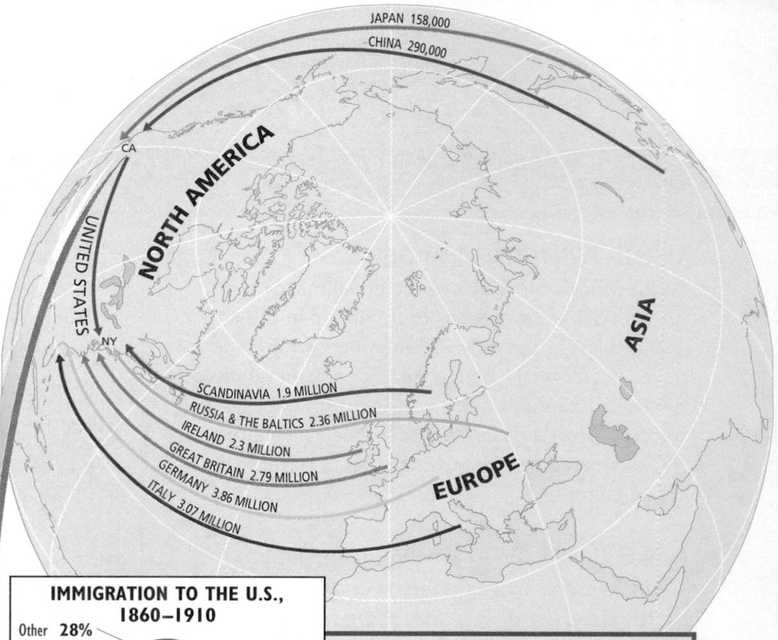

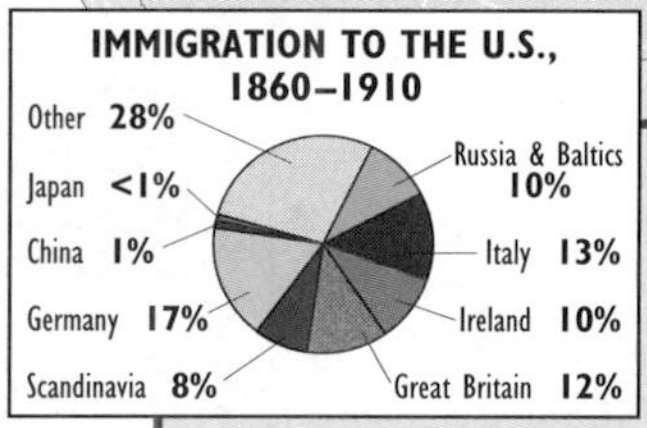

JAPAN 158,000
CHINA 290,000

CA
NORTH AMERICA
UNITED STATES
NY
SCANDINAVIA 1.9 MILLION
RUSSIA & THE BALTICS 2.36 MILLION
IRELAND 2.3 MILLION
GREAT BRITAIN 2.79 MILLION
GERMANY 3.86 MILLION
ITALY 3.07 MILLION
EUROPE
ASIA

IMMIGRATION TO THE U.S., 1860–1910

Other 28%
Japan <1%
China 1%
Germany 17%
Scandinavia 8%
Russia & Baltics 10%
Italy 13%
Ireland 10%
Great Britain 12%

Compared to European immigrants, immigrants from Asia had to travel twice as far to reach the United States. The vast majority of Chinese immigrants in the late 19th century came from the province of Guangdong. Although most initially settled along the Pacific coast, particularly in the San Francisco area, some eventually journeyed across the United States. In 1870 a Massachusetts factory owner began to recruit Chinese laborers from California to take the place of striking workers. As this practice caught on, more Chinese Californians made the trek to the east coast. Today the thriving Chinatowns of Boston, New York, and San Francisco are all the results of the 19th century journeys from Guangdong.

From Across the Pacific to the Atlantic Coast

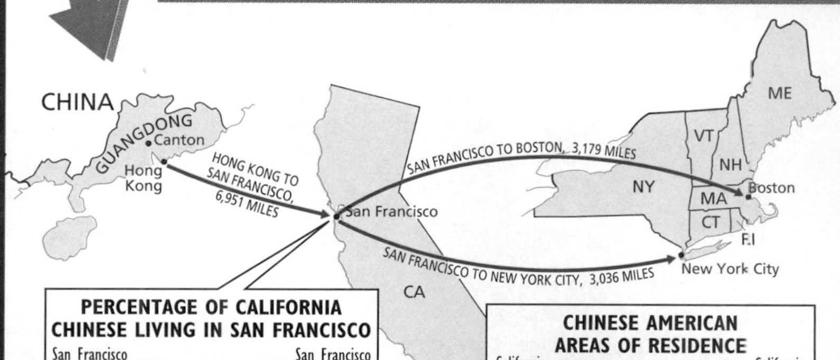

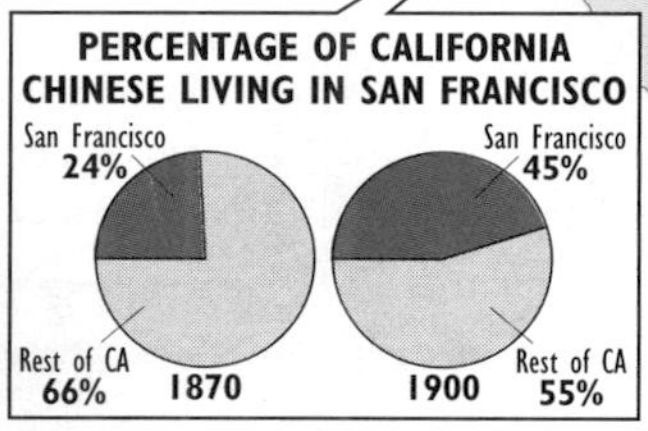

CHINA
GUANGDONG
Canton
Hong Kong
HONG KONG TO SAN FRANCISCO, 6,951 MILES
San Francisco
SAN FRANCISCO TO BOSTON, 3,179 MILES
SAN FRANCISCO TO NEW YORK CITY, 3,036 MILES
CA
ME
VT
NH
NY
MA
CT
Boston
R.I.
New York City

PERCENTAGE OF CALIFORNIA CHINESE LIVING IN SAN FRANCISCO

San Francisco 24%
Rest of CA 66%
1870

San Francisco 45%
Rest of CA 55%
1900

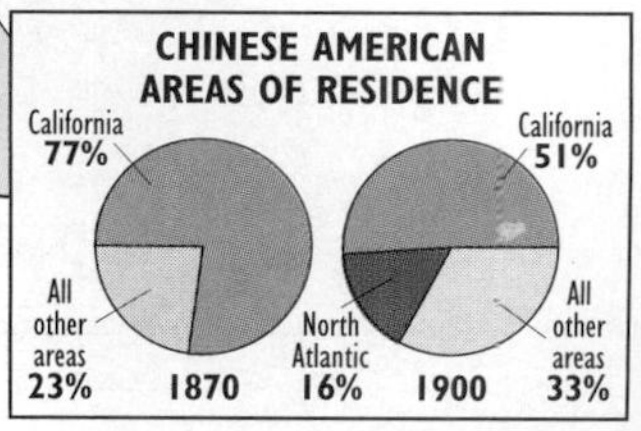

CHINESE AMERICAN AREAS OF RESIDENCE

California 77%
All other areas 23%
1870

California 51%
North Atlantic 16%
All other areas 33%
1900

Conquering Distance Across the West

Map labels (states/territories): WA, OR, ID, MT, ND, MN, WI, MI, SD, WY, NE, IA, NV, UT, CO, KS, MO, IL, IN, KY, CA, ARIZONA TERRITORY, NEW MEXICO TERRITORY, OKLAHOMA TERR., INDIAN TERR., AR, TN, TX, LA, MS, AL

Cities: Seattle, Portland, Walla Walla, Boise, Sacramento, San Francisco, Salt Lake City, Los Angeles, Yuma, Tucson, El Paso, Cheyenne, Laramie, Denver, Ogallala, Omaha, Santa Fe, Pueblo, Dodge City, Wichita, Abilene, Salina, Coffeyville, Kansas City, St. Joseph, Sedalia, St. Louis, Des Moines, Minneapolis, St. Paul, Chicago, Bismarck, Miles City, Ft. Buford, Ft. Smith, Dallas, Ft. Worth, Houston, San Antonio, New Orleans, Hannibal & St. Joseph

Railroads/trails: GREAT NORTHERN, NORTHERN PACIFIC, UNION PACIFIC, CENTRAL PACIFIC, SOUTHERN PACIFIC, DENVER & RIO GRANDE, ATLANTIC & PACIFIC, KANSAS PACIFIC, TOPEKA & SANTA FE, ATCHISON, SHORTLINE, OREGON, PONY EXPRESS, OVERLAND STAGE, BUTTERFIELD, OVERLAND MAIL, GOODNIGHT - LOVING CATTLE TRAIL, CHISHOLM CATTLE TRAIL, WESTERN CATTLE TRAIL, SHAWNEE TRAIL, TEXAS & PACIFIC, SANTA FE - FT. SMITH TRAIL, SANTA FE TRAIL, LOWER EMIGRANT TRAIL, ST. JOSEPH & GRAND ISLAND, MISSOURI, KANSAS, & TEXAS

Ethnic settlement / Indian reservation labels: NEZ PERCE, SIOUX, GERMAN, NORWEGIAN, SWEDISH, IRISH, FINNISH, DANISH, DUTCH, POLISH, CZECH, FRENCH, SHOSHONE, PAIUTE, ARAPAHO, NAVAJO, HOPI, APACHE, CHEROKEE, CREEK, SEMINOLE, CHICKASAW, CHOCTAW, CHINESE, MEXICAN, claimed by Texas

Legend
- Railroad
- Cattle trail
- Other trail
- Area settled by 1890
- DUTCH Ethnic settlement area
- SIOUX Indian reservation

Scale: 0 — 200 — 400 Miles; 0 — 200 — 400 Kilometers
Albers Equal Area Projection

As the railroads and western population increased, many small towns grew into thriving cities within a few short years. Many followed the pattern of Omaha, Nebraska. The small settlement of Omaha, which was a popular stopping point for settlers headed to Colorado, officially became a town in 1857. After the first tracks of the Union Pacific Railroad were laid there in 1865, Omaha's population soared. Located in the heart of cattle country, the city developed a thriving meat-processing industry in the 1880s. This new industry attracted many settlers, particularly poor immigrants from southern and central Europe.

POPULATION OF OMAHA

Year	Population
1860	1,833
1900	102,555

Omaha

WESTERN POPULATION GROWTH, 1860–1910

Year	% Foreign born	% Native born	Total
1860	29%	71%	619,000 total
1870	32%	68%	991,000 total
1880	28%	72%	1,801,000 total
1890	25%	75%	3,134,000 total
1900	20%	80%	4,309,000 total
1910	20%	80%	7,082,000 total

- 25% % Foreign born
- 75% % Native born

Chart information from *Historical Statistics of the United States*, *World Book Encyclopedia*, and Ronald Takaki's *Strangers from a Different Shore*.

MAKING CONNECTIONS
Literature

One of the best-known series of books on the personal lives of the settlers who conquered distance was written by Laura Ingalls Wilder. Wilder's stories of growing up on the Plains during the late 19th century became best-sellers during the 20th century. Among her most popular works is the classic *Little House on the Prairie*, which was the basis for a hit television series. In recent years more historians have begun to value the Wilder books as examples of the daily lives of settlers.

■ Ask students if they have read any of the works of Laura Ingalls Wilder. Ask what they learned about prairie life from their reading.

POLITICS AND PROTEST

1865–1910

Chapter Overview

America in the late 1800s was characterized not only by rapid industrialization and modernization, but also by political scandals and government corruption that were tied to party patronage. As industry expanded, the gap between the lavish lifestyles of the rich and the living conditions of laborers widened. Low wages and long hours prompted many workers to join labor organizations to fight for reform. Likewise, farmers who felt disfranchised in the new industrial order organized politically to protect their interests. And Americans throughout society supported reform in government service.

Chapter Planning Guide

CHAPTER 16	CORE RESOURCE BOOKLETS	AUDIOVISUAL AV RESOURCES	PROGRAM RESOURCES
INTRODUCTION pp. 484–485	■ Literature Worksheet 16 ■ Building Your Portfolio Worksheet 5		
TEACHING THE CHAPTER pp. 486–501	■ Graphic Organizer 16 ■ Social Studies Skills Worksheet 16 ■ Geography Worksheet 16 ■ Outline Map 9	■ Everyday Life in America Transparency and Worksheet 16	■ *Eyewitness and Others,* Volume 2: Readings 20, 24, 29
REVIEW AND ASSESSMENT pp. 502–503	■ Chapter 16 Daily Quizzes ■ Review Worksheet 16 ■ Chapter 16 Tests ■ Alternative Assessment Forms		■ Test Generator

Additional Resources

BOOKS FOR TEACHERS

Filippelli, Ronald L. ed. *Labor Conflict in the United States: An Encyclopedia.* Garland Publishers, 1990. Guide to major events in labor history.

McMath, Robert C. *American Populism: A Social History, 1877–1898.* Hill & Wang, 1993. Social history of the agrarian revolt in the late 19th century.

Painter, Nell I. *Standing at Armageddon: The United States, 1877–1919.* Norton, 1989. U.S. political and labor history.

Smith, Page. *The Rise of Industrial America.* Viking Penguin, 1990. Covers social history of the late 1800s.

BOOKS FOR STUDENTS

Goodwyn, Lawrence. *The Populist Moment: A Short History of the Agrarian Revolt in America.* Oxford University Press, 1978. Detailed history of 19th-century agrarian revolt.

*Jones, Mother. *The Autobiography of Mother Jones.* Ed. by Mary F. Parton. C. H. Kerr, 1990.

Meltzer, Milton. *Bread & Roses: The Struggle of American Labor, 1865–1915.* Facts on File, 1990. Discusses the formative years of the American labor movement.

* for students reading below grade level

MULTIMEDIA MATERIALS

The 1880s. Video, 32 min. Kaw Valley/SSSS. Describes politics and popular culture.

Populism: Where Historians Disagree. 2 filmstrips. Random House Media. Presents opposing viewpoints on Populist party.

The Pullman Strike. Video, 20 min. Multi-Media Productions/SSSS. Describes major events in labor conflict.

THEMES IN AMERICAN HISTORY

USE WITH PAGES
484–485

*L*isted on the right are the themes emphasized in Chapter 16. The questions in boldface type stimulate critical thinking and provide students with an opportunity to discuss the themes within a broadened context. The questions also appear in the pupil's edition on p. 484.

■ DEMOCRATIC VALUES

What actions might citizens take to bring about change in society? Students might mention supporting reform candidates for political office; supporting organized groups that are working for change such as labor unions and political parties; and protests, riots, or other radical violent actions.

■ CULTURAL DIVERSITY

How might political and economic conditions unite different groups in society? Students might mention that laborers in different fields and those of different ethnic backgrounds might come together to fight for better conditions or to support sympathetic political parties or candidates. Farmers and wage earners might unite to call for changes in economic policies that hurt both groups.

How might they divide groups? Students might mention that groups might be divided by competition for jobs, by conflicting needs or goals, or by political policies that affect the groups differently.

CHAPTER STRATEGIES FOR MEETING INDIVIDUAL NEEDS

LIMITED ENGLISH PROFICIENT LEARNERS

As students read through the chapter, have them work in small groups to pick an illustration from each section. Ask groups to write an extended caption explaining each illustration's significance and tying it to the section content.

TACTILE/KINESTHETIC LEARNERS

Organize students into small groups to prepare skits of key events of labor and agrarian protest in the late 1800s. Call on groups to perform their skits.

LEARNERS HAVING DIFFICULTY

Have students work in pairs to construct an annotated outline, section by section, as they read through the chapter. Call on volunteers to present and explain their outlines.

AUDITORY LEARNERS

Have students prepare dramatic readings of important speeches or articles by labor leaders or politicians highlighted in the chapter.

VISUAL LEARNERS

Ask students to sketch a variety of items representative of this period to make a museum display. Students may use labor propaganda, clothing, letters, song lyrics, diary excerpts, maps, books, and other items.

GIFTED LEARNERS

Direct students to report on the major events in this chapter by creating the front page of a newspaper containing headlines and articles on labor conflicts and government corruption.

■ **UNDERSTANDING
THE MAIN IDEA**

Read aloud the Understanding the Main Idea paragraph. Call on volunteers to explain how the second industrial revolution changed the U.S. and write their answers on the chalkboard. Then ask students to predict what actions Americans might take, who believed they had not received their fair share of prosperity. List students' responses on a flip chart or butcher paper. Then have them evaluate their responses after they read the chapter.

 THEMES
Have students work individually or in small groups to answer the questions under Themes. Save students' responses so that they can compare them with their responses after studying the chapter. (See p. 483B for suggested answers.)

■ **THE TIME LINE**

Point out that major economic depressions began in 1873 and again in 1893 and that some of the events recorded on the time line were related to these economic downturns. Have students copy the time line, adding other important events as they read the chapter.

■■ Ask students how difficult times might cause people to change their economic strategies and outlook.

CORE RESOURCES

• **Graphic Organizer 16**
• **Literature
  Worksheet 16**
• **Outline Map 9**
• **Building Your Port-
  folio Worksheet 5**

484

ABOUT THE ILLUSTRATION

In the late 1800s it was not uncommon for young children to work in factories. Tell students that the children in this photograph are working at a mill in Macon, Georgia. Because they were small, children often were made to climb onto the spinning machines to mend broken threads or replace empty bobbins. Ask students to assume the role of union leaders and write letters to the editor in which they protest the dangerous conditions under which children work and demand a change in child labor laws.

Chapter 16

1865–1910

POLITICS AND PROTEST

▼ **FOCUS**

UNDERSTANDING
THE MAIN IDEA

Rapid industrialization and westward expansion helped transform the United States into a prosperous, modern nation. However, many Americans believed that they had not received their fair share of prosperity. Ignored by the major political parties, these Americans organized to protect their own interests or became involved in the political process to win reform.

 THEMES

■ **DEMOCRATIC VALUES**
What actions might citizens take to bring about change in society?

■ **CULTURAL DIVERSITY**
How might political and economic conditions unite different groups in society? How might they divide groups?

1869	1883	1886	1892	1894
Knights of Labor founded.	Pendleton Civil Service Act passed.	Haymarket Riot occurs.	Populist party founded.	Pullman strike occurs.

Refer students to the Commentary on Jacksonian democracy on p. 241. Have them identify the changes and opportunities that Jacksonian democracy "promised" to society. List these on a flip chart or butcher paper. Save the list for students to review at the close of chapter study.

■■ LINK TO THE PAST ▶

By the late 1800s the promise of Jacksonian democracy was little more than a distant, vain hope for many Americans. To them it appeared that all political power lay in the hands of a few wealthy people. Winning a share of power and prosperity, they realized, would take action on their part.

Child factory laborers

In the 1873 novel *The Gilded Age,* by Mark Twain and Charles Dudley Warner, a Washington observer tries to explain to a young friend why Congress takes so long to get down to business each legislative session:

> 66 The first preliminary it always starts out on, is to clean itself, so to speak. It will arraign [accuse] two or three dozen of its members, or maybe four or five dozen, for taking bribes to vote for this and that and the other bill last winter. . . . One of our Congresses can never rest easy until it has thoroughly purified itself of all blemishes. 99

Astounded, his young friend asks whether Congress ever worries that it will expel so many members that it can no longer do business. "Why I did not say Congress would expel anybody," the man replies. "But good God we *try* them, don't we!"

> 66 They appoint a committee to investigate, and that committee hears evidence three weeks. . . . They don't acquit, they don't condemn. They just say, "Charge not proven." It leaves the accused in a kind of a shaky condition before the country, it purifies Congress, it satisfies everybody. 99

In real life, of course, it did not satisfy everyone. Many Americans were deeply troubled by the abuses of wealth and power that seemed to characterize the era. Some people called for political reform. Others—such as industrial workers and farmers—took matters into their own hands, organizing to protect their interests.

UMW emblem, 1890

MAKING CONNECTIONS

Literature
"I consider it one of the most astonishing novels that was ever written," Mark Twain wrote in a column in a New York newspaper. Although some critics agreed that the representation of congressional life and corruption in *The Gilded Age* was probably accurate, others called it vicious and shocking.

■■ Have interested students read *The Gilded Age* and report on what aspects of the book might have caused such criticism.

PRIMARY SOURCE

Description of Change: excerpted and bracketed
Rationale: excerpted to focus on main idea; bracketed to clarify meaning

PRIMARY SOURCE

Description of Change: excerpted
Rationale: excerpted to focus on main idea

PREVIEW WORKSHOP

Following is a list of the significant people and terms in this section. You may wish to use this list as a section preview.

- Charles Guiteau
- Chester A. Arthur
- Grover Cleveland
- Benjamin Harrison

People
- Schuyler Colfax
- Samuel J. Tilden
- Rutherford B. Hayes
- James A. Garfield

Terms
- Gilded Age
- Tweed Ring
- Pendleton Civil Service Act
- mugwumps

FOCUS OBJECTIVES

- Explain why many Americans called for civil service reform.

- Analyze why critics believed that the Pendleton Civil Service Act would accomplish little.

- Describe how President Harrison dealt with the reform programs of President Cleveland.

BUILDING VOCABULARY

The term *graft* has similar meanings in horticulture and politics. In work with plants, a part from one plant is grafted onto another so that it eventually becomes a permanent part of that plant. In politics the term is used to designate money obtained fraudulently, because it usually results from illegal practices "grafted" to the official duties of an officeholder.

PRIMARY SOURCE

Description of Change: excerpted
Rationale: excerpted to focus on main idea

CORE RESOURCES

• **Section 1 Daily Quiz**

486

Section 1

RESTORING HONEST GOVERNMENT

FOCUS

- **Why did many Americans call for civil service reform?**
- **Why did critics believe that the Pendleton Civil Service Act would accomplish little?**
- **How did President Harrison deal with the reform programs of President Cleveland?**

Few contemporary observers had anything good to say about the late-19th-century political scene. Historian Henry Adams noted that "the period was poor in purpose and barren in results." Many Americans agreed with Adams, viewing their elected representatives as little better than a bunch of crooks. Infuriated, these Americans demanded political reforms.

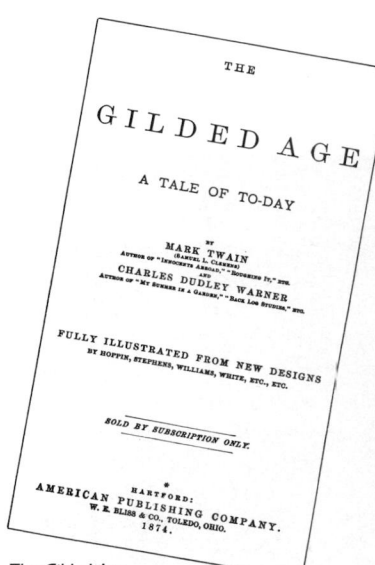

THE

GILDED AGE

A TALE OF TO-DAY

BY

MARK TWAIN
(SAMUEL L. CLEMENS)
AUTHOR OF "INNOCENTS ABROAD," "ROUGHING IT," ETC.
AND
CHARLES DUDLEY WARNER
AUTHOR OF "MY SUMMER IN A GARDEN," "BACK LOG STUDIES," ETC.

FULLY ILLUSTRATED FROM NEW DESIGNS
BY HOPPIN, STEPHENS, WILLIAMS, WHITE, ETC., ETC.

SOLD BY SUBSCRIPTION ONLY.

HARTFORD:
AMERICAN PUBLISHING COMPANY.
W. E. BLISS & CO., TOLEDO, OHIO.
1874.

The Gilded Age

GRAFT AND CORRUPTION

Mark Twain and Charles Dudley Warner titled their novel about post–Civil War America *The Gilded Age* to make a point. Twain and Warner believed that, like the base material that hides beneath the glittering gold surface of a gilded picture frame, corruption and greed lurked below the polite and prosperous luster of late-19th-century American society. The image struck a chord, and the era became known as the **Gilded Age**.

The authors had ample evidence to support their view—particularly in the area of politics. Politicians of both parties—and at every level of government—made pious speeches about the great honor of holding public office. Yet they often showed more interest in taking advantage of their positions to plunder the public treasury than in serving the public good.

Twain and Warner took as their main target the national political scene. But corruption was no less widespread on state and local levels, where powerful political machines prevailed. Among the most notorious was Tammany Hall, the Democratic party machine that controlled New York City government. Tammany Hall's reputation for graft and corruption was launched by William Marcy Tweed, who along with his cronies—the **Tweed Ring**—robbed the city treasury of some $200 million between 1865 and 1871.

It is doubtful that any of the later bosses ever exceeded Tweed's take, but graft remained one of the Gilded Age's best roads to riches—one the bosses vigorously defended. "Everybody is talkin' these days about Tammany men growin' rich on graft," complained boss George Washington Plunkitt, "but nobody thinks of drawin' the distinction between honest graft and dishonest graft."

    ❝ There's an honest graft, and I'm an example of how it works. . . . My party's in power in the city, and it's goin' to undertake a lot of public improvements. Well, I'm tipped off, say, that they're going to lay out a new park at a certain place. . . . I go to that place and I buy up all the land I can in the neighborhood. Then the board of this or

MOTIVATING: STUDENT EXPERIENCES

Have students identify any local, state, or federal political corruption or scandals of which they are aware. Have volunteers describe the public reaction to these events. Ask students about any reforms that the scandals prompted. Tell students that Section 1 deals with government corruption and attempts at reform in the late 1800s.

Teaching the Section

CIVIL SERVICE REFORM

Have students write letters, as Americans living in the Gilded Age, to their senator or representative. Letters should express their views of conditions in government and should explain why civil service reform is needed. Tell students to use examples from the text to support their arguments. Have each student exchange his or her letter with a classmate, who will read the letter aloud and offer a spoken response, in the role of a senator or representative, to the points it raises. Students may wish to include their letters in their portfolios.

▶

POLITICAL PATRONAGE

THROUGH OTHERS' EYES

In late-19th-century America, local politicians were often the only champions of the urban poor or the newly arrived immigrant. British writer H. G. Wells noted this aspect of patronage when he visited Alderman Kenna, a powerful political boss in Chicago. Wells wrote:

66*He is very kind to all his crowd. He helps them when they are in trouble, even if it is trouble with the police. He helps them find employment when they are down on their luck. He stands between them and the impacts of an unsympathetic and altogether too careless social structure in a sturdy and almost parental way. I can quite believe what I was told, that in the lives of many of these rough undesirables he's almost the only decent influence. He gets wives well treated, and he has an open heart for children.* 99

that makes its plan public, and there is a rush to get my land. . . . Ain't it perfectly honest to charge a good price and make a profit on my investment and foresight? . . . Well, that's honest graft. 99

SCANDAL IN THE WHITE HOUSE

City bosses were not the only masters at graft and corruption, however. Politicians in Washington, D.C., played the same games—often for even higher stakes. This fact was brought home during Ulysses S. Grant's years in the White House.

Grant's first term in office was marred by several scandals. In 1869 his brother-in-law helped financier Jay Gould attempt to corner the gold market. The attempt failed, pushing several investors—though not Gould—into financial ruin. Then in 1872 an even greater scandal surfaced, one involving Grant's vice president, Schuyler Colfax. In 1867, directors of the Union Pacific Railroad had formed the Crédit Mobilier Company and then had awarded the company contracts to build a

section of the transcontinental railroad. Crédit Mobilier overcharged Union Pacific by more than $20 million. These excess profits went straight into the pockets of Crédit Mobilier's stockholders, many of whom were members of Congress, including then–Speaker of the House Colfax. Although this scandal transpired before Grant became president, it tarnished his administration's image.

Critics charged that the corruption in Grant's administration was in large part the result of the spoils system (see Chapter 7). Rather than award civil service jobs on the basis of patronage, they asked, why not let ability be the deciding factor? Let applicants who received the highest grades on competitive examinations, the reformers proposed, get the jobs.

■■ **Convinced that the spoils system led to political corruption, many Americans called for civil service reform.**

Civil service reform was the battle cry of New York *Tribune* editor Horace Greeley, Grant's Liberal Republican opponent in the 1872 presidential race. The Liberal Republican party was formed by Republicans shocked over the Grant scandals and tired of Reconstruction. The Democrats, hoping to benefit from the split in the Republican party, threw their support to Greeley.

▼ **This New York newspaper cartoon satirized the corrupt politicians of the times.**

WHO STOLE THE PEOPLES MONEY ? — DO TELL. N.Y.TIMES.   'TWAS HIM.

THROUGH OTHERS' EYES

Alderman Kenna's largess was made possible by graft. Corruption, however, was almost a given for Chicago aldermen. A lawyer charged in 1894 that 66 of Chicago's 68 aldermen could be bought. He knew this, he said, "because I have bought them myself."

PRIMARY SOURCE

Description of Change: excerpted
Rationale: excerpted to focus on main idea

HISTORICAL SIDELIGHTS

"Shaking the Plum Tree"
Pennsylvania Republican boss Matthew Quay called the awarding of patronage jobs after an election "shaking the plum tree." What fell were political plums—government jobs that paid well but involved little work. This term, which is American in origin, probably derives from the 17th-century British slang word *plum,* meaning £1,000 (a good deal of money at that time).

Teaching the Section

REFORM AND ITS CRITICS

Call on students to play the following roles in a press conference on the Pendleton Civil Service Act: Samuel Tilden, Rutherford B. Hayes, Roscoe Conkling, and James G. Blaine. Ask each participant to present a brief statement of his public position on the act. Then have the class, acting as the press, question each participant about the reasons for his position, his record and sincerity, and his opinion on whether reform can work.

HARRISON VERSUS CLEVELAND

Assign students to work in pairs to role-play presidents Cleveland and Harrison on Harrison's inauguration day. Tell each pair to conduct a conversation in which Cleveland proudly recounts his record on political reform, and Harrison tells Cleveland how he intends to reward his supporters. Have volunteers re-create their conversations for the class. Ask students to assess the impact that Harrison's actions would have on Cleveland's reforms.

HISTORICAL SIDELIGHTS

Many Scandals

The Crédit Mobilier scandal proved to be only the tip of the iceberg of corruption in Grant's administration. For example, Secretary of War William W. Belknap collected annual bribes from traders who held the profitable rights to trade with Native Americans and with frontier army posts. And Grant's private secretary, Orville E. Babcock, was found to have connections to the "Whisky Ring," a group of liquor distillers who had bilked the government of millions of dollars in taxes.

🌐 GLOBAL CONNECTIONS

The roots of civil service go back as far as the early river civilizations of Asia. The running of the irrigation systems in these civilizations necessitated bureaucracies of clerks, secretaries, and royal advisers. However, China had the first centralized, hierarchical civil service based on competitive examinations.

Liberal Republicans viewed the Crédit Mobilier scandal as a nail in Grant's political coffin. But Grant, playing once again on his image as a war hero, easily won reelection. Disheartened and worn out, Greeley died just three weeks after the election. His party did not last much longer, and it seemed that civil service reform, too, had been dealt a death blow. However, continued exposure of corruption in the second Grant administration breathed new life into the movement.

🅣HE STRUGGLE FOR REFORM

Hoping to make the corruption of the Grant years a campaign issue, the Democrats nominated New York governor Samuel J. Tilden as their presidential candidate in 1876. Tilden had won national attention by helping break up the corrupt Tweed Ring. But the Republicans rode to victory with their nominee: Ohio governor Rutherford B. Hayes, known for his support of civil service reform (see Chapter 13 for details on election).

President Hayes's efforts at reform soon drew the wrath of his own party. The Republicans had split into two factions—nicknamed the Stalwarts and the Half-breeds—over the issue of patronage. The Stalwarts, led by the haughty Senator Roscoe Conkling of New York, strongly opposed reform. Conkling referred to the proposed merit system for government jobs as "snivel service." The Half-breeds, led by James G. Blaine of Maine, claimed to support reform, but they also wanted to control patronage jobs.

Hayes chose not to run for reelection in 1880. At the Republican Convention, the two factions battled to control the party ticket. The Half-breeds won, naming James A. Garfield as the party's presidential candidate. To appease the Stalwarts, they placed Conkling's political ally Chester A. Arthur on the ticket as the vice presidential nominee.

Garfield edged out his Democratic rival, Civil War veteran General Winfield Scott Hancock, by fewer than 40,000 votes. But his victory was short-lived. On July 2, 1881, Charles Guiteau (guh-TOH), a disappointed and mentally unstable government job seeker, shot Garfield. The deranged Guiteau believed that killing Garfield would further the Stalwart cause. The shooting had the opposite effect. When Garfield died in September, Chester A. Arthur, though a Stalwart, sympathetically responded to the calls for reform.

In 1883 President Arthur helped gain passage of the **Pendleton Civil Service Act**, which established a Civil Service Commission to administer competitive examinations to those seeking government jobs. The act was an important step toward reform because it enacted into law the idea that federal jobs below the policy-making level should be filled by merit. Critics charged, however, that the act was of limited value because it covered only about 10 percent of federal jobs.

▪▪ Critics argued that the Civil Service Act covered too few federal jobs to be effective.

Angered by Arthur's reform efforts, many Stalwarts refused to support his bid for the 1884 Republican presidential nomination. Instead, they cast their lot with James Blaine, the leader of the Half-breeds. Blaine's nomination angered

PRESIDENTIAL LIVES

RUTHERFORD B. HAYES
1822–1893

in office 1877–1881

At the time of his election to the presidency, Rutherford B. Hayes was a veteran of many years in politics. He had served as Cincinnati's city solicitor, as a U.S. congressman, and as governor of Ohio for three terms. But he found the presidency hard work. "I am heartily tired of this life of bondage, responsibility, and toil," he told his wife. After one term he gladly returned to private life.

RB Hayes

Practice

GUIDED PRACTICE

Organize the class into two groups. Take turns asking one group to identify the advances in political reform during the late 1800s and the other group the setbacks to it. List responses on the chalkboard. Ask volunteers to summarize the period in one sentence, based on the information on the chalkboard.

INDEPENDENT PRACTICE

Direct students to select one of the advances or setbacks in political reform listed in the Guided Practice and write a headline and accompanying news story about their selected topic that might have appeared in a newspaper in the late 1800s. Students may wish to include their news stories in their portfolios.

Review and Assessment

REVIEW Ask volunteers to summarize in a short statement the main ideas of Section 1. Write responses on the chalkboard. Have students select one statement and write a paragraph that includes supporting details. Students may wish to include their paragraphs in their portfolios. Then assign the Section 1 Review on p. 490.

ASSESS Assign the **Section 1 Daily Quiz** in *Core Resources.* ▶

PRESIDENTIAL LIVES

JAMES A. GARFIELD
1831–1881

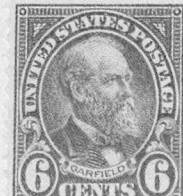

in office 1881

James A. Garfield was the last president to be born in a log cabin. Garfield enjoyed his years in Congress but did not look forward to life in the White House. He called the presidency "a bleak mountain" and forecast that "I am bidding good-bye to private life and to a long series of happy years which I fear terminate in 1880." The following year, Garfield lay dead from an assassin's bullet.

James A. Garfield.

CHESTER A. ARTHUR
1829–1886

in office 1881–1885

Chester A. Arthur much preferred the social side of the presidency to paperwork. Arthur loved life in the executive mansion. "He wanted the best of everything," an employee recalled, "and wanted it served in the best manner." Tall and handsome, with impeccable manners, Arthur was called Gentleman Boss by his political followers, and in the White House he became known as the Prince of Hospitality.

Chester A. Arthur

Republican reformers, who charged that the candidate "wallowed in spoils like a rhinoceros in an African pool." Dubbed "**mugwumps**" (the Algonquian word for big chiefs), these reformers threw their support to the Democratic candidate, Grover Cleveland. Like Tilden, Cleveland had gained national attention when, as governor of New York, he opposed Tammany Hall. Mudslinging, rather than a discussion of the issues, marked the campaign. But in the end Cleveland won.

ADVANCES AND SETBACKS

Proclaiming that "a public office is a public trust," Cleveland entered the White House determined to promote political reform and end the days when government jobs were given only in reward for political favors. Toward this end, he doubled the number of federal jobs requiring civil service exams.

Although his stand on reform angered some party leaders, Cleveland won the Democratic presidential nomination in 1888. To oppose him, the Republicans chose Benjamin Harrison of Indiana, a grandson of the ninth president, William Henry Harrison. After a dirty campaign, Cleveland won the popular election by some 100,000 votes. But Harrison came out on top in electoral votes, thus winning the race.

The new president and Congress quickly set out to reward their supporters, thereby weakening the reform efforts of Cleveland. The Republicans filled practically every job not on the civil service list with members of their own party. The 1890 Republican Congress spent so freely for Civil War pensions and other pet projects that it became known as the Billion Dollar Congress.

▪▪ President Harrison weakened the reform efforts of President Cleveland.

HISTORICAL SIDELIGHTS

Cleveland Wins New York
Cleveland should have enjoyed strong support in New York in 1884. However, his fights with Tammany Hall while he was governor caused the Democratic machine's Irish leaders to offer only a lukewarm endorsement. But when a Blaine supporter called the Democrats the party of "Rum, Romanism, and Rebellion," some Irish Americans considered the remark to be nativist and switched their votes to Cleveland. Their support was enough to deprive Blaine of New York's electoral votes—and the presidency.

HISTORICAL SIDELIGHTS

Citizen Blaine
Although candidate Blaine was charged with public corruption in the 1884 campaign, his supporters emphasized his morality in private life. This caused one mugwump to suggest that the voters "remand Mr. Blaine to the private life which he is so eminently fitted to adorn."

RETEACH Pair students and randomly assign each pair one of the headings in the section. Have pairs write three questions about the material under their assigned heading. Then have pairs present their questions to the entire group to answer.

Closure

Have volunteers explain Henry Adams's statement on p. 486 that the late 19th century was "poor in purpose and barren in results." Ask students whether they agree or disagree with this characterization. Encourage them to cite examples to support their opinions.

Extension

CREATE Have interested students create political cartoons about a scandal of the Grant administration or the Tweed Ring in New York City.

INVESTIGATE Have students research and report on the federal civil service system today.

SECTION REVIEW ANSWERS

IDENTIFY

For significance, see the following pages:
Gilded Age (p. 486)
Tweed Ring (p. 486)
Schuyler Colfax (p. 487)
Samuel J. Tilden (p. 488)
Rutherford B. Hayes (p. 488)
James A. Garfield (p. 488)
Charles Guiteau (p. 488)
Chester A. Arthur (p. 488)
Pendleton Civil Service Act (p. 488)
mugwumps (p. 489)
Grover Cleveland (p. 489)
Benjamin Harrison (p. 489)

1. *belief that spoils system led to graft and political corruption*
2. *According to critics, it covered too few federal jobs to be effective.*
3. *Harrison's rewarding of supporters weakened Cleveland's reforms.*
4. *Editorials might mention that the spoils system leads to political corruption, and that the scandals of Grant's administration resulted from the spoils system.*
5. *Guiteau believed killing Garfield would end movement for civil service reform; rallied Arthur to help gain passage of Pendleton Civil Service Act.*

490

PRESIDENTIAL LIVES

GROVER CLEVELAND
1837–1908

in office 1885–1889 and 1893–1897

Called Uncle Jumbo by his family, Grover Cleveland was a large and genial man. Because he was so insistent about government reform, however, his enemies called him His Obstinacy.

A bachelor, Cleveland was accused in the campaign of 1884 of fathering a child out of wedlock. Refusing to participate in the mudslinging, Cleveland replied: "The other side can have a monopoly of all the dirt in this campaign." The New York *World* defended Cleveland, giving four reasons for supporting the candidate: "1. He is an honest man; 2. He is an honest man; 3. He is an honest man; 4. He is an honest man."

BENJAMIN HARRISON
1833–1901

in office 1889–1893

Grandson of a president and son of a congressman, Benjamin Harrison was often compared to earlier Harrisons, much to his displeasure. Once when he was introduced at a political gathering as the grandson of President William Henry Harrison, "Little Ben" immediately retorted, "I want it understood that I am the grandson of nobody. I believe that every man should stand on his own merits."

Indeed, as president, Harrison was unlike his grandfather. Although Harrison was an effective public speaker, close up he seemed aloof. One official dubbed him the "White House Iceberg."

SECTION 1 REVIEW

IDENTIFY and explain the significance of the following: Gilded Age, Tweed Ring, Schuyler Colfax, Samuel J. Tilden, Rutherford B. Hayes, James A. Garfield, Charles Guiteau, Chester A. Arthur, Pendleton Civil Service Act, mugwumps, Grover Cleveland, Benjamin Harrison.

1. MAIN IDEA What led many Americans to call for civil service reform?

2. MAIN IDEA Why was the Pendleton Civil Service Act criticized?

3. CONTRASTING How did President Harrison's reform record differ from that of President Cleveland?

4. WRITING TO PERSUADE Imagine you are Horace Greeley. Write an editorial stating what is wrong with the spoils system and why Grant should be defeated in the 1872 election.

5. IDENTIFYING CAUSE AND EFFECT Why did Charles Guiteau assassinate President Garfield? Why can it be said that Guiteau's action did not have its intended effect?

Chapter 16

SECTION 2

*Introducing
the Section*

PREVIEW WORKSHOP

Following is a list of the significant people, places, and terms in this section. You may wish to use this list as a section preview.

People
- Terence V. Powderly
- Mary Harris Jones

Places
- Haymarket Square
- Homestead steel plant
- Pullman sleeping-car factory

Terms
- company town
- scrip
- Knights of Labor
- Great Upheaval

- Haymarket Riot
- anarchists
- blacklists
- yellow-dog contracts
- lockouts
- strikebreakers
- American Federation of Labor

Section 2

LABOR STRIVES TO ORGANIZE

FOCUS
- **What was working life like for industrial laborers in the late 19th century?**
- **What weakened support for the labor movement?**
- **How did the government respond to labor disputes in the 1890s?**

Preoccupied with political reform, the government overlooked one of the major trends of the late 1800s—the growing gulf between the haves and the have-nots. By 1890 close to 75 percent of the nation's wealth was controlled by just 10 percent of the population. At the same time, nearly 50 percent of American industrial workers lived below the poverty line. Demanding the right to share in the country's prosperity, some workers organized labor unions.

South Carolina textile mill worker, c. 1890

THE NEW WORKING CLASS

The demand for labor soared under the new industrial order. Millions of workers were needed to staff factories, construct machines, furnish raw materials, and transport and sell finished goods. This great demand was met, in large part, by the flood of immigrants who came to the United States during the 1800s. By 1900 one third of the country's industrial workers were foreign-born.

These immigrant workers were joined by hundreds of thousands of rural Americans who moved to the cities in search of jobs. Among this group were thousands of African Americans from the South who came to the North in hope of securing industrial work. Though the postwar South was home to many industries—textiles, tobacco, lumber, coal, and iron—African Americans were barred

from most factory jobs. Almost all southern textile workers were white and native-born. Cigar factories did rely on African American workers—women cleaned and sorted the leaves, men made the cigars—but their numbers were few. In 1891, only some 7,400 southern blacks held industrial jobs. Most African Americans, like most southerners, remained tied to the land and impoverished.

► Sorting tobacco leaves in cigar factories was grueling, tedious work. The strong fumes often caused painful eye disorders.

FOCUS OBJECTIVES
- Describe the working life of industrial laborers in the late 19th century.
- Analyze what weakened support for the labor movement.
- Explain how the government responded to labor disputes in the 1890s.

CORE RESOURCES
- **Social Studies Skills Worksheet 16**
- **Geography Worksheet 16**
- **Section 2 Daily Quiz**

VOICES IN HISTORY

In 1880 German immigrant John Ehmann described conditions in the Cincinnati meat-packing industry, in which he served as a butcher: "Besides the dangers of chopping fingers, rheumatism seizes every butcher; their limbs become stiff at thirty-five and they are unfit for the trade. . . . Few of them have any opportunity to learn English. . . . Some, who have been in this country for 15 years, cannot talk in English, and have some difficulty to understand it. These men say that the . . . conditions under which they are employed, are not those of Germany, but purely of American growth."

Southern blacks hoped conditions would be better in the North. But industrial employment remained out of reach for most. The best jobs still went to native-born whites or to immigrants. African American men—even those with skills—generally found themselves confined to the dirtiest or most dangerous work or to such service-related jobs as gardening or driving coaches.

African American women in northern cities competed with poor immigrant women for domestic jobs and unskilled factory work. Most women—African American or immigrant—worked because they had to work. As a state official in Massachusetts noted, "a family of workers can always live well, but the man with a family of small children to support, unless his wife works also, has a small chance of living properly." The ranks of women workers more than doubled between 1870 and 1890 as wives, daughters, and sisters labored to put food on the table. By 1900, women accounted for about 15 percent of the labor force—some five million workers.

The number of children in the work force doubled during this period for the same reason. By 1890 close to 20 percent of American children between ages 10 and 15—some 1.5 million in all—worked for wages. In the textile mills of North Carolina, for example, one in every four workers was a child. The ratio was much lower in Massachusetts mills—1 in 20. In other places, countless boys and girls worked in garment factories or at home, making clothing or other items by the piece. Others labored in the nation's mines, canneries, and shoe factories, or they roamed the streets shining shoes, selling newspapers, collecting scrap, running errands, or delivering packages.

▲ In the 1870s the Knights of Labor campaigned for legislation to protect child workers. But children continued to experience wretched working conditions throughout the next few decades.

WORKING CONDITIONS

Children in the labor force faced terrible conditions. In some textile mills, for instance, children worked 12-hour shifts—often at night—for pennies a day. But all industrial workers, regardless of age, sex, or race, labored long hours for little pay. Conditions were especially rough for unskilled workers. Most unskilled male laborers worked at least 10 hours a day, 6 days a week, for less than $10 a week. Many African American, Mexican American, and Asian American men worked the same number of hours for even lower wages. And employers made few allowances for women and children, expecting them to work the same number of hours as men for sometimes as little as half the pay.

Such long hours left workers exhausted at the end of the day. And fatigue increased the danger in already unsafe working surroundings. In 1881 alone, some 30,000 railroad workers were killed or injured on the job. Most employers felt no responsibility for work-related deaths and injuries and made little effort to improve workplace safety.

Teaching the Section

THE NEW WORKING CLASS

Call on volunteers to role-play the following figures in the late 1800s: African American coal miner, child textile-mill worker, Russian laundress, Mexican American cannery worker, Chinese American cook, male and female Hungarian shoe-factory workers, female Italian garment worker, German American railroad worker. Ask the volunteers to explain their jobs, working conditions, family economic situations, and job opportunities. Have the class respond as late 1800s citizens by writing letters to the editor regarding what they have learned about the plight of these workers. (Some students might wish to take the roles of labor union leaders, settlement house workers, or Social Darwinists in writing their letters.) Select students to read their letters aloud. Students may wish to include their letters in their portfolios.

▶

Workers who lived in a **company town**, a town where a company owned the housing and the businesses, faced special problems. These workers usually received their wages in **scrip**—paper money that could be used only to pay rent to the company or to buy goods at company stores. Prices at company stores were usually much higher than at regular stores, and workers often spent whole paychecks on necessities like food and clothing.

> ■■ For most industrial laborers, working life meant long hours of toil for little pay and few benefits.

THE KNIGHTS OF LABOR

As conditions worsened, workers clamored for change. They knew that alone they could do little. But if they banded together, the factory owners, the politicians, and the capitalists on New York's Wall Street would have to listen. Workers formed a number of local unions in the first half of the 1800s, but after 1850, organizing efforts went national.

One of the earliest national unions was the **Knights of Labor**, founded in 1869 by nine Philadelphia garment workers led by Uriah

▼ Terence V. Powderly is shown here surrounded by other influential leaders of the Knights of Labor.

Stephens. It remained largely a white male organization until 1879, when Terence V. Powderly, an Irish Catholic machinist and mayor of Scranton, Pennsylvania, became its leader. Under his leadership the Knights' membership mushroomed.

Powderly wanted the Knights of Labor to attract workers who were often excluded from other unions. He therefore opened the union's doors to both skilled and unskilled laborers. He also welcomed thousands of women into the union's ranks. A number of women, such as Mary Harris Jones, played prominent roles in the Knights of Labor.

Born in Cork, Ireland, in 1830, Mary Harris came to the United States as a young child. She married George Jones, a union supporter, in 1861.

BIO GRAPHY

Widowed six years later, she devoted herself to the labor movement. In the 1870s, at the invitation of Powderly, she became an organizer for the Knights of Labor. Declaring that her place was "wherever there is a fight," she organized strikes, marches, and demonstrations. Her activities earned her the title "the most dangerous woman in America." But because she looked more motherly than radical, most people called her Mother Jones.

Mary Harris Jones

Jones was sentenced to 20 years in jail for her part in a 1912 West Virginia strike, but a public outcry caused the governor of the state to free her. Mother Jones continued fighting for the rights of America's working people until her death, at age 100, in 1930.

Powderly also opened the union to African Americans. By the mid-1880s the Knights claimed some 60,000 black members. At the Knights' 1886 national convention in Richmond, Virginia, African American delegate Frank Ferrell told the crowd:

> 66 One of the objects of our Order is the abolition of these distinctions which are maintained by creed or color. . . . My experience . . . [has] taught me that we have worked so far successfully toward the extinction of these regrettable distinctions. 99

Teaching the Section

LABOR MOVEMENT WEAKENED

Organize students into groups of three to role-play a "broadcast journalist" conducting a short interview with a labor union official and a factory manager in 1886 about the causes of the Great Upheaval, its effect on the general public, and its potential consequences for workers and their union. Suggest that the labor leader and the manager may agree on some points and disagree on others. Have groups present their interviews to the class.

GOVERNMENT SIDES WITH BUSINESS

Have students construct a flowchart that illustrates the causes, events, government response, and effects of the Homestead and Pullman strikes. Call on a volunteer to draw his or her flowchart on the chalkboard and have class members modify and add to it as necessary. Students may wish to include their flowcharts in their portfolios.

VOICES IN HISTORY

Isaac Myers, the head of the first national African American workers' organization, the Colored National Labor Union, founded in 1869, believed that unionization was the only way to protect employment opportunities for blacks. Without strong unions, he said, African Americans would be forced out of the skilled trades and consigned to be "the sweepers of shavings, the scrapers of pitch and the carriers of mortar."

GLOBAL CONNECTIONS

The first eight-hour day agreements, signed in the 1850s, were won by unions representing skilled construction workers in the Australian cities of Melbourne and Sydney. A leader of the Melbourne eight-hour movement, Dr. Thomas Embling, coined the phrase "eight hours labor, eight hours recreation, eight hours rest," which, with various adjustments, became the rallying cry for American workers demanding a shorter working day.

Not all African American Knights, however, agreed with Ferrell's assessment. "The white Knights of Labor prevent me from getting employment because I am a colored man," complained a mason from North Carolina, "although I belong to the same organization." Still, the Knights did more than other early unions to try to meet the needs of African American workers.

The Knights were not equality-minded when it came to everyone, however. Although Powderly welcomed some European immigrants to the union, he, like many working-class Americans, actively opposed Chinese workers, claiming they stole jobs from white Americans. At his urging, for instance, West Coast branches of the Knights of Labor vigorously campaigned for passage of the Chinese Exclusion Act.

Powderly led the Knights of Labor for 15 years. Under his leadership, the union fought for temperance, the eight-hour workday, equal pay for equal work, and an end to child labor. By 1886, the union boasted a membership of more than 700,000.

THE GREAT UPHEAVAL

The Knights' phenomenal growth was due in part to the great railroad strike of 1877 and to a successful strike that the Knights had launched against railroad baron Jay Gould in 1884. Both strikes made workers more willing to press for the better working conditions being championed by the Knights. In 1886, as the nation entered a year of intense strikes and violent labor confrontations that would become known as the **Great Upheaval,** the Knights were riding the crest of immense popularity.

By 1886, American workers were primed for action. An economic depression in the early 1880s had led to massive wage cuts. Workers needed—and demanded—relief. When negotiations with management failed, many workers took direct action. By the end of 1886, some 1,500 strikes, involving more than 400,000 workers, had swept the nation. Many of these strikes turned violent, as angry strikers clashed head-on with their employers and the police. Perhaps the most notorious of these confrontations was the **Haymarket Riot**.

The seeds for the Haymarket Riot were sown when some 40,000 Chicago workers struck on May 1, 1886. The strike was launched by the local craft unions, but it soon fell under the leadership of a group of political radicals and **anarchists** (people who oppose all forms of government). On May 3 a confrontation between the police and the strikers picketing the McCormick harvester plant left two strikers dead. In protest, the strikers called a meeting for the next day in Chicago's Haymarket Square. Peaceful and sparsely attended, the rally was about to break up when nearly 200 police officers appeared. Suddenly a bomb exploded in the midst of the police. The police responded with gunfire. When the smoke cleared, more than 70 people lay wounded. The day's rioting also resulted in the deaths of seven police officers and one civilian.

The police arrested eight well-known anarchists—only one of whom had attended the meeting—charging them with incitement to murder. All eight

▼ Printed in both English and German, posters asked workingmen to "appear in full force" at Chicago's Haymarket Square on May 3, 1886, to protest the killing of two strikers. When an unknown person threw a bomb, violence quickly erupted.

Practice

GUIDED PRACTICE

Write the following headings on the chalkboard: *The New Working Class of the Late 1800s* and *Working Conditions in the Late 1800s*. Ask students to brainstorm information on these two topics. Enter their responses under the appropriate heading. Then ask students to use information on the chalkboard to make two generalizations, one on the new working class, the other on its working conditions.

INDEPENDENT PRACTICE

Have students use the information from the Guided Practice to write a pamphlet from Terence V. Powderly evaluating the conditions of the working class and encouraging workers to join the union. Students may wish to include their pamphlets in their portfolios.

Review and Assessment

REVIEW Divide the class into groups of three. Assign each group member one of the Focus questions to answer. Then have group members meet with others assigned the same question to come to a consensus on their answer. Have members reconvene in their original groups to share their answers. Then assign the Section 2 Review on p. 496.

ASSESS Assign the **Section 2 Daily Quiz** in *Core Resources*. ▶

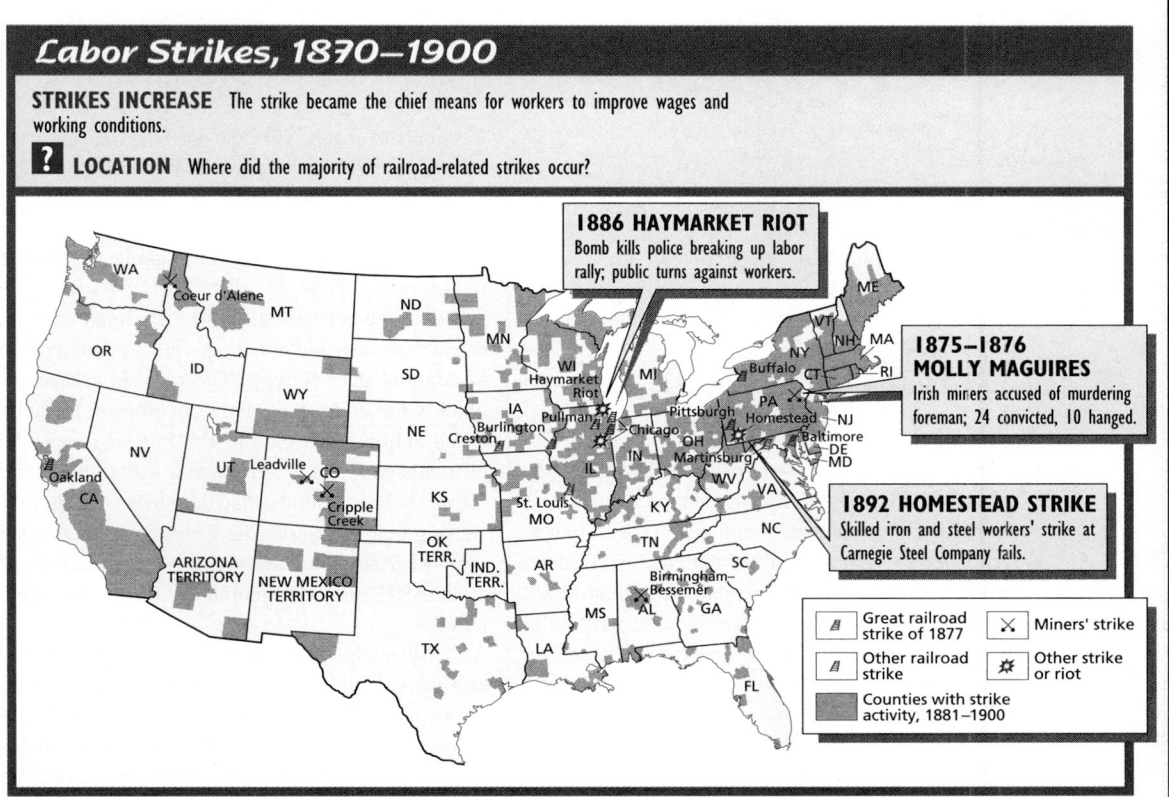

Labor Strikes, 1870–1900

STRIKES INCREASE The strike became the chief means for workers to improve wages and working conditions.

? **LOCATION** Where did the majority of railroad-related strikes occur?

1886 HAYMARKET RIOT
Bomb kills police breaking up labor rally; public turns against workers.

1875–1876 MOLLY MAGUIRES
Irish miners accused of murdering foreman; 24 convicted, 10 hanged.

1892 HOMESTEAD STRIKE
Skilled iron and steel workers' strike at Carnegie Steel Company fails.

Legend:
- Great railroad strike of 1877
- Other railroad strike
- Counties with strike activity, 1881–1900
- Miners' strike
- Other strike or riot

Map Caption Answer
the Midwest

HISTORICAL SIDELIGHTS

Baseball Players' Revolt The first major U.S. labor-management conflict that involved professional sports occurred during the baseball players' revolt of 1889–1890. In 1885 the players formed the Brotherhood of Professional Baseball Players—the first union of professional athletes—to negotiate contracts and salaries with club owners. In 1889, after making little headway in negotiations with team owners, the Brotherhood broke away and formed its own league. National League owners, however, put pressure on the new league's financial backers. The league and the Brotherhood quickly collapsed.

PRIMARY SOURCE

Description of Change: excerpted and bracketed
Rationale: excerpted to focus on main idea; bracketed to clarify meaning

BUILDING VOCABULARY

The use of *blacklists* dates to medieval times. Black books were used by early British universities to record cases of student misconduct. Merchants later used similar books to list the names of people who were poor credit risks.

were found guilty; four went to the gallows. On the final day of the trial, one of the defendants warned:

> ❝ I have told [Chicago Police] Captain Schaack, and I stand by it, "if you cannonade us, we shall dynamite you." You laugh! Perhaps you think, "you'll throw no more bombs"; but let me assure you I die happy on the gallows, so confident am I that the hundreds and thousands to whom I have spoken will remember my words; . . . they will do the bomb throwing! ❞

But worker activism actually decreased by the close of the year. Emboldened by the Haymarket conviction, employers struck back. They drew up **blacklists**—lists of union supporters—that they shared with one another. Blacklisted workers found it almost impossible to get jobs. Many employers also made job applicants sign agreements—called **yellow-dog contracts** by the workers—promising not to join unions. When these measures failed and workers struck anyway, many companies instituted **lockouts**, barring workers from the plant, and brought in nonunion **strikebreakers**, often African

Americans or others who felt abandoned by the unions. As labor suffered repeated defeats and as the tide of public sentiment turned against workers, union membership—including the Knights'—shrank.

Many of the workers who remained in unions were in skilled trades. Alarmed by the violence of 1886 and by the response of the employers, these workers broke ranks with the unskilled and joined the newly formed **American Federation of Labor** (AFL), founded by Samuel Gompers in 1886. The AFL was a collection of independent skilled craft unions committed to working together to advance the interests of skilled workers (see Chapter 17).

▦ Support for the labor movement was weakened by the violence of the 1886 strikes.

*T*HE HOMESTEAD AND PULLMAN STRIKES

After a few years of relative peace, industrial unrest broke out again in 1892. At Andrew

RETEACH Organize students into groups and assign each group a subsection of the section. Have each group develop several questions and answers about the main ideas in its assigned material. Then have each group quiz another group.

Closure

Ask volunteers to offer words and phrases describing the working conditions and concerns of the working class in the late 1800s. List responses on the chalkboard. Then have students evaluate if and how well the labor movement addressed these conditions and concerns.

Extension

ANALYZE Have students research and report on Allan Pinkerton and the role of his detectives in labor disputes.

CREATE Have students research and create a visual display including sketches and political cartoons of the labor strikes during this period.

PRIMARY SOURCE
Description of Change: excerpted
Rationale: excerpted to focus on main idea

IDENTIFY

For significance, see the following pages:
company town (p. 493)
scrip (p. 493)
Knights of Labor (p. 493)
Terence V. Powderly (p. 493)
Mary Harris Jones (p. 493)
Great Upheaval (p. 494)
Haymarket Riot (p. 494)
anarchists (p. 494)
blacklists (p. 495)
yellow-dog contracts (p. 495)
lockouts (p. 495)
strikebreakers (p. 495)
American Federation of Labor
* (p. 495)*

LOCATE

For locations, see the map on p. 495.

1. *long hours, unsafe conditions, low pay, few benefits*
2. *Strike-related violence weakened union support.*
3. *business—blacklists, yellow-dog contracts, lockouts, and strikebreakers; government—broke strikes with troops*
4. *might mention eight-hour workday, no wage cuts, better treatment; will raise morale, productivity*
5. *opened membership to unskilled and skilled workers, women, African Americans but excluded Chinese immigrants*

▲ **Pullman strikers in 1894 blocked trains, sabotaged railroad switches, and drove engineers from railway cars to protest wage cuts.**

Carnegie's Homestead steel plant in Pennsylvania, manager Henry Clay Frick announced a wage cut. In June the workers went on strike. Frick responded by instituting a lockout and hiring some 300 detectives to guard the plant. A violent clash between strikers and the detectives in early July resulted in 16 deaths. The violence soon spread to other plants. Order was restored only after state militiamen were called in.

Labor disputes sparked more violence in 1894. On May 11, 1894, workers at the Pullman sleeping-car factory in Chicago went on strike. The owner, George Pullman, had cut wages while refusing to lower rents or prices at the stores in his company town. Eugene V. Debs, head of the American Railway Union (ARU), backed the Pullman strikers. Urging other union members to boycott all trains that included Pullman cars, Debs proclaimed:

> ❝ The struggle . . . has developed into a contest between the producing classes and the money power of the country. We stand upon the ground that the workingmen are entitled to a just proportion of the proceeds of their labor. ❞

The railroad companies came to George Pullman's rescue by threatening to fire any worker who refused to handle Pullman cars. In response, railroad workers tied up rail traffic throughout the Midwest. The railroad companies quickly turned to the federal government for help. By attaching mail cars to the Pullman cars, the railroads gave the government a way to block the strike on the grounds that the strikers were preventing mail delivery. The government demanded that the ARU end the strike. When Debs and other ARU officials ignored the order, they were jailed.

Meanwhile, President Cleveland ordered federal troops into Chicago on July 4, sparking violence that left scores dead or wounded and produced hundreds of thousands of dollars in property damage. Within a few days, however, the troops had restored order. In the process, the Pullman strike had been broken and the ARU destroyed.

■■ During the 1890s the government sided with business against the labor unions.

SECTION 2 REVIEW

IDENTIFY and explain the significance of the following: company town, scrip, Knights of Labor, Terence V. Powderly, Mary Harris Jones, Great Upheaval, Haymarket Riot, anarchists, blacklists, yellow-dog contracts, lockouts, strikebreakers, American Federation of Labor.

LOCATE and explain the importance of the following: Haymarket Square, Homestead steel plant, Pullman sleeping-car factory.

1. **MAIN IDEA** Describe working life for most industrial laborers in late-19th-century America.

2. **MAIN IDEA** How did the strikes of 1886 weaken the labor movement?

3. **ASSESSING CONSEQUENCES** How did business and the government respond to labor activism in the late 1800s?

4. **WRITING TO EXPRESS A VIEWPOINT** Imagine you are a member of an industrial workers' union in the late 1800s. Write a proposal for changes in work rules and conditions to present to management. State why you think these changes should be made.

5. **EVALUATING** Why might it be said that the Knights of Labor's recruitment policies under Powderly seem contradictory?

496

Section 3

FARMERS, POPULISM, AND DEPRESSION

FOCUS
- **What problems did American farmers face during the late 1800s?**
- **What did the Grange and Alliance movements and the Populist party hope to achieve?**
- **Why did the Populists fail in the 1896 election?**

Farm family, 1881

America's farmers suffered many hardships during the late 1800s. Like industrial workers, farmers organized to win their share of prosperity. This drive to organize culminated in the founding of the People's, or Populist, party. A severe economic depression helped the Populists gain strength during the early 1890s. However, the party's later focus on a single issue—free silver—led to its downfall.

THE FARMERS' PLIGHT

The development of the new industrial order offered fresh opportunities for American farmers. The rapidly growing population in the industrial centers needed feeding. The farmers responded, each year raising more crops and animals. Unfortunately for the Americans, farmers in Great Britain, Russia, Canada, Argentina, Australia, and other nations did the same. Soon prices tumbled as supply exceeded demand. But railroad freight charges continued to spiral upward, as did the cost of new machinery. As farm profits plunged, many farmers bought more land and increased production. Greater production, however, only pushed prices even lower.

To make matters worse, almost all farm families had borrowed money to pay for their land or to buy new equipment, generally putting their farms up as security. Those who could not repay the loans lost their farms. Many ended up as tenant farmers, paying rent to the new owners. Others were forced to become farm laborers.

■■ In the late 1800s, farmers were burdened with crushing debt as the prices of farm products fell and costs increased.

To farmers, the situation seemed terribly unfair. The merchants who sold farm equipment and other supplies were making money. Also prospering were the bankers who lent farmers money and the railroads that hauled the farmers' grain and livestock to market. All that the farmers had to show for long days of backbreaking labor were rising debts. Something had to be done.

THE GRANGE MOVEMENT

In an effort to better their lot, farmers organized. The first major farmers' organization, the Patrons of Husbandry, or the **National Grange**, was founded by Oliver Hudson Kelley in 1867. Kelley set up the Grange primarily as a social organization. But as membership increased and farmers'

MOTIVATING:
PRIOR KNOWLEDGE

Call on a volunteer to review the methods industrial laborers in the late 19th century used to protest their working conditions and low wages, and list them on the chalkboard. Then tell students this section deals with methods American farmers used in the late 1800s in attempting to gain a share of the country's prosperity. Have students compare laborers' and farmers' approaches as they study the section.

𝒯eaching the 𝒮ection

FARMERS' PLIGHT

Tell students to imagine that they have been selected to speak before a Senate committee on the plight of debt-ridden farmers in the Midwest. Have students prepare a compelling description of the problems farmers face. Have volunteers read their statements to the class. Encourage students to respond to the statements in the role of senators from eastern, southern, and Great Plains states.

🌐 GLOBAL CONNECTIONS

Cooperative retailing was established by the Rochdale Society of Equitable Pioneers, which opened a store in Rochdale, England, in 1844. The store provided quality goods at reasonable prices for members, and profits were shared among members in proportion to the value of purchases they made. Membership in the society was open to all, regardless of race, sex, religion, or political affiliation. And each member had one vote in decision making. In the mid-1870s the National Grange attempted to organize its cooperatives according to the Rochdale system.

Map Caption Answer
hay and dairy, grapes, potatoes, wheat, oats, tomatoes

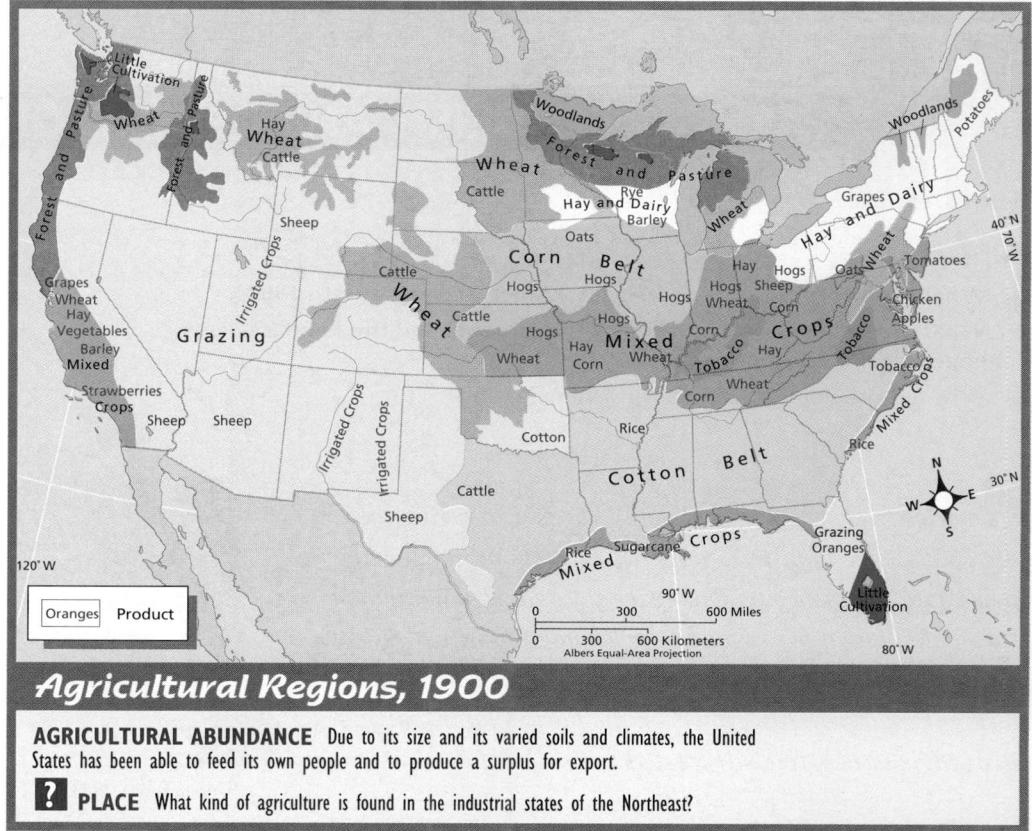

Agricultural Regions, 1900

AGRICULTURAL ABUNDANCE Due to its size and its varied soils and climates, the United States has been able to feed its own people and to produce a surplus for export.

❓ PLACE What kind of agriculture is found in the industrial states of the Northeast?

financial problems grew, the Grange began tackling economic and political issues.

To lower costs, some Grange members formed **cooperatives**. Cooperative members sold their products directly to big-city markets and bought farm equipment and other goods in large quantities at wholesale prices—thereby cutting costs. But the Grange's main focus was on forcing states to regulate railroad freight rates. In the early 1870s, responding to pressure from farmers, the state legislatures of Illinois, Iowa, Minnesota, and Wisconsin passed "Granger laws," which set up state commissions to fix maximum railroad rates.

Many railroads challenged the Granger laws in the courts. In a victory for farmers, the United States Supreme Court in *Munn* v. *Illinois* (1877) declared that state legislatures had the right to regulate businesses—like railroads—that involved the public interest. But 10 years later the Court, in *Wabash* v. *Illinois,* qualified its decision. State governments, the Court ruled, had no power to regulate traffic that moved across state boundaries. Only the federal government had that right.

This decision led directly to the passage of the **Interstate Commerce Act** in 1887. The act prohibited railroads from giving secret rebates, or refunds, to large shippers or from charging more for short hauls than for long hauls over the same line. It also stated that railroad rates had to be "reasonable and just." To monitor railroad activities, the act created the **Interstate Commerce Commission** (ICC). But the ICC had little power to enforce its rulings. When it took railroads to court for violating the law, the courts almost always ruled in the railroads' favor.

𝒯HE ALLIANCE MOVEMENT

While the Grange was struggling to win the fight for railroad legislation, a more powerful farm organization—the **Farmers' Alliance**—arose. Beginning in Texas in 1877, the Alliance movement quickly spread. Debt-ridden farm families grasped the Alliance message of solidarity and hope like a drowning person clinging to a log. By

Have students imagine they are reporters: some are attending an Alliance rally, some a Grange rally, and others a Populist party rally. Have them write newspaper articles detailing the goals of the movement, the methods proposed to achieve these goals, and any special activities taking place at the rally. Have volunteers from each group present their articles to the class. Then, on the basis of the articles, have students compare and contrast the Grange, Alliance, and Populist movements. Students may wish to include their newspaper articles in their portfolios.

POPULIST PARTY PLATFORM

Call on volunteers to list the planks of the Populist party platform. Then divide the class, calling on one half to defend the platform, the other to argue against it. Conclude the debate by discussing why the Populist party did not succeed in the election of 1896.

▶

▲ **African American farmers joined the Colored Farmers' Alliance to protect their interests against monopolies and unfair freight prices. Shown here are Virginia homesteaders during the 1890s.**

1890 the movement claimed some 400,000 members in three organizations: the National Farmers' Alliance of the Northwest, the all-white Southern Alliance, and the Colored Farmers' Alliance.

Alliance leaders traveled the country, urging people to take action. Among the most effective was Mary Elizabeth Lease from Kansas. "The great common people of this country are slaves, and monopoly is the master," she told her audiences:

66 The politicians said we suffered from overproduction. Overproduction, when 10,000 little children, so statistics tell us, starve to death every year in the United States. . . . We will stand by our homes and stay by our fireside by force if necessary, and we will not pay our debts to the loan-shark companies until the government pays its debts to us. 99

Like the Grange, the Alliance organized cooperatives to buy equipment and to market farm products. It also offered farmers low-cost insurance and lobbied for tougher bank regulations, government ownership of the railroads, and a **graduated income tax** that taxed higher incomes at a higher rate.

■■ **The Grange and Farmers' Alliance movements sought economic and political gains for farmers.**

THE MONEY QUESTION

The Alliance also echoed the demand that farmers had been making since the end of the Civil War: expand the money supply by printing more greenbacks, the paper money used during the war. The resulting inflation would benefit farmers by allowing them to charge more for their farm products and by making it easier for them to repay their bank loans.

Such prospects alarmed eastern bankers. They wanted the money supply tied to the **gold standard**. Under this system, each dollar was equal to and redeemable for a set amount of gold, and the amount of money in circulation was limited by the amount of gold held in the U.S. Treasury.

Siding with the bankers, the government began withdrawing greenbacks from circulation. Farmers responded by demanding that the government back the money supply with silver (which was plentiful in the West) as well as with gold. Bowing to pressure, Congress passed the **Bland-Allison Act** in 1878 and the **Sherman Silver Purchase Act** in 1890. Both acts required the government to buy silver each month and mint it into coins. But because the government bought so little silver, the money supply did not increase noticeably.

Disappointed, Alliance members threw themselves into the 1890 elections, supporting any candidate who accepted their pro-farmer programs. The results were remarkable. Alliance-backed candidates won 38 U.S. congressional seats, 4 southern governorships, and numerous other political offices.

THE POPULIST PARTY

Elated, Alliance leaders sought to build on these successes by forming a new political party. At a national convention in St. Louis in February 1892, a gathering of farmers, labor leaders, and reformers founded the People's party, which became more commonly known as the **Populist party**. Politician and author Ignatius Donnelly of Minnesota opened the convention with a thunderous address:

66 We meet in the midst of a nation brought to the verge of moral, political, and material ruin. Corruption dominates the ballot-box, the Legislatures, the Congress. . . . We seek to restore the government of the Republic to the hands of the "plain people." 99

CULTURAL PATTERNS

Although northern Grangers tried to convince their southern counterparts of the value of organizing African American farmers, the Patrons of Husbandry refused to admit black members. When confronted by similar discrimination in the Alliance movement, African Americans organized their own farm groups, such as the Colored Farmers' Alliance and the National Colored Alliance. However, rivalry between these groups weakened them. So did opposition from the Southern Alliance and other whites, who opposed any effort to unite southern blacks. In the 1890s these factors led to the collapse of some African American farm organizations and to the absorption of others into white organizations.

PRIMARY SOURCES

Description of Change: excerpted
Rationale: excerpted to focus on main idea

Practice

GUIDED PRACTICE

Create a three-column chart on the chalkboard to compare the goals, methods, and results of the Grange and Alliance movements and the Populist party. Call on volunteers to fill in the chart.

HISTORICAL SIDELIGHTS

World's Columbian Exposition

As the depression loomed over the nation, Chicago was host to the World's Columbian Exposition, designed to pay tribute to American enterprise. The exposition's buildings and exhibits highlighted American technical and cultural achievements. It included a Women's Building that housed displays illustrating the accomplishments of America's "new woman." Responding to the charge that the exposition's managers had ignored African Americans' contributions to the nation, a special day was set aside at which Frederick Douglass was the principal speaker.

COOPERATIVE LEARNING

Organize students into six groups and assign to each group one of the following topics: Government Corruption, Political Reform, Labor Organizes, The Great Upheaval, Farmers Organize, The Election of 1896. Have groups work as editorial boards to develop the front page of a special-edition newspaper on their assigned subject. Display completed front pages on the bulletin board.

INDEPENDENT PRACTICE

Have students write letters, as farmers in the late 1800s, to an industrial worker. Letters should stress problems that farmers and workers share, list the goals of the Grange or Alliance movements or the Populist party, and explain how industrial workers can benefit by supporting these goals. Students may wish to include their letters in their portfolios.

PRESIDENTIAL LIVES

WILLIAM McKINLEY
1843–1901

in office 1897–1901

William McKinley used presidential power so effectively that a Republican newspaper concluded: "No executive in the history of the country . . . has given a greater exhibition of his influence over Congress." Even his political enemies respected his tact and persuasiveness. Speaker of the House Tom Reed said of him, with envy, "My opponents in Congress go at me tooth and nail, but they always apologize to William when they are going to call him names."

A courteous manner characterized McKinley in private life as well. He was devoted to protecting and caring for his wife Ida, who suffered headaches and seizures that often kept her from fulfilling her role as First Lady. He stayed close to her during state dinners and receptions. If she fainted, he would tend to her and yet carry right on with conversation so as not to embarrass her.

William McKinley

The party platform echoed Grange and Alliance demands: a graduated income tax, bank regulation, government ownership of railroad and telegraph companies, and the free coinage of silver. Appealing to the labor and reform votes, the platform also called for immigration restrictions, a shorter workday, and voting reforms.

■■ **The Populist party platform addressed many of the concerns of farmers, laborers, and political reformers.**

Review and Assessment

REVIEW Have students create fliers or handbills for the Alliance, Grange, or Populist movement that list farmers' problems in the late 1800s and spell out the goals and methods of the movement. Select students to explain their fliers or handbills to the class. Then assign the Section 3 Review on p. 501.

ASSESS Assign the **Section 3 Daily Quiz** in *Core Resources.*

The Populists nominated James B. Weaver to run in the 1892 presidential election against Republican Benjamin Harrison, the incumbent, and Democrat Grover Cleveland, the former president who had lost to Harrison in the 1888 election. Weaver had run for president—and lost—on the Greenback party ticket in 1880. Cleveland won the 1892 election. But the Populist party elected 3 senators, 11 congressmen, 3 governors, and numerous state legislators. And Weaver polled a very respectable one million popular votes, carrying four western states and 22 electoral votes.

DEPRESSION, DISCONTENT, AND GOLD

In May 1893, only two months after Cleveland took office, one of the country's leading railroad companies failed. The failure triggered a financial panic on Wall Street that sent stock prices plunging. The country quickly slid into an economic depression. By the end of 1893, some three million people were unemployed—100,000 in Chicago alone. In New York City 20,000 homeless people sought shelter in jails. Strikes and protests swept the country.

The depression had many causes, including a worldwide financial panic. But President Cleveland chose to focus on one—the Sherman Silver Purchase Act, which required the government to pay for silver purchases with Treasury notes redeemable in either gold or silver. As new silver finds decreased the value of the metal, people rushed to exchange their notes for gold. This action put a terrible strain on the Treasury's gold reserves. To protect the gold standard and to restore confidence in the economy, Cleveland called for repeal of the Sherman Silver Purchase Act. Congress complied in October 1893.

THE ELECTION OF 1896

Cleveland's actions salvaged the gold standard, but they did not end the debate on the money supply. Silver became a central issue in the 1896 election.

The Republicans gave the presidential nomination to Ohio governor William McKinley and adopted a conservative platform upholding the gold standard. A deeply split Democratic party

500

RETEACH Organize students into four groups and assign each group one of the section's Essential Points. Have groups outline the material that their Essential Point covers. Then have a spokesperson from each group present his or her group's outline to the other groups.

Closure

Retrieve the list from the Link to the Past activity that opened the chapter. Ask students how well the principles of Jacksonian democracy had been fulfilled by the late 1800s. Encourage them to cite evidence to support their opinions. Ask students whether they would have been optimistic or pessimistic after the election of 1896 about achieving the promise of Jacksonian democracy for America.

Extension

CREATE Have students create campaign posters for a Populist party candidate at the state or national level in the 1892 election. Display posters in the classroom.

RESEARCH Have students research the life of Mary Elizabeth Lease and prepare an oral report on their findings.

▶ **While Bryan traveled 13,000 miles and gave 600 speeches during the 1896 campaign, McKinley stayed home and received visitors on the front porch of his Ohio home. Ribbons from McKinley's campaign are shown here.**

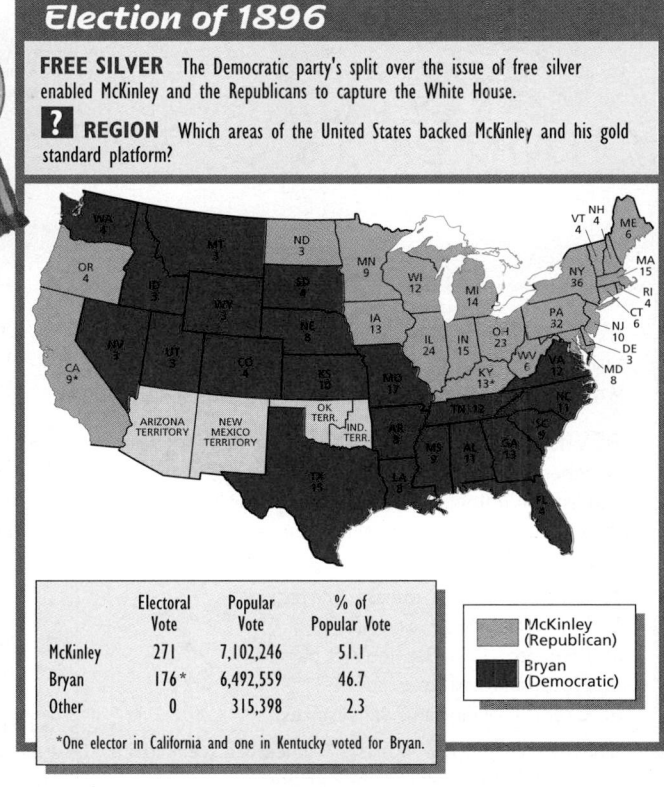

Election of 1896

FREE SILVER The Democratic party's split over the issue of free silver enabled McKinley and the Republicans to capture the White House.

? **REGION** Which areas of the United States backed McKinley and his gold standard platform?

	Electoral Vote	Popular Vote	% of Popular Vote
McKinley	271	7,102,246	51.1
Bryan	176*	6,492,559	46.7
Other	0	315,398	2.3

*One elector in California and one in Kentucky voted for Bryan.

■ McKinley (Republican)
■ Bryan (Democratic)

rejected President Cleveland, finally nominating free-silver advocate William Jennings Bryan, a two-term congressman from Nebraska. The Populists—their free-silver platform taken up by the Democratic party—threw their support to Bryan.

Bryan swept the South and much of the West, but he made no headway at all in the urban industrial East or in the mixed industrial and farm states of the Midwest. When the popular votes were counted, McKinley had edged out Bryan by some 500,000 votes. The Populists were in shock—free silver had proved too weak an issue for a national campaign, and urban workers and immigrants had found little that had appealed to them in the Populists' agenda.

The election defeat and the arrival of better times for farmers essentially ended the power of the Populist party. It nevertheless stands as the first example of a large-scale effort by a disadvantaged group in the modern industrial era to use the political process to advance its interests. Furthermore, the

Populist platform laid the groundwork for future reform (see Chapter 17). As Populist leader Mary Elizabeth Lease noted in 1914, "The seeds we sowed out in Kansas did not fall on barren ground."

■ **New prosperity among farmers and the decline of the free-silver issue led to the collapse of the Populist party.**

Map Caption Answer
the industrial East, California and Oregon, the agricultural Midwest

SECTION REVIEW ANSWERS

IDENTIFY

For significance, see the following pages:
cooperatives (p. 498)
Interstate Commerce Act (p. 498)
Interstate Commerce Commission (p. 498)
Mary Elizabeth Lease (p. 499)
graduated income tax (p. 499)
gold standard (p. 499)
Bland-Allison Act (p. 499)
Sherman Silver Purchase Act (p. 499)
Populist party (p. 499)
James B. Weaver (p. 500)
William McKinley (p. 500)
William Jennings Bryan (p. 501)

1. foreign competition, falling prices, rising costs, heavy debt, loss of farms
2. organize farmers to increase economic and political power, railroad and business regulation; voiced concerns of farmers, laborers, government reformers
3. South and West; East and Midwest
4. needed unity for economic, political gains; groundwork for future reform
5. Farmers hoped inflation would make it easier to pay debts; inflation would cheapen money and shrink bank profits.

■ ■ SECTION 3 REVIEW

IDENTIFY and explain the significance of the following: cooperatives, Interstate Commerce Act, Interstate Commerce Commission, Mary Elizabeth Lease, graduated income tax, gold standard, Bland-Allison Act, Sherman Silver Purchase Act, Populist party, James B. Weaver, William McKinley, William Jennings Bryan.

1. **MAIN IDEA** What serious problems did American farmers face in the late 19th century?

2. **MAIN IDEA** What were the main goals of the Grange and Farmers' Alliance movements? What did the Populist party try to accomplish through its political platform?

3. **GEOGRAPHY: REGION** What regions of the nation did William Jennings Bryan win in the 1896 election? In what areas did he poll the fewest votes?

4. **WRITING TO EXPLAIN** Imagine you are Mary Elizabeth Lease in 1914. Write an essay explaining why the Alliance movement was necessary and describe the legacy of the Populist party.

5. **ANALYZING** Why did expansion of the money supply appeal to farmers but not to eastern bankers?

Return to the Themes section on p. 484. Have students discuss these again and compare their original responses with those given now. (See p. 483B for suggested answers.)

Chapter Review Answers

WRITING A SUMMARY
See Essential Points in each section for main ideas.

REVIEWING CHRONOLOGY
2, 5, 3, 1, 4
Synthesizing
because it involved wage dispute, management refused to recognize union, and it ended in violent confrontation

IDENTIFYING PEOPLE AND IDEAS

1. *name of late-19th-century novel that was used to label the era*
2. *cronies of Boss Tweed who ran New York's Tammany Hall*
3. *disgruntled government job seeker who killed President Garfield*
4. *Democratic president known for his reform efforts and honesty*
5. *"Mother Jones," strong labor activist from 1870s to 1930*
6. *leader of Knights of Labor who greatly expanded union membership*
7. *company practice barring workers from plant where they were employed*
8. *organizations formed by farmers to directly market their products and cut costs by volume purchases of equipment and other goods*

9. *effective Alliance and Populist party leader*
10. *system in which each dollar was equal to a set amount of gold and the money supply was limited by the amount of gold in the U.S. Treasury*

UNDERSTANDING MAIN IDEAS

1. *Workers faced dangerous working conditions, low pay, and long hours. Farmers had huge debts from falling farm prices and rising costs.*
2. *believed that the spoils system led to political corruption*

3. *Government backed business. For example, Cleveland sent troops to stop 1894 Pullman strike.*
4. *addressed concerns such as graduated income tax, expansion of money supply, immigration restriction, and a shorter workday*
5. *the return of prosperity and decline of the free-silver issue*

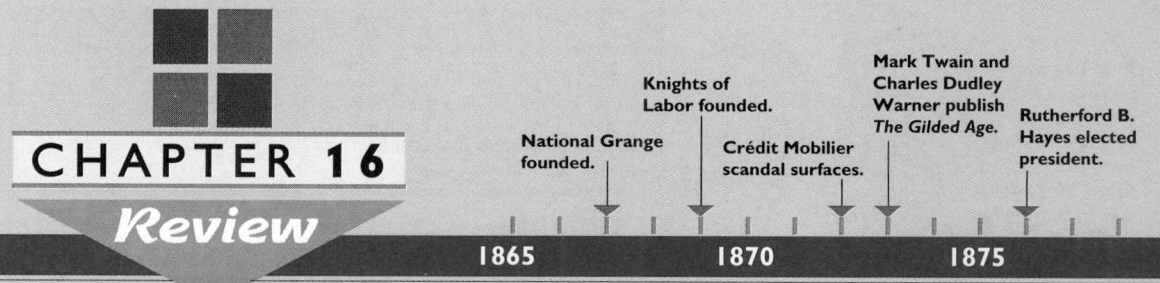

CHAPTER 16
Review

National Grange founded.
Knights of Labor founded.
Crédit Mobilier scandal surfaces.
Mark Twain and Charles Dudley Warner publish *The Gilded Age*.
Rutherford B. Hayes elected president.

1865 — 1870 — 1875

WRITING A SUMMARY
Using the essential points of the chapter as a guide, write a summary of the chapter.

REVIEWING CHRONOLOGY
Number your paper 1 to 5. Study the time line above, and list the following events in the order in which they happened by writing the first next to 1, the second next to 2, and so on. Then complete the activity.

1. Sherman Silver Purchase Act passed.
2. National Grange founded.
3. Pendleton Civil Service Act passed.
4. Homestead strike occurs.
5. Crédit Mobilier scandal surfaces.

Synthesizing How was the Homestead steel strike typical of many strikes of the period?

IDENTIFYING PEOPLE AND IDEAS
Explain the historical significance of each of the following people or terms.

1. Gilded Age
2. Tweed Ring
3. Charles Guiteau
4. Grover Cleveland
5. Mary Harris Jones
6. Terence V. Powderly
7. lockouts
8. cooperatives
9. Mary Elizabeth Lease
10. gold standard

UNDERSTANDING MAIN IDEAS
1. What problems did American industrial workers and farmers face in the late 1800s?
2. Why did some Americans support civil service reform?
3. What position did the government take in the labor disputes of the late 1800s?
4. How did the Populist party represent the interests of farmers, laborers, and political reformers?
5. What caused the Populist party to lose the 1896 election?

📋 REVIEWING THEMES
1. **Democratic Values** What steps did reformers take to bring about political and economic change in American society in the late 1800s?

2. **Cultural Diversity** How were different groups of people united by changing economic and political conditions? How were they divided?

THINKING CRITICALLY
1. **Hypothesizing** How might workers have gained more ground if the strikes of 1886 had not become so violent?
2. **Analyzing** Why did the Interstate Commerce Act and the Sherman Silver Purchase Act represent only partial victories for reformers?
3. **Evaluating** How did the focus of reform efforts change from the 1870s to the 1890s?

STRATEGY FOR SUCCESS
Review the Skills Handbook entry on Reading Charts and Graphs beginning on page 996. Then study the graph below. What might account for the dramatic change in Knights' membership before and after 1886?

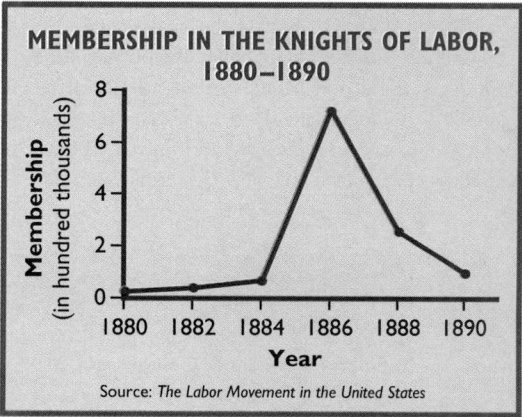

MEMBERSHIP IN THE KNIGHTS OF LABOR, 1880–1890

Membership (in hundred thousands)

1880 1882 1884 1886 1888 1890
Year

Source: *The Labor Movement in the United States*

WRITING ABOUT HISTORY
Writing to Explain Imagine you are Mary Harris Jones and have been invited to be the guest speaker at a rally for the Alliance movement. Write a speech explaining how the Alliance can use the techniques of unions such as the Knights of Labor.

REVIEWING THEMES

1. organized into farm groups, labor unions, and political parties; pushed for legislation; supported reform candidates for office
2. Farmers united into the Grange and Alliance movements; unions formed that included a variety of people; the Populist party tried to unite farmers, laborers, and reformers. But hard times also caused workers to go on strike and to oppose new immigrants; farmers battled merchants, bankers, and railroads.

THINKING CRITICALLY

1. The public might have been more sympathetic to workers' plight, employers less hostile to worker demands, and government less inclined to keep peace by using force.
2. ICC created but had little power to regulate railroads. Although Sherman Silver Purchase Act required government silver purchases, little silver was bought.
3. Reform efforts of the 1870s focused on political reform—ending corruption and graft; by the 1890s the focus shifted to economic reform to help farmers and laborers.

STRATEGY FOR SUCCESS

The recruitment practices of Powderly and the strike against Jay Gould increased membership up to 1886, then the violence of the Great Upheaval caused it to drop.

WRITING ABOUT HISTORY

Speeches might mention that Alliance can help farmers by providing means to pay debts and offering lobbying power; should try to unite all farmers across racial and regional lines.

USING PRIMARY SOURCES

Students should note the agricultural problems described in the passage, but that even when these problems were not present, the overwhelming problem of mortgage debt was always there.

LINKING HISTORY AND GEOGRAPHY

Most strikes occurred in the Midwest, because it was the hub of heavy industry and railroad activity.

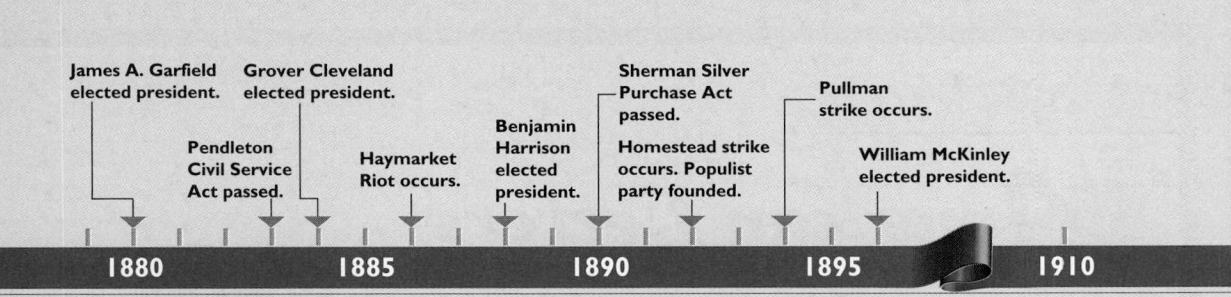

James A. Garfield elected president.

Grover Cleveland elected president.

Pendleton Civil Service Act passed.

Haymarket Riot occurs.

Benjamin Harrison elected president.

Sherman Silver Purchase Act passed.

Homestead strike occurs. Populist party founded.

Pullman strike occurs.

William McKinley elected president.

1880   1885   1890   1895   1910

USING PRIMARY SOURCES

In the late 19th century, farmers faced a variety of problems, from unpredictable weather and pests to railroad price-fixing. Read the poem below, written by a Georgia farmer in 1890. Then explain how it reflects the problems that led to the formation of farmers' groups. What was the most severe problem?

> "We worked through spring and summer,
>   through winter and through fall;
> But the mortgage worked the hardest
>   and the steadiest of them all;
> It worked on night and Sunday, it
>   worked each holiday;
> It settled down among us and it never
>   went away.
>
> Whatever we kept from it seemed
>   almost as bad as theft;
> It watched us every minute and ruled
>   us right and left
> The rust and blight was with us
>   sometimes, and sometimes not;
> The dark brown scowling mortgage was
>   forever on the spot.
>
> The weevil and the cut worm, they
>   went as well they came;
> The mortgage stayed forever, eating
>   hearty all the same
> It nailed up every window, stood
>   guard at every door;
> And happiness and sunshine made their
>   place with us no more. "

LINKING HISTORY AND GEOGRAPHY

Review the map on page 495. In which region did most labor strikes take place? Why do you think this was so?

BUILDING YOUR PORTFOLIO

Complete the following projects independently or cooperatively.

1. **SOCIAL CONFLICT** In chapters 14 and 15 you explored social conflicts arising from westward expansion and immigration. Building on that experience, imagine you are an African American from the rural South seeking a job in a northern industrial city. Write a short play that describes the competition for urban jobs and the problems you are facing in securing employment.

2. **TECHNOLOGY AND INDUSTRY** In chapters 14 and 15 you were a land speculator planning a railhead in Nebraska. Building on that experience, imagine that your town is a reality and has become a thriving railroad hub linking cattle ranchers, farmers, and area manufacturers and merchants to eastern markets. Local members of the Grange are up in arms over the cost of shipping their products by rail. Prepare a speech to deliver to the state legislature supporting passage of a series of Granger laws.

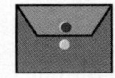

3. **REFORM** In Chapter 15 you portrayed a settlement-house worker. Building on that experience, imagine you are a labor leader organizing a union in the late 1800s. Create a poster designed to persuade women, African Americans, and recent immigrants to join the union.

BUILDING YOUR PORTFOLIO

Have students refer to **Building Your Portfolio Worksheet 5**, assigned at the beginning of Unit 5. Use the worksheet to help students monitor their progress on the portfolio projects.

Assessment

Core Resources
- Review Worksheet 16
- Chapter 16 Tests
- Alternative Assessment Forms

Test Generator

MARK TWAIN'S AMERICA

SETTING THE SCENE

First published in serial form in *The Atlantic Monthly* during 1875, *Life on the Mississippi* (1883) recounts Twain's apprenticeship as a riverboat pilot. Twain tells how in many journeys up and down the Mississippi he gains the intimate knowledge of the river that a pilot needs. The story concludes with a triumph, but also with a tragedy. Twain achieves his boyhood dream of becoming a pilot, but the Civil War ends the pilot's way of life on the river.

In *The Gilded Age* (1873), Twain and Warner skillfully skewer political corruption and introduce one of the great characters in American humor: Colonel Beriah Sellers. Part confidence artist and part dreamer, Sellers constantly schemes to make a fortune. His schemes are as questionable as the actions of a crooked politician, but they are so vast, wild, and imaginative that everyone is taken in. By portraying Sellers in such a loving fashion, Twain recognizes the role that such speculators played in building the United States.

UNIT 5

American Letters

Mark Twain's America

Samuel Langhorne Clemens—Mark Twain to generations of readers—remains one of America's greatest humorists and chroniclers of the American character. In the following two selections, Twain explores life in two very different settings—the Mississippi River and Washington, D.C.

▲ **Mark Twain**

From *Life on the Mississippi*

by Mark Twain

The river's earliest commerce was in great barges—keelboats, broadhorns. They floated and sailed from the upper rivers to New Orleans, changed cargoes there, and were tediously warped and poled back by hand. A voyage down and back sometimes occupied nine months. In time this commerce increased until it gave employment to hordes of rough and hardy men; rude, uneducated, brave, suffering terrific hardships with sailor-like stoicism; heavy drinkers, coarse frolickers in moral sties like the Natchez-under-the-hill of that day, heavy fighters, reckless fellows, every one, elephantinely jolly, foul-witted, profane, prodigal of their money, bankrupt at the end of the trip, fond of barbaric finery, prodigious braggarts; yet, in the main, honest, trustworthy, faithful to promises and duty, and often picturesquely magnanimous.

By and by the steamboat intruded. Then, for fifteen or twenty years, these men continued to run their keelboats downstream, and the steamers did all of the upstream business, the keelboatmen selling their boats in New Orleans, and returning home as deck-passengers in the steamers.

But after a while the steamboats so increased in number and in speed that they were able to absorb the entire commerce; and then keelboating died a permanent death. The keelboatman became a deckhand, or a mate, or a pilot on the steamer; and when steamer-berths were not open to him, he took a berth on a Pittsburgh coal-flat, or on a pine raft constructed in the forests up toward the sources of the Mississippi.

In the heyday of the steamboating prosperity, the river from end to end was flanked with coal-fleets and timber-rafts, all managed by hand, and employing hosts of the rough characters whom I have been trying to describe. . . .

By way of illustrating the keelboat talk and manners, and that now departed and hardly remembered raft life, I will throw in, in this place, a chapter from a book which I have been working at. . . . The book is a story which details some passages in the life of an ignorant village boy, Huck Finn, son of the town drunkard. . . . He has run away from his persecuting father, and from a persecuting good widow who wishes to make

▼ *Mississippi riverboat*

a nice, truth telling respectable boy of him; and with him a slave of the widow's has also escaped. They have found a fragment of a lumber-raft (it is high water and dead summer-time), and are floating down river by night, and hiding in the willows by day— bound for Cairo, [Illinois,] whence the Negro will seek freedom in the heart of the free states. But, in the fog, they have passed Cairo without knowing it. By and by they begin to suspect the truth, and Huck Finn is persuaded to end the dismal suspense by swimming down to a huge raft which they have seen in the distance ahead of them, creeping aboard under cover of the darkness, and gathering the needed information by eavesdropping: . . .

I swum down along the raft till I was most abreast the campfire in the middle, then I crawled aboard and inched along and got in among some shingles on the weather side of the fire. There was thirteen men there—they was the watch on deck of course. And a mighty rough-looking lot, too. . . .

The man they called Ed said the muddy Mississippi water was wholesomer to drink than the clear water of the Ohio; he said that if you let a pint of this yaller Mississippi water settle, you would have about a half to three-quarters of an inch of mud in the bottom, according to the stage of the river, and then it warn't no better than Ohio water—what you wanted to do was to keep it stirred up—and when the water was low, keep mud on hand to put in and thicken the water up the way it ought to be.

The Child of Calamity said that was so; he said there was nutritiousness in the mud, and a man that drunk Mississippi water could grow corn in his stomach if he wanted to. He says:

"You look at the graveyards; that tells the tale. Trees won't grow worth shucks in a Cincinnati graveyard, but in a Sent Louis graveyard they grow upwards of eight hundred foot high. It's all on account of the water the people drunk before they laid up. A Cincinnati corpse don't richen a soil any." ❖

From *The Gilded Age*

by Mark Twain and Charles Dudley Warner

Every individual you encounter in the City of Washington almost—and certainly every separate and distinct individual in the public employment, from the highest bureau chief, clear down to the maid who scrubs the Department halls . . . —represents Political Influence. Unless you can get the ear of a Senator, or a Congressman, or a Chief of a Bureau or Department, and persuade him to use his "influence" in your behalf, you cannot get an employment of the most trivial nature in Washington. Mere merit, fitness and capability, are useless baggage to you without "influence." The population of Washington consists pretty much entirely of government employés and the people who board them.

There are thousands of these employés, and they have gathered there from every corner of the Union and got their berths through the intercession (command is nearer the word) of the Senators and Representatives of their respective States. It would be an odd circumstance to see a girl get employment at three or four dollars a week . . . without any political grandee to back her, but merely because she was worthy, and competent, and a good citizen of a free country that "treats all persons alike." Washington would be mildly thunderstruck at such a thing as that. If you are a member of Congress, (no offence,) and one of your constituents who doesn't know anything, and does not want to go into the bother of learning something, and has no money, and no employment, and can't earn a living, comes besieging you for help, do you say, "Come, my friend, if your services were valuable you could get employment elsewhere—don't want you here?" Oh, no. You take him to a Department and say, "Here, give this person something to pass away the time at—and a salary"— and the thing is done. You throw him on his country. He is his country's child, let his country support him. There is something good and motherly about Washington, the grand old benevolent National Asylum for the Helpless. ❖

THINKING AND WRITING ABOUT LITERATURE

1. Toward which group does Mark Twain seem most sympathetic—the Mississippi boatmen or the public servants in Washington? Provide evidence to support your answer.
2. Twain and Charles Dudley Warner published *The Gilded Age* in 1873. What events in Washington might have influenced the tone of the book?

PRIMARY SOURCES
Description of Change: excerpted and bracketed **Rationale:** excerpted for space considerations; bracketed to clarify meaning

THINKING AND WRITING ABOUT LITERATURE

1. *the Mississippi boatmen; Twain describes the boatmen as rude and uneducated but honest, trustworthy, and hardworking; the public servants in Washington, according to Twain, get paid for doing nothing*
2. *scandals in President Ulysses S. Grant's first administration (see pp. 485–88), including the Crédit Mobilier scandal, which surfaced in 1872*

INTERPRETING ECONOMIC DATA

Guide students through the discussion of how to interpret economic data and then have them complete the Practicing the Strategy exercise. Point out that *Historical Statistics of the United States,* the yearly editions of *Statistical Abstract of the United States,* and other reports contain economic data useful for interpreting historical trends. Have students analyze a table in one of these books or from another source and create a chart or graph to express a historical trend. Then have students restate in a written summary the economic information contained in their charts or graphs.

PRACTICING THE STRATEGY

1. *amount of raw steel produced, in millions of short tons, for the years 1870, 1880, 1890, and 1900*
2. *a substantial increase in each decade—more than double the total of the previous one*
3. *that the last decades of the 19th century witnessed a boom in steel production in the U.S.*

Strategies for Success

INTERPRETING ECONOMIC DATA

The ability to interpret economic data broadens your understanding of historical developments, such as the impact of new technologies. A great deal of information about the economy—production, prices, income, and so on—can be found in statistical charts and graphs. But data, to be useful, must be analyzed and interpreted. The data in a given chart or graph is like a snapshot that shows one specific angle on the economy or segment of the economy. When interpreting economic statistics, take into consideration what you know about the overall economy or that segment of the economy for the period under study.

How to Interpret Economic Data

1. **Read the chart or graph.** Identify the type of data included in the chart or graph and the categories, amounts, and time intervals in which the data are presented. Determine the purpose of the chart or graph. Review, if necessary, Reading Charts and Graphs beginning on page 996.
2. **Find significant trends.** Study the actual numbers or values, noting increases and decreases and looking for significant trends.
3. **Use the information.** Ask yourself: What do these statistics tell me? Compare and contrast the data in an effort to understand the trends and changes. Then draw conclusions and form hypotheses based on your analysis.

Applying the Strategy

Advances in the communications industry helped transform the U.S. economy in the late 19th century. As the chart on this page indicates, telegraph and telephone networks—measured in miles of telegraph wire laid and in number of telephones in use—saw dramatic expansion in the last 25 years of the century. Both means of communication depended heavily on the use of copper for wire. The graph shows that copper mining underwent a similar dramatic expansion during the last 30 years of the 19th century.

The fact that communications and copper mining both experienced rapid expansion during the late 1800s suggests an economic link between the two industries. Higher demand for copper may have spurred mining efforts and thus led to an increase in the available supply. But remember to keep in mind the bigger historical picture. Consider, for example, the possible roles of the expansion of the nation's railroad system, which helped link western mining regions to the rest of the country, and of the growth of the electric power industry, which was the largest user of copper.

Practicing the Strategy

Study the data in the graph on page 459. Then, on a separate sheet of paper, answer the following questions.
1. What type of information is presented in the graph?
2. What trend in the data does the graph show?
3. What possible conclusions can be drawn from the information presented in the graph?

EXPANSION OF COMMUNICATIONS INDUSTRY, 1875–1900		
Year	Number of Telephones	Miles of Telegraph Wire
1875	3,000*	179,000
1880	48,000	234,000
1885	156,000	462,000
1890	228,000	679,000
1895	340,000	803,000
1900	1,356,000	933,000

*Data for 1876
Source: *Historical Statistics of the United States*

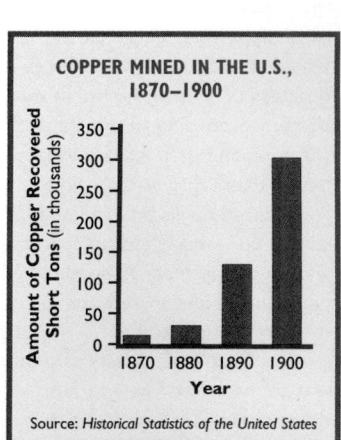

COPPER MINED IN THE U.S., 1870–1900

Source: *Historical Statistics of the United States*

BUILDING YOUR PORTFOLIO

Each portfolio project described below is the culmination of the Building Your Portfolio activities in the chapter reviews of Unit 5. First, decide whether you wish students to work individually or in groups on these unit projects. Then permit each student to choose the project on which he or she desires to

work. Provide students with copies of **Building Your Portfolio Worksheet 5** from *Core Resources*. This worksheet will guide students step by step to complete their projects.

BUILDING YOUR PORTFOLIO

Outlined below are three projects. Independently or cooperatively, complete one and use the products to demonstrate your mastery of the historical concepts involved.

1 SOCIAL CONFLICT
Westward expansion, immigration, and industrialization often created conflicts between different groups in American society. Using the portfolio materials you designed in chapters 14, 15, and 16, develop a series of dramatic sketches and monologues that address these

conflicts and explore the *positive* consequences of cultural diversity for society.

2 TECHNOLOGY AND INDUSTRY
In the late 1800s technological advances and the growth of industry dramatically changed the appearance of the American city as well as the life-styles and work habits of its citizens. Using the portfolio materials you designed in chapters 14, 15, and 16, prepare a presentation highlighting the development of your Nebraska town from small railhead to thriving city. Be sure to include an indication of

the problems that you faced and some of the solutions.

3 REFORM
American society changed rapidly at the end of the 19th century, leading to a host of social, economic, and political problems. Using the portfolio materials you designed in chapters 15 and 16, hold a meeting between business leaders, labor organizers, and urban reformers to discuss what social reforms are needed, and how these reforms can be accomplished with the cooperation of all the groups involved.

Videodisc Review

In assigned groups, develop an outline for a video collage of America in the years between 1860 and 1910. Choose images that best illustrate the major topics of the period. Write a script to accompany the images. Assign narrators to different parts of the script, and present your video collage to the class.

Further Reading

Andrist, Ralph K. *The Long Death: The Last Days of the Plains Indians.*

Macmillan (1993). History of the struggle of the Plains Indians.

Barth, Gunther. *City People: The Rise of Modern City Culture in Nineteenth-Century America.* Oxford (1980). Analysis of the spread of big-city culture.

Brown, Dee. *Bury My Heart at Wounded Knee.* Holt (1970). A history of the American West through Native American eyes.

Jones, Jacqueline. *The Dispossessed: America's Underclasses from the Civil War to the Present.* Harper-Collins (1992). An overview of poverty in America.

Katz, William L. *The Black West.* Open Hand (1987). History of the African American pioneers who helped develop the West.

Luchetti, Cathy, and Carol Olwell. *Women of the West.* Orion (1982). Firsthand accounts of women's lives in the West taken from photographs, diaries, and letters.

Schlereth, Thomas J. *Victorian America: Transformations in Everyday Life 1876–1915.* HarperCollins (1991). Detailed historical overview of the impact of immigration, expansion, and industrialization on American society.

PORTFOLIO ASSESSMENT

1. *Sketches and monologues should review consequences of conflicts between Indians and non-Indians over land, the problems encountered by southern and eastern European immigrants, and labor conflicts between white northerners and black migrants.*

2. *Presentations should show the impact on the town of railroad expansion, new technologies and sources of power, and railroad price-fixing.*

3. *Meeting should explore the urban problems that the settlement-house and labor movements sought to abolish.*

A World Power ❖ 1897–1920

UNIT OVERVIEW

By the turn of the century, many Americans had begun to focus on the economic and social problems that accompanied industrialization and urban growth. Some reformers fought for social change; others sought to reform government at all levels. As the world's major powers pursued imperialist policies, the U.S. also sought to extend its influence in the Pacific, the Caribbean, Latin America, and Asia. And, ultimately the U.S. became embroiled in the conflict that imperialism and nationalism caused in Europe itself. At the end of World War I, President Wilson tried to negotiate a just peace, but the treaty was rejected by the Senate.

CORE RESOURCES

- **American Almanac Poster** and **Worksheet 6**
- **Building Your Portfolio Worksheet 6**
  You may wish to preview the Unit 6 Review and Building Your Portfolio performance assessment activities on p. 617.

Using the American Almanac Posters

Begin the unit by displaying the American Almanac Poster and discussing entries with students. In addition to the worksheet, the annotations that follow provide additional information about the entries and suggest questions and activities.

Then, as students study the unit, have them work in small groups to create their own almanacs—using the same six headings—on pieces of butcher paper. At the end of the unit, call on groups to display and discuss their almanacs.

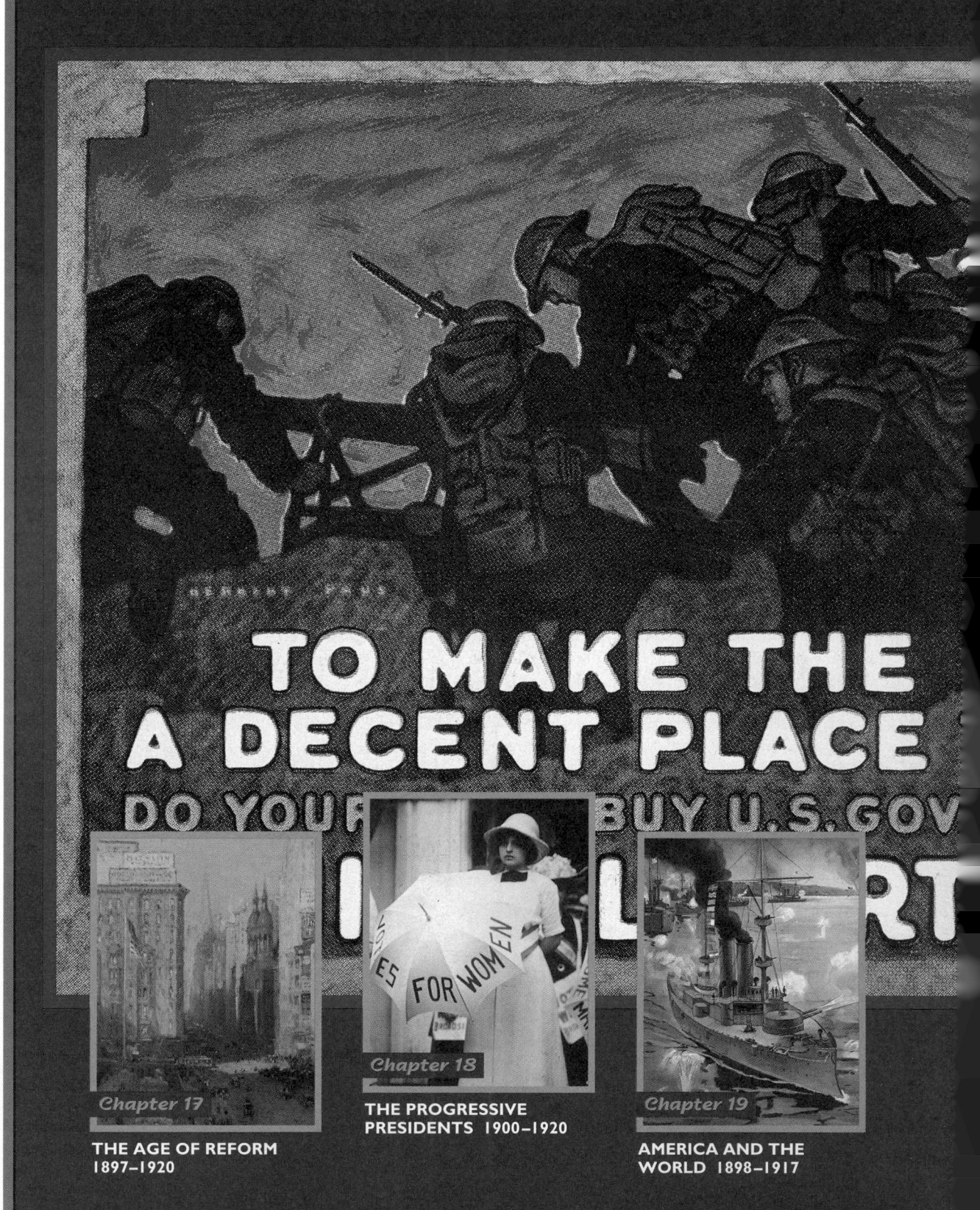

Chapter 17
THE AGE OF REFORM
1897–1920

Chapter 18
THE PROGRESSIVE
PRESIDENTS 1900–1920

Chapter 19
AMERICA AND THE
WORLD 1898–1917

The American People

Mention that the rate of urbanization was rapid in the first 20 years of the 1900s. A report published by the Census Bureau in 1921 showed that 51 percent of the population lived in urban areas.

■■ Ask students to research the population count that made up an urban area in the early 1900s and in the 1990s.

Off to Work

Point out that in 1900 unskilled male laborers earned 10¢ per hour on average, and young girls working a loom at a textile factory often took home as little as $2 for a 50- to 55-hour week.

■■ Have students who work compare their pay rates with the pay rates of 1900.

At Your Leisure

Cy Young was elected to the National Baseball Hall of Fame in 1937. Today, at the end of each baseball season, the Cy Young Award is given to the outstanding pitcher in each major league.

■■ Have students identify and discuss other awards named for famous people.

Firsts in Science and Technology

Henson had accompanied Peary on a number of expeditions prior to the one that took them to the North Pole. "I cannot get along without him," Peary commented.

■■ Ask students what might motivate them to take part in a voyage of exploration.

The Automobile

Point out that the automobile was very much a part of American life by the beginning of the 1920s. One of every four American families bought or sold a car each year.

■■ Ask students what impact the automobile has had on life today.

The Latest Looks

By 1920 factory-made, ready-to-wear clothes in standardized sizes were available in most clothing stores.

■■ Ask students to describe today's "latest looks."

UNIT

A World Power

1897–1920

6

By the turn of the century, many Americans had turned their attention to economic and social problems, which had accompanied rapid industrialization and urban growth. Some reformers fought for social change, while others worked to reform all levels of government. As the other major powers pursued policies of economic and political imperialism, the United States also sought to extend its influence abroad. The United States tried to avoid the conflict that imperialism and nationalism caused in Europe, but the nation was eventually drawn into World War I. At war's end President Wilson worked to negotiate a just peace.

◀ Liberty Loan poster, World War I

WORLD WAR I
1914–1920

Chapter 20

THE AGE OF REFORM

1897–1920

THE AMERICAN NATION VIDEODISC PROGRAM
A variety of still images, short videos, and activities are available for you to use as you teach this chapter. See Correlation to *The American Nation Videodisc Program* for barcode correlations and suggestions for using the program.

Chapter Overview

By the beginning of the 20th century, the U.S. was witnessing the benefits—as well as the ills—of industrialization and rapid urbanization. Americans from all walks of life focused on the basic economic and social inequities that existed in the nation. Muckraking journalists exposed corrupt political and corporate practices as well as racial and economic injustices, while novelists and intellectuals publicized social problems and theorized about solutions. Social reformers fought for changes in the workplace and tackled problems in housing and public health, and issues of personal morality. Nonwhite reformers organized to address problems of discrimination and prejudice, but with mixed results.

Chapter Planning Guide

CHAPTER 17	CORE RESOURCE BOOKLETS	AUDIOVISUAL RESOURCES	PROGRAM RESOURCES
INTRODUCTION pp. 510–511	■ Building Your Portfolio Worksheet 6	■ Everyday Life in America Transparency and Worksheet 17	
TEACHING THE CHAPTER pp. 512–529	■ Graphic Organizer 17 ■ Social Studies Skills Worksheet 17 ■ Literature Worksheet 17 ■ Geography Worksheet 17 ■ Outline Map 9	■ Linking Geography and History Transparencies and Worksheets 11A, 13A	■ Art in American History Transparency and Worksheet 20 ■ *Eyewitnesses and Others*, Volume 2: Readings 18, 26, 30
REVIEW AND ASSESSMENT pp. 530–531	■ Chapter 17 Daily Quizzes ■ Review Worksheet 17 ■ Chapter 17 Tests ■ Alternative Assessment Forms		■ Test Generator

Additional Resources

BOOKS FOR TEACHERS

Brasch, Walter M. *Forerunners of Revolution: Muckrakers & the American Social Conscience.* University Press of America, 1990. Examines role of muckrakers.

Davis, Allen F. *Spearheads for Reform: The Social Settlements & the Progressive Movement, 1890 to 1914.* Rutgers University Press, 1985. Scholarly history of the Progressive movement.

Rosenberg, Rosalind. *Divided Lives: American Women in the Twentieth Century.* Hill and Wang, 1992. History of the 20th-century women's movement.

BOOKS FOR STUDENTS

Brady, Kathleen. *Ida Tarbell: Portrait of a Muckraker.* University of Pittsburgh Press, 1989. Biography of Tarbell.

Schneider, Carl and Dorothy Schneider. *American Women in the Progressive Era, 1900–1920.* Facts on File, 1992. History of women in the Progressive Era.

*Tames, Richard. *Nineteen Hundred to Nineteen Nineteen.* Watts, 1991. Photographic history of the first two decades of the 20th century.

*for students reading below grade level

MULTIMEDIA MATERIALS

Muckrakers and Reformers. Sound filmstrip, 10 min. Multi-Media Productions/SSSS. Examines goals of reformers.

The Progressive Era: Reform Works in America. Video, 23 min. Britannica. Examines the Progressive Era.

Progressives, Populists and Reform in America (1890–1917). Video, 32 min. Guidance Associates/SSSS. Primary sources show reformers' work.

THEMES IN AMERICAN HISTORY

USE WITH PAGES 510–511

Listed on the right are the themes emphasized in Chapter 17. The questions in boldface type stimulate critical thinking and provide students with an opportunity to discuss the themes within a broadened context. The questions also appear in the pupil's edition on p. 510.

■ ECONOMIC DEVELOPMENT

How might state governments justify regulating how businesses treat workers? Students might suggest that a state is obligated to protect the rights of all its citizens, even within the workplace.

■ DEMOCRATIC VALUES

How might reform groups help extend opportunities to all citizens? Students might note that by calling attention to social and economic injustices, reform groups can heighten public awareness of important issues, which may result in increased pressure on local, state, or national business or political leaders for widespread change.

■ CONSTITUTIONAL HERITAGE

How might reform movements lay the groundwork for constitutional change? Students might suggest that reform efforts could bring to light concerns about issues so basic to American society that some people might believe constitutional change to be the appropriate remedy. Once the general public is made aware of such issues, a ground swell of support may build for constitutional amendments that will institute needed changes.

CHAPTER STRATEGIES FOR MEETING INDIVIDUAL NEEDS

LIMITED ENGLISH PROFICIENT LEARNERS

As students read through the chapter, have them work in pairs to select an illustration from each section. Ask pairs to write an extended caption for each illustration, explaining its relation to the section content. You may also wish to involve these students in the simulated 1905 strike activity.

TACTILE/KINESTHETIC LEARNERS

Encourage students to act out a 1905 union strike against a factory. Students may want to create banners, signs, and other visuals to use in their presentation.

LEARNERS HAVING DIFFICULTY

Organize students in pairs to create biography cards of the chapter's key people and groups. Have one side list the name of the person or group and the other list pertinent actions, events, and issues. Encourage students to use the cards to quiz each other.

AUDITORY LEARNERS

Have students assume roles of the persons quoted in the chapter's primary sources. Allow time for them to dramatize the quotes before the class.

VISUAL LEARNERS

Invite students to view a sound filmstrip such as *Muckrakers and Reformers* (see Multimedia Materials, p. 509A). Then have students write a muckraking story based on information in the chapter.

GIFTED LEARNERS

Have students create a pictorial exhibit titled "Progressive Reformers," showing the actions of each reformer and his or her impact on society.

510

ABOUT THE ILLUSTRATION

Tell students that the 1913 painting by C. C. Cooper of New York City's Fifth Avenue illustrates typical conditions in large cities in the U.S. in the early 1900s. Ask students to study the illustration and to write a short paragraph describing the conditions they see in this painting and suggesting reasons why people in the early 1900s might have sought to change these conditions.

Chapter 17

THE AGE OF REFORM

1897–1920

FOCUS

UNDERSTANDING THE MAIN IDEA

A new reform mood swept the United States during the early 1900s. With great optimism and faith in scientific efficiency, reformers set out to conquer the negative effects of industrialization and rapid urbanization: unsafe working conditions, long hours, poor wages, and slum housing.

THEMES

■ **ECONOMIC DEVELOP-MENT** How might state governments justify regulating how businesses treat workers?

■ **DEMOCRATIC VALUES** How might reform groups help extend opportunities to all citizens?

■ **CONSTITUTIONAL HERITAGE** How might reform movements lay the groundwork for constitutional change?

1900	1904	1909	1912	1919
ILGWU established.	National Child Labor Committee formed.	NAACP founded.	Massachusetts passes minimum-wage law.	Eighteenth Amendment ratified.

Call on volunteers to review the social and economic changes brought on by the growth of American business and industry in the Gilded Age. Ask other volunteers to describe how the reform work of Jane Addams and of supporters of the Social Gospel movement addressed some of these problems.

■■ LINK TO THE PAST

While the Gilded Age had promoted industrial development and generated great profits for some, it had also created many problems. The Populist movement had brought to the nation's attention the plight of farmers and urban workers. Gilded Age reformers like Jane Addams and the men and women involved in the Social Gospel movement had worked to improve conditions for the urban poor.

Fifth Avenue in New York, 1913

In 1906 Upton Sinclair published *The Jungle,* a novel about the meat-packing industry in Chicago. In an effort to alert the public to what he saw as the consequences of capitalist greed, Sinclair described industry practices in graphic detail:

> ❝ There was never the least attention paid to what was cut up for sausage. . . . There would be meat that had tumbled out on the floor, in the dirt and sawdust. . . . There would be meat stored in great piles in rooms; and the water from leaky roofs would drip over it, and thousands of rats would race about on it. . . . These rats were nuisances, and the packers would put poisoned bread out for them, they would die, and then rats, bread, and meat would go into the hoppers together. ❞

Sinclair's images were so vivid that they made some readers physically sick. "I aimed at the public's heart," Sinclair remarked, "and by accident I hit it in the stomach." In response to *The Jungle,* Americans demanded federal laws prohibiting unhealthful conditions in food-processing industries.

The Jungle was part of a reform movement that swept the country in the early 20th century. Most reformers recognized the benefits of industrialism, but they were intent on correcting its abuses.

Urban child collecting firewood

MAKING CONNECTIONS

Literature

In 1905 President Theodore Roosevelt and Congress were locked in battle over legislation about impurities in food. Alarmed by reading page proofs of *The Jungle* sent to him by a senior partner of the company that was about to publish the book, Roosevelt launched an investigation of the stockyards, then publicly released part of the findings. When the public responded with outrage, Roosevelt threatened congressional opponents that he would release even more lurid parts of the book unless they acted. As a result, Congress passed the Pure Food and Drug Act and the Meat Inspection Act.

PRIMARY SOURCE

Description of Change: excerpted
Rationale: excerpted to focus on main idea

FOCUS OBJECTIVES

- List some of the goals of progressivism.

- Explain why some women were attracted to the Progressive movement.

- Identify the roles that muckrakers, writers, and intellectuals played in the Progressive movement.

Section 1

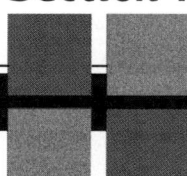

THE PROGRESSIVE MOVEMENT

F O C U S

- **What were some of the goals of progressivism?**
- **Why were many women attracted to the Progressive movement?**
- **What roles did muckrakers, writers, and intellectuals play in the Progressive movement?**

*I*n spite of its name, the Progressive movement—the reform effort that swept the nation between 1900 and 1920—was not a single movement united behind a single goal. Rather it was a collection of reform-minded individuals and groups dedicated to bettering life in the United States. Building on Populist efforts and the work of 19th-century reformers, the progressives publicized the ills of industrial society and sought to remedy them.

SAMUEL
GOMPERS
President
American Federation
of Labor

COURT HOUSE
Thursday, June 3
7:45 P. M.
SUBJECT:
Shorter Work Day

Announcement of an AFL
meeting, 1897

THE PROGRESSIVE SPIRIT

By the early 1900s industrialization had transformed the United States. Much of the transformation was positive: economic growth, new goods and services, and an expanding middle class. However, economic growth also widened the gap between the rich and the poor and contributed to unsafe working conditions and crowded cities. These ills led to a spirit of reform known as **progressivism**.

This concern over the effects of industrialization was by no means new. In the late 1800s Populists had protested unfair or corrupt corporate practices and had pressed for government legislation to stop them. Populism, however, was mainly a rural movement. Progressivism, on the other hand, focused on urban problems, such as unsafe working conditions, bad sanitation, and corrupt political machines.

Progressives carried on the Populists' struggle to "restore government to the people" by proposing election reforms that would enable people to participate more fully in running their government (see

◄ **In the early 1900s most major labor unions excluded women, even though they made up nearly one fourth of the work force. Seamstresses, such as these shown here, often formed their own unions to fight for better working conditions.**

Ask volunteers to recall the goals of the Populists in the late 1800s; write student responses on the chalkboard. Explain that this section identifies the goals of other reformers who were determined to halt the negative effects of industrialization in urban America.

Teaching the Section

PROGRESSIVES' GOALS

Pair students to role-play Populist and progressive reformers. Tell each pair to discuss similarities and differences in their goals for reform. Choose pairs to re-create their conversations for the class. Then ask each student to write a summary sentence about the goals of progressivism. Have students read their sentences aloud.

◀ The progressive spirit also influenced a new school of artists during the early 1900s. Known as the Ash Can School for the gritty and realistic subjects of their paintings, the movement included such artists as George Bellows, Robert Henri, John Sloan, George Luks, William Glackens, and Everett Shinn. Many of their paintings, such as George Bellows's *Lone Tenement* (1909), shown at left, depicted the ugly tenements and tough living conditions of poor urban neighborhoods.

Chapter 18). Some progressives believed that the cure for democracy's ills was more democracy.

Progressives also repeated the Populists' demand for a curb on corporate power. Toward this end, they promoted legislation that prohibited monopolies and enabled smaller businesses to compete successfully in the economy.

Like Populists and the Social Gospel ministers, progressives were inspired by the spirit of social justice. To cap the skyrocketing incomes of the rich, they took up the Populists' demand for a federal graduated income tax. They also supported the Populists' cry for an eight-hour workday. In addition, they sought to institute minimum wages, assure safe working conditions, and end child labor.

The progressive spirit was deeply infused with idealism. Theodore Roosevelt, who would become a leading progressive, aptly reflected this idealism when he wrote:

❝ If we wish to do good work for our country, we must be unselfish, disinterested, sincerely desirous of the well-being of the commonwealth, and capable of devoted adherence to a lofty ideal. ❞

This idealism extended to a firm belief in the power of science and technology to solve social problems. The progressive philosopher John Dewey urged reformers to gather data about society's ills through observation and experimentation and then test solutions. Progressives, assisted by universities, initiated many social research projects.

▪▪ Progressives sought a more democratic government, a check on corporate power, and solutions to social problems.

Although people from all walks of life participated in reform efforts during the Progressive Era, many progressives were native born, middle or upper class, and college educated. Men and women of the urban middle class—social workers, engineers, writers, teachers, doctors, ministers, lawyers, and small-business owners were particularly attracted to progressivism. This class had grown from some 750,000 in 1870 to around 10 million by 1910. In the words of Kansas editor William Allen White, by the 1900s Populism had "shaved its whiskers, washed its shirt, put on a derby, and moved up into the middle class."

Many middle-class women were attracted to the Progressive movement for the same reason earlier generations of women had assisted reform efforts: reform work provided them with one of the

▲ Shown here is a group of Vassar women from the 1920s.

MAKING CONNECTIONS
Sociology
Middle-class women reformers believed that the problems brought about by industrial growth had a direct impact on family life. They insisted that government should assume a greater responsibility for the economic well-being of citizens, particularly women and children.

PRIMARY SOURCE
Description of Change: excerpted
Rationale: excerpted to focus on main idea

▪▪ Ask students if they think it is possible for a president to adhere to such high ideals without politics getting in the way.

Teaching the Section

PROGRESSIVE WOMEN

Ask three volunteers to role-play middle-class women of the early 1900s. Have other students work in small groups to write questions they would ask the women in order to gain a better understanding of their reasons for becoming involved in the Progressive movement. Invite representatives of each group to ask the role-players their questions.

THE MUCKRAKERS

Organize the class into four groups, each group representing the editorial board of a new "muckraking" magazine for the early 1900s. Have each group choose a name for its magazine, draft a statement of purpose to appear in the magazine, and choose titles for five articles to appear in the first issue. Ask a student from each group to present its ideas to the class. Then ask the groups how other writers and intellectuals reinforced the work of the muckrakers.

Graph Caption Answer
about 40 percent

MAKING CONNECTIONS

Literature

Roosevelt used the term *muckraker* in a 1906 speech. His reference was to a character in John Bunyan's 17th-century English classic *Pilgrim's Progress* who was too busy raking the filth on the floor to look up and accept a celestial crown.

BIO GRAPHY PERSONALITIES IN HISTORY

Tarbell's extensively researched articles were compiled into two volumes. Her work aroused public interest and resulted in federal investigations of the Standard Oil Company. That company was dissolved in 1911 under the Sherman Antitrust Act. Although Tarbell gained her fame in her 40s as a writer for *McClure's* magazine, she was the author of numerous articles and books, including several books about Abraham Lincoln. She was planning a new book when she died at age 86.

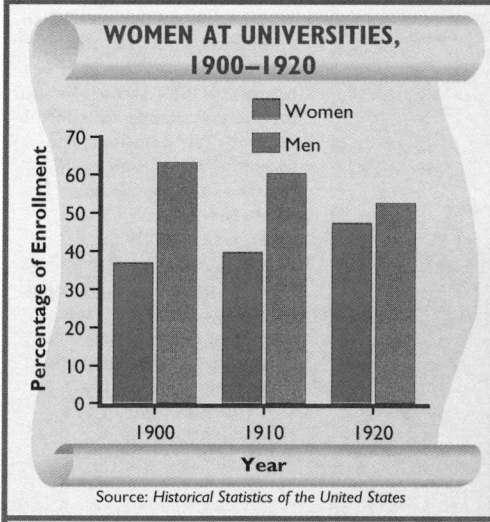

WOMEN AT UNIVERSITIES, 1900–1920

Source: *Historical Statistics of the United States*

INCREASING ENROLLMENT Roughly 2.3 percent of young adults attended colleges and universities in 1900. By 1920 the number had risen to some 4.7 percent. Over this period women made up an increasing proportion of college students.

? **BUILDING GRAPH SKILLS** In 1910, approximately what percentage of university students were women?

few acceptable avenues for influencing politics and society. Although the number of women enrolled in colleges increased during the early 1900s, women's career options were limited. Reform work provided college-educated women with a way to apply their knowledge of medicine, psychology, sociology, and other disciplines. Some women made careers of reform work; others volunteered their time through associations such as the General Federation of Women's Clubs, the Women's Trade Union League, and the National Association of Colored Women.

▪▪ Not only did reform work provide women with a way to influence social change, it was one of the few career opportunities open to college-educated women.

INSPIRATION FOR REFORM

Progressive journalists helped spread the reform message. Newly founded mass-circulation magazines like *McClure's, Munsey's,* and *Cosmopolitan* filled their pages with stories that explored

---

corruption in politics and business as well as such social problems as slums and child labor.

The progressive journalists were relentless in their assaults on social evils, leading Theodore Roosevelt to complain: "Men with a muck-rake are often indispensable to the well-being of society, but only if they know when to stop raking the muck." The vivid image stuck, and the journalists became known as **muckrakers**—a name they accepted with obvious pride.

▲ *McClure's* featured the work of many prominent authors and journalists, including Rudyard Kipling and Ray Stannard Baker.

McClure's publication of "Tweed Days in St. Louis" by journalists Lincoln Steffens and Claude Wetmore in October 1902 marked the beginning of the muckraking school of journalism. The article exposed the political machine in St. Louis, comparing corrupt city government there with New York City's government under Boss Tweed. *McClure's* went on to publish many articles on political and corporate corruption, poor working conditions, and slum life.

BIO GRAPHY In November 1902, *McClure's* ran the first installment of Ida Tarbell's "History of the Standard Oil Company." Tarbell, the daughter of an independent oil producer, was born in western Pennsylvania in 1857. She grew up admiring the independent oil man "whose ear was attuned to Fortune's call, and who had the daring and the energy to risk everything." Tarbell was deeply angered when John D. Rockefeller's Standard Oil Company began swallowing up independent oil companies. When her father went bankrupt and his partner committed suicide, 15-year-old Tarbell blamed Rockefeller.

In 1876 Tarbell entered Allegheny College, the only female in a freshman class of 40 "hostile or indifferent" males. Soon after graduation she moved to Paris and began her career

Ida Tarbell

Practice

GUIDED PRACTICE

Call on students to identify the types of people who were attracted to progressivism. List their responses on the chalkboard and then review the list, asking why each type of person might be interested in reform.

INDEPENDENT PRACTICE

Have students choose one of the types from the Guided Practice chalkboard list and in the role of such a person write a short essay titled "Why I Am a Progressive." Students may wish to include their essays in their portfolios.

Review and Assessment

REVIEW Have students copy the names of persons listed in the Preview Workshop on p. 512 and write a brief statement about each individual's contribution to progressive reform. Then assign the Section 1 Review on p. 516.

ASSESS Assign the **Section 1 Daily Quiz** in *Core Resources.*
▶

▲ Standard Oil's practice of swallowing up independent oil companies is sharply criticized in this editorial cartoon.

as a writer. By the 1890s she was writing a popular biographical series for *McClure's.*

In 1900 the magazine's reform-minded founder, Scotch-Irish immigrant S. S. McClure, assigned her to investigate Standard Oil. "Out with you. Look, see, report," he urged. "Don't do it," warned her father, knowing too well the power of Standard Oil to punish its enemies. But she went ahead, publishing her findings in a series of 18 articles. Month after month she attacked Standard Oil's business practices:

❝ One of the most depressing features . . . is that instead of such methods arousing contempt, they are more or less openly admired. . . . There is no gaming table in the world where loaded dice are tolerated, no athletic field where men must not start fair. Yet Mr. Rockefeller has systematically played with loaded dice. . . . Business played in this way loses all its sportsmanlike qualities. It is fit only for tricksters. ❞

McClure's readers shared Tarbell's outrage, hailing her as "a modern Joan of Arc" and "the Terror of the Trusts." One reader even called her series "the *Uncle Tom's Cabin* of today." Later, Rockefeller biographer Allan Nevins would call it "the most spectacular success of the muckraking school of journalism, and its most enduring achievement."

Meanwhile, muckraking books poured off the presses. In *The Octopus* (1901) Frank Norris exposed the ways in which railroads misused their vast power. Lincoln Steffens continued to document

political corruption in urban America in *The Shame of the Cities* (1904). Jack London wrote *The Iron Heel* (1907) to warn that bloody revolution might result if something was not done to curb capitalism's abuses.

Only a few progressives, however, concerned themselves with racial justice. One who did was Ray Stannard Baker. Baker traveled around the nation in 1904, examining the plight of African Americans. He found that African Americans were segregated, routinely robbed of their right to vote, and otherwise discriminated against. Worst of all, lynchings still took place. In *Following the Color Line* (1908), Baker described a lynching in Springfield, Ohio:

❝ The worst feature of all in this Springfield lynching was the apathy of the public. No one really seemed to care. A "nigger" had been hanged: what of it? But the law itself had been lynched. What of that? . . . If ever there was an example of good citizenship lying flat on its back . . . , Springfield furnished an example of that condition. ❞

■■ **Muckrakers exposed political and corporate corruption, difficult working conditions, crowded slums, and racial injustice.**

EXPLORING SOCIAL PROBLEMS

Like the muckraking journalists, novelists and intellectuals explored the darker side of the new industrial order's effect on people's behavior and values. Theodore Dreiser, in novels such as *Sister Carrie* (1900) and *The Financier* (1912),

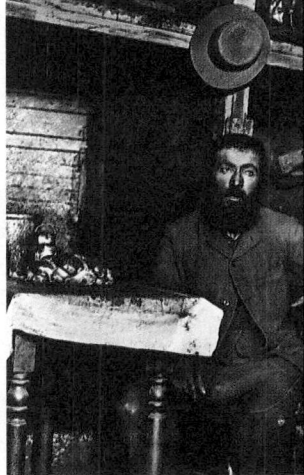

▲ Slum life was a frequent target of muckrakers. This 1910 photograph shows a Jewish immigrant in the home he has made in a coal cellar.

CULTURAL PATTERNS

Mary Church Terrell, Oberlin College graduate and first president of the National Association of Colored Women (NACW), fought for equal rights and suffrage for all women. But she believed that she and other professional African American women had a special obligation to help those "to whom they are bound by ties of race and sex." Under her leadership, the NACW established kindergartens and day nurseries for the children of black working mothers, fought for employment opportunities for black women, and sought equality in the criminal justice system.

RETEACH Organize students into groups and assign each group a subsection of Section 1. Have each group develop several questions and answers about the main ideas in its assigned material. Then have each group quiz the other groups with its list of questions.

Closure

Call on one volunteer to read aloud Theodore Roosevelt's words on p. 513 and another to read Jane Addams's statement on p. 516. Ask students to identify similarities between the two statements. Then discuss ways in which they reflected the ideals of progressive reform.

Extension

ANALYZE Have students read one of the fiction or nonfiction works noted in the section and report on it to the class.

EVALUATE Suggest that students find examples of muckraking in current newspapers and magazines. Display the stories in the classroom. Then have students debate the pros and cons of this type of journalism.

PRIMARY SOURCE
Description of Change: excerpted and bracketed
Rationale: excerpted to· focus on main idea; bracketed to clarify meaning

SECTION REVIEW ANSWERS

IDENTIFY

For significance, see the following pages:
progressivism (p. 512)
John Dewey (p. 513)
muckrakers (p. 514)
Lincoln Steffens (p. 514)
Ida Tarbell (p. 514)
S. S. McClure (p. 515)
Ray Stannard Baker (p. 515)
Theodore Dreiser (p. 515)
Herbert Croly (p. 516)
Jane Addams (p. 516)

1. *through more democratic government, checks on corporate power, a federal graduated income tax, labor reforms, and research projects to solve social problems*
2. *political and corporate corruption; difficult working conditions, crowded slums, racial injustice*
3. *offered avenues for influencing politics and society, ways to apply college education; few other career options*
4. *Articles will vary but should offer a solution to the social problem selected.*
5. *Both supported legislation prohibiting corrupt business practices, proposed election reforms, supported graduated income tax and eight-hour workday.*

◄ **Jane Addams joined the settlement-house movement in order to provide college-educated women like herself an opportunity to "learn of life from life itself." Her settlement house in Chicago became a model for social reforms in child labor, health care, urban renewal, and public education.**

depicted workers brutalized by low wages and business owners driven by greed.

Progressive intellectuals proposed solutions. In *The Promise of American Life* (1909), political theorist Herbert Croly praised Alexander Hamilton's call, over a century earlier, for a strong, activist central government. But instead of promoting the interests of only the business class, as Hamilton had favored, Croly held that the government should promote the welfare of all its citizens by expanding opportunities.

Social thinkers urged citizens to take responsibility as well. Jane Addams, by now well known for her settlement-house work among Chicago's immigrants, argued in *Democracy and Social Ethics* (1902) that democracy meant more than the right to vote. It demanded a society that showed concern for the well-being of everyone:

❝ This is the penalty of a democracy—that we are bound to move forward or [slip backward] together. None of us can stand aside; our feet are mired in the same soil, and our lungs breathe the same air. ❞

■■ **Progressive writers and intellectuals publicized social problems and offered theories on how to solve them.**

Although progressives like Addams and Croly wanted to change American society, they remained committed to democracy. Most progressives sought reforms of local government, businesses, and city life to ensure that the full promise of democracy became available to all citizens.

S E C T I O N **1** R E V I E W

IDENTIFY and explain the significance of the following: progressivism, John Dewey, muckrakers, Lincoln Steffens, Ida Tarbell, S. S. McClure, Ray Stannard Baker, Theodore Dreiser, Herbert Croly, Jane Addams.

1. **MAIN IDEA** In what ways did progressives hope to reform society?
2. **MAIN IDEA** What types of political and social evils did muckrakers expose through their writings?
3. **RECOGNIZING POINTS OF VIEW** Why were middle-class women attracted to the Progressive movement and reform activities?
4. **WRITING TO INFORM** Imagine you are a progressive writer or intellectual in the early 20th century. Write an article for *McClure's* proposing a solution to a social problem of the new industrial order.
5. **COMPARING** In what ways were the goals of Populists and progressives similar?

Section 2

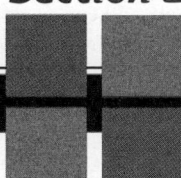

REFORMING THE NEW INDUSTRIAL ORDER

FOCUS
- **How did progressives try to reform the workplace?**
- **How did the Supreme Court respond to social legislation?**
- **Which labor organizations represented workers in the Progressive Era? How did these organizations differ?**

The new industrial order changed American society in deep and disturbing ways. Many workers felt victimized by unhealthful working conditions, poor wages, and long workdays. At times progressive reformers and labor organizations joined forces, but more often they organized their own campaigns to improve conditions for workers.

IWW songbook

The Granger Collection, New York

REFORMING THE WORKPLACE

As progressives explored working conditions firsthand, they saw men and women laboring long hours, often in dangerous jobs. In 1900 the average laborer worked nearly 10 hours a day, 6 days a

▼ Child laborers, such as these shown in a textile mill, often worked in unsafe conditions.

week for about $1.50 a day. Women and children workers were paid even less.

Social reformers had long argued that the conditions women and children faced in the workplace undermined home and family life. Progressives and labor-union activists campaigned for laws prohibiting or limiting child labor and improving conditions for women workers. Florence Kelley was one of the women who worked tirelessly for this cause, helping to persuade the Illinois legislature in 1893 to prohibit child labor and to limit the number of hours women could work. In 1904 she helped organize the National Child Labor Committee, which worked to persuade state legislatures to pass laws against employing young children. By 1912 the committee had helped 39 states pass child labor laws. Some states even limited older children's employment to 8 or 10 hours a day and barred them from working at night or in dangerous occupations. But enforcement of such laws was lax. Many employers, claiming that their business success depended on cheap child labor, simply refused to obey the laws and continued to hire child workers.

Progressives also campaigned for laws that would force factories to limit the long hours employers demanded of their adult workers, men

FOCUS OBJECTIVES
- Explain how progressives tried to reform the workplace.
- Analyze the Supreme Court's response to social legislation.
- Cite labor organizations that represented workers in the Progressive Era and identify how they differed.

GLOBAL CONNECTIONS

Like many other progressive goals, the impetus for child labor reform reached America from Europe. Great Britain passed the first child labor law in 1802, but because it did not provide for enforcement it had little effect. A more effective attack on the use of child labor was Charles Dickens's novel *Oliver Twist,* which was published in the 1830s and widely read in Britain and America. Not until 1900, however, was the International Association for Labour Legislation established in Switzerland to promote child labor reform throughout the world.

MOTIVATING:
STUDENT EXPERIENCES

Ask students to name tasks they have performed or jobs they have held for which they have been paid money. Ask them what job conditions they had hoped to have. Then discuss working conditions they would find unacceptable. Tell students that in this section they will learn about progressive reformers' campaigns to improve workers' conditions in the early 1900s.

Teaching the Section

REFORMING THE WORKPLACE

Encourage students to write letters to a 1904 state legislator from the viewpoint of a progressive reformer demanding laws to improve the workplace. Instruct students to suggest specific changes they would make and to provide information to back up their demands. Ask volunteers to read their letters aloud. Students may wish to include their letters in their portfolios.

VOICES IN HISTORY

Long before the Triangle Company fire, women had been trying to improve conditions in the shirtwaist industry. A strike by some 20,000 to 30,000 workers, mostly young female immigrants, brought the industry to a halt in the winter of 1909–10. Theresa Malkiel, a Russian immigrant, stated her feelings about the strike: "There is nothing dishonest in standing up for one's bread. We must warn the newcomers that us girls are out on strike because our boss is paying starvation wages. . . . This land is one big union, and us children were taught very early that united we stand and divided we fall."

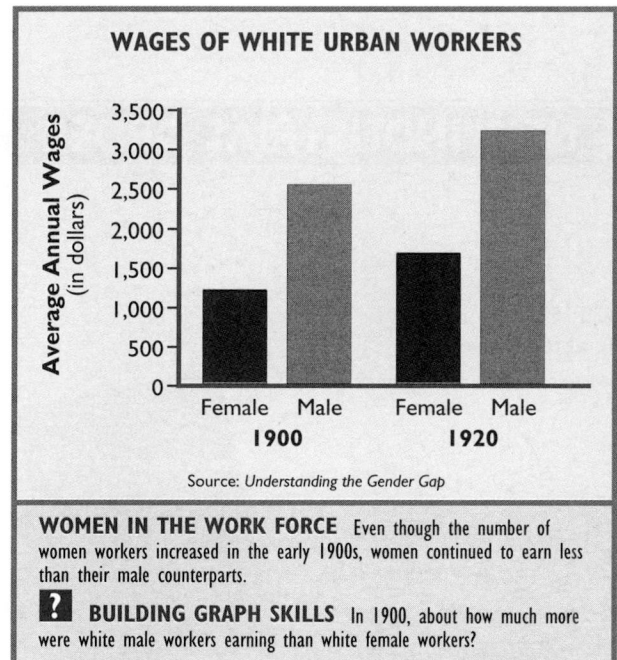

WAGES OF WHITE URBAN WORKERS

Average Annual Wages (in dollars)

1900: Female, Male
1920: Female, Male

Source: *Understanding the Gender Gap*

WOMEN IN THE WORK FORCE Even though the number of women workers increased in the early 1900s, women continued to earn less than their male counterparts.

? **BUILDING GRAPH SKILLS** In 1900, about how much more were white male workers earning than white female workers?

and women alike. In 1903, Florence Kelley helped lobby the Oregon legislature to pass a law limiting women laundry workers to 10 hours a day. Earlier, Utah had enacted a law that limited working days in dangerous occupations like mining and smelting to 8 hours. Other states passed similar laws.

Wages were another target for progressives. Of the some 30 million men and 8 million women employed in 1910, about one third lived in poverty. In 1912, in response to progressive agitation, Massachusetts passed the nation's first minimum-wage law—setting base wages for women and children. Gradually, other states followed suit.

But it would not be until 1938 that the nation passed a minimum-wage law for all workers.

Progressives also worked to improve workplace safety. Tragic events in March 1911 catapulted the need for such reforms onto the front pages of the nation's newspapers.

Late in the afternoon on Saturday, March 25, some 500 employees—most of them young Jewish or Italian immigrant women—were completing their six-day workweek at New York City's Triangle Shirtwaist Company. Shortly before quitting time, as they rose from their crowded worktables and started to leave, a fire erupted in a rag bin. Within moments the entire eighth floor of the 10-story building was ablaze. Escape quickly became impossible—there were only two stairways, and most of the exit doors were locked. Leaping from high windows became the last, desperate way out. Some 60 workers took it—to their death.

Through the night, weeping family members wandered among the crushed bodies on the sidewalk, looking for their loved ones. In all, more than 140 people perished in the Triangle fire, victims of a thoroughly unsafe workplace. Rose Schneiderman, a Women's Trade Union League organizer, argued that only a strong working-class movement could bring real change to the workplace. She noted:

❝ This is not the first time girls have been burned alive in the city. Each week I must learn of the untimely death of one of my sister workers. Every year thousands of us are maimed. The life of men and women is so cheap and property is so sacred. There are so many of us for one job it matters little if 143 of us are burned to death. ❞

▼ Rose Schneiderman's impassioned speech (below) after the Triangle Shirtwaist Company's fire (left) marked the beginning of sweeping reforms that improved factory safety regulations.

THE SUPREME COURT'S RESPONSE

Choose nine students to represent Supreme Court justices. Organize the rest of the class into four groups. Two groups should prepare briefs for and against New York's law regulating the workday of bakers. The other two groups should do the same for the Oregon law regulating the workday of female employees. In each case, after each side presents its brief, the justices should discuss the legal and social issues and make their ruling. Conclude the activity by asking the class to hypothesize about why the Court struck down reform in New York but upheld it in Oregon. *(In the Oregon case, the Court was persuaded by Brandeis's brief showing how long hours harmed women. In the New York case, the need for the law was not supported by evidence.)*

THE LABOR UNIONS

Organize the class into small groups. Ask half the groups to write brochures outlining the benefits of becoming a member of the AFL. Have the other groups do the same for the IWW. Ask one volunteer from each group to present the argument in that group's brochure to the class. Ask students what might make a worker choose one union over the other.

▶

But it did matter. The public outcry was so great that it pressured lawmakers to pass protective legislation. The New York legislature responded by enacting the nation's strictest fire safety code.

■■ **Progressives sought laws to end child labor, limit working hours, raise wages, and improve safety.**

𝒯HE COURT'S RESPONSE

As more states passed laws regulating businesses, owners fought back through the courts—even to the Supreme Court. Owners appealed to the Fourteenth amendment to the Constitution, which prohibits states from depriving any person of "life, liberty, or property, without due process of law." They claimed that laws that limited their businesses deprived them of their "property" unfairly.

The Supreme Court sided with business owners and declared much of the early social legislation unconstitutional. The Court also ruled that some social legislation violated the constitutional "liberty" of workers by denying them **freedom of contract**. In 1905, for example, in *Lochner* v. *New York,* the Court overturned the New York law limiting bakers' workdays to 10 hours, declaring that the law robbed workers of their "liberty of contract." Workers, the Court argued, should be free to accept any conditions of employment that business owners required—including 14- or 16-hour workdays.

The Court did uphold some social legislation, however. In 1908, in *Muller* v. *Oregon,* an employer challenged the 10-hour workday law Florence Kelley had helped push through the Oregon legislature. Kelley and her co-worker, Josephine Goldmark, swung into action to convince the Court to uphold this hard-won law. Goldmark gathered data for the brief, or legal argument, to defend the law. Kelley recruited Goldmark's brother-in-law, the brilliant Boston lawyer Louis D. Brandeis, to argue the case. The "Brandeis Brief" broke new legal ground. In addition to making sound legal points, the brief included extensive evidence of the bad effects that working long hours had on women's health and well-being. This social research not only convinced the Court to uphold the Oregon law but became a model for the defense of other social legislation.

◀ **Josephine Goldmark**

▶ **Louis Brandeis**

The Granger Collection, New York

■■ **On the grounds of property rights and freedom of contract, the Supreme Court struck down much—but not all—progressive legislation.**

𝐿ABOR UNIONS

Progressive reformers were not the only ones fighting for workers' rights. Labor unions continued to battle for better conditions and for the

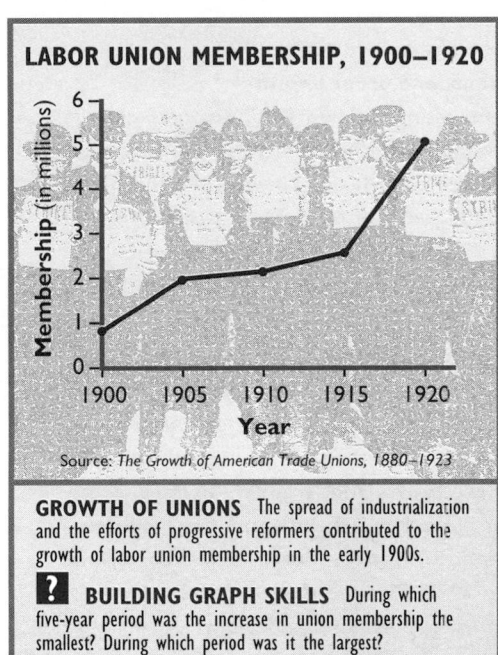

LABOR UNION MEMBERSHIP, 1900–1920

Source: *The Growth of American Trade Unions, 1880–1923*

GROWTH OF UNIONS The spread of industrialization and the efforts of progressive reformers contributed to the growth of labor union membership in the early 1900s.

❓ **BUILDING GRAPH SKILLS** During which five-year period was the increase in union membership the smallest? During which period was it the largest?

MAKING CONNECTIONS

Sociology

Brandeis argued in *Muller* v. *Oregon* that women's work hours should be limited because "women are fundamentally weaker than men." In making its decision, the Court noted that women would always depend on men for "protection." Despite the sexism of the argument and the decision, both of which mirrored male attitudes of the time, the outcome benefited working women by limiting their work hours and by breaking with the legal principle that employers had sole control over the terms of employment. Yet the decision had the undermining effect of reinforcing social stereotypes of women.

■■ Ask students if they think this argument could be successfully used today in a court of law.

HISTORICAL SIDELIGHTS

"The People's Attorney"

Brandeis was known as "the people's attorney" because of his support of public causes such as offering life insurance at affordable rates for workers. His support of progressive reforms was a factor in his becoming in 1916 the first Jew to be appointed to the Supreme Court.

Graph Caption Answer
1905–1910; 1915–1920

Practice

GUIDED PRACTICE

Work with students to develop on the chalkboard a web diagram, using *Progressive Reforms* as the hub of the diagram. Then have students complete the diagram by listing conditions that led to progressive reforms in the workplace. Review the completed web with the class, asking students to elaborate on each condition it contains.

INDEPENDENT PRACTICE

Instruct students to choose one of the conditions listed in the Guided Practice web diagram and, in the role of a progressive reformer, to write a letter to the editor protesting the situation and suggesting what should be done about it. Students may wish to include their letters in their portfolios.

Review and Assessment

REVIEW Have students work in small groups to locate in the text the persons and terms listed in the Preview Workshop. Guide students to discuss and write explanations of how each person and term is related to industrial reform. Then ask groups to exchange papers and compare answers. Then assign the Section 2 Review on p. 521.

ASSESS Assign the **Section 2 Daily Quiz** in *Core Resources*.

THROUGH OTHERS' EYES

The economic development of the Southwest was due in large part to Mexican immigrant labor. One historian estimates that during the first several decades of the 1900s, agricultural labor in the Southwest was 65 to 85 percent Mexican. And from 1900 to 1940 Mexican workers were 60 percent of common labor in mines and 60 to 90 percent of the extra gangs employed by 18 western railroads. Mexico, in turn, benefited; between 1917 and 1927 Mexican laborers in the U.S. sent an average of $10 million a year to relatives back home.

PRIMARY SOURCE

Description of Change: excerpted

Rationale: excerpted to focus on main idea

---

closed shop—a workplace where the employer hires only union members. Most union members favored "working within the system." They wanted to change how workers were treated, but they did not want to threaten capitalism's very existence. Some union members wanted to replace capitalism with an economic system that workers controlled. Many in this group favored **socialism**, the system under which the government or worker cooperatives, not private interests, own factories, utilities, and transportation and communications systems.

The AFL. The major labor organization in these years remained the American Federation of Labor (AFL). The AFL stood firmly for working within the system. Under Samuel Gompers' leadership, AFL membership grew from some 500,000 in 1900 to about 2 million in 1914. But the AFL excluded most unskilled workers—the majority of whom were Eastern European immigrants or African Americans. This left most urban workers without organized support.

IMMIGRANT WORKERS

THROUGH OTHERS' EYES

*P*rogressive reformers won shorter workdays, better working conditions, and other improvements for many U.S. workers. But such changes were unknown to the immigrants who crossed the border from Mexico to work the railroads, mines, and fields of the southwestern United States. These immigrant workers experienced both poor working conditions and prejudice. In 1910 the Mexican newspaper **Diario del Hogar** wondered what drove "our workingmen, so attached to the land, to abandon the country [Mexico], even at the risk of the Yankee contempt with which they are treated on the other side of the Bravo [Rio Grande]." Indeed, some Mexican laborers were assaulted or lynched. Venustiano Carranza, Mexico's president from 1917 to 1920, claimed that 114 Mexicans had been murdered across the border.

◀ **AFL seal, about 1890**

One AFL union that did try to assist unskilled workers was the International Ladies' Garment Workers Union (ILGWU). Established in 1900 in New York City, it sought to unionize workers—mainly Jewish and Italian immigrant women—employed in sewing shops like the Triangle Shirtwaist Company.

In order to organize workers, union leaders generally planned a strike to establish the union's power to negotiate for workers. The International Ladies' Garment Workers Union used this tactic in November 1909 when it staged the "Uprising of the Thirty Thousand." Thousands of women garment workers heeded the union's call and walked off their jobs to demand that their companies recognize the ILGWU as their union.

The strike lasted through the bitter winter. Hard-pressed strikers received generous aid from progressive groups such as the Women's Trade Union League, an organization of well-to-do women who supported the efforts of working women to form unions.

The strike's results were mixed. Most employers agreed to many of the ILGWU's demands. The employers, however, were determined to run **open shops**—or nonunion workplaces. Thus, they refused to recognize the union—the ILGWU's most important demand.

The IWW. While Gompers and his AFL trade unions negotiated with business owners for worker gains, a new union emerged with a different agenda. The Industrial Workers of the World (IWW), founded in Chicago in 1905, opposed capitalism. Its leader, "Big Bill" Haywood, proclaimed IWW's aim. Referring to the Continental Congress that had declared American independence, Haywood asserted:

   ❝ Fellow workers, this is the continental congress of the working class. We are here to confederate the workers of this country into a working-class movement that shall have for its purpose the emancipation of the working class from the slave bondage of capitalism. ❞

RETEACH Organize students into groups and assign individuals or pairs the task of outlining subsections. Have students exchange outlines and use them to ask questions of other members of their group.

Closure

Ask volunteers to state which industrial reform accomplished by the progressives they consider to be most important and why. Discuss students' responses with the class.

Extension

RESEARCH Invite students to research the growth of the AFL (now AFL–CIO) from the time covered in this section to the present. Then ask students to create a time line showing their findings.

COMPARE Challenge students to investigate their state's child labor laws and, using Labor Department information, to compare the laws with those in the early 1900s.

▶ **Employers often used armed guards to remove picketing workers. This photograph shows local militiamen aiming their guns at strikers in Lawrence, Massachusetts.**

Haywood denounced the AFL's cooperation with business owners and its failure to include unskilled workers. He vowed to organize migrant farm workers, miners, lumber workers, and textile workers to overthrow the capitalist system. In addition to enlisting African American, Hispanic American, and Asian American workers, the IWW actively recruited women workers and the wives of male workers. An IWW newspaper expressed optimism about the role of union women:

66 The advent of women side by side with men in strikes, will soon develop a fighting force that will end capitalism and its horrors in short order. . . . The industrial union movement seeks to develop the fighting quality of both sexes. 99

The Wobblies, as the members of the IWW came to be called, pursued their goals through general strikes, boycotts, and industrial sabotage. Their greatest hour came in 1912 when they led 20,000 workers in a strike against the textile mills of Lawrence, Massachusetts, to protest a 30-cent wage cut. After a bitter and much publicized two-month strike, the mill owners gave in.

Success was short-lived, however. Several later IWW-led strikes failed miserably. Most Americans grew fearful of IWW's aims, and the government cracked down on the union with increasing force. Disagreements among Wobbly leaders also weakened IWW's power. Within a few years the IWW collapsed and eventually faded from power. The AFL trade unions continued to flourish, but the majority of American industrial workers remained outside the union movement.

▪▪ **The AFL worked within the system and focused on skilled workers, while the IWW opposed capitalism and focused on unskilled workers.**

PRIMARY SOURCE

Description of Change: excerpted
Rationale: excerpted to focus on main idea

SECTION REVIEW ANSWERS

IDENTIFY

For significance, see the following pages:
Florence Kelley (p. 517)
Rose Schneiderman (p. 518)
freedom of contract (p. 519)
Josephine Goldmark (p. 519)
Louis D. Brandeis (p. 519)
closed shop (p. 520)
socialism (p. 520)
Samuel Gompers (p. 520)
open shops (p. 520)
"Big Bill" Haywood (p. 520)

1. *to end young child labor, to limit working hours and improve workplace safety, and to set minimum wages for women and children*
2. *unconstitutional because they interfered with property rights of owners and denied workers freedom of contract*
3. *AFL worked within the system; IWW opposed cooperation with business owners; sought to overthrow the capitalist system.*
4. *Letters should describe working conditions that contributed to the disaster and how they would be different after legislation was passed to protect workers.*
5. *Students might suggest government regulation of the workplace and strong unions that protect workers while allowing employers to still make a profit.*

▪▪ ▪▪ S E C T I O N   **2**   R E V I E W

IDENTIFY and explain the significance of the following: Florence Kelley, Rose Schneiderman, freedom of contract, Josephine Goldmark, Louis D. Brandeis, closed shop, socialism, Samuel Gompers, open shops, "Big Bill" Haywood.

1. **MAIN IDEA** What kinds of laws to improve the workplace did progressives seek?

2. **MAIN IDEA** What reasons did the Supreme Court use to justify striking down some progressive legislation?

3. **CONTRASTING** How did the goals of the AFL differ from those of the IWW?

4. **WRITING TO DESCRIBE** Imagine you are a worker in New York City's Triangle Shirtwaist Company in March 1911. Write a letter to a friend that describes work conditions before and after the fire.

5. **USING HISTORICAL IMAGINATION** If you were a progressive in the early 1900s, how would you balance the needs of employers with the needs of employees?

PREVIEW WORKSHOP

Following is a list of the significant people and terms in this section. You may wish to use this list as a section preview.

People
- Lawrence Veiller
- Frances Willard
- W.E.B. Du Bois

Terms
- Woman's Christian Temperance Union
- Eighteenth Amendment
- National Association for the Advancement of Colored People
- Society of American Indians

FOCUS OBJECTIVES

- Describe steps reformers took to try to solve urban problems.

- Identify the actions taken by African American and Native American progressives to address discrimination.

- Explain why the Progressive movement had mixed results for immigrants.

HISTORICAL SIDELIGHTS

Man with a Mission
Lawrence Veiller was only 28 years old when he hit upon a plan to bring the tenement housing problem to the public's attention. He set up a Tenement Housing Exhibition in New York. His cardboard model of the Canal Street slum demonstrated the conditions in which 2,781 residents shared 264 toilets and not one bathtub. Among the thousands of viewers was Theodore Roosevelt, then governor of New York. He told Veiller, "Tell me what you want and I will help you get it."

CORE RESOURCES

- **Literature Worksheet 17**
- **Section 3 Daily Quiz**

AV RESOURCES

- **Linking Geography and History Transparencies** and **Worksheets 11A, 13A**

522

Section 3

REFORMING SOCIETY

FOCUS

- **What steps did reformers take to try to solve urban problems?**
- **What actions did African American and Native American progressives take to address discrimination?**
- **Why can it be said that the Progressive movement had mixed results for immigrants?**

Progressive reformers were convinced that as citizens they were responsible for the well-being of their communities. While most white progressives concentrated on improving housing, public health, and personal morality, African American and Native American progressives organized to fight discrimination. Other progressives, motivated by nativist sentiments, set out to change immigrants' cultures.

Woman doing laundry, about 1910

REFORMING CITY LIFE

By 1920, for the first time in U.S. history, more than 50 percent of Americans lived in cities. As urban populations soared, the ability of cities to provide garbage collection, safe and affordable housing, health care, police and fire protection, and adequate public education was stretched to the breaking point.

Cleaning up the city. What cities needed, some reformers announced, was "municipal housekeeping," a campaign to make the cities a more healthful and livable home for all residents. "The community is one great family," explained Louise DeKoven Bowen, the president of Chicago's Woman's City Club, and "each member of it is bound to help the other." The Woman's City Club, other women's clubs, various men's clubs, and reform organizations enlisted the aid of local governments to clean up the cities. Some organizations took the cleanup campaign literally, working to rid the cities of garbage. Other reform organizations worked for better housing or to improve public education.

Progressive reformers published articles and books documenting urban problems, even assigning blame for them in some cases. For example, Lawrence Veiller (VYL-uhr), a settlement-house worker, lashed out at irresponsible tenement owners "who for the sake of a large profit on their investments sacrifice the health and welfare of countless thousands."

Veiller campaigned tirelessly for improved housing. In 1901 he succeeded in getting the New York State Tenement House bill passed. The law banned construction of dark and airless tenements. New buildings had to be constructed around an open courtyard that would let in light and air. The law also required that new buildings contain one bathroom for each apartment or for every three rooms, rather than one or two for an entire floor, as was the common practice. Housing reformers in other states used the New York law as a model for their own legislative proposals.

Teaching the Section

URBAN REFORM

Organize students into small groups. Have each group use drawing paper and markers to design a plan for a dream city of the early 1900s. Direct students to label and annotate proposed buildings and land uses. Then call on volunteers from each group to present their plan, citing the urban problems they have addressed and their proposed solutions for those problems.

In another campaign to make the cities more-healthful places to live, a group of physicians and reform-minded citizens formed the National Tuberculosis Association. The association focused on education and on lobbying the government to fund special hospitals to treat victims of tuberculosis. Thanks in part to this effort, by 1915 the death rate from TB had dropped significantly.

Other reformers campaigned for more city parks and playgrounds to provide safe places for children to play. The playground developed earlier at Jane Addams's Hull House in Chicago served as the model, and by 1920, millions of dollars had been spent establishing playgrounds.

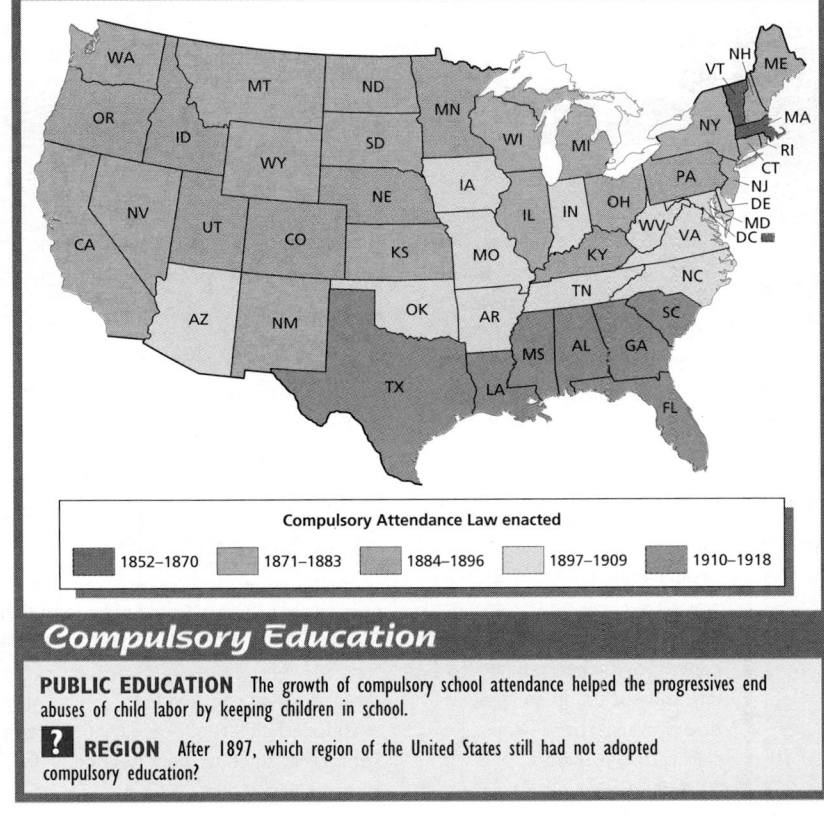

Compulsory Attendance Law enacted

| ■ 1852–1870 | ■ 1871–1883 | ■ 1884–1896 | ■ 1897–1909 | ■ 1910–1918 |

Compulsory Education

PUBLIC EDUCATION The growth of compulsory school attendance helped the progressives end abuses of child labor by keeping children in school.

? **REGION** After 1897, which region of the United States still had not adopted compulsory education?

City planning. Progressives firmly believed that cleaned-up cities would produce better citizens. Out of this belief grew the city-planning movement. The first National Conference on City Planning was held in 1909. Through wise planning, its members hoped, the spread of slums could be halted and cities could be beautified. Beautiful cities and imposing public architecture, they argued, would instill patriotism among the immigrant population.

In 1909 Daniel Burnham, a leading architect and city planner, produced a magnificent plan for redesigning Chicago, the first comprehensive plan to redesign an American city. The centerpiece of Burnham's vision for Chicago was a soaring city hall that would inspire all residents to be good citizens. "Make no little plans," said Burnham. "They have no magic to stir men's blood."

City-planning commissions in Washington, D.C., Cleveland, and San Francisco also engaged Burnham to

◀ **Daniel Burnham**

◀ **Daniel Burnham's plan for Chicago included wide intersecting streets similar to the ones he saw in Paris.**

COOPERATIVE LEARNING

Have students work in groups of three to portray members of a city commission that is formulating a plan for urban reform. One member should be in charge of urban services, another of health and education, and another of moral reform. Encourage groups to present their plans to the class.

■■ Ask students if they have participated in any projects to beautify their community.

AV **TRANSPARENCY**

Linking Geography and History Transparency and **Worksheet 11A**

Changing Ways

THE ORPHAN TRAINS

LINK TO TODAY

An organization called the Orphan Train Heritage Society of America was formed in 1986. Since then, dozens of former "train orphans" have gathered together to share their stories and to make sure that lessons of the orphan train movement are not forgotten.

THINKING CRITICALLY

Have students read the quote from the Children's Aid Society on p. 524. Then read to them the following quote from a 72-year-old former train orphan. "New York missed a good thing when they shipped out so many talented people." Ask students which statement they agree with more and the reasons for their choice.

PRIMARY SOURCE

Description of Change: excerpted
Rationale: excerpted to focus on main idea

Changing Ways

THE ORPHAN TRAINS

In the late 1800s and early 1900s, periodic economic downswings left many people unable to provide for their families. Urban immigrants faced desperate poverty. Many children of broken families, or whose parents could not provide for them, roamed the streets of New York and other eastern cities.

Many of these children died; others ended up in orphanages. But most found a way to survive on the streets. They shined shoes, sold newspapers, or picked pockets by day and curled up to sleep in doorways, garbage heaps, or outhouses at night.

Progressives and other reformers pitied the abandoned children. But they also feared that without parents to teach them right from wrong, the children posed a danger to society. As the Children's Aid Society warned:

> 66 They will vote—they will have the same rights as we ourselves though they have grown up ignorant of moral principle. . . . Let society beware, when the vicious, reckless multitude of New York boys, swarming now in every foul alley and low street, come to know their power and use it! 99

The founding director of the Children's Aid Society, the minister Charles Loring Brace,

▲ Children whose parents could no longer care for them often were sent to orphanages. Some remained there until they were old enough to take care of themselves; others were placed in homes or ran away.

devised a plan to provide for abandoned children. Brace reasoned that since farmers needed laborers and street urchins needed homes, why not bring these adults and children together? By 1914 the Society had transported some 116,000 children on "orphan trains" from eastern cities to a very different life on farms in New England, the South, and the Midwest.

Photojournalist Jacob Riis, a supporter of the Society, described how "big-hearted farmers" came from miles away to meet the trains and choose from the "little troop[s]" of children. "Night falls," he wrote, "upon a joyous band returning home over the quiet country road, the little stranger snugly stowed among his new friends, one of them already, with home and life before him."

Despite this idealized picture, there were problems. Some critics justifiably charged

that the Society failed to turn away farmers who were looking for no more than cheap labor. Others condemned the lack of adequate follow-up supervision. They argued that such safeguards were necessary to protect children from being taken advantage of economically or abused physically. Still others accused the Society of "dumping" New York's juvenile delinquents. As a result, some states passed laws restricting the placement of children in foster homes across state borders.

Whatever the shortcomings of the program, it provoked a long and fruitful debate on how the nation could provide for abandoned or orphaned children. Before the first orphan train departed in 1854, child-welfare workers saw institutionalization as the only option. By 1900 "placing out"—finding homes for children—had become the preferred solution.

MORAL REFORM

Have students work in pairs to write a newspaper editorial either supporting or opposing prohibition or motion pictures. Then ask each student in each pair to write a letter to the editor, taking the opposite view. Select pairs to read their editorials and letters to the class. Students may wish to include their letters in their portfolios.

▶

develop grand schemes for their cities. His plans were never fully realized, but some, such as those for Washington, D. C., were a success. Above all, his efforts helped people realize that city planning—parks, building codes, sanitation standards, and zoning—was a necessary function of municipal government.

■■ **Progressives sought to clean up the cities by enlarging the function of government to include housing standards, public health, and city planning.**

URBAN MORAL REFORM

Progressives also wanted to "clean up" what they considered to be immoral behavior. Toward this end, they pushed for prohibition—a ban on the manufacture and sale of alcoholic beverages—and for the closing of the nation's saloons. Reformers believed that prohibition and the elimination of saloons would have several benefits. These reforms would lessen social problems by removing what reformers viewed as two of the chief causes of unemployment: crime and the breakup of families. Such actions would also limit the powers of brewery and liquor interests, groups that exercised considerable influence over the government.

▲ While serving as president of the WCTU, Frances Willard also helped organize the Prohibition party in 1882.

The Anti-Saloon League (ASL) and the **Woman's Christian Temperance Union** (WCTU), an offshoot of the mid-19th-century temperance movement, led the crusade against alcohol. By 1902 the ASL had branches in 39 states with 200 paid staff members. It sent out thousands of volunteer speakers, many of them Protestant ministers, to spread the anti-saloon message in the nation's churches.

Billy Sunday, an ex-ballplayer and a Presbyterian minister, preached that the saloon was "the sum of all villainies," and "the parent of crimes and the mother of sins." Frances Willard, who presided over the WCTU from 1879 to 1898, described the zeal she felt as she led a prayer meeting in a saloon early in her career:

> 66 Kneeling on that sawdust floor, with a group of earnest hearts around me, and behind them, filling every corner and extending out into the street, a crowd of unwashed, unkempt, hard-looking drinking men, I was conscious that perhaps never in my life, save beside my sister Mary's dying bed, had I prayed as truly as I did then. 99

A brilliant organizer and magnetic public speaker, Willard eventually made the WCTU a powerful national force for temperance, moral purity, and the rights of women.

Drawing on Americans' spirit of patriotic sacrifice, prohibitionists achieved their goal during World War I. The **Eighteenth Amendment**, which Congress passed in 1917 and the states ratified in 1919, barred the manufacture, sale, or importation of alcoholic beverages. The amendment proved unpopular and difficult to enforce, however, and was repealed in 1933 (see Chapter 22).

The growing popularity of the newly invented motion picture gave urban reformers another source of danger to worry about. The first movie to tell a story, *The Great Train Robbery,* was

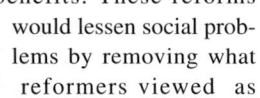

▼ Movie theaters attracted large crowds by showing action films such as *The Great Train Robbery*. Early cowboy stars gained worldwide fame from these movie westerns.

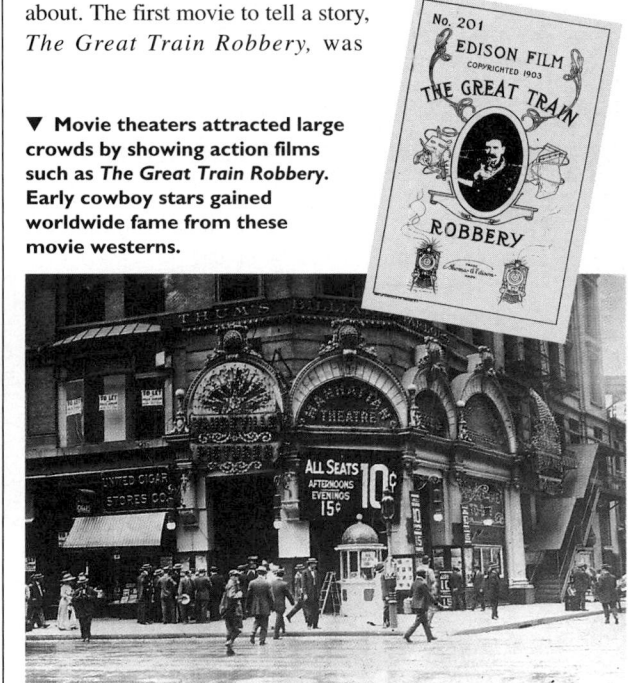

PRIMARY SOURCE
Description of Change: excerpted
Rationale: excerpted to focus on main idea

HISTORICAL SIDELIGHTS

A Flamboyant Preacher

Billy Sunday was born in Ames, Iowa, in 1862. After completing high school and holding a variety of odd jobs, he joined the Chicago White Sox baseball team in 1883. For the next eight years he played professional baseball in Chicago, Philadelphia, and Pittsburgh. During this time he experienced a religious conversion. He became a revivalist preacher and was ordained in the Presbyterian church in 1903. Sunday, a flamboyant preacher, gained a huge following and purportedly accumulated a fortune from the offerings of his followers.

Teaching the Section

DISCRIMINATION AND PREJUDICES

Organize students into small groups. Ask half the groups to outline a speech to be given by an African American progressive. Ask the other half to outline a speech to be given by an American Indian progressive. Tell students that the speeches should express their feelings as African Americans or American Indians about progressive reform and should advocate methods to be used to draw attention to their community's needs. Then stage a rally for reform with volunteers from each group giving the speeches.

PRIMARY SOURCES

Description of Change: excerpted

Rationale: excerpted to focus on main idea

■■ Ask students how the concerns about movies voiced in the primary source (column 1) compare to concerns about movies today.

BIOGRAPHY PERSONALITIES IN HISTORY

While at Atlanta University in 1897, Du Bois began what he called his "real life work." He began a scientific study of the problems of city blacks, collecting facts to support his theories. His intent was to study and publish the findings of one aspect of African American life each year for 10 years. After the 10-year cycle had been repeated 10 times, 100 years of research material about African American life would be available as a source for scholars and government leaders. After 10 years, however, lack of funds brought the work to an end.

---

produced in 1903, and by 1910, millions of Americans were attending the movies each week. In 1916 the *New York Times* could declare that films were the fifth-largest U.S. industry.

To the urban poor a 5- to 10-cent movie ticket provided cheap, readily available entertainment. But many middle-class Americans believed that movies—especially the steamy romances—and movie houses were immoral and sources of temptation, particularly for the young. As one writer of the time reported:

> **66** The pictures thrown upon the luminous curtain of the stage have been declared extremely corrupting to the idle young people lurking in the darkness before it. The darkness itself has been held a condition of inexpressible depravity and a means of allurement to evil. **99**

Declaring that moviegoing "softens the mental fibre and saps the character," reformers demanded that motion pictures be censored. Several states and cities set up censorship boards to ban movies they considered immoral. In 1909 the movie industry began to censor itself.

■■ **Reformers sought to improve American morals by working for prohibition and censorship of movies.**

---

*T*HE LIMITS OF PROGRESSIVISM

For nonwhites the Progressive movement had mixed results. While most progressives were concerned about the plight of the poor, few white progressives devoted very much energy to the problems of discrimination and prejudice against African Americans and American Indians. Some progressives even expressed openly racist sentiments against these groups. Many African Americans and American Indians, however, drew on progressive ideas to develop programs appropriate to their own communities.

BIOGRAPHY

One of the most influential black leaders to emerge during this period was W.E.B. Du Bois (doo BOYS). Born in 1868 in Great Barrington, Massachusetts, Du Bois graduated from Fisk University, a black school in Nashville, Tennessee. He then studied history in Germany and at Harvard University. In 1895 he became the first African American to earn a doctorate from Harvard. Two years later he was hired as a professor of history and economics at Atlanta University, a leading African American college, where he taught until 1910.

By the early 1900s Du Bois was recognized as a brilliant thinker and strong advocate of African American civil rights and culture. He believed that the opportunity for a college education, as well as vocational training, would best ensure progress for African Americans. He also believed that African Americans should be politically active in the struggle for racial equality.

Throughout his life Du Bois maintained a passionate interest in Africa, which he regarded as the spiritual homeland of all blacks. In his influential book *The Souls of Black Folk* (1903), Du Bois eloquently expressed his dual identity as both African and American:

> **66** One feels his two-ness—an American, a Negro, two souls, two thoughts, two unreconciled strivings, two warring ideals. . . .
>
> The history of the American Negro is the history of this strife. . . . He would not Africanize America. . . . He would not bleach the Negro soul in a flood of white Americanism. . . . He simply wishes to make it possible for a man to be both a Negro and an American, without being cursed and spit upon. **99**

W.E.B. Du Bois

In the 1920s, in an effort to forge greater unity among blacks and to promote pride in their African heritage, Du Bois organized a series of Pan-African congresses, which attracted black leaders from around the world.

During the 1930s and 1940s, Du Bois continued his career as a scholar and political activist. By the 1950s he had embraced socialism—which attracted many prominent American intellectuals, both black and white—for its promise

IMMIGRANTS AND PROGRESSIVES

Set up two student "face-off" panels: Ask one panel to assume roles of progressives in the early 1900s and the other panel to represent immigrants. Have the members of each panel discuss how to help the immigrant poor from that panel's point of view. Encourage the rest of the class to question and challenge panel members on their positions. Close the discussion by asking the progressive panel to list proposals on the chalkboard and the immigrant panel to support or reject each proposal and explain why.

of social justice. In 1961, at age 93, Du Bois joined the Communist party and moved to Ghana, where he died two years later.

The fight for racial justice. In 1909, in an effort to end racial discrimination, Du Bois, along with leading white progressives such as Jane Addams, helped found the **National Association for the Advancement of Colored People** (NAACP). Through its magazine, *The Crisis,* which Du Bois edited, the NAACP publicized cases of racial inequality and called for social reforms that would ensure equal rights for African Americans.

The NAACP also worked through the courts to end restrictions on voting and on other civil rights. In 1915 it won its first major victory in *Guinn* v. *United States.* In this case the Supreme Court outlawed the "grandfather clause." Southern states used this clause to ensure that suffrage requirements designed to keep blacks from voting would not apply to whites. Two years later, NAACP lawyers won *Buchanan* v. *Warley,* which overturned a

▶ Du Bois served as editor of *The Crisis* from 1910 to 1932. This monthly magazine focused on issues important to African Americans.

THE CRISIS
A RECORD OF THE DARKER RACES

Louisville, Kentucky, law requiring racially segregated housing. As a result, similar laws were struck down across the country. Since then the NAACP has continued to fight for blacks' legal rights.

Another important organization in the struggle for racial justice during this period was the National Urban League. Founded in 1910 by concerned blacks and whites, the League worked to improve job opportunities and housing for urban

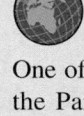

GLOBAL CONNECTIONS

One of the main purposes of the Pan-African congresses was to garner support for the independence of the African colonies of European nations. At these conferences Du Bois continued to condemn the exploitation of Africa by imperialist countries and called for the dismantling of the French and British colonial empires.

Map Caption Answer
the South

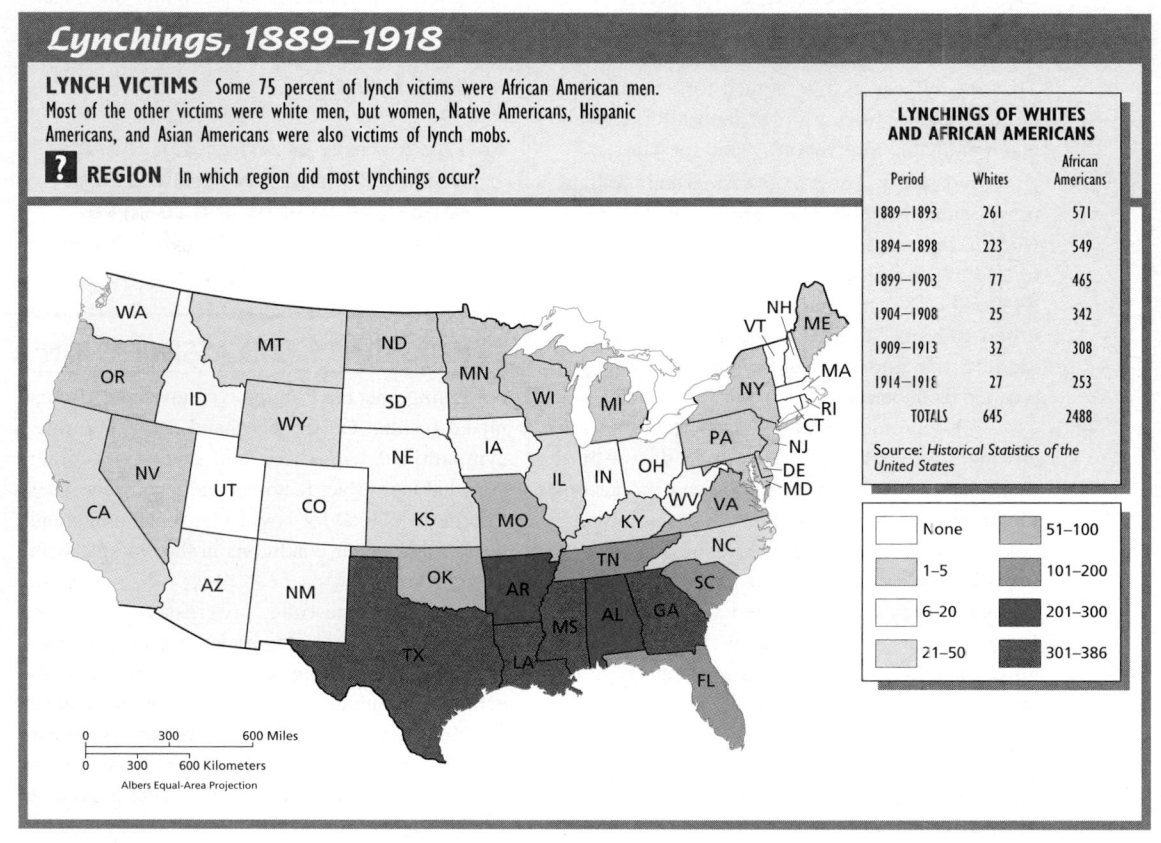

Lynchings, 1889–1918

LYNCH VICTIMS Some 75 percent of lynch victims were African American men. Most of the other victims were white men, but women, Native Americans, Hispanic Americans, and Asian Americans were also victims of lynch mobs.

? REGION In which region did most lynchings occur?

LYNCHINGS OF WHITES AND AFRICAN AMERICANS

Period	Whites	African Americans
1889–1893	261	571
1894–1898	223	549
1899–1903	77	465
1904–1908	25	342
1909–1913	32	308
1914–1918	27	253
TOTALS	645	2488

Source: *Historical Statistics of the United States*

None
1–5
6–20
21–50
51–100
101–200
201–300
301–386

0   300   600 Miles
0   300   600 Kilometers
Albers Equal-Area Projection

Practice

GUIDED PRACTICE

Create an outline on the chalkboard, using *Reforming Society* as the title and the section's subheads as the main topics. Leave space under each subhead. Call on students to list details that might appear under each main topic and add them to the outline.

THINKING CRITICALLY

Recognizing Prejudice

In his First Annual Message (1901), President Theodore Roosevelt spoke in favor of the assimilation of Indians, calling for an end to their rights of heritage and for the breakup of their tribal lands. Roosevelt said Native Americans should conform to white customs and that their need for anything beyond a vocational education was "very limited." Ask students how the attitude of the government's chief executive may have kept many American Indians from accepting assimilation.

HISTORICAL SIDELIGHTS

Immigration Restriction

Business leaders opposed restricting immigration for the same reason that the labor unions supported it— immigrants were a source of low-paid unorganized workers. Many southerners opposed restriction because they hoped to attract immigrant workers. By 1910, however, cultural issues and concerns caused many opposition groups to begin to lean toward restrictions on immigration.

AV TRANSPARENCY

Linking Geography and History Transparency and Worksheet 13A

INDEPENDENT PRACTICE

Ask students to choose a main topic and accompanying details from the outline developed in the Guided Practice and use them to write a subsection of an encyclopedia article that might appear under an entry titled "Social Reform."

Review and Assessment

REVIEW Have students use the Essential Points of the section to write an essay that explains how the progressives worked to reform society. Then assign the Section 3 Review on p. 529.

ASSESS Assign the **Section 3 Daily Quiz** in *Core Resources*.

---

blacks. One of its chief goals was to help African American migrants from the South adjust to life in northern cities. Today the National Urban League carries on its efforts to end racial discrimination and to aid the disadvantaged.

The NAACP and the National Urban League made possible some important gains for black citizens. Nevertheless, most African Americans still faced discrimination and denial of equal rights. The long struggle to eliminate racism continued.

▪▪ **Black leaders and organizations such as the NAACP and the National Urban League fought for racial justice. But racism continued to haunt American life.**

American Indian progressives. Most Indian rights advocates initially supported the Dawes Act of 1887 (see Chapter 14), which encouraged American Indians to abandon reservation life and become private landowners. By the early 20th century, however, it was clear that this policy had led many Indians to lose their property to land speculators and fall deeper into poverty. Thus, many progressives argued for a more gradual approach: slowing down land allotment and maintaining the reservation system for a time.

In 1911 a group of 50 American Indians, most of them middle-class professional men and women, formed the **Society of American Indians** to address the problems facing Indians. One of its members, Seneca historian Arthur C. Parker, urged Indians "to strike out into the duties of modern life and . . . find every right that had escaped them before."

While some members supported strengthening tribal values, most favored complete assimilation. The Society publicized the accomplishments of famous Indians such as Olympic gold medalist Jim Thorpe and lobbied against the use of such derogatory terms as "buck" and "squaw." They also discussed ways to improve Indian health, education, civil rights, and local government. But the Society's moderate positions on most issues led to disputes among members, thus weakening the organization.

One member, Dr. Carlos Montezuma, a Yavapai-Apache, urged the Society to criticize the Bureau of Indian Affairs for mismanaging

▲ As a founder of the Society of American Indians, Gertrude S. Bonnin fought to protect Indians in Oklahoma from exploitation. There, land speculators used every possible tactic to secure oil leases to valuable Indian property.

reservations. Most Society members refused to take such a strong antigovernment stand, and the group's influence dwindled after 1923. While the Society did not last long, it provided a forum for Indian leaders and a basis for later attempts to improve conditions for Indians.

▪▪ **The Society of American Indians worked to improve the image of American Indians and to solve the problems they faced.**

IMMIGRANTS AND ASSIMILATION

For immigrants the Progressive movement also had mixed results. On the one hand, many reformers sympathized with the plight of the newcomers crowded into urban factories and tenements. These reformers lobbied for laws to improve immigrants' lives and to better conditions in the workplace and in city slums.

At the same time, progressives criticized immigrants, accusing them of immoral behavior— of drinking, gambling, and other vices. They also denounced immigrant support for big-city political machines. As a result, some native-born Americans with progressive ideals also favored restricting immigration. Madison Grant was a case in point. In 1916 Grant, a prominent New Yorker, published

RETEACH Organize students into small work groups to reread the Focus questions on p. 522. Have students answer each question in round-robin style, with one student in each group recording the answers. Then have volunteers read their groups' answers.

Closure

Discuss how actions of early 1900s reformers still affect life in the 1990s. Ask students to name and comment on programs and organizations begun in the Progressive Era that continue to affect society today. Have students comment on which of the many reforms they think had the greatest impact on future generations.

Extension

INVESTIGATE Have students research reformers who are questioning the impact of TV and movies on society today. Have them compare the present-day crusade with reformers' efforts in the Progressive Era.

COMPARE Have students find newspaper and magazine articles about recent immigrants. Have them write a paper comparing the experiences of today's immigrants with those of the immigrants of the early 1900s.

The Passing of the Great Race. In this book he expressed racist opinions about African Americans, Jews, and immigrants from southern and eastern Europe. Yet Grant was also a progressive who supported urban planning and other reforms.

Many progressives believed immigrants should be "Americanized" as quickly as possible. Americanizing, though, often meant trying to reshape them in the mold of the native-born Protestant majority. Russian immigrant Eugene Lyons described the effects of this process in *Assignment in Utopia*:

66 We sensed a disrespect for the alien traditions in our homes and came unconsciously to resent and despise those traditions . . . because they seemed [impossible] barriers between ourselves and the adopted land. 99

▲ In 1890 Arnold Genthe photographed this Chinese immigrant family on an outing in San Francisco.

The Granger Collection, New York

Not all progressives viewed immigrants with suspicion, however. Some, like Jane Addams, welcomed the diverse culture that immigrant groups were helping to create. The philosopher Horace Kallen in his 1924 book on culture and democracy also envisioned a nation that would be home to a number of distinctive cultures.

In addition, the immigrant poor and the political bosses who represented them supported middle-class progressives when they fought for practical reforms such as worker protection and public-health programs. On such issues the big-city political machines sometimes played a key role. For example, a New York State legislative committee set up to investigate factory conditions after the Triangle fire won strong backing from New York City's immigrant-based democratic machine.

■■ **Immigrants supported progressive reformers on practical health and welfare issues.**

PRIMARY SOURCE
Description of Change: excerpted and bracketed
Rationale: excerpted to focus on main idea; bracketed to clarify meaning

SECTION REVIEW ANSWERS

IDENTIFY
For significance, see the following pages:
Lawrence Veiller (p. 522)
Woman's Christian Temperance Union (p. 525)
Frances Willard (p. 525)
Eighteenth Amendment (p. 525)
W.E.B. Du Bois (p. 526)
National Association for the Advancement of Colored People (p. 527)
Society of American Indians (p. 528)

1. *enlarging the function of government to include housing standards, public health, and city planning*
2. *through prohibition, censorship of movies*
3. *African Americans founded organizations such as NAACP to fight for racial justice. Native Americans founded Society of American Indians to solve common problems.*
4. *Pamphlets might mention efforts to protect workers, public-health programs, and housing regulations; or accusations of immoral behavior and morality, racism.*
5. *to lessen social problems by removing what they considered one of the chief causes*

■ ■
SECTION 3 REVIEW

IDENTIFY and explain the significance of the following: Lawrence Veiller, Woman's Christian Temperance Union, Frances Willard, Eighteenth Amendment, W.E.B. Du Bois, National Association for the Advancement of Colored People, Society of American Indians.

1. **MAIN IDEA** What approach did progressives use to clean up American cities?
2. **MAIN IDEA** How did reformers attempt to improve American morality?
3. **MAIN IDEA** How did African Americans and Native Americans attempt to fight racism and discrimination?
4. **WRITING TO EXPLAIN** Imagine you are an immigrant. Write a brief pamphlet for other immigrants that attempts to explain why you do or do not support the Progressive movement.
5. **ANALYZING** Why did progressives support prohibition and the elimination of saloons?

Return to the Themes section on p. 510. Have students discuss these again and compare their original responses with those given now. (See p. 509B for suggested answers.)

Chapter Review Answers

WRITING A SUMMARY
See Essential Points in each section for main ideas.

REVIEWING CHRONOLOGY
5, 2, 4, 3, 1
Evaluating
created public outcry for new legislation to protect workers

IDENTIFYING PEOPLE AND IDEAS
1. *urban reform movement inspired by spirit of social justice*
2. *reformer and co-worker of Florence Kelley who helped research the "Brandeis Brief"*
3. *progressive journalists who exposed racial injustice and corruption in government and business*
4. *organizer of National Child Labor Committee who worked to prohibit child labor and to limit working hours for women*
5. *principle that workers had right to accept any conditions of employment that business owners required*
6. *architect who developed first comprehensive plan to redesign an American city*
7. *system under which government or worker cooperatives own businesses*
8. *reformer who worked for a law that set standards for urban housing*
9. *president of WCTU (1879–98)*
10. *organization formed by Native Americans, most of whom favored assimilation; worked to improve image, solve problems*
11. *muckraker who documented urban political corruption in The Shame of the Cities*

UNDERSTANDING MAIN IDEAS
1. *Women worked through reform organizations, wrote books and articles, and urged laws to correct social evils; one of the few ways in which they could influence social change and use their education, and one of the few careers open to them.*
2. *Muckrakers exposed corruption, urban social problems, and racial injustice. Writers and intellectuals attacked social problems and offered ideas for their solution.*
3. *child labor, long hours, low wages, unsafe working conditions*
4. *worked to clean up and beautify cities; passed housing laws, building codes, public-health measures; campaigned for parks and playgrounds*
5. *founded organizations to help fight racial injustice, improve image, and solve their unique problems*

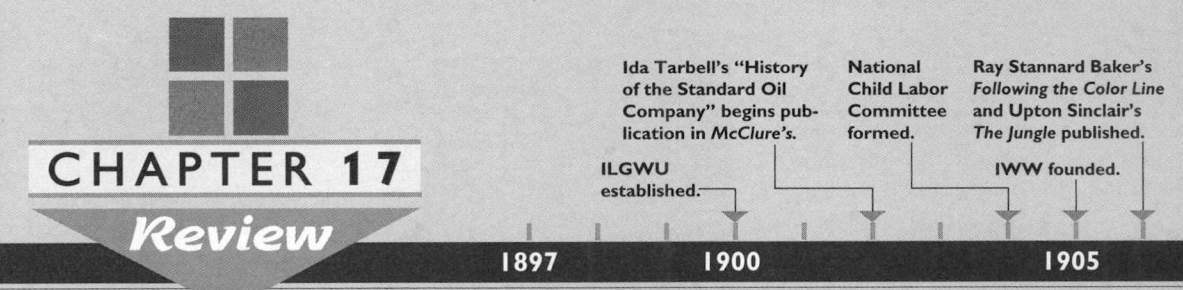

CHAPTER 17
Review

Ida Tarbell's "History of the Standard Oil Company" begins publication in *McClure's*.

National Child Labor Committee formed.

Ray Stannard Baker's *Following the Color Line* and Upton Sinclair's *The Jungle* published.

ILGWU established.

IWW founded.

1897   1900   1905

WRITING A SUMMARY
Using the essential points of the chapter as a guide, write a summary of the chapter.

REVIEWING CHRONOLOGY
Number your paper 1 to 5. Study the time line above, and list the following events in the order in which they happened by writing the first next to 1, the second next to 2, and so on. Then complete the activity below.

1. Eighteenth Amendment ratified.
2. IWW founded.
3. Massachusetts passes minimum-wage law.
4. NAACP founded.
5. National Child Labor Committee formed.

Evaluating What effect did the Triangle Shirtwaist Company fire have on improving workplace safety?

IDENTIFYING PEOPLE AND IDEAS
Explain the historical significance of each of the following people or terms.

1. progressivism
2. Josephine Goldmark
3. muckrakers
4. Florence Kelley
5. freedom of contract
6. Daniel Burnham
7. socialism
8. Lawrence Veiller
9. Frances Willard
10. Society of American Indians
11. Lincoln Steffens

UNDERSTANDING MAIN IDEAS
1. In what ways did women work for progressive goals? Why were they so active in the Progressive movement?
2. What roles did muckrakers, writers, and intellectuals play in the reform movement?
3. Which labor issues did reformers hope to remedy through legislation?
4. What actions did progressive reformers take to improve conditions in cities?
5. What steps did African American and Native American progressives take to address the problems facing their communities?

REVIEWING THEMES
1. **Economic Development** Why did states pass laws to protect workers' rights?
2. **Democratic Values** How did progressives propose to extend opportunities to all citizens? Were they successful in these efforts? Why or why not?
3. **Constitutional Heritage** How did progressives help win passage of the Eighteenth Amendment?

THINKING CRITICALLY
1. **Analyzing** How did industrialization influence progressive reform efforts?
2. **Hypothesizing** How might the course of reform have been different if the Supreme Court had supported more early social legislation?
3. **Contrasting** How did the AFL and the IWW differ in their views on the scope and nature of labor reform?

STRATEGY FOR SUCCESS
Review the Strategies for Success on Interpreting Economic Data on page 506. Study the two graphs below. This information was compiled as an average for all industries in the period from 1900 to 1910. What conclusions can you draw from the graph data about the impact of progressivism?

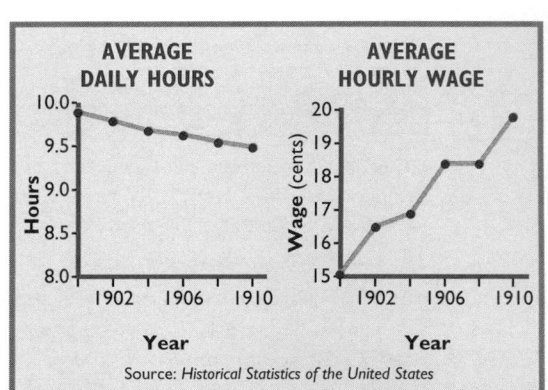

AVERAGE DAILY HOURS

Hours

10.0 — 9.5 — 9.0 — 8.5 — 8.0

1902 1906 1910

Year

AVERAGE HOURLY WAGE

Wage (cents)

20 — 19 — 18 — 17 — 16 — 15

1902 1906 1910

Year

Source: *Historical Statistics of the United States*

REVIEWING THEMES

1. because of pressure on legislatures from reformers to pass such laws
2. by proposing election reforms that would enable people to participate more fully in running their government, by promoting legislation to curb corporate power, by seeking social justice; generally successful because many of their reforms were enacted; however, racist attitudes and lack of respect for ethnic differences marred the record of many progressive reformers
3. by campaigning vigorously for prohibition and elimination of saloons

THINKING CRITICALLY

1. Industrialization contributed to labor abuses and overcrowding, which increased urban problems but also fostered respect for progress; reformers focused on correcting urban problems and believed science and technology could help solve these problems.
2. might have reduced conflicts between employers and workers, led to faster and greater improvement of working conditions
3. AFL worked within system, negotiating with business owners and focusing on skilled workers; IWW opposed capitalism and focused on the needs of unskilled workers.

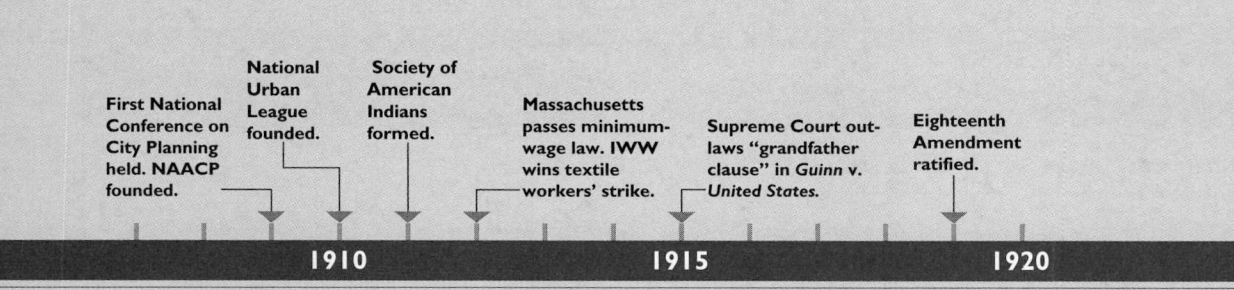

First National Conference on City Planning held. NAACP founded.

National Urban League founded.

Society of American Indians formed.

Massachusetts passes minimum-wage law. IWW wins textile workers' strike.

Supreme Court outlaws "grandfather clause" in *Guinn* v. *United States.*

Eighteenth Amendment ratified.

1910   1915   1920

WRITING ABOUT HISTORY

Writing to Persuade Imagine you are the young Boston lawyer Louis D. Brandeis. Write a closing argument attempting to convince the Supreme Court to uphold laws that guarantee workers' rights. Include specific examples of working conditions to support your arguments.

USING PRIMARY SOURCES

In 1905 W.E.B. Du Bois wrote to an African American student who was discouraged about the career opportunities that would be available to her. Read the following excerpt from his letter and write a summary of his advice to her.

> ❝ *I have heard that you are a young woman of some ability but that you are neglecting your school work because you have become hopeless of trying to do anything in the world. I am very sorry for this. . . .*
>
> *There are in the U.S. today tens of thousands of colored girls who would be happy beyond measure to have the chance of educating themselves that you are neglecting. If you train yourself as you easily can, there are wonderful chances of usefulness before you: you can join the ranks of 15,000 Negro women teachers, of hundreds of nurses and physicians, of the growing number of clerks and stenographers. . . . Ignorance is a cure for nothing. Get the very best training possible & the doors of opportunity will fly open before you as they are flying before thousands of your fellows. On the other hand every time a colored person neglects an opportunity, it makes it more difficult for others of the race to get such an opportunity. Do you want to cut off the chances of the boys and girls of tomorrow?* ❞

LINKING HISTORY AND GEOGRAPHY

Review the map on compulsory education on page 523. Note that most states adopted compulsory attendance laws for school-aged children during the 19th century, but 19 states did not do so until after 1896. Where are most of these 19 states located? Drawing on what you have learned in previous chapters, what factors might help explain the link between geographic region and the timing of passage of compulsory attendance laws for school-aged children?

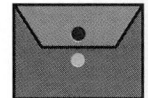
BUILDING YOUR PORTFOLIO

Complete the following projects independently or cooperatively.

1. **REFORM** Imagine you are a progressive reformer in the early 1900s. Write an editorial for *McClure's, Cosmopolitan,* or another progressive magazine that addresses an urban problem in government, business, the workplace, or the community. Be sure that your editorial suggests a possible solution to the problem. Editorials might examine political machines, corporate abuses, poor working conditions, or public-health concerns.

2. **DEMOCRATIC RIGHTS** Imagine you are a progressive reformer working to promote women's rights. Prepare a speech on women's rights to deliver at an Independence Day celebration. Be sure that the speech outlines the various problems and concerns faced by women in the early 1900s and indicates how progressive reformers intend to address these problems and concerns.

THE PROGRESSIVE PRESIDENTS

1900–1920

Chapter Overview

In an effort to improve life for all Americans, the progressives sought to curb corrupt politicians and to mobilize the power of government to improve society. Initial efforts were at the local level, but the spirit of reform soon spread to all levels of government.

Theodore Roosevelt, William Howard Taft, and Woodrow Wilson all used the office of the president to further the aims of progressivism. Some gains were made in cleaning up government and regulating big business, but by 1916 much still remained to be done.

THE AMERICAN NATION VIDEODISC PROGRAM A variety of still images, short videos, and activities are available for you to use as you teach this chapter. See Videodisc Resources in the Core Resources Binder for barcode correlations and suggestions for using the program.

Chapter Planning Guide

CHAPTER 18	CORE RESOURCES	AUDIOVISUAL RESOURCES	PROGRAM RESOURCES
INTRODUCTION pp. 532–533	■ Literature Worksheet 18 ■ Building Your Portfolio Worksheet 6	■ Everyday Life in America Transparency and Worksheet 18	
TEACHING THE CHAPTER pp. 534–553	■ Graphic Organizer 18 ■ Social Studies Skills Worksheet 18 ■ Geography Worksheet 18 ■ Outline Map 9	■ *The American Nation* Videodisc: Yosemite National Park	■ *Eyewitnesses and Others,* Volume 2: Reading 28
REVIEW AND ASSESSMENT pp. 554–555	■ Chapter 18 Daily Quizzes ■ Review Worksheet 18 ■ Chapter 18 Tests ■ Alternative Assessment Forms		■ Test Generator

Additional Resources

BOOKS FOR TEACHERS

Broderick, Francis L. *Progressivism at Risk: Electing a President in 1912.* Greenwood Press, 1989. Issues surrounding the 1912 presidential election.

Cashman, Sean D. *America in the Age of the Titans.* New York University Press, 1988. A thorough account of the Progressive Era.

Giese, James R. *The Progressive Era: The Limits of Reform.* 2nd ed. Social Science Education Consortium, 1989. A review of progressive reforms.

BOOKS FOR STUDENTS

Cooper, John Milton, Jr. *Pivotal Decades.* Norton, 1990. Reviews historical developments from 1900 to 1920.

*Fritz, Jean. *Bully for You, Teddy Roosevelt!* Putnam, 1991. Award-winning author explores the life of TR.

*Whitelaw, Nancy. *Theodore Roosevelt Takes Charge.* Albert Whitman, 1992. Chronicles the life of Theodore Roosevelt.

* for students reading below grade level

MULTIMEDIA MATERIALS

TR & His Times. Video, 58 min. PBS. A study of the life and times of Theodore Roosevelt.

The United States in the 20th Century: 1900–1912. Video, 12 min. Coronet Instructional Films. Focuses on the administrations of Roosevelt and Taft.

The United States in the 20th Century: 1912–1920. Video, 12 min. Coronet Instructional Films. Examines the presidency of Woodrow Wilson.

ᎢHEMES IN AMERICAN HISTORY

USE WITH PAGES
532–533

Listed on the right are the themes emphasized in Chapter 18. The questions in boldface type stimulate critical thinking and provide students with an opportunity to discuss the themes within a broadened context. The questions also appear in the pupil's edition on p. 532.

■ DEMOCRATIC VALUES

What are some ways in which government can restore political power to the people? Students might suggest that government could restore power to the people by allowing more people to vote, by filling more offices by election instead of by appointment, and by allowing voters a more direct voice in shaping the laws that affect them. Limiting the power of government officials by making them more accountable to the voters who elected them also increases the people's political power.

■ ECONOMIC DEVELOPMENT

How can government regulate business practices without discouraging free enterprise? Students might suggest that a democratically elected government has an obligation to the public that empowers it. This obligation may include some oversight of business practices in the public interest, such as protecting consumers from harmful products or protecting businesses from dishonest competitors. Such business regulation provides for the general welfare without disrupting the free enterprise system.

■ CONSTITUTIONAL HERITAGE

How might people use constitutional change to reform politics and society? Students might suggest that government officials may not always meet the wants or needs of the majority—or even a large minority—of society, and that they may sometimes be more responsive to other powerful interests. In such cases people may call for a constitutional amendment to accomplish a reform. Students may note that reform achieved through amendment is more permanent than change accomplished by laws, which might be changed later or voided by the Supreme Court.

ᏟHAPTER STRATEGIES FOR MEETING INDIVIDUAL NEEDS

LIMITED ENGLISH PROFICIENT LEARNERS

Have students work in small groups to create flyers, banners, and signs that represent various points of view on the issues discussed in the chapter.

TACTILE/KINESTHETIC LEARNERS

Have students work in small groups to create an annotated, illustrated map of the National Parks system. Display the map on the bulletin board.

LEARNERS HAVING DIFFICULTY

Encourage students to write answers to the questions in each section's Focus. Then have them use these answers to write a brief summary of the chapter.

AUDITORY LEARNERS

Guide students to use the books listed on p. 531A to prepare dramatic readings on issues discussed in the chapter—tariff reform, business regulation, conservation, and women's suffrage, for example.

VISUAL LEARNERS

Ask students to review the chapter and other texts on the progressives to locate illustrations that represent the presidencies of Roosevelt, Taft, and Wilson. Call on volunteers to present and explain their selections.

GIFTED LEARNERS

Encourage students to write and present speeches that might have been given by Roosevelt, Taft, or Wilson on one of the issues discussed in the chapter.

USING THE CHAPTER FOCUS

■ UNDERSTANDING THE MAIN IDEA

Have students read the Understanding the Main Idea paragraph. Then ask them to suggest what kinds of reform legislation a progressive president like Roosevelt, Taft, or Wilson might propose or support in order to carry the reform agenda to the national level. List student responses on a flip chart. As students read the chapter, have them review and revise the list.

 **THEMES**
Have students work individually or in small groups to answer the questions under Themes. Save students' responses so that they can compare them with their responses after studying the chapter. (See p. 531B for suggested answers.)

■ THE TIME LINE

Have students list the time-line entries in their notebooks. Then, as they read the chapter, have them note what impact each event or incident on the time line had on the advance of progressivism.

CORE RESOURCES

- **Graphic Organizer 18**
- **Literature Worksheet 18**
- **Building Your Portfolio Worksheet 6**

AV RESOURCES

- **Everyday Life in America Transparency and Worksheet 18**

ABOUT THE ILLUSTRATION

Rallies similar to this one were held frequently by supporters of women's suffrage. On March 3, 1913, the day of Wilson's inauguration, the new president was almost upstaged by some 5,000 suffragists who marched down Pennsylvania Avenue. Ask students how they would react if they were members of a group that was denied the same rights as other Americans.

Chapter 18

1900–1920

THE PROGRESSIVE PRESIDENTS

FOCUS

UNDERSTANDING THE MAIN IDEA

Many progressives sought to extend their reform efforts to government itself. They wanted to take power away from corrupt political machines and mobilize the power of the government to improve American life. On the national level, presidents Theodore Roosevelt, William Howard Taft, and Woodrow Wilson tried in varying degrees to implement the progressive reform agenda.

THEMES

■ **DEMOCRATIC VALUES**
What are some ways in which government can restore political power to the people?

■ **ECONOMIC DEVELOPMENT** How can government regulate business practices without discouraging free enterprise?

■ **CONSTITUTIONAL HERITAGE** How might people use constitutional change to reform politics and society?

1901	1906	1910	1912	1914	1920
William McKinley assassinated.	Pure Food and Drug Act passed.	Mann-Elkins Act passed.	Progressive party formed.	Federal Trade Commission created.	Nineteenth Amendment ratified.

LINK TO THE PAST

Have volunteers recall and identify some of the strategies used by 19th-century reformers and record student responses on the chalkboard. Then, as they read the chapter, ask students to compare the chalkboard list to strategies used by the progressives.

■■ LINK TO THE PAST ▶

Various efforts to reform society had occupied American women and men throughout the 19th century. Reformers had campaigned to end slavery, to secure women's rights, and to correct the problems caused by industrialization and urbanization. Similar new efforts at reform engaged many middle-class Americans early in the 20th century.

Suffrage rally, 1912

HISTORICAL SIDELIGHTS
A Stepping-Stone?
Lincoln Steffens described Roosevelt's work as police commissioner as "pitiless reorganization and absolute publicity." Indeed, it seemed to many people that publicity was all-important to Roosevelt and that the commission was simply a stepping-stone to higher office. That office, Steffens and Riis suspected, was the presidency.

*O*n the morning of May 6, 1895, two progressive reporters, Jacob Riis and Lincoln Steffens, waited eagerly outside New York City police headquarters. The new head of the city's four-member police commission, Theodore Roosevelt, was due to arrive any minute. The reporters eagerly wished to find out Roosevelt's plans for reforming New York's notoriously corrupt police department.

Riis and Roosevelt were already friends and political allies. Five years before, Riis had gained national attention for his book *How the Other Half Lives,* in which he documented the grim reality of slum life in New York City. Roosevelt wrote to Riis, requesting a meeting, saying, "I have read your book, and I have come to help."

Now Roosevelt would have the chance to reform the nation's largest police force. Arriving at police headquarters, he called the two reporters into his office, leaving his fellow commissioners outside. Motioning Riis and Steffens to sit down, he said, "Now then, what'll we do?" As Steffens later recalled, "It was just as if we three were the Police Board." Within days Roosevelt had fired the police chief and had begun to clean up the department. By the end of the summer, fellow commissioner Avery Andrews noted, "The whole country . . . was talking about Theodore Roosevelt."

Six years later, Roosevelt was president of the United States. He brought to the White House the same boundless energy and progressive spirit he had demonstrated as police commissioner. Under Roosevelt's leadership progressivism moved from state and local politics into the national arena.

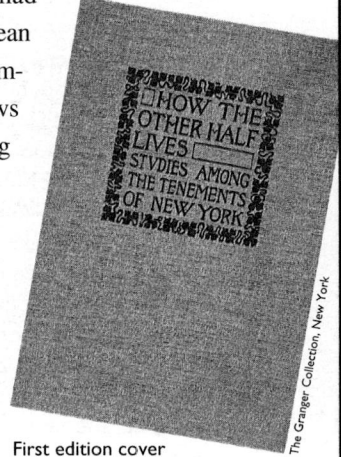

First edition cover of Riis's book

The Granger Collection, New York

FOCUS OBJECTIVES

- Describe the forms that government corruption took.

- Identify election reforms supported by progressives to make government more democratic.

- List reforms enacted in city and state governments during the Progressive Era.

VOICES IN HISTORY

A speaker of the Assembly in Wisconsin, Irvine L. Lenroot, described how corporate interests worked against Wisconsin's reform governor La Follette. "It was . . . generally understood in the Assembly that any member favoring the bill [that La Follette favored] could better his financial condition if he was willing to vote against it." Lenroot went on to say that "a prominent member stated that he did not dare to vote for the bill, because he was at the mercy of the railroad companies, and he was afraid they would ruin his business by advancing his rates."

CORE RESOURCES

- **Literature Worksheet 18**
- **Section 1 Daily Quiz**

534

PREVIEW WORKSHOP

Following is a list of the significant people, places, and terms in this section. You may wish to use this list as a section preview.

People
- Samuel M. Jones
- Tom Johnson
- Robert M. La Follette

Places
- Wisconsin

Terms
- direct primary
- Seventeenth Amendment
- initiative
- referendum
- recall
- Wisconsin Idea

MOTIVATING: STUDENT EXPERIENCES

Ask the class how candidates are selected for offices in school groups. As volunteers explain each group's process, have students evaluate how democratic each process is. Tell students that in this section they will discover how the process for selecting government officials became more democratic in the early 20th century.

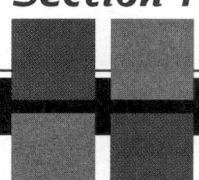

Section 1

REFORMING GOVERNMENT

FOCUS

- **What forms did government corruption take?**
- **What election reforms did progressives support to make government more democratic?**
- **What reforms were enacted in city and state governments during the Progressive Era?**

*P*rogressives did not limit their reform efforts to social ills. They also tackled the task of curbing the political power of the privileged few and removing the corrupt political machines that served them. Toward this end, progressives sought changes in the electoral process that would restore political power to the people.

New York political boss Charles Murphy voting, 1916

GOVERNMENT CORRUPTION

Theodore Roosevelt and other progressive reformers found corruption at all levels of government, from city hall to Washington, D.C. As Lincoln Steffens so graphically reported in *The Shame of the Cities,* urban political machines demanded bribes from anyone wanting to do business with city government.

In Philadelphia, for instance, in order to secure jobs teachers had to pay the political machine $120 of the first $141 they earned. In Pittsburgh, public jobs went to contractors who paid bribes. Of course, they were allowed to pad their bills to make up the losses. One Pittsburgh political boss even opened his own paving firm so that he could take the lion's share of contracts himself—at inflated prices.

Government corruption did not stop at the city level. City machines were often linked to Democratic or Republican state machines. The state machines catered to "special interests," making deals with the railroads, the lumber industry, or anyone else who wanted tax breaks or other favors

from state legislatures. In return, the machines expected generous gifts, often in the form of "campaign contributions."

At the federal level some U.S. senators, who were often put in power by state machines, accepted bribes to vote the way corporations wished. In 1906 the progressive writer David Graham Phillips began

▲ This 1926 cartoon, entitled *The National Gesture,* satirizes the widespread practice of receiving bribes among government officials.

CORRUPT GOVERNMENT

Divide the class into fourths to write letters to the editor. Two groups' letters should explain why as taxpayers or business owners they object to political machines in their city government. Students in the other groups should explain why they believe state or national government to be corrupt and undemocratic. Select students from each group to read their letters aloud.

STRENGTHENING DEMOCRACY

Ask students to list the election reforms that progressive reformers accomplished. Record responses on the chalkboard. Then ask volunteers to explain how each reform made government more democratic and responsive to the people rather than to special interests. Students may wish to consult the letters they wrote in the previous activity to speculate how each reform might address the issues they raised in their letters.

CITY AND STATE REFORM

Organize students into small groups to discuss progressive reform in city and state government. Direct half the groups to analyze the relationship between business and reform of city government. Have the other groups analyze how the Wisconsin Idea reflected progressive ideas about making government serve the people rather than the special interests. Call on a spokesperson from each group to report its findings to the class. ▶

---

publishing articles that described how special interests influenced American politics. In "The Treason of the Senate," he wrote:

> 66 The greatest single hold of "the interests" is the fact that they are the "campaign contributors." . . . Who pays the big election expenses of your congressman, of the men you send to the legislature to elect senators? Do you imagine those who foot those huge bills are fools? Don't you know that they make sure of getting their money back, with interest? 99

■■ **Corrupt political bosses and machines accepted bribes from special interests in return for government favors.**

ELECTION REFORMS

Government corruption outraged reformers. To restore honest government, they demanded, "Give the government back to the people!" Only when government heeded the public's voice, they believed, could the problems of American life be remedied.

One way progressives sought to break the powers of the bosses and the special interests was to reform the election process. First, they wanted to take the job of choosing candidates for office away from the machines. Therefore, progressives pushed for the **direct primary**—a nominating election in which voters choose the candidates who will later run in a general election. Wisconsin adopted the direct primary in 1903, and by 1916 most other states had followed suit.

Next, progressives proposed to change the method of electing U.S. senators. At the time, the U.S. Constitution mandated that state legislatures elect senators. To progressives, this law made it easy for the bosses to control government. By 1912 the progressive tide had grown strong enough to pass the **Seventeenth Amendment**, which was ratified the next year. The amendment authorized voters to elect their senators directly.

As another step toward more democratic government, the progressives sought to reform the voting process. At the time, each political party

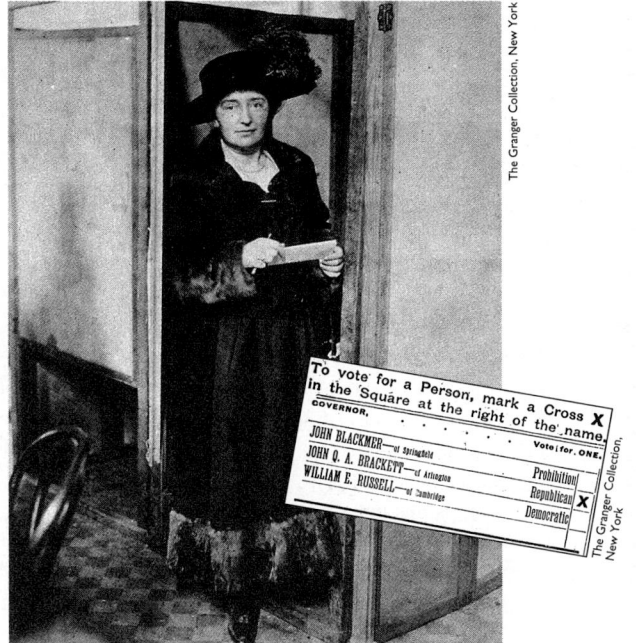

▲ Progressives reformed the voting process by eliminating colored ballots. With the secret ballot, people could cast their vote without revealing their party preference.

printed its own ballot in a distinctive color. On Election Day the colored ballots made it easy to see how people voted. Without secrecy, voters could be pressured to support certain candidates. To lessen this threat, progressives proposed using the secret ballot. Developed in Australia, the ballot lists all candidates on a single sheet of paper and is printed at public expense. By 1910 most states had switched to the secret ballot.

Finally, progressives urged states to adopt three other election reforms: initiative, referendum, and recall. The **initiative** gives voters the power to initiate, or introduce, legislation. If a certain percentage of voters in a state (usually 5 to 15 percent) petition their legislature to enact a measure, the legislature has to consider it. The **referendum** is a companion to the initiative. By securing a specified number of signatures on a petition, voters can compel the legislature to place a measure on the ballot. The **recall** enables voters to remove an elected official from office by calling for a new election.

■■ **Progressives supported the direct primary, the direct election of U.S. senators, the secret ballot, and the initiative, referendum, and recall.**

PRIMARY SOURCE

Description of Change: excerpted

Rationale: excerpted to focus on main idea

🌐 GLOBAL CONNECTIONS

Because Australia led the way in instituting the secret ballot, it sometimes is referred to as the *Australian* ballot. Adopted first by the colonial government of Victoria in 1856, it spread over western Australia by 1879. During the 1870s it was also adopted in New Zealand, Britain, Canada, and Belgium. The first American states to introduce the secret ballot were Massachusetts and Kentucky in 1888.

HISTORICAL SIDELIGHTS

Election Reform

Referendums and initiatives were not new devices. Massachusetts in 1780 allowed referendums for constitutional ratification. In 1831 the Swiss were first to use referendums to approve laws. They also instituted the initiative in 1845. The recall has more modern origins. It first appeared in the Los Angeles city charter in 1903.

Practice

GUIDED PRACTICE

On the chalkboard draw a two-column chart with *Mayor/Council* and *Commission* as headings. Ask students to provide information about these two forms of city government as you add their responses in the appropriate column.

INDEPENDENT PRACTICE

Have students use the information from the chart developed in the Guided Practice to write a paragraph explaining which form of government they think is the more efficient. Suggest that students read and compare their paragraphs. Students may wish to include their paragraphs in their portfolios.

Review and Assessment

REVIEW Ask students to create an outline of Section 1, using the essential points as their main topic headings. Then assign the Section 1 Review on p. 537.

ASSESS Assign the **Section 1 Daily Quiz** in *Core Resources*.

HISTORICAL SIDELIGHTS

Golden Rule at Work

As a manufacturer of oil-well machinery, Jones treated his employees according to the Golden Rule. The workday was eight hours, and workers kept track of their own time. Workers received a week's paid vacation, Christmas bonuses, and free lunches. Jones also provided a park and a company band for recreation and entertainment.

HISTORICAL SIDELIGHTS

A Popular Party Boss

Not all urbanites welcomed progressive efforts at reform. In ethnic neighborhoods political bosses were often the only people who seemed willing to stand up for immigrants. One popular but corrupt party boss was Long Island mayor Patrick Jerome Gleason, an Irish immigrant who amassed a large following by fighting big businesses that took advantage of the working class. His most lasting legacy was construction of a school in an Irish American community. Amid the protests of his supporters, he was removed from office after it was revealed that he profited financially from the venture.

REFORMING CITY GOVERNMENT

Efforts to reform government were not motivated solely by a desire for more democracy. Businesspeople supported reform because the costs of political corruption had become too great. John Patterson of the National Cash Register Company argued that individuals "skilled in business management and social service" should run "municipal affairs on a strict business basis." Many agreed. As a result, good-government campaigns put a large number of reform mayors into office. Two of the most successful were elected in Ohio: Samuel M. Jones and Tom Johnson. Both were self-made men who had amassed their fortunes early and then in mid-life had traded business for politics.

Samuel M. "Golden Rule" Jones got his nickname from his belief in the biblical Golden Rule—"Do unto others as you would have them do unto you." Seeking to apply this principle to government, Jones successfully ran for mayor of Toledo in 1897. Over the next seven years he overhauled the police force, improved municipal services, set a minimum wage for city workers, and opened kindergartens for children.

During this same period, Tom Johnson served as Cleveland's mayor. A former streetcar magnate, he knew personally how closely business interests were tied to political bosses, and he worked to sever those ties. His success led writer Lincoln Steffens to call Johnson "the best mayor of the best governed city in the United States."

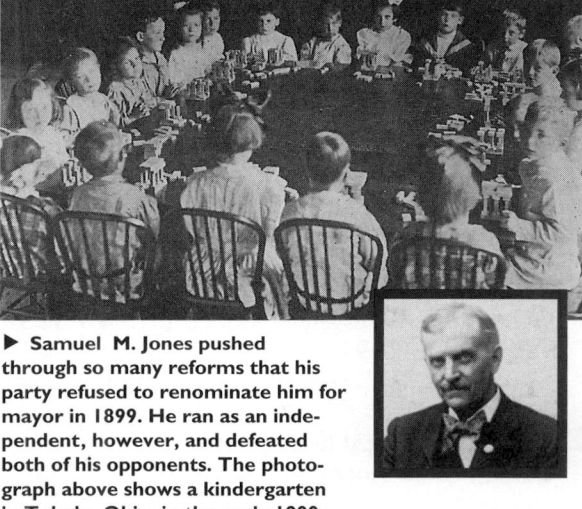

▶ Samuel M. Jones pushed through so many reforms that his party refused to renominate him for mayor in 1899. He ran as an independent, however, and defeated both of his opponents. The photograph above shows a kindergarten in Toledo, Ohio, in the early 1900s.

A few charismatic mayors alone, however, could not conquer entrenched corruption. Many reformers came to believe that only a change in the structure of city government could break the political machines. The typical city government of the time consisted of a mayor and a city council made up of aldermen. Each alderman was the elected leader of one of the wards into which a city was divided. Under this system a political machine could easily elect its own people.

Oddly enough, it was a hurricane that struck Galveston, Texas in 1900—killing some 6,000 people and destroying the city—that produced an alternative to this system. The city's government could not cope with the emergency, so the state legislature named a five-person city commission to

▶ The disastrous hurricane that struck Galveston, Texas, in 1900 led to a new structure of government.

RETEACH Direct students to summarize the section by writing a sentence for each of the major headings. Call on volunteers to read their summaries to the group.

Closure

Read the following statement to the class: *In America's cities business was often the friend of government reform, but at the state level, business was often its foe.* Ask students whether they agree or disagree with this assessment and to cite evidence from the section to support their opinions.

Extension

RESEARCH Suggest that students research and write a biographical sketch of one of the reform politicians or progressive writers discussed in Section 1.

INVESTIGATE Encourage students to interview a local official about the structure of local government. Suggest that they also ask about operating procedures that safeguard against graft and corruption. Ask them to present their findings to the class.

rebuild the area. The commissioners were experts in their fields, not party loyalists, and citizens praised the commission as more honest and efficient than the previous city government. By 1913, city commissions ran more than 350 U.S. cities.

The desire for increased government efficiency also gave rise to city managers. These were expert administrators hired to run cities as they might run a business. National Cash Register's John Patterson pushed for a city-manager government in Dayton, Ohio, after a flood devastated the city in 1913.

Corporate leaders like Patterson claimed that city managers and city commissions would get politics out of city government. In fact, these reforms often increased the political clout of business leaders and reduced the power of the poor.

■■ **Many American cities elected reform mayors, formed city commissions, and hired city managers to increase government efficiency.**

REFORMING STATE GOVERNMENT

The spirit of reform also affected many state governments. In Wisconsin, Governor Robert M. "Fighting Bob" La Follette instituted reforms that turned Wisconsin into what Theodore Roosevelt would call "the laboratory of democracy."

 Born in June 1855 in Primrose, Wisconsin, La Follette worked his way through college and law school. Although a loyal Republican, he found himself at odds with

Wisconsin's Republican machine, which railroad and lumber interests dominated. After serving as a county district attorney and as a U.S. congressman in the late 1800s, he signaled his break with the party machine by refusing a bribe by a party boss.

La Follette emerged early in the progressive movement as one of its most energetic leaders. Elected governor in 1900, he vigorously backed a reform program—soon known as the **Wisconsin Idea**—that became a model for other states. First, La Follette brought the direct primary to Wisconsin. He then prodded the state legislature to increase taxes on the railroads and the public utilities—gas, electric, and streetcar companies—and to create commissions to regulate these companies in the public interest. La Follette also got laws passed to curb excessive lobbying and backed labor legislation, the conservation of Wisconsin's natural resources, and other social legislation. In 1905 the Wisconsin legislature elected La Follette to the U.S. Senate, where he battled for reform until his death in 1925.

Robert M. La Follette

■■ **La Follette's Wisconsin Idea provided a model for reforming local and state government and regulating big business.**

SECTION REVIEW ANSWERS

IDENTIFY

For significance, see the following pages:
direct primary (p. 535)
Seventeenth Amendment (p. 535)
initiative (p. 535)
referendum (p. 535)
recall (p. 535)
Samuel M. Jones (p. 536)
Tom Johnson (p. 536)
Robert M. La Follette (p. 537)

LOCATE

For location, see the map on pp. 1016–1017.

1. direct primary; direct election of U.S. senators; secret ballot; initiative, referendum, recall
2. by electing reform mayors, forming city commissions, and hiring city managers
3. A city commission of experts replaced the political machine, which could not deal with the crisis—other cities adopted city commissions.
4. Articles might describe bribery of government officials and how special interests influence legislation.
5. direct primary, tax increases on railroads and public utilities, regulatory commissions, laws to curb excessive lobbying, support for labor legislation, conservation of natural resources, other social legislation; because their aim was to restore government by and for the people

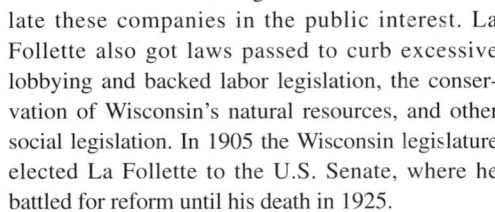

■ SECTION 1 REVIEW

IDENTIFY and explain the significance of the following: direct primary, Seventeenth Amendment, initiative, referendum, recall, Samuel M. Jones, Tom Johnson, Robert M. La Follette.

LOCATE and explain the importance of the following: Wisconsin.

1. **MAIN IDEA** What measures did progressives suggest to make government more democratic?
2. **MAIN IDEA** How did many U.S. cities try to increase government efficiency and lessen corruption?
3. **GEOGRAPHY: HUMAN-ENVIRONMENT INTERACTION** How did the Galveston hurricane help produce a new political structure for cities?
4. **WRITING TO INFORM** Imagine you are David Graham Phillips. Write an article describing political corruption at the local, state, and federal levels.
5. **ANALYZING** What reforms made up the Wisconsin Idea? Why can it be said that these reforms are examples of the progressive spirit?

PREVIEW WORKSHOP

Following is a list of the significant people and terms in this section. You may wish to use this list as a section preview.

People
■ Theodore Roosevelt

Terms
■ arbitration
■ Square Deal
■ Elkins Act
■ Hepburn Act
■ Meat Inspection Act
■ Pure Food and Drug Act
■ Newlands Reclamation Act
■ reclamation

Section 2

ROOSEVELT AND THE SQUARE DEAL

F O C U S

■ **What was the Square Deal?**

■ **How did Theodore Roosevelt fight corruption in business?**

■ **What steps did Roosevelt take to protect the environment?**

Theodore Roosevelt brought progressivism into the White House. Taking office after the assassination of President William McKinley, Roosevelt was elected in his own right in 1904. During his two terms as president, he promoted the regulation of big business and helped preserve natural resources for future generations.

Assassination of
President McKinley, 1901

ROOSEVELT BECOMES PRESIDENT

In 1900 President McKinley ran for reelection with Theodore Roosevelt as his running mate. The Democrats again nominated William Jennings Bryan and made free silver their campaign issue. But in 1900 most Americans felt prosperous, and McKinley and Roosevelt sailed to victory. Then on September 6, 1901, anarchist Leon Czolgosz shot McKinley. A week later the president died, and Roosevelt became the nation's chief executive.

Theodore Roosevelt was born in 1858 into a wealthy New York family. A sickly child, he built up his strength through rigorous exercise. From his father, he acquired a love of the outdoors, a strong sense of fair play, and concern for the less fortunate. As a student at Harvard University, he developed a taste for history and politics. After graduating, Roosevelt won election to the New York state legislature, where he served from 1882 to 1884. As a legislator he earned a reputation as a moderate but energetic reformer.

Toward the end of his third term, Roosevelt's wife, Alice Lee, died following childbirth. Deeply saddened, he did not seek reelection. Instead he headed for his ranch in the Dakota Territory. Roosevelt spent much of the next two years ranching and writing history books, including what would become the four-volume *Winning of the West.* The harsh winter of 1885–86, however, forced him out of the cattle business and back to New York. In December 1886 he married childhood friend Edith Kermit Carow.

In the 1890s Roosevelt served in a variety of local, state, and federal positions. Then, during the Spanish-American War in 1898 (see Chapter 19), he helped organize a volunteer cavalry unit—the Rough Riders—and went off to fight in Cuba. He returned a war hero that same year and was elected governor of New York.

As governor, Roosevelt worked to reform government and to regulate big business. Angered by the governor's progressive efforts, conservative Republican party leaders tried to ease Roosevelt out of state office by having him run as vice president on the McKinley ticket in 1900. Alarmed, the conservative senator Mark Hanna warned that there would be "only one life between

Theodore Roosevelt

Ask students to recall and list in their notebooks the political reforms promoted by the Populists in the late 1800s. Then, as they read this section, direct students to note if and how the progressives enacted these Populist goals.

*T*eaching the *S*ection

A SQUARE DEAL

Suggest that students imagine they are speech writers for Teddy Roosevelt. Ask them to write a campaign speech explaining the aims of, and outlining the proposed programs of, the Square Deal. Call on volunteers to deliver their speeches to the class. Students may wish to include their speeches in their portfolios.

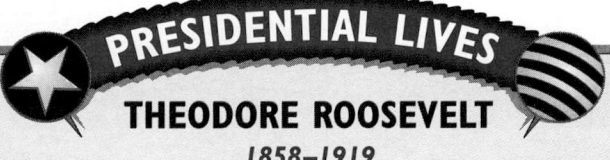

PRESIDENTIAL LIVES

THEODORE ROOSEVELT
1858–1919

in office
1901–1909

Theodore Roosevelt relished the limelight. As one of his children remarked, Roosevelt always wanted to be "the bride at every wedding."

This hero of the Rough Riders became a legend in his own time. Roosevelt always lived life to the hilt. "No President has ever enjoyed himself as much as I have enjoyed myself," he claimed. An old friend explained Roosevelt's great love of life: "You must

always remember that the President is about six [years old]."

His energy was legendary. For example, when the French ambassador once visited the White House, he and the president played tennis, jogged, and then worked out. Roosevelt turned to his guest and asked, "What would you like to do now?" "If it's just the same with you, Mr. President," said the ambassador, "I'd like to lie down and die."

Theodore Roosevelt

VOICES IN HISTORY

Lincoln Steffens was of the opinion that Roosevelt had no real ideals. "You don't stand for anything fundamental," he once scornfully told the president. "All you represent is the square deal." "That's it," Roosevelt retorted. "That's my slogan: the square deal." What Steffens had meant as an insult, Roosevelt gleefully seized upon as his administration's catchphrase.

this madman and the Presidency." When Roosevelt moved into the White House a year later, Hanna exclaimed to a colleague, "My God, that . . . cowboy in the White House!"

Teddy, or TR, as he was now commonly called, loved hunting and sports. Only 42 years old, he brought a new style to the presidency. Journalist William Allen White described him as a "rumbling, roaring . . . tornado of a man." His no-nonsense style and toothy grin made him a favorite target of political cartoonists.

*T*HE SQUARE DEAL

Unlike the presidents of the Gilded Age, who generally took a hands-off approach to government, Roosevelt believed that the president should use his office as a "bully pulpit" to speak out on vital issues. Roosevelt brought dynamic leadership to the progressive movement.

Soon after Roosevelt became president, a labor dispute helped define his approach to the office. In 1902 some 150,000 Pennsylvania coal miners struck for higher wages and recognition of the United Mine Workers union. But the mine owners—mostly railroad companies—would not negotiate.

Roosevelt urged the two sides to accept **arbitration**—to let a third party settle the dispute. When the mine owners refused, the president threatened to take over the mines. The mine

owners backed down. The arbitrators gave both the miners and the mine owners part of what they wanted. The compromise was a landmark: For the first time, the federal government had intervened in a strike to protect the interests of the workers and the public. Satisfied, Roosevelt pronounced the compromise a square deal.

The **Square Deal** became Roosevelt's 1904 campaign slogan. He promised to "see to it that every man has a square deal, no less and no more." This pledge summed up Roosevelt's belief in balancing the interests of labor, business, and consumers. Roosevelt's Square Deal called for limiting the power of trusts, promoting public health and safety, and improving working conditions.

The president was so popular with voters that no Republican dared challenge him for the 1904 nomination. In the election, Roosevelt easily defeated his Democratic opponent, Judge Alton Parker of New York.

■■ **Roosevelt's Square Deal pledged fair treatment for business, workers, and the public.**

*R*EGULATING BUSINESS

One of Roosevelt's goals during both terms in office was to regulate large corporations. While he considered big business essential to the nation's growth, he also believed companies should behave responsibly.

Teaching the Section

ROOSEVELT THE TRUSTBUSTER

Organize the class to debate the following question: *Roosevelt—Does He Deserve the Title "Trustbuster"?* Ask students from both sides of the question to state their views. Suggest that students consider whether a president who left trusts intact unless they were "bad" was a genuine trustbuster.

ENVIRONMENTAL PROTECTION

Have students work in small groups to create a four-page pictorial essay on environmental-protection activity during Roosevelt's presidency. Ask volunteers from each group to present and explain their group's essay to the class.

"We don't wish to destroy corporations," he said, "but we do wish to make them subserve the public good."

Trustbusting. In 1902 the president put this philosophy into practice. He directed the attorney general to sue the Northern Securities Company, which monopolized railroad shipping in the Northwest. In 1904 the Supreme Court ruled that the monopoly violated the Sherman Antitrust Act and therefore ordered the corporation dissolved. Encouraged by this victory, Roosevelt's administration went on a "trustbusting" campaign, filing 44 suits against business combinations deemed "bad." It was not size that mattered, Roosevelt declared, but whether a trust was good or bad for the public as a whole. As he put it, "We draw the line against misconduct, not against wealth."

The Roosevelt administration also promoted railroad regulation. At the president's urging, Congress passed two laws that turned the Interstate Commerce Commission (ICC) into a significant regulatory agency. The first, the 1903 **Elkins Act**, forbade shippers from accepting rebates (money secretly given back to shippers in return for their business). The second, the 1906 **Hepburn Act**, authorized the ICC to set railroad rates and to regulate other companies engaged in interstate commerce, such as pipelines and ferries.

Protecting the consumer. Roosevelt was also concerned about the food and drug industries. By the early 1900s clear evidence existed that some drug companies, meat packers, and food processors were selling dangerous products. Some drug companies sold ineffective over-the-counter medicines that contained dangerous drugs such as cocaine or morphine. Exposing drug industry abuses, journalist Samuel Hopkins Adams wrote:

❝ Gullible America will spend this year some seventy-five millions of dollars in the purchase of patent [over-the-counter]

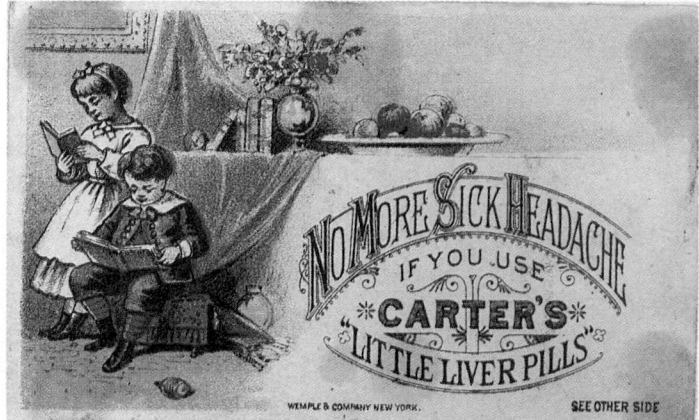

▲ The Pure Food and Drug Act tried to prevent drug manufacturers from making false or exaggerated claims about their products. This advertisement, for example, promises the user will be spared from headaches after taking Carter's liver pills.

medicines. . . . It will swallow huge quantities of alcohol, an appalling amount of opiates and narcotics. ❞

The drug companies' claims that their "health tonics" could cure everything from baldness to cancer, Adams charged, amounted to fraud.

In response to these abuses and those of the food industry, Roosevelt and Congress enacted two consumer-protection laws in 1906. The **Meat Inspection Act** required government inspection of meat shipped from one state to another. The **Pure Food and Drug Act** forbade the manufacture, sale, or transportation of food and patent medicine containing harmful ingredients. The law also required that containers of food and medicines carry ingredient labels.

■■ **Roosevelt fought corruption in business by breaking up illegal trusts and regulating railroads and the food and drug industries.**

Protecting the environment. The president may have achieved his most enduring legacy in the field of conservation. He recognized that America's natural resources were limited and that the needs of business had always taken precedence over the environment. "In the past, we have admitted the right of the individual to injure the future of the Republic for his own present profit," he charged. "The time has come for a change."

Practice

GUIDED PRACTICE

On the chalkboard write *Roosevelt's Square Deal.* Underneath, draw a three-column chart with these headings: *Problem, Promise,* and *Action.* Help students to complete the chart with entries that relate Roosevelt's Square Deal promises and philosophy to the actions he took to address the problems of the early 1900s.

INDEPENDENT PRACTICE

Have students use the information in the Guided Practice chart to "grade" ("A" to "F") Theodore Roosevelt as a reform president and to write paragraphs explaining their evaluations. Students may wish to include their evaluations in their portfolios.

Review and Assessment

REVIEW Direct students to create an annotated time line of domestic affairs during the Roosevelt presidency. Students may wish to include their time lines in their portfolios. Then assign the Section 2 Review on p. 542.

ASSESS Assign the **Section 2 Daily Quiz** in *Core Resources.* ▶

Never content with mere talk, Roosevelt withdrew from sale millions of acres of public land and set aside some 150 million acres as forest reserves. At his urging, Congress created national parks and wildlife sanctuaries and in 1902 passed the **Newlands Reclamation Act**. The act allowed money from the sales of public land to be used for irrigation and **reclamation**—the process of making damaged land productive again. Moreover, a 1908 White House conference on conservation led to the creation of a National Conservation Commission to study natural resource issues and to the establishment of conservation agencies in 41 states.

■■ **Roosevelt saved public lands from destructive development and created wildlife sanctuaries and national parks.**

Then and Now — NATIONAL PARKS

In the late 1800s government, industry, and most Americans still believed there was no end to the nation's natural resources. Between the 1850s and the 1870s alone, millions of acres of public land were sold cheaply or even given away to mining, logging, and railroad companies for development.

However, an increasing number of Americans, including Theodore Roosevelt, believed the country's lands and wildlife were being recklessly destroyed. During his years in office, President Roosevelt fought for programs to protect public land and historic sites.

Many opposed Roosevelt's efforts, believing the economic value of the reserved land outweighed the need to conserve it. But in 1916, largely as a result of Roosevelt's efforts, Congress created the National Park Service to maintain and oversee the country's 10 national parks and 21 national monuments. Today, the National Park Service manages some 355 sites on 80 million acres of land.

Although the number and size of parks have increased tremendously since Roosevelt's day, one problem facing the Park Service remains unchanged. The agency is still caught between those who wish to preserve and expand park land and those who want to use the parks' resources.

▲ Yellowstone National Park was established in 1872. Shown here is a detail from Thomas Moran's painting of the park, *Grand Canyon of the Yellowstone.*

Conservationists charge that clear-cutting, strip mining, and overdevelopment are destroying wildlife habitats and old-growth forests. Logging and mining interests counter that the demand for wood and mineral products—not to mention the protection of thousands of industry jobs—requires the use of park resources. Lawmakers are caught in the middle, hoping to please voters on both sides of the issue.

Lawmakers—and Park Service officials—also face the problem of trying to maintain the parks while containing costs. More than 250 million people visit the national parks annually, and some officials argue that the visitors are literally "loving the parks to death." To counteract the strain on park resources, officials have proposed that visitation be limited in certain popular parks.

The future of the national parks is far from settled. But all sides in the debate might well consider Teddy Roosevelt's words: "A nation is obligated to manage its resources for the greatest good of the greatest number over the long run."

Then and Now

Point out that the first director of the National Park Service was Stephen T. Mather, a Chicago businessman. After seeing the impact of overgrazing on Yosemite National Park, Mather wrote a letter noting his concerns to Secretary of the Interior Frank Lane. Lane later invited Mather to run the parks.

THE AMERICAN NATION VIDEODISC PROGRAM

Yosemite National Park

| 1B | 08593 | 4:04 |

Map Caption Answer
(for map on p. 542)
Alaska

RETEACH Ask students to draw a chart with the following column headings: *Trustbusting, Protecting the Consumer, Protecting the Environment.* Have students complete the chart by listing the actions that Roosevelt took in these three areas.

Closure

Have students write a paragraph that answers the following questions: *What do you think was the single most important action taken by President Roosevelt? Why?* Ask volunteers to present and defend their paragraphs.

Extension

COMPARE Encourage students to research the federal government's involvement in conservation today and compare it with the government's role in environmental issues during the early 1900s.

RESEARCH Ask students to research editorial cartoons about Teddy Roosevelt and present their findings to the class.

SECTION REVIEW ANSWERS

IDENTIFY

For significance, see the following pages:
Theodore Roosevelt (p. 538)
arbitration (p. 539)
Square Deal (p. 539)
Elkins Act (p. 540)
Hepburn Act (p. 540)
Meat Inspection Act (p. 540)
Pure Food and Drug Act (p. 540)
Newlands Reclamation Act (p. 541)
reclamation (p. 541)

1. to limit the power of trusts, promote public health and safety, and improve working conditions
2. broke up illegal trusts, regulated railroads and other companies engaged in interstate commerce, regulated food and drug industries
3. required government inspection of meat shipped between states; forbade the manufacture, sale, or transportation of food and patent medicine with harmful ingredients
4. Reports might state that land was destroyed by industry. Action plan might advise creating forest reserves, wildlife sanctuaries, and national parks.
5. Possible positions: miners might favor it because government protected the workers; owners might oppose it because it forced them to negotiate.

National Parks and Conservation

NATIONAL PARK SYSTEM The park system, which includes the national parks, national monuments, and national historic parks, protects the nation's cultural and historic sites as well as its natural wonders.

❓ PLACE Which state has the greatest land area set aside in national parks?

SECTION 2 REVIEW

IDENTIFY and explain the significance of the following: Theodore Roosevelt, arbitration, Square Deal, Elkins Act, Hepburn Act, Meat Inspection Act, Pure Food and Drug Act, Newlands Reclamation Act, reclamation.

1. **MAIN IDEA** What did Roosevelt pledge to accomplish through the Square Deal?
2. **MAIN IDEA** What actions did Roosevelt take against trusts and railroads?
3. **MAIN IDEA** How did the Meat Inspection Act and Pure Food and Drug Act try to protect consumers?
4. **WRITING TO EXPLAIN** Imagine you are a member of the National Conservation Commission. Write a report to the president, evaluating the impact that business has had on natural resources and offering a plan of action for protecting those resources.
5. **TAKING A STAND** Roosevelt's handling of the Pennsylvania coal miners' strike represented a new approach to labor relations. Take a stand either on the side of the miners or the mine owners and explain how that group might feel about Roosevelt's solution.

PREVIEW WORKSHOP

*Following is a list of the significant
people and terms in this section.
You may wish to use this list as a
section preview.*

■ Joseph Cannon
■ George Norris
■ Woodrow Wilson
■ Eugene Debs

People
■ William Howard Taft
■ Nelson Aldrich
■ Richard Ballinger
■ Gifford Pinchot

Terms
■ Mann-Elkins Act
■ Sixteenth Amendment
■ New Nationalism
■ New Freedom

FOCUS OBJECTIVES

■ Describe the reforms
carried out by President
Taft.

■ Explain why Taft lost the
progressives' support.

■ Examine the result of
the 1912 election.

Section 3

REFORM UNDER TAFT

FOCUS
■ **What reforms did President Taft carry out?**
■ **Why did Taft lose the progressives' support?**
■ **What was the result of the 1912 election?**

*A*lthough a financial panic and sharp depression
hit the nation in 1907, President Roosevelt
remained popular. The Republican nomination was
his for the asking, but having served almost two
full terms, he chose not to run again. The
Republicans then turned to William Howard Taft,
who easily won the 1908 election. In some ways,
Taft carried on Roosevelt's reform program.
But as his term wore on, progressives became
more and more unhappy with his actions.

Taft and Sherman
campaign banner, 1908

TAFT TAKES OFFICE

At the 1908 Republican convention, Roosevelt
supported his secretary of war, William Howard
Taft, who won the nomination on the first ballot.
The Democrats again nominated William Jennings
Bryan, whose prolabor platform won the backing
of the American Federation of Labor. Despite
labor's support, the Democrats lost the election by
a wide margin.

From the start it was clear that Taft would be
a different sort of president than Roosevelt.
Roosevelt enjoyed being in the public eye. Taft
was just the opposite. "I don't like politics," he
once wrote. "I don't like the limelight."

A smart but cautious man, Taft stressed the
limits on his power as president, rather than his
potential for leadership. Nevertheless, he chalked

up an impressive list of accomplishments. His
administration filed 90 antitrust suits, more than
twice the number begun under Roosevelt. At Taft's
urging, Congress passed the **Mann-Elkins Act** in
1910, extending the regulatory powers of the
Interstate Commerce Commission to telephone and
telegraph companies.

Taft also advanced the cause of conservation.
He added vast areas to the nation's forest reserves.
Taft also supported reforms to aid working people.
With his approval, Congress created the
Department of Labor to enforce labor laws. It also
passed mine-safety laws and established an eight-
hour workday for employees of companies holding
contracts with the federal government.

The Taft administration was partly responsible, too, for the adoption of the **Sixteenth
Amendment**. Proposed in 1909 and ratified in
1913, the amendment authorizes a national tax

CORE RESOURCES

• **Section 3 Daily Quiz**

Teaching the Section

TAFT THE REFORMER

Ask for volunteers to state Roosevelt's reform achievements. Have students write the responses in their notebooks. Then, as students read this section, direct them to compare the reform record of William Howard Taft with that of Roosevelt.

On the chalkboard draw a four-column chart with the following headings: *Business Regulation, Conservation, Labor Issues, Economic Policy.* Call on volunteers to enumerate Taft's actions in these areas as you note their responses in the appropriate column. Then have students use the information in the chart to write a paragraph summarizing Taft's achievements as a reformer. Students may wish to include their summaries in their portfolios.

HISTORICAL SIDELIGHTS

Duty-Free Art

Some people saw the Payne-Aldrich Tariff as an example of how wealthy business leaders controlled conservatives in the Senate. As evidence they pointed to the fact that imported fine art was one of the few items exempted from the tariff. This exemption allowed Americans to bring works of art from Europe duty-free. For example, J. Pierpont Morgan, the banker and financier, saved a fortune in tariffs on the importation of his European art collection, which was valued at some $20 million.

HISTORICAL SIDELIGHTS

An Expected Firing

Pinchot was not surprised at being fired, and he held no animosity toward Taft for taking such action. Taft, Pinchot said, "was perfectly justified in firing me. I had asked for it and I could not complain."

■■ Ask students to discuss whether they would risk losing a job over a matter of principle.

PRESIDENTIAL LIVES

WILLIAM H. TAFT
1857–1930

in office
1909–1913

William Taft was an unhappy president—at heart a judge, not a politician. He seemed ill suited for public office, dozing off at official dinners or Cabinet meetings, forgetting names, procrastinating, and being tactless at the worst moments. When leaving the White House, he welcomed incoming President Woodrow Wilson by saying, "I'm glad to be going. This is the lonesomest place in the world."

What Taft really wanted was a seat on the U.S. Supreme Court. Taft had had a distinguished legal career, serving as U.S. solicitor general, as a federal judge, as a president of the American Bar Association, and as a law professor at Yale University. In 1921 Taft got his wish—he was appointed chief justice of the Supreme Court. "Presidents come and go," a happy Taft said, "but the Court goes on forever."

based on individual income. Progressives had long supported such a tax as a way to fund needed government programs in a fair manner.

■■ Taft's administration supported the Mann-Elkins Act, conservation programs, labor reforms, and the Sixteenth Amendment.

TAFT ANGERS THE PROGRESSIVES

Despite these reforms, Taft lost the support of progressive Republicans. The split between the president and the progressives began in April 1909 with the passage of a tariff bill.

Both Taft and the progressives favored tariff reductions to lower the prices of consumer goods. Some members of Congress, however, wanted high tariffs to protect American industry. They won out when the House sent a low-tariff bill to the Senate, and Nelson Aldrich of Rhode Island turned it into a high-tariff measure.

Taft could have vetoed the bill, now called the Payne-Aldrich Tariff, or he could have pressured Aldrich to change the rates. But Taft lacked the political skill to oppose conservative Republicans in Congress. Despite his misgivings, he signed the bill. To make matters worse, he proceeded to call it the best tariff ever passed. Outraged progressives accused Taft of betraying the reform cause.

Progressives also attacked Taft for sabotaging Roosevelt's conservation program. The dispute revolved around Taft's secretary of the interior, Richard Ballinger, who believed that the Roosevelt administration had exceeded its authority when it stopped the sale of public land. Ballinger approved the sale of a vast tract of coal-rich Alaska timberland. The head of the U.S. Forest Service, Gifford Pinchot (PIN-shoh), an ardent conservationist and Roosevelt's friend, attacked Ballinger for favoring private interests over conservation. Taft warned Pinchot to stop criticizing Ballinger. When Pinchot did not stop, Taft fired him.

For progressives the Ballinger-Pinchot affair signaled Taft's weakness on conservation.

▼ This cartoon appeared in the *Tacoma News Tribune* in 1909 and satirizes Taft's awkward position in the Ballinger-Pinchot affair.

Although his administration later restored the Alaska land to the federal forest reserve, the episode hurt the Republicans in the 1910 congressional elections. For the first time in 16 years, the Republicans lost control of the House of Representatives.

◀ The Progressive, or Bull Moose, party held its convention in Chicago on August 5, 1912. Delegates paraded through the aisles, singing "Onward Christian Soldiers," and unanimously nominated Theodore Roosevelt for president. Souvenirs from the Bull Moose campaign are shown here.

■■ **Taft lost progressive support when he signed the Payne-Aldrich Tariff and fired conservationist Gifford Pinchot.**

Taft made one particularly dangerous enemy—Theodore Roosevelt, who broke with Taft over the Pinchot controversy. In the congressional elections of 1910, Roosevelt campaigned for progressive Republicans who opposed Taft and the party's conservative wing. In a speech at Osawatomie (oh-suh-WAHT-uh-mee), Kansas, Roosevelt offered his **New Nationalism**—a bold program of social legislation calling for tough laws to protect workers, ensure public health, and regulate business. He declared:

❝ The true friend of property, the true conservative, is he who insists that property shall be the servant and not the master of the commonwealth. . . . The citizens of the United States must effectively control the mighty commercial forces which they have themselves called into being. ❞

Government, Roosevelt said, must become the "steward of the public welfare." His call for a more activist federal government represented a far more liberal position than he had taken as president. Delighted, reformers hailed the New Nationalism as a revival of the progressive spirit.

THE REPUBLICAN PARTY DIVIDES

Not long before Roosevelt's speech, a bitter dispute in Congress had further deepened the gulf between Taft and the progressives. In the spring of 1910, progressive Republicans in Congress launched a major attack on Speaker of the House Joseph ("Uncle Joe") Cannon of Illinois, a conservative Republican.

Cannon, a 73-year-old tobacco-chewing poker player, was one of Washington's most powerful politicians. As Speaker he ruled the House with an iron hand, appointing all House committees and naming their chairmen. As head of the powerful Rules Committee, which determined the order of business in the House, Cannon prevented bills he opposed from even reaching the House floor for debate.

Progressives charged that Cannon used his great power to block reform legislation. ("Not one cent for scenery," he had growled in dismissing a call for environmental protection.) In March 1910 Congressman George Norris of Nebraska, a progressive, began an effort to break Cannon's power. Norris proposed that in the future, House members elect the Rules Committee and that the Speaker be excluded from membership.

After a heated debate, Norris's motion passed. A year later, the House also stripped the Speaker of the power to appoint members of the other committees—a major progressive victory. Throughout this bitter dispute, Taft refused to take sides, further alienating progressives.

By 1912 the conservative and the progressive wings of the Republican party were deeply divided. Theodore Roosevelt, by now completely at odds with Taft, decided to run again for the presidency. Borrowing a prizefighting term, he proclaimed: "My hat is in the ring." Roosevelt won almost every Republican state primary, including the one in Taft's own state, Ohio.

At the convention the Taft forces, firmly in control of the party machinery, refused to seat many of Roosevelt's delegates. When Taft won the nomination, Roosevelt's supporters angrily walked out, and held their own convention, adopting a platform based on the New Nationalism and nominating Roosevelt as their presidential candidate. Thus was born the Progressive party, also known as the Bull Moose party after Roosevelt declared that he felt "fit as a bull moose" to run.

Practice

GUIDED PRACTICE

Ask for volunteers to identify the major legislation and issues of Taft's administration. Write their responses on the chalkboard. Guide students to arrange the information on the chalkboard into two columns in their notebooks, one column

headed *Positive Impact on Reform* and the other headed *Negative Impact on Reform*. Then invite students to share and compare their lists.

INDEPENDENT PRACTICE

Have students use the information from the Guided Practice to create election posters or editorial cartoons that express their views of Taft as a progressive reformer. Students may wish to include their work in their portfolios.

Review and Assessment

REVIEW Suggest that students write the main ideas of the section in the form of newspaper headlines. Ask for volunteers to present their headlines, and have the class discuss what might be included in articles that accompany the headlines. Then assign the Section 3 Review on p. 547.

ASSESS Assign the **Section 3 Daily Quiz** in *Core Resources.*

VOICES IN HISTORY

French political writer Charles Oster, who came to America to observe the 1912 election, commented on the difficulties Taft had faced during his presidency in following someone with the personality of Roosevelt: "Mr. Taft was not the kind of President the people needed in 1908. The rank and file felt this even when they elected him. Since his election that feeling has increased. . . . The people wanted a fighter . . . a Jefferson or a Jackson, and Mr. Taft is not of that type. . . . With all the good he has done in awakening the country from a long sleep and . . . with all the popularity he won by such a course, Mr. Roosevelt was an overpowering adversary for Mr. Taft."

PRIMARY SOURCE

Description of Change: excerpted
Rationale: excerpted to focus on main idea

Chart Caption Answer
1912

Map Caption Answer
(for map on p. 547)
California, with 11 for Roosevelt, 2 for Wilson

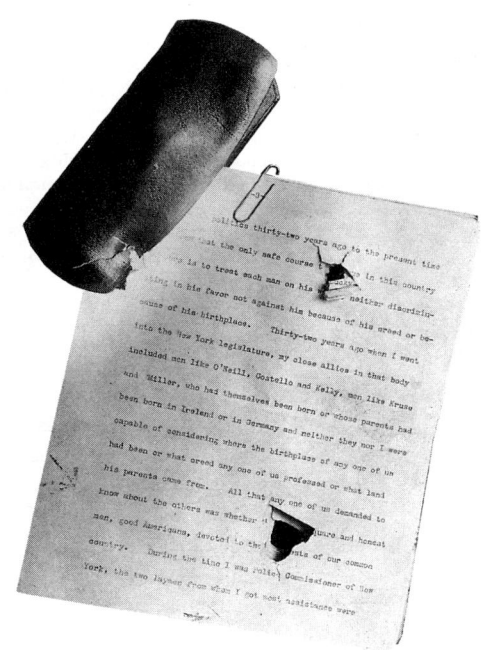

▲ **Part of the speech**
Theodore Roosevelt delivered on October 14, 1912, and the eyeglass case he carried are shown here. Notice the bullet holes made during the attempted assassination.

Roosevelt's candidacy, however, almost ended on October 14, 1912, when a deranged man shot him in the chest during a campaign stop. Roosevelt finished his planned speech, despite the bullet lodged in his body. This reckless display of courage reinforced his image as a larger-than-life hero.

■■ **When Roosevelt failed to win the 1912 Republican presidential nomination, he formed the Progressive party.**

A DEMOCRATIC VICTORY IN 1912

Although Roosevelt's campaign continued to pick up steam, the division in the Republican party practically assured a Democratic victory. Roosevelt and Taft were likely to split the Republican vote, while Democrats united behind one candidate. Their choice was Governor Woodrow Wilson of New Jersey, who ran on a platform calling for tariff reduction, banking reform, laws benefiting wage earners and farmers, and stronger antitrust legislation.

Wilson, a native of Virginia and a political newcomer, had long nurtured dreams of high office. In college he had made calling cards proclaiming "Thomas Woodrow Wilson, Senator from Virginia." He eventually became a professor at Princeton University in New Jersey and later served as its president. He was elected governor in 1910. In his short time as governor, he fought the state's Democratic party bosses and pushed through laws regulating business. As an outspoken reformer and eloquent speaker, Wilson was the presidential choice of progressives in the Democratic party.

In the 1912 campaign, Wilson brilliantly captured the nation's reform mood. His program, the **New Freedom**, called for a revival of small business and a return to an America where people were free from the control of big business and government. Wilson asserted:

❝ The only way that government is kept pure is by keeping . . . channels open, so that . . . there will constantly be coming new blood into the veins of the body politic. ❞

RISE OF THE SOCIALIST PARTY
Number of Socialist Votes, 1900–1920

Election Year	1900	1904	1908	1912	1916	1920
Presidential	87,814	402,283	420,793	900,672	585,113	919,799
Gubernatorial	0	73,914	13,694	386,828	125,907	230,907
Congressional	8,021	138,201	113,450	1,599,420	770,230	1,128,200

Sources: *Congressional Quarterly's Guide to U.S. Elections* (for gubernatorial and congressional),
Historical Statistics of the United States (for presidential)

THE SOCIALIST CHALLENGE Dramatic social changes at the turn of the century spurred the popularity of the prolabor, reform-minded Socialist party.

❓ **BUILDING GRAPH SKILLS** In which year did Socialist candidates obtain the largest number of overall votes?

Have students work in groups and assign individuals or pairs the task of outlining subsections. Have students exchange outlines and use them to ask questions of other members of their group.

Close

Write the following statement on the chalkboard: *Taft was a conservative, not a progressive.* Ask students to present arguments that support or challenge the statement.

Extension

INVESTIGATE Encourage students to investigate other significant third-party or independent presidential candidates, such as George Wallace and H. Ross Perot, and to report on the role they played in presidential elections.

ANALYZE Have students research the New Nationalism program and analyze how it represented the ideals and principles of progressivism.

Although Wilson shared the progressive belief in government as an agent of reform, he believed that making government too strong could stifle individual freedom. He believed that the goal of reform should be to rid the system of corruption so that free competition could flourish, without significantly altering the system itself. In this regard he differed from Roosevelt and especially from another candidate for president, Eugene Debs of the Socialist party. The Socialist party supported radical economic reforms, including public ownership of all major industries. The party had done very well in the 1910 elections.

In Debs, Wilson, and Roosevelt, American voters had a choice of three strong reform-minded candidates. Even Taft supported some reform programs, although he appeared to represent a more conservative viewpoint.

As expected, Wilson won the election, receiving 435 electoral votes to 88 for Roosevelt and 8 for Taft. Debs won over 900,000 popular votes but no electoral votes. Out of more than 15 million votes cast, the three reform candidates received some 11 million. Some 1,200 Socialist candidates, including 79 mayors, were elected to offices across the country, reflecting the desire for new approaches to government. Although Wilson won just six million popular votes, he took office with a strong mandate for reform.

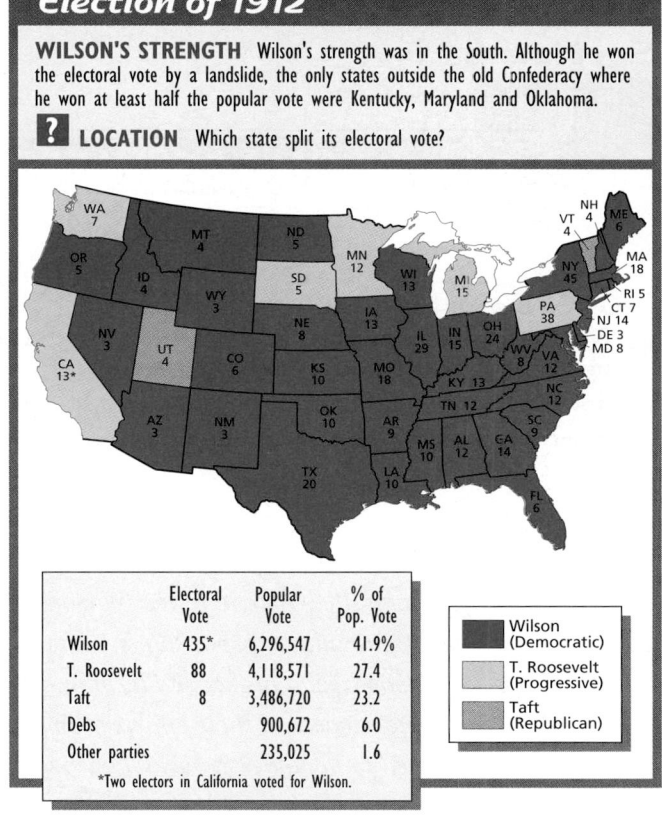

Election of 1912

WILSON'S STRENGTH Wilson's strength was in the South. Although he won the electoral vote by a landslide, the only states outside the old Confederacy where he won at least half the popular vote were Kentucky, Maryland and Oklahoma.

? LOCATION Which state split its electoral vote?

	Electoral Vote	Popular Vote	% of Pop. Vote
Wilson	435*	6,296,547	41.9%
T. Roosevelt	88	4,118,571	27.4
Taft	8	3,486,720	23.2
Debs		900,672	6.0
Other parties		235,025	1.6

*Two electors in California voted for Wilson.

- Wilson (Democratic)
- T. Roosevelt (Progressive)
- Taft (Republican)

■■ **The split in the Republican vote and the public support for reform enabled Woodrow Wilson to win the 1912 presidential election.**

IDENTIFY

For significance, see the following pages:
William Howard Taft (p. 543)
Mann-Elkins Act (p. 543)
Sixteenth Amendment (p. 543)
Nelson Aldrich (p. 544)
Richard Ballinger (p. 544)
Gifford Pinchot (p. 544)
New Nationalism (p. 545)
Joseph Cannon (p. 545)
George Norris (p. 545)
Woodrow Wilson (p. 546)
New Freedom (p. 546)
Eugene Debs (p. 547)

1. *supported Mann-Elkins Act, conservation programs, labor reforms, Sixteenth Amendment (income tax)*
2. *signed Payne-Aldrich Tariff, was accused of sabotaging Roosevelt's conservation program*
3. *It split the Republican vote, practically assuring a Democratic victory.*
4. *Speeches should explain New Nationalism (tough laws to protect workers, ensure public health, and regulate business) and should criticize Taft's control of the Republican party.*
5. *no, because Taft's administration extended reforms begun under TR, filed more than twice the number of antitrust suits, preserved much land, did more for labor than TR*

■□
□■

SECTION 3 REVIEW

IDENTIFY and explain the significance of the following: William Howard Taft, Mann-Elkins Act, Sixteenth Amendment, Nelson Aldrich, Richard Ballinger, Gifford Pinchot, New Nationalism, Joseph Cannon, George Norris, Woodrow Wilson, New Freedom, Eugene Debs.

1. **MAIN IDEA** What contributions did the Taft administration make to reform?
2. **MAIN IDEA** What actions caused Taft to lose the support of progressives?
3. **MAIN IDEA** How did the Progressive party help determine the outcome of the 1912 presidential election?
4. **WRITING TO EXPRESS A VIEWPOINT** Imagine you are Teddy Roosevelt. Write a speech explaining your plan of action and why you formed the Progressive party.
5. **DISTINGUISHING FACT FROM OPINION** Supporters of the Progressive party believed that Taft had not lived up to the progressive ideals of the Roosevelt administration. Comparing Taft's reform record to Roosevelt's, was this a fair assessment? Why or why not?

FOCUS OBJECTIVES

■ Outline the achieve-
ments of the Wilson
administration in the
areas of tariff and bank-
ing reforms and business
regulation.

■ Explain how women
won the right to vote.

■ Determine the major
success of progressivism.

PRIMARY SOURCE

Description of Change:
excerpted
Rationale: excerpted to
focus on main idea

548

Section 4

WILSON'S "NEW FREEDOM"

FOCUS

■ **What did the Wilson administration achieve in the areas of tariff
and banking reforms and business regulation?**

■ **How did women win the right to vote?**

■ **What was the major success of progressivism?**

*D*uring the 1912 campaign, Woodrow Wilson pledged to restore
opportunity in American life. Once in office, Wilson moved to lower
tariffs, reform banking, regulate corporations, and aid farmers and
wage earners. As Wilson began his second term in office, progressives could claim some success in their efforts to improve American
life. Yet much remained to be done. Progressives had barely begun
to clean up government and regulate business, women still did not
have the right to vote, and the pledge of equal opportunity for all
Americans remained unfulfilled.

Suffragist demonstrating in front of
the White House, about 1916

REFORM ON MANY FRONTS

On March 4, 1913, President Wilson gave his first
inaugural address in which he eloquently summed
up the spirit of the progressive reform movement:

66 We have been proud of
our industrial achievements,
but we have not . . . stopped
. . . to count the . . . fearful
physical and spiritual cost to
the men and women and children upon whom the . . .
weight and burden of it all has
fallen. . . . This is not a day of
triumph; it is a day of dedication. Here muster, not the
forces of party, but the forces
of humanity. 99

A month later, Wilson presented his legislative agenda. It included tariff and banking
reforms and stronger antitrust laws. Opposed by
business groups and lobbyists, Wilson used all his
skill to rally support for his program, both in
Congress and among the American people.

Wilson's first priority
was to lower tariffs, long a goal
of the Democratic party's southern agrarian wing. Well aware
that big business had blocked
tariff reduction during Taft's
presidency, Wilson mounted a
public campaign to undermine
the business lobby and overcome Senate opposition. His

◄ **Woodrow Wilson is shown
delivering his first inaugural
address on March 4, 1913.**

Teaching the Section

TARIFF AND BANKING REFORM

Organize students into small groups and suggest that they imagine they are public-relations advisers to President Wilson. Inform groups that their task is to develop a media campaign to "sell" to the American public Wilson's reforms for tariff and banking. Invite groups to present and explain their campaigns to the class.

▶

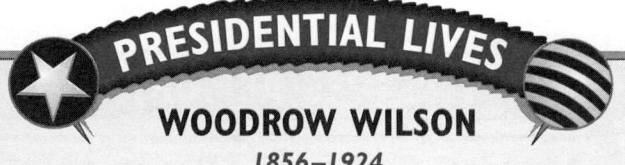

PRESIDENTIAL LIVES

WOODROW WILSON
1856–1924

**in office
1913–1921**

Woodrow Wilson had a reputation for being very serious and often inflexible. He hated political compromise and at times would oppose legislation he originally proposed if it was amended by someone else. He once told a political associate, "I am sorry for those who disagree with me. . . . Because I know they are wrong."

Yet, despite his public image, Wilson often surprised his close associates with

sudden displays of humorous behavior. Once when Wilson was riding in the country with a Secret Service agent, they passed a small boy on the road. "Did you see what that boy did?" Wilson said to the agent, very seriously "He made a face at me." Then the president asked, "Did you see what I did?" "No, Sir," said the agent. With a boyish grin, Wilson replied, "I made a face right back!"

strategy worked. In 1913 Congress passed the **Underwood Tariff Act**, which reduced tariffs to their lowest levels in 50 years. To make up for the lost revenue, the bill imposed a graduated income tax, taxing people with high incomes at a higher rate than those with low incomes.

Next on Wilson's agenda was banking. At the time, there was no central fund that banks could borrow from to prevent collapse during financial panics. Thus, when many people withdrew their deposits at the same time, banks commonly failed. Reform was clearly necessary, but Americans disagreed on how to change the banking system. Conservative business groups wanted to give the nation's large private banks more control. In contrast, many Democrats and progressive Republicans wanted the government to run the system.

The **Federal Reserve Act** of 1913, which Wilson helped pass, combined these two views. It created a three-level banking system. At the top was the Federal Reserve Board, a group appointed by the president and charged with running the system. At the second level were 12 Federal Reserve banks, under mixed public and private control. These "bankers' banks" served other banks rather than individuals. At the third level were private banks, which could borrow from the Federal Reserve banks at interest rates set by the Board.

■■ Wilson worked to secure passage
of the Underwood Tariff Act and
the Federal Reserve Act.

WILSON AND BIG BUSINESS

Having achieved important tariff and banking reforms, Wilson turned to business regulation. He wanted to limit the power of monopolies, which he viewed as a threat to small business. Toward this end, he backed passage of the **Clayton Antitrust Act** of 1914. This act clarified and extended the 1890 Sherman Antitrust Act by clearly stating what corporations could not do. For example, companies could not sell goods below cost to drive competitors out of business. They also could not buy competing companies' stock to create a monopoly.

The Wilson administration also backed the creation of the **Federal Trade Commission** (FTC). The FTC, which Congress established in 1914, was

◀ This 1913 cartoon portrays Wilson's use of antitrust legislation to protect small businesses from the unfair competition of monopolies and other large corporations.

Teaching the Section

REGULATING BUSINESS, AIDING WORKERS

Randomly assign students the following characters: owner of big business, farmer, union member, railroad worker, federal worker. Have students write 25-word telegrams to President Wilson, urging him to support legislation that affects their characters. Then ask a representative of each character to read his or her telegram to the class.

Changing Ways

THE ARMORY SHOW

SETTING THE SCENE

A number of the American artists involved in the Armory Show were no strangers to controversy or negative criticism. In 1908 they had taken part in an exhibition called "Eight American Painters." The works on display, many of which had been rejected the previous year by the National Academy of Design, featured realistic portrayals of the seedier side of city life—barrooms, back alleys, and so on. As a result, critics contemptuously referred to these eight artists as the "Ash Can School."

THINKING CRITICALLY

Point out that new developments in the arts commonly cause controversy. Have students write a paragraph on why some people might find such new developments unsettling.

■■ Ask students if they can identify recent examples of art or pop culture that caused controversy.

Changing Ways   THE 1913 ARMORY SHOW

The progressive reform spirit influenced art as well as economic policies in the early 1900s. Just as industry reformers attacked business trusts, progressive artists tackled the leading American museums' monopoly in determining which paintings and sculptures the public saw.

Resistant to change, the mainstream art community in America was hostile to the "radical" ideas and techniques of the growing modern art movement in Europe. Modernists such as Picasso, Van Gogh, Matisse, and Cézanne offered a new art style, which blurred the lines between reality and fantasy.

Resolved to introduce the American public to modern art, a small group of independent artists formed the Association of American Painters and Sculptors (AAPS) in 1912. The group planned an international exhibition, combing galleries and studios in Munich, Berlin, Paris, and the Hague for works to display. On February 17, 1913, the International Exhibition of Modern Art opened in the 69th Regiment Armory in New York City. The Armory Show presented some 1,300 works by both European and American artists.

Newspaper reporters raved about the show, calling it "an event not to be missed."

▲ The Armory Show introduced contemporary European artists and works of art, such as Marcel Duchamp's *Nude Descending a Staircase,* to a curious, but often puzzled, American public.

Art critics were not so kind. They blasted Van Gogh as "unskilled" and Cézanne as "absolutely without talent." As for Duchamp's *Nude Descending a Staircase,* they described it as "a lot of disused golf clubs and bags" and "an explosion in a shingle factory."

Ironically, the critics' remarks boosted attendance, which exceeded the organizers' wildest dreams. People came primarily to gape. "I remember one woman becoming so hysterical with laughter," an artist recalled, "that she actually rolled over on the floor—I also remember [AAPS president] Arthur B. Davies taking Teddy Roosevelt through the show— Roosevelt waved his arms and stomped through the Galleries pointing at pictures and saying 'That's not art!' 'That's not art!'"

Even if it failed to enchant Americans with modern art, the Armory Show was a huge success in terms of attendance and publicity. Before the show moved to Chicago, AAPS honored its "friends and enemies" in the press with a beefsteak dinner. Glasses were raised; speeches were made; diners sang and danced. One critic summed up the general mood: "It was a good show, but don't do it again."

WOMEN AND THE VOTE

Ask students to write newspaper editorials supporting or opposing ratification of the Nineteenth Amendment. Suggest that their editorials might also include commentary on the tactics of the women's movement, the impact that women's suffrage would have on American democracy, or changes the vote might bring for women. Ask volunteers to read their editorials to the class. Students may wish to include their editorials in their portfolios.

THE PROGRESSIVE LEGACY

Organize students into groups of four or five and ask them to list the political, social, and economic accomplishments of the progressives. Instruct each group to use its list to review progressive reform and to draft a statement indicating what it believes to be the progressives' major success. Tell the groups that they must achieve consensus among their members on the statement. Have representatives of each group read its statement to the class and briefly summarize how it was developed. Then use the groups' statements to reach a class determination about the progressives' most important legacy. Also ask the class what it believes to be the most significant shortcoming of progressive reform. (*Students may suggest its implicit racism or its imposition of white middle-class values on ethnic groups.*)

authorized to investigate corporations and issue "cease and desist orders" to those engaged in unfair or fraudulent practices and to use the courts to enforce its rulings. Among the abuses the FTC targeted were mislabeled products and false claims.

■■ **Wilson backed passage of the Clayton Antitrust Act and creation of the Federal Trade Commission.**

WILSON AND WORKERS

The Wilson administration also supported legislation to aid working people. The **Federal Farm Loan Act** provided low-interest loans to farmers. The Clayton Antitrust Act included a provision that affirmed labor's right to strike so long as property was not irreparably damaged. The **Adamson Act** reduced the workday for railroad workers from 10 to 8 hours, with no cut in pay. This law not only won applause from reformers but avoided a threatened railroad strike. With Wilson's support, Congress also passed the **Federal Workmen's Compensation Act**, which provided benefits to federal workers injured on the job.

The Wilson administration was less successful in the campaign against child labor. For years progressives had wanted to get young children out of the mills, factories, and mines (see Chapter 17). As labor organizer Mother Jones later recalled:

❝ Every day little children came into Union Headquarters, some with their hands off, . . . some with their fingers off at the knuckle. They were stooped little things, round shouldered and skinny. Many were not over ten years of age. ❞

Faced with rising protests against child labor from the National Consumers' League and other groups, Congress passed the **Keating-Owen Child Labor Act** in 1916. This act, which had Wilson's backing, outlawed the interstate sale of products produced by child labor. In 1918, however, the Supreme Court declared the law unconstitutional because it restricted commerce instead of directly outlawing child labor. Another law, passed in 1919, met the same fate. Not until the 1930s would the United States outlaw child labor.

THE STRUGGLE FOR WOMEN'S SUFFRAGE

Another part of the progressive agenda—the campaign for women's suffrage—faced strong opposition. Liquor interests feared that women would vote for prohibition. Businesses feared that the vote would empower women to demand better wages and working conditions. When one state senator expressed the widely held belief that the vote would rob women of their beauty and charm, a suffragist retorted:

❝ We have women working in the foundries. . . . Women in the laundries . . . stand for 13 or 14 hours in the terrible steam and heat with their hands in hot starch. Surely these women won't lose any

WOMEN'S SUFFRAGE

In 1902 the first International Woman Suffrage Conference was held in Washington, D.C. The United States was among the nations represented that had not yet granted women national suffrage. Swedish delegate Emmy Evald remarked that in her homeland women had voted on some level since 1736. She then went on to point out the contradictions in the American situation:

❝ **You** can not trust the ballot into the hands of women teachers in the public schools but you give it to men who can not read or write. You can not trust the ballot to women who are controlling millions of [dollars] and helping support the country but you give it to loafers and vagabonds who know nothing, have nothing and represent nothing. You can not trust the ballot in the hands of women who are the wives and daughters of your heroes but you give it to those who are willing to sell it for a glass of beer and you trust it in the hands of anarchists. ❞

📀 **AMERICAN CIVICS CITIZENSHIP SKILLS**

Videocassette or Videodisc: Segment 1

Segment 1, Side A

Search Chapter 1

PRIMARY SOURCES

Description of Change: excerpted
Rationale: excerpted to focus on main idea

THROUGH OTHERS' EYES

The international nature of the suffrage movement was underscored when conference delegates agreed to establish a permanent organization, the International Woman Suffrage Alliance. Its first meeting, held in Berlin in 1904, was attended by delegates from Australia, Britain, Denmark, Germany, the Netherlands, Norway, Sweden, and the United States.

PRIMARY SOURCE

Description of Change: excerpted and bracketed
Rationale: excerpted to focus on main idea; bracketed to clarify meaning

Practice

GUIDED PRACTICE

Work with students to summarize Wilson's progressive reform accomplishments by creating on the chalkboard a three-column chart with the headings *Issue, Action,* and *Impact.* Ask students to provide and explain entries for the chart.

INDEPENDENT PRACTICE

Have students write letters to Washington during the Wilson administration urging their senator or representative to support one of the actions listed in the Guided Practice. Letters should explain why the writer believes the action is needed and what he or she expects its impact to be. Students may wish to include their letters in their portfolios.

Review and Assessment

REVIEW Have students work together to develop a list of five words that characterize progressivism. Ask students to use these words to write a paragraph that discusses Wilson's accomplishments as a progressive president. Then assign the Section 4 Review on p. 553.

ASSESS Assign the **Section 4 Daily Quiz** in *Core Resources.*

COOPERATIVE LEARNING

Organize students into three groups to create an illustrated time line of important events during the administrations of the three progressive presidents. Assign each group one of the administrations, and suggest that group members share tasks—research, artwork, writing, and so on. Have each group present its time line.

VOICES IN HISTORY

Wilson's racial policies caused the NAACP in August 1913 to send him an open letter: "Should ten millions of our citizens say that their civic liberties and rights are not safe in your hands? To ask the question is to answer it. They desire a 'New Freedom' too, Mr. President."

Map Caption Answer
the West

more of their beauty and charm by putting a ballot in a ballot box once a year than they are likely to lose standing in foundries or laundries all year. **"**

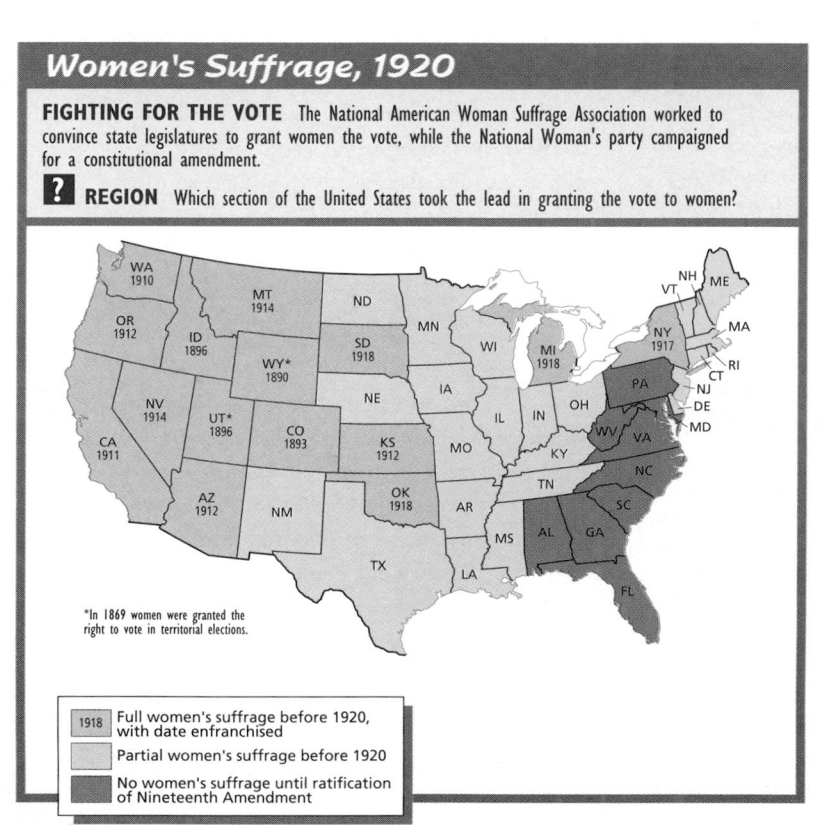

▲ Alice Paul

One leading force in the suffrage movement was the National American Woman Suffrage Association, or NAWSA, founded in 1890. Its first two presidents, Elizabeth Cady Stanton and Susan B. Anthony, distrusted party politics because of Republican leaders' failure after the Civil War to press for voting rights for women as well as for African Americans. As a result, they took a nonpartisan, local approach, trying to get state legislatures to grant women the vote. They achieved few successes in their first few years of lobbying, however.

In 1913 Alice Paul, a militant young Quaker suffragist, broke away from NAWSA and formed another organization, the Congressional Union for Woman Suffrage, which in 1916 became the National Woman's party. The party focused on passing an amendment to the Constitution guaranteeing women the right to vote.

Paul, who had studied in England, favored the British suffragists' more political approach. Thus when Wilson and the Democratic party failed to support woman suffrage in the 1916 election, the Woman's party campaigned against them. Wilson won, but narrowly. (See Chapter 20 for more on the election.)

Paul also favored using the attention-getting protest tactics employed by British suffragists. For example, in January 1917, with Wilson reelected, the Woman's party began round-the-clock picketing of the White House in an effort to pressure Wilson to support a suffrage amendment. They held banners asking, "Mr. President, What Will You Do for Woman Suffrage?" and "How Long Must Women Wait for Liberty?" Many were arrested. Some went on hunger strikes in prison.

Meanwhile, the NAWSA, energized by the leadership of the highly skilled organizer Carrie Chapman Catt, continued to follow traditional political means to attain voting rights. Launching what came to be called her "Winning Plan" in 1916, the NAWSA won a string of successes for suffrage at the state level. After the United States entered World War I in 1917, leaders of the movement—along with millions of American women—lent strong support to the war effort. Their patriotism helped weaken opposition to women's suffrage. By 1919 thirty states had granted women full or partial voting rights. Finally, in 1919, the U.S. Congress passed the **Nineteenth Amendment**, granting women full voting rights. It was ratified in 1920.

Carrie Chapman Catt cautioned, however, that the vote was only an "entering wedge." Women still had to

Women's Suffrage, 1920

FIGHTING FOR THE VOTE The National American Woman Suffrage Association worked to convince state legislatures to grant women the vote, while the National Woman's party campaigned for a constitutional amendment.

? **REGION** Which section of the United States took the lead in granting the vote to women?

*In 1869 women were granted the right to vote in territorial elections.

1918	Full women's suffrage before 1920, with date enfranchised
	Partial women's suffrage before 1920
	No women's suffrage until ratification of Nineteenth Amendment

RETEACH Suggest that students work together to divide and assign the section material according to headings and subheadings. Ask each student to write a question on the content of his or her assigned heading or subheading. Then use the questions to quiz the group on the section.

*C*losure

Ask students to write several sentences explaining which of the three presidents discussed in the chapter has the best claim to the title "progressive." Invite volunteers to reveal and defend their choices.

*E*xtension

INVESTIGATE Have students investigate and report on Carrie Chapman Catt's "Winning Plan."

EVALUATE Suggest that students evaluate the success of progressive reform by responding to the following statement: *The progressives identified the problems but offered few working solutions.*

force their way through the "locked door" of political decision making.

■■ **In 1920, with ratification of the Nineteenth Amendment, American women won their long battle for the right to vote.**

*C*OMMENTARY

The Progressive Legacy

Although scholars agree that the progressive movement left a lasting legacy, they often disagree over how to define that legacy. Many scholars have noted that progressivism was primarily supported by fairly conservative, middle-class, white Americans trying to maintain some level of political and economic power. Many of the successes and shortcomings of the movement can be tied to its origins in the white middle class.

Progressivism made great strides in many areas; however, some of the economic and political reforms of the movement failed to bring about the radical changes anticipated. Such policies as the creation of the Federal Reserve System and implementation of a federal income tax did improve the government's ability to regulate the economy and pay for new programs. Yet, many regulations on businesses fell short of reforming the capitalist system; corporations were eventually able to use the regulations to their own advantage. Corporations also benefitted by being able to operate in the more orderly, predictable environment that regulation provided. On the political front, reforms such as

the initiative, referendum, and recall were primarily used on the local level and thus had little impact on broad questions of national public policy.

One of progressivism's most successful elements, the settlement-house movement, improved opportunities for women, brought great urban reform, and eased the plight of European immigrants. However, most settlement-house workers neglected to address the problems of African Americans, many of whom were new migrants from the rural South.

The progressive presidents showed little interest in racial issues. President Wilson was the least sympathetic to African American concerns. During his administration numerous bills designed to institute segregation were submitted to Congress. Although none passed, Wilson issued an executive order segregating eating and restroom facilities for federal employees. Wilson justified this policy by arguing that it prevented friction between white and black workers, but African Americans denounced it as racist.

Despite these shortcomings, however, progressives took real strides toward making the new industrial society more just and orderly. Their efforts to end child labor, to protect workers and consumers, and to promote conservation profoundly influenced the nation. Their greatest legacy, however, was in demonstrating that America's democratic system could respond and adapt to changes in American life.

■■ **Although progressivism fell short of some of its goals and failed to address racism, it made industrial society more just and humane.**

SECTION REVIEW ANSWERS

IDENTIFY

For significance, see the following pages:
Underwood Tariff Act (p. 549)
Federal Reserve Act (p. 549)
Clayton Antitrust Act (p. 549)
Federal Trade Commission (p. 549)
Federal Farm Loan Act (p. 551)
Adamson Act (p. 551)
Federal Workmen's Compensation Act (p. 551)
Keating-Owen Child Labor Act (p. 551)
Alice Paul (p. 552)
Carrie Chapman Catt (p. 552)
Nineteenth Amendment (p. 552)

1. *by passage of the Underwood Tariff Act and the Federal Reserve Act*
2. *supported Clayton Antitrust Act and creation of FTC*
3. *granted women full voting rights*
4. *Paragraphs might mention: improvements in business regulation, education, women's opportunities, urban reform, immigrant aid, more just and humane industry, failure to address racism, and falling short of some goals.*
5. *Despite business opposition, Wilson passed his legislative agenda including support for labor's right to strike and help for farmers, railroad workers, federal employees, and child laborers.*

■■ **SECTION 4 REVIEW**

IDENTIFY and explain the significance of the following: Underwood Tariff Act, Federal Reserve Act, Clayton Antitrust Act, Federal Trade Commission, Federal Farm Loan Act, Adamson Act, Federal Workmen's Compensation Act, Keating-Owen Child Labor Act, Alice Paul, Carrie Chapman Catt, Nineteenth Amendment.

1. **MAIN IDEA** How did Wilson hope to reduce tariffs and reform the banking system?
2. **MAIN IDEA** How did the Wilson administration attempt to regulate business?
3. **MAIN IDEA** What did the passage of the Nineteenth Amendment accomplish?
4. **WRITING TO EVALUATE** From a current perspective, write a paragraph evaluating the legacy of progressivism.
5. **ANALYZING** How successful was Wilson in enlisting the "forces of humanity" to help farmers, railroad and federal workers, and child laborers?

Return to the Themes section on p. 532. Have students discuss these again and compare their original responses with those given now. (See p. 531B for suggested answers.)

Chapter Review Answers

WRITING A SUMMARY
See Essential Points in each section for main ideas.

REVIEWING CHRONOLOGY
3, 5, 1, 4, 2
Analyzing
obtained funds based on ability to pay by authorizing a graduated income tax; sought to eliminate corruption by providing for direct election of senators

IDENTIFYING PEOPLE AND IDEAS

1. *reform giving voters power to introduce legislation*
2. *reform mayor of Toledo, nicknamed "Golden Rule"*
3. *law authorizing ICC to establish railroad rates and to regulate other companies engaged in interstate commerce*
4. *process of making damaged land productive*
5. *Taft's secretary of interior, opposed restrictions on sale of public land*
6. *Roosevelt's program of social legislation calling for tough laws to protect workers, ensure public health, and regulate business*
7. *Speaker of the House who used his power to block reform legislation*

8. *reform legislation passed under Wilson, creating Federal Reserve Board and Federal Reserve banks*
9. *reduced the workday for railroad workers from 10 to 8 hours for same pay*
10. *militant Quaker suffragist who formed National Woman's party*

UNDERSTANDING MAIN IDEAS
1. *because composed of experts, not party loyalists, who made honest, efficient decisions for cities*

2. *provided a model for reform in government and for regulating big business*
3. *Both promoted reform in business, for the environment, and on behalf of labor.*
4. *The Payne-Aldrich Tariff and the Ballinger-Pinchot affair convinced TR that Taft was too conservative. TR wanted to push for further reform.*
5. *Clayton Antitrust Act helped define what business could not do; FTC investigated offending corporations and used courts to enforce its rulings.*
6. *that America's democratic system could respond and adapt to changes in American life*

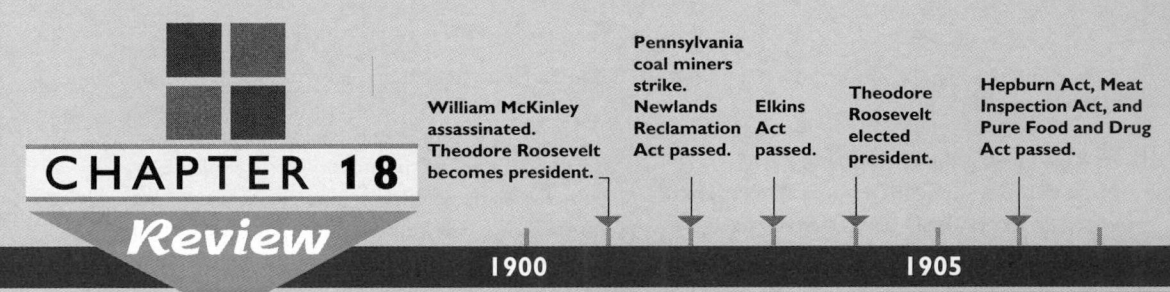

CHAPTER 18
Review

William McKinley assassinated. Theodore Roosevelt becomes president.

Pennsylvania coal miners strike. Newlands Reclamation Act passed.

Elkins Act passed.

Theodore Roosevelt elected president.

Hepburn Act, Meat Inspection Act, and Pure Food and Drug Act passed.

1900   1905

WRITING A SUMMARY
Using the essential points of the chapter as a guide, write a summary of the chapter.

REVIEWING CHRONOLOGY
Number your paper 1 to 5. Study the time line above, and list the following events in the order in which they happened by writing the first next to 1, the second next to 2, and so on. Then complete the activity below.

1. Progressive party formed.
2. Nineteenth Amendment ratified.
3. Pennsylvania coal miners strike.
4. Federal Trade Commission created.
5. William Howard Taft elected president.

Analyzing How did the Sixteenth and Seventeenth amendments promote reform?

IDENTIFYING PEOPLE AND IDEAS
Explain the historical significance of each of the following people or terms.

1. initiative
2. Samuel M. Jones
3. Hepburn Act
4. reclamation
5. Richard Ballinger
6. New Nationalism
7. Joseph Cannon
8. Federal Reserve Act
9. Adamson Act
10. Alice Paul

UNDERSTANDING MAIN IDEAS
1. Why were city commissions effective at achieving efficiency in city government?
2. How did the Wisconsin Idea lay the foundation for further reforms?
3. In what ways were Theodore Roosevelt and William Howard Taft similar in their approaches to reform?
4. Why did Roosevelt challenge Taft in 1912?
5. What were the effects of the Clayton Antitrust Act and the creation of the Federal Trade Commission on the regulation of business?
6. What was the progressive movement's greatest legacy?

⭐ REVIEWING THEMES
1. **Democratic Values** How did reformers seek to curb political corruption and to make government more democratic in the early 20th century?
2. **Economic Development** How did President Roosevelt attempt to regulate business without discouraging free enterprise?
3. **Constitutional Heritage** How might reformers have used the Nineteenth Amendment as a means of accomplishing reform in politics and business?

THINKING CRITICALLY
1. **Synthesizing** How did Roosevelt bring dynamic leadership to the progressive movement at the city, state, and national levels?
2. **Evaluating** How did the controversy over tariffs contribute to Taft's defeat in the 1912 election?
3. **Analyzing** What interests worked against the campaign for women's suffrage in the early 20th century?
4. **Hypothesizing** How might life have been different for African Americans if Wilson had pursued a different racial policy?

STRATEGY FOR SUCCESS
Review the Skills Handbook entry on Reading a Time Line on page 991. Then study the time-line entries below, which focus on the years from 1908 to 1912. What cause-and-effect relationship is suggested by the sequence of events listed? How did the events of 1910 relate to those of 1912?

1908	William Howard Taft elected president.
1909	Payne-Aldrich Tariff passed. Taft fires Gifford Pinchot.
1910	Republicans lose control of House of Representatives.
1912	Roosevelt forms Progressive party. Woodrow Wilson elected president.

WRITING ABOUT HISTORY
Writing to Evaluate Write an essay evaluating the progressives' record on racial issues.

REVIEWING THEMES

1. through election reforms to make government more directly responsible to the people, such as direct primary; direct election of U.S. senators; secret ballot; and initiative, referendum, and recall
2. Roosevelt limited trustbusting and regulation only to those companies behaving irresponsibly.
3. by encouraging women to vote for female reform candidates and for legislation giving women equality in the labor force

THINKING CRITICALLY

1. fought for political, economic, and social reform as head of New York City's police commission, New York state legislator, governor of New York, and president
2. Taft's signing of high-tariff bill outraged progressives, who threw support to Roosevelt. Resulting party division led to Taft's election defeat.
3. liquor interests and businesses that feared women would demand better wages and working conditions
4. might have made advances sooner and more easily if Wilson had not instituted segregation for federal employees

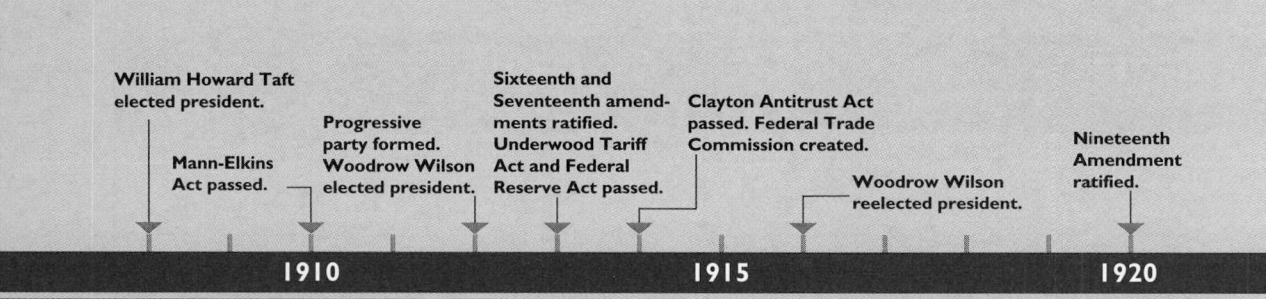

William Howard Taft elected president.

Mann-Elkins Act passed.

Progressive party formed. Woodrow Wilson elected president.

Sixteenth and Seventeenth amendments ratified. Underwood Tariff Act and Federal Reserve Act passed.

Clayton Antitrust Act passed. Federal Trade Commission created.

Woodrow Wilson reelected president.

Nineteenth Amendment ratified.

1910 — 1915 — 1920

USING PRIMARY SOURCES

In 1906 Upton Sinclair published *The Jungle*, a biting attack on the industrial practices and unsanitary conditions in the Chicago stockyards. Read the following excerpt, which describes the manufacture and processing of canned goods in "Packingtown" (Chicago). Then, in a paragraph, explain how publication of this book might have influenced the passage of the Meat Inspection Act.

> ❝ *"Deviled ham" . . . was made out of the waste ends of smoked beef that were too small to be sliced by the machines; and also tripe, dyed with chemicals so that it would not show white, and trimmings of hams and corned beef, and potatoes, skins and all. . . . All this ingenious mixture was ground up and flavored with spices to make it taste like something. Anybody who could invent a new imitation had been sure of a fortune, . . . but it was hard to think of anything new in a place where . . . men welcomed tuberculosis in the cattle they were feeding, because it made them fatten more quickly; and where they bought up all the old rancid [stale] butter . . . rechurned it with skim milk, and sold it in bricks in the cities!* ❞

Chicago stockyards, 1919

LINKING HISTORY AND GEOGRAPHY

Study the map on page 552. What might explain the link between geographic region and the granting of women's suffrage?

Sample ballot, 1892

BUILDING YOUR PORTFOLIO

Complete the following projects independently or cooperatively.

1. **REFORM** In Chapter 17 you portrayed a progressive reformer addressing a problem in your city. Building on that experience, write a platform for the Progressive party that translates the problems of political machines, women's suffrage, business regulation, and worker protection into specific reforms your party hopes to institute.

2. **DEMOCRATIC RIGHTS** In Chapter 17 you portrayed a progressive reformer preparing a speech on women's rights to deliver at an Independence Day celebration. Building on that experience, imagine you are the editor of a labor union newspaper. Write an editorial indicating why you believe that progressives are not adequately addressing the needs of working-class women.

AMERICA AND THE WORLD

1898–1917

THE AMERICAN NATION VIDEODISC PROGRAM
A variety of still images, short videos, and activities are available for you to use as you teach this chapter. See Correlation to *The American Nation Videodisc Program* for barcode correlations and suggestions for using the program.

Chapter Overview

In the late 1800s and early 1900s, the U.S. sought to extend its influence in the Pacific, Latin America, the Caribbean, and Asia. In its drive to become a world power, the U.S. adopted a program of economic and political imperialism. It fought a war with Spain and gained control of Cuba and added the Philippines, Hawaii, and Puerto Rico to its territorial possessions. To link its growing empire, the U.S. built the Panama Canal. To successfully compete with the European powers for trade in Asia, the U.S. formulated the Open Door policy in China. In the Western Hemisphere, U.S. military power protected American business investments in other nations.

Chapter Planning Guide

CHAPTER 19	CORE RESOURCE BOOKLETS	AUDIOVISUAL AV RESOURCES	PROGRAM RESOURCES
INTRODUCTION pp. 556–557	■ Building Your Portfolio Worksheet 6		
TEACHING THE CHAPTER pp. 558–579	■ Graphic Organizer 19 ■ Social Studies Skills Worksheet 19 ■ Literature Worksheet 19 ■ Geography Worksheet 19 ■ Outline Maps 1, 2, 8, 11, 12, 13, 20, 21, 24	■ *The American Nation Videodisc: The Panama Canal* ■ Linking Geography and History Transparency and Worksheet 15 ■ Everyday Life in America Transparency and Worksheet 19	■ *Eyewitnesses and Others*, Volume 2: Readings 13, 23
REVIEW AND ASSESSMENT pp. 580–581	■ Chapter 19 Daily Quizzes ■ Review Worksheet 19 ■ Chapter 19 Tests ■ Alternative Assessment Forms		■ Test Generator

Additional Resources

BOOKS FOR TEACHERS

Hall, Linda B. and Don M. Coerver. *Revolution on the Border: The United States and Mexico, 1910–1920.* University of New Mexico Press, 1988. Account of the Mexican Revolution in the U.S.–Mexico borderlands.

LaFeber, Walter. *Panama Canal: The Crisis in Historical Perspective.* Oxford University Press, 1990. Historical perspective of the Panama Canal.

O'Toole, G. J. *The Spanish War: An American Epic, 1898.* Norton, 1986. History of the war and its impact on U.S. foreign policy.

BOOKS FOR STUDENTS

Dolan, Edward F. *Panama & the United States: Their Canal, Their Stormy Years.* Watts, 1990. History of Panama and Panama–U.S. relations from years as a Spanish colony through 1990.

*Marrin, Albert. *The Spanish-American War.* Atheneum, 1991. Explores causes and consequences of war, yellow journalism, and Teddy Roosevelt's role.

Paterson, Thomas G. and Stephen G. Rabe, eds. *Imperial Surge: The United States Abroad, the 1890s–Early 1900s.* Heath, 1992. Explores U.S. imperialism in the 1890s and early 1900s.

* for students reading below grade level

MULTIMEDIA MATERIALS

Becoming a Modern Nation. Video, 28 min. Video Knowledge. Traces U.S. history from Spanish-American War to World War I.

The Lure of Empire: America Debates Imperialism. Video, 27 min. Learning Corporation of America. Dramatizes the debate over the Spanish-American War and U.S. foreign policy in the Pacific.

The Splendid Little War. Video, 55 min. Belle Grove. Uses newsreels, reenactments, and period music to tell the story of the Spanish-American War.

THEMES IN AMERICAN HISTORY

USE WITH PAGES 556–557

Listed on the right are the themes emphasized in Chapter 19. The questions in boldface type stimulate critical thinking and provide students with an opportunity to discuss the themes within a broadened context. The questions also appear in the pupil's edition on p. 556.

■ GLOBAL RELATIONS

Why might a country acquire overseas colonies? Students may explain that overseas colonies could provide resources or markets for a country's economic activities. A country might want to colonize another nation in order to achieve the political control it thinks necessary to serve its economic interests there. It also might want colonies in order to resettle some of its population, or for international prestige.

Why might a country resist becoming a colony? Students may suggest that a country might resist colonization because it wants to maintain its political independence or control its own resources.

■ ECONOMIC DEVELOPMENT

How might foreign investors influence a country's economy? Students might suggest that by purchasing land and businesses in foreign countries, foreign investors can come to dominate certain industries. They also might influence another economy by making loans to private businesses in a country, by financing infrastructure improvements, and otherwise creating jobs.

What problems might arise from these investments? Students may suggest that problems could develop if foreign investors try to exert political or economic influence over another nation or deprive its citizens of opportunities to develop their own economy.

■ DEMOCRATIC VALUES

Does the acquisition of colonies conflict with democratic principles? Why or why not? Students might suggest that a colonizing country can establish democratic governments in its colonies. On the other hand, students might indicate that the very act of imposing a system of government on another limits its citizens' freedom to choose their own institutions and form of government.

CHAPTER STRATEGIES FOR MEETING INDIVIDUAL NEEDS

LIMITED ENGLISH PROFICIENT LEARNERS

Organize the class into three groups. Have one group write questions about the People in the Preview Workshop for each section, while other groups write questions about the Places and Terms. Have groups pose their questions to the class.

TACTILE/KINESTHETIC LEARNERS

Direct students to work in groups to make color-coded world maps. Maps should show the locations of U.S. colonies and of countries in which the U.S. intervened militarily or practiced dollar diplomacy.

LEARNERS HAVING DIFFICULTY

Direct students to create a three-column chart for each section labeled *What I Already Know, What I Expect to Learn, What I Learned.* Have them complete columns one and two for each Focus question. After they complete the section, have students fill in column three.

AUDITORY LEARNERS

Have students make an audiotape script—titled "Imperialism Yes! Imperialism No!"—of quotes from the chapter defending, expressing concern about, or opposing U.S. expansion. Suggest that students write brief introductions to the quotes.

VISUAL LEARNERS

Have students create a booklet in the style of a newsmagazine's "People" section, highlighting the various people who took part in the events of this period.

GIFTED LEARNERS

Encourage students to conduct research and write an essay comparing Americans' belief in manifest destiny to U.S. imperialism. Essays should note how these ideas influenced U.S. domestic and foreign policy.

USING THE CHAPTER FOCUS

 **UNDERSTANDING THE MAIN IDEA**

Call on a volunteer to read aloud the Understanding the Main Idea paragraph and to define the term *foreign policy*. Then ask students why Americans might have believed that the U.S. had a greater right to exercise its power and influence in the Western Hemisphere than did Spain or other major European powers. Encourage students to speculate about possible reasons for growing U.S. interest in the Pacific, the Caribbean, and Latin America.

THEMES

Have students work individually or in groups to answer the questions under Themes. Save students' responses so that they can compare them with their responses after studying the chapter. (See p. 555B for suggested answers.)

■ **THE TIME LINE**

Invite students to convert time-line entries into newspaper headlines. As they read the part of the chapter that pertains to each headline, have students write brief newspaper articles that explain the who, what, when, where, and why of each event.

CORE RESOURCES

• **Graphic Organizer 19**
• **Outline Maps 1, 2, 8, 11, 12, 13, 20, 21, 24**
• **Building Your Portfolio Worksheet 6**

556

ABOUT THE ILLUSTRATION

Pictures of battle scenes, such as the one below, received front-page coverage during the Spanish-American War. Newspapers sent journalists overseas to wire dispatches of the most exciting events. News of the Battle of Manila Bay was hard to obtain because the telegraph cable that could have immediately relayed news of the American victory was cut. It was not until May 9, more than a week after the battle, that Dewey officially cabled news of his victory to the U.S. Ask students to compare the coverage of this battle with news coverage of a recent world event, and to speculate about the impact of accurate and immediate news accounts on public opinion.

Chapter 19

AMERICA AND THE WORLD

1898–1917

FOCUS

UNDERSTANDING THE MAIN IDEA

In the waning years of the 19th century, the United States established itself as a world power by defeating Spain and acquiring Spain's last colonies in the Western Hemisphere. The progressive presidents asserted a strong foreign policy, acting to promote U.S. economic and security interests in the Pacific, the Caribbean, Asia, and Latin America.

THEMES

■ **GLOBAL RELATIONS** Why might a country acquire overseas colonies? Why might a country resist becoming a colony?

■ **ECONOMIC DEVELOPMENT** How might foreign investors influence a country's economy? What problems might arise from these investments?

■ **DEMOCRATIC VALUES** Does the acquisition of colonies conflict with democratic principles? Why or why not?

1898	1899	1904	1910	1915
Spanish-American War begins.	U.S. annexes Philippines.	Russo-Japanese War begins.	The Mexican Revolution starts.	Wilson sends marines into Haiti.

Ask students to recall key points of the Monroe Doctrine and the reasons that President Monroe issued it in 1823. Write their responses on the chalkboard. Ask them for examples of domestic concerns in the early and mid-1800s that might have distracted American attention from foreign affairs. Ask students to speculate about the role industrialization might have played in reawakening Americans' interest in foreign affairs. Point out that in this chapter, students will see how America's view of its role in the world changed in the late 1800s and early 1900s, and how these changes influenced the way its leaders made and carried out foreign policy.

■■ **LINK TO THE PAST** ▶

President James Monroe issued the Monroe Doctrine in 1823 as a warning to European powers to keep out of the Americas. But for much of the 19th century, the United States was too involved in domestic affairs to enforce the doctrine.

MAKING CONNECTIONS
Music
Dewey's victory at Manila Bay made him an instant hero and the subject of a wildly popular song that included these lines:

O Dewey was the morning
  Upon the first of May,
And Dewey was the Admiral
  Down in Manila Bay. . . .
And Dewey feel discouraged?
  I Dew not think we Dew.

Battle of Manila Bay

Dawn was just breaking as the American fleet, its flags flying, steamed across lovely Manila Bay, in the Philippines. It was early morning, May 1, 1898—just 11 days after the United States had declared war on Spain. Commodore George Dewey stood on the bridge of his flagship, *Olympia,* his eyes trained on the Spanish guns aimed at his ships from the shore and from the small Spanish fleet anchored in the harbor.

Sighting the Americans, the Spanish opened fire. Shortly after 5:30 A.M., Commodore Dewey gave an order to his flagship captain: "You may fire when you are ready, Gridley." The boom and flash of naval guns exploded through the bay. Shells crashed into several Spanish vessels, and they erupted into flames.

The Battle of Manila Bay had begun, the first battle of the Spanish-American War. It marked America's emergence on the world stage at the end of the 19th century. Throughout most of the century, Americans had followed George Washington's advice and remained aloof from foreign entanglements. Indeed, as late as 1889, Congressman Henry Cabot Lodge of Massachusetts wrote: "Our relations with foreign nations today fill but a slight place in American politics." But this would soon change as the United States became deeply involved in events abroad, from nearby Cuba and Mexico to distant China.

U.S. soldiers question Filipino women, 1899.

FOCUS OBJECTIVES

- Explain what fueled the quest for overseas territory.

- Analyze why the U.S. declared war on Spain.

- Determine the outcome of the Spanish-American War for the U.S. and for Spain.

HISTORICAL SIDELIGHTS

Influence of Sea Power

Alfred Thayer Mahan's *Influence of Sea Power Upon History, 1660–1783,* was one of the most influential books of the era. Mahan's ideas received strong support from Massachusetts congressman Henry Cabot Lodge, who was fond of telling people that sea power was essential to "the greatness of every splendid people."

Section 1

WAR WITH SPAIN

F O C U S
- **What fueled the quest for overseas territory?**
- **Why did the United States declare war on Spain?**
- **What was the outcome of the Spanish-American War for the United States and Spain?**

In the late 1800s the United States emerged as the world's leading industrial producer and agricultural exporter. This economic success encouraged the nation to establish overseas colonies, just as the European powers were doing. The United States hoped colonization would provide new markets for its goods and new sources of raw materials. U.S. involvement in Samoa and a short war with Spain in 1898 increased the American role in the Pacific and the Caribbean.

Recruiter, 1898

THE IMPULSE FOR IMPERIALISM

In March 1889 seven warships—one British, three German, and three American—faced off in the South Pacific harbor of Apia, in present-day Western Samoa. But before a shot could be fired, a typhoon struck, destroying all but the British ship. What brought these three powerful nations to the brink of war? **Imperialism**: the quest for colonial empires.

Between 1876 and 1915, vast areas of Africa, Asia, and Latin America fell under the control of a handful of industrialized nations locked in a race to acquire overseas colonies. Great Britain, the leading imperialist power, had colonies flung so far across the globe that the British could boast, "The sun never sets on the British Empire."

What lay behind this wave of imperialism? The desire for power and prestige played a role, but it was also a matter of economics. Industrial workers, aided by efficient machines and abundant capital, produced far more goods than could be consumed at home. In response, industrialists turned to Africa, Asia, and Latin America for new

◀ **Samoan families lived in grass-thatched huts, such as this one in Pago Pago.**

MOTIVATING: PRIOR KNOWLEDGE

Ask volunteers to recall the economic role that the American colonies played in the British empire in the 1600s and 1700s. *(markets for British goods and sources of raw materials)* Display a world map, and have students speculate on what areas might be targets for similar American economic activity in the late 1800s and early 1900s.

Teaching the Section

IMPERIALISM

Have students work in groups to create a list of the reasons for U.S. interest in becoming an imperial power at the turn of the century. *(industrialization and increased dependence on world trade, desire for overseas military bases and fueling stations, interest in spreading U.S. political system and Christianity)* Direct groups to label each reason as an economic, strategic, cultural, or political motive for imperialism and to identify in the section an example of each reason in practice. Then ask groups to share their lists and examples with the class and discuss them.

---

customers and new sources of raw materials. The telegraph, steamship, and railroad made even the remotest areas potential markets. To protect these new markets from competition, industrialized nations launched a campaign of colonization.

Although American enthusiasm for overseas expansion never matched that of the Europeans, support grew during the late 1800s. Some supporters, like Alfred Thayer Mahan of the U.S. Naval College, argued that overseas territories would make the United States more powerful and provide sites for naval bases and steamship fueling stations from which to conduct trade. Others claimed that the United States had a duty to spread its political system and the Christian religion to other parts of the world. This belief often went hand-in-hand with feelings of racial superiority. In his widely read book *Our Country* (1885), Josiah Strong, a Protestant minister and social reformer, proclaimed that Anglo-Saxons (people of English ancestry) had a special mission:

> 66 God, with infinite wisdom and skill, is training the Anglo-Saxon race for an hour sure to come in the world's future. . . .
>
> Then this race . . . the representative, let us hope, of the largest liberty, the purest Christianity, the highest civilization . . . will spread itself over the earth. 99

▪▪ The quest for empire was fueled by strategic, economic, and cultural motives.

It was the desire for naval bases and fueling stations, rather than cultural or religious concerns, that led the United States, Great Britain, and Germany to square off in Samoa in 1889. The Samoans realized that this competition put them in grave danger. In 1898 Te'o Tuvale, a government official, warned his fellow Samoans:

> 66 Be kind and don't start a war in Samoa, because if you do the Three Powers [Britain, Germany, and the United States] will take over the conduct of the country and your orators and Chiefs and things that you have been accustomed to will be of no further use. 99

Te'o Tuvale's prophecy was fulfilled the next year when, in the face of overwhelming European and U.S. military might, Samoans surrendered their government. The United States won control over Eastern Samoa, and Germany was granted control over Western Samoa. Today Western Samoa is independent, while Eastern (or American) Samoa remains a U.S. territory (see map on page 564).

CONFLICT IN CUBA

The Caribbean island of Cuba, just 90 miles from the Florida Keys, provided a testing ground for U.S. imperialism. In the late 1800s Cuba simmered with unrest. Along with its Caribbean neighbor Puerto Rico, it was the last of the Spanish colonies in the Americas. Since 1868, Cubans had launched a series of unsuccessful revolts against Spanish rule. To put down the rebellion, the Spanish government exiled many leaders of the independence movement. Foremost among these exiles was the Cuban poet José Martí, who was forced out of Cuba in 1871 and again in 1879.

From his exile in New York, Martí wrote poems and newspaper articles promoting Cuban independence. He also urged Cuban exiles to mount an invasion of Cuba:

▲ José Martí

> 66 Let us rise up at once with a final burst of heartfelt energy. . . . Let us rise up for the true republic, those of us who, with our passion for right and our habit of hard work, will know how to preserve it. 99

When Cubans launched another revolt in February 1895, Martí and other exiles joined them. Martí became a martyr for Cuban independence when he was killed a month later in a battle with Spanish soldiers.

In 1896 Spain sent General Valeriano Weyler to put down the uprising. Within days Weyler had imprisoned thousands of farmers in concentration camps to prevent them from supplying the rebels. Over the next two years, starvation and disease claimed the lives of perhaps 200,000 Cubans.

The American press branded Weyler "the Butcher." William Randolph Hearst's *Journal* and Joseph Pulitzer's *World*, two New York City newspapers, outdid each other in publicizing Spanish atrocities. In 1897 Hearst sent artist

---

Teaching the **Section**

WAR WITH SPAIN

Work with the class to develop a chalkboard list of reasons that the U.S. went to war with Spain. Discuss each reason as it is recorded on the chalkboard. Then have students imagine they are newspaper editors in 1898 and have them write editorials calling for war with Spain. Ask students to read their editorials aloud. Students may wish to include their editorials in their portfolios.

THE WAR'S OUTCOME

Have students work in groups to discuss the outcomes of the Spanish-American War for the U.S. and Spain and then report to the class about whether they think those outcomes justified U.S. participation in this war.

■■ Direct students to list circumstances or reasons they believe would justify U.S. military intervention in another country today.

Frederic Remington to Cuba to send back drawings that vividly documented Spanish cruelty. Hearst hoped to sell more newspapers, but he also hoped to horrify Americans into agitating for war against Spain.

Finding nothing to draw, Remington reportedly cabled Hearst: "EVERYTHING IS QUIET. THERE IS NO TROUBLE HERE. THERE WILL BE NO WAR. WISH TO RETURN." Hearst was said to have replied: "PLEASE REMAIN. YOU FURNISH THE PICTURES AND I'LL FURNISH THE WAR."

In addition to U.S. horror at Spanish atrocities, threats to U.S. investments in Cuba convinced many that the United States should aid the Cuban rebels. In the face of mounting war fever, President William McKinley, himself a veteran of the Civil War, struggled to remain neutral and to resist committing American troops. "I have been through one war. I have seen the dead piled up, and I do not want to see another," he explained.

But early in 1898, two shattering events forced his hand. First, on February 9 Hearst's *Journal* printed a letter written by Spain's minister to the United States, Enrique Dupuy de Lôme. The letter, which had been intercepted by a Cuban spy and sold to Hearst, ridiculed President McKinley as "weak, and a bidder for the admiration of the crowd."

Americans were outraged at the Spaniard's remarks, which the *Journal* called "the worst insult to the United States in its history." Then on February 15 the American battleship *Maine*—sent to Havana, Cuba, to protect U.S. lives and property—blew up, killing 260 sailors. "DESTRUCTION OF THE WAR SHIP MAINE WAS THE WORK OF AN ENEMY!" screamed the *Journal*'s headline. Though it was later determined that a fire in a coal bin had probably caused the explosion, many Americans blamed Spain. "Remember the *Maine*! And to hell with Spain!" became a familiar chant.

Spain tried to calm tensions by agreeing to a U.S.–proposed peace plan. But it was too late. On April 11 President McKinley bowed to public pressure and asked Congress to intervene in Cuba "in the name of humanity, in the name of civilization, and in behalf of endangered American interests."

On April 20 Congress recognized Cuban independence and voted to use U.S. military force to help Cuba attain it. Congress also adopted the **Teller Amendment**, which stated that the United States claimed no "sovereignty, jurisdiction, or control" over Cuba. Once Cuba won its independence from Spain, the amendment promised, the United States would "leave the government and control of the Island to its people."

■■ **To protect U.S. investments and to help Cuba overthrow Spanish rule, the United States declared war on Spain in April 1898.**

WAR WITH SPAIN

The first battles of the **Spanish-American War** were not fought in nearby Cuba, but halfway around the world, in the Spanish-held Philippine Islands. Weeks before war was declared, Assistant Secretary of the Navy Theodore Roosevelt had, without authorization, cabled Commodore George Dewey, commander of the U.S. Navy's Asiatic fleet anchored at Hong Kong. Roosevelt ordered Dewey to prepare his ships for offensive action in the Philippines.

On May 1, 1898, less than two weeks after war was declared, Dewey's fleet easily defeated the small Spanish fleet guarding the Philippine city of Manila. In order to capture the city itself, Dewey obtained the support of a rebel army of Filipino patriots led by Emilio Aguinaldo (ahg-ee-NAHL-doh). Filipinos had been fighting for independence from Spain for two years. Now, along with U.S. soldiers, they attacked and captured Manila. Cut off by Commodore Dewey's warships and surrounded by Aguinaldo's forces, Spanish forces in the Philippines surrendered on August 14, 1898.

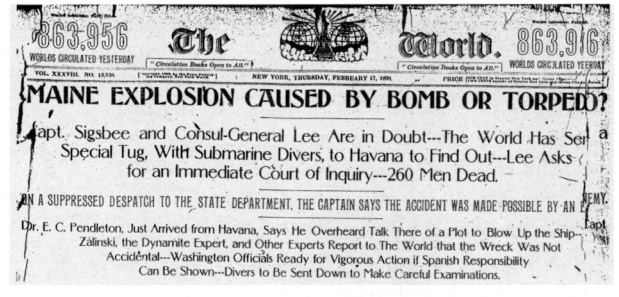

▲ The United States found it difficult to maintain its neutrality in the Cuban-Spanish conflict amid the public outrage triggered by sensationalized news reports. This headline appeared in Joseph Pulitzer's *World*.

Practice

GUIDED PRACTICE

List the following on the chalkboard: *Spanish rule in Cuba, Hearst and Pulitzer newspaper stories, U.S. investments in Cuba, De Lôme letter,* and *sinking of the* Maine. Call on students to describe the role that each factor played in encouraging the U.S. to declare war on Spain.

INDEPENDENT PRACTICE

Ask students to choose an item from the Guided Practice and to write a paragraph that supports or disputes it as a good reason for declaring war on Spain. Students may wish to include their paragraphs in their portfolios.

Review and Assessment

REVIEW Have students work in pairs to create time lines of the events in this section, making sure to leave out at least four key events. Instruct pairs to exchange time lines, to identify the missing events, and to enter them in the appropriate places on the time lines. Then assign the Section 1 Review on p. 562.

ASSESS Assign the **Section 1 Daily Quiz** in *Core Resources*. ▶

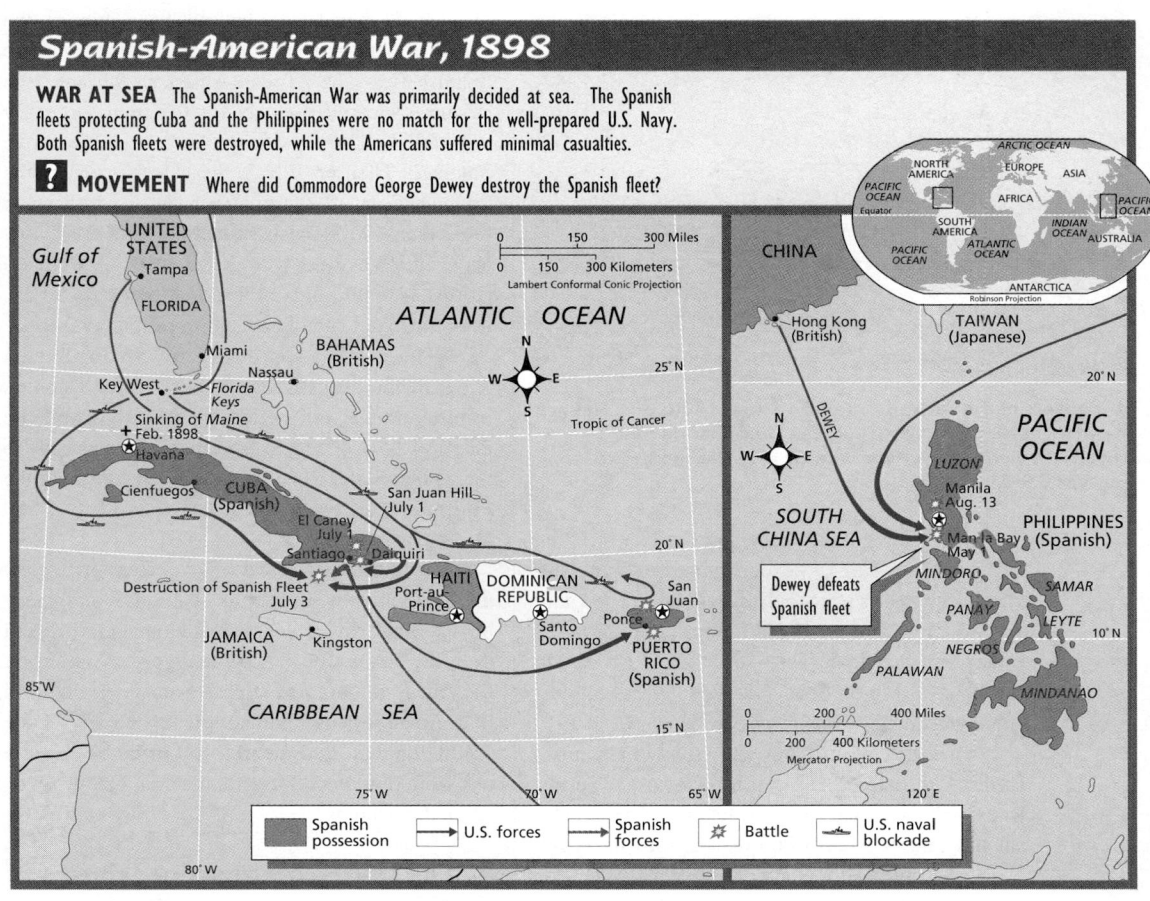

Spanish-American War, 1898

WAR AT SEA The Spanish-American War was primarily decided at sea. The Spanish fleets protecting Cuba and the Philippines were no match for the well-prepared U.S. Navy. Both Spanish fleets were destroyed, while the Americans suffered minimal casualties.

? **MOVEMENT** Where did Commodore George Dewey destroy the Spanish fleet?

Victory in Cuba would not come quite as easily as it had in the Philippines. With a regular army of only some 28,000 soldiers, the U.S. War Department was unprepared for land battles. Thousands of volunteers raced to enlist, but how could they be trained and equipped overnight? With little training and outfitted in heavy wool uniforms (the only ones that army storehouses could supply), U.S. troops sailed for tropical Cuba in mid-June. For rations, the men were issued canned corned beef that was supposed to keep in any weather. "Well," reported one soldier, "it commenced to explode. We had to throw it all overboard." Another soldier described life once the troops arrived in Cuba:

66 Heavy rains pouring down, no tents for cover, . . . standing in trenches in a foot of water and mud, day and night. . . . Ration issue consisting of a slice of sow belly, hardtack, and some grains of coffee. . . . Then came the issue of fleece-lined underwear in a 132 [degree] climate. . . . Then came on malaria. 99

▲ Emilio Aguinaldo, shown wearing a vest, sat for this photograph with his advisers in 1896.

RETEACH Organize students into groups and assign each group a subsection of the section. Have each group develop several questions and answers about the main ideas in its assigned material. Then have each group quiz the other groups with its questions.

Closure

Ask students to assess whether or not America's involvement in war with Spain was part of the mission outlined by Josiah Strong in the quote on p. 559. Require students to explain and defend their opinions.

Extension

INTERPRET

Have students research Cuban poet José Martí's poems or essays about the U.S. and interpret them for the class.

INVESTIGATE

Students might investigate the lives and activities of the "founders" of yellow journalism: Joseph Pulitzer and William Randolph Hearst.

SECTION REVIEW ANSWERS

IDENTIFY

For significance, see the following pages:
imperialism (p. 558)
Te'o Tuvale (p. 559)
José Martí (p. 559)
Valeriano Weyler (p. 559)
William Randolph Hearst (p. 559)
William McKinley (p. 560)
Enrique Dupuy de Lôme (p. 560)
Teller Amendment (p. 560)
Spanish-American War (p. 560)
George Dewey (p. 560)
Emilio Aguinaldo (p. 560)

LOCATE

For locations, see the maps on pp. 561 and 564.

1. *new markets for growing industries, bases and fueling stations to reach and protect those markets*
2. *sensational reports of Spanish atrocities, threats to U.S. investments in Cuba, Dupuy de Lôme's letter, destruction of the Maine, public pressure*
3. *U.S. gained Puerto Rico, Guam, and Philippines; Spain lost its last American and Pacific colonies.*
4. *Poems should express feelings of Cuban people under what they saw as oppressive Spanish rule.*
5. *Both published newspapers that sensationalized Spanish actions, thus provoking Americans toward war.*

▲ Soldiers of the African American 9th and 10th cavalries are shown here during the Battle of Las Guásimas on June 24, 1898. This victory paved the way for American forces to capture Santiago.

The major American land actions in Cuba began on July 1 as U.S. troops mounted an assault on the Spanish stronghold of Santiago. Their aim was to capture the heights above Santiago—El Caney and San Juan Hill—so that they could aim their guns down on Spanish troops. One U.S. division overcame Spanish forces at El Caney.

In what would become the war's most famous battle, Lieutenant Colonel Teddy Roosevelt (who had resigned his naval post) led a cavalry unit of some 1,000 men toward the garrison on San Juan Hill. Composed largely of athletes from eastern colleges, miners, cowboys, Native Americans, ranchers, and would-be adventurers, the unit was known as the Rough Riders.

Since their horses had not been shipped, the Rough Riders had to charge on foot under intense Spanish fire. The African American 9th and 10th cavalries cleared the way for the final surge. By nightfall U.S. troops controlled the ridge above Santiago. Then on July 3, the U.S. Navy sank the Spanish fleet off the coast of Cuba, resulting in more than 400 Spanish casualties. With their navy crushed, two weeks later, on July 17, Spanish troops in Cuba surrendered. Meanwhile, U.S. troops also defeated Spanish troops in Puerto Rico.

The war proved costly for Spain. By the terms of the peace treaty, Spain granted Cuba its independence and ceded Puerto Rico and the Pacific island of Guam (see map on page 564) to the United States. Spain also gave up control of the Philippines in return for a U.S. payment of $20 million.

By gaining control of overseas territories, the United States secured its position as an imperialist and world power. Expansionists expressed delight, but many Americans were troubled by the quest for empire. Furthermore, the United States paid a heavy human toll for the war. Some 5,400 soldiers died, nearly 400 in battle and the rest from dysentery, typhoid, malaria, yellow fever, or food poisoning.

■■ **The United States gained most of Spain's overseas territory through victory in the Spanish-American War.**

 SECTION 1 REVIEW

IDENTIFY and explain the significance of the following: imperialism, Te'o Tuvale, José Martí, Valeriano Weyler, William Randolph Hearst, William McKinley, Enrique Dupuy de Lôme, Teller Amendment, Spanish-American War, George Dewey, Emilio Aguinaldo.

LOCATE and explain the importance of the following: American Samoa; Santiago, Cuba; Manila, Philippines; Puerto Rico; Guam.

1. **MAIN IDEA** What led the United States and other industrial powers to turn to imperialism?
2. **MAIN IDEA** What factors caused the United States to become involved in the Spanish-American War?
3. **GEOGRAPHY: PLACE** What territories did the United States gain as a result of the Spanish-American War? How did the war affect Spain?
4. **WRITING TO CREATE** Imagine you are Cuban revolutionary José Martí. Write a poem supporting Cuban independence from Spain.
5. **EVALUATING** How did publishers William Randolph Hearst and Joseph Pulitzer influence the United States to declare war on Spain in 1898?

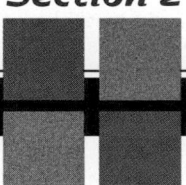

PREVIEW WORKSHOP

Following is a list of the significant people, places, and terms in this section. You may wish to use this list as a section preview.

People
- William Howard Taft
- Kalakaua
- Liliuokalani

- John Hay
- Matthew Perry

Places
- Hawaii
- Taiwan
- Korea
- Beijing, China
- Yokohama, Japan

Terms
- annex
- Philippine Government Act
- Jones Act of 1916
- spheres of influence
- Open Door policy
- Boxer Rebellion
- Russo-Japanese War

Section 2

EXPANSION IN THE PACIFIC

FOCUS
- **How did the United States deal with Filipino calls for independence?**
- **Why did the U.S. government annex Hawaii?**
- **What role did the United States play in China?**
- **What kind of relationship developed between Japan and the United States in the late 1800s and early 1900s?**

America's war with Spain began over Cuba. But, in addition to establishing a U.S. presence in the Caribbean, the war extended the U.S. presence in Asia and the Pacific. After the war, the United States established political control over the Philippines and added Hawaii to its colonial holdings. The United States also became further involved in affairs in China and took a new interest in Japan.

Hawaiian coin

FOCUS OBJECTIVES
- Describe how the U.S. dealt with Filipino calls for independence.
- Explain why the U.S. government annexed Hawaii.
- Determine the role the U.S. played in China.
- Analyze the relationship that developed between Japan and the U.S. in the late 1800s and early 1900s.

HISTORICAL SIDELIGHTS
The Philippines
When news reached the U.S. of Dewey's victory at Manila Bay, humorist Finley Peter Dunne quipped that Americans weren't sure if the Philippines "were islands or canned goods."

UPROAR OVER THE PHILIPPINES

When Dewey's fleet steamed into Manila Bay in 1898, few Americans even knew where the Philippines were. President McKinley confessed that before he consulted a globe, he could not locate the islands "within two thousand miles." The Philippines—a group of islands—cover some 100,000 square miles in the Pacific Ocean, southeast of the Chinese coast. Now that the Philippines were "flung into [U.S.] arms by Dewey's guns," Americans faced an urgent question: Should Filipinos be forced to accept U.S. rule?

The debate over annexation. The debate over whether the United States should **annex**, or take control of, the Philippines was rooted in the larger controversy over imperialism raging across the country.

▶ Filipino women are shown winnowing, or separating, rice on Palawan Island.

People questioned whether it was proper or wise for the United States to annex any foreign territory and rule its government and its people.

Expansionists argued forcefully in favor of annexation. In addition to making a case for annexation for commercial and naval reasons, some believed that the United States would bring democracy to the Philippines. Others held that the United States had to rule the Philippines to keep out European powers. Charles Denby, a former American

CORE RESOURCES
- **Geography Worksheet 19**
- **Section 2 Daily Quiz**

AV RESOURCES
- **Linking Geography and History Transparency and Worksheet 15**

MOTIVATING: STUDENT EXPERIENCES

Ask students to locate the Philippines, Japan, and China on a wall map. Ask students to discuss the current relationship between the U.S. and these countries. Then tell students that this section reviews the relationship between the U.S. and these countries in the late 1800s and early 1900s.

PRIMARY SOURCES

Description of Change: excerpted
Rationale: excerpted to focus on main idea

HISTORICAL SIDELIGHTS

McKinley's Decision
President McKinley agonized over whether to recognize Filipino independence or to annex the islands. His ultimate support for annexation reflected widely held attitudes of the time about America's superiority and its duty to spread its culture to other parts of the world. "We could not leave [the Filipinos] to themselves—they were unfit for self-government," McKinley later reported. In addition, he said, America had a responsibility "to educate the Filipinos, and uplift and civilize and Christianize them, and by God's grace to do the best we could by them."

AV TRANSPARENCY

Linking Geography and History Transparency and **Worksheet 15**

Map Caption Answer
American Samoa

Teaching the Section

ANNEXATION OR INDEPENDENCE

Organize 12 students into two groups of 6 students each, leaving remaining students to form a large third group. Assign the two small groups the roles of witnesses appearing before a congressional committee considering annexation of the Philippines. Ask one small group to present arguments in favor of annexation and the other to give arguments against it. Have the large group act as the congressional panel: they are to listen to arguments of witnesses, ask questions, and finally vote for or against annexation. Then reorganize groups to allow other class members to act as congressional witnesses for a hearing on the annexation of Hawaii.

---

foreign minister to China, warned opponents of annexation that times had changed:

> 66 I recognize the existence of a national sentiment in accordance with . . . Washington's Farewell Address, which is against the acquisition of foreign territory; but . . . circumstances are changed. . . . We have a great commerce to take care of. We have to compete with the commercial nations of the world in far-distant markets. Commerce, not politics, is king. 99

Opponents of American imperialism responded that, by annexing the Philippines and denying its independence, the United States would violate its own ideals expressed in the Declaration of Independence. In June 1898, opponents of U.S. imperialism formed the Anti-Imperialist League, which proclaimed:

> 66 We regret that it has become necessary in the land of Washington and Lincoln to reaffirm that all men, of whatever race

or color, are entitled to life, liberty, and the pursuit of happiness. . . . We insist that the subjugation of any people is "criminal aggression" and open disloyalty to the distinctive principles of our Government. 99

After a fierce debate, the Senate narrowly approved the treaty annexing the Philippines on February 6, 1899. The vote was 57 to 27, barely reaching the two-thirds majority required.

Conquest and early rule. Filipinos, however, did not want to exchange one master for another—gaining independence from Spain only to lose it to the United States. Emilio Aguinaldo had already set up a provisional Filipino government and proclaimed himself president of the Philippine Republic. Now he warned that Filipinos would go to war if "American troops attempt to take forcible possession. Upon their heads will be all the blood which may be shed."

For the next three years, Filipino independence fighters and U.S. soldiers fought for control of the Philippines. U.S. forces captured Aguinaldo in March 1901. When Filipino resistance continued, however, U.S. forces implemented a concentration camp policy as Weyler had done in Cuba. By the time U.S. forces crushed the rebellion in 1902, the cost in Filipino lives was horrendous, estimated in the hundreds of thousands. More than 4,000 U.S. soldiers lost their lives.

In 1902 the U.S. Congress passed the **Philippine Government Act**, also known as the Organic Act. The act decreed that the Philippines would be ruled by a governor and a two-house legislature. The United States would appoint the governor and the legislature's upper house. After peace was

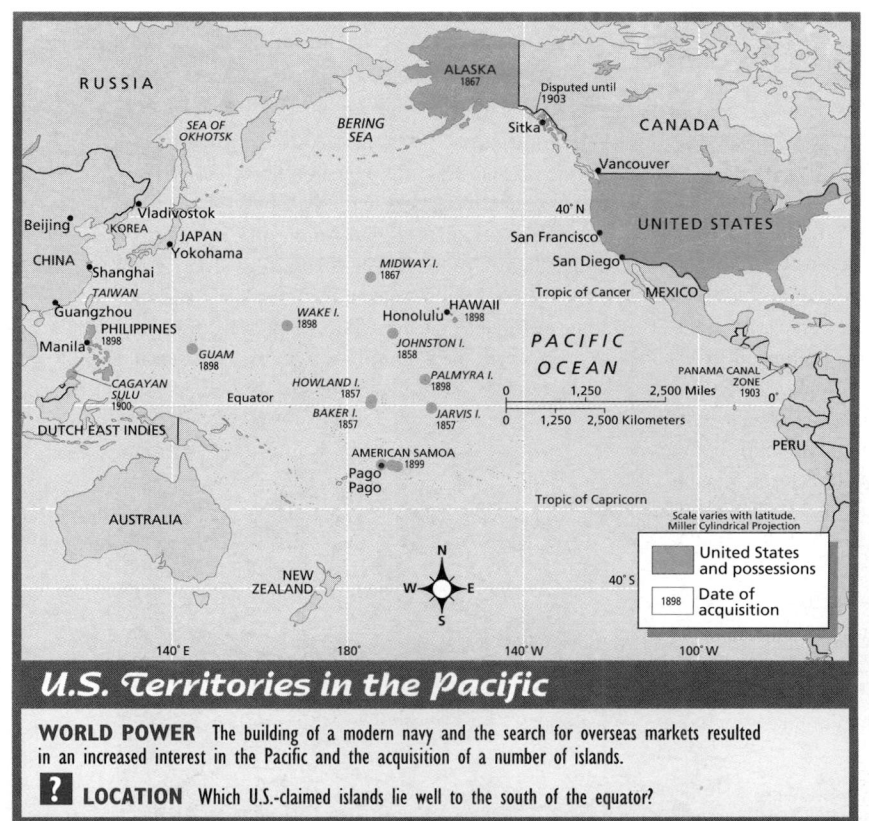

RUSSIA
ALASKA 1867
Disputed until 1903
SEA OF OKHOTSK
BERING SEA
Sitka
CANADA
Vancouver
Beijing
Vladivostok
KOREA
JAPAN
Yokohama
40° N
UNITED STATES
San Francisco
CHINA
Shanghai
TAIWAN
MIDWAY I. 1867
San Diego
Guangzhou
WAKE I. 1898
Honolulu
HAWAII 1898
Tropic of Cancer
MEXICO
PHILIPPINES 1898
Manila
GUAM 1898
JOHNSTON I. 1858
PACIFIC OCEAN
PANAMA CANAL ZONE 1903
CAGAYAN SULU 1900
Equator
HOWLAND I. 1857
PALMYRA I. 1898
0   1,250   2,500 Miles
0°
DUTCH EAST INDIES
BAKER I. 1857
JARVIS I. 1857
0   1,250   2,500 Kilometers
PERU
AMERICAN SAMOA 1899
Pago Pago
Tropic of Capricorn
AUSTRALIA
Scale varies with latitude. Miller Cylindrical Projection
United States and possessions
NEW ZEALAND
40° S
1898 Date of acquisition
140° E   180°   140° W   100° W

U.S. Territories in the Pacific

WORLD POWER The building of a modern navy and the search for overseas markets resulted in an increased interest in the Pacific and the acquisition of a number of islands.

❓ **LOCATION** Which U.S.-claimed islands lie well to the south of the equator?

ANNEXING HAWAII

Organize small groups of students to serve as staff members of a U.S. senator. Have the groups prepare memos on the annexation of Hawaii. Memos should outline the issue's history, summarize public opinion in the U.S. and Hawaii, present the arguments for and against annexation, assess the political consequences of each action, and recommend a position for the senator to take. After each staff has reported its recommendation, have the class vote on whether or not to annex Hawaii.

▲ To suppress the Filipino uprising, the United States sent approximately 70,000 troops to the Philippines in 1899. This cartoon shows Emilio Aguinaldo's government crushed by American military might.

restored, Filipino voters would be allowed to elect the legislature's lower house.

Judge William Howard Taft became the first American governor of the Philippines. Taft authorized the construction of public schools, roads, and railroads and improved medical care and sanitation. As the United States reduced and then removed tariffs on Filipino products, U.S. trade with the Philippines flourished.

But Filipinos still lacked the independence for which they had fought so long. The **Jones Act of 1916** gave Filipinos the right to elect both houses of their legislature but stated that independence would have to wait until Congress declared that "a stable government" had been established. The wait would be a long one. The United States finally granted independence to the Philippines on July 4, 1946, nearly half a century after American and Spanish naval guns had shattered the early morning silence of Manila Bay.

■■ **Despite Filipino calls for independence, the United States annexed the Philippines and delayed independence until 1946.**

*A*CQUIRING HAWAII

Renewed interest in expansion after the Spanish-American War led to demands for U.S. annexation of the Hawaiian Islands, nearly 4,000 miles east of the Philippines. The United States had long been interested in Hawaii for its strategic location along trade routes to China and for its fertile lava-enriched soil. In the 1820s Protestant missionaries from New England traveled to the islands to convert Hawaiians to Christianity. The missionaries' descendants remained, becoming major landholders. By the 1870s Americans living in Hawaii controlled land and trade and exercised growing influence over the Hawaiian government.

When the Hawaiian king, Kalakaua (kah-LAH-KAH-ooh-ah), sought to restrict American influence in 1886, some 400 American businessmen, planters, and traders in Hawaii formed the secret Hawaiian League. Their aim was to overthrow the monarchy and persuade the United States to annex Hawaii.

In 1887 the League forced Kalakaua to sign a new constitution that made the Hawaiian monarch only a figurehead and limited native Hawaiians'

▶

MAKING CONNECTIONS
Economics
The McKinley Tariff Act of 1890 caused huge financial losses for Hawaiian sugar planters. The act placed a bounty on U.S.-grown sugar, in effect subsidizing the U.S. sugar industry and causing sugar prices to plummet. As a result, Hawaiian planters lost some $12 million. This loss caused an even greater desire for Hawaiian annexation among sugar planters, who wanted the benefits that U.S. sugar producers had gained.

BUILDING VOCABULARY
The term *figurehead* originally identified the carved figures attached to the bows of sailing ships. These ornaments, although attractive, had no practical use. Today the term refers to a person who is a boss or chief in name only.

▼ After 1900, pineapples began to rival sugarcane as Hawaii's most important crop. Many of the laborers on Hawaiian plantations were from China, Japan, Korea, and the Philippines.

Teaching the Section

THE U.S. AND CHINA

Draw a door on the chalkboard, and call on volunteers to cite the three principles outlined in Hay's Open Door policy as you write them on the door. Then ask students whether or not the American response to the

Boxer Rebellion was consistent with the Open Door policy. Ask students to speculate about the motives behind the U.S. response.

U.S.–JAPAN RELATIONSHIP

Work with students to develop a cause-and-effect chart on the chalkboard that illustrates the relationship between the U.S. and Japan from the mid-1800s to 1907. Begin by writing *Perry Arrives in Japan* at the top of the chalkboard and *Russo-Japanese War* at the bottom. Then have students fill in the missing cause-effect relationships and add arrows to link causes and effects. Have students use the chart to explain U.S. views of Japan in the late 1800s and early 1900s.

BIO GRAPHY **PERSONALITIES IN HISTORY**

Liliuokalani was the first and only Hawaiian queen. One of the reasons she agreed to give up her throne was to win pardons for loyal supporters who had been jailed during a revolt to restore her to the throne. In her later life she tried unsuccessfully to obtain federal reimbursement for her property losses. The Hawaiian legislature eventually voted her an annual pension of $4,000. She also received income from a sugar plantation. The Queen wrote "Aloha Oe," meaning "Farewell to Thee," one of Hawaii's most popular songs.

PRIMARY SOURCE

Description of Change: excerpted
Rationale: excerpted to focus on main idea

right to hold office in their own country. Hawaiians criticized what they called the "Bayonet Constitution." That same year, the United States succeeded in getting Kalakaua to grant rights to use Pearl Harbor for a U.S. naval base.

Hawaiian resentment intensified as American interests continued to lobby Washington to annex Hawaii. Then in 1891 Kalakaua died. Succeeding him was his sister, Liliuokalani (li-lee-uh-woh-kuh-LAHN-ee), champion of Hawaiian nationalism, who pledged to regain "Hawaii for Hawaiians."

Liliuokalani was born into a Hawaiian ruling family in 1838. As a young girl she saw the monarchy reclaim Hawaiian independence after a brief British takeover. She would never forget the pride she felt as the Hawaiian flag was again raised over her native land.

Queen Liliuokalani

Early in her reign, Queen Liliuokalani began working to overturn the Bayonet Constitution and replace it with one that would return power to native Hawaiians. In 1893 she announced her plans to publish a new constitution. The announcement caused the annexationists to swing into action. Forming a Committee of Safety, they forcibly occupied government buildings, declared the end of the monarchy, and set up a provisional government of their own. U.S. Marines stood by as the American foreign minister to Hawaii recognized the provisional government. A deeply saddened Queen Liliuokalani signed a paper giving up her throne:

❝ I, Liliuokalani, . . . protest against any and all acts done against myself and the constitutional government of the Hawaiian kingdom. . . . Now, to avoid any collision of armed forces and perhaps the loss of life, I do, under this protest, and impelled by said forces, yield my authority until such time as the government of the United States shall . . . undo the action of its representatives and reinstate me. ❞

▶ **Ivory vases and brightly colored fans were some of the many items sold through the lucrative China trade. The fan shows the seaport town of Huang-pu, where American ships took aboard Chinese goods.**

The U.S. government never reinstated Liliuokalani. But recognizing that native Hawaiians overwhelmingly opposed annexation, it did not annex Hawaii until 1898. Liliuokalani lived out the rest of her life in Honolulu, a proud reminder of Hawaii's past. She died in 1917 after a severe stroke and was buried in the Royal Mausoleum.

■■ **American settlers' response to Queen Liliuokalani's reforms and a renewed interest in overseas colonies led to the U.S. annexation of Hawaii.**

AMERICAN INVOLVEMENT IN CHINA

The United States had originally become interested in Hawaii because it was the gateway to the China trade. This trade had begun in 1784 when a U.S. trading ship, the *Empress of China*, sailed for the port of Guangzhou (Canton). In 1843 China officially opened five ports to trading ships from the United States and Europe.

For the next 50 years, China's rulers struggled to balance American and European interests to keep them from overrunning the country. In 1895, however, the Chinese government was overrun from another direction. Japan attacked and defeated China, winning from it the large island of Taiwan (Formosa), territory on China's Liaotung Peninsula, and control of Korea.

European powers quickly took advantage of China's weakened position. Great Britain, France, Germany, and Russia pressured the Chinese government to carve the country into separate **spheres of influence**—ports or regions where a particular country would have exclusive rights over trade, mines, and railroads.

Peabody and Essex Museum, Salem, Massachusetts

GUIDED PRACTICE

Draw a four-column chart on the chalkboard with the headings *Country, Policy Goals, Actions,* and *Effects.* In the first column list *Philippines, Hawaii, China,* and *Japan.* Have students complete the chart by describing the goals of U.S. foreign policy toward each country, the tactics used to achieve those goals, and the impact of U.S. actions on that country.

INDEPENDENT PRACTICE

Ask students to use the information in the Guided Practice to create a political cartoon about American policy toward one of the countries in the chart. Tell students to draw their cartoons from the viewpoint of a citizen from the country they select. Students may wish to include their cartoons in their portfolios.

Review and Assessment

REVIEW Direct students to use the section's four Essential Points as main topics for an outline titled "Expansion in the Pacific." Have students add subtopics to the outline. Then assign the Section 2 Review on p. 568.

ASSESS Assign the **Section 2 Daily Quiz** in *Core Resources.*

▶

The United States feared it would be squeezed out of the China trade. In 1899 Secretary of State John Hay responded by inaugurating an **Open Door policy,** which called for all nations to have equal access to trade and investment in China. Senator Henry Cabot Lodge concluded: "We ask no favors; we only ask that we shall be admitted to that great market upon the same terms with the rest of the world."

In September 1899 Hay began sending a series of Open Door notes to the European powers and Japan. The notes asked them to agree to three principles: (1) to keep all ports in their spheres open to all nations; (2) to allow Chinese officials to collect all tariffs and duties; and (3) to guarantee equal railroad, harbor, and tariff rates in their spheres to all nations trading in China. When the European nations and Japan did not reject the principles outright, Hay announced that the Open Door policy had been accepted.

Chinese resentment of foreigners continued to grow, however. It erupted in the spring of 1900, when a Chinese secret society—the "Fists of Righteous Harmony"—launched a rebellion to drive the "foreign devils" out of the country. They attacked Western missionaries and traders in northern China, killing about 300. Supported by some Chinese government officials, the "Boxers"—the name Westerners gave them because of the "Fists" in their Chinese name—laid siege to the large walled-in foreign settlement in the capital at Beijing (Peking). For eight weeks the siege continued until finally, in August, an international force rescued the foreigners.

The **Boxer Rebellion** ended, but John Hay feared that Japan and other nations would use it as an excuse to seize more Chinese territory. In a second series of Open Door notes, he pressured the foreign powers to observe open trade throughout China and to preserve China's right to rule its own territory. China retained its territory but had to pay foreign powers $333 million in damages for losses sustained during the Boxer Rebellion.

■■ The United States worked to maintain its trading rights in China through the Open Door policy.

An Emerging Japan

Japan's 1894 invasion of China marked Japan's emergence as an imperial power. A mere 41 years earlier Japan had ended its almost complete isolation from the rest of the world. From 1639 to the 1850s Japanese rulers had allowed only one Dutch trading ship a year to enter the country. However, Japan's foreign policy had suddenly changed in 1853, when Commodore Matthew Perry of the United States sailed his squadron of black-hulled warships, bristling with guns, into Edo (Tokyo) Bay. President Millard Fillmore had ordered Perry to persuade Japan to open its doors to trade with the rapidly industrializing West. The gifts Perry presented to Japan's rulers symbolized the industrial age: a telegraph transmitter and a model train.

Perry's warships and industrial wonders forced the Japanese to yield to Western demands for trade. But they also convinced Japanese rulers that they must modernize their country—build up its military might and its industry. If they did not, they reasoned, foreigners might gain control of their nation.

Japan rapidly transformed itself into an industrial power and built up its army and navy. Within four decades Japan had become a winner in the struggle for empire rather than a victim of it, as its war with China, and later with Russia, proved.

Japan and Russia were rivals for Chinese territories—especially for Korea and for the fertile soil and mineral riches of Manchuria in northern

▲ Almost a year after Perry presented gifts to the Japanese, U.S. ships were allowed to trade in the ports of Hakodate and Shimoda.

MAKING CONNECTIONS

Geography

By 1911 there were more than 50 treaty ports in China in which Westerners were granted the right of extraterritoriality. This meant that they were not subject to the laws of China.

VOICES IN HISTORY

Some Chinese officials were suspicious of U.S. and European efforts to open relations with China. One Chinese official observed of foreign diplomats that they "think only of profit, and with the meretricious hope of profit they beguile the Chinese people." Have students give their own opinions about whether profit was the main goal of U.S. foreign policy in Asia at that time.

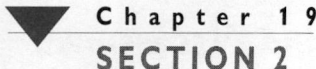
RETEACH Organize students who require reteaching into groups. Ask half the groups to write headlines reflecting the events that took place in the U.S., the Philippines, Hawaii, China, or Japan. Have the remaining groups write two- or three-paragraph news stories explaining each headline.

Closure

Read aloud the quotation by Congressman Henry Cabot Lodge in 1889 on p. 557. Encourage students to explain and cite examples of why this statement was no longer true by 1907.

Extension

COMPARE Have students write a paper that compares manifest destiny with imperialism, explaining the similarities and differences between the two.

INVESTIGATE Have students investigate the terms of the treaty between Japan and Russia that was negotiated by Roosevelt and that won him the Nobel Peace Prize.

Chart Caption Answer
Students should weigh the reasons for U.S. involvement and its consequences.

SECTION REVIEW ANSWERS

IDENTIFY

For significance, see the following pages:
annex (p. 563)
Philippine Government Act (p. 564)
William Howard Taft (p. 565)
Jones Act of 1916 (p. 565)
Kalakaua (p. 565)
Liliuokalani (p. 566)
spheres of influence (p. 566)
John Hay (p. 567)
Boxer Rebellion (p. 567)
Matthew Perry (p. 567)
Russo-Japanese War (p. 568)

LOCATE

For locations, see the map on p. 564.

1. *annexed islands, crushed rebellion, set up government, delayed independence until 1946*
2. *Liliuokalani's plan to replace the Bayonet Constitution, revolt by U.S. settlers*
3. *to protect U.S. trade opportunities*
4. *Reports might suggest that Japan's growing power threatens U.S. influence in China and the Pacific.*
5. *Answers should weigh economic and political benefits against loss of sovereignty.*

U.S. IMPERIALISM

	U.S. Involvement	Interim Status	Current Status
Samoa	Agreement divides islands between U.S. and Germany (1899)	German Samoa achieves independence (1962)	American Samoa under U.S. control
Philippines	Ceded to U.S. (1898)	Philippine Government Act defines government (1902) Declared a commonwealth (1935)	Independent republic (1946)
Cuba	American forces occupy Cuba (1898)	Platt Amendment authorizes U.S. intervention (1902)	Independent republic (1934)
Puerto Rico	Ceded to U.S. (1898)	Foraker Act establishes government (1900) Application for statehood (1924)	Declared a commonwealth (1952)
Hawaii	U.S. annexation (1898)	Application for statehood (1937)	50th state (1959)

Sources: *An Encyclopedia of World History, Webster's New Geographical Dictionary*

AMERICAN EXPANSIONISM U.S. economic and security interests extended into Asia, the Pacific, the Caribbean, and Latin America at the turn of the century.

? **ASSESSING CONSEQUENCES** Using one of the countries on the chart as a case study, trace U.S. involvement and its consequences for the country's current status.

China. In February 1904, Japanese troops attacked Russian forces in Manchuria, starting the **Russo-Japanese War**. President Theodore Roosevelt watched the war closely. If Japan won, it might grow dangerously strong. If Russia won, it might cut off U.S. trade with Manchuria.

By May 1905 the Japanese had won a series of crucial battles, and they asked Roosevelt to negotiate peace with Russia. Roosevelt brought representatives of the two countries together at Portsmouth, New Hampshire, where they pounded out a treaty. It granted neither side all it wanted and left both dissatisfied. But it did end the war, and it won the Nobel Peace Prize for Roosevelt.

Aware that Japan might now turn its expansionist eye toward the Pacific, including the U.S.–held Philippines, Roosevelt decided to demonstrate American military might. In late 1907 he sent a fleet of 4 destroyers and 16 battleships, painted a dazzling white, on a 46,000-mile world cruise. The "Great White Fleet" sailed into the Japanese port of Yokohama, where it underscored Roosevelt's later boast that now "the Pacific was as much our home waters as the Atlantic."

■■ **The United States came to see Japan, newly emergent as a modern world power, as a rival for influence in China and the Pacific.**

SECTION 2 REVIEW

IDENTIFY and explain the significance of the following: annex, Philippine Government Act, William Howard Taft, Jones Act of 1916, Kalakaua, Liliuokalani, spheres of influence, John Hay, Boxer Rebellion, Matthew Perry, Russo-Japanese War.

LOCATE and explain the importance of the following: Hawaii; Taiwan; Korea; Beijing, China; Yokohama, Japan.

1. **MAIN IDEA** How did the United States respond to Filipino demands for independence?
2. **MAIN IDEA** What events led to the U.S. annexation of Hawaii?
3. **MAIN IDEA** What did the Open Door policy attempt to accomplish in China?
4. **WRITING TO EXPLAIN** Imagine you are a U.S. diplomat in Japan in 1905. Write a report to President Roosevelt, explaining why the United States should reevaluate its relationship with Japan.
5. **TAKING A STAND** Do you think the United States is ever justified in annexing a foreign territory? Give reasons for your answer.

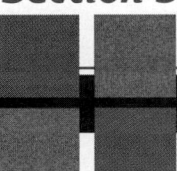

PREVIEW WORKSHOP

Following is a list of the significant people, places, and terms in this section. You may wish to use this list as a section preview.

People
- Leonard Wood
- Carlos Finlay

Places
- Guantánamo Bay
- Panama Canal
- Colombia
- Venezuela
- Dominican Republic
- Nicaragua
- Haiti

Terms
- Platt Amendment

- protectorate
- Foraker Act
- Jones Act of 1917
- Clayton-Bulwer Treaty
- Hay-Pauncefote Treaty
- Hay-Herrán Treaty
- Hay–Bunau-Varilla Treaty
- Roosevelt Corollary
- dollar diplomacy

Section 3

EXPANSION IN LATIN AMERICA

FOCUS

- **How did the United States deal with Cuba and Puerto Rico after the Spanish-American War?**
- **What events cleared the way for construction of the Panama Canal?**
- **How did presidents Roosevelt, Taft, and Wilson enforce the Monroe Doctrine?**

From 1898 onward, as American power grew in the Pacific, the U.S. role in Latin America expanded as well. Cuba came under U.S. control, while Puerto Rico became an out-and-out American possession. The United States built a canal across the Isthmus of Panama in these years, and the U.S. presence was felt throughout Latin America.

President Theodore Roosevelt at Panama Canal site

FOCUS OBJECTIVES

- Determine how the U.S. dealt with Cuba and Puerto Rico after the Spanish-American War.

- Identify the events that cleared the way for construction of the Panama Canal.

- Explain how presidents Roosevelt, Taft, and Wilson enforced the Monroe Doctrine.

GOVERNING CUBA AND PUERTO RICO

Both Cuba and Puerto Rico hoped that the peace treaty ending the Spanish-American War would bring independence from Spain followed by the speedy departure of American troops. After all, the Teller Amendment had pledged to Cuba that the United States would allow Cubans to control their government. But Cubans and Puerto Ricans were disappointed. Wanting to restore order quickly in both countries and thus protect U.S. investments, President McKinley set up military governments to rule the islands.

McKinley appointed General Leonard Wood governor of Cuba in 1899. Wood authorized the construction of schools and a sanitation system. U.S. Army doctors Walter Reed and William Gorgas had called for the sanitation system to reduce the mosquito population. Carlos Finlay

▲ Carlos Finlay

(feen-LY), a Cuban doctor, had theorized that mosquitoes spread yellow fever. He was right. Once built, the system all but eliminated the disease.

Wood also presided over the writing of a new constitution that limited Cuba's independence. The U.S. Congress agreed to remove American troops only if Cuba made the **Platt Amendment** part of its constitution. The Platt Amendment (1) limited Cuba's freedom to make treaties with other countries; (2) authorized the United States to intervene in Cuban affairs as it saw necessary; and (3) required Cuba to sell or lease land to the United States for naval and fueling stations. This last clause eventually led to the establishment of the U.S. Navy base at Guantánamo Bay (see map on page 578). In effect, the Platt Amendment made Cuba an American **protectorate**: America promised to protect Cuba from other nations but reserved the right to intervene in Cuba's affairs.

In 1902, after Cuba reluctantly accepted the Platt Amendment, U.S.

MOTIVATING: LINK TO TODAY

Ask students to describe what they know about the relationships that exist between the U.S. and Cuba, Puerto Rico, or Panama today. Then tell students that in this section they will gain some insights into why those relationships are what they are today.

Teaching the Section

CUBA AND PUERTO RICO

List on the chalkboard the three clauses of the Platt Amendment. Ask volunteers to identify the goal of U.S. policy in Cuba and how the clauses of the Platt Amendment furthered this goal. Then have volunteers suggest possible advantages and disadvantages for Cuba of U.S. intervention. Have them speculate about why Cubans were reluctant to agree to the Platt Amendment. Then have students explain how and why the U.S. treated Puerto Rico differently from Cuba.

troops left. But a U.S. presence remained at the naval base at Guantánamo Bay, which was leased in 1903. Over the next three decades, the United States intervened in Cuba several times. It pressured Cuba into accepting policies favorable to U.S. investors and sent in troops when it decided that the Cuban government could not keep order. The Platt Amendment remained in force until 1934, when America renounced its right to intervene in Cuba. Even then, however, U.S. influence over Cuban affairs remained great.

For Puerto Rico, U.S. policy followed a different course. No Teller Amendment guaranteed independence for Puerto Rico, so the United States ruled the island as a territory like Samoa or the Philippines in the Pacific. But just how these new territories were to be governed raised a thorny legal question for the United States. Were the people of these territories entitled to all the rights of U.S. citizens?

No, ruled the Supreme Court in 1901. The Court argued that the new territories were not fully part of the United States. Therefore, Congress could choose which rights to extend them. The Court affirmed the **Foraker Act** of 1900, which called for Puerto Rico's governor and upper house of the legislature to be appointed by the United States and a lower house to be elected by Puerto Ricans.

The **Jones Act of 1917** made Puerto Ricans American citizens and gave them the right to elect both houses of their legislature. In 1952 Puerto

▲ After Puerto Rico became a U.S. territory, the government built new public schools such as the one shown here.

▶ The Panama Canal was built by the United States between 1904 and 1914. Shown here are laborers who helped construct the canal.

Rico became a self-governing commonwealth of the United States, which retains ties of citizenship and trade with the mainland.

■■ After the Spanish-American War, the United States retained a strong influence in Cuba, and Puerto Rico became a U.S. territory.

*T*HE PANAMA CANAL

With such vital interests in both the Caribbean and the Pacific, the United States looked for a way to cut the travel time between the seas. The long and hazardous voyage around Cape Horn at the southern tip of South America took several weeks. In response the United States proposed digging a canal through a narrow neck of land in Central America to allow the U.S. Navy to police both seas.

Early steps toward a canal. The idea for such a canal was not new. As far back as 1517, Vasco Núñez de Balboa had proposed that a canal be dug across the 50-mile-wide Isthmus of Panama. In 1850 the United States and Great Britain had drawn up the **Clayton-Bulwer Treaty**, proposing an equal partnership to build and run a Central American canal, but they never acted on it. In the 1880s a French company actually worked on a canal across the Isthmus. But after less than 10 years and the loss of some 20,000 lives and more than $280 million, the French abandoned the effort. Deadly tropical diseases, repeated landslides, and bankruptcy killed the project.

Finally, in 1901 President Theodore Roosevelt decided that "after four centuries of conversation" by other countries, it was time for the United States to act. He instructed Secretary of State John Hay to negotiate with Great Britain

Changing Ways

A PATH BETWEEN THE SEAS

On August 15, 1914, the SS *Ancon* completed the first passage through the Panama Canal, a 51-mile-long ribbon of waters connecting the Caribbean Sea and the Pacific Ocean. The voyage marked the completion of what Theodore Roosevelt called "the greatest task of its own kind that has ever been performed in the world at all!"

Americans began working on the canal in 1904. Roosevelt was eager "to make the dirt fly" in Panama, but harsh working conditions and shortages hampered U.S. efforts from the start. Then in late 1904 a serious outbreak of yellow fever hit. By early 1905 the project was at a near standstill.

To put the project back on track, Roosevelt appointed John F. Stevens as chief engineer and architect. Stevens tackled the technical problems, while army colonel Dr. William C. Gorgas worked on improving living conditions. Gorgas, who had helped rid Cuba of tropical diseases, had drinking water purified and buildings screened. Then, to destroy the breeding places of the mosquitoes that transmit yellow fever and malaria, he had swamps drained and standing water coated with oil. By 1906 yellow fever had almost been eliminated. Malaria was under control by 1913.

Panama Canal Zone

Map: CARIBBEAN SEA, Río Chagres, Colón, Cristóbal, Gatún Locks, Gatún Lake, CANAL ZONE, Panama Canal, Río Chagres, Gaillard Cut, Continental Divide, PANAMA, Pedro Miguel Locks, Miraflores Locks, Balboa, Panama, Fort Amador, PACIFIC OCEAN, 80° W, 79°30' W, 9° N, 0 5 10 Miles, 0 5 10 Kilometers, Lambert Conformal Conic Projection

STRATEGIC INTERESTS Because it took the U.S. naval vessel *Oregon* 66 days to sail from San Francisco around Cape Horn to Key West during the Spanish-American War, pressure increased to build a U.S.–controlled canal through Central America.

? LOCATION If you enter the Panama Canal from the Caribbean Sea on the Atlantic side, which direction will you travel to exit on the Pacific Ocean?

Canal construction soon resumed in force. More than 60 giant steam shovels bit into the land, digging out nearly 160 trainloads of earth each day. Workers numbered more than 43,000, many of whom were recruited from the British West Indies.

Originally, the canal was designed to be built at sea level, but the difficulty of moving millions of tons of dirt and rock prompted a new design—an elevated waterway using locks. One group of workers dredged an approach channel and built a dam and locks on the Atlantic side. Another group dredged a passage from the Pacific through the Bay of Panama and constructed two smaller sets of locks. The hardest job fell to another group, which had to blast an eight-mile-long path through the mountainous Continental Divide. Geologic faults, heavy rains, and shifting earth caused frequent and often fatal avalanches. But finally, on October 10, 1913, President Wilson signaled crews to dynamite the protective dike at the south end of the canal. In a dramatic finale, water from the two sides rushed together—85 feet above sea level.

The human and economic costs of building the canal were staggering: some 6,000 workers died and about $366 million was spent. But the seemingly impossible had become a reality. The United States—and the rest of the world—now had a "Path Between the Seas."

Changing Ways

A PATH BETWEEN THE SEAS

LINK TO TODAY

The Panama Canal became a vacation destination for wealthy Americans. In 1913, some 20,000 U.S. tourists went to Panama to see the engineering marvel under construction.

■■ Ask students if the Panama Canal is a popular vacation site for U.S. tourists today. Why or why not?

Map Caption Answer
southeast

HISTORICAL SIDELIGHTS

The Big Ditch
In the U.S. the Panama Canal was also known as the "Big Ditch." It lopped some 7,800 miles off the trip between New York City and San Francisco, and it reduced travel time by three weeks. William Gorgas's work in clearing the canal zone of yellow fever proved beneficial in the U.S. as well. Cities such as New Orleans and Mobile implemented the sanitation practices that Gorgas pioneered in order to control infectious diseases.

Teaching the Section

THE PANAMA CANAL

Work with students to create on the chalkboard a time line of the events that cleared the way for the construction of the Panama Canal. Then have students use the time line to write paragraphs explaining how President Roosevelt "took the Canal and let Congress debate." Students may wish to include their paragraphs in their portfolios.

THREE PRESIDENTS AND THE MONROE DOCTRINE

Select three students to role-play presidents Roosevelt, Taft, and Wilson. Organize remaining students into groups to act as journalists from the U.S. and various Latin American countries. Each group should prepare questions for a press conference and interview the three presidents about similarities and differences in their application of the Monroe Doctrine in Latin America and the effects of these actions.

HISTORICAL SIDELIGHTS

Canalimony

Although Roosevelt considered the taking of the canal an achievement equal in magnitude to the Louisiana Purchase or the acquisition of Texas, some American political leaders had second thoughts about how Colombia had been treated. In 1922, the U.S. government paid $25 million to Colombia, an expenditure which many labeled "conscience money" or "canalimony."

COOPERATIVE LEARNING

Organize students into five groups. Within four of the groups assign each student a different Latin American country discussed in the section. Assign the remaining students the role of U.S. diplomats. Have the students of each Latin American group discuss the fairness of the Roosevelt Corollary and dollar diplomacy from their country's perspective and compose a written alternative to these U.S. policies. Then add one or more U.S. diplomats to each group and have the groups negotiate with him or her for acceptance of their policy alternatives.

---

to end the partnership set up by the Clayton-Bulwer Treaty. In the resulting **Hay-Pauncefote Treaty**, Britain agreed that the United States could build the canal by itself and have "exclusive management and policing of it." In return, the United States promised to keep the canal open to all the world's vessels in wartime as well as in peacetime.

Hay then began negotiations with the Republic of Colombia—of which Panama was then a part. In 1903 the **Hay-Herrán Treaty** was drafted. In return for a 99-year lease on a six-mile strip of land across the Isthmus, the United States agreed to pay Colombia $10 million and a yearly rental of $250,000. But holding out for better terms, Colombia's senate adjourned without ratifying the treaty. A furious President Roosevelt accused the Colombians of blackmail and swore that they must not be allowed "to bar one of the future highways of civilization."

▲ John Hay served as secretary of state from 1898 until his death in 1905.

Revolution in Panama. Events in Panama soon turned in Roosevelt's favor. Key Panamanian leaders who wanted the canal built began plotting revolution against the Colombian government. Helping them was Philippe Bunau-Varilla (boo-noh-vah-ree-yah), the former chief engineer for the French canal-building attempt.

Bunau-Varilla traveled to Washington to get American support for the revolution. On October 9, 1903, he met privately with President Roosevelt. Exactly what was said at the meeting remains unknown, but on November 2 the U.S. gunboat *Nashville* arrived in Panama. The following day, Panamanians began their rebellion. U.S. Marines prevented Colombian forces from reaching the rebels.

On November 4, 1903, the victorious rebels set up a new government and declared Panama an independent nation. Acting with lightning speed, the United States two days later recognized the

▲ This 1903 cartoon shows Roosevelt digging the Panama Canal and throwing dirt in the direction of Colombia, the country that had refused to ratify an earlier canal treaty.

Republic of Panama, and Hay began negotiating a new canal treaty with Panama's special envoy, Bunau-Varilla. The **Hay–Bunau-Varilla Treaty** gave the United States complete and unending sovereignty over a 10-mile-wide Canal Zone.

Did the United States engineer the Panamanian revolution? The facts remain obscure, but President Theodore Roosevelt later boasted, "I took the Canal Zone and let Congress debate." It is clear that U.S. aid to the Panamanian rebels and America's immediate recognition of Panama as an independent nation served American interests and made the Panama Canal possible. American trade and naval power grew stronger because of it, allowing the United States to extend its economic and political interests in Latin America.

▪▪ **The Panamanian revolution and a favorable treaty cleared the way for the United States to build and retain control of the Panama Canal.**

*A*PPLYING THE MONROE DOCTRINE

The American interventions in Cuba, Puerto Rico, and Panama were only three instances in a long history of U.S. involvement in Latin America. As far back as 1823, the Monroe Doctrine had cast the United States as protector

GUIDED PRACTICE

Construct on the chalkboard a three-column chart with the headings *Big Stick, Dollar Diplomacy,* and *Democratic Governments.* Have volunteers define each policy, identify the president who followed it, list how it was carried out, and identify countries targeted by each. Write the information on the chart.

INDEPENDENT PRACTICE

Have students write letters to the president as a citizen of one of the countries listed in the Guided Practice. Letters should support or denounce that president's policies toward their country. Students may wish to include their letters in their portfolios.

REVIEW Guide students to make an annotated time line for the period from 1898 to 1914, showing key events in the history of U.S–Latin American relations during that time period. Then assign the Section 3 Review on p. 574.

ASSESS Assign the **Section 3 Daily Quiz** in *Core Resources.*

▶

of the hemisphere. But for much of the century the doctrine was little more than an idle threat. This changed following the Spanish-American War, as presidents Theodore Roosevelt, William H. Taft, and Woodrow Wilson actively enforced the Monroe Doctrine in an effort to protect U.S. interests in Latin America (see map on page 578).

The Roosevelt Corollary. Latin America, with its wealth of raw materials and potential consumers, attracted a flood of European and American capital during the late 1800s. Much of this capital was in the form of high-interest bank loans. Although many Latin American countries welcomed the loans, difficulty in repaying them often resulted in foreign intervention. In 1902, for example, Great Britain, Germany, and Italy blockaded and attacked Venezuelan ships and ports when the nation failed to repay its loans. President Roosevelt quickly warned the three European powers not to seize any Venezuelan land and convinced them to settle the issue through arbitration.

Roosevelt's actions sent a clear signal that he intended to enforce the Monroe Doctrine. Roosevelt underscored this point in 1904 when the Dominican Republic proved unable to repay its European lenders. Fearing that the Europeans would use force to collect the loans, he issued the **Roosevelt Corollary** to the Monroe Doctrine:

> 66 If a nation . . . keeps order and pays its obligations, it need fear no interference from the United States. Chronic wrongdoing . . . in the Western Hemisphere . . . may force the United States, however reluctantly, . . . to the exercise of an international police power. 99

Without seeking approval from any Latin American nation, Roosevelt assumed the role of "international police officer" in the Western Hemisphere. He had applied in practice the West African proverb he loved to quote: "Speak softly and carry a big stick; you will go far."

Next, Roosevelt convinced the Dominican government to accept U.S. assistance. The United States pledged to use American armed forces to stop any European country from seizing Dominican territory. In exchange, the Dominican government agreed to let the United States collect all Dominican customs duties and turn half over to

YANKEE IMPERIALISM

THROUGH OTHERS' EYES

*A*lthough much of Latin America had at first favored the Monroe Doctrine, support for the policy began to dwindle by the early 1900s. As Peruvian diplomat Francisco García Calderón noted, the Monroe Doctrine took "an aggressive form with Mr. [Theodore] Roosevelt, the politician of the 'big stick.'" Writing in 1913, García Calderón chronicled the list of recent U.S. interventions in Panama, Cuba, the Dominican Republic, and Venezuela. As a result of this "Yankee imperialism," he claimed, "everywhere the Americans of the North are feared" and "hostility against the Anglo-Saxon invaders assumes the character of a . . . crusade." In the view of Mexican scholar Luis Quintanilla, the Roosevelt Corollary had twisted the Monroe Doctrine "from a case of America vs. Europe" to one of "United States vs. America."

foreign creditors. In 1916, when civil disturbances racked the Dominican Republic, the United States government sent in marines. They did not leave until eight years later, in 1924.

■■ **The Roosevelt Corollary established a greater U.S. role in Latin America.**

Some Latin American countries objected to Roosevelt's policy. They argued that every country should maintain control over its own affairs. Some Latin American countries issued a declaration stating that debts owed to other countries could not be collected by force. But despite Latin American protests, intervention continued.

Dollar diplomacy. Roosevelt's successor as president, William H. Taft, further extended U.S. influence in Latin America. Taft favored "substituting dollars for bullets"—economic influence for military force—as a means of protecting U.S.

RETEACH For each subsection in the section, have students write a sentence that summarizes the main idea. Select students to read their statements aloud. Have the group choose the best summary sentence for each subsection.

Closure

Organize students into groups to decide how the following statement applied to U.S. actions in each of the countries discussed in this section: *The purpose of U.S. foreign policy is to promote and protect U.S. economic or political interests.*

Extension

CREATE Have students create political cartoons that illustrate U.S. policy in Latin America from 1891 to 1914. Students should present and interpret their cartoons for the class.

RESEARCH Direct students to research and report on the steps taken to return the canal to Panama in the year 2000.

Graph Caption Answer
about $1.2 billion

IDENTIFY

For significance, see the following pages:
Leonard Wood (p. 569)
Carlos Finlay (p. 569)
Platt Amendment (p. 569)
protectorate (p. 569)
Foraker Act (p. 570)
Jones Act of 1917 (p. 570)
Clayton-Bulwer Treaty (p. 570)
Hay-Pauncefote Treaty
(p. 572)
Hay-Herrán Treaty (p. 572)
Hay–Bunau-Varilla Treaty
(p. 572)
Roosevelt Corollary (p. 573)
dollar diplomacy (p. 574)

LOCATE

For locations, see the map on p. 578.

1. *Cuba became a U.S. protectorate; Puerto Rico became a U.S. territory, then a self-governing commonwealth.*
2. *enabled U.S. to build and control Panama Canal*
3. *All three sent in troops. Taft encouraged U.S. investment; Wilson, democratic government as a stabilizing force.*
4. *Speeches might mention the right of each country to maintain control over its own affairs and resources.*
5. *Teller Amendment would have guaranteed Puerto Rico's independence and thus limited the range of U.S. intervention.*

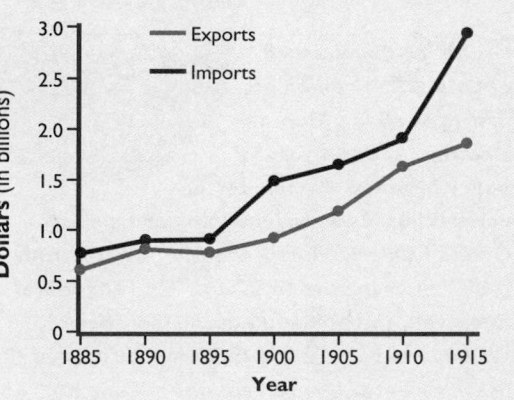

U.S. TRADE AND TERRITORIAL EXPANSION

Dollars (in billions) — Exports / Imports

Source: *Historical Statistics of the United States*

U.S. FOREIGN TRADE As the United States emerged as a world power, it began to acquire overseas colonies. One consequence of this territorial expansion was the rapid increase of U.S. exports and imports to and from these new overseas markets.

? **BUILDING GRAPH SKILLS** What was the difference in the value of U.S. exports and imports by 1915?

interests in Latin America (see map on page 578). To implement this policy, which came to be called **dollar diplomacy**, Taft suggested replacing European loans with American ones. Increasing U.S. economic power, Taft argued, would reduce the chances of European intervention. By 1914 U.S. capital in Latin America had grown to over $1.6 billion, mainly invested in railroads, mines, and banana and sugar plantations.

Nicaragua was one of the places that Taft put dollar diplomacy to the test. At the invitation of the Nicaraguan president, American bankers made loans totaling $1.5 million to Nicaragua in 1911. The following year, Taft sent more than 2,000 marines to crush a revolt and to protect the U.S. investments that had poured in.

Taft's successor, President Woodrow Wilson, believed that democratic governments, not U.S. dollars, would keep European powers out of Latin America. To keep Germany from taking control of strategic Caribbean territory, Wilson sent marines to several Caribbean countries to put down rebellions and establish constitutional governments. In 1915, when revolution shook Haiti, Wilson sent in marines. Haiti was forced to accept a treaty giving the United States powers in running the Haitian government, and the marines stayed until 1934. Some 1,500 Haitians died resisting U.S. control.

■■ **Taft's dollar diplomacy and Wilson's military interventions increased U.S. political and economic influence in Latin America.**

SECTION 3 REVIEW

IDENTIFY and explain the significance of the following: Leonard Wood, Carlos Finlay, Platt Amendment, protectorate, Foraker Act, Jones Act of 1917, Clayton-Bulwer Treaty, Hay-Pauncefote Treaty, Hay-Herrán Treaty, Hay–Bunau-Varilla Treaty, Roosevelt Corollary, dollar diplomacy.

LOCATE and explain the importance of the following: Guantánamo Bay, Panama Canal, Colombia, Venezuela, Dominican Republic, Nicaragua, Haiti.

1. **MAIN IDEA** How did the U.S. relationship with Cuba and Puerto Rico change after the Spanish-American War?

2. **MAIN IDEA** Why did the United States support the Panamanian rebels and recognize the Republic of Panama?

3. **CONTRASTING** How did presidents Roosevelt, Taft, and Wilson apply the Monroe Doctrine in Latin America?

4. **WRITING TO PERSUADE** Imagine you are a political leader in a Latin American country during this period. Write a speech seeking to persuade the U.S. government not to interfere in the affairs of your country.

5. **HYPOTHESIZING** How might U.S. policy toward Puerto Rico have been different if the Teller Amendment had been extended to apply to that territory?

PREVIEW WORKSHOP

Following is a list of the significant people in this section. You may wish to use this list as a section preview.

■ Francisco "Pancho" Villa
■ Emiliano Zapata
■ Álvaro Obregón
■ John J. Pershing

People
■ Porfirio Díaz
■ Francisco Madero
■ Victoriano Huerta
■ Venustiano Carranza

Section 4

CONFLICT WITH MEXICO

FOCUS

■ **How did the Mexican Revolution affect relations between the United States and Mexico?**

■ **Why did the United States intervene in Mexico?**

■ **Why did tensions between the two countries remain strong during Carranza's presidency?**

*D*ollar diplomacy played a significant role in another Latin American country: Mexico. Though many Mexicans uneasily referred to the United States as "the Colossus of the North," economic ties between the two countries increased in the late 19th century. But the Mexican Revolution of 1910 threatened these ties, bringing the two countries to the brink of war.

American artillery along the Mexican border, 1916

THE MEXICAN REVOLUTION

Dollars helped tie Mexico and the United States closer together in the late 19th century, thanks to Mexico's president, Porfirio Díaz. Díaz, who with the political support of wealthy landowners ruled Mexico for more than 30 years, offered special concessions to attract foreign investment. By 1908, U.S. companies controlled three quarters of all Mexican mining operations. Total U.S. investments amounted to almost $1 million by 1913.

Foreign investors helped develop Mexico's economy by building railroads that linked Mexico to U.S. and other foreign markets. But foreign investors and Díaz's friends profited the most from economic growth. Little trickled down to workers and peasants. Indeed, Díaz's policies helped wealthy Mexicans and foreigners take land away from peasants. As a result, most Mexicans—mainly landless peasants and struggling urban workers—lived in poverty.

In 1910 Díaz used force and fraud to defeat opposition candidate Francisco Madero. Peasants, workers, and the middle class, angry at the lack of political democracy, rallied behind Madero in armed revolt against Díaz beginning in November. The rebels defeated Díaz's troops in key cities in northern and central Mexico, forcing Díaz into exile in Paris in 1911. In Mexico's first democratic elections in 30 years, Madero won the presidency.

Madero sought to establish a democratic government, but few agreed on the details. The revolutionary leaders who had supported Madero against

▼ **Women served in military roles during the Mexican Revolution. This 1911 photograph shows a group of female revolutionaries armed with rifles.**

FOCUS OBJECTIVES

■ Analyze how the Mexican Revolution affected relations between the U.S. and Mexico.

■ Explain why the U.S. intervened in Mexico.

■ Determine why tensions between the two countries remained strong during Carranza's presidency.

GLOBAL CONNECTIONS

The favoritism that the Díaz government showed to foreign interests gave rise to a popular saying in Mexico: "Mexico, mother of foreigners and stepmother of Mexicans." British and American companies controlled Mexico's oil industry. U.S. companies dominated the mining industry, and French and Spanish investors owned many textile factories. A variety of foreign companies had sugar, banana, rubber, and tobacco plantations, on which crops were grown for export to the U.S.

575

MOTIVATING: PRIOR KNOWLEDGE

Have students read the section's introductory paragraph. Note that a colossus is a statue or person of gigantic size and power. Ask students to apply what they have learned about U.S. actions in other parts of Latin America to speculate about whether "Colossus of the North" is positive or negative.

THE MEXICAN REVOLUTION

Assign each of nine volunteers these identities: Porfirio Díaz, Pancho Villa, Francisco Madero, Victoriano Huerta, Venustiano Carranza, Emiliano Zapata, Henry Lane Wilson, Woodrow Wilson, John J. Pershing. Have volunteers line up in any order and without identifying their character explain why and how "he" participated in the revolution and how his actions affected U.S.–Mexican relations. As volunteers present their statements, have students list the speaker's identity on a sheet of paper. When the activity is complete, have students check their lists for accuracy.

HISTORICAL SIDELIGHTS

Wilson vs. Wilson

President Wilson was furious at the part played by U.S. ambassador Henry Lane Wilson in the overthrow of the Madero government. In 1913 the president had Wilson recalled. Despite private investments by Americans totaling more than $1 billion, President Wilson announced that he was "not the servant of those who wish to enhance the value of their Mexican investments."

GLOBAL CONNECTIONS

The British regarded President Wilson's opposition to Huerta as impractical and unreasonable. However, the British feared the growing power of Germany and thought that maintaining American goodwill was important in case war broke out in Europe. The British foreign office agreed to advise Huerta to retire from office and recalled its minister from Mexico.

PRIMARY SOURCE

Description of Change: excerpted
Rationale: excerpted to focus on main idea

Díaz thought Madero's plan did not go far enough in such areas as returning land to the peasants. Others, including conservative military officers and wealthy landowners, thought the plan went too far.

Complicating this situation was Henry Lane Wilson, the U.S. ambassador, who did not believe Madero could protect U.S. investments in Mexico. Wilson overstepped his diplomatic role by arranging for factions opposed to Madero to meet and discuss Madero's overthrow. In 1913, backed by wealthy landowners and foreign business interests, General Victoriano Huerta (WER-tah) seized control of the government and had Madero thrown into jail. Huerta's soldiers shot Madero when, they alleged, he attempted to escape.

Madero's murder outraged President Woodrow Wilson. He angrily refused to recognize Huerta, calling his regime a "government of butchers." Civil war raged in Mexico as revolutionary armies battled to drive Huerta out. President Wilson adopted a policy of "watchful waiting," hoping that the revolutionaries would be successful. He also authorized arms sales to the revolutionaries, while refusing to allow arms sales to Huerta's forces.

■■ **The Mexican Revolution strained U.S.–Mexican relations as the fighting disrupted Mexico's government and society.**

▲ **Pancho Villa, center, and Emiliano Zapata, right, are shown with their followers in the presidential palace in Mexico City.**

Huerta's soldiers arrested several crew members from the USS *Dolphin*. The U.S. sailors had gone ashore for supplies at the Mexican port of Tampico. The Americans were released unharmed, but Wilson pursued the matter. He backed the American admiral, who demanded an apology and a public ceremony in which Mexico would "hoist the American flag in a prominent position and salute it with twenty-one guns." Huerta made the apology but refused to perform the ceremony.

On April 20 President Wilson went before Congress:

❝ I . . . come to ask your approval that I should use the armed forces of the United States . . . to obtain from General Huerta and his adherents the fullest recognition of the rights and dignity of the United States, even amidst the distressing conditions now unhappily obtaining in Mexico. ❞

Before Congress could act, Wilson learned that a German ship bearing arms for Huerta was heading for the Mexican port of Veracruz. He ordered the U.S. Navy to land marines at Veracruz, take the customs house, and prevent the weapons from being delivered. By the time Congress voted Wilson the authority to use force, the order had been carried out.

AMERICAN INTERVENTION

Four major revolutionary armies continued to fight Huerta. But their leaders—Venustiano Carranza (bay-noos-TYAHN-oh kahr-RAHN-sah), Francisco "Pancho" Villa, Emiliano Zapata, and Álvaro Obregón (oh-bray-GAWN)—were not united. Two of the leaders, Carranza and Villa, actually hated each other. Although the revolutionaries controlled territory throughout Mexico, Wilson worried that they would never be able to defeat Huerta.

In 1914 an incident occurred that gave Wilson an excuse to intervene directly. On April 9,

At this critical stage Argentina, Brazil, and Chile—sometimes called the "ABC powers"—organized a conference at Niagara Falls, Ontario, to resolve the crisis. The conference urged Huerta to resign. Since his forces were losing, he complied and fled to Spain. In August 1914 Carranza marched into Mexico City. For the next year the revolutionary generals battled each other for control of the presidency.

■■ **The United States intervened in Mexico to help overthrow the antirevolutionary Huerta government.**

CARRANZA IN POWER

In 1915 Carranza assumed the presidency, and American forces withdrew from Veracruz. The United States recognized Carranza's government in the same year, after he guaranteed that Mexico would respect foreign lives and property.

Venustiano Carranza, with his trim white goatee and his "gentlemanly bearing," hardly fit anyone's picture of a typical revolutionary. Born in 1859 in the state of Coahuila (koh-uh-WEE-luh) in northern Mexico, he was over 50 years old when he took up the rebel cause.

Carranza, who owned a large, profitable ranch, had held many government offices under Díaz. But in 1908 Díaz and Carranza clashed, and three years later, Carranza joined Madero's fight to overthrow Díaz. After Madero was deposed, Carranza helped defeat Huerta's forces. He used his experience as head of a revolutionary army and his considerable political talents to gain the presidency of Mexico.

▲ **Venustiano Carranza**

Carranza's presidency was marked by conflict. Pancho Villa, who had hoped for U.S. support against Carranza, decided to retaliate against the Americans for recognizing Carranza as president. Villa communicated his plans to rebel leader Emiliano Zapata:

66 We have decided not to fire a bullet more against Mexicans, our brothers, and to prepare and organize ourselves to attack the Americans in their own dens and make them know that Mexico is a land for the free and a tomb for thrones, crowns, and traitors. 99

In March 1916 some 500 of Villa's men crossed the border to raid Columbus, New Mexico. Villa's men burned and looted the surprised town and the army post located there. Seventeen Americans—nine civilians and eight soldiers—were killed, while more than a hundred Mexicans died. Villa hoped the raid would provoke American intervention in Mexico that would, in turn, undermine Carranza's regime. He did not have to wait long for his expected result.

Without Carranza's approval President Wilson ordered a military expedition into Mexico to capture Villa "dead or alive." A week after Villa's raid, General John J. Pershing led a force of some 5,800 soldiers into Chihuahua, Villa's home state. Although Pershing later increased his troop size to more than 10,000 men, Villa still eluded capture. The deeper Pershing pushed into Mexican territory, the more the Mexicans resented the Americans.

A battle between Mexican and U.S. troops in June brought the United States and Mexico to the brink of war. Carranza ordered Mexican troops to prevent U.S. soldiers from advancing any farther south into Mexico. When one of Pershing's cavalry units attempted to pass through the town

▲ In 1916 President Wilson sent U.S. soldiers into Mexico to capture revolutionary leader Pancho Villa, "dead or alive."

PRIMARY SOURCE

Description of Change: excerpted
Rationale: excerpted to focus on main idea

HISTORICAL SIDELIGHTS

Carranza in Office
Carranza was a moderate political reformer who opposed the sweeping social changes that Zapata and Villa favored. After he became president, Carranza did little to institute the far-reaching land reforms that the Constitution of 1917 called for.

VOICES IN HISTORY

The Mexican Revolution created a great upsurge of immigration to the U.S. Some Mexicans emigrated when their towns were occupied by rebel troops; others, such as Señora Flores de Andrade, went to the U.S. hoping to support the revolution. Flores de Andrade left Chihuahua, Mexico, for El Paso, Texas, in 1906 to raise money and arms to overthrow Díaz. After Madero's execution, however, she grew disenchanted with the struggle, noting with bitterness in the 1920s that "the revolution promised a great deal to the Mexican people but hasn't accomplished anything."

Practice

GUIDED PRACTICE

Write the following statement on the chalk-board: *Concern for U.S. investments justified U.S. intervention in Mexico.* Have volunteers react to this statement as you write key phrases of their responses on the chalkboard. Then change the statement to read: *Concern for Mexican investments justifies Mexican intervention in the U.S.* Compare student reactions to this statement with reactions to the first statement.

INDEPENDENT PRACTICE

Invite students to imagine that they are Mexican citizens in 1916. Have them write letters to friends in the U.S., explaining how they feel about U.S. intervention in Mexico during the revolution.

Review and Assessment

REVIEW Ask students to create cause-and-effect charts showing events of the Mexican Revolution and effects of those events on U.S.–Mexican relations. Students may wish to include their charts in their portfolios. Then assign the Section 4 Review on p. 579.

ASSESS Assign the **Section 4 Daily Quiz** in *Core Resources*.

Map Caption Answer
Panama, Nicaragua, Cuba, Haiti, Dominican Republic

HISTORICAL SIDELIGHTS

Constitution of 1917

The 1917 Constitution gave the Mexican government the right to redistribute land from wealthy landowners to peasants, provided factory workers with minimum wages and the right to strike, allowed the president to deport foreigners, limited the powers of the Catholic Church, and provided for free and compulsory public schools.

AV TRANSPARENCY

Linking Geography and History Transparency and **Worksheet 15**

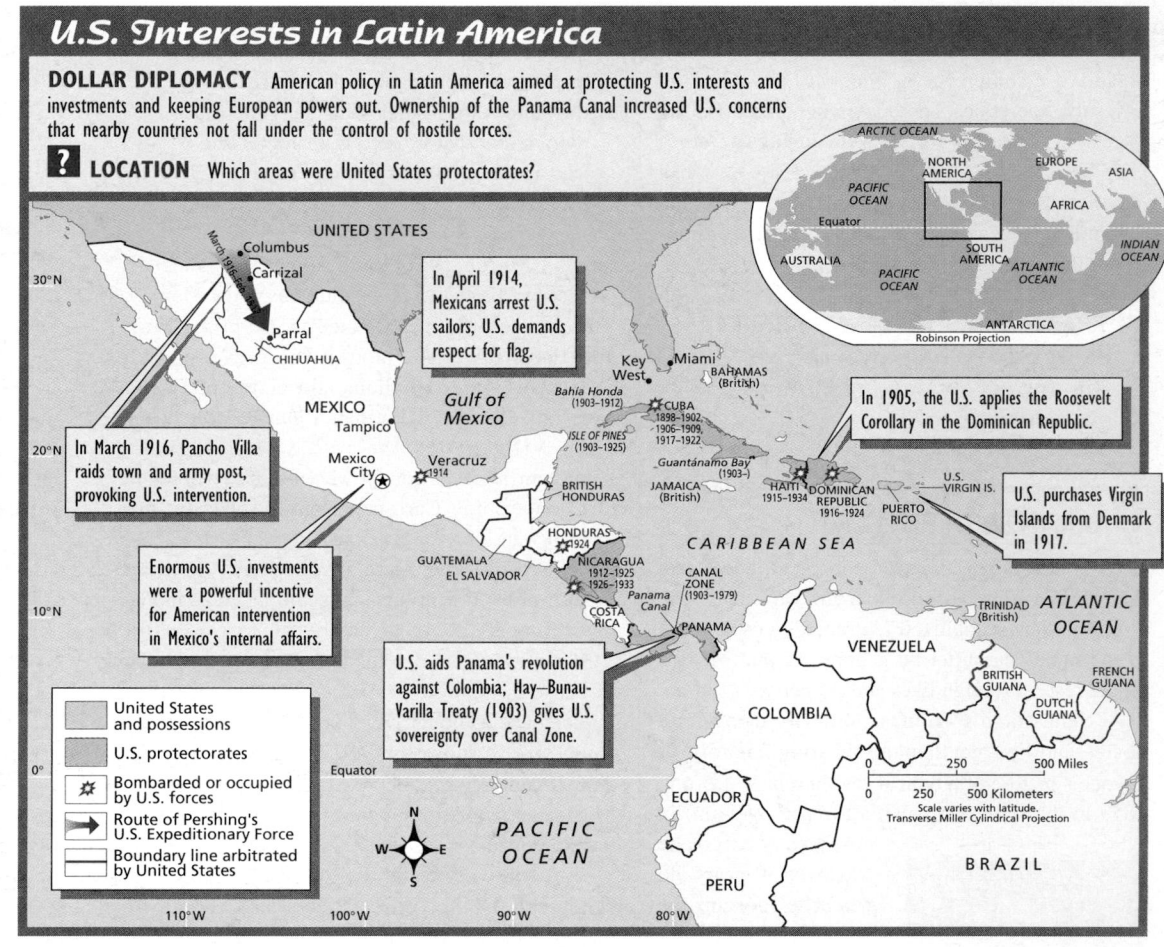

U.S. Interests in Latin America

DOLLAR DIPLOMACY American policy in Latin America aimed at protecting U.S. interests and investments and keeping European powers out. Ownership of the Panama Canal increased U.S. concerns that nearby countries not fall under the control of hostile forces.

? LOCATION Which areas were United States protectorates?

In April 1914, Mexicans arrest U.S. sailors; U.S. demands respect for flag.

In March 1916, Pancho Villa raids town and army post, provoking U.S. intervention.

Enormous U.S. investments were a powerful incentive for American intervention in Mexico's internal affairs.

U.S. aids Panama's revolution against Colombia; Hay–Bunau-Varilla Treaty (1903) gives U.S. sovereignty over Canal Zone.

In 1905, the U.S. applies the Roosevelt Corollary in the Dominican Republic.

U.S. purchases Virgin Islands from Denmark in 1917.

United States and possessions
U.S. protectorates
Bombarded or occupied by U.S. forces
Route of Pershing's U.S. Expeditionary Force
Boundary line arbitrated by United States

---

of Carrizal, the commander of the Mexican garrison refused passage. Instead of bypassing the town, the U.S. commander chose to enter Carrizal, and a battle ensued.

By early September 1916 nearly 150,000 U.S. National Guardsmen were stationed along the Mexican border. The prospect of armed conflict with Mexico was extremely unpopular in the United States, however, particularly in view of the events in Europe and on the high seas that threatened to pull the United States into World War I (see Chapter 20). Wilson backed down. In exchange for withdrawing U.S. troops, Wilson asked Carranza to adopt a measure that would allow the United States to intervene in Mexico to protect U.S. investments. Carranza refused to limit Mexican sovereignty in this way. Realizing that the threat of war increased with every day U.S. troops remained in Mexico, Wilson ordered U.S. troops withdrawn in January 1917.

In that same year, Carranza approved a sweeping new constitution for Mexico, but he would not have much time to put its provisions in place. In 1920 he was overthrown and killed by forces loyal to another revolutionary leader—Álvaro Obregón. Obregón and subsequent Mexican presidents gradually implemented the new constitution. This constitution would have important repercussions for U.S. oil companies operating in Mexico in the 1930s (see Chapter 25).

■■ **Villa's raid on a U.S. town and army post and Carranza's refusal to grant the United States the right to protect American investments raised tensions between the United States and Mexico to a dangerous pitch.**

RETEACH Ask students, working in pairs, to write sentences that explain how each person listed in the Preview Workshop is related to the main idea of the subsection in which the person is mentioned.

Closure

Have students reread the warning on p. 559 by Samoan leader Te'o Tuvale to his fellow Samoans and speculate about whether Mexican president Venustiano Carranza would have agreed with it. Have students suggest ways in which Carranza might have reworded Tuvale's statement to reflect Mexico's experience with the U.S.

Extension

CREATE Ask students to investigate the railroads that linked Mexico to U.S. and foreign markets and then to create a map showing these railroads.

RESEARCH Direct students to research the life and legend of Pancho Villa. Have students report to the class on how American movies have characterized Villa and compare these characterizations to what their investigation has revealed about him.

COMMENTARY

Expansion in Perspective

In the years from 1890 to 1920, America's global involvement expanded enormously. In some cases this involvement meant actual military intervention and colonial rule of foreign territories. Although new territory and influence benefited the United States, many Americans believed that overseas expansion helped foreign countries as well. Many supporters of imperialism viewed Samoa, the Philippines, Puerto Rico, and other non-European countries as economically backward and uncivilized. Arguing from this point of view, American imperialists asserted that Americans had a responsibility to bring democracy, prosperity, and order to the world's nonindustrialized nations.

But did U.S. imperialism succeed in bringing all of these benefits to foreign countries? In Cuba, Puerto Rico, and the Philippines, better sanitation, education, roads, transportation, and public health followed the American flag. And in some cases, such as in Venezuela, U.S. diplomatic actions prevented European countries from colonizing Latin American territory.

U.S. economic and military interventions, however, rarely brought order or democracy to politically troubled countries. For example, U.S. dollar diplomacy in Nicaragua did not prevent a revolt, and the United States military brutally suppressed the Filipino independence movement.

Although designed to create democracy, the U.S. military governments that were established in many countries often denied citizens a basic democratic right: political representation.

U.S. attempts to spread American culture sometimes came at the expense of the other country's culture. In Puerto Rico, for example, the U.S. government ordered that English—instead of the native Spanish—be used in classrooms. English was used in order to make Puerto Ricans—in the words of Manuel Maldonado-Denis—"good North American citizens." Maldonado-Denis, a Puerto Rican who grew up under this system, recalled that "Puerto Rican students had to daily swear loyalty to the North American flag in English" and sing "songs in English composed to inspire patriotism in North American students." In this way, Maldonado-Denis concluded, the United States attempted "to rob us of every source of identification with all that is Puerto Rican."

U.S. economic expansion also created resentment against the United States around the world. The millions of dollars that U.S. banks and businesses poured into oil wells, mines, plantations, and railroad projects in poor nations gave the United States control of those nations' natural resources. The people in these nations grew angry as they watched their resources and the profits from them flow into the United States. The efforts of these countries to regain control of their own resources would provide a continuing source of tension between them and the United States.

SECTION REVIEW ANSWERS

IDENTIFY

For significance, see the following pages:
Porfirio Díaz (p. 575)
Francisco Madero (p. 575)
Victoriano Huerta (p. 576)
Venustiano Carranza (p. 576)
Francisco "Pancho" Villa (p. 576)
Emiliano Zapata (p. 576)
Álvaro Obregón (p. 576)
John J. Pershing (p. 577)

1. *strained U.S.–Mexican relations as fighting disrupted Mexican government and society*
2. *to help overthrow the anti-revolutionary Huerta government*
3. *border raid on U.S. town by Villa's men; brought U.S. and Mexico to the brink of war*
4. *Letters might state that Díaz's policies helped wealthy Mexicans and foreigners take land away from peasants and contributed to poverty in Mexico.*
5. *help—brought public health, education, transportation, and political improvements; hurt—military intervention restricted political representation, cultural domination created resentment, economic domination created resentment and drained wealth.*

SECTION 4 REVIEW

IDENTIFY and explain the significance of the following: Porfirio Díaz, Francisco Madero, Victoriano Huerta, Venustiano Carranza, Francisco "Pancho" Villa, Emiliano Zapata, Álvaro Obregón, John J. Pershing.

1. **MAIN IDEA** How did the Mexican Revolution impact relations between the United States and Mexico?

2. **MAIN IDEA** Why did President Wilson ask Congress for authority to use the military in Mexico?

3. **IDENTIFYING CAUSE AND EFFECT** What event during Carranza's presidency provoked U.S. intervention in Mexico? What effect did U.S. intervention have on relations between the two countries?

4. **WRITING TO EXPLAIN** Imagine you are a landless peasant in Mexico after the overthrow of Porfirio Díaz. Write a letter to a relative in the United States explaining why you took part in the revolution.

5. **SYNTHESIZING** How did U.S. intervention both help and hurt other countries?

WORLD WAR I

1914–1920

THE AMERICAN NATION
VIDEODISC PROGRAM
A variety of still images, short videos, and activities are available for you to use as you teach this chapter. See Correlation to *The American Nation Videodisc Program* for barcode correlations and suggestions for using the program.

Chapter Overview

War erupted in 1914 because nationalism and territorial rivalries had turned Europe into a cauldron of hatred. Initially declaring itself neutral, the U.S. slowly was dragged into the conflict. In 1917 the U.S. abandoned its neutrality and entered the war on the Allied side. To aid the nation's war effort, President Wilson called for the complete mobilization of American society.

In November 1918 the warring parties signed an armistice and brought the conflict to an end. President Wilson then moved to forge what he hoped would be a just peace. But the final treaty was a mass of compromises, which the U.S. Senate refused to ratify.

Chapter Planning Guide

CHAPTER 20	CORE RESOURCE BOOKLETS	AUDIOVISUAL [AV] RESOURCES	PROGRAM RESOURCES
INTRODUCTION pp. 584–585	■ Geography Worksheet 20 ■ Building Your Portfolio Worksheet 6	■ Everyday Life in America Transparency and Worksheet 20	■ *Eyewitnesses and Others*, Volume 2: Reading 35
TEACHING THE CHAPTER pp. 586–611	■ Graphic Organizer 20 ■ Social Studies Skills Worksheet 20 ■ Literature Worksheet 20 ■ Outline Maps 14, 15, 16, 17, 18, 19	■ *The American Nation* Videodisc: Weaponry and Warfare ■ Linking Geography and History Transparency and Worksheet 16	■ Art in American History Transparency and Worksheet 21 ■ *Eyewitnesses and Others*, Volume 2: Readings 32, 33, 34
REVIEW AND ASSESSMENT pp. 612–613	■ Chapter 20 Daily Quizzes ■ Review Worksheet 20 ■ Chapter 20 Tests ■ Alternative Assessment Forms		■ Test Generator

Additional Resources

BOOKS FOR TEACHERS

Bruce, Anthony. *An Illustrated Companion to the First World War.* Viking Penguin, 1990. Overview of World War I.

Coffman, Edward M. *The War to End All Wars: The American Military Experience in World War I.* University of Wisconsin Press, 1986. Account of American military in World War I.

Schneider, Dorothy and Carl J. *Into the Breach: American Women Overseas in World War I.* Viking Penguin, 1991. Story of the American women who took part in World War I.

BOOKS FOR STUDENTS

* Bosco, Peter. *World War I.* Facts on File, 1991. Overview of WWI.

Freidel, Frank. *Over There: The Story of America's First Great Overseas Crusade.* Temple University Press, 1990. Illustrated account of American involvement in the war.

Hoehling, A. A. *The Last Voyage of the Lusitania.* Outlet Book Co., 1991. Account of the incident that helped to draw the U.S. into the war.

Marshall, S. L. *World War I.* Houghton Mifflin, 1985. Review of military, political, and social aspects of the war.

* for students reading below grade level

MULTIMEDIA MATERIALS

The American Diary—The Price of Peace. Video, 24 min. Aims Media. Reviews U.S. role in the Great War and the struggle for a lasting peace.

The Great War—1918. Video, 60 min. PBS. American involvement in the war told through letters and diaries of soldiers.

Men of Bronze. Video, 58 min. Films Incorporated. Reviews the role of African American soldiers in World War I.

THEMES IN AMERICAN HISTORY

USE WITH PAGES 584–585

Listed on the right are the themes emphasized in Chapter 20. The questions in boldface type stimulate critical thinking and provide students with an opportunity to discuss the themes within a broadened context. The questions also appear in the pupil's edition on p. 584.

■ GLOBAL RELATIONS

Why might a country be drawn into an international conflict in spite of efforts to remain neutral? Students might suggest that ties to other nations, such as trade and diplomatic agreements, might make neutrality difficult. The way that the warring nations treat the neutral country might also make it difficult to stay out of the conflict.

■ ECONOMIC DEVELOPMENT

How might fighting a war affect a nation's economy? Students might suggest that war would require increased production of weapons and other military materiel. It might require controls, such as rationing, to make sure that needed materiel are available for the war effort. Rationing and increased war production might result in reduced availability of consumer goods. A war might also bring new workers into the work force to replace workers who enter the armed services.

■ DEMOCRATIC VALUES

How might war affect a government's respect for its citizens' rights? Students might suggest that government efforts to increase wartime national security and to unite the nation behind a war effort could lead to the suppression of dissent. Such actions might result in restrictions of free speech and assembly and other basic rights.

CHAPTER STRATEGIES FOR MEETING INDIVIDUAL NEEDS

LIMITED ENGLISH PROFICIENT LEARNERS

Organize students in pairs to create information cards on the key people, places, and terms introduced in each section. One side of the card should list a name or term; the other side should provide a definition or pertinent biographical, geographical, and historical information.

TACTILE/KINESTHETIC LEARNERS

Have students work in small groups to sketch key events and scenes of American involvement in World War I. Call on volunteers to use their sketches for a "slide show" presentation on the war years.

LEARNERS HAVING DIFFICULTY

Organize students in pairs to construct an annotated outline, section by section, as they read the chapter. Have pairs compare their outlines.

AUDITORY LEARNERS

Suggest that students listen to recordings, or read aloud the lyrics, of American songs that were popular during World War I. Then have students discuss what the songs reveal about life during the war years.

VISUAL LEARNERS

Organize students into four groups and assign each group one of the sections in the chapter. Direct groups to identify a symbol or photograph from the text that best illustrates the main theme of their assigned section. Have each group present and explain its choice.

GIFTED LEARNERS

Ask students to list and describe the major turning points in U.S. foreign affairs from 1914 to 1920. Guide them to evaluate the U.S. response at each point and to identify possible alternative actions that could have been taken.

USING THE CHAPTER FOCUS

■ UNDERSTANDING THE MAIN IDEA

Ask students to read the Understanding the Main Idea paragraph. Then call on volunteers to suggest things that a government might do to mobilize a nation's economy to meet a national emergency, and how government might also mobilize public support. Write responses on a flip chart and retain them. At the close of the chapter, have students review and refine their responses.

 THEMES

Have students work individually or in small groups to answer the questions under Themes. Save students' responses so that they can compare them with their responses after studying the chapter. (See p. 583B for suggested answers.)

■ THE TIME LINE

Ask students to copy time-line entries into their notebooks. As students read the chapter, have them write the causes and effects of each event. After they complete the chapter, have students compare their cause-and-effect lists.

CORE RESOURCES

- **Graphic Organizer 20**
- **Geography Worksheet 20**
- **Outline Maps 14, 15, 16, 17, 18, 19**
- **Building Your Portfolio Worksheet 6**

AV RESOURCES

- **Everyday Life in America Transparency** and **Worksheet 20**

ABOUT THE ILLUSTRATION

Much of Houplines, France, was destroyed before the British finally took the city in a battle on April 9, 1918. Many cities throughout Europe were left decimated by the war. Have students find in magazines or newspapers photographs of cities that have been severely damaged by recent conflicts.

Chapter 20

1914–1920

WORLD WAR I

FOCUS
■

UNDERSTANDING THE MAIN IDEA

When war enveloped Europe, the United States tried to remain neutral. In 1917, however, the United States joined the Allied cause. The government quickly moved to mobilize the economy and to build public support for the war. Then when the fighting stopped, Wilson worked to shape a just peace. He failed, however, to win congressional support for the treaty he helped write.

THEMES

- **■ GLOBAL RELATIONS** Why might a country be drawn into an international conflict in spite of efforts to remain neutral?

- **■ ECONOMIC DEVELOPMENT** How might fighting a war affect a nation's economy?

- **■ DEMOCRATIC VALUES** How might war affect a government's respect for its citizens' rights?

1914	1915	1917	1918	191
Archduke Franz Ferdinand assassinated.	German U-boat sinks *Lusitania*.	Congress declares war.	Wilson introduces Fourteen Points.	Treaty of Versailles

Have volunteers review the 19th-century record of U.S. neutrality in European conflicts. Then ask students to speculate as to why remaining neutral would be more difficult for the U.S. in the early 20th century. *(U.S. was considered a major power; new technology had made world "smaller" and increased ties among nations; U.S. had various diplomatic and economic ties with European nations; new immigrants might put pressure on government to become involved in European affairs.)*

■ LINK TO THE PAST ▷

In his farewell address President Washington had warned against entangling American "peace and prosperity in the toils of European ambition." The United States had long heeded this advice and tried to remain neutral. But isolation became increasingly difficult as the nation emerged as a world power in the early 1900s.

Houplines, France, 1918

On the morning of July 29, 1914, Americans opened their newspapers to screaming headlines announcing the outbreak of war in Europe. The *New York Tribune* proclaimed: "AUSTRIA DECLARES WAR, RUSHES VAST ARMY INTO SERBIA; RUSSIA MASSES 80,000 MEN ON BORDER."

Most Americans reacted with stunned disbelief. Many were grateful that the Atlantic Ocean separated them from Europe. Urging Americans not to take sides, President Wilson attempted to steer a neutral course among the warring nations. With the passing months, however, neutrality became more difficult for the United States. Step by step, events pushed America closer to involvement. Finally, in the spring of 1917, the United States entered the fighting on the side of the Allies—one of some 30 nations on five continents formally to join the war. Before it ended, the war claimed the lives of over 8.5 million people and left some 21 million wounded or maimed.

World War I profoundly affected the American home front. It spurred government regulation of the economy, triggered a great northward migration of African Americans, and unleashed ugly forces of suspicion—even attacks—against dissenters.

President Wilson hoped that a new world order would arise from the ashes of the war. Yet, ironically, when the shooting stopped, the victors imposed a harsh peace on Germany, and the United States refused to join the League of Nations, the organization that embodied Wilson's hopes.

Red Cross unit

HISTORICAL SIDELIGHTS

An Unexpected War

The American public was surprised by the outbreak of war in part because, before August 1914, American newspapers devoted relatively less space to foreign affairs than did European newspapers. After the war's outbreak, however, the American press provided readers with fuller coverage of events than could be obtained anywhere else in the world.

FOCUS OBJECTIVES

■ Examine the tensions that helped bring about the war in Europe.

■ Describe what life was like in the trenches.

■ Analyze why most Americans found it difficult to remain "impartial in thought" concerning the war.

■ Explain how the warring nations' naval strategies challenged American neutrality.

PREVIEW WORKSHOP

Following is a list of the significant people, places, and terms in this section. You may wish to use this list as a section preview.

People
■ Archduke Franz Ferdinand
■ Gavrilo Princip

Places
■ Austria-Hungary
■ Bosnia and Herzegovina
■ Alsace-Lorraine
■ Balkans
■ Belgium

Terms
■ Pan-German movement
■ Pan-Slavic movement

■ militarism
■ Triple Alliance
■ Triple Entente
■ Allied Powers
■ Central Powers
■ First Battle of the Marne
■ no-man's land
■ trench warfare
■ Battle of the Somme

Section 1

WORLD WAR I BREAKS OUT

FOCUS

■ **What tensions helped bring about the war in Europe?**

■ **What was life in the trenches like?**

■ **Why did most Americans find it difficult to remain "impartial in thought" concerning the war?**

■ **How did the warring nations' naval strategies challenge American neutrality?**

Soldier and horse in gas masks

By the early 1900s nationalism, territorial rivalries, and militarism had turned Europe into a powder keg of hatred and petty jealousies. An assassination in a small Balkan state provided the spark that ignited this explosive mix. Within weeks, war gripped the whole continent. Everyone expected the conflict to end quickly, but it sank into a deadly stalemate. The United States declared neutrality, but the personal feelings of many Americans and the actions of the warring nations tested the country's stand.

THE ORIGINS OF THE WAR

While the Wilson administration grappled with the problems created by the Mexican Revolution, another dangerous international situation developed in Europe. On the surface Europe appeared peaceful—after all, no major conflicts had erupted since the 1870s. Furthermore, many European nations had endorsed the recommendations of two international peace conferences that arbitration be used to settle disputes among nations. But most European governments paid no more than lip service to arbitration and international cooperation. Fear, distrust, and petty jealousies often ruled their relations with other nations.

Nationalism and territorial rivalries.
At the root of the problem was the intense nationalism that engulfed Europe. Nationalism proved especially strong in northern, central, and eastern

Europe. There the **Pan-German movement**, led by Germany, sought to unite all German-speaking peoples under one flag. In direct opposition, Russia supported the **Pan-Slavic movement**, which sought to bring together all the Slavic peoples of central and eastern Europe. These movements seemed destined to come into conflict, since many Slavs lived in Austria-Hungary, a part of the German world.

Another source of tension in Europe was territorial rivalry. European nations, large and small, coveted land held by their neighbors. In 1908, for example, Austria-Hungary annexed Bosnia and Herzegovina. The annexation angered Serbia, which also had designs on the small Balkan province. Other countries, too, eyed neighboring territories. Russia wanted ice-free harbors in the Baltic Sea and access for Russian warships from the Black Sea into the Mediterranean. Germany, the major Baltic power, opposed Russia's ambitions. France wanted to recover Alsace-Lorraine, a

CORE RESOURCES

• **Geography Worksheet 20**
• **Section 1 Daily Quiz**

AV RESOURCES

• *The American Nation Videodisc: Weaponry and Warfare*

MOTIVATING:
LINK TO TODAY

Ask students what they know about the recent history of the Balkans and tensions that have existed there. As students read the section, have them compare the recent history of the Balkans to the situation there at the outbreak of World War I.

Teaching the Section

CAUSES OF THE WAR

On the chalkboard draw a word web with *World War I* at the center and *Alliances, Assassination of Archduke Franz Ferdinand, Militarism, Nationalism,* and *Imperialism* around it. Then ask volunteers to explain how each satellite word or phrase helped bring about World War I.

▶

French area the Germans had conquered in 1871, and Italy desired nearby territories belonging to Austria-Hungary.

Militarism and alliances. This dizzying tangle of territorial claims helped generate a spirit of **militarism**, or glorification of armed strength, across the continent. Each nation built up its army and navy against the military threat posed by its neighbors. Military buildup quickly turned into an arms race as each nation tried to develop weapons more powerful than those of its neighbors.

European nations also sought to strengthen their military positions through alliances. Germany, Austria-Hungary, and Italy formed the **Triple Alliance**. Great Britain, France, and Russia joined in the **Triple Entente**. In the treaties that cemented these alliances, the members usually promised to aid any other member who came under attack from an outside power.

The spark that led to war. These alliances helped maintain a balance of power, but they also meant that even a minor incident could provoke a war. Many observers feared that if such an incident occurred, it would be in the Balkans—a region so unstable that some called it "the powder keg of Europe." Observers also agreed that the incident would likely involve nationalist rivalries. As German general Helmuth von Moltke (MAWLT-kuh) remarked in 1912:

> 66 A European war is bound to come sooner or later, and then it will . . . be a struggle between Teuton [German] and Slav. It is the duty of all states who uphold the banner of German spiritual culture to prepare for this conflict. But the attack must come from the Slavs. 99

The attack came in 1914. In June of that year, Archduke Franz Ferdinand, the heir to the Austro-Hungarian throne, paid a goodwill visit to Sarajevo (SAHR-uh-ye-voh), the capital of Bosnia and Herzegovina. As Franz Ferdinand's open motor car proceeded along the city's streets, Serbian nationalist Gavrilo Princip (PREENT-seep) stepped out of the crowd and fired two shots, killing the archduke and his wife, Sofie.

Suspecting—correctly—that the Serbian government knew of Princip's plans, Austria-Hungary declared war on Serbia. The declaration drew each side's allies into the conflict. Russia sided with Serbia; Germany, with Austria-Hungary. Within a week France and Great Britain had declared war on Austria-Hungary and Germany. Despite membership in the Triple Alliance, Italy remained neutral until 1915, when it joined France, Great Britain, Russia, and the other **Allied Powers** against the **Central Powers** of Germany, Austria-Hungary, the Ottoman Empire (Turkey), and Bulgaria. Eventually some 30 nations would take sides in the Great War.

■■ Nationalism, territorial rivalries, militarism, and military alliances created tensions that led to war.

▼ Archduke Franz Ferdinand, his wife, and their children pose for a royal family picture.

▶ Gavrilo Princip was 19 years old when he assassinated Franz Ferdinand. He was arrested and sentenced to 20 years—the maximum prison penalty for someone under 20 years old.

PRIMARY SOURCE

Description of Change: excerpted and bracketed

Rationale: excerpted to focus on main idea; bracketed to clarify meaning

HISTORICAL SIDELIGHTS

The Pig War

Among the issues that strained relations between Serbia and Austria-Hungary was the "Pig War," an economic struggle that had enormous political implications. In 1905 Serbia attempted to reduce its almost total dependence on trade with Austria-Hungary by signing a customs agreement with Bulgaria. Austria-Hungary responded by banning imports of Serbian livestock—Serbia's largest export. The country's success in developing other markets in Egypt, Greece, Turkey, and Germany for its goats and pigs fanned Serbian nationalism. Austria-Hungary, on the other hand, was humiliated and angered by its inability to dominate the Serbs.

HISTORICAL SIDELIGHTS

Serbian Involvement?

Princip was an agent of a radical nationalist group called "The Black Hand" or "Union or Death." It was believed that the group had ties to Serbian intelligence agencies, and a high-ranking intelligence officer may have planned the archduke's assassination.

*T*eaching the *S*ection

NAVAL STRATEGIES

Organize students into small groups to study the map on p. 588. Have them use the map to identify and list the countries that comprised the Allied Powers and the Central Powers. Then ask students to use the map to write a paragraph explaining how geography influenced the naval strategies of each side.

GLOBAL CONNECTIONS

The conflict in the Balkans quickly developed into a world war in part because the major belligerents were imperial powers. Soldiers from all over the British Empire, including Canada, India, Australia, and New Zealand, fought under the British flag. French fighting forces were bolstered by troops from French colonies in Africa. And Germany kept thousands of British and African troops busy by waging a hit-and-run campaign in its East African possessions.

Map Caption Answer
on the Eastern Front

MAKING CONNECTIONS
Geography

After the outbreak of war the Russian authorities renamed St. Petersburg *Petrograd* because they felt the original name sounded too Germanic. In 1924 the city was renamed *Leningrad* in memory of the Bolshevik leader V. I. Lenin.

*T*HE EARLY WEEKS OF THE WAR

In 1905, accepting the inevitability of a European war, German military leaders had developed a plan for swift victory. The plan called for German forces to skirt the heavily defended Franco-German border, march through then-neutral Belgium, and invade France across the practically unguarded Belgian border before Great Britain could move its forces across the English Channel. With France and Britain knocked out of the war, Germany could focus on defeating Russia.

On August 3, 1914, the Germans launched their plan, surging into Belgium. German military leaders expected to reach the French border quickly and then sweep across northern France toward Paris. Like their kaiser (ruler), Wilhelm II, they believed that the war would end "before the leaves have fallen from the trees." But thanks to

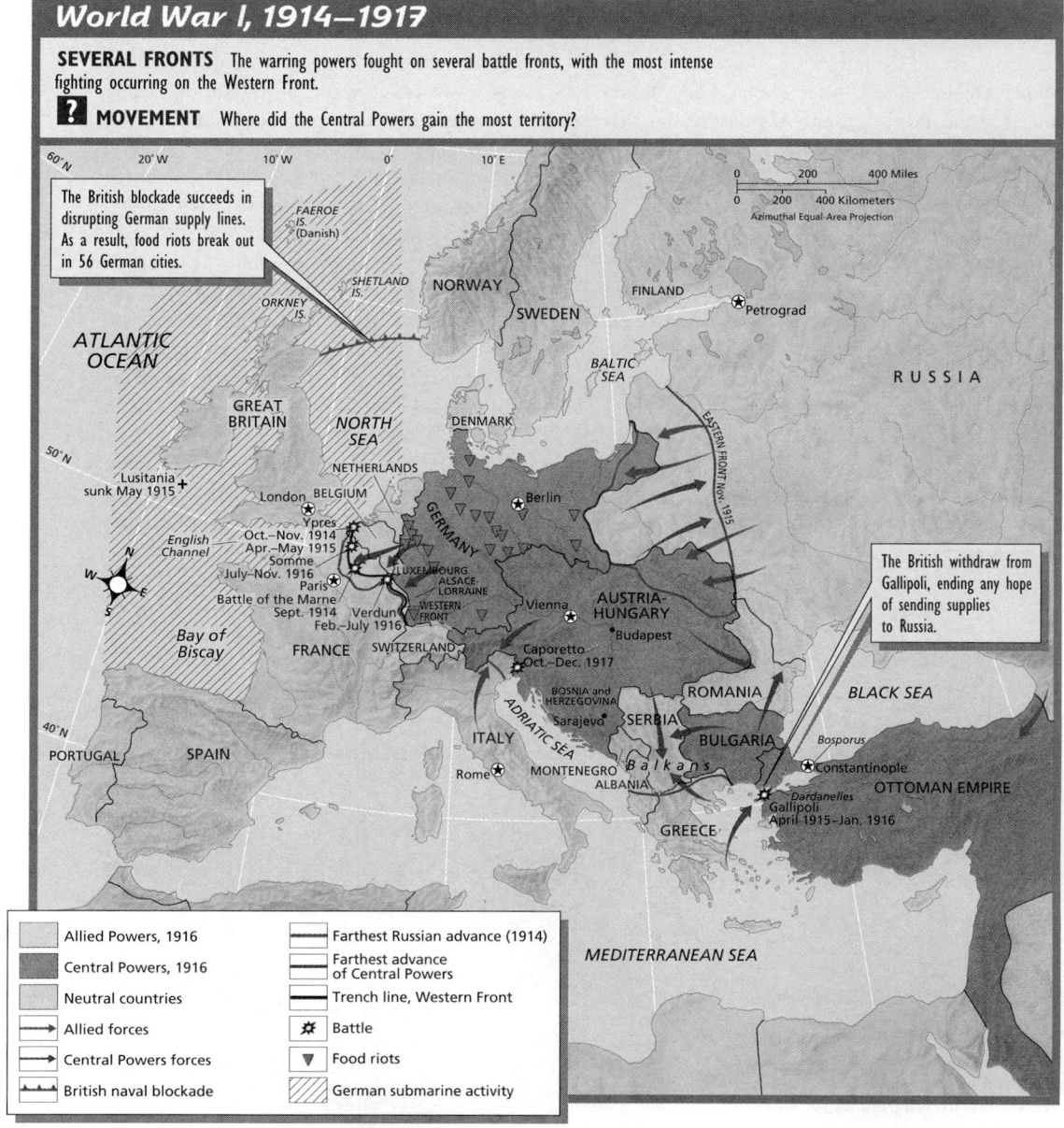

World War I, 1914–1917

SEVERAL FRONTS The warring powers fought on several battle fronts, with the most intense fighting occurring on the Western Front.

? **MOVEMENT** Where did the Central Powers gain the most territory?

The British blockade succeeds in disrupting German supply lines. As a result, food riots break out in 56 German cities.

The British withdraw from Gallipoli, ending any hope of sending supplies to Russia.

▢	Allied Powers, 1916	—	Farthest Russian advance (1914)
▢	Central Powers, 1916		Farthest advance of Central Powers
▢	Neutral countries	—	Trench line, Western Front
→	Allied forces	✳	Battle
→	Central Powers forces	▼	Food riots
∿	British naval blockade	▨	German submarine activity

LIFE IN THE TRENCHES

Have students work in small groups to produce a radio newscast titled "A Day in the Trenches." The newscast should include eyewitness accounts or interviews with soldiers about their daily lives and commentary from military experts on how new weapons technology has affected warfare and life in the trenches. If cassette recorders are available, groups may wish to record their newscasts, complete with sound effects. Invite groups to present their newscasts to the class.

the small Belgian army's fierce resistance, the Germans spent nearly three weeks fighting their way across Belgium. As a result, General Joseph Joffre (zhawfruh), the French commander, had time to rush troops to the Belgian border, and the British had time to transport some 90,000 troops to northern France.

These measures managed to slow the German advance but did not stop it. The Germans' superior military might pushed the French and the British back to the Marne River in northeast France. Against heavy odds, the French and the British stopped the Germans early in September 1914 at the **First Battle of the Marne.** From roughly Ypres (eepruh) to Verdun, the German line fell back some 40 miles (see map on page 588). The French and the British launched a counteroffensive but were unable to dislodge the Germans. The Germans had no better luck advancing against the Allies. As 1914 drew to a close, leaders of both sides realized that there would be no quick victory.

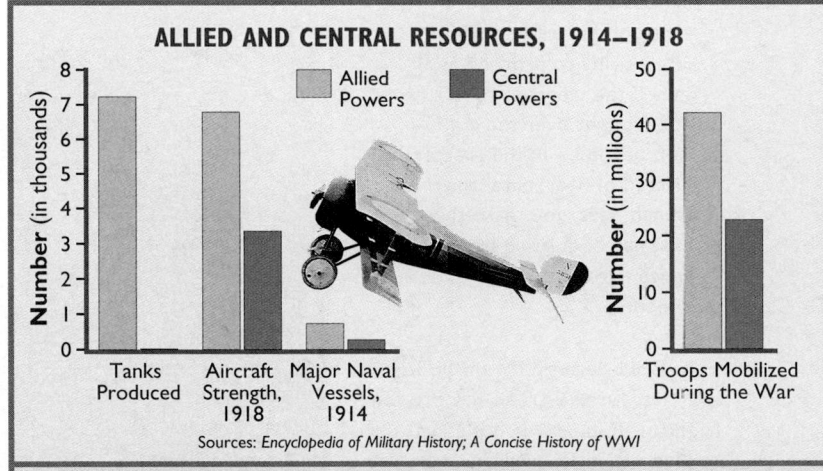

ALLIED AND CENTRAL RESOURCES, 1914–1918

Sources: *Encyclopedia of Military History; A Concise History of WWI*

COMPARATIVE STRENGTHS At the beginning of the war, Germany had the majority of aircraft and was the second greatest naval power. However, the Allied countries mobilized more troops and were able to use their economic resources to surpass Germany in overall war production.

? BUILDING GRAPH SKILLS What was the total aircraft strength in 1918?

▲ This 1914 photograph shows German soldiers traveling to the western front in a train marked with the inscription "A trip to Paris—See you again on the boulevard."

WAR REACHES A STALEMATE

By early 1915 both armies dug in along a front running some 400 miles from the North Sea to the Swiss border. Holed up in trenches and separated by a thin strip of territory called **no-man's land,** both sides struggled to advance.

Trench warfare. Even the most hardened soldier had never encountered anything like **trench warfare.** Britain's field marshal Lord Kitchener lamented, "I don't know what is to be done—this isn't war." In this war most battles began with deafening artillery fire. Then as the smoke and dust from the cannonade cleared, one army would charge the enemy trenches. Most soldiers who succeeded in getting through the barbed wire and land mines strewn across no-man's land were cut down by a hail of bullets from the enemy trenches. In the **Battle of the Somme** in 1916, for example, the British suffered some 60,000 casualties in a single day! All told, this four-month-long battle claimed more than a million dead and wounded.

Maneuvering in the trenches was nightmarish. As British soldier Charles Carrington wrote:

❝ When moving about in the trenches you turn a corner every few yards, which makes it seem like walking in a maze. It is

HISTORICAL SIDELIGHTS
Taking a Cab
The French had so few trucks in which to transport their troops that reinforcements at the Battle of the Marne were rushed from Paris to the front lines in Parisian taxicabs.

Graph Caption Answer
about 10,000

BUILDING VOCABULARY
The original *no-man's land* was a wasteland used for public executions outside the north wall of 14th-century London. Because no one wanted to claim ownership of this strip of ground strewn with the bones of executed criminals, it became known as *no-man's land.* The term was first used in the military sense around 1900.

Teaching the Section

ATTITUDES ABOUT THE WAR

Ask students to presume that the year is 1915 and that their ancestors immigrated to America from one of the combatant nations of World War I. Direct them to write letters to President Wilson expressing their opinions about America's neutrality policy. Ask representatives of the various ethnic backgrounds to read their letters to the class. Then have the class generalize about why Americans found it difficult to feel impartial about this war. Students may wish to include their letters in their portfolios.

CHALLENGES TO AMERICAN NEUTRALITY

Pair students and ask half the pairs to portray American and German diplomats and the other half, American and British diplomats. Have each "American" draft a note protesting the other country's naval actions and deliver it to the other student. That "diplomat" should return a response that explains and defends that country's naval strategy. Select pairs to read their exchanges to the class.

PRIMARY SOURCES

Description of Change: excerpted
Rationale: excerpted to focus on main idea

BUILDING VOCABULARY

In its developmental stages, the tank was called a *landship*. However, to conceal its identity, the weapon was given the code name *tank* and transported under a tarpaulin marked "portable water tank." By the time the vehicle was used in combat, it was commonly referred to as a *tank*.

MAKING CONNECTIONS

Science

Chlorine gas was the first chemical weapon used in World War I. The far more potent phosgene, produced by the interaction of chlorine and carbon monoxide in sunlight, was introduced later. By the end of the war, however, dichlorodiethyl sulfide was the most common chemical weapon. Better known as "mustard gas" because of its color and smell, it blinded, blistered skin, and seared lungs. Soldiers who survived mustard gas attacks commonly suffered skin, vision, and breathing disorders for years after the war.

impossible to keep your sense of direction and infinitely tiring to proceed at all. When the trenches have been fought over the confusion becomes all the greater. Instead of neat, parallel trench lines, you make the best use of existing trenches which might run in any direction. 〞

Even during lulls in the fighting, life in the trenches proved frightful. Rats and lice plagued the soldiers. Rain flooded the trenches, drenching the soldiers in mud. Artillery fire frequently prevented burial of the dead for days, and exploding shells often unearthed corpses buried earlier. Such unsanitary conditions bred disease, and sickness claimed nearly as many men as bombs and bullets did. The only way out of the trenches, a British soldier observed, was on a stretcher.

New weapons. New weapons added to the horror of trench warfare. The Germans' machine guns fired hundreds of rounds per minute, felling advancing Allied troops like a scythe cutting wheat. The Allies introduced the tank partly to counter the machine gun's deadly impact. First used at the Battle of the Somme in September 1916, the tank produced the intended effect. It

▲ A British tank force is shown here fighting near Amiens, France, in August 1918.

scared the Germans "out of their wits," one British soldier reported, and made them "scuttle like frightened rabbits."

But perhaps the most feared new weapon introduced during World War I was poison gas. No whistling shell announced a gas attack. The green mist silently drifted over the trenches, and the soldiers had only seconds to slip on their gas masks. Any delay meant a slow, suffocating death. After watching a comrade die of poison gas, soldier-poet Wilfred Owen wrote:

〝 But someone still was yelling out
    and stumbling,
And floundr'ring like a man in fire
    or lime . . .
Dim, through the misty panes and
    thick green light,
As under a green sea, I saw him
    drowning. 〞

▪▪ Heavy casualties, unsanitary conditions, and fearful new weapons made trench warfare a horrible experience.

▲ Soldiers fought much of World War I from trenches. There they struggled to protect themselves from artillery fire, exposure to all types of weather, and disease and unsanitary conditions.

Continued stalemate. While new military technology produced horrendous casualties on both sides, it did little to break the stalemate on the

Practice

GUIDED PRACTICE

On the chalkboard write phrases identifying the major events covered in this section, leaving space between each phrase. Tell students that these phrases are headlines for news stories. Choose one headline and ask volunteers to give details that might appear in a news story accompanying the headline.

INDEPENDENT PRACTICE

Direct students to choose one of the headlines written on the chalkboard for the Guided Practice activity. Have them first list details about events and then convert these details into a news story that would accompany their selected headlines. Students may wish to include their news stories in their portfolios.

Review and Assessment

REVIEW Have students summarize the major points of the section by writing a paragraph using people, places, and terms listed in the Preview Workshop on p. 586. Ask volunteers to read their summaries to the class. Then assign the Section 1 Review on p. 592.

ASSESS Assign the **Section 1 Daily Quiz** in *Core Resources*.

▶

western front. From 1915 to the spring of 1917, both armies launched offensives that gained them a few miles of territory, which more often than not they quickly lost.

As the months passed, many people wondered whether the fighting would ever stop. They began to suggest that only the intervention of the United States could bring the war to an end.

AMERICAN NEUTRALITY

At the outbreak of the war, most Americans had expressed surprise and horror. After the initial shock, however, Americans tended to look on the war as a faraway conflict that did not involve the United States. As one American diplomat wrote: "Again and ever I thank Heaven for the Atlantic Ocean."

Not surprisingly, then, President Wilson received strong support when he announced a policy of neutrality. All Americans, he urged, ought to be "neutral in fact as well as in name . . . impartial in thought as well as action." Wilson thought that by taking a neutral stance, the United States might help to negotiate a settlement to the conflict. He pursued this goal throughout 1915 and 1916, but without success.

As the war dragged on, most Americans remained neutral in action, but few could claim to be impartial in thought. Some 28 million Americans—almost 30 percent of the population—were immigrants or the children of immigrants. Many men and women of German, Austrian, Hungarian, or Turkish background sympathized with the Central Powers. So did many Irish Americans anxious to free Ireland from Great Britain's rule.

Most Americans, however, backed the Allies. Ties of ancestry, language, and culture bound many Americans to Britain. Strong, long-established links to France also existed. After all, the French had helped Americans win their War of Independence. The British also bolstered American support for the Allies through a skillful propaganda campaign, which painted Germans as brutal warmongers.

▪▪ The U.S. government remained neutral, but most Americans—because of ancestral ties or national sympathies—favored one side or the other.

Challenges to American neutrality. Despite its policy of neutrality, the United States could not remain untouched by the war. When the war began, the British navy blockaded the German coast and planted explosive mines across the North Sea. The British even stopped American ships bound for ports in neutral countries and examined cargos—including the mail—for goods that might ultimately be destined for Germany. The United States protested, charging that British actions violated American neutrality.

American hostility toward Great Britain faded, however, in the face of German submarine, or U-boat, warfare. Early in 1915 the Germans established a "war zone" around Great Britain. Any ships entering this zone, even those from neutral nations, were liable to U-boat attack. In response, Wilson warned that the United States would, in accordance with international laws of neutrality, hold Germany accountable for any injury to American lives or property on the high seas.

On March 28, 1915, a U-boat sank a British liner in the Irish Sea, killing more than 100 people, including an American. While the United States debated its response, a far more serious incident occurred. On May 7, 1915, a U-boat patrolling off the Irish coast torpedoed the British passenger liner *Lusitania*. The dead included 128 Americans. The *New York Herald* accused the Germans of "piracy on the high seas," and the *New York Times* called the Germans "savages drenched with blood." Outraged Americans agreed. German leaders justified their actions, declaring that they had placed advertisements in U.S. newspapers warning Americans against sailing into the war zone. They also charged that the *Lusitania* was carrying

▶ The *Lusitania*'s 1915 voyage announcement carried a warning from the German Embassy against Atlantic sea travel.

RETEACH Organize students into groups and assign each group one of the Focus questions on p. 586. Have group members discuss and write an answer to their question. Ask group representatives to share their answers with the other groups.

Closure

Write this statement on the chalkboard: *Peace in Europe was as difficult to maintain as was American neutrality once war had broken out.* Call on volunteers to cite and evaluate arguments in support of and in opposition to the statement.

Extension

RESEARCH Have students research and report on one of the new weapons of World War I.

CREATE Ask students to assume the role of a World War I European soldier in the trenches and compose a poem that expresses the soldier's feelings about the war.

SECTION REVIEW ANSWERS

IDENTIFY

For significance, see the following pages:
Pan-German movement (p. 586)
Pan-Slavic movement (p. 586)
militarism (p. 587)
Triple Alliance (p. 587)
Triple Entente (p. 587)
Archduke Franz Ferdinand (p. 587)
Gavrilo Princip (p. 587)
Allied Powers (p. 587)
Central Powers (p. 587)
First Battle of the Marne (p. 589)
no-man's land (p. 589)
trench warfare (p. 589)
Battle of the Somme (p. 589)

LOCATE

For locations, see the map on p. 588.

1. *nationalism, territorial rivalries, militarism, alliances*
2. *violated American neutrality, led to U.S. outrage and Wilson's demand that Germany stop unrestricted submarine warfare*
3. *No. Most favored one side or the other because of ancestral ties or national sympathies.*
4. *Diary entries might mention casualties, the effect of weather, unsanitary conditions, and new weapons.*
5. *Responses might suggest that digging in was defensive and that new weapons made attacks horribly costly in human lives.*

▲ The *Lusitania* was photographed shortly before its fateful voyage from New York in 1915.

armaments for England—an accusation that later proved true.

Nevertheless, Wilson fired off an angry protest to the German government, demanding specific pledges against unrestricted submarine warfare. Secretary of State William Jennings Bryan, charging that the president's protest amounted to an ultimatum, resigned. Bryan argued that the United States could not issue ultimatums and remain neutral. The country, he warned, would eventually be drawn into the war.

■■ **British and German naval activities violated the rights of neutral nations and led to American protests.**

THE SINKING OF THE *LUSITANIA*

Germany's Baron von Schwarzenstein offered the following response to the outrage over the sinking of the *Lusitania*:

❝❞t was only *after England declared the whole North Sea a war zone . . . that Germany with precisely the same right declared the waters around England a war zone and announced her purpose of sinking all hostile commercial vessels found therein. . . . In the case of the Lusitania the German Ambassador even further warned Americans through the great American newspapers against taking passage thereon. Does a pirate act thus? Does he take pains to save human lives? . . . Nobody regrets more sincerely than we Germans the hard necessity of sending to their deaths hundreds of men. Yet the sinking was a justifiable act of war. . . . The scene of war is no golf links, the ships of belligerent powers no pleasure places. . . . We have sympathy with the victims and their relatives, of course, but did we hear anything about sympathy . . . when England adopted her diabolical plan of starving a great nation?* **❞❞**

SECTION **1** REVIEW

IDENTIFY and explain the significance of the following: Pan-German movement, Pan-Slavic movement, militarism, Triple Alliance, Triple Entente, Archduke Franz Ferdinand, Gavrilo Princip, Allied Powers, Central Powers, First Battle of the Marne, no-man's land, trench warfare, Battle of the Somme.

LOCATE and explain the importance of the following: Austria-Hungary, Bosnia and Herzegovina, Alsace-Lorraine, Balkans, Belgium.

1. **MAIN IDEA** What factors contributed to the outbreak of World War I?
2. **MAIN IDEA** What effect did Britain and Germany's naval strategies have on American neutrality?
3. **RECOGNIZING POINTS OF VIEW** Did the U.S. government's policy of neutrality reflect the views of most Americans? Why or why not?
4. **WRITING TO DESCRIBE** Imagine you are a British soldier at the front during 1916. Write a diary entry that describes the conditions you experience during trench warfare.
5. **ANALYZING** How might trench warfare and new weapons have contributed to the stalemate on the western front?

Section 2

THE UNITED STATES GOES TO WAR

FOCUS
- **Why did the United States finally enter the war?**
- **Why did the United States institute a draft?**
- **What part did the American military play in the Allied war effort?**

*G*ermany's continued violations of American neutrality drew the United States into World War I on the Allied side in 1917. The Americans' entry came none too soon for the Allies, who faced a desperate military situation. As U.S. forces poured into Europe the tide turned. The Germans slowly fell back, and in November 1918 the warring parties signed an armistice. The four-year nightmare had finally ended.

World War I poster

FOCUS OBJECTIVES
- Explain why the U.S. finally entered the war.
- Determine why the U.S. instituted a draft.
- Describe the part played by the American military in the Allied war effort.

THE ROAD TO WAR

The sinking of the *Lusitania* brought the conflict in Europe closer to home for many Americans. Even so, most still hoped the United States could stay out of the war. Further challenges to American neutrality, however, were not long in coming. In August 1915 two Americans died when a German submarine sank the *Arabic,* another British liner. Then in March 1916 the French passenger vessel *Sussex* was attacked, injuring several Americans. In a sternly worded message to the German government, President Wilson threatened to sever diplomatic ties if Germany did not abandon unrestricted submarine warfare. The German government responded with the *Sussex* **pledge**, a renewal of an earlier promise not to sink liners without warning or without assuring the passengers' safety.

Wilson's actions criticized. Most Americans supported Wilson's approach. However, a number of prominent politicians, including former president Theodore Roosevelt, accused Wilson of not doing enough. Wilson, "that infernal skunk

in the White House," Roosevelt complained, had adopted a course of inaction and was little better than a "coward and weakling."

Others accused Wilson of abandoning neutrality. Former secretary of state William Jennings Bryan argued that Wilson's commercial and trade policies helped the Allies. As secretary of state, Bryan had discouraged American bankers from

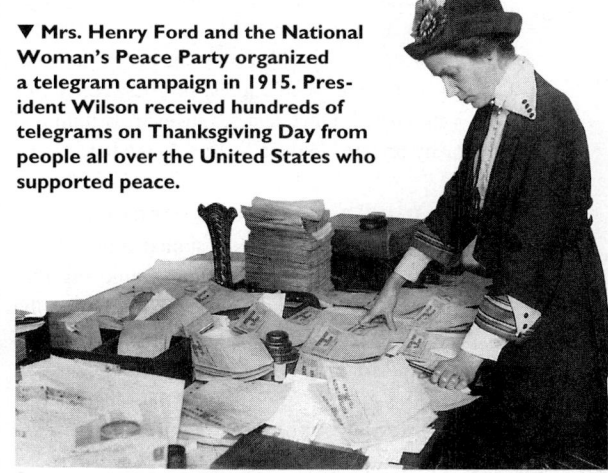

▼ **Mrs. Henry Ford and the National Woman's Peace Party organized a telegram campaign in 1915. President Wilson received hundreds of telegrams on Thanksgiving Day from people all over the United States who supported peace.**

MOTIVATING: PRIOR KNOWLEDGE

Ask students to write a brief response to this question: Basing your answer on what you learned in Section 1, tell what you think might have drawn the U.S. into the war. Ask volunteers to read and explain their responses. Then remind students to check the accuracy of their responses as they read this section.

▲ These Girl Scouts helped the war effort by collecting peach pits. The pits could be ground into a charcoal powder and placed in gas masks to help filter out the poisonous fumes during gas attacks.

making loans to either side, but this policy was soon abandoned. Bryan's successor at the State Department, Robert Lansing, encouraged trade in war materials, especially with the Allies. By 1916, arms sales to the Allies stood at some $500 million, about 80 times the amount sold in 1914.

Preparedness and peace. Bryan's fears increased when Wilson launched a military "preparedness" program. The **National Defense Act**, passed in June 1916, increased the number of soldiers in the regular army from some 90,000 to about 175,000, with an ultimate goal of about 223,000 men. It also set the size of the National Guard at some 450,000 troops and provided for their training. Another bill, passed two months later, appropriated $313 million to build up the navy.

President Wilson assured Americans that he had not abandoned neutrality. Running on the slogan "He Kept Us Out of War," Wilson won reelection in 1916, narrowly defeating the Republicans' Charles Evans Hughes.

Wilson still hoped to negotiate a settlement to the war. In a January 1917 speech, he called for "peace without victory." A lasting peace, he said, had to be one between equals, not between victor and vanquished. Once again, however, Britain and Germany rejected Wilson's effort to mediate.

Diplomatic relations broken. On February 1, 1917, Germany resumed full-scale U-boat warfare. The Germans were gambling that their U-boat fleet could defeat the Allies before the Americans joined the war. Wilson, as he had threatened, broke off diplomatic relations. He also ordered the arming of American merchant ships sailing into the war zone. Nonetheless, German torpedoes sank five American ships.

The publication on March 1, 1917, of an intercepted cable from German foreign secretary Arthur Zimmermann to the German minister in Mexico further heightened tensions. The **Zimmermann Note**, as the cable was quickly dubbed, instructed the minister that if the United States declared war on Germany, he was to propose to Mexico that it enter an alliance with Germany. With German support, the cable went on, Mexico could "reconquer the lost territory in New Mexico, Texas, and Arizona."

As the weeks passed, Wilson reluctantly concluded that the United States could not stay out of the conflict. On April 2, 1917, the president addressed Congress, asking them to vote on a declaration of war.

CONGRESS DECLARES WAR

A hushed Congress heard Wilson condemn Germany's submarine warfare for its "wanton and wholesale destruction." Wilson, however, did not rest his case solely on the evils of U-boat warfare. He summoned Americans to a crusade for a better world:

> 66 We are glad . . . to fight thus for the ultimate peace of the world and for the liberation of its peoples, . . . for the rights of nations great and small and the privilege of men everywhere to choose their way of life. . . . The world must be made safe for democracy. 99

At these words, cheers and applause rang through the Capitol. A somber Wilson later told an aide: "My message today was a message of death for our young men. How strange it seems to applaud that."

■■ U-boat activity and the interception of the Zimmermann Note led the United States to declare war on Germany.

The Senate declared war on April 4; the House, two days later. The vote was not unanimous—6 senators and 50 representatives opposed the declaration. Congresswoman Jeannette Rankin of Montana was among the opposition. "I want to stand by my country," she explained, "but I cannot vote for war."

THE ROAD TO WAR

Organize students into groups, and instruct them to list all the factors that they think contributed to the entry of the U.S. into World War I. Then ask groups to rank their lists from most to least significant factors. Ask groups to present their lists and explain the reasoning for their rankings. As a whole class discuss the differences in groups' rankings.

THE DRAFT

Guide students to hold a "town meeting" on the Selective Service Act. Ask some students to make statements of support for the draft, presenting the reasons for it. Others should state the reasons for their opposition to the draft. When all the speeches have been made, allow the "town" to vote on whether or not it is willing to support the draft.

■■ Ask students if they favor or oppose a draft as an appropriate device for a democratic nation to maintain its military.

▶

Born in Missoula, Montana, in 1880, Rankin was a committed pacifist, social worker, and leader of the women's suffrage movement. In 1916 she became the first woman elected to Congress, and in 1918 she played a key role in the passage of the Nineteenth Amendment. However, with Allied victory only days away, Rankin lost her bid for a Senate seat in the November 1918 elections.

Elected to the House again in 1940, Rankin continued to speak out against the draft and military spending, casting the only vote against the United States' entry into World War II. That vote cost her reelection in 1942. She did not give up her pacifism, however. In January 1968, at age 87, Rankin led a march on Washington, D.C., to protest the Vietnam War.

Jeannette Rankin

MOBILIZING AMERICAN MILITARY POWER

In his war message on April 2, President Wilson pledged all the nation's "material resources" to the Allied war effort. But what the Allies most urgently needed were fresh troops. Few Americans, however, rushed to volunteer for military service.

On May 18, 1917, Congress responded by passing the **Selective Service Act**, which required men between ages 21 and 30 to register with local draft boards. (The age range was later changed to 18–45) By the end of the war, some 24 million men had registered, and some 2.8 million had been drafted. In fact, more than half of the almost 4.8 million Americans who served in the armed forces were draftees.

Many who supported conscription argued that the draft would help build a more democratic America by bringing together soldiers from different backgrounds. In reality, Native Americans, African Americans, Mexican Americans, and many foreign-born soldiers faced discrimination.

Most foreign-born soldiers, for example, were assigned to segregated units where they were taught civics and English. Congress did, however, offer citizenship to the some 10,000 Native Americans who served during the war.

The more than 370,000 African American recruits experienced particularly harsh discrimination. They were blocked from service in the marines and limited to kitchen duties in the navy. Most African Americans in the army were confined to all-black support units commanded by white officers. And African American draftees sent to army training camps in the South often faced harassment from local whites.

Pressure from the NAACP and other African American organizations convinced the army to open up more opportunities for black soldiers. A school was established to train African American officers, and more blacks were assigned combat duty. The army, however, made no effort to integrate blacks and whites in the same units.

■■ **The United States instituted the draft to bring the armed services up to full force.**

▲ Approximately 1,400 African American officers served during World War I. This officer was stationed in Saint-Dizier, France.

PERSONALITIES IN HISTORY

Many other members of the suffrage movement also were pacifists, and they strongly supported Rankin's stand on the war. But some—most notably Carrie Chapman Catt, the head of the National American Woman Suffrage Association—advised Rankin to support the war because they felt that a woman casting an antiwar vote might hurt their cause.

VOICES IN HISTORY

There was disagreement in the African American community about whether blacks should serve in the military. Some African Americans saw service as a way to end prejudice and discrimination. The major African American newspaper, the *Chicago Defender*, noted, "The colored soldier who fights side by side with the white American . . . will hardly be begrudged a fair chance when the victorious armies return." The editors of the *Messenger*, however, disagreed. "Since when has the subject race come out of a war with its rights and privileges accorded for such participation?" they challenged.

PRIMARY SOURCE
Description of Change:
excerpted
Rationale: excerpted to
focus on main idea

HISTORY
in the Making

THE DOUGHBOY'S PACK

SETTING THE SCENE

In many ways the experiences of average soldiers in World War I differed from those in previous wars. Point out that some of the supplies provided to U.S. troops, such as steel helmets and gas masks, were responses to what then was called modern warfare.

A MORAL WEAPON?

Tell students that Germans first used poison gas as an offensive weapon in 1915 and that the British soon copied their example. Although used throughout the war by both sides, poison gas was a disappointment to some military commanders because its effectiveness depended heavily on weather conditions. For example, shifting winds might carry the deadly gas back over the very soldiers who launched it. It came to be regarded as an impractical weapon, but not necessarily an unethical one. Point out that the use of chemical weapons today is regarded by many nations as an atrocity.

OVER THERE

With mobilization well under way, American troops sailed to France as part of the American Expeditionary Force (AEF). The first U.S. troops, under the command of General John J. Pershing, reached France in late June 1917. On July 4, thousands of "Yanks," cheered on by huge crowds, marched through Paris to the tomb of the Marquis de Lafayette, the French hero of the American Revolution. "Lafayette, we are here!" proclaimed one of Pershing's aides.

Lieutenant Edward F. Graham wrote home about the sense of purpose that he—and many other soldiers—felt:

66 The desperate contest between justice and empire . . . is now on. You should be proud to have me . . . participate in the

HISTORY
in the Making

BY DR. PAUL BOYER

The Doughboy's Pack

History is much more than a study of dates, documents, or facts about influential people. Ordinary objects also leave a historical record about an event or an era. For example, common items provided to soldiers during a war tell a story about how that war was fought.

During World War I the American infantryman—or doughboy, as he was nicknamed—wearily trudged across European battlefields carrying all his necessary equipment inside a canvas "field kit" strapped to his back. Some of the items provided to American soldiers in World War I are shown on these pages. Examine the photographs carefully. What can we learn about the combat experiences of World War I soldiers by studying what they carried?

Begin with the field kit. Examine the cartridge belt attached at waist level. Notice the individual pockets. Each compartment held 10 rounds of ammunition. The around-the-

▶ Soldier equipped with gas mask and steel helmet

waist design with pockets was adopted during World War I because of automatic weapons. Rifles could now fire as many as five bullets per minute, and a soldier needed easy access to large amounts of ammunition during the heat of battle. The cartridge belt served this purpose.

Next notice the shovel strapped to the field kit, with its blade encased inside a protective flap. Until 1918 most of the war on the western front was fought from the trenches. Consequently, digging equipment was a necessity. Each squad shared a variety of tools: shovels, hand axes, pickaxes, and wire cutters. Wire cutters were particularly essential to the needs of World War I infantry. Before a soldier could

reach the enemy's trenches, he had to clear a path through coils of sharp barbed wire. Getting even a small cut from the rusty barbs could prove dangerous—infections in a minor wound often led to the amputation of an arm or a leg.

Now examine the photograph of the American soldier wearing the gas mask and steel helmet. Chlorine gas and mustard gas were greatly feared weapons introduced during World War I. The gas mask struggle as a part of the human wall against a second Dark Ages. **99**

As the weeks went by, American troops arrived in France in ever-swelling numbers. To supply and maintain them, army engineers built docks and railroads and strung up networks of telephone and telegraph lines. They also constructed camps, ammunition dumps, storage sheds, and hospitals.

Some 10,000 American women worked in these hospitals. Emily Vuagniaux, an Army Medical Corps nurse, described life in a battlefield hospital:

66 We . . . have worked . . . sometimes 18 hours straight. I have the operating room and they run four tables day and night and have between 200 and 300 patients right off the field, so you may know we are quite close in. **99**

PRIMARY SOURCE
Description of Change: excerpted
Rationale: excerpted to focus on main idea

filtered out poisonous fumes that could suffocate or blind a soldier. The odd-looking rubber contraption was hot and uncomfortable, but crucial to survival. The soldier's steel helmet, as you can see, extended to the top of the ear line. The helmet was designed to help prevent head wounds. A soldier was particularly vulnerable to such injuries when he first peered out from a trench—just before going "over the top."

Next look at a soldier's vital "mess" equipment. The oval "meat can" served as both a skillet and a plate. Sturdy metal containers protected two days' worth of rations from rain, rats, and insects. A doughboy carried two portions of hard biscuits called hardtack. The condiment can had separate compartments for coffee, sugar, and salt. Above the condiment can is a bacon tin. In addition to such supplies, a soldier carried emergency rations such as stringy beef, scornfully called "monkey

meat" by many soldiers. From this mess equipment and the simple nature of the rations, we can assume that a doughboy's supply lines were within a short distance of each squad. More-substantial meals were prepared by a company cook, who followed the combat units.

In addition to the items shown here, an infantryman carried a tent, tent poles, a rain poncho, a bayonet, a blanket, a sewing kit, socks, identification tags, a compass, and a flashlight. On a long march a World War I soldier might have cursed his heavy pack. But he also knew his burden could mean the difference between life and death.

▲ **Field kit**

◀ **Bacon tin**

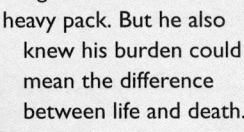

◀ **Condiment can**

▲ **Meat can**

DRUDGERY AND DISCOMFORT

Fully loaded, a doughboy's field kit, including his uniform, weighed between 70 and 90 pounds. U.S. soldiers wore heavy woolen uniforms in every season. Bulky winter overcoats, when drenched by the rain, added even more weight to a soldier's burden.

LINK TO TODAY

Suggest that students make a list of all the items shown on these pages and described in the feature. Ask them to identify items that are probably still necessary for soldiers today. (*shovel, helmet, canteen, gas mask, tent, poncho*)

THINKING CRITICALLY

Ask students if they think certain weapons used in warfare can be regarded as humane or moral while others are immoral. Then ask students if they see any contradiction in this idea, pointing out that most offensive weapons are designed to kill one's opponents.

Teaching the Section

AMERICAN CONTRIBUTIONS TO VICTORY

Ask students to imagine that they are journalists covering the war for an American newspaper. Direct them to write a commentary on American contributions to the Allied victory. The commentary should be titled "Could the Allies Have Won the War Without Us?" Ask volunteers to read their commentaries to the class. Students may wish to include their commentaries in their portfolios.

▲ Ambulance drivers were responsible for transporting wounded soldiers from the battlefield to hospitals behind the front lines. Many of the ambulance units included women drivers and mechanics.

Thousands more American women went to Europe as volunteers for the Red Cross, the YMCA, or other agencies.

Merchant vessels, escorted by American warships, transported troops, supplies, and volunteers through the submarine-infested North Atlantic. This **convoy system** proved quite effective. Of the more than two million American soldiers who crossed the Atlantic, not one died as the result of an enemy attack on the high seas. Other American warships patrolled the western Atlantic and laid some 70,000 mines in a lethal 240-mile necklace across the North Sea from Norway to the Orkney Islands off Great Britain. This barrier made life hazardous for German U-boats trying to return to their bases.

THE END OF THE WAR

The Americans' entry into the war came none too soon for the Allies. In an effort to break the deadlock on the western front, the Allies had launched an offensive in the summer of 1917. It failed, shattering the Allied troops' already shaky morale. That fall, mutinies broke out in French units all along the front. In October the Central Powers crashed through Italian lines at Caporetto, on the border between Italy and Austria-Hungary (see map on page 588). Only the arrival of Allied reinforcements saved Italy from collapse.

Worse news arrived from Russia. The Russian people, dissatisfied with working and living conditions, had overthrown the czar in March 1917. Political turmoil continued until November, when the **Bolsheviks**, a branch of the Russian Communist party, seized power. The Bolshevik leader, Vladimir Ilich Lenin, opposed the war. The Bolsheviks signed the **Treaty of Brest-Litovsk** with the Central Powers in March 1918, leaving the Central Powers free to mass their forces on the western front.

Germany's last bid for victory. On March 21, 1918, some one million German troops launched a do-or-die offensive against the Allies. The Germans were backed by some 6,000 heavy guns, including "Big Berthas" capable of firing 250- to 300-pound shells 74 miles. By late May the Germans had pushed the Allies back to the Marne River, only 50 miles from Paris.

General Pershing had originally insisted that American troops fight as a separate army under their own commanders. In light of the situation, however, he agreed to join a unified Allied army under the command of Marshal Ferdinand Foch of France. The introduction of American forces proved decisive. In a last-ditch defense of Paris, American troops helped the French stop the Germans at Château-Thierry on June 3–4. Nearby, a division of American marines counterattacked, recapturing Belleau Wood and two other villages. After fierce fighting, the German advance was halted, and Paris was saved.

On July 15 the Germans threw everything into a final assault around Reims. But the Allied lines held, and Foch ordered a counterattack three days later. The charge, spearheaded by American

Practice

GUIDED PRACTICE

Create a chalkboard chart titled *Aiding the Allies* and list the following items in its left column: *Robert Lansing, National Defense Act, Selective Service Act, American Expeditionary Force, John Pershing,* and *Convoy System.* Ask volunteers to explain how each entry aided the Allies' cause and record their responses in the chart's right column.

INDEPENDENT PRACTICE

Ask students to select the entry from the Guided Practice chart that they think was most important in aiding the Allies. Then direct students to write a paragraph explaining their choice.

Review and Assessment

REVIEW Organize students in small groups to create a four-page pictorial essay titled "The United States and World War I: 1915–1918." Have groups present and explain their essays to the class. Then assign the Section 2 Review on p. 600.

ASSESS Assign the **Section 2 Daily Quiz** in *Core Resources.*

▶

---

troops, pushed the Germans back. The tide had turned in favor of the Allies.

▪▪ With the assistance of American troops, the Allies turned the tide against the Germans.

Allied victory. In the late summer Foch seized the initiative, ordering a major offensive along the entire western front. Over the next three months, the Allies pushed deep into German-held territory.

In this offensive the Americans fought as a separate army under Pershing's command and led the attack that pushed the Germans back at Saint-Mihiel, France, in September 1918. The Americans next drove toward Sedan, the French rail center that the Germans had held since 1914. For more than a month the Americans pushed northward along the

Meuse River and through the rugged Argonne Forest, facing artillery and machine-gun fire all the way. The Americans suffered some 120,000 casualties on this drive, but by November they had reached and occupied the hills around Sedan.

Lieutenant Edward Graham was one of the casualties. By the time he died, he no longer saw the war as a noble venture. In his last letter he described it as incomprehensible:

❝ This is a cowering war—pigmy man huddles in little holes and caves praying to escape the blows of the giant who pounds the earth with blind hammers. ❞

African American troops played a major role in the Argonne offensive. Members of the 369th Infantry, an African American regiment whose men hailed from New York, so distinguished

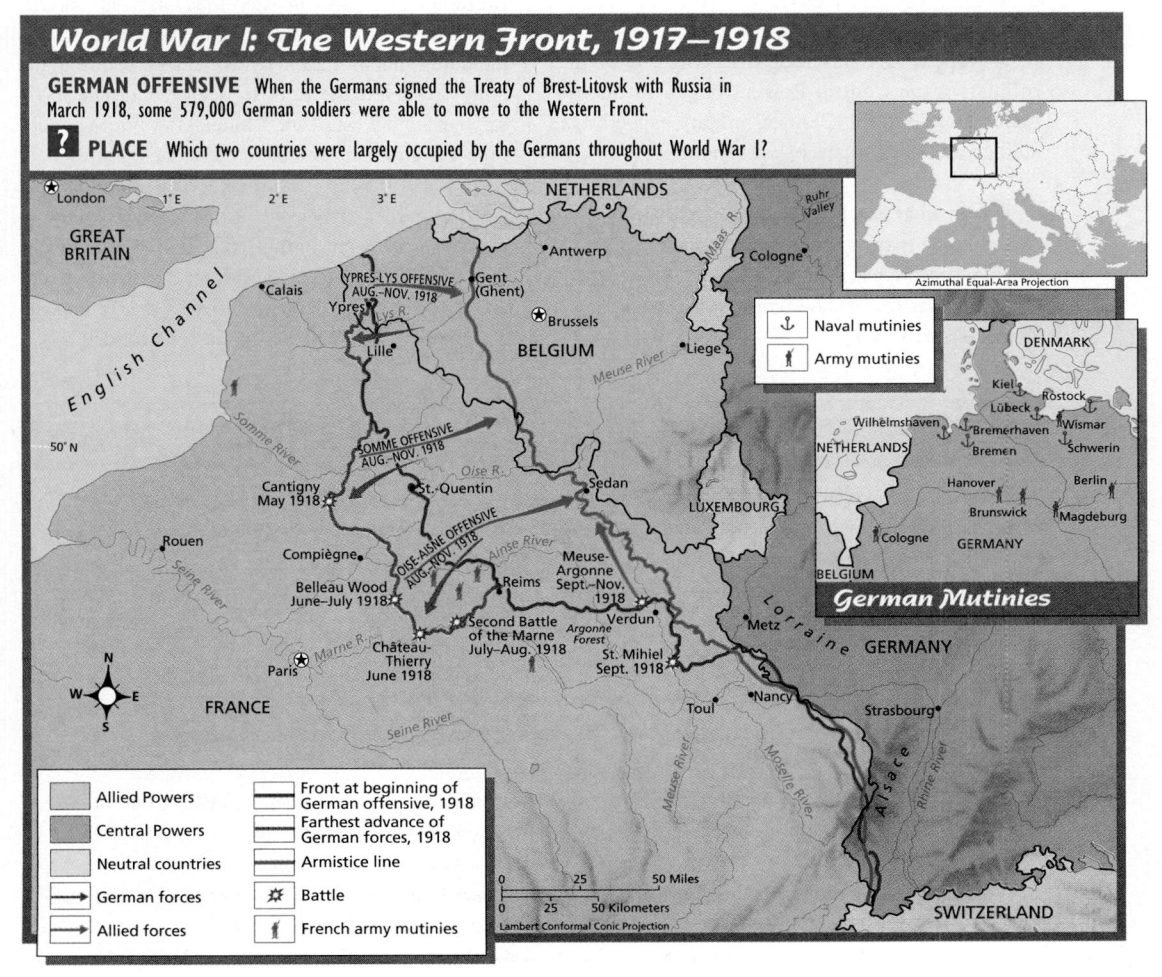

World War I: The Western Front, 1917–1918

GERMAN OFFENSIVE When the Germans signed the Treaty of Brest-Litovsk with Russia in March 1918, some 579,000 German soldiers were able to move to the Western Front.

? **PLACE** Which two countries were largely occupied by the Germans throughout World War I?

Legend:
- Allied Powers
- Central Powers
- Neutral countries
- German forces
- Allied forces
- Front at beginning of German offensive, 1918
- Farthest advance of German forces, 1918
- Armistice line
- Battle
- French army mutinies
- Naval mutinies
- Army mutinies

German Mutinies

AV TRANSPARENCY
Everyday Life in America Transparency and **Worksheet 20**

PRIMARY SOURCE
Description of Change: excerpted
Rationale: excerpted to focus on main idea

Map Caption Answer
Belgium and France

HISTORICAL SIDELIGHTS
The Air War
While ground troops grimly struggled for territory yard by yard, the air forces engaged in spectacular aerial "dogfights" high overhead. The U.S. Army Air Service boasted a number of pilots called "aces." The most famous of these was Eddie Rickenbacker. An auto racer who had driven several times in the Indianapolis 500, Rickenbacker began the war as a driver attached to General Pershing's staff. Flying a French-built Spad 13, a wood-and-fabric plane with a top speed of over 200 miles per hour, Rickenbacker shot down 26 German planes.

AV TRANSPARENCY
Linking Geography and History Transparency and **Worksheet 16**

RETEACH Ask students, working in pairs, to write sentences that explain how each entry in the Preview Workshop relates to the main idea of the subsection in which it is located. Have pairs share their sentences with the group.

Closure

Direct students to create an annotated time line showing the 10 major events of American involvement in World War I. Call on volunteers to present their time lines and justify their choice of events.

Extension

COMPARE Students may wish to examine why it is difficult for a country to remain neutral in time of war. Suggest that they compare the events leading up to the War of 1812 with the process by which the U.S. was drawn into World War I.

RESEARCH Have students research and report on the contributions of African Americans or women to the AEF during World War I.

PRIMARY SOURCE

Description of Change: excerpted
Rationale: excerpted to focus on main idea

SECTION REVIEW ANSWERS

IDENTIFY

For significance, see the following pages:
Sussex pledge (p. 593)
Robert Lansing (p. 594)
National Defense Act (p. 594)
Zimmermann Note (p. 594)
Jeannette Rankin (p. 594)
Selective Service Act (p. 595)
John J. Pershing (p. 596)
convoy system (p. 598)
Bolsheviks (p. 598)
Treaty of Brest-Litovsk
  (p. 598)
Ferdinand Foch (p. 598)
armistice (p. 600)

LOCATE

For locations, see the maps on pp. 588 and 599.

1. U-boat activity, interception of Zimmermann Note
2. to bring the military to full strength so the Allies would have urgently needed fresh troops
3. Students may cite racial discrimination and harassment, segregated units, restricted opportunity in armed forces.
4. Memos might mention influx of American warships, troops, and supplies in helping the Allies.
5. U.S. might not have been provoked to enter the war, and so Allies might have been defeated.

▲ **The armistice ending the war was signed in this railway passenger car on November 11, 1918.**

themselves that the French awarded them the *Croix de Guerre* (kwahd i GER), or "Cross of War," a French military honor.

Repeatedly hammered during the Allied offensive, the Central Powers began to disintegrate. Morale in the German military sagged. One soldier, anxious for peace, wrote home:

 In what way have we sinned, that we should be treated worse than animals? Hunted from place to place, cold, filthy . . . we are destroyed like vermin. Will they *never* make peace? "

Mutinies broke out in both the German army and navy. German civilians took to the streets demanding food, not war. Realizing that the war was lost, Wilhelm II fled to the Netherlands in early November. The following day, Germany's new government agreed to an **armistice**, or cease-fire.

On November 8, 1918, German representatives were summoned to Compiègne (kohmp-YAYN), the Allied headquarters, to hear the armistice terms. The Allies demanded that the Germans evacuate France, Belgium, Luxembourg, and Alsace-Lorraine. They also insisted that Germany surrender an enormous amount of war materials, including much of their naval fleet. In addition, the Allies reserved the right to occupy German territory east and west of the Rhine. After brief negotiations the Germans agreed to these harsh terms.

Early on the morning of November 11, the warring parties signed the armistice, and at 11 A.M. the cease-fire went into effect. The constant crashing of guns was replaced, according to one American, by a "silence [that] was nearly unbearable." The Great War, at long last, had ended.

SECTION 2 REVIEW

IDENTIFY and explain the significance of the following: *Sussex* pledge, Robert Lansing, National Defense Act, Zimmermann Note, Jeannette Rankin, Selective Service Act, John J. Pershing, convoy system, Bolsheviks, Treaty of Brest-Litovsk, Ferdinand Foch, armistice.

LOCATE and explain the importance of the following: Caporetto, Château-Thierry, St. Mihiel, Sedan, Meuse River, Compiègne.

1. **MAIN IDEA** What actions provoked the United States to declare war on Germany?

2. **MAIN IDEA** Why did the United States pass the Selective Service Act?

3. **ANALYZING** What evidence suggests that conscription did not make America more democratic?

4. **WRITING TO INFORM** Imagine you are Secretary of State Robert Lansing. Write a memorandum to President Wilson that summarizes the effect the American entry into the war had on Allied efforts.

5. **HYPOTHESIZING** How might the war in Europe have been different if Germany had abandoned U-boat warfare?

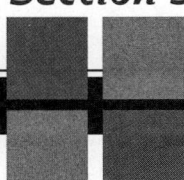

PREVIEW WORKSHOP

Following is a list of the significant people and terms in this section. You may wish to use this list as a section preview.

People
- William McAdoo
- Herbert Hoover
- Bernard Baruch
- Carrie Chapman Catt
- Harriot Stanton Blatch
- Victor Berger

Terms
- Food Administration
- Fuel Administration
- Railroad Administration
- War Industries Board
- National War Labor Board
- Great Migration
- Committee on Public Information
- Espionage Act
- Sedition Act

Section 3

THE WAR AT HOME

FOCUS OBJECTIVES

- List the steps taken by the federal government to mobilize the economy for war.

- Describe how the labor force changed during the war.

- Explain how the government stifled dissent and rallied support for its wartime policies.

F O C U S

- **What steps did the federal government take to mobilize the economy for war?**
- **How did the labor force change during the war?**
- **How did the government stifle dissent and rally support for its wartime policies?**

Once the United States entered the war, President Wilson quickly moved to mobilize the nation. The government set up programs to finance the war, to conserve scarce resources, and to redirect industry and labor toward wartime production. Wilson also launched a huge propaganda campaign to mobilize support for the war effort. But as the government whipped up enthusiasm for the war, intolerance of antiwar opinion spread across the land.

Irving Berlin song sheet, 1918

MOBILIZING THE ECONOMY

At the outset of the war, Wilson had noted that "there are no armies in this struggle; there are entire nations armed." To "arm" the nation, Wilson realized, the economy had to be put on a wartime footing.

The first step in this process was raising money to pay for the war, which eventually cost Americans more than $33 billion. The government raised money through four Liberty Bond issues during the war and one Victory Bond issue after the armistice. Posters, parades, and rallies promoted each bond issue. "Every person who refuses to subscribe . . . is a friend of Germany," declared William McAdoo, secretary of treasury and Wilson's son-in-law, and "is not entitled to be an American citizen." With pressure like this behind them, these promotions were a huge success, raising some $23 billion for the war.

The government also planned to raise money by increasing taxes. This proved more difficult than selling bonds. Congress debated a new tax program for months, finally reaching agreement in October 1917. The new taxes on business incomes and large personal incomes produced about $9 billion for the war—much less than expected.

Mobilizing the economy for war entailed more than raising money, however. It also involved coordinating the actions of government, business,

▲ Movie stars Douglas Fairbanks, Mary Pickford, and Charlie Chaplin lent their support to a Liberty Bond drive in Philadelphia.

CULTURAL PATTERNS

Many African Americans readily subscribed to Liberty Bond drives, even if they had little money to spare. In 1917, for example, bond drives among African American soldiers raised about $800,000. As historians Arthur E. Barbeau and Florette Henri noted, African Americans willingly bought bonds because "*Liberty* was a beautiful word to [people] only a generation removed from slavery."

CORE RESOURCES

- **Social Studies Skills Worksheet 20**
- **Section 3 Daily Quiz**

Ask students what actions they think would be necessary to prepare the nation to fight a war. Then ask how each action might affect daily life. List their answers on a flip chart. As students read the section, have them compare their responses to the nation's World War I experiences.

Teaching the Section

BOND RALLIES

Have students work in small groups to write a "You Are There" newscast of a war bond rally. Newscasts should include descriptions of the activities as well as interviews with celebrities supporting the rally and with Americans planning to buy bonds. Then invite group members to "broadcast" their newscasts to the class.

MOBILIZING THE ECONOMY

Organize students into groups of four or five. Tell groups that they are President Wilson's economic advisory panel, which has been charged with drawing up a plan to prepare the nation's economy for wartime. Suggest that they divide their plan into three parts—raising money, organizing resources, and organizing industry and labor. Then call on groups to present and explain their plans to the class.

HISTORICAL SIDELIGHTS

Conservation Tactics

To get Hoover's conservation message across to the American people, about 500,000 Food Administration representatives went door to door, handing homemakers cards that requested their cooperation in conserving food.

HISTORICAL SIDELIGHTS

No Idle Threat

Government intimidation to gain wartime cooperation was not limited to the steel industry. During a difficult meeting with automobile executives, Bernard Baruch telephoned the head of the government's Railroad Administration and, within earshot of the executives, asked him to "take down the names of the following factories, and I want you to stop every wheel going in and out." The executives quickly accepted Baruch's suggestions.

and industry. This was done through a multitude of federal war boards. While the federal government never took complete control of the economy, it exercised sweeping economic power through these various agencies. It set the prices and production levels of hundreds of commodities and regulated businesses crucial to the war effort.

CONSERVING FOOD AND FUEL

Among the most successful of the federal war boards were the **Food Administration** and the **Fuel Administration**, which were charged with regulating the production and supply of these essential resources. To direct the Food Administration, Wilson chose Herbert Hoover, a prosperous mining engineer who had managed a food-relief campaign for war-stricken Belgium. Hoover saw his task as twofold: to encourage increased agricultural production and to conserve existing food supplies.

To stimulate wartime production, Hoover guaranteed farmers high prices. Farm production soared. For example, farmers upped wheat production, harvesting some 921 million bushels in 1919—a dramatic increase over the 1917 figure of some 637 million bushels.

Announcing that "food will win the war," Hoover called on Americans to reduce their food consumption by observing wheatless and meatless days. To supplement their diets,

▲ **Herbert Hoover, director of the Food Administration**

he suggested they plant "victory gardens" filled with vegetables. The campaign proved very effective—without, as Hoover proudly noted, forced rationing.

The Fuel Administration director, Harry Garfield, the son of the former president, took a similar course of action, encouraging people to observe heatless Mondays. Garfield was not averse to using force, however. When the nation ran short of coal in early 1918, he closed all factories east of the Mississippi for several days.

ORGANIZING INDUSTRY

Hundreds of other boards and agencies regulated industrial production and distribution. For example, the **Railroad Administration**, run by William McAdoo, reorganized the railroads, setting limits on transportation rates and workers' wages.

The work of all these boards was coordinated by the government's central war agency, the **War Industries Board** (WIB). Its director, Wall Street banker Bernard Baruch, had overall responsibility for allocating scarce materials, establishing production priorities, and setting prices. Baruch preferred to persuade business leaders to comply with his wishes. However, when steel owners refused to cut prices, the government threatened to take over their foundries and mills.

At first many business leaders were critical of Wilson's economic mobilization programs. Government intervention, they argued, would permanently damage the American free-enterprise system. As profits soared, however, they ceased to complain.

■■ **The government mobilized for war by setting up programs to raise money, conserve scarce resources, and coordinate government, business, and industry.**

MOBILIZING LABOR

Organized labor moved quickly to gain its share of wartime prosperity. With hundreds of thousands of men drafted into the army and with European immigration slowed to a trickle, industry found itself desperately short of labor as it geared up for the war effort. Taking advantage of this situation, unionized workers across the country went on strike, demanding higher wages and other benefits. Nearly 4,500 strikes involving more than one million workers occurred in 1917 alone. The tactic worked—over the war years, working conditions substantially improved.

To ensure that the voice of labor received a hearing, President Wilson established the **National War Labor Board** (NWLB) in April 1918. Composed of representatives from business and labor, the NWLB arbitrated disputes between workers and employers. In the more than 1,200

THE WARTIME LABOR FORCE

Write the following on the chalkboard, leaving space between each: *Unionization, Women, Immigration,* and *Migration.* Ask volunteers to explain how each of these elements was a factor in creating a wartime labor force. Write a summary of their explanations below the appropriate heading. Then ask students to use the chalkboard information to write a summary paragraph about changes that occurred in the American labor force during World War I. Students may wish to include their paragraphs in their portfolios.

SHAPING PUBLIC OPINION

Conduct class referenda on the creation of the Committee on Public Information and on the passage of the Espionage Act and the Sedition Act. Before each vote, ask volunteers to explain each item and have students discuss whether it is appropriate and necessary in order to rally public support for the war. When the referenda are complete, call on students to explain and defend their votes.

▶

▲ Many American women helped the war effort by working in munitions factories and other industries. Here, a woman loads cartridges for rifles.

cases that it heard, the board ruled in favor of labor more often than not. In this climate of official support, union membership grew rapidly. AFL membership, for instance, rose from some 2 million in 1916 to roughly 3.2 million by 1919. By the end of the decade, some 15 percent of the nonagricultural work force was unionized.

The labor shortage that helped strengthen unions also brought about changes in the work force. The number of women working outside the home grew by about 6 percent during the war. Many of these women took traditionally male jobs. They worked as automobile mechanics, truck drivers, bricklayers, metalworkers, or railroad engineers. In all, some 1.5 million American women worked in industry during the war. Like Norma B. Kastl, an interviewer with a women's service bureau, many women considered employment their patriotic duty:

❝ The navy is taking on women as yeomen to do shore duty. . . . Every girl that becomes a yeoman can have the satisfaction of knowing that she is releasing, as from prison, some sailor who had been fuming . . . because he had to spend his days in an office instead of on the deck of a destroyer. ❞

Women also helped plan wartime mobilization. Carrie Chapman Catt, a women's suffrage leader, sat on the Women's Committee of the Council of National Defense, a civilian agency organized to support the war effort. Harriot Stanton Blatch, the daughter of Elizabeth Cady Stanton, headed the Food Administration's Speakers' Bureau.

Women's war efforts helped produce one very important political change—the passage of the Nineteenth Amendment. President Wilson, who had wavered on woman suffrage, threw his support behind the amendment in recognition of women's wartime contributions. "The greatest thing that came out of the war," Carrie Chapman Catt later noted, "was the emancipation of women, for which no man fought."

THE GREAT TREK NORTH

The labor shortage that drew women into the work force also spurred immigration from Mexico. Fleeing the Mexican Revolution and lured by southwestern employers who depended on Mexican labor, some 150,000 men and women migrated from Mexico to the United States during the war. Most took agricultural, mining, or railroad jobs in Arizona, California, Colorado, New Mexico, or Texas. But some headed northward for better-paying jobs in such industrial centers as Chicago and Cleveland.

Job opportunities and the prospect of higher wages also brought about one of the most important population shifts in American history—the **Great Migration** of African Americans from the South to northern cities between 1915 and 1930. Persuaded by recruitment agents sent by the Pennsylvania Railroad and other large employers, hundreds of thousands of African Americans moved northward during the war years (estimates range from 200,000 to 550,000). African American newspapers strongly encouraged the migration: "Get out of the South," declared an editorial in the Chicago *Defender.* "Come north . . . The *Defender* says come."

▪▪ **The wartime labor shortage brought large numbers of women, Mexican immigrants, and African Americans into the work force.**

HISTORICAL SIDELIGHTS

The Volunteer Spirit
African American women who wanted to support the war effort by helping the troops in Europe faced a roadblock of prejudice. Many African American nurses expressed their readiness to serve at the front. The Red Cross, however, ignored their offer. Even so, some evidence suggests that perhaps 300 African American nurses served in battlefield hospitals.

PRIMARY SOURCE

Description of Change: excerpted
Rationale: excerpted to focus on main idea

Practice

GUIDED PRACTICE

Create on the chalkboard a chart titled *Organizing the Home Front*. Ask volunteers to identify actions taken to mobilize the home front to fight World War I. Ask other students to explain the consequences of each action as you record their responses.

INDEPENDENT PRACTICE

Tell students to choose an action from the Guided Practice chart and to write a newspaper editorial about it. Editorials should first explain the action to readers and then either support or challenge it as vital to America's war effort. Students may wish to include their editorials in their portfolios.

Review and Assessment

REVIEW Have students work in small groups to draw up plans for a nonfiction book on the American home front during World War I. Suggest that they include the following: a table of contents and brief descriptions of maps, charts, graphs, and other illustrations. Then assign the Section 3 Review on p. 605.

ASSESS Assign the **Section 3 Daily Quiz** in *Core Resources*.

▲ National guardsmen were called in to preserve the peace during the East St. Louis race riot in July 1917.

African Americans went to the North with great hope. But for many, life in the North proved harsh. Although they enjoyed a better standard of living than they had in the South, racial violence remained a serious problem. The most brutal wartime racial incident occurred in East St. Louis, Illinois, on July 2, 1917. White rioters—egged on by spectators—rampaged through black neighborhoods in an orgy of burning and shooting that left at least 39 dead. Shocked and angered, many African Americans asked themselves why they should fight for freedom in Europe when they enjoyed so little at home.

Mobilizing Attitudes

Many Americans—for religious, political, or personal reasons—believed that the United States should have stayed out of the conflict. President Wilson, who wanted all Americans to support the war effort, established the **Committee on Public Information** (CPI) in the spring of 1917. Headed by George Creel, a progressive journalist, the CPI waged a vigorous propaganda campaign to sell the war to Americans.

At first much of the material that the CPI put out was based on fact but censored to present an upbeat picture of the war. Very quickly, however, the CPI began churning out raw propaganda, picturing the Germans as evil monsters. Hollywood joined in, producing movies such as *The Claws of the Hun, The Prussian Cur,* and *The Kaiser, the Beast of Berlin.* These titles vividly illustrate the message the CPI tried to convey.

CPI pamphlets warned citizens to be on the lookout for German spies. Dozens of "patriotic organizations," with names like the American Protective League and the American Defense Society, sprang up. These groups spied, tapped telephones, and opened mail in an effort to ferret out "spies and traitors."

These groups targeted almost anyone who called for peace, questioned the Allies' progress, or criticized the government's policies. They were particularly hard on German Americans, many of whom lost their jobs. Sometimes this anti-German sentiment took absurd turns. German books vanished from library shelves, schools stopped teaching German language courses, and German music disappeared from concert programs. People even renamed German-sounding items: sauerkraut became liberty cabbage, dachshunds became liberty pups, and hamburger became Salisbury steak.

Vigilantes publicly humiliated people of German heritage by forcing them to kiss the flag, recite the Pledge of Allegiance, or buy war bonds. Sometimes the vigilantes turned violent. In March 1918 John H. Wintherbotham, a midwestern representative for the government's Council of National Defense, reported:

66 All over this part of the country men are being tarred and feathered and some are being lynched. . . . These cases do not get into the newspapers nor is an effort

◄ Wartime posters inspired people to purchase savings stamps for their country.

ever made to punish the individuals concerned. In fact, as a rule, it has the complete backing of public opinion. 🙶🙶

SUPPRESSING DISSENT

Even in this hysterical atmosphere, some Americans continued to oppose the war. Quaker and Mennonite men, committed by faith to nonviolence, refused to take up arms. Considered traitors by many Americans, they faced violence and abuse.

Pacifists like Congresswoman Jeannette Rankin, Senator Robert La Follette, and settlement-house leader Jane Addams never stopped calling for peace. But such declarations held little sway with Wilson, who heaped contempt on the pacifists for their "stupidity."

The Socialist party, too, proclaimed its unalterable opposition to the war. To most party members, the war used the laboring masses as cannon fodder in a capitalist struggle for control of world markets. The Industrial Workers of the World (IWW), the radical labor union, had a similar view of the war and led strikes in a number of war-related industries.

To silence dissenters, Congress passed the **Espionage Act** in June 1917 and the **Sedition Act** a year later. These measures not only outlawed acts of treason but also made it a crime to "utter, print, write, or publish any disloyal . . . or abusive language" criticizing the government, the flag, or the military. Opposition to the draft, to war-bond drives, or to the arms industry also became a crime.

■■ **The Committee on Public Information rallied support for the war, while the Espionage and Sedition acts crushed antiwar dissent.**

More than 1,000 people—including some 200 members of the IWW—were convicted of violating these laws. Victor Berger, a Socialist congressman from Wisconsin, received a 20-year sentence for publishing antiwar articles in his newspaper, the Milwaukee *Leader*. The Socialist party leader Eugene V. Debs went to prison for 10 years for making a speech against the war.

Many Americans, even some who supported the war, believed that the Espionage and Sedition acts violated the First Amendment. The Supreme Court, however, disagreed. In the landmark case *Schenck* v. *United States* (1919), Justice Oliver Wendell Holmes wrote:

🙶🙶 The question . . . is whether the words used are used in such circumstances and are of such a nature as to create a clear and present danger. . . . When a nation is at war many things that might be said in time of peace . . . will not be endured [and] no Court could regard them as protected by any constitutional right. 🙶🙶

This decision was meant to apply to extraordinary circumstances like war. Unfortunately, intolerance of unpopular ideas continued long after the war had ended.

■■ **S E C T I O N   3   R E V I E W**

IDENTIFY and explain the significance of the following: William McAdoo, Food Administration, Fuel Administration, Herbert Hoover, Railroad Administration, War Industries Board, Bernard Baruch, National War Labor Board, Carrie Chapman Catt, Harriot Stanton Blatch, Great Migration, Committee on Public Information, Espionage Act, Sedition Act, Victor Berger.

1. **MAIN IDEA** How did the U.S. government mobilize the economy for war?
2. **MAIN IDEA** What effect did wartime labor shortage have on the work force?
3. **MAIN IDEA** What steps did the government take to shape and control public opinion during the war?
4. **WRITING TO EXPLAIN** Imagine you are an American opposed to the war. Write a newspaper editorial, outlining your reasons for opposing the Committee on Public Information.
5. **EVALUATING** Do you think the U.S. government was justified in taking control of the economy during the war? Why or why not?

FOCUS OBJECTIVES

■ Identify the two major
issues addressed by
Wilson's peace plan.

■ Explain why Wilson was
forced to compromise
on his Fourteen Points.

■ Determine why the
Senate rejected the
Treaty of Versailles.

■ Evaluate the impact of
the war on Europe and
on the Middle East.

PREVIEW WORKSHOP

*Following is a list of the significant
people, places, and terms in this
section. You may wish to use this
list as a section preview.*

People
■ Vittorio Orlando
■ David Lloyd George
■ Georges Clemenceau
■ Henry Cabot Lodge

Places
■ Czechoslovakia
■ Yugoslavia
■ Finland
■ Estonia
■ Latvia
■ Lithuania
■ Poland
■ Saar

Terms
■ Fourteen Points
■ self-determination
■ Big Four
■ reparations
■ Treaty of Versailles
■ mandate system
■ irreconcilables
■ reservationists
■ Balfour Declaration

Section 4

THE LEAGUE OF NATIONS

F O C U S
■ **What two major issues did Wilson's peace plan address?**
■ **Why was Wilson forced to compromise on his Fourteen Points?**
■ **Why did the Senate reject the Treaty of Versailles?**
■ **What impact did the war have on Europe and the Middle East?**

*P*resident Wilson developed a program for a just peace
even before the war ended. This program served as the
focus of the Paris Peace Conference in 1919. Wilson had to
compromise on many of the points, but the final treaty
included the heart of his peace program—the League of
Nations. The U.S. Senate, however, rejected the treaty.
Without American membership, the League of Nations
proved inadequate to solve the world's postwar problems.

Versailles, site of peace-treaty signing

WILSON'S FOURTEEN POINTS

News of the armistice on November 11, 1918, set
off a joyful celebration in the United States.
Wilson shared the people's great happiness at the
Allied victory, but he knew that the task of forging
a just peace lay ahead.

This challenge had long been on Wilson's
mind. Late in 1917 he had invited a group of
scholars to advise him on peace terms. Drawing
from their work, Wilson had developed a program
for world peace, which he had presented to
Congress on January 8, 1918. He called his program the **Fourteen Points** because it contained 14
points, or principles.

Nine of the points dealt with the
issue of **self-determination**—the right
of people to govern themselves—and
with the various territorial disputes
created by the war. Other points
focused on what Wilson considered the
causes of modern war: secret diplomacy, the arms race, violations of freedom of the seas, and trade barriers. But
the final point—the establishment of
the League of Nations—was the heart
of Wilson's program.

◄ **Jubilant Americans celebrate
Armistice Day in Washington, D.C.,
in 1918.**

Teaching the Section

WILSON'S PEACE PLAN

Choose a student to read aloud the excerpt on p. 594 from Wilson's speech of April 1917. Have a volunteer list his principles for a just peace as expressed in the excerpt. Ask other students to explain how Wilson's Fourteen Points addressed each of these principles. Then have the class examine the provisions of the treaty and compare them with his principles. Conclude by asking why Wilson was forced to compromise on his Fourteen Points.

■■ In his peace plan Wilson aimed to settle territorial disputes and to end the causes of modern war.

Congress and the American public warmly received the Fourteen Points. The reaction of the Allies, however, proved lukewarm. Moreover, the German government, labeling Wilson an "American busybody," rejected the program.

However, as the war turned against them, the Germans sued for a peace settlement based on the Fourteen Points. Wilson had to push and prod the Allies, but they eventually agreed. After the armistice a peace conference was set for January 1919 in Paris. To make sure that the talks focused on his peace program, Wilson attended the conference.

THE PARIS PEACE CONFERENCE

On December 4, 1918, Wilson boarded the *George Washington* for his precedent-setting trip to Europe—he was the first president to cross the Atlantic while in office. As the ship steamed out of New York harbor, a huge crowd gave Wilson a rousing send-off. His reception at the French port of Brest some nine days later proved no less enthusiastic. And on a triumphal tour through France, Britain, and Italy, people welcomed him as a conquering hero. Elated by the cheering throngs, Wilson convinced himself that he had a mandate to shape the peace according to the Fourteen Points.

While Wilson and his fellow leaders gathered to discuss peace, the world was far from peaceful. Across central and eastern Europe, various ethnic groups, now liberated from Austro-Hungarian or Russian rule, clashed over territory. Defeated, Germany teetered on the brink of civil war. In Russia, Bolsheviks fought off the czarists' challenge. The Allied powers—including America—had become entangled in the Russian conflict, sending troops to support the czarists' effort to overthrow the Bolsheviks.

The other delegates at the conference refused to let Wilson dictate the peace terms. Italy's prime minister, Vittorio Orlando, came to Paris only to make sure his nation got the territories it had been promised on entering the war in 1915. David Lloyd George, Britain's prime minister, had just won an election with such slogans as "Hang the Kaiser." He had no intention of showing generosity

▲ Pictured here are David Lloyd George of England, Italian foreign minister Naron Sonnino, Georges Clemenceau of France, and Woodrow Wilson of the United States.

toward the Germans or of giving up Britain's naval supremacy by accepting Wilson's idea of "freedom of the seas."

The French premier, Georges Clemenceau, wanted to ensure France's security by crushing Germany. Distrustful of Wilson's idealism, Clemenceau growled: "God gave us his Ten Commandments, and we broke them. Wilson gave us his Fourteen Points—we shall see."

As the conference opened on January 18, 1919, Wilson expressed great enthusiasm for the task ahead. But the demands of the other members of the **Big Four**—as Wilson, Orlando, Lloyd George, and Clemenceau became known—soon wore Wilson down. The others insisted that Germany bear the financial cost of the war by making huge payments, called **reparations**, to the Allies. They also wanted several secret spoils-of-war treaties honored. Such demands violated practically every one of the points of President Wilson's peace plan.

Wilson had two options: he could either compromise or walk out. Indeed, at one point he ordered the *George Washington* to stand by to return him to the United States. But he realized that leaving would be an admission of failure. He also feared that without a comprehensive peace agreement, the Bolshevik Revolution might spread from Russia into the already politically unstable regions of central and eastern Europe. More than anything else, however, he wanted to see the creation of the League of Nations. The League, he

HISTORICAL SIDELIGHTS
The Tiger

Perhaps the most formidable member of the Big Four was French premier Georges Clemenceau. At age 78, Clemenceau still commanded fear and respect, as his nickname, "the Tiger," indicated. He had begun his political career in the early 1870s, during the Franco-Prussian War. France's humiliating defeat in that conflict was seared into his memory, and he made no secret that he intended to use the Versailles conference to get revenge on Germany.

HISTORICAL SIDELIGHTS
Against Reparations

A British newspaper's demand that Germany "pay [reparations] until the pips squeak" echoed the sentiments of a majority of people in Europe. Yet one voice against this course of action was British economist John Maynard Keynes. In his book *The Economic Consequences of the Peace* (1919), Keynes argued that, first and foremost, the devastated economies of Europe had to be rebuilt. Forcing Germany to pay reparations, he maintained, would only delay that work.

Teaching the Section

THE SENATE REJECTS THE TREATY

Organize students into groups to role-play President Wilson, Senator Lodge, and a news reporter who has brought them together on a radio program. Tell each reporter to interview the president and the senator about their positions on the Treaty of Versailles and to explore possibilities for compromise. Select groups to re-create their interviews for the class. Then discuss the roles that principle and compromise play in resolving conflict, using the treaty issue as an example.

■■ Ask students to describe how the ability to compromise might affect family, school, and peer relationships.

---

believed, would remedy any injustices the treaty might contain. Wilson stayed on.

■■ **Allied demands that Germany pay war damages and that secret treaties be honored forced Wilson to compromise.**

THE TREATY OF VERSAILLES

After six months of debate, the delegates agreed to a peace treaty. The official signing of the **Treaty of Versailles** took place in the magnificent palace of Versailles, just outside Paris, on June 28, 1919. Publicly, the American delegation expressed satisfaction with the document. In private, however, they voiced a different opinion. Secretary of State Robert Lansing confided that he felt "disappointment, . . . regret, and . . . depression." He continued:

66 The terms of peace appear immeasurably harsh and humiliating. . . . Resentment and bitterness, if not desperation, are bound to be the consequences of such provisions. . . . We have a treaty of peace, but it will not bring permanent peace because it is founded on the shifting sands of self-interest. 99

According to the treaty, Germany's colonies and the Ottoman Empire (Turkey) were divided among the Allied nations, as specified in the spoils-of-war treaties. At Wilson's insistence, however, the treaty established a **mandate system** that required the new colonial rulers to report on their administration to the League of Nations. To satisfy nationalist longings in central and eastern Europe, the peace treaty also created the new nations of Czechoslovakia and Yugoslavia. (Finland, Estonia, Latvia, Lithuania, and Poland also emerged from the war as independent nations—Poland after nearly 150 years of domination by outside powers.)

The treaty proved a bitter pill for the Germans. Not only did Germany lose its colonies, but France also reclaimed Alsace-Lorraine and won 15-year control of the Saar, an industrial region of Germany rich in coal

Map

Lost by Germany
Lost by Bulgaria
Lost by Austria-Hungary
Lost by Russia
Lost by Ottoman empire
British mandate
French mandate
Occupied by Allies

In 1922 the Bolsheviks were firmly in control of Russia, and they organized the Union of Soviet Socialist Republics.

Europe and the Middle East After World War I

END OF EMPIRE Four empires had collapsed by the end of the First World War—the Russian, German, Austro-Hungarian, and Ottoman.

❓ **LOCATION** How many countries were created from or received land that had belonged to Russia before the war?

THE IMPACT OF THE WAR

Encourage students to imagine that they are living in Belgium, France, Germany, Russia, or the former Ottoman Empire immediately after World War I. Ask students to write letters to relatives in the U.S., noting the impact that the war has had on the area in which they live. Call on volunteers to read their letters to the class. Students may wish to include their letters in their portfolios.

▶

and iron. In addition, Germany was disarmed, forced to admit full guilt for the war, and assessed billions of dollars in reparations.

Harsh as this treatment was, it would have been much worse but for Wilson's moderating influence. He steadfastly opposed some of the more extreme Allied demands. And, above all, the president made sure that the treaty included a covenant creating the League of Nations.

▲ The first informal meeting of the League of Nations met in Geneva in 1920.

Headquartered in Geneva, the League consisted of a permanent administrative staff; an assembly, where each member nation had one vote; and a council, or executive body. The council was intended to have five permanent members—France, Great Britain, Italy, Japan, and the United States—and four other members that were periodically elected by the assembly.

The League Covenant required member nations to try to resolve disputes peacefully. If negotiations failed, the nations were to observe a waiting period before going to war. If any member nation failed to follow this procedure, the council could apply economic pressure and even recommend the use of force against the offending nation. The heart of the League Covenant—Article 10—required each member nation to "respect and preserve" the independence and territorial integrity of all other member nations.

THE TREATY IN THE SENATE

Returning to America in July 1919, President Wilson worked to win the Senate's consent to the Treaty of Versailles. He believed that he could count on the votes of most Democratic senators, but he would need solid support from Republicans to gain the required two-thirds majority. He faced a difficult task, for most Republican senators had doubts about the treaty. Fourteen of them—called the **irreconcilables**—would have nothing to do with the League of Nations and flatly rejected the treaty. The other 35 Republican senators—the

reservationists—said they could support the treaty if the League Covenant were amended. They particularly objected to Article 10, which seemed to commit the United States to go to war in defense of any League member that came under attack. The Senate's constitutional power to declare war must be protected, they insisted.

Wilson's only hope for consent was to win over close to 20 reservationists. Gaining their support, however, meant compromising on the League, which Wilson refused to do. The more his advisers urged compromise, the more rigid Wilson became.

Henry Cabot Lodge of Massachusetts, head of the Senate Committee on Foreign Relations and Wilson's longtime enemy, led the reservationists. Lodge, too, refused to budge. Playing for time, he bottled up the treaty in the Foreign Relations Committee through the summer of 1919. Angry and frustrated, Wilson took his case to the people. Although he was not feeling well, Wilson began a grueling 9,500-mile speaking tour on September 4. In city after city he ardently defended the treaty. To Wilson's satisfaction, the crowds grew more enthusiastic as the tour went on. Lodge, however, remained unmoved. "The only people who have votes on the treaty," he declared, "are here in the Senate."

On the night of September 25, after an impassioned speech in Pueblo, Colorado, Wilson complained of a splitting headache. His worried doctor ordered him back to Washington, D.C. A few days later, Wilson collapsed from a near-fatal stroke. Wilson lived out the rest of his term in seclusion in the White House, cut off from practically everyone except his wife and his closest aides. Moody, suspicious, and increasingly out of touch with reality, Wilson refused all suggestions of compromise on the treaty.

In November, Lodge presented the treaty, with a list of 14 reservations, to the Senate. Wilson ordered Democratic senators to vote no on the document, thereby rejecting it. The treaty without the list of reservations met the same fate at the hands of the irreconcilables and reservationists. In March

Practice

GUIDED PRACTICE

Work with students to create on the chalkboard a time line of Wilson's efforts to obtain a just peace in Europe. Call on students to offer events to place on the time line.

INDEPENDENT PRACTICE

Ask students to choose an event from the Guided Practice time line and write an editorial that either supports or opposes that event in the process of framing, negotiating, or ratifying terms of peace. Students may wish to include their editorials in their portfolios.

Review and Assessment

REVIEW Tell students to imagine that they are soldiers just returned from Europe. Ask them to write letters to President Wilson, explaining why they are for or against ratification of the Treaty of Versailles. Ask volunteers from both sides to read their letters to the class. Then assign the Section 4 Review on p. 611.

ASSESS Assign the **Section 4 Daily Quiz** in *Core Resources*.

COOPERATIVE LEARNING

Organize students in small work groups to design a "debate page" on the ratification of the Treaty of Versailles. Pages should include statements on the major issues involved in the conflict over ratification, interviews with ordinary Americans, editorial cartoons, and so on. Allow time for groups to present and discuss their pages.

HISTORICAL SIDELIGHTS

The End of the League
After Wilson's electoral defeat, his supporters periodically brought up the subject of American membership in the League of Nations. In 1923 President Warren G. Harding gave them his final reply. The issue, he said, was "dead. . . . Let it rest in the deep grave to which it has been consigned." Wilson, the architect of the League, died a few months later in February 1924.

PRIMARY SOURCE

Description of Change: excerpted
Rationale: excerpted to focus on main idea

Graph Caption Answer
(for graph on p. 611)
Russia, Germany

◀ On his 65th birthday Woodrow Wilson was photographed for the first time since his stroke.

1920 another vote on Lodge's version of the treaty failed, although a number of Democrats broke ranks and sided with the reservationists. A few weeks later, Wilson vetoed a congressional resolution declaring the United States at peace with the Central Powers. There would be no peace treaty, he insisted, without the League of Nations.

■■ **Wilson's refusal to compromise on the League Covenant led to U.S. rejection of the Treaty of Versailles.**

Wilson clutched at the 1920 election as his one remaining hope. He urged the nation to make the election a "great and solemn referendum" on the League Covenant. Americans, however, wanted to put the war and troublesome European problems behind them, and in November they gave the Republican party a landslide victory. By the time Wilson left office, the League of Nations had been established, but without the participation of the United States.

THE GLOBAL IMPACT OF THE WAR

While U.S. leaders debated whether or not to accept the Treaty of Versailles, the Europeans struggled to recover from the war. The destruction and human suffering were almost incomprehensible. In all, over 8.5 million died in battle, and another 21 million were wounded. Germany, with some 6 million dead and wounded, and Russia, with nearly 7 million casualties, suffered the greatest losses. (In contrast, the United States armed forces counted some 112,000 dead.) To add further misery, the influenza epidemic of 1918–1919 killed some 27 million worldwide.

The war had left the industry and agriculture of much of continental Europe in ruins. Northern France was completely destroyed. As British economist John Maynard Keynes observed:

> 66 For mile after mile nothing was left. No building was habitable and no field fit for the plow. . . . One devastated area was exactly like another—a heap of rubble, a morass of shell-holes, and tangle of wire. 99

Those businesses still operating could not produce enough to meet demand, and rampant inflation resulted. In Germany, food shortages were so extreme that it proved almost impossible to keep track of prices.

▼ Verdun was just one of the many cities reduced to rubble by bombing attacks during the war.

▼ American soldiers who fell in France are still remembered and honored in this cemetery.

Germany, reeling from the harsh terms of the treaty, seethed with unrest. Throughout the continent, nations vied with one another over territories they thought the treaty ought to have ceded to them. In the Middle East, Arab nations, which had sided with the Allies in hopes of winning their independence from the Ottoman Turks, found themselves living under French and British mandates. Tensions in the region heightened after Britain issued the **Balfour Declaration** in 1917, declaring British support for a Jewish homeland in Palestine.

The new world order, which so many hoped would arise from the ashes of World War I, never materialized. Instead, as historian J. M. Winter noted, "The old order reasserted its will, distributed the spoils of war, and left unresolved the problems which had led to . . . war in 1914."

■■ **The war, which destroyed a generation of young men and left much of Europe in ruins, resolved few prewar issues.**

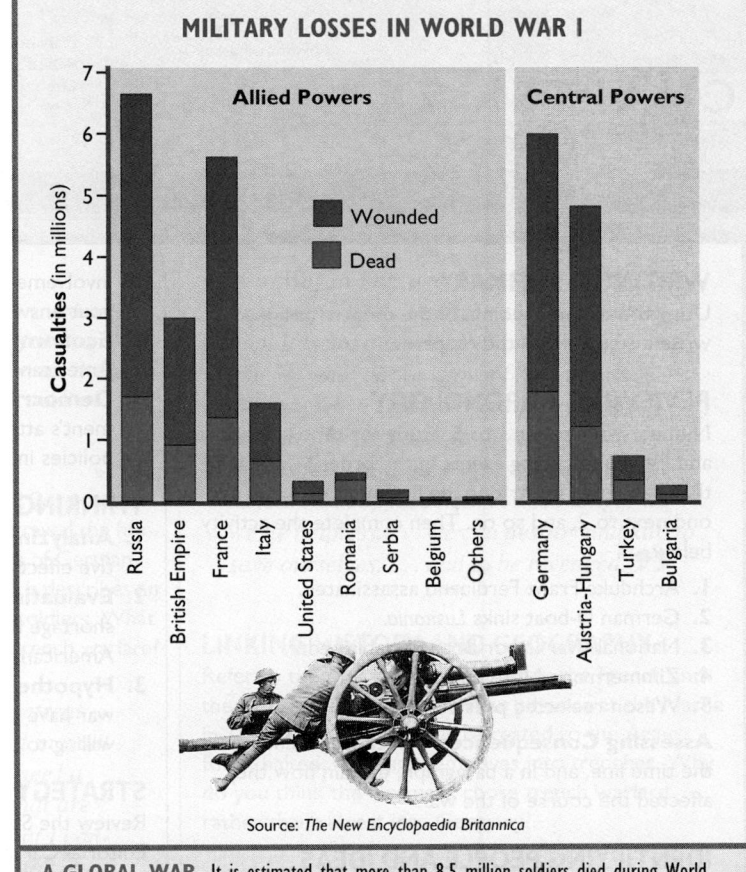

MILITARY LOSSES IN WORLD WAR I

Allied Powers   Central Powers

Casualties (in millions)

■ Wounded
■ Dead

Russia, British Empire, France, Italy, United States, Romania, Serbia, Belgium, Others, Germany, Austria-Hungary, Turkey, Bulgaria

Source: *The New Encyclopaedia Britannica*

A GLOBAL WAR It is estimated that more than 8.5 million soldiers died during World War I; an even higher number suffered from battle-inflicted wounds.

? **BUILDING GRAPH SKILLS** Which Allied power had the highest number of total casualties? Which Central power had the highest casualties?

■ ■
■ ■
SECTION 4 REVIEW

IDENTIFY and explain the significance of the following: Fourteen Points, self-determination, Vittorio Orlando, David Lloyd George, Georges Clemenceau, Big Four, reparations, Treaty of Versailles, mandate system, irreconcilables, reservationists, Henry Cabot Lodge, Balfour Declaration.

LOCATE and explain the importance of the following: Czechoslovakia, Yugoslavia, Finland, Estonia, Latvia, Lithuania, Poland, Saar.

1. **MAIN IDEA** What did Wilson's peace plan hope to accomplish?
2. **MAIN IDEA** What Allied demands forced Wilson to compromise on his Fourteen Points?
3. **ASSESSING CONSEQUENCES** What were some of the effects of the war on Europe and the Middle East?
4. **WRITING TO EXPRESS A VIEWPOINT** Imagine you are a reservationist in the U.S. Senate. Prepare a speech stating your reasons for not supporting ratification of the Treaty of Versailles.
5. **SYNTHESIZING** What aspects of the Treaty of Versailles lend support to Secretary of State Robert Lansing's observation that it was "founded on the shifting sands of self-interest"?

THE SPANISH–AMERICAN WAR

SETTING THE SCENE

SETTING THE SCENE

José Martí was a leader in the drive for Cuban independence from Spain. Twice exiled from the island for his political activities, he eventually took up residence in New York City. There he continued to work for freedom for his homeland, founding the Cuban Revolutionary party in 1892. Accompanied by a few party members, he staged a revolt on the island three years later. He was killed by Spanish troops two days after writing the diary entry that is excerpted on p. 614.

Like Martí, Lola Rodríguez de Tió was exiled from her homeland because of her political activities. Settling in New York, she became friends with Martí and helped him plan the Cuban revolt of 1895. Her desire for freedom for all peoples of the Caribbean, expressed in her poetry and in her actions, earned her the name "Daughter of the Isles."

UNIT 6

American Letters

The Spanish–American War

As a result of the Spanish-American War, the United States won territories in the Caribbean and the Pacific. In the following selections, Cuban poet and essayist José Martí, Puerto Rican poet Lola Rodríguez de Tió, an anonymous Mexican American poet, and American writers Mark Twain and Edgar Lee Masters explore the meaning of the war for the Caribbean and the United States.

▲ **Lola Rodriguez de Tió**

Diary Entry

by José Martí

[April 25, 1895.] Day of combat. Straight through the woods we are drawing close, already in the claws of Guantanamo. . . . The breast swells with fond reverence and overpowering affection at the sight of the vast landscape of the loved river. We cross it, near a *ceiba* tree, and after greeting a patriot family, overjoyed to see us, we enter the open wood, with sweet sun, rain-washed leaves. As over a carpet go our horses, so thick is the grass. All is garland and leaf, and through the openings, to the right, the green of the cleared fields is visible on the other bank, sheltered and compact. . . . Here as everywhere I am touched by the affection with which we are received, and the unity of soul which will not be allowed to coalesce [grow together], and which will not be recognized, and which will be overridden, harming, at least with the harm of delay, the Revolution in the impulse of its first year. The spirit I sowed, is that which has borne fruit, and that of the Island, and with it, and guiding ourselves by it, we will soon triumph, and with a better victory and for a better peace. ❖

The Song of Borinquen

by Lola Rodríguez de Tió

Awake, Borinqueños,[1]
   for they've given the signal!

Awake from your sleep
   for it's time to fight!

Come! The sound of cannon
   will be dear to us.

At that patriotic clamor
   doesn't your heart burn?

Look! The Cuban will soon be free,
   the machete will give him freedom.

The drum of war announces in its beating
   that the thicket is the place, the meeting place!

Most beautiful Borinquen, we have to follow Cuba;
   you have brave sons who want to fight!

Let us no more seem fearful!
Let us no more, timid, permit our enslavement!

We want to be free already
   and our machete is well sharpened!

Why should we, then, remain so asleep
   and deaf, asleep and deaf to that signal?

▼ *General Toral surrenders the city of Santiago to General Shaftner in 1898.*

There's no need to fear, Ricans, the sound of cannon,
for saving the homeland is the duty of the heart!

We want no more despots! Let the tyrant fall!
Women, likewise wild, will know how to fight!

We want freedom and our machete will give it to us!

Let's go, Puerto Ricans, let's go already,
for LIBERTY is waiting, ever so anxious! ❖

1 Borinqueños are Puerto Ricans. The word is adapted from
Borinquén, the Native American name for Puerto Rico.

The Voice of the Hispano

Anonymous

Many are the opinions
Against the Hispanic people
And they accuse them of betraying
The American government.

Making an experiment,
They will be disillusioned,
Our brave native men
Do not refuse to be soldiers.

It matters not what is said
Or how our fame is insulted,
As they will fight with pleasure
For the American eagle.

They accuse our native people
Of being rabble,
But they have not proven to be so
On the battlefield.

Like good countrymen
And faithful Americans,
We will free them from that yoke
The humble Cubans. ❖

From To the Person Sitting in Darkness

by Mark Twain

There have been lies; yes, but
they were told in a good cause.
We have been treacherous; but
that was only in order that real
good might come out of apparent
evil. True, we have crushed a
deceived and confiding people; we

have turned against the weak and the friendless who
trusted us; we have stamped out a just and intelligent
and well-ordered republic; we have stabbed an ally in
the back and slapped the face of a guest; we have
bought a Shadow from an enemy that hadn't it to sell;
we have robbed a trusting friend of his land and
liberty; . . . but each detail was for the best. ❖

"Harry Wilmans" From Spoon River Anthology

by Edgar Lee Masters

I was just turned twenty-one,
And Henry Phipps, the Sunday-school superintendent,
Made a speech in Bindle's Opera House.
"The honor of the flag must be upheld," he said,
"Whether it be assailed by a barbarous tribe of
    Tagalogs[1]
Or the greatest power in Europe."
And we cheered and cheered the speech and the flag
    he waved
As he spoke.
And I went to the war in spite of my father,
And followed the flag till I saw it raised
By our camp in a rice field near Manila,
And all of us cheered and cheered it.
But there were flies and poisonous things;
And there was the deadly water,
And the cruel heat,
And the sickening, putrid food. . . .
Following the flag,
Till I fell with a scream, shot through the guts.
Now there's a flag over me in Spoon River!
A flag! A flag! ❖

1 a people of central Luzon, Philippines

THINKING AND WRITING ABOUT LITERATURE

1. José Martí had just returned to Cuba from his exile in New York
   when he wrote this diary entry. Which phrases show that he
   missed Cuba in his absence?
2. Like Martí, Lola Rodríguez de Tió lived in New York and wrote
   in support of independence from Spain. Whose model does she
   urge Puerto Ricans to follow?
3. In the anonymous poem, what does the author believe Mexican
   American soldiers will prove?
4. Mark Twain's controversial essay and Edgar Lee Masters's poem
   use irony to express the authors' views of the war. Describe
   both authors' perspectives on the war.

PRIMARY SOURCES

Description of Change:
excerpted, bracketed, and
footnoted
Rationale: excerpted for
space considerations; bracketed and footnoted to clarify
meaning

THINKING AND WRITING ABOUT LITERATURE

1. "fond reverence," "overpowering affection," "the
   loved river," "sweet sun"
2. that of the Cubans, who
   had already taken up arms
   against Spain
3. their bravery, patriotism,
   and loyalty to the U.S. government; that Mexican
   Americans are not "rabble"
4. Twain believes that the
   U.S. has deceived its
   wartime allies (the
   Philippines, Cuba, Puerto
   Rico) and robbed them of
   their liberty. Masters
   believes that Harry
   Wilmans's death was in
   vain and did nothing to
   promote "the honor of the
   flag."

RECOGNIZING STEREOTYPES

Guide students through the discussion of how to recognize stereotypes and then have them complete the Practicing the Strategy exercise. Note that stereotypes, though inaccurate, often arise from actual historical events. Have students review the discussion of Francisco "Pancho" Villa's raid on Columbus, New Mexico, on pp. 577–578. Ask students to speculate about what stereotype of Mexicans Villa's raid may have helped create in the U.S. (the *bandido*) Discuss how this stereotype might distort an understanding of Villa's motivations for the raid and how it might affect the treatment of Mexican Americans.

PRACTICING THE STRATEGY

1. African Americans

2. The poster presents different stereotypes of African Americans. Two of the images portray African Americans as dancers or musicians, a common stereotype in a society that cast blacks as entertainers while also denying them opportunities in other areas. One image shows African Americans as destructive and violent, another widespread stereotype.

Strategies for Success

RECOGNIZING STEREOTYPES

A stereotype is a generalization or oversimplification about a group or culture. Stereotypes deny individual differences by attributing the same characteristics to every member in a group: All poor people are lazy. All Irish drink too much. All African Americans are good athletes. All girls have difficulty with math and science. Most stereotypes are negative and often lead to discrimination and prejudice.

How to Recognize Stereotypes

1. **Examine the message.** Pay close attention to how a person or group is portrayed. Identify generalizations that lack supporting facts. Ask yourself: Are the same qualities being attributed to all individuals in a group?
2. **Note words that signal stereotyping.** Watch for clue words such as *all, always, never,* or *every* that allow no exceptions; their use may signal stereotyping.
3. **Detect bias or prejudice.** Note any bias or tone that indicates prejudice toward the subjects being described.
4. **Use your knowledge.** In evaluating general statements about people, apply what you have learned from your studies or through direct experience with individual classmates, your family members, or others.

Applying the Strategy

In the following passage, Samuel Bryan, an Anglo American sociologist, describes Mexican immigrants in the United States in 1912:

66 Socially and politically the presence of large numbers of Mexicans in this country gives rise to serious problems. . . . They . . . are slow to learn English, . . . move readily from place to place, and do not acquire or lease land to any extent. But their most unfavorable characteristic is their inclination to . . . live in a clannish manner. 99

Bryan's description is an example of the kind of stereotyping that breeds prejudice. First, he lumps together all Mexican immigrants—and, by implication, all Mexican Americans. He ignores the fact that in many areas of the United States stable, prosperous Mexican American communities existed long before Anglo settlement. Second, he blames immigrants for conditions that are a product of their immigrant status. Like members of other immigrant groups, Mexicans often found many jobs closed to them. One area in which they could find work was farm labor. Because farm labor is seasonal, Mexican farm workers were forced to move often in search of crops to harvest. This migratory existence, coupled with the low wages typical of such farm work, made it difficult for many Mexican immigrants to buy land.

Practicing the Strategy

Study the song poster below. Then, on a separate sheet of paper, answer the following questions.
1. What group is pictured in this song poster?
2. Why can this song poster be considered an example of stereotyping?

BUILDING YOUR PORTFOLIO

Each portfolio project described below is the culmination of the Building Your Portfolio activities in the chapter reviews of Unit 6. First, decide whether you wish students to work individually or in groups on these unit projects. Then permit each student to choose the project on which he or she desires to work. Provide students with copies of **Building Your Portfolio Worksheet 6** from *Core Resources*. This worksheet will guide students step by step to complete their projects.

BUILDING YOUR PORTFOLIO

Outlined below are four projects. Independently or cooperatively, complete one and use the products to demonstrate your mastery of the historical concepts involved.

1 REFORM

In the late 19th century the transformation of the United States from a rural economy to an industrialized, urban society created numerous social problems. In response, the Progressive party sought reforms. Using the portfolio materials you designed in chapters 17 and 18, create a series of Progressive party campaign posters that outline the party's reform goals.

2 DEMOCRATIC RIGHTS

Historians note that progressivism was primarily a white, middle-class movement and thus did not address many of the concerns of working-class women. Using the portfolio materials you designed in chapters 17 and 18, conduct a debate between a white, middle-class progressive and a working-class woman on whether the progressive emphasis on women's suffrage best serves the needs of all women.

3 GLOBAL RELATIONS

The expansionist policies of the United States in the 19th century led to the establishment of U.S. overseas colonies, increased foreign investment, and conflicts with foreign powers. Using the portfolio materials you designed in chapters 19 and 20, create a world map showing areas of U.S. colonization, investment, and conflict through World War I.

4 WAR

The Spanish-American War and World War I brought the United States onto the world stage. Using the portfolio materials you designed in chapters 19 and 20, prepare a speech for delivery to Congress, outlining some of the costs and benefits of America's international role.

Videodisc Review

In assigned groups, develop an outline for a video collage of America in the years between 1897 and 1920. Choose images that best illustrate the major topics of the period. Write a script to accompany the images. Assign narrators to different parts of the script, and present your video collage to the class.

Further Reading

Ettinger, Albert M., and A. Churchill Ettinger. *A Doughboy with the Fighting 69th.* White Mane (1992). Reminiscence of World War I by a soldier of the 69th Rainbow Division.

Hall, Linda B., and Don M. Coerver. *Revolution on the Border: The United States and Mexico, 1910–1920.* University of New Mexico Press (1990). Examines the role that trade and investment played in U.S.–Mexico relations.

Liliuokalani. *Hawaii's Story by Hawaii's Queen.* Charles E. Tuttle (1991). Firsthand account of 19th-century Hawaii.

Schneider, Dorothy, and Carl J. Schneider. *Into the Breach.* Viking (1991). Examines the participation of American women in World War I.

Tuchman, Barbara W. *The Guns of August.* Bantam (1989). Analysis of the events of August 1914 that propelled Europe into World War I.

PORTFOLIO ASSESSMENT

1. *Campaign posters should show Progressive support of women's suffrage, and reform of political machines, business corruption, poor working conditions, and public health.*
2. *Debates should describe Progressive support of shorter working hours for women, stricter workplace safety standards, and temperance. Debates should also show the importance of higher wages and better working conditions for women workers.*
3. *World maps should show U.S. occupation of Cuba; acquisition of Eastern Samoa, the Philippines, Puerto Rico, and Hawaii; construction of the Panama Canal; intervention in the Dominican Republic, Haiti, and Mexico; investment in Nicaragua and China; Perry's contact with Japan and the voyage of the "Great White Fleet"; and World War I battles in Europe.*
4. *Speeches should address the economic benefits for the U.S. of new colonies, the political benefits for the colonies, and the problems of opposition movements in the colonies.*

Prosperity and Crisis ❖ 1920–1945

UNIT OVERVIEW

The prosperity of the 1920s introduced millions of Americans to mass production and mass culture. Rapid change caused social upheaval and led many to question traditional values. In 1929 the U.S. plunged into the worst economic depression in history. Facing unemployment, hunger, and homelessness, Americans looked to President Roosevelt and his New Deal programs for help. Recovery was slow, but the economy fully re-vived when the U.S. entered World War II. By 1945 the U.S. was the most powerful nation in the free world.

CORE RESOURCES

- **American Almanac Poster** and **Worksheet 7**
- **Building Your Portfolio Worksheet 7**
  You may wish to preview the Unit 7 Review and Building Your Portfolio performance assessment activities on p. 775.

Using the American Almanac Posters

Begin the unit by displaying the American Almanac Poster and discussing entries with students. In addition to the worksheet, the annotations that follow provide additional information about the entries and suggest questions and activities.

Then, as students study the unit, have them work in small groups to create their own almanacs—using the same six headings—on pieces of butcher paper. At the end of the unit, call on groups to display and discuss their almanacs.

Chapter 21
A TURBULENT DECADE
1919–1929

Chapter 22
THE JAZZ AGE
1920–1930

Chapter 23
THE GREAT DEPRESSION
1929–1933

America's Music and Dance

Swing, the popular music of the 1930s and 1940s, gave rise to a new language called *jive. Cats* were musicians known for *kicking out,* or improvising, when they played. *Alligators,* or devotees of swing, often could be seen *cuttin' the rug,* or dancing.

▪▪ Have students identify and explain some terms associated with today's popular music.

At Your Leisure

Most comic-book heroes were outsiders, often aliens, mutations, or technological creations disguised in some way so that they could pass unnoticed in everyday life. They revealed their true nature only when society was threatened by danger or evil.

▪▪ Ask students why comic-book heroes such as Superman and Batman are still popular today.

Fashion Plate

Point out that the life-styles of young, wealthy people—"glamour girls" and "men about town"—attracted a great deal of publicity and often influenced the fashions of society at large.

▪▪ Ask students who, if anyone, influences their fashion decisions.

The Cost of Living

Other 1930s clothes prices: women's—leather shoes, $1.79; raincoat, $2.69; wool sweater, $1.69; men's—shirt, 47¢; silk tie, 55¢; shoes, $3.85.

▪▪ Ask students to investigate today's prices of the items listed.

Firsts in America

Earhart's other flying achievements included first nonstop solo flight from Honolulu to California, and a number of altitude and speed records.

▪▪ Ask students to identify the flight "firsts" that are being accomplished today.

Sports Extra

Owens's feat stood until Carl Lewis matched it at the 1984 Los Angeles Olympics.

The Silver Screen

Mention that Temple began her movie career at the age of 3 and appeared in some 25 films during the 1930s. She retired from movies at age 21. In later years she served as ambassador to the UN, Ghana, and Czechoslovakia.

▪▪ Ask students what child stars are popular today.

UNIT 7

Prosperity and Crisis

1919–1945

The prosperity of the 1920's introduced millions of Americans to mass produced goods and mass culture and led many to question traditional values. By the end of the decade, however, the nation had plunged into the Great Depression. Facing unemployment and poverty, millions of Americans turned to President Roosevelt and his New Deal. But economic recovery remained slow until the United States entered World War II. By 1945 the United States was the world's most powerful nation.

◄ President Roosevelt, radio broadcast, 1937

Chapter 24

THE NEW DEAL
1933–1940

Chapter 25

BETWEEN THE WARS
1921–1941

Chapter 26

AMERICANS IN WORLD WAR II 1941–1945

A TURBULENT DECADE

1919–1929

*C*hapter *O*verview

In the years immediately after World War I, the U.S. went through a brief but painful economic recession, labor strikes, and the anti-Communist hysteria known as the "Red Scare." Hoping for a return to the prosperity of the prewar period, voters elected Warren G. Harding, Calvin Coolidge, and then Herbert Hoover as president. Conservative Republicans dominated American politics throughout the decade despite political scandals. Immigrants and racial, ethnic, and religious groups experienced increased hostility during this period.

> **THE AMERICAN NATION VIDEODISC PROGRAM**
> A variety of still images, short videos, and activities are available for you to use as you teach this chapter. See *Correlation to The American Nation Videodisc Program* for barcode correlations and suggestions for using the program.

*C*hapter *P*lanning *G*uide

CHAPTER 21	CORE RESOURCE BOOKLETS	AUDIOVISUAL RESOURCES	PROGRAM RESOURCES
INTRODUCTION pp. 620–621	■ Building Your Portfolio Worksheet 7	■ Everyday Life in America Transparency and Worksheet 21	
TEACHING THE CHAPTER pp. 622–639	■ Graphic Organizer 21 ■ Social Studies Skills Worksheet 21 ■ Literature Worksheet 21 ■ Geography Worksheet 21 ■ Outline Map 9	■ Linking Geography and History Transparency and Worksheet 17	■ *Eyewitnesses and Others*, Volume 2: Readings 36, 37, 42, 43
REVIEW AND ASSESSMENT pp. 640–641	■ Chapter 21 Daily Quizzes ■ Review Worksheet 21 ■ Chapter 21 Tests ■ Alternative Assessment Forms		■ Test Generator

*A*dditional *R*esources

BOOKS FOR TEACHERS

Cott, Nancy F. *The Grounding of Modern Feminism.* Yale University Press, 1987. Analysis of the campaign for women's suffrage.

Harrison, Alferdteen, ed. *Black Exodus: The Great Migration from the Great American South.* University Press of Mississippi, 1992. Story of the black migration from the South to the urban North.

Leuchtenburg, William E. *The Perils of Prosperity: 1914–32.* University of Chicago, 1958. Distinguished historian's classic study.

BOOKS FOR STUDENTS

Green, Harvey. *The Uncertainty of Everyday Life, 1915–1945.* HarperCollins, 1992. In-depth look at life in the U.S. before, during, and after the "Turbulent Twenties."

* Lawler, Mary. *Marcus Garvey.* Holloway, 1990. Biography of the leader of the Back-to-Africa movement.

* Wade, Linda R. *Warren G. Harding.* Children's Press, 1989. An easy-to-read biography of the 29th president.

* for students reading below grade level

MULTIMEDIA MATERIALS

The Age of Ballyhoo. Video, 52 min. Republic/SSSS. Cultural history of the 1920s. Includes newsreels of Sacco and Vanzetti.

The Big Red Scare of 1919–1920. Video, 10 min. Multi-Media Productions/SSSS. Traces the origins of anti-Communist and anti-immigrant hysteria in 1919 and 1920.

The Reckless Years. Video, 39 min. Guidance Associates/SSSS. Chronicles the twenties with maps, graphs, cartoons, and historical photographs.

THEMES IN AMERICAN HISTORY

USE WITH PAGES 620–621

*L*isted on the right are the themes emphasized in Chapter 21. The questions in boldface type stimulate critical thinking and provide students with an opportunity to discuss the themes within a broadened context. The questions also appear in the pupil's edition on p. 620.

■ DEMOCRATIC VALUES

How might a democratic government respond to a perceived threat of revolution? Students might suggest that even a democratic government may try to stifle dissent if many people feel that a revolution threatens their way of life. In such a situation a government might try to intimidate or even to imprison people believed to be responsible for the threat.

■ CULTURAL DIVERSITY

In what ways might ethnic and racial groups respond to acts of discrimination? Students might suggest that members of such groups might try to work together to form their own communities or work to eliminate discrimination by changing attitudes and laws.

■ ECONOMIC DEVELOPMENT

What actions should the federal government take to promote economic prosperity? Students might suggest that the government could pass laws that promote economic development or relax existing regulations that might inhibit development.

CHAPTER STRATEGIES FOR MEETING INDIVIDUAL NEEDS

LIMITED ENGLISH PROFICIENT LEARNERS

Have students work in small groups to role-play interviews with the presidential candidates discussed in Chapter 21. Interviews should show the main differences in candidates and parties.

TACTILE/KINESTHETIC LEARNERS

Have students create campaign buttons, posters, and placards for the Hoover or Smith presidential campaign of 1928. Campaign materials should show differences between candidates and parties.

LEARNERS HAVING DIFFICULTY

Have students work in pairs and pick three events in each section. Then have them write two or three sentences explaining the importance of each event. As a class, create a time line showing all events.

AUDITORY LEARNERS

Have students prepare a radio broadcast of the news of the decade using the events on the chapter time line on pp. 640–641 as ideas for news items.

VISUAL LEARNERS

Have students prepare an advertisement or poster for a movie titled *The 1920s,* which shows key events in those turbulent years and stars key figures in the history of the period.

GIFTED LEARNERS

Have students write an essay comparing the anti-immigrant sentiment of the 1920s with the nativism of the Know-Nothing party of the 1850s.

USING THE CHAPTER FOCUS

■ UNDERSTANDING THE MAIN IDEA

Call on a volunteer to read aloud the Understanding the Main Idea paragraph and define the term *probusiness*. Explain that "normalcy" was a term coined by one of the probusiness Republican presidents discussed in this chapter. Have students speculate what this word might mean and why it might be interpreted differently by white war veterans, African Americans, Native Americans, and immigrants.

■ THEMES

Have students work individually or in small groups to answer the questions under Themes. Save students' responses so that they can compare them with their responses after studying the chapter. (See p. 619B for suggested answers.)

■ THE TIME LINE

Direct students to copy the time-line entries in their notebooks. After they have read about each event on the time line, have them draw an editorial cartoon that focuses on each event.

CORE RESOURCES

• Graphic Organizer 21
• Outline Map 9
• Building Your Portfolio Worksheet 7

AV RESOURCES

• Everyday Life in America Transparency and Worksheet 21

ABOUT THE ILLUSTRATION

On September 16, 1920, around the noon lunch hour, a driver parked a horse and wagon along the curb on Wall Street. Within five minutes the wagon exploded, instantly killing more than 30 people. Hundreds were injured in the blast, and damage to buildings and other property was estimated between a half a million and two million dollars. Although the bomber was never found, police and other officials believed that radicals were to blame for the crime. Ask students to speculate why radicals might have chosen Wall Street for such an act. Then tell students that it was events such as this that characterized the 1920s as a "turbulent decade."

Chapter 21

1919–1929

A TURBULENT DECADE

▼ **FOCUS**

UNDERSTANDING THE MAIN IDEA

The end of World War I ushered in a period of economic and social instability. Voters, eager to return to "normalcy," elected probusiness Republican presidents, and as the 1920s progressed, prosperity returned. Not all, however, shared the benefits of this economic renewal. Organized labor lost ground, and Native Americans, African Americans, and immigrants faced discrimination.

THEMES

■ **DEMOCRATIC VALUES**
How might a democratic government respond to a perceived threat of revolution?

■ **CULTURAL DIVERSITY**
In what ways might ethnic and racial groups respond to acts of discrimination?

■ **ECONOMIC DEVELOP-MENT** What actions should the federal government take to promote economic prosperity?

1919	1921	1924	1927	1928
Palmer raids begin.	Congress limits immigration.	Congress grants Native Americans citizenship.	Sacco and Vanzetti executed.	Herbert Hoover elected president.

MAKING CONNECTIONS
Sociology

Although many Americans yearned for a return to life as they imagined it in prewar America, industrialization had changed forever the way Americans lived. In 1899 electricity powered only about 2 percent of U.S. factories; by 1919 it powered some 31 percent. In 1920 over eight million cars bumped and lurched down U.S. roads, an increase of about 300 percent from 1915. Such developments created opportunities for a radically different life-style for many Americans in the 1920s. Old beliefs and attitudes, however, proved more resistant to change.

The end of World War I brought joyous celebration. As author Malcolm Cowley wrote, "We danced in the streets, embraced old women and pretty girls, swore blood brotherhood with soldiers in little bars, drank with our elbows locked in theirs, reeled through the streets with bottles of champagne." But this joy proved short-lived.

For many Americans life after the war did not appear promising. War veterans returned home to find few jobs available. Those who did find work soon discovered that soaring prices ate up their earnings. Economic and social problems increased. Strikes broke out across the nation, and violent race riots exploded in many American cities. Fueled by wartime fears, anti-immigrant feelings raised social tensions. Looking back on the first years after the war, author and journalist Ray Stannard Baker remarked, "I can recall no period in which life in America looked bleaker."

Aftermath of Wall Street bombing, 1920

World War I veteran with his family, 1919

FOCUS OBJECTIVES

- Describe what economic conditions were like after the war.

- Identify how workers reacted to hard times.

- Explain why many Americans feared that a Communist revolution was at hand.

- Analyze what the Sacco and Vanzetti case revealed about America in the early 1920s.

PREVIEW WORKSHOP

Following is a list of the significant people, places, and terms in this section. You may wish to use this list as a section preview.

People

- Ole Hanson
- Edwin Curtis
- A. Mitchell Palmer
- Emma Goldman

- Nicola Sacco
- Bartolomeo Vanzetti

Places

- Seattle, Washington
- Boston, Massachusetts

Terms

- demobilization
- Red Scare
- Palmer raids

Section 1

POSTWAR TROUBLES

F O C U S

- **What were economic conditions like after the war?**
- **How did workers react to hard times?**
- **Why did many Americans fear that a Communist revolution was at hand?**
- **What did the Sacco and Vanzetti case reveal about America in the early 1920s?**

Children in 1916 supporting their striking relatives

The horrors of World War I shocked and disillusioned many Americans. The war, wrote novelist John Dos Passos, had been a "waste of time, waste of money, waste of lives, waste of youth." In response, many Americans tried to return to the way things had been before the war. But there was no going back. Instead of a return to the "old ways," the nation faced economic hardship and social strife.

DEMOBILIZATION

Under the best of conditions, **demobilization**, the shift from a wartime to a peacetime footing, is not an easy task for a nation. The process is made more difficult when the shift is rapid, as was the case after World War I. The war's end caught the

▲ After World War I, millions of veterans scrambled for available jobs. American Legion employment offices, such as this one in Los Angeles, tried to find work for veterans.

American government by surprise—literally. Trains carrying new recruits to boot camp were stopped en route. Within a year some four million soldiers returned to civilian life.

Women were urged to give up their jobs to make room for returning veterans. "The same patriotism which induced women to enter industry during the war should induce them to vacate their positions," declared the New York labor federation. Most of the women who did not respond to patriotic appeals were forced out of jobs traditionally held by men. As a result, the percentage of women in the work force in 1920 fell slightly below what it had been in 1910.

Adding to employment worries was a sky-rocketing cost of living. With peace at hand, consumers went on a spending spree, making purchases they had put off during the war. As the demand for goods outpaced supply, prices soared until the cost of goods and services in 1920 was about twice that of 1914.

Soon, however, this trend reversed as the deep but brief recession of 1920–1921 struck and

MOTIVATING:
PRIOR KNOWLEDGE

Ask volunteers to describe what life had been like before the war for many people in small-town, rural America. Have students recall the beliefs many had held during the war about what it would accomplish. Tell students this section examines both why the war left many Americans disillusioned and how they reacted to this disillusionment.

Teaching the Section

POSTWAR ECONOMICS

Have students work in groups to prepare skits for a radio show in which a reporter interviews a panel consisting of a female factory worker, housewife/consumer, midwestern grain farmer, and returning war veteran. Each panelist should explain how demobilization has affected his or her life.

▶

prices fell. Demobilization was one of the factors behind the recession. During the war millions of Americans worked in war industries. But at war's end the government canceled more than $2 billion in war contracts. Factories responded by cutting back production and laying off workers. By 1921 some 5 million workers—more than 10 percent of the labor force—were unemployed, and the economy was shrinking.

A farm crisis contributed to the economic problems. Farmers had benefited from wartime markets in Europe. As European farm production revived, however, these markets dried up and farm prices fell. According to the Department of Agriculture, wheat, for example, dropped from $2.16 a bushel in 1919 to less than a dollar a bushel in 1922. Burdened with debt, hundreds of thousands of American farmers lost ownership of their land during the 1920s.

■■ **After the war the cost of living soared, but prices soon fell as a recession took hold and unemployment increased.**

LABOR STRIFE

In 1919, however, Americans were still struggling with rapidly rising prices for food, clothing, and shelter. Workers watched in dismay as runaway inflation ate up their wartime financial gains. Angry and frustrated, they asked for higher wages and shorter hours. But management ignored labor's pleas. In response, many workers walked off the job. In 1919 alone, unions called more than 3,600 strikes—involving more than four million workers.

◀ **Strikes became commonplace in the years after World War I, as workers demanded better wages and conditions. Here, mounted policemen break up a group of Philadelphia strikers in 1919.**

The Seattle general strike. The first strike of 1919 occurred in January, when some 35,000 shipyard workers in Seattle, Washington, walked off the job, demanding higher wages and a shorter workday. Within two weeks 110 local unions voted to join the shipyard workers in a general strike.

The general strike began on February 6 at 10 A.M. An eerie calm fell over the city as 60,000 workers left their jobs. "It was," declared one shipyard worker, "the most beautiful thing I ever seen!"

Alarmed at such a show of unity, Seattle newspapers blamed immigrants, calling the strikers "muddle-headed foreigners" and "riffraff from Europe intent on terrorizing the community." Mayor Ole Hanson denounced the strike as the work of Bolsheviks and called in troops to prevent unrest. But no violent incidents occurred. Instead, the well-disciplined strikers took steps to preserve order and to make sure that food and essential services were available to the community. Nevertheless, the strikers came under increased public pressure to go back to work. After five days they ended the strike without winning any of their demands.

Although the strike had been peaceful, anti-labor forces tried to convince the public that Seattle had been on the brink of revolution. Mayor Hanson told the national press:

▲ **The Seattle Union Record published a special edition on February 6, 1919, announcing the beginning of the general strike.**

❝ Revolution . . . doesn't need violence. The general strike . . . is of itself the weapon of revolution, all the more dangerous because quiet. To succeed, it must suspend everything. . . . That is to say, it puts the government out of operation. And that is all there is to revolt—no matter how achieved. ❞

Many people believed these charges. In the end the Seattle strike helped turn public opinion against organized labor.

GLOBAL CONNECTIONS

By early 1915 orders for food to supply the Allies increased demand for U.S. farm products, which meant high prices for crops at home and abroad. Many U.S. farmers borrowed heavily to buy more land and machinery in order to expand production. After the war, overseas demand for U.S. food products dropped sharply, leaving farmers with huge surpluses and lower market prices as they struggled to repay their loans.

MAKING CONNECTIONS

Literature
American author John Dos Passos noted the spirit of change that threatened many Americans after the war: "Any spring is a time of overturn, but then Lenin was alive, the Seattle general strike had seemed the beginning of the flood. . . . Currents of energy seemed breaking out everywhere as young guys climbed out of their uniforms. . . . In every direction the countries of the world stretched out starving and angry, ready for anything turbulent and new."

PRIMARY SOURCE

Description of Change: excerpted
Rationale: excerpted to focus on main idea

Teaching the Section

LABOR STRIFE

Organize students into three groups. Assign each group one of the following strikes: Seattle shipyard workers, Boston police, steel workers. Have groups imagine they are workers who participated in these strikes. Ask each group to write a letter to their local newspaper explaining their reasons for striking, their opinion of government and public reaction to the strike, the way the strike has been portrayed in the newspapers, and how they feel about the strike's outcome.

■■ Have students give examples of ways they or the American public in general have been affected by media coverage of a controversial issue today. Consider talk shows as well as newspaper and TV news reports.

◀ **An important issue during the Boston police strike was whether public employees had the right to strike. When policemen refused to report to work, civilians took over traffic control and other public safety jobs.**

return to work. Curtis, however, refused to reinstate them. Instead, he hired a new force made up of unemployed veterans. Union sympathizers protested. Unmoved, Coolidge backed the commissioner, proclaiming that "there is no right to strike against the public safety by anybody, anywhere, any time." Coolidge's words made him an overnight hero in conservative circles.

The Boston police strike. In September 1919 another strike, this time by the Boston police force, further inflamed antilabor sentiments. The Boston police had recently formed a union to seek better pay and working conditions. Although police in other cities had unionized without incident, Boston's police commissioner, Edwin Curtis, refused to recognize the union. Instead, he fired 19 officers for engaging in union activities. In response, some 75 percent of the police force went on strike.

Public order collapsed. Journalist William Allen White described the first night of the strike:

    66 The devil was loose in Boston. . . . Little knots of boys and young men began wandering through the streets. . . . By midnight, the . . . crowds had formed one raging mob, a drunken, noisy, irresponsible mob. . . . Someone threw a loose paving stone through a store window about one o'clock. The tension snapped. . . . By two o'clock, looting had begun. **99**

After two nights of violence, Governor Calvin Coolidge called in the state militia to restore order. The city's newspapers denounced the strikers as "agents of Lenin" and the strike as a "Bolshevist nightmare." The public also came out firmly against the strike. Recognizing that their cause was doomed, the police voted unanimously to

The steel strike. Two weeks after the trouble in Boston, the most important strike of 1919 began. In late September some 365,000 steelworkers—many of them immigrants—walked off the job, demanding recognition of their union and protesting low wages and long working hours. This massive walkout threatened to shut down the steel industry.

For years the major steel companies had fought efforts to unionize steelworkers. Now the companies did everything in their power to break the strike. In an effort to divide labor along ethnic lines, they portrayed foreign workers as radicals and called on "loyal" Americans to return to work.

▼ **During the steel strike, Pittsburgh policemen arrested dozens of protesters. In a notice printed in several languages, the *Pittsburgh Chronicle Telegraph* declared the strike a failure and urged strikers to go back to work.**

The Strike Has Failed

RED SCARE AND PALMER RAIDS

Have students identify the reasons for the fear of communism in 1919 and 1920. Then ask students why immigrants and foreigners were particular targets during the Red Scare. Conclude by asking volunteers to take the role of 1920s Americans and to give 15-second statements about why they think a Communist revolution is at hand.

■■ Ask students whether they think a period of hysteria like the Red Scare could happen in the U.S. today and, if so, what groups might be targets. If not, what safeguards would prevent it?

THE TRIAL OF SACCO AND VANZETTI

Divide the class in half to prepare radio news commentaries on the Sacco and Vanzetti trial. Direct each student in the first group to support the conviction of Sacco and Vanzetti. Direct those in the other group to protest the conviction. Call on volunteers to present their commentaries. Then discuss what the case revealed about America in the early 1920s. ▶

The steel bosses also brought in thousands of African Americans and Mexican Americans as replacement workers, and they hired armed thugs to attack the strikers. Strikers were jailed, beaten, or shot. Faced with such tactics, union leaders called off the strike on January 9, 1920. Labor had suffered a crushing defeat. It would be 15 years before unions again tried to organize workers in heavy industry.

■■ **Workers responded to hard times by striking for higher pay and better working conditions, but their efforts largely failed.**

THE RED SCARE

The 1919 strikes were prompted primarily by labor's desire for a fair deal. However, many Americans saw labor unrest as proof that Russia's Bolshevik Revolution of 1917, with its call for a worldwide revolution of workers, was spreading to American shores. This fear of communism reached fever pitch in 1919 and 1920, a period of anti-Communist hysteria known as the **Red Scare**.

Although Communists and Socialists comprised only a tiny fraction of the country's population, some Americans saw "Reds" everywhere. They even implied that Communists controlled many women's organizations. Peace groups, such as the Women's International League for Peace and Freedom, came under particularly strong attack. Antiradical fears reached such heights that several elected members of the New York State Assembly were expelled because they were members of the Socialist party. As journalist Walter Lippmann sarcastically noted:

❝ The people are shivering in their boots over Bolshevism, they are far more afraid of Lenin [the Bolshevik leader] than they ever were of the Kaiser [Wilhelm II, who ruled Germany during World War I]. We seem to be the most frightened lot of victors that the world ever saw. ❞

■■ **The Bolshevik Revolution and the strikes of 1919 led many Americans to fear that a Communist revolution was at hand.**

▲ This cartoon entitled *Put Them Out & Keep Them Out* appeared in the *Philadelphia Inquirer* in 1919 and expressed the fear that Bolshevism was creeping into American society.

The Palmer raids. In 1919 a rash of bomb scares seemed to justify Americans' fears. In April, alert postal clerks discovered 36 bombs in the mail addressed to such prominent citizens as John D. Rockefeller, Supreme Court justice Oliver Wendell Holmes, and Postmaster General Albert Burleson. Then less than a month later, several bombings occurred, one of which damaged the front of Attorney General A. Mitchell Palmer's house. The assailant, an Italian anarchist, died in the blast.

Newspapers began demanding harsh action against radicals. One paper even called for "a few free treatments in the electric chair." Attorney General Palmer, hoping to further his presidential ambitions, responded by launching an anti-Red crusade. He created a special government office to

◀ A. Mitchell Palmer

HISTORICAL SIDELIGHTS

A State of Terror
In their zeal to root out the "Reds" in American society, government agents had little respect for their suspects' rights. For example, Justice Department officials beat an alleged Communist while newspaper reporters watched. The reporters were warned that they would be prosecuted if they reported what they had seen. A professor whose "crime" was teaching algebra in Russian was beaten by government agents. Two men accused of being anarchists were detained and tortured at the Justice Department until one killed himself. Reformer Frederic Howe remarked: "Few people would believe the extent to which private hates and prejudices were permitted to usurp government powers."

PRIMARY SOURCE

Description of Change: excerpted and bracketed
Rationale: excerpted to focus on main idea; bracketed to clarify meaning

Practice

GUIDED PRACTICE

Write the following headlines on the chalk-board: *Boston Commissioner Locks Out Police, Federal Officials Arrest 6000 Suspected Radicals, Sacco and Vanzetti Die.* Organize students into two groups. Instruct one group to outline the causes of

each event described in the headlines and the other group to outline the effects of the events. Have groups present their outlines to the class.

INDEPENDENT PRACTICE

Have individuals use the headlines and the outlines created in the Guided Practice to write a news story on one of the events. Students may wish to include their news stories in their portfolios.

Review and Assessment

REVIEW Have students work in pairs to create graphic organizers that link the following events in a cause-and-effect relationship: recession of 1920–21, labor unrest, Red Scare, trial of Sacco and Vanzetti. Then assign the Section 1 Review on p. 627.

ASSESS Assign the **Section 1 Daily Quiz** in *Core Resources.*

PRIMARY SOURCE

Description of Change: excerpted

Rationale: excerpted to focus on main idea

BIO GRAPHY | PERSONALITIES IN HISTORY

Goldman was deeply troubled by what she saw in Russia. As a strong advocate of free speech, she was outraged when she saw "people raided, imprisoned, and shot for their *ideas!*" She requested and got an interview with Lenin where she confronted him with her concerns. Her decision to speak out in the American press against the Bolsheviks led to isolation and rejection by her former radical friends.

THINKING CRITICALLY

Recognizing Prejudice

Webster Thayer, the presiding judge in the Sacco-Vanzetti trial, said of Vanzetti: "This man, although he may not actually have committed the crime . . . is . . . the enemy of our existing institutions. . . . The defendant's ideals are cognate [consistent] with crime." Have students identify the prejudices toward immigrants and radicals expressed in this quote and explain why it is possible that Sacco and Vanzetti did not get a fair trial.

gather information on radical activities and put J. Edgar Hoover, the future head of the FBI, in charge.

Palmer's most dramatic action was a series of raids to capture alleged radicals. The **Palmer raids** began in November 1919 and peaked on January 2, 1920, when federal officials arrested thousands of suspected radicals in 33 cities nationwide. As journalist Frederick Lewis Allen wrote:

> ❝ Over six thousand men were arrested in all, . . . often without any chance to learn what was the explicit charge against them. . . . In Detroit, over a hundred men were herded into a bull-pen measuring twenty-four by thirty feet and kept there for a week. . . . In Hartford, while the suspects were in jail the authorities took the further precaution of arresting . . . all visitors who came to see them. ❞

Most of those arrested were poor immigrants newly arrived in the country. In most cases, there was no real evidence against them. In fact, although the government claimed that radicals were "armed to the teeth," only three pistols were seized in the raids.

BIO GRAPHY

Emma Goldman. During the Red Scare hundreds of foreigners suspected of radical activities were deported to Russia. Among the deportees was Emma Goldman, a noted feminist, writer, and speaker.

Goldman was born in 1869 in Lithuania, a nation that was then part of Russia. Raised in a traditional Jewish family, Goldman was an independent, determined girl who often clashed with her authoritarian father. When she was 15, her

Emma Goldman

father arranged for her to marry a man she did not love. But as she later wrote, "I would not listen to his schemes; I wanted to study, to know life, to travel. Besides, I never would marry for anything but love." So at age 16, Goldman immigrated to the United States.

The young Goldman settled in Rochester, New York, where she took a factory job. Gradually she grew disillusioned with the treatment of foreigners and workers in the United States. In 1889 at age 20, she moved to New York City and entered the world of radical politics. She soon became famous for her fiery speeches. After one such speech in 1893, she was convicted of inciting a riot and sent to prison for a year.

In 1906 Goldman started a radical monthly called *Mother Earth.* In its pages she presented articles on a wide range of topics, from birth control to modern art and literature. Above all, she used the magazine as a forum to defend freedom of speech.

In 1917 Goldman was arrested again, this time for opposing the draft. Two years later, at the height of the Red Scare, she was released from prison and deported to Russia. Like many other radicals, she was eager to see revolutionary Russia up close. "At last . . . ," she wrote, "I would behold . . . the land freed from political and economic masters." Instead of a free land, however, she found a country where freedom of expression was severely limited. Disenchanted, Goldman left Russia in 1921 and spent the rest of her life speaking and writing in Europe.

By mid-1920 public hysteria over radicalism was dying down. The fearful predictions of A. Mitchell Palmer and others that a Communist revolution was close at hand proved to be unfounded. Furthermore, many Americans had never supported the witch-hunting tactics employed by many of the anti-Communist crusaders.

SACCO AND VANZETTI

Although the Red Scare passed, hostility toward foreigners and radicals persisted. This hostility was evident during the 1921 trial of two Italian anarchists, Nicola Sacco and Bartolomeo Vanzetti. Accused of committing murder during a payroll robbery at a factory outside Boston, they were convicted and sentenced to death.

The verdict outraged defenders of civil liberties. They argued that the two men had been

◄ **American poet Edna St. Vincent Millay was one of many protesters during the Sacco and Vanzetti trial.**

convicted not because of the evidence presented but because they were immigrants and radicals. Even the trial judge had shown bias by declaring that the men's anarchist beliefs were grounds for conviction.

The verdict and subsequent appeals drew worldwide attention. In Paris, New York City, and elsewhere, thousands of people marched in protest. Noted writers and artists rallied to the cause. Calling them "victims of race and national prejudice and class hatred," labor unions contributed to Sacco and Vanzetti's defense fund. The protesters

called for a new trial, but all these pleas failed. On August 23, 1927, Sacco and Vanzetti were executed.

Many Americans believed that radicals like Sacco and Vanzetti deserved to be punished for their views, while others saw them as heroes and martyrs. Historians still debate whether Sacco and Vanzetti were guilty or innocent. All agree, however, that the case reflected the deep divisions tearing at American society in the postwar era.

■■ **The Sacco and Vanzetti case underscored a hostility in the United States toward foreigners and radicals following the war.**

Ben Shahn, Bartolomeo Vanzetti and Nicola Sacco (1931–1932)

▶ **In the early 1930s immigrant artist Ben Shahn created a series of paintings about the events surrounding the Sacco and Vanzetti trial.**

SECTION **1** REVIEW

IDENTIFY and explain the significance of the following: demobilization, Ole Hanson, Edwin Curtis, Red Scare, A. Mitchell Palmer, Palmer raids, Emma Goldman, Nicola Sacco, Bartolomeo Vanzetti.

LOCATE and explain the importance of the following: Seattle, Washington; Boston, Massachusetts.

1. **MAIN IDEA** How did the end of World War I affect the economy?
2. **MAIN IDEA** How did workers respond to deteriorating economic conditions after the war? Were their efforts successful?
3. **IDENTIFYING CAUSE AND EFFECT** What events led to the Red Scare? What were some of the Red Scare's consequences?
4. **WRITING TO INFORM** Imagine you are a reporter covering the Sacco and Vanzetti case. Write an article exploring the public debate surrounding the anarchists' arrest and conviction.
5. **ANALYZING** Why can it be said that international events had a strong impact on American society in the postwar years?

FOCUS OBJECTIVES

■ Explain why voters elected Warren G. Harding president in 1920.

■ Analyze how the economy fared under Harding.

■ Assess the presidency of Calvin Coolidge.

■ Describe some effects of the Republicans' probusiness policies.

BUILDING VOCABULARY

The word *nostrum* means a "usually questionable remedy or scheme." It also refers to a medicine with secret ingredients recommended without scientific proof of its effectiveness.

PRIMARY SOURCE

Description of Change: excerpted and bracketed **Rationale:** excerpted to focus on main idea; bracketed to clarify meaning

628

Section 2

THE REPUBLICANS IN POWER

F O C U S
■ **Why did voters elect Warren G. Harding president in 1920?**
■ **How did the economy fare under Harding?**
■ **What kind of president was Calvin Coolidge?**
■ **What were some effects of the Republicans' probusiness policies?**

Tired of social strife, voters in the 1920 election rejected the party of Woodrow Wilson and elected Republican Warren G. Harding president. Although the Harding years ended in scandal, Harding's Republican successor, Calvin Coolidge, restored a sense of integrity to the White House. As a result, voters elected another Republican president—Herbert Hoover—in 1928.

1924 campaign slogan favoring big business

THE ELECTION OF 1920

With the country in turmoil and Republican voters united once again, Republican leaders felt confident of victory in the 1920 presidential election. As their candidate they nominated Senator Warren G. Harding of Ohio. Harding lacked Woodrow Wilson's razor-sharp intelligence, but he was pleasant and friendly.

Harding ran on a probusiness, antilabor platform that promised tax revision, higher tariffs, limits on immigration, and some aid to farmers. What pleased war-weary voters

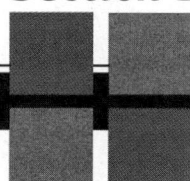

◄ **With this 1920 campaign ribbon, the Republican party in Pennsylvania urged voters to support the "whole Republican ticket."**

the most, however, was Harding's call for a return to "normalcy":

   ❝ America's present need is not heroics but healing, not nostrums [quack cures] but normalcy, not revolution but restoration, . . . not surgery but serenity, . . . not submergence in internationality but sustainment in triumphant nationality. **❞**

In contrast, the Democratic candidate, Governor James M. Cox of Ohio, bowed to pressure from President Wilson and stressed support for the League of Nations.

   The nation's farmers, suffering from falling farm prices, threw their support behind Harding. Many in the middle class, tired of labor strikes and high taxes, also voted Republican. Americans cast their vote for "normalcy," giving Harding some 60 percent of the popular vote.

■■ **Anxious for stability after the war and the social strife of the Wilson years, American voters elected a Republican president.**

MOTIVATING: STUDENT EXPERIENCES

Name a recent or current U.S. president. On a sheet of paper, have students rate the president's performance as good, fair, or poor and list the criteria they used to make their judgments. Ask volunteers to explain their criteria. Tell students to use their criteria to rate the presidents they will read about in this section.

Teaching the Section

THE ELECTION OF 1920

Ask students to explain why a campaign that promised "a return to normalcy" would appeal so strongly to American voters in 1920. Have students speculate how the term "normalcy" could be interpreted by each of these groups: manufacturers, farmers, nativists, isolationists, union workers. Then have students take on the role of a member of one of the groups discussed above and write a paragraph titled "How I Voted in 1920 and Why." Call on volunteers to read their paragraphs to the class. Ask class members to guess the roles of the readers. Students may wish to include their paragraphs in their portfolios.

▶

THE HARDING ADMINISTRATION

From his first day in office, Harding set a very different tone from that of the somber Wilson. Journalist Frederick Lewis Allen commented on the change:

> 66 For four long years the gates of the White House had been locked and guarded with sentries. Harding's first official act was to throw them open, to permit . . . sight-seers to roam the grounds and flatten their noses against the executive window-panes. . . . The act seemed to symbolize the return of the government to the people. 99

Focus on the economy. What the Harding administration came to symbolize, however, was—as Harding put it—"less government in business

PRESIDENTIAL LIVES

WARREN G. HARDING
1865–1923

in office
1921–1923

A genial, sociable man, Warren G. Harding was fond of drinking and spending time with his friends. He was the sort "to play poker with all Saturday night," one associate recalled. Under Harding, the White House had more the atmosphere of an Elks or Moose lodge than a stately executive mansion. Liquor flowed freely at Harding's parties, despite Prohibition.

Harding, who did not like being president, compared his position to being in jail. Believing that he was unsuited for the job, he once remarked that he was "a man of limited talents from a small town."

▲ President Harding's cabinet was photographed on the White House lawn at its first meeting in 1921. Secretary of State Charles Evans Hughes is seated to Harding's right, while Vice President Calvin Coolidge is seated to his left.

and more business in government." His probusiness cabinet included such successful businessmen as Secretary of the Treasury Andrew W. Mellon and Secretary of Commerce Herbert Hoover.

These men believed that government should not interfere with the economy except to aid business. As a result, the administration had two main economic goals: to reduce the national debt and to promote economic growth.

Wartime spending had driven up the national debt from some $1 billion in 1914 to more than $25 billion in 1919. To eliminate the debt, the head of the newly created Bureau of the Budget, Charles Dawes, set out to slash spending. In 1922, his first year on the job, Dawes succeeded in turning the annual deficit into a surplus.

To achieve the second goal—economic growth—Secretary Mellon proposed eliminating the high wartime taxes imposed on the wealthy. If "government takes away an unreasonable share," he argued, "the incentive to work is no longer there and slackening of effort is the result." Furthermore, he claimed, if taxes were lower, the rich would have more money to invest and the economy would grow. The benefits, Mellon said, would then trickle down to the middle and lower classes in the form of jobs and higher wages. In response to Mellon's program, Congress cut taxes on wealthy Americans during the 1920s.

By 1923 Harding's economic policy appeared to be working. The postwar slump was over, unemployment was low, and most sectors of the economy had entered a period of tremendous growth. Not all sectors were flourishing, however.

PRIMARY SOURCE
Description of Change: excerpted
Rationale: excerpted to focus on main idea

HISTORICAL SIDELIGHTS
Small-town Values
Harding won a landslide victory in 1920 in part because he seemed to stand for many of the values associated with small-town life. Harding's speeches often emphasized that he was a small-town boy who made good. "I grew up in a village of six hundred . . . and I have often referred to it as a fine illustration of the opportunities of American life," Harding said. "There is more happiness in the American village than any other place on the face of the earth." Many voters in 1920 could identify with Harding's roots and dreamed that they too could become self-made successes.

Teaching the **Section**

THE ECONOMY UNDER HARDING

Select a volunteer to explain Harding's philosophy of "less government in business and more business in government." Have other students cite ways that Harding addressed each goal. Then ask students to state their opinions of Harding's policies. Have the class assess the economy's health under Harding.

MAKING CONNECTIONS

Economics

Another signal, besides the "sick industries," that not all was well with the U.S. economy during the 1920s was the very uneven distribution of the prosperity generated by the government's economic policies. One-tenth of 1 percent of the families at the top received as much income as the bottom 42 percent of families.

HISTORICAL SIDELIGHTS

Veterans' Bureau Scandal

One of the typical schemes of Veterans' Bureau director Charles Forbes was to give a St. Louis firm a contract to build new hospitals in exchange for substantial kickbacks. He also made money by selling some $3 million worth of government bed sheets and other hospital supplies to a Boston company for about $600,000.

The coal industry fell on hard times as oil became a popular fuel source. The producers of cotton and wool textiles suffered because of competition from new synthetic fabrics, such as rayon. These and other "sick industries" signaled that not all was well in the economy.

■■ **The Harding administration's probusiness policies helped fuel an economic boom, but not all sectors of the economy benefited.**

The Harding scandals. Midway through Harding's term, most Americans seemed happy with the nation's course. Yet talk of corruption had begun to haunt the Harding administration. A group of Harding's friends—known as the Ohio Gang—had followed him to Washington and were using their connections with the president to enrich themselves at the public's expense.

The first scandal came to light in the spring of 1923, when it was discovered that Charles Forbes, director of the Veterans' Bureau and Harding's close friend, had received millions of dollars as the result of corrupt schemes. Harding was deeply worried over the Forbes scandal and other signs of wrongdoing in his administration. In June 1923 he confessed to journalist William Allen White, "I have no trouble with my enemies. I can take care of my enemies all right. [It's my] friends . . . that keep me walking the floor nights." Soon after talking to White, Harding set out on an extended tour of the West. In San Francisco on August 2, he died.

After Harding's death other scandals surfaced. In 1924 Attorney General Harry Daugherty,

◀ Teapot Dome and other scandals tarnished the reputation of the Harding administration.

Harding's right-hand man, was forced to resign after it was discovered he had been taking bribes. Next erupted the **Teapot Dome scandal**, which took its name from a government oil reserve in Teapot Dome, Wyoming. According to a Senate investigation, Secretary of the Interior Albert Fall had received loans, cash, and cattle for leasing the oil reserve—along with another reserve in California—to private oil companies. Fall was convicted of accepting bribes and jailed in 1926— the first cabinet member to be imprisoned for crimes committed while in office.

COOLIDGE TAKES CHARGE

After Harding's death Vice President Calvin Coolidge succeeded to the presidency. Immediately he began working to limit the damage from the Harding scandals and to restore the reputation of the presidency.

Coolidge easily won the Republican presidential nomination in 1924. On the 103rd ballot the Democrats, divided between rural and urban wings and split over issues such as prohibition, chose John W. Davis, a corporate lawyer. Both parties faced strong opposition from the Progressive party's nominee, Robert La Follette. Backed by angry farmers and workers, the Progressive platform denounced federal policies favoring business and called for more aid to working people.

Despite these rumblings of discontent, Coolidge won by a landslide, receiving 15.7 million votes to Davis's 8.4 million. La Follette received about 4.8 million votes. Although the Progressive party faded from the scene when La Follette died soon after the election, its strong showing made it clear that not all Americans agreed with the Republicans' emphasis on big business.

In some ways Calvin Coolidge seemed an unlikely man to win the support of so many Americans. Stern

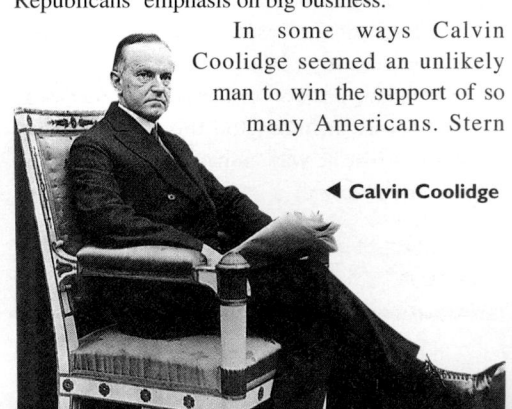

◀ Calvin Coolidge

PRESIDENTIAL LIVES

CALVIN COOLIDGE
1872–1933

in office 1923–1929

Vermont-born Calvin Coolidge had a stern face and quiet, unemotional manner that made him seem the very picture of cold New England granite. According to his wife Grace, once at a Washington dinner party another guest told Coolidge she had bet that she could make him say at least three words to her. Tight-lipped as usual, Coolidge replied, "You lose."

"Silent Cal" could be as frugal—or even stingy—as he was quiet. Sometimes rather than buying presents, he sent out the boxes of cigars that he himself had received as gifts. Coolidge even refused to share the contents of the stream in front of his vacation home in South Dakota. One day he observed a stranger catching fish from the stream. Coolidge sent a Secret Service agent after the man to retrieve the fish, stating bluntly, "They are my fish."

and unemotional, he was known as Silent Cal. His often sour expression inspired one wit's comment that Coolidge looked as if he had been weaned on a pickle. Yet because Coolidge's no-nonsense manner and frugal habits recalled a simpler era, many Americans found him reassuring.

A staunch conservative, Coolidge was even more probusiness than Harding. "The business of America is business," he once declared. "The man who builds a factory builds a temple. The man who works there worships there." Coolidge favored legislation to aid business but generally opposed laws to help farmers or workers, arguing that such legislation stifled private initiative and harmed the economy.

Coolidge also took a tightfisted approach to government spending. In the name of economy, he vetoed a bonus bill designed to aid World War I veterans (Congress passed the bill over his veto). He also vetoed a bill designed to boost farm prices by authorizing the government to buy surplus crops and sell them abroad.

Despite these vetoes the president remained popular and almost certainly could have won reelection in 1928. Instead, to almost everyone's surprise, he announced he would not run.

▪▪ **Coolidge was a conservative, probusiness president whose no-nonsense style won the support of most Americans.**

𝒯HE ELECTION OF 1928

In 1928 the Republicans nominated Secretary of Commerce Herbert Hoover for president. Hoover had a reputation for skill and efficiency. His strongest asset, though, was the nation's apparent prosperity after eight years of Republican rule. In a campaign speech he declared:

❝ The poorhouse is vanishing from among us. We have not yet reached the goal, but, given a chance to go forward with the policies of the last eight years, we shall soon . . . be in sight of the day when poverty will be banished from this nation. ❞

▲ By the 1928 election Herbert Hoover was known for his integrity and humanitarian ideals.

After a bitter fight the Democrats nominated Governor Alfred E. Smith of New York, a moderate progressive. The party's choice signaled a shift in Democratic strategy—a response, in part, to the Progressive party's strength in the 1924 election. Smith's core support came from urban immigrant voters. By nominating Smith, the Democrats hoped to be seen as "the party of progress and liberal thought," as Franklin Roosevelt put it. Yet Smith had several political liabilities. He was Roman Catholic, he opposed prohibition, and he had ties

Practice

GUIDED PRACTICE

Draw on the chalkboard a two-column chart with the headings *Harding Administration* and *Coolidge Administration*. Call on students to list the ways that each administration approached the country's economy. Write responses in the appropriate column.

INDEPENDENT PRACTICE

Direct students to use the chart developed in the Guided Practice to write a paragraph that compares Harding's and Coolidge's economic policies and that concludes with a generalization about the effects of Republicans' probusiness policies. Students may wish to include their paragraphs in their portfolios.

Review and Assessment

REVIEW Have students work in pairs to prepare memorials to Harding and Coolidge, highlighting key events in the administration of each and listing their policy successes and failures. Then assign the Section 2 Review on p. 633.

ASSESS Assign the **Section 2 Daily Quiz** in *Core Resources*.

 GLOBAL CONNECTIONS

The Fordney-McCumber Tariff Act had a terrible effect on world trade. The act blocked Europe from selling goods to the U.S., and as a result of retaliatory tariffs imposed by Europe on the U.S., American goods were no longer sold to Europe. In addition, by preventing U.S. war loans from being repaid in goods, the tariff created serious economic problems for European governments—problems that would later help bring down their economies during the global depression of the 1930s.

HISTORICAL SIDELIGHTS

Division over the ERA

Women who opposed the ERA because they feared it would invalidate protective legislation found allies among conservative groups such as the National Council of Catholic Women. The members of this organization believed the amendment "seriously menaced . . . the unity of the home and family life" and went against the "essential differences in rights and duties" of the sexes.

---

to New York City's Tammany Hall. All these points stirred strong opposition to Smith's candidacy, especially in the South.

Riding on Smith's handicaps and the economy's strength, Hoover won 58 percent of the popular vote. Smith lost his own state as well as several southern states that went Republican for the first time since Reconstruction. However, Smith did well in the nation's largest cities. His appeal to these voters offered the Democrats hope for the future.

■■ Herbert Hoover sailed to victory in 1928 on the strength of the economy and his opponent's political liabilities.

---

*T*HE EFFECTS OF REPUBLICAN POLICIES

During the 1920s the Republican administrations' probusiness policies helped promote economic growth. Yet these policies also had negative effects on the environment and on many working people.

Business growth and prosperity. One reason for the economic boom that began in 1923 was the availability of surplus capital, in part due to tax cuts. This capital allowed old industries to grow rapidly and new ones to enter the ranks of the corporate giants. The 1920s also saw more than 1,000 **mergers**—the combining of two or more companies. Business favored mergers because they brought greater efficiency and higher profits. By 1930, some 200 corporations owned nearly half the nation's corporate wealth. The government, with its favorable attitude toward business, encouraged this process of consolidation and made little effort to enforce antitrust laws.

▲ As early as 1917, the corner of 42nd St. and Madison Ave. in New York City was often congested with heavy auto traffic.

This rapid industrial growth was not without its drawbacks, however. Chemical wastes poured into the nation's rivers and lakes. Cities witnessed increased traffic congestion and air pollution. Yet few Americans saw these consequences of industrial development as problems.

Labor and farming. Workers did not share significantly in business's good fortune during the 1920s. From 1923 to 1929, business profits increased some 60 percent. Over the same period, workers' incomes grew by only about 10 percent. Many workers in "sick industries" even faced pay cuts and unemployment. Farmers were also hit hard, as the postwar slump in farm prices continued into the 1920s.

To help farmers, Congress passed the **Fordney-McCumber Tariff Act** of 1922. The act levied high duties on imported farm products in an effort to boost domestic crop prices. But it brought little relief. Farmers still faced shrinking markets, low prices, high interest rates, and crushing debts.

Organized labor also suffered during the 1920s as the government and courts sought to roll back the gains of the Progressive Era. Federal courts, for example, upheld "yellow-dog contracts," which required employees to promise not to join a union. At the same time, business leaders promoted a policy known as the **American Plan**. The plan called for open shops—factories in which workers could choose not to join unions and management did not have to negotiate with union leaders. As a result, union membership shrank from a high of more than 5 million in 1920 to some 3.6 million in 1923. Without the backing of strong unions, many people continued to work long hours for low wages under often unsafe conditions.

■■ Republican policies contributed to business growth and general prosperity, but many workers and farmers suffered.

---

*T*HE EQUAL RIGHTS AMENDMENT

Regulating hours, working conditions, and wages for women and children had been an important part of the progressive agenda. However, in the 1920s women debated the desirability of such protective legislation. This debate came about because of the National Woman's party's efforts on behalf of the

Equal Rights Amendment, introduced into Congress in 1923. Had it passed, the amendment would have given men and women "equal rights throughout the United States." One of the amendment's effects would have been to invalidate protective legislation.

The amendment drew most of its support from middle-class and professional women. They argued that protective legislation discouraged employers from hiring women. Furthermore, they argued, limitations on working hours kept women out of many highly paid jobs.

Opponents of the amendment supported protective legislation as necessary to protect women—few of whom belonged to unions—and their families. Mary Anderson, director of the U.S. Women's Bureau, asserted:

> ❝ Women who are wage earners, with one job in the factory and another in the home, have little time and energy left to carry on the fight to better their economic status. They need the help of . . . labor laws. ❞

Pauline Newman of the Women's Trade Union League observed that before protective legislation women "were 'free' and 'equal' to work long hours for starvation wages, or free to leave the job and starve!"

Protective legislation did hamper women working in male-dominated occupations. However, few working-class women were employed in such occupations. Thus, they withheld their support for the amendment, which they viewed as benefiting

only middle-class and upper-class women who had the training to enter the professions or skilled trades.

The debate over these issues created deep divisions in the women's movement. It would continue to divide women's organizations until the 1960s.

█ █ The debate over the Equal Rights Amendment divided women's groups.

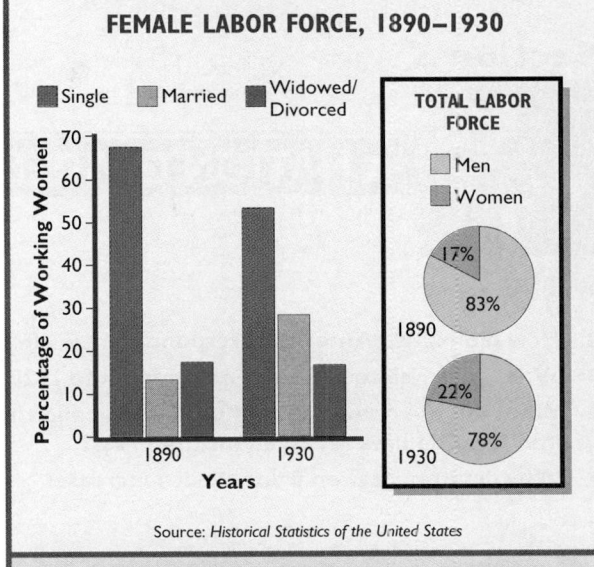

FEMALE LABOR FORCE, 1890–1930

Source: *Historical Statistics of the United States*

WOMEN AT WORK Not only did the size of the female labor force grow by 1930, its makeup also changed. By 1930 some 30 percent of working women were married, up from just over 10 percent in 1890.

? BUILDING GRAPH SKILLS Women made up what percentage of the total labor force in 1890? in 1930?

**█ █
S E C T I O N 2 R E V I E W**

IDENTIFY and explain the significance of the following: Warren G. Harding, Andrew W. Mellon, Herbert Hoover, Charles Dawes, Teapot Dome scandal, Albert Fall, Calvin Coolidge, Alfred E. Smith, mergers, Fordney-McCumber Tariff Act, American Plan.

1. **MAIN IDEA** Why did American voters elect a Republican president in 1920?
2. **MAIN IDEA** What qualities did President Coolidge possess that won the support of most Americans in the 1920s?
3. **ASSESSING CONSEQUENCES** What effect did the probusiness policies of Harding and Coolidge have on the economy?
4. **WRITING TO PERSUADE** Imagine you are a Republican campaigning for Herbert Hoover in 1928. Write a handbill you would distribute to urge other voters to support your candidate.
5. **ANALYZING** Why were women's groups divided over support of the Equal Rights Amendment?

PREVIEW WORKSHOP

*Following is a list of the significant
people and terms in this section.
You may wish to use this list as a
section preview.*

People
■ A. Philip Randolph
■ Marcus Garvey

Terms
■ Immigration Act of 1924

FOCUS OBJECTIVES

■ Describe how Native
Americans responded to
new efforts to seize tribal land.

■ Summarize factors that
gave rise to black nationalism in the 1920s.

■ Analyze what the revival
of the Ku Klux Klan and
the passage of new
immigration laws
revealed about the
1920s.

■ Explain why immigration
from Mexico increased.

PRIMARY SOURCE

Description of Change:
excerpted
Rationale: excerpted to
focus on main idea

CORE RESOURCES

• **Literature
  Worksheet 21**
• **Section 3 Daily Quiz**

AV RESOURCES

• **Linking Geography
  and History
  Transparency** and
  Worksheet 17

Section 3

A NATION DIVIDED

FOCUS

■ **How did Native Americans respond to new efforts to seize tribal land?**
■ **What gave rise to black nationalism in the 1920s?**
■ **What did the revival of the Ku Klux Klan and the passage of new
  immigration laws reveal about the 1920s?**
■ **Why did immigration from Mexico increase?**

*Although many Americans prospered during the 1920s, deep social
and racial divisions still plagued American life. Native Americans,
African Americans, and Mexican immigrants all struggled for a
place in American society. As African Americans continued to
migrate to northern cities, racial tensions increased. The
Ku Klux Klan encouraged bigotry not only against African
Americans but also against foreigners. Responding to the
national mood, Congress passed laws limiting immigration.*

Ku Klux Klansman

NATIVE AMERICAN LIFE

For Native Americans the 1920s brought some
recognition of the difficulties they faced. The
Dawes Act, which attempted to "Americanize"

▲ **Native Americans carry water from a government well
in Arizona.**

Indians by dividing tribal land into individual
plots (see Chapter 14) had clearly failed. The
act's allotment policies—as the Board of Indian
Commissioners acknowledged—had often been
"a short cut to the separation of . . . Indians from
their land and cash."

In the 1920s Native Americans successfully
organized to fight new efforts to take tribal land.
Native American leaders stopped the Harding
administration's attempt to buy back all tribal land.
Then in 1922 the different Pueblo tribes of the
Southwest organized against the Bursum Bill,
which was designed to legalize non–Native
American claims to Pueblo land. Furthermore, the
bill would limit the power of tribal governments.
The Pueblos appealed to all Americans:

   66 This bill will destroy our common life
and will rob us of everything which we hold
dear—our lands, our customs, our traditions. Are the American people willing to
see this happen? **99**

Teaching the Section

AMERICAN INDIAN RIGHTS

Ask students to analyze the effectiveness of American Indians' efforts to retain their land. Have them list evidence that the government was beginning to listen to their interests and evidence that improvements in policy still needed to be made.

▶

Many Americans were not. The Pueblos won the support of the General Federation of Women's Clubs and of anthropologists, as well as the support of many other influential men and women. As a result, the *New York Times* could write in January 1923 that the bill was "happily, dead."

In 1924 Congress granted citizenship to all Native Americans, partly in recognition of those who had fought in World War I. But citizenship did not soften the harsh effects of poverty that many Native Americans continued to experience.

■■ **Native Americans organized to fight efforts to take their lands.**

*A*FRICAN AMERICANS MOVE NORTH

During the 1920s some 800,000 African Americans joined the hundreds of thousands who had moved to the North during World War I. By 1930 the North's African American population had reached almost 2.5 million, more than double its size in 1910. Large African American communities sprang up in Chicago, Detroit, New York City, and other

▲ A neighborhood strewn with rubble reveals the tragic aftermath of the Chicago race riots in 1919.

northern cities. Harlem, a section of New York City with a large black population, proudly styled itself "the capital of Black America."

The North, however, was not free of bigotry. African Americans who had risked their lives in Europe "to make the world safe for democracy" confronted lynch mobs. Others faced discrimination, and as demands for labor eased, African Americans were the first to lose their jobs.

At times, racial tensions erupted violently. One of the worst outbreaks occurred in Chicago in July 1919. The trouble began when a white man

VOICES IN HISTORY

Not all American Indians were pleased by the government's decision to grant them citizenship. Tuscarora chief Clinton Rickard feared his people would lose their status as a sovereign tribe. "We had a great attachment to our style of government. We wished to remain treaty Indians and preserve our ancient rights. There was no great rush among my people to go out and vote in white man's elections. Anyone who did so was denied the privilege of becoming a chief."

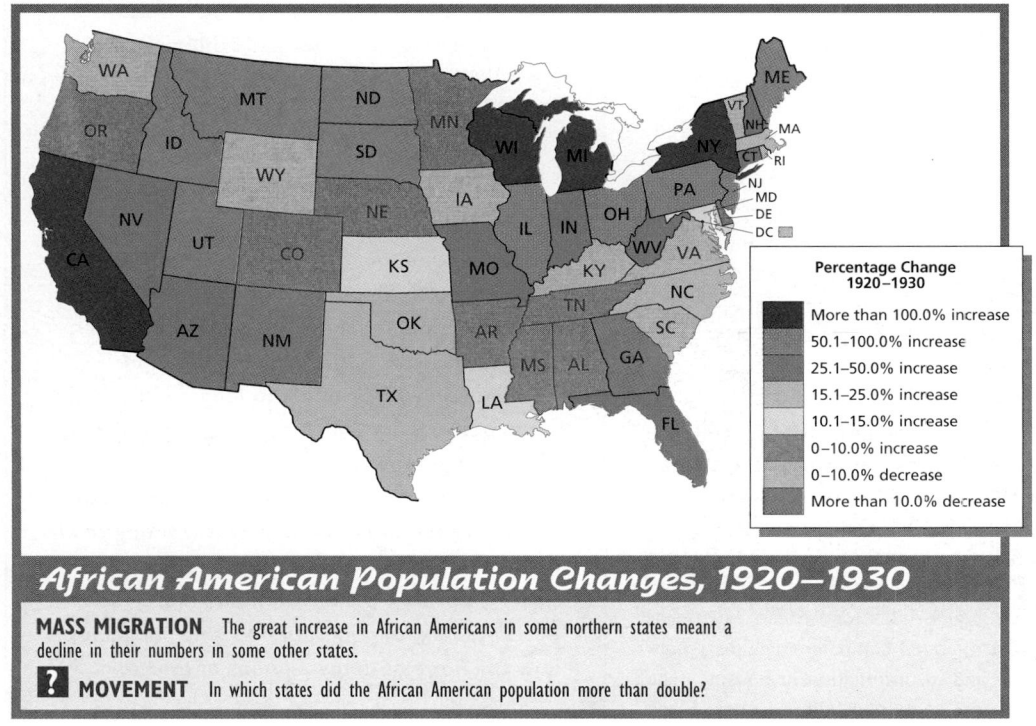

African American Population Changes, 1920–1930

Percentage Change 1920–1930

- More than 100.0% increase
- 50.1–100.0% increase
- 25.1–50.0% increase
- 15.1–25.0% increase
- 10.1–15.0% increase
- 0–10.0% increase
- 0–10.0% decrease
- More than 10.0% decrease

MASS MIGRATION The great increase in African Americans in some northern states meant a decline in their numbers in some other states.

❓ **MOVEMENT** In which states did the African American population more than double?

Teaching the Section

RISE OF BLACK NATIONALISM

Invite each student to imagine that he or she is editor of a 1920s African American newspaper. Direct students to write editorials for their newspapers that describe the status of African Americans in the 1920s and that express opinions on the programs and goals of Marcus Garvey. Select students to read their editorials to the class. Students may wish to include their editorials in their portfolios.

THE KKK AND IMMIGRATION QUOTAS

Draw a two-column chart on the chalkboard with the headings *Ku Klux Klan* and *Immigration Act of 1924*. Ask students to list the groups that were discriminated against by the KKK or through passage of the act. List responses on the chart. Then ask students what the chart suggests about the national attitude toward racial and ethnic groups in the 1920s.

HISTORICAL SIDELIGHTS
Pullman Porters

In the 1920s sleeping-car porters had high status in the African American community. Porters were relatively well paid, and such jobs were often the only ones open to black college graduates. However, compared with unionized white railroad workers, porters were grossly underpaid. Beginning in 1925, A. Philip Randolph led the porters in a 12-year fight to get the Pullman Company to recognize their union.

PRIMARY SOURCES
Description of Change: excerpted and bracketed
Rationale: excerpted to focus on main idea; bracketed to clarify meaning

HISTORICAL SIDELIGHTS
Garvey's Charisma

Garvey was an inspired entrepreneur and promoter who drew by some estimates anywhere from a half a million to two million people to the UNIA. Huge crowds attended Garvey's parades, at which members of his African Legion carried the tricolor UNIA flag. Garvey said the flag was black for the race, red for the blood of the race, and green for the hope of the race.

▲ The NAACP began as an interracial coalition fighting for African Americans' rights. James Weldon Johnson, seated behind the desk, served as executive secretary of the NAACP from 1920 to 1930. Johnson was also a noted author and songwriter.

threw rocks at an African American teenager swimming in Lake Michigan. The boy drowned. The fight that broke out between whites and blacks on shore spread to the rest of the city. The rioting continued for more than a week. White gangs fueled much of the violence as they prowled the slums, attacking African Americans and destroying property. By the time order was restored, 38 people had been killed and 537 injured.

By late 1919, some 25 race riots had erupted around the country. In June 1921, at least 30 people died during a race riot in Tulsa, Oklahoma. One resident described attacks on the black section of town:

> 66 People were seen to flee from their burning homes, some with babes in their arms and leading crying and excited children. . . . [A] machine gun . . . was raining bullets down on our section. 99

Faced with continued violence and discrimination, many African Americans organized to defend their rights. The National Association for the Advancement of Colored People (NAACP) stepped up its legal battle to win equal rights for African Americans and mounted campaigns against lynching and discrimination in housing. The unions' continued failure to help black

workers led labor activist A. Philip Randolph to found the Brotherhood of Sleeping Car Porters in 1925. It became a powerful voice for black workers.

*B*LACK NATIONALISM

Frustrated by the slow pace of change, some African Americans lost hope of ever achieving equality in the United States. What African Americans needed, they said, was a nation of their own. Foremost among these black nationalists was Marcus Garvey.

Garvey, a native of Jamaica, founded the Universal Negro Improvement Association (UNIA) in 1914. UNIA had two main goals: to foster African Americans' economic independence by establishing black-owned businesses and to create an independent black homeland in Africa. "We

THE BACK–TO–AFRICA MOVEMENT

Marcus Garvey's Back-to-Africa movement drew many followers both in America and in Africa. In 1922 a representative of the king of Abyssinia (Ethiopia) read the following message to a Universal Negro Improvement Association (UNIA) convention:

THROUGH OTHERS' EYES

> 66 *A*ssure them [Garvey's followers] of the cordiality with which I invite them back to the home land, particularly those qualified to help solve our big problems and to develop our vast resources. Teachers, artisans, mechanics, writers, musicians, professional men and women—all who are able to lend a hand in the constructive work which our country so deeply feels, and greatly needs.
>
> Here we have abundant room and great opportunities and here destiny is working to elevate and enthrone a race which has suffered slavery, poverty, persecution and martyrdom, but whose expanding soul and growing genius is now the hope of many millions of mankind. 99

shall now organize," Garvey told the delegates to UNIA's first international convention, "to plant the banner of freedom on the great continent of Africa."

A charismatic speaker, Garvey urged African

▲ **Marcus Garvey**

Americans to draw on their African heritage. He asserted that before Europeans were civilized:

> ❝ Africa was peopled with a race of cultured black men, who were masters in art, science and literature. . . . Why, then, should we lose hope? Black men, you were once great; you shall be great again. Lose not courage, lose not faith, go forward. ❞

To foster economic independence, Garvey founded the Black Star Steamship Company in 1919. He urged African Americans to invest in his company so that they "may exert the same influence on the world as the white man does today." Garvey promised investors huge returns, but the company never turned a profit. In 1925 Garvey was jailed for mail fraud in connection with his fund-raising activities. President Coolidge pardoned him in 1927 but ordered him deported. He died in 1940, still clinging to his dream.

Garvey's movement declined after he was jailed. Nevertheless, as one newspaper said in 1927, "He made black people proud. . . . He taught them that black is beautiful." Although other African American leaders, such as W.E.B. Du Bois, shared Garvey's belief in racial pride and solidarity, they opposed his Back-to-Africa movement. They insisted that African Americans should fight for justice and equality in American society.

▪▪ **Continued discrimination and a growing sense of black pride led to the rise of black nationalism.**

𝓣HE RETURN OF THE KU KLUX KLAN

To some degree, racism and discrimination during the 1920s reflected a broader repressive mood in American society. More and more, native-born Protestant Americans distrusted people who seemed different. One sign of this growing intolerance was the resurgence of the Ku Klux Klan.

Like the Klan of post–Civil War days, the new Klan, established in 1915 at Stone Mountain, Georgia, used kidnappings, beatings, and lynchings to terrorize African Americans in the South. However, the Klan also grew rapidly outside the South. In northern and midwestern towns and cities, the Klan targeted not only blacks but also radicals, immigrants, Catholics, and Jews, as well as such threats to traditional moral values as divorce.

The Klan grew slowly at first, but as the Red Scare took hold, membership soared. Reaching its peak in the mid-1920s, the Klan had perhaps as many as five million members. At mass rallies white-robed Klan members burned crosses and spoke out against people and ideas they considered "undesirable." Klan views also influenced politics, helping candidates win elections in such states as Louisiana, Oklahoma, Ohio, Texas—even Oregon. The Klan was particularly powerful in Indiana.

After 1925, however, the Klan declined, and by 1930 its membership had dropped to some 9,000. Rising prosperity and the end of the Red Scare diminished the Klan's appeal, but other factors also contributed. One was the conviction of an Indiana Klan leader—Grand Dragon David Stephenson—for second-degree murder. Another was the discovery that Klan promoters were getting rich from membership fees and the sale of regalia. Nevertheless, the Klan did not die out; it continues to spread its message of white supremacy.

▲ **Ku Klux Klan members taught racist attitudes to their children. Here, a baby is being enrolled into the Klan on Independence Day, 1927.**

Practice

GUIDED PRACTICE

Draw a two-column chart on the chalkboard with the headings *Expectations* and *Realities*. In the first column have students list some of the expectations American Indians, African Americans, and Mexican Americans had about how they should be treated in the U.S. In the second column have students identify ways in which those expectations were or were not met.

INDEPENDENT PRACTICE

Invite students to assume the role of an American Indian, African American, or a Mexican American and use the information from the charts created in the Guided Practice to write letters to friends discussing the realities of their lives in the 1920s.

Review and Assessment

REVIEW Ask groups of students to prepare a series of interview questions they could use to gather information from various racial and ethnic groups about life in the 1920s. Have groups exchange their papers and answer the questions they receive. Then assign the Section 3 Review on p. 639.

ASSESS Assign the **Section 3 Daily Quiz** in *Core Resources.*

VOICES IN HISTORY

The Immigration Act of 1924 angered the Japanese, who saw the quotas as discrimination based on race. In a "Message from Japan to America," the *Japan Times and Mail* complained that the law "stamps Japanese as of an inferior race."

■■ Ask students if they think that anti-immigrant sentiment exists in America today. Consider attitudes toward recent non-European immigrant groups.

COOPERATIVE LEARNING

Organize students into groups. Assign each group one of these nationalities: Chinese, Italian, Japanese, Mexican, Russian. Have groups imagine they are immigrants living in the U.S. in 1924. Have each group create an editorial, a letter to the president, and an editorial cartoon reacting to the rise in KKK membership and to the Immigration Act of 1924.

Map Caption Answer
Arizona

Immigration Restrictions

During the 1920s the Klan also played on anti-immigrant feelings. Many Americans feared that the country was being overrun by immigrants—in 1920 nearly a quarter of the population was foreign-born or nonwhite. Furthermore, the number of immigrants, which had declined during the war, was once again rising, increasing from some 140,000 in 1919 to some 805,000 in 1921. This dramatic growth, coupled with the widespread belief that immigrants held radical views and took jobs from native-born Americans, led to demands for limits on immigration.

In 1921 Congress passed a law limiting the number of immigrants from each country allowed into the United States. The quota was set at 3 percent of each nationality already in the country in 1910, except for Asians, who were excluded altogether. (Immigration from nations in the Western Hemisphere was not limited.) The **Immigration Act of 1924** reduced the quota to 2 percent of the 1890 figures for each national group. This change worked against southern and eastern Europeans because in 1890 most Americans traced their origins to England, Ireland, or northern Europe. While the 1924 law did not exclude Asians, it set the annual quota at only 100 Chinese and 100 Japanese immigrants. In 1925 the restrictions reduced the total number of new immigrants from Europe, Africa, Asia, and Australia to some 153,000.

■■ **The revival of the Ku Klux Klan and new limits on immigration revealed continued hostility toward racial and ethnic groups.**

▲ **"Ellis Island Blues" was one of many songs written in the 1920s about the flood of immigrants to the United States after World War I.**

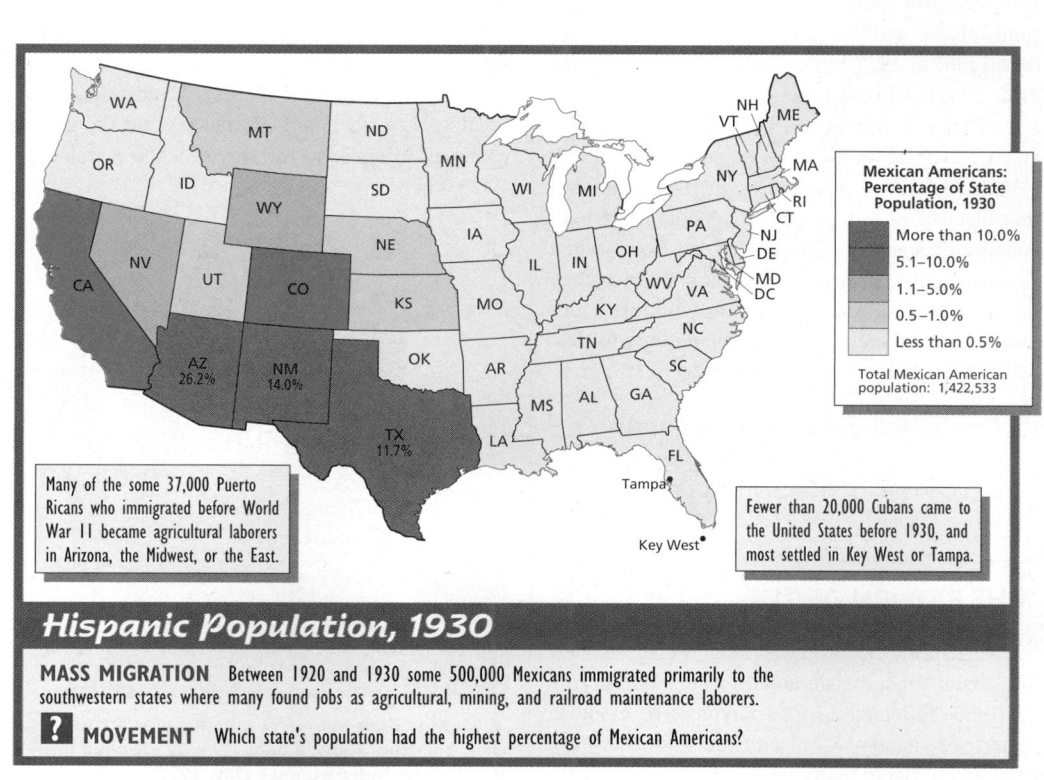

Many of the some 37,000 Puerto Ricans who immigrated before World War II became agricultural laborers in Arizona, the Midwest, or the East.

Fewer than 20,000 Cubans came to the United States before 1930, and most settled in Key West or Tampa.

Mexican Americans: Percentage of State Population, 1930

- More than 10.0%
- 5.1–10.0%
- 1.1–5.0%
- 0.5–1.0%
- Less than 0.5%

Total Mexican American population: 1,422,533

AZ 26.2%
NM 14.0%
TX 11.7%

Hispanic Population, 1930

MASS MIGRATION Between 1920 and 1930 some 500,000 Mexicans immigrated primarily to the southwestern states where many found jobs as agricultural, mining, and railroad maintenance laborers.

? MOVEMENT Which state's population had the highest percentage of Mexican Americans?

RETEACH Have students work in groups, assigning individuals or pairs the task of outlining subsections of Section 3. Have students exchange outlines and use them to ask questions of other members of their group.

Closure

Have students explain why the phrase "Turbulent Twenties" fits the 1920s and have them suggest other phrases for the decade that might describe the experiences of the racial and ethnic groups living in the U.S. at that time.

Extension

COMPARE Have students compare and report on the KKK of the Reconstruction South, the KKK of the 1920s, and the Klan today.

INVESTIGATE Have students research and report on African American, Mexican American, or other migration to their city or state in the 1920s.

MEXICAN AMERICAN MIGRATION

In the Southwest, employers, particularly in agriculture, railroad construction, and mining, encouraged Mexican immigration, which was not affected by the restrictive legislation of the 1920s. Few people were arriving from Europe and Asia, and southwestern employers were eager to keep a steady flow of workers to fill low-wage jobs. As a result, during the 1920s some 500,000 immigrants arrived from Mexico, where wages were far lower.

Those who took agricultural jobs not only had to accept low pay but many also had to live in ramshackle labor camps. One observer noted:

  ❝ Shelters were made of almost every conceivable thing—burlap, canvas, palm branches. . . . We found one woman carrying water in large milk pails from the irrigation ditch. . . . This is evidently all the water which they have in camp. ❞

In the 1920s many Mexican immigrants also moved into urban areas. Some were drawn to well-paying factory jobs in cities such as Chicago and Detroit and established new centers of Mexican population in the Midwest. Most, however, migrated to cities in the Southwest—particularly Los Angeles, El Paso, and San Antonio (see map on page 638). Usually the men came alone, and once established, they sent for their wives and children. Many brought other relatives as well, reestablishing extended family networks. These networks helped new arrivals find jobs and housing.

Because of economic hardship, many families allowed their young, unmarried daughters to work outside the home. Many found employment in bakeries, hotels, and laundries, while others worked as maids. Their newfound independence, as one Mexican immigrant woman sadly noted, brought young women "into conflict with their parents. They learn . . . about the outside world, learn how to speak English, and then they become ashamed of their parents who brought them up here." Despite such conflicts, these new immigrants contributed to the mosaic of cultures that helps define American life.

■■ **The promise of jobs drew Mexican immigrants, who were not subject to restrictive quotas, to cities in the Southwest and Midwest.**

▲ Mexican American Victor Villaseñor wrote *Rain of Gold*, a book about his family's experiences as immigrants to California in the 1920s. Shown here is the 1929 wedding of his parents, Juan Salvador and Lupe.

PRIMARY SOURCE
Description of Change: excerpted
Rationale: excerpted to focus on main idea

SECTION REVIEW ANSWERS

IDENTIFY
For significance, see the following pages:
A. Philip Randolph (p. 636)
Marcus Garvey (p. 636)
Immigration Act of 1924 (p. 638)

1. *successfully organized to appeal for public support and to fight measures such as Bursum Bill*
2. *slow pace of change, continued violence and discrimination, and growing sense of pride inspired by leaders such as Marcus Garvey*
3. *revival of KKK, race riots, passage of Immigration Act of 1924*
4. *Diary entries might mention the lure of employment in agriculture, railroad construction, and mining in the Southwest or in factories in the Midwest.*
5. *Students might mention urban population growth, formation of black communities in major cities, eruption of racial tensions, and organization by African Americans to fight lynching and discrimination in housing and employment.*

■■   **S E C T I O N   3   R E V I E W**

IDENTIFY and explain the significance of the following: A. Philip Randolph, Marcus Garvey, Immigration Act of 1924.

1. **MAIN IDEA** In what way did Native Americans fight government attempts to take tribal land?
2. **MAIN IDEA** What factors contributed to the rise of black nationalism?
3. **MAIN IDEA** What events in the 1920s revealed continued hostility toward racial and ethnic groups?
4. **WRITING TO EXPLAIN** Imagine you are a Mexican immigrant in the 1920s. Write a diary entry that explains why you moved to the Southwest or to the Midwest.
5. **EVALUATING** What effect did the migration of African Americans have on the North?

Chapter Review Answers

WRITING A SUMMARY
See Essential Points in each section for main ideas.

REVIEWING CHRONOLOGY
1, 3, 5, 2, 4
Hypothesizing
Scandals might have discredited Harding's probusiness policies and have led to election of a Democrat.

IDENTIFYING PEOPLE AND IDEAS
1. *shift from wartime to peacetime footing*
2. *police commissioner whose refusal to recognize union led to Boston police strike*
3. *period of anti-Communist hysteria, 1919–20*
4. *feminist writer, speaker, and founder of* Mother Earth *who was deported to Russia*
5. *treasury secretary who proposed taxes reduced on wealthy to spur economic growth*
6. *scandal in which government oil reserve in Wyoming was leased to private oil companies*
7. *combining two or more companies to achieve higher profits and greater efficiency*
8. *business leaders' policy favoring open shops, which discouraged union membership*
9. *black nationalist who founded UNIA and supported creation of black homeland in Africa*
10. *act limiting number of immigrants from southern and eastern Europe, Africa, Asia, and Australia into the United States*

UNDERSTANDING MAIN IDEAS
1. *consumers went on spending spree, thus increasing demand; led to cancellation of war contracts, cutbacks in factory production, layoffs of workers, and drop in farm prices*
2. *failed to achieve goals of higher wages and shorter hours; fear of revolution, antilabor propaganda*
   helped turn public opinion against organized labor
3. *Both favored reduction in government spending, minimal interference in the economy, lower taxes, limits on immigration, and probusiness laws.*
4. *industries that did not share in 20s prosperity; coal industry suffered as oil became more popular fuel than coal; cotton and wool textiles suffered because of competition from new synthetic fibers.*
5. *events—economic problems, strikes, Red Scare, race riots, rise of KKK; attitudes—anti-immigrant sentiment, racial discrimination, fear of anarchists and Communists*

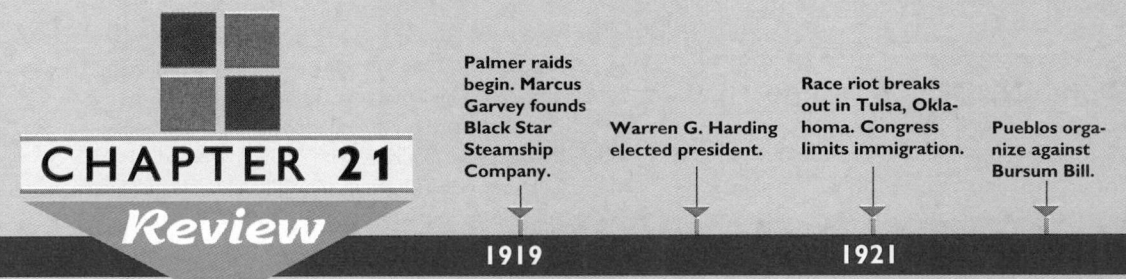

CHAPTER 21
Review

Palmer raids begin. Marcus Garvey founds Black Star Steamship Company.

Warren G. Harding elected president.

Race riot breaks out in Tulsa, Oklahoma. Congress limits immigration.

Pueblos organize against Bursum Bill.

1919   **1921**

WRITING A SUMMARY
Using the essential points of the chapter as a guide, write a summary of the chapter.

REVIEWING CHRONOLOGY
Number your paper 1 to 5. Study the time line above, and list the following events in the order in which they happened by writing the first next to 1, the second next to 2, and so on. Then complete the activity below.

1. Palmer raids begin.
2. Calvin Coolidge elected president.
3. Congress limits immigration.
4. Sacco and Vanzetti executed.
5. Equal Rights Amendment introduced into Congress.

Hypothesizing How might political events have been different during the 1920s if President Harding had not died?

IDENTIFYING PEOPLE AND IDEAS
Explain the historical significance of each of the following people or terms.

1. demobilization
2. Edwin Curtis
3. Red Scare
4. Emma Goldman
5. Andrew W. Mellon
6. Teapot Dome scandal
7. mergers
8. American Plan
9. Marcus Garvey
10. Immigration Act of 1924

UNDERSTANDING MAIN IDEAS
1. Why did the cost of living soar after the war? How did demobilization lead to recession and an increase in unemployment?
2. What were the results of the 1919 strikes in Seattle and Boston?
3. How were Warren G. Harding and Calvin Coolidge alike in their approaches to government?
4. What were the "sick industries" during the 1920s? Why did they fail to benefit from the economic boom?
5. What events and attitudes led to increased social tensions during the 1920s?

🏛 REVIEWING THEMES
1. **Democratic Values** What steps did the federal government take during the 1920s to reduce the perceived threat of revolution?
2. **Cultural Diversity** In what ways did Native Americans, African Americans, and Mexican Americans respond to discrimination?
3. **Economic Development** How did Republican probusiness policies attempt to stimulate the economy?

THINKING CRITICALLY
1. **Synthesizing** Why did many Americans vote Republican in the 1920, 1924, and 1928 presidential elections?
2. **Analyzing** Why did many farmers fail to benefit from the economic boom of the 1920s?
3. **Evaluating** Do you think women's groups that opposed the Equal Rights Amendment were justified? Why or why not?

STRATEGY FOR SUCCESS
Review the Strategies for Success on Recognizing Stereotypes on page 616. Then read the following passage from a 1926 article by Hiram Wesley Evans, the Imperial Wizard of the Ku Klux Klan. What group is the subject of this passage? Why can Evans's characterization be considered an example of stereotyping?

> ❝ The alien . . . is unalterably fixed in his instincts, character, thought, and interests by centuries of racial selection and development. . . . He thinks first for his own people, works only with and for them, . . . considers himself always one of them, and never an American. ❞

WRITING ABOUT HISTORY
Writing to Evaluate Write an essay evaluating the impact of the Sacco and Vanzetti case on public opinion.

REVIEWING THEMES

1. Courts acted against unions by supporting "yellow-dog contracts," attorney general launched crusade against and deported suspected radicals, Congress restricted immigration.
2. Native Americans—organized and gained support to keep tribal lands; African Americans—fought for legal rights, supported black nationalism; Mexican Americans—formed communities and family networks in urban areas
3. reduced national debt and lowered taxes to free capital for investment, vetoed bills that increased government spending, encouraged mergers

THINKING CRITICALLY

1. 1920—tired of social strife, war, and higher taxes; 1924—supported probusiness policies that led to economic boom; 1928—favored strong economy that Hoover promised to continue
2. Farmers suffered because of shrinking markets, falling prices, high interest rates on loans, crushing debts, and failure of high tariff laws to bring relief.
3. Answers should weigh the goals of ERA in helping women compete in male-dominated occupations against the benefits of protective legislation in regulating hours, working conditions, and wages for women not protected by unions.

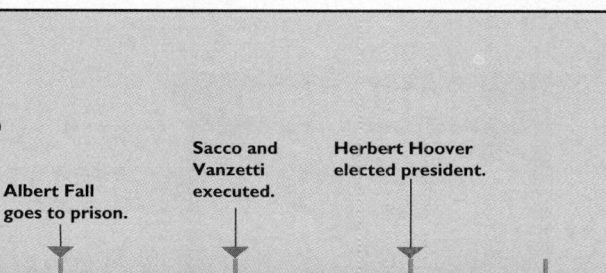

1923		1925		1927		1929

Harding dies. Equal Rights Amendment introduced into Congress.

Congress grants Native Americans citizenship. Immigration Act of 1924 passed. Calvin Coolidge elected president.

A. Philip Randolph founds Brotherhood of Sleeping Car Porters.

Albert Fall goes to prison.

Sacco and Vanzetti executed.

Herbert Hoover elected president.

USING PRIMARY SOURCES

In 1925 more than 11,000 textile workers went on strike in Passaic, New Jersey, to demand better working conditions and higher wages. Read the following excerpt from "The War in Passaic" written by labor activist Mary Heaton Vorse. Then write a paragraph summarizing the author's views of the strike.

❝ Half the picket line is composed of young people. Mothers with children by the hand, older women and high-school boys and girls stream along, their heads thrown back, singing. . . . Passaic sprawling in its winter slush and snow watches its mill-workers make a full-hearted protest against the intolerable conditions in the mills, against the inhuman and unbearable wage cut. . . .

The mayor of Passaic menaced the strikers with a force of three hundred mounted policemen. . . . They charged a crowd of 3,000 strikers, bludgeoned many men, women, and children, and smashed with deliberate intent the persons and cameras of the news photographers. . . . The strikers, armed with gas masks, helmets, and their unbending courage, defied the police successfully—and paraded in peace. . . .

The present Passaic strike is only a phase of the long fight of the textile workers for organization and a living wage. . . . When there is such want and suffering, when conditions of toil are so degrading, when the places that human beings live in are so indecent, it becomes the concern of the public at large to make its power felt and to see that this state of things is altered. ❞

LINKING HISTORY AND GEOGRAPHY

Study the African American and Hispanic population maps on pages 635 and 638. Write a brief summary of the population trends shown on each map. Then prepare a list of possible factors that might help explain the population distributions.

Passaic strikers

BUILDING YOUR PORTFOLIO

Complete the following projects independently or cooperatively.

1. **THE ECONOMY** Imagine you are a World War I veteran in 1919. Write a letter to your senator, explaining why you feel the federal government should help you secure a job. Your letter might mention your concerns about low wages, the high cost of living, and the few employment opportunities available in the postwar economy.

2. **CULTURE AND SOCIETY** Imagine you are an immigrant artist on the staff of Emma Goldman's radical magazine *Mother Earth* in the late 1920s. Create a cover illustration for an upcoming issue that expresses your views about one of the following: the Red Scare, the Sacco and Vanzetti case, labor strikes, or the Equal Rights Amendment.

LAND USE

HISTORICAL SIDELIGHTS

The Novel Soybean

The nutritious soybean was originally introduced to the United States as a novelty item around 1804. By 1900 some farmers began to produce the crop for livestock grazing, then later for industrial uses and for cattle feed. Soybeans were not used in products for human consumption until after the 1930s, when German chemists developed a method of removing the unpleasant taste and odor from soybean oil.

BUILDING VOCABULARY

In recent years the term *agribusiness* has been used to describe the development of large-scale, commercial farming ventures. The term was first used in 1955 by Assistant Secretary of Agriculture John H. Davis to describe the "vertical integration of agriculture through a company's control of the production, processing, and marketing of farm products."

America's GEOGRAPHY

LAND USE

FOR thousands of years Americans have used the land to grow crops. Many Native American groups cultivated crops on small plots of land long before the arrival of Europeans. In the early days of the republic, most farmers continued to grow food crops on small farms, although many large plantations in the South used the land to grow great quantities of tobacco and cotton. By the late 19th century, improved farm machinery and pesticides allowed farmers to grow larger quantities of food on smaller plots of land. Despite changes in farming techniques, some aspects of American farming have remained the same. For instance, corn is still the primary food crop grown in America—just as it was in the earliest civilizations.

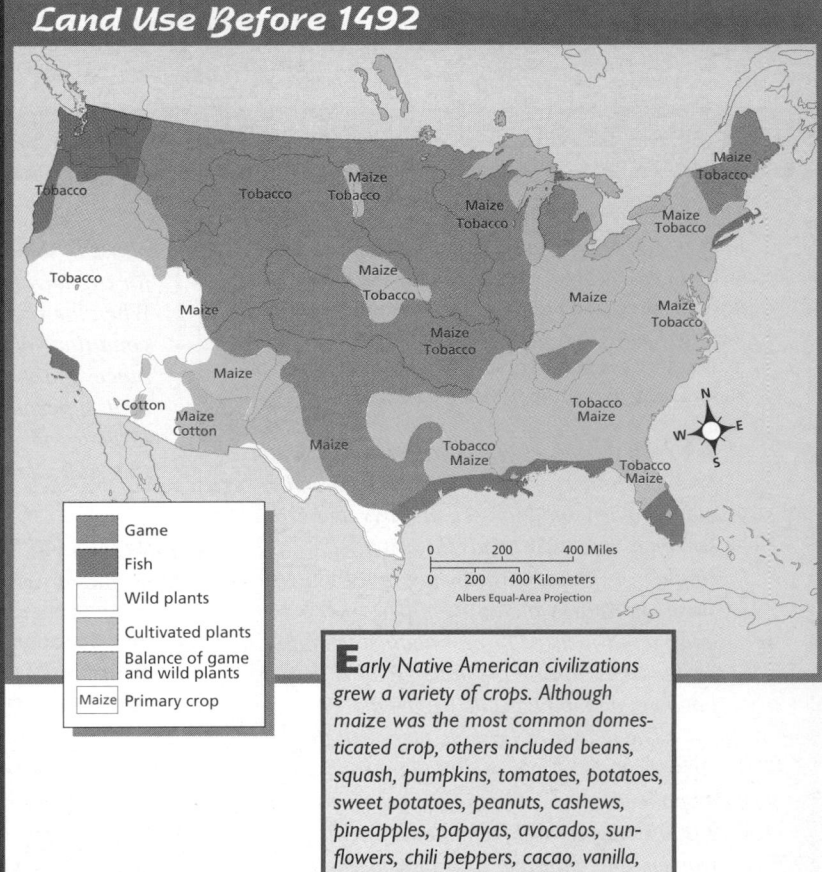

Land Use Before 1492

	Game
	Fish
	Wild plants
	Cultivated plants
	Balance of game and wild plants
Maize	Primary crop

Early Native American civilizations grew a variety of crops. Although maize was the most common domesticated crop, others included beans, squash, pumpkins, tomatoes, potatoes, sweet potatoes, peanuts, cashews, pineapples, papayas, avocados, sunflowers, chili peppers, cacao, vanilla, tobacco, indigo, and cotton.

The multipurpose, high-protein soybean has become the agricultural wonder of the 20th century. By 1991 it was the second most-popular crop in the United States. Soybeans are used in the processing of cattle feed, fertilizer, insect sprays, and paint, as well as in food products such as soy sauce, soy milk, baby food, cereals, processed meats, and tofu.

AGRICULTURAL PRODUCTION, 1910–1991

	1910	1991
CORN (in bushels)	2.85 billion	7.75 billion
WHEAT (in bushels)	625 million	1.98 billion
COTTON (in bales)	11.61 million	17.5 million
TOBACCO (in pounds)	1.05 billion	1.66 billion
SOYBEANS (in bushels)	< 50,000	1.99 billion

Sources: *Historical Statistics of the United States, Statistical Abstract of the United States.*

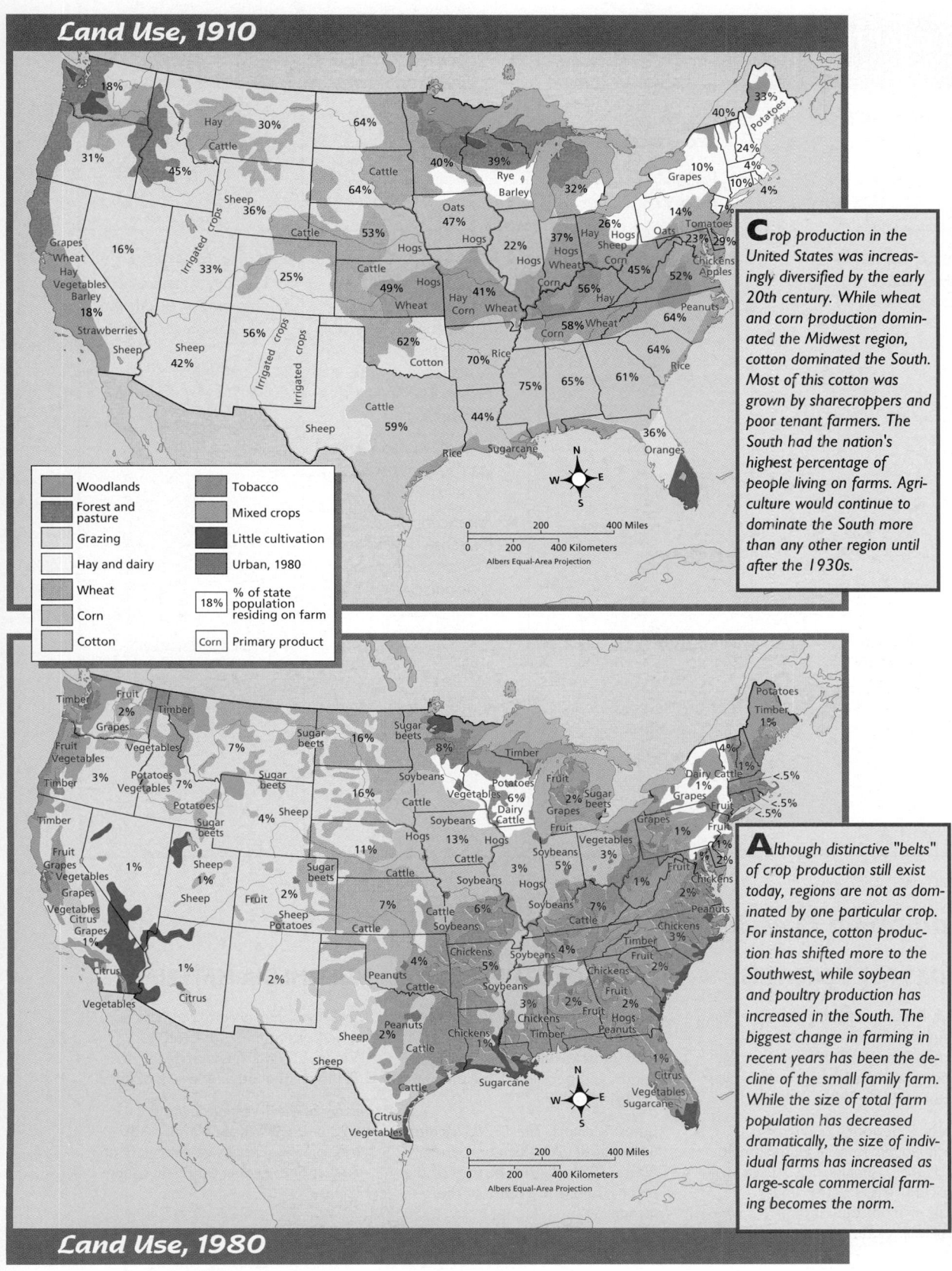

Land Use, 1910

Legend:
- Woodlands
- Forest and pasture
- Grazing
- Hay and dairy
- Wheat
- Corn
- Cotton
- Tobacco
- Mixed crops
- Little cultivation
- Urban, 1980
- 18% — % of state population residing on farm
- Corn — Primary product

Land Use, 1980

Crop production in the United States was increasingly diversified by the early 20th century. While wheat and corn production dominated the Midwest region, cotton dominated the South. Most of this cotton was grown by sharecroppers and poor tenant farmers. The South had the nation's highest percentage of people living on farms. Agriculture would continue to dominate the South more than any other region until after the 1930s.

Although distinctive "belts" of crop production still exist today, regions are not as dominated by one particular crop. For instance, cotton production has shifted more to the Southwest, while soybean and poultry production has increased in the South. The biggest change in farming in recent years has been the decline of the small family farm. While the size of total farm population has decreased dramatically, the size of individual farms has increased as large-scale commercial farming becomes the norm.

HISTORICAL SIDELIGHTS

Farm Monopolies

Small family farms have been disappearing from the American scene at a rapid rate. In 1986 the Congressional Office of Technology Assessment predicted that by the year 2000 about 50,000 large farms would control at least 75 percent of all food production in the United States.

CHAPTER 22

THE JAZZ AGE

1920–1930

THE AMERICAN NATION VIDEODISC PROGRAM
A variety of still images, short videos, and activities are available for you to use as you teach this chapter. See Correlation to *The American Nation* Videodisc Program for barcode correlations and suggestions for using the program.

Chapter Overview

The decade of the 1920s was one of rapid technological change, a booming economy, flappers, jazz bands, the Charleston, and the Harlem Renaissance. Fueled by a postwar economy that grew at an unprecedented rate, the prosperity of the 1920s introduced millions of Americans to mass-produced goods as well as to mass culture. This rapid change caused social upheaval, leading many Americans to question traditional values.

Chapter Planning Guide

CHAPTER 22	CORE RESOURCE BOOKLETS	AV AUDIOVISUAL RESOURCES	PROGRAM RESOURCES
INTRODUCTION pp. 644–645	■ Literature Worksheet 22 ■ Building Your Portfolio Worksheet 7		
TEACHING THE CHAPTER pp. 646–665	■ Graphic Organizer 22 ■ Social Studies Skills Worksheet 22 ■ Geography Worksheet 22	■ *The American Nation* Videodisc: The Film Age; Prohibition; Automobile Assembly Line; The 1920s: Americans on the Move; The Wright Brothers ■ Everyday Life in America Transparency and Worksheet 22 ■ *American Civics Citizenship Skills* Videocassette or Videodisc	■ Art in American History Transparencies and Worksheets 22, 23, 26, 27, 28 ■ *Eyewitnesses and Others,* Volume 2: Readings 38, 39
REVIEW AND ASSESSMENT pp. 666–667	■ Chapter 22 Daily Quizzes ■ Review Worksheet 22 ■ Chapter 22 Tests ■ Alternative Assessment Forms		■ Test Generator

Additional Resources

BOOKS FOR TEACHERS

Smith, Page. *Redeeming the Time, Vol. 8: A People's History of the 1920s and the New Deal.* Viking Penguin, 1991. Early chapters provide a vivid picture of the 1920s.

Vincent, Theodore G. *Voices of a Black Nation: Political Journalism in the Harlem Renaissance.* Africa World Press, 1991. Primary sources from the Harlem Renaissance.

BOOKS FOR STUDENTS

Lewis, David L. *When Harlem Was in Vogue.* Oxford University Press, 1989. Narrative of major events, trends, and people during the 1920s in Harlem.

*Tames, Richard. *The 1920s (Picture History of the 20th Century Series).* Watts, 1991. Picture history of the major issues and events of the decade.

* for students reading below grade level

MULTIMEDIA MATERIALS

The Story of Henry Ford: Famous Americans of the 20th Century. Video, 55 min. Questar/SSSS. Explores the life and legacy of Ford.

History of the Twentieth Century, 1920–1929. Video, 60 min. ABC Video/SSSS. Expansive overview of Al Capone, Prohibition, and other topics.

THEMES IN AMERICAN HISTORY

USE WITH PAGES
643–644

Listed on the right are the themes emphasized in Chapter 22. The questions in boldface type stimulate critical thinking and provide students with an opportunity to discuss the themes within a broadened context. The questions also appear in the pupil's edition on p. 644.

■ ECONOMIC DEVELOPMENT

How might increased consumer spending help improve a nation's economy? Students might consider that as more consumers buy products, factories and other businesses earn more money. This might lead to increased production and thus to more employment, which would provide citizens with income to consume even more products. This consumerism might spur growth in many industries.

■ TECHNOLOGY AND SOCIETY

How might new technology transform people's lives? Students may cite technological advances of which they are aware and mention the impact of those advances on their lives.

■ CULTURAL DIVERSITY

How might the cultural traditions of a particular area or group conflict with or contribute to a national culture? Students might give examples of how regional or ethnic customs, such as fashion or music, might influence a national culture. Students might also discuss how some customs may conflict with a nation's traditional mainstream values.

CHAPTER STRATEGIES FOR MEETING INDIVIDUAL NEEDS

LIMITED ENGLISH PROFICIENT LEARNERS

Have students role-play a young person during the 1920s, such as a flapper, a singer in a musical, or a writer, and tell what life was like during this period.

TACTILE/KINESTHETIC LEARNERS

Organize students into small groups to create scripts for a 1920s drama or comedy radio program that includes creative sound effects. Call on groups to present their programs.

LEARNERS HAVING DIFFICULTY

Discuss with students the meaning of key terms in the chapter, encouraging them to offer definitions. Then have students use the key terms to write a brief summary of the chapter.

AUDITORY LEARNERS

Direct students to research and bring to class a record or tape that illustrates the music or radio programs of the 1920s.

VISUAL LEARNERS

Have students create a magazine advertisement on a popular product of the "Roaring Twenties."

GIFTED LEARNERS

Organize students into small groups to prepare a script for a documentary film on the changes that took place in U.S. society during the Jazz Age.

USING THE CHAPTER FOCUS

■ UNDERSTANDING THE MAIN IDEA

Ask a volunteer to read aloud the Understanding the Main Idea paragraph. Ask students to suggest what changes may have created social conflict in the 1920s. Ask students if they think that the 1990s are also marked by social conflict and, if so, what changes might have caused it.

■ THEMES

Have students work individually or in small groups to answer the questions under Themes. Save students' responses so that they can compare them with their responses after studying the chapter. (See p. 643B for suggested answers.)

■ THE TIME LINE

Remind students that World War I helped to bring about massive social, political, and technological changes in the U.S. Then encourage students to speculate on the relationships between postwar changes and the events on the time line. Have students review their speculations as they read the chapter.

CORE RESOURCES

- Literature Worksheet 22
- Graphic Organizer 22
- Building Your Portfolio Worksheet 7

644

ABOUT THE ILLUSTRATION

In the 1920s white northerners first heard jazz music in whites-only nightclubs, such as Chicago's Sunset Club and Harlem's Cotton Club. Although attracted by the music, white audiences also came to see the floor shows, such as the one shown below. In Prohibition-era America, these nightclubs allowed alcohol and offered more-risqué performances than Broadway shows. Draw students' attention to the racial composition of the audience and the performers in the photograph below. Ask students to speculate about the social differences between blacks and whites that this photo reveals.

Chapter 22

1920–1930

THE JAZZ AGE

FOCUS

UNDERSTANDING THE MAIN IDEA

Jazz, the upbeat musical form developed by African Americans, helped give the 1920s a unique character. The automobile, advertising, radio programs, and movies also influenced American life. Artists and writers portrayed an American society growing more urban and "modern." Many Americans found the changes of the 1920s unsettling, and the decade was marked by social conflict.

THEMES

- **ECONOMIC DEVELOPMENT** How might increased consumer spending help improve a nation's economy?

- **TECHNOLOGY AND SOCIETY** How might new technology transform people's lives?

- **CULTURAL DIVERSITY** How might the cultural traditions of a particular area or group conflict with or contribute to a national culture?

1920	1925	1926	1927	1928
First radio stations go on the air.	Scopes trial held in Dayton, Tennessee.	Langston Hughes's *Weary Blues* published.	Charles Lindbergh completes first nonstop flight from New York to Paris.	Amelia Earhart crosses Atlantic Ocean by plane.

Ask volunteers to recall the sacrifices made by Americans during World War I. Then have students speculate about how life might have changed for Americans after the Great War and write their responses on a flip chart. Tell students that this chapter focuses on daily life in America after the war. As students read the chapter, have them compare their responses to the information given in the chapter.

◨▢ **LINK TO THE PAST**

Americans had cut back on purchasing goods during World War I. With the war over, men and women were eager to buy the new products that postwar American industry offered in abundance.

Jazz floor show in Chicago, 1924

*A*n avalanche of new products transformed the lives of Americans in the 1920s—none more so than the automobile. The automobile changed the way Americans worked, socialized, and ran their households. It also helped change social roles for women. As early as 1907 a poem celebrated the growing independence of women who drove:

> 66 Like the breeze in its flight, or
> the passage of light,
> Or swift as the fall of a star.
> She comes and she goes in a nimbus
> of dust
> A goddess enthroned on a car.
> The maid of the motor, behold her
> erect
> With muscles as steady as steel.
> Her hand on the lever and always
> in front
> The girl in the automobile. 99

New forms of entertainment, including the wildly popular jazz bands, amused Americans in the generally prosperous 1920s. Radio programs, talking pictures, musical performances, and sporting events also entertained millions. But the decade was not all amusement. A small group of writers and artists revitalized American arts with their sober reflections on the war, race relations, and the nature of American society.

Life magazine cover, 1926

The Granger Collection, New York

*Following is a list of the significant
people and terms in this section.
You may wish to use this list as a
section preview.*

People
- Henry Ford
- Frederick W. Taylor
- Robert Lynd
- Helen Lynd

Terms
- assembly line
- scientific management

FOCUS OBJECTIVES

- List the factors that led to the economic boom of the 1920s.

- Identify the processes that changed work habits during the twenties.

- Describe how the automobile affected American life.

- Analyze the developments that stimulated consumerism.

Section 1

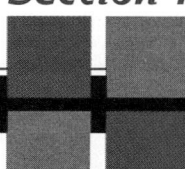

BOOM TIMES

FOCUS

- **What factors led to the economic boom of the 1920s?**
- **Which processes changed work habits during the twenties?**
- **How did the automobile affect American life?**
- **What developments stimulated consumerism?**

The economy prospered in the 1920s. In 1928 wages were a third higher than they had been in 1914. The gross national product climbed from $70 billion in 1922 to $100 billion just seven years later. Prosperity was accompanied by changes in the workplace and a new automobile age. Salespeople sold cars and a host of other products through aggressive campaigns that aimed to turn the United States into a nation of consumers.

Automobile advertisement, 1920

PROSPERITY AND PRODUCTIVITY

Many factors led to the boom times of the 1920s. One was the Republicans' probusiness stance. Another was abundant supplies of energy—coal, oil, natural gas, and waterpower, as well as a vast network of electrical power plants. Between 1920 and 1929 fuel oil output doubled, and annual electrical production went from some 56 billion to 114 billion kilowatt-hours. By 1930 over two thirds of all U.S. homes had electricity.

The widespread availability of electricity created a demand for a dizzying array of new electrical appliances—washing machines, sewing machines, cake mixers, and food grinders. Radio and phonograph sales boomed. Chemical companies also tempted consumers, offering a variety of products made from plastic, rayon, acetate, and other new "wonder" materials. In 1930, textile mills produced more than 118 million pounds of rayon and acetate yarns—more than 13 times the 1920 production level.

A new production technique—the **assembly line**—helped factories churn out goods faster. Around 1913, after adapting techniques used in the slaughterhouses

► **The Ford Motor Company introduced assembly-line techniques in its factories as early as 1913. This photograph of a Ford factory was taken in 1924. Henry Ford is shown in the inset.**

MOTIVATING: PRIOR KNOWLEDGE

Call on volunteers to cite events or developments of the early years of the 20th century that might have helped spur an economic boom during the 1920s. *(general probusiness stance, wartime economic expansion, efforts to modernize industry)* List responses on the chalkboard. As students read, have them compare the chalkboard list to the causes of the economic boom that are noted in the section.

Teaching the Section

ECONOMIC BOOM

Organize students into small groups to create a poster or collage that illustrates the major factors that led to the economic boom of the 1920s. Have them write captions for their poster or collage. Then have volunteers explain each group's artwork to the class. Conclude by asking students if any reasons for the boom were not illustrated in the groups' art.

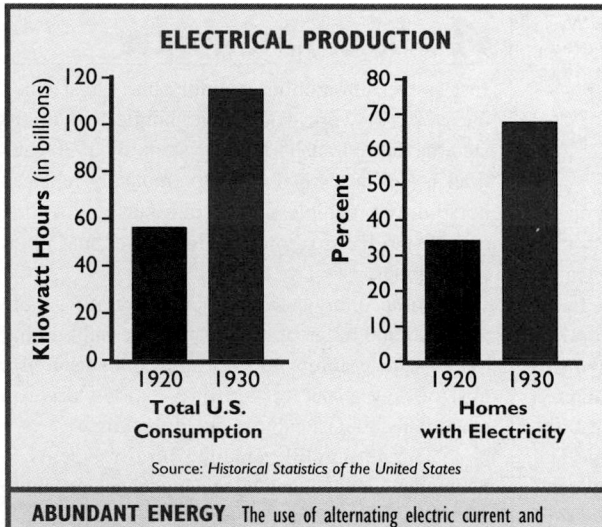

ELECTRICAL PRODUCTION

Kilowatt Hours (in billions)

Total U.S. Consumption — 1920, 1930

Homes with Electricity (Percent) — 1920, 1930

Source: *Historical Statistics of the United States*

ABUNDANT ENERGY The use of alternating electric current and powerful transformers allowed electricity to be transmitted over great distances. As a result, electrical use increased dramatically during the 1920s.

? **IDENTIFYING CAUSE AND EFFECT** By about what percentage did electrical consumption increase from 1920 to 1930?

of Chicago, Henry Ford introduced the assembly line in his Detroit automobile plant. Workers stood in one spot as partially assembled automobiles moved past them on a conveyor belt timed to advance precisely six feet per minute. Bit by bit, workers assembled the 5,000 parts of a Model T, or "Tin Lizzie," until the finished product could be driven out of the factory. Machinery did much of the work of producing individual parts and carrying them to workers. Boasted Ford:

> 66 Every piece of work in the shop moves; it may move on hooks, on overhead chains . . . it may travel on a moving platform, or it may go by gravity, but the point is that there is no lifting or trucking. . . . No workman has anything to do with moving or lifting anything. 99

The assembly line cut the engine assembly time for a Model T in half. Other large car manufacturers quickly followed Ford's lead and installed assembly lines. But few small companies could afford the expense of building or maintaining the new technology. Unable to compete, many were driven out of business. Soon the industry was dominated by three big corporations: Ford, General Motors, and Chrysler.

The assembly line allowed manufacturers to reduce the prices of cars, bringing them within reach of ordinary American families. Automobile registrations during the twenties rose from 8 million to 26 million—an average of one car for every five citizens.

In the 1920s the auto industry was the nation's biggest business. This new industrial giant consumed huge quantities of steel, glass, rubber, and other materials. Gasoline, formerly a troublesome by-product of the petroleum industry, became the industry's most-valued product. By 1929 over one million people labored in the automobile industry or a related business.

▪▪ **Probusiness policies, ample energy, new industries, and the assembly line fueled the economic boom of the 1920s.**

*C*HANGES IN WORK

Although assembly lines increased productivity, they had a human cost. Little technical skill was needed to "work the line." Thus, many higher-paid skilled laborers were thrown out of work. But even the people who found jobs on the line suffered. The work was deadening, leading many to quit within a few weeks. To counter the high turnover, Ford limited the workday to eight hours and doubled wages to an unheard-of $5 a day.

Both of these bold steps were welcomed. However, as the wife of one Ford worker noted, the pay increase did not change working conditions:

> 66 The chain system [assembly line] you have is a *slave driver! My God!* Mr. Ford. My husband has come home & thrown himself down & won't eat his supper—so done out! Can't it be remedied? . . . That $5 a day is a blessing—a bigger one than you know but *oh* they earn it. 99

The innovations of "Fordism" were more than matched by those of another movement, "Taylorism." The movement's creator, Frederick W. Taylor, called his approach **scientific management**.

Chart Caption Answer
about 100 percent

HISTORICAL SIDELIGHTS
Engineering
Henry Ford led the way in improving assembly-line techniques. By 1914 the assembly process was refined to the point that a Model T's engine could be built in about 6 hours. Constructing a complete chassis took just 1½ hours. By the time the Model T was discontinued in 1927, approximately 15 million had been sold.

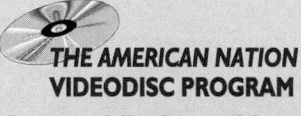

THE AMERICAN NATION VIDEODISC PROGRAM

Automobile Assembly Line

2A   39871   :26

PRIMARY SOURCE
Description of Change: excerpted
Rationale: excerpted to focus on main idea

PRIMARY SOURCE
Description of Change: excerpted and bracketed
Rationale: excerpted to focus on main idea; bracketed to clarify meaning

Teaching the S*ection*

CHANGES IN THE WORKPLACE

Instruct each student to write a letter to an employer from the perspective of a 1920s factory employee, explaining how scientific management and changes in technology have transformed working conditions. Have students read their letters aloud. Ask volunteers to respond to the letters as a 1920s employer would. Students may wish to include their letters in their portfolios.

CAR CULTURE

Organize students into small groups to create charts listing the positive effects and the negative effects of the automobile during the 1920s. Then have representatives from each group create a class chart on the chalkboard. Conclude by asking the class to decide if the automobile was a benefit or a liability for the people of the 1920s.

CULTURAL PATTERNS

Mexican immigrants found jobs at Ford Motor Company plants during World War I. But because of the postwar recession, Ford sent some 3,000 Mexican auto workers back to Mexico in 1920. This forced repatriation slowed Mexican immigration for a time, but by 1923 it had increased. Mexican workers were being drawn to work in factories in Chicago, Detroit, and Pittsburgh. The high rate of Mexican immigration in the 1920s led some labor groups to call for quotas on Mexican immigrants, but such efforts failed.

THE AMERICAN NATION VIDEODISC PROGRAM

The 1920s: Americans on the Move

1B   50587   :34

◀ **Frederick W. Taylor pioneered techniques used to increase workers' output.**

It was based on the idea that every kind of work could be broken down into a series of smaller tasks. Trained observers conducted "time-and-motion" studies to identify these tasks and then set rates of production that people and machines had to meet. Soon "efficiency experts" were applying Taylor's methods to many areas of business.

The assembly line and scientific management changed the types of jobs available to workers. While the number of factory jobs grew only slightly during the 1920s, openings for such white-collar jobs as manager, clerical worker, and salesperson increased from slightly more than 10 million to more than 14 million. Because most of these jobs required that applicants have at least a high-school education, few newly arrived immigrants qualified. Discriminatory hiring practices also closed most of these jobs to African Americans.

Changes in technology affected domestic labor as well. Electrical appliances transformed housework for those who could afford them. Before the introduction of appliances, servants did the laundry and heavy cleaning in most middle- and upper-class homes. With the introduction of electrical appliances, many middle-class housewives took over the jobs they had previously supervised. As a result, many servants were forced to find new employment.

As more families bought cars, housewives also began taking over their families' transportation needs. Before many middle- and upper-class families had cars, their groceries and other supplies had been delivered to their homes. The automobile allowed housewives to drive to grocery stores and other shops. Thus, like household servants, delivery people often found their jobs in jeopardy.

▪▪ **Scientific management and new technology transformed working conditions in the 1920s.**

A LAND OF AUTOMOBILES

Just as the automobile assembly line transformed the world of work, so the automobile revolutionized the entire transportation system. By 1930 cars, trucks, and buses had almost completely replaced horse-drawn vehicles. Even railroads and trolley cars lost riders to Ford's "Tin Lizzie" and other automobiles.

To accommodate the increased traffic, more than 400,000 miles of new roads were built during the decade. Alongside the highways sprouted a host of new structures—filling stations, drive-in restaurants, tourist cabins, and billboards.

The automobile enabled rural residents to have greater contact with their neighbors and more access to shopping and leisure activities. Cars linked rural regions to urban areas, making it easier for rural residents to relocate to the booming cities and for city dwellers to visit the country. At the same time, however, the automobile contributed to the depopulation of America's inner

▼ **With some nine million automobiles in use by 1920, more and more families explored the country in their cars. Shown here is an advertisement encouraging motorists to take the Apache Trail Motor Tour through Arizona's National Reserve.**

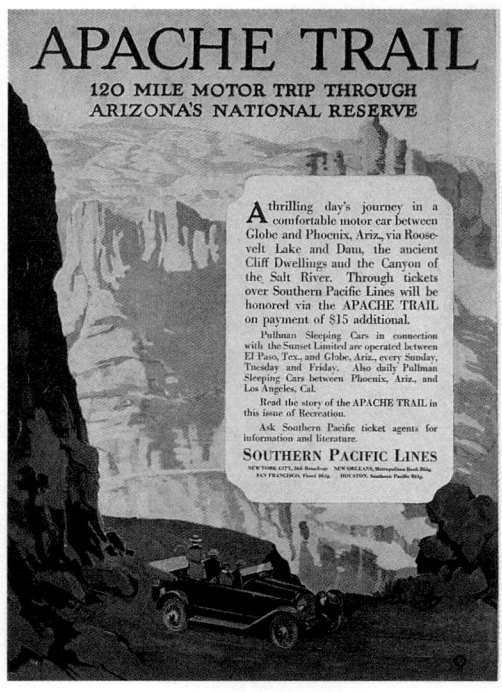

ADVERTISING AND CONSUMERISM

Have students work in pairs to write a slogan or jingle that illustrates the factors that stimulated consumerism in the 1920s. Have pairs present their jingles to the class.

▪▪ Ask students how, and in what forms, advertising influences their lives today.

▶

Changing Ways

HITTING THE ROAD

In the 1920s, as millions of Americans purchased automobiles, a new craze swept the nation—the "autotouring" vacation. Guidebooks urged Americans to hit the road:

“ Does father crave to fish for trout and bass and pike and musky? Take him auto-touring. Does sister want to dip in the surf . . . or see the world? Take her automobile vacationing. . . . Does mother sigh for a rest from daily routines? Take her touring. . . . Does baby need fresh mountain air far from flies and heat? Take him auto-camping. ”

Freed from travel restrictions imposed by the schedules and routes of passenger trains, car owners took to the road to see America.

Most motor tourists were city dwellers who vacationed in the country to "get away from it all." But in getting away, they often took a lot of "it" with them. Camping gear for the typical autotourist included a tent, gas stove, heater, cooking utensils, pots and pans, folding table and chairs, blankets, and even beds.

Autotourists tended to camp together and had a culture all their own. They often dressed in ways that led observers to marvel and to gawk at the same time. One reporter wrote:

▲ Families took advantage of new government autocamps while traveling on the road. This photograph shows a family camping in the 1920s.

“ It was amazing what colorful combinations the knickered rovers [autotourists] managed to attain. They wore veils of all descriptions, flowing Egyptian veils and even gas masks [to keep out road dust]. They wore paper hats that tied under their chins, caps trimmed with the tails of squirrels, skins of rattlesnakes, and quills of porcupines. ”

At first farmers welcomed these visitors from the city. Autotourists broke the isolation of rural life and seemed likely customers for farm produce. But instead of buying fruits and vegetables, vacationers often snitched them from trees and fields. Sometimes campers even milked farmers' cows! They also dumped their garbage on farmers' land. Soon signs banning autotouring appeared in rural areas. One such sign read:

“ Trespassers will B persecuted to the full extent of 2 mongrel dogs which neve was over sochible to strangers and 1 doubl brl shot gun which ain't loaded with sofa pillors. ”

National and state park services, along with town governments, stepped in to keep local people and visitors from clashing. These agencies set up free autocamps to provide tourists with welcome comforts, while keeping them off private land. Electric lighting made it possible for motorists to arrive and set up camp after dark, and gas ranges eliminated the need for firewood.

The heyday of autotourism passed as the prosperity of the 1920s gave way to the depression of the 1930s. But its legacy can be seen today in the continuing appeal of sight-seeing and camping vacations and in the popularity of recreational vehicles.

---

*P*ractice

GUIDED PRACTICE

Construct a word web on the chalkboard by first writing the word *automobile* and circling it. Then draw lines radiating from the circle and call on volunteers to cite how the automobile affected America in the 1920s. Add students' responses to the web.

INDEPENDENT PRACTICE

Direct students to create word webs similar to the one constructed in the Guided Practice activity using *work processes* and *advertising* as the circled terms. Students may wish to include their word webs in their portfolios.

*R*eview and *A*ssessment

REVIEW Call on volunteers to give short statements summarizing the main ideas of Section 1. Write responses on the chalkboard. Have students select one statement and write a paragraph that includes supporting details from the section. Then assign the Section 1 Review on p. 651.

ASSESS Assign the **Section 1 Daily Quiz** in *Core Resources.*

MAKING CONNECTIONS

Sociology

Middletown was a pioneering sociological study. The Lynds were the first to apply the methods of cultural anthropology to the study of a Western city. The Lynds returned to Muncie in the 1930s to study the impact of the Great Depression on the city, publishing their findings in their book *Middletown in Transition: A Study in Cultural Conflicts* (1937).

PRIMARY SOURCE

Description of Change: excerpted and bracketed
Rationale: excerpted to focus on main idea; bracketed to clarify meaning

**AMERICAN CIVICS
CITIZENSHIP SKILLS**

**Videocassette or
Videodisc: Segment 6**

Segment 6, Side B

Search Chapter 3

cities. Suburbs, now more accessible than ever, attracted thousands of middle-class families.

The automobile also transformed family life. Cars enabled families to enjoy simple drives in the country and elaborate camping trips. The automobile created new social opportunities for teenagers as well. Sociologists Robert Lynd and Helen Lynd, whose book *Middletown* (1929) chronicled life in Muncie, Indiana, wrote:

> 66 The extensive use of this new tool [the automobile] by the young has enormously extended their mobility and the range of alternatives before them; joining a crowd motoring over to a dance . . . twenty miles away may be a matter of a moment's decision, with no one's permission asked. 99

But the automobile had negative effects as well. Critics claimed that cars reduced people's sense of neighborliness. The Lynds observed that "since the advent of the automobile and the movies" Muncie families and neighbors no longer spent "long summer evenings and Sunday afternoons on the porch or in the side yard." Also, by the twenties, cars were already causing pollution, traffic jams, and parking problems. Most serious was the steadily climbing accident rate.

▶ **Advertisements often stressed the ease of operation or low maintenance of the device being offered for sale. This ad for an "unusually quiet" refrigerator appeared in 1927.**

▼ **Salespeople proudly display a host of new home electrical appliances that proved wildly popular in the 1920s.**

■■ **Cars revolutionized the nation's transportation system, eased rural isolation, aided suburban growth, and changed family and community relations.**

*C*REATING CONSUMERS

Advertising, which became big business in the 1920s, fueled the demand for cars and other consumer goods. Before World War I, money spent on advertising had totaled some $500 million yearly. By 1929 the total had soared to more than $3 billion. Ads were everywhere. Commercial messages bombarded potential buyers not only in magazines and newspapers but also on billboards and over the new medium of radio.

Advertisements, most of which targeted women, used psychology to play on consumers' hopes and fears. Ads for Borden's milk, for instance, warned mothers that "Hardly a family—well-to-do and poor alike—escapes the menace of malnutrition. Your own child may fall victim to this insidious evil."

Companies used slogans, jingles, and testimonials by celebrities to fix product names in

LADIES HOME JOURNAL

It hasn't a single belt, fan or drain pipe....

It always works perfectly and never needs oiling

GE Refrigerator
GENERAL ELECTRIC

customers' minds. Eleanor Roosevelt (whose husband, Franklin D. Roosevelt, was then governor of New York) praised Cream of Wheat, which their son John had eaten since babyhood. The cereal, she was quoted as saying, "has undoubtedly played its part in building his robust physique."

As the number of products expanded to meet the growing demand, new chain stores sprang up around the country. For example, the A & P grocery chain grew from some 3,000 stores in 1922 to about 14,000 by 1925. The chain grocery stores, which slowly replaced the corner markets, stocked a wide variety of new products. The chain stores could do so because cellophane, a transparent wrapping material first produced in the United States in 1924, and quick-freezing techniques preserved fresh foods longer and allowed them to be shipped over longer distances.

Effective merchandising depended above all on clever salespeople. "There are always some people that you can sell anything to if you hammer them hard enough," claimed a car dealer. Door-to-door salespeople hawked everything from cleaning supplies to encyclopedias.

People also bought more because of easy credit. Before the 1920s, consumers bought only a few expensive items, such as pianos and sewing machines, on the installment plan. By mid-decade,

▲ Chain grocery stores did not completely replace the neighborhood grocery. Immigrants continued to shop at family-run groceries such as this one, owned by Antonio and Angeline Tortolano. At such stores customers could buy ethnic foods and talk to shopkeepers in their native language.

buyers purchased about 75 percent of cars on credit. The practice soon spread to many other items. As a car dealer noted:

> 66 To keep America growing we must keep Americans working, and to keep Americans working we must keep them wanting; wanting more than the bare necessities; wanting the luxuries and frills that make life so much more worthwhile, and installment selling makes it easier to keep Americans wanting. 99

■■ **Advertising, merchandising, and installment buying encouraged consumerism.**

SECTION 1 REVIEW

IDENTIFY and explain the significance of the following: assembly line, Henry Ford, Frederick W. Taylor, scientific management, Robert Lynd, Helen Lynd.

1. **MAIN IDEA** What factors contributed to the economic prosperity of the 1920s?
2. **MAIN IDEA** What innovations transformed working conditions in the late 1920s?
3. **ASSESSING CONSEQUENCES** How did the invention of the automobile change the way Americans lived?
4. **WRITING TO INFORM** Imagine you are the president of a chain store. Prepare for your board of directors a brief summary of how the company plans to attract new customers.
5. **ANALYZING** Why can it be said that the technological and business innovations of the 1920s had both positive and negative consequences for American society?

FOCUS OBJECTIVES

■ List the most popular forms of entertainment during the 1920s.

■ Describe the ways young women of the 1920s departed from traditional female behavior.

■ Analyze the debate over Prohibition and Fundamentalism and what it revealed about American society.

CULTURAL PATTERNS

In the 1920s local radio stations developed programs for ethnic audiences that reinforced the cultures of ethnic communities. In 1926, Chicago had four radio stations devoted to such programs, which aired music and news from immigrants' homelands. In Los Angeles, the Mexican American barrio listened to *corridos* (folk ballads) on KMPC's popular Spanish-language program.

CORE RESOURCES

• **Geography Worksheet 22**
• **Section 2 Daily Quiz**

AV **RESOURCES**

• *The American Nation* **Videodisc: The Film Age; Prohibition; The Wright Brothers**

PREVIEW WORKSHOP

Following is a list of the significant people and terms in this section. You may wish to use this list as a section preview.

People
■ Babe Ruth
■ Helen Wills
■ Gertrude Ederle
■ Jim Thorpe

■ Charles Lindbergh
■ Amelia Earhart
■ Aimee Semple McPherson
■ John Scopes

Terms
■ flappers
■ Volstead Act
■ Twenty-first Amendment
■ Fundamentalism

Section 2

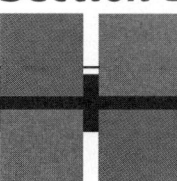

LIFE IN THE TWENTIES

F O C U S

■ **What were the most popular forms of entertainment during the 1920s?**

■ **In what ways did young women of the 1920s depart from traditional female behavior?**

■ **What did the debate over Prohibition and Fundamentalism reveal about American society in the 1920s?**

The decade of the 1920s has been called the gateway to modern America. For the first time a truly national mass culture emerged in the United States. Commercial radio linked Americans from coast to coast. Instant communications not only entertained people but also informed them about serious developments. The emerging mass culture also brought changes in women's roles and caused conflicts over traditional values.

Matinee idol Rudolph Valentino

POPULAR ENTERTAINMENT

Boom times in the United States meant that many—though not all—Americans had bigger paychecks and more free time than in years past. To help fill their leisure hours, many Americans turned to radio and movies.

Commercial radio arose in the twenties. The first stations, Detroit's WWJ and Pittsburgh's KDKA, went on the air in 1920. By 1929, more than 800 stations reached some 10 million homes—more than a third of the nation's households. "There is radio music in the air, every night, everywhere," gushed a San Francisco newspaper. "Anybody can hear it at home on a receiving set." Along with music, radio stations broadcast sports events, news, and comedy shows.

By the end of the decade, two networks, the National Broadcasting Company (NBC) and the Columbia Broadcasting System (CBS), aired their programs nationwide. Households across the land tuned in to the same programs.

Movies proved equally popular, having grown in both length and complexity since their beginnings in the 1890s. The earliest movie

◀ **Advances in technology made radio more accessible to Americans during the 1920s. This photograph shows a young woman tuning in to a program on her radio set in 1922.**

Call on volunteers to identify radio programs they have listened to or movies they have seen in recent weeks. Then have students discuss what they know about the beginnings of radio and the motion-picture industry. Tell students that this section focuses on the development of radio and the film industry in the U.S., and on other social developments in the 1920s.

▲ Moviegoers during the 1920s stood in line to see romance films starring John Gilbert and Greta Garbo, action films with Douglas Fairbanks, or comedies featuring Charlie Chaplin.

▶ As motion pictures grew in popularity, theater owners built lavish movie palaces with elaborate balconies, box seats, and a pit for live orchestral music.

theaters—called nickelodeons because of the five-cent admission—attracted mainly working-class and immigrant audiences. By the 1920s, lavish movie palaces with names like the Roxy, the Bijou, and the Ritz, were attracting middle-class audiences as well. The more-luxurious theaters had velvet drapes, plush carpets, uniformed ushers, and great theater organs to accompany the silent films. The mass appeal of movie theaters impressed journalist Lloyd Lewis:

66 In the "de luxe" [movie] house every man is a king and every woman a queen. Most of these cinema palaces sell all their seats at the same price,—and get it; the rich man stands in line with the poor. . . . In this suave atmosphere, the differences . . . that determine our lives outside are forgotten. All men enter these portals equal, and thus the movies are perhaps a symbol of democracy. 99

In 1927 Warner Brothers released the first feature-length "talkie," *The Jazz Singer,* starring Al Jolson. Silent-screen stars with high squeaky voices soon found themselves unemployed. In their places emerged new actors with distinctive and appealing voices, among them Gary Cooper and Clara Bow. The advent of sound also led to new film forms, including musicals and newsreels,

short films summing up the news of the day. In 1929 some 80 million Americans flocked to the theaters each week.

■■ **Americans turned to radio and movies for entertainment during the 1920s.**

CELEBRITIES AND HEROES

When movie star Rudolph Valentino died in 1926 at age 31, mourners lined up for blocks to view his body. In this era of mass culture, actors became instant celebrities. So did other figures in the public eye, especially athletes and pilots.

One sports favorite was Babe Ruth. Ruth dominated baseball from 1920 to 1935, during which time he led the New York Yankees to four World Series championships. In 1927 the spindle-legged, pigeon-toed ball player astounded the sports world with a record 60 home runs. Hard-hitting tennis star Helen Wills wowed audiences

▲ During his long career, Babe Ruth hit 714 home runs—a record not broken until 1974.

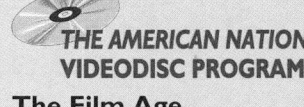

PRIMARY SOURCE

Description of Change: excerpted and bracketed
Rationale: excerpted to focus on main idea; bracketed to clarify meaning

HISTORICAL SIDELIGHTS

Harlem Globetrotters Probably the first mass-appeal U.S. basketball team was the all-black Harlem Globetrotters. Orginally called the Savoy Big Five, they first played their games in Chicago's Savoy Ballroom. In 1927, when the ballroom became a skating rink, they took the name Harlem Globetrotters and scheduled all their games on the road. But they became so good that fewer and fewer teams were willing to play them. After winning the World Basketball Tournament in 1940, they adopted the show tactics for which they are best known today.

Teaching the Section

POPULAR ENTERTAINMENT IN THE 1920s

Organize students into small groups to create a script for a newsreel that describes popular forms of entertainment in the 1920s. Have them use details from the section in their scripts. Ask volunteers from each group to present their scripts to the class.

THE TWENTIES

Richard Müller-Freienfels, a German professor and writer, studied industrialization and the mass culture that emerged in the early 20th century. Here is his description of American life in the 1920s:

THROUGH OTHERS' EYES

“*All the men seem to be clothed by the same tailor, and all the women seem to have bought their hats at the same shop. . . . The most remarkable thing is that even the people impress one as having been standardized. All these clean-shaven men, all these girls, with their doll-like faces, which are generally painted, seem to have been produced somewhere in a Ford factory, not by the dozen but by the thousand. In no other country are the individuals reduced to such a dead-level as in the United States, and this appears all the more remarkable when we reflect that nowhere [else] is there such a . . . mixture of races and peoples.*”

and captured more major tennis championships than any other woman in the world. Wills won the U.S. Open title seven times and Wimbledon eight times. Swimmer Gertrude Ederle broke the world record when she swam the English Channel in 1926 at age 19. She went on to set more than 20 U.S. swimming records and to win several medals in the 1924 summer Olympics.

Few athletes of the 1920s, however, enjoyed greater fame than Jim Thorpe. Born in 1888 in Oklahoma, he was of Sauk, Fox, Irish, and French ancestry. Thorpe attended the Carlisle Indian School in Pennsylvania. There he played every intercollegiate sport the school offered.

After he left Carlisle, Thorpe began training for the Olympics. At the 1912 games, held in Stockholm, Sweden, he became the first contestant to win both the pentathlon and the decathlon. "Sir, you are the greatest athlete

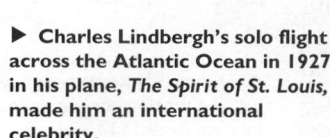

Jim Thorpe

in the world," said the Swedish king as he presented Thorpe with his gold medals. "Thanks, King," replied Thorpe with a grin.

A year later Thorpe's triumph turned to ashes. The news became public that he had played semiprofessional baseball for money. (At the time, Olympic athletes had to be amateurs.) Officials erased his name from Olympic record books and confiscated his awards. Many people felt that Thorpe had been treated unfairly; he had not realized that playing baseball for money would disqualify him from track competition.

Thorpe went on to a respectable career in major-league baseball and in the 1920s enjoyed several spectacular years playing professional football. In his later years, which were clouded by illness, he tried to become a movie actor. Not until 1982, 29 years after his death, did an Olympic committee restore his medals.

Probably the greatest celebrity of the 1920s was pilot Charles Lindbergh. In May 1927 he took off in a small single-engine plane, aiming to win a $25,000 prize that had been offered to the first pilot

▶ Charles Lindbergh's solo flight across the Atlantic Ocean in 1927 in his plane, *The Spirit of St. Louis,* made him an international celebrity.

THE NEW WOMAN

Encourage students to imagine they are listening to a 1920s radio talk show on the topic "What's With Today's Young Women?" Ask volunteers to "call" the show with their comments and views to either support or challenge the "new woman's" departure from traditional behavior.

■■ Ask students to compare women's dress and behavior today with the flappers of the 1920s.

PROHIBITION

Have students choose a role (immigrant, religious leader, social reformer, and so on) and write editorials defending or opposing the Volstead Act. Call on volunteers to read their editorials. Use editorials to launch a class discussion on the cultural conflicts revealed by the Prohibition debate.

▶

to fly nonstop from New York to Paris. After flying solo for 33 1/2-hours, he landed in France. Americans were delirious with joy. New Yorkers threw a ticker-tape parade for Lindbergh, and President Coolidge received the modest young man at the White House. Lindbergh's flight offered exciting glimpses of a coming era of air travel. The next year, pilot Amelia Earhart became the first woman to cross the Atlantic Ocean by plane.

THE "NEW WOMAN"

Two of the many changes in the 1920s were in women's dress and behavior. Influenced by popular actresses and by the independence of working-class women, some young women exercised new freedom in how they dressed and behaved. These women stopped wearing heavy corsets and started wearing shorter skirts and transparent silk hose. Actress Colleen Moore explained that these changes in dress represented a new independence for women:

> 66 Long skirts, corsets, and flowing tresses have gone. . . . The American girl will see to this. She is independent, a thinker [who] will not follow slavishly the ordinances of those who in the past have decreed this or that for her to wear. 99

People began to call the era's "new women" **flappers**. Flappers enjoyed defying traditional standards of womanly behavior. They wore their dresses daringly short, bobbed their hair, and wore makeup. They also drove cars, participated in sports, and smoked cigarettes.

Flappers gloried not only in their social freedom but also in their economic independence. Young women increasingly worked outside the home, which gave them more freedom to meet people and save money for themselves. If they married, however, they were expected to quit their paid employment and to fulfill their roles as wives and mothers. As Samuel Gompers, leader of the AFL, made clear in 1921 when he described the winner of the first Miss America beauty pageant, the homemaker was still the ideal of American womanhood:

> 66 She represents the type of womanhood America needs—strong, red-blooded, able

to shoulder the responsibilities of home-making and motherhood. It is in her type that the hope of the country resides. 99

■■ **The "new woman" of the twenties defied conventions in dress and behavior.**

A CRISIS OF VALUES

Many Americans found the social changes of the 1920s more troubling than exciting. For them conservative values and traditional ways of life remained important. Despite the spread of mass culture, many citizens' lives still centered on family, church, and neighborhood, and religion remained a vital part of American culture.

For these traditionalists, the flapper symbolized the unwelcome changes overtaking the country in the 1920s. With their unconventional dress and behavior, flappers rejected traditional values. To conservatives, the popularity of romantic movies and cheek-to-cheek dancing seemed signs of increasing immorality. Most critics blamed these "modern" habits on cities, noting with anxiety that radio and movies spread city ways to even the remotest rural areas. Anxiety increased when the census of 1920 revealed that for the first time, more than half of the U.S. population lived in metropolitan areas. In the face of these tremendous changes, arguments raged over such issues as alcohol and religion.

Prohibition. Progressive reformers had called for a ban on alcohol to combat such urban problems as family violence, crime, and poverty (see Chapter 17). Baptists, Methodists, and other Protestants also opposed drinking. Furthermore, during World War I, many reformers had advocated prohibition as a war measure. Playing on widespread anti-German sentiment, they had noted that German Americans owned

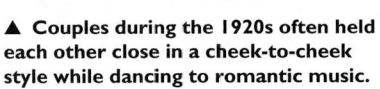
▲ Couples during the 1920s often held each other close in a cheek-to-cheek style while dancing to romantic music.

HISTORICAL SIDELIGHTS

Amelia Earhart
Born in Atchison, Kansas, in 1897, Amelia Earhart first became interested in flying during World War I while serving as a Red Cross volunteer at a Canadian military hospital. Intrigued by stories told by the members of the Royal Flying Corps, she began flying lessons in 1920. Earhart disappeared in 1937 on an attempted around-the-world flight.

PRIMARY SOURCE

Description of Change: excerpted and bracketed
Rationale: excerpted to focus on main idea; bracketed to clarify meaning

BUILDING VOCABULARY

The origin of the term *flapper* is obscure. The term may have been applied to teenage girls because their pigtails flapped when they walked. The term also may have arisen because flappers wore their boots with the hooks unfastened, so each boot would "flap" against the other as they walked.

PRIMARY SOURCE

Description of Change: excerpted
Rationale: excerpted to focus on main idea

Teaching the Section

FUNDAMENTALISM

Call on volunteers to role-play witnesses before the grand jury deliberating on whether or not John Scopes should be indicted. Some "witnesses" should present the Fundamentalist viewpoint, while others should support Scopes's position. Have the rest of the class act as the grand jury and make a decision on the indictment.

Conclude by asking students to discuss how the Scopes trial symbolized cultural conflict in the 1920s.

■■ Ask students what issues cause cultural conflict in society today.

BUILDING VOCABULARY

The term *bootlegging,* which came into use in the mid-1800s, derives from the smugglers' trick of concealing illegal items in the legs of their boots. During the 1920s the label was applied to smugglers of illegal liquor.

 ## GLOBAL CONNECTIONS

Canada benefited greatly from Prohibition in the U.S. New hotels, bars, and steamboats on the Canadian side of the border, which catered to thirsty American tourists, gave the economy a huge boost. And the more than one million gallons of spirits sold for "export"—in other words, smuggled to the U.S.—produced huge profits for the Canadian liquor monopolies and impressive tax revenues for the Canadian government.

 *THE AMERICAN NATION* VIDEODISC PROGRAM

Prohibition

2A 37756 :37

▲ **Federal agents such as Izzy Einstein and Moe Smith often went undercover and tried to purchase alcohol in speakeasies. When the alcohol was served, the agents made their arrests.**

many of the large breweries. They had also pointed out that drinking reduced the efficiency of soldiers and workers. After the Eighteenth Amendment made the manufacture, sale, and transportation of alcoholic beverages illegal in January 1919, Congress passed the **Volstead Act** in October 1919 to enforce the amendment. America entered the era of Prohibition.

In some regions Prohibition was strictly enforced, and drinking declined. But in many parts of the country, especially among immigrants, college students, and some city dwellers, Prohibition was extremely unpopular and widely ignored. Many people treated the reform as an annoyance, if not a joke. They frequented speakeasies, made their own wine or liquor, and bought bootleg (illegal) alcohol that had been smuggled from Canada or the West Indies.

Bootlegging became one of the decade's booming businesses. Criminal gangs in the large cities controlled liquor sales. Gang leaders gained the cooperation of law enforcement officials by bribing or threatening them. Al Capone, the boss of Chicago's underworld, commanded a small army of heavily armed mobsters. He and other gangsters made millions of dollars.

Gangs branched out to seize control of gambling establishments, houses of prostitution, and dance halls. They also made money through "protection" rackets, collecting money from owners of stores and other businesses by threatening violence if their victims failed to pay.

Prohibition had some positive consequences. Alcoholism declined and so did the number of deaths from alcohol-related causes. Prohibition's negative results, however, drew more attention. Prohibition led to a widespread breakdown of law and order and turned millions of otherwise law-abiding citizens into lawbreakers. Prohibition would later be repealed with the ratification of the **Twenty-first Amendment** in 1933.

Fundamentalism. The increasing popularity of a Protestant movement called **Fundamentalism** also revealed deep cultural conflicts in 1920s America. Fundamentalists believed that every word of the Bible should be regarded as literally true. They attacked Christian "liberals" who had accepted modern scientific learning, such as the theory of evolution. This "modernism," said Fundamentalists, weakened Christianity and contributed to the moral decline of the nation.

Revivalist preachers of the "old-time religion" found an eager audience, both in rural areas and in urban areas where traditional values remained strong. Billy Sunday, who had long preached against alcohol, drew huge crowds to his tent revivals. People were spellbound by Sunday's showmanship and his rousing attacks on dancing, card playing, and drinking. When Prohibition went into effect, he held a funeral service for "John Barleycorn," who personified alcohol, and declared that "the reign of tears is over."

Another popular revivalist of the 1920s was Aimee Semple McPherson, whose practice of faith healing and message of love attracted thousands to her International Church of the Foursquare Gospel, headquartered in Los Angeles. Most of her followers were city dwellers of modest income, many of them recent migrants from the Midwest. Outfitted in her signature white dress, white shoes, and blue cape,

▼ **Aimee Semple McPherson preached for nearly 20 years in a Los Angeles temple that her supporters built at a cost of $1.5 million.**

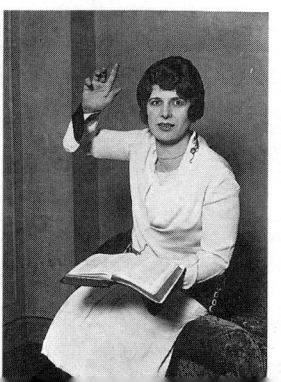

Practice

GUIDED PRACTICE

Organize students into small groups and direct each group to write dramatic headlines for each of the section's main topics. Have group representatives present their headlines to the class. Then ask the class to select the best headlines and develop brief outlines for newspaper stories to accompany those headlines.

INDEPENDENT PRACTICE

Tell students to use one of the outlines developed in the Guided Practice activity to write a newspaper story on that aspect of life in the U.S. during the 1920s. Students may wish to include their newspaper stories in their portfolios.

Review and Assessment

REVIEW Call on students to take turns answering the Focus questions on p. 652. For each question, record the responses on the chalkboard until no further details can be provided. Then assign the Section 2 Review on p. 658.

ASSESS Assign the **Section 2 Daily Quiz** in *Core Resources*.

▶

Then and Now — CENSORSHIP

The Roaring Twenties was a time of short skirts, bathtub gin, gambling, jazz, and the first talking movies. It was a time when old taboos were challenged one after the other. Alarmed and outraged by what they saw as the breakdown of the nation's moral standards, many community, religious, and government groups took action.

These activists pulled from library and store shelves books and magazines that used foul language, discussed sex frankly, or supported radical political ideas. U.S. Customs officials labeled many foreign books obscene and seized them, including the novel *Ulysses* by Irish author James Joyce.

Groups also targeted the movie industry. Several states and dozens of communities formed censorship boards to ban movies deemed unsuitable for young people. To both stem the tide of censorship and address public concerns over movie content, Hollywood set up in 1924 its own review board, a forerunner of today's movie-rating system, to screen movie content.

The American Civil Liberties Union and other groups opposed these growing

▲ Although James Joyce's *Ulysses* was initially banned, a later federal court ruling declared that it was not obscene and was a true work of literature.

restrictions on the content of movies and literature. They argued that such censorship violated the Constitution's First Amendment, which guarantees freedom of speech and freedom of the press.

Today the battle between censorship and freedom of speech continues. The National Endowment for the Arts (NEA), for example, has come under attack for funding artists whose works some consider obscene. But while some critics judge the art as obscene and unsuitable for public funding, the artists defend their right to freedom of expression. The NEA and other agencies are caught in the middle of the battle.

Several rock and rap musicians have also come under fire for recording songs that contain violent lyrics or lyrics that degrade women. In response, the Recording Industry Association of America has begun placing warning labels on any recordings that contain lyrics that might be unsuitable for minors. But many people believe voluntary labeling is not enough. In 1992, for instance, Washington State banned the sale and distribution of certain recordings to minors.

Is such censorship a violation of free speech or a needed form of protection? American society and U.S. courts continue to struggle with this question.

Then and Now

Ask students how they feel about censorship and restraints on free expression in general. Have them name movies or records they know of that have been censored. Take a survey of class attitudes toward censorship by asking students to anonymously vote "for" or "against" censorship.

HISTORICAL SIDELIGHTS

Verdict Reversed
Scopes appealed his conviction, and in 1927 the Tennessee supreme court reversed the verdict on a technicality—the judge had set a fine higher than the law prescribed. However, the court upheld the anti-evolution law, which remained on Tennessee's statute books until the 1960s.

McPherson addressed her followers' concerns about the new doctrines of "communism, socialism, and jazz-ism." McPherson also used radio and magazines to spread her fundamentalist message.

The Scopes trial. Fundamentalism went on trial in a famous court case in July 1925. Earlier that year the Tennessee legislature had outlawed the teaching of Charles Darwin's theory of evolution—a prime target of Fundamentalists—in the state's public schools. To test the law's constitutionality, the American Civil Liberties Union offered to defend any Tennessee schoolteacher who would challenge the statute. John Scopes, a shy high-school biology teacher from Dayton, accepted the offer.

The trial took place in a circus atmosphere. As the trial began in Dayton, the little town was overrun by reporters, farmers in mule-drawn wagons, and big-city lawyers. Scopes's chief defense attorney was salty Clarence Darrow, a famous criminal lawyer from Chicago. The prosecution's star witness was the elderly William Jennings Bryan, the former Democratic presidential candidate and secretary of state.

RETEACH Have students work in small groups to chart the major ideas and events presented in the section. Direct each group to indicate on its chart how each item addresses one of the section's Focus questions.

Closure

Ask students to explain why their textbook (on p. 652) characterizes the 1920s as "the gateway to modern America." Require that they give examples to support their explanations.

Extension

COMPARE Ask students to make an oral report comparing the role sports and entertainment played in 1920s American life to the role these pastimes play today.

INVESTIGATE Have students investigate how Canada and Mexico responded to U.S. Prohibition.

PRIMARY SOURCE

Description of Change: excerpted and bracketed
Rationale: excerpted to focus on main idea; bracketed to clarify meaning

SECTION REVIEW ANSWERS

IDENTIFY

For significance, see the following pages:
Babe Ruth (p. 653)
Helen Wills (p. 653)
Gertrude Ederle (p. 654)
Jim Thorpe (p. 654)
Charles Lindbergh (p. 654)
Amelia Earhart (p. 655)
flappers (p. 655)
Volstead Act (p. 656)
Twenty-first Amendment (p. 656)
Fundamentalism (p. 656)
Aimee Semple McPherson (p. 656)
John Scopes (p. 657)

1. *radio and movies*
2. *broke conventional rules of dress and behavior, had social and economic independence*
3. *Their differences exposed a division between traditional religious values and new values based on science.*
4. *negative—bootlegging, gang control of liquor sales, "protection" rackets; positive—decrease in alcoholism and alcohol-related deaths*
5. *sports figures—instant celebrities because of influence of mass culture; revivalists—popular because changes threatened traditional values*

► Clarence Darrow (right) devoted a large part of his legal career to defending the "underdog." This photograph shows him with John Scopes in 1925.

▼ Because the theory of evolution implied that human beings had descended from ape-like creatures, the Scopes trial became known as the "Monkey Trial."

THE CHICAGO DAILY NEWS.
SCOPES "GUILTY" IN APE CASE

The Scopes trial exposed a deep division in American society between traditional religious values and new values based on scientific ways of thought. Bryan represented the many Americans who felt that the theory of evolution contradicted deeply held religious beliefs. Speaking before the trial to an audience of local admirers, Bryan declared:

> **❝** Our purpose and our only purpose is to vindicate [uphold] the right of parents to guard the religion of their children against efforts made in the name of science to undermine faith in supernatural religion. **❞**

Darrow, on the other hand, expressed the views of many other Americans when he attacked the Tennessee law as a threat to free expression. In one of his courtroom speeches, he warned his listeners that "today it is the public school teachers, tomorrow the private, the next day the preachers and the lecturers, the magazines, the books, the newspapers."

Darrow's arguments failed to sway the jury. They found Scopes guilty and fined him $100. The verdict seemed a victory for Fundamentalists. But press accounts of the trial, which often portrayed Bryan and his cause as narrow-minded, colored many people's views of Fundamentalism.

■■ **The debate over Prohibition and Fundamentalism revealed a crisis of values in 1920s America.**

SECTION 2 REVIEW

IDENTIFY and explain the significance of the following: Babe Ruth, Helen Wills, Gertrude Ederle, Jim Thorpe, Charles Lindbergh, Amelia Earhart, flappers, Volstead Act, Twenty-first Amendment, Fundamentalism, Aimee Semple McPherson, John Scopes.

1. **MAIN IDEA** What two forms of entertainment were most popular among Americans during the 1920s?
2. **MAIN IDEA** How did the flapper represent the "new woman" of the 1920s?
3. **IDENTIFYING VALUES** In what ways did the differing views of Clarence Darrow and William Jennings Bryan in the Scopes trial reflect the clash in values of 1920s America?
4. **WRITING TO INFORM** Write an essay explaining the negative and positive consequences of Prohibition.
5. **HYPOTHESIZING** What social factors might account for the popularity of sports figures and revivalists during the 1920s?

PREVIEW WORKSHOP

Following is a list of the significant people, places, and terms in this section. You may wish to use this list as a section preview.

People
- Joseph "King" Oliver
- Langston Hughes
- Marian Anderson
- Paul Robeson
- Rose McClendon

- Ernest Hemingway
- Diego Rivera
- Alfred Stieglitz

Places
- Harlem

Terms
- Harlem Renaissance
- Lost Generation
- planned obsolescence

Section 3

A CREATIVE ERA

FOCUS

- **How did African Americans contribute to the arts during the Harlem Renaissance?**
- **Who were the Lost Generation writers, and how did they get their name?**
- **What factors influenced artists and designers of the 1920s?**
- **How did mass media and advertising affect American culture in the 1920s?**

Louis Armstrong

The decade of the 1920s was a period of great creative energy. African American musicians transformed popular music by introducing the nation to jazz. A new generation of writers explored the problems of postwar American life and the experience of being black. Mexican muralists brought their paintings of social protest to the United States. And new currents in art and architecture swept the nation.

FOCUS OBJECTIVES

- Explain how African Americans contributed to the arts during the Harlem Renaissance.
- Identify the Lost Generation writers and explain how they got their name.
- Describe the factors that influenced artists and designers in the 1920s.
- Analyze how mass media and advertising affected American culture in the 1920s.

MUSIC AND DANCE

The 1920s has been called the Jazz Age because this was the period when jazz, with its richly complex rhythms, first won a wide following. Jazz originated among African Americans in the South, especially in New Orleans. By the late 1800s, jazz had emerged from a blend of West African and Latin American rhythms, African American spirituals and blues, and European harmonies.

Joseph "King" Oliver, an early jazz great, helped spread jazz northward by moving from New Orleans to Chicago and founding the Creole Jazz Band. In 1922 the great jazz trumpeter Louis Armstrong joined Oliver in Chicago. Pianist and composer Ferdinand "Jelly Roll" Morton also moved north.

As it became popular on a national level, jazz was adapted in various ways. White musicians—among them the cornetist and pianist Bix Beiderbecke—incorporated jazz rhythms in their music. George Gershwin's *Rhapsody in Blue,* which

▶ Ferdinand "Jelly Roll" Morton began his career playing ragtime piano in New Orleans. Later, he moved to Chicago where he formed the recording group Red Hot Peppers.

CORE RESOURCES

- **Literature Worksheet 22**
- **Section 3 Daily Quiz**

AV RESOURCES

- **Everyday Life in America Transparency and Worksheet 22**

MOTIVATING:
LINK TO TODAY

Call on volunteers to explain how artists, writers, and musicians influence American society today. Tell students that this section will describe the influences of artists, writers, and musicians on mass culture during the 1920s.

▲ During the 1920s jazz music such as "Tin Roof Blues" and "If You Knew Susie Like I Know Susie" became popular hits.

premiered in 1924, "translated" jazz into symphonic form. Jazz also influenced many classical musicians, including such noted composers as Igor Stravinsky and Aaron Copland.

The big bands, both black (Fletcher Henderson's and Duke Ellington's, for instance) and white (such as Paul Whiteman's), popularized jazz for dancing, creating faster and bouncier dances set to jazz rhythms. This new kind of jazz swept the nation via phonograph records, radio, and the movies. Young men and their flapper partners shocked their elders by dancing cheek-to-cheek fox-trots. The Charleston, originally an African dance performed by slaves, became *the* dance of the twenties.

While jazz became universal in the 1920s, it continued to express the particular sadness, pain, and joy of black America. African American poet Langston Hughes noted that through jazz, African Americans were saying "Why should I want to be white? I am a Negro—and beautiful!"

■■ **Jazz became widely popular during the 1920s, influencing many other forms of music.**

𝐴 BLACK RENAISSANCE

African American writers, artists, actors, and musicians in the 1920s expressed a growing black pride. Nowhere was this pride more evident than in the New York City neighborhood of Harlem, the nation's leading African American community. So many important African American writers, musicians, and artists lived in Harlem that this period of artistic development is known as the **Harlem Renaissance**.

The 1920s was a decade of achievement for African American musicians. They popularized not

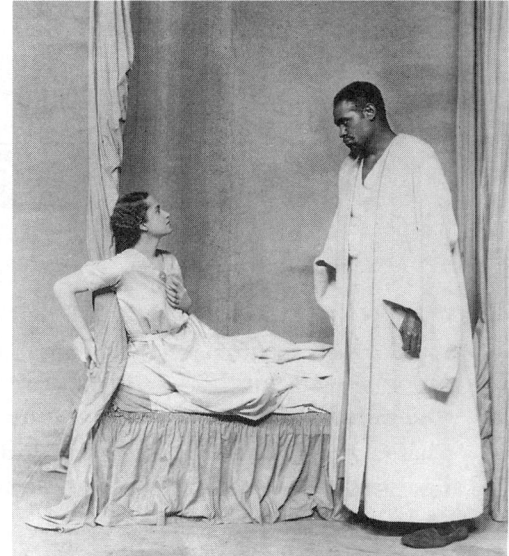

▲ In the 1920s Paul Robeson won fame as an actor in such plays as Shakespeare's *Othello*.

only jazz but also blues and religious songs known as spirituals. In 1920 Mamie Smith's recording of "Crazy Blues" made popular the moody melodies of blues for white audiences. Bessie Smith, "the Empress of the Blues," toured widely and made many blues recordings. Marian Anderson, a gifted singer who began her operatic career in the 1920s, and Paul Robeson, singer and actor, incorporated spirituals in their repertoires.

In an era when African Americans were limited in the theatrical roles they were allowed to play, blacks produced and staged several enormously successful Broadway musicals, including Eubie Blake's *Shuffle Along* (1921). African American actors also achieved fame. Charles Gilpin played the title role in Eugene O'Neill's drama *Emperor Jones* in 1920. Paul Robeson made history in 1924 by becoming the first black actor to play a leading role opposite a white actress.

BIO A lead-
GRAPHY ing African American actress of the 1920s was Rose McClendon. Born in 1884 in South Carolina, McClendon moved to New York City as a child. She took part in church

Rose McClendon

HARLEM RENAISSANCE

Ask a volunteer to provide a dramatic reading of Langston Hughes's poem on pp. 661–662 and ask other volunteers to offer interpretations of its meaning. Then have students assume the role of an African American artist, writer, actor, or musician involved in the Harlem Renaissance. Invite them to write an essay or poem explaining how the Harlem Renaissance is an expression of their identity as blacks and as Americans. Have volunteers read their articles to the class. Students may wish to include their writings in their portfolios.

▶

---

plays but did not become a professional actress until her thirties, after winning a scholarship to the American Academy of Dramatic Art.

McClendon first won fame in *Deep River,* a "native opera with jazz" staged in 1926. Even the simple act of descending a staircase won her praise from critics and fellow actors alike. In later years she played in the Pulitzer Prize–winning tragedy *In Abraham's Bosom,* about a would-be reformer; the first production of *Porgy,* set in Charleston, South Carolina; and *Never No More,* the story of a lynching. Her last role was in Langston Hughes's *Mulatto.*

In addition to directing plays at the Harlem Experimental Theatre, Rose McClendon helped found the Negro People's Theatre in Harlem in 1935. The organization increased opportunities for black actors and playwrights.

As important and impressive as African American contributions to movie and stage were during the Harlem Renaissance, it was above all a literary movement. Black novelists and poets produced work marked by bitterness and defiance but also by joy and hope. In his novel *Home to Harlem* (1928), Jamaica-born Claude McKay explored the excitement and stresses of Harlem life for a returned black soldier. Nella Larsen, born in Chicago of West Indian and Danish ancestry, described the quest for racial identity in her novel *Quicksand* (1928).

Among the most-famous Harlem poets were Langston Hughes and Countee Cullen. Hughes's *Weary Blues* (1926) and Cullen's *Color* (1925) viewed African American life and the African cultural heritage with sensitivity. In the poem "I, Too," Hughes sums up black pride in a few powerful lines:

> ❝ I, too, sing America.
>
> I am the darker brother.
> They send me to eat in the kitchen
> When company comes,
> But I laugh,
> And eat well,
> And grow strong.

Harlem Renaissance, 1920s

HARLEM'S EXPANSION Migrants came to New York City from the South and the islands of the West Indies. During the 1920s, some 25 percent of Harlem's black population was foreign born.

? PLACE What was the extent of African American settlement in Harlem in 1920?

Famous club where Duke Ellington and other black entertainers perform for whites-only audiences.

This branch library features exhibits by African American artists and poetry readings by Countee Cullen.

Site of Marcus Garvey's UNIA rallies

W.E.B. Du Bois sometimes lectures here, and the Krigwa Players stage plays by African Americans.

Countee Cullen's column, "The Dark Tower," provides the name for this Harlem literary salon.

Johnson's 1922 anthology, *The Book of Negro Poetry,* helps launch the Harlem Renaissance. His parties draw noted intellectuals, such as Paul Robeson and Clarence Darrow.

- ■ Black settlement in Harlem, 1920
- ■ Black settlement in Harlem, 1930
- ■ Areas predominantly African American
- ■ Point of interest

Map Caption Answer *from 130th St. to 145th St., and from 5th Ave. to 8th Ave.*

HISTORICAL SIDELIGHTS
Discrimination in Radio

While the radio networks employed black guest performers during the 1920s, they did not hire African Americans as actors or technicians. In addition, some radio programs, such as *Amos 'n' Andy,* in which black characters were portrayed by white actors, contributed to the stereotyping of African Americans.

CULTURAL PATTERNS

African American writer Jessie Fauset served as literary editor of the NAACP's journal, *The Crisis,* in the 1920s. *The Crisis* published many of the Harlem Renaissance writers for the first time. Fauset's encouragement of young writers and her willingness to accept experimental work supported African American exploration of black themes.

PRIMARY SOURCE
Description of Change: excerpted
Rationale: excerpted to focus on main idea

Teaching the **Section**

THE LOST GENERATION

Have students write journal entries from the perspective of young people of the 1920s explaining why they are disillusioned with life in postwar America. Have volunteers share their entries in class. Use these presentations as a starting point for a class discussion on why Gertrude Stein chose the term *lost generation* to characterize young American writers' anger and disappointment in 1920s society.

PRIMARY SOURCE
Description of Change: excerpted
Rationale: excerpted to focus on main idea

HISTORICAL SIDELIGHTS

Americans in Paris

For some members of the Lost Generation, the disillusionment with American society was so complete that they went into exile and lived abroad. Many—Ernest Hemingway among them—gravitated to Paris. Indeed, some scholars have suggested that during the 1920s the French capital was the center of the American literary world. The headquarters for most American writers in Paris was Shakespeare and Company, a bookstore and lending library run by American Sylvia Beach. Hemingway considered Shakespeare and Company "a wonderful place," and he visited it practically every day during his time in Paris.

▲ **Langston Hughes**

Tomorrow,
I'll be at the table
When company comes.
Nobody'll dare
Say to me,
"Eat in the kitchen,"
Then.

Besides,
They'll see how beautiful I am
And be ashamed—

I, too, am America. 99

▪▪ **African American musicians, actors, and writers in the 1920s flourished, creating a cultural movement known as the Harlem Renaissance.**

*T*HE LOST GENERATION

The creative spirit of the 1920s expressed itself not only in jazz, but also in the literature of the decade. Many younger writers of the time were haunted by the death and destruction of World War I and scornful of middle-class consumerism and the superficiality of the postwar years. "You are all a lost generation," said poet Gertrude Stein to one such writer, Ernest Hemingway. The label stuck, and scholars refer to writers of the era as the **Lost Generation**.

Ernest Hemingway spent much of his life in France, Spain, and Cuba. During World War I, he and several other young writers became ambulance drivers as a way to experience and develop an understanding of war. Hemingway was seriously wounded while serving at the Italian front. Later, he expressed his anger at war's futility in such novels as *The Sun Also Rises* (1926) and *A Farewell to Arms* (1929). In a famous passage from the latter book, a war veteran explains what the war means to him:

66 I was always embarrassed by the words sacred, glorious, and sacrifice and the expression in vain. We had heard them . . . and had read them . . . now for a long time, and I had seen nothing sacred, and the things that were glorious had no glory and the sacrifices were like the stockyards at Chicago if nothing was done with the meat except to bury it. 99

Disillusionment with World War I echoed in the works of other Lost Generation writers, including John Dos Passos's *Three Soldiers* (1919) and *Manhattan Transfer* (1925).

Another Lost Generation writer, F. Scott Fitzgerald, was the foremost chronicler of the youthful Jazz Age. In his first novel, *This Side of Paradise* (1920), Fitzgerald described the life of rich college students bored by fast living and hard liquor. In *The Great Gatsby* (1925), Fitzgerald portrayed the emptiness of life devoted to a frenzied struggle to make money and win social status in Prohibition-era America. Sinclair Lewis, another writer who criticized American society, satirized middle-class life in *Main Street* (1920) and *Babbitt* (1922).

The journalist and critic Henry L. Mencken championed the new writers. In his magazine *The American Mercury,* Mencken publicized novelists who satirized middle-class Americans, whom he ridiculed as "the booboisie." Mencken made fun of Republican politicians, fundamentalist Christians, rural southerners, residents of small towns, and many other groups.

▪▪ **Gertrude Stein called Ernest Hemingway and other postwar writers "a lost generation" because of their anger and sense of loss.**

▲ Diego Rivera painted many murals that focused on workers and their relationship to industrial production. Shown here is *Entry to the Mine.*

OTHER CURRENTS IN ART AND DESIGN

The artistic vitality of the 1920s can also be seen in the work of U.S. artists and designers as they confronted the machine age and reflected its influence on American society. They chronicled factories, new technology, workers, and urban landscapes.

Painting and photography. Many American painters of the 1920s depicted urban, industrial settings. Edward Hopper's New York City scenes convey a sense of loneliness. *Early Sunday Morning* (1930) shows a row of darkened stores and a street empty of people. New York City intrigued Georgia O'Keeffe, too. In the 1920s she painted pictures of its factories and tenements. Later she would move to New Mexico, paint dramatic pictures of flowers, and capture the stark beauty of the Southwest.

Photography came into its own as an art form in the early 1900s. Alfred Stieglitz (STEEG-luhts), more than anyone else, gave it new status. Stieglitz's New York gallery influenced many other American artists. In addition to striking portraits of people, his own subjects included airplanes, skyscrapers, and crowded city streets. Charles Sheeler, a photographer and painter, won fame for the "portraits of machinery" he produced for the Ford Motor Company, which commissioned him to photograph its plant near Detroit, Michigan, in 1927.

Another renaissance of the 1920s took place in Mexico and was later brought to the United States by its major artists. This artistic movement stressed American Indian traditions and the ideals of the Mexican Revolution of 1910. The artists emphasized the nobility of ordinary people—peasants and other workers—and the tyranny of wealthy capitalists. Their favorite medium was the monumental public mural because, in the words of artist José Clemente Orozco (oh-rohs-koh), "it cannot be hidden away for the benefit of a certain privileged few. It is for the people. It is for *ALL.*"

The movement's three major artists—known in Mexico as *los tres grandes,* or "the big three"—were Orozco, David Alfaro Siqueiros (see-KAY-rohs), and Diego Rivera. Each first became known in Mexico in the 1920s and painted murals in the United States in the early 1930s. Orozco

Addison Gallery of American Art, Phillips Academy, Andover, MA

▲ This 1928 painting by Edward Hopper is called *Manhattan Bridge Loop.*

HISTORICAL SIDELIGHTS

Politics and Art

In 1932 Diego Rivera began work on a mural at Rockefeller Center in New York City. Titled *Man at the Crossroads,* the mural proposed that socialism was the route humanity should take. That a work of art espousing such a view was housed in a building named for one of America's richest capitalists caused a huge controversy. Rivera was ordered to stop work on the mural. In 1934, in what Rivera called "an act of cultural vandalism," the mural was destroyed.

HISTORICAL SIDELIGHTS

Top of the Art World

Georgia O'Keeffe and Alfred Stieglitz were married, and they had a great respect for each other's talent. Stieglitz described O'Keeffe's paintings as "wonders." In *Radiator Building, Night, New York* (see p. 664), O'Keeffe emblazoned Stieglitz's name in a red neon sign, placing him at the top of the art world.

*P*ractice

GUIDED PRACTICE

Call on volunteers to identify the major developments in American arts during the 1920s. List responses on the chalkboard, asking students to provide background information on each item.

INDEPENDENT PRACTICE

Have students use the list developed in the Guided Practice to construct an annotated time line on American artistic creativity in the 1920s. Students may wish to include their time lines in their portfolios.

*R*eview and *A*ssessment

REVIEW Have students write 10 questions about Section 3 on individual note cards with the answers on the reverse side. Then divide students into groups of four. Ask them to use their note cards to question the other members of the group. Then assign the Section 3 Review on p. 665.

ASSESS Assign the **Section 3 Daily Quiz** in *Core Resources*.

GLOBAL CONNECTIONS

Industrial design originated at the Bauhaus, a school of design founded by architect Walter Gropius in Germany in 1919. Emphasizing simple, practical designs and attention to craftsmanship, the Bauhaus had a worldwide impact. Its influence was especially marked in the U.S., where some of its members came to teach after the Nazis closed the school in the early 1930s.

PRIMARY SOURCE

Description of Change: excerpted
Rationale: excerpted to focus on main idea

COOPERATIVE LEARNING

Divide the class into groups of four. Assign each group one of these topics on the 1920s to research: music, literature, sports, art. Have groups use their research to create a mural. Students in each group should share assignments among themselves; some might be responsible for research, others for mural design, and still others for writing text to explain the mural.

---

created several murals for American universities, many featuring heroic figures who helped humanity. In Los Angeles, Siqueiros painted large-scale murals outdoors, "in the free air," as he put it. Diego Rivera focused on workers' problems and industrial development in his U.S. murals. In a mural at the Detroit Institute of Art, which Rivera painted in 1932, his subject was, fittingly, assembly-line workers in automobile factories.

Industrial design. The machine age that inspired artists also gave rise to a new professional field: industrial design. Spreading from Germany to the United States in the 1920s, industrial design aimed to create objects that were pleasing to look at as well as functional.

Industrial designers, working with such new materials as stainless steel and plastics, developed a wide range of products with a "modern" look. The designers developed streamlining—contours that reduced resistance—for trains, planes, ships, and cars. They also applied streamlining to objects that did not even move, such as radios, clocks, and appliances.

Manufacturers quickly learned that a new design for what was essentially the same product boosted sales. They had discovered what came to be called **planned obsolescence**—making products specifically designed to go out of style and to be replaced by the purchase of an up-to-date model. Auto manufacturers were among the first to take advantage of planned obsolescence. In the early 1920s General Motors introduced the ideas of the yearly model change and the trade-in. Thereafter, many American families routinely traded in their "old" models and bought new cars every year.

Architecture. Industrial design, which combined function and visual appeal, had its counterpart in the world of architecture. Louis Sullivan and Frank Lloyd Wright inspired many other architects to embrace the idea that a building ought to use the materials and follow the forms most suitable to the building's purpose. The structure that most clearly illustrated this principle was the skyscraper, with its clean-cut vertical lines, its use of steel and concrete, its many glass windows, and its relative freedom from ornamentation.

New York City, whose population density and expensive real estate made it more cost effi-

▲ Georgia O'Keeffe (inset) painted this scene, entitled *Radiator Building, Night, New York,* in 1927.

cient to build upward than outward, witnessed a boom in skyscraper construction during the 1920s. Builders began construction of two landmarks—the Chrysler Building and the Empire State Building.

Civic boosters loved the skyscrapers, but critics voiced their doubts. For example, a verse of the time protested:

❝ THE
S K Y -
SCRAPER
T A L L
I S   A
WONDER
TO ALL
A THING
TOADMIRE
BEYOND
QUESTION
Butoh!downbelowwherepedestriansgo
itcertainlyaddstocongestion ❞

*C*OMMENTARY

A Standardized Culture?

What were the social effects of the new mass media and mass marketing of the 1920s? Most historians agree that mass media and mass marketing helped produce a standardized middle-class culture. Movies, radio, advertising, and

RETEACH For each subsection in the section, have students write a sentence that summarizes the main idea. Select students to read their sentences aloud. Have the group choose the best summary sentence for each subsection.

Closure

Encourage students to create poems, songs, or posters that explain why the period from 1920 to 1929 might be called a creative era. Have volunteers present and explain their work. Students may wish to include their poems, songs, or posters in their portfolios.

Extension

ANALYZE Have students investigate and analyze the ways in which jazz influenced classical musicians such as Igor Stravinsky and Aaron Copland.

RESEARCH Encourage students to read further about one of the persons listed in the Preview Workshop and report on that person's contributions during the 1920s.

magazines such as *The Saturday Evening Post* and *Time* reached every corner of the nation. These new forms of media promoted middle-class ways by presenting an ideal world of middle-class families very similar in behavior and values. Mass marketing promoted standardization by offering customers a limited range of choices among soap and appliance brands, car models, and food products. Rather than relying on local or regional goods, people all over the country used largely the same products.

Historians recognize, however, that mass media and mass marketing also changed life for Americans by acquainting them with the cultures of other groups of Americans. For example, many people—rich and poor, urban and rural—listened and danced to African American–influenced music and dance, and some white Americans enjoyed reading the works of Harlem Renaissance writers. Many middle-class women adopted forms of behavior previously associated with working-class women, such as wearing makeup and smoking.

The mass media also helped strengthen working-class, immigrant, and African American cultures. Musical recordings by African Americans, Mexican Americans, and others preserved traditional musical forms. Immigrant and working-class neighborhood movie theaters served as community meeting places. Some local radio stations devoted their programs exclusively to ethnic audiences, offering ethnic music and local news as well as news about the immigrants'

homelands. Ethnic newspapers continued to fulfill their role of helping to preserve the immigrants' languages and ethnic identities.

While most middle-class families bought the same brands at chain stores, most working-class and immigrant families continued to buy from their local corner groceries. These local grocers, who usually shared the ethnicity of their patrons, extended credit to their customers. The grocers sold traditional ethnic ingredients such as Italian macaroni, Jewish kosher meats, or Asian delicacies, which the chain stores rarely carried. These corner groceries thus allowed ethnic Americans to maintain traditional diets. Furthermore, these corner stores served as places where people could meet, swap news, and gossip.

The mass media thus helped maintain ethnic cultures while they promoted middle-class values. And when middle-class Americans all over the country copied the style of life presented by the movies, network radio, and mass magazines, they were adopting ways influenced by different cultural perspectives. In short, the mass media and mass marketing not only supported traditional ways but also helped to spread new ways of thinking and acting throughout the nation.

■■ **Mass media and mass marketing promoted both new and standardized modes of behavior. At the same time, the mass media also helped sustain traditional cultures.**

SECTION REVIEW ANSWERS

IDENTIFY

For significance, see the following pages:
Joseph "King" Oliver (p. 659)
Langston Hughes (p. 660)
Harlem Renaissance (p. 660)
Marian Anderson (p. 660)
Paul Robeson (p. 660)
Rose McClendon (p. 660)
Ernest Hemingway (p. 662)
Lost Generation (p. 662)
Diego Rivera (p. 663)
Alfred Stieglitz (p. 663)
planned obsolescence (p. 664)

LOCATE

For location, see the map on p. 661.

1. through music—especially jazz—theater, art, and literature
2. because they were discouraged by World War I and disillusioned with middle-class values; Gertrude Stein
3. both glorified life of ordinary people and created public mural art that all could view
4. Radio reached a broader audience and presented a world of traditional, middle-class values. Some stations also reinforced ethnic customs by directing programs to ethnic audiences.
5. They challenged middle-class values and criticized capitalism.

SECTION 3 REVIEW

IDENTIFY and explain the significance of the following: Joseph "King" Oliver, Langston Hughes, Harlem Renaissance, Marian Anderson, Paul Robeson, Rose McClendon, Ernest Hemingway, Lost Generation, Diego Rivera, Alfred Stieglitz, planned obsolescence.

LOCATE and explain the importance of the following: Harlem.

1. **MAIN IDEA** In what ways did the artists of the Harlem Renaissance contribute to American culture?

2. **MAIN IDEA** Why were Ernest Hemingway and other young writers of the 1920s called "a lost generation"? Who coined this phrase?

3. **MAIN IDEA** What characteristics did the work of artists and photographers of the 1920s have in common?

4. **WRITING TO EVALUATE** How did radio help people maintain long-held customs?

5. **ANALYZING** Why might black artists, writers of the Lost Generation, and other painters and photographers of the 1920s be considered social critics?

Chapter Review Answers

WRITING A SUMMARY

See Essential Points in each section for main ideas.

REVIEWING CHRONOLOGY

2, 5, 1, 3, 4
Assessing Consequences
popularized sound in movies, resulting in emergence of actors with appealing voices; led to development of new film forms, such as musicals and newsreels

IDENTIFYING PEOPLE AND IDEAS

1. *technique that sped up product assembly*
2. *Frederick W. Taylor's method of breaking down jobs into smaller tasks so as to improve work efficiency*
3. *sociologist who chronicled life in Muncie, Indiana, in the book* Middletown *(1929)*
4. *Native American athlete who won pentathlon and decathlon in 1912 Olympics*
5. *first pilot to fly nonstop from New York to Paris*
6. *Protestant movement believing in literal truth of Bible*
7. *period of African American artistic flowering centered in New York City*
8. *African American theater actor and director*
9. *Mexican muralist whose work focused on workers' problems and on industrial development*
10. *making products that are designed to go out of style*

UNDERSTANDING MAIN IDEAS

1. *Middle-class Americans embraced new musical forms, new products, and new forms of behavior popularized by mass media and advertising.*
2. *disillusionment with World War I, superficiality of middle-class life and emptiness of life devoted merely to making money and winning social status*
3. *popular actresses, independence of working-class women, advertisements, and the automobile*
4. *With more leisure time and more money to spend, Americans sought new ways to entertain themselves, thus encouraging growth of the entertainment industry.*
5. *popularized music such as jazz and blues, and dances such as the Charleston; promoted black cultural pride in literature, theater, and other fields*

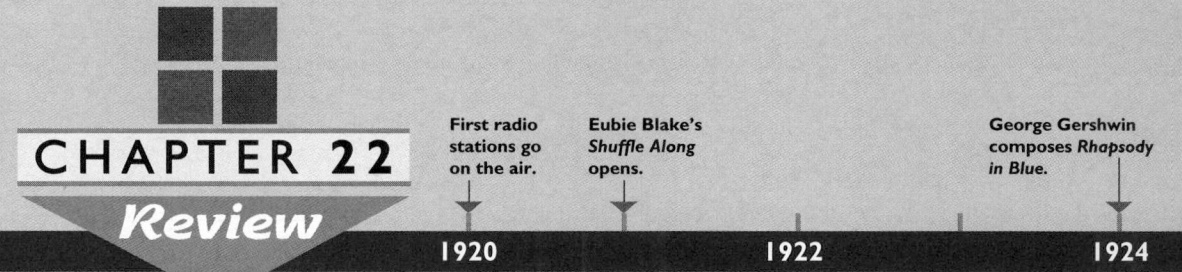

CHAPTER 22
Review

First radio stations go on the air.	Eubie Blake's *Shuffle Along* opens.		George Gershwin composes *Rhapsody in Blue*.
1920	1922		1924

WRITING A SUMMARY
Using the essential points of the chapter as a guide, write a summary of the chapter.

REVIEWING CHRONOLOGY
Number your paper 1 to 5. Study the time line above, and list the following events in the order in which they happened by writing the first next to 1, the second next to 2, and so on. Then complete the activity below.

1. Scopes trial held in Dayton, Tennessee.
2. Eubie Blake's *Shuffle Along* opens.
3. *The Jazz Singer* released.
4. Robert Lynd and Helen Lynd's *Middletown* issued.
5. George Gershwin composes *Rhapsody in Blue*.

Assessing Consequences How did *The Jazz Singer* influence the development of American entertainment?

IDENTIFYING PEOPLE AND IDEAS
Explain the historical significance of each of the following people or terms.

1. assembly line	6. Fundamentalism
2. scientific management	7. Harlem Renaissance
3. Helen Lynd	8. Rose McClendon
4. Jim Thorpe	9. Diego Rivera
5. Charles Lindbergh	10. planned obsolescence

UNDERSTANDING MAIN IDEAS
1. How was middle-class life in the 1920s changed by mass media and advertising?
2. What postwar problems did the Lost Generation deal with in their literature?
3. What influences led women to exercise new freedom in dress and behavior?
4. How did the prosperity of the 1920s influence American entertainment?
5. What contributions did African Americans make to the changing American culture of the 1920s?

REVIEWING THEMES
1. **Economic Development** How did advertising, merchandising, and installment buying help the nation's economy in the 1920s?
2. **Technology and Society** How did new technology affect Americans' lives at work and at home?
3. **Cultural Diversity** How did the mass media help preserve ethnic cultures?

THINKING CRITICALLY
1. **Analyzing** How did increased productivity and consumerism pave the way for future environmental problems?
2. **Synthesizing** Why might the Model T be an appropriate symbol for the 1920s?
3. **Evaluating** How did social changes contribute to the popularity of religious revivals?

STRATEGY FOR SUCCESS
Review the Skills Handbook entry on Taking a Test on page 1002. Below is a sample multiple-choice question that might be asked about Chapter 22. Write a paragraph summarizing how you would arrive at the correct answer.

The aspect of industrial design that most increased sales was
    a. scientific management.
    b. advertising.
    c. planned obsolescence.
    d. streamlining.

Ford automobile plant, 1921

 **REVIEWING THEMES**

1. fueled demand for more and new products, which stimulated production and employment
2. Assembly line, scientific management, and new products changed working conditions and types of jobs available to American workers; new appliances and automobiles allowed middle-class women to manage households without servants.
3. radio programs aimed at ethnic audiences played traditional music, offered news of the homeland, and—along with ethnic newspapers—used the immigrants' languages

THINKING CRITICALLY

1. Increased factory production and automobile traffic began a chain of environmental pollution that has continued to the present.
2. represented changes in production methods and in use of postwar industrial materials; led to transformation of transportation system and of social structure, roles, and values
3. Modern concepts and behavior alarmed many conservatives; revivalists spoke to conservatives' fears and supported traditional values.

STRATEGY FOR SUCCESS

Correct answer is "c." Students should discuss how "a" and "b" can be quickly eliminated because they are not aspects of industrial design; "d" would not necessarily affect sales.

WRITING ABOUT HISTORY

Letters might mention that concerns about teaching evolution have forced the school to eliminate Darwin's theories from curriculum.

USING PRIMARY SOURCES

Paragraphs should consider how Paul Robeson's accomplishments inspired other African Americans to succeed.

LINKING HISTORY AND GEOGRAPHY

Answers might mention that the clustering of African Americans from different backgrounds encouraged the exchange of artistic ideas.

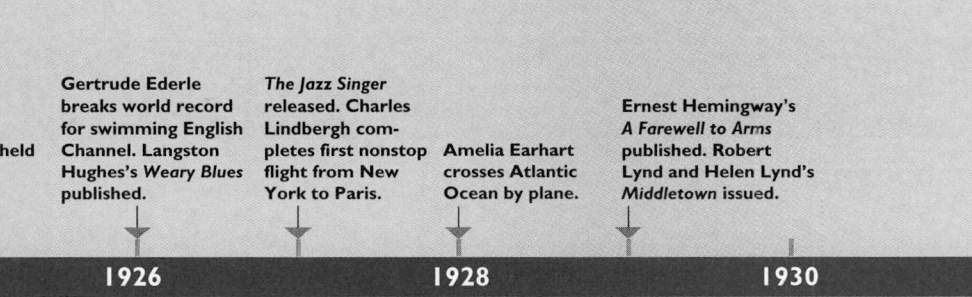

Scopes trial held in Dayton, Tennessee.	Gertrude Ederle breaks world record for swimming English Channel. Langston Hughes's *Weary Blues* published.	The Jazz Singer released. Charles Lindbergh completes first nonstop flight from New York to Paris.	Amelia Earhart crosses Atlantic Ocean by plane.	Ernest Hemingway's *A Farewell to Arms* published. Robert Lynd and Helen Lynd's *Middletown* issued.
	1926		**1928**	**1930**

WRITING ABOUT HISTORY

Writing to Explain Imagine you are a high school principal at the time of the Scopes trial. Write a letter to parents, outlining the issues involved in the trial and explaining how the verdict will affect next year's science curriculum.

USING PRIMARY SOURCES

Harlem was the social, cultural, and entertainment capital for many African Americans during the 1920s. In the following excerpt, Howard "Stretch" Johnson talks about the black basketball teams popular in the 1920s and about the influence of Paul Robeson, one of the Harlem Renaissance's major figures. Write a paragraph explaining how Robeson influenced African Americans in the 1920s.

❝ *The Renaissance Big Five basketball team was a part of [the Harlem Renaissance]. . . .*

My father was a very fine professional basketball player. He played with a group called the Puritans, which later became the Renaissance Big Five. . . .

Paul Robeson played with Alpha fraternity against my father when my father was playing with St. Christopher's, another semipro team that was popular in the '20s. Paul was a great figure. People used to swarm around him when he walked out on the street. He was the inspiration in every walk of life. Those blacks who went in for law had respect for his being a Phi Beta Kappa at Columbia University. Those who aspired to be successful in the athletic field had him as an exemplar [model] with his record at Rutgers, where he got fifteen varsity letters—more varsity A's than any individual who ever went to Rutgers—in football, basketball, track, and baseball. ❞

LINKING HISTORY AND GEOGRAPHY

Refer to the map on page 661. What factors might explain the birth of the Harlem Renaissance during the 1920s?

Young women in Harlem

 **BUILDING YOUR PORTFOLIO**

Complete the following projects independently or cooperatively.

1. **THE ECONOMY** In Chapter 21 you portrayed an unemployed veteran. Building on that experience, imagine you are a prosperous business owner in the 1920s. Create an advertisement for a new household product aimed at the expanding consumer market. Your ad might use psychology, slogans, jingles, or celebrity testimonials to sell your product.

2. **CULTURE AND SOCIETY** In Chapter 21 you portrayed an immigrant artist. Building on that experience, imagine you are an African American artist during the Harlem Renaissance. Create a dance, jazz poem, or painting that expresses cultural pride in your African American heritage.

 **BUILDING YOUR PORTFOLIO**

Have students refer to **Building Your Portfolio Worksheet 7**, assigned at the beginning of Unit 7. Use the worksheet to help students monitor their progress on the portfolio projects.

*A*ssessment

Core Resources
• Review Worksheet 22
• Chapter 22 Tests
• Alternative Assessment Forms
Test Generator

THE GREAT DEPRESSION

1929–1933

Chapter Overview

The excesses of the 1920s, the stock market crash of 1929, and a global economic downturn led to the greatest economic depression in U.S. history. During the Great Depression millions of Americans faced unemployment and hunger. President Herbert Hoover's attempts to deal with the devastation of the Great Depression failed. In 1932 voters elected Franklin Delano Roosevelt to the presidency with hopes that his promised New Deal would solve America's social and economic problems.

THE AMERICAN NATION VIDEODISC PROGRAM
A variety of still images, short videos, and activities are available for you to use as you teach this chapter. See Correlation to *The American Nation Videodisc Program* for barcode correlations and suggestions for using the program.

Chapter Planning Guide

CHAPTER 23	CORE RESOURCE BOOKLETS	AUDIOVISUAL AV RESOURCES	PROGRAM RESOURCES
INTRODUCTION pp. 668–669	■ Literature Worksheet 23 ■ Building Your Portfolio Worksheet 7		
TEACHING THE CHAPTER pp. 670–689	■ Graphic Organizer 23 ■ Social Studies Skills Worksheet 23 ■ Geography Worksheet 23 ■ Outline Maps 1, 2, 9, 11	■ *The American Nation* Videodisc: The Great Depression; Boulder Dam ■ Everyday Life in America Transparency and Worksheet 23	■ *Eyewitnesses and Others*, Volume 2: Readings 41, 44, 47
REVIEW AND ASSESSMENT pp. 690–691	■ Chapter 23 Daily Quizzes ■ Review Worksheet 23 ■ Chapter 23 Tests ■ Alternative Assessment Forms		■ Test Generator

Additional Resources

BOOKS FOR TEACHERS

Galbraith, John Kenneth. *The Great Crash of 1929.* Houghton Mifflin, 1988. Recounts the financial aspects of the crash.

Garraty, John A. *The Great Depression.* Harcourt Brace, 1986. Overview of causes and consequences of the depression.

Klingaman, William K. *Nineteen Twenty-Nine: The Year of the Great Crash.* HarperCollins, 1990. Account of the effects of the crash.

BOOKS FOR STUDENTS

Fausold, Martin L. *The Presidency of Herbert C. Hoover.* University Press of Kansas, 1985. Overview of Hoover's presidency and life.

Meltzer, Milton. *Brother, Can You Spare a Dime?* Facts on File, 1990. Discusses trauma of the depression.

* Schraff, Anne E. *The Great Depression and The New Deal.* Watts, 1990. Explores effects of crash and FDR's programs.

* for students reading below grade level

MULTIMEDIA MATERIALS

Brother Can You Spare a Dime? History in Action. Video, 20 min. Films for the Humanities/SSSS. Depicts causes and effects of the depression.

The Great Depression: Witness to History. Video, 15 min. Guidance Associates/SSSS. Chronicles effects of the depression on everyday life.

Roll of Thunder, Hear My Cry. Video, 115 min. SSSS. Portrays the struggle of southern black landowners during the Great Depression.

THEMES IN AMERICAN HISTORY

USE WITH PAGES 668–669

Listed on the right are the themes emphasized in Chapter 23. The questions in boldface type stimulate critical thinking and provide students with an opportunity to discuss the themes within a broadened context. The questions also appear in the pupil's edition on p. 668.

■ ECONOMIC DEVELOPMENT

What factors might cause an economic depression? Students might mention factors such as: overproduction by industries, overuse of credit in place of money, ineffective government economic policies, inequities in the distribution of wealth.

■ GEOGRAPHIC DIVERSITY

How might an economic crisis affect people's choices of where to live? Students might cite that people in regions where there is a scarcity of jobs might move to regions where more jobs are available. For example, impoverished farmers might move into urban areas to find work, or laid-off industrial workers might seek employment in other cities. Job scarcity might also force families to separate.

■ CULTURAL DIVERSITY

How and why might various ethnic groups be affected differently by an economic depression? Students should note that members of some ethnic groups might be laid off before other workers. Because of prejudice and historic disparities in wealth, opportunity, and status, members of these groups might be more drastically affected by such unemployment.

CHAPTER STRATEGIES FOR MEETING INDIVIDUAL NEEDS

LIMITED ENGLISH PROFICIENT LEARNERS

Pair students and have pairs select an illustration from each section in the chapter. Have them write or recite new captions for their selections that explain the significance of the illustrations, tying each one to the section content.

TACTILE/KINESTHETIC LEARNERS

Ask students to choose a specific group of people who were upset with Hoover's policies during the Great Depression. Then have students create banners, signs, and other visuals that people at the time might have used to object to Hoover's actions.

LEARNERS HAVING DIFFICULTY

Have students work in pairs to write answers to the Focus questions in each section. Then have students use their answers to write a brief chapter summary.

AUDITORY LEARNERS

Call on students to assume the roles of persons listed in the chapter's Preview Workshops. Ask them to tell the class the contribution of each person during the depression years.

VISUAL LEARNERS

Have students create posters, charts, and maps that depict the effects of the Great Depression on everyday life in America.

GIFTED LEARNERS

Have students list and describe each of the policies Hoover instituted to deal with the depression. Ask each student to research one of these policies, evaluate its merits and failings, and report his or her findings to the class.

USING THE CHAPTER FOCUS

■ **UNDERSTANDING THE MAIN IDEA**

Call on a volunteer to read aloud the Understanding the Main Idea paragraph. Ask students to name ways in which a severe economic depression might affect people's lives. List their responses on a flip chart or a sheet of butcher paper. Have students evaluate their answers at the end of the chapter.

■ **THEMES**
Have students work individually or in small groups to answer the questions under Themes. Save students' responses so that they can compare them with their responses after studying the chapter. (See p. 667B for suggested answers.)

■ **THE TIME LINE**

Point out that placing high tariffs on goods coming into the country is one way a government might react to internal economic crises. Ask students what event on the time line signaled that the U.S. was facing economic difficulties in the late 1920s. Have students copy the time line and annotate it with references to the nation's social and economic decline as they read the chapter.

CORE RESOURCES

- **Graphic Organizer 23**
- **Literature Worksheet 23**
- **Outline Maps 1, 2, 9, 11**
- **Building Your Portfolio Worksheet 7**

668

ABOUT THE ILLUSTRATION

As the depression hit, Mexican Americans, who were the nucleus of California's farm labor force, formed unions and went on strike against wage reductions. Among the largest was a strike of 18,000 cotton pickers in the San Joaquin Valley in October 1933. The sign in the photograph refers to Pixley, California, where two strikers were killed and several wounded when their union hall was riddled by rifle fire. Despite such violent opposition to their demands, the strikers won a 15-cent increase to 75 cents per 100 pounds of cotton picked. Ask students what "aid" the governor sent to Pixley and how they think the women on the truck might have felt about the governor's "aid."

Chapter 23

1929–1933

THE GREAT DEPRESSION

FOCUS

UNDERSTANDING THE MAIN IDEA

In 1929 the stock market crashed, causing financial ruin for millions of Americans. The collapse of the stock market was one of several factors that gave rise to the Great Depression. When President Hoover's efforts to revive the economy failed, Americans elected a Democratic president, Franklin D. Roosevelt, to reverse the country's economic decline.

THEMES

■ **ECONOMIC DEVELOPMENT** What factors might cause an economic depression?

■ **GEOGRAPHIC DIVERSITY** How might an economic crisis affect people's choices of where to live?

■ **CULTURAL DIVERSITY** How and why might various ethnic groups be affected differently by an economic depression?

THE GOVERNOR SENDS "AID TO PIXLEY" 24 DEPUTY SHERIFFS 11 HIGHWAY PATROLMEN

WE WANT FOOD!

1929	1930	1931	1932
Stock market crashes.	Smoot-Hawley Tariff passed.	Scottsboro Boys case begins.	Franklin Roosevelt elected president.

Suggest that a volunteer recall the causes and results of the economic boom of the 1920s. *(Probusiness economic policies of Harding and Coolidge led to a boom in certain industries, which resulted in more products being available and affordable to many Americans.)* Then tell students that in this chapter they will analyze how the attitudes and actions of people in the 1920s led to the Great Depression.

HISTORICAL SIDELIGHTS
Money Pool

In a desperate attempt to save the stock market, six bankers from New York's largest banks met on the fateful Thursday afternoon of October 24, 1929. They formed a pool of $240 million—along with an additional $100 million from other financial firms—to buy stocks, hoping to reverse the panic selling. Although their actions did drive the market up briefly, their efforts failed. Later, they sold most of the stocks they bought, making a profit for themselves.

LINK TO THE PAST

The economic boom of the 1920s gave most Americans tremendous faith in the future. For many Americans, prosperity seemed limitless; however, the prosperity was unevenly distributed. The life-style of the Jazz Age also led to enormous debt.

Thursday, October 24, 1929, dawned windy and cool in New York City. Employees of the New York Stock Exchange buttoned their overcoats as they hurried down Wall Street to work. In the first few hours of stock trading, share prices fell sharply. At first, investors remained calm. The market had been shaky in recent weeks but had always resumed its upward trend. Today was different, though. As prices continued to fall, panic struck. Frantic orders to sell stock came pouring in.

All across America, grim-faced investors watched as stock tickers reported the alarming news. The plunge in prices was wiping out the life savings of millions of Americans who had invested in stocks. "One saw men looking defeat in the face," said an eyewitness. "[It was] the smash-up of the hopes of years."

The economic prosperity of the 1920s was over, and the worst economic depression in U.S. history had begun. Over the next several years the American people faced widespread unemployment and poverty. By the time of the 1932 election, they were desperate for a change.

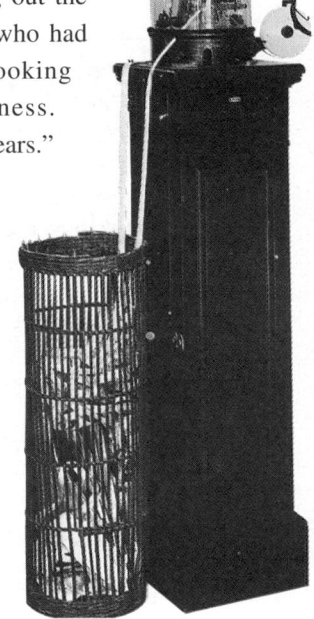

Mexican American women bound for picket line in the San Joaquin Valley, California, cotton strike, 1933

Ticker tape machine

FOCUS OBJECTIVES

■ Explain why many Americans invested in the stock market in the 1920s.

■ Analyze the causes of the stock market crash of 1929.

■ List the factors that gave rise to the Great Depression.

CORE RESOURCES

• **Section 1 Daily Quiz**

AV RESOURCES

• *The American Nation Videodisc: The Great Depression*

PREVIEW WORKSHOP

Following is a list of the significant terms in this section. You may wish to use this list as a section preview.

Terms
■ bull market
■ bear market
■ margin buying
■ Black Thursday
■ Black Tuesday
■ gross national product
■ Great Depression
■ Smoot-Hawley Tariff
■ business cycle

MOTIVATING: PRIOR KNOWLEDGE

Call on volunteers to list on the chalkboard warning signs that the U.S. economy was "sick" in the 1920s. Ask students why few people paid attention to these warning signs. Point out that this section explains why the 1929 stock market crash was a direct result of the excesses of the 1920s and analyzes the factors that gave rise to the Great Depression.

Section 1

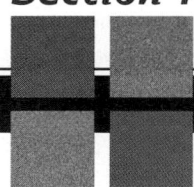

PROSPERITY SHATTERED

F O C U S

■ **Why did many Americans invest in the stock market in the 1920s?**

■ **What caused the stock market crash of 1929?**

■ **What factors gave rise to the Great Depression?**

Throughout the generally prosperous 1920s, isolated voices warned of problems with the American economy. Some people pointed to the farm crisis and to "sick" industries as problems in need of attention. Yet despite these warnings, most Americans believed that the economy would continue to thrive. Then came the stock market crash of 1929. Stock prices plunged, and investors lost billions of dollars. U.S. industries, already showing signs of weakness, almost ground to a halt.

Newspaper headline, October 1929

"GET RICH QUICK"

Few Americans other than farmers and the poor worried about the nation's economic health in the late 1920s. Many Americans agreed with Herbert Hoover that the nation was "nearer to the final triumph over poverty than ever before in the history of any land."

This sense of confidence was reflected in the stock market. Stock sales had risen steadily for several years. As demand rose, so did stock prices. Many experts saw no end to the **bull market**—the upward trend in stock prices (as opposed to a **bear market**, or downward trend). Business leaders, such as General Motors executive John J. Raskob, urged Americans to invest, claiming that anyone who put $15 a month in the stock market for 20 years would end up with $80,000—a fortune at the time.

By the late 1920s, stock speculation—"playing" the market by buying and selling to make a quick profit—was widespread. Although speculation fueled economic growth, it also created problems. Rapid buying and selling inflated the prices of stocks to the point that many stocks were selling for more than they were really worth. This speculative buying was fine as long as demand was high, but if investor confidence weakened, prices would tumble.

The situation was made shakier still by **margin buying**—purchasing stocks with borrowed money. Many speculators put up as little as 10 percent of the price of a stock, borrowing the rest. Margin buying worked as long as the bull market continued. If prices fell, though, investors would find themselves deep in debt with no way to pay off their loans. It was a very risky venture.

Although consumer confidence in the market remained high throughout the summer of 1929, a few gloomy voices were heard. In early September, stock analyst Roger Babson wrote: "Sooner or later a crash is coming, and it may be terrific." Some shrewd investors saw the writing on the wall and began to sell their stocks, but most people remained confident in the market. As one eyewitness wrote: "Money is king—but there is something else. It is a high, wild time, a time of riotous spirits and belief in magic rather than cold calculation."

INVESTING IN THE MARKET

Invite students to assume the role of stock-brokers in the late 1920s. Have them work in groups to write brochures aimed at potential investors, explaining why this is a good time to invest. After groups present their brochures, ask class members which brochure would most encourage them to invest in the stock market and why.

CAUSES OF THE CRASH

Discuss with students the concept of scarcity and the relationship between the availability of an item and its value. Ask students to apply this concept to explain the effect that the great speculative demand for stocks had on share prices in the late 1920s. Then ask students to predict what might happen to share prices if a great number of shares were offered for sale over a short period of time. Have a volunteer explain how the practice of margin buying increased the supply of stocks for sale as prices started down, and the further effect this had on prices. Conclude by inviting students to write letters to friends in the role of 1920s stock speculators, explaining why they sold their stock during the crash of 1929. Ask students to read their letters to the class. Students may wish to include their letters in their portfolios.

■■ **Hoping to earn enormous profits from rising stock prices, many Americans invested in the stock market.**

THE STOCK MARKET CRASHES

The magic faltered on October 24, 1929—**Black Thursday**. Large investors, made nervous by various factors, including rising interest rates, suddenly began to sell their shares. The dumping of so much stock on the market jolted investor confidence and caused prices to plunge. Panic gripped Wall Street. A *New York Times* reporter described the crash:

❝ It came with a speed and ferocity that left men dazed. The bottom simply fell out of the market. . . . The streets were crammed with a mixed crowd—agonized little speculators, . . . sold-out traders, . . . inquisitive individuals and tourists seeking . . . a closer view of the national catastrophe. . . . Where was it going to end? ❞

Black Thursday was only the opening stage of a long downward spiral. Prices dropped still lower the following week, as more investors sold their stocks. On October 29—**Black Tuesday**—prices sank to a shocking new low as investors dumped over 16 million shares of stock on the market.

As prices plunged, brokers fired off frantic telegrams to the customers who owed them money. The brokers demanded cash to cover their loans. Unable to raise the funds, thousands of people were forced to sell their stocks at huge losses. Many investors were wiped out. By mid-November the average value of leading stocks had been cut in half, and stockholders had lost some $30 billion. By year's end stock losses exceeded the total cost of U.S. involvement in World War I.

■■ **Speculative buying drove stock prices above their real value. When large-scale selling occurred in October 1929, the market crashed.**

THE DEPRESSION BEGINS

In the first months after the stock market crash, business leaders and public officials insisted that the setback was minor and temporary. President Hoover declared: "We have now passed the worst and . . . shall rapidly recover." But optimistic statements could not conceal the grim truth. By late 1930 it was clear that a major economic depression was under way in the United States and throughout the rest of the world.

From late 1929 to 1933 the U.S. economy sank steadily. In 1929, the last boom year of the period, America's **gross national product**—the total value of all goods and services produced in a given year—reached $103 billion. In 1933, at the depth of the depression, it fell below $56 billion. Over that same period, average income for Americans fell by half. By 1932 the auto and steel industries were producing at just a small fraction of their capacity. Factories and mines stood idle. Railroad cars sat silent and empty. Many companies shut down, and millions of workers lost their jobs.

The banking industry was also hard hit by the

THE CRASH

Company	High Price Sept. 3, 1929	Low Price Nov. 13, 1929
American Telephone and Telegraph	304	197¼
General Electric	396¼	168⅛
General Motors	72¾	36
Montgomery Ward	137⅞	49¼
United States Steel	261¾	150
Woolworth	100⅜	52¼

Source: *Only Yesterday*

FROM RICHES TO RAGS In the days following the stock market crash on October 29, 1929, stock prices continued to fall. Average stock prices reached their lowest point for the year on November 13, 1929, slightly two months after they had reached the high point for the year on September 3.

❓ **BUILDING GRAPH SKILLS** Which company's stock lost the greatest number of points between September 3 and November 13, 1929?

VOICES IN HISTORY

Just weeks after Black Thursday, African American teenager Gordon Parks lost his job as a bellboy, a position he needed to put himself through high school. "By the first week of November. . . I was without a job. . . . Finally, on the seventh of November I went to school and cleaned out my locker, knowing it was impossible to stay on. A piercing chill was in the air as I walked back to the rooming house. The hawk had come. I could already feel his wings shadowing me." Toward the end of the Great Depression, Parks became an award-winning photographer.

Graph Caption Answer
General Electric

𝒯eaching the 𝒮ection

THE DEPRESSION BEGINS

Begin a chart on the chalkboard under the heading *Conditions Contributing to the Great Depression*. Call on students to cite the factors that contributed to the Great Depression as you add them to the chart. *(crash of 1929, global economic downturn, debt, easy credit policies, high tariffs, the business cycle, unequal distribution of income)* Then call on volunteers to explain how each factor contributed to the Great Depression.

GLOBAL CONNECTIONS

The global depression left many national governments short of funds. By 1930 the Soviet Union was so short of money that government officials sold 21 paintings from its famous Hermitage Museum to American millionaire Andrew Mellon. The $7 million that the Soviets earned was desperately needed as unemployment grew there.

THE AMERICAN NATION VIDEODISC PROGRAM

The Great Depression

```
|||||||||||||||||||||||||||
2A    25392    3:24
```

▲ Panicked by the 1929 stock market crash, many bank depositors stood in long lines to withdraw their money. This photograph was taken in New York City.

depression. After the stock market crash, many debt-ridden investors and businesses could not repay their loans, leaving banks with no incoming funds. Fearing bank failures, many depositors panicked and withdrew their savings. Under the combined weight of these factors, the banking system collapsed.

Between 1930 and 1932 more than 5,000 U.S. banks failed. Customers who went to their banks to withdraw savings often found the doors barred and their money gone. Because bank deposits were not insured, many people lost their life savings. The collapse of one big New York City bank in 1930 wiped out roughly $180 million in savings by some 400,000 depositors, including many poor immigrants.

WHAT CAUSED THE DEPRESSION?

The stock market crash of 1929 jolted the American economy and destroyed individual fortunes, but it alone did not cause the **Great Depression**, the deep economic downturn that gripped the United States between 1929 and the beginning of World War II. At the time, many observers, including President Hoover, blamed the depression on the state of the world economy following World War I. The global economy had suffered enormous setbacks because of the massive war debts incurred by European countries. But this, like the stock market crash, was only a contributing factor. Today economists and historians agree that the root causes of the Great Depression lay in numerous factors, including the American economic system itself.

The troubling twenties. Although the 1920s appeared to be a decade of unlimited

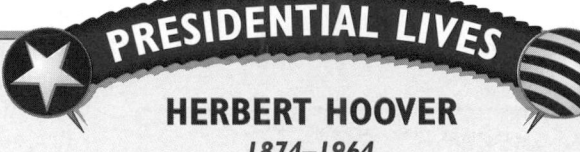

PRESIDENTIAL LIVES

HERBERT HOOVER
1874–1964

in office
1929–1933

As a young man Herbert Hoover was shy and awkward, but very hardworking. Born into a Quaker family in Iowa, he was left an orphan at age nine. He had few friends in college and would wander around with his eyes glued to the ground as if to avoid people. As one of his few friends noted, he had a habit of standing "with one foot thrust forward, jingling the keys in his trouser pocket," chuckling sometimes, but rarely laughing out loud. Even in the White House he remained self-conscious and shy.

After college Hoover rapidly built a career as a successful mining engineer and business consultant. By the age of 40 he was a millionaire. His role as coordinator of food relief during World War I also gave him a reputation as a kind and humanitarian leader. After his presidency he continued to work in public service and wrote many books and articles.

"There is little importance to men's lives," he wrote, "except the accomplishments they leave to posterity."

Herbert Hoover

Practice

GUIDED PRACTICE

Ask students to choose the main events in Section 1. List these events on the chalkboard. Have students develop newspaper headlines, such as the one shown on p. 670, that could be used to describe each event, and write these headlines on the chalkboard. Work with students to develop a list of details that would appear in an article accompanying each headline.

INDEPENDENT PRACTICE

Direct each student to choose one of the headlines and the accompanying details developed in the Guided Practice. Have them write an article that might appear under the headline. Students may wish to include their newspaper articles in their portfolios.

Review and Assessment

REVIEW Have half the students write a letter to the editor in 1929, explaining why they invested in the stock market and how the crash affected them. Have the others write a business article on factors that led to the depression. Select students to read their work aloud. Then assign the Section 1 Review on p. 674.

ASSESS Assign the **Section 1 Daily Quiz** in *Core Resources*. ▶

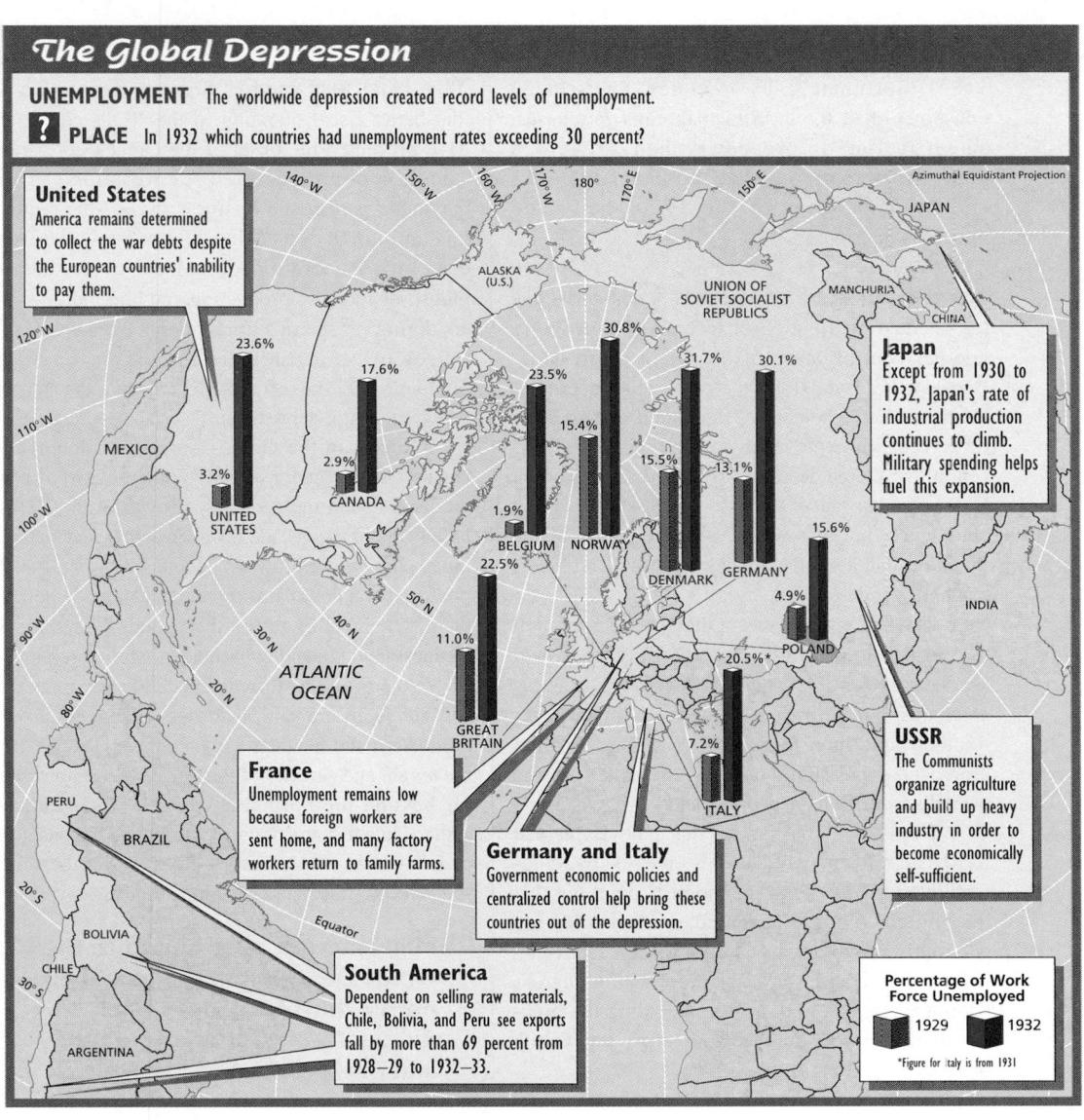

The Global Depression

UNEMPLOYMENT The worldwide depression created record levels of unemployment.

? PLACE In 1932 which countries had unemployment rates exceeding 30 percent?

Azimuthal Equidistant Projection

United States
America remains determined to collect the war debts despite the European countries' inability to pay them.

Japan
Except from 1930 to 1932, Japan's rate of industrial production continues to climb. Military spending helps fuel this expansion.

France
Unemployment remains low because foreign workers are sent home, and many factory workers return to family farms.

Germany and Italy
Government economic policies and centralized control help bring these countries out of the depression.

USSR
The Communists organize agriculture and build up heavy industry in order to become economically self-sufficient.

South America
Dependent on selling raw materials, Chile, Bolivia, and Peru see exports fall by more than 69 percent from 1928–29 to 1932–33.

Percentage values shown: 23.6% (United States), 3.2% (UNITED STATES), 17.6%, 2.9% (CANADA), 23.5%, 30.8%, 15.4%, 1.9%, 31.7%, 30.1%, 15.5%, 13.1% (BELGIUM/NORWAY/DENMARK/GERMANY), 22.5% (BELGIUM), 15.6%, 4.9% (POLAND), 11.0% (GREAT BRITAIN), 20.5%*, 7.2% (ITALY)

Percentage of Work Force Unemployed
 1929 ▮ 1932
*Figure for Italy is from 1931

THE GREAT DEPRESSION ▦ 673

673

---

economic prosperity, many analysts place primary blame for the Great Depression on economic practices in the 1920s. These practices produced quick profits for some but in the long run contributed to economic chaos. Farm prices, for example, dropped in the 1920s. By the end of the decade, mining, textiles, construction, and other industries were also beginning to suffer.

Another disturbing trend was the widespread dependence on credit. In the late 1920s, the federal government encouraged borrowing by keeping interest rates low. The Republican administrations of the time reasoned that an easy-credit policy would promote business. Easy credit enabled consumers to buy goods when they did not actually have the money to pay for them. This was not a problem when the economy was booming. Once the economy began to slow and the government raised interest rates, however, many consumers could not pay their debts. After the crash many businesses stopped extending credit altogether.

In 1931 one department store even tried to turn the "credit crunch" to its advantage. While inviting customers to shop and spend as much as they wanted to, it advertised that it would accept only cash. The store claimed to be protecting its patrons from falling into debt. This approach depended on the hope that consumers would keep spending in the face of a depression.

Map Caption Answer
Germany, Denmark, Norway

MAKING CONNECTIONS
Sociology
In the late 1920s, installment credit was used to purchase three of every five cars as well as 80 percent of all radios. During the last half of the decade, outstanding installment indebtedness more than doubled—to $3 billion.

🌐 GLOBAL CONNECTIONS
The Smoot-Hawley Tariff raised duties by as much as 50 percent on foreign products entering the U.S. But this action did not alleviate economic conditions in the U.S., and it accelerated the spreading worldwide depression. After the crash Americans stopped investing in Europe, and the tariff severely cut the amount of goods that Europeans could sell in the U.S. Other countries subsequently passed high tariffs of their own, and all countries suffered as a result.

RETEACH Organize students into small groups. Tell each group to divide the section material, by subsections, among its members. Direct students to write questions about the main ideas presented in their assigned material. Have group members quiz one another with the questions.

*C*losure

Have students, in small groups, review the causes of the Great Depression. Then have each group determine which of the causes it thinks was the biggest factor in precipitating the economic crisis. Ask volunteers from each group to explain their group's choice. Discuss each group's choice and reasoning with the rest of the class.

*E*xtension

CREATE Invite students to create a diagram showing the business cycle. Have them write a paragraph explaining the normal business cycle and describing how the cycle differed during the Great Depression.

RESEARCH Suggest that students research and report on worldwide economic conditions in late 1930.

SECTION REVIEW ANSWERS

IDENTIFY

For significance, see the following pages:
bull market (p. 670)
bear market (p. 670)
margin buying (p. 670)
Black Thursday (p. 671)
Black Tuesday (p. 671)
gross national product (p. 671)
Great Depression (p. 672)
Smoot-Hawley Tariff (p. 674)
business cycle (p. 674)

1. *belief that quick profits could be made by buying and selling stock while prices were rising*
2. *inflated stock prices above their real value*
3. *Nervousness and loss of confidence caused some investors to sell shares, driving down prices and confidence, which led to panic sales; prices plunged and the market crashed.*
4. *Essays might mention the stock market crash of 1929, declining farm prices, weakening of industries, global economic downturn, poor economic practices of the 1920s leading to excess consumer debt, unequal distribution of income, overproduction.*
5. *Answers might note that real wealth was in the hands of very few people. Many other Americans enjoyed "abundance" only because of easy credit that resulted in heavy indebtedness for large segments of the population.*

Unfortunately, by 1931 few debt-ridden consumers had the cash to make any purchases. The illusion of prosperity had prevented many from realizing that the benefits of the economic policies of the 1920s had been unevenly distributed.

A mismanaged economy. Economists cite the unequal distribution of income in America as another central cause of the Great Depression. Between 1923 and 1929 the disposable income of the wealthiest 1 percent of the nation increased by 63 percent while the income of the poorest 93 percent of the nation decreased by 4 percent. As writer Upton Sinclair noted: "The . . . depression is one of abundance, not of scarcity. . . . The cause of the trouble is that a small class has the wealth, while the rest have the debts."

This income gap meant that a large portion of the population did not have the buying power needed to boost the economy. According to many economists, if workers had received better wages for their labor and farmers better prices for their crops, the depression would have been less severe or perhaps could have been avoided.

Even the global factors that Hoover blamed for the depression could have been eased by more-farsighted U.S. policies. Economists point out that the United States contributed to the worldwide economic downturn by slapping high tariffs on imported goods. Even after the crash, Congress continued to pass high tariffs, including the highest in U.S. history, the **Smoot-Hawley Tariff** of 1930.

The business cycle. Some economists argue that better fiscal planning in the 1920s could not have prevented the onset of the Great Depression. These economists view depressions as an inevitable part of the **business cycle**—the regular ups and downs of business in a free-enterprise economy. According to business-cycle theory, industries increase production and hire more workers during prosperous times so that eventually surpluses pile up. Industries then cut back on production and lay off workers, causing the start of a recession or a depression.

Events in the Great Depression support the business-cycle theory in part. While a wave of new products fueled the economic growth of the 1920s, by the end of the decade fewer Americans were buying expensive goods. Most people who wanted such products, and could afford them, had already bought them. The inability to sell their goods caused many businesses to fail and contributed to the depression.

According to this theory, however, once the surplus goods are sold, industries again gear up for production and the depression comes to an end. But the *length* and *severity* of the Great Depression went far beyond the normal rhythms of the business cycle. Thus it seems incorrect to blame the business cycle—or any one factor—for causing the most severe economic depression in U.S. history.

■■ **Many factors contributed to the Great Depression: the global economic downturn, debt, the unequal distribution of wealth, and overproduction.**

■ SECTION 1 REVIEW

IDENTIFY and explain the significance of the following: bull market, bear market, margin buying, Black Thursday, Black Tuesday, gross national product, Great Depression, Smoot-Hawley Tariff, business cycle.

1. **MAIN IDEA** What factors encouraged many Americans to participate in the bull market of the 1920s?
2. **MAIN IDEA** How did speculation affect stock prices?
3. **IDENTIFYING CAUSE AND EFFECT** What caused the large-scale selling of stocks in October 1929? What effect did this have on the stock market?
4. **WRITING TO EXPLAIN** Write an essay outlining the factors that contributed to the Great Depression.
5. **ANALYZING** Considering the economic developments of the 1920s, how accurate was Upton Sinclair's statement that the depression was "one of abundance, not of scarcity"?

674

PREVIEW WORKSHOP

Following is a list of the significant people and terms in this section. You may wish to use this list as a section preview.

People
■ Josefina Fierro de Bright
■ James Hilton
■ James T. Farrell
■ Nathanael West

■ William Faulkner

Terms
■ *mutualistas*
■ breadlines
■ shantytowns

Section 2

HARD TIMES

FOCUS OBJECTIVES

■ Explain how unemployment affected Americans in the 1930s.

■ Describe urban and rural living conditions during the Great Depression.

■ Identify what Americans did for entertainment during the period.

FOCUS

■ **How did unemployment affect Americans in the 1930s?**
■ **What were urban and rural living conditions like during the Great Depression?**
■ **What did Americans do for entertainment during the period?**

The Great Depression of the 1930s was not the first depression in American history, but it was by far the worst. It lasted for most of the decade, and during that time millions of Americans lost their jobs and sank into poverty. In cities and in rural areas, many people suffered from hunger, homelessness, and despair. Life was not all bleak during the depression, though. Movies, radio, and popular fiction helped lift American spirits.

Unemployed worker, 1930

HISTORICAL SIDELIGHTS

Falling Incomes
Typical of the depression's effects on workers was that a New York subway conductor who earned more than $2,000 per year in 1930 was earning just over $1,200 two years later.

"WORK IS WHAT I WANT"

Perhaps the clearest sign of the deepening depression was a sharp rise in unemployment. In 1929 some 1.5 million Americans were unemployed; three years later that figure had risen to some 12 million, as ailing and failed businesses laid off their employees. To poet Langston Hughes, it seemed "everybody in America was looking for work."

By 1932, industrial output had fallen to about half that of 1929, resulting in massive layoffs. Even for those who managed to keep their jobs, wages fell dramatically—in some cases to as low as 10 cents an hour. Factory workers' average annual income fell by nearly one third between 1929 and 1933. For the first time in years, immigration to the United States greatly decreased. One despondent Slavic immigrant told a reporter in 1932: "If you had told me, when I come to this country that now I live like this, I shot you dead."

African Americans faced especially difficult times, as economic troubles added to the problem of racial discrimination they already faced. When

factories laid off employees, black workers were often the first to go. In several cities as much as 25 to 40 percent of African Americans were out of work by 1933. One study of Chicago unemployment patterns noted the general view among whites that blacks "should not be hired as long as there are white men without work."

African American women, who made up the vast majority of domestic servants, also suffered

◄ Thousands of unemployed workers gathered before the White House on March 6, 1930, to protest for better unemployment policies.

CORE RESOURCES

• **Literature Worksheet 23**
• **Section 2 Daily Quiz**

AV RESOURCES

• **Everyday Life in America Transparency** and **Worksheet 23**

MOTIVATING: STUDENT EXPERIENCES

Ask students how the unemployment rate affects a person's chances of getting a job. Then ask students to describe the psychological impact unemployment might have on a person. Tell them that in this section they will learn how the Great Depression's high unemployment affected Americans.

Teaching the Section

AMERICANS OUT OF WORK

Organize the class into groups of five. Have each group develop a skit demonstrating the effects of unemployment during the Great Depression on a white male factory worker, a black female domestic worker, a white female worker, a black male factory worker, and an immigrant male worker. Have the groups perform their skits before the class.

LIFE IN THE CITY

Ask students to create editorial cartoons illustrating the plight of people living in cities during the Great Depression. Cartoons might focus on ways that people sought relief and on the conditions they faced. Ask volunteers to present and interpret their cartoons for the class. Students may wish to include their cartoons in their portfolios.

Map Caption Answer
South Dakota

HISTORICAL SIDELIGHTS

Selling Apples

In 1930 the International Apple Shippers Association, searching for a way to get rid of surplus apples, decided to sell the apples on credit to Americans without jobs. The jobless then became street vendors and tried to sell the apples for five cents each, hoping to earn an income. By the end of 1930 there were about 6,000 apple vendors on the streets of New York.

PRIMARY SOURCE

Description of Change: excerpted
Rationale: excerpted to focus on main idea

HISTORICAL SIDELIGHTS

Racial Violence

As the depression worsened so did acts of violence against African Americans. Hilton Butler, a writer for the *New Republic,* reported that black firemen on the railroads in Mississippi were being shot because white workers wanted their jobs. He wrote: "Mississippi, in its own primitive way, had begun to deal with the unemployment problem. . . . Dead men not only tell no tales but create vacancies."

Unemployment Relief

DOUBLE TROUBLE In the early 1930s a disastrous drought struck the agricultural states of the Great Plains, adding to the difficulties caused by the depression.

? PLACE Which state had the highest percentage of its people receiving unemployment?

Percentage of Total State Population Receiving Unemployment Relief
- More than 25 percent
- 21-25 percent
- 16-20 percent
- 11-15 percent
- Less than 11 percent

massive unemployment. Without regular work, many would stand on street corners and try to obtain work as maids. Two black women, Ella Baker and Marvel Cooke, referred to this method of hiring as the "Bronx Slave Market." In an investigative article they wrote for *The Crisis,* they described a typical scene:

66 Rain or shine, cold or hot, you will find them there—Negro women, old and young—sometimes bedraggled, sometimes neatly dressed . . . waiting expectantly for Bronx housewives to buy their strength and energy. 99

Since many employers could hire women more cheaply than men, the percentage of women in the work force actually increased in the 1930s. Most were employed as office workers or domestic servants. But as the percentage of women in the work force rose overall, the percentage of employed African

American women actually fell because of increased competition in domestic and agricultural work.

Some unemployed workers took to selling apples on the street, where on a good day a seller might earn $1.15, causing President Hoover to claim, "Many people have left their jobs for the more profitable one of selling apples." But few people in the depression had any choice over how or where they worked. Some even hitchhiked or hopped freight trains across the country to find jobs.

▪▪ **During the depression one fourth of the work force lost their jobs. Many had to seek work wherever they could find it.**

*L*IFE IN THE CITY

The impact of the depression spread all across America, hitting people in cities and on farms and disrupting family life. Some of the most-lasting images of the period came from urban America, as the depression hit many cities hard. During the early 1930s the federal government did little to aid local communities.

City governments, religious groups like the Salvation Army, and charitable organizations such as the Red Cross tried to take on the burden of providing direct relief to the needy. Neighbors also helped one another. One African American woman told a visitor: "My neighbors helps me, by bringin' me a little to eat, when they knows I ain't got nothin' in the house to cook."

Mexican American communities formed *mutualistas,* or mutual-aid societies, to help local residents. Some Chinese American

▲ **In the 1930s many couples participated in dance marathons to win money. Some marathons would last for days, until all but one couple dropped from exhaustion.**

LIFE ON THE FARM

Have students work in pairs to write two 1933 newspaper editorials: one discussing the farm crisis, and one calling for help for tenant farmers in the South. Have volunteer pairs read their editorials to the class; then discuss ways in which the farmers were trying to cope with their problems.

▲ Shantytowns appeared outside many towns and cities during the early 1930s. Shown here is a Hooverville in New York City.

communities set out open barrels of rice so that people could draw from them privately, without asking for handouts. Harlem residents organized "rent parties"—large social gatherings that charged a small admission to help pay someone's monthly rent.

Across the country, people engaged in a daily struggle to feed themselves and their children. Haggard men and women waited in **breadlines** for bowls of soup and pieces of bread. When one hungry schoolchild was told to go home for lunch, she replied: "It won't do any good. . . . This is my sister's day to eat." Hunger was so widespread that by 1932 one out of every five children in New York City suffered from malnutrition. Meager diets caused some Americans to suffer long-term health effects in the form of stunted growth, weak bones, and dental problems.

In addition to hunger, homelessness was a serious urban problem during the depression. **Shantytowns**—collections of makeshift shelters built out of packing boxes, scrap lumber, corrugated iron, and other thrown-away items—rose up outside most cities. Blaming an unresponsive president for their plight, the homeless mockingly referred to these shantytowns as Hoovervilles and the newspapers they often slept under as Hoover blankets.

▪▪ **With little help from the federal government, urban communities struggled to provide for the hungry and homeless.**

LIFE ON THE FARM

The depression also struck hard at rural America, as the farm crisis of the 1920s turned into a disaster in the 1930s. People in the cities needed food but could not pay for it. As demand for farm products shrank, prices plummeted, and farmers found themselves with more goods than they could sell. While people went hungry in the cities, farmers in some areas were forced to let crops rot in the fields and to slaughter excess livestock they could not afford to feed.

As their incomes fell, many farmers were unable to keep up their mortgage payments. While banks foreclosed on farms all across America, some communities banded together to fight back. Often when a bank held a foreclosure auction to sell off a family's possessions, neighbors would

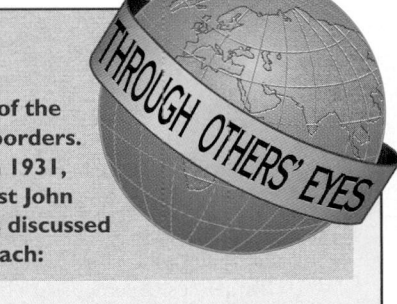

DEPRESSION WORLDWIDE

The depression of the 1930s knew no borders. In a radio talk in 1931, British economist John Maynard Keynes discussed its worldwide reach:

THROUGH OTHERS' EYES

❝*The slump in trade and employment and the business losses . . . are as bad as the worst which have ever occurred in the modern history of the world. No country is exempt. The privation [hardship] and—what is sometimes worse—the anxiety which exist today in millions of homes all over the world is extreme. In the three chief industrial countries of the world, Great Britain, Germany, and the United States, I estimate that probably 12 million industrial workers stand idle. But I am not sure that there is not even more human misery today in the great agricultural countries of the world—Canada, Australia, and South America, where millions of small farmers see themselves ruined by the fall in the prices of their products, so that their receipts after harvest bring them in much less than the crops have cost them to produce.*❞

Teaching the Section

MEXICAN AMERICANS AND THE DEPRESSION

Have students stage an organizational meeting of a branch of El Congreso. Call on volunteers to voice examples of discrimination against migrant workers in the Southwest. Then have students suggest actions that the organization might take to fight the discrimination. Have a volunteer list the organization's proposed actions on the chalkboard.

PRIMARY SOURCE

Description of Change: excerpted
Rationale: excerpted to focus on main idea

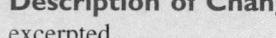

BIO GRAPHY PERSONALITIES IN HISTORY

El Congreso shifted its goals from militant activism to support of a united national front when the U.S. entered World War II. This change in focus led to the disbanding of the congress, but group leaders found themselves under federal investigation for ties to the Communist party in the years after the war. Anticipating that she would be arrested, Josefina Fierro de Bright left the United States to avoid incriminating friends and associates with her testimony.

arrive and bid absurdly low prices, such as 25 cents for a plow. In a particularly noteworthy example, a farm with an $800 mortgage was sold for $1.90. After the auction they would then give the goods back to the farm family. Furthermore, farmers quickly warned off anyone who made serious bids. This tactic was so successful that several farm states, beginning with Iowa in 1933, passed foreclosure moratorium laws.

Conditions were especially bleak for tenant farmers in the South, where most rural residents already faced crippling poverty. As cotton prices fell from 16 cents per pound in 1929 to below 6 cents in 1931, many tenant farmers, mostly African Americans, were virtually ruined. Some were even forced off the land they had lived on all their lives. While farmers in the Midwest faced an overabundance of food, southern cotton farmers faced scarcity due to poor soil and lack of money to buy food. Gracie Turner, a sharecropper's wife, testified to the hardships of tenant life in the 1930s:

▲ Shown here is a meeting in Los Angeles, around 1940, of the group known as El Congreso, which helped organize Hispanic migrants to fight for better conditions.

> 66 That's all there is to expect—work hard and go hungry part time. . . . This year's been so hard we had to drop our burial insurance. . . . All it costs is twenty-five cents . . . but they don't come many twenty-five cents in this house. 99

Migrant farm workers in the Southwest, most of them recent immigrants, also encountered difficulties. As relief costs soared, local authorities chose the cheaper policy of paying Mexican migrants to return to their native land. During the 1930s some 500,000 people of Mexican descent—some of them U.S. citizens—were pressured into leaving the states. Those who remained often faced discrimination and poor working conditions.

▶ **Josefina Fierro de Bright**

BIO GRAPHY Some of the Mexican American families who stayed during the depression helped organize resistance to discrimination in the Southwest. One such organizer was Josefina Fierro de Bright, the daughter of migrants who had fled revolution in Mexico to settle in California. The experience of growing up during the depression in the midst of poverty and ethnic discrimination had a profound effect on her. As with many children of the depression, Fierro's life was very unstable. Her family had to move often, causing Fierro to change schools eight times. But throughout the hard times her mother always encouraged her to strive for success. "Rely on yourself, be independent," Mrs. Fierro advised. She also emphasized the importance of getting an education.

In 1938, at age 18, Josefina Fierro entered the University of California at Los Angeles. She planned to study medicine, but activism on behalf of the Mexican American community soon took up most of her time. With the aid of her husband, activist Hollywood

FAMILY LIFE AND THE DEPRESSION

Tell students to imagine they are living in the 1930s and their families are suffering great hardship. Ask students to write a journal entry describing how the Great Depression has affected their lives and how they and family members are coping with their difficulties. Ask volunteers to read their journal entries to the class. Students may wish to include their journal entries in their portfolios.

▶

screenwriter John Bright, she began to lead boycotts of companies that did business in Mexican American communities but did not hire Mexican American workers. Enlisting financial support from a few well-known movie stars, Fierro de Bright also started a radio program for Spanish-speaking audiences.

These activities brought her to the attention of a Mexican American group called El Congreso, which was organizing Hispanic migrants to resist oppressive conditions. In 1939 El Congreso leaders asked Fierro de Bright to help them establish a branch in Los Angeles. Over the next few years, she worked tirelessly, leading marches and hunger strikes, lobbying for expanded relief programs for Hispanic Americans, and encouraging bilingual education for migrant children. "I used to work so hard it used to kill me," she recalled. But throughout her life she never forgot the lessons her mother instilled in her during those early years of the depression. Those memories spurred her efforts to improve the lives of all working people.

■■ **Rural farm workers faced increased hardship during the depression. Some were forced to leave their land.**

FAMILY LIFE IN THE 1930s

On farms and in cities, family members often pulled together and helped one another cope with their difficulties. They shared food and money and provided the support and encouragement their relatives needed to get through hard times. In many cases, relatives doubled up in small houses, and young adults moved back in with their parents.

▼ Life was difficult for many families during the depression as they struggled to make ends meet. The strain is clearly evident in the faces of these migrant children and their mother.

Economic hardship took its toll on families, however. Some eventually broke apart under the strain. The divorce rate rose during the depression. Many young people put off getting married and starting their own families, which caused marriage and birthrates to decline, especially during the early years of the depression. Looking back on those years, a Chicago schoolteacher remarked:

66 Do you realize how many people in my generation are not married? . . . It wasn't that we didn't have a chance. I was going with someone when the Depression hit. We probably would have gotten married. . . . Suddenly he was laid off. It hit him like a ton of bricks. And he just disappeared. 99

Life was certainly not easy for women during the depression. In the face of economic hardship, the mothers of hard-hit depression families often played roles of quiet heroism. Such daily challenges as putting food on the table and making clothes and shoes last for one more year brought constant worry. As one woman remarked: "I figured every which way I could to make ends meet . . . but some of [those] ends just wouldn't meet. They just couldn't be stretched far enough to meet." In rural and small-town households, women revived old crafts such as soap making and bread making. Others took jobs outside the home to help support their families.

COMMENTARY

The Psychological Impact of the Depression

The Great Depression affected Americans in countless ways. Some of these effects—such as hunger and homelessness—were temporary for most people. When the depression ended, most Americans got back on their feet. Other effects, though, were longer lasting. In fact, the depression had a major long-term impact on the behavior and the outlook of the millions of Americans who struggled through hard times.

The term *depression* could just as easily describe the mood of the country as well as the economy in the 1930s. More than 20,000 Americans committed suicide in 1932, a 28 percent increase over 1929. For middle-class and well-to-do Americans, many of whom had never

HISTORICAL SIDELIGHTS

A People Displaced
Estimates on the number of Mexican Americans repatriated during the 1930s vary from a quarter of a million to half a million. Approximately half of those repatriated were born in America. The treatment of Mexican Americans by U.S. officials in the 1930s increased Mexican American distrust of the U.S. government.

MAKING CONNECTIONS

Health
The effect of the depression on children was illustrated in the following report by the chief of the Children's Bureau, Department of Labor, which appeared in the *New York Times* on June 18, 1932: "A check-up of the [Chicago] city schools revealed today that 11,000 hungry children are being fed by teachers . . . [who themselves] are seriously handicapped by the failure of the Board of Education to pay them."

Teaching the Section

POPULAR CULTURE IN THE 1930S

Have students work in groups to create an "Entertainment Section" for a newspaper of the 1930s that describes the forms of popular culture during the period. Suggest that they include critics' columns. Post the sections; then call on volunteers to list their choices for a week's entertainment on the chalkboard.

■■ Remind students that in the 1930s there were no televisions, computers, or video games. Ask them which entertainment options of the 1930s they would enjoy the most if they had to choose today. Have students explain their choices.

---

known poverty, the depression was a cruel blow. Many would never forget the shame they felt at being unemployed, losing their businesses or homes, and being unable to provide for their families. The attitude of an unemployed teacher in New Orleans was typical: "If with all the advantages I've had, I can't make a living, I'm just no good, I guess. I've given up ever amounting to anything. It's no use."

The depression had a devastating effect on the unemployed. Many men whose lives had been dominated by work did not know what to do without a job. They often spent their days just dawdling around the house or roaming the streets. The depression proved equally severe on working women who lost their jobs, especially those who were single or whose families depended on two incomes to survive. Many parents who could not support their families were consumed by guilt and self-doubt.

Even after the depression, the memories of those lean years remained vivid. Habits of scrimping and saving, of making every penny count, would stay with members of this generation for the rest of their lives. A strong desire for financial stability and material comforts shaped the outlook of many Americans who came of age during the depression.

POPULAR CULTURE IN THE THIRTIES

Even during hard times, Americans found ways to enjoy themselves. Many people took up inexpensive pastimes, such as reading and playing games at home. Movies and radio also offered a temporary release from economic worries.

The sound explosion. Movies were a big hit during the depression. Talking pictures, which had begun to replace silent films in the late 1920s, enthralled audiences, who flocked to the new movie theaters cropping up in nearly every town. Among the most popular movies of the early 1930s were gangster films, which portrayed tough guys fighting their way to the top against all odds. Likewise, strong women, such as Bette Davis, Greta Garbo, Mae West, and Marlene Dietrich, lit up the screen, reinforcing the theme of survival in a difficult world.

▲ Hollywood musicals flourished during the depression. In order to take their minds off their troubles, audiences flocked to see upbeat films such as *Gold Diggers of 1933.*

Meanwhile, upbeat musicals like *Gold Diggers of 1933,* featuring the song "We're in the Money," and comedies portraying the hilarious antics of comedians like the Marx Brothers proved very popular. Movie cartoons also brightened the 1930s, thanks to Walt Disney's Mickey Mouse and Donald Duck characters. Often, Disney cartoons were as popular with movie audiences as the feature films they preceded.

As the movie business flourished, radio also enjoyed its golden age. Radio was immensely popular because it offered free entertainment at home.

▲ This couple, seated beside their radio, entertained themselves by listening to their favorite radio programs.

Practice

GUIDED PRACTICE

Create a two-column chart on the chalkboard with the headings *Urban Life* and *Rural Life*. Call on volunteers to list the impact the depression had on people living in urban and rural communities and add their responses to the chart.

INDEPENDENT PRACTICE

Ask students to assume the role of an urban or rural dweller during the Great Depression. Have them use information from the chart in the Guided Practice activity to write a letter to President Hoover explaining why they need help dealing with the Great Depression. Students may wish to include their letters in their portfolios.

Review and Assessment

REVIEW Have students write a table of contents and an illustration list for a book titled *Hard Times.* Tell them the book should focus on the effects of unemployment, urban and rural living conditions, family life, and recreational activities during the Great Depression. Then assign the Section 2 Review on p. 682.

ASSESS Assign the **Section 2 Daily Quiz** in *Core Resources.* ▶

Then and Now — BASEBALL

By the 1930s baseball was the country's favorite sport and a symbol of American culture, just as it is today. But baseball in the 1930s was in some ways much different from the game we know now.

To be a baseball fan in the 1930s meant taking trips out to the ballpark. Without television to bring the game into people's homes, fans either listened to games on the radio or headed for their local baseball stadium to root for the home team. Games were held only in the daytime until 1930—the year the first night game was held in a major-league park.

Depression-era fans watched such players as home-run king Babe Ruth and pitcher Walter "Boom Boom" Beck. They cheered players who had higher batting averages and hit more home runs than today's players. The ballparks were often smaller than today's stadiums. And the day games favored batters because they could see the ball more clearly during the day than today's players can at night.

However, the biggest difference between baseball then and now was who could play the game. Professional baseball was still racially segregated in the 1930s. White owners maintained a so-called gentleman's agreement not to sign black players. So African Americans formed clubs and leagues of their own.

The Negro National League (NNL) fielded teams in the East such as the Newark Eagles and the New York Black

▲ Baseball increased in popularity during the 1930s thanks to the skills of players such as Babe Ruth and Lou Gehrig. This painting by Morris Kantor, *Baseball at Night,* depicts a game from 1934.

Yankees. The Negro American League (NAL) covered the South and Midwest with clubs like the Kansas City Monarchs and the Chicago American Giants. Players included Hall of Fame pitcher Satchel Paige and William "Judy" Johnson. Turnouts at Paige's games could be as large as any in the majors.

Although they would not sign black players, white club owners rented their ballparks to black teams when white teams were on the road. In fact, it was under just such an arrangement that the Kansas City Monarchs pioneered a portable lighting system and held the first night games in a major-league park. The Monarchs' night games drew such good crowds that within a few years scores of other ballparks also installed lighting.

In the off-season, Satchel Paige and many other baseball players—both black and white—played in Mexico, Cuba, and other countries. Like most Americans in the 1930s, baseball players needed all the money they could earn—their salaries, especially in the black leagues, provided just enough to get by. Today's off-season training camps and million-dollar contracts were unheard of during the depression. Salaries, team rosters, ballparks, and media coverage are all very different today. But the most important element—the enjoyment the game brings—remains the same.

Then and Now

In general the American public reacted negatively to President Hoover's handling of the depression. In the 1931 World Series, for example, Hoover was booed when he threw out the first ball. While Hoover's popularity plummeted, Babe Ruth's increased. In 1930 Babe Ruth's salary was $80,000. When he was told that his salary was greater than President Hoover's, Ruth said, "Well, I had a better year than he did."

AV **TRANSPARENCY**
Everyday Life in America Transparency and **Worksheet 23**

RETEACH Organize the class into small groups and assign each group a subsection. Direct each group to develop questions about the main ideas in its subsection. Then have each group exchange its questions with another group and work to answer the questions it receives.

Closure

Refer students to President Hoover's quotation on p. 676: "Many people have left their jobs for the more profitable one of selling apples." Ask students how this statement might reflect the economic conditions of the Great Depression and the attitude of the Hoover administration toward those conditions.

Extension

COMPARE Ask students to research and report on a previous economic depression (1784, 1837, 1893) and compare the similarities and differences between them.

RESEARCH Invite interested students to research the music of Woody Guthrie. Have them give an oral report (with recorded music) or write an essay explaining why Guthrie's songs were popular in the 1930s.

PRIMARY SOURCE

Description of Change: excerpted and bracketed
Rationale: excerpted to focus on main idea; bracketed to clarify meaning

SECTION REVIEW ANSWERS

IDENTIFY

For significance, see the following pages:
mutualistas *(p. 676)*
breadlines *(p. 677)*
shantytowns *(p. 677)*
Josefina Fierro de Bright *(p. 678)*
James Hilton *(p. 682)*
James T. Farrell *(p. 682)*
Nathanael West *(p. 682)*
William Faulkner *(p. 682)*

1. *massive unemployment; wages and earnings dropped for workers, especially minorities, but employment of women rose*
2. *surplus in Midwest, scarcity in South, hardship everywhere; drop in farm income led to foreclosures, evictions*
3. *cities hit hard, received little federal aid; people formed mutual-aid societies, helped hungry with free food; homeless formed shantytowns*
4. *Outlines might mention movies, radio programs, and literature, giving examples in each area.*
5. *Although some families pulled together for support, others broke apart as a result of divorce, loss of self-esteem, or suicide. Marriage and birth rates declined.*

During the 1930s the number of radio sets in the United States rose from some 12 million to about 28 million. The most popular programs allowed listeners to forget the hardships of reality. Like the voice of a comforting friend, the opening of a favorite program captured listeners:

> 66 Return with us now to those thrilling days of yesteryear . . . [sound of hoofbeats] . . . From out of the West comes a fiery horse with the speed of light, a cloud of dust, and a hearty 'Hi-yo Silver'—The Lone Ranger rides again! 99

Heroes such as the Lone Ranger, Little Orphan Annie, and the Shadow always triumphed over evil, offering a hopeful message to listeners.

Literature in the early 1930s. The public's desire for entertainment also gave rise to new forms of popular literature. Magazines and comic books offered cheap and accessible forms of entertainment, presenting fantastic heroes such as Superman and Tarzan. One of the best-selling magazines of the time, *Reader's Digest,* presented a selection of condensed articles from various magazines. For families on a limited budget, this "all-purpose" magazine seemed ideal.

Many of the most popular novels of the era also offered escapism. In James Hilton's *Lost Horizon* (1933), a weary traveler stumbles upon a peaceful, prosperous utopia hidden in the mountains of Tibet. The idea of discovering a perfect world appealed to many readers.

Not all fiction of the 1930s was escapist, however. James T. Farrell portrayed the grim

◄ **William Faulkner used his experiences growing up in Oxford, Mississippi, to create the mythical Yoknapatawpha County—a setting that appeared frequently in his novels.**

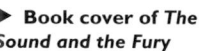
▶ **Book cover of *The Sound and the Fury***

life of Chicago's Irish immigrants in his *Studs Lonigan* trilogy (1932–1935), while Nathanael West presented the American dream as a nightmare in *Miss Lonelyhearts* (1933). William Faulkner, in novels such as *The Sound and the Fury* (1929) and *As I Lay Dying* (1930), tragically portrayed small-town life in fictional Yoknapatawpha County, Mississippi. Faulkner's novels later earned him the Nobel Prize for literature in 1949 and two Pulitzer prizes—one in 1955 and another in 1963.

■■ During the 1930s Americans enjoyed many forms of popular culture, including movies, radio programs, and literature.

SECTION 2 REVIEW

IDENTIFY and explain the significance of the following: *mutualistas, breadlines, shantytowns, Josefina Fierro de Bright, James Hilton, James T. Farrell, Nathanael West, William Faulkner.*

1. **MAIN IDEA** How did the depression affect the work force?
2. **MAIN IDEA** What impact did the Great Depression have on living conditions in rural areas?
3. **MAIN IDEA** How were urban communities affected by the Great Depression? In what ways did individuals and communities try to cope?
4. **WRITING TO DESCRIBE** Imagine you are a magazine editor researching a story on popular culture during the 1930s. Write an outline for an article that describes popular forms of entertainment during this period.
5. **EVALUATING** How did economic hardship alter family life in the 1930s?

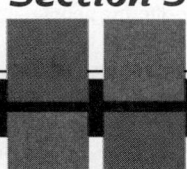

PREVIEW WORKSHOP

Following is a list of the significant people and terms in this section. You may wish to use this list as a section preview.

People
- Andrew Mellon
- A. J. Muste
- Franklin Delano Roosevelt
- Eleanor Roosevelt

Terms
- rugged individualism
- Agricultural Marketing Act
- Home Loan Bank Act
- Reconstruction Finance Corporation
- Bonus Army

Section 3

HOOVER FAILS

FOCUS

- **What beliefs shaped President Hoover's response to the depression?**
- **What effect did the Hoover administration's economic policies have on the depression?**
- **Why did Hoover lose the election of 1932?**

When the depression began, many Americans had great faith in Herbert Hoover. His skills as a businessman and as an administrator inspired confidence. Under his direction the government undertook some important measures to fight the depression. But they were not enough to end the crisis. As a result, voters in the election of 1932 rejected Hoover in favor of his Democratic opponent, Franklin D. Roosevelt.

Republican campaign button, 1932

HOOVER'S PHILOSOPHY

The most urgent task confronting President Hoover was to ease the human suffering caused by the depression. Prior to the crash most Americans believed that the government should not interfere in the free-enterprise system. Immediately after the crash, the *New York Times* advised that "the fundamental prescriptions for recovery [are] such homely things as savings . . . and hopeful waiting for the turn." Within a few months, however, the worsening crisis led to calls for the federal government to provide direct relief—food, clothing, shelter, and money—to the needy. Hoover rejected the idea of such government aid, stating:

❝ I do not believe that the power and duty of the [federal] Government ought to be extended to the relief of individual suffering. . . . The lesson should be constantly enforced that though the people support the Government the Government should not support the people. ❞

Direct federal relief, Hoover argued, would create a vast bureaucracy, inflate the federal budget, and undermine the self-respect of people receiving the aid. Instead, Hoover urged Americans to lift themselves up through hard work and strength of character.

Hoover's political beliefs stemmed from the notion of **rugged individualism**—the idea that

▼ Unemployed workers protested in New York's Times Square in 1933. Demonstrators carried signs indicating they were willing to work for $1 a week.

FOCUS OBJECTIVES

- Describe the beliefs that shaped President Hoover's response to the depression.

- Analyze the effect the Hoover administration's economic policies had on the depression.

- Explain why Hoover lost the election of 1932.

PRIMARY SOURCE
Description of Change: excerpted and bracketed
Rationale: excerpted to focus on main idea; bracketed to clarify meaning

CORE RESOURCES

- **Social Studies Skills Worksheet 23**
- **Geography Worksheet 23**
- **Section 3 Daily Quiz**

AV RESOURCES

- *The American Nation Videodisc: Boulder Dam*

**MOTIVATING:
LINK TO TODAY**

Point out that in 1992 President George Bush was faced with many of the same problems that President Herbert Hoover faced 60 years earlier. Point out that, in part, both men lost their reelection bids because of economic problems of their day.

Teaching the Section

HOOVER'S BELIEFS

Organize students into small groups to act as speechwriters for President Herbert Hoover. Have each group write a speech for the president, explaining his philosophy about the role of the federal government in ending the depression. Call on group representatives to present their speeches to the class.

HISTORICAL SIDELIGHTS

Unemployment Relief

In January 1932 Walter Gifford, Hoover's director of the Committee for Unemployment Relief at the time, told a Senate subcommittee that "federal aid would be a disservice to the unemployed . . . and that the situation can be better handled as it is being handled." When members of the subcommittee wanted to know on what he based his optimistic beliefs, Gifford responded that they were based on telephone conversations with state representatives of the president's committee. But when the senators asked Gifford how many people were actually unemployed and needy, he was unable to provide any data.

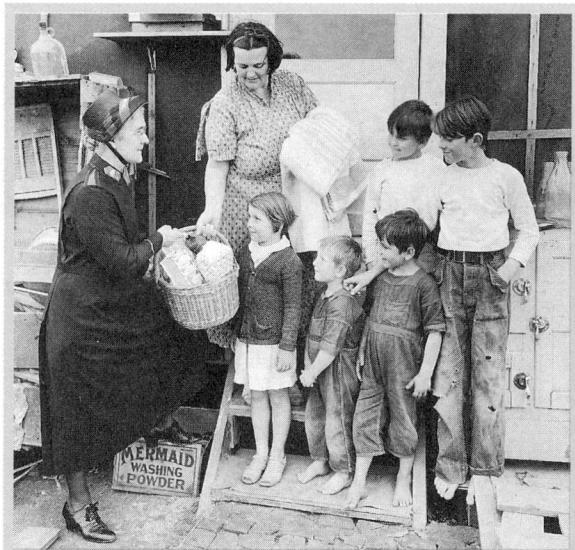

▲ Private charities and organizations such as the Salvation Army helped families in need of assistance by bringing them food and clothing.

▼ Nurses, such as this one in Maryland, often went door-to-door offering people free medical assistance.

success comes through individual effort and private enterprise. He believed that private charities and local communities, not the federal government, could best provide for those in need. "A voluntary deed," said Hoover, "is infinitely more precious to our national ideas and spirit than a thousandfold poured from the Treasury."

Hoover was not alone in his beliefs. Millions of Americans agreed that voluntary efforts were preferable to government intervention. It soon became clear, however, that voluntary efforts alone could not deal with the scale of the depression. Communities and private charities lacked the resources to cope with the ever-rising tide of human misery. Local governments were forced to stretch already inadequate funds to cover growing numbers of needy families. By 1933, for example, families on public welfare in New York City were paid just $23 a month.

In 1930 Hoover appointed the Committee for Unemployment Relief to assist state and local relief efforts. The committee, however, did little beyond urging Americans to contribute more to charity. The human misery of the depression continued practically unchecked.

■■ **Hoover's belief in rugged individualism led him to oppose direct federal relief for those in need.**

ℬ OOSTING THE ECONOMY

Although critics would later charge that Hoover's relief plans failed because he did not get the government involved, Hoover was not totally opposed to the government intervening in the economy. In fact, despite his opposition to direct public relief, Hoover's administration played a

▲ President Hoover addressed 250 leaders of finance, industry, and commerce in August 1932. In his speech, Hoover asked business leaders to assume more responsibility for improving the economy.

HOOVER'S POLICIES

Select several volunteers to take turns playing Herbert Hoover at a press conference. Have the rest of the class portray reporters, asking Hoover to explain the economic policies and measures he is taking to end the depression. List the policies and measures on the chalkboard. Then have students choose one policy or measure and write an editorial explaining why that policy or measure is having little effect on the depression. Students may wish to include their editorials in their portfolios.

▶

more active role in attempting to shape the economy than any previous administration had.

Stimulating the economy. Within weeks of the stock market crash, Hoover called a White House conference of top business, labor, and political leaders. The *New York Times* hailed the meeting as a step in the right direction, noting:

> 66 [It is] the largest gathering of noted heads of industrial and other corporations in Washington since the resources of the nation were marshalled for participation in the World War! 99

Hoover urged these leaders to maintain employment and wages voluntarily as a step toward reviving business activity and promoting recovery. At the same time, he issued cheerful public statements designed to boost confidence and get the economy going again.

Unfortunately, most people did not share Hoover's optimism. Many became very cynical toward the administration as trust in government and in business declined. Moaned the chairman of the Republican National Committee: "Every time an administration official gives out an optimistic statement about business conditions, the market immediately drops."

At Hoover's request, Congress funded several public-works programs, among them the giant Hoover Dam on the Colorado River. Hoover expected these projects to achieve two goals: (1) to stimulate business by providing contracts for construction and materials and (2) to provide relief by employing jobless workers. Overall, he approved some $800 million in public-works funding. Yet the crisis was so great that even this large amount had little impact on the depression.

Coping with the farm crisis. Hoover also took some steps to ease the plight of farmers. As crop prices fell, Hoover instructed the Federal Farm Board—created through the **Agricultural Marketing Act** of 1929—to buy up surplus wheat, corn, cotton, and other farm products. Officials believed that reducing crop supplies would cause prices to rise. The government could store these commodities and then sell them when prices were higher. The scheme did not work. Farmers at first refused to limit production. Instead, they reacted to low prices by growing more crops. In 1931 the Farm Board stopped buying surplus crops, having already spent some $180 million.

Just as he opposed direct relief for jobless factory workers, Hoover resisted giving direct aid to desperate farmers. He did try to aid farmers indirectly, though, by recommending passage of the **Home Loan Bank Act** in 1932. The act provided money to savings banks, building and loan associations, and insurance companies for low-interest mortgages. Hoover believed that the act would reduce foreclosures on homes and farms and thus allow more farmers to keep their land. He also believed that the act would encourage home construction, boosting employment and increasing the flow of money through the economy.

The Reconstruction Finance Corporation. Hoover also tried to stimulate the economy through the **Reconstruction Finance Corporation** (RFC), created by Congress in February 1932. The RFC lent large sums to railroads, insurance companies, banks, and other financial institutions. By strengthening these key businesses through federal loans, Hoover hoped to reduce bank failures and create more jobs.

By the end of Hoover's term, RFC loans had helped a number of large corporations avoid collapse. Yet the economy continued to decline, in part because the RFC offered too little, too late. It was created while the depression was in full swing, and it provided no direct aid to industries or

◀ Hoover Dam on the Colorado River was completed in 1936. It is the main source of hydroelectric power in the Southwest.

PRIMARY SOURCE
Description of Change: excerpted and bracketed
Rationale: excerpted to focus on main idea; bracketed to clarify meaning

HISTORICAL SIDELIGHTS
Building Hoover Dam
The hundreds of people who came to Las Vegas, Nevada, in 1930 to work on the construction of the nearby Hoover Dam often found conditions as bad as in the places from which they came. Just north of Las Vegas, tents and shacks housed hundreds of men, women, and children. When work started in April, the companies that were constructing the dam provided wooden barracks for about 480 single men. People with families, however, were responsible for their own housing until Boulder City, a permanent town, was built. Besides the danger of the actual construction work, workers faced the problem of the unbearable summer heat, which resulted in many heat-related deaths.

THE AMERICAN NATION
VIDEODISC PROGRAM
Boulder Dam

1B   52402   :34

Teaching the Section

THE 1932 ELECTION

Have students work in pairs. Have one student assume the role of an interviewer and the other the role of a former Hoover supporter who is voting for FDR in the 1932 election. Ask student pairs to develop interviews in which the voter explains why he or she is voting for FDR. Call on volunteers to present their interviews to the class.

PRIMARY SOURCE
Description of Change: excerpted
Rationale: excerpted to focus on main idea

to small businesses, which continued to fail at an alarming rate.

Critics attacked the RFC's trickle-down approach to economic recovery. They argued that money lent to big business would not filter down quickly enough to help the real victims of the depression—ordinary citizens. As one economist put it, this was like putting fertilizer on the branches of a tree—rather than on the roots—to help the tree grow. A more effective approach, said critics, would be to funnel money directly to those in need. This would increase consumers' buying power and thereby stimulate business. Newspaper columnist Walter Lippmann reflected popular sentiments when he wrote:

> 66 It is hard for the country to realize that this era of easy finance is over. . . . In respect to government finance, as in respect to so many other things, Congress and the people of the country have radically to readjust their minds. 99

Government activism. Although President Hoover's policies failed to end the Great Depression, the RFC and other measures—such as the Home Loan Bank Act and funding for public works—represented a major shift in government policy. To a greater degree than ever before, the president and Congress accepted the idea that the federal government can and should do something to boost the economy in times of crisis.

In the early 1930s Treasury Secretary Andrew Mellon had advised the traditional do-nothing approach. He even argued that a short depression would be good for the country because "it will purge the rottenness out of the system." But as the depression became more severe, the government took unprecedented steps to promote recovery. Unfortunately, these measures were not sufficient to halt the downward trend. As Americans continued to suffer, they increasingly blamed their plight on Herbert Hoover.

▲ Andrew Mellon

▦ **Hoover's limited measures to end the depression did little to ease the crisis.**

RUMBLINGS OF DISCONTENT

By 1932 Hoover was the most hated man in America. His appearance in movie newsreels provoked boos and catcalls from audiences. And he made little effort to win public support by changing his aloof manner or stiff, boring speeches. "This is not a showman's job," Hoover remarked. "I will not step out of character."

As confidence in Hoover eroded, radical political parties grew more vocal. Both the Communist party and the Socialist party condemned the capitalist system that they believed created the depression. Both parties helped organize several mass protests in the early 1930s. Socialist leader A. J. Muste gathered the jobless into Unemployed Leagues to demand work. The Communist party encouraged labor-union activism and led strikes by migrant farm workers.

A Most Vicious Circle

▲ As the depression worsened, more and more people began to blame President Hoover for their troubles. This cartoon appeared June 1931 in the *Albany News.*

THE COUNTRY SPEAKS OUT

Call on students to identify specific groups who were unhappy about Hoover's handling of the depression. List these groups on the chalkboard. Then ask students to imagine themselves as a member of one of these groups and to write a letter to the Republican party, stating his or her frustration with the Hoover administration. Call on volunteers to read their letters to the class. Students may wish to include their letters in their portfolios.

▲ Shown here is lawyer Samuel Leibowitz (left) meeting with Heywood Patterson, one of the principal defendants in the Scottsboro case.

The party also helped expose racial injustice. In 1931 an all-white jury in Scottsboro, Alabama, sentenced eight of nine black youths aged 13 to 21 years to death on a highly questionable rape charge. The Communist party helped supply legal defense for the "Scottsboro Boys" and organized mass demonstrations to overturn the convictions.

Many desperate Americans responded to communist and socialist calls for direct action. Early in 1932, thousands of unemployed men demanding work participated in a hunger march on the Ford auto plant near Detroit. Four were killed when police opened fire. In Seattle, 5,000 unemployed protestors seized a public building. After two days local officials finally forced them out.

Some activism was spontaneous, reflecting the desperation of the times. In rural areas people armed with clubs, pitchforks, and shotguns confronted officials trying to foreclose on homes. Farmers destroyed crops and blocked roads to prevent food from being shipped to market, hoping that limiting food supplies would push prices up. "They say blockading the highway's illegal," an Iowa farmer said. "Seems to me there was a Tea Party in Boston that was illegal too."

The biggest protest was staged by more than 10,000 World War I veterans and their families in May 1932. They came to Washington, D.C., to support a veterans' bonus bill then before Congress. The bill would have granted the veterans—many of whom were unemployed—early payment of pension bonuses due to them for their service during the war. This group was soon dubbed the **Bonus Army**.

At first, officials allowed the Bonus Army demonstrators to live in empty government buildings and to camp in an open area across the Potomac River. When Congress rejected the bonus bill, most of the demonstrators returned home. But about 2,000 veterans stayed, defying orders to leave. In a clash with authorities, two veterans and two policemen were killed. The police requested aid, and President Hoover ordered the army to disperse the squatters.

In late July the army moved in with machine guns, tanks, and tear gas. One woman recalled her husband's experience that day:

> 66 My husband went to Washington. To march with . . . the bonus boys. He was a machine gunner in the war. He'd say them . . . Germans gassed him in Germany. And [then] his own government . . . gassed him and run him off the country up there with a water hose, half drowned him. 99

▲ More than 10,000 veterans marched to Washington, D.C., in May 1932 to petition Congress for full and immediate payment of pension bonuses earned during World War I.

HISTORICAL SIDELIGHTS
Protests
Encouraged by the Communist party, a group of 500 armed farmers in England, Arkansas, asked a Red Cross administrator for food. When told that there were no more food requisition blanks, the farmers invaded the town's stores. Alarmed, the merchants gave the farmers $900 worth of food.

PRIMARY SOURCE
Description of Change: excerpted and bracketed
Rationale: excerpted to focus on main idea; bracketed to clarify meaning

HISTORICAL SIDELIGHTS
The Scottsboro Boys
The convictions of the "Scottsboro Boys" were overturned twice by the Supreme Court—in 1932 because of inadequate legal representation, and again in 1935 because African Americans were excluded from Alabama juries. The state retried and reconvicted five of the defendants. The case was not finally settled until 1950, when four of the defendants were paroled and the last escaped to Michigan, where officials refused to return him to prison in Alabama.

Practice

GUIDED PRACTICE

Organize the class into the delegates at a Democratic platform committee meeting. Call on the delegates to list the failures of the Hoover administration and to develop a list of measures the Democratic party will undertake to overcome those failures.

INDEPENDENT PRACTICE

Have students create an editorial cartoon based on the list developed in the Guided Practice. Cartoons should either attack Hoover's failures or support Roosevelt. Students may want to include their cartoons in their portfolios.

Review and Assessment

REVIEW Have students use the section's Essential Points to write a paragraph telling why Hoover was not reelected in 1932. Then assign the Section 3 Review on p. 689.

ASSESS Assign the **Section 3 Daily Quiz** in *Core Resources*.

Commanded by General Douglas MacArthur (later a hero in World War II), the troops drove the veterans from the buildings, broke up their encampment, and burned their shacks. Hundreds were injured and three killed, including an 11-week-old baby. Many Americans found the government's treatment of the veterans shocking. Across the nation, anger against Hoover grew. As the election of 1932 approached, Americans joked bitterly, "In Hoover we trusted and now we are busted."

■■ Public unrest grew as the depression worsened and Hoover mishandled the Bonus Army protest.

*T*HE ELECTION OF 1932

In the summer of 1932, with elections scheduled for the fall, the Republicans reluctantly renominated Herbert Hoover as their presidential candidate. With public sentiment running strongly against the Republicans, no other member of the party was eager for the nomination. The Democrats, sensing victory, chose Franklin Delano Roosevelt of New York as their candidate.

The Democratic challenger. Roosevelt—who often went by his initials, FDR—was a determined and skillful politician. Born into a wealthy and prestigious family, his background suggested that he would be more likely to identify with the wealthy than with working-class citizens. He could easily have become a Wall Street power broker, but instead he chose a career in public service.

FDR was highly influenced by the progressivism of his distant cousin, former president Theodore Roosevelt, and by that of the former president's niece Eleanor Roosevelt, who married FDR in 1905. Her earnest belief in social reform impressed the young FDR. Mrs. Roosevelt would become one of his most important political assets. A fellow Democrat once said of the relationship between Franklin and Eleanor Roosevelt: "Any good things he may have done during his political career are due to her and any mistakes he may have made are due to his not taking up the matter with his wife."

FDR ran as a vice-presidential candidate in 1920, but his political career appeared to be over when he was paralyzed from the waist down by polio in 1921. Yet with the help of his wife, he overcame his physical challenges and was elected governor of New York in 1928. As governor he gained high marks for his imaginative state relief programs that had instituted unemployment benefits and supported failing industries. In accepting his party's nomination for president, Roosevelt issued a call for a new style of government, declaring:

▼ Franklin D. Roosevelt's support of innovative relief programs while governor of New York made him a strong contender for the 1932 Democratic party presidential nomination (below). The photograph at right shows him campaigning in 1932.

Closure

Draw two columns on the chalkboard. Title one *Pros* and the other *Cons*. Call on students to list the pros and cons of government intervention in economic affairs during the depression. Ask students whether or not they would have supported government intervention and to defend their positions.

Extension

EVALUATE Have students locate and read Hoover's "Rugged Individualism" speech. Ask them to evaluate it from the viewpoint of an industry leader and from the viewpoint of a factory worker.

ANALYZE Suggest that students research the proposals of Coxey's Army in 1894. Ask students to analyze whether those proposals might have provided solutions for the Great Depression.

---

66 Republican leaders not only have failed in material things, they have failed in national vision, because in disaster they have held out no hope. . . . I pledge you, I pledge myself, to a new deal for the American people. 99

A change in leadership. The 1932 campaign had one key issue—the depression. While Hoover tried to defend his policies, he realized he had little chance of victory. Roosevelt continually attacked Hoover's record and called for major policy changes, including direct federal relief for the needy, a massive public-works program, and federal regulation of the stock market to prevent fraud. Roosevelt promised to seek a fairer distribution of wealth and to put the political and economic system at "the service of the people."

On election day, Roosevelt and his running mate, John Nance Garner of Texas, carried 42 states, capturing 23 million popular votes and 472 electoral votes to Hoover's 16 million popular votes and 59 electoral votes. The Democrats won decisive majorities in both houses of Congress, solidifying gains they had already made in the congressional election of 1930. As a result, Roosevelt was confident that his programs would have strong support in Congress.

In the 1920s most Americans had credited the Republicans for the era's glowing prosperity. In 1932, voters made it clear that the Republicans would have to take the blame for the depression.

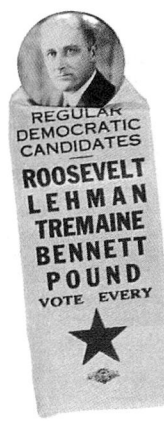 

▲ These Roosevelt campaign artifacts were used during the 1932 presidential election.

Many of those who voted for Roosevelt were really voting against Herbert Hoover. But other Americans saw in Roosevelt the kind of dynamic personality they believed could lead the country out of its troubles. Roosevelt had promised a "new deal." During the four months between Election Day and Roosevelt's inauguration on March 4, 1933, Americans waited hopefully to see how the new president would carry out his campaign pledge.

■■ **Hoover lost the election of 1932 because voters were upset by the Republicans' handling of the depression and were inspired by Franklin Roosevelt's confidence.**

■ **SECTION 3 REVIEW**

IDENTIFY and explain the significance of the following: rugged individualism, Agricultural Marketing Act, Home Loan Bank Act, Reconstruction Finance Corporation, Andrew Mellon, A. J. Muste, Bonus Army, Franklin Delano Roosevelt, Eleanor Roosevelt.

1. **MAIN IDEA** Why did President Hoover rely on local and voluntary efforts and oppose direct federal relief for those in need?

2. **MAIN IDEA** What measures did the Hoover administration support to end the depression? Why did they fail?

3. **MAIN IDEA** Why did public unrest grow during the Hoover administration?

4. **WRITING TO EXPRESS A VIEWPOINT** Imagine you are a campaign worker for Franklin Delano Roosevelt. Write a campaign poster explaining why voters should support your candidate in the 1932 election.

5. **HYPOTHESIZING** How might the events of the early 1930s have been different if the Hoover administration had supported direct federal relief?

Return to the Themes section on p. 668. Have students discuss these again and compare their original responses with those given now. (See p. 667B for suggested answers.)

Chapter Review Answers

WRITING A SUMMARY
See Essential Points in each section for main ideas.

REVIEWING CHRONOLOGY
1, 5, 3, 2, 4
Evaluating
The committee urged Americans to contribute more to charity.

IDENTIFYING PEOPLE AND IDEAS
1. *downward trend in stock prices*
2. *Treasury Secretary who advised the traditional do-nothing approach to depression*
3. *October 29, 1929, day when more than 16 million shares of stock were sold*
4. *mutual-aid societies formed by Mexican American communities to fight the depression*
5. *collections of makeshift shelters used by the homeless*
6. *activist who lobbied for expanded relief programs for Hispanic Americans*
7. *author who portrayed grim life of Chicago's Irish immigrants in* Studs Lonigan *trilogy*
8. *belief that success comes through individual effort and private enterprise*

9. *measure designed to aid farmers by providing money for low-interest mortgages*
10. *veterans who protested in Washington, demanding early payments of pension bonuses*

UNDERSTANDING MAIN IDEAS
1. *speculation for quick profits, ease of margin buying, and confidence in the bull market; speculative buying drove stock prices above their real value, causing large-scale selling, panic, and crash*

2. *The banking system collapsed as debt-ridden investors defaulted on loans and panic drove depositors to withdraw their savings.*
3. *Economic hardship caused many families to break apart and many young people to put off getting married and starting their own families.*
4. *began limited public-works programs, bought farm surpluses, supported Home Loan Bank Act, created RFC*
5. *Some joined radical political parties, which became more vocal and helped organize mass protests; farmers blocked food shipments in rural areas; Bonus Army marched on Washington, D.C.*

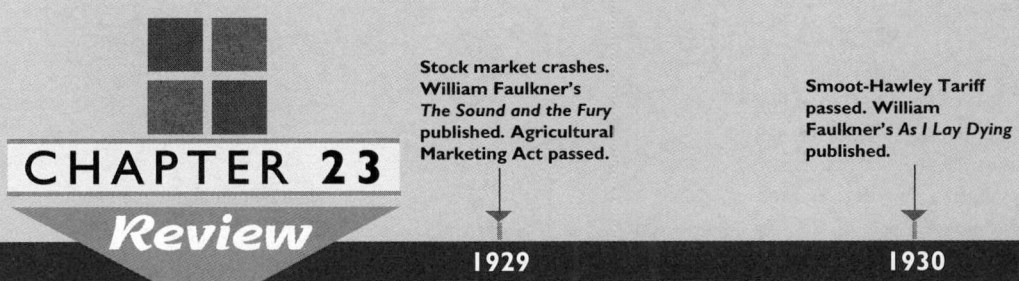

CHAPTER 23
Review

Stock market crashes. William Faulkner's *The Sound and the Fury* published. Agricultural Marketing Act passed.

Smoot-Hawley Tariff passed. William Faulkner's *As I Lay Dying* published.

1929   **1930**

WRITING A SUMMARY
Using the essential points of the chapter as a guide, write a summary of the chapter.

REVIEWING CHRONOLOGY
Number your paper 1 to 5. Study the time line above, and list the following events in the order in which they happened by writing the first next to 1, the second next to 2, and so on. Then complete the activity below.
1. Stock market crashes.
2. Bonus Army marches on Washington, D.C.
3. Scottsboro Boys case begins.
4. James Hilton's *Lost Horizon* and Nathanael West's *Miss Lonelyhearts* published.
5. Smoot-Hawley Tariff passed.

Evaluating How did Hoover's appointment of the Committee for Unemployment Relief show his support for rugged individualism?

IDENTIFYING PEOPLE AND IDEAS
Explain the historical significance of each of the following people or terms.
1. bear market
2. Andrew Mellon
3. Black Tuesday
4. *mutualistas*
5. shantytowns
6. Josefina Fierro de Bright
7. James T. Farrell
8. rugged individualism
9. Home Loan Bank Act
10. Bonus Army

UNDERSTANDING MAIN IDEAS
1. What factors led Americans to invest in the stock market during the 1920s? Why did the stock market crash in 1929?
2. How did the depression affect the banking industry?
3. What effect did the depression have on family life in the 1930s?
4. What measures did President Hoover take to stimulate the economy?
5. What are some of the ways in which people expressed their discontent during the depression?

⭐ REVIEWING THEMES
1. **Economic Development** What factors caused the Great Depression?
2. **Geographic Diversity** How did the depression influence where people lived during the 1930s?
3. **Cultural Diversity** How were African Americans and Mexican Americans affected differently by the depression?

THINKING CRITICALLY
1. **Evaluating** How did the depression affect the behavior and outlook of Americans who struggled through those hard times?
2. **Analyzing** Why did Hoover oppose direct federal relief to the needy?
3. **Synthesizing** What major policy changes did Franklin Roosevelt propose during the 1932 presidential campaign?

STRATEGY FOR SUCCESS
Review the Skills Handbook entry on Distinguishing Fact from Opinion on page 990. Then read the following excerpt, in which the editor of the Johnstown *Tribune* warns the city of dangers to be expected from the arrival of the Bonus Army. What opinions does the editor have about the marchers? How might they differ from the opinions of one of the marchers?

> 66 In any group of the size of the Bonus Army, made up of men gathered from all parts of the country, without discipline, without effective leadership in a crisis, . . . there is certain to be a mixture of undesirables—thieves, plug-uglies [thugs], degenerates. . . . The community must protect itself from the criminal fringe of the invaders. 99

WRITING ABOUT HISTORY
Writing to Create Write a poem or lyrics for a song that would reflect the mood of Americans struggling with the depression.

REVIEWING THEMES

1. 1929 stock market crash, downturn in global economy, poor economic practices of 1920s, decline in farm prices, weakening of major industries, overuse of credit, unequal distribution of income, and overproduction
2. Unemployed people moved across country to find jobs; relatives doubled up in small houses; young adults moved back in with their parents.
3. African American workers were typically the first to be laid off, black domestic servants lost jobs because of increased competition from white women, many Mexican American agricultural workers in the Southwest were forced to repatriate.

THINKING CRITICALLY

1. Many would never forget the shame of unemployment, of losing their businesses or homes, or of being unable to provide for families. A strong desire for financial security and material comforts shaped the outlook of many.
2. He thought it would create a vast bureaucracy, inflate federal budget, and undermine self-respect of people receiving aid.
3. direct federal relief for the needy, a massive public-works program, federal regulation of stock market to prevent fraud, and a fairer distribution of wealth

STRATEGY FOR SUCCESS

that the group has no discipline or leadership, that it poses a danger, that it includes criminal elements; marchers might view their group as heroic veterans, marching for a just cause

WRITING ABOUT HISTORY

Poems or songs might recall more prosperous times past, mention despair over present hardships, or express attitudes about the future.

USING PRIMARY SOURCES

a warning that a violent revolution could come from the ranks of the unemployed

LINKING HISTORY AND GEOGRAPHY

Delaware, Maine, New Hampshire, North Carolina, Vermont, Virginia; factors might include differences among the states in their basic industries and economic activities, and the movement of people into or out of the state in search of employment

---

1931 — Herbert Hoover appoints Committee for Unemployment Relief. Scottsboro Boys case begins.

1932 — Home Loan Bank Act passed. RFC created. Bonus Army marches on Washington, D.C. Franklin Roosevelt elected president.

1933 — James Hilton's *Lost Horizon* and Nathanael West's *Miss Lonelyhearts* published.

USING PRIMARY SOURCES

As the depression continued into the winter of 1932, the growing numbers of unemployed forced to seek relief in soup kitchens became a familiar sight. In her poem "Bread Line," which was published in January 1932, Florence Converse attempted to make sense of this tragedy. Read the following excerpt from the poem. What point is the poet trying to make?

66 *What's the meaning of this queue,*
Tailing down the avenue,
Full of eyes that will not meet
The other eyes that throng the street—
The questing eyes, the curious eyes,
Scornful, popping with surprise
To see a living line of men
As long as round the block, and then
As long again? . . .

. . . .

What's the meaning in these faces
Modern industry displaces,
Emptying the factory
To set the men so tidily
Along the pavement in a row?
Now and then they take a slow
Shuffling step, straight ahead,
As if a dead march said:
"Beware! I'm not dead."

. . . .

A spark can creep, a spark can run;
Suddenly a spark can wink
And send us down destruction's brink.

. . . .

What if our slow-match have caught
Fire from a burning thought?
What if we should be destroyed
By our patient unemployed? 99

LINKING HISTORY AND GEOGRAPHY

Refer to the map on page 676. Which states had the smallest percentage of people receiving unemployment benefits? What factors might account for variations in the number of people receiving unemployment assistance?

Breadline

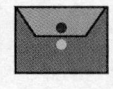 BUILDING YOUR PORTFOLIO

Complete the following projects independently or cooperatively.

1. **THE ECONOMY** In chapters 21 and 22 you dealt with the postwar economic downswing and the upswing of the 1920s. Building on that experience, imagine you are a cartoonist in 1929. Create an editorial cartoon that criticizes the investment practices that led to the stock market crash.

2. **GLOBAL RELATIONS** Imagine you are a journalist in the 1930s at the height of the Great Depression. Create a series of newspaper headlines that describe the effects of the depression both in the United States and around the world. Headlines might mention stories about individual families, homelessness and food shortages, unemployment, Hoover's political problems, or international trade issues.

BUILDING YOUR PORTFOLIO

Have students refer to **Building Your Portfolio Worksheet 7**, assigned at the beginning of Unit 7. Use the worksheet to help students monitor their progress on the portfolio projects.

Assessment

Core Resources
• Review Worksheet 23
• Chapter 23 Tests
• Alternative Assessment Forms
Test Generator

THE NEW DEAL

1933–1940

Chapter Overview

When FDR became president in 1933, he attacked the depression with a series of bold new government programs collectively known as the New Deal. Laws were designed to restart the economy through relief, recovery, and reform programs. Projects targeted jobless and needy Americans from urban factory workers to rural farmers. Even the arts benefited from government programs that provided work. Criticism of New Deal programs came from both the left and right. African Americans and other ethnic groups benefited from New Deal programs but faced continued discrimination.

THE AMERICAN NATION VIDEODISC PROGRAM A variety of still images, short videos, and activities are available for you to use as you teach this chapter. See Correlation to *The American Nation Videodisc Program* for barcode correlations and suggestions for using the program.

Chapter Planning Guide

CHAPTER 24	CORE RESOURCE BOOKLETS	AUDIOVISUAL RESOURCES	PROGRAM RESOURCES
INTRODUCTION pp. 692–693	■ Building Your Portfolio Worksheet 7	■ Everyday Life in America Transparency and Worksheet 24	■ *Eyewitnesses and Others,* Volume 2: Reading 49
TEACHING THE CHAPTER pp. 694–719	■ Graphic Organizer 24 ■ Social Studies Skills Worksheet 24 ■ Literature Worksheet 24 ■ Geography Worksheet 24 ■ Outline Map 9	■ *The American Nation* Videodisc: Serving the Nation; Marian Anderson	■ Art in American History Transparencies and Worksheets 23, 29, 30, 31, 32, 33 ■ *Eyewitnesses and Others,* Volume 2: Readings 40, 45, 47, 48
REVIEW AND ASSESSMENT pp. 720–721	■ Chapter 24 Daily Quizzes ■ Review Worksheet 24 ■ Chapter 24 Tests ■ Alternative Assessment Forms		■ Test Generator

Additional Resources

BOOKS FOR TEACHERS

Leuchtenburg, William E. *Franklin D. Roosevelt and the New Deal.* Harper-Collins, 1963. A noted historian's scholarly treatment of the years 1932–1940.

Reiman, Richard A. *The New Deal & American Youth: Ideas & Ideals in a Depression Decade.* University of Georgia Press, 1992. Examines role of youth in New Deal.

Rosenbaum, Herbert D. and Elizabeth Bartelme, eds. *Franklin D. Roosevelt: The Man, the Myth, the Era, 1882–1945.* Greenwood, 1987. Biography of FDR.

BOOKS FOR STUDENTS

Allen, Frederick L. *Since Yesterday.* HarperCollins, 1986. Reissue of a classic political and social history of the 1930s.

Daniel, Pete, et al. *Official Images: New Deal Photography.* Smithsonian, 1987. Dramatic images of New Deal photographs accompanied by essays analyzing propaganda techniques used by federal agencies.

*Freedman, Russell. *Franklin Delano Roosevelt.* Houghton Mifflin, 1992. An award-winning biography of FDR by a distinguished writer of nonfiction for young adults.

* for students reading below grade level

MULTIMEDIA MATERIALS

Franklin D. Roosevelt: The Speeches Collection. Video, 40 min. MPI Home Video/SSSS. Includes a speech to CCC workers and a teacher's guide on Roosevelt.

The Great Depression. Video, 31 min. Guidance Associates/SSSS. Traces the depression from 1929 to 1939 and shows how the New Deal changed the power and scope of the federal government.

You May Call Her Madam Secretary. Video, 57 min. Vineyard Video Productions/SSSS. Documents the life of Frances Perkins, the first woman cabinet member.

THEMES IN AMERICAN HISTORY

USE WITH PAGES 692–693

Listed on the right are the themes emphasized in Chapter 24. The questions in boldface type stimulate critical thinking and provide students with an opportunity to discuss the themes within a broadened context. The questions also appear in the pupil's edition on p. 692.

■ ECONOMIC DEVELOPMENT

How can the federal government aid economic recovery? Students might suggest that the federal government could establish programs that encourage businesses to expand and hire workers, provide direct relief to the needy, and sponsor public-works and other projects to employ people.

■ CONSTITUTIONAL HERITAGE

Why might government interference in the economy be considered unconstitutional? Students might recall that the powers enumerated in the Constitution give the federal government little direct control over private businesses unless those businesses are involved in interstate commerce. The federal government might exceed such limits in laws or policies that impact local economic activity.

■ CULTURAL DIVERSITY

What role might the arts play in reflecting ethnic and cultural diversity? Students might mention that novels and plays may reflect the thoughts and experiences of different ethnic groups; paintings might portray scenes of ethnic life; and music may reflect the diversity of traditions within various regions and culture groups.

CHAPTER STRATEGIES FOR MEETING INDIVIDUAL NEEDS

LIMITED ENGLISH PROFICIENT LEARNERS

Organize students into eight groups to create news headlines for the years 1933–1940. Assign each group a different year. Have groups review the chapter to find at least two events that took place during their assigned year. Students should write their headlines on poster paper and create a New Deal collage or bulletin board.

TACTILE/KINESTHETIC LEARNERS

Have students work in groups to prepare skits showing the way the New Deal changed the life of a jobless banker, an unemployed factory worker, or an artist.

LEARNERS HAVING DIFFICULTY

Organize students into groups to create an "Alphabet Soup" directory of New Deal programs, listing them in alphabetical order with two or three sentences explaining each program's purpose.

AUDITORY LEARNERS

Direct students to interview people who lived during the 1930s to determine their opinions of Roosevelt and New Deal programs. Students might prepare audiotapes of their interviews.

VISUAL LEARNERS

Ask students to imagine they are artists employed by the Federal Arts Project. Have them design a symbol or a poster for a New Deal program.

GIFTED LEARNERS

Have students research and write an essay explaining how FDR's New Deal changed forever the role of government in American life.

USING THE CHAPTER FOCUS

 **UNDERSTANDING THE MAIN IDEA**
Call on a volunteer to read aloud the Understanding the Main Idea paragraph. Then ask students to draw on what they have learned about the early depression years to speculate on the problems the New Deal would try to solve.

THEMES
Have students work individually or in small groups to answer the questions under Themes. Save students' responses so that they can compare them with their responses after studying the chapter. (See p. 691B for suggested answers.)

■ **THE TIME LINE**
Direct students' attention to the entries for 1939 and 1940. Ask students who have read the books noted, or other books of the 1930s, to discuss major themes and approaches of literature of the time.

CORE RESOURCES

• **Graphic Organizer 24**
• **Social Studies Skills Worksheet 24**
• **Outline Map 9**
• **Building Your Portfolio Worksheet 7**

AV **RESOURCES**

• **Everyday Life in America Transparency** and **Worksheet 24**

ABOUT THE ILLUSTRATION

Murals in public buildings, such as the one in this post office, became quite common during the New Deal era. As the government sponsored the construction of new public buildings, it also employed artists to paint murals in them. The program not only provided artists with jobs, but it also helped expose their work to audiences throughout the country. Have students draw sketches for a mural to be painted on a wall in their school. Suggest that their sketches reflect a message about some aspect of their daily lives.

Chapter 24

1933–1940

THE NEW DEAL

FOCUS

UNDERSTANDING THE MAIN IDEA

To help the nation recover from the Great Depression of the 1930s, President Franklin Roosevelt created a series of programs known as the New Deal. These reforms improved the economy and expanded the role of government in economic life. The government provided jobs to thousands of unemployed workers and provided direct relief to the needy.

THEMES

■ **ECONOMIC DEVELOP-MENT** How can the federal government aid economic recovery?

■ **CONSTITUTIONAL HERITAGE** Why might government interference in the economy be considered unconstitutional?

■ **CULTURAL DIVERSITY** What role might the arts play in reflecting ethnic and cultural diversity?

1933	1935	1936	1937	1939	1940
▼ New Deal launched.	▼ CIO organized.	▼ *Gone with the Wind* published.	▼ GM strike begins.	▼ *The Grapes of Wrath* published.	▼ *Native Son* published.

LINK TO THE PAST

Have students give examples of ways the Hoover administration attempted to deal with the Great Depression and write their responses on the chalkboard. *(called on volunteer organizations, local governments to provide assistance to the needy; urged creation of Reconstruction Finance Corporation and passage of Home Loan Bank Act)* Then explain why Hoover's approach was described as "very cautious" and ask students to speculate how government might take a more active role in shaping the economy.

LINK TO THE PAST

The prosperous economic times of the 1920s had come to a devastating end with the stock market crash of 1929 and the Great Depression. President Hoover's administration had been very cautious in dealing with the economic crisis. By electing Franklin Roosevelt in 1932, the nation appeared ready for the federal government to take a more active role in shaping the economy.

HISTORICAL SIDELIGHTS
FDR's Inaugural

Franklin Delano Roosevelt was the last president required to wait four months to take office after being elected. By 1933 the day had long passed when transportation networks and winter travel were obstacles to a new president reaching the capital. So the Constitution's Twentieth Amendment, adopted in 1933, stipulated that the president's term in office should begin and end on January 20 instead of on March 4.

PRIMARY SOURCE
Description of Change: excerpted
Rationale: excerpted to focus on main idea

By 1933, Americans had endured three years of economic depression—each year more desperate than the last. On his last day in office, President Hoover was heard to sigh, "We are at the end of our string. There is nothing more we can do." But the new president, Franklin Delano Roosevelt, did not share this despair. In his inaugural address he offered the American people hope:

> **66** First of all let me assert my firm belief that the only thing we have to fear is fear itself—nameless, unreasoning, unjustified terror which paralyzes needed efforts to convert retreat into advance. . . . This Nation asks for action, and action now. **99**

Roosevelt's words rang out across the land, lifting Americans from despair and stirring their hopes. Some half a million letters in support of the new president poured into the White House.

Roosevelt's program had three general aims: *relief,* to ease the plight of citizens in economic distress; *recovery,* to restore the economy to health; and *reform,* to correct ills and injustices in American society. Despite much confusion, inefficiency, and political conflict, Roosevelt's measures proved enormously powerful and far-reaching. They restored public hope, aided the unemployed, and gave the government a central role in regulating business and the economy and promoting public welfare.

Post office mural, *Evening on the Farm,* by Orr C. Fisher

National Recovery Administration symbol

FOCUS OBJECTIVES

- Identify the New Deal programs that tackled the banking, farm, and home owners' crises.

- Describe how the New Deal provided relief for the unemployed.

- Explain the effect the New Deal had on the Tennessee Valley region.

PREVIEW WORKSHOP

Following is a list of the significant people, places, and terms in this section. You may wish to use this list as a section preview.

People
- Frances Perkins
- Harry L. Hopkins

Places
- Tennessee River Valley

Terms
- New Deal
- bank holiday
- Emergency Banking Act
- Federal Deposit Insurance Corporation
- Farm Credit Administration
- Home Owners Loan Corporation
- Federal Emergency Relief Administration
- Civil Works Administration
- Civilian Conservation Corps
- National Industrial Recovery Act
- Public Works Administration
- National Recovery Administration
- Agricultural Adjustment Act
- subsidies
- Southern Tenant Farmers' Union
- Tennessee Valley Authority

Section 1

RESTORING HOPE

F O C U S

- **What New Deal programs tackled the banking, farm, and home owners' crises?**
- **How did the New Deal provide relief for the unemployed?**
- **What effect did the New Deal have on the Tennessee Valley region?**

Roosevelt wasted no time making good his pledge of "action, and action now." As soon as he arrived in the Oval Office, he confidently proposed programs that would strengthen the nation's teetering banking system and provide relief for the needy. Soon he moved on to attack the deep-seated problems that plagued agriculture and industry. One project would transform an entire region of the country.

New Yorker
magazine cover, 1933

ROOSEVELT CONFRONTS THE EMERGENCY

Roosevelt's optimism proved contagious. "The whole country is with him," noted humorist Will Rogers, "just so he does something. If he burned down the Capitol, we would cheer and say, 'Well, we at least got a fire started anyhow.'" People were ready for action, even if it meant making mistakes along the way.

Roosevelt did indeed get a fire started. With the help of the Brain Trust, the advisory group that he had formed in 1932 while still governor of New York, the energetic new president drew up 15 relief and recovery measures, his promised "new deal for the American people." Immediately after taking office on March 5, Roosevelt called Congress into special session. Over the next 100 days, Congress approved all 15

measures, which made up the heart of the president's **New Deal** program.

Roosevelt started with the nation's banks, which were in serious trouble. The day after his inauguration, he issued a proclamation closing every bank in the nation for a few days. This so-called **bank holiday** was designed to stop massive withdrawals. On Thursday, March 9, Congress took only a few hours to pass the **Emergency Banking Act**,

▶ Americans listened as Roosevelt discussed important issues in one of his many radio broadcasts.

Ask students to identify what they know from newspapers, magazines, and television about federal government programs to assist the needy. Have students list responses in their notebooks. Suggest that, as they read the section, students compare items on their lists to the programs instituted by the Roosevelt administration during the New Deal.

*T*eaching the *S*ection

BANKING, FARM, AND HOME OWNERS' CRISES

Organize students into three groups. Assign one group banking, another farm problems, and the third the home owners' crisis. Have each group imagine they are members of the Roosevelt brain trust. Direct groups to prepare "fireside chats" for Roosevelt to deliver to the nation, explaining their assigned problem, steps the administration is taking to solve it, and reasons the public should support these policies. Have each group choose a "Roosevelt" to deliver its "chat" to the class.

■■ Have students describe some of the ways presidents today use the media to present policies or programs to the public. ▶

THE GREATEST MAN OF THE AGE

J. B. Murray, a young Australian, came to the United States in 1926. He spent the next 11 years working in California orchards, oil fields, and ranches. When Franklin Roosevelt was nominated for the presidency in 1932, Murray became an eager observer of American politics.

*"*F*or myself,"* he later wrote in a book about his travels titled American Trails, *"I believed in Roosevelt completely, and became engrossed with his campaign. He travelled to distant cities, and into the farming country, and wherever he went left hope behind him. The man's charm of manner and quiet confidence and strength were irresistible."* Murray noted that Roosevelt's *"personality flooded the countryside like warm sunshine. . . . The country listened spellbound to [his] clear, confident voice, which assured all that a new era was commencing."* Murray concluded, *"Listening to his radio talks, I had already marked him down as the greatest man of the age."*

THROUGH OTHERS' EYES

Corporation (FDIC) in June 1933. This reform insured each bank deposit up to $2,500. (Today, the figure is $100,000 per account.)

Roosevelt then turned his attention to the plight of the farmers. On March 28 he issued an executive order to create the **Farm Credit Administration**, to provide low-interest, long-term loans to farmers. Congress obliged, and with these loans, farmers paid off mortgages and overdue taxes, bought back lost farms, and purchased needed seed, fertilizer, and equipment. In April, Roosevelt asked Congress to create the **Home Owners Loan Corporation** (HOLC) to address the problem of home owners who could not meet their mortgage payments. Again, Congress obliged. By June 1936 the HOLC had saved the homes of some one million American families by granting them low-interest, long-term mortgage loans.

■■ **The bank holiday and FDIC restored public trust in banks, while the FCA and HOLC provided loans to farmers and home owners.**

---

which authorized the government to examine all banks and allow those that were financially sound to reopen. Roosevelt hoped that the act would restore public confidence in the banking system.

Caught without cash, Americans scrambled to find substitutes for it during the bank holiday. Many used subway and bus tokens, postage stamps, and IOUs. On Sunday evening, March 12, some 60 million anxious Americans tuned in their radios to hear the president explain how the bank holiday would protect their money. In this first of many "fireside chats"—radio broadcasts from the White House—Roosevelt urged people to reinvest in banks. "I can assure you that it is safer to keep your money in a reopened bank than under the mattress," he advised.

The next morning, as banks began reopening, more than $1 billion in deposits flowed into the system. Confidence in banks increased still more when Congress created the **Federal Deposit Insurance**

*R*ELIEF FOR THE NEEDY

Along with these measures the Roosevelt administration also launched a large-scale program of direct relief to the nation's 13 million unemployed. In many ways Roosevelt's direct-relief program completed the agenda that reformers had been trying to get the government to support since the Progressive Era. Through the efforts of Eleanor Roosevelt and Democratic National Committee member Molly Dewson, the president brought in many long-time reformers to direct his programs, including Secretary of Labor Frances Perkins.

In May 1933, at Roosevelt's request, Congress established the **Federal Emergency Relief Administration** (FERA) with half a billion dollars for relief aid to be funneled directly to state and local agencies. One of FDR's most trusted advisers, Harry L. Hopkins, headed the FERA program.

Have students explain what leadership qualities FDR had that Murray admired. Then ask students why such qualities were especially useful in the midst of the depression.

PRIMARY SOURCE
Description of Change: excerpted and bracketed
Rationale: excerpted to focus on main idea; bracketed to clarify meaning

 **GLOBAL CONNECTIONS**

Bank failures in the U.S. were followed by bank failures abroad. Europe's flagging economy sank even further in May 1931 with the failure of Austria's largest private bank. Its collapse had a ripple effect throughout eastern Europe.

HISTORICAL SIDELIGHTS
Fireside Chats
During his 12 years as president, FDR gave 30 fireside chats. All began with the greeting "My friends . . ." and were presented in a way that seemed both personal and caring. One historian has said that FDR was like "a father talking about public affairs while sitting with his family in the living room."

ᴦeaching the Section

RELIEF FOR THE UNEMPLOYED

Call on volunteers to briefly outline the purposes of the FERA, CWA, and CCC and to explain why each was considered a relief program. Then organize students into three groups and assign to each group one of the programs listed above. Have each group prepare a press release that explains to prospective recipients how they can partici-pate in the program and how they will ben-efit. Have groups present their press releas-es to the class. Encourage other members of the class to act as reporters and ask the pre-senters questions about their programs.

HISTORICAL SIDELIGHTS

The CCC

CCC workers earned $30 a month in pay, $22 of which was automatically sent home to their families. Although workers took part in forest-fire prevention, mosquito control, and dam and road building, their pri-mary task was tree planting. Of all the trees planted in the first 175 years of the nation's history, more than half were planted by the CCC.

■■ In April 1938, 78 per-cent of the electorate ques-tioned in a Gallup Poll favored making the CCC a permanent part of govern-ment. Ask students how they feel about the value of such a program today.

THE AMERICAN NATION VIDEODISC PROGRAM

Serving the Nation

```
2A    20156    2:54
```

A Washington newspaper reported the eagerness of the FERA director to get relief to the needy:

> 66 The half-billion dollars for direct relief of States won't last a month if Harry L. Hopkins, the new relief administrator, main-tains the pace he set yesterday in disbursing more than $5,000,000 during his first two hours in office. 99

By 1935 the total of such direct federal relief aid had risen to some $3 billion. At one point nearly eight million American families were surviving on public assistance.

Americans, however, disliked this kind of aid. They wanted jobs, not handouts. So Hopkins orga-nized the **Civil Works Administration** (CWA) to create jobs. Most of these were "make-work" pro-jects such as raking leaves and picking up park litter. From 1933 to 1934, the CWA paid some $750 mil-lion in wages to some four million men and women.

To aid unemployed young men between ages 18 and 25, Congress established the **Civilian Conservation Corps** (CCC) in 1933. Initially, some 250,000 young men left their homes and went to army camps for CCC training. Once trained, they spread out into the nation's forests, where they planted trees, cleared underbrush, laid out park trails, and developed campgrounds and beaches. For their efforts they earned a dollar a day. Most of their

earnings were sent back home to help their families. Said one CCC veteran of the experience:

> 66 I really enjoyed it. I had three wonderful square meals a day. . . . They sure made a man out of ya, because you learned that every-body here was equal. There was nobody bet-ter than another in the CCC's. 99

During its nearly 10-year life, the CCC enrolled more than 2.5 million young men and planted millions of trees, most in the South and the Southwest. The program earned back much of its cost in the value it added to the nation's forests.

■■ **Through the FERA, the CWA, and the CCC, the New Deal granted direct relief to the unemployed and created jobs.**

Hᴇʟᴘɪɴɢ THE NATION RECOVER

While New Deal relief programs aided needy Americans, the Roosevelt administration also pur-sued recovery programs to revive the economy. Roosevelt saw relief as a short-term remedy; recovery was his long-term goal.

To stimulate recovery in business and indus-try, the Roosevelt administration poured money into the economy through federal loans and gov-ernment spending—a process sometimes called "priming the pump." Many of the New Deal recovery programs were based on the theories of noted economist John Maynard Keynes, who argued that for a nation to recover fully from a depression, the government had to spend money to create jobs and boost investment.

One of the chief ways in which the Roosevelt administration attempted to prime the economy's pump was through the **National Industrial Recovery Act** (NIRA), which Congress passed in June 1933. The act was designed to stimulate industrial and business activity and reduce unemployment by stabilizing prices, raising wages, limiting workers' hours, and providing jobs. To help achieve these goals,

◄ Some 2.5 million jobless young men were employed by the CCC from 1933 to 1943. During the decade they worked on projects designed to preserve and restore the nation's natural resources.

HELPING THE NATION RECOVER

Call on students to review the major recovery programs of the New Deal. Suggest that they note the recovery legislation passed by Congress, the agencies that were established as a result, and any criticisms that were leveled against the recovery programs. Then ask students to select a program and design a bumper sticker that supports or opposes that program. Ask volunteers to present and explain their bumper stickers to the class.

THE IMPACT OF THE TVA

Organize students into groups of five and have groups imagine they are the editorial board of a newspaper published in the Tennessee Valley. Have the boards draw up an editorial reply to critics of the Tennessee Valley Authority, pointing out how the program transformed social and economic life throughout the Tennessee River Valley. Have groups present and defend their editorials.

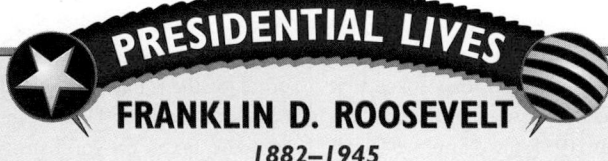

PRESIDENTIAL LIVES

FRANKLIN D. ROOSEVELT
1882–1945

in office
1933–1945

Franklin D. Roosevelt

"Mr. Roosevelt is a unique figure in the modern world: the one statesman . . . who seems able to relax," wrote one journalist about the charismatic leader. Indeed, FDR always appeared to be warm, energetic, and easygoing, despite the enormous pressures that faced his administration. His optimistic outlook may have helped in his recuperation from polio.

The president always hid his private thoughts behind his dazzling smile. One of his speech writers commented that one could never tell what was going on in FDR's "heavily forested interior." Yet, the president relied heavily on instinct and idealism in making decisions. Political ideology held little value for him. His warm style and compassionate manner, expressed in his weekly "fireside chats," helped win support for many of his programs. Years after the depression many Americans would remember FDR almost as a beloved family member.

---

the NIRA created two new federal agencies—the **Public Works Administration** (PWA) and the **National Recovery Administration** (NRA).

The PWA, under the leadership of Secretary of the Interior Harold Ickes, provided jobs and stimulated business activity by contracting with private firms to construct roads, public buildings, and other public-works projects. Between 1933 and 1939, the PWA spent more than $4 billion on some 34,000 projects.

The NIRA's other arm, the NRA, attempted to promote recovery by encouraging businesses to draw up "codes of fair competition." Under these codes, competing businesses agreed to work together to stabilize prices, wages, hours, and production levels. Businesses were able to do this because the NIRA had suspended antitrust laws. To help protect labor through this period of business self-regulation, Section 7(a) of the NIRA guaranteed workers the "right to organize and bargain collectively through representatives of their own choosing . . . free from the interference, restraint or coercion of employers."

Under the direction of former army general Hugh S. Johnson, the NRA began on a wave of popular enthusiasm. Parades of workers marched through cities displaying the NRA banner—a blue eagle clutching lightning bolts in its claw, with the slogan "We Do Our Part." Johnson compared the NRA to a fighting army:

> **66** This campaign is a frank dependence on the power and the willingness of the American people to act together as one person in an hour of great danger. . . . The Blue Eagle is a symbol of industrial solidarity and self-government. **99**

But enthusiasm soon faded. Businesses did not always obey the codes. Workers complained that the codes held their wages down, while consumers

▲ Roosevelt's approach to government was to recommend a new program, try it, and if it failed, then "admit it frankly and try another." His approach is satirized in this 1934 cartoon.

HISTORICAL SIDELIGHTS
The PWA

Major PWA projects included the Triborough Bridge and the Queens-Midtown Tunnel in New York City, the Golden Gate Bridge in San Francisco, and the Grand Coulee Dam in Washington state. Other PWA projects administered the building or restoration of about 5,900 school buildings, 13,000 playgrounds, 2,500 hospitals, and 1,000 airports.

HISTORICAL SIDELIGHTS
Opposition to the NRA

The most outspoken opponents of the NRA were the leaders of the larger industries. Henry Ford, for example, refused to have the "Roosevelt buzzard [the Blue Eagle emblem] on my cars."

PRIMARY SOURCE
Description of Change: excerpted
Rationale: excerpted to focus on main idea

Practice

GUIDED PRACTICE

Draw on the chalkboard a four-column chart with the headings *Measure, Why Needed, Who Benefited, Effects.* In the first column, list major New Deal legislation and agencies discussed in this section. Then help the class to complete the chart.

INDEPENDENT PRACTICE

Have students choose one of the New Deal programs listed in the chart developed in the Guided Practice activity. Ask them to write letters to President Roosevelt from the viewpoint of a person affected by that program, explaining the impact it has had on his or her life. Students may wish to include their letters in their portfolios.

Review and Assessment

REVIEW Have students work in pairs to list and classify each New Deal program in this section as a relief or a recovery program. Have each group identify the relief program and the recovery program that it thinks had the greatest impact on people's lives and explain its choices. Then assign the Section 1 Review on p. 699.

ASSESS Assign the **Section 1 Daily Quiz** in *Core Resources.*

HISTORICAL SIDELIGHTS

A Diverse Organization

The STFU was unusual in its ability to bring together people of various backgrounds. In addition to attracting both black and white farmers, the movement was aided by radical farm labor organizers and fundamentalist members who used religious songs and imagery to inspire the group. African Americans A. B. Brookins and John Handcock, for instance, transformed the gospel tune "We Shall Not Be Moved" into an STFU protest song.

MAKING CONNECTIONS

Geography

When it was completed, the TVA operated a system of dams draining an area of some 40,000 square miles. The dams transformed the Tennessee River into a waterway some 300 feet wide, navigable by large ships for about 650 miles from Knoxville, Tennessee, to Paducah, Kentucky.

Map Caption Answer

Tennessee, Alabama, Kentucky, Mississippi border

---

complained that the codes pushed prices up. As people lost confidence in the NRA, they joked that it stood for "National Run Around" and "No Recovery Allowed." In 1935 the Supreme Court declared the NIRA (and the NRA) unconstitutional.

AGRICULTURAL RECOVERY

To raise farm prices and increase farmers' purchasing power, Roosevelt proposed that farmers cut production. Congress passed the **Agricultural Adjustment Act** (AAA) in May 1933, which established the Agricultural Adjustment Administration (AAA). The AAA paid farmers to reduce their output of cotton, wheat, corn, hogs, rice, tobacco, dairy products, and other commodities. The money for these payments, or **subsidies**, came from taxes levied on food processors, including meat packers, canners, and flour millers.

In one year the plan reduced the cotton crop by more than three million bales, raising cotton prices. Such increased income gave cotton growers and large-scale farmers more cash to spend, thus stimulating overall economic recovery. New Deal supporters pointed to these favorable results as proof of the value of sound federal planning. But critics of the New Deal farm program pointed out that the taxes on food processors were passed along to consumers in the form of higher prices. Thus, while farmers' incomes rose, the purchasing power of city dwellers declined.

Critics also charged that farmers with large land-holdings benefited far more from the AAA than did small farmers. Often when large landowners cut production, they forced sharecroppers off their land and kept all of the government payments for themselves. Thus, the poorest farmers were forced into deeper poverty. In response, a group of Arkansas sharecroppers, both black and white, formed the **Southern Tenant Farmers' Union** (STFU) in 1934. The union lobbied the government to halt tenant evictions and to force landowners to share payments with the farmers who rented land. Within one year the STFU had grown to more than 10,000 members.

Early in 1936, the Supreme Court struck down the AAA on the grounds that the processing tax was unconstitutional. This decision, like its ruling against the NIRA and NRA, reflected

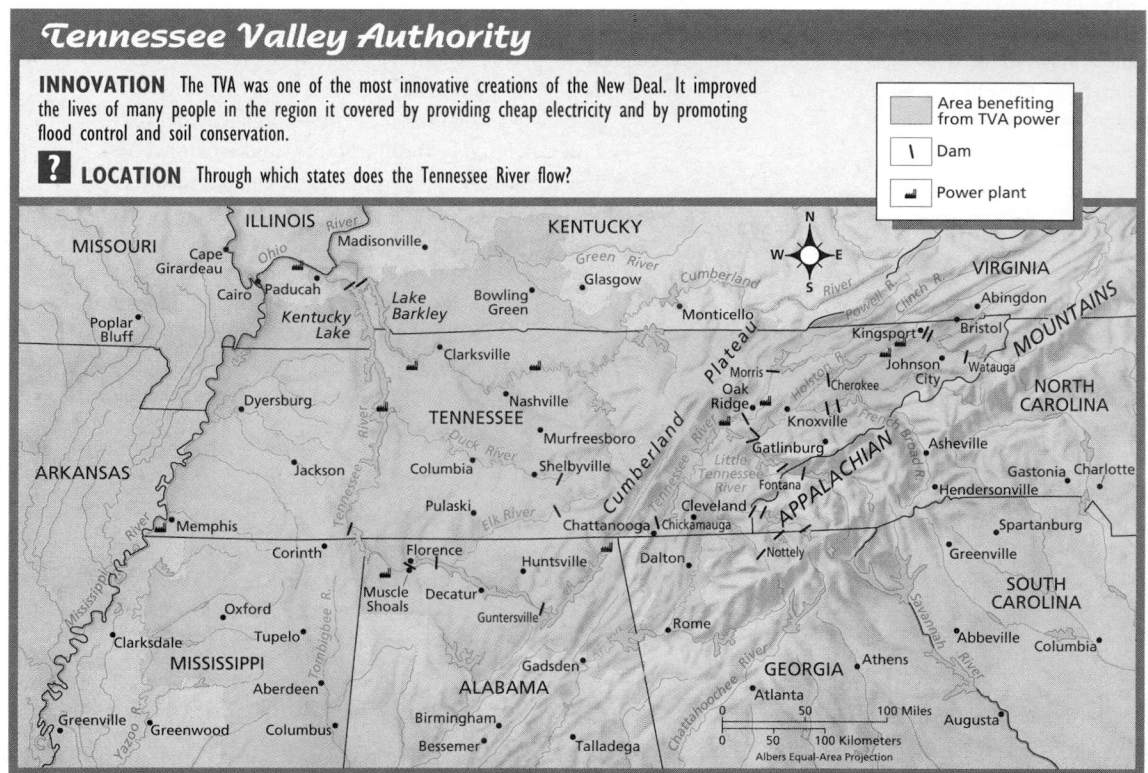

Tennessee Valley Authority

INNOVATION The TVA was one of the most innovative creations of the New Deal. It improved the lives of many people in the region it covered by providing cheap electricity and by promoting flood control and soil conservation.

? LOCATION Through which states does the Tennessee River flow?

Legend:
- Area benefiting from TVA power
- \ Dam
- Power plant

the Supreme Court's opposition to growing government power.

■■ To stimulate economic recovery, Congress passed the NIRA to help business and industry and the AAA to aid agriculture.

REVITALIZING A REGION

The most monumental of all the early New Deal programs was the Tennessee Valley project, which sought to revitalize the seven-state region drained by the Tennessee River and its tributaries (see map on page 698). This rural area was scarred by over-cut forests and frequent flooding. Poverty, malnutrition, disease, and illiteracy plagued its two million residents.

The **Tennessee Valley Authority** (TVA), created in May 1933, transformed the economic and social life of the region. Under the guidance of David E. Lilienthal, the TVA built 38 dams and several power stations that provided electricity, flood control, and recreational facilities for the region. Other TVA projects combated malaria, illiteracy, and soil erosion and tried to improve the region's standard of living, which had barely changed since Reconstruction.

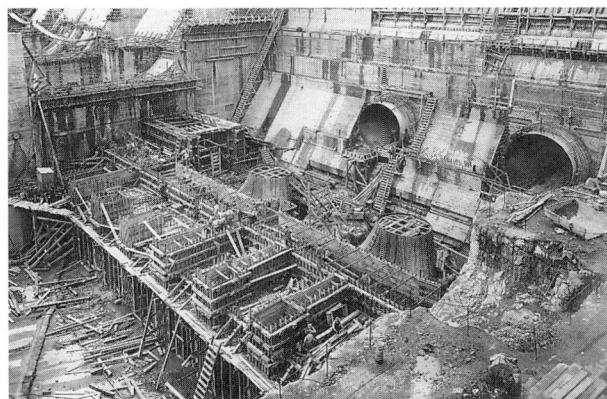

▲ The TVA's system of hydroelectric plants, dams, and navigation channels covers an area of some 41,000 square miles. Shown here is the construction of Norris Dam.

Critics denounced the TVA as overuse of government power. Shareholders in private utility companies, who feared it would cut into their dividends, brought several court cases against the TVA. The Supreme Court, however, refused to strike down the TVA. Probably the best known of the "alphabet soup" of programs created during Roosevelt's First Hundred Days, the TVA remains one of the New Deal's most enduring successes.

■■ The TVA transformed economic and social conditions throughout the Tennessee River Valley.

SECTION 1 REVIEW

IDENTIFY and explain the significance of the following: New Deal, bank holiday, Emergency Banking Act, Federal Deposit Insurance Corporation, Farm Credit Administration, Home Owners Loan Corporation, Frances Perkins, Federal Emergency Relief Administration, Harry L. Hopkins, Civil Works Administration, Civilian Conservation Corps, National Industrial Recovery Act, Public Works Administration, National Recovery Administration, Agricultural Adjustment Act, subsidies, Southern Tenant Farmers' Union, Tennessee Valley Authority.

LOCATE and explain the importance of the following: Tennessee River Valley.

1. **MAIN IDEA** How did the Roosevelt administration attempt to restore confidence in the banking system? What New Deal measures provided loans to farmers and home owners?

2. **MAIN IDEA** Which New Deal programs granted direct relief to the unemployed and created jobs? Which programs helped business, industry, and agriculture?

3. **GEOGRAPHY: REGION** Describe the physical characteristics of the Tennessee River Valley.

4. **WRITING TO INFORM** Imagine you are a resident of the Tennessee River Valley in 1935. Write a letter to a critic of the TVA, outlining the positive ways in which the TVA has transformed the region where you live.

5. **ANALYZING** How are the economic theories of John Maynard Keynes evident in the approach that the Roosevelt administration took toward reviving the economy?

FOCUS OBJECTIVES

- Identify the criticisms aimed at the New Deal.

- Explain what enabled Roosevelt to win reelection easily in 1936.

- Describe how Roosevelt tried to prevent the Supreme Court from overturning his programs.

- Analyze how the Second New Deal benefited labor and agriculture.

Section 2

NEW CHALLENGES

F O C U S

- **What criticisms were aimed at the New Deal?**
- **What enabled Roosevelt to win reelection easily in 1936?**
- **How did Roosevelt try to prevent the Supreme Court from overturning his programs?**
- **How did the Second New Deal benefit labor and agriculture?**

*Once the furious activity of the First Hundred Days ended,
the nation anxiously waited to see how well the New Deal
would work. Critics were quick to speak out. Rather than slowing the New Deal down, however, these critics made the
administration more determined to enact still another series of
innovative programs that created jobs, provided security for
older Americans, and improved labor and farming conditions.*

Townsend Plan sign near Weslaco, Texas

CRITICS OF THE NEW DEAL

Criticism of the New Deal came from both the left and the right of the political spectrum. Liberal and radical critics on the left argued that the New Deal was not going far enough in providing relief, recovery, and reform. Conservatives on the right charged that the New Deal was going too far—pushing government into areas where it had no right to interfere. Conservatives also worried about the heavy costs of the New Deal. Although FDR had campaigned for a balanced budget in 1932, the federal deficit rose from roughly $1.3 billion in 1933 to some $3.5 billion in 1936.

Most conservative complaints came from the American Liberty League, made up largely of Republican business interests and disenchanted Democrats led by Al Smith, who accused New Deal supporters of "irresponsible ravings against million-aires and big business." The League complained that the New Deal measures were destroying both the Constitution and free enterprise and would drive the nation into bankruptcy.

Among the others who opposed the New Deal was Dr. Francis E. Townsend of California. Townsend wanted the government to grant a pension of $200 a month to every American over 60 years old. All recipients were to spend the pensions within 30 days and thus pump money into the

▲ Huey Long

MOTIVATING: LINK TO TODAY

Have students name some programs promoted by the current U.S. president and identify ways opponents of these programs make their views known. *(newscasts, talk shows, editorials, voting or lobbying against a program in Congress)* Ask students to describe the ways the president today attempts to counteract such actions.

Teaching the Section

NEW DEAL CRITICS

Organize a portion of the class into four groups. Assign groups the following roles: American Liberty League, Huey Long supporters, conservative business interests and wealthy Americans, and Roosevelt administration officials. Have the first three groups list their criticisms of the New Deal, reasons for these criticisms, and their alternatives. Have groups give their lists to the Roosevelt group to prepare responses. Then choose a moderator from the class and have all groups select a spokesperson to participate in a radio "Crossfire" debate on the merits of the New Deal. After the debate, the class can decide which group most persuasively argued its position.

---

economy. Father Charles E. Coughlin, the "radio priest," broadcast a similar message from his pulpit in Michigan. He urged the government to nationalize all banks and return to the silver standard.

Huey Long, "the Kingfish," a colorful but corrupt senator from Louisiana, probably had the most radical plan. Like Robin Hood, Long wanted to take from the rich and give to the poor. He claimed that he had done just that as governor of Louisiana, when he had helped the poor by building public housing, roads, and schools and by providing free textbooks to students. Actually, he had financed his state's public-works projects not by taking from the rich, but by imposing higher taxes on everyone—including the poor. In addition, Long and his friends had often profited personally from the projects.

In 1933 Senator Long proposed a radical new kind of relief program, which he called **Share-Our-Wealth**. The program would empower the government to confiscate wealth from the rich through taxes and then provide a guaranteed minimum income and a home to every American family. Long even had his own theme song:

> 66 Ev'ry man a king, ev'ry man a king,
> For you can be a millionaire,
> There's enough for all people to share.
> When it's sunny June and December too,
> Or in the wintertime or spring:
> There'll be peace without end,
> Ev'ry neighbor a friend,
> With ev'ry man a king. 99

In spite of Long's reputation for corruption, the Share-Our-Wealth program drew a great deal of popular support. Some critics suspected that Long harbored dreams of becoming a dictator. Such fears led the Communist party and the Socialist party to denounce Long even though his program promised to redistribute wealth. Bolstered by popular support, Long soon threatened to challenge Roosevelt as a third-party candidate in the 1936 election. But both this threat and the Share-Our-Wealth program died when an assassin killed Long in 1935.

■■ Some critics accused the New Deal of pushing government power too far, while others wanted to expand it further.

THE SECOND NEW DEAL

In the midterm elections of 1934, the Democrats picked up more seats in Congress. The victory, coupled with pressure from the left, encouraged New Deal planners to initiate more public-works programs, a social security plan, and wage and hour improvements for laborers. This series of programs would eventually come to be called the **Second New Deal**. While still providing relief and pursuing recovery, the Second New Deal would increasingly emphasize reform.

The Works Progress Administration. A works program, the **Works Progress Administration** (WPA), began in April 1935 under the direction of Harry Hopkins. The CWA had ended the previous year, yet unemployment was still high. Millions of American families remained on relief rolls. To create jobs for them, Congress allotted $5 billion for the WPA.

Over the eight years of its life, the WPA employed an estimated 14 million people, with about 2 million working for it at any given time. Workers engaged in a variety of tasks. Male blue-collar workers built or rebuilt a total of some 350 airports, more than 100,000 public buildings, some 78,000 bridges, and about 500,000 miles of roads. White-collar workers took on research projects and teaching jobs. The WPA had a special division for women, but the program often discriminated against women by paying them lower wages than men. On most projects male workers received $5 a day while female workers received only $3 for the same job.

▼ The WPA employed many women, such as this weaver from Kansas, in a variety of jobs.

HISTORICAL SIDELIGHTS

Townsend and Coughlin Townsend was an elderly California doctor whose organization, Old-Age Revolving Pensions, Ltd., had a membership of more than 500,000 by 1935. Radio priest Father Coughlin reached an estimated audience of 10 million weekly. Despite their popularity, neither Townsend nor Coughlin made a significant impact on national public policy. Most observers dismissed the Townsend plan as unfeasible. And Coughlin's following began to dwindle as his sermons became increasingly anti-Semitic in the late 1930s.

PRIMARY SOURCE

Description of Change: excerpted
Rationale: excerpted to focus on main idea

MAKING CONNECTIONS

Literature Robert Penn Warren's Pulitzer Prize–winning novel *All the King's Men* (1946) was loosely based on the life and career of Huey Long.

Teaching the Section

THE SECOND NEW DEAL

Encourage students to imagine they are New Deal planners. Have them write a report, for presentation to President Roosevelt, indicating why a Second New Deal is necessary, outlining the problems the country still faces, and the steps they intend to take to solve these problems. Call on volunteers to read their reports to the class. Students may wish to include their reports in their portfolios.

The WPA tried to help struggling young people between the ages of 16 and 25 by establishing the **National Youth Administration** (NYA), a "junior WPA." The NYA gave young people part-time jobs that provided money to help them stay in school. Within a year the NYA was providing aid to half a million people.

Social Security. Another cornerstone of the Second New Deal was the **Social Security Act**, which Congress passed in August 1935. The act contained three major provisions. First, it provided unemployment insurance for workers who lost their jobs. The funds for this insurance came from a payroll tax on businesses. Second, the act provided pensions for retired workers over age 65. The money for these pensions came from two sources—a payroll tax on employers and a tax on employees' wages. Third, in a shared federal-state program, the act provided payments to the blind, disabled, and elderly and to wives and children of male workers who had died.

At first the Social Security Act covered only a limited segment of the work force. Farmers and the self-employed were excluded, as well as domestic workers, some 60 percent of whom were African American women. Coverage broadened over the years, however, and the Social Security Act became the model for a wide range of public social welfare programs.

Other programs. Underlying Roosevelt's Second New Deal was the president's belief that the government had not yet "weeded out the overprivileged and . . . effectively lifted up the underprivileged." To help the underprivileged, Roosevelt issued an executive order in May 1935 establishing the **Rural Electrification Administration** (REA). The REA extended power lines into isolated rural areas. Within a few years, only 1 farm in 10 lacked electricity.

Roosevelt also went after public utility companies. He charged that many of them were able to set higher prices than their costs justified—and thus make excessive profits—because they held monopolies over gas and electricity. To reform this system, Congress passed a law giving the government the right to regulate interstate production, transmission, and sale of gas and electricity.

Roosevelt also went after the rich, declaring that tax laws had not done enough "to prevent an unjust concentration of wealth and economic

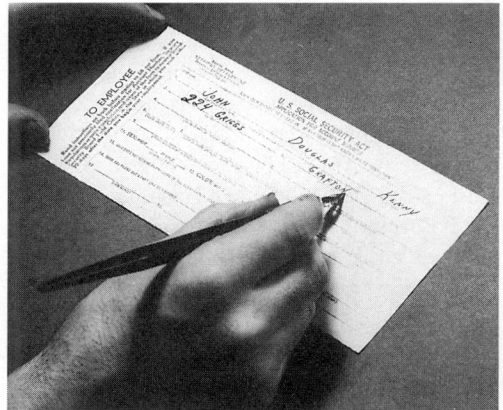

▲ **The Social Security Act marked an unprecedented step in providing relief to the unemployed and elderly. In this photograph, a man named John Kenny fills out one of the first applications for a social security number.**

power." In response, Congress passed the Revenue Act of 1935. Often referred to as the **Wealth Tax Act**, it sharply increased taxes on the nation's richest people. Corporations had to pay an "excess profits" tax if they made an annual profit greater than 10 percent. A year later, Congress increased corporate taxes again. Business complained bitterly that the tax increase discouraged business expansion.

*T*HE ELECTION OF 1936

By 1936 the depression still lingered. Some 9 million workers lacked regular jobs, and 3.5 million remained on the WPA or the CCC rolls. Many factories remained closed or operated at far less than full capacity. Still, America had made some progress. Since 1932 the national income had jumped from roughly $43 billion to more than $80 billion and unemployment had dropped by nearly three million.

In June 1936 the Democrats enthusiastically nominated Roosevelt for a second term. Labor unions, farmers, those on relief, and even many Republicans also endorsed him. For the first time since Reconstruction, most African Americans living in the North abandoned their traditional ties to the Republican party—"the party of Lincoln"—to support the Democrats. The Republicans nominated the capable but unexciting governor of Kansas, Alfred M. Landon. The Republican platform condemned the New Deal,

ROOSEVELT REELECTED

Have students work in pairs to prepare an interview between a reporter and President Roosevelt in which the president explains what enabled him to win reelection in 1936. Select pairs to conduct their interviews for the class.

▶

NEW DEAL PROGRAMS

Year	First New Deal	Provisions
1933	Emergency Banking Act	Gave administration right to regulate banks.
1933	Farm Credit Administration (FCA)	Extended loans to farm owners to refinance loans.
1933	Economy Act	Aimed at balancing the budget.
1933	Civilian Conservation Corps (CCC)	Employed young men on public-works projects.
1933	Federal Emergency Relief Administration (FERA)	Provided relief to the needy.
1933	Agricultural Adjustment Act of 1933 (AAA)	Paid farmers to reduce crops; funded by processing tax later declared unconstitutional.
1933	Tennessee Valley Authority (TVA)	Constructed dam and power projects to improve Tennessee Valley Region.
1933	Home Owners Loan Corporation (HOLC)	Loaned money to home owners to refinance mortgages.
1933	Banking Act of 1933	Created FDIC and prohibited banks from selling stock or financing corporations.
1933	Federal Deposit Insurance Corporation (FDIC)	Insured deposits in individual bank accounts.
1933	National Industrial Recovery Act (NIRA)	Established NRA and a series of fair-competition codes for businesses.
1933	National Recovery Administration (NRA)	Regulated industry and raised wages and prices.
1933	Public Works Administration (PWA)	Set up public-works projects to increase employment and business activity.
1933	Civil Works Administration (CWA)	Provided federal jobs to the unemployed.
1934	Securities and Exchange Commission	Regulated securities market.
1934	Federal Housing Administration (FHA)	Insured bank loans for building and repairing homes.

Year	Second New Deal	Provisions
1935	Works Progress Administration (WPA)	Employed people to do public works, research, and artistic projects.
1935	Soil Conservation Service	Promoted control and prevention of soil erosion.
1935	Rural Electrification Administration (REA)	Provided electricity to rural areas lacking public utilities.
1935	National Youth Administration (NYA)	Provided job training and part-time jobs to students.
1935	National Labor Relations Act (Wagner-Connery Act)	Recognized rights of labor to organize and bargain collectively; regulated labor practices.
1935	Social Security Act	Provided unemployment benefits, pensions for the elderly, and survivor's insurance.
1935	Revenue Act of 1935 (Wealth Tax Act)	Increased taxes on the wealthy.
1937	Farm Security Administration (FSA)	Provided loans to help tenant farmers buy land.
1938	Agricultural Adjustment Act of 1938 (AAA)	Increased government regulation of crop production and payments to farmers.
1938	Revenue Act of 1938	Increased taxes on wealthy businesses.
1938	Fair Labor Standards Act	Established minimum wage of 40 cents per hour and maximum work week of 40 hours for businesses in interstate commerce.

Source: *Encyclopedia of American History*

RELIEF, RECOVERY, AND REFORM Franklin Roosevelt proposed a wide number of programs to aid in the nation's recovery after he assumed office in 1933. These programs became the First New Deal. Two years later he outlined a broader program of social reform in the Second New Deal.

? **BUILDING GRAPH SKILLS** Which New Deal programs were aimed primarily at helping farmers?

𝒯eaching the 𝒮ection

ROOSEVELT AND THE SUPREME COURT

Have students work in groups and imagine they are newspaper editors in 1937 shortly after Roosevelt asked Congress to grant him the power to appoint additional Supreme Court justices. Have each group prepare an editorial, accompanied by an editorial cartoon, expressing an opinion on Roosevelt's attempt to "pack" the Court.

■■ Have students speculate how the U.S. legal system might be different today if Roosevelt had won his battle to pack the Court and how the American public would react to such a proposal from the president today.

but called for few specific changes in New Deal programs. The Republicans did promise to balance the budget and to reduce federal power by returning more power to the states.

Roosevelt's opponents—mainly business interests upset by new regulations and corporate taxes, conservative newspaper editors, and rich Americans angered by high taxes—renewed their charges that Roosevelt ignored the Constitution. They pointed out that the Supreme Court had overturned the NRA, AAA, and five other key New Deal measures. American individualism, free enterprise, and private property, they insisted, were being abandoned for socialism. Some even charged falsely that the Social Security Act would require everyone to wear metal dog tags!

President Roosevelt entered the fight with great zest. In accepting renomination, he pledged to stay on the course the New Deal had set. He won a smashing victory—with some 28 million popular votes to Landon's 17 million. Roosevelt carried every state but Maine and Vermont—the most lopsided victory in more than a century. The Democrats increased their majorities in both houses of Congress. The coalition that Democrats forged in the election—farmers, southern whites, city dwellers, industrial workers, and northern blacks—would hold together for many elections to come.

■■ **The Democrats, forging a powerful coalition of groups who benefited from the New Deal, easily reelected Roosevelt in 1936.**

𝐑OOSEVELT AND THE SUPREME COURT

Flushed with his triumph and convinced of the power that a solidly Democratic Congress gave him, Roosevelt moved to "reform" the Supreme Court. Angered that the Court had declared several New Deal measures unconstitutional, Roosevelt called attention to the ages of the justices, labeling them "Nine Old Men" (six were 70 or older), and accused them of being stuck in the "horse and buggy" days in their thinking.

In February 1937, two weeks after his second inauguration, Roosevelt asked Congress to grant him the power to appoint one new justice for each of those 70 or older, up to six new justices. The Supreme Court needed "a persistent infusion of new blood," he argued. Roosevelt's proposal triggered a storm of protest across the nation. Critics—Democrats as well as Republicans—charged that this unprecedented "court-packing" would tamper with the delicate balance of legislative, executive, and judicial powers. Dorothy Thompson, a popular political columnist, denounced Roosevelt's scheme as a move toward dictatorship:

❝ If the American people accept this last audacity of the President without letting out a yell to high heaven, they have ceased to be jealous of their liberties and are ripe for ruin. This is the beginning of a pure personal government. ❞

▶ The negative attitude that many members of the Supreme Court had toward New Deal reforms is satirized in the cartoon *Nine Old Men.*

Congress resoundingly denied Roosevelt's request. But this was just one battle in a war that FDR would eventually win. The Supreme Court soon upheld the Social Security Act and the National Labor Relations Act. Many Americans concluded that the justices had decided to become more agreeable to prevent a drastic reform of the Court itself. "A switch in time saves nine," people joked. Over the next four years, seven justices died or retired and were replaced by Roosevelt appointees. By 1945 eight of the nine justices were Roosevelt appointees.

■■ Roosevelt tried to "pack" the Supreme Court with six new members in order to protect his New Deal programs.

▲ As unions became better organized and membership grew, the number of strikes increased. A 1937 sit-down strike is shown above. Workers for a New York City vending company (right) also went on strike later that same year.

ᴛHE SECOND NEW DEAL AND LABOR

When the Supreme Court declared the NIRA unconstitutional in May 1935, it struck down Section 7(a), which protected the rights of labor unions. Two months later, however, Congress passed the National Labor Relations Act, also called the **Wagner-Connery Act**, to guarantee labor's right to organize unions and to bargain for better wages and working conditions.

The American Federation of Labor (AFL) continued its efforts to organize workers, including those in such mass-production industries as steel and automobiles. But the AFL did not move fast enough to please gruff, shaggy-browed John L. Lewis, the intimidating leader of the United Mine Workers union. In 1935 Lewis and several other like-minded labor leaders organized the **Congress of Industrial Organizations** (CIO), which tried to unite workers in various industries.

The new CIO unions included all workers, skilled and unskilled, in a given industry. For example, the United Auto Workers (UAW) represented all workers in automotive plants.

Previously, different AFL craft unions had represented different types of autoworkers, such as electricians, welders, or metalworkers. Now all auto workers negotiated as a single powerful union. And in contrast to many AFL branches, the CIO welcomed African American, immigrant, and female members.

The organizing efforts of both the AFL and the CIO resulted in a wave of strikes. One of the most bitter strikes was waged against General Motors (GM) in the winter of 1936–37. The UAW had been trying to unionize GM factories, but the company had been fighting the union's efforts. Meanwhile, GM workers were growing increasingly frustrated with frequent layoffs, abuses of power by management, and work speedups. On December 31, 1936, this frustration led to a **sit-down strike**.

Instead of leaving the automotive plants, workers occupied the factories and pledged to remain until management met their demands. Wives, daughters, and female workers formed the Women's Auxiliary and the Women's Emergency

Practice

GUIDED PRACTICE

Make a four-column chart on the Second New Deal. Label the columns *Measures, Goals, Who Benefited, Criticisms.* Have volunteers complete the chart. Then ask students which of these measures they think had the most long-lasting effects.

INDEPENDENT PRACTICE

Have students select one of the Second New Deal programs from the chart developed in the Guided Practice activity. Then ask them to compose lyrics to a song or rap that illustrate the benefits or criticisms of their selected program. Students may wish to include their work in their portfolios.

Review and Assessment

REVIEW Have pairs of students write two or three sentences identifying groups who might have supported each of these New Deal programs and explaining why critics might have opposed them: WPA/NYA, Social Security Act, Wealth Tax Act, Wagner-Connery Act, second AAA. Then assign the Section 2 Review on p. 707.

ASSESS Assign the **Section 2 Daily Quiz** in *Core Resources.*

MAKING CONNECTIONS

Economics

The sit-down strike had two advantages over other tactics. It prevented owners from replacing strikers with newly hired workers. Owners also delayed taking violent actions against sit-down strikers for fear the attacks might result in damage to their buildings.

PRIMARY SOURCE

Description of Change: excerpted
Rationale: excerpted to focus on main idea

HISTORICAL SIDELIGHTS

FSA Avoids Discrimination

Because FSA leader Will Alexander insisted that no discrimination exist in the treatment of applicants for the loans made by the agency, thousands of African Americans were able to own farms for the first time.

🌐 GLOBAL CONNECTIONS

FDR also had his admirers abroad. British political scientist Harold Laski said of the New Deal: "Success or failure, it bears . . . the hallmarks of great leadership. Improvised in haste, devised under the grim pressure of crisis. . . . It stands out in remarkable . . . contrast to the economic policy of any other capitalist government in the world."

Brigade to picket outside the plants in support of the union. Many women felt their lives were changed by this experience. They soon took up the cause of equal pay for men and women in the auto industry. Said one female activist:

> 66 I'm living for the first time with a definite goal. . . . Just being a woman isn't enough anymore. I want to be a human being with the right to think for myself. 99

Finally, after six weeks, General Motors gave in and granted the UAW the right to organize GM workers. Within eight months the UAW membership grew to some 400,000. Owing in part to the Wagner-Connery Act, total union membership shot up from about 4 million in 1936 to some 9 million in 1939.

■■ **The Wagner-Connery Act guaranteed the rights of labor, increasing union membership and activity.**

THE SECOND NEW DEAL AND FARMERS

The Second New Deal also brought relief for farmers. When the Supreme Court struck down the Agricultural Adjustment Act in January 1936, Congress created another program to replace it. Like the AAA, the new program aimed to keep farm prices high by cutting crop production. To avoid opposition from the Supreme Court, however, Congress combined crop reduction with a soil conservation plan—a legitimate governmental activity.

The Second New Deal also sought to help tenant farmers, sharecroppers, and migrant farm workers. The rise of the Southern Tenant Farmers' Union had brought a backlash of violence against sharecroppers by landowners and authorities in the South, forcing some union members to conduct their activities in secrecy. Then in 1936 the union organized

▶ These members of the Southern Tenant Farmers' Union are shown attending a union meeting. Both African Americans and European Americans belonged to the STFU.

▲ The depression left many African Americans struggling to find work. This photograph shows people from Memphis, Tennessee, being transported to Arkansas for a day's work in the cotton fields.

a series of strikes by cotton pickers in five states. In 1937 Congress created the **Farm Security Administration** (FSA) to make low-interest, long-term loans to tenant farmers and sharecroppers to buy farms. The FSA also established camps where migrant farm workers could find shelter and medical care.

The Roosevelt administration recognized that the soil conservation program did not do enough to limit farm production. So in 1938 Congress passed a second Agricultural Adjustment Act. The government continued to pay farmers to withdraw land from production and to practice conservation, but it also authorized the Department of Agriculture to limit the amount of specific crops that could be brought to market each year. When harvests exceeded these limits, the government stored the surpluses until prices rose. Farmers cooperating in this program could get government loans based on the value of their stored crops.

RETEACH Organize students so that approximately the same number are assigned to each subsection of the section. Direct each student to write a question about the material in his or her assigned subsection. Then use the questions to quiz the entire group.

Closure

Write the following statement by FDR on the chalkboard: *"Government has a final responsibility for the well-being of its citizenship. If private cooperative endeavor fails to provide work for willing hands and relief for the unfortunate . . . government . . . must make fitting response."* Have students explain how FDR, in the Second New Deal, carried out the views expressed in this statement.

Extension

CONTRAST Have students contrast the lives and views of Huey Long and Dr. Francis E. Townsend and identify examples of how some of their views were reflected in New Deal programs.

INTERPRET Have students read three historians' views of FDR's plan to reorganize the Supreme Court and write an essay titled "FDR's Court Packing: Major Mistake or Calculated Risk That Paid Off?"

All in all, New Deal agricultural policy compiled a mixed record. Farm income did rise from 1933 to 1937, but critics pointed out that higher farm prices not only hurt consumers but also caused American farm products to lose out in highly competitive foreign markets. Critics also complained about the large cost of farm subsidies. But the farm legislation of the 1930s had some successes. It helped many farmers escape economic disaster, saved homes, and increased the fertility of millions of acres of land through conservation programs.

■■ **The Second New Deal increased farm income; aided tenant farmers, sharecroppers and migrant workers; and encouraged soil conservation.**

*B*USINESS SLUMP, POLITICAL SETBACKS

During 1936 and early 1937, the economy seemed to be improving, but in August 1937 it again plunged downward. Stung by criticism of excessive government spending, Roosevelt had begun cutting back on New Deal relief and public-works programs in 1936. Unfortunately, private industry was not yet strong enough to employ those dropped from government rolls because of the cutbacks. In addition, withholding Social Security taxes from workers' paychecks further reduced the flow of money into the economy. By the autumn of 1937, factories were closing and unemployment was rising. Republicans called this period of economic activity "Roosevelt's recession."

President Roosevelt and Congress again primed the economic pump by increasing government lending and spending. The Reconstruction Finance Corporation rescued troubled businesses. The Works Progress Administration quickly doubled the number of workers on its payroll from some 1.5 million to about 3 million. By the fall of 1938, unemployment had declined and industrial production had increased.

As the 1938 midterm elections drew near, Roosevelt decided to reenergize the New Deal (and to punish Democrats who had voted against his Supreme Court reform plan) by opposing conservative Democrats in Congress who did not support the Second New Deal. He actually urged voters to turn these Democrats out of office!

Just as his "court-packing" scheme had backfired, however, so did his attempt to "purge" the Democratic party. All but one member of Congress whom Roosevelt opposed won reelection. Moreover, voters elected still more Democrats who opposed New Deal programs. Adding to Roosevelt's dismay, the Republicans gained 7 seats in the Senate and 80 in the House. Though the Democrats still maintained majorities in both houses of Congress, their margin was much narrower. Faced with increasing criticism from all sides, FDR decided not to propose any new reforms in 1939, marking an end to the New Deal era.

SECTION REVIEW ANSWERS

IDENTIFY

For significance, see the following pages:
Francis E. Townsend (p. 700)
Charles E. Coughlin (p. 701)
Huey Long (p. 701)
Share-Our-Wealth (p. 701)
Second New Deal (p. 701)
WPA (p. 701)
NYA (p. 702)
Social Security Act (p. 702)
REA (p. 702)
Wealth Tax Act (p. 702)
Alfred M. Landon (p. 702)
Wagner-Connery Act (p. 705)
CIO (p. 705)
sit-down strike (p. 705)
FSA (p. 706)

1. *Conservatives claimed that it took government power too far; liberals claimed that it did not go far enough in providing relief, recovery, and reform.*
2. *guaranteed rights of labor; increased farm income, aided farm workers, encouraged soil conservation*
3. *to protect his New Deal programs*
4. *Pamphlets should be aimed at farmers, southern whites, city dwellers, industrial workers, and northern blacks and should outline benefits of the New Deal.*
5. *Those who criticized the New Deal for not providing enough relief revealed liberal values of the left; those who criticized it as ruining the free-enterprise system revealed conservative values of the right.*

■ **SECTION 2 REVIEW**

IDENTIFY and explain the significance of the following: Francis E. Townsend, Charles E. Coughlin, Huey Long, Share-Our-Wealth, Second New Deal, Works Progress Administration, National Youth Administration, Social Security Act, Rural Electrification Administration, Wealth Tax Act, Alfred M. Landon, Wagner-Connery Act, Congress of Industrial Organizations, sit-down strike, Farm Security Administration.

1. **MAIN IDEA** What charges did some critics level against the New Deal?
2. **MAIN IDEA** How did the Wagner-Connery Act benefit labor? How did other Second New Deal programs benefit agriculture?
3. **MAIN IDEA** Why did Roosevelt try to "pack" the Supreme Court with six new members?
4. **WRITING TO EXPRESS A VIEWPOINT** Imagine you are a Democratic campaign worker during the 1936 election. Write a campaign pamphlet aimed at the "Roosevelt coalition," explaining why you think FDR should be reelected.
5. **IDENTIFYING VALUES** How did criticisms of the New Deal reveal the values held by the left and the right?

Following is a list of the significant people, places, and terms in this section. You may wish to use this list as a section preview.

People
■ Marian Anderson
■ Robert C. Weaver
■ Mary McLeod Bethune
■ Antonio Luhan
■ John Collier

■ Dorothea Lange

Places
■ Dust Bowl

Terms
■ American Indian Defense Association
■ Indian Reorganization Act
■ Okies

FOCUS OBJECTIVES

■ Explain how African Americans fared during the New Deal era.

■ Identify the gains Native Americans made during the 1930s.

■ Describe the effect the Dust Bowl had on the Southwest population.

THINKING CRITICALLY

Recognizing Prejudice
Ask students to explain how the responses of Harold Ickes and Eleanor Roosevelt to the DAR's treatment of Anderson helped fight prejudice. Suggest that students consider how the responses of these two prominent people might have influenced ordinary Americans or made it easier for others to stand up against bigotry.

THE AMERICAN NATION VIDEODISC PROGRAM

Marian Anderson

2A   38876   :32

Section 3

LIFE IN THE NEW DEAL ERA

F O C U S
■ **How did African Americans fare during the New Deal era?**
■ **What gains did Native Americans make during the 1930s?**
■ **What effect did the Dust Bowl have on the Southwest population?**

African Americans, Native Americans, Mexican Americans, and displaced farmers remained among the nation's poorest groups during the depression years. They faced not only economic hardship but also prejudice and hostility. The New Deal, however, did make some efforts to help these groups.

Thomas Hart Benton's *Ploughing It Under*, 1939

A STRUGGLE FOR AFRICAN AMERICANS

New Deal programs succeeded to a large degree in helping African Americans economically. Some programs, however, were tainted by discrimination. The FERA and later the WPA became the greatest sources of relief and work for African American males. Some 200,000 young black men flocked to the CCC, where they found work and training, though they were strictly segregated from whites. The TVA employed black workers, but they were not allowed to live in the model towns built by the TVA. NRA codes often set lower wages for blacks than for whites, a practice that led some African American leaders to call the NRA the "Negro Run Around" or "Negroes Ruined Again." Social Security also discriminated indirectly against African Americans since most were agricultural or domestic workers not eligible for benefits.

The discrimination evident in the programs was reflective of social attitudes. The depression increased racial tensions in the country, especially in the South. Twenty-four black people were lynched in 1933 alone. Fearing political backlash from the South, Roosevelt did little to support legislation that might bring civil equality for African Americans, such as a federal antilynching law sponsored by the NAACP. Eleanor Roosevelt, however, became a champion of racial justice. Black leaders often commented on Mrs. Roosevelt's unusual ability to understand the struggles of African Americans. "We [whites] are largely to blame" for poverty among the black community, she once said. It was her goal to see educational and economic opportunities open up for African Americans.

Interior Secretary Harold Ickes, a former president of the Chicago NAACP, also tried to respond to the concerns of African Americans. When the Daughters of the American Revolution (DAR) refused to let the gifted black concert singer Marian Anderson perform in their

Teaching the Section

A NEW DEAL FOR AFRICAN AMERICANS?

Have students work in groups to role-play a meeting of FDR's black cabinet. Direct groups to discuss the New Deal's positive and negative impact on African Americans. Have group representatives report the results of the discussions. Then have the class use these reports to write a memo to FDR about the inequalities and benefits of the New Deal programs for African Americans, and ways in which the programs might be improved.

■■ Ask students why the depression increased racial tensions and whether they think economic conditions affect race relations today.

▶

◀ When Marian Anderson (inset) was denied the use of concert facilities at Constitution Hall, she gave a free concert from the steps of the Lincoln Memorial on Easter Sunday, 1939.

Constitution Hall, both Ickes and Mrs. Roosevelt reacted strongly. Roosevelt resigned her longtime membership in the DAR, stating that "to remain as a member implies approval of that action." She and Ickes then arranged for Anderson to give a free concert at the Lincoln Memorial, which attracted an audience of some 75,000.

Long before this incident, Ickes had brought in several prominent African Americans to advise his department on racial matters, including Robert C. Weaver, the first African American to obtain a Ph.D. in economics from Harvard. Weaver was just one of many African Americans who received high-level government jobs during the New Deal era. FDR named more than 100 blacks to major departments of the federal government, more than any other president since Ulysses S. Grant. These appointees included a wide variety of experts, from legal scholars to educators, social workers, and newspaper editors.

A core group of African American government officials evolved into the Federal Council on Negro Affairs, which became known as the black cabinet or the black brain trust. According to Robert Weaver, their "common cause was to maximize the participation of blacks in all phases of the New Deal." They met weekly at the home of Mary McLeod Bethune, the dynamic director of the Division of Negro Affairs in the National Youth Administration.

BIO GRAPHY Mary McLeod Bethune's journey to prominence in Washington began in 1875 in Mayesville, South Carolina, where she was born the 15th of 17 children to farmers who had once been slaves. The young girl's chances for an education seemed slim, since the Mayesville school was for whites only. But with the aid of a Presbyterian mission school and a series of scholarships, she eventually attended the Moody Bible Institute in Chicago. Bethune originally intended to become a missionary in Africa but soon found her mission to be educating African American children. She once said of her decision:

❝ The drums of Africa still beat in my heart. They will not let me rest while there is a single Negro boy or girl without a chance to prove his [or her] worth. ❞

In 1904 she founded a primary school for black girls in Florida, which eventually evolved into Bethune-Cookman College, a four-year coeducational institution with a predominantly African American student body.

Bethune became involved with numerous African American groups, including the NAACP and the Urban League. In 1935 she helped unite all national organizations for African American women into the National Council of Negro Women. Through her work with this association, she became close friends with Eleanor Roosevelt, who insisted that Bethune be appointed to work with the NYA. Bethune fought hard, though not always successfully, to rid the NYA of

Mary McLeod Bethune

VOICES IN HISTORY

Arthur Mitchell became the nation's first black Democratic congressman in 1934. In a speech the following year he observed: "Mr. Roosevelt has appointed more Negroes to responsible governmental positions than the last three Republican administrations taken together. . . . I believe that under this administration the Negroes . . . have the best opportunity that has come to them during my lifetime."

PRIMARY SOURCE

Description of Change: excerpted and bracketed
Rationale: excerpted to focus on main idea; bracketed to clarify meaning

BIO GRAPHY **PERSONALITIES IN HISTORY**

In 1904 when Bethune started her school in a rented house in Daytona Beach, Florida, she had five students and almost no money. Three years later she moved the school to Faith Hall, a building constructed on land that had once been used as a town dump. By 1923 the school had 600 students and joined with the Methodist church's Cookman Institute to eventually become Bethune-Cookman College.

Teaching the Section

INDIAN REORGANIZATION ACT

Call on volunteers to review and summarize the Dawes General Allotment Act (see Chapter 14). Then ask the class to explain how the Indian Reorganization Act shifted the focus of the federal government's American Indian policy. Conclude by asking students to assume the role of Indians and write a letter to the editor on the problems they face in revitalizing their culture. Select students to read their letters to the class. Students may wish to include their letters in their portfolios.

■■ Have students report on the ways that American Indians today are reviving and celebrating their cultural heritage.

VOICES IN HISTORY

Critics of the Indian Reorganization Act like Rupert Costo, a Cahuilla, felt that it did not offer American Indians true self-government. He resented the fact that "any plans the Indians might have for . . . self-government would have to be first submitted to the interior secretary or commissioner of Indian affairs for supervision and approval." Sioux critic Ramon Roubideaux argued that "self-government by permission is no self-government at all."

---

racism. Although Bethune left government service after the NYA ended in 1944, she continued to work on behalf of civil rights and educational opportunities for young African Americans until her death in 1955.

■■ **African Americans gained economic assistance and a voice in government during the New Deal. But little progress was made toward ending discrimination.**

A NEW DEAL FOR AMERICAN INDIANS

As the New Deal era began, life for many American Indians was very bleak. A late 1920s report on Indian life across the country listed numerous problems that plagued their communities. Inadequate housing, poor health care, and malnutrition left many of the nation's more than 300,000 Indians easy prey for epidemics.

Native Americans argued that their culture had been stripped away by measures like the Dawes Act (see Chapter 14), which had ended tribal government and authorized the sale of tribal land to individuals. Antonio Luhan, a member of the Taos Pueblo in New Mexico, described how government policies and the Bureau of Indian Affairs commissioners who enforced them overwhelmed traditional Indian culture:

❝ We had Commissioners against us who tried to stop our ceremony dances and our [religious] dances. They nearly destroy us; call our ways bad or immoral or something, and put in the paper they are going to stop us. ❞

In the 1920s Luhan had shown a white social worker named John Collier the poor living conditions in Native American communities. Deeply moved, Collier founded the **American Indian Defense Association**, which fought to protect Indians' religious freedom and tribal property. For the next decade Collier championed Indian reform efforts. In 1933 President Roosevelt appointed Collier as the new commissioner of Indian Affairs. Almost immediately Collier tried to change the government's direction by revitalizing American Indian life and culture. "Anything less than to let Indian culture live on would be a crime against the earth itself," Collier declared.

To put these reform ideas into law, Congress passed the **Indian Reorganization Act** of 1934. Reversing the Dawes Act policy, the new law tried to revive tribal rule. The act provided funds to start tribal business ventures and to pay for the college education of young Native Americans. It also ordered Congress "to promote the study of Indian civilization and preserve and develop . . . Indian arts, crafts, skills, and traditions."

▲ The Indian Reorganization Act encouraged Native Americans to preserve their cultural traditions. Shown here is Angelia La Moose, a young girl in the Flathead tribe, wearing traditional Flathead dress.

◀ This 1930 photograph shows a home on the San Xavier Indian Reservation in Arizona.

THE DUST BOWL

Read the following statements to the class: 1) *Thousands of Okies leave Dust Bowl for California*; 2) *Migrant farm workers face falling wages and increasing unemployment*; 3) *Wages of migrant farm workers stabilize*. Direct students to write two or three sentences detailing the causes that might have brought about these effects. Call on volunteers to read and discuss the causes they have identified.

▶

Critics complained that Collier had not obtained enough input from the tribes themselves in formulating policies and that the programs decreased the power of women in some tribes. Still, two thirds of the nation's Native American tribes voted to participate in the new programs.

■■ **New Deal policies encouraged Native Americans to reclaim and revitalize their cultural heritage.**

⊤HE STRUGGLE FOR A PLACE IN THE SUN

Toward the end of the 1930s, a billboard appeared on Route 66 just outside Tulsa, Oklahoma, that proclaimed: "NO JOBS in California. If YOU are looking for work—KEEP OUT!" The message was clear. The market for migrant workers on the West Coast was glutted. The sign was directed at the thousands of migrant farmers from the Midwest who traveled to California in the mid-1930s. Driven off their land by the forces of nature, they sought a better life in the Southwest.

The Dust Bowl. In the mid-1930s a severe drought struck the Great Plains—the Texas and Oklahoma panhandles and parts of Colorado, New Mexico, and Kansas. As the topsoil loosened and dried, winds picked it up and turned this 50-million-acre region into a wasteland. Throughout the **Dust Bowl**, as the region came to be called, wind-borne dust clouds darkened the skies at noon and buried fences and farm machinery. Dust crept into houses through tiny cracks; ships reported great dust clouds hundreds of miles out to sea. One Texas farmer recalled:

> 66 If the wind blew one way, here came the dark dust from Oklahoma. Another way and it was the gray dust from Kansas. Still another way, the brown dust from Colorado and New Mexico. Little farms were buried. And the towns were blackened. 99

To prevent future dust bowls, the Department of Agriculture started extensive programs in soil-erosion control. The most dramatic was a shelterbelt of some 217 million trees that CCC workers planted. This windbreak stretched through the Great Plains from Texas to Canada.

By 1939 the amount of dried-out farmland had decreased dramatically. But it was too late to save the many Dust Bowl farmers who had already

(continued on page 714)

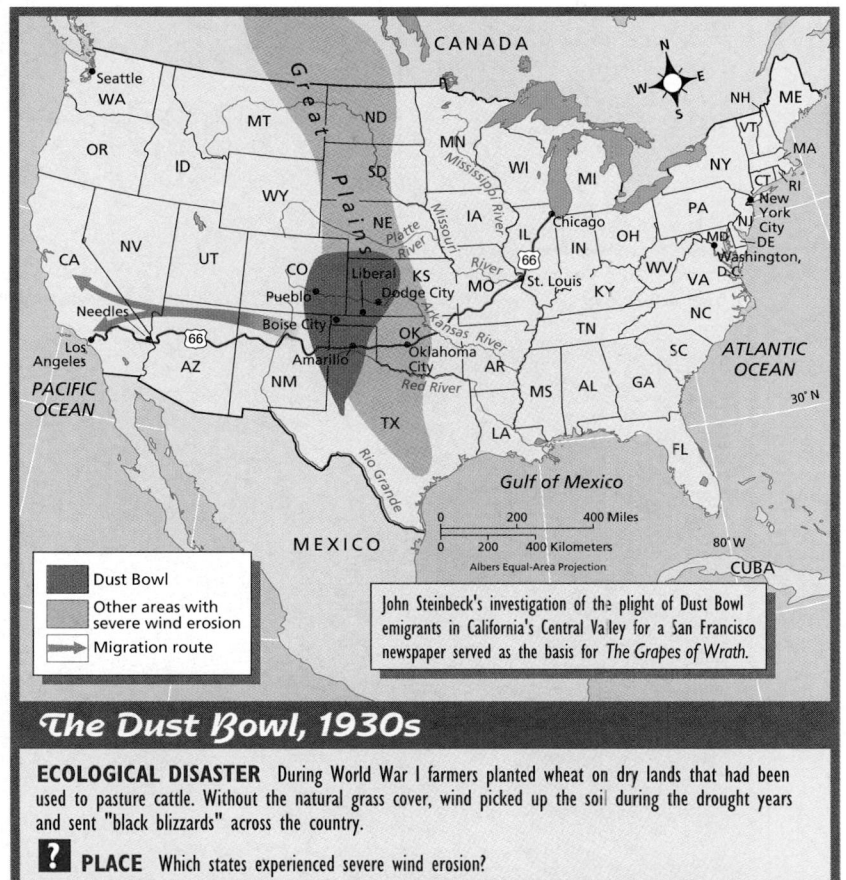

John Steinbeck's investigation of the plight of Dust Bowl emigrants in California's Central Valley for a San Francisco newspaper served as the basis for *The Grapes of Wrath*.

The Dust Bowl, 1930s

ECOLOGICAL DISASTER During World War I farmers planted wheat on dry lands that had been used to pasture cattle. Without the natural grass cover, wind picked up the soil during the drought years and sent "black blizzards" across the country.

❓ **PLACE** Which states experienced severe wind erosion?

PRIMARY SOURCE
Description of Change: excerpted
Rationale: excerpted to focus on main idea

HISTORICAL SIDELIGHTS
Dust Storms
A March 1935 dust storm blew away twice the amount of dirt dug up during the construction of the Panama Canal. A month later a dust storm in the Texas panhandle destroyed wheat worth an estimated $20 million.

HISTORICAL SIDELIGHTS
Stopping Erosion
The shelterbelt plan—which was Roosevelt's own—was roundly criticized. Governor "Alfalfa Bill" Murray of Oklahoma, for example, scoffed that the plan was "like trying to grow hair on a bald head." But, much to the surprise of Murray and other critics, the shelterbelt succeeded in slowing erosion.

Map Caption Answer
TX, OK, KS, NE, SD, ND, MT

HISTORY
in the Making

PHOTOGRAPHING THE DEPRESSION

SETTING THE SCENE
The primary mission of the FSA was to provide mortgages for farm families and labor camps for migrant workers. However, Roosevelt and the FSA wisely saw that documenting the tragedies of farm families could influence public opinion.

HISTORY
in the Making

BY DR. PAUL BOYER

Photographing the Depression

Many Americans at first were suspicious of the New Deal programs. The tradition of self-reliance ran deep in the United States. President Roosevelt believed that opponents of federal relief programs might change their minds if they saw the frightful conditions under which migrant farm workers and city dwellers lived. With Roosevelt's encouragement numerous federal agencies, including the Department of the Interior, the Works Progress Administration (WPA), the Department of Agriculture, and the Farm Security

Administration (FSA), hired photographers in the 1930s to travel across the country and document the lives of ordinary Americans.

No agency used photography more effectively than the FSA, whose staff amassed

more than 250,000 images of American life during the depression. Roy E. Stryker, head of the FSA historical section, assembled an all-star team of photographers that included Walker Evans, Ben Shahn, Arthur Rothstein, and Dorothea Lange.

▶ Russell Lee photographed these carrot field workers in Santa Maria, Texas, waiting to begin their day.

◀ In Missouri, 1939, Arthur Rothstein captured the mood of this sharecropper's child after the boy's family had been evicted from their land.

To make sure his photographers were prepared, Stryker often tutored them before sending them out on assignment. For example, former print journalist Carl Mydans was set to "go South and 'do cotton'" for the FSA. Learning that Mydans knew virtually nothing about the subject, Stryker postponed the trip. Mydans recalled what happened next:

66 We sat down and we talked almost all day about cotton. We went to lunch and we went to dinner, and we talked well into the night. He [Stryker] talked about cotton as an agricultural product, cotton as a commercial product, the history of cotton in the South, what cotton did to the history of the U.S.A. and how it affected areas outside the U.S.A. By the end of that evening, I was ready to go off and photograph cotton! 99

▶ *Migrant Mother* **is one of Dorothea Lange's most famous photographs of the depression.**

Other photographers, such as Dorothea Lange, were already well grounded in understanding the social and economic forces that shaped rural Americans' lives in the 1930s. Lange often traveled for weeks at a time, working up to 14 hours a day. One of her most famous photographs, *Migrant Mother,* showed an exhausted single mother whose children subsisted chiefly on vegetables they scavenged from California fields. When it appeared in 1936, *Migrant Mother* inspired Californians to defy powerful growers' associations and insist on decent, government-sponsored housing for seasonal harvesters.

Migrant Mother was not the only photograph to fulfill Roosevelt's goal of gaining support for government programs. From 1936 to 1941, FSA photographs were widely published in government pamphlets and in *Time, Life,* and other magazines. The pictures prompted an outpouring of congressional and public support for federal relief.

Today, the FSA photographs are housed in the Library of Congress and provide an invaluable source of information for historians. They are a detailed visual record of the 1930s that allows researchers today to "see" life in depression America. These photographs have thus enabled historians and citizens alike to step back in time to a crucial period in our history.

◀ **Ben Shahn photographed these rural West Virginia residents heading into Scotts Run to obtain food from relief workers in 1935.**

MORE ABOUT FSA STAFF

Roy Stryker was an economics professor at New York's Columbia University when he was asked to start the FSA's historical section. The first photographer he hired was one of his students, Arthur Rothstein. Rothstein shot dramatic photos of the Dust Bowl storms. After a brief stay at the FSA, Carl Mydans became one of the first staff photographers at *Life*. But Stryker continued to influence Mydans's work. "I often hear Stryker's voice guiding me when I make pictures," Mydans once said. FSA photographer Ben Shahn is perhaps better known today for his paintings on themes of social concern.

PRIMARY SOURCE

Description of Change: excerpted and bracketed
Rationale: excerpted to focus on main idea; bracketed to clarify meaning

THINKING CRITICALLY

Ask students in what ways the photographs taken for the FSA were both art and propaganda. Have students explain who the audience might have been for these photographs and what the images hoped to teach.

Practice

GUIDED PRACTICE

Direct students' attention to the photographs featured in History in the Making on pp. 712–713. Guide them in analyzing these photographs by asking them to follow these steps: 1) Determine the subject; 2) Study the details; 3) Determine the photographer's viewpoint; 4) Using information developed in the first three steps, determine the usefulness of the photographs as a historical record of life in the depression.

INDEPENDENT PRACTICE

Direct students to select another photograph from this section. Have them analyze their selection according to the steps outlined in the Guided Practice activity. Call on volunteers to present and discuss their analyses.

Review and Assessment

REVIEW Have students in groups of four role-play a conversation among an African American, an American Indian, a Mexican American, and a Filipino in which they contrast their experiences in the 1930s. Select groups to re-create their conversations for the class. Then assign the Section 3 Review on p. 715.

ASSESS Assign the **Section 3 Daily Quiz** in *Core Resources*.

PRIMARY SOURCE

Description of Change: excerpted
Rationale: excerpted to focus on main idea

HISTORICAL SIDELIGHTS

Backbreaking Work

Many California land-owners hired Filipino workers to do "stoop labor"—strenuous hand work that involved a great deal of bending over. These landowners argued that Filipinos were well suited to stoop work because of their small size. One Japanese farmer noted that in his fields, "the Fils do all the stoop labor. They are small and work fast." Yet many Filipino workers suffered from severe back problems because of their work. One Filipino migrant recalled that "at night, I'd feel all kinds of pain in my body—my back, my arm." Another worker complained, "Many people think that we don't suffer from stoop work, but we do."

▲ Many Japanese Americans on the West Coast were also among those who competed for work as migrant field laborers. These men labored in sugar fields.

66 When we moved to California, we would work after school. Sometimes we wouldn't go. "Following the crops," we missed much school. Trying to get enough money to stay alive the following winter, the whole family picking apricots, walnuts, prunes. . . . We were taken advantage of quite a bit by the labor contractor and the crew pusher. 99

lost their land. Packing their meager belongings into battered old cars or trucks, they headed west on Route 66, bound for what they saw as a land of promise—California and other parts of the West Coast. There they hoped to find work picking crops. Thousands of them made the trek, and since many came from Oklahoma, they picked up the nickname **Okies**. Once they reached the West Coast, however, they found themselves in desperate competition with other farm laborers looking for work.

Competition for migrant work. Even before the Dust Bowl refugees started arriving, Mexican Americans had been having a hard time finding work in the West. Like African Americans, Mexican Americans often found themselves the victims of discrimination in many New Deal programs. For example, although the CCC did not segregate Mexican Americans, some complained that they were harassed by camp officials, denied clothing, and assigned to kitchen duty more often than non-Hispanics.

Many families continued to seek what little work they could find as migrant farm laborers. A 1935 California survey found that the average income of Mexican American families had fallen below $300 a year. César Chávez, who later became a noted labor leader, recalled growing up in a depression-era migrant family:

Mexican Americans also faced job competition from Filipino laborers. During the 1920s the Filipino population of California had grown to more than 30,000. Like Mexican American migrants, most Filipinos worked in agriculture. When the depression hit, both groups faced tough economic times, but the Filipino workers attempted to combat decreasing wages by organizing. Throughout the early 1930s the Filipino Labor Union launched a series of strikes to protest wage reductions. In 1936 the American Federation of Labor sponsored the Field Workers Union, a combined organization for Mexican American and Filipino laborers.

The unions were able to keep wages from falling too much. However, as more Okies arrived, competition for migrant work increased. Thus life for all migrants remained difficult.

■■ **Dust Bowl refugees moved to the West, where they competed with Mexican Americans and Filipinos for migrant farm work.**

Picturing THE FACE OF THE DEPRESSION

The grim experiences of migrants and others in rural America provided rich subject matter for documentary filmmakers and photographers. These artists created a memorable visual record of the New Deal era. Better than any words could do, their images of the slumped shoulders of

RETEACH Have students work in small groups to chart the major ideas and events presented in the section. Direct each group to indicate on its chart how each item addresses one of the section's Focus questions. Have groups compare their completed charts.

Closure

Lead the class in a debate on the following question: *Was the New Deal a new deal for America's minorities?*

Extension

INTERPRET Have students pick five photographs from collections taken during the 1930s, such as Arthur Rothstein's *The Depression Years,* and prepare an oral report explaining what can be learned about the depression from each picture.

RESEARCH Direct students to research the lives and careers of the members of Roosevelt's black cabinet.

▲ FSA photographer Carl Mydans captured the devastation of soil erosion in Kentucky in 1936.

unemployed men, the staring faces of children, and the worried expressions of prematurely aged women conveyed the human suffering of the era.

In 1936 and 1937 the filmmaker Pare Lorentz directed two documentary films on the era. *The River* depicts the TVA and its effect on the surrounding regions, while *The Plow That Broke the Plains* portrays the devastation of the Dust Bowl. Using few images of people, the films rely heavily on background music and an unseen narrator to enhance the visual images of the depression's impact on the landscape.

In the late 1930s the Farm Security Administration recruited a group of photographers to record American rural life. These photographers included Walker Evans, who depicted life among sharecroppers in rural Alabama; African American Gordon Parks, who later became a filmmaker; international photojournalist Margaret Bourke-White; and Dorothea Lange, probably the best-known of the FSA photographers.

 Lange was one of the most talented photographers of the depression era. Born in Hoboken, New Jersey, she decided in her late teens to become a photographer. After studying the craft for several years, she set out to tour the world and record her impressions. Lange was out of money by the time she reached San Francisco, however, so she stayed and opened a portrait studio.

When the depression struck, Lange began to take pictures of the homeless men wandering the streets of San Francisco. Soon the federal government hired her to photograph migrant farmers in California. Her pictures, which carry captions in the farmers' own words, revealed the migrants' poverty and suffering, as well as their great dignity. Lange's most famous picture, *Migrant Mother* (see page 713), is considered a masterpiece.

During World War II, Lange continued her documentary work by taking pictures of Japanese Americans in California internment camps. Later she produced photo essays for *Life* magazine and traveled the world taking pictures. By the time of her death in 1965, she ranked as one of the world's foremost photographers.

The Granger Collection, New York

Dorothea Lange

SECTION REVIEW ANSWERS

IDENTIFY

For significance, see the following pages:
Marian Anderson (p. 708)
Robert C. Weaver (p. 709)
Mary McLeod Bethune (p. 709)
Antonio Luhan (p. 710)
John Collier (p. 710)
American Indian Defense Association (p. 710)
Indian Reorganization Act (p. 710)
Okies (p. 714)
Dorothea Lange (p. 715)

LOCATE

For location, see the map on p. 711.

1. Although many New Deal programs benefited African Americans, others discriminated directly or indirectly.
2. reversed Dawes Act policy, tried to revive tribal rule, provided funds for business ventures and college educations, encouraged the study and preservation of Native American culture
3. Erosion, severe drought, and winds combined to dry and loosen farmland topsoil.
4. Diary entries might mention the desperate competition with Mexican Americans and Filipinos for migrant farm work.
5. Both groups created visual records of the depression's misery through their photographic images.

■ SECTION 3 REVIEW

IDENTIFY and explain the significance of the following: Marian Anderson, Robert C. Weaver, Mary McLeod Bethune, Antonio Luhan, John Collier, American Indian Defense Association, Indian Reorganization Act, Okies, Dorothea Lange.

LOCATE and explain the importance of the following: Dust Bowl.

1. **MAIN IDEA** How did the New Deal affect African Americans during the 1930s?
2. **MAIN IDEA** How did the Indian Reorganization Act benefit Native Americans?
3. **LINKING HISTORY AND GEOGRAPHY** What factors caused the Dust Bowl during the 1930s?
4. **WRITING TO DESCRIBE** Imagine you are an Okie migrating west in 1939. Write a diary entry describing your experiences on the West Coast.
5. **ANALYZING** How did filmmakers, such as Pare Lorentz, and photographers, such as Dorothea Lange, serve as social critics during the 1930s?

PREVIEW WORKSHOP

Following is a list of the significant people and terms in this section. You may wish to use this list as a section preview.

People

- Margaret Mitchell
- John Steinbeck
- Zora Neale Hurston
- Richard Wright
- Aaron Copland
- Thomas A. Dorsey

- Benny Goodman
- Robert Sherwood
- Lillian Hellman
- Thornton Wilder
- Jacob Lawrence
- Georgia O'Keeffe
- Anna "Grandma" Moses

Terms

- Federal Project No. 1
- Federal Writers' Project
- regionalists

MOTIVATING: STUDENT EXPERIENCES

Have students give examples of ways that music and the other arts reflect concerns present in American society today. Then have students speculate how the concerns of the depression might have affected the work of people in the arts in the 1930s.

Section 4

THE NEW DEAL AND THE ARTS

FOCUS

- **How did Federal Project No. 1 aid writers and artists?**
- **What were many novels like in the late 1930s?**
- **What common themes were often heard and seen in music, plays, and paintings of the New Deal era?**

In attempting to put Americans back to work, the Roosevelt administration did not forget about those who worked in the arts. The WPA established a series of programs to employ writers, actors, musicians, painters, and other artists. Meanwhile literature in the late 1930s began to turn from escapist fantasies to realistic portrayals of the depression, while musicians, playwrights, and painters searched for uniquely American subject matter.

1936 poster for WPA production, *Macbeth*

THE WPA PROGRAMS

All workers struggled with unemployment in depression-era America, including artists. Without an audience that could afford to buy their work, most of the nation's writers, stage actors, musicians, and painters lost their means of earning an income. Like workers in other fields, they sought relief from the government. In February 1935 a few writers picketed federal offices in New York City, carrying signs that read "CHIL-DREN NEED BOOKS. WRITERS NEED BREAD. WE DEMAND PROJECTS."

Later that year, the WPA set aside some $300 million to create **Federal Project No. 1**. This program tried to encourage pride in American culture by aiding unemployed artists in the fields of writing, theater, music, and visual arts.

The WPA's **Federal Writers' Project** (FWP) hired some 6,600 unemployed writers to produce a variety of works, including state travel guides and histories of various ethnic groups. Others conducted oral-history interviews with hundreds of elderly former slaves. Historians still use these sources to study slave life. Members of the project also studied American folklore and wrote down folktales. These eventually became the basis for the best-selling *Treasury of American Folklore* (1944). The FWP eventually won praise as the "biggest literary project in history," producing more than 1,000 books

◄ **Unemployed and striking actors picketed outside the hotel where heads of the regional, state, and national offices of the WPA met in July 1939.**

FEDERAL PROJECT NO. 1

Ask volunteers to describe the ways writers, actors, musicians, and artists were employed during the New Deal. Have students speculate how the New Deal's art programs changed the role of the arts in everyday life and affected the public's perception of artists and the arts.

■■ Ask students in what ways the federal government supports the arts today.

THE ARTS OF THE NEW DEAL ERA

Organize the class into four groups and assign one of the following art forms to each group: novels, plays, music, and paintings. Direct each group to create a chart or other graphic organizer to present the artists, works, trends, and themes of the New Deal era in its assigned art form. Encourage groups to illustrate their graphic organizers. After each group has shown and explained its graphic organizer to the class, ask volunteers to describe the themes and characteristics that these organizers have identified as common to American novels and other literary, performing, and fine arts during the Great Depression.

▶

---

and pamphlets. It also helped launch the careers of numerous writers who went on to great success, such as John Steinbeck and Richard Wright.

The WPA's Federal Theatre Project hired unemployed actors, directors, designers, stagehands, and playwrights to encourage theatrical productions. It entertained millions of Americans, bringing productions to many small towns that had never experienced live theater. The Federal Music Project hired musicians to form orchestras and present some 4,000 musical productions per month to audiences across the country. It also hired music researchers to write down popular American folk songs. The Federal Arts Project hired unemployed artists and designers to produce posters for New Deal programs and to teach art in public schools. Others painted murals on public buildings constructed by the PWA.

■■ **Federal Project No. 1 employed various writers and artists and spread their work throughout the country.**

LITERATURE IN THE LATE 1930s

American interest in romantic fiction continued into the late 1930s. One of the best-selling novels of the decade was Margaret Mitchell's *Gone with the Wind* (1936), a sweeping story of the Old South during the Civil War and Reconstruction. Many depression-era readers could relate to the turmoil faced by the novel's main character, Scarlett O'Hara, who survives war and economic chaos. Her uplifting closing line, "After all, tomorrow is another day," inspired readers of the 1930s.

By the end of the decade, many writers had incorporated the experiences of the depression into their works. John Steinbeck, a writer employed by the FWP, produced a gripping picture of the depression era in *The Grapes of Wrath* (1939). The story follows the fortunes of a desperately poor Dust Bowl family as they travel to California:

❝ As the dark caught them, they clustered like bugs near to shelter and to water. And because they were lonely . . . , because they had all come from a place of sadness and . . . were all going to a new mysterious place, they huddled together. ❞

▲ Some three years in the planning, MGM's production of *Gone with the Wind* was the most eagerly awaited and top-grossing film of 1939.

As it was for the real Okies, life in California is lonely and harsh for Steinbeck's fictional migrant family. Like *Gone with the Wind,* however, Steinbeck's novel includes a hopeful note, as the head of the family, Ma Joad, optimistically states, "They ain't gonna wipe us out. Why, we're the people—we go on."

Other novels described the experiences of ethnic minorities in the era. African American anthropologist Zora Neale Hurston wrote *Their Eyes Were Watching God* (1937), which explores a black woman's search for fulfillment in rural Florida. Richard Wright offered a grim picture of black urban life in *Native Son* (1940), which

◀ *Native Son* by Richard Wright

▶ *Their Eyes Were Watching God* by Zora Neale Hurston

VOICES IN HISTORY

A number of writers gained fame in the 1930s, including Albert Halper, the son of poor Jewish immigrants from Lithuania. Halper's writing reflected on depression-era society. "I am sorry for many things in life," he wrote in 1934. "I am sorry for the small folk who live thin twisted lives, who have to hold onto their job and look alive when the big chief passes by. I am sorry for the broken men who stand against buildings when the wind howls down the street and the snow whirls past the arc lamps. I am sorry . . . for all my old buddies down at the Post Office—the whites, the Negroes, and the Filipinos, who stand hour on hour tossing mail."

PRIMARY SOURCE
Description of Change: excerpted
Rationale: excerpted to focus on main idea

*P*ractice

GUIDED PRACTICE

Tell students to imagine they are reporters preparing to interview one of the artists in this section. Work with students to develop a series of questions they would like the artist to answer.

INDEPENDENT PRACTICE

Have students select one of the people listed in the Preview Workshop. Then ask students to use the questions developed in the Guided Practice activity as the basis for a magazine "profile" of their chosen subject.

*R*eview and *A*ssessment

REVIEW Have students work in small groups to create a four-page pictorial essay titled "A Reflection of the Times: The Art of the 1930s." Call on volunteers to display and discuss their essays. Then assign the Section 4 Review on p. 719.

ASSESS Assign the **Section 4 Daily Quiz** in *Core Resources*.

MAKING CONNECTIONS

Art

Painter George Biddle once said FDR had "done more for painters in this country than anybody else ever did—not only by feeding them . . . but by establishing the idea that paintings are a good thing to have around, and that artists are important."

COOPERATIVE LEARNING

Organize students into four-person groups consisting of a scriptwriter, caption writer, designer, and artist. Direct them to create plans for a museum exhibit titled "The Arts in the 1930s." Groups can design exhibits on literature, music, plays, paintings, or photography, with each group creating a floor plan, description of works, captions for displays, and tour-guide script for its exhibit.

AV TRANSPARENCY

Everyday Life in America Transparency and **Worksheet 24**

PRIMARY SOURCE

Description of Change: excerpted
Rationale: excerpted to focus on main idea

---

chronicles the journey of a young African American man lost in a racist world where he can never succeed. *Native Son* explores several themes that haunted the 1930s, including class differences, socialism, racism, and urban despair.

■■ **Many novels of the late 1930s reflected the experiences of the depression.**

---

*P*ERFORMING ARTS IN THE NEW DEAL ERA

American music of the late 1930s increasingly tried to capture uniquely American sounds. As WPA researchers wrote down American folk songs and folktales, composer Aaron Copland used these themes as the basis for his most popular compositions, including *Billy the Kid* (1938).

▲ **Paper fan depicting singer Mahalia Jackson**

Interest in African American music continued throughout the 1930s. Black gospel, a cross between jazz and traditional spirituals, gained popularity through the work of African American composer Thomas A. Dorsey —whose songs included "Precious Lord, Take My Hand"—and singers such as Sister Rosetta Tharpe and Mahalia Jackson. Jackson recalled that some ministers initially objected to this new style of music:

66 They didn't like the hand-clapping and the stomping and they said we were bringing jazz into the church and it wasn't dignified. Once at church one of the preachers got up in the pulpit and spoke out against me. I got right up, too. I told him I was born to sing gospel music. 99

Jazz continued its rise in popularity, largely because of the development of swing, a smooth big-band style popular in dance halls. The style derived its name from Duke Ellington's 1932 hit "It Don't Mean a Thing If It Ain't Got That Swing." White conductor Benny Goodman helped popularize swing in the late 1930s. He also broke new ground in popular music by integrating his shows with both black and white performers. Meanwhile, other bands, such as those of Count Basie and Glenn Miller, kept the swing sound alive throughout the 1930's.

On the theatrical stage, plays with social significance—that is, plays that dealt with the nation's labor and class problems—drew large audiences. Robert Sherwood's *The Petrified Forest* (1935) attacked the "petrified forest" of ideas destroying America. Lillian Hellman's *The Little Foxes* (1939) exposed the upper-class greed that many believed was undermining America. By the end of the decade, popular plays, like popular music, focused increasingly on American traditions and values. Two examples are Thornton Wilder's *Our Town* (1938), a heartwarming drama of life and death in a small American town around 1900, and William Saroyan's *The Time of Your Life* (1939), which celebrates the diversity of urban America.

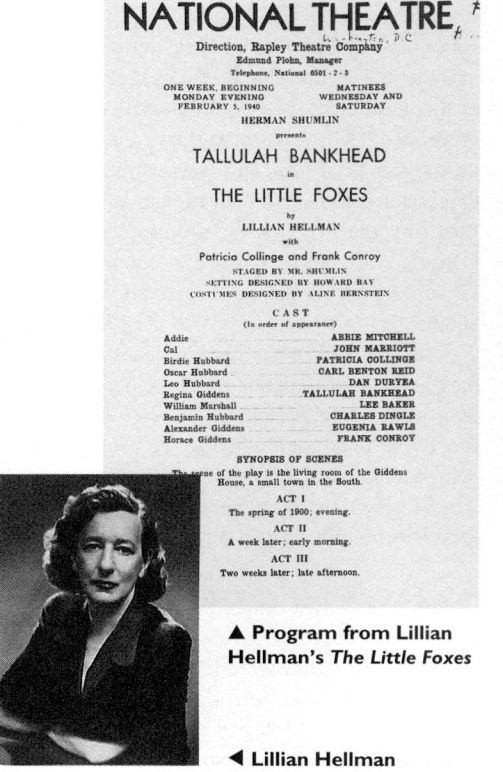

▲ **Program from Lillian Hellman's *The Little Foxes***

◄ **Lillian Hellman**

■■ Music—folk songs, gospel, and jazz—and plays—socially significant and traditional—reflected uniquely American styles and themes.

PAINTERS EXAMINE LOCAL CULTURE

Like American writers, painters recorded a variety of memorable American images during the depression. Harlem artist Jacob Lawrence portrayed the daily lives of African American heroes, such as Frederick Douglass and Harriet Tubman, while New Mexico artist Georgia O'Keeffe painted haunting images of the southwestern desert landscape.

Perhaps reflecting the New Deal's focus on farmers' problems, many artists of the era looked to rural America for their subject matter. A group of midwestern artists known as the **regionalists** stressed local folk themes and customs. The regionalists included artists such as Thomas Hart Benton of Missouri, John Steuart Curry of Kansas, and Grant Wood of Iowa.

These artists reminded urban art lovers of America's rural traditions. Wood always insisted that his best ideas "came while milking a cow." The most famous of the regionalist paintings is probably Wood's *American Gothic,* which depicts a stern farmer, pitchfork in hand,

▲ Paintings of rustic scenes, such as *Sugaring Off* by Anna "Grandma" Moses, were typical of regionalists and other folk artists of the depression era.

standing beside a sad-eyed woman in front of a humble farmhouse.

As interest in regional culture grew, people rediscovered the richness of American folk art, such as handmade quilts and woodcarvings. Many obscure folk artists, including the elderly painter Anna "Grandma" Moses, became wellknown during this period.

■■ American painters, led by the regionalists, explored a diversity of local folk life.

■■

SECTION 4 REVIEW

IDENTIFY and explain the significance of the following: Federal Project No. 1, Federal Writers' Project, Margaret Mitchell, John Steinbeck, Zora Neale Hurston, Richard Wright, Aaron Copland, Thomas A. Dorsey, Benny Goodman, Robert Sherwood, Lillian Hellman, Thornton Wilder, Jacob Lawrence, Georgia O'Keeffe, regionalists, Anna "Grandma" Moses.

1. **MAIN IDEA** Why was Federal Project No. 1 created?
2. **MAIN IDEA** What contribution did regionalists make to American painting?
3. **COMPARING** What common themes did music and plays of the 1930s share?
4. **WRITING TO CREATE** Write a promotional piece for *The Grapes of Wrath, Their Eyes Were Watching God,* or *Native Son* that shows how the novel reflects the experiences of the depression.
5. **ANALYZING** How were the experiences of African Americans expressed artistically during the New Deal era?

Chapter Review Answers

WRITING A SUMMARY

See Essential Points in each section for main ideas.

REVIEWING CHRONOLOGY

4, 5, 2, 1, 3
Assessing Consequences
gained appointment to NYA, which she tried to rid of racism; facilitated work of Federal Council on Negro Affairs, a core group of African American government officials

IDENTIFYING PEOPLE AND IDEAS

1. Roosevelt's relief, recovery, and reform program
2. FDR's labor secretary
3. money paid to farmers to reduce output of goods
4. African American anthropologist and author of Their Eyes Were Watching God
5. 1935 revenue act that increased taxes on the wealthy
6. protest whereby workers occupy factories until labor demands are met
7. black brain-trust member and New Deal adviser on racial matters
8. commissioner of Indian Affairs who championed Indian reform efforts
9. Great Plains region

turned into wasteland during 1930s by soil erosion and drought
10. Louisiana senator who proposed Share-Our-Wealth program

UNDERSTANDING MAIN IDEAS

1. to restore public confidence in the banking system
2. First New Deal focused on direct relief and recovery programs, Second New Deal on social reform.
3. increased purchasing power and farm prices through AAA, revitalized rural areas through TVA

and REA, provided farm loans through FSA, began soil-erosion control and conservation programs through CCC
4. African Americans—found relief and work mainly through FERA and WPA, appointed to some government offices, faced discrimination in some New Deal programs; Native Americans—revitalized cultural heritage through the Indian Reorganization Act
5. Both created visual records of the depression—Lorentz through documentary films, Lange through photographs.

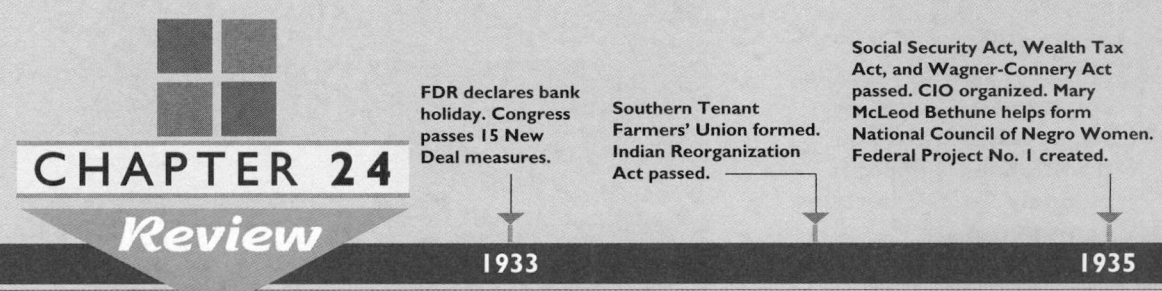

CHAPTER 24
Review

FDR declares bank holiday. Congress passes 15 New Deal measures.

Southern Tenant Farmers' Union formed. Indian Reorganization Act passed.

Social Security Act, Wealth Tax Act, and Wagner-Connery Act passed. CIO organized. Mary McLeod Bethune helps form National Council of Negro Women. Federal Project No. 1 created.

1933   **1935**

WRITING A SUMMARY

Using the essential points of the chapter as a guide, write a summary of the chapter.

REVIEWING CHRONOLOGY

Number your paper 1 to 5. Study the time line above, and list the following events in the order in which they happened by writing the first next to 1, the second next to 2, and so on. Then complete the activity below.

1. Aaron Copland composes *Billy the Kid*.
2. CIO organized.
3. Richard Wright's *Native Son* published.
4. FDR declares bank holiday.
5. Indian Reorganization Act passed.

Assessing Consequences How did Mary McLeod Bethune help maximize the participation of African Americans in the New Deal?

IDENTIFYING PEOPLE AND IDEAS

Explain the historical significance of each of the following people or terms.

1. New Deal
2. Frances Perkins
3. subsidies
4. Zora Neale Hurston
5. Wealth Tax Act
6. sit-down strike
7. Robert C. Weaver
8. John Collier
9. Dust Bowl
10. Huey Long

UNDERSTANDING MAIN IDEAS

1. What was the purpose of the bank holiday and the FDIC?
2. How were the economic and social programs of the Second New Deal different from those of the First New Deal?
3. What steps did the government take in the 1930s to aid farmers?
4. How did the New Deal affect African Americans and Native Americans?
5. What contributions did Pare Lorentz and Dorothea Lange make to the New Deal era?

REVIEWING THEMES

1. **Economic Development** How did the Roosevelt administration attempt to promote economic recovery?
2. **Constitutional Heritage** Why might the Supreme Court have declared some New Deal measures unconstitutional?
3. **Cultural Diversity** How did writers and artists of the 1930s reflect the ethnic and cultural diversity of the nation?

THINKING CRITICALLY

1. **Analyzing** Why did some conservative and liberal critics oppose the New Deal?
2. **Evaluating** Do you think that Roosevelt was justified in trying to "pack" the Supreme Court? Why or why not?
3. **Assessing Consequences** How did WPA programs enrich American culture during the 1930s?

STRATEGY FOR SUCCESS

Review the Skills Handbook entry on Identifying the Main Idea beginning on page 988. Examine the photograph below, taken by Margaret Bourke-White in 1937. These residents of Louisville, Kentucky, are waiting in a relief line to receive aid. What contrasts can you see between the experiences of the people in the line and the message on the billboard behind them?

REVIEWING THEMES

1. enacted measures to safeguard banking system, provided loans to home owners, granted direct relief and jobs to unemployed, spurred economic growth through "pump priming," passed laws protecting labor and benefiting farmers
2. may have believed that some New Deal measures interfered with American individualism, free enterprise, or private property rights
3. Novelists described ethnic experiences, composers integrated music with ethnic themes, playwrights celebrated urban diversity, and artists focused on ethnic heroes and stressed local folk customs.

THINKING CRITICALLY

1. Some conservatives said measures were destroying free enterprise and driving the nation into bankruptcy. Some liberals argued that the New Deal was not going far enough.
2. Evaluations should balance Supreme Court arguments to overturn some New Deal measures against FDR's reasons for protecting his programs.
3. WPA financed researchers who wrote down American folktales and folk songs; sponsored interviews with former slaves; spread theater, music, and art to rural areas; launched careers of writers and other artists.

STRATEGY FOR SUCCESS

People in line do not seem to enjoy the "world's highest standard of living"; they are ethnically diverse, sad-looking, and struggling, unlike the smiling white middle-class family on the billboard behind them.

WRITING ABOUT HISTORY

Charts may vary but should include the following: banks—Emergency Banking Act, FDIC; farmers—second AAA, FCA, AAA, TVA, REA, FSA; labor—CCC, PWA, NRA, Wagner-Connery Act; business—NRA, PWA, CWA, WPA.

USING PRIMARY SOURCES

that workers were intimidated by the company bosses after they joined the CIO; that the CIO will increase wages and improve working conditions

LINKING HISTORY AND GEOGRAPHY

forced Dust Bowl farmers to migrate; many went to the West, where they found themselves in competition for jobs with other migrant workers

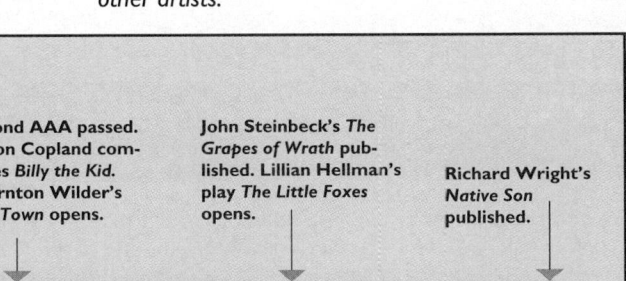

Margaret Mitchell's *Gone with the Wind* **published. FDR reelected president.**

FDR tries to "pack" Supreme Court. Farm Security Administration created. GM strike begins.

Second AAA passed. Aaron Copland composes *Billy the Kid.* **Thornton Wilder's** *Our Town* **opens.**

John Steinbeck's *The Grapes of Wrath* **published. Lillian Hellman's play** *The Little Foxes* **opens.**

Richard Wright's *Native Son* **published.**

1937   **1939**

WRITING ABOUT HISTORY

Writing to Classify Create a chart that classifies the programs of the New Deal according to whether they were designed primarily to help banks, farmers, labor, or business.

USING PRIMARY SOURCES

Mexican American Jesse Perez worked for the meat-packing industry in Chicago in 1939, during a time when the CIO was attempting to organize workers in the stockyards. Read the following statement, which comes from an interview Perez did at that time with a member of the Federal Writers' Project. What does Perez have to say about the company's treatment of workers who joined the union during this time? How does Perez view the CIO?

> 66 *I was first to wear CIO button; ever since I start wearing the button they start to pick. I can butcher, but they don't give me job. . . . So when I start telling the boys we have a union for them, almost all join right away. We talk all the time what the union going to do for us, going to raise wages, stop speed-up. The bosses watch and they know it's a union coming.*
>
> *So every day they start saying we behind in the work. They start speeding up the boys more and more every day. . . . We told bosses we working too fast, can't keep up. The whole gang, thirteen men, all stop. Bosses say, we ain't standing for nothing like this. Four days later they fire the whole gang, except two. We took the case in the labor board and . . . now all who was fired got work.*
>
> *Now the bosses try to provoke strike before CIO get ready. . . . We know what they do, we don't talk back, got to watch out they don't play tricks like that.* 99

LINKING HISTORY AND GEOGRAPHY

Describing the effects of the Dust Bowl, John Steinbeck wrote: "The Western States are nervous under the beginning change. . . . A half-million people moving over the country; a million more, restive [restless] to move; ten million more feeling the first nervousness." How did the Dust Bowl influence population shifts in the Southwest?

Scene from the film *The Grapes of Wrath,* 1939

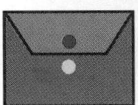 **BUILDING YOUR PORTFOLIO**

Complete the following projects independently or cooperatively.

1. **THE ECONOMY** In chapters 21, 22, and 23, you examined the U.S. economy in the 1920s. Building on that experience, imagine you are a New Deal legislator. Write a proposal for a new public works project. Your proposal should describe what the project is, how workers and businesses will benefit, and why your project will be useful to society in terms of relief, recovery, or reform.

2. **CULTURE AND SOCIETY** In chapters 21 and 22 you explored U.S. society in the 1920s. Building on that experience, imagine you are an author in the 1930s. Write a short, realistic passage for your novel that describes the Dust Bowl's effect on your main character.

 **BUILDING YOUR PORTFOLIO**

Have students refer to **Building Your Portfolio Worksheet 7,** assigned at the beginning of Unit 7. Use the worksheet to help students monitor their progress on the portfolio projects.

Assessment

Core Resources
• Review Worksheet 24
• Chapter 24 Tests
• Alternative Assessment Forms
Test Generator

CHAPTER 25

BETWEEN THE WARS

1921–1941

THE AMERICAN NATION VIDEODISC PROGRAM

A variety of still images, short videos, and activities are available for you to use as you teach this chapter. See Correlation to *The American Nation* Videodisc Program for barcode correlations and suggestions for using the program.

Chapter Overview

After World War I many nations expected that the U.S. would take a leadership position in world affairs. But the prospects of becoming entangled in another war led the U.S. to limit its leadership role to diplomatic and disarmament conferences. Instead, U.S. attention was focused on affairs at home and in Latin America. However, the worldwide economic depression promoted the rise of dictators in Europe, which made American isolation from European affairs more difficult to maintain and eventually resulted in involvement in another world war.

Chapter Planning Guide

CHAPTER 25	CORE RESOURCE BOOKLETS	AV AUDIOVISUAL RESOURCES	PROGRAM RESOURCES
INTRODUCTION pp. 722–723	■ Building Your Portfolio Worksheet 7	■ Everyday Life in America Transparency and Worksheet 25	
TEACHING THE CHAPTER pp. 724–739	■ Graphic Organizer 25 ■ Social Studies Skills Worksheet 25 ■ Literature Worksheet 25 ■ Geography Worksheet 25 ■ Outline Maps 1, 2, 14, 15, 19, 20, 21	■ *The American Nation* Videodisc: U.S. Warships in Havana Harbor	
REVIEW AND ASSESSMENT pp. 740–741	■ Chapter 25 Daily Quizzes ■ Review Worksheet 25 ■ Chapter 25 Tests ■ Alternative Assessment Forms		■ Test Generator

Additional Resources

BOOKS FOR TEACHERS

Alonso, Harriet H. *Peace As a Women's Issue.* Syracuse University Press, 1993. Covers the history of the women's peace movement from the 19th century to modern times.

Black, George. *The Good Neighbor.* Pantheon, 1988. Account of U.S. relations with Central America and the Caribbean.

Scott, William R. *The Sons of Sheba's Race.* Indiana University Press, 1992. In-depth description of the role of African Americans in Italy's war with Ethiopia.

BOOKS FOR STUDENTS

* Allen, Peter. *The Origins of World War II.* Watts, 1992. Part of Witness to History Series; includes illustrations.

Jenkins, Tony. *Nicaragua and the United States: Years of Conflict.* Watts, 1989. Traces the history of U.S. foreign policy in Nicaragua from the 19th century to the present.

Overy, Richard. *The Road to War.* Random House, 1990. Highly readable account of the events leading up to World War II.

* for students reading below grade level

MULTIMEDIA MATERIALS

A New Germany: 1933–1939, Vol. I. Video, 52 min. Thames Television/SSSS. Documentary footage of the major political and economic events that led to the spread of Nazism.

Prelude to War: 1935–1939. Video, 25 min. Aims/SSSS. Narrates events leading to Hitler's rise in Germany, the Spanish Civil War, and Japan's aggression toward China.

Seeds of Discord: 1933–1936. Video, 25 min. Aims/SSSS. Covers the rise of Stalin, Hitler, and Mussolini.

U.S. Intervention in Latin America: Witness to History. Video, 15 min. Guidance Associates/SSSS. Analyzes history of U.S. relations with Latin America.

USE WITH PAGES 722–723

Listed on the right are the themes emphasized in Chapter 25. The questions in boldface type stimulate critical thinking and provide students with an opportunity to discuss the themes within a broadened context. The questions also appear in the pupil's edition on p. 722.

■ GLOBAL RELATIONS

How might nations work together to promote world peace? Students may suggest that nations could agree to set limits on weapons, enter into treaties, or form international organizations to monitor world problems.

■ ECONOMIC DEVELOPMENT

What economic problems might wars create? Students may mention that the loss of lives and the destruction of homes, businesses, factories, and transportation networks disrupt a nation's economy. As a result, unemployment might rise, and there may be a shortage of consumer goods.

What political problems might result from these economic difficulties? Economic problems might create dissatisfaction among citizens, which could possibly lead to changes in government policies and leadership.

■ DEMOCRATIC VALUES

What conditions might give rise to a dictatorship? Students may mention that economic downturns might cause citizens to turn to strong leaders to solve a nation's problems. In turn, such a government might use an economic crisis as an excuse to assert more control over its citizens. The presence of a strong military might enable that government to increase its power, while the absence of stable political parties might weaken opposition to the government's restrictions of people's rights.

CHAPTER STRATEGIES FOR MEETING INDIVIDUAL NEEDS

LIMITED ENGLISH PROFICIENT LEARNERS

Have students work in groups to create a visual display for the bulletin board that describes the people involved in and the important events leading to World War II.

TACTILE/KINESTHETIC LEARNERS

Organize the class into groups and have each group create a skit that examines and dramatizes the difficult decisions that different nations' policymakers faced between the wars.

LEARNERS HAVING DIFFICULTY

After students have read the chapter, have them work in pairs, assigning each pair an Essential Point from the chapter. Ask pairs to expand on their topic by writing brief explanations or creating visuals. Have pairs share their explanations or visuals.

AUDITORY LEARNERS

Assign each student to research a person presented in the chapter. Then have students present short biographical sketches to the class, and have other students guess the identity of the person presented.

VISUAL LEARNERS

Have students study the illustrations in this chapter. Ask them to do library research to locate additional images that relate to the chapter content and to share their findings with the class.

GIFTED LEARNERS

Organize students into groups, assigning each of the chapter's sections to two groups. Have each group develop a debate that covers one of the main ideas presented in the section. Ask each pair of groups to present its debate to the class.

USING THE CHAPTER FOCUS

■ UNDERSTANDING THE MAIN IDEA

Have students identify some domestic problems that confront the U.S. today. *(health and welfare issues, homelessness, crime, unemployment)* Write students' responses on the chalkboard. Ask students to speculate how similar problems in some European nations during the 1920s and 1930s could have created conditions that led to war. Have students check the accuracy of their speculations as they read the chapter.

★ THEMES

Have students work individually or in small groups to answer the questions under Themes. Save students' responses so that they can compare them with their responses after studying the chapter. (See p. 721B for suggested answers.)

■ THE TIME LINE

Have students copy in their notebooks the time line at the bottom of the page. As they read the chapter, have students prepare brief articles about each time-line event that might appear in an encyclopedia. Students should also suggest illustrations that might accompany their articles.

CORE RESOURCES

• **Graphic Organizer 25**
• **Outline Maps 1, 2, 14, 15, 19, 20, 21**
• **Building Your Portfolio Worksheet 7**

AV RESOURCES

• **Everyday Life in America Transparency and Worksheet 25**

ABOUT THE ILLUSTRATION

By 1932 the National Socialist, or Nazi, party was the strongest of Germany's seven major political parties. The Nazis attracted almost 14 million of nearly 37 million votes cast in the July election and gained 230 of 608 seats in the Reichstag, the German parliament. This photograph shows supporters of the Nazi party, which in 1933 Hitler declared the only political party legally allowed to operate in Germany. Ask students to speculate what might motivate such enthusiastic support for Hitler's antidemocratic party.

Chapter 25

1921–1941

BETWEEN THE WARS

▼ FOCUS

UNDERSTANDING THE MAIN IDEA

After World War I many Americans hoped to focus on matters at home. Unfortunately, the depression touched off global economic problems. The rise of dictators in Europe set the stage for another war. Dictators also came to power in several Latin American countries. Other countries in Latin America, such as Nicaragua and Mexico, attempted to reduce U.S. influence.

★ THEMES

■ **GLOBAL RELATIONS** How might nations work together to promote world peace?

■ **ECONOMIC DEVELOPMENT** What economic problems might wars create? What political problems might result from these economic difficulties?

■ **DEMOCRATIC VALUES** What conditions might give rise to a dictatorship?

1921	1926	1931	1933	1939
Washington Conference begins.	Augusto Sandino organizes revolt in Nicaragua.	Japan invades Manchuria.	Adolf Hitler becomes chancellor of Germany.	World War II starts.

▶ LINK TO THE PAST

Call on volunteers to recall the impact the Great Depression had on the U.S. Ask students to speculate why economic hardships might cause Americans to resist military involvement in Europe and Asia and to consider what nonmilitary steps the U.S. might take to reduce international tensions and to promote world peace.

▶ LINK TO THE PAST

World War I and the depression created chaos in Europe. Germany was required to pay substantial war reparations, while other European countries owed the United States large war debts. After the war many Americans called for an end to foreign military involvements.

"One word . . . describes the whole feeling in America to-day, and that is *disillusionment* [disappointment]: disillusionment in the leaders, disillusionment in the business men, disillusionment in politics," wrote a friend to British prime minister David Lloyd George in January 1932. This feeling of pessimism arose from the economic strains of the depression and the international chaos caused by World War I. Instead of bringing peace, the end of the war ushered in a period of economic and political instability in Europe.

Many Americans feared that involvement in European affairs might draw the United States into another war. In 1937 the magazine *Christian Century* estimated that "ninety-nine Americans out of a hundred would today regard as an imbecile anyone who might suggest that, in the event of another European war, the United States should again participate in it." In general, the United States backed down from military intervention in foreign countries in the 1920s and 1930s. American efforts on the world stage focused on reducing weapons and improving relations with Latin America.

Nevertheless, conditions brewing in Europe and Asia would soon doom hopes for world peace. In Italy, Germany, and Spain, ruthless dictators came to power by promising to make their countries great through foreign conquest. In Japan, militaristic dreams of empire threatened U.S. interests in China and the Pacific. When the aggressor nations formed an alliance, the stage was set for global war.

Nazi parade watchers, 1932

The Granger Collection, New York

Antiwar sheet music, 1940

FOCUS OBJECTIVES

- Explain why the U.S. pursued an isolationist foreign policy after World War I.

- Describe how the U.S. tried to promote world peace in the 1920s and 1930s.

- Analyze how war debts and reparations affected European countries after World War I.

CORE RESOURCES

• Section 1 Daily Quiz

PREVIEW WORKSHOP

Following is a list of the significant people, places, and terms in this section. You may wish to use this list as a section preview.

People
- Emily Greene Balch
- Charles Evans Hughes

Places
- Manchuria

Terms
- isolationism
- unilateralism
- disarmament
- Five Power Agreement
- Four Power Treaty
- Nine Power Treaty
- Kellogg-Briand Pact
- debtor nation
- creditor nation
- moratorium

MOTIVATING: LINK TO TODAY

Ask students to give examples of ways that the U.S. promotes world peace today. Then tell students that this section explains how the U.S. attempted to reduce world tensions between 1921 and 1941.

Section 1

THE SEARCH FOR PEACE

F O C U S

- **Why did the United States pursue an isolationist foreign policy after World War I?**

- **How did the United States try to promote world peace in the 1920s and 1930s?**

- **How did war debts and reparations affect European countries after World War I?**

Profoundly disillusioned by the Great War, the United States sought to promote world peace during the 1920s. Fear of becoming involved in another war caused Americans to try to avoid conflict at any cost. As the world slipped into an economic depression and as dictators rose to power in Europe in the 1930s, however, isolation from the world's problems proved increasingly difficult for the United States.

Peace activists, 1940

LEGACIES OF WORLD WAR I

Over 8 million people, including more than 112,000 Americans, had died fighting in the Great War. Yet, because of the postwar chaos in Europe and the founding of a Communist government in the Soviet Union, Americans did not believe that the war had made the world "safe for democracy." The Women's International League for Peace and Freedom summed up the nation's doubts: "War to end war has proved a failure. The war is won, yet nowhere is there peace, security or happiness."

Americans worried about being dragged into another foreign conflict. "We ask only to live our own life in our own way, in friendship and sympathy with all, in alliance with none," declared Senator Hiram W. Johnson in 1922. Such sentiments led the United States to follow a policy of partial **isolationism**, or withdrawal from world affairs, in the 1920s and 1930s.

Isolationists did not want to cut off the United States completely from the affairs of the rest of the world. They merely wanted to avoid what Thomas Jefferson had called "entangling alliances" that could drag the United States into another war. Isolationists also supported U.S. **unilateralism**, that is, one-sided or independent action in foreign affairs.

Isolationism and unilateralism led the United States to shun membership in international organizations set up after the war, such as the League of Nations and the Permanent Court of International Justice (the World Court).

Presidents Coolidge, Hoover, and Roosevelt all proposed that the United States join the World Court, created to solve international disputes. Public opinion, however, ran strongly against membership. The Senate set strict terms for joining in order to guard its right to make treaties. The nations that already belonged to the World Court rejected the Senate's terms, and the matter was dropped.

AN ISOLATIONIST POLICY

Direct students to prepare a short speech to deliver before a class "Senate," explaining why the U.S. should pursue an isolationist policy after World War I. Have volunteers deliver their speeches to the class. Students may wish to include their speeches in their portfolios.

PROMOTING PEACE

Draw on the chalkboard a four-column chart with the headings: *Five Power Agreement, Four Power Treaty, Nine Power Treaty, Kellogg-Briand Pact.* Complete the chart by having students indicate the nations that signed each treaty and provide its terms. Then have volunteers explain how each treaty was intended to contribute to world peace.

WAR DEBTS AND REPARATIONS

Call on three volunteers to represent government officials from the U.S., Germany, and a U.S. ally after World War I. Ask each official to state his or her government's position on war debts and reparations, explaining how the issue is affecting his or her nation. Have remaining class members act as a tribunal to question the officials and challenge their positions. Ask the tribunal to determine an equitable solution to the issue.

▶

■■ **To avoid being drawn into European wars, the United States pursued an isolationist foreign policy after World War I.**

PROMOTING PEACE

Instead of joining international peacekeeping organizations, the United States used diplomacy to promote world peace. American peace groups urged the U.S. government to bring world leaders together to negotiate **disarmament**, or limiting their weapons. Jane Addams, Emily Greene Balch, Jeannette Rankin, and other leaders of the women's movement played important roles in these peace efforts. For their organizing efforts in the United States and abroad, both Addams (in 1931) and Balch (in 1946) received the Nobel Peace Prize.

The Washington Conference. In Washington, D.C., beginning in November 1921, the United States hosted an international conference on naval disarmament and Pacific security. The meeting was organized by Charles Evans Hughes, the U.S. secretary of state. Born in April 1862, he had served as governor of New York and almost won the 1916 presidential election against Woodrow Wilson. After this crushing defeat—Hughes had gone to bed on election night believing himself the victor only to wake and learn he had lost the nation's most important office by a scant 23 electoral votes—he turned to the issue of world peace. Ironically, he supported American entry into the League of Nations, the brainchild of his old enemy Wilson.

Charles Evans Hughes

At the Washington Conference Hughes surprised the other delegates with his bold proposal that the major powers scrap 78 large warships amounting to almost 1.9 million tons. He also called for a 10-year "naval holiday" during which no battleships or battle cruisers would be built.

Hughes proposed that the United States, Great Britain, and Japan scrap enough large warships to bring their naval strength into a ratio of 5:5:3. That is, Great Britain and the United States would be equal in naval strength, with a large-warship tonnage of roughly 525,000 each, while Japan would have some 315,000 tons. Italy and France would both be limited to some 175,000 tons. This plan became known as the **Five Power Agreement**. Marveled one observer: "Secretary Hughes sank in 35 minutes more ships than all the admirals of the world have sunk in . . . centuries."

The Washington Conference produced other important agreements as well. In the **Four Power Treaty**, Japan, Great Britain, France, and the United States pledged to respect one another's territory in the Pacific. The **Nine Power Treaty**, which included the nations that signed the Five Power agreement as well as the Netherlands, Portugal, Belgium, and China, guaranteed China's territorial integrity and promised to uphold the Open Door policy.

Japan's navy minister, Admiral Kato Tomosaburo, declared that the conference had created "a new order of seapower." He explained Japan's support for disarmament:

> ❝ Japan is ready for the new order of thought—the spirit of international friendship and cooperation for the greater good of humanity—which the Conference has brought about. ❞

For a time the Washington Conference agreements eased tensions in Asia. Japan withdrew, at least partially, from the Shandong (Shantung) Peninsula it had invaded in 1914 and from parts of Siberia it had occupied during the Russian Revolution. In 1930 Japan's agreement to extend

▲ **Delegates from Great Britain, France, Belgium, Italy, the Netherlands, Portugal, China, Japan, and the United States attended the Washington Conference.**

HISTORICAL SIDELIGHTS

Women for Peace
To promote world peace and women's rights, Jane Addams and other women activists founded the Women's International League for Peace and Freedom (WILPF) in 1919. Addams became its international leader, lobbying alongside Emily Greene Balch, secretary-treasurer of the WILPF, for peace accords in Geneva.

PRIMARY SOURCE

Description of Change: excerpted
Rationale: excerpted to focus on main idea

BIO GRAPHY PERSONALITIES IN HISTORY

Charles Evans Hughes served twice on the Supreme Court. First appointed by President William Howard Taft, Hughes left the bench to try for the presidency against Woodrow Wilson and lost by a slender margin. He became the chief justice of the Supreme Court during President Herbert Hoover's term and remained in that position for over a decade.

Practice

GUIDED PRACTICE

Organize students into small groups, and direct each group to write a dramatic headline for a newspaper story on each of the section's main topics. Have each group present its headlines, and then ask the class to devel-op a brief outline for a newspaper story on each topic.

INDEPENDENT PRACTICE

Tell students to use one of the headlines their group wrote in the Guided Practice activity and the related class outline to write a newspaper story on an aspect of the U.S. effort to promote world peace after World War I. Students may wish to include their stories in their portfolios.

Review and Assessment

REVIEW Have students use the Essential Points of the section as main headings of an outline titled "The Search for Peace." Ask them to use details from the section to add subheads to the outline. Then assign the Section 1 Review on p. 727.

ASSESS Assign the **Section 1 Daily Quiz** in *Core Resources.*

HISTORICAL SIDELIGHTS

Sanctions Against Japan

Although Secretary of State Henry L. Stimson supported economic sanctions against Japan, President Hoover rejected such a penalty. Hoover believed that sanctions would lead to U.S. involvement in a war in a region not vital to U.S. security.

COOPERATIVE LEARNING

Organize students into groups of three to prepare to teach the content that appears under each of the section's three main headings. Each group member should select one of the headings and create a teaching tool, such as an editorial cartoon, newspaper headline, or flowchart, that emphasizes the main idea under their assigned heading. Direct students to create a different teaching tool for each heading. Ask groups to present their plans to the class.

PRIMARY SOURCE

Description of Change: excerpted
Rationale: excerpted to focus on main idea

the holiday on warship construction marked the high point of postwar international cooperation.

Unsuccessful efforts. On April 6, 1927, the 10th anniversary of America's entry into World War I, the French foreign minister, Aristide Briand (ah-ree-steed bree-ahn), proposed that France and the United States enter into an agreement to outlaw war as a means of resolving their differences. The U.S. secretary of state, Frank Kellogg, made a counter-proposal that the pact include all nations. Sixty-two countries eventually signed the **Kellogg-Briand Pact**, which outlawed war "as an instrument of national policy" but allowed countries to go to war in self-defense. Unfortunately, the treaty lacked provisions for enforcement. One U.S. senator remarked that the treaty was "as effective to keep down war as a carpet would be to smother an earthquake."

■■ Through diplomatic conferences and international agreements the United States worked for world peace.

The pact's weaknesses became clear in September 1931. Japan, whose military leaders were gaining influence, violated all the international agreements and invaded the Chinese territory of Manchuria (see map on page 739). This invasion launched a bloody war between Japan and China. Although many Americans called for

▲ Suffragist and peace activist Carrie Chapman Catt praised the Kellogg-Briand Pact and lobbied Congress for its passage.

▲ These Japanese cavalrymen were photographed in Manchuria in December 1931, some three months after the war between China and Japan had begun.

an economic boycott of Japan, U.S. leaders refused to support sanctions against the Japanese. The failure of diplomacy to prevent Japanese aggression marked the end of attempts at international agreements. Preoccupied by the Japanese invasion and the worldwide economic depression, delegates of the League of Nations' 1932 World Disarmament Conference went home without agreeing to reduce weapons.

WAR DEBTS AND REPARATIONS

The issue of war debts also weakened peace efforts. In the late 1800s European investors had financed U.S. industrial growth, making the United States a **debtor nation** with respect to Europe. After 1914, however, the United States became a **creditor nation**. At the start of World War I, U.S. banks lent money to Great Britain and France so that they could buy armaments in the United States. The U.S. government granted billions more in credit to the Allies. By 1920 the Allies owed more than $10 billion to the United States.

The debtor nations argued that their debts to the United States should be wiped out. David Lloyd George, who had been the British prime minister when the United States entered the war, said:

❝ The United States did not from first to last make any sacrifice or contribution remotely comparable to those of her European Associates, in life, limb, money, material or trade, towards the victory which she shared with them. ❞

RETEACH Organize students into small groups. Tell each group to divide the section material, by subsections, among its members. Direct students to write questions about the main ideas presented in their assigned material. Have group members quiz one another with the questions.

Closure

Read students the following statement made by President Coolidge after World War I: "The world has had enough of the curse of hatred and selfishness, of destruction and war. . . . For the healing of the nations there must be good will and charity, confidence and peace." Have volunteers explain how American foreign policy in the 1920s reflected this attitude.

Extension

RESEARCH Have students research and report on the Japanese conquest of Manchuria.

INVESTIGATE Have students investigate and prepare an oral report on the economic hardships in Germany that were created by reparations.

U.S. officials rejected appeals from Great Britain, France, and Italy to cancel all their war debts. However, the U.S. government reduced the interest rates on the loans and canceled part of the debts. Still, the only way the Allies could pay their war debts to the United States was to collect reparations, or damages, from defeated Germany. In 1921 a reparations commission had set total German reparations at 132 billion gold marks ($32 billion). The Germans bitterly condemned the reparations as too harsh. Chancellor Joseph Wirth paid part of the reparations by borrowing money from Great Britain. The German government also printed paper money, causing massive inflation as the value of the German mark plunged.

In 1931, as the worldwide depression deepened, President Herbert Hoover declared a year's **moratorium**, or halt, on reparation and war-debt payments. The moratorium, however, only prolonged the crisis. Most of the war debts remained

▲ During the 1920s rapid inflation in Germany made most currency worthless. This woman used several million-mark notes to start a breakfast fire.

unpaid. By 1934 none of the debtor nations except Finland could make even a token payment.

America's efforts to collect the war debts sowed resentment in Europe. In Germany the economic hardships created by the reparations made people especially bitter. With his country near financial collapse, Adolf Hitler, a young German politician, hatched a plot to overthrow the German government in 1923. The plot failed, and Hitler was sent to jail. The next year, an international plan temporarily eased Germany's economic crisis by providing loans and extending German debt payments. Continuing German anger over reparations, however, would help bring Hitler to power 10 years later.

▪▪ **Europeans resented America's efforts to collect war debts. German anger over reparations helped Adolf Hitler gain support.**

SECTION REVIEW ANSWERS

IDENTIFY
For significance, see the following pages:
isolationism (p. 724)
unilateralism (p. 724)
disarmament (p. 725)
Emily Greene Balch (p. 725)
Charles Evans Hughes (p. 725)
Five Power Agreement (p. 725)
Four Power Treaty (p. 725)
Nine Power Treaty (p. 725)
Kellogg-Briand Pact (p. 726)
debtor nation (p. 726)
creditor nation (p. 726)
moratorium (p. 727)

LOCATE
For location, see the map on p. 739.

1. *because of public opinion and disillusionment with the Great War's failure to bring peace and security to Europe*
2. *supported diplomatic conferences; proposed naval armaments reductions; signed international agreements*
3. *U.S. efforts to collect war debts from the Allies caused them to press Germany for reparations payments, which created hardships and resentment in Germany and helped bring Hitler to power.*
4. *Essays might mention goals of disarmament and reduction of tensions in Asia and specific agreements.*
5. *lacked provisions for enforcement, so could not stop Japanese aggression*

■■ **S E C T I O N 1 R E V I E W**

IDENTIFY and explain the significance of the following: isolationism, unilateralism, disarmament, Emily Greene Balch, Charles Evans Hughes, Five Power Agreement, Four Power Treaty, Nine Power Treaty, Kellogg-Briand Pact, debtor nation, creditor nation, moratorium.

LOCATE and explain the importance of the following: Manchuria.

1. **MAIN IDEA** Why did the United States partially withdraw from world affairs in the 1920s and 1930s?

2. **MAIN IDEA** What steps did the United States take to work for world peace?

3. **ASSESSING CONSEQUENCES** How did war debts and reparations affect Germany and other European countries?

4. **WRITING TO INFORM** Imagine you are a delegate to the Washington Conference in 1921. Write an essay outlining the goals and accomplishments of the conference.

5. **ANALYZING** Why was the Kellogg-Briand Pact unsuccessful in resolving the conflict in Manchuria?

FOCUS OBJECTIVES

■ Explain how U.S. rela-
tions with Latin America
changed in the 1930s.

■ Describe how the Great
Depression affected
Latin American coun-
tries.

■ Identify the role played
by the U.S. in
Nicaraguan politics.

■ Describe how the U.S.
responded when Mexico
took over the Mexican
oil industry.

PRIMARY SOURCE

Description of Change:
excerpted
Rationale: excerpted to
focus on main idea

Section 2

RELATIONS WITH LATIN AMERICA

FOCUS

■ **How did U.S. relations with Latin America change in the 1930s?**
■ **How did the Great Depression affect Latin American countries?**
■ **What role did the United States play in Nicaraguan politics?**
■ **How did the United States respond when Mexico took over the
  Mexican oil industry?**

*In the 1920s and 1930s the United States preferred to use eco-
nomic influence—dollar diplomacy—rather than military force to
protect its interests in Latin America. For example, conflict
between the Mexican government and U.S. oil companies was
solved through diplomacy. However, when U.S. interests faced
threats in Nicaragua, America sent in the marines.*

Woman picking coffee beans in
El Salvador

THE GOOD NEIGHBOR

While the United States tried to avoid war in
Europe, presidents Coolidge, Hoover, and
Roosevelt all tried to improve relations with Latin
American countries. Before his inauguration,
Hoover toured Latin America to promote goodwill.
Franklin D. Roosevelt spelled out the **Good
Neighbor policy** in his inaugural speech of 1933:

66 In the field of world policy I would dedicate this nation to the policy of the good neighbor—the neighbor who resolutely respects
himself and, because he does so, respects the
rights of others. 99

To back up his words, Roosevelt in 1934
canceled the Platt Amendment, by which the
United States had claimed the right to intervene in
Cuba's affairs. Two years later he gave up the U.S.
claim to intervene unilaterally in Panama.
Roosevelt also withdrew marines from Haiti,
where they had been stationed as an occupying

force since 1915. However, in economic matters
the United States often behaved more like an over-
bearing landlord than a good neighbor.

U.S. investors played a powerful, and sometimes negative, role in Latin America. After World
War I, large U.S. companies increased their investments in banana, coffee, and sugar plantations in
Central America and the Caribbean.

■■ **In the 1930s the United States
pledged to reduce military
intervention in Latin America.
U.S. business investment
continued, however.**

The largest of the American companies was
the United Fruit Company, which owned millions
of acres in Central America and the Caribbean. In
Guatemala it was the largest landowner, exporter,
and employer. Besides establishing plantations,
United Fruit and other companies built roads and
railroads and controlled the ports and shipping
lines necessary to export their products. They also
tied these regions to the world economy, though

RELATIONS WITH LATIN AMERICA

Direct students to assume the role of FDR and prepare a script for a "fireside chat" explaining how his Good Neighbor policy will change U.S. relations with Latin America. Have volunteers deliver their talks. Students may wish to include their scripts in their portfolios.

DEPRESSION AFFECTS LATIN AMERICA

Organize students into small groups to create cause-and-effect charts showing the relationship between the depression, the rise of caudillos, and U.S. foreign policy in Latin America. Then have each group compare its chart with events in Nicaragua.

NICARAGUA AND MEXICO

Have students work in groups to create scripts for a short radio news commentary on U.S. involvement in Nicaraguan and Mexican politics in the 1930s. Commentaries should focus on similarities and differences in U.S. policy toward each country. After each group has "broadcast" its commentary, ask each student to write a paragraph assessing whether Roosevelt's policies toward Mexico showed that the U.S. had become a "good neighbor." ▶

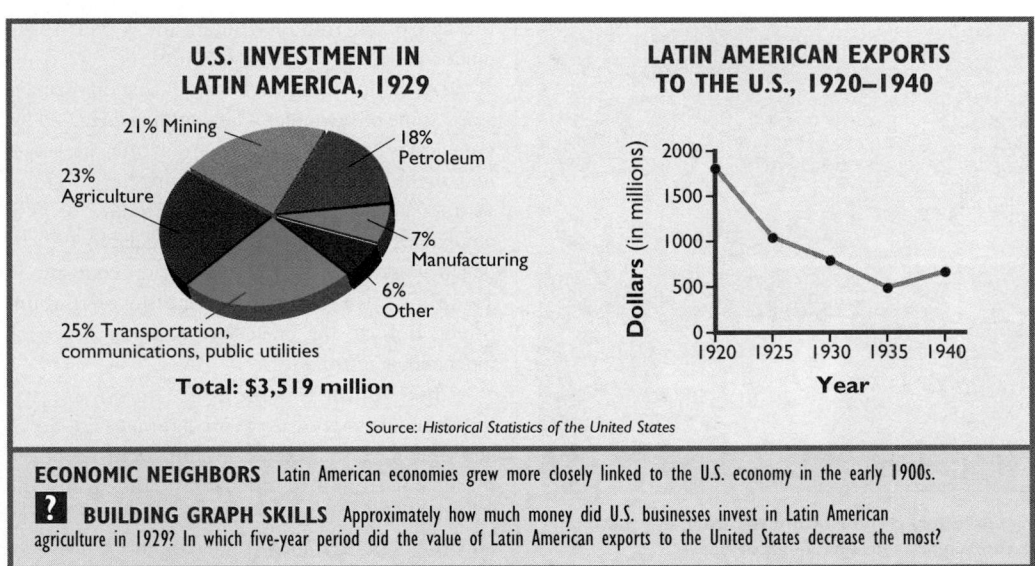

ECONOMIC NEIGHBORS Latin American economies grew more closely linked to the U.S. economy in the early 1900s.

? BUILDING GRAPH SKILLS Approximately how much money did U.S. businesses invest in Latin American agriculture in 1929? In which five-year period did the value of Latin American exports to the United States decrease the most?

profits went mostly to the corporations and wealthy Latin Americans.

In addition to their economic importance in Latin America, the U.S. companies had political power. They made alliances with Latin American landowners and politicians and often played a role in governing the countries in which they operated. The economic and political powers of the large American companies earned them the resentment of many Latin Americans. Chilean poet Pablo Neruda (nay-ROO-thah) wrote:

66 The Fruit Company, Inc.
reserved for itself the most
    succulent,
the central coast of my own land,
the delicate waist of America.
It rechristened its territories
as the "Banana Republics." 99

"Banana republics" were countries run largely to serve the interests of the foreign companies that grew bananas and other crops.

THE RISE OF DICTATORS

The Wall Street crash of 1929 sent shock waves through Latin America. Worldwide depression meant lower prices for coffee, bananas, and other crops on which Latin American economies depended. In El Salvador, coffee prices fell so low

that some plantation owners did not bother to harvest the 1930 coffee crop. Farm wages dropped to eight cents a day.

As workers lost their jobs, the gulf between Latin America's small class of wealthy landowners and the large class of poor landless people widened. The U.S. diplomat Major A. R. Harris commented on the inequality he noted between the classes in El Salvador in 1931:

66 The first thing one observes . . . is the number of expensive automobiles on the streets. . . . There seems to be nothing between these high-priced cars and the ox-cart with its barefooted attendant. . . . Roughly 90 percent of the wealth of the country is held by about one-half of one percent of the population. 99

In countries throughout the region, the difficult 1930s brought **caudillos** (kow-THEE-yohs) to power. These caudillos were military leaders who used force to maintain order. In 1932 the caudillo Maximiliano Hernández Martínez brutally crushed a revolt by peasants in El Salvador's hard-hit coffee-growing region. Thousands of peasants were massacred.

During the 1930s caudillos also came to power in Cuba, the Dominican Republic, Guatemala, and Honduras. U.S. diplomats sometimes denounced the caudillos' methods of staying in power: bans on opposition parties and restrictions

MAKING CONNECTIONS

Sociology
American journalist Carleton Beals traveled through Guatemala in the late 1920s. There he saw railway passengers crammed into second-class coaches and seated on the floor because there were far more cars for carrying bananas than for passengers. When asked about it, Guatemalan President José María Orellana replied, "Yes, bananas are the yellow gold of Guatemala."

PRIMARY SOURCES

Description of Change: excerpted
Rationale: excerpted to focus on main idea

THE AMERICAN NATION VIDEODISC PROGRAM

U.S. Warships in Havana Harbor

2A   41576   :32

Practice

GUIDED PRACTICE

Write *Relations with Latin America* on the chalkboard and circle it. Then draw lines radiating from the circle. Ask students to cite events that affected U.S.–Latin American relations after World War I. As you write each event on a line, ask students to explain how and why it affected those relations.

INDEPENDENT PRACTICE

Have students choose one of the events cited in the Guided Practice activity and, in the role of an American businessperson or a Latin American nationalist, write a newspaper editorial attacking or defending U.S. actions and policy. Students may wish to include their editorials in their portfolios.

Review and Assessment

REVIEW Organize students into four groups and assign each group one of the section's four subsections. Ask each group to create an editorial cartoon that illustrates the Essential Point of their assigned subsection. Have the class interpret each group's cartoon. Then assign the Section 2 Review on p. 731.

ASSESS Assign the **Section 2 Daily Quiz** in *Core Resources*.

HISTORICAL SIDELIGHTS

Dominican Dictator

Rafael Trujillo Molina, dictator in the Dominican Republic, rose to power through the National Guard. He "won" the 1930 presidential election with more votes than registered voters. While in office he promoted his nine-year-old son, Ramfis, to the rank of brigadier general. Trujillo had a hand in Dominican affairs until his assassination in 1961.

VOICES IN HISTORY

At the Havana Conference in January 1928, Latin American leaders criticized U.S. intervention in Nicaragua. Later, on August 4, 1928, Sandino warned in a letter to 15 Latin American presidents: "Do the Latin American governments think perhaps that the Yankees would be content with the conquest of Nicaragua alone? Have these governments perhaps forgotten that among twenty-one American republics six have already lost their sovereignty? Panama, Puerto Rico, Cuba, Haiti, Santo Domingo, and Nicaragua."

▲ **U.S. Army cooks buy produce from Nicaraguan vendors. The baskets contain papayas and alligator pears.**

on freedom of speech. However, the United States often supported the caudillos, since they created favorable environments for U.S. businesses.

■■ **The depression wrecked Latin American economies, caused social unrest, and helped bring caudillos to power in many countries.**

INTERVENTION IN NICARAGUA

The United States played a large role in Nicaraguan politics throughout the 1920s and 1930s. In 1925 General Emiliano Chamorro (chah-MAWR-roh) overthrew the government, sparking a bitter civil war.

The United States refused to recognize Chamorro. In May 1926 President Coolidge sent in the marines to protect U.S. commercial interests. He also sent Henry Stimson, a long-time public official, to negotiate an end to the civil war. Stimson brought the two sides together and they negotiated a peace treaty in May 1927. More important, Stimson called for the abolition of Nicaraguan armed forces. U.S. troops would then train a new Nicaraguan National Guard to maintain order after the withdrawal of U.S. forces.

Augusto César Sandino (sahn-DEE-noh), a general who opposed Chamorro, refused to accept Stimson's proposal. Born in 1893, Sandino was the son of an Indian woman and a well-to-do landowner.

After attending high school, Sandino supervised some of his father's landholdings. He fled his hometown in 1920 to avoid arrest after he shot a man in the leg during a fight. During the next three years, Sandino worked as a mechanic for U.S. companies in Honduras and Guatemala. In 1923 he began working for a U.S.–owned oil company in Tampico, Mexico. There Sandino read about Simon Bolívar, the great hero of Latin American independence struggles.

In 1926, after his return to Nicaragua, Sandino organized a revolt against Chamorro and Chamorro's successor, Adolfo Díaz. He hoped to rid Nicaragua of the Americans, whom he viewed as invaders, and to allow ordinary Nicaraguans to control their country's land and wealth. He planned to help workers and peasants "exploit our own natural resources for the benefit of the Nicaraguan family in general."

Sandino's army, which varied from as few as 30 to as many as 3,000, proved a tough adversary for the U.S. Marines. Although the Americans used aerial bombing for the first time against Sandino's forces, they could not completely destroy the army, which relied on sympathetic farmers to feed and house them.

The marines never defeated Sandino. The war became increasingly costly for the United States in the midst of the depression. In 1933 President Hoover withdrew the last of the U.S. troops. A year later, the commander of the U.S.–trained National Guard, General Anastasio Somoza, ordered Sandino's assassination. With Sandino dead, organized resistance to Somoza and his military evaporated. Somoza forced out the Nicaraguan president in 1936 and took over the presidency the next year. With U.S. backing, Somoza and other members of his family ruled Nicaragua almost without interruption until the Sandinista revolution (named for Sandino) overthrew the dynasty in 1979.

▲ **Augusto César Sandino**

RETEACH Organize students into small groups and have them assign one Focus question to each member. Direct students to prepare brief answers to the questions and to share their answers with their group.

Closure

Ask students to evaluate how "good" a "neighbor" the U.S. was with Latin America in the 1920s and 1930s.

Extension

INVESTIGATE Have students investigate and report on how caudillos came to power in Cuba, the Dominican Republic, Guatemala, or Honduras during the 1930s.

COMPARE Have students research the everyday lives of the poor and the rich in Latin America in the 1930s and write a report that compares and contrasts the two.

■■ **The United States opposed Sandino and trained the National Guard, which helped bring Somoza to power.**

RELATIONS WITH MEXICO

The most severe test of the Good Neighbor policy came when Mexico's president, Lázaro Cárdenas (KAHR-thay-nahs), began to **nationalize**, or assert government control over, the country's oil industry in March 1938. Although the Mexican Constitution of 1917 proclaimed that Mexico controlled all its underground resources (see Chapter 19), U.S. and British firms had continued to own and operate oil companies in Mexico. When the foreign companies refused to meet the demands of Mexican oil workers for higher wages and better working conditions, however, President Cárdenas nationalized the oil fields.

U.S. oil companies hotly criticized the Mexican seizure of their property. They pressed the U.S. State Department to resist the nationalization. Some called for action to oust Cárdenas. Meanwhile, the U.S. ambassador to Mexico, Josephus Daniels, argued for a compromise between the Mexican government and the oil companies. He urged the United States to recognize Mexico's right to control its oil resources but added that U.S. companies should be compensated for the property they had lost.

▲ President Lázaro Cárdenas (center) is shown with Britain's minister to Mexico (left) and Mexico's secretary of foreign relations (right) shortly before diplomatic relations between Mexico and Great Britain were broken in May 1938.

Most Mexicans supported Cárdenas's bold action against the oil companies. Mexicans worried, however, that the United States might invade Mexico to restore U.S. oil companies' property rights. With events in Europe and Asia looking increasingly threatening, however, Roosevelt decided to maintain good relations with Mexico. He acknowledged Mexico's right to control its own resources and urged the oil companies to reach an agreement with the Mexican government for fair compensation. Mexico agreed to the compromise and began payments in 1939.

■■ **Roosevelt resisted calls from oil companies for U.S. intervention to protect their interests in Mexico.**

SECTION 2 REVIEW

IDENTIFY and explain the significance of the following: Good Neighbor policy, caudillos, Maximiliano Hernández Martínez, Emiliano Chamorro, Henry Stimson, Augusto César Sandino, Adolfo Díaz, Anastasio Somoza, Lázaro Cárdenas, nationalize, Josephus Daniels.

LOCATE and explain the importance of the following: El Salvador, Nicaragua.

1. **MAIN IDEA** How did the United States hope to secure its interests in Latin America after World War I?

2. **MAIN IDEA** What effect did the Great Depression have on Latin America?

3. **IDENTIFYING CAUSE AND EFFECT** How did the United States intervene in Nicaraguan politics throughout the 1920s and 1930s? What was the effect of this intervention?

4. **WRITING TO PERSUADE** Imagine you are Josephus Daniels in 1938. Write a memorandum to President Roosevelt recommending U.S. policy toward Mexico after the oil fields were nationalized.

5. **EVALUATING** Why did Augusto César Sandino organize a revolt against Díaz?

FOCUS OBJECTIVES

- List the factors that led to the rise of dictatorships after World War I.

- Explain how other countries responded to German aggression.

- Describe the events that caused World War II.

- Explain how the U.S. moved closer to becoming involved in World War II.

Section 3

THE ROAD TO WAR

FOCUS

- **What led to the rise of dictatorships after World War I?**
- **How did other countries respond to German aggression?**
- **What caused World War II?**
- **How did the United States move closer to becoming involved in World War II?**

America's isolationist stand faced a severe test when dictators came to power in Italy, Germany, Spain, and Japan in the 1920s and 1930s. Americans tried to stay out of European affairs. Neutrality proved difficult, however, as France and other nations fell before German armies, Great Britain battled for its life, and Japan expanded its territory in Asia.

Japanese women raising money for the war in China

THE RISE OF DICTATORSHIPS

Most European nations after World War I faced inflation and unemployment, which caused political and social unrest. Disagreements over how to solve these problems led to violent clashes between Communists and conservatives. Right-wing military leaders came to power in several countries by promising to end the chaos.

Mussolini in Italy. Although Italy had been on the winning side when World War I ended, many Italians felt they had not benefited from the Treaty of Versailles. Thousands of Italian soldiers returned home after the war only to find themselves jobless. Many joined the Italian Communist party, which urged Italian peasants to take over land and Communist workers to seize factories.

To smash the Communist party and promote his own rise to power, Benito Mussolini founded the **Fascist party** in 1921. The Fascists believed that a military-dominated government should control all aspects of society. Beginning in 1921,

bloody clashes between Communists and Fascists created a situation bordering on civil war. In October 1922 Mussolini led an army of his followers, whose black uniforms gave them the name **Blackshirts**, in a march on Rome. With the support of nationalists, who wanted to strengthen Italy, and of businesspeople who opposed the Socialists and Communists, the Fascists occupied the city.

▲ **Benito Mussolini** (center), shown here with his followers during their march on Rome, was known as *Il Duce* (eel DOO-chay), or "the leader."

Teaching the Section

RISE OF DICTATORSHIPS

The king appointed Mussolini prime minister and granted him dictatorial powers. Mussolini limited freedom of speech, arrested political opponents, and restricted voting rights. Acting on a pledge to make Italy an imperial power, Mussolini sent Italian forces into the African nation of Ethiopia in 1935 (see map on page 736). The small, poorly equipped Ethiopian army proved no match for the Italian dive-bombers and machine guns. The U.S. Congress, fearful of being drawn into the conflict, passed a neutrality act banning arms shipments to both sides. Such an embargo hurt Ethiopia more than Italy, which continued to receive weapons from Germany and oil from U.S. companies.

African Americans raised money to send relief and medical aid to the Ethiopians. Thousands of African Americans volunteered to fight in Ethiopia, but pressure from the U.S. government forced Ethiopia to reject such support. This lack of support convinced other fascist countries, such as Germany, that aggression would go unpunished.

Hitler in Germany. In 1932 Adolf Hitler's National Socialist party, or **Nazi party**, won more than 40 percent of the vote, and Hitler became chancellor the next year. While in prison, Hitler had written *Mein Kampf* (*My Struggle*), which laid out his plans to restore German power. Hitler blamed Jews, intellectuals, and Communists for Germany's decline. The book won him many supporters, especially among the middle class and the unemployed ruined by inflation and the depression.

Hitler's government, called the Third Reich (the Third Empire), claimed dictatorial powers. Hitler prohibited Jews and non-Nazis from holding government positions, outlawed strikes, and made military service mandatory. Nazi storm troopers, known as **Brownshirts** because of the color of their uniforms, crushed all political opposition.

Hitler's tight control over German industry strengthened the economy and reduced unemployment, allowing him to rearm the country in violation of the Treaty of Versailles. Hitler declared:

> ❝ The buildup of the armed forces is the most important precondition for . . . political power. . . . How is this political power to be used when it is won? . . . Maybe fighting for new export possibilities, maybe . . . conquest of new *Lebensraum* [space for expansion] in the East. ❞

◀ During the 1930s Nazi posters, such as the one shown here, appealed to those who longed to see Germany restored to its former position as a world power.

In March 1936, German troops moved into the Rhineland (see map on page 736). Two years later they overran Austria. Hitler then turned toward the Sudetenland (soo-DAYT-uhn-land), in western Czechoslovakia, where more than three million German-speaking people lived. Hitler demanded that Czechoslovakia turn over the region to Germany. Czechoslovakia refused Hitler's demand.

Meanwhile, Hitler's **anti-Semitism**, or hatred of Jews, became official government policy. He deprived Jews of their German citizenship and authorized the destruction of Jewish property. On November 9, 1938, Nazi thugs burned down synagogues and destroyed Jewish businesses. Known as *Kristallnacht*, "the night of broken glass," the violence provided a chilling preview of the still more-terrible fate that awaited European Jews and others who fell victim to Hitler's murderous rule. Despite outrage at these events, however, most Americans remained unwilling to intervene in Germany or to encourage Jewish immigration.

Franco in Spain. Spain did not escape the spread of fascism. In the 1930s Spain faced bitter political conflicts. In 1931 a constitution that limited the power of the military and the Catholic church went into effect. It called for such reforms as universal suffrage, nationalization of public utilities, and land for peasants.

Their power threatened by the liberal reforms, conservative military men united under the leadership of General Francisco Franco. In July 1936 the Fascist army officers tried to overthrow the government, starting the **Spanish Civil War** between Fascists and Loyalists.

HISTORICAL SIDELIGHTS

The "Brown Condor"
African American pilot John Robinson was the only American volunteer in the war in Ethiopia. Known as the "Brown Condor," news of his exploits against Mussolini's Blackshirts created excitement in the African American community. When Robinson returned to the U.S. in 1936, he promoted the Ethiopian cause and praised Haile Selassie, the "brave and noble leader" of Ethiopia.

[AV] TRANSPARENCY
Everyday Life in America Transparency and **Worksheet 25**

PRIMARY SOURCE
Description of Change: excerpted and bracketed
Rationale: excerpted to focus on main idea; bracketed to clarify meaning

Teaching the Section

RESPONSE TO GERMAN AGGRESSION

Have students write an official statement from the point of view of a policymaker attending the Munich Conference to explain why the European powers settled on the policy of appeasement. Call on volunteers to read their statements. Then ask students to assess the sincerity of European leaders who argued that appeasement would maintain peace. Ask students to cite evidence to support their assessments.

GLOBAL CONNECTIONS

Between 1900 and 1930 Japan became a major exporter of raw silk, and about half of Japan's peasants depended on its production. During the Great Depression silk prices dropped about 50 percent, dealing a blow to the Japanese economy and impoverishing many peasants. This development became a prime factor in discrediting the policies and leaders of the 1920s and laid the foundation for Japanese militarism.

THROUGH OTHERS' EYES

As Italian and German troops invaded Spain, some Americans recognized the urgency of the Spanish situation. Henry L. Stimson pleaded against Roosevelt's refusal to sell arms to Spain: "If this Loyalist Government is overthrown, it is evident now that its defeat will be solely due to the fact that it has been deprived of its rights to buy . . . the munitions necessary for its defense."

PRIMARY SOURCE

Description of Change: excerpted and bracketed
Rationale: excerpted to focus on main idea; bracketed to clarify meaning

After almost three years of fighting, Franco took over the national government with German and Italian military aid. The Soviet Union aided the Loyalists, but Roosevelt's fears of being drawn into a European war kept the United States from sending aid.

Individual Americans, however, did join the fight against fascism. Some 3,000 Americans joined the Abraham Lincoln Brigade, one of several international brigades made up of volunteers who went to Spain. Ernest Hemingway, who covered the Spanish Civil War, expressed his support for the Loyalist cause in the powerful novel *For Whom the Bell Tolls* (1940).

THE SPANISH CIVIL WAR

After the Spanish Civil War, many Loyalists remained bitter over the failure of Western nations to support their cause. In 1940 Julio Alvarez del Vayo, a wartime diplomat for the defeated Spanish Republic, charged that this lack of support had cost the Loyalists the war:

❝*A*part from Russia, from whom she was able, for a time, to buy arms, Republican Spain had no great powers at her side to supply her with men and munitions. . . . Alone, abandoned to their fate, . . . the Spanish people fought for nearly three years against the armed might of the totalitarian states. . . .

My one desire is to show what it would have meant to the Western democracies to have had in Spain a certain ally ready to defend the liberty and dignity of Europe against all attempts at domination and oppression. If . . . Republican Spain had not been defeated, the present war [World War II] would never have begun. . . .

No, it was not Spanish democracy that failed. It was the other democracies who failed to save democratic Spain, as they will one day learn to their cost. ❞

▲ Shown here are Spanish Loyalists leaving Madrid to fight a rebel army advancing on the city.

Militarists in Japan. As German aggression threatened Europe, Japanese expansion loomed in Asia (see map on page 739). Although Japan had moved toward democracy in the 1920s, the leaders of Japan's military forces remained independent of the government. These military men wanted to lessen Japan's reliance on foreign imports, to reduce the influence of Western countries in Asia, and to promote Japanese expansion throughout Asia.

The creation of a Japanese empire in Asia would give Japan direct control over territories that produced rubber, petroleum, iron, and timber. Worsening economic conditions in Japan strengthened the appeal of the militarists' position.

Japan's 1931 invasion of Manchuria signaled its imperial ambitions. In 1934 and 1935, breaking their Washington Conference pledges, the Japanese began a rapid naval buildup. On July 7, 1937, Japanese and Chinese troops clashed near Beijing (Peking). This incident soon developed into a full-scale war. Japan occupied northern China and launched devastating bombing raids against Chinese cities. Although the League of Nations and the United States condemned Japan's actions, they failed to check Japanese expansion.

■■ **In Italy, Germany, Spain, and Japan, postwar problems brought military dictators to power in the 1920s and 1930s.**

THE RESPONSE TO FASCISM

The spread of fascism in Asia and Europe caused a shake-up in international diplomatic relationships. The most surprising of these realignments was the shift in U.S.–Soviet relations. The Soviets were concerned about curbing the Japanese, who had massed troops in nearby Manchuria. Hoping "to avert the Japanese danger," Soviet foreign affairs commissar Maksim Litvinov mended diplomatic fences with the United States. In November 1933, after years of hostility between the two countries, the United States formally recognized the Soviet Union.

The fascist powers also formalized their ties. In 1936 the rest of Europe trembled when Germany and Italy formed a military alliance. The two countries became known as the **Axis powers**, which later included Japan.

Roosevelt called for European leaders to meet and resolve their conflicts peacefully. Hitler and Mussolini joined British prime minister Neville Chamberlain and French premier Édouard Daladier (dah-lahd-yay) at Munich in September 1938. The four leaders at the **Munich Conference** signed a pact giving Germany control of the Sudetenland. The European leaders had opted for a policy of **appeasement**, or giving in to demands in an effort to avoid larger conflicts. Many politicians underestimated Hitler's expansionist goals, believing that Hitler sought only to remedy what he considered wrongs created by the Treaty of Versailles. But other politicians, such as Winston Churchill of Great Britain, feared that appeasement would only encourage Hitler to take more territory. Britain and other nations in Europe sped up their rearmament.

■■ European leaders tried to appease Hitler to avoid war.

Most Americans denounced the actions of the Axis powers, but isolationism remained strong. American pacifists—religious groups such as the Mennonites and the Society of Friends (Quakers) and organizations such as the Committee on the Cause and Cure of War—urged U.S. leaders to reject war as a means of solving conflicts.

A series of neutrality laws passed by Congress from 1935 to 1939 expressed Americans' desire for peace. The neutrality laws (1) prohibited the shipment of U.S. munitions to warring nations, (2) required warring nations that bought goods from America to transport these goods in their own ships, and (3) forbade Americans to travel on the vessels of warring nations.

Not all Americans endorsed neutrality. Many urged the United States to help the nations under attack. If America allowed aggression to go unpunished, they warned, the United States might one day find itself surrounded by powerful enemies.

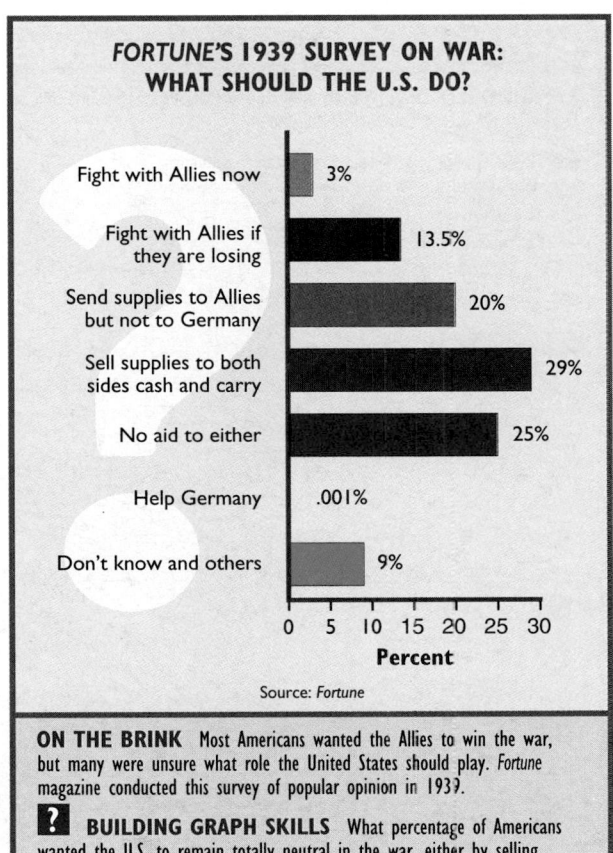

FORTUNE'S 1939 SURVEY ON WAR: WHAT SHOULD THE U.S. DO?

	Percent
Fight with Allies now	3%
Fight with Allies if they are losing	13.5%
Send supplies to Allies but not to Germany	20%
Sell supplies to both sides cash and carry	29%
No aid to either	25%
Help Germany	.001%
Don't know and others	9%

Source: *Fortune*

ON THE BRINK Most Americans wanted the Allies to win the war, but many were unsure what role the United States should play. *Fortune* magazine conducted this survey of popular opinion in 1939.

? **BUILDING GRAPH SKILLS** What percentage of Americans wanted the U.S. to remain totally neutral in the war, either by selling supplies to both sides or by refusing to aid either side?

By 1937 President Roosevelt had become convinced that the United States must resist aggression. In October he urged other countries to quarantine, or isolate, expansionist countries. Most Americans, however, were not yet ready to accept U.S. involvement in the quarantine. Proof of this position came in December 1937, when Japanese planes attacked the U.S. gunboat *Panay* and three U.S. oil tankers on China's Yangtze (YANG-SEE) River (Chang Jiang). Several U.S. citizens were killed, and many were wounded. Yet a public opinion poll showed that 54 percent of Americans thought the United States should withdraw from China rather than risk becoming involved in a war.

WAR!

U.S. public opinion slowly changed, however, as German aggression continued. In March 1939, Hitler's armies occupied all of Czechoslovakia. Hitler also proposed to annex the Polish port city of

Teaching the Section

CAUSES OF WORLD WAR II

Write the following on the chalkboard: *World War II Begins.* Ask students to offer events that led to World War II. Using student responses, create a time line of these events on the chalkboard. Then have students suggest policies that world leaders could have employed that might have avoided the German invasion of Poland and the outbreak of war. *(Responses might include calls for arms reduction in Europe, further appeasement, involvement of League of Nations in a settlement, tougher stance toward Germany, preventive war against Germany.)* Discuss each response with the class.

Map Caption Answer
Poland held land between Germany and East Prussia.

HISTORICAL SIDELIGHTS

The Baltic States

The Soviet occupation of Lithuania, Latvia, and Estonia was briefly interrupted in 1941, when Hitler invaded the Soviet Union and occupied the Baltic States. By 1945, however, the three countries were once again under Soviet control. All three states attempted to repel the Soviet takeover, but many members of the opposition were killed or deported to labor camps in Siberia. By 1988 the three republics organized protests favoring sovereignty, and in late 1989 and early 1990, non-Communist governments emerged. In 1990 the new governments declared their intentions to secede from the Soviet Union and became independent the next year after the collapse of the USSR.

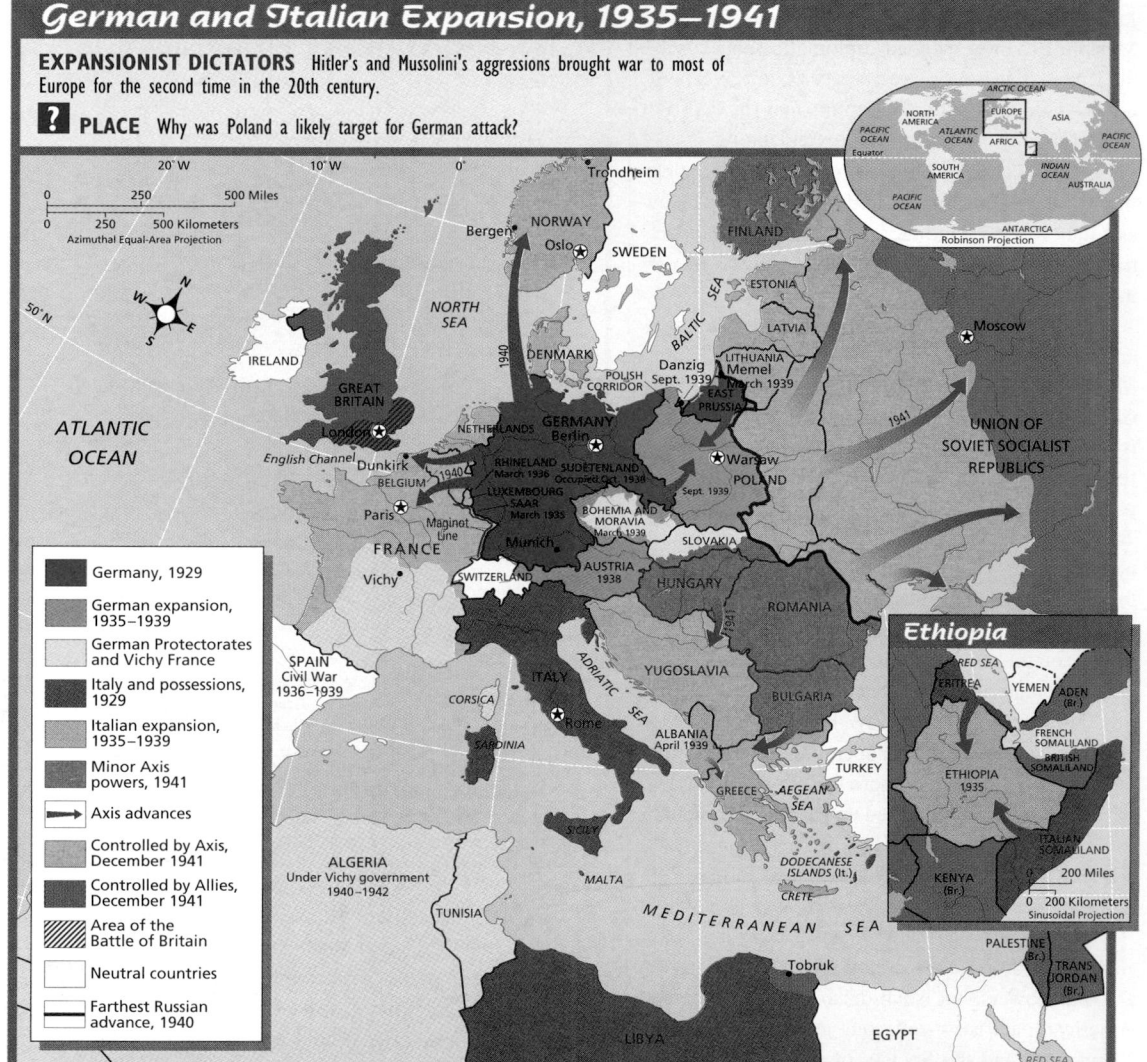

German and Italian Expansion, 1935–1941

EXPANSIONIST DICTATORS Hitler's and Mussolini's aggressions brought war to most of Europe for the second time in the 20th century.

? PLACE Why was Poland a likely target for German attack?

Germany, 1929
German expansion, 1935–1939
German Protectorates and Vichy France
Italy and possessions, 1929
Italian expansion, 1935–1939
Minor Axis powers, 1941
Axis advances
Controlled by Axis, December 1941
Controlled by Allies, December 1941
Area of the Battle of Britain
Neutral countries
Farthest Russian advance, 1940

Ethiopia

Danzig (DAN-sig), but the Poles refused. In addition, Mussolini's troops invaded Albania on April 7.

Awakening at long last to their common peril, Great Britain and France announced that a German attack upon Poland would mean war and called on the Soviet Union to join them in resisting further aggression. Instead, on August 23, 1939, the Soviet Union signed a **nonaggression pact** with Nazi Germany. This surprising union came about in part because of a secret clause in the pact in which the two nations agreed to divide Poland between them.

On September 1, 1939, German bombers and armored divisions crashed across the border into Poland. Two days later, Great Britain and France declared war on Germany. World War II had begun. Soviet troops, meanwhile, invaded Poland from the east, occupied the independent nations Estonia, Latvia, and Lithuania, and demanded the right to establish military bases in Finland. When Finland refused, the Soviet Union attacked the small nation and soon annexed part of its territory.

■■ **Allied appeasement failed to halt German aggression. In 1939 the German invasion of Poland sparked World War II.**

▲ This 1939 cartoon satirizes the lack of trust between Germany and the Soviet Union, even after the two nations signed the nonaggression pact.

Roosevelt took steps to aid the European countries under siege. Some three weeks after the German invasion of Poland, he urged Congress to amend the neutrality act that barred the export of munitions. After a six-week debate, Congress agreed on a compromise. The new law allowed any nation to buy munitions from the United States but required that the goods be shipped on foreign vessels.

The European conflict loomed as a major issue in the 1940 election. Both candidates—Roosevelt, who sought a third term, and Republican Wendell Willkie—promised to keep America out of the conflict. In a radio talk on September 3, 1939, Roosevelt pledged: "As long as it remains in my power to prevent, there will be no blackout of peace in the United States."

Roosevelt won his bid for an unprecedented third term. In spite of his public promises to pursue peace, however, he became increasingly alarmed by Japanese and German aggression. He began to view American involvement as unavoidable and started a campaign to prepare U.S. defenses for the likely conflict.

By the end of 1940, U.S. supplies flowed to Great Britain. The British, however, had little cash

to pay for needed war materials. Roosevelt proposed that the United States lend or lease arms and other supplies to the British and the other Allies. Congress passed the **Lend-Lease Act** in March 1941. It appropriated $7 billion for ships, planes, tanks, and other supplies to non-Axis countries.

■■ **The United States took its first step toward involvement in the growing European conflict by extending aid to the Allies.**

CONTINUING AGGRESSION

While Hitler carried on his **blitzkrieg** (BLITS-kreeg), or "lightning war," against Poland, the French mobilized. In May 1940, German armored divisions, supported by fighter planes and bombers, crashed through the **Maginot Line**, a line of defenses along the French border with Germany. The Germans occupied France; the Netherlands, Belgium, Luxembourg (known as the Low Countries); Denmark; and Norway.

Germany established a puppet government in France headed by Philippe Pétain (pay-tan) and headquartered in the town of Vichy (VISH-ee). A secret French organization known as the Resistance continued to oppose the Germans. In London, French general Charles de Gaulle headed a committee called "Free France," which organized opposition against the Germans.

With the fall of France, Great Britain stood alone. On May 10, 1940, Winston Churchill

▲ Members of the Resistance continued to fight the Germans after the fall of France. This French girl was part of a patrol that hunted down German snipers in Paris late in 1944.

Practice

GUIDED PRACTICE

Organize students into small groups and assign each group one of the following: Italy, Germany, Spain. Ask groups to create cause-and-effect charts that show why and how dictators came to power in each coun-try. Call on volunteers from each group to draw the group's chart on the chalkboard.

INDEPENDENT PRACTICE

Ask students to use the information in the Guided Practice to develop maps that illus-trate the rise of dictatorships in Europe in the 1930s. Students should label each coun-try, identify the dictator and/or parties that came to power in the 1920s and 1930s, and annotate their maps with information from the Guided Practice charts.

Review and Assessment

REVIEW Write the following statement on the chalkboard: *Americans found it diffi-cult to avoid foreign entanglements because* . . . . Call on a volunteer to list one reason. Then call on another student to add another reason. Write students' responses on the chalkboard. Then assign the Section 3 Review on p. 739.

ASSESS Assign the **Section 3 Daily Quiz** in *Core Resources.*

 GLOBAL CONNECTIONS

The U.S. embargo caused dissension among Japan's leaders. The embargo effec-tively ended oil shipments to Japan, which realized that its oil reserves would not see it through a major war. Japan's cabinet settled on a plan of working toward preparedness for war while simultaneously attempting a negotiated set-tlement. According to the plan, if the diplomatic mea-sures proved unsuccessful, Japan would enter into hos-tilities against the U.S., Britain, and the Nether-lands. Emperor Hirohito opposed the plan and advo-cated peace over war. Although the U.S. was aware of the plan because it had cracked Japan's diplomatic codes, it was unaware of the dissension among Japanese leaders.

PRIMARY SOURCE

Description of Change: excerpted

Rationale: excerpted to focus on main idea

▲ **RAF combat pilots are shown rushing to their planes to fight German bombers somewhere over French territory.**

became prime minister. With a rare gift for leader-ship, Churchill rallied the British:

> 66 Hitler knows that he will have to break us in this island or lose the war. . . . Let us therefore brace ourselves to our duties, and so bear ourselves that, if the British Empire and its Commonwealth last for a thousand years, men will still say, "This was their finest hour." 99

On June 10 Italy declared war on France and Great Britain. In August, Hitler unleashed his bombers against Great Britain. The outnumbered British Royal Air Force (RAF) flew day and night to combat the German blitzkrieg.

TENSIONS MOUNT IN THE ATLANTIC

In the face of continuing German attacks, U.S. aid to the Allies gradually increased. By the spring of 1941, German and Italian submarines were turning the North Atlantic into a graveyard of ships. In April, U.S. airplanes and naval vessels began to patrol the Atlantic, notifying British warships of the location of German ships.

A few months later, Roosevelt issued "shoot-on-sight" orders to U.S. warships operat-ing in the North Atlantic "safety zone" America had established in 1939. U.S. warships also began to accompany merchant vessels as far as Iceland. In November, Congress voted to allow U.S. mer-chant vessels to enter combat areas. Roosevelt armed the merchant vessels and provided them with gun crews.

With the United States moving rapidly toward undeclared war with Germany, Roosevelt and

Churchill met secretly off the coast of Newfoundland in August 1941. The two leaders agreed to a series of principles for international relations. Known as the **Atlantic Charter**, the agreement (1) pledged that the United States and Great Britain would forego territorial expansion, (2) affirmed their respect for the right of every nation to choose its own form of government, and (3) called for freedom of international trade and equal access to raw materials for all countries. Once the war was over, the charter declared, aggressor states should be disarmed, and all nations should work together to rid the world of fear and want.

THE GROWING THREAT FROM JAPAN

As war raged in Europe, Japan added to its conquests in Asia. In July 1941, Japanese troops occupied French Indochina (see map). President Roosevelt immediately froze all Japanese assets in the United States and approved an embargo on shipments of gasoline, machine tools, scrap iron, and steel to Japan. Japan retaliated by freezing all U.S. assets in areas under its control. As a result, trade between the United States and Japan practically ended.

As U.S. resistance to Japanese aggression grew stronger, Japan's war leaders secretly planned an attack on the United States. Even as the plan went forward, however, a Japanese peace mission visited Washington. On November 20, 1941, this mission demanded that the United States (1) unfreeze Japanese assets, (2) supply Japan's gaso-line needs, and (3) cease all aid to China. To help prevent further Japanese expansion in China, the United States had made China eligible for lend-lease aid earlier in the year.

The United States had no intention of accept-ing the Japanese demands. However, U.S. diplo-mats kept up the appearance of continuing negotiations with Japan to allow more time to pre-pare U.S. defenses in the Pacific. By this time the United States had succeeded in breaking the secret code used to send messages between Tokyo and the Japanese mission in Washington, D.C. The Americans knew that the Japanese planned a strike, although they did not know where. The challenge was, as Secretary of War Henry Stimson wrote in his diary, "how we should maneuver them into the position of firing the first shot without allowing too much danger to ourselves."

RETEACH For each subsection in Section 3, have students write a sentence that summarizes the main idea. Select students to read their statements aloud. Have the reteaching group choose the best summary sentence for each subsection.

Closure

Ask students to explain why this section is titled The Road to War. Have them provide evidence from the section that supports such a title.

Extension

INVESTIGATE Instruct students to investigate the immigration of German intellectuals and scientists to the U.S. before World War II.

RESEARCH Invite students to research and report on *Kristallnacht*.

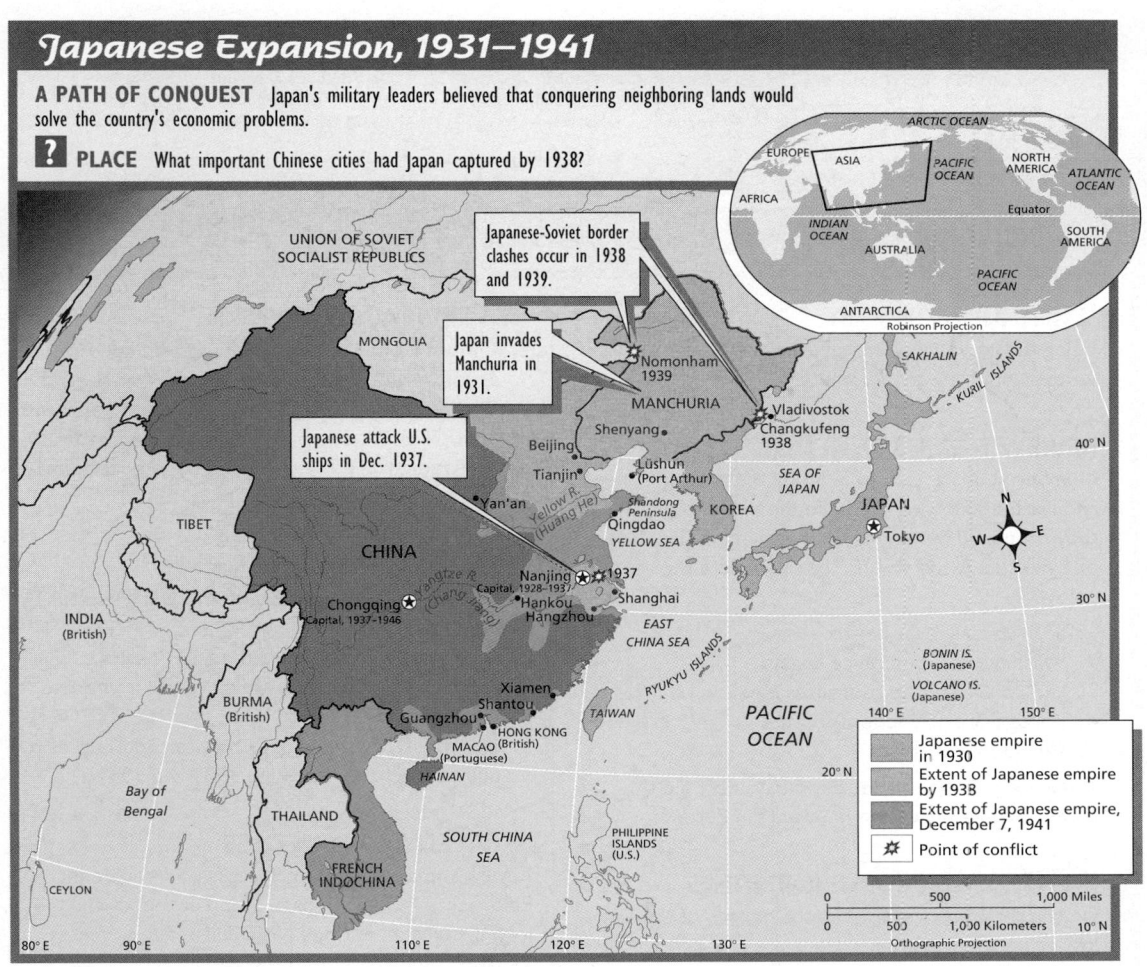

Japanese Expansion, 1931–1941

A PATH OF CONQUEST Japan's military leaders believed that conquering neighboring lands would solve the country's economic problems.

? PLACE What important Chinese cities had Japan captured by 1938?

SECTION REVIEW ANSWERS

IDENTIFY

For significance, see the following pages:
Benito Mussolini (p. 732)
Fascist party (p. 732)
Blackshirts (p. 732)
Adolf Hitler (p. 733)
Nazi party (p. 733)
Brownshirts (p. 733)
anti-Semitism (p. 733)
Kristallnacht (p. 733)
Francisco Franco (p. 733)
Spanish Civil War (p. 733)
Axis Powers (p. 735)
Munich Conference (p. 735)
appeasement (p. 735)
Winston Churchill (p. 735)
nonaggression pact (p. 736)
World War II (p. 736)
Lend-Lease Act (p. 737)
blitzkrieg (p. 737)
Maginot Line (p. 737)
Atlantic Charter (p. 738)

LOCATE

For locations, see the maps on pp. 736 and 739.

1. appeasement; to avoid war
2. failure of appeasement policy; German invasion of Poland
3. extended aid to the Allies through agreements such as the Lend-Lease Act
4. Articles might mention the effects of inflation, unemployment, and political and social unrest.
5. A firmer response might have prevented further German aggression.

SECTION 3 REVIEW

IDENTIFY and explain the significance of the following: Benito Mussolini, Fascist party, Blackshirts, Adolf Hitler, Nazi party, Brownshirts, anti-Semitism, *Kristallnacht,* Francisco Franco, Spanish Civil War, Axis powers, Munich Conference, appeasement, Winston Churchill, nonaggression pact, Lend-Lease Act, blitzkrieg, Maginot Line, Atlantic Charter.

LOCATE and explain the importance of the following: Ethiopia; Rhineland; Sudetenland; Munich, Germany; Yangtze River (Chang Jiang); Albania; Poland; Finland; French Indochina.

1. **MAIN IDEA** What policy did European countries follow in negotiations with Hitler? Why?
2. **MAIN IDEA** What factors led to war in 1939?
3. **MAIN IDEA** What step brought the United States closer toward involvement in the war?
4. **WRITING TO EVALUATE** Imagine you are an American reporter in Europe during the 1920s and 1930s. Write an article that accounts for the rise of dictatorships after World War I.
5. **HYPOTHESIZING** How might events in Europe have been different if European leaders had not decided on an appeasement policy with Hitler?

9. 1939 agreement between Germany and the Soviet Union in which both countries agreed not to attack the other
10. British politician who opposed appeasement

UNDERSTANDING MAIN IDEAS
1. fears of entangling alliances and war; growth of dictatorships, failure of appeasement policy to halt Axis aggression
2. economic—increased investments and internal improvements that tied Latin America to world economy; political—made alliances with landowners

and politicians, supported caudillos and military intervention to protect U.S. interests
3. refusal of oil companies to meet workers' demands for better wages and working conditions, right to control Mexican resources
4. hoped to avoid war; feared appeasement would encourage Hitler to seize more land
5. U.S. and Great Britain would forego territorial expansion, respect the right of every nation to self-government, and call for equal access to trade and raw materials; it established principles for building peace in postwar era.

DEVELOPING THEMES

Return to the Themes section on p. 722. Have students discuss these again and compare their original responses with those given now. (See p. 721B for suggested answers.)

Chapter Review Answers

WRITING A SUMMARY
See Essential Points in each section for main ideas.

REVIEWING CHRONOLOGY
2, 4, 1, 3, 5
Assessing Consequences
Hitler took advantage of appeasement policy and continued the territorial aggression that led to war.

IDENTIFYING PEOPLE AND IDEAS
1. one-sided action in foreign affairs
2. U.S. women's movement leader who received Nobel Peace Prize
3. plan reducing naval strength of U.S., Great Britain, Japan, Italy, and France
4. Latin American military leaders who used force to maintain order
5. Nicaraguan general who led revolt against Díaz
6. assert government control over an industry
7. anti-Semitic author of Mein Kampf, head of Nazi party, and dictator of Germany
8. "the night of broken glass" in 1938 when Nazis destroyed synagogues and Jewish businesses

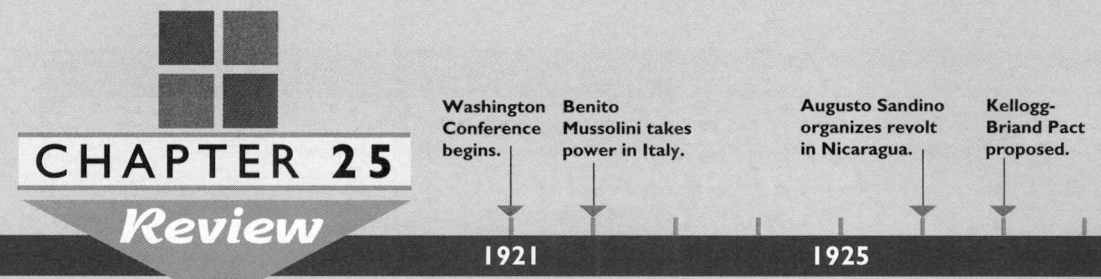

CHAPTER 25
Review

| Washington Conference begins. | Benito Mussolini takes power in Italy. | Augusto Sandino organizes revolt in Nicaragua. | Kellogg-Briand Pact proposed. |

1921   1925

WRITING A SUMMARY
Using the essential points of the chapter as a guide, write a summary of the chapter.

REVIEWING CHRONOLOGY
Number your paper 1 to 5. Study the time line above, and list the following events in the order in which they happened by writing the first next to 1, the second next to 2, and so on. Then complete the activity below.

1. Spanish Civil War begins.
2. Washington Conference begins.
3. Lázaro Cárdenas nationalizes Mexican oil fields.
4. Kellogg-Briand Pact proposed.
5. World War II starts.

Assessing Consequences What effect did the Munich Conference have on events in Europe?

IDENTIFYING PEOPLE AND IDEAS
Explain the historical significance of each of the following people or terms.

1. unilateralism
2. Emily Greene Balch
3. Five Power Agreement
4. caudillos
5. Augusto César Sandino
6. nationalize
7. Adolf Hitler
8. *Kristallnacht*
9. nonaggression pact
10. Winston Churchill

UNDERSTANDING MAIN IDEAS
1. What factors encouraged the growth of isolationism in the United States after World War I? What events in the 1930s convinced U.S. leaders to abandon the policy?
2. What economic and political role did the United States play in Latin America?
3. Why did Lázaro Cárdenas nationalize Mexican oil fields in 1938?
4. Why did some European leaders favor a policy of appeasement toward Hitler? Why did others oppose it?
5. What were the provisions of the Atlantic Charter? Why was it adopted?

REVIEWING THEMES
1. **Global Relations** In what ways did countries promote world peace after World War I?
2. **Economic Development** What economic and political problems emerged after World War I?
3. **Democratic Values** How did the fascist dictatorships in Europe limit civil liberties?

THINKING CRITICALLY
1. **Analyzing** How did Benito Mussolini rise to power?
2. **Evaluating** What were the goals of Japan's militarists? Why did they want to create a Japanese empire in Asia?
3. **Synthesizing** How did American approaches to neutrality change between 1935 and 1941?

STRATEGY FOR SUCCESS
Review the Strategies for Success on Interpreting Editorial Cartoons on page 332. Then study the following cartoon, entitled *New Kind of Pump Priming*. What is the cartoonist's message?

Pump Priming—New Style

REVIEWING THEMES

1. formed organizations such as League of Nations and World Court; held diplomatic conferences to negotiate disarmament; reached agreements protecting countries' borders and outlawing war
2. economic—loss of lives and property, war debts and reparations, unemployment and inflation; political—rise of caudillos in Latin America and right-wing dictatorships in Europe and Asia
3. limited freedom of speech, political dissent, and voting rights; persecuted Jews

THINKING CRITICALLY

1. supported by businesspeople and nationalists, who feared the radical politics that emerged from Italy's postwar social unrest
2. to lessen Japan's reliance on foreign imports, to reduce Western influence in Asia, and to create an empire; to give Japan control over territories that produced needed raw materials
3. Early laws limited arms trade with warring nations. After 1939 U.S. increased military and other aid to Allies and increased U.S. military and economic pressure on Germany and Japan.

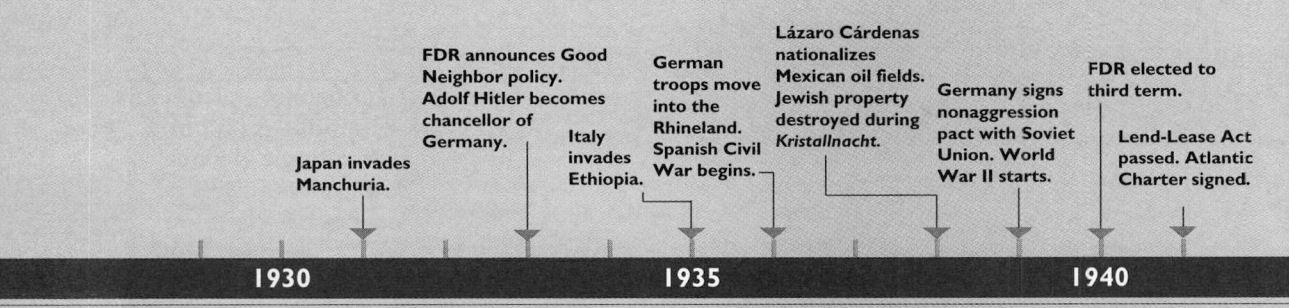

Japan invades Manchuria.

FDR announces Good Neighbor policy. Adolf Hitler becomes chancellor of Germany.

Italy invades Ethiopia.

German troops move into the Rhineland. Spanish Civil War begins.

Lázaro Cárdenas nationalizes Mexican oil fields. Jewish property destroyed during *Kristallnacht*.

Germany signs nonaggression pact with Soviet Union. World War II starts.

FDR elected to third term.

Lend-Lease Act passed. Atlantic Charter signed.

1930   **1935**   **1940**

WRITING ABOUT HISTORY

Writing to Describe Imagine you are a Loyalist during the Spanish Civil War. Write a letter to an American friend describing the events during that period.

USING PRIMARY SOURCES

President Roosevelt's proposal of the Lend-Lease Act aroused fierce debate in Congress. Read the following excerpt from isolationist Burton K. Wheeler, a Republican senator from Montana, who argued against passing the measure. What reasons does he give for his stand?

> ❝ *Never before have the American people been asked or compelled to give . . . so completely of their tax dollars to any foreign nation. Never before has the Congress of the United States been asked by any President to violate international law. . . . Never before has the United States given to one man the power to strip this nation of its defenses. . . .*
>
> *Approval of this legislation means war, open and complete warfare. I, therefore, ask the American people before they . . . accept it—Was the last World War worthwhile?*
>
> *If it were, then we should lend and lease war materials. If it were, then we should lend and lease American boys. President Roosevelt has said we would be repaid by England. We will be. . . . Our boys will be returned—returned in caskets, maybe; returned with bodies maimed; returned with minds warped and twisted by sights of horrors and the scream and shriek of high-powered shells.* ❞

LINKING HISTORY AND GEOGRAPHY

After World War I, France built the Maginot Line, a line of fixed fortifications to protect its border with

Germany. French military commanders felt this series of forts would repel a German attack. Study the map below, which shows the German invasion of France in 1940. How did the German army defeat this French strategy?

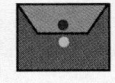

BUILDING YOUR PORTFOLIO

Complete the following projects independently or cooperatively.

1. GLOBAL RELATIONS In Chapter 23 you portrayed a journalist examining the global effects of the Great Depression. Building on that experience, imagine your assignment is to evaluate the new political trends of the 1930s. Create a chart that compares the similarities and differences among fascist dictators around the world.

2. WAR Imagine you are a diplomat at the 1938 Munich Conference. Write a speech aimed at convincing the Allies to abandon their policy of appeasement toward Germany's Adolf Hitler. Your speech might mention *Kristallnacht*, Hitler's repressive domestic policies, German aggression into the Rhineland and Austria, and your opposition toward granting the Sudetenland to Hitler.

AMERICANS IN WORLD WAR II

1941–1945

Chapter Overview

The Japanese attack on Pearl Harbor drew the U.S. into World War II. In early 1942 the Allies suffered defeats in the Pacific and Europe, but by year's end the tide began to turn. At home, Americans rallied to support the war effort, and the lives of minorities and women were affected. Japanese Americans were interned in relocation camps. African Americans, Mexican Americans, and women entered the wartime work force, but experienced discrimination. Allied invasions of North Africa, Italy, and France and bombardment of German cities led to Germany's surrender. The atomic bomb ended the war with Japan. After the war, the horrors of the Holocaust were revealed, and new power alignments emerged.

THE AMERICAN NATION VIDEODISC PROGRAM A variety of still images, short videos, and activities are available for you to use as you teach this chapter. See Correlation to *The American Nation Videodisc Program* for barcode correlations and suggestions for using the program.

Chapter Planning Guide

CHAPTER 26	CORE RESOURCE BOOKLETS	AUDIOVISUAL (AV) RESOURCES	PROGRAM RESOURCES
INTRODUCTION pp. 742–743	■ Social Studies Skills Worksheet 26 ■ Building Your Portfolio Worksheet 7	■ Everyday Life in America Transparency and Worksheet 26	■ *Eyewitnesses and Others*, Volume 2: Reading 50
TEACHING THE CHAPTER pp. 744–769	■ Graphic Organizer 26 ■ Literature Worksheet 26 ■ Geography Worksheet 26 ■ Outline Maps 1, 2, 14, 15, 16, 19, 20, 21, 24	■ *The American Nation* Videodisc: Beyond the Home Front; Japanese Americans in Relocation Camps ■ Linking Geography and History Transparencies and Worksheets 18, 19	■ *Eyewitnesses and Others*, Volume 2: Readings 51, 52, 53, 54, 55, 56, 57
REVIEW AND ASSESSMENT pp. 770–771	■ Chapter 26 Daily Quizzes ■ Review Worksheet 26 ■ Chapter 26 Tests ■ Alternative Assessment Forms		■ Test Generator

Additional Resources

BOOKS FOR TEACHERS

Bernstein, Alison R. *American Indians and World War II.* University of Oklahoma Press, 1991. Survey of the contributions of Native Americans to the war effort and how the war's aftermath affected Indian affairs.

Hilberg, Raul. *Perpetrators, Victims, Bystanders.* HarperCollins, 1993. A noted historian of the Holocaust looks at Holocaust agents, victims, and collaborators and documents the inaction of the Allies.

Keegan, John. *The Second World War.* Viking Penguin, 1990. A comprehensive history of World War II by a military historian.

BOOKS FOR STUDENTS

Devaney, John. *America Fights the Tide, 1942.* Walker, 1991. Chronicles the year 1942 on the battlefield from the American, German, Japanese, British, and Russian perspectives.

* Meltzer, Milton. *Never to Forget.* HarperCollins, 1991. An introduction to the Holocaust.

Time-Life Books Editors. *WW II: Time–Life Books History of the Second World War.* Prentice-Hall, 1989. Amply illustrated overview of World War II.

* Whitman, Sylvia. *V Is for Victory.* Lerner, 1993. A compendium of facts about the home front.

* for students reading below grade level

MULTIMEDIA MATERIALS

Hiroshima and Nagasaki. Video, 20 min. Zenger/SSSS. Examines the question of whether Truman's decision to drop the bomb on Japan was justified.

The Holocaust: A Teenager's Experience. Video, 30 min. United Learning/SSSS. Holocaust survivor David Bergman tells the story of his years in work camps and death camps, using archival footage and drawings.

The Home Front—1940 to 1945. 3 videos, 180 min. Reader's Digest/SSSS. Documents daily life on the American home front.

THEMES IN AMERICAN HISTORY

USE WITH PAGES 742–743

Listed on the right are the themes emphasized in Chapter 26. The questions in boldface type stimulate critical thinking and provide students with an opportunity to discuss the themes within a broadened context. The questions also appear in the pupil's edition on p. 742.

■ GLOBAL RELATIONS

How might nations coordinate civilian and military resources to win a global war? Students might discuss the difficulties of devising a joint military and supply strategy on which each country can agree. They should, however, recognize the necessity of instituting a multinational command to coordinate the war effort. Students should also point out that each nation would more tightly control production and distribution of goods and information.

■ CULTURAL DIVERSITY

Why might wartime patriotism lead to discrimination against certain groups? Students may suggest that such discrimination could arise because people might question the loyalty of recent immigrants from countries with which a nation is at war. As an example, students might cite the discrimination that German Americans faced in the United States during World War I.

■ TECHNOLOGY AND SOCIETY

What political and moral concerns might a government take into account when developing a potentially destructive technology? Students might note political concerns about the establishment of peace and national security, and the widespread international anxiety that might result when such a technology exists. They might cite moral concerns associated with establishing or maintaining peace through the use or threat of destructive force, and of developing a technology that could have highly destructive effects.

CHAPTER STRATEGIES FOR MEETING INDIVIDUAL NEEDS

LIMITED ENGLISH PROFICIENT LEARNERS

Have pairs of students prepare telephone conversations between World War II soldiers stationed in various parts of the world and family members at home. Conversations should focus on the experiences and feelings of the soldier and family member. Volunteers should dramatize their conversations for the class.

TACTILE/KINESTHETIC LEARNERS

Organize students into small groups and have them select interviews from Studs Terkel's *The Good War: An Oral History of World War II* to dramatize for the class.

LEARNERS HAVING DIFFICULTY

Organize students into groups to create slogans or posters encouraging U.S. civilians to support the war effort by increasing productivity at work, buying war bonds, conserving food, or working against ethnic and racial discrimination.

AUDITORY LEARNERS

Pair students and have them create lists of questions they can use to interview friends, relatives, or others who were teenagers or adults during World War II about their memories of this period. Have students conduct the interviews and compare responses.

VISUAL LEARNERS

Have students create recruitment posters for branches of the armed forces. Posters should encourage Americans to serve their country and explain the importance of an Allied victory.

GIFTED LEARNERS

Direct students to write an essay explaining why they think events such as the Holocaust or the internment of Japanese Americans should be taught in U.S. history classes and what lessons they teach.

USING THE CHAPTER FOCUS

■ UNDERSTANDING THE MAIN IDEA

Call on a volunteer to read aloud the Understanding the Main Idea paragraph. Then ask students to speculate about the challenges the U.S. would face in fighting World War II and the contributions the U.S. could make to the war's outcome.

THEMES
Have students work individually or in small groups to answer the questions under Themes. Save students' responses so that they can compare them with their responses after studying the chapter. (See p. 741B for suggested answers.)

■ THE TIME LINE
Direct students to copy the time line in their notebooks. As they study the chapter, ask them to write details about each time-line event and then to write a summary of each event. At the close of the chapter, call on volunteers to read their summaries to the class.

CORE RESOURCES

- **Graphic Organizer 26**
- **Social Studies Skills Worksheet 26**
- **Outline Maps 1, 2, 14, 15, 16, 19, 20, 21, 24**
- **Building Your Portfolio Worksheet 7**

AV RESOURCES

- **Everyday Life in America Transparency and Worksheet 26**

ABOUT THE ILLUSTRATION

"The attack yesterday on the Hawaiian Islands has caused severe damage to American naval and military forces. Very many American lives have been lost," reported President Roosevelt as he detailed for Congress the devastating outcome of the Japanese attack. The scene below—fuel tanks exploding at the demolished seaplane base at Kaneohe Bay on the east coast of Oahu—depicts one outcome of the surprise attack that stunned Americans. Have students describe how they think they might have felt in December 1941 upon hearing the sudden news on the radio of the bombing of Pearl Harbor.

Chapter 26

AMERICANS IN WORLD WAR II

1941–1945

FOCUS

UNDERSTANDING THE MAIN IDEA

In December 1941 the Japanese bombed Pearl Harbor, bringing the United States into World War II. Americans and their allies battled the Axis powers on land in Europe and North Africa and on sea in the Atlantic, Pacific, and Mediterranean. By August 1945 the Allies defeated the Axis powers, but only after heavy casualties and the atomic bombing of two Japanese cities.

THEMES

- **GLOBAL RELATIONS** How might nations coordinate civilian and military resources to win a global war?

- **CULTURAL DIVERSITY** Why might wartime patriotism lead to increased discrimination against certain groups?

- **TECHNOLOGY AND SOCIETY** What political and moral concerns might a government take into account when developing a potentially destructive technology?

1941	1942	1943	1944	1945
Japanese attack Pearl Harbor.	Bataan Death March occurs.	Zoot-suit riots break out.	D-Day invasion begins.	Japan surrenders.

LINK TO THE PAST

Have a volunteer define the term *neutrality*. Then call on volunteers to recall the reasons for American reluctance to become involved in World War II. *(disillusionment over results of World War I and concern about domestic affairs and recovery from the depression)*

LINK TO THE PAST

The German invasion of Poland in 1939 launched World War II. By 1940, much of Western Europe had fallen to Germany, while Japan expanded its hold on Asia. For a time, the United States maintained its neutrality. Lend-lease aid to the Allies, beginning in 1941, however, marked an important step in U.S. involvement in the conflict.

Aftermath of Japanese attack on Hawaii, 1941

Shortly before 8:00 A.M. on December 7, 1941, the message *"Tora! Tora! Tora!"* was radioed to Japanese carrier ships approaching Hawaii. The signal "Tora," meaning "tiger," launched the long-planned Japanese air-and-sea attack on the U.S. naval base at Pearl Harbor. The heart of America's Pacific Fleet was anchored there, and more than a hundred U.S. planes lined nearby airfields.

Within seconds after the attack began, explosions from bombs and torpedoes turned Pearl Harbor into a blazing inferno. When the assault ended less than two hours later, almost 20 American warships and nearly 200 aircraft had been destroyed. Among some 2,400 American dead were 1,103 sailors entombed on the *Arizona* when the battleship sank.

The bombing shocked and united Americans. Ann Hoskins, a Connecticut newspaper owner, noticed that before the attack "there was great tension and feelings between people not to intervene. But the minute Pearl Harbor happened, there was utter unity." The next day, a somber President Roosevelt described December 7 as "a date which will live in infamy" and called on Congress for a declaration of war against Japan.

Air Force officers, Hawaii, 1941

Section 1

EARLY DIFFICULTIES

FOCUS

- **What obstacles did the United States face when it first entered the war?**
- **In which three battles did the Allies halt Japan's advance in the Pacific?**
- **What were two major turning points in the western theater of operations?**
- **What forms did Allied cooperation take?**

*D*eeply angered by the bombing of Pearl Harbor, Congress and the American people overwhelmingly supported President Roosevelt's call for war against Japan. Great Britain declared war on Japan as well. On December 11, Japan's allies, Germany and Italy, declared war on the United States, and Congress recognized a state of war with those two nations. World War II had now vastly expanded.

Army nurses evacuated from Bataan

AXIS ADVANTAGES

When the United States entered the war, the Axis powers had two big advantages. First, Germany, Italy, and Japan had already secured firm control of the areas they had invaded. The United States thus faced a long, drawn-out fight on several fronts, including Western Europe, the Pacific, the Mediterranean, and Northern Africa.

Second, Germany was better prepared for war. Since 1933 it had been rearming and building airfields, barracks, and military training centers. By the mid-1930s, the Nazis had converted most of the German economy to military production. In contrast, the United States had not begun to prepare for war until 1940, when President Roosevelt called for more money to be devoted to military production. Even then, however, the country's preparations were limited.

■■ When the United States entered the war, it faced the problems of fighting on many fronts and a lack of preparation.

◄ **Three U.S. sailors in Chicago read about the Japanese attack on Pearl Harbor.**

Ask students if they have seen any movies about World War II and to explain how they reacted to these films. Tell students that in this section they will learn about how, after the attack on Pearl Harbor, the U.S. and the Allies cooperated to overcome the powerful offensives mounted by the Axis.

U.S. OBSTACLES

Have volunteers identify Axis strengths and U.S. weaknesses at the time the U.S. entered the war. List responses on the chalkboard. (*Axis strengths: firm control of areas invaded, military preparedness; U.S. weaknesses: necessity to fight on many fronts, lack of preparation for war*) Ask students to speculate about what the U.S.

and its allies might do to counter the Axis powers' advantages. Write their responses on the chalkboard.

▶

Hitler, Mussolini, and the Japanese war leaders hoped they could win the conflict before the United States—fighting a two-ocean war—could mobilize its enormous resources. After the Pearl Harbor attack, one Hitler aide warned:

66 We have just one year to cut off Russia from her American supplies. . . . If we don't succeed and the munitions potential of the United States joins up with the manpower potential of the Russians, the war will enter a phase in which we shall only be able to win it with difficulty. 99

𝒲AR IN THE PACIFIC

Japan's assault on Pearl Harbor was only part of a giant offensive throughout the Pacific region. In December the Japanese launched attacks on several other American islands, on the Philippines, and on various British possessions. By the end of the month, Japan controlled Guam, Wake Island, the British colony of Hong Kong, and Thailand.

The year 1942 brought more Japanese victories. In January, Japanese forces took Manila, the capital of the Philippines. The next month, they overran the British naval base at Singapore, and in the **Battle of the Java Sea**, they crushed a fleet of American, British, Dutch, and Australian warships (see map on page 746). By April, Japan had conquered most of the Netherlands East Indies, with its supplies of oil, tin, rubber, and other vital war materials. The Japanese were also driving the British out of Burma.

In the Philippines a small force of Americans and Filipinos under General Douglas MacArthur, commander of U.S. Army troops in the Far East, mounted a heroic but hopeless resistance against the Japanese. After the surrender of Manila, MacArthur's forces withdrew to the Bataan Peninsula across Manila Bay. In March, MacArthur was ordered to Australia but vowed, "I shall return."

Fighting against overwhelming odds, the hungry, sick, exhausted survivors who remained on Bataan surrendered in April. Japanese soldiers forced the some 70,000 survivors to march through the jungle on their way to prison camp. Some 10,000 died on what came to be called the **Bataan Death March** (see map on page 771). U.S. and Filipino soldiers received brutal treat-

JAPAN DECLARES WAR

The day after the Japanese attack on Pearl Harbor, Emperor Hirohito made a speech that was relayed around the world. In it he laid out Japan's reasons for declaring war on the United States and Great Britain:

66 *𝐵oth America and Britain . . . have aggravated the disturbances in East Asia. . . . These two powers, inducing other countries to follow suit, increased military preparations on all sides of Our Empire. . . . They have obstructed by every means Our peaceful commerce, and finally resorted to a direct severance [cutting off] of economic relations. . . . Patiently have We waited and long have We endured, in hope that Our Government might retrieve the situation in peace. But Our adversaries [enemies], showing not the least spirit of conciliation, have unduly delayed a settlement. . . . Our Empire for its existence and self defense has no other recourse but to appeal to arms and to crush every obstacle in its path.* 99

ment at the hands of the Japanese: prisoners were beaten, shot, or prevented from drinking water. The bravery of the Filipino defenders at Bataan inspired thousands of Filipino Americans to enlist in the armed forces. In 1942 alone some 16,000 Filipino Americans in California joined the fight.

By the summer of 1942, the Japanese were poised to strike west at India, south at Australia, and east through Hawaii at the Pacific coast of the United States. At this crucial point, however, the Allies succeeded in halting the Japanese advance in the Pacific. The U.S. Pacific Fleet, commanded by Admiral Chester Nimitz, helped turn the tide with three battles.

The first battle began on May 7, 1942, in the Coral Sea, off the northeastern coast of Australia. A Japanese force on its way to attack Port Moresby, New Guinea, seized Tulagi (too-LAHG-ee) Island,

THROUGH OTHERS' EYES

Ask students to list the reasons Hirohito gives for declaring war. Then have students give reasons why the Allies might reject the validity of Hirohito's explanation.

PRIMARY SOURCE
Description of Change: excerpted
Rationale: excerpted to focus on main idea

PRIMARY SOURCE
Description of Change: excerpted and bracketed
Rationale: excerpted to focus on main idea; bracketed to clarify meaning

VOICES IN HISTORY

On the Bataan Peninsula, U.S. and Filipino soldiers fought valiantly together. Stories of Filipino bravery at Bataan led to better treatment of Filipinos in the U.S. One California Filipino observed, "No longer on the streetcar do I feel myself in the presence of my enemies. We Filipinos are the same— it is Americans that have changed in their recognition of us."

Teaching the Section

ALLIES HALT JAPANESE IN PACIFIC

Organize students into small groups. Assign each group one of these battles: Coral Sea, Midway, or Guadalcanal. Tell groups their job is to give a military briefing to the press on their assigned battle. The briefing should review the war in the Pacific up to the bat-tle, identify the battle's location, describe the military action, note the battle's outcome, and explain how it furthered the Allied cause. Select groups to present their briefings to the class.

HISTORICAL SIDELIGHTS

Battle of the Coral Sea
The Battle of the Coral Sea initiated a new era in modern naval warfare. For the first time in modern naval battle, the warring fleets, which centered around aircraft carriers, never came close enough to exchange fire. The carriers served as takeoff and landing stations for dive bombers, fighters, and torpedo planes. Japanese aircraft destroyed the American carrier *Lexington*. U.S. planes sank the Japanese carrier *Shoho*.

AV **TRANSPARENCY**

Linking Geography and History Transparency and **Worksheet 19**

▲ Shown here are American and Filipino soldiers at the start of the grueling Bataan Death March in April 1942. Thousands died on the march to a Japanese prison camp.

one of the Solomons. But before the Japanese force could reach its destination, a joint British-American naval force intercepted it. Planes from U.S. carriers damaged a Japanese carrier and destroyed one carrier and several aircraft. The **Battle of the Coral Sea** was an important victory for the Allies. Although the Allies lost a carrier, the battle stopped the Japanese advance on Australia.

The second naval battle took place early in June 1942. Japan, seeking to crush the U.S. Pacific Fleet, launched a two-pronged attack. One unit succeeded in occupying two of the Aleutian Islands, near Alaska. This move was

Map Caption Answer
most of the Netherlands East Indies

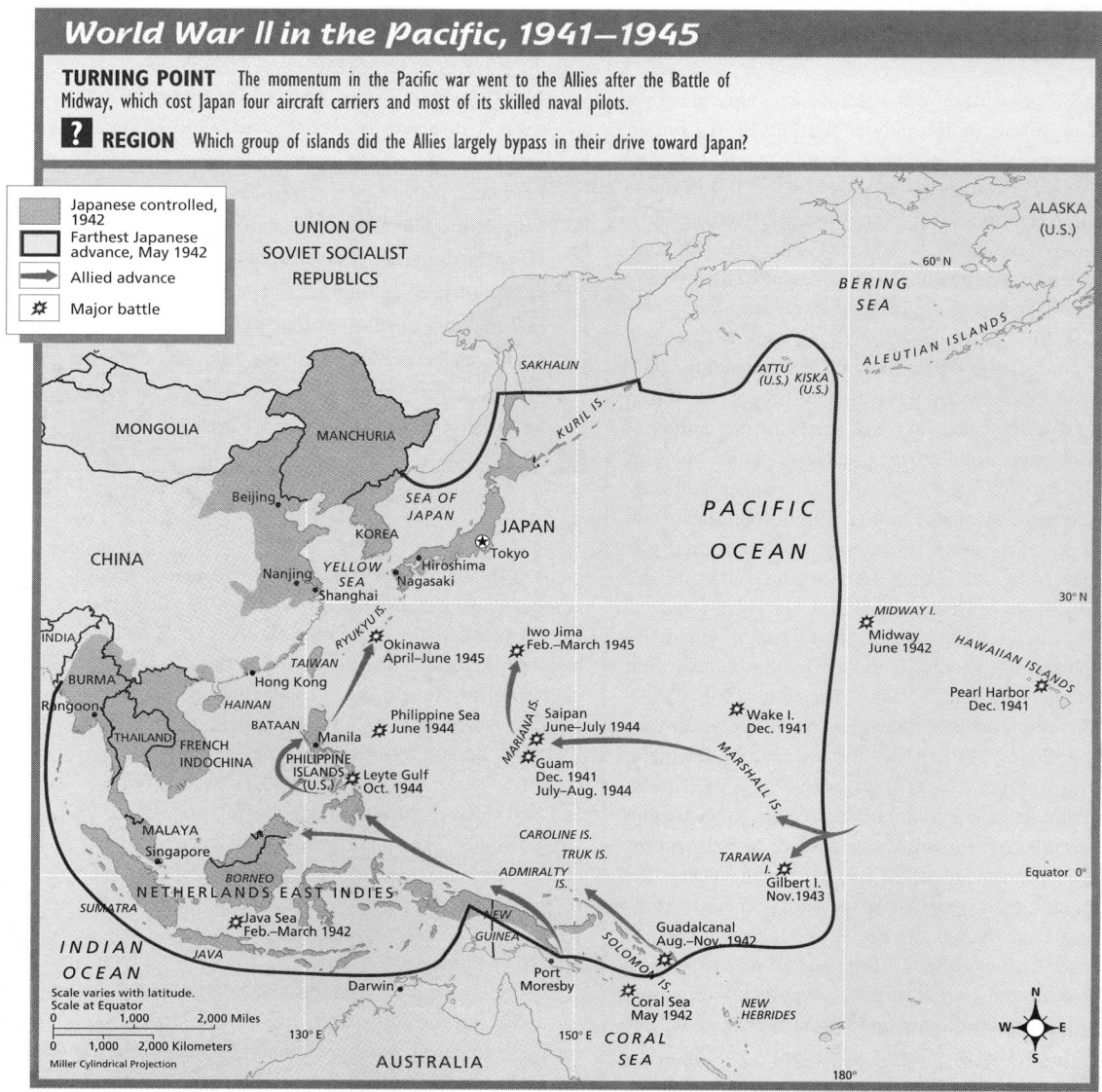

World War II in the Pacific, 1941–1945

TURNING POINT The momentum in the Pacific war went to the Allies after the Battle of Midway, which cost Japan four aircraft carriers and most of its skilled naval pilots.

? **REGION** Which group of islands did the Allies largely bypass in their drive toward Japan?

Have students explain how Germany benefited from the advance into the Soviet Union *(expanded industrial and agricultural base)* and what Germany expected to gain from its North African offensive. *(Suez Canal, Middle East oil fields)* Ask why these goals were important to Germany's war effort. Then ask students to explain how supply problems influenced the outcome of battles at El Alamein and Stalingrad and why these battles are considered turning points in the war. Conclude by having students speculate about how the war might have been different if the Allies had lost either battle.

▲ Although U.S. forces won the Battle of Midway in June 1942, the islands did not escape damage. Japanese bombers hit military installations, including the oil tank shown here.

designed to divert American ships to the north while the Japanese carried out their second offensive, an attack on Midway, two small islands northwest of Hawaii. The United States, however, knew of the Japanese strategy because American experts had broken the Japanese fleet code. Nimitz was therefore able to assemble U.S. aircraft carriers and destroyers north of Midway to fend off the Japanese attack.

Americans and Japanese clashed from June 3 to June 6. U.S. fighters, dive-bombers, and torpedo planes sank four Japanese aircraft carriers and shot down many enemy planes. The American victory at the **Battle of Midway** proved crucial. Japan lost not only ships and planes but also a number of skilled pilots, many of whom had taken part in the Pearl Harbor attack. The battle provided the Americans with valuable experience in naval air warfare and gave people confidence in the carrier-based strike force.

After the Battle of Midway, the United States successfully launched its first offensive. In August 1942, American marines waded ashore at Guadalcanal, another of the Solomon Islands. For six desperate months, with a heavy loss of life, they clung to a toehold around the airport, repelling Japanese attacks from the air, the sea, and the surrounding jungle.

In November the Japanese sent a huge fleet to the Solomons, hoping to regain Guadalcanal. The American fleet defeated the Japanese in a bloody battle. Guadalcanal was secure. The tide of battle in the Pacific had finally turned in the Allies' favor.

■■ The Allies stopped the Japanese Pacific offensive in the battles of Coral Sea, Midway, and Guadalcanal.

ᗷIGHTING IN EUROPE AND THE MEDITERRANEAN

By the time of the attack on Pearl Harbor, the Axis powers, which now included Hungary, Romania, and Bulgaria, firmly controlled much of the western theater of operations—Europe and the lands around the Mediterranean. Yugoslavia and Greece had been occupied, and southern Europe was firmly under the Axis boot. Throughout most of 1942, the Axis powers racked up one victory after another.

The Germans and their allies scored victories on many different fronts. German submarines, or U-boats, controlled the Atlantic Ocean, sinking Allied military and merchant ships and nearly cutting off British supply lines. In the first half of 1942, German U-boats sank almost 500 ships off the eastern seaboard of the United States.

In Europe, German troops had penetrated far into the Soviet Union after their initial attack in June 1941. As the Germans advanced, the Soviets lost many industrial centers as well as rich grainfields in the Ukraine (see map on page 748). In the summer of 1942, the Germans pushed toward the oil fields of southern Russia. They also laid siege to Stalingrad (now known as Volgograd). The city mobilized its defenses. For months the men, women, and children defending the city suffered a nightmare of shell fire and starvation.

In North Africa, Italian forces had launched an invasion in 1940. When British troops later began to inflict heavy damage on the Italians, Hitler sent in the German *Afrika Korps* under commander Erwin Rommel.

▼ Erwin Rommel (left) was commander of the German *Afrika Korps* in North Africa.

BUILDING VOCABULARY

The term *U-boat* comes from a German word *unterseeboot,* or undersea boat. The term referred to a German submarine. During World War II, the Germans built more than 1,100 U-boats. By war's end, the Allies had sunk over 600 of them.

𝒯eaching the 𝒮ection

ALLIED COOPERATION

Have students work in pairs to create a graphic organizer that shows the forms Allied cooperation took, including lend-lease programs, joint strategic planning, and agreement on war aims. Have volunteers present their charts. Conclude by having students write paragraphs explaining why joint strategic planning and shared war aims were essential for an Allied victory. Select students to read their paragraphs to the class. Students may wish to include their paragraphs in their portfolios.

Map Caption Answer

Italy

COOPERATIVE LEARNING

Organize students into groups of five. Direct them to use the maps on pp. 746 and 748 and the chapter text to create on butcher paper a wall-size illustrated time line that shows the major World War II battles in Europe, North Africa, and the Pacific. In order to emphasize that some battles in both theaters were taking place simultaneously, ask groups to place the battles in Europe and North Africa above the time line and those in the Pacific below the time line. Students should also note the outcome of each battle on their time lines. Encourage students to divide tasks so that one student locates the battles on the maps, one locates the outcome of each battle in the text, one adds the information to the time line, and the others provide the illustrations.

AV TRANSPARENCY

Linking Geography and History Transparency and **Worksheet 18**

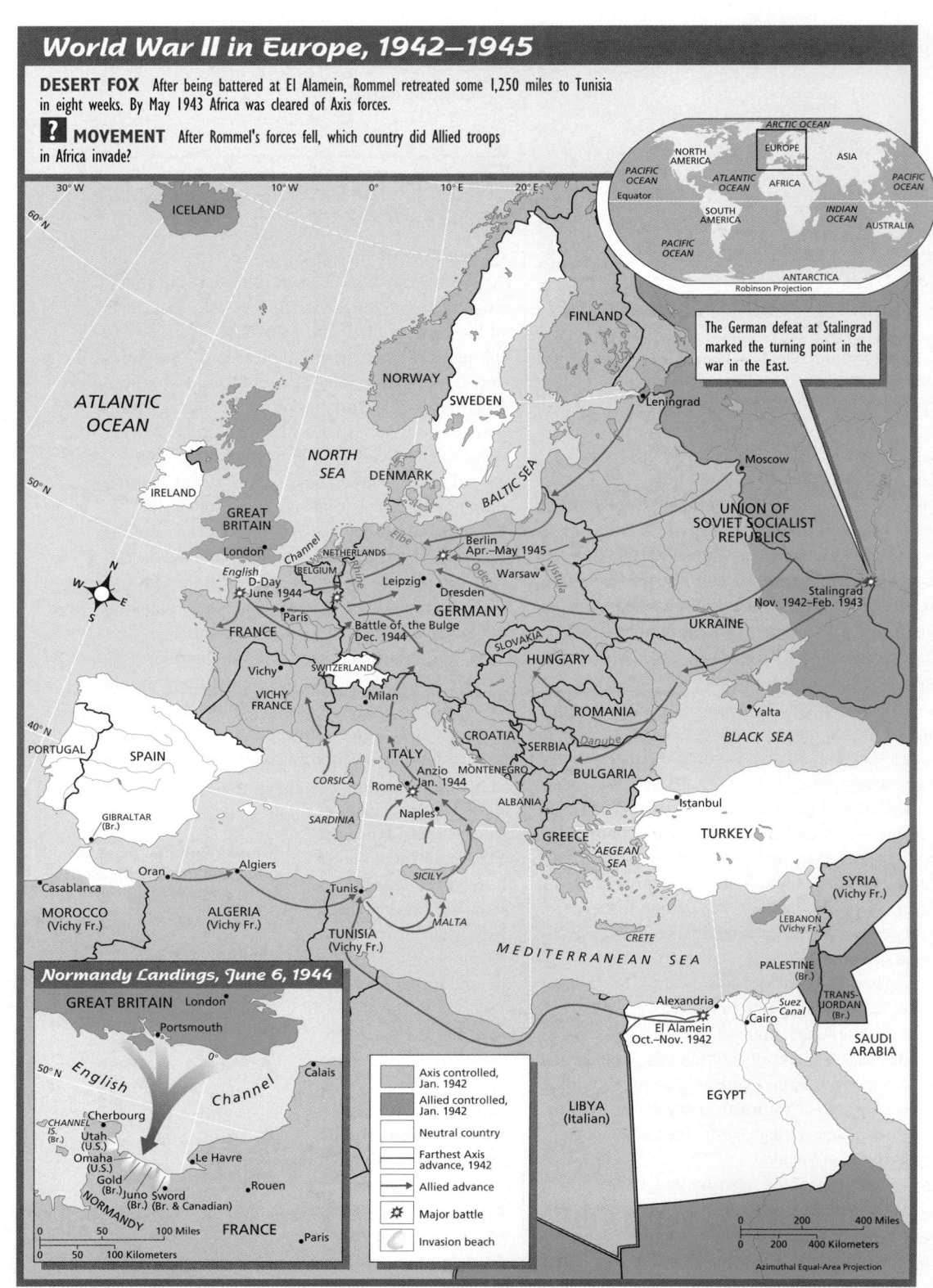

World War II in Europe, 1942–1945

DESERT FOX After being battered at El Alamein, Rommel retreated some 1,250 miles to Tunisia in eight weeks. By May 1943 Africa was cleared of Axis forces.

? **MOVEMENT** After Rommel's forces fell, which country did Allied troops in Africa invade?

The German defeat at Stalingrad marked the turning point in the war in the East.

Normandy Landings, June 6, 1944

Axis controlled, Jan. 1942	
Allied controlled, Jan. 1942	
Neutral country	
Farthest Axis advance, 1942	
→ Allied advance	
✿ Major battle	
Invasion beach	

▶ Soldiers in Britain's Eighth Army are shown here in defensive positions during the Battle of El Alamein. This battle stood in marked contrast to the highly mobile fighting characteristic of the war in North Africa.

▼ Soviet forces laid siege to Stalingrad for 17 months before the German army surrendered in February 1943. Shown here is part of the ruined city shortly after it was liberated.

Rommel, known as the Desert Fox, had advanced as far as El Alamein, Egypt, by July 1942. His troops were ready for a final thrust at the Suez Canal and the oil fields of the Middle East (the European designation for Northeast Africa and Southwest Asia). At the same time, Axis aircraft all but forced British naval craft out of the Mediterranean. In order to reach Egypt, the Middle East, and India, Britain had to send its ships thousands of miles around Africa.

Despite the British forces' transport problems, it was Rommel who suffered most from shortages of men and supplies. The British, led by General Bernard Montgomery, turned this to their advantage. In October, Montgomery attacked, pushing Rommel's *Afrika Korps* steadily westward out of Egypt and into Libya by November. The British victory in the **Battle of El Alamein** helped turn the corner for the Allies in North Africa.

Another turning point came in the fall of 1942, when the Soviets attacked German troops in Stalingrad. Throughout a terrible winter the Germans hung on, forbidden by Hitler to surrender. Trapped in the ruined city with few supplies and little food, the Axis troops finally surrendered in February 1943. After the **Battle of Stalingrad**, less than one third of the original German force of almost 300,000 remained alive. Galina Utkina, a Russian woman, recalled the crucial role Soviet women played in defeating the Germans:

ff Anti-aircraft battalions, air-force regiments and signalling units were made up entirely of women. When the battle reached the city itself, women fought along-side the men. 99

The Allied victories at El Alamein and Stalingrad broke the momentum of the Axis advance. Said British prime minister Winston Churchill: "Before Alamein we never had a victory. After Alamein we never had a defeat."

▪▪ **Setbacks for the Axis powers at El Alamein and Stalingrad were turning points in World War II.**

ALLIED COOPERATION

How had the Allies managed to overcome the powerful offensives mounted by the Axis in both theaters of the war? The ability of the United States to harness its human and industrial resources helped the Allied effort. Through the lend-lease program the United States shipped vast quantities of munitions to its allies. By the end of the war, lend-lease aid totaled more than $50 billion. Of this vast sum, over 60 percent went to Great Britain.

Allied cooperation, which involved joint strategic planning, also helped turn the tide. Just

RETEACH Have students work in groups, assigning individuals or pairs the task of outlining subsections. Have students exchange outlines and use them to ask questions of other members of their group.

*C*losure

Call on volunteers to explain how the U.S. and the Allies dealt with the challenges of fighting a war on many fronts. In their explanations, students should consider the war strategies agreed upon by FDR and Churchill in Washington.

*E*xtension

COMPARE Have students research and write reports comparing the challenges of weather, climate, and terrain that Allied soldiers faced fighting in North Africa and on Pacific islands.

INTERPRET Through their cartoons and writings, journalists Bill Mauldin and Ernie Pyle kept Americans informed about the war. Have students read and present to the class examples of their work.

SECTION REVIEW ANSWERS

IDENTIFY

For significance, see the following pages:
Battle of the Java Sea
(p. 745)
Douglas MacArthur (p. 745)
Bataan Death March (p. 745)
Battle of the Coral Sea
(p. 746)
Battle of Midway (p. 747)
Erwin Rommel (p. 747)
Bernard Montgomery
(p. 749)
Battle of El Alamein (p. 749)
Battle of Stalingrad (p. 749)
unconditional surrender
(p. 750)
Joseph Stalin (p. 750)

LOCATE

For locations, see maps on pp. 746, 748, and 771.

1. *in the battles of the Coral Sea, Midway, Guadalcanal*
2. *German defeats at El Alamein, Stalingrad*
3. *Axis had converted economy to military production and had securely occupied territory. U.S. had to fight on many fronts and had not begun to prepare for war until the summer of 1940.*
4. *Memos might mention lend-lease exchanges, joint strategic planning, and agreement on war aims.*
5. *Japan lost ships, planes, and skilled pilots, while U.S. gained confidence and experience in naval air warfare.*

two weeks after the assault on Pearl Harbor, Churchill and Roosevelt met in Washington, D.C., together with their top military commanders and technical aides. The two leaders and their staffs agreed that defeating the Axis powers in Europe would be the first Allied priority. For the time being, Allied strategy in the Pacific would be defensive rather than offensive.

To formalize their alliance, representatives of 26 Allied countries, calling themselves the United Nations, met in Washington, D.C. On January 1, 1942, they signed the Joint Declaration, which had been drafted by Roosevelt and Churchill. In it the Allies (1) promised full military and economic cooperation in the war effort, (2) agreed that none of them would make a separate peace with the Axis powers, and (3) endorsed the war aims outlined by Roosevelt and Churchill in the Atlantic Charter (see Chapter 25).

Throughout the war Churchill and Roosevelt met several times. At Casablanca, Morocco, in January 1943, the two leaders agreed to demand the **unconditional surrender** of their enemies. In other words, if the Axis powers gave up, they would have to do so on the Allies' terms. Churchill and Roosevelt also agreed that the Allies should attack Hitler on a second front in order to relieve pressure on the Soviet Union (the first front). The Allies decided to open the second front by invading southern Europe by way of North Africa and the Mediterranean island of Sicily.

▲ **Chinese leader Chiang Kai-shek (left), President Roosevelt (center), and British prime minister Winston Churchill (right) are shown at the Cairo Conference in November 1943.**

At Cairo in November 1943, Roosevelt and Churchill met with Chiang Kai-shek of China. The leaders outlined Allied strategy against Japan and made plans to restore Japanese-held territories after the war. At Tehran, Iran, shortly afterward, Roosevelt and Churchill met for the first time with Soviet leader Joseph Stalin. Stalin gave his support for Allied war plans.

▪▪ Cooperation among the Allies took the form of lend-lease exchanges, joint strategic planning, and agreement on war aims.

SECTION 1 REVIEW

IDENTIFY and explain the significance of the following: Battle of the Java Sea, Douglas MacArthur, Bataan Death March, Battle of the Coral Sea, Battle of Midway, Erwin Rommel, Bernard Montgomery, Battle of El Alamein, Battle of Stalingrad, unconditional surrender, Joseph Stalin.

LOCATE and explain the importance of the following: Pearl Harbor, Guam, Wake Island, Hong Kong, Thailand, Bataan, Coral Sea, Midway Islands, Guadalcanal, Ukraine, Stalingrad, El Alamein, Casablanca.

1. **MAIN IDEA** Where did the Allies stop the Japanese Pacific offensive?
2. **MAIN IDEA** What two German setbacks were turning points for the Allies in World War II?
3. **CONTRASTING** What advantages did the Axis powers have over the United States at the beginning of the war?
4. **WRITING TO INFORM** Imagine you are a participant in one of the early wartime conferences. Write a memorandum to the Allies, giving examples of cooperative efforts that could help them win the war.
5. **LINKING HISTORY AND GEOGRAPHY** What was the significance of the American victory at the Battle of Midway for both Japan and the United States?

Chapter 26

SECTION 2

Introducing the Section

PREVIEW WORKSHOP

Following is a list of the significant people and terms in this section. You may wish to use this list as a section preview.

People
- James F. Byrnes
- Thomas E. Dewey
- Norman Mineta
- A. Philip Randolph

Terms
- War Production Board
- Selective Training and Service Act
- internment
- Fair Employment Practices Committee
- braceros
- zoot-suit riots

Section 2

THE HOME FRONT

FOCUS

- **How did the United States mobilize for war?**
- **Why were Japanese Americans interned during the war?**
- **What gains did African Americans and Mexican Americans make during the war?**
- **What changes did World War II bring for American women?**

Seamstresses making flags and banners

*A*lthough World War II was fought on the battlefields of Europe, Asia, and North Africa, American farms and factories also helped win the war. As the United States mobilized its resources for combat, the entertainment industry helped sustain morale. For Japanese Americans the war resulted in confinement in remote camps. For African Americans, Mexican Americans, and women, the conflict brought both new opportunities and reminders that discrimination and inequality still existed in American society.

MOBILIZING FOR WAR

After the Japanese attack at Pearl Harbor plunged the United States into war, America switched from a peacetime to a wartime economy. Engineer R. W. Danischefsky noted how quickly factory orders came in: "At the time of Pearl Harbor [December 7, 1941] we had five projects in Michigan. By the end of December we had forty-two." To fill these vital orders, union leaders agreed not to organize strikes during the war.

A production boom. The United States soon became the Allies' biggest armaments supplier. Between 1940 and 1945, U.S. war plants produced millions of planes, tanks, jeeps, and guns. Shipbuilders produced thousands of ships, creating a powerful navy and merchant marine.

War production helped create an economic boom. The number of jobless workers, still over 2.5 million in 1942, sank to fewer than 700,000 in 1944. Earnings nearly doubled between 1939 and 1945. People who had stood in breadlines a decade

◀ **After the bombing of Pearl Harbor, many existing factories were converted to wartime production. The Firestone Tire & Rubber Company, for example, made antiaircraft guns, tank and submarine parts, and gas masks, as well as tires for all military vehicles.**

FOCUS OBJECTIVES

- Describe how the U.S. mobilized for war.
- Explain why Japanese Americans were interned during the war.
- Determine what gains African Americans and Mexican Americans made during the war.
- Examine the changes World War II brought for American women.

MAKING CONNECTIONS

Economics
Due to increased demands of wartime production during the war years, the weekly earnings of a typical factory worker rose from about $25 to about $47.

CORE RESOURCES

- **Social Studies Skills Worksheet 26**
- **Literature Worksheet 26**
- **Section 2 Daily Quiz**

AV RESOURCES

- ***The American Nation Videodisc: Beyond the Home Front; Japanese Americans in Relocation Camps***
- **Everyday Life in America Transparency and Worksheet 26**

AMERICANS IN WORLD WAR II ▌▌ 751

**MOTIVATING:
PRIOR KNOWLEDGE**

Have volunteers recall the ways the American home front was mobilized to contribute to the war effort during World War I. List student responses on a flip chart. After students complete the section, have them compare the flip-chart list with ways Americans at home contributed to the World War II war effort.

Graph Caption Answer
approximately $240 billion

HISTORICAL SIDELIGHTS

American Indian Contributions

Many American Indians contributed both money and resources to the war effort. For example, Uchee and Creek Indians voted to purchase $400,000 in war bonds, while the Quapaws made a $1 million donation to the war effort and had to be persuaded to accept war bonds in return. A Sioux tribal council voted to postpone receipt of a $5 million government settlement. The Klamath called for building an airfield on their reservation in Oregon to be used for training pilots. The United Pueblos volunteered all of their cars and trucks for the delivery of war-related supplies.

earlier now worked overtime and brought home fat paychecks.

The boom also led to vast population shifts. More than four million workers left their homes to find work in war-industry factories in other states. Sharecroppers, tenant farmers, and others eking out a living on farms flocked to the centers of wartime production—shipyards on the Gulf and Pacific coasts and factories in the Midwest and West. The West especially witnessed phenomenal economic and population growth during the war. The federal government spent billions of dollars to build western factories and military bases. This wartime spending helped the West become a major industrial region after World War II.

American farms also achieved marvels of productivity. Although many agricultural workers went off to fight in the war or to work in wartime factories, productivity remained high. During the war years U.S. farmers produced enough food to supply the American people and the Allies overseas.

Government expansion. Mobilizing for war led to a greatly expanded federal government. The number of federal employees grew from almost one million in 1940 to nearly three million by 1945. The Office of War Mobilization (OWM) coordinated all government agencies involved in producing and distributing civilian goods. Its powerful director, James F. Byrnes, was sometimes called the "assistant president."

The **War Production Board** (WPB) directed the conversion of existing factories to wartime production and supervised the building of new plants. The WPB assigned raw materials to industry, including scrap iron from factories and recyclable tin, aluminum, and fats (used in bullets) from homes.

The WPB (and later the OWM) also coordinated the production and distribution of consumer goods. For instance, it diverted nylon to making parachutes. The WPB even regulated clothing styles in order to save fabric; canceled for the duration of the war were cuffs on men's trousers and pleats in women's skirts.

▶ **After the war began, the government conserved valuable resources by establishing rationing programs. Students at Wilson Senior High in Washington, D.C., are shown learning how to use the latest ration book.**

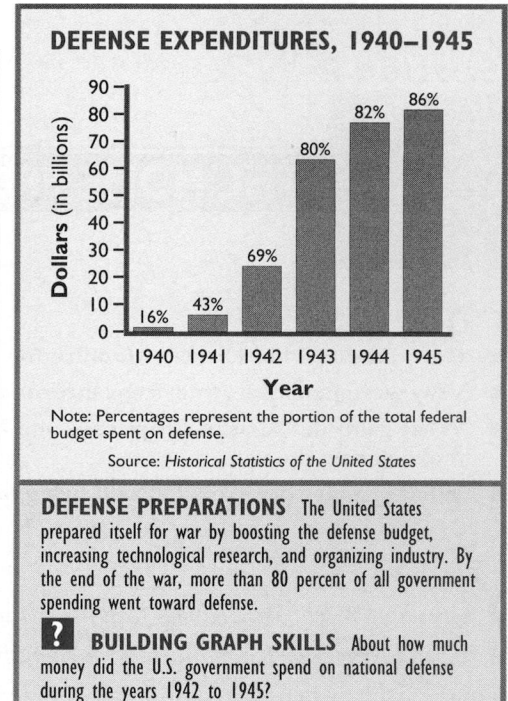

DEFENSE EXPENDITURES, 1940–1945

Note: Percentages represent the portion of the total federal budget spent on defense.

Source: *Historical Statistics of the United States*

DEFENSE PREPARATIONS The United States prepared itself for war by boosting the defense budget, increasing technological research, and organizing industry. By the end of the war, more than 80 percent of all government spending went toward defense.

? BUILDING GRAPH SKILLS About how much money did the U.S. government spend on national defense during the years 1942 to 1945?

Directing the economy. The government also extended its control over the economy. In order to pay for the war, the government increased by more than 10 times the number of Americans who had to pay income tax. The new taxes included most middle- and lower-income groups for the first time. The rest of the money came from borrowing, mainly through war bonds.

The sale of war bonds also helped the government deal with another major concern—keeping inflation down. When incomes remain high but few consumer items are available for people to buy, prices go up and inflation results. Selling war bonds offered one way of siphoning off excess income, thus keeping inflation down.

Organize students into seven groups. Assign to each group one of the following roles: factory owner, factory worker, farmer, federal employee, taxpayer, consumer, and draft board member. Have each group discuss—and select a representative to explain to the class—ways that his or her group is contributing to the war effort and how the group has been affected by the expansion of government control that accompanied mobilization.

■■ Examine with students reasons that such agencies as the War Production Board were necessary. Ask students if they think Americans today would accept the same regulation of the economy in the event of war.

▶

The government took other anti-inflationary steps as well. One was rationing, which reduced consumer demand by limiting how much people could buy. The measure also cut civilian purchases of products needed for the war effort. Rationed items included gasoline, heating fuel, tires, coffee, sugar, meat, butter, and canned goods. The government also tried to keep wages and prices down. At first it froze wages, but when the cost of living rose, the government allowed wages to rise by 15 percent.

Raising an army. Along with increased production and expanded government controls, gearing up for war meant recruiting soldiers. In 1940, before the attack on Pearl Harbor, the United States passed the **Selective Training and Service Act**, which provided for the first peacetime draft in American history. The law required the registration of all men between ages 21 and 35 (age limits later extended from 18 to 37). Local draft boards determined fitness and deferred men for family, religious, or health reasons.

Of the some 15 million members of the armed services during World War II, about two thirds were draftees and the rest volunteers, including more than 300,000 women. Women enrolled in the Women's Auxiliary Army Corps (WAACs), Women's Airforce Service Pilots (WASPs), or auxiliary branches of the navy (WAVES), coast guard (SPARS), and marines. They worked as nurses, did office work, drove vehicles, and ferried planes in order to free men for active duty.

While most women military personnel served on the home front, women in the Army Nurse Corps (ANC) and Navy Nurse Corps (NNC) tended wounded soldiers overseas. Eunice Hatchitt, a nurse who served at Bataan, described the terrible conditions and heavy casualties:

66 Days and nights were an endless nightmare, until it seemed we couldn't stand it any longer. Patients came in by the hundreds, and the doctors and nurses worked continuously under the tents amid the flies and heat and dust. We had from eight to nine hundred victims a day. 99

■■ **The United States mobilized for war by increasing production, expanding government control of the economy, and raising an army.**

▶ The armed services actively recruited women. After registering and receiving vaccinations, WAAC recruits (below) emerge with duffel bags containing their uniforms.

The urgency of the war effort convinced President Roosevelt, who had led the nation since 1933, to run for an unprecedented fourth term. As the 1944 campaign drew near, Roosevelt told an aide, "God knows I don't want to [run]. but I may find it necessary." Roosevelt won the nomination with little opposition; his vice-presidential candidate was a Missouri senator, Harry S. Truman.

The Republicans chose Thomas E. Dewey, governor of New York, who had won fame as a district attorney for prosecuting racketeers. However, he lacked Roosevelt's charisma and experience and was defeated by an electoral vote of 99 to Roosevelt's 432.

PROMOTING THE WAR

As it mobilized the nation's resources, the government also worked to keep morale high. This was especially important in the early days of the war, when Allied troops faced many setbacks. The government encouraged the media to do their part. Moviemakers, songwriters, and radio station programmers responded by urging all-out participation in the war effort.

HISTORICAL SIDELIGHTS
Rationing
Every American family had a ration coupon book, distributed each month by some 5,600 ration boards at neighborhood schools. Each person was allowed 64 "red" points a month for the purchase of such foods as meat, butter, and fats. Various cuts of meat required different numbers of points, but on average Americans could buy about two pounds of meat a week. Each person was also allowed 48 "blue" points toward purchase of processed foods, such as ketchup, and canned foods, such as peas and beans. Grocery store shelves were lined with tags that displayed the items' prices and point values.

THE AMERICAN NATION VIDEODISC PROGRAM
Beyond the Home Front

| 2A | 31486 | 3:29 |

PRIMARY SOURCE
Description of Change: excerpted
Rationale: excerpted to focus on main idea

Teaching the Section

PROMOTING THE WAR

Organize students into groups and ask them to outline a script for a radio report on how the media and entertainment industries are promoting the war effort. Groups might also include appropriate interviews in their reports. Select volunteers to "broadcast" their group's reports.

HISTORICAL SIDELIGHTS
Patriotism

Support for the U.S. war effort ran so high that fans began singing "The Star-Spangled Banner" at the beginning of ball games, a tradition that continues today.

HISTORICAL SIDELIGHTS
Japanese Relocation

Support among Californians for Japanese relocation came in part from wartime hysteria and in part from resentment of Japanese Americans' success as merchants, fruit and vegetable farmers, and fishers. Some Japanese Americans fought relocation in the courts. Gordon Hirabayashi in Washington state refused to report to an evacuation center. He argued: "As an American citizen, I wanted to uphold the principles of the Constitution, and the . . . evacuation orders which singled out a group on the basis of ethnicity violated them."

THE AMERICAN NATION VIDEODISC PROGRAM

Japanese Americans in Relocation Camps

```
2A    43252    :49
```

Movie stars advertised war bonds and traveled overseas to entertain the troops. Hundreds of war movies poured out of Hollywood. Some patriotic films, such as *So Proudly We Hail*—about army nurses in the Philippines—built support for the war. Striking a lighter note were comedies like Bob Hope's *Caught in the Draft.* A few films, such as *Wake Island* and *Report from the Aleutians,* offered realistic views of combat. Most, however, romanticized American and other Allied soldiers and stereotypically portrayed the Japanese as treacherous, the Germans as fanatical, and the Italians as cowardly.

Radio stations broadcast both war news and entertainment. Radio correspondents such as Edward R. Murrow and Eric Sevareid gave on-the-scene accounts of war-ravaged Europe. A new federal agency, the Office of War Information (OWI), controlled the flow of war news at home.

Wartime musical hits included "Remember Pearl Harbor" and "Praise the Lord and Pass the Ammunition!" But the biggest hits of the period did not deal directly with the war. African American musicians—including trumpeter Dizzy Gillespie, sax player Charlie Parker, and piano player Thelonious Monk—popularized a new form of jazz, called bebop, or bop. Also popular were such sentimental songs as "White Christmas," which expressed Americans' longing for a return to peace.

The war also affected popular radio serials. Radio stations abandoned spy and sabotage programs for the duration of the war. Some even banned certain sound effects, such as wailing sirens, to avoid alarming listeners.

On the whole, World War II enjoyed broad support. Convinced that the cause was just, most Americans put up with shortages, planted "victory gardens" to conserve food, and bought millions of dollars worth of war bonds. Many families proudly displayed window banners with a star—a blue one for a loved one in the service, a gold one to commemorate a death in combat.

JAPANESE AMERICAN RELOCATION

By and large, World War II did not produce the kind of home-front intolerance that erupted during World War I. One tragic exception was the forced relocation and imprisonment, or **internment**, of Japanese Americans living on the Pacific coast. In September 1945, U.S. State Department adviser Eugene Rostow called internment "a tragic and dangerous mistake" and argued that "its motivation and its impact on our system of law deny every value of democracy."

When Pearl Harbor was bombed, about 119,000 people of Japanese ancestry lived in Washington, Oregon, and California. Of these, about a third, the Issei (EE-SAY), had been born in Japan and were regarded by the U.S. government as aliens ineligible for U.S. citizenship. The rest, the Nisei (NEE-SAY), had been born in the United States and were thus American citizens.

People of Japanese ancestry had long suffered racial discrimination in the United States. Laws prevented Japanese immigrants from becoming citizens, and prejudice restricted the kinds of jobs they and their descendants could hold and the neighborhoods where they could live.

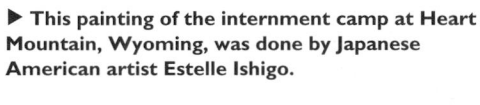

▶ This painting of the internment camp at Heart Mountain, Wyoming, was done by Japanese American artist Estelle Ishigo.

◀ Toyo Miyatale photographed this scene in Los Angeles in the early days of World War II. With their belongings piled high on the sidewalk, Japanese Americans wait for the buses that will take them to a relocation assignment center.

JAPANESE RELOCATION

Have students write letters to the editor from the viewpoint of a Japanese American who is about to be interned in a relocation camp. Letters should protest the reasons for internment, explain how internment will disrupt the writer's life, and explain why, as Eugene Rostow noted (p. 754), "its motivation and its impact on our system of law deny every value of democracy." Call on volunteers to read their letters to the class.

Students may wish to include their letters in their portfolios.

■■ Ask students if they think internment of any minority group could happen today. Have students identify legal and other resources that a target group might use to resist such an action.

▶

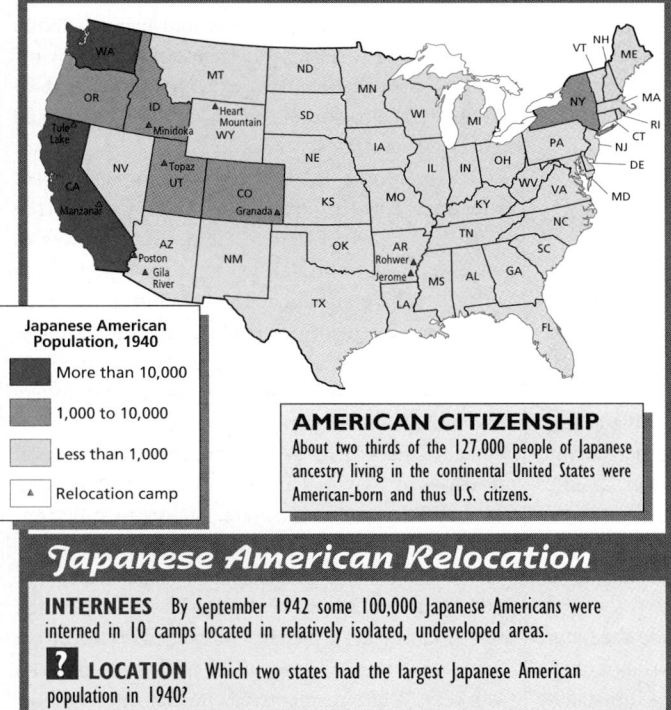

Japanese American Population, 1940

- ■ More than 10,000
- ■ 1,000 to 10,000
- □ Less than 1,000
- ▲ Relocation camp

AMERICAN CITIZENSHIP
About two thirds of the 127,000 people of Japanese ancestry living in the continental United States were American-born and thus U.S. citizens.

Japanese American Relocation

INTERNEES By September 1942 some 100,000 Japanese Americans were interned in 10 camps located in relatively isolated, undeveloped areas.

? **LOCATION** Which two states had the largest Japanese American population in 1940?

young Mineta fearfully watched his neighbors being taken away for questioning by the FBI. He recalled bitterly that "they had done nothing; the only thing that they had done was to be born of Japanese ancestry."

Ten years old when his family was uprooted, Mineta wore his Cub Scout uniform on the train, hoping that it would show his loyalty to the United States. After six months in a barracks at the Santa Anita racetrack in southern California, Mineta's family was interned with some 10,000 others at a hastily built camp at Heart Mountain, Wyoming. "These camps were all barbed wire, guard towers, searchlights," recalled Mineta. "They were concentration camps. There's no question about it."

After the war Mineta attended college, became an insurance agent, and went into local politics in San Jose. In 1974 he was elected to the House of Representatives, where he served on several committees and introduced legislation seeking reparations for Japanese American internees.

Like most other internees, Mineta deplored what had happened, but his patriotism never wavered:

> 66 Despite the color of our hair and skin, despite the shape of our eyes, the U.S. was our country. I remember how my parents reminded us of that fact. Just before our family was evacuated, my father . . . said, "No matter what happens, *this* is your home." 99

Patriotism, and the desire to disprove accusations of disloyalty, inspired many young men in the camps to volunteer for military duty (in segregated units).

When war came, prejudice turned into near hysteria. There was no evidence of disloyalty on the part of any Issei or Nisei. Strong anti-Japanese sentiments among some vocal politicians and residents of western states, however, persuaded the federal government to remove people of Japanese descent from the West Coast. In February 1942 they were ordered to detention camps in Wyoming, Utah, and other states. Here most were imprisoned until 1945—an action upheld by the Supreme Court in 1944.

■■ **Because of prejudice and war hysteria, Japanese Americans living on the West Coast were interned in relocation camps.**

Relocation profoundly disrupted the lives of Japanese Americans. They were forced to leave hurriedly, abandoning or selling their homes and businesses at rock-bottom prices. A government estimate later put Japanese American property losses at $400 million.

One imprisoned Japanese American was Norman Mineta, a Nisei from San Jose, California. On the day of the Pearl Harbor bombing, the

Norman Mineta

BIO
GRAPHY

VOICES IN HISTORY

Mary Tsukamoto and most of the community of Florin, California, were sent to an internment camp in Arkansas. There she reflected on what had happened: "Though we had lost Florin, hope doggedly stayed with us. . . . I tried to understand the meaning of my existence in this camp. . . . Though the U.S. was at war with both Germany and Italy, only we citizens of Japanese ancestry had been subjected to this cruelty by our own government. Our only guilt was that we were of the Japanese race."

Map Caption Answer
California and Washington

AV **TRANSPARENCY**
Everyday Life in America Transparency and **Worksheet 26**

PRIMARY SOURCE
Description of Change: excerpted
Rationale: excerpted to focus on main idea

Teaching the Section

WARTIME GAINS AND LIMITS

Create a chalkboard chart with columns headed *African Americans* and *Mexican Americans* and rows titled *Opportunities* and *Limitations*. Organize students into groups to discuss the war's consequences for each ethnic group. Then have the groups work together, using information gained from their discussions to complete the chalkboard chart. Conclude by asking students to hypothesize about why the wartime period was marked by racial unrest.

WOMEN IN THE WAR EFFORT

Organize students into groups to create a short segment for a World War II newsreel on women's contributions to the war effort. Segments should include narration, brief scenes of women at work, and comments from women, their supervisors, and their coworkers about women workers and about changes the war has brought to the workplace and to women's lives. Have each group present its newsreel segment to the class.

One Nisei combat team, the 442nd, fought in Europe and became one of the most decorated units in the armed services. Several thousand Japanese Americans also served in the Military Intelligence Service as interpreters and translators in the Pacific.

THE MARCH ON WASHINGTON

For African Americans, World War II brought both continued discrimination and greater opportunities. Many blacks moved into better-paying industrial jobs and played a key role in the military effort. About a million black soldiers served in the armed forces, including several thousand women in the Women's Auxiliary Army Corps. However, despite their protests, African Americans continued to serve in segregated units and until 1943 were kept out of combat. Blacks were usually restricted to menial work.

The millions of black Americans in the labor force in the 1940s also played an important home-front role in the war effort. But they had to struggle to gain acceptance. Many war plants would not hire blacks or would employ them only as janitors. And despite labor leaders' no-strike pledge, some white workers staged strikes, called "hate strikes," to keep black workers out of high-paying factory jobs.

In 1941, before the United States entered the war, African American labor leader A. Philip Randolph planned a march on Washington, D.C., to protest discrimination against black workers.

▲ African Americans served with distinction during the war. These pilots at a training center in Tuskegee, Alabama, study a map before going aloft in 1943.

President Roosevelt wanted to prevent the march, which Randolph predicted would bring 100,000 protesters to the Capitol. Randolph called it off after Roosevelt issued an executive order forbidding racial discrimination in defense plants and government offices.

To enforce the order, the government created the **Fair Employment Practices Committee** (FEPC). The FEPC investigated companies to make sure that all qualified applicants, regardless of race, were considered. The committee, however, lacked enforcement powers and could not prevent the widespread abuses. In addition, African Americans still had to struggle for equality in pay and promotion.

As in World War I, many blacks moved northward to work in war plants. In crowded cities, they faced discrimination in housing. Resulting tensions sometimes led to outbursts of violence against African Americans. In Detroit in 1943, some 25,000 white workers violated the wartime no-strike pledge and staged a hate strike to protest the promotion of African American workers. White residents of one Detroit neighborhood tried to prevent blacks from moving into the newly constructed Sojourner Truth Housing Project. In June of the same year, 25 blacks and 9 whites died in several days of rioting after a fight between blacks and whites at Belle Isle, a popular Detroit park, spread to other parts of the city.

Despite these incidents, most African Americans supported the war. Educator and civil rights activist Mary McLeod Bethune noted that African Americans "feel that the fight against fascism is their fight too," because they realized "that their persecution would be even worse under Hitler."

THE ZOOT–SUIT RIOTS

For Mexican Americans, as for blacks, World War II brought both opportunities and problems. More than 300,000 Mexican Americans served in the military, and 17 earned the Congressional Medal of Honor. The 88th Division, an elite combat unit known as the "Blue Devils," consisted mostly of Mexican Americans.

Mexican Americans also helped meet home-front labor needs. University of Texas history professor Carlos E. Castañeda served as assistant to the chairman of the FEPC and worked to

GUIDED PRACTICE

Work with the class to develop two lists on the chalkboard—one of the positive changes the war had on the lives of minorities and women on the home front and the other reflecting the negative effects.

INDEPENDENT PRACTICE

Have students pick one of the positive or negative outcomes listed in the Guided Practice activity and create an editorial cartoon that illustrates the experience. Students may wish to include their editorial cartoons in their portfolios.

REVIEW Organize a role-play in which volunteers represent a factory owner, farmer, entertainer, journalist, Japanese American, Mexican American, African American, and woman worker. Have remaining students interview the role-players about the war years. Then assign the Section 2 Review on p. 758.

ASSESS Assign the **Section 2 Daily Quiz** in *Core Resources.*
▶

▲ These Mexican American infantrymen are being trained to use the rapid-firing Garand rifle at a U.S. Army camp. Because many of these soldiers spoke Spanish, army trainers gave instructions in both English and Spanish.

improve working conditions for Mexican Americans in Texas. In 1945 the FEPC ordered a major Texas oil company to discontinue its hiring and promotion practices that discriminated against Hispanics.

As a result of similar FEPC actions, and the pressing need for workers, many factories opened up jobs to Mexican Americans. Many Mexican Americans moved from the Southwest to industrial centers in the Midwest and on the West Coast. Under a 1942 agreement between the United States and Mexico, thousands of Mexican farm and railroad workers—known as **braceros**—came north to work in the Southwest during World War II.

But prejudice and discrimination against Hispanics in jobs, housing, and recreation facilities caused bitter resentment. Relations grew especially hostile in Los Angeles. Mexican American youths had adopted the fad of wearing zoot suits—long jackets, pegged trousers, and wide-brimmed hats. In the summer of 1943, sailors roamed the city attacking zoot-suiters in what came to be known as the **zoot-suit riots**. The government eventually clamped down on the sailors, but not before they had viciously beaten many Mexican Americans.

A citizens' committee later determined that the attacks were motivated by racial prejudice. The committee also placed partial responsibility on the police, who had responded to the riots by arresting Mexican Americans, and on biased newspaper reports.

■■ **African Americans and Mexican Americans won better factory jobs during the war but continued to face widespread discrimination.**

Rosie the Riveter

During the depression, the government discouraged women, especially married women, from working. The government now urged them to enter the job market to replace departing servicemen and to help win the war against fascism. One government poster showed a woman worker in bandanna and overalls. The caption read: "I'm Proud . . . my husband <u>wants</u> me to do my part." Advertisements and a popular song promoted "Rosie the Riveter," the symbol of patriotic women defense workers.

From 1940 to 1944 the number of women in the labor force increased by more than four million. Women worked in war plants and replaced men in a host of jobs ranging from newspaper reporting to truck driving. Many of these new workers were married women who were taking jobs outside the home for the first time. Many women already in the paid work force left traditional "women's work" as domestics and other service jobs to work in factories.

■■ **World War II increased women's participation in the paid labor force and allowed them to move into traditionally male jobs.**

Women's participation in the war effort gave many of them a new sense of pride and self-worth. One woman aircraft worker finally felt a sense of achievement after feeling "average" at other jobs:

66 Foremen from other departments come to my machine to ask me to do some work for them if I have time because they say I'm the best countersinker in the vast building! At forty-nine I've at last become not better than average, but the best! 99

HISTORICAL SIDELIGHTS

Women in the Work Force

In the auto industry the number of women production workers went from 1 in 20 in 1940 to 1 in 5 by 1944. However, many women were not offered specialized on-the-job training and were assigned to low-wage jobs. In addition, women workers faced hissing and whistling from their male counterparts. One female machine shop worker noted: "It was very rough for a while, but we were determined to stay, and eventually, the majority of men learned to accept us and respect us as co-workers."

PRIMARY SOURCE

Description of Change: excerpted
Rationale: excerpted to focus on main idea

RETEACH Ask students, working in pairs, to write sentences that explain how each entry in the Preview Workshop is related to the main idea of the subsection in which it is located. Have pairs share their sentences with the group.

Closure

Write these World War II slogans on the chalkboard: *Pay your Taxes, Beat the Axis; Back the Attack with War Bonds;* and *Don't Let Them Catch Us with Our Plants Down.* Ask students to explain how each slogan reflects the U.S. war effort on the home front.

Extension

ANALYZE Interested students can read the decisions in the two Supreme Court cases—*Hirabayashi* v. *United States* (1943) and *Korematsu* v. *United States* (1944)—which established the legality of the U.S. internment of Japanese Americans and write papers commenting on the decisions.

RESEARCH Ask students to research the work of the United Service Organization (USO) during World War II.

SECTION REVIEW ANSWERS

IDENTIFY

For significance, see the following pages:
James F. Byrnes (p. 752)
War Production Board (p. 752)
Selective Training and Service Act (p. 753)
Thomas E. Dewey (p. 753)
internment (p. 754)
Norman Mineta (p. 755)
A. Philip Randolph (p. 756)
Fair Employment Practices Committee (p. 756)
braceros (p. 757)
zoot-suit riots (p. 757)

1. *increased industrial production and put production and distribution under government control, financed war and fought inflation by extending income tax to more Americans and by selling war bonds*

2. *increased women's participation in paid labor force, allowed women to move into traditionally male jobs*

3. *because prejudice and war hysteria made some Americans question the loyalty of Japanese Americans*

4. *Letters might weigh movement into better-paying jobs, service in armed forces against discrimination and struggles for equality in pay and promotion.*

5. *encouraged media to promote war effort, created OWI; supported the war effort, planted "victory gardens," and bought war bonds*

▼ These young women worked as welders in a war plant.

▲ Vultee Aircraft was one of the first aircraft plants to employ a large number of women workers. These Vultee workers are preparing a Vengeance Dive-Bomber for spray painting in August 1942.

A government study in 1942 praised women workers, noting that factories "were practically unanimous in reporting that on the whole the work done by women was considered equal to that of men." Nevertheless, women encountered discrimination. Women workers continued to be paid less than men for the same work. African American women and women over 40 found few employers willing to hire them. Although Frances Perkins, long a supporter of women workers, continued to head the Department of Labor during the war years, wartime federal agencies did little to enforce equal treatment for women workers.

In spite of women's achievements, it was widely assumed—by many women as well as men—that most of the jobs women held during the war were temporary. A manager of a shipyard predicted that "these women who are willing . . . to lend a hand with the war will be the . . . office personnel of . . . the future." The message was clear: in traditionally "masculine" jobs, women were wanted as emergency helpers, not as competition.

SECTION 2 REVIEW

IDENTIFY and explain the significance of the following: James F. Byrnes, War Production Board, Selective Training and Service Act, Thomas E. Dewey, internment, Norman Mineta, A. Philip Randolph, Fair Employment Practices Committee, braceros, zoot-suit riots.

1. MAIN IDEA What steps did the United States take to shift from a peacetime to a wartime economy?

2. MAIN IDEA How did World War II change life for American women?

3. HYPOTHESIZING Why did the United States forcibly relocate and imprison Japanese Americans living on the West Coast?

4. WRITING TO EVALUATE Imagine you are either an African American or a Mexican American during World War II. Write a letter to your representative in Congress, evaluating the gains you have made during the war.

5. IDENTIFYING CAUSE AND EFFECT What did the U.S. government do to keep morale high during World War II? How did most Americans respond to the government's actions?

Section 3

DEFEAT OF THE AXIS POWERS

FOCUS
- **What did the Allied offensive in North Africa achieve?**
- **How did the Allies gain final victory in Europe?**
- **What was the chief objective of Allied assaults in the Pacific?**
- **Why and when did Japan surrender?**

*A*merican supplies and troops began to make a difference in the war by late 1942. But it would take over two more years of hard fighting to defeat the Axis powers. The Allied invasions of North Africa, Italy, and France and the fierce bombardments of German cities forced Germany to surrender in May 1945. In the Pacific, meanwhile, the United States seized Japanese-held islands, including the Philippines. Atomic attacks devastated Japan, and it surrendered in August 1945.

Liberation of Paris, 1944

ALLIED ATTACKS IN THE MEDITERRANEAN

The Allies agreed soon after Pearl Harbor that they would open up a second front against the Axis powers in order to relieve pressure on the Soviet Union. At Churchill's urging, they focused this attack on the Mediterranean region—what Churchill called the "soft underbelly" of the Axis territory.

Axis surrender in North Africa. In November 1942, after the British had driven the Germans and Italians into Libya, another Allied force landed in French Northwest Africa in an invasion code-named Operation Torch (see map on page 748). General Dwight D. Eisenhower commanded the invasion force, which consisted of American and British soldiers. As the soldiers established beachheads in Morocco and Algeria, Allied planes and ships cut Axis supply lines from Italy. Then, during the winter of 1942–43, the two Allied land forces—one from the west and the other from the east—began squeezing the Axis troops into a trap between them.

Several fierce battles took place in Tunisia. Finally, in May 1943, the Axis force of some

◄ **"We are out to win the war in the quickest and most economical way,"** U.S. Army chief of staff George C. Marshall (right) declared in 1943. Marshall was photographed with General Dwight D. Eisenhower in North Africa in June 1943.

FOCUS OBJECTIVES
- Analyze the achievements of the Allied offensive in North Africa.
- Explain how the Allies gained final victory in Europe.
- Determine the chief objective of Allied assaults in the Pacific.
- State why and when Japan surrendered.

 GLOBAL CONNECTIONS

Almost a half-million survivors of the Afrika Corps in North Africa, as well as the first prisoners taken in the Italian campaign, were brought to POW camps in the U.S. and Canada. Many of the POWs were put to work on peanut farms in Florida and in logging camps in West Virginia. The prisoners came to admire the American farmer's way of life. Many POWs returned to the U.S. after the war and obtained U.S. citizenship.

CORE RESOURCES
- **Section 3 Daily Quiz**

AV RESOURCES
- **Linking Geography and History Transparencies and Worksheets 18, 19**

AMERICANS IN WORLD WAR II ■■ 759

MOTIVATING: PRIOR KNOWLEDGE

Ask students to identify on a map areas held by the Allies and by the Axis powers in late 1942. Have students review the war's turning points and describe how they think Americans at home and on the battlefields might have felt about the war at that time.

Teaching the **Section**

THE NORTH AFRICAN OFFENSIVE

Ask for volunteers to role-play a military news briefing in Washington, D.C., to report the successful completion of the Allies' North African campaign. Roles should include: a press officer to coordinate the briefing; staff officers to brief the press on battle locations, tactics, and other geo-

graphic aspects; and field officers and soldiers to relate their battlefield experiences. The remainder of the class should portray newspaper reporters at the briefing, asking questions about the information presented and about the potential significance of the victory on the course of the war in Europe.

MAKING CONNECTIONS
Science

Sonar stands for *"so*und *na*vigation and *r*anging"—a method of locating and judging the distance of underwater objects by analyzing the sound waves they deflect or give off. Scientists had developed sonar to locate icebergs, but after the outbreak of World War I British and U.S. scientists concentrated their research on using sonar to locate enemy submarines.

HISTORICAL SIDELIGHTS
Dummy Installations

The Allies successfully hid the D-Day landing point through an operation code-named *Fortitude*. While the real invasion force secretly prepared for the Normandy landing, other troops distracted the enemy by mustering in crowded fields in southeastern England accompanied by fake ammunition dumps, hospitals, field kitchens, and artillery made of wood and canvas.

250,000 men surrendered. The Allies now controlled much of the Mediterranean. This victory also gave American troops valuable combat experience, especially in amphibious assaults.

■■ **The conquest of North Africa gave the Allies increased control over the Mediterranean.**

The invasion of Italy. North Africa offered a gateway to the Italian island of Sicily. Allied leaders decided to invade it next in order to clear the Axis forces out of the central Mediterranean and acquire a launching pad for an invasion of the Italian mainland.

Battling high winds and difficult seas, almost half a million troops landed in July 1943 and subdued Sicily in a little over a month. The Italian king named a new prime minister to replace Benito Mussolini and ordered Mussolini's arrest. The Germans, however, were determined not to surrender the peninsula. They took Mussolini to Germany and then set up a base for him in northern Italy.

In September the Italian government signed an armistice with the Allies. Two days later the Allies invaded southern Italy to attack the Germans. Although the Allies took Naples on October 1, they soon bogged down. Hoping to outflank Nazi troops near Rome, they landed to the south at Anzio in January 1944 (see map on page 748); but their attack failed, and they were pinned down for months. Not until June 1944 did the Allies march into Rome, which became the first Axis capital to fall.

American and British forces then began driving slowly north. They were joined by small units of troops from more than 25 countries. After months of bitter mountain warfare, the German occupiers were finally defeated. Mussolini was captured in late April and shot by Italian partisans.

◄ **World War II Victory Medal**

*V*ICTORY IN EUROPE

During the months of fighting in the Mediterranean region, the Allies were waging campaigns on several other fronts as well. Although they faced a determined enemy, they eventually overcame all resistance.

Sea and air assaults. In the Atlantic, German U-boats continued to take a staggering toll of Allied ships, lives, and supplies. Not until 1943 did the **Battle of the Atlantic** begin to turn in the Allies' favor. An important factor was the refinement of sonar equipment, which uses sound waves to detect underwater objects. The Allies also developed fast escort ships for convoys and air-bombed German U-boats and submarine yards. By 1944 the Allies had won the Battle of the Atlantic.

In the air, too, 1943 was an important year for the Allies. They intensified their campaign of strategic bombing aimed at destroying German military production and at undermining the morale of the German people. British Royal Air Force (RAF) planes flew chiefly at night, dropping their bombs in the general area of a given target. American aircraft concentrated on precision bombing in daylight raids. By 1944, bombers rained tons of explosives on German factories, supply lines, and military centers. Many German civilians died in these raids.

The invasion of France. Victory in the Battle of the Atlantic and air assaults on Germany paved the way for Operation Overlord—the long-awaited Allied invasion of German-occupied France. Commanded by General Eisenhower, it had involved years of planning. The Allies put in place a system of dummy installations and false clues to convince the Germans that the invasion would take place near Calais.

Instead, the Allies landed to the south, in Normandy. On **D-Day**, June 6, 1944, nearly 5,000 troop transports, landing craft, and warships carried some 150,000 American, British, and Canadian soldiers across the English Channel. Overhead, planes dropped close to 23,000 airborne troops and bombed roads, bridges, and German troop concentrations. Sergeant Ralph G. Martin recalled that "everything was confusion" during the landing made in pounding surf:

Ask students to reread p. 750 on the Allied war aims that FDR and Churchill agreed upon in Washington, D.C., and Casablanca. Then have volunteers recall the situation in the Soviet Union in 1943 and explain why opening a second front was desirable. *(relieve pressure on the Soviets)* Have students analyze how the Italian campaign would further that aim. *(Germany would be forced to move troops from other* *places in Europe to defend Italy, which could help the Soviets to regain lost territory.)*

Pair students to create a teaching tool to chronicle events in Europe that led to the Allied victory, from the invasion of Italy in July 1943 to Germany's surrender in May 1945. Tell each pair to first decide whether to organize this information on a map, on a flowchart or other graphic organizer, or on a time line. Select pairs to present their work to the class. Then ask volunteers to assess the contribution of naval and air power to the Allies' victory. ▶

THE NEW YORK TIMES.

ALLIED ARMIES LAND IN FRANCE IN THE HAVRE-CHERBOURG AREA; GREAT INVASION IS UNDER WAY

The Granger Collection, New York

▲ The *New York Times* announced the Allied invasion of France on June 6, 1944. After landing at Normandy, these American members of the invasion force rest under a cliff before advancing inland.

> 66 Units were mixed up, many of them leaderless, most of them not being where they were supposed to be. Shells were coming in all the time; boats burning; vehicles with nowhere to go bogging down, getting hit; supplies getting wet; boats trying to come in all the time, some hitting mines, exploding. 99

The Germans had fortified the Normandy beaches with concrete bunkers, tank traps, and mines. But the Allied disinformation campaign had done its job. Hitler refused to send reinforcements, believing that the main invasion would occur elsewhere. Although the Allies met determined opposition, they penetrated 15 miles into France in less than a week. Aided by the French Resistance, the Allies drove steadily eastward. They liberated Paris on August 25, 1944. By early September they had landed over two million troops in western Europe. Another Allied force drove northward through France from the Mediterranean. Meanwhile, Soviet troops pressed Germany from the east.

A German counterattack.

Although Germany's situation was grave, Hitler would not give up. In September 1944 the Germans launched their first V-2s, long-range rockets aimed at cities in England and Belgium. Once launched, these bombs could not be shot down without causing considerable damage.

By September 1944 the Allies had crossed the German border. As they paused to bring in sup-plies and to regroup, the Germans launched their last counterattack. In heavy snow, they drove against the Allies in the thickly wooded Ardennes region of Belgium and northern France, pushing them westward to create a dangerous bulge in the Allied lines. In the resulting **Battle of the Bulge**, some 200,000 Germans attacked an initial American force of around 80,000. Because many of the regular troops had been transferred to other areas, much of the fighting was done by "cooks, clerks, mechanics, and radio operators," one American soldier remembered.

Allied generals rushed reinforcements to the front, and the Allies pushed the Germans back. Artillery-man Francis Tsuzuki, whose Japanese American battalion pursued the Germans, remembered that "the Germans were retreating so fast. At times we were moving . . . more than 100 miles a day." By January 1945 it was clear that the German offensive had failed. In February Roosevelt, Churchill, and Stalin met at the **Yalta Conference** to plan for the postwar peace. At the conference the leaders agreed to divide and occupy Germany and outlined plans for a new international peace organization.

Last days. During the early months of 1945, Allied bombers continued to blast German industrial and population centers, including Dresden, Leipzig, and Berlin. One of the most devastating—and controversial—attacks hit Dresden in February. This beautiful old city, of little strategic value, was packed with refugees fleeing from the war-torn areas. In one massive two-day attack, Allied bombers caused the worst firestorms of the war. Total civilian deaths have been estimated at between 30,000 and 60,000.

▲ The Allied bombing of Dresden, Germany, killed many civilians and left many famous buildings in ruins. Shown here is the damage to the Zwinger Museum, which housed a priceless art collection.

HISTORICAL SIDELIGHTS

Bombing of Dresden

While much of Dresden was destroyed by the Allied bombing raids, many of its art treasures were not, since the German government had hidden them outside the city. Although Soviet troops took the art collection in 1945, much of it was returned in the mid-1950s. The damaged Zwinger Museum shown in the photograph on this page was one of the few 18th-century structures that survived the bombing raids.

PRIMARY SOURCE

Description of Change: excerpted

Rationale: excerpted to focus on main idea

Teaching the *Section*

WAR IN THE PACIFIC

Have students work in groups and assume the roles of American military commanders in the Pacific. Ask each group to prepare a briefing explaining the military strategy of island-hopping and its importance. "Commanders" should also create outline maps of the Pacific and locate and label the islands that were involved in the island-hopping strategy. Have volunteers present each group's "briefings" and maps. Then have the class summarize why the recapture of islands was critical to Allied strategy in the Pacific.

 GLOBAL CONNECTIONS

The Coast Watchers

During World War II, Australians living on remote islands in the South Pacific served as the eyes of the Allies. The Australians informed them by radio of Japanese troop movements and rescued shipwrecked sailors and Allied pilots shot down at sea.

BIO GRAPHY **PERSONALITIES IN HISTORY**

Throughout the early part of 1942, MacArthur disagreed with the U.S. strategy that emphasized Germany's defeat, and he called for a "Japan first" strategy. In mid-1943 MacArthur began his plan for the reconquest of the Philippines. When it was suggested that Admiral Nimitz's forces undertake the campaign, MacArthur bristled and continued to promote himself for the task. Then in 1944, when military leaders questioned the necessity of reconquering the Philippines, he successfully campaigned for his point of view. When MacArthur finally received the go-ahead, he waded onto Leyte beach and made a brief speech. "This is the Voice of Freedom, General MacArthur speaking. People of the Philippines: I have returned!"

In March, Allied troops from the west crossed the Rhine and drove into the heart of Germany. By then, Soviet troops occupied much of Eastern Europe. Churchill wanted the Allies to push east as far and as fast as possible because he worried that the Russians might later lay claim to territories they seized. But Eisenhower, who did not want military strategy determined by political considerations, halted the Allied advance at the Elbe River in April. The Soviet army agreed to halt momentarily east of Berlin.

On April 30, 1945, Hitler committed suicide in his bunker deep under the ruins of Berlin. As Soviet troops occupied the city, German armies all over Europe stopped fighting. American sergeant Mack Morriss described the grim mood of the fallen city: "There is a feeling that here has ended not only a city but a nation, that here a titanic force has come to catastrophe." Germany surrendered unconditionally on May 7. The next day, known as V-E (Victory in Europe) Day, marked the formal end of a brutal war that had held Europe in its grip for more than five years.

■■ **After winning the Battle of the Atlantic and bombing Germany, the Allies invaded France. Germany surrendered in May 1945.**

---

*P*ACIFIC OFFENSIVES

In the Pacific, as in the western theater of operations, the Allies went on the offensive by 1943. The planned attack on Japan had two components: (1) air, land, and naval forces would seize Japanese-held islands in the central Pacific and set up air bases there; (2) combined forces would retake New Guinea and then the Philippines. The ultimate objective, of course, was to come within striking distance of Japan itself.

Island-hopping. As early as 1942, the American high command had adopted a policy of **island-hopping**. This meant that troops would attack and seize only certain strategic Japanese-held islands, rather than try to recapture all of them. Japanese garrisons on bypassed islands would be cut off from supplies and troop reinforcements.

In the central Pacific, an island-hopping offensive began in November 1943 in the Gilbert Islands (see map on page 746). Army troops easily took Makin Island. Tarawa Island proved more difficult. Because of a coral reef encircling the island, the marines who landed there, according to Sergeant John Bushemi, had to wade in to the beach "in the face of murderous Japanese fire, with no protection." Almost 1,000 marines lost their lives, and some 2,000 were wounded before the island was secure.

The next important series of landings targeted the Marshall Islands, north of the Gilberts. Here Americans captured several key bases from which they bombed the Truk Islands, the headquarters of the Japanese fleet.

By the summer of 1944, Americans advanced to the Mariana Islands. In June, under cover of intense air and naval bombardment from nearby carriers, landing craft swept in to the beaches of Saipan. The Japanese, determined to take a stand, sent out a big fleet to stop this offensive. In the resulting **Battle of the Philippine Sea**, the United States won a decisive victory, downing hundreds of Japanese planes while only losing some 80 U.S. planes.

Saipan and Guam fell in July and August, respectively. U.S. victories here were especially crucial. The islands provided airstrips from which American bombers could launch missions against the islands of Japan.

Reconquering the Philippines. Despite these setbacks, Japanese resistance proved just as fierce when the Allies began their New Guinea–Philippines campaign in June 1943. Douglas MacArthur, who had earlier evacuated the Philippines, commanded U.S. forces.

BIO GRAPHY MacArthur was born in 1880, the son of distinguished general Arthur MacArthur. After graduating first in his class from West Point, young MacArthur served in the Philippines and was wounded twice in World War I. From

Douglas MacArthur

JAPAN SURRENDERS

As a class, discuss the reasons why Japan surrendered after the bombing of Hiroshima and Nagasaki. Then have students debate this statement: *President Truman's decision to drop the atomic bomb on Japan was a wise one.*

▶

Changing Ways
THE NAVAJO CODE TALKERS

During World War II Native Americans served in several branches of the U.S. armed forces. Their languages allowed them to play a unique role in the Signal Corps, the communication units responsible for coding and sending classified military information. On the basis of the success of a few Native American army groups in code work, the Marine Signal Corps decided in March 1942 to organize a unit composed entirely of Navajos. The marines believed that the Navajo language would be unfamiliar to the Japanese, and thus would provide an unbreakable code. They quickly assembled a group of Navajo soldiers for the job.

The new unit devised and memorized a special Navajo dictionary containing 413 military terms. For example, the Navajo word for

"chicken hawk" meant dive-bomber in the code; "humming-bird" meant fighter plane; and "iron fish" meant submarine. Armed with this new code, the Navajo "Code Talkers" first went into action in the fall of 1942 in the Pacific.

Soon after the Code Talkers arrived on the front lines, U.S. field commanders reported that the Navajos' methods reduced the time

▲ Corporal Henry Bake, Jr., (left) and Private George H. Kirk (right) were two members of the Navajo Code Talkers. They are shown operating a portable radio set behind front lines in the Solomon Islands in1943.

needed for decoding and encoding messages by half. As radio operators tracking Japanese movements, the Navajos often had to work in especially dangerous conditions behind enemy lines. "The Navajo Code Talkers have proved to be excellent Marines, intelligent, industrious, efficient," one officer wrote. Another remarked, "Were it not for the Navajos, the Marines would never have taken Iwo Jima."

By August 1943 nearly 200 Navajos were participating in the Code Talker program, and by the war's end more than 400 had served in the Marine Signal Corps. Their codes completely baffled the Japanese and were never broken. Though the Navajo Code Talkers made up only a small part of the Allied forces, their contributions to the war effort were invaluable.

Changing Ways

THE NAVAJO CODE TALKERS

SETTING THE SCENE

Japan had been able to crack every code the United States devised until civil engineer Philip Johnston came up with the idea of using the Navajos as code talkers. He had learned Navajo while his parents were Protestant missionaries among the Navajos. Realizing the need for secret communications from his own experiences in World War I, Johnston believed that the Navajo language would be well suited to sending secret messages. He persuaded the marines to test his idea.

1919 to 1922 he was superintendent of West Point. He took part in the attack on the Bonus Army marchers of 1932 (see Chapter 23), justifying the violence by claiming that Communists were behind this veterans' protest. After serving as a military adviser in the Philippines for several years, MacArthur was recalled to active duty in the summer of 1941. Eventually he was given command of all U.S. Army units in the Pacific.

In many respects, MacArthur was an excellent strategist. No one doubted his courage. But he was also arrogant, and though he demanded absolute loyalty from his subordinates, he did not hesitate to disagree with his superiors.

In the Allied drive to recapture the Philippines, MacArthur led U.S. and Australian troops in a series of landings along the north coast of New Guinea. By late July 1944 they had reached the western end of this large island. Allied forces also took smaller islands nearby, such as the Admiralty Islands.

By the fall of 1944, with New Guinea secure and with its newly won bases in the Marianas, the United States was ready to invade the Philippines.

Practice

GUIDED PRACTICE

Work with students to prepare a time line on the chalkboard to combine the events in the Pacific and Europe that led to the end of World War II. For each event on the time line, have students describe its effect on the Allied war effort.

INDEPENDENT PRACTICE

Have each student pick three events from the Guided Practice time line that he or she considers critical to Allied victory either in Europe or in the Pacific. Instruct students to write a paragraph to justify each choice. Students may wish to include their paragraphs in their portfolios.

Review and Assessment

REVIEW Select students to assume the roles of General Eisenhower, General MacArthur, and President Truman at a "Meet the Press" radio newscast. Have other students serve as members of the press, questioning the panel on the events that led to victory. Then assign the Section 3 Review on p. 765.

ASSESS Assign the **Section 3 Daily Quiz** in *Core Resources*.

HISTORICAL SIDELIGHTS

Kamikaze Pilots

The kamikaze pilots went through a ritual-like procedure before takeoff that included a last toast, farewell bids by onlookers, and writing last letters home. The goals of the kamikazes were spelled out in the First Order to the Kamikazes: "It is absolutely out of the question for you to return alive. Your mission involves certain death. Your bodies will be dead, but not your spirits."

MAKING CONNECTIONS

Science

Scientists from all over the world participated in the Manhattan Project. Among them was German American physicist Maria Mayer, who had come to the U.S. in 1930. Mayer later became the first woman to receive the Nobel Prize in theoretical physics for her contribution to proving the shell-model theory of the nucleus of an atom. This theory posits that the nucleus is made up of concentric shells of protons and neutrons.

PRIMARY SOURCE

Description of Change: excerpted
Rationale: excerpted to focus on main idea

Allied forces poured onto the beaches of the island of Leyte in October. The Japanese navy's counterattack led to the **Battle of Leyte Gulf**, the last, largest, and most decisive naval engagement in the Pacific. The battle was a disaster for the Japanese, who lost four carriers, two battleships, and several cruisers. From this time on, the Japanese fleet no longer seriously threatened the Allies.

Allied troops, aided by Filipino guerrillas, fanned out over the islands of the Philippines. Overcoming bitter opposition, they entered Manila in February 1945 and subdued most Japanese defense forces within weeks. "I'm a little late," said MacArthur, "but we finally came."

■■ **Island-hopping and the reconquest of the Philippines brought the Allies within bombing distance of Japan's cities.**

VICTORY IN THE PACIFIC

These Pacific victories gave the United States bases to launch B-29 bombers against the Japanese home islands. In a series of devastating night attacks, U.S. planes hit most of the country's major cities. The worst raid, over Tokyo in March 1945, created firestorms that destroyed much of the city.

▼ A few hours after U.S. Marines captured Iwo Jima, naval landing crafts delivered tons of supplies to the island. The slippery volcanic ash made it difficult for marines to keep their footing while carrying the heavy crates.

Japanese civilian morale sagged, but the country's military leaders refused to surrender. In February 1945, when marines attacked Iwo Jima—only 750 miles from Tokyo—they met strong resistance. U.S. marines struggled to take Mount Suribachi, which the Japanese held with a strong system of tunnels and bunkers. The Battle of Iwo Jima lasted nearly a month. Some 4,000 marines were killed, while the Japanese lost more than 20,000.

On April 1 the largest landing force in Pacific history invaded Okinawa, about 350 miles from Japan. Allied soldiers drove the Japanese forces to the southern tip of the island. The **Battle of Okinawa** was perhaps the bloodiest of the Pacific war, with U.S. casualties estimated at 49,000 and Japanese losses at over 100,000. Meanwhile, a 700-plane squad of **kamikaze**, or suicide planes, damaged 13 U.S. destroyers. (*Kamikaze* is a Japanese word meaning "divine wind.")

By early April 1945, however, American victory in the Pacific was near. But President Roosevelt did not live to see the end of hostilities with Japan. The world was stunned when he died suddenly on April 12. The new president, Harry S. Truman, wrote candidly about his bewilderment:

▲ The sudden death of President Roosevelt shocked many Americans. A weeping Sergeant Graham Jackson plays "Going Home" on his accordion as the president's casket passes by.

❝ I did not know what reaction the country would have to the death of a man whom they all practically worshipped. I was worried about the reaction of the Armed Forces. . . . I knew the President had a great many meetings with Churchill and Stalin. I was not familiar with any of these things. ❞

Within weeks, however, Truman faced a grave decision. Should the Allies invade Japan or use a fearsome new weapon, the atomic bomb?

RETEACH Organize students so that a roughly equal number are assigned to each subsection of Section 3. Direct each student to write a question about the material in his or her assigned subsection. Then use the questions to quiz the entire group.

Closure

Ask students whether they agree with the statement below and to give evidence to support their opinion. Then ask them how they might change the statement to make it more accurate or specific: *The U.S. made a contribution to the Allied victory.*

Extension

RESEARCH Have students research the Manhattan Project and the role of its lead physicist, Robert Oppenheimer.

INTERPRET Have students listen to recordings of the wartime speeches of Winston Churchill and Franklin Roosevelt and draw conclusions about why these speeches had such a powerful, positive effect on their listeners.

Germany's surrender had freed Allied forces for the war in the Pacific, but Japan remained a formidable opponent with a well-trained army and strong defenses—despite repeated Allied bombings.

The United States' new weapon had been developed by the top-secret **Manhattan Project**, whose scientists had been working on a bomb since 1942. The scientists successfully tested their bomb at Alamogordo, New Mexico, on July 16, 1945. The very next day, Truman met with Allied leaders at Potsdam, south of Berlin. On July 26 they demanded Japan's unconditional surrender, which Japan rejected.

Truman decided to give the order to use atomic weapons against Japan. On August 6 a U.S. plane called the *Enola Gay* dropped an atomic bomb on Hiroshima. It flattened a huge area of the city and killed more than 75,000 people. Three days later the United States dropped the second atomic bomb on Nagasaki. The Japanese estimated that the total number of deaths caused by both bombs—including those who died later from burns and radiation poisoning—was 240,000.

A day before the bombing of Nagasaki, the Soviet Union had declared war on Japan and began an invasion of Manchuria. The Japanese soon

▲ This aerial photograph shows the devastation in Hiroshima after the atomic bomb was dropped. The watch shown was found in the wreckage, its hands frozen at 8:15—the exact time of the explosion.

offered to surrender. Despite the unconditional surrender demand, the Allies accepted a big condition: the emperor could remain on his throne. The formal surrender was signed on September 2, 1945, aboard the battleship *Missouri* in Tokyo Bay.

■■ After the U.S. atomic bombings of Hiroshima and Nagasaki, Japan surrendered in August 1945.

SECTION REVIEW ANSWERS

IDENTIFY
For significance, see the following pages:
Dwight D. Eisenhower (p. 759)
Battle of the Atlantic (p. 760)
D-Day (p. 760)
Battle of the Bulge (p. 761)
Yalta Conference (p. 761)
island-hopping (p. 762)
Battle of the Philippine Sea (p. 762)
Battle of Leyte Gulf (p. 764)
Battle of Iwo Jima (p. 764)
Battle of Okinawa (p. 764)
kamikaze (p. 764)
Harry S. Truman (p. 764)
Manhattan Project (p. 765)

LOCATE
For locations, see the maps on pp. 746 and 748.

1. increased control over Mediterranean, opened way for invasion of Italy
2. bombing of Germany, invasion of Germany from east and west
3. by island-hopping and reconquest of Philippines; to bring Allies within bombing distance of Japan
4. Essays should mention continued resistance despite military reverses and low civilian morale; surrendered after the dropping of atomic bombs on Hiroshima and Nagasaki, which caused great destruction and loss of life.
5. Diary entries will vary but should describe the battle selected.

SECTION 3 REVIEW

IDENTIFY and explain the significance of the following: Dwight D. Eisenhower, Battle of the Atlantic, D-Day, Battle of the Bulge, Yalta Conference, island-hopping, Battle of the Philippine Sea, Battle of Leyte Gulf, Battle of Iwo Jima, Battle of Okinawa, kamikaze, Harry S. Truman, Manhattan Project.

LOCATE and explain the importance of the following: Sicily, Anzio, Normandy, Dresden, Elbe River, Gilbert Islands, Marshall Islands, Mariana Islands, New Guinea, Leyte, Iwo Jima, Okinawa, Hiroshima, Nagasaki.

1. **MAIN IDEA** What did the Allies accomplish through the military campaign in North Africa?
2. **MAIN IDEA** What events forced Germany to surrender in 1945?
3. **GEOGRAPHY: LOCATION** How did the Allies attempt to regain control of the Pacific? What was the overall aim of this military strategy?
4. **WRITING TO EXPLAIN** Write an essay that explains when and why Japan surrendered.
5. **USING HISTORICAL IMAGINATION** Imagine you are a soldier on either the European or the Pacific front. Write a diary entry that describes conditions you experienced in one of the battles mentioned in the text.

PREVIEW WORKSHOP

Following is a list of the significant people, places, and terms in this section. You may wish to use this list as a section preview.

People
■ Elie Wiesel

Places
■ Kuril Islands

■ Sakhalin Island
■ Taiwan
■ Hainan

Terms
■ Holocaust
■ genocide
■ superpowers

**MOTIVATING:
LINK TO TODAY**

Ask students how they think Truman's decision to drop the atomic bomb affected prospects for world peace. Ask volunteers if they think the world today is made more secure or less so by the existence of nuclear weapons. Tell students that in this section they will examine this and other consequences of World War II.

FOCUS OBJECTIVES

■ Examine the costs of World War II.

■ Explain what the Holocaust was and describe how it affected European Jews.

■ Analyze the international consequences of World War II.

Section 4

THE PRICE OF VICTORY

FOCUS
■ **What were some of the costs of World War II?**
■ **What was the Holocaust? How did it affect European Jews?**
■ **What were the international consequences of World War II?**

After years of struggle and sacrifice, World War II ended in victory for the Allies. But the price was high. The toll in lives and property was without precedent. Most alarming was the knowledge—fully revealed only after the defeat of Germany—that Hitler had tried to exterminate all the Jews of Europe. Along with peace came many uncertainties about the future.

Soviet civilians mourn dead soldiers.

COSTS OF THE WAR

The United States and its allies achieved their war aims. Germany's murderous Nazi regime was destroyed. Japanese expansion in Asia was halted and the nation's military warlords overthrown. But the toll in death, suffering, and destruction was appallingly high.

World War II was the most devastating war the world has ever known. When it finally ended,

hundreds of cities, from London to Tokyo, lay in ruins. Beautiful churches and palaces were reduced to rubble, and priceless works of art had gone up in smoke. Millions of people lacked heat, electricity, running water, adequate food, or means of traveling from one place to another. In some regions, mile upon mile of field and forest had been reduced to utter desolation.

There is no way of estimating the value of property loss, but two examples indicate its extent. In Düsseldorf, Germany, more than 90 percent of homes could not be lived in. The cities of Kiev and Minsk in the Soviet Union had to be completely rebuilt.

The war took more lives than any other conflict in history and brought untold suffering to civilians. According to one estimate, some 30 million noncombatants lost their lives from bombing, shelling, disease, or starvation. Millions more were injured, were weakened by malnutrition, or lost everything they owned. The Soviet Union and

◄ **Britain's Coventry Cathedral was one of many churches virtually destroyed by bombing attacks during the war. This ceremony was held among the church ruins in February 1941.**

CORE RESOURCES

• **Section 4 Daily Quiz**

COSTS OF WAR

Have students, using the text and chart on p. 767, compare the costs of war for the European and Asian combatants with the costs of war for the U.S. Ask students to explain why the U.S. and France had fewer military deaths than many of the other major combatants and why the U.S. had the fewest civilian deaths.

THE HOLOCAUST

Have students explain why the Holocaust is called genocide. *(not random or sporadic killing, but a deliberate, carefully planned and carried out attempt to destroy Europe's Jews)* Organize students into small groups to identify factors that allowed the Holocaust to take place *(history of anti-Semitism in Europe, Nazi propaganda against Jews, assistance or apathy of non-Jews, inaction of Allied leaders)* and to explain how each contributed to the genocide.

INTERNATIONAL CONSEQUENCES

Write *The Consequences of War* on the chalkboard. Call on volunteers to cite consequences of World War II for both sides and write responses on the chalkboard. Direct students to use the list to write a paragraph explaining the war's short- and long-term effects on the world's people. Have volunteers read their paragraphs to the class. Students may wish to include their paragraphs in their portfolios.

Chart Caption Answer
Soviet Union

 GLOBAL CONNECTIONS

As the Nazis implemented their racial policies, Hitler taunted the international community to accept the Jews desperately seeking refuge. "I can only hope," he said, "that the other world which has such deep sympathy . . . will . . . convert this sympathy into practical aid." However, the Évian Conference in July 1938 sent a clear message to Hitler that the Jews had few protectors. Conceived by FDR, the conference brought to Évian, France, delegates from 32 nations. Each explained why it could not accept any Jews. Australia's delegate stated "We don't have a racial problem and we don't want to import one." Venezuela did not want to disturb its "demographic equilibrium." In the end only the Dominican Republic responded positively. It offered to accept 100,000 Jews.

DEATHS IN WORLD WAR II		
Country	Military Deaths	Civilian Deaths
ALLIED POWERS		
British Commonwealth	373,372	92,673
France	213,324	350,000
Poland	123,178	5,675,000
Philippines	27,000	91,000
United States	292,131	6,000
Soviet Union	11,000,000	7,000,000
Yugoslavia	305,000	1,200,000
AXIS POWERS		
Bulgaria	10,000	10,000
Germany	3,500,000	780,000
Hungary	200,000	290,000
Italy	242,232	152,941
Japan	1,300,000	672,000
Romania	300,000	200,000
Source: *Encyclopedia Britannica*		

THE WAR TO END ALL WARS World War II had an enormous global impact. Tens of thousands of men, women, and children died from causes directly related to the war, and untold numbers lost their homes and livelihoods.

❓ BUILDING GRAPH SKILLS Which country had the highest overall casualties?

When Germany occupied France and other countries of Western Europe, and attacked Poland and the Soviet Union, it extended its control over additional thousands of Jews. Now Hitler's war against this people entered a new phase—one of utter savagery. In many regions special squads of German soldiers rounded up Jews and shot them. Elsewhere, Jews were forced into cities and isolated in ghettos. In 1941 the Germans began constructing camps specifically for the purpose of **genocide**—the deliberate annihilation of an entire people. Hitler and senior Nazi officials called this extermination program the "final solution of the Jewish question."

Major death camps were Auschwitz (OWSH-vits), Treblinka, and Majdanek, all in Poland. Here Jewish men, women, and children were transported in sealed railroad cars, marched into rooms disguised as shower facilities, and gassed. Their bodies were then cremated. All told, some six million Jews—two thirds of the Jewish population of Europe—perished.

China were especially hard hit. As in World War I, U.S. civilian losses were relatively light. In economic terms, armaments and other military costs probably totaled over $1 trillion.

■■ **World War II resulted in more deaths and destroyed more property than any other war in history.**

THE HOLOCAUST

No other wartime civilian deaths caused more horror than those of the **Holocaust**, Nazi Germany's systematic slaughter of European Jews. Before the war, Hitler had forced Jews out of most professions and had stripped them of their civil rights (see Chapter 25). The Nazis' goal was a Germany that was *Judenrein*—free of Jews. The Nazi authorities at first encouraged emigration, and about two thirds of all German and Austrian Jews left their countries. Many of those who remained were imprisoned in concentration camps such as Dachau (DAHK-ow) and Buchenwald (BOO-kuhn-wawld).

▲ These survivors of the large concentration camp in Evensee, Austria were photographed in May 1945 after their liberation by U.S. soldiers.

Practice

GUIDED PRACTICE

Work with students to develop a flowchart on the chalkboard that shows the stages and developments of the Nazis' plan for a Germany free of Jews.

INDEPENDENT PRACTICE

Ask students to use the information from the Guided Practice activity to write three journal entries from the viewpoint of a Holocaust survivor. One entry should describe the Nazis' actions toward Jews *before* the war; another, *during* the war; and the last, the psychological effects of the Holocaust on its survivors. Students may wish to include their journal entries in their portfolios.

Review and Assessment

REVIEW Have students write a script for a documentary called "The Legacies of World War II." Assign groups the following topics: the costs of war, the Holocaust, the changing balance of power, the beginning of the atomic age. Another group should write an introduction, segment transitions, and conclusion. Then assign the Section 4 Review on p. 769.

HISTORICAL SIDELIGHTS

The *St. Louis*

Although the U.S. could have offered a safe haven to many thousands of Jews fleeing Nazi persecution early in the war, it did not. In 1940 a ship called the *St. Louis* carrying 900 German Jewish refugees tried to land at U.S. ports, but the ship was denied entry. Eventually it returned to Germany, where most of its passengers were sent to Nazi death camps.

PRIMARY SOURCE

Description of Change: excerpted

Rationale: excerpted to focus on main idea

HISTORICAL SIDELIGHTS

A Memorial Museum

In April 1993 the U.S. Holocaust Memorial Museum opened in the nation's capital. The federal government donated the museum's site, which lies near the Washington Monument, to the U.S. Holocaust Memorial Council, an organization set up in 1980 by Congress to create a living memorial to the Holocaust's victims. The museum was built entirely through private donations. Its design incorporates powerful symbols of the death camps— the barbed-wire fences and the guard towers.

The Nazis' pitiless slaughter extended to other peoples, too. Other victims, numbering in the millions, included Gypsies, Poles, the mentally disabled, religious dissidents, and homosexuals. Communists, Socialists, and other political and religious opponents of the Nazi regime faced imprisonment and death as well.

When the Allies liberated the death camps, they found thousands of starving survivors. One was Elie Wiesel, a Romanian-born writer. Having been sent first to Auschwitz and then to Buchenwald, he was an emaciated youth of 16 when freed. Hospitalized for two weeks, he recovered. His writings, however, express the deep psychological scars left on concentration camp survivors:

> 66 One day I was able to get up, after gathering all my strength. I wanted to see myself in the mirror hanging on the opposite wall. I had not seen myself since the ghetto.
>
> From the depths of the mirror, a corpse gazed back at me.
>
> The look in his eyes, as they stared into mine, has never left me. 99

▪▪ The Holocaust took the lives of six million Jews—two thirds of European Jewry.

Why were the Nazis able to carry out the monstrous genocide? They built on a long history of anti-Semitism in Europe stretching back to the Middle Ages. A barrage of Nazi propaganda against Jews whipped up this anti-Semitism. Some non-Jews in countries occupied by the Nazis assisted or failed to prevent the Nazis from sending their Jewish fellow citizens off to the death camps. Others, however, heroically worked to save Jewish lives.

Another factor underlying the Holocaust was the lack of direct action by the Allies. Although reports of mass exterminations surfaced as early as 1941, the Allies believed the reports to be exaggerated. As a result, Allied nations did not open their doors to greater numbers of refugees or attempt to destroy rail lines that led to the death camps.

▶ British prime minister Winston Churchill (left), President Roosevelt (center), and Soviet leader Joseph Stalin (right) met at Yalta in 1945 to discuss territorial divisions after the war.

A NEW BALANCE OF POWER

By the time of the Yalta Conference, the political balance of power had clearly shifted. The United States had confirmed its position as the world's strongest nation. Its western European allies, notably Great Britain, had been weakened by the war. The Soviet Union, in spite of the devastation it had undergone, emerged from the war as a mighty force. For the next several decades, the United States and the Soviet Union, as **superpowers**, would dominate the world.

Much of the Soviet Union's new power was based on the territory it had occupied in Eastern Europe during the war. At the Yalta Conference, Roosevelt and Churchill had secretly agreed to accept the Soviet occupation of Poland in return for Stalin's vague promise of eventual free elections. When this agreement later became public, some critics blamed Roosevelt and Churchill for giving in to Stalin's demands. But with Soviet troops in control of Poland, they had little choice. Furthermore, Roosevelt wanted to assure Russia's entry into the war against Japan.

By the end of the war, the Soviet Union had absorbed the Baltic nations of Estonia, Latvia, Lithuania, and parts of Czechoslovakia and Romania. After Japan's surrender, the Soviet Union also took control of former Japanese territory, including the Kuril Islands and half of Sakhalin Island, which lie north of Japan. Defeated Japan also lost Inner Mongolia, Manchuria, and the islands of Taiwan (Formosa) and Hainan to China.

▪▪ Among the many consequences of World War II were the emergence of two superpowers and territorial realignments.

RETEACH For each subsection in Section 4, have students write a sentence that summarizes the main idea. Select students to read their statements aloud. Have the reteaching group choose the best summary sentence for each subsection.

*C*losure

Ask students what they think was the most enduring legacy of World War II for the U.S. *(Students might mention superpower status, new relationships with former allies and enemies, arms race.)*

*E*xtension

DEBATE Have students research and debate the following statement: *Eisenhower's decision to stop his invasion of Germany at the Elbe River set the stage for Soviet dominance of Eastern Europe.*

EVALUATE Have students consult David Wyman's *The Abandonment of the Jews* and write essays on why American leaders did not act on their knowledge of the Holocaust.

COMMENTARY

Using the Atomic Bomb

President Franklin Roosevelt approved research on the development of an atomic bomb after Albert Einstein and other scientists warned him in 1939 that Germany might be working on such a weapon. But by early 1945, with Germany defeated, some Manhattan Project scientists opposed using the bomb against Japan or urged a demonstration of its powers first. Nevertheless, with President Truman's approval, atomic bombs were dropped on two Japanese cities, with massive civilian casualties. Was Truman's action justified, or was it a grave error?

Truman defended his decision by noting Japan's refusal to surrender unconditionally. The atomic bomb, he claimed, had prevented a costly American invasion of Japan. He also linked the atomic bomb to Pearl Harbor. "The Japanese began the war," said Truman. "They have been repaid manyfold."

Some historians have questioned Truman's explanations. They point out that the U.S. had broken the Japanese secret code, so Truman knew that Tokyo was sending out urgent peace feelers by way of Moscow. These scholars also note Stalin's pledge at Yalta to enter the war against Japan within three months of Germany's surrender—in other words, by early August. Victory was possible, these historians argue, without the dropping of the atomic bomb and without a U.S. invasion.

These historians suggest several reasons for Truman's decision. They point out that the barriers

against attacking civilians had already been broken by Nazi rocket attacks and by the Allied firebombing of Dresden, Hamburg, Tokyo, and other cities. They contend that Truman feared postwar investigations if he failed to use the bomb after spending millions to build it.

Above all, these scholars argue, Truman dropped the bomb not only to end the war but also to demonstrate America's atomic might and thus strengthen America's postwar position in dealing with the Soviet Union. "The dropping of the atomic bomb," one historian argued, "was not so much the last military act of the second World War, as the first major operation of the cold diplomatic war with Russia."

Other historians, however, point to Japan's wartime atrocities and to the bitter-end defense of Okinawa. They note that top military leaders in Tokyo fiercely opposed the peace overtures and favored a desperate defense of the home islands. We simply do not know, these historians insist, what precise role the atomic bomb played in ending the war.

While the debate over Truman's decision continues, all historians agree on its long-range effects: a deadly nuclear arms race. In the postwar years, the United States, the Soviet Union, and other nations built vast arsenals of nuclear weapons and missiles. Even after the risk of global nuclear war faded, the danger that smaller nations would develop nuclear weapons remained, and massive quantities of radioactive waste threatened environmental safety. Truman's fateful decision of 1945 had consequences few anticipated at the time.

IDENTIFY

For significance, see the following pages:
Holocaust (p. 767)
genocide (p. 767)
Elie Wiesel (p. 768)
superpowers (p. 768)

LOCATE

For locations, see the map on p. 746.

1. *caused more deaths and destroyed more property than any other war in history*
2. *took the lives of six million Jews—two thirds of European Jewry—and left deep psychological scars on concentration camp survivors*
3. *the weakening of Western Europe, emergence of U.S. and Soviet Union as two superpowers, Soviet occupation of Eastern Europe*
4. *Letters might mention emaciated appearance of survivors, execution chambers within camps, and large number of Jews annihilated.*
5. *Students should balance the number of lives saved in avoiding an invasion of Japan with the devastation brought about by the bomb's use.*

S E C T I O N 4 R E V I E W

IDENTIFY and explain the significance of the following: Holocaust, genocide, Elie Wiesel, superpowers.

LOCATE and explain the importance of the following: Kuril Islands, Sakhalin Island, Taiwan, Hainan.

1. **MAIN IDEA** Why was World War II the most devastating war the world has ever known?
2. **MAIN IDEA** How did the Holocaust affect European Jews?
3. **ASSESSING CONSEQUENCES** Summarize the international consequences of World War II.
4. **WRITING TO DESCRIBE** Imagine you are a soldier who has helped liberate one of the German death camps. Write a letter home that describes what you saw there.
5. **TAKING A STAND** Do you think the United States was justified in using the atomic bomb against Japan? Give reasons for your answer.

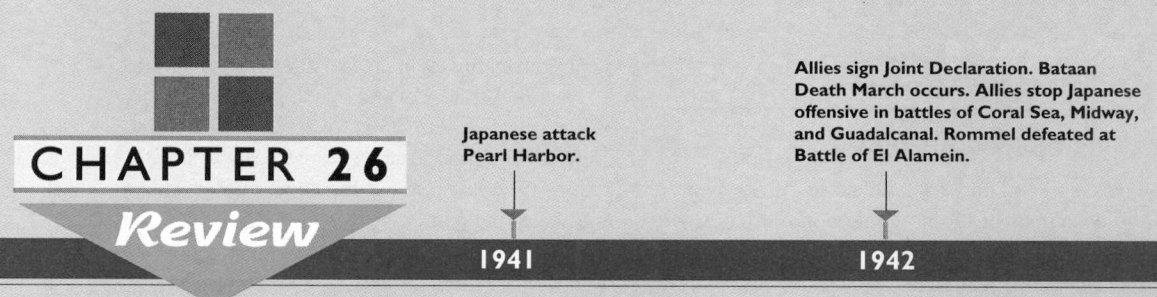

CHAPTER 26
Review

Japanese attack
Pearl Harbor.

1941

Allies sign Joint Declaration. Bataan
Death March occurs. Allies stop Japanese
offensive in battles of Coral Sea, Midway,
and Guadalcanal. Rommel defeated at
Battle of El Alamein.

1942

DEVELOPING THEMES

Return to the Themes section on p. 742. Have students discuss these again and compare their original responses with those given now. (See p. 741B for suggested answers.)

Chapter Review Answers

WRITING A SUMMARY

See Essential Points in each section for main ideas.

REVIEWING CHRONOLOGY

5, 1, 3, 2, 4
Assessing Consequences
removed Japanese fleet as threat to Allies in Pacific

IDENTIFYING PEOPLE AND IDEAS

1. *commander of U.S. forces in Pacific*
2. *battle that provided Americans with experience in naval air warfare and created confidence in carrier-based strike force*
3. *Mexicans who came to the U.S. to work*
4. *agency that directed conversion of existing U.S. factories to wartime production and supervised building of new plants*
5. *Japanese American interned during WW II; as a member of Congress he worked for reparation payments for other internees*
6. *June 6, 1944, date of Allied invasion of France*
7. *strategy of attacking strategic Pacific islands while bypassing others*
8. *Japanese suicide planes*
9. *deliberate annihilation of an entire people*

10. *Romanian-born writer who survived Auschwitz and Buchenwald*

UNDERSTANDING MAIN IDEAS

1. *through Japan's bombing of Pearl Harbor; war declarations by Germany and Italy; secure occupied territory and factories already converted to war production*
2. *increased wartime production, expanded federal bureaucracy through WPB and OWM, directed economy, extended taxes and sold war bonds, instituted rationing on specific goods, passed Selective Service Act; urged all-out participation in war effort, publicized war aims, provided pro-war entertainment*
3. *African Americans and Mexican Americans gained factory jobs and fought in the armed services. Women took over jobs traditionally held by male workers, increasing female participation in paid labor force.*
4. *refined sonar equipment, developed fast escort ships for convoys, air-bombed German U-boats and submarine yards*
5. *sent Jews to concentration camps, rounded up Jews and shot them, sent Jews and other victims to camps designed for genocide*

WRITING A SUMMARY

Using the essential points of the chapter as a guide, write a summary of the chapter.

REVIEWING CHRONOLOGY

Number your paper 1 to 5. Study the time line above, and list the following events in the order in which they happened by writing the first next to 1, the second next to 2, and so on. Then complete the activity below.

1. Allies sign Joint Declaration.
2. D-Day invasion begins.
3. Zoot-suit riots break out.
4. FDR dies.
5. Japanese attack Pearl Harbor.

Assessing Consequences What was the effect of the Allied victory at the Battle of Leyte Gulf?

IDENTIFYING PEOPLE AND IDEAS

Explain the historical significance of each of the following people or terms.

1. Douglas MacArthur
2. Battle of Midway
3. braceros
4. War Production Board
5. Norman Mineta
6. D-Day
7. island-hopping
8. kamikaze
9. genocide
10. Elie Wiesel

UNDERSTANDING MAIN IDEAS

1. How was the United States drawn into World War II? What advantages did the Axis Powers have over the United States at the beginning of the war?
2. What steps did the U.S. government take to mobilize for war? What did the media do to keep morale high?
3. What gains did African Americans, Mexican Americans, and women make during the war?
4. How did the Allies win the Battle of the Atlantic?
5. How did the Nazis carry out the Holocaust?

REVIEWING THEMES

1. **Global Relations** How did the Allies pool their resources to win World War II?
2. **Cultural Diversity** How did wartime conditions

lead to increased discrimination against Japanese Americans?
3. **Technology and Society** What political and moral issues did the development of atomic weapons raise?

THINKING CRITICALLY

1. **Analyzing** What actions did the Allies take to win the war in Europe?
2. **Synthesizing** What were the final costs and consequences of World War II?
3. **Evaluating** Why was the atomic bomb used against Japan? What effect did the use of this weapon have on the war in the Pacific?

WRITING ABOUT HISTORY

Writing to Classify Create a time line listing the important battles and other events leading to the Allied victory in the Pacific.

STRATEGY FOR SUCCESS

Review the Skills Handbook entry on Identifying Cause and Effect beginning on page 989. Then study the poster below, which was issued by the U.S. government during World War II. What cause-and-effect relationship does the poster suggest?

1. instituted lend-lease program, engaged in joint strategic plannings, signed the Joint Declaration, agreed on war aims during conferences at Casablanca, Cairo, Tehran, and Yalta
2. Prejudice and war hysteria led many to question the loyalty of people of Japanese descent, resulting in an internment policy.
3. political—concerns over control of atomic weapons and fears of arms race; moral—doubts over use of weapons of such devastating power

THINKING CRITICALLY

1. seized control of Mediterranean, won Battle of the Atlantic, launched offensives on southern, western, and eastern fronts, stepped up bombing of German cities
2. destroyed hundreds of cities, left millions destitute, incurred military costs of probably over $1 trillion, caused nearly 40 million casualties; made U.S. and Soviet Union into superpowers, caused territorial realignments
3. to prevent loss of lives from American invasion of Japan; brought about Japan's surrender, ended war in Pacific

WRITING ABOUT HISTORY

Time lines should include battles of the Coral Sea, Midway, and Guadalcanal in 1942; island-hopping in Gilbert Islands in 1943; battles of Philippine Sea, Saipan, Guam, and Leyte Gulf in 1944; battles of Iwo Jima and Okinawa and use of atomic bomb against Hiroshima and Nagasaki in 1945.

STRATEGY FOR SUCCESS

Careless talk in front of someone who might be a spy could lead to Allied military disaster.

USING PRIMARY SOURCES

Essays might express students' feelings of pity, anger, disgust, and sorrow.

Allied leaders meet at Casablanca, Cairo, and Tehran. Soviets defeat Axis troops at Stalingrad. Allies conquer North Africa. Zoot-suit riots break out.

Allies capture Rome. D-Day invasion begins. Japanese navy defeated at Battle of Leyte Gulf. Germans launch V-2 rockets. FDR reelected president. Allied and German troops clash at Battle of the Bulge.

Allies meet at Yalta. Allies win battles of Iwo Jima and Okinawa. FDR dies. Germany surrenders. U.S. drops atomic bombs on Hiroshima and Nagasaki. Japan surrenders.

1943   **1944**   **1945**

USING PRIMARY SOURCES

After the war, survivors of German concentration camps began to reveal to the world the horrors suffered by Jews and other prisoners. Read the following excerpt from *The Holocaust Kingdom* (1963), written by Alexander Donat, a survivor of Majdanek. Then write an essay expressing your feelings about what you have read.

66 *Usually they were taken there [to the gas chamber] at night, but once I saw the operation in broad daylight. . . . Through a crack in the wall we saw a long procession of living skeletons slowly emerging from Barrack Nineteen on their way to the gate. It was the way we would look in another two, four, or six weeks: it was the way it all ended. Majdanek was an industrial factory for producing corpses: death, the destruction of the greatest number of prisoners in the shortest time at the lowest cost was Majdanek's purpose. Life was treated as something . . . essentially worthless; in fact, contemptible. Death was our constant companion and not a terrible one, for quite often one wished passionately for it. It was life that was terrible, the long, agonizing process of parting from it after it had been shorn of dignity. Life in Majdanek was reduced to its basic elements.* 99

LINKING HISTORY AND GEOGRAPHY

After Allied forces on the Bataan Peninsula surrendered in April 1942, the Japanese ordered them to assemble at Mariveles and then march to San Fernando. From there the prisoners were shipped north by train. Study the map of the Bataan Death March in the next column. About how far did the prisoners have to march to reach San Fernando? About how far did they travel by train? What was their final destination? Why is it not possible to assess the difficulty of the journey from this map?

LINKING HISTORY AND GEOGRAPHY

about 60 miles; more than 20 miles; Camp O'Donnell; terrain, weather conditions, and availability of supplies cannot be determined from the map

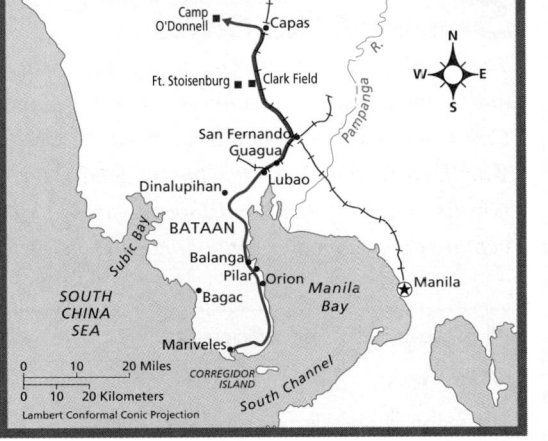

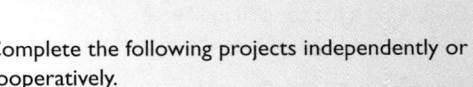

BUILDING YOUR PORTFOLIO

Complete the following projects independently or cooperatively.

1. **GLOBAL RELATIONS** In chapters 23 and 25 you portrayed a journalist. Building on that experience, imagine you are a member of a peace organization in the United States. Write an essay on ways to resolve international conflicts without war.

2. **WAR** In Chapter 25 you portrayed a diplomat at the beginning of the war. Building on that experience, imagine you are on a government committee examining the effects of the war. Compile statistics that illustrate the effects.

3. **CULTURE AND SOCIETY** In chapters 21, 22, and 24 you explored U.S. society in the 1920s and 1930s. Building on that experience, imagine you are a woman factory worker during World War II. Create a series of journal entries expressing your feelings about life on the home front.

BUILDING YOUR PORTFOLIO

Have students refer to **Building Your Portfolio Worksheet 7**, assigned at the beginning of Unit 7. Use the worksheet to help students monitor their progress on the portfolio projects.

Assessment

Core Resources
• Review Worksheet 26
• Chapter 26 Tests
• Alternative Assessment Forms
Test Generator

SONGS OF THE CITIES

SETTING THE SCENE

Claude McKay and Jean Toomer greatly influenced the development of the Harlem Renaissance. Born in Jamaica, McKay was already a poet of note when he came to the U.S. in 1912. His concentration on the everyday life of African Americans and his angry denunciation of racism set the focus and tone for much Harlem Renaissance literature. Toomer's experimental novel *Cane* (1923) caused a sensation among the young African American artists who became the nucleus of the Harlem Renaissance. It also raised for the first time many of the themes that occupied Harlem Renaissance writers.

Sinclair Lewis employed a mixture of realism and satire to depict his view of life in American small towns. He won the Nobel Prize for Literature in 1930, the first American writer to be awarded the honor.

Toshio Mori's "Lil' Yokohama" was set in the cities of Oakland and San Leandro on San Francisco Bay. The author lived in the Bay area all of his life, with two exceptions. The first was a brief period in which he played professional baseball for the Chicago Cubs; the second was for three years during World War II, when he was confined to an internment camp in Utah.

UNIT 7

Songs of the Cities

The Roaring Twenties was an era of cities, when economic prosperity and technological innovations led to a boom in skyscraper construction. Cities continued to expand throughout the Great Depression and World War II. Harlem Renaissance poets Claude McKay and Jean Toomer, novelist Sinclair Lewis, and Japanese American writer Toshio Mori capture the dynamic growth of the cities in the following selections.

▲ Jean Toomer

A Song of the Moon

by Claude McKay

The moonlight breaks upon the city's domes,
And falls along cemented steel and stone,
Upon the grayness of a million homes,
Lugubrious[1] in unchanging monotone.

Upon the clothes behind the tenement,
That hang like ghosts suspended from the lines,
Linking each flat to each indifferent,
Incongruous[2] and strange the moonlight shines.

There is no magic from your presence here,
Ho, moon, sad moon, tuck up your trailing robe,
Whose silver seems antique and so severe
Against the glow of one electric globe.

Go spill your beauty on the laughing faces
Of happy flowers that bloom a thousand hues,
Waiting on tiptoe in the wilding spaces,
To drink your wine mixed with sweet drafts of dews. ❖

---
1 melancholy
2 not harmonious

From *The Blue Meridian*

by Jean Toomer

The prairie's sweep in flat infinity,
The city's rise is perpendicular to farthest star,
I stand where the two directions intersect,
At Michigan Avenue and Walton Place,[1]

Level with my countrymen,
Right-angled to the universe.

It is a new America,
To be spiritualized by each new American,
To be taken as a golden grain
And lifted, as the wheat of our bodies,
To matter uniquely man.
I would give my life to see inscribed
Upon the arch of our consciousness
These aims: Growth, Transformation, Love,
That we might become heart-centered towards
 one another,
Love-centered towards God, dedicated to the creation
 of a higher type of man, growing up to Him.
Let new eyes see this statue in the bay,
Let this be quarantine to unbend dreams,
Let old eyes see it in Wall Street and the Loop,[2]
And through this clearing house
Let all pass checks who may. ❖

---
1 streets in downtown Chicago
2 Chicago's downtown

From *Babbitt*

by Sinclair Lewis

The towers of Zenith aspired above the morning mist; austere [simple] towers of steel and cement and limestone, sturdy as cliffs and delicate as silver rods. They were neither citadels nor churches, but frankly and beautifully office-buildings.

The mist took pity on the fretted [eroded] structures of earlier generations: the Post Office with its shingle-tortured mansard,[1] the red brick minarets [towers] of hulking old houses, factories with stingy and sooted windows, wooden tenements colored like mud. The city was full of such grotesqueries,[2] but the clean towers were thrusting them from the business center, and on the farther hills were shining new houses, homes—they seemed—for laughter and tranquillity.

Over a concrete bridge fled a limousine of long sleek hood and noiseless engine. These people in evening clothes were returning from an all-night rehearsal of a Little Theater play. . . . Below the bridge curved a railroad, a maze of green and crimson lights. The New York Flyer boomed past, and twenty lines of polished steel leaped into the glare.

In one of the skyscrapers the wires of the Associated Press were closing down. The telegraph operators wearily raised their celluloid eye-shades after a night of talking with Paris and Peking. Through the building crawled the scrubwomen, yawning, their old shoes slapping. The dawn mist spun away. Cues [lines] of men with lunch-boxes clumped toward the immensity of new factories, sheets of glass and hollow tile, glittering shops where five thousand men worked beneath one roof, pouring out the honest wares that would be sold up the Euphrates[3] and across the veldt.[4] The whistles rolled out in greeting a chorus cheerful as the April dawn; the song of labor in a city built—it seemed—for giants. ❖

1 a sloping roof
2 things that are not harmonious
3 river in Southwest Asia
4 grassland of southern Africa

From *Lil' Yokohama*

by Toshio Mori

In Lil' Yokohama, as the youngsters call our community, we have twenty-four hours every day . . . and morning, noon, and night roll on regularly just as in Boston, Cincinnati, Birmingham, Kansas City, Minneapolis, and Emeryville.

When the sun is out, the housewives sit on the porch or walk around the yard, puttering with this and that, and the old men who are in the house when it is cloudy or raining come out on the porch or sit in the shade and read the newspaper. The day is hot. All right, they like it. The day is cold. All right, all right. The people of Lil' Yokohama are here. *Here, here,* they cry with their presence just as the youngsters when the teachers call the roll. And when the people among people are sometimes missing from Lil' Yokohama's roll, perhaps forever, it is another matter; but the news belongs here just as does the weather.

Today young and old are at the Alameda ball grounds to see the big game: Alameda Taiiku *vs.* San Jose Asahis. The great Northern California game is under way. Will Slugger Hironaka hit that southpaw from San Jose? Will the same southpaw make the Alameda sluggers stand on their heads? It's the great question. . . .

It is Sunday evening in Lil' Yokohama, and the late dinners commence. Someone who did not go to the game asks, "Who won today?" "San Jose," we say. "Oh, gee," he says. "But Slugger knocked another home run," we say. "What again? He sure is good!" he says. "Big league scouts ought to size him up." "Sure," we say.

Tomorrow is a school day, tomorrow is a work day, tomorrow is another twenty-four hours. In Lil' Yokohama night is almost over. On Sunday nights the block is peaceful and quiet. . . .

Something is happening to the Etos of the block. All of a sudden they turn in their old '30 Chevrolet for a new Oldsmobile Eight! They follow this with a new living-room set and a radio and a new coat of paint for the house. On Sundays the whole family goes for an outing. Sometimes it is to Fleishhacker Pool or to Santa Cruz. It may be to Golden Gate Park or to the ocean or to their relatives in the country. . . . They did not strike oil or win the sweepstakes. Nothing of the kind happens in Lil' Yokohama, though it may any day. . . . What then? ❖

PRIMARY SOURCES

Description of Change: excerpted, bracketed, and footnoted

Rationale: excerpted for space considerations; bracketed and footnoted to clarify meaning

THINKING AND WRITING ABOUT LITERATURE

1. *domes, steel and stone, gray homes, tenement clotheslines; because the poet thinks the moon illuminates only ugliness in the city*

2. *growth, transformation, and love*

3. *The new buildings are simple, sturdy, delicate, and clean, and the old buildings are complicated, "hulking," mud-colored, and grotesque. Lewis is contrasting the city's present and past.*

4. *to show that Japanese Americans live just like other Americans*

THINKING AND WRITING ABOUT LITERATURE

1. What features of the city does Claude McKay describe? Why do you think he wants the moon to shine somewhere else?

2. What are the three things Jean Toomer wishes city dwellers to aspire to?

3. How does Sinclair Lewis describe Zenith's buildings? What do you think he means to show by contrasting the old and new buildings?

4. Why does Toshio Mori describe the daily activities of the Japanese American neighborhood of Lil' Yokohama?

RECOGNIZING PROPAGANDA

Guide students through the discussion of how to recognize propaganda and then have them complete the Practicing the Strategy exercise. Point out that in times of national crisis propaganda messages became especially intense in the U.S. Have students work in groups to identify the intended message, the images used, and the techniques employed in the following examples of propaganda: the World War I propaganda posters on pp. 593 and 604; the New Deal poster on p. 693 and sign on p. 700; and the World War II recruiting poster on p. 753. Then have them create posters that could have been used during Operation Desert Storm to build support for the war. Ask students to evaluate how effective one another's posters are.

Strategies for Success

Will you give at least 10% of your pay in War Bonds?

RECOGNIZING PROPAGANDA

Propaganda is a form of mass communication designed to sway people's attitudes and actions. It appeals primarily to emotion, not reason, using language, symbols, and images. Propaganda is favored by totalitarian regimes, which use it to control the hearts and minds of their people. But propaganda is not always used for sinister purposes. Democracies employ propaganda to discredit their enemies and to gain citizen support for particular policies. Special-interest groups use it in lobbying for or against legislation, and politicians use it in campaigning for election. The following techniques are often used in propaganda:

- **Card-stacking** means presenting just one side of a story. Examples include the selective use of statistics and the parading of opinion as fact.
- **Name-calling** is attaching offensive labels to opponents to cast them in a negative light.
- **Sloganeering** is repetition of catchy, but often empty, statements instead of real arguments.
- **Bandwagon** involves begging support for a cause merely because it is popular. This technique relies on peer pressure to conform.
- **Endorsements** are testimonials by famous people who urge support of a cause. Propagandists hope that people will transfer their liking or respect for the celebrity to the cause.

How to Recognize Propaganda

1. **Look, listen, and read carefully.** Analyze the message being conveyed, noting the use of emotionally charged words. Also examine any imagery: propaganda can be visual.
2. **Recognize the technique used.** Identify the technique being employed (such as card-stacking or name-calling).
3. **Consider the purpose.** Ask yourself: Who is sending the message and why? Decide who is its intended audience and what reaction it is meant to provoke.

Applying the Strategy

During World War II the U.S. government used propaganda techniques to build support for the war. For example, patriotic posters used emotional appeals to encourage people to buy war bonds. The World War II poster in the next column pictures a women with her children. The picture and the words "I gave a man!" are meant to play on workers' emotions and to make them feel guilty if they do not buy war bonds.

The government also used propaganda techniques to recruit women for the nation's defense industry, sounding the theme that "it's a woman's war, too." A government brochure of the time, which used the bandwagon approach and one-sided descriptions of factory labor, read: "Millions of women find war work pleasant and as easy as running a sewing machine, or using a vacuum cleaner."

Practicing the Strategy

Read the statement below, made in 1927 by Joseph Goebbels (who later became Hitler's propaganda minister) in commemoration of the German soldiers who died in World War I. Then, on a separate sheet of paper, answer the questions that follow.

> **"** We think of the two million who grow pale in the graves of Flanders and Poland. . . . We think of . . . all those who gave their lives upon the altar of the future so that Germany might be established again. . . . Retaliation! Retaliation! The day is dawning! . . . We greet you, dead ones. Germany is beginning to glow anew in the dawn of your blood. . . . Let sound the march-beat . . . for freedom! The army of the dead marches with you, you storm troop soldiers, into a better future. **"**

1. What is the message of the excerpt? At whom is it aimed?
2. What clues identify this passage as propaganda?

BUILDING YOUR PORTFOLIO

Each portfolio project described below is the culmination of the Building Your Portfolio activities in the chapter reviews of Unit 7. First, decide whether you wish students to work individually or in groups on these unit projects. Then permit each student to choose the project on which he or she desires to work. Provide students with copies of **Building Your Portfolio Worksheet 7** from *Core Resources*. This worksheet will guide students step by step to complete their projects.

BUILDING YOUR PORTFOLIO

Outlined below are four projects. Independently or cooperatively, complete one and use the products to demonstrate your mastery of the historical concepts involved.

1 THE ECONOMY
The excesses of the 1920s helped trigger the Great Depression. The federal government attempted to get the economy moving through the New Deal. Using the portfolio materials you designed in chapters 21, 22, 23, and 24, create a mural that depicts the economic trends between 1920 and 1940. Your mural might portray the effects of unemployment, consumerism, the depression, or the New Deal.

2 CULTURE AND SOCIETY
American society changed rapidly from the 1920s to the 1940s. Using the portfolio materials you designed in chapters 21, 22, 24, and 26, create a radio program that highlights the issues of the period. Shows might include news of the day, a jazz presentation from the 1920s, a book review from the 1930s, or an interview with women workers from the 1940s.

3 GLOBAL RELATIONS
The world experienced severe economic, political, and social unrest in the years leading up to World War II. Using the portfolio materials you designed in chapters 23, 25, and 26, conduct a debate with representatives from several nations about global relations after World War II. Debates should center around the issue of how the United States should respond in the future to the rise of dictators in other parts of the world.

4 WAR
World War II brought tragedy to millions of people around the world. Using the portfolio materials you designed in chapters 25 and 26, create a design for a war memorial to the victims of World War II. Memorials might commemorate soldiers, prisoners of war, victims of the Holocaust, or civilians killed in the war.

Videodisc Review
In assigned groups, develop an outline for a video collage of American life in the years between 1920 and 1945. Choose images that best illustrate the major topics of the period. Write a script to accompany the images. Assign narrators to different parts of the script, and present your video collage to the class.

Further Reading
Anderson, Jervis. *This Was Harlem: A Cultural Portrait, 1900–1950.* Farrar Straus Giroux (1993). Story of Harlem in the first half of the 20th century.

Berenbaum, Michael. *The World Must Know: The History of the Holocaust as Told in the United States Holocaust Memorial Museum.* Little, Brown (1993). Pictorial and eye-witness history of the Holocaust.

Cohen, Stan. *V for Victory.* Pictorial Histories (1991). Overview of the effect of World War II on Americans on the home front.

Cook, Haruko Taya, and Theodore F. Cook. *Japan at War.* New Press (1992). Accounts of war's effect on the Japanese.

McElvaine, Robert S. *The Great Depression: America, 1929–1941.* Times Books (1984). Overview of the Great Depression.

PORTFOLIO ASSESSMENT

1. *Murals should show the post–World War I bust, the boom period during the 1920s, the stock market crash of 1929, and the Great Depression.*

2. *Radio programs should show students' mastery of one of the following topics: the reasons for the spread of anti-Communist hysteria during the Red Scare; labor problems in the 1920s; the original proposal of the Equal Rights Amendment; the influence of jazz in the 1920s; the impact of the Dust Bowl; or the experiences of women workers during World War II.*

3. *Debates should trace the economic problems leading to the rise of dictators before World War II, U.S. participation in diplomatic conferences between the wars, and the policy of appeasement.*

4. *War memorial designs should show the casualties of Kristallnacht, the Holocaust, the bombing of Hiroshima and Nagasaki, or other military and civilian casualties.*

Postwar America ❖ 1945–1975

UNIT OVERVIEW

The U.S. emerged from World War II as the richest and most influential nation in the world. Affluence, abundance, and optimism characterized the postwar period. But the Cold War and the nuclear age contributed to a sense of uncertainty during this time. And in the midst of prosperity, widespread poverty existed. The nation's disfranchised citizens raised other concerns about the reality of the American dream. Similar disillusionment underscored the national debate over the Vietnam War. By the mid-1970s, many Americans were questioning long-standing and cherished perceptions about their country.

CORE RESOURCES

• **American Almanac Poster** and **Worksheet 8**
• **Building Your Portfolio Worksheet 8**
  You may wish to preview the Unit 8 Review and Building Your Portfolio performance assessment activities on p. 895.

Using the American Almanac Posters

Begin the unit by displaying the American Almanac Poster and discussing entries with students. In addition to the worksheet, the annotations that follow provide additional information about the entries and suggest questions and activities.

Then, as students study the unit, have them work in small groups to create their own almanacs—using the same six headings—on pieces of butcher paper. At the end of the unit, call on groups to display and discuss their almanacs.

Chapter 27
THE POSTWAR YEARS
1945–1952

Chapter 28
DECADE OF CONTRASTS
1950–1960

Chapter 29
THE SIXTIES
1960–1970

The American People

The soaring birthrate from 1946 to 1964 became known as the baby boom. The expanding economy meant that couples could afford larger families. But in the 1970s and 1980s, baby boomers found competition for jobs stiffer than it was for their parents.

■■ Have students check a current almanac to determine the birthrate today.

America's Music

Point out that the British invasion greatly influenced American rock music. Yet the Beatles identified African American musicians, such as Chuck Berry, as major influences on their music.

■■ Ask students to identify bands from other countries that they listen to today.

In Style

Point out that many young people in the 1960s, unlike previous generations, were unwilling to adopt the hairstyles and fashions of their parents.

■■ Ask students whether it is important to create their own look or if they dress much like their parents.

TV Generation

Show a video of a popular TV show from the 1950s or 1960s. Ask students about their impressions of the program and how it differs from shows today.

■■ Ask students if they are influenced by the ways that characters behave on TV.

Firsts on Earth and in Space

More than one fifth of the world's population watched the *Apollo 11* moon landing on TV via satellite.

■■ Call on volunteers to suggest what events might attract a large TV audience today.

The Shrinking Dollar

Point out that prices of consumer goods and services rise even during periods of economic stability.

■■ Ask students what a pair of jeans costs today.

The Sporting Life

Mention that Robinson's "first" also signaled the end of the black baseball leagues. As major league clubs rushed to sign black players, African American ball clubs folded.

■■ Call on volunteers to identify the social barriers in sports that are being challenged today.

UNIT

Postwar America

8

1945–1975

The United States emerged from world War II as the world's most powerful nation. The affluence and optimism of the period was tempered by the sense of uncertainty brought by the Cold War and the nuclear age. And in the midst of prosperity, widespread poverty existed. Disfranchised citizens also raised questions about the reality of the American dream, and disillusionment underscored the debate over the Vietnam War. By the mid-1970s, many Americans were questioning cherished perceptions about their country.

◄ American teenagers, 1950s

Chapter 30

WAR IN VIETNAM
1954–1975

THE POSTWAR YEARS

1945–1952

Chapter Overview

The end of World War II thrust the U.S. into the position of world leadership. While dealing with its own postwar readjustments, the U.S. joined with other allies in occupying Germany and Japan and in organizing the United Nations. A breakdown in U.S.–Soviet relations launched a Cold War and generated a renewed fear of communism at home and abroad. America "fought" the Cold War by providing massive aid to Europe and through economic, political, and military involvement in East Asia and the Middle East.

THE AMERICAN NATION VIDEODISC PROGRAM
A variety of still images, short videos, and activities are available for you to use as you teach this chapter. See Correlation to *The American Nation* Videodisc Program for barcode correlations and suggestions for using the program.

Chapter Planning Guide

CHAPTER 27	CORE RESOURCE BOOKLETS	AUDIOVISUAL RESOURCES	PROGRAM RESOURCES
INTRODUCTION pp. 778–779	■ Literature Worksheet 27 ■ Building Your Portfolio Worksheet 8	■ Everyday Life in America Transparency and Worksheet 27	
TEACHING THE CHAPTER pp. 780–801	■ Graphic Organizer 27 ■ Social Studies Skills Worksheet 27 ■ Geography Worksheet 27 ■ Outline Maps 1, 2, 9, 14, 15, 17, 18, 20	■ *The American Nation* Videodisc: Jackie Robinson; MacArthur in Korea ■ Linking Geography and History Transparency and Worksheet 20	■ Art in American History Transparencies and Worksheets 34, 35 ■ Eyewitnesses and Others, Volume 2: Reading 58
REVIEW AND ASSESSMENT pp. 802–803	■ Chapter 27 Daily Quizzes ■ Review Worksheet 27 ■ Chapter 27 Tests ■ Alternative Assessment Forms		■ Test Generator

Additional Resources

BOOKS FOR TEACHERS

Blair, Clay. *The Forgotten War: America in Korea 1950–1953.* Doubleday, 1989. Chronicles international political history of Korean War.

Brands, H.W. *Inside the Cold War: Loy Henderson & the Rise of the American Empire, 1918–1961.* Oxford University Press, 1991. History of the development of the Cold War.

McCullough, David. *Truman.* Simon & Schuster, 1992. A prize-winning biography of political and private life of Harry S. Truman.

BOOKS FOR STUDENTS

Chafe, William H. *The Unfinished Journey: America Since World War II.* Oxford University Press, 1991. American society after 1945.

Halliday, Jon, and Bruce Cumings. *Korea: The Unknown War.* Pantheon, 1988. Examines the war from the perspectives of both North and South Korea.

* Leavell, Perry. *Harry S. Truman.* Chelsea House, 1988. Part of "World Leaders, Past and Present" series.

* for students reading below grade level

MULTIMEDIA MATERIALS

The Cold War: Witness to History. Video, 15 min. Guidance Associates/SSSS. Surveys Cold War conflicts in the aftermath of World War II.

For All the People: The Harry S. Truman Library. Video, 29 min. SSSS. Archival footage and selected speeches survey the Truman era.

Korea: MacArthur's War With Truman. Video, 40 min. Zenger/SSSS. Archival footage, maps, and contemporary images document issues of Korean War.

THEMES IN AMERICAN HISTORY

USE WITH PAGES 778–779

Listed on the right are the themes emphasized in Chapter 27. The questions in boldface type stimulate critical thinking and provide students with an opportunity to discuss the themes within a broadened context. The questions also appear in the pupil's edition on p. 778

■ GLOBAL RELATIONS

What international and domestic problems might a rivalry between two powerful nations create? Students might mention that the rivalry could lead to military escalation and global competition. The rivalry might create the need for a strong foreign aid program and a robust defense industry at home. Students might disagree about whether this situation would create jobs or drain resources from a nation's economy.

■ TECHNOLOGY AND SOCIETY

How might a society respond to the development of potentially destructive technology? Students might point out that some people would support such technology, arguing that it would enhance a nation's power and status in the world. Opponents might argue that it could generate fear and distrust among nations and heighten world tensions.

■ DEMOCRATIC VALUES

How might individuals be affected by a government's limitation of civil liberties? Students might provide examples of a government limiting such civil liberties as freedom of speech, the right to due process of law, and the right to privacy. Examples might include government restrictions on the free flow of information during a time when some perceive a nation's security to be threatened, or the effects a government's intelligence-gathering activities might have on citizens' due process rights or privacy rights.

CHAPTER STRATEGIES FOR MEETING INDIVIDUAL NEEDS

LIMITED ENGLISH PROFICIENT LEARNERS

Have students develop clue cards for the people listed in the Preview Workshops. Call on volunteers to present their clues and ask others to identify each person. After each person has been identified, have students select one and write an introduction that might be used by someone honoring that person.

TACTILE/KINESTHETIC LEARNERS

Have students create a series of skits that demonstrate the fears of Americans during the Red Scare period of the late 1940s and the early 1950s.

LEARNERS HAVING DIFFICULTY

Have students recite answers to the Main Idea questions in each Section Review. Then have them write a brief summary of each section.

AUDITORY LEARNERS

Have students research speeches and/or quotations about the Cold War by George Kennan, George C. Marshall, Dean Acheson, Joseph Stalin, and Harry S. Truman. Have students prepare dramatic readings of their selections.

VISUAL LEARNERS

Organize students into small groups to prepare illustrated flowcharts showing the tensions and hostilities that resulted from the Cold War.

GIFTED LEARNERS

Direct students to create a scrapbook of Truman's written and verbal statements. Have students divide the scrapbook into sections that correlate to the chapter's sections. Assign students to write generalizations about the historical significance of each section's quotes.

USING THE CHAPTER FOCUS

■ UNDERSTANDING THE MAIN IDEA

Call on a volunteer to read aloud the Understanding the Main Idea paragraph. Ask students to speculate on what problems a country might face in rebuilding from the devastation of war. Write students' responses on the chalkboard and ask them to evaluate their responses as they read the chapter.

 THEMES

Have students work individually or in small groups to answer the questions under Themes. Save students' responses so that they can compare them with their responses after studying the chapter. (See p. 777B for suggested answers.)

■ THE TIME LINE

Instruct students to copy the time-line entries into their notebooks. As students read about each event on the time line, have them create cause-and-effect flowcharts for each time-line entry.

CORE RESOURCES

• **Graphic Organizer 27**
• **Literature Worksheet 27**
• **Outline Maps 1, 2, 9, 14, 15, 17, 18, 20**
• **Building Your Portfolio Worksheet 8**

AV RESOURCES

• **Everyday Life in America Transparency** and **Worksheet 27**

ABOUT THE ILLUSTRATION

Joyful welcomes of returning military personnel, such as the scene shown below, were common after the war. But such happy reunions were often tinged with anxiety because the psychological impact of the war was great for soldiers and civilians alike. Soldiers who had experienced the horrors of war, and who had not seen their families for years, had to readjust to civilian and family life and become reacquainted (or sometimes acquainted) with their children. Women who had worked outside the home for the first time during the war faced potentionally new roles within their families. Ask students to write a diary entry from the perspective of a postwar American soldier or civilian, detailing the hopes and fears that person has about the coming years.

Chapter 27   1945–1952

THE POSTWAR YEARS

▼ FOCUS

UNDERSTANDING THE MAIN IDEA

After World War II many nations struggled to rebuild their war-torn economies. In the United States, wartime production led to a postwar boom. On the international front, however, tensions between the United States and the Soviet Union grew. In 1950, in the midst of the increasing threat of nuclear disaster, the Korean War erupted.

THEMES

■ **GLOBAL RELATIONS** What international and domestic problems might a rivalry between two powerful nations create?

■ **TECHNOLOGY AND SOCIETY** How might a society respond to the development of a potentially destructive technology?

■ **DEMOCRATIC VALUES** How might individuals be affected by a government's limitation of civil liberties?

1945	1947	1948	1950	1952
Nuremberg trials begin.	Truman Doctrine proposed.	Racial discrimination banned in military and in federal hiring.	North Korea invades South Korea.	U.S. occupation of Japan ends.

Call on volunteers to recall the principles of the Atlantic Charter and write their responses on the chalkboard. *(U.S. and Great Britain would renounce territorial expansion. Every nation has a right to choose its own form of government. There should be freedom of international trade and equal access to raw materials for all countries. Aggressor states should be disarmed, and all nations should work together to rid the world of want and fear.)* As students read the chapter have them compare the charter's provisions for world peace with events and developments in the postwar world.

■■ LINK TO THE PAST

The Churchill-Roosevelt Atlantic Charter of 1941 had called for a free world in which all nations were able to choose their own governments. The agreement, however, did not end imperialism. It took World War II to end Japanese imperialism in Asia and to weaken European colonialism in Asia, Africa, and the Middle East.

Returning U.S. soldiers, 1946

*T*he United States emerged from World War II a world power. Americans realized, however, that with this new role came new challenges. Praising the "brave millions [of soldiers] homeward bound," General Douglas MacArthur in September 1945 urged all Americans "to preserve in peace what we won in war."

In their fight against fascism, American soldiers had helped liberate the surviving victims of Nazi concentration camps. Leon Bass, an African American soldier, believed that the Nazi death camps and the Holocaust had important lessons to teach Americans: "If this could happen [in Germany], it could happen anywhere. It could happen to me. It could happen to black folks in America." Horrified by the Holocaust and inspired by their advances during the war, many African Americans took up the fight for civil rights with increased energy.

The lessons learned from World War II, however, proved difficult to put into practice because of postwar economic chaos and the threat of an all-out nuclear war between the United States and the Soviet Union. Despite the creation of a new international organization to promote peace, Soviet-American tensions escalated and new conflicts broke out. By 1950 the United States was involved in yet another war, this time in Korea.

Soldiers with captured Nazi flag

HISTORICAL SIDELIGHTS

Double Victory
The NAACP's Walter White noted that "World War II has immeasurably magnified the Negro's awareness of the disparity between the American profession and practice of democracy." African Americans began calling for a "Double V"—victory over fascism overseas and over racism at home. During the war, NAACP membership increased about 900 percent to more than 500,000 Americans.

Chapter 27

SECTION 1

Introducing the Section

FOCUS OBJECTIVES

- Describe how Germany and Japan were governed after the war.

- Explain what the war crimes trials accomplished.

- Analyze why the United Nations was founded.

HISTORICAL SIDELIGHTS

The Potsdam Conference

Although they were shaping the postwar world, the conferees at Potsdam showed their very human natures. At first Truman was drawn to Stalin but was put off by Churchill, whom he considered long-winded. At one party Truman provided violin and piano entertainment, which Churchill hated. He got even by having a Royal Air Force band play loud music all through dinner at a party he hosted.

CORE RESOURCES

• **Section 1 Daily Quiz**

780

PREVIEW WORKSHOP

PREVIEW WORKSHOP

Following is a list of the significant people and terms in this section. You may wish to use this list as a section preview.

People
- Adolf Eichmann
- Josef Mengele
- Klaus Barbie
- Hideki Tōjō
- Trygve Lie
- Eleanor Roosevelt

Terms
- Potsdam Conference
- *zaibatsu*
- Nuremberg trials
- United Nations

MOTIVATING: PRIOR KNOWLEDGE

Call on a volunteer to describe the U.S. attitude about involvement in world affairs prior to its entrance into World War II. *(generally isolationist)* Ask students to speculate on why U.S. involvement in World War II might have changed that policy. Tell students that this section describes how the U.S. participated in reshaping the world after the war.

Section 1

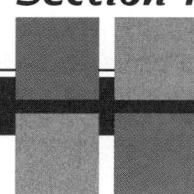

HEALING THE WOUNDS OF WAR

FOCUS

- **How were Germany and Japan governed after the war?**
- **What did the war crimes trials accomplish?**
- **Why was the United Nations founded?**

***M**any Americans gained confidence from the Allied victory. "The war and the victory showed us what we could do in the world," summed up Melville Grosvenor, a magazine editor. Americans now realized that the United States had to take a leading role in the world. One urgent task was dealing with the human suffering and political chaos resulting from the war. The United States worked with the other Allies to restore peace by occupying Germany and Japan and by creating a new international organization, the United Nations.*

United Nations flag

OCCUPATION RULE

After the war Germany and Japan lay in ruins, their wartime governments shattered. A German actress, Hildegard Knef, described a German town "without houses, without windowpanes, without roofs; holes

Allied Occupation Zones, 1945

in the asphalt, rubble, rubbish, rats." An American GI noted that in the area around Tokyo, "there was practically nothing left; the rubble did not even look like much." A Japanese American soldier remarked of the devastation: "Tokyo was all flattened, and people were living in holes with corrugated roofs. They were desperate for food." With the fighting over, Germany and Japan now faced the task of rebuilding their governments, economies, and cities under the watchful eyes of the Allies.

The occupation of Germany. The first overseas conference that President Harry S. Truman attended after Roosevelt's death—the **Potsdam Conference** in July 1945—laid the foundation for Germany's postwar status. Truman, Churchill (later replaced by new prime minister Clement Attlee), and Stalin met in Potsdam, Germany, to approve the details of their joint occupation of Germany. The leaders divided Germany into four occupation zones. The British, the French, and the Americans each took control of a zone in the western, industrialized part of Germany. The Soviets agreed to control the poorer,

GOVERNMENT IN GERMANY AND JAPAN

Have students create charts comparing the systems of government set up in Germany and Japan after World War II. Have volunteers present their charts. Then discuss possible reasons that Germany and Japan were governed differently.

■■ Ask students how they would react if another nation occupied the U.S.

THE WAR CRIMES TRIALS

Organize students into groups and invite each to imagine that it is a tribunal presiding at war crimes trials after World War II. Ask groups to develop lists of standards, behaviors, and principles against which it will measure defendants who appear before it. Have representatives of each group present and explain its list.

THE UNITED NATIONS

Head five columns on the chalkboard with the five W's: *What, When, Why, Where,* and *Who.* Have students explain the purpose of the United Nations by offering statements for each heading.

▶

▲ **This 1946 photograph shows Emperor Hirohito (top) in the Japanese Diet, or legislature, in Tokyo. Hirohito unveiled the new constitution and announced the transfer of his power to the Japanese people and the abolition of the armed forces.**

more rural, eastern zone. The four powers also set up occupation zones in Austria and agreed to administer jointly the city of Berlin, deep in the Soviet zone.

In order to bring stability to the German zones, the occupying powers pledged to crush the Nazi party, reestablish local governments, and rebuild German industry. In addition, the Allies agreed to resettle German refugees.

The conference attendees recognized that the joint occupation of Germany would require cooperation. However, Soviet occupation of much of Eastern Europe created tensions among the Allies. Stalin demanded that the Allies recognize Soviet-backed Poland's claims to German territory it had occupied during the war. The other Allies reluctantly agreed but grew increasingly concerned about Soviet expansion in Eastern Europe. Another source of tension was the Soviet Union's demand for immediate reparations from Germany.

The occupation of Japan. Postwar Japan also faced massive challenges in its attempts to rebuild. Its economy lay in shambles, and Hiroshima and Nagasaki had been devastated by atom bombs. The United States administered

defeated Japan, occupying the island nation from 1945 to 1952.

In addition to helping rebuild the Japanese economy, the United States worked to end Japanese militarism and to create a democratic government. During the occupation Emperor Hirohito remained in the imperial palace, but he became merely a figurehead. Supreme Commander Douglas MacArthur, his staff, and the new Japanese congress ran the country.

Under MacArthur's direction, Japan demobilized more than five million troops and adopted a new constitution in 1947. The constitution set up a democratic system of government, which extended voting rights to women and established separation of church and state. The constitution abolished the Japanese army and navy and prohibited Japan from ever again becoming a military power. Although the constitution bore the clear stamp of American influence, it won support from the Japanese people.

The Japanese also undertook important economic reforms in this period. One program transferred land to Japanese farmers. The government also allowed labor unions to organize and broke up the *zaibatsu*, the huge corporations run by single families that had monopolized the Japanese economy. These political and economic reforms laid the foundation for Japan's tremendous postwar economic recovery.

■■ **After World War II the Allies occupied Germany and Japan and set up new governments in these countries.**

*T*HE WAR CRIMES TRIALS

After the war the Allies also addressed the issue of war crimes. All agreed that convicted German war criminals must be punished for starting the war and for the Holocaust. By the same token, Japanese war criminals were to be punished for the mistreatment of prisoners of war and for other atrocities committed in Bataan and China.

The German war crimes trials—known as the **Nuremberg trials** because they took place in Nuremberg, the former rallying place of Hitler's Nazi party—began in November 1945. Before an international military tribunal, witnesses gave chilling accounts of Nazi atrocities, including the torture and murder of millions of Jews, Gypsies,

Practice

GUIDED PRACTICE

Write the main events of the section in headline form on the chalkboard, one at a time. Then choose one of the headlines, and call on volunteers to give details about the event in the headline, as you write responses on the chalkboard.

INDEPENDENT PRACTICE

Instruct students to select one of the headlines from the Guided Practice, list the details of the event, and then use the details to write a news story that might accompany the headline. Students may wish to include their news stories in their portfolios.

Review and Assessment

REVIEW Have students use the section's Essential Points as the main topics of an outline. Direct them to complete the outline by adding subtopics. Then assign the Section 1 Review on p. 783.

ASSESS Assign the **Section 1 Daily Quiz** in *Core Resources*.

GLOBAL CONNECTIONS

After the war many European countries began their own search for Nazi sympathizers. Norway, France, Holland, Belgium, and Denmark all attempted to purge their governments of those suspected of collaborating with the enemy during the war. Thousands were arrested, prison terms and death sentences were handed out, and thousands more were banned from pursuing their professions.

PRIMARY SOURCE

Description of Change: excerpted
Rationale: excerpted to focus on main idea

HISTORICAL SIDELIGHTS

Nazi War Criminals

Adolf Eichmann was tracked down by Israeli agents in 1960 in Argentina. They took him to Israel, where a court tried him for war crimes and crimes against humanity. He was found guilty and hanged. An autopsy established that Josef Mengele, who had fled to Brazil, probably died while swimming. Klaus Barbie, who had escaped to Bolivia, eventually stood trial in Lyons, France. He was found guilty of crimes against humanity and sentenced to life imprisonment, the maximum punishment.

Chart Caption Answer

Security Council

782

▲ Allied judges at the Nuremberg trials brought German war criminals to justice. Hermann Göring, commander of the German air force during the war, is shown on the witness stand on May 13, 1946. He later committed suicide in jail.

and others. Marie Vaillant, a concentration camp survivor, testified:

> 66 For months, for years we had one wish only: the wish that some of us would escape alive, in order to tell the world what the Nazi convict prisons were like. . . . There was the systematic . . . urge to use human beings as slaves and to kill them when they could work no more. 99

In September 1946 the tribunal announced its first verdicts. The court had tried 21 Nazi leaders on four charges: planning the war, committing war crimes, committing other crimes against humanity, and conspiring to commit the crimes. Eleven Nazi leaders were sentenced to death; seven received jail sentences; and three were acquitted.

In other trials held in the U.S. occupation zone, thousands of former Nazi officials were tried and jailed, fined, or barred from public office. However, many Nazis—including Adolf Eichmann, the architect of the Jewish extermination program; Josef Mengele (MENG-ge-luh), Auschwitz's "Angel of Death"; and Klaus Barbie, known as the "Butcher of Lyons" for his cruel acts in that French city—escaped immediate prosecution by concealing their identities and fleeing to Latin America.

In the Tokyo war crimes trials, an international tribunal tried more than 20 war leaders. Seven were sentenced to death, including Hideki Tōjō, the wartime premier.

Many Americans, shocked by the evidence of war crimes, argued that more German and Japanese officials should have been punished. Nevertheless, the judges observed legal procedures and tried to avoid acting vengefully. In fact, the trials did set important precedents for international law and the conduct of war. The chief lesson was that nations and individuals can be held accountable for their actions during war. Many countries now accept the principle that war crimes cannot be excused on the grounds that those responsible were "just following orders."

■■ War crimes trials in Germany and Japan established the principle of individual responsibility for wartime conduct.

THE UNITED NATIONS

During the war, the Allies had met several times to map out strategies to defeat the Axis Powers. In

DECISION–MAKING BODIES OF THE UNITED NATIONS

Body	Function
General Assembly	Sets policies.
Security Council	Resolves diplomatic, military, and political disputes.
Economic and Social Council	Deals with human welfare and fundamental rights and freedoms.
International Court of Justice	Handles international legal disputes.
Trusteeship Council	Supervises territories that are not independent.
Secretariat	Performs routine administrative work of the UN.

Sources: *Encyclopedia of American History; Funk & Wagnalls New Encyclopedia*

MULTINATIONAL COOPERATION The United Nations was established in order to give every member nation a voice in international affairs. The General Assembly includes over 150 countries and uses five official languages—English, Russian, French, Spanish, and Chinese.

❓ **ANALYZING** Which body of the United Nations is responsible for monitoring military aggressions between nations?

RETEACH Ask students, working in pairs, to write sentences that explain how each entry in the Preview Workshop is related to the topic of the subsection in which it is located. Have pairs share their sentences with the reteaching group.

Closure

Ask volunteers to explain what Melville Grosvenor meant by his statement in the section opener on p. 780. Have other students provide details from the section that show his views were an accurate assessment of American foreign policy after the war.

Extension

ANALYZE Have students locate and read the Preamble to the Charter of the United Nations. Have them write an essay comparing the UN preamble to the Preamble of the United States Constitution.

CREATE Ask students to imagine they are teenagers in Germany or Japan after World War II. Have them write a poem or rap that reflects their feelings about another nation occupying their country.

1944, delegates from the United States, Great Britain, the Soviet Union, and China met at Dumbarton Oaks, an estate in Washington, D.C. There they worked out a proposal for a postwar international organization called the **United Nations** (UN). Through the UN, the Allies hoped to continue their alliance by working together to promote world peace.

In April 1945, delegates from 50 nations met in San Francisco to draw up the Charter of the United Nations. The delegates took just eight weeks to write the document. The charter established six bodies: (1) the General Assembly in which all countries shape policy, (2) the Security Council to address military and political problems, (3) the Economic and Social Council, (4) the International Court of Justice, (5) the Trusteeship Council to administer territories, and (6) the Secretariat—headed by the secretary-general—to administer the UN. As permanent members of the Security Council, the United States, the Soviet Union, Great Britain, France, or China could veto any action the UN proposed.

Soon afterward, the Senate overwhelmingly approved American membership in the UN. More than 60 percent of Americans approved of U.S. membership. On October 24, now observed as United Nations Day, the UN officially came into existence when the 29th country approved the UN charter. The UN established its headquarters in New York City. Trygve Lie (TRIG-vuh LEE) of Norway served as the UN's first secretary-general.

From the outset, UN delegates realized that building world peace required both diplomatic and economic cooperation. Eleanor Roosevelt, who served as a U.S. representative to the UN and helped shape the Universal Declaration of Human Rights, explained:

> 66 Security requires both control of the use of force and the elimination of want. No people are secure unless they have the things needed not only to preserve existence, but to make life worth living. . . . All peoples throughout the world must know that there is an organization where their interests can be considered and where justice and security will be sought for all. 99

Early critics of the UN insisted that it was doomed to fail because it had no real power to enforce its own decisions. Nevertheless, most Americans were as optimistic as President Truman, who noted in 1945: "This charter points down the only road to enduring peace. There is no other."

▲ **Eleanor Roosevelt chaired the UN Human Rights Commission from 1946 to 1951. She helped draft the Universal Declaration of Human Rights in 1948.**

■■ **The United Nations was founded to promote peaceful cooperation among the nations of the world.**

SECTION REVIEW ANSWERS

IDENTIFY

For significance, see the following pages:
Potsdam Conference (p. 780)
zaibatsu (p. 781)
Nuremberg trials (p. 781)
Adolf Eichmann (p. 782)
Josef Mengele (p. 782)
Klaus Barbie (p. 782)
Hideki Tōjō (p. 782)
United Nations (p. 783)
Trygve Lie (p. 783)
Eleanor Roosevelt (p. 783)

1. *that nations and individuals are accountable for their wartime actions*
2. *to promote international cooperation in the interests of world peace*
3. *Germany—divided into four occupation zones, Nazi party crushed and local governments and industry rebuilt and refugees resettled; Japan—democratic constitution adopted that ended militarism, economy reformed, zaibatsu were broken up*
4. *Letters might mention devastation, economic chaos, and social, economic, and political reforms.*
5. *Students might suggest that such issues affect national security, international relations, and world peace.*

SECTION **1** REVIEW

IDENTIFY and explain the significance of the following: Potsdam Conference, *zaibatsu*, Nuremberg trials, Adolf Eichmann, Josef Mengele, Klaus Barbie, Hideki Tōjō, United Nations, Trygve Lie, Eleanor Roosevelt.

1. **MAIN IDEA** What principle did the war crimes trials in Germany and Japan establish?
2. **MAIN IDEA** What was the purpose of the United Nations?
3. **COMPARING** How did the Allied powers govern Germany and Japan after World War II?
4. **WRITING TO DESCRIBE** Imagine you are a Japanese American soldier in Tokyo in 1946. Write a letter home that describes conditions in Japan after the war.
5. **ANALYZING** Why do you think the United Nations deals with economic and social issues in addition to its peacekeeping efforts?

FOCUS OBJECTIVES

■ Describe how the American economy fared after the war.

■ Explain how the Taft-Hartley Act affected unions.

■ Cite the most important issues in the 1948 election.

HISTORICAL SIDELIGHTS

Mexican American Discrimination

Some Mexican American veterans faced discrimination upon their return. In one notorious case, a white funeral home owner in Texas refused to hold services for Felix Longoria, a Mexican American soldier killed in the Pacific. Many Texans were outraged, and U.S. senator Lyndon B. Johnson arranged for Longoria to be buried in Arlington National Cemetery.

AV TRANSPARENCY

Everyday Life in America Transparency and **Worksheet 27**

CORE RESOURCES

• **Section 2 Daily Quiz**

AV RESOURCES

• *The American Nation* **Videodisc: Jackie Robinson**
• **Everyday Life in America Transparency** and **Worksheet 27**

PREVIEW WORKSHOP

Following is a list of the significant people and terms in this section. You may wish to use this list as a section preview.

People
■ Sadie Alexander
■ J. Strom Thurmond
■ Henry Wallace
■ Thomas Dewey

Terms
■ GI Bill of Rights
■ Employment Act
■ Council of Economic Advisors
■ Taft-Hartley Act
■ Committee on Civil Rights
■ Dixiecrats
■ Fair Deal

Section 2

THE CHALLENGES OF PEACE

FOCUS
■ **How did the American economy fare after the war?**
■ **How did the Taft-Hartley Act affect unions?**
■ **What were the most important issues in the 1948 election?**

During the difficult transition from war to peace, Americans were apprehensive. Returning veterans were "worried sick about post-war joblessness," according to Fortune *magazine. Many African American, Mexican American, and women workers feared they would lose the economic gains they had made during the war.*

Homecoming, 1945

THE PROBLEMS OF DEMOBILIZATION

At war's end, troop ships headed home. By mid-1946 over nine million servicemen and women had been discharged. The troops received a hero's welcome, but their return also sparked concern. Could the economy absorb all these new workers? The government soon cancelled $23 billion in military contracts, hitting hard the shipyards, munitions factories, aircraft plants, and military bases.

Postwar measures. To prevent a depression and to help war-weary veterans make the difficult transition to civilian life, Congress passed the Servicemen's Readjustment Act of 1944, commonly known as the **GI Bill of Rights**. The act provided pensions and government loans to help veterans start businesses and buy homes or farms. Under the GI Bill, thousands of veterans also received money for tuition, books, and living expenses while they attended college.

▶ Under the GI Bill, many veterans received financial aid to pursue a college education or industrial training. Howard Timian of Milwaukee is shown here studying for an engineering course.

To ensure economic growth, Congress also passed the **Employment Act** of 1946. The act promised that the government would promote full employment and production. It also established the **Council of Economic Advisers** to counsel the president on economic policy.

Despite widespread fears, the postwar depression never materialized. Employment remained high, as plants that had been making tanks and bombers began to produce consumer goods. With world agricultural output shattered by the war, U.S. food exports also remained high. In addition, Americans now began spending the money they had saved from their wartime paychecks.

THE POSTWAR ECONOMY

Organize students into small groups to create a plan for a two-page magazine spread titled "The American Postwar Economy." Ask groups to write brief summaries of articles that might appear in the spread to explain how veterans, farmers, consumers, and members of ethnic groups fared in the postwar economy.

Ask volunteers to list the provisions of the Taft-Hartley Act. Then have students play the role of business owner or union worker and write a letter to the editor, explaining their support for or their objections to the Taft-Hartley Act. Call on volunteers with opposing viewpoints to read their letters to the class. Students may wish to include their letters in their portfolios.

▶

▲ A. Philip Randolph and Eleanor Roosevelt are shown here at a 1946 rally at Madison Square Garden to save the Fair Employment Practices Committee. Congress later abolished the committee.

Not all was rosy on the economic front, however. Government measures encouraged employers to give priority in hiring to veterans. The fears of many women, African Americans, and Mexican Americans were realized as they lost their jobs to returning veterans. During the war these workers had been encouraged to take jobs in vital defense factories. African Americans had been protected from job discrimination by the Fair Employment Practices Committee. Soon after the war, however, Congress abolished the committee.

Many workers were also hit hard by inflation. With the lifting of most wartime price controls in 1946, prices soared. Meat prices zoomed so high that some markets began selling horsemeat. Blaming the Truman administration, angry consumers called the president "Horsemeat Harry."

■■ **Despite fears of a depression, the American economy prospered after the war, though inflation hurt many workers.**

Labor unrest. As inflation worsened, people took matters into their own hands. Workers who had sacrificed during the depression and the war now craved a better standard of living. Freed of their wartime no-strike pledge, millions of workers walked off the job to win wage increases and to preserve some wartime price controls. In 1946—the most strike-filled year in U.S. history after 1919—almost five million workers walked the picket lines.

President Truman, though a backer of labor unions, opposed these strikes because he feared they would disrupt the economy. In April 1946, when some 400,000 coal miners went on strike, Truman ordered the army to establish government

control of the mines. United Mine Workers' president John L. Lewis retorted: "You can't dig coal with bayonets." After the courts slapped heavy fines on the union, though, Lewis ordered the miners back to work. When confronted with striking railway workers, Truman threatened to end the strike by drafting the strikers into the army. Faced with Truman's threat, union leaders negotiated an end to the strike.

To reduce the strength of organized labor, Congress—under Republican control since the 1946 elections—passed an antiunion bill in 1947. This law, known as the **Taft-Hartley Act**, allowed courts to end some strikes, outlawed closed-shop agreements (which required union membership for employment), restricted unions' political contributions, and required union officers to swear they were not Communists. President Truman vetoed the bill, but Congress passed it over his veto.

The Taft-Hartley Act stirred angry debate. Conservative supporters argued that the law corrected unfair advantages granted to labor in the Wagner-Connery Act (see Chapter 24). Prolabor opponents denounced it as a "slave labor law."

The act limited the tactics unions could use. Despite these restrictions, however, organized labor continued to make some gains in the postwar years. For example, in 1948 General Motors and the United Automobile Workers (UAW) signed a contract tying wage increases to cost-of-living increases. Union contracts also began to include provisions for such benefits as retirement pensions and health insurance.

■■ **The Taft-Hartley Act placed a variety of restrictions on labor unions.**

◀ The cartoon *Three Men on a Horse* appeared on February 24, 1953. Union leaders John L. Lewis, Walter Reuther, and George Meany ride toward the Taft-Hartley Act, hoping to axe some of its restrictions on labor unions.

VOICES IN HISTORY

During World War II and immediately after, Asian American plantation workers in Hawaii organized unions to win better wages and working conditions. Unions lobbied state legislators, who in 1946 passed a law giving the agricultural workers the right to collective bargaining. Saburo Fujisaki, a Nisei union member, explained the union's success: "We had a territory-wide political machine organized. We elected two members of the union to the House of Representatives. We gained respect because we could get votes for people who otherwise couldn't get elected. What we couldn't win across the bargaining table, we decided we'd seek through the Territorial Legislature."

HISTORICAL SIDELIGHTS
Gains for African American Women

By 1953, some 60 percent of the degrees from black colleges were granted to women, as compared to about 35 percent for all women graduating from all colleges in the same time period.

Teaching the Section

ISSUES IN THE 1948 ELECTION

Call on volunteers to represent Truman supporters, Dixiecrats, and Progressives during the 1948 election campaign. Have role-players argue the major campaign issues and list their positions on the chalkboard. Then discuss why many Americans expected Truman to lose the election of 1948. Ask students to explain how they would have voted in the election.

THE 1948 ELECTION

By 1948 inflation, high taxes, and labor unrest had eroded public support for Truman. His approval rating stood at 35 percent in March, down from 60 percent the previous year. "To err is Truman," people joked. But Truman was determined to prove his critics wrong. His stand on civil rights for African Americans became an important issue in the 1948 campaign.

The Committee on Civil Rights. In 1946 African American civil rights groups urged Truman to take action against the racism that stained American society. They pointed out that most African Americans in the South were prevented from voting through the use of poll taxes. Blacks throughout the nation faced segregation in schools and buses and discrimination in housing and employment. And in many areas African Americans continued to be lynched, a crime that local courts often ignored. Efforts to battle these conditions met a wall of white resistance.

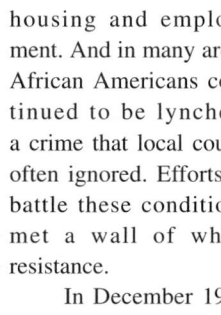

▲ **Shown here are African American demonstrators outside the convention hall at the 1948 Democratic Convention in Philadelphia.**

In December 1946 Truman, distressed by these reports, set up the **Committee on Civil Rights** to examine the issue. The committee's 15 members included African American lawyer Sadie Alexander; Dr. Channing Tobias, director of the Phelps-Stokes Fund, which supported educational opportunities for African Americans; General Electric's president Charles Wilson; and Franklin Roosevelt, Jr.

The committee's report, "To Secure These Rights," appeared in October 1947. The report documented widespread civil rights abuses, including discrimination against black veterans and an increase in Ku Klux Klan violence. The committee urged Congress to pass an antilynching law and an anti-poll-tax measure and to end discrimination in federal agencies and the military. The report also called for an end to racial segregation in interstate transportation.

When Truman did not immediately act on the report's recommendations, African American leader A. Philip Randolph threatened to launch a campaign of civil disobedience if the military remained segregated. The tactic worked. In July 1948 Truman issued executive orders banning racial discrimination in the military and in federal hiring. He also took steps to end employment discrimination by companies working under government contracts.

White southern Democrats were outraged at African American demands for civil rights and at Truman's actions. Senator Olin Johnston of South Carolina angrily warned that the South's electoral votes "won't be for Truman. They'll be for somebody else. He ain't going to be re-elected."

The Democratic convention. Despite Senator Johnston's bluster, southern opposition did not prevent Truman from winning the nomination at the Democratic convention in July. Senator Alben W. Barkley of Kentucky was selected to be Truman's running mate. The Democrats hoped to appeal to the former New Deal coalition of farmers, unionized workers, big-city ethnic groups, and African Americans. The Democratic platform called for repeal of the Taft-Hartley Act; an increase in federal aid for housing, education, and agriculture; and broader social security benefits. It also included a strong civil rights plank.

The civil rights issue split the Democratic party. Southern delegates threatened to walk out of the convention. Declaring "LET 'EM WALK," the NAACP argued:

❝ There is no room . . . for compromise. . . . Those Democrats who say the

▼ **Misled by early returns, the *Chicago Daily Tribune* published an early election-night edition announcing Dewey as the winner.**

Practice

GUIDED PRACTICE

Ask students to imagine they are advisers to President Truman. Have them name postwar problems that Truman will have to address. List the problems on the chalkboard. Then discuss how each problem might be handled.

INDEPENDENT PRACTICE

Have students choose a problem listed in the Guided Practice and, in their role as advisers to President Truman, have them write a memorandum to the president, explaining the problem and suggesting a solution. Students may wish to include their memorandums in their portfolios.

Review and Assessment

REVIEW Write the following items on the chalkboard: *Demobilization, Taft-Hartley Act,* and *1948 election.* Have students work in groups of three to develop cause-and-effect charts centering on each item. Then assign the Section 2 Review on p. 788.

ASSESS Assign the **Section 2 Daily Quiz** in *Core Resources.*

▶

President's recommendation of such a program is a "stab in the back" of the South are saying they do not choose to abide by the Constitution. They are also saying . . . that the whole section of our nation believes as they do. . . . We *know* it is not true! 🙶

After bitter debate the delegates adopted the civil rights plank. Southern delegates stormed out of the convention. They formed the States' Rights party—nicknamed the **Dixiecrats**—which called for continued racial segregation. The Dixiecrats nominated Governor J. Strom Thurmond of South Carolina as their presidential candidate. These explosive divisions were an opening skirmish in a mighty struggle against racism that would soon sweep over the nation.

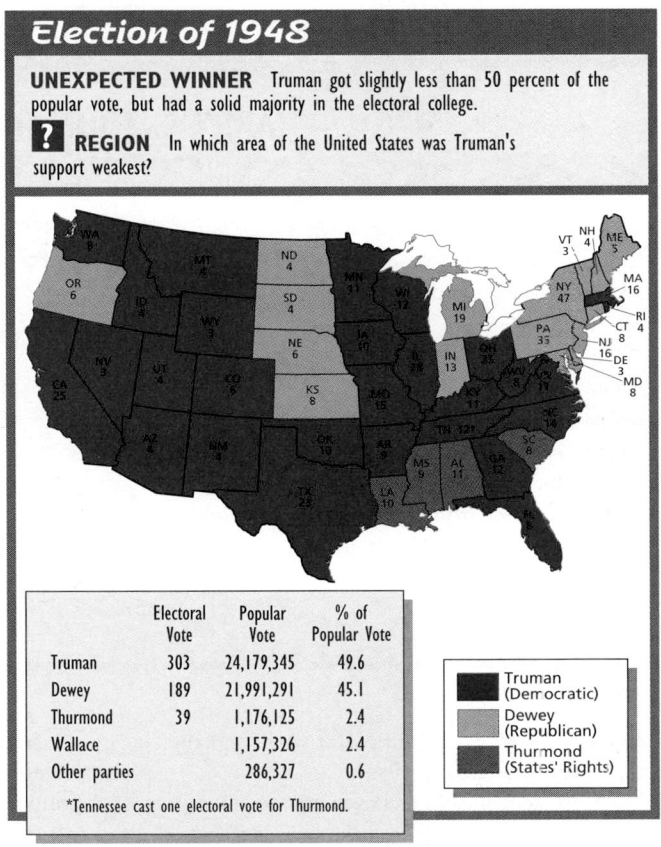

Election of 1948

UNEXPECTED WINNER Truman got slightly less than 50 percent of the popular vote, but had a solid majority in the electoral college.

❓ REGION In which area of the United States was Truman's support weakest?

	Electoral Vote	Popular Vote	% of Popular Vote
Truman	303	24,179,345	49.6
Dewey	189	21,991,291	45.1
Thurmond	39	1,176,125	2.4
Wallace		1,157,326	2.4
Other parties		286,327	0.6

*Tennessee cast one electoral vote for Thurmond.

Truman (Democratic)
Dewey (Republican)
Thurmond (States' Rights)

Map Caption Answer
Northeast

HISTORICAL SIDELIGHTS

Whistle-Stop Campaign

President Truman wanted to take his message directly to the people. For 33 days, beginning in September 1948, Truman traveled some 31,000 miles by train, speaking from the rear platform of the train to people in towns across the country. No presidential candidate had ever traveled so far and none would ever again attempt such a campaign by railroad. In a letter to his sister, Truman wrote: "It will be the greatest campaign any President ever made. Win, lose, or draw people will know where I stand."

The gulf widens. A different issue caused another break within the Democratic party. Troubled by Truman's antilabor actions in 1946, former vice president Henry Wallace and other liberal New Dealers left the Democratic party to found the Progressive party. This group, which was not related to the Progressive party of the early 1900s, called for an extension of the New Deal and for friendly relations with the Soviet Union. The American Communist party supported the Progressive party.

With the Democrats' votes split three ways, the Republicans were confident of victory. They nominated Governor Thomas Dewey of New York as their presidential candidate and Earl Warren, the popular governor of California, as Dewey's running mate. Opinion polls and most newspapers predicted a Dewey victory.

But Truman ran an energetic campaign, attacking the conservatism of the Republicans and the radicalism of the Progressives. As he crisscrossed the country, criticizing the "do-nothing" Republican Congress, crowds began to chant, "Give 'em hell, Harry." In one of the great upsets of U.S. political history, Truman won, gaining 49

percent of the popular vote to Dewey's 45 percent. Black voters helped Truman carry several key states. Workers, farmers, and ethnic voters generally supported Truman, proving that the political coalition that had supported Franklin Roosevelt in the 1930s still held.

■■ **Civil rights and labor issues splintered the Democratic party. Truman, however, ran a tough campaign and won the 1948 election.**

THE FAIR DEAL

Heartened by his victory, Truman urged Congress to continue Roosevelt's New Deal reforms. Proclaiming that "every segment of our population . . . has a right to expect from our government a fair deal," Truman proposed new reforms, which he labeled the **Fair Deal**. Truman's Fair Deal proposed full employment, higher minimum wages, a national health insurance program, affordable

RETEACH Organize students into groups and assign each group a subsection of Section 2. Have each group develop several questions and answers about the main ideas in its assigned material. Then have each group quiz the other groups with its questions.

Closure

Ask students to explain in their own words why they think the author titled this section "The Challenges of Peace." *(Student responses should tie economic, political, and civil rights issues to the transition from war to peace.)*

Extension

COMPARE Have students develop a chart that compares the restrictions imposed on unions by the Taft-Hartley Act of 1947 with the rights they gained under the Wagner Labor Relations Act of 1935.

CREATE Have students create buttons, campaign literature, banners, and other election materials for each of the candidates in the 1948 election.

SECTION REVIEW ANSWERS

IDENTIFY

For significance, see the following pages:
GI Bill of Rights (p. 784)
Employment Act (p. 784)
Council of Economic Advisors (p.784)
Taft-Hartley Act (p. 785)
Committee on Civil Rights (p. 786)
Sadie Alexander (p. 786)
Dixiecrats (p. 787)
J. Strom Thurmond (p. 787)
Henry Wallace (p. 787)
Thomas Dewey (p. 787)
Fair Deal (p. 787)

1. *Economy prospered because of high employment and consumer spending spree, but end of price controls brought inflation that hurt workers.*
2. *reduced the power of labor by allowing courts to end strikes, outlawing closed-shop agreements, and restricting unions' political contributions*
3. *Many lost their jobs to returning veterans.*
4. *Commentaries might mention inflation, high taxes, civil rights, and labor unrest.*
5. *pressure from African American civil rights groups, the findings of the Committee on Civil Rights, Randolph's threat of civil disobedience*

PRESIDENTIAL LIVES

HARRY S. TRUMAN
1884–1972

in office 1945–1953

Harry S. Truman was known to be an honest politician who always spoke his mind. His very direct manner of speaking shocked many people, but impressed others. Once Truman wrote a letter to a music critic who had written a harsh review of a recital by the president's daughter Margaret. In addition to calling the critic "a frustrated old man who never made a success," the president informed him that "I never met you, but if I do

you'll need a new nose." While some considered this response inappropriate, public opinion strongly supported Truman's defense of his daughter.

While Truman was quick to defend his family and others, he often downplayed his own abilities as president. Many years after he left office he told an interviewer, "I wasn't one of the great Presidents; but I had a good time trying to be one."

Harry S. Truman

U.S. Postage 8 cents

---

housing construction, aid to farmers, and the expansion of welfare benefits.

Most Republicans, and even conservatives in Truman's own party, opposed the president's program. Nevertheless, Truman managed to push through some of his reforms. Between 1949 and 1952 Congress extended social security benefits to some 10 million more people, raised the minimum wage from 40 to 75 cents an hour, and approved programs to clear slums. Congress also expanded federal programs to promote flood control, hydroelectric power, and irrigation.

Overall, though, the Fair Deal had limited success amid an increasingly conservative postwar political climate. Congress failed to repeal the Taft-Hartley Act or to pass a civil rights bill. Most of the New Dealers had resigned from Truman's cabinet in disappointment, leaving business leaders and military men who had little enthusiasm for the Fair Deal. These domestic issues also unfolded against the backdrop of other pressing concerns that had international implications: conflict with the Soviet Union and almost hysterical fears of communism.

SECTION 2 REVIEW

IDENTIFY and explain the significance of the following: GI Bill of Rights, Employment Act, Council of Economic Advisers, Taft-Hartley Act, Committee on Civil Rights, Sadie Alexander, Dixiecrats, J. Strom Thurmond, Henry Wallace, Thomas Dewey, Fair Deal.

1. **MAIN IDEA** What effect did the end of World War II have on the U.S. economy?
2. **MAIN IDEA** What restrictions did the Taft-Hartley Act place on unions?
3. **MAIN IDEA** How did the end of the war affect women, African American, and Mexican American workers?
4. **WRITING TO INFORM** Imagine you are a political correspondent covering the 1948 election. Write a magazine commentary that outlines the most important issues in the campaign.
5. **ANALYZING** What convinced Truman to desegregate the military and to end discrimination in federal jobs?

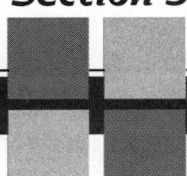

Section 3

THE COLD WAR BEGINS

FOCUS
■ **What caused the Cold War?**
■ **What did the United States hope to accomplish through
the Marshall Plan?**
■ **What effects did the Cold War have on American society?**

Soon after World War II, the wartime alliance between the
United States and the Soviet Union collapsed. The two
countries, at odds because of competing global objectives
and different economic and political systems, fought over
control of Europe and access to atomic energy.

Berlin airlift, 1948

THE ROOTS OF THE COLD WAR

An intense rivalry between the United States and
the Soviet Union began after World War II. With
once-mighty Germany, Japan, and Great Britain in
ruins, only the United States and the Soviet Union
were left to struggle for international dominance.
Their competition for global power and influence,
which came to be known as the **Cold War**, was
waged mostly on political and economic fronts
rather than on the battlefield. Nevertheless, the
threat of all-out war was always present.

The origins of the Cold War lay in profound
economic, political, and philosophical differences
between the two nations. Most Americans, committed to the principles of democratic government,
individual freedom, and a capitalist economy,
deeply opposed the Soviet system.

Founded on Communist ideology, the Soviet
system included a state-run economy, one-party
rule, suppression of religion, and the use of force
to crush opposition. Until his death in 1953, dictator Joseph Stalin ruled the Soviet Union with an
iron hand.

Stalin looked with a mixture of envy and
horror at powerful America with its capitalist
system, its industrial might, and its atomic bombs.
Soviet propagandists endlessly denounced
American "imperialism" and U.S. capitalists'
"oppression" of the laboring masses. The Soviets
pointed to racial discrimination in the U.S. to
discredit America's boasts of freedom and
democracy.

Soviet expansionism after World War II
fueled American mistrust. During World War II the
Soviets had taken over the Baltic states of
Lithuania, Latvia, and Estonia. Then they captured
large areas of Poland and Romania. By war's end
the Soviets also controlled Manchuria.

After the war, Stalin made clear his determination to maintain Soviet influence in Eastern
Europe, claiming the need for a buffer zone of
"friendly nations" on the U.S.S.R.'s western border. He stripped eastern Germany of some 40 percent of its industrial equipment, installed
pro-Soviet governments in Poland and Romania,
and worked to establish Communist rule throughout Eastern Europe. The countries under Soviet
control became known as **satellite nations**.

FOCUS OBJECTIVES
■ Identify what caused the
Cold War.

■ Explain what the United
States hoped to accom-
plish through the
Marshall Plan.

■ Analyze the effects the
Cold War had on
American society.

MAKING CONNECTIONS
Language Arts
The term *Cold War* first
appeared in print in 1947,
when Walter Lippmann's
The Cold War, a study of
American-Soviet relations,
was published.

PRIMARY SOURCE
Description of Change:
excerpted and bracketed
Rationale: excerpted to
focus on main idea; bracketed to clarify meaning

CORE RESOURCES

• **Literature
Worksheet 27**
• **Geography
Worksheet 27**
• **Section 3 Daily Quiz**

AV RESOURCES

• **Linking Geography
and History
Transparency** and
Worksheet 20

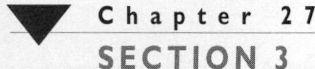
MOTIVATING: LINK TO TODAY

Ask students if they think that the dissolution of the Soviet Union has eliminated concern about nuclear war and the spread of communism in the world today. Point out that in this section they will learn how such fears sparked the Cold War and how they affected postwar Americans.

Teaching the Section

ROOTS OF THE COLD WAR

Organize the class into two groups. Direct one group to assume the roles of Soviet students and the other the roles of American students after World War II. Have students work in pairs to write letters explaining why they think the other group is responsible for the Cold War. Ask Soviet students to address their letters to Truman and American students to write to Stalin. Call on pairs to read their letters to the class. Then work with the class, using their letters to reach some general conclusions about the roots of the Cold War.

HISTORICAL SIDELIGHTS
Cold War Tensions

Time, in reporting Stalin's speech, described it as "the most warlike pronouncement uttered by any top-rank statesman since V-J Day."

HISTORICAL SIDELIGHTS
Iron Curtain

In February 1945, thirteen months before Churchill spoke of the Iron Curtain at Fulton, Missouri, Nazi propaganda minister Joseph Goebbels used the phrase *iron screen* with reference to Russia. The image that inspired their use of similar terms was probably the fireproof iron curtains long used in European theaters.

PRIMARY SOURCE
Description of Change: excerpted
Rationale: excerpted to focus on main idea

Concerned about Stalin's actions, the United States, Great Britain, and France solidified their control of West Germany and revived its industries. The United States also pressured Stalin to withdraw Soviet forces from Iran, the oil-rich Middle Eastern nation that the Soviets had occupied during the war. In April 1946 Stalin finally agreed to withdraw his troops.

In February of the same year, however, Stalin had made a tough speech—dubbed the "Declaration of World War III" by Supreme Court justice William Douglas—proclaiming that capitalism and communism could never coexist. Winston Churchill, Britain's wartime prime minister, answered Stalin in March with an equally tough speech delivered in Fulton, Missouri. Churchill declared that a Soviet "Iron Curtain has descended across the Continent," isolating Western Europe from Soviet-dominated Eastern Europe. Churchill called for closer cooperation between Great Britain and America to check Soviet power.

Churchill's speech was well received in Washington. At the time, George Kennan, a State Department official and Soviet expert, advised similar action. Kennan argued that the Soviet Union's long-term aim was to defeat capitalism and expand the Soviet sphere of influence. He believed that the Soviets would be persistent, yet cautious, expanding only when there were few risks. Kennan explained how American foreign policy could thus stop the spread of communism:

66 The Soviet pressure against the free institutions of the Western world is something that can be contained by the . . . vigilant application of counterforce at a series of constantly shifting geographical and political points. . . . The Russians look forward to a duel of infinite duration. 99

Kennan's **containment** doctrine, which aimed to contain, or restrict, Soviet expansion, became the basis for U.S. Cold War strategy. Many Americans, unwilling to return to the appeasement policy of the 1930s, applauded Kennan's stand against communism.

▪▪ **The origins of the Cold War lay in U.S.–Soviet global competition, conflicting economic and political systems, and mutual distrust.**

*T*HE DEADLOCK OVER ATOMIC WEAPONS

The United States and the Soviet Union soon became locked in a dispute over the control of atomic weapons. This standoff terrified many Americans, who feared a nuclear war. Most people shared lawyer David E. Lilienthal's 1946 assessment that "the awful strength of atomic power . . . directly affects every man, woman, and child in the world." Recognizing this fact, the UN created a commission to draw up a plan for the control of nuclear arms early in 1946.

At the commission's first meeting, U.S. representative Bernard Baruch called for the creation of a special UN agency with the authority to inspect any nation's atomic-energy installations. This proposal, known as the **Baruch Plan**, would impose penalties on countries violating international controls. Until such a plan was in place, Baruch said, the United States would not reveal any atomic-energy secrets or give up its atomic weapons. At the time, American physicists were developing more-powerful nuclear bombs.

Working feverishly on its own bomb, the Soviet Union rejected all inspection and enforcement provisions. With neither country willing to compromise, hopes for international control of

▼ In July 1946 the United States conducted atomic bomb tests in Bikini Atoll in the western Pacific Ocean. These tests were intended to measure the effects of atomic bombs on warships.

▶

atomic energy died. When the Soviet Union tested its first atomic bomb in 1949, fears of a nuclear-arms race became reality.

Despite the failure of the Baruch Plan, the United States achieved some success in controlling nuclear weapons. Atomic-energy scientists and U.S. peace organizations, such as the Women's International League for Peace and Freedom, urged the U.S. government to establish civilian, rather than military, control of atomic energy. Responding to these appeals, Congress in August 1946 passed the **Atomic Energy Act**. The act set up the Atomic Energy Commission (AEC) under civilian control to oversee nuclear weapons research and to promote peacetime uses of atomic energy. Its main activity, however, became supporting the government's nuclear weapons program.

CONTAINMENT AROUND THE WORLD

As prospects for U.S.–Soviet cooperation dimmed, the Truman administration pursued a more aggressive policy toward the Soviet Union. The U.S. containment policy first took shape in Greece, where a civil war had broken out in 1946. Communist-led rebels battled the Greek monarchy, which relied on military and financial support from Great Britain. In early 1947, however, the British announced that they could no longer continue their aid to Greece. Without aid it seemed likely that Greece's pro-Western government would fall to the Communists and the country would come under Soviet control.

Containment in the Mediterranean. At the same time, the Soviet Union pressured Turkey to give up sole control of the Dardanelles, a narrow strait linking the Black Sea and the Mediterranean. President Truman knew that control of this area would give the Soviets a dominant position in the eastern Mediterranean and would threaten the security of the Suez Canal. In a somber speech before Congress on March 12, 1947, Truman declared: "It must be the policy of the United States to support free peoples who are resisting attempted subjugation [conquest] by armed minorities or by outside pressures."

This statement, which became known as the **Truman Doctrine**, made no mention of the Soviet Union, though clearly Truman had devised it with the Soviets in mind. Agreeing with Truman's

sentiments, Congress soon voted $400 million to aid Greece and Turkey. This action was only a prelude, however, to the more massive foreign-aid program that soon followed.

Containment in Europe. After World War II, European economies were in shambles. In 1948 Germany produced only 45 percent of the goods it had produced before the war. To make matters worse, the winter of 1946–47 brought the worst blizzards in some 50 years. Starvation and chaos loomed. Some Americans believed that the United States should help Europe. They feared that such desperate economic conditions would make Europe more vulnerable to Soviet influence.

Secretary of State George C. Marshall shared this belief. Born in Uniontown, Pennsylvania, in 1880, Marshall graduated from Virginia Military Institute and joined the army. During World War I he served under General Pershing. As army chief of staff during World War II, he attended the Casablanca, Yalta, and Potsdam conferences.

After the war Marshall served briefly as a U.S. envoy to China before Truman appointed him secretary of state in 1947. In a speech at Harvard University on June 5, 1947, Marshall warned that if steps were not taken soon, Europe faced "economic, social, and political" collapse. He then called for a major U.S. effort to promote European recovery "to permit the emergence of political and social conditions in which free institutions can exist." At the same time, Marshall warned that any attempt to block recovery or exploit Europe's difficulties for political ends would face strong American opposition.

George C. Marshall

After Marshall's speech, Truman asked Congress for $17 billion in economic aid for Europe. Truman's request sparked heated debate throughout the United States. Supporters argued that such aid would contain communism by restoring Europe's economic health and would help the U.S. economy as Europeans purchased American goods and military hardware. Opponents said the United States could not afford to "carry Europe on its back."

GLOBAL CONNECTIONS

Although Roosevelt and Churchill had agreed in 1945 to full collaboration in the field of atomic energy between the U.S., the United Kingdom, and Canada, the passage of the Atomic Energy Act terminated virtually all U.S. communications about atomic energy. Truman and Congress felt that the U.S. should keep information about atomic energy to itself since it was valuable and dangerous information. In 1947, feeling betrayed by the Atomic Energy Act, members of Britain's Labour Cabinet called for Britain to begin work on its own atomic bomb.

Teaching the Section

THE MARSHALL PLAN

Call on volunteers to role-play George Marshall and his state department advisers. Have remaining students work in small groups to develop interview questions to ask Marshall and his advisers about the Marshall Plan. Tell students that the interview should focus on the aims of the Marshall Plan and the part it plays in Truman's overall Cold War strategy. Have each group select a representative for a panel to interview the Marshall group. Conclude by asking all students to write a newspaper article that recaps the interview.

■■ Ask students what types of aid the U.S. provides to other countries today.

🌐 GLOBAL CONNECTIONS

Under Soviet pressure, Czechoslovakia, Poland, Romania, and other satellite countries of Eastern Europe refused to participate in the Marshall Plan. Soviet foreign minister V.M. Molotov explained his objections to the Marshall Plan when he said it was, "nothing but a vicious American scheme for using dollars to buy its way [into the affairs of Europe]."

HISTORICAL SIDELIGHTS
The Berlin Airlift

When the Soviet Union blocked off Berlin, it left more than 2 million German citizens, and Allied forces as well, with enough food for only about 36 days, and enough coal for 45. U.S. general Lucius Clay asked for 4,500 tons of supplies a day to be airlifted, knowing that even this amount would not be enough to sustain Berlin during the winter months. By the end of the airlift, British and American aircraft had delivered, in over 277,000 flights, more than 2 million tons of food, fuel, machinery, and other supplies.

PRIMARY SOURCE
Description of Change: excerpted
Rationale: excerpted to focus on main idea

▲ The first cargo of sugar transported under the Marshall Plan is unloaded from the S.S. *Araby* in London in February 1949.

A turning point in the debate came early in 1948, when pro-Soviet Communists overthrew the government of Czechoslovakia. Jolted into action by the coup, Congress passed the European Recovery Act, or **Marshall Plan**, in April 1948. The plan, based on Marshall's recommendations, provided some $12 billion in aid to Western Europe over the next four years. For his efforts Marshall won the Nobel Peace Prize in 1953.

■■ **The Marshall Plan aimed to contain the spread of communism by easing economic hardship in Europe.**

CRISIS IN BERLIN

The non-Soviet zone of Germany grew stronger as a result of the Marshall Plan. In early June 1948, Great Britain, France, and the United States announced plans to combine their occupation zones and support the formation of a new West German government.

The Berlin airlift. The Soviets, deeply fearful of renewed German power, opposed this action. On June 24, 1948, the Soviets suddenly blocked all roads, canals, and railways linking Berlin and western Germany, cutting off shipments of food, fuel, and other crucial supplies to the city. The Soviets hoped to drive the Western powers out of Berlin and to delay the formation of a West German government. Berlin had become a pawn in the Cold War chess game.

The British and the Americans responded to the Soviet action with the **Berlin airlift**. Over the next 10 months, U.S. and British planes carried more than two million tons of food and supplies to the people of West Berlin. As one Berliner recalled, the airlift became a lifeline to the rest of the world:

❝ Early in the morning, when we woke up, the first thing we did was listen to see whether the noise of aircraft engines could be heard. That gave us the certainty that we were not alone, that the whole civilized world took part in the fight for Berlin's freedom. ❞

The success of the Berlin airlift proved a huge embarrassment to the Soviet Union. In May

▲ As tensions mounted, American military police in Berlin warily faced their Soviet counterparts across the dividing line between the Allied and Soviet zones.

THE COLD WAR AT HOME

Direct students to create a web that illustrates the nation's domestic response to the Cold War. Students should write and circle the term *Cold War*. At the end of lines emanating from the circle, students should indicate the ways that the government responded at home to the Cold War. Have volunteers present their webs. Then have class members explain how each government response on the webs illustrates the national climate of concern about communism. Students may wish to include their webs in their portfolios.

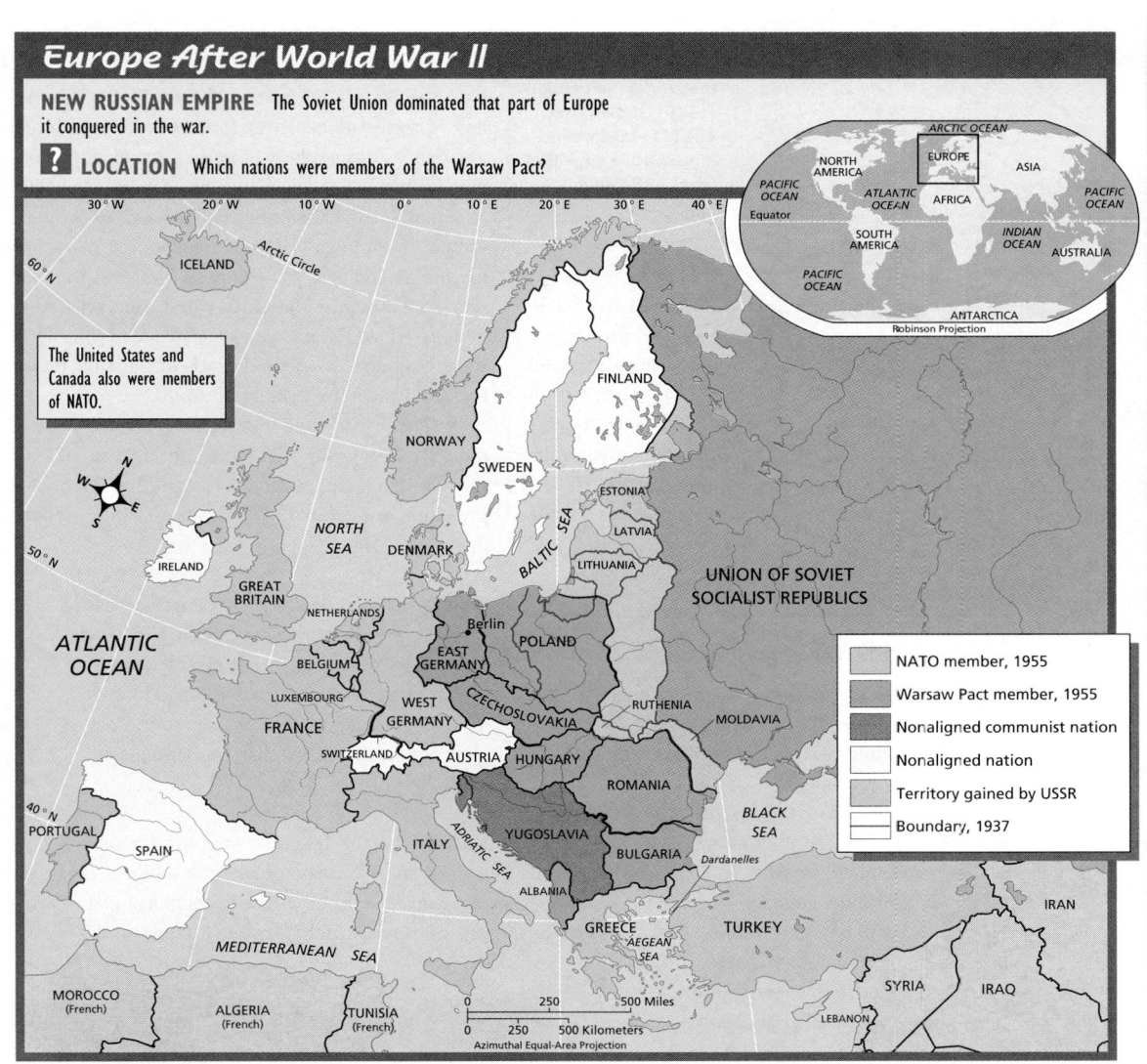

Europe After World War II

NEW RUSSIAN EMPIRE The Soviet Union dominated that part of Europe it conquered in the war.

? LOCATION Which nations were members of the Warsaw Pact?

The United States and Canada also were members of NATO.

Legend:
- NATO member, 1955
- Warsaw Pact member, 1955
- Nonaligned communist nation
- Nonaligned nation
- Territory gained by USSR
- Boundary, 1937

Map Caption Answer
U.S.S.R., Poland, East Germany, Czechoslavakia, Hungary, Romania, Bulgaria, Albania

HISTORICAL SIDELIGHTS
NATO

The signing of the NATO treaty marked a radical departure from U.S. tradition. It was the nation's first peacetime military alliance in over 150 years. President Truman ranked NATO (along with the Marshall Plan) as one of the proudest achievements of his presidency. He was convinced that had NATO been in existence in 1914 and 1939, the world would have been spared two world wars.

AV TRANSPARENCY

Linking Geography and History Transparency and **Worksheet 20**

1949 the Soviets lifted the blockade. On May 9 the Federal Republic of Germany, known as West Germany, was founded. In response, the Soviets set up the German Democratic Republic—East Germany—in the Soviet zone. The division of Germany would last for more than 40 years as a result of Cold War rivalries.

The Western alliance. After the Berlin crisis the United States shifted its attention in Europe from economic recovery to military preparedness. In April 1949 nine Western European nations joined the United States, Canada, and Iceland in a military alliance called the **North Atlantic Treaty Organization**, or NATO.

Under the terms of the NATO treaty, known as the Atlantic Pact, each member nation pledged to defend the others in the event of an outside attack. When Truman submitted the treaty for Senate ratification, debate focused on whether the agreement would allow the United States to go to war without an act of Congress. Concern over this same issue had helped keep the United States out of the League of Nations. This time, however, fear of Soviet expansionism outweighed other concerns. In July 1949 the Senate ratified the treaty.

In 1951 General Dwight D. Eisenhower became the supreme commander of NATO forces. As its contribution to NATO, the United States

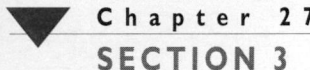

Practice

GUIDED PRACTICE

Lead the class in interpreting the cartoon on p. 794. (You may wish to review with students the Strategies for Success on Interpreting Editorial Cartoons on p. 332.) Ask students how caricature, symbols, and labels convey the message in this cartoon.

INDEPENDENT PRACTICE

Direct students to use the techniques discussed in the Guided Practice to create an editorial cartoon about Cold War tensions between the Soviet Union and the U.S. in the 1940s and 1950s. Tell students that their cartoons may be from either the Soviet or the U.S. viewpoint. Students may wish to include their cartoons in their portfolios.

Review and Assessment

REVIEW Direct students to create cause-and-effect charts which show the causes and effects of the Cold War in Europe and at home. Then assign the Section 3 Review on p. 795.

ASSESS Assign the **Section 3 Daily Quiz** in *Core Resources*.

VOICES IN HISTORY

Although the NAACP accused the Communist party of exploiting race issues, many African Americans were attracted by its message. As one Communist organizer explained, "All my life I'd been sweated and stepped-on and Jim-Crowed. . . . All of a sudden, I had found organizations in which Negroes and whites sat together, and worked together, and knew no difference of race or color."

PRIMARY SOURCE

Description of Change: excerpted
Rationale: excerpted to focus on main idea

HISTORICAL SIDELIGHTS

The Hollywood Ten
During the Hollywood investigation, HUAC interviewed some of the biggest names in the industry, including studio mogul Jack L. Warner, Walt Disney, Gary Cooper, and Ronald Reagan (then an actor involved in the Screen Actors Guild), all of whom testified about Communists in the movie industry.

The Granger Collection, New York

◀ **This U.S. cartoon, entitled *Banner of the Non-Soviet Union* (1949), shows that NATO was formed in response to Allied fears of Soviet aggression.**

stationed troops in Europe and gave massive military aid to its European allies. The Soviet Union responded in 1955 by forming its own military alliance with other Communist countries in Eastern Europe. This alliance came to be called the **Warsaw Pact**.

THE COLD WAR AT HOME

The Cold War had important consequences within the United States. As a result of Cold War pressures, the United States streamlined its military to allow for peacetime rearmament. In July 1947 Congress replaced the War Department with the Department of Defense, combining the leadership of the army, navy, and air force under the Joint Chiefs of Staff. In addition, Congress set up the **National Security Council** (NSC) to advise the president on strategic matters and established the **Central Intelligence Agency** (CIA) to gather information overseas.

Another Red scare. The Cold War also aroused fears of communism at home. Although Truman opposed communism abroad, some Republicans accused him of allowing Communists in the American government. Responding to such charges, Truman set up the Loyalty Review Board in 1947 to investigate all federal employees. By the end of 1951, more than 20,000 federal workers had been investigated, some 2,000 had resigned, and more than 300 had been fired as "security risks." In most cases the government did not allow dismissed employees to respond to the charges against them.

Meanwhile, Congress cracked down on the Communist party. Leading the anti-Communist crusade in Congress was the

House Committee on Un-American Activities (HUAC), originally established in 1938 to investigate fascist groups in the United States. HUAC held a series of hearings to question the political allegiances of members of peace organizations, liberal political groups, and labor unions. In 1947, responding to charges that Hollywood was riddled with Communists, HUAC investigated people in the movie industry. A group of film directors and writers, known as the **Hollywood Ten**, refused to answer HUAC's questions and went to jail. They were blacklisted—denied work in the film industry—and saw their careers destroyed.

The hysteria generated by HUAC spread quickly. One group that spoke out against HUAC, the Women's International League for Peace and Freedom, argued in 1949 that the hearings violated democratic rights:

❝ Fully recognizing the danger of fascist and communist totalitarianism, the League believes that such forces can be best opposed by open discussion and by the strengthening of our own democratic procedures, rather than by attempts at direct control. ❞

Because of the league's support for progressive causes, the FBI investigated the national organization and several of its local chapters. The investigation scared many potential members away.

▲ **A delegation of Hollywood personalities attended a meeting of HUAC on October 27, 1947. Humphrey Bogart, Lauren Bacall, and Sterling Hayden were among those present.**

RETEACH For each subsection in the section, have students write a sentence that summarizes the main idea. Select students to read their statements aloud. Have the class choose the best summary sentence for each subsection.

Closure

Ask a volunteer to explain George Kennan's quote on p. 790. Call on students to provide examples of how the U.S. containment policy was implemented around the world, examples of how the Soviet Union responded to containment, and examples of how Americans at home reacted to the Soviet response.

Extension

ANALYZE Have students research and report on a Soviet satellite nation of their choice, analyzing its political, economic, and/or geographical importance to the Soviet Union.

COMPARE Have students create a chart comparing the U.S. government's response to the Red Scare during the Cold War with its response to the Red Scare following World War I.

HUAC investigations had a similar effect on labor unions and many political groups.

The search for spies. HUAC also investigated individuals accused of spying for the Soviets. In 1948 Whittaker Chambers, who had been a member of the Communist party, accused Alger Hiss of being a Communist spy. Chambers told HUAC that Hiss, a New Deal lawyer who had joined the State Department in 1936, had given him secret State Department documents to pass on to the Soviets.

Hiss denied the charges, but persistent questioning by HUAC member Richard Nixon, a young Republican congressman from California, revealed apparent inconsistencies in Hiss's testimony. In 1950 Hiss was convicted of perjury (lying under oath) and sentenced to five years in prison.

Another notorious spy case also helped fuel domestic fears of communism. In 1951 a U.S. court convicted two Americans, Julius and Ethel Rosenberg, of giving the Soviets atomic-energy secrets during World War II. Defenders of the Rosenbergs claimed that the two were innocent victims of anti-Communist hysteria. Despite worldwide protests on their behalf, however, the Rosenbergs were executed in June 1953. Historians have found evidence for the guilty verdict against Julius Rosenberg but agree that the death sentences were extreme reactions in the nervous Cold War climate.

Other anti-Communist measures included the **Internal Security Act**, passed in 1950. The act

▲ Escorted by a U.S. marshal (left), Julius and Ethel Rosenberg are shown on March 8, 1951, awaiting the result of their trial on charges of conspiracy to commit espionage.

required party members and organizations to register with the federal government. It also imposed strict controls on immigrants suspected of being Communist sympathizers. The anti-Communist hysteria of these years shattered many lives and careers. Today many historians look back on this period as one of the bleakest in American history.

■■ **Cold War anti-communism led to efforts to expose alleged Communists in the United States, creating a climate of fear and suspicion.**

SECTION REVIEW ANSWERS

IDENTIFY
For significance, see the following pages:
Cold War (p. 789)
satellite nations (p. 789)
George Kennan (p. 790)
containment (p. 790)
Baruch Plan (p. 790)
Atomic Energy Act (p. 791)
Truman Doctrine (p. 791)
George C. Marshall (p. 791)
Marshall Plan (p. 792)
Berlin airlift (p. 792)
NATO (p. 793)
Warsaw Pact (p. 794)
NSC (p. 794)
CIA (p. 794)
HUAC (p. 794)
Hollywood Ten (p. 794)
Internal Security Act (p. 795)

LOCATE
For locations, see the map on p. 793.

1. *U.S.–Soviet global competition, conflicting economic, political, and philosophical systems, mutual distrust*
2. *to contain communism by easing economic hardship in Europe*
3. *suspicion about and investigation of many individuals and groups*
4. *Letters might mention fears of communism and restrictions on civil liberties.*
5. *by applying counterforce at points of Soviet pressure through Truman Doctrine, Marshall Plan, Berlin airlift, and NATO*

SECTION 3 REVIEW

IDENTIFY and explain the significance of the following: Cold War, satellite nations, George Kennan, containment, Baruch Plan, Atomic Energy Act, Truman Doctrine, George C. Marshall, Marshall Plan, Berlin airlift, NATO, Warsaw Pact, National Security Council, Central Intelligence Agency, House Committee on Un-American Activities, Hollywood Ten, Internal Security Act.

LOCATE and explain the importance of the following: Greece, Turkey, Dardanelles, Federal Republic of Germany (West Germany), German Democratic Republic (East Germany).

1. **MAIN IDEA** What factors gave rise to the Cold War?
2. **MAIN IDEA** What was the purpose of the Marshall Plan?
3. **ASSESSING CONSEQUENCES** What impact did the Cold War have on U.S. society?
4. **WRITING TO EXPRESS A VIEWPOINT** Imagine you are a court reporter at either the Alger Hiss trial or the trial of Ethel and Julius Rosenberg. Write a letter to a friend abroad explaining the significance of one of the trials.
5. **SYNTHESIZING** How did the U.S. government put George Kennan's containment doctrine into practice?

Following is a list of the significant people, places, and terms in this section. You may wish to use this list as a section preview.

People
- David Ben-Gurion
- Ralph Bunche
- Chiang Kai-shek
- Mao Zedong
- Kim Il Sung
- Syngman Rhee
- Dean Acheson
- Douglas MacArthur

Places
- Palestine
- Israel
- Gaza Strip
- West Bank
- Taiwan
- People's Republic of China
- 38th parallel
- Pusan
- Seoul
- Yalu River

Terms
- Zionism
- Long March

FOCUS OBJECTIVES

- Analyze why Israel and Arab nations went to war.
- Explain how Communists came to power in China.
- Examine what led to the division of Korea.
- Identify who fought in the Korean War.

BUILDING VOCABULARY

The term *Zionism* is derived from the word *Zion*, a hill in Jerusalem on which Solomon's temple stood.

HISTORICAL SIDELIGHTS

A Noble Name
David Ben-Gurion was born David Gruen. He later adopted the ancient Hebrew name Ben-Gurion.

CORE RESOURCES
- **Social Studies Skills Worksheet 27**
- **Section 4 Daily Quiz**

AV RESOURCES
- *The American Nation Videodisc:*
MacArthur in Korea

796

Section 4

THE COLD WAR TURNS HOT

FOCUS
- **Why did Israel and Arab nations go to war?**
- **How did Communists come to power in China?**
- **What led to the division of Korea?**
- **Who fought in the Korean War?**

World War II had weakened the grip of European nations on their colonies and spheres of influence in the Middle East and Asia. After the war these former colonies struggled to set up their own governments. The United States became involved in the conflict between Israel and several Arab nations in the Middle East. Concerns over the spread of communism led the United States to support the Nationalists in their struggle against the Communists in China. By 1950 Cold War rivalries drew the United States into outright war in Korea.

U.S. soldiers in Korea, 1952

MIDDLE EAST TENSIONS

Soon after World War II, tensions flared in Palestine, a region at the eastern end of the Mediterranean claimed by both Jews and Arabs. Since World War I, Great Britain had ruled Palestine under a League of Nations mandate. Unable to resolve conflicting claims over the territory, Britain in 1947 turned the problem over to the United Nations. The UN came up with a plan to divide Palestine into two states—one for Jews, the other for Arabs—but Arabs rejected the proposal.

The proposal was a victory for **Zionism**, the movement calling for a Jewish homeland in Palestine. Zionist leader David Ben-Gurion

▲ **David Ben-Gurion**

(ben-goohr-YAWN), born in Plonsk, Russia, in 1886, had fought for just this outcome since the early 1900s. Idealistic and determined, Ben-Gurion sailed to Palestine in 1906. Expelled in 1915 for Zionist activities, he went to the United States to raise money and recruit volunteers among the American Jewish community.

During World War II, Ben-Gurion supported the Allied struggle against Hitler but continued to organize Jewish resistance in Palestine. After the war, Ben-Gurion helped develop land, resettle Jewish refugees, and organize covert activities against British and Arab rule.

With the UN's decision to divide Palestine, Great Britain agreed to give up its control of the region. On May 14, 1948, the last of

Teaching the Section

WAR IN THE MIDDLE EAST

Pair students to chronicle events that aroused or increased tensions between Jews and Arabs in the Middle East. Select pairs to list their events on the chalkboard. Then ask volunteers to indicate which events on the chalkboard lists they think were the most important factors in bringing war to the Middle East in 1948. Have the class discuss and evaluate the volunteers' selections.

Ask students to describe the status of this area of the world today.

Israel in June 1948

Territory Israel gained by January 1949

Territory Israel held after 1949 armistice

Boundary of British Mandate of Palestine, 1922–1948

★ Capital city

UN Partition

Israeli territory

Arab territory

Jerusalem (International Zone)

PALESTINE

EGYPT

1947

Israel, 1949

SUCCESS STORY The memory of the Holocaust and the struggle to create a Jewish state unified the Israelis in a common cause.

? PLACE Which river divides the West Bank from Jordan?

counted on an impressive arsenal bought in part with the millions of dollars that poured in from the American Jewish community.

In 1948 war broke out between Israel and Arab nations over the disputed territory of Palestine.

In an effort to end the war, the UN sent a mediator, Count Folke Bernadotte of Sweden, to the Middle East. Bernadotte negotiated a shaky cease-fire, but within months he was assassinated by Israeli extremists. In 1949 a second UN mediator, the American diplomat Ralph Bunche, persuaded both sides to accept an armistice. For his efforts Bunche won the Nobel Peace Prize in 1950—

▲ **Ralph Bunche**

the first African American to receive that honor.

The 1949 agreement gave Israel more territory than the earlier UN partition plan had, but it divided Jerusalem into Arab and Israeli zones. The plan gave Egypt control of the Gaza Strip, while Jordan took over the West Bank of the Jordan River. The Arab countries, however, still refused to recognize the state of Israel. Also left unresolved was the fate of the Arabs remaining in Israel and the hundreds of thousands of Arabs who had fled or had been driven out of Israel.

Before the territorial agreements were finalized, Israel held its first parliamentary elections in January 1949. Ben-Gurion became prime minister, a post he held almost continuously until 1963. At his death in 1973, Ben-Gurion was hailed as the chief architect of the state of Israel.

COMMUNIST VICTORY IN CHINA

While the conflict between Arabs and Israelis escalated after World War II, tensions also came to a head in China. The seeds of the conflict were planted in the 1920s. Chiang Kai-shek's Kuomintang (KMT), or Nationalist party, battled the

the British forces withdrew. Ben-Gurion and other Jewish leaders promptly proclaimed the new state of Israel. Both Truman and Stalin immediately recognized the new nation.

The Arab states, however, did not recognize Israel, since they wanted Palestine to remain an Arab country. Armies from the Arab states of Egypt, Lebanon, Jordan (called Transjordan until 1949), Syria, and Iraq attacked Israel. Although vastly outnumbered in the Arab-Israeli war, Israeli forces under Ben-Gurion's overall command captured and held much of Palestine. Israeli soldiers

Teaching the Section

COMMUNISM IN CHINA

Organize the class into two groups. Direct students from one group to each write a journal entry from the viewpoint of Chiang Kaishek explaining why Chinese Communists won control of China. Have students in the remaining group write their journal entries from the viewpoint of Mao Zedong. Call on volunteers from each group to read their entries to the class.

Students may wish to include their journal entries in their portfolios.

THE ARAB RESPONSE

Musa Alami, an Arab lawyer and diplomat from Palestine, promoted Palestinian nationalism and unity among the Arab states. After the Arab-Israeli war, Alami published a book, *The Lesson of Palestine* (1949), which examined the causes of the war:

THROUGH OTHERS' EYES

❝*T*he British were the prime causers of the disaster. . . . They were assisted by the Americans and the Russians. . . . We found ourselves face to face with the Jews, and entered into battle with them to decide the future; and in spite of what the British, the Americans, and the Russians had done, it was still within our power to win the fight.

The Arabs failed to defend Palestine. . . . We worked on a local basis, without unity, without totality, without a general command, our defense disjointed and our affairs disordered, every town fighting on its own and only those in areas adjacent to the Jews entering the battle at all. . . . The natural result of all this was disaster and the loss of Palestine. ❞

Chinese Communists. KMT forces held most of northern China, and Communist soldiers controlled parts of southern and central China. But in 1931, when Japan invaded Manchuria, the KMT and the Communists declared a truce and joined forces against the Japanese.

In 1934, however, Chiang broke the truce when he launched what he hoped would be the final battles against the Communist-controlled areas of the south. The KMT forces were successful. From 1934 to 1935 some 100,000 Communists marched nearly 6,000 miles to northern China. Known as the **Long March**, this exodus

helped cement Mao Zedong's leadership of the Chinese Communist party and led to the establishment of a strong base in the north.

Chiang's attacks on the Communists kept him from devoting full attention to stopping further Japanese aggression. By the early 1930s the Japanese controlled Manchuria, Inner Mongolia, and parts of northern China. To prevent the loss of more Chinese territory to the Japanese, a group of KMT soldiers kidnapped Chiang in 1936 and released him only after he agreed to join forces with the Communists against the Japanese. This cooperation continued throughout World War II.

At war's end, however, the conflict resumed. During World War II the Communists had prevented the Japanese from controlling all of northwest China. This effective resistance, plus the reforms that Mao instituted to give land to poor peasants, won more support for the Communists and recruits for their army.

The United States, which had long supported Chiang, did not want to see China become a Communist country. During and after World War II the United States sent economic and military aid, including troops, to China to unite the country under the KMT. Truman sent George Marshall to China in 1946 to arrange a truce, but neither side would compromise.

Although Chiang had helped modernize China by building railroads, roads, and factories, his government was becoming increasingly unpopular. The fight against the Japanese had wrecked the Chinese economy, and the Chinese people faced soaring inflation. Chiang seemed unresponsive to these economic problems. In addition, Chiang made no efforts at land reform to help the desperately poor peasants. Moreover, he presided over an increasingly corrupt and authoritarian government that banned all other political parties. As opposition to Chiang mounted, Mao's forces gained control of most of the country by 1949.

Realizing his defeat, Chiang and his army retreated to the island of Taiwan, off the coast of southeast China. The Chinese Communists established the People's Republic of China. Dismayed by the Communist victory, the United

▲ **Nationalist forces kidnapped Chiang Kai-shek in 1936. This photograph of Chiang with his wife was taken after his release.**

THE COLD WAR AND KOREA

Organize the class into small groups. Tell each group to create a time line or graphic organizer that illustrates how developments in Korea after World War II were part of the overall Cold War struggle between the Soviet Union and the U.S. over the spread and containment of communism. Have students from each group present and interpret its creation to the class. Then ask volunteers to summarize why Korea was divided.

THE KOREAN WAR

Direct students to create a flowchart that shows the course of the Korean War and that indicates at what points various fighting forces entered the war. Call on volunteers to present their flowcharts. Students may wish to include their flowcharts in their portfolios.

▶

States continued to recognize the Nationalists as China's legal government. The Chinese seat on the UN Security Council, granted to Chiang's Taiwan government after World War II, remained in Nationalist hands until 1971.

■■ **In 1949, after a long struggle with Nationalist forces, Chinese Communists under Mao Zedong won control of China.**

*T*HE KOREAN WAR

Meanwhile, political tensions rose in Korea, a peninsula jutting southward from the northeast corner of China. The Japanese had ruled Korea from 1910 to 1945 but had been driven out by Soviet and American troops at the end of World War II. In 1945 the Allies divided Korea into two parts—North Korea and South Korea—with the border between the two countries set at the **38th parallel**. Soviet forces occupied the North, and American troops held the South.

This division was meant to be temporary, but Cold War tensions cemented it. In 1948 North Korea and South Korea set up separate governments, each claiming to rule the entire country. Communist North Korea, led by Kim Il Sung, became known as the People's Republic of Korea. Kim's government, a Communist dictatorship, redistributed land to poor peasants and nationalized most industries. Although Kim's government limited freedom of speech, it expanded education and established formal equality for women. South Korea, under President Syngman Rhee (SING-muhn REE), called itself the Republic of Korea. The southern republic faced economic and political instability after World War II.

Anxious that South Korea not fall to the Communists as China had, the United States built up the South Korean army as a counterbalance to the Soviet-trained northern forces. By 1949 both the United States and the Soviet Union had pulled their troops out of Korea. The pullout left only the two Korean armies tensely facing each other across the 38th parallel.

■■ **After World War II, Korea was divided into Soviet and American occupation zones. In 1948 North Korea and South Korea established separate governments.**

The Korean War

Legend:
- 0 50 100 Miles
- 0 50 100 Kilometers
- Conic Projection
- → UN forces
- → Communist forces

Map labels: CHINA, MANCHURIA, U.S.S.R., Chongjin, Chosan, Yalu River, NORTH KOREA, Hungnam, Farthest UN advance, Oct.–Nov. 1950, SEA OF JAPAN, Armistice line, July 1953, Pyongyang, Kaesong, Panmunjom, Boundary set by Allies after World War II, YELLOW SEA, Inchon, Seoul, UN landings, Sept. 1950, SOUTH KOREA, Farthest Chinese/North Korean advance, Jan. 1951, Taegu, Pusan, Farthest North Korean advance, Sept. 1950, Korea Strait. Latitude lines: 42° N, 40° N, 38° N, 36° N, 34° N. Longitude lines: 124° E, 126° E, 128° E, 130° E.

Inset: Robinson Projection world map with ARCTIC OCEAN, EUROPE, ASIA, NORTH AMERICA, ATLANTIC OCEAN, AFRICA, PACIFIC OCEAN, Equator, SOUTH AMERICA, INDIAN OCEAN, AUSTRALIA, ANTARCTICA.

CHINESE INTERVENTION Fearing UN forces would cross the Yalu River into Manchuria, the Chinese entered the war and invaded Korea.

? MOVEMENT How far north of the 38th parallel did the UN forces advance?

Practice

GUIDED PRACTICE

Create on the chalkboard a three-column chart with the headings *Middle East, China, Korea*. Call on students to list ways in which the U.S. or the Soviet Union, or both, affected the conflicts that developed in each area.

INDEPENDENT PRACTICE

Have students refer to the Guided Practice chart and write a journal entry from the viewpoint of an Arab, Israeli, Chinese, or Korean explaining how their country has been affected by the Cold War.

Review and Assessment

REVIEW Write each of the main headings in the section in headline form on the chalkboard. Have students write brief details that might appear in a newspaper article under the headline. Then assign the Section 4 Review on p. 801.

ASSESS Assign the **Section 4 Daily Quiz** in *Core Resources.*

HISTORICAL SIDELIGHTS

Woman War Correspondent

The American journalist Marguerite Higgins won a Pulitzer Prize in 1951 for her coverage of the Korean War. In her book, *War in Korea: The Report of a Woman Combat Correspondent* (1951), Higgins explained why the Chinese waited so long to enter the war: "The Chinese stayed out of the war just as long as there was any hope that the North Koreans could lick us on their own. That hope came very close to reality until the Inchon landing suddenly changed the picture."

PRIMARY SOURCE

Description of Change: excerpted and bracketed
Rationale: excerpted to focus on main idea; bracketed to clarify meaning

THE AMERICAN NATION VIDEODISC PROGRAM

MacArthur in Korea

```
2A    46063    1:15
```

Chart Caption Answer
passed Marshall Plan, began Berlin airlift, joined NATO, intervened in Korea

---

The war begins. After repeated clashes between North Korean and South Korean troops, the North Korean army invaded South Korea on June 25, 1950. A perceived shift in American policy may have encouraged the invasion. Earlier that year Secretary of State Dean Acheson had given a speech defining America's "defensive perimeter" against the spread of communism in Asia. This perimeter, an imaginary line stretching from Alaska to the Philippines, did not include Korea. Thus it appeared that the United States would not defend South Korea against invasion.

In an emergency session the UN Security Council called for an immediate cease-fire. (At the time the Soviets were boycotting the Security Council over its refusal to admit Communist China, so their delegate was not on hand to veto the UN resolution.) Two days later, on June 27, President Truman pledged U.S. support for South Korea. That same day, the Security Council adopted a U.S.–sponsored resolution branding North Korea an "aggressor" and calling on UN members to come to South Korea's defense. Truman later explained: "I felt certain that if South Korea was allowed to fall, Communist leaders

MAJOR EVENTS OF THE COLD WAR	
Year	**Event**
1945	Korea divided into two zones, one occupied by United States and the other by Soviet Union.
1948	U.S. Congress approves Marshall Plan to provide some $12 billion in aid to Western Europe over next four years.
	Soviet Union blocks routes between Berlin and West Germany. Western powers meet blockade with Berlin airlift.
	North Korea and South Korea establish separate governments.
	United States and Soviet Union recognize Israel.
1949	NATO formed.
	Chinese Communists win control of China.
1950	Korean War begins when North Korea invades South Korea.
	China enters Korean War.
1955	Warsaw Pact signed.

Sources: *Encyclopedia of American History; Encyclopedia of World History*

STRUGGLE FOR SUPREMACY The United States and the Soviet Union fought to establish political supremacy across the globe through both diplomatic and military means.

? ANALYZING How did the United States attempt to counteract the influence of the Soviet Union?

---

would be emboldened to override nations closer to our own shores."

Bitter fighting. Acting under the UN resolution, Truman ordered U.S. air and ground forces into action under the command of General Douglas MacArthur. Truman also ordered the U.S. Seventh Fleet to protect Taiwan. Although 15 other UN members contributed assistance, the United States and South Korea played the major role in resisting North Korea's aggression.

At first, however, the onslaught of North Korean forces and their Soviet-made tanks was overwhelming. Outgunned and outmanned, the U.S. and South Korean troops fell back. One soldier, Sergeant Raymond Remp, recalled his first encounter with the North Korean army:

66 Someone fired a green flare, and [the enemy] saw us. . . . They were right on top of us in the hills, firing down on us. . . .
Some colonel—don't know who—said, "Get out the best way you can." . . .
All day and night we ran like antelopes. We didn't know our officers. They didn't know us. We lost everything we had. 99

By August the North Koreans had overrun nearly all of South Korea. The U.S. and South Korean forces were backed into a small area around Pusan, in southeast Korea (see map on page 799).

On September 15, 1950, however, MacArthur launched a powerful counterattack. Coming ashore at Inchon, near the 38th parallel, MacArthur's forces swept inland, recapturing Seoul (SOHL), the capital of South Korea. At the same time, a strong UN army, now well equipped and supported from the air, attacked from the south. Caught in a huge trap, North Koreans surrendered by the thousands. Others fled north across the 38th parallel, with UN forces in hot pursuit. By late October the UN army had reached the Yalu River, the boundary between North Korea and China.

But again the tide turned. Late in November, China entered the war on North Korea's side, sending some 300,000 troops across the Yalu. Chinese foreign minister Zhou Enlai (JOH ENLY) explained why China had intervened:

66 The U.S. imperialists have adopted a hostile attitude towards us . . . while paying

RETEACH Write each person's name from Identify in the Section 4 Review on a separate slip of paper. Have each student select one of the slips of paper and explain orally that person's role in the events presented in the section.

Closure

Have volunteers summarize why the U.S. became involved in the conflicts in the late 1940s between the Israelis and Arabs in the Middle East, between the Nationalists and Communists in China, and between North and South Korea in the early 1950s. Then ask students if they think the U.S. should have the responsibility for protecting nations from attack by other nations.

Extension

ANALYZE Have students conduct further research into the conflict between Truman and MacArthur over escalating the war in Korea. Have students analyze each person's position and write an essay in which they defend the actions of each.

RESEARCH Have students research and report on the Long March. Encourage them to use maps or other graphics.

lip service to non-aggression and non-intervention. From the information we got, they wanted to calm China first and after occupying North Korea, they will come to attack China. **99**

Outnumbered and with their lines dangerously extended, the UN forces fell back. After desperate fighting and heavy losses in the bitter winter cold, MacArthur's troops finally established a stable defensive line near the 38th parallel.

■■ **During the Korean War, UN forces—mainly U.S. and South Korean soldiers—fought North Korean and Chinese troops.**

The great debate. With China now involved, MacArthur called for a major expansion of the war. He proposed to blockade China's coast, bomb the Chinese mainland, and "unleash" Chiang's Nationalist forces to invade mainland China. This plan stirred fierce public debate. Supporters said it would bring victory in Korea and overthrow the Chinese Communists. Opponents argued that an attack on China could bring the Soviet Union into the conflict and trigger World War III.

President Truman strongly opposed MacArthur's plan because he did not want the war in Korea to lead to another world war. MacArthur, however, refused to accept the Korean War as a limited conflict. Publicly criticizing the president, MacArthur appealed to

▲ **In September 1950, U.S. soldiers used hand grenades to remove the remaining North Korean forces from Seoul.**

Republican leaders in Congress. He also delivered an ultimatum to the enemy—demanding unconditional surrender—thereby upsetting Truman's plans for peace negotiations. As commander in chief of the military, Truman removed MacArthur from his post in April 1951. General Matthew Ridgway replaced MacArthur as commander of the UN forces.

By the summer of 1951, the war had settled into a stalemate. Bitter fighting continued, but little territory changed hands. Combat in Korea's mountainous terrain became intensely frustrating as the American death toll mounted. Under these circumstances American public opinion gradually turned against the war. The Korean conflict would soon become a major issue in the 1952 presidential election.

PRIMARY SOURCE
Description of Change: excerpted
Rationale: excerpted to focus on main idea

SECTION REVIEW ANSWERS

IDENTIFY
For significance, see the following pages:
Zionism (p. 796)
David Ben-Gurion (p. 796)
Ralph Bunche (p. 797)
Chiang Kai-shek (p. 797)
Long March (p. 798)
Mao Zedong (p. 798)
Kim Il Sung (p. 799)
Syngman Rhee (p. 799)
Dean Acheson (p. 800)
Douglas MacArthur (p. 800)

LOCATE
For locations, see the maps on pp. 797, 799 and 1012–1013.

1. *because of conflict over Palestine*
2. *Korea divided into Soviet and American zones*
3. *UN forces, made up mainly of U.S. and South Korean soldiers, fought North Koreans and Chinese*
4. *Essays should mention the effects of World War II, U.S. involvement, Chiang's policies, Mao's reforms, and the war between the Communists and Nationalists.*
5. *Students might mention the possibility of overthrowing Communists in Korea and China or the chance that war would have involved more countries.*

■■   **S E C T I O N   4   R E V I E W**

IDENTIFY and explain the significance of the following: Zionism, David Ben-Gurion, Ralph Bunche, Chiang Kai-shek, Long March, Mao Zedong, Kim Il Sung, Syngman Rhee, Dean Acheson, Douglas MacArthur.

LOCATE and explain the importance of the following: Palestine, Israel, Gaza Strip, West Bank, Taiwan, People's Republic of China, 38th parallel, Pusan, Seoul, Yalu River.

1. **MAIN IDEA** Why did war break out between Israel and Arab states in 1948?

2. **MAIN IDEA** How did the end of World War II affect Korea?

3. **MAIN IDEA** What forces fought in the Korean War?

4. **WRITING TO EXPLAIN** Write an essay explaining how the Communists gained control of China in 1949.

5. **HYPOTHESIZING** How do you think the Korean War would have proceeded if MacArthur had been allowed to expand the war into China?

CHAPTER 27
Review

🎖 DEVELOPING THEMES

Return to the Themes section on p. 778. Have students discuss these again and compare their original responses with those given now. (See p. 777B for suggested answers.)

Chapter Review Answers

WRITING A SUMMARY
See Essential Points in each section for main ideas.

REVIEWING CHRONOLOGY
5, 1, 3, 2, 4
Identifying Cause and Effect
Answers will vary but should make the cause and effect of events clear.

IDENTIFYING PEOPLE AND IDEAS

1. *postwar organization formed to promote international cooperation*
2. *first UN secretary-general*
3. *1944 measure that helped veterans make transition to civilian life*
4. *African American lawyer appointed to Committee on Civil Rights in 1946*
5. *States' Rights party formed by southern Democrats to oppose Truman on civil rights*
6. *Eastern European countries under Soviet control after WW II*
7. *State Department official who proposed containment doctrine*
8. *1946 act that set up civilian control over atomic energy research*
9. *ardent Zionist and first prime minister of Israel*
10. *leader of Communist party in China*

UNDERSTANDING MAIN IDEAS

1. *occupied Germany and Japan and set up new governments; held war crimes trials; helped found UN*
2. *Employment and food exports remained high as plants produced goods to meet consumer spending spree; soaring prices caused inflation.*
3. *urged Truman to ban discrimination in military and in federal hiring, served on Committee on Civil Rights, threatened civil disobedience; white southern Democrats formed new party*
4. *inflation, high taxes, and labor unrest; ran an energetic campaign attacking Republican conservatives, "do-nothing" Congress, and Progressives while keeping support of workers and ethnic voters*
5. *to protect its borders from feared U.S. invasion*

CHAPTER 27 *Review*

Potsdam Conference held. Nuremberg trials begin. UN charter drafted. Korea divided into two zones.	Employment Act and Atomic Energy Act passed. Coal miners go on strike. Committee on Civil Rights appointed. Baruch Plan proposed.	Japan adopts new constitution. Taft-Hartley Act passed. Truman Doctrine proposed. NSC and CIA established. HUAC investigates movie industry.
1945	**1946**	**1947**

WRITING A SUMMARY
Using the essential points of the chapter as a guide, write a summary of the chapter.

REVIEWING CHRONOLOGY
Number your paper 1 to 5. Study the time line above, and list the following events in the order in which they happened by writing the first next to 1, the second next to 2, and so on. Then complete the activity below.
1. Committee on Civil Rights appointed.
2. Israel declares its independence.
3. Truman Doctrine proposed.
4. North Korea invades South Korea.
5. UN charter drafted.

Identifying Cause and Effect Select two events on the time line, and in a paragraph, explain the cause-and-effect relationship between them.

IDENTIFYING PEOPLE AND IDEAS
Explain the historical significance of each of the following people or terms.

1. United Nations
2. Trygve Lie
3. GI Bill of Rights
4. Sadie Alexander
5. Dixiecrats
6. satellite nations
7. George Kennan
8. Atomic Energy Act
9. David Ben-Gurion
10. Mao Zedong

UNDERSTANDING MAIN IDEAS
1. How did the United States work with other Allies to restore peace after World War II?
2. Why did postwar fears of a depression never materialize? What effect did the lifting of wartime price controls have on the economy?
3. How did African Americans work for civil rights in the late 1940s? What effect did these actions have on the 1948 election?
4. What factors caused public support for President Truman to plunge by 1948? How did he win the 1948 election?
5. Why did China enter the Korean War on the side of North Korea?

🎖 REVIEWING THEMES
1. **Global Relations** What international and domestic tensions resulted from the conflict between the United States and the Soviet Union?
2. **Technology and Society** How did the development of atomic energy affect the United States?
3. **Democratic Values** How did the U.S. government's response to Cold War pressures lead to limitations on civil liberties?

THINKING CRITICALLY
1. **Problem Solving** What steps did the U.S. government take after World War II to make the transition from war to peace?
2. **Analyzing** How did the Taft-Hartley Act attempt to place restrictions on the tactics unions could use to win improvements?
3. **Synthesizing** What were the main causes of the Cold War? How did the Cold War get played out in Korea?

STRATEGY FOR SUCCESS
Review the Strategies for Success on Recognizing Propaganda on page 774. Then read the excerpt below, which comes from an address by J. Edgar Hoover warning of the dangers of communism. What clues identify this passage as propaganda?

> 66 The Communist Party of the United States . . . is far better organized than were the Nazis. . . . They [the Communists] are seeking to weaken America just as they did . . . when they were aligned with the Nazis. Their goal is the overthrow of our government. 99

WRITING ABOUT HISTORY
Writing to Explain Imagine you are an American diplomat in China during 1946. Write a memorandum to President Truman, explaining the reasons for the mounting opposition to Chiang Kai-shek after World War II.

REVIEWING THEMES

1. *international*—Cold War, arms race, military confrontations or conflicts in Berlin and Middle East and Asia; *domestic*—spread of anti-Communist hysteria
2. created struggle between those who argued that technology would strengthen U.S. defenses and those who feared that spread of nuclear weapons might lead to war
3. Federal employees lost their jobs without being allowed to respond to charges against them. Other government investigations also infringed on free speech and privacy rights in the hunt for suspected Communists.

THINKING CRITICALLY

1. acted to help veterans reenter civilian life, promoted full employment and production, controlled labor unrest, and promoted civil rights
2. allowed courts to end strikes; outlawed closed-shop agreements; restricted unions' political contributions
3. competition between U.S. and U.S.S.R., competing economic, political, and philosophical models, mutual distrust; Communist North Korea, U.S.S.R., and China battled South Korea, U.S., and UN forces

---

1948 — Racial discrimination banned in military and in federal hiring. Marshall Plan passed. Berlin airlift begins. Israel declares its independence. Dixiecrats formed. Truman elected president.

1949 — NATO established. Middle East agreements reached. Communists gain control of China.

1950 — Alger Hiss convicted of perjury. Internal Security Act passed. North Korea invades South Korea.

1951 — Julius and Ethel Rosenberg convicted.

1952 — U.S. occupation of Japan ends.

USING PRIMARY SOURCES

Attempts to find alleged Communists spread to every level of government. In 1946 President Truman nominated David Lilienthal to head the U.S. Atomic Energy Commission. During Lilienthal's confirmation hearings, Senator Kenneth D. McKellar of Tennessee accused the nominee of being a Communist sympathizer. In Lilienthal's eloquent reply below, how did he defend himself against the charge?

> 66 *I believe—and I conceive the Constitution of the United States to rest . . . upon the fundamental proposition of the integrity of the individual. . . .*
>
> *Any form of government, therefore, and any other institutions which . . . exalt the state or any other institutions above the importance of men, which place arbitrary power over men as a fundamental tenet [belief] of government are contrary to that conception, and, therefore, I am deeply opposed to them.*
>
> *The communistic . . . form of government falls within this category. . . . The fundamental tenet of communism is that the state is an end in itself, and that therefore the powers which the state exercises over the individual are without any ethical standard to limit them.*
>
> *That I deeply disbelieve. . . .*
>
> *I deeply believe in the capacity of democracy to surmount any trials that may lie ahead, provided only that we practice it in our daily lives.*
>
> *And among the things we must practice is this: that while we seek fervently to ferret out the subversive and anti-democratic forces in the country, we do not at the same time, by hysteria . . . and other unfortunate tactics, besmirch [soil] the very cause that we believe in.* 99

LINKING HISTORY AND GEOGRAPHY

Refer to the map on page 797. What effect did the 1949 armistice have on both Israeli and Arab territorial boundaries?

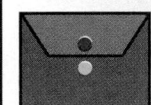

BUILDING YOUR PORTFOLIO

Complete the following projects independently or cooperatively.

1. **THE COLD WAR** Imagine that you are a U.S. delegate to the UN conference in San Francisco in 1945. Write a memorandum to the U.S. Senate, detailing world conditions in 1945 that call for the formation of an association of world nations and urging U.S. participation in such an association.

2. **THE GOVERNMENT AND THE ECONOMY** Imagine you are a member of the Department of Labor. Prepare a chart that shows how the U.S. government is assisting returning soldiers through programs designed to help them find civilian jobs, attain college educations, or own their own homes.

3. **CIVIL RIGHTS** Imagine you are a reporter covering the Committee on Civil Rights. Research and prepare a radio piece on why the committee was formed, who its members are, and what it has documented in its official report, "To Secure These Rights."

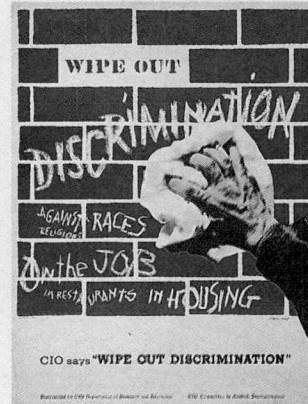

CIO says "WIPE OUT DISCRIMINATION"

DECADE OF CONTRASTS

1950–1960

Chapter Overview

In 1952 Republican Dwight D. Eisenhower was elected president, breaking the Democrats' 20-year hold on the White House. During Eisenhower's presidency Americans continued to focus on the Cold War. As the 1950s drew to a close, however, it seemed possible that U.S.–Soviet relations might improve.

On the domestic front the 1950s were years of great prosperity. Millions of middle-class Americans, living in comfortable suburbs, enjoyed a rising standard of living. But not all shared in this prosperity. Many non-whites continued to endure prejudice and poverty. By the end of the 1950s, however, some African Americans had begun to push for equality of opportunity.

THE AMERICAN NATION VIDEODISC PROGRAM
A variety of still images, short videos, and activities are available for you to use as you teach this chapter. See Correlation to *The American Nation* Videodisc Program for barcode correlations and suggestions for using the program.

Chapter Planning Guide

CHAPTER 28	CORE RESOURCE BOOKLETS	AUDIOVISUAL AV RESOURCES	PROGRAM RESOURCES
INTRODUCTION pp. 804–805	■ Literature Worksheet 28 ■ Building Your Portfolio Worksheet 8		■ *Eyewitnesses and Others,* Volume 2: Reading 62
TEACHING THE CHAPTER pp. 806–827	■ Graphic Organizer 28 ■ Social Studies Skills Worksheet 28 ■ Geography Worksheet 28 ■ Outline Maps 1, 2, 9, 16, 17, 18, 20	■ *The American Nation* Videodisc: McCarthy and McCarthyism; Bomb Shelters; The Growth of Suburbia; The Interstate Highway System; The Salk Polio Vaccine ■ Linking Geography and History Transparencies and Worksheets 11B,17A, 20, 21 ■ Everyday Life in America Transparency and Worksheet 28 ■ *American Civics Citizenship Skills* Videocassette or Videodisc	■ Art in American History Transparencies and Worksheets 36, 37 ■ *Eyewitnesses and Others,* Volume 2: Readings 59, 60, 61
REVIEW AND ASSESSMENT pp. 828–829	■ Chapter 28 Daily Quizzes ■ Review Worksheet 28 ■ Chapter 28 Tests ■ Alternative Assessment Forms		■ Test Generator

Additional Resources

BOOKS FOR TEACHERS

Halberstam, David. *The Fifties.* Random House, 1993. An exhaustive, highly readable review of the decade.

Inglis, Fred. *The Cruel Peace.* Basic Books, 1993. Study of the myths and realities of the Cold War.

BOOKS FOR STUDENTS

Oakley, J. Ronald. *God's Country: America in the Fifties.* Barricade Books, 1990. Entertaining and informative look at the decade.

*Tames, Richard. *The 1950s: Picture History of the 20th Century.* Watts, 1990. Review of the major issues and events of the decade.

* for students reading below grade level

MULTIMEDIA MATERIALS

The Age of Anxiety. Video, 24 min. AIMS Media. Reviews the Eisenhower years.

Postwar Hopes, Cold War Fears. Video, 58 min. PBS. Examination of how the Cold War influenced life in the U.S. during the 1950s.

THEMES IN AMERICAN HISTORY

USE WITH PAGES 804–805

Listed on the right are the themes emphasized in Chapter 28. The questions in boldface type stimulate critical thinking and provide students with an opportunity to discuss the themes within a broadened context. The questions also appear in the pupil's edition on p. 804.

■ ECONOMIC DEVELOPMENT

How might an economic boom affect population growth and residential patterns? Students might suggest that economic prosperity could encourage parents to have more children and to seek more affluent neighborhoods, resulting in migration from the cities to the suburbs.

■ CULTURAL DIVERSITY

How can people demonstrate diversity in a society that emphasizes conformity? Students may point out that some people might openly rebel against society. Other people might take a more subtle approach by maintaining ethnic traditions, dressing in nonconformist ways, or challenging mainstream ideas.

■ DEMOCRATIC VALUES

How might a group of people seek to change laws that discriminate against them? Students might suggest that people could challenge those laws in court, stage public protests, and otherwise pressure elected officials to make changes.

CHAPTER STRATEGIES FOR MEETING INDIVIDUAL NEEDS

LIMITED ENGLISH PROFICIENT LEARNERS

Encourage pairs of students to compile a "Then and Now" list about life in the 1950s. Tell them to list key elements of life in the 1950s under the first category. Under the second category, they should indicate whether that element is the same now or explain how it is different.

TACTILE/KINESTHETIC LEARNERS

Have students work in small groups to prepare skits depicting two or three key events of the 1950s. Call on groups to perform their skits.

LEARNERS HAVING DIFFICULTY

Have students work in pairs to create index cards on the key people, places, and terms listed in the chapter's Preview Workshops. One side of the card should list the person, place, or term; the other side should provide pertinent information about the person, place, or term.

AUDITORY LEARNERS

Pair students and assign each pair a person mentioned in the chapter. Have pairs write statements that their assigned person might have said. Call on volunteer pairs to read their statements and have the class identify the person.

VISUAL LEARNERS

Encourage students to use materials in the school and public libraries to locate and photocopy illustrations for a collage that portrays the title of the chapter. Ask volunteers to present and explain their collages to the class.

GIFTED LEARNERS

Direct students to research the impact of the Cold War on everyday life in the U.S. Suggest that they present their findings in an illustrated report.

USING THE CHAPTER FOCUS

■ UNDERSTANDING THE MAIN IDEA

Call on a volunteer to read aloud the Understanding the Main Idea paragraph. Then ask students to speculate, based on information in the main idea paragraph, what major developments and trends characterized America during the 1950s. List student responses on a flip chart. Have students evaluate their responses after they have completed the chapter.

★ THEMES

Have students work individually or in small groups to answer the questions under Themes. Save students' responses so that they can compare them with their responses after studying the chapter. (See p. 803B for suggested answers.)

■ THE TIME LINE

Have students review the time line and point out the entries that concern the Cold War and the entries that concern the civil rights movement. Ask students to construct time lines of the major events of these topics as they read the chapter.

CORE RESOURCES

- **Graphic Organizer 28**
- **Literature Worksheet 28**
- **Outline Maps 1, 2, 9, 16, 17, 18, 20**
- **Building Your Portfolio Worksheet 8**

ABOUT THE ILLUSTRATION

Point out that the drive for desegregation in the South in part grew out of the experiences of African American military personnel. While serving overseas many African Americans had come into contact with societies different from their own, societies that seemed to pay no heed to their race. African Americans who served in Korea fought in integrated units and returned to the U.S. determined to end racial discrimination and segregation at home. Have students assume the role of the African American airman in the photograph. Ask them to write a journal entry that describes how he might feel about the segregated waiting room.

■■ Ask students what methods they might use to combat segregation in public facilities.

Chapter 28   1950–1960

DECADE OF CONTRASTS

▼ FOCUS
■■

UNDERSTANDING THE MAIN IDEA

Though the Korean War came to an end, the Cold War continued in the 1950s, increasing Americans' fears of communism and nuclear war. Meanwhile most Americans experienced economic prosperity, leading white middle-class Americans to move away from cities into suburbs. Popular culture, including television, encouraged conformity, but some groups challenged the practices of American society, especially discrimination against African Americans.

★ THEMES

■ **ECONOMIC DEVELOP-MENT** How might an economic boom affect population growth and residential patterns?

■ **CULTURAL DIVERSITY** How can people demonstrate diversity in a society that emphasizes conformity?

■ **DEMOCRATIC VALUES** How might a group of people seek to change laws that discriminate against them?

1953	1954	1955	1957	1960
Korean War ends.	Supreme Court issues ruling in *Brown v. Board of Education*.	Montgomery bus boycott begins.	*On the Road* published.	U-2 incident occurs.

United States airman at
Atlanta Terminal Station, 1956

LINK TO THE PAST

The end of World War II renewed Americans' optimism about the future. Soon, however, the country was caught up in a Cold War with the Soviet Union. President Truman's commitment to contain the spread of communism led the United States into the Korean War and heightened suspicion that there were Communist spies in America.

HISTORICAL SIDELIGHTS
A Reluctant Candidate

The Democrats and the Republicans both had sought Eisenhower as a presidential candidate in 1948, but he rejected their appeals. Only his announcement that he was a Republican prevented a similar situation from developing in 1952. Republican leaders finally got him to agree to run in 1952 by appealing to his soldier's sense of duty.

*I*n 1952, after 20 years of Democratic rule in the White House, Americans chose Republican Dwight D. Eisenhower for president, echoing the campaign chant "We Like Ike." The Eisenhower era, which occupied much of the 1950s, saw continued conflict in many parts of the world. However, the emergence of new leadership in the Soviet Union raised hopes for a thaw in the Cold War. At home the 1950s brought widespread economic prosperity. The United States had long been the world's richest, most productive nation. Now millions of middle-class Americans enjoyed a rising standard of living, leading many to move away from cities and rural areas into suburbs.

American life was not all rosy, however. Cold War tensions and nuclear-war fears disturbed much of the nation. Moreover, economic prosperity was not shared equally. Rural residents, African Americans, Hispanic Americans, and Native Americans continued to endure poverty and prejudice. By the mid-1950s, however, a new generation of African Americans started to achieve some successes in the long struggle for the equality of opportunity promised in the Fourteenth Amendment.

Watching a 3-D movie, 1953

FOCUS OBJECTIVES

- Identify the impact of the Korean War's outcome on Korea.

- Determine what led to the downfall of Senator Joseph McCarthy.

- Analyze how President Eisenhower handled threats to U.S. interests in Iran, Guatemala, and Egypt.

- Explain how the U-2 incident affected the arms race.

PREVIEW WORKSHOP

Following is a list of the significant people, places, and terms in this section. You may wish to use this list as a section preview.

People
- Dwight D. Eisenhower
- Adlai E. Stevenson
- Joseph McCarthy
- Margaret Chase Smith
- Nikita Khrushchev

Places
- Iran
- Guatemala
- Suez Canal

Terms
- hydrogen bomb
- *Sputnik*
- National Aeronautics and Space Administration
- National Defense Education Act
- brinkmanship
- Eisenhower Doctrine

Section 1

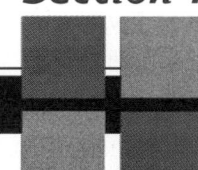

COLD WAR FEARS

F O C U S

- **How did the outcome of the Korean War affect Korea?**
- **What led to Senator Joseph McCarthy's downfall?**
- **How did President Eisenhower handle threats to U.S. interests in Iran, Guatemala, and Egypt?**
- **How did the U-2 incident affect the arms race?**

*S*oon after his victory in the 1952 presidential election, Dwight D. Eisenhower kept his campaign promise to end the Korean conflict. But the Cold War continued, generating fears of nuclear weapons and stirring suspicions that Communists had infiltrated every part of American life. On the world stage the Eisenhower administration developed an aggressive policy to fight the spread of communism, while taking steps to improve diplomatic relations with the Soviet Union.

Eisenhower campaign bumper sticker, 1952

CORE RESOURCES

- Section 1 Daily Quiz

AV RESOURCES

- *The American Nation Videodisc:* McCarthy and McCarthyism; Bomb Shelters
- *Linking Geography and History Transparency* and *Worksheet 20*

THE GENERAL VS. THE EGGHEAD

As 1952 began, President Truman found himself confronted with a host of problems. The Korean War had ground to a bloody stalemate, and peace talks were making little progress. Republicans saw their chance to break the Democrats' 20-year hold on the White House by choosing popular World War II hero General Dwight D. Eisenhower as their presidential candidate. Conservative senator Richard M. Nixon of California served as his running mate.

Truman, recognizing that he had little support even within his own party, decided not to run for reelection. The Democrats selected Governor Adlai E. Stevenson of Illinois as their candidate. Stevenson defended the Fair Deal and Truman's foreign policies. Many voters, however, viewed him as an intellectual out of touch with the common people. Some jokingly referred to Stevenson as an "egghead"—"someone with more brains than hair."

Stevenson also could not match Eisenhower's patriotic appeal. Eisenhower reassured voters that America would remain strong throughout the Cold War. The hero of World War II promised to resist communism and end the Korean War. A triumphant Eisenhower received 55 percent of the popular vote and swept the electoral count 442 to 89.

▼ During the 1952 presidential election, Dwight Eisenhower had promised voters, "I shall go to Korea." Eisenhower fulfilled the promise a month after his presidential victory. Here he is shown eating lunch with his old army outfit.

MOTIVATING:
PRIOR KNOWLEDGE

Call on volunteers to identify the causes of the Korean War. Point out that in this section, students will learn that the causes of the war were left unresolved and the international tensions that brought about American involvement in the war continued to influence U.S. foreign policy throughout the 1950s.

Teaching the Section

THE END OF THE KOREAN WAR

Ask groups of students to imagine they are State Department representatives on a tour of Korea shortly after the signing of the Korean War armistice. Have each group write a report for department officials detailing the impact of the war on Korea, the terms of the armistice, and how the war's outcome might affect future U.S. relations with China and Korea. Call on volunteers to present group reports to the class.

▶

KOREAN WAR ENDS, FEAR CONTINUES

The new president quickly fulfilled his promise to end the war. Eisenhower used military force to get peace negotiations moving. He stepped up bombing raids on North Korea in May 1953 and dropped ominous hints that he would use nuclear weapons, if necessary, to end the conflict.

On July 27, 1953, negotiators agreed to an armistice that divided Korea into two nations, Communist North Korea and anti-Communist South Korea, roughly at the 38th parallel—the prewar dividing line. Some Americans questioned whether this outcome in a distant war justified U.S. losses—some 54,000 dead and 103,000 wounded. More than 1.5 million Chinese and Koreans had also died in the conflict. For years after the war, U.S. relations with China and North Korea remained strained.

■■ **The armistice that ended the Korean War created two nations divided at the 38th parallel: North Korea and South Korea.**

The Korean conflict heightened the fears of some that communism was gaining ground in the United States. This anxiety continued even after the war ended. Many Americans became convinced that spies and Communist sympathizers were everywhere. Joseph McCarthy, a U.S. senator from Wisconsin, helped fuel these suspicions.

Senator McCarthy came to public attention in 1950, when he claimed to have a list of known Communists who worked at the State Department. Although he never produced the list, dozens of federal employees lost their jobs after being labeled as "security risks." McCarthy used his position as chairman of the Senate Permanent Subcommittee on Investigations to wage war against alleged "Communist sympathizers" in the federal government. With almost no supporting evidence, McCarthy questioned the patriotism—and ruined the reputations—of hundreds of government workers. Many Americans, terrified of communism and the power of the Soviet Union, supported his crusade.

McCarthy's popularity and ruthlessness made many politicians wary of challenging him. One who did, however, was Margaret Chase Smith, a Republican senator from Maine. Smith was born in the small mill town of Skowhegan, Maine, in 1897. When her husband, Republican congressman Clyde Smith, died in 1940, voters chose her to complete his congressional term.

After four full terms in the house, Smith won a seat in the Senate in 1948, becoming the first woman to be elected to both houses of Congress. Sixteen years later, she became the first woman to seek the Republican nomination for president. When she left the Senate in 1973, her colleagues praised her as a "woman of courage." Smith once said of public service:

Margaret Chase Smith

❝ It must be a complete dedication to the people and to the nation with full recognition that every human being is entitled to courtesy and consideration, that constructive criticism is not only to be expected but sought, that smears are not only to be expected but fought, that honor is to be earned but not bought. ❞

McCARTHY'S DOWNFALL

In 1950 Smith and several other senators issued the "Declaration of Conscience," which condemned those who had turned the Senate into "a forum of hate and character assassination." While she never mentioned McCarthy by name, everyone knew she was referring to him. Few others joined in the condemnation, however. Even President Eisenhower refused to criticize McCarthy.

Most of the critics who did speak out came from the arts or the media. In *The Crucible* (1953), playwright Arthur Miller drew parallels between McCarthyism and the Salem witchcraft trials of 1692. On the television program *See It Now,* newscaster Edward R. Murrow questioned McCarthy's tactics. "We cannot defend freedom abroad," Murrow cautioned, "by deserting it at home." While some viewers praised Murrow, others bombarded him with hate mail.

BIO GRAPHY PERSONALITIES IN HISTORY

Smith's challenge of McCarthy was entirely in character, for she had a reputation as a woman of independent mind. On what she termed "dramatic" issues—the budget, for example—Smith readily broke party ranks and voted with the Democrats. After one such vote she came under attack from Republican conservatives. The *Chicago Tribune* went so far as to suggest that she should be "read out of the party."

PRIMARY SOURCE

Description of Change: excerpted
Rationale: excerpted to focus on main idea

🌐 GLOBAL CONNECTIONS

While Asian immigration to the U.S. increased after the end of the Korean War, many Chinese immigrants found themselves targets of suspicion. In 1955 Everett F. Drumwright, U.S. consul general in Hong Kong, charged that Chinese Communists were infiltrating the U.S. Acting on these allegations, federal officials began to crack down on illegal immigration in Chinese American communities.

Teaching the Section

THE ARMY–McCARTHY HEARINGS

Tell students to imagine that they are TV news anchors reporting on the Army-McCarthy hearings. Have them write a 90-second report or commentary on the hearings for the evening news broadcast. Scripts should identify the personalities involved, describe the major incidents, and detail the outcomes. Some students may wish to act as newscasters and "broadcast" their scripts to the class. Use these presentations as a starting point for a class discussion on how the hearings led to McCarthy's downfall. Students may wish to include their scripts in their portfolios.

In 1954 McCarthy's committee investigated charges that Communists had gained a foothold in the U.S. Army. Each day a vast television audience, sometimes as many as 20 million people, tuned in to the Army-McCarthy hearings. In the circus-like proceedings, McCarthy repeatedly interrupted and ridiculed witnesses. One victim of this treatment complained that McCarthy "acted like the gangster in a B movie rubbing out someone who had got in his way."

Television exposure of McCarthy's bullying tactics, contrasted with the calm, dignified behavior of army chief counsel Joseph Welch, soon turned public opinion against the senator. At one point when Welch criticized McCarthy for his wild charges, the audience in the hearing room broke into applause. A few months later, the Senate—by a vote of 67 to 22—condemned McCarthy for conduct unbecoming a senator.

■■ **McCarthy's behavior during the Army-McCarthy hearings cost him public support.**

NUCLEAR ANXIETY

Americans' fear of nuclear war heightened as the Soviet Union and the United States raced to develop more-powerful nuclear weapons. In 1950 American scientists began work on a **hydrogen bomb**, or H-bomb, which they said would be 1,000 times more powerful than the atomic bomb dropped on Hiroshima and Nagasaki in World War II. The first H-bomb test in 1952 completely vaporized a small island in the Pacific. Some nine months later, the Soviet Union tested its own H-bomb. J. Robert Oppenheimer, one of the creators of the atomic bomb, cautioned:

❝ [The United States and the Soviet Union] are like two scorpions in a bottle, each capable of killing the other but only at the risk of his own life. . . . The atomic clock ticks faster and faster. ❞

▲ In the 1950s schools across America held air-raid drills like this one, though such measures would have been of little value in an actual nuclear attack.

As concerns about nuclear war grew, the government launched a campaign to calm public fears. The federally sponsored book *How to*

THE NUCLEAR ARMS RACE

THROUGH OTHERS' EYES

The testing of increasingly powerful and destructive nuclear weapons by the United States and the Soviet Union in the 1950s alarmed national leaders around the world. In April 1954 Jawaharlal Nehru, Prime Minister of India, voiced his fears:

❝ The United States of America and the Union of Soviet Socialist Republics, we are told, possess this [nuclear] weapon and each of these countries has during the last two years effected test explosions, unleashing impacts which in every respect were far beyond those of any weapons of destruction known to man. . . . We know that its use threatens the existence of man and civilization as we know it. . . . There can be little doubt about the deep and widespread concern in the world . . . about these weapons and their dreadful consequences. But concern is not enough. . . . We must endeavor with faith and hope to promote all efforts that seek to bring to a halt this drift to what appears to be the menace of total destruction. ❞

NUCLEAR ANXIETY

Invite students to imagine that they are a social studies class in the 1950s. Hold a "current events" discussion about proposals for a nuclear test ban. Remind students to keep in mind the Cold War tensions and nuclear anxieties of the time as they role-play the class discussion. Conclude by having students, in their 1950s role, vote on whether they favor or oppose a ban on nuclear testing.

▶

Changing Ways AMERICANS GO UNDERGROUND

As Cold War tensions and Americans' fear of a Soviet nuclear attack increased in the 1950s, a civil defense craze swept the United States. In 1951 the Federal Civil Defense Administration began a campaign to educate the public on what to do in a nuclear attack. Pamphlets, films, television shows, magazines, and the "Duck and Cover" program for children all encouraged citizens to protect themselves. For example, the *Survival Under Nuclear Attack* booklet urged:

▶ **During the 1950s many children learned about civil defense through the "Duck and Cover" program.**

BERT *the* TURTLE *
says
DUCK *and* COVER
* STAR OF THE OFFICIAL U.S. CIVIL DEFENSE FILM "DUCK AND COVER"
FEDERAL CIVIL DEFENSE ADMINISTRATION

Harry S Truman Library

> ❝ You can live through an atom bomb raid and you won't have to have a Geiger counter, protective clothing, or special training in order to do it. The secrets of survival are: KNOW THE BOMB'S TRUE DANGERS. KNOW THE STEPS YOU CAN TAKE TO ESCAPE THEM. ❞

Americans' fear increased in 1954 when the U.S. *Bravo* hydrogen-bomb tests in the Pacific Ocean revealed the far-reaching effects of nuclear fallout. The crew of a Japanese fishing boat 85 miles away from the test site developed radiation sickness. People realized that no one would be safe in a nuclear attack. "The alternatives," one civil defense official said, "are to dig, die, or get out." No one wanted to die, and with little warning of incoming missiles, evacuating would not be possible. So some Americans began to dig, constructing backyard fallout shelters.

Pamphlets like the *Family Fallout Shelter* promoted do-it-yourself home shelters. *Life* magazine even presented building a shelter as a father-and-son project. Shelter manufacturers also sprang up, selling their concrete and steel igloos at county fairs for about $1,500. The typical shelter contained flashlights, a first-aid kit, battery radio, chemical toilet, and two-week supply of food (mainly canned meats and vegetables) and water. Most shelters were furnished with only metal bunk beds or cots, a table, and chairs, but some had all the comforts of home. One man in Austin, Texas, spent $90,000 on his luxury shelter.

Some people also purchased guns to keep out anyone who tried to enter their shelter during a raid. This survivalist view led many to question the ethics of home bomb shelters. Did they represent unbridled—and dangerous—individualism? But before this issue could be resolved, the civil defense craze passed. In 1963 the United States, the Soviet Union, and Great Britain signed a treaty ending above-ground nuclear testing. The fear of fallout diminished, and demand for bomb shelters rapidly decreased.

Changing Ways

AMERICANS GO UNDERGROUND

SETTING THE SCENE

Calls for a civil defense program against nuclear attack came soon after the bombings of Hiroshima and Nagasaki. The scheme taken most seriously during these early days of the atomic age was urban dispersal—the resettling of people in small communities in the country's vast open spaces. Protection in place—the construction of bomb shelters—replaced dispersal as the most-favored civil defense program during the 1950s.

PRIMARY SOURCE

Description of Change: excerpted
Rationale: excerpted to focus on main idea

THE AMERICAN NATION VIDEODISC PROGRAM
Bomb Shelters

2A   48004   :43

Survive an Atomic Bomb, for example, offered suggestions on how to live through a nuclear attack. Some Americans put these recommendations to use by building backyard bomb shelters. Schoolchildren went through air-raid drills in which they crawled under their desks to protect themselves from radiation.

While a nuclear attack remained a grim possibility, radioactive fallout—a by-product of nuclear explosions—already posed a threat. American and Soviet H-bomb tests had spewed tons of radioactive material into the atmosphere. In 1957 Congress held a special hearing on the dangers of radioactive fallout. Defense officials

Teaching the Section

FOREIGN POLICY CONCERNS

Write the following headings on the chalk-board: *Latin America, Middle East, Eastern Europe.* Call on volunteers to identify events that took place in these regions during the 1950s, noting their replies under the appropriate heading. Then ask students to explain how the Eisenhower administration responded to each event. Write answers next to the appropriate event. Have students use information on the chalkboard to discuss how and why U.S. responses to these events differed.

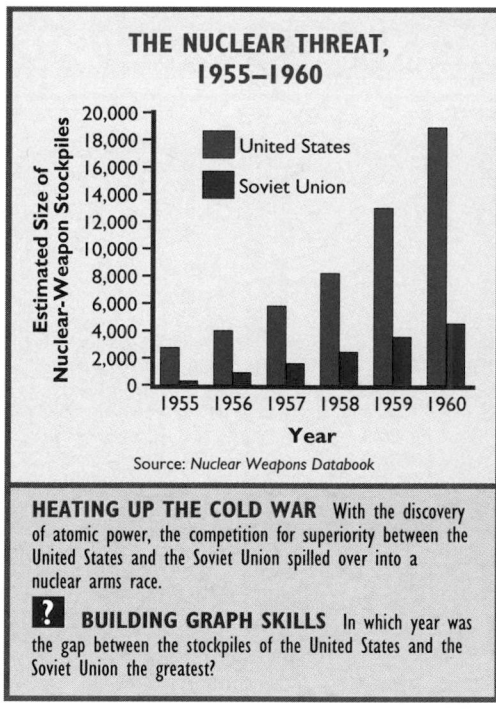

THE NUCLEAR THREAT, 1955–1960

Estimated Size of Nuclear-Weapon Stockpiles

■ United States
■ Soviet Union

20,000 / 18,000 / 16,000 / 14,000 / 12,000 / 10,000 / 8,000 / 6,000 / 4,000 / 2,000 / 0

1955 1956 1957 1958 1959 1960

Year

Source: Nuclear Weapons Databook

HEATING UP THE COLD WAR With the discovery of atomic power, the competition for superiority between the United States and the Soviet Union spilled over into a nuclear arms race.

? **BUILDING GRAPH SKILLS** In which year was the gap between the stockpiles of the United States and the Soviet Union the greatest?

claimed nuclear testing was perfectly safe, but many scientists argued that radiation released during the tests presented a serious danger to the environment and possibly increased the risk of cancer in human beings. Soon the fear of radiation led to an organized campaign against nuclear test- ing. In 1957 a group of Americans, including well- known doctor Benjamin Spock, organized the Committee for a Sane Nuclear Policy (SANE). SANE urged the United States to begin negotiations with the Soviet Union to end nuclear tests. Within a year SANE had grown to more than 25,000 members in some 130 chapters across the country.

The arms race surged on, however, especially after the Soviet Union launched the satellite *Sputnik* into orbit around the earth in October 1957. Many Americans feared that this launch proved the United States was falling behind the Soviets in technological development. Eisenhower urged Congress to expand American space tech- nology by establishing the **National Aeronautics and Space Administration** (NASA). In 1958 NASA sent the first American satellite, *Explorer I,* into orbit. That same year Congress approved the **National Defense Education Act**, which appro- priated millions of dollars to improve education in science, mathematics, and foreign languages.

ℱIGHTING COMMUNISM ABROAD

The Eisenhower administration viewed nuclear arms and technology as central to the govern- ment's priority of ending Communist expansion. Secretary of State John Foster Dulles called for the liberation of all nations that had fallen under Soviet control since 1945. To fulfill this aim, the United States would have to confront Communist aggression and not back down—even if that meant going all the way to the brink of war. "The ability to get to the verge without getting into war is the necessary art," Dulles said. This policy of **brinkmanship** rested on the threat of massive retaliation, including the use of nuclear weapons. Eisenhower, however, proved less confrontational than Dulles's policy might have suggested. Instead, he pursued U.S. aims by more covert—secret— means and by diplomacy.

Covert war and the CIA. Eisenhower tested his covert approach to the Cold War in Iran. Shortly after coming to power in 1951, Iranian pre- mier Mohammad Mosaddeq (MAWS-ad-dek) nation- alized British-owned oil fields in Iran. After Eisenhower took office he suspended aid to Iran, fearing that nationalization would endanger Western oil purchases. Eisenhower also authorized a covert action by the CIA to organize a military coup against the Iranian leader. The plan, called Operation Ajax, succeeded in having Mosaddeq arrested and replaced with the young pro- American Shah of Iran, Reza Pahlavi (ri-ZAH PAL- uh-vee). While Eisenhower achieved his goal of removing Mosaddeq, this interference in Iranian affairs sowed seeds of anti-American feelings in that country.

In 1954 Eisenhower ordered another covert action, this time in Latin America, where the United States had often intervened in the past. In

"Don't Be Afraid—I Can Always Pull You Back"

◀ **The policy of brinkmanship was sati- rized in this 1956 car- toon. Secretary of State John Foster Dulles is shown push- ing Uncle Sam to the brink of war.**

From Herblock's Special For Today (Simon & Schuster, 1958)

THE U-2 INCIDENT

Organize students into small groups to role-play national security advisors to President Eisenhower. Tell each group to prepare a short report to brief the president about the U-2 incident. Briefings should contain the following elements: 1) background information about the flights and why they were instituted; 2) explanations about what has happened to this flight; 3) suggestions about how to explain this incident to the Soviets. Have groups present their briefings to the class. Then have half the class prepare Eisenhower's message to Khrushchev and the other half prepare Khrushchev's response.

▶

1954 the Guatemalan president, Jacobo Arbenz Guzmán, took possession of uncultivated sections of Guatemala's largest plantations—including those of the American-owned United Fruit Company—to redistribute among the rural poor.

United Fruit Company executives accused the Guatemalan president of being a Communist sympathizer. Eisenhower called on the CIA to gather a small army to oust Arbenz. The CIA-led forces bombed the capital in May 1954 and installed a new pro-U.S. government, which quickly reversed Arbenz's reform program. But American intervention in Guatemala stirred up bitter resentment throughout Latin America.

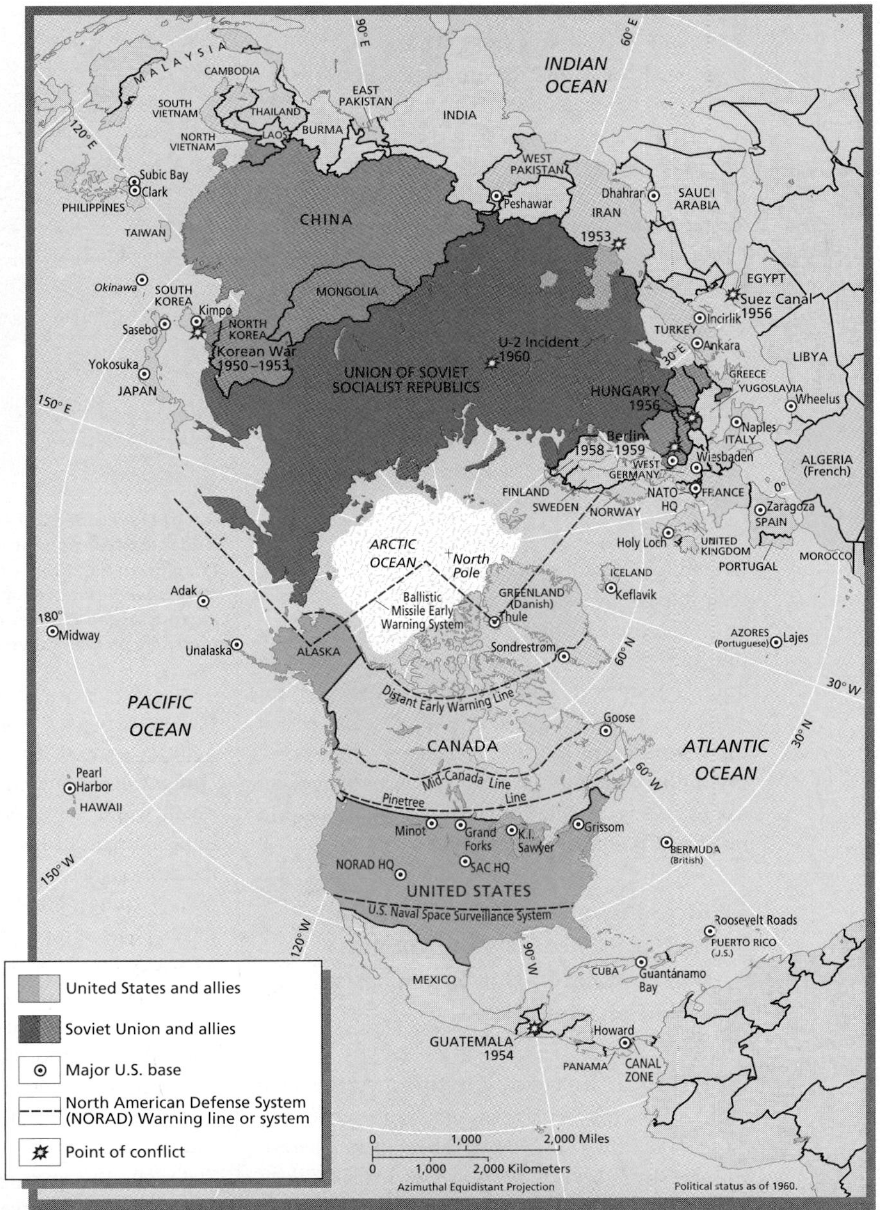

The Suez crisis. In some cases, Eisenhower used diplomacy rather than covert actions to influence foreign policy. In 1955 the American government offered Egypt financial help to build a large dam at Aswan on the Nile River. However, when Egyptian leader Gamal Abdel Nasser also sought assistance from the Soviet Union, the United States canceled its promised aid. Nasser then seized the Suez Canal, a foreign-owned waterway that linked the Mediterranean and Red seas (see map on page 905). Egypt would use canal tolls to build the Aswan Dam, Nasser declared.

Nasser's nationalization of the canal posed many problems, including a threat to the Western oil trade. Egypt also refused to allow ships bound for Israel to pass through the canal. Late in October 1956, Israel launched an attack into Egyptian territory toward the Suez Canal. Great Britain and France, claiming they were protecting

Cold War Defenses

CONTAINMENT The United States ringed the globe with alliances and military bases in an effort to prevent the spread of communism.

? LOCATION What system did the United States put into place to provide the first warning of a Soviet attack?

Legend:
- United States and allies
- Soviet Union and allies
- ⊙ Major U.S. base
- - - - North American Defense System (NORAD) Warning line or system
- ✳ Point of conflict

0   1,000   2,000 Miles
0   1,000   2,000 Kilometers
Azimuthal Equidistant Projection   Political status as of 1960.

AV TRANSPARENCY

Linking Geography and History Transparency and **Worksheet 20**

HISTORICAL SIDELIGHTS

Hawaii and the Cold War

Although the location of Hawaii was a strategic advantage for the U.S., it was not granted statehood until 1959 in part because of the fear of communism. The islands' most powerful union, the International Longshoremen's and Warehousemen's Union, was rumored to be under Communist control. Many members of Congress also were reluctant to create a state with an Asian American majority population that would likely elect Asian Americans to Congress. Indeed, after statehood, Hawaiians elected the first Chinese American senator, Hiram Leong Fong, and a Japanese American congressman, Daniel Ken Inouye.

Map Caption Answer
Ballistic Missile Early Warning System

*P*ractice

GUIDED PRACTICE

Work with the class to create on the chalkboard a time line of events in U.S.–Soviet relations from the Korean War to the U-2 incident. Place each event above or below the line according to class discussion of whether it eased or increased tensions.

INDEPENDENT PRACTICE

Direct students to select an event from the time line developed in the Guided Practice activity. Have them write an "op-ed" column, from the viewpoint of a newspaper columnist living in the 1950s, on how their selected event will affect U.S.–Soviet relations. Call on volunteers to read and discuss their columns. Students may wish to include their columns in their portfolios.

*R*eview and *A*ssessment

REVIEW Provide students with copies of the Preview Workshop list. Direct students to use its people, places, and terms to write a paragraph on Cold War fears in the U.S. Ask volunteers to read their paragraphs to the class. Then assign the Section 1 Review on p. 813.

ASSESS Assign the **Section 1 Daily Quiz** in *Core Resources*.

HISTORICAL SIDELIGHTS

Marines to Lebanon

Nationalist fervor swept across the Middle East in the wake of the Suez crisis. In 1958 a group of army officers killed the king of Iraq and set up a nationalist government. The president of Lebanon, fearing that the new Iraqi government would try to incite unrest in his country, asked the U.S. for assistance. Invoking the Eisenhower Doctrine, the U.S. ordered the marines to Lebanon. As the troops waded ashore, they were greeted by shocked Lebanese sunbathers, who had no idea what was happening.

PRIMARY SOURCE

Description of Change: excerpted
Rationale: excerpted to focus on main idea

MAKING CONNECTIONS

Literature

One outcome of Khrushchev's denunciation of Stalin was a more liberal attitude toward art and artists. For example, the ban on Aleksandr Solzhenitsyn's *One Day in the Life of Ivan Denisovich,* a novel about life in one of Stalin's terrible prison camps, was lifted.

---

the canal, seized the Mediterranean end of the waterway a few days later. The Soviet Union threatened war if the three nations did not withdraw from Egypt at once.

The United States faced the difficult choice of either supporting its allies—Britain, France, and Israel—or siding with Egypt and the Soviet Union. In the end, Eisenhower supported a UN resolution calling for an immediate cease-fire and the withdrawal of the invading troops. He explained:

> 66 If the United Nations once admits that international disputes can be settled by using force, then we will have destroyed the foundation of the organization and our best hope of establishing a world order. 99

Grudgingly, Britain, France, and Israel withdrew their forces, and the crisis eased.

The Soviet Union's support of Egypt during the Suez crisis bolstered the Soviets' position among the Arab nations. To counter Soviet influence in the Middle East, the president issued the **Eisenhower Doctrine** in January 1957, offering military aid and in some instances American troops to any Middle East nation seeking help in resisting Communist aggression.

■■ **Eisenhower used the CIA to protect U.S. interests in Iran and Guatemala. In the Suez Crisis, he relied on diplomacy.**

Uprising in Eastern Europe. At the same time that the Suez crisis was unfolding, an equally dangerous situation was developing in Eastern Europe. In February 1956 Soviet leader Nikita Khrushchev stunned political observers by denouncing his predecessor, Joseph Stalin, who had died in 1953, for many ruthless crimes. Observers hoped that this move signaled a new era of reform for the Soviet Union and Eastern Europe. Later in 1956, Polish reformers tested Khrushchev by calling for greater political freedom.

Inspired by the example of Poland, thousands of Hungarians took to the streets in late October to demand reform. Moderates seized control of the Hungarian government and called for a Western-style democracy in their nation and for Hungary's secession from the Warsaw Pact. Khrushchev

▲ On November 2, 1956, Hungarian rebels in Budapest triumphantly waved the tricolored Hungarian flag atop a captured Russian tank. Two days later Soviet troops occupied the main square in front of the Houses of Parliament, where this photograph was taken.

responded with crushing force. On November 4, heavily armed Soviet troops moved into the Hungarian capital, Budapest, and smashed the revolt within days. A new pro-Soviet government imposed martial law and executed or imprisoned the rebel leaders.

Throughout their struggle the Hungarian rebels pleaded for help from the West. Eisenhower worried, however, that intervention in Eastern Europe would lead to all-out nuclear war with the Soviets. He condemned the Soviets' actions but refused to aid the rebels. He did, however, help ease immigration laws to allow more Eastern European refugees into the United States. As a result, some 40,000 Hungarians fled to the United States after the uprising.

To some observers Eisenhower's lack of support for the rebels indicated a retreat from Dulles's talk of liberating Communist-controlled countries. But most of the American public supported Eisenhower, whom they reelected by a landslide against Adlai Stevenson in November 1956.

*H*OPES RAISED, HOPES DASHED

Near the end of the decade, the United States and the Soviet Union moved to improve their diplomatic relations. In 1959 Vice President Nixon

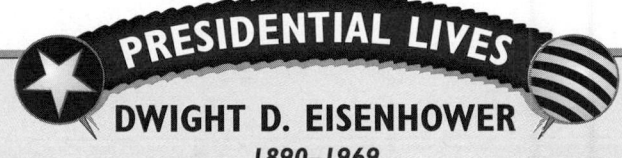

PRESIDENTIAL LIVES

DWIGHT D. EISENHOWER
1890–1969

in office 1953–1961

U.S. 6ᶜ POSTAGE

DWIGHT D. EISENHOWER

Dwight Eisenhower built his army career slowly. He graduated from West Point in 1915 and worked in an Army camp in Pennsylvania during World War I. Throughout the years between the first and second world wars he moved around the globe, from Panama to the Philippines, becoming a master organizer and coordinator.

In charge of Allied military forces in North Africa in 1943, "he now became," a British colleague explained, "the chairman of a company of great power and resources." As president, Eisenhower continued his military habits of shared leadership. "No man can be a Napoleon in modern war," the president once said. "I don't believe this government was set up to be operated by any one acting alone."

Dwight Eisenhower [signature]

---

visited the Soviet Union and Premier Khrushchev came to the United States. Touring Iowa farms, Pittsburgh steel plants, and Hollywood movie studios, the jovial Khrushchev charmed the American media. In Des Moines he jokingly told reporters, "We have beaten you to the moon, but you have beaten us in sausage making." He and Eisenhower agreed to meet at a summit conference in Paris the following year to discuss arms reductions.

In May 1960, however, just before the Paris conference was to open, Khrushchev announced that an American U-2—a high-altitude spy plane—had been shot down over the Soviet Union. At first American officials insisted that it was a weather-research plane that had strayed off course. But the captured pilot, Francis Gary Powers, admitted he had been on a spying mission.

Khrushchev refused to go ahead with the summit unless the United States halted such spying missions and apologized for past flights. Eisenhower promised that the U-2 flights would stop but did not apologize. Khrushchev refused to meet with Eisenhower again. The brief thaw in the Cold War had come to an abrupt end.

■■ **The U-2 incident halted arms-reduction talks between Khrushchev and Eisenhower.**

■□
□■ SECTION **1** REVIEW

IDENTIFY and explain the significance of the following: Dwight D. Eisenhower, Adlai E. Stevenson, Joseph McCarthy, Margaret Chase Smith, hydrogen bomb, *Sputnik,* National Aeronautics and Space Administration, National Defense Education Act, brinkmanship, Eisenhower Doctrine, Nikita Khrushchev.

LOCATE and explain the importance of the following: Iran, Guatemala, Suez Canal.

1. **MAIN IDEA** How did the armistice that ended the Korean War affect Korea?
2. **MAIN IDEA** What effect did the U-2 incident have on relations between the United States and the Soviet Union?
3. **COMPARING** What various tactics did Eisenhower use to protect U.S. interests abroad?
4. **WRITING TO PERSUADE** Imagine you are a reporter covering the Army-McCarthy hearings. Write a commentary explaining why Senator McCarthy should be removed from office.
5. **EVALUATING** What actions by the Soviet Union and the United States heightened Americans' fears of nuclear war?

PREVIEW WORKSHOP

Following is a list of the significant people and terms in this section. You may wish to use this list as a section preview.

People
■ Oveta Culp Hobby
■ George Meany

Terms
■ modern Republicanism
■ Relocation Act
■ termination
■ Highway Act
■ baby boom
■ automation
■ Landrum-Griffin Act
■ urban renewal

Section 2

THE AFFLUENT SOCIETY

F O C U S

■ **What was the economy like in the 1950s?**
■ **How did the population shift during the decade?**
■ **What was early television programming like?**
■ **How did the work force change in the 1950s?**

*D*uring Eisenhower's presidency a rapidly growing economy brought prosperity to many Americans. Newly prosperous whites left the cities for the suburbs, while the rural poor flocked to urban areas in search of jobs. The growth of the suburbs and the spread of television helped create a consumer culture that many of the poorer members of society could not enjoy. Changes in the workplace and the work force also helped transform American society during the 1950s.

Advertisement for TV dinner

MODERN REPUBLICANISM

President Eisenhower took office in 1953 determined to change the federal government. He pledged to cut the bureaucracy, to curb what he called the "creeping socialism" of the New Deal, to balance the budget, and to reduce government regulation of the economy.

In the first year of his presidency, Eisenhower cut thousands of government jobs and pared billions of dollars from the federal budget. To reduce government influence over the economy, he cut government farm subsidies and turned over federally owned coastal lands for private development.

But despite his pledge to curb "creeping socialism," Eisenhower left the basic social and economic programs of the New Deal–Fair

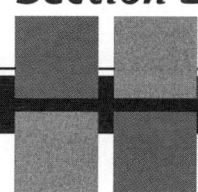

Deal era intact. Under his administration, social security and unemployment benefits expanded, and the minimum wage increased. Eisenhower established the Department of Health, Education, and Welfare, under the supervision of Texan Oveta Culp Hobby. The president also supported the largest increase in educational spending up to that time. This approach to domestic affairs, which Eisenhower described as "conservative when it comes to money and liberal when it comes to human beings," became known as **modern Republicanism**.

Providing funding for social programs, defense, and other government obligations undermined Eisenhower's pledge to balance the federal budget.

◀ As secretary of Health, Education, and Welfare, Oveta Culp Hobby lobbied for legislation providing for a national polio vaccination program.

MOTIVATING:
STUDENT EXPERIENCES
Encourage students to tell what they know about life in the 1950s from books, magazines, television programs, and discussions with older family members. Note their responses on a flip chart. After students read the section, have them review and adjust the list.

Teaching the *Section*

THE 1950s ECONOMY
Organize students into small groups and direct groups to prepare a statement that responds to the following question: *The 1950s—Good Times or Not?* Tell groups to consider such factors as the rate of economic growth, the role of government, who benefited, and who did not. Call on volunteers from each group to present and explain their group's statement to the class.

Only three of the eight budgets he presided over were balanced. Furthermore, during his years in office the federal debt grew by about 9 percent, to $291 billion.

*T*HE "GOOD" YEARS

For many Americans the 1950s was a decade of economic prosperity. The post–World War II spending spree that began in the late 1940s continued into the 1950s. Defense spending, triggered by the Korean War, also boosted growth in the early 1950s. Unemployment and inflation rarely edged above 5 percent. By the mid-1950s more than 60 percent of Americans were earning a "middle-class" income, at that time considered $3,000–$10,000 annually. Never before, the popular media declared, had so many people enjoyed such prosperity. "This is a new kind of capitalism," declared the *Reader's Digest,* "capitalism for the many, not for the few."

Not everyone shared in the good times, however. A 1957 study found nearly 40 million Americans living below or near the poverty line of $3,000 for a family of four. Almost half of the nation's poor lived in rural areas, where they suffered from poor nutrition, inadequate medical care, and lack of education.

■■ The 1950s saw rapid economic expansion and prosperity for many, but the prosperity was not evenly distributed.

*P*EOPLE ON THE MOVE

The 1950s was a decade of geographic mobility. Millions of newly prosperous whites, especially young couples, moved to the suburbs that developers built around the nation's cities. At the same time, many poor rural citizens migrated to the cities in search of a better life.

The urban communities. Most of the rural residents who moved to the cities to escape poverty found little improvement in their economic status. By 1960 more than 20 million city dwellers were living in poverty.

While large numbers of poor rural whites flocked to the cities, African Americans consti-

▲ **Puerto Rican immigrants developed strong community organizations in their New York neighborhoods. Here, Puerto Rican boys play in the game room of the Good Neighbor Church and Community Center located in Manhattan.**

tuted the single largest group in the rural-to-urban movement. In a continuation of the Great Migration, which had begun during World War I (see Chapter 20), African Americans left the South for the industrial cities of the North. This northward movement peaked in the mid-1950s, with the African American population of some northern cities growing by about 2,000 each week.

Wide-scale unemployment caused many Puerto Ricans to leave the island for the mainland. Some 40,000–50,000 migrated annually in the 1950s. About 70 percent of Puerto Rican migrants settled in New York City. Many Mexicans also moved to the United States in order to find work. While most immigrants from Mexico had previously settled in rural areas, the new immigrants tended to settle in cities such as Los Angeles, Denver, El Paso, Phoenix, and San Antonio. By 1960 about 80 percent of Hispanic Americans were living in cities.

Relocation under pressure. Thousands of American Indians also moved to the cities in the 1950s. But unlike other migrants, Indians did so under federal pressure. To promote the assimilation of American Indians into mainstream society, the Eisenhower administration supported passage of the **Relocation Act** of 1956. The act

▶ **In 1958, American Indians protested when the federal government seized reservation land for a power project in Niagara Falls. This Tuscarora boy was photographed as he walked the picket line.**

MUST YOU TAKE EVERY THING THE INDIANS OWN??

AV TRANSPARENCY
Linking Geography and History Transparencies and **Worksheets 11B, 17A**

MAKING CONNECTIONS
Sociology
Poverty in the 1950s was not limited to any particular racial or ethnic group, but certain kinds of people seemed more likely to be poor. For example, nearly one half of all families headed by a woman or someone over the age of 65 were poor. And some 60 percent of poor families were headed by people who had only a grade-school education. Nearly 50 percent of all nonwhite Americans lived in poverty, however.

Teaching the Section

POPULATION SHIFTS

Have students work in small groups to write a script for a five-minute documentary on the population changes that took place in the 1950s. Suggest that students integrate information from the map on p. 816 into their scripts. If video equipment is available, groups may wish to record their documentaries. Call on volunteers to present their documentaries to the class.

CULTURAL PATTERNS

Although thousands of American Indians relocated to the cities during the 1950s, many eventually returned to the reservations. Native Americans joked that you could send an Indian to the moon without making any arrangements for his return. Just tell him he was being relocated, and he would find his own way home!

Map Caption Answer
the South

 **TRANSPARENCY**

Linking Geography and History Transparency and **Worksheet 21**

THE AMERICAN NATION VIDEODISC PROGRAM

The Growth of Suburbia

```
2B    00599   2:57
```

urged Native Americans to move to urban areas. It even set up relocation offices in major cities to assist newcomers. Many feared that this would deplete the reservations of future leaders and destroy tribal cultures. Oglala Lakota activist Gerald One Feather recalled:

> 66 The relocation program had an impact on our . . . government at Pine Ridge [South Dakota]. Many people who could have provided [our] leadership were lost because they had motivation to go off the reservation to find employment or obtain an education. Relocation drained off a lot of our potential leadership. 99

To hasten relocation, the government adopted a policy of termination in 1953. **Termination** involved ending on a tribe-by-tribe basis the reservation system and most federal funding for Native Americans. Various tribal groups launched protests and lawsuits against the termination policy, considering it an attempt to wipe out Native American communities. By 1958 the Eisenhower administration backed down, saying it would no longer support legislation "to terminate tribes without their consent."

The suburbs. As more poor migrants settled in the cities, many more-prosperous city residents moved to the suburbs. By the end of the decade,

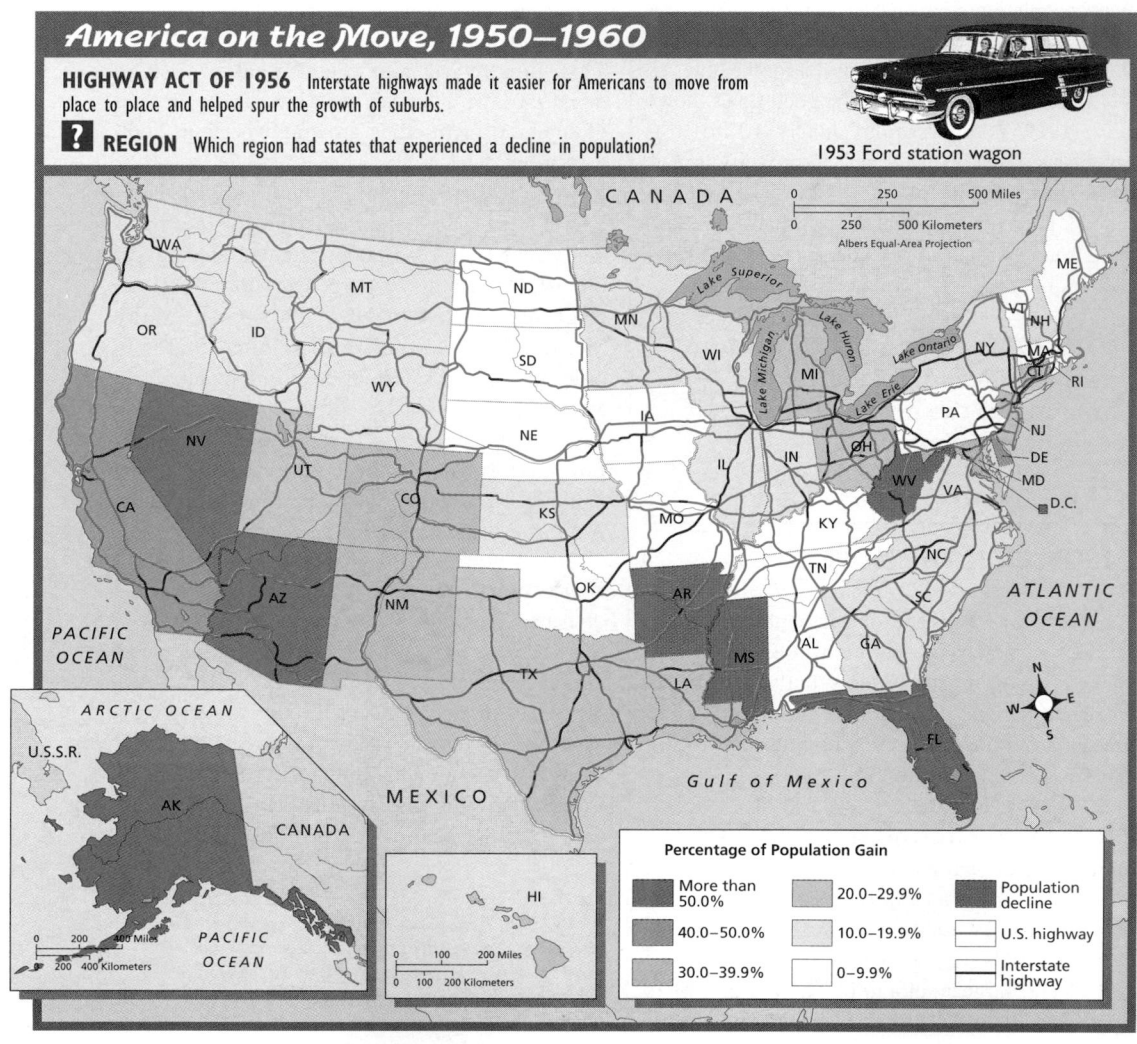

America on the Move, 1950–1960

HIGHWAY ACT OF 1956 Interstate highways made it easier for Americans to move from place to place and helped spur the growth of suburbs.

❓ **REGION** Which region had states that experienced a decline in population?

1953 Ford station wagon

Percentage of Population Gain

- More than 50.0%
- 40.0–50.0%
- 30.0–39.9%
- 20.0–29.9%
- 10.0–19.9%
- 0–9.9%
- Population decline
- U.S. highway
- Interstate highway

CONSUMPTION AND CONFORMITY

Call on a student to read aloud the statement by Henry Steele Commager on p. 817 (near top of column 2). Ask students to cite evidence in the section that supports or challenges Commager's statement. Note responses on the chalkboard. Then use the information on the board as the starting point for a class discussion on the validity of Commager's view of American values in the 1950s.

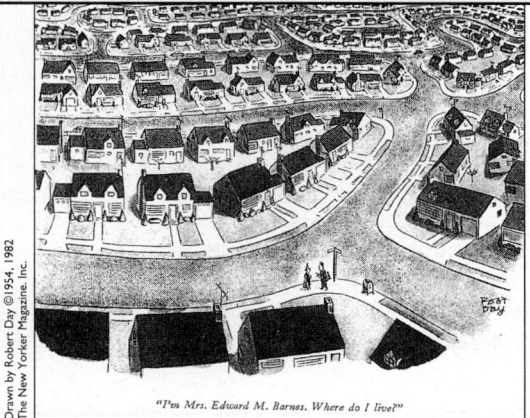

Drawn by Robert Day ©1954, 1982
The New Yorker Magazine, Inc.

"I'm Mrs. Edward M. Barnes. Where do I live?"

▲ This cartoon satirizing life in the suburbs appeared in *The New Yorker* in 1954.

close to 60 million Americans—one third of the total population—lived in the suburbs. Many of these suburbs were planned communities.

Suburban growth took off in part because more Americans could afford to purchase homes. Veterans had access to low-interest mortgages from such government agencies as the Veterans Administration (VA) and the Federal Housing Administration (FHA). Private savings and loan associations, too, offered mortgages on relatively easy terms. In addition, the **Highway Act** of 1956 greatly expanded the nation's highway systems, making it easier for suburban residents to commute to jobs in the cities.

The growth of suburbs was also spurred by an expanding population. During the depression and World War II years, many people had postponed getting married or starting a family. After the war, Americans began to get married at earlier ages and in greater numbers than they had for generations. They also had more children. The soaring birth rate accounted for more than 90 percent of the 30-million increase in the population during the 1950s. The decade, many observers said, had experienced nothing less than a **baby boom**.

■■ Poor whites, African Americans, Hispanic Americans, and American Indians moved to the cities, while many middle-class Americans moved to the suburbs.

Consumption and Conformity

Suburbanization and prosperity changed the way many Americans lived. Seemingly secure in their jobs and confident of increasing incomes,

Americans went on a buying spree, purchasing between five and seven million new automobiles and an array of household appliances each year.

With an increase in consumerism came a rising emphasis on conformity. Suburban neighbors worked hard to "keep up with the Joneses," that is, to make sure that they had as many modern conveniences as their neighbors. Scholar Henry Steele Commager noted how conformity affected American values: "What is the new loyalty? It is, above all, conformity. It is the uncritical and unquestioning acceptance of America as it is."

Children became an important focus of suburban life, largely because of the baby boom. The baby boom also led to an emphasis on child rearing, focusing on the role of mothers. Popular magazines, advertisements, and self-help books depicted the ideal wife and mother as a full-time homemaker who devoted all of her energy to making her family happy (and buying all the latest household gadgets). Contrary to these popular images, however, the number of working mothers actually *increased* during the 1950s. By the end of the decade, some 39 percent of all women with children ages 6 to 17 worked for wages outside the home.

While it had long been common for mothers of poor families to work for wages, an increasing number of women in the work force were middle-class mothers. Despite the popular media's image of the typical middle-class family as a stay-at-home

CHANGES IN MATERIAL STANDARDS OF LIVING, 1940–1955

Households Owning	1940	1955
Automobile	50.0%	71.0%
Television Set	0.0%	76.1%
Refrigerator	44.0%	94.1%
Washing Machine	46.0%	84.1%
Clothes Dryer	0.0%	9.2%
Vacuum Cleaner	38.0%	64.3%

Sources: *The Overworked American; 1956 Statistical Abstract; An Economic History of Women in America; The Proud Decades*

"THE GOOD LIFE" After World War II many American consumers rushed to buy the latest in modern conveniences.

❓ **BUILDING GRAPH SKILLS** Which item experienced the greatest increase in ownership?

MAKING CONNECTIONS
Geography

The great surge in suburban housing construction was led by William Levitt. An admirer of Henry Ford, Levitt in the late 1940s adapted mass-production techniques to the building of communities of modestly priced, small, almost identical single-family homes. By the end of the 1950s, other contractors had jumped on the bandwagon, and such developments dotted the outskirts of every major American city.

Chart Caption Answer
television set

Teaching the Section

TELEVISION IN THE 1950s

Call on volunteers to role-play a panel of 1950s network television programming executives who are presenting their new programs at a news conference. Have the rest of the class act as reporters and ask the panel questions on the social relevance of the programs, whether or not the programs accurately reflect life in America, and if and how the programs support American values.

■■ Conclude the role-play activity by asking students to identify in what ways the television programs of the 1950s differ from those of today.

FOR WHITE WHITE WASHES WITHOUT RED HANDS
DUZ GIANT ECONOMY SIZE
I've Gone Back to DUZ!
DUZ DOES EVERYTHING

▶ The stereotypical "happy housewife" was often used in 1950s advertisements to sell household products to female shoppers.

wife supported by a well-employed husband, some families needed a second income to share in the middle-class consumer culture. Many of the jobs held by these women were part-time or low-level jobs with little long-term career potential.

Just as the reality of working mothers conflicted with media images of the suburban housewife, so too did the reality of domestic life. Though advertisements portrayed the full-time suburban homemaker as happy and satisfied, many experts argued that isolation at home made women "bored stiff," especially after their children left home. Indeed, many stay-at-home suburban mothers longed to pursue career opportunities once their children were older. Writer Benita Eisler recalled:

❝ For our generation of housewives and mothers, "getting it over with" was our promise to a future deferred. We would "do something" with our college education (or finish it) when we "got out from under" diapers, formulas, car pools. ❞

Church attendance soared in the 1950s. Religious worship promoted social stability in these unsettled postwar years. For uprooted Americans streaming to the suburbs, church membership provided a sense of belonging.

Atomic fear also spurred the upsurge of religion. The young evangelist Billy Graham, whose crusades drew vast audiences in the 1950s, often warned of the nuclear danger in urging Americans to turn to God. The Reverend Norman Vincent Peale assured Americans in his best-selling book *The Power of Positive Thinking* that God could help them overcome fear and feelings of weakness.

Further, in these frightening Cold War years, America's piety underscored the contrast with the atheistic Soviet Union. In this spirit, Congress added the phrases "In God We Trust" and "Under God" to the nation's currency and the Pledge of Allegiance, respectively.

THE GOLDEN AGE OF TELEVISION

Television helped to reinforce both consumerism and mythical images of American life. By the end of the 1950s, 46 million households owned at least one television set.

Advertising played a major role in television programming. By 1960, advertisers were spending $1.6 billion trying to convince viewers to buy their products. Often one business would sponsor a show, such as *General Electric Theatre* and *Kraft Television Theatre,* so that viewers immediately connected the program with a company. This monopoly on advertising also gave many companies great control over program content. During the height of McCarthyism, some sponsors had actors and writers fired from shows because of their suspected political beliefs.

Sporting events, comedies, variety programs, and quiz shows—such as the World Series, *Your Show of Shows,* and *The $64,000 Question*—shared the airwaves with serious dramas in the early years of television. The most popular program of the decade was the comedy *I Love Lucy,* starring Lucille Ball and Desi Arnaz. Thousands of fans tuned in every week to witness Lucy's slapstick antics.

▼ In 1993, *TV Guide* magazine rated the *I Love Lucy* show as the best sitcom in television history.

CHANGES IN THE WORK FORCE

Encourage students to imagine they are members of an AFL–CIO study group preparing a report on changes in the work force. Suggest that they address the following in their reports: how and why the nature of work changed, which new groups of workers joined the labor force, and how and why organized labor should change its tactics and goals to keep pace with these changes. Call on volunteers to present their reports to the class. Students may wish to include their reports in their portfolios.

▶

Then and Now PESTICIDES

The production and use of chemical pesticides and fertilizers soared in the 1950s. One insecticide in particular was hailed as a modern miracle—dichlorodiphenyltrichloroethane (DDT). DDT and similar pesticides promised farmers increased crop yields and reduced labor expenses. Consumers would benefit as well with higher quality food at a lower cost. These modern chemicals seemed to be a dream come true.

But amid all the praise, Rachel Carson, a former biologist with the U.S. Fish and Wildlife Service, asked, "What has already silenced all the voices of spring in countless towns in America?" In 1962 Carson sent the world a startling message in her book *Silent Spring.* She warned that the indiscriminate use of pesticides, particularly DDT, killed wildlife and polluted the environment. Carson cited a Michigan town that sprayed DDT to kill beetles attacking the town's elm trees. When the elm leaves fell in the fall, they were eaten by worms, which were then eaten by robins. By early spring, almost all the robins in the city were dead.

Today, views on the use of DDT and other pesticides have changed dramatically. Public opinion and that of the scientific community now firmly stand behind many of Carson's ideas.

▲ Workers spray pesticides on fruit trees.

Since the 1960s, possible evidence of cancer and other health problems in field workers and children exposed to DDT has surfaced. And traces of DDT have been found in penguins and seals in Antarctica and in whales off the coast of Greenland—areas far removed from any application of the chemical.

As a result, in 1972 the Environmental Protection Agency (EPA) ordered a ban on domestic uses of DDT, and by the mid-1980s the agency had made addressing pesticide pollution a priority. Now the chemical industry, research scientists, and environmental groups are experimenting with a variety of natural biological controls, such as fungi, bacteria, and "beneficial" insects, to destroy harmful pests.

Carson died in 1964, too soon to see the results of her efforts. Her concerns and warnings inspired a generation of Americans to work toward finding ecologically safe pesticides and fertilizers.

Though television grew in popularity, it proved a very selective mirror, showing primarily white, middle-class, suburban experiences. Poverty, if shown at all, was a problem all but solved. Working women, ethnic minorities, and inner-city life rarely appeared. When they did, it was usually in a way that reinforced stereotypes.

One of the era's most controversial programs was the popular comedy about black urban life, *Amos 'n' Andy.* The show began as a radio program with two white men creating the voices of black characters. When the show moved to television, African American actors took over the roles; but to many viewers, the characters reflected white stereotypes of the black community. The NAACP launched a protest against the program. Others joined in the protest, and in 1953 *Amos 'n' Andy* left the air. In 1966 the network banned it from being shown in reruns.

■■ **Television provided a variety of programs but often reinforced stereotypes of ethnic groups, women, and American life.**

Controversy followed the publication of *Silent Spring.* The chemical industry questioned Carson's credentials as a scientist, while some critics charged that she seemed to care more about insects and birds than humans. Other people, however, called for the government to look into Carson's claims. A commission established by President John F. Kennedy confirmed Carson's findings in 1963.

AMERICAN CIVICS CITIZENSHIP SKILLS

Videocassette or Videodisc: Segment 5

Segment 5, Side B

Search Chapter 2

HISTORICAL SIDELIGHTS
"Vast Wasteland"
By the end of the 1950s, some people had begun to decry the deterioration in the quality of television programming. For example, Newton N. Minow, chairman of the FCC, likened television programming to a ■■"vast wasteland."

Mention that 30 years later Minow still regarded television as a wasteland and, worse, a danger to children. Ask students to explain whether they agree or disagree.

Practice

GUIDED PRACTICE

On the chalkboard construct a chart with *Moving to the City, Forced Movement,* and *Moving to the Suburbs* as horizontal headings, and *Who, Why,* and *Impact* as vertical headings. Call on volunteers to offer entries for the chart and note their responses.

INDEPENDENT PRACTICE

Have students work individually to create charts, similar to that constructed in the Guided Practice activity, on life in America during the 1950s. Suggest that they use such horizontal headings as *Economic Growth, Poverty and Prosperity, Population Changes, Consumerism, Television,* and *Changes in the Workplace.*

Review and Assessment

REVIEW Suggest that students write the main ideas of the section in the form of newspaper headlines. Ask volunteers to present their headlines to the class. Then assign the Section 2 Review on p. 821.

ASSESS Assign the **Section 2 Daily Quiz** in *Core Resources.*

MAKING CONNECTIONS
Economics

By the end of the 1950s, some 600 corporations—less than one half of 1 percent of all corporations in the U.S.—accounted for more than 50 percent of all corporate income.

PRIMARY SOURCE

Description of Change: excerpted
Rationale: excerpted to focus on main idea

MAKING CONNECTIONS
Sociology

Most women—some 65 percent by 1960—worked in what was called the "pink collar ghetto." This was a work setting in which the majority of employees were women holding low-paying jobs with little opportunity for promotion.

CHANGES IN THE WORKPLACE

Many of the social shifts in America were related to shifts in the work force. Large corporations prospered during the decade as some 5,000 companies merged to form larger organizations.

Automation. American factories were also changing. Throughout the 1950s companies introduced machines that could perform industrial operations faster and more efficiently than human workers could. This process of **automation** greatly increased productivity. But automation also reduced the number of manufacturing jobs. Many workers began to fear an automated future, as one popular song noted:

> 66 I walked, walked, walked into the
> foreman's office.
> To find out what was what.
> I looked him in the eye and said,
> "What goes?"
> And this is the answer I got:
> His eyes turned red, then green,
> then blue
> And it suddenly dawned on me—
> There was a robot sitting in the seat
> Where the foreman used to be. 99

Automation also affected America's farms as new machinery boosted production while reducing the labor force. While farm productivity

▲ Ford Motor Company closed its Somerville, Massachusetts, plant in 1958. Over 1,000 employees were directly affected by the decision.

increased from 1950 to the 1960s, the farm population shrank from 23 million to 15.6 million.

As the number of manufacturing and farming jobs decreased, professional and service jobs increased. Huge new corporations required a multitude of managers, supervisors, and clerical workers. Furthermore, the spending spree of the 1950s created millions of retail jobs. Many of the newly created service jobs were in occupations traditionally filled by women, such as nursing, teaching, retail sales, and clerical work. By 1960, women made up about one third of the total work force. But many women continued to earn much less than men in the same fields, and few received promotions to management jobs.

The new union style. Changes in the work force also influenced organized labor. Boosted in part by the merger of the AFL and CIO in 1955, union membership grew steadily in the mid-1950s, peaking at some 18.5 million in 1956.

To help workers get their fair share of economic prosperity, union leaders abandoned efforts at economic, political, and social reforms in favor of achieving gains in wages and benefits. In order to do so, they sought accommodation, rather than confrontation, with management. George Meany, the AFL–CIO's first president, boasted that he had never led a strike. Further, he said he had no interest in reforming society. His only goal, he stated, was to ensure "an ever rising standard of living" for his members.

Many unions fought for and won guaranteed annual wages and cost-of-living adjustments—automatic pay raises linked to the rate of inflation. In return, unions made concessions, such as accepting automation plans or changes in work rules or production levels.

In the late 1950s newspapers reported corruption and links to organized crime among some union officials. Congress attempted to crack down on union corruption by passing the **Landrum-Griffin Act** of 1959, which banned ex-convicts from holding union offices, required frequent elections of officers, and regulated the investment of union funds. The negative publicity hurt union membership, which steadily declined after 1957.

▪▪ **The work force changed through automation, an increase in professional and service jobs, and a new approach by union leaders.**

RETEACH Organize students so that a roughly equal number are assigned to each subsection of Section 2. Direct each student to write a question about the material in his or her assigned subsection. Then use the questions to quiz the entire group.

Closure

Ask students to use evidence from the section to support or challenge the use of the phrase *the affluent society* as a description of Americans in the 1950s.

Extension

INVESTIGATE Have pairs of students investigate information about 1950s television programs. Have pairs write a brief synopsis—length, major characters, plot line, and so on—for each program.

CREATE Have students work individually or in small groups to design a poster promoting or criticizing President Eisenhower's modern Republicanism. Call on volunteers to explain their posters.

URBAN RENEWAL

The changing work force also affected those moving to the cities. Automation had eliminated many of the semiskilled jobs traditionally taken by city newcomers. Skilled workers often found that their way to better jobs was blocked by discrimination.

Nowhere was discrimination more obvious than in housing. Prevented by poverty and by discriminatory real-estate practices from moving into newer neighborhoods, African Americans, Hispanics, and Native Americans were generally limited to crowded tenements and old housing in the poorest neighborhoods. Eventually, however, these neighborhoods provided a sense of community for those who lived there. Local stores, churches, and social clubs gave structure to the lives of those struggling to adjust to the cities. As one resident of El Barrio, New York's Puerto Rican neighborhood, observed:

66 This is our neighborhood. . . . We consider this part of the city to be ours. . . . The stores, barbershops, restaurants, butcher shops, churches, funeral parlors, . . . everything is all Latino. 99

Government officials, however, saw only neglected, shabby buildings. To improve inner-city housing, the federal government proposed **urban renewal** programs to replace old, run-down inner-city buildings with new ones. Across the country the government bulldozed older urban neighborhoods to

▲ A poor family crowds into the kitchen of a small tenement in Harlem, New York City.

make way for some 417,000 low-income public housing units. Most of these units were cramped apartments, so small, one resident said, "You feel like you can't breathe." The new high-rise buildings also had a cold, impersonal atmosphere. The sense of community that people had felt in the old neighborhoods was gone.

PRIMARY SOURCE
Description of Change: excerpted
Rationale: excerpted to focus on main idea

SECTION REVIEW ANSWERS

IDENTIFY

For significance, see the following pages:
Oveta Culp Hobby (p. 814)
modern Republicanism (p. 814)
Relocation Act (p. 815)
termination (p. 816)
Highway Act (p. 817)
baby boom (p. 817)
automation (p. 820)
George Meany (p. 820)
Landrum-Griffin Act (p. 820)
urban renewal (p. 821)

1. *Poor whites, African Americans, Hispanics, and Native Americans moved to cities; many in middle class moved to suburbs.*
2. *automation, increase in professional and service jobs, new approach by union leaders*
3. *because of economic expansion and spreading prosperity; emphasis on conformity and consumerism*
4. *Articles might argue that TV perpetuates ethnic stereotypes, rarely shows women with careers, portrays families as white, middle-class suburbanites with wage-earning father and homemaker mother.*
5. *crowded minorities into run-down tenements; replaced old neighborhoods with public housing that lost community atmosphere*

■ **S E C T I O N   2   R E V I E W**

IDENTIFY and explain the significance of the following: Oveta Culp Hobby, modern Republicanism, Relocation Act, termination, Highway Act, baby boom, automation, George Meany, Landrum-Griffin Act, urban renewal.

1. **MAIN IDEA** How did the American population shift during the 1950s?
2. **MAIN IDEA** What changes occurred in the work force during the 1950s?
3. **IDENTIFYING CAUSE AND EFFECT** Why are the 1950s considered boom years? How were American values affected by the economic boom?
4. **WRITING TO EVALUATE** Imagine you are a television critic during the 1950s. Write an article for *TV Guide* that assesses the portrayal of ethnic groups, women, and families on television.
5. **HYPOTHESIZING** What effect did discrimination in housing have on ethnic groups? Why were some ethnic communities upset with urban renewal programs?

PREVIEW WORKSHOP

Following is a list of the significant people, places, and terms in this section. You may wish to use this list as a section preview.

People
- Thurgood Marshall
- Rosa Parks
- Martin Luther King, Jr.
- Orval Faubus

- Ralph Ellison
- Jack Kerouac

Places
- Topeka, Kansas
- Montgomery, Alabama
- Little Rock, Arkansas

Terms
- *Brown* v. *The Board of Education of Topeka*

- Montgomery Improvement Association
- "Little Rock Nine"
- Civil Rights Act of 1957
- Beats
- silent generation
- juvenile delinquency
- rock 'n' roll

FOCUS OBJECTIVES

- Explain why the *Brown* v. *Board of Education* decision and the Montgomery bus boycott were major turning points for the civil rights movement.

- Determine what the Central High School crisis demonstrated about some white southerners' attitudes toward desegregation.

- Describe how teenagers rebelled against the conformity of the 1950s.

822

Section 3

VOICES OF DISSENT

FOCUS

- **Why were the *Brown* v. *Board of Education* decision and the Montgomery bus boycott major turning points for the civil rights movement?**
- **What did the Central High School crisis demonstrate about some white southerners' attitudes toward desegregation?**
- **How did teenagers rebel against the conformity of the 1950s?**

*A*lthough politics and popular culture in the 1950s emphasized conformity, a few voices spoke out against the system. African Americans, tired of segregation and discrimination, launched the civil rights movement to demand equality. Meanwhile writers, including the Beats, and a new style of music called rock 'n' roll sowed the seeds of rebellion in teenagers.

Rebel Without a Cause movie poster

*B*ROWN v. BOARD

The NAACP had long waged a campaign against segregation in education, a practice upheld by the Supreme Court's 1896 "separate but equal" doctrine in *Plessy* v. *Ferguson* (see Chapter 13). The NAACP had been able to open some all-white universities and graduate schools to African American students by demonstrating that in most cases separate educational facilities for black students were far inferior to the facilities established for whites only. But the Court continued to maintain that segregation in and of itself was legal.

In 1952 a group of cases that challenged segregation in public schools came before the Supreme Court in the form of *Brown* v. *The Board of Education of Topeka*. The case involved Linda Brown, a young African American student from Topeka, Kansas. Segregation in Topeka's schools prevented her from attending an all-white elementary school a short walk from her home. Instead, she had to travel a long distance over dangerous railroad tracks to get to an all-black school.

Arguing on Brown's behalf, NAACP lawyer Thurgood Marshall introduced data that suggested segregation psychologically damaged African American students by lowering their self-esteem.

▼ **Thurgood Marshall (center) discussed legal strategies for fighting school segregation cases with other NAACP attorneys in 1954.**

MOTIVATING:
LINK TO TODAY

Ask students who they think are today's voices of dissent in the U.S. Encourage students to identify the issues protested and the methods used by these persons. Then, as students read the section, have them compare the nature of dissent in the 1990s to dissent in the 1950s.

Teaching the Section

THE CIVIL RIGHTS MOVEMENT

Encourage students to imagine they are involved in the civil rights struggle in the South during the mid-1950s. Have them write a letter to a friend, explaining how they think the Supreme Court decision in *Brown* v. *Board of Education* and the Montgomery bus boycott will affect the civil rights movement and life for African Americans in the future. Call on volunteers to read their letters to the class. Students may wish to include their letters in their portfolios.

Marshall's arguments greatly influenced the Court's ruling, which was issued on May 17, 1954. Written by Chief Justice Earl Warren, the unanimous decision declared that segregation generated

> 66 a feeling of inferiority . . . that may affect [children's] hearts and minds in a way unlikely ever to be undone. . . . In the field of education the doctrine of "separate but equal" has no place. Separate educational facilities are inherently unequal. 99

Many Americans praised the decision as a long overdue step toward ending segregation entirely. Scholar Allison Davis hailed it as the salvation of American industry because it would create more skilled black workers: "The survival of the United States seems to depend upon its developing the ability of millions of our citizens whose capacities have been crippled by segregation."

Some states moved quickly to end school segregation. Many white southern leaders, however, reacted to the decision with alarm. The governor of Virginia, for instance, vowed to use every legal means at his command to maintain segregated schools in his state. Because of the resistance from the South, the Supreme Court issued a ruling in 1955 calling on the federal district courts to end school segregation "with all deliberate speed."

THE MONTGOMERY BUS BOYCOTT

The NAACP next aimed at ending segregation on southern transportation systems, beginning their efforts in Montgomery, Alabama. Local NAACP leaders had been looking for a test case to challenge the practice of forcing African American citizens to ride in the back of buses. On December 1, 1955, Rosa Parks, a black seamstress, provided them with their case when she refused to give up her bus seat to a white passenger.

BIO GRAPHY Born in 1913 in Tuskegee, Alabama, Rosa Parks moved to the Montgomery area at a young age. Her mother was determined that Parks would receive a good education. Montgomery did not have a high school for black students, so her parents sent her to the laboratory school at Alabama State College. Because discrimination prevented her from finding a job that matched her education, she found work as a seamstress. She also became involved in the civil rights movement, holding office in the Montgomery chapter of the NAACP.

In the late 1950s Parks moved to Detroit, where she began working for Congressman John Conyers in 1967. She has continued her commitment to civil rights action and has won numerous awards, including the NAACP's Spingarn Medal, recognizing the "highest or noblest achievement" by an African American.

Rosa Parks

Parks's refusal to give up her seat led to her arrest and conviction for violating the city's segregation laws. In protest, Montgomery's 50,000 African Americans organized a boycott against the bus system. The **Montgomery Improvement Association** (MIA), a group of local civil rights leaders, persuaded the community to continue the boycott while the NAACP and Parks fought her conviction in the courts.

The MIA chose as its spokesperson Martin Luther King, Jr., a 26-year-old Baptist minister who was new to the town. An energetic and charismatic speaker, King could inspire large audiences. His ability to move people helped hold the African American community together as the bus boycott dragged on for months.

White racists tried every method from intimidation to physical violence to break the boycott. White vigilantes attacked and beat boycotters and bombed the houses of King and other MIA leaders. Many boycotters—including Rosa Parks—lost their jobs. But King urged the black community not to respond to violence with more violence. Finally, the peaceful protest worked. In November 1956 the Supreme Court declared both the Montgomery and the Alabama segregation laws unconstitutional. By the end of the year, Montgomery had a desegregated bus system, and the civil rights movement had a new leader—Martin Luther King, Jr.

The successful struggle of thousands of Montgomery blacks to win their basic human rights marked a blow to racism—and to the general fear of standing up against those in power engendered by Cold War hysteria in America. Not surprisingly, Martin Luther King, Jr., was accused of being a Communist by many who opposed the movement. Some southern whites, however, reluctantly accepted that change had to

HISTORICAL SIDELIGHTS

A Southern Manifesto
In 1956 more than 100 southern members of Congress issued a "Southern Manifesto" condemning the Supreme Court's *Brown* ruling as "a clear abuse of judicial power." Only 23 southern members of the House and only 3 southern senators, Lyndon Johnson of Texas among them, refused to sign the document.

HISTORICAL SIDELIGHTS

Spreading the Word
To publicize the boycott, Jo Ann Robinson, a teacher at Alabama State College, stayed up all night printing 35,000 handbills, which she and some of her students distributed throughout the city on the morning of December 2. A local white reporter got one of the handbills and wrote a story on the boycott for his newspaper's December 4 edition. This further helped spread word of the boycott to local African Americans.

Teaching the *Section*

CENTRAL HIGH SCHOOL CRISIS

Have students work together to produce a *You Are There* program on the events surrounding the desegregation of Central High School in Little Rock. Assign students roles such as reporters, politicians, African American students, white students, school officials, members of the National Guard, African American bystanders, liberal white bystanders, and white segregationists. After students have presented their program, have them discuss the impact of the Central High crisis on the attitudes of whites and African Americans toward segregation.

▲ In response to a 1956 court ruling, Dallas buses were ordered to end segregation. Shown here is an employee of the Dallas Transit Company removing a separate seating sign from the rear of a bus.

come. As a South Carolina newspaper declared, "Segregation is going—it's all but gone. . . . The South can't reverse the trend." Even so, other white southerners fought to delay change for as long as possible.

■■ *Brown* v. *Board of Education* and the Montgomery bus boycott marked the first steps toward ending segregation in the South.

SHOWDOWN IN LITTLE ROCK

Despite the Supreme Court rulings, school desegregation in the South moved slowly. By the end of the 1956–57 school year, the vast majority of southern school systems remained segregated. In Arkansas, however, school desegregation was progressing with relatively little opposition. Two of the three southern school districts that began desegregation in 1954 were in Arkansas. The Little Rock school board was the first

in the South to announce it would comply with the *Brown* decision.

Little Rock's desegregation plan was set to begin in September 1957 with the admission of nine black students to the all-white Central High School. However, Governor Orval Faubus, about to embark on a bid for reelection, came out against the desegregation plan. The night before school was to start, he ordered the Arkansas National Guard to surround Central High. He did so, he claimed, to protect the school from attacks by armed protesters. "It will not be possible to restore or to maintain order . . . if forcible integration is carried out tomorrow in the schools of this community," he warned.

No real danger existed, but Faubus's claims panicked everyone. Elizabeth Eckford did not receive a message that instructed the black students to stay home. When she attempted to enter the school, a mob of angry whites and a line of armed National Guardsmen met her. She described the ordeal:

❝When I got in front of the school, . . . I didn't know what to do. . . . Just then the guards let some white students through. . . . I walked up to the guard who had let [them] in. . . . When I tried to squeeze past him, he raised his bayonet, and then the other guards moved in. . . . Somebody [in the crowd] started yelling, "Lynch her! Lynch her!"❞

For nearly three weeks the National Guard prevented the students, now known as the "**Little Rock Nine**," from entering the school. Then, under

▶ Elizabeth Eckford bravely walked alone through a crowd of angry, jeering whites before she was turned away from entering Little Rock's Central High School.

TEENAGE REBELLION

Organize students into small groups and direct groups to draw up plans for a special insert titled "How Teenagers Are Rebelling in the 1950s" for a current-affairs magazine. Suggest that groups include in their plans items such as ideas for cover design, a table of contents with brief synopses of articles, and a list of illustrations that might be used. Groups should present and explain their plans to the class.

■■ Ask students to identify the ways in which young people rebel against conformity today.

▶

▲ On November 4, 1957, leaders of the Arkansas branch of the NAACP appeared in court to fight an ordinance forcing them to turn over confidential records. State president Daisy Bates (second from the left) played a central role in helping the Little Rock Nine integrate Central High School.

court order, Faubus removed the National Guard. When the nine attempted to enter the school on September 23, the white mob rioted. Deploring the "disgraceful occurrences" at Central High, President Eisenhower ordered some 1,000 federal troops to Little Rock. On September 25, 1957, under the troops' fixed bayonets, the Little Rock Nine finally entered Central High.

In the midst of the Little Rock crisis, President Eisenhower signed the **Civil Rights Act of 1957**. This act, the first civil rights law since Reconstruction, made it a federal crime to prevent qualified persons from voting. It also set up the federal Civil Rights Commission to investigate violations of the law. A follow-up law, passed in 1960, strengthened the courts' powers to protect blacks' voting rights. But prejudice and discrimination remained a fact of life for most African Americans. Much remained to be done before they could claim victory in the struggle for civil rights.

■■ **The Central High crisis in Little Rock showed that some southern whites were not willing to comply with desegregation.**

QUESTIONING CONFORMITY

While the African American community in the South was challenging segregation, other groups were beginning to question the American culture of consumption and conformity. One such group included a handful of writers and scholars who

sought to expose what one called the "crack in the picture window" of society.

A number of novelists depicted the experiences of those facing poverty and discrimination. In Ralph Ellison's *Invisible Man* (1952), an African American man searches for his place in a society at once both hostile and indifferent to him. His struggle reflects that of many people left out of mainstream society:

❝I am an invisible man. . . . I am a man of substance, of flesh and bone, fiber and liquids—and I might even be said to possess a mind. I am invisible, understand, simply because people refuse to see me. ❞

Other critics attacked suburban society and the corporate mentality of America. Harvard economist John Kenneth Galbraith warned privileged Americans in *The Affluent Society* (1958) that they were ignoring pressing social issues in their pursuit of material possessions and comfort.

Sociologists William Whyte, C. Wright Mills, and David Riesman criticized the new corporate system. Whyte in *The Organization Man* (1956) and Mills in *White Collar* (1951) argued that the need to conform in a large corporation was wiping out the independent spirit of workers. Riesman argued that the country was facing "a silent revolution against work" because work no longer had meaning for people. Many younger Americans were beginning to agree with him.

The **Beats**, a small but influential group of writers and poets, challenged both the literary

▲ Ralph Ellison received the National Book Award in 1953 for his novel *Invisible Man*.

MAKING CONNECTIONS

Literature

While African Americans remained "invisible" to many in white society during the 1950s, their voices were heard by a wider audience in the literary world. In 1950 poet Gwendolyn Brooks became the first African American to win a Pulitzer Prize—for her collection of poems titled *Annie Allen*. Lorraine Hansberry won the New York Drama Critics Circle Award for *A Raisin in the Sun* (1959), her play about an African American family's struggle to obtain decent housing.

PRIMARY SOURCE

Description of Change: excerpted
Rationale: excerpted to focus on main idea

Practice

GUIDED PRACTICE

List the five major headings of the section on the chalkboard, one at a time. Inform students that these are headlines for news stories. Invite volunteers to suggest the main points for each story as you note their responses under the appropriate heading.

INDEPENDENT PRACTICE

Direct students to select one headline listed in the Guided Practice activity. Have them use information on the chalkboard to write a news story to accompany the headline. Call on volunteers to read their stories to the class.

Review and Assessment

REVIEW Direct students to read through the section and note all the words that imply dissent. Encourage students to select three of the words and use them to write paragraphs that summarize the section. Then assign the Section 3 Review on p. 827.

ASSESS Assign the **Section 3 Daily Quiz** in *Core Resources*.

COOPERATIVE LEARNING

Organize students into groups of three and assign each group member one of the chapter's sections. Have group members list all the items mentioned in their sections that they might want to include in a time capsule for the 1950s. Then have group members work together to develop a group list of 10 items. Call on group representatives to present and justify their selections.

HISTORICAL SIDELIGHTS

A Rising Star
Richard Valenzuela, a 17-year-old musician from the Los Angeles area, signed his first recording contract in the late 1950s. At the same time, he changed his surname to Valens so that white disk jockeys would be able to pronounce it. His first two records sold well, especially in the barrios of the big cities, and he appeared to be on the verge of stardom. However, he died in a plane crash in 1959. The biographical movie *La Bamba* (1987) secured Valens's position as a pioneer in the fusion of Mexican American music with mainstream rock 'n' roll.

conventions of the day and the life-styles of the middle class. Allen Ginsberg's poem "Howl," for instance, raged against the nuclear threat and the conventions of corporate America. The Beats wrote as they lived—without form, plot, planning, or revision. One of the best-known Beat works, Jack Kerouac's novel *On the Road* (1957), was written in a continuous three-week-long session at the typewriter. Kerouac celebrated the search for individual identity and the rejection of stability. One sentence in the novel caught the essence of the Beat philosophy: "We gotta go and never stop going till we get there."

A "SILENT GENERATION"?

Despite many parents' fears, the Beats never grew into a mass movement among young people. Indeed, many observers dubbed the middle-class youth of the 1950s the **silent generation** because of their seeming willingness to conform to consumer culture without protest. Despite the outward appearance of conformity, however, many young people were beginning to question society and to rebel in subtle ways.

Literature and films. Many young people discontented with suburban life found meaning in literature and films. Some identified with Holden Caulfield, the main character of J.D. Salinger's *The Catcher in the Rye* (1951). Disgusted by the hypocrisy of the adult world, Holden declared it "crumby" and "phony." Other young people turned

to satirical magazines, such as *MAD,* which dedicated itself to making fun of everything associated with "the American way of life." Many parents worried that reading such magazines would increase **juvenile delinquency**—antisocial behavior by the young.

Several of the most popular films of the decade reflected images of juvenile delinquency and young, angry rebels frustrated with life. Often their anger was directed not at any one particular thing, but at all of society in general. In the 1953 film *The Wild One,* a character asks the young gang leader played by Marlon Brando what he is rebelling against. Brando snarls back, "Whadda ya got?" This image of the rebel with no direction was reinforced in 1955's *Rebel Without a Cause,* starring James Dean, Natalie Wood, and Sal Mineo as teenagers confused about the values of their suburban families. Many teenagers could identify with that confusion.

The rock rebellion. Many teenagers tried to escape the conformity of suburbia through a new type of music called **rock 'n' roll**. This reworking of black rhythm and blues produced a raw sound very different from many tunes of the day, and teenagers claimed it as their own. Cleveland disc jockey Alan Freed coined the term *rock 'n' roll* in 1951, when he started a rhythm-and-blues show aimed at young white audiences. Soon the sound caught on across the country.

Elvis Presley, a truck driver from Memphis, Tennessee, emerged as rock's leading talent. With his sullen good looks, wild body movements, and blues-influenced vocal style, Presley sent shock waves through the white middle class. African American musicians such as Little Richard, Chuck Berry, and Fats Domino, as well as Hispanic performers like Ritchie Valens, profoundly influenced early rock 'n' roll.

Many parents immediately disliked rock 'n' roll. Some critics called it immoral. Others simply dismissed

◀ **Teenagers tuned to Dick Clark's** *American Bandstand* **to listen to the latest rock 'n' roll records and watch the newest groups perform.**

Closure

Point out that the word *repose* may mean "calm," "tranquility," or "peace." Then write the following on the chalkboard: *The 1950s were years of repose.* Direct students to use information from the section to debate whether or not this characterization of the 1950s in the U.S. is accurate.

Extension

EVALUATE Have students evaluate the social impact of art in the 1950s by writing a review of one of the books or movies mentioned in the section.

COMPARE Ask students to compare the aims and methods of the abolitionists of the mid-1800s to those of civil rights workers of the 1950s.

◀ Ritchie Valens

◀ Fats Domino

▲ Elvis Presley

it as useless noise, pointing out that the lyrics of many popular rock songs did not seem to make any sense, such as in the Silhouettes' 1957 hit "Get a Job":

> ❝ Sha da da da
> Sha da da da da
> Bah do
> Bah yip yip yip yip yip yip yip yip
> Mum mum mum mum mum mum
> Get a job. ❞

Rock 'n' roll also upset many people by seeming to break down the walls of racial segregation. White rockers such as Presley, Jerry Lee Lewis, and Buddy Holly shared the airwaves, and often the stage, with noted black artists. While southern officials were worried about sending black and white teenagers to school together, many of those same teens were listening to the same radio stations and sneaking off to attend the same integrated concerts.

▪▪ **Teenagers challenged conformity through literature, films, and rock 'n' roll.**

PRIMARY SOURCE
Description of Change: excerpted
Rationale: excerpted to focus on main idea

SECTION REVIEW ANSWERS

IDENTIFY

For significance, see the following pages:
Brown v. The Board of Education of Topeka (p. 822)
Thurgood Marshall (p. 822)
Rosa Parks (p. 823)
Montgomery Improvement Association (p. 823)
Martin Luther King, Jr. (p. 823)
Orval Faubus (p. 824)
"Little Rock Nine" (p. 824)
Civil Rights Act of 1957 (p. 825)
Ralph Ellison (p. 825)
Beats (p. 825)
Jack Kerouac (p. 826)
silent generation (p. 826)
juvenile delinquency (p. 826)
rock 'n' roll (p. 826)

LOCATE

For locations, see the map on pp. 1016–1017.

1. *first steps toward ending segregation in the South*
2. *They were unwilling to comply with desegregation.*
3. *that segregation lowered black students' self-esteem*
4. *Stories might refer to conformity and influence of literature, films, and rock 'n' roll.*
5. *Speeches might mention history of segregation, recent successes, and hope for the future.*

■■ ␣ **S E C T I O N ␣ 3 ␣ R E V I E W**

IDENTIFY and explain the significance of the following: *Brown v. The Board of Education of Topeka,* Thurgood Marshall, Rosa Parks, Montgomery Improvement Association, Martin Luther King, Jr., Orval Faubus, "Little Rock Nine," Civil Rights Act of 1957, Ralph Ellison, Beats, Jack Kerouac, silent generation, juvenile delinquency, rock 'n' roll.

LOCATE and explain the importance of the following: Topeka, Kansas; Montgomery, Alabama; Little Rock, Arkansas.

1. **MAIN IDEA** What impact did the decision in *Brown* v. *Board of Education* and the Montgomery bus boycott have on the civil rights movement?

2. **MAIN IDEA** What did events in Little Rock show about attitudes of some southern whites toward school desegregation?

3. **RECOGNIZING POINTS OF VIEW** What arguments did members of the civil rights movement use to help overturn the "separate but equal" doctrine?

4. **WRITING TO EXPRESS A VIEWPOINT** Write a short story involving a teenage character who expresses his or her view of 1950s society.

5. **USING HISTORICAL IMAGINATION** Imagine you are a member of the Montgomery Improvement Association in 1956. Write a speech you would deliver to the community urging them to continue the boycott against the bus system.

Chapter Review Answers

WRITING A SUMMARY

See Essential Points in each section for main ideas.

REVIEWING CHRONOLOGY

3, 4, 2, 5, 1
Assessing Consequences
intensified arms race, led to creation of NASA and to launching of Explorer I

IDENTIFYING PEOPLE AND IDEAS

1. *first woman elected to both houses of Congress; McCarthy critic*
2. *policy of confronting Communist aggression by going to brink of war*
3. *Iranian premier overthrown by CIA plot*
4. *policy giving military aid to Middle East nations fighting Communist aggression*
5. *1959 law passed to crack down on union corruption*
6. *name given to soaring birthrate during 1950s*
7. *policy ending reservation system*
8. *NAACP lawyer who argued* Brown v. Board of Education of Topeka
9. *first black students enrolled at Central High School in 1957*
10. *group of writers who challenged literary conventions and middle-class life-styles*

828

UNDERSTANDING MAIN IDEAS

1. *formalized Korea's division into two nations, heightened U.S. fears of communism*
2. *McCarthy's powerful position in Senate, fear of communism; widespread criticism of his tactics, loss of public support after Army-McCarthy hearings*
3. *domestic life—caused suburban growth and baby boom, led to fears of juvenile delinquency, increased consumerism, encouraged conformity; workplace—led to corporate mergers and to automation, created new professional and service jobs, increased number of women in work force*
4. *successes—*Brown v. The Board of Education of Topeka, *which declared segregated schools illegal; Montgomery bus boycott, which led to Supreme Court declaration that Montgomery and Alabama segregation laws were unconstitutional; setbacks—Central High School crisis, which showed that many white southerners were not willing to obey the law, though Eisenhower reaffirmed federal authority*
5. *Teenagers used them to rebel against the conformity of the culture.*

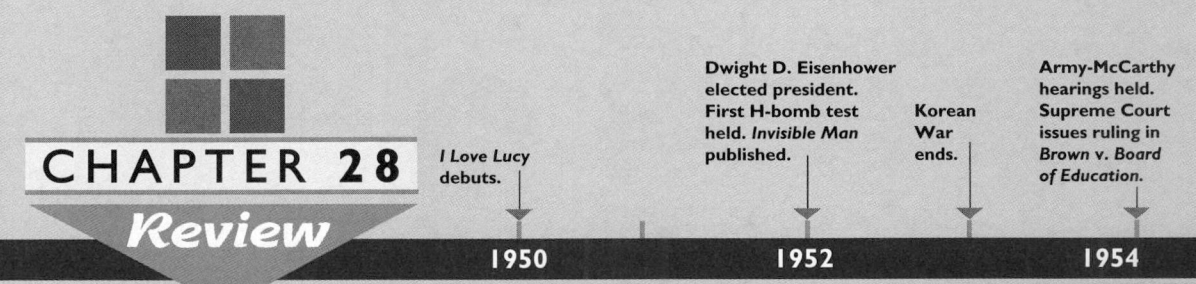

CHAPTER 28
Review

Dwight D. Eisenhower elected president. First H-bomb test held. *Invisible Man* published.

I Love Lucy debuts.

Korean War ends.

Army-McCarthy hearings held. Supreme Court issues ruling in *Brown v. Board of Education.*

1950   1952   1954

WRITING A SUMMARY
Using the essential points of the chapter as a guide, write a summary of the chapter.

REVIEWING CHRONOLOGY
Number your paper 1 to 5. Study the time line above, and list the following events in the order in which they happened by writing the first next to 1, the second next to 2, and so on. Then complete the activity below.

1. U-2 incident occurs.
2. Montgomery bus boycott begins.
3. First H-bomb test held.
4. Army-McCarthy hearings held.
5. *On the Road* published.

Assessing Consequences How did the launch of *Sputnik* affect the United States?

IDENTIFYING PEOPLE AND IDEAS
Explain the historical significance of each of the following people or terms.

1. Margaret Chase Smith
2. brinkmanship
3. Mohammad Mosaddeq
4. Eisenhower Doctrine
5. Landrum-Griffin Act
6. baby boom
7. termination
8. Thurgood Marshall
9. "Little Rock Nine"
10. Beats

UNDERSTANDING MAIN IDEAS
1. How did the end of the Korean War affect Korea and the United States?
2. What factors led to the rise of McCarthyism? What events brought about McCarthy's downfall?
3. How did the economic prosperity of the 1950s affect both domestic life and the workplace?
4. What were some of the major successes and setbacks in ending segregated education in the 1950s?
5. How did literature, films, and music affect middle-class teenagers in the 1950s?

REVIEWING THEMES
1. **Economic Development** How were population shifts affected by the economic boom of the 1950s?

2. **Cultural Diversity** How did some people attempt to rebel against the conformity of the 1950s?
3. **Democratic Values** How did Native Americans and African Americans fight discrimination during this decade?

THINKING CRITICALLY
1. **Analyzing** What strategies did President Eisenhower use to fight the spread of communism? Where were these strategies used?
2. **Evaluating** What events contributed to Americans' fears of nuclear war? How were these fears reduced?
3. **Synthesizing** What was the popular image of a mother's role in society during the 1950s? How did this image conflict with reality?

STRATEGY FOR SUCCESS
Review the Strategies for Success on Recognizing Fallacies in Reasoning on page 220. Examine the following excerpt, written by a white southerner opposed to the forced integration of schools. Then analyze the excerpt for a fallacy in reasoning.

> **❝** Much of the legislation enacted in the Southern states . . . has been aimed basically at preserving domestic tranquillity as well as racial integrity. This is especially true in the fields of education and recreation, where indiscriminate mingling of the races is bound to bring discord and strife. . . . The closing of such institutions in many cases would be the sensible alternative to the emotional, social, and physical upheaval which would follow on the heels of forced race mixing. **❞**

WRITING ABOUT HISTORY
Writing to Classify Create a time line that lists the important events of the civil rights movement in this period.

REVIEWING THEMES

1. *Poor whites, African Americans, Hispanics, and Native Americans moved from rural areas to industrial cities in North, Northeast, or Southwest; many middle-class whites moved to suburbs.*
2. *by protesting in the civil rights movement, and by supporting nonconformist literature, films, and rock 'n' roll*
3. *Native Americans fought termination and relocation programs. African Americans fought TV stereotypes, challenged segregation in courts and through boycotts, and worked for civil rights legislation.*

THINKING CRITICALLY

1. *brinkmanship and threat of massive retaliation in Korea, covert wars in Iran and Guatemala, diplomacy during Suez crisis and Hungarian uprising*
2. *building of H-bomb, launch of Sputnik, U-2 incident; through government campaigns, hearings, and activism to decrease nuclear weapons*
3. *that a woman should be a perfect wife, mother, and full-time homemaker; isolation at home made domestic life boring, need for second income increased number of working mothers*

STRATEGY FOR SUCCESS

The author attributes social upheaval to a single cause, integration, and then concludes that closing the schools is the solution.

WRITING ABOUT HISTORY

Time lines should include Brown v. Board of Education, the Montgomery bus boycott, the Central High School crisis, and the Civil Rights acts of 1957 and 1960.

USING PRIMARY SOURCES

Beethoven and Tchaikovsky were classical composers; song reflects desire to break away from musical traditions like theirs and embrace music that is more like rhythm and blues—with energy and a driving beat.

LINKING HISTORY AND GEOGRAPHY

Alaska gave U.S. close contact with Soviet Union and Asia, while Hawaii gave U.S. a better location from which to defend the Pacific Ocean.

AFL merges with CIO. Montgomery bus boycott begins.

Suez crisis occurs. Soviet troops invade Budapest, Hungary.

Sputnik launched. Federal troops ordered to Little Rock. On the Road published.

Explorer I launched.

U-2 incident occurs.

| 1956 | 1958 | 1960 |

USING PRIMARY SOURCES

Rock 'n' roll music of the 1950s often reflected a desire to break away from old traditions and be more daring. Read the following lyrics from Chuck Berry's "Roll Over Beethoven" (1956). Who are Beethoven and Tchaikovsky? How do the lyrics of the song reflect rebellion and a break from the past?

> 66 *Well, I'm gonna write a little letter,*
> *gonna mail it to my local D.J.*
> *Yes, it's a jumpin' little record I want*
> *my jockey to play*
> *Roll over Beethoven, I gotta hear it*
> *again today*
> *You know my temp'rature's risin' and*
> *the juke box blowin' a fuse*
> *My heart's beatin' rhythm and my soul*
> *keeps a singin' the blues*
> *Roll over Beethoven and tell*
> *Tchaikovsky the news.* 99

Chuck Berry

LINKING HISTORY AND GEOGRAPHY

Alaska and Hawaii became the 49th and 50th states of the union, respectively, in 1959. Study the map in the next column. What strategic advantages of these two areas might have lent support for their statehood during the Cold War?

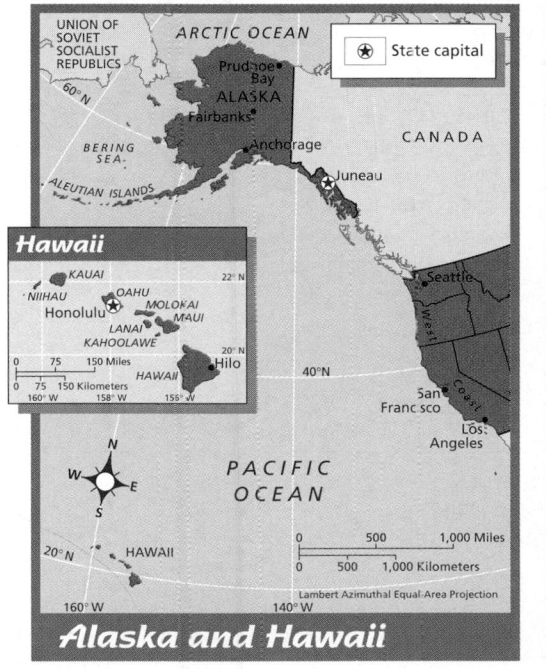

★ State capital

Hawaii

Alaska and Hawaii

BUILDING YOUR PORTFOLIO

Complete the following projects independently or cooperatively.

1. **THE COLD WAR** In Chapter 27 you served as a UN conference delegate. Building on that experience, prepare a speech outlining UN goals.

2. **CIVIL RIGHTS** In Chapter 27 you were a reporter covering the Committee on Civil Rights. Building on that experience, develop an outline of the civil rights movement from 1945 to 1960.

3. **POPULAR CULTURE** Imagine you are a magazine editor. Create a photo essay that reflects cultural changes in the 1950s.

BUILDING YOUR PORTFOLIO

Have students refer to **Building Your Portfolio Worksheet 8**, assigned at the beginning of Unit 8. Use the worksheet to help students monitor their progress on the portfolio projects.

Assessment

Core Resources
- Review Worksheet 28
- Chapter 28 Tests
- Alternative Assessment Forms

Test Generator

THE SIXTIES

1960–1970

Chapter Overview

The 1960s were a time of immense change. President John F. Kennedy took office promising to take the country across a "new frontier." His successor, Lyndon Johnson, pushed a profusion of social legislation designed to transform the U.S. into a "Great Society."

The civil rights movement continued the struggle for racial equality, finally gaining ground through the passage of important civil rights and voting rights laws. However, some movement members felt that progress was too slow and called for more militancy.

The 1960s also saw cultural conflict as many young Americans challenged traditional institutions and forms of expression, launching a counterculture of their own.

THE AMERICAN NATION VIDEODISC PROGRAM
A variety of still images, short videos, and activities are available for you to use as you teach this chapter. See Correlation to *The American Nation Videodisc Program* for barcode correlations and suggestions for using the program.

Chapter Planning Guide

CHAPTER 29	CORE RESOURCE BOOKLETS	AUDIOVISUAL RESOURCES	PROGRAM RESOURCES
INTRODUCTION pp. 830–831	■ Literature Worksheet 29 ■ Building Your Portfolio Worksheet 8	■ Everday Life in America Transparency and Worksheet 29	
TEACHING THE CHAPTER pp. 832–857	■ Graphic Organizer 29 ■ Social Studies Skills Worksheet 29 ■ Geography Worksheet 29 ■ Outline Maps 1, 2, 9, 12, 13, 14	■ *The American Nation Videodisc:* The Peace Corps; John F. Kennedy's Berlin Speech; The Assassination of John F. Kennedy; VISTA Volunteers; Martin Luther King, Jr.; Malcolm X; César Chávez; The Women's Rights Movement ■ Linking Geography and History Transparency and Worksheet 17B	■ Art in American History Transparency and Worksheet 39 ■ *Eyewitnesses and Others,* Volume 2: Readings 64, 65, 66, 67, 68, 71
REVIEW AND ASSESSMENT pp. 858–859	■ Chapter 29 Daily Quizzes ■ Review Worksheet 29 ■ Chapter 29 Tests ■ Alternative Assessment Forms		■ Test Generator

Additional Resources

BOOKS FOR TEACHERS

Blum, John M. *Years of Discord: American Politics and Society.* Norton, 1992. Highly readable narrative of the period.

Friedan, Betty. *It Changed My Life: Writings on the Women's Movement.* Dell, 1991. Essays on a major social movement of the 1960s.

Powledge, Fred. *Free at Last?* HarperCollins, 1992. The civil rights movement through first-person accounts.

BOOKS FOR STUDENTS

*Archer, Jules. *The Incredible Sixties.* Harcourt Brace, 1986. Key events, figures, and movements.

Carson, Clayborne, et al., eds. *Eyes on the Prize Civil Rights Reader.* Viking Penguin, 1991. Accounts of the black struggle for freedom.

Haskins, James, and Kathleen Benson. *The Sixties Reader.* Viking, 1988. Uses primary sources to outline the history of the 1960s.

* for students reading below grade level

MULTIMEDIA MATERIALS

Making Sense of the Sixties: Breaking Boundaries, Testing Limits. Video, 60 min. PBS. A study of the 1960s' youth rebellion and counterculture.

The Second American Revolution, Part II. Video, 58 min. PBS. Details the assault on segregation.

Women in American Life: 1955–1977. Video, 25 min. National Women's History Project. Charts the dramatic changes in women's lives.

THEMES IN AMERICAN HISTORY

USE WITH PAGES 830–831

*L*isted on the right are the themes emphasized in Chapter 29. The questions in boldface type stimulate critical thinking and provide students with an opportunity to discuss the themes within a broadened context. The questions also appear in the pupil's edition on p. 830.

■ GLOBAL RELATIONS

How might foreign policy decisions undermine domestic programs? Students may suggest that foreign policy decisions might require costly measures, such as economic aid to other countries or military spending, that divert resources from domestic programs.

■ DEMOCRATIC VALUES

How might protests help expand democracy? Students might mention that protests could expand democracy by expressing the discontent of groups who feel left out of the political process and/or by calling attention to their problems. In response the government might pass laws or implement policies that expand democracy to empower such groups.

■ CULTURAL DIVERSITY

What are some institutions and traditions that might come under fire by groups questioning conformity? Students might consider institutions such as schools, government agencies, the military, the family, and churches. Traditions might include such things as art, literature, music, styles of dress and hair, language, manners, and life-styles.

CHAPTER STRATEGIES FOR MEETING INDIVIDUAL NEEDS

LIMITED ENGLISH PROFICIENT LEARNERS

Pair students and have them create lists of questions they can use to interview friends, teachers, or others who were teenagers or adults during the 1960s about their memories and feelings about this period. Have students conduct the interviews and compare responses.

TACTILE/KINESTHETIC LEARNERS

Have students work in small groups to sketch the key events and scenes of the 1960s. Ask groups to use their sketches to develop a "slide show" or a mural about the decade.

LEARNERS HAVING DIFFICULTY

Organize students into four groups and assign each group one section's Focus questions. Have groups discuss and write answers to their assigned questions. Then have each group share its answer with the other groups.

AUDITORY LEARNERS

Have students listen to a variety of popular music from the 1960s. (Most public libraries should have a wide selection of period recordings.) Ask students to explain to the class what the music discloses about life during the decade.

VISUAL LEARNERS

Organize students in small groups to design a symbol or logo that represents life in the U.S. in the 1960s. Encourage groups to share their symbols or logos.

GIFTED LEARNERS

Encourage students to write an essay analyzing the role that religion played in the 1960s civil rights movement.

USING THE CHAPTER FOCUS

■ UNDERSTANDING THE MAIN IDEA

Call on a volunteer to read aloud the Understanding the Main Idea paragraph. Then point out that many of the changes of the 1960s continue to have an impact on life in the U.S. today. Ask students to note, as they read the chapter, the changes, developments, and innovations of the 1960s that have influenced their lives.

THEMES

Have students work individually or in small groups to answer the questions under Themes. Save students' responses so that they can compare them with their responses after studying the chapter. (See p. 829B for suggested answers.)

■ THE TIME LINE

Review the time-line entries with students. Point out that some people saw the election of Kennedy as the beginning of a time of hope, and Woodstock as the last act of this period of promise. As students study the chapter, ask them to note the events that marked the rise and decline of hope and promise in the 1960s.

CORE RESOURCES

- **Graphic Organizer 29**
- **Literature Worksheet 29**
- **Outline Maps 1, 2, 9, 12, 13, 14**
- **Building Your Portfolio Worksheet 8**

AV RESOURCES

- **Everday Life in America Transparency and Worksheet 29**

ABOUT THE ILLUSTRATION

Some 200,000 people surrounded the Reflecting Pool, between the Washington and Lincoln memorials, at the culmination of the March on Washington on August 28, 1963. The media had predicted that such an event—at the time the largest political gathering in U.S. history—would result in violence. But, buoyed by Martin Luther King, Jr.'s magnificent "I Have a Dream" speech, the crowd remained remarkably peaceful. Point out that President Kennedy and other politicians initially opposed the march because they believed it would result in adverse publicity for the civil rights movement. Then ask students how effective they think such mass demonstrations are in bringing about social change.

Chapter 29

1960–1970

THE SIXTIES

FOCUS

UNDERSTANDING THE MAIN IDEA

The 1960s marked a decade of great change in America. The promise of President John Kennedy's administration was cut short by his assassination. But the new president, Lyndon Johnson, ushered in major social reforms through the Great Society programs, while civil rights leaders finally gained some ground in the struggle for equality. Their success inspired other groups, including some middle-class women and college students, to challenge traditional society.

THEMES

- **■ GLOBAL RELATIONS** How might foreign policy decisions undermine domestic programs?

- **■ DEMOCRATIC VALUES** How might protests help expand democracy?

- **■ CULTURAL DIVERSITY** What are some institutions and traditions that might come under fire by groups questioning conformity?

1960	1962	1964		1968	1969
John F. Kennedy elected president.	Cuban missile crisis erupts.	Freedom Summer launched.		Martin Luther King, Jr., assassinated.	Woodstock Music Festival occurs.

⬛▶ LINK TO THE PAST

Create a two-column flip chart with the headings *Civil Rights* and *Challenge to Conformity*. Ask students to identify the major events and developments in the struggle for civil rights and the challenge to conformity during the 1950s. Write their responses on the flip chart. *(Civil Rights: 1954—Brown v. Board of Education; 1955–56—Montgomery bus boycott; 1957—Central High School crisis in Little Rock, Civil Rights Act. Challenge to Conformity: scholarly and fictional works; movies, such as* The Wild One *and* Rebel Without a Cause; *and rock 'n' roll music.)* As students study the chapter, have them add related entries for the 1960s.

⬛ LINK TO THE PAST ▶

During the Eisenhower era the Cold War intensified. On the domestic front the civil rights movement gained momentum from the Supreme Court ruling on school desegregation and from the success of the Montgomery bus boycott. By the end of the 1950s, the popular culture's emphasis on conformity and consumerism came under attack from the Beats and rock 'n' roll.

March on Washington for civil rights, 1963

In 1960, voters chose the youngest man ever elected president, the 43-year-old John F. Kennedy, to succeed one of the oldest presidents up to that time, the 70-year-old Dwight Eisenhower. Kennedy brought a spirit of youth and hope to the nation—a spirit reflected in the dramatic changes of the 1960s. The civil rights movement continued its success, winning expansion of voting rights for African Americans and further breaking down the walls of segregation in the South. Other groups, such as Mexican Americans, Native Americans, and women, also pressed for fairer treatment. Throughout America the generation raised after World War II started to question traditional society through organized protests, music, and the creation of a counterculture.

On the foreign front, the Cold War reached its most dangerous crisis when the United States and the Soviet Union came to the brink of nuclear war in Cuba. Afterward, both nations worked to ease tensions between them. During this period, the United States also increased its involvement in Latin America and Vietnam. As the Vietnam conflict shifted funding from domestic programs, such as President Lyndon Johnson's Great Society reforms, discontent grew within American society. By the end of the 1960s, much of the idealism that began the decade was lost in the wake of violence and division.

African dashiki, worn by American youths in the 1960s

FOCUS OBJECTIVES

- Describe how the Kennedy administration tried to boost the economy.

- Explain the purpose of flexible response.

- Identify the events that sparked the Cuban missile crisis and analyze how it changed Soviet-American relations.

HISTORICAL SIDELIGHTS

A New Beginning

The spirit of change in America was symbolized by the contrast between the outgoing and incoming presidents at Kennedy's inauguration. Eisenhower huddled in a heavy overcoat to combat the chill January air. Kennedy, wearing no topcoat, radiated energy and appeared the very embodiment of youth. The difference between the two provided a vivid illustration of the theme of Kennedy's inaugural address.

CORE RESOURCES

• Section 1 Daily Quiz

AV RESOURCES

• *The American Nation* Videodisc: The Peace Corps; John F. Kennedy's Berlin Speech

PREVIEW WORKSHOP

Following is a list of the significant people, places, and terms in this section. You may wish to use this list as a section preview.

People
- Richard Nixon
- John F. Kennedy
- Fidel Castro

Places
- Cuba
- Bay of Pigs
- San Cristobal

Terms
- New Frontier
- Equal Pay Act
- flexible response
- Peace Corps

- Alliance for Progress
- Berlin Wall
- Limited Nuclear Test Ban Treaty
- "hot line"

Section 1

THE NEW FRONTIER

FOCUS

- **How did the Kennedy administration try to boost the economy?**
- **What was the purpose of flexible response?**
- **What events sparked the Cuban missile crisis? How did the crisis change Soviet-American relations?**

President Eisenhower's successor, the 43-year-old John F. Kennedy, brought fresh vigor to the office, promising that his administration would be a "new frontier." On the domestic front, he boosted the economy, mostly by increasing spending on defense and space exploration. Internationally, he first stood firm against the Soviets, then tried to ease Soviet-American tensions. In November 1963, Kennedy's presidency ended suddenly and tragically, its bright promise largely unfulfilled.

President John F. Kennedy and Jacqueline Kennedy in 1961

A NEW BEGINNING

As 1960 began, many voters were looking for someone to inject new life into the White House. Economic recession in the late 1950s, coupled with the Soviet Union's advances in space technology, led many people to fear that the country was falling behind its counterparts.

As expected, the Republicans chose Richard Nixon as their presidential candidate in the upcoming election. His solid performance as Eisenhower's vice president had won him wide support among Republican party members. Trying to appeal to a wide variety of voters, he downplayed his past roles in conservative causes such as the investigations of the House Committee on Un-American Activities.

Senator John F. Kennedy of Massachusetts eventually emerged as the Democratic candidate. The Irish American Kennedy promised to "get America moving again." Voters were impressed with his charm, wit, good looks, and war record. But as a Roman Catholic, he faced falling victim to the same prejudices that had hurt Al Smith's presidential bid in 1928. To neutralize concerns about his religion, Kennedy assured voters that he believed firmly in the separation of church and state.

◀ The second of four televised debates between Senator John F. Kennedy and Vice President Richard Nixon took place on October 7, 1960.

Call on volunteers to recall the aims of the domestic agendas of presidents Roosevelt, Truman, and Eisenhower. *(Roosevelt: providing relief, economic recovery, and economic reform during the depression; Truman: extending the New Deal; Eisenhower: balancing liberal social programs with conservative financial policies)*

Then tell students that this section explains President Kennedy's New Frontier agenda, which, on the domestic front, included attempts to boost the economy and to address social problems such as poverty. As students read the section, have them compare the major aims of Kennedy's domestic programs with those of his predecessors.

Nixon led in the polls until the first of four televised debates. Tired and gaunt after an illness, Nixon seemed nervous and uneasy before the cameras. Kennedy, on the other hand, appeared fit, confident, and relaxed. The election was close. Kennedy and his running mate, Lyndon B. Johnson of Texas, defeated Nixon and his running mate, Henry Cabot Lodge, Jr., of Massachusetts, by a margin of fewer than 120,000 popular votes. Their electoral victory was more decisive—303 to 219.

Kennedy was the youngest person ever elected president. His youth helped provide the theme to his inaugural address:

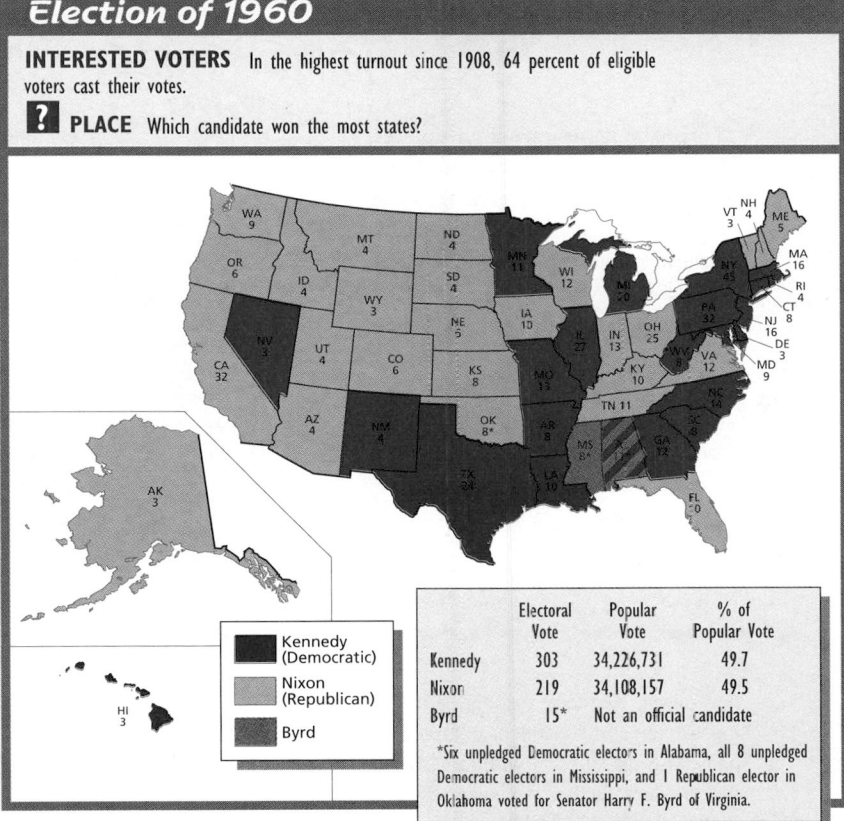

Election of 1960

INTERESTED VOTERS In the highest turnout since 1908, 64 percent of eligible voters cast their votes.

? PLACE Which candidate won the most states?

	Electoral Vote	Popular Vote	% of Popular Vote
Kennedy	303	34,226,731	49.7
Nixon	219	34,108,157	49.5
Byrd	15*	Not an official candidate	

*Six unpledged Democratic electors in Alabama, all 8 unpledged Democratic electors in Mississippi, and 1 Republican elector in Oklahoma voted for Senator Harry F. Byrd of Virginia.

Legend:
- Kennedy (Democratic)
- Nixon (Republican)
- Byrd

66 Let the word go forth . . . that the torch has been passed to a new generation of Americans. . . . The energy, the faith, the devotion which we bring to this endeavor will light our country and all who serve it. . . . And so, my fellow Americans—ask not what your country can do for you—ask what you can do for your country. 99

THE DOMESTIC FRONTIER

Kennedy stocked his cabinet with young, well-educated men, including his brother Robert as attorney general. These advisers shared the belief that government should offer solutions to national and global problems. Since Kennedy had once compared these problems to a "new frontier," his agenda became known as the **New Frontier**.

One of the first domestic challenges that Kennedy faced was stimulating the economy. To help revive the economy, the president called for an increase in government spending, giving defense and space programs top priority. This emphasis reflected Cold War concerns. In April 1961 Soviet cosmonaut Yuri Gagarin had completed the first orbital space flight, sparking fears that the United States was falling behind in the space race. In late May 1961 Kennedy responded by challenging the nation to "commit itself to achieving the goal, before this decade is out, of landing a man on the moon and returning him safely to earth."

By the end of 1961, inflation was down, but unemployment was still relatively high. Kennedy hoped to keep inflation down and further the recovery by getting labor and business to agree to informal wage and price controls. Businesses had been granting higher wages to workers and then passing the costs on to consumers in the form of higher prices. Kennedy urged businesses to limit prices in return for workers agreeing to fewer pay raises. When U.S. Steel dramatically raised prices in 1962 after workers had agreed to accept small

Map Caption Answer
Nixon, with 26 to Kennedy's 22; Byrd won 2

MAKING CONNECTIONS
Science
Although public attention focused on NASA's manned space flights, unmanned flights also broadened knowledge of space. In August 1962, for example, NASA launched *Mariner 2* on a journey to Venus. Nearly 16 weeks later, NASA received a 42-minute radio transmission that provided valuable information about that mysterious planet.

PRIMARY SOURCE
Description of Change: excerpted
Rationale: excerpted to focus on main idea

Teaching the Section

BOOSTING THE ECONOMY

On the chalkboard draw a three-column chart with *Concern, Action,* and *Outcome* as headings. Under *Action* make the following entries: *spending on defense and the space program increased; voluntary price and wage controls suggested; cut in personal and corporate taxes proposed; status of women in America examined by presidential commission.* Call on volunteers to identify the causes and consequences of these actions, and note their suggestions in the appropriate columns. Then use the chart as the starting point for a class discussion to explore how each action was intended to boost the economy, and to assess the effectiveness of the administration in this area.

THE AMERICAN NATION VIDEODISC PROGRAM

The Peace Corps

2B   35399   1:00

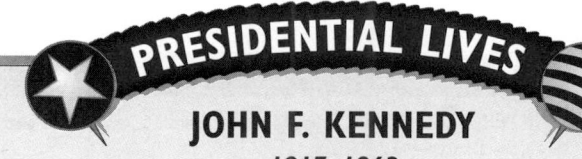

PRESIDENTIAL LIVES

JOHN F. KENNEDY
1917–1963

in office 1961–1963

Throughout his career in politics, John F. Kennedy presented an image of youth and vigor. Kennedy always looked younger than his years. On several occasions after he entered Congress he was mistaken for a page boy. Once, while he was a senator, a guard tried to stop him from using a special telephone with the warning: "Sorry, mister, these are reserved for the Senators."

Although Kennedy was frequently photographed in sporting activities such as football, sailing, and

swimming, his athletic image hid the severe physical pain he suffered through most of his adult life. During World War II he suffered a severe back injury after his naval vessel sank. For the rest of his life, Kennedy would endure extreme pain from this injury and from the effects of Addison's disease. His brother Robert once recalled that "at least one half of the days that he spent on this earth were days of intense physical pain." Publicly, however, he seldom displayed signs of physical strain.

pay raises, Kennedy responded in anger, threatening to cancel government contracts with the company. U.S. Steel soon withdrew the price hike, but the incident further weakened Kennedy's already shaky relationship with the business community.

■■ **Kennedy helped stimulate the economy through increased federal spending, especially in space and defense programs.**

Kennedy also had problems getting cooperation from Congress. A coalition of southern Democrats and conservative Republicans in Congress blocked about two thirds of the president's domestic programs. Early in 1963 Kennedy proposed a $13.5 billion reduction in personal and corporate taxes to boost consumer spending and business investment. Congress, however, was not convinced that tax cuts were wise. As 1963 drew to a close, the tax-cut proposal remained tied up in the Senate.

One area of domestic policy that Congress did support involved women's rights. Kennedy appointed a presidential commission to examine the status of women in America. The

commission report, completed in 1963, noted that while the number of working women in America had increased in recent years, women still faced discrimination in hiring and received less pay than men for the same jobs.

The president responded by issuing an order requiring the civil service to grant jobs "solely on the basis of ability to meet the requirements of the position, and without regard to sex." The commission report also led to passage of the **Equal Pay Act** in June 1963, which made it illegal for employers to pay female workers less than male workers for the same job.

▼ On June 10, 1963, President Kennedy signed into law the Equal Pay Act, which required that women receive pay equal to that of men for performing the same job.

Call on a volunteer to explain the strategy of flexible response and to list the military options it provided for dealing with international crises. Next, have students identify nonmilitary actions Kennedy supported in order to prevent the expansion of communism. Then create on the chalkboard a chart of international events discussed in the section. Ask students to cite how, and to what degree, the Kennedy administration applied military and nonmilitary options to each event and add students' responses to the chart.

KENNEDY AND THE COLD WAR

In foreign affairs Kennedy tended to follow the Cold War policies of his predecessors. As a World War II veteran, he shared Eisenhower's belief in the need for military strength; but unlike his predecessors, Kennedy did not want to rely primarily on the threat of nuclear weapons to deter Communist expansion. He preferred to have a range of options open in case of international crises—a strategy called **flexible response**. To expand the nation's options, the Kennedy administration continued the nuclear arms buildup started under Eisenhower and strengthened conventional forces. In addition, the government established special military units like the Green Berets to assist nations struggling to combat communist rebels.

▲ By 1967 some 10,200 Peace Corps volunteers worked in rural communities throughout the world. Shown here is Molly Heit, a schoolteacher in Peru who taught her students how to earn extra money by weaving simple tapestries for tourists.

■■ **Flexible response offered a variety of options for dealing with international conflict.**

Kennedy also supported nonmilitary options to prevent Communist expansion. Economic aid to developing countries, he realized, could serve to strengthen their societies and block Soviet intervention. Toward this end, he introduced a number of assistance programs designed to help the developing nations of Africa, Asia, and Latin America. Foremost among these programs was the **Peace Corps**, which sent volunteers to work for two years in developing countries.

The president also introduced a program to expand economic aid to Latin America. The **Alliance for Progress** offered billions of dollars in aid to participating nations. In exchange for money, the countries were expected to develop democratic reforms and encourage capitalism. The alliance was a disappointment, however. By 1963 most of the money that had been given to participating countries was in the hands of corrupt politicians, and few Latin American leaders had enacted reforms. One Latin American writer, Victor Alba, blamed the program's failure on its inability to mobilize the poor majority in Latin American countries:

66 We know who killed the Alliance: the oligarchic governments of Latin America. . . . We know who supplied the poison: the bureaucrats and technicians. And we know who would have defended it if anyone had bothered to let them know that it existed and needed defenders: the people. 99

THE BAY OF PIGS

Latin America was a special target for aid from the United States because the Soviet Union had recently gained a foothold there. In 1959 an uprising led by Fidel Castro succeeded in overthrowing the Cuban dictator, Fulgencio Batista. Many Americans applauded Castro's success, believing he would bring democracy to Cuba. Castro, however, quickly established a Communist-style dictatorship with strong ties to the Soviet Union.

Fidel Castro

Teaching the Section

CUBAN MISSILE CRISIS

Call on volunteers to present a current affairs program on the Cuban missile crisis. One student might act as program moderator/interviewer, others might play the show's guests—such as representatives of the governments involved and policy experts. Still others might act as television reporters offering background stories and reports on developments in the crisis. Remaining class members should "phone in" questions for the show's guests.

INTERNATIONAL CRISES

Pair students and ask each pair to develop a paragraph that explains how the Bay of Pigs, the Berlin Wall, and the Cuban missile crisis were related. Select pairs to read their paragraphs aloud and have the class evaluate each pair's analysis of how these events were connected.

THE AMERICAN NATION VIDEODISC PROGRAM

John F. Kennedy's Berlin Speech

```
2B    43456    :42
```

When Kennedy took office, a plan to overthrow Castro was already in the works. The plan called for an invasion of Cuba by a group of anti-Castro Cuban refugees trained and financed by the Central Intelligence Agency (CIA). Kennedy gave the green light for the plan to proceed.

The invasion was a disaster. When the nearly 1,500 rebels came ashore at Cuba's Bay of Pigs on April 17, 1961, they were quickly pinned down by Cuban forces. The U.S. naval and air support that the rebels expected never materialized—at the last minute Kennedy vetoed any direct U.S. involvement. Equally damaging, the invasion failed to spark a popular uprising among the Cuban people. It took Cuban military forces less than 72 hours to crush the invasion and take some 1,200 surviving rebels prisoner.

Kennedy accepted full responsibility for the failed invasion, but his gesture did little to quiet criticism. One American journalist complained that the Bay of Pigs had made the United States look "like fools to our friends, rascals to our enemies, and incompetents to the rest." The invasion also drove Cuban leaders closer to the Soviets.

▲ To halt the flow of refugees into West Berlin, East Germans set up blockades along subway and elevated rail lines and cut off key crossing points between both sectors. This photograph shows one view of the Berlin Wall in October 1961.

THE BERLIN CRISIS

The Bay of Pigs convinced Soviet leader Nikita Khrushchev that Kennedy was weak and could be intimidated. During a summit meeting in June 1961, Khrushchev issued an ultimatum: the West must recognize the sovereignty of Communist East Germany and remove all troops from West Berlin.

Kennedy refused, saying that he intended to honor the United States' commitment to defend West Berlin. The situation worsened in mid-August, when the East Germans threw up a barbed-wire barrier across Berlin, cutting off traffic between East and West Berlin. Kennedy responded by sending more American troops to the city. The Soviets also bolstered their military forces there. For a few days American and Soviet soldiers eyed each other nervously across the barbed wire.

Tensions gradually eased when it became clear that the real goal of Khrushchev's ultimatum had been fulfilled. The barrier had halted the exodus of East Germans, who during the summer of 1961 had fled to the West through Berlin at a rate of some 1,000 per day. In time the East Germans replaced the barbed wire with a wall of gray concrete and watchtowers. The **Berlin Wall** became the most recognizable symbol of the Cold War.

THE MISSILES OF OCTOBER

After Berlin, Khrushchev continued to try to test America's commitment to containment, leading to the Cold War's greatest crisis. To ward off another invasion, Fidel Castro asked the Soviet Union to provide him with defensive weapons. The Soviets complied and also offered *offensive* weapons— nuclear missiles that could reach major cities of the eastern United States.

CIA officials monitored the Soviet arms buildup in Cuba throughout the summer of 1962. But they did not grasp the full extent of the buildup until October 14, when an American U-2 spy plane photographed numerous missile launching pads near the Cuban town of San Cristobal. Additional U-2 flights over the island located

Practice

GUIDED PRACTICE

Ask students to suggest what the word *frontier* means to them, noting their responses on the chalkboard. Then lead them in a discussion of why Kennedy chose this word to describe his presidential agenda. List conclusions reached on the chalkboard.

INDEPENDENT PRACTICE

Direct students to use the information developed in the Guided Practice activity to design a poster, logo, or bumper sticker that symbolizes Kennedy's New Frontier. Students may wish to include their designs in their portfolios.

Review and Assessment

REVIEW Encourage students to imagine that they are TV newscasters in 1963. Direct them to write a brief commentary on how well President Kennedy has lived up to the ideals of his New Frontier. Call on volunteers to present their commentaries to the class. Then assign the Section 1 Review on p. 838.

ASSESS Assign the **Section 1 Daily Quiz** in *Core Resources*.

▶

---

more missiles, all of which appeared to be aimed at the United States.

On October 22 Kennedy ordered a naval blockade of Cuba to prevent further deliveries of Soviet weapons. He also demanded that the Soviets remove the missiles. Khrushchev promised to challenge the blockade, calling it "outright banditry." Over the next two days, nuclear war loomed on the horizon. In a frenzy of activity, Soviet military advisers armed the missiles in Cuba. American B-52 bombers armed with nuclear weapons prepared for battle. Meanwhile, Soviet ships sailed toward the blockade line.

Suddenly, on October 24, many of the Soviet ships stopped short of the blockade line, turned, and sailed home. "We're eyeball to eyeball," said Secretary of State Dean Rusk, "and I think the other fellow just blinked." On October 28 Khrushchev agreed to dismantle the missile bases in response to Kennedy's promise not to invade

Cuba. Kennedy also secretly agreed to remove American missiles from some foreign sites.

The event marked a historic turning point in Soviet-American relations. Sobered by their brush with nuclear war, Kennedy and Khrushchev sought to ease tensions between their countries. Kennedy declared that it was time to write a new chapter in the Cold War:

> 66 If we are to open new doorways to peace, if we are to seize this rare opportunity for progress, if we are to be as bold and farsighted in our control of weapons as we have been in their invention, then let us now show all the world on this side of the wall and the other that a strong America also stands for peace. 99

In 1963 the United States, the Soviet Union, and Great Britain signed a **Limited Nuclear Test**

PRIMARY SOURCE
Description of Change: excerpted
Rationale: excerpted to focus on main idea

HISTORICAL SIDELIGHTS
At the Brink of War
A number of incidents during the missile crisis brought the superpowers to the very brink of nuclear war. Without orders from Moscow, Soviet troops in Cuba shot down an American U-2. After another U-2 violated Soviet airspace to the north of Alaska, U.S. fighters armed with nuclear weapons took off to protect the plane. In the midst of the crisis, the U.S. Air Force also launched a test missile, which the Soviets thought might be an American first strike. "It was something of a miracle," journalist Tad Szulc commented later, "that we were spared a nuclear war."

Cuban Missile Crisis

1. Aug. 22: Kennedy confirms reports of Russian technicians and supplies arriving in Cuba.

2. Oct. 14: Aerial surveillance reveals missile on launching pads.

3. Oct. 22: Kennedy addresses nation about Soviet threat and announces "quarantine" (blockade) of Cuba.

4. Oct. 23: Khrushchev warns that U.S. actions could lead to thermonuclear war.

5. Oct. 27: Kennedy accepts Khrushchev's proposal to end the crisis: Soviets will remove missiles and U.S. will end blockade and promise not to invade Cuba.

6. Oct. 28: Khrushchev announces that weapons will be returned to the Soviet Union.

⚓ U.S. navy base
✈ U.S. air force base
▽▽ U.S. blockade
⌶ Soviet missile site

NINETY MILES AWAY The United States needed to control the sea lanes to Cuba in order to stop delivery of Soviet missiles, which if launched from Cuba could hit U.S. cities some 2,000 miles away.

❓ **LOCATION** Which bodies of water did the U.S. Navy patrol to enforce the blockade?

Map Caption Answer
Atlantic Ocean, Gulf of Mexico, Caribbean Sea

RETEACH Organize students into small groups and assign each group a subsection of Section 1. Direct each group to develop questions about the main ideas in its subsection. Then have each group exchange its questions with another group and work together to answer the questions it receives.

Closure

Lead the class in a discussion of the following statement: *Both in person and in practice, Kennedy was little different from Eisenhower.*

Extension

ANALYZE Have students consult newspapers and magazines of the time to analyze the impact of television on the 1960 presidential election.

INVESTIGATE Ask students to trace the development of the Peace Corps from its creation to the present day. Have them present their findings in an oral report.

PRIMARY SOURCE
Description of Change: excerpted and bracketed
Rationale: excerpted to focus on main idea; bracketed to clarify meaning

SECTION REVIEW ANSWERS

IDENTIFY

For significance, see the following pages:
Richard Nixon (p. 832)
John F. Kennedy (p. 832)
New Frontier (p. 833)
Equal Pay Act (p. 834)
flexible response (p. 835)
Peace Corps (p. 835)
Alliance for Progress (p. 835)
Fidel Castro (p. 835)
Berlin Wall (p. 836)
Limited Nuclear Test Ban Treaty (p. 837)
"hot line" (p. 838)

LOCATE

For locations, see the map on p. 837.

1. *through increased spending, suggesting wage and price controls and tax cuts*
2. *a range of options, short of nuclear confrontation, to deal with international conflict*
3. *much of the U.S. exposed to Soviet missiles launched from there*
4. *Reports might mention wage and hiring discrimination and recommend ways to correct inequities.*
5. *believed in military strength but gave greater support to nonmilitary programs to contain communism*

CUBAN MISSILE CRISIS

In October 1962 President Kennedy issued an ultimatum to the Soviet Union, demanding that it remove all its missiles from Cuba. For several days the world held its breath as it teetered on the brink of nuclear war. In the end, the Soviets agreed to remove the missiles. Soviet Premier Nikita Khrushchev relates his memory of the crisis:

❝ It had been, to say the least, an interesting and challenging situation. The two most powerful nations of the world had been squared off against each other, each with its finger on the button. You'd have thought that war was inevitable. But both sides showed that if the desire to avoid war is strong enough, even the most pressing dispute can be solved by compromise. . . . I'll always remember the late President [Kennedy] with deep respect because, in the final analysis, he showed himself to be sober-minded and determined to avoid war. He didn't let himself become frightened, nor did he become reckless. He didn't overestimate America's might, and he left himself a way out of the crisis. . . . It was a great victory for us, though, that we had been able to extract from Kennedy a promise that neither America nor any of her allies would invade Cuba. **❞**

Ban Treaty to end the testing of nuclear bombs in the atmosphere and under water. A "**hot line**" was also set up between the United States and the Soviet Union. This direct telephone connection enabled leaders of the two countries to communicate directly during a crisis.

■■ The Bay of Pigs and Berlin Wall crises led to the Cuban missile crisis, after which the United States and Soviet Union worked harder for peace.

 SECTION 1 REVIEW

IDENTIFY and explain the significance of the following: Richard Nixon, John F. Kennedy, New Frontier, Equal Pay Act, flexible response, Peace Corps, Alliance for Progress, Fidel Castro, Berlin Wall, Limited Nuclear Test Ban Treaty, "hot line."

LOCATE and explain the importance of the following: Cuba, Bay of Pigs, San Cristobal.

1. **MAIN IDEA** How did President Kennedy attempt to stimulate the economy?
2. **MAIN IDEA** What was the advantage of the Kennedy administration's foreign-policy strategy of flexible response?
3. **LINKING HISTORY AND GEOGRAPHY** Why were Americans so concerned with the missile buildup in Cuba?
4. **WRITING TO INFORM** Imagine you are a member of the presidential commission assigned to examine the status of women in America. Write a report that summarizes the findings of the commission and presents recommendations for change.
5. **ANALYZING** How did President Kennedy's approach to foreign affairs differ from that of his predecessors?

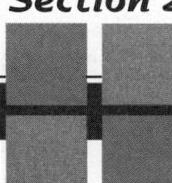

PREVIEW WORKSHOP

Following is a list of the significant people, places, and terms in this section. You may wish to use this list as a section preview.

People
- Lyndon Johnson
- Lee Harvey Oswald
- Juan Bosch

Places
- Dominican Republic

Terms
- Warren Commission
- War on Poverty
- Office of Economic Opportunity
- Great Society
- Medicare

- Medicaid
- Elementary and Secondary School Education Act
- Omnibus Housing Act
- Housing and Urban Development Act

Section 2

JOHNSON'S GREAT SOCIETY

FOCUS
- **What were the four major concerns of the Great Society programs?**
- **How did the Warren Court decisions affect individual rights?**
- **How did foreign policy concerns affect President Johnson's domestic programs?**

*O*n *November 22, 1963, John Kennedy's presidency ended when he was gunned down in Dallas. The new president, Lyndon Johnson, pledged himself to the "ideas and ideals" that Kennedy had "so nobly represented." Johnson sponsored a series of social programs designed to transform American society. These triumphs on the domestic scene, however, were soon overshadowed as foreign policy problems caused Johnson's presidency to unravel.*

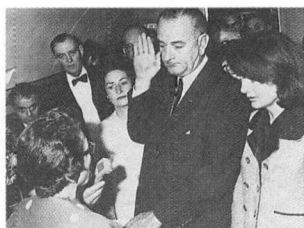

LBJ taking the presidential oath in Dallas, 1963

FOCUS OBJECTIVES
- Identify the four major concerns of the Great Society programs.
- Explain how the Warren Court decisions affected individual rights.
- Determine how foreign policy concerns affected President Johnson's domestic programs.

THE AMERICAN NATION VIDEODISC PROGRAM

The Assassination of John F. Kennedy

2B   44810   :32

TRAGEDY IN DALLAS

Kennedy knew he would have to campaign hard to win reelection in 1964. In November 1963 he traveled to Texas to try to bolster his support there. In Dallas on November 22, enthusiastic crowds lined the route of Kennedy's open-car motorcade from the airport. At about 12:30 P.M., as the motorcade moved through the downtown area, shots rang out. Kennedy slumped over, mortally wounded. Within hours Vice President Lyndon Johnson was sworn in as president. Over the next four days, the nation came together to mourn the dead president. Millions watched the funeral on television. Many Americans felt that the death of the youthful, vibrant Kennedy had also killed something in them. "We'll never be young again," Kennedy staffer Daniel Patrick Moynihan sadly observed.

Within hours of the shooting, the Dallas police had seized Lee Harvey Oswald as a suspect. Two days after his arrest, while he was being moved from one jail to another, Oswald was shot to death by nightclub owner Jack Ruby.

This strange turn of events caused many people to question whether Oswald had acted alone in killing the president or whether he had been part of a larger conspiracy. To end speculation, President Lyndon Johnson named a commission, headed by Chief Justice Earl Warren, to investigate the assassination. The **Warren Commission**, which spent 10 months reviewing the evidence, concluded that there was no evidence of conspiracy: both Oswald and Ruby had acted alone.

JOHNSON TAKES OVER

President Lyndon Johnson appeared very different from the wealthy, charismatic Kennedy. Born in the hill country of central Texas, Johnson grew up in a household that knew, in turn, poverty and relative prosperity. Brash, ambitious, and hardworking, Johnson rose rapidly through the Democratic party ranks. By the time he won election to the Senate in 1948, he was a major power in the party.

A master of compromise, Johnson seemed to always find the middle course on which most

CORE RESOURCES
- **Social Studies Skills Worksheet 29**
- **Section 2 Daily Quiz**

AV RESOURCES
- *The American Nation* Videodisc: The Assassination of John F. Kennedy; VISTA Volunteers

Teaching the Section

THE GREAT SOCIETY

On the chalkboard draw a two-column chart with *Concerns* and *Actions* as headings. Call on volunteers to list what the Johnson administration believed were the major social problems in the U.S. during the 1960s, noting their suggestions in the first column. *(poverty, civil rights, health care, education, urban renewal)* Ask other students to identify the programs launched by Johnson to address these concerns. Write student responses in the second column. (Note that civil rights legislation is the subject of Section 3.) Then use the chart as a starting point for a class discussion on the impact of Johnson's domestic agenda on the U.S. today.

people could agree. This mastery of the political process, coupled with his years of experience in Washington, enabled Johnson to manage the transition of power with considerable skill and tact. Kennedy's cabinet and advisers stayed on to lend continuity to the Johnson administration.

Announcing in his first cabinet meeting in January 1964 that "the day is over when top jobs are reserved for men," Johnson pledged to add 50 more women to high government offices. Some of his choices included consumer advocate Betty Furness, economists Alice Rivlin and Penelope Thunberg, and Texas legislator Barbara Jordan. Although Johnson was able to appoint only 27 women to high offices, his strong support for women's rights marked a significant break with past administrations.

The new president also promised to appoint more Mexican Americans to high positions. He assigned Vicente T. Ximenes (he-MAY-nays) to chair a presidential committee on Mexican American affairs. Other top appointments went to Héctor P. García, a Texas advocate for Mexican American veterans, and to Raul H. Castro, a noted attorney who later became the first Mexican American governor of Arizona.

As 1964 began, Johnson focused his legislative efforts on three areas: tax cuts, civil rights, and poverty. Within weeks he had persuaded Congress to adopt Kennedy's tax program, which cut personal and corporate income taxes by 4 percent. He then pressured members of Congress to enact the long-stalled civil rights bill (see Section 3) and a comprehensive program to fight poverty.

*T*HE WAR ON POVERTY

In 1962, social activist Michael Harrington published *The Other America,* a well-documented study of poverty in the United States. The best-selling book shattered the popular notion that all Americans had benefited from the prosperity of the 1950s. Harrington reported that more than 42 million Americans lived on less than $1,000 per year. He issued a direct challenge for leaders to face the reality of poverty:

❝ [The poor exist] within the most powerful and rich society the world has ever known. Their misery has continued while the majority of the nation talked of itself as being "affluent." . . . In this way tens of millions of human beings became invisible. They dropped out of sight and out of mind. . . . How long shall we ignore this underdeveloped nation in our midst? ❞

Harrington also noted that racism still kept many ethnic groups, especially African Americans, in poverty. He warned that the end of legalized segregation would not change the economic condition of most poor blacks. "The laws against color can be removed," he wrote, "but that will leave the poverty that is the historic . . . consequence of color. As long as this is the case, being born a Negro will continue to be the most profound disability that the United States imposes upon a citizen."

President Johnson responded to such concerns by declaring an "unconditional war on poverty in America." To launch his **War on Poverty**, Johnson sent to Congress a bill calling for the establishment of the **Office of Economic Opportunity** (OEO), with a budget of $1 billion, to coordinate a series of new antipoverty programs. These programs included the Job Corps, a work training program for young people between the ages of 16 and 21; Head Start, an education program for preschoolers from low-income families; and VISTA (Volunteers in Service to America), a domestic version of the Peace Corps. The bill passed Congress in late August 1964.

Whereas Kennedy had trouble pushing legislation through Congress, Johnson fulfilled all the major legislative goals of his first term within eight months. Comparing the two administrations, Texas journalist Liz Carpenter concluded: "Kennedy

▲ VISTA volunteers donated their time and talent to aid poor Americans in the United States and in U.S. territories having limited public services. Shown here is an elementary schoolteacher in the U.S. Virgin Islands.

THE WARREN COURT AND INDIVIDUAL RIGHTS

List on the chalkboard the Supreme Court cases discussed on p. 842. Then have students work in pairs to write newspaper headlines that state how the decision in each case strengthened individual rights. Call on pairs to read their headlines to the class. Use the headlines as a starting point for a discussion of how the Warren Court during the Johnson years shaped the electoral and criminal justice systems of today.

Ask students whether they think that American society has benefited as a result of these reforms.

FOREIGN POLICY AND THE GREAT SOCIETY

Encourage students to assume the role of Americans who strongly support President Johnson's Great Society programs. Direct them to write a letter to the president, expressing their thoughts about how his increased involvement in foreign affairs will affect the Great Society. Call on volunteers to read their letters aloud. Students may wish to include their letters in their portfolios. ▶

inspired . . . Johnson delivered." Opinion polls showed that Americans were overwhelmingly impressed with Johnson's achievements.

JOHNSON'S VISION FOR AMERICA

Riding this wave of popularity, Johnson easily won the Democratic presidential nomination for the 1964 election. He selected Hubert Humphrey, a liberal senator from Minnesota, as his running mate. Adopting a platform that rejected Eisenhower's modern Republicanism, the Republicans chose Barry Goldwater, a conservative senator from Arizona, as their presidential nominee, with New York congressman William E. Miller as his running mate.

Goldwater and Johnson campaign dolls, 1964

Johnson won by a landslide, taking 61 percent of the popular vote and 486 electoral votes to Goldwater's 52. The Democrats further increased their majority in both the House and the Senate. The last president to receive such a mandate was Franklin Roosevelt in 1936.

The plan. Long before the election, Johnson had mapped out plans for his presidency. He saw his major task as building a **Great Society**. In this Great Society, he said, poverty and racial injustice would end. All children would have access to an education that enriched their knowledge and enhanced their talents. The cities would serve not only people's physical needs, but also their desire for culture and their "hunger for community." In short, in the Great Society people would be "more concerned with the quality of their goals than the quantity of their goods."

After his election Johnson moved quickly to make the Great Society a reality. While civil rights was a major part of the Great Society legislation, other issues included health care, education, and urban renewal.

The programs. In 1965 Johnson persuaded Congress to establish **Medicare**, a national health insurance program for people over age 65.

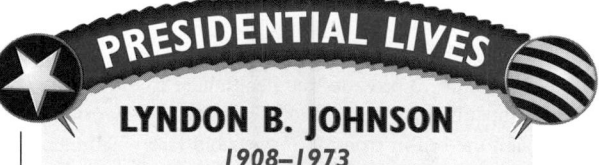

PRESIDENTIAL LIVES

LYNDON B. JOHNSON
1908–1973

in office
1963–1969

Many observers saw Lyndon Johnson as the stereotypical Texas politician—loud, brash, and slightly uncouth. Johnson loved to intentionally shock observers with his language, stories, and behavior. Once during an interview he lifted up his shirt for a photographer to display his scar from gall bladder surgery.

Johnson was also a very physical politician. He would shake people's hands until his own bled and slap others on their backs in a friendly gesture. Fellow senators joked that Johnson had two techniques for getting another senator's attention. There was the Half-Johnson—"when he just put a hand on your shoulder"—and the Full-Johnson—"when he put his arm clear around you and thrust his face close to yours." But Johnson's techniques got results.

He was known as a workaholic who drove himself and his staff to exhaustion to complete multiple tasks. "What's the hurry?" one senator asked another about Johnson's busy schedule. "Rome wasn't built in a day." The other senator replied, "No, but Lyndon Johnson wasn't foreman on that job."

MAKING CONNECTIONS
Communications

During the 1964 campaign, Johnson's supporters aired a television commercial that the *New York Times* has called "probably the most controversial . . . of all time." Intended to imply that the conservative Goldwater was a warmonger, it showed a young girl standing alone in a field, plucking petals from a flower. As the girl plucked each petal, a background voice recited a countdown. At "zero," the picture faded into the mushroom cloud of a nuclear explosion. The voiceover then said: "Vote for President Johnson. . . . The stakes are too high for you to stay home." Critics labeled the commercial "dirty politics." It was quickly withdrawn.

Practice

GUIDED PRACTICE

Write the following topic headings on the chalkboard: *Civil Rights, Health Care, Education, Urban Renewal, Individual Rights.* Call on volunteers to identify the major developments in these areas that took place during the Johnson administration and note their responses under the appropriate heading.

INDEPENDENT PRACTICE

Have students select one of the topics listed in the Guided Practice activity and create editorial cartoons or write poems or rap songs to illustrate the developments listed under their selected topic heading. Students may wish to include their work in their portfolios.

Review and Assessment

REVIEW Direct students to use the section's headings as the main topics for an outline of the section. Have students use the text under each heading to add details to their outline. Students may wish to include their outlines in their portfolios. Then assign the Section 2 Review on p. 843.

ASSESS Assign the **Section 2 Daily Quiz** in *Core Resources*.

HISTORICAL SIDELIGHTS

Master of Symbolism

Making use of symbolism as he had with the Medicaid bill signing, Johnson signed the Elementary and Secondary School Education Act in the one-room schoolhouse he had attended as a boy, with his first teacher, Kate Dietrich, looking on.

PRIMARY SOURCES

Description of Change:
excerpted and bracketed
Rationale: excerpted to focus on main idea; bracketed to clarify meaning

MAKING CONNECTIONS

Political Science

The Warren Court also made controversial decisions on freedom of speech and freedom of the press. In a number of cases the Court refined the definition of what could be regarded as obscene—essentially materials that had no redeeming artistic, scholastic, or social qualities. And in *New York Times Co.* v. *Sullivan* (1964), the Court said that published material about a public official, even though it contained falsehoods, could not be considered libelous unless it was written with malice or reckless disregard for the truth.

Congress also authorized funds for states to set up **Medicaid** to provide free health care to the needy. Johnson traveled to Independence, Missouri, to sign the bill in front of 81-year-old Harry Truman, who had first proposed federally funded health insurance in his Fair Deal program.

Johnson also asked Congress to take action on funding for education. In a moving speech, he recalled:

> ❝ My first job after college was as a teacher in Cotulla, Texas, in a small Mexican American school. . . . Somehow you never forget what poverty and hatred can do when you see its scars on the hopeful face of a young child. . . . It never even occurred to me in my fondest dreams that I might have the chance to help the sons and daughters of those students and to help people like them all over this country.
>
> But now I do have that chance—and I'll let you in on a secret: *I mean to use it.* ❞

Congress responded by passing the **Elementary and Secondary School Education Act** of 1965, which provided $1.3 billion in aid to schools in impoverished areas.

Pushing on, Johnson persuaded Congress to pass the **Omnibus Housing Act** in 1965, followed by the **Housing and Urban Development Act** of 1968. The acts authorized billions of dollars for urban renewal and housing assistance for low-income families. They also established the Department of Housing and Urban Development (HUD) to oversee all federal housing programs. Robert C. Weaver, a member of the New Deal's "black brain trust" headed this new department, making him the first African American member of a presidential cabinet. Weaver declared that the new programs had made Americans aware that "our cities were filled with poorly housed, badly educated, underemployed, desperate, unhappy Americans."

▲ President Johnson congratulates Robert Weaver after he is sworn in as secretary of HUD.

▪▪ **Civil rights, health care, education, and urban renewal were the major concerns of the Great Society programs.**

Great Society laws poured out of Congress at an incredible rate. It was the most hectic period of legislative activity since Franklin Roosevelt's first 100 days.

THE WARREN COURT DECISIONS

Like the Johnson administration, the Supreme Court of the 1960s reflected a spirit of activism. Under the leadership of Chief Justice Earl Warren, the Court sought to continue the trend begun with the 1954 desegregation decision in *Brown* v. *Board of Education* of defining and extending individual rights.

In addition to outlawing segregation across the nation, the Court tried to extend equality in the voting booth with the "one person, one vote" principle. In many congressional districts, sparsely populated rural areas had the same number of representatives as densely populated urban areas. In *Baker* v. *Carr* (1962), however, the Court ruled that election districts should contain approximately equal numbers of voters in order to offer fairly equal representation for everyone.

The Court also issued a series of decisions protecting the rights of those accused of crimes. *Gideon* v. *Wainwright* (1963) required the states to provide lawyers, at public expense, for impoverished defendants charged with serious crimes. *Escobedo* v. *Illinois* (1964) granted accused persons the right to have a lawyer present during police interrogations. *Miranda* v. *Arizona* (1966) said that accused persons must be informed of their rights at the time of their arrests.

Many people saw the Supreme Court's actions as an attempt to build a society more firmly committed to the principle of equality for all, but many others were outraged by such decisions. The Court had overstepped its authority, critics charged, by making law rather than interpreting it. Some went so far as to accuse the chief justice of "high crimes and misdemeanors," erecting billboards that proclaimed "IMPEACH EARL WARREN!" One critic declared:

> ❝ Earl Warren has sinned too grandly for [impeachment]. He has defiled our jurisprudence and made war against the public order. . . . The bench over which he presides has made a mockery of the Supreme Court's appointed function. ❞

RETEACH For each subsection in the section, have students write a sentence that summarizes the main idea. Select students to read their sentences aloud. Have the students choose the best summary sentence for each subsection.

Closure

Ask students to explain whether they think that Lyndon Johnson upheld the "ideas and ideals" represented by John F. Kennedy. Students should support their position with examples from the text.

Extension

EVALUATE Have students research Head Start, a cornerstone program of the War on Poverty. Ask them to evaluate the program by arguing for or against it on the basis of quality, cost, and results.

INVESTIGATE Encourage students to investigate one of the Warren Court cases discussed on p. 842. Have them present their findings in a report to the class.

■■ **The Warren Court's controversial decisions strengthened individual rights.**

*F*OREIGN POLICY AND THE GREAT SOCIETY

While the Great Society was taking shape, foreign affairs also drew President Johnson's attention. In addition to dealing with the Vietnam conflict inherited from Kennedy (see Chapter 30), he became involved in the affairs of the Dominican Republic (see map on page 837). The nation's democratically elected president, Juan Bosch, had been ousted by a military coup in 1963. The new leader never really gained control of the country, and in April 1965, factions within the military rebelled, demanding Bosch's return. The American ambassador, believing that Bosch had fallen under Communist influence, insisted that Johnson intervene to "prevent another Cuba."

Johnson responded promptly, sending in a force of some 22,000 marines. With American support, troops loyal to the military government gained the upper hand and the situation stabilized. In 1966, after relatively free and fair elections put a conservative, pro-American government in power, Johnson withdrew the marines.

Many people in Latin America condemned American intervention in the Dominican Republic, labeling it gunboat diplomacy. Even those who

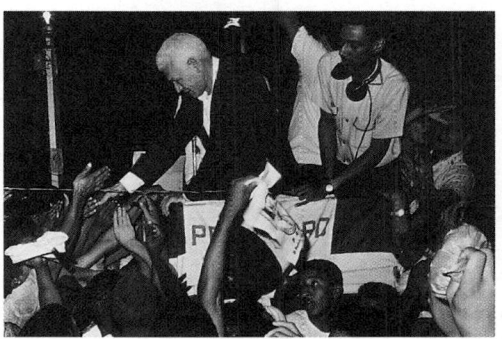

▲ Juan Bosch is shown here on December 18, 1962, two days before being elected president of the Dominican Republic. A military coup removed him from power less than one year later.

supported Johnson's action did so reluctantly. In the United States, however, the majority of the public backed Johnson, praising his aggressive stand against the threat of Communist expansion.

By the spring of 1965 Johnson was also focusing more of his attention on the Vietnam War. As the conflict in Vietnam consumed more of his time, his attention to Great Society programs decreased. In 1966 the government spent about 18 times more on the Vietnam War than it did on the War on Poverty. Citing such statistics, civil rights leader Martin Luther King, Jr., declared that the Great Society had been "shot down on the battlefields of Vietnam."

■■ **Foreign policy concerns drew federal funding and President Johnson's attention away from Great Society programs.**

■■ **SECTION 2 REVIEW**

IDENTIFY and explain the significance of the following: Lyndon Johnson, Lee Harvey Oswald, Warren Commission, War on Poverty, Office of Economic Opportunity, Great Society, Medicare, Medicaid, Elementary and Secondary School Education Act, Omnibus Housing Act, Housing and Urban Development Act, Juan Bosch.

LOCATE and explain the importance of the following: Dominican Republic.

1. **MAIN IDEA** What four major concerns did the Great Society programs address?
2. **MAIN IDEA** How did events in Vietnam and Latin America affect President Johnson's domestic programs?
3. **IDENTIFYING VALUES** How did President Johnson's programs reflect values from his early life?
4. **WRITING TO EXPLAIN** Write an essay explaining how the Warren Court decisions strengthened individual rights.
5. **EVALUATING** Why do you think Michael Harrington believed that ending legalized segregation would not change the economic condition of most poor African Americans?

FOCUS OBJECTIVES

- Identify the major tactic of the early civil rights movement and explain how it generated public support for the movement.

- List the events that helped expand legislation on civil rights and voting rights.

- Describe how African American frustration was expressed in the late 1960s.

- Cite other civil rights movements that were inspired by the African American civil rights movement.

Following is a list of the significant people, places, and terms in this section. You may wish to use this list as a section preview.

People
- Malcolm X
- César Chávez

Places
- Greensboro, North Carolina
- Birmingham, Alabama
- Albany, Georgia
- Selma, Alabama
- Memphis, Tennessee

Terms
- Southern Christian Leadership Conference
- nonviolent resistance
- sit-in
- Student Nonviolent Coordinating Committee
- Congress of Racial Equality
- Freedom Riders
- March on Washington
- Civil Rights Act of 1964
- Freedom Summer
- Voting Rights Act
- Black Power
- Kerner Commission
- United Farm Workers
- Chicano movement
- American Indian Movement

Section 3

THE CIVIL RIGHTS MOVEMENT

FOCUS

- **What was the major tactic of the early civil rights movement? How did it generate public support for the movement?**
- **What events helped expand legislation on civil rights and voting rights?**
- **How was African American frustration expressed in the late 1960s?**
- **What other civil rights movements were inspired by the African American civil rights movement?**

As the 1960s began, southern civil rights leaders called for new efforts in the struggle for racial equality. These efforts won passage of important civil rights and voting rights laws in 1964 and 1965. However, some young members of the movement believed that progress was too slow. In the mid-1960s, frustration over the lack of progress exploded into violence in black neighborhoods. Meanwhile, other groups, inspired by African American activism, fought for their rights.

Martin Luther King, Jr., 1963

NONVIOLENCE IN ACTION

After the success of the Montgomery bus boycott (see Chapter 28), southern civil rights leaders met in Atlanta, Georgia, in 1957 to discuss future strategy. They expanded the Montgomery Improvement Association (MIA) into the **Southern Christian Leadership Conference** (SCLC), an alliance of church-based African American organizations dedicated to ending discrimination. The leader of the MIA, the Reverend Martin Luther King, Jr., led the new organization. The SCLC pledged to use **nonviolent resistance** in its protests. Nonviolent resistance required that protesters never resort to violence, even when others attacked them. King called it meeting "the forces of hate with the power of love."

Many non-SCLC members soon took up nonviolent protests on their own. On February 1,

1960, four African American college students sat down at the "whites only" lunch counter of a Greensboro, North Carolina, department store. The management refused to serve them, but they returned the following day, vowing to continue the **sit-in** protest until they received service. News of the Greensboro sit-in quickly spread, and within weeks students began similar demonstrations in cities throughout the South. In April 1960 the leaders of these demonstrations founded the **Student Nonviolent Coordinating Committee** (SNCC, pronounced "snick"), a loose association of student activists from throughout the South.

White response to the sit-ins tested the students' commitment to nonviolence. White racists taunted the demonstrators, dumping food and drinks on them. Sometimes the harassment escalated into physical attacks. But the demonstrators never resorted to violence. By the end of the year, many

Ask students to identify the actions they would be willing to take to protest laws that they felt were unjust. List their responses on a flip chart. As students read the section, have them compare their list to the actions taken in the 1960s in the struggle for civil rights.

Teaching the *Section*

NONVIOLENT TACTICS

Organize students into small groups to role-play leaders of a workshop for civil rights workers in the use of nonviolent tactics. Direct them to develop a handout for the workshop on the tactic of nonviolence. Tell them that handouts should include a definition of nonviolence and some examples of nonviolent action that might be used in the civil rights struggle. Call on groups to instruct the class on nonviolent tactics and to explain why learning and using this approach can benefit the civil rights movement.

▶

MAKING CONNECTIONS
Political Science
The Freedom Rides were designed to test the Supreme Court decision of *Boynton* v. *Virginia* (1960), which held that segregated interstate bus terminals were illegal. "Our intention was to provoke the southern authorities into arresting us and thereby prod the Justice Department into enforcing the law of the land," CORE leader James Farmer said.

Map Caption Answer
Rock Hill, Anniston, Birmingham, Montgomery

restaurants and other eating establishments across the South had been integrated.

■■ **Early civil rights activists used nonviolent resistance to push for equal rights.**

THE FREEDOM RIDES

The success of the sit-ins inspired the **Congress of Racial Equality** (CORE), a northern-based civil rights group, to launch a protest against segregation in interstate transportation. In May 1961 an integrated group of **Freedom Riders** set off from Washington, D.C., for a trip through the South.

Outside the town of Anniston, Alabama, a white mob firebombed one of the two buses carrying the group members and beat the riders as they tried to escape. The riders on the other bus were attacked in Birmingham. When the bus company refused to carry the passengers any farther, CORE called off the ride. Immediately, Nashville SNCC members stepped in to complete the rest of the trip. SNCC leader Diane Nash explained why:

66 If the Freedom Riders had been stopped as a result of violence, I strongly felt that the future of the movement was going to be cut short. The impression would have been that whenever a movement starts, all [you have to do] is attack it with massive violence and the blacks [will] stop. 99

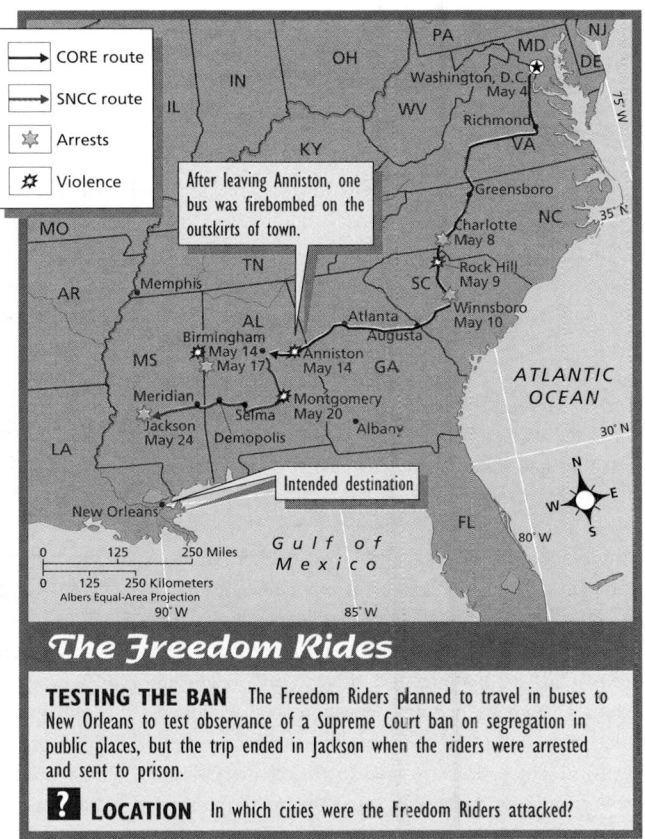

CORE route
SNCC route
✡ Arrests
✷ Violence

After leaving Anniston, one bus was firebombed on the outskirts of town.

Intended destination

The Freedom Rides

TESTING THE BAN The Freedom Riders planned to travel in buses to New Orleans to test observance of a Supreme Court ban on segregation in public places, but the trip ended in Jackson when the riders were arrested and sent to prison.

❓ **LOCATION** In which cities were the Freedom Riders attacked?

SNCC sent additional Freedom Riders to Birmingham, where they were quickly arrested by the city commissioner of public safety, T. Eugene "Bull" Connor, and dumped across the state line. The students made their way back to Birmingham and convinced the bus line to take them to Montgomery, where they were once again attacked by a mob. Under pressure from civil rights leaders, Attorney General Robert Kennedy sent federal marshals to protect the riders on the rest of their journey. In Jackson, Mississippi, however, state officials arrested the riders. Outraged by the arrests, hundreds of other protesters tried to carry on the rides. Over the summer more than 300 Freedom Riders traveled the South to protest segregation. In response, Robert Kennedy pressured the Interstate Commerce Commission (ICC) into strengthening its desegregation regulations.

PRIMARY SOURCE
Description of Change: excerpted and bracketed
Rationale: excerpted to focus on main idea; bracketed to clarify meaning

◄ **Stunned Freedom Riders gather outside their bus after it was firebombed by a white mob. In all, 12 people were taken to an Anniston hospital for treatment.**

Teaching the *Section*

INCREASED PUBLIC SUPPORT

Divide the class in half. Then encourage half the students to imagine they are civil rights workers in the South. Have them write letters to a friend, detailing a Freedom Ride, James Meredith's efforts to enroll at the University of Mississippi, or incidents in Birmingham, Alabama, during SCLC protests there. Have the other members of the class read the letters and write a return letter stating how their opinion of the civil rights movement was affected by what they read. Call on volunteers to read their letters to the class.

HISTORICAL SIDELIGHTS

The Roots of Nonviolence

King's philosophy of non-violence was influenced by many sources, including the Social Gospel writers, Henry David Thoreau, and the teachings of the African American churches. King's primary model for nonviolent civil disobedience came from the Indian nationalist leader Mohandas K. Gandhi, who helped his country gain independence from Great Britain in 1947. Gandhi called his version of nonviolent resistance *Satyagraha,* which he defined as "the vindication of truth not by infliction of suffering on the opponent but on one's self."

THE AMERICAN NATION VIDEODISC PROGRAM

Martin Luther King, Jr.

```
2B    39585    2:09
```

SUCCESSES AND SETBACKS

The civil rights movement saw many successes; it also saw many setbacks. Despite Supreme Court rulings, many educational institutions remained segregated. In 1962 the NAACP obtained a court order requiring the University of Mississippi to admit African American applicant James Meredith. President Kennedy dispatched federal marshals to ensure that Meredith arrived safely at school. When word got out on the evening of September 30 that Meredith was on campus, a riot broke out that left two people dead. Meredith registered the next day and attended classes the rest of the year under the protection of armed guards.

Events elsewhere tested the effectiveness of nonviolent resistance as a protest tactic. In Albany, Georgia, civil rights organizations staged numerous nonviolent protests against discrimination, but Police Chief Laurie Pritchett was prepared for them. Calling his method of law enforcement meeting "nonviolence with nonviolence," Pritchett quietly arrested all of the protesters without resorting to violence. He arranged to fill all the jails in the surrounding areas with prisoners and continued to fill them for as long as possible, causing the Albany movement to virtually stall out.

Nonviolent resistance proved more effective in Birmingham. In April 1963 the SCLC launched a series of boycotts, sit-ins, and marches to protest the city's segregation laws. Hundreds of demonstrators, including Martin Luther King, Jr., were arrested and jailed. The protests continued to grow until May, when Bull Connor ordered the police to attack the marchers, many of them schoolchildren, with high-pressure fire hoses, dogs, and nightsticks. Scenes of these attacks appeared in newspapers and on television throughout the world, increasing support for the civil rights movement.

■■ **Mob violence against civil rights activists increased public support for the movement.**

THE MARCH ON WASHINGTON

Early in June, President Kennedy urged the passage of a broad new civil rights act designed to end segregation. To show support for Kennedy's civil rights bill, African American leaders called for a huge march on Washington, D.C. On August 28, 1963, more than 200,000 people gathered at the Lincoln Memorial, where they heard Martin Luther King, Jr., deliver one of the most moving speeches

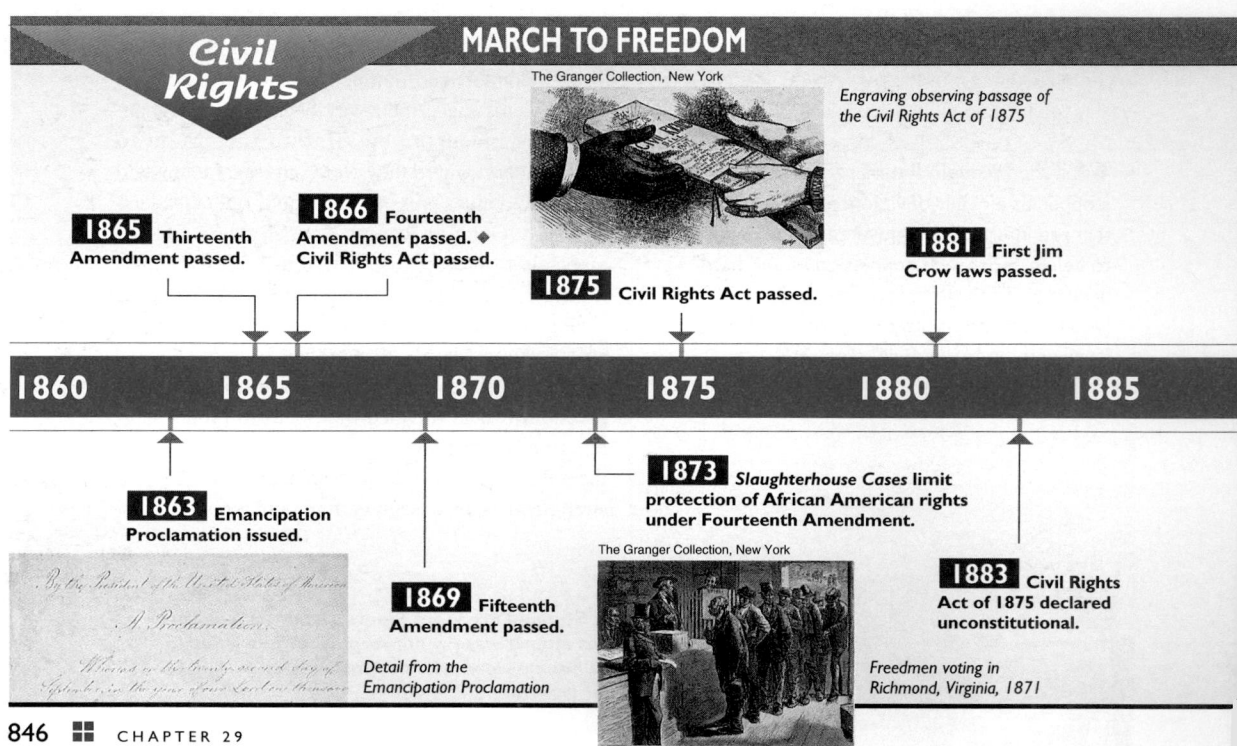

Civil Rights — **MARCH TO FREEDOM**

The Granger Collection, New York

Engraving observing passage of the Civil Rights Act of 1875

1865 Thirteenth Amendment passed.

1866 Fourteenth Amendment passed. ◆ Civil Rights Act passed.

1875 Civil Rights Act passed.

1881 First Jim Crow laws passed.

1860   1865   1870   1875   1880   1885

1863 Emancipation Proclamation issued.

1873 *Slaughterhouse Cases* limit protection of African American rights under Fourteenth Amendment.

1869 Fifteenth Amendment passed.

1883 Civil Rights Act of 1875 declared unconstitutional.

By the President of the United States of America
A Proclamation...

Detail from the Emancipation Proclamation

The Granger Collection, New York

Freedmen voting in Richmond, Virginia, 1871

THE MARCH ON WASHINGTON

Have students work in groups to present an "on location" newscast at the March on Washington that includes interviews with federal officials, organizers, speakers, and other participants. Newscasts should conclude with a summary of the reasons for the march and an assessment of whether or not it was a success. Have group members "broadcast" their newscasts to the class.

▶

in American history. Repeating the phrase "I have a dream," King spoke of a nation in which all Americans would live in harmony (see page 1010).

Other speakers, such as A. Philip Randolph, gave eloquent testimony to the long struggle for civil rights in America. SNCC leader John Lewis warned that the younger generation of demonstrators were determined not to give up their struggle until equality was a true reality:

> 66 By the force of our demands, our determination and our numbers, we shall splinter the segregated South into a thousand pieces, and put them back together in the image of God and democracy. 99

The success of the **March on Washington** raised the spirits of civil rights workers everywhere. But their joy proved short-lived. In mid-September a bomb exploded in a Birmingham church, killing four young African American girls. Then in November an assassin's bullet cut down President Kennedy. The new president, Lyndon Johnson, urged Congress to pass Kennedy's civil rights bill. The **Civil Rights Act of 1964** barred discrimination in employment and in public accommodations and gave the Justice Department the power to bring lawsuits to enforce school desegregation.

■■ **The March on Washington helped bring about passage of the Civil Rights Act of 1964.**

ƎREEDOM SUMMER AND SELMA

As Congress debated the Civil Rights Act, movement leaders turned their attention to voter registration. In June 1964 they launched **Freedom Summer**, a campaign to register African American voters. It involved nearly 1,000 volunteers, many of them white northerners. Freedom Summer focused on Mississippi, a state with a black population of 45 percent, but where only 5 percent of African Americans were on the voting rolls.

Mississippi had a reputation for racial violence, growing out of the state's many lynchings in the early 20th century and the murder of 14-year-old African American Emmett Till in 1955. Violence quickly struck the Freedom Summer campaign. On June 21 Michael Schwerner and Andrew Goodman, two white New Yorkers, and James Chaney, a black Mississippian, were abducted and killed. Shocked volunteers carried on, but many local blacks feared they would also become the victims of violence if they registered.

Students at Tuskegee Institute

1909 NAACP founded.

1900 New York City race riot occurs.

1908 Ray Stannard Baker's *Following the Color Line* published.

| 1890 | 1895 | 1900 | 1905 | 1910 |

1895 Ida Wells-Barnett publishes lynching study.

The Granger Collection, New York

Ida Wells-Barnett

1896 Plessy v. Ferguson supports segregation.

1906 Teddy Roosevelt discharges entire black regiment in Brownsville, Texas. ◆Atlanta race riot occurs.

1910 National Urban League founded.

Teaching the Section

EXPANDING VOTER REGISTRATION

Write the following on the chalkboard, leaving space between each entry: *Freedom Summer, Selma's Bloody Sunday, Voting Rights Act.* Call on volunteers to explain how each is related to expanding African American voter registration and write their responses below the corresponding entry. Then direct students to write a summary statement explaining the impact of these events on African American voter registration. Have students compare their statements.

By the end of the summer, only 1,600 African Americans had been added to the voting rolls.

In early 1965, civil rights workers launched a similar registration drive in Selma, Alabama. They invited King, who had won the Nobel Peace Prize the previous year, to lead them. For days African Americans attempted to register at election commission offices in the Selma area, only to face beatings and arrests. Civil rights leaders responded by calling for a protest march from Selma to Montgomery. On Sunday, March 7, some 600 people started on the 50-mile trek.

Just outside Selma, police attacked the marchers. One eight-year-old girl in the march recalled the scene: "I saw those horsemen coming toward me and they had those awful masks on; they rode right through the cloud of tear gas. Some of them had clubs, others had ropes, or whips, which they swung about them like they were driving cattle." Stunned by the fierceness of this attack, thousands of Americans poured into Selma to show support for the marchers. President Johnson was also shocked by Selma's "Bloody Sunday." On March 15, before a joint session of Congress, he asked for speedy passage of a voting rights bill. All Americans, he said, ought to take up the struggle for civil rights, for "it's . . . all of us who must overcome the crippling legacy of bigotry and injustice. And we *shall* overcome."

A week later, under the protection of federal marshals and the National Guard, the marchers completed their journey. Five months later Congress passed the **Voting Rights Act** of 1965, which put the entire registration process under federal control. Within days of the act's passage, federal examiners descended on the South to sign up new African American voters. By 1968 over half of all eligible African Americans in the South were registered.

Freedom Summer, Selma's Bloody Sunday, and the Voting Rights Act of 1965 expanded African American voter registration.

*B*LACK POWER

As the civil rights movement grew, many African Americans questioned the effectiveness of nonviolence. Some felt that they should be able to use violence for self-defense. Others began to question the desirability of integration altogether. Adopting the slogan **Black Power**, many of these leaders argued that African Americans should mobilize to gain economic and political power. Some also argued that since white society caused racism, only separation from white society would enable African

MARCH TO FREEDOM

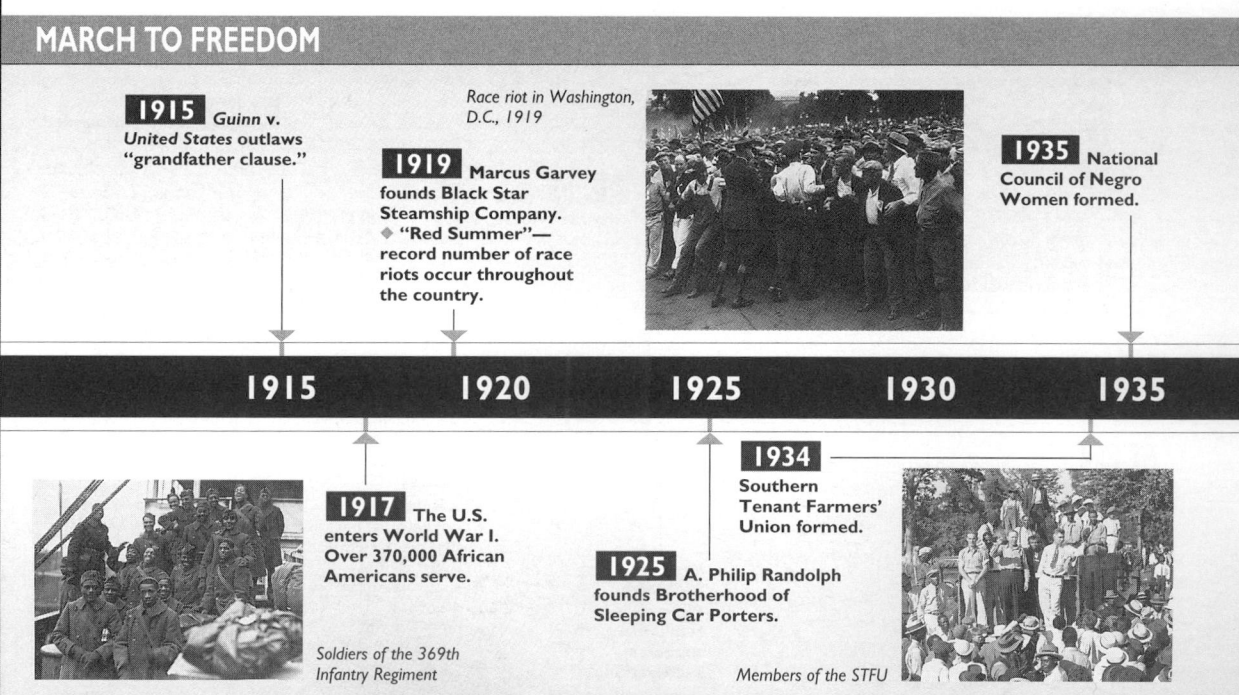

1915 *Guinn v. United States* outlaws "grandfather clause."

1919 Marcus Garvey founds Black Star Steamship Company.
♦ "Red Summer"— record number of race riots occur throughout the country.

Race riot in Washington, D.C., 1919

1935 National Council of Negro Women formed.

1915   1920   1925   1930   1935

1917 The U.S. enters World War I. Over 370,000 African Americans serve.

Soldiers of the 369th Infantry Regiment

1925 A. Philip Randolph founds Brotherhood of Sleeping Car Porters.

1934 Southern Tenant Farmers' Union formed.

Members of the STFU

GROWING AFRICAN AMERICAN FRUSTRATION

Draw a line down the center of the chalkboard. To the left of the line, enter the heading *Prior to the Voting Rights Act of 1965;* to the right, enter the heading *After the Voting Rights Act of 1965.* Ask volunteers to identify the distinctive characteristics of the African American struggle for civil rights in these two time periods. *(non-violence before, confrontation after)* Note their responses in the appropriate column.

(Students may wish to consult the "March to Freedom" time line on pp. 846–850.) Then have students write a sentence explaining why the civil rights movement changed after 1965. Encourage students to share and discuss their sentences.

OTHER CIVIL RIGHTS MOVEMENTS

Have students role-play a Mexican American farm worker or a Native American activist and write a journal entry explaining their struggle for equal rights, indicating how that struggle has been influenced by the African American civil rights movement. Call on volunteers to read and discuss their journal entries. Students may wish to include their journal entries in their portfolios. ▶

Americans to obtain such power. Although the Black Power slogan was not widely used until the late 1960s, it represented the ideas of many earlier African American leaders, including Marcus Garvey (see Chapter 21) and Malcolm X, a black nationalist who rose to prominence in the early civil rights era.

BIO GRAPHY Malcolm X was born Malcolm Little in Nebraska in 1925. His father was a Baptist minister and organizer for Marcus Garvey. After his father died and his mother succumbed to mental illness, the family was disrupted. Moving first to Michigan and then to Massachusetts, the young Malcolm drifted into a life of crime, eventually ending up in prison. While in prison, he embraced the teachings of Elijah Muhammad's Nation of Islam, or Black Muslims, an offshoot of the orthodox Islamic faith.

Malcolm X

Freed in 1952, Malcolm rejected the name Little, handed down to him from some former slaveholder, and used "X" to symbolize his lost African surname. He soon became a leading minister for the Nation of Islam. A powerful orator, Malcolm X championed black separatism and called for freedom to be brought about "by any means necessary." The time for nonviolence had passed, he argued:

> 66 You're getting a new generation that has been growing right now, and they're beginning to think with their own minds and see that you can't negotiate up on freedom nowadays. If something is yours by right, then fight for it or shut up. If you can't fight for it, then forget it. 99

Malcolm X broke with the Black Muslims in 1964 after a pilgrimage to the Islamic holy city of Mecca. Turning away from separatism, he converted to orthodox Islam and began calling for unity among all people. This break set off a bitter struggle between Malcolm X and the Nation of Islam. In February 1965, Black Muslim assassins gunned down Malcolm X.

Other young activists, however, carried on some of his ideas. In 1966, college students Huey P. Newton and Bobby Seale founded the Black Panther party in Oakland, California, to promote self-determination in the black community. Asserting that blacks could not trust white police officers to protect them, the Black Panthers armed themselves and established citizen patrols to monitor the streets. "War can only be abolished through war," they declared. Although the Black Panthers

---

BIO GRAPHY **PERSONALITIES IN HISTORY**

While in Mecca, Malcolm X observed pilgrims of all races worshipping and socializing together in complete harmony. This made him realize his beliefs that all whites were "devils" and that integration could never work might be flawed. When he returned to the U.S., he talked not of a separate black state, but of "a society in which people can live like human beings on the basis of equality."

THE AMERICAN NATION VIDEODISC PROGRAM
Malcolm X

2B   28273   4:20

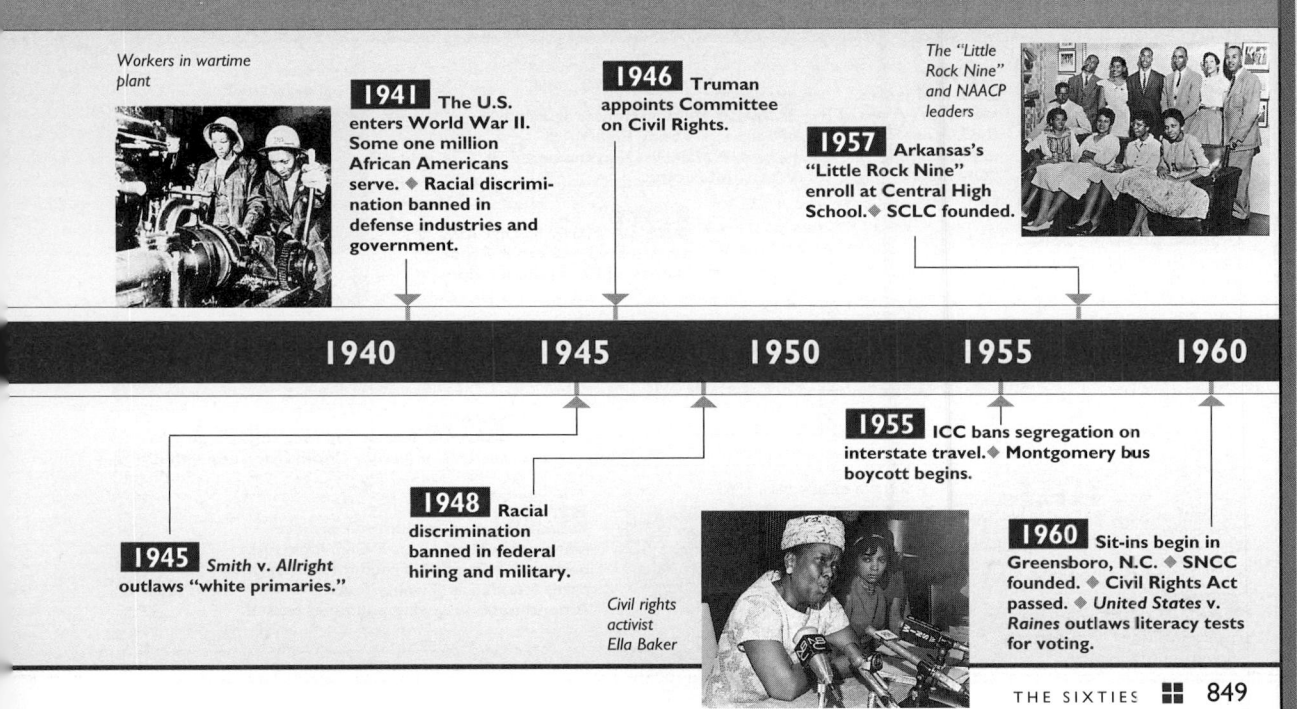

Workers in wartime plant

1941 The U.S. enters World War II. Some one million African Americans serve. ◆ Racial discrimination banned in defense industries and government.

1946 Truman appoints Committee on Civil Rights.

The "Little Rock Nine" and NAACP leaders

1957 Arkansas's "Little Rock Nine" enroll at Central High School. ◆ SCLC founded.

1940   1945   1950   1955   1960

1945 *Smith v. Allright* outlaws "white primaries."

1948 Racial discrimination banned in federal hiring and military.

Civil rights activist Ella Baker

1955 ICC bans segregation on interstate travel. ◆ Montgomery bus boycott begins.

1960 Sit-ins begin in Greensboro, N.C. ◆ SNCC founded. ◆ Civil Rights Act passed. ◆ *United States v. Raines* outlaws literacy tests for voting.

Practice

GUIDED PRACTICE

Write on the chalkboard the eight subsection titles of Section 3 and inform students that these are topics for news stories that will appear in a magazine special feature titled "The Civil Rights Movement." Call on volunteers to develop brief story outlines for each topic, noting their suggestions on the chalkboard under the appropriate title.

INDEPENDENT PRACTICE

Direct students to select one of the outlines developed in the Guided Practice activity and to use it to write a news story. Students might also suggest illustrations to accompany their stories. Students may wish to include their stories in their portfolios.

Review and Assessment

REVIEW Ask students to construct an annotated and illustrated map of the 1960s civil rights movement. Suggest that they use the map on p. 845 as a model. Then assign the Section 3 Review on p. 851.

ASSESS Assign the **Section 3 Daily Quiz** in *Core Resources.*

HISTORICAL SIDELIGHTS

The Roots of a Name

AIM was founded, in part, because the other American Indian organizations in the area were run by boards dominated by whites. The founders, uncertain what to call the new organization, listened to the advice of older, respected tribal members. "Well, you keep saying that you *aim* to do this, you *aim* to do that. Why don't you call it AIM, the American Indian Movement?" the elders suggested.

THE AMERICAN NATION VIDEODISC PROGRAM

César Chávez

|||||||||
2B   38963   :21

were involved in numerous confrontations with police, many African Americans admired their boldness.

FIRE IN THE STREETS

Frustration among poor inner-city African Americans fueled much of the support for the Black Power movement. Despite the successes of the civil rights movement, discrimination still plagued the lives of most African Americans. In August 1965 frustration became revolt when a routine arrest by Los Angeles police in the black neighborhood of Watts broke into a riot that raged for six days. When the National Guard finally restored order, 34 people were dead, hundreds were injured, and almost 4,000 had been arrested.

Over the next two years, more than 100 riots broke out in cities across the country. The worst erupted in Detroit, where 43 people lost their lives. A federal report by the **Kerner Commission** charged that white racism was largely responsible for the tensions that led to the riots. "Our nation," the report warned, "is moving toward two societies, one black, one white—separate and unequal."

Seeking to address the frustration of the late 1960s, Martin Luther King, Jr., started to embrace some of the Black Power movement's ideas, such as the need for African Americans to gain economic power. He also became increasingly upset that funding that might have gone for the War on Poverty was being used for the war in Vietnam (see Chapter 30). In March 1968 he called for a Poor People's March on Washington to protest this misuse of government funding.

Before the Poor People's March took place, King went to Memphis, Tennessee, to show his support for a garbage workers' strike. On the evening of April 4, 1968, the man who was the symbol of nonviolence met a violent end when a sniper killed him. Within hours of King's death, black neighborhoods all over the country exploded in outrage. A week of rioting left 46 dead and thousands injured.

■■ **The Black Power movement and the riots of the late 1960s demonstrated growing frustration among African Americans.**

OTHERS INSPIRED BY THE MOVEMENT

King's tragic death and the divisions within the civil rights movement during the 1960s sometimes

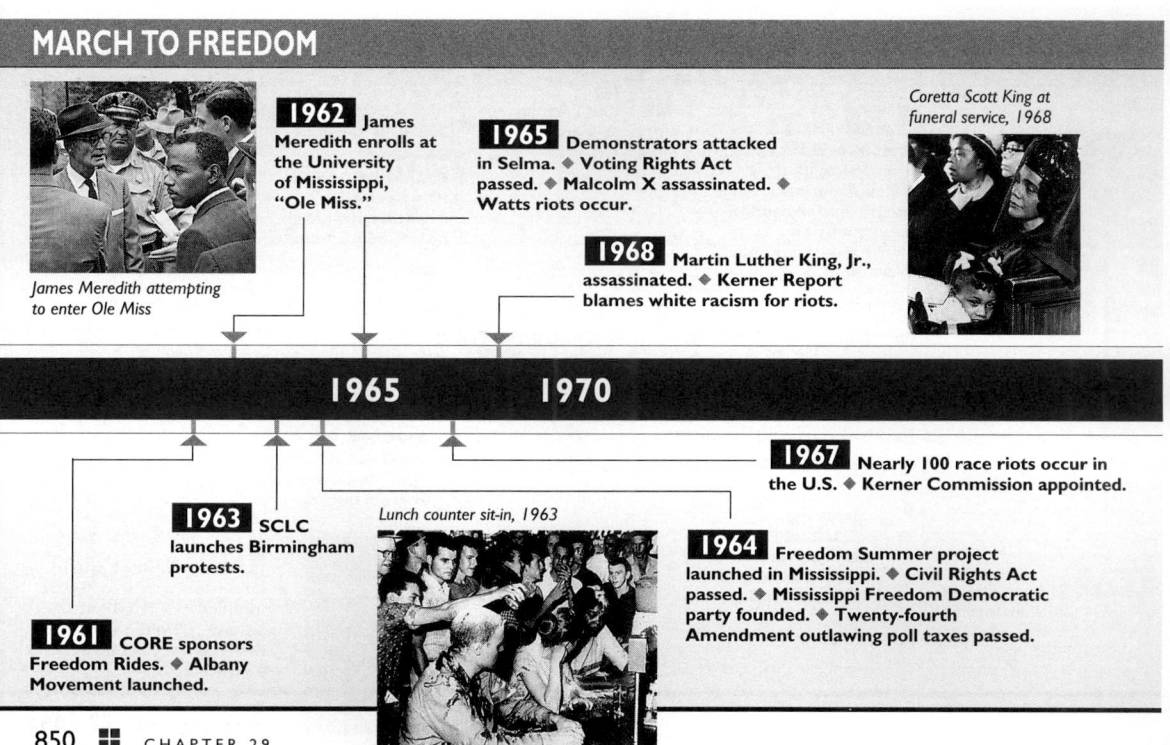

MARCH TO FREEDOM

James Meredith attempting to enter Ole Miss

1962 James Meredith enrolls at the University of Mississippi, "Ole Miss."

1965 Demonstrators attacked in Selma. ◆ Voting Rights Act passed. ◆ Malcolm X assassinated. ◆ Watts riots occur.

1968 Martin Luther King, Jr., assassinated. ◆ Kerner Report blames white racism for riots.

Coretta Scott King at funeral service, 1968

1965   **1970**

1967 Nearly 100 race riots occur in the U.S. ◆ Kerner Commission appointed.

1963 SCLC launches Birmingham protests.

Lunch counter sit-in, 1963

1964 Freedom Summer project launched in Mississippi. ◆ Civil Rights Act passed. ◆ Mississippi Freedom Democratic party founded. ◆ Twenty-fourth Amendment outlawing poll taxes passed.

1961 CORE sponsors Freedom Rides. ◆ Albany Movement launched.

Closure

Have students discuss whether the civil rights movement accomplished its goals. Have them cite evidence from the section to support their judgments.

Extension

COMPARE Have students write a biographical essay on Martin Luther King, Jr. and Malcolm X comparing their approaches to the civil rights struggle.

INVESTIGATE Have students investigate the work of *La Raza Unida* and present their findings in an oral report.

---

obscure the movement's gains. It also inspired other groups, such as Mexican Americans and American Indians, to demand better treatment. During the 1960s a group that would become the **United Farm Workers** (UFW), led by César Chávez, began to organize Western migrant workers, most of whom were Mexican Americans, to win better wages and working conditions. In 1965 Chávez called a strike of California grape pickers and launched a nationwide boycott of grapes picked by nonunion workers. By 1970 the UFW had won most of its demands.

As in the African American civil rights movement, many younger members of the Mexican American movement began demanding more-radical action. Young Mexican American college students organized the **Chicano movement,** which emphasized pride in Mexican culture and heritage. Such pride was reflected in the numerous Mexican American political parties that sprang up around the country, most notably *La Raza Unida* ("the united race"), founded in 1970.

Some American Indians organized into the Red Power movement, which demanded, among other things, that the U.S. government pay tribes for lands that had been taken from them illegally. In 1968 three Minnesota Chippewas organized the **American Indian Movement** (AIM), which would become the major force in the Red Power movement during the 1970s (see Chapter 31).

In 1969 a group of Red Power advocates occupied the abandoned federal prison on Alcatraz Island near San Francisco. The protesters offered to buy the island from the government with beads and cloth—the same price paid by the Dutch for Manhattan Island. The occupation of Alcatraz lasted for many months, until federal authorities finally removed the protesters by force.

All these movements emphasized ethnic pride and group loyalty. Popular culture in the 1950s had promoted the message that to be truly "American" meant to be white and middle class. In the 1960s, African Americans, Hispanics, American Indians and other groups insisted that the meaning of American must expand to include all citizens equally, not just one favored group.

The rise of these movements also raised a central question: Could oppressed groups discover their own identities and promote their own interests yet at the same time retain a sense of citizenship and belonging to the larger American society? This important question still confronts us today.

> ■■ **The civil rights movement inspired other groups, such as Mexican Americans and American Indians, to fight for their rights.**

SECTION 3 REVIEW

IDENTIFY and explain the significance of the following: Southern Christian Leadership Conference, nonviolent resistance, sit-in, Student Nonviolent Coordinating Committee, Congress of Racial Equality, Freedom Riders, March on Washington, Civil Rights Act of 1964, Freedom Summer, Voting Rights Act, Black Power, Malcolm X, Kerner Commission, United Farm Workers, César Chávez, Chicano movement, American Indian Movement.

LOCATE and explain the importance of the following: Greensboro, North Carolina; Birmingham, Alabama; Albany, Georgia; Selma, Alabama; Memphis, Tennessee.

1. **MAIN IDEA** What tactic did members of the early civil rights movement use to fight for equal rights? What effect did this tactic have on public opinion?

2. **MAIN IDEA** What event helped bring about passage of the Civil Rights Act of 1964? What incidents helped expand African American voter registration?

3. **MAIN IDEA** How did the African American civil rights movement affect other ethnic movements?

4. **WRITING TO EXPRESS A VIEWPOINT** Imagine you are a Freedom Rider. Write a letter to the editor of a southern newspaper explaining why you feel it is necessary to complete the rides.

5. **TAKING A STAND** Take a stand in support of either Martin Luther King, Jr.'s method of negotiation and nonviolent resistance or Malcolm X's method of separation and self-defense. State the strengths and possible effects of that method on the civil rights movement.

SECTION REVIEW ANSWERS

IDENTIFY

For significance, see the following pages:
SCLC (p. 844)
nonviolent resistance (p. 844)
sit-in (p. 844)
SNCC (p. 844)
CORE (p. 845)
Freedom Riders (p. 845)
March on Washington (p. 847)
Civil Rights Act of 1964 (p. 847)
Freedom Summer (p. 847)
Voting Rights Act (p. 848)
Black Power (p. 848)
Malcolm X (p. 849)
Kerner Commission (p. 850)
United Farm Workers (p. 851)
César Chávez (p. 851)
Chicano movement (p. 851)
AIM (p. 851)

LOCATE

For locations, see the map on p. 845.

1. *nonviolent resistance; increased support for movement as violence against activists grew*
2. *March on Washington; Freedom Summer, Selma's Bloody Sunday, Voting Rights Act*
3. *inspired Mexican Americans and Native Americans to fight for rights*
4. *Letters might mention the need to stand up to mob violence and support desegregation laws.*
5. *Answers will vary but should note differences in goals and methods of each.*

PREVIEW WORKSHOP

Following is a list of the significant people and terms in this section. You may wish to use this list as a section preview.

People
■ Timothy Leary
■ Roy Lichtenstein
■ Claes Oldenberg

■ Andy Warhol
■ Betty Friedan
■ Gloria Steinem
■ Jimi Hendrix
■ Bob Dylan

Terms
■ generation gap
■ hippies

■ counterculture
■ pop art
■ National Organization for Women
■ British Invasion
■ Woodstock

FOCUS OBJECTIVES

■ Describe how hippies rebelled against traditional society.

■ Discuss what the revived women's movement did for women.

■ Explain how rock music impacted the 1960s.

 GLOBAL CONNECTIONS

The strike at Berkeley was the first major action of a student revolt that spread across the world during the 1960s. In cities as distant—and different—as Prague, Paris, and Tokyo, young people rose up to challenge the existing social and political order. Some came incredibly close to bringing about radical change. The French student uprising in May and June 1968, for example, almost toppled the government of President Charles de Gaulle.

CORE RESOURCES

• Section 4 Daily Quiz

AV **RESOURCES**

• *The American Nation Videodisc: The Women's Rights Movement*
• *Everday Life in America Transparency* and *Worksheet 29*

Section 4

CULTURE AND COUNTERCULTURE

F O C U S
■ **How did hippies rebel against traditional society?**
■ **What did the revived women's movement do for women?**
■ **How did rock music impact the 1960s?**

"*The times they are a-changin',*" *declared singer Bob Dylan in 1963. He was not referring to the civil rights movement alone. Many young people, rejecting the values of their parents' generation, embraced new styles of music and dress and new ways of life. Others challenged American traditions, including religious practices and the role of women in society. The result was a reinvention of culture that eventually affected the entire nation.*

Hippie, 1967

THE COUNTERCULTURE

The youth rebellion that began in the 1950s with the Beats and rock 'n' roll evolved into a broad movement in the 1960s that challenged the beliefs and traditions of older generations. Growing up during an era of Cold War fears, massive civil rights protests, and the Vietnam War led many children of the baby boom to question the values of American society and to blame their parents for creating the problems that plagued the country. This **generation gap** between the baby boomers and their elders grew ever wider as the decade wore on.

Shaking the ivory tower. The first audible rumblings of the 1960s youth movement occurred on college campuses among white middle-class students. Many felt frustrated by the impersonal academic bureaucracy and by the conservative curriculum offered at universities. To them, traditional courses seemed out of touch with the real world.

In 1964 discontent exploded into protest at the University of California at Berkeley. Some 70 percent of the students went on strike. Instead of attending classes, they rallied, held sit-ins, and picketed university administration buildings. Their intention, they declared, was to "Shut This Factory Down." By 1965 such chants were echoing from college campuses across the nation.

◄ **Five hundred policemen were present during the Berkeley student protests in December 1964. Some demonstrators who staged a sit-in were arrested and hauled off to jail.**

MOTIVATING:
LINK TO TODAY

Ask students to discuss the characteristics of today's youth culture. Guide their discussion by mentioning such cultural elements as fashion, music, art, literature, and so on. Note on a flip chart the major components of the youth culture identified in the discussion. As students read the section, have them compare today's youth culture with the counterculture of the 1960s.

Teaching the Section

THE COUNTERCULTURE

Organize students into groups of six to develop skits on the counterculture. Suggest that two students assume the roles of white middle-class college students, two play hippies, and two take the roles of older people. In the skits the students and hippies should defend their values and life-styles and explain why they have chosen to follow them. The older people should question the validity of these values and life-styles. Call on groups to perform their skits.

▶

As the Vietnam War escalated in the late 1960s, campus activism increased still more. One woman who participated in the student movement at Columbia University recalled the mood of the students:

❝ There was an incredible exhilaration, that here we were making history, changing the world. . . . Everybody believed that this university would never be the same, that society would be . . . changed, that there'd be a revolution in the United States within five years, and a whole new social order. ❞

While some students wanted to change the world, others rebelled by rejecting everything connected with mainstream America, what they called the Establishment. Instead, these **hippies**—as they soon became known—sought to create an alternative life-style, a **counterculture**.

Elements of the counterculture. Like the Beats before them, hippies rejected the materialism and work ethic of past generations in favor of simplicity and doing "your own thing." Many hippies indulged in behavior intended to shock older Americans, such as public displays of nudity and the use of profanity. Most searched for new physical experiences by engaging in permissive sexual behavior or by experimenting with mind-altering drugs, such as LSD (lysergic acid diethylamide), or "acid."

Timothy Leary, a Harvard professor who was fired in 1963 for using LSD with his students, became the drug's leading advocate. Leary invited people to "tune in, turn on, drop out." Many followed his advice. But there was a high price to pay for the experimentation of the era, as reported cases of sexually transmitted diseases and drug addiction increased at an alarming rate.

Some hippies "dropped out" of society by joining rural communes, where they attempted to live collectively in harmony with nature. They rejected most modern conveniences, grew their own food, and shared all property. Some formed their own hippie neighborhoods in run-down urban areas, such as the **Haight-Ashbury** district of San Francisco.

▦ **Hippies rebelled against traditional society by forming their own counterculture.**

▲ **The Haight-Ashbury district of San Francisco attracted hippies of all ages. This photograph was taken in May 1968.**

QUESTIONING AMERICAN SOCIETY

The counterculture movement reflected a growing sense of skepticism in America. In the 1960s many Americans, even those not active in the counterculture movement, were beginning to question the value of conformity. Many institutions, including traditional churches, came under scrutiny. In the mid-1950s, over 80 percent of Americans said religion could answer all or most of modern society's problems. By 1969, however, 70 percent said that religion was *losing* its influence on American life, leading *Time* magazine to ask, "Is God Dead?"

Americans, especially the young, did not necessarily lack spiritual faith, but many lost confidence in the ability of the established churches of their parents to provide spiritual assurance in the modern world. The challenges of the nuclear age, some felt, had made conventional religious answers irrelevant. Reflecting the search for alternative answers, the number of college courses in religion—and enrollment in them—grew dramatically, as did interest in Eastern religions such as Zen Buddhism.

The questioning of tradition even extended into the art world. Many new visual artists argued that the art world had become a slave to elite tastes

PRIMARY SOURCE
Description of Change: excerpted
Rationale: excerpted to focus on main idea

BUILDING VOCABULARY

Hippie, which came into popular use in the mid-1960s, is a derivation of the word *hip,* meaning "knowing," or "aware." Some language scholars think that *hip* derives from the West African word *hipi,* which means "to be aware."

VOICES IN HISTORY

Many hippies became interested in American Indian dress and culture. Many American Indians, however, were not pleased with this fascination. Peter Nuvamsa, Sr., recalled that when a group of hippies visited his Hopi village, they "offended our way of life. . . . They hugged each other and kissed in public as if they didn't have anything else to do. . . . I went out there and spoke to some of them. I said, 'Why are you here? Why do you behave this way, doing anything that comes into your head? We do not like the way you are behaving. It's not our way.'"

—Quote from "Hopis and the Love Generation" by Peter Nuvamsa, Sr., from *Hopi Voices: Recollections, Traditions and Narratives of the Hopi Indians,* edited by Harold Courlander.

Teaching the *Section*

THE WOMEN'S MOVEMENT REVIVED

Organize students into small groups to act as leaders of the National Organization for Women (NOW). Direct them to develop a mission statement that explains why the women's movement needs to be revived, describes the role of NOW in that process, and outlines what the organization hopes to achieve—politically, socially, and economically—for women. Ask groups to volunteer to read their statements. Discuss and evaluate each statement after it is presented.

---

and prejudices. Artists created works only to please a few cultured critics, not to appeal to the majority of non-artists.

As the 1960s began, a number of New York painters and sculptors emerged who wanted to make art more accessible to the general public. They accomplished their goals by using "found objects"—tin cans, furniture, cardboard packaging, cartoon strips, and other everyday articles—as the subjects of their works. The leading proponents of this method, called **pop art**, included Roy Lichtenstein and Claes Oldenberg. Many of Lichtenstein's huge paintings were done in comic-strip style, complete with speech balloons. Oldenberg used a variety of materials to make giant sculptures of such things as hamburgers, toothpaste tubes, and clothespins.

The best-known pop artist, however, was Andy Warhol. His most notable paintings included oversize soup cans, rows of green soda bottles, and a garishly colored rendering of a photograph of Marilyn Monroe reproduced multiple times. Initially, Warhol painted by hand. However, he soon switched to a stencil-printing process called silk screen. Finally, he simply did designs that an army of assistants then reproduced. Warhol's message, that everything—even art—can be mass-produced, both glorified and mocked consumerism. Warhol once predicted that "In the future everyone will be famous for 15 minutes," reflecting consumers' constant desires for new products.

A REVIVED WOMEN'S MOVEMENT

One of the most lasting legacies of the 1960s was its challenge to traditional views of women. After years of inaction, the women's movement experienced a widespread revival.

Sparks of unrest. This revival was sparked in part by the publication of Betty Friedan's *The Feminine Mystique* (1963), which rejected the popular notion that women were content with the roles of wife, mother, and homemaker. Many women, she charged, felt stifled by the "comfortable concentration camp" of domestic life:

> 66 Each suburban wife struggled with it alone. As she made the beds, shopped for groceries, matched slipcover material, ate peanut butter sandwiches with her children, chauffeured Cub Scouts and Brownies, . . . she was afraid to ask even of herself the silent question—"Is this all?" 99

Other women agreed with Friedan. Her book helped motivate women to demand greater opportunities and fairer treatment in the workplace. Although the Civil Rights Act of 1964 outlawed sexual discrimination in employment, the government seemed reluctant to deal with women's grievances. As a result, in 1966 Friedan and other feminists founded the **National Organization for Women** (NOW) to lobby for women's rights. Women began to stand up for themselves in a variety of ways. Some held consciousness-raising sessions to improve their self-esteem. Others took direct action. In 1968, for example, some feminists disrupted the Miss America pageant, charging that beauty contests degraded women.

▶ Pop artists helped make art more accessible to the general public by selecting images that reflected everyday life. Andy Warhol, for example, painted these oversize soup cans in 1965.

Andy Warhol, Campbell's Soup, 1965

Roy Lichtenstein

◀ Many of Roy Lichtenstein's paintings were drawn in a flamboyant, comic-strip style.

A MUSICAL REVOLUTION

Pair students and invite them to imagine that they are American young people during the 1960s. Direct each pair to create a message for a time capsule, to be opened in the 1990s, that describes their music and explains how it was influenced by the developments of their time. Select a number of pairs to read their messages to the class. Then have students compare music as a reflection of social conditions and change in the 1960s to the social role of current musical forms in contemporary society.

BY DR. ALICE KESSLER-HARRIS

Social History

Until relatively recently, most American history textbooks focused on political history, recounting the deeds of the nation's political, military, and social leaders. Today, however, textbooks have begun to place a greater emphasis on social history.

What is social history? Some 50 years ago the well-known British historian G. M. Trevelyan described social history as "the history of a people with the politics left out." Social historians studied people's private lives rather than political events. They concentrated on the household, giving details about the daily lives of men, women, and children. Though colorful, this history failed to explain larger historical themes.

But social history changed in the 1960s. The civil rights movement, antiwar protests, and the women's movement inspired a new generation of historians. In order to explain how these protest movements arose, historians began studying how African Americans, women, and ethnic groups other than white Protestants contributed to American history. Focusing on ordinary people—workers, women, city dwellers, farmers, immigrants—social historians set out to expand the history of the United States.

To do so, these historians sought out new sources and used new methods to reconstruct the daily lives and thoughts of ordinary people. Earlier historians had analyzed only written sources left by political and intellectual leaders. The new social historians uncovered new sources—workers' speeches and letters, oral histories, autobiographies, songs, folklore, reports of chari-

▲ *Roll, Jordan, Roll*, an example of social history by Eugene D. Genovese, explores plantation life in the pre–Civil War South.

table societies, and ethnic and immigrant newspapers. These historians used statistical methods to study how people voted, where they moved, what they ate and drank, how they spent and saved their money, and the size of their families.

The new social historians have created a body of work whose strength lies in its respect for cultural diversity. Their work explores the values and ideas that Americans of different racial, ethnic, and class backgrounds share and do not share. For example, Julia Kirk Blackwelder's *Women of the Depression: Caste and Culture in San Antonio, 1929–39* (1984) shows how people's racial and ethnic backgrounds helped them cope with economic distress.

The new social history also explores the social institutions—families, schools, churches, and so on—that both preserve traditional values and help introduce new ones. This history, however, goes beyond the "old" social history by using social institutions to help explain broader political, economic, or technological changes. For example, Kenneth Jackson's *Crabgrass Frontier* (1985) explains that American families' preference for detached homes of their own helped lead to the growth of suburbs—an important economic and geographic change.

The best social history combines research on political and economic institutions with research on how ordinary people think and act. This combination helps us understand politics and the forces that ultimately create change. In doing so, the new social historians can rightly claim to have updated Trevelyan's definition of social history by creating a history of all Americans with the politics mixed in.

SOCIAL HISTORY

SETTING THE SCENE

The 1960s revival in American social history was fired, in part, by exposure to the works of European social historians. The French *Annales* school of historians emphasized the impact of long-term trends, such as how wheat harvests affected peasant life over a particular time period. In Britain a group of historians focused on the rise of the working class and its role in history. Such research encouraged some young American historians to look at subjects in a different way.

COOPERATIVE LEARNING

Organize students into groups of six and ask each to create a social history time capsule for the 1960s. Group members should divide tasks: some might research suitable items for the capsule, others might "re-create" written or visual items. Call on groups to present and discuss their time capsules.

Practice

GUIDED PRACTICE

Write the four subsection titles on the chalkboard and inform students that these are headings of segments for a magazine article on cultural developments in the 1960s. Ask students what points they would include for each segment and note their ideas under the appropriate heading.

INDEPENDENT PRACTICE

Direct each student to use the information on the chalkboard to write one segment of the article framed in the Guided Practice activity. Encourage students to illustrate, or suggest illustrations for, their segments.

Review and Assessment

REVIEW Have students write 10 questions on Section 4 on individual note cards with the answers on the reverse side. Then divide students into groups of four. Ask them to use their note cards to question the other members of the group. Then assign the Section 4 Review on p. 857.

ASSESS Assign the **Section 4 Daily Quiz** in *Core Resources.*

**THE AMERICAN NATION
VIDEODISC PROGRAM**

**The Women's Rights
Movement**

```
1B      48258     :32
```

BIO GRAPHY **PERSONALITIES IN HISTORY**

Gloria Steinem was not the first feminist in her family. Her grandmother, Pauline Steinem, served as the president of the Ohio Women's Suffrage Association in the early 1900s and was one of two American delegates to the conference held by the International Council of Women in 1908.

AV TRANSPARENCY

Everyday Life in America Transparency and **Worksheet 29**

HISTORICAL SIDELIGHTS

The Counterculture Declines

Television images of Haight-Ashbury had drawn to the counterculture hundreds of misfits, drug peddlers, and others who had little interest in peace and happiness. Violence, not love, soon ruled the streets of the hippie mecca. In the fall of 1967, the leaders of the counterculture celebrated "Death of Hippie," a funeral procession through Haight-Ashbury.

856

A new generation. Many young women who had participated in the civil rights movement and counterculture realized that they faced just as much sexual discrimination in those realms as they did in mainstream society. One activist recalled a friend telling her that "you'll never be a radical as long as you don't see how the system affects *you.* You always think it affects other people." By the late 1960s more women inspired by other movements were beginning to stand up for their own rights. One woman who became so inspired was journalist Gloria Steinem.

BIO GRAPHY Gloria Steinem was born on March 25, 1934, in Toledo, Ohio. In 1946 her parents divorced. She spent most of her teenage years taking care of her invalid mother. In 1952 Steinem entered Smith College, where she graduated with honors. "I loved Smith," she recalled. "They gave you three meals a day to eat, and all the books you wanted to read—what more could you want?" Steinem's love of reading and writing led to her desire to become a journalist.

In 1968 she started writing a political column for *New York* magazine, which brought her into contact with activists such as César Chávez and African American Communist Angela Davis. Later that year she wrote her first openly feminist article, "After Black Power, Women's Liberation," which established her as an advocate of the movement. In 1971 she helped found the National Women's Political Caucus to encourage women to run for political office. That same year, she became editor of a new magazine for women entitled *Ms.*

Gloria Steinem

"There is nothing outside of [the movement]," Steinem said. "I once thought I would do this for two or three years and go home to my real life." But she has continued to be a leader in the women's movement, writing several books, lobbying for causes such as the passage of the Equal Rights Amendment (see Chapter 31), and helping found numerous organizations for women, including the Coalition of Labor Union Women and Women Against Pornography.

■■ **The 1960s revival of the women's movement challenged traditional views of women.**

---

*M*USICAL REVOLUTION

All of the social and political movements of the 1960s marched to new forms of music. A compelling influence on the youth rebellion of the 1950s, rock 'n' roll continued to reflect social change in the 1960s, while it branched out into a variety of new forms.

The year 1964 marked the musical **British Invasion**—the arrival of such English bands as the Beatles and the Rolling Stones. Drawing on rock 'n' roll and African American blues for inspiration, these bands created a vibrant, powerful new style of music. Meanwhile, African American artists, many sponsored by Motown Records of Detroit, were experimenting with enhanced blendings of traditional black music. The unique and widely popular style they created became known as the "Motown sound."

The use of electrically amplified instruments, especially the electric guitar, inspired musicians to try innovative—and very loud—sounds on audiences. Seattle native Jimi Hendrix was the master

▼ Jimi Hendrix, shown here performing in 1970, was one of the most innovative rock 'n' roll guitarists to emerge during the late 1960s.

▲ Folk music by artists such as Joan Baez was also popular during the 1960s.

RETEACH List on the chalkboard the terms from the Preview Workshop at the beginning of this section. Have students respond to the section's Focus questions with sentences containing the terms.

Closure

Refer students to the quote by Bob Dylan that opens the section. Have students discuss the relevance of Dylan's statement by reviewing the changes that took place during the 1960s.

Extension

CREATE Have students create a collage of the counterculture. Suggest that they use 1960s slogans or song titles as captions for their collages. Call on volunteers to present and explain their collages.

CONDUCT Ask students to conduct an interview with an older relative about life in the 1960s. Have students present their findings in an oral report.

of the electric guitar in the 1960s. Folk music also inspired a new type of rock sound as singers such as Joan Baez and Bob Dylan created lyrics that sent a political message to listeners, such as in this 1962 Dylan hit:

> 66 How many years can a mountain exist
> before it's washed to the sea?
> Yes, 'n' How many years can some
> people exist
> before they're allowed to be free?
> Yes, 'n' How many times can a man
> turn his head
> pretending he just doesn't see?
> The answer, my friend, is blowin'
> in the wind,
> The answer is blowin' in the wind. 99

In the late 1960s, as the Vietnam War continued to rage, rock music became more openly political. Dylan, Baez, and other musicians popular with counterculture performed songs that bitterly criticized the war.

Rock music would be the focal point of an event that marked the beginning of the end for the counterculture movement—the Woodstock Music Festival. In August 1969 some 300,000 young people descended on rural upstate New York for the three-day festival. Despite driving rain, knee-deep mud, and severe shortages of food and water, the concert remained a peaceful gathering as listeners reveled in the music of rock's top performers.

▲ In spite of traffic jams, water shortages, lack of public conveniences, and rain, the Woodstock Music Festival in August 1969 was an overwhelming success.

Woodstock was more than just a rock concert. It was a celebration of the era, marking the high point of the counterculture movement. Some four months later, at a free concert held at Altamont Raceway near San Francisco, a security team beat a young African American fan to death in full view of the stage. The idealistic spirit of the youth movement seemed to die with him.

■■ **Rock music followed the movements of the 1960s and marked the high point of the counterculture at Woodstock.**

PRIMARY SOURCE
Description of Change: excerpted
Rationale: excerpted to focus on main idea

SECTION REVIEW ANSWERS

IDENTIFY

For significance, see the following pages:
generation gap (p. 852)
hippies (p. 853)
counterculture (p. 853)
Timothy Leary (p. 853)
pop art (p. 854)
Roy Lichtenstein (p. 854)
Claes Oldenberg (p. 854)
Andy Warhol (p. 854)
Betty Friedan (p. 854)
National Organization for Women (p. 854)
Gloria Steinem (p. 856)
British Invasion (p. 856)
Jimi Hendrix (p. 856)
Bob Dylan (p. 857)
Woodstock (p. 857)

1. *to create an alternative life-style that rejected traditional values*
2. *caused women to question and challenge traditional roles and views*
3. *brought an examination of traditional values, created a generation gap, increased rates of drug addiction and sexually transmitted diseases*
4. *Articles should note how music reflected social and political changes of the decade.*
5. *commented on consumerism, rejected traditional styles of art elite*

SECTION 4 REVIEW

IDENTIFY and explain the significance of the following: generation gap, hippies, counterculture, Timothy Leary, pop art, Roy Lichtenstein, Claes Oldenberg, Andy Warhol, Betty Friedan, National Organization for Women, Gloria Steinem, British Invasion, Jimi Hendrix, Bob Dylan, Woodstock.

1. **MAIN IDEA** Why did hippies form their own counterculture?
2. **MAIN IDEA** What effect did the revival of the women's movement have on traditional views of women?
3. **ASSESSING CONSEQUENCES** What consequences did the youth rebellion of the 1960s have on society?
4. **WRITING TO EVALUATE** Imagine you are a music critic in 1969. Write an article that evaluates the relationship between rock 'n' roll music and the events of the 1960s.
5. **SYNTHESIZING** How did the various works of pop artists reflect American culture in the 1960s?

Chapter Review Answers

WRITING A SUMMARY

See Essential Points in each section for main ideas.

REVIEWING CHRONOLOGY

4, 3, 5, 2, 1

Evaluating

spurred U.S. government to support War on Poverty

IDENTIFYING PEOPLE AND IDEAS

1. Kennedy's agenda, designed to offer solutions to national and global problems
2. program that sent volunteers to work in developing countries
3. Communist dictator of Cuba
4. commission headed by Chief Justice Earl Warren that concluded there was no evidence of conspiracy in Kennedy assassination
5. democratically elected president of Dominican Republic who was ousted by a 1963 military coup
6. method of protest that forbids use of violence
7. 1965 measure that placed voter registration under federal control
8. movement organized to emphasize pride in Mexican culture and heritage
9. division between baby boomers and older Americans

10. journalist and editor of Ms. magazine who helped found the National Women's Political Caucus

UNDERSTANDING MAIN IDEAS

1. by applying the principle of flexible response, attempted to overthrow Castro through Bay of Pigs invasion, upheld U.S. commitment to West Berlin, and opposed Soviet missiles in Cuba; by supporting nonmilitary options such as the Peace Corps and Alliance for Progress in developing countries
2. to resolve social problems in the U.S.; through legislative efforts and government programs

3. belief that members of these groups should be proud of their heritages and should fight to correct injustices against them
4. through shocking behavior, use of mind-altering drugs, formation of communes or hippie neighborhoods, rejection of traditional values and behaviors
5. won equal pay for equal work through Equal Pay Act, demanded greater opportunities and fairer treatment in work force and other rights; through NOW and similar organizations

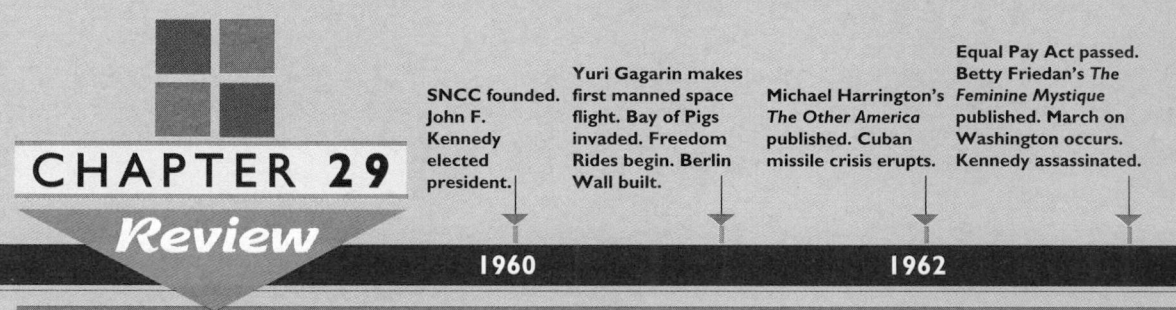

CHAPTER 29
Review

SNCC founded. John F. Kennedy elected president.

Yuri Gagarin makes first manned space flight. Bay of Pigs invaded. Freedom Rides begin. Berlin Wall built.

Michael Harrington's *The Other America* published. Cuban missile crisis erupts.

Equal Pay Act passed. Betty Friedan's *The Feminine Mystique* published. March on Washington occurs. Kennedy assassinated.

1960   **1962**

WRITING A SUMMARY

Using the essential points of the chapter as a guide, write a summary of the chapter.

REVIEWING CHRONOLOGY

Number your paper 1 to 5. Study the time line above, and list the following events in the order in which they happened by writing the first next to 1, the second next to 2, and so on. Then complete the activity below.

1. Woodstock Music Festival occurs.
2. American Indian Movement organized.
3. Betty Friedan's *The Feminine Mystique* published.
4. Freedom Rides begin.
5. Medicare and Medicaid established.

Evaluating How did Michael Harrington's book *The Other America* influence American domestic policy?

IDENTIFYING PEOPLE AND IDEAS

Explain the historical significance of each of the following people or terms.

1. New Frontier
2. Peace Corps
3. Fidel Castro
4. Warren Commission
5. Juan Bosch
6. nonviolent resistance
7. Voting Rights Act
8. Chicano movement
9. generation gap
10. Gloria Steinem

UNDERSTANDING MAIN IDEAS

1. How did the Kennedy administration propose to deter Communist expansion?
2. What was the purpose of the Great Society? How did President Johnson propose to make the Great Society a reality?
3. What did the Brown Power, Red Power, and Black Power movements have in common?
4. How did young people rebel against conformity during the 1960s?
5. What gains did women make during the 1960s? How did they make these gains?

REVIEWING THEMES

1. **Global Relations** How did events overseas undermine the Great Society programs?
2. **Democratic Values** How did the Freedom Rides, sit-ins, and other peaceful civil rights protests help expand democracy?
3. **Cultural Diversity** What institutions and traditions were challenged in the late 1960s?

THINKING CRITICALLY

1. **Evaluating** How did the Warren Court's decisions in *Gideon* v. *Wainwright*, *Escobedo* v. *Illinois*, and *Miranda* v. *Arizona* strengthen individual rights?
2. **Synthesizing** In what ways did African Americans express frustration over their slow progress in achieving civil rights?
3. **Analyzing** What contribution did music and pop art make to society in the 1960s?

STRATEGY FOR SUCCESS

Review the Skills Handbook entry on Reading Charts and Graphs beginning on page 996. Study the graph below, which shows the number of drug arrests reported between 1960 and 1970. In which year did the number of arrests first exceed 100,000? About how many arrests were reported in 1970?

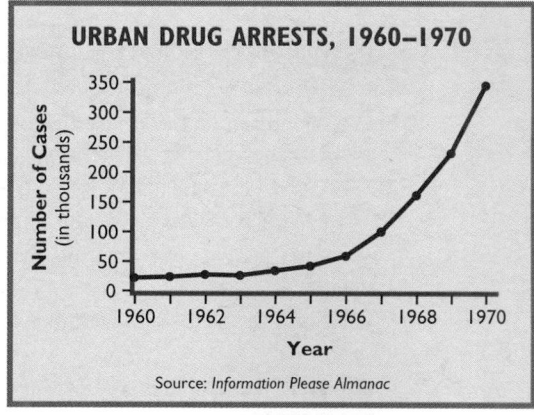

URBAN DRUG ARRESTS, 1960–1970

Number of Cases (in thousands)

Year

Source: *Information Please Almanac*

 **REVIEWING THEMES**

1. *Conflicts in Dominican Republic and in Vietnam drew federal funding and Johnson's attention away from domestic programs.*
2. *drew attention to segregation in South, inspired protests in other areas, attracted public support for civil rights movement, led to laws expanding civil rights and voting rights*
3. *universities; churches; materialism; work ethic; traditional attitudes and values as expressed in life-styles, art, and music*

THINKING CRITICALLY

1. *Gideon—states had to provide lawyers for poor defendants charged with serious crimes; Escobedo—accused had the right to have a lawyer present during interrogations; Miranda—accused had to be informed of rights at time of arrest*
2. *formed Black Power movement to champion black separatism and use of violence, if necessary, to fight for equal rights*
3. *music—reflected events of 1960s; pop art—commented on consumerism of period, made art more accessible to public*

STRATEGY FOR SUCCESS
1967; about 350,000

WRITING ABOUT HISTORY
Essays should contrast Johnson's background and his skill in political compromise with Kennedy's.

USING PRIMARY SOURCES
Students might mention lack of modern conveniences, high levels of disease and infant mortality, and low life-expectancy rates on the reservation.

LINKING HISTORY AND GEOGRAPHY
feared close proximity to U.S. of Soviet allies, refused to compromise on missiles in Cuba, sent troops to Dominican Republic to oppose Bosch

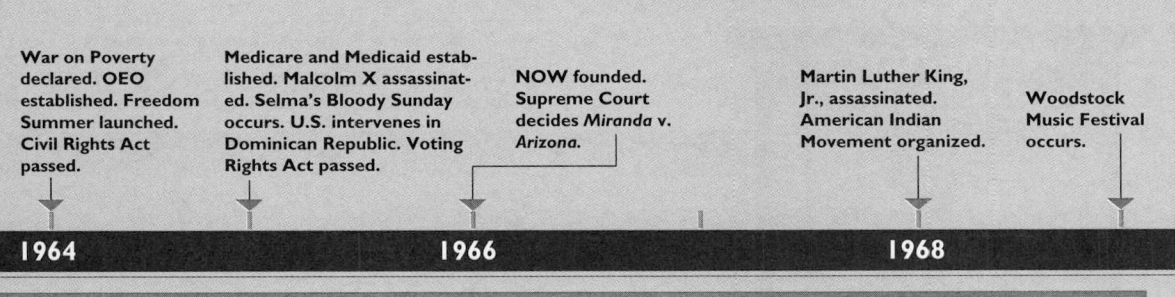

War on Poverty declared. OEO established. Freedom Summer launched. Civil Rights Act passed.

Medicare and Medicaid established. Malcolm X assassinated. Selma's Bloody Sunday occurs. U.S. intervenes in Dominican Republic. Voting Rights Act passed.

NOW founded. Supreme Court decides *Miranda* v. *Arizona*.

Martin Luther King, Jr., assassinated. American Indian Movement organized.

Woodstock Music Festival occurs.

1964   1966   1968

WRITING ABOUT HISTORY
Writing to Evaluate Write an essay that evaluates the different leadership styles of Lyndon Johnson and John F. Kennedy.

USING PRIMARY SOURCES
Native Americans were one ethnic group in the 1960s whose problems were not addressed by the U.S. government. Read the following excerpt, which comes from an article published in the *New Republic* in 1965, describing conditions on the Pine Ridge Reservation in South Dakota. Then write a paragraph summarizing what you have read.

> 66 *Practically none of the houses on the reservation has electricity. Half of the houses are without wells nearby; Poverty-Program workers are discovering people hauling water fifteen miles. Indoor plumbing or telephone service is rare. . . .*
>
> *There is a great deal of illness at Pine Ridge. . . . The infant mortality rate is twice that of the nation's, and infectious diseases among small children are a major problem. The incidence of tuberculosis is seventeen times that for the rest of the country. The life expectancy for a person at Pine Ridge is thirty-eight years, compared with sixty-two years nationally. . . .*
>
> *The solution to the Indian problem still is dimly seen to lie in pouring the Indians into the big cities where they will intermingle with everyone else. But the city planners are trying to figure out how to get people out of the cramped city and back into the countryside. If the administration does not pull hard to redevelop these rural areas, it will end up merely fanning the flames in the cities.* 99

LINKING HISTORY AND GEOGRAPHY
Refer to the map on page 837. How did geography influence U.S. policy toward Cuba and the Dominican Republic?

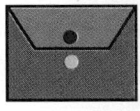 **BUILDING YOUR PORTFOLIO**

Complete the following projects independently or cooperatively.

1. CIVIL RIGHTS In chapters 27 and 28 you served as a reporter covering the civil rights movement. Building on that experience, write a memorandum to the manager of your station explaining why the station should provide coverage of the civil rights efforts of African Americans, Hispanic Americans, Native Americans, and women.

2. THE GOVERNMENT AND THE ECONOMY In Chapter 27 you prepared a chart of government programs designed to help WWII veterans. Building on that experience, imagine you are a member of Johnson's Great Society. Prepare an illustrated pamphlet that describes government efforts in areas such as health care, urban renewal, or education.

3. POPULAR CULTURE In Chapter 28 you prepared a photo essay on American culture during the 1950s. Building on that experience, imagine you are a reporter for *Rolling Stone*, assigned to write an article about the first two decades of rock 'n' roll. Prepare a family tree of rock music, using photos to trace the influence of rhythm and blues, jazz, folk, country, and the British Invasion on American music up to 1970.

 **BUILDING YOUR PORTFOLIO**
Have students refer to **Building Your Portfolio Worksheet 8**, assigned at the beginning of Unit 8. Use the worksheet to help students monitor their progress on the portfolio projects.

Assessment

Core Resources
• Review Worksheet 29
• Chapter 29 Tests
• Alternative Assessment Forms
Test Generator

*U*RBAN AMERICA

HISTORICAL SIDELIGHTS
Hollywood

The growth of Los Angeles in the 1920s and 1930s was largely because of the expansion of the motion picture industry in Hollywood. The Nestor Company built Hollywood's first film studio in 1911, and numerous other companies followed suit. Most film studios were attracted to the Los Angeles area because of its mild, dry climate and proximity to natural scenery that was ideal for outdoor filming.

America's GEOGRAPHY

URBAN AMERICA

*A*S more people moved into the cities and suburbs after World War II, metropolitan areas —large cities or groups of cities and their surrounding areas—arose. The city of Los Angeles is typical of the 20th-century metropolis. In the 1920s most of the land inside the official city limits was not developed. As the city grew, it engulfed numerous surrounding areas. By the 1980s the Los Angeles metropolitan area encompassed some 80 smaller cities. Like many urban-dwellers, Los Angeles–area residents generally live outside the city and commute to work. This has led to the observation that Los Angeles, like many other metropolitan areas, is in fact "a hundred suburbs in search of a city."

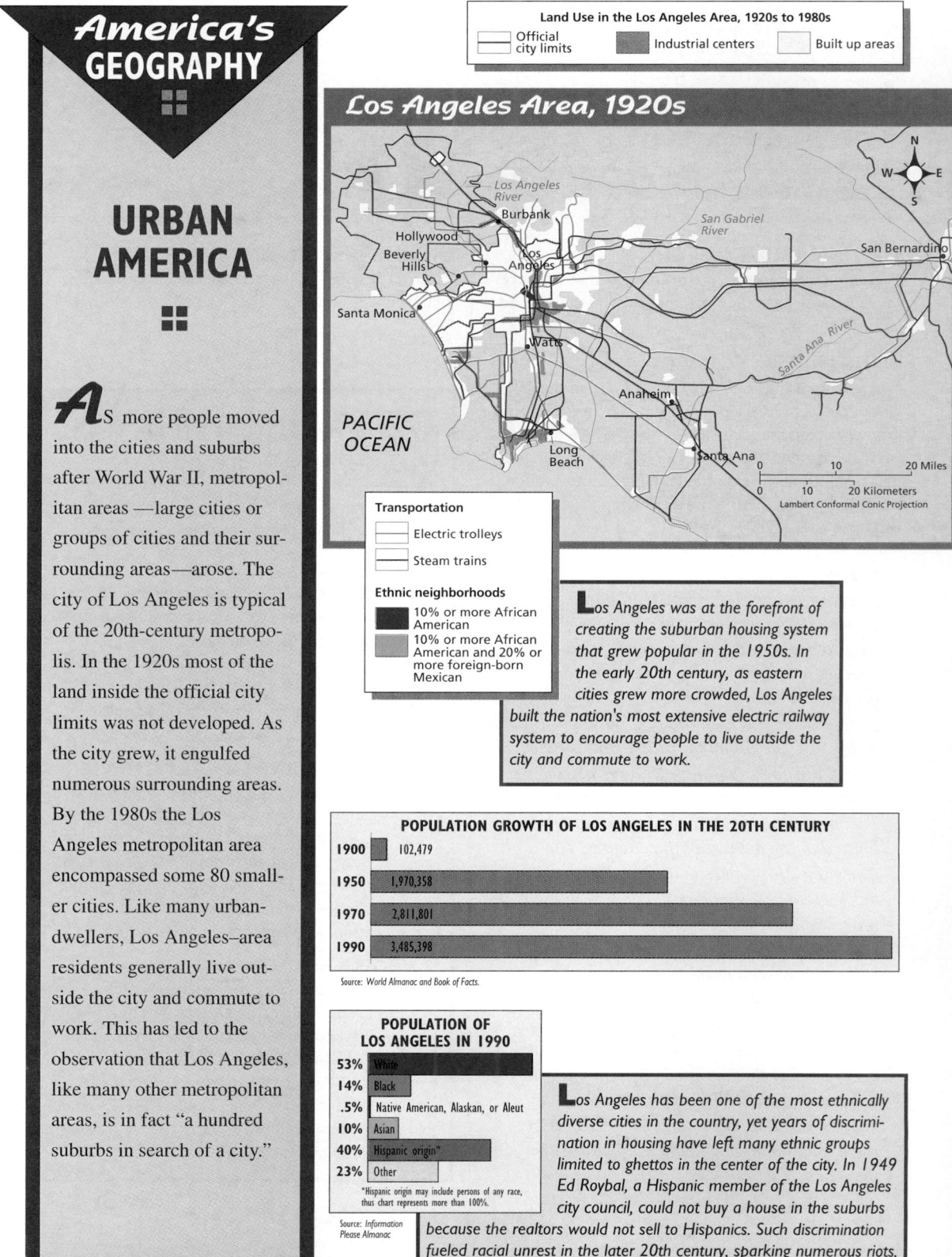

Land Use in the Los Angeles Area, 1920s to 1980s
Official city limits | Industrial centers | Built up areas

Los Angeles Area, 1920s

Los Angeles River · Burbank · Hollywood · Beverly Hills · Los Angeles · San Gabriel River · San Bernardino · Santa Monica · Watts · Anaheim · PACIFIC OCEAN · Long Beach · Santa Ana · Santa Ana River

0 10 20 Miles
0 10 20 Kilometers
Lambert Conformal Conic Projection

Transportation
Electric trolleys
Steam trains

Ethnic neighborhoods
10% or more African American
10% or more African American and 20% or more foreign-born Mexican

*L*os Angeles was at the forefront of creating the suburban housing system that grew popular in the 1950s. In the early 20th century, as eastern cities grew more crowded, Los Angeles built the nation's most extensive electric railway system to encourage people to live outside the city and commute to work.

POPULATION GROWTH OF LOS ANGELES IN THE 20TH CENTURY

Year	Population
1900	102,479
1950	1,970,358
1970	2,811,801
1990	3,485,398

Source: World Almanac and Book of Facts.

POPULATION OF LOS ANGELES IN 1990

%	Group
53%	White
14%	Black
.5%	Native American, Alaskan, or Aleut
10%	Asian
40%	Hispanic origin*
23%	Other

*Hispanic origin may include persons of any race, thus chart represents more than 100%.

Source: Information Please Almanac

*L*os Angeles has been one of the most ethnically diverse cities in the country, yet years of discrimination in housing have left many ethnic groups limited to ghettos in the center of the city. In 1949 Ed Roybal, a Hispanic member of the Los Angeles city council, could not buy a house in the suburbs because the realtors would not sell to Hispanics. Such discrimination fueled racial unrest in the later 20th century, sparking numerous riots, such as the Watts riot of 1965 and the south central riots of 1992.

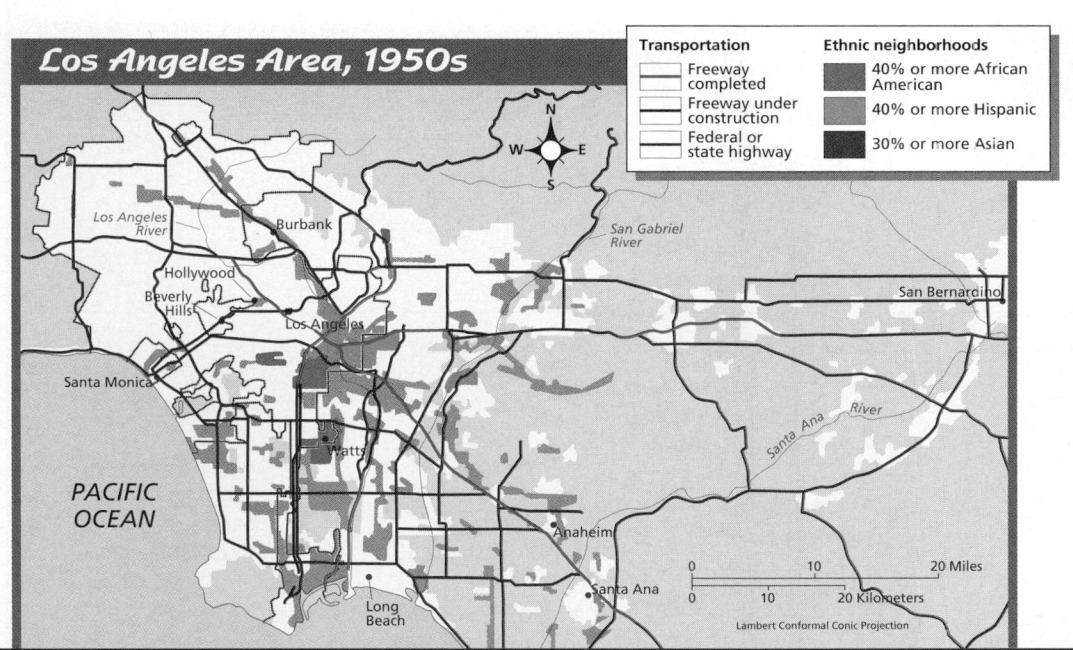

Los Angeles Area, 1950s

Transportation	Ethnic neighborhoods
Freeway completed	40% or more African American
Freeway under construction	40% or more Hispanic
Federal or state highway	30% or more Asian

By the 1940s automobiles had replaced the railway system as the preferred means of transportation in Los Angeles. Construction of a huge freeway network encouraged automobile use, but it also led to a rise in smog pollution—a problem that plagues many cities today. While Los Angeles has grown rapidly, it has also faced numerous problems caused by its geography. The dry climate has contributed to several brush fires in recent years. Lack of an adequate water supply led to the construction of Owens River Aqueduct in 1913, followed by the California Aqueduct in 1973. Los Angeles also lies in an area of heavy earthquake activity. The city has been rocked by numerous earthquakes, including one in January 1994 that killed more than 50 people.

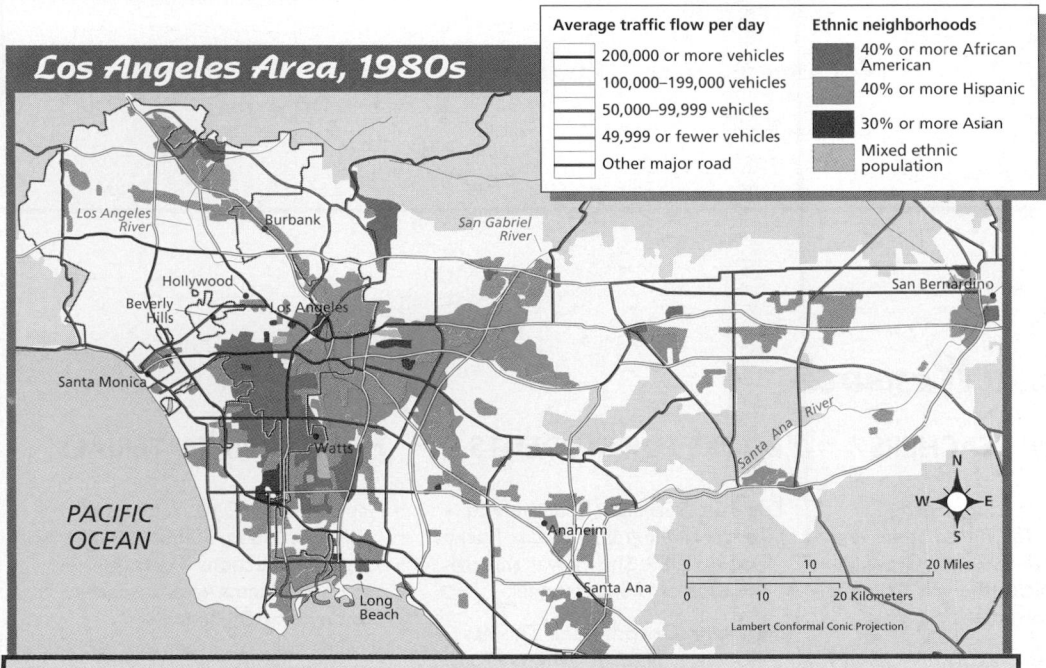

Los Angeles Area, 1980s

Average traffic flow per day	Ethnic neighborhoods
200,000 or more vehicles	40% or more African American
100,000–199,000 vehicles	40% or more Hispanic
50,000–99,999 vehicles	30% or more Asian
49,999 or fewer vehicles	Mixed ethnic population
Other major road	

By the mid–1980s Los Angeles was the second-largest city in America. Many citizens, worried that the city was growing too rapidly, campaigned for measures to slow growth and improve urban conditions. In 1986 the city passed a measure that cut in half the amount of land available to developers for construction. Also in the mid–1980s the city began working on plans to improve public transportation with a new train and subway system.

HISTORICAL SIDELIGHTS
Freeways

As the traffic flow in large cities increased in the 20th century, so did the expansion of freeways—also called superhighways. These are limited-access, multi-lane highways designed for high-speed traffic. The word *freeway,* which was coined in the 1930s to refer to non-toll roads, now simply refers to the free flow of traffic on these highways. Thus some so-called freeways carry toll charges.

WAR IN VIETNAM

1954–1975

Chapter Overview

In the early 1950s American containment policy focused on Asia. To prevent a Communist victory in Vietnam, the U.S. first supported France's attempts to reestablish rule over its former colony. The U.S. then aided the anti-Communist government of South Vietnam, under attack from the Communist north. Escalating U.S. military involvement failed to produce victory and provoked dissension at home. The Vietnam War ended in 1975, when Communist forces took over South Vietnam.

Chapter Planning Guide

CHAPTER 30	CORE RESOURCE BOOKLETS	AUDIOVISUAL AV RESOURCES	PROGRAM RESOURCES
INTRODUCTION pp. 862–863	▪ Geography Worksheet 30 ▪ Building Your Portfolio Worksheet 8		
TEACHING THE CHAPTER pp. 864–889	▪ Graphic Organizer 30 ▪ Social Studies Skills Worksheet 30 ▪ Literature Worksheet 30 ▪ Outline Map 21	▪ *The American Nation* Videodisc: Vietnam and the Media ▪ Everyday Life in America Transparency and Worksheet 30 ▪ *American Civics Citizenship Skills* Videocassette or Videodisc	▪ *Eyewitnesses and Others,* Volume 2: Readings 69, 70 ▪ Art in American History Transparency and Worksheet 45
REVIEW AND ASSESSMENT pp. 890–891	▪ Chapter 30 Daily Quizzes ▪ Review Worksheet 30 ▪ Chapter 30 Tests ▪ Alternative Assessment Forms		▪ Test Generator

Additional Resources

BOOKS FOR TEACHERS

Herring, George C. *America's Longest War: The United States and Vietnam, 1950–1975.* McGraw-Hill, 1986. Chronicles the war from earliest U.S. involvement.

Karnow, Stanley. *Vietnam: A History.* Viking Penguin, 1984. Companion to the PBS Series "Vietnam: A Television History."

BOOKS FOR STUDENTS

Edelman, Bernard. *Dear America: Letters Home from Vietnam.* Pocket Books, 1989. Shows war through the eyes of U.S. personnel.

*Hoobler, Dorothy, and Thomas Hoobler. *Vietnam: Why We Fought.* Knopf, 1990. History of Vietnam's foreign relations.

* for students reading below grade level

MULTIMEDIA MATERIALS

How Far from Home: Veterans after Vietnam. Video, 30 min. Northern Light Productions. Portrays the many problems veterans faced upon returning home.

Vietnam: Chronicle of a War. Video, 88 min. CBS. Walter Cronkite traces history of U.S. involvement.

ᴛHEMES IN AMERICAN HISTORY

USE WITH PAGES 862–863

*L*isted on the right are the themes emphasized in Chapter 30. The questions in boldface type stimulate critical thinking and provide students with an opportunity to discuss the themes within a broadened context. The questions also appear in the pupil's edition on p. 862.

■ GLOBAL RELATIONS

How might global conditions lead one nation to intervene in the affairs of another? Student responses should consider differences in nations' foreign-policy goals, economic interests, and national values. Responses might also reflect students' individual values and beliefs.

■ CONSTITUTIONAL HERITAGE

Why might one branch of government fear another branch becoming too strong? Students should note that the balance of power between branches and the system of checks and balances would be jeopardized.

■ DEMOCRATIC VALUES

What are the limits to the government's responsibility to keep the public informed? Students should consider national security interests versus the need for open government in a democratic system. The development of the atomic bomb during World War II might be a point for debate.

In a democracy, what limits are there to a people's right to protest government actions? Students might suggest that citizens must protest through legal means—peaceful demonstrations, boycotts, elections, recalls, etc.

ᴄHAPTER STRATEGIES FOR MEETING INDIVIDUAL NEEDS

LIMITED ENGLISH PROFICIENT LEARNERS

Have pairs of students write down the boldfaced terms and define them with sketches or short phrases. Ask partners to take turns asking each other questions that use the terms.

TACTILE/KINESTHETIC LEARNERS

Have students work in groups to develop two skits, one illustrating U.S. soldiers' Vietnam experiences, and the other showing confrontation at home between hawks and doves.

LEARNERS HAVING DIFFICULTY

Have pairs of students write brief answers to the questions in each section Focus and two or three sentences summing up each section. Then have them write a short summary of the chapter.

AUDITORY LEARNERS

Have students prepare dramatic readings of important quotations and other critical parts of each section of the chapter.

VISUAL LEARNERS

Have students view a videotape or movie on the Vietnam War. Then have small groups of students make a flowchart showing major events of the war. Students should then list the domestic responses to each event in the chart.

GIFTED LEARNERS

Have students list and describe major turning points in the war. Ask them to evaluate the U.S. response at each point, deciding whether the response should have included withdrawal.

USING THE CHAPTER FOCUS

■ UNDERSTANDING THE MAIN IDEA

Call on a volunteer to read the Understanding the Main Idea paragraph aloud. Ask students what they know about Vietnam from movies, TV programs, and books. List students' comments on a flip chart or butcher paper and have students evaluate their comments after they complete the chapter.

THEMES

Have students work individually or in small groups to answer the questions under Themes. Save students' responses so that they can compare them with their responses after studying the chapter. (See p. 861B for suggested answers.)

■ THE TIME LINE

Point out that events such as the Geneva Conference in 1954 and the unrest that grew in South Vietnam after Diem took power in 1955 heightened Cold War tensions and U.S. fears of the spread of communism. These events helped shape U.S. decisions to increase America's involvement in Vietnam.

Have students note the length of U.S. troop deployment in Vietnam. Ask them to compare it to American involvement in other conflicts (World War I, 1917–1918; World War II, 1941–1945; Korea, 1950–1953).

CORE RESOURCES

- **Graphic Organizer 30**
- **Geography Worksheet 30**
- **Outline Map 21**
- **Building Your Portfolio Worksheet 8**

ABOUT THE ILLUSTRATION

A marine officer takes shelter during the struggle for Hue, one of the most bitter battles of the war. North Vietnamese briefly captured the city in early 1968. U.S. Marines played a decisive role in helping South Vietnamese troops retake the city. In the rubble-strewn streets, U.S. soldiers had a difficult time locating and identifying the enemy. Have students study the marine's expression and stance. Ask them what emotions they think the soldier is feeling.

Chapter 30

1954–1975

WAR IN VIETNAM

FOCUS

UNDERSTANDING THE MAIN IDEA

Most U.S. leaders expected the war in Vietnam to end quickly once U.S. troops and equipment entered the conflict. They did not dream that some 2.6 million Americans would serve in a war that dragged on for more than a decade. Nor did they imagine that antiwar protests would grow to the proportions they did.

THEMES

■ **GLOBAL RELATIONS** How might global conditions lead one nation to intervene in the affairs of another?

■ **CONSTITUTIONAL HERITAGE** Why might one branch of government fear another branch becoming too strong?

■ **DEMOCRATIC VALUES** What are the limits to the government's responsibility to keep the public informed? In a democracy, what limits are there to a people's right to protest government actions?

1954	1955	1965	1973	1975
Geneva Conference held.	Diem comes to power in South Vietnam.	U.S. sends combat troops to Vietnam.	Cease-fire declared.	Saigon falls.

Have students list the reasons that led the U.S. to fight in Korea. Write students' answers on a flip chart or butcher paper and save it. As you move through the chapter, compare the reasons for U.S. involvement in Korea with those for American involvement in Vietnam.

▰▰ LINK TO THE PAST

The United States had taken the position of opposing the spread of communism anywhere in the world. U.S. troops had recently fought against Communist forces in Korea. Now Americans became involved in a similar war in Vietnam, where the Vietnamese had won their independence from the French a few years earlier.

MAKING CONNECTIONS

Literature
Have students compare Graham Greene's description of the young U.S. adviser with the soldier shown in the photograph. Ask students whether the photograph and Greene's description match.

PRIMARY SOURCE
Description of Change: excerpted
Rationale: excerpted to focus on main idea

A U.S. Marine officer takes cover.

In Graham Greene's novel *The Quiet American* (1955), the narrator sits in a Vietnamese café thinking about a new arrival, the American "adviser" Alden Pyle. According to the narrator, the young American "seemed incapable of harm":

> ❝ Perhaps only ten days ago he had been walking back across the Common in Boston, his arms full of the books he had been reading in advance on the Far East and the problems of China. He didn't even hear what I said; he was absorbed already in the dilemmas of Democracy and the responsibilities of the West; he was determined—I learnt that very soon—to do good, not to any individual person but to a country, a continent, a world. ❞

Greene's Alden Pyle closely resembles the American advisers sent to South Vietnam in the 1950s. This "quiet American," wading into the rough sea of post–World War II Southeast Asia, typifies the early American self-image in Vietnam: confident, serious, and eagerly committed to building a model democracy.

This sense of idealism was grounded in the effort to save Vietnam and the rest of the world from communism, even at great cost to America. The eventual cost—years of war and more than 60,000 Americans dead or missing—was higher than most believed possible. And despite the sacrifices, Vietnam was not "saved." In the war's wake, Americans were left to ponder how early idealism ended in what has been called "a tragedy of epic dimensions."

Vietnam Women's Memorial

FOCUS OBJECTIVES

- Describe why China and then France sought control of Vietnam.

- Explain why the U.S. refused to back Vietnamese independence in the 1940s and 1950s.

- Identify the reasons why President Kennedy increased U.S. involvement in Vietnam.

Section 1

BACKGROUND TO CONFLICT

F O C U S

- **Why did China and then France want to control Vietnam?**
- **Why did the United States refuse to back Vietnamese independence in the 1940s and 1950s?**
- **Why did President Kennedy increase U.S. involvement in Vietnam?**

For centuries invaders coveted the fertile river deltas and coastal lowlands of Vietnam. First China and later France conquered and ruled Vietnam. But the deep desire of the Vietnamese people to be free could not be overcome. During World War II, France began to lose its grip on Vietnam. And as the war came to a close, Vietnamese Communists fought for power, hoping to establish an independent nation. This threat of a Communist takeover soon drew the United States into the conflict.

French colonial occupation in Saigon

THE GEOGRAPHIC SETTING

Fishhook-shaped Vietnam is the easternmost country of Southeast Asia—8,000 miles across the Pacific from the west coast of the United States. It

▲ **Vietnam is one of the world's largest producers of rice, cultivating more than 12 million acres each year.**

is slightly smaller than California, covering 127,207 square miles of mostly hills and dense forests. Lying south of China, Vietnam is bordered on the west by Laos and Cambodia. Its coastline stretches along the Gulf of Tonkin, the South China Sea, and the Gulf of Thailand (see map on page 865).

The population of Vietnam is centered mostly in two areas: the Red River Delta in the far north and the Mekong (MAY-KAWNG) Delta in the south. The Mekong Delta is Vietnam's richest agricultural region, specializing in rice cultivation. Hanoi is the major city of the north and the country's capital, while Ho Chi Minh City (previously South Vietnam's capital, Saigon) is the largest city in the south. Other cities, such as the ports Da Nang and Hue (WAY), are located on the narrow coastal lowlands of central Vietnam.

To the north of the Mekong Delta are the central highlands, sparsely populated and mostly covered by forest. Farther north, the Annamite Mountains form the jagged backbone of Vietnam. Their rugged peaks and dense rain forest separate much of Vietnam from neighboring Laos.

Teaching the Section

THE GEOGRAPHY OF VIETNAM

Have students work in small groups to draw maps of Vietnam, including major rivers, mountain ranges, highlands, ports, cities, and delta regions. Display the maps on the wall. Call on groups to suggest geographic characteristics of Vietnam that might cause China and France to want to control it. Ask what geographic characteristics might make such control difficult.

CHINESE OCCUPATION

The moist tropical climate of the deltas and coastal lowlands has allowed Vietnamese farmers to grow several crops of rice a year. It was this agricultural abundance that tempted China to invade the Red River Delta around 200 B.C. For more than a thousand years, the Chinese struggled to maintain control over northern and central Vietnam. But the Vietnamese resisted, finally winning limited independence from China in A.D. 939.

In the 1400s China tried to reassert control over Vietnam. A Vietnamese military leader named Le Loi employed guerrilla warfare to defeat the Chinese invaders. Using tactics similar to those later used against the French and Americans, Le Loi's rebels worked as peasants by day; by night they took up arms to attack the Chinese. By 1428 the rebels had driven the Chinese from the country and won independence for Vietnam. Le Loi became the new emperor.

FRENCH OCCUPATION

Vietnam again lost its independence in the surge of European imperialism in the mid-1800s. This time the invaders were French, attracted by the promise of gaining access to Asian trade and of making new Catholic converts.

Despite the stubborn resistance of the Vietnamese, French military power ultimately won out. In 1883 the Vietnamese were forced to grant France complete control of the country. France later combined Vietnam with Laos and Cambodia to form French Indochina, one of France's richest possessions.

■ **The Chinese and later the French sought control of Vietnam's rich farmlands and trade.**

Ho Chi Minh and Vietnamese independence. Like the Chinese, the French gained control of the land but not the hearts of the Vietnamese. Nationalist feelings remained strong.

Indochina

A TROPICAL PENINSULA The nations of Indochina occupy a peninsula stretching from the mainland of Southeast Asia deep into the tropical waters of the South China Sea.

? RELATIVE LOCATION How might Vietnam's location have contributed to its long history of foreign invasion?

Foremost among the nationalists was Nguyen That Thanh (en-gy-EN TAHT TAHN), a world wanderer and man of many names, whose last alias was Ho Chi Minh (HOH CHEE MIN)—"He Who Enlightens."

Ho was born in central Vietnam in 1890, the son of a poor country scholar. In 1911, calling himself Van Ba (Third Son), he got a job as cook on a French merchant ship. After spending a few years at sea, he decided to settle in London. There, while working as a pastry cook in a hotel, Ho learned the English language (he was already fluent in French).

From London, Ho went to Paris, where he soon emerged as a leader of Vietnamese nationalists living in France. Ho joined the French socialists but

BUILDING VOCABULARY

In this instance *Indo* refers to India. Due to the influence of India in the region, some areas in Asia, such as Indochina, came to be labeled in part by their location relative to India.

Map Caption Answer
Its access to land and water trade routes and its climate suited to rice production made it attractive to foreign invaders.

HISTORICAL SIDELIGHTS
Ho's Early Request
In 1919 Ho, who was living in France at the time, petitioned the Paris Peace Conference to consider the cause of the Vietnamese people. He asked that the principles of national self-determination enunciated in Wilson's Fourteen Points be applied to Indochina. But Ho was not successful in getting the Big Four to consider his appeal.

*P*ractice

GUIDED PRACTICE

Have volunteers identify periods of external or internal conflict for Vietnam. List the periods on the chalkboard and review them, asking students to provide details about each period.

INDEPENDENT PRACTICE

Using the list developed in the Guided Practice, have students prepare illustrated time lines showing the periods of conflict in Vietnam. Students may wish to include their time lines in their portfolios.

*R*eview and *A*ssessment

REVIEW Have students create an outline of the major points in Section 1. Then assign the Section 1 Review on p. 869.

ASSESS Assign the **Section 1 Daily Quiz** in *Core Resources.*

---

meanwhile, did not want to see Vietnam handed over completely to the Communists.

A cease-fire was agreed to, but no definite political settlement was achieved. Vietnam was temporarily divided at the 17th parallel (17° north latitude). North of the 17th parallel, the Vietminh held undisputed power; south of the line, remnants of the French-controlled government resumed authority. Vietminh forces would withdraw to the north; French forces would withdraw to the south. General elections to reunify the country were scheduled for July 1956. Alarmed that the Communists would likely win a nationwide election, the United States refused to endorse the agreement.

---

*T*HE REGIME OF NGO DINH DIEM

President Eisenhower estimated that Ho might win a general election by as much as four to one. Still, he hoped that southern Vietnam, at least, might be kept non-Communist. Who could stand against Ho? One possibility was Ngo Dinh Diem (en-GOH DIN de-EM), a former government official under the French. Though lacking Ho's charisma, Diem was enough of a nationalist to be a credible Vietnamese leader.

Diem takes power in the south. Ngo Dinh Diem was strongly anti-Communist. He had spent several years in the United States, where his political views attracted powerful backers. In 1955 Diem became president of the newly established Republic of Vietnam (South Vietnam) following a rigged election—in Saigon, Diem got more than 605,000 votes from the 450,000 registered voters! But Diem knew that he had no chance of winning a nationwide election against Ho. Thus, he refused to call an election in the south when the July 1956 date set by the Geneva Conference rolled around.

Diem, a Roman Catholic, was unpopular from the start. The large Buddhist population resented the favoritism he showed toward Catholics. Peasants disliked his land policies, which favored wealthy landholders. And almost everyone objected that power was solely in the grip of Diem's family. Above all, people feared his ruthless efforts to root out his political enemies. Diem's hated security forces routinely tortured and imprisoned opponents.

By the late 1950s armed revolution had erupted in the south. In 1959, military assistance began

flowing from the north to the Vietminh who had stayed in the south. In 1960 the southern Vietminh formed the National Liberation Front (NLF). The NLF's main goal was the overthrow of the Ngo Dinh Diem regime. Members of this rebel force were called **Vietcong** (Vietnamese Communists) by their opponents, but not all NLF supporters were Communists.

Many peasants joined the ranks of the NLF, some because of government repression. Others joined out of fear: the NLF, like Diem's forces, used terrorist tactics, assassinating hundreds of government officials. Soon much of the countryside was under Vietcong control.

America's involvement deepens. John F. Kennedy, who became president in 1961, fully subscribed to the domino theory. He also was eager to bolster America's image in the world—an image that had been tarnished by the failed Bay of Pigs invasion and the Soviets' raising of the Berlin Wall early in his presidency (see Chapter 29). Coming to the aid of South Vietnam, which Kennedy had once called the "cornerstone of the Free World in Southeast Asia," provided America with a chance to assert its power.

When Kennedy took office, some 700 U.S. military advisers were in South Vietnam training

▼ Ngo Dinh Diem paces the floor of his Saigon palace after crushing an attempt to overthrow his regime in the spring of 1955.

RETEACH Have students work in small groups to answer the questions in the section Focus. Assign each group member a question. Have members share answers with one another.

Closure

Have students reflect on Vietnam's history until 1963. Then ask if they agree with President Kennedy's statement that Vietnam was the "cornerstone of the Free World in Southeast Asia."

Extension

EVALUATE Have interested students evaluate and report on George Kennan's attitude toward U.S. involvement in Vietnam.

RESEARCH Have students research and report on Vietnam's Joan of Arc, Trieu Au, who fought for independence from China in the third century A.D.

Diem's army. Over the course of his administration, Kennedy increased that number to more than 16,000. As Vietcong attacks mounted, Kennedy authorized U.S. forces to engage in direct combat. As a result, the number of Americans killed or wounded climbed from 14 in 1961 to nearly 500 in 1963.

■■ **President Kennedy saw U.S. involvement in Vietnam as a way to halt the spread of communism and strengthen America's image in the world.**

Diem's overthrow. The situation was also escalating politically. South Vietnam's Buddhist leaders now openly opposed Diem's regime. Diem was waging a brutal campaign of repression against Buddhists. Hundreds had been arrested, and many had been killed in the crackdown. In response, several Buddhist monks publicly set themselves on fire. These grisly protests shocked Americans, and U.S. officials in Saigon threatened to withdraw support for Diem unless he ended the repression.

When Diem refused to comply, U.S. leaders gave quiet encouragement to a group of young South Vietnamese army officers plotting Diem's overthrow. The plotters struck in November 1963, murdering both Diem and his brother. Diem's violent assassination upset U.S. advisers, who had been prepared to fly Diem out of the country.

▲ On June 11, 1963, Quang Duc set himself on fire at a busy intersection in Saigon. He was the first of several Buddhist monks who killed themselves to protest Diem's policies.

Kennedy's doubts increase. Diem's overthrow did nothing to ease Kennedy's growing concern over America's involvement in Vietnam. In an interview shortly before Diem's fall, Kennedy had said of the South Vietnamese: "In the final analysis it is their war. They are the ones who have to win or lose it." But we will never know how Kennedy might have handled the situation. Three weeks after Diem's murder, Kennedy himself was assassinated in Dallas.

SECTION 1 REVIEW

IDENTIFY and explain the significance of the following: Ho Chi Minh, Vietminh, domino theory, Ngo Dinh Diem, Vietcong.

LOCATE and explain the importance of the following: Vietnam, China, Red River Delta, Mekong Delta, Hanoi, Saigon, central highlands, Annamite Mountains, Dien Bien Phu.

1. **MAIN IDEA** Why did President Truman refuse Ho's requests for help against the French?
2. **MAIN IDEA** What led President Kennedy to increase U.S. involvement in Vietnam?
3. **LINKING HISTORY AND GEOGRAPHY** What attracted the Chinese and the French to Vietnam?
4. **WRITING TO PERSUADE** Imagine you are an adviser to President Eisenhower in 1959. On the basis of what you would know at the time, prepare a statement outlining the pros and cons of U.S. involvement in Vietnam. Then, in a paragraph, make a policy recommendation.
5. **USING HISTORICAL IMAGINATION** In the 1941 Atlantic Charter, President Roosevelt and British Prime Minister Churchill pledged "to see sovereign rights and self-government restored to those who have been forcibly deprived of them." Imagine that you are Ho. Write a letter to President Truman explaining why America should honor this pledge in Vietnam.

VOICES OF CHANGE

HISTORICAL SIDELIGHTS

Biblical Themes

Some critics have noticed strong Biblical themes in "The Times They Are A-Changin'." "The waters" mentioned in the first verse may refer to the Flood described in Genesis, the first book of the Bible. Images of Old Testament prophets are evoked in the second verse by mention of "writers and critics/Who prophesize." And the battle that will shake windows and rattle walls, mentioned in the third verse, may refer back to Joshua and the Battle of Jericho. The last verse rephrases in a number of ways the lines from the book of Matthew: "But many that are first shall be last; and the last shall be first." This song, one critic concluded, could have been written only by someone well versed in the Bible.

HISTORICAL SIDELIGHTS

Poets' Mecca

Ferlinghetti founded the City Lights Bookstore in San Francisco in 1953. Open until midnight on weekdays and until 2 A.M. on weekends, it quickly became a gathering place for local poets. Through the bookstore, Ferlinghetti published the work of many Beat writers in a paperback series called "Pocket Poets."

UNIT 8

American Letters

Voices of Change

In many ways the postwar years were a troubled time. Americans confronted serious issues, from Cold War fears and war to racial prejudice and social injustice. Singer-songwriter Bob Dylan, San Francisco Beat poet Lawrence Ferlinghetti, African American poet Naomi Long Madgett, and Native American poet-novelist James Welch were among the writers who explored these problems and tensions.

The Times They Are A-Changin'

by Bob Dylan

Come gather 'round people
Wherever you roam
And admit that the waters
Around you have grown
And accept it that soon
You'll be drenched to the bone.
If your time to you
Is worth savin'
Then you better start swimmin'
Or you'll sink like a stone
For the times they are a-changin'.

Come writers and critics
Who prophesize with your pen
And keep your eyes wide
The chance won't come again
And don't speak too soon
For the wheel's still in spin
And there's no tellin' who
That it's namin'.
For the loser now
Will be later to win
For the times they are a-changin'.

Come senators, congressmen
Please heed the call
Don't stand in the doorway
Don't block up the hall

For he that gets hurt
Will be he who has stalled
There's a battle outside
And it is ragin'.
It'll soon shake your windows
And rattle your walls
For the times they are a-changin'.

Come mothers and fathers
Throughout the land
And don't criticize
What you can't understand
Your sons and your daughters
Are beyond your command
Your old road is
Rapidly agin'.

Please get out of the new one
If you can't lend your hand
For the times they are a-changin'.

The line it is drawn
The curse it is cast
The slow one now
Will later be fast
As the present now
Will later be past
The order is
Rapidly fadin'.
And the first one now
Will later be last
For the times they are a-changin'. ❖

▼ *Civil rights demonstrators attacked with high-pressure water hoses, 1963*

▼ *Flower power, 1967*

▲ *Voter registration march to Montgomery, Alabama, 1965*

From **I Am Waiting**

by Lawrence Ferlinghetti

I am waiting for my number to be
    called
and I am waiting
for the living end
and I am waiting
for dad to come home
his pockets full
of irradiated silver dollars
and I am waiting
for the atomic tests to end
and I am waiting happily
for things to get much worse
before they improve
and I am waiting
for the Salvation Army to take
    over
and I am waiting
for the human crowd
to wander off a cliff somewhere
clutching its atomic umbrella
and I am waiting
for Ike to act
and I am waiting
for the meek to be blessed
and inherit the earth. . .
and I am waiting for forests and
    animals
to reclaim the earth as theirs
and I am waiting
for a way to be devised
to destroy all nationalisms
without killing anybody
and I am waiting
for linnets[1] and planets to fall like
    rain
and I am waiting for lovers and
    weepers
to lie down together again
in a new rebirth of wonder. . . . ❖

1 birds of the finch family

Midway

by Naomi Long Madgett

I've come this far to freedom and
    I won't turn back.
I'm climbing to the highway from
    my old dirt track.
  I'm coming and I'm going
  And I'm stretching and
    I'm growing
And I'll reap what I've been
    sowing or my skin's not
    black.

I've prayed and slaved and waited
    and I've sung my song.
You've bled me and you've starved
    me but I've still grown
    strong.
  You've lashed me and you've
    treed me
  And you've everything but
    freed me
But in time you'll know you need
    me and it won't be long.

I've seen the daylight breaking
    high above the bough.
I've found my destination and I've
    made my vow;
  So whether you abhor me
  Or deride me or ignore me,
Mighty mountains loom before me
    and I won't stop now. ❖

Plea to Those Who Matter

by James Welch

You don't know I pretend my
    dumb.
My songs often wise, my bells
    could chase
the snow across these whistle-
    black plains.
Celebrate. The days are grim. Call
    your winds
to blast these bundled streets and
    patronize
my past of poverty and 4-day
    feasts.

Don't ignore me. I'll build my face
    a different way,
a way to make you know that I am
    no longer
proud, my name not strong
    enough to stand alone.
If I lie and say you took me for a
    friend,
patched together in my thin bones,
will you help me be cunning and
    noisy as the wind?

I have plans to burn my drum,
    move out
and civilize this hair. See my nose?
    I smash it
straight for you. These teeth? I
    scrub my teeth
away with stones. I know you help
    me now I matter.
And I—I come to you, head down,
    bleeding from my smile,
happy for the snow clean hands of
    you, my friends. ❖

THINKING AND WRITING ABOUT LITERATURE

1. Why do you think "The Times They Are A-Changin'" became
    an anthem for the youth movement of the 1960s?
2. What image does Lawrence Ferlinghetti paint of life in the 1950s?
3. To whom are the speakers in Naomi Long Madgett's and James
    Welch's poems addressing their message? How are the speakers'
    attitudes similar? How are they different?

PRIMARY SOURCES

Description of Change:
excerpted and footnoted
Rationale: excerpted for
space considerations; footnoted to clarify meaning

THINKING AND WRITING ABOUT LITERATURE

1. *because it celebrates the
new ideas and beneficial
changes that young people
can bring about*
2. *in a state of waiting for an
atomic disaster and subsequent rebirth to occur*
3. *White Americans; both
express an awareness of
past injustices and a determination to overcome
them; Madgett describes
the determination of an
African American who will
not let her spirit be broken;
Welch describes an
American Indian who feels
that he must transform
himself and deny his own
heritage in order to become
accepted by society.*

CONDUCTING AN INTERVIEW

Guide students through the discussion of how to conduct an interview and then have them complete the Practicing the Strategy exercise. Point out that oral histories are often invaluable sources of material for historians researching the daily lives of people of a particular era. Have students imagine that they are historians in the year 2030. Have them prepare a short list of questions that would give them information about the daily lives of American students in the 1990s. Then have students use these questions to interview another student. Ask students to write a short report summarizing the results of the interview.

PRACTICING THE STRATEGY

Students' lists will vary but might include such questions as the following: How old were you when the Vietnam War began? When and why did you begin to oppose the war? Can you describe a peace demonstration or march in which you participated? Do you know anyone who served in the armed forces in Vietnam? Since the war, have your views of it changed?

Strategies for Success

CONDUCTING AN INTERVIEW

Historians often conduct interviews with people who witnessed or participated in historical events. Such interviews are called oral histories and are considered primary sources.

One of the largest oral history collections was compiled in the 1930s by the Federal Writers' Project of the WPA. Project members interviewed former slaves to gather their recollections of life in the South under slavery and during Reconstruction. The accounts were first published in 1944 in *Lay My Burden Down*. Historian Charles A. Beard described the accounts as "literature more powerful than anything I have read in fiction."

Effective interviewing involves more than just talking to people. To get the most from an interview, conduct it carefully and accompany it with prior research as well as follow-up analysis.

How to Conduct an Interview

1. **Identify and research the topic.** Gather information on your topic as the basis for questions.
2. **Set up an interview.** Contact the interviewee; identify yourself, state clearly the purpose of the interview, and schedule a convenient time and place to conduct it. Ask whether you may tape-record the interview.
3. **Prepare questions.** Formulate questions to get at the information you need. Plan the interview so that questions logically follow one another.
4. **Conduct the interview.** Be an active listener. Allow responses that go beyond your specific questions, but keep the interview on the topic.
5. **Analyze the interview.** Review and summarize the interview's content, noting what was said with emphasis. Identify statements that are representative of the person's overall views.

Applying the Strategy

Read the following excerpt from Studs Terkel's oral history *Working*. The speaker is Nora Watson, a staff writer for a publisher of health-care literature. Then decide what questions Terkel might have asked to obtain such responses.

> 66 Jobs are not big enough for people. It's not just the assembly line worker whose job is too small for his spirit, you know? . . .
>
> I had expected to put the energy and enthusiasm and the gifts that I may have to work—it isn't happening. They expect less than you can offer. Token labor. . . . I know I'm vegetating and being paid to do exactly that. . . . But then you walk out with no sense of satisfaction. . . . I'm being had. Somebody has bought the right to you for eight hours a day. . . . You know what I mean? 99

Terkel probably began his interview with a question like "How do you spend your workday?" He then may have inquired about how demanding and rewarding the job is. Given Nora Watson's dissatisfaction, his follow-up questions probably encouraged her to reflect further on feeling "underemployed."

Practicing the Strategy

Several oral histories have been written based on interviews with ground and air troops, nurses, support personnel, reporters, and other people who were in Vietnam. But the war can be remembered from many points of view. Prepare a list of questions to use in conducting interviews with people who participated in the antiwar movement. Use chapters 29 and 30 as background for the period.

▼ Studs Terkel

BUILDING YOUR PORTFOLIO

Each portfolio project described below is the culmination of the Building Your Portfolio activities in the chapter reviews of Unit 8. First, decide whether you wish students to work individually or in groups on these unit projects. Then permit each student to choose the project on which he or she desires to work. Provide students with copies of **Building Your Portfolio Worksheet 8** from *Core Resources*. This worksheet will guide students step by step to complete their projects.

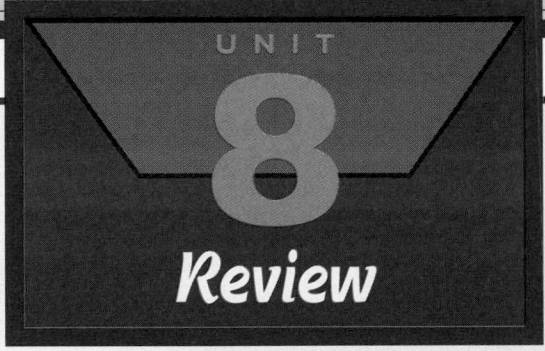

UNIT

8

Review

BUILDING YOUR PORTFOLIO

Outlined below are four projects. Independently or cooperatively, complete one and use the products to demonstrate your mastery of the historical concepts involved.

1 **THE COLD WAR**
In 1945, representatives of 50 world nations created the United Nations. Using the portfolio materials you designed in chapters 27, 28, and 30, write a report to President Nixon in 1973 recommending or condemning continued U.S. membership in the United Nations. Your report should explain why the United States originally joined the United Nations and evaluate the decision in light of world events between 1945 and 1973.

2 **CIVIL RIGHTS**
To many Americans, the greatest strides in civil rights came in the 30 years after World War II. African Americans, Hispanic Americans, Americans with disabilities, women, and other groups made progress in securing rights long guaranteed others. Using the portfolio materials you designed in chapters 27, 28, 29, and 30, rehearse and then present your 15-minute news program to the class, making sure the program accomplishes the goals you set and follows your plan of production.

3 **THE GOVERN-MENT AND THE ECONOMY**
In the postwar era, the United States government became increasingly involved in managing and influencing the American economy. Using the portfolio materials you designed in chapters 27 and 29, create a visual display of the different areas of the economy in which the government plays a role. Make sure your display shows how each type of government involvement affects the lives of average citizens.

4 **POPULAR CULTURE**
In the 1950s and 1960s, advances in science and technology, population growth and shifts, and a rising standard of living helped transform the daily lives of Americans. Using the materials you designed in chapters 28 and 29, present to the class a slide show documenting the changes in everyday life from the 1950s to the 1960s.

Videodisc Review

In assigned groups, develop an outline for a video collage of postwar America. Choose images that best illustrate the major topics of the period. Write a script to accompany the images. Assign narrators to different parts of the script, and present your video collage to the class.

Further Reading

Chafe, William H. *Civilities and Civil Rights.* Oxford (1981). Overview of the formative years of the civil rights movement.

Hampton, Henry, and Steve Fayer. *Voices of Freedom.* Bantam (1990). Oral history of the civil rights movement.

Knox, Donald. *The Korean War: Uncertain Victory.* Harcourt (1988). Oral history of war.

O'Neil, Doris C., ed. *Life—The '60s.* Bullfinch Press (1989). An overview of the 1960s from a social history perspective.

Thompson, Robert Smith. *The Missiles of October.* Simon & Schuster (1992). The story of the Cuban missile crisis.

Young, Marilyn B. *The Vietnam Wars, 1945–1990.* HarperCollins (1991). History of the Vietnam War and its aftermath.

PORTFOLIO ASSESSMENT

1. Reports should describe the postwar problems that led to the creation of the UN, the UN's role during the 1950s, and the structure of the UN.

2. News programs should show, for each of the following, the influence on the struggle for civil rights: the postwar Committee on Civil Rights, the Brown v. Board of Education *ruling and Montgomery bus boycott of the 1950s, Freedom Rides and other movements of the 1960s, and the Vietnam War.*

3. Visual displays should show the postwar employment and veteran assistance programs, including the GI Bill; and Johnson's Great Society programs of the 1960s, including Medicare and education and housing programs.

4. Slide shows should present the development of rock 'n' roll, the Beat poets and rebelliousness in the 1950s, and the counterculture and British invasion of the 1960s.

Modern Times ❖ 1970–the Present

UNIT OVERVIEW

President Nixon took action to improve relations with China and the Soviet Union, but the Watergate scandal forced his resignation. His successors, Ford and Carter, grappled with challenges confronting the nation, including a growing sense of discontent. Reagan rode this wave of dissatisfaction into office in 1981 with a conservative agenda. He cut government social programs, lowered taxes, and increased military spending. Bush continued Reagan's policies but failed to pull the U.S. out of its recession. He lost his reelection bid to Clinton in 1992. As Clinton took office, many nations looked to the U.S. for guidance in finding their place in a new world order that followed the collapse of the Soviet Union and the end of the Cold War.

CORE RESOURCES

- **American Almanac Poster** and **Worksheet 9**
- **Building Your Portfolio Worksheet 9**
  You may wish to preview the Unit 9 Review and Building Your Portfolio performance assessment activities on p. 985.

Using the American Almanac Posters

Begin the unit by displaying the American Almanac Poster and discussing entries with students. In addition to the worksheet, the annotations that follow provide additional information about the entries and suggest questions and activities.

Then, as students study the unit, have them work in small groups to create their own almanacs—using the same six headings—on pieces of butcher paper. At the end of the unit, call on groups to display and discuss their almanacs.

Chapter 31
FROM NIXON TO CARTER 1970–1980

Chapter 32
REAGAN, BUSH, AND CLINTON 1980–Present

The American People

Mention that between 1980 and 1990, the Asian American population more than doubled, while the number of Hispanic Americans increased by 53 percent.

▪▪ Direct students to research the fastest-growing ethnic groups in the U.S. today.

The Environment

Earth Day became a worldwide celebration, with an estimated 200 million people in 140 countries participating in 1990. The major purpose of Earth Day was to heighten awareness of environmental issues.

▪▪ Ask students who have been involved with environmental issues to share their experiences.

A Healthy Body

A 1990 survey found that only 32 percent of Americans aged 18 to 25 smoked cigarettes—down from 50 percent in 1976.

▪▪ Ask students if they have changed their eating habits as a result of recent research.

Up in the Sky

Dr. Mae Jemison became the first African American woman astronaut when she took part in a space-shuttle mission in September 1992.

▪▪ Ask students what qualities they think an astronaut should have.

Wide World of Sports

Point out that Aaron ended his career with 755 home runs, a record that many experts believe is unassailable.

▪▪ Ask students whether individual records have any importance in team sports.

Changing Times

Note that a 1990 Census Bureau survey showed that men and women were marrying at a later age than at any other time in the 20th century—about age 26 for men and nearly 24 for women.

▪▪ Ask students what they think are the advantages of waiting until they are older to marry.

At Your Leisure

A recent survey showed that 62 percent of U.S. households owned a videocassette recorder and a similar percentage of households subscribed to cable television.

▪▪ Have students prepare a one-month chart that shows how much time they spend watching movies, videos, and TV.

UNIT 9

Modern Times

1970–the Present

President Nixon's foreign policy successes brought improved relations with the Soviet Union and China, but the Watergate scandal forced him to resign. A growing sense of discontent characterized the administrations of Nixon's successors, Ford and Carter. Reagan and his conservative agenda rode this wave of dissatisfaction into office in 1981. Although Bush continued Reagan's policies, the economy faltered, and Bush lost his reelection bid to Clinton in 1992. As Clinton took office, many nations looked to the United States for guidance in finding their place in the new era that emerged following the collapse of the Soviet Union.

◀ President Reagan and Soviet leader Gorbachev, Moscow, 1988

Chapter 33

AMERICA IN TODAY'S WORLD
1970–Present

FROM NIXON TO CARTER

1970–1980

Chapter Overview

The 1970s began with great political and social change as President Nixon attempted to deal with pressing domestic problems while improving relations with China and developing a policy of détente with the Soviet Union. But the Watergate scandal forced Nixon to resign. His successor, Gerald Ford, grappled unsuccessfully with many of the domestic issues. In 1976 the nation turned to Jimmy Carter to restore its faith in government. But persistent inflation and Middle East turmoil eroded the public's confidence in Carter. The 1970s was a decade of gains for women, ethnic groups, and Americans with disabilities.

THE AMERICAN NATION VIDEODISC PROGRAM A variety of still images, short videos, and activities are available for you to use as you teach this chapter. See Correlation to *The American Nation* Videodisc Program for barcode correlations and suggestions for using the program.

Chapter Planning Guide

CHAPTER 31	CORE RESOURCE BOOKLETS	AUDIOVISUAL AV RESOURCES	PROGRAM RESOURCES
INTRODUCTION pp. 898–899	■ Building Your Portfolio Worksheet 9	■ Everyday Life in America Transparency and Worksheet 31	
TEACHING THE CHAPTER pp. 900–923	■ Graphic Organizer 31 ■ Social Studies Skills Worksheet 31 ■ Literature Worksheet 31 ■ Geography Worksheet 31 ■ Outline Maps 1, 2, 9, 17, 18, 19, 21	■ *The American Nation* Videodisc: The First Landing on the Moon; Nixon in China; The Constitution in Crisis; Richard Nixon Resigns; Ford Pardons Nixon; César Chávez; The Women's Rights Movement ■ Linking Geography and History Transparencies and Worksheets 12B, 13B ■ *American Civics Citizenship Skills* Videocassette or Videodisc	■ Art in American History Transparencies and Worksheets 40, 41, 42, 43 ■ *Eyewitnesses and Others*, Volume 2: Readings 72, 73, 76, 77
REVIEW AND ASSESSMENT pp. 924–925	■ Chapter 31 Daily Quizzes ■ Review Worksheet 31 ■ Chapter 31 Tests ■ Alternative Assessment Forms		■ Test Generator

Additional Resources

BOOKS FOR TEACHERS

Ambrose, Stephen E. *Nixon: Ruin and Recovery, 1973–1990.* Simon & Schuster, 1992. Includes Nixon's private writings and conversations.

Barone, Michael. *Our Country: The Shaping of America from Roosevelt to Reagan.* Free Press, 1990. Chronicles political and social events.

BOOKS FOR STUDENTS

* Feinberg, Barbara S. *Watergate: Scandal in the White House.* Watts, 1990. Part of the Twentieth-Century American History series.

Woodward, Bob, and Carl Bernstein. *All the President's Men.* Simon and Schuster, 1987. Watergate history by Pulitzer Prize–winning journalists who uncovered the scandal.

MULTIMEDIA MATERIALS

Modern U.S. History, Unit 3: 1969–1981. Video, 46 min. Guidance Associates/SSSS. Focuses on important events of Nixon, Ford, and Carter presidencies.

Watergate: The Secret Story. Video, 94 min. CBS/SSSS. Overview of the Watergate break-in and its aftermath.

* for students reading below grade level

THEMES IN AMERICAN HISTORY

USE WITH PAGES 898–899

Listed on the right are the themes emphasized in Chapter 31. The questions in boldface type stimulate critical thinking and provide students with an opportunity to discuss the themes within a broadened context. The questions also appear in the pupil's edition on p. 898.

■ ECONOMIC DEVELOPMENT

How might a nation's choice of energy sources affect its economy? Students might suggest that if a nation relies too heavily on one source of energy, and the supply decreases or cost rises dramatically, the economy could be adversely affected. Students might suggest economic consequences such as higher prices for items manufactured through the use of that energy source or reduced consumption of the source itself, resulting in unemployment in industries related to the source.

■ GLOBAL RELATIONS

How might opening relations with one nation help improve relations with another nation? Students might suggest that if one nation opens relations with another country, that act could also lead to better ties with the other country's allies. In addition, the other country's enemies might seek improved relations with the first nation, so that their enemy will not have better relations with the first nation than they do.

■ CONSTITUTIONAL HERITAGE

Why is it dangerous for one branch of government to withhold information from another branch of government? Students might suggest that by withholding information, one branch could make it more difficult for another branch to carry out its responsibilities under the Constitution. They might note that withholding information therefore could upset the balance of powers as outlined in the Constitution.

CHAPTER STRATEGIES FOR MEETING INDIVIDUAL NEEDS

LIMITED ENGLISH PROFICIENT LEARNERS

Place students into one of three groups and assign each group to represent presidents Nixon, Ford, or Carter. Have students in each group create at least two journal entries that might have been written by their assigned person during his presidency.

TACTILE/KINESTHETIC LEARNERS

Have students create a classroom display or bulletin-board collage that illustrates the diversity in the U.S. population. Then have students give brief talks describing the struggles and achievements of diverse groups during the 1970s.

LEARNERS HAVING DIFFICULTY

Organize students into four groups. Assign each group one section of the chapter. Have each group develop questions and answers about the main ideas in their section. Then have each group quiz the other groups with its questions.

AUDITORY LEARNERS

Have students choose a quote from the chapter text, read the quote aloud, and then paraphrase the quote, explaining its relationship to the chapter content.

VISUAL LEARNERS

Have students study the illustrations and accompanying captions in the chapter. Then have students write a paragraph describing what they believe to be the three most important events that helped shape society in the 1970s.

GIFTED LEARNERS

Have students use magazine and newspaper headlines, stories, and editorial cartoons to create a pictorial museum of the Nixon, Ford, and Carter presidencies. Then have students act as museum tour guides and give oral presentations of the accomplishments and failures of each president.

USING THE CHAPTER FOCUS

■ UNDERSTANDING THE MAIN IDEA

Call on a volunteer to read aloud the Understanding the Main Idea paragraph. Ask students what factors cause people to lose confidence in a president. List students' responses on a flip chart. After students have read the chapter, have them note which factors caused people to lose confidence in the three presidents who held office during the 1970s.

 THEMES
Have students work individually or in small groups to answer the questions under Themes. Save students' responses so that they can compare them with their responses after studying the chapter. (See p. 897B for suggested answers.)

■ THE TIME LINE

Ask students to write the time-line entries in their notebooks. Have students take notes about each event as they read about it in the chapter. Then have students use the time-line entries as headlines and write articles to accompany their headlines that might appear in a newsmagazine. Students might also suggest illustrations to include with their articles.

CORE RESOURCES

• **Graphic Organizer 31**
• **Outline Maps 1, 2, 9, 17, 18, 19, 21**
• **Building your Portfolio Worksheet 9**

AV RESOURCES

• **Everyday Life in America Transparency and Worksheet 31**

ABOUT THE ILLUSTRATION

In 1976, celebrations of the Bicentennial—the 200th anniversary of the Declaration of Independence on July 4, 1776—were carried on throughout the country. Many events became major historical projects that lasted throughout the year. Ask students if they or any older family members have any mementos from the Bicentennial (these may even include Bicentennial quarters). Have volunteers bring in mementos to share with the class. Ask students how they think the Bicentennial might have affected American morale in the mid-1970s.

Chapter 31

1970–1980

FROM NIXON TO CARTER

 **FOCUS**

UNDERSTANDING THE MAIN IDEA

Vice President Gerald Ford became president when the Watergate scandal forced Richard Nixon to resign in 1974. Ford lost the 1976 presidential election, however, to Democrat Jimmy Carter. The legacy of the civil rights movement continued through activism by numerous groups that had faced discrimination. Affirmative action programs and busing, however, brought about a white backlash.

 THEMES

■ **ECONOMIC DEVELOP-MENT** How might a nation's choice of energy sources affect its economy?

■ **GLOBAL RELATIONS** How might opening relations with one nation help improve relations with another nation?

■ **CONSTITUTIONAL HER-ITAGE** Why is it dangerous for one branch of government to withhold information from another branch of government?

1970	1974	1976	1979
First Earth Day celebration held.	Nixon resigns presidency.	Jimmy Carter elected president.	Iran hostage crisis begins.

:: LINK TO THE PAST *Throughout the 1960s the United States increased its involvement in the Vietnam War. As the war escalated, so did criticism of the conflict. A weary and unpopular Lyndon Johnson decided not to run for reelection in 1968. Republican Richard Nixon won the election, promising to end the war in Vietnam and to restore "law and order" to society.*

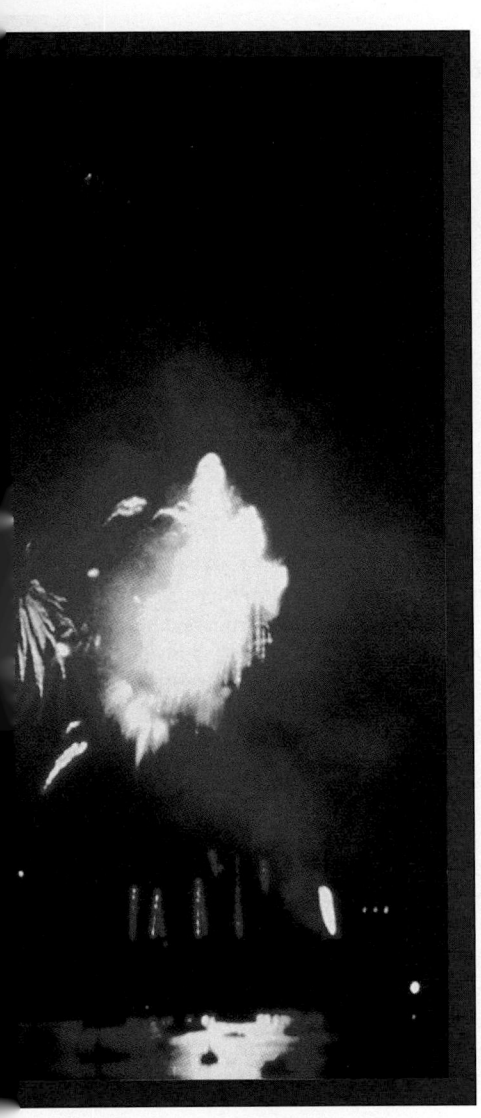

Scene from 1976 bicentennial celebration

"*G*ood evening. This is the thirty-seventh time I have spoken to you from this office." President Richard Nixon's voice cracked with emotion as he addressed the American people on August 8, 1974. Less than two years earlier, he had won reelection in a landslide victory. Now he was announcing his resignation. Facing impeachment for his role in the Watergate affair, the most serious scandal ever to hit the White House, Richard Nixon became the first U.S. president to resign.

Vice President Gerald Ford served out the remainder of Nixon's term. In 1976 the nation elected a Democratic president, Jimmy Carter—a Washington outsider whose promise of honesty in government appealed to many Americans. Carter's popularity soon plummeted, however, and he was voted out of office after one term.

Amid these political twists and turns, American society changed rapidly as many people moved to the Southwest and new waves of immigrants arrived from Latin America and Asia. In addition, the African American civil rights movement continued to influence other groups seeking equal rights—particularly women, Hispanic Americans, people with disabilities, and American Indians.

Gas station sign, 1973

FOCUS OBJECTIVES

- Examine how President Nixon tried to reverse the liberal trends of the Kennedy-Johnson years.

- Describe what caused the energy crisis of the early 1970s.

- List the factors that contributed to the growth of the environmental movement.

- Identify President Nixon's main foreign-policy goal.

THE AMERICAN NATION VIDEODISC PROGRAM

The First Landing on the Moon

2B   51971   :29

900

PREVIEW WORKSHOP

Following is a list of the significant people, places, and terms in this section. You may wish to use this list as a section preview.

People
- Warren Burger
- Leonid Brezhnev
- Salvador Allende
- Golda Meir

Places
- Israel
- Egypt
- Jordan
- Syria

Terms
- silent majority
- Family Assistance Plan
- southern strategy
- stagflation
- Organization of Petroleum Exporting Countries
- Environmental Protection Agency
- Occupational Safety and Health Administration
- Clean Air Act
- Water Quality Improvement Act
- realpolitik
- Strategic Arms Limitation Talks
- détente

Section 1

THE NIXON YEARS

FOCUS

- **How did President Nixon try to reverse the liberal trends of the Kennedy-Johnson years?**
- **What caused the energy crisis of the early 1970s?**
- **What factors contributed to the growth of the environmental movement?**
- **What was President Nixon's main foreign-policy goal?**

President Nixon tried to steer the nation away from the liberalism of the Kennedy-Johnson years. His conservative agenda, however, was undermined by a Democratic Congress and by serious domestic problems, including a stagnant economy. In foreign affairs, though, the president had greater success. Nixon chalked up his most important achievement by easing tensions with the Communist world.

Chinese leader Mao Zedong and President Richard Nixon

COURTING THE SILENT MAJORITY

On July 20, 1969, Americans cheered as *Apollo 11* astronauts Neil Armstrong and Edwin "Buzz" Aldrin landed their lunar module on the moon. Stepping onto the moon's surface, Armstrong declared, "That's one small step for man, one giant leap for mankind." President Nixon and many other Americans hoped that the leap signaled a shift away from the troubles of the 1960s.

Much of Nixon's support came from middle-class voters weary from the social upheaval of the 1960s. Nixon called these people the **silent majority**—"the forgotten Americans, the non-shouters, the non-demonstrators." He won their votes by pledging to restore law and order and to cut back Democratic programs. Many critics of Johnson's Great Society policies charged that the programs had failed to significantly decrease poverty in America. Instead, critics insisted, these policies had created a complex, inefficient bureaucracy that made people dependent upon the federal government. The welfare system came under particular attack, as the number of welfare recipients climbed from some 3.1 million in 1960 to some 9.7 million in 1970.

◄ Astronauts Neil Armstrong and Edwin "Buzz" Aldrin made the first lunar landing in 1969. By 1973, five additional Apollo flights had explored the surface of the moon.

Call on volunteers to name some of the social reforms of the Johnson years. *(Students might cite voting and civil rights legislation; and health, housing, education, and antipoverty programs.)* Tell students that in this section they will learn how Nixon attempted to reverse the social trends of the 1960s while setting precedents in foreign affairs.

Teaching the Section

NIXON REVERSES TRENDS

Organize students into "White House domestic policy advisory groups" on poverty, civil rights, law and order, and the economy. Assign one group to analyze each of these areas. Tell the groups to summarize developments in their policy area during the 1960s and to suggest actions that the new president might take to reverse the liberal trends of the Kennedy-Johnson years. Ask representatives from each advisory group to "present" its findings and recommendations to President Nixon. Then call on group members or other students to explain how or why each of Nixon's actions in these areas was intended to achieve his desired result.

▶

Under the existing welfare system, most families received the bulk of aid in the form of services, such as Medicaid. Nixon proposed replacing this system with the **Family Assistance Plan** (FAP), which would guarantee families a minimum income. Supporters of FAP argued that giving money directly to families would cut down on government service programs and the bureaucracy that went with them. Critics, however, charged that such direct aid would only make poor families even more dependent on the federal government. After a heated battle, the Senate rejected the FAP.

In addition to trying to reform the federal bureaucracy, Nixon promised not to ask for any new civil rights legislation. This move was part of the Republicans' **southern strategy**—a plan to win conservative southern white voters away from the Democratic party. As part of this plan, Nixon also delayed pressuring southern schools to desegregate. When the Supreme Court ruled in a 1971 case that busing could be used to integrate schools, Nixon denounced the decision.

The southern strategy also influenced the president's choice of justices for the Supreme Court. Nixon claimed that the liberal rulings of the Warren Court had encouraged lawlessness in America. Such lawlessness, he argued, was demonstrated by a series of prison riots in the late 1960s and the early 1970s. Among the most serious of these was the 1971 rebellion at New York's Attica prison, which resulted in the death of 40 prisoners and guards. When Chief Justice Warren retired in 1969, Nixon appointed a conservative justice, Warren Burger, to head the Court. Two other Nixon nominees to the Court were rejected by the Senate, but the president eventually appointed three more conservative justices: Harry Blackmun, Lewis Powell, and William Rehnquist.

▪▪ **Nixon tried to reverse liberal trends by cutting back on civil rights legislation and appointing conservative justices to the Supreme Court.**

TACKLING THE ECONOMY

Reversing the liberal policies of the 1960s was not Nixon's only objective. He also had to tackle a faltering economy. Although the United States had enjoyed an economic boom during the 1960s, by the time Nixon took office the economy was in trouble. High levels of government spending on social programs and on the Vietnam War had led to a recession and growing unemployment. Normally in times of high unemployment, inflation goes down. Yet in the 1970s, inflation and unemployment

PRESIDENTIAL LIVES

RICHARD M. NIXON
1913–1994

in office
1969–1974

Richard Milhous Nixon rose to the top ranks of the Republican party through hard work and intense ambition. Growing up in a poor family in California made Nixon determined to be a success and never to give up.

One of the more famous examples of Richard Nixon's ability to bounce back from political challenges came during the 1952 presidential election. Nixon, who was Dwight Eisenhower's vice presidential running mate, had been accused of accepting personal gifts from wealthy businessmen. He went on national television to deny the charges. In what came to be called the "Checkers speech," Nixon admitted to accepting one personal gift. "You know what it was?" the candidate asked. "It was a little cocker spaniel dog . . . black, white, and spotted, and our little girl Tricia, the six-year-old, named it Checkers. . . . And I just want to say this, right now, that regardless of what they say about it, we're going to keep it." The Checkers speech won wide public support and saved Nixon from being dropped from the Republican ticket.

Richard Nixon

Teaching the Section

THE ENERGY CRISIS

Begin a flowchart on the chalkboard headed *Events Leading to the 1973–74 Energy Crisis.* Call on students to cite events that contributed to the energy crisis and list their responses on the flowchart. Call on volunteers to interpret the cause-and-effect relationships in the chart.

▪▪ Ask students to speculate about how their lives might be affected if the nation suffered a similar energy crisis today.

GLOBAL CONNECTIONS

In response to the Arab oil squeeze, nations around the world undertook energy-saving measures. The Netherlands restricted motorists to two and a half gallons of gas per week. Norway banned Sunday driving. Britain cut street lighting in half, restricted heating and lighting in commercial buildings, and banned small planes from flying on Sunday. France lowered speed limits on highways and imposed an 11 P.M. signoff for weeknight TV. Greece limited Sunday driving to alternate Sundays.

Graph Caption Answer
1979–1981; 2.5 billion

PRIMARY SOURCE

Description of Change: excerpted
Rationale: excerpted to focus on main idea

HISTORICAL SIDELIGHTS

U.S. Gas Hikes
Gasoline shortages led to long lines at gas stations. Accustomed to paying about 30 cents for a gallon of gas, Americans suddenly faced gas prices near a dollar per gallon.

---

both rose. This phenomenon is called **stagflation.**

In August 1971 Nixon took a drastic step to curb inflation by imposing wage and price controls—temporary freezes on wages, prices, and rents. Many people were surprised by the action, since Nixon had long opposed the use of such controls. Labor leaders feared that wage freezes would hurt those earning the lowest wages. AFL–CIO president George Meany called it "Robin Hood in reverse, because it robs from the poor and gives to the rich."

Nixon, however, was bowing to political reality. Only by taking bold action on the economy could he hope to win the upcoming presidential election. The strategy worked. Inflation slowed, and Nixon was reelected in 1972. When he eased controls the following year, though, inflation shot up again. By August 1974 the annual inflation rate had reached 12 percent. A homemaker from Chicago reflected public sentiments about the economy:

  66 You always used to think in this country that there would be bad times followed by good times. Now, maybe it's bad times followed by hard times followed by harder times. **99**

THE ENERGY CRISIS

The surging cost of oil was a major cause of inflation during the 1970s. Since World War II the U.S. economy had become increasingly dependent on foreign oil. By the early 1970s the United States was importing one third of its oil needs.

To get higher prices for their oil, several oil-exporting nations, mainly Arab countries, had formed the **Organization of Petroleum Exporting Countries** (OPEC) in 1960. In the fall of 1973, amid a new Arab-Israeli war, OPEC quadrupled oil prices. Many Arab countries cut off oil shipments to the United States as retaliation for

---

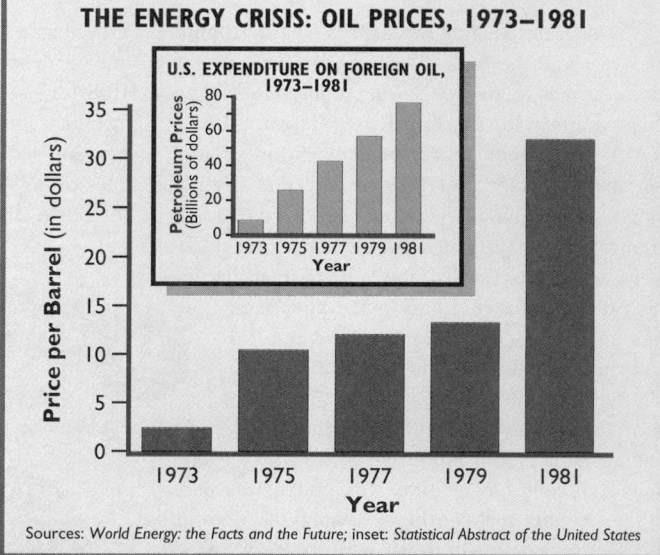

THE ENERGY CRISIS: OIL PRICES, 1973–1981

U.S. EXPENDITURE ON FOREIGN OIL, 1973–1981

Sources: *World Energy: the Facts and the Future*; inset: *Statistical Abstract of the United States*

OPEC'S OIL Throughout the 1970s the U.S. government struggled to ease the problems caused by skyrocketing oil prices. These efforts were largely unsuccessful because American dependence on foreign oil continually increased.

? **BUILDING GRAPH SKILLS** Between which two-year period did the United States experience its biggest increase in oil prices? Approximately how many barrels of foreign oil were purchased in 1975?

U.S. support of Israel. Although the Arabs lifted their embargo after a few months, the price of oil remained high. Some Americans charged that oil companies were keeping prices artificially high to boost their profits.

The oil embargo and the price hikes caused an energy crisis in the United States during the winter of 1973–74. As the cost of gasoline, heating oil, and electricity soared, some parts of the country experienced severe hardship. One Detroit hospital told its patients to stay in bed to keep warm. "We had so little oil left that we just had to cut back the thermostats," noted one hospital official. "In storage rooms and areas with no patients, it got as low as 40 degrees."

Responding to the crisis, President Nixon announced a program to make the United States less dependent on foreign oil. He called for energy conservation and signed a bill authorizing construction of a pipeline to bring oil south from Alaska. Nevertheless, America's dependence on oil imports grew throughout the 1970s.

▪▪ **The Arab oil embargo and price hikes of 1973 helped provoke an energy crisis in the United States.**

Call on students to identify the major environmental issues of the 1970s. *(air pollution, water pollution, nuclear power)* Direct each student to create an editorial cartoon that might have appeared in a newspaper of the time, expressing concern about one of these issues. Give students an opportunity to review one another's cartoons. Then use the cartoons to spark a class discussion about the relationship between public awareness and the growth of the environmental movement in the 1970s. Conclude by asking students to assess the impact of education and awareness on the environmental movement today. Students may wish to include their editorial cartoons in their portfolios.

NIXON'S FOREIGN POLICY

Write *realpolitik* and *détente* on the chalkboard. Ask volunteers to define them and to describe the role they played in Nixon's foreign policy. Have the class assess the degree to which each approach was a departure from the foreign policies of other Cold War presidents. Then ask students to explain how Nixon's efforts to improve relations with China and the Soviet Union were part of his main foreign-policy goal and how they reflected a realpolitik strategy. ▶

*C*LEANING UP THE ENVIRONMENT

When Nixon took office, few Americans seemed worried about the environment. Two events soon helped increase concern, however. The first was a massive oil spill off the coast of Santa Barbara, California, in 1969. The second was the first Earth Day celebration in April 1970. Across the country huge crowds took part in "teach-ins" and other activities designed to raise awareness of environmental problems. At an Earth Day event in New York City's Central Park, Episcopal bishop Paul Moore told a group of schoolchildren: "Unless we stop stealing, exploiting, and ruining nature for our own gain, we will lose everything."

In 1970 Congress responded to growing public concern over the environment by approving the creation of the **Environmental Protection Agency** (EPA), a federal agency with power to enforce environmental laws. Congress also approved the creation of the **Occupational Safety and Health Administration** (OSHA) to enforce laws protecting workers from dangerous or unhealthy working conditions. That same year, Congress passed two laws to limit pollution. The **Clean Air Act** set air-quality standards and tough emissions guidelines for car manufacturers. The **Water Quality Improvement Act** made oil companies pay some of the cleanup costs of oil spills and set limits on the discharge of industrial pollutants into water.

■■ **Public concern over air and water quality, coupled with events like Earth Day, fueled the growth of the environmental movement in the 1970s.**

The government also increased support for the use of nuclear energy to replace oil and coal sources. As a relatively clean source of energy that did not eat up limited natural resources, nuclear power seemed to many energy experts to be "the only practicable energy source in sight adequate to sustain our way of life and to promote our economy." By January 1974, 42 nuclear power plants were in operation and over 160 more were under construction or in the planning stages. Yet many critics worried that the risks of a nuclear accident outweighed the advantages of nuclear power.

◀ As concerns over the environment grew, U.S. cities began to stage Earth Day celebrations. Shown here is the 1970 Earth Day event in New York City's Central Park.

*F*OREIGN AFFAIRS UNDER NIXON

Although domestic issues demanded much of Nixon's attention, his main interest was foreign affairs. Working closely with his national security adviser, Henry Kissinger, Nixon sought to reshape U.S. foreign policy and leave his mark on world affairs.

The Nixon–Kissinger approach. Nixon and Kissinger shared a belief in **realpolitik** ("practical politics")—an approach to foreign policy that emphasized national interests over moral or ethical concerns. Applying realpolitik meant that national interests, rather than ideals such as democracy and human rights, should be the guiding force in American foreign policy. Therefore, governments allied with the United States should receive American support, even if they were not democratic.

The chief goal of the Nixon-Kissinger foreign policy was to establish a balance of power among the world's five major powers: the United States, the Soviet Union, Western Europe, Japan, and the People's Republic of China. As Nixon explained in 1972:

❝ The only time in the history of the world that we have had any extended period of peace is when there has been a balance of power. It is when one nation becomes infinitely more powerful in relation to its potential competitors that the danger of war arises. ❞

HISTORICAL SIDELIGHTS
Earth Day
The first Earth Day was the idea of Wisconsin senator Gaylord Nelson. Credited as the unofficial beginning of today's environmental movement, Earth Day has been held every year since its beginning in 1970 and has evolved into a worldwide event.

PRIMARY SOURCE
Description of Change: excerpted
Rationale: excerpted to focus on main idea

Practice

GUIDED PRACTICE

Ask students to make a headline from each of the section's main headings. List headlines on the chalkboard. Have the class select one headline and use it to create an outline for a news story that might appear with that headline.

INDEPENDENT PRACTICE

Direct students to choose one of the outlines developed in the Guided Practice and to use the information to write a news story. Students may wish to include their news stories in their portfolios.

Review and Assessment

REVIEW Have students work in small groups to create graphic organizers for each Essential Point in the section. Ask group members to present and explain their graphic organizers. Then assign the Section 1 Review on p. 905.

ASSESS Assign the **Section 1 Daily Quiz** in *Core Resources*.

THE AMERICAN NATION VIDEODISC PROGRAM
Nixon in China

```
2B    45667    :29
```

PRIMARY SOURCE

Description of Change: excerpted
Rationale: excerpted to focus on main idea

HISTORICAL SIDELIGHTS

The CIA and Chile

Following the overthrow of Allende, it was alleged that the CIA had spent $8 million supporting Chilean opposition newspapers, political parties, and right-wing extremist groups. In 1974 Kissinger testified before the Senate Foreign Relations Committee that the money was spent to keep political parties alive, not to overthrow the government. Congressional investigations in 1975 concluded that the CIA's actions were "striking but not unique."

Map Caption Answer
(for map on p. 905)
Iran hostage crisis, Soviet invasion of Afghanistan

■■ **Nixon's main foreign-policy goal was to achieve a balance of power that would help reduce international conflict.**

Relations with China and the Soviets.

As part of this strategy, President Nixon sought improved relations with the People's Republic of China. By the 1970s China and the Soviet Union—though both still Communist—had become bitter enemies. Nixon believed that improved ties with China would enhance American power in Asia and further divide the Communist world.

Nixon visited China in 1972 in an effort to ease more than 20 years of hostility. The two nations agreed to work together to promote peace in the Pacific region and to develop trade relations and cultural and scientific ties. Furthermore, Nixon promised eventual withdrawal of U.S. forces from Taiwan. This move helped decrease Chinese support for the North Vietnamese. Although many American conservatives were shocked by Nixon's trip, it gave the president leverage to promote a new policy with the Soviet Union.

In May 1972, three months after visiting China, Nixon flew to Moscow for talks with Soviet leader Leonid Brezhnev (BREZSH-nef). The two agreed to promote trade and to cooperate on other issues of mutual concern. At the time, Nixon declared, "There must be room in this world for two great nations with different systems to live together and work together."

Nixon and Brezhnev also signed a treaty limiting nuclear weapons. This treaty, the product of the **Strategic Arms Limitation Talks** (SALT), limited the number of intercontinental nuclear missiles—those capable of traveling long distances to other continents—each nation could have. Although the SALT treaty did not end the arms race, it was a small first step in reducing the nuclear threat. As a result of the peace talks, the United States and the Soviet Union entered into a period of **détente**—the lessening of military and diplomatic tensions between countries.

Trouble spots.

In general, Nixon and Kissinger paid little attention to countries that were not of direct strategic importance to the United States. One exception was the South American nation of Chile. In 1970 Chile elected a Socialist president, Salvador Allende (ah-YAYN-day). Fearing that Allende planned to turn Chile into "another Cuba"—a Communist ally to the Soviet Union—Nixon tried to topple the Allende government. He cut off aid to Chile and provided funds to Allende's opponents in the Chilean military. He also instructed the CIA to disrupt economic and political life in the country. In September 1973 the Chilean army killed Allende and set up a military dictatorship. To many observers, American actions in Chile represented a serious abuse of power.

Shortly after the Chilean coup, conflict erupted in the Middle East. Six years earlier, in 1967, Israel had crushed its Arab neighbors—Egypt, Jordan, and Syria—in the Six-Day War. Embittered by their defeat, the Arab states continued to harass Israel, and Israel continued to strike back. Israeli prime minister Golda Meir recalled the tension between her country and its Arab neighbors:

▲ Golda Meir

❝ For years we had been shouting "peace" and hearing the echo "war" come back from the other side. . . . The only time that Arab states were prepared to recognize the existence of . . . Israel was when they attacked it in order to wipe it out. ❞

This simmering conflict was fueled by Cold War competition, with the Soviets providing aid to their Arab allies while the United States gave most of its support to Israel. Then, in October 1973, Egypt and Syria invaded Israel, seeking to recover land lost in the 1967 war. The attack, which came during the Jewish holiday of Yom Kippur, caught the Israelis by surprise. They soon launched a counterattack, however, that threatened Egypt's capital, Cairo. Facing defeat, Egypt called on the Soviet Union for help.

When the Soviets threatened to send troops into the region, President Nixon put all U.S. forces on alert. A major military confrontation seemed possible. Within days, however, the superpowers persuaded the Arabs and the Israelis to accept a cease-fire. Détente had survived its first critical test, but prospects for a lasting peace in the Middle East remained in doubt.

RETEACH Have students work in groups and assign individuals or pairs the task of outlining subsections of the section. Have students exchange outlines and use them to ask questions of other members of their group.

Closure

On the chalkboard write: *As president, Richard Nixon achieved greater success in foreign affairs than he did with domestic issues.* Call on students to give arguments supporting or contesting the statement.

Extension

RESEARCH Have students research Nixon's trip to China in newsmagazines of the period and analyze the political significance of the trip.

INVESTIGATE Have students investigate the circumstances surrounding the CIA's disruption of Chile's economic and political life and write a paper explaining why many observers considered the disruption to be a serious abuse of power.

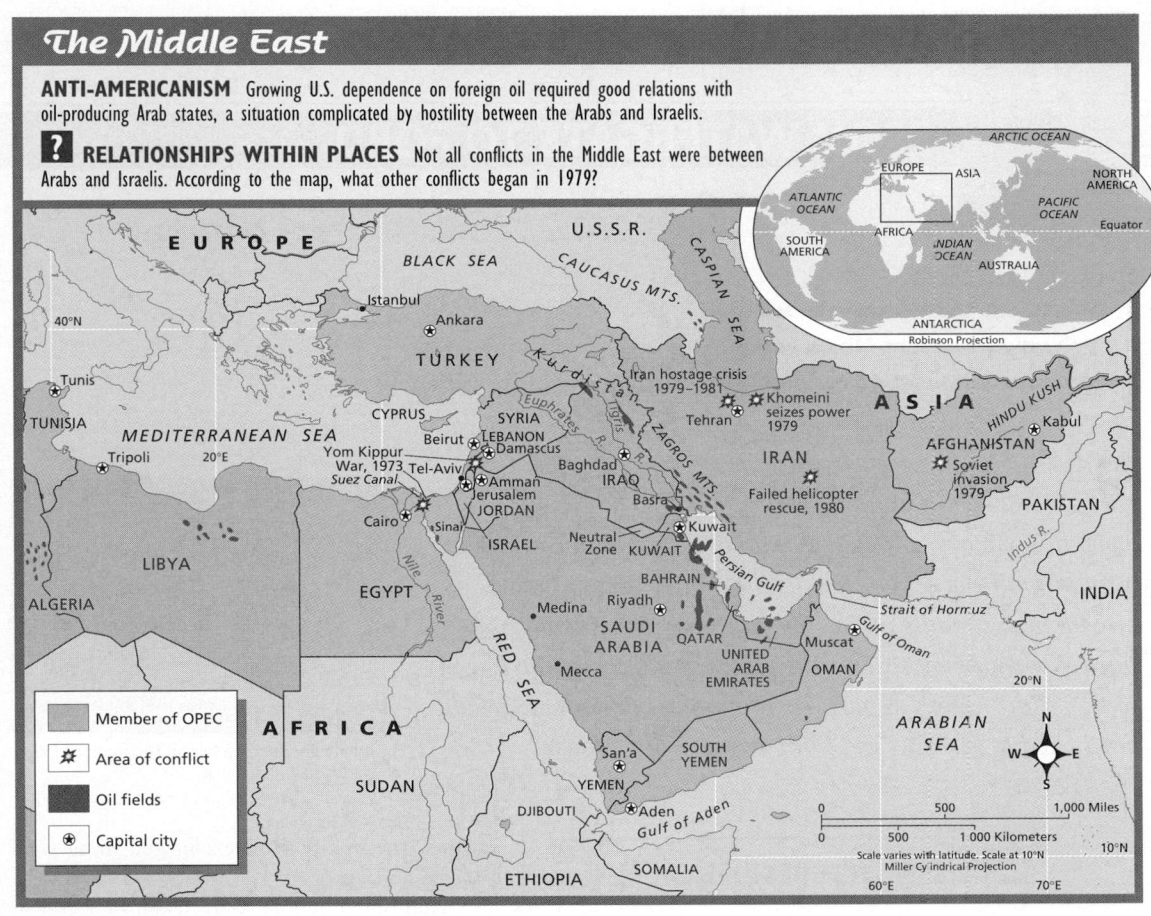

The Middle East

ANTI-AMERICANISM Growing U.S. dependence on foreign oil required good relations with oil-producing Arab states, a situation complicated by hostility between the Arabs and Israelis.

? RELATIONSHIPS WITHIN PLACES Not all conflicts in the Middle East were between Arabs and Israelis. According to the map, what other conflicts began in 1979?

Legend:
- Member of OPEC
- ✿ Area of conflict
- Oil fields
- ✶ Capital city

SECTION 1 REVIEW

IDENTIFY and explain the significance of the following: silent majority, Family Assistance Plan, southern strategy, Warren Burger, stagflation, Organization of Petroleum Exporting Countries, Environmental Protection Agency, Occupational Safety and Health Administration, Clean Air Act, Water Quality Improvement Act, realpolitik, Leonid Brezhnev, Strategic Arms Limitation Talks, détente, Salvador Allende, Golda Meir.

LOCATE and explain the importance of the following: Israel, Egypt, Jordan, Syria.

1. **MAIN IDEA** What steps did President Nixon take to reverse the liberal policies of the Kennedy and Johnson administrations?

2. **MAIN IDEA** What factors provoked an energy crisis in the United States in 1973?

3. **IDENTIFYING CAUSE AND EFFECT** What events fueled the growth of the environmental movement in the 1970s?

4. **WRITING TO EVALUATE** Imagine you are a member of the National Security Council. Write a memorandum that outlines President Nixon's main foreign-policy goal and evaluates how this goal was threatened by events in the Middle East.

5. **ANALYZING** What was unique about the economy during the early 1970s? How did Nixon propose to deal with this situation?

FOCUS OBJECTIVES

- Describe the Watergate scandal.

- Explain why President Nixon resigned.

- Identify the problems President Ford faced during his presidency.

HISTORICAL SIDELIGHTS

Enemies List

The White House "enemies list" contained some 200 names, including politicians, actors, university presidents, and other well-known figures. The White House conducted background investigations on these people in an attempt to find damaging material that could be leaked to newspapers. Senator Edward Kennedy and Speaker of the House Carl Albert were among those on the list.

PRIMARY SOURCE

Description of Change: excerpted
Rationale: excerpted to focus on main idea

CORE RESOURCES

- **Social Studies Skills Worksheet 31**
- **Section 2 Daily Quiz**

AV RESOURCES

- *The American Nation* Videodisc: **The Constitution in Crisis; Richard Nixon Resigns; Ford Pardons Nixon**

Section 2

FROM WATERGATE TO FORD

FOCUS
- **What was the Watergate scandal?**
- **Why did President Nixon resign?**
- **What problems did President Ford face during his presidency?**

*N*ixon's second term, which began with a sweeping reelection victory, ended less than two years later with his resignation from office. Just as the words Teapot Dome sum up the scandals of Warren Harding's presidency, the word Watergate represents the political abuses of the Nixon years. With Nixon's departure from office, President Gerald Ford tried to restore credibility to the White House.

Headline announcing Nixon resignation, 1974

CRISIS IN THE PRESIDENCY

Years after Richard Nixon left office, Henry Kissinger reflected on the presidency of his former boss:

  ❝ Nixon had three goals: to win by the biggest electoral landslide in history; to be remembered as a peacemaker; and to be accepted by the "Establishment" as an equal. He achieved all these objectives at the end of 1972 and the beginning of 1973. And he lost them all two months later—partly because he turned a dream into an obsession. ❞

This obsession began before Nixon won his landslide victory in the 1972 election. Nixon increasingly worked to extend and to maximize his power. He shifted much of the authority of the cabinet, whose appointment required Senate approval, to his personal White House staff. He also hid vital information from Congress and the public. When the news media criticized Nixon's

actions, the White House charged them with biased reporting.

Additional actions were taken in secret to help ensure Nixon's reelection. In 1969 Nixon ordered his staff to compile an "enemies list"—made up of critics opposed to his policies—and then tried to ruin their reputations. Two years later, in reaction to Daniel Ellsberg's leak of the Pentagon Papers (see Chapter 30), Nixon set up a secret unit called "the plumbers." This group, which included former agents of the CIA and FBI, was ordered to stop leaks and carry out a variety of illegal actions in the name of "national security."

By 1972 these secret activities had mushroomed into a full-scale effort to ensure Nixon's reelection—no matter what it took. This campaign, which involved criminal activity and electoral "dirty tricks," along with subsequent attempts to cover them up, became known as **Watergate**. The scandal took its name from the Watergate building in Washington, D.C. In June 1972 five men carrying wiretap equipment and other spying devices were caught breaking into the Watergate offices of the Democratic National Committee. It was soon

Teaching the Section

WATERGATE SCANDAL

Provide the following statement to students: *Compared to the nation's social, economic, and foreign-policy problems in the 1970s, Watergate was an event that did not justify the attention it received.* Organize students into groups to discuss and react to this statement. Ask a representative from each group to report any conclusions it reached.

Then continue with a general class discussion on the statement, calling on individual students to agree or disagree with the groups' conclusions about the importance of the Watergate scandal and to explain their opinions.

▶

▲ Bob Woodward (left) and Carl Bernstein (right) were two *Washington Post* reporters who investigated the link between the Nixon White House and the Watergate break-in. This photograph was taken in April 1973.

discovered that these men had ties to the White House and were being paid with funds from Nixon's campaign organization, the Committee to Re-elect the President (CREEP).

The administration denied any link to the break-in, calling it a "third-rate burglary." But two *Washington Post* reporters, Bob Woodward and Carl Bernstein, kept digging for the truth. A high-level source, known only as "Deep Throat," revealed that White House officials and CREEP had hired 50 agents to sabotage the Democrats' chances in the 1972 election.

■■ **The Watergate scandal implicated the Nixon administration in illegal activities, which officials later tried to cover up.**

THE WATERGATE INVESTIGATION

Woodward and Bernstein's astonishing revelations did not prevent Nixon's reelection. But by the spring of 1973, both the judicial and the legislative branches of government were investigating Watergate. Senator Sam Ervin of North Carolina led the investigations for the Senate. One of the first witnesses to testify was James McCord, an ex-CIA agent who had taken part in the Watergate break-in. McCord admitted that top White House officials had helped plan the break-in and later tried to cover it up. This testimony broke the case wide open.

WATERGATE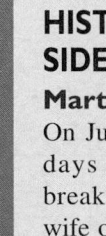

Foreign journalists were particularly interested in the Watergate case. Many noted that similar scandals exposed by journalists in their countries were often ignored because the popular press had little political influence. For example, although the French followed the Watergate investigation with great interest, an alleged French government attempt to wiretap the offices of a weekly newspaper, *Le Canard Enchaîné*, drew little attention. After Nixon's resignation, French journalist André Fontaine commented in the newspaper *Le Monde*:

❝We no longer knew it, we no longer wanted to believe it. But there's still at least one nation on this earth where the law, decidedly, is stronger than men, where, just named by the President, some judges were capable of making some decisions against him. . . .

The idea that the President of the United States must give up his place to the liberties he took with the truth doesn't leave [Americans] astonished. As for the Watergate scandal, we have heard much that the wiretapping at **Le Canard** is only a weak replica, the fact is that France has had some others . . . .

Our old . . . countries . . . have become very indulgent toward sins. But the Americans, despite the excesses of competition and counterculture . . . haven't yet loosened the cocoon of moralism, into which the puritans put their political life. **❞**

The biggest bombshells were yet to come. In May, live television coverage of the Senate hearings began. Across the nation millions of Americans sat glued to their sets as senators grilled witnesses and compiled evidence of official misconduct. Eventually several top White House officials went to jail. Still, Nixon's role in Watergate remained unclear. Time and again, a key member of the Watergate committee, Senator

---

Teaching the *Section*

THE ROAD TO RESIGNATION

Work with the class to create on the chalkboard a flowchart listing the events that eventually led to the resignation of President Nixon. Begin the flowchart with the creation of Nixon's "enemies list" in 1969 and carry it through "the plumbers" unit; events of the Watergate break-in, investigation, and cover-up; the Saturday Night Massacre; and the resignation itself in 1974. As the class offers items for the flowchart, call on students to suggest how each event had an impact on the powers and rights established for government and the people under the Constitution.

**THE AMERICAN NATION
VIDEODISC PROGRAM**

Richard Nixon Resigns

2B   47518   1:01

PRIMARY SOURCE

Description of Change:
excerpted
Rationale: excerpted to
focus on main idea

VOICES IN HISTORY

Worldwide opinions on the results of Watergate varied. One French businessman declared, "The French press is *lamentable,* but the American press is even worse. It's *scandaleux* that your country's press is powerful enough—and irresponsible enough—to politically assassinate one of your greatest presidents." Meanwhile, a British lawyer said, "Watergate didn't really surprise me. After all, corruption is standard practice in American politics. But I still don't understand why it took you two years to get rid of Nixon."

Howard Baker of Tennessee, asked: "What did the president know and when did he know it?" In June, Nixon's former White House counsel John Dean gave the stunning answer: the president himself had ordered the cover-up.

Nixon denied the charge, and there seemed to be no way to prove it. Then another witness revealed that Nixon had secretly tape-recorded his conversations in the White House! In the tapes, investigators believed, lay the truth behind Watergate. The Justice Department's special prosecutor, Archibald Cox, demanded that Nixon turn over the tapes. Citing "executive privilege," Nixon refused on the grounds that release of the tapes would endanger national security.

In the midst of this controversy, the Justice Department dealt the administration another blow. In October 1973 it charged Vice President Spiro Agnew with bribe-taking and income-tax evasion. Agnew pleaded no contest and resigned in exchange for minimal punishment. Nixon then nominated Gerald Ford, the Republican leader in the House of Representatives, as vice president.

*N*IXON RESIGNS

Shortly before Agnew resigned, a federal judge ordered Nixon to release the tapes. The president refused to comply. On October 20, after Special Prosecutor Cox demanded that he obey the judge, Nixon ordered Attorney General Elliot Richardson to fire Cox. Both the attorney general and Deputy Attorney General William Ruckelshaus resigned rather than obey the order. The task of firing Cox then fell to Robert Bork, the solicitor general, who complied. This series of events, known as the **Saturday Night Massacre**, outraged the public and led to increased calls to impeach Nixon.

Nixon finally agreed to release some of the White House tapes. Vital segments were missing, however, and Nixon again resisted turning over the whole set. It was only months later—after the Supreme Court ordered Nixon to turn over all the tapes—that Americans found out the truth: Nixon had directed the Watergate cover-up and had authorized illegal activities. Still, Nixon refused to step down. The House Judiciary committee responded by approving a series of impeachment charges against him. Facing almost certain conviction, Nixon decided to resign. On August 8, 1974, he spoke to the nation:

▲ Gerald Ford was sworn in as the nation's 38th president as his wife, Betty, watches.

❝ I have never been a quitter. To leave office before my term is completed is opposed to every instinct in my body. But as president I must put the interests of America first. . . . Therefore, I shall resign the presidency effective at noon tomorrow. **❞**

▪▪ President Nixon resigned rather than face impeachment for his role in covering up the Watergate affair.

On August 9, 1974, Vice President Gerald Ford was sworn in as the 38th president of the United States. He then nominated Governor Nelson Rockefeller of New York for vice president, and Congress confirmed his choice. For the first time in history, both the president and the vice president held office by appointment.

*C*OMMENTARY

The Larger Meaning of Watergate

Watergate was not the first scandal to taint the presidency. The administration of Ulysses S. Grant, a century before Nixon, was stained by financial scandal. So, too, was the presidency of Warren G. Harding. But Watergate was different. Nixon was the first president to resign from office and the first since Andrew Johnson in 1868 to

NIXON RESIGNS

Have students debate the issue—*Resolved: that President Nixon should have been forced to face charges, despite the fact that he resigned.* Have a volunteer list on the chalkboard the major points of each side. Conclude by conducting a class referendum on the issue, calling on individual students to explain their votes.

FORD'S PROBLEMS

With one student serving as moderator and several others acting as political analysts, stage a TV round-table discussion of the domestic and foreign-policy problems of the Ford administration. Remaining class members should act as the studio audience, asking questions of the panel during the program's "commercial breaks." Conclude by having students use the knowledge gained from the discussion to write editorials on the eve of the 1976 election, evaluating Gerald Ford's presidency. Students may wish to include their editorials in their portfolios.

▶

face a serious threat of impeachment. Unlike Johnson, Nixon's troubles did not result from a power struggle with Congress but from charges of criminal activity.

Furthermore, Watergate did not involve typical political misconduct, such as taking bribes. It challenged the very basis of our constitutional government. Nixon tried to place the presidency above the rule of law and above the constitutional system of balance of powers. Afterward, Congress would try to clean up government corruption by passing several laws, including some limiting the amount of money individuals and corporations could contribute to a political candidate.

Watergate tested our system of constitutional government to the limit, but the system held firm. Vigorous investigative journalism and strong action by the courts and Congress exposed the criminal activities of the Watergate conspirators and forced a president to resign. Watergate underscored the fact that the United States is a government of law, not of individuals.

ƒORD TRIES TO REUNITE THE NATION

The new president, Gerald Ford, was gifted with the common touch. As leader of the Republicans in the House, he had won the respect of colleagues in both parties for his honesty and unassuming manner. "I'm a Ford, not a Lincoln," he once joked.

But President Ford lost much of this early goodwill when, a month after taking office, he granted Nixon a full pardon. Overnight Ford's popularity rating dropped from 72 percent to 49 percent. His critics charged that now the full truth about Watergate would never emerge. They pointed to the double standard that allowed Nixon to go free while his co-conspirators were punished. Many people suspected that the pardon had been agreed upon in advance in exchange for Nixon's resignation. President Ford denied this charge. He defended the pardon by saying that a public trial would have prolonged the bitterness and division produced by Watergate. He had acted, he said, to heal "the wounds of the past."

A week later, Ford took another controversial step by offering partial amnesty to Vietnam draft evaders and military deserters who agreed to reaffirm their allegiance to the United States and spend two years performing public service. Supporters of the Vietnam War felt the pardon was unfair to soldiers who had served their country. Meanwhile, only a handful of people accepted the president's offer. Some war resisters, like Dee Knight, contrasted the conditional pardon with the full pardon granted Nixon:

❝ We knew the clemency was proclaimed just to offset the Nixon pardon, which was an insult. We weren't criminals, and Nixon was, but Ford proposed to pardon Nixon unconditionally while offering "alternative punishment" to us. ❞

ƒORD'S TROUBLES CONTINUE

Ford soon ran into other problems, including conflicts with the Democratic majority in Congress. A moderate conservative, Ford vetoed a number of social-welfare bills sponsored by Democrats. In fact, he vetoed more bills than any other president had in such a short time. As Ford's relations with Congress worsened, he found it increasingly difficult to implement his policies.

One of Ford's main goals was to combat inflation, which was being fueled by the energy

▼ The energy crisis increased the price of many consumer goods in the United States. To win public support for his anti-inflation program, President Ford issued buttons with initials representing "Whip Inflation Now."

🅞 **THE AMERICAN NATION VIDEODISC PROGRAM**
Ford Pardons Nixon

| 2B | 50431 | :41 |

PRIMARY SOURCE
Description of Change: excerpted
Rationale: excerpted to focus on main idea

HISTORICAL SIDELIGHTS
Betty Ford's Activism
While President Ford was embroiled in domestic and foreign affairs, First Lady Betty Ford was drawing attention to important health issues. She was willing to break the silence about health issues that many people were reluctant to discuss. She publicly discussed her bout with breast cancer and urged women to take steps to detect tumors in their early stages. After leaving the White House, and after revealing her own addiction to alcohol and pills, Ford became an advocate in 1978 for the treatment of drug and alcohol abuse.

Practice

GUIDED PRACTICE

Write the following statement by Richard Nixon on the chalkboard: *"When the president does it, that means that it is not illegal."* Ask students to name actions of Nixon that they regard as illegal. List responses on the chalkboard.

INDEPENDENT PRACTICE

Have students choose one of the actions cited in the Guided Practice activity and write an entry for their personal journal on the day that the action became public. Tell students that their journal entries should include their reactions and feelings about the news and a reflection on the action's potential significance for the nation. Students may wish to include their journal entries in their portfolios.

Review and Assessment

REVIEW Have students write a letter to President Ford explaining why they will or will not vote for him in the 1976 election. Students should give details from the section to support their viewpoint. Have volunteers with opposing opinions read and defend their letters before the class. Then assign the Section 2 Review on p. 911.

ASSESS Assign the **Section 2 Daily Quiz** in *Core Resources.*

BIOGRAPHY
PERSONALITIES IN HISTORY

After retiring from politics, Jordan took a position at the Lyndon Baines Johnson School of Public Affairs at the University of Texas at Austin, where she served as a faculty adviser, minority recruiter, and teacher. Explaining her decision to leave politics, Jordan said, "I thought that my role now was to be one of the voices in the country defining where we were, where we were going, what the policies were that were being pursued, and where the holes in those policies were. I felt I was more in an instructive role than a legislative role."

PRIMARY SOURCE

(for source on p. 911)
Description of Change: excerpted
Rationale: excerpted to focus on main idea

PRESIDENTIAL LIVES

GERALD R. FORD
1913–

in office
1974–1977

Gerald Ford faced the difficult task of restoring the nation's confidence in government after the Watergate crisis. Most observers believed that Ford was uniquely qualified to remove the taint of scandal from the White House. Throughout his career he had been known as an honest and likable politician. "The nicest thing about Jerry Ford," said Senator Robert P. Griffin, "is that he doesn't have any enemies." Indeed, when Ford first heard about President Nixon's "enemies list," he responded that "anybody who can't keep his enemies in his head has too many enemies."

Gerald R. Ford

EXPERIENCE COUNTS
Elect Gerald R. FORD in '76

Unlike many politicians, Ford made friends because he always maintained a fair-minded attitude. He was never vengeful when he lost or arrogant when he won. He acquired this attitude from years of playing sports, especially football. He had been a star player for the University of Michigan and received several offers to play for professional teams. Instead he worked his way through law school as a coach and entered politics. Sports remained an influential part of his life, however. He was the most athletic president in the White House since Teddy Roosevelt.

---

crisis and the soaring cost of oil. Like Nixon, Ford tried to curb inflation by cutting federal spending, but this threw the country into a recession and prolonged the nation's economic woes.

In foreign affairs, Ford also continued many of Nixon's policies, including détente. Gradually, however, U.S.–Soviet relations began to unravel. One problem was Soviet emigration policy, which restricted the freedom of Jews and political dissidents to leave the country. When members of Congress criticized this policy, the Soviets canceled a proposed U.S.–Soviet trade pact. Over the next few years, relations continued to sour.

Ford also tried to maintain American influence in Southeast Asia. Toward that end, he requested $722 million in military aid for Cambodia and South Vietnam. But Congress, opposed to further military ventures in Southeast Asia, turned down Ford's request. Then, in May 1975, Cambodian Communists

seized the *Mayaguez,* an unarmed U.S. cargo ship. In response, Ford launched a military action to free the vessel and its crew. Forty-one Americans were killed in the effort to release the 39 crew members. While some applauded the president's actions, others criticized it as hasty and ill-timed. As facts later revealed, the *Mayaguez* crew had already been released when the troops were sent.

▼ Cambodian Communists seized an unarmed U.S. cargo ship, the *Mayaguez,* in May 1975. President Ford called the action piracy and sent U.S. Marines to free the vessel and its crew.

Closure

Return students' attention to Nixon's statement cited in the Guided Practice: "When the president does it, that means that it is not illegal." Ask students whether they agree or disagree with Nixon's point of view. Inform students that Nixon expressed the view in 1977, after he had resigned. Ask students what his actions during Watergate suggest about his views on this subject while he was president.

Extension

COMPARE Have students review the impeachment of President Andrew Johnson and write an essay comparing and contrasting the charges against Johnson with those against President Nixon.

ANALYZE Have students write a paper analyzing the public perceptions of government after Watergate and explaining why most presidents since Ford have campaigned as Washington outsiders.

■■ **Ford clashed with Congress over domestic and foreign policy. During his term U.S.–Soviet relations began to unravel.**

THE ELECTION OF 1976

At the 1976 Republican convention, Ford narrowly won the party's nomination over his more conservative challenger, Ronald Reagan of California. To balance the ticket, the convention nominated conservative senator Robert Dole of Kansas for vice president. At the Democratic convention, Jimmy Carter—a former governor of Georgia—won the nomination, with Senator Walter Mondale of Minnesota as his running mate. Congresswoman Barbara Jordan of Texas gave the keynote address at the Democratic convention.

 Jordan brought a strong sense of moral authority to the Democratic party. Born in 1936, she grew up in Houston, Texas. She excelled in school and eventually received a law degree from Boston University. In 1966 Jordan became the first African American woman elected to the Texas senate. There her tireless efforts on behalf of social reform won praise from President Lyndon Johnson, who noted, "She proved that black is beautiful before we knew what it meant."

In 1972 Jordan was elected to the U.S. House of Representatives, where she soon gained a reputation as a skilled legislator and brilliant orator. She played a key role in drawing up impeachment charges against President Nixon. At one point Jordan declared: "I am not going to sit here and be an idle spectator to the . . . destruction of the Constitution." Despite her outstanding record in Congress, in 1978 Jordan announced that she would not run for a fourth term. As a political analyst and adviser, however, she played a prominent role in national affairs until her death in early 1996.

Barbara Jordan

In her speech to the 1976 Democratic convention, Jordan declared:

> 66 We cannot improve on the system of government handed down to us by the founders of the Republic, but we can find new ways to implement that system and realize our destiny. 99

The idea of a new approach to government was central to Jimmy Carter's campaign. Little known outside the South, Carter ran as a Washington outsider untainted by Watergate. He promised never to lie to the American people and openly noted that he was a born-again Christian whose religious ethics strongly shaped his political actions. "You can't divorce religious beliefs and public service," he said. In a close election, he captured 297 electoral votes to Ford's 240. After eight years of Republican rule, the Democrats returned to the White House. Many hoped that Carter would be able to reverse the public's mistrust of government.

■■ ## SECTION 2 REVIEW

IDENTIFY and explain the significance of the following: Watergate, Bob Woodward, Carl Bernstein, Sam Ervin, James McCord, John Dean, Archibald Cox, Gerald Ford, Saturday Night Massacre, Jimmy Carter, Barbara Jordan.

1. **MAIN IDEA** Why did President Nixon choose to resign from office in 1974?
2. **MAIN IDEA** What difficulties did President Ford face during his time in office?
3. **ASSESSING CONSEQUENCES** What was the significance of the Watergate investigation?
4. **WRITING TO INFORM** Imagine you are an investigative reporter for the *Washington Post*, covering the Watergate scandal. Write an article that outlines the major events in the scandal and the investigation leading up to President Nixon's resignation.
5. **HYPOTHESIZING** How might events have been different if Ford had not pardoned Nixon?

FOCUS OBJECTIVES

■ Identify the critical
domestic issues facing the
Carter administration.

■ Examine how Carter's
foreign policy differed
from Nixon's.

■ Explain why Cold War
tensions rose under
President Carter.

■ Analyze how the Iran
hostage crisis affected
Carter's presidency.

Section 3

CARTER: THE OUTSIDER AS PRESIDENT

F O C U S
■ **What critical domestic issues faced the Carter administration?**
■ **How did Carter's foreign policy differ from Nixon's?**
■ **Why did Cold War tensions rise under President Carter?**
■ **How did the Iran hostage crisis affect Carter's presidency?**

Family member awaiting return
of hostages in Iran

*O*n January 20, 1977, Jimmy Carter took the oath as the 39th
president of the United States. Initially a popular president, Carter
enjoyed some notable successes. But serious problems—including
persistent inflation and conflict in the Middle East—eventually
helped erode the president's popularity. In 1980 he lost his bid for
a second term.

*A*N "OPEN ADMINISTRATION"

During the presidential campaign, Carter had
promised, if elected, to stay in touch with the people. He quickly showed his intentions to keep that
promise. Following his inauguration, the president
and his family walked down Pennsylvania Avenue
to the White House, rather than make the trip in a
limousine surrounded by Secret Service.

The Carter style. Carter brought a folksy
style to the White House, abandoning much of the
pomp and ceremony of previous presidents.
Contributing to this informal tone was his colorful
family, who became the subject of much public
interest. The news media reported on the activities
of Carter's young daughter, Amy, and on the views
of his outspoken mother, Miss Lillian. Carter's
wife, Rosalynn, received even more attention as
one of his most trusted advisers. Although critics
questioned his wife's influence on policy, the president insisted that she play a prominent role in
White House affairs.

Early on, Carter took several steps that indicated a new approach to government. On his first
full day in office, he announced an unconditional
pardon for most Vietnam-era draft evaders, moving beyond the conditional pardon offered by
President Ford. This gesture helped heal lingering
divisions over the war. Carter also held several

◀ **The Carter family attracted almost as much
media attention as the president. Shown here are
President Carter with his wife, Rosalynn, and his
young daughter, Amy.**

Teaching the Section

CARTER'S DOMESTIC ISSUES

Tell each student to choose what he or she believes to be the nation's most pressing domestic problem in the late 1970s and to prepare a message to President Carter, expressing his or her concerns about that issue. Then choose a volunteer to represent Jimmy Carter and conduct a town meeting at which students deliver their messages to the president. Students may wish to include their messages in their portfolios.

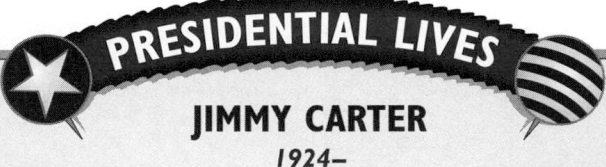

PRESIDENTIAL LIVES

JIMMY CARTER
1924–

in office
1977–1981

The common reaction to Georgia governor Jimmy Carter's announcement that he was running for president was "Jimmy who?" Few people outside of his home state were familiar with the peanut farmer from Plains. Soon, however, voters began to discover that there was much more to this southern politician than his large grin. A highly ranked graduate of the United States Naval Academy, Carter had worked as a nuclear engineer before entering politics.

Carter had a balanced, modern rela-

tionship with his wife. Rosalynn Carter took an active and public role in political affairs, traveling around the world to represent her husband's views. Meanwhile Jimmy Carter shared the household chores, such as cooking, caring for their daughter, and grocery shopping. One interviewer was shocked to see the candidate sewing a button onto his own jacket during the presidential campaign. When asked if he always did his own sewing, Carter simply mumbled with thread in mouth, "Uh-huh."

Jimmy Carter

"town meetings" and radio and television call-in sessions to keep in touch with the people. Unlike Richard Nixon, Jimmy Carter seemed determined to keep his administration open to public view.

Carter's economic policy. One of Carter's first tasks was to stimulate the economy, which was just beginning to emerge from several years of recession. Some eight million Americans—7.8 percent of the work force—were unemployed. The unemployment rate among African Americans and Hispanic Americans was 13 percent.

To revive the economy and create jobs, Carter implemented a series of economic measures, including a corporate tax cut. The Carter administration's policies helped reduce unemployment slightly, but they also fueled inflation, which reached 13.3 percent by 1979. To curb inflation, Carter called for voluntary wage and price controls, along with cuts in funding for social services. But Carter's anti-inflation program produced more unemployment. By the summer of 1980, the economy was once again mired in recession.

Facing the energy crisis. A major cause of the nation's economic woes was the high cost of imported oil. To reduce the nation's oil dependence, Congress created the **Department of Energy** in 1977. The following year it passed the

National Energy Act to relax controls on the price of natural gas. Despite these efforts, world events continued to affect the nation's energy supply.

In January 1979 a revolution in Iran disrupted world oil shipments. A few months later, OPEC raised the price of oil 50 percent, leading to another U.S. energy crisis (see the chart on page 902). As gasoline supplies dwindled, many gas stations closed or reduced their hours. Tempers flared as frustrated drivers had to wait hours to fill

▼ High energy costs hurt many groups during the late 1970s, including farmers. On February 6, 1979, protesting farmers drove their tractors down Pennsylvania Avenue to demonstrate in front of the White House.

Teaching the Section

FOREIGN–POLICY DIFFERENCES

Pair students to prepare discussions between presidents Carter and Nixon about their foreign policies. Within their dialogues each "president" should explain his approach to foreign policy, state why he thinks it is the better approach, and find fault with the other's approach. Select pairs to re-create their dialogues for the class.

■■ Ask students whether national self-interest or concern for human rights should guide American foreign policy today.

HISTORICAL SIDELIGHTS

The China Syndrome

Public doubts about the safety of nuclear power were exacerbated by the movie *The China Syndrome,* which had been released about two weeks before the Three Mile Island incident. The movie's plot involved a utility company's attempt to cover up a serious accident at a power plant similar to Three Mile Island.

GLOBAL CONNECTIONS

Brigadier General Omar Torrijos of Panama said that if the U.S. Senate had failed to ratify the treaties, Panama would have resorted to "violent liberation" of the canal zone, including the possibility of closing the Panama Canal.

AMERICAN CIVICS
CITIZENSHIP SKILLS

Videocassette or
Videodisc: Segment 7

Segment 7, Side A

Search Chapter 4

PRIMARY SOURCE

Description of Change:
excerpted
Rationale: excerpted to focus on main idea

▲ After the disaster at Three Mile Island, residents staged protests that questioned the safety of nuclear power. Protesters urged the government to explore alternative energy sources, such as solar power.

their gas tanks. Some people responded by driving less and by embracing other energy-saving measures, such as installing solar heaters in their homes.

In the midst of the oil crisis, another event dramatized America's energy problems. In late March 1979 a nuclear reactor failed at the Three Mile Island power plant in Pennsylvania, nearly causing a catastrophic nuclear meltdown—the melting of the reactor's core. This incident stirred public fears about nuclear power.

■■ **An economic recession and an energy crisis were among the serious domestic issues facing the Carter administration.**

*H*UMAN RIGHTS AND FOREIGN POLICY

As Carter struggled with difficult domestic issues, he was also charting a new course in foreign affairs. Rejecting the realpolitik of the Nixon years, Carter tried to inject moral principles into American foreign policy. Reflecting on past administrations, he declared:

❝ We are deeply concerned . . . by the . . . subtle erosion in the focus and morality of our foreign policy. Under the Nixon-Ford administration, there has evolved a kind of secretive "Lone Ranger" foreign policy—

a one-man policy of international adventure. This is not an appropriate policy for America. ❞

Carter's new approach was most evident in the area of **human rights**—the rights of all people to freedom from unlawful detention or torture. Declaring that "our commitment to human rights must be absolute," Carter called for strong diplomatic and economic pressure on countries that violated human rights.

Not surprisingly, many dictatorships that repressed the rights of their people strongly opposed Carter's policy. Some American diplomats also had doubts. They warned that such meddling in the domestic affairs of other countries might increase world tensions. The United States would resent meddling by other nations in *its* domestic affairs, they pointed out.

■■ **Carter moved away from Nixon's foreign policy of realpolitik to emphasize moral principles and respect for human rights.**

Carter's stand on the Panama Canal caused even greater controversy. He supported Panama's right to control the canal zone and pushed for passage of the **Panama Canal treaties**, which granted Panama control over canal operations by the year 2000 while safeguarding U.S. security interests. Critics charged that Carter was "giving away" the canal. "We built it, we paid for it, it's ours, and . . . we are going to keep it!" declared conservative Republican Ronald Reagan.

Gradually, however, public opinion shifted in Carter's favor, and after a long and bitter debate,

▲ Through the Panama Canal treaties, President Carter proposed that the United States give control of the canal zone to Panama by the year 2000.

the Senate narrowly ratified the treaties in 1978. In Latin America, where U.S. control over the canal had long been a sore point, the treaties met with general approval.

CARTER AND THE COLD WAR

Carter's stance on the Panama Canal issue signaled a more flexible approach to relations with developing countries. Carter hoped the approach would improve America's image and diminish the appeal of communism. His policy was evident in Africa, where the United States and the Soviet Union were jockeying for influence among the continent's newly independent states.

Unlike Nixon and Ford, who showed little interest in Africa, Carter tried to win friends among African nations by helping them sort out their problems in their own way. One Carter official noted, "It is not a sign of weakness to recognize that we alone cannot dictate events elsewhere. It is rather a sign of maturity in a complex world."

Carter's ambassador to the United Nations, former civil rights activist Andrew Young, tried to reach out to black African states. He criticized white imperialism in Africa, condemned South Africa's policy of **apartheid** (racial segregation), and supported black majority rule in Rhodesia (now Zimbabwe).

Carter's flexible approach helped smooth relations in Africa and ease Cold War conflict. The easing of tensions was short-lived, however. In December 1979 Soviet troops invaded the country of Afghanistan to install a pro-Soviet leader. The invasion put Soviet troops within striking distance of major oil routes.

Labeling the invasion a threat to peace, President Carter warned the Soviets to withdraw. When they refused, he cut grain sales to the Soviet Union and announced a boycott of the 1980 Summer Olympics in Moscow. Congress also postponed the signing of a key U.S.–Soviet arms-control treaty. Finally, the president warned that any Soviet military action in the Persian Gulf would provoke a military response by the United States.

Although the U.S. improved relations with developing countries, Cold War tensions increased when the Soviets invaded Afghanistan.

CARTER AND THE MIDDLE EAST

Not long before the Soviet invasion of Afghanistan, Carter engineered his chief foreign-policy triumph: a Middle East peace accord. Carter had taken office in 1977 amid fears of another Egyptian-Israeli war. Egyptian president Anwar Sadat (sah-DAHT) and Israeli premier Menachem Begin (muh-NAHK-uhm BAY-gin) met for peace talks, but those talks deadlocked.

Anwar Sadat received a great deal of criticism from the leaders of other Arab nations for attempting any peace talks with Israel. Sadat was born in the small village of Mit Abu-Kum on the Nile Delta in 1918. His childhood was heavily influenced by his close-knit family and the local Imam (religious leader), who taught him the principles of the Islamic faith. Soon after graduating from the Egyptian Military Academy in 1938, Sadat joined a group of rebels who wanted to rid Egypt of its constitutional monarchy, which was under British control.

Sadat went to prison in the 1940s for his efforts to liberate Egypt. After being released from prison, he joined the rebel forces who finally overthrew the monarch in 1952. Thereafter Sadat played a central role in shaping Egyptian policy, finally

▲ **Anwar Sadat**

◀ As U.S. ambassador to the United Nations, **Andrew Young** condemned apartheid and sympathized with the concerns of developing nations. His actions made him a controversial figure, and he was forced to resign in 1979.

Practice

GUIDED PRACTICE

Create a four-cell chart on the chalkboard with columns labeled *Successes* and *Failures* and rows labeled *Foreign* and *Domestic*. Have the class assess Carter's handling of each event discussed in the section and list that event in the appropriate cell.

INDEPENDENT PRACTICE

Instruct students to choose an event from one of the cells in the Guided Practice chart and create an editorial cartoon that reflects Carter's handling of that situation. Students may wish to include their editorial cartoons in their portfolios.

Review and Assessment

REVIEW Ask students to imagine they voted for Carter in 1976. Have them write a journal entry explaining why they voted for Jimmy Carter. Then instruct them to write a second journal entry citing issues that affected the way they voted in 1980. Then assign the Section 3 Review on p. 917.

ASSESS Assign the **Section 3 Daily Quiz** in *Core Resources.*

PRIMARY SOURCE

Description of Change: excerpted and bracketed
Rationale: excerpted to focus on main idea; bracketed to clarify meaning

PRIMARY SOURCE

Description of Change: excerpted
Rationale: excerpted to focus on main idea

HISTORICAL SIDELIGHTS

Carter and the Soviets

According to Tass, the Soviet press agency, the reason for Carter's defeat in the 1980 presidential election was his hard-line approach toward the Soviet Union. Tass also claimed that the U.S. boycott of the Summer Olympics in Moscow had severely damaged the Carter administration. After Reagan's victory Soviet Premier Nikolai Tikhonov expressed hope that Reagan would call for a "constructive approach" that would lead to improvement in U.S.–Soviet relations.

Map Caption Answer
(for map on p. 917)
Minnesota and Hawaii

---

becoming president in 1970. As president he played a key role in Middle East events, including trying to pave the road to peace. When Sadat visited Israel in 1977, Premier Begin remarked:

> 66 The time of the flight between Cairo and Jerusalem is short . . . [but] the distance between them . . . until yesterday, quite large. . . . Sadat passed this distance with heartfelt courage. . . . We, the Jews, know how to appreciate this courage. 99

But Sadat always downplayed his own role in bringing about peace. He considered his actions a collective effort by the entire country. To him, all Egyptians shared responsibility for the nation's future. He once said:

> 66 Responsibility cannot be relegated to certain individuals, no matter how good your opinion of them might be; neither can it be confined to groups of people, however good their intentions may be. Responsibility is the entire people's property. 99

In September 1978 Sadat met with Begin and Carter at Camp David, the presidential retreat in Maryland. There, after 12 days of negotiations, the three agreed on a framework for peace, which became known as the **Camp David Accords**. As a result of their efforts, Sadat and Begin shared the Nobel Peace Prize for 1978. The following year, the two leaders signed a formal peace treaty ending 30 years of war between Egypt and Israel. At the emotion-filled ceremony, each quoted the prophet Isaiah: "And they shall beat their swords into plowshares and their spears into pruning hooks."

The accords did not meet universal approval. Some supporters of Israel accused President Carter of favoring the Arabs in order to appease Arab oil-exporting nations, such as Saudi Arabia. Sadat drew the wrath of other Arab nations, furious at his "betrayal" for making peace with Israel. In 1981, members of an Islamic fundamentalist group within the Egyptian army assassinated Sadat while he was reviewing a military parade.

CARTER'S POPULARITY FALLS

Although Carter had chalked up some notable successes as president, by 1980 only 21 percent of Americans approved of his performance. Nixon's approval rating had not fallen this low even during the depths of Watergate. Carter's drop in popularity was partly due to his lack of political experience. But his troubles also lay in the nature of the problems he faced. The energy crisis, inflation, unemployment, Middle East conflict, and Cold War tensions were highly complicated issues that defied simple solutions. Of all the difficulties he faced, however, none was more damaging than the **Iran hostage crisis**.

Iran had long been regarded as critical to U.S. security in the Middle East. In the 1950s the United States had helped overthrow Iran's leader and restore Shah Reza Pahlavi to power (see Chapter 28). Although the shah's regime was very repressive, the United States always supported him. In 1979, however, followers of a militant Islamic leader, the Ayatollah Khomeini (eye-uh-TOH-luh koh-MAY-nee), forced the shah to flee the country. The new government was outraged when President Carter allowed the shah into the United States for medical treatment. On November 4, 1979, in an effort to force the shah's return to Iran for trial, Iranian militants seized 53 American hostages at the U.S. embassy in Tehran, Iran's capital.

Month after month, the hostage crisis dragged on. In April 1980 a rescue mission failed when U.S. military helicopters crashed in the Iranian desert, killing eight Americans. As frustration over the crisis mounted, public anger at Carter also grew. Many felt that his inability to free the hostages signaled America's decline as a symbol of power. Even one Carter aide admitted that "Khomeini would not have touched the Soviet Embassy."

Echoing these thoughts during the 1980 presidential election campaign, the Republican candidate, Ronald Reagan, attacked Carter as a weak president who had presided over a decline in American power. Reagan's promise to "make America strong

▶ **American hostage in Iran**

RETEACH Organize students so that a roughly equal number are assigned to each subsection of the section. Direct each student to write a question about the material in his or her assigned subsection. Then use the questions to quiz the entire group.

Closure

Discuss the advantages and disadvantages of electing a president who is considered an outsider. Ask students to suggest how Carter's outsider status may have influenced his domestic and foreign-policy strategies.

Extension

CONDUCT Ask students to conduct interviews with parents, teachers, or others who experienced the energy crisis of the late 1970s. Have students report their findings to the class in the form of anecdotes.

RESEARCH Have students research additional information about the Camp David Accords and write a summary that identifies the details of the agreement between Egypt and Israel.

again" struck a chord with voters. He and his running mate, George Bush, easily won the election, capturing 489 electoral votes to Carter and Mondale's 49. An independent candidate, John Anderson, failed to capture any electoral votes, but did win almost 7 percent of the popular vote, further reflecting public frustration with the administration. For the first time since 1952, the Republicans won control of the Senate, while the Democrats' majority in the House dropped somewhat.

After his defeat Carter continued to negotiate for the release of the hostages. On January 20, 1981, after 444 days in captivity, the hostages were finally freed, just moments after Ronald Reagan was sworn in as president.

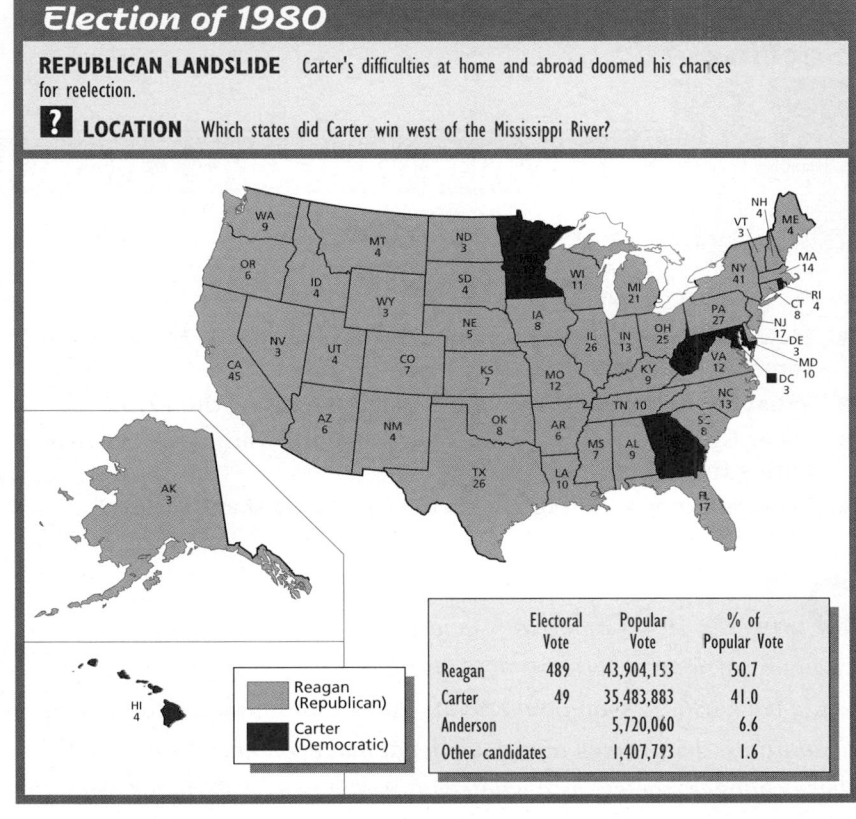

Election of 1980

REPUBLICAN LANDSLIDE Carter's difficulties at home and abroad doomed his chances for reelection.

? LOCATION Which states did Carter win west of the Mississippi River?

	Electoral Vote	Popular Vote	% of Popular Vote
Reagan	489	43,904,153	50.7
Carter	49	35,483,883	41.0
Anderson		5,720,060	6.6
Other candidates		1,407,793	1.6

Reagan (Republican)

Carter (Democratic)

■■ **The Iran hostage crisis contributed to Carter's defeat in the 1980 election.**

■■   S E C T I O N **3** R E V I E W

IDENTIFY and explain the significance of the following: Rosalynn Carter, Department of Energy, National Energy Act, human rights, Panama Canal treaties, Andrew Young, apartheid, Anwar Sadat, Menachem Begin, Camp David Accords, Iran hostage crisis, Ayatollah Khomeini, Ronald Reagan, John Anderson.

LOCATE and explain the importance of the following: Iran, South Africa, Rhodesia (Zimbabwe), Afghanistan.

1. **MAIN IDEA** What two serious domestic issues did President Carter face?
2. **MAIN IDEA** How did the Carter administration's approach to the Cold War influence events overseas? What event caused Cold War tensions to increase?
3. **CONTRASTING** Contrast the Carter administration's approach to foreign policy with the Nixon administration's approach.
4. **WRITING TO EXPLAIN** Imagine you are a political analyst covering the 1980 presidential election. Write an essay explaining why Carter has been defeated.
5. **TAKING A STAND** Was Carter right in supporting the Panama Canal treaties? Why or why not?

PREVIEW WORKSHOP

*Following is a list of the significant
people and terms in this section.
You may wish to use this list as a
section preview.*

People
■ Patricia Harris
■ Russell Means

Terms
■ League of United Latin
  American Citizens
■ Rehabilitation Act
■ Education for All
  Handicapped Children Act
■ affirmative action
■ *University of California* v.
  Bakke

■ Education Amendments Act
■ *Roe* v. *Wade*
■ Equal Rights Amendment
■ zero population growth
■ Sunbelt
■ Voting Rights Act of 1975
■ Bilingual Education Act

FOCUS OBJECTIVES

■ Analyze how the civil
  rights movement contin-
  ued in the 1970s and
  describe how some
  whites responded.

■ Explain what American
  Indian leaders fought for
  during the 1970s.

■ Identify the issues that
  both encouraged and
  divided the women's
  movement during the
  1970s.

■ Describe how the new
  immigrants in the 1970s
  helped shape society.

**THE AMERICAN NATION
VIDEODISC PROGRAM**

César Chavéz

2B   38963   :21

CORE RESOURCES

• **Literature
  Worksheet 31**
• **Section 4 Daily Quiz**

AV **RESOURCES**

• *The American Nation
  Videodisc: César
  Chávez; The
  Women's Rights
  Movement*
• **Linking Geography
  and History
  Transparencies** and
  Worksheets 12B, 13B

918

Section 4

A DECADE OF SOCIAL CHANGE

F O C U S

■ **How did the civil rights movement continue in the 1970s? How did
  some whites respond?**
■ **What did American Indian leaders fight for during the 1970s?**
■ **What issues both encouraged and divided the women's movement
  during the 1970s?**
■ **How did the new immigrants in the 1970s help shape society?**

*During the 1970s American society underwent important social
changes. African Americans made further gains, despite a growing
white backlash. Hispanic Americans, American Indians, people with
disabilities, and women also made legal and economic strides. Amid
these changes, society as a whole was evolving as Americans were
living longer and moving more often, and new immigrants were
swelling the population.*

A woman with visual impairment
demonstrating for civil rights

THE LEGACY OF THE CIVIL
RIGHTS MOVEMENT

The 1970s brought some progress in the area of civil
rights. Though a 1975 Civil Rights Commission
report found that many African Americans were still
being kept from voting by various means, by the end
of the 1970s over 4,500 African Americans held
elective office—three times the number in 1969.
The roster of elected black officials in 1978 included
16 members of the House of Representatives and
170 mayors, including those of Los Angeles,
Atlanta, Detroit, and Washington, D.C.

As new African American leaders gained
political experience, they formed strong alliances
and effective lobbies. They also worked hard to get
out the black vote, a key factor in Jimmy Carter's
electoral victory in 1976. As president, Carter
helped open the doors of the federal government to
African Americans, naming more blacks to federal
jobs than any previous president. In addition to his

choice of Andrew Young as UN ambassador,
Carter appointed the first African American
woman to a cabinet post—Patricia Harris as secretary of Housing and Urban Development.

During the 1970s Hispanic Americans also
began to reap some rewards for their political
struggles of the previous decade. Between 1974
and 1987 the number of elected Hispanic officials
in the United States more than doubled. Growing
numbers of Hispanic Americans were appointed to
federal jobs, while Hispanic groups such as
LULAC—**League of United Latin American
Citizens**—mounted lobbying efforts and helped
raise national awareness of Hispanic concerns. In
California the United Farm Workers won a key
victory in 1975 with the passage of a state law
extending legal protection to migrant farm workers. In addition, the Southwest Voter Registration
Education Project helped Hispanic Americans register to vote.

Americans with disabilities also made their
voices heard in the 1970s. Why, they asked, should

Teaching the **Section**

CIVIL RIGHTS

Have students work in small groups to conceptualize and complete a graphic organizer that summarizes gains made by African Americans, Hispanic Americans, and Americans with disabilities during the 1970s. Ask volunteers from each group to present and explain its graphic organizer to the class. Then discuss with the class why some white Americans might have objected to some of these gains, and how they expressed their objections.

▶

▲ These demonstrators in San Francisco protested lack of access to public transportation by blocking buses during rush hour.

their tax dollars help build public facilities that people in wheelchairs or people with visual disabilities could not easily use? In response to protests, state and local governments passed laws requiring wheelchair ramps and special parking spaces at public facilities. Many public facilities also put up signs in braille to help the visually impaired. Congress joined these efforts by passing the **Rehabilitation Act** in 1973, which forbade discrimination in jobs, education, or housing because of physical disabilities. In 1975 it passed the **Education for All Handicapped Children Act**, which required public schools to provide education for children with physical and mental disabilities.

■■ **The legacy of the civil rights movement continued in the growing political clout of African Americans, Hispanic Americans, and people with disabilities.**

A WHITE BACKLASH

The expansion of civil rights during the 1970s was the result of both public and private efforts. In an effort to uphold federal laws against discrimination, the Civil Rights Division of the Department of Justice sued corporations and labor unions to end unfair employment practices. Many schools and businesses also instituted **affirmative action** programs, whereby ethnic minorities and women were given preference in hiring and admission to make up for previous discrimination.

But the 1970s also brought a white backlash against this aspect of the civil rights movement. Some white citizens complained that affirmative action programs were depriving them of their own rights. One of the first targets of white anger was court-ordered busing to achieve school desegregation. Busing met with strong opposition in a number of cities, most notably Boston. One angry white Bostonian, Jimmy Kelley, warned: "You heard of the Hundred Years War? This will be the eternal war. It will be passed down from father to son."

By the fall of 1974, violent protests against busing had erupted in Boston. Many people were injured in the riots. Yet despite the risks, many

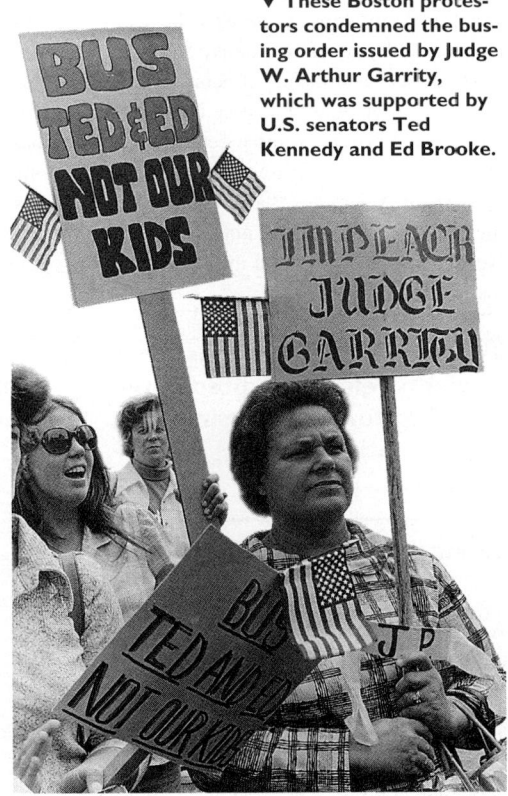

▼ These Boston protestors condemned the busing order issued by Judge W. Arthur Garrity, which was supported by U.S. senators Ted Kennedy and Ed Brooke.

Teaching the Section

AMERICAN INDIANS ORGANIZE

Organize the class into small groups and tell them to assign group members to be either TV journalists or American Indians in the 1970s. Direct the "journalists" to interview one or more of the "American Indians" about their opinions of the American Indian Movement (AIM) and its tactics. Journalists also should ask subjects for their opinions about other methods that were used in the 1970s for achieving American Indian rights.

PRIMARY SOURCES

Description of Change: excerpted
Rationale: excerpted to focus on main idea

VOICES IN HISTORY

At age 16, Russell Means transferred from a racially mixed school to a school whose population was comprised almost entirely of whites. There, he grew angry at the taunting and daily insults he received from his classmates. "I guess I was sort of what you'd call a boy named Sioux," he has been quoted as saying. "Every time some wise guy would mouth off I'd figger I had to defend myself for bein' Indian. I got to know what it was like to hate to see it rain."

■■ Ask students what they think Means meant by his last sentence. *(probably that, as an American Indian, he was the victim of prejudicial slurs that referred to stereotypical Indian rain dances)*

[AV] **TRANSPARENCY**
Linking Geography and History Transparency and **Worksheet 12B**

---

black parents believed that busing was necessary. As one African American woman, Rachel Twymon, told her two children who were being bused to a previously all-white school:

> 66 I'm afraid this isn't going to be an easy year for either of you. You're going to be called a lot of ugly names. You're going to be spat at, maybe pushed around some. But it's not the first time this has happened and it won't be the last. It's something we have to go through—something *you* have to go through—if this city is ever going to get integrated. 99

By the late 1970s the busing controversy had quieted down, but anger over affirmative action continued. Many whites argued that affirmative action programs led to reverse discrimination. In 1978 the Supreme Court handed down an important ruling on affirmative action. In *University of California* v. *Bakke,* the Court ruled that a white man, Allan Bakke, had been unfairly denied admission to medical school on the basis of quotas—systems that set aside a fixed number of places for certain groups of people, in this case, African Americans. Although the Court did not rule out all forms of affirmative action, it did strike down quotas as a means of achieving racial equality. In a bitter dissent Justice Thurgood Marshall recalled the history of three centuries of racial discrimination in America and its toll on generations of African Americans: "The dream of America as the great melting pot has not been realized for the Negro; because of his skin color he never even made it into the pot."

■■ **White backlash against civil rights reform erupted in the 1970s, fueled by busing and affirmative action.**

---

*A*MERICAN INDIANS ORGANIZE

As part of the broad movement for civil rights, American Indians also began to organize, to seek redress in the courts, and to engage in commercial ventures. Young urban Indians launched the American Indian Movement (AIM) in 1968, calling for a renewal of Native American culture and recognition of Native American rights. In 1972,

some 500 AIM members, protesting what they called the "Trail of Broken Treaties," temporarily occupied the Bureau of Indian Affairs (BIA) in Washington, D.C.

One of the leaders of the BIA occupation was Russell Means, a longtime Indian activist. Born in 1940 on the Pine Ridge Sioux Reservation of South Dakota, Means spent much of his childhood in the San Francisco Bay area. By 1970 he had become a prominent figure in AIM.

▲ **Russell Means**

In 1973 Means helped lead AIM's most dramatic action—the seizure of the trading post on the Sioux reservation in Wounded Knee, South Dakota. Here in 1890, U.S. cavalry units had killed more than 300 Sioux. For 71 days AIM members and U.S. marshals engaged in a grim standoff. Finally, after two people had been killed and one wounded, the government agreed to consider AIM's grievances, and the siege came to an end.

While AIM's confrontational tactics captured headlines and television attention, other American Indian leaders worked to renew tribal life by quieter means, including court action. The Taos Pueblo Indians of New Mexico recovered 48,000 acres of land, including the sacred Blue Lake. American Indians in Maine, claiming that more than half of the state had been illegally taken from them, won from Congress an $81.5 million award and the right to purchase up to 300,000 acres. Tribal groups in Alaska, South Dakota, Washington, and elsewhere either regained ancient lands or received large payments from the government for lands illegally taken from them. These cases were handled by the Indians Claims Commission, a federal agency set up in 1946.

American Indians also benefited from a 1961 federal law designed to encourage economic development on reservations. Under this law, many tribes established a variety of business ventures, such as factories, processing plants, and resorts. Some of the income from these businesses went to improve conditions on reservations. Tribal schools and colleges, for example, improved as a result of the new prosperity.

◄ The lumber mill and power project depicted in these photographs are among the many businesses established by American Indian tribes.

Reflecting growing pride among American Indians, the number of persons who identified themselves as Indian to federal census-takers surged from fewer than 800,000 in 1970 to nearly 2 million in 1990. Despite the gains, however, American Indians remained among the poorest of citizens and continued to grapple with many social problems.

■■ **During the 1970s Indian leaders worked to improve conditions for American Indians and to regain tribal lands.**

𝒯HE WOMEN'S MOVEMENT GAINS MOMENTUM

The women's movement made many advances in the 1970s as leaders worked to shape public policy and elect more women to public office. Many all-male colleges opened their doors to women, while other universities instituted courses in women's studies. In 1972 Congress passed the **Education Amendments Act**, which outlawed sexual discrimination in higher education.

The following year, the Supreme Court handed down a landmark decision affecting women. In the case ***Roe v. Wade***, the Court overturned a state law limiting women's access to abortion. The Court ruled that a woman and her doctor, not the state, should make such decisions. While most feminists hailed *Roe* v. *Wade* as a victory, opponents protested that the ruling violated the right to life of the unborn.

The 1970s also saw a major battle over the **Equal Rights Amendment** (ERA), the proposed constitutional amendment barring discrimination on the basis of sex (see Chapter 21). The ERA received strong support from the National Organization for Women (NOW) and other women's groups. In testimony before Congress, feminist leader Gloria Steinem asserted:

❝ Women suffer second-class treatment from the moment they are born. They are expected to *be* rather than achieve, to function biologically rather than learn. A brother, whatever his intellect, is more likely to get the family's encouragement and education money, while girls are often pressured to conceal ambition and intelligence. ❞

Congress passed the ERA in 1972, but the amendment still required the approval of at least 38 states. At first, ratification seemed certain, but by

▼ During a news conference, National Women's Political Caucus leaders Gloria Steinem, Bella Abzug, Shirley Chisholm, and Betty Friedan announced their goal to increase the number of women delegates to the 1972 presidential conventions.

Chapter 31
SECTION 4

Practice

GUIDED PRACTICE

Begin a word web by writing *Social Change in the 1970s* in the center of the chalkboard and drawing a circle around it. Draw lines emanating from the circle. Have students add the significant social changes of the 1970s to the end of each line.

INDEPENDENT PRACTICE

Instruct students to select a topic from the word web developed in the Guided Practice activity and to write a paragraph summarizing that change from the perspective of a person who experienced it. Students may wish to include their summaries in their portfolios.

Review and Assessment

REVIEW Have students use the Essential Points of the section to write a paragraph explaining how the civil rights successes of one group may affect other groups. Then assign the Section 4 Review on p. 923.

ASSESS Assign the **Section 4 Daily Quiz** in *Core Resources.*

VOICES IN HISTORY

Some American Indian women were among those who felt that the leaders of NOW did not represent their views. Lorelei DeCora Means, a Winnebago/Minneconjou Lakota activist, explained: "We are *American Indian* women, in that order. We are oppressed, first and foremost, as American Indians, as peoples colonized by the United States of America, *not* as women. . . . We tend to view those who come to us wanting to form alliances on the basis of . . . 'more important' issues to be a little less than friends, especially since most of them come from the Euroamerican population which benefits most directly from our ongoing colonization."

AV TRANSPARENCY

Linking Geography and History Transparency and Worksheet 13B

922

◄ Phyllis Schlafly was one of the most vocal critics of the ERA during the 1970s and the 1980s.

the 1982 deadline set by Congress, the ERA was still three states short of ratification. As a result, it failed to become law.

The women's movement made many political gains; however, it also alienated many women who viewed it as a movement primarily for privileged white women. Many women from working-class and ethnic communities felt that the leaders of NOW could not identify with the problems they faced every day.

The movement also alienated many middle-class women who felt that it downgraded the family and condemned women who chose to be full-time homemakers. These women viewed *Roe* v. *Wade* and the ERA as threats to traditional family life. Critics warned that the ERA would "nullify any laws that make any distinction between men and women." Eventually, they claimed, men and women would even be forced to share public restrooms! When the ERA failed to win ratification, conservative critic Phyllis Schlafly proclaimed: "The defeat of the Equal Rights Amendment is the greatest victory for women's rights since the woman's suffrage movement of 1920."

▪▪ The women's movement was encouraged by legislation such as the ERA, but the issues alienated many women from the movement.

A CHANGING POPULATION

As different groups in American society worked for change, the society itself was evolving. Thanks to medical advances, Americans were living longer, a phenomenon referred to as the "graying of America." At the same time, the birthrate was dropping sharply, to an average of two births per woman. For years, experts had been promoting this level of **zero population growth** (ZPG)—a birthrate that replaces the existing population but does not increase it—in hopes of preventing overpopulation.

The divorce rate continued to rise during the 1970s. In 1979, 5.3 divorces were registered per 1,000 Americans, up from 2.2 in 1960. Increasingly, many Americans were abandoning the idea that marriage was necessarily a lifelong commitment.

Americans also moved more often in the 1970s than in the past. During the decade a growing number of Americans migrated from the North and the East to the **Sunbelt** states of the South and the West, seeking a warmer climate and a more suburban life-style. This migration caused the population growth of California, Texas, and Florida to outpace that of the rest of the nation.

Another key factor in America's evolution during this period was continued immigration, mostly from Asia and Latin America. Most Latin American immigrants came from Mexico, but a sizable number also came from the Caribbean. In 1980, for example, nearly 120,000 Cubans fled the

▲ Many multigenerational Asian families, such as the one pictured here, immigrated to the United States in the 1970s.

922 ▪▪ CHAPTER 31

RETEACH Organize students into small groups and assign each a subsection of the section. Tell each group to compose a poem, song, or rap that expresses the theme of its subsection. Have each group perform its composition.

Closure

Ask students to explain why this section is titled "A Decade of Social Change." Ask them to give examples from the text to support their explanations.

Extension

SYNTHESIZE Have students research the controversy surrounding the passage of the Bilingual Education Act of 1974 and write a paper that synthesizes the controversy's issues.

ANALYZE Have students write an essay analyzing why busing was seen as a natural extension of the 1954 Supreme Court ruling in *Brown* v. *Board of Education*.

Communist island for the United States, settling mainly in the Miami area. Economically successful, Cuban Americans became an important interest group in American politics.

Of the 1.6 million immigrants from Asia in the 1970s, most came from the Philippines and South Korea. China, which opened the way for emigration after President Nixon's visit, supplied some of the new Asian population as well. Many of these Chinese immigrants were highly skilled and well-educated professionals fleeing political persecution. Despite their backgrounds, however, some of these immigrants found when they arrived that their inability to speak English, as well as discrimination, kept them from obtaining well-paying jobs. The experiences of Wei-Chi Poon, a biology professor from China, and her husband, a skilled architect, were not unique. Neither knew any English when they immigrated to the United States. As a result, she worked in a laundry for $1.85 an hour, while he took on two low-paying jobs.

Congress tried to aid such immigrants by passing two new laws. The **Voting Rights Act of 1975** required states and communities with large numbers of non-English speakers to print voting materials in various foreign languages. The **Bilingual Education Act** of 1974 encouraged public schools to provide instruction to students in their

▲ The Bilingual Education Act of 1974 encouraged public schools, such as the one shown here, to provide students with instruction in their primary languages while they learned English.

primary languages while they learned English. Although some critics opposed bilingual education—charging that it slowed the assimilation of immigrants into American life—there was little question that the United States was becoming an increasingly multicultural society. Coping with new immigrants, both legal and illegal, would remain an important issue for America.

■■ **Large-scale Asian and Latin American immigration during the 1970s prompted support for bilingual education.**

SECTION 4 REVIEW

IDENTIFY and explain the significance of the following: Patricia Harris, League of United Latin American Citizens, Rehabilitation Act, Education for All Handicapped Children Act, affirmative action, *University of California v. Bakke*, Russell Means, Education Amendments Act, *Roe v. Wade*, Equal Rights Amendment, zero population growth, Sunbelt, Voting Rights Act of 1975, Bilingual Education Act.

1. **MAIN IDEA** Why did American Indians begin to organize during this period?

2. **MAIN IDEA** What influence did the Asian and Latin American immigrants in the 1970s have on American society?

3. **IDENTIFYING CAUSE AND EFFECT** How did the impact of the civil rights movement continue into the 1970s? How did some whites respond to this legacy?

4. **WRITING TO EXPRESS A VIEWPOINT** Imagine you are a political observer of the women's movement. Write an essay that summarizes the impact of *Roe v. Wade* and the ERA on the movement.

5. **LINKING HISTORY AND GEOGRAPHY** Why did many Americans move to the Sunbelt states during the 1970s? What effect did this migration have on population patterns?

9. Native American activist and AIM leader
10. Supreme Court decision overturning state law limiting access to abortion

UNDERSTANDING MAIN IDEAS
1. domestic—followed conservative agenda on law-and-order issues, civil rights, economy; foreign—initiated realpolitik policy, détente with Soviet Union and opening to China
2. illegal activities by Nixon administration to ruin enemies and win reelection; led to Nixon's resignation and eroded public trust in government

3. domestic—conflicts over social welfare programs, inflation; foreign—relations with Soviet Union, Mayaguez incident
4. abandoned pomp and ceremony of previous presidents, adopted folksy style, held public forums to keep in touch with people; lack of political experience and failure to resolve economy, energy crisis, and Iran hostage crisis
5. increased political participation and legislation concerning special issues, provided new opportunities through affirmative action programs; concerns that civil rights reform deprived whites of their own rights

Chapter Review Answers

WRITING A SUMMARY
See Essential Points in each section for main ideas.

REVIEWING CHRONOLOGY
2, 3, 1, 4, 5
Evaluating
increased Soviet-American tensions, cut oil supplies to U.S., involved U.S. in the region's search for solutions

IDENTIFYING PEOPLE AND IDEAS
1. middle-class voters weary from social upheaval of 1960s
2. measure setting air quality standards and emissions guidelines for car manufacturers
3. Socialist president of Chile overthrown with U.S. help
4. series of events on October 20, 1973, that increased calls to impeach Nixon
5. congresswoman who gave keynote address at Democratic convention in 1976
6. policy of racial segregation in South Africa
7. Egyptian president who participated in Camp David Accords
8. 1973 act that forbade discrimination in jobs, education, or housing because of physical disabilities

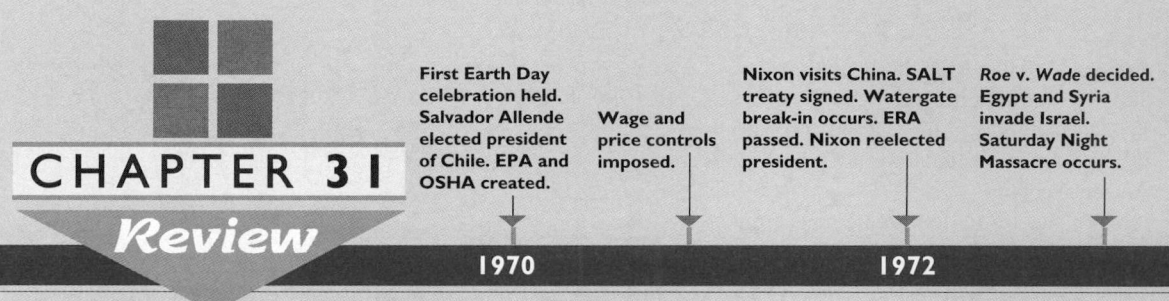

CHAPTER 31
Review

First Earth Day celebration held. Salvador Allende elected president of Chile. EPA and OSHA created.	Wage and price controls imposed.	Nixon visits China. SALT treaty signed. Watergate break-in occurs. ERA passed. Nixon reelected president.	Roe v. Wade decided. Egypt and Syria invade Israel. Saturday Night Massacre occurs.

1970 **1972**

WRITING A SUMMARY
Using the essential points of the chapter as a guide, write a summary of the chapter.

REVIEWING CHRONOLOGY
Number your paper 1 to 5. Study the time line above, and list the following events in the order in which they happened by writing the first next to 1, the second next to 2, and so on. Then complete the activity below.

1. Bilingual Education Act passed.
2. First Earth Day celebration held.
3. Watergate break-in occurs.
4. Panama Canal treaties ratified.
5. Iran hostage crisis begins.

Evaluating How did the Arab-Israeli war affect the United States?

IDENTIFYING PEOPLE AND IDEAS
Explain the historical significance of each of the following people or terms.

1. silent majority
2. Clean Air Act
3. Salvador Allende
4. Saturday Night Massacre
5. Barbara Jordan
6. apartheid
7. Anwar Sadat
8. Rehabilitation Act
9. Russell Means
10. Roe v. Wade

UNDERSTANDING MAIN IDEAS
1. How did Nixon's domestic and foreign policies differ from those of his predecessors?
2. What was the origin of the Watergate scandal? What long-term effects did this scandal have on the United States?
3. What domestic and foreign problems did Ford face during his administration?
4. How did Carter attempt to keep his pledge of an "open administration"? Why did he fail to win reelection in 1980?
5. How did the expansion of the civil rights movement during the 1970s affect ethnic groups, women, and people with disabilities? What caused white backlash during this period?

REVIEWING THEMES
1. **Economic Development** How did U.S. dependence on foreign oil affect the economy?
2. **Global Relations** What effect did Nixon's visit to China have on U.S.–Soviet relations?
3. **Constitutional Heritage** Why did Nixon refuse to turn over his White House tapes to the Justice Department? How did his refusal challenge the basis of constitutional government?

THINKING CRITICALLY
1. **Analyzing** What steps did the government take during the 1970s to clean up the environment?
2. **Synthesizing** What domestic and foreign policy actions by Nixon interfered with democratic rights?
3. **Evaluating** Do you think a government is justified in basing a policy of foreign affairs on the principle of human rights? Explain your answer.

WRITING ABOUT HISTORY
Writing to Create Imagine you are a member of the environmental movement. Design a poster for the first Earth Day celebration that illustrates your concerns about the environment.

STRATEGY FOR SUCCESS
Review the Strategies for Success on Conducting an Interview on page 894. Imagine you are a reporter covering the Camp David Accords during 1978. Prepare a list of three questions to use in conducting an interview with either Anwar Sadat or Menachem Begin.

Sadat, Carter, and Begin signing the Camp David Accords, 1978

1. Cost of oil fueled inflation and drove up prices of gasoline, heating oil, and electricity; embargo sparked energy crisis, led to concerns over environment, and increased government funding for alternative energy sources.

2. gave Nixon leverage to negotiate SALT treaty, enter into détente

3. because of belief in "executive privilege" and claim that their release would endanger national security; set presidency above law and balance of powers

THINKING CRITICALLY

1. created EPA to enforce environmental laws and OSHA to protect health of workers, passed Clean Air Act and Water Quality Improvement Act, increased support for alternative energy sources

2. domestic—"dirty tricks" campaign, Watergate break-in, refusal to release White House tapes, Saturday Night Massacre; foreign—overthrow of Allende government in Chile

3. Students should balance benefits of basing a foreign policy on moral issues with concerns that such a policy would provoke resentment in other countries and increase world tensions.

WRITING ABOUT HISTORY

Posters will vary but should express concerns over the environmental issue selected.

STRATEGY FOR SUCCESS

Students' lists will vary but might include questions similar to the following: What were your reasons for beginning negotiations? How does this treaty help your country? How do you think this treaty will be accepted by the people in your country?

USING PRIMARY SOURCES

that implementation of court-ordered busing is difficult and can lead to unwieldy transportation problems

LINKING HISTORY AND GEOGRAPHY

Nevada and Arizona; South and West

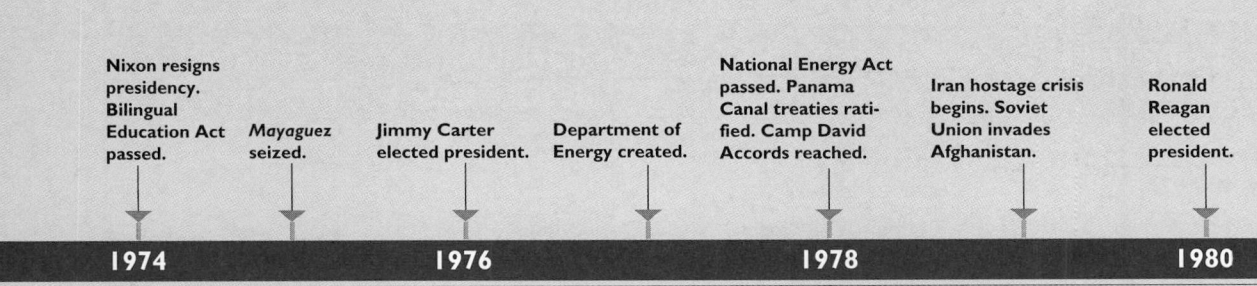

| Nixon resigns presidency. Bilingual Education Act passed. | Mayaguez seized. | Jimmy Carter elected president. | Department of Energy created. | National Energy Act passed. Panama Canal treaties ratified. Camp David Accords reached. | Iran hostage crisis begins. Soviet Union invades Afghanistan. | Ronald Reagan elected president. |

1974   1976   1978   1980

USING PRIMARY SOURCES

During the 1970s, court-ordered busing was seen as one way of overcoming racial segregation. Read the following excerpt from an account about the effect of busing on West Charlotte High School in Virginia. What is the message of this piece?

❝ The district judge . . . made it clear that he wanted socioeconomic integration as well as racial integration. . . .

We are presently operating under [a court] order which forbids any change in assignment of a lottery-chosen white student assigned to West Charlotte High even if his family moves away from the area in which he was chosen. This has resulted in some bizarre transportation problems. In one case, we had to assign a driver and bus to pick up one pupil whose family built a new home and moved to the far northerly end of the county, more than 25 miles from West Charlotte High School. ❞

Young antibusing protester

LINKING HISTORY AND GEOGRAPHY

Study the map in the next column, which shows population changes in the United States from 1970 to 1980. Which states had the greatest population growth? Which regions were most affected by population growth?

Percentage Increase in Population
- More than 50.0%
- 25.0%–50.0%
- 15.0%–24.9%
- 5.0%–14.9%
- Less than 5.0%
- Loss

BUILDING YOUR PORTFOLIO

Complete the following projects independently or cooperatively.

1. POLITICS Imagine you are a *Washington Post* reporter covering the Senate investigations into the Watergate affair. Write a short article outlining the constitutional issues involved in the Watergate break-in, cover-up, and news coverage.

2. THE ECONOMY Imagine you are an economist in the 1970s. Create a flow chart that shows how increases in oil prices overseas ultimately affect the cost of consumer goods in the United States.

3. GLOBAL RELATIONS Imagine you are a United Nations delegate from an emerging nation. Conduct an interview with the secretary-general on the role the United Nations should play in establishing a world balance of power amid Cold War conflicts.

BUILDING YOUR PORTFOLIO

Have students refer to **Building Your Portfolio Worksheet 9**, assigned at the beginning of Unit 9. Use the worksheet to help students monitor their progress on the portfolio projects.

Assessment

Core Resources
- Review Worksheet 31
- Chapter 31 Tests
- Alternative Assessment Forms

Test Generator

REAGAN, BUSH, AND CLINTON

1980–the Present

THE AMERICAN NATION
VIDEODISC PROGRAM
A variety of still images, short
videos, and activities are available for you
to use as you teach this chapter. See
Correlation to *The American Nation*
Videodisc Program for barcode correlations
and suggestions for using the program.

Chapter Overview

In the 1980s America elected conservative president Ronald Reagan, who supported cutting taxes and social programs in order to boost the economy. Although Reagan initially took a hard line against the Soviet Union, he welcomed the easing of tensions after Soviet reformer Mikhail Gorbachev came to power. In 1988 Reagan's vice president, George Bush, was elected president. Bush rose in popularity after the U.S. and its allies defeated Iraq in the Persian Gulf War. But lingering economic problems eroded his popularity and helped Democrat Bill Clinton win the 1992 election. Despite early-term setbacks, Clinton won reelection in 1996, the first Democratic president since Franklin Delano Roosevelt to win two terms.

Chapter Planning Guide

CHAPTER 32	CORE RESOURCE BOOKLETS	AUDIOVISUAL (AV) RESOURCES	PROGRAM RESOURCES
INTRODUCTION pp. 926–927	■ Literature Worksheet 32 ■ Building Your Portfolio Worksheet 9		
TEACHING THE CHAPTER pp. 928–951	■ Graphic Organizer 32 ■ Social Studies Skills Worksheet 32 ■ Geography Worksheet 32 ■ Outline Maps 1, 2, 8, 9, 12, 15, 17	■ *The American Nation* Videodisc: U.S. Troops in the Persian Gulf; A Nation of Immigrants; Early Computer Robot ■ Linking Geography and History Transparencies and Worksheets 11C, 13B, 22 ■ Everyday Life in America Transparency and Worksheet 32 ■ *American Civics Citizenship Skills* Videocassette or Videodisc	■ Art in American History Transparencies and Worksheets 47, 48, 49 ■ *Eyewitnesses and Others,* Volume 2: Readings 74, 75, 78
REVIEW AND ASSESSMENT pp. 952–953	■ Chapter 32 Daily Quizzes ■ Review Worksheet 32 ■ Chapter 32 Tests ■ Alternative Assessment Forms		■ Test Generator

Additional Resources

BOOKS FOR TEACHERS

Campbell, Colin, et al., eds. *The Bush Presidency.* Chatham House, 1991. A thoughtful collection of early assessments of Bush administration.

Wills, Garry. *Reagan's America.* Viking Penguin, 1988. Biography focusing on how Reagan's political philosophy took shape and influenced America.

BOOKS FOR STUDENTS

* Bratman, Fred. *War in the Persian Gulf.* Millbrook Press, 1991. Chronicles the Persian Gulf War.

* Bentley, P. F. *Clinton: Portrait of Victory.* Warner Books, 1993. Pictorial history of 1992 presidential election.

* for students reading below grade level

MULTIMEDIA MATERIALS

A Line in the Sand. Video, 50 min. ABC News/SSSS. Presents the background of the Iraqi invasion of Kuwait and looks at the role of oil in Middle East politics.

History of the 80s. 10 videos, 60 min. each. ABC News/SSSS. Each video documents a different year in the decade, focusing on both foreign and domestic issues.

THEMES IN AMERICAN HISTORY

USE WITH PAGES 926–927

*L*isted on the right are the themes emphasized in Chapter 32. The questions in boldface type stimulate critical thinking and provide students with an opportunity to discuss the themes within a broadened context. The questions also appear in the pupil's edition on p. 926.

■ ECONOMIC DEVELOPMENT

What positive and negative effects might measures that cut taxes, social programs, and business regulations have on a nation's economy? Students might suggest that cuts in social programs could reduce government spending and that cuts in taxes and business regulations could stimulate the economy and provide more jobs. They might also note, however, that tax cuts might result in deficit spending. Regulatory cuts could allow business corruption, and social program cuts might lead to increases in crime, poverty, and other social problems.

■ DEMOCRATIC VALUES

How might the use of modern technology increase democratic participation in an election? Students might point out that radio, television, and computer-generated mass mailings could help inform voters about political issues. Communications technology, such as telephones, faxes, and voice mail, could allow voters greater contact with candidates.

CHAPTER STRATEGIES FOR MEETING INDIVIDUAL NEEDS

LIMITED ENGLISH PROFICIENT LEARNERS

Organize students into four groups. Have each group compile a list of the achievements and the failures of the Reagan, Bush, and Clinton presidencies. Have students share their lists.

TACTILE/KINESTHETIC LEARNERS

Organize students into groups to prepare a military briefing for the press—including maps—to show U.S. military operations in Operation Desert Storm.

LEARNERS HAVING DIFFICULTY

Organize students into groups to create posters, campaign slogans, or bumper stickers for the presidential campaigns discussed in this chapter.

AUDITORY LEARNERS

Have students poll classmates, friends, and family members on the 10 most pressing problems of the 1990s. Have students compare answers and identify differences in responses based on age, gender, and race.

VISUAL LEARNERS

Have students create a design for an exhibit for the presidential library of Reagan, Bush, or Clinton. Exhibits should highlight events that took place during the administration chosen.

GIFTED LEARNERS

Have students write an essay comparing economic policies and attitudes toward business in the 1980s with such attitudes and policies in the late 1800s or in the 1920s.

USING THE CHAPTER FOCUS

■ UNDERSTANDING THE MAIN IDEA

Call on a volunteer to read aloud the Understanding the Main Idea paragraph. Then ask students why they think the economy is such an important issue for voters. Have students compare the problems troubling Americans in the 1980s and early 1990s to their concerns in the years following World War II.

THEMES

Have students work individually or in small groups to answer the questions under Themes. Save students' responses so that they can compare them with their responses after studying the chapter. (See p. 925B for suggested answers.)

■ THE TIME LINE

Have students list in their notebooks the names of the three presidents noted on the time line. Ask them to chart the domestic and foreign policies of each president as they read the chapter. At the close of the chapter, have students write summary statements on each president and how his policies affected Americans.

CORE RESOURCES

- **Graphic Organizer 32**
- **Social Studies Skills Worksheet 32**
- **Literature Worksheet 32**
- **Outline Maps 1, 2, 8, 9, 12, 15, 17**
- **Building Your Portfolio Worksheet 9**

926

ABOUT THE ILLUSTRATION

During the first day of the 100-hour ground campaign in the Persian Gulf War, the 101st Airborne Division launched the largest helicopter assault in history. The 101st was comprised of some 17,000 soldiers, of whom about 900 were women. The photograph shows U.S. soldiers dropped into combat positions from Black Hawk helicopters.

Have students speculate about the challenges of fighting a war on desert terrain. Suggest that they consider such factors as the effects of heat and sand on equipment and armaments, and problems of road building, camouflage, and visibility of supply lines.

Chapter 32

1980–the Present

REAGAN, BUSH, AND CLINTON

FOCUS

UNDERSTANDING THE MAIN IDEA

President Ronald Reagan entered office in 1981 with a series of conser-vative reforms for the economy and foreign relations. His vice president, George Bush, won the presidency in 1988. Plagued by economic and political problems, Bush lost to Democrat Bill Clinton in the 1992 election. Though initially troubled by political failures, Clinton presided over an economic resurgence and easily won reelection in 1996. As he prepared to lead the country up to the twenty-first century, Americans grappled with issues such as increased immigration, urban racial tensions, and the spread of AIDS.

THEMES

■ **ECONOMIC DEVELOPMENT** What positive and negative effects might measures that cut taxes, social programs, and business regulations have on a nation's economy?

■ **DEMOCRATIC VALUES** How might the use of modern technology increase democratic participation in an election?

1981	1984	1988	1991	1992	1994
Sandra Day O'Connor appointed to Supreme Court.	Ronald Reagan reelected president.	George Bush elected president.	Operation Desert Storm launched.	Bill Clinton elected president.	Republicans gained control of the House and Senate.

⬛▶ LINK TO THE PAST

Have students recall how the Iran hostage crisis and economic problems affected President Carter's bid for reelection. Tell students this chapter discusses the Reagan, Bush, and Clinton presidencies and the domestic and foreign-policy challenges that each administration faced.

▦ LINK TO THE PAST

Public frustration with government grew in the 1970s as the Watergate scandal broke, the energy crisis emerged, and the economy continued to weaken. As a result, Democrat Jimmy Carter, who promised to reform government, was elected president. The Iran hostage crisis and runaway inflation, however, undermined his presidency, contributing to a Republican victory in the 1980 election.

HISTORICAL SIDELIGHTS
Late Bloomer
Ronald Reagan had not always been a conservative or a Republican. He voted four times for FDR for president and later said that he had been "a near-hopeless hemophilic liberal" during the New Deal era. He began to embrace conservative causes in the 1940s.

ntering the White House on a wave of discontent, Ronald Reagan promised to set the nation on a new course with lower taxes, fewer federal regulations, cuts in social programs, and increased military spending. A former Hollywood actor, Reagan was well suited for the television age. Often called "the Great Communicator," he projected a sense of confidence and patriotism that reassured Americans troubled by the nation's mounting economic problems and weakened world image. Television observer John Corry noted of Reagan: "His voice is his greatest weapon. It is not an orator's voice. It is husky, and sometimes it fades to a whisper. Meanwhile, it is extraordinarily intimate. Mr. Reagan does not speak to audiences; he speaks to individuals."

Reagan's vice president, George Bush, was elected president in 1988. Bush's greatest achievements were on the international front. Under his administration, the United States launched a successful invasion of Panama and played a primary role in crushing the Iraqi takeover of Kuwait. Bush's domestic record was less impressive, however. By the time he ran for reelection in 1992, the country was beset by an ailing economy and other domestic problems. In a campaign that saw the rise of independent candidate H. Ross Perot and an increased role for women, Bush lost to baby-boom Democrat Bill Clinton, who won reelection in 1996 pledging to "build a bridge to the twenty-first century."

Operation Desert Storm, 1991

President Bush visiting U.S. troops

PREVIEW WORKSHOP

Following is a list of the significant people, places, and terms in this section. You may wish to use this list as a section preview.

People
■ José Napoleón Duarte

■ Geraldine Ferraro
■ Sandra Day O'Connor
■ Oliver North

Places
■ Nicaragua
■ El Salvador
■ Grenada

Terms
■ New Right
■ Moral Majority
■ Reaganomics
■ Strategic Defense Initiative
■ Solidarity
■ Sandinistas
■ contras

■ Gramm-Rudman-Hollings Act
■ Tax Reform Law
■ insider trading
■ *glasnost*
■ *perestroika*
■ Intermediate-Range Nuclear Forces Treaty
■ Iran-contra affair

FOCUS OBJECTIVES

■ Explain Reaganomics and describe how it affected the country.

■ Analyze why the Reagan administration considered events in Nicaragua and El Salvador to be important.

■ Identify the economic problems that plagued the country during the late 1980s.

■ Describe the Iran-contra affair.

Section 1

THE REAGAN MOVEMENT

F O C U S

■ **What was Reaganomics? How did it affect the country?**

■ **Why did the Reagan administration consider events in Nicaragua and El Salvador important?**

■ **What economic problems plagued the country during the late 1980s?**

■ **What was the Iran-contra affair?**

*R*onald Reagan's 1980 presidential victory reflected the growing conservative mood of the nation. Adopting Reagan's programs, Congress cut taxes and reduced federal regulation of the economy. As a result, the economy boomed in the mid-1980s. Toward the end of the decade, however, political scandals and a soaring federal deficit troubled the nation.

President Ronald Reagan with his wife, Nancy

CORE RESOURCES

• **Geography Worksheet 32**
• **Section 1 Daily Quiz**

AV RESOURCES

• **Linking Geography and History Transparency** and **Worksheet 22**

THE NEW RIGHT

A former Democrat turned conservative Republican, Ronald Reagan appealed to a wide range of voters who were disenchanted with liberal politics. Reagan's strongest support, however, came from the political conservatives of the **New Right**. At the forefront of the New Right was Reverend Jerry Falwell's **Moral Majority**—a fundamentalist Christian organization founded in 1978.

◀ **The Reverend Jerry Falwell's Moral Majority encouraged churchgoers to register to vote and support conservative causes.**

President Reagan and the New Right shared the same political goals. Both supported school prayer, a strong defense, and free-market economic policies. Both opposed abortion, the Equal Rights Amendment, gun control, and busing to achieve racial balance in schools.

In addition to helping elect Reagan president, New Right conservatives were largely responsible for the Republicans gaining control of the Senate in 1980. They also played a significant role in shaping Republican policy throughout the decade. Although Jerry Falwell disbanded the Moral Majority in the late 1980s, New Right conservatives continued to exert a strong influence in the Republican party.

REAGANOMICS IN ACTION

President Reagan entered office with a comprehensive economic program already mapped out. This plan, dubbed **Reaganomics**, was based on the

Teaching the Section

REAGANOMICS

Organize students into six groups. Assign half the groups the role of Reagan supporters and the remaining groups the role of Reagan critics. Have all groups prepare a cost/benefit analysis of Reaganomics. Next to each cost and each benefit have groups indicate who might have been hurt and who might have benefited by these changes.

Then convene a panel of representatives from all the groups to conduct a "Crossfire" roundtable debate on Reaganomics. Have the remainder of the class act as the audience, challenging and asking questions about the positions of panel members.

supply-side economics argument that lowering the top income tax rates would spur economic growth. Supporters of Reaganomics claimed that people would invest their tax savings in businesses, thereby creating jobs, increasing consumer spending, and generating higher tax revenues. Congress responded to Reagan's program by passing a three-year plan to cut federal income taxes by 25 percent.

Congress also supported another part of Reagan's economic plan—drastic cuts in government regulation of industries such as television, trucking, airlines, and banking. The Reagan administration's probusiness, antiregulation stance was typified by the Department of Interior's handling of public lands. Against the objections of environmentalists, Secretary of the Interior James Watt leased huge areas of the seafloor to private companies searching for oil and gas. He also leased federal lands to coal companies.

At first, Reaganomics seemed to work. By 1983 the inflation rate had dropped to a manageable 4 percent. Americans went on a shopping spree similar to those in the 1920s and 1950s. Business revived, the stock market soared, and the future looked bright.

Critics were quick to point out that not all Americans benefited equally from the recovery. Deep cuts in social programs—an important element in Reaganomics—hurt the poor. And although employment rose overall, joblessness remained high among African Americans and Hispanic

Americans, especially unskilled workers in the inner cities. Unemployment among factory workers in the Midwest, once America's industrial heartland, also remained high. As a result, homelessness increased dramatically.

Critics also charged that Reagan's tax cuts favored the wealthy and that spending cuts and deregulation weakened programs that protected consumers, the needy, and the environment. They also warned that big tax cuts combined with increased military spending (another important element of Reaganomics) would produce enormous deficits in the federal budget.

■■ Reaganomics stimulated the economy by cutting taxes and industrial regulations, but critics claimed the policies hurt the poor and increased the federal deficit.

*R*EAGAN AND THE COLD WAR

The Reagan administration's emphasis on increased military spending was in part a reflection of Ronald Reagan's strong anti-Communist views. He took a hard line against the Soviet Union, even branding it an "evil empire." To counter the Soviet threat, Reagan called for new weapons systems and an increased U.S. presence in such areas as the Indian Ocean and the Persian Gulf.

HISTORICAL SIDELIGHTS
Cuts Affect Poor
The cuts in social programs fell most heavily on the poor. Some of the deepest cuts were in programs such as food stamps, child nutrition, job training, Aid to Families with Dependent Children (AFDC), public service jobs, and low-income housing. A half-million working female heads of households lost child assistance benefits, while 70 percent of the savings in the food stamp programs came from cuts to families already living below the poverty line.

VOICES IN HISTORY

Many of Reagan's policies disturbed African American leaders. These policies included Reagan's support of tax-exempt status for segregated private schools, his initial refusal to endorse the extension of the 1965 Voting Rights Act, the Justice Department's opposition to affirmative action programs, and the administration's attempt to weaken the Civil Rights Commission. Taken together, these actions led the National Urban League to characterize the Reagan presidency as "the most hostile administration in the last 50 years."

PRESIDENTIAL LIVES

RONALD REAGAN
1911–

in office
1981–1989

One of Reagan's political gifts was a sharp wit. After his first debate with Jimmy Carter in the 1980 election, a reporter asked if he had been nervous appearing on stage with the president. "No, not at all," Reagan replied, then referred to his past career as an actor: "I've been on the same stage with John Wayne."

Reagan's wit helped reassure the nation after a lone gunman shot him on

March 30, 1981. As the wounded president was wheeled into the operating room, he looked around at the surgeons and quipped, "Please assure me that you are all Republicans!" While he was recuperating in intensive care, Reagan sent several humorous notes to his staff members, including one that read, "If I had had this much attention in Hollywood, I'd have stayed there!"

Ronald Reagan

REAGAN AND THE COLD WAR

Pair students and ask them to write several sentences explaining how each of these events affected U.S.–Soviet relations: Soviets refuse to withdraw troops from Afghanistan; Reagan calls for SDI; Soviet-backed Polish government closes down Solidarity; Korean airliner is shot down over Soviet air space; U.S. sends nuclear weapons to England and Germany; Soviets boycott 1984 Olympics. Then have each pair choose one event and create two editorial cartoons that show how the event might have been viewed by the Reagan administration and by Soviet leaders. Have volunteer pairs interpret their cartoons for the class.

HISTORICAL SIDELIGHTS

Star Wars

Director George Lucas's 1977 high-tech space fantasy *Star Wars* provided some popular phrases for Reagan as well as for his critics. The film's villain Darth Vader ruled the "evil empire," a phrase Reagan used to describe the Soviet Union.

Critics of the president's Strategic Defense Initiative believed it to be as much a fantasy as was the movie. Some scientists called SDI impractical and costly, and doubted its feasibility, arguing that some attacking missiles would always get through the space-based shield. They also predicted that its computers would fail and its rockets misfire. By 1988 this criticism had convinced Congress to drastically cut SDI's funding. Despite the criticism, some scholars argue that SDI had one unexpected, positive consequence: Fear of SDI's potential made the Soviets more willing to take part in disarmament talks.

PRIMARY SOURCE

Description of Change: excerpted
Rationale: excerpted to focus on main idea

New weapons. From 1981 to 1985 the Pentagon's budget grew from some $150 billion to about $250 billion. Much of the money went to fund nuclear weapons. Reagan's first secretary of state, Alexander Haig, suggested that "nuclear warning shots" might be useful in a conventional war.

The talk of nuclear war stirred public fear. In town meetings and state referendums, voters urged a freeze on the testing and deployment of nuclear weapons. Many Americans marched in rallies to show their support for the proposals.

To blunt the nuclear-freeze movement, Reagan proposed the **Strategic Defense Initiative** (SDI), a space-based missile-defense system, in March 1983. SDI quickly stirred controversy. Critics labeled it "Star Wars," after the popular 1977 movie, saying it rested on untested technology and was probably unworkable. They also warned that SDI research would intensify the arms race. Reagan countered that SDI would be a weapon for peace—one that killed weapons, not people. In a national address he proclaimed:

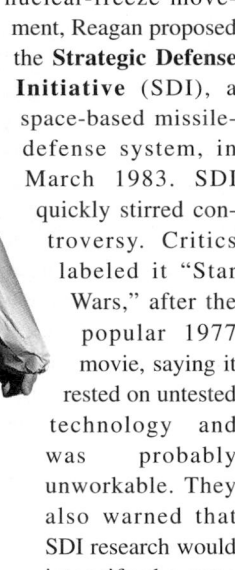

▲ In Boston in 1979 this woman protests the use of nuclear power.

> 66 I call upon the scientific community in our country, those who gave us nuclear weapons, to turn their great talents now to the cause of mankind and world peace: to give us the means of rendering these nuclear weapons impotent and obsolete. 99

U.S.–Soviet relations. Even before President Reagan took office, U.S.–Soviet relations had cooled because of the Soviet Union's 1979 invasion of Afghanistan (see map on page 905). Relations deteriorated further when, in August 1980, Polish workers in Gdansk and Szczecin (SHCHET-seen) staged a series of massive

▲ Many Americans, particularly those of Polish descent, supported the Solidarity movement. These Boston residents marched to show their support.

strikes to protest high prices and to demand the right to form trade unions free from government or Communist party control. At first, things went well for the strikers. In late August, faced with the threat of a nationwide general strike, the Polish government legalized independent union activity. Labor activists responded by voting on September 17 to form the independent trade union **Solidarity**, under the leadership of Lech Walesa (vah-LEN-suh), an electrician at a Gdansk shipyard who had helped launch the initial strikes.

Then, in December 1981, the Soviet-backed government changed its stand and instituted martial law. Government troops shut down Solidarity centers and arrested union leaders. Expecting resistance, Soviet troops prepared to brutally "restore order" as they had in Hungary in 1956 and in Czechoslovakia in 1968. Warning the Soviet Union not to invade Poland, Reagan called for new trade restrictions against the Soviets. Moscow heeded the warning and stayed out of Poland.

Tensions flared again in 1983. On September 30, the Soviets shot down a Korean airliner over Soviet airspace, killing all 269 passengers, including many Americans. Despite international outcries, the Soviets defended their action, claiming the plane had been spying. Later that year, when the United States sent new nuclear missiles to England and Germany, the Soviets walked out of arms-control talks. When the Soviets boycotted the 1984 Summer Olympics in Los Angeles, relations between the two superpowers sank to their lowest point in years.

REAGAN AND LATIN AMERICA

Tell students to imagine that the Senate Foreign Relations Committee will recommend whether to appropriate funds to support the president's policies in Central America. Assign a group to role-play the committee and other groups to represent the Reagan administration, U.S. opposition groups, the governments of Nicaragua and El Salvador, and the insurgents in each nation. Each group should prepare a statement on the situation in one or both countries from its perspective, explaining why events there are or are not important to the U.S. Then have a member of each group testify, the "committee" make a recommendation, and the class vote on funding Reagan's Central American policies. Call on students to explain their votes.

▶

REAGAN AND LATIN AMERICA

Fearing that the developing nations of Latin America would fall under the influence of the Soviet Union, President Reagan increased U.S. involvement in the region, particularly the Central American countries of Nicaragua and El Salvador.

In 1979, Nicaraguan rebels known as **Sandinistas** had overthrown the dictatorship of Anastasio Somoza Debayle, whose family had ruled Nicaragua since the 1930s. Soon after Reagan took office, he cut all U.S. aid to Nicaragua on the grounds that the Sandinistas were backed by the Soviet bloc. He also charged that the Sandinistas were exporting revolution by shipping Cuban and Soviet weapons to rebels in El Salvador. The Sandinistas reacted to U.S. pressure by strengthening their ties to the Soviet bloc. Reagan then decided to support the Nicaraguan **contras**, a large army recruited, financed, and armed by the CIA. Hoping the revolutionary group would overthrow the Sandinista government, Reagan called the contras "freedom fighters" and compared them to the founders of the United States.

Many Americans opposed the CIA-sponsored war against the Sandinistas, fearing another Vietnam in Central America. Reflecting such concerns, Congress began restricting funds for the contras late in 1984. But, as the nation would soon learn, the White House continued to finance the contras despite the congressional ban, using funds secretly contributed by wealthy supporters and foreign governments.

The Reagan administration also found itself pulled into events in El Salvador. In 1979 a group of young military officers seized power in the country, instituting a brutally repressive government. The army and special death squads killed and tortured opposition leaders. Soon fighting erupted between

HISTORICAL SIDELIGHTS
Solidarity
In the early 1980s, after Solidarity's leaders were imprisoned and martial law was imposed on Poland, the union movement went underground. It emerged again in 1989, when the government sanctioned its existence and allowed it to campaign for political power in the nation's freest elections since 1945. The next year Walesa became Poland's president.

GLOBAL CONNECTIONS
Opposition to Reagan's Central American policy came from the closest Latin American neighbor to the U.S. In June 1983 Mexican writer Carlos Fuentes, speaking at Harvard's commencement, admonished the U.S.: "Because we are your true friends, we will not permit you to conduct yourselves in Latin American affairs as the Soviet Union conducts itself in Central European and Central Asian affairs."

Map Caption Answer
Grenada, Panama, Honduras, El Salvador

Central America and the Caribbean, 1980s

SPREAD OF COMMUNISM The domino theory influenced Reagan's policy in Latin America.

? LOCATION Which countries did the United States invade or send troops to during the 1980s?

1986: Duvalier is ousted; political instability follows.

1980–1992: Civil war between U.S.-backed Salvadoran government and leftist guerrillas supported by Cuba and Nicaragua.

1981–1987: United States aids the anti-Sandinista Contras in Nicaragua; civil war ends in 1990.

Communist country

⚘ Guerrilla activity or civil war

👤 U.S. military presence or intervention

ECONOMIC PROBLEMS

Work with the class to develop a list on the chalkboard of the economic problems facing the U.S. in the late 1980s. (*huge budget deficits, insider trading, stock market crash, failure of S & Ls and banks*) Have volunteers explain why each was a serious economic problem. Then ask students to assess whether or not Reaganomics contributed to these problems and to explain why or why not.

▲ The surrender of the Nicaraguan National Guard to the Sandinistas in July 1979 marked the end of the Somoza regime. Citizens celebrated the rebel victory by dragging a statue of Somoza through the streets of downtown Managua.

government forces and rebels demanding radical reform.

In 1984, José Napoleón Duarte, a moderate, won election by promising reforms and an end to the civil war. Eager to prevent a rebel victory that might allow El Salvador to fall under Soviet influence, the Reagan administration offered Duarte military and economic aid and sent advisers to train government troops. The civil war raged on, however, until intense international pressure forced both sides to sign a peace treaty in 1992.

■■ **Central America, especially Nicaragua and El Salvador, became a flashpoint in the struggle between the United States and the Soviet Union.**

*R*EAGAN REELECTED

Despite criticisms of his policies, President Reagan remained popular. His emphasis on patriotism and national pride struck a responsive chord with many Americans. While Carter was haunted by his failures and setbacks, the public seemed quick to forgive and forget any mishaps or scandals in Reagan's administration.

Adding to Reagan's popularity was a small-scale military action in 1983. On the tiny Caribbean island of Grenada, a military group overthrew the government and killed the prime minister. Several Caribbean nations requested U.S. intervention. On October 25, 1983, some 2,000 U.S. Marines and

Army Rangers went ashore on Grenada, unseated the coup leaders, and set up a government favorable to the United States.

Soon after the Grenada invasion, Reagan announced that he would seek a second term in 1984, with George Bush again as his running mate. Former vice president Walter Mondale won the Democratic nomination. He picked Congresswoman Geraldine Ferraro of New York as his running mate. Ferraro thus became the first woman to run on a major party presidential ticket. Some predicted Ferraro's presence would increase support for the Democratic party among women.

Republicans had been taking steps to enhance the role of women in their party. Reagan appointed several women to high public offices, including Elizabeth Dole as secretary of transportation, Margaret Heckler as secretary of health and human services, and Jeane Kirkpatrick as head of the U.S. delegation to the United Nations—the first woman to hold the post. In 1981 Reagan had also appointed the first woman ever to serve on the Supreme Court—conservative justice Sandra Day O'Connor. Republicans also sought the support of women who felt abandoned by the feminist movement. The percentage of female delegates to the Republican convention increased from 24 percent in 1980 to 44 percent in 1984. In the end, Ferraro's presence did not add many votes for the Democrats. On election day, Reagan received 54.5 million popular votes to Mondale's 37.6 million. The Republicans swept the electoral vote, 525 to 13.

▼ The invasion of Grenada began in October 1983, when U.S. troops landed on the island.

COLD WAR THAW

Call students' attention to the photograph of Reagan and Gorbachev on p. 934. Have them write an imaginary memoir in which one of these men recalls his thoughts at the meeting. Call on students to read their memoirs to the class. Students may wish to include their memoirs in their portfolios.

THE IRAN-CONTRA AFFAIR

Pair students to develop graphic organizers that link the Reagan administration's foreign policies in Iran with its policies in Central America. Select pairs to explain their organizers to the class. Then ask students if they believe these activities were proper. Have students speculate about why the Iran-contra affair of the 1980s did not produce results similar to the Watergate scandal of the 1970s.

▶

SIGNS OF TROUBLE

One issue that arose during the election was the growing conservative emphasis of the Supreme Court. When Chief Justice Warren Burger retired in 1986, Reagan elevated Associate Justice William Rehnquist to chief justice. To fill Rehnquist's position, Reagan nominated conservative Antonin Scalia. When another justice retired in 1987, Reagan nominated Robert Bork, a federal judge and law professor who held a far narrower interpretation of the Bill of Rights than the Court had upheld in recent years.

Bork's views alarmed many people, including many senators. By a 58–42 vote, the Senate rejected Bork, handing Reagan a crushing loss. His next choice, Douglas Ginsberg, withdrew after press reports that he had smoked marijuana as a law professor. At last Reagan found a conservative judge who could also win Senate confirmation, Anthony Kennedy of California.

The failure of the Bork nomination was one of several signs that the "Reagan Revolution" was starting to weaken. Of special concern was the federal deficit, which had reached over $200 billion in 1985. Seeking to balance the budget with forced spending cuts, Congress passed the Balanced Budget and Emergency Control Act in 1985. Called the **Gramm-Rudman-Hollings Act** after its sponsors, the law required automatic across-the-board cuts in government spending when the deficit exceeded a certain amount. Other legislation took aim at specific problems. The **Tax Reform Law** of 1986, for example, wiped out many rules that gave certain groups special tax breaks.

The stock market also showed signs of trouble. Reagan's tax cuts and business deregulation had stimulated a stock market boom, but with this boom came a wave of illegal **insider trading**—the use of confidential financial information by stockbrokers for personal gain. Several large brokerage firms pleaded guilty to illegal activities and faced severe penalties. These scandals eroded investor trust in stockbrokers.

Then, on October 19, 1987, after several years of growth, the stock market crashed. On paper, stock losses totaled almost $1 trillion. The value of Eastman Kodak stock fell by more than 30 percent. Other major corporations experienced similar sharp drops in their stocks' values.

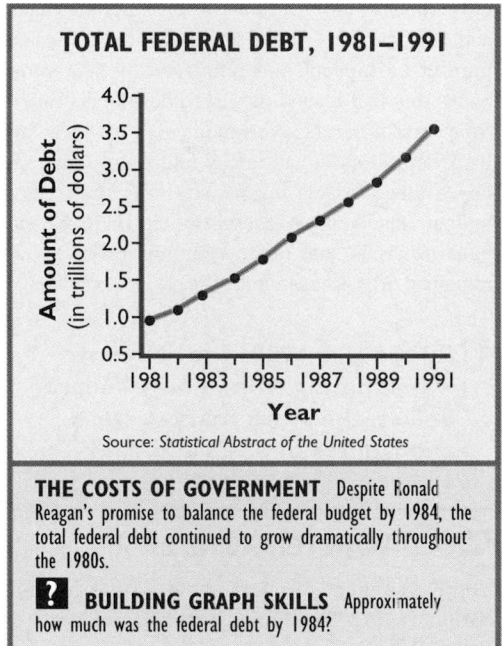

TOTAL FEDERAL DEBT, 1981–1991

Source: Statistical Abstract of the United States

THE COSTS OF GOVERNMENT Despite Ronald Reagan's promise to balance the federal budget by 1984, the total federal debt continued to grow dramatically throughout the 1980s.

❓ BUILDING GRAPH SKILLS Approximately how much was the federal debt by 1984?

In another sign of economic trouble, a crisis hit the nation's savings and loan (S&L) and banking industries in the late 1980s and early 1990s. Freed of federal regulation, banks and S&Ls, especially in the Southwest, had made risky loans to

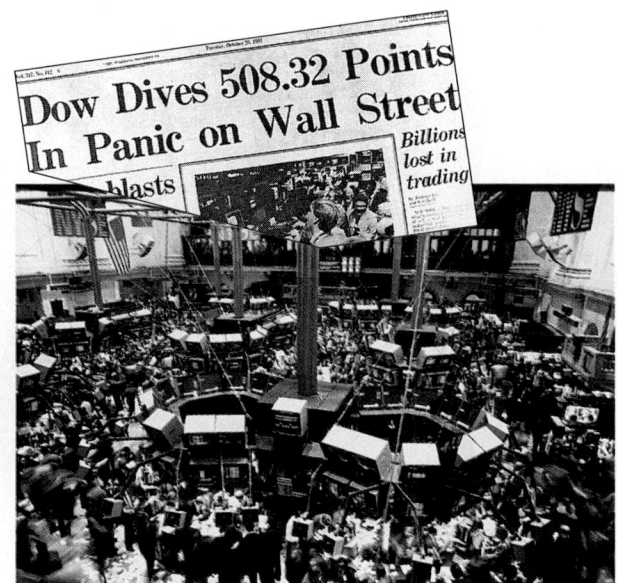

Dow Dives 508.32 Points In Panic on Wall Street

Billions lost in trading

▲ Investors lost billions of dollars during the stock market crash of October 1987. Shown here is the frantic scene on the floor of the New York Stock Exchange on the day of the crash, as traders tried to sell shares and cut losses.

HISTORICAL SIDELIGHTS
Tax Reform Law
The 1986 Tax Reform Law removed many low-income Americans from the tax rolls. It eliminated some tax deductions, such as those for most interest payments, reduced the amounts taxpayers could deduct for business entertainment, and cut back the benefits that corporations gained from tax credits and depreciation. However, the law also lowered the maximum income tax rate for wealthy Americans from 50 to 28 percent and lowered the tax rate for corporations.

HISTORICAL SIDELIGHTS
S&L Crisis
Deregulation gave the S&L industry greater freedom to invest depositors' funds in high-risk ventures and to make high-risk loans. Without the oversight of government regulators, some S&L officials mismanaged—or used for their own benefit—the savings of thousands of unsuspecting depositors. For example, a group of California S&L officials enjoyed the use of two $17 million jets on which they flew family and friends to condominiums bought with depositors' money.

Practice

GUIDED PRACTICE

Assume the role of a radio talk show host. Group students to represent big business owners, Republican and Democratic party workers, homeless people, immigrants from the Soviet Union, African Americans and Hispanic Americans, environmental groups, and industrial workers. Ask these Americans to "call in" to the talk show to give their opinions on the Reagan era. As students give their opinions, write their responses on the chalkboard.

INDEPENDENT PRACTICE

Have students pick an opinion of a talk show "caller" with whom they agreed or disagreed and write a letter to the radio station, either supporting or challenging the caller's opinion about the Reagan presidency.

Review and Assessment

REVIEW Have pairs of students create a "report card" for the Reagan years, giving the president foreign- and domestic-policy grades and including a paragraph about areas that need improvement or that are commendable. Select pairs to summarize their evaluations for the class. Then assign the Section 1 Review on p. 935.

ASSESS Assign the **Section 1 Daily Quiz** in *Core Resources*. ▶

 GLOBAL CONNECTIONS

After the summit between Reagan and Gorbachev, Gorbachev recalled how he asked Reagan if he still considered the Soviet Union the evil empire: "He [Reagan] said no, and he said that within the walls of the Kremlin . . . in the heart of the evil empire. We take note of that. As the ancient Greeks said, 'Everything flows, everything changes.'"

HISTORICAL SIDELIGHTS

Iran-contra Update

One month before leaving office, President Bush pardoned six former Reagan administration officials who had been charged or convicted in the Iran-contra scandal. The men faced such charges as perjury, obstructing congressional investigations, and withholding information from Congress. In giving the pardons, Bush said that "whether their actions were right or wrong," the six had acted from patriotism.

PRIMARY SOURCE

Description of Change: excerpted
Rationale: excerpted to focus on main idea

PRIMARY SOURCE

(for source on p. 935)
Description of Change: excerpted and bracketed
Rationale: excerpted to focus on main idea; bracketed to clarify meaning

---

developers to build office towers, shopping malls, and other projects. In the late 1980s the real-estate market collapsed, and hundreds of S&Ls and banks that had loaned money to developers failed. Since the federal government insures S&L and bank depositors, it had to pay billions of dollars to cover these losses, further straining the federal budget. The soaring federal deficit, the S&L and banking crisis, and other economic problems all remained after Reagan left office.

■■ **By the late 1980s the economy was suffering from a huge federal deficit, the stock market crash, and failures of S&Ls and banks.**

COLD WAR TENSIONS EASE

There was more to cheer about on the international front. The most significant event of Reagan's second term was a dramatic easing of Cold War hostilities. When Mikhail Gorbachev became leader of the Soviet Union in 1985, a new era of Soviet history began. With his nation burdened by a failing economy, a repressive political system, and heavy military costs, Gorbachev introduced a policy of openness, called *glasnost* (GLAZS-nuhst), that promised more freedom for

▲ On June 1, 1988, President Ronald Reagan and Soviet leader Mikhail Gorbachev embraced during a Moscow ceremony celebrating ratification of the INF Treaty.

the Soviet people. Equally dramatic was *perestroika* (per-uh-STROY-kuh)—Gorbachev's plan to restructure the Soviet economy and government. On the economic front, he called for increased foreign trade and reduced military spending. The revenues from these changes were to be used to modernize factories.

To further his domestic goals and defuse the costly Cold War conflict, Gorbachev pursued détente with the United States. In 1987, after a series of meetings between Gorbachev and President Reagan, the Soviet Union and the United States signed the **Intermediate-range Nuclear Forces** (INF) **Treaty**. This treaty eliminated all medium-range nuclear weapons from Europe. Gorbachev also withdrew Soviet troops from Afghanistan. Addressing the United Nations in 1988, Gorbachev said:

> 66 The use or threat of force no longer can or must be an instrument of foreign policy. . . . All of us, and primarily the stronger of us, must exercise self-restraint and totally rule out any outward-oriented use of force. 99

In May 1988, as the Senate prepared to ratify the INF Treaty, Reagan flew to Moscow. As television cameras whirred, the U.S. president and the Soviet leader embraced like old friends.

■■ **During Reagan's second term U.S.–Soviet relations improved dramatically as Gorbachev instituted *glasnost* and *perestroika*.**

THE IRAN-CONTRA AFFAIR

As relations with the Soviet Union improved, the Reagan administration continued to face problems in the Middle East and Latin America. These frustrations led to the most serious crisis to hit the Reagan White House—the **Iran-contra affair**.

After Congress cut off funds for the contras' war against Nicaragua's Sandinista government, the Reagan administration sought other sources of funding. At the time, the White House was secretly bargaining with Iran for the release of U.S. hostages held by pro-Iranian groups in Lebanon. As part of the bargain, the administration shipped more than 500 antitank missiles to

Iran by way of Israel. Without informing Congress, the administration used the profits from these arms sales to pay for weapons and supplies for the contras.

When the arms sales became known in 1986, Reagan appointed a committee to investigate. The committee cleared Reagan of any direct involvement but heavily criticized other White House officials, some of whom resigned. The secret funding of the contra war soon leaked out as well. It was revealed that Lieutenant Colonel Oliver North, a White House aide, had funneled millions of dollars from the Iranian arms sales to the contras after Congress had forbidden aid. In 1987, House and Senate committees investigated the affair. North admitted that he and his secretary, Fawn Hall, had destroyed key documents. But North emotionally insisted that he had acted out of loyalty and patriotism.

In its report the congressional committee denounced North's activities and criticized the loose White House management style that had allowed North to operate as he did. The chairman of the Senate committee, Senator Daniel Inouye of Hawaii, countered North's claim that he was just following orders. Said Inouye:

66 [The] colonel was well aware that he was subject to the Uniform Code of Military Justice. . . . And that code makes it abundantly clear that orders of a superior

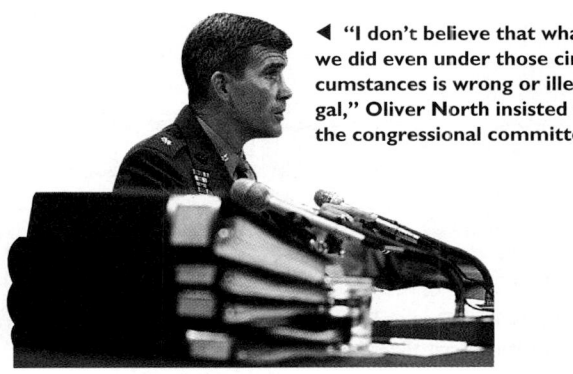

◀ **"I don't believe that what we did even under those circumstances is wrong or illegal,"** Oliver North insisted to the congressional committee.

officer must be obeyed by subordinate members—but it is lawful orders. . . . In fact, it says members of the military have an obligation to disobey unlawful orders. **99**

In 1988 a court-appointed special prosecutor filed criminal charges against North and President Reagan's national security adviser, Admiral John Poindexter. North was convicted on various charges, including the destruction of government documents and lying to Congress. The conviction was later reversed on a legal technicality.

■■ In the Iran-contra affair, White House aides provided illegal funding for the Nicaraguan contras through arms sales to Iran.

■■ **SECTION 1 REVIEW**

IDENTIFY and explain the significance of the following: New Right, Moral Majority, Reaganomics, Strategic Defense Initiative, Solidarity, Sandinistas, contras, José Napoleón Duarte, Geraldine Ferraro, Sandra Day O'Connor, Gramm-Rudman-Hollings Act, Tax Reform Law, insider trading, *glasnost, perestroika,* Intermediate-range Nuclear Forces Treaty, Iran-contra affair, Oliver North.

LOCATE and explain the importance of the following: Nicaragua, El Salvador, Grenada.

1. **MAIN IDEA** How did Reagan's economic policies both help and hurt the country?

2. **MAIN IDEA** What factors weakened the U.S. economy during the late 1980s?

3. **ANALYZING** Imagine you are a citizen of El Salvador in the early 1980s. Describe the political situation in your country and explain why you think the United States is intervening in your country's affairs.

4. **WRITING TO INFORM** Imagine you are a member of the congressional committee appointed to investigate the Iran-contra affair. Write a letter to your constituents that summarizes the results of the investigation.

5. **ASSESSING CONSEQUENCES** How did each political party try to appeal to women voters in the 1984 presidential election?

Chapter 32

SECTION 2

Introducing the Section

FOCUS OBJECTIVES

- Explain how Operation Desert Storm differed from previous American military conflicts.

- Identify some of the domestic problems President Bush faced.

- Analyze how the 1992 election reflected the concerns of voters.

CORE RESOURCES

- **Section 2 Daily Quiz**

AV RESOURCES

- ***The American Nation Videodisc: U.S. Troops in the Persian Gulf***
- ***American Civics Citizenship Skills Videocassette or Videodisc: Segment 4***

PREVIEW WORKSHOP

Following is a list of the significant people, places, and terms in this section. You may wish to use this list as a section preview.

People
- Jesse Jackson
- Michael Dukakis
- George Bush
- Saddam Hussein
- Clarence Thomas
- Anita Hill
- Bill Clinton
- Hillary Rodham Clinton
- H. Ross Perot
- Ruth Bader Ginsburg
- Newt Gingrich

Places
- Iraq
- Kuwait

Terms
- Operation Desert Storm
- sexual harassment

Section 2

FROM BUSH TO CLINTON

FOCUS

- **How did Operation Desert Storm differ from previous American military conflicts?**
- **What were some of the domestic problems President Bush faced?**
- **How did the 1992 election reflect voter concerns?**

In 1988 Vice President George Bush was elected president. Bush's popularity soared after U.S. troops defeated the Iraqis in the Persian Gulf War. But Bush faced many challenges at home, including a persistent recession that contributed to his defeat by Democrat Bill Clinton in 1992. Clinton entered office in 1993 to the optimistic theme song "Don't Stop Thinking About Tomorrow." The youthful Democrat had reason to be optimistic, having just won a close, hard-fought election. He won reelection by a comfortable margin in 1996.

Female soldier during Operation Desert Storm

THE 1988 ELECTION

With the popular Reagan prohibited from running for a third term, the Democrats hoped to regain the White House in 1988. African American leader Jesse Jackson, who had run in 1984, was among a large group seeking the Democratic nomination. Jackson hoped to attract a "Rainbow Coalition"—a diverse group of voters representing all races, classes, and creeds. As a candidate in 1984, Jackson had helped generate the largest turnout of African American voters ever for a Democratic primary.

By 1988 Jackson's appeal had expanded to encompass a wide range of voters. On "Super Tuesday," the largest single day of primary voting, Jackson won more votes than any other candidate. Governor Michael Dukakis of Massachusetts, however, won the most delegates and eventually gained the nomination. Dukakis, the son of Greek immigrants, selected Senator Lloyd Bentsen of Texas as his running mate. Vice President George Bush won the Republican presidential nomination with young Indiana senator Dan Quayle as his running mate.

The 1988 presidential campaign proved to be one of the harshest in recent years. Initially, Bush tried to appeal to voters' sense of optimism

◄ Seeking to unite a "Rainbow Coalition" of voters, Jesse Jackson ran for the Democratic party's presidential nomination in both 1984 and 1988.

936

Ask volunteers to recall their experiences watching, hearing, or reading about Operation Desert Storm and the Persian Gulf War. Ask how they felt about their country and their president during the conflict. Have them speculate on why presidential popularity usually increases during a war just as it decreases during economic hard times.

Teaching the Section

THE 1988 ELECTION

Ask students to assume the role of voters in the 1988 election. Have them write a letter to the editor expressing their reactions to the negative ads used in the campaign. Call on volunteers to read their letters to the class. Students may wish to include their letters in their portfolios.

▶

by promising "a kinder and gentler nation." In the campaign's final weeks, however, most of the Republican ads focused on negative issues. For instance, one commercial attacked Dukakis's record on the environment by showing scenes of Massachusetts' heavily polluted Boston Harbor.

The most controversial Republican advertising campaign, however, was designed to sway voters troubled by the rising crime rate, which had jumped by over 12.5 percent between 1984 and 1988. A series of television and print ads painted Dukakis as weak on crime by associating him with convicted murderer Willie Horton. While out on a weekend pass under a Massachusetts prison program, Horton had attacked a Maryland couple. Since he was African American, some critics charged that the ads played on fears of black criminals and were racist.

Dukakis resisted using similarly negative ads in his own campaign. Instead, he tried to convince voters of his skills as a manager, arguing that the election should be about competence. This approach did not work, however. In the November election, the Bush-Quayle ticket won 426 electoral votes to the Dukakis-Bentsen ticket's 112. But the Democrats did increase their majorities in both houses of Congress and kept control of most state legislatures.

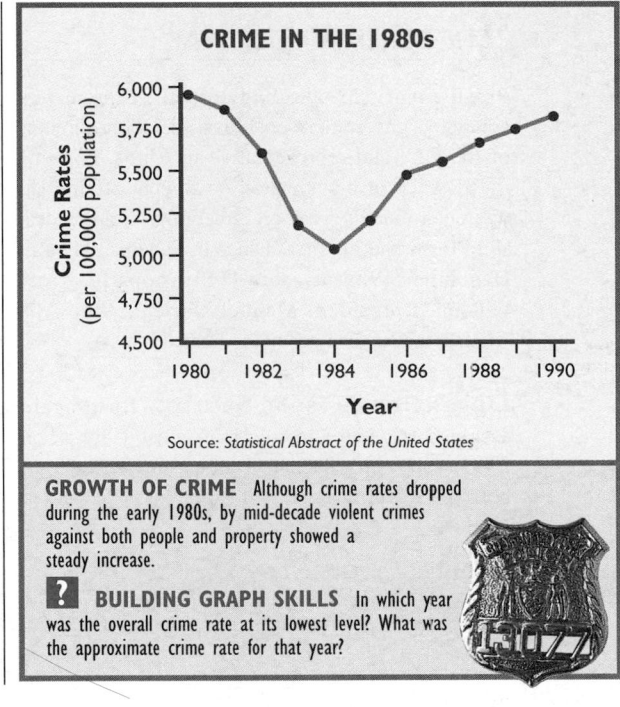

CRIME IN THE 1980s

Source: *Statistical Abstract of the United States*

GROWTH OF CRIME Although crime rates dropped during the early 1980s, by mid-decade violent crimes against both people and property showed a steady increase.

? BUILDING GRAPH SKILLS In which year was the overall crime rate at its lowest level? What was the approximate crime rate for that year?

Election of 1988

LOW VOTER TURNOUT Only some 50 percent of those eligible voted in 1988, the lowest percentage since the election of 1924.

? LOCATION Which candidate carried Washington, D.C.?

▼ 1988 campaign button

	Electoral Vote	Popular Vote	% of Popular Vote
Bush	426	48,886,097	53.4
Dukakis	111	41,809,074	45.6
Other candidates	1	899,638	1.0

■ Bush (Republican)
■ Dukakis (Democratic)

*West Virginia cast 1 electoral vote for Senator Lloyd Bentsen of Texas

Graph Caption Answer
1984; about 5,000 crimes per 100,000 people

Map Caption Answer
Dukakis

THINKING CRITICALLY

Recognizing Prejudice
Skillful use of misleading and negative ads helped Bush to portray Dukakis as soft on crime. The Willie Horton ad, for example, blamed Dukakis for the incident when in fact the Massachusetts prison furlough program that had allowed Horton out of jail on a weekend pass was set up by Dukakis's Republican predecessor. Have students identify the racial stereotype used in the Willie Horton ad and suggest reasons why critics labeled such ads racist.

■■ Have students give examples of negative campaigning in local or state elections. Ask students how they think this type of advertising affects the election process.

AMERICAN CIVICS
CITIZENSHIP SKILLS

Videocassette or Videodisc: Segment 3

Segment 3, Side A

Search Chapter 3

Teaching the Section

THE PERSIAN GULF WAR

Organize students into small groups to prepare skits in which male and female veterans of the Gulf War explain to veterans of World War II and the Vietnam War how the Persian Gulf War was different from those conflicts. Have the other veterans in the skit react, or respond with questions, to the Gulf War veterans' explanations.

VOICES IN HISTORY

The quick American victory in the Persian Gulf War changed the way the U.S. was viewed by many foreign nations. An Asian diplomat in Beijing, China, observed that before the Gulf War, "America was regarded as a paper tiger. . . . It was beaten like a wet rat in Vietnam and because of this we tended to underestimate it. But the Gulf War has changed all that."

HISTORICAL SIDELIGHTS

Coalition Builder
Prior to the Gulf War, Bush worked skillfully to build support for the war among Arab nations, traditional U.S. allies, and the American public. Twenty-eight nations provided troops or naval forces. Arab states in the coalition included Egypt, Syria, and Saudi Arabia, while former enemies like the Soviet Union and old allies Britain, France, and Canada also took part. The day after the air war began, an ABC poll reported that 83 percent of the American people supported the war.

THE PERSIAN GULF WAR

President Bush, who had served in numerous appointed government positions, including director of the CIA and representative to China, concentrated much of his attention on foreign affairs. He was determined to reassert America's world leadership. Bush had his first chance in Panama, when in December 1989 he sent U.S. troops to arrest Panama's president Manuel Noriega, who was wanted on drug charges in the United States.

Operation Desert Storm. Bush again assumed a leadership role in August 1990 when Iraq, led by ruler Saddam Hussein, invaded neighboring Kuwait, a major oil producer. The United

THE GULF WAR

THROUGH OTHERS' EYES

Although the Persian Gulf War was brief, many people were caught in the crossfire, including the residents of Israel. To retaliate against UN forces, Iraq launched an attack on Israel. Sari Nusseibeh, a Palestinian philosopher living in Israel when fighting broke out, recalled his impressions as the war raged:

It was January 29, 13 days since the aerial bombardment in the Gulf War had started. For fully two weeks we had been placed under a total 24-hour curfew, interspersed only by three two-hour intervals in which we were allowed to do our shopping. All of us—my wife, my three children, and myself—had taken to sleeping together on the floor of the sitting-dining area of our apartment. This way we kept each other company through the Scud [missile] scares (. . . we wondered each time where the rockets would fall, and what deadly poison they might be carrying). . . .

For almost two weeks we lived in a state of suspension between TV scenes of missiles hitting Iraqi targets and footage of missiles flying over our heads.

Nations condemned the attack, imposed economic sanctions on Iraq, and set a deadline for Iraq's withdrawal from Kuwait. As the January 15, 1991, deadline neared, military forces representing the United States, Britain, France, Egypt, and Saudi Arabia prepared for war. In all, some 690,000 allied troops—including some 540,000 Americans—amassed along the border of Kuwait. On January 16, the allied forces began bombing attacks on Iraqi forces and military and industrial installations.

The ground assault began on February 23. Within days the Iraqis had been driven back, and Kuwait's ruling al-Sabah family returned to power. American casualties included some 150 killed and 450 wounded, while an estimated 100,000 Iraqis died. U.S. air attacks also severely damaged the Iraqi capital, Baghdad, and other cities. Many hailed the success of **Operation Desert Storm** and applauded the leadership of General Colin Powell, chair of the Joint Chiefs of Staff, and Secretary of Defense Richard Cheney. The commander of U.S. forces, General H. Norman Schwarzkopf, received a hero's welcome in New York City. Bush's approval rating soared following the war.

A unique war. Operation Desert Storm differed from previous American military engagements. It was won almost entirely by the use of high-tech weaponry. Television reporters also provided unprecedented coverage of the war, including live coverage of the air assaults. As Americans sat glued to their television sets, news correspondent Bernard Shaw reported the first allied bombings on Iraq:

This is [pause] something is happening outside. . . . The skies over Baghdad have been illuminated. We're seeing bright flashes going off all over the sky.

Military technology quickly became the star of the show as coverage of the war expanded. The technological nature of the war highlighted another unique aspect of Operation Desert Storm—the significant role played by women. More than 35,000 American women served in the Persian Gulf conflict—some 6 percent of U.S. troops. Eleven American women soldiers were killed and two taken prisoner. Though the U.S. military banned women from serving as combat pilots, they served in almost every other capacity—including flying support planes and working on missile crews.

OPERATION DESERT STORM

Point out that the Persian Gulf War was a popular war with the American public and that it boosted President Bush's popularity. Have students speculate about how both the high-tech nature of the battles and live television coverage might have contributed to public enthusiasm. Have students suggest other factors that added to public support. *(Students may suggest support for Bush's aims, dislike of Saddam Hussein, the limited duration of the conflict and the comparatively low numbers of American casualties.)*

▶

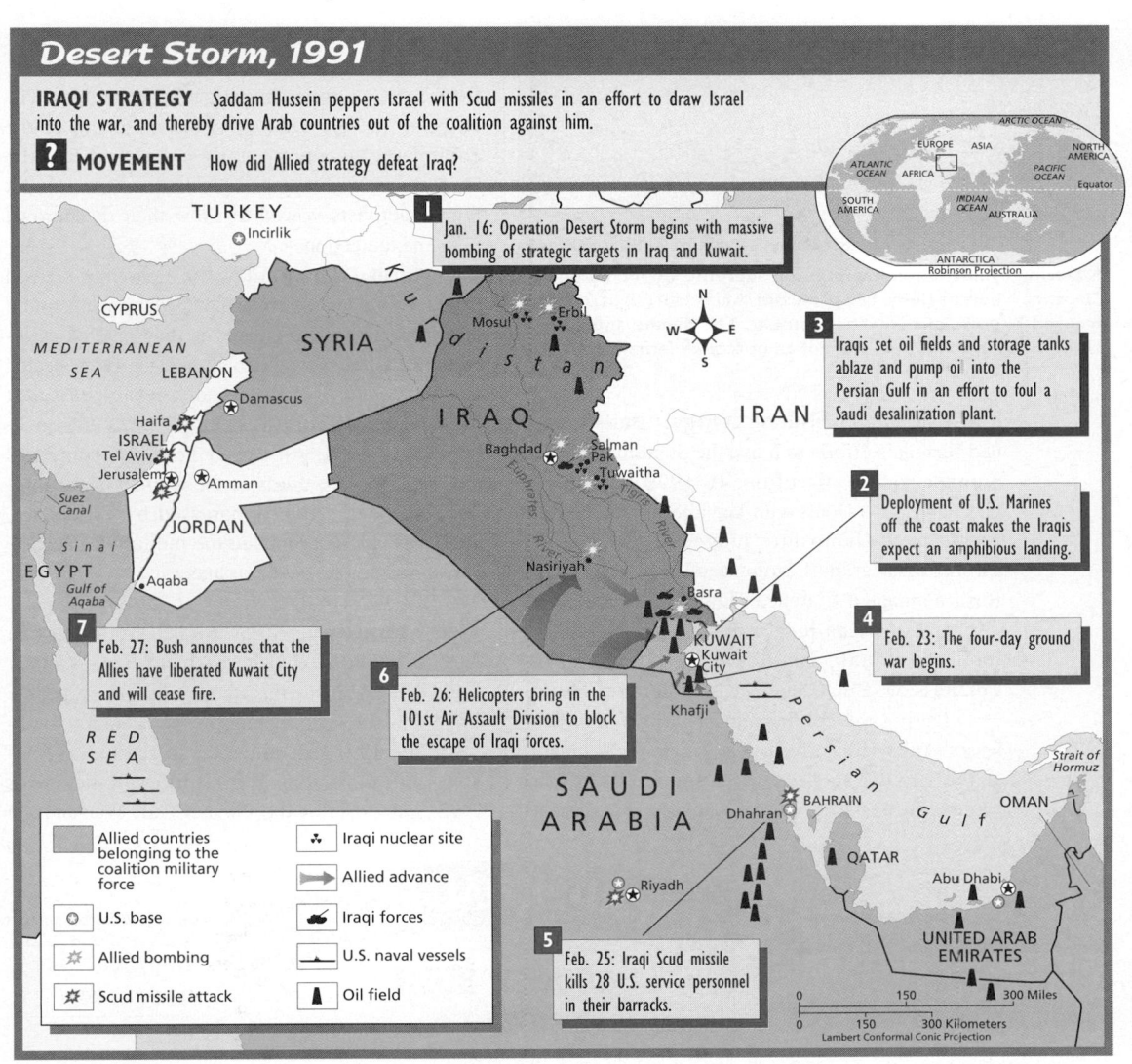

Desert Storm, 1991

IRAQI STRATEGY Saddam Hussein peppers Israel with Scud missiles in an effort to draw Israel into the war, and thereby drive Arab countries out of the coalition against him.

? MOVEMENT How did Allied strategy defeat Iraq?

1 Jan. 16: Operation Desert Storm begins with massive bombing of strategic targets in Iraq and Kuwait.

3 Iraqis set oil fields and storage tanks ablaze and pump oil into the Persian Gulf in an effort to foul a Saudi desalinization plant.

2 Deployment of U.S. Marines off the coast makes the Iraqis expect an amphibious landing.

4 Feb. 23: The four-day ground war begins.

7 Feb. 27: Bush announces that the Allies have liberated Kuwait City and will cease fire.

6 Feb. 26: Helicopters bring in the 101st Air Assault Division to block the escape of Iraqi forces.

5 Feb. 25: Iraqi Scud missile kills 28 U.S. service personnel in their barracks.

Allied countries belonging to the coalition military force / U.S. base / Allied bombing / Scud missile attack / Iraqi nuclear site / Allied advance / Iraqi forces / U.S. naval vessels / Oil field

The role of women in Desert Storm and the nature of the war caused many people to question the usefulness of banning women from combat. With technology playing an increasingly significant role in modern warfare, critics charged, physical differences between men and women would become less important than technological skill. During the previous years the number of women in the military had increased to the point that U.S. Air Force colonel Douglas Kennett commented that his branch of the service "couldn't go to war without women and we couldn't win without them." In August 1991 the Senate removed the ban on women serving as combat pilots, but continued to limit service in ground battles.

▪▪ Operation Desert Storm was unique for its use of high-tech weaponry, live television coverage, and use of women soldiers.

PROBLEMS AT HOME

Bush's successes in foreign affairs won him popularity and international praise, but some critics charged that he was neglecting problems at home. As the 1992 presidential campaign approached, domestic issues, particularly the economy and a growing political controversy, troubled the public and undermined the president's support.

Map Caption Answer
by outflanking Iraq's main forces, precipitating their retreat

HISTORICAL SIDELIGHTS
Women in the Gulf War

The Gulf War provided many new jobs for women in the military. Female helicopter pilots carried supplies to the front and female mechanics maintained tanks, coordinated water supplies, and worked as truck drivers and cargo handlers. Women also served as intelligence specialists, paratroopers, flight controllers, shipboard navigators, and ground-crew chiefs. However, women were barred from flying fighters and holding permanent assignments on carriers, destroyers, and submarines during the war.

THE AMERICAN NATION VIDEODISC PROGRAM

U.S. Troops in the Persian Gulf

2B   49621   :28

Teaching the Section

THE THOMAS–HILL HEARINGS

Have students explain why the Thomas-Hill hearings had such a strong impact on the debate about sexual harassment. Ask students whether they think the discussion of this issue that followed the hearings is likely to have any long-lasting effect on the relationships between men and women in the workplace.

Point out that in recent years increased attention has been paid to sexual harassment of high school students by their classmates. Ask volunteers to define what they perceive sexual harassment to be. Ask students if they think it is a problem in their school.

▲ During confirmation hearings for Supreme Court nominee Clarence Thomas (left), law professor Anita Hill (right) accused Thomas of sexual harassment. The Senate approved Thomas's nomination, in spite of an outcry by female activists.

The Thomas-Hill hearings. Bush continued Reagan's efforts to move the Supreme Court in a conservative direction. In 1990 he filled a vacancy on the Court with David Souter, a conservative New Hampshire judge. In 1991, when Thurgood Marshall announced his retirement, Bush nominated Clarence Thomas, a conservative African American judge and former head of the federal Equal Employment Opportunity Commission (EEOC), to take his place.

During the confirmation hearings, law professor Anita Hill, a former associate of Thomas's at the EEOC, accused the nominee of **sexual harassment**—the use of unwelcome sexual

language or behavior that creates a hostile working environment. In televised hearings, the Senate Judiciary Committee investigated her charges. The bullying tactics used by some members of the committee outraged many women. After the Senate narrowly approved the Thomas nomination, female activists vowed to show their disapproval in the next election.

Across the country the hearings stirred debate about sexual harassment. Many women told of experiencing harassment as they entered male-dominated fields. The debate became more heated after news broke of wide-scale sexual harassment of female officers at a naval convention in September 1991. An earlier Pentagon study had revealed that two thirds of the women in the military had been sexually harassed by colleagues. Such revelations prompted the military to increase punishment of sexual harassment.

The economy. Many women confessed that they tolerated sexual harassment because they could not afford to lose their jobs. Many people could relate to such feelings as the economy weakened. The 1991 federal deficit surged to $282 billion, with more than $350 billion predicted for 1992. The costs of the Persian Gulf War and the

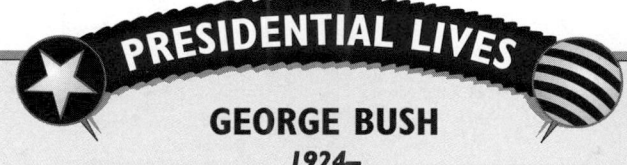

PRESIDENTIAL LIVES

GEORGE BUSH
1924–

in office 1989–1993

Following the popular and charismatic Ronald Reagan was not easy for George Bush. Throughout the 1988 campaign he was constantly fighting "the wimp factor"—the accusation that he was a weak politician and a better follower than leader. This charge seemed particularly ironic for Bush, who had bravely served as a pilot in World War II.

At the age of 18, George Bush became one of the youngest commissioned pilots in the navy. He flew 58 missions in all and

was shot down once. Bush's experiences in war may have contributed to his strong interest in foreign affairs. During his presidency, memories of World War II came back to him when he considered committing troops to battle. "When it came time for me to send our kids . . . to the Middle East," he once said, "I thought back on my own experiences in combat and what it was like to be shot at. . . . Having been in combat rounded out my awareness of the human cost of war."

bailout of the S&L and banking industries added to the deficit.

The trade gap persisted as well. Though the trade deficit had declined from its 1990 high of almost $102 billion, in 1991 it still stood at about $66 billion. Japan's massive annual sales of automobiles and electronic goods to U.S. consumers accounted for a large portion of the gap. On a 1992 trade mission to Japan, President Bush and U.S. business leaders tried with little success to persuade the Japanese to increase imports from the United States.

Adding to these economic woes, a recession hit in 1990. As the economy faltered, unemployment rose. States facing budget deficits cut their welfare programs. The number of Americans living below the poverty line grew by more than two million in 1990. The recession hung on throughout 1992, complicating President Bush's reelection hopes.

■■ Domestically, Bush faced troubles over the Thomas-Hill hearings and the sagging economy.

WINDS OF CHANGE

Despite the nation's economic woes, President Bush was still riding a wave of popularity from the Persian Gulf War as 1991 ended. One of the few Democrats willing to challenge him in the 1992 election was Governor William "Bill" Clinton of Arkansas.

Bill Clinton was born in 1946 in Hope, Arkansas, shortly after the death of his father. His mother, Virginia, later married Roger Clinton, an abusive alcoholic. Clinton's childhood experiences of dealing with poverty and a troubled home life shaped his outlook on the world. When he met President John Kennedy in 1963, Clinton decided on a political career. After receiving a bachelor's degree in international affairs from Georgetown University, he studied at Oxford University in England and gained a law degree from Yale University.

▲ Bill Clinton

At Yale he met Hillary Rodham, a law student who later served as counsel to the House Judiciary Committee considering the impeachment of Nixon. They married in 1975. Three years later Clinton became the nation's youngest governor when he was elected to lead Arkansas. As a baby boomer, Clinton reflected many traits of his generation. He opposed the war in Vietnam and for a time tried to avoid being drafted. Influenced by the idealism of the Kennedy era and by the civil rights movement, he believed strongly in the value of diversity and equality.

Hillary Rodham Clinton, a feminist influenced by the women's movement, enjoyed a successful legal career while furthering her husband's political career. As first lady of Arkansas, Hillary Rodham Clinton served on several influential committees, including one that developed a ground-breaking education-reform program.

Some observers noted that Hillary Rodham Clinton was qualified to run for president herself. Acknowledging his wife's key role, Bill Clinton said during the 1992 campaign that voters would be getting "two for the price of one" if he were elected president. As became apparent after the election, however, many Americans were uncomfortable with the idea of a president's wife in a policy-making role.

▲ **Hillary Rodham Clinton advised her husband on a number of key issues during the 1992 presidential campaign.**

THE 1992 ELECTION

After years of low voter participation, people turned out in droves in 1992 to make their voices heard. Candidates used public forums such as television talk shows and radio call-in programs to answer questions directly from the public. A master of this electronic format was independent presidential candidate H. Ross Perot.

Perot, a billionaire from Texas who ran as an outsider, promised to bring a populist reform movement to Washington, D.C., by decreasing the influence of political lobbyists and by giving the public a greater voice in government. He also promised to use his skills as a businessman to cut spending and balance the budget. Perot's message appealed to many voters worried about the economy.

Teaching the Section

THE 1992 ELECTION

Organize students into groups of three to write a letter to President Bush explaining why they think he lost the 1992 election, a second letter to Ross Perot explaining what they think his election campaign accomplished, and a third letter to President Clinton explaining why they think he won and what issues he should focus on in the 1990s. Have groups share their letters with the class. Then have students debate the following statement: *Given the concerns of American voters, there was nothing George Bush could have done to win the 1992 presidential election.*

Perot's popularity reflected the feelings of many voters that politicians were out of touch. One group of voters who insisted on being heard were women, especially those outraged by the Thomas-Hill hearings. Shortly after the hearings, activist Eleanor Smeal had declared: "The Senate did more in one week to underscore the critical need for more women in the Senate than feminists have been able to do in 25 years." Women responded by running for public office in record numbers.

The increase in women candidates led the press to dub 1992 "the year of the woman." Many of these candidates won election. Four prominent women Democrats gained U.S. Senate seats, including Patty Murray of Washington and African American Carol Moseley-Braun of Illinois. California filled both of its Senate seats with women—Barbara Boxer and Dianne Feinstein.

In the presidential race, Bill Clinton's message of economic and social reform paid off. Clinton and his running mate, Senator Al Gore of Tennessee, won 43 percent of the popular vote and 370 electoral votes to the Bush-Quayle ticket's 38 percent of the popular vote and 168 electoral votes. Although Perot and his running mate, Admiral William Stockdale, failed to pick up any electoral votes, they captured 19 percent of the popular vote—more than any independent presidential ticket since that of Theodore Roosevelt in 1912.

■■ **The 1992 election saw increased voter participation, numerous reform candidates, and the election of baby boomer Bill Clinton.**

CLINTON TAKES OFFICE

Once in office, Clinton put together a diverse cabinet. His appointees included Mexican American Henry Cisneros as secretary of housing and urban affairs and African Americans Ron Brown and Joycelyn Elders as secretary of commerce and surgeon general, respectively. Other women appointees included Press Secretary Dee Dee Myers, Attorney General Janet Reno, and Secretary of Health and Human Services Donna Shalala. Clinton also chose Ruth Bader Ginsburg to fill a vacancy on the Supreme Court.

As his presidency began, Clinton suffered a series of setbacks. An elaborate plan to reform the nation's health-care system, drafted by a task force headed by Hillary Rodham Clinton, died in Congress. In addition, both Clintons faced charges of past financial improprieties, including their

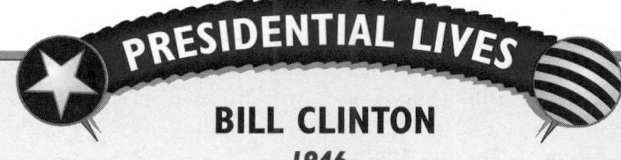

PRESIDENTIAL LIVES

BILL CLINTON
1946–

in office 1993–

Bill Clinton's presidency marked many firsts in the White House. He was the first president born in the post–World War II era and the first president from Arkansas. Clinton was also the first president to play the saxophone at his own inaugural celebration.

Clinton's career goal as a young teenager was to become a jazz musician. He was heavily influenced by African American jazz artists and early rock 'n' roll stars such as Elvis Presley. He excelled at playing the

saxophone and was offered numerous music scholarships to college after he graduated from high school. Although Clinton went on to make a career in politics, he frequently used his musical talents in campaigns, such as during the 1992 presidential election when, wearing dark glasses, he played the saxophone on a popular late-night talk show. Despite his love of music, Clinton believes that he made the right career choice. "I would have been a very good musician," he once noted, "but not a great one."

Bill Clinton

Practice

GUIDED PRACTICE

Work with the class to develop two lists on the chalkboard—one listing the accomplishments of the Clinton administration and another listing its problems.

INDEPENDENT PRACTICE

Using the information from the lists developed in the Guided Practice activity, have students imagine they are encyclopedia writers in the year 2010. Have each write an entry on the Clinton presidency. Students may wish to include their entries in their portfolios.

Review and Assessment

REVIEW Organize students into groups to prepare a time line of the key events in this section. Ask each group to select for its time line three events that helped Clinton win the 1992 election and three that helped him win the 1996 election. Have groups explain their choices. Then assign the Section 2 Review on p. 944.

ASSESS Assign the **Section 2 Daily Quiz** in *Core Resources*.
▶

tangled involvement in a failed Arkansas real-estate development called Whitewater. Then in 1996 came charges that the White House had improperly obtained FBI files on Republicans.

Amid these distractions, Clinton confronted a range of global challenges, among them fighting in Bosnia and Northern Ireland and emerging democracy in Russia. Clinton also wrestled with an upsurge of terrorism (see Chapter 33).

THE CLINTON PRESIDENCY

President Clinton focused on economic recovery, and his efforts showed some signs of paying off. In August 1993 Congress narrowly passed a budget act which combined tax increases and spending cuts to reduce the national debt.

The medicine worked, over time. The 1996 deficit dropped to about $145 billion, half that of 1992. Unemployment went down to 5.4 percent, a ten-year low, and inflation hovered under 3 percent. As investors gained confidence, the stock market boomed.

Not all economic news—especially that in Clinton's first few years—was rosy, however. The trade deficit remained high (see Chapter 33). And as corporations pushed for greater efficiency, they fired thousands of employees. Both white-collar and blue-collar workers lost their jobs as AT&T, IBM, GM, and other corporations cut their payrolls. In addition, many of the new jobs that were created during the Clinton years were low-paying, unskilled positions. In the inner cities, with their large black and Hispanic populations, even these jobs were scarce. The gap between the wealthiest and poorest Americans continued to widen.

Encouraged by Clinton's early setbacks, Republicans geared up for the 1994 midterm election. Many Republican candidates signed a "Contract with America" pledging a balanced-budget amendment and other reforms.

On election day, the Republicans won a stunning victory, gaining control of the House and the Senate. Newt Gingrich of Georgia became house speaker. The Christian Coalition, a political lobby founded by television evangelist Pat Robertson, helped back this conservative resurgence.

■■ **Concerned with early failures in the Clinton administration, voters gave Republicans control of**

both the House and the Senate in the 1994 midterm elections.

CAMPAIGN 1996

Despite the results of the 1994 midterm elections, Clinton's popularity improved as the economy boomed. Describing the healthy financial conditions that had allowed Clinton to survive the 1994 midterm elections, economist David Wyss commented, "If you look at the economy during the Clinton administration, you have to say that it's been a success. We have low inflation, full employment, and steady growth. This is really just about the best of all [economic] worlds."

The president's stock rose higher as the Republican Congress failed to enact key measures in its Contract with America and tried to cut popular social and environmental programs. As Clinton and the Republican Congress battled over a budget bill in 1995, the federal government briefly shut down. Voters blamed the Republicans, and Newt Gingrich's popularity plummeted.

Clinton also benefited from divisions among Republicans, who split over issues such as taxes, budget cuts, government regulations, and social issues. These divisions sharpened as the 1996 presidential campaign began. Among a large field of Republican candidates, Senator Bob Dole of Kansas emerged victorious from the primaries and tried to unite his party's competing factions.

The Race. A disabled World War II veteran, Dole faced concerns about his age. At 73, voters wondered, was he out of touch? Could he handle the demands of the presidency? Resigning from the Senate, Dole proved an ineffective campaigner. "He never . . . offered the sustained and layered argument that precedes the applause line," concluded political analyst Peggy Noonan. "He just declared things—And there'll be no more crime in a Dole Administration—and waited for people to clap as he cleared his throat."

▲ **Newt Gingrich**

VOICES IN HISTORY

The welfare reform bill, which replaced federal programs with state grants and cut off aid after a certain number of years, stirred harsh criticism. New York senator Daniel Patrick Moynihan commented, "If you think things can't be worse, just you wait until there are a third of a million children in the streets. That's what you're talking about—children on grates, because there is no money in the states and cities to care for them. It is a social risk that no sane person would take, and I mean that." Clinton, however, largely defended the measure, insisting, "Today we have a historic opportunity to make welfare what it was meant to be: a second chance, not a way of life."

HISTORICAL SIDELIGHTS

Ross Perot's Second Campaign

Ross Perot again ran for president in 1996 as an independent candidate. With the economy faring well, however, he won just 9 percent of the popular vote—roughly half of his take in the 1992 election. Many observers thought Perot would take even less than 9 percent.

RETEACH Have students work in groups, assigning individuals or pairs the task of outlining subsections. Have students exchange outlines and use them to ask questions of other members of their group.

Closure

Ask students if they believe that bipartisan cooperation will take place after the election of 1996. If students seem pessimistic, ask them to offer ways politicians might foster bipartisan efforts.

Extension

RESEARCH Have students research and report on weapons, military tactics and strategies, media coverage, the role of allies, or key personalities in the Persian Gulf War.

COMPARE Have students research the issue of women in combat and write papers expressing their feelings on the topic.

SECTION REVIEW ANSWERS

IDENTIFY

For significance, see the following pages:
Jesse Jackson (p. 936)
Michael Dukakis (p. 936)
George Bush (p. 936)
Saddam Hussein (p. 938)
Operation Desert Storm (p. 938)
Clarence Thomas (p. 940)
Anita Hill (p. 940)
sexual harassment (p. 940)
Bill Clinton (p. 941)
Hillary Rodham Clinton (p. 941)
H. Ross Perot (p. 941)
Ruth Bader Ginsburg (p. 942)
Newt Gingrich (p. 943)

LOCATE

For locations, see the map on p. 939.

1. *high-tech weaponry, TV coverage from within Iraq, women's roles*
2. *Thomas-Hill hearings and the economy*
3. *new uses of media increased voter participation, support for reform, independent candidates*
4. *Essays should note women's roles in Desert Storm, Thomas-Hill hearings, and 1992 election.*
5. *increased African American participation, united variety of voters; "outsider" status, grass-roots movement, variety of support*

▲ Clinton-Dole debate, 1996

Clinton, meanwhile, seized the middle ground on many issues. The president echoed the Republicans in calling for economic growth, smaller government, anti-crime programs, and middle-class tax relief. He urged tougher school discipline and a crackdown on "deadbeat dads" who failed to provide child support. Clinton also echoed Republican critics of the nation's welfare system. The president and Republican leaders both called for welfare reform that would limit benefits, introduce work requirements, and shift programs from the federal government to the states. Clinton signed such a bill in August 1996.

On issues such as environmental protection, gun control, and programs for the elderly, however, Clinton highlighted the difference between himself and his Republican opponent. By arguing for the protection of both long-standing and new social programs, he presented himself as more caring and humane than Dole. Another issue dividing the two candidates was tobacco. Clinton advocated stricter measures to discourage smoking, particularly among the young. Dole, by contrast, despite overwhelming medical evidence, questioned whether tobacco was really addictive.

The Result. Clinton's approach proved successful, and he became the first Democrat since Franklin Delano Roosevelt to win a full second term. Though his was not a landslide victory, he won 50 percent of the popular vote and 379 electoral votes. Dole, who had gone on a grueling 96 hour multistate tour in the last days of the campaign, took 41 percent of the popular vote and 159 electoral votes.

Though a few of Newt Gingrich's "Freshman Class of 1994" failed to win reelection, the Republicans won a majority in both the House and the Senate. This was the first time that a Democrat had been elected to the presidency while the Republicans won both the House and the Senate, and the event seemed to send a message supporting a working bipartisan government.

As he approached his second term, President Clinton echoed this bipartisan theme, "proclaim[ing] that the vital center is alive and well." He pledged to provide health insurance to children and the unemployed, fix parts of the welfare bill, connect classrooms to the Internet, and repair crumbling schools.

Many observers described Clinton's proposals as "small steps" intended to avoid the political overreach that had doomed much of his first term.

SECTION 2 REVIEW

IDENTIFY and explain the significance of the following: Jesse Jackson, Michael Dukakis, George Bush, Saddam Hussein, Operation Desert Storm, Clarence Thomas, Anita Hill, sexual harassment, Bill Clinton, Hillary Rodham Clinton, H. Ross Perot, Ruth Bader Ginsburg, Newt Gingrich.

LOCATE and explain the importance of the following: Iraq, Kuwait.

1. **MAIN IDEA** What was unique about Operation Desert Storm?
2. **MAIN IDEA** What were two domestic issues that plagued President Bush?
3. **CONTRASTING** Why was the 1992 election different from any other in recent history?
4. **WRITING TO EXPLAIN** Analysts refer to 1992 as "the year of the woman." Considering women's roles in events during 1991, 1992, and 1993, write an essay explaining why the early 1990s might be called "the years of the women."
5. **ASSESSING CONSEQUENCES** What impact did Jesse Jackson's "Rainbow Coalition" campaign have on the 1984 and 1988 elections? How were the Jackson campaigns similar to that of H. Ross Perot in 1992?

PREVIEW WORKSHOP

*Following is a list of the significant
people, places, and terms in this
section. You may wish to use this
list as a section preview.*

People
- Rodney King
- Nelson Mandela
- Wilma Mankiller
- Bill Gates

Places
- Haiti
- Los Angeles
- Miami

Terms
- Immigration Act
- Family and Medical Leave
Act
- AIDS

- Americans with Disabilities
Act
- space shuttle
- Internet
- cyberspace

Section 3

AMERICA IN THE 1990s

FOCUS
- **How did immigration patterns of the 1990s affect the United States?**
- **What were some problems urban Americans confronted?**
- **How did government and businesses attempt to help working parents?**
- **What health challenges did the nation face?**

*Leaving behind the 1980s, Americans faced both promising
trends and pressing social problems. The 1990 U.S. census
revealed a population that was increasingly urban, southern
and western, and immigrant. Americans worked to overcome
the economic problems and racial divisions that fractured many
cities in the 1990s. Meanwhile, the rising costs of health
care and the spread of AIDS contributed to the nationwide
health-care crisis.*

Rally supporting AIDS research

A NEW WAVE OF IMMIGRATION

In November 1991, U.S. Coast Guard vessels intercepted boatloads of Haitians bound for the United
States. A military coup had ousted Haiti's first
democratically elected president, Jean-Bertrand
Aristide. As political and economic chaos spread,
thousands of Haitians sailed to the United States.

However, bound by a 1981 agreement with
Haiti and facing economic troubles of its own, the
United States began to return the Haitians to their
home country. Many politicians criticized the government's policy. "Returning Vietnamese, Russian
Jews, Cubans, Nicaraguans and others back to the
repressive countries from which they were fleeing
would have been unthinkable," declared Senator

Connie Mack of Florida. "How can we justify it
for Haitians?"

The Haitian issue underscored the continuing
debate within the United States over immigration.
The 1990 census revealed that more immigrants
had come to the United States in the 1980s than in
any decade since 1910, and more than 80 percent

▶ The U.S. Coast Guard intercepted Haitian
refugees, such as the family shown here, and took
them to a temporary "tent-city" at Guantánamo
Bay Naval Base. Some 2,500 refugees were housed
at this base before being returned to Haiti.

FOCUS OBJECTIVES

- Explain how immigration
patterns of the 1990s
affected the U.S.

- Identify some problems
urban Americans
confronted.

- Analyze how govern-
ment and businesses
attempted to help work-
ing parents.

- Describe health chal-
lenges the nation faced.

HISTORICAL
SIDELIGHTS

Immigration
In 1991 the U.S. accepted
over 1.8 million legal immigrants, more than all the
other industrialized nations
combined. Over two thirds
of these immigrants set-
tled in just seven states.
California led with 40 percent of all immigrants.
Texas, New York, Florida,
Illinois, New Jersey, and
Arizona also absorbed large
immigrant populations.

CORE RESOURCES

- **Literature
Worksheet 32**
- **Section 3 Daily Quiz**

AV RESOURCES

- **The American Nation
Videodisc: A Nation
of Immigrants; Early
Computer Robot**
- **Linking Geography
and History
Transparencies** and
Worksheets 11C, 13B
- **Everday Life in
America Trans-
parency** and
Worksheet 32

MOTIVATING:
LINK TO TODAY

Have volunteers name the most pressing economic and social problems they think Americans face in the 1990s. List responses on a flip chart. At the end of the section study, have students review the chart and add to, delete, or otherwise revise their list.

Teaching the Section

IMMIGRATION PATTERNS

Organize students into groups to brainstorm reasons for the rise in opposition to immigration in the 1990s and then list the benefits of immigration for U.S. business and industry. Have each group use its lists to debate the merits of open immigration and to reach a group consensus on the issue. Then have each group write a two-minute radio editorial explaining its position. Have each group choose a representative to air its views. After each presentation, allow time for dissenting opinion.

■■ Ask students how they think the sluggish economy of the early 1990s influenced the way Americans felt about immigration at that time.

VOICES IN HISTORY

The 1990 census counted some 290,000 Haitian Americans in the U.S. Counting undocumented immigrants, however, yields a larger figure. One expert has estimated the Haitian American population at around 1.2 million. Most Haitian Americans are concentrated in southern Florida and New York. Commented Haitian American Joel Dreyfuss, "We are cabdrivers and college professors, schoolteachers and police officers, stockbrokers and baby sitters, soldiers and politicians, bankers and factory workers." He complained, however, that many people saw Haitian Americans as merely "boat people."

AV TRANSPARENCY

Linking Geography and History Transparency and **Worksheet 13B**

of them came from Asia, Latin America, and the Caribbean. This influx of immigrants alarmed many native-born Americans. Many blamed immigrants for taking jobs from native-born residents. Some also argued that the presence of large numbers of immigrants willing to work for lower wages served to keep wages down for all workers.

Supporters of immigration offered a different view. They argued that immigrants created new businesses that revitalized urban areas and helped the economy. In addition, supporters of immigration noted that many recent immigrants, most notably those from India, the Philippines, China, and Korea, on average had more schooling than either native-born Americans or European immigrants. Asian immigrants, they pointed out, made up about one third of all engineers in California's center of computer technology, the Silicon Valley.

■■ **Opposition to immigration increased in the 1990s, although immigrants made many contributions to U.S. businesses and industries.**

President Bush recognized these benefits and signed the **Immigration Act** of 1990. The new law changed U.S. immigration policy by increasing the number of immigrants and doubling the number of skilled workers allowed into the United States each year. The act also authorized special visas for foreign investors interested in establishing businesses in economically depressed areas of the country.

In 1996 during Clinton's first term, Congress passed an immigration bill to fight the continuing problem of illegal immigration by strengthening control of the borders. Much of the Immigration and Naturalization Service's increased control efforts focus on the area around San Diego, California—a point where almost half of all illegal immigrants enter the United States.

The 1996 immigration bill also contained provisions aimed at keeping new immigrants off welfare rolls. For example, sponsors of immigrants must have incomes at least 125 percent above the poverty level. The bill also prevents legal immigrants who are not U.S. citizens from receiving most forms of welfare benefits. Many believe this provision will encourage immigrants to become citizens. Already the number of naturalizations has increased from some 500,000 in 1994 to 1,000,000 in 1995.

If current trends hold, the United States will witness increased immigration in the coming years. Thus, Americans will continue to grapple with the question of whether to welcome immigrants.

CITIES OF DIVERSITY

Conflicts experienced by immigrants included the riots that erupted in April 1992 in south central Los Angeles. The area exploded in violence after the acquittal of four white police officers accused of beating Rodney King, an African American. Most of the violence affected neighborhood residents and businesses as many people were beaten and robbed. Some looters specifically targeted Korean-owned businesses.

The riots disheartened people who had worked to improve relations among African

▶ Tension flared between the African American and Cuban American communities in Miami after Nelson Mandela, shown here, spoke favorably of Fidel Castro.

URBAN PROBLEMS

Organize students into groups to assume the roles of members of a big-city mayor's task force on urban affairs. Have groups create public service announcements for TV or radio explaining to suburban listeners what the problems of America's cities are, the causes of these problems, and why everyone within the listening area should be concerned about such problems. Groups might also construct alternative scenarios for cities of the future—one in which urban problems worsen, and one in which steps are taken to solve them.

▶

Americans, Hispanic Americans, and Asian Americans in Los Angeles. Sylvia Castillo, a Mexican American community activist who was a target of the violence, noted, "I was outraged by the verdict and had always struggled against racism. All I could think was: 'Why are they [rioters] doing this to me?'" Rodney King himself urged people to "try to work it out" peacefully, asking, "Can we all get along?" Most residents in south central Los Angeles did not take part in the riots, and many people braved the violence to rescue victims.

Miami, Florida, deemed the "new Ellis Island" by psychologist Marvin Dunn, also experienced increased immigration and racial tensions. In 1992 Miami had more foreign-born residents—including Cubans, Haitians, Nicaraguans, and Peruvians—than any other city in the United States. Boosted by a thriving tourist industry, the city's economy had boomed in recent years, but it had also seen three riots since 1980.

Tension in Miami was particularly strong between Cuban Americans and African Americans. In 1990, black leaders began a national boycott of Miami's convention facilities after Cuban American city officials snubbed South African leader Nelson Mandela. Mandela had made favorable remarks about Fidel Castro, Cuba's Communist leader whose regime many Cuban Americans had fled. After Hispanic American businesspeople agreed to hire more African Americans and patronize black-owned businesses, black leaders ordered an end to the boycott.

Economic problems compounded many urban problems. Some analysts argued that bad economic conditions contributed to the Los Angeles riots. Once home to major companies such as Bethlehem Steel and Goodyear, Los Angeles lost over 200,000 jobs in 1991 alone. Such loss of inner-city jobs was repeated across the country. Many of the companies that left the inner cities relocated to the suburbs, changing the faces of both the cities and the suburbs. Many suburban areas now contain more office space than midtown Manhattan. While this development means more jobs for suburban areas, inner-city residents despair of again attracting the industries that could reduce unemployment in their communities.

■■ **Inner cities experienced racial conflicts and lost jobs to the suburbs in the 1980s and 1990s.**

WORK AND FAMILY

Many observers expressed concern about the growing number of single-parent families in the 1980s and 1990s. From 1970 to 1991 the number of children living in single-parent households more than doubled. In 1991 some 20 percent of all white children, 60 percent of all African American children, and 30 percent of all Hispanic children lived with one parent, usually their mothers.

Most single parents faced serious financial burdens. Patricia Mull, a Los Angeles seamstress who stretched her income to send her daughter to private school, described the stress she faced: "I worry about the rent. I worry if I can make the payment in time. I worry if I have enough money

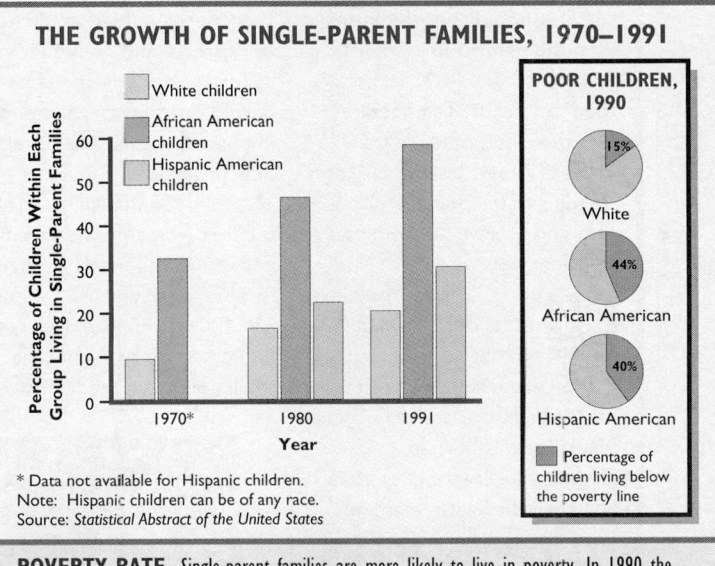

THE GROWTH OF SINGLE-PARENT FAMILIES, 1970–1991

- White children
- African American children
- Hispanic American children

Percentage of Children Within Each Group Living in Single-Parent Families

Year: 1970*, 1980, 1991

POOR CHILDREN, 1990

- White — 15%
- African American — 44%
- Hispanic American — 40%
- Percentage of children living below the poverty line

* Data not available for Hispanic children.
Note: Hispanic children can be of any race.
Source: *Statistical Abstract of the United States*

POVERTY RATE Single-parent families are more likely to live in poverty. In 1990 the poverty rate for single-parent Hispanic families was 68 percent, for single-parent African American families about 67 percent, and for single-parent white families nearly 45 percent.

? **BUILDING GRAPH SKILLS** What was the percent increase in African American children living in single-parent families from 1970 to 1980? What percent of Hispanic American children lived below the poverty line in 1990?

HISTORICAL SIDELIGHTS

Korean Americans

Experts point to a variety of reasons for the success of Korean immigrants in the U.S. Many Korean newcomers were middle class and well educated. In 1990 78 percent of the 2,500 Korean fruit-and-vegetable store owners in New York City had college educations. Many also had access to capital to start their own businesses, usually borrowing from relatives or from mutual savings associations set up in the U.S.

AV **TRANSPARENCY**

Linking Geography and History Transparency and **Worksheet 11C**

◎ **THE AMERICAN NATION VIDEODISC PROGRAM**

A Nation of Immigrants

2B   23298   2:45

Graph Caption Answer
about 14 percent; 40 percent

HISTORICAL SIDELIGHTS

Children in Poverty

Between 1960 and 1988, the poverty rate among children rose from 15 percent to more than 20 percent. Almost all the increase came in the 1980s.

Teaching the Section

HELP FOR WORKING PARENTS

Have students imagine they are members of a lobby group favoring government and business support for day care. Have students write speeches they would use to explain to Congress and/or private businesses why the need for such services is growing, who would benefit from such services, and why the federal government and businesses should provide financial support for such services. Call on volunteers to present their speeches. Students may wish to include their speeches in their portfolios.

AMERICAN INDIAN RENEWAL: A CASE STUDY

SETTING THE SCENE

Water rights are a key issue for many American Indian groups. The Shoshonis and Arapahos on the Wind River Reservation in Wyoming turned to the courts to help them reclaim their water rights. In a 1989 case, the Supreme Court upheld their right to one third of the water that originates on their reservation. A former Shoshoni tribal councilman noted: "We're simply protecting our sacred, sovereign rights. A lot of people in the West aren't accustomed to seeing Indians stand up for themselves."

BIO GRAPHY **PERSONALITIES IN HISTORY**

Wilma Mankiller's distinctive last name came from an 18th-century warrior ancestor. As chief of the second largest Indian nation in the U.S., Mankiller works with a $52 million annual budget to run health clinics, businesses, and cultural programs. In 1990 Mankiller signed an agreement with the U.S. government that gave the Cherokee nation direct control of $6.1 million in federal funding.

Changing Ways
AMERICAN INDIAN RENEWAL: A CASE STUDY

The economic problems facing the United States in the 1980s and 1990s presented special problems for the nation's nearly two million American Indians, more than 20 percent of whom lived on or near reservations. As in earlier years, joblessness, lack of education, and poor health care made life hard for many Indians. But cultural renewal, economic ventures, and successful claims of treaty rights offered promise.

The Shoshoni-Bannock Indians of Fort Hall Reservation in Idaho were among the Indians who successfully pressed their treaty claims. In 1990, using the terms of an 1868 treaty with the United States, the Shoshoni-Bannock Indians won the right to use water from the Snake River to irrigate their farmlands. The decision was the result of more than 25 years of American Indian efforts to win greater political autonomy and achieve economic self-sufficiency.

BIO GRAPHY
Wilma Mankiller, chief of the 108,000–strong Cherokee Nation, launched one of the most significant renewal efforts. Mankiller was born in Tahlequah, Oklahoma, in 1945. She spent her early years on a farm, where her family faced economic hardships and lived without indoor plumbing or electricity.

When Mankiller was 12, the farm failed after two drought years. Her family then moved to San Francisco, California, under the Bureau of Indian Affairs' relocation program. The adjustment to city life was difficult for Mankiller, who recalled, "One day I was [in Oklahoma] and the next day I was trying to deal with the mysteries of television, indoor plumbing, neon lights and elevators."

She soon became active in the American Indian Movement, which inspired her to become more involved in her community. In the mid-1970s Mankiller moved back to Oklahoma. She completed college and began working to promote economic growth in the Cherokee Nation. Stressing self-esteem and community self-help, Mankiller helped develop rural water systems, improve housing, and develop new businesses.

In 1985 Mankiller became the first woman principal chief, and in 1987 she won a tough four-way race and a subsequent runoff election. Mankiller compared her job to "running a small country, a medium-size

Wilma Mankiller

▲ The Shoshoni-Bannock Indians successfully sued the U.S. government in 1990 to reclaim irrigation rights that had been guaranteed to them in an 1868 treaty.

corporation, and being a social worker." In addition to helping Cherokee communities create new jobs and provide better health care, the Cherokee Nation sponsored a program to teach students how to read and write the Cherokee language. "I can't help but feel hopeful about our future," Mankiller noted in her 1990 State of the Nation address:

❝ I think the strongest thing I see as I travel around to Cherokee communities and talk with people is their tenacity [persistence]. Despite everything that's happened to our people throughout history we've managed to hang on to our culture, we've managed to hang on to our sense of being Cherokee. ❞

left for other things. I worry about money every day, every night."

Many two-parent families shared Mull's concerns as they struggled to balance job and family responsibilities. More than 60 percent of married women worked outside the home in 1995, up from about one third in 1960. The increase in single-parent families and in families with both parents in the work force created the need for affordable day care. Employers increasingly began to realize that family concerns affected the job performance of their employees. To help employees balance work and family, a coalition of businesses in 1992 announced a program to build more day-care and elder-care centers across the country.

The U.S. government also recognized the need to help working families. In February 1993, two weeks after his inauguration, President Clinton signed into law the **Family and Medical Leave Act**, which President Bush had twice vetoed. The legislation requires large companies to provide workers up to 12 weeks of unpaid leave for family and medical emergencies without losing their medical coverage or their jobs.

This legislation reflected the significant changes in attitudes toward work and family that have occurred in the 1990s. Florence Skelly, the vice chairperson of a market-research firm, noted in 1993 that "rather than trying to climb the economic ladder, people are becoming more concerned with relationships and family and community involvement."

■■ Government and businesses issued new policies to help working parents juggle home and work life.

HEALTH IN THE 1990s

Between 1970 and 1993, U.S. spending on health care rose from more than $74 billion to some $884 billion. The aging population, soaring physicians' fees, higher insurance costs, and more-expensive medical equipment accounted for much of this increase. Rising medical costs hit the poor and those without health insurance especially hard.

Fueling the health crisis in the 1990s was the alarming spread of Acquired Immune Deficiency Syndrome, or **AIDS**. This is the final

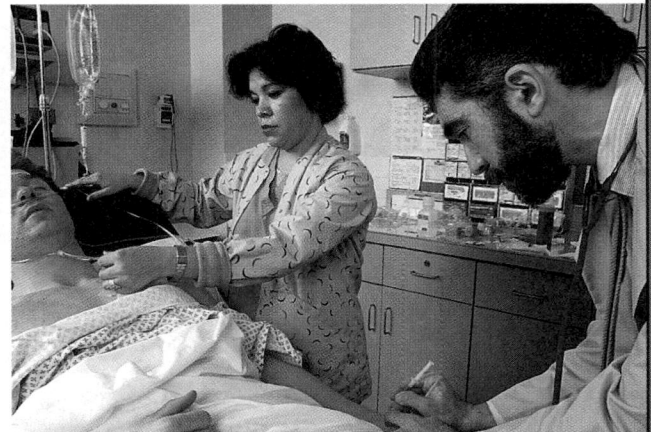

▲ The rising costs of health insurance, doctor's fees, and improved medical equipment created a health-care crisis during the 1990s.

deadly stage of an illness caused by the human immunodeficiency virus, or HIV. By March 1993 some one million people had been infected with HIV, and by 1996 AIDS had claimed the lives of more than 320,000 Americans. In 1993 AIDS was the leading cause of death among men ages 25–44 in 64 U.S. cities. New AIDS cases reported for women more than tripled between 1986 and 1990.

AIDS has left almost no continent untouched. In the African nation of Zambia, President Kenneth Kaunda's son died of AIDS. In 1991, basketball star Earvin "Magic" Johnson of the Los Angeles Lakers announced that he had tested positive for HIV. Other celebrities struck by the disease have included movie star Rock Hudson and tennis legend Arthur Ashe.

The World Health Organization (WHO) estimated in 1995 that some 1.3 million persons worldwide had full-blown AIDS. The organization predicts that some 40 million people will be carriers of HIV by the year 2000.

Some activists accused the United States government of responding too slowly and with too little research money to the AIDS crisis. The Food and Drug Administration responded to these criticisms by speeding up the approval of several drugs for the treatment of AIDS.

A major step forward for disabled citizens came in July 1990, when President George Bush signed into law the **Americans with Disabilities Act**. The act prohibits discrimination against people with mental or physical disabilities—including diseases such as AIDS—in employment, transportation, telephone services, and public buildings.

*P*ractice

GUIDED PRACTICE

Work with students to create a list on the chalkboard of challenges facing Americans in the 1990s. Have students rank these items in order from highest to lowest priority, justifying their choices.

INDEPENDENT PRACTICE

Have students pick a challenge from the Guided Practice list and write a paragraph that describes the challenge and notes progress, or lack of progress, made toward meeting it. Students may wish to include their paragraphs in their portfolios.

*R*eview and *A*ssessment

REVIEW Have students write a letter to a friend in another country describing the concerns and challenges facing Americans in the 1990s and describing, where applicable, the steps presidents Bush or Clinton took to address the challenges. Select students to read their letters to the class. Then assign the Section 3 Review on p. 951.

ASSESS Assign the **Section 3 Daily Quiz** in *Core Resources.*

AV TRANSPARENCY

Everyday Life in America Transparency and **Worksheet 32**

COOPERATIVE LEARNING

Organize students into small groups. Have each group draw a picture or write a description of a technological development that might enhance their quality of life. Have students take on roles as writers, artists, or presenters to prepare a model or poster explaining their choice to the class.

THE AMERICAN NATION VIDEODISC PROGRAM

Early Computer Robot

| 2A | 40641 | :27 |

PRIMARY SOURCE

(for source on p. 951)
Description of Change: excerpted
Rationale: excerpted to focus on main idea

PRIMARY SOURCE

(for source on p. 951)
Description of Change: excerpted and bracketed
Rationale: excerpted to focus on main idea; bracketed to clarify meaning

950

▼ This demonstrator showed support for the Americans with Disabilities Act during a 1990 rally in New York City.

The act also requires companies with 25 or more employees to remove structural barriers in offices.

■■ **The rising costs of health care and the spread of AIDS led to a health crisis in the 1990s.**

*T*ECHNOLOGY AND SOCIETY

The 1980s and 1990s brought advances in space technology. In 1981 the National Aeronautics and Space Administration (NASA) launched the first reusable space vehicle—a **space shuttle.** NASA suffered a grave setback in 1986, when the shuttle *Challenger* exploded shortly after lift-off. All seven crew members perished, including social studies teacher Christa McAuliffe, who would have been the first civilian in space.

Despite this tragedy, NASA forged ahead. With the end of the Cold War, the space agency focused on commercial and scientific projects more than military efforts. The Hubble Space Telescope, launched in 1990 and repaired in 1993, transmitted vital astronomical information and breathtaking photos from deep space. In 1994 came a joint U.S.-Russian space mission.

BIO GRAPHY

Of all the technological advances of these years, the rapid growth of personal computers (PCs) loomed especially large. A leader in this revolution was William "Bill" Gates. Born in Seattle in 1955, Gates began programming at thirteen. In 1974, while a student at Harvard, he devised a PC operating system. A year later he cofounded the Microsoft Corporation to develop computer software. The first IBM personal computer, introduced in 1981, utilized a Microsoft operating system, MS-DOS. By 1986, when Microsoft went public, it was a world leader in providing PC software.

By then, PCs were transforming American life. By the mid-1990s most business offices and public institutions were computerized, and nearly 40 percent of American homes had PCs. Students from grade school to college were using computers for many purposes. In libraries, bulky reference books gave way to CD-ROM computer disks. Physicians could instantly access information on the latest medical research via Medline, a computerized database. Typesetting machines disappeared as books, magazines, and newspapers were printed directly from computer disks. Computers also proved to be a great boon to the disabled, who used them to communicate in a number of ways.

Bill Gates's home near Seattle, Washington, illustrates some of the ways in which technology might eventually transform private life. In the huge hillside home, which includes about 100 internal microcomputers, technology exists to serve and delight, with intricate remote control systems regulating music, entertainment, and even paintings! Each visitor to the house is issued an electronic pin, which stores information and tracks motion. The pins cue the computer system to route

Bill Gates

calls for a particular guest to the nearest phone and to set the lights along the visitor's path to the desired brightness.

The **Internet,** a vast, computer-based communications and information system, enabled users to communicate worldwide, join discussion

---

RETEACH Have students work in small groups to chart the major subjects and events presented in the section. Direct each group to indicate on its chart how each item addresses one of the section's Focus questions.

Closure

Have students use the section's main headings to create a graphic organizer that depicts America in the 1990s. Call on volunteers to present their graphic organizers to the class. Then hold a class discussion in which students explain what they think has been the greatest challenge to Americans in the 1990s.

Extension

ANALYZE Have students research a social issue of the 1990s, such as AIDS, drug abuse, teenage violence, gun control, or police brutality, and report on its causes and experts' recommendations for addressing this problem.

INTERPRET Have students read *Equal Rights for Americans with Disabilities* by Frank Bowe and create a Bill of Rights for Americans with disabilities.

---

groups, and gather information from countless databases. The World Wide Web, developed by Swiss scientists in the early 1990s, linked a wide array of internet sites offering texts, animations, and graphics covering an almost infinite array of topics. Some observers hoped the so-called "information highway"—the Internet and the World Wide Web—would bring people from different social classes, cultures, and countries together. In *The Road Ahead*, his book on computer technology, Bill Gates offered this hope:

> 66 The information highway is going to break down boundaries and may promote a world culture, or at least a sharing of cultural activities and values. The highway will also make it easy for patriots, even expatriates, deeply involved in their own ethnic communities to reach out to others with similar interests no matter where they may be located. 99

Almost a decade earlier, in 1981, writer William Gibson coined the term "cyberspace" for the new computer realm. Wrote Gibson in 1996:

> 66 The [World Wide Web] is not what it was six months ago; in another six months it will be something else again. It was not planned; it simply happened. . . . It is happening the same way cities happen. It _is_ a city. 99

One use of the World Wide Web that promises to aid historical research is the National Digital Library (NDL), which was begun by the Librarian of Congress, James H. Billington. With money raised from private sources and with some government funding, the NDL plans to have 5 million items available on the Library of Congress's web site by the year 2000. Each item displayed on screen will be a digitized image of the original. Among the items already on line are documents and photographs relating to the history of African Americans, the Civil War, women's suffrage, the Great Depression and World War II.

But computers have not brought utopia. The social problems plaguing American society soon appeared in cyberspace as well. In the Telecommunications Act of 1996, Congress tried to regulate indecency on the Internet. A federal court quickly struck down key provisions of this law, however, as a violation of First Amendment free speech rights.

In addition to fears about the kinds of material circulating through cyberspace, some observers worried that a fully computerized society would not need human workers. Such fears were probably exaggerated, since new technologies typically create more jobs than they eliminate. But in the interval between job loss and the emergence of new jobs, severe disruptions can occur. In fact, job layoffs remained high, affecting about 8 percent of workers during the period 1993–1995. Other people worried that computers would deepen social divisions as well-to-do, well-educated Americans mastered the new technology, while poorer citizens lagged behind. Like all new technologies, the computer held both vast promise and troubling challenges for the future.

■■ SECTION 3 REVIEW
■■

IDENTIFY and explain the significance of the following: Immigration Act, Rodney King, Nelson Mandela, Wilma Mankiller, Family and Medical Leave Act, AIDS, Americans with Disabilities Act, space shuttle, Bill Gates, Internet, cyberspace.

LOCATE and explain the importance of the following: Haiti, Los Angeles, Miami.

1. **MAIN IDEA** What economic and urban problems did inner-city workers and families face?
2. **MAIN IDEA** How did AIDS impact the nation?
3. **MAIN IDEA** How have computers transformed American life?
4. **WRITING TO PERSUADE** Imagine you are the owner of a medical clinic. Write a speech that convinces listeners in your community that a health-care crisis exists in the 1990s.
5. **EVALUATING** How has NASA impacted science and technology?

Chapter Review Answers

WRITING A SUMMARY
See Essential Points in each section for main ideas.

REVIEWING CHRONOLOGY
4, 3, 1, 5, 2
Analyzing
to force Congress to balance the budget through a series of spending cuts if spending went over a certain level

IDENTIFYING PEOPLE AND IDEAS
1. *Polish independent trade union*
2. *CIA-sponsored army attempting to overthrow Nicaraguan Sandinistas*
3. *first woman to run on major party presidential ticket*
4. *stockbrokers' use of confidential financial information for personal gain*
5. *Iraqi ruler whose invasion of Kuwait led to Persian Gulf War*
6. *African American whose beating by police led indirectly to Los Angeles riot*
7. *law increasing numbers of immigrants allowed into U.S.*
8. *Cherokee leader who worked to promote American Indian causes*
9. *fatal disease caused by HIV virus*
10. *Founder of the Microsoft Corporation*

UNDERSTANDING MAIN IDEAS

1. *increased military spending, proposed new weapons systems such as MX and SDI, instituted trade restrictions against Soviet Union, increased involvement in Nicaragua and El Salvador*
2. *Persian Gulf War, growth of deficit, large trade gap, S&L bailout, worsening economy, Thomas-Hill hearings*
3. *deficit, recession, role and treatment of women, reform of government*
4. *helped economy by creating new businesses and contributing to high-tech industries*
5. *urban—racial conflicts, loss of inner-city jobs; health—aging population, rising medical insurance costs, spread of AIDS*

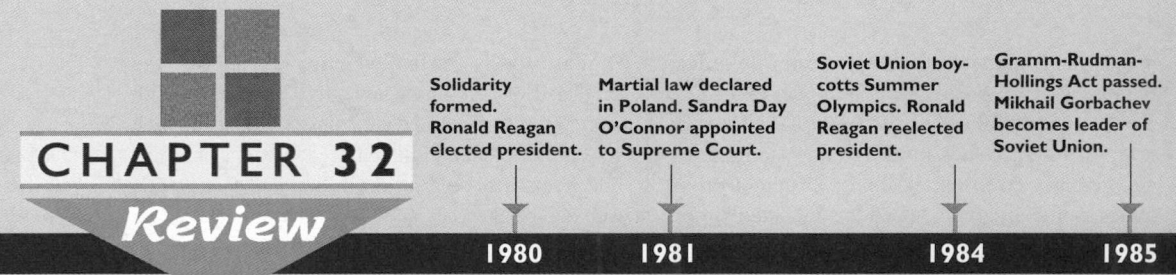

	Solidarity formed. Ronald Reagan elected president.	Martial law declared in Poland. Sandra Day O'Connor appointed to Supreme Court.	Soviet Union boycotts Summer Olympics. Ronald Reagan reelected president.	Gramm-Rudman-Hollings Act passed. Mikhail Gorbachev becomes leader of Soviet Union.
	1980	1981	1984	1985

CHAPTER 32
Review

WRITING A SUMMARY
Using the essential points of the chapter as a guide, write a summary of the chapter.

REVIEWING CHRONOLOGY
Number your paper 1 to 5. Study the time line above, and list the following events in the order in which they happened by writing the first next to 1, the second next to 2, and so on. Then complete the activity below.

1. INF Treaty ratified.
2. Bill Clinton elected president.
3. Soviet Union boycotts Summer Olympics.
4. Solidarity formed.
5. Thomas-Hill hearings occur.

Analyzing What was the purpose of the Gramm-Rudman-Hollings Act?

IDENTIFYING PEOPLE AND IDEAS
Explain the historical significance of each of the following people or terms.

1. Solidarity
2. contras
3. Geraldine Ferraro
4. insider trading
5. Saddam Hussein
6. Rodney King
7. Immigration Act
8. Wilma Mankiller
9. AIDS
10. Bill Gates

UNDERSTANDING MAIN IDEAS
1. How did the Reagan administration fight the Cold War?
2. What challenges did President Bush face during his term?
3. What important issues did Americans discuss during the 1992 election campaign?
4. What benefits did the arrival of immigrants in the 1990s have for the United States?
5. What urban problems and health challenges did Americans face during the early 1990s?

★ REVIEWING THEMES
1. **Economic Development** What effects did Reaganomics have on the country?

2. **Democratic Values** In what ways might technological advances help increase voter participation in the election process?

THINKING CRITICALLY
1. **Comparing and Contrasting** How did the scandal surrounding the Iran-contra affair prove both similar to and different from the Watergate scandal?
2. **Analyzing** How did improved relations affect the United States and the Soviet Union?

STRATEGY FOR SUCCESS
Review the Strategies for Success entry on Comparing Points of View on page 420. Then read the following two excerpts from the 1984 presidential campaign. The first is from a speech by Jesse Jackson. The second is from a Republican commercial for Ronald Reagan. How do these two selections reflect different views of America?

> **❝** Our flag is red, white and blue, but our nation is rainbow—red, yellow, brown, black and white. . . . America is not like a blanket—one piece of unbroken cloth, the same color, the same texture, the same size. America is more like a quilt—many patches, many pieces, many colors, many sizes, all woven and held together by a common thread. . . .
>
> Even in our fractured state, all of us count and fit somewhere. . . . We have not proven that we can win or make progress without each other. We must come together. **❞**

> **❝** In a town not too far from where you live, a young family has just moved into a new home. Three years ago, even the smallest house seemed completely out of reach. Right down the street, one of the neighbors has just bought himself a new car, with all the options. The factory down the river is working again. Not long ago, people were saying it probably would be closed forever. . . . Life is better. America is back. **❞**

REVIEWING THEMES

1. increased investment, higher employment, reduced inflation, cut social and environmental programs, large federal budget deficits
2. Students might mention widespread use of public formats such as TV talk shows and radio call-in programs to involve voters and heighten their awareness of the issues.

THINKING CRITICALLY

1. similar—involved secret and illegal actions, led to investigations by Congress, resulted in resignations of key White House officials; different—did not lead to impeachment charges against Reagan nor undermine his presidency
2. U.S.—eased fears of nuclear war; Soviet Union—helped focus on glasnost and perestroika

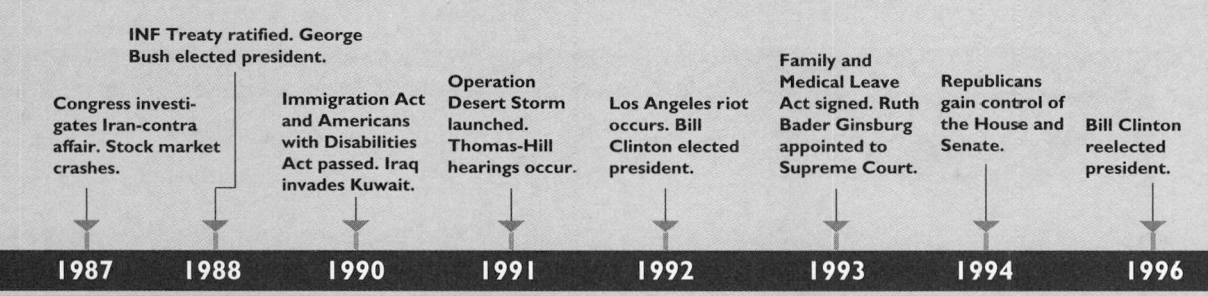

1987	1988	1990	1991	1992	1993	1994	1996
Congress investigates Iran-contra affair. Stock market crashes.	INF Treaty ratified. George Bush elected president. Immigration Act and Americans with Disabilities Act passed. Iraq invades Kuwait.		Operation Desert Storm launched. Thomas-Hill hearings occur.	Los Angeles riot occurs. Bill Clinton elected president.	Family and Medical Leave Act signed. Ruth Bader Ginsburg appointed to Supreme Court.	Republicans gain control of the House and Senate.	Bill Clinton reelected president.

WRITING ABOUT HISTORY

Writing to Explain Write an essay that explains the significance of the passage of the Americans with Disabilities Act.

USING PRIMARY SOURCES

After the Los Angeles riot, African American Willie L. Williams became the city's new chief of police. In an interview shortly after the riots, Williams expressed his impressions of African American concerns in Los Angeles. Read the following excerpt from the interview. According to Williams, what do African Americans want from police, and how has crime affected their neighborhoods?

66 *The African-American community wants strong, tough, honest, fair policing. There is no African-American community in America that does not want to see police there. The people want to be treated fairly. They want to be treated honestly and with dignity. . . .*

Crime also has a long-term effect on the community because it drives out the mom-and-pop businesses, the corner stores, where a lot of shopping is done. It drives out the source of income for the teenagers and the young adults who don't have a lot of skills or are just going to school to learn skills. It often drives out the source of income for parents who may be living and working at home and working in the area. The cost of crime in the African-American community cannot be underestimated. 99

LINKING HISTORY AND GEOGRAPHY

Refer to the maps on page 917 and page 937. Which states did the Democratic party win in 1988 that it did not win in 1980?

Willie L. Williams

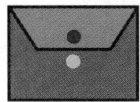

BUILDING YOUR PORTFOLIO

Complete the following projects independently or cooperatively.

1. **POLITICS** In Chapter 31 you were a reporter covering Watergate. Building on that experience, imagine you are covering the Iran-contra affair. Create a flow chart that traces the Iran-contra transfer of weapons, money, and supplies.

2. **BUSINESS AND TRADE** Imagine you are the director of a private agency that assists immigrant businesspeople. Prepare a speech on how immigrant businesses are helping to boost your city's economy.

3. **THE ECONOMY** In Chapter 31 you examined oil prices and inflation. Building on that experience, imagine you are one of President Reagan's economic advisers. Prepare a pamphlet describing the principles and goals of Reaganomics.

$\mathcal{A}$ DIVERSE COUNTRY

HISTORICAL SIDELIGHTS
Segregation

In some U.S. cities ethnic and cultural diversity has managed to carry over into individual neighborhoods. But despite advances in civil rights and the diversity of ethnic representation in America, areas in the United States remain racially segregated. A 1992 study of black and white residential patterns found the least segregated cities in the nation to be Jacksonville, NC; Lawton, OK; and Anchorage, AK.

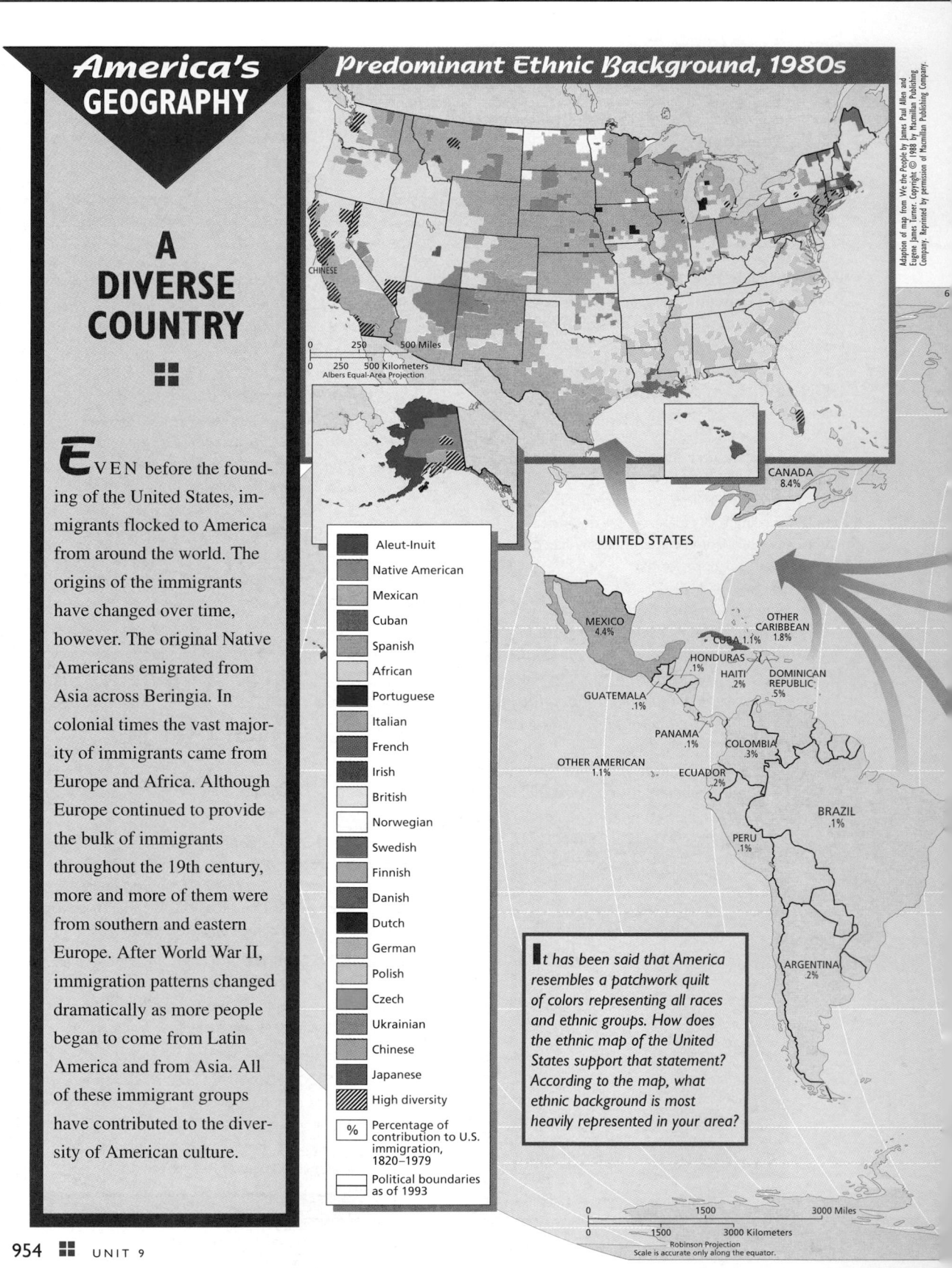

America's
GEOGRAPHY

Predominant Ethnic Background, 1980s

Adaption of map from *We the People* by James Paul Allen and Eugene James Turner. Copyright © 1988 by Macmillan Publishing Company. Reprinted by permission of Macmillan Publishing Company.

A DIVERSE COUNTRY

$\blacksquare\blacksquare$

$\mathbf{E}$VEN before the founding of the United States, immigrants flocked to America from around the world. The origins of the immigrants have changed over time, however. The original Native Americans emigrated from Asia across Beringia. In colonial times the vast majority of immigrants came from Europe and Africa. Although Europe continued to provide the bulk of immigrants throughout the 19th century, more and more of them were from southern and eastern Europe. After World War II, immigration patterns changed dramatically as more people began to come from Latin America and from Asia. All of these immigrant groups have contributed to the diversity of American culture.

Legend:
- Aleut-Inuit
- Native American
- Mexican
- Cuban
- Spanish
- African
- Portuguese
- Italian
- French
- Irish
- British
- Norwegian
- Swedish
- Finnish
- Danish
- Dutch
- German
- Polish
- Czech
- Ukrainian
- Chinese
- Japanese
- High diversity
- % Percentage of contribution to U.S. immigration, 1820–1979
- Political boundaries as of 1993

CHINESE

UNITED STATES

CANADA 8.4%

MEXICO 4.4%

OTHER CARIBBEAN 1.8%

CUBA 1.1%

HONDURAS .1%

HAITI .2%

DOMINICAN REPUBLIC .5%

GUATEMALA .1%

PANAMA .1%

COLOMBIA .3%

OTHER AMERICAN 1.1%

ECUADOR .2%

PERU .1%

BRAZIL .1%

ARGENTINA .2%

It has been said that America resembles a patchwork quilt of colors representing all races and ethnic groups. How does the ethnic map of the United States support that statement? According to the map, what ethnic background is most heavily represented in your area?

0   250   500 Miles
0   250   500 Kilometers
Albers Equal-Area Projection

0   1500   3000 Miles
0   1500   3000 Kilometers
Robinson Projection
Scale is accurate only along the equator.

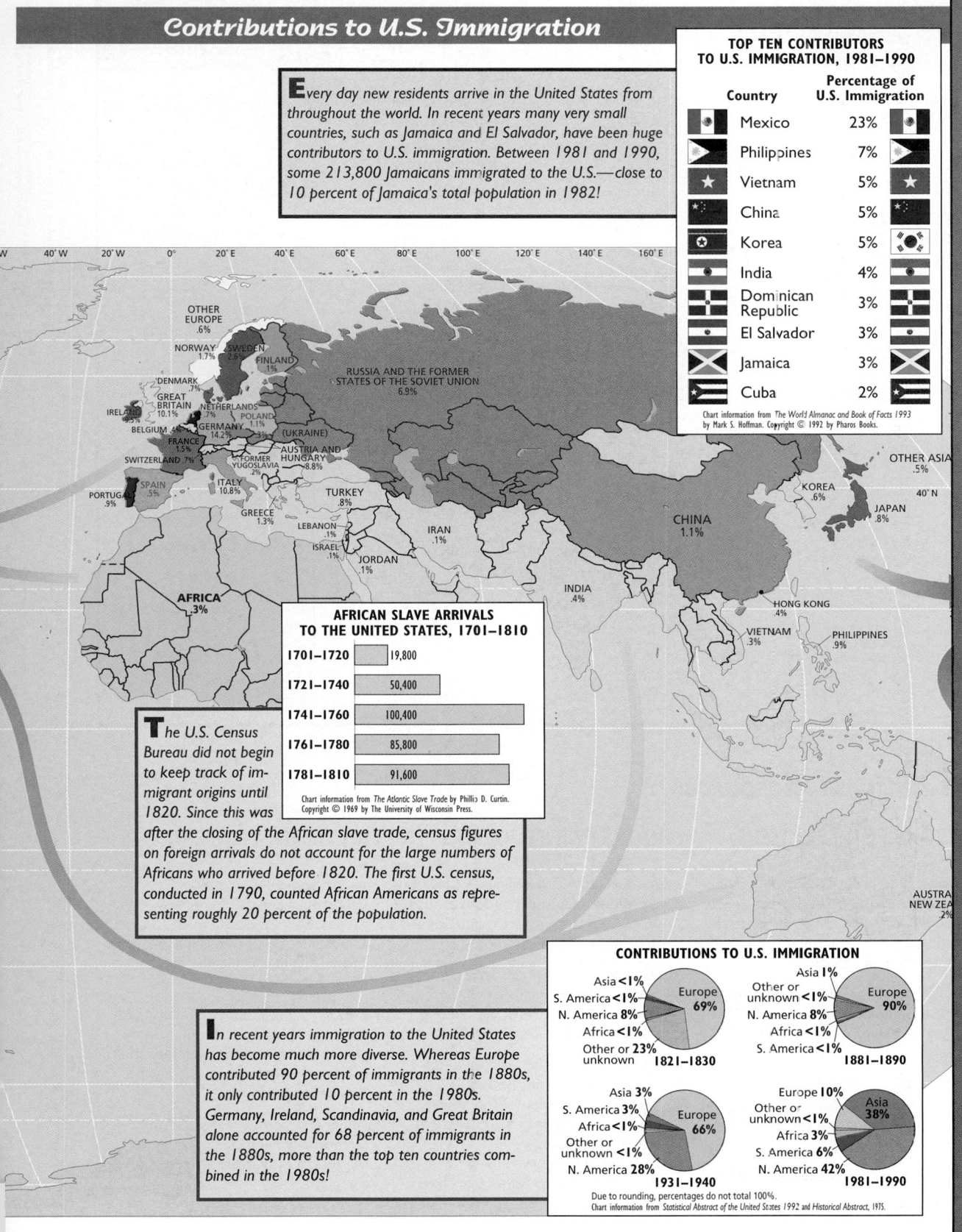

Contributions to U.S. Immigration

Every day new residents arrive in the United States from throughout the world. In recent years many very small countries, such as Jamaica and El Salvador, have been huge contributors to U.S. immigration. Between 1981 and 1990, some 213,800 Jamaicans immigrated to the U.S.—close to 10 percent of Jamaica's total population in 1982!

TOP TEN CONTRIBUTORS TO U.S. IMMIGRATION, 1981–1990

Country	Percentage of U.S. Immigration
Mexico	23%
Philippines	7%
Vietnam	5%
China	5%
Korea	5%
India	4%
Dominican Republic	3%
El Salvador	3%
Jamaica	3%
Cuba	2%

Chart information from *The World Almanac and Book of Facts 1993* by Mark S. Hoffman. Copyright © 1992 by Pharos Books.

VOICES IN HISTORY

Israeli writer Ehud Yonay, commenting on America's continuing appeal to immigrants and tourists, wrote in 1977, "One comes to the United States—always, no matter how often—to see the future. It's what life in one's own country will be like five, ten, twenty years from now."

AFRICAN SLAVE ARRIVALS TO THE UNITED STATES, 1701–1810

Period	Arrivals
1701–1720	19,800
1721–1740	50,400
1741–1760	100,400
1761–1780	85,800
1781–1810	91,600

Chart information from *The Atlantic Slave Trade* by Phillip D. Curtin. Copyright © 1969 by The University of Wisconsin Press.

The U.S. Census Bureau did not begin to keep track of immigrant origins until 1820. Since this was after the closing of the African slave trade, census figures on foreign arrivals do not account for the large numbers of Africans who arrived before 1820. The first U.S. census, conducted in 1790, counted African Americans as representing roughly 20 percent of the population.

In recent years immigration to the United States has become much more diverse. Whereas Europe contributed 90 percent of immigrants in the 1880s, it only contributed 10 percent in the 1980s. Germany, Ireland, Scandinavia, and Great Britain alone accounted for 68 percent of immigrants in the 1880s, more than the top ten countries combined in the 1980s!

CONTRIBUTIONS TO U.S. IMMIGRATION

1821–1830
- Asia <1%
- S. America <1%
- N. America 8%
- Africa <1%
- Other or unknown 23%
- Europe 69%

1881–1890
- Asia 1%
- Other or unknown <1%
- N. America 8%
- Africa <1%
- S. America <1%
- Europe 90%

1931–1940
- Asia 3%
- S. America 3%
- Africa <1%
- Other or unknown <1%
- N. America 28%
- Europe 66%

1981–1990
- Europe 10%
- Other or unknown <1%
- Africa 3%
- S. America 6%
- N. America 42%
- Asia 38%

Due to rounding, percentages do not total 100%.
Chart information from *Statistical Abstract of the United States 1992* and *Historical Abstract, 1975*.

955

*A*MERICA IN TODAY'S WORLD

1970–the Present

*C*hapter *O*verview

The collapse of the Soviet Union and the fall of communism heralded the coming of a new era. But the post-Communist world proved as fraught with danger as the world of the Cold War. The nations of the world had to find their place and their role in an ever-growing, interdependent global economy. At the same time they faced such pressing problems as diminishing energy resources, environmental pollution, overpopulation, famine, the spread of drugs, and rising crime rates. Many world leaders looked to the U.S. for guidance in the search for solutions to these problems.

THE AMERICAN NATION VIDEODISC PROGRAM A variety of still images, short videos, and activities are available for you to use as you teach this chapter. See Correlation to *The American Nation* Videodisc Program for barcode correlations and suggestions for using the program.

*C*hapter *P*lanning *G*uide

CHAPTER 33	CORE RESOURCE BOOKLETS	AUDIOVISUAL **AV** RESOURCES	PROGRAM RESOURCES
INTRODUCTION pp. 956–957	■ Literature Worksheet 33 ■ Building Your Portfolio Worksheet 9	■ Linking Geography and History Transparency and Worksheet 23	
TEACHING THE CHAPTER pp. 958–979	■ Graphic Organizer 33 ■ Social Studies Skills Worksheet 33 ■ Geography Worksheet 33 ■ Outline Maps 1, 2, 6, 8, 12, 13, 14, 16, 19, 20, 24, 25	■ *The American Nation* Videodisc: The Maiden Flight of the Concorde; Images of America; The Peace Corps ■ Linking Geography and History Transparency and Worksheet 24 ■ Everyday Life in America Transparency and Worksheet 33	
REVIEW AND ASSESSMENT pp. 980–981	■ Chapter 33 Daily Quizzes ■ Review Worksheet 33 ■ Chapter 33 Tests ■ Alternative Assessment Forms		■ Test Generator

*A*dditional *R*esources

BOOKS FOR TEACHERS

Brown, Lester R., et al. *State of the World 1996.* W. W. Norton, 1996. Draws on wide range of research and statistics to review some of the major global challenges.

Diuk, Nadia, and Adrian Karatnycky. *New Nations Rising.* Wiley, 1993. Reviews the forces reshaping the former Soviet Union.

Halberstam, David. *The Next Century.* Updated ed. Avon, 1992. Analyzes global economy on the eve of the 21st century.

BOOKS FOR STUDENTS

Epping, Randy C. *A Beginner's Guide to the World Economy.* Random House, 1992. Offers concise explanations of world economic issues.

Kronenwetter, Michael. *Taking a Stand Against Human Rights Abuses.* Watts, 1990. Reviews the current status of human rights in the world.

* Smith, Brenda. *The Collapse of the Soviet Union.* Lucent Books, 1993. Traces the breakup of the Soviet Union and explores the challenges facing the region.

* for students reading below grade level

MULTIMEDIA MATERIALS

The Environment—New Global Concerns. Video, 20 min. New York Times/SSSS. Discusses such issues as destruction of the rain forests, ozone depletion, and the greenhouse effect.

Pacific Horizons: Economic Change and Challenge. 2 videos, 28 min. Close-Up Foundation/SSSS. Examines the growing importance of the Pacific Rim nations.

Whither Democracy? Video, 57 min. Democracy Films/SSSS. Examines the future of democracy around the globe.

THEMES IN AMERICAN HISTORY

USE WITH PAGES 956–957

Listed on the right are the themes emphasized in Chapter 33. The questions in boldface type stimulate critical thinking and provide students with an opportunity to discuss the themes within a broadened context. The questions also appear in the pupil's edition on p. 956.

■ ECONOMIC DEVELOPMENT

How might economic influence be more important than military strength in determining the political power of nations? Students may mention that a nation with little military strength could be very powerful in the global community if it controlled large amounts of trade with other nations. Its political power would be further heightened if it controlled products or resources on which other nations were heavily dependent.

■ GLOBAL RELATIONS

What might nations do to resolve global conflicts in other regions? Students might mention actions such as using embargoes to apply political and economic pressure on nations involved in the conflicts, trying to negotiate cease-fire or settlement agreements between warring nations, or direct intervention with military force—either independently or as part of a larger international effort to restore peace to a region.

■ TECHNOLOGY AND SCIENCE

How might technological advances both hinder and help the environment? Students might point out that some technological advances have created machinery, products, and processes that have polluted, exploited, and otherwise harmed the environment. Other technological advances, however, have resulted in the development of more environmentally sensitive products and in more efficient use of scarce resources.

CHAPTER STRATEGIES FOR MEETING INDIVIDUAL NEEDS

LIMITED ENGLISH PROFICIENT LEARNERS

Have pairs of students list the key issues in the chapter. Tell each pair to prioritize its list, from the issue it believes most important to the issue it believes least important. Have pairs defend their rankings when they compare their lists.

TACTILE/KINESTHETIC LEARNERS

Have students construct a number of wall maps to illustrate some of the issues discussed in the chapter, such as the state of the economy or the state of the environment. Encourage students to consult *The New State of the Earth Atlas* (Touchstone, 2nd ed., 1995), edited by Joni Seager, for ideas.

LEARNERS HAVING DIFFICULTY

Discuss the meaning of the boldfaced terms in the chapter with students, encouraging them to offer definitions. Then have students use these terms to write a brief summary of the chapter.

AUDITORY LEARNERS

Have students prepare a brief oral presentation on an issue discussed in the chapter. After each presentation, have listeners write a summary of the major points covered. Encourage students to compare their summaries.

VISUAL LEARNERS

Have students use library resources to locate visual materials that illustrate the titles of the four sections of this chapter. Call on volunteers to present and explain their selections.

GIFTED LEARNERS

Have students write an essay titled "The World on the Threshold of the 21st Century." Suggest that they focus on four themes—politics, economics, the environment, and technology.

ABOUT THE ILLUSTRATION

On November 9, 1989, the East German government began to dismantle the Berlin Wall. The image of the wall coming down became a symbol of the fall of communism throughout Europe. Encourage students to imagine they are East Germans witnessing the fall of the wall. Ask them to describe what they might have felt upon seeing this event. Have students research old news stories about the fall of the Berlin Wall and write a short essay summarizing global responses to the event.

Chapter 33

1970–the Present

AMERICA IN TODAY'S WORLD

FOCUS

UNDERSTANDING THE MAIN IDEA

In the 1990s, world leaders faced the task of reorganizing relations in the post–Cold War world. As Japan and other countries gained economic power, many Americans feared that the United States would lose its place as the leading world power. Meanwhile, many world leaders worried about the effects of global pollution and health hazards such as drugs, overpopulation, and famine.

THEMES

■ **ECONOMIC DEVELOPMENT** How might economic influence be more important than military strength in determining the political power of nations?

■ **GLOBAL RELATIONS** What might nations do to resolve global conflicts in other regions?

■ **TECHNOLOGY AND SOCIETY** How might technological advances both hinder and help the environment?

1972		1986	1989	1992	1993
Terrorists attack Israeli athletes at Munich Olympics.		Chernobyl nuclear accident occurs.	Berlin Wall falls.	Operation Restore Hope launched.	NAFTA ratified.

Ask students to identify the key events that signaled the thawing of the Cold War in the late 1980s. *(reforms of Soviet leader Mikhail Gorbachev, series of meetings between Gorbachev and President Reagan)* Then have students speculate how the end of the Cold War might affect U.S. foreign relations. Ask students to review and adjust their speculations as they read the chapter.

⬢⬢ LINK TO THE PAST ▶

Cold War tensions decreased somewhat in the 1970s as President Nixon negotiated détente with Soviet leaders. But in the early 1980s U.S.– Soviet relations deteriorated as the Soviets became embroiled in turmoil in Poland, and the United States increased its activities in Central America. Relations began to improve, however, after the reform-minded Mikhail Gorbachev became leader of the Soviet Union in 1985.

*G*lasnost and *perestroika* marked the beginning of the end of the Cold War. World leaders now face the task of reshaping the international order in a new era—an era that is hardly peaceful. Bitter conflicts have erupted in many countries, and urgent economic and social problems spill beyond national borders. The most serious of these problems include nationalist conflicts in the former Soviet Union, trade disputes, an exploding world population, dwindling energy resources, and environmental hazards. And while industrialized nations continue to enjoy high standards of living, the developing world faces grinding poverty, malnutrition, and even famine. The task of deciding how the United States will address these global concerns is one of the greatest challenges facing Americans today.

Although the world's problems are great, encouraging signs have emerged that the global community is prepared to tackle important issues. Organizations such as the United Nations and Amnesty International have tried to bring people together from around the globe to find solutions to pressing problems. Meanwhile brave individuals throughout the world are speaking out for justice and peace. As the leading superpower in the world, the United States is at the forefront of these efforts.

Dismantling the Berlin Wall, 1989

Bumper sticker

HISTORICAL SIDELIGHTS
A Global Challenge

In his inaugural address, given in January 1993, President Bill Clinton reflected on the excitement, promise, and challenge of living in a global community: "Communications and commerce are global, investment is mobile, technology is almost magical, and ambition for a better life is now universal. We earn our livelihood in America today in peaceful competition with people all across the earth. Profound and powerful forces are shaking and remaking our world. And the urgent question of our time is whether we can make change our friend."

PREVIEW WORKSHOP

Following is a list of the significant people, places, and terms in this section. You may wish to use this list as a section preview.

People
- Boris Yeltsin
- Yasir Arafat
- Yitzhak Rabin
- Daw Aung San Suu Kyi
- Carlos Ximenes Belo
- Jose Ramos-Horta

Places
- Azerbaijan
- Somalia
- Bosnia and Herzegovina

Terms
- German reunification
- Commonwealth of Independent States
- Operation Restore Hope

FOCUS OBJECTIVES

- Identify the events that marked the end of the Cold War.

- Explain how the end of the Cold War affected regional conflicts.

- Describe how terrorist activity changed in the 1990s.

- Examine the role of the United Nations in the post–Cold War era.

Section 1

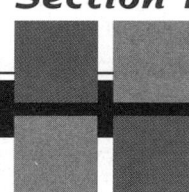

A NEW ERA

FOCUS

- **What events marked the end of the Cold War?**
- **How did the end of the Cold War affect regional conflicts?**
- **How did terrorist activity change in the 1990s?**
- **What role has the United Nations played in the post–Cold War era?**

Mikhail Gorbachev's reform efforts in the Soviet Union led to the end of the Cold War—and eventually to the breakup of the Soviet Union. In early 1991, President Bush reflected on the promise of a new era free from Cold War pressures. "Now we can see . . . the very real prospect of a new world order," he declared, "a world in which freedom and respect for human rights find a home among all nations." But in recent years, conflict, crisis, and disorder have often seemed the norm.

Confrontation in Tiananmen Square, China, 1989

THE OLD ORDER FADES

Historians still debate how far Mikhail Gorbachev intended to go with the economic and political reform of the Soviet system. Undoubtedly, he meant to institute real change. But many argue that it is unlikely he foresaw the end result—the breakup of the Soviet Union and the collapse of Communist rule. Once set in motion, however, Gorbachev's reforms took on a life of their own.

Gorbachev's efforts to modernize and expand the Soviet economy led to a dramatic easing of Cold War tensions with the United States (see Chapter 32). They also indirectly assisted the democratic movements that swept Eastern and Central Europe in 1989 and 1990. No longer willing or able to bear the costs of propping up Communist regimes around the world, the Soviet Union announced in 1989 that it was adopting a policy of nonintervention in Eastern Europe. Thus the Soviets did nothing when Poland and Hungary held free elections and the Communist governments in Czechoslovakia and Romania fell.

◀ **Pro-democracy demonstrations, such as the one shown here, helped bring on the collapse of Communist party rule in Russia.**

CORE RESOURCES

- **Social Studies Skills Worksheet 33**
- **Section 1 Daily Quiz**

AV RESOURCES

- **Linking Geography and History Transparency and Worksheet 24**

Teaching the Section

THE END OF THE COLD WAR

Have students work in small groups to write scripts for a five-minute television news story on the fall of communism in Eastern Europe and the Soviet Union. Suggest that groups include in their scripts ideas for visuals to illustrate the story. Ask groups to present and discuss their news stories. Then lead the class in a discussion on how the fall of the Soviet Union has affected American foreign policy.

The Breakup of the Soviet Sphere, 1991

NATIONALISM The Soviets had kept a firm lid on nationalist sentiments. The collapse of the Soviet empire unleashed bitter ethnic and religious conflicts.

? LOCATION The U.S.S.R. and some of the nations in the former Soviet sphere broke up. Which nation was reunited?

Legend:
- Commonwealth of Independent States
- Independent republics
- Former East European satellite of Soviet Union
- Boundary of former Soviet Union

Map Caption Answer
Germany

AV TRANSPARENCY
Linking Geography and History Transparency and **Worksheet 24**

CULTURAL PATTERNS

Though many Americans admired Mikhail Gorbachev, by 1991 many Soviet citizens had become disenchanted with his reform program. A public opinion poll released in the spring of the year found that close to 40 percent of respondents would not have supported *perestroika* if they could have foreseen the outcome.

The Soviets also did nothing when pro-democracy demonstrations broke out in East Germany in the fall of 1989. Throughout the fall, tens of thousands of East Germans fled to the West through Hungary. Then in October demonstrators forced Communist leader Erich Honecker to resign. Hoping to restore calm, the East German government opened the Berlin Wall on November 9 and lifted restrictions on travel to the West. But it was already too late; the pressure for **German reunification**—the reuniting of East and West Germany as one nation—was too great. After free elections, the two nations were united as the Federal Republic of Germany on October 3, 1990, without opposition from Gorbachev.

By 1991 Gorbachev had problems of his own in the Soviet Union. Alarmed by the pace of reforms, Communist hard-liners attempted to oust him. Their coup collapsed quickly, but Gorbachev's days in power were numbered. On December 1 the Ukrainians voted for independence. A week later the presidents of Ukraine, Russia, and Belarus declared that the Soviet Union was "ceasing its existence" and formed the **Commonwealth of Independent States** (CIS). On December 25 Gorbachev resigned as president of the Soviet Union and turned over control of the armed forces to Boris Yeltsin, the president of Russia. The Soviet Union was no more. Eventually the former Soviet republics of Armenia, Azerbaijan, Kazakhstan, Kyrgyzstan, Moldova, Tajikistan, Turkmenistan, Uzbekistan, and Georgia joined the CIS.

Russia faced political turmoil and hard economic times as it struggled toward democracy and a free-market system. By September 1993 Russia was so unstable that Boris Yeltsin temporarily suspended the constitution and dissolved

Teaching the *Section*

REGIONAL CONFLICTS

List the following regions on the chalkboard: *Commonwealth of Independent States, Africa, Eastern Europe, Middle East.* Refer students to the regional map on p. 959 and the world map on pp. 1012–1013, and ask volunteers to identify conflicts that took place within the listed regions in the early 1990s. Note their responses under the appropriate chalkboard headings. Then discuss how the disintegration of the Soviet Union might have contributed to events in each of these regions. Ask students to explain why the collapse of Soviet military power might have contributed to instability within Eastern Europe and the former republics of the Soviet Union.

GLOBAL CONNECTIONS

Ethnic and regional disputes in such places as the former Yugoslavia and the Horn of Africa caused a huge population displacement. A report issued in late 1993 by the UN High Commissioner for Refugees noted that violence across the world had forced some 19.7 million refugees to flee their countries. The report further stated that some 24 million people were internal refugees—they had fled their homes for safe havens elsewhere in their own countries.

VOICES IN HISTORY

Some of the violence in South Africa resulted from differences between the predominantly Zulu Inkatha movement and the African National Congress (ANC), whose members were from numerous tribes. ANC leaders insisted that tribal differences had to be put aside. "The message has always been clear—that we are South Africans first," one leader stated. "Tribalism is a devil that we must destroy."

Parliament, sparking a power struggle. In a 1996 presidential election, Yeltsin, despite poor health, defeated a former communist who favored a return to centralized rule.

■■ The collapse of communism in Eastern Europe, the fall of the Berlin Wall, and the breakup of the Soviet Union marked the end of the Cold War.

In contrast, pro-democracy reformers in China met a different fate. In May 1989 students and others took to Beijing's streets to protest Communist party policies. On June 4 the government sent soldiers and tanks against the peaceful protesters gathered in Tiananmen Square. Estimates of the number of protesters killed range from a few hundred to more than a thousand. In the 1990s China abandoned a centrally controlled economy in favor of capitalist free enterprise, but human-rights abuses persisted.

*R*EGIONAL CONFLICTS

As the Cold War fades, regional conflicts have intensified. The end of Communist rule in Eastern Europe unleashed bitter ethnic and local disputes that had formerly been kept in check by Communist authorities. Bosnia, in a region that was once Yugoslavia, was torn by fighting between Serbs, Croatians, and Slovenes.

In the former Soviet Union itself, the 15 newly independent republics experienced conflict as different groups struggled for power and self-rule. Russia and Ukraine argued over control of the Black Sea fleet, while Christians in the former Soviet republic of Armenia battled with Muslims in neighboring Azerbaijan (az-uhr-by-JAHN).

On a brighter note, a new era dawned in South Africa when decades of white-only rule came to an end. In 1994 South Africa held elections in which all races could vote. Nelson Mandela, who had spent years in prison, won the presidency. Despite conflict between rival political and ethnic groups, South Africa's future looked hopeful.

Elsewhere in Africa, however, turmoil reigned, worsened by famine and grinding poverty. Civil war raged in Zambia, Liberia, Mali, and Somalia. In Nigeria a series of coups beginning in 1983 gave rise to a brutal military dictatorship. In December 1992 United Nations forces, including many Americans, launched **Operation Restore Hope** to provide relief to famine-stricken Somalia. Fighting among rival clans in that country had prevented relief workers from getting food and other supplies to starving Somalis. By 1995, when the last UN forces left, the country had no central government, and Somalia's suffering continued. The failed Somalia operation showed the limits of international intervention in desperately poor societies torn by conflict.

■■ Regional conflicts in the former Soviet Union and in Africa have increased since the end of the Cold War.

In the Middle East instability also threatens many nations, as Islamic fundamentalists battle for political power. However, hopes for peace between Palestinians and Israelis were renewed in September 1993, when Palestinian leader Yasir Arafat and Israeli prime minister Yitzhak Rabin signed a peace accord. President Clinton, who oversaw the signing of the agreement at the White House, approvingly referred to it as a "historic and honorable compromise."

The peace process suffered a setback in 1995, when a young Israeli ultra-nationalist assassinated Yitzhak Rabin. In 1996 elections Benjamin Netanyahu came to power pledging a tougher line on peace negotiations. U.S. secretary of state Warren Christopher worked hard to keep the peace process alive, but new outbreaks of violence

▲ During the 1990s Somalia was torn apart by civil war, famine, and poverty. In December 1992, UN forces helped stabilize the political situation to ensure that food and supplies reached starving people.

THE THREAT OF TERRORISM

Organize students into groups to discuss the problem of international terrorism. Tell the groups to consider in their discussions such topics as the nature of international terrorism, recent changes in terrorist tactics, and the impact that terrorism could have on the U.S. and on American citizens. Ask representatives of the groups to share their conclusions with the class.

WORKING FOR PEACE

Organize students into three groups. Have each group imagine it is the United Nations Security Council in the early 1990s. Assign each group the task of formulating a plan to resolve regional conflicts in one of the following areas: Somalia, South Africa, or the former states of Yugoslavia. Suggest to students that their plans may include a variety of solutions, from organizing international boycotts to sending in peacekeeping forces.

Have a representative from each group share its plan with the class.

▶

HISTORY in the Making

DR. PAUL BOYER

The Freedom of Information Act

Under the Freedom of Information Act (FOIA), anyone is supposed to be able to examine the records of U.S. federal agencies. Many people expected the FOIA to be particularly useful for scholars of political history. In reality, however, many scholars have found their use of the law severely limited by government red tape.

The congressional call for the Freedom of Information Act originated during the 1950s, when Senator Joseph McCarthy accused numerous government employees of harboring Communist sympathies. Several members of Congress began to push for an act that would allow easy access to government files on people accused of being Communists. By the time Congress passed the law in 1966, all government files were supposed to be open to the public unless national security needs clearly justified their exclusion.

Many government officials, however, claimed that the FOIA interfered with Cold War politics. In some circumstances, they argued, foreign agents might be reluctant to pass information on to American agencies for fear that the information might be made public through the FOIA. As a result of such concerns, numerous amendments were made to the

FOIA to grant agencies exemptions from the law. Critics argue that such exemptions, coupled with the complicated way the government handles FOIA requests, have made the law virtually useless. This situation has been particularly troubling to scholars of political history, who cannot fairly evaluate government actions without inside information.

In the post–Cold War era, many observers have begun to press for an overhaul of the FOIA. One strong supporter of FOIA reform has been former Middle East journalist Terry Anderson. Anderson was captured by Islamic terrorists in 1985 and held hostage until December 1991. After his release, Anderson attempted

▲ Terry Anderson tried to use the FOIA to obtain information for his 1993 book *Den of Lions.*

to use the FOIA to research a book about his captivity. Anderson wrote to 10 agencies requesting information on himself, his fiancée, two other hostages held with him, and an Islamic group implicated in the hostage crisis.

Anderson received no useful information from his requests. Some agencies tried to delay answering for as long as possible. Others sent him information that did not relate to his requests or that came from public news reports he could easily have obtained elsewhere. In some cases, when he did receive classified documents, they were so heavily edited that they were useless. For example, one agency sent him 62 pages of documents, of which, Anderson found, "26 were totally blank, 20 showed only addresses with all the text [blacked out], 3 were newspaper reports, and 3 were reports on terrorism outside the Middle East."

As more people push for reform of the law they say is "outmoded by Cold War assumptions," scholars are hopeful that government documents will become more accessible. If reform of the FOIA opens new files to researchers, it may allow historians to examine and evaluate the Cold War period in a new light.

HISTORY in the Making

THE FREEDOM OF INFORMATION ACT

SETTING THE SCENE

Recent statistics show that the FBI is one of the most difficult agencies from which to pry information. In 1990 the agency dealt with nearly 19,000 requests for information. Some 78 percent of these requests were closed without releasing any documents. Such requests, the FBI stated, were incorrectly filed or sought information that was not available. Further, the average time for handling a request—whether information was released or not—ran about 340 days, and the agency had a backlog of more than 9,000 unanswered applications. With new requests running at more than 15,000 a year, FBI compliance with FOIA is unlikely to improve.

THINKING CRITICALLY

Mention that agencies often reject requests for information in the interests of "national security." Ask students to explain in which situations, if any, this might be a valid reason for denying access to government documents.

*P*ractice

GUIDED PRACTICE

Write on the chalkboard the four subsection titles and inform students that these are topics for news stories. Call on volunteers to develop brief story outlines for each topic, noting their suggestions under the appropriate title.

INDEPENDENT PRACTICE

Direct students to use one of the outlines developed in the Guided Practice activity to write a news story on global developments and concerns after the fall of communism. Students may wish to include their stories in their portfolios.

*R*eview and *A*ssessment

REVIEW Have students work in small groups to create a four-page pictorial essay titled "The Post-Communist World—Promise and Challenge." Call on volunteers to display and discuss their essays. Then assign the Section 1 Review on p. 963.

ASSESS Assign the **Section 1 Daily Quiz** in *Core Resources.*

HISTORICAL SIDELIGHTS
Getting the Message Out

In 1988 Amnesty International organized the "Human Rights Now!" tour—a series of rock concerts that mixed music with the organization's message. The tour played in 15 nations on five continents and drew an audience close to one million people. A "highlights" video broadcast of the tour was later seen by an estimated one billion people in 58 nations.

PRIMARY SOURCE
Description of Change: excerpted
Rationale: excerpted to focus on main idea

---

between Israeli soldiers and Palestinians in September 1996 made it clear that the future was far from certain in this troubled region.

*T*ERRORISM

With the end of the Cold War, terrorist activity has increased throughout the world. According to one group of experts, the number of terrorist acts rose by 11 percent from 1991 to 1992. Terrorism has been a global problem for many years. The 1972 Summer Olympics in Munich, West Germany, were marred when eight Arab terrorists killed two Israeli athletes and took nine others hostage. The standoff ended in a gun battle that left 15 people dead.

American leaders have been quick to respond to international terrorism linked directly to a particular nation. In 1986 President Reagan ordered a bombing attack on Libya after evidence tied that country's leader, Muammar Qaddafi (kuh-DAHF-ee), to an attack on a West Berlin nightclub that killed one American serviceman and injured many others. In the summer of 1993, President Clinton ordered the bombing of Iraqi Intelligence Service

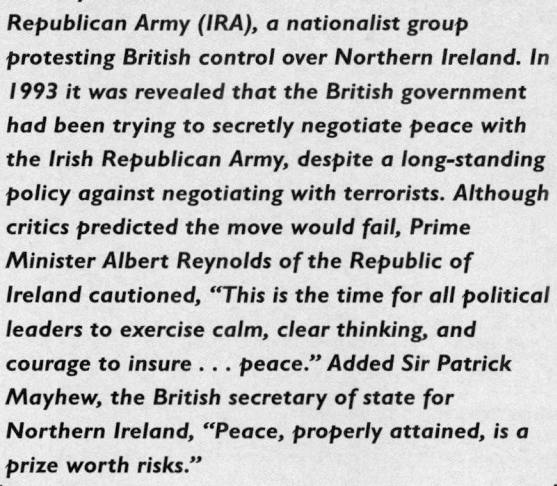

NEGOTIATING WITH TERRORISTS

*O*ne of the most-active terrorist organizations of the late 20th century has been the Irish Republican Army (IRA), a nationalist group protesting British control over Northern Ireland. In 1993 it was revealed that the British government had been trying to secretly negotiate peace with the Irish Republican Army, despite a long-standing policy against negotiating with terrorists. Although critics predicted the move would fail, Prime Minister Albert Reynolds of the Republic of Ireland cautioned, "This is the time for all political leaders to exercise calm, clear thinking, and courage to insure . . . peace." Added Sir Patrick Mayhew, the British secretary of state for Northern Ireland, "Peace, properly attained, is a prize worth risks."

THROUGH OTHERS' EYES

---

headquarters after the FBI uncovered an Iraqi plot to assassinate former president George Bush.

In recent years, however, terrorism by groups and individuals has grown dramatically. Some of this terrorist activity has been directed at the United States. On February 26, 1993, a bomb blast rocked the World Trade Center in New York City, killing six people and injuring more than a thousand. The suspects arrested in the bombing were all tied to an Egyptian fundamentalist leader linked to several terrorist acts. In 1996 a truck bomb in Saudi Arabia killed 19 American servicemen and wounded 280. Terrorism in the air also took a grievous toll. In 1988 a bomb destroyed a Pan Am flight over Lockerbie, Scotland, killing all 259 aboard, including many Americans. The bomb was traced to two Libyans, but Libya's Muammar Qaddafi refused to extradite them for trial.

Domestic terrorism was especially chilling. In April 1995 a truck bomb destroyed a federal building in Oklahoma City, killing 169. Two men with ties to anti-government militia groups were soon charged with the crime. A year later, the FBI arrested Theodore Kaczynski, a loner with a grievance against modern technology, and charged him with a series of mail-bombings. Then, during the 1996 Summer Olympics in Atlanta, a bomb killed one and injured more than 100.

Terrorism, the weapon of the weak against the powerful, raises agonizing dilemmas. The challenge of defending society against terrorists without endangering Americans' constitutional rights poses a major challenge.

■■ **Terrorist activity by small groups has been increasingly aimed at the United States.**

*P*ROMOTING PEACE

With the end of the Cold War, many hope that the United Nations will at last become the international force for peace that its planners had envisioned. By 1992, thousands of UN forces were serving on peacekeeping missions throughout the world. In places such as Cambodia and El Salvador, UN peacekeepers played a successful role.

The United Nations compiled a mixed record, however, in dealing with the most-dangerous situations, as in Somalia. In Bosnia and Herzegovina, a former state of Yugoslavia, ethnic fighting among Serbs, Croatians, and Muslims left some 150,000 people dead or missing by the end of 1993. Although the United Nations and NATO sent peacekeeping forces to the area and launched an investigation into alleged Serbian war crimes, the fighting continued.

As the Bosnian Serbs seized land, bombed cities, and killed or expelled Bosnian Muslims, the Clinton administration at first did little. By 1995, however, as the tide turned against the Bosnian Serbs, Clinton took a stronger role. The United States and NATO cooperated in bombing Bosnian Serb positions, and in November 1995 the United States brought the leaders of the warring factions to Dayton, Ohio, to hammer out a peace accord. The resulting agreement provided for a multi-ethnic Bosnian federation, war crimes trials, and elections, which were held in the fall of 1996. In addition, Clinton sent some 15,000 Americans to Bosnia to join the NATO troops in enforcing the Dayton accords. But ethnic hatreds in Bosnia ran deep, and the fate of the U.S. peace initiative remained uncertain.

■■ **The United Nations has played the role of peacekeeper in the post–Cold War era, with mixed results.**

Efforts at promoting world peace have not been limited to the UN. Since the end of the Cold War, many private organizations have also pursued efforts to build a more peaceful and just world order. From 1945 to 1990, the number of private organizations concerned with international issues grew from under 3,000 to more than 13,000. The London-based Amnesty International, for example, publicizes cases of political repression and torture throughout the world.

Individuals have also played vital roles in this effort. The roster of men and women who have won the Nobel Peace Prize reflects the international nature of the struggle to create a better world. Recent winners have ranged from Daw Aung San Suu Kyi (**daw awng sahn sue chee**) of Burma, who resisted her country's oppressive military leaders, to Carlos Ximenes Belo and Jose Ramos-Horta of East Timor, who have worked against the repression that the people of the former Portuguese colony faced after Indonesia took over the country. Rather than oppressing its citizens, Suu Kyi declared that the ideal government must:

▲ **Daw Aung San Suu Kyi**

66 observe . . . the concepts of truth, righteousness, and loving kindness. It is government based on these very qualities that the people of Burma are seeking in their struggle for democracy. 99

 SECTION 1 REVIEW

IDENTIFY and explain the significance of the following: German reunification, Commonwealth of Independent States, Boris Yeltsin, Operation Restore Hope, Yasir Arafat, Yitzhak Rabin, Daw Aung San Suu Kyi, Carlos Ximenes Belo, Jose Ramos-Horta.

LOCATE and explain the importance of the following: Azerbaijan, Somalia, Bosnia and Herzegovina.

1. **MAIN IDEA** What three events signaled the end of the Cold War? What effect did the end of the Cold War have on regional conflicts?

2. **MAIN IDEA** How has terrorism changed in recent years?

3. **MAIN IDEA** How has the United Nations worked to promote peace in the post–Cold War era? Why can it be said that the United Nations has had a mixed record in achieving its goal?

4. **WRITING TO PERSUADE** Imagine you are a member of the Nobel Prize committee. Write a speech to persuade members of the committee to nominate Oscar Arias Sanchez or Daw Aung San Suu Kyi for the Nobel Peace Prize.

5. **TAKING A STAND** Do you think it is best for groups such as the United Nations to handle international crises in the post–Cold War period? Why or why not?

FOCUS OBJECTIVES

■ Explain what supporters of the North American Free Trade Agreement hope it will accomplish.

■ Describe how some Americans have proposed to combat foreign economic competition.

■ Discuss the effect of the exportation of U.S. mass culture.

MAKING CONNECTIONS

Economics

Trade among Asian nations recently has grown dramatically. By the end of the 1980s, for example, close to 40 percent of Asian exports went to other Asian countries. Further, about 50 percent of Pacific air cargo moved between Asian countries. And about half the freight handled by the port of Singapore came from its Asian neighbors.

PRIMARY SOURCE

Description of Change: excerpted
Rationale: excerpted to focus on main idea

CORE RESOURCES

• Section 2 Daily Quiz

AV RESOURCES

• *The American Nation* Videodisc: The Maiden Flight of the Concorde

Section 2

A GLOBAL ECONOMY

FOCUS
■ **What do supporters hope the North American Free Trade Agreement will accomplish?**
■ **How have some Americans proposed to combat foreign economic competition?**
■ **What has been the effect of the exportation of U.S. mass culture?**

*B*illions of dollars' worth of international trade links the major industrial nations. This interweaving of economies produced both benefits and tensions. As the U.S. trade deficit grows, many U.S. government and business leaders have argued that the answer lies in joining North American countries into a unified trading alliance. Others have argued for protectionist legislation.

Japanese assembly worker

*I*NTERNATIONAL TRADE

In the fall of 1992, American journalist Bruce W. Nelan observed:

❝ Just as wars—two World Wars and, equally important, the Cold War—dominated the geopolitical map of the 20th century, economics will rule over the 21st. All the big questions confronting the world in the century ahead are basically economic. ❞

Much evidence supports this view. Today the United States is only one of several economic superpowers. The nations of the Pacific Rim and the European Union, in particular, provide stiff competition.

The **Pacific Rim** nations, which include Australia, China, Indonesia, Japan, Macao, Malaysia,

▲ As president of the EC's European Commission, Jacques Delors pushed for passage of the Maastricht Treaty.

New Zealand, Papua New Guinea, Philippines, Singapore, South Korea, and Taiwan, have played an expanding role in the global economy in recent decades. In 1994, for instance, goods from the Pacific Rim accounted for 39 percent of all imports to the United States. Japan alone provided for 18 percent of U.S. imports. The Pacific Rim's reputation for producing high-quality, low-priced automobiles, computers, telecommunications equipment, TVs, VCRs, and other goods helped spur demand.

The **European Union**—the Western European trading bloc created by the European Community (EC)—was formed in 1993 with ratification of the **Maastricht Treaty**. By the terms of the treaty, the members of the European Union—at the time of ratification, Belgium, Denmark, France, Germany, Great Britain, Greece, Ireland, Italy, Luxembourg, the Netherlands, Portugal, and Spain—represent a powerful economic and political

MOTIVATING:
STUDENT EXPERIENCES

Call on volunteers to identify everyday items that were not made in the U.S. and have them note the origin of these items. (*clothes made in Central American or Asian countries, athletic shoes made in Taiwan or Korea, audio components made in Asia, autos made in Japan or Europe*) Point out that such items illustrate the focus of this section—that the U.S. participates in a global economy.

Teaching the Section

FREE TRADE

Organize the class into small groups. Have half the groups represent supporters of the North American Free Trade Agreement and the other half represent opponents of the agreement. Have groups list reasons why they support or oppose the agreement. Have one volunteer from each group present its views to the rest of the class. After each group has presented its views, have the class vote on whether or not they would have supported NAFTA.

▲ In recent years high-quality Japanese products such as televisions, radios, and other electronic equipment have captured a large share of the U.S. market.

force. The Union is designed to allow for the free movement of goods, labor, and capital among member nations. The treaty also calls for greater cooperation on such matters as health, education, foreign policy, culture, and crime. Some predict that a full political union—the "United States of Europe," which could include as many as 20 member states—will eventually form. If this were to happen, the European Union would be the world's largest trading bloc.

By 1993, concern over economic competition from Europe and the Pacific Rim led to growing support for U.S. ratification of the **North American Free Trade Agreement** (NAFTA). The agreement, which President Bush signed in December 1992 and Congress ratified in November 1993, provides for a lowering of trade barriers between the United States, Mexico, and Canada.

■■ Supporters hope that the North American Free Trade Agreement will help counter economic competition from the European Union and the Pacific Rim.

*M*ULTINATIONAL CORPORATIONS

Many Americans also worry about the effects of foreign investment in the United States. The global economy is increasingly dominated by **multinational corporations** that invest money in a variety of business ventures around the globe. U.S. media and entertainment companies have been a favorite of foreign investors. For example, in 1989 Japan's SONY Corporation bought Columbia Pictures, a major Hollywood movie studio, for $3.4 billion. Not to be outdone, Japan's Matsushita Electric Industrial Company, a leading electronics company, bought MCA, Inc., a major U.S. entertainment company, for some $6.5 billion. Meanwhile, a German corporation bought RCA Records, and Australian tycoon Rupert Murdoch gained control of the 20th-Century Fox film studio and of a media empire that included *TV Guide* magazine.

Sometimes these multinational corporations bring economic benefits to the United States. Leading Japanese corporations, for example, have opened factories in the United States. Honda operates a major plant in Marysville, Ohio. The U.S. branch of Mitsubishi, a Japanese electronics giant, employs some 50,000 American workers. Such plants boost the U.S. economy, although most of the profits go to the parent corporations in Japan.

Just as foreign companies invest in the United States, many American businesses are expanding their investments in other countries. For example, the New York–based International Telephone and Telegraph (ITT), which began as a communications company, expanded its investments until, by the 1990s, it held major interests in such diverse businesses as hotels, finance, food processing, insurance, and real estate. ITT investments were spread throughout the world, from Bolivia to France. Other corporations such as General Motors, Texaco, and International Business Machines (IBM) also operate worldwide.

▲ Multinational corporations have opened several manufacturing plants in the United States. Shown here are workers in the Honda automobile factory in Marysville, Ohio.

Teaching the Section

DEBATING TRADE POLICY

Encourage students to suggest what steps the government might take to combat foreign economic competition and to improve U.S. economic competitiveness. Then discuss the possible international consequences of such steps.

EXPORTING MASS CULTURE

Draw on the chalkboard a two-column chart, titled *Exporting American Mass Culture*, with *Pros* and *Cons* as column headings. Call on volunteers to suggest entries for the chart and write their responses in the appropriate column. Then ask students to use information in the chart to write a brief essay on the pros and cons of the export of mass culture. Students may wish to include their essays in their portfolios.

▪▪ Refer students to the Jamaican journalist's statement on p. 968. Ask students if they agree or disagree that U.S. movies and TV programs may give a distorted view of life in the U.S. Have students give examples of movies or TV programs to support their view.

Graph Caption Answer
EC

HISTORICAL SIDELIGHTS

Rebuilding Japan
Recently declassified government documents indicate that the U.S. government fostered the trade problems the U.S. is experiencing with Japan today. To prevent Japan from falling to communism, the Truman and Eisenhower administrations took steps to ensure its economic stability. Eisenhower encouraged Japan to export goods to the U.S. by negotiating trade agreements highly favorable to the Japanese and by urging American companies to buy Japanese goods.

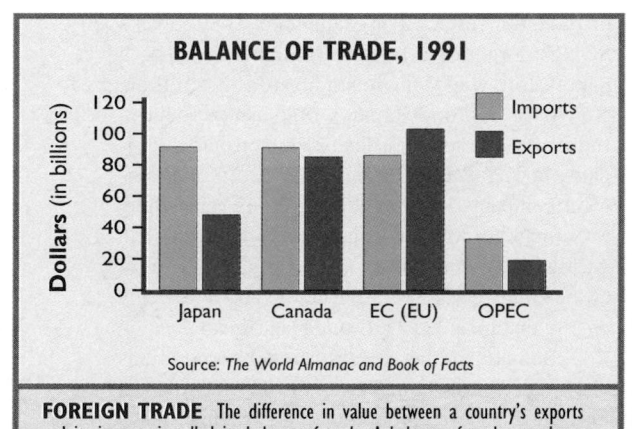

BALANCE OF TRADE, 1991

Source: *The World Almanac and Book of Facts*

FOREIGN TRADE The difference in value between a country's exports and its imports is called its balance of trade. A balance of trade may be either positive or negative in value.

? **BUILDING GRAPH SKILLS** Which group exported more goods than it imported, resulting in a positive balance of trade?

*D*EBATING TRADE POLICY

The complex webs of international trade weave powerful bonds among nations. Sometimes, however, trade relations fall out of balance. In 1994, for example, the United States ran a deficit of $8 billion in its trade with EC nations. The overall U.S. trade gap with all nations in 1994 stood at some $150 billion. In the face of this huge gap, some Americans advocated **protectionism**—higher tariffs and stricter barriers against foreign imports—to encourage U.S. industry and protect jobs from foreign competition.

Protectionist sentiments fueled opposition to the ratification of the North American Free Trade Agreement. Such critics as former presidential candidates H. Ross Perot and Jesse Jackson opposed NAFTA, arguing it would encourage American businesses to invest more money in Mexico, where wages are lower and environmental laws weaker. Yet over 60 percent of U.S. business executives polled in 1992 said that the advantages of free trade in promoting economic activity and efficiency outweighed the costs.

Sometimes, imbalances between trading partners produce tensions. Such strains have occurred, for example, between the United States and two of its Pacific Rim trading partners: Japan and China. In 1988 the U.S. trade deficit with Japan soared to a then all-time high of $54 billion, as more and more Americans purchased Japanese products,

especially automobiles. In 1970 Japanese imports accounted for only 5 percent of the U.S. auto market; by 1990, the Japanese held 28 percent of the market. Despite President Bush's 1992 trade mission to Japan (see Chapter 32), the trade gap remained.

One 1992 poll showed that Americans considered Japan "the greatest threat to the U.S.'s dominant position in world affairs in the 21st century." As "Buy American" campaigns spread, some people have resorted to "Japan bashing," blaming all of America's economic woes on that nation.

Others urged the United States to imitate Japan's investment strategy. For example, although Japan's economy is only about two thirds the size of the U.S. economy, Japanese businesses invest more in new plants and updated equipment than U.S. companies do. In America a larger slice of corporate profits goes directly to stockholders. Some critics have suggested Americans cut back on consumption and invest more wealth in modern technology.

▼ Some 1,000 members of the United Auto Workers Union Local 595 in Linden, New Jersey, attended a rally to protest both foreign imports and Japanese criticism of U.S. workers.

GUIDED PRACTICE

Work with groups to develop a list of questions to ask a local business leader concerning the impact of foreign investment, imports, and trade agreements on the U.S. economy. Topics might include how foreign investments and imports affect the U.S. economy, whether the business leader supports or opposes trade agreements with other countries and why, and the business leader's recommendations for increasing America's global competitiveness.

INDEPENDENT PRACTICE

Organize students into small groups and have groups use the list developed in the Guided Practice activity to conduct an interview with a local business leader. Have groups present the results of their interviews to the rest of the class.

REVIEW Have students write 10 questions on Section 2 on individual note cards with the answers on the reverse side. Then divide students into groups of four. Ask them to use their note cards to question the other members of the group. Then assign the Section 2 Review on p. 968.

ASSESS Assign the **Section 2 Daily Quiz** in *Core Resources*.

▶

Other observers saw Japan's educational system as a key to its economic success and called on U.S. schools to follow the Japanese model by providing more instruction in basic skills and technical training. Some advocated year-long schooling, again following the Japanese pattern. Other educators, however, noted that Japanese schools place heavy emphasis on rote memorization, and little on creativity.

The impulse to copy Japan's model faded by 1993 as Japan faced a severe recession, caused in part by the tight hold of powerful monopolies on Japan's economy. To promote recovery and foster competition, Prime Minister Mirohiro Hosokawa, who took office in August 1993, proposed deregulation of the nation's key industries.

As the 1990s wore on, China emerged as another trading partner with whom America had a trade imbalance. The Clinton administration worked to increase U.S. exports to China, as well as other nations, and to challenge Chinese trading practices Americans considered unfair. U.S. trade negotiator Charlene Barshefsky made eight trips to Beijing from 1993 through 1995. Among other issues, Barshefsky demanded that Beijing stop Chinese companies' illegal copying of U.S. movies, compact disks, and computer software. Although the U.S. trade gap with China totaled $3.3 billion in June 1996—exceeding the gap with Japan for the first time—the administration claimed success when the overall U.S. trade gap declined by some 14 percent during the first half of 1996.

As trading tensions with China increased, Sino-American relations suffered. In March 1996, when China threatened to interfere in elections in Taiwan, President Clinton ordered U.S. aircraft carriers to nearby waters. Relations improved somewhat, but remained uneasy, as Clinton's first term ended. The importance of foreign trade in the post–Cold War era made clear that in the future, relations among the industrialized nations would increasingly revolve around economic issues rather than traditional military or territorial rivalries.

▲ The Japanese model of education has attracted many admirers in the United States. Shown here are students from Kojimachi Junior High School.

■■ Protectionism and improved education have been some remedies proposed to combat foreign economic competition.

EXPORTING U.S. MASS CULTURE

While America's international trade deficit has remained high in the 1990s, one U.S. product is increasingly in demand. American mass culture—movies, pop music, and television shows—has won fans throughout the world. By 1990, mass culture was one of America's most profitable exports, with annual sales of over $5 billion. The sales of American TV shows in Europe alone totaled some $600 million a year. The U.S. music industry earned about 70 percent of its revenues from overseas sales. Said a British economics journal in 1989: "America is to entertainment what . . . Saudi Arabia is to oil."

American consumer products, from McDonald's hamburgers and Coca-Cola to Levi's blue jeans, have been snapped up by people the world over. The overseas division of the McDonald's Corporation, for instance, has grown enormously. In 1992 McDonald's opened more restaurants overseas—including one in Beijing, China—than it did in the United States. Of McDonald's $30 billion sales in 1995, over $14 billion was generated by its some 9,000 restaurants in foreign nations.

VOICES IN HISTORY

Jack Lang, France's Minister of Culture during the 1980s, was one of the most vocal critics of the export of American mass culture. Leaders of the American entertainment business, Lang charged, were nothing more than cultural "imperialists" who wanted "to impose a uniform way of life on the entire planet." Lang used his office to push for increased funding to French artists and for at least 60 percent of programming on French television to be French-produced. Such actions, he suggested, were the only way to protect French culture from the "mass-culture superpower," the U.S.

RETEACH Have students work in small groups to chart the major ideas presented in the section. Direct each group to indicate on its chart how each item addresses one of the section's Focus questions.

Closure

Have students use information from the section to write a brief paragraph that explains the meaning of the term *economic interdependence.* Call on volunteers to read their paragraphs to the class. Students may wish to include their paragraphs in their portfolios.

Extension

RESEARCH Encourage students to use almanacs and statistical abstracts to research U.S. international trade over the last five years. Have them present their findings in an illustrated chart.

CREATE Have students work in small groups to create posters that support or oppose the "Buy American" campaign. Call on groups to display and explain their posters.

PRIMARY SOURCE
Description of Change: excerpted
Rationale: excerpted to focus on main idea

IDENTIFY
For significance, see the following pages:
Pacific Rim (p. 964)
European Union (p. 964)
Maastricht Treaty (p. 964)
North American Free Trade Agreement (p. 965)
multinational corporations (p. 965)
protectionism (p. 966)
Morihiro Hosokawa (p. 967)

1. *increased support for economic alliance and relaxation of trade barriers between U.S., Canada, and Mexico*
2. *protectionism, investment of corporate profits in new factories and modern technology, improved education*
3. *helped U.S. economy but also provoked worries that it suffocated local cultures and distorted images of U.S.*
4. *Memos might mention the trade deficit and Japan's growing investments in the U.S.*
5. *Students should balance the impact of foreign investments on national economies with concerns that most profits are returned to the parent corporations in other countries.*

► **American consumer products such as fast food, clothing, and movies have spread throughout the world. This American restaurant, for example, is in Bangkok, Thailand.**

Some foreign intellectuals worry that U.S. mass culture will suffocate their own cultures. How can traditional music and food, along with other cultural elements, survive in an environment that values American rock'n'roll and hamburgers so much? They also worry that Hollywood movies and television shows give the world a distorted impression of life in the United States. Deploring the effects of American television on his fellow citizens, a Jamaican journalist wrote:

&6 Because of what they see on television, everyone in Jamaica thinks . . . that everything in America is wonderful. Shows like *Dallas* make it look like the land of milk and honey. It makes people think that money and material wealth are the only ways to be rich in this world. 99

But the shared global culture has advantages as well. Television links the entire world through orbiting communications satellites. Events in one nation are instantly transmitted around the globe. Thus events like natural disasters quickly produce a global outpouring of sympathy and help.

■■ **The export of U.S. mass culture has helped the U.S. economy, but critics worry that it distorts images of the United States.**

SECTION 2 REVIEW

IDENTIFY and explain the significance of the following: Pacific Rim, European Union, Maastricht Treaty, North American Free Trade Agreement, multinational corporations, protectionism, Morihiro Hosokawa.

1. **MAIN IDEA** How have U.S. economic policies been affected by the European Union and by the Pacific Rim nations?
2. **MAIN IDEA** What remedies have been proposed to fight foreign economic competition?
3. **MAIN IDEA** What effect has the export of U.S. mass culture had on the United States and other countries?
4. **WRITING TO EXPLAIN** Imagine you are a U.S. economic adviser on trade with Japan. Write a memo that summarizes some of the economic reasons for the strained relationship between the United States and Japan.
5. **ANALYZING** Why might multinational corporations have both positive and negative effects on the global economy?

PREVIEW WORKSHOP

Following is a list of the significant people, places, and terms in this section. You may wish to use this list as a section preview.

People
■ Chico Mendes

Places
■ Chernobyl
■ Antarctica

Terms
■ geothermal power
■ biomass
■ ecosystem
■ global warming
■ ozone layer
■ ultraviolet solar radiation
■ chlorofluorocarbons
■ acid rain
■ recycling

■ Third UN Conference on the Law of the Sea
■ Montreal Protocol on Ozone Depletion
■ Earth Summit
■ Green parties

Section 3

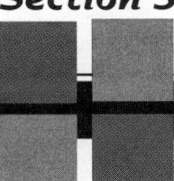

ENERGY AND THE ENVIRONMENT

FOCUS OBJECTIVES

■ Explain what has renewed interest in alternative energy sources and conservation.

■ Identify some major environmental problems facing the world today.

■ Examine some solutions that have been proposed to deal with environmental concerns.

FOCUS

■ **What has led to renewed interest in alternative energy sources and conservation?**

■ **What are some of the major environmental problems facing the world today?**

■ **What are some of the solutions that have been proposed to deal with environmental concerns?**

*O*f the many problems facing the United States and the rest of the world in the 1990s, some of the most pressing relate to energy use and the environment. Environmentalists warn that the earth's reserves of oil, gas, and coal—the fossil-based energy sources that once seemed unlimited—threaten to run out someday. Many also note that industrialization has taken a toll on the natural environment. In future decades, the combination of population growth and environmental pollution could make life more difficult.

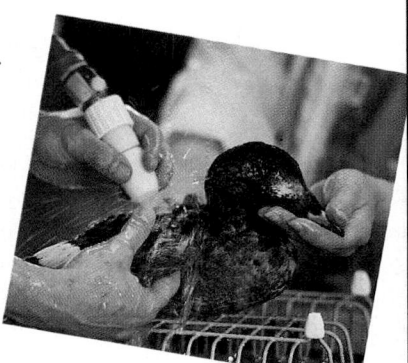

Cleaning waterfowl after the Alaska oil spill, 1989

ENERGY CONSUMPTION

It was in the 1970s that a sense of crisis about the world's energy supply first gripped America (see Chapter 31). Spurred by government regulations, scientists began to conduct research on more energy-efficient cars, furnaces, and air conditioners. Despite conservation efforts, however, global consumption of energy continues to rise under the pressure of population growth, urbanization, and industrial expansion. In 1991 the world consumed an amount of energy equivalent to that of over 535 billion barrels of oil. The United States, which is home to about 5 percent of the world's population, accounted

for nearly 25 percent of this consumption. Some 40 percent of U.S. energy came from oil, 23 percent from natural gas, 22 percent from coal, 8 percent from alternative sources such as solar or hydroelectric power, and 7 percent from nuclear power.

In the late 1970s and 1980s, thanks to federal rules, lower speed limits, and rising prices at the pump, average automobile gasoline mileage improved in the United States. In the 1990s, however, as speed limits crept up and Americans traded in their fuel-efficient compacts for larger cars, vans, and light trucks, per capita gasoline consumption increased.

◄ **Some environmentalists suggest that solar-powered automobiles, such as the one shown here, may one day replace those fueled by gasoline.**

CORE RESOURCES

• **Literature Worksheet 33**
• **Section 3 Daily Quiz**

AV RESOURCES

• *The American Nation* **Videodisc: Images of America**
• **Linking Geography and History** **Transparency** and **Worksheet 23**
• **Everyday Life in America Transparency** and **Worksheet 33**

MOTIVATING: STUDENT EXPERIENCES

Call on volunteers to identify programs that their community supports to preserve and protect the environment. Note responses on a flip chart. As students read the section, have them compare their local environmental concerns and solutions to those in the global community.

 GLOBAL CONNECTIONS

The Soviet Union's drive to develop nuclear power has left a terrible legacy. Accidents like that at Chernobyl, test explosions of nuclear bombs, and the indiscriminate dumping of nuclear waste in landfills and at sea have made radioactive contamination "the number one environmental problem in [Russia]," an adviser to Boris Yeltsin noted. "The way we . . . dealt with the whole issue of nuclear power, . . . was irresponsible and immoral," he concluded.

VOICES IN HISTORY

Paiakan, a leader of the Kayapó Indians of the Amazon, provided one description of the interrelated nature of life in the rain forest: "The forest is one big thing; it has people, animals, and plants. There is no point saving the animals if the forest is burned down; there is no point saving the forest if the people and animals who live in it are killed or driven away."

Teaching the Section

ALTERNATIVE ENERGY SOURCES

Call on volunteers to identify the various sources of energy mentioned in the section and note their responses on the chalkboard. Discuss with students the advantages and disadvantages of each energy source, noting the major points of the discussion on the chalkboard under the appropriate source. Then ask students to use the chalkboard information to write a generalization on why scientists find it necessary to continue the search for alternative sources of energy. Have students compare their generalizations.

In the early post–World War II years, nuclear power seemed an answer to the nation's energy needs. Journalists predicted that nuclear-power plants would generate electricity "too cheap to meter." But the nuclear-power industry was in serious trouble by the 1990s. A 1986 accident at the Chernobyl nuclear-power plant near Kiev, Ukraine (see map on page 971), sent a cloud of radioactivity drifting across Europe and made the surrounding land unsafe for human life. The Chernobyl disaster pumped 50 times more radioactive material into the environment than the bombs dropped on Hiroshima and Nagasaki combined in 1945.

The Chernobyl incident, coming in the wake of the 1979 Three Mile Island accident (see Chapter 31), heightened public anxiety over nuclear power. Some began to call for increased funding for research on alternative energy sources such as solar power, **geothermal power** (geysers and hot springs), wind power, **biomass** (materials such as wood or waste products that can be burned or used to make fuel), and hydrogen. In addition, many U.S. utility companies—spurred by government tax breaks and other incentives—have launched successful energy conservation programs designed to reduce consumer demand and increase the efficiency of energy production.

▪▪ **Increases in global energy use and concern over the safety of nuclear-power plants have led to renewed interest in conservation and alternative energy sources.**

FOREST LIFE

As scientists search for new forms of energy, many environmentalists focus on protecting the world's remaining forests and wildlife. Owing to population growth, industrialization, and expanding commercial agriculture and livestock operations, forests are disappearing at an alarming rate. In northern Maine, for example, timber companies clear-cut vast forests, leaving only a narrow "beauty strip" of trees along rivers, lakes, and highways. And, according to the United Nations Food and Agriculture Organization, almost 42 million acres of forests in tropical regions were lost per year between 1981 and 1990.

▲ **Clearing a piece of Amazon rain forest has become a controversial action now that people understand the importance of trees to the larger ecosystem.**

Experts warn that forests are vital to the larger **ecosystem**—the interaction of living beings with their environment. Forests help prevent floods and soil erosion. Trees also absorb carbon dioxide; therefore, as forests vanish, more carbon dioxide is released into the atmosphere, contributing to pollution and global warming (see page 972). Of special concern is the disappearance of the tropical rain forests that are home to about half the world's plant and animal species. As the forests vanish, some species may be lost forever.

The debate over forest destruction is not a simple one. In economically depressed Maine, some 112,000 jobs depend directly or indirectly on the logging industry. In poor nations, rain-forest lands are also viewed as a source of jobs and revenue. Business and agricultural interests in developing nations argue that it is unfair for environmentalists in the industrialized world to ask poor nations to make heavy economic sacrifices to preserve the rain forests.

 The conflict over the rain forests can be bitter, even deadly. In the 1980s, Brazilian Chico Mendes, whose family made their living from tapping the sap from rubber trees, organized a campaign against the destruction of the Amazon rain forest by ranchers seeking grazing land for their cattle. Mendes, who was born Francisco Alves Mendes Filho in 1944, grew up

Chico Mendes

PROTECTING FOREST LIFE

Organize students into small groups to act as environmentalists who have been given the task of preparing an oral presentation on why it is necessary to protect endangered species and the rain forests. Have each group suggest methods that can be used to focus attention on these problems. Select groups to make their presentations to the class.

▶

with a deep appreciation and understanding of nature. "I became an ecologist long before I had ever heard the word," he once recalled.

In the 1960s, South American leaders instituted a plan to burn off much of the rain forest to make room for industrialization and large-scale agriculture. To oppose this destruction Mendes organized workers who tapped rubber trees and otherwise used the rain forest in environmentally responsible ways. With nonviolent methods of resistance, such as human blockades to stop heavy equipment, the workers focused the world's attention on the disappearing Amazon rain forest.

Map Caption Answer
Africa, Asia, and Europe

MAKING CONNECTIONS
Biology
The International Council for Bird Preservation reports that of the approximately 9,000 bird species that inhabit the world, more than 10 percent face extinction and about another 70 percent are in decline. Howard Youth of the Worldwatch Institute notes that "birds are often accurate indicators of overall imbalances in a habitat that affect other species."

AV **TRANSPARENCY**
Linking Geography and History Transparency and **Worksheet 23**

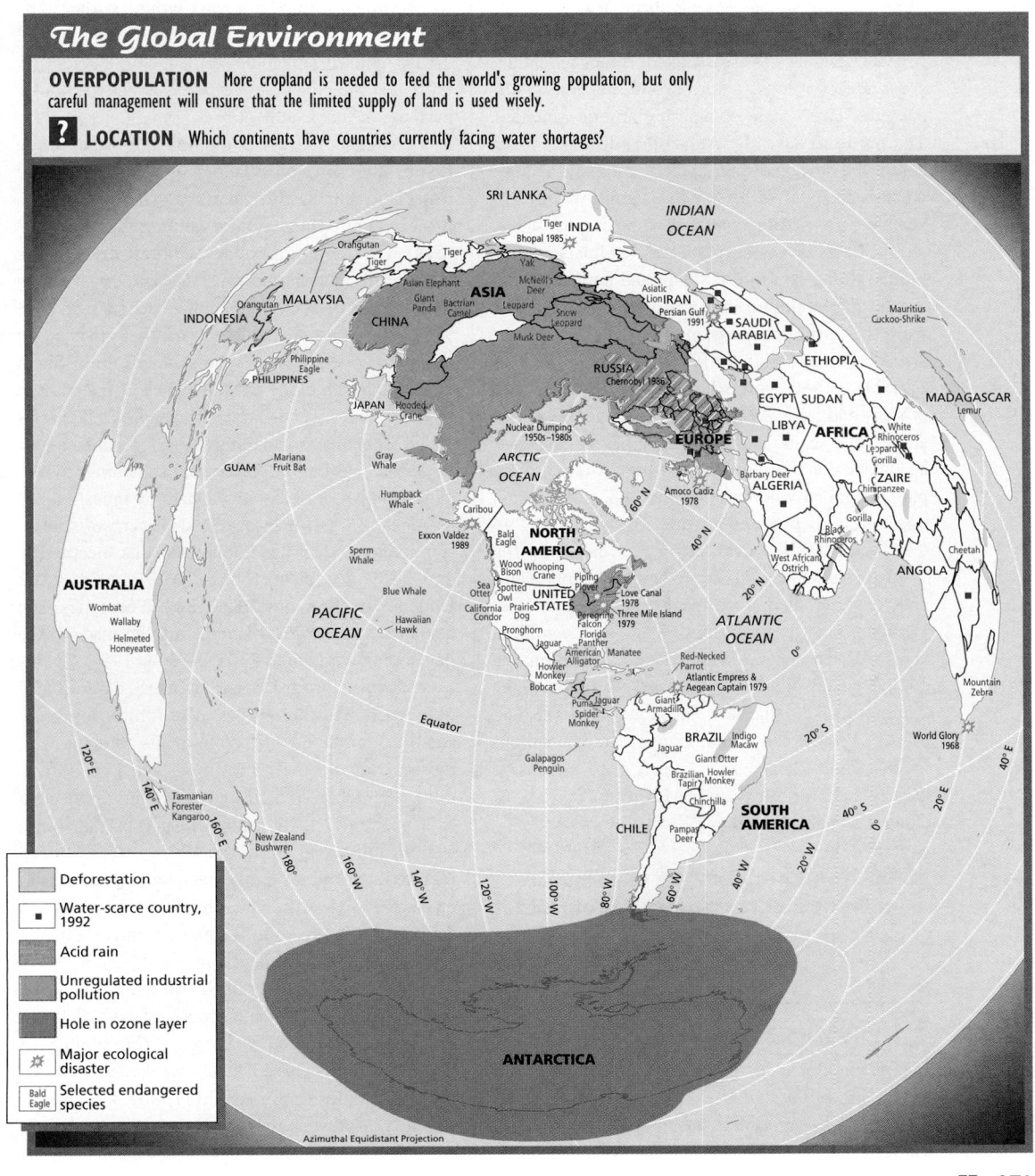

The Global Environment

OVERPOPULATION More cropland is needed to feed the world's growing population, but only careful management will ensure that the limited supply of land is used wisely.

❓ **LOCATION** Which continents have countries currently facing water shortages?

Legend:
- Deforestation
- Water-scarce country, 1992
- Acid rain
- Unregulated industrial pollution
- Hole in ozone layer
- Major ecological disaster
- Selected endangered species (Bald Eagle)

Azimuthal Equidistant Projection

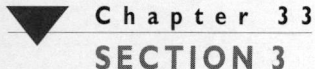
SOLUTIONS FOR ENVIRONMENTAL PROBLEMS

Organize students into groups to assume the role of an editorial board for an environmental magazine. Ask the "editors" to prepare a table of contents for an issue on proposed solutions to environmental problems, including recycling, urban planning, and international cooperation. Groups should prepare short summaries of each article and might also suggest visuals to accompany their articles.

Teaching the Section

ENVIRONMENTAL HAZARDS

Write the term *environmental hazards* on the chalkboard and circle it. Draw lines emanating from the circle. Then ask students to identify the environmental hazards that are threatening human health and survival. *(global warming, thinning of ozone layer, acid rain)* Write responses at the ends of lines. Call on volunteers to explain the causes and effects of each hazard. Close by discussing how such environmental hazards can cause conflict as well as mutual concern among nations.

MAKING CONNECTIONS

Science

Most scientists agree that the phenomenon of global warming is real, but they disagree as to its cause. While some charge that it is the result of increased emissions of harmful gases produced by industrialization, others argue that recent climate changes are no different from earlier fluctuations that were the result of purely natural processes.

THE AMERICAN NATION VIDEODISC PROGRAM

Images of America

```
1A    50231    :35
```

PRIMARY SOURCE

Description of Change: excerpted

Rationale: excerpted to focus on main idea

Still, the burning of the rain forest continued. In 1988 Mendes declared:

> **❝** In the last half century Amazônia has never seen so many fires as in 1988. They are burning everything. Our airports were closed one week in 1987 because of the smoke. This year they were closed one month for the same reason. . . . Amazônia is nothing but smoke. How it hurts! **❞**

In 1988 Mendes was assassinated. A rancher and his son were convicted of the crime, but many suspected a large-scale conspiracy among ranchers. The battle to save the Amazon and other forests continues, however, spurred on by estimates that the world's tropical forests will be gone within 115 years if deforestation continues at the current rate.

Efforts at saving plants and animals are not limited to the rain forests. Plant and animal species around the world are in grave danger of extinction from the explosion of human population and the spread of cities and industry (see map on page 971). Individuals and groups have worked to slow this process and save at least some endangered species and unique scenic areas. For example, Greenpeace, an international environmental organization, campaigns against whaling, and the U.S. government has acted to protect unique lands. The 1994 California Desert Protection Act enlarged the Joshua Tree and Death Valley National Monuments and converted them to national parks. Then in 1996 President Clinton took steps to protect 1.7 million acres of Utah canyon lands where a Dutch mining company held valuable coal leases. By invoking the Antiquities Act—the law Theodore Roosevelt had used to protect the Grand Canyon from development—Clinton was able to create the Canyons of the Escalante National Monument without Congressional approval.

▪▪ Environmentalists are working to prevent deforestation and to protect species from extinction.

ENVIRONMENTAL POLLUTION

The rise in global energy consumption and the continued loss of the world's forests have led to growing concerns over **global warming**, the increase in the temperature of the earth's atmosphere. Global warming results from the greenhouse effect. With the spread of automobiles, cities, and factories, the earth's atmosphere has become heavily polluted with carbon dioxide and other gases that allow solar radiation to reach the earth's surface while preventing heat from escaping. This process is intensified by the burning of fossil fuels and by the cutting and burning of forests. Scientists warn that over time the greenhouse effect could cause temperate areas to become so hot that crops would wither. The melting of the polar ice caps could flood coastal areas, jeopardizing many cities. Some scientists think that the greenhouse effect is already seriously harming the environment.

A related danger is the thinning of the **ozone layer**—the thin veil of molecules some 10 to 30 miles above the earth's surface. These molecules protect against **ultraviolet solar radiation** (UV rays). UV rays can cause skin cancer, damage marine life, and harm crops. To date, most ozone thinning has been over Antarctica (see map on page 971). But environmentalists warn that other areas, like the ozone layer over the southern tip of South America, are thinning as well. Much of the damage to the ozone layer has been caused by chemicals called **chlorofluorocarbons** (CFCs)—combinations of carbon, chlorine, fluorine, and sometimes hydrogen—pumped into the atmosphere by industrialized nations. CFCs, which are used in aerosol sprays, refrigerator and air-conditioner coolants, electronics, and plastics, can no longer be produced in the United States and most industrialized countries. The chemical can, however, continue to be made in the developing world until 2005.

A third hazard of atmospheric pollution is **acid rain**. As factories and automobiles spew chemical pollutants, these pollutants combine with the moisture in the atmosphere and later fall as rain, often far from their places of origin. This acid rain gradually kills trees and makes lakes and streams unfit for fish. In the 1980s and the 1990s, regions as distant as the Appalachian Mountains in eastern North America, the lakes in northern Canada, and the mountains of central Europe showed the effects of acid rain.

Acid rain has provoked conflict between the United States and Canada. Smoke from Michigan factories is believed to increase rain acidity in Canada. As the United States weakened environmental standards during the 1980s, Canadians strongly protested that this action harmed their environment.

Practice

GUIDED PRACTICE

Call on volunteers to identify major energy and environmental challenges that the nation faces today. List responses on the chalkboard, asking students to provide background information on each item.

INDEPENDENT PRACTICE

Have students choose one of the challenges listed in the Guided Practice activity to create a full-page, illustrated magazine or newspaper advertisement that focuses on their selected item. Students may wish to include their advertisements in their portfolios.

Review and Assessment

REVIEW Suggest that students write the main ideas of the section in the form of newspaper headlines. Ask volunteers to present their headlines to the class and have the class suggest details for news stories that might accompany the headlines. Then assign the Section 3 Review on p. 974.

ASSESS Assign the **Section 3 Daily Quiz** in *Core Resources.*

▶

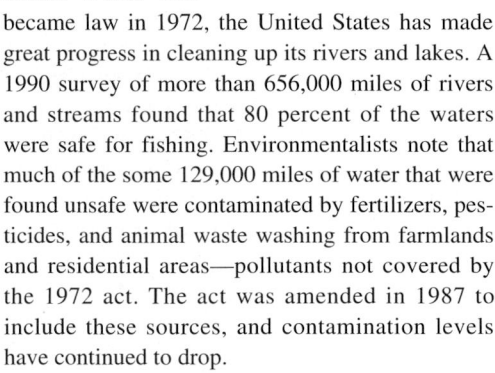

▶ Acid rain not only injures trees and lakes but also damages buildings and monuments. This statue in Rome has gradually deteriorated from being exposed to acid rain.

The United States has a better record in dealing with water pollution. Since the Clean Water Act became law in 1972, the United States has made great progress in cleaning up its rivers and lakes. A 1990 survey of more than 656,000 miles of rivers and streams found that 80 percent of the waters were safe for fishing. Environmentalists note that much of the some 129,000 miles of water that were found unsafe were contaminated by fertilizers, pesticides, and animal waste washing from farmlands and residential areas—pollutants not covered by the 1972 act. The act was amended in 1987 to include these sources, and contamination levels have continued to drop.

Pollution from oil spills also presents serious problems. Spills, such as the 1989 Exxon *Valdez* accident along the coast of Alaska, kill countless fish and waterfowl and cost millions of dollars to clean up. As a result, environmentalists and many government leaders are calling for stricter controls.

■■ **Environmentalists and government leaders are working to reverse the effects of global warming, ozone depletion, acid rain, and water pollution.**

*R*ECYCLING AND URBAN GROWTH

As environmental awareness grows, **recycling**—the collection and processing of used items for reuse—has been winning support. Recycling serves two important purposes: it reuses scarce natural resources, and it reduces the mountain of solid waste that must be burned in incinerators, buried in overflowing landfills, dumped into the sea, or shipped to disposal facilities in poorer nations.

By 1991 some 4,000 curbside recycling programs were underway in the United States, a 250

percent increase over the 1989 figure. The nation recycled an estimated 14 percent of its solid waste in 1991. The United States lags behind other industrialized nations in recycling, however. Japan, for example, recycles 50 percent of its paper and 54 percent of its glass.

The concern over recycling is related to urban growth. Experts predict that there will be at least 21 cities with populations of 10 million or more by the year 2000. Eighteen of these cities will be in poor, developing nations. The enormous amount of garbage created in these urban areas threatens the future of the residents. One expert estimates that an excess of garbage is risking the health of 40 percent of the urban population in the developing world.

Many cities are instituting innovative waste-management systems. In Cairo, Egypt, some 30,000 Zabaleens (Christians from southern Egypt) use horse-drawn carriages to collect garbage from the city. They then sort through the garbage and sell the reusable material. Thrown-away food goes to feed pigs. Waste products are used to fertilize crops. Scrap metal, glass, paper, and plastic are recycled.

One recycling expert notes that Cairo's system has economic as well as environmental benefits:

> ❝ Zabaleens make as much as three times the average income in Cairo. In many developing countries, up to 2 percent of the population is supported directly or indirectly by refuse from the upper 20 percent of the population. ❞

▲ Growing populations have overburdened the sanitation resources of many cities. Some cities have loaded their garbage on barges and tried to export it to other areas—often without success. The governor of Florida, for example, refused to allow this New York barge to dock in his state.

HISTORICAL SIDELIGHTS

Products from Garbage
Industries have found creative uses for recycled materials. Sawdust, wood scraps, plastic bags, and industrial shrink-wrap have been combined to make a wood substitute. One brand of hiking shoe contains what was previously rubber tires, plastic bottles, and white paper. And the garment industry has even found a way to make sweaters and underwear from plastic soda bottles!

PRIMARY SOURCE

Description of Change: excerpted
Rationale: excerpted to focus on main idea

COOPERATIVE LEARNING

Organize students into small work groups to create a "debate page" on one of the environmental issues discussed in the section. Suggest that pages include pro and con statements on the issue, the views of "people in the street," editorial cartoons, and maps where appropriate. Direct group members to allocate the various tasks—research, writing, artwork, design, and so on—among themselves. Allow time for groups to present and discuss their pages.

RETEACH List on the chalkboard the terms from the Preview Workshop at the beginning of this section. Have students respond to the section's Focus questions with sentences containing the terms.

*C*losure

Ask students to develop a list of world environmental challenges and to compare it to the U.S. list developed in the Guided Practice. Then refer students to the statement by the Worldwatch Institute on p. 974. Call on students to indicate whether or not the lists they have developed support the statement.

*E*xtension

INVESTIGATE Encourage students to investigate and report on an alternative energy source under development at the present time.

EVALUATE Ask students to research and evaluate the impact of the Green parties in solving environmental problems. Have them present their conclusion in an oral report.

SECTION REVIEW ANSWERS

IDENTIFY

For significance, see the following pages:
geothermal power (p. 970)
biomass (p. 970)
ecosystem (p. 970)
Chico Mendes (p. 970)
global warming (p. 972)
ozone layer (p. 972)
ultraviolet solar radiation (p. 972)
chlorofluorocarbons (p. 972)
acid rain (p. 972)
recycling (p. 973)
Third UN Conference on the Law of the Sea (p. 974)
Montreal Protocol on Ozone Depletion (p. 974)
Earth Summit (p. 974)
Green parties (p. 974)

LOCATE

For locations, see the map on p. 971.

1. *by promoting conservation and by showing new interest in alternative energy sources*
2. *destruction of forests and animal species, global warming, thinning of ozone layer, acid rain*
3. *Letters might mention recycling, urban planning, and international cooperation.*
4. *Students may point to international cooperation through conferences and agreements, Green parties, and the great number of environmental organizations in the world.*

Other cities, such as Juarez City, Mexico, have instituted similar systems. As a result, many urban planners, such as Donella Meadows, are cautiously optimistic about the future. "If humans manage brilliantly starting very soon," she advises, "it is possible the world might look better than it does now."

THE WORLD RESPONDS

Growing environmental dangers have stirred the international community to action. For instance, in the 1982 agreements issued by the **Third UN Conference on the Law of the Sea**, participating nations pledged to protect the marine environment of coastal waters and to make the oceans "the common heritage of mankind."

Confronted with what many people consider to be the urgent danger of ozone depletion, the international community again took action. The **Montreal Protocol on Ozone Depletion**, signed in Montreal, Canada, in 1987, set standards for reducing the emission of CFCs and other gases that threatened the ozone layer. In 1990, as evidence of ozone depletion grew more alarming, this agreement was made even stricter. Ninety-three nations pledged to halt CFC production entirely within the decade, and more ozone-damaging chemicals were added to the banned list. In addition, the industrialized nations pledged $240 million to enable developing nations to purchase alternatives to CFCs.

In 1992, the 20th anniversary of the first United Nations conference on the environment, the UN sponsored the United Nations conference on Environment and Development—dubbed the **Earth Summit**—in Rio de Janeiro, Brazil. The conference attracted some 35,000 participants, including delegations from 178 nations and some 1,200 private environmental organizations. At the conference, U.S. representatives hedged on supporting several proposals they considered unrealistic, including a promise to cut carbon dioxide emissions to a certain level by the year 2000. Yet the conference yielded some significant compromises and increased hopes for future agreements.

The rise in environmental awareness has also been evident in the growth of private organizations and lobbying groups, such as the international Worldwatch Institute. In Europe, environmentalist political parties, such as the **Green parties** of Britain and Germany, have gained influence as public concern over the environment has increased. These groups have tried to work together to promote international cooperation and concern about the environment. As the Worldwatch Institute noted in 1992: "In an environmentally interdependent world, no country can separate its fate from that of the world as a whole."

New waste-management systems, recycling, and international cooperation are among the solutions promoted to control global environmental hazards.

SECTION 3 REVIEW

IDENTIFY and explain the significance of the following: geothermal power, biomass, ecosystem, Chico Mendes, global warming, ozone layer, ultraviolet solar radiation, chlorofluorocarbons, acid rain, recycling, Third UN Conference on the Law of the Sea, Montreal Protocol on Ozone Depletion, Earth Summit, Green parties.

LOCATE and explain the importance of the following: Chernobyl, Antarctica.

1. **MAIN IDEA** How did utility companies, the public, and the government respond to global increases in energy consumption and to fears over the safety of nuclear power?

2. **MAIN IDEA** What are some of the environmental problems facing the world in the 1990s?

3. **WRITING TO PERSUADE** Imagine you are a member of the Worldwatch Institute. Write a letter to the head of a foreign nation, outlining possible solutions to control environmental hazards.

4. **IDENTIFYING VALUES** Provide support for the view that the international community values a healthy environment.

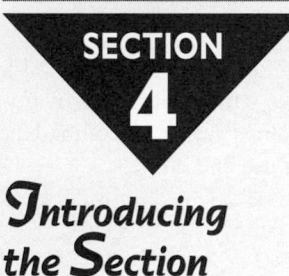

Chapter 33

SECTION 4

Introducing the Section

PREVIEW WORKSHOP

Following is a list of the significant people, places, and terms in this section. You may wish to use this list as a section preview.

People
- Indira Gandhi

Places
- Peru
- Bangladesh
- Ethiopia
- Sudan

Terms
- Peace Corps

Section 4

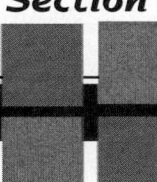

ADDRESSING GLOBAL ILLS

FOCUS
- **What has contributed to a worldwide increase in crime in recent decades?**
- **What are some of the countries that are experiencing particularly high rates of population growth?**
- **What are some of the causes of famine in the developing world?**

While protection of the environment is an urgent global task, humankind faces many other problems as well. The expansion of the international drug trade has contributed to a worldwide increase in crime. Meanwhile, many developing nations are suffering from famine and the effects of overpopulation—a problem experts predict will worsen in the next century. Many nations continue to look to the United States for help and guidance in solving these problems.

Afghan farmer collecting opium

DRUGS AND CRIME

As urbanization has increased worldwide, so has drug use and violent crime. The international drug trade is a multibillion dollar operation. In countries such as Peru, Colombia, Burma, Laos, and Thailand, drug lords often amass great wealth, exert vast political influence, and control their own military forces. Consequently, many governments have had trouble combating the drug trade. Although the campaign against drug abuse proved frustrating, it went on. In 1995, for example, under pressure from the United States, police in Colombia rounded up the leaders of a powerful drug ring that dominates the world cocaine market.

Drug use varies from country to country. A 1992 United Nations report noted: "Abuse of heroin is soaring in a number of regions, and cocaine, once abused mainly in the Americas and Europe, now threatens Africa, the Near and Middle East, South and Southeast Asia and the

South Pacific." While overall drug use in the United States declined somewhat in the 1980s, the use of a cheap but deadly form of cocaine called crack increased. Use of injected drugs, particularly heroin, helped spread AIDS in many countries. Two thirds of the AIDS patients in Italy and France have been heroin addicts.

As the worldwide drug traffic has grown, so has crime. A 1986 UN survey found a 120 percent increase in drug-related crimes worldwide from the preceding decade. The same report found a 30 percent increase in murder worldwide and a 22 percent increase in thefts. In the United States, for example, violent crime rose by almost 33 percent from 1982 to 1991. Crime also has risen dramatically in the former Soviet Union since the end of Communist party rule. Violent crime in Moscow jumped nearly 90 percent in 1989. Said one Moscow citizen, echoing sentiments often heard in American cities: "Moscow was a safe city when I was growing up, but it isn't any more. There are thieves on the streets these days, all kinds of criminals."

FOCUS OBJECTIVES
- Determine what has contributed to a world-wide increase in crime in recent decades.
- Identify countries that are experiencing particularly high rates of population growth.
- Examine causes of famine in the developing world.

HISTORICAL SIDELIGHTS
Russian Crime Rates
Rising crime rates were a problem throughout Russia during the early 1990s. In 1992 there were 2.76 million registered crimes in Russia, an increase of some 27 percent over 1991. Government officials expected the number of crimes to rise by about 600,000 annually over the next two years. One of the most alarming developments noted by officials was the rise in the number of young criminal offenders. Minors—people under age 16—committed about 200,000 crimes in 1992. And from 1988 to 1992, the number of Russian criminals aged 14 or 15 increased by over 50 percent.

CORE RESOURCES
- **Geography Worksheet 33**
- **Section 4 Daily Quiz**

AV RESOURCES
- **The American Nation Videodisc: The Peace Corps**

AMERICA IN TODAY'S WORLD ■ 975

975

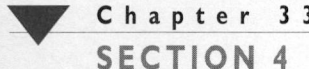
MOTIVATING:
PRIOR KNOWLEDGE

Ask students to use information they have gathered from newspapers, magazines, and television news programs to identify major social challenges facing the world today. Note their responses on a flip chart. As students read the section, have them complete the chart by adding details about the challenges.

Teaching the Section

DRUGS AND CRIME

Pair students and ask them to create a graphic organizer that illustrates the world-wide causes and consequences of drug trafficking. Call on pairs to present their graphic organizers and have students speculate how the world's nations might combat the problems of the drug trade and rising crime rates.

■■ Ask students what measures, if any, their community has taken to combat the problems of drug use and crime.

Map Caption Answer
Africa

MAKING
CONNECTIONS
Science

UN analysts have projected that if growth rates remain constant, the world population will stand at an incredible 694 billion by the year 2150. This translates into a population density of 12,100 people for every square mile of land.

The State of the World

POPULATION GROWTH At the 1995 rate of growth—1.6 percent—the world's population will double to some 10.5 billion people in less than 45 years. In Africa, where the annual growth rate is 2.8 percent, the population will double in less than 25 years.

? **LOCATION** Which continent has the highest rate of population growth and the most countries with an average calorie supply 25 percent below recommended levels?

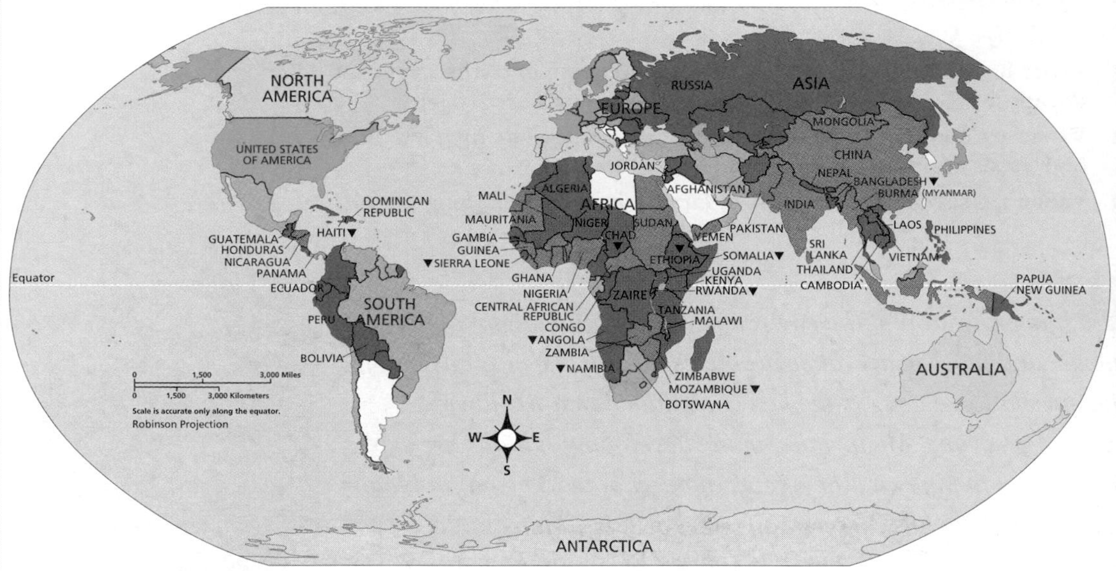

Estimated Average Yearly Infant Mortality Rates for Selected Nations 1990–1995 (deaths per 1,000 live births)	
Finland	5
United States	8
Romania	19
China	27
Mexico	36
Algeria	61
India	88
Mali	159

Rich Nations and Poor Nations, 1993

Per Capita GNP, 1993
- Less than $300
- $300–$750
- $751–$2,500
- $2,501–$6,000
- $6,001–$9,000
- $9,001–$20,000
- $20,001–$30,000

▼ Calorie supply 25% below recommended levels, 1988

Population, 1993
total population: 5,544,000,000 (growth rate: 1.6%)

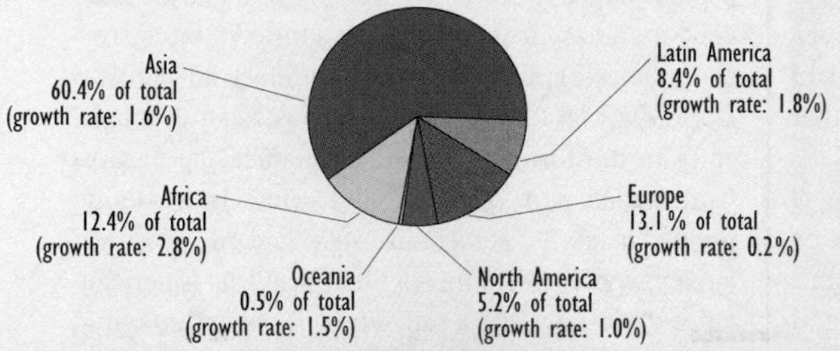

- Asia 60.4% of total (growth rate: 1.6%)
- Africa 12.4% of total (growth rate: 2.8%)
- Oceania 0.5% of total (growth rate: 1.5%)
- North America 5.2% of total (growth rate: 1.0%)
- Europe 13.1% of total (growth rate: 0.2%)
- Latin America 8.4% of total (growth rate: 1.8%)

Estimated Cumulative HIV Infections, June 1994	
North America; Western Europe; Australia, New Zealand	1.5 million
Central America, South America, and Caribbean	2 million
Sub-Saharan Africa	10 million +
India and Southeast Asia	2.5 million +
Eastern Europe and former USSR; East Asia, West Asia, North Africa; Oceania	200,000 +

Pair students to construct a line, bar, or pie graph that shows a population trend in the world or in a specific country or region discussed in the section. Remind pairs to choose a type of graph appropriate to the trend they wish to measure. Encourage students to be creative in designing their graphs. Select pairs to present their graphs to the class.

Organize students into small groups to act as members of a UN commission on world hunger. Have groups prepare a brief report that identifies areas of the world where famine exists and explains why famine is a problem in these areas. Groups might wish to include in their report graphics such as outline maps to locate affected areas. Have groups present their reports to the class. Then call on volunteers to offer possible solutions to the problem of famine and note their responses on the chalkboard. Have groups add a final paragraph to their reports that discusses how world hunger might be alleviated.

▶

In America, the picture was not all bleak. Despite widespread fears of ever-rising crime rates, U.S. crime statistics improved as the 1990s wore on. From 1992 to 1994, the number of serious crimes reported in America fell by 5 percent; in 1995 violent crime fell another 9 percent. The greatest decline was in cities of more than 1 million population. Experts credited the decline both to beefed-up law enforcement and to an improving economy.

■■ An increase in the international drug trade has led to an increase in crime worldwide.

POPULATION EXPLOSION

Many of the world's toughest problems have been made worse by a massive increase in population. By 1995 the world's population stood at 5.7 billion, and it was growing by a rate of three people every second. Much of this growth has been concentrated in the developing world. While the population of the industrialized nations grew by less than 1 percent a year, in many developing nations the population grew by 2 or 3 percent. Experts predict that India's population will jump from 936 million in 1995 to 1.3 billion by 2020; Mexico's, from 94 million to 136 million; and Bangladesh's, from 128 million to 210 million. By 2020, Africa is expected to account for about 18 percent of the world's population, in contrast to 9 percent in 1950.

One key to limiting population growth in developing countries, some argue, is to advance the status of women. Former Indian prime minister Indira Gandhi, who was assassinated in 1984, wrote in 1980:

❝ Men and most women are unaware of the potential ability of women. Their lives are entrapped by pre-conceived notions and attitudes from birth onwards. . . . A lower status for women, or lesser opportunity for women, is a handicap for the growth of mankind as a whole. **❞**

As women gain equality of rights and opportunity, Gandhi believed, they will no longer be valued primarily for their ability to produce children.

■■ India, Mexico, Bangladesh, and the developing nations of Africa are expected to experience high rates of population growth in the coming decades.

WORLD HUNGER

Rapid population growth has worsened food shortages in some countries. In addition, differences in wealth produce wide variations in diet and nutrition within countries and between countries. In the United States, malnutrition is still a problem among the poor, particularly those in rural areas, even though most Americans enjoy a high standard of living.

By contrast, famine plagues many countries, including Bangladesh and the African countries of Ethiopia, Sudan, and Somalia. From the 1950s to the 1990s, rainfall declined sharply in northern Africa. Civil wars in some famine-stricken countries made the situation even worse by preventing relief workers from reaching victims. Worldwide in the early 1990s, an average of 37,000 children under age five died *each day* of starvation, diarrhea, and diseases associated with malnutrition and poor health care.

Increasing the likelihood of food shortages is the fact that the world's grain production declined in the late 1980s, despite advances in agricultural productivity. This was due in part to the fact that in Latin America and elsewhere, commercial farms producing beef, pork, and poultry for the world

POVERTY AND NUTRITION

State	% Below Poverty Line	% Receiving Food Stamps/ Lunch Programs
Mississippi	25.7	19.5
Louisiana	23.6	16.8
New Mexico	20.9	10.0
Arkansas	19.6	9.5
Alabama	19.2	11.2

Source: *Statistical Abstract of the United States*

WHEN ENDS DON'T MEET In 1990 some 14 percent of the U.S. population was living below the poverty line, while 9 percent participated in the Federal Food Stamp and National School Lunch programs.

? **BUILDING GRAPH SKILLS** In which state was the percentage of population living below the poverty line but not receiving food assistance the greatest?

MAKING CONNECTIONS
Health
An observer of the famine in Somalia described the possible long-term impact of malnutrition on children: "Within weeks after refeeding begins, even those adults who were on the verge of death will have largely recovered. But children, especially those under five, can carry the scars for life. They can go blind from lack of vitamin A. They may never achieve their full height. Girls may never be able to safely bear children . . . and mental function is often impaired."

PRIMARY SOURCE
Description of Change: excerpted
Rationale: excerpted to focus on main idea

Chart Caption Answer
New Mexico

Practice

GUIDED PRACTICE

Have students turn to p. 976. Call on volunteers to use the information from the charts and the map to make generalizations about relative GNP, the spread of HIV, infant mortality rates, and population growth. Write students' generalizations on the chalkboard.

INDEPENDENT PRACTICE

Have students use the generalizations from the Guided Practice activity to write a song or poem titled "State of the World." Students may wish to include their compositions in their portfolios.

Review and Assessment

REVIEW Pair students and have pairs develop a list of the challenges, in order of significance, facing the world as it moves toward the 21st century. Have pairs present and defend their lists. Then assign the Section 4 Review on p. 979.

ASSESS Assign the **Section 4 Daily Quiz** in *Core Resources*.

Then and Now

Early in 1992 the Peace Corps sent its first volunteers to Eastern Europe. Most of these volunteers taught English to Eastern Europeans, who saw mastery of English as the key to entering the western capitalist world.

THE AMERICAN NATION VIDEODISC PROGRAM

The Peace Corps

| 2B | 35399 | 1:00 |

VOICES IN HISTORY

Some people in developing countries objected to the presence of Peace Corps volunteers, but this view was not shared by everyone. Rodrigo Carazo Odio, former president of Costa Rica, noted: "The Peace Corps volunteer helps present another face of the American people from the Marine who also arrived [here]. . . . We're cultivating mutual understanding."

Then and Now — THE PEACE CORPS

When President John F. Kennedy launched the **Peace Corps** program in 1961, hundreds of young Americans eager to help the United States win the Cold War joined the program. In its first year some 900 volunteers served in 16 host countries, where they started projects to improve agricultural output, literacy rates, and sanitation. At its height in the mid-1960s, the Peace Corps had more than 10,000 volunteers, serving in over 50 countries in Asia, Africa, and Latin America. During the 1970s, budget cuts and decreased recruitment efforts caused the number of Peace Corps volunteers to drop to some 6,000 recruits.

In the 1980s the agency reorganized and increased its emphasis on helping people gain skills in technology and free enterprise. This reorganization led to a change in the kind of volunteer recruited by the Peace Corps. The typical Peace Corps volunteers in the 1960s tended to be a young person in his or her twenties, fresh out of college, who volunteered for a stint before going on to other careers. Few volunteers in the 1960s had any previous work

experience. The Peace Corps often served as a training ground for the volunteers, many of whom continued to work in public service. One such volunteer was Julia Chang Bloch, who joined the Peace Corps in 1964 after graduating from the University of California at Berkeley. Bloch later became a Peace Corps recruiter and continued to work in overseas service. In 1981, as assistant administrator of the Food for Peace and Voluntary

▲ Peace Corps volunteers in the Philippines

Assistance program, she became the highest-ranking Asian American in the Reagan administration.

"Certainly the Peace Corps was the first step for me in . . . a career in overseas aid and development," Bloch notes. "When I was an undergraduate . . . I had thought I might be a journalist, having majored in communications and public policy. But there are several hundred like me that I could point to."

In recent years, fewer Peace Corps volunteers have been recent college graduates. The Peace Corps has increased its efforts to recruit older volunteers, including retired persons, who possess special skills and experience needed in developing countries. In the 1960s as many as 85 percent of Peace Corps volunteers were under age 26. Today that figure has dropped to just over 50 percent.

The ending of the Cold War in the 1990s has also brought about a shift in the program's focus. The Peace Corps is now being invited into countries that were once part of the Soviet bloc. In November 1992 the first group of volunteers went to Russia. Many of them are teaching the Russians about capitalism and how to run small businesses. One of the first volunteers to go to Russia was a retired U.S. military officer, Charles Bennett, who had once trained as a navigator for nuclear-bombing missions against the Soviet Union. Bennett reflected on the changing times: "I had a military flavor to my life. The idea was to . . . kill the enemy and not be friends. But now the big threat is over. . . . Here I am now eating dinner [with] people I was willing to turn into dust."

RETEACH Organize students into small groups and assign each group a subsection of Section 4. Direct each group to develop questions about the main ideas in its subsection. Then have each group exchange its questions with another group and work to answer the questions it receives.

Closure

Have students work in groups to put together a time capsule of a dozen or so items that represent the state of the world at the close of the 20th century. Call on groups to describe their items and explain why they chose them.

Extension

INVESTIGATE Ask students to investigate the steps the U.S. government is taking to combat the drug trade at home and abroad. Have them present their findings in an oral report.

CREATE Have students research and report on what steps are being taken to deal with hunger in the U.S.

market expanded into rain-forest lands or into agricultural acreage formerly devoted to growing grain. The grain that is still produced in these nations increasingly goes to feed livestock rather than human populations.

■■ **Overpopulation, drought, civil wars, and a decreased grain supply have contributed to severe famines in the developing world.**

As these concluding chapters have made clear, America and the world face many hazards as a new century dawns. Recent decades, however, have brought encouraging developments as well as urgent problems. Most encouraging of all has been the end of the Cold War and the declining threat of global nuclear holocaust.

Throughout our history, we Americans have faced great challenges. As we accept our role as citizens, cultivate a deepened sense of community, and understand our common interest in addressing our common problems, we shall surely prove equal to the challenges ahead, just as other Americans have in centuries past.

COMMENTARY

America's Role in a New Era

The end of the Cold War has not ended the world's problems. In many parts of the world, true democracy remains the dream of a few. A key question of the 1990s has been whether democratic nations can convince the rest of the world of democracy's appeal as they try to help solve the world's social and economic ills. This goal will be accomplished not by military or economic might, but by the power of ideas.

The United States must play a central role in this effort. Some of the earliest English settlers in America believed they were lighting a beacon that would show the way to a new era in human history. With the American Revolution and the establishment of a democratic government, the idea of America as a world leader took on new meaning. Of course, the nation has often failed to live up to its professed ideals. Many groups have been excluded from the promise of democracy. But gradually, over the years, the United States has slowly and painfully tried to achieve a fuller and more complete understanding of the meaning of democracy and individual freedom.

Despite a shifting balance of global power and changing economic realities, the appeal of individual freedom, democratic self-government, and opportunity for all remains as strong as ever, especially to those denied them by repressive rulers or by grinding poverty. The vision of democracy and freedom can still inspire men and women to acts of great courage and heroism.

As has always been true in our history, the shape of the future will be determined by the willingness of men and women to plunge into the fray and grapple with tough problems. In this book you have learned of our nation's history up to the present. The next chapters in this still-unfolding story will be yours to write.

SECTION REVIEW ANSWERS

IDENTIFY

For significance, see the following pages:
Indira Gandhi (p. 977)
Peace Corps (p. 978)

LOCATE

For locations, see the map on p. 976.

1. *increase in worldwide drug trade*
2. *expected to increase at a rate much higher than that of the industrialized world*
3. *overpopulation, drought, civil wars, decreased grain supply*
4. *Essays might mention the large amounts of money to be gained in the international drug trade, power of drug lords, increased drug use in some countries.*
5. *Answers may vary but students should consider the goals of democracy and define the role of the U.S. in achieving those goals worldwide.*

■■ **S E C T I O N 4 R E V I E W**

IDENTIFY and explain the significance of the following: Indira Gandhi, Peace Corps.

LOCATE and explain the importance of the following: Peru, Bangladesh, Ethiopia, Sudan.

1. **MAIN IDEA** What has contributed to the worldwide increase in crime in recent decades?

2. **MAIN IDEA** How are the populations of India, Mexico, Bangladesh, and the developing nations of Africa expected to change in the coming years?

3. **IDENTIFYING CAUSE AND EFFECT** What factors have contributed to severe famines in the developing world?

4. **WRITING TO INFORM** Write an essay that explores the reasons why the drug trade became an international phenomenon during the 1990s.

5. **EVALUATING** What role do you think the United States should play in today's world? Give reasons for your answer.

Chapter Review Answers

WRITING A SUMMARY

See Essential Points in each section for main ideas.

REVIEWING CHRONOLOGY

4, 2, 3, 5, 1
Analyzing
Programs would slow population increase, which contributes to famine and other problems.

IDENTIFYING PEOPLE AND IDEAS

1. *head of Russian Republic who replaced Gorbachev*
2. *UN effort to provide famine relief for Somalia*
3. *treaty which weakened economic barriers and planned a unified monetary system for Europe*
4. *policy of higher tariffs and stricter barriers against foreign imports*
5. *Japanese prime minister who favored deregulation of key industries to improve competition*
6. *Brazilian environmentalist who opposed destruction of Amazon rain forests*
7. *gradual warming of earth brought about by atmospheric pollution*
8. *chemical pollutants combined with moisture in atmosphere*
9. *environmentalist political parties in Britain and Germany*

10. *Indian prime minister who argued that improving women's status would help limit population in developing countries*

UNDERSTANDING MAIN IDEAS

1. *collapse of communism in Eastern Europe, fall of Berlin Wall, breakup of Soviet Union; led to increased conflicts in former Soviet Union*
2. *advocated protectionism, free trade combined with economic planning, reduced consumption, increased*

investment, improved education, encourage American consumers to buy domestic goods
3. *solar power, geothermal power, wind power, biomass, hydrogen; rise in use of energy, fears of nuclear power*
4. *loss of rain forests, endangered species, global warming, destruction of ozone layer, acid rain; recycling, urban planning, international cooperation*
5. *overpopulation, drought, civil wars, decreased food supply, increasing drug trade and use*

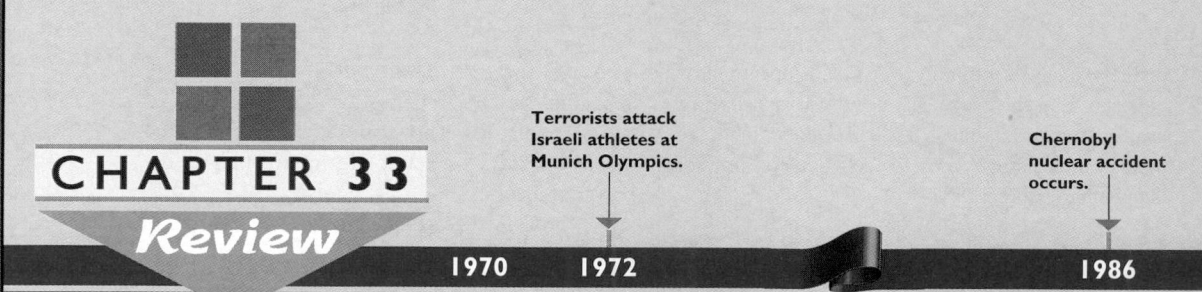

CHAPTER 33
Review

Terrorists attack Israeli athletes at Munich Olympics.

Chernobyl nuclear accident occurs.

1970   1972   1986

WRITING A SUMMARY
Using the essential points of the chapter as a guide, write a summary of the chapter.

REVIEWING CHRONOLOGY
Number your paper 1 to 5. Study the time line above, and list the following events in the order in which they happened by writing the first next to 1, the second next to 2, and so on. Then complete the activity below.

1. NAFTA ratified.
2. Berlin Wall falls.
3. Commonwealth of Independent States formed.
4. Chernobyl nuclear accident occurs.
5. Operation Restore Hope launched.

Analyzing Why do you think Indira Gandhi believed it was important to establish family-planning programs in India?

IDENTIFYING PEOPLE AND IDEAS
Explain the historical significance of each of the following people or terms.

1. Boris Yeltsin
2. Operation Restore Hope
3. Maastricht Treaty
4. protectionism
5. Morihiro Hosokawa
6. Chico Mendes
7. global warming
8. acid rain
9. Green parties
10. Indira Gandhi

UNDERSTANDING MAIN IDEAS
1. What events marked the end of the Cold War? What impact did the end of the Cold War have on conflicts around the world?
2. What various ways did the American government and public propose to deal with increasing foreign economic competition?
3. What are some alternative energy sources scientists proposed during the 1990s? Why were these energy sources necessary?
4. What global environmental problems divided nations during this period? What solutions were offered?
5. What were some of the problems that developing nations experienced during the 1990s?

REVIEWING THEMES
1. **Economic Development** How might economic influence increase the political power of the European Union and Pacific Rim nations?
2. **Global Relations** What role did the United Nations play in resolving global conflicts during the 1990s?
3. **Technology and Society** In what ways has technology proved both beneficial and harmful to the environment in recent decades?

THINKING CRITICALLY
1. **Analyzing** How did the end of the Cold War affect old global divisions?
2. **Evaluating** How might environmental policies possibly endanger jobs and the economy?
3. **Hypothesizing** What global problems might leaders in the 21st century need to face?

STRATEGY FOR SUCCESS
Review the Strategies for Success on Interpreting Editorial Cartoons on page 332. Then study the following cartoon, which appeared in the *Los Angeles Times* in 1975. What is the cartoonist's message?

WRITING ABOUT HISTORY
Writing to Inform Write a pamphlet that describes one contribution made to world peace or the environment by an international organization.

REVIEWING THEMES

1. Multinational corporations and role in trade might lead to greater influence over politics in other countries.
2. sent peacekeeping forces into troubled areas, launched Operation Restore Hope, investigated allegations of Serbian war crimes
3. beneficial—has led to alternative energy sources, recycling; harmful—has caused atmospheric pollution, global warming, thinning of ozone layer, acid rain, loss of animal species

THINKING CRITICALLY

1. ended some old political divisions and created new ones based on economic alliances
2. Some policies, such as those that protect forest life, might cut jobs and harm industries that benefit from the destruction of the environment.
3. Students might mention terrorism, pollution, drug trade, overpopulation, and world hunger.

STRATEGY FOR SUCCESS

The cartoonist believes that leaders of multinational corporations have no loyalty to a specific country but serve only selfish economic interests.

WRITING ABOUT HISTORY

Pamphlets will vary but might mention the UN, Amnesty International, Greenpeace, Worldwatch, or Green parties.

USING PRIMARY SOURCES

Because environmental problems are so immediate, this movement relies on civil disobedience to harass its targets and to increase public awareness.

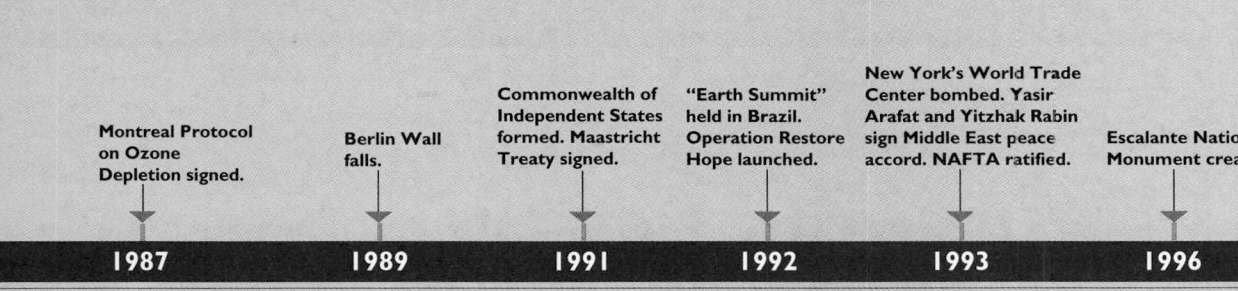

					New York's World Trade Center bombed. Yasir	
Montreal Protocol on Ozone Depletion signed.	Berlin Wall falls.	Commonwealth of Independent States formed. Maastricht Treaty signed.	"Earth Summit" held in Brazil. Operation Restore Hope launched.	Arafat and Yitzhak Rabin sign Middle East peace accord. NAFTA ratified.	Escalante Nation Monument crea
1987	**1989**	**1991**	**1992**	**1993**	**1996**

USING PRIMARY SOURCES

In the early 1980s a new environmental movement, symbolized by groups such as Earth First!, emerged. The movement abandoned conservative protests against corporations in favor of more-radical actions, such as tree sitting, inserting spikes into trees, and destroying logging equipment. Read the following excerpt from the book *Green Rage*, which profiles this movement. How do radical environmentalists justify the methods they use?

❝ In general, however, radical environmentalism has no pretensions of being a mass movement and does not expect the huge demonstrations the civil rights and antiwar movements produced. It aims to harass more than obstruct, with the hope that the public awareness it generates will do the rest. . . .

A more important difference in strategy stems from the extreme urgency of the environmental crisis. . . . For the "constituency" of the biocentric civil rights movement, however, there is often no tomorrow. Once an old-growth forest is cut, it will not grow back for hundreds of years, if ever. Once a species becomes extinct the battle is lost. This sense of urgency often motivates the use of ecological civil disobedience, not to make far-reaching changes in society's views of the environment, but merely to buy time for legal redress or for the emergence of public pressure. ❞

LINKING HISTORY AND GEOGRAPHY

Study the map in the right column, which shows the number of nations in Africa affected by hunger and food shortages, as measured by daily calorie intake. How many African nations have food supplies averaging less than 1,950 calories per person per day?

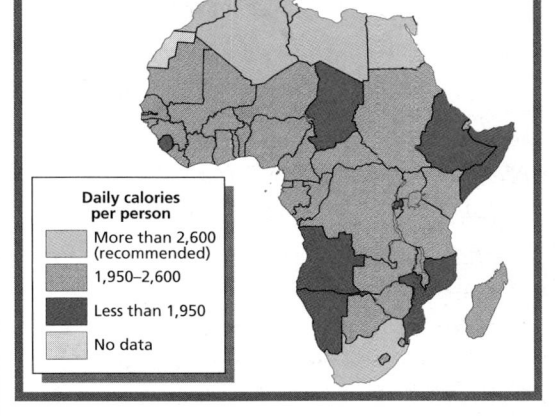

Daily calories per person

More than 2,600 (recommended)

1,950–2,600

Less than 1,950

No data

LINKING HISTORY AND GEOGRAPHY

eight nations

BUILDING YOUR PORTFOLIO

Complete the following projects independently or cooperatively.

1. **GLOBAL RELATIONS** In Chapter 31 you portrayed a delegate to the United Nations. Building on that experience, write a speech explaining what effects the end of the Cold War has had on your nation. Your speech should indicate both the benefits of the end of the Cold War and any negative consequences—such as increased regional or local conflicts—for your nation.

2. **BUSINESS AND TRADE** In Chapter 32 you portrayed the director of a private agency assisting immigrant businesspeople. Building on that experience, imagine you are advising your clients on international trade. Research the advantages and disadvantages of free-trade agreements, such as the North American Free Trade Agreement, and then develop a policy statement to deliver to your clients.

BUILDING YOUR PORTFOLIO

Have students refer to **Building Your Portfolio Worksheet 9**, assigned at the beginning of Unit 9. Use the worksheet to help students monitor their progress on the portfolio projects.

Assessment

Core Resources
- Review Worksheet 33
- Chapter 33 Tests
- Alternative Assessment Forms

Test Generator

Stories of Diversity

SETTING THE SCENE

As a child, Jimmy Santiago Baca was abandoned by his parents. He lived with his grandparents and with other relatives in New Mexico, running away when he was ten. Eventually he began to write poetry and graduated from the University of New Mexico. Believing that his success gave him the ability and responsibility to help others, he established a scholarship fund for young writers and worked to rebuild houses and to find jobs for the unemployed.

UNIT 9

American Letters

Stories of Diversity

More than 10 million immigrants arrived on American shores between 1970 and 1989, most of them from Asia or Latin America. In the following selections, Chinese American author Gish Jen, Mexican American poet Jimmy Santiago Baca, and Philippine-born novelist Jessica Hagedorn explore the struggles of characters who are fully American yet retain ties to their country of origin.

▲ **Jimmy Santiago Baca**

From *Typical American*

by Gish Jen

"We are family," echoed Helen.

"Team," said Ralph. "We should have name. The Chinese Yankees. Call Chang-kees for short."

"Chang-kees!" Everyone laughed.

Ball games became even more fun. Theresa explained how the

▼ **Portrait of a Chinese Family (1985), by Tomie Arai**

Yankees had lost the Series to the Dodgers the year before; they rooted for a comeback. "Let's go Chang-kees!" This was in the privacy of their apartment, in front of their newly bought used Zenith TV; the one time they went to an actual game, people had called them names and told them to go back to their laundry. They in turn had sat impassive as the scoreboard. Rooting in their hearts, they said later. Anyway, they preferred to stay home and watch. "More comfortable." "More convenient." "Can see better," they agreed.

These were the same reasons Ralph advocated buying a car.

"Seems like someone's becoming[1] one-hundred-percent American-ized," Theresa kidded.

"What's so American? We had a car, growing up. Don't you remember?" Ralph argued that in fact this way they could avoid getting too Americanized. "Everywhere we go, we can keep the children inside. Also they won't catch cold."

"I thought we agreed the children are going to be American," puzzled Helen.

Ralph furrowed his brow. When Callie turned three they had decided that Mona and Callie would learn English first, and then Chinese. This was what Janis and Old Chao were planning on doing with Alexander; Janis didn't want him to have an accent. For Ralph and Helen, it was a more practical decision. Callie had seemed confused by *outside people* sometimes understanding her and sometimes not. Playing with other children in the park, she had several times started to cry, and once or twice to throw things; she had lost a doll this way, and a dragon. Also, one grabby little boy had, in an ensuing ruckus, lost some teeth. . . .

Now Ralph drummed his fingers. He stopped and smiled.

"And what better way to Americanize the children than to buy a car!" ❖

---

1 Italics indicate words spoken in Chinese.

from "Martín IV," Martín and Meditations on the South Valley

by Jimmy Santiago Baca

On visiting days with aunts and
    uncles,
I was shuttled back and forth—
between Chavez bourgeois in the
    city
and rural Lucero sheepherders,
new cars and gleaming furniture
and leather saddles and burlap
    sacks,
noon football games and six packs
    of cokes
and hoes, welfare cards and
    bottles of goat milk.

I was caught in the middle—
between white skinned, English
    speaking altar boy
at the communion railing,
and brown skinned, Spanish
    speaking plains nomadic child
with buffalo heart groaning under-
    world earth powers,
between Sunday brunch at a
    restaurant
and burritos eaten in a tin-roofed
    barn,
between John Wayne on the
    afternoon movie
rifle butting young Braves,
and the Apache whose red
    dripping arrow
was the altar candle in praise of
    the buck
just killed.

Caught between Indio-Mejicano
    rural uncles
who stacked hundred pound sacks
    of pinto beans
on boxcars all day, and worked
    the railroad tracks
behind the Sturgis sheds, who
    sang Apache songs
with accordions, and Chavez
    uncles and aunts

who vacationed and followed the
    Hollywood model
of My Three Sons for their own
    families,
sweeping the kitchen before
    anyone came to visit,
looking at photo albums in the
    parlor. ❖

"Luna Moth" from *Dogeaters*

by Jessica Hagedorn

Without warning, [my mother]
cheerfully announces she is sending me to school in America and
moving there with me for an
indefinite period. I am ecstatic, at
first. Everyone else is stunned. My
father cannot stop her—my
mother has inherited money from
her father and pays for our passage to America. We settle first in
New York, then Boston. I convince myself I am not homesick,
and try not to bring up my father
or brother when I speak. My
mother actually sells a few paintings. The months turn into years.
"Are we going to stay here
forever?" I finally ask her. She
looks surprised. "I don't know
about you, but I love the cold
weather. Go back to Manila if you
want. Tell Raul I miss him more
than he could ever imagine." She
smiles one of her cryptic smiles.
"But he'll have to visit me here if
he wants to see me—" her voice

trails off. . . .

When I finally come home to
Manila to visit, my father warns
me not to bother visiting our old
house. "You'll be disappointed.
Memories are always better."
Smiling apologetically, he tells me
reality will diminish the grandeur
of my childhood image of home.
I take his picture with my new
camera, which later falls in the
swimming pool by accident. The
camera is destroyed, along with
my roll of film. I decide to visit
our old house . . . anyway, borrowing a car from Mikey. Pucha
goes with me; she loves riding
around in cars and doesn't need
any excuse. . . .

My father is right. The house
with its shuttered windows looks
smaller than I remember, and
dingy. The once lush and sprawling
garden is now a forlorn landscape
of rocks, weeds, and wild ferns.
The bamboo grove has been cut
down. "Let's go," Pucha whispers,
impatient and uninterested. An old
man with bright eyes introduces
himself as Manong Tibo, the care-
taker. He unlocks door after door
for us, pulling aside cobwebs,
warning us to be careful. Rotting
floorboards creak under the
weight of our footsteps. "My bed-
room," I say to the old man, who
nods. I am overwhelmed by melancholy at the sight of the empty
room. A frightened mouse dashes
across the grimy tiled floor. ❖

PRIMARY SOURCES

Description of Change:
excerpted, bracketed, and
footnoted
Rationale: excerpted for
space considerations; bracketed and footnoted to clarify
meaning

THINKING AND WRITING ABOUT LITERATURE

1. *They buy a television,
    watch baseball games,
    teach their children to
    speak English first, and
    decide to buy a car. They
    continue to speak Chinese.*
2. *One side represents main-
    stream American life and
    the other represents his
    ethnic heritage and the
    lifestyles of many Mexican
    Americans. He seems to
    prefer his Lucero relatives,
    who represent traditional
    ways of life.*
3. *Her old house is aban-
    doned and is smaller and
    dirtier than she remem-
    bers. She does not seem
    completely happy in the
    U.S. because she asks,
    "Are we going to stay here
    forever?"*

THINKING AND WRITING ABOUT LITERATURE

1. How do Gish Jen's characters become "Americanized"? What
    aspects of Chinese culture do they retain?
2. In Baca's poem, what two different ways of life do the two sides
    of the speaker's family represent? Which do you think he
    prefers? Why?
3. Why is Jessica Hagedorn's character disappointed when she sees
    her old home? Do you think she is happy in the United States?

EVALUATING NEWS STORIES

Guide students through the discussion of how to evaluate news stories and then have them complete the Practicing the Strategy exercise. Ask students to imagine that they are newspaper reporters in the 1980s or 1990s and have them write a news story on one of the following topics: the Moral Majority, the Strategic Defense Initiative, the L.A. riots, Operation Desert Storm, the confirmation hearings of Clarence Thomas, the "Year of the Woman," or the *Challenger* disaster. Each news story should include a headline, date, and byline and should have a lead paragraph answering the questions *who, what, when, where,* and *how.* Students should make use of newspaper and magazine reports, books, and interviews when preparing their stories.

PRACTICING THE STRATEGY

Essays will vary according to the topics chosen. Each should include an evaluation of the issue as covered by both print and broadcast media, describing the depth of coverage, presence (if any) of bias in the reporting, and the impact of the story on the student.

Strategies for Success

EVALUATING NEWS STORIES

Information today comes at us in a flood—from talk shows to tabloids, from the morning headlines to the nightly news. Today's news reporting will become the basis of tomorrow's history, so evaluating news stories contributes to your understanding of current history. News sources, which collectively are called the news media, can be divided into two groups: *broadcast media* and *print media.*

▲ Bill Clinton jamming on *The Arsenio Hall Show,* 1992

Broadcast Media

Broadcast media include television and radio. Television is, by far, the dominant medium for news. Surveys show that Americans are much more inclined to watch TV news than to read a daily newspaper. Television, like no other medium, presents the opportunity to witness history in the making. TV and radio can provide on-the-spot, around-the-clock coverage, creating a sense of immediacy. Also, both increasingly offer "instant

analysis" to go with their reporting. Broadcasters like CNN, the 24-hour all-news cable network, and "talk radio" have greatly expanded the amount and kind of news available over the air.

Print Media

Print media include newspapers, weekly newsmagazines like *Newsweek* and *Time,* and other publications that cover current events. Newspapers, particularly such big-city dailies as the *New York Times* or the *Chicago Tribune,* give detailed accounts of national and world events as they occur. Newsmagazines, which have more time to prepare their stories, specialize in in-depth analyses of issues.

How to Evaluate News Media

To evaluate news reporting, ask questions like the following:

- **Coverage.** Is the subject treated superficially or in-depth? Does the reporting include information on the background to a story? Does it explore long-range implications of events?
- **Fairness and accuracy.** Does the reporting stick to the facts? Is it fair and balanced? Is there any recognizable bias in the coverage?
- **Immediacy and interest.** How close in time is the reporting to the event? Have there been new develop-

ments since the story was written or broadcast? Is the news presented in an interesting way?

Applying the Strategy

Choose a topic that is frequently in the news and that has been covered both in print and on radio and TV. Evaluate recent reporting on the issue in terms of the categories listed above. First, examine how well the reporting covers the *why* and *how* of the event, as well as the *who, what, when,* and *where.* Remember that each story has a wider context, a past and a future; good reporting will bring out these connections. Second, consider whether the story is told objectively. Every reporter has a point of view, so be alert for any expression of bias. Finally, note whether any late-breaking developments have changed the situation as last reported. Evaluate the reporting for the level of interest it creates, keeping in mind that a complex subject such as a financial scandal may be hard to present in exciting images or film footage.

Practicing the Strategy

Choose another current topic and examine reporting about it by each of the following: a TV network news program, a major daily newspaper, a public-radio program, and a national weekly newsmagazine. Write a brief essay evaluating the treatment of the issue or event by the different news media, describing the depth of the coverage offered by each, the presence of bias in any of the reporting, and the impact of the story on you.

BUILDING YOUR PORTFOLIO

Each portfolio project described below is the culmination of the Building Your Portfolio activities in the chapter reviews of Unit 9. First, decide whether you wish students to work individually or in groups on these unit projects. Then permit each student to choose the project on which he or she desires to work. Provide students with copies of **Building Your Portfolio Worksheet 9** from *Core Resources*. This worksheet will guide students step by step to complete their projects.

BUILDING YOUR PORTFOLIO

Outlined below are four projects. Independently or cooperatively, complete one and use the products to demonstrate your mastery of the historical concepts involved.

1 POLITICS

The Watergate scandal and the Iran-contra affair challenged the foundation of constitutional government. Using the portfolio materials you designed in chapters 31 and 32, write an editorial that examines the ways in which the Watergate scandal was both similar to and different from the Iran-contra affair.

2 THE ECONOMY

Stagflation and the effects of the energy crisis are only two of the economic problems presidents Nixon, Ford, and Carter struggled with in the 1970s. In the 1980s President Reagan attempted to stimulate the economy through conservative reforms. Using the portfolio materials you designed in chapters 31 and 32, discuss the different ways in which economic actions affect people by presenting your chart and pamphlet to the class.

3 GLOBAL RELATIONS

During the 1970s and 1980s, the United States opened negotiations with China, improved relations with the Soviet Union, and witnessed the end of the Cold War and the breakup of the Soviet Union. Regional and local conflicts emerged, however, as new nations were torn apart by ethnic and religious struggles. Using the portfolio materials you designed in chapters 31 and 33, conduct a panel discussion about the new world order that highlights the sometimes conflicting interests of the superpowers, industrialized nations, and developing nations.

4 BUSINESS AND TRADE

In the last several decades, the U.S. economy has become increasingly global in scope. Using the portfolio materials you designed in chapters 32 and 33, prepare a presentation on the role of immigrants and immigrant businesses in strengthening America's position in the global economy.

PORTFOLIO ASSESSMENT

1. *Editorials should demonstrate an understanding of the roots and consequences of the Watergate scandal and the Iran-contra affair.*
2. *Charts and pamphlets should show the effects of rising oil prices on the U.S. economy in the 1970s and the goals and effects of Reaganomics in the 1980s.*
3. *The panel discussion should show an understanding of the effect on other nations of the Cold War rivalry between the U.S. and the Soviet Union.*
4. *Presentations should show the impact of immigrant businesses on local economies and the potential effects of the North American Free Trade Agreement and the Maastricht Treaty.*

Videodisc Review

In assigned groups, develop an outline for a video collage of America in the years between 1970 and the present. Choose images that best illustrate the major topics of the period. Write a script to accompany the images. Assign narrators to different parts of the script, and present your video collage to the class.

Further Reading

Edelstein, Andrew J., and Kevin McDonough. *The Seventies: From Hot Pants to Hot Tubs.* Dutton (1990). Social history of the 1970s.

Johnson, Haynes. *Sleepwalking through History: America in the Reagan Years.* Norton (1991). Overview and critical analysis of the Reagan years.

Moore, Jim, with Rick Ihde. *Clinton: Young Man in a Hurry.* The Summit Group (1992). Biography detailing the rise of Bill Clinton to become the 42nd president of the United States.

Virga, Vincent. *The Eighties: Images of America.* Edward Burlingame Books (1992). Photographic essay on life in the United States during the 1980s.

Woodward, Bob, and Carl Bernstein. *The Final Days.* Simon & Schuster (1976). Chronicle of the last days of Richard Nixon's presidency.

Reference
SECTION

Your understanding and appreciation of the past will grow as your study skills improve. This Skills Handbook contains instruction on critical thinking strategies and social studies skills that will help you gain a fuller understanding of American history. It explains, for example, how to identify cause and effect and how to distinguish fact from opinion. The lessons in the Handbook equip you to handle historical sources, time lines, maps, and graphs, as well as build your vocabulary and sharpen your research, writing, and test-taking abilities.

1 IDENTIFYING THE MAIN IDEA

In the study of history, the ability to identify what is central is a key to understanding any complex event or issue. *Boyer's The American Nation* is designed to help you focus on the main ideas in American history. The paragraph titled Understanding the Main Idea that introduces each chapter and the Focus Questions that begin each section are intended to guide your reading. The essential points—the blue summary statements placed throughout the text—highlight and reinforce the main ideas presented.

But not everything you read is structured like *Boyer's The American Nation.* Applying the following guidelines will help you identify the main ideas in what you read.

HOW TO IDENTIFY THE MAIN IDEA

1. **Read introductory material.** Read the title and the introduction, if there is one. They often point to the main ideas to be covered.

2. **Have questions in mind.** Formulate questions that you think might be answered by the material. Having such questions in mind will focus your reading.

3. **Note the outline of ideas.** Pay attention to any headings or subheadings. They may provide a basic outline of the major ideas.

4. **Distinguish supporting details.** As you read, distinguish sentences providing supporting details from the general statements they support. A trail of facts may lead to a conclusion that expresses a main idea.

APPLYING YOUR SKILL

Read the following paragraph, from the subsection in Chapter 3 titled "The Pilgrims," to identify its main idea.

The Metropolitan Museum of Art

    66 Conflicts over religious doctrine had raged in England since 1534 when Henry VIII broke with the Roman Catholic church to form the Church of England (Anglican church). Henry's motives had been primarily personal—the pope had refused to grant him a divorce from his first wife. At heart still a Roman Catholic, he had created a

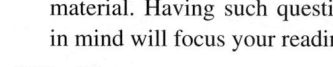

church that remained largely Catholic in form. This deeply troubled many English Christians, who longed for a truly Protestant church. **"**

As the lead sentence indicates, the paragraph focuses on religious conflicts in England. Details about Henry VIII and the origin of the Anglican church are included to provide a background to the disputes. The main idea is best captured in the concluding sentence: There was no "truly Protestant church" in England, and this fact greatly upset those who wanted such a church.

PRACTICING YOUR SKILL

Now read the last paragraph of the subsection on the Pilgrims (pages 66–67), then answer the following questions.

1. What is the paragraph's main idea? How does the author support that idea?
2. What is the relationship of the main ideas of this paragraph and the paragraph on the Church of England? Combine them into one statement that summarizes the subsection.

2   IDENTIFYING CAUSE AND EFFECT

Identifying and understanding cause-and-effect relationships is crucial to the study of history. To investigate why an event took place, and what else happened as a result of that event, historians ask questions such as: What is the immediate activity that triggered the event? What is the background leading up to the event? Who were the people involved?

HOW TO IDENTIFY CAUSE AND EFFECT

1. Look for clues. Certain words and phrases are immediate clues to the existence of a cause-and-effect relationship. Note the examples that follow:

CLUE WORDS AND PHRASES

Cause	Effect
as a result of	aftermath
because	as a consequence
brought about	depended on
inspired	gave rise to
led to	originating from
produced	outcome
provoked	outgrowth
spurred	proceeded from
the reason	resulting in

2. Identify the relationship. Read carefully to identify how events are related. Writers do not always state the link between cause and effect. Sometimes a reader of history has to infer the cause or the effect.

3. Check for complex connections. Beyond the immediate cause and effect, check for other, more complex connections. Note, for example, whether (1) there were additional causes of a given effect, (2) a cause had multiple effects, and (3) these effects themselves caused further events.

APPLYING YOUR SKILL

The diagrams on page 990 present an important cause-and-effect relationship among the events leading up to the American Revolution. Because of the costs incurred in the French and Indian War, Parliament levied taxes on the colonies to raise revenue—taxation that led colonists

The Granger Collection, New York

PRACTICING YOUR SKILL

1. the Pilgrims' search for religious toleration; details about life in the Netherlands and Pilgrim leader's response to their new life
2. The main idea of the paragraph on the Church of England—its creation—provides the cause for the main idea of the paragraph on the Pilgrims—their search for religious toleration. Student statements should express an understanding of the reasons the Pilgrims sought to settle in Virginia.

| **Cause** Britain incurs huge debt from the French and Indian War. | ➡ | **Effect** Parliament raises taxes on the colonies. | | **Cause** Britain incurs huge debt from the French and Indian War. | ➡ | **Effect/Cause** Parliament raises taxes on the colonies. | ➡ | **Effect** Colonists protest taxation without representation in Parliament. |

PRACTICING YOUR SKILL

Students should chart and describe a recent historical development in terms of cause and effect, demonstrating a knowledge of the connections between the actions and the outcomes.

to cry, "No taxation without representation!" A diagram of the first part of this relationship is shown above. The diagram at the top of the next column adds the relationship between the British taxation of colonists and the colonial protests, showing how an effect may in turn become a cause. Such diagrams provide a graphic way of seeing complex relations of events.

PRACTICING YOUR SKILL

From your knowledge of recent American history, choose a sequence of events shaped by cause-and-effect relationships. Draw a chart showing the relationships between the actions and the outcomes. Then write a paragraph that explains the connections.

 DISTINGUISHING FACT FROM OPINION

Historical sources may contain facts and opinions. Sources such as letters, diaries, and speeches usually express personal views. The ability to distinguish facts from opinions is essential to judge the soundness of an argument or the reliability of a historical account.

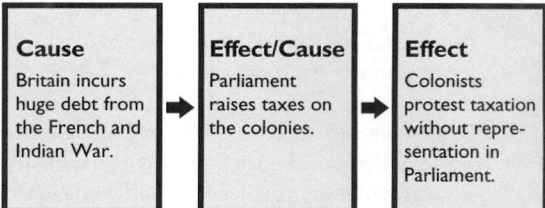

little aided by invention or imagination, but sure in conclusion. 🍃

Jefferson's assessment—that Washington was neither brilliant nor particularly imaginative as a thinker, but that he possessed sound judgment and decisiveness—is clearly an opinion. Note the comparative words and phrasing: *great . . . without being of the first order, . . . sounder, . . . slow in operation.*

HOW TO DISTINGUISH FACT FROM OPINION

1. **Identify the facts.** Ask yourself: Can it be verified? Determine whether the idea can be checked for accuracy in a source such as an almanac or encyclopedia. If so, it is probably factual; if not, it probably contains an opinion.

2. **Identify the opinions.** Look for clues that signal a statement of opinion: phrases such as *I think* and *I believe,* comparative words like *greatest* and *more important,* and value-laden words like *extremely* and *ridiculous* imply a judgment, and thus an opinion.

APPLYING YOUR SKILL

Read the following description of George Washington by Thomas Jefferson:

🍃 His mind was great and powerful, without being of the very first order; . . . no judgment was ever sounder. It was slow in operation, being

PRACTICING YOUR SKILL

1. *Fact: Washington listened to his officers' advice.*
2. *word clues: best, certainly, more judiciously, slow*

PRACTICING YOUR SKILL

Read the excerpt below, in which Jefferson further evaluates Washington as a commander in battle. Then answer the questions that follow.

🍃. . . Hence the common remark of his officers, of the advantage he derived from councils of war, where hearing all suggestions, he selected whatever was best; certainly no General ever planned his battles more judiciously [carefully]. But if deranged [disrupted] during the course of the action, . . . he was slow in re-adjustment. 🍃

1. What fact (or facts) does Jefferson mention in his description of Washington?
2. Which words provide clues to Jefferson's opinion of Washington as a commander?

4 READING A TIME LINE

Chronology has been called "the skeleton of history." Knowing the chronological order of historical events—that is, the sequence in which they occurred—is essential to understanding them. A time line is a visual framework representing the chronology of a particular historical period. It enables you to see at a glance what happened when. Studying a time line involves seeing relationships between events as well as remembering important dates.

HOW TO READ A TIME LINE

1. **Determine its framework.** Note the years covered and the intervals of time into which the time line is divided.
2. **Study the sequence of events.** Study the order in which the events appear on the time line, noting especially the length of time between events.
3. **Supply missing information.** Think about the people, places, and other events associated with each item on the time line. In this way you can "flesh out" the framework.
4. **Note relationships.** Ask how an event relates to earlier or later events. Look for cause-and-effect relationships and long-term developments.

APPLYING YOUR SKILL

Study the time line below. It lists important events in the history of World War II in the Pacific.

1941	1942	1945
▼	▼	▼
Japan invades Indochina. U.S. declares embargo against Japan. Japanese attack Pearl Harbor.	Battle of Midway occurs.	U.S. drops bombs on Hiroshima and Nagasaki. Japan surrenders.

When more than one event is listed for the same year, they are stacked with the earliest on top. The entries for 1941 illustrate the background to the surprise attack on Pearl Harbor.

PRACTICING YOUR SKILL

From the time line above, answer the following.

1. What other events might belong on this time line for the years between the attack on Pearl Harbor and the dropping of the atomic bombs?
2. What cause-and-effect relationship is suggested by the sequence of entries for 1945?

 ## 5 BUILDING VOCABULARY

In your study of history, you may encounter many new and unfamiliar words. But with regular effort you can master unfamiliar words and turn reading history into an opportunity to enlarge your vocabulary. Following the steps outlined here will assist you in building your vocabulary.

HOW TO BUILD VOCABULARY

1. **Identify unusual words.** As you read, list words that you cannot pronounce or define.
2. **Study context clues.** Study the sentence and paragraph where you find the new term. This setting, or context, may give you clues to the word's meaning through examples or a definition using more familiar words.

3. **Use the dictionary.** Use a dictionary to learn how to say the words on your list and what they mean.
4. **Review new vocabulary.** Look for ways to use the new words—in homework assignments, conversation, or classroom discussions. The best way to master a new word is to use it.

PRACTICING YOUR SKILL

1. What is context? How can it provide clues to a word's meaning?
2. As you read the next chapter, list any unusual words that you find. Write down what you think each word means, then check your definitions against those in a dictionary.

PRACTICING YOUR SKILL

1. Students might suggest: *Manhattan Project begins (1942); Battle of the Coral Sea (1942); Guadalcanal regained (1943); Battle of Leyte Gulf (1944); Philippines reconquered (1944).*
2. *that the bombing of Hiroshima and Nagasaki brought about Japan's surrender*

PRACTICING YOUR SKILL

1. *the setting, such as the sentence or paragraph, in which a word is found; either by providing a familiar synonym or an example of what it means*
2. *Students should list and define any new vocabulary words in the next chapter, then check their definitions against those in a dictionary.*

6

Questions about history as well as geography can be answered by consulting maps. Maps convey a wealth of varied information through colors, lines, symbols, and labels. To read and interpret maps, you must be able to understand their language and symbols.

TYPES OF MAPS

A map is an illustration drawn to scale of all or part of the earth's surface. Types of maps include *physical maps, political maps,* and *special-purpose maps.* Physical maps illustrate the natural landscape of an area—the landforms that mark the earth's surface. Physical maps often use shading to show relief—the existence of mountains, hills, and valleys—and colors to show elevation, or the height above or below sea level. The map of the United States on pages 1014–15 is a physical map.

Political maps illustrate political units such as states and nations, employing lines to mark boundaries, dots for major cities, and stars or stars within circles for capitals. The map of the United States on pages 1016–17 is a political map. Political maps are used also to show information such as territorial changes or military alliances. Special-purpose maps present specific information such as the routes of explorers, the outcome of an election, regional economic activity, or population density. The "Election of 1860" and "The Underground Railroad" maps on these pages are special-purpose maps.

MAP FEATURES

Most maps have a number of features in common. Familiarity with these basic elements makes reading any map easier.

Titles, legends, and labels. A map's title tells you what the map is about. It often includes information on what area is shown and what time period is being represented. The *legend,* or key, explains any special symbols, colors, or shadings used on the map. Labels designate things such as political and geographic place-names as well as physical features like mountain ranges, oceans, and rivers.

Directions and distances. Most maps in this textbook have a *compass rose,* or directional indicator, like the one on "The Underground Railroad" map. The compass rose indicates the four cardinal points: *N* for north, *S* for south, *E* for east, and *W* for west. You can also find intermediate directions—northeast, southeast, southwest, and northwest—using the compass rose. This helps in describing the *relative location* of a place—its location relative to another point of reference. (If a map has no compass rose, assume that north is at the top, east is to the right, and so on.)

Many maps in this textbook include a scale, showing both miles and kilometers, to help you relate distances on the map to actual distances on the earth's surface. You can use a scale to find the distance between any two points.

The global grid. The *absolute location* of any place on the earth is given in terms of *latitude* (number of degrees north or south of the equator) and *longitude*

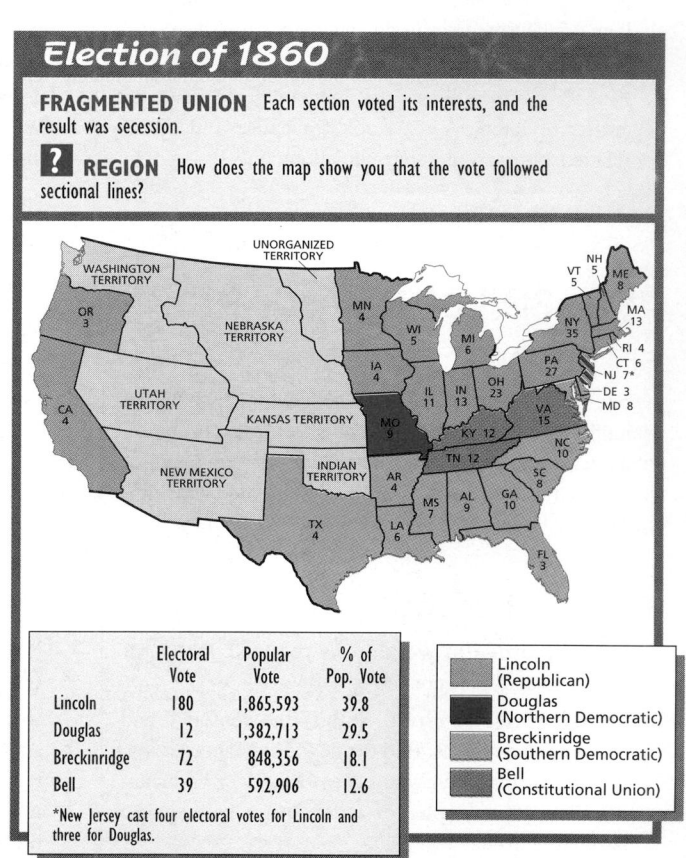

Election of 1860

FRAGMENTED UNION Each section voted its interests, and the result was secession.

? REGION How does the map show you that the vote followed sectional lines?

	Electoral Vote	Popular Vote	% of Pop. Vote
Lincoln	180	1,865,593	39.8
Douglas	12	1,382,713	29.5
Breckinridge	72	848,356	18.1
Bell	39	592,906	12.6

*New Jersey cast four electoral votes for Lincoln and three for Douglas.

Lincoln (Republican)
Douglas (Northern Democratic)
Breckinridge (Southern Democratic)
Bell (Constitutional Union)

(number of degrees east or west of the prime meridian). The *global grid* is created by the intersecting lines of latitude *(parallels)* and lines of longitude *(meridians)*. In *Boyer's The American Nation,* grid lines sometimes are indicated by tick marks near the edge of the map. Many maps also have *locator maps* (right), which place the area of focus in a larger context, showing it in relation to the entire United States, or the world.

▶ **The maps on these two pages are special-purpose maps. On the page opposite is an Albers projection. Above right is a locator map, and below is an example of a tilted perspective.**

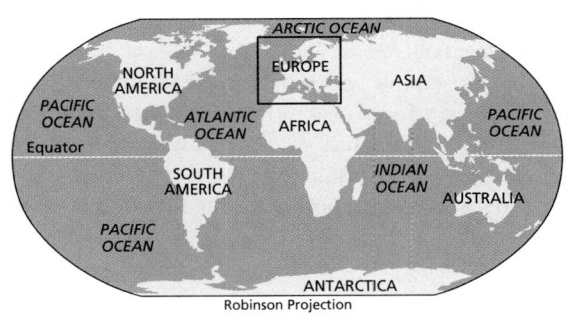

Robinson Projection

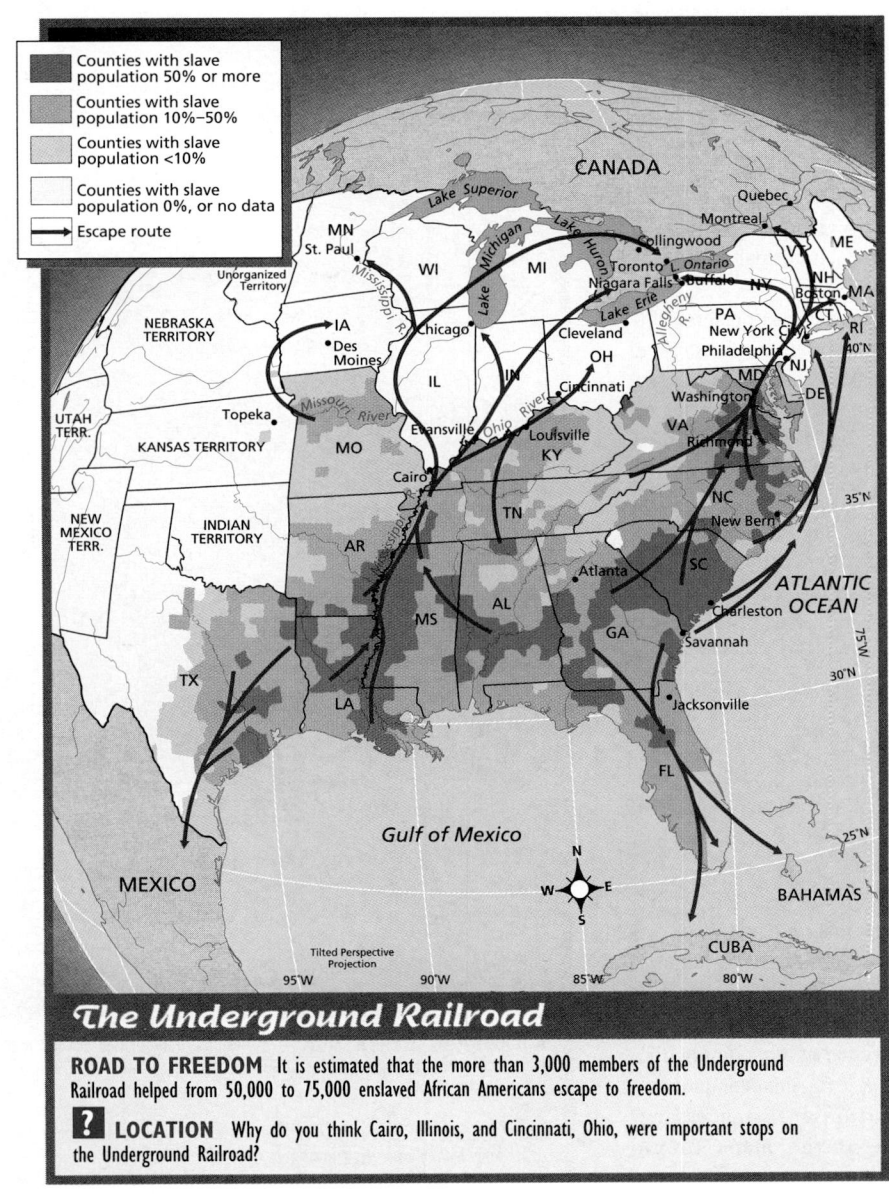

The Underground Railroad

ROAD TO FREEDOM It is estimated that the more than 3,000 members of the Underground Railroad helped from 50,000 to 75,000 enslaved African Americans escape to freedom.

❓ LOCATION Why do you think Cairo, Illinois, and Cincinnati, Ohio, were important stops on the Underground Railroad?

Map projections. Because the earth is a sphere, it is most accurately represented by a three-dimensional globe. The task of *cartographers,* or mapmakers, is to depict that globe on a flat surface as accurately as possible—to, in the words of 16th-century mapmaker Gerardus Mercator, square the circle. Cartographers do this by transferring the curved coordinates of the globe onto the flat surface in a systematic way. These two-dimensional views of the earth's surface are called *projections.*

To flatten the curved coordinates of a globe, cartographers must squeeze or stretch the global grid of parallels and meridians. Thus every map projection, and therefore every map, distorts to some extent at least one of the following aspects: (1) the shape of land areas, (2) their relative sizes, (3) directions, or (4) distances. Mapmakers choose the projection that least distorts what they wish to show. Most projections in *Boyer's The American Nation* fall into two broad categories: conformal and equal area.

Conformal projections preserve the shape and scale of small areas around a point or a line. They cannot, however, preserve the shape of large countries or continents because scale varies from point to point. For example, in a world map using a Mercator conformal projection, sizes and shapes are accurate along the equator but distorted toward the poles. As a result, Greenland and South America appear to be the same size even though South America is actually nine times as large as Greenland. The Transverse Mercator projection used on the "French and Indian War" map on page 92 and the "Lexington and Concord" map on page 114 are examples of conformal projection.

Equal-area projections show the relative sizes of different countries or continents quite accurately—a square inch or centimeter of paper represents the same number of square miles or kilometers of ground at any point on the map. But the price for this standardization is a distortion of distances and shapes. Most of the maps found in *Boyer's The American Nation* are equal-area projections, with Albers Equal-Area projections being the most common. The Albers projection is used on most of the U.S. maps—including all of the special-purpose maps like the "Election of 1860"—because it is effective in showing, with a minimum of distortion, large countries with east-west orientations.

Not all of the projections used in this textbook are conformal or equal area. The Robinson projection, used for the locator maps, is an effective compromise between the two categories. It minimizes distortions in size, shape, distance, and direction, although without preserving complete accuracy in any aspect. Other projections are used to give unique perspectives. "The

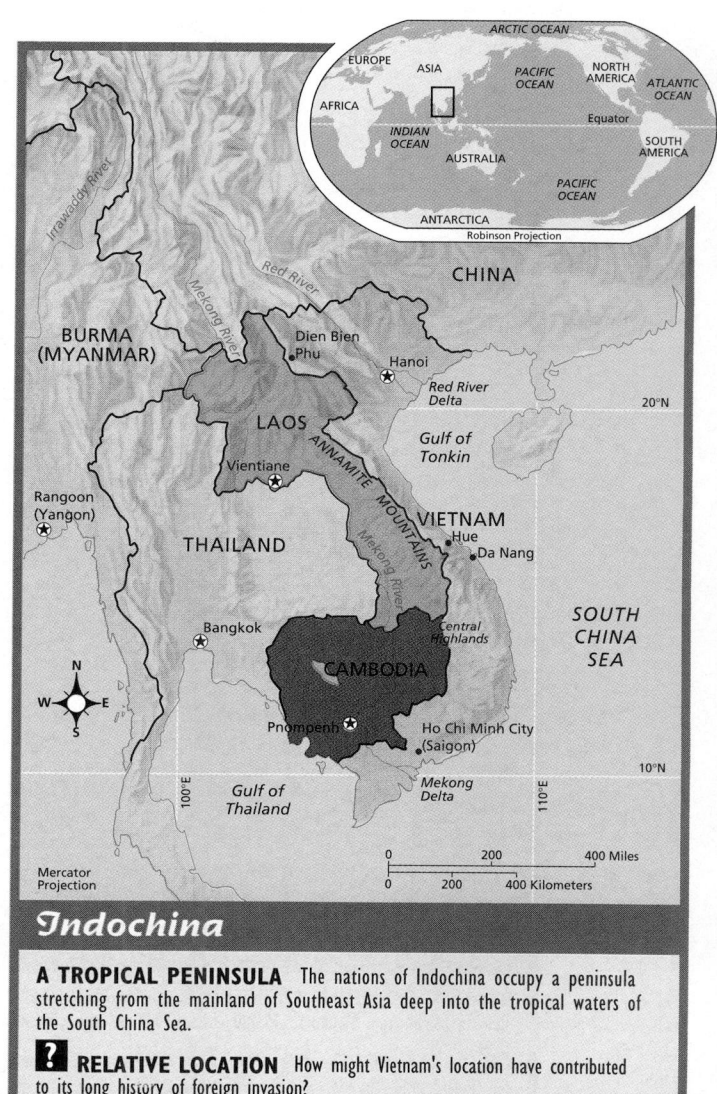

Indochina

A TROPICAL PENINSULA The nations of Indochina occupy a peninsula stretching from the mainland of Southeast Asia deep into the tropical waters of the South China Sea.

? RELATIVE LOCATION How might Vietnam's location have contributed to its long history of foreign invasion?

Underground Railroad" map on page 993 uses a *tilted perspective*. Compare the map to the Albers projection "Election of 1860" map on page 992. Note how the size and shape of the southern states are fairly accurate while the states and territories to the north and west are distorted on the tilted-perspective map. The perspective serves to draw attention to the southern states, the primary focus of the map.

HOW TO READ A MAP

1. **Determine the focus of the map.** Read the map's title and labels to determine the map's focus—its subject and the geographic area it covers.

2. **Study the map legend.** Read the legend and become familiar with any special symbols, lines, colors, and shadings used on the map.

3. **Check directions and distances.** Use the directional indicator and scale as needed to determine direction, location, and distance.

4. **Check the grid lines.** Refer to lines of longitude and latitude, or to a locator map, to fix the area in its larger context.

5. **Determine the projection.** Determine what projection is being used for the map, especially whether it is an equal area or a conformal projection. Ask yourself why this kind of projection has been chosen for the particular map, keeping in mind what its advantages or drawbacks are.

6. **Study the map.** Study the map's basic features and details, keeping its purpose in mind. If it is a special-purpose map, study the specific information being presented.

APPLYING YOUR SKILL

Study the map of Indochina on the opposite page. Use the locator map to determine the region's global location and to help you understand why the region is also called Southeast Asia. The locator map allows you to determine that Indochina is across the Pacific Ocean from the United States. Note that because the map has lines of longitude and latitude and a scale, you can find the absolute locations of each of the national capitals and compare the relative sizes of the countries. The scale even allows you to compare the size of the countries to your state.

This map combines both physical and political features in one map. Note how the use of relief clearly shows the mountains and coastal lowlands. Trace the Red River and Mekong River to their deltas and determine into what bodies of water each flows.

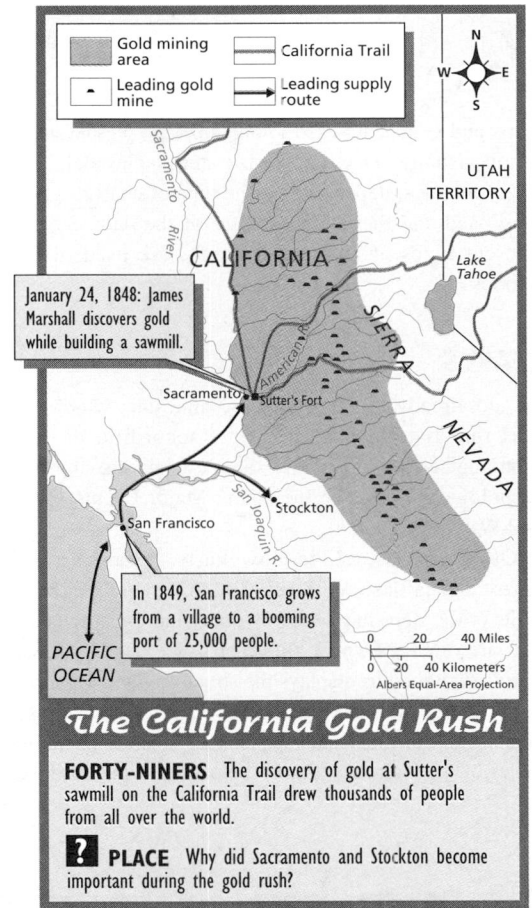

The California Gold Rush

FORTY-NINERS The discovery of gold at Sutter's sawmill on the California Trail drew thousands of people from all over the world.

? **PLACE** Why did Sacramento and Stockton become important during the gold rush?

Study the borders of the countries that make up Indochina. Note for which countries the Mekong River serves as a border. Also note that Laos is an entirely landlocked country, while Vietnam, on the other hand, has hundreds of miles of coastline on the Gulf of Tonkin, South China Sea, and Gulf of Thailand. Vietnam also has a lengthy mountainous border to its north and west—a geographic fact that has been very important in its history.

PRACTICING YOUR SKILL

For each of the special-purpose maps in this lesson—"Election of 1860" on page 992, "The Underground Railroad" on page 993, and "The California Gold Rush" on this page—answer the following questions.

1. What is the special focus of the map?
2. How is a map helpful in presenting this information?
3. What special symbols, if any, are used on the map?
4. What do the color variations or different lines indicate?

PRACTICING YOUR SKILL

1. **(a)** *state-by-state presidential election results in 1860*
   (b) *the routes escaping slaves took to gain their freedom*
   (c) *the extent of gold mining in California*
2. **(a)** *The clustering of colors for each candidate shows sectional differences.*
   (b) *The scale of the map shows how far slaves had to travel to gain their freedom, and the arrows show that some fled to other countries.*
   (c) *The color and the clustering of the gold mine symbols shows the gold rush area.*
3. **(a)** *none*
   (b) *arrows to show routes*
   (c) *symbol to represent leading gold mines and arrows to show California Trail and supply routes*
4. **(a)** *support for different presidential candidates*
   (b) *percentages of slaves in certain counties and the different routes*
   (c) *trails and supply routes and extent of gold mining*

7 **READING CHARTS AND GRAPHS**

Charts and graphs are used to organize and present information visually. They categorize and display data in a variety of ways, depending on the type of chart or graph being used and the subject matter of the data. Several different types of charts and graphs are used in this textbook.

CHARTS

You are already familiar with the time line, which is a chart that lists historical events according to their chronological order. For an example of another kind of chronological chart, see the chart "Major Events of the Cold War" on page 800.

Other charts include flowcharts, organizational charts, and tables. A *flowchart* shows a sequence of events or the steps in a process. Cause-and-effect relationships are often shown by flowcharts (see page 990). An *organizational chart* displays the structure of an organization, indicating the ranking or function of its internal parts and the relationships between them. "Decision-Making Bodies of the United Nations" (below left) is an example

of an organizational chart. A *table* is a single, or more often, multicolumn chart that presents data in categories that are easy to understand and compare. Tables, such as "Changes in Material Standards of Living, 1940–1955" (below right), are effective in displaying statistics that vary greatly or would be cumbersome in graph form.

HOW TO READ A CHART

1. **Read the title.** Read the title to identify the focus or purpose of the chart.

2. **Study the chart's parts.** Read the chart's headings, subheadings, and labels to identify the categories used and the specific data given for each category.

3. **Analyze the details.** When reading quantities, note increases or decreases in amounts. When reading dates, note intervals of time. When viewing an organizational chart, follow directional arrows or lines.

4. **Put the data to use.** Form generalizations or draw conclusions based on the data.

DECISION–MAKING BODIES OF THE UNITED NATIONS

Body	Function
General Assembly	Sets policies.
Security Council	Resolves diplomatic, military, and political disputes.
Economic and Social Council	Deals with human welfare and fundamental rights and freedoms.
International Court of Justice	Handles international legal disputes.
Trusteeship Council	Supervises territories that are not independent.
Secretariat	Performs routine administrative work of the UN.

Sources: *Encyclopedia of American History; Funk & Wagnalls New Encyclopedia*

MULTINATIONAL COOPERATION The United Nations was established in order to give every member nation a voice in international affairs. The General Assembly includes over 150 countries and uses five official languages—English, Russian, French, Spanish, and Chinese.

? **ANALYZING** Which body of the United Nations is responsible for monitoring military aggressions between nations?

CHANGES IN MATERIAL STANDARDS OF LIVING, 1940–1955

Households Owning	1940	1955
Automobile	50.0%	71.0%
Television Set	0.0%	76.1%
Refrigerator	44.0%	94.1%
Washing Machine	46.0%	84.1%
Clothes Dryer	0.0%	9.2%
Vacuum Cleaner	38.0%	64.3%

Sources: *The Overworked American; 1956 Statistical Abstract; An Economic History of Women in America; The Proud Decades*

"THE GOOD LIFE" After World War II many American consumers rushed to buy the latest in modern conveniences.

? **BUILDING GRAPH SKILLS** Which item experienced the greatest increase in ownership?

◀ The chart "Decision-Making Bodies of the United Nations" is an organizational chart. "Changes in Material Standards of Living, 1940–1955" is a table.

GRAPHS

There are several types of graphs; each has certain advantages in displaying data for a particular emphasis. A *line graph* plots changes in quantities over time. A line graph has a horizontal axis and a vertical axis. One axis generally lists numbers or percentages, while the other axis is marked off in periods of time. The line is created by plotting data on the grid formed by the intersecting axes and then connecting the dots. "Total Immigration to the U.S., 1860–1900" is an example of a line graph. A *bar graph* can be used to display changes in quantities over time. But most often bar graphs are used to compare quantities within categories. For example, the bar graphs in the "Allied and Central Resources, 1914–1918" chart on this page compare the military resources of the Allied and Central powers during World War I. A *pie graph,* or *circle graph,* displays proportions by showing sections of a whole like slices of a pie, with the whole equaling 100 percent. "Population in the South, 1860" on page 998 features two pie graphs.

HOW TO READ A GRAPH

1. **Read the title.** Read the title to identify the subject and purpose of the graph. Note the kind of graph, remembering what each kind is designed to emphasize.

2. **Study the labels.** To identify the type of information presented in the graph, read the labels that define each axis, bar, or section of the graph.

3. **Analyze the data.** Note increases or decreases in quantities. Look for trends, relationships, and changes in the data.

4. **Put the data to use.** Use the results of your analysis to form generalizations and to draw conclusions.

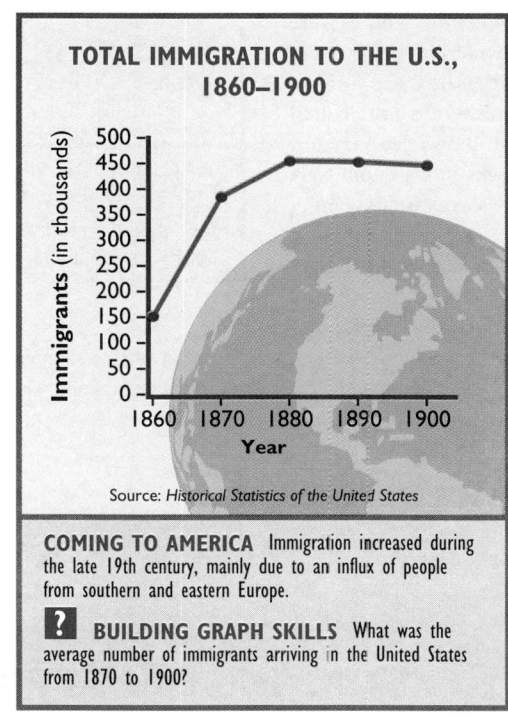

TOTAL IMMIGRATION TO THE U.S., 1860–1900

Source: *Historical Statistics of the United States*

COMING TO AMERICA Immigration increased during the late 19th century, mainly due to an influx of people from southern and eastern Europe.

? **BUILDING GRAPH SKILLS** What was the average number of immigrants arriving in the United States from 1870 to 1900?

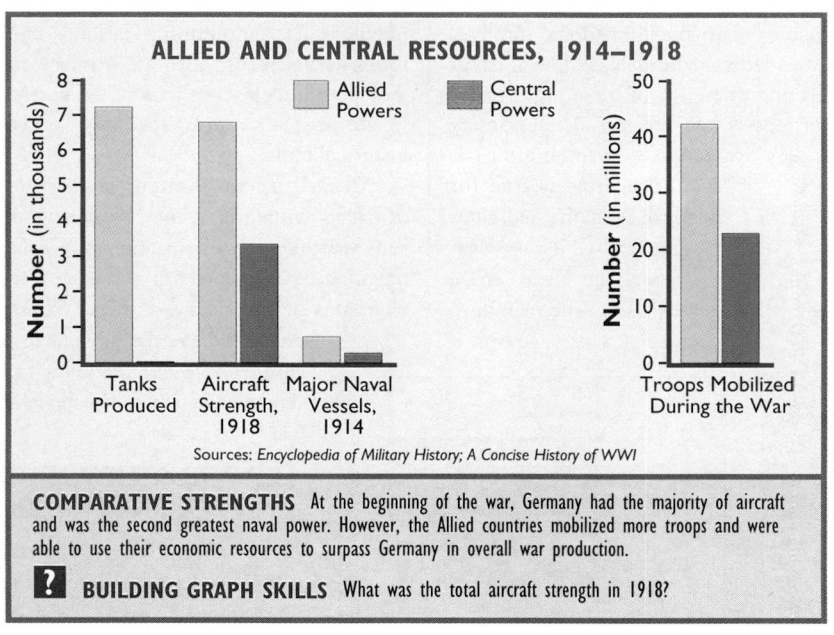

ALLIED AND CENTRAL RESOURCES, 1914–1918

Sources: *Encyclopedia of Military History; A Concise History of WWI*

COMPARATIVE STRENGTHS At the beginning of the war, Germany had the majority of aircraft and was the second greatest naval power. However, the Allied countries mobilized more troops and were able to use their economic resources to surpass Germany in overall war production.

? **BUILDING GRAPH SKILLS** What was the total aircraft strength in 1918?

APPLYING YOUR SKILL

Study the pie graphs on the South's population on the eve of the Civil War. From the first graph you can see that relatively few whites were slaveholders; for every one who was, about three were not. But it also shows that very few blacks in the South were *not* slaves (only about 1 in 17). The second graph focuses on a small segment of the southern population—slaveholding households. The graph shows that of this segment of the population nearly 75 percent had fewer than 10 slaves, while only 3 percent had 50 or more.

PRACTICING YOUR SKILL

Use the line graph on page 997 to answer the following questions.

POPULATION IN THE SOUTH, 1860

Total Population

- 47%
- 1%
- 2%
- 16%
- 34%

Slaveholding Households

- 72%
- 1%
- 2%
- 25%

Legend (Total Population):
- Nonslaveholding whites
- Slaveholding whites
- Slaves
- Free blacks
- Others

Legend (Slaveholding Households):
- Less than 10 slaves
- 10–49 slaves
- 50–99 slaves
- 100 or more slaves

Sources: Historical Statistics of the United States; Slavery and the Southern Economy; The Black American Reference Book

SLAVERY IN THE SOUTH Although slavery played an important part in the southern economy, only a small minority of southerners owned slaves.

? **BUILDING GRAPH SKILLS** Which group made up the largest section of the population in the South? What percent of all slaveholders owned 50 or more slaves?

---

1. What type of data is illustrated, and what intervals are used for the horizontal axis and the vertical axis?
2. Which decade shows the greatest increase in immigration to the United States? At what number (approximately) does the level of immigration begin to level out? In what year does this occur?
3. What generalizations or conclusions can you draw from the information in this graph?

PRACTICING YOUR SKILL

1. *The line graph shows the number of immigrants to the U.S. from 1860 to 1900; the intervals on the horizontal axis are 10 years, and the intervals on the vertical axis are 50,000 people.*
2. *The decade of 1860–69 shows the greatest increase in immigration; immigration begins to level out at roughly 450,000 in 1880.*
3. *Students might conclude from this line graph that immigration to the U.S. tripled from 1860 to 1880 and that almost two million immigrants came to the U.S. in the late 1800s.*

8 STUDYING PRIMARY AND SECONDARY SOURCES

There are many sources of firsthand historical information, including diaries, letters, editorials, and legal documents such as wills and titles. All of these are *primary sources*. Newspaper reports, too, are considered primary sources, although they are generally written after the fact. The same is true for personal memoirs and autobiographies, which are usually written late in a person's life. The paintings,

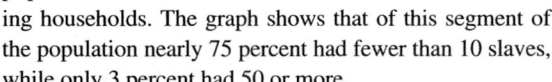

photographs, and editorial cartoons that comprise history's visual record also are primary sources. Because they permit a close-up look at the past—a chance to get inside people's minds—primary sources are valuable historical tools.

Secondary sources are descriptions or interpretations of events written after the events have occurred by persons who did not participate in the events. History books, biographies, encyclopedias, and other reference works are examples of secondary sources. Writers of secondary sources have the advantage of knowing the long-range consequences of events. This knowledge helps shape their analyses.

HOW TO STUDY PRIMARY AND SECONDARY SOURCES

1. **Study the material carefully.** Consider the nature of the material. Is it verbal or visual? Is it based on firsthand

information or on the accounts of others? Note the major ideas and supporting details.

2. Consider the audience. Ask yourself: For whom was this message meant originally? Whether a message was intended, for instance, for the general public or for a specific, private audience may have influenced its style or content.

3. Check for bias. Watch for words or phrases that signal a one-sided view of a person or event.

4. When possible, compare sources. Study more than one source on a topic if available. Comparing sources gives you a more complete, balanced account.

PRACTICING YOUR SKILL

1. What distinguishes secondary sources from primary sources?
2. What advantage do secondary sources have over primary sources?
3. Why should you consider the original audience of a historical source?
4. Of the following, identify which are primary and which are secondary sources: a newspaper, a private journal, a biography, an editorial cartoon, a deed to property, a snapshot of a family on vacation, a magazine article about the history of the West, an autobiography.

9 CREATING AN OUTLINE

An outline is a tool for organizing information. It is a logical summary that presents the main points of what you have read or plan to communicate. An outline is an important part of preparing to write a paper. An essay outline, for example, would highlight the main ideas that you intend to express and sketch the details that you want to include for support. An outline is only a skeletal structure. It must be fleshed out in use. But if an outline is thorough and well thought out, it makes writing the final product much easier.

HOW TO CREATE AN OUTLINE

1. Order your material. Decide what you want to emphasize or focus on. Order or classify your material with that in mind. Determine what information belongs in an introduction, what should make up the body of your paper, and what to leave for the conclusion.

2. Identify main ideas. Identify the main ideas to be highlighted in each section. Make these your outline's main headings.

3. List supporting details. Determine the important details or facts that support each main idea. Rank and list them as subheadings, using additional levels of subheadings as necessary. Subheadings must come in pairs, at the least: no *A*'s without *B*'s, no *1*'s without *2*'s.

4. Put your outline to use. Structure your essay or report according to your outline. Each main heading, for instance, might form the basis for a topic sentence to begin a paragraph. Subheadings would then

make up the content of the paragraph. In a more lengthy paper, each subheading might be the main idea of a paragraph.

The sample outline below could have been used in preparation for writing about the Louisiana Purchase. Note the several levels of headings that rank the parts of the outline.

I. Republicans favor westward expansion
  A. Settlement of the Trans-Appalachian West
  B. Access to the Mississippi River
    1. Importance of the port of New Orleans
    2. France regains control of Louisiana
      a. Threat to American trade
      b. Obstacle to U.S. westward expansion
II. Jefferson negotiates with France
  A. U.S. diplomats purchase Louisiana
  B. Why France made the sale
    1. Napoléon fails to build empire
      a. Need for naval base in West Indies
      b. Revolt in Saint Domingue (Haiti)
      c. French fail to regain Haiti
    2. Napoléon needs money for war plans

PRACTICING YOUR SKILL

Read the subsection in Chapter 17 titled "Urban Moral Reform" (pages 525–26). Then, using the information you have gained here, create an outline that you could use in writing about this subject.

1. *Secondary sources are not firsthand accounts; they are written at a later time by persons not involved in the events they describe.*
2. *Secondary sources can provide a perspective broader than that available in primary sources.*
3. *The style or content of a message may have been shaped to elicit a particular response from its original, intended audience.*
4. *primary: newspaper, private journal, editorial cartoon, deed to property, snapshot, autobiography; secondary: biography, magazine article about the history of the West*

PRACTICING YOUR SKILL

Student outlines will vary, but main idea should sum up progressive moral reform. Subheadings might include: support of prohibition (ASL and WCTU lead crusade against alcohol; Eighteenth Amendment ratified in 1919) and support of movie censorship (states and cities set up censorship boards; movie industry institutes self-censorship in 1909).

To complete research papers or special projects, you may need to use resources other than this textbook. Conducting research generally requires you to seek out the resources available in a library.

FINDING INFORMATION

To find a particular book, you need to know how libraries organize their materials. Books of fiction are alphabetized according to the last name of the author. To classify nonfiction books, libraries use the Dewey decimal system and the Library of Congress system. Both systems assign each book a *call number* that tells you its classification.

To find the number, look in the library's *card catalog*. The catalog lists books by author, by title, and by subject. If you know the author or title of the book, finding it is simple. If you do not know this information, or if you just want to find any book about a general subject, look up that subject heading. Some libraries have computerized card catalogs, which can make searching for specific information easier.

Librarians can assist you in using the card catalog and direct you to a book's location. They can also suggest additional resources.

USING RESOURCES

In a library's reference section, you will find encyclopedias, specialized dictionaries, atlases, almanacs, and indexes to recent material in magazines and newspapers. Encyclopedias often will be your best resource. Encyclopedias include biographical sketches of important historical figures; geographic, economic, and political data on individual nations, states, and cities; and discussions of historical events and religious, social, and cultural issues. Entries often include cross-references to related articles.

Specialized dictionaries exist for almost every field. Historical dictionaries such as *The Concise Dictionary of American History* include definitions of historical terms as well as brief descriptions of important laws, court cases, social movements, and more. Geographical

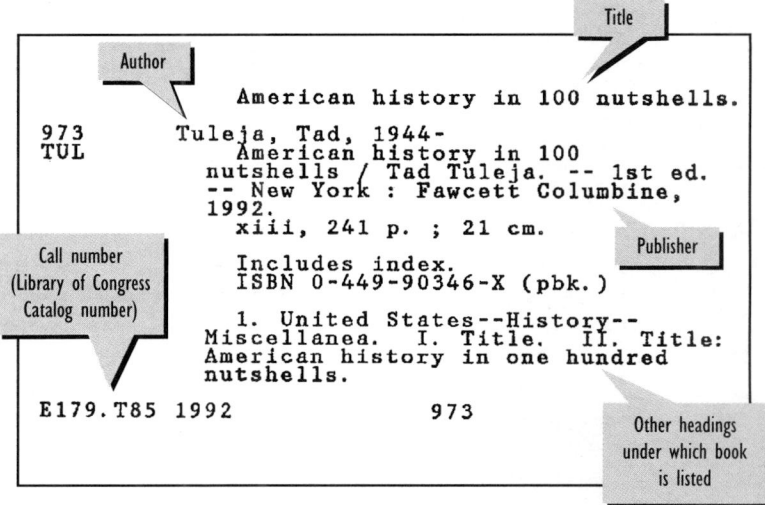

dictionaries—or *gazetteers*—list significant natural physical features and place-names. Pronunciation guides, statistical data, and brief descriptions are also included. *Atlases* contain maps and visual representations of geographic data.

To find up-to-date facts about a subject, you can use almanacs, yearbooks, and periodical indexes. References like *The World Almanac and Book of Facts* include historical information and a variety of statistics about population, the environment, sports, and so on. Encyclopedia yearbooks keep up with recent, significant developments not fully covered in encyclopedia articles.

Periodical indexes, especially *The Readers' Guide to Periodical Literature,* can help you locate articles published in magazines. The *New York Times Index* catalogs the news stories published in the *Times,* the U.S. daily newspaper with perhaps the most in-depth coverage of national and world events.

PRACTICING YOUR SKILL

1. In what two ways are nonfiction books classified?
2. What kinds of references contain information about geography?
3. Where would you look to find recent coverage of a political or social issue?
4. Would you look in an encyclopedia, an atlas, or an American history dictionary to find each of the following items? (a) the latitude of Guatemala (b) a biography of Julius Caesar (c) the purpose of the Taft-Hartley Act (d) the major industries of Cleveland, Ohio

---

PRACTICING YOUR SKILL

1. *Dewey decimal and Library of Congress systems*
2. *gazetteers, encyclopedias, atlases, and almanacs*
3. *The Readers' Guide to Periodical Literature, the* New York Times Index, *encyclopedia yearbooks, or almanacs*
4. **(a)** *atlas*
   (b) *encyclopedia*
   (c) *American history dictionary*
   (d) *encyclopedia*

WRITING A PAPER

Boyer's The American Nation provides you with numerous writing opportunities. Section reviews have writing exercises (labeled Writing to Inform, Writing to Persuade, and so on) that give you the chance to write about a historical subject with a particular focus in mind. Chapter reviews contain additional opportunities for writing.

WRITING WITH A PURPOSE

Always keep your purpose for writing in mind. That purpose might be to analyze, to evaluate, to synthesize, to inform, to persuade, to hypothesize, or to take a stand. As you begin, your purpose will determine the most appropriate approach to take; and when you are done, it will help you evaluate how well you have succeeded.

Each different purpose for writing requires its own form, tone, and content. The point of view you are adopting will shape what you write, as will your intended audience. For example, you would take a different tone when writing to a president from the tone you would use with a relative.

HISTORICAL IMAGINATION

Many writing opportunities in *Boyer's The American Nation* ask you to create a specific type of writing, such as a diary entry, a letter, a newspaper editorial, a poem, or an advertisement. Often such writing about history involves using historical imagination—that is, writing from the perspective of a person living *then* rather than *now*. An assignment may require, for instance, that you address a particular historical figure, such as a former president, or that you write as if living through a specific historical crisis.

HOW TO WRITE A PAPER

Each writing opportunity provided in this textbook will have specific directions about what and how to write. But whether you are writing a diary entry describing your experiences as a western pioneer or an essay about the significance of the frontier, you should follow certain basic steps. The guidelines outlined in the second column (which apply especially to longer papers) can help you plan and improve your writing.

SOME TYPES OF WRITING

- A **diary** is an informal, personal log of your experiences and recollections (or those of someone else in history). Entries are dated and consist of brief accounts of the day's happenings and your reactions.

- A **letter** is a personal communication meant for a specific individual.

- An **advertisement** is an announcement to promote a product or event. Effective ads are direct and to the point, using memorable language, such as jingles and slogans, to highlight important features.

- A newspaper **editorial** is a public statement of an opinion or point of view. It takes a stand on an issue and gives reasons for that stand.

---

1. **Identify your purpose in writing.** Read the directions carefully to identify the purpose for your writing. Keep that purpose in mind as you plan and write your paper.

2. **Consider your audience.** When writing for a specific audience, choose the tone and style that will best communicate your message.

3. **Create an outline.** Think and plan before you begin writing your first draft. Organize themes, main ideas, and supporting details into an outline.

4. **Collect information.** Do research if necessary. Your writing will be more effective if you have many details at hand.

5. **Write a first draft and evaluate it.** In your first draft, remember to use your outline as a guide. Each paragraph should express a single main idea or set of related ideas, with details for support. Be careful to show the relationships between ideas and to use proper transitions—sentences that build connections between paragraphs.

6. **Review and edit.** Revise and reorganize your draft as needed to make your points. Improve sentences by adding appropriate adjectives and adverbs. Make your writing clearer by changing the length or structure of awkward sentences. Replace inexact

PRACTICING YOUR SKILL

1. *the purpose; determines the most appropriate approach to take and helps the writer evaluate the finished product*
2. *determines format and tone of one's writing*
3. *reorganize sections, add appropriate adjectives and adverbs, change the length and structure of sentences, replace inexact words, and check for proper spelling, punctuation, and grammar*

PRACTICING YOUR SKILL

1. *by eliminating choices you know are wrong*
2. *helps in estimating how much time to take per section or question, anticipating difficult areas, and pacing through the test*
3. *Answers might include: consistent study habits, rest, keeping up with assignments, taking careful notes, reviewing material, concentrating on the test, ignoring distractions, and following all directions.*

wording with more precise word choices. Then check for proper spelling, punctuation, and grammar.

7. **Write your final version.** Prepare a neat, clean final version. Appearance is important; it may not affect the quality of your writing itself, but it can affect the way your writing is perceived and understood.

PRACTICING YOUR SKILL

1. What factor—more than any other—should affect how and what you write? Why?
2. Why is it important to consider the audience for whom you are writing?
3. What steps should you take to edit a first draft?

12 TAKING A TEST

When it comes to taking a test, for history or any other subject, nothing can take the place of preparation. A good night's sleep added to consistent study habits give you a far better chance for success than hours of late-night, last-minute cramming.

But keeping your mind focused on the test and free from distractions is not all you can do to improve your test scores. Mastering some basic test-taking skills can also help. Keeping up with your daily reading assignments and taking careful notes as you read can turn taking a test into a mere matter of review. Reviewing material that you already know takes less time—and causes less stress—than trying to learn something new under pressure.

▲ *Homework by Winslow Homer*

You will face several basic types of questions on U.S. history tests: multiple choice, matching, and essay. In answering multiple-choice questions, eliminate any answers that you know are wrong; this will narrow your field of choice. When doing a matching exercise, first go through the entire list, matching those that you are sure of. Then study any that remain.

Read essay questions carefully so that you know exactly what you are being asked to write. If time permits, make an outline of the main ideas and supporting details that you plan to include in your essay. Keep your answer clear and brief, but cover all necessary points.

HOW TO TAKE A TEST

1. **Prepare beforehand.** This all-important step not only involves studying and reviewing the material prior to the test. It also means being physically rested and mentally focused on the day of the test.

2. **Follow directions.** Read all instructions carefully. Listen closely, particularly if you are being told the directions rather than being given written instructions.

3. **Preview the test.** Skim through the entire test to determine how much time you have for each section. Try to anticipate which areas of the examination will be the most difficult for you. You may wish to allow yourself more time to work on the more difficult sections.

4. **Concentrate on the test.** Do not "watch the clock," but stay aware of the time. If you do not know an answer, move on to the next question. It is best to answer as many questions as you can within the time limit.

5. **Review your answers.** If you have time, return to questions that you skipped or were unsure of and work on them. Review your essays to catch and correct any mistakes in spelling, punctuation, or grammar.

PRACTICING YOUR SKILL

1. How can you improve your chances on multiple-choice questions?
2. Why is it important to skim through the entire test before you begin?
3. Name three things that can help you in taking a test.

Thomas Jefferson's First Inaugural Address

March 4, 1801

Friends and Fellow Citizens...

All . . . will bear in mind this sacred principle, that though the will of the majority is in all cases to prevail, that will to be rightful must be reasonable; that the minority possess their equal rights, which equal law must protect, and to violate would be oppression. Let us, then, fellow citizens, unite with one heart and one mind. Let us restore to social intercourse [dealings] that harmony and affection without which liberty and even life itself are but dreary things. And let us reflect that, having banished from our land that religious intolerance under which mankind so long bled and suffered, we have yet gained little if we countenance [allow] a political intolerance as despotic, as wicked, and capable of as bitter and bloody persecutions. . . . But every difference of opinion is not a difference of principle. We have called by different names brethren of the same principle. We are all Republicans; we are all Federalists. If there be any among us who would wish to dissolve this Union or to change its republican form, let them stand undisturbed as monuments of the safety with which error of opinion may be tolerated where reason is left free to combat it. I know, indeed, that some honest men fear that a republican government cannot be strong, that this government is not strong enough; but would the honest patriot, in the full tide of successful experiment, abandon a government which has so far kept us free and firm on the theoretic [hypothetical] and visionary fear that this government, the world's best hope, may by possibility want energy to preserve itself? I trust not. I believe this, on the contrary, the strongest government on earth. I believe it the only one where every man, at the call of the law, would fly to the standard of the law, and would meet invasions of the public order as his own personal concern. Sometimes it is said that man cannot be trusted with the government of himself. Can he, then, be trusted with the government of others? Or have we found angels in the forms of kings to govern him? Let history answer this question.

Let us, then, with courage and confidence pursue our own Federal and Republican principles, our attachment to union and representative government. Kindly separated by nature and a wide ocean from the exterminating havoc of one quarter of the globe; too high-minded to endure the degradations of the others; possessing a chosen country, with room enough for our descendants to the thousandth and thousandth generation; entertaining a due sense of our equal right to the use of our own faculties, to the acquisitions of our own industry, to honor and confidence from our fellow citizens, resulting not from birth, but from our actions and their sense of them; enlightened by a benign religion, professed, indeed, and practiced in various forms, yet all of them inculcating [implanting] honesty, truth, temperance, gratitude, and the love of man; acknowledging and adoring an overruling Providence, which by all its dispensations proves that it delights in the happiness of man here and his greater happiness hereafter—with all these blessings, what more is necessary to make us a happy and a prosperous people? Still one thing more, fellow citizens—a wise and frugal government, which shall restrain men from injuring one another, shall leave them otherwise free to regulate their own pursuits of industry and improvement, and shall not take from the mouth of labor the bread it has earned. This is the sum of good government, and this is necessary to close the circle of our felicities [good intentions].

About to enter, fellow citizens, on the exercise of duties which comprehend [include] everything dear and valuable to you, it is proper you should understand what I deem the essential principles of our government and consequently those which ought to shape its administration. I will compress them within the narrowest compass they will bear, stating the general principle, but not all its limitations. Equal and exact justice to all men, of whatever state or persuasion religious or political; peace, commerce, and honest friendship with all nations, entangling alliances with none; the support of the state governments in all their rights, as the most competent administrations for our domestic concerns and the surest bulwarks [defenses] against anti-republican tendencies; the preservation of the general government in its whole constitutional vigor, as the sheet anchor [main support] of our peace at home and safety abroad; a jealous care of the right of election by the people—a mild and safe corrective of abuses which are lopped by the sword of revolution where peaceable remedies are unprovided; absolute acquiescence in [submission to] the decisions of the majority, the vital principle of republics, from which [there] is no appeal but to force, the vital principle and immediate parent of despotism; a well-disciplined militia, our best reliance in peace and for the first moments of war, till regulars may relieve them; the supremacy of the civil over the military authority; economy in the public expense, that labor may be lightly burdened; the honest payment of our debts and sacred preservation of the public faith; encouragement of agriculture, and of commerce as its handmaid; the diffusion of information and arraignment [bringing up] of all abuses at the bar of the public reason; freedom of religion; freedom of the press; and freedom of person under the protection of the *habeas corpus,** and trial by juries impartially selected. These principles form the bright constellation which has gone before us and guided our steps through an age of revolution and reformation. The wisdom of our sages and blood of our heroes have been devoted to their attainment. They should be the creed of our political faith, the text of civic instruction, the touchstone by which to try the services of those we trust; and should we wander from them in moments of error or of alarm, let us hasten to retrace our steps and to regain the road which alone leads to peace, liberty, and safety.

I repair, then, fellow citizens, to the post you have assigned me. With experience enough in subordinate offices to have seen the difficulties of this the greatest of all, I have learned to expect that it will rarely fall to the lot of imperfect man to retire from this station with the reputation and the favor which bring him into it. Without pretensions to that high confidence you reposed in our first and greatest revolutionary character [Washington] whose pre-eminent services had entitled him to the first place in his country's love and destined for him the fairest page in the volume of faithful history, I ask so much confidence only as may give firmness and effect to the legal administration of your affairs. I shall often go wrong through defect of judgment. When right, I shall often be thought wrong by those whose positions will not command a view of the whole ground. I ask your indulgence for my own errors, which will never be intentional, and your support against the errors of others, who may condemn what they would not if seen in all its parts. The approbation [approval] implied by your suffrage is a great consolation to me for the past, and my future solicitude [concern] will be to retain the good opinion of those who have bestowed it in advance, to conciliate [win over] that of others by doing them all the good in my power, and to be instrumental to the happiness and freedom of all.

Relying, then, on the patronage of your good will, I advance with obedience to the work, ready to retire from it whenever you become sensible how much better choice it is in your power to make. And may that Infinite Power which rules the destinies of the universe lead our councils to what is best, and give them a favorable issue for your peace and prosperity. ❖

Habeas corpus: legal provision guaranteeing a prisoner or detainee the right to be informed of the cause of his or her detention, as a protection against illegal imprisonment.

HISTORICAL DOCUMENT

The Monroe Doctrine

December 2, 1823

At the proposal of the Russian Imperial Government, made through the minister of the Emperor residing here, a full power and instructions have been transmitted to the minister of the United States at St. Petersburg to arrange by amicable negotiations the respective rights and interests of the two nations on the northwest coast of this continent. A similar proposal had been made by His Imperial Majesty to the government of Great Britain, which has likewise been acceded [agreed] to. The government of the United States has been desirous by this friendly proceeding of manifesting the great value which they have invariably attached to the friendship of the Emperor and their solicitude to cultivate the best understanding with his government. In the discussions to which this interest has given rise and in the arrangements by which they may terminate the occasion has been judged proper for asserting, as a principle in which the rights and interests of the United States are involved, that the American continents, by the free and independent condition which they have assumed and maintain, are henceforth not to be considered as subjects for future colonization by any European powers. . . .

The citizens of the United States cherish sentiments the most friendly in favor of the liberty and happiness of their fellow men on that side of the Atlantic [in Europe]. In the wars of the European powers in matters relating to themselves we have never taken any part, nor does it comport with our policy to do so. It is only when our rights are invaded or seriously menaced that we resent injuries or make preparation for our defense. With the movements in this hemisphere we are of necessity more immediately connected, and by causes which must be obvious to all enlightened and impartial observers. The political system of the allied powers [Holy Alliance]* is essentially different in this respect from that of America. This difference proceeds from that which exists in their respective governments; and to the defense of our own, which has been achieved by the loss of much blood and treasure, and matured by the wisdom of their most enlightened citizens, and under which we have enjoyed unexampled felicity, this whole nation is devoted. We owe it, therefore, to candor and to the amicable relations existing between the United States and those powers to declare that we should consider any attempt on their part to extend their system to any portion of this hemisphere as dangerous to our peace and safety. With the existing colonies or dependencies of any European power, we have not interfered and shall not interfere. But with the governments who have declared their independence and maintained it, and whose independence we have, on great consideration and on just principles, acknowledged, we could not view any interposition for the purpose of oppressing them, or controlling in any other manner their destiny, by any European power in any other light than as the manifestation of an unfriendly disposition toward the United States. In the war between those new governments and Spain, we declared our neutrality at the time of their recognition, and to this we have adhered, and shall continue to adhere, provided no change shall occur which,

*Holy Alliance: alliance between France, Austria, Russia, and Prussia.

in the judgment of the competent authorities of this government, shall make a corresponding change on the part of the United States indispensable to their security.

The late events in Spain and Portugal show that Europe is still unsettled. Of this important fact no stronger proof can be adduced [offered] than that the allied powers should have thought it proper, on any principle satisfactory to themselves, to have interposed by force in the internal concerns of Spain. To what extent such interposition may be carried, on the same principle, is a question in which all independent powers whose governments differ from theirs are interested, even those most remote, and surely none more so than the United States. Our policy in regard to Europe, which was adopted at an early stage of the wars which have so long agitated that quarter of the globe, nevertheless remains the same, which is, not to interfere in the internal concerns of any of its powers; to consider the government *de facto* [such as it is] as the legitimate government for us; to cultivate friendly relations with it, and to preserve those relations by a frank, firm, and manly policy, meeting in all instances the just claims of every power, submitting to injuries from none. But in regard to those continents [North and South America] circumstances are eminently and conspicuously different. It is impossible that the allied powers should extend their political system to any portion of either continent without endangering our peace and happiness; nor can anyone believe that our southern brethren [Latin Americans], if left to themselves, would adopt it of their own accord. It is equally impossible, therefore, that we should behold such interposition in any form with indifference. If we look to the comparative strength and resources of Spain and those new governments and their distance from each other, it must be obvious that she can never subdue them. It is still the true policy of the United States to leave the parties to themselves, in the hope that other powers will pursue the same course. ❖

The Seneca Falls Declaration of Sentiments

July 19–20, 1848

When, in the course of human events, it becomes necessary for one portion of the family of man to assume among the people of the earth a position different from that which they have hitherto occupied, but one to which the laws of nature and of nature's God entitle them, a decent respect to the opinions of mankind requires that they should declare the causes that impel them to such a course.

We hold these truths to be self-evident: that all men and women are created equal; that they are endowed by their Creator with certain inalienable rights; that among these are life, liberty, and the pursuit of happiness; that to secure these rights governments are instituted, deriving their just powers from the consent of the governed. Whenever any form of government becomes destructive of these ends, it is the right of those who suffer from it to refuse allegiance to it, and to insist upon the institution of a new government, laying its foundation on such principles, and organizing its powers in such form, as to them shall seem most likely to effect their safety and happiness. Prudence, indeed, will dictate that governments long established should not be changed for light and transient causes; and accordingly all experience has shown that mankind are more disposed to suffer while evils are sufferable [bearable], than to right themselves by abolishing the forms to which they were accustomed. But when a long train of abuses and usurpations [seizures] pursuing invariably the same object evinces [reveals] a design to reduce them under absolute despotism, it is their duty to throw off such government, and to provide new guards for their future security. Such has been the patient sufferance [suffering] of the women under this government, and such is now the necessity which constrains them to demand the equal station to which they are entitled.

The history of mankind is a history of repeated injuries and usurpations on the part of man toward woman, having in direct object the establishment of an absolute tyranny over her. To prove this, let facts be submitted to a candid world. . . .

Having deprived her of this first right of a citizen, the elective franchise [right to vote], thereby leaving her without representation in the halls of legislation, he has oppressed her on all sides.

He has made her, if married, in the eye of the law, civilly dead. . . .

Now, in view of this entire disfranchisement [loss of right to vote] of one half of the people of this country, their social and religious degradation—in view of the unjust laws above mentioned, and because women do feel themselves aggrieved, oppressed, and fraudulently deprived of their most sacred rights, we insist that they have immediate admission to all the rights and privileges which belong to them as citizens of the United States.

In entering upon the great work before us, we anticipate no small amount of misconception, misrepresentation, and ridicule; but we shall use every instrumentality [means] within our power to effect our object. We shall employ agents, circulate tracts [pamphlets], petition the state and national legislatures, and endeavor to enlist the pulpit and the press in our behalf. We hope this convention will be followed by a series of conventions embracing every part of the country. . . .

Resolutions

Resolved, That all laws which prevent woman from occupying such a station in society as her conscience shall dictate, or which place her in a position inferior to that of man, are contrary to the great precept of nature, and, therefore, of no force or authority.

Resolved, That woman is man's equal—was intended to be so by the Creator, and the highest good of the race demands that she should be recognized as such. . . .

Resolved, That woman has too long rested satisfied in the circumscribed [narrow] limits which corrupt customs and a perverted [misdirected] application of the Scriptures have marked out for her, and that it is time she should move in the enlarged sphere which her great Creator has assigned her.

Resolved, That it is the duty of the women of this country to secure to themselves their sacred right to the elective franchise.

Resolved, That the equality of human rights results necessarily from the fact of the identity [sameness of essential character] of the race in capabilities and responsibilities. . . .

Resolved, therefore, That, being invested by the Creator with the same capabilities, and the same consciousness of responsibility for their exercise, it is demonstrably the right and duty of woman, equally with man, to promote every righteous cause by every righteous means; and especially in regard to the great subjects of morals and religion, it is self-evidently her right to participate with her brother in teaching them, both in private and in public, by writing and by speaking, by any instrumentalities proper to be used, and in any assemblies proper to be held. . . .

Resolved, That the speedy success of our cause depends upon the zealous and untiring efforts of both men and women, for the overthrow of the monopoly of the pulpit, and for the securing to women an equal participation with men in the various trades, professions, and commerce. ❖

The Emancipation Proclamation

January 1, 1863

**BY THE PRESIDENT OF
THE UNITED STATES OF AMERICA**

A Proclamation

Whereas on the twenty-second day of September, A.D. 1862, a proclamation was issued by the President of the United States, containing, among other things, the following, to wit [namely]:

"That on the first day of January, A.D. 1863, all persons held as slaves within any state or designated part of a state, the people whereof shall then be in rebellion against the United States, shall be then, thenceforward, and forever free; and the executive government of the United States, including the military and naval authority thereof, will recognize and maintain the freedom of such persons and will do no act or acts to repress such persons or any of them, in any efforts they may make for their actual freedom.

"That the Executive will on the first day of January aforesaid, by proclamation, designate the states and parts of states, if any, in which the people thereof, respectively, shall then be in rebellion against the United States; and the fact that any state or the people thereof shall on that day be in good faith represented in the Congress of the United States by members chosen thereto at elections wherein a majority of the qualified voters of such states shall have participated shall, in the absence of strong countervailing [opposing] testimony, be deemed conclusive evidence that such state and the people thereof are not then in rebellion against the United States."

Now, therefore, I, Abraham Lincoln, President of the United States, by virtue of the power in me vested as Commander-in-Chief of the Army and Navy of the United States in time of actual armed rebellion against the authority and government of the United States, and as a fit and necessary war measure for suppressing said rebellion, do, on this first day of January, A.D. 1863, and in accordance with my purpose so to do, publicly proclaimed for the full period of one hundred days from the first day above mentioned, order and designate as the states and parts of states wherein the people thereof, respectively, are this day in rebellion against the United States the following, to wit:

Arkansas, Texas, Louisiana (except the parishes of St. Bernard, Plaquemines, Jefferson, St. John, St. Charles, St. James, Ascension, Assumption, Terrebonne, Lafourche, St. Mary, St. Martin, and Orleans, including the city of New Orleans), Mississippi, Alabama, Florida, Georgia, South Carolina, North Carolina, and Virginia (except the forty-eight counties designated as West Virginia, and also the counties of Berkeley, Accomac, Northampton, Elizabeth City, York, Princess Anne, and Norfolk, including the cities of Norfolk and Portsmouth), and which excepted parts are for the present left precisely as if this proclamation were not issued.

And by virtue of the power and for the purpose aforesaid, I do order and declare that all persons held as slaves within said designated states and parts of states are, and henceforward shall be, free; and that the executive government of the United States, including the military and naval authorities thereof, will recognize and maintain the freedom of said persons.

And I hereby enjoin [order] upon the people so declared to be free to abstain from all violence, unless in necessary self-defense; and I recommend to them that, in all cases when allowed, they labor faithfully for reasonable wages.

And I further declare and make known that such persons of suitable condition will be received into the armed service of the United States to garrison forts, positions, stations, and other places, and to man vessels of all sorts in said service.

And upon this act, sincerely believed to be an act of justice, warranted by the Constitution upon military necessity, I invoke the considerate judgment of mankind and the gracious favor of Almighty God. ❖

Abraham Lincoln's Gettysburg Address

November 19, 1863

Four score and seven years ago our fathers brought forth on this continent a new nation, conceived in liberty, and dedicated to the proposition that all men are created equal.

Now we are engaged in a great civil war, testing whether that nation, or any nation so conceived and so dedicated can long endure. We are met on a great battlefield of that war. We have come to dedicate a portion of that field as a final resting place for those who here gave their lives that that nation might live. It is altogether fitting and proper that we should do this.

But, in a larger sense, we cannot dedicate—we cannot consecrate [make holy]—we cannot hallow—this ground. The brave men, living and dead, who struggled here, have consecrated it far above our poor power to add or detract. The world will little note nor long remember what we say here, but it can never forget what they did here. It is for us, the living, rather, to be dedicated here to the unfinished work which they who fought here have thus far so nobly advanced. It is rather for us to be here dedicated to the great task remaining before us—that from these honored dead we take increased devotion to that cause for which they gave the last full measure of devotion; that we here highly resolve that these dead shall not have died in vain; that this nation, under God, shall have a new birth of freedom; and that government of the people, by the people, for the people, shall not perish from the earth. ❖

The Fourteen Points

January 8, 1918

Gentlemen of the Congress:

It will be our wish and purpose that the processes of peace, when they are begun, shall be absolutely open and that they shall involve and permit henceforth no secret understandings of any kind. The day of conquest and aggrandizement is gone by; so is also the day of secret covenants entered into in the interest of particular governments and likely at some unlooked-for moment to upset the peace of the world. It is this happy fact, now clear to the view of every public man whose thoughts do not still linger in an age that is dead and gone, which makes it possible for every nation whose purposes are consistent with justice and the peace of the world to avow now or at any other time the objects it has in view.

We entered this war because violations of right had occurred which touched us to the quick and made the life of our own people impossible unless they were corrected and the world secured once for all against their recurrence. What we demand in this war, therefore, is nothing peculiar to ourselves. It is that the world be made fit and safe to live in; and particularly that it be made safe for every peace-loving nation which, like our own, wishes to live its own life, determine its own institutions, be assured of justice and fair dealing by the other peoples of the world as against force and selfish aggression. All the peoples of the world are in effect partners in this interest, and for our own part we see very clearly that unless justice be done to others it will not be done to us. The program of the world's peace, therefore, is our program; and that program, the only possible program, as we see it, is this:

I. Open covenants of peace, openly arrived at, after which there shall be no private international understandings of any kind but diplomacy shall proceed always frankly and in the public view.

II. Absolute freedom of navigation upon the seas, outside territorial waters, alike in peace and in war, except as the seas may be closed in whole or in part by international action for the enforcement of international covenants.

III. The removal, so far as possible, of all economic barriers and the establishment of an equality of trade conditions among all the nations consenting to the peace and associating themselves for its maintenance.

IV. Adequate guarantees given and taken that national armaments will be reduced to the lowest point consistent with domestic safety.

V. A free, open-minded, and absolutely impartial adjustment of all colonial claims, based upon a strict observance of the principle that in determining all such questions of sovereignty the interests of the populations concerned must have equal weight with the equitable claims of the government whose title is to be determined.

VI. The evacuation of all Russian territory and such a settlement of all questions affecting Russia as will secure the best and freest cooperation of the other nations of the world in obtaining for her an unhampered and unembarrassed opportunity for the independent determination of her own political development and national policy and assure her of a sincere welcome into the society of free nations under institutions of her own choosing; and, more than a welcome, assistance also of every kind that she may need and may herself desire. The treatment accorded Russia by her sister nations in the months to come will be the acid test of their good will, of their comprehension of her needs as distinguished from their own interests, and of their intelligent and unselfish sympathy.

VII. Belgium, the whole world will agree, must be evacuated and restored, without any attempt to limit the sovereignty which she enjoys in common with all other free nations. No other single act will serve as this will serve to restore confidence among the nations in the laws which they have themselves set and determined for the government of their relation with one another. Without this healing act the whole structure and validity of international law is forever impaired.

VIII. All French territory should be freed and the invaded portions restored, and the wrong done to France by Prussia in 1871 in the matter of Alsace-Lorraine, which has unsettled the peace of the world for nearly fifty years, should be righted, in order that peace may once more be made secure in the interest of all.

IX. A readjustment of the frontiers of Italy shall be effected along clearly recognizable lines of nationality.

X. The peoples of Austria-Hungary, whose place among the nations we wish to see safeguarded and assured, should be accorded the freest opportunity of autonomous development.

XI. Rumania, Serbia, and Montenegro should be evacuated; occupied territories restored; Serbia accorded free and secure access to the sea; and the relations of the several Balkan states to one another determined by friendly counsel along historically established lines of allegiance and nationality; and international guarantees of the political and economic independence and territorial integrity of the several Balkan states should be entered into.

XII. The Turkish portions of the present Ottoman Empire should be assured a secure sovereignty, but the other nationalities which are now under Turkish rule should be assured an undoubted security of life and an absolutely unmolested opportunity of autonomous development, and the Dardanelles should be permanently opened as a free passage to the ships and commerce of all nations under international guarantees.

XIII. An independent Polish state should be erected which should include territories inhabited by indisputably Polish populations, which should be assured a free and secure access to the sea, and whose political and economic independence and territorial integrity should be guaranteed by international covenant.

XIV. A general association of nations must be formed under specific covenants for the purpose of affording mutual guarantees of political independence and territorial integrity to great and small states alike.

In regard to these essential rectifications [righting] of wrong and assertions of right we feel ourselves to be intimate partners of all the governments and peoples associated together against the Imperialists. We cannot be separated in interest or divided in purpose. We stand together until the end.

For such arrangements and covenants we are willing to fight and to continue to fight until they are achieved; but only because we wish the right to prevail and desire a just and stable peace such as can be secured only by removing the chief provocations to war, which this program does not remove. We have no jealousy of German greatness, and there is nothing in this program that impairs it. We grudge her no achievement or distinction of learning or of pacific [peaceful] enterprise such as have made her record very bright and very enviable. We do not wish to injure her or to block in any way her legitimate influence or power. We do not wish to fight her either with arms or with hostile arrangements of trade if she is willing to associate herself with us and the other peace-loving nations of the world in covenants of justice and law and fair dealing. We wish her only to accept a place of equality among the peoples of the world—the new world in which we now live,—instead of a place of mastery.

Neither do we presume to suggest to her any alteration or modification of her institutions. But it is necessary, we must frankly say, and necessary as a preliminary to any intelligent dealings with her on our part, that we should know whom her spokesmen speak for when they speak to us, whether for the Reichstag [German legislature] majority or for the military party and the men whose creed is imperial domination.

We have spoken now, surely, in terms too concrete to admit of any further doubt or question. An evident principle runs through the whole program I have outlined. It is the principle of justice to all peoples and nationalities, and their right to live on equal terms of liberty and safety with one another, whether they be strong or weak. Unless this principle be made its foundation no part of the structure of international justice can stand. The people of the United States could act upon no other principle; and to the vindication of this principle they are ready to devote their lives, their honor, and everything that they possess. The moral climax of this the culminating and final war for human liberty has come, and they are ready to put their own strength, their own highest purpose, their own integrity and devotion to the test. ❖

Martin Luther King, Jr.'s "I Have A Dream" Speech

August 28, 1963

Five score years ago, a great American, in whose symbolic shadow we stand, signed the Emancipation Proclamation. This momentous decree came as a great beacon light of hope to millions of Negro slaves who had been seared in the flames of withering injustice. It came as a joyous daybreak to end the long night of captivity.

But one hundred years later, we must face the tragic fact that the Negro is still not free. One hundred years later, the life of the Negro is still sadly crippled by the manacles of segregation and the chains of discrimination. One hundred years later, the Negro lives on a lonely island of poverty in the midst of a vast ocean of material prosperity. One hundred years later, the Negro is still languished in the corners of American society and finds himself an exile in his own land. So we have come here today to dramatize an appalling condition.

In a sense we have come to our nation's Capital to cash a check. When the architects of our republic wrote the magnificent words of the Constitution and the Declaration of Independence, they were signing a promissory note to which every American was to fall heir. This note was a promise that all men would be guaranteed the unalienable rights of life, liberty, and the pursuit of happiness.

It is obvious today that America has defaulted on this promissory note insofar as her citizens of color are concerned. Instead of honoring this sacred obligation, America has given the Negro people a bad check; a check which has come back marked "insufficient funds." But we refuse to believe that the bank of justice is bankrupt. We refuse to believe that there are insufficient funds in the great vaults of opportunity of this nation. So we have come to cash this check—a check that will give us upon demand the riches of freedom and the security of justice.

We have also come to this hallowed spot to remind America of the fierce urgency of *now*. This is no time to engage in the luxury of cooling off or to take the tranquilizing drug of gradualism. *Now* is the time to make real the promises of democracy. *Now* is the time to rise from the dark and desolate valley of segregation to the sunlit path of racial justice. *Now* is the time to open the doors of opportunity to all of God's children. *Now* is the time to lift our nation from the quicksands of racial injustice to the solid rock of brotherhood.

It would be fatal for the nation to overlook the urgency of the moment and to underestimate the determination of the Negro. This sweltering summer of the Negro's legitimate discontent will not pass until there is an invigorating autumn of freedom and equality. Nineteen sixty-three is not an end, but a beginning. Those who hope that the Negro needed to blow off steam and will now be content will have a rude awakening if the nation returns to business as usual. There will be neither rest nor tranquility in America until the Negro is granted his citizenship rights. The whirlwinds of revolt will continue to shake the foundations of our nation until the bright day of justice emerges.

But there is something that I must say to my people who stand on the warm threshold which leads into the palace of justice. In the process of gaining our rightful place we must not be guilty of wrongful deeds. Let us not seek to satisfy our thirst for freedom by drinking from the cup of bitterness and hatred. We must forever conduct our struggle on the high plane of dignity and discipline. We must not allow our creative protest to degenerate into physical violence. Again and again we must rise to the majestic heights of meeting physical force with soul force.

The marvelous new militancy which has engulfed the Negro community must not lead us to a distrust of all white people, for many of our white brothers, as evidenced by their presence here today, have come to realize that their destiny is tied up with our destiny and their freedom is inextricably bound to our freedom. We cannot walk alone.

And as we walk, we must make the pledge that we shall march ahead. We cannot turn back. There are those who are asking the devotees of civil rights, "When will you be satisfied?"

We can never be satisfied as long as the Negro is the victim of the unspeakable horrors of police brutality.

We can never be satisfied as long as our bodies, heavy with the fatigue of travel, cannot gain lodging in the motels of the highways and the hotels of the cities.

We cannot be satisfied as long as the Negro's basic mobility is from a smaller ghetto to a larger one.

We can never be satisfied as long as a Negro in Mississippi cannot vote and a Negro in New York believes he has nothing for which to vote.

No, no, we are not satisfied, and we will not be satisfied until justice rolls down like waters and righteousness like a mighty stream.

I am not unmindful that some of you have come here out of great trials and tribulations. Some of you have come fresh from narrow jail cells. Some of you have come from areas where your quest for freedom left you battered by the storms of persecution and staggered by the winds of police brutality. You have been the veterans of creative suffering. Continue to work with the faith that unearned suffering is redemptive.

Go back to Mississippi, go back to Alabama, go back to South Carolina, go back to Georgia, go back to Louisiana, go back to the slums and ghettos of our Northern cities, knowing that somehow this situation can and will be changed. Let us not wallow in the valley of despair.

I say to you today, my friends, that in spite of the difficulties and frustrations of the moment I still have a dream. It is a dream deeply rooted in the American dream.

I have a dream that one day this nation will rise up and live out the true meaning of its creed: "We hold these truths to be self-evident; that all men are created equal."

I have a dream that one day on the red hills of Georgia the sons of former slaves and the sons of former slaveowners will be able to sit down together at the table of brotherhood.

I have a dream that one day even the state of Mississippi, a desert state sweltering with the heat of injustice and oppression, will be transformed into an oasis of freedom and justice.

I have a dream that my four little children will one day live in a nation where they will not be judged by the color of their skin but by the content of their character.

I have a dream today.

I have a dream that one day the state of Alabama, whose governor's lips are presently dripping with the words of interposition and nullification, will be transformed into a situation where little black boys and black girls will be able to join hands with little white boys and white girls and walk together as sisters and brothers.

I have a dream today.

I have a dream that one day every valley shall be exhalted, every hill and mountain shall be made low, the rough places will be made plain, and the crooked places will be made straight, and the glory of the Lord shall be revealed, and all flesh shall see it together.

This is our hope. This is the faith with which I return to the South. With this faith we will be able to hew out of the mountain of despair a stone of hope. With this faith we will be able to transform the jangling discords of our nation into a beautiful symphony of brotherhood.

With this faith we will be able to work together, to pray together, to struggle together, to go to jail together, to stand up for freedom together, knowing that we will be free one day.

This will be the day when all of God's children will be able to sing with new meaning, "My country 'tis of thee, sweet land of liberty, of thee I sing. Land where my fathers died, land of the Pilgrims' pride, from every mountainside, let freedom ring."

And if America is to be a great nation, this must become true. So let freedom ring from the prodigious hilltops of New Hampshire. Let freedom ring from the mighty mountains of New York. Let freedom ring from the heightening Alleghenies of Pennsylvania!

Let freedom ring from the snowcapped Rockies of Colorado! Let freedom ring from the curvaceous peaks of California! But not only that; let freedom ring from Stone Mountain of Georgia! Let freedom ring from Lookout Mountain of Tennessee!

Let freedom ring from every hill and molehill of Mississippi. From every mountainside, let freedom ring.

When we let freedom ring, when we let it ring from every village and every hamlet, from every state and every city, we will be able to speed up that day when all of God's children, black men and white men, Jews and Gentiles, Protestants and Catholics, will be able to join hands and sing in the words of the old Negro spiritual, "Free at last! Free at last! Thank God Almighty, we are free at last!" ❖

ATLAS

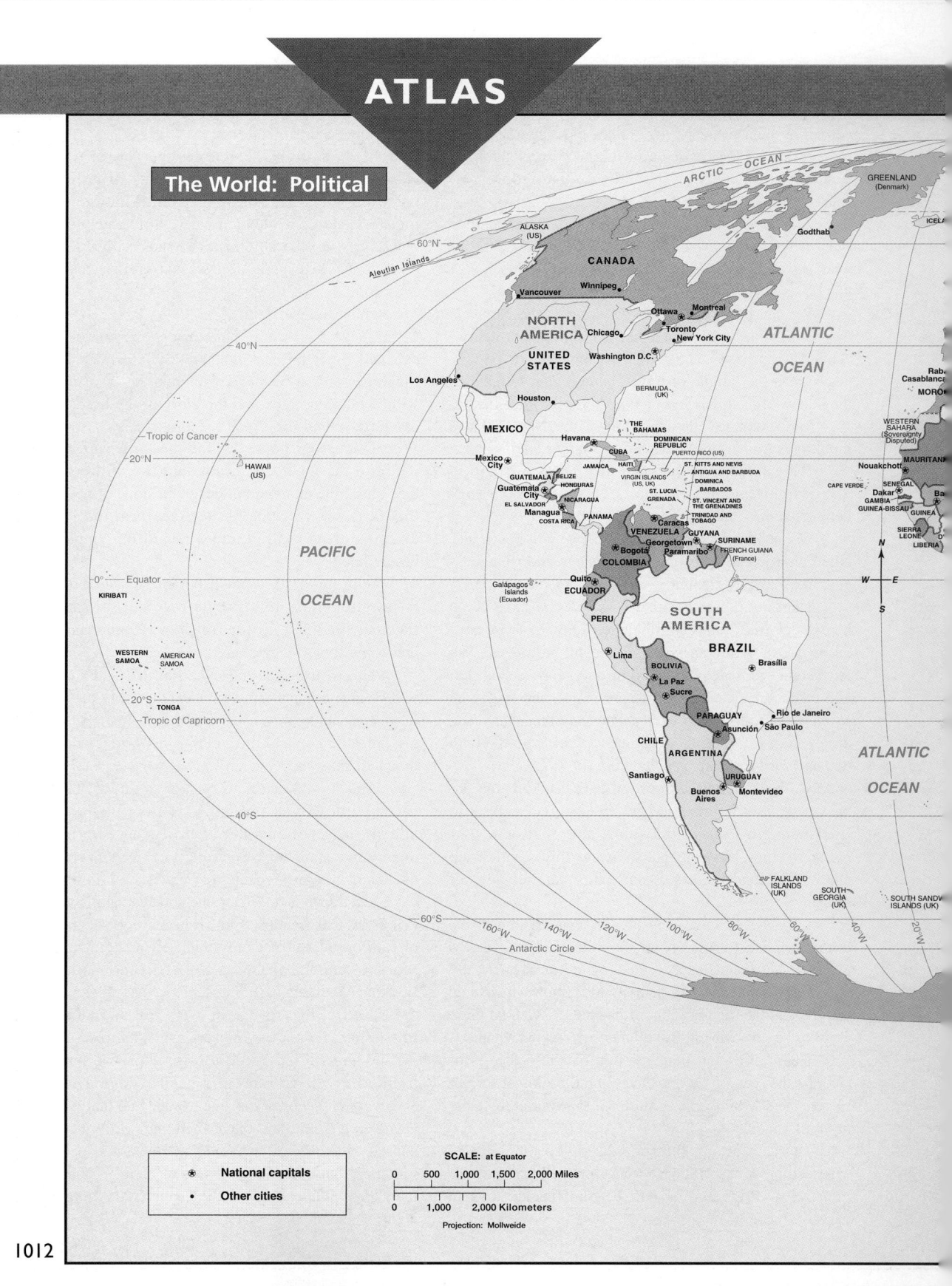

The World: Political

ARCTIC OCEAN

GREENLAND (Denmark)

ICELA

60°N

ALASKA (US)

Godthab

Aleutian Islands

CANADA

Vancouver Winnipeg

NORTH AMERICA

Ottawa Montreal

Toronto

Chicago New York City

Washington D.C.

ATLANTIC OCEAN

40°N

UNITED STATES

Los Angeles

Rab
Casablanca
MORO

Houston

BERMUDA (UK)

WESTERN SAHARA (Sovereignty Disputed)

MEXICO

THE BAHAMAS

Tropic of Cancer

Havana DOMINICAN REPUBLIC

CUBA PUERTO RICO (US)

Nouakchott MAURITAN

20°N

Mexico City

JAMAICA HAITI ST. KITTS AND NEVIS
ANTIGUA AND BARBUDA
VIRGIN ISLANDS (US, UK) DOMINICA
ST. LUCIA
BARBADOS
ST. VINCENT AND THE GRENADINES
TRINIDAD AND TOBAGO

HAWAII (US)

GUATEMALA BELIZE

Guatemala City HONDURAS

EL SALVADOR NICARAGUA

Managua PANAMA

COSTA RICA

Caracas

VENEZUELA GUYANA

CAPE VERDE SENEGAL
Dakar
GAMBIA
GUINEA-BISSAU
GUINEA

SIERRA LEONE
LIBERIA

Georgetown SURINAME

PACIFIC

Bogota Paramaribo FRENCH GUIANA (France)

N

COLOMBIA

0° Equator

Galápagos Islands (Ecuador)

Quito
ECUADOR

W   E

OCEAN

KIRIBATI

PERU

SOUTH AMERICA

S

WESTERN SAMOA AMERICAN SAMOA

BRAZIL

Lima

BOLIVIA Brasília

20°S TONGA

La Paz
Sucre

Tropic of Capricorn

PARAGUAY Rio de Janeiro

Asunción São Paulo

CHILE ARGENTINA

ATLANTIC

Santiago URUGUAY

Buenos Aires Montevideo

OCEAN

40°S

60°S 160°W 140°W 120°W 100°W 80°W 60°W 40°W 20°W

FALKLAND ISLANDS (UK)

SOUTH GEORGIA (UK)

SOUTH SANDW ISLANDS (UK)

Antarctic Circle

⊛ National capitals

• Other cities

SCALE: at Equator

0   500   1,000 1,500 2,000 Miles

0   1,000   2,000 Kilometers

Projection: Mollweide

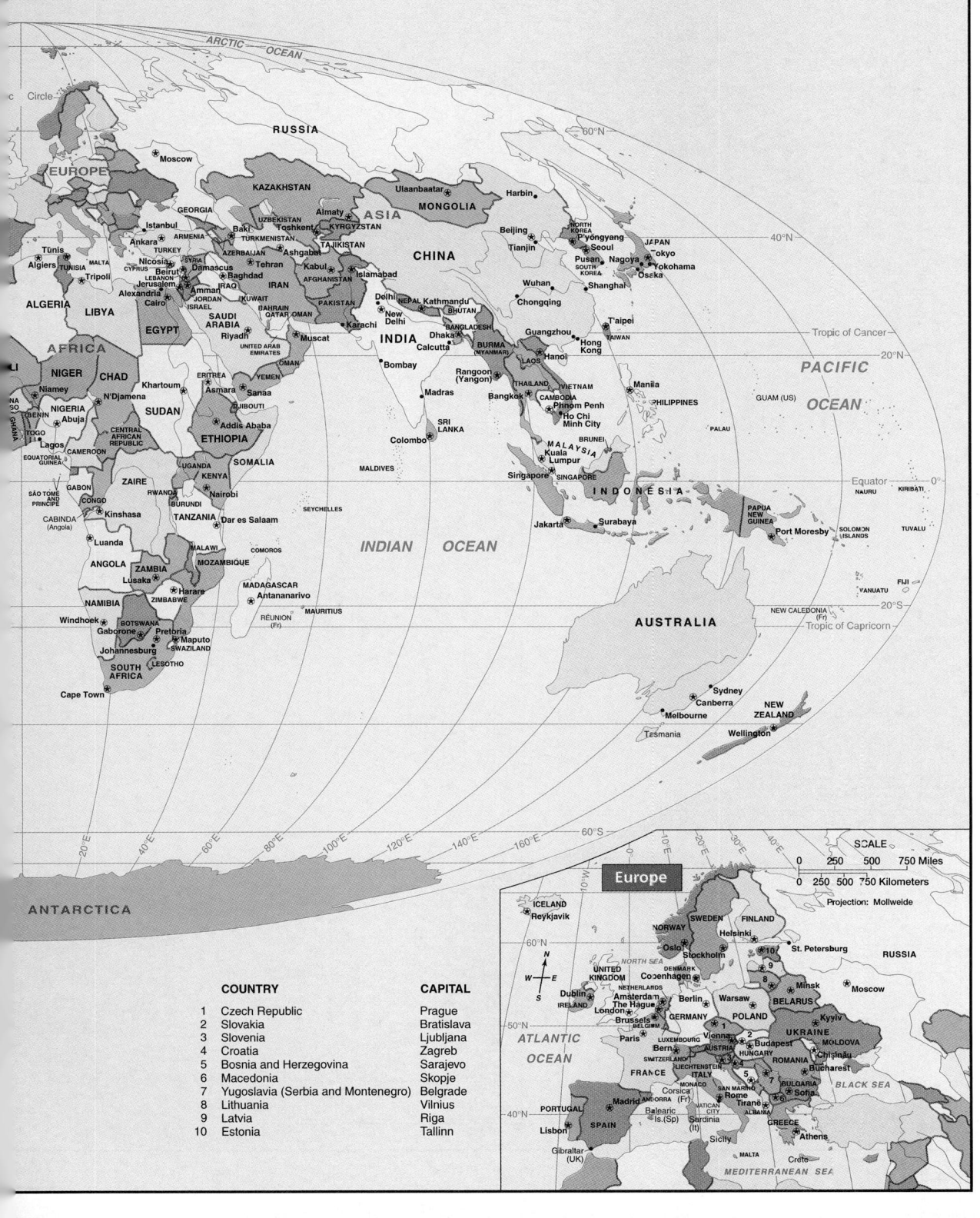

	COUNTRY	CAPITAL
1	Czech Republic	Prague
2	Slovakia	Bratislava
3	Slovenia	Ljubljana
4	Croatia	Zagreb
5	Bosnia and Herzegovina	Sarajevo
6	Macedonia	Skopje
7	Yugoslavia (Serbia and Montenegro)	Belgrade
8	Lithuania	Vilnius
9	Latvia	Riga
10	Estonia	Tallinn

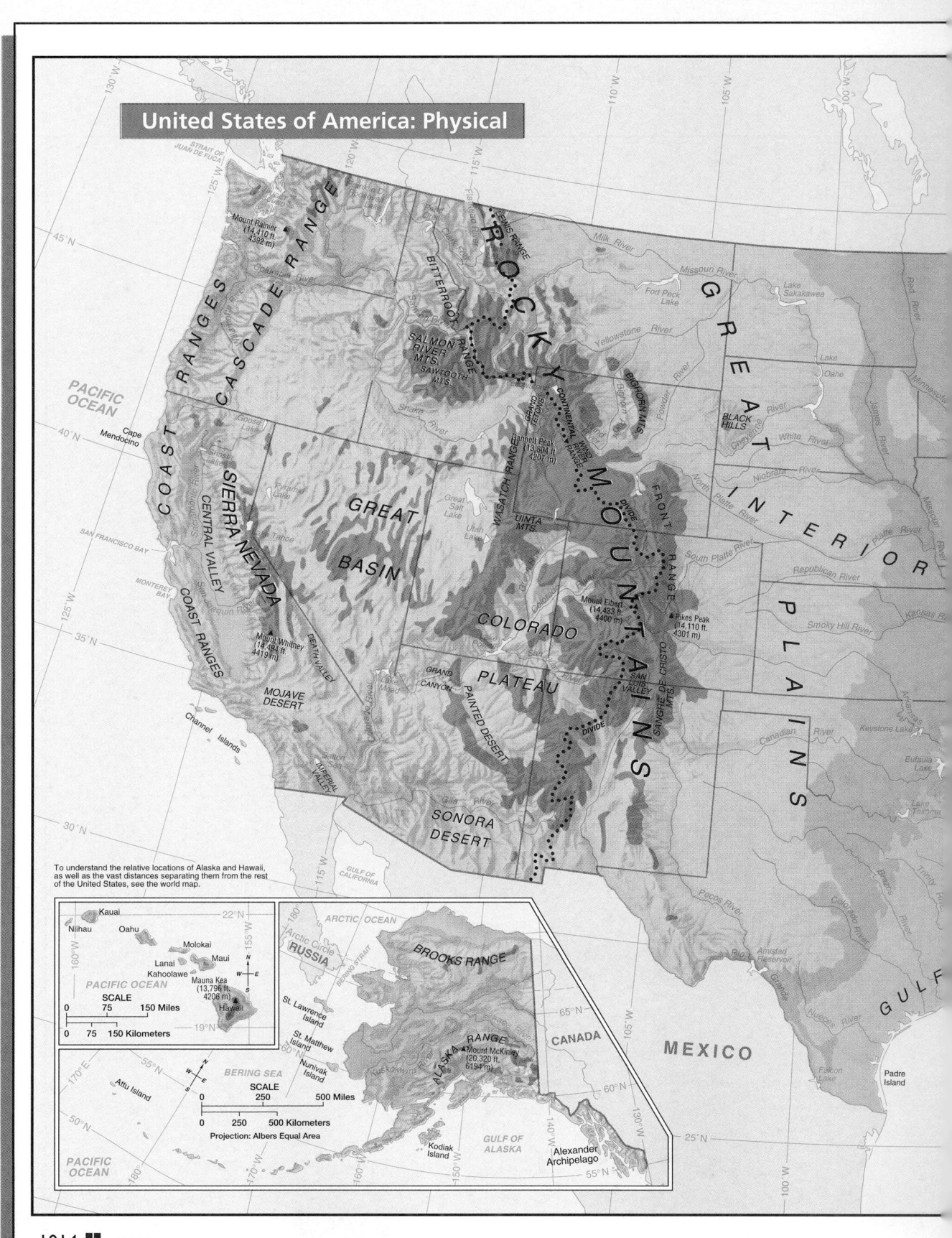

United States of America: Physical

STRAIT OF JUAN DE FUCA

PACIFIC OCEAN

Cape Mendocino

SAN FRANCISCO BAY

MONTEREY BAY

COAST RANGES

CASCADE RANGE

Mount Rainier (14,410 ft. 4392 m)

BITTERROOT RANGE

SALMON RIVER MTS.

SAWTOOTH MTS.

ROCKY MOUNTAINS

Milk River

Missouri River

Fort Peck Lake

Lake Sakakawea

Yellowstone River

Powder River

Bighorn River

BIGHORN MTS.

GRAND TETONS

CONTINENTAL DIVIDE

Snake River

Hannah Peak (13,804 ft. 4207 m)

GREAT INTERIOR PLAINS

Lake Oahe

White River

BLACK HILLS

Cheyenne River

Niobrara River

North Platte River

SIERRA NEVADA

CENTRAL VALLEY

COAST RANGES

Pyramid Lake

Tahoe

GREAT BASIN

Great Salt Lake

Utah Lake

WASATCH RANGE

UINTA MTS.

FRONT RANGE

Mount Elbert (14,433 ft. 4400 m)

Pikes Peak (14,110 ft. 4301 m)

South Platte River

Republican River

Smoky Hill River

Kansas R.

Sacramento River

San Joaquin River

Mount Whitney (14,494 ft. 4419 m)

DEATH VALLEY

MOJAVE DESERT

Channel Islands

IMPERIAL VALLEY

COLORADO PLATEAU

GRAND CANYON

PAINTED DESERT

Colorado River

SANGRE DE CRISTO MTS.

SAN LUIS VALLEY

DIVIDE

Canadian River

Keystone Lake

Arkansas River

Eufaula Lake

Lake Texoma

Gila River

SONORA DESERT

Pecos River

Rio Grande

Red River

Brazos River

Colorado River

Trinity River

GULF

Amistad Reservoir

MEXICO

Falcon Lake

Padre Island

To understand the relative locations of Alaska and Hawaii, as well as the vast distances separating them from the rest of the United States, see the world map.

GULF OF CALIFORNIA

Kauai
Niihau
Oahu
Molokai
Lanai   Maui
Kahoolawe
Mauna Kea (13,796 ft. 4206 m)
Hawaii

PACIFIC OCEAN

SCALE

0   75   150 Miles

0   75   150 Kilometers

ARCTIC OCEAN

Arctic Circle

RUSSIA

BERING STRAIT

BROOKS RANGE

St. Lawrence Island

St. Matthew Island

Nunivak Island

ALASKA RANGE

Mount McKinley (20,320 ft. 6194 m)

CANADA

GULF OF ALASKA

Kodiak Island

Alexander Archipelago

BERING SEA

SCALE

0   250   500 Miles

0   250   500 Kilometers

Projection: Albers Equal Area

Attu Island

PACIFIC OCEAN

CANADA

MESABI RANGE

Isle Royale

Lake Superior

Lake Huron

Lake Michigan

Wisconsin River

Mississippi River

Des Moines River

Illinois River

P L A I N S

Lake of the Ozarks

OZARK PLATEAU

OUACHITA MTS.

Wabash River

Scioto River

Ohio River

Lake Barkley

Kentucky Lake

White River

Mississippi River

Red River

Sabine River

Toledo Bend Reservoir

C O A S T A L   P L A I N

Tombigbee River

Pearl River

Alabama R.

Chattahoochee River

Chandeleur Islands

Mississippi Delta

GULF OF MEXICO

Lake Ontario

Finger Lakes

St. Lawrence River

St. Lawrence Seaway

ADIRONDACK MTS.

Lake Champlain

GREEN MTS.

WHITE MTS.

LONGFELLOW MTS.

St. John River

Penobscot River

Cape Cod

LONG ISLAND SOUND

Long Island

Allegheny River

Susquehanna River

P L A T E A U

CATSKILL MTS.

Delaware R.

Potomac River

Monongahela R.

A L L E G H E N Y

Kanawha River

BLUE RIDGE MOUNTAINS

CUMBERLAND PLATEAU

Cumberland River

GREAT SMOKY MTS.

Tennessee River

Chattahoochee River

Oconee River

Savannah River

Altamaha River

Sea Islands

A T L A N T I C   C O A S T A L   P L A I N

DELAWARE BAY

CHESAPEAKE BAY

Roanoke River

PAMLICO SOUND

Cape Hatteras

ATLANTIC OCEAN

Okefenokee Swamp

FLORIDA PENINSULA

Cape Canaveral

Lake Okeechobee

The Everglades

Cape Sable

Florida Keys

STRAITS OF FLORIDA

THE BAHAMAS

CUBA

90° W

85° W

80° W

75° W

70° W

65° W

60° W

50° N

45° N

40° N

35° N

30° N

25° N

70° W

75° W

80° W

85° W

90° W

65° W

ELEVATION	
Feet	Meters
13,120	4,000
6,560	2,000
1,640	500
656	200
(Sea level) 0 Below sea level	0 (Sea level) Below sea level

Ice cap

N
W — E
S

SCALE

0   250   500 Miles

0   250   500 Kilometers

Projection: Albers Equal Area

United States of America: Political

PACIFIC OCEAN

WASHINGTON
Olympia ★ Seattle
Tacoma
Spokane
STRAIT OF JUAN DE FUCA
PUGET SOUND
Franklin D. Roosevelt Lake
Pond Oreille
Portland
Salem ★
Eugene
OREGON
Columbia River

Cape Mendocino

Goose Lake
Shasta Lake
Pyramid Lake

IDAHO
Boise ●

Helena ★
MONTANA
Fort Peck Lake
Yellowstone River
Billings
Flathead Lake
Missouri River

NORTH DAKOTA
Bismarck ★
Fargo

Yellowstone Lake
Snake River
Pocatello ●

WYOMING
Casper ●
Cheyenne ★

Great Salt Lake
Salt Lake City ●
Utah Lake ● Provo

SOUTH DAKOTA
Pierre ★
Sioux Falls

NEBRASKA
Omaha ●
Lincoln ★

NEVADA
Reno ●
Carson City ★
Lake Tahoe

Concord
Berkeley ● Sacramento ★
Oakland
San Francisco ● Stockton
Hayward ● Modesto
Sunnyvale ● Fremont
San Jose

SAN FRANCISCO BAY
MONTEREY BAY

Fresno ●

CALIFORNIA
Bakersfield ●

UTAH

COLORADO
Lakewood ● ★ Aurora
Denver
Colorado Springs ●

Green River

Lake Powell

KANSAS
Wichita ●

Kansas City
Topeka ★

San Joaquin River

Oxnard
Glendale Pasadena
Los Angeles ● Pomona
Inglewood ● San Bernardino
Torrance ● Ontario
Long ● Riverside
Beach Fullerton
Garden Grove ● Anaheim
Huntington Beach ● Santa Ana
San Diego

Channel Islands

Las Vegas ●

Lake Mead
Colorado River

Salton Sea

Gila River

ARIZONA

Glendale ●
Phoenix ★ ● Scottsdale
● Mesa

Tucson ●

Santa Fe ★

Albuquerque ●

NEW MEXICO

GULF OF CALIFORNIA

El Paso ●

Amarillo ●

Lubbock ●

Abilene ●
Odessa ●

Canadian River

Pecos River

OKLAHOMA
Oklahoma City ●
Keystone Lake
Tulsa
Eufaula Lake

Lake Texoma

Irving ● ● Garland
Fort Worth ● ● Dallas
Arlington

Waco ●

TEXAS
Brazos River
Colorado River
Austin ★

MEXICO
Rio Grande
Amistad Reservoir

San Antonio ●

Laredo ●

Houston
Pasadena

Corpus Christi ●

Padre Island

To understand the relative locations of Alaska and Hawaii as well as the vast distances separating them from the rest of the United States, see the world map.

Kauai
Niihau
Oahu
Honolulu ★ Molokai
Lanai Maui
HAWAII Kahoolawe
PACIFIC OCEAN
SCALE
0   75   150 Miles
0   75   150 Kilometers
Hawaii

ARCTIC OCEAN
Arctic Circle
RUSSIA
BERING STRAIT

St. Lawrence Island
Nome ●
St. Matthew Island
Nunivak Island

ALASKA
Yukon River
Fairbanks ●

Anchorage ●

CANADA

GULF OF ALASKA

Kodiak Island

Juneau ★

Alexander Archipelago

BERING SEA
Attu Island
SCALE
0   250   500 Miles
0   250   500 Kilometers
Projection: Albers Equal Area

Aleutian Islands

PACIFIC OCEAN

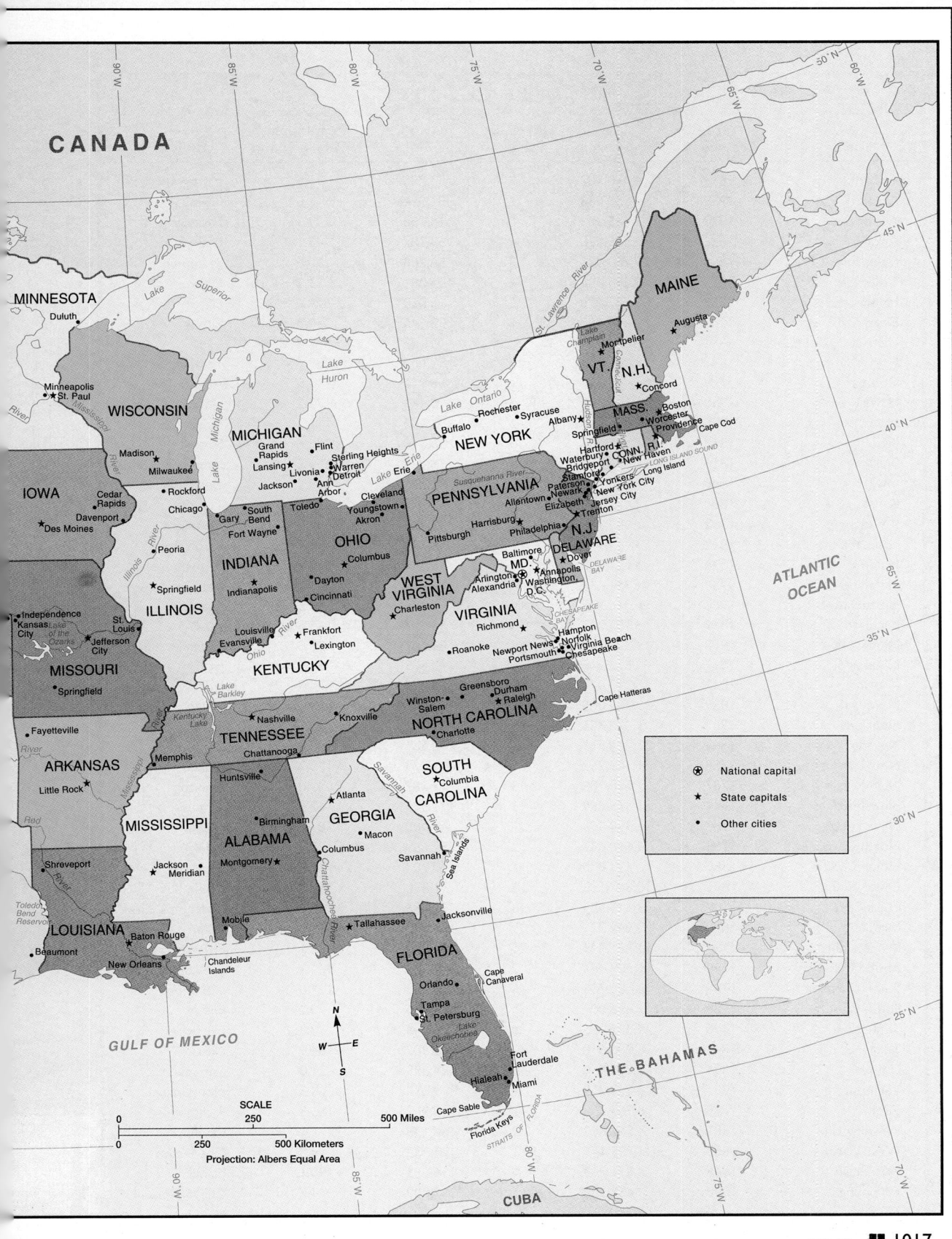

CANADA

MINNESOTA
• Duluth

• Minneapolis
★ St. Paul

WISCONSIN

• Madison
• Milwaukee
• Rockford

IOWA
• Cedar
Rapids
• Davenport
★ Des Moines

• Chicago
• Peoria

ILLINOIS
★ Springfield

MICHIGAN
Grand
Rapids • Flint
Lansing ★ • Sterling Heights
• Warren
Jackson • • Livonia
• Detroit
Ann
Arbor

Gary • South
Bend
Fort Wayne •

INDIANA
• Indianapolis

• Toledo
Cleveland •
Youngstown •
Akron •

OHIO
• Columbus

• Dayton
• Cincinnati

Lake Superior

Lake Huron

Lake Michigan

Lake Ontario

NEW YORK
• Buffalo
• Rochester
• Syracuse
• Albany ★

Lake Erie

Susquehanna River

PENNSYLVANIA
• Harrisburg
• Pittsburgh

MAINE
• Augusta ★

Montpelier •
VT. ★ N.H.
★ • Concord

St. Lawrence River

Lake Champlain

MASS. • Boston
Springfield • Worcester •
Hartford • Providence •
Waterbury • CONN. R.I.
Bridgeport • • New Haven
Stamford • • Long Island
Paterson • • Yonkers Long Island
Newark • • New York City
Allentown • Elizabeth • Jersey City
• Trenton

Cape Cod

LONG ISLAND SOUND

• Philadelphia
N.J.
• Dover
DELAWARE

Baltimore •
MD. • Annapolis
Arlington ★ • Washington,
Alexandria • D.C. ⊛

DELAWARE
BAY

ATLANTIC
OCEAN

WEST
VIRGINIA
• Charleston

VIRGINIA
• Richmond

CHESAPEAKE
BAY

Ohio River

Louisville •
Evansville •
• Frankfort ★
• Lexington

KENTUCKY

Hampton •
Roanoke • Newport News • • Norfolk
Portsmouth • • Virginia Beach
• Chesapeake

Lake Barkley

Kentucky Lake

• Fayetteville

• Memphis

ARKANSAS
• Little Rock ★

★ Nashville
• Knoxville

TENNESSEE
• Chattanooga

• Huntsville

Winston- • Greensboro
Salem Durham
• Raleigh ★
NORTH CAROLINA
• Charlotte

Cape Hatteras

Independence •
Kansas • • St.
City • Louis
• Jefferson
City

MISSOURI
• Springfield

Lake
of the
Ozarks

Illinois River

Mississippi River

Missouri River

Red River

Lake
Okeechobee

Cape Canaveral

SOUTH
CAROLINA
• Columbia ★

Savannah River

GEORGIA
• Macon
• Atlanta ★

Sea Islands

MISSISSIPPI
• Jackson ★
• Meridian

ALABAMA
• Birmingham
• Montgomery ★

• Columbus

• Savannah

Chattahoochee River

Shreveport •

LOUISIANA
• Baton Rouge ★
• Beaumont
• New Orleans

Mobile •

Chandeleur
Islands

★ Tallahassee
• Jacksonville

FLORIDA

• Orlando

Tampa •
• St. Petersburg

Cape
Canaveral

Toledo
Bend
Reservoir

GULF OF MEXICO

Fort
Lauderdale •
Hialeah • • Miami

Cape Sable

Florida Keys

THE BAHAMAS

STRAITS OF FLORIDA

CUBA

N
W ⊕ E
S

SCALE
0   250   500 Miles
├────┼────┼────┤
0   250   500 Kilometers
Projection: Albers Equal Area

⊛ National capital
★ State capitals
• Other cities

FACTS ABOUT THE STATES					
State	Year of Statehood	1990 Population	Reps. in Congress	Area (sq. mi.)	Population Density (sq. mi.)	Capital
Alabama	1819	4,040,587	7	51,705	79.6	Montgomery
Alaska	1959	550,043	1	591,004	1.0	Juneau
Arizona	1912	3,665,228	6	114,000	32.3	Phoenix
Arkansas	1836	2,350,725	4	53,187	45.1	Little Rock
California	1850	29,760,021	52	158,706	190.8	Sacramento
Colorado	1876	3,294,394	6	104,091	31.8	Denver
Connecticut	1788	3,287,116	6	5,018	678.4	Hartford
Delaware	1787	666,168	1	2,045	340.8	Dover
District of Columbia	—	606,900	—	69	9,882.8	—
Florida	1845	12,937,926	23	58,664	239.6	Tallahassee
Georgia	1788	6,478,216	11	58,910	111.9	Atlanta
Hawaii	1959	1,108,229	2	6,471	172.5	Honolulu
Idaho	1890	1,006,749	2	83,564	12.2	Boise
Illinois	1818	11,430,602	20	56,345	205.6	Springfield
Indiana	1816	5,544,159	10	36,185	154.6	Indianapolis
Iowa	1846	2,776,755	5	56,275	49.7	Des Moines
Kansas	1861	2,477,574	4	82,277	30.3	Topeka
Kentucky	1792	3,685,296	6	40,410	92.8	Frankfort
Louisiana	1812	4,219,973	7	47,752	96.9	Baton Rouge
Maine	1820	1,227,928	2	33,265	39.8	Augusta
Maryland	1788	4,781,468	8	10,460	489.2	Annapolis
Massachusetts	1788	6,016,425	10	8,284	767.6	Boston
Michigan	1837	9,295,297	16	58,527	163.6	Lansing
Minnesota	1858	4,375,099	8	84,402	55.0	St. Paul
Mississippi	1817	2,573,216	5	47,689	54.9	Jackson
Missouri	1821	5,117,073	9	69,697	74.3	Jefferson City
Montana	1889	799,065	1	147,046	5.5	Helena
Nebraska	1867	1,578,385	3	77,355	20.5	Lincoln
Nevada	1864	1,201,833	2	110,561	10.9	Carson City
New Hampshire	1788	1,109,252	2	9,279	123.7	Concord
New Jersey	1787	7,730,188	13	7,787	1,042.0	Trenton
New Mexico	1912	1,515,069	3	121,593	12.5	Santa Fe
New York	1788	17,990,455	31	49,108	381.0	Albany
North Carolina	1789	6,628,637	12	52,669	136.1	Raleigh
North Dakota	1889	638,800	1	70,702	9.3	Bismarck
Ohio	1803	10,847,115	19	41,330	264.9	Columbus
Oklahoma	1907	3,145,585	6	69,956	45.8	Oklahoma City
Oregon	1859	2,842,321	5	97,073	29.6	Salem
Pennsylvania	1787	11,881,643	21	45,308	265.1	Harrisburg
Rhode Island	1790	1,003,464	2	1,212	960.3	Providence
South Carolina	1788	3,486,703	6	31,113	115.8	Columbia
South Dakota	1889	696,004	1	77,116	9.2	Pierre
Tennessee	1796	4,877,185	9	42,144	118.3	Nashville
Texas	1845	16,986,510	30	266,807	64.9	Austin
Utah	1896	1,722,850	3	84,899	21.0	Salt Lake City
Vermont	1791	562,758	1	9,614	60.8	Montpelier
Virginia	1788	6,187,358	11	40,767	156.3	Richmond
Washington	1889	4,866,692	9	68,139	73.1	Olympia
West Virginia	1863	1,793,477	3	24,232	74.5	Charleston
Wisconsin	1848	4,891,769	9	56,153	90.1	Madison
Wyoming	1890	453,588	1	97,809	4.7	Cheyenne

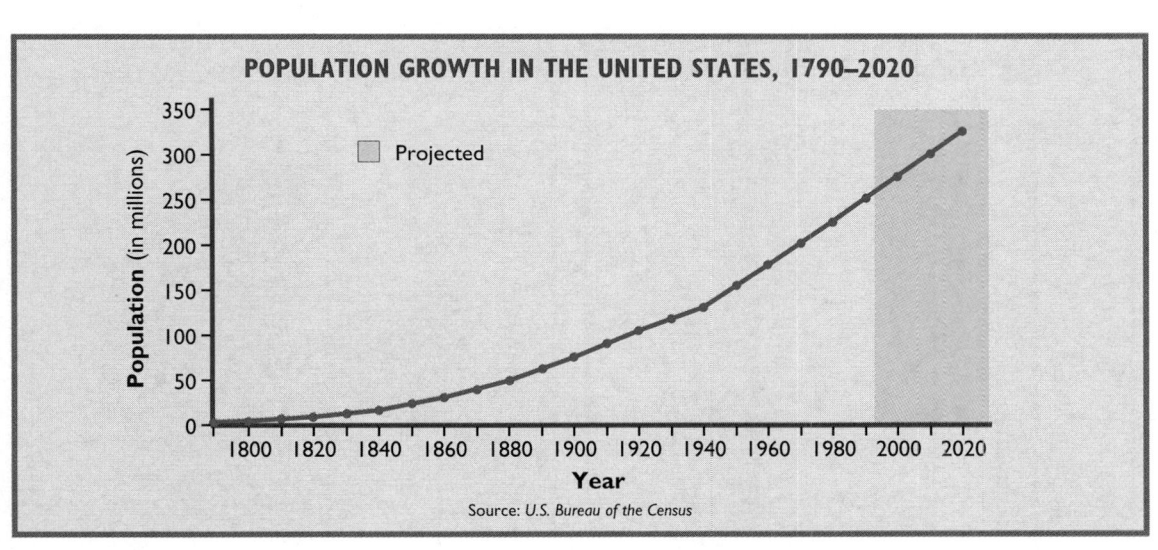

POPULATION GROWTH IN THE UNITED STATES, 1790–2020

Population (in millions) / Year

Projected

Source: U.S. Bureau of the Census

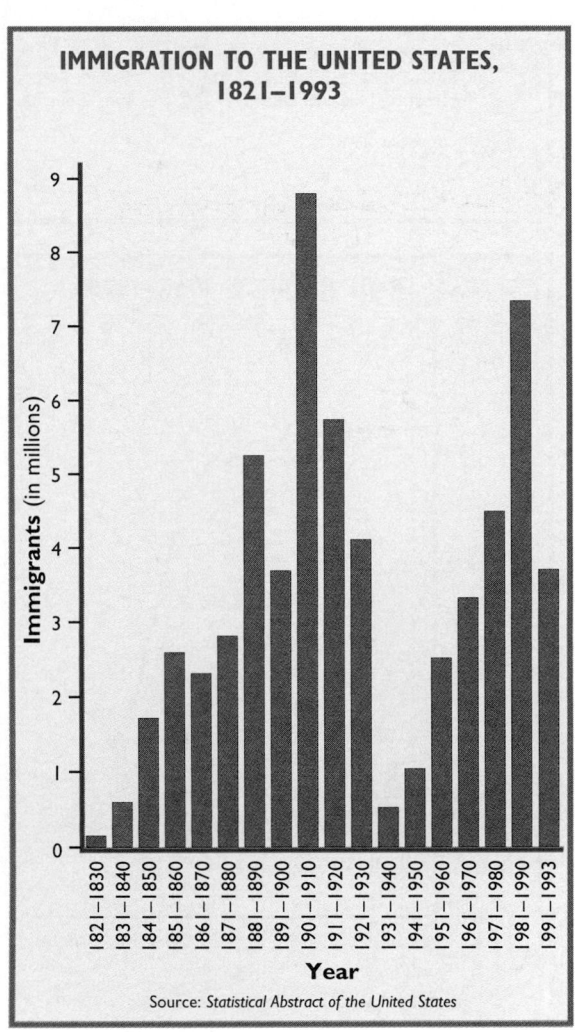

IMMIGRATION TO THE UNITED STATES, 1821–1993

Immigrants (in millions) / Year

Source: Statistical Abstract of the United States

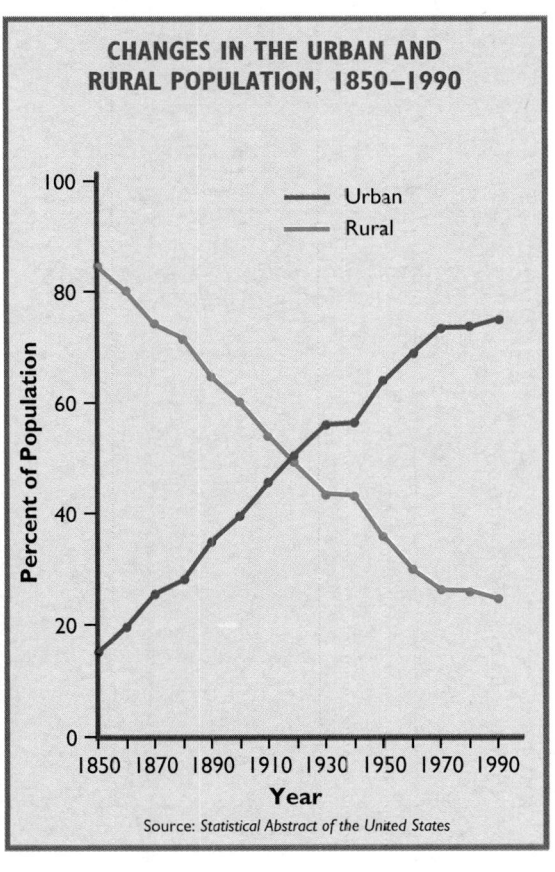

CHANGES IN THE URBAN AND RURAL POPULATION, 1850–1990

Percent of Population / Year

Urban
Rural

Source: Statistical Abstract of the United States

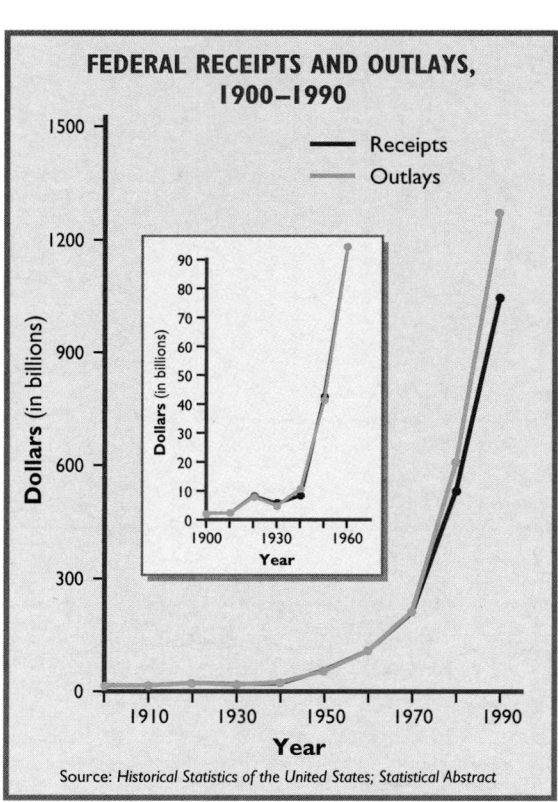

FEDERAL RECEIPTS AND OUTLAYS, 1900–1990

— Receipts
— Outlays

Dollars (in billions)

Year

Source: *Historical Statistics of the United States; Statistical Abstract*

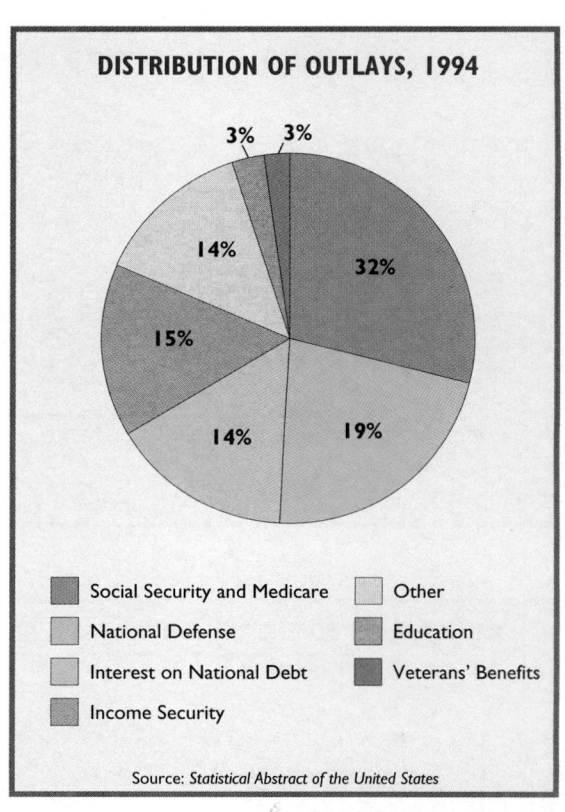

DISTRIBUTION OF OUTLAYS, 1994

3% 3%
14%
32%
15%
14% 19%

Social Security and Medicare
National Defense
Interest on National Debt
Income Security
Other
Education
Veterans' Benefits

Source: *Statistical Abstract of the United States*

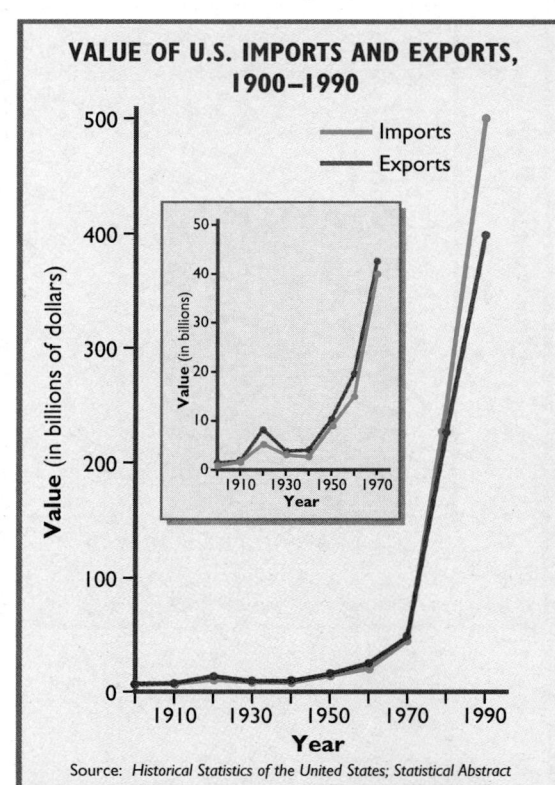

VALUE OF U.S. IMPORTS AND EXPORTS, 1900–1990

— Imports
— Exports

Value (in billions of dollars)

Year

Source: *Historical Statistics of the United States; Statistical Abstract*

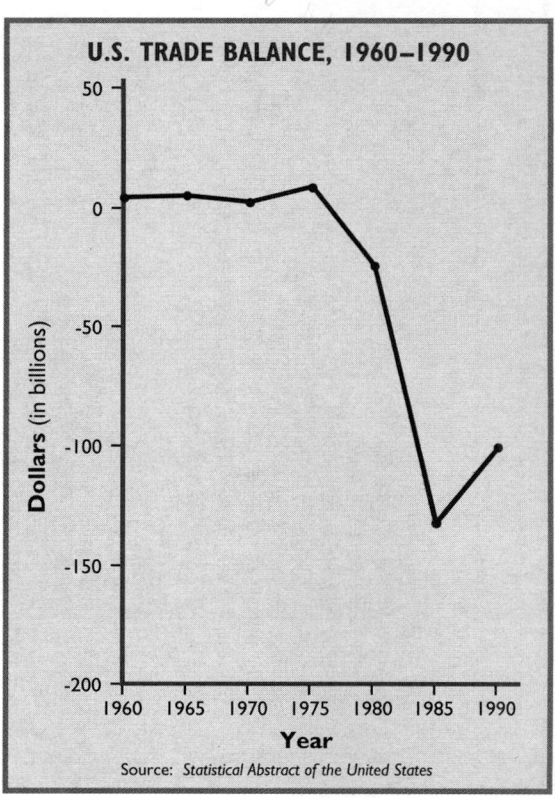

U.S. TRADE BALANCE, 1960–1990

Dollars (in billions)

Year

Source: *Statistical Abstract of the United States*

PRESIDENTS OF THE UNITED STATES

No.	Name	Born–Died	Years In Office	Political Party	Home State	Vice President
1	George Washington	1732–1799	1789–97	None	VA	John Adams
2	John Adams	1735–1826	1797–1801	Federalist	MA	Thomas Jefferson
3	Thomas Jefferson	1743–1826	1801–09	Republican*	VA	Aaron Burr
						George Clinton
4	James Madison	1751–1836	1809–17	Republican	VA	George Clinton
						Elbridge Gerry
5	James Monroe	1758–1831	1817–25	Republican	VA	Daniel D. Tompkins
6	John Quincy Adams	1767–1848	1825–29	Republican	MA	John C. Calhoun
7	Andrew Jackson	1767–1845	1829–37	Democratic	TN	John C. Calhoun
						Martin Van Buren
8	Martin Van Buren	1782–1862	1837–41	Democratic	NY	Richard M. Johnson
9	William Henry Harrison	1773–1841	1841	Whig	OH	John Tyler
10	John Tyler	1790–1862	1841–45	Whig	VA	
11	James K. Polk	1795–1849	1845–49	Democratic	TN	George M. Dallas
12	Zachary Taylor	1784–1850	1849–50	Whig	LA	Millard Fillmore
13	Millard Fillmore	1800–1874	1850–53	Whig	NY	
14	Franklin Pierce	1804–1869	1853–57	Democratic	NH	William R. King
15	James Buchanan	1791–1868	1857–61	Democratic	PA	John C. Breckenridge
16	Abraham Lincoln	1809–1865	1861–65	Republican	IL	Hannibal Hamlin
						Andrew Johnson
17	Andrew Johnson	1808–1875	1865–69	Republican	TN	
18	Ulysses S. Grant	1822–1885	1869–77	Republican	IL	Schuyler Colfax
						Henry Wilson
19	Rutherford B. Hayes	1822–1893	1877–81	Republican	OH	William A. Wheeler
20	James A. Garfield	1831–1881	1881	Republican	OH	Chester A. Arthur
21	Chester A. Arthur	1830–1886	1881–85	Republican	NY	
22	Grover Cleveland	1837–1908	1885–89	Democratic	NY	Thomas A. Hendricks
23	Benjamin Harrison	1833–1901	1889–93	Republican	IN	Levi P. Morton
24	Grover Cleveland		1893–97	Democratic	NY	Adlai E. Stevenson
25	William McKinley	1843–1901	1897–1901	Republican	OH	Garrett A. Hobart
						Theodore Roosevelt
26	Theodore Roosevelt	1858–1919	1901–09	Republican	NY	
						Charles W. Fairbanks
27	William Howard Taft	1857–1930	1909–13	Republican	OH	James S. Sherman
28	Woodrow Wilson	1856–1924	1913–21	Democratic	NJ	Thomas R. Marshall
29	Warren G. Harding	1865–1923	1921–23	Republican	OH	Calvin Coolidge
30	Calvin Coolidge	1872–1933	1923–29	Republican	MA	
						Charles G. Dawes
31	Herbert Hoover	1874–1964	1929–33	Republican	CA	Charles Curtis
32	Franklin D. Roosevelt	1882–1945	1933–45	Democratic	NY	John Nance Garner
						Henry Wallace
						Harry S. Truman
33	Harry S. Truman	1884–1972	1945–53	Democratic	MO	
						Alben W. Barkley
34	Dwight D. Eisenhower	1890–1969	1953–61	Republican	KS	Richard M. Nixon
35	John F. Kennedy	1917–1963	1961–63	Democratic	MA	Lyndon B. Johnson
36	Lyndon B. Johnson	1908–1973	1963–69	Democratic	TX	
						Hubert H. Humphrey
37	Richard M. Nixon	1913–1994	1969–74	Republican	CA	Spiro T. Agnew
						Gerald R. Ford
38	Gerald R. Ford	1913–	1974–77	Republican	MI	Nelson A. Rockefeller
39	Jimmy Carter	1924–	1977–81	Democratic	GA	Walter F. Mondale
40	Ronald Reagan	1911–	1981–89	Republican	CA	George Bush
41	George Bush	1924–	1989–1993	Republican	TX	J. Danforth Quayle
42	Bill Clinton	1946–	1993–	Democratic	AR	Albert Gore, Jr.

*The Republican party of the third through sixth presidents is not the party of Abraham Lincoln, which was founded in 1854.

LEADING SUPREME COURT CASES

1. MARBURY V. MADISON

5 U.S. (1 Cranch) 137 (1803)

WHAT WAS THIS CASE ABOUT?

The story. In early 1801 the Federalist party had been defeated in the presidential and congressional elections. However, the winners of the election were not due to take office until March 4. In the meantime the Federalists chose a number of supporters as justices of the peace in the District of Columbia. These people were nominated by the outgoing president and confirmed by the Senate at the last minute—on March 3. But no one could take office until his commission had been delivered. The next day when the new president, Thomas Jefferson, took over, he found that the previous secretary of state, John Marshall, had not had time to deliver all of the commissions. Jefferson immediately ordered his new secretary of state, James Madison, not to deliver the rest.

William Marbury, one of the people whose commission was not delivered, sued Madison. Marbury took advantage of a law passed by Congress that allowed him to make this kind of complaint directly to the Supreme Court. He asked the Court to order Madison to deliver the commission even though this request meant disobeying the president. Marbury probably expected the Court to do as he asked because John Marshall had been appointed chief justice of the Supreme Court.

The question. As Chief Justice Marshall saw it, the question before the Court had three parts. First, did Marbury have a right to receive the commission? Second, if he did have a right to the commission, was the government now required to make amends? Finally, if the government was required to make amends, would it have to order Madison to deliver Marbury's commission, as Marbury requested?

The issues. Chief Justice Marshall wanted the Court to be able to decide if laws passed by Congress were constitutional. Whether or not the Court had this power of judicial review had not yet been decided. Marshall posed the question before the Court in the way he did in order to discuss judicial review.

HOW WAS THE CASE DECIDED?

Two years later, the Court ruled against ordering Madison to deliver Marbury's commission.

WHAT DID THE COURT SAY ABOUT GOVERNMENTAL POWERS?

The Court's reasoning went through three steps:

Step 1. Pointing to a law passed by Congress, which told how District of Columbia justices of the peace should be appointed, the Court said that Marbury had a right to the commission.

Step 2. The Court said that when government officials hurt people by neglecting legal duties, our laws require that a remedy be found for the injury.

Step 3. Marbury had asked that the Supreme Court order Madison to deliver the commission. Here Chief Justice Marshall did something surprising. He said a court could issue such an order, but this was not the right court to issue it.

Marbury had taken advantage of a law passed by Congress that allowed complaints such as his to be taken straight to the Supreme Court. However, Chief Justice Marshall said that this law was unconstitutional. The Constitution mentions several kinds of cases that can be brought straight to the Supreme Court. All other kinds of cases must go through lower courts first. Marbury's lawsuit, said the chief justice, was one of the kinds of cases that must go through lower courts first. It did not matter that Congress had passed a law saying something different, because the Constitution is a higher law.

Marshall's cleverly written opinion gave up the power, granted by Congress, of hearing lawsuits such as Marbury's before lower courts had heard them. But the way that Marshall gave up this power was to claim for the Court an even greater power—the power of judicial review, or the power to decide if laws made by Congress are allowed by the Constitution.

WHAT IMPLICATIONS DID THIS CASE HAVE FOR THE FUTURE?

Without judicial review, Congress would decide for itself on the constitutionality of the laws it passed. By writing the opinion in *Marbury* v. *Madison,* Marshall changed all that forever. By deciding on the constitutionality of the other two branches' actions, the Supreme Court is the nation's final authority on the meaning of the Constitution.

2. MARTIN V. HUNTER'S LESSEE

14 U.S. (I Wheat) 304 (1816)

WHAT WAS THIS CASE ABOUT?

The story. In 1777, during the Revolutionary War, Virginia had passed a law saying that the land of people who were still loyal to England no longer belonged to them. One person affected by this law was Lord Fairfax. When he died in England in 1781, his Virginia lands passed to his American relative, Thomas Martin. But Virginia gave Fairfax's land to David Hunter.

Thomas Martin considered himself the true owner of the land. Hunter disagreed and rented it to someone else. Naturally, the renter (called the "lessee") tried to have Martin evicted. Virginia's highest court ruled that Hunter owned the land.

Martin appealed his case to the United States Supreme Court. He reminded the Court of the treaties between America and England, which promised to protect the rights of British subjects who had owned property in America before the Revolution. Because of these treaties, he said, Virginia's 1777 law was not valid. The Supreme Court agreed. It sent the case back to the Virginia court with orders to change its decision.

But the Virginia court denied that the Supreme Court had the authority to tell a state court what to do. So, Martin asked the Supreme Court to reverse the Virginia court's judgment.

The question. In cases that involve the federal Constitution, laws, and treaties, does the Constitution give federal courts the power to reverse state court judgments?

The issues. *Marbury* v. *Madison* gave the Supreme Court the power of judicial review, but it did not settle the issue of how far the power of judicial review extends. In *Marbury* v. *Madison,* one of the other branches of the federal govern-

ment had been overruled, but in this case, Martin asked the Supreme Court to overrule one of the branches of a state government.

HOW WAS THE CASE DECIDED?

In 1816, in an opinion written by Justice Joseph Story, the Supreme Court did what Martin asked. It reversed the judgment of the Virginia court.

WHAT DID THE COURT SAY ABOUT GOVERNMENTAL POWERS?

Justice Story thought that the Constitution gave the Supreme Court the power to reverse state courts in cases involving the federal Constitution, laws, and treaties. To explain his decision, he first tried to show why various objections to his view were mistaken. One objection was that the Constitution does not affect the state governments, but only the people in them. Justice Story pointed out that the Constitution is "crowded" with provisions that affect the state governments. Another objection was that if federal judges had the power of final decision about the meaning of the federal Constitution, laws, and treaties, they might abuse it. Justice Story explained that the power of final decision has to be put somewhere.

Finally, Justice Story asserted the need for uniformity. If federal judges were not allowed to reverse state court judgments, then state courts in each of the different states might interpret the federal Constitution, laws, and treaties in different ways.

WHAT IMPLICATION DID THIS CASE HAVE FOR THE FUTURE?

Under the Constitution, power is divided into two levels, state and national. Our history is full of various kinds of conflicts between the states and the national government. Usually, as in *Martin* v. *Hunter's Lessee,* the national government has won these conflicts. Thus, there has been a slow drift of power from the states to the national government. Justice Story, however, did not claim that federal courts could overrule state courts in all cases. He said only that they could overrule state courts in cases involving the United States Constitution, laws, and treaties.

3. MCCULLOCH V. MARYLAND

17 U.S. (4 Wheat) 304 (1819)

WHAT WAS THIS CASE ABOUT?

The story. In 1791 Congress passed a law that set up a Bank of the United States. An attempt to renew the bank's charter in 1811 failed. A number of states took advantage of this situation to charter their own banks.

After the War of 1812, the federal government needed money to pay for the war. But instead of being able to borrow money from one central bank, it had to deal with many state banks. Thus, Congress set up a Second Bank of the United States in 1816. The states opposed the new national bank, and several states passed laws that hindered it. For instance, they heavily taxed branches of the national bank within their borders. When the Maryland branch of the national bank refused to pay the taxes, Maryland sued the bank's cashier, James McCulloch. A year later, the legal battle reached the Supreme Court.

The question. As Chief Justice John Marshall saw it, the question before the Court had two parts. Does the Constitution give Congress the power to establish a national bank? If so, does the Constitution allow Maryland to tax that bank?

The issues. The question of whether or not Congress had the power to establish a bank was not new. In 1791, after Congress had passed the bill setting up the First Bank of the United States, President Washington had asked his cabinet for advice. He saw that Article 1, Section 8, of the Constitution, which lists the powers of Congress, does not mention the power to charter a bank. On the other hand, it states that besides the listed powers, Congress may also make all laws that are "necessary and proper" for carrying out the listed powers.

Thomas Jefferson and Alexander Hamilton presented Washington with sharply opposing views. Hamilton considered the power to charter a bank constitutional because it had "a natural relation" to the powers of collecting taxes and regulating trade. By contrast, Jefferson said that while the power to charter a bank may be "convenient" for carrying out this power, it was not "necessary," and thus was unconstitutional. Finding Hamilton's argument more convincing, Washington signed the bill. Now, Maryland wanted the Supreme Court to interpret the Constitution in the way that Washington had rejected.

HOW WAS THE CASE DECIDED?

Led by Chief Justice Marshall, the Court ruled that the Constitution allowed Congress to establish a national bank but that it did not allow Maryland to tax the bank.

WHAT DID THE COURT SAY ABOUT GOVERNMENTAL POWERS?

Jefferson's argument against the First Bank of the United States had rested on a narrow interpretation of the word "necessary" in the "necessary and proper" clause. The state of Maryland used the same argument. Marshall, however, said that Maryland's interpretation of the Constitution was not broad enough. In ordinary speech, he explained, when it is said that certain means are "necessary" to an end, it usually does not mean that the end cannot be achieved without them. Rather it means that they are "calculated to produce" the end. The power to charter a bank is calculated to help carry out the other constitutional powers, so the Constitution permits it.

The second question before the Court was whether or not the Constitution allows Maryland to tax the national bank. Marshall said that if the states could tax one of the federal government's activities, they could tax any of them. But "the power to tax," said Marshall, "involves the power to destroy." This could not be permitted because the "supremacy clause" in Article VI states that the Constitution and laws of the federal government come before state constitutions and laws.

WHAT IMPLICATIONS DID THIS CASE HAVE FOR THE FUTURE?

As new cases arise, members of the Supreme Court try to settle them by using principles that have been developed in earlier cases. What principles does this case involve?

The principle of implied powers. Some powers given the federal government by the Constitution are listed. These are called enumerated powers. Others, called implied powers, are understood as given because they are needed to help carry out the enumerated powers.

The principle of national supremacy. The federal government has only those powers that are enumerated and implied in the Constitution. But when the federal government is using powers that do belong to it, the states must give way.

4. DRED SCOTT V. SANDFORD

60 U.S. (19 How.) 393 (1857)

WHAT WAS THIS CASE ABOUT?

The story. In 1833 Dred Scott was purchased by an army doctor named John Emerson. As the army transferred Emerson from post to post, Scott went with him. First they went to Illinois; later they moved to the Wisconsin Territory. When Emerson was transferred yet again, he sent Scott to Missouri, a slave state, to live with his wife, Irene Sanford Emerson. She inherited Scott when her husband died in 1843.

At this time, slavery was illegal in Illinois and in Wisconsin Territory. Scott believed that because he had lived for five years on free soil, he should be free.

In 1846 Emerson moved to New York and left Scott with sons of Scott's original owner. One son, a lawyer, opposed the extension of slavery. He helped Scott file a lawsuit asking the Missouri courts to declare Scott free.

In 1852 the Supreme Court of Missouri ruled against Scott. In 1854, however, Scott's original lawsuit was revived by lawyers who wanted to see the issue of slavery in the territories resolved. Scott's case got on the docket of the Federal Circuit Court of Missouri and worked its way to the Supreme Court.

The question. Roger B. Taney, the chief justice, saw the case as asking two questions. First, does the Constitution give an African American the right to start a suit in a federal court? Second, does the Constitution allow Congress to make a law that takes slaves away from people who bring them into a free territory?

The issues. If African Americans are U.S. citizens, then they must have all of the rights of other citizens. Therefore, the first question before the court involved the Constitution's definition of a citizen.

If slaves are property, then Congress faces the same limits when it makes a law about slavery as when it makes a law about property. Therefore, the second question before the Court involved what kinds of limits the Constitution puts on laws about property.

HOW WAS THE CASE DECIDED?

The Court ruled that the Constitution denied blacks the right to sue in federal court and denied Congress the power to make a law freeing slaves brought into a free territory.

WHAT DID THE COURT SAY ABOUT CONSTITUTIONAL RIGHTS?

One theme of the Court's opinion was the relation between race and citizenship, and the opinion reflected the prejudices of the day. Taney said that African Americans had "none of the rights and privileges" of citizens. This statement was especially startling because it applied to free blacks as well as to slaves. Taney ignored the important fact that many states considered free blacks state citizens, and Article III Section 2 of the Constitution gives the federal courts jurisdiction over various kinds of suits involving state citizens.

The other theme of Taney's opinion concerned slavery. The 5th Amendment states that no one may be "deprived of life, liberty, or property, without due process of law." First, the chief justice reasoned that because slaves are "property," slaves cannot be taken away without "due process of law." Second, he reasoned that a law taking away citizens' property just because they have entered a free territory cheats them of their "due process of law." Taney concluded that the Missouri Compromise was unconstitutional.

WHAT IMPLICATIONS DID THIS CASE HAVE FOR THE FUTURE?

By the time the Court made its decision, the Kansas-Nebraska Act had already canceled the Missouri Compromise's ban on slavery in certain federal territories. Therefore, it might seem that the Court's judgment that the Missouri Compromise was unconstitutional did not matter. But the Kansas-Nebraska Act was unpopular with people who opposed the extension of slavery. Many of them would have liked to have seen a return to something like the Missouri Compromise. The Court's decision, however, made such a return impossible and heated up the controversy over slavery in the territories.

Furthermore, because of this case, merely freeing the slaves was not enough to guarantee their citizenship. Not until 1868, when the 14th Amendment was passed, did the Constitution guarantee African Americans citizenship.

---

5. LOCHNER V. NEW YORK

198 U.S. 45 (1905)

WHAT WAS THIS CASE ABOUT?

The story. In 1897 the New York legislature passed a law that regulated the number of hours that employees in a bakery could be required, or allowed, to work. Why was such a law needed? The legislature thought that workers could be made to agree to work long hours because they were afraid of losing their jobs. Even if they wanted to work such long hours, the legislature thought that they should not be allowed to do so. Bakery work is very hard and very hot, and working long hours would hurt the workers' health.

Lochner, a bakery owners convicted of violating the law, appealed. He said that the law was unconstitutional because it took away his liberty to make a contract. Lochner said that liberty of contract is promised by a clause in the 14th Amendment that says that no state may "deprive any person of life, liberty, or property, without due process of law."

The question. Is it a violation of the 14th Amendment for a state to limit the number of hours that employees may work?

The Issues. State governments have a general power—called the police power— to make regulations that support the safety, health, morals, and general welfare of their citizens. The basic issue in this case is how the Constitution might limit state governments' police power.

Various amendments set limits on the states,

but the most general is the "due process" clause of the 14th Amendment. To apply this clause to the New York bakery law, the Supreme Court had to decide: Which freedoms are meant by the word *liberty?* What is promised by the guarantee of "due process of law"?

HOW WAS THE CASE DECIDED?

In an opinion written by Justice Rufus Wheeler Peckham, the Court ruled that the law limiting the hours of labor in bakeries was unconstitutional.

WHAT DID THE COURT SAY ABOUT GOVERNMENTAL POWERS?

Peckham argued that the New York legislature's interference with liberty of contract was improper. Peckham did not mean that the Constitution forbids all interference with liberty of contract. In fact, he stressed that the Court had approved a similar Utah law that said that no one could work more than eight hours a day in an underground mine "except in cases of emergency, where life or property is in imminent danger." Such uses of the police power, he said, were "fair, reasonable, and appropriate." They regulate liberty without taking it away. By contrast, he argued, New York's interference with liberty of contract was "unreasonable" and had nothing to do with safety, morals, or general welfare, and was not necessary to protect health.

WHAT IMPLICATIONS DID THIS CASE HAVE FOR THE FUTURE?

Even though the Court tries to use the same principles over and over, sometimes its members change their minds about controversial issues. Four justices disagreed with the *Lochner* ruling. The most interesting dissenting opinion was written by Justice Oliver Wendell Holmes. "This case," he said, "is decided upon an economic theory [laissez-faire] which a large part of the country does not entertain." According to this theory a person has "liberty to do what he likes so long as he does not interfere with the liberty of others to do the same." He went on to say that he thought that the decision was for the citizens and their legislators; his duty as a judge was to see if the theory was in the Constitution.

Over the years the membership of the Supreme Court changed. In the 1940s the Court began to reverse all of the precedents it had set in cases like *Lochner.* By the 1960s this process was complete. As Justice Huge Black said in a 1963 case, *Ferguson* v. *Skrupa,*

> The doctrine that prevailed in Lochner . . . that due process authorizes courts to hold laws unconstitutional when they believe the legislature has acted unwisely—has long since been discarded. We have returned to the original constitutional proposition that courts do not substitute their social and economic beliefs for the judgment of legislative bodies.

6. PLESSY V. FERGUSON AND BROWN V. BOARD OF EDUCATION

163 U.S. 537 (1896) and 347 U.S. 483 (1954)

WHAT WERE THESE CASES ABOUT?

The stories. These two cases illustrate a profound change in the legality of racial segregation. *Plessy* v. *Ferguson* begins with a law that required all railway companies in Louisiana to provide "separate but equal" accommodations for European American and African American passengers. A group of people who thought the law was unfair recruited Homer Plessy to get arrested in order to test the law. Plessy entered a train and took an empty seat in an all-white coach. When he refused to move to an all-black coach, he was arrested and jailed. In his defense he said that the 1890 law was unconstitutional. The case eventually worked its way up to the Supreme Court.

More than 50 years later an African American named Oliver Brown and his family moved into a white neighborhood in Topeka, Kansas. The Browns assumed that their daughter would attend the neighborhood school. Instead, the school board ordered her to attend a distant all-black school that was supposedly "separate but equal." Saying that school segregation violated the 14th Amendment to the Constitution, Mr. Brown sued the school board.

The question. The question raised by the Court was the same in both cases. Do racially segregated facilities violate the "equal protection" clause of the 14th Amendment?

The issues. The 14th Amendment is one of several amendments that were passed soon after the Civil War to guarantee the freedom of African Americans and to protect them from unfair treatment. The wording of the equal protection clause is: "No State shall . . . deny to any person within its jurisdiction the equal protection of the laws." But just what does this wording forbid? Louisiana in *Plessy* argued that separate railway carriages could be equal. For instance, they could be equally clean and equally safe. In *Brown,* Kansas said much the same thing, claiming that their all-black and all-white schools were equal in the skill of their teachers, the quality of their buildings, and so on.

In the days of racial segregation the claim that segregated facilities were equal in tangible, or measurable, features was almost always a terrible lie. But the issue facing the Court went deeper. Even if things were made equal in racially segregated facilities, was there something inherently unequal about segregation?

HOW THE CASE WAS DECIDED?

In *Plessy* v. *Ferguson,* the Court ruled that the 14th Amendment's equal protection clause allows racial segregation. In *Brown* v. *Board of Education,* the Court unanimously ruled that the clause does not allow racial segregation.

WHAT DID THE COURT SAY ABOUT CONSTITUTIONAL RIGHTS?

Justice Henry Billings Brown wrote the Court's opinion in *Plessy.* He admitted that the purpose of the 14th Amendment was "to enforce the absolute equality of the two races before the law." But he said that this statement meant political equality, not social equality. In his view, neither African Americans nor European Americans wanted the races to mingle. Brown said that the argument that separate facilities implied that blacks were inferior was false.

In *Brown* the Court's opinion was written by Chief Justice Earl Warren. Separation of African American schoolchildren from European American schoolchildren of the same age and ability, he said, "generates a feeling of inferiority as to their status in the community that may affect their hearts and minds in a way unlikely ever to be undone:' He said that when racial segregation is required by law, the harm is even greater. It makes no difference that "the physical facilities and other 'tangible' factors may be equal."

WHAT IMPLICATIONS DID THESE CASES HAVE FOR THE FUTURE?

In *Brown* v. *Board of Education* the Court did not say that the "separate but equal" doctrine had no place anywhere. It said that the doctrine had no place in public education. This statement, although limited, influenced future cases.

Taken together, *Plessy* and *Brown* show the flexibility of the Constitution's legal principles whose interpretations may change as society changes. The decision in *Plessy* was not unanimous. In a dissenting opinion, Justice John Marshall Harlan declared "Our Constitution is color-blind, and neither knows nor tolerates classes among its citizens." Eventually Harlan's dissent became the law of the land.

7. GIDEON V. WAINWRIGHT

372 U.S. 436 (1963)

WHAT WAS THIS CASE ABOUT?

The story. Clarence Earl Gideon was accused of breaking and entering a Florida poolroom and stealing. When Gideon's case came to trial he could not afford a lawyer, and he asked that the court pay for one. The judge refused, and Gideon was found guilty. While in prison, Gideon asked the U.S. Supreme Court to review his case. He claimed that by refusing to appoint a lawyer to help him, Florida had violated rights promised him by the 6th and 14th Amendments.

The question. Is it a violation of the 6th or 14th Amendment to deny a poor person accused of a major crime the free assistance of a lawyer?

The Issues. The 6th Amendment promises certain rights to people accused of crimes. One promise is that "the accused shall enjoy the right . . . to have the Assistance of Counsel [a lawyer] for his defense." By itself this amendment requires that poor people be provided with free lawyers in fed-

eral trials. Gideon, however. was accused of breaking state laws and was tried in a state court. But the 14th Amendment promises that states will not deprive people of life, liberty, or property without due process of law. Jailed, Gideon had been deprived of liberty. Had this liberty been taken away without due process of law?

HOW WAS THE CASE DECIDED?

In a unanimous opinion written by Justice Hugo Black, the Court ruled in Gideon's favor.

WHAT DID THE COURT SAY ABOUT CONSTITUTIONAL RIGHTS?

Members of the Court based their decision that the Constitution requires the appointment of lawyers for the poor on two different view of the 14th Amendment. One is the incorporation view, which holds that the purpose of the due process clause is to take the first eight amendments in the Bill of Rights and incorporate them into state court procedures. The second is the fundamental liberties view, which holds that "due process of law" means "whatever is necessary for justice." What is necessary for justice may not include every promise in the first eight amendments, but it may include promises that go beyond anything in the first eight amendments. In *Gideon* v. *Wainwright* the justices came to the same conclusion by different means.

Justice Black, who wrote the Court's opinion, had to tailor it to accommodate both the incorporation view and the fundamental liberties view. The opinion was a compromise. It said that the 6th Amendment's promise of the "assistance of counsel" is necessary for a fair trial in any court, but it did not say that due process covers every other promise in the first eight amendments.

WHAT IMPLICATIONS DOES THIS CASE HAVE FOR THE FUTURE?

Gideon v. *Wainwright* was one of several Supreme Court cases guaranteeing that the government would pay lawyers to help poor people accused of crimes. The Criminal Justice Act of 1964, signed into law the year after the Gideon decision, provided funding.

8. MIRANDA V. ARIZONA

384 U.S. 436 (1966)

WHAT WAS THIS CASE ABOUT?

The story. On March 13, 1963, a woman was kidnapped near Phoenix, Arizona. Ernesto Miranda was arrested for the crime, and the victim picked him out from a police lineup. Two officers then took him to a room to question him. Although at first Miranda denied the crime, after a short time he gave a detailed oral confession. He then made and signed a written confession.

At the trial the officers testified that they had warned Miranda that anything he might say could be used against him in court and that Miranda had understood. The officers also said that he had confessed without any threats or force. They admitted, however, that they had not told Miranda about his right to silence or legal assistance. Miranda was found guilty. Eventually, he appealed to the U.S. Supreme Court.

The question. Is it a violation of the 5th, 6th, or 14th Amendment to use a confession from someone who has not been informed of the constitutional rights to silence and legal assistance?

The issues. The 6th Amendment promises the assistance of a lawyer to defendants in criminal trials in federal courts and the 14th Amendment applies this promise to the states. Another promise about the way trials are conducted is given in the 5th Amendment: "No person . . . shall be compelled [forced] in any criminal case to be a witness against himself." Thus the 5th Amendment gives a person the right to be silent. Without such a right, innocent people could be tortured until they confessed.

One issue is the point at which 5th and 6th Amendment rights begin. Do they begin only at the trial? Or do these rights begin earlier?

A deeper issue concerns the meaning of being forced to be a witness against oneself. Perhaps keeping a person ignorant of his or her rights is a kind of force. If so, then it violates the 5th Amendment.

HOW WAS THE CASE DECIDED?

By only a five to four majority, the Supreme Court ruled that taking Miranda's confession without informing him of his rights to silence and legal assistance had deprived him of these rights.

WHAT DID THE COURT SAY ABOUT CONSTITUTIONAL RIGHTS?

With regard to the first issue, the Court ruled that an accused person's 5th and 6th Amendment rights begin as soon as the person is arrested. With regard to the second issue, the Court said that failing to inform the accused of his or her rights is a violation of these rights.

Today, if prisoners are not informed of their rights, then judges will rule that what the accused tells the police may not be used as evidence in court, nor can any evidence police find that was based on what the accused said. The arrest may still be valid; it is only the accused person's statements that cannot be used.

WHAT IMPLICATIONS DOES THIS CASE HAVE FOR THE FUTURE?

Miranda v. *Arizona* has been one of the Supreme Court's most controversial cases because it deals with the delicate balance between protecting the accused and protecting society. Even the Court split five to four. Among the general public the most hotly debated aspect of the decision has been the rule that confessions given by accused people who have not been informed of their rights may not be used as evidence. The Court made this rule to prevent innocent people from being found guilty. Some people accept this reasoning. Others think that the rule prevents guilty people from being convicted.

9. UNITED STATES V. NIXON

418 U.S. 683 (1974)

The story. During the investigation of the Watergate burglary the president's lawyer, John Dean, testified before the Senate that the president had helped plan the cover-up from the beginning. Nixon denied it, but then another witness revealed that Nixon had secretly tape-recorded every conversation that had ever taken place in his office. The tapes would show whether or not Nixon was telling the truth.

By 1974 criminal charges had been filed

against seven members of the Nixon administration. Although Nixon was not charged, he was listed as one of the people involved in the conspiracy. The special prosecutor in charge of the case at the time, Leon Jaworski, asked Nixon to let him hear the tapes. Nixon had already ordered a previous special prosecutor fired for asking the same thing, and to no one's surprise, Nixon refused again. However, Jaworski persisted. He asked the federal district court for help. When the judge ordered Nixon to release the tapes to the court for secret examination, Nixon disobeyed.

Refusing the special prosecutor's request caused a sandal, but disobeying the judge's order caused a constitutional crisis—a tug of war between two branches of government. Could a president defy a federal judge?

Nixon claimed that he could. As president, he said, he had an executive privilege of keeping presidential communications confidential. He also said that the privilege was absolute, which meant that nobody could override it for any reason. Because of the urgency of the case, the U.S. Supreme Court agreed to skip over the Court of Appeals in order to settle the case immediately.

The question. Does the Constitution give the president an absolute executive privilege?

The issues. President Nixon gave two arguments for his position. His first argument was that the principle of separation of powers requires that the executive and judicial branches be totally independent of each other. If presidents had to obey judges who ordered them to release evidence, this independence would be destroyed.

His second argument was that the secrecy of communications between a president and his advisers is necessary for the president to be able to look after the public good. Nixon said that is a president's advisers knew that anything they said could be repeated to the public, they might not give him good advice for fear what people would think. Nixon said that if a president didn't receive good advice, it would be harder to carry out the duties of the office as spelled out in the Constitution.

HOW WAS THE CASE DECIDED?

In a decision written by Chief Justice Warren Burger, the Court ruled that executive privilege is not absolute and that Nixon had to turn over the tapes as he had been ordered.

WHAT DID THE COURT SAY ABOUT GOVERNMENTAL POWERS?

The Court examined each of the president's two arguments in turn. One was that preservation of the separation of powers requires the executive and judicial branches to be totally independent. Total independence means that the president does not have to obey court orders to release evidence. The chief justice rejected this claim. The Constitution is based on separation of powers, but under this separation it gives each power or branch a job of its own to do. If the president could withhold evidence from the courts, the courts could not do the job given them by the Constitution. "The powers," concluded the chief justice, "were not intended to operate with absolute independence."

Nixon's second argument was that communications between the president and his advisers need to be confidential for the sake of the public good. Burger admitted that sometimes confidentiality, or secretiveness, is important. But it only applies in specific instances. When communications are about diplomatic or military secrets, confidentiality is of the utmost importance. On the other hand, when communications concern other subjects, confidentiality might not be important at all. Burger concluded that in presidential claims of executive privilege, the need for confidentiality must be balanced against competing needs on a case-by-case basis.

In *United States* v. *Nixon* the need for confidentiality competed with the need to find out the truth in a criminal trial. The purpose of criminal justice, said Burger, "is that guilt shall not escape or innocence suffer." But finding out the truth in a criminal trial requires that courts have all the evidence, even if it includes presidential communications. In this case the courts needed the information on the tapes to carry out their duty. When the need to find out the truth in the Watergate trial was weighed against President Nixon's need for confidentiality, confidentiality lost. Confidentiality might have won had the tapes been about diplomatic or military secrets or had they not contained crucial evidence. Moreover, the district court had not even planned to make the complete tapes public. It had planned to examine them in secret and only the parts that were necessary for the trial would be used in open court.

WHAT IMPLICATIONS DOES THIS CASE HAVE FOR THE FUTURE?

If the president had defied the Supreme Court as he had defied the district court, it would have been an important sign for the future. One reason is that the courts have no enforcement powers of their own. They depend on the executive branch to enforce court orders. If the executive branch defies a court order, the courts have no recourse. Another reason is that successful defiance of the Supreme Court would call the entire idea of judicial review into question. The judicial branch has been established as the final judge of the meaning of the Constitution, and defiance by the president would be like saying the executive branch is its own final judge.

Nixon did not defy the Supreme Court. He obeyed, not out of respect for judicial review, but out of self interest. He feared that unless he gave in, the Senate would remove him from office. Even so, the evidence of the tapes turned out to be so damaging (the tapes showed that he had been part of the cover-up) that Nixon felt that he had to resign or the House would start impeachment proceedings.

What principles emerge from this case? The Court did not say whether or not such a thing as executive privilege exists. However, it clearly stated that there is no such thing as an absolute executive privilege. The Court put forth the following principles:

The president's need for confidentiality must be weighed against competing needs, such as the needs of the criminal justice system.

In disputed cases this weighing may be done by the federal courts.

Conflicts over executive privilege will probably continue to arise. For example, presidents have claimed executive privilege over 50 times just since 1952. In most of these cases they claimed the privilege in order to avoid giving Congress information that it had requested. However, so long as the two principles listed above are accepted by all parties—particularly that the final decision is made by the judicial branch—theses conflicts have much less chance of hurting the nation.

10. ROE V. WADE

410 U.S. 113 (1973)

WHAT WAS THIS CASE ABOUT?

The story. In 1970 Norma McCorvey, an unmarried pregnant woman living in Texas, sought to obtain a legal abortion in a medical facility. Because of Texas' antiabortion statutes, no licensed physician would agree to perform the abortion. Financially unable to travel to another state with less-restrictive abortion laws, McCorvey faced either continuing an unwanted pregnancy or having the procedure performed in a nonmedical facility, which, she believed, would endanger her life.

McCorvey claimed that the Texas antiabortion laws were unconstitutional in that they interfered with her right of personal privacy that is protected by the 9th and 14th Amendments. She took legal action, naming the Dallas County district attorney, Henry Wade, in her lawsuit. Throughout the case, McCorvey used the pseudonym Jane Roe.

The question. Is it a violation of a person's right to privacy for a state to prevent a woman from terminating a pregnancy through an abortion?

The issues. The 14th Amendment says that "No state shall make or enforce any law which shall abridge the privileges . . . of citizens of the United States . . . nor deny to any person . . . the equal protection of the laws." The 9th Amendment states that "The enumeration in the Constitution of certain rights shall not be construed to deny or disparage others retained by the people." Do these amendments encompass and protect a woman's right to a legal abortion?

HOW WAS THE CASE DECIDED?

In an opinion written by Justice Harry Blackmun, the Court ruled that the 14th Amendment's due process guarantee of personal liberty guarantees the right to personal privacy. This guarantee protects a woman's decision about abortion and assures that a state's laws do not abridge, or diminish, this right. The vote was seven to two.

WHAT DID THE COURT SAY ABOUT CONSTITUTIONAL RIGHTS?

In ruling that a state cannot prevent a woman from terminating a pregnancy during the first three months, the Court relied on citizens' right of privacy. Justice Blackmun stated in his opinion that "This right of privacy, whether it be founded in the Fourteenth Amendment's concept of personal liberty and restrictions upon state action, as we feel it is, or . . . in the 9th Amendment's reservation of rights to the people, is broad enough to encompass a woman's decision whether or not to terminate her pregnancy." In its ruling, however, the Court recognized the right of a state to regulate abortions as a pregnancy progressed. During the first three months of a pregnancy, a woman has an unrestricted right to an abortion, although a state can prevent abortions by nonphysicians.

During the second trimester, a state can regulate abortions to protect a woman's health. Only in the final three months of a pregnancy can a state forbid an abortion, unless it is necessary to protect a woman's health.

The ruling also said that a state cannot adopt a theory of when life begins. This prevents a state from giving a fetus the same rights as a newborn.

In 1965 the Court said in *Griswold* v. *Connecticut* that restrictions on the availability of contraceptives violated the constitutional right to privacy. This right—the basis for the Court's ruling in *Roe* v. *Wade*—thus became a pivotal issue in cases that challenged abortion laws.

WHAT IMPLICATIONS DOES THIS CASE HAVE FOR THE FUTURE?

In the decades following the ruling, related cases have been decided that some people claim weaken the legislative impact of *Roe* v. *Wade.* In *Harris* v. *McRae* (1980), the Court ruled that the federal and local governments did not have to pay for abortions for women on welfare, even if the abortions were necessary for medical reasons. Critics of this ruling claimed that women who could not afford the procedure would, like Jane Roe, be faced with either continuing an unwanted pregnancy or resorting to dangerous measures to terminate it. The ruling in *Webster* v. *Reproductive Health Services* (1989), added more restrictions on the availability of abortions.

11. REGENTS OF THE UNIVERSITY OF CALIFORNIA V. BAKKE

438 U.S. 265 (1978)

WHAT WAS THIS CASE ABOUT?

The story. Allan Bakke twice applied to the medical school at the University of California, Davis during the years the medical school operated two different admissions programs. Since the Civil Rights Act of 1964, there had been pressure for schools and other institutions to provide special admissions programs for minority students. There were, however, no specific guidelines on how to accomplish this.

At the University of California, Davis medical school, 84 of the 100 places in the incoming class were filled from the regular program, while 16 were set aside for the special program, which used a quota system. The regular program was for students of all races, so long as they met admission requirements, including a minimum grade point average. Only members of racial minorities could apply through the special program, and their grades did not have to meet the minimum.

Bakke, a white male, applied through the regular program and was turned down. He thought he had been unfairly treated because in both years, students had been admitted through the special program whose grades and test scores were much lower than his. He sued the state university system. Bakke said the special program, established to fulfill the racial quota, violated his 14th Amendment right to equal protection of the law.

The California Supreme Court made two rulings. One said that Davis's admission system was illegal and ordered Bakke admitted. The other ordered that in the future, admissions decisions must not take race into consideration. The California university system appealed to the U.S. Supreme Court.

The questions. First, does the use of a racial quota in admissions violate the equal protection clause of the 14th Amendment? Second, does the equal protection clause require that race be completely ignored? The U.S. Supreme Court had to consider these questions separately, because there might be ways of taking race into account that do not involve quotas.

The issues. Historically, most racial discrimination in our country has hurt members of racial minorities. Bakke complained about a different kind of discrimination. Sometimes called reverse discrimination, it hurt members of the racial majority in order to help members of racial minorities. If the Constitution is "color-blind," then both forms of racial discrimination are unconstitutional.

The 14th Amendment was primarily written because African Americans who had recently been freed from slavery needed protection from discrimination by the white majority. This fact suggests that the equal protection clause protects racial minorities more than the racial majority. On the other hand, what the amendment actually says is that no state may deny to any person the equal protection of the laws. This fact suggests that the equal protection clause gives the same protection to people of all races. The intent seems to have been to protect minorities, but the wording does not specify this intent.

HOW WAS THE CASE DECIDED?

The Court agreed that the use of a racial quota in admissions was unconstitutional and ordered that Bakke should be admitted. But the Court rejected the idea that an admissions system may never pay any attention to race.

WHAT DID THE COURT SAY ABOUT CONSTITUTIONAL RIGHTS?

Justice Lewis Powell wrote the Court's opinion. He said that the equal protection clause does not completely prohibit states from taking race into account when they are making laws and official policies but that it does make the consideration of race "suspect," or suspicious. When such a law or policy is challenged in court, judges must apply a two-part test. First, are the purposes of the law or policy legitimate? Second, is the consideration given to race necessary to achieve these purposes? California told the Court that its racial quota had four purposes.

Purpose 1. To correct the shortage of racial minorities in medical schools and among doctors. Justice Powell said that this purpose was not acceptable. "Preferring members of any one group for no reason other than race or ethnic origin is discrimination for its own sake."

Purpose 2. To counteract the effects of racial discrimination in society. Justice Powell said that this was an acceptable purpose. He approved of helping people who belong to groups that have been hurt by past discrimination. However, he said that helping them by hurting others is right only when it makes up for hurts that those specific others have done to them. There was no evidence that Bakke had ever discriminated against people of racial minorities.

Purpose 3: To increase the number of doctors who will be willing to practice medicine in communities where there are not enough doctors. This purpose was also acceptable. However, California had not shown that racial quotas were needed to accomplish this purpose.

Purpose 4. To improve education by making the student body more diverse. This purpose, too, was acceptable. But Justice Powell pointed out that racial diversity is only one aspect of overall diversity and that racial quotas are not the only way to increase racial diversity.

WHAT IMPLICATIONS DOES THIS CASE HAVE FOR THE FUTURE?

This decision showed how sharply the members of the Court disagreed about reverse discrimination. Furthermore, Powell stressed that the Court's decision concerned only reverse racial discrimination. He warned that reverse sexual discrimination may or may not have to be treated the same way. Although in a 1982 case *Mississippi University for Women* v. *Hogan,* for example, the Court ruled that it was unconstitutional for a state-run school of nursing to refuse admission to men.

---

12. TEXAS V. JOHNSON

491 U.S. 397 (1989)

WHAT WAS THIS CASE ABOUT?

The story. Heated political protests and demonstrations, reminiscent of the widespread antiwar protests of the 1960s and 70s, ensued during the 1984 Republican National Convention held in Dallas, Texas. Many of the protesters were voicing their opposition to the policies of the administration of President Ronald Reagan. Outside Dallas City Hall, where some of the demonstrators had gathered, Gregory Lee Johnson set a U.S. flag on fire as a means of political protest.

Johnson was arrested and charged with the desecration of a venerated object, a Texas law that made it a crime to desecrate a state or national flag. Johnson was convicted and sentenced to one year in prison and fined $2,000. The Texas Court of Criminal Appeals, however, reversed the conviction, maintaining that Johnson's burning of the flag was a form of symbolic speech and, therefore, protected by the First Amendment. The state of Texas then appealed to the U.S. Supreme Court. Oral arguments were presented in March 1989. The Court announced its decision on June 21.

The question. Does the First Amendment protect the desecration of the U.S. flag as a form of symbolic speech?

The issues. The First Amendment states, in part, that "Congress shall make no law . . . abridging the freedom of speech." But what actions can be included under the term speech? According to the Texas Court of Criminal Appeals, which overturned Johnson's conviction, burning a flag falls under this protected term. The Texas Court stated, "Given the context of an organized demonstration, speeches, slogans, and the distribution of literature, anyone who observed . . . would have understood the message. . . . The act for which [Johnson] was convicted was clearly 'speech' contemplated by the First Amendment. . . ." Texas, however, argued that its interest was in preserving the flag as a symbol of national unity and in preventing breaches of the peace. It was now up to the Supreme Court to decide the validity of Johnson's conviction.

HOW WAS THE CASE DECIDED?

In an opinion written by Justice William Brennan, the Supreme Court ruled that Johnson's conviction was inconsistent with the First Amendment. In other words, Johnson was within his constitutional rights when he burned the U.S. flag in protest. The Court's vote was five to four.

WHAT DID THE COURT SAY ABOUT CONSTITUTIONAL RIGHTS?

In *Texas* v. *Johnson*, Justice Brennan concluded that Johnson's act was "expressive conduct" in that he was attempting to "convey a . . . message."

Thus, burning the flag as a form of symbolic speech is protected by the First Amendment. According to Brennan, "Government may not prohibit the expression of an idea simply because society finds the idea itself offensive."

Citing Texas' interest in preventing breaches of the peace and preserving the flag as a symbol of national unity, Justice Brennan stated that Johnson's expression posed no threat to the peace and that the burning of the flag did not endanger the flag's status as a national symbol. As a result, Texas' statute prohibiting the desecration of a venerated object was declared unconstitutional.

WHAT IMPLICATIONS DOES THIS CASE HAVE FOR THE FUTURE?

Critics of the Court's ruling in *Texas* v. *Johnson* argued that the Court had interpreted the term speech too broadly. Since *Texas* v. *Johnson*, the Supreme Court has had other opportunities to reiterate its position that symbolic speech, or "nonverbal expression," is indeed protected by the First Amendment. In direct response to the Court's controversial ruling in *Texas*, the U.S. Congress passed the Flag Protection Act of 1989. The Supreme Court ruled this act unconstitutional in *The United States* v. *Eichman* (496 U.S. 310) in June 1990.

---

13. BOARD OF EDUCATION OF KIRYAS JOEL VILLAGE SCHOOL DISTRICT V. GRUMET

114 U.S. 2481 (1994)

WHAT WAS THIS CASE ABOUT?

The story. New York's Village of Kiryas Joel is home to more than 10,000 members of the Satmar Hasidic religious sect, a strict form of Judaism. The Satmars shun most modern conveniences and wear distinctive clothing. The Satmars employ strict interpretations of the Torah, speak Yiddish, and have special dietary restrictions.

Once an undeveloped subdivision of Monroe, New York, Kiryas Joel was incorporated as a self-governing village in 1977. When it seceded from Monroe, Kiryas Joel's boundaries were drawn to include only Satmar families. The village's children attended private religious schools. Because these schools could not adequately accommodate Kiryas Joel's more than 100 children with disabilities, in 1989 the state created a public-school district specifically for these children. Citing the First Amendment, Louis Grumet, then president of the New York Association of School Boards, challenged the legality of a state-funded district created to serve the children of a religious group. The State of New York ruled against the Kiryas Joel School District. The Supreme Court heard the case in March 1994.

The question. Did the legislature act constitutionally when it established a state-funded school district for the children with disabilities of the Village of Kiryas Joel, a religious enclave?

The issues. This was not the first time that the fate of Kiryas Joel's children with disabilities was in the hands of the Supreme Court. The Monroe-Woodbury Central School District's attempt to provide special services to these children was discontinued after the Court's ruling in *Aguilar* v. *Felton* (1985) declared that public-school teachers could not be sent into private religious schools. After Aguilar, some Satmar families tried sending their children to Monroe's nearby public schools, but the children were "traumatized" by ridicule from non-Satmar children. When the families then claimed that their children were legally entitled to special programs currently unavailable, the state created a special school district for the Village of Kiryas Joel.

The key issues in *Kiryas Joel* v. *Grumet* were the children's entitlement to receive needed special programs, the First Amendment's establishment clause, which calls for the separation of church and state, and the role of the state in accommodating religion to "alleviate special burdens."

HOW WAS THE CASE DECIDED?

In an opinion written by Justice David Souter, the Supreme Court ruled that creating a special school district for a religious enclave incorporated as a village to exclude all but its practitioners violated the establishment clause of the First Amendment.

WHAT DID THE COURT SAY ABOUT CONSTITUTIONAL RIGHTS?

Justice Souter wrote that "The Constitution allows the state to accommodate religious needs by alleviating special burdens. . . ." This, however, "is not a principle without limits . . . Neutrality among religions must be honored." Justice Souter's argument against Kiryas Joel centered on the establishment clause of the First Amendment, which ensures that a state act with neutrality toward religion. In other words, a state cannot favor "one religion over another" or "religion to irreligion." There was no way of knowing whether another group in a similar situation would be granted the same privilege as Kiryas Joel. In addition, according to the Court, the Village of Kiryas Joel had other alternatives to pursue to alleviate its "burden." For example, the Monroe-Woodbury Central School District could legally offer an appropriate program at a "neutral" site to serve the children with disabilities.

Justice Kennedy noted a "fine line between the voluntary association that leads to a political community comprised of people who share a common religious faith, and the forced separation that occurs when the government draws explicit political boundaries on the basis of peoples' faith."

WHAT IMPLICATIONS DOES THIS CASE HAVE FOR THE FUTURE?

While the government cannot "endorse" or "advance" religion, it must also protect the rights of all, regardless of religion. Some people believe that the Supreme Court contradicts itself in its efforts to abide by these tenets. In his dissent, Justice Antonin Scalia echoed that criticism: "The Founding Fathers would be astonished to find that the Establishment Clause—which they designed 'to insure that no one powerful sect . . . could use political or governmental power to punish dissenters'—has been employed to prohibit . . . American accommodation of the religious practices . . . of a tiny minority sect. . . . Once this Court has abandoned text and history as guides, nothing prevents it from calling religious toleration the establishment of religion." The case of Kiryas Joel made it clear that a religious group cannot be granted its own government-funded school district. What will continue to be debated is whether the government's obligation to protect the rights of all is counter to the Court's ruling.

GAZETTEER

A

Abilene   Town in east-central Kansas. Railhead town during the cattle boom of the late 19th century. (39°N 97°W) *m445*

Afghanistan   Country of southwest-central Asia. Invaded by the Soviet Union in 1979. Capital: Kabul. (33°N 63°E) *m905, m1012–13*

Alabama (AL)   State in the southern U.S. Admitted as a state in 1819. Capital: Montgomery. (33°N 87°W) *m1016–17*

Alaska (AK)   U.S. state in northwest North America. Became a territory in 1912 (first organized in 1884) and a state in 1959. Capital: Juneau. (64°N 150°W) *m1016–17*

Albania   Country in southeast Europe on the Adriatic Sea. Invaded by Italy in 1939. Capital: Tiranë. (41°N 20°E) *m736, m959, m1012–13*

Albany   City in southwestern Georgia. Scene of civil rights protests in the 1960s. (31°N 84°W) *m845*

Alsace-Lorraine   Region between France, Germany, Belgium, and Switzerland. Part of the German Empire, 1871–1918; returned to France by the Treaty of Versailles, 1919. (48°N 7°E) *m588*

American River   River in north-central California whose gold-bearing waters started the gold rush of 1849. (38°N 120°W) *m325*

American Samoa   Unincorporated territory of the U.S. in the southern Pacific Ocean. Administered by the U.S. since 1899. (14°S 170°W) *m564*

Annamite Mountains   Range of mountains that runs north-south through Vietnam. (17°N 105°E) *m865*

Anzio   Town in central Italy. In World War II Allied troops landed at Anzio in January 1944. (41°N 12°E) *m748*

Appomattox Courthouse   Virginia town where General Lee surrendered to General Grant, ending the Civil War. *m387*

Arizona (AZ)   State in southwestern U.S. Became a territory in 1863 and a state in 1912. Capital: Phoenix. (34°N 113°W) *m1016–17*

Arkansas (AR)   State in south-central U.S. Admitted as a state in 1836. Capital: Little Rock. (35°N 93°W) *m1016–17*

Armenia   Republic; member of the Commonwealth of Independent States. Formerly part of the USSR. Independent in 1991. Capital: Yerevan. (41°N 44°E) *m959, m1012–13*

Atlanta   Major southern city, capital of Georgia. During the Civil War it was captured and burned by General Sherman, 1864. (33°N 84°W) *m387*

Austria-Hungary   Former monarchy in central Europe. Consisted of Austria, Hungary, Bohemia, and parts of Poland, Romania, Yugoslavia, and Italy. Formed in 1867; lasted until 1918. (47°N 12°E) *m588*

Azerbaijan   Republic; member of the Commonwealth of Independent States. Formerly part of the USSR. Independent in 1991. Capital: Baki. (40°N 47°E) *m959, m1012–13*

B

Baghdad   Capital of Iraq. Scene of U.S. bombings during the Persian Gulf War. (33°N 44°E) *m940*

Bahamas   Country in the Atlantic Ocean consisting of hundreds of islands. Gained independence from Great Britain in 1973. Capital: Nassau. (26°N 76°W) *m41, m1012–13*

Balkans   Countries that occupy the Balkan Peninsula, including Albania, Bulgaria, Greece, Romania, the former Yugoslavia, and northwestern Turkey. (43°N 24°E) *m588*

Baltimore   Maryland city northeast of Washington, D.C., on upper Chesapeake Bay. (39°N 76°W) *m75*

Bangladesh   Country in southern Asia. Formerly part of Bengal, it became part of Pakistan in 1947. In 1971 it became a separate nation. Capital: Dacca. (24°N 90°E) *m1012–13*

Barbary states   North African states of Algiers, Tunis, Tripoli, and Morocco. Some warred with the U.S. in the early 1800s. *m212*

Bataan   Peninsula of western Luzon, Philippines. In World War II U.S. and Philippine troops surrendered to the Japanese, April 1942. U.S. forces recaptured the peninsula in February 1945. *m746*

Bay of Pigs   Bay on southwest coast of Cuba. Site of the failed 1961 invasion by Cuban exiles trained by the CIA. (22°N 81°W) *m837*

Beijing   Capital of China. (40°N 116°E) *m25, m564*

Belarus   Republic in Eastern Europe; member of the Commonwealth of Independent States. Formerly part of the USSR. Independent in 1991. Capital: Minsk. (53°N 25°E) *m959, m1012–13*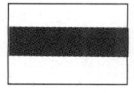

Belgium   Country in northwest Europe. Invaded by Germany in 1914 and 1940. Scene of the Battle of the Bulge. Capital: Brussels. (51°N 3°E) *m588, m1012–13*

Beringia   Land bridge formed during the last Ice Age between Siberia and what is today Alaska. (65°N 170°W) *m4*

Berlin   Capital and largest city of Germany. Divided into East Berlin and West Berlin in 1945. Reunited in 1989. (52°N 13°E) *m736, m780, m793*

Birmingham   City in north-central Alabama. Scene of several civil rights protests. (33°N 86°W) *m845*

Black Sea   Inland sea between Europe and Asia. (43°N 32°E) *m29*

Bosnia and Herzegovina   Country annexed to Austria-Hungary in 1908 and Yugoslavia in 1918. Capital: Sarajevo. (44°N 17°E) *m588, m959, m1012–13*

Boston   Massachusetts capital on Massachusetts Bay founded in the 17th century. Leading center of anti-British sentiment in the 18th century and antislavery thought in the 19th century. (42°N 71°W) *m129*

Brazil Republic in eastern South America. Largest country on the continent; ruled by Portugal from 1500 to 1822. Empire until 1889. Capital: Brasília. (9°S 53°W) *m971, m1012–13*

Buffalo City in western New York at the eastern end of Lake Erie on the Canadian border. End point of the Erie Canal. (43°N 79°W) *m233*

Cahokia Settlement founded by the Mississippian culture near present-day St. Louis, Missouri. (38°N 90°W) *m15*

California (CA) State in western U.S. Admitted as a free state in 1850. Capital: Sacramento. (38°N 121°W) *m1016–17*

Cambodia Republic in southeast Asia. Independent in 1954. Scene of fighting during Vietnam War. Capital: Pnompenh. (12°N 104°E) *m865, m1012–13*

Canada Country in northern North America. Settled by English and French colonists. Ceded to Great Britain in 1763. Declared equal partner of Great Britain, 1931. Capital: Ottawa. (50°N 100°W) *m214, m1012–13*

Cape of Good Hope Cape on southern tip of Africa. First rounded by Bartolomeu Dias in 1488. (34°S 18°E) *m29*

Cape Verde Islands Group of islands in Atlantic Ocean that were settled by the Portuguese in the mid–15th century; became a colony in 1495. Gained independence in 1975. Capital: Praia. (15°N 26°W) *m29, m1012–13*

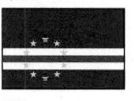

Caporetto Town in Slovenia. Scene of World War I defeat of Italian troops in December 1917. *m588*

Casablanca City in northwest Morocco. Founded by the Portuguese in the 16th century. Scene of World War II Allied conference. (33°N 7°W) *m748*

Chancellorsville Town in northeastern Virginia where a major Civil War battle was fought in May 1863. Union forces were defeated by Confederate troops. *m377*

Chapultepec Fort in Mexico City, Mexico; scene of U.S. victory during the Mexican War. (19°N 99°W) *m313*

Château-Thierry Town in northern France where Allied forces stopped German advance in World War I. (49°N 3°E) *m599*

Chernobyl City in north-central Ukraine where a nuclear power plant exploded in 1986. (51°N 30°E) *m971*

Chesapeake Bay Inlet of Atlantic Ocean in Virginia and Maryland. (38°N 76°W) *m75*

Cheyenne Wyoming state capital since 1869. Railhead town during the cattle boom of the 19th century. (41°N 104°W) *m445*

Chicago City in northeastern Illinois on Lake Michigan. Major port and third largest U.S. city. (41°N 87°W) *m233, m495*

Chile Country in southwest South America colonized by Spain in 1541; became independent in 1818. Capital: Santiago. (35°S 72°W) *m582, m1012–13*

China (Official name: People's Republic of China) Country in eastern Asia. After a bitter civil war (1946–49), became a Communist republic; nationalists fled to Taiwan. Capital: Beijing. (36°N 93°E) *m564, m865, m1012–13*

Cincinnati City in southwestern Ohio. (39°N 84°W) *m253*

Colombia Country in northwest South America. Capital: Bogotá. (3°N 72°W) *m578, m1012–13*

Colorado (CO) State in southwestern U.S. Became a territory in 1861 and a state in 1876. Capital: Denver. (39°N 107°W) *m1016–17*

Columbus Capital of Ohio. (40°N 83°W) *m1016–17*

Compiègne City in northern France. Armistice ending World War I signed nearby on November 11, 1918. (49°N 2°E) *m599*

Concord Town in northeastern Massachusetts in which (along with Lexington) the first fighting of the Revolutionary War was fought. (42°N 71°W) *m114*

Connecticut (CT) State in northeastern U.S., one of the original Thirteen Colonies. Admitted as a state in 1788. Capital: Hartford. (41°N 73°W) *m1016–17*

Coral Sea Part of the southwest Pacific Ocean. Scene of Allied naval victory during World War II. (13°S 150°E) *m746*

Cuba Island country in the Caribbean about 90 miles south of Florida. Capital: Havana. (22°N 79°W) *m837, m1012–13*

Cuzco Former capital of Inca Empire in Peru. (13°S 72°W) *m15*

Czechoslovakia Country in central Europe formed in 1918. Communist forces gained control of it in 1948 and kept power until 1989. In 1993 peacefully divided into Czech Republic (Capital: Prague) and Slovakia (Capital: Bratislava). (49°N 16°E) *m608, m736, m959, m1012–13*

Dardanelles Strait dividing Europe and southwest Asia. (40°N 26°E) *m793*

Deadwood City in western South Dakota. Founded after gold was discovered in Deadwood Gulch in 1876. (44°N 103°W) *m450*

Delaware (DE) State in eastern U.S., one of the original Thirteen Colonies. In 1787 became first state to ratify the Constitution. Capital: Dover. (38°N 75°W) *m1016–17*

Dien Bien Phu Town in northwestern Vietnam where French troops were defeated by Vietminh troops in 1954, leading to the end of French involvement in Indochina. (21°N 102°E) *m865*

District of Columbia (DC) Federal district of the U.S., seat of federal government since 1800. (39°N 77°W) *m1016–17*

Dodge City Kansas cattle town during the cattle boom of the 19th century. (37°N 100°W) *m445*

Dominican Republic Island country in the Caribbean. Makes up eastern part of island of Hispaniola. Capital: Santo Domingo. (19°N 70°W) *m578, m1012–13*

Dresden City in east-central Germany. Bombed during World War II. (51°N 13°E) *m748*

Dust Bowl Drought-ridden region in the 1930s that included parts of Texas, Oklahoma, Colorado, New Mexico, and Kansas. *m711*

East Berlin *See* Berlin.

Egypt Country in northeast Africa on the Mediterranean Sea. Capital: Cairo. (27°N 27°E) *m797, m905, m1012–13*

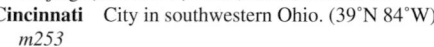

El Alamein   Town in northern Egypt on the Mediterranean Sea. Scene of World War II defeat of German Afrika Korps. *m748*

Elbe River   River in central Europe. (52°N 11°E) *m748*

El Salvador   Country in Central America. Capital: San Salvador. (14°N 89°W) *m578, m932, m1012–13*

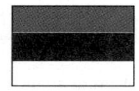

England   Region of the United Kingdom, comprising most of the southern part of the island of Great Britain. Capital: London. (51°N 1°W) *m19*

Estonia   Country in northeast Europe. Annexed to the USSR in 1940. Became independent in 1991. Capital: Tallinn. (59°N 25°E) *m608, m959, m1012–13*

Ethiopia   Country in eastern Africa; formerly Abyssinia. Capital: Addis Ababa. (7°N 38°E) *m736, m976, m1012–13*

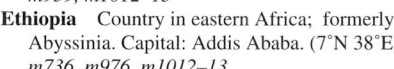

Federal Republic of Germany   *See* Germany

Finland   Country in northeast Europe. Capital: Helsinki. (62°N 26°E) *m608, m736, m1012–13*

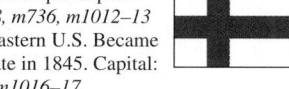

Florida (FL)   State in southeastern U.S. Became a territory in 1822 and a state in 1845. Capital: Tallahassee. (30°N 84°W) *m1016–17*

Fort Duquesne   Scene of French defeat by the British in 1758. Eventually became Pittsburgh. *m92*

Fort Sumter   Fort in Charleston, South Carolina, harbor. Attack here by Confederate forces began the Civil War. (32°N 80°W) *m366*

France   Country in western Europe. French Revolution of 1789 overthrew the monarchy. Capital: Paris. (46°N 0°) *m19, m588, m748*

Fredericksburg   City in northeastern Virginia. Scene of Civil War battle in 1862. Union forces defeated by Confederate army. (38°N 77°W) *m377*

French Indochina   Former French territory in southeast Asia, 1946–55. (17°N 105°E) *m739*

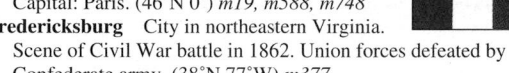

Gaza Strip   Narrow coastal strip along the Mediterranean Sea. Controlled by Egypt, 1948–67, and by Israel, 1967–present. (31°N 34°E) *m797*

Genoa   City in northwestern Italy. Major trading center since Roman times. (44°N 10°E) *m29*

Georgia (GA)   State in southeastern U.S., one of the original Thirteen Colonies. Admitted as a state in 1788. Capital: Atlanta. (32°N 84°W) *m1016–17*

Georgia   Republic; member of the Commonwealth of Independent States. Formerly part of the USSR. Independent in 1991. Capital: T'bilisi. (42°N 43°E) *m959, m1012–13*

German Democratic Republic   *See* Germany

Germany   Country in western Europe. Fascist during the 1930s and 1940s. Divided into German Democratic Republic (East Germany) and Federal Republic of Germany (West Germany) after World War II. Reunified in 1990. Capital: Berlin. (51°N 8°E) *m736, m793, m959, m1012–13*

Gettysburg   Town in southern Pennsylvania. Scene of major Union victory in the Civil War. Abraham Lincoln delivered Gettysburg Address here in 1863. (40°N 77°W) *m377*

Ghana   Republic in western Africa. Ancient African trading kingdom. Capital: Accra. (8°N 2°W) *m26, m1012–13*

Gila River   River with source in western New Mexico; flows across southern Arizona. (33°N 110°W) *m315*

Gilbert Islands   Group of islands in the central Pacific Ocean. Scene of World War II battle. Capital: Tarawa. (0°174°E) *m746*

Goliad   Town in south-central Texas. Mission and *presidio* established by the Spanish in 1749. Texas forces defeated near here by Mexican troops during the Texas Revolution. (28°N 97°W) *m308*

Great Britain   Kingdom in western Europe. Consists of England, Scotland, and Wales. Capital: London. (54°N 4°W) *m1012–13*

Greece   Balkan country in southern Europe with numerous islands. Fought civil war, 1946–49. Capital: Athens. (39°N 21°E) *m793, m1012–13*

Greensboro   City in northern North Carolina. Scene of first 1960s sit-in to protest segregation. (36°N 79°W) *m845*

Grenada   Country in the Caribbean made up of the island of Grenada and the southern Grenadines. Capital: St. George's. (12°N 61°W) *m932*

Guadalcanal   One of the Solomon Islands in the Pacific Ocean. Scene of heavy fighting during World War II. (9°S 158°E) *m746*

Guam   Pacific island that became U.S. territory after the Spanish-American War. Capital: Agana. (14°N 143°E) *m746*

Guangdong   Province in southeast China. (23°N 113°E) *m482*

Guantánamo Bay   Bay on southeastern coast of Cuba. U.S. naval station established in 1903. (19°N 75°W) *m578*

Guatemala   Republic in Central America. Capital: Guatemala City. (15°N 91°W) *m811, m1012–13*

Gulf of Tonkin   Part of the South China Sea east of northern Vietnam. (20°N 108°E) *m873*

Hainan   Island located in the South China Sea, separated from Leizhou Peninsula by a narrow strait. Part of the Chinese province of Guangdong. (19°N 109°E) *m746*

Haiphong Harbor   Harbor of a city in northeast Vietnam on the Red River delta near the Gulf of Tonkin. Mined by U.S. forces during the Vietnam War (1972). (21°N 107°E) *m873*

Haiti   Island country in the Caribbean located on the western part of the island of Hispaniola. Former U.S. protectorate. Capital: Port-au-Prince. (19°N 72°W) *m578, m932, m1012–13*

Hampton   City in southeastern Virginia opposite Norfolk on Hampton Roads, the outlet of three rivers into Chesapeake Bay. Settled by colonists from Jamestown in 1610, the city was sacked by the British in the War of 1812. (37°N 76°W) *m1016–17*

Hanoi   Capital of Vietnam. (21°N 106°E) *m865*

Harlem   Section of New York City in northern Manhattan bordering on the Harlem and East rivers. Influx of blacks beginning in 1910 made it one of America's largest African American communities. (40°N 74°W) *m661*

Hawaii (HI)   U.S. state in the central Pacific Ocean comprising the Hawaiian Islands. Admitted as a state in 1959. Capital: Honolulu. (20°N 157°W) *m564, m1016–17*

Hiroshima   Japanese city; U.S. dropped the first atomic bomb used in warfare on the city in August 1945. (34°N 132°E) *m746*

Hispaniola   Columbus and his crew established the colony of La Navidad here in 1492; today comprises the countries of the Dominican Republic and Haiti. (17°N 73°W) *m41*

Hong Kong   British crown colony located on the coast of China southeast of Guangzhou. Will become administrative region of China at end of the 20th century. Capital: Victoria. (21°N 115°E) *m746*

Iberian Peninsula   Peninsula of southwest Europe comprising Spain and Portugal. Separated from the rest of Europe by the Pyrenees and from Africa by the Strait of Gibraltar. (40°N 5°W) *m19*

Idaho (ID)   State in northwestern U.S. Admitted as a state in 1890. Capital: Boise. (44°N 115°W) *m1016–17*

Illinois (IL)   State in north-central U.S. Admitted as a state in 1818. Capital: Springfield. (40°N 90°W) *m1016–17*

Indiana (IN)   State in north-central U.S. Admitted as a state in 1816. Capital: Indianapolis. (40°N 86°W) *m1016–17*

Indian Territory   Former territory in south-central United States. In 1834 it was set aside by the government as a home-land for forcibly displaced Native Americans. Western section, which became Oklahoma Territory, was opened to white set-tlement in 1889. In 1907 Indian Territory was merged with Oklahoma Territory to form the state of Oklahoma. (36°N 98°W) *m244*

Iowa (IA)   State in north-central U.S. Admitted as a state in 1846. Capital: Des Moines. (42°N 94°W) *m1016–17*

Iran   Country in southwest Asia where 53 Americans were held hostage during the Carter administration and which fought a long war with Iraq. Capital: Tehran. (31°N 53°E) *m905, m1012–13*

Iraq   Country in southwest Asia. Iraq's invasion of Kuwait led to UN–imposed economic sanctions and to war with the U.S. and the Allies in 1991. Capital: Baghdad. (32°N 43°E) *m905, m940, m1012–13*

Ireland   Located in the British Isles, Ireland is divided between Northern Ireland (Capital: Belfast), which is part of Great Britain, and the independent Republic of Ireland (Capital: Dublin). (54°N 8°W) *m1012–13*

Israel   Country in southwest Asia on the eastern Mediterranean coast that Jews established after the UN division of Palestine in 1948. Capital: Jerusalem. (32°N 34°E) *m797, m905, m1012–13*

Italy   Country in southern Europe, which fought on the side of the Allies in World War I. During World War II it was allied with Germany. Capital: Rome. (44°N 11°E) *m1012–1013*

Iwo Jima   Small Pacific island that the Americans captured in World War II after heavy fighting with the Japanese. *m746*

Jamaica   Island country in the Caribbean, which Columbus visited in 1494. It became a British colony in 1655 and an important sugar producer. Capital: Kingston. (18°N 78°W) *m41, m1012–13*

Jamestown   First successful English colony in America. *m57*

Japan   Chain of islands in the western Pacific Ocean. World War II military ally of Germany and Italy. Two of its cities devastated by atomic bombs. Since the war, has played a central role in the global economy. Capital: Tokyo. (37°N 134°E) *m739, m746, m1012–13*

Jerusalem   Capital of Israel, located in the east-central part of the country in the West Bank. Considered a holy place by Jews, Moslems, and Christians, the city was occupied as far back as the fourth millennium B.C. (31°N 35°E) *m25, m797*

Jordan   Country of southwest Asia. Capital: Amman. (30°N 38°E) *m797, m905, m1012–13*

Jordan River   River of southwest Asia rising in Syria and flowing about 200 miles south through the Sea of Galilee to the northern end of the Dead Sea. (32°N 36°E) *m797*

Kansas (KS)   Territory in central U.S., created by Kansas-Nebraska Act in 1854, in which the issue of slavery was to be determined on the basis of popular sovereignty. Admitted to the Union as a free state in 1861. Capital: Topeka. (38°N 99°W) *m345, 1016–17*

Kazakhstan   Republic; member of the Commonwealth of Independent States. Formerly part of the USSR. Independent in 1991. Capital: Almaty. (49°N 59°E) *m959, m1012–13*

Kentucky (KY)   State in east-central U.S. Admitted as a state in 1792. Capital: Frankfort. (37°N 87°W) *m1016–17*

Kings Mountain   Site of Tory defeat in South Carolina (1780). (35°N 81°W) *m129*

Korea   Peninsula and former country of eastern Asia between the Yellow Sea and the Sea of Japan. Officially divided into two independent nations, North Korea and South Korea, in 1945. (38°N 128°W) *m564, m799*

Kuril Islands   Island chain of extreme eastern Russia extend-ing about 750 miles in the Pacific Ocean between Kamchatka Peninsula and northern Hokkaido, Japan. (46°N 149°E) *m746*

Kuwait   Oil-rich country on the northeast Arabian Peninsula at the head of the Persian Gulf. Invaded by Iraq, it was liberated by the Allies in the Persian Gulf War (1991) Capital: Al Kuwait. (29°N 48°E) *m940, m1012–13*

Kyrgyzstan   Republic; member of the Commonwealth of Independent States. Formerly part of the USSR. Independent in 1991. Capital: Bishkek. (42°N 28°E) *m959, m1012–13*

L

La Navidad First Spanish settlement established by Columbus and named in honor of Christmas Day—the day it was founded in 1492. (19°N 72°W) *m41*

Lake Erie One of the Great Lakes, linked with the Hudson River by the New York State Barge Canal. *m214*

Latin America Central and South America; settled by Spain and Portugal. *m231*

Latvia Country of northern Europe on the Baltic Sea. Capital: Riga. (57°N 24°E) *m1012–13*

Lexington One of two northeastern Massachusetts towns (along with Concord) where the first fighting of the Revolutionary War took place. (42°N 71°W) *m114*

Leyte Island of the east-central Philippines, north of Mindanao. (10°N 125°E) *m746*

Liberia Country on west coast of Africa founded in 1817 by the American Colonization Society for the resettlement of freed African Americans. Capital: Monrovia. (6°N 10°W) *m1012–13*

Line of Demarcation Line established in 1493 to divide the claims in the Americas of Spain and Portugal. *m45*

Lithuania Country of northern Europe on the Baltic Sea; declared independence from USSR in March 1990. Capital: Vilnius. (55°N 23°E) *m959, m1012–13*

Little Rock Capital of Arkansas, located in the central part of the state. Federal troops were sent there in 1957 to enforce a 1954 U.S. Supreme Court ruling against segregation in the public schools. (34°N 92°W) *m1016–17*

Los Angeles City of southern California. Center of a sprawling metropolitan area. (34°N 118°W) *m1016–17*

Louisiana (LA) One of the southeastern states carved out of the Louisiana territory. Admitted as a state in 1812. Capital: Baton Rouge. (31°N 93°W) *m1016–17*

Lowell Massachusetts city on the Merrimack River northwest of Boston. (42°N 71°W) *m253*

M

Madeira Islands Archipelago in the northeast Atlantic Ocean west of Morocco. Islands are a part of Portugal. (33°N 16°W) *m29*

Maine (ME) State in the northeastern U.S. Admitted as a state in 1820. Capital: Augusta. (45°N 70°W) *m1016–17*

Mali Country of western Africa. Capital: Bamako. (15°N 0°) *m26, m1012–13*

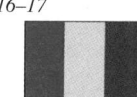

Manchuria Region of northeast China, which was invaded by Japan in 1931. (48°N 125°E) *m739*

Manila Capital and largest city of the Philippines, located on southwest Luzon Island and Manila Bay, inlet of the South China Sea. (14°N 121°E) *m564*

Mariana Islands Group of 15 islands in the western Pacific Ocean, east of the Philippines. Guam, the largest island of the group, is a U.S. territory; other islands are a self-governing commonwealth under U.S. protection. *m746*

Marshall Islands Self-governing island group in the central Pacific Ocean. Capital: Majuro. (10°N 165°E) *m746*

Maryland (MD) State in east-central U.S., one of the original Thirteen Colonies. Admitted as a state in 1788. Capital: Annapolis. (39°N 76°W) *m1016–17*

Massachusetts (MA) State in northeastern U.S., one of the original Thirteen Colonies. Admitted as a state in 1788. Capital: Boston. (42°N 72°W) *m1016–17*

Mediterranean Sea Large sea bordered by southern Europe, southwest Asia, and northern Africa. (32°N 13°E) *m1012–13*

Mekong Delta Located in northern Vietnam, the delta has formed where the Mekong River empties into the South China Sea. Fertile rice-growing region. (18°N 104°E) *m865*

Memphis Tennessee city on the Mississippi River near the Mississippi border. Founded and named (1819) by Andrew Jackson. (35°N 90°W) *m1016–17*

Meuse River River in western Europe flowing from northeast France through southern Belgium and the southeast Netherlands to the North Sea. (50°N 5°E) *m599*

Mexican Cession Area that Mexico ceded to the U.S. at the end of the Mexican War, comprising the present-day states of California, Nevada, and Utah, and parts of Arizona, Colorado, and New Mexico. *m315*

Mexico Republic in North America, bounded on the north by the U.S. and on the south by Guatemala and British Honduras. Capital: Mexico City. (23°N 104°W) *m1012–13*

Miami City in southeastern Florida located on Biscayne Bay. (25°N 80°W) *m1016–17*

Michigan (MI) State in north-central U.S. Admitted as a state 1837. Capital: Lansing. (46°N 87°W) *m1016–17*

Midway Islands Islands northwest of Hawaii occupied by the United States Navy in 1867; site of an important U.S. naval victory in World War II. (28°N 179°W) *m746*

Minnesota (MN) State in north-central U.S. Admitted as a state in 1858. Capital: St. Paul. (46°N 90°W) *m1016–17*

Mississippi (MS) State in southeastern U.S. Admitted as a state in 1817. Capital: Jackson. (32°N 89°W) *m1016–17*

Missouri (MO) State in central U.S. Admitted as a state in 1821. Capital: Jefferson City. (38°N 93°W) *m237, m1016–17*

Mogadishu Located on the Indian Ocean; capital and largest city of Somalia. *m25*

Moldova Republic; member of the Commonwealth of Independent States. Formerly part of the USSR. Independent in 1991. Capital: Chişinău. *m959, m1012–13*

Montana (MT) State in northwestern U.S. Admitted as a state in 1889. Capital: Helena. (47°N 112°W) *m1016–17*

Monterey City in western California, south of San Francisco on Monterey Bay. (36°N 122°W) *m313*

Montgomery Capital of Alabama. Capital of the Confederate States of America, February to May 1861. (32°N 86°W) *m1016–17*

Munich City in southeastern Germany founded in 1158, long the center of Bavaria. City was largely rebuilt after extensive Allied bombing in World War II. (48°N 11°E) *m736*

N

Nagasaki Japanese city; 1945 site of the second atom-bombing by the U.S., ending World War II. (32°N 130°E) *m746*

Nebraska (NE) State in central U.S. Admitted as a free state in 1867. Capital: Lincoln. (41°N 101°W) *m1016–17*

Nevada (NV)   State in western U.S. Organized as a separate territory in 1861 and admitted as a state in 1864. Capital: Carson City. (39°N 117°W) *m1016–17*

New Guinea   Island in the southwest Pacific Ocean north of Australia. Western half is part of Indonesia; eastern half forms the major portion of Papua New Guinea. (5°S 140°E) *m746*

New Hampshire (NH)   State in northeastern U.S., one of the original Thirteen Colonies. Admitted as a state in 1788. Capital: Concord. (44°N 71°W) *m1016–17*

New Jersey (NJ)   State in eastern U.S.; one of the original Thirteen Colonies. Admitted as a state in 1787. Capital: Trenton. (40°N 75°W) *m1016–17*

New Mexico (NM)   State in southwestern U.S.; originally Zuni country, ceded to the U.S. by Mexico in 1848; organized as a territory that included Arizona and part of Colorado in 1850; admitted as a state in 1912. Capital: Santa Fe. (34°N 107°W) *m1016–17*

New Orleans   City in southeastern Louisiana between the Mississippi River and Lake Pontchartrain. Founded in 1718, it became the capital of a French colony in 1722 and passed to the U.S. as part of the Louisiana Purchase of 1803. (30°N 90°W) *m209*

New York (NY)   State in northeastern U.S. One of the original Thirteen Colonies. Admitted as a state in 1788. Capital: Albany. (42°N 78°W) *m1016–17*

Nicaragua   Country of Central America on the Caribbean Sea and the Pacific Ocean. Columbus spotted its Caribbean coastline in 1502, and the first European settlements were made by Spain in 1524. Capital: Managua. (12°N 86°W) *m578, m932, m1012–13*

Nogales   City in southern Arizona, south of Tucson on the Mexican border and adjacent to Nogales, Mexico. (31°N 111°W) *m52*

Normandy   Northern French province that was the site of the D-Day invasion during World War II. (49°N 0°) *m748*

North Carolina (NC)   State in southeastern U.S. One of the original Thirteen Colonies. Admitted as a state in 1789. Capital: Raleigh. (35°N 81°W) *m1016–17*

North Dakota (ND)   State in north-central U.S. Admitted as a state in 1889. Capital: Bismarck. (47°N 102°W) *m1016–17*

North Korea   (Official name: Democratic People's Republic of Korea) Country on east coast of Asia, bounded on north by China, on east by Sea of Japan, on south by South Korea, and on west by the Yellow Sea and Korea Bay. Capital: P'yongyang. (40°N 127°E) *m799, m1012–13*

North Vietnam   *See* Vietnam

Northwest Territory   Region of the north-central U.S., extending from the Ohio and Mississippi rivers to the Great Lakes. Area was ceded to the U.S. in 1783; became a territory in 1787 and later was split up into the present-day states of Ohio, Indiana, Illinois, Michigan, Wisconsin, and part of Minnesota. Control over the territory was a major issue in the War of 1812. *m142*

Nueces River   Texas river that Mexicans claimed was the boundary between Mexico and Texas. (28°N 98°W) *m313*

Ogallala   Nebraska city on the South Platte River, 52 miles west of North Platte. (41°N 101°W) *m445*

Ohio (OH)   State in north-central U.S. Originally part of the Northwest Territory; admitted as a state in 1803. Capital: Columbus. (40°N 83°W) *m1016–17*

Okinawa   Japanese island captured by U.S. forces in World War II after heavy losses on both sides. (26°N 128°E) *m746*

Oklahoma (OK)   State in south-central U.S. Except for its panhandle, Oklahoma formed part of the Louisiana Purchase; was organized as a territory in 1890 and became a state in 1907. Capital: Oklahoma City. (36°N 98°W) *m1016–17*

Oregon (OR)   State in northwestern U.S. Admitted as a state in 1859. Capital: Salem. (43°N 122°W) *m1016–17*

Oregon Country   Region encompassing all the land from the California border to Alaska and from the Pacific Ocean to the Rocky Mountains; held jointly by Great Britain and the U.S., 1818–46, when the international boundary was fixed at the 49th parallel. *m229*

Oswego   City in north-central New York at the mouth of the Oswego River on Lake Ontario northwest of Syracuse. (43°N 76°W) *m92*

Palestine   Often called the Holy Land, historical region in Southwest Asia between the eastern Mediterranean and the Jordan River, now divided between Israel and Jordan. (31°N 35°E) *m797*

Panama   Country in southern Central America occupying the Isthmus of Panama. Capital: Panama City. (8°N 81°W) *m578, m1012–13*

Panama Canal   Ship canal, about 51 miles long, crossing the Isthmus of Panama in the Canal Zone and connecting the Caribbean Sea with the Pacific Ocean. Opened to traffic on August 15, 1914. *m571*

Pearl Harbor   Port in the Hawaiian Islands where the American Pacific fleet was destroyed by a Japanese surprise attack in 1941. (21°N 158°W) *m746*

Pennsylvania (PA)   State in eastern U.S., one of the original Thirteen Colonies. Admitted as a state in 1787. Capital: Harrisburg. (41°N 78°W) *m1016–17*

People's Republic of China   *See* China

Persian Gulf   Arm of the Arabian Sea between the Arabian Peninsula and southwestern Iran in southwest Asia. (27°N 50°E) *m940*

Peru   Republic in western South America, bounded on north by Ecuador and Colombia, on east by Brazil and Bolivia, on southern tip by Chile, and on west by the Pacific Ocean. Capital: Lima. (10°S 75°W) *m976, m1012–13*

Philippines, Republic of the   Archipelago of about 7,100 islands, lying approximately 500 miles off the southeast coast of Asia. Capital: Manila. (14°N 125°E) *m561, m1012–13*

Pikes Peak   Mountain, 14,110 feet high, in Rocky Mountains in central Colorado. (38°N 105°W) *m450*

Pittsburgh   City in Pennsylvania, located at the point where the joining of the Allegheny and Monongahela rivers forms the Ohio River. Fort Duquesne was built on the site by the French c. 1750 and fell to the British in 1758, when it was renamed Fort Pitt. (40°N 80°W) *m233*

Plymouth   Site in Massachusetts where the Pilgrims first landed in North America in 1620. (42°N 70°W) *m69*

Poland   Country of central Europe bordering on the Baltic Sea. Capital: Warsaw. (52°N 17°E) *m608, m736, m959, m1012–13*

Portugal   Country of southwest Europe on the western Iberian Peninsula. It includes the Madeira Islands and the Azores in the Atlantic Ocean. Capital: Lisbon. (38°N 9°W) *m19, m1012–13*

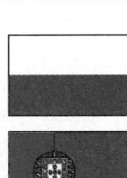

Puerto Rico (PR)   Island east of Cuba and southeast of Florida, ceded to the U.S. after the Spanish-American War; self-governing commonwealth. Capital: San Juan. (18°N 67°W) *m561, m1012–13*

Pusan   City in southeastern South Korea on Korea Strait. Developed into a major port during the Japanese occupation of Korea, 1910–45. (35°N 129°E) *m799*

Quebec   First permanent French settlement in North America, now a city in eastern Canada on the St. Lawrence River. (47°N 71°W) *m92*

Red River   River of southeast Asia that rises in southern China and flows about 730 miles, generally south, through Vietnam to a fertile delta on the Gulf of Tonkin. (22°N 104°E) *m865*

Rhineland   Region along the Rhine River in western Germany. (50°N 6°E) *m736*

Rhode Island (RI)   State in northeastern U.S., one of the original Thirteen Colonies. Admitted as a state in 1790. Capital: Providence. (41°N 71°W) *m1016–17*

Rhodesia   Region of south-central Africa south of Zaire, comprising modern-day Zambia and Zimbabwe. (18°S 29°E) *m1012–13*

Richmond   State capital, in the east-central part of Virginia on the James River. Strategically important in the American Revolution. Capital of the Confederacy in the Civil War and major objective of the Union Army; fell in 1865. (37°N 77°W) *m366*

Rio Grande   "Great River" that forms the border between Texas and Mexico. (26°N 98°W) *m313*

Roanoke   Island off the coast of North Carolina where two early English settlements failed. (36°N 77°W) *m57*

Russia   Country in Eastern Europe and Northwest Asia. Formerly part of USSR. Independent in 1991. Member of the Commonwealth of Independent States. Capital: Moscow. (61°N 60°E) *m1012–13*

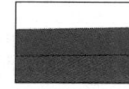

Saar   River, about 150 miles long, rising in northeast France and flowing north and northwest to the Moselle River in western Germany. River's valley is also known as the Saar Basin. *m608*

Sagres   Portuguese town in which Prince Henry ("the Navigator") built a school of navigation in the 15th century. *m29*

Sahara   Vast desert of northern Africa extending east from the Atlantic coast to the Nile Valley and south from the Atlas Mountains to the region of the Sudan. (23°N 1°W) *m26*

Saigon   Present-day Ho Chi Minh City. Largest city of Vietnam, in the southern part of the country near the South China Sea; formerly capital of South Vietnam. (10°N 106°E) *m865*

St. Augustine   City in northeastern Florida on the Atlantic Ocean, south-southeast of Jacksonville. Founded by the Spanish in 1565, it is the oldest permanent European settlement in the U.S. (30°N 81°W) *m52*

St. Lawrence River   River in southeast Canada flowing about 750 miles northeast from Lake Ontario along the Ontario–New York border and through southern Quebec to the Gulf of St. Lawrence. (48°N 69°W) *m57, m92*

St. Mihiel   Village in northeast France on the Meuse River east of Paris. World War I battle here (1918) was the first major American offensive led by General John J. Pershing. (49°N 5°E) *m599*

Sakhalin Island   Island of southeast Russia in the Sea of Okhotsk north of Hokkaido, Japan. (52°N 144°E) *m746*

Salem   City northeast of Boston. Founded in 1626, it is noted as the site of witchcraft trials, 1692, and of Nathaniel Hawthorne's *House of the Seven Gables.* (42°N 71°W) *m69*

San Antonio   City in south Texas. (29°N 98°W) *m308*

San Diego   City in southern California on San Diego Bay, an inlet of the Pacific Ocean near the Mexican border. (33°N 117°W) *m52*

San Francisco   City in western California on a peninsula between the Pacific Ocean and San Francisco Bay. Discovery of gold nearby in 1848 changed the city from a small community into a thriving boomtown. (37°N 122°W) *m52*

Santa Fe   Capital of New Mexico, in the north-central part of the state northeast of Albuquerque. Important city in Spanish America, it became the territorial capital in 1851 and state capital in 1912. (35°N 106°W) *m52*

Santiago   Cuban seaport captured by American forces during the Spanish-American War. (20°N 76°W) *m561*

Saudi Arabia   Country on the Arabian Peninsula in southwest Asia, bordered on the north by Jordan, Iraq, and Kuwait; the world's second-largest producer of oil. Capital: Riyadh. (22°N 46°E) *m940, m1012–13*

Savannah   U.S. city on east coast of Georgia captured by General Sherman during Civil War, 1864. (32°N 81°W) *m387*

Seattle   Washington city bounded by Puget Sound and Lake Washington. First settled in the 1850s; prospered after the coming of the railroad in 1884 and became a boomtown during the Alaskan gold rush of 1897. (47°N 122°W) *m445*

Sedan   Town of northeast France on the Meuse River near the Belgian border. Site of important battle in World War I. (50°N 5°E) *m599*

Selma   Alabama city west of Montgomery. In 1965 was the site of a voter-registration drive led by Rev. Martin Luther King, Jr. (32°N 87°W) *m845*

Seoul   Capital and largest city of South Korea, in the northwest section of the country. Twice occupied by Communist forces during the Korean War. (37°N 127°E) *m799*

Shiloh   Locality in southwestern Tennessee east of Memphis. Site of civil war battle, 1862, which claimed more than 10,000 casualties on both sides. *m382*

Sicily   Italian island in the Mediterranean taken by Allied forces prior to the occupation of Italy during World War II. (37°N 13°E) *m748*

Sierra Leone   Country in western Africa on the Atlantic coast. First visited by the Portuguese in the 1460s; region became a British protectorate in 1896 and achieved independence in 1961. Capital: Freetown. (8°N 12°W) *m29*

Somalia   Country of extreme eastern Africa on the Gulf of Aden and the Indian Ocean. Capital: Mogadishu. (3°N 44°E) *m1012–13*

South Africa   Country of southern Africa on the Atlantic and Indian oceans. Pretoria is the administrative capital, Cape Town the legislative capital, and Bloemfontein the judicial capital. (28°S 25°E) *m1012–13*

South Carolina (SC) State in southeastern U.S., one of the original Thirteen Colonies. Admitted as a state in 1788. First state to secede from the Union (1860). Capital: Columbia. (34°N 81°W) *m1016–17*

South Dakota (SD) State in north-central U.S. Constituted the southern part of the Dakota Territory; admitted as a state in 1889. Capital: Pierre. (44°N 102°W) *m1016–17*

South Korea (Official name: Republic of Korea) Country on east coast of Asia, bounded on north by North Korea, on east by the Sea of Japan, on south by the Korea Strait, and on west by the Yellow Sea. Capital: Seoul. (36°N 128°E) *m1012–13*

South Vietnam *See* Vietnam

Spain Country in southwest Europe, occupying the greater part of the Iberian Peninsula and including the Balearic and Canary islands. Capital: Madrid. (40°N 4°W) *m1012–13*

Spice Islands Present-day Moluccas. Group of islands in eastern Indonesia between Celebes and New Guinea. Islands were settled by the Portuguese but taken in the 17th century by the Dutch, who used them as the base for their monopoly of the spice trade. *m29*

Stalingrad Present-day Volgograd (renamed in 1961). City of southwest Russia on the Volga River. (48°N 42°E) *m748*

Sudan Country in northeast Africa south of Egypt. Capital: Khartoum. (14°N 28°E) *m976, m1012–13*

Sudetenland Historical region of northwest Czechoslovakia along the Polish border. Seized by the Germans in September 1938, it was restored to Czechoslovakia in 1945. *m736*

Suez Canal International waterway in the Middle East seized by Egypt in 1956. British, French, and Israeli troops unsuccessfully attempted to end Egyptian control. (31°N 32°E) *m811*

Sutter's Fort Fortified town built by John Sutter on California's American River in 1839. *m325*

Syria Country in southwest Asia on the eastern Mediterranean coast. Capital: Damascus. (35°N 37°E) *m905, m1012–13*

Taiwan (Official name: Republic of China) Formerly Formosa. Country off the southeast coast of China made up of the island of Taiwan, the Pescadores, and other smaller islands. Capital: Taipei. (37°N 112°E) *m564, m746, m1012–13*

Tajikistan Republic; member of the Commonwealth of Independent States. Formerly part of the USSR. Independent in 1991. Capital: Dushanbe. (39°N 69°E) *m1012–13*

Tennessee (TN) State in south-central U.S. Admitted as a state in 1796. Capital: Nashville. (36°N 88°W) *m1016–17*

Tenochtitlán Ancient name of Mexico City, which with Texcoco and Tlacopán formed the Aztec confederacy and became the capital of the Aztec empire. (19°N 99°W) *m15*

Texas (TX) State in south-central U.S., bounded on south by Gulf of Mexico and Mexico. Known as the Lone Star State because it was an independent republic (1836–45) whose flag featured a single star. Capital: Austin. (31°N 101°W) *m1016–17*

Thailand Formerly Siam. Country in southeast Asia on the Gulf of Thailand. Was occupied by the Japanese in World War II and was a strong supporter of the U.S. in the Vietnam War. Capital: Bangkok. (16°N 101°E) *m746, m1012–13*

Tikal Ancient Mayan city, in present-day northern Guatemala, northeast of Petén Itza; excavation and restoration of ruins began in 1956. *m15*

Timbuktu Town in Mali, in western Africa near the Niger River; reached height of prosperity as commercial and cultural center under Songhai rule c. 1500. (16°N 3°W) *m26*

Topeka Capital of Kansas, in the northeastern part of the state west of Kansas City. (39°N 95°W) *m1016–17*

Turkey Country in southwest Asia and southeast Europe between the Mediterranean and the Black seas. Capital: Ankara. (38°N 32°W) *m793, m1012–13*

Turkmenistan Republic; member of the Commonwealth of Independent States. Formerly part of the USSR. Independent in 1991. Capital: Ashgabat. (40°N 56°E) *m959, m1012–13*

Ukraine Republic; member of the Commonwealth of Independent States. Formerly part of the USSR. Independent in 1991. Central theater of warfare in both world wars. Capital: Kiev. (49°N 30°E) *m748, m959, m1012–13*

United Kingdom of Great Britain and Northern Ireland *See* Great Britain

United States of America Federal republic, North America, bounded on north by Canada and (in Alaska) the Arctic Ocean, on east by the Atlantic Ocean, on south by Mexico and the Gulf of Mexico, and on west by the Pacific Ocean. Capital: Washington, D.C. (38°N 110°W) *m1012–13, m1016–17*

Utah (UT) State in western U.S. First explored by Coronado expedition, 1540. Admitted as a state in 1896. Capital: Salt Lake City. (39°N 112°W) *m1016–17*

Uzbekistan Republic; member of the Commonwealth of Independent States. Formerly part of the USSR. Independent in 1991. Capital: Toshkent. (42°N 60°E) *m959, m1012–13*

Venezuela Country in northern South America on the Caribbean Sea. Capital: Caracas. (8°N 65°W) *m578, m1012–13*

Venice City in northeast Italy on islets within a lagoon in the Gulf of Venice, wide inlet of the northern Adriatic Sea. (45°N 12°E) *m29*

Vermont (VT) State in northeastern U.S., one of the original Thirteen Colonies. Admitted as a state in 1791. Capital: Montpelier. (44°N 73°W) *m1016–17*

Vicksburg   City in western Mississippi on bluffs above the Mississippi River west of Jackson. During the Civil War it was besieged (1862–63) and finally captured by Union troops led by Ulysses S. Grant. (42°N 85°W) *m382*

Vietnam   Southeast Asian country (divided into North Vietnam and South Vietnam between 1954 and 1975) where United States and South Vietnamese forces fought a war against the Communist North Vietnamese. Capital: Hanoi. (18°N 107°E) *m865, m1012–13*

Virginia (VA)   State in eastern U.S., one of the original Thirteen Colonies. Admitted as a state in 1788. Capital: Richmond. (37°N 80°W) *m1016–17*

W

Wake Island   Island in the western Pacific Ocean between Hawaii and Guam. Annexed by the U.S. in 1898, it was a commercial air base and later a military base, held by the Japanese from 1941 to 1945. (19°N 167°E) *m746*

Waltham   Massachusetts city west of Boston. Site of first paper mill in U.S. and first power loom for manufacture of textiles. (42°N 71°W) *m253*

Washington (WA)   State in northwestern U.S., bounded on north by Canadian province of British Columbia and on west by the Pacific Ocean. Admitted as a state in 1889. Capital: Olympia. (47°N 121°W) *m1016–17*

Washington, D.C.   Capital of the United States, on the Potomac River between Virginia and Maryland and coextensive with the District of Columbia. Leading international political and educational center. (39°N 77°W) *m214*

West Berlin   *See* Berlin

West Virginia (WV)   State in east-central U.S. Admitted as a state in 1863. Part of Virginia until the area refused to endorse the Ordinance of Secession in 1861. Capital: Charleston. (39°N 81°W) *m1016–17*

Willamette Valley   Fertile agricultural region of Oregon, first settled in the 1830s by pioneers traveling west along the Oregon Trail. *m319*

Wisconsin (WI)   State in north-central U.S. Admitted as a state in 1848. First settled by the French, region was ceded to Great Britain in 1763 and became part of the Northwest Territory in 1787. Capital: Madison. (44°N 91°W) *m1016–17*

Wyoming (WY)   State in northwestern U.S. Organized as the Wyoming Territory in 1868 and admitted as a state in 1890. Capital: Cheyenne. (43°N 108°W) *m1016–17*

Y

Yalu River   River forming part of the North Korea–China border. (41°N 126°E) *m799*

Yangtze River   Longest river of China and of Asia, flowing about 3,450 miles from Xizang (Tibet) to the East China Sea. (30°N 117°E) *m739*

Yokohama   Japanese city in southeast Honshu, on the western shore of Tokyo Bay. Almost entirely destroyed by an earthquake and fire in 1923, again largely destroyed by U.S. bombing in World War II. (35°N 139°E) *m564*

Ysleta   First permanent Spanish colony in Texas, founded in 1681. (31°N 106°W) *m52*

Yugoslavia   Former country in southeast Europe bordering on the Adriatic Sea. It was formed in 1918 as the Kingdom of Serbs, Croats, and Slovenes after the collapse of the Austro-Hungarian Empire and renamed Yugoslavia in 1929. Today the name is claimed by Serbia and Montenegro. (44°N 17°E) *m608, m959, m1012–13*

Yukon Territory   Territory of northwest Canada east of Alaska. Region first explored by fur traders in the 1840s and acquired by Canada from the Hudson Bay Company in 1870. Capital: Whitehorse. (63°N 135°W) *m450*

GLOSSARY

This Glossary contains terms you need to understand as you study American history. After each term there is a brief definition or explanation of the meaning of the term as it is used in *Boyer's The American Nation.* The page number refers to the page on which the term is introduced in the textbook.

Phonetic Respelling and Pronunciation Guide

Many of the key terms in this textbook have been respelled to help you pronounce them. The letter combinations used in the respellings throughout the narrative are explained in the following phonetic respelling and pronunciation guide. The guide is adapted from *Webster's Ninth New Collegiate Dictionary, Webster's New Geographical Dictionary,* and *Webster's New Biographical Dictionary.*

MARK	AS IN	RESPELLING	EXAMPLE
a	alphabet	a	*AL-fuh-bet
ā	Asia	ay	AY-zhuh
ä	cart, top	ah	KAHRT, TAHP
e	let, ten	e	LET, TEN
ē	even, leaf	ee	EE-vuhn, LEEF
i	it, tip, British	i	IT, TIP, BRIT-ish
ī	site, buy, Ohio	y	SYT, BY, oh-HY-oh
	iris	eye	EYE-ris
k	card	k	KARD
ō	over, rainbow	oh	oh-vuhr, RAYN-boh
ů	book, wood	ooh	BOOHK, WOOHD
o	all, orchid	aw	AWL, AWR-kid
ŏi	foil, coin	oy	FOYL, KOYN
aů	out	ow	OWT
ə	cup, butter	uh	KUHP, BUHT-uhr
ü	rule, food	oo	ROOL, FOOD
yü	few	yoo	FYOO
zh	vision	zh	VIZH-uhn

A syllable printed in small capital letters receives heavier emphasis than the other syllable(s) in a word.

abolitionists   People who wanted to put an end to slavery. **78**

acid rain   Atmospheric pollution that gradually kills trees and makes lakes unfit for marine life. **972**

Adamson Act   Federal law reducing the workday for railroad workers from 10 to 8 hours with no decrease in wages. **551**

Adams-Onís Treaty (1819)   Agreement in which Spain transferred East Florida to the U.S. for $5 million and the U.S. promised to drop its claim to Texas. **230**

affirmative action   Programs giving preference to ethnic minorities and women in jobs or school admission to make up for past discrimination. **919**

African diaspora   Forcible resettlement of millions of African people to the Americas from the 1500s through the 1800s. **30**

Agricultural Adjustment Act (AAA)   Federal law passed in 1933 to reduce farmers' output, increase crop prices, and establish the Agricultural Adjustment Administration. **698**

Agricultural Marketing Act (1929)   Federal law that created the Federal Farm Board, an agency to help ease the plight of farmers by buying farm surpluses. **685**

AIDS   Acquired Immune Deficiency Syndrome, the final deadly stage of an illness believed to be caused by the human immunodeficiency virus (HIV). **949**

Albany Plan of Union (1754)   Benjamin Franklin's plan to unite the colonies through a loose confederation aimed at promoting their defense. **91**

Alien and Sedition Acts (1798)   Series of laws passed by the Federalists to protect the country from foreign influence, limit Republican power, and silence government critics. **202**

Alliance for Progress   President Kennedy's policy of sending economic aid to Latin America; designed to encourage democratic reforms and to promote capitalism. **835**

Allied Powers   World War I alliance that included France, Great Britain, Russia, Italy, and later the United States. **587**

American Anti-Slavery Society   First national antislavery organization devoted to immediate abolition, formed in 1833 by both black and white abolitionists. **294**

American Colonization Society Group founded by prominent northerners and southerners in 1817 to persuade slaveholders to free their slaves and transport them to Liberia. **265**

American Federation of Labor (AFL) Organization of independent skilled craft unions founded in 1886 by Samuel Gompers. **495**

American Indian Defense Association Organization that fought to protect religious freedom and tribal property for Native Americans. **710**

American Indian Movement (AIM) Organization, founded in 1968 by Minnesota Chippewas, that became the major force in the Red Power movement during the 1970s. **851**

American Plan Policy, promoted by business leaders during the 1920s, that called for open shops. **632**

Americans with Disabilities Act (1990) Federal law that prohibits discrimination against people with mental or physical disabilities. **949**

American System Henry Clay's federal program for economic development; it included a national bank, a protective tariff, and a national transportation system. **227**

amnesty Official pardon for crimes committed against the government. **395**

anarchists People who oppose all forms of government. **494**

annex Action by which one country takes control of another country or territory. **563**

Antifederalists Individuals who feared a powerful national government and opposed ratification of the U.S. Constitution. **150**

anti-Semitism Hatred of Jews. **733**

apartheid Racial segregation; former racial policy in South Africa. **915**

appeasement Policy of giving in to demands of a country or countries in an effort to avoid major conflicts. **735**

arbitration Hearing in which a third party settles a dispute. **539**

armistice Cease-fire. **600**

Articles of Confederation Agreement, ratified in 1781, in which the 13 colonies established a government of states with each state retaining power over its own affairs. **140**

assembly line Manufacturing technique in which a product is passed along a line of workers and assembled in stages. **646**

assimilation Cultural absorption of a group. **434**

Atlantic Charter (1941) Joint declaration of principles for international relations, agreed to by the United States and Great Britain. **738**

Atomic Energy Act (1946) Federal law that placed the Atomic Energy Commission under civilian control to oversee nuclear weapons research and to promote peacetime uses of atomic energy. **791**

automation Manufacturing process that used machines to perform industrial operations faster and more efficiently than human labor. **820**

Axis powers Military alliance of Germany, Italy, and Japan during World War II. **735**

baby boom Soaring birth rate between 1946 and 1964. **817**

Bacon's Rebellion (1676) Uprising by Virginia settlers, disgruntled over taxes and land, that included attacking Indians, looting wealthy plantations, and burning Jamestown. **77**

balance of trade Difference in value between trade exports and imports. **83**

Balfour Declaration (1917) Statement issued by Great Britain declaring its support for a Jewish homeland in Palestine. **611**

bank holiday (1933) New Deal proclamation that temporarily closed every U.S. bank to stop massive withdrawals. **694**

bank notes Paper money issued by banks in place of gold or silver. **192**

Baruch Plan (1946) Proposal submitted to the UN Atomic Energy Commission for international control of atomic energy. **790**

Bataan Death March (1942) Forced march of Allied prisoners on the Bataan peninsula to a Japanese detention camp, during which thousands died. **745**

Battle of Antietam (1862) Civil War battle that helped bolster northern confidence while dashing Confederate hopes of winning European support. **378**

Battle of Bunker Hill (1775) Revolutionary War battle in which British troops defeated Patriot forces atop two hills overlooking Boston Harbor. **116**

Battle of Camden (1780) Revolutionary War battle in which British troops defeated Patriot forces in South Carolina. **131**

Battle of Chancellorsville (1863) Confederate victory during the Civil War that resulted in the death of General Stonewall Jackson. **379**

Battle of El Alamein (1942) British victory in Egypt during World War II that broke the momentum of the Axis advance in North Africa. **749**

Battle of Fallen Timbers (1794) Decisive battle in the Northwest Territory in which U.S. troops defeated a confederation of Native Americans, weakening Indian resistance on the frontier. **197**

Battle of Fredericksburg (1862) Confederate victory during the Civil War that cost Union troops more than 12,000 casualties and led to General Burnside's replacement. **378**

Battle of Gettysburg (1863) Union victory during the Civil War that halted General Lee's invasion of the North. **379**

Battle of Iwo Jima (1945) Allied victory in the Pacific during World War II in which Japanese forces lost more than 20,000 troops. **764**

Battle of Leyte Gulf (1944) Decisive naval victory for the Allies during World War II that eliminated the Japanese fleet as a threat in the Pacific. **764**

Battle of Midway (1942) Allied naval victory that helped halt the major Japanese offensive in the Pacific during World War II. **747**

Battle of New Orleans (1815) Battle in which American troops defeated British forces after the War of 1812 had officially ended. **214**

Battle of Okinawa (1945) Allied victory in the Pacific during World War II in which Japanese forces lost more than 100,000 troops. **764**

Battle of Rosebud (1876) Battle against U.S. Army in which Native Americans gained confidence in their fighting force. **429**

Battle of San Jacinto (1836) Texan victory over Mexican troops that resulted in the Mexican government granting Texas its independence. **309**

Battle of Saratoga (1777) Patriot victory, during Revolutionary War, that convinced France to support the American fight for independence. **130**

Battle of Seven Pines (1862) Civil War battle in which Confederate general Johnston was seriously wounded and succeeded by Robert E. Lee. **377**

Battle of Shiloh (1862) Costly Civil War battle in which General Grant's troops defeated Confederate forces. **381**

Battle of Stalingrad (1942–43) Soviet defeat of German troops during World War II that broke the momentum of the Axis advance in Europe. **749**

Battle of the Atlantic World War II naval war fought between German U-boats and the Allied navy and air force. **760**

Battle of the Bulge (1944)   World War II battle in which Allied forces repulsed the final German offensive. **761**

Battle of the Coral Sea (1942)   Allied naval victory during World War II in which a joint British-American naval force stopped the Japanese advance on Australia. **746**

Battle of the Java Sea (1942)   World War II naval battle in which the Japanese navy defeated a fleet of American, British, Dutch, and Australian warships. **745**

Battle of the Little Bighorn (1876)   Native American victory that resulted in the death of U.S. Army general Custer and all the men in his detachment. **429**

Battle of the Philippine Sea (1944)   Decisive Allied naval and air victory over the Japanese during WorldWar II. **762**

Battle of the Somme (1916)   World War I battle in which the British lost some 60,000 troops in a single day. **589**

Battle of the Thames (1813)   American victory during the War of 1812 that helped break the British hold on the Northwest Territory. **214**

Battle of Tippecanoe (1811)   Battle in Indiana Territory between U.S. troops and a confederation of Native Americans; ended in defeat for the Indians and made William Henry Harrison a hero. **212**

Battle of Trenton (1776)   Revolutionary War battle in which Washington's army attacked and defeated Hessian soldiers stationed at Trenton, New Jersey. **128**

Battle of Vincennes (1779)   Revolutionary War battle in the West in which Patriot troops recaptured a British fort and went on to take control of western lands. **131**

Battle of Yorktown (1781)   Revolutionary War battle in which Patriot troops defeated British forces under General Cornwallis, effectively ending the war. **132**

Bear Flag Revolt (1846)   Uprising by U.S. settlers in California against Mexican rule in which they declared California an independent republic. **313**

bear market   Downward trend in stock prices. **670**

Beats   Small but influential group of writers and poets who challenged literary conventions and the life-style of the middle class in the 1950s. **825**

benevolent societies   Organizations formed during the turn of the century to support and aid new immigrants. **469**

Beringia   Former land bridge between Siberia and present-day Alaska used by Paleo-Indians to cross from Asia into North America. **4**

Berlin airlift (1948)   Joint effort by U.S. and British air forces to deliver food and supplies into West Berlin after the Soviets blocked all routes into the city. **792**

Berlin Wall   Concrete barrier built in 1961 to cut off traffic between East Berlin and West Berlin. **836**

bicameral   Legislature made up of two houses. **147**

Big Four   During World War I, term for U.S. president Woodrow Wilson, French premier Georges Clemenceau, Italian prime minister Vittorio Orlando, and British prime minister David Lloyd George. **607**

Bilingual Education Act (1974)   Federal law encouraging public schools to provide instruction to students in their native languages until they learned English. **923**

bill of attainder   Law that punishes a person by fine, imprisonment, or seizure of property without a court trial. **163**

Bill of Rights (1791)   First 10 amendments to the Constitution that protect individual liberties. **191**

biomass   Materials, such as wood or waste products, that can be burned or used to make fuel. **970**

black codes   Laws adopted by former Confederates after the Civil War to limit the freedom of former slaves. **398**

blacklists   Lists of union supporters drawn up by employers for the purpose of denying jobs to union workers. **495**

Black Power   African American movement that focused on gaining control of economic and political power to achieve equal rights, by force if necessary. **848**

Blackshirts   Followers of Benito Mussolini. **732**

Black Thursday   October 24, 1929; day investors caused a panic on Wall Street by selling their shares. **671**

Black Tuesday   October 29, 1929; day the stock market crashed. **671**

Bland-Allison Act (1878)   Federal law passed in response to pressure from farmers; required the government to buy and mint silver each month. **499**

blitzkrieg   German word for war carried on with great speed and force, used to describe Hitler's "lightning war" against Poland in World War II. **737**

Bolsheviks   Branch of the Russian Communist party that seized power in 1917 following the overthrow of the czar. **598**

bonanza farm   Large-scale farm usually owned by a large company and run like a factory. **441**

Bonus Army   Name given to World War I veterans who marched on Washington, D.C., in 1932 to support a bill granting veterans early payment of pension bonuses. **687**

bosses   Powerful political party leaders who used political machines and patronage to control elections. **469**

Boston Massacre (1770)   Clash in Boston between an angry crowd of colonists and British soldiers that resulted in the death of five colonists. **110**

Boston Tea Party (1773)   Protest against British tax on tea in which colonists dumped tea into Boston Harbor. **111**

bourgeoisie   The middle class; originated in the Middle Ages and was made up of merchants and bankers. **20**

Boxer Rebellion (1900)   Revolt by a Chinese secret society attempting to drive foreigners out of China. **567**

braceros   Mexican farm workers who came to work in the Southwest during World War II and after. **757**

breadlines   Lines formed by people waiting for free food, such as those that occurred during the Great Depression. **677**

brinkmanship   Policy promoted by Secretary of State Dulles during the 1950s, which called for threatening all-out war in order to confront Communist aggression. **810**

British Invasion   Revolution in popular music inspired by the 1964 arrival of English rock bands such as the Beatles and the Rolling Stones. **856**

Brownshirts   Nazi storm troopers. **733**

Brown* v. *The Board of Education of Topeka (1952)   Supreme Court case challenging segregation in public schools; in it the Court ruled that separate educational facilities were unequal. **822**

bull market   Upward trend in stock prices. **670**

Bureau of Indian Affairs   Federal agency established within the War Department in 1824 to administer Native American reservations. **427**

business cycle   Regular ups and downs of business in a free-enterprise economy. **674**

cabinet   Heads of government departments who are appointed by, and serve as advisers to, the president. **191**

Camp David Accords (1978)   Middle East peace agreement drafted by the U.S., Egypt, and Israel. **916**

capitalism   Economic system based on a free market and private ownership of property. **192**

carpetbaggers Northern Republicans who moved south after the Civil War to help freedpeople or to profit financially from unsettled conditions under Reconstruction governments. **406**

caudillos Latin American military leaders during the 1930s who used force to maintain order. **729**

Cayuse War First of a series of Indian wars in Oregon Country that began in 1847 after the murder of missionaries Marcus and Narcissa Whitman and 12 others by Cayuse Indians. **322**

Central Intelligence Agency (CIA) Federal agency created to gather information overseas. **794**

Central Powers World War I alliance led by Germany, Austria-Hungary, the Ottoman Empire (Turkey), and Bulgaria. **587**

Charter of 1606 Document, issued by King James I of England, that licensed the Plymouth Company and the London Company to organize settlements in Virginia. **59**

checks and balances System giving each branch of the federal government the means to restrain the powers of the other two branches. **155**

Chicano movement Brown Power movement organized by young Mexican American college students to emphasize pride in Mexican culture and heritage. **851**

Chinese Exclusion Act (1882) Federal law that denied U.S. citizenship to people born in China and prohibited the immigration of Chinese laborers. **471**

chlorofluorocarbons (CFCs) Compounds, containing carbon, chlorine, fluorine, and sometimes hydrogen; they are suspected of damaging the ozone layer. **972**

circumnavigate To sail around the world. **45**

Civilian Conservation Corps (CCC) New Deal agency established in 1933 to employ men on conservation projects. **696**

civil liberties People's rights as individuals against the power of the government. **163**

Civil Rights Act of 1866 Federal law that granted full civil rights, but not voting rights, to everyone born in the U.S. **400**

Civil Rights Act of 1957 Federal law that made it a federal crime to prevent qualified persons from voting. **825**

Civil Rights Act of 1964 Federal law that barred discrimination in employment and public facilities and gave the Justice Department the power to enforce school desegregation. **847**

Civil Rights Bill of 1875 Federal law that prohibited discrimination by businesses serving the public. **408**

Civil Works Administration (CWA) New Deal agency designed to create jobs during the Great Depression. **696**

Clayton Antitrust Act (1914) Federal law that clarified and extended the 1890 Sherman Antitrust Act. **549**

Clayton-Bulwer Treaty (1850) Agreement between the U.S. and Great Britain that proposed an equal partnership in building and running a Central American canal. **570**

Clean Air Act (1970) Federal law that set air-quality standards and tough emissions guidelines for car manufacturers. **903**

closed shop Workplace where the employer hires only union members. **520**

Cold War Competition between the U.S. and the Soviet Union for global power and influence. **789**

Columbian exchange Transfer of people, ideas, plants, animals, and diseases among the Americas, Europe, Asia, and Africa; initiated by Columbus's voyages. **44**

Committee of Correspondence Massachusetts group formed in the 1770s to inform the colonies about British policies. **111**

Committee on Civil Rights Group established by President Truman in 1946 to document civil rights abuses. **786**

Committee on Public Information (CPI) Agency established in 1917 that waged a vigorous propaganda campaign to convince Americans to support the war effort. **604**

commonwealth Political unit founded on law in which members are expected to work together for the common good. **69**

Commonwealth of Independent States (CIS) International organization of sovereign states organized in 1991 by Russia, Ukraine, and Belarus. Other former Soviet republics later became members. **959**

company town Community where housing and businesses are owned by one firm. **493**

Compromise of 1850 Resolution proposed by Henry Clay that temporarily settled differences between the North and the South over slavery issues. **342**

Compromise of 1877 Deal between leading Republicans and southern Democrats that gave the presidency to Rutherford B. Hayes in 1876 in exchange for a promise not to use the military to enforce Reconstruction laws in the South. **408**

Comstock Lode Rich Nevada silver vein that was the center of frantic prospecting beginning in 1859. **449**

concurrent powers Powers granted jointly in the United States Constitution to the federal government and the state government. **154**

Congress of Industrial Organizations (CIO) Labor group organized in 1935 to unite workers in various industries. **705**

Congress of Racial Equality (CORE) Northern-based civil rights group that launched a protest against segregation in interstate transportation in 1961. **845**

conquistadors Spanish soldiers who helped conquer the Americas. **46**

conscription Compulsory draft into military service. **368**

conspicuous consumption Lavish spending to increase social prestige. **473**

Constitutional Convention Meeting called in 1787 and held in Philadelphia to strengthen the government, during which delegates wrote and adopted the U.S. Constitution. **145**

containment Cold War strategy proposed by George Kennan to stop the spread of communism. **790**

contras Nicaraguan army recruited, financed, and armed by the CIA to overthrow the Sandinistas. **931**

Convention of 1818 Agreement by which Great Britain and the U.S. set the U.S.–Canadian border at the 49th parallel west to the Rocky Mountains. **229**

convoy system Use of armed escort vessels to accompany unarmed vessels transporting troops or supplies. **598**

cooperatives Groups that pool members' resources to sell products directly to urban markets and buy goods at wholesale prices. **498**

Copperheads Northern Democrats who sympathized with the South during the Civil War. **375**

corporation Type of business in which the money needed to run the company is obtained by selling shares of stock. **462**

cotton gin Machine invented by Eli Whitney in 1793 to separate seeds from cotton fiber. **234**

Council of Economic Advisers Federal agency created by the Employment Act of 1946 to counsel the president on economic policy. **784**

counterculture Culture that holds values and beliefs different from those of established society; for example, the culture of the hippies in the 1960s. **853**

covenant Contract. **69**

creditor nation Country that loans money to other nations. **726**

Crittenden Compromise Civil War–era plan to resolve conflict between North and South by calling for the westward extension of the Missouri Compromise line through the remaining territories. **364**

crop-lien system Arrangement in which sharecroppers offered crops to merchants in exchange for supplies. **411**

Crusades Series of wars between 1096 and the late 1200s in which Christian crusaders fought Muslims for control of the Holy Land. **19**

cultural diffusion Process of spreading cultural practices or beliefs from one group to another. **8**

Dawes General Allotment Act (1887) Federal law that established private ownership of Indian land. **434**

D-Day June 6, 1944; day when Allied soldiers crossed the English Channel to begin their invasion of France. **760**

debtor nation Country that owes money to other nations. **726**

Declaration of Independence (1776) Document adopted by the Second Continental Congress that justified and outlined reasons for the American separation from Great Britain. **118**

Declaratory Act (1766) Law passed by Parliament that asserted the right of Great Britain to make laws governing its American colonies. **108**

defoliants Chemicals designed to strip land of vegetation. **873**

delegated powers Powers granted to the federal government in the U.S. Constitution. **154**

demobilization Shift from wartime preparations to a peacetime economy. **622**

denominations Religious groups consisting of a number of local congregations. **283**

Department of Energy Federal agency created in 1977 to reduce U.S. dependence on oil. **913**

depression Sharp drop in business activity accompanied by rising unemployment. **143**

détente Lessening of military and diplomatic tensions between countries. **904**

Diamond Sutra First known printed book, China, A.D. 868. **24**

direct primary Nominating election in which voters choose candidates to run in a general election. **535**

disarmament Reduction or limitation in the amount of a nation's military weapons. **725**

dissenters People who disagree with opinions expressed by the majority. **68**

dividends Portions of a company's profits received by its stockholders. **462**

Dixiecrats States' Rights party formed by southern Democrats in 1948; supported continued racial segregation. **787**

doctrine of nullification Theory of the states' right to refuse to obey any act passed by Congress that they consider unconstitutional. **245**

dollar diplomacy President Taft's policy of using economic influence, rather than military force, to protect U.S. interests in Latin America. **574**

domestication Adaptation and control of plants and animals. **8**

domino theory Foreign policy principle of the 1950s and the 1960s stating that if one country fell to communism, neighboring countries would also fall. **867**

doves People who support negotiation and compromise and who oppose war. **876**

Dred Scott **decision** (1857) Supreme Court case in which Scott, a slave, was declared not to be a citizen and therefore not able to bring a suit for his freedom in U.S. courts. **350**

drivers Slave assistants who helped overseers supervise other slaves. **269**

dry farming Techniques to conserve moisture in areas of little rainfall. **440**

Dust Bowl Fifty-million–acre region in the Great Plains that suffered a severe drought in the mid-1930s. **711**

duty Tax on imports. **106**

Earth Summit (1992) United Nations Conference on Environment and Development held in Rio de Janeiro, Brazil, in 1992. **974**

economies of scale Principle of buying supplies in bulk and producing goods in large quantities to lower production costs and increase profits. **463**

ecosystem Interaction of living beings with the environment. **970**

Education Amendments Act (1972) Federal law prohibiting sexual discrimination in higher education. **921**

Education for All Handicapped Children Act (1975) Federal law requiring public schools to provide education for children with physical and mental disabilities. **919**

Eighteenth Amendment (1919) Constitutional amendment that barred the manufacture, sale, or importation of alcoholic beverages; repealed by Twenty-first Amendment. **525**

Eisenhower Doctrine (1957) Policy designed to counter Soviet influence in the Middle East by offering military aid to those nations seeking help in resisting Communist aggression. **812**

elastic clause "Necessary and proper" clause that allows Congress to expand its powers beyond those limits outlined in the U.S. Constitution. **157**

electors People selected by state legislatures to cast electoral votes for president and vice president. **150**

Elementary and Secondary School Education Act (1965) Federal law that provided $1.3 billion to aid schools in impoverished areas. **842**

Elkins Act (1903) Federal law that prohibited shippers from accepting rebates. **540**

Emancipation Proclamation Decree freeing all slaves living in those areas of the Confederacy that were still in rebellion against the U.S. as of January 1, 1863. **384**

Embargo Act (1807) Measure that stopped shipments of food and other American products to all foreign ports in an effort to maintain U.S. neutrality in European conflicts. **211**

Emergency Banking Act (1933) Federal law authorizing only banks that were financially sound to reopen after the New Deal bank holiday. **694**

Employment Act (1946) Post–World War II law that established the Council of Economic Advisers and pledged the promotion of full employment and production. **784**

empresarios Businesspeople who agreed to recruit and take responsibility for new settlers in Texas in return for land grants from Mexico. **307**

encomienda System that gave Spanish colonists the right to have a certain number of Indians work for them. **40**

Enforcement Acts Three acts passed by Congress between 1870 and 1871 allowing the government to use military force to stop violence against African Americans. **407**

Enlightenment Intellectual movement of the 18th century that rejected traditional political, social, and religious ideas and emphasized human reason and progress. **84**

environment Physical surroundings. **5**

Environmental Protection Agency (EPA) Federal agency created in 1970 to enforce environmental laws. **903**

Equal Pay Act (1963) Federal law that made it illegal for employers to pay female workers less than male workers for the same job. **834**

Equal Rights Amendment (ERA) Proposed constitutional amendment barring discrimination on the basis of sex. **921**

escalation Increase or buildup of military forces or weapons. **871**

Espionage Act (1917)   Federal law designed to silence dissenters during World War I. **605**

European Union   Western European trading bloc formed by the European Community in 1993 with ratification of the Maastricht Treaty. **964**

Exodusters   Black settlers who moved west during the late 1800s to find economic and political freedom. **439**

ex post facto **law**   Law passed "after the deed"; sets a penalty for an act that was not illegal when committed. **163**

factory system   Manufacturing system that cuts costs and increases output by relying on machines to do the work. **235**

Fair Deal   President Truman's proposed reforms after the 1948 election; for example, a national health insurance program. **787**

Fair Employment Practices Committee (FEPC)   Federal commission created in 1941 to prevent job discrimination based on race or ethnic background. **756**

Family and Medical Leave Act (1993)   Federal law requiring large companies to provide workers up to 12 weeks of unpaid leave for family and medical emergencies without losing their medical coverage or jobs. **949**

Family Assistance Plan (FAP)   President Nixon's proposal to replace the welfare system with a plan that would guarantee families a minimum income. **901**

Farm Credit Administration   New Deal agency created in 1933 to give farmers low-interest, long-term loans. **695**

Farmers' Alliance   Powerful farm organization formed in 1877 that lobbied to help farmers economically and politically. **498**

Farm Security Administration (FSA)   New Deal agency created in 1937 to help tenant farmers and sharecroppers buy farms through low-interest, long-term loans. **706**

Fascist party   Political party, founded by Benito Mussolini in 1921, that supported a military-dominated government in control of all aspects of Italian society. **732**

Federal Deposit Insurance Corporation (FDIC)   New Deal agency created in 1933 to insure bank savings deposits. **695**

Federal Emergency Relief Administration (FERA)   New Deal agency created in 1933 to funnel relief aid directly to state and local agencies. **695**

Federal Farm Loan Act   Federal law proposed during President Woodrow Wilson's administration that provided low-interest loans to farmers. **551**

federalism   Division and sharing of powers between a strong central government and state governments. **146**

Federalist, The   Essays written to support ratification of the U.S. Constitution; also called *Federalist Papers*. **150**

Federalists   Members of a political party who advocated strong national government and favored ratification of the U.S. Constitution. **149**

Federal Project No. 1   New Deal program established in 1935 to aid unemployed artists. **716**

Federal Reserve Act (1913)   Federal law that created a three-level banking system controlled by both private banks and the government. **549**

Federal Trade Commission (FTC)   Government agency established in 1914 to enforce antitrust laws and to investigate corporations engaged in unfair or fraudulent practices. **549**

Federal Workmen's Compensation Act   Federal law providing benefits to federal workers injured on the job. **551**

Federal Writers' Project (FWP)   Program that hired unemployed writers to produce a variety of cultural works. **716**

feudalism   System in the Middle Ages in which nobles pledged military assistance and loyalty to rulers in return for land and protection. **17**

Fifteenth Amendment (1869)   Constitutional amendment that guaranteed that the right to vote could not be denied because of race. **404**

First Battle of Bull Run (1861)   Confederate victory at Manassas Junction, outside of Washington, D.C., that proved the Civil War would last longer than a few months. **371**

First Battle of the Marne (1914)   World War I battle in which French and British forces stopped the German advance in northeast France. **589**

First Continental Congress (1774)   Meeting of delegates from 12 colonies to discuss grievances against Great Britain, including those resulting from the Intolerable Acts. **113**

Five Power Agreement (1921)   Arrangement between the U.S., Great Britain, France, Italy, and Japan to set limits on each nation's naval strength. **725**

flappers   "New women" whose dress and conduct after World War I defied traditional standards of womanly behavior. **655**

flexible response   Strategy adopted by the Kennedy administration of keeping a range of options open for dealing with international crises. **835**

Food Administration   Government agency responsible for regulating production and supply of food during World War I. **602**

Foraker Act (1900)   Federal law outlining the organization of Puerto Rico's government. **570**

Fordney-McCumber Tariff Act (1922)   Federal law that placed high duties on imported farm products in an effort to boost domestic crop prices and to help farmers. **632**

forty-niners   Nickname for gold-seekers who went to California, beginning in 1849, to seek their fortune. **324**

Four Power Treaty (1921)   Agreement between the U.S., Great Britain, France, and Japan to respect one another's territory in the Pacific. **725**

Fourteen Points (1918)   President Wilson's program for world peace after World War I that contained 14 principles, including the creation of the League of Nations. **606**

Fourteenth Amendment (1866)   Constitutional amendment that granted full citizenship, civil rights, and equal protection under the law to African Americans. **401**

Freedmen's Bureau   Organization established by Congress in 1865 to aid southerners left homeless by the war and to help ex-slaves. **400**

freedom of contract   Right of workers and employers to agree to certain conditions of employment. **519**

Freedom Riders   Integrated group who protested segregation in interstate transportation in 1961. **845**

Freedom Summer   Campaign to register African American voters during the summer of 1964. **847**

freemen   People who enjoy full political and civil liberties. **69**

Freeport Doctrine (1858)   Position, held by Stephen Douglas, that people in a territory have the power to prohibit slavery by refusing to pass local laws necessary to make a slave system work. **353**

Free-Soil party   Political party, formed by antislavery Whigs and Democrats in 1848, that opposed the expansion of slavery into the territories. **339**

French Revolution   Revolt beginning in Paris in 1789 that led to the overthrow of the monarchy and the creation of a new French Republic. **195**

Fuel Administration   Government agency responsible for regulating production and supply of fuel during World War I. **602**

Fugitive Slave Act   Law passed as part of the Compromise of 1850 that made it a federal crime to assist runaway slaves. **343**

Fundamental Orders of Connecticut (1639)   First written constitution in the colonies; adopted by Thomas Hooker's congregation in its Connecticut Valley settlement. **72**

Fundamentalism   Protestant movement whose followers believe in a literal interpretation of the Bible. **656**

G

Gadsden Purchase (1853) Agreement by which the U.S. acquired Mexico's territory south of the Gila River in present-day Arizona and New Mexico for $10 million. **315**

gang labor Work system in which groups of slaves performed specialized jobs. **270**

General Court Massachusetts Bay Colony's elected legislature, which made laws for the colony. **69**

generation gap Difference in years, attitudes, and cultural beliefs between generations; applied to baby boomers and their elders during the 1960s. **852**

genocide Deliberate annihilation of an entire people. **767**

geothermal power Alternative energy source from the earth's interior, such as from geysers and hot springs. **970**

German reunification Reuniting of East Germany and West Germany as one nation in 1990. **959**

GI Bill of Rights (1944) Servicemen's Readjustment Act, which provided pensions and government loans to help veterans start their own businesses, buy homes or farms, and attend college. **784**

Gilded Age Name applied to post–Civil War America to describe the corruption and greed that lurked below the surface of industrial society. **486**

glasnost Policy of openness introduced in the Soviet Union by Mikhail Gorbachev in 1985. **934**

global warming Gradual increase in the temperature of the earth's atmosphere. **972**

Glorious Revolution (1688) Bloodless English rebellion in which the Catholic king James II was replaced by the Protestant rulers Mary and William. **84**

glyph Picture or symbol used in the Olmec and other picture writing systems. **11**

gold standard Monetary system in which each dollar is equal to and redeemable for a set amount of gold. **499**

Good Neighbor policy FDR's policy of promoting goodwill toward Latin America. **728**

government bonds Certificates issued by a government in exchange for loans. **192**

graduated income tax System in which the rate of taxation varies according to income. **499**

Gramm-Rudman-Hollings Act (1985) Federal law requiring across-the-board cuts in government spending when the deficit exceeds a certain point. **933**

Great Awakening Period of religious revival that swept through the colonies in the mid-18th century. **84**

Great Compromise (1787) Plan approved at the Constitutional Convention in which each state, regardless of size, was given an equal voice in the upper house, while representation in the lower house was determined by population. **147**

Great Depression Deep economic downturn that gripped the U.S. between 1929 and the beginning of World War II. **672**

Great Migration Mass movement of Puritans from England to the Americas beginning in 1630. **68** Mass movement of African Americans from the South to the North between 1915 and 1930. **603**

Great Society President Lyndon Johnson's economic and social programs during the 1960s. **841**

Great Upheaval (1886) Year of intense worker strikes and violent labor confrontations in the U.S. **494**

Green parties Environmentalist political parties in Europe. **974**

gross national product Total value of all goods and services produced by a country in a given year. **671**

guerrilla warfare Military tactic of using hit-and-run skirmishes while avoiding direct battles. **131**

H

Haight-Ashbury San Francisco district known for its hippie population during the mid-1960s. **853**

hajj Pilgrimage. **26**

hard-rock mining Technique that involved sinking deep mine shafts to get at ore in quartz veins. **452**

Harlem Renaissance Period of African American artistic development during the 1920s in New York City's Harlem. **660**

Hartford Convention (1814) Meeting of New England Federalists who debated seceding from the Union and negotiating a separate peace with Great Britain during the War of 1812. **215**

hawks People who support war or a warlike policy. **876**

Hay–Bunau-Varilla Treaty (1903) Agreement with Panama giving U.S. control over a 10-mile-wide Canal Zone. **572**

Hay-Herrán Treaty (1903) Proposed agreement with Colombia that would have given the U.S. a lease to build a canal in Panama. **572**

Haymarket Riot (1886) Violent confrontation in Chicago between workers, anarchists, and police that helped turn public support against the labor movement. **494**

Hay-Pauncefote Treaty (1901) Agreement with Great Britain by which the U.S. could build and control a Central American canal. **572**

Hepburn Act (1906) Federal law that authorized the Interstate Commerce Commission to set railroad rates and to regulate other companies engaged in interstate commerce. **540**

Highway Act (1956) Federal law that expanded the nation's highway systems. **817**

hippies Name given to people in the 1960s who rejected everything connected with mainstream America. **853**

Ho Chi Minh Trail Network of jungle paths used by the North Vietnamese to move weapons and supplies to the Vietcong in South Vietnam. **872**

Hollywood Ten Group of film directors and writers who went to jail rather than answer questions from the House Committee on Un-American Activities. **794**

Holocaust Systematic slaughter of European Jews by the Nazis during World War II. **767**

Home Loan Bank Act (1932) Federal law that provided money to savings banks, building and loan associations, and insurance companies for low-interest mortgages. **685**

Home Owners Loan Corporation (HOLC) New Deal agency created in 1933 to grant low-interest, long-term mortgage loans to home owners. **695**

Homestead Act (1862) Federal law that gave public land to any citizen willing to live on the Great Plains and cultivate the land for five years. **436**

horizontal integration Method of expanding a company by buying other companies involved in the same business. **463**

"hot line" Telephone connection between the U.S. and the Soviet Union that allowed leaders to communicate directly during a crisis. **838**

House Committee on Un-American Activities (HUAC) Congressional committee established in 1938 to investigate anti-American propaganda. **794**

House of Burgesses Virginia's colonial governing assembly. **77**

Housing and Urban Development Act (1968) Federal law that, along with the Omnibus Housing Act, provided money for urban renewal and created the Department of Housing and Urban Development. **842**

human rights Basic rights and freedoms to which all people are entitled, including freedom from unlawful detention or torture. **914**

hunter-gatherers   People who moved from place to place in search of game and edible plants. **5**

hydraulic mining   Technique that uses water pressure to remove mountains of gravel, exposing the minerals underneath. **452**

hydrogen bomb   Weapon approximately 1,000 times more powerful than the atomic bomb. **808**

Immigration Act (1990)   Federal law that updated U.S. immigration laws from the 1960s and increased the number of immigrants allowed into the United States each year. **946**

Immigration Act of 1924   Federal law reducing the immigration quota for each nationality to 2 percent of the 1890 figures. **638**

Immigration Restriction League   Group founded in 1894 by well-to-do Bostonians who sought to impose a literacy test on all immigrants. **471**

impeachment   Formal charge of wrongdoing or misconduct brought against a government official. **155**

imperialism   Practice of extending the power of a nation by direct territorial acquisition of colonial empires. **558**

impressment   Practice of kidnapping and forcing people into public service; used by Great Britain in the late 1700s and early 1800s to secure sailors for the British navy. **196**

indentured servant   Person who agreed to work for a specified time for the person who paid his or her way to America. **61**

Indian Removal Act (1830)   Federal law that provided for the relocation of Indian nations living east of the Mississippi River to Indian Territory in present-day Oklahoma. **243**

Indian Reorganization Act (1934)   Federal law that sought to revive tribal rule by funding tribal business ventures and paying for the college education of Native Americans. **710**

Industrial Revolution   Shift from hand production to machine production that began in Great Britain in the mid-1700s. **234**

inflation   Rise in prices resulting from an increase in the amount of money in circulation relative to the amount of goods available for sale. **58**

initiative   Election reform that gives voters the power to introduce legislation. **535**

insider trading   Use of confidential financial information by stockbrokers for personal gain. **933**

interchangeable parts   Parts made in large quantities that can be substituted for other parts during construction of a final product. **234**

Intermediate-range Nuclear Forces (INF) **Treaty** (1987)   Agreement that eliminated all medium-range nuclear weapons from Europe and set up inspection procedures to enforce provisions of the treaty. **934**

internal improvements   Advances in transportation networks such as roads and canals, undertaken at public expense. **228**

Internal Security Act (1950)   Federal law that required Communist party members and organizations to register with the federal government. **795**

Internet   A worldwide computer-based communications and information system. **950**

internment   Imprisonment; practice of forced relocation applied to Japanese Americans living on the West Coast after Pearl Harbor. **754**

Interstate Commerce Act (1887)   Federal law that regulated railroad freight rates and created an agency to monitor railroad activities. **498**

Interstate Commerce Commission (ICC)   Organization created by the Interstate Commerce Act to oversee railroad companies, but having little power of enforcement. **498**

Intolerable Acts (1774)   Series of laws passed by Great Britain to punish Massachusetts for the Boston Tea Party, while strengthening British control over the colonies; also called the Coercive Acts. **111**

Iran-contra affair   Name given to the illegal actions taken by White House aides in the 1980s to fund Nicaraguan contras. **934**

Iran hostage crisis (1979–81)   Period during which 53 Americans in Iran were seized by followers of militant Islamic leader Ayatollah Khomeini in an attempt to force the return of Shah Reza Pahlavi from exile in the U.S. **916**

Iroquois League   Confederation of Indian tribes formed in the 15th or 16th century; also called the Six Nations. **91**

irreconcilables   Fourteen Republican senators who opposed the League of Nations and rejected the Treaty of Versailles after World War I. **609**

island-hopping   Allied military tactic during World War II in which certain strategic Japanese-held islands in the Pacific were seized, while others were bypassed. **762**

isolationism   Policy of avoiding international political or economic alliances; followed by the U.S. during most of the 1920s and 1930s. **724**

Jay's Treaty (1794)   Treaty in which Great Britain agreed to abandon its forts in the Northwest Territory in exchange for U.S. payment of debts owed to the British. **197**

Jim Crow laws   State laws adopted in the South that were designed to enforce segregation. **413**

joint-stock companies   Companies in which investors share the start-up and maintenance costs as well as profits or losses. **59**

Jones Act of 1916   Law that gave Filipinos the right to elect both houses of their legislature, but delayed independence until a stable government was established. **565**

Jones Act of 1917   Law that granted U.S. citizenship to Puerto Ricans and gave them the right to elect both houses of their legislature. **570**

judicial review   Supreme Court's right to determine whether laws violate the U.S. Constitution. **157**

Judiciary Act of 1789   Law that created the federal court system, including district courts, circuit courts of appeals, and the Supreme Court. **191**

juvenile delinquency   Antisocial behavior by the young that is subject to legal action. **826**

K

kamikaze   Japanese planes during World War II assigned to suicide missions against Allied ships. **764**

Kansas-Nebraska Act (1854)   Federal law that established popular sovereignty in newly organized territories and overturned the Missouri Compromise. **347**

Keating-Owen Child Labor Act (1916)   Proposed federal law that outlawed the interstate sale of products produced by child labor. **551**

Kellogg-Briand Pact (1927)   Agreement signed by 62 nations that outlawed war as an instrument of national policy but allowed countries to declare war in self-defense. **726**

Kentucky and Virginia Resolutions   State resolutions passed between 1798 and 1799 that declared states should be the final judge of whether a law was unconstitutional. **202**

Kerner Commission Federal Commission that investigated the 1960s riots and reported that white racism was responsible for the violence. **850**

Klondike Gold Rush Flood of prospectors to the Klondike district of Canada's Yukon Territory in the late 1890s in search of gold. **450**

Knights of Labor National union founded in 1869 that consisted of skilled and unskilled workers. **493**

Know-Nothings Name given to members of the nativist American party prominent during the 1850s. **262**

Kristallnacht "Night of broken glass," November 9, 1938, when Nazis burned down synagogues and destroyed Jewish businesses in Germany. **733**

laissez-faire capitalism Theory that opposes government regulation of economic matters. **462**

Land Ordinance of 1785 Federal law that established a system for surveying western lands by townships and selling smaller parcels to the public. **141**

Landrum-Griffin Act (1959) Federal law designed to reduce corruption in labor unions. **820**

land speculators People who buy land expecting a quick profit from its resale. **91**

League of United Latin American Citizens (LULAC) Hispanic group that lobbied for national awareness of Hispanic concerns and issues. **918**

Lecompton Constitution (1857) Proslavery Kansas constitution that gave voters the right to decide whether more slaves could enter the territory, but not the means to interfere with slavery already present. **349**

Lend-Lease Act (1941) Law that appropriated money for the U.S. to lend or lease arms and other supplies to non-Axis countries. **737**

Lewis and Clark expedition (1804–06) Expedition responsible for mapping the boundaries of the Louisiana Territory and cataloging its natural resources. **208**

limited liability Legal guarantee whereby stockholders are not held responsible for a corporation's debt. **462**

Limited Nuclear Test Ban Treaty (1963) Agreement by the U.S., the Soviet Union, and Great Britain to end the testing of nuclear bombs in the atmosphere or under water. **837**

literacy tests Tests requiring proof of a person's ability to read in order to vote; used in southern states to deny voting rights to African Americans. **412**

"Little Rock Nine" Name given to the African American students who were admitted to an all-white school in Arkansas in 1957. **824**

lockouts Tactic used by employers of barring workers from plants until concessions from workers are obtained. **495**

long drives Overland treks on which cowboys herded cattle from ranches to rail lines. **444**

Long March Exodus of 1934–35 when Communist Chinese marched nearly 6,000 miles to northern China, helping cement Mao Zedong's leadership of the party. **798**

Long Walk Forced march of Navajos to Bosque Redondo, a reservation in eastern New Mexico, following their surrender in early 1864. **435**

loose construction Theory set forth by Alexander Hamilton that the federal government possesses all powers not specifically forbidden by the U.S. Constitution. **193**

Lost Generation Name given by Gertrude Stein to writers of the 1920s whose works expressed disillusionment after World War I. **662**

Louisiana Purchase (1803) U.S. purchase from France of Louisiana for some $15 million. **206**

Lowell girls Single women who worked in the textile mills of Lowell, Massachusetts, in the early 19th century. **257**

Loyalists Americans loyal to Great Britain during the Revolutionary War; also called Tories. **119**

Maastricht Treaty Agreement between European countries that weakened economic barriers and made plans to create a unified monetary system in Europe; ratified in 1993. **964**

Maginot Line Line of defenses built by the French after World War I along their border with Germany. **737**

Magna Carta (1215) Charter signed by King John that limited the power of the English monarch, guaranteed basic liberties for nobles, and protected trade. **20**

mandate system Provision of the Treaty of Versailles that required new colonial rulers to report to the League of Nations on their administration of former Central Power territories. **608**

Manhattan Project Top-secret U.S. project begun in 1942 in which scientists developed the first atomic bomb. **765**

manifest destiny Phrase coined in 1845 to express the belief that the U.S. was destined to extend its boundaries westward to the Pacific Ocean. **306**

Mann-Elkins Act (1910) Federal law that extended the regulatory powers of the Interstate Commerce Commission to telephone and telegraph companies. **543**

manor Land a noble received from the ruler under the feudal system in exchange for military assistance and loyalty. **17**

Marbury v. *Madison* (1803) Legal case in which the Supreme Court first exercised its right of judicial review. **204**

March on Washington (1963) Demonstration in Washington, D.C., called by African American leaders to show support for President Kennedy's civil rights bill. **847**

margin buying Purchasing stock with borrowed money. **670**

Mariposa War (1850–51) California raids by the Miwoks and the Yokuts to reclaim Native American lands taken over by miners. **327**

market revolution Creation of profitable national markets during the 1800s brought about by new transportation systems and regional specialization. **234**

Marshall Plan (1948) U.S. program that provided some $12 billion in economic aid to Western Europe after World War II; also called the European Recovery Act. **792**

mass production Manufacture of large quantities of goods, usually by machines. **234**

mass transit Public transportation systems, such as commuter trains and subways, that made it possible for workers to live farther away from their jobs. **472**

Mayflower Compact (1620) Document that established Plymouth Colony as a self-governing colony based on the majority rule of male church members. **67**

Meat Inspection Act (1906) Federal consumer-protection law that required the government inspection of interstate meat shipments. **540**

Medicaid State programs established in 1965 and funded by Congress to provide free health care to the needy. **842**

Medicare Great Society program established in 1965 to provide national health insurance for people over age 65. **841**

mercantilism Economic policy based on the view that a nation's power depended on maintaining a favorable balance of trade by exporting more goods than it imported. **83**

mergers Combining of two or more companies to achieve greater efficiency and higher profits. **632**

Mesoamerica Area that includes Central America and the southern and central regions of Mexico; also called Middle America. **10**

Mexican Cession (1848) Area surrendered by Mexico to the U.S. in the Treaty of Guadalupe Hidalgo; included the present-day states of California, Nevada, and Utah, and parts of Arizona, Colorado, and New Mexico. **315**

Mexican War (1846–48) Conflict between Mexico and the U.S. brought about by the U.S. annexation of Texas and its quest for more territory. **312**

middle class Social class that occupies a position between the wealthy and the poor. **256**

Middle Passage Voyage made by slave ships from Africa across the Atlantic Ocean during which many slaves suffered and died. **78**

militarism Glorification of armed strength and aggressive military preparedness. **587**

minutemen Members of the colonial militia who promised to be ready at a minute's notice. **114**

Missouri Compromise (1820) Act that maintained the balance of slave and free states in Congress by admitting Missouri as a slave state and Maine as a free state, while prohibiting the spread of slavery in the territories to areas north of latitude 36°30′. **238**

modern Republicanism Name given to President Eisenhower's attempt to balance liberal domestic reforms with conservative spending during the 1950s. **814**

monopoly Exclusive control, such as in trade or industry, that eliminates competition. **28, 462**

Monroe Doctrine (1823) U.S. government policy statement in which the Americas were declared off-limits to European expansion. **231**

Montgomery Improvement Association (MIA) Group of civil rights leaders in Montgomery, Alabama, whose members included Martin Luther King, Jr. **823**

Montreal Protocol on Ozone Depletion (1987) International agreement that set standards for reducing the emission of CFCs and other gases. **974**

Moral Majority Fundamentalist Christian political organization founded in 1978 by Reverend Jerry Falwell. **928**

moratorium Authorized period of delay in paying a debt or fulfilling a legal obligation. **727**

Morrill Act (1862) Federal law that gave land to states to establish agricultural colleges. **436**

mountain men Name given to fur trappers in the Far West. **318**

muckrakers Nickname given by President Theodore Roosevelt to progressive journalists in the early 1900s who exposed political and social evils. **514**

"mugwumps" Nickname for Republican reformers who supported Democratic candidate Grover Cleveland in the 1884 presidential election. **489**

multinational corporations Companies that invest money in a variety of international business ventures. **965**

Munich Conference (1938) Meeting attended by government leaders from Great Britain, Italy, France, and Germany in which a pact was signed giving Germany control of the Sudetenland. **735**

mutualistas Mutual-aid societies formed by Mexican American communities to help local residents. **676**

National Aeronautics and Space Administration (NASA) Federal agency established in 1958 to direct American space exploration. **810**

National Association for the Advancement of Colored People (NAACP) Civil rights organization founded in 1909 to work for various social reforms that would benefit African Americans and end racial discrimination. **527**

national bank Central bank with branches in major cities. **192**

national debt Money owed by the federal government to its creditors. **192**

National Defense Act (1916) Military "preparedness" program established prior to World War I that increased the size of the National Guard and the U.S. regular army. **594**

National Defense Education Act (1958) Federal law that appropriated money to improve education in science, math, and foreign languages. **810**

National Energy Act (1978) Federal law that relaxed controls on the price of natural gas in an effort to ease U.S. dependence on foreign oil. **913**

National Grange Farmers' group founded in 1867 as a social organization that grew into a political force; also called Patrons of Husbandry. **497**

National Industrial Recovery Act (NIRA) Federal law passed in 1933 to stimulate industrial and business activity and to reduce unemployment. **696**

nationalism Sense of pride or loyalty to a nation. **226**

nationalize To assert government control or ownership over a business or industry. **731**

National Organization for Women (NOW) Group founded by feminists in 1966 to promote equal rights for women. **854**

National Recovery Administration (NRA) Federal agency that encouraged businesses to draw up "codes of fair competition" as one means of achieving business recovery during the Great Depression. **697**

National Security Council (NSC) Organization created in 1947 by Congress to advise the president on strategic matters. **794**

National War Labor Board (NWLB) Group of representatives from business and labor who arbitrated disputes between workers and employers during World War I. **602**

National Youth Administration (NYA) New Deal agency that provided part-time jobs to people between the ages of 16 and 25. **702**

nativism Policy of favoring native-born Americans over immigrants. **261**

Navigation Acts (1651) Series of mercantilist laws designed to increase English merchants' profits by limiting direct trade between English colonies and other European nations. **83**

Nazi party Political party, led by Adolf Hitler, that controlled Germany from 1933 to 1945; also called the National Socialist party. **733**

New Deal President Franklin Roosevelt's program of providing relief and recovery to the U.S. during the Great Depression. **694**

New England Way Cooperation between church and state that was the basis for the Puritan commonwealth. **69**

New Freedom Name given to Woodrow Wilson's progressive program of reform as proposed during the 1912 presidential election. **546**

New Frontier President John Kennedy's political, social, and economic programs of the early 1960s. **833**

new immigrants People, mostly southern and eastern Europeans, who came to the United States in the late 1800s and early 1900s. **466**

Newlands Reclamation Act (1902) Federal law that allowed money from the sale of public land to be used for irrigation and reclamation. **541**

New Nationalism Name given to Theodore Roosevelt's program of social legislation first proposed during the 1910 congressional elections. **545**

New Right Conservatives who showed increased political influence during the 1980s. **928**

Nine Power Treaty (1921) Agreement arising from the Washington Conference that guaranteed China's territorial integrity and promised to uphold the Open Door policy. **725**

Nineteenth Amendment (1920) Constitutional amendment that granted women full voting rights. **552**

no-man's land Thin strip of territory along the Western Front that separated opposing armies during World War I. **589**

nonaggression pact (1939) Temporary alliance in which Germany and the Soviet Union agreed to divide Poland between them. **736**

nonimportation agreements Documents signed by colonial merchants promising not to buy or import British goods. **107**

Non-Intercourse Act (1809) Federal law that prohibited U.S. trade with Great Britain and France. **212**

nonviolent resistance Strategy of peaceful protest. **844**

North American Free Trade Agreement (NAFTA) International treaty ratified in 1993 to relax trade barriers between the U.S., Canada, and Mexico. **965**

North Atlantic Treaty Organization (NATO) Alliance formed in 1949 whose member nations agreed to protect one another in the event of attack. **793**

Northwest Ordinance (1787) Federal law that established a system for governing the Northwest Territory; also called the Land Ordinance of 1787. **142**

northwest passage Northern water route from Europe to Asia sought by early European explorers. Many European claims in North America resulted from the search for such a route. **56**

Northwest Territory Area organized in 1787 that extended north of the Ohio River to the Great Lakes and west of Pennsylvania to the Mississippi River. **142**

Nuremberg trials Trials of Nazi war criminals by the Allies that began in 1945. **781**

Occupational Safety and Health Administration (OSHA) Federal agency created in 1970 to protect workers from unhealthful working conditions. **903**

Office of Economic Opportunity (OEO) Government agency formed in 1964 to coordinate antipoverty programs, including the Job Corps, VISTA, and Head Start. **840**

Okies Negative term for farmers, many from Oklahoma, who migrated in 1939 to the West Coast to find work. **714**

old immigrants People, generally Protestants from northwestern Europe, who came to the U.S. between 1800 and 1880. **466**

Olive Branch Petition (1775) Final plea for peace sent by the Second Continental Congress to King George III. **116**

Omnibus Housing Act (1965) Federal law that, together with the Housing and Urban Development Act of 1968, provided money for urban renewal and housing assistance for low-income families. **842**

Open Door policy (1899) U.S. policy, proposed by Secretary of State John Hay, that called for all nations to have equal access to trade and investment in China. **567**

open range Grazing land that the government allowed cattle ranchers to use in the late 1800s. **446**

open shops Nonunion workplaces. **520**

Operation Desert Storm (1991) U.S. military mission that joined allies in driving Iraqi forces from Kuwait. **938**

Operation Restore Hope (1992) United Nations plan to ensure that relief efforts reached famine-stricken Somalia. **960**

Operation Rolling Thunder U.S. bombing campaign against military targets in North Vietnam that began in 1965. **872**

Orders in Council (1807) British acts that forbade neutral vessels from trading with France or from entering ports under French control. **211**

Oregon Country Disputed area of Pacific Northwest occupied jointly by the U.S. and Great Britain after the War of 1812. **229**

Oregon Trail Route to Oregon Country during the 1800s. **318**

Organization of Petroleum Exporting Countries (OPEC) Group of oil-producing countries, mainly Arab, formed in 1960 to get higher prices for oil exports. **902**

override Constitutional power that allows Congress to overrule a presidential veto with a two-thirds vote. **155**

overseers People who supervise workers. **269**

ozone layer Thin veil of molecules, located some 10 to 30 miles above the earth's surface, that protects the earth from UV rays. **972**

pacification Military tactic used by U.S. troops during the Vietnam War that involved moving residents to refugee camps and burning their villages. **874**

Pacific Railway Act (1862) Federal law that gave land for development of a transcontinental railroad. **436**

Pacific Rim Countries on the western edge of the Pacific Ocean. **964**

Paleo-Indians First people who crossed Beringia into North America during the last Ice Age. **4**

Palmer raids (1919–20) Raids to capture alleged radicals; launched by Attorney General A. Mitchell Palmer during the Red Scare. **626**

Panama Canal treaties (1978) Agreements granting Panama control over canal operations by the year 2000. **914**

Pan-German movement German plan prior to World War I to unite all German-speaking peoples under one flag. **586**

Panic of 1819 Economic collapse caused in part by the Second Bank of the United States' attempt to curb lending policies of state banks. **236**

Pan-Slavic movement Russian plan to bring together all Slavic peoples of central and eastern Europe, in direct opposition to the Pan-German movement of the early 1900s. **586**

partnerships Business enterprises that are owned by two or more people who are responsible for the businesses' debts. **462**

patio **process** Mining technique developed in Mexico and South America during the 1700s that used mercury to extract silver from ore; used in the western U.S. **449**

Peace Corps Program established by President John Kennedy in the early 1960s that sends volunteers to developing countries. **835**

Pendleton Civil Service Act (1883) Federal law that created a Civil Service Commission to administer competitive examinations to those seeking government jobs. **488**

Pentagon Papers Secret government documents, published in 1971, that showed how the government had misled Americans about the Vietnam War. **882**

peons   Landless laborers, mostly Indians, who worked on Spanish haciendas. **53**

perestroika   Mikhail Gorbachev's plan to restructure the Soviet economy and government during the late 1980s. **934**

pet banks   State banks that received deposits of federal funds because of their officers' loyalty to the Democratic party and to President Andrew Jackson. **247**

philanthropy   Charitable efforts to promote public welfare, such as financing libraries, museums, and art galleries; endowing universities; and establishing theater or music groups. **474**

Philippine Government Act (1902)   Federal law decreeing that the Philippines would be ruled by a governor and a two-house legislature. **564**

Pilgrims   People who left England because of religious conflict and sailed aboard the *Mayflower* to North America, where they founded Plymouth Colony in 1620. **66**

Pinckney's Treaty (1795)   Agreement negotiated with Spain that set the southern boundary of the U.S. near Florida at the 31st parallel. **197**

planned obsolescence   Practice of making products that are designed to go out of style. **664**

Platt Amendment   Addition to Cuba's constitution, enacted in 1902 and renounced in 1934, that gave the U.S. greater control over Cuban affairs. **569**

Plessy v. Ferguson (1896)   Supreme Court case in which the court upheld segregation by ruling that "separate but equal" facilities did not violate the Fourteenth Amendment. **414**

political machines   Political organizations, headed by bosses, that used appointments to government jobs to control elections. **469**

poll taxes   Fixed taxes imposed on every voter by southern states in an effort to deprive African Americans of the right to vote. **412**

Pontiac's Rebellion (1763)   Indian war led by Ottawa chief Pontiac against settlers of western lands. **105**

pop art   Art form begun in the 1960s that uses everyday objects as subject matter or in the works themselves. **854**

popular sovereignty   Right of the people to rule, used as an argument for letting citizens of each new territory decide whether to permit slavery there. **339**

Populist party   Political party founded by farmers, labor leaders, and reformers in 1892; also called the People's party. **499**

Potsdam Conference (1945)   Overseas meeting attended by the U.S., Britain, and the Soviet Union that laid the foundation for Germany's postwar status. **780**

Pottawatomie Massacre (1856)   Revenge attack by antislavery raiders, led by John Brown on proslavery settlers along Pottawatomie Creek in Kansas. **348**

precedent   Action that may serve as a guide for future, similar actions. **190**

Proclamation of 1763   Declaration issued by Great Britain that barred settlement west of the Appalachian Mountains. **105**

progressivism   Reform movement concerned with curing the ills caused by industrialization. **512**

prohibition   Legal ban on the manufacture, transportation, and sale of alcoholic beverages. **289**

proprietorships   Small businesses owned by individuals or families. **462**

protectionism   Practice of imposing higher tariffs and stricter barriers against foreign exports in an effort to encourage Americans to purchase domestic goods. **966**

protectorate   Country dependent on another for protection. **569**

Protestant Reformation   Religious upheaval in Europe begun by Martin Luther in 1517 to protest corruption in the Roman Catholic church. **57**

Public Works Administration (PWA)   New Deal agency established in 1933 that contracted with private firms to construct roads, public buildings, and similar projects. **697**

Pueblo Revolt (1680)   Attacks by the Pueblo Indians that temporarily drove the Spanish from New Mexico. **51**

Pure Food and Drug Act (1906)   Federal consumer-protection law that provided for government inspection of food and drugs. **540**

Puritans   English Protestants who sought to "purify" the Anglican church of Catholic rituals and traditions. **66**

Quartering Act (1765)   Law enacted by Parliament requiring the colonists to house and supply British troops. **109**

Quebec Act (1774)   Law enacted by Parliament extending Quebec's boundaries south to the Ohio River and granting full religious rights to French Roman Catholics. **112**

Qur'an   Holy book of Islam. **23**

railhead   Town located along a railroad; long cattle drives usually ended there. **445**

Railroad Administration   Federal agency that reorganized railroads and set limits on transportation rates and workers' wages during World War I. **602**

Reaganomics   President Ronald Reagan's economic program built on big tax cuts to encourage business investment. **928**

realpolitik   Approach to foreign policy, adopted by Henry Kissinger and President Richard Nixon, that emphasized national interests over moral or ethical concerns. **903**

recall   Election reform that allows voters to remove an elected official from office by calling for a new election. **535**

reclamation   Process of making damaged land productive. **541**

Reconquista   Ongoing battle to recapture Spanish lands from the Moors that ended in 1492. **22**

Reconstruction   Rebuilding of the former Confederate states to reunite the nation. **395**

Reconstruction Acts (1867)   Federal laws that gave radical Republicans military control of the South. **402**

Reconstruction Finance Corporation (RFC)   Federal agency created in 1932 to stimulate the economy by lending money to railroads, insurance companies, banks, and other financial institutions. **685**

recycling   Collection and processing of used items for reuse. **973**

Red Scare (1919–20)   Period of anti-Communist hysteria after the Bolshevik Revolution in Russia. **625**

referendum   Election reform that allows voters to place a measure on the ballot. **535**

regionalists   Midwestern artists popular in the 1930s who stressed local folk themes and customs in their work. **719**

rehabilitation   Treatment to restore someone to a useful and constructive place in society. **287**

Rehabilitation Act (1973)   Federal law forbidding discrimination in education, in jobs, or in housing because of physical disabilities. **919**

Relocation Act (1956)   Federal law passed to relocate Native Americans to urban areas. **815**

Renaissance   Rebirth of European art and learning spurred by the Crusades. **20**

rendezvous system   Arrangement to cut costs and increase profits in the Rocky Mountain fur trade by having trappers gather once a year to sell furs and buy supplies. **318**

reparations   Payments of damages. **607**

republic   Form of government in which leaders receive authority from citizens to make and enforce laws. **138**

reservationists   Republican senators who would support the Treaty of Versailles only if the League Covenant were amended. **609**

reserved powers   Powers kept by the states because they are not specifically granted to the federal government or denied to the states by the U.S. Constitution. **154**

right of deposit   Right to temporarily unload goods at a port without paying a duty. **198**

rock 'n' roll   Popular music introduced in the 1950s that reworked black rhythm and blues. **826**

Roe v. *Wade* (1973)   Supreme Court case that overturned a state law limiting a woman's access to an abortion. **921**

Roosevelt Corollary (1904)   Policy that extended the Monroe Doctrine by allowing the U.S. a greater role in maintaining peace and order in the Western Hemisphere. **573**

rotation in office   Periodic replacement of officeholders. **241**

rugged individualism   Idea that success comes through individual effort and private enterprise. **683**

Rural Electrification Administration (REA)   New Deal agency that brought electricity to isolated rural areas. **702**

Rush-Bagot Agreement (1817)   Disarmament plan between the U.S. and Great Britain that limited each nation's military presence on the Great Lakes to a few armed ships. **229**

Russo-Japanese War (1904–05)   War between Russia and Japan that began with a Japanese attack on Russian forces in Manchuria. **568**

Sand Creek Massacre (1864)   Slaughter of Cheyenne Indians by U.S. troops in Colorado Territory. **427**

Sandinistas   Nicaraguan rebels who overthrew the dictatorship of Anastasio Somoza Debayle in 1979. **931**

Santa Fe Trail   Trail between Missouri and Santa Fe, New Mexico, important for taking merchandise to the West. **317**

satellite nations   Countries under the control of the Soviet Union. **789**

Saturday Night Massacre (1973)   Resignation and firing of top government officials who refused to aid President Richard Nixon in the Watergate cover-up. **908**

scalawags   Southern whites who backed the Union and supported Reconstruction after the Civil War. **406**

scientific management   Theory, promoted by Frederick W. Taylor, that every kind of work could be broken into a series of smaller tasks and that rates of production could be set for each component task. **647**

scrip   Paper money that workers in company towns received as wages. **493**

search-and-destroy missions   Military attacks that involve looking for and annihilating hidden enemy troops. **873**

Second Battle of Bull Run (1862)   Union defeat during the Civil War that led to General McClellan's appointment as commander of Union forces in the east. **377**

Second Continental Congress (1775)   Convention held in Philadelphia during which the delegates established the Continental Army and chose George Washington as its commander. **114**

Second Great Awakening   Renewal of religious faith that swept the U.S. beginning in the 1790s. **282**

Second New Deal   Government programs passed after the 1934 elections that provided relief and recovery but emphasized reform. **701**

Second Seminole War (1835–1842)   Resistance by the Seminoles to their removal from Florida; cost more money and lives than any other Indian war in U.S. history. **244**

sectionalism   Loyalty to a particular area of the country. **198**

sedition   Act of stirring up discontent or rebellion against a government or other lawful authority. **202**

Sedition Act (1918)   Federal law enacted during World War I that made written criticism of the government a crime. **605**

segregation   Separation of the races. **413**

Selective Service Act (1917)   Federal law that required men to register with local draft boards. **595**

Selective Training and Service Act (1940)   Federal law that provided for America's first peacetime draft. **753**

self-determination   Right of people to govern themselves. **606**

Seneca Falls Convention (1848)   Meeting held in Seneca Falls, New York, that marked the birth of the organized women's rights movement in the U.S. **298**

separation of powers   Allotment of powers between the legislative, executive, and judicial branches of government to prevent any one branch from becoming too powerful. **155**

Separatists   Radical group of Puritans, including the Pilgrims, who separated from the Church of England and came to North America seeking religious freedom. **66**

serfs   People who lived on a feudal manor and worked the lord's land in exchange for crops and protection. **17**

settlement houses   Community centers in poor neighborhoods that provided food, shelter and other services. **476**

Seven Days' Campaign (1862)   Civil War battle in which Confederate troops forced General McClellan to retreat before he could take Richmond. **377**

Seventeenth Amendment (1913)   Constitutional amendment that provided for the direct election of United States senators. **535**

sexual harassment   Use of unwelcome sexual language or behavior that creates a hostile working environment. **940**

shantytowns   Makeshift shelters built by homeless people; for example, the Hoovervilles that were built during the Great Depression. **677**

sharecropping   Arrangement under which a sharecropper agreed to work a parcel of land in return for a share of the crop, a cabin, seed, tools, and a mule. **410**

Share-Our-Wealth (1933)   Radical relief program proposed by Senator Huey Long to empower the government to confiscate wealth from the rich through taxes and provide a guaranteed minimum income and home to every family. **701**

Shays's Rebellion (1786–87)   Farmers' revolt against high taxes and heavy debts, led by Daniel Shays. **144**

Sherman Antitrust Act (1890)   Federal law that declared monopolies and trusts illegal. **464**

Sherman Silver Purchase Act (1890)   Federal law that required the government to buy silver each month and mint it into coins. **499**

silent generation   Name given to middle-class youth of the 1950s who seemed willing to conform to consumer culture without protest. **826**

silent majority   Name given by President Richard Nixon to middle-class voters weary from the social upheaval of the 1960s. **900**

sit-down strike   Work stoppage in which workers occupy factories until management meets their demands. **705**

sit-in   Strategy of nonviolent protest in which a group enters a public place and refuses to leave. **844**

Sixteenth Amendment (1913)   Constitutional amendment that authorized an individual income tax. **543**

Smoot-Hawley Tariff (1930)   High-tariff law that contributed to the global economic downturn of the 1930s. **674**

Social Darwinism   Theory, proposed in the late 1800s, that society progressed through competition, with the fittest rising to positions of wealth and power. **462**

Social Gospel   Movement by Protestant ministers in the late 1800s that called for people to apply Christian principles to address social problems. **477**

socialism   System under which government or worker cooperatives own all means of production and distribution. **520**

Social Security Act (1935)   Federal law that provided a system of unemployment compensation and retirement pensions. **702**

Society of American Indians   Organization formed by Native Americans to address Indian problems. **528**

Solidarity   Polish independent trade union and social movement that was formed in 1980. **930**

Sons of Liberty   Secret groups of Patriots formed in 1765 to oppose the Stamp Act and to protest British authority in the colonies. **107**

Southern Christian Leadership Conference (SCLC)   Alliance of church-based African American organizations formed in 1957 and dedicated to ending discrimination. **844**

southern strategy   President Richard Nixon's plan to woo conservative southern white voters away from the Democratic party by cutting back on new civil rights legislation. **901**

Southern Tenant Farmers' Union (STFU)   Arkansas sharecroppers who lobbied government in 1934 to halt tenant evictions and to force landowners to share payments with tenants. **698**

space shuttle   Reusable space vehicle first launched by NASA in 1981. **951**

Spanish-American War (1898)   War declared by the U.S. on Spain to protect U.S. investments and to help Cuba overthrow Spanish rule. **560**

Spanish Armada   Spanish naval force defeated by England in 1588. **58**

Spanish Civil War   War that began in 1936 between Fascists and Loyalists in Spain. **733**

specie   Gold or silver coins that a bank held to back up its notes. **226**

Specie Circular (1836)   Executive order issued by President Andrew Jackson instructing the Treasury to accept only gold and silver as payment for public land. **247**

spheres of influence   Ports or regions in a nation where a foreign country retains exclusive rights over trade, mines, and railroads. **566**

spirituals   Songs that are rich in Biblical lore. **275**

spoils system   Political practice, introduced by Andrew Jackson, of giving government jobs to supporters. **241**

Sputnik (1957)   Satellite launched by the Soviet Union that led the U.S. to focus more on technological development. **810**

Square Deal   Theodore Roosevelt's 1904 presidential campaign slogan pledging fair treatment for business, workers, and the public. **539**

stagflation   Economic condition in which inflation is accompanied by unemployment. **902**

Stamp Act (1765)   Law enacted by Parliament that placed a tax on all printed matter in the colonies. **106**

Stamp Act Congress (1765)   Delegates from nine colonies who gathered in New York City to seek repeal of the Stamp Act and to deny Parliament's right to tax the colonies. **107**

stock   Certificates of ownership in a company. **462**

stockholders   Owners of certificates in a corporation who receive a certain percentage of the corporation's profits through dividends. **462**

Strategic Arms Limitation Talks (SALT)   Agreement between the U.S. and the Soviet Union, limiting the number of intercontinental nuclear missiles each nation could have. **904**

Strategic Defense Initiative (SDI)   Space-based missile-defense system proposed by President Ronald Reagan in the 1980s to blunt the nuclear-freeze movement; also called "Star Wars." **930**

strict construction   Theory set forth by Thomas Jefferson that the federal government possesses only those powers that the U.S. Constitution specifically allows. **193**

strike   Tactic used by labor unions in which workers refuse to work until employers meet union demands. **258**

strikebreakers   Nonunion workers brought in by a company to replace striking workers. **495**

Student Nonviolent Coordinating Committee (SNCC)   Association formed in 1960 by student activists from throughout the South. **844**

subsidies   Payments made to farmers to reduce their production of a crop or commodity. **698**

subsistence farming   Growing just enough crops for survival. **8**

suburbs   Residential areas beyond city limits that came about partly as a result of mass transit. **473**

suffrage   Right to vote. **299**

Sugar Act (1764)   Law enacted by Parliament that set an import tax on foreign sugar, molasses, and other goods to the colonies. **106**

Sunbelt   Southern and western states having warm climates and suburban life-styles. **922**

superpowers   Nations that possess great power and become dominant in global politics. **768**

supremacy clause   Clause in the U.S. Constitution stating that the federal constitution and all federal laws outrank state constitutions and state laws. **155**

Sussex **pledge** (1916)   Promise by Germany not to sink ocean liners without warning or without assuring the passengers' safety. **593**

Swahili   Bantu language spoken by people in East Africa. **25**

Taft-Hartley Act (1947)   Federal law that extended government regulation of labor unions and included a provision allowing courts to end strikes. **785**

Tariff Act of 1816   Federal law that placed a 25 percent duty on most imported factory goods. **227**

tariffs   Taxes on goods. **148**

task system   System in which plantation slaves were given specific duties each day. **81**

Tax Reform Law (1986)   Federal law that eliminated special tax breaks for certain groups. **933**

Tea Act (1773)   Law enacted by Parliament that allowed the British East India Company to sell tea directly to American agents without paying certain duties. **111**

Teapot Dome scandal (1926)   Scandal in which Secretary of the Interior Albert Fall was convicted of accepting bribes for leasing the government oil reserve in Teapot Dome, Wyoming, to private oil companies. **630**

Teller Amendment (1898)   Act that stated the U.S. claimed no sovereignty, jurisdiction, or control over Cuba. **560**

temperance movement   Reform efforts to curb or limit alcohol consumption. **288**

Tennessee Valley Authority (TVA)   New Deal agency created in 1933 to develop power stations and dams throughout the Tennessee River Valley. **699**

termination   Government policy during the 1950s designed to end the reservation system. **816**

Tet offensive (1968)   North Vietnamese attack on South Vietnam during Tet, the Vietnamese New Year. **879**

Texas longhorn Hardy breed of cattle developed by the 1850s that helped make long drives possible. **444**

Texas Revolution (1835) Revolt against Mexico by Tejanos and American settlers in Texas after the loss of state power. **308**

Third UN Conference on the Law of the Sea (1982) International conference in which participating nations agreed to protect the world's oceans. **974**

Thirteenth Amendment (1865) Constitutional amendment that abolished slavery. **398**

38th parallel Border between North Korea and South Korea set by the Allies in 1945. **799**

Three-Fifths Compromise (1787) Agreement made at the Constitutional Convention that counted only three fifths of the slave population in determining total state population. **148**

Toleration Act (1649) Maryland colonial law that guaranteed religious freedom to all Christians. **74**

Tonkin Gulf Resolution (1964) Act that gave the president authority to take all necessary measures to repel an armed attack against U.S. forces. **870**

total war Strategy used in the Civil War of striking at the enemy's economic resources in addition to fighting enemy troops. **387**

Townshend Acts (1767) Law enacted by Parliament that placed duties on goods imported by the colonies. **109**

Trail of Tears (1838) Forced relocation of Cherokees from Georgia to Indian Territory, during which many died. **244**

Trans-Appalachian West Area between the Appalachian Mountains and the Mississippi River. **205**

transcendentalists New England intellectuals who believed people could attain perfection and could acquire knowledge about God, self, and the universe. **285**

treason Offense of openly attempting to overthrow a government to which a person owes allegiance, or of killing or personally harming the head of that government or his or her family. **164**

Treaty of Brest-Litovsk (1918) Agreement signed by the Bolsheviks in which Russia made a separate peace with the Central Powers and withdrew from World War I. **598**

Treaty of Fort Laramie (1851) Agreement that set boundaries for Native American groups and allowed the U.S. government to build roads and forts through Indian Territory. **321**

Treaty of Ghent Agreement signed in 1814 that ended the War of 1812. **214**

Treaty of Greenville (1795) Agreement with Native Americans that gave the U.S. title to Native American lands that make up much of present-day Ohio and part of Indiana. **197**

Treaty of Guadalupe Hidalgo Agreement ending the Mexican War in 1848 by which Mexico ceded Texas and the rest of its western territory. **313**

Treaty of Medicine Lodge (1867) Agreement that ended a long-standing war between the Sioux and the U.S. **428**

Treaty of Paris (1783) Agreement signed by Great Britain and the U.S. granting the U.S. independence, territory, and fishing rights. **132**

Treaty of Tordesillas (1494) Agreement that divided control over new territories in the Americas between Spain and Portugal. **45**

Treaty of Versailles (1919) Agreement ending World War I that provided for the establishment of the League of Nations. **608**

trench warfare Strategy used during World War I in which opposing armies fought from behind fixed fortifications. **589**

Triple Alliance Military alliance formed by Germany, Austria-Hungary, and Italy prior to World War I. **587**

Triple Entente Military alliance formed by Great Britain, France, and Russia prior to World War I. **587**

Truman Doctrine U.S. policy of giving military and financial aid to those countries resisting Communist rule. **791**

trunk lines Major railroads connected to surrounding areas by feeder or branch lines. **459**

trust Group of companies that give control of their stock to a board of directors, which then runs the companies as a single enterprise. **462**

Tweed Ring Corrupt political organization that controlled New York City government during the Gilded Age. **486**

Twelfth Amendment (1804) Constitutional amendment that requires electors to vote for presidential and vice-presidential candidates on separate ballots. **203**

Twenty-first Amendment (1933) Constitutional amendment that repealed Prohibition. **656**

Twenty-sixth Amendment (1971) Constitutional amendment that lowered the voting age from 21 to 18. **884**

U

ultraviolet solar radiation (UV rays) Radiation from the sun that can cause skin cancer, damage marine life, and harm crops. **972**

unconditional surrender Arrangement whereby the loser agrees to the terms of the victor. **750**

Underground Railroad Network that helped slaves escape to the North or Canada before the Civil War. **273**

Underwood Tariff Act (1913) Federal law that reduced tariffs to their lowest levels in 50 years. **549**

unilateralism One-sided or independent action in foreign affairs. **724**

United Farm Workers (UFW) Organization of migrant workers formed to win better wages and working conditions. **851**

United Nations (UN) International organization formed in 1945 to work for world peace. **783**

University of California v. *Bakke* (1978) Supreme Court decision that struck down quotas as a means of achieving racial equality; in institutions of higher learning, for example. **920**

urban renewal Programs designed to replace or restore run-down inner-city buildings. **821**

U.S. Department of Agriculture Government agency created in 1862 to help farmers. **440**

utopias Ideal communities. **284**

V

vertical integration Strategy whereby one company acquires other companies that provide materials and services necessary to the first company. **463**

veto Power to reject a proposed law. **155**

viceroy Governor who rules a country in place of a king. **39**

Vietcong Vietnamese Communists. **868**

Vietminh Resistance movement organized by Ho Chi Minh in 1941; also known as the League for the Independence of Vietnam. **866**

Vietnamization President Richard Nixon's plan to end the Vietnam War by turning over the fighting to the South Vietnamese army and withdrawing U.S. troops. **881**

Virginia Plan James Madison's proposal during the Constitutional Convention of shifting power away from the states toward a central government. **146**

Virginia Statute for Religious Freedom (1786) Virginia state law that called for separation of church and state. **139**

Volstead Act (1919)   Federal law that enforced the Eighteenth Amendment (Prohibition). **656**

Voting Rights Act (1965)   Federal law that put voter registration under government control. **848**

Voting Rights Act of 1975   Federal law requiring states and communities with large numbers of non-English speakers to print voting materials in various foreign languages. **923**

Wagner-Connery Act (1935)   Federal law that guaranteed labor's right to organize unions and bargain for better wages and working conditions. **705**

War Industries Board (WIB)   U.S. agency during World War I responsible for allocating scarce materials, establishing production priorities, and setting prices. **602**

war of attrition   Civil War strategy of wearing down the Confederates through constant attack. **386**

War on Poverty   President Lyndon Johnson's Great Society programs designed to end poverty in the U.S. **840**

War Powers Act (1973)   Federal law limiting the president's power to send U.S. troops to foreign conflicts. **888**

War Production Board (WPB)   Government agency during World War II that directed the conversion of existing factories to wartime production. **752**

Warren Commission   Group assigned in 1963 to investigate the assassination of President John Kennedy. **839**

Warsaw Pact (1955)   Alliance formed by the Soviet Union and other Communist countries in Eastern Europe. **794**

Water Quality Improvement Act (1970)   Federal law requiring oil companies to pay some oil spill cleanup costs and setting limits on discharge of industrial pollutants into water. **903**

Watergate   Name given to government scandal that began in 1972 and led to President Richard Nixon's resignation in 1974. **906**

Wealth Tax Act (1935)   Federal law that sharply increased taxes on the rich. **702**

Whiskey Rebellion (1794)   Uprising by western Pennsylvania farmers against a tax on whiskey. **194**

Wilmot Proviso (1846)   Proposed constitutional amendment that would have banned slavery in all lands acquired from Mexico. **339**

Wisconsin Idea   Program of progressive reforms proposed by Wisconsin governor Robert M. "Fighting Bob" La Follette during the early 1900s. **537**

Woman's Christian Temperance Union (WCTU)   Reform group in favor of temperance, moral purity, and the rights of women. **525**

Woodstock (1969)   Three-day rock concert in upstate New York that was one of the high points of the counterculture movement. **857**

Worcester **v.** *Georgia* (1832)   Supreme Court decision that forbade the state of Georgia to seize Cherokee lands. **244**

Works Progress Administration (WPA)   New Deal agency formed in 1935 to create jobs for people on relief. **701**

Wounded Knee Massacre (1890)   Massacre that occurred between the Sioux on Wounded Knee Creek and the army sent to confiscate the Indians' rifles. **432**

writ of *habeas corpus*   Legal document that forces a jailer to release a person from prison unless the person has been formally charged with, or convicted of, a crime. **164**

writs of assistance   Search warrants issued to aid customs officers in the search for smuggled goods. **109**

XYZ affair (1797)   Foreign policy scandal in which the French sought bribes from U.S. diplomats before beginning treaty negotiations. **201**

Yalta Conference (1945)   Postwar peace meeting between the U.S., Britain, and the Soviet Union in which plans were made to divide and occupy Germany. **761**

yellow journalism   Newspaper stories that featured sensationalized reporting. **478**

yellow-dog contracts   Agreements many job applicants signed, promising not to join unions. **495**

yeoman farmers   Small farmers who own and cultivate their own land. **267**

zaibatsu   Huge corporations run by single families that had monopolized the Japanese economy prior to World War II. **781**

zero population growth (ZPG)   Birthrate that replaces existing population but does not increase it. **922**

Zimmermann Note (1917)   Document that showed that Germany was trying to establish a military alliance with Mexico. **594**

Zionism   Movement, originally intended to promote the founding of a Jewish national state, that called for a Jewish homeland in Palestine. **796**

zoot-suit riots (1943)   Racial attacks by U.S. sailors on Mexican American youths in Los Angeles. **757**

INDEX

circle graph, 997
circumnavigate, 45, *m45*
CIS. *See* Commonwealth of Independent States
Cisneros, Henry, 942
cities: in colonial America, 76; culture in, 478-79, *p478, p479;* growth of, in 1800s, 235, *c235, m473, c508,* 772-73; impact of railroads, 459; impact of skyscrapers, 472, 664; impact of technology, 472-73, *p472;* middle classes in, 474-75, *p474;* planning in, 523, *p523,* 525; poor in, 475, *p475;* population of, *c360, c361,* 860; reforms in, 476-77, *p477,* 522-23, *p523,* 536-37; upper classes in, 473-74, *p473. See also* specific cities
city-states, East African, 25-27, *m26*
Civilian Conservation Corps (CCC), 696, *p696, c703,* 708
civil liberties, 163
Civil Rights Act (1866), 400-01, *p401,* 409
Civil Rights Act (1957), 825
Civil Rights Act (1964), 847, 854
Civil Rights Bill (1875), 408, *p408*
Civil Rights Cases (1883), 413-14
civil rights movement: and affirmative action, 919; backlash against, 919-20, *p919;* and *Brown* v. *The Board of Education,* 822-23, 842; Committee on Civil Rights, 786; events in, *c846-50, p892, p893;* Freedom Rides in, 845, *m845, p845;* and Freedom Summer, 847-48; for Hispanic Americans, 851, 918; legacy of, 918-19; and March on Washington, *p830-31,* 846-47; under Martin Luther King, Jr., 823, 844, *p844,* 850; Montgomery bus boycott in, 823-24, *p823;* for Native Americans, 851, 920-21; nonviolence in, 844; and people with disabilities, 918-19, *p919;* and segregation fight in Little Rock, 824-25, *p824, p825;* successes and setbacks in, 846. *See also* women's rights movement
Civil War: African Americans in, 334, *p369,* 384-85, *p385;* American Indians in, 334, 369; armies in, 368-69, *p373, p390, p391;* battles in, *p362-63,* 371-72, *p371,* 376-88, *m377, p378, p379, p386, m387, p387;* casualties of, *p389;* comparison of sides, 366-68, *c367;* consequences of, 389, 394-95; and Crittenden Compromise, 364; declaration of sides in, 366, *m366;* European response to, 367, 372-73; fall of Fort Sumter in, 365, *p365;* literature of, 419; Mexican Americans in, 369; military experience in, 335, 373-74, 391; northern opposition to, 374-75, *p374, p375;* strategies in, 372-73, 383; surrender in, 388, *p388;* war in the West, 380-82, *m382;* women in, 334, 369-70, *p370*

Civil Works Administration (CWA), 696, *c703*
Clansman, The (Dixon), 409
Clapton, Eric, 276
Clark, Dick, *p826*
Clark, George Rogers, 131, 132
Clark, William, 208-09, *m209*
Clay, Henry: and American System, 227; and election of 1824, 238-39; and election of 1832, 247; and Latin American rebellions, 230; and Missouri Compromise, 238; as secretary of state, 239; and slavery issue, 340-42; and tariff issue, 246; and Texas annexation, 311; and War of 1812, 212; as Whig, 248
Clayton Antitrust Act (1914), 549
Clayton-Bulwer Treaty (1850), 570
Clean Air Act (1970), 903
Clean Water Act (1972), 973
clear-cutting, 89
Clemenceau, Georges, 607, *p607*
Clemens, Samuel Langhorne. *See* Twain, Mark
Clermont (steamboat), *p232,* 233
Cleveland, Grover, 490, *p490;* in election of 1984, 489; and immigration, 471; and labor movement, 496
Cleveland, OH: African American school in, 290; planning in, 523, 525
Clifford, Clark, 878
Clifton, Peter, 269, 272
Clinton, Bill, 941, *p941,* 944, *p944;* appointments of, 942; and bombing of Iraqi Intelligence Service, 962; and Bosnian crisis, 963; economy under, 943-44; in election of 1992, *p240,* 927, 943; and Family and Medical Leave Act, 949; and health care reform, 942; and Middle East accord, 960
Clinton, George, *m129,* 132, 150
Clinton, Hillary Rodham, 941-42, *p941*
closed shop, 520
Clovis points, 7, *p7*
Coalition of Labor Union Women, 856
cocaine, 975
Cold War, 789, *c800, m811;* and Berlin crisis, 792-94, *p792,* 836; and Carter, 915; communism in China, 797-99; containment in, 791-92; and Cuban missile crisis, 836-38, *m837;* deadlock over atomic weapons in, 790-91, *p790;* defenses, *m811;* and détente, 904, 935; and domino theory, 866-67; end of, 979; and Eastern Europe, 812, *p812;* and Eisenhower, 810-12; and Ford, 910; and Freedom of Information Act, 961; and Kennedy, 835; and Korean War, 799-801, *m799, p801,* 807; Middle East tensions in, 796-97, *m797;* and Nixon, 903-04; and nuclear bombs, 808-10, *p808, c810;* and Reagan, 930-31, 935; roots of, 789-90; in U.S., 794-95, *p794, p795*
Colfax, Schuyler, 487
Collier, John, 710

Collins, Elizabeth, 451
Colonial America: agriculture in, 60-61, 74, 75-76, 87, *p87;* cities in, 86-87, *p86;* life in, 100-01, *c100, p100-01;* cost of protecting, *c106;* education in, 76, 100; growth of, 86-87; indentured servants in, 61, 74-75, *p75;* Indian relations in, 60-61, 88-91; logging in, 89; pioneer life in, 1, *p1,* 87, *p87;* protests in, 106-08, *c111;* religion in, 69-70, 73, 84-85, 139; territorial expansion of, 104-05, *m105;* trade in, 75-76, 83, *p83,* 106-12; witchcraft in, 70-71, *p70. See also* specific colonies
Color (Cullen), 661
Colorado: mining in, 449, 451; Sand Creek Massacre in, 427, *m428*
Colored Farmers' Alliance, *p499*
Columbia, 975
Columbia Broadcasting System (CBS), 652
Columbian exchange, *m34-35,* 43-44, *c43*
Columbus, Bartolomé, 40
Columbus, Christopher, 10, 37, *p36-37, p38,* 38-40; colonizing efforts of, 40-41; journal of, 39; legacy of, 43-44; voyages of, 39-40, *m41*
Comanches: and horse, 44; and Indian Wars, 425, 426, 427; in Texas, 51, 307
Committee for a Sane Nuclear Policy (SANE), 810
Committee for Unemployment Relief, 684
Committee of Correspondence, 111
Committee on Civil Rights, 786
Committee on Public Information (CPI), 604
Committee on the Cause and Cure of War, 735
Committee to Re-elect the President (CREEP), 907
Common Sense (Paine), 117, *p117,* 119
commonwealth, 69-71
Commonwealth of Independent States (CIS), creation of, 959-60, *m959*
communications, advances in, 459-60, 951
communism: in Asia, 797-99, 866-68; and McCarthyism, 807-08; and Red Scare, 625-26, *p625,* 794-95, *p794*
Communist party (U.S.): and Progressive party, 787; and Red Scare, 625-26, *p625,* 794-95, *p794;* and Scottsboro case, 687; and Share-Our-Wealth program, 701
company town, 493
Comparing and Contrasting, xxi
compass rose, 992
Compromise of 1850, 342-43
Compromise of 1877, 408
computers, 950-51; UNIVAC I, 777
Comstock Lode, 449, 452
Concord, Battle of, *p113,* 114, *m114*
concurrent powers, 154, *c154*

Confederate States of America, 356, *m366;* army of, 368-69, *p368, p390,* 391, *p391;* fall of Fort Sumter, 365, *p365;* resources of, 366-67, *c367;* war strategy of, 372-73

Confederation, weaknesses in, 142-43, 145

conformal projections, 994

Confucius, 24

Congress, 166: and Army-McCarthy hearings, 807-08; and House Committee on Un-American Activities, 794-95; and Iran-contra affair, 935-36, *p936;* powers of, 169; and Reconstruction, 399-404, *m400, p402, p404;* and Thomas-Hill hearings, 941, *p941;* and Watergate investigation, 907-08. *See also* specific acts

Congressional Quarterly, 168

Congressional Union for Woman Suffrage, 552

Congress of Industrial Organizations (CIO), 705

Congress of Racial Equality (CORE), 845

Conjure Woman (Chesnutt), 479

Conkling, Roscoe, 488

Connecticut: industrialization in, 253, *m253;* and Quebec Act, 112; settlement of, *m69,* 72-73

Connolly, Maureen "Little Mo," 777

Connor, T. Eugene "Bull," 845

conquistadors, 46-49

conscription. *See* draft

Consequences, Assessing, xxii

conservation: in New Deal, 696, *p696;* under Taft, 543, 544; under Theodore Roosevelt, 540-41, *p541, m542*

Considerations on This Trade and Finances of the Kingdom (Whately), 105

conspicuous consumption, 473

constitution(s), state, 138-39

Constitution Handbook, 160-85

Constitution, U.S., *p160;* text of, 166-84; amendments to, 163, *c163, c164;* completing, 148-49; drafting of, *p156;* evaluating, 152; federalism in, 153-55; federalist vs. antifederalist position on, 149-50; flexibility of, 156-57; and Great Compromise, 147; and New Jersey Plan, 147; ratification of, 150-51, *p151, m159,* 163; separation of powers in, 155-56; signing of, *p136-37;* and Three-Fifths Compromise, 147-48; and Virginia Plan, 146, 147. *See also* Bill of Rights

Constitutional Convention, 145-46, 153

Constitutional Union party, 354-55

consumer protection, under Theodore Roosevelt, 540

containment, 790-92

Continental Army: African Americans in, 124-25; establishment of, 114; shortages in, 124; soldiers of, 130

Continental Congress: First, 113-14;

Second, 114, 116, *p117,* 118, *p121,* 124, 138, 143, *p143*

Continentals, 143, *p143*

contras, 931, *m932,* 935-36

Convention of 1818, 229, *m229*

Converse, Florence, 691

convoy system, in World War I, 598

Conwell, Russell H., 462

Coolidge, Calvin, *p630,* 631, *p631;* and labor relations, 624; succession to presidency, 630-31

cooperatives, 498

Cooper, Gary, 653

Cooper, James Fenimore, 222

Cooper, Thomas, 245

Copeland, John, 353-54

Copland, Aaron, 660, 718

Copperheads, 375, *p375*

Coral Sea, Battle of the (1942), 745-46, *m746*

Corbin, Margaret, 125

Cornish miners, 450-51

Cornish, Samuel, 293, *p293*

Cornwallis, Charles, 128, *m129;* surrender of, 131-32, *p132*

Coronado, Francisco Vásquez de, 46, *m57*

corporation, 462

corruption: in government, 486-87, 534-35; under Grant, 487-89

Corry, John, 927

Corsi, Edward, 468

Cortés, Hernán, 46-48, *p46,* 54, *m57*

Cortina, Juan Nepomuceno, 316

cost of living: in 1800s, 222; in 1920s, 618; in 1970s, 777; post–World War I, 618, 622-23

cotton: and crop-lien system, 411; expansion of production, 263, *m264, p359;* and Indian Removal Act, 243; and market revolution, 233, 234, 236; production of, 263, *p279, c416, c642, m642, m643*

cotton gin, 234, *m264*

Coughlin, Father Charles E., 701

Council of Economic Advisers, 784

counterculture, 852-53, *p852*

coureurs de bois, 88

covenant, 69

cowboys, 447; African American, 447, *p447;* on long drives, 444-45; Mexican American, 447, *p447; vaquero* origins of, 53

Cowley, Malcolm, 621

Cox, Archibald, 908

Cox, Jacob, 408

Cox, James M., 628

crack (cocaine), 975

Craddock, Thomas, 115

Crane, Stephen, 479

Crawford, William, and election of 1824, 238-39

Crazy Horse. *See* Ta-sunko-witko

credit, dependence on, in 1920s, 673

Crédit Mobilier Company, 487

creditor nation, 726

Creeks: in Civil War, 369; removal of, 242, 245; and Tecumseh, 212;

and War of 1812, *m214*

Creel, George, 604

Crick, Francis, 777

crime: and drugs, 975: as issue in 1988 election, 938; in Moscow, 975, 977; in 1920s, 656; in 1980s, 938, *c938;* and Warren Court, 842

criollos, 53

Cripple Creek, CO, 451

Critical Thinking Skills, xx-xxiv

Crittenden Compromise, 364

Crittenden, John J., 364, *p364,* 366

Croatians, 960, 962

Croghan, George, 104, 105

Croly, Herbert, 516

Cromwell, Oliver, 68

Cronkite, Walter, 879-80

crop-lien system, 411

Crows, 426, 427

Crucible, The (Miller), 807

Crum, George, 223

Crusades, 19-20, *m19, p20*

Cruz, Juana Inés de la, 55

Crystal Globe (Cetron and Davies), 967

Cuba: as U.S. protectorate, *c568,* 569-70; and Bay of Pigs, 836-37; and Columbus, *m41;* early Indian settlements in, 39; early U.S. interests in, 346; missile crisis in, 836-38, *m837;* and Spanish-American War, 559-62

Cuban Americans: and Bay of Pigs, 836; in Miami, 947

Cuban missile crisis, 836-38, *m837*

Cuernavaca, Mexico. 54

Cullen, Countee, 661

cultural diffusion, 8

Cumberland Road, 228

currency, problems in early 1800s, 226, 227-28

Currier and Ives, print by, *p232*

Currier, Nathaniel, print by, *p234*

Curry, John Steuart, 719

Custer Battlefield National Monument, 431

Custer Died for Your Sins (Deloria), 431

Custer, George Armstrong, 428-29, 430-31, *p430*

Custis, Martha Dandridge, *p116*

Cuzco, Peru, 12

cyberspace, 951

Czech Americans, 466, *m483, m954*

Czechoslovakia: fall of Communist government in, 958, *m959;* German aggression toward, 735-36; post–World War I, 608, *m608;* post–World War II, 768; Solidarity in, 931

Czolgosz, Leon, 538, *p538*

Dachau, Germany, 767

da Gama, Vasco, 31

Daladier, Édouard, 735

European Community (EC), U.S. trade with, 966, *c966. See also* European Union

European Recovery Act (1948), 792, *p792*

European Union (EU), 964-65

Evald, Emmy, 551

Evaluating, xxiv

Evans, Hiram Wesley, 640

Evans, John, 427

Evans, Priscilla Merriam, 454

Evans, Walker, 712, 715

evolution, theory of, and Scopes trial, 657-58, *p658*

Exodusters, 439

ex post facto law, 163

Fact from Opinion, Distinguishing, xxiii, 990

factories, 235, *c367*, 646-48, 671, 675, 705, 752, 784-85, *p964*, 965; African Americans and, 491-92, 675, 756, 785; child labor in, 257, *p257, p484-85*, 492, *p492*, 517, *p517*, 551; new working class in, 491-93; southern, 264, *c367*, 411; wages in, 508; women workers in, *p254-55*, 257-58, 492, *p512*, 517-18, 757-58, 785; working conditions in, *p254-55*, 257-58, 492-93, *p492*, 517-19, *p518. See also* labor movement; strikes

factory system, 235

Fair Deal, 787-88

Fair Employment Practices Committee (FEPC), 756, 757

Fair Labor Standards Act (1938), *c703*

Fallacies in Reasoning, Recognizing, 220

Fall, Albert, 630

Fallen Timbers, Battle of (1794), 197, *p197*

fall line, 252, *m252*

fallout shelters, 809

Falwell, Jerry, 928, *p928*

Family and Medical Leave Act (1993), 949

Family Assistance Plan (FAP), 901

family life: 75-76, 256, 475; on farms, 262, 442-43; in New England, 71-72; in 1930s, 679; in 1950s, 817-18; in 1990s, 947, 949, *c949;* on ranches, 446-47; under slavery, 274-75

Farewell to Arms, A (Hemingway), 662

Farm Credit Administration (FCA), 695, *c703*

farmers: 16, 71-72, 234, 497, 503; and Alliance movement, 498-99, *p503;* and bonanza farms, 441-42, *p441;* in early civilizations, 8, 10-13, 14; in Far West, 318-19; and Grange movement, 497-98; and Great Depression, 677-78, 685, 698, 706-07, 711-15; and

Populist party, 499-501; protests by, 76-77, 143-44, *p913;* southern, 75-77, 266-67, 410-11; tenant, 410-11, 497; in Texas, 307, 309; and western settlement, 436-43. *See also* agriculture; sharecropping

Farmers' Alliance, 498-99

Farm Security Administration (FSA), *c703*, 706, 712-13, 715

Farragut, David, 367, 381

Farragut, George, 130

Farrell, James T., 682

fascism: in Germany, 733; in Italy, 732-33; in Spain, 733-34; world response to, 734-35

Fascist party, 732-33

Faubus, Orval, 824

Faulkner, William, 682, *p682*

Federal Arts Project, 717

Federal Council on Negro Affairs, 709

Federal Deposit Insurance Corporation (FDIC), 695, *c703*

Federal Emergency Relief Administration (FERA), 695-96, *c703*, 708

Federal Farm Board, 685

Federal Farm Loan Act, 551

Federal Housing Administration (FHA), *c703*, 817

federalism, 146-47, 153-55, 170

Federalist, The, 150, *p150*, 157, 162

Federalist party, 149-51; and Alien and Sedition Acts, 202; collapse of, 228; and election of 1796, 200; and election of 1800, 203; and Hartford Convention, 215; and the judiciary, 204; and Kentucky and Virginia Resolutions, 202-03; and Louisiana Purchase, 205; and sectionalism, 198-99

Federalists, 149-51

Federal Music Project, 717

Federal Project No. 1, 716

Federal Reserve Act (1913), 549

Federal Theatre Project, 717

Federal Trade Commission (FTC), 549, 551

Federal Workmen's Compensation Act, 551

Federal Writers' Project (FWP), 716-17

Feinstein, Dianne, 943

Feminine Mystique, The (Friedan), 854

Ferdinand, Franz, 587, *p587*

Ferdinand II of Aragon, 22, *p22*, 39, 40

Ferlinghetti, Lawrence, 893

Ferraro, Geraldine, 897, 933

Ferrell, Frank, 493

feudalism, 17-19

Fierro de Bright, Josefina, 678-79, *p678*

Fifteenth Amendment (1870), 403-04, *p404*, 409, 412; text of, 180

Fifth Amendment (1791), 177, *c191*, 519

"Fifty-four forty or fight," 320

Filipino Labor Union, 714

Filipinos: during Great Depression, 714; immigration of, 946, *p946;* literature

of, 983; in Spanish-American War, *p557*, 560, *p561, p563*, 564-65; in World War II, 745, *p746*, 764

Fillmore, Millard, 342, *p342*, 349, 567

Financier, The (Dreiser), 515

Finland: post–World War I, 608; Soviet aggression toward, 736

Finlay, Carlos, 569, *p569*

Finley, James, 282-83

Finley, Martha, 478

Finney, Charles Grandison, 283, 284

First Amendment (1791), 177, *c191*

First Continental Congress (1774), 113

First Inaugural Address (Jefferson), 1003-04

Fisher, Orr C., mural by, *p692-93*

Fisk University Jubilee Singers, *p418*

"Fists of Righteous Harmony," 567

Fitzgerald, F. Scott, 662

Fitzhugh, George, 266

Five Power Agreement (1921), 725

flappers, 655, *p655*

flatboats, 232

flexible response, 835

Florida: and Adams-Onís Treaty, *m229*, 230; and Cotton Kingdom, *m264;* immigration to, *m638;* and Indian removal, 244, *m244;* and Pinckney's Treaty, 197; racial tensions in, 947; secession of, 356, 364; and Second Seminole War, 244; and Senator Connie Mack, 945; Spanish explorations of, 45, 50, *p50;* Spanish missions in, *m52;* as Spanish territory, 50, 197, *m209*, 212; and Treaty of Paris (1763), 104; and Treaty of Paris (1783), 132

flowchart, 996

Foch, Ferdinand, 598

folktales, African American, 277, *p277*

Following the Color Line (Baker), 515

Fong, Hiram L., 777

Fontaine, André, 907

Food Administration, 602, *p602*, 603

Foraker Act (1900), 570

Forbes, Charles, 630

Ford, Betty, *p908*

Ford, Gerald R., 910, *p910;* criticisms of, 909; domestic policy of, 909-10, *p909;* in election of 1976, 911; foreign policy of, 910, *p910;* nomination as vice president, 908; as president, 899, 908, *p908*

Ford, Henry, *p646*, 647

Ford, Henry (Mrs.), *p593*

Ford Motor Company, 646-47, *p646*

Fordney-McCumber Tariff Act (1922), 632

Forrest, Nathan Bedford, 407

Forster, William Edward, 354

Fort Duquesne, 92, *m92*

Forten, Charlotte, 412-13

Fort Hall Reservation, 948

Fort McHenry, 214, *m214*

Fort Sumter, fall of, 365, *p365*

Fort William Henry, 92, *m92*

forty-niners, 324-27, *p324, m325, p325*

Fort Yuma, 327

For Whom the Bell Tolls (Hemingway), 734

Four Power Treaty (1921), 725, *p725*

Fourteen Points (1918), 606; text of, 1008-10

Fourteenth Amendment (1868), 401, 409, 519; text of, 179-80

Fourth Amendment (1791), 177, *c191*

Fox Indians, 196

France: aid to American colonies, 130; North American colonies of, 88, *m88;* early claims of, 56-58, *m57;* and European Union, 964; explorations of, *m57;* and French and Indian War, 91-93, *m92;* and heroin, 975; involvement in China, 566; occupation of Vietnam, *p864,* 865-68, *p867;* response to fascism, 735; at Washington Conference, 725; and World War I, *p584-85,* 586-87, 588, *m588,* 589; and World War II, 760-61, *p761;* and the XYZ affair, 200-01, *p201*

Franco, Francisco, rise of, 733-34

Franklin, Aretha, 276, 776, *p776*

Franklin, Benjamin, 100-01, *p100,* 132; and Albany Plan of Union, 91; and bifocals, 100, *p100;* as delegate to Constitutional Convention, 146

Franklin, John Hope, 210

Frederick Douglass's Paper (newspaper), 294

Fredericksburg, Battle of (1862), 378

Freed, Alan, 826

Freedmen's Bureau, 335, *p392-93,* 400, *m400*

freedom of contract, 519

Freedom of Information Act (1966), 961

Freedom Riders (1961), 845, *m845*

Freedom's Journal, 222, 293

Freedom Summer (1964), 847-48

Freeman, Daniel, *p436*

freemen, 69

Freeport Doctrine (1858), 353

Free-Soil party, 348; in election of 1848, 339

Frémont, John C., 313, 349

French and Indian War, 91-93, *m92*

French Huguenots, 81

French Indochina: Japanese occupation of, 738, *m738*

French Revolution, 195-96, *p195*

Frick, Henry Clay, 496

Friedan, Betty, 854, *p921*

Fuel Administration, 602

Fugitive Slave Act (1850), 343, 344-45, *p344, p345*

Fulbright, J. William, 878

Fuller, Margaret, 285

Fulton, Robert, 232-33

Fundamentalism, 656-57

Fundamental Orders of Connecticut (1639), 72

Furness, Betty, 840

Gable, Clark, 618

Gadsden, James, 315

Gadsden Purchase (1853), 315, *m315*

Gagarin, Yuri, 833

Gage, Thomas, 110, 114

Galbraith, John Kenneth, 825

Galveston, TX, reforms in, 536-37, *p536*

Gálvez, Bernardo de, *m129,* 130, *p130*

Gam Saan (Gold Mountain), 326

Gandhi, Indira, 977

gang labor, 270

Gannett, Deborah Sampson, 125

Garbo, Greta, 680, *p680*

García Calderón, Francisco, 573

García, Héctor P., 840

Garfield, Harry, 602

Garfield, James A., 489, *p489;* and election of 1880, 488; and Reconstruction, 408

Garland, Hamlin, 443, *p443,* 454

Garner, John Nance, 689

Garnet, Henry Highland, 292, *p292*

Garreau, Joel, 947

Garrison, Nicholas, painting by, *p64-65*

Garrison, William Lloyd: and equal rights for women, 296; launch of the *Liberator,* 293; opposition to, 294-95; and passage of Fifteenth Amendment, 404

Garrity, W. Arthur, *p919*

Garvey, Marcus, 636-37, *p637*

Gates, Bill, 950, *p950*

gazetteers, 1000

Gehrig, Lou, 681

General Court, 69

General Federation of Women's Clubs, 514, 635

generation gap, 852

Genet, Edmond, 196, *p196*

Geneva Conference (1954), 867-68

Genoa, Italy, 20, 28-29, *m29*

genocide, 767

Genthe, Arnold, photograph by, *p529*

Gentilz, Theodore, painting by, *p316*

geography: of Africa, *m583;* of agriculture, 642-43, *m642-43;* of Asia, *m583;* of Australia, *m583;* of cities, *m860, m861;* of Europe, *m583;* five themes of, 9; and immigration, 482, *m482-83, m954-55;* and imperialism, 582-83, *m582-83;* and industrialization, 252-53, *m252-53;* of North America, *m582;* and railroads, 253, *m253;* regions, 360-61, *m360-61;* and schools, *m360-61;* of South America, 582, *m582;* of the West, 186-87, *m186-87, m483*

George, Henry, 457

George III (England), 113-14, *p113,* 116, 118, 146

Georgia (CIS), *m959,* 960

Georgia (U.S.): in Civil War, 386-88; Great Awakening in, 85; secession of, 356, 364; settlement of, 83, *p83*

geothermal power, 970

German Americans, 81, 82, *c259,* 260-62, 309-10, 466, 469, *c482, m482, m483,* 591, *m954*

German reunification (1990), 959

Germany: and Berlin airlift, *p789,* 792, *p792;* foreign investment in, *c582-83;* Green party in, 974; and Holocaust, 767-68; impact of war debt and reparations on, 726-27, *p727;* inflation in, 727, *p727;* involvement in China, 566-67; and Maastricht Treaty, 964-65; Nazis in, *p722-23,* 733, *p733,* 734-35, *m736;* post–World War II occupation of, 780-81, 789; reunification, 959; signing of nonaggression pact with Soviet Union, 736; and World War I, 587, 588-89, *m588,* 591-92, 593, *p612;* in World War II, 735-38, 747, *p747, m748,* 749, *c767,* 761-62

Geronimo, *m428,* 432-33

Gershwin, George, 659-60

Gettysburg Address, The (Lincoln), 380, 1008

Gettysburg, Battle of (1863), 379-81, *p379, p381*

Ghana, 26, *m26*

Ghost Dance, 429, *p429,* 432

GI Bill of Rights (1944), 784, *p784*

Gideon v. Wainwright (1963), 842, 1028

Gilbert, Sir Humphrey, 59

Gilded Age, The (Twain and Warner), 485, 486, *p486,* 505

Gillespie, Dizzy, 754

Gilpin, Charles, 660

Gingrich, Newt, 943-44, *p943*

Ginsberg, Douglas, 933

Ginsburg, Ruth Bader, *p165,* 943

Gladden, Washington, 477

glasnost, 934, 957

Glass, Hugh, 318

Glidden, Joseph, 448

global grid, 993

global warming, 972

Glorious Revolution (1688), 84

Glory-Hunter (Van de Water), 431

glyph, 11

Golden Hind (ship), 58

Goldman, Emma, 626, *p626*

Goldmark, Josephine, 519, *p519*

gold rush, in California, 323, 324-27, *p324, m325, p325*

gold standard, 499, 500

Goldwater, Barry M., 841

Gompers, Samuel, 495, 520, 655

Gone with the Wind (Mitchell), 717, *p717*

Goodman, Andrew, 847

Goodman, Benny, 618, 718

Good Neighbor policy, 728-29

Gorbachev, Mikhail, 934, *p934,* 957, 958-59

Gordon, John B., 377

Gore, Al, 943

Gorgas, William C., 569, 571

"Gospel of Wealth," 477

Gould, Jay, 487, 494

Taylor, Zachary, 339, *p339*; in election of 1848, *p338, 339*; and Mexican War, 312-13
Tea Act (1773), 111
Teapot Dome scandal (1926), 630, *p630*
technological innovations: and impact on business, 458-60; and impact on city, 472-73; in 1980s and 1990s, 950-51; and people with disabilities, 951
Tecumseh, 212, *p212, 217, 1033-34
Tejanos, 307
Telecommunications Act of 1996, 951
telecommunications device for the deaf (TDD), 951
telegraph, 459
telephone: development of, 423, *p458, 460;* in households, 509; impact on women, 460
television: in households, 776, *p776*, 897; influence of, 968; in 1950s, 818-19, *p818*
Teller Amendment (1898), 560
temperance movement, 288-89, *p288, m303,* 525
tenant farmers: and industrialization, 497; in Great Depression, 678; in New South, 410-11, *p411*
tenements, 473, 475, *p475, p821;* and housing reforms, 522
Tennessee: in New Deal, *m698, 699, c703,* 708; secession of, 366
Tennessee Valley Authority (TVA), *m698,* 699, *p699, c703,* 708
Tenochtitlán (Mexico City) 12, 47
Tenth Amendment (1791), 178, *c191*
Tenure of Office Act (1867), 402-03
termination policy, 816
term limits, 943
terrorism, 962
Tesla, Nikola, 461
Test, Taking a, 1002
Tet offensive (1968), 879-80
Texas: U.S. settlement of, 307; annexation of, 305, 311-12, *m315;* in Civil War, 369, 382; cotton in, 263, *m264;* Dust Bowl in, 711, *m711;* French in, 309; Germans in, 309-310; life in Republic of, 309-10, *p309;* Mexican Americans in, 307, 310, 316; Mexican migration to, *m638,* 639, *p639,* 756-57, 815; Mexican settlement of, 307; and Mexican War, 311-12, *m313,* 314, 315-16; Native Americans in, 307; and Reconstruction, *m402;* Republic of, 309-10, *p309;* revolution in, 308-09, *m308;* secession of, 356, 364, *m366;* slavery in, 338-39, 340, *m340, m345;* Spanish settlement of, 51, *p53;* Tejanos in, 307, 310, 316
Texas Revolution (1835), 308-09, *m308*
Texas v. *Johnson,* 1033-34
textiles, 235, 252-53, *m252-53, 257*
Thailand: and drug trade, 975; in World War II, 745
Thames, Battle of the (1813), 214

Tharpe, Sister Rosetta, 718
Thayendanegea, 125, *p125*
theater: African American, 660-61; and New Deal, 718-19
Their Eyes Were Watching God (Hurston), 717
Themes in American History, xviii-xix
Third Amendment (1791), 177, *c191*
Third UN Conference on the Law of the Sea (1982), 974
Thirteenth Amendment (1865), 398; text of, 179
38th parallel, 799
Thomas, Clarence, 940, *p940, 942*
Thomas Jefferson: An Intimate History (Brodie), 207
Thomas, Seth, 235
Thompson, Dorothy, 704
Thompson, Joseph S., *p290*
Thoreau, Henry David, 285, 312, 354
Thorpe, Jim, 528, 654, *p654*
Three-Fifths Compromise (1787), 147-48
Three Mile Island, PA, disaster at, 914, *p914*
Thunberg, Penelope, 840
Thurmond, J. Strom, 787
Tiananmen Square, *p958,* 960
Tiger, Jerome, painting by, *p229*
Tikal, Guatemala, 11
Tilden, Samuel J., 408, 488
Till, Emmett, 847
Tillman, Ben, 408
tilted perspective, 995
Timbuktu, Mali, *m26,* 27
Time Line, Reading a, 991
"Times They Are A-Changin', The" (Dylan), 852, 892
Timucuas, 50
"Tippecanoe and Tyler too," 249
Tippecanoe, Battle of (1811), 212
Titusville, PA, 460
tobacco, in English colonies, 60-61, 75-76, *c76*
Tobias, Channing, 786
Tocqueville, Alexis de, 281, 287
Todd, Mary, 352, 366
Toleration Act (1649), 74
Toltecs, 11-12
Tompkins, Sally Louisa, 370, *p370*
Tom Thumb (locomotive), 233
Tonkin Gulf Resolution (1964), 870-71; repeal of, 882
Toomer, Jean, 772, *p772*
Tories, 119. *See also* Loyalists
total war, 387-88
"To the Hon. J. Winthrop, Esq." (Warren), 218-19
"To the Person Sitting in Darkness" (Twain), 615
Townsend, Francis E., 700
Townshend Acts (1767), 109-11, *c111*
Townshend, Charles, 109, *p109*
trade: balance of, 83, *c966;* colonial, 76, 83, 106-12; foreign investment and, 582, *c582-83, m582-83;* gap in, 941; international, 964-65; in Middle Ages, 19-20, *m29;* and NAFTA, 965, 966-

67; and tariff of 1816, 227-28; and territorial expansion, *c574;* U.S.–Japan, 966-67
trading kingdoms, African, 25-27, *m26*
Trail of Tears (1838), 244-45, *m244*
Trans-Appalachian West, 186, 205
transcendentalists, 285, 312, 354
transcontinental railroad, 436, 437, 438, *p438,* 459
Transjordan, relation with Israel, 797
transportation: and growth of railroads, 459; in Los Angeles, CA, 861, *m861*
transportation revolution, 232-33, *m233*
Travels of Sir John Mandeville, 30
treason, 164
Treasury Department, creation of, 191
Treasury of American Folklore, 716
Treaty of Brest-Litovsk (1918), 598
Treaty of Fontainebleau (1762), 93
Treaty of Fort Laramie (1851), 321, 426
Treaty of Fort Laramie (1868), 428
Treaty of Ghent (1814), 214-15, 227
Treaty of Greenville (1795), 197
Treaty of Guadalupe Hidalgo (1848), 313, 314, 315, 326
Treaty of Medicine Lodge (1867), 428
Treaty of Paris (1763), 93, 103, 104
Treaty of Paris (1783), 132, 143; effects of, *m139*
Treaty of Tordesillas (1494), 45
Treaty of Versailles (1919), 608-10
Treaty on European Union. *See* Maastricht Treaty
Treblinka, Poland, 767
Tredegar Iron Works, 264
trench warfare, 589-90, *p590*
Trenton, Battle of (1776), 128, *p128, m129*
Trevelyan, G. M., 855
Triangle Shirtwaist Company fire, 518-19, 529
Triple Alliance, 587
Triple Entente, 587
Tripoli, Libya, 211, *m212*
Troy Female Seminary, 291
Truman Doctrine, 791
Truman, Harry S., 788, *p788,* 803; and atomic bomb, 765, 769; in election of 1944, 753; in election of 1948, 786-87, *p786, m787;* and Fair Deal, 787-88; foreign policy of, 791-94; and Korean War, 799-801; and labor relations, 785; succession to presidency, 764; and UN, 782-83
Trumbull, John, painting by, *p132*
Trumbull, Lyman, 403
trunk lines, 459
trust, 462
trustbusting, 464, 540
Truth, Sojourner, 294, *p294,* 299, 300
Tubman, Harriet, 274, *p274,* 369
Tula, Mexico, 11, *p11*
Tulagi Island, in World War II, 745
Tulsa, OK, race riot in, 636
Tunis, 211, *m212*

ACKNOWLEDGMENTS

For permission to reprint copyrighted material, grateful acknowledgment is made to the following sources:

Brandt & Brandt Literary Agents, Inc.: Quotation from commencement speech by Carlos Fuentes at Harvard University, June 1983. Copyright © 1983 by Carlos Fuentes.

Harold Courlander: From "Hopis and the Love Generation" by Peter Nuvamsa, Sr., from *Hopi Voices: Recollections, Traditions and Narratives of the Hopi Indians,* edited by Harold Courlander. Copyright © 1982 by Harold Courlander. Published by The University of New Mexico Press, Albuquerque.

Democratic National Committee: Television advertisement for the 1964 reelection campaign of President Lyndon B. Johnson.

Elizabeth H. Dos Passos: Quotation by John Dos Passos about the spring of 1919 from *The Perils of Prosperity, 1914–1932* by William E. Leuchtenburg.

Doubleday, a division of Bantam Doubleday Dell Publishing Group, Inc.: From "The Chinese Intervention" from *War in Korea: The Report of a Woman Combat Correspondent* by Marguerite Higgins. Copyright 1951 by Marguerite Higgins.

Lance Fujisaki: From "Saburo Fujisaki: An Oral History," Asian American Studies 129 paper by Lance Fujisaki, University of California, Berkeley, Spring 1983.

Barbara Jordan: Quotation by Barbara Jordan on her decision to leave politics from *Epic Lives: One Hundred Black Women Who Made a Difference,* edited by Jessie Carney Smith.

Lorelei DeCora Means: Quotation by Lorelei DeCora Means from speech about American Indian women delivered during International Women's Week at the University of Colorado, Boulder, April 1985.

Montgomery Advertiser, AL: Quotation from an interview with Rosa Parks from *Montgomery Advertiser,* February 24, 1982. Copyright © 1982 by Montgomery Advertiser.

National Wildlife Federation: From "Sacred Rights" by Mark Wexler from *National Wildlife,* June/July 1992. Copyright © 1992 by National Wildlife Federation.

New Republic, Inc.: From investigative report by Hilton Butler on the shooting of black firemen in Mississippi from *The New Republic,* 1930. Copyright 1930 by New Republic, Inc.

The New York Times Company: Excerpt from an article by Warren Hoge, correspondent in Nicaragua, 1983, from *The New York Times.* Copyright © 1983 by The New York Times Company.

Ohio Historical Society: Quotation by Pauline Taylor, an African American steelworker organizer in Youngstown, Ohio, and quotation by German immigrant John Ehmann, a Cincinnati butcher, from *No Strength Without Union: An Illustrated History of Ohio Workers, 1803–1980* by Raymond Boryczka and Lorin Lee Cary. Copyright © 1982 by Ohio Historical Society.

Penthouse International, Ltd.: Quotation from interview with Vernon Bellecourt by Richard Ballad from *Penthouse,* July 1973. Copyright © 1973 by Penthouse International, Ltd.

Texas A&M University Press: From "František Branecký" and "Josef Šilar" from *Czech Voices: Stories from Texas in the Amerikán Národní Kalendář*, translated and edited by Clinton Machann and James W. Mendl, Jr. Copyright © 1991 by Clinton Machann and James W. Mendl, Jr.

Time Inc.: From "It Takes More Than Food to Cure Starvation" by Michael D. Lemonick from *Time*, December 21, 1992. Copyright © 1992 by Time Inc.

Mary Tsukamoto and Elizabeth Pinkerton: From "Internment at Jerome, Arkansas" from *We the People: A Story of Internment in America* by Mary Tsukamoto and Elizabeth Pinkerton. Copyright © 1987 by Mary Tsukamoto and Elizabeth Pinkerton.

Verso, an imprint of Routledge, Chapman & Hall, Inc.: Quotation by Paiakan, Kayapó leader, from "The Ecology of Justice" from *The Fate of the Forest: Developers, Destroyers and Defenders of the Amazon* by Susanna Hecht and Alexander Cockburn. Copyright © 1989 by Susanna Hecht and Alexander Cockburn.

Ling-chi Wang: From unpublished manuscript "Politics of Assimilation and Repression: History of the Chinese in the United States, 1940–1970" by Ling-chi Wang, Asian American Studies Library, University of California, Berkeley.

The Washington Post: Quotation by Alexei Yablokov from "Sacrificed to the Superpower" by Michael Dobbs from *The Washington Post*, September 20-26, 1993. Copyright © 1993 by The Washington Post.

The Washington Times: From "North Korea in Gulf 'shock'" by Michael Breen from *The Washington Times*, March 12, 1991. Copyright © 1991 by News World Communications, Inc.

REFERENCES:

Quotation by a Jasper County, Mississippi, man from "Education" from *Encyclopedia of Southern Culture: Volume 1, Agriculture–Environment*. Published by the University of North Carolina, 1989.

Excerpt from *The Unknown Soldiers: Black American Troops in World War I* by Arthur E. Barbeau and Florette Henri. Published by Temple University, 1974.

Quotation by President José María Orellana of Guatemala from "Mattresses for Bananas" from *Banana Gold* by Carleton Beals. Published by J. B. Lippincott Company, 1932.

Excerpt about treatment of Filipinos in the United States during World War II from *I Have Lived with the American People* by Manuel Buaken. Published by Caxton Printers, 1948.

Quotation by Russell Means from *The Road to Wounded Knee* by Robert Burnette and John Koster. Published by Bantam Books, 1974.

Quotation by Ramon Roubideaux, Sioux, from *To Be an Indian: An Oral History*, edited by Joseph H. Cash and Herbert T. Hoover. Published by Holt, Rinehart and Winston, Inc., 1971.

ACKNOWLEDGMENTS

For permission to reprint copyrighted material, grateful acknowledgment is made to the following sources:

Addison Wesley Longman Ltd.: From "The Words of the Griot Mamadou Kouyaté" from *Sundiata: An Epic of Old Mali* by D. T. Niane, translated by G. D. Pickett. English translation copyright © 1965 by Longmans, Green and Co. Ltd.

Víctor Alba: From *Alliance Without Allies: The Mythology of Progress in Latin America* by Víctor Alba. Copyright © 1965 by Víctor Alba.

Terry Anderson: From "My Paper Prison" by Terry Anderson from *The New York Times*, April 4, 1993.

Archives of American Art, Smithsonian Institution: Excerpt by Carl Mydans from interview with Richard K. Doud, April 19, 1964.

Richard Atkinson: Quotation by Richard Atkinson from "Beginning of the Road" by Garry Wills from *Time*, July 20, 1992.

The Atlantic: From "Bread Line" by Florence Converse from *The Atlantic Monthly*, January 1932. Copyright 1932 by The Atlantic Monthly.

Ayer Company Publishers Inc.: From *Ark of Empire: The American Frontier, 1784–1803* by Dale Van Every.

Banco de México and Dolores Olmedo: From "America Must Discover Her Own Beauty," an unpublished manuscript dated August 3, 1930, by Diego Rivera from The Bertram Wolfe Collection of the Hoover Institution. Copyright © by the Banco de México.

Ann Banks: From "Jesse Perez" by Betty Burke from *First-Person America*, edited and with an introduction by Ann Banks. Copyright © 1980 by Ann Banks.

Beacon Press, Boston: From *The Broken Spears* by Miguel Leon-Portilla. Copyright © 1962, 1990 by Beacon Press.

Chuck Berry: From lyrics from "Roll Over Beethoven" by Chuck Berry.

Bethune-Cookman College Archives: Quotation by Mary McCleod Bethune.

Robert Bly: From "The United Fruit Co." by Pablo Neruda from *Neruda and Vallejo: Selected Poems*, chosen and translated by Robert Bly. Copyright © 1974 by Robert Bly. Published by Beacon Press, 1974.

Brassey's, Inc.: From "This Was D-Day" by Sgt. Ralph G. Martin from *Yank: The Story of World War II as Written by the Soldiers* by the Staff of *Yank*, the Army Weekly. Copyright © 1984 by Yank Productions, Inc.

Curtis Brown Ltd.: Quotation by Antonio Luhan from "Commissioner Collier Is on Our Side" from *Winter in Taos* by Mabel Dodge Luhan. Copyright © 1933 by Mabel Dodge Luhan.

Peter N. Carroll: Quotation by a Chicago housewife from "The Loss of Connection" and quotation by Ralph E. Lapp, energy expert, from "Pinch, Squeeze, Crunch, or Crisis" from *It Seemed Like Nothing Happened: America in the 1970s* by Peter N. Carroll. Copyright © 1982 by Peter Carroll.

The Caxton Printers, Ltd.: From "Lil' Yokohama" from *Yokohama, California* by Toshio Mori. Copyright © 1949 by The Caxton Printers, Ltd.

Sheyann Webb Christburg: Quotation by eight-year-old Sheyann Webb from "The Turbulent Sixties" from *The Enduring Vision: A History of the American People* by Paul S. Boyer et al.

Conservatory of American Letters: From "Guerrilla War" from *The Awkward Silence* by W. D. Ehrhart. Copyright © 1980 by W. D. Ehrhart.

Crisis Publishing Co., Inc.: From "The Bronx Slave Market" by Ella Baker and Marvel Cooke from *The Crisis*, vol. 42, November 1935. Copyright © 1935 by Crisis Publishing Co., Inc.

Daughters of the Utah Pioneers: From "Journal of Priscilla Merriman Evans" from *Heart Throbs of the West* and *Our Pioneer Heritage*, both edited by Kate B. Carter.

Helen Davie: "The Skyscraper" from *Problems of City Life* by Maurice R. Davie. Copyright 1932 by Maurice R. Davie.

Devin-Adair Publishers, Inc., Old Greenwich, Connecticut, 06870: From "The Case Against Forced Integration" from *The Case for the South* by William D. Workman, Jr. Copyright © 1960 by Devin-Adair Publishers, Inc. All rights reserved.

Mrs. Alexander Donat: From *The Holocaust Kingdom: A Memoir* by Alexander Donat. Copyright © 1963, 1965 by Alexander Donat.

Doubleday, a divison of Bantam Doubleday Dell Publishing Group, Inc. : Quotation by Joseph Goebbels from *The Goebbels Diaries: 1942–1943* by Louis P. Lochner. Copyright 1948 by The Fireside Press, Inc. From "Can Wars Be Just?" by Sari Nusseibeh from *But Was It Just?: Reflections on the Morality of the Persian Gulf War* by Jean Bethke Elshtain et al., translated by Peter Heinegg, edited by David E. Decosse. Copyright © 1992 by Jean Bethke Elshtain, Stanley Hauerwas, Sari Nusseibeh, and George Weigel. From *The Blue Eagle from Egg to Earth* by Hugh S. Johnson. Copyright 1935 by Hugh S. Johnson. From *When Heaven and Earth Changed Places: A Vietnamese Woman's Journey from War to Peace* by Le Ly Hayslip. Copyright © 1989 by Le Ly Hayslip and Charles Jay Wurts.

Facts on File, Inc., New York: From "Origin of Fire," from "The Origin of the Iroquois Nations," and from "The Strange Origin of Corn" from *Voices of the Winds: Native American Legends* by Margot Edmonds and Ella E. Clark. Copyright © 1989 by Margot Edmonds and Ella E. Clark.

Farrar, Straus & Giroux, Inc.: From "Cabo Haitiano to Dos Rios" from *The America of José Martí*, translated by Juan de Onís. Copyright © 1954 by The Noonday Press, Inc.; copyright renewed © 1982 by Farrar, Straus & Giroux, Inc.

The Forum: Quotation by a Slav immigrant from "Relief and Revolution" by Charles R. Walker from *The Forum*, 73, August 1932.

Dan Freedman and Jacqueline Rhoads: From "Jacqueline Navarra Rhoads" from *Nurses in Vietnam: The Forgotten Veterans*, edited by Dan Freedman and Jacqueline Rhoads. Copyright © 1987 by Dan Freedman and Jacqueline Rhoads.

Grove Press, Inc.: From "The India of My Dreams" from *My Truth* by Indira Gandhi, presented by Emmanuel Pouchpadass. Copyright © 1980 by Editions Stock. First published in English in 1981 by Vision Books Pvt. Ltd., New Delhi, in collaboration with Editions Stock, Paris.

Harcourt Brace & Company: From "Harlem" from *You Must Remember This: An Oral History of Manhattan from the 1890's to World War II* by Jeff Kisseloff. Copyright © 1989 by Jeff Kisseloff.

HarperCollins Publishers, Inc.: From "Greed" from *1929: The Year of the Great Crash* by William K. Klingaman. Copyright © 1989 by William K. Klingaman. From "The Buffalo Go" from *American Indian Mythology* by Alice Marriot and Carol K. Rachlin. Copyright © 1968 by Alice Marriot and Carol K. Rachlin. From *The American People: Creating a Nation and a Society*, Second Edition, by Gary B. Nash et al. Copyright © 1990 by HarperCollins Publishers.

Harvard University Press: From *A Sor Juana Anthology*, translated by Alan S. Trueblood. Copyright © 1988 by the President and Fellows of Harvard College.

James A. Henretta: Quotation by a Chicago schoolteacher from "Family Values" and quotation by a coal miner's daughter from "Herbert Hoover and the Great Depression" from *America's History* by James A. Henretta et al. Copyright © 1987 by The Dorsey Press.

Henry Street Settlement and Munson-Williams-Proctor Institute: From "Statements by artists 1963" from *1913 Armory Show 50th Anniversary Exhibition*, 1963, organized by Munson-Williams-Proctor Institute and sponsored by Henry Street Settlement, New York. Copyright © 1963 by Henry Street Settlement, New York, and Munson-Williams-Proctor Institute, Utica, New York.

Hill and Wang, a division of Farrar, Straus & Giroux, Inc.: From *Night* by Elie Wiesel, translated by Stella Rodway. Copyright © 1960 by MacGibbon & Kee; copyright renewed © 1988 by The Collines Publishing Group.

Houghton Mifflin Co.: From *Silent Spring* by Rachel Carson. Copyright © 1962 by Rachel L. Carson; copyright renewed © 1990 by Roger Christie. From *The Autobiography of Will Rogers*, edited by Donald Day. Copyright 1949 by Houghton Mifflin Co. From *Typical American* by Gish Jen. Copyright © 1991 by Gish Jen.

Howe Brothers Publishers: Excerpt by Gerald One Feather from *Indian Self-Rule: First-Hand Accounts of Indian-White Relations from Roosevelt to Reagan*, edited by Kenneth R. Philp. Published by Howe Brothers Publishers, 1986.

Independent Woman: Quotation by female aircraft worker from "Comments on 'Womanpower 4F'" from *Independent Woman*, November 1943 and quotation by a shipyard manager from "Anchors Aweigh!" by Beatrice Oppenheim from *Independent Woman*, March 1943. Published by the Washington National Federation of Business and Professional Women's Clubs, Inc.

Vera John-Steiner: "The Song of Borinquén" by Lola Rodríguez de Tió from *Borinquén: An Anthology of Puerto Rican Literature*, edited by María Teresa Babín and Stan Steiner.

Charles H. Kerr & Company, Chicago: From "The March of the Mill Children" from *The Autobiography of Mother Jones*, edited by Mary Field Parton. Copyright 1925, © 1972 by Charles H. Kerr & Company.

Heirs to the Estate of Martin Luther King, Jr., c/o Writers House, Inc. as agent for the proprietor: "I Have a Dream" by Martin Luther King Jr. Copyright © 1963 by Martin Luther King, Jr.; copyright renewed © 1991 by Coretta Scott King. From sermon opposing the Vietnam War by Martin Luther King, Jr. Copyright © 1967 by Martin Luther King, Jr.; copyright renewed © 1995 by Coretta Scott King.

Alfred A. Knopf, Inc.: From "I, Too" from *Selected Poems* by Langston Hughes. Copyright 1926 by Alfred A. Knopf, Inc.; copyright renewed 1954 by Langston Hughes.

Kodansha International Ltd.: From *War-Wasted Asia: Letters, 1945–1946*, edited by Otis Cary. Copyright © 1975 by Kodansha International Ltd. All rights reserved.

Maya Ying Lin: Quotation about the Vietnam Veterans Memorial designed by Maya Ying Lin.

Macmillan Ltd.: From "Economy (1931)" from *The Collected Writings of John Maynard Keynes: Volume IX, Essays in Persuasion*. Originally published as "The Problem of Unemployment—II" in the *Listener*, January 4, 1931.

Naomi Long Madgett: "Midway" from *Star by Star* by Naomi Long Madgett. Copyright © 1965 by Naomi Long Madgett. Published by Harlo Press in 1965, Evenill in 1970, and Lotus in 1972.

The Magnes Press: From *"I Egypt": Aspects of President Anwar Al-Sadat's Political Thought* by Raphael Israeli. Copyright © 1981 by the Magnes Press, The Hebrew University.

Wilma Mankiller: From "State of the Nation Address" to the Cherokee Nation by Wilma Mankiller. Copyright © 1990 by Wilma Mankiller.

McIntosh and Otis, Inc.: From *America's Immigrants: Adventures in Eyewitness History* by Rhoda Hoff. Copyright © 1967 by Rhoda Hoff.

The Archives of Claude McKay, Carl Cowl, Administrator: "A Song of the Moon" from *Selected Poems of Claude McKay*. Published by Harcourt Brace & Company, 1979.

David McKay Company, Inc., a Subsidiary of Random House, Inc.: From *The Long Shadow of Little Rock* by Daisy Bates. Copyright © 1962 by Daisy Bates.

The Middle East Institute: From "The Lesson of Palestine" by Musa Alami from *The Middle East Journal*, vol. 3, October 1949. Copyright 1949 by The Middle East Institute.

Le Monde: From "Sacrilege" by André Fontaine from *Le Monde*, August 10, 1974. Copyright © 1974 by Le Monde.

Patricia Mull: Quotation by Patricia Mull from "What $152 a Week Buys" by Nancy Gibbs from *Time*, September 10, 1990. Copyright © 1990 by Patricia Mull.

Multimedia Product Development, Chicago, IL: From "Erma's Story" from *Making Do: How Women Survived the '30s* by Jeane Westin. Copyright © 1976 by Jeane Westin. All rights reserved.

NAACP: From advertisement "Let 'Em Walk" by the NAACP.

The Nation magazine: From "The War in Passaic" by Mary Heaton Vorse from *The Nation*, March 17, 1926. Copyright 1926 by The Nation Company, L.P.

National Rainbow Coalition: From "The Rainbow Coalition" speech by Jesse Jackson to the Democratic Convention, July 17, 1984.

New Directions Publishing Corporation: From "Martín IV" from *Martín & Meditations on the South Valley* by Jimmy Santiago Baca. Copyright © 1986, 1987 by Jimmy Santiago Baca. From "I Am Waiting" from *A Coney Island of the Mind* by Lawrence Ferlinghetti. Copyright © 1958 by Lawrence Ferlinghetti. From "Dulce et Decorum Est" from *The Collected Poems of Wilfred Owen*. Copyright © 1963 by Chatto & Windus, Ltd.

The New Republic: From "The De Luxe Picture Palace" by Lloyd Lewis from *The New Republic*, vol. 58, March 27, 1929. Copyright 1929 by The New Republic. From "More Lost Indians" by James Ridgeway from *The New Republic*, December 11, 1965. Copyright © 1965 by Harrison-Blaine of New Jersey, Inc.

The New York Times Company: From "Televised Debate Between Ronald Reagan and Walter F. Mondale" by John Corry from *The New York Times*, October 9, 1984. Copyright © 1984 by The New York Times Company. From "Volunteers from U.S. in Business in Russia" by Steven Erlanger from *The New York Times*, April 6, 1993. Copyright © 1993 by The New York Times Company.

Newsweek, Inc.: Quotation by Hugh Austin from "Business and Finance" from *Newsweek*, November 19, 1973. Copyright © 1973 by Newsweek, Inc. All rights reserved.

W. W. Norton & Company, Inc.: From "The Teflon Years: Electronic Culture" from *Sleepwalking Through History: America in the Reagan Years* by Haynes Johnson. Copyright © 1991 by Haynes Johnson.

Oakland Museum: From *Westward to Promontory: Building the Union Pacific Across the Plains and Mountains* by Barry B. Combs. Copyright © 1969 by Oakland Museum.

Palladium Limited Partnership: Excerpt from "The Lone Ranger" radio script.

Pantheon Books, a division of Random House, Inc.: From "Luna Moth" from *Dogeaters* by Jessica Hagedorn. Copyright © 1990 by Jessica Hagedorn.

Pathfinder Press: From "OAAU Founding Rally" and from "Short Statements: Fight or Forget It" from *By Any Means Necessary: Speeches, Interviews, and a Letter by Malcolm X*. Copyright © 1970, 1992 by Betty Shabazz and Pathfinder Press.

Penguin Books, Ltd.: From "Assorted Monsters" from *The Travels of Sir John Mandeville*, translated by C.W.R.D. Moseley (Penguin Classics, 1983). Copyright © 1983 by C.W.R.D. Moseley.

Penguin Books USA Inc.: From *Movin' on Up* by Mahalia Jackson, with Evan McLeod Wylie. Copyright © 1966 by Mahalia Jackson and Evan McLeod Wylie. Published by Hawthorne Books, New York, 1966.

Peters Fraser & Dunlop Group Ltd.: From "The First Tanks in Action, 15 September 1916" by Bert Chaney from *People at War, 1914–1918* by Michael Moynihan. Published by David and Charles, 1973.

Princeton University Press: Quotation regarding Charles E. Hughes from *Toward a New Order of Sea Power: American Naval Policy and the World Scene, 1918–1922* by Harold and Margaret Sprout. Published by Princeton University Press, 1943, 1946.

Publishers Weekly: From interview with Gloria Steinem from *Publishers Weekly*, August 12, 1983. Copyright © 1983 by R. R. Bowker Company.

The Putnam Publishing Group: From "Their Finest Hour," a speech delivered to the House of Commons, June 18, 1940, by Winston Churchill from *Blood, Sweat, and Tears* by The Right Honorable Winston S. Churchill. Copyright © 1941 by Winston S. Churchill. From *Duarte: My Story* by José Napoleón Duarte, with Diana Page. Copyright © 1986 by José Napoleón Duarte. From "The Yom Kippur War" from *My Life* by Golda Meir. Copyright © 1975 by Golda Meir.

Rainy Day Press: Quotation by Lucy Ann Henderson Deady from *The Lockley Files: Conversations with Pioneer Women* by Fred Lockley, compiled and edited by Mike Helm.

The Reader's Digest Association, Inc.: From "The Spread of Grass-Roots Capitalism" by Edward Maher from *Reader's Digest*, June 1955. Copyright © 1955 by The Reader's Digest Association, Inc.

Estate of Erich Maria Remarque: From *All Quiet on the Western Front* by Erich Maria Remarque. "Im Westen Nichts Neues" copyright 1928 by Ullstein A. G.; copyright renewed © 1956 by Erich Maria Remarque. "All Quiet on the Western Front" copyright 1929, 1930 by Little, Brown and Company; copyright renewed © 1957, 1958 by Erich Maria Remarque. All rights reserved.

Republican National Committee: From "Morning in America" advertisement for Ronald Reagan 1984 presidential campaign.

Roosevelt University, Labor Education Division: From "Automation" by Joe Glazer from *Songs of Work and Freedom*, edited by Edith Fowke and Joe Glazer. Published by Roosevelt University, Labor Education Division, 1960.

Scribner, a Division of Simon & Schuster, Inc.: From *A Farewell to Arms* by Ernest Hemingway. Copyright 1929 by Charles Scribner's Sons; copyright renewed © 1957 by Ernest Hemingway.

SIGI Productions, Inc.: Quotations by Arthur Komori and by Francis Tsuzuki from *"I Can Never Forget": Men of the 100th/442nd* by Thelma Chang. Copyright © 1991 by SIGI Productions, Inc.

Siglo XXI Editores S.A. de C.V.: From "Atahualpa" from *El primer nueva corónica y buen gobierno* by Rolena Adorno and John Murra. Copyright © 1980 by Siglo XXI Editores.

Simon & Schuster: Adapted from map "United States: Ethnic Population, 1980's" from *We the People* by James Paul Allen and Eugene James Turner. Copyright © 1988 by Macmillan Publishing Company. From "The Buckle and the Horseshoe Nail" from *Adventures in the Unknown Interior of America* by Cabeza de Vaca, edited by Cyclone Covey. Copyright © 1961 by The Crowell-Collier Publishing Company. From

From *Filipinos: Forgotten Asian Americans, a Pictorial Essay, 1763–circa 1963* by Fred Cordova. Published by Kendall/Hunt Publishing Co., 1983.
"The persecutions become intolerable" from *Concentration Camps USA: Japanese Americans and World War II* by Roger Daniels. Published by Holt, Rinehart and Winston, Inc., 1971.

From "The Lost Pioneers of the West" by Hugh Dellios from the *Chicago Tribune*, April 4, 1993.

Quotation by General Tran Do on the political outcome in the United States of the Tet Offensive.

From *Black Reconstruction in America* by W.E.B. Du Bois. Published by Atheneum Publishers, 1935.

From Dwight Eisenhower's diary about Kim Roosevelt, October 1953.

From "Black Power Strikes" from *The Making of Black Revolutionaries* by James Forman. Published by Open Hand Publishing Inc., 1985.

Quotation by Phuong Hoang from "Better to Die at Sea Than to Remain: 1975–1976" from *Hearts of Sorrow: Vietnamese-American Lives* by James M. Freeman. Published by Stanford University Press, 1989.

Quotation by Señora Flores de Andrade from *The Mexican Immigrant: His Life Story* by Manuel Gamio. Published by the University of Chicago Press, 1931.

Quotation by a Cuban professor and quotation by Cuban journalist Carlo Franqui from "The Pearl of the Antilles" from *The Cuban Americans* by Renèe Gernand. Published by Chelsea House Publishers, a division of Main Line Book Co., 1988.

Quotations from Latin American sources about the Alliance for Progress from *Remembering America: A Voice from the Sixties* by Richard N. Goodwin. Published by Little, Brown and Company, 1988.

From *On the Shore: Young Writer Remembering Chicago* by Albert Halper. Published by Viking Press, 1934.

Quotation by a black soldier from *Vietnam: Why We Fought* by Dorothy and Thomas Hoobler. Published by Alfred A. Knopf, Inc., 1990.

Quotation by Ton That Tung and excerpt from President Richard Nixon's diary from *Vietnam: A History* by Stanley Karnow. Published by Viking Penguin, a division of Penguin Books USA Inc., 1983.

Quotation by Zack Miller describing Bill Pickett from *The Black West* by William Loren Katz. Published by Ethrac Publications, Inc., 1987.

From "The Roosevelt Experiment" by Harold J. Laski from *The Atlantic Monthly*, vol. 153, no. 2, February 1934.

Quotations from interviews with Vernon Jordon of the Urban League and James Farmer of CORE about Richard Nixon and the race issue from "Washington" from *The Promised Land: The Great Black Migration and How It Changed America* by Nicholas Lemann. Published by Alfred A. Knopf, Inc., 1991.

"Special Problems of the Depression" from *Interpretations, 1931–1932* by Walter Lippmann. Copyright 1932 by Walter Lippmann.
Eleanor Smeal: Excerpt by Eleanor Smeal on the Senate's role in the Thomas–Hill hearings.
Society for the Advancement of Education: From "An American Tragedy: The Internment of Japanese-Americans During World War II" by Norman Y. Mineta from *USA Today*, vol. 112, no. 2468, May 1984. Copyright © 1984 by Society for the Advancement of Education.
Special Rider Music: From lyrics from "Blowin' in the Wind" by Bob Dylan. Copyright © 1962 by Warner Bros. Music; copyright renewed © 1990 by Special Rider Music. All rights reserved. International copyright secured. From lyrics from "The Times They Are A-Changin'" by Bob Dylan. Copyright © 1963, 1964 by Warner Bros. Music; copyright renewed © 1991 by Special Rider Music. All rights reserved. International copyright secured.
Staniels Associates on behalf of Edwin P. Hoyt: From *Japan's War: The Great Pacific Conflict, 1853 to 1952* by Edwin P. Hoyt. Copyright © 1986 by Edwin P. Hoyt.
Gloria Steinem: Quotations by Gloria Steinem about the women's movement.
Betty Lee Sung: From "The Pioneer Chinese" from *Mountain of Gold: The Story of the Chinese in America* by Betty Lee Sung. Copyright © 1967 by Betty Lee Sung.
Syracuse University Press: From "Freedom of Thought and Speech" statement at 1949 annual meeting of the Women's International League for Peace and Freedom in *Peace as a Women's Issue: A History of the U.S. Movement for World Peace and Women's Rights* by Harriet Hyman Alonso. Copyright © 1993 by Syracuse University Press.
Charles M. Tatum: "The Voice of the Hispano" (anonymous), translated by Charles M. Tatum. Copyright © 1982 by Charles M. Tatum.
Time Inc.: From "The Century Ahead: How the World Will Look in 50 Years" by Bruce W. Nelan from *Time*, Fall 1992. Copyright © 1992 by Time Inc.
Times Books Ltd.: Quotation about Mansa Mūsā from *The World: An Illustrated History*, edited by Geoffrey Parker. Copyright © 1986 by Times Books Limited.
Margaret Truman and SCG, Inc., 381 Park Ave., So., NYC, NY 10016: From *Memoirs by Harry S. Truman: Years of Trial and Hope*. Copyright © 1956 by Time Inc. Published by Doubleday and Company.
United Feature Syndicate, Inc.: From "En Route to London, January 5 (1946)" from *My Day, Volume II: The Post-War Years* by Eleanor Roosevelt, edited by David Emblidge. Copyright © 1990 by Pharos Books.
United Nations Development Programme, Division of Information: From "The Value in Wastes" by Carl Bartone from *Decade Watch*, September 1988. Copyright © 1988 by the United Nations Development Programme.
The University of North Carolina Press: From "Tore Up and a-Movin'" from *These Are Our Lives* by the Federal Writers' Project. Copyright © 1939 by The University of North Carolina Press.
University of Washington Press: From *Island: Poetry and History of Chinese Immigrants on Angel Island, 1910–1940* by Him Mark Lai et al. Copyright © 1991 by University of Washington Press.
U.S. News & World Report: Quotation by Sylvia Castillo from "The Untold Story of the L.A. Riot" from *U.S. News & World Report*, May 31, 1993. Copyright © 1993 by U.S. News & World Report.
Warner/Chappell Music, Inc.: From lyrics from "Get a Job" by Earl Beal, Richard Lewis, and Raymond Edwards. Copyright © 1957 and renewed © 1985 by Windswept Pacific Entertainment Co. d/b/a Longitude Music Co. All rights reserved.
James Welch c/o Elaine Markson Literary Agency, Inc.: From "Plea to Those Who Matter" from *Riding the Earthboy 40* by James Welch. Copyright © 1990 by James Welch.
Willie L. Williams: Quotation by Los Angeles police chief Willie L. Williams from "We Have to Start Talking to Each Other" by Daniel S. Levy from *Time*, May 11, 1992. Copyright © 1992 by Willie L. Williams.
Yale Collection of American Literature, Beinecke Rare Book and Manuscript Library, Yale University: From "Blue Meridian" from *Cane* by Jean Toomer. Copyright 1923 by Boni & Liveright; copyright renewed © 1951 by Jean Toomer.
Yale University Press: From "Learning to Be a Miner" and from "The Voyage to California" from *Gold Seeker: Adventures of a Belgian Argonaut during the Gold Rush Years* by Jean-Nicolas Perlot, translated by Helen Harding Bretnor, edited by Howard R. Lamar. Copyright © 1985 by Yale University Press.

REFERENCES:

From 1924 statement by the American Federation of Labor regarding the case of Sacco and Vanzetti from *Redeeming the Time,* Vol. 8, by Page Smith. Published by McGraw-Hill Book Company, 1987.
From "The Stock Market Crash" by Elliott V. Bell from *The New York Times,* October 24, 1929.
Quotation by Ruth Smith on Congress from "Victories Were Captured by G.O.P., Not the Party's Platform" by Richard L. Berke from *The New York Times,* November 10, 1994.
From *Fear, War, and the Bomb: Military and Political Consequences of Atomic Energy* by P.M.S. Blackett. Published by Whittlesey House, New York, 1949.
Excerpt by attorney Brent Bozell about Earl Warren from *The National Review.*
Excerpt from "The Blessing of Time Sales" by Walter Engard from *Motor,* vol. 49, no. 112, April 1928.
From a letter by a friend of David Lloyd George from *The Truth About Reparations and War-Debts* by The Right Honorable David Lloyd George. Published by William Heinemann Ltd., 1932
Quotation about Lyndon B. Johnson from *With No Apologies: The Personal and Political Memoirs of United States Senator Barry Goldwater* by Barry Goldwater. Published by Greenwillow Books, a division of William Morrow & Company.
From *The Rattling Chains: Slave Unrest and Revolt in the Ante-bellum South* by Nicholas Halasz.
From "Before the Colors Fade: Last of the Rough Riders" by V. C. Jones from *American Heritage Magazine,* August 1969.
Quotation by Jim Kelley about fighting for his neighborhood from *From Brown to Bakke: The Supreme Court and School Integration* by J. Harvey Wilkinson.
From "Still 'A Little Left of Center'" by Anne O'Hare McCormick from *The New York Times,* June 21, 1936.
Quotation by a Panhandle county sheriff from "Race, Labor, and the Frontier" from *Anglos and Mexicans in the Making of Texas, 1836-1986* by David Montejano. Copyright © 1987 by University of Texas Press.
From letter by Manuel Mier y Terán to the Mexican Minister of War, Pueblo Viejo, November 14, 1829, from *Terán and Texas: A Chapter in Texas-Mexican Relations* by Ohland Morton (Austin, 1948).
Excerpt about the Bay of Pigs from *The New York Times.*
From "Bare-Bones Imbroglio: Repatriating Indian Remains and Sacred Artifacts" by Dean Peerman from *The Christian Century,* October 17, 1990.
From Vice-President Quayle's remarks about Murphy Brown and family values from "Digging a Divide" by Anna Quindlen from *The New York Times,* June 14, 1992.
Quotation by an African American woman from *The American Slave: Georgia Narratives,* Part 1, vol. 12, edited by George P. Rawick. Published by Greenwood Publishing Group.
From *Texas* by Ferdinand Roemer, 1935, translated by Oswald Mueller. Published by the German-Texan Heritage Society, 1983.
From "The Twelve Principles of EPIC (End Poverty In California)" from *The EPIC Plan for California* by Upton Sinclair. 1934 Pamphlet.
From *The Peoples of Southern Nigeria* by Percy Talbot. Published by Oxford University Press, London.
Quotation about Harry Hopkins from "Money Flies" from the *Washington Post.*
Quotation about Senator Joe McCarthy by James Wechsler from the *New York Post.*
From *German Student's War Letters* by A. F. Wedd. Published by Cambridge University Press, 1979.
From "The Question of Reburial: How the Crow Creek archaeologists view the question of reburial" by P. Willey from *Early Man Magazine,* Autumn 1981. Published by Center of American Archeology.
From *The Experience of World War I* by J. M. Winter. Published by Oxford University Press, New York, 1989.

PHOTO CREDITS Abbreviations used: (t) top, (c) center, (b) bottom, (l) left, (r) right, (bckgd) background, (bdr) border.
Front Cover: © Tony Stone Images, Reza Estakhrian.
Front Matter and Table of Contents: Page i, iii, v(t), © Tony Stone Images, Reza Estakhrian; (b), Dallas & John Heaton/The Stock Shop; vi(l), Colonial Williamsburg Foundation; (tr), Peter Newark's Western Americana; (br), Robert Rubic/St. Paul's Chapel, Parish of Trinity Church, City of New York; vii(t), The Shelburne Museum, Shelburne, Vermont, detail of the painting "Conestoga Wagon" by Thomas Birch, Photograph by Ken Burris; (b), Courtesy of The Charleston Museum, Charleston, South Carolina; viii(t), Southern Historical Collection, Wilson Library, University of North Carolina; (b), The Granger Collection, New York;ix(t), Peter Newark's Western Americana; (b), Nebraska State Historical Society; x(t), National Museum of American Art, Smithsonian Institution, lent by the U.S. Department of the Interior, Office of the Secretary/Art Resource, NY; (cl), The Bettmann Archive; (cr), Theodore Roosevelt Collection, Harvard College Library; (b), Culver Pictures; xi, The Granger Collection, New York; xii(t), UPI/Bettmann; (c), UPI/Bettmann Newsphotos; (b), UPI/Bettmann; xiii(l), C. W. Owen/Black Star; (r), NASA; xiv, xv, Courtesy of John Harold, HRW photo by Lance Shriner; xxi(t), U.S. War Dept. General Staff photo #1650SB-75 in the National Archives; (bl), Marie Ueda/Leo de Wys, Inc.; (br), Peter Newark's Western Americana; xxii, Library of Congress; xxiii(t), American Museum of Natural History; (b), Collections of the Virginia Historical Society, Richmond, VA; xxiv(all), Library of Congress.
Unit 1: 0-1, E.T. Archive, British Museum; 0(l), Steve Vidler/Leo de Wys, Inc.; (r), Rare Books and Manuscripts Division, The New York Public Library, Astor, Lenox and Tilden Foundations; 1, Print Collection, Miriam and Ira D. Wallach Division of Art, Prints and Photographs, New York Public Library, Astor, Lenox and Tilden Foundations.
Chapter 1: 2-3, Steve Vidler/Leo de Wys, Inc.; 3(b), National Maritime Museum London; 4, John & Ann Mahan; 5(t), Wolfgang Kaehler; (b), E. R. Degginger/Animals Animals/Earth Scenes; 6(t), Ken Graham; (cl), Patti Murray/Earth Scenes; (c), Elizabeth H. Walker; (cr), John Lemker/Earth Scenes; (b), Doug Wechsler/Earth Scenes; 7(l, r), Finley-Holiday Films/Page Museum; (b), Marty Cordano/Future Image; 8(t), The Botanical Museum of Harvard University; (b), Arizona State Museum, University of Arizona; 10, Dallas & John Heaton/The Stock Shop; 11(t), Courtesy Department of Library Services, American Museum of Natural History; 11(bl), Robert Frerck/Odyssey Productions; (br), Marie Ueda/Leo de Wys, Inc.; 12(l), Explorer/Mary Evans Picture Library; (r), D. Finnin/American Museum of Natural History; 13, Arizona State Museum, University of Arizona; 14(t), Rich Buzzelli/Tom Stack & Associates; (b), George Gerster/Comstock; 17(both), E.T. Archive, British Library; 18, E.T. Archive, Abbey of Monteoliveto Maggiore, Siena; 20, E.T. Archive, Musee Conde, Chantilly; 21(t), E.T. Archive, University Library, Istanbul; (b), Ancient Art & Architecture Collection; 22, Robert Frerck/Odyssey Productions; 23, Boltin Picture Library; 24, The Granger Collection, New York; 27, Giraudon/Art Resource, NY; 28(t), Erich Lessing/Art Resource, NY; (b), Scala/Art Resource, NY; 29(both), Library of Sint-Baafskathedraal, Ghent; 30, Scala/Art Resource, NY; 31, The Granger Collection, New York; 34(l), Finley-Holiday Films/Page Museum; (r), Marty Cordano/Future Image; 35, ©1979 by The Metropolitan Museum of Art, Gift of J. Pierpoint Morgan, 1900.
Chapter 2: 36-37, Rare Books and Manuscripts Division, The New York Public Library, Astor, Lenox and Tilden Foundations; 37, Mary Evans Picture Library; 38(t), The Granger Collection, New York; (b), © 1979 by The Metropolitan Museum of Art, Gift of J. Pierpoint Morgan, 1900; 39, Reproduced by permission of The Huntington Library, San Marino, California; 40, Antonio Mercado/Art Resource, NY; 42, Photo by C. Chesek/J. Becket, Courtesy Department of Library Services, American Museum of Natural History; 45, Bodleian Library, Oxford, Ms. Arch. Selden A.1, 67R (detail); 46(l), E.T. Archive; (r), E.T. Archive, Piti Palace, Florence; 47, Mary Evans Picture Library; 48(tl, lc), Boltin Picture Library; (c), American Social History Project; (cr, tr), Boltin Picture Library; (b), The Mansell Collection; 49, © Michael Holford/Library of Escorial, Spain; 50(t), Mark Nohl, courtesy New Mexico Magazine; (b), Culver Pictures; 51(l), North Wind Picture Archives/Harcourt Brace & Company Library; (r), Cat #7832, Hawikuh Glaze Polychrome Jar, CA. 1860. Douglas Kahn/Museum of Indian Arts and Culture/Laboratory of Anthropology, Santa Fe; 53(t), Bob Daemmrich Photo; (c), Jack Parsons; (b), The Granger Collection, New York; 54, D. Donne Bryant; 55, The Granger Collection, New York; 56(t), New York Public Library/Rare Book Room; (b), Mary Evans Picture Library; 58, E.T. Archive, National Maritime Museum London; 59(l), Courtesy of the John Carter Brown Library at Brown University; (r), Library of Congress; 60(t), National Portrait Gallery, Smithsonian Institution, Washington, DC/Art Resource, NY; (b), Ashmolean Museum, Oxford; 61, The Granger Collection, New York; 63, British Museum/Michael Holford.
Chapter 3: 64-65, I.N. Phelps Stokes Collection, Miriam and Ira D. Wallach Division of Art, Prints and Photographs, New York Public Library, Astor, Lenox and Tilden Foundations; 65(b), Metropolitan Museum of Art, Bequest of Jacob Ruppert, 1939; 66(t), Rare Books and Manuscripts Division, The New York Public Library, Astor, Lenox and Tilden Foundations; (b), Courtesy of the Pilgrim Society, Plymouth, Massachusetts; 67, Joslyn Art Museum, Omaha, Nebraska; 68(t, bl), Courtesy, Peabody Essex Museum, Salem, Mass., Courtesy of the Pilgrim Society, Plymouth, Massachusetts; 69(t), The Granger Collection, New York; (b), Courtesy of the Pilgrim Society, Plymouth, Massachusetts; 70, Peabody Essex Museum; 72(tl, tr), The Granger Collection, New York; (b), The Connecticut Historical Society, Hartford, Connecticut; 73, Culver Pictures; 74(t), Maryland Historical Society, Baltimore, Maryland; (b), Enoch Pratt Free Library, Philadelphia; 75, © British Museum; 76(t), The Metropolitan Museum of Art, gift of Edgar William and Bernice Chrysler Garisch, 1963; 76(bckgd), The Granger Collection, New York; 77, Culver Pictures; 78(t), Rare Books and Manuscripts Division, The New York Public Library, Astor, Lenox and Tilden Foundations; (b), National Maritime Museum London; 79(bckgd), Photographs and Prints Division, Schomburg Center for Research in Black Culture, The New York Public Library, Astor, Lenox and Tilden Foundations; 80(t), Fine Arts Museums of San Francisco, gift of Mr. and Mrs. John D. Rockefeller 3rd; (b), Public Record Office, Crown Copyright, reproduced with the permission of the Controller of Her Brittanic Majesty's Stationery Office PRO# C05/398; 81, Colonial Williamsburg Foundation; 82, Courtesy Winterthur Museum; 83(t), Rare Books and Manuscripts Division, The New York Public Library, Astor, Lenox and Tilden Foundations; (b), Arents Collection, The New York Public Library, Astor, Lenox and Tilden Foundations; 84, Courtesy Winterthur Museum; 85, Mary Evans Picture Library; 86(t), Missouri Historical Society Museum Collections; (b), The Dietrich American Foundation Philadelphia, PA. Photo by Will Brown, Philadelphia, PA; 87, Courtesy American Antiquarian Society; 88, Rare Books and Manuscripts Division, The New York Public Library, Astor, Lenox and Tilden Foundations; 89, Joan Menschenfreund/The Stock Market; 90(t), Courtesy of the Rhode Island Historical Society; (b), Rare Books and Manuscripts Division, The New York Public Library, Astor, Lenox and Tilden Foundations; 93, Washington/Custis/Lee Collection, Washington and Lee University, Lexington, VA; 94, Museum of the Fur Trade, Chadron, Nebraska; 95, Photographs and Prints Division, Schomburg Center for Research in Black Culture, The New York Public Library, Astor, Lenox and Tilden Foundations; 96, Jerry Jacka Photography, Courtesy of The Heard Museum, Phoenix, AZ; 98, The New York Public Library, Stokes Collection.
Unit 2: 100-101, Independence National Historical Park Collection; 100(l), (detail), The Historical Society of Pennsylvania; (r), U. S. Capitol. 101, (detail), National Gallery of Art, Washington/Everett/CSU Archives.
Chapter 4: 102-103, The Historical Society of Pennsylvania. 103(b), Library of Congress; 104(t), Colonial Williamsburg Foundation; (b), Courtesy of the Hunt Institute for Botanical Documentation, Carnegie Mellon University, Pittsburgh, PA; 106(t), Rare Books and Manuscripts Division, The New York Public Library, Astor, Lenox and Tilden Foundations; (b), The Granger Collection, New York; 106-107(r), Rare Books and Manuscripts Division, The New York Public Library, Astor, Lenox and Tilden Foundations; 107 (t), Robert D. Rubic/Rare Books and Manuscripts Division, The New York Public Library, Astor, Lenox and Tilden Foundations; (bl), The Granger Collection, New York, (br), The Historical Society of Pennsylvania; 108, The Library Company of Philadelphia; 109(both), The Granger Collection, New York; 110(l), Peter Newark's American Pictures; (r), Stock Montage; 113(t), Library of Congress; (b), The Mansell Collection; 114, Mt. Vernon Ladies Association; 115, The Bettmann Archive; 116, Washington/Custis/Lee Collection, Washington and Lee University, Lexington, VA; 117(t), The Historical Society of Pennsylvania; (bl), National Portrait Gallery, Smithsonian Institution, Washington, DC/ Art Resource, NY; (br), Library of Congress; 118, Courtesy of the Massachusetts Historical Society; 120-123(bdr), The Bettmann Archive; 121, The Historical Society of Pennsylvania; 124, 125(t), Library of Congress; (b), New York State Historical Association, Cooperstown; 126, Library of Congress; 127(t), The Granger Collection, New York; (b), Anne S. K. Brown Military Collection, Brown University Library; 128, The Dietrich American Foundation, photograph by Will Brown, Philadelphia, PA; 129, New Hampshire Historical Society; 130(l), Independence National Historical Park Collection; (r), Giraudon/Art Resource, NY; (c), The Historic New Orleans Collection, 7accession no. 1991.34.15; 131(both), The Granger Collection, New York; 132, Yale University Art Gallery, Trumbull Collection; 134, The Granger Collection, New York; 135(l), Ted Spiegel/Black Star; (r), Anne S. K. Brown Military Collection, Brown University Library.
Chapter 5: 136-137, U.S. Capitol; 137(b), U.S. Supreme Court; 138(t), Rare Books And Manuscripts Division, The New York Public Library, Astor, Lenox and Tilden Foundations; (b), Stock Montage; 140, Courtesy Winterthur Museum; 141, Ted Spiegel; 143, Courtesy Winterthur Museum; 144, 145(t), Stock Montage; (b), I.N. Phelps Stokes Collection, Miriam and Ira D. Wallach Division of Art, Prints and Photographs, The New York Public Library, Astor, Lenox and Tilden Foundations; 147(tl), Portrait File, Miriam and Ira D. Wallach Division of Art, Prints and Photographs, The New York Public Library, Astor, Lenox and Tilden Foundations; (tr), National Archives; (b), Bettmann; 148, Louis Schwarz; 149(t), Courtesy of the John Carter Brown Library at Brown University; (b), Library of Congress; 150, 151, The Granger Collection, New York; 152, George F. Mobley/© National Geographic Society; 153(t), Courtesy Winterthur Museum; (b), New York Public Library; 154, Stock Montage; 155(all), National Archives; 156, National Archives; 157, Courtesy, Supreme Court of the United States, The Supreme Court Historical Society; 160, 160-185 (bdr) The Bettmann Archive; 162(l), U.S. Postal Service/Harcourt Brace & Company; (r), U.S. Postal Service/Harcourt Brace & Company; 165(b), Ken Heinen/AP / Wide World; 186(b), Everett/CSU Archives.
Chapter 6: 188-189, Everett/CSU Archives, National Gallery of Art, Washington, DC; 189, Bequest of Mrs. J. Insely Blair in memory of Mr. and Mrs. J. Insely Blair, Museum of the City of New York, 52.100.39; 190(t), Robert Rubic/St. Paul's Chapel, Parish of Trinity Church, City of New York; (b), The Free Library of Philadelphia; 191, The Granger Collection, New York; 192(t), National Portrait Gallery, Smithsonian Institution, Washington, DC, Gift of Henry Cabot Lodge/Art Resource, NY; (b), Larry Stevens/Nawrocki Stock Photo; 193(t), U.S. Postal Service/Harcourt Brace & Company; (b), United States History, Local History and Genealogy Division, The New York Public Library, Astor, Lenox and Tilden Foundations; 194, The Granger Collection, New York; 195(t), Mickey Osterreicher/Black Star for Harcourt Brace & Company; (b), The Mansell Collection; 196(t), Courtesy, Peabody Essex Museum, Salem, Mass.; (b), Culver Pictures; 197(t), Peter Newark's Western Americana; (b), Ohio Historical Society; 198, The Historical New Orleans Collection, accession no. 1971.40; 199(l), Abbey Aldrich Rockefeller Folk Art Center, Williamsburg, VA; (r), The Metropolitan Museum of Art, Bequest of Susan W. Tyler, 1979 (1979.395); 200, Museum of American Political Life, University of Hartford, photo by Sally Anderson-Bruce; 201(t), The Bettmann Archive; (c), U.S. Postal Service/Harcourt Brace & Company; (b), United States History, Local History and Genealogy Division, The New York Public Library, Astor, Lenox and Tilden Foundations; 202, Virginia State Library and Archives; 203(t), Peter Newark's American Pictures; (b), The Hamilton Grange/National Park Service; 204, Nawrocki Stock Photo; 205, Peter Newark's Western Americana; 206(t), The Granger Collection, New York; (b), The Amistad Research Center, Tulane University, photographed by Dennis R. Whitehead; 207, Jack McGuire/Washington Stock Photo; 209, Fred J. Maroon; 210(t), U.S. Postal Service/Harcourt Brace & Company; 210(b), United States History, Local History and Genealogy Division, The New York Public Library, Astor, Lenox and Tilden Foundations; 211, Courtesy of The Mariners' Museum, Newport News, VA; 212, National Portrait Gallery, Smithsonian Institution, Washington, DC/Art Resource, NY; 213(t), U.S. Postal Service/Harcourt Brace & Company; (b), United States History, Local History and Genealogy Division, The New York Public Library, Astor, Lenox and Tilden Foundations; 215, Peter Newark's Military Pictures; 217, Jim Hays/Unicorn Stock Photos; 218, Bequest of Winslow Warren, Courtesy of Museum of Fine Arts, Boston, MA; 219, The Library Company of Philadelphia.
Unit 3: 222-223, Art Resource, NY; 222(l), (detail), The Boatmen's National Bank, St. Louis, Missouri; (r, c), The Bettmann Archive; 223, (detail), Archives Division - Texas State Library.
Chapter 7: 224-225, The Boatmen's National Bank, St. Louis, Missouri. 225(b), National Portrait Gallery, Smithsonian Institution, Washington, DC/Art Resource, NY; 226, The Granger Collection, New York; 227, The Cincinnati Historical Society; 228, M. and M. Karolik Collection, Courtesy Museum of Fine Arts, Boston; 229, Courtesy of the National Museum of the American Indian, Smithsonian Institution, neg. #23/6992; 230(t), U.S.

From "The Roosevelt Magic" from *The LIFE History of the United States, Volume 11, 1933–1945: New Deal and Global War* by William E. Leuchtenburg. Published by Time Inc., 1964.

From a letter to his sister by President Truman from "Fighting Chance" from *Truman* by David McCullough. Published by Simon & Schuster, 1992.

From *On Politics: A Carnival of Buncombe* by H. L. Mencken, edited by Malcolm Moos. Published by Vintage Books, NY, 1960.

Quotation by Tuscarora chief Clinton Rickard from "A Twentieth-Century Indian Voice" from *Native American Testimony*, edited by Peter Nabokov. Copyright © 1978, 1991 by Peter Nabokov.

Quotation by Blade Nzimande, African National Congress leader, from "Mandela Urges an End to Zulu Tribalism" from *The New York Times*, October 25, 1993.

Quotation by George Biddle from *The Roosevelt I Knew* by Frances Perkins. Published by Viking Penguin, Inc., 1946.

Quotation by Rupert Costo, Cahuilla, from *Indian Self-rule*, edited by Kenneth R. Philp. Published by Howe Brothers, Salt Lake City, UT, 1986.

From "A Letter to the Rulers of Latin America, August 4, 1928" by Augusto Sandino from *Sandino: The Testimony of a Nicaraguan Patriot, 1921–1934*, compiled and edited by Sergio Ramírez, edited and translated by Robert Edgar Conrad. Published by Princeton University Press, 1990.

Quotation by Frederic Howe from *America Enters the World: A People's History of the Progressive Era and World War I: Volume Seven* by Page Smith. Copyright © 1985 by Page Smith.

Quotation by Amanda Burks from *The Long Trail: How Cowboys & Longhorns Opened the West* by Gardner Soule. Published by McGraw-Hill Book Company, 1976.

From editorial about Joseph Stalin's speech from *The New York Times*, February 9, 1946.

From "First Order to the Kamikazes" from "It was a Fight to the Finish" from *The American Heritage Picture History of World War II* by C. L. Sulzberger and the Editors of *American Heritage*. Published by American Heritage Publishing Co., Inc., 1966.

Quotation by Gordon Hirabayashi from *Strangers from a Different Shore: A History of Asian Americans* by Ronald Takaki. Published by Little, Brown and Company, 1989.

From *A Colored Woman in a White World* by Mary Church Terrell.

Quotation by a French businessman and quotation by a British lawyer from Preface from *Watergate: A Crisis for the World* by James Trezise, James Glen Stovall, and Hamid Mowlana. Published by Pergamon Press, England, 1980.

Quotation by President Rodrigo Carazo Odio of Costa Rica from "Excerpts from Interviews with Foreign Leaders" from *Making a Difference: The Peace Corps at Twenty-Five*, edited by Milton Viorst. Published by Weidenfeld & Nicolson, New York, a Division of Wheatland Corporation, 1986.

From "Men at War: An Interview with Shelby Foote" from *The Civil War: An Illustrated History* by Geoffrey C. Ward et al. Published by Alfred A. Knopf, Inc., 1990.

Quotation by Theodore Roosevelt from "A Progressive Foreign Policy, 1900–1921" by Lloyd Gardner from *From Colony to Empire: Essays in the History of American Foreign Relations*, edited by William Appleman Williams. Published by John Wiley & Sons, Inc., 1972.

NOTES

Notes

Notes

NOTES

NOTES

NOTES

NOTES

NOTES